Volume IV includes one General Article and book-length, detailed interpretations of 1 and 2 Maccabees, Job, and Psalms.

BOOKS OF THE BIBLE

Robert Doran, the author of the Introduction, Commentary, and Reflections on the books of 1 and 2 Maccabees, is Professor of Religion at Amherst College, Amherst, Massachusetts. Professor Doran's other works include *Temple Propaganda: The Purpose and Character of 2 Maccabees*. He is an Associate Editor of *Catholic Biblical Quarterly*.

Carol A. Newsom, the author of the Introduction, Commentary, and Reflections on the book of Job, is Associate Professor of Old Testament at the Candler School of Theology, Emory University, Atlanta, Georgia. Among other works, she co-edited *The Women's Bible Commentary* and was an Associate Editor of *Harper's Bible Commentary*.

J. Clinton McCann Jr., the author of the Introduction, Commentary, and Reflections on the book of Psalms, is Evangelical Associate Professor of Biblical Interpretation, Eden Theological Seminary, St. Louis, Missouri. His previous works include *A Theological Introduction to the Book of Psalms: The Psalms as Torah* and commentaries on Psalms in *Texts for Preaching: A Lectionary Commentary Based on the NRSV—Year C*.

THE GENERAL ARTICLE

Introduction to Hebrew Poetry. Adele Berlin, Robert H. Smith Professor of Hebrew Bible and Associate Provost for Faculty Affairs, University of Maryland, College Park, Maryland.

THE NEW INTERPRETER'S® BIBLE

IN TWELVE VOLUMES

VOLUME FOUR

EDITORIAL BOARD

THE NEW INTERPRETER'S® BIBLE

GENERAL ARTICLES
&
INTRODUCTION, COMMENTARY, & REFLECTIONS
FOR EACH BOOK OF THE BIBLE
INCLUDING
THE APOCRYPHAL / DEUTEROCANONICAL BOOKS
IN
TWELVE VOLUMES

VOLUME
IV

ABINGDON PRESS
Nashville

THE NEW INTERPRETER'S® BIBLE
VOLUME IV

Copyright © 1996 by Abingdon Press

This book is printed on recycled, acid-free paper.

Library of Congress Cataloging-in-Publication Data

The New Interpreter's Bible: general articles & introduction,
    commentary, & reflections for each book of the Bible, including the
Apocryphal/Deuterocanonical books.
        p. cm.
        Full texts and critical notes of the New International Version and
    the New Revised Standard Version of the Bible in parallel columns.
        Includes bibliographical references.
        ISBN 0-687-27817-1 (v. 4: alk. paper)
        1. Bible—Commentaries.   2. Abingdon Press.   I. Bible.   English.
New International. 1994. II. Bible. English. New Revised
Standard. 1994.
BS491.2.N484 1994
220.7'7—dc20   94-21092
                                                                                     CIP

PUBLICATION STAFF
President and Publisher: Neil M. Alexander
Managing Editor: Michael E. Lawrence
Project Director: Jack A. Keller, Jr.
Assistant Editor: Eli D. Fisher, Jr.
Production Editor: Linda S. Allen
Designer: J. S. Laughbaum
Copy Processing Manager: Sylvia S. Marlow
Composition Specialist: Kathy M. Harding
Publishing Systems Analyst: Glenn R. Hinton
Prepress Manager: William E. Gentry
Prepress Systems Technicians: Thomas E. Mullins
                                        J. Calvin Buckner
Director of Production Processes: James E. Leath
Scheduling: Laurene M. Brazzell
                Tracey D. Seay
Print Procurement Coordinator: David M. Sanders

98 99 00 01 02 03 04 05—10 9 8 7 6 5 4 3 2

MANUFACTURED IN THE UNITED STATES OF AMERICA

CONSULTANTS

NEIL M. ALEXANDER
President and Publisher
The United Methodist Publishing House
Nashville, Tennessee

OWEN F. CAMPION
Associate Publisher
Our Sunday Visitor
Huntington, Indiana

MINERVA G. CARCAÑO
Minister-in-Charge
South Valley Cooperative Ministry
Albuquerque, New Mexico

V. L. DAUGHTERY, JR.
Pastor
Park Avenue United Methodist Church
Valdosta, Georgia

SHARON NEUFER EMSWILER
Pastor
First United Methodist Church
Rock Island, Illinois

JUAN G. FELICIANO VALERA
Pastor
Iglesia Metodista "Juan Wesley"
Arecibo, Puerto Rico

CELIA BREWER MARSHALL
Lecturer
University of North Carolina at Charlotte
Charlotte, North Carolina

NANCY C. MILLER-HERRON
Attorney and clergy member of the
Tennessee Conference
The United Methodist Church
Dresden, Tennessee

ROBERT C. SCHNASE
Pastor
First United Methodist Church
McAllen, Texas

BILL SHERMAN
Pastor
Woodmont Baptist Church
Nashville, Tennessee

RODNEY T. SMOTHERS
Pastor
Central United Methodist Church
Atlanta, Georgia

WILLIAM D. WATLEY
Pastor
St. James African Methodist Episcopal Church
Newark, New Jersey

TALLULAH FISHER WILLIAMS
Pastor
Trinity United Methodist Church
Mt. Prospect, Illinois

SUK-CHONG YU
Pastor
San Francisco Korean United Methodist Church
San Francisco, California

CONTRIBUTORS

ELIZABETH ACHTEMEIER
Adjunct Professor of Bible and Homiletics
Union Theological Seminary in Virginia
Richmond, Virginia
(Presbyterian Church [U.S.A.])
Joel

LESLIE C. ALLEN
Professor of Old Testament
Fuller Theological Seminary
Pasadena, California
(Baptist)
1 & 2 Chronicles

GARY A. ANDERSON
Associate Professor of Religious Studies
University of Virginia
Charlottesville, Virginia
(The Roman Catholic Church)
Introduction to Israelite Religion

DAVID L. BARTLETT
Lantz Professor of Preaching and
Communication
The Divinity School
Yale University
New Haven, Connecticut
(American Baptist Churches in the U.S.A.)
1 Peter

ROBERT A. BENNETT, PH.D.
Cambridge, Massachusetts
(The Episcopal Church)
Zephaniah

ADELE BERLIN
Robert H. Smith Professor of Hebrew Bible
Associate Provost for Faculty Affairs
University of Maryland
College Park, Maryland
Introduction to Hebrew Poetry

BRUCE C. BIRCH
Professor of Old Testament
Wesley Theological Seminary
Washington, DC
(The United Methodist Church)
1 & 2 Samuel

PHYLLIS A. BIRD
Associate Professor of Old Testament
Interpretation
Garrett-Evangelical Theological Seminary
Evanston, Illinois
(The United Methodist Church)
The Authority of the Bible

C. CLIFTON BLACK
Associate Professor of New Testament
Perkins School of Theology
Southern Methodist University
Dallas, Texas
(The United Methodist Church)
1, 2, & 3 John

JOSEPH BLENKINSOPP
John A. O'Brien Professor of Biblical Studies
Department of Theology
University of Notre Dame
Notre Dame, Indiana
(The Roman Catholic Church)
Introduction to the Pentateuch

M. EUGENE BORING
I. Wylie and Elizabeth M. Briscoe Professor of
New Testament
Brite Divinity School
Texas Christian University
Fort Worth, Texas
(Christian Church [Disciples of Christ])
Matthew

WALTER BRUEGGEMANN
William Marcellus McPheeters Professor of Old Testament
Columbia Theological Seminary
Decatur, Georgia
(United Church of Christ)
Exodus

DAVID G. BUTTRICK
Professor of Homiletics and Liturgics
The Divinity School
Vanderbilt University
Nashville, Tennessee
(United Church of Christ)
The Use of the Bible in Preaching

RONALD E. CLEMENTS
Samuel Davidson Professor of Old Testament
King's College
University of London
London, England
(Baptist Union of Great Britain and Ireland)
Deuteronomy

RICHARD J. CLIFFORD
Professor of Old Testament
Weston School of Theology
Cambridge, Massachusetts
(The Roman Catholic Church)
Introduction to Wisdom Literature

JOHN J. COLLINS
Professor of Hebrew Bible
The Divinity School
University of Chicago
Chicago, Illinois
(The Roman Catholic Church)
Introduction to Early Jewish Religion

ROBERT B. COOTE
Professor of Old Testament
San Francisco Theological Seminary
San Anselmo, California
(Presbyterian Church [U.S.A.])
Joshua

FRED B. CRADDOCK
Bandy Distinguished Professor of Preaching and New Testament, Emeritus
Candler School of Theology
Emory University
Atlanta, Georgia
(Christian Church [Disciples of Christ])
Hebrews

TONI CRAVEN
Professor of Hebrew Bible
Brite Divinity School
Texas Christian University
Fort Worth, Texas
(The Roman Catholic Church)
Introduction to Narrative Literature

JAMES L. CRENSHAW
Robert L. Flowers Professor of Old Testament
The Divinity School
Duke University
Durham, North Carolina
(Baptist)
Sirach

KEITH R. CRIM
Pastor
New Concord Presbyterian Church
Concord, Virginia
(Presbyterian Church [U.S.A.])
Modern English Versions of the Bible

R. ALAN CULPEPPER
Dean
The School of Theology
Mercer University
Atlanta, Georgia
(Southern Baptist Convention)
Luke

KATHERYN PFISTERER DARR
Associate Professor of Hebrew Bible
The School of Theology
Boston University
Boston, Massachusetts
(The United Methodist Church)
Ezekiel

ROBERT DORAN
Professor of Religion
Amherst College
Amherst, Massachusetts
1 & 2 Maccabees

THOMAS B. DOZEMAN
Professor of Old Testament
United Theological Seminary
Dayton, Ohio
(Presbyterian Church [U.S.A.])
Numbers

JAMES D. G. DUNN
Lightfoot Professor of Divinity
Department of Theology
University of Durham
Durham, England
(The Methodist Church [Great Britain])
1 & 2 Timothy; Titus

ELDON JAY EPP
Harkness Professor of Biblical Literature
and Chairman of the Department of Religion
Case Western Reserve University
Cleveland, Ohio
(The Episcopal Church)
Ancient Texts and Versions of the New Testament

KATHLEEN ROBERTSON FARMER
Professor of Old Testament
United Theological Seminary
Dayton, Ohio
(The United Methodist Church)
Ruth

CAIN HOPE FELDER
Professor of New Testament Language
and Literature
The School of Divinity
Howard University
Washington, DC
(The United Methodist Church)
Philemon

TERENCE E. FRETHEIM
Professor of Old Testament
Luther Seminary
Saint Paul, Minnesota
(Evangelical Lutheran Church in America)
Genesis

FRANCISCO O. GARCÍA-TRETO
Professor of Religion and Chairman of the
Department of Religion
Trinity University
San Antonio, Texas
(Presbyterian Church [U.S.A.])
Nahum

CATHERINE GUNSALUS GONZÁLEZ
Professor of Church History
Columbia Theological Seminary
Decatur, Georgia
(Presbyterian Church [U.S.A.])
*The Use of the Bible in Hymns, Liturgy,
and Education*

JUSTO L. GONZÁLEZ
Adjunct Professor of Church History
Columbia Theological Seminary
Decatur, Georgia
(The United Methodist Church)
*How the Bible Has Been Interpreted in
Christian Tradition*

DONALD E. GOWAN
Robert Cleveland Holland Professor of Old
Testament
Pittsburgh Theological Seminary
Pittsburgh, Pennsylvania
(Presbyterian Church [U.S.A.])
Amos

JUDITH MARIE GUNDRY-VOLF
Assistant Professor of New Testament
Fuller Theological Seminary
Pasadena, California
(Presbyterian Church [U.S.A.])
Ephesians

DANIEL J. HARRINGTON
Professor of New Testament
Weston School of Theology
Cambridge, Massachusetts
(The Roman Catholic Church)
Introduction to the Canon

RICHARD B. HAYS
Associate Professor of New Testament
The Divinity School
Duke University
Durham, North Carolina
(The United Methodist Church)
Galatians

THEODORE HIEBERT
Professor of Hebrew Bible
McCormick Theological
Seminary
Chicago, Illinois
(Mennonite Church)
Habakkuk

CARL R. HOLLADAY
Professor of New Testament
Candler School of Theology
Emory University
Atlanta, Georgia
*Contemporary Methods of Reading the
Bible*

MORNA D. HOOKER
Lady Margaret's Professor of Divinity
The Divinity School
University of Cambridge
Cambridge, England
(The Methodist Church [Great Britain])
Philippians

DAVID C. HOPKINS
Professor of Old Testament
Wesley Theological Seminary
Washington, DC
(United Church of Christ)
Life in Ancient Palestine

DENISE DOMBKOWSKI HOPKINS
Professor of Old Testament
Wesley Theological Seminary
Washington, DC
(United Church of Christ)
Judith

LUKE T. JOHNSON
Robert W. Woodruff Professor of New
Testament and Christian Origins
Candler School of Theology
Emory University
Atlanta, Georgia
(The Roman Catholic Church)
James

WALTER C. KAISER, JR.
Colman Mockler Distinguished Professor
of Old Testament
Gordon-Conwell Theological Seminary
South Hamilton, Massachusetts
(The Evangelical Free Church of America)
Leviticus

LEANDER E. KECK
Winkley Professor of Biblical Theology
The Divinity School
Yale University
New Haven, Connecticut
(Christian Church [Disciples of Christ])
Introduction to The New Interpreter's Bible

CHAN-HIE KIM
Professor of New Testament and Director of
Korean Studies
The School of Theology at Claremont
Claremont, California
(The United Methodist Church)
Reading the Bible as Asian Americans

RALPH W. KLEIN
Dean and Christ Seminary-Seminex Professor of
Old Testament
Lutheran School of Theology at Chicago
Chicago, Illinois
(Evangelical Lutheran Church in America)
Ezra; Nehemiah

MICHAEL KOLARCIK
Assistant Professor
Regis College
Toronto, Ontario
Canada
(The Roman Catholic Church)
Book of Wisdom

WILLIAM L. LANE
Paul T. Walls Professor of Wesleyan
and Biblical Studies
Department of Religion
Seattle Pacific University
Seattle, Washington
(Free Methodist Church of North America)
2 Corinthians

ANDREW T. LINCOLN
Department of Biblical Studies
University of Sheffield
Sheffield, England
(The Church of England)
Colossians

J. CLINTON MCCANN, JR.
Evangelical Associate Professor of
Biblical Interpretation
Eden Theological Seminary
St. Louis, Missouri
(Presbyterian Church [U.S.A.])
Psalms

ABRAHAM J. MALHERBE
Buckingham Professor of New Testament
Criticism and Interpretation, Emeritus
The Divinity School
Yale University
New Haven, Connecticut
(Church of Christ)
*The Cultural Context of the New Testament:
The Greco-Roman World*

xii

CONTRIBUTORS

W. EUGENE MARCH
Arnold Black Rhodes Professor of Old
Testament
Louisville Presbyterian Theological Seminary
Louisville, Kentucky
(Presbyterian Church [U.S.A.])
Haggai

JAMES EARL MASSEY
Dean Emeritus and
Distinguished Professor-at-Large
The School of Theology
Anderson University
Preacher-in-Residence, Park Place Church
Anderson, Indiana
(Church of God [Anderson, Ind.])
*Reading the Bible from Particular Social
Locations: An Introduction;
Reading the Bible as African Americans*

J. MAXWELL MILLER
Professor of Old Testament
Candler School of Theology
Emory University
Atlanta, Georgia
(The United Methodist Church)
Introduction to the History of Ancient Israel

PATRICK D. MILLER
Charles T. Haley Professor of Old Testament
Theology
Princeton Theological Seminary
Princeton, New Jersey
(Presbyterian Church [U.S.A.])
Jeremiah

FREDERICK J. MURPHY
Associate Professor and Chair of the
Department of Religious Studies
College of the Holy Cross
Worcester, Massachusetts
(The Roman Catholic Church)
Introduction to Apocalyptic Literature

CAROL A. NEWSOM
Associate Professor of Old Testament
Candler School of Theology
Emory University
Atlanta, Georgia
(The Episcopal Church)
Job

GEORGE W. E. NICKELSBURG
Professor of Christian Origins and Early Judaism
School of Religion
University of Iowa
Iowa City, Iowa
(Evangelical Lutheran Church in America)
*The Jewish Context of the New
Testament*

IRENE NOWELL
Associate Professor of Religious Studies
Benedictine College
Atchison, Kansas
(The Roman Catholic Church)
Tobit

KATHLEEN M. O'CONNOR
Professor of Old Testament Language,
Literature, and Exegesis
Columbia Theological Seminary
Decatur, Georgia
(The Roman Catholic Church)
Lamentations

GAIL R. O'DAY
Almar H. Shatford Associate Professor of Homiletics
Candler School of Theology
Emory University
Atlanta, Georgia
(United Church of Christ)
John

BEN C. OLLENBURGER
Associate Professor of Old Testament
Associated Mennonite Biblical Seminaries
Elkhart, Indiana
(Mennonite Church)
Zechariah

DENNIS T. OLSON
Associate Professor of Old Testament
Princeton Theological Seminary
Princeton, New Jersey
(Evangelical Lutheran Church in America)
Judges

CAROLYN OSIEK
Professor of New Testament
Department of Biblical Languages
and Literature
Catholic Theological Union
Chicago, Illinois
(The Roman Catholic Church)
Reading the Bible as Women

SAMUEL PAGÁN
Evangelical Seminary of Puerto Rico
San Juan, Puerto Rico
(Christian Church [Disciples of Christ])
Obadiah

SIMON B. PARKER
Associate Professor of Hebrew Bible and
Harrell F. Beck Scholar in Hebrew Scripture
The School of Theology
Boston University
Boston, Massachusetts
(The United Methodist Church)
*The Ancient Near Eastern Literary
Background of the Old Testament*

PHEME PERKINS
Professor of New Testament
Boston College
Chestnut Hill, Massachusetts
(The Roman Catholic Church)
Mark

DAVID L. PETERSEN
Professor of Old Testament
The Iliff School of Theology
Denver, Colorado
(Presbyterian Church [U.S.A.])
Introduction to Prophetic Literature

CHRISTOPHER C. ROWLAND
Dean Ireland's Professor of the Exegesis
of Holy Scripture
The Queen's College
Oxford, England
(The Church of England)
Revelation

ANTHONY J. SALDARINI
Professor of Biblical Studies
Boston College
Chestnut Hill, Massachusetts
(The Roman Catholic Church)
Baruch; Letter of Jeremiah

J. PAUL SAMPLEY
Professor of New Testament and
Christian Origins
The School of Theology and The Graduate Division
Boston University
Boston, Massachusetts
(The United Methodist Church)
1 Corinthians

JUDITH E. SANDERSON
Assistant Professor of Hebrew Bible
Department of Theology and Religious Studies
Seattle University
Seattle, Washington
*Ancient Texts and Versions of the Old
Testament*

EILEEN M. SCHULLER
Associate Professor
Department of Religious Studies
McMaster University
Hamilton, Ontario
Canada
(The Roman Catholic Church)
Malachi

FERNANDO F. SEGOVIA
Associate Professor of New Testament
and Early Christianity
The Divinity School
Vanderbilt University
Nashville, Tennessee
(The Roman Catholic Church)
Reading the Bible as Hispanic Americans

CHRISTOPHER R. SEITZ
Associate Professor of Old Testament
The Divinity School
Yale University
New Haven, Connecticut
(The Episcopal Church)
Isaiah 40–66

CHOON-LEONG SEOW
Associate Professor of Old Testament
Princeton Theological Seminary
Princeton, New Jersey
(Presbyterian Church [U.S.A.])
1 & 2 Kings

MICHAEL A. SIGNER
Abrams Professor of Jewish Thought and
Culture
Department of Theology
University of Notre Dame
Notre Dame, Indiana
*How the Bible Has Been Interpreted in
Jewish Tradition*

MOISÉS SILVA
Professor of New Testament
Westminster Theological Seminary
Philadelphia, Pennsylvania
(The Orthodox Presbyterian Church)
Contemporary Theories of Biblical Interpretation

DANIEL J. SIMUNDSON
Professor of Old Testament
Luther Seminary
Saint Paul, Minnesota
(Evangelical Lutheran Church in America)
Micah

ABRAHAM SMITH
Assistant Professor of New Testament
and Christian Origins
The School of Theology
Boston University
Boston, Massachusetts
(The National Baptist Convention, USA, Inc.)
1 & 2 Thessalonians

DANIEL L. SMITH-CHRISTOPHER
Associate Professor of Theological Studies
Department of Theology
Loyola Marymount University
Los Angeles, California
(The Society of Friends [Quaker])
Daniel; Bel and the Dragon; Prayer of Azariah; Susannah

MARION L. SOARDS
Professor of New Testament Studies
Louisville Presbyterian Theological Seminary
Louisville, Kentucky
(Presbyterian Church [U.S.A.])
Acts

ROBERT C. TANNEHILL
Academic Dean and Harold B. Williams
Professor of Biblical Studies
Methodist Theological School in Ohio
Delaware, Ohio
(The United Methodist Church)
The Gospels and Narrative Literature

GEORGE E. TINKER
Associate Professor of Cross-Cultural Ministries
The Iliff School of Theology
Denver, Colorado
(Evangelical Lutheran Church in America)
Reading the Bible as Native Americans

W. SIBLEY TOWNER
The Reverend Archibald McFadyen Professor of
Biblical Interpretation
Union Theological Seminary in Virginia
Richmond, Virginia
(Presbyterian Church [U.S.A.])
Ecclesiastes

PHYLLIS TRIBLE
Baldwin Professor of Sacred Literature
Union Theological Seminary
New York, New York
Jonah

GENE M. TUCKER
Professor of Old Testament, Emeritus
Candler School of Theology
Emory University
Atlanta, Georgia
(The United Methodist Church)
Isaiah 1–39

CHRISTOPHER M. TUCKETT
Rylands Professor of Biblical Criticism
and Exegesis
Faculty of Theology
University of Manchester
Manchester, England
(The Church of England)
Jesus and the Gospels

RAYMOND C. VAN LEEUWEN
Professor of Religion and Theology
Eastern College
Saint Davids, Pennsylvania
(Christian Reformed Church in North America)
Proverbs

ROBERT W. WALL
Professor of Biblical Studies
Department of Religion
Seattle Pacific University
Seattle, Washington
(Free Methodist Church of North America)
Introduction to Epistolary Literature

DUANE F. WATSON
Associate Professor of New Testament Studies
Department of Religion and Philosophy
Malone College
Canton, Ohio
(The United Methodist Church)
2 Peter; Jude

RENITA J. WEEMS
Associate Professor of Hebrew Bible
The Divinity School
Vanderbilt University
Nashville, Tennessee
(African Methodist Episcopal Church)
Song of Songs

SIDNIE A. WHITE
Assistant Professor of Religion
Department of Religion
Albright College
Reading, Pennsylvania
(The Episcopal Church)
Esther; Additions to Esther

VINCENT L. WIMBUSH
Professor of New Testament and
    Christian Origins
Union Theological Seminary
New York, New York
(Progressive National Baptist Convention, Inc.)
*The Ecclesiastical Context of the New
    Testament*

N. THOMAS WRIGHT
Lecturer in New Testament Studies
Fellow, Tutor, and Chaplain
Worcester College
Oxford, England
(The Church of England)
Romans

GALE A. YEE
Associate Professor of Old Testament
Department of Theology
University of Saint Thomas
Saint Paul, Minnesota
(The Roman Catholic Church)
Hosea

FEATURES OF
THE NEW INTERPRETER'S® BIBLE

The general aim of *The New Interpreter's Bible* is to bring the best in contemporary biblical scholarship into the service of the church to enhance preaching, teaching, and study of the Scriptures. To accomplish that general aim, the design of *The New Interpreter's Bible* has been shaped by two controlling principles: (1) form serves function, and (2) maximize ease of use.

General articles provide the reader with concise, up-to-date, balanced introductions and assessments of selected topics. In most cases, a brief bibliography points the way to further exploration of a topic. Many of the general articles are placed in volumes 1 and 8, at the beginning of the coverage of the Old and New Testaments, respectively. Others have been inserted in those volumes where the reader will encounter the corresponding type of literature (e.g., "Introduction to Prophetic Literature" appears in Volume 6 alongside several of the prophetic books).

Coverage of each biblical book begins with an "Introduction" that acquaints the reader with the essential historical, sociocultural, literary, and theological issues necessary to understand the biblical book. A short bibliography and an outline of the biblical book are found at the end of each Introduction. The introductory sections are the only material in *The New Interpreter's Bible* printed in a single wide-column format.

The biblical text is divided into coherent and manageable primary units, which are located within larger sections of Scripture. At the opening discussion of any large section of Scripture, readers will often find material identified as "Overview," which includes remarks applicable to the large section of text. The primary unit of text may be as short as a few verses or as long as a chapter or more. This is the point at which the biblical text itself is reprinted in *The New Interpreter's Bible*. Dealing with Scripture in terms of these primary units allows discussion of important issues that are overlooked in a verse-by-verse treatment. Each scriptural unit is identified by text citation and a short title.

The full texts and critical notes of the New International Version and the New Revised Standard Version of the Bible are presented in parallel columns for quick reference. (For the Apocryphal/Deuterocanonical works, the NIV is replaced by The New American Bible.) Since every translation is to some extent an interpretation as well, the inclusion of these widely known and influential modern translations provides an easy comparison that in many cases will lead to a better understanding of a passage. Biblical passages are set in a two-column format and placed in green tint-blocks to make it easy to recognize them at a glance. The NAB, NIV and NRSV material is clearly identified on each page on which the text appears.

Immediately following each biblical text is a section marked "Commentary," which provides an exegetical analysis informed by linguistic, text-critical, historical-critical, literary, social-scientific, and theological methods. The Commentary serves as a reliable, judicious guide through the text, pointing out the critical problems as well as key interpretive issues.

The exegetical approach is "text-centered." That is, the commentators focus primarily on the text in its final form rather than on (a) a meticulous rehearsal of problems of scholarship associated with a text, (b) a thorough reconstruction of the pre-history of the text, or (c) an exhaustive rehearsal of the text's interpretive history. Of course, some attention to scholarly problems, to the pre-history of a text, and to historic interpretations that have shaped streams of tradition is important in particular cases precisely in order to illumine the several levels of meaning in the final form of the text. But the *primary* focus is on the canonical text itself. Moreover, the Commentary not only describes pertinent aspects of the text, but also teaches the reader what to look for in the text so as to develop the reader's own capacity to analyze and interpret the text.

Commentary material runs serially for a few paragraphs or a few pages, depending on what is required by the biblical passage under discussion.

Commentary material is set in a two-column format. Occasional subheads appear in a bold green font. The next level of subdivisions appears as bold black fonts and a third level as black italic fonts. Footnotes are placed at the bottom of the column in which the superscripts appear.

Key words in Hebrew, Aramaic, or Greek are printed in the original-language font, accompanied by a transliteration and a translation or explanation.

Immediately following the Commentary, in most cases, is the section called "Reflections." A detailed exposition growing directly out of the discussion and issues dealt with in the Commentary, Reflections are geared specifically toward helping those who interpret Scripture in the life of the church by providing "handles" for grasping the significance of Scripture for faith and life today. Recognizing that the text has the capacity to shape the life of the Christian community, this section presents multiple possibilities for preaching and teaching in light of each biblical text. That is, instead of providing the preacher or teacher full illustrations, poems, outlines, and the like, the Reflections offer *several* trajectories of possible interpretation that connect with the situation of the contemporary listeners. Recognizing the power of Scripture to speak anew to diverse situations, not all of the suggested trajectories could be appropriated on any one occasion. Preachers and teachers want some specificity about the implications of the text, but not so much specificity that the work is done for them. The ideas in the Reflections are meant to stimulate the thought of preachers and teachers, not to replace it.

Three-quarter width columns distinguish Reflections materials from biblical text and Commentary.

Occasional excursuses have been inserted in some volumes to address topics of special importance that are best treated apart from the flow of Commentary and Reflections on specific passages. Set in three-quarter width columns, excursuses are identified graphically by a green color bar that runs down the outside margin of the page.

Occasional maps, charts, and illustrations appear throughout the volumes at points where they are most likely to be immediately useful to the reader.

CONTENTS
VOLUME IV

THE FIRST BOOK OF MACCABEES

INTRODUCTION, COMMENTARY, AND REFLECTIONS
BY
ROBERT DORAN

THE FIRST BOOK OF
MACCABEES

INTRODUCTION

The first and second books of the Maccabees describe the revolt of the Jews in Judea against the Seleucid Empire in the second century BCE. They are two separate works, as 2 Maccabees is not the sequel to 1 Maccabees but an independent telling of the same events. Both works, in different ways, deal with the problem of how Jews were to maintain their own cultural and religious identity within the larger empire of the Seleucids. Both works show how friction grew between the inhabitants of Judea and the Seleucid monarch Antiochus IV Epiphanes, until he decided to outlaw the practice of Judaism within Judea, leading to the profanation of the Temple in Jerusalem. In response to this attack on their culture and religion, various groups of Jews rose up in revolt, spearheaded by the Maccabean family. First Maccabees begins with the actions of Antiochus IV against the Jews and the profanation of the Temple, and it focuses on the first generation of the Maccabees, sometimes called the Hasmoneans, from the father Mattathias through his sons Judas, Jonathan, and Simon. During this time, the Temple was retaken and purified, and the independence of Judea was proclaimed in 142/41 BCE. The narrative ends with the death of Simon in 135/34 BCE. The narrative of 2 Maccabees is preceded by two letters addressed by the Jews in Judea to the Jews in Egypt, requesting that the Egyptian Jews celebrate the Feast of the Purification of the Temple—i.e., the Feast of Hanukkah. The first letter is dated to 124 BCE, while the second purports to be written in the time of Judas Maccabeus. The narrative portion of 2 Maccabees begins in the reign of Antiochus IV's predecessor, Seleucus IV. It provides more details about events leading up to the oppression of Judea in Jerusalem, highlights the martyrdom of Jewish resisters, and concentrates on the figure of Judas Maccabeus. The account ends while Judas is still alive after the defeat of the Seleucid commander Nicanor in 161 or 160 BCE.

HISTORICAL BACKGROUND

The Ancient Near Eastern Setting. Once the dust had settled from the battles over who would inherit Alexander the Great's conquests, three major powers had emerged in the eastern Mediterranean: the Macedonian Empire, the Ptolemaic Empire based in Egypt, and the Seleucid Empire. The Seleucid Empire was the true heir to the Achaemenid, or Persian, Empire. It stretched from the western coast of Asia Minor to present-day Afghanistan and was the largest of the Hellenistic kingdoms. The Seleucid Empire also lay claim to Coelesyria, which the Ptolemaic Empire had controlled since 301 BCE. Size brought its own problems, and the Seleucid kings would see their territory whittled away during the third century BCE. In the west, partly as a result of the Celtic invasions in Asia Minor in 278–277 BCE, various states in Asia Minor arose—Bithynia, Pontus, Cappadocia, and the Attalids at Pergamum. In the east, Bactria and Parthia seceded. Although the Seleucid kings kept an interest in their Iranian possessions, no doubt for reasons of military defense, they did not maintain as strong an influence as in Syria and Mesopotamia. Antiochus III reasserted Seleucid authority in Iran during his expedition there (212–205/4 BCE), for

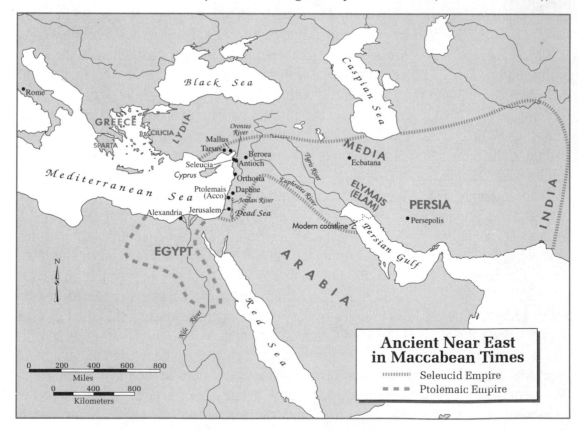

Ancient Near East in Maccabean Times

⋅⋅⋅⋅⋅⋅⋅ Seleucid Empire
■ ■ ■ Ptolemaic Empire

which he assumed the title "Great King," but Parthia and Bactria remained unconquered, and Seleucid control of eastern Iran remained rather superficial. Antiochus III also sought to restore Seleucid control over western Asia Minor and marched into Coelesyria in 202 BCE. He seized control of Coelesyria, Phoenicia, and Palestine with a decisive victory over the Ptolemaic forces at Panium in 200 BCE.

Antiochus's attempt to restore the Seleucid kingdom to its former glory failed, however, for a new player had entered the power game in the eastern Mediterranean. Rome, however hesitatingly and clumsily, was emerging as the dominant force. By its victories over Philip V of Macedonia at Cynoscephalae in 197 BCE, over Philip's son Perseus at Pydna in 168 BCE, and finally over the Achaean League in 146 BCE, Rome gained complete control of Macedonia and Greece. Antiochus III also fell before the Romans at Magnesia in 190 BCE, and the subsequent Treaty of Apamea in 188 BCE took away most of his possessions in Asia Minor and saddled him with a heavy indemnity. When Antiochus IV attempted to extend Seleucid influence into Egypt, the Roman envoy C. Popillius Laenas delivered to him the senate's order that he leave Egypt, and he did so in humiliation. Rome was the dominant power in the East from the second century on. The weaker party in any dispute would appeal to Rome, and Rome's representatives were frequently in the East investigating conflicts and advising the senate on solutions.

The Ptolemaic and Seleucid empires would continue, however, although wracked by dynastic struggles between rival claimants to the throne. The Seleucid Empire ended when Pompey the Great annexed Syria in 64 BCE; the Ptolemaic Empire formally lasted longer, ending when Cleopatra VII committed suicide in 30 BCE. While weak, these empires could still muster impressive forces. Antiochus VII Sidetes invaded Judea in 135/34 BCE, besieging Jerusalem and reinstating Seleucid rule, if only for a brief time. Later, about 112 BCE, John Hyrcanus could not resist the incursions of Antiochus IX Cyzicenus. When Alexander Jannaeus, king of Judea 103–76 BCE, tried to extend his territory west to the port of Ptolemais (Akko) early in his reign, he was decisively defeated by Ptolemy IX Soter II (Lathyrus); later, about 88 BCE, he was defeated by the Seleucid monarch Demetrius III Eucaerus.

Judea. When Antiochus III defeated the Ptolemaic forces at Panium in 200 BCE, he forthwith gained control of the small city-state of Judea. Judea had been ruled by the Ptolemies for over a century, but the details of its administration remain very hazy, since the sources at our disposal are not concerned with these sociopolitical questions.[1] Following is a discussion of the main narrative sources used to search out life in pre-Maccabean Jerusalem.

(1) First Maccabees provides almost no details of Judean life before the revolt. It does mention that there were some anonymous "renegades" who wanted Jews to conform to

---

1. A full listing of these sources can be found in the work by Lester L. Grabbe, *Judaism from Cyrus to Hadrian*, 2 vols. (Minneapolis: Fortress, 1992), and in the revised edition of Emil Schürer, *The History of the Jewish People in the Age of Jesus Christ*, rev. ed., 4 vols. (Edinburgh: T. & T. Clark, 1973–87). The interested reader may consult the full discussion in those works.

the way of life of the nations round about and so had a gymnasium built in Jerusalem (1 Macc 1:11-15).

(2) Second Maccabees provides more details about the high priests in Jerusalem and their role in the building of a gymnasium. It gives names and events not otherwise recorded.

(3) The Jewish historian Josephus, writing at the end of the first century CE, provides information about Jerusalem in the pre-Maccabean period in his works *The Jewish War* and *Antiquities of the Jews.* The latter work in particular includes citations of official letters by Seleucid rulers about the Jews. It also contains a narrative about one Jewish family, the Tobiads, which is usually called the Tobiad romance.[2] This story tells of the rise to prominence of Joseph the Tobiad, who took over the role of tax collector for the Egyptian Ptolemies from his uncle, the miserly high priest Onias. Josephus tells the story in a most confusing way, but some scholars believe that they can glean some historical data from this fanciful account and date the events to the rule of Ptolemy III Euergetes (246–221 BCE). According to this story, the seven oldest sons of Joseph fought against their younger half brother, Hyrcanus, and this rivalry was in part responsible for the Seleucids' intervening in Judah to offset the Ptolemaic connections of Hyrcanus.

(4) The last part of the canonical book of Daniel also recounts the events preceding and during the reign of Antiochus IV in the visions of Daniel 7–12. The events are cast in the form of a symbolic vision, with the kings of the south, the Ptolemies, waging war against the kings of the north, the Seleucids. The exact significance of some of the references is unclear.

(5) The first book of *Enoch,* a pseudepigraphic work (portions of which have been found among the Dead Sea Scrolls), also recounts in symbolic form the history of Israel up to the time of the Maccabees (*1 Enoch* 83–90). Here the symbols are of animals fighting against one another.

(6) The work of Jesus ben Sira, a teacher in Jerusalem around 190–170 BCE, evidences a deep concern for the role of wisdom in creation. True wisdom comes from God, and Ben Sira identifies divine wisdom with the Torah, or Law of Moses (Sir 24:8-29). He places great emphasis on proper worship in the Temple.

From these various sources, then, scholars attempt to piece together a sense of what life was like in Judea in the third century BCE, and what happened there.

From a decree found in Josephus, we know that Antiochus III affirmed the right of the Jews to live according to their ancestral religion.[3] He also mentioned that the Jews had a "council" (γερουσία *gerousia*), but we do not know precisely who its members were (probably wealthy aristocracy) or how they were chosen. Although Antiochus does not mention the high priest in his letter, the Greek historian Hecataeus of Abdera, who wrote around 300 BCE, stated that the high priest was a leading figure in civil as well as religious matters. Hecataeus's work is reported by a later Greek writer of the first century BCE,

---

2. Josephus *Antiquities of the Jews* 12.157-236.
3. Ibid., 12.138-146.

Diodorus Siculus.[4] In his idealized picture of the Jews, Hecataeus wrote that Moses appointed priests to be "judges in all major disputes, and entrusted to them the guardianship of the laws and customs. For this reason the Jews never have a king, and authority over the people is regularly vested in whichever priest is regarded as superior to his colleagues in wisdom and virtue. They call this man the high priest, and believe he acts as a messenger to them of God's commandments."[5]

Ben Sira (50:1-21) also lavishes praise on the high priest of his own day, Simon son of Onias, and notes how Simon built the walls of the temple enclosure and fortified the city against siege. The Tobiad romance has the high priest in charge of paying tribute to the Ptolemies, although the point of the story is the transfer of this power to a non-priest, Joseph the Tobiad. Scholars have deduced from this that the high priest was the only authority in Judea, but we do not know whether the Ptolemies or the Seleucids installed another imperial functionary alongside the high priest.

Nothing much changed through the transfer of power from the Ptolemies to the Seleucids. However, the defeat of Antiochus III by the Romans in 190 BCE put the Seleucid Empire under a heavy indemnity. The description of the attempt by Seleucus IV, Antiochus's successor, to obtain money from the Jerusalem Temple as told in 2 Maccabees 3 should be seen in the light of the Seleucid emperor's need for money to keep up payment of that indemnity. More important, the author of 2 Maccabees recounts how Jason, the brother of the high priest Onias III, outbid his brother to take from him the office of high priest (2 Macc 4:7-10). We do not know if previously every high priest had to pay for reinstatement at the advent of a new ruler, but the accession of Antiochus IV saw the bestowal of the high priesthood on the highest bidder. The narrative of 2 Maccabees in particular forces us to consider the competition and rivalries among various groups in pre-Hasmonean Jerusalem. Following is a highlight of important areas for the reader to keep in mind while working through 1 and 2 Maccabees.

Factions in Jerusalem. In any discussion of the causes of the rebellion in Judea, one has to remember that the small state of Judea (traveling about twenty miles in any direction from Jerusalem would take one outside its territory) was ruled by wealthy priestly and lay families. At times, this situation is described as an ideal one: "the holy city was inhabited in unbroken peace and the laws were strictly observed" (2 Macc 3:1 NRSV). The high priest is described by Sirach as being surrounded by the whole congregation, lifting up their hands and voices in unison and harmony as they worshiped God (Sir 50:1-21). Such an idyllic picture is, however, rudely countered by the descriptions of factional fighting and murder committed by one group against another (see, e.g., 2 Macc 4:3).

Several influential families can be identified from the sources: the Oniad family of Zadokite high priests, Onias III and Jason (2 Macc 3:1; 4:7); the Bilgah family, Simon, Menelaus, and Lysimachus (2 Macc 3:4; 4:23-29); the Hakkoz family, John and Eupolemus

4. Diodorus Siculus 40.3.1-8.
5. Ibid., 40.3.5.

(1 Macc 8:17; 2 Macc 4:11); the Jehoiaribs, i.e., the Hasmonean family; the family of Jakim, Alcimus (1 Macc 7:5); and the Tobiads.[6] Although the Tobiads, who were lay leaders and not priests, do not appear at all in 1 and 2 Maccabees, Josephus in one account describes how the sons of Tobias urged Antiochus IV to invade Jerusalem.[7] It is also important to keep in mind that other wealthy lay families vied for power and prestige in Judea. As for the priestly families, it seems significant that the chronicler, in the lists of ancestral houses of the priests apart from the high priest Zadok, mentions the other four families (1 Chr 24:7, 10, 12, 14). Hakkoz's descendants were barred from the priesthood after the return from exile because their family name could not be found in the genealogical entries (Ezra 2:61-63), but their presence in the list in Chronicles as well as their diplomatic activity in the second century BCE (2 Macc 4:11; 1 Macc 8:17) attests to their continued prominence. From the narrative in 2 Maccabees, one can see how the Bilgah family seized the opportunity offered by the split in the Zadokite family between Onias and his brother Jason and how the Hakkoz family sided with the Hasmoneans, while Alcimus of the family of Jakim pursued his own quest for power. Thus the causes of the Maccabean revolt must be seen as having arisen from the competition between ambitious families in the small city-state of Judea.

There are other signs that all was not well in Judea. The discoveries at Qumran have shown that discontent was present in the third century BCE. In *1 Enoch* 1–16, part of a pseudepigraphic work dated to the third century BCE, a story similar to that of Gen 6:1-8 is told of how angels from heaven brought sin and pollution upon the earth. The story is paradigmatic for the way the author of *1 Enoch* and his community viewed their world as one of disorder and confusion. Later, in the second century BCE, the author of the book of Daniel depicted the history of the world from the Babylonians to the Greeks as chaotic and bestial (Daniel 7). Within Judaism itself there was dissension over the cultic calendar as seen in the book of *Jubilees,* which favors a solar instead of a lunar-solar calendar. There was debate over other legal questions as well, if 4QMMT found at Qumran is to be dated early. Even the traditionalist Ben Sira includes in his work a prayer for the deliverance of Jerusalem and the Jewish nation from foreign oppression (Sir 36:1-22). Within both 1 and 2 Maccabees we also meet a group called the Hasideans (1 Macc 2:42; 7:13; 2 Macc 14:6). We do not know who they were, but their choice of name—"pious," "loyal ones"—suggests that they thought others were not so pious and loyal as they. The *Damascus Document* also hints that members of its exclusivist group were found throughout Judea.[8] Clearly, not everyone thought that all was well in Judea.

Persecution by Antiochus IV. The accounts of the persecution enforced by Antiochus IV Epiphanes differ in 1 and 2 Maccabees. Here is a schematic outline of the events:

6. Josephus *Antiquities of the Jews* 12.158-236.
7. Josephus *The Jewish War* 1.31-32.
8. CD 12:19.

Figure 1: A Synoptic Chart of Antiochus's Persecution

1 Maccabees	2 Maccabees
1. "Renegades" ask to be like other nations; they build a gymnasium.	The high priest Jason asks to build a gymnasium as a way to adopt the Greek way of life. The high priest Menelaus commits acts of sacrilege, which lead to an uprising of the people.
2. An arrogant Antiochus IV invades Egypt, plunders it, and then plunders Jerusalem and the Temple.	After Antiochus IV's second invasion of Egypt, a civil war breaks out between Jason and Menelaus. In response to this, a bestial Antiochus plunders the Temple.
3. Two years later, a military garrison is set up in Jerusalem.	Antiochus installs governors in Judea and in Samaria. He then commands another attack on Jerusalem.
4. Sometime later, Antiochus IV imposes a cult on Judea, profanes the Temple, and prohibits the Mosaic Law.	Finally, Antiochus IV outlaws Judaism in Judea, profanes the Temple, and installs another cult.
5. When news reaches Antiochus that the Temple has been recaptured and purified by the Jews, he dies.	Antiochus IV dies before the Temple is purified.

The two accounts are basically the same, but with important differences that will be discussed in the commentary. Both accounts agree that some Jews built a gymnasium and that Antiochus IV imposed a cult on Jerusalem. The characterization of Antiochus IV differs in both. In 1 Maccabees, Antiochus IV is arrogant from the start and seeks to impose a unified worship and behavior throughout his empire. In 2 Maccabees, he is at first portrayed neutrally, then as sympathetic, but finally as enraged against the Jews. Second Maccabees shows that the cult was imposed after a series of disturbances and uprisings in Jerusalem, and it places much of the blame on the unruly passions of the emperor. On the other hand, 1 Maccabees states that the cult was imposed because the emperor wished all nations to be the same and to give up their particular customs (1 Macc 1:41-42). Antiochus is thus portrayed in 1 Maccabees as zealous in the spread of Hellenization, of striving to conform everyone to Greek customs, while in 2 Maccabees he is shown initially as encouraging the adoption of Greek customs by some Jews.

It must be said that Antiochus IV was not a Hellenizing zealot. He certainly wanted to keep the Seleucid Empire together, but all evidence suggests that he encouraged the maintenance of local customs and traditions and did not seek to suppress them. We should see as rhetorical polemic, therefore, the statement in 1 Macc 1:41 concerning a decree to force all peoples to abandon their customs. However, we should also be sensitive to the pressure there must have been to learn the ways of the Seleucids. The Seleucid monarch was extremely powerful, and it would have been in the best interests of rulers within his empire to be on good terms with him. What we find is that during the reigns of Antiochus III and Antiochus IV a number of older cities were recognized as *poleis* (πόλεις), i.e., Greek cities, and were renamed. Obviously this was thought to be a beneficial step for the cities concerned—indeed, a goal to strive for.

The high priest Jason must have thought so, because he had Jerusalem renamed as Antioch-at-Jerusalem (2 Macc 4:9, 19) and built a gymnasium, an exercise and educational establishment that every "decent" Greek city was supposed to have. One must also recognize, however, that we know almost nothing about what this process of renaming entailed. Did the renaming of an ancient city like Jerusalem as Antioch-at-Jerusalem necessarily signify the adoption of a new constitution? Was the *gerousia* under Antiochus III different from that under Antiochus IV and his successors? Earlier scholars argued that, theoretically, if not in practice, a new constitution was adopted, but the minimal evidence seems to support the continuance of older customs. In addition, nothing indicates that citizenship in Antioch-at-Jerusalem was limited to wealthy friends of Jason. As for the gymnasium, we simply do not know what its curriculum was; evidence from what took place in Athens should be applied cautiously to Jerusalem, since each city controlled its own educational process. What we do know is that the people in the gymnasium would have been taught to speak Greek, as well as to carry out the exercises and sports that any well-reared Greek citizen would have learned. The emperor would certainly have had interpreters available, but the ability to become a member of the club by partaking in gymnastic exercises and by conversing in Greek would no doubt have made for a more amicable relationship with the powerful monarch. Moreover, the renaming of Jerusalem around 175 BCE and the building of a gymnasium brought about no local upheaval, even though the author of 2 Maccabees sees it as the start of the Hellenization and the religious factionalism it produced (2 Macc 4:11-17).

The trouble developed following a series of events. Factional war broke out between the high priest Menelaus and the former high priest Jason while Antiochus IV was campaigning in Egypt. Antiochus's reaction to this revolt was to enter Jerusalem by force, massacre the population, and pillage the Temple (2 Macc 5:1-21). Antiochus appointed overseers in Jerusalem and over the Samaritans (2 Macc 5:22-23). Later, there were two more missions against Jerusalem, one by Apollonius, captain of the Mysians (1 Macc 1:29-35; 2 Macc 5:24-26), and one by Geron the Athenian, to compel the Jews to abandon their laws (1 Macc 1:44-51; 2 Macc 6:1-2). Since these missions were probably not mere whims, it seems safe to conclude that the populace of Jerusalem and Judea was considered by the Seleucid authorities to be restless and that the decision to stamp out forcibly the practice of Judaism was the final step in a series of unsuccessful attempts to settle affairs in Jerusalem. Indeed, the persecution was limited to Judea, Samaria (2 Macc 6:2), and neighboring Greek cities (2 Macc 6:8-9). Jews in other major cities of the Seleucid Empire, such as Antioch, were not, so far as we know, affected.

The persecution aimed at every aspect of Jewish observance. Torah scrolls were burned, circumcision was forbidden, and the sabbath was not to be observed. Jews were forced to participate at pagan festivals and compelled to eat pork. Observance of Torah was outlawed under threat of death. The Temple was profaned and turned into a temple for pagan festivals.

A great deal of energy has been spent trying to pinpoint exactly which cult was imposed upon Jerusalem by Antiochus IV. The sources tell us that the temple was dedicated to Zeus Olympios (2 Macc 6:2), that a desolating sacrilege and an altar were placed on top of the altar of burnt offering in the temple courtyard (1 Macc 1:54, 59; 4:43-44), and that both the king's birthday and the feast day of the god Dionysos were celebrated monthly (2 Macc 6:7). There may also have been temple prostitutes (2 Macc 6:4). The term "desolating sacrilege" (βδέλυγμα ἐρημώσεως *bdelygma erēmōseōs*, 1 Macc 1:54) is the same as that found in Dan 9:27; 11:31, where the Hebrew (שקוצים משמם *šiqqûṣîm měšōmēm*) is a play on the name "Ba'al Shamen," or "Lord of Heaven," the Syrian counterpart of Zeus Olympios. Based on this, some scholars have argued that the cult was Syro-Canaanite, assuming that one cult substituted for another. However, 1 Macc 1:47 speaks of many altars, sacred precincts, and shrines for idols, and 2 Macc 10:2 details that altars had been built in the public square of Jerusalem and also that there were sacred precincts. Rather than the imposition of the worship of one god in place of Yahweh, it seems that the worship of many gods, including Dionysus and Zeus Olympios, took place. Thus regular paganism, characterized by the worship of many gods and goddesses, was introduced.

Antiochus IV would later change his mind and revoke the persecution (2 Macc 11:27-33), but the enigma still remains as to why he started a policy so at variance with the usual workings of the Hellenistic world, wherein states normally respected the existing gods and cultic practices of the various cities. Antiochus III and Seleucus IV had supported the cult in Jerusalem. Scholars have attempted to find a specific answer to the problem. Suggestions that Antiochus was either crazy or a zealous Hellenizer do not explain why only this small area of his kingdom was affected. Goldstein has suggested that Antiochus IV, a former hostage in Rome, was attempting to set up an empirewide Antiochian citizenship similar to Roman civic and religious programs, but his ingenious theory lacks supporting data.[9] Other scholars have sought an explanation from within the factions in Jerusalem. E. Bickermann argued brilliantly that the initiative for the persecution came from the "Hellenizers" in Jerusalem, who wanted to reform Judaism and remove the barriers that separated Jews from Gentiles;[10] the persecution of opponents would have followed Jewish models of persecution such as that carried out by Jehu (2 Kings 9–10). V. Tcherikover did not follow the notion of a Reform Judaism, but stressed that the

9. Jonathan A. Goldstein, *I Maccabees*, AB 41 (Garden City, N.Y.: Doubleday, 1976) 104-21.
10. Elias Bickermann, *The God of the Maccabees: Studies on the Meaning and Origin of the Maccabean Revolt*, SJLA 32 (Leiden: Brill, 1979).

Hellenizers were an upper-class elite, whereas the common people were staunchly anti-Hellenistic.[11] He speculated that the people, led by the legal and spiritual leaders, the scribes, attempted to throw out both Jason and Menelaus; it was their pious revolt that led to Antiochus's persecution and the installation of a Syrian military colony, which set up its own worship in the Jerusalem Temple. Goldstein agreed with both Bickermann, in holding that the religion imposed was a kind of polytheistic Judaism, and Tcherikover, in that the religion was brought in by Antiochus's military colony in Jerusalem, a colony made up of Jewish soldiers who followed that kind of practice.[12] K. Bringmann stressed that, while Menelaus created the new religion in line with the Syrian military colony, Antiochus issued the orders primarily to consolidate his own power and to provide a stable source of revenue.[13]

I have emphasized that Antiochus IV, when he gained the Seleucid throne in 175 BCE, quickly knew that the Ptolemies were eager to renew hostilities to regain Coelesyria. The Ptolemies would have invaded in 180 BCE if Ptolemy V Epiphanes had not been assassinated. Once his widow had died in 176 BCE, the new government did little to conceal its hostile intentions and, in fact, finally attacked in late 170 or early 169 BCE. In this atmosphere of hostility on his southern border, Antiochus IV would have wished to have a region favorable to him and so acceded to Jason's request to rename Jerusalem. The gymnasium with its attached *ephebium* would have trained young men in military exercises for possible use as auxiliary forces. When Antiochus IV was rebuffed from Egypt by the Romans in 168 BCE, he may have felt even more strongly the need for a secure southern border and hence the imposition of paganism in Judea. However, I would not wish to hold that Antiochus was guided only by political concerns, as one cannot easily separate religion and politics in the ancient world. Rather, Antiochus IV may have heard stories that the Jews had a misanthropic attitude toward other nations, as stated even in the positive account of Hecataeus of Abdera, who wrote that "as a result of their expulsion from Egypt, [Moses] introduced an unsocial and intolerant mode of life."[14] Antiochus may have decided that this aspect of religious polity had to be suppressed. Why this institution of paganism required the burning of the books of the Law, the prohibition of circumcision, and the end of the daily offering in the Temple remains an enigma. Given the meager quality of our sources and their highly polemical stance, scholars will continue to debate and put forward explanations.

The Sequel to the Revolt. The last event recorded in 1 and 2 Maccabees is the death of Simon Maccabeus in 135/34 BCE. It is hinted that he was succeeded by his son John Hyrcanus, who would rule from 135/34 to 104 BCE. After repulsing the attempted coup of his brother-in-law Ptolemy, John was forced to submit to Seleucid forces under Antiochus

11. V. Tcherikover, *Hellenistic Civilization and the Jews* (Philadelphia: Jewish Publication Society, 1961).

12. Jonathan A. Goldstein, *II Maccabees*, AB 41A (Garden City, N.Y.: Doubleday, 1983) 98-112.

13. K. Bringmann, *Hellenistische Reform und Religionsverfolgung in Judäa: Eine Untersuchung zur jüdisch-hellenistische Geschichte (175–163 v. Chr)* (Göttingen: Vandenhoeck and Ruprecht, 1983).

14. Diodorus Siculus 40.3.4.

VII Sidetes and to pay tribute. After Antiochus died in 129 BCE while campaigning against Parthia, the Seleucid throne remained weak, and John Hyrcanus seized the opportunities offered by this Syrian weakness. During the course of his thirty-year reign, the territory of Judea expanded enormously to the east, north, and south. Early in his career, John captured two fortified towns in Transjordan: Medeba and Samoga. Then he turned north and captured Shechem and Mount Gerizim; he also subdued the Samaritans and destroyed their temple. Then he marched south to Idumea and captured its two main cities, Adora and Marisa. Late in his reign, he conquered the Macedonian colony at Samaria and also captured Scythopolis. The details of how John accomplished this expansion are debated, in part because the dating of a document preserved by Josephus is disputed.[15] Does it belong early in John's reign at the time of Antiochus VII or later, during the reign of Antiochus IX? If later, then John Hyrcanus's forces are seen to be weak and unable to resist Seleucid attacks. We know that John Hyrcanus hired mercenaries, but how many and how effective a fighting force are unknown.[16] Could he have successfully controlled the area he is said to have conquered without some support from the native populations? Hyrcanus was certainly the strong man of the area, but how were the forcibly circumcised Idumeans so compliantly integrated into the Jewish way of life?[17] Although facing some internal opposition in his thirty-year reign,[18] Hyrcanus succeeded in forging a Jewish state such as had not existed from pre-exilic times. Josephus lavishly praises him and states that he was the only person to unite in himself the roles of ruler, priest, and prophet.

Hyrcanus's son, Aristobulus I, ruled for one year (104–103 BCE). He continued the policy of expansion and appropriated Galilee.[19] Aristobulus is said by Josephus to have transformed the government into a kingdom and to have put the diadem on his own head.[20] His successor, his brother Alexander Jannaeus (103–76 BCE), was continually embroiled in foreign and domestic wars. Josephus gives a list of the territory conquered by Alexander: northern Transjordan; most of the coastal cities as far north as Caesarea, Idumea, Samaria, and Galilee—a kingdom almost as large as Solomon's.[21] Such a major territorial expansion raises questions about the identity of those persons introduced into the new realm. Aristobulus is said to have forced inhabitants of Galilee who wished to remain in the country to be circumcised and to live according to the laws of the Jews.[22] During the expansion under Alexander Jannaeus, the city of Pella is said to have been razed because its inhabitants would not promise to accept and practice the ancestral customs of the Jews.[23] These statements raise the question of what being a "Jew" meant. Did it mean merely that the conquered cities were to be under the control of

15. Josephus *Antiquities of the Jews* 14.249-250.
16. See ibid., 13.249.
17. See ibid., 13.257-258; 15.253-256.
18. Josephus *The Jewish War* 1.67-68.
19. See Josephus *Antiquities of the Jews* 13.318-319.
20. Ibid., 13.301.
21. Ibid., 13.395-397.
22. Ibid., 13.318-319.
23. Ibid., 13.397.

Dates: BCE	Seleucid[1] Calendar	Events:	References: 1 Maccabees	2 Maccabees	Daniel
333–323		Conquests of Alexander the Great	1:1-9		7:7; 11:3-4
202		Antiochus III invades Coelesyria, begins Fifth Syrian War			
200		Antiochus III defeats Ptolemy V at Paneas			11:5
198		Antiochus III controls Coelesyria, including Judea; Jews allowed to live by their own law			
196		Onias III becomes high priest			
190		Roman army defeats Antiochus III at Magnesia			11:18
		Treaty of Apamea; Antiochus V taken as hostage to Rome			
187		Death of Antiochus III, succeeded by Seleucus IV			11:19
180		Ben Sira finishes his writings			
		Heliodorus's attempt to loot the Temple		3:1-40	11:20
		Simon schemes against Onias		4:1-6	
175	137	Death of Seleucus IV, accession of Antiochus IV	1:10-15	4:7	7:8, 23-25; 11:21
		Jason appointed high priest (Onias deposed)		4:7	9:26a; 11:22?
		Hellenization of Jerusalem begins		4:7-17	
172		Menelaus appointed high priest (Jason deposed)		4:23-50	
171/170		Sixth Syrian War between Antiochus IV and Ptolemy VI			
170/169		Antiochus IV invades Egypt	1:16-19		
169	143	Syrian attack on Jerusalem	1:20-28[2]	5:11-14	11:28
168		Antiochus IV's second invasion of Egypt;		5:1	11:29
		Roman ultimatum to withdraw obeyed;			11:30a
		Jason's coup attempt		5:5-10	
167	145	Second Syrian attack on Jerusalem:			9:26b; 11:30b
		Massacre by Apollonius	1:29-32	5:21-26	9:12-14?
		Construction of the citadel (Akra)	1:33-40		
		Enforced Hellenization by Antiochus IV	1:41-50		
		Judaism outlawed, Temple defiled	1:51-64	6:1-10	9:27; 11:31-35; 12:11
		Maccabean revolt in Modein	2:1-28		
		Slaughter of innocents on sabbath	2:29-38		
		Guerilla attacks led by Mattathias	2:39-48	6:11	
166	146	Death of Mattathias	2:49-70		
		Martyrdoms of Eleazar, seven brothers, and mother		6:12–7:42	
		Judas becomes leader of the revolt	3:1-9	8:1-8	
		Judas's early victories:	3:10-26	8:5	
		Apollonius defeated at Lebonah	3:10-12		
		Seron defeated at Beth-horon	3:13-26		
165	147	Antiochus IV's campaign to Persia	3:27-37		
		Victory over Seleucid armies led by Ptolemy, Nicanor, and Gorgias	3:38–4:25	8:8-29; 11:1-15	
164	148	Amnesty offer gained by Menelaus			
		First expedition of Lysias	4:28-35	11:1-15	
	148	Peace negotiations of Lysias and the role of the Romans		11:16-21, 34-38	
	149	Death of Antiochus IV, accession of Antiochus V Eupator (Lysias regent)[3]	6:1-17	9:1-29; 10:10-11	11:40-45
		Cleansing and rededication of the Temple	4:36-61	10:1-9	
		Restoration of ancestral customs by Antiochus V		11:22-26	

Dates: BCE	Seleucid[1] Calendar	Events:	1 Maccabees	2 Maccabees	Daniel
		Jewish defensive campaigns:			
		Idumea	5:3-5, 65a	10:14-23	
		Ammon	5:6-8		
		Gilead	5:9-13, 24-51	8:30-33; 10:24-38; 12:17-31	
		Galilee	5:14-23		
		Philistia	5:65b-68		
		Siege of the citadel by Judas	6:18-27		
162	150	Seleucid invasion led by Lysias:	6:28-63	13:1-26[4]	
		Execution of Menelaus		13:3-8	
		Battle near Modein		13:9-17	
		Siege of Beth-zur	6:28-31, 49-50	13:18-22	
		Battle at Beth-zechariah	6:32-47		
		Siege of Jerusalem	6:48-54		
		Peace made with Lysias	6:55-63	13:23-26	
161	151	Demetrius I ascends:	7:1-7	14:1-2	
		Lysias and Antiochus IV executed			
		First Seleucid campaign led by Bacchides:	7:8-25		
		Alcimus appointed high priest	7:9-18	14:3-10	
		Seleucid invasion led by Nicanor:	7:26-50	14:11–15:37	
		Defeated by Judas at Caphar-salama		End of 2 Maccabees	
		Defeated by Judas at Adasa			
		Judas's Treaty with Rome	8:1-32		
160	152	Second Seleucid campaign by Bacchides:	9:1-53		
		Death of Judas Maccabeus at Elasa	9:18		
		Jonathan appointed "ruler and leader"	9:28-31		
159	153	Death of Alcimus; no high priest appointed	9:54-57		
157		Third Seleucid campaign by Bacchides:	9:58-73		
		Siege of Bethbasi	9:62-69		
		Peace made with Jonathan	9:70-73		
152	160	Revolt of Alexander Balas (Epiphanes)	10:1-14		
		Jonathan appointed high priest	10:15-21		
		Demetrius makes overtures to Jonathan	10:22-47		
151		Alexander defeats Demetrius (who is slain)	10:48-50		
150	162	Alexander weds Cleopatra	10:51-66		
147	165	Demetrius II invades Seleucia	10:67-68		
		Jonathan defeats Apollonius at Jamnia	10:69-89		
145	167	Ptolemy VI of Egypt defeats Alexander Balas; Demetrius II made king	11:1-19		
		Jonathan's alliance with Demetrius II	11:20-38, 41-53		
		Trypho sets up Antiochus VI as king	11:39-40, 54-56		
		Jonathan's alliance with Antiochus VI	11:57–12:38		
		Trypho usurps the throne	12:39		
143		Jonathan slain by Trypho	12:40-53; 13:23 30		
		Simon becomes leader	13:1-22		
142	170	Simon's alliance with Demetrius II; Judean independence	13:31-42		
		Simon conquers Gazara	13:43-48		
141	171	Citadel in Jerusalem captured	13:49-53		
140	172	Demetrius II captured and imprisoned	14:1-3		
		Diplomacy with Rome and Sparta	14:16-24		
		Simon appointed high priest	14:25-49		
138	174	Antiochus VII grants rights to Simon	15:1-9		
		Antiochus VII defeats Trypho	15:10-14		
		Renewed ties with Rome	15:15-24		
		Campaign led by Cendebeus against Jews	15:37–16:10		
135/34	177	Simon and sons murdered by Ptolemy	16:11-17		
		John Hyrcanus becomes high priest	16:18-24		

1. Dates given in 1 or 2 Maccabees.
2. 1 Maccabees records this attack following Antiochus's first invasion of Egypt, 2 Maccabees following his second invasion.
3. 1 Maccabees places the death of Antiochus IV after the cleansing of the Temple.
4. Dated 149 (163 BCE) in 2 Maccabees.

the king of Judea? Or did it mean, as the requirement of circumcision suggests, that the conquered population was to be treated as resident aliens in the land, following the commands of Exod 12:48; 22:20; and throughout Deuteronomy? What was their status vis-à-vis the citizens of Judea? Who would determine that all the male inhabitants of every village were circumcised? The incorporation of so many towns with different cultural traditions would have sparked a debate over what it meant to be a Jew—a native-born citizen of Judea, or one who was circumcised and followed the requirements of the resident alien, or someone who was circumcised and followed all the Torah?

THE ETHICS OF VIOLENCE

War dominates these books. They include stories of incredible courage under torture, as in the stories of Eleazar and the mother who encouraged her seven sons to die rather than transgress the Mosaic Law (2 Macc 6:18–7:42). There are stories of great daring, as in the story of another Eleazar who attempted to attack and kill the king and so end the battle. Eleazar fought through the ranks of the opposing army and killed an elephant on which he thought the king was riding, even though he knew that it would mean his own death, sacrificing his own life for those of his comrades and his nation (1 Macc 6:43-46). The story of Razis (2 Macc 14:37-46) shows a man ready to die rather than be captured, a mentality that was much admired in the ancient world. As Euripides the Greek playwright said, "Not death is evil, but a shameful death."[24] There are stories of night raids and tactical maneuvers, the stuff of which thrilling movies are made.

But woven into these accounts is a much more disquieting thread, for we find stories in which whole towns are razed. Throughout the accounts of the battles against neighboring cities in Gilead runs the refrain "and killed every male by the edge of the sword" (1 Macc 5:28 NRSV; see also 1 Macc 5:35, 51). Cities are burned to the ground. In one grisly scene, the army of Judas as well as the men, women, and children they are bringing back to Judea walk over the bodies of their slain enemies (1 Macc 5:51). In another scene, a lake near a town seems to be running over with the blood of those slain by the Maccabean forces (2 Macc 12:13-16). The delight in the destruction of human life seems almost palpable.

These stories imitate those found in the book of Judges. In trying to understand the ethics of violence in the books of the Maccabees, the analysis that Susan Niditch has made of the war accounts in the Hebrew Scriptures is very informative.[25] Niditch categorizes some of the narratives of the destruction of whole cities, in particular the killing of human beings, as narratives that portray the Israelites as instruments of God's justice, requiting the sins and misdeeds of their opponents. We see just such an attitude in the books of the Maccabees, as the Gentiles are consistently depicted as attempting to destroy the

24. Euripides *Fragments,* as quoted by Epictetus *Discourses* 2.1.
25. S. Niditch, *War in the Hebrew Bible: A Study of the Ethics of Violence* (New York: Oxford, 1993).

Maccabean forces without provocation (1 Macc 5:1; 2 Macc 12:2). Such an attitude also lies behind the ethnic cleansing that Simon pursues as he forces the inhabitants of Gazara and Beth-zur to leave; in the case of Gazara, he purifies the city (1 Macc 13:43-47; 11:65-66). The campaigns are also seen as purifying God's land of idol worship.

There are other instances in the books of Maccabees that fit Niditch's category of the ideology of expediency, an ideology in which force is used to instill terror. When the citizens of Antioch rebel against King Demetrius, Jonathan brutally suppresses the uprising as his troops fan out through the city and kill about one hundred thousand persons (1 Macc 11:41-51). Here Jonathan is portrayed as using brutal tactics to stop the revolt quickly. His tactics succeed, and he wins great renown.

For those who have been reared in the just-war tradition, which justifies waging war only as a last resort and prohibits attacking innocent civilians and annihilating defeated enemies, these stories do not provide an example that we would wish to follow. The books of the Maccabees are replete with judgments on their opponents as barbarous, godless, and sinful. There is no attempt to see the opponents as fellow human beings. War and the defeat of the enemy are glorified. In reading these stories, then, we have to realize that they tell us a great deal, not about how we ought to behave, but about what kind of group produced them. As Niditch states, "the more stable a group or person is, the surer they are of their identity, the less likely they are to be warlike, and the less rigid and totalistic their war ideologies are likely to be."[26] We can begin to understand that the communities out of which these books came felt themselves to be under attack and knew that their existence depended on building up their own self-esteem by denigrating their opponents. When we read these books, then, we can empathize with the protagonists in their struggles and seek to understand their point of view, but without sympathizing with their war practices and their demonization of their enemies. What reading these books should do is strengthen our commitment to explore ways to implement policies that embody the perspective of just-war theory. We should not be anesthetized by these stories of slaughter, but resolve that war and violence should be the last resort to settle conflicts, and that conflict will never make us forget that our enemies are human. If wars and conflicts result from insecurity and a sense of injustice, we must work to bring social justice and fair treatment to all nations and peoples. We must strive to bolster the self-image of all.

The books of 1 and 2 Maccabees also force readers to confront the problem of self-defense versus pacificism, particularly in the narrative of Jews who, despite attempting to live their lives in solitude, are hunted down and killed (1 Macc 2:29-41). Within this narrative, the right to defend oneself and one's country is strikingly affirmed. What we have to remember in reading these books is that there were no constraints on the emperor's will. If he wanted to, he could order the execution of all who opposed his will. The non-violent techniques used by Gandhi in India and by Martin Luther King, Jr., in the United States worked to a certain extent because both India under British rule and the United States are societies in

26. Ibid., 21.

which the rule of law constrains what leaders and police can do. Such techniques would have been of no avail in the Seleucid regime. To preserve one's own heritage and culture when threatened, one had to defend oneself. There was no escape. These books on war, therefore, while they affirm the right of a society to defend itself by recourse to war, do not address the question of the right of an individual in today's society to object conscientiously to serving in the military. That is another issue.

Finally, these books about war and events of the public arena reflect a male perspective. Women appear even less than in works like the *Iliad.* We learn that Jonathan and Simon had sons, but no mention is made of their wives. When women do appear in the stories, it is in the role of mother, as in the martyrdom stories (1 Macc 1:60; 2 Macc 6:10; 7), or as an image to describe social upheaval with the women leaving their houses and being seen in the streets (2 Macc 3:19-21). These are very male-dominated works.

THE DATING OF EVENTS

How to harmonize the dates given in the books of Maccabees has long puzzled commentators. Chronology in the study of Judaism is always complicated by the fact that the lunar-solar calendar was never perfect, being off by about ten days. Moreover, when trying to chart the events recounted in 1 and 2 Maccabees, scholars have been faced with inconsistencies between the two books (e.g., while 1 Macc 6:20 dates Lysias's second expedition to 150 of the Seleucid era, 2 Macc 13:1 dates it to 149 of the Seleucid era). Further confusion sets in when we realize that there were two systems for calculating the dates of the Seleucid era, which was held to begin from the conquest of Babylonia by Seleucus I. One system started the year following the Macedonian calendar, which began in the autumn, and so year 1 of the Seleucid Macedonian system would correspond to the time of autumn 312 to autumn 311 BCE. The second system, following the Babylonian calendar, started the year in spring, and so year 1 of the Seleucid Babylonian system would be from spring 311 to spring 310 BCE. The author of 1 Maccabees uses the Jewish names of the months (1:54; 4:52; 7:43, 49; 14:27; 16:14) and places the Festival of Booths in the seventh month (10:21), presuming a system beginning in spring. However, he dates the death of Antiochus IV to the year 149 of the Seleucid era (6:16), whereas the Babylonian cuneiform tablets, which also use a calendar that begins in spring, date Antiochus's death in 148 of the Seleucid era. Scholars have outlined three solutions to keep all the dates in balance and maintain the basic reliability of the sources:

(1) There is one system of dating in 1 Maccabees that begins in autumn 312.[27] According to this chronology, the suppression of Jewish worship would have begun in 168 BCE, and the Temple would have been purified in December 165 BCE. One problem for this solution is found at 10:21, where the Feast of Booths is said to occur in Tishri, the seventh month, presupposing a calendar beginning in spring.

(2) There are two systems of dating in 1 Maccabees, one for internal Jewish events, like

27. K. Bringmann, *Hellenistische Reform und Religionsverfolgung in Judäa,* 15-40; J. VanderKam, "Hanukkah: Its Timing and Significance According to 1 and 2 Maccabees," *JSP* (1987) 23-40.

festivals, that begins, like the Seleucid Babylonian system, in spring 311 BCE, and one for external events, such as the dates for Seleucid expeditions, that is based on the Seleucid Macedonian system, which began in autumn 312 BCE.[28] According to this chronology, Antiochus's persecution would have begun in 167 BCE, and the Temple would have been purified in December 164 BCE.

(3) There are two systems of dating in 1 Maccabees, as in theory 2, except that the calendar for dating internal Jewish events would have begun in spring 312 BCE.[29] According to this system, the suppression of Jewish worship would be dated to 168 BCE and the purification of the Temple to 165 BCE.

Deciding upon one from among these theories is exceedingly complex. Bickermann's theory, theory 2, is the one most widely accepted and the one followed in this commentary. Most scholars hold that the author of the epitome in 2 Maccabees followed the Seleucid Macedonian system.

STYLE, WORLDVIEW, AND DATE

First Maccabees opens with a prologue that speaks of Alexander the Great and his exploits (1 Macc 1:1-10), but the narrative covers events from sometime after the accession of Antiochus IV Epiphanes in 175 BCE until the death of Simon Maccabeus in 135/34 BCE. Furthermore, the book is structured around the Hasmonean family. After a description of the apostasy of some from Judaism and the subsequent persecution when Antiochus tries to force all peoples to abandon their native customs (1:41), the narrative focuses on the patriarch Mattathias and his three sons—Judas, Jonathan, and Simon—as they lead the fight against those who wish to do away with their ancestral religion.

Style. Although 1 Maccabees gives the appearance of a straightforward narrative, it is not so straightforward as it seems. The author intersperses various documents into the narrative to provide the proper aura of documentation required to foster belief in the historical correctness of the account. (The authenticity of some of these documents has been disputed. See the Overview of 1 Macc 8:1-32 and Commentary on 1 Macc 10:22-45; 12:1-23 for details.) Yet this is a narrative interspersed with traditional poetic passages and whose syntax imitates that of narrative sections of the Hebrew Scriptures. It is, then, a narrative that consciously aims at incorporating its story into the tradition of the Hebrew Scriptures. It is not a retelling of Hebrew Scriptures as, for example, the pseudepigraphic book of *Jubilees,* which recounts the primeval history of humanity and the history of God's chosen people up to the time of Moses, or as the *Temple Scroll* from Qumran,[30] which restates much of the legislation from Exodus, Leviticus, and Deuteronomy. Rather, 1 Maccabees perceives the events it tells as another reenactment of the events of the Hebrew Scriptures. This is seen in the way the author views the execution of the Hasideans in

---

28. E. Bickermann, *The God of the Maccabees,* 155-58.
29. L. Grabbe, "Maccabean Chronology: 167–164 or 168–165 BCE?" *JBL* 110 (1991) 59-74.
30. 11QTemple.

7:16 as being in accordance with the words of Ps 79:2-3—that is, the author sees the words of the psalm actualized in the events of his own day. This view of present-day events reflecting the Scriptures can be compared to the way the Qumran covenanters and the authors of the Gospels interpret the psalms and the prophets as talking about events in their own history. The author has not written a simple presentation of facts, but has woven a highly textured narrative.

That the syntax of 1 Maccabees reflects the narrative sections of the Hebrew Scriptures can be seen in the opening sentence, which begins as so many Hebrew narratives (e.g., Joshua, Judges, Ruth, 2 Samuel) begin and is then followed by a string of clauses all connected by "and." In addition, the Greek of 1 Maccabees is filled with Semitisms much like those in the LXX. There are also places in the text where one can understand what is going on if one presupposes that an original Hebrew text has been misunderstood or mistranslated (e.g., 9:2; possibly 3:37; and the enigmatic transliteration at 14:27). All this has led scholars to posit that 1 Maccabees was originally written in Hebrew and that our present text is a translation, while the original Hebrew text is missing. The Greek translator follows closely the translation style of other portions of the Hebrew Scriptures, so that one can often reconstruct what the original Hebrew text would have looked like. As the discoveries at Qumran have shown, writings in Hebrew were plentiful at this time, and so a writing in Hebrew should not surprise us.

The author also at times shows the inner connections of incidents by inserting literary linkages. For example, at 1 Macc 3:37, the author states that Antiochus IV was going through the upper provinces and then repeats the phrase at 6:1, thus binding Antiochus into the whole first series of actions and successes of the Hasmoneans. The same technique of intercalation is used to set the alliance of Jonathan with Rome between two attacks by commanders of Demetrius (11:63; 12:24). The author also carefully places in the narrative the documents that show the growing prestige and power of the Hasmoneans.

Even though the original text of 1 Maccabees was probably written in Hebrew, one should be aware of what a careful job the Greek translator has done. He shows considerable awareness of the Greek translation of the Hebrew Scriptures, but also is able to show connections in his choice of Greek phrasing and sections. For example, the use of the same root for the verb and the noun at 2:42 and 7:12 ("there united [συνήχθησαν *synēchthēsan*] . . . a company [συναγωγή *synagōgē*]"; "there appeared [ἐπισυνήχθησαν *episynēchthēsan*] . . . a group [*synagōgē*]") and the repetition of the same phrases throughout 7:1-25 bind the section together (see also 9:58-73). It is, for the most part, a thoughtful translation.

Worldview. That the author of the books of Maccabees wrote in Hebrew in imitation of the style of the Hebrew Scriptures was no accident. The author consciously set out to show how the Maccabean revolt closely followed ancestral traditions. Particularly noteworthy is the way the author has spliced the narrative with poetic compositions that echo traditional psalms of lament and rejoicing. Just as the author of the Gospel of Luke used hymns in the opening chapters of his work to give his Gospel a traditional flavoring, so too did this earlier author. The author also models his heroes on biblical antecedents. Mattathias's opening act of rebellion explicitly echoes that of Phinehas in Num 25:6-13. Mattathias, as he lies dying, gives his testament, as Jacob had done (Genesis 49), and commissions his sons just as Moses had commissioned Joshua (Deut 31:7-23; Josh 1:6-9) and David had commissioned Solomon (1 Chr 22:13; 28:20). The Maccabeans are also related to the former judges of Israel. The most explicit reference to these judges is at 9:73, where Jonathan is said to "judge" Israel; Jonathan's election to succeed Judas also shows the influence of Jephthah's election (Judg 10:18; 11:6-11). The structural principle of the book of Judges is that when the Israelites do what is wrong in the eyes of the Lord, they are punished, but when they cry out, the Lord raises up someone to deliver them, and the land is at peace while that judge lives (Judg 2:16-18; 3:7-11). That same principle is operative in 1 Maccabees. Judas turns away God's anger (3:8) as he becomes the savior of Israel (9:21), under whom the land is at peace—if only for a while (7:50). When the land is in great distress after Judas's death, Jonathan is chosen to lead the people, and he succeeds so well that the sword no longer hangs over Israel (9:73). When destruction again threatens after Jonathan's capture, Simon takes command, and soon the country is at peace again (14:4). The ideology of the Judges also appears in the way towns are put under the ban and whole towns and their inhabitants are destroyed (5:28, 35, 44). Judas acts toward Ephron in accordance with the regulations of Deut 20:10-15 (1 Macc 5:45-51), and Simon's ethnic cleansing of Gazara/Gezer (1 Macc 13:47-48) attempts to follow the command not to have any covenant with the inhabitants of the land and to tear down their altars (Deut 7:1-6; Judg 2:1-2). The author of 1 Maccabees also frequently uses the term "foreigners" (ἀλλόφυλοι *allophyloi*) to describe the Gentiles (3:41; 4:12, 22, 26, 30; 5:15, 66, 68; 11:68, 74), a term often found in Judges and 1 Samuel.

It is also important to note how the Jewish enemies of the Hasmoneans are characterized: They are the lawless (1 Macc 2:44; 3:5-6; 7:5; 9:23, 58, 69), the workers of lawlessness (1 Macc 3:6; 9:23), sinners (1 Macc 2:44, 48, 62), and impious persons (1 Macc 3:8; 6:21; 7:5-9; 9:73). More significantly, they are "renegades" (παράνομοι *paranomoi*; see 1 Macc 1:11; 10:61; 11:21), a term used to describe those who would lead Israel astray (Deut 13:12-15), to characterize those who attacked and raped the Levite's concubine and so started a civil war (Judg 19:22), and to describe the followers of Jeroboam, who brought on the split of David's kingdom (2 Chr 13:7). The author of 1 Maccabees uses only these labels to describe the Jewish opponents of the Hasmoneans—with one exception, Alcimus. Except for the high priest Alcimus, the enemies' names would be forever forgotten if not for 2 Maccabees. The author thus uses labels effectively to emphasize that the Hasmonean party is right and its enemies wrong, to set up a strong us/them dichotomy.

The author of 1 Maccabees thus frames his narrative in biblical imagery. His heroes have been raised up by God to defend the people, just like the judges before them. The Hasmoneans are skillfully portrayed as upholding the traditional ancestral faith while their enemies are destroyers of the social fabric, those who bring in foreign ways. The opposition to foreigners extends to the Seleucids and to the Ptolemies, but not to the Romans. The

Romans are portrayed as trustworthy and loyal, whereas the Ptolemies and the Seleucids are consistently untrustworthy. This may evidence a proper lack of knowledge of the Roman way of handling affairs, but it also shows how the author is willing to view in a favorable light anyone who does not attempt to wrest away Israel's independence, for this is the aim of the author—to celebrate the gaining of independence—and this is what he means by proclaiming the Hasmoneans the family through whom deliverance was given to Israel (5:62; cf. 13:41-42).

Date. It is not known who wrote 1 Maccabees, when or where it was written, or when it was translated into Greek. Since Josephus seems to base his account on the Greek version, it must have been translated sometime before the end of the first century CE. The fact that it was written in Hebrew, as well as the accuracy of some of its geographical data, suggests that it was composed in Israel. Its style of writing suggests someone well-versed in the traditional Scriptures of Israel. The erudite echoing of the Hebrew Scriptures suggests someone from the scribal class, or someone educated by a teacher like Sirach.

Scholars have consistently used two factors in determining a date for 1 Maccabees: its pro-Hasmonean stance and its concluding sentence, which refers to the annals of the high priesthood of John Hyrcanus (who ruled until 104 BCE). Bar-Kochva has suggested that the author, by the vividness and accuracy of his descriptions of the battles of Judas, must have been an eyewitness to the events and was, therefore, writing early in the reign of John Hyrancus.[31] However, a vivacious writing style and accurate geography can be achieved by others besides eyewitnesses. Most scholars have combined the above two factors to suggest a date late in Hyrcanus's reign or just after his death. S. Schwartz has argued, however, that the pro-Hasmonean stance of the author and his keeping of foreigners at arm's length are in conflict with what we know happened during the lengthy reign of Hyrcanus and his successors, when whole groups were incorporated into the area controlled by Hyrcanus. (For details on the reign of John Hyrcanus, see the section "Historical Background," above.) Schwartz therefore proposed a date early in Hyrcanus's reign, before such assimilation began. Schwartz's point is well taken, but the conclusion to the book still sounds as it if were written after the death of John Hyrcanus; thus Schwartz proposes that it was added later.[32] I would suggest that one should look more carefully at the assumption that the work is pro-Hasmonean. It clearly approves the gaining of independence, describes the Hasmonean founders as biblical heroes, and claims that they were the family through whom deliverance came to Israel. It is striking, however, that the author portrays Simon as having died while drunk at a banquet, which need not have been mentioned. There is also contrast between the utopian picture of Roman government in chapter 8 and the one-man rule imposed by Simon (14:41-45). Therefore, 1 Maccabees may be seen as a critique of the developments that had taken place under Hyrcanus and his successors, opposing the assimilation of non-Jews (which Schwartz points to), and the increasingly regal life-style of the Hasmoneans. Thus it is plausible to date 1 Maccabees to shortly after the death of John Hyrcanus.

31. Bezalel Bar-Kochva, *Judas Maccabeus* (Cambridge: Cambridge University Press, 1988).
32. S. Schwartz, "Israel and the Nations Roundabout: 1 Maccabees and the Hasmonean Expansion," *Journal of Jewish Studies* 42 (1991) 16-30.

FIRST AND SECOND MACCABEES IN JEWISH AND CHRISTIAN TRADITION

The events recounted in 1 and 2 Maccabees were, and are, celebrated in the Jewish community with the Feast of Hanukkah. In that festival, God's miraculous deliverance of the covenant people from their oppressors is remembered. The message of Hanukkah has been meaningful to a community that has sought to preserve its traditional beliefs and customs in an often hostile environment. Such a community could always look back and recall how the Seleucid kings had tried to stamp out Judaism, but were prevented from doing so by God's working through the Maccabees. In this way, the community could be reassured that it would never be deserted by God. Particularly symbolic of that deliverance is a story found not in 1 and 2 Maccabees, but in the later rabbinic tradition. This story recounts how the Jews, when they retook the city of Jerusalem and were preparing to reinstate proper worship in the Temple, found only one jar of oil for the temple lamps, which would have lasted but a single day. Miraculously, that one jar kept the lamps lighted for eight days. Enemies had tried to snuff out Judaism, but it had survived. This tradition also extolled the martyrdom accounts, particularly that of the mother and her seven sons (2 Maccabees 7), which was expanded by naming the mother Hannah and by the addition of more grisly torments for the martyrs. Much later, the heroism of the Maccabees in resisting oppression and defending their own culture and religion was especially meaningful in the nineteenth-century Zionist movement.

Early Christian communities also found the message of 1 and 2 Maccabees congenial. Not only could this record of events be used to validate the book of Daniel as prophetic and true, but also the story of a community faithful to God's commandments in the face of an idolatrous oppressor resonated with the life situation of many Christians in the Roman Empire. The books were particularly recommended for their martyrdom accounts. The feast of the Maccabean martyrs was celebrated at Antioch in Syria; at Carthage in North Africa, center of a Christian community determined not to be polluted by the contagion of the outside world, the martyrs were extolled. The great Christian thinker of the third century CE, Origen of Alexandria, wrote to exhort Christians to undergo martyrdom: "What dead person could be more deserving of praise than he who of his own choice elected to die for his religion? This is what Eleazar did, who welcoming death with honor rather than life with ignominy, went up to the rack to die of his free choice" (see 2 Macc 6:19).[33] The characters in 1 and 2 Maccabees still provide examples of endurance to what one believes in, even if that endurance means death.

33. Origen *To the Martyrs* 22.

BIBLIOGRAPHY

Bar-Kochva, Bezalel. *Judas Maccabeus.* Cambridge: Cambridge University Press, 1988. A fascinating analysis of the battles in 1 Maccabees by a military historian of the Hellenistic period. Essential reading for these battle scenes.

Bickerman, Elias. *The God of the Maccabees: Studies on the Meaning and Origin of the Maccabean Revolt.* SJLA 32. Leiden: Brill, 1979. A ground-breaking work, first published in German in 1937, on the background of the persecution.

Bringmann, Klaus. *Hellenistische Reform und Religionsverfolgung in Judäa: Eine Untersuchung zur jüdisch-hellenistische Geshichte (175–163 v. Chr).* Göttingen: Vandenhoeck and Ruprecht, 1983. Bringmann stresses the political and economic factors at play in the intervention by Antiochus IV.

Doran, Robert. *Temple Propaganda: The Purpose and Character of 2 Maccabees.* Washington, D.C.: Catholic Biblical Association, 1981. This work places 2 Maccabees in its literary and historiographical setting.

Geller, M. J. "New Information on Antiochus IV from Babylonian Astronomical Diaries," *BSO(A)S* 54 (1991) 1-4. Provides in handy format the diary entries pertinent to the Maccabean revolt.

Goldstein, Jonathan A. *1 Maccabees.* AB 41. Garden City, N.Y.: Doubleday, 1976.

———. *2 Maccabees.* AB 41A. Garden City, N.Y.: Doubleday, 1983. An erudite commentary whose comments on particular verses are worth consulting, but which is marred at times by overarching theories.

Grabbe, Lester L. *Judaism from Cyrus to Hadrian.* 2 vols. Minneapolis: Fortress, 1992. A survey of all the relevant materials; includes a bibliography.

Harrington, Daniel J. *The Maccabean Revolt: Anatomy of a Biblical Revolution.* Wilmington, Del.: Michael Glazier, 1988.

Momigliani, Arnaldo. "The Second Book of Maccabees," *CP* 70 (1975) 81-88. Makes the festivals in 2 Maccabees central to its explanation.

Mørkholm, Otto. *Antiochus IV of Syria.* Copenhagen: Gyldendalske Boghandel, 1966. Important for reconstructing a more balanced view of Antiochus IV.

Schürer, Emil. *The History of the Jewish People in the Age of Jesus Christ (175 BC–AD 135).* 3 vols. Revised by G. Vermes, F. Millar, M. Goodman. Edinburgh: Clark, 1973–87. An excellent reference book.

Sievers, Joseph. *The Hasmoneans and Their Supporters: From Mattathias to the Death of John Hyrcanus.* Atlanta: Scholars Press, 1991. A sensible attempt to reconstruct the history of this turbulent period.

Tcherikover, Victor. *Hellenistic Civilization and the Jews.* Philadelphia: Jewish Publication Society, 1961. First published in Hebrew in 1931 and later revised, this book contains a wealth of information. It and Bickerman's book still guide most scholarly treatments.

OUTLINE OF 1 MACCABEES

I. 1 Maccabees 1:1–2:70, Mattathias

    A. 1:1-64, The Persecution
        1:1-10, Introductory Scene
        1:11-15, The Apostasy

1 MACCABEES 1:1–2:70

MATTATHIAS

1 MACCABEES 1:1-64, THE PERSECUTION

1 Maccabees 1:1-10, Introductory Scene

NAB

1 After Alexander the Macedonian, Philip's son, who came from the land of Kittim, had defeated Darius, king of the Persians and Medes, he became king in his place, having first ruled in Greece. ² He fought many campaigns, captured fortresses, and put kings to death. ³ He advanced to the ends of the earth, gathering plunder from many nations; the earth fell silent before him, and his heart became proud and arrogant. ⁴ He collected a very strong army and conquered provinces, nations, and rulers, and they became his tributaries. ⁵ But after all this he took to his bed, realizing that he was going to die. ⁶ He therefore summoned his officers, the nobles, who had been brought up with him from his youth, to divide his kingdom among them while he was still alive. ⁷ Alexander had reigned twelve years when he died.

⁸ So his officers took over his kingdom, each in his own territory, ⁹ and after his death they all put on royal crowns, and so did their sons after them for many years, causing much distress over the earth.

¹⁰ There sprang from these a sinful offshoot, Antiochus Epiphanes, son of King Antiochus, once a hostage at Rome. He became king in the year one hundred and thirty-seven of the kingdom of the Greeks.

The basic text used here is the Greek as found in W. Kappler, *Maccabaeorum liber I* (Göttingen: Vandenhoeck & Ruprecht, 1936).
1, 2: Omit tēs gēs; so LXX^{A,MSS}; dittog from v 3.

NRSV

1 After Alexander son of Philip, the Macedonian, who came from the land of Kittim, had defeated[a] King Darius of the Persians and the Medes, he succeeded him as king. (He had previously become king of Greece.) ²He fought many battles, conquered strongholds, and put to death the kings of the earth. ³He advanced to the ends of the earth, and plundered many nations. When the earth became quiet before him, he was exalted, and his heart was lifted up. ⁴He gathered a very strong army and ruled over countries, nations, and princes, and they became tributary to him.

5After this he fell sick and perceived that he was dying. ⁶So he summoned his most honored officers, who had been brought up with him from youth, and divided his kingdom among them while he was still alive. ⁷And after Alexander had reigned twelve years, he died.

8Then his officers began to rule, each in his own place. ⁹They all put on crowns after his death, and so did their descendants after them for many years; and they caused many evils on the earth.

10From them came forth a sinful root, Antiochus Epiphanes, son of King Antiochus; he had been a hostage in Rome. He began to reign in the one hundred thirty-seventh year of the kingdom of the Greeks.[b]

a Gk adds *and he defeated*   b 175 B.C.

COMMENTARY

The opening verses of 1 Maccabees locate the events the author is going to narrate within the larger framework of history. The passage is in some sense one long sentence, since the ten verses are a series of main clauses all connected by the particle "and" (καί *kai*). The end of the passage is indicated by the repetition of the phrase "came out of"; just as Alexander came out, so also Antiochus came out. This grammatical style reflects Hebrew syntax, and the opening words of 1 Maccabees ("and [he] came out" [καὶ ἐγένετο *kai egeneto*]) are the same as those found at the beginning of Joshua, Judges, Ruth, and 2 Samuel in the LXX. The work is thus squarely placed in the Jewish historiographical tradition.

1:1. Alexander began his journey of conquest from Pella, the capital of Macedonia, in the spring of 334 BCE. The author has Alexander leave the land of the Kittim, a word used variously in the Old Testament. At Gen 10:4 and 1 Chr 1:7, the Kittim are the descendants of Yavan and thus Japheth. Jeremiah 2:10 locates the sites of the Kittim as one extreme of the world, while Ezek 27:6 has them as trading partners of Tyre. In these two passages the Kittim are often identified with Cyprus; Josephus similarly identifies the Kittim as being from Kition, a Phoenician city on the island of Cyprus.[34] Balaam predicts in his fourth oracle that ships shall come from Kittim and oppress Asshur and Eber (Num 24:24). Here again the Kittim are a maritime force, and Eber might be interpreted as the Hebrews (see Gen 10:21-24). Perhaps deriving from this use, Kittim became a term in later apocalyptic texts to designate a far-off people who will wage war. At Dan 11:30, the Kittim are the Romans, who shame Antiochus IV, and in *Jub.* 24:28-29 they are an ultimate enemy who will confront the accursed Philistines. In the *Pesher on Habakkuk* from Qumran,[35] the Kittim have dominion over Israel and appear to be the Romans; in the *War Scroll* from Qumran, they are the last world power to oppress God's people.[36] Elsewhere in 1 Maccabees, Perseus, king of Mace-

donia, is described as being the king of the Kittim (1 Macc 8:5). Thus, although the author of 1 Maccabees calls the Macedonians "Kittim," one may suggest that this term is no neutral geographical indicator but that even in 1 Maccabees the term carries the overtones of an oppressive world power.

Alexander's success was enormous. He first defeated a Persian army led by satraps at Granicus in northwest Asia Minor (in spring 334 BCE), then one led by King Darius himself at Issus in southeast Asia Minor in autumn 333. From there he moved to conquer the Syrian coast (332) and occupy Egypt in the winter of 332/331 BCE, before returning to defeat decisively King Darius at Gaugmela in northern Iraq in late 331. Darius fled to the Median capital of Ecbatana while Alexander occupied Babylon and Persia. Darius hastily retreated further, but was finally arrested and killed by his own satraps. The last Achaemenid was dead, and Alexander was master of Asia. But he was still not content; he pushed on through present-day northern Iran and Afghanistan to Pakistan and the Punjab valley before turning back; he died at Babylon on June 10, 323 BCE. While he may not have conquered the ends of the earth—his western ambitions remained unfulfilled—Alexander had united a formidable empire, inaugurating the Hellenistic world.

1:2-4. At v. 2, Alexander is said to have slain "the kings of the earth." In fact, Alexander was usually not cruel to those he defeated, except in the case of the usurper Bessus. The author of Maccabees describes the normal behavior of victors (cf. 2 Kgs 25:6-7). After Alexander's conquests, the land is said to be at peace, a phrase found frequently in 1 Maccabees (7:50; 9:57; 11:38, 52; 14:4). It is used here to describe the absence of war. The phrase is used in the Hebrew Scriptures as well, particularly in the book of Judges. After the Israelites had repented of worshiping other gods, the Lord sent them deliverers in the persons of Othniel and Ehud, who defeated the enemies and left the land at "rest" (see Judg 3:11, 30), and under the good king Asa, the land was said to have been "at rest" (2 Chr 14:1). The phrase as used here, however, seems to fit better

---

34. Josephus *Antiquities of the Jews* 1.28.
35. See 1 QpHab 2:12–6:12.
36. See 1QM 1:2; 15:2A.

the context of its use at Zech 1:11, where the angels of the Lord who have patrolled the earth report that the whole earth is at peace, a peace that is oppressive to Israel.

The greatness of Alexander's success is said to have "lifted up" his heart. In the Hebrew Bible, this phrase symbolizes arrogance, as when King Jehoash of Judah, who became too cocksure, went to battle against the king of Israel and was defeated (2 Kgs 14:10; 2 Chr 25:19). Obadiah predicts doom to Edom, whose proud heart has "lifted it up" (Obad 3). Daniel so characterizes the king of the south, Ptolemy IV, after his early victory over Antiochus III, whereas Antiochus ultimately prevails over Egypt (Dan 11:12). Thus the phrase "his heart was lifted up" is a hint that something bad is going to happen to Alexander.

All the countries must pay tribute. The phrase again echoes the LXX (Josh 19:48a; Judg 1:28-31, 33, 35) and encapsulates the loss of independence of all the various conquered peoples.

1:5-9. At the height of his power, Alexander is suddenly struck down. Many stories circulated as to the cause of Alexander's death. Some claim that Alexander was poisoned.[37] Others relate that he died after drinking too strong unmixed wine.[38] Plutarch and Arrian report that his death came after a feverish sickness and discount other suggestions.[39] The author of 1 Maccabees does not detail how Alexander died, but the suddenness of the event at the height of his power suggests divine judgment (cf. the oracle of Isaiah against Babylon [Isa 14:5-21] or that of Obadiah against Edom [Obad 1-4]). The death of Antiochus IV was also seen as divine punishment. The same language ("to fall sick" [ἔπεσεν ἐπὶ τὴν κοίτην καὶ ἔγνω ὅτι ἀποθνῄσκει *epesen epi ten koiten kai egnō hoti apothnēskei*] lit., "to fall on his bed," "perceive/realize that he was dying") is used to describe Antiochus IV when he hears the news of the victorious Judas Maccabeus (1 Macc 6:8-9).

First Maccabees depicts Alexander as dividing his kingdom among his followers. This is similar to what is found in the late work of Ps-Callisthenes, who portrays Alexander, on his deathbed, writing a will.[40] Diodorus reports that when asked to whom he left the kingdom, Alexander said, "To the strongest."[41] By contrast, the author of 1 Maccabees links the rulers of his own day with that proud ruler. He describes an orderly transition of power, whereas, in fact, there were many long, hard-fought campaigns among rival leaders. Only in 306 BCE did Antigonus and his son Demetrius, who then ruled jointly over much of Greece, Asia Minor, and Syria, assume the diadem, and they were followed in this a year later by Ptolemy and Seleucus.

1:10. "A sinful root" comes forth from these kings. By using the term "root" (ῥίζα *rhiza*), the author intimates the beginning of future troubles. (The same image is used at Isa 14:29, when King Ahaz of Judea dies.) Antiochus IV Epiphanes was the youngest son of Antiochus III, "the Great." After the Romans decisively defeated Antiochus III at the battle of Magnesia (190 BCE), this youngest son was handed over to the Romans as a hostage. Antiochus III was succeeded in 187 BCE by his older son, Seleucus IV. Around 176, the Romans exchanged Antiochus for Seleucus IV's son Demetrius. On Seleucus IV's death in 175 BCE, Antiochus seized the opportunity to gain control of the kingdom in place of his brother's son. "The one hundred thirty-seventh year" of the Seleucid kingdom would be 176–175 BCE; a cuneiform king-list from Babylon presents Antiochus IV as the immediate successor of Seleucus IV in September 175. The reference to Antiochus as a hostage in Rome intimates that there are other powers in the world besides the successors of Alexander and looks forward to the favorable description of the Romans in chapter 8.

37. Arrian *Anabasis* 7.27.
38. Diodorus Siculus 17.117.
39. Plutarch *Alexander* 75-77; Arrian *Anabasis* 7.25-26.

40. Pseudo-Callisthenes *Life of Alexander* 3:33. This account of the life of Alexander was written in part to glorify the foresight of Alexander and to promote the city of Alexandria.
41. Diodorus Siculus 17.117.

1 Maccabees 1:11-15, The Apostasy

NAB	NRSV
[11] In those days there appeared in Israel men who were breakers of the law, and they seduced many people, saying: "Let us go and make an alliance with the Gentiles all around us; since we separated from them, many evils have come upon us." [12] The proposal was agreeable; [13] some from among the people promptly went to the king, and he authorized them to introduce the way of living of the Gentiles. [14] Thereupon they built a gymnasium in Jerusalem according to the Gentile custom. [15] They covered over the mark of their circumcision and abandoned the holy covenant; they allied themselves with the Gentiles and sold themselves to wrongdoing.	[11]In those days certain renegades came out from Israel and misled many, saying, "Let us go and make a covenant with the Gentiles around us, for since we separated from them many disasters have come upon us." [12]This proposal pleased them, [13]and some of the people eagerly went to the king, who authorized them to observe the ordinances of the Gentiles. [14]So they built a gymnasium in Jerusalem, according to Gentile custom, [15]and removed the marks of circumcision, and abandoned the holy covenant. They joined with the Gentiles and sold themselves to do evil.

COMMENTARY

1:11-13. After the prologue, with its emphasis on the arrogance and sudden death of Alexander the Great, the detailed narrative opens with an account of apostasy. These verses again are filled with biblical allusions. "Certain renegades" echoes Deut 13:12-15, which describes certain renegades who lead astray the inhabitants of a town by saying, "Let us go and worship other gods" (Deut 13:13 NRSV). The civil war against the Benjaminites started when "certain renegades" attacked and raped the concubine of a Levite (Judg 19:22). The division between the northern kingdom of Israel and the southern kingdom of Judah started because "certain renegades" encouraged Jeroboam to defy Solomon's son Rehoboam (2 Chr 13:7). The theme of being like the nations is also linked to wrongdoing in the Bible (Exod 34:15; Deut 7:2-4; 1 Sam 8:4-8). Second Kings 17:7-18 gives a long reflection on why the northern kingdom was captured by Assyria, the primary reason being that the Israelites followed the ways of the nations round about them. At 1 Macc 1:15, the Judeans "abandoned the holy covenant" (διαθήκης ἁγίας *diathēkēs hagias*; a verb found with this meaning at Deut 13:10, 13; 32:15; Josh 22:18-19, 23, 29) and join with the Gentiles (lit., "yoke themselves" [ἐζευγίσθησαν *ezeugisthēsan*]; see Num 25:3; Ps 106:28, where Israel yoked itself to Baal of Peor). They "sold themselves

to do evil" (ἐπράθησαν τοῦ ποιῆσαι τὸ πονηρόν *eprathēsan tou poiēsai to ponēron*) as the Israelites of the northern kingdom had done before them (2 Kgs 17:17) and also the wicked King Ahab (1 Kgs 21:20, 25).

1:14-15. The renegades built a gymnasium. Second Maccabees 4:7-17 fills out the details of this undertaking. The educational, social, and physical exercise complex that composed the gymnasium was the hallmark of a Greek city, and so building one in Jerusalem signaled a rejection of traditional Jewish customs. They "removed the marks of circumcision," an operation first described at some length by a Latin author, Celsus.[42] The apostle Paul also suggests that such an operation was possible: "Was anyone at the time of his call already circumcised? Let him not seek to remove the marks of circumcision" (1 Cor 7:18 NRSV). Since the Greek ideal of beauty viewed circumcision as a mutilation, and since the custom was for athletes in Greek games to compete in the nude, some strove to remove the marks of circumcision. It is unlikely, however, that all the Jews, including priests, who exercised in the Jerusalem gymnasium underwent this operation. Other contemporary descriptions of the apostasy

42. Celsus *On Medicine* 7.25.

(Dan 11:32; 2 Macc 4:7-17; *Jub.* 30; *1 Enoch* 90:6-9) make no mention of it. The literal translation, "made foreskins for themselves," shows that the author of 1 Maccabees has wrought a trenchant metaphor to describe his opponents as complete apostates, acting against the covenantal regulation: "This is my covenant, which you shall keep, between me and you and your offspring after you: Every male among you shall be circumcised. . . . Any uncircumcised male who is not circumcised in the flesh of his foreskin shall be cut off from his people; he has broken my covenant" (Gen 17:10, 14 NRSV).

1 Maccabees 1:16-28, The Visitation of Antiochus IV

NAB

[16]When his kingdom seemed secure, Antiochus proposed to become king of Egypt, so as to rule over both kingdoms. [17] He invaded Egypt with a strong force, with chariots and elephants, and with a large fleet, [18] to make war on Ptolemy, king of Egypt. Ptolemy was frightened at his presence and fled, leaving many casualties. [19] The fortified cities in the land of Egypt were captured, and Antiochus plundered the land of Egypt.

[20] After Antiochus had defeated Egypt in the year one hundred and forty-three, he returned and went up to Israel and to Jerusalem with a strong force. [21] He insolently invaded the sanctuary and took away the golden altar, the lampstand for the light with all its fixtures, [22] the offering table, the cups and the bowls, the golden censers, the curtain, the crowns, and the golden ornament on the façade of the temple. He stripped off everything, [23] and took away the gold and silver and the precious vessels; he also took all the hidden treasures he could find. [24] Taking all this, he went back to his own country, after he had spoken with great arrogance and shed much blood.

[25] And there was great mourning for Israel, in
    every place where they dwelt,
[26] and the rulers and the elders groaned.
    Virgins and young men languished,
      and the beauty of the women was disfigured.
[27] Every bridegroom took up lamentation,
    she who sat in the bridal chamber
      mourned,
[28] And the land was shaken on account of its
    inhabitants,
    and all the house of Jacob was covered with
    shame.

NRSV

[16]When Antiochus saw that his kingdom was established, he determined to become king of the land of Egypt, in order that he might reign over both kingdoms. [17]So he invaded Egypt with a strong force, with chariots and elephants and cavalry and with a large fleet. [18]He engaged King Ptolemy of Egypt in battle, and Ptolemy turned and fled before him, and many were wounded and fell. [19]They captured the fortified cities in the land of Egypt, and he plundered the land of Egypt.

[20]After subduing Egypt, Antiochus returned in the one hundred forty-third year.[a] He went up against Israel and came to Jerusalem with a strong force. [21]He arrogantly entered the sanctuary and took the golden altar, the lampstand for the light, and all its utensils. [22]He took also the table for the bread of the Presence, the cups for drink offerings, the bowls, the golden censers, the curtain, the crowns, and the gold decoration on the front of the temple; he stripped it all off. [23]He took the silver and the gold, and the costly vessels; he took also the hidden treasures that he found. [24]Taking them all, he went into his own land.

    He shed much blood,
      and spoke with great arrogance.
[25] Israel mourned deeply in every community,
[26] rulers and elders groaned,
    young women and young men became faint,
      the beauty of the women faded.
[27] Every bridegroom took up the lament;
    she who sat in the bridal chamber was
      mourning.
[28] Even the land trembled for its inhabitants,
    and all the house of Jacob was clothed with
      shame.

[a] 169 B.C.

COMMENTARY

1:16-19. The war between the Seleucid and the Ptolemaic empires began when the guardians of Ptolemy VI Philometor moved to invade Seleucid territory and recapture Syria and Palestine (late 170 or early 169 BCE). Antiochus IV reacted swiftly and won a decisive victory near Pelusium, on the Mediterranean coast near the border of Egypt. Antiochus seems to have tried to install his sister's son, Ptolemy VI, in power, with himself as Ptolemy's regent. The author of 1 Maccabees describes Antiochus IV, however, as being as ambitious as Alexander the Great to extend his empire and to gain plunder.

1:20-24a. No reason is given by the author for this sudden violent attack on Jerusalem in the autumn of 169 BCE. No doubt the author wishes it to be seen as the result of the Judeans' forsaking of the covenant, although he also accuses Antiochus IV of arrogance. In 2 Macc 5:1-26, the attack of Antiochus is placed after his second invasion of Egypt and is seen as being caused by factional fighting within Jerusalem, which Antiochus understands as a rebellion against his authority. The Babylonian astronomical diaries recount that in November/December 169 Antiochus IV confiscated funds from the Esagil (temple) in Babylon. Polybius also writes that Antiochus sacrilegiously pillaged the temples.[43] The desecration of the Jerusalem Temple must be seen, therefore, as part of a policy of Antiochus IV to gain additional monies. The actions as described in 1 Maccabees, however, do seem to go beyond simply taking funds from a temple.

Antiochus IV "entered the sanctuary"—i.e., the inner courts of the Temple, not the holy of holies. According to 3 Macc 1:9-12, a king was allowed to enter the sanctuary, but not the holy of holies. Antiochus took away the altar of incense (see Exod 30:1-10), the lamp stand (see Exod 25:31-40), the table of showbread (see Exod 25:23-30), the incense dishes, and the libation bowls (see Exod 25:29). The curtain referred to seems to be the curtain before the holy of holies, where the ark of the covenant had stood (Exod 26:31-35). Thus, while Antiochus IV is not said to have himself entered the holy of holies,[44] taking the curtain would have been seen as an act of desecration (cf. Mark 15:38, where, at the death of Jesus, the curtain is torn from top to bottom). "The crowns" refers to decorations on the Temple, as at 4:57, and perhaps to the clasps of gold on the curtains, as at Exod 36:13. "The hidden treasures" perhaps was money left in the Temple on deposit. Antiochus IV, known to Greek historians such as Polybius as having sought to restore his fortunes through robbing various temples, did a thorough job at Jerusalem.

1:24b-28. The narrator here breaks into poetic format, with parallelism between the constituent parts—for example, "shed much blood"/"spoke with arrogance"; "land"/"house of Jacob." Just as traditional imagery was often used in the narrative, so also this poem, in traditional lament format, draws on traditional style. One might compare it with the way the author of the Gospel of Luke uses hymns in the opening chapters to create an atmosphere of traditional piety. The author of 1 Maccabees, by the use of such a traditional format, thus shows respect for tradition and arouses sympathy for the presentation among hearers or readers.

---

44. Josephus insists that Pompey the Great was the first foreigner to enter the holy of holies. See *Antiquities of the Jews* 14.71-72; *The Jewish War* 1.152.

43. Polybius 30.26.9.

1 Maccabees 1:29-40, The Occupation of Jerusalem

NAB	NRSV
29 Two years later, the king sent the Mysian commander to the cities of Judah, and he came	29Two years later the king sent to the cities of Judah a chief collector of tribute, and he came to Jerusalem with a large force. 30Deceitfully he spoke peaceable words to them, and they believed him; but he suddenly fell upon the city, dealt it
1, 29: (*apesteilen ho basileus*) *ton mysarkēn* (*eis tas poleis Iouda*); so 2 Mc 5, 24; Greek translator mistook Hebrew *rō'š hămûšîm* for *rō'š hammissîm* (=*arkonta phorologias*, "chief collector of tribute").	

NAB

to Jerusalem with a strong force. ³⁰ He spoke to them deceitfully in peaceful terms, and won their trust. Then he attacked the city suddenly, in a great onslaught, and destroyed many of the people in Israel. ³¹ He plundered the city and set fire to it, demolished its houses and its surrounding walls, ³² took captive the women and children, and seized the cattle. ³³ Then they built up the City of David with a high, massive wall and strong towers, and it became their citadel. ³⁴ There they installed a sinful race, perverse men, who fortified themselves inside it, ³⁵ storing up weapons and provisions, and depositing there the plunder they had collected from Jerusalem. And they became a great threat.

³⁶ The citadel became an ambush against the
sanctuary,
and a wicked adversary to Israel at all
times.
³⁷ And they shed innocent blood around the
sanctuary;
they defiled the sanctuary.
³⁸ Because of them the inhabitants of Jerusalem
fled away,
and she became the abode of strangers.
She became a stranger to her own offspring,
and her children forsook her.
³⁹ Her sanctuary was as desolate as a
wilderness;
her feasts were turned into mourning,
Her sabbaths to shame,
her honor to contempt.
⁴⁰ Her dishonor was as great as her glory had
been,

NRSV

a severe blow, and destroyed many people of Israel. ³¹He plundered the city, burned it with fire, and tore down its houses and its surrounding walls. ³²They took captive the women and children, and seized the livestock. ³³Then they fortified the city of David with a great strong wall and strong towers, and it became their citadel. ³⁴They stationed there a sinful people, men who were renegades. These strengthened their position; ³⁵they stored up arms and food, and collecting the spoils of Jerusalem they stored them there, and became a great menace,

³⁶ for the citadel*ᵃ* became an ambush against the
sanctuary,
an evil adversary of Israel at all times.
³⁷ On every side of the sanctuary they shed
innocent blood;
they even defiled the sanctuary.
³⁸ Because of them the residents of Jerusalem
fled;
she became a dwelling of strangers;
she became strange to her offspring,
and her children forsook her.
³⁹ Her sanctuary became desolate like a desert;
her feasts were turned into mourning,
her sabbaths into a reproach,
her honor into contempt.
⁴⁰ Her dishonor now grew as great as her glory;
her exaltation was turned into mourning.

ᵃ Gk *it*

COMMENTARY

Antiochus IV had been able to conquer Egypt so successfully in his first campaign in part because Rome was engaged in fighting Perseus, king of Macedon, who was defeated on June 22, 168 BCE. When the opposition to Antiochus IV in Egypt proclaimed Ptolemy VIII Euergetes II and Cleopatra to be joint rulers, Antiochus's protégé joined with them. So Antiochus once again laid siege to Alexandria. But this time the Romans intervened,

and the Roman ambassador C. Popillius Laenas came before Antiochus to deliver an ultimatum for him to withdraw all his forces from Egypt and Cyprus. Antiochus had to submit to the superior power of Rome and ignominiously return to Syria. An Egyptian priest, Hor, had recorded a dream he had that Antiochus and his army would leave Egypt by July 30, 168 BCE, and his dream was confirmed by events.

1:29-31. The expression "a chief collector of tribute" is usually interpreted in the light of 2 Macc 5:24, where this figure is identified as Apollonius, captain of the Mysians. The Greek translator might easily have misread the Hebrew "chief collector of tribute" (שׂר המוסים *śar hammûsîm*) as "captain of the Mysians" (שׂר המיסים *śar hammîssîm*).

The sending of a force to strengthen the city of Jerusalem would seem to fit in with the strategic necessity of defending Antiochus's southern border with Egypt. This strengthening of Jerusalem, however, is described as oppression by the author of 1 Maccabees. As the text now stands, Antiochus's intent is to collect tribute, just as Alexander had taken tribute (1:4), and an official comes with a large force, just as Antiochus IV had invaded Egypt before plundering it (1:17, 19). The enemies of the Jews are described as using peaceable words to work deceit (this negative description of enemies is found elsewhere in 1 Maccabees; e.g., 7:10, 15, 27-30; 10:46; 11:2-3). The author of 2 Maccabees intensifies the heinousness of the deed by having the invasion take place on a sabbath. Many inhabitants are slaughtered, and the city is looted, burned, and left defenseless by the destruction of its walls (cf. Jer 51:58).

1:32. There is a sudden change from the third-person singular to the third-person plural. The third-person plural can be used in place of the passive tense, or it may be that the large force mentioned in v. 29 is considered not collectively now but as being made up of individuals. (This latter phenomenon is seen in 2 Kgs 25:5 LXX: "the army [sing.] of the Chaldeans pursued the king, and they overtook him.")

The women, children, and livestock are groups distinct from the fighting males. When the tribes of Reuben and Gad wished to stay in the land of Jazer and Gilead and not cross over the Jordan, Moses allowed them to leave their little ones, their wives, their flocks, and all their livestock behind, but all men armed for war had to cross over to help conquer the promised land (Num 32:25-27; cf. Deut 3:19). Exodus 20:17 and Deut 5:21 classify women and livestock as possessions. Taking away the women and children ensures that the city will not reproduce itself and survive; taking the livestock removes the means of sustenance. The combination of women, children, and livestock, therefore, represents the life of a town.

1:33. According to 2 Macc 5:5, this whole operation was motivated by an attempt by the former high priest Jason to gain control of Jerusalem after hearing a false rumor that Antiochus IV had died. Although the destruction of its walls would strip the city of its defenses, in order to provide some security "the city of David" was fortified and became the occupying force's citadel. There was a citadel in Jerusalem in Persian times, which seems to have been located north of the temple area (Neh 7:2), and this citadel had apparently been destroyed prior to the time of Antiochus IV. According to 2 Macc 4:12, there was, indeed, a citadel in Jerusalem before the persecution of Antiochus IV. This citadel seems to have been within the city of David (2 Macc 5:5), since Jonathan later built a barrier between the citadel and the city (1 Macc 12:36). In 1 Macc 1:33, "citadel" parallels the fortified "city of David," and so it should perhaps be taken in the more general sense of "stronghold," rather than referring to the citadel within the city.

1:34-35. In the citadel was stationed "a sinful race, perverse men." The two phrases are in apposition. "Perverse men" refers to 1:11, with the biblical resonance of renegades and apostates from Judaism. "A sinful nation" is found at Isa 1:4 in a bitter reproach against a rebellious Israel:

> Ah, sinful nation,
>   people laden with iniquity,
> offspring who do evil,
>   children who deal corruptly,
> who have forsaken the LORD,
>   who have despised the Holy One of Israel,
>   who are utterly estranged! (NRSV)

Those living in the citadel, therefore, would seem to be Jews who did not rebel against Antiochus IV. They are characterized as a "snare," using a term by which Joshua had described the nations left in the land (Josh 23:13), and with which Hosea (5:1) and Jeremiah (5:26; cf. Ps 119:110) had described sinners within Israel.

1:36-40. The author again breaks into a poetic lament, wherein the verses evidence strong parallelism. The language echoes Lam 5:2: "Our inheritance has been turned over to strangers, our homes to aliens," as well as the oracle against Jerusalem uttered by Amos: "I will turn your feasts into mourning,/ and all your songs into lamentation" (Amos 8:10 NRSV; cf. Lam 5:15-18). It stresses the gap between those who now dwell in Jerusalem and true Israelites, connects these

events with the destruction of Jerusalem in 587 BCE, and depicts the author as the true upholder of Israelite tradition.

1 Maccabees 1:41-64, The Imposition of Paganism

NAB

⁴¹ Then the king wrote to his whole kingdom that all should be one people, ⁴² each abandoning his particular customs. All the Gentiles conformed to the command of the king, ⁴³ and many Israelites were in favor of his religion; they sacrificed to idols and profaned the sabbath.

⁴⁴ The king sent messengers with letters to Jerusalem and to the cities of Judah, ordering them to follow customs foreign to their land: ⁴⁵ to prohibit holocausts, sacrifices, and libations in the sanctuary, to profane the sabbaths and feast days, ⁴⁶ to desecrate the sanctuary and the sacred ministers, to build pagan altars and temples and shrines, ⁴⁷ to sacrifice swine and unclean animals, ⁴⁸ to leave their sons uncircumcised, and to let themselves be defiled with every kind of impurity and abomination, ⁴⁹ so that they might forget the law and change all their observances. ⁵⁰ Whoever refused to act according to the command of the king should be put to death.

⁵¹ Such were the orders he published throughout his kingdom. He appointed inspectors over all the people, and he ordered the cities of Judah to offer sacrifices, each city in turn. ⁵² Many of the people, those who abandoned the law, joined them and committed evil in the land. ⁵³ Israel was driven into hiding, wherever places of refuge could be found.

⁵⁴ On the fifteenth day of the month Chislev, in the year one hundred and forty-five, the king erected the horrible abomination upon the altar of holocausts, and in the surrounding cities of Judah they built pagan altars. ⁵⁵ They also burnt incense at the doors of houses and in the streets. ⁵⁶ Any scrolls of the law which they found they tore up and burnt. ⁵⁷ Whoever was found with a scroll of the covenant, and whoever observed the law, was condemned to death by royal decree. ⁵⁸ So they used their power against Israel, against

NRSV

⁴¹Then the king wrote to his whole kingdom that all should be one people, ⁴²and that all should give up their particular customs. ⁴³All the Gentiles accepted the command of the king. Many even from Israel gladly adopted his religion; they sacrificed to idols and profaned the sabbath. ⁴⁴And the king sent letters by messengers to Jerusalem and the towns of Judah; he directed them to follow customs strange to the land, ⁴⁵to forbid burnt offerings and sacrifices and drink offerings in the sanctuary, to profane sabbaths and festivals, ⁴⁶to defile the sanctuary and the priests, ⁴⁷to build altars and sacred precincts and shrines for idols, to sacrifice swine and other unclean animals, ⁴⁸and to leave their sons uncircumcised. They were to make themselves abominable by everything unclean and profane, ⁴⁹so that they would forget the law and change all the ordinances. ⁵⁰He added,ᵃ "And whoever does not obey the command of the king shall die."

⁵¹In such words he wrote to his whole kingdom. He appointed inspectors over all the people and commanded the towns of Judah to offer sacrifice, town by town. ⁵²Many of the people, everyone who forsook the law, joined them, and they did evil in the land; ⁵³they drove Israel into hiding in every place of refuge they had.

⁵⁴Now on the fifteenth day of Chislev, in the one hundred forty-fifth year,ᵇ they erected a desolating sacrilege on the altar of burnt offering. They also built altars in the surrounding towns of Judah, ⁵⁵and offered incense at the doors of the houses and in the streets. ⁵⁶The books of the law that they found they tore to pieces and burned with fire. ⁵⁷Anyone found possessing the book of the covenant, or anyone who adhered to the law, was condemned to death by decree of the king. ⁵⁸They kept using violence against Israel, against those

ᵃ Gk lacks *He added*   ᵇ 167 B.C.

NAB

those who were caught, each month, in the cities. [59] On the twenty-fifth day of each month they sacrificed on the altar erected over the altar of holocausts. [60] Women who had had their children circumcised were put to death, in keeping with the decree, [61] with the babies hung from their necks; their families also and those who had circumcised them were killed. [62] But many in Israel were determined and resolved in their hearts not to eat anything unclean; [63] they preferred to die rather than to be defiled with unclean food or to profane the holy covenant; and they did die. Terrible affliction was upon Israel.

NRSV

who were found month after month in the towns. [59] On the twenty-fifth day of the month they offered sacrifice on the altar that was on top of the altar of burnt offering. [60] According to the decree, they put to death the women who had their children circumcised, [61] and their families and those who circumcised them; and they hung the infants from their mothers' necks.

[62] But many in Israel stood firm and were resolved in their hearts not to eat unclean food. [63] They chose to die rather than to be defiled by food or to profane the holy covenant; and they did die. [64] Very great wrath came upon Israel.

COMMENTARY

The author now describes the measures undertaken by Antiochus IV to impose control over Judea, measures that meant the abolition of the observance of the law in Judea. The author of 1 Maccabees states that these measures were part of a general plan to homogenize all the peoples (v. 41). Antiochus's effort may be seen as hubris against God, with perhaps an allusion to Gen 11:6, where God sees that humans are one people and one language and are conspiring to act against heaven, and so scatters them. The same kind of homogenizing effort is also found in Daniel 3, where Nebuchadnezzar is said to have set up a golden statue and to have commanded all "peoples, nations, and languages" to worship it. Antiochus IV was the first Seleucid king to use the title "god manifest" (Ἐπιφανής θεός *Epiphanēs theos*); from his depictions on coins, he appears to have had a particular devotion to Olympian Zeus, rather than to Apollo, as had been customary among the Seleucids. Daniel 11:37-38 speaks of Antiochus's honoring the god of fortresses (Zeus Olympios) rather than "the gods of his ancestors, or to the one beloved by women" (NRSV; Tammuz); it is also suggested that Antiochus considered himself greater than these other gods. However, there is no evidence that Antiochus IV attempted to stamp out the customs and traditional religious observances of other nations; in fact, he seems to have promoted local customs. Such a move by Antiochus IV to abolish the religious practice of a people would have been deeply at odds with the usual practice of the time, whereby ancient states respected the existing gods and cultic practices of differing localities.

Nevertheless, Antiochus is consistently portrayed as instigating the abolition of Jewish observances. Both biblical and extra-biblical sources indicate that the attack on Jewish observances emanated from Antiochus himself. At Dan 11:30-31, he is said to "take action against the holy covenant" (NRSV) and to send forces to profane the Temple. The first-century BCE historian Diodorus Siculus relates how Antiochus VII Sidetes was told by his friends:

> Antiochus, called Epiphanes, on defeating the Jews had entered the innermost sanctuary of the god's temple, where it was lawful for the priest alone to enter. He found there a marble statue of a heavily bearded man seated on an ass, with a book in his hands. He supposed it to be an image of Moses, the founder of Jerusalem and organizer of the nation. Moses was the person who had ordained for the Jews their misanthropic and lawless customs. Since Epiphanes was shocked by such hatred directed against all mankind, he had set himself to break down their traditional practices.[45]

This incredibly untrue depiction evidences some of the anti-Jewish nonsense circulating about the Jews. Later, in a letter to Lysias, his guardian,

45. Diodorus Siculus 34/35.1.3-4.

Antiochus V reversed this prohibition against Judaism (see 2 Macc 11:23-25), which he attributes to his father.

The letters of the king (v. 44) complete the agenda of the renegades mentioned in v. 11—to follow after other customs (1:11; cf. Deut 13:2). The text makes clear that this meant the abandonment of all that was distinctive of Judaism— Jewish festivals, daily offerings, sabbaths, circumcision, kosher laws—but it is not clear exactly what replaced them. Elias Bickermann suggests that the religion was a Hellenistic reform of Judaism, whereby the worship of the God of the Jews was replaced by the cult of Ba'al Shamen ("Lord of the Heavens"); the desolating sacrilege in 1 Macc 1:54 is a translation of the term at Dan 11:31 (השקוץ משומם *haššiqqûs̆ mĕs̆ômēm*), which is a pun on the word *Shamen*.[46] Jonathan Goldstein suggests that the divine triad of Zeus, Athena, and Dionysus was worshiped.[47] However, these suggestions remain highly speculative. What we do know is that (1) the Temple was dedicated to Zeus Olympios (2 Macc 6:2); (2) unlawful sacrifices were made on the altar of burnt offering (1 Macc 1:59; 2 Macc 6:5); (3) other altars were placed in the cities of Judea (1 Macc 1:54) and in the agora of Jerusalem (2 Macc 10:2); (4) feasts of Dionysus were celebrated, as was the king's birthday (2 Macc 6:7); (5) pigs were sacrificed, as was frequently done in Greek religious practices. We do not know whether cultic statues were set up, although later writers make this claim.[48] The proliferation of altars and the various festivals suggest that, rather than the cult of one particular deity or trio of deities, what was established was the worship of various gods and goddesses.[49]

1:45. "Burnt offerings and sacrifices and drink offerings" refer to the burnt offerings, grain offerings, and drink offerings that were to be offered daily, on sabbaths, and on feast days (see Numbers 28–29). "To profane sabbaths" was to become guilty of death (Exod 31:12-17; cf. Neh 13:17-18; Ezek 20:13, 16).

1:46-49. The term "priests" (ἅγιοι *hagioi*) literally means "holy ones" (Latin manuscripts read "holy things"). What is being described is the elimination of the distinction between clean and unclean, which is so much a part of the Torah. The sanctuary is no longer the only holy place (Lev 17:1-9; Deut 12:2-14), the most holy place in Israel (Ezek 45:3), but there are to be other altars and other offering places, and the offering of swine and other unclean animals signifies the end of the kosher laws of Leviticus 11. The prohibition of circumcision made a Jewish male's body uncovenanted (Gen 17:11). Thus the distinguishing marks of the religious culture of Judea—sacred time, sacred space, sacred food, and sacred body—were eliminated (the language "to make themselves abominable" reflects the language of Lev 11:43-44; 20:25-26).

1:50. The change from indirect speech to direct speech heightens the sense of immediacy and impending threat. The Greek word for "command" (ῥῆμα *rhēma*) is frequently found in the Greek translation of the Bible for what God says in the Torah (e.g., Lev 17:2; Num 30:1 [LXX 30:2]; Deut 12:32 [LXX 13:1]; 25:58; 31:9).

1:51. The opening words of v. 41 are repeated. This verse further describes the way in which Antiochus's decree was to be implemented.

1:52-53. Many of the people are said to follow the king's order (v. 42) to forsake their ancestral tradition. At Dan 11:30, Antiochus is said to "pay heed to those who forsake the holy covenant" (NRSV; cf. Prov. 28:4: "Those who forsake the law praise the wicked, but those who keep the law struggle against them" [NRSV]). Just as the successors of Alexander caused many evils on the land (1:9), so also did those who now forsake the law.

Only those who resist the king's command deserve the name of "Israel." Where they fled is not specified, but more than 150 cave complexes have been discovered in the Judean foothills, southwest of Jerusalem. Hewn into the chalk rock, parts of these cave complexes are connected by low and narrow passages. The entrances to the various segments of the complex could be blocked and defended from the inside; there were water installations, areas for storage rooms, and means of providing ventilation. These complexes would have been fully operational at the time of the Jewish revolts against Rome in 66–70 and 132–135 CE, but they

46. Elias Bickermann, *The God of the Maccabees: Studies on the Meaning and Origin of the Maccabean Revolt,* SJLA 32 (Leiden: Brill, 1979) 61-75.
47. Jonathan Goldstein, *I Maccabees,* AB 41 (Garden City, N.Y.: Doubleday, 1976) 148-58.
48. See Jerome *Commentary on Daniel* 8:14-15; 11:31, citing Porphyry, a pagan philosopher and historian of the late third century CE.
49. F. Miller, "The Background to the Maccabean Revolution: Reflections on Martin Hengel's 'Judaism and Hellenism,' " *JJS* 29 (1978) 1-21.

were also in use, if not quite so elaborately, during the Hellenistic period. As Amos Kloner states, "The warrens appear to have been of local design and execution, and their integration within and around settlements points to their extensive use during the Hellenistic and Roman periods."[50] (The hiding places are also mentioned at 1 Macc 2:29-31.)

1:54-59. The fifteenth day of Chislev, the ninth month in the Jewish calendar, would be about the middle of December. The author of 2 Maccabees as well as the author of 1 Maccabees would date the removal of this sacrilege on the 25th day of Chislev (1 Macc 4:52, 54; 2 Macc 10:5). The author of 2 Maccabees follows the schema whereby punishment and reward fall on the same day, and so connects the profanation of the Temple with the feast of Antiochus's birthday (25 Chislev), rather than with the actual erection of the abomination of desolation. The book of Daniel speaks of the removal of the daily burnt offering (Dan 8:11) and the setting up of the desolating abomination (Dan 9:27; 11:31). The erection of altars throughout the towns of Judea and the burning of incense in the streets signify the ways in which all the community of Judea was to be involved in this transformation. Demosthenes says that one should fill the streets with the savor of sacrifice,[51] and a decree from Asia Minor in the late second century BCE speaks of both the official sacrifice and the household sacrifice to honor the goddess Artemis on her feast day.[52] One might compare the action of King Josiah against such practices (2 Kgs 23:4-20).

The word for "books" (βιβλία *biblia*) in v. 56 is the same word used for "letters" in v. 44. Perhaps the author suggests that the "books"—

that is, letters—of the king replace the "books" of the law. The burning of the book of the law might be compared to the cutting and burning of Jeremiah's scroll by King Jehoiakim (Jeremiah 36).

1:60-63. The author has chosen to highlight the execution of women here not only to show the cruelty of the persecutors, but also to symbolize the attempt to destroy the traditions of the Jews (cf. 2 Macc 6:10). Since it is through women that a people continues, the gruesome sight of babies and mothers executed together strongly signifies the stamping out of a people.

In v. 62, the language is that of war and siegecraft. Interestingly, the resistance of those who do not obey the king's command is signified by their not eating unclean food. The same concern occurs in the book of Daniel, where Daniel and his companions, captives in the service of Nebuchadnezzar, king of Babylon, refuse to eat the royal rations of food and wine so as not to defile themselves (Dan 1:8-16). When Antiochus IV defiles sacred spaces and sacred times, some Jews do not allow their "covenanted" bodies to be breached by ingesting unclean food. The result of both actions—the womens' actions to covenant their sons and the men's to not eat unclean food—is the same: death.

1:64. The time of wrath upon Israel is recognized by Mattathias (1 Macc 2:49) and is taken away by the actions of Judas Maccabeus (1 Macc 3:8). The author here follows a pattern whereby the sins of Israel bring on the wrath of God, but their repentance prompts God to send a deliverer. The pattern of sin/repentance/deliverance is strongly expressed in Judg 2:11-14; 3:7-10. The "wrath of the Lord" is also prominent in the accounts of the reasons for God's punishment and exile of Israel (2 Kgs 17:7-18) and Judah (2 Kgs 21:14-15; 22:16-17; 23:26-27).

50. Amos Kloner, "Underground Hiding Complexes from the Bar Kokhba War in the Judean Shephelah," *BA* 46 (1983) 219.

51. Demosthenes *Oration* 21.51; cf. Aristophanes *Birds* 1233.

52. *Sylloge Inscriptionum Graecarum*, ed. W. Dittenberger, 4 vols. (Leipzig: Hirzel, 1915–24) 2:695.

REFLECTIONS

Wars, with their attendant violence and oppression, are not merely about geographical boundaries. Perhaps even more, wars concern questions of cultural identity. We may never know exactly what prompted Antiochus IV to attempt to stamp out the ancestral religious traditions of Judea in 167 BCE. He may have wanted to eliminate any opposition in an area near the border with Egypt, or he may have been venting his anger at being humiliated by the Romans on an available target. Why these motives entailed systematic destruction of the religion of Judea is unclear. The author of 1 Maccabees has presented the conflict as a question of self-determination and does not mention the Roman setback to Antiochus IV in Egypt. Rather, Antiochus is portrayed as a powerful monarch who tries to impose his will on a much smaller nation. The Jews, who stood firm, are depicted as wishing to maintain their cultural traditions. Several issues arise as one ponders this narrative.

1. The question of minority rights immediately comes to mind as one reads the account of the oppression of the Jews under Antiochus. Within a large, multi-cultural nation, how are the rights and ethnicity of the minority to be respected and protected? The issue is exemplified particularly when one discusses religion in the public schools. If the holy days of the majority group are discussed in school by a teacher (e.g., Christian feasts, like Christmas), should the teacher not also discuss the holy days of other religions, like Judaism, Islam, and Hinduism? If prayer were to be allowed in public schools, should the prayers of all religious groups be said along with those of the religion of the majority? The issue becomes particularly acute when an element of a minority's religious practice seems to run counter to the majority culture. If peyote, a hallucinogenic drug, is sacred to Native American worship, can the majority culture decide the use of this substance should be prohibited because it is a drug? What if a religious group practices animal sacrifice? Should they be allowed to perform a sacrifice in public? How far does the majority need to go to respect minority rights?

2. The author of 1 Maccabees paints Antiochus IV as a hubristic propagandist for his own gods and so demonizes him. All war propaganda does the same. The Germans during World War I were called "pillaging, raping Huns." All communists became tarred with the slogan "Better dead than Red." Politicians regularly accuse their opponents of being "socialist" or, inversely, "fascist." Such a temptation to demonize and to ostracize opponents as "the other" is always present when conflict or disagreement arises, but it is a tendency that should be resisted. The rhetoric of violence, of estrangement, must be eschewed if common ground is to be found among all peoples. Successful diplomatic negotiations may, in fact, hinge on treating one's opponent with respect.

3. The author of 1 Maccabees skillfully uses language to portray the Maccabees as righteous upholders of traditional Jewish religion and contrasts their opponents as evil to draw boundaries around who is a "real" Jew. The members of any group will not always agree with each other on everything, but the rhetoric can quickly escalate into polarized language whereby one group hurls anathemas at the other. Are Sunni Muslims true Muslims, or are only Shiites true Muslims? Does one group have a monopoly on salvation? Can one Christian group agree to disagree with another without setting up barriers between them? When discussing such questions, we must not neglect to determine what are the social causes of division. Ecumenical dialogue almost requires as a prerequisite a social stability that brings with it the confidence to allow others to be different.

1 MACCABEES 2:1-70, THE CAREER OF MATTATHIAS

1 Maccabees 2:1-14, The Family of Mattathias

NAB	NRSV
2 In those days Mattathias, son of John, son of Simeon, a priest of the family of Joarib,	**2** In those days Mattathias son of John son of Simeon, a priest of the family of Joarib,

NAB

left Jerusalem and settled in Modein. ² He had five sons: John, who was called Gaddi; ³ Simon, who was called Thassi; ⁴ Judas, who was called Maccabeus; ⁵ Eleazar, who was called Avaran; and Jonathan, who was called Apphus. ⁶ When he saw the sacrileges that were being committed in Judah and in Jerusalem, ⁷ he said: "Woe is me! Why was I born to see the ruin of my people and the ruin of the holy city, and to sit idle while it is given into the hands of enemies, and the sanctuary into the hands of strangers?

⁸ "Her temple has become like a man disgraced,
⁹   her glorious ornaments have been carried off
        as spoils,
    Her infants have been murdered in her streets,
        her young men by the sword of the enemy.
¹⁰ What nation has not taken its share of her
        realm,
        and laid its hand on her possessions?
¹¹ All her adornment has been taken away.
        From being free, she has become a slave.
¹² We see our sanctuary and our beauty
        and our glory laid waste,
    And the Gentiles have defiled them!
¹³   Why are we still alive?"

¹⁴ Then Mattathias and his sons tore their garments, put on sackcloth, and mourned bitterly.

2, 7: (kai) kathisai (ekei): so LXX^{A, MSS}; Vet Lat^{MSS}.

NRSV

moved from Jerusalem and settled in Modein. ²He had five sons, John surnamed Gaddi, ³Simon called Thassi, ⁴Judas called Maccabeus, ⁵Eleazar called Avaran, and Jonathan called Apphus. ⁶He saw the blasphemies being committed in Judah and Jerusalem, ⁷and said,

    "Alas! Why was I born to see this,
        the ruin of my people, the ruin of the holy
          city,
    and to live there when it was given over to
        the enemy,
    the sanctuary given over to aliens?
⁸ Her temple has become like a person without
        honor;ᵃ
⁹   her glorious vessels have been carried into
        exile.
    Her infants have been killed in her streets,
        her youths by the sword of the foe.
¹⁰ What nation has not inherited her palacesᵇ
        and has not seized her spoils?
¹¹ All her adornment has been taken away;
        no longer free, she has become a slave.
¹² And see, our holy place, our beauty,
        and our glory have been laid waste;
    the Gentiles have profaned them.
¹³   Why should we live any longer?"

14Then Mattathias and his sons tore their clothes, put on sackcloth, and mourned greatly.

ᵃ Meaning of Gk uncertain   ᵇ Other ancient authorities read *has not had a part in her kingdom*

COMMENTARY

2:1-5. The vague time reference "in those days" does not allow one to specify when Mattathias decided enough was enough—before the plundering of Jerusalem by Apollonius (1 Macc 1:29) or after? Before the decrees of the king (1:41) or after? Before the erection of the abomination of desolation (1 Macc 1:54) or after? Modein, seven miles east of Lydda and seventeen miles northwest of Jerusalem, lay in the mountains. It is described later as the ancestral home of Mattathias and his family (1 Macc 2:70; 9:19). This makes all the more intriguing the notice that Mattathias resided in Jerusalem and that he was

not there only on priestly duty for an appointed cycle (cf. Zechariah, the father of John the Baptist, in Luke 1:8). What does such information tell us about Mattathias's social status, wealth, and relationship to those other priests, who participated in the gymnasium at Jerusalem (2 Macc 4:14-15)? No data are available to answer these questions, but one can safely assume that Mattathias was not an ignorant country priest. According to 1 Chr 24:7, the house of Jehoiarib, whom the writer of 1 Maccabees names Joarib (v. 1), had the first of the twenty-four priestly courses in the temple service. The surnames of the five sons of Jehoiarib/Joarib remain enigmatic; "Maccabeus" most likely means "Hammerer."

2:6-13. Mattathias breaks into a lament similar to the laments found in Mic 7:1 and Jer 4:31. The language also echoes that of Lam 2:11; 3:48; 4:10, as well as that of the personal lament of Jer 15:10-21. In place of the phrase "to live there," many Greek manuscripts read "and they sat there," where the sense would be of someone sitting among ruins (cf. Lam 1:1; Hag 1:4).

Since it is unusual to compare a building to a man, some manuscripts read "people" instead of "temple." Cities are frequently personified and said to be ashamed (e.g., Nah 3:1-17; Jer 50:11-12). The language of honor and shame was also used in connection with the destruction of Jerusalem in 587 BCE (Jer 51:51). The parallel line in v. 9a speaks of the taking away of the Temple's glorious accoutrements. One might see the image of a properly outfitted man versus a man in hand-me-down clothing (cf. Lam 4:1-2, 7-8).

The poetic parallelism of 9bc is clear: infants//youths; killed//by the sword. The pride of a city is its children. A city renews itself through the children of its citizens; without them a city dies. The image of fainting children and slain youth is poignantly expressed in the laments over the destruction of Jerusalem in 587 BCE:

> The young and the old are lying
> on the ground in the streets;
> my young women and my young men
> have fallen by the sword;
> in the day of your anger you have killed them,
> slaughtering without mercy.
> (Lam 2:21 NRSV; cf. 2:11)

The author continues using traditional images of war, looting, and slavery in vv. 9-11.

Like earlier writers, the author of this lament mourns over the wasted beauty of the city (v. 12). "Our holy and beautiful house,/ where our ancestors praised you,/ has been burned by fire,/ and all our pleasant places have become ruins" (Isa 64:11 NRSV; cf. Lam 1:10; Dan 11:31-32). From the first-person singular of v. 7, the lament moves to the first-person plural as Mattathias's lament becomes that of the faithful Israelite.

2:14. The donning of sackcloth is another traditional ritual act of mourning. Jacob put on sackcloth when he thought that his son Joseph had been killed by wild animals (Gen 37:34), and David ordered his men to put on sackcloth when he heard of Abner's death (2 Sam 3:31). The author of 1 Maccabees, by this concatenation of traditional images, metaphors, and ritual action, paints Mattathias as a staunch upholder of ancestral custom.

1 Maccabees 2:15-28, The Actions at Modein

NAB

15 The officers of the king in charge of enforcing the apostasy came to the city of Modein to organize the sacrifices. 16 Many of Israel joined them, but Mattathias and his sons gathered in a group apart. 17 Then the officers of the king addressed Mattathias: "You are a leader, an honorable and great man in this city, supported by sons and kinsmen. 18 Come now, be the first to obey the king's command, as all the Gentiles and the men of Judah and those who are left in Jerusalem have done. Then you and your sons shall be numbered among the King's Friends, and shall be enriched with silver and gold and many gifts." 19 But Mattathias answered in a loud voice: "Although all the Gentiles in the king's realm obey him, so

NRSV

15The king's officers who were enforcing the apostasy came to the town of Modein to make them offer sacrifice. 16Many from Israel came to them; and Mattathias and his sons were assembled. 17Then the king's officers spoke to Mattathias as follows: "You are a leader, honored and great in this town, and supported by sons and brothers. 18Now be the first to come and do what the king commands, as all the Gentiles and the people of Judah and those that are left in Jerusalem have done. Then you and your sons will be numbered among the Friends of the king, and you and your sons will be honored with silver and gold and many gifts."

19But Mattathias answered and said in a loud

NIV

that each forsakes the religion of his fathers and consents to the king's orders, [20] yet I and my sons and my kinsmen will keep to the covenant of our fathers. [21] God forbid that we should forsake the law and the commandments. [22] We will not obey the words of the king nor depart from our religion in the slightest degree."

[23] As he finished saying these words, a certain Jew came forward in the sight of all to offer sacrifice on the altar in Modein according to the king's order. [24] When Mattathias saw him, he was filled with zeal; his heart was moved and his just fury was aroused; he sprang forward and killed him upon the altar. [25] At the same time, he also killed the messenger of the king who was forcing them to sacrifice, and he tore down the altar. [26] Thus he showed his zeal for the law, just as Phinehas did with Zimri, son of Salu.

[27] Then Mattathias went through the city shouting, "Let everyone who is zealous for the law and who stands by the covenant follow after me!" [28] Thereupon he fled to the mountains with his sons, leaving behind in the city all their possessions.

NRSV

voice: "Even if all the nations that live under the rule of the king obey him, and have chosen to obey his commandments, everyone of them abandoning the religion of their ancestors, [20] I and my sons and my brothers will continue to live by the covenant of our ancestors. [21] Far be it from us to desert the law and the ordinances. [22] We will not obey the king's words by turning aside from our religion to the right hand or to the left."

[23] When he had finished speaking these words, a Jew came forward in the sight of all to offer sacrifice on the altar in Modein, according to the king's command. [24] When Mattathias saw it, he burned with zeal and his heart was stirred. He gave vent to righteous anger; he ran and killed him on the altar. [25] At the same time he killed the king's officer who was forcing them to sacrifice, and he tore down the altar. [26] Thus he burned with zeal for the law, just as Phinehas did against Zimri son of Salu.

[27] Then Mattathias cried out in the town with a loud voice, saying: "Let every one who is zealous for the law and supports the covenant come out with me!" [28] Then he and his sons fled to the hills and left all that they had in the town.

COMMENTARY

2:15-18. Although Mattathias and his sons left Jerusalem, they could not escape the decrees of the king (1:51). The scene stresses the separation of Mattathias and his sons from those who actively support the king's program. Nevertheless, the king's officers address Mattathias respectfully as a powerful clan leader and suggest that others follow his lead. In return, Mattathias and his family will obtain the privilege of membership in the royal court (1 Macc 10:65; 11:27) and wealth.

2:19-22. Mattathias answers by contrasting his kinsfolk's unswerving devotion to the covenant with the apostasy of all others. The author uses traditional language, not "turning aside . . . to the right hand or to the left," the language Moses had used when he instructed the Israelites to follow the path of God's commandments (Deut 5:32-33). Those who have "chosen to obey [the king's] commandments" have forgotten what Moses said

and brought on the curses written in the book of Deuteronomy (Deut 29:25-28).

2:23-26. Mattathias's attachment to his ancestral traditions is further demonstrated by his action toward an apostate Jew, recalling how Phinehas, the grandson of Aaron, acted during the wandering of the Israelites in the desert (Num 25:6-15). The Israelite males had been led astray by their non-Israelite wives to worship other gods, and one Israelite male defiantly brought a Midianite woman to his tent in the sight of Moses. In retribution, Phinehas speared both the man and the woman (Num 25:1-8). Through his zeal, Phinehas averted a plague on Israel, and a perpetual priesthood was granted to him and his descendants (Num 25:8-9, 12-13; Ps 106:28-31; Sir 45:23-25). By using this model, the author of Maccabees suggests not only that Mattathias is the real priestly descendant of Phinehas, but also that the action of Mattathias will avert the persecution of the Jews and that his descendants will be duly rewarded.

2:27-28. The hills to which Mattathias and his sons flee are probably those to the northeast of Modein, near Gophna and bordering on Samaria.

Second Maccabees 5:27, with no mention of Mattathias or Modein, portrays Judas Maccabeus as fleeing to the wilderness. He and his sons leave everything they own (v. 28) rather than "leave" the law and the ordinances (v. 21).

1 Maccabees 2:29-48, The Exploits of Mattathias

NAB

29 Many who sought to live according to righteousness and religious custom went out into the desert to settle there, 30 they and their sons, their wives and their cattle, because misfortunes pressed so hard on them.

31 It was reported to the officers and soldiers of the king who were in the City of David, in Jerusalem, that certain men who had flouted the king's order had gone out to the hiding places in the desert. 32 Many hurried out after them, and having caught up with them, camped opposite and prepared to attack them on the sabbath. 33 "Enough of this!" the pursuers said to them. "Come out and obey the king's command, and your lives will be spared." 34 But they replied, "We will not come out, nor will we obey the king's command to profane the sabbath." 35 Then the enemy attacked them at once; 36 but they did not retaliate; they neither threw stones, nor blocked up their own hiding places. 37 They said, "Let us all die without reproach; heaven and earth are our witnesses that you destroy us unjustly." 38 So the officers and soldiers attacked them on the sabbath, and they died with their wives, their children and their cattle, to the number of a thousand persons.

39 When Mattathias and his friends heard of it, they mourned deeply for them. 40 "If we all do as our kinsmen have done," they said to one another, "and do not fight against the Gentiles for our lives and our traditions, they will soon destroy us from the earth." 41 On that day they came to this decision: "Let us fight against anyone who attacks us on the sabbath, so that we may not all die as our kinsmen died in the hiding places."

42 Then they were joined by a group of Hasideans, valiant Israelites, all of them devout followers of the law. 43 And all those who were fleeing from the disaster joined them and sup-

NRSV

29At that time many who were seeking righteousness and justice went down to the wilderness to live there, 30they, their sons, their wives, and their livestock, because troubles pressed heavily upon them. 31And it was reported to the king's officers, and to the troops in Jerusalem the city of David, that those who had rejected the king's command had gone down to the hiding places in the wilderness. 32Many pursued them, and overtook them; they encamped opposite them and prepared for battle against them on the sabbath day. 33They said to them, "Enough of this! Come out and do what the king commands, and you will live." 34But they said, "We will not come out, nor will we do what the king commands and so profane the sabbath day." 35Then the enemy[a] quickly attacked them. 36But they did not answer them or hurl a stone at them or block up their hiding places, 37for they said, "Let us all die in our innocence; heaven and earth testify for us that you are killing us unjustly." 38So they attacked them on the sabbath, and they died, with their wives and children and livestock, to the number of a thousand persons.

39When Mattathias and his friends learned of it, they mourned for them deeply. 40And all said to their neighbors: "If we all do as our kindred have done and refuse to fight with the Gentiles for our lives and for our ordinances, they will quickly destroy us from the earth." 41So they made this decision that day: "Let us fight against anyone who comes to attack us on the sabbath day; let us not all die as our kindred died in their hiding places."

42Then there united with them a company of Hasideans, mighty warriors of Israel, all who offered themselves willingly for the law. 43And all who became fugitives to escape their troubles joined them and reinforced them. 44They organ-

a Gk they

NIV

ported them. [44] They gathered an army and struck down sinners in their anger and lawbreakers in their wrath, and the survivors fled to the Gentiles for safety. [45] Mattathias and his friends went about and tore down the pagan altars; [46] they also forcibly circumcised any uncircumcised boys whom they found in the territory of Israel. [47] They put to flight the arrogant, and the work prospered in their hands. [48] They saved the law from the hands of the Gentiles and of the kings and did not let the sinner triumph.

NRSV

ized an army, and struck down sinners in their anger and renegades in their wrath; the survivors fled to the Gentiles for safety. [45] And Mattathias and his friends went around and tore down the altars; [46] they forcibly circumcised all the uncircumcised boys that they found within the borders of Israel. [47] They hunted down the arrogant, and the work prospered in their hands. [48] They rescued the law out of the hands of the Gentiles and kings, and they never let the sinner gain the upper hand.

COMMENTARY

After Mattathias's dramatic revolt comes a discussion of what he achieved. First, however, is told the story of another group who wished to have no part in the changes to their ancestral traditions. Will Mattathias behave like them?

2:29-38, The Seekers After Righteousness and Justice. The Judean wilderness was a traditional hiding place (see 1 Sam 23:14, where David hides from Saul). It also came to symbolize the place where Israel had covenanted with God (see Jer 2:2-3; Hos 2:14-15). First Maccabees describes the group that flees there in traditional terms, usually given in the order "justice and righteousness" (see, e.g., Jer 22:15; 23:5; Ezek 18:27; 33:14, 19; 45:9). Zephaniah 2:3 exhorts the people to do justice and seek righteousness and humility so that they might perhaps be hidden on the day of the Lord's wrath. Qumran covenanters were exhorted in their *Community Rule* to do truth and righteousness and justice.[53] In a description of God's renewing the land, the Isaianic tradition foretells that justice will dwell in the wilderness and righteousness in the fruitful field (Isa 32:16).

In contrast to Mattathias and his followers, who left everything behind in the city, this group takes all the elements of social living with them—sons, wives, and livestock (note how for this patriarchal author wives came after sons, but at least before livestock). "Troubles" here refers to the evil being done in the land by those who have forsaken the law (1 Macc 1:52-53). This effort to set up an alternate

social existence is opposed by the people in Jerusalem, the city of David, which has now become the center of apostasy (1:33-40; 2:18; for more on the hiding places, see Commentary on 1:53).

The seekers after righteousness choose to die "in their innocence" (ἐν τῇ ἁπλότητι ἡμῶν *en tē haplotēti hēmōn*). The same word is found concerning Daniel (1 Macc 2:60) and has the overtones of integrity and sincerity (1 Chr 29:17; Wis 1:1). Those who sought justice (v. 29) are destroyed unjustly. "Heaven and earth" are frequently invoked to witness covenant violations (Deut 4:26; 30:19; 31:28; 32:1; Isa 1:2). The total annihilation of humans and livestock recalls the tradition of the ban (Josh 6:21; 1 Sam 15:3; 22:19); it is also similar to the victory stele of Mesha, the ninth-century BCE king of Moab.[54] A variation on this story is told in 2 Macc 6:11. There the group assembles for sabbath worship and is not said to have left on a permanent basis; this account states that all were burnt to death. Another similar story is found in the *Testament of Moses* 9. There Taxo, from the tribe of Levi, upon witnessing the evils that have come upon the nation, exhorts his seven sons never to transgress God's commandments and advises them to fast for three days and then to go into a cave in the open country and wait to die rather than submit to apostasy. The mind-set is that one should flee from all contact with contagion and sin, and the only way to avoid them completely is to commit suicide.

53. CD 1:5; 8:2.

54. James B. Pritchard, ed., *Ancient Near Eastern Texts Relating to the Old Testament (ANET)*, 3rd ed. with supplement (Princeton: Princeton University Press, 1969) 321.

2:39-41, The Response of Mattathias and His Friends. The language of v. 39 reflects the ritual mourning for the dead (as in 1:25-27), establishing a rhetorical bond between Mattathias and his group and those seekers of righteousness who had died. Mattathias is consciously depicted as surrounded by his friends, in contrast to the king and his closest companions, called the king's friends (see, e.g., 1 Macc 2:8; 3:38; 6:10). The language of v. 40 catches the sense of a group caught in a quandary and coming to a decision in a time of crisis ("each said to his neighbor" as at Judg 6:29; 10:18; 2 Kgs 7:3, 9; Jdt 7:4; 1 Macc 3:43). The community aspect of the decision is further enhanced by the reference to "brothers," by the use of the first-person plural, and by the repetition of "our." One might also note how the singular for "life" is used—not "for our lives," but "for our life," as though the community has one life. The result is a community-based decision that, in these particular circumstances and in order to maintain the community's existence, defensive warfare on the sabbath will be allowed. Bar-Kochva has cogently pointed out that previously there had not been any ban against warfare on the sabbath, otherwise Jews could not have served in Hellenistic armies (as they certainly did).[55] Nonetheless, the emphasis in both this and the previous passage is on defense on the sabbath in particular (2:32, 34, 38, 41), not just on any day; there were many who opposed any kind of warfare on the sabbath. The pseudepigraphic book of *Jubilees* states that anyone who made war on the sabbath should die,[56] a position maintained by some into the first century CE. Allowing oneself to be killed by refusing to fight on the sabbath was considered a pious act.[57] Both the emphasis on this being a community-based decision and its rhetorical placement (between the preceding pious opponents of Antiochus and the succeeding attachment of the Hasideans to Mattathias) illustrate the author's attempts to link the Hasmoneans to the most Torah-observant traditions.

2:42-48, The Deeds of Mattathias. These verses describe the consequences of Mattathias's

action in killing the king's officer and fleeing to the hills (cf. 1 Macc 2:24-28). The connecting particle "then" (τότε *tote*; the same word is used to start v. 29) suggests that the decision to resist even on the sabbath brought in these supporters—i.e., the decision to defend oneself on the sabbath is ratified by important members of the community.

2:42-43. A group called the Hasideans now join Mattathias and his followers. Some manuscripts read "Judeans," but "Hasideans" appears the preferable reading ('Ασιδαῖοι [*Asidaioi*] reflects the Aramaic חסידיא [*ḥasîdayyā'*] and the Hebrew חסידים [*ḥasîdîm*], "pious," "loyal ones"). The author of 1 Maccabees, in discussing the execution of some Hasideans (7:12-17), quotes Ps 79:2 (where the Hebrew term [*ḥasîdîm*] is found) to describe their fate. The transliteration suggests that the Hasideans were a well-known group, but their exact identity has evoked much scholarly discussion. Are they to be connected with "the wise ones" of Dan 11:33 or with those described allegorically in *1 Enoch* 90:6-9? Are they to be linked to the Essenes or to the Pharisees? The term "Hasidean" itself draws upon traditional terminology, where those loyal to God are referred to as *ḥasîdîm*. In 2 Macc 14:6, Judas Maccabeus is said to be the leader of the Hasideans, whereas here and at 1 Macc 7:13 the Maccabees are distinguished from them. The phrase translated "mighty warriors" (ἰσχυροὶ δυνάμει *ischyroi dynamei*) is also used to describe Judas Maccabeus in his fitness to lead the army after Mattathias's death (2:66). The word has overtones of leadership when it is used in 1 Chronicles to describe the heads of ancestral houses (1 Chr 5:24; 7:2, 5, 7, 9, 11). This quality of leadership is also evident in 1 Macc 7:13, where the Hasideans are said to be first among the sons of Israel. The Hasideans are thus a distinguished people, and their willingness to offer their own lives for the sake of the law responds to Mattathias's call to all who are zealous for the law to follow him (2:27). In 1 Maccabees, then, the Hasideans are neither pacifist nor apocalyptic, but important folk devoted to the law. Besides them come others. The translation "to escape their troubles" (cf. 2:29) must be seen in the light of 1:52-53: the group is fleeing from the evil in the land.

2:44-48. Describing the rebels as an army may be a trifle grandiose, but they were an effective

55. B. Bar-Kochva, *Judas Maccabeus* (Cambridge: Cambridge University Press, 1989) 474-81.

56. *Jub.* 50:12-13.

57. M. D. Goodman and A. J. Holladay, "Religious Scruples in Ancient Warfare," *Classical Quarterly* 36 (1986) 151-71. See also Josephus *Against Apion* 1, 212.

fighting force that set out to redress what had taken place. The phrase "sinners and renegades" echoes the terms used of the group stationed in the Akra (1:34). The survivors of this counterattack now fully join the Gentiles, as they had sought to do early (see 1:11-15). Mattathias destroys the pagan altars built in the towns around Judea. Mattathias also undoes the king's ban of circumcision (1:48). The pursuit of the "sons of arrogance" (author's trans.) recalls the arrogance of Antiochus IV (1:21, 24). Just as the king tried to make Israel forget the law

(1:49) and destroyed the books of the law (1:56-57), so also Mattathias now rescues the law. Mattathias's actions recall those of Judith, who, before cutting off the head of the Assyrian commander Holofernes, prayed, "Now indeed is the time for aiding your heritage" (Jdt 13:5 NAB). "Gain the upper hand" is literally "did not give horn to the sinner." The horn is a traditional symbol of strength (cf. 1 Kgs 22:11; Ps 148:14). Sirach complains that the kings of Judah abandoned the law and gave their horn to others and their glory to a foreign nation (49:4-5).

REFLECTIONS

This account of the exploits of Mattathias emphasizes how he and his friends overturn the damage done to ancestral traditions by the arrogant decrees of Antiochus IV. The narrative evinces solidarity with those who went down into the wilderness and were executed, but has Mattathias and his group choose another course in order to prevent complete annihilation of their cause. As such, the narrative forces us to ask questions about the proper use of violence. The rebels who went down to the desert certainly had not planned a guerrilla campaign, or they would not have taken along their families and livestock. They simply wanted to be left alone. Would they have defended themselves if attacked on a day other than the sabbath? Although the narrative does not give us the answer, wanting instead to emphasize the heinous nature of the crime, it nonetheless raises the issue of pacifism. (For further reflections, see the section "The Ethics of Violence" in the Introduction, 16-18.)

1 Maccabees 2:49-70, The Death of Mattathias

NAB	NRSV
49 When the time came for Mattathias to die, he said to his sons: "Arrogance and scorn have now grown strong; it is a time of disaster and violent anger. 50 Therefore, my sons, be zealous for the law and give your lives for the covenant of our fathers.	49Now the days drew near for Mattathias to die, and he said to his sons: "Arrogance and scorn have now become strong; it is a time of ruin and furious anger. 50Now, my children, show zeal for the law, and give your lives for the covenant of our ancestors.
51 "Remember the deeds that our fathers did in their times, and you shall win great glory and an everlasting name. 52 Was not Abraham found faithful in trial, and it was reputed to him as uprightness? 53 Joseph, when in distress, kept the commandment, and he became master of Egypt. 54 Phinehas our father, for his burning zeal, received the covenant of an everlasting priesthood.	51"Remember the deeds of the ancestors, which they did in their generations; and you will receive great honor and an everlasting name. 52Was not Abraham found faithful when tested, and it was reckoned to him as righteousness? 53Joseph in the time of his distress kept the commandment, and became lord of Egypt. 54Phinehas our ancestor, because he was deeply zealous, received the covenant of everlasting priesthood. 55Joshua, because he fulfilled the command, became a judge in Israel. 56Caleb, because he testified in the assembly, received an inheritance in the land. 57David, because he was mer-

NAB

55 Joshua, for executing his commission,
    became a judge in Israel.
56 Caleb, for bearing witness before the assembly,
    received an inheritance in the land.
57 David, for his piety,
    received as a heritage a throne of everlasting
    royalty.
58 Elijah, for his burning zeal for the law,
    was taken up to heaven.
59 Hananiah, Azariah and Mishael, for their faith,
    were saved from the fire.
60 Daniel, for his innocence,
    was delivered from the jaws of lions.
61 And so, consider this from generation to
    generation,
    that none who hope in him shall fail in
    strength.
62 Do not fear the words of a sinful man,
    for his glory ends in corruption and worms.
63 Today he is exalted, and tomorrow he is not to
    be found,
    because he has returned to his dust,
    and his schemes have perished.
64 Children! be courageous and strong in keeping
    the law,
    for by it you shall be glorified.

65 "Here is your brother Simeon who I know is a wise man; listen to him always, and he will be a father to you. 66 And Judas Maccabeus, a warrior from his youth, shall be the leader of your army and direct the war against the nations. 67 You shall also gather about you all who observe the law, and you shall avenge the wrongs of your people. 68 Pay back the Gentiles what they deserve, and observe the precepts of the law."

69 Then he blessed them, and he was united with his fathers. 70 He died in the year one hundred and forty-six, and was buried in the tombs of his fathers in Modein, and all Israel mourned him greatly.

NRSV

ciful, inherited the throne of the kingdom forever. 58Elijah, because of great zeal for the law, was taken up into heaven. 59Hananiah, Azariah, and Mishael believed and were saved from the flame. 60Daniel, because of his innocence, was delivered from the mouth of the lions.

61"And so observe, from generation to generation, that none of those who put their trust in him will lack strength. 62Do not fear the words of sinners, for their splendor will turn into dung and worms. 63Today they will be exalted, but tomorrow they will not be found, because they will have returned to the dust, and their plans will have perished. 64My children, be courageous and grow strong in the law, for by it you will gain honor.

65"Here is your brother Simeon who, I know, is wise in counsel; always listen to him; he shall be your father. 66Judas Maccabeus has been a mighty warrior from his youth; he shall command the army for you and fight the battle against the peoples.[a] 67You shall rally around you all who observe the law, and avenge the wrong done to your people. 68Pay back the Gentiles in full, and obey the commands of the law."

69Then he blessed them, and was gathered to his ancestors. 70He died in the one hundred forty-sixth year[b] and was buried in the tomb of his ancestors at Modein. And all Israel mourned for him with great lamentation.

[a] Or of the people   [b] 166 B.C.

COMMENTARY

As did other great leaders in giving farewell addresses, Mattathias gathers his sons to deliver his last will and testament (cf. Jacob, Genesis 49; Moses, Deuteronomy 33; Joshua, Joshua 23; Samuel, 1 Samuel 12; and David, 1 Kings 2). The death of Mattathias contrasts with that of Alexander the Great (1:6-9). Whereas Alexander's successors brought evil upon the land, however, Mattathias's sons will bring a renewal of ancestral traditions.

2:49-50. The same formula used of Jacob (Gen 47:29) and David (1 Kgs 2:1) is used here: "When the days drew near for x to die. . . ." The arrogance of Antiochus has been mentioned before (1:21, 24), as has the "anger" toward Israel (1:64). Mattathias entreats his sons that just as he had burned with zeal (2:24-26), so also must they act.

2:51-60. In Mattathias's exhortation of his sons to give their lives for the covenant, the author of 1 Maccabees provides a list of the great actions of the past. Covenants or treaties made between two parties usually followed a standard structure: a list of the stipulations of the treaty, requirements for the deposit and public reading of the covenant, and the list of witnesses to the covenant. The covenant would usually begin with a historical prologue, which would describe the previous relationships between the two parties, particularly the benevolent acts of a suzerain toward his vassals or the rebellion of a vassal or his ancestors against the suzerain. This historical element is well represented in the covenant scene of Joshua 24, and it provides the opening framework for the book of Deuteronomy, a work steeped in covenantal concerns that is, on some level, a testament of Moses before his death. At Deut 32:7-14, Moses appeals to the people to remember how God had acted properly toward them, and that they had been unmindful of the rock that bore them, forgetful of the God who had birthed them (Deut 32:18). Joshua also recounts to the people all that they have seen God do and encourages them to observe the commandments (Josh 23:2-6). The list in 1 Maccabees urges the sons to remember how God had acted faithfully toward covenant partners in the past, when those partners had acted faithfully in return. Mattathias's list of those persons worthy of imitation is interesting both for who is included and who is not. Contrasted with the list of famous men in Sirach 44–50, Mattathias omits, among others, Enoch, Noah, Isaac, Jacob, Moses, Aaron, Solomon, Elisha, Isaiah, Hezekiah, and Josiah. The author of 1 Maccabees thus lists a select group of heroes—and no heroines.

2:52. The author links the testing of Abraham, when he is commanded to slay his son Isaac (Genesis 22), with the present situation, drawing especially on the phrase from Gen 15:6, where Abraham's faith in God is credited to him as righteousness. Because of this verse, Abraham became a paradigm of faithfulness (cf. Rom 4:3). The book of *Jubilees* lists many tests in which Abraham was found faithful (*Jub.* 17:17-18), beginning with a famine in the land of Chaldea and his rejection of idol worship. Pseudo-Philo also has a story in which Abraham in Chaldea is thrown into a fiery furnace because he rejects idols.[58] The testing of Abraham parallels the situation the Maccabees now find themselves in.

2:53. Joseph's rejection of the attempted seduction by Potiphar's wife (Genesis 39) is retold in *Jub* 39:1-10. There Joseph resists because "he remembered the Lord and the words which Jacob, his father, used to read" (*Jub* 39:6). Joseph, through his gift of dream interpretation, becomes lord of Egypt in Gen 41:40-45. With this example, the author of 1 Maccabees suggests that faithfulness leads to exaltation and rule.

2:54. Phinehas has already been cited as the model for Mattathias's zeal (1 Macc 2:26). Here Mattathias claims to be a descendant of Phinehas and thereby sets the stage for later Hasmonean claims to high priestly station (see also Sir 45:23-26).

2:55. "Because he fulfilled the command" might also be translated "when he had completed the task." Joshua was commissioned by Moses (Num 27:18-23) and by God (Josh 1:2-9), and his role is glorified in Sir 46:1-7. After Joshua conquered the promised land and divided it among the Israelite tribes, he gathered all the tribes at Shechem and made a covenant with the people to turn away from other gods and to serve Yahweh alone. Although Joshua is not explicitly called a "judge" (κριτής *kritēs*) in 1 Maccabees, elsewhere he is reported to have made "statutes and ordinances" (חק ומשפט *ḥōq ûmišpāṭ*; LXX νόμον καὶ κρίσιν *nomon kai krisin*; see Josh 24:25), and he is the first leader mentioned in the book of Judges (1:1–2:10). He is put on the list because he conquered the land, and, as mentioned in the Introduction, the author of 1 Maccabees draws heavily on the language and ideology of the book of Judges.

2:56. Caleb, along with Joshua, reported positively about the land he and others were sent to

---

58. Pseudo-Philo *Biblical Antiquities* 6.

spy out (Numbers 14). Caleb and Joshua were the only representatives allowed to enter the promised land. Caleb, of the tribe of Nun, settled around Hebron (Josh 14:6-15). The author of 1 Maccabees again ties reward to the land to faithful discharge of duty. (Sirach speaks of Caleb and Joshua opposing the assembly to prevent them from sinning [Sir 46:7-10]).

2:57. That David was rewarded because he was "merciful" (ἔλεος *eleos*) seems out of place in this list. Perhaps one should see behind *eleos* the Hebrew word denoting acts of covenant faithfulness (חסד *ḥesed*). As such, *eleos* would reflect what David said in his song of thanksgiving (2 Sam 22:21-25). David's trust in God is clearly stated in his fight against Goliath (1 Sam 17:45-47). That David's dynasty would last forever is promised in 2 Sam 7:13-16 (see also Psalm 89; Sir 47:2-11). Although John Hyrcanus would later lay claim to the title of king, the author of 1 Maccabees does not bestow such a title on any of the Hasmoneans, but gives them only the title "leader" (ἡγούμενος *hēgoumenos*, 14:35).

2:58. Elijah, the great miracle-working prophet of the ninth century BCE, appeared when King Ahab of Israel began to worship the Canaanite storm god Baal. Baal was believed to bring life-giving rain to restore fertility to the land. Elijah showed the futility of worshiping Baal by proclaiming that Yahweh would bring a drought on the land; in a dramatic contest with the priests of Baal, Elijah proved that Yahweh is the real bestower of health and fertility (1 Kgs 17:1–18:46). Elijah proclaimed his zeal for God at Mount Horeb (1 Kgs 19:1-14) where Yahweh appeared to him not in a mighty wind or an earthquake or fire, but in a whisper, assuring Elijah that there were others in Israel who had not worshiped Baal (1 Kgs 19:11-18). In keeping with Elijah's fiery confrontation with the storm god Baal, Elijah was taken up to heaven in a chariot of fire during a whirlwind (2 Kings 2).

2:59-60. In Daniel 3, when King Nebuchadnezzar made a huge golden statue that he commanded all peoples and nations to serve, Shadrach, Meshach, and Abednego, Jewish captives of the Babylonians (Dan 1:6-7), refuse to worship the idol. They are denounced to the king and thrown into a fiery furnace, in which they are miraculously preserved. This miracle prompts

Nebuchadnezzar to honor the God of the Jews and to promote them in Nebuchadnezzar's service.

In Daniel 6, envious opponents plot to destroy the innocent and praiseworthy Daniel through his obedience to his God. Accordingly, they require that everyone in the whole kingdom worship only the king, Darius, for thirty days. When Daniel ostentatiously disobeys the command, he is thrown into a den of lions, but is saved by an angel of God. Daniel's accusers are forthwith gobbled up by the lions, the king himself honors Daniel's God, and Daniel prospers.

One might suggest reasons why these models were chosen. Abraham is the father of the Jews. Joseph and Joshua rose to important positions, whereas Caleb received an inheritance in the land. Phinehas and David represent the two major institutions in Israel: priesthood and monarchy. Elijah was victorious against idol worship, and Daniel and his three companions overcame the commands to worship idols of Persian kings, the forerunners of the Seleucid rulers.

2:61-64. The author uses traditional sentiments to draw a conclusion from the historical examples: "Do not put your trust in princes,/ in mortals, in whom there is no help./ When their breath departs, they return to the earth;/ on that very day their plans perish" (Ps 146:3-4 NRSV; cf. 1 Sam 2:4-5; Ps 26:1; Isa 14:14-21). An exhortation to abide by the covenant follows on this conclusion. When Moses was about to die, he summoned Joshua and used the same exhortation, so that Joshua would lead the people into the promised land (Deut 31:7, 23; Josh 1:5-9, 18).

2:65-68. Mattathias now plans for the future, and the author shows in some sense the organization of the rest of the book, in inverse order, around Judas and Simon. Interestingly, Jonathan is not mentioned, nor is he given a hymn in the narrative, as are Judas (3:3-9) and Simon (14:4-15).

2:65. The most praise is given to Simon, here called Simeon. He replaced Mattathias as leader of the family and is described with the attributes of a leader ("wise in counsel"), somewhat like the ideal leader described in Isa 9:6. This Simeon contrasts with Simeon, the son of Jacob, into whose council Jacob hopes never to come (Gen 49:6), whereas Simon is lauded as a wise leader (14:4-15).

2:66. Judas is to be the commander in chief. Instead of "battle against the peoples," one might translate "battle for the tribes," on the analogy with 1 Macc 3:2, where the same syntax is used in "fight for Israel." Judas is to be the standard bearer in fighting on Israel's behalf.

2:67-68. The final injunctions of Mattathias, in a chiastic pattern, are intended to unite the Torah observers and to urge them to take vengeance on their enemies, the Gentiles. The language resonates with that of Moses' final injunctions (Deut 32:43-47), as well as with the words of the divine warrior at Isa 59:18: "According to their deeds, so will he repay;/ wrath to his adversaries, requital to his enemies" (NRSV). The conflict is set up between the Jewish people and the Gentiles, and it brings to a fitting close this introduction to the body of the work; the first chapter was concerned to point out the attempt to eradicate Jewish ancestral traditions by the Gentiles, and the second the response to that attempt.

2:69-70. Again using traditional language, the death of Mattathias is described in a way similar to the description of Jacob's death (Gen 49:28-29, 33; 50:10). Mattathias is "gathered to his ancestors," as were Moses (Deut 32:50), the generation of Joshua (Judg 2:11), and the husband of Judith (Jdt 16:22); the phrase also occurs in the prediction of the death of the good king Josiah (2 Kgs 22:20) and in the story of Bel and the Dragon (Bel and the Dragon 1). The mourning of all Israel, here for Mattathias, is recorded also when all Israel mourns over the defiled sanctuary (1 Macc 4:39) and at the deaths of Judas (1 Macc 9:20) and Jonathan (1 Macc 13:26).

REFLECTIONS

As we read of the determination of Mattathias to resist with force the attack on Judaism by Antiochus IV, we might pause to consider the long tradition in the West concerning "just" warfare. Under what conditions should one go to war, and how should one conduct oneself in war? Moral and legal standards have been set up as to whether force should be used in a given instance. In considering what these standards may be, one might ponder these questions:

(1) Who has the authority to declare war? One answer might be that only the legally constituted ruling authority, such as the United States Congress or the United Nations.

(2) What circumstances lead to the outbreak of war? The presumption should be that a nation will not go to war. We should in no way seek to harm our neighbor. A nation should not embark on war for any reasons of revenge or self-aggrandizement, but to right some injustice, to defend itself, and to restrain wrongdoing. War is permissible to protect innocent life, to secure basic human rights, and to ensure that one can lead a decent existence. Those who go to war should have as their aim the restoration of peace. Thus nations should choose war only as a last resort after every other avenue to ensure peace or to right the wrong has been exhausted. Whoever goes to war should have a reasonable hope of success, for otherwise lives will be endangered and lost for no purpose.

(3) What is acceptable conduct toward armed belligerents and toward unarmed civilians? Under no circumstances, according to just-war theory, can unarmed civilians be targeted. If attacked, one should attempt to restrain but not to annihilate the enemy. This criterion becomes increasingly difficult to observe once the possibility of nuclear warfare appears.

When we look at the actions of Mattathias and his sons in the light of these criteria, we see that they were undergoing a massive attack on their standard of living and on their cultural existence. The author has gone out of his way to exaggerate the evil intention of Antiochus IV to eradicate Judaism. By describing the massacre of the seekers after righteousness, the author shows that there was no alternative; one could not even opt out of society. The high priest, not Mattathias, was the leader of Judah, but the high priest is not shown as being directly opposed to the actions of Antiochus IV (see 2 Maccabees 4). The author of 1 Maccabees thus grants Mattathias a different kind of leadership from that of the high priest. Major members of society, the Hasideans, rally behind Mattathias's leadership. More important, Mattathias is cloaked in the mantle of divine authority, since his actions are so closely linked to those of the divinely inspired Phinehas. While this obviates the problem of Mattathias's not being a duly appointed leader, the narrative also poses other problems. Many persons may lay claim to divinely inspired leadership, but how is one to judge the validity of their claim?

The narrative also raises questions about how a war should be conducted. When Mattathias is depicted as forcing all citizens of Judea to be circumcised (1 Macc 2:46), this action could be interpreted as going beyond the limits set by the requirements for just conduct in war. Within our own day, the development of weapons of mass destruction, of missiles that can be sent long distances and not always with pinpoint accuracy, forces us to wonder whether any war can ever be just according to the traditional criteria of just war. Will not such weapons of mass destruction inevitably cause the deaths of civilians?

JUDAS MACCABEUS

1 MACCABEES 3:1-9, HERO OF HIS PEOPLE

NAB

3 Then his son Judas, who was called Maccabeus, took his place. ² All his brothers and all who had joined his father supported him, and they carried on Israel's war joyfully.

³ He spread abroad the glory of his people,
    and put on his breastplate like a giant.
He armed himself with weapons of war;
    he planned battles and protected the camp
        with his sword.
⁴ In his actions he was like a lion,
    like a young lion roaring for prey.
⁵ He pursued the wicked, hunting them out,
    and those who troubled his people he
        destroyed by fire.
⁶ The lawbreakers were cowed by fear of him,
    and all evildoers were dismayed.
By his hand redemption was happily achieved,
⁷   and he afflicted many kings;
He made Jacob glad by his deeds,
    and his memory is blessed forever.
⁸ He went about the cities of Judah
    destroying the impious there.
He turned away wrath from Israel
⁹   and was renowned to the ends of the earth;
    he gathered together those who were
        perishing.

NRSV

3 Then his son Judas, who was called Maccabeus, took command in his place. ²All his brothers and all who had joined his father helped him; they gladly fought for Israel.

³ He extended the glory of his people.
    Like a giant he put on his breastplate;
he bound on his armor of war and waged
        battles,
    protecting the camp by his sword.
⁴ He was like a lion in his deeds,
    like a lion's cub roaring for prey.
⁵ He searched out and pursued those who broke
        the law;
    he burned those who troubled his people.
⁶ Lawbreakers shrank back for fear of him;
    all the evildoers were confounded;
    and deliverance prospered by his hand.
⁷ He embittered many kings,
    but he made Jacob glad by his deeds,
    and his memory is blessed forever.
⁸ He went through the cities of Judah;
    he destroyed the ungodly out of the land;[a]
    thus he turned away wrath from Israel.
⁹ He was renowned to the ends of the earth;
    he gathered in those who were perishing.

[a] Gk *it*

COMMENTARY

3:1-2. The author stresses that Judas is the son of Mattathias. Following the death of his father, Judas assumes the role of leader of the resistance to Antiochus's policy. He is joined by all who had rallied to his father.

3:3-9. Whereas in the first two chapters the author used poetry to describe the distress of Israel, he now uses poetry to laud Judas.

3:3-6. The text first emphasizes that Judas fights for his people, not for himself. Judas is described in bigger-than-life terms, as he single-handedly defends the camp. The traditional image of the warrior is that of a lion, used of Judah (Gen 49:9), God (Isa 31:4; cf. Hos 5:14; 11:10; Amos 3:4-8), and the enemies of Israel (Jer 4:7; 5:6). Given the references in the poem to Jacob/Israel (3:7-8), as well as the previous resonances between Jacob and Mattathias in giving their last will and testament, the linkage with Judah seems strong. The image of "burning" the troublers of Israel reflects also the wrath of divine judgment (Isa 66:15; Obadiah 18). "Those who troubled his people" are probably Jews (see 7:22). The phrase recalls Elijah, who, when King Ahab called him the troubler of Israel, responded that it was not he but Ahab who troubled Israel (1 Kgs 18:18). Achar (i.e., Achan), who violated the holy war conditions by taking booty from what had been consecrated to God at the capture of Jericho (Joshua 7), is also called the troubler of Israel (1 Chr 2:7). Judas's actions here resemble those of Mattathias (2:47).

3:7-8. Verse 7 has a play on words between "embittered" (ἐπίκρανεν *epikranen*) and "made glad" (εὔφρανεν *euphranen*). Judas embittered (*epikranen*) many kings, but he made glad (*euphranen*) Jacob. Judas's destruction of the ungodly from the land of Judah recalls the campaigns of Joshua when he conquered the promised land (Joshua 10–11). Just as the description of the renegades at 1 Macc 1:11 recalls Deuteronomy 13, so also Judas's destruction of the ungodly (v. 8) alludes to Deuteronomy 13, which commands Israel to destroy anyone advocating idol worship. The anger of the Lord, which had fallen on Israel (1:64; 2:49), is "turned away," as the author again relies on traditional language (see Num 25:4; 2 Chr 12:12; 29:10; 30:8; Ps 106:23; Ezek 10:14; Dan 9:16; Hos 14:4; Zech 1:2).

3:9. Judas's renown stretches to the ends of the earth, as will Simon's (14:10). Israel, which had been driven into hiding (1:53), is now brought back. The gathering-in of those who had been dispersed is a theme found earlier (e.g., Isa 11:12; 27:13, where God is going to bring back the people who have been dispersed to other lands).

1 MACCABEES 3:10-26, JUDAS'S FIRST VICTORIES

1 Maccabees 3:10-12, Victory Against Apollonius

NAB	NRSV
¹⁰ Then Apollonius gathered the Gentiles, together with a large army from Samaria, to fight against Israel. ¹¹ When Judas learned of it, he went out to meet him and defeated and killed him. Many fell wounded, and the rest fled. ¹² Their possessions were seized and the sword of Apollonius was taken by Judas, who fought with it the rest of his life.	10Apollonius now gathered together Gentiles and a large force from Samaria to fight against Israel. ¹¹When Judas learned of it, he went out to meet him, and he defeated and killed him. Many were wounded and fell, and the rest fled. ¹²Then they seized their spoils; and Judas took the sword of Apollonius, and used it in battle the rest of his life.

COMMENTARY

Apollonius, who has not been mentioned before, appears abruptly without introduction. At 10:69, the governor of Coelesyria is called Apollonius. In 2 Maccabees, three people are named Apollonius: Apollonius of Tarsus, son of Menestheus, who was the governor of Coelesyria and

Phoenicia (2 Macc 3:5; 4:4); Apollonius, the captain of the Mysians (5:24); and Apollonius, son of Gennaeus, a local governor (12:2). Josephus identifies the Apollonius of 1 Macc 3:10 as the governor of Samaria.[59] The author of 1 Maccabees makes no effort to identify Apollonius further, which might suggest that he was well-known or that "Apollonius" is recognized as a Greek name.

This Apollonius was able to muster a fighting force from the district of Samaria, most probably from people of Gentile origin who had settled there (cf. 2 Kgs 17:24-41). Here is a clear instance in which "Israel," for the author of 1 Maccabees,

refers not to the geographical northern kingdom, but to those persons whom he considers to be the followers of ancestral tradition—specifically, those who have joined with the Maccabees.

No details of where the encounter took place are given; most likely it was an ambush as against Seron, somewhere between Shechem and the Gophna Hills. (Cf. the summary account of Judas's exploits at the start of his career in 2 Macc 8:5-7.) The author describes the event like a single combat between Judas and Apollonius, much like the fight between David and Goliath (1 Sam 17:40-54), when David took the sword of Goliath (1 Sam 17:51) and the Philistines were routed.

59. Josephus *Antiquities of the Jews* 12.287; see also 12.261.

1 Maccabees 3:13-26, Victory Against Seron

NAB

13 But Seron, commander of the Syrian army, heard that Judas had gathered many about him, an assembly of faithful men ready for war. 14 So he said, "I will make a name for myself and win glory in the kingdom by defeating Judas and his followers, who have despised the king's command." 15 And again a large company of renegades advanced with him to help him take revenge on the Israelites. 16 When he reached the ascent of Beth-horon, Judas went out to meet him with a few men. 17 But when they saw the army coming against them, they said to Judas: "How can we, few as we are, fight such a mighty host as this? Besides, we are weak today from fasting." 18 But Judas said: "It is easy for many to be overcome by a few; in the sight of Heaven there is no difference between deliverance by many or by few; 19 for victory in war does not depend upon the size of the army, but on strength that comes from Heaven. 20 With great presumption and lawlessness they come against us to destroy us and our wives and children and to despoil us; 21 but we are fighting for our lives and our laws. 22 He himself will crush them before us; so do not be afraid of them." 23 When he finished speaking, he rushed suddenly upon Seron and his army, who were crushed before him. 24 He pursued Seron down the descent of Beth-horon into the plain. About eight hundred of their men fell, and the

NRSV

13When Seron, the commander of the Syrian army, heard that Judas had gathered a large company, including a body of faithful soldiers who stayed with him and went out to battle, 14he said, "I will make a name for myself and win honor in the kingdom. I will make war on Judas and his companions, who scorn the king's command." 15Once again a strong army of godless men went up with him to help him, to take vengeance on the Israelites.

16When he approached the ascent of Beth-horon, Judas went out to meet him with a small company. 17But when they saw the army coming to meet them, they said to Judas, "How can we, few as we are, fight against so great and so strong a multitude? And we are faint, for we have eaten nothing today." 18Judas replied, "It is easy for many to be hemmed in by few, for in the sight of Heaven there is no difference between saving by many or by few. 19It is not on the size of the army that victory in battle depends, but strength comes from Heaven. 20They come against us in great insolence and lawlessness to destroy us and our wives and our children, and to despoil us; 21but we fight for our lives and our laws. 22He himself will crush them before us; as for you, do not be afraid of them."

23When he finished speaking, he rushed suddenly against Seron and his army, and they were

NAB

rest fled to the country of the Philistines. ²⁵ Then Judas and his brothers began to be feared, and dread fell upon the Gentiles about them. ²⁶ His fame reached the king, and all the Gentiles talked about the battles of Judas.

NRSV

crushed before him. ²⁴They pursued them[a] down the descent of Beth-horon to the plain; eight hundred of them fell, and the rest fled into the land of the Philistines. ²⁵Then Judas and his brothers began to be feared, and terror fell on the Gentiles all around them. ²⁶His fame reached the king, and the Gentiles talked of the battles of Judas.

[a] Other ancient authorities read *him*

COMMENTARY

3:13-14. Seron, although described as the commander of the Syrian army, was most likely one of the commanders of the mercenary garrisons in the region. He commanded a more formidable fighting force than Apollonius had. Seron decides, on his own initiative, to put down Judas's uprising and so gain a reputation.

3:15. Seron's army comprises "godless men." In 1 Maccabees, "godless" (ἀσεβής *asebēs*) usually refers to those Jews whom the author considers apostates (3:8; 6:21; 7:5, 9; 9:25, 73). They have joined Seron's force, and their aim is the opposite of Mattathias's exhortation to his sons (2:67).

3:16. The public road Seron takes up the steep ascent to the mountain plateau—about twelve miles northwest of Jerusalem, between the villages of Lower and Upper Beth-horon—is extremely treacherous because of its winding narrowness, and yet not as bad as other possible routes from the west to Jerusalem. It lies near the Gophna Hills, where Judas and his forces were concentrated.

3:17-22. The objection of Judas's troops to fighting against this large army may result from their long wait in ambush, but the author of 1 Maccabees phrases the whole exchange in traditional language. The stipulations for waging war in Deuteronomy 20 emphasize that Israel should not fear enemies with larger forces, for God is with Israel (Deut 20:1-4). This theme is dear to the author of Deuteronomy, as seen at Deut 7:7-8, where God states that Israel was chosen not because it was more numerous than any other people, but because God loved Israel, and at Deut

9:1-3, where God promised that the Israelites would defeat the more powerful nations in the promised land because God would be with them. This remains an important theme throughout the deuteronomic history. The phrase "to save by many or by few" echoes the words of Jonathan, the son of Saul, as he initiates the first victory of the Israelites over the Philistines (1 Sam 14:6). It is also reminiscent of the story of Gideon in Judges 7, where with a drastically reduced number of troops so that Israel would not claim credit for the victory, Gideon prevails because God fights with him. (See also the prayer of Judith before she sets out to confront Holofernes [Jdt 9:7-11], and her song of victory after killing him [Jdt 16:11].) Unlike the OT examples, however, the author of 1 Maccabees avoids using the terms "Lord" and "God" and uses "heaven" as a substitute.

The author contrasts the aggression of the enemy against the whole community with the defensive nature of Judas's own stance to preserve the ancestral traditions (vv. 20-21). The author thus has Judas claim that he fights in a just cause. God is portrayed as the divine warrior, as in the Song of Moses (Exod 15:3, 7).

3:23-24. The surprise attack brings the desired result. The estimate of 800 slain is modest compared to other battles. "The land of the Philistines" refers to the Hellenized cities on the southern coastal plain, although they were no longer so called. Sirach uses the term "Philistine" to refer to a nation his soul detests (Sir 50:26), so the phrase probably carried pejorative connotations as a non-Israelite area.

3:25-26. The fame of Judas expands, just as God promised to the Israelites in the desert that the nations would tremble at the report of Israel's deeds (Deut 2:25), and as the fame of David spread to all lands after his defeat of the Philistines (1 Chr 14:17).

REFLECTIONS

1. The author, using traditional language, themes, and poetry, continues to portray the Maccabees as being steeped in, and upholders of, their traditional religion. He also seeks to show that they are not terrorists, but freedom fighters. As such, they claim that God is on their side, working through them to restore rightful worship. The symbiosis of divine and human action is particularly clear where the verb "crush" (συντρίβω *syntribō*) is used to describe God's action in v. 22 and to describe the act committed upon Seron, following Judas's attack, in v. 23. Judas is portrayed as a hero for his nation to emulate. One can only admire the courage of Judas and his small band as they fight to maintain their right to worship their God. Such constancy in the face of attack is admirable. However, we must also learn to be cautious when confronted with such a heroic figure. The inherent glorification of warfare, of the warrior as the hero to be emulated and imitated, rather than uplifting those who seek to redress a situation through mediation and arbitration, can lead to a glorification of violence in society. We must constantly remind ourselves that the presumption should always be against warfare, against the taking of life. So, although Judas and his followers fought against extermination of their culture, their actions must be seen as a last resort when all other efforts for peace had failed, and must not lead to a glorification of violence. One should hope that a well-trained army would never need to be so used.

2. The claim "God is with us" brings its own problems. German soldiers in Hitler's army went into battle with "God is with us" inscribed on their belt buckles. Such an attitude raises the stakes, since it polarizes a situation into us versus them, where only one side can be right and no room is left for mediation and arbitration. Religious and political leaders need to be extremely cautious in so invoking the deity as to demonize their adversaries. One can see the problem in the way Judas is portrayed as searching out lawbreakers, burning those who troubled his people, and destroying the ungodly out of the land (1 Macc 3:5, 8). Who determines what is ungodly? The zeal of Judas here prefigures that of the Inquisition in tracking down heretics, or of those who sought out "witches" in Puritan Massachusetts. Judas has gone over from defensive action, from acting so as to be able to serve God in his own way, to offensive action, destroying anyone who does not agree with his interpretation of how the law should be obeyed. Even though we may be inspired by Judas's constancy in faith, nevertheless we must be wary of adopting all the attitudes encapsulated in the narrative.

1 MACCABEES 3:27–4:35, MAJOR SELEUCID COUNTERATTACKS

1 Maccabees 3:27-37, The King's Decision

NAB	NRSV
27 When Antiochus heard about these events, he was angry; so he ordered a muster of all the forces of his kingdom, a very strong army. 28 He opened	27When King Antiochus heard these reports, he was greatly angered; and he sent and gathered all the forces of his kingdom, a very strong army.

NAB

his treasure chests, gave his soldiers a year's pay, and commanded them to be prepared for anything. ²⁹ He then found that this exhausted the money in his treasury; moreover the income from the province was small, because of the dissension and distress he had brought upon the land by abolishing the laws which had been in effect from of old. ³⁰ He feared that, as had happened more than once, he would not have enough for his expenses and for the gifts that he had previously given with a more liberal hand than the preceding kings. ³¹ Greatly perplexed, he decided to go to Persia and levy tribute on those provinces, and so raise a large sum of money. ³² He left Lysias, a nobleman of royal blood, in charge of the king's affairs from the Euphrates River to the frontier of Egypt, ³³ and commissioned him to take care of his son ·Antiochus until his own return. ³⁴ He entrusted to him half of the army, and the elephants, and gave him instructions concerning everything he wanted done. As for the inhabitants of Judea and Jerusalem, ³⁵ Lysias was to send an army against them to crush and destroy the power of Israel and the remnant of Jerusalem and efface their memory from the land. ³⁶ He was to settle foreigners in all their territory and distribute their land by lot.

³⁷ The king took the remaining half of the army and set out from Antioch, his capital, in the year one hundred and forty-seven; he crossed the Euphrates River and advanced inland.

NRSV

²⁸He opened his coffers and gave a year's pay to his forces, and ordered them to be ready for any need. ²⁹Then he saw that the money in the treasury was exhausted, and that the revenues from the country were small because of the dissension and disaster that he had caused in the land by abolishing the laws that had existed from the earliest days. ³⁰He feared that he might not have such funds as he had before for his expenses and for the gifts that he used to give more lavishly than preceding kings. ³¹He was greatly perplexed in mind; then he determined to go to Persia and collect the revenues from those regions and raise a large fund.

32He left Lysias, a distinguished man of royal lineage, in charge of the king's affairs from the river Euphrates to the borders of Egypt. ³³Lysias was also to take care of his son Antiochus until he returned. ³⁴And he turned over to Lysias*a* half of his forces and the elephants, and gave him orders about all that he wanted done. As for the residents of Judea and Jerusalem, ³⁵Lysias was to send a force against them to wipe out and destroy the strength of Israel and the remnant of Jerusalem; he was to banish the memory of them from the place, ³⁶settle aliens in all their territory, and distribute their land by lot. ³⁷Then the king took the remaining half of his forces and left Antioch his capital in the one hundred and forty-seventh year.*b* He crossed the Euphrates river and went through the upper provinces.

a Gk *him*   *b* 165 B.C.

COMMENTARY

According to the author of 1 Maccabees, the Jewish uprising is the determining factor of all the policies of the Seleucid king. In reality, the small Jewish revolutionary force was no match for the Seleucid army. Even the author of 1 Maccabees must admit that, whenever the Seleucid army is fully directed against Judea, it is victorious (1 Macc 6:33-54; 9:1-17). In fact, Antiochus IV mustered his forces to take effective control of the eastern satrapies, and not because of the revolt led by Judas, which was dealt with by Lysias, a subordinate. The Parthian kingdom began to expand gradually under Mithridates I of Parthia (175–138 BCE), so that at the death of Antiochus IV (164 BCE), it covered the whole of Iran and subsequently Mesopotamia. Antiochus's expedition, if not directly against the Parthians, was designed to hold together the Seleucid kingdom.

3:27-28. Antiochus's reaction is typical of Seleucid kings and their allies, who are frequently described as becoming angry (5:1; 6:28; 9:69; 11:22; 15:36). They are not as in control of their emotions as a wise leader should be. Often pay was given in advance to encourage and boost the soldiers' morale, but a year's pay would be very unusual. By connecting it to the expedition against Judea, the author heightens the importance of Judas's uprising.

3:29. The Seleucid Empire, through the Treaty of Apamea in 188 BCE, had lost its provinces in western Asia Minor and was forced to pay a heavy indemnity. The final payment of the indemnity had been made in 173 BCE and was no longer a consideration by the time of the events of this chapter, which occurred after 166 (2:70). Nevertheless the empire was still without funds and sorely needed to shore up its treasury in whatever way it could. The Seleucids, starting with Antiochus III, had tended to use temple funds to replenish their own depleted resources.[60] Antiochus IV was lavish in his expenditures, and no doubt he found temple treasuries a convenient target from which to refill his coffers. In fact, Antiochus IV died shortly after attempting to despoil the sanctuary of Artemis in Elam.[61] The author of 1 Maccabees associates the depletion of funds with the interference of Antiochus IV in changing the laws of all the nations (1:41), although, as mentioned previously, there is no evidence that Antiochus made any such change outside of Judea.

3:30. Antiochus IV was munificent toward the Greek temples in Delos, Athens, and elsewhere. Polybius tells us that "in the sacrifices he furnished to cities and in the honors he paid to the gods he surpassed all those who had been kings before him. This is shown by the temple to Olympian Zeus at Athens and the statues around the altar at Delos."[62] Polybius in particular stresses Antiochus IV's extravagance, saying that he would suddenly give unexpected presents to people he had never met before.[63]

3:31. "Persia" refers to the entire territory of historical Persia. The author of 1 Maccabees thus connects the king's decision to go to Persia with the expense needed to outlay an expedition against the Jewish uprising, and so enhances the latter's importance.

3:32-33. The "royal lineage" is not necessarily a blood relationship, as "kinsman of the king" was

a title given to a high-ranking courtier (see 2 Macc 11:1). Lysias was appointed regent and deputy to the king in the western districts. Antiochus V Eupator, who at this time was about seven or eight years old, was co-regent with his father in case anything happened on the eastern expedition (see 2 Macc 9:23-25).

3:34. Antiochus IV would almost certainly have taken elephants, an important part of his army, on the eastern expedition. Theoretically, the Treaty of Apamea forbade the Seleucids to possess war elephants. The Greek text, in giving the impression that all the elephants remained with Lysias, underscores the importance of the confrontation with Judas. Presumably, Lysias would have much to worry about in administering the Seleucid Empire, but the author highlights the events in Judea.

3:35-36. The author dramatizes Antiochus's command about Judea with the blanket order to destroy all the residents of Judea and Jerusalem. Earlier the author had stressed that Antiochus had strong support from many in Judea (1:52) and that a Seleucid garrison had been established in Jerusalem (1:33-35). Antiochus clearly did not want to destroy those supporters. Rather, the author reflects the perception of Judas's band that this was a life-and-death struggle for the survival of their culture, a perception that builds on the fate of the seekers after righteousness (2:38). The irony is that Lysias is sent to stamp out the strength of Israel, while the reader knows that this strength is from heaven (3:19) and thus cannot be stamped out.

Antiochus IV is said to intend to set up military settlements in Judea, thus abolishing the *polis* of Antioch-in-Jerusalem (2 Macc 4:9, 19), as well as revoking any privileges that had previously been bestowed on the citizens of Judea. The author of 1 Maccabees makes no mention of such a *polis* or of such privileges. Either he did not know of them, or he wanted to erase them completely from memory. The author once again emphasizes only the dire straits that Judea was placed in, as well as the tyrannous character of Antiochus IV.

3:37. Antiochus IV left on his eastward march in 165 BCE. Opinions differ as to whether it was in early or late summer; the answer depends on whether the co-regency of his son Antiochus V, which lasted eighteen months, be-

---

60. Polybius 10:27; Diodorus Siculus 28:3; 29:15; Strabo 16.1.18; Justin *Epitome* 32.2.1-2.
61. Polybius 31.9.1-4.
62. Ibid., 26.1.10-11; cf. 29.24.13.
63. Ibid., 26.1.9.

gan when Antiochus IV left for Persia or a little earlier. Also, the exact date of Antiochus IV's death is unknown; his death became known in Babylon sometime between November 20 and December 18, 164 BCE.

1 Maccabees 3:38–4:25, The Battle Against Nicanor and Gorgias

1 Maccabees 3:38-60, Preparations for Battle

NAB

[38] Lysias chose Ptolemy, son of Dorymenes, and Nicanor and Gorgias, capable men among the King's Friends, [39] and with them he sent forty thousand men and seven thousand cavalry to invade the land of Judah and ravage it according to the king's orders. [40] Setting out with all their forces, they came and pitched their camp near Emmaus in the plain. [41] When the merchants of the country heard of their fame, they came to the camp, bringing fetters and a large sum of silver and gold, to buy the Israelites as slaves. A force from Idumea and from Philistia joined with them.

[42] Judas and his brothers saw that the situation had become critical now that armies were encamped within their territory; they knew of the orders which the king had given to destroy and utterly wipe out the people. [43] So they said to one another, "Let us restore our people from their ruined estate, and fight for our people and our sanctuary!"

[44] The assembly gathered together to prepare for battle and to pray and implore mercy and compassion.

[45] Jerusalem was uninhabited, like a desert;
    not one of her children entered or came
        out.
The sanctuary was trampled on,
    and foreigners were in the citadel;
    it was a habitation of Gentiles.
Joy had disappeared from Jacob,
    and the flute and the harp were silent.

[46] Thus they assembled and went to Mizpah near Jerusalem, because there was formerly at

NRSV

[38] Lysias chose Ptolemy son of Dorymenes, and Nicanor and Gorgias, able men among the Friends of the king, [39] and sent with them forty thousand infantry and seven thousand cavalry to go into the land of Judah and destroy it, as the king had commanded. [40] So they set out with their entire force, and when they arrived they encamped near Emmaus in the plain. [41] When the traders of the region heard what was said to them, they took silver and gold in immense amounts, and fetters,[a] and went to the camp to get the Israelites for slaves. And forces from Syria and the land of the Philistines joined with them.

[42] Now Judas and his brothers saw that misfortunes had increased and that the forces were encamped in their territory. They also learned what the king had commanded to do to the people to cause their final destruction. [43] But they said to one another, "Let us restore the ruins of our people, and fight for our people and the sanctuary." [44] So the congregation assembled to be ready for battle, and to pray and ask for mercy and compassion.

[45] Jerusalem was uninhabited like a wilderness;
    not one of her children went in or out.
The sanctuary was trampled down,
    and aliens held the citadel;
    it was a lodging place for the Gentiles.
Joy was taken from Jacob;
    the flute and the harp ceased to play.

[46] Then they gathered together and went to Mizpah, opposite Jerusalem, because Israel formerly had a place of prayer in Mizpah. [47] They fasted that day, put on sackcloth and sprinkled ashes on their heads, and tore their clothes. [48] And they opened the book of the law to inquire into

3, 40: (kai) apēran (syn): so LXXA,MSS.
3, 41: (dynamis) Idoumaias (kai gēs): conj.; Greek translator mistook Hebrew 'ēdōm for 'ărām.

a Syr: Gk Mss, Vg slaves

NAB

Mizpah a place of prayer for Israel. [47] That day they fasted and wore sackcloth; they sprinkled ashes on their heads and tore their clothes. [48] They unrolled the scroll of the law, to learn about the things for which the Gentiles consulted the images of their idols. [49] They brought with them the priestly vestments, the first fruits, and the tithes; and they brought forward the nazirites who had completed the time of their vows. [50] And they cried aloud to Heaven: "What shall we do with these men, and where shall we take them? [51] For your sanctuary has been trampled on and profaned, and your priests are in mourning and humiliation. [52] Now the Gentiles are gathered together against us to destroy us. You know what they plot against us. [53] How shall we be able to resist them unless you help us?" [54] Then they blew the trumpets and cried out loudly.

[55] After this Judas appointed officers among the people, over thousands, over hundreds, over fifties, and over tens. [56] He proclaimed that those who were building houses, or were just married, or were planting vineyards, and those who were afraid, could each return to his home, according to the law. [57] Then the army moved off, and they camped to the south of Emmaus. [58] Judas said: "Arm yourselves and be brave; in the morning be ready to fight these Gentiles who have assembled against us to destroy us and our sanctuary. [59] It is better for us to die in battle than to witness the ruin of our nation and our sanctuary. [60] Whatever Heaven wills, he will do."

NRSV

those matters about which the Gentiles consulted the likenesses of their gods. [49]They also brought the vestments of the priesthood and the first fruits and the tithes, and they stirred up the nazirites[a] who had completed their days; [50]and they cried aloud to Heaven, saying,

"What shall we do with these?
Where shall we take them?
[51] Your sanctuary is trampled down and profaned,
and your priests mourn in humiliation.
[52] Here the Gentiles are assembled against us to destroy us;
you know what they plot against us.
[53] How will we be able to withstand them,
if you do not help us?"

[54]Then they sounded the trumpets and gave a loud shout. [55]After this Judas appointed leaders of the people, in charge of thousands and hundreds and fifties and tens. [56]Those who were building houses, or were about to be married, or were planting a vineyard, or were fainthearted, he told to go home again, according to the law. [57]Then the army marched out and encamped to the south of Emmaus.

[58]And Judas said, "Arm yourselves and be courageous. Be ready early in the morning to fight with these Gentiles who have assembled against us to destroy us and our sanctuary. [59]It is better for us to die in battle than to see the misfortunes of our nation and of the sanctuary. [60]But as his will in heaven may be, so shall he do."

[a] That is *those separated* or *those consecrated*

COMMENTARY

3:38-41, On the Seleucid Side. 3:38. To emphasize the importance of this battle, the author of 1 Maccabees reports that Lysias, the deputy king, oversaw the arrangements appointing a triumvirate to lead the Seleucid forces against Judas. The author of 2 Maccabees, on the other hand, states that Philip, the Seleucid official in charge of Jerusalem (2 Macc 5:22), appealed for help from Ptolemy, the governor of Coelesyria and Phoenicia, who appointed Nicanor, leader of a large army, with Gorgias as his deputy (2 Macc 8:8-9). The more circumstantial account in 2 Macc

8:9-36, with its well-defined chain of command (rather than a triumvirate), is more likely. Nicanor, as one of the king's first friends (2 Macc 8:9), may have governed one of the important coastal regions. Gorgias later became governor of Idumea after the purification of the Temple (2 Macc 12:32).

3:39. The figures seem exaggerated. Second Maccabees reports that the army comprised only 20,000 soldiers (2 Macc 8:9), a number that may reflect the battles of David against the Arameans

(2 Sam 10:6, 18). Such a large cavalry force would not have been of much use in the hills of Judea.

3:40. Emmaus, literally "Ammaus," is about 20 miles west-northwest of Jerusalem. According to 1 Macc 9:50, Emmaus lay within the province of Judea. At the eastern edge of the Aijalon Valley, this position controlled the western entrances to Jerusalem and provided easy access to the rear. It was a fertile land with good water supply, and so it was an excellent choice for a camp for a long period.

3:41. Merchants were used as contractors in Hellenistic army camps, but the authors of 1 and 2 Maccabees (2 Macc 8:11) stress the enemy's evil intentions by relating that they were slave traders. Also, since Nicanor's force came from Syria, it has been suggested that they were joined by forces from Idumea, not Syria. The original Hebrew may have read "Idumea" (אדם 'ĕdôm) rather than "Syria" (ארם 'ărām). This is bolstered by the fact that the defeated enemy will flee to Idumea (1 Macc 4:15).

3:42-60, On the Jewish Side. 3:42. Judas and his brothers learn of the large force massed to attack. The phrase "misfortunes had increased" (ἐπληθύνθη τὰ κακά eplēthynthē ta kaka) recalls the era of chaos immediately following Alexander's death (1:9). The term "final destruction" (ἀπώλειαν καὶ συντέλειαν apōleian kai synteleian) refers to Antiochus's commands to dismantle Judea and turn it into a military colony (vv. 35-36). Although the Israelites had frequently sinned against God in previous times, God had not made an end of them (Jer 4:27; 5:10, 18; Ezek 11:13-21). Hope thus remains for the beleaguered forces of Judas.

3:43-44. The same emphasis on community, signified by each speaking to the other, is also found at 2:40. The members of each group exhort those of the other to fight, just as Joab had exhorted his brother Abishai when they were surrounded by their enemies (2 Sam 10:11-12; 1 Chr 19:12-13). The exhortation also echoes the promise of Amos that the fallen booth of David will be raised up (Amos 9:11), as well as the hope expressed in Jeremiah that God will build up the people and not tear them down, plant them and not pluck them up (Jer 24:6; 42:10). Preparations for war must be paralleled by prayer and petition.

3:45. The author breaks into a lament over Jerusalem, perhaps as an explanation for why the troops assembled at Mizpah (v. 46). Note the parallel style, typical of the poetry of the Hebrew Bible.

3:46. Mizpah has been identified with a site eight miles north of Jerusalem. It was here that the Israelites assembled to punish the tribe of Benjamin for the rape of the Levite's concubine (Judges 20–21). Here, also, Samuel assembled all the people to repent and fast, and God aided the Israelites in winning a great victory over the Philistines (1 Sam 7:5-11). Since Jerusalem cannot be seen from Mizpah, the term "opposite" may be used loosely as, for example, at 1 Macc 6:32, where Beth-zechariah is said to be "opposite" Beth-zur, even though the two sites are ten kilometers apart. Or "opposite" could translate the Hebrew word נגד (neged), which can mean "like," "comparable to" (cf. Gen 2:18, 20). Mizpah is not far from the Beth-horon ascent, and so an army could easily retreat into the Gophna Hills from this site.

3:47. Fasting, putting on sackcloth, sprinkling ashes on the head, and tearing clothes are all traditional mourning customs. Although often elements of mourning past events or catastrophes, such deeds also were signs of repentance intended to avert divine punishment for past misdeeds—see, for example, the reactions of Ahab, when he heard Elijah's prediction of how his dynasty would fall (1 Kgs 21:27); the whole community of Israel, before confessing their sins and those of their ancestors (Neh 9:1); and the king of Nineveh, when he heard Jonah's prophecy (Jonah 3:5).

3:48. This verse is extremely difficult to translate. The NRSV translation, "to inquire into those matters about which the Gentiles consulted the likenesses of their gods," not only is difficult to justify grammatically, but also suggests an analogy between the Torah and idol worship that the author of 1 Maccabees would have been unlikely to make. Some Greek manuscripts read, "about which the Gentiles sought to write/paint on them the images of their idols," indicating that books of the law that had been defiled were unrolled to remind God of the iniquities that had been performed (1:56-57). This variant reading, although attempting to make sense of the text, is not easy to justify. Public mourning is often accompanied by public reading of the Torah in adherence to the covenant (Neh 9:1-3). But no mention is made of such painting in 1 Macc 1:56-57. Neither does this reading do justice to the Greek preposition περί (*peri*), which means "concerning." Moreover, a book or scroll is unrolled so that it can be read. A better translation of this verse would be: "They unrolled the book of the Torah concerning those things about which they were inquiring, namely, the Gentiles and the likenesses of their idols." This would mean that the assembled congregation read those sections of the Torah that told how the Gentiles and their idols were to be dealt with (e.g., Deuteronomy 4; 7). The reading of the law may also be compared with the consultation of the Lord before battle (Judg 20:18; 1 Sam 23:2; 2 Sam 5:19, 23).

3:49. The priestly vestments mentioned here are those used for service in the Temple (Exod 28:40-43; 39:1). The *War Scroll* from Qumran suggests that the vestments the priests wore for battle could not be brought into the Temple,[64] and so distinguishes between two sets of vestments. First fruits, which may have included the firstborn of clean animals (see Exod 13:12-15; 34:22-26; Lev 23:17-20; Deut 12:6-18), were obligatory offerings brought during the Second Temple period around the Feast of Weeks or the Feast of Tabernacles. First fruits and tithes were the portion of the priests and Levites (Exod 23:19*a*; Num 18:13; Deut 18:4) and, by the second century BCE, normally would have been offered only at the Temple in Jerusalem. Mizpah is thus depicted here as an alternate Jerusalem, since Jerusalem was defiled and under the control of the Seleucids and their followers.

There were different kinds of tithes: some were allotted to the sanctuary (Lev 27:30-33), some to the Levites (Num 18:21-24), and some to the offerers themselves to eat in the presence of the Lord (Deut 14:22-28). God had promised through the prophet Malachi that if the people gave tithes to the sanctuary, God would bless them with fruitfulness (Mal 3:10), and Tobit is described as diligently obeying the law about tithing and even surpassing it to the extent of giving a second and a third tithe (Tob 1:6-8; see also the mention of tithes and first fruits in 2 Chr 31:5-12; Neh 12:44; 13:5, 10; Jdt 11:13).

The mention of the Nazirites is another indication that Mizpah is considered a substitute for Jerusalem. At the end of their vows, Nazirites had to present themselves at the Temple in order to show that their obligations had been discharged by cutting their hair and offering a sacrifice (Num 6:13-20).

3:50-53. Once again, the author of 1 Maccabees breaks into poetry, here a community lament and prayer for help, echoing the language of 1:39-40; 2:12; 3:35; and 3:45. The appeal for help is found frequently in the psalms (e.g., Pss 20:2; 35:2; 38:22; 62:7; 94:17; 108:12; 121:1-2).

3:54. Trumpets were to be sounded before going to war "so that you may be remembered before the LORD your God and saved from your enemies" (Num 10:9 NRSV).[65]

3:55-57. The division of the army (v. 55) follows the example of Jethro's advice to Moses (Exod 18:21, 25) and Moses' actual division of the people (Deut 1:15), but it differs from the account of Judas's division of the troops in 2 Macc 8:22. Since the division is not used in describing the strategy of the battle, the author is portraying Judas as a traditionalist, a portrayal that continues with the description of his actions in v. 56, which are based in the regulations of Deuteronomy (Deut 20:5-8). The movement of the camp should be seen as in tandem with the action of Gorgias (1 Macc 4:1-5), not as preceding it. Judas left Mizpah, and Gorgias set out for Mizpah independently of each other. By leaving Mizpah, Judas resolved to use the element of surprise, even without the advantage of Gorgias's leaving the camp.

3:58-60. Judas's speech reflects the one that the priest is assigned to give to the Israelites before going to war (Deut 20:2-4). The Qumran *War Scroll* also recounts a speech by the priest, wherein the phrase "be courageous" (lit., "be powerful sons") is found (see also 2 Sam 2:7; 13:28).[66] Judas encourages his soldiers with the same sentiments found at 1 Macc 2:7. The description of the strength of the Seleucid forces, followed by the move from a defensive posture at Mizpah to a more offensive move toward the enemy's camp, leads to this rather despairing assessment of the outcome: Better to die fighting (v. 59). Nevertheless, Judas ends with a strong

64. See 1QM 7:11-12.

65. Cf. IQM 10:7.
66. See 1QM 15:7.

conditional statement: "One never knows, God might help us and we could win" (see v. 60).

The author thus keeps the reader in suspense as to what will happen.

1 Maccabees 4:1-25, The Battle at Emmaus

NAB

4 Now Gorgias took five thousand infantry and a thousand picked cavalry, and this detachment set out at night ² in order to attack the camp of the Jews and take them by surprise. Some men from the citadel were their guides. ³ Judas heard of it, and himself set out with his soldiers to attack the king's army at Emmaus, ⁴ while the latter's forces were still scattered away from the camp. ⁵ During the night Gorgias came into the camp of Judas, and found no one there; so he began to hunt for them in the mountains, saying, "They are fleeing from us."

⁶ But at daybreak Judas appeared in the plain with three thousand men, who lacked such armor and swords as they would have wished. ⁷ They saw the army of the Gentiles, strong and breastplated, flanked with cavalry, and made up of expert soldiers. ⁸ Judas said to the men with him: "Do not be afraid of their numbers or dread their attack. ⁹ Remember how our fathers were saved in the Red Sea, when Pharaoh pursued them with an army. ¹⁰ So now let us cry to Heaven in the hope that he will favor us, remember his covenant with our fathers, and destroy this army before us today. ¹¹ All the Gentiles shall know that there is One who redeems and delivers Israel."

¹² When the foreigners looked up and saw them marching toward them, ¹³ they came out of their camp for battle, and the men with Judas blew the trumpet. ¹⁴ The battle was joined and the Gentiles were defeated and fled toward the plain. ¹⁵ Their whole rearguard fell by the sword, and they were pursued as far as Gazara and the plains of Judea, to Azotus and Jamnia. About three thousand of their men fell.

¹⁶ When Judas and the army returned from the pursuit, ¹⁷ he said to the people: "Do not be greedy for the plunder, for there is a fight ahead of us, ¹⁸ and Gorgias and his army are near us on the mountain. But now stand firm against our

4, 15: (tōn pedíōn tēs) Ioudaias (kai Azōtou; so LXXᴬ,ᴹˢˢ).

NRSV

4 Now Gorgias took five thousand infantry and one thousand picked cavalry, and this division moved out by night ²to fall upon the camp of the Jews and attack them suddenly. Men from the citadel were his guides. ³But Judas heard of it, and he and his warriors moved out to attack the king's force in Emmaus ⁴while the division was still absent from the camp. ⁵When Gorgias entered the camp of Judas by night, he found no one there, so he looked for them in the hills, because he said, "These men are running away from us."

⁶At daybreak Judas appeared in the plain with three thousand men, but they did not have armor and swords such as they desired. ⁷And they saw the camp of the Gentiles, strong and fortified, with cavalry all around it; and these men were trained in war. ⁸But Judas said to those who were with him, "Do not fear their numbers or be afraid when they charge. ⁹Remember how our ancestors were saved at the Red Sea, when Pharaoh with his forces pursued them. ¹⁰And now, let us cry to Heaven, to see whether he will favor us and remember his covenant with our ancestors and crush this army before us today. ¹¹Then all the Gentiles will know that there is one who redeems and saves Israel."

¹²When the foreigners looked up and saw them coming against them, ¹³they went out from their camp to battle. Then the men with Judas blew their trumpets ¹⁴and engaged in battle. The Gentiles were crushed, and fled into the plain, ¹⁵and all those in the rear fell by the sword. They pursued them to Gazara, and to the plains of Idumea, and to Azotus and Jamnia; and three thousand of them fell. ¹⁶Then Judas and his force turned back from pursuing them, ¹⁷and he said to the people, "Do not be greedy for plunder, for there is a battle before us; ¹⁸Gorgias and his force are near us in the hills. But stand now against our enemies and fight them, and afterward seize the plunder boldly."

NAB

enemies and overthrow them. Afterward you can freely take the plunder."

¹⁹ As Judas was finishing this speech, a detachment appeared, looking down from the mountain. ²⁰ They saw that their army had been put to flight and their camp was being burned. The smoke that could be seen indicated what had happened. ²¹ When they realized this, they were terrified; and when they also saw the army of Judas in the plain ready to attack, ²² they all fled to Philistine territory.

²³ Then Judas went back to plunder the camp, and his men collected much gold and silver, violet and crimson cloth, and great treasure. ²⁴ As they returned, they were singing hymns and glorifying Heaven, "for he is good, for his mercy endures forever." ²⁵ Thus Israel had a great deliverance that day.

NRSV

19Just as Judas was finishing this speech, a detachment appeared, coming out of the hills. ²⁰They saw that their army*a* had been put to flight, and that the Jews*a* were burning the camp, for the smoke that was seen showed what had happened. ²¹When they perceived this, they were greatly frightened, and when they also saw the army of Judas drawn up in the plain for battle, ²²they all fled into the land of the Philistines. ²³Then Judas returned to plunder the camp, and they seized a great amount of gold and silver, and cloth dyed blue and sea purple, and great riches. ²⁴On their return they sang hymns and praises to Heaven—"For he is good, for his mercy endures forever." ²⁵Thus Israel had a great deliverance that day.

a Gk *they*

COMMENTARY

4:1-5. The Seleucids decide to try a surprise night assault against the assembly at Mizpah, about which the Syrians have been informed. The Syrians were guided through the Judean hills by scouts from the Jerusalem citadel, probably Jews who were not of Judas's persuasion. In his hubris, Gorgias thinks the Jews are fleeing, but to the contrary, Judas is preparing to attack.

4:6-18. Judas's forces, which number 3,000 men (cf. 7:40; 9:5), are outmatched more than thirteen to one. Judas's forces are not fully equipped, in contrast to the heavily armed Seleucid forces. Judas's rallying cry, using the language of Deut 1:21, again recalls that of the priest before battle (Deut 20:3-5; the prayer of the priest before battle in the Qumran *War Scroll* also alludes to the defeat of Pharaoh [1QM 11:9-10]). Judas prays that their cry will be heard, just as the prayer of the suffering Israelites in Egypt was heard by God, who remembered the covenant with Abraham, Isaac, and Jacob (Exod 2:23-24). Further, when David defeated Goliath, it was known in all the earth that "there is a God in Israel" (1 Sam 17:46 NRSV). Thus with his appeal to the faith of his troops and the tactical advantage

of attacking from the hills, Judas wins a convincing victory and puts the enemy to flight.

4:15. Gazara, about four and one-half miles northwest of Emmaus, was the closest Seleucid fort (1 Macc 7:45). If Gorgias's forces included Idumeans (see Commentary on 1 Macc 3:42), some of the force retreated homeward. Azotus is biblical Ashdod, whose territory extended to near Gazara (1 Macc 14:34). The flight, therefore, was to the north, the south, and the east.

4:16-18. Having won the battle, Judas and his troops regroup. Second Maccabees 8:26, however, gives an alternate reason for their stopping the pursuit: The next day was the sabbath (probably due to that author's desire to emphasize Judas's Torah observance).

4:19-22. Returning from the plateau around Mizpah, Gorgias and his expeditionary force see from the burning camp that the battle is over. Judas had exhorted his soldiers not to be frightened (4:8), but that is now the reaction of the enemy. The author also suggests that Judas's army was as ready for battle as ever, and this fierceness results in the enemy's flight.

4:23-25. Once all danger is past, the Israelites are free to plunder the enemy camp. The riches have been brought in part by slave traders (3:41). Blue and purple are the famous "Tyrian" dyes. The pair "blue and purple," like "silver and gold," is found frequently in the Hebrew Scriptures to describe the rich furnishings of the Temple (e.g., Exod 25:4; 35:23, 25, 35). In this case, these colors probably refer to the outer clothing of the infantry and the cavalry. Polybius described the cavalry of Antiochus IV, as they paraded in the festival of Daphnae, as wearing purple outer garments, some of which were golden and adorned with figures.[67] The Israelites celebrate their victory by marching home (presumably to Mizpah) to the sound of hymns (Pss 106:1; 107:1; 136:1; cf. 2 Chr 20:21). The battle account is thus framed liturgically by the penitential service (3:47) and this chant of victory. The author's closing comment draws once more on traditional language (Exod 14:13; 1 Sam 11:13; 19:5; 2 Kgs 13:5).

67. Polybius 30.25.10.

REFLECTIONS

1. The author has emphasized through his liturgical frame for the whole battle around Emmaus the importance of prayer and repentance if one is to succeed. The forces of Judas are seen as totally devoted to God's law, and this inner conviction drives them to victory. In contrast, the Seleucid forces are given no inner resolve; they are simply obeying the vengeful orders of the king and, with their slave traders, are hoping to gain wealth. In our own time we have seen how hard it is even for the most advanced military power to defeat an army that is driven to defend its own homeland. The narrative here in 1 Maccabees makes us reflect on how a major military power should use its power in the world. Antiochus IV's pique at being rebuffed is clearly not a model for any commander in chief to follow. Nor is the decision to utterly annihilate one's opponent, no matter how great the provocation may be. Rather, greatness is shown not by excessive use of force, but by benevolent treatment. Only the really strong can afford to be gracious. The message of this narrative should be that one should not try to impose solutions, but should try to gather all parties together to see if, by patient diplomacy, disagreements can be resolved.

2. The Seleucid Empire encompassed a great deal of territory and many different cultures and races, and it finally broke apart as different regions sought independence. How can one nation allow its diverse cultural groups the freedom to express their own individual spirit, to maintain their own cultural identities, and yet not cause the nation to so split apart that it cannot hang together? How can the diverse groups learn to respect each other's traditions and cultures? This problem has been present since the growth of nationalism in the nineteenth century. If one tries to suppress cultural differences and create a homogeneous society, eventually the dam holding back these repressed feelings will break. One solution for such divisions might be for us all to try to learn more about one another's traditions and cultures. We need to seize every opportunity to teach children, youth, and adults about the many religious traditions that make up the fabric of society, and so to bring them to understand other perspectives and not ignorantly reject them as "other."

1 Maccabees 4:26-35, The Campaign of Lysias

NAB	NRSV
26 But those of the foreigners who had escaped went and told Lysias all that had occurred. 27 When he heard it he was disturbed and dis-	26Those of the foreigners who escaped went and reported to Lysias all that had happened. 27When he heard it, he was perplexed and dis-

couraged, because things in Israel had not turned out as he intended and as the king had ordered.

28 So the following year he gathered together sixty thousand picked men and five thousand cavalry, to subdue them. 29 They came into Idumea and camped at Beth-zur, and Judas met them with ten thousand men. 30 Seeing that the army was strong, he prayed thus:

"Blessed are you, O Savior of Israel, who broke the rush of the mighty one by the hand of your servant David and delivered the camp of the Philistines into the hand of Jonathan, the son of Saul, and his armor-bearer. 31 Give this army into the hands of your people Israel; make them ashamed of their troops and their cavalry. 32 Strike them with fear, weaken the boldness of their strength, and let them tremble at their own destruction. 33 Strike them down by the sword of those who love you, that all who know your name may hymn your praise."

34 Then they engaged in battle, and about five thousand of Lysias' men fell in hand-to-hand fighting. 35 When Lysias saw his ranks beginning to give way, and the increased boldness of Judas, whose men were ready either to live or to die bravely, he withdrew to Antioch and began to recruit mercenaries so as to return to Judea with greater numbers.

couraged, for things had not happened to Israel as he had intended, nor had they turned out as the king had ordered. 28But the next year he mustered sixty thousand picked infantry and five thousand cavalry to subdue them. 29They came into Idumea and encamped at Beth-zur, and Judas met them with ten thousand men.

30When he saw that their army was strong, he prayed, saying, "Blessed are you, O Savior of Israel, who crushed the attack of the mighty warrior by the hand of your servant David, and gave the camp of the Philistines into the hands of Jonathan son of Saul, and of the man who carried his armor. 31Hem in this army by the hand of your people Israel, and let them be ashamed of their troops and their cavalry. 32Fill them with cowardice; melt the boldness of their strength; let them tremble in their destruction. 33Strike them down with the sword of those who love you, and let all who know your name praise you with hymns."

34Then both sides attacked, and there fell of the army of Lysias five thousand men; they fell in action.[a] 35When Lysias saw the rout of his troops and observed the boldness that inspired those of Judas, and how ready they were either to live or to die nobly, he withdrew to Antioch and enlisted mercenaries in order to invade Judea again with an even larger army.

[a] Or and some fell on the opposite side

COMMENTARY

4:26-27. The plans of Antiochus (3:34-36) and his deputy Lysias are frustrated, as Lysias admits here; Antiochus makes the same admission at 6:8. This theme of "man proposes but God disposes" runs throughout the book.

4:28-29. The phrase "the next year" raises questions. If one dates Antiochus's march to the eastern satrapies in late 165 BCE, then this decision would have occurred in late 164 BCE. This length of time is surprising, and the author of 1 Maccabees makes no attempt to fill in the gap. From letters preserved in 2 Maccabees 11, however, we learn that Antiochus IV, at the prompting of the high priest Menelaus, offered amnesty to the Jews in March 164 BCE, by which they could enjoy

their own laws as formerly (2 Macc 11:27-33). Lysias and Ptolemy Macron seem to have been brokers to the peace terms (2 Macc 11:16-21; 2 Macc 10:12). These peace negotiations would have taken place during this time covered by the phrase "the next year." The author of 1 Maccabees makes no mention of these negotiations because he insists on painting his Jewish enemies, as well as Lysias and Antiochus, as implacably opposed to Judas and true Judaism. Why the negotiations failed is not known. The increase in Judas's forces from 3,000 in 4:6 to 10,000 in 4:29, even allowing for inflated figures, suggests that Judas had used the time to recruit.

According to the author, Lysias assembles an

even larger force of infantry than does Ptolemy, but with fewer cavalry (3:38), no doubt anticipating a battle in the Judean hills. Lysias also chooses a new route. Instead of the approach from the west, he moves into the Judean hills from the southeast, through Idumea and Mt. Hebron. Beth-zur, where they encamped, was on Judea's southern border with Idumea (1 Macc 4:61; 14:33) and has been identified with Khirbet el Tabeiqa. (According to 2 Macc 11:5-6, Lysias besieges Beth-zur.)

4:30-33. Judas's prayer first remembers and thanks God for past victories before asking for help in the present situation. The word for "Philistines" (αλλοφύλοι *allophyloi,* v. 30) is the same as the word for "foreigners" in v. 26, so the examples of David (1 Samuel 17) and Jonathan (1 Sam 14:1-15) are appropriate in a battle against armies invading the land. In the requests for help (vv. 31-33), Judas calls his group "your people Israel," "those who love you," and "all who know your name," whereas his opponents remain unnamed, a generic enemy. Judas calls on the divine warrior to instill fear into their enemy, and they will praise God as did Moses and the Israelites (Exodus 15).

4:34-35. "Rout" (τροπή *trope*) should be translated "reversal." If 5,000 soldiers had fallen, presumably there would have been a panicked retreat, but Lysias is here described as withdrawing in an organized way (2 Macc 11:16 describes a panicked flight). In reality, Lysias, as vice regent, may have received news of Antiochus IV's death and decided to return to Antioch to act as regent for Antiochus V. This is not suggested by the author of 1 Maccabees, who records the king's death after the purification of the Temple.

The Maccabees are shown to be ready (cf. 4:21), cast in a heroic mode as prepared to die with honor. They stand in marked contrast to the shameful behavior of their enemy, who turn and run (4:35). Their action corresponds to the prayer of Judas that the enemy be ashamed of their troops and cavalry (4:31-32). A further contrast is made between Judas and his men, who fight for their country, and those who fight for money with no inner conviction (4:35). The very brevity of the battle scene, as compared to the lengthy prayer of Judas, suggests that the author is hazy about the details.

1 MACCABEES 4:36-61, THE CLEANSING OF THE TEMPLE

NAB

36 Then Judas and his brothers said, "Now that our enemies have been crushed, let us go up to purify the sanctuary and rededicate it." 37 So the whole army assembled, and went up to Mount Zion. 38 They found the sanctuary desolate, the altar desecrated, the gates burnt, weeds growing in the courts as in a forest or on some mountain, and the priests' chambers demolished. 39 Then they tore their clothes and made great lamentation; they sprinkled their heads with ashes 40 and fell with their faces to the ground. And when the signal was given with trumpets, they cried out to Heaven.

41 Judas appointed men to attack those in the citadel, while he purified the sanctuary. 42 He chose blameless priests, devoted to the law; 43 these purified the sanctuary and carried away the stones of the Abomination to an unclean place.

NRSV

36Then Judas and his brothers said, "See, our enemies are crushed; let us go up to cleanse the sanctuary and dedicate it." 37So all the army assembled and went up to Mount Zion. 38There they saw the sanctuary desolate, the altar profaned, and the gates burned. In the courts they saw bushes sprung up as in a thicket, or as on one of the mountains. They saw also the chambers of the priests in ruins. 39Then they tore their clothes and mourned with great lamentation; they sprinkled themselves with ashes 40and fell face down on the ground. And when the signal was given with the trumpets, they cried out to Heaven.

41Then Judas detailed men to fight against those in the citadel until he had cleansed the sanctuary. 42He chose blameless priests devoted to the law, 43and they cleansed the sanctuary and

NAB

44 They deliberated what ought to be done with the altar of holocausts that had been desecrated. 45 The happy thought came to them to tear it down, lest it be a lasting shame to them that the Gentiles had defiled it; so they tore down the altar. 46 They stored the stones in a suitable place on the temple hill, until a prophet should come and decide what to do with them. 47 Then they took uncut stones, according to the law, and built a new altar like the former one. 48 They also repaired the sanctuary and the interior of the temple and purified the courts. 49 They made new sacred vessels and brought the lampstand, the altar of incense, and the table into the temple. 50 Then they burned incense on the altar and lighted the lamps on the lampstand, and these illuminated the temple. 51 They also put loaves on the table and hung up the curtains. Thus they finished all the work they had undertaken.

52 Early in the morning on the twenty-fifth day of the ninth month, that is, the month of Chislev, in the year one hundred and forty-eight, 53 they arose and offered sacrifice according to the law on the new altar of holocausts that they had made. 54 On the anniversary of the day on which the Gentiles had defiled it, on that very day it was reconsecrated with songs, harps, flutes, and cymbals. 55 All the people prostrated themselves and adored and praised Heaven, who had given them success.

56 For eight days they celebrated the dedication of the altar and joyfully offered holocausts and sacrifices of deliverance and praise. 57 They ornamented the façade of the temple with gold crowns and shields; they repaired the gates and the priests' chambers and furnished them with doors. 58 There was great joy among the people now that the disgrace of the Gentiles was removed. 59 Then Judas and his brothers and the entire congregation of Israel decreed that the days of the dedication of the altar should be observed with joy and gladness on the anniversary every year for eight days, from the twenty-fifth day of the month Chislev.

60 At that time they built high walls and strong towers around Mount Zion, to prevent the Gentiles from coming and trampling over it as they had done before. 61 Judas also placed a garrison

NRSV

removed the defiled stones to an unclean place. 44They deliberated what to do about the altar of burnt offering, which had been profaned. 45And they thought it best to tear it down, so that it would not be a lasting shame to them that the Gentiles had defiled it. So they tore down the altar, 46and stored the stones in a convenient place on the temple hill until a prophet should come to tell what to do with them. 47Then they took unhewn[a] stones, as the law directs, and built a new altar like the former one. 48They also rebuilt the sanctuary and the interior of the temple, and consecrated the courts. 49They made new holy vessels, and brought the lampstand, the altar of incense, and the table into the temple. 50Then they offered incense on the altar and lit the lamps on the lampstand, and these gave light in the temple. 51They placed the bread on the table and hung up the curtains. Thus they finished all the work they had undertaken.

52Early in the morning on the twenty-fifth day of the ninth month, which is the month of Chislev, in the one hundred forty-eighth year,[b] 53they rose and offered sacrifice, as the law directs, on the new altar of burnt offering that they had built. 54At the very season and on the very day that the Gentiles had profaned it, it was dedicated with songs and harps and lutes and cymbals. 55All the people fell on their faces and worshiped and blessed Heaven, who had prospered them. 56So they celebrated the dedication of the altar for eight days, and joyfully offered burnt offerings; they offered a sacrifice of well-being and a thanksgiving offering. 57They decorated the front of the temple with golden crowns and small shields; they restored the gates and the chambers for the priests, and fitted them with doors. 58There was very great joy among the people, and the disgrace brought by the Gentiles was removed.

59Then Judas and his brothers and all the assembly of Israel determined that every year at that season the days of dedication of the altar should be observed with joy and gladness for eight days, beginning with the twenty-fifth day of the month of Chislev.

60At that time they fortified Mount Zion with high walls and strong towers all around, to keep

a Gk whole   b 164 B.C.

NAB

there to protect it, and likewise fortified Beth-zur, that the people might have a stronghold facing Idumea.

4, 61: Omit *auto tērein* after *ochyrōsen*: so LXX^{MSS}, P^{MSS}; dittog.

NRSV

the Gentiles from coming and trampling them down as they had done before. [61]Judas[a] stationed a garrison there to guard it; he also fortified Beth-zur to guard it, so that the people might have a stronghold that faced Idumea.

[a] Gk *He*

COMMENTARY

After his victories, Judas goes up to Mt. Zion. The victory march to God's holy mountain is part of an ancient mythic pattern describing the battles of the divine warrior, as exemplified in the great hymn of victory at Exodus 15. The Temple is where God dwells, the connecting point where heaven and earth meet, a stabilizing force for the maintenance of the proper order of creation. With the Temple desecrated, the world of the Jews was askew; therefore, it was essential that the Temple be reconsecrated and the world put right.

4:36-37. The enemies have been crushed by the divine warrior (v. 30; cf. Exod 15:3). The term "dedicate" or "renew" (ἐγκαινίζω *egkainizō*) is used to describe Solomon's dedication of the Temple (1 Kgs 8:63; 2 Chr 7:5 LXX), the dedication of the Temple under Ezra (Ezra 6:16-17), Asa's repair of the altar (2 Chr 15:8), and Nehemiah's dedication of the walls of Jerusalem (Neh 12:27). The expression "go up" (ἀναβαίνω *anabainō*) is the language of the psalms (Pss 24:3; 121:4). The wholeness of the community is emphasized as all the army goes up. So, too, when Solomon dedicated the Temple, all the people of Israel assembled (1 Kgs 8:1-5).

4:38. The author refers to the desecration described earlier (1:31; 2:12). He draws on descriptions of a defeated city to heighten the emotional effect: Micah had foretold how the temple mount would become a wooded height (Mic 3:12), and Isaiah graphically depicted the desolate state of a destroyed land (Isa 34:13-15). The author moves from the outer court, with its altar, to the inside of the Temple, with its courts and chambers (1 Chr 9:23-24; 28:11-18).

4:39-40. The mourning ritual is described as it was at 1 Macc 2:70; 3:47. The trumpets are to be blown to serve as a reminder before God (Num 10:1-10). The scene is reminiscent of the restoration of temple worship under Asa (2 Chr 15:8-15), when trumpets and horns were blown as the people renewed their covenant.

4:41. The citadel, called the Akra, overlooked the sanctuary from the south (see 1:33). It was still under the enemy's control, and thus troops were required to protect the priests purifying the Temple.

4:42-43. The purity required of priests is described in Leviticus 21. Priests are to delight in the law, as God delights in covenant faithfulness (Mic 7:18; for a statement of such delight, see Psalm 118). The defiled stones were part of the desolating sacrilege (1:54; cf. Jer 32:34), like the stones in a leper's house (Lev 14:40); thus they had to be put in a place that must be avoided if one is to remain ritually pure.

4:44-46. The altar of burnt offering could not be treated like the altars of idols (Deut 12:2-3). It was sacred and yet desecrated. So, just as the remaining parts of the bull used for a purification offering are still sacred, even though they have absorbed the sanctuary's impurities and must be put in a clean place (Lev 4:11-12), so also the altar can be kept on the temple hill—a clean place—until a prophet determines what should be done (see 14:41; Deut 18:15, 18-19).

The phrase "until a prophet arises" has sometimes been given an eschatological interpretation because of phrases found in the Qumran literature: "[the men of holiness] should not depart from any council of the law . . . but shall be ruled by the first directives which the men of the Community began to be taught until the prophet comes and the Messiahs of Aaron and Israel."[68]

68. 1QS 9:10-11. See also the Messianic Anthology, 4Q175, where Deut 18:18-19 is quoted.

In the *Damascus Document* from Qumran, there seem to be two moments, for God raised up "the Teacher of Righteousness," but one still had to wait until there arose "he who teaches justice at the end of days."[69] This last figure may be identified with the eschatological high priest, the Messiah of Aaron,[70] since part of the role of priests was the teaching of the law (Deut 33:10). Since the phrase at 1 Macc 4:46 (and 14:41) echoes the language of Deut 18:15, there is no need to read it as eschatological. It is also similar to the phrase found at Ezra 2:63 (= Neh 7:65), "until there should be a priest to consult Urim and Thummim" (NRSV), which has no eschatological meaning. Thus the author of 1 Maccabees expects the proper restoration of a normal functioning community, and such communities have a prophet. The phrase at 1 Maccabees envisions that when God sends a prophet, as God had promised for every generation (Deut 18:15-19), the prophet will solve all the knotty problems. The author longs for the restoration of the time when the full functioning community of Judah had priests, kings, and prophets, with the prophet functioning as a counterweight to the power of the king (see 1 and 2 Kings). It is interesting that the author of 1 Maccabees speaks of a prophetic figure rather than a priest or a teacher; perhaps it may hint at the author's view of his own role.

4:47-51. The altar is rebuilt according to the regulations found in Exodus and Deuteronomy (Exod 20:25; Deut 27:5-6). The temple furnishings, stripped away by Antiochus IV (1 Macc 1:21-24), are restored according to the stipulations of Exodus 25–27.

69. CD 1.1; 6.11.
70. See 4Q 541.

4:52-55. On December 14, 164 BCE, the birthday of Antiochus IV (see 1:59; 2 Macc 6:7), the daily offering was resumed (Exod 29:38-42). When Daniel had asked how long the prohibition on the regular burnt offering would last, the angel had responded, "For two thousand three hundred evenings and mornings" (Dan 8:14 NRSV), or 1,150 days, about three and a half years, which corresponds roughly to the extent of the desecration of the sanctuary, according to 1 Macc 1:54–4:55. The correspondence of time was taken as an indication that God was behind the action. The rejoicing is similar to that at the dedication of Solomon's Temple (2 Chr 5:11-14) and at the dedication of the city wall by Nehemiah (Neh 12:27). Under Judas, deliverance prospered (3:60) and is confirmed in the restoration of the temple worship.

4:56-59. The Feast of Dedication is patterned after the Feast of Tabernacles (Lev 23:33-36) and the dedication of the Temple by Solomon (1 Kings 8) and Hezekiah (2 Chronicles 29). Mention of burnt offerings (Lev 6:8-13), sacrifices of well-being (Leviticus 3), and thanksgiving offerings (Lev 7:11-15) is also made at Hezekiah's restoration of worship (2 Chr 29:31-35). The Temple is restored to its former glory, and the disgrace is removed (cf. 1:39-40). Judas, his brothers, and "all the assembly of Israel" (all true believers) determine that this feast should be an annual celebration.

4:60-61. The author concludes this section by describing the defensive measures taken to ensure that the Gentiles would not repeat what they had done at Jerusalem (1:31; 3:45, 51), or attack from the south (4:29). The refortified walls are not those of the whole of Jerusalem, but of the temple mount itself. The Akra remained in enemy hands.

REFLECTIONS

Solomon's prayer at the dedication of the first Temple in Jerusalem shows an awareness that if heaven and earth cannot contain God, still less could the Temple that Solomon had built (1 Kgs 8:27). Yet a community requires a place to gather in order to worship together. When a church building or other place of worship is destroyed by a hurricane or by a fire, the community rallies around the congregation and starts to find ways to rebuild. We all need a familiar place, familiar songs and practices. Whenever there is a change in liturgy, opposition arises, as in the sixteenth-century Year of Grace rebellion in England and the opposition to the Second Vatican Council decision to replace Latin with the vernacular in Roman Catholic worship. Some worshiping communities still prefer the resonances of the King James Version of the Bible to more accurate contemporary translations. People like what is familiar, what is traditional. That is how the community is accustomed to meeting God. The reintroduction of purified worship in the Temple reflects that same human tendency, for religion is not just intellectual—the whole person is involved. That means that we are moved by the hymns and the familiar gestures and words of prayer, by the familiar sights and sounds, the traditional stories. Through such human interaction, the religious culture is transmitted from one generation to another.

1 MACCABEES 5:1-68, WARS WITH NEIGHBORS

OVERVIEW

This section deals with raids across the Jordan, into Galilee, to the south, and in the coastal plain. The attacks are said to be in response to the hostile posture of neighboring peoples, a hostility that parallels that encountered by the Israelites when they entered the land (Josh 9:1-2; 11:1-5), as well as the resistance to rebuilding the Temple after the exile (Ezra 4–5). Psalm 48:4-7 speaks of the panic of kings gathered together against Zion when they behold the Temple as a symbol and focus of the people's commitment to the covenant worship.

1 Maccabees 5:1-8, Battles in Idumea and Ammon

NAB

5 When the Gentiles round about heard that the altar had been rebuilt and the sanctuary consecrated as before, they were very angry. ² So they decided to destroy the descendants of Jacob who were among them, and they began to massacre and persecute the people. ³ Then Judas attacked the sons of Esau at Akrabattene in Idumea, because they were blockading Israel; he defeated them heavily, overcame and despoiled them. ⁴ He also remembered the malice of the sons of Baean, who had become a snare and a stumblingblock to the people by ambushing them along the roads. ⁵ He forced them to take refuge in towers, which he besieged; he vowed their annihilation and burned down the towers along with all the persons in them. ⁶ Then he crossed over to the Ammonites, where he found a strong army and a large body of people with Timothy as their leader. ⁷ He fought many battles with them, routed them, and struck them down. ⁸ After seizing Jazer and its villages, he returned to Judea.

5, 5: (tous pyrgous) auton: so LXX^MSS, Vet Lat; or omit autēs: so P^MSS.

NRSV

5 When the Gentiles all around heard that the altar had been rebuilt and the sanctuary dedicated as it was before, they became very angry, ²and they determined to destroy the descendants of Jacob who lived among them. So they began to kill and destroy among the people. ³But Judas made war on the descendants of Esau in Idumea, at Akrabattene, because they kept lying in wait for Israel. He dealt them a heavy blow and humbled them and despoiled them. ⁴He also remembered the wickedness of the sons of Baean, who were a trap and a snare to the people and ambushed them on the highways. ⁵They were shut up by him in their^a towers; and he encamped against them, vowed their complete destruction, and burned with fire their towers and all who were in them. ⁶Then he crossed over to attack the Ammonites, where he found a strong band and many people, with Timothy as their leader. ⁷He engaged in many battles with them, and they were crushed before him; he struck them down. ⁸He also took Jazer and its villages; then he returned to Judea.

^a Gk her

COMMENTARY

5:1-2. The neighboring Gentiles become angry, as Antiochus IV had been angered (3:27), and their plan, like his (3:35), is to destroy the Jews. This time, however, the efforts are directed not at the strong Judas, but at the weaker Jews living in foreign domains.

5:3-5. First, Judas moves against the Idumeans. The "descendants of Esau" are described in the book of *Jubilees* as being angry with Esau for reconciling with Jacob (Genesis 35), and they attack Jacob and his sons (*Jubilees* 37–38). The reference to the descendants of Jacob (v. 2) conjures up this ancient rivalry with Esau. Akrabattene may refer to the area southwest of the Dead Sea, the ascent of Akrabbin (Num 34:4). Josephus, however, mentions an area called Akrabattene in Samaria, near the region of Gophna.[71] It is unknown exactly who the sons of Baean are. Baean is the name given in the LXX to one of the towns of Moab (Num 32:3). Could it, therefore,

refer to the Moabites? One might recall how Joshua warned the Israelites about not joining to the nations round about, for they would then be a snare and a trap (Josh 23:11-13), and that the daughters of Moab had led Israel astray (Num 25:1-3; Ps 106:28-39). Whatever group is meant, one should note how the language here is that of the ban, the vow to complete destruction, which one finds in Numbers and Joshua.

5:6-8. In 1 Maccabees, Timothy seems to be a local ruler of the Ammonites, whereas in 2 Maccabees (8:30-33; 9:3; 10:24) a Timothy is said to be a high Seleucid official (2 Maccabees seems to have exaggerated the importance of Timothy). Jazer (Num 21:32) was near Heshbon in the Transjordan. If Akrabattene is situated in Idumea, then Judas is pictured as making a counterclockwise movement from Idumea through Moab to Ammon, following the course laid out in the book of Numbers. Such a parallel may explain the use of the ancient names. (See Reflections at 5:63-68.)

---

71. Josephus *The Jewish War* 2.234-235, 568.

---

1 Maccabees 5:9-54, Battles in Galilee and Gilead

NAB	NRSV
[9] The Gentiles in Gilead assembled to attack and destroy the Israelites who were in their territory; these then fled to the stronghold of Dathema. [10] They sent a letter to Judas and his brothers saying: "The Gentiles around us have combined against us to destroy us, [11] and they are preparing to come and seize this stronghold to which we have fled. Timothy is the leader of their army. [12] Come at once and rescue us from them, for many of us have fallen. [13] All our kinsmen who were among the Tobiads have been killed; the Gentiles have carried away their wives and children and their goods, and they have slain there about a thousand men."	9Now the Gentiles in Gilead gathered together against the Israelites who lived in their territory, and planned to destroy them. But they fled to the stronghold of Dathema, 10and sent to Judas and his brothers a letter that said, "The Gentiles around us have gathered together to destroy us. 11They are preparing to come and capture the stronghold to which we have fled, and Timothy is leading their forces. 12Now then, come and rescue us from their hands, for many of us have fallen, 13and all our kindred who were in the land of Tob have been killed; the enemy*a* have captured their wives and children and goods, and have destroyed about a thousand persons there."
[14] While they were reading this letter, suddenly other messengers, in torn clothes, arrived from Galilee to deliver a similar message: [15] that the inhabitants of Ptolemais, Tyre, and Sidon, and the whole of Gentile Galilee had joined forces to destroy them. [16] When Judas and the people heard	14While the letter was still being read, other messengers, with their garments torn, came from Galilee and made a similar report; 15they said that the people of Ptolemais and Tyre and Sidon, and all Galilee of the Gentiles,*b* had gathered together
	a Gk *they* *b* Gk *aliens*

NAB

this, a great assembly convened to consider what they should do for their unfortunate kinsmen who were being attacked by enemies.

[17] Judas said to his brother Simon: "Choose men for yourself, and go, rescue your kinsmen in Galilee; I and my brother Jonathan will go to Gilead."

[18] In Judea he left Joseph, son of Zechariah, and Azariah, leader of the people, with the rest of the army to guard it. [19] "Take charge of these people," he commanded them, "but do not fight against the Gentiles until we return." [20] Three thousand men were allotted to Simon, to go into Galilee, and eight thousand men to Judas, for Gilead.

[21] Simon went into Galilee and fought many battles with the Gentiles. They were crushed before him, [22] and he pursued them to the very gate of Ptolemais. About three thousand men of the Gentiles fell, and he gathered their spoils. [23] He took with him the Jews who were in Galilee and in Arbatta, with their wives and children and all that they had, and brought them to Judea with great rejoicing. [24] Judas Maccabeus and his brother Jonathan crossed the Jordan and marched for three days through the desert. [25] There they met some Nabateans, who received them peacefully and told them all that had happened to the Jews in Gilead: [26] "Many of them have been imprisoned in Bozrah, in Bosor near Alema, in Chaspho, Maked, and Carnaim"—all of these are large, fortified cities— [27] "and some have been imprisoned in the other cities of Gilead. Tomorrow their enemies plan to attack the strongholds and to seize and destroy all these people in one day."

[28] Thereupon Judas suddenly changed direction with his army, marched across the desert to Bozrah, and captured the city. He slaughtered all the male population, took all their possessions, and set fire to the city. [29] He led his army from that place by night, and they marched toward the stronghold of Dathema. [30] When morning came, they looked ahead and saw a countless multitude of people, with ladders and devices for capturing the stronghold, and beginning to attack the people within. [31] When Judas perceived that the struggle had begun and that the noise of the battle was

5, 31: (hē kraugē) tou polemou: so Vet Lat MSS, V.

NRSV

against them "to annihilate us." [16] When Judas and the people heard these messages, a great assembly was called to determine what they should do for their kindred who were in distress and were being attacked by enemies.[a] [17] Then Judas said to his brother Simon, "Choose your men and go and rescue your kindred in Galilee; Jonathan my brother and I will go to Gilead." [18] But he left Joseph, son of Zechariah, and Azariah, a leader of the people, with the rest of the forces, in Judea to guard it; [19] and he gave them this command, "Take charge of this people, but do not engage in battle with the Gentiles until we return." [20] Then three thousand men were assigned to Simon to go to Galilee, and eight thousand to Judas for Gilead.

[21] So Simon went to Galilee and fought many battles against the Gentiles, and the Gentiles were crushed before him. [22] He pursued them to the gate of Ptolemais; as many as three thousand of the Gentiles fell, and he despoiled them. [23] Then he took the Jews[b] of Galilee and Arbatta, with their wives and children, and all they possessed, and led them to Judea with great rejoicing.

[24] Judas Maccabeus and his brother Jonathan crossed the Jordan and made three days' journey into the wilderness. [25] They encountered the Nabateans, who met them peaceably and told them all that had happened to their kindred in Gilead: [26] "Many of them have been shut up in Bozrah and Bosor, in Alema and Chaspho, Maked and Carnaim"—all these towns were strong and large— [27] "and some have been shut up in the other towns of Gilead; the enemy[c] are getting ready to attack the strongholds tomorrow and capture and destroy all these people in a single day."

[28] Then Judas and his army quickly turned back by the wilderness road to Bozrah; and he took the town, and killed every male by the edge of the sword; then he seized all its spoils and burned it with fire. [29] He left the place at night, and they went all the way to the stronghold of Dathema.[d] [30] At dawn they looked out and saw a large company, which could not be counted, carrying ladders and engines of war to capture the stronghold, and attacking the Jews within.[e] [31] So Judas saw

[a] Gk them [b] Gk those [c] Gk they [df] Gk lacks of Dathema. See verse 9 [e] Gk and they were attacking them

resounding to heaven with trumpet blasts and loud shouting, [32] he said to the men of his army, "Fight for our kinsmen today."

[33] He came up behind them with three columns blowing their trumpets and shouting in prayer. [34] When the army of Timothy realized that it was Maccabeus, they fell back before him, and he inflicted on them a crushing defeat. About eight thousand of their men fell that day. [35] Then he turned toward Alema and attacked and captured it; he killed all the male population, plundered the place, and burned it down. [36] From there he moved on and took Chaspho, Maked, Bosor, and the other cities of Gilead.

[37] After these events Timothy assembled another army and camped opposite Raphon, on the other side of the stream. [38] Judas sent men to spy on the camp, and they reported to him: "All the Gentiles around us have rallied to him, making a very large force; [39] they have also hired Arabs to help them, and have camped beyond the stream, ready to attack you." So Judas went forward to attack them.

[40] As Judas and his army were approaching the running stream, Timothy said to the officers of his army: "If he crosses over to us first, we shall not be able to resist him; he will certainly defeat us. [41] But if he is afraid and camps on the other side of the river, we will cross over to him and defeat him."

[42] But when Judas reached the running stream, he stationed the officers of the people beside the stream and gave them this order: "Do not allow any man to pitch a tent; all must go into battle." [43] He was the first to cross to the attack, with all the people behind him, and the Gentiles were crushed before them; they threw away their arms and fled to the temple enclosure at Carnaim. [44] The Jews captured that city and burnt the enclosure with all who were in it. So Carnaim was subdued, and Judas met with no more resistance.

[45] Then he assembled all the Israelites, great and small, who were in Gilead, with their wives and children and their goods, a great crowd of people, to go into the land of Judah. [46] When they reached Ephron, a large and strongly fortified city along the way, they found it impossible to encircle

5, 35: (apeklinen eis) Alema (kai): so LXXMSS; cf P and v 26.

that the battle had begun and that the cry of the town went up to Heaven, with trumpets and loud shouts, [32]and he said to the men of his forces, "Fight today for your kindred!" [33]Then he came up behind them in three companies, who sounded their trumpets and cried aloud in prayer. [34]And when the army of Timothy realized that it was Maccabeus, they fled before him, and he dealt them a heavy blow. As many as eight thousand of them fell that day.

[35]Next he turned aside to Maapha,[a] and fought against it and took it; and he killed every male in it, plundered it, and burned it with fire. [36]From there he marched on and took Chaspho, Maked, and Bosor, and the other towns of Gilead.

[37]After these things Timothy gathered another army and encamped opposite Raphon, on the other side of the stream. [38]Judas sent men to spy out the camp, and they reported to him, "All the Gentiles around us have gathered to him; it is a very large force. [39]They also have hired Arabs to help them, and they are encamped across the stream, ready to come and fight against you." And Judas went to meet them.

[40]Now as Judas and his army drew near to the stream of water, Timothy said to the officers of his forces, "If he crosses over to us first, we will not be able to resist him, for he will surely defeat us. [41]But if he shows fear and camps on the other side of the river, we will cross over to him and defeat him." [42]When Judas approached the stream of water, he stationed the officers[b] of the army at the stream and gave them this command, "Permit no one to encamp, but make them all enter the battle." [43]Then he crossed over against them first, and the whole army followed him. All the Gentiles were defeated before him, and they threw away their arms and fled into the sacred precincts at Carnaim. [44]But he took the town and burned the sacred precincts with fire, together with all who were in them. Thus Carnaim was conquered; they could stand before Judas no longer.

[45]Then Judas gathered together all the Israelites in Gilead, the small and the great, with their wives and children and goods, a very large company, to go to the land of Judah. [46]So they came to Ephron. This was a large and very strong town

a Other ancient authorities read Alema   b Or scribes

NAB

it on either the right or the left; they would have to march right through it. ⁴⁷ But the men in the city shut them out and blocked up the gates with stones. ⁴⁸ Then Judas sent them his peaceful message: "We wish to cross your territory in order to reach our own; no one will harm you; we will only march through." But they would not open to him.

⁴⁹ So Judas ordered a proclamation to be made in the camp that everyone make an attack from the place where he was. ⁵⁰ When the men of the army took up their positions, he assaulted the city all that day and night, and it was delivered to him. ⁵¹ He slaughtered every male, razed and plundered the city, and passed through it over the slain.

⁵² Then they crossed the Jordan to the great plain in front of Beth-shan; ⁵³ and Judas kept rounding up the stragglers and encouraging the people the whole way, until he reached the land of Judah. ⁵⁴ They ascended Mount Zion in joy and gladness and offered holocausts, because not one of them had fallen; they returned in safety.

NRSV

on the road, and they could not go around it to the right or to the left; they had to go through it. ⁴⁷But the people of the town shut them out and blocked up the gates with stones.

⁴⁸Judas sent them this friendly message, "Let us pass through your land to get to our land. No one will do you harm; we will simply pass by on foot." But they refused to open to him. ⁴⁹Then Judas ordered proclamation to be made to the army that all should encamp where they were. ⁵⁰So the men of the forces encamped, and he fought against the town all that day and all the night, and the town was delivered into his hands. ⁵¹He destroyed every male by the edge of the sword, and razed and plundered the town. Then he passed through the town over the bodies of the dead.

⁵²Then they crossed the Jordan into the large plain before Beth-shan. ⁵³Judas kept rallying the laggards and encouraging the people all the way until he came to the land of Judah. ⁵⁴So they went up to Mount Zion with joy and gladness, and offered burnt offerings, because they had returned in safety; not one of them had fallen.

COMMENTARY

The action now moves to the north, with Judas and his brothers rescuing Jews from their Gentile neighbors and bringing them back to Judah.

5:9-20, The Attack of the Gentiles and Judas's Response. 5:9-13. Gilead is the region east of the Jordan. The location of Dathema is uncertain (4:29 places it a night's journey from Bozrah). The language of destruction is the same as that used by Antiochus IV (3:35). The situation of the Jews in Gilead is depicted in terms similar to that of the Gibeonites in Josh 10:1-11. The land of Tob was southeast of the sea of Galilee, in northern Gilead, from whence Jephthah the judge came (Judg 11:3; cf. 2 Sam 10:6, 8). However, the text literally reads "in the lands of Toubias," which refers to southern Gilead.

5:14-15. The messengers come "with their garments torn," a sign of having traveled a long distance (cf. Josh 9:3-15, where the Gibeonites tricked Joshua into thinking that they had traveled

a long distance by wearing such clothing). Torn clothes could also be the sign of messengers bringing bad news, as when the news of the capture of the ark by the Philistines was brought to Eli (1 Sam 4:12), or when Saul's death was reported to David by a man "with his clothes torn and dirt on his head" (2 Sam 1:2 NRSV).

"Galilee of the Gentiles" (Isa 9:1; 8:23 MT) refers to the seacoast towns of Ptolemais, Tyre, and Sidon. The term used for "Gentiles" (ἀλλόφυλος allophylos) often signifies "Philistines" in the LXX.

5:16-20. The Maccabees are constantly portrayed as consulting the people (2:41; 4:44). The great assembly resonates with the crowd that gathered at the dedications of the Temple under Solomon (1 Kgs 8:65; 2 Chr 7:8), Hezekiah (2 Chr 30:13), and Ezra (Ezra 10:1), as well as Nehemiah's assembly to stop the oppression of the Jewish poor (Neh 5:7). The term "assembly" (ἐκκλησία ekklēsia) translates a basic Hebrew term (קהל qāhāl) that signifies the community of Israel. At this assembly, Judas divides his forces to deal with the emergencies facing the people. Presumably Azariah is one of those "leaders of the people" whom Judas had appointed (3:55).

When a prohibition like the one Judas makes in v. 19 is given, the reader knows that eventually it will be broken. It is broken at 5:55-62.

5:21-23, The Conflict in Galilee. Simon's activity is quickly summarized but glorified highly. The number of dead corresponds to the force under Simon's control (v. 22). Ptolemais is also known as Acco or Acre. Arbatta is otherwise unknown; a Narbatta lay south of Mt. Carmel in the neighborhood of Caesarea, and perhaps this is meant here.[72] The return (v. 23) is almost liturgical in character, as the men, women, and children all return to Judea with merriment and festivity. In the book of Isaiah, the ransomed of the Lord are described as returning to Zion in the same way (Isa 51:11).

5:24-44, Judas in Gilead. In contrast to Simon's activity, which is described in a very summary fashion, Judas and Jonathan are given much more attention.

5:24-27. The Nabateans at this time were nomadic traders based in southern Transjordan. While the author suggests that Judas was on friendly terms with them, 2 Maccabees records a battle before peace is reached (2 Macc 12:11-12). The cities (v. 26) are located east and north of the River Yarmuke in Transjordan. They are described in terms reminiscent of the description of the towns of the promised land (Num 13:28). The Jews are to be destroyed, as had been threatened earlier by Antiochus IV (3:35) and the Gentiles in Gilead (5:9).

5:28-44. The author now proceeds to list victories of Judas against the Gentiles of Gilead. All the towns listed in v. 26, except for Alema, are dealt with. The string of victories here recalls those of Joshua (Josh 10:28-43). Judas burns towns with fire as Joshua burned Jericho (Josh 6:24) and Ai (Josh 8:28), and takes their spoils. Note the repetition at vv. 28, 35, and 51, where the destruction of three different centers is told in basically the same terms.

5:31. The townspeople of Dathema, under threat of annihilation, cry out to God. A similar phrase is used of the people of the Philistine city

Ekron when the ark of the covenant is put in its midst and causes death and pestilence among the inhabitants (1 Sam 5:12). The trumpets sound the alarm as directed (Num 10:6), and the great shout adds to the din of warfare, as one side tries to intimidate the other. (See 1 Sam 4:5-6, where the great shout that goes up from the Israelites' camp when the ark of the Lord is brought to it frightens the Philistines.)

5:33-34. The division of the army into three companies occurs frequently in the OT: Gideon divided his forces into three (Judg 7:16), as did Abimelech (Judg 9:43), Saul (1 Sam 11:11), and David (2 Sam 18:2). The *War Scroll* from Qumran also divides the Sons of Light into three arrays against the Sons of Darkness.[73] Battle and prayer are combined as before when the Israelites had assembled at Mizpah against the invasion of Ptolemy, Nicanor, and Gorgias (3:43-54). In Solomon's prayer at the dedication of the Temple in Jerusalem, he asked that when the Israelites went out to battle and prayed facing Jerusalem and the Temple, God would hear them (1 Kgs 8:44-45; 2 Chr 6:34-35). Thus "to cry out in prayer" may refer to a battle cry like the one in Judg 7:18, " 'For the LORD and for Gideon!' " (NRSV), or to a watchword like that at 2 Macc 13:15, "God's Victory" (NAB). Once again, the number of dead corresponds to the number of Judas's men.

5:35-36. These verses describe a series of victories told in shorthand as Judas deals with the besieged towns of Gilead. The location of Maapha is unknown; it may refer to Mizpah of Gilead.

5:37-44. The battle against the last city, Carnaim, is described here. Timothy is introduced as someone whom the reader has already encountered, suggesting that he is the Timothy of 5:6. His force is described as numerous, with Arabs as mercenaries. The enemy looks for a sign to see whether Judas and his forces are eager to fight. A similar tactic is used by Jonathan, the son of King Saul, when he sees God's hand behind the answer that the Philistine guards give to him. He knows that God has given them into his hand when they tell him to come up to them, rather than come down to Jonathan themselves (1 Sam 14:6-15). As in Jonathan's case, fear comes upon the enemy of Judah, a fear sent by God as

---

72. See Josephus *The Jewish War* 2.291, 509.

73. See 1QM 8.

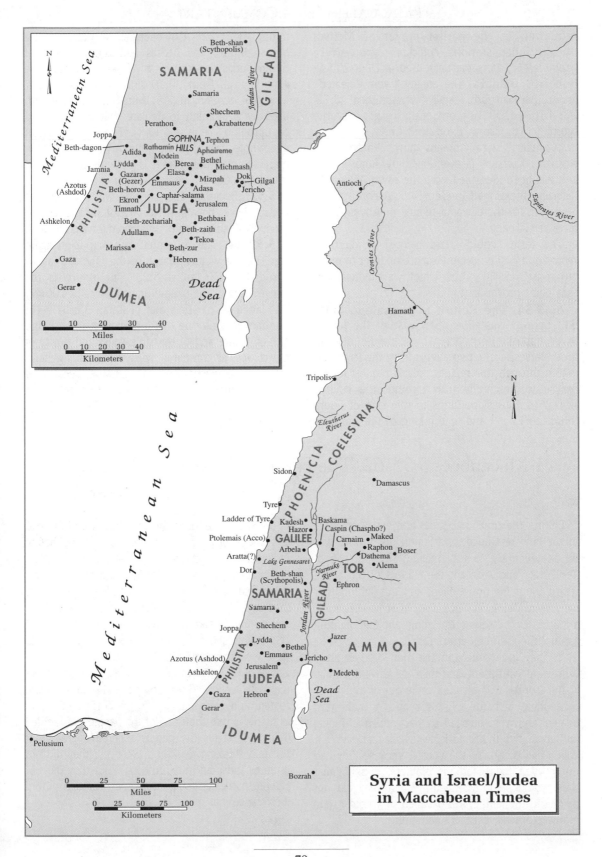

Inset map labels:

Beth-shan (Scythopolis)
SAMARIA
GILEAD
Mediterranean Sea
N
Samaria
Shechem
Perathon
Akrabattene
Jordan River
Joppa
GOPHNA
Tephon
Beth-dagon
Rathamin HILLS
Aphaireme
Adida
Modein
Bethel
Lydda
Berea
Michmash
Jamnia
Gazara (Gezer)
Elasa
Mizpah
Dok
Beth-horon
Emmaus
Adasa
Gilgal
Ekron
Caphar-salama
Jericho
Azotus (Ashdod)
Timnath
JUDEA
Jerusalem
Ashkelon
Beth-zechariah
Bethbasi
Adullam
Beth-zaith
Marissa
Beth-zur
Tekoa
Gaza
Adora
Hebron
Gerar
IDUMEA
Dead Sea
PHILISTIA

0 10 20 30 40
Miles
0 10 20 30 40
Kilometers

Main map labels:

Antioch
Euphrates River
Orontes River
Hamath
Tripolis
Eleutherus River
PHOENICIA
COELESYRIA
Sidon
Damascus
Tyre
Ladder of Tyre
Kadesh
Baskama
Hazor
Caspin (Chaspho?)
Ptolemais (Acco)
GALILEE
Carnaim
Maked
Arbela
Raphon
Boser
Aratta(?)
Lake Gennesaret
Dathema
Alema
Dor
Beth-shan (Scythopolis)
Yarmuk River
TOB
GILEAD
Ephron
SAMARIA
Samaria
Jordan River
Shechem
Joppa
Jazer
AMMON
Lydda
Bethel
Emmaus
Jericho
Azotus (Ashdod)
Jerusalem
Ashkelon
Medeba
JUDEA
Gaza
Hebron
Dead Sea
Gerar
Mediterranean Sea
IDUMEA
Pelusium
Bozrah
N

0 25 50 75 100
Miles
0 25 50 75 100
Kilometers

Syria and Israel/Judea in Maccabean Times

requested in the earlier prayer at Mizpah (4:32). Judas stations "officers" (γραμματεῖς grammateis), the same term used in Deut 20:5-9; Josh 1:10; 3:2 LXX. The enemy "were defeated" (συντρίβω syntribō), literally "were crushed" (3:22-23; 4:10, 14, 30, 36), one of the author's favorite words (cf. its use at Exod 15:3 LXX).

"Carnaim" literally means "horns," a symbol of strength. Karnaim is mentioned by Amos (6:13) and has been identified with the town Ashteroth-karnaim, mentioned in Gen 14:5. According to 2 Macc 12:26, there was a temple of Atargatis/Astarte at Carnaim.

The term "could stand before" (ὑποστῆναι hypostēnai) is the same verb used earlier to mean "to resist" (5:40). Thus Timothy's prediction at that point proves true.

5:45-54, The Return to Jerusalem. 5:45-51. Ephron was nine miles east of the Jordan River, opposite Beth-shan. The scene described in these verses recalls two events from the Israelites' march through this region. Judas's request for his people to peacefully pass through the land is similar to Moses' petitions to the king of Edom (Num 20:14-17) and to the king of the Amorites

(Num 21:21-22). However, since Judas cannot bypass Ephron, as Moses had the kingdom of Edom, Judas destroys it, as Moses conquered the Amorites (cf. Deut 20:10-15). Ephron is "razed" (ἐκριζόω ekrizoō; lit., "uprooted"), the same verb used by Zephaniah to declare that Ekron would be uprooted (Zeph 2:4 LXX). The final image of the whole group of men, women, and children marching over the corpses is particularly grisly and triumphalistic.

5:52. Beth-shan (Scythopolis) was west of the Jordan. Note how 2 Macc 12:29-31 stresses the goodwill of the citizens of Scythopolis toward the Jews.

5:53-54. The triumphal return to Zion again parallels the victory march of the Divine Warrior (Exod 15:1-17), as at 5:23. The return is the in-gathering of the people prayed for at Ps 106:47. The language parallels that of Isaiah 35; 51:9-11. The fact that no one had died was seen as a sign of God's care and of the sinlessness and purity of the troops, as compared with the exodus generation, whose warriors had all perished because of their lack of trust in God's power to defeat their enemy (Numbers 13–14; Deut 1:34-36; 2:16). (See Reflections at 5:63-68.)

1 Maccabees 5:55-62, The Failure of Joseph and Azariah

NAB

55 During the time that Judas and Jonathan were in the land of Gilead, and Simon his brother was in Galilee opposite Ptolemais, 56 Joseph, son of Zechariah, and Azariah, the leaders of the army, heard about the brave deeds and the fighting that they were doing. 57 They said, "Let us also make a name for ourselves by going out and fighting against the Gentiles around us."

58 They gave orders to the men of their army who were with them, and marched toward Jamnia. 59 But Gorgias and his men came out of the city to meet them in battle. 60 Joseph and Azariah were beaten, and were pursued to the frontiers of Judea, and about two thousand Israelites fell that day. 61 It was a bad defeat for the people, because they had not obeyed Judas and his brothers, thinking that they would do brave deeds. 62 But they did not belong to the family of those men to whom it was granted to achieve Israel's salvation.

NRSV

55Now while Judas and Jonathan were in Gilead and their[a] brother Simon was in Galilee before Ptolemais, 56Joseph son of Zechariah, and Azariah, the commanders of the forces, heard of their brave deeds and of the heroic war they had fought. 57So they said, "Let us also make a name for ourselves; let us go and make war on the Gentiles around us." 58So they issued orders to the men of the forces that were with them and marched against Jamnia. 59Gorgias and his men came out of the town to meet them in battle. 60Then Joseph and Azariah were routed, and were pursued to the borders of Judea; as many as two thousand of the people of Israel fell that day. 61Thus the people suffered a great rout because, thinking to do a brave deed, they did not listen to Judas and his brothers. 62But they did not belong to the family of those men through whom deliverance was given to Israel.

a Gk his

COMMENTARY

The reversal suffered by Joseph and Azariah is in stark contrast to the success of Judas and Simon. They rashly seek to make a name for themselves as Seron (3:14) and David had (2 Sam 8:13; 1 Chr 17:8). Jamnia was also a center of opposition to the Jews (2 Macc 12:8-9).

The same word (ἐτροπώθη *etropōthē,* "reversal") used to describe the conquest of Carnaim is used here to tell of the reversal of Joseph and Azariah (v. 61). Just as the Israelites did not listen to Moses, but went up to fight against the inhabitants of the promised land (Num 14:40-45; Deut 1:41-44), so also Joseph and Azariah do not listen to Judas and his brothers. And just as God raised

up judges to deliver Israel (Judg 2:16-18), so also Judas and his brothers are to bring deliverance (v. 62). The contrast between the two groups recalls the revolt of Korah against the authority of Moses and Aaron in the wilderness (Numbers 16). The phrase "not belong to the family" (οὐκ ἦσαν ἐκ τοῦ σπέρματος *ouk ēsan ek tou spermatos*; lit., "not of the seed of") is found at Num 16:40 to state that only direct descendants of Aaron shall approach to offer incense before the Lord. Here, it indicates that the Maccabees have been divinely appointed to bring deliverance to Israel. (See Reflections at 5:63-68.)

1 Maccabees 5:63-68, Further Successes

NAB

63 The valiant Judas and his brothers were greatly renowned in all Israel and among all the Gentiles, wherever their name was heard; 64 and men gathered about them and praised them.

65 Then Judas and his brothers went out and attacked the sons of Esau in the country toward the south; he took Hebron and its villages, and he destroyed its strongholds and burned the towers around it. 66 He then set out for the land of the Philistines and passed through Marisa. 67 At that time some priests fell in battle who had gone out rashly to fight in their desire to distinguish themselves. 68 Judas then turned toward Azotus in the land of the Philistines. He destroyed their altars and burned the statues of their gods; and after plundering their cities he returned to the land of Judah.

NRSV

63The man Judas and his brothers were greatly honored in all Israel and among all the Gentiles, wherever their name was heard. 64People gathered to them and praised them.

65Then Judas and his brothers went out and fought the descendants of Esau in the land to the south. He struck Hebron and its villages and tore down its strongholds and burned its towers on all sides. 66Then he marched off to go into the land of the Philistines, and passed through Marisa.[a] 67On that day some priests, who wished to do a brave deed, fell in battle, for they went out to battle unwisely. 68But Judas turned aside to Azotus in the land of the Philistines; he tore down their altars, and the carved images of their gods he burned with fire; he plundered the towns and returned to the land of Judah.

[a] Other ancient authorities read *Samaria*

COMMENTARY

5:63-64. Just as David's fame increased (1 Sam 18:30), so also does that of Judas and his brothers, as foretold in the hymn to Judas (3:9).

5:65-66. Judas had previously fought against the sons of Esau (5:3) and then traveled counterclockwise northward on the eastern side of the Jordan. Now he fights against them in the south and travels clockwise to the coastal plain. Marisa lies to the west of Hebron.

5:67-68. These priests, like Joseph and Azariah (v. 61), seek to do brave deeds as had Judas and Simon (5:56). They act "unwisely" by not heeding the determination of the assembly (v. 16). Judas, on the contrary, is completely successful (3:6). He follows the commands of Deuteronomy (Deut 7:5, 25; 12:3) in dealing with idols, just as Hezekiah (2 Chr 31:1) and Josiah (2 Chr 34:3-7) had done.

REFLECTIONS

This chapter with its stories of the battles against neighboring peoples is chilling. As well as being intended to destroy idols, justification for the war is provided in that the Gentiles started the persecution of the Israelites. The actions of Judas and his followers, however, go far beyond any criteria for just conduct of war. In their first engagement, they put their enemies under the ban (5:5), the vow to total destruction. This language is kept up through the repetition of "killed every male by the edge of the sword; then he seized all its spoils and burned it with fire" (5:28 NRSV; cf. vv. 35, 51), as well as the burning of idols (5:44, 68). The tradition of putting one's enemies under the ban is one of the most troubling ethical issues in the OT.

The Hebrew Scriptures have been the inspiration for concern for the weaker members of a society—for widows, orphans, and children (Exod 22:21-24)—and passages from the Bible have inspired those who seek social justice for the oppressed. Passages such as Amos 5:24 have become slogans for advancement: "Let justice roll down like waters,/ and righteousness like an ever-flowing stream" (NRSV). The exodus story of liberation from slavery has been used by African American slaves and by liberation theologians as a model for the plight and the hope of the oppressed.

Yet there is a tradition of violence within the Bible, a tradition used by the Puritans in the American colonies to inspire the colonists to extirpate the Native Americans. How is one to reconcile the respect for life shown in the Bible with the command by God to annihilate every living thing, both humans and animals (1 Sam 15:3)?

Susan Niditch, in exploring these issues, describes two uses of the ban.[74] The most difficult instances to understand are those when the Israelites pledge their enemies as a sacrifice to God in exchange for God's leading them to victory (see, e.g., Num 21:2-3). Niditch suggests that such passages must be put within a sacrificial context, in which human beings are the most precious offering to God. This practice of human sacrifice is condemned by the dominant threads of the OT (Deut 12:31; Lev 18:21), but not by threads within Israelite culture itself. A number of scholars have suggested that child sacrifice was part of a state-sponsored cult within ancient Israel until the reforms of the Judean king Josiah in the seventh century BCE.

The second group of traditions about the ban are those that treat the ban as evidence of God's justice, a way of uprooting the sources of impurity and idolatry that might infect Israel. When Achan transgresses God's covenantal demands and takes some of the things devoted to the Lord, he and his family are put under the ban and destroyed, in order to eradicate that sin from Israel's midst (Joshua 7). In 1 Maccabees, the destruction of the Gentiles is seen as punishment for their determination to wipe out Israel (1 Macc 5:1-2, 9, 27). Although Judas does not kill every breathing thing (cf. Josh 10:28, 30, 32, 35-37, 39, 40; 11:11, 14) but only every male, one must still note what this implies. In that culture, the father was believed to provide the seed, whereas the mother provided the matter. By killing every male, Judas was destroying that city's race. In addition, no mention is made of the women and girls, although Num 31:15-18 provides that young girls who had not yet slept with a man be kept alive and assimilated into the Israelite camp. What will happen to these defenseless women in the towns of Gilead after the Maccabees leave? Although the author of 1 Maccabees insists that Judas and Simon bring back not only the Jewish men but also their wives and children

---

74. S. Niditch, *War in the Hebrew Bible: A Study of the Ethics of Violence* (New York: Oxford University Press, 1993).

(5:23, 45), the enemies' wives and female children are not worth discussing. The most horrifying image is that of 5:51, where the returning men, women, and children are depicted as walking over the corpses of their enemies.

Whether or not the actions in 1 Maccabees happened in precisely the way described, what is important to note is the way language is being used to engender an implacable hostility toward one's enemy—they are to be exterminated. This is how one is to deal with neighbors.

What steps can one take to break down such prejudicial attitudes? One must first teach against the dehumanizing of one's enemy, and decry those elements of one's tradition that do so. Rather than seeing one's own racial, religious, or sexual group as having the right to impose its views and behaviors on all others, one must seek out those elements of commonality that unite diverse groups. We must not resort to ethnic cleansing or social ostracism, wherein certain groups are excluded from entering "our" domain. Rather than accepting the position that "whoever is not with me is against me" (Matt 12:30 NRSV; cf. Luke 11:23), we might take the position that "whoever is not against us is for us" (Mark 9:40 NRSV; cf. Luke 9:50). Rather than restricting the command to love one another (cf. John 13:34), one might extend the notion of neighbor to include the hated "Samaritan" (see Luke 10:25-37).

1 MACCABEES 6:1-17, THE DEATH OF ANTIOCHUS IV

NAB

6 As King Antiochus was traversing the inland provinces, he heard that in Persia there was a city called Elymais, famous for its wealth in silver and gold, 2 and that its temple was very rich, containing gold helmets, breastplates, and weapons left there by Alexander, son of Philip, king of Macedon, the first king of the Greeks. 3 He went therefore and tried to capture and pillage the city. But he could not do so, because his plan became known to the people of the city 4 who rose up in battle against him. So he retreated and in great dismay withdrew from there to return to Babylon.

5 While he was in Persia, a messenger brought him news that the armies sent into the land of Judah had been put to flight; 6 that Lysias had gone at first with a strong army and been driven back by the Israelites; that they had grown strong by reason of the arms, men, and abundant possessions taken from the armies they had destroyed; 7 that they had pulled down the Abomination which he had built upon the altar in Jerusalem; and that they had surrounded with high walls both the sanctuary, as it had been before, and his city of Beth-zur.

8 When the king heard this news, he was struck

NRSV

6 King Antiochus was going through the upper provinces when he heard that Elymais in Persia was a city famed for its wealth in silver and gold. 2Its temple was very rich, containing golden shields, breastplates, and weapons left there by Alexander son of Philip, the Macedonian king who first reigned over the Greeks. 3So he came and tried to take the city and plunder it, but he could not because his plan had become known to the citizens 4and they withstood him in battle. So he fled and in great disappointment left there to return to Babylon.

5Then someone came to him in Persia and reported that the armies that had gone into the land of Judah had been routed; 6that Lysias had gone first with a strong force, but had turned and fled before the Jews;[a] that the Jews[b] had grown strong from the arms, supplies, and abundant spoils that they had taken from the armies they had cut down; 7that they had torn down the abomination that he had erected on the altar in Jerusalem; and that they had surrounded the sanctuary with high walls as before, and also Beth-zur, his town.

a Gk them   b Gk they

NAB

with fear and very much shaken. Sick with grief because his designs had failed, he took to his bed. ⁹ There he remained many days, overwhelmed with sorrow, for he knew he was going to die.

¹⁰ So he called in all his Friends and said to them: "Sleep has departed from my eyes, for my heart is sinking with anxiety. ¹¹ I said to myself: 'Into what tribulation have I come, and in what floods of sorrow am I now! ¹² Yet I was kindly and beloved in my rule.' But I now recall the evils I did in Jerusalem, when I carried away all the vessels of gold and silver that were in it, and for no cause gave orders that the inhabitants of Judah be destroyed. ¹³ I know that this is why these evils have overtaken me; and now I am dying, in bitter grief, in a foreign land."

¹⁴ Then he summoned Philip, one of his Friends, and put him in charge of his whole kingdom. ¹⁵ He gave him his crown, his robe, and his signet ring, so that he might guide the king's son Antiochus and bring him up to be king. ¹⁶ King Antiochus died in Persia in the year one hundred and forty-nine.

¹⁷ When Lysias learned that the king was dead, he set up the king's son Antiochus, whom he had reared as a child, to be king in his place; and he gave him the title Eupator.

NRSV

8When the king heard this news, he was astounded and badly shaken. He took to his bed and became sick from disappointment, because things had not turned out for him as he had planned. ⁹He lay there for many days, because deep disappointment continually gripped him, and he realized that he was dying. ¹⁰So he called all his Friends and said to them, "Sleep has departed from my eyes and I am downhearted with worry. ¹¹I said to myself, 'To what distress I have come! And into what a great flood I now am plunged! For I was kind and beloved in my power.' ¹²But now I remember the wrong I did in Jerusalem. I seized all its vessels of silver and gold, and I sent to destroy the inhabitants of Judah without good reason. ¹³I know that it is because of this that these misfortunes have come upon me; here I am, perishing of bitter disappointment in a strange land."

14Then he called for Philip, one of his Friends, and made him ruler over all his kingdom. ¹⁵He gave him the crown and his robe and the signet, so that he might guide his son Antiochus and bring him up to be king. ¹⁶Thus King Antiochus died there in the one hundred forty-ninth year.ᵃ ¹⁷When Lysias learned that the king was dead, he set up Antiochus the king'sᵇ son to reign. Lysiasᶜ had brought him up from boyhood; he named him Eupator.

ᵃ 163 B.C.   ᵇ Gk *his*   ᶜ Gk *He*

COMMENTARY

The news of the death of Antiochus IV was announced in Babylon in November–December 164 BCE, before the cleansing of the Temple. The author of 1 Maccabees, however, places Antiochus's death after the Temple has been purified and after Judas and Simon have defeated neighboring peoples and brought back threatened Jews to Judah and Mt. Zion. By modeling the narrative on Joshua's conquest of the land, the author suggests that Judas and his group have cleansed the land along with the Temple. Thus Antiochus defiled both the Temple and the land, whereas Judas restored both. Then, appropriately, the persecutor dies while repenting of what he had done. Such a reward for dastardly deeds fits well with the scheme of Deuteronomy, which presumes that

the good flourish but the wicked suffer (Deut 7:11). (For other accounts of Antiochus's death, see Dan 11:40-45; 2 Macc 1:13-17; 9:1-29; Polybius 31.9; Appian *Syriaca* 66.)

6:1-4. The author uses exactly the same language as at 3:37 to describe Antiochus's journey to the eastern satrapies, and so he sees this section as a fitting conclusion to the events narrated in between. Elymais (Elam) was properly the mountainous country west of Persia. The temple attacked by Antiochus was that of Artemis/Aphrodite/Nanaia. Strabo narrates how Mithradates I of Parthia (175–138 BCE) later attacked this same temple.⁷⁵ Nowhere else is it mentioned

75. Strabo 16.1.18.

that Alexander visited this temple of Artemis. He would not simply have left weapons behind, but would have dedicated them to the goddess. Whereas Alexander is shown to be respectful of this temple and Artemis worship, Antiochus is disdainful. A battle need not have taken place, since the citizens' readiness to fight may have caused a retreat, just as Gorgias retreated (4:21-22).

6:5-7. Before reaching Babylon, Antiochus receives reports that Judas has undone his design. The message is a summary of 1 Maccabees 3–4. The phrase "been routed" recalls the defeat of the army led by Ptolemy, Nicanor, and Gorgias (4:1-25). Lysias's campaign (3:28-35) is mentioned; the "plunder" that Judas captured is recalled (3:12; 4:23). The strength of the Jewish army reminds the reader that Judas's forces had grown from 3,000 (4:6) to more than 11,000 (5:20). The phrase "torn down the abomination" recalls the purification of the Temple (4:43-47; the rebuilding of the fortification was described at 4:60-61). In effect, all of Antiochus's plans have been thwarted.

6:8-13. Antiochus's reaction to news from Judea has changed from anger (3:27) to perplexity and discouragement (4:27) and now to astonishment and fear (6:8). The author of 1 Maccabees, since his map of the world centers on Judea, views Antiochus IV's death as caused by his failure in Judea. While the Jews rejoice (4:58; 5:54), Antiochus lies in distress, finally realizing that he is dying (v. 9).

Unlike Mattathias's last words, which looked to the future (2:49-68), Antiochus's last words are repentance of past deeds. Antiochus's reflections on the complete reversal of his fortunes use images like those in Psalm 42 (1 Macc 6:11), a prayer for help. Antiochus was in fact a benefactor through his building projects and support of traditional customs in other parts of his empire and the Mediterranean world. His policy toward Judea was an aberration of his normal behavior.

The repentance ascribed to Antiochus IV (vv. 12-13) is similar to that ascribed to the wicked Judean king Manasseh in the Prayer of Manasseh, an apocryphal composition from around the first century BCE. Manasseh, portrayed in the Bible as the most wicked king of Judah (2 Kgs 21:1-18), is said to have repented of his sins while in exile and to have composed a prayer of entreaty (see 2 Chr 33:18-19, even though 2 Chronicles does not provide the prayer). The present apocryphal prayer fills that gap. Antiochus is seen to repent of his misdeeds (1:20-28; 3:35). He is said to die in a "strange land." Persia did lie in his own kingdom, but the author stresses the pathos of his death: To die away from one's homeland and one's ancestors was to be cut off from a proper resting place. (A similar fate befalls the high priest Jason in 2 Macc 5:9-10.)

6:14-17. In contrast to the description of Alexander's properly providing for his succession by dividing his kingdom (1:6), Antiochus is described as leaving behind a mess. He names Philip as ruler of the kingdom and guardian of his son without any mention that he had appointed Lysias over half his kingdom and as guardian (3:32-33) and had left him half the forces. The following division within the kingdom is therefore placed at Antiochus's feet. The author seems unaware that Antiochus's son was already co-regent and suggests rather that Lysias's action in elevating him to rule is improper.

The date given for Antiochus's death, the 149th year (163 BCE), is wrong according to the Babylonian reckoning of the Seleucid era, which counted from March–April 311 BCE and according to which Antiochus IV died in the year 148. If the Seleucid era is reckoned according to a Macedonian form that began in September–October 312 BCE, Antiochus would have died in the year 149. Scholars have suggested, therefore, that dates for events of royal Seleucid history are given in 1 Maccabees according to the Macedonian form of the Seleucid era.

REFLECTIONS

Antiochus IV is described as having died bitter and disappointed. The author of 1 Maccabees states that Antiochus had thought on a grand scale of uniting all his kingdom as one people, all having the same customs (1 Macc 1:41-42). It was a plan on the magnitude of Napoleon's or Hitler's or of the uniting of European nations under one command. But such a vision of unity was ultimately a vision of uniformity, achieved at the expense of diversity and freedom. Yet one must also recognize the value of striving for unity, of seeking to avoid the conflicts and tensions that arise out of difference. Diversity also carries responsibility, the need to respect the values and traditions of others, the need not to strive to homogenize everything or to maintain that everything and everybody who does not agree with you is wrong. Unity that respects diversity is a worthwhile goal, but one hard to keep in sight. A start can be made by fighting not to be led, or rather misled, by stereotypes.

1 MACCABEES 6:18-63, ATTACKS UNDER ANTIOCHUS V EUPATOR

OVERVIEW

The death of Antiochus IV did not bring any respite, according to the author of 1 Maccabees, from attacks from the Seleucids. The letter preserved at 2 Macc 11:22-26, if written at the accession of Antiochus V, would suggest that

amnesty was granted at the death of Antiochus IV. The author of 1 Maccabees allows for no such respite, however. The Hasmoneans are depicted as pursuing their goal of winning independence from the Seleucid monarch.

1 Maccabees 6:18-31, The Pre-Invasion Events

NAB

18 The men in the citadel were hemming in Israel around the sanctuary, continually trying to harm them and to strengthen the Gentiles. 19 But Judas planned to destroy them, and called all the people together to besiege them. 20 So in the year one hundred and fifty they assembled and stormed the citadel, for which purpose he constructed catapults and other devices. 21 Some of the besieged escaped, joined by impious Israelites; 22 they went to the king and said:

"How long will you fail to do justice and avenge our kinsmen? 23 We agreed to serve your father and to follow his orders and obey his edicts. 24 And for this the sons of our people have become our enemies; they have put to death as many of us as they could find and have plundered our estates. 25 They have acted aggressively not only against us, but throughout their whole territory. 26 Look! They have now besieged the citadel in Jerusalem in order to capture it, and they have fortified the sanctuary and Beth-zur. 27 Unless you

6, 24: Omit *kai periekathēnto ep' autēn:* misplaced gloss or variant; cf v 26.

NRSV

18Meanwhile the garrison in the citadel kept hemming Israel in around the sanctuary. They were trying in every way to harm them and strengthen the Gentiles. 19Judas therefore resolved to destroy them, and assembled all the people to besiege them. 20They gathered together and besieged the citadel[a] in the one hundred fiftieth year;[b] and he built siege towers and other engines of war. 21But some of the garrison escaped from the siege and some of the ungodly Israelites joined them. 22They went to the king and said, "How long will you fail to do justice and to avenge our kindred? 23We were happy to serve your father, to live by what he said, and to follow his commands. 24For this reason the sons of our people besieged the citadel[c] and became hostile to us; moreover, they have put to death as many of us as they have caught, and they have seized our inheritances. 25It is not against us alone that they have stretched out their hands; they have also attacked all the lands on their borders. 26And see, today they have encamped against the citadel in

[a] Gk *it* [b] 162 B.C. [c] Meaning of Gk uncertain

NAB

quickly forestall them, they will do even worse things than these, and you will not be able to stop them."

28 When the king heard this he was angry, and he called together all his Friends, the officers of his army, and the commanders of the cavalry. 29 Mercenary forces also came to him from other kingdoms and from the islands of the seas. 30 His army numbered a hundred thousand foot-soldiers, twenty thousand cavalry, and thirty-two elephants trained for war. 31 They passed through Idumea and camped before Beth-zur. For many days they attacked it; they constructed siege-devices, but the besieged made a sortie and burned these, and they fought bravely.

NRSV

Jerusalem to take it; they have fortified both the sanctuary and Beth-zur; 27unless you quickly prevent them, they will do still greater things, and you will not be able to stop them."

28The king was enraged when he heard this. He assembled all his Friends, the commanders of his forces and those in authority.[a] 29Mercenary forces also came to him from other kingdoms and from islands of the seas. 30The number of his forces was one hundred thousand foot soldiers, twenty thousand horsemen, and thirty-two elephants accustomed to war. 31They came through Idumea and encamped against Beth-zur, and for many days they fought and built engines of war; but the Jews[b] sallied out and burned these with fire, and fought courageously.

[a] Gk those over the reins   [b] Gk they

COMMENTARY

6:18. The citadel remains under enemy control, manned primarily by the Seleucid garrison. They continue to harass the Jews in the temple area (cf. 4:60-61) and are involved in other actions aimed at defeating the Hasmoneans.

6:19-20. The Gentiles round about had determined to destroy the race of Jacob in their midst (5:1-2), and likewise Judas resolves to destroy the Gentile group within Judea. The author emphasizes the community aspect of the assembly—all the people (i.e., the true Israelites) are gathered to participate in the siege. The siege probably began in spring 162 BCE, "in the one hundred fiftieth year," according to the Babylonian reckoning of the Seleucid era, which the Jews used to date their annual events; this year spanned April 162 BCE to March 161 BCE. The "siege towers," possibly a stage for artillery machines, may have been spoils from earlier victories.

6:21-27. The siege prompts a delegation to the new king. The "ungodly Israelites" are the opposite of those who had joined Mattathias (3:2) and like those who accompanied Seron. Note that no names are given; they are simply categorized as the godless. The author of 1 Maccabees opens the speech of the ungodly like a complaint found often in the psalms: "How long will you fail to

do justice and to avenge our kindred?" (v. 22; cf. Pss 13:1-2; 74:10; 94:3). The speech contains phrases used earlier to describe this group (1:43-44). The godless are said to follow "strange" (ἀλλότριος *allotrios*) customs (1:44); those who were "found" (εὑρίσκω *heuriskō*) not doing so were "put to death" (ἀποθνήσκω *apothnēskō*; 1:50, 57). Now they complain that their countrymen "have become hostile" (lit., "were estranged" from us), that they "have put to death" as many as they "have caught" (lit., "found"). In this context, these Jews complain that they, who followed strange customs, have been turned into strangers and what they had done to Jews who kept the tradition is now being done to them. They have lost their inheritance because they have become strangers/foreigners/aliens.

Verses 25-26 provide a summary of the events described in chapter 5, wherein the forces under Judas are seen as moving outside the territorial limits of Judea and attacking forces in Idumea, Galilee, and Gilead. What is justified in 1 Maccabees 5 as a defensive measure to protect oppressed Jews is described by their enemies as offensive warfare; the fortifying of Beth-zur and Mt. Zion (4:60-61) is seen as preparation for battle. The difference in perception shows how actions can be misinterpreted, particularly when there is suspicion, and lead to the breakdown of any negotiations. Verse 27 is a prophecy of what will happen under Simon, who will establish control over Joppa, extend the borders of his nation, and gain control of the citadel and evict those who dwell within it (13:11, 43-50; 14:5-6).

6:28-31. Antiochus V Eupator was actually only about eleven years old at this time, and Lysias remained in control. The author repeats the language describing Antiochus IV (3:27) to hint at the troubles to come. The size of the army assembled is enormous—larger than was possible for the Seleucid army. The exaggerated size of this army highlights the seriousness with which Judas is now being taken and the increased danger to Judas's army. The army takes the same southern route that Lysias had taken previously (4:29). The "engines of war" (see 6:20) are siege devices. According to this account, Beth-zur will not be captured until after the battle of Beth-zechariah (vv. 49-50). It is unlikely, however, that the Seleucids would have marched toward Jerusalem and left a fortified city at their rear to harass them. (Indeed, 2 Macc 13:18-25 describes a series of battles at Beth-zur, but no attack on Jerusalem.)

1 Maccabees 6:32-47, The Battle at Beth-zechariah

NAB

32 Then Judas marched away from the citadel and moved his camp to Beth-zechariah, on the way to the king's camp. 33 The king, rising before dawn, moved his force hastily along the road to Beth-zechariah; and the armies prepared for battle, while the trumpets sounded. 34 They made the elephants drunk on grape and mulberry wine to provoke them to fight. 35 The beasts were distributed along the phalanxes, each elephant having assigned to it a thousand men in coats of mail, with bronze helmets, and five hundred picked cavalry. 36 These anticipated the beast wherever it was; and wherever it moved, they moved too and never left it. 37 A strong wooden tower covering each elephant, and fastened to it by a harness, held, besides the Indian mahout, three soldiers who fought from it. 38 The remaining cavalry were stationed on one or the other of the two flanks of the army, to harass the enemy and to be protected from the phalanxes. 39 When the sun shone on the gold and bronze shields, the mountains gleamed with their brightness and blazed like flaming torches. 40 Part of the king's army extended over the heights, while some were on low ground, but they marched forward steadily and in good order. 41 All who heard the noise of their numbers, the tramp of their marching, and the clashing of the arms, trembled; for the army was very great and strong.

42 Judas with his army advanced to fight,

6, 34: For *edeixan=hir'û*, read *hirwû*, conj; cf 3 Mc 5, 2.
6, 37: (*andres dynameōs*) *treis* (*hoi polemountes*): conj; the Greek translator read Hebrew *šĕlôšîm* (*triakonta*: so LXXMSS)for *šālišîm?*

NRSV

32Then Judas marched away from the citadel and encamped at Beth-zechariah, opposite the camp of the king. 33Early in the morning the king set out and took his army by a forced march along the road to Beth-zechariah, and his troops made ready for battle and sounded their trumpets. 34They offered the elephants the juice of grapes and mulberries, to arouse them for battle. 35They distributed the animals among the phalanxes; with each elephant they stationed a thousand men armed with coats of mail, and with brass helmets on their heads; and five hundred picked horsemen were assigned to each beast. 36These took their position beforehand wherever the animal was; wherever it went, they went with it, and they never left it. 37On the elephants[a] were wooden towers, strong and covered; they were fastened on each animal by special harness, and on each were four[b] armed men who fought from there, and also its Indian driver. 38The rest of the cavalry were stationed on either side, on the two flanks of the army, to harass the enemy while being themselves protected by the phalanxes. 39When the sun shone on the shields of gold and brass, the hills were ablaze with them and gleamed like flaming torches.

40Now a part of the king's army was spread out on the high hills, and some troops were on the plain, and they advanced steadily and in good order. 41All who heard the noise made by their multitude, by the marching of the multitude and

[a] Gk *them* [b] Cn: Some authorities read *thirty*; others *thirty-two*

and six hundred men of the king's army fell. [43] Eleazar, called Avaran, saw one of the beasts bigger than any of the others and covered with royal armor, and he thought the king must be on it. [44] So he gave up his life to save his people and win an everlasting name for himself. [45] He dashed up to it in the middle of the phalanx, killing men right and left, so that they fell back from him on both sides. [46] He ran right under the elephant and stabbed it in the belly, killing it. The beast fell to the ground on top of him, and he died there.

[47] When the Jews saw the strength of the royal army and the ardor of its forces, they retreated from them.

the clanking of their arms, trembled, for the army was very large and strong. [42] But Judas and his army advanced to the battle, and six hundred of the king's army fell. [43] Now Eleazar, called Avaran, saw that one of the animals was equipped with royal armor. It was taller than all the others, and he supposed that the king was on it. [44] So he gave his life to save his people and to win for himself an everlasting name. [45] He courageously ran into the midst of the phalanx to reach it; he killed men right and left, and they parted before him on both sides. [46] He got under the elephant, stabbed it from beneath, and killed it; but it fell to the ground upon him and he died. [47] When the Jews[c] saw the royal might and the fierce attack of the forces, they turned away in flight.

[c] Gk they

COMMENTARY

6:32-39. Judas encamps his troops at Beth-zechariah, about six miles north of Beth-zur. Lysias thus marches his army out to meet them (vv. 33); the author provides a vivid description of their march (vv. 35-39). The war elephant was the centerpoint for each formation, its flanks defended by one thousand infantry, with five hundred cavalry protecting the infantry. Each formation/phalanx thus operated independently (v. 36); the role of the cavalry was to protect the phalanxes (v. 38). The infantries' armor and shields provide a blazing sight (v. 39).[76]

6:40-47. 6:40-42. As the valley narrowed, troops had to be assigned to secure the ridges. The orderly advance ensures that no gaps would appear in the phalanx that could be exploited. In spite of the impressive appearance of Lysias's army, Judas and his army attack (v. 42), killing six hundred Seleucid soldiers. Those who fall are probably the advance group whose role would be to locate ambushes.[77]

6:43-46. Judas's brother Eleazar (see 2:5), in an act of bravery, kills the royal elephant; it is highly unlikely that a Seleucid king would be riding on the elephant. Eleazar, like Judas himself (3:6; 9:21), dies to save his people and wins proper fame, as contrasted to Joseph and Azariah (5:57). Eleazar's action reflects the ideal warrior, the virtue of self-sacrifice for the cause.[78]

6:47. The author does not state outright that Judas was defeated, but only that the Jews "turned away" (ἐκκλίνω *ekklinō*) in flight. The same Greek verb is used in Num 20:21 LXX to describe how Israel turned away from Edom when the Edomites, refusing to give the Israelites passage through the land, confront them heavily armed. The same verb is found also at Deut 20:3, where the Israelites are exhorted not to turn away from their enemies. This strategic withdrawal, where discretion is the better part of valor, perhaps intimates that the main body of the Seleucid army was not engaged. (In 2 Macc 13:22, Judas wins a victory over Lysias.)

---

76. Polybius notes that armies used to polish their arms to cause apprehension. See Polybius 11.9.1-2.

77. See Josephus *Antiquities of the Jews* 12.372.

78. Such heroism is exemplified in the classics by the stand of Leonidas and the Spartans at Marathon to hold back the Persian forces. See Herodotus 7.207-228.

1 Maccabees 6:48-54, The Siege of Jerusalem

NAB

48 A part of the king's army went up to Jerusalem to attack them, and the king established camps in Judea and at Mount Zion. 49 He made peace with the men of Beth-zur, and they evacuated the city, because they had no food there to enable them to stand a siege, for that was a sabbath year in the land. 50 The king took Beth-zur and stationed a garrison there to hold it. 51 For many days he besieged the sanctuary, setting up artillery and machines, fire-throwers, catapults and mechanical bows for shooting arrows and slingstones. 52 The Jews countered by setting up machines of their own, and kept up the fight a long time. 53 But there were no provisions in the storerooms, because it was the seventh year, and the tide-over provisions had been eaten up by those who had been rescued from the Gentiles and brought to Judea. 54 Few men remained in the sanctuary; the rest scattered, each to his own home, for the famine was too much for them.

NRSV

48The soldiers of the king's army went up to Jerusalem against them, and the king encamped in Judea and at Mount Zion. 49He made peace with the people of Beth-zur, and they evacuated the town because they had no provisions there to withstand a siege, since it was a sabbatical year for the land. 50So the king took Beth-zur and stationed a guard there to hold it. 51Then he encamped before the sanctuary for many days. He set up siege towers, engines of war to throw fire and stones, machines to shoot arrows, and catapults. 52The Jews[a] also made engines of war to match theirs, and fought for many days. 53But they had no food in storage,[b] because it was the seventh year; those who had found safety in Judea from the Gentiles had consumed the last of the stores. 54Only a few men were left in the sanctuary; the rest scattered to their own homes, for the famine proved too much for them.

a Gk *they*   *b* Other ancient authorities read *in the sanctuary*

COMMENTARY

The king now starts to undo what Judas had accomplished (see 4:60-61): He captures Beth-zur and besieges Jerusalem; the terms used for the siege devices are the same as for those Judas had used against the citadel (6:20).

Because of the "sabbatical year," when the land was not worked (Exod 23:11; Lev 25:3-7), the Jews had not been able to set aside enough provisions and thus are unable to withstand the siege (vv. 49, 53). Such food shortages most likely occurred in the year following the sabbatical year. Moreover, the refugees brought from Galilee and Gilead (5:23, 54) had helped to deplete the supplies before the new harvest after the sabbatical year could be gathered in. This section ends with a traditional way of breaking off after a battle (cf. Judg 9:55; 1 Sam 26:25).

1 Maccabees 6:55-63, The End of the Assault by Antiochus V Eupator

NAB

55 Lysias heard that Philip, whom King Antiochus, before his death, had appointed to train his son Antiochus to be king, 56 had returned from Persia and Media with the army that accompanied the king, and that he was seeking to take over the

NRSV

55Then Lysias heard that Philip, whom King Antiochus while still living had appointed to bring up his son Antiochus to be king, 56had returned from Persia and Media with the forces that had gone with the king, and that he was trying to

NAB

government. [57] So he hastily resolved to withdraw. He said to the king, the leaders of the army, and the soldiers: "We are growing weaker every day, our provisions are scanty, the place we are besieging is strong, and it is our duty to take care of the affairs of the kingdom. [58] Therefore let us now come to terms with these men, and make peace with them and all their nation. [59] Let us grant them freedom to live according to their own laws as formerly; it was on account of their laws, which we abolished, that they became angry and did all these things."

[60] The proposal found favor with the king and the leaders; he sent peace terms to the Jews, and they accepted. [61] So the king and the leaders swore an oath to them, and on these terms they evacuated the fortification. [62] But when the king entered Mount Zion and saw how the place was fortified, he broke the oath he had sworn and gave orders for the encircling wall to be destroyed. [63] Then he departed in haste and returned to Antioch, where he found Philip in possession of the city. He fought against him and took the city by force.

NRSV

seize control of the government. [57]So he quickly gave orders to withdraw, and said to the king, to the commanders of the forces, and to the troops, "Daily we grow weaker, our food supply is scant, the place against which we are fighting is strong, and the affairs of the kingdom press urgently on us. [58]Now then let us come to terms with these people, and make peace with them and with all their nation. [59]Let us agree to let them live by their laws as they did before; for it was on account of their laws that we abolished that they became angry and did all these things."

[60]The speech pleased the king and the commanders, and he sent to the Jews[a] an offer of peace, and they accepted it. [61]So the king and the commanders gave them their oath. On these conditions the Jews[b] evacuated the stronghold. [62]But when the king entered Mount Zion and saw what a strong fortress the place was, he broke the oath he had sworn and gave orders to tear down the wall all around. [63]Then he set off in haste and returned to Antioch. He found Philip in control of the city, but he fought against him, and took the city by force.

[a] Gk them   [b] Gk they

COMMENTARY

6:55-57. The confusion that the author had seen as being brought on by the death of Antiochus IV (1 Macc 6:14-17) now begins to manifest itself as a power struggle between Antiochus IV's generals. Whereas the author has been emphasizing that the Jews had no provisions (6:49-53), suddenly Lysias claims that the reason for pulling out is that the Seleucid army is low on food. Perhaps the sabbatical year had affected the besiegers' ability to find provisions for the large army locally. Lysias does not explicitly refer to the advance of Philip, but his listeners must have known even from the vague phrasing that something important was afoot. Josephus specifies that Lysias's speech, given by order of the king, intentionally misrepresents the true reason for their withdrawal.[79]

79. Josephus *Antiquities of the Jews* 12.379-381.

6:58-59. The expression "let us come to terms" (δῶμεν δεξιάς *dōmen dexias*) is literally, "give the right [i.e., good] hand." This is the first mention of peace negotiations in 1 Maccabees. From the correspondence collected in 2 Macc 11:16-38 (particularly vv. 27-32), one can deduce that peace negotiations had already been initiated during the reign of Antiochus IV. No mention is made of these overtures in 1 Maccabees, however, possibly because they involved Jewish groups other than the Maccabees. For the author of 1 Maccabees, only the Maccabees count as Jews; other groups are either naive (1 Macc 7:12-18) or part of the "godless." Lysias seeks to reverse the decrees of Antiochus IV (1:41, 44).

6:60-63. Lysias's proposal pleases the king, who guarantees it with an oath (cf. 8:21), but who then proceeds to break this sacred promise once the Jews have evacuated the temple mount.

The Seleucids have already been depicted as deceitful (1:30), and the narrative will continue to show them to be untrustworthy (7:10-18, 27; 11:2). The wall Judas Maccabeus had built around the sanctuary (4:60) was destroyed, but there is no mention that the temple service restored by

Judas was interfered with. Lysias returns home and defeats Philip.[80]

80. 2 Macc 9:29 states that Philip fled to Egypt, but Josephus (*Antiquities of the Jews* 12.386) holds that Philip was captured and put to death by Eupator.

REFLECTIONS

The Seleucids are shown as finally being forced to negotiate with the Hasmoneans when news reached them that they were under threat from another quarter. The advice of Lysias to come to terms and let the Jews live under their own laws is good advice. However, the Seleucids feel that they are in a position of strength and so are not bound by the negotiated terms. We must reflect on how each of us is bound by contracts made, and how we too should feel bound to honor such contracts, which have been negotiated in good faith, even if later conditions change. Should not a company honor the retirement benefits it has promised to its employees? Are not employees required to give an honest day's work for an honest day's pay? Negotiations have to be entered into in good faith, and once completed must be respected.

1 MACCABEES 7:1-25, THE EXPEDITION OF BACCHIDES AND ALCIMUS

OVERVIEW

This section is held together by certain repetitions of phrases and plays on words that are important to note. Alcimus and others bring charges against the people (v. 6), and Alcimus returns to the king and brings charges against Judas and his followers (v. 25). When Alcimus is commanded to take "vengeance" (ἐκδίκησισ *ekdikēsis*) on the sons of Israel (v. 9), the group of scribes "seek just peace terms" (v. 12; ἐκζητῆσαι δίκαια *ekzētēsai dikaia*), and the Hasideans, first among the sons

of Israel, say that Alcimus "will not harm" (οὐκ ἀδικήσει *ouk adikēsei*) the people (v. 14). Alcimus swears that he "will not seek evil" (οὐκ ἐκζητήσομεν κακόν *ouk ekzētēsomen kakon*, v. 15). The execution of the Hasideans is thus the first step in the fulfillment of the king's command and is followed by other damage on the sons of Israel (v. 23). In response, Judas takes vengeance on those who had deserted him (v. 24). This section is thus a unity.

1 Maccabees 7:1-7, The New King, Demetrius

NAB	NRSV
7 In the year one hundred and fifty-one, Demetrius, son of Seleucus, set out from Rome, arrived with a few men in a city on the seacoast, and began to rule there. ² As he was preparing to enter the royal palace of his ancestors, the soldiers seized Antiochus and Lysias to	**7** In the one hundred fifty-first year[a] Demetrius son of Seleucus set out from Rome, sailed with a few men to a town by the sea, and there began to reign. ²As he was entering the royal palace of his ancestors, the army seized Antiochus

a 161 B.C.

NAB

bring them to him. ³ When he was informed of this, he said, "Do not show me their faces." ⁴ So the soldiers killed them, and Demetrius sat on the royal throne.

⁵ Then all the lawless and impious men of Israel came to him. They were led by Alcimus, who desired to be high priest. ⁶ They made this accusation to the king against the people: "Judas and his brothers have destroyed all your friends and have driven us out of our country. ⁷ So now, send a man whom you trust to go and see all the havoc Judas has done to us and to the king's land, and let him punish them and all their supporters."

NRSV

and Lysias to bring them to him. ³But when this act became known to him, he said, "Do not let me see their faces!" ⁴So the army killed them, and Demetrius took his seat on the throne of his kingdom.

5Then there came to him all the renegade and godless men of Israel; they were led by Alcimus, who wanted to be high priest. ⁶They brought to the king this accusation against the people: "Judas and his brothers have destroyed all your Friends, and have driven us out of our land. ⁷Now then send a man whom you trust; let him go and see all the ruin that Judas*a* has brought on us and on the land of the king, and let him punish them and all who help them."

a Gk *he*

COMMENTARY

7:1. Demetrius I Soter, the son of Seleucus IV and nephew of Antiochus IV Epiphanes, had been a hostage at Rome under the terms of the Treaty of Apamea. When he perceived the crisis in leadership after the death of Antiochus IV, he asked permission of the Roman senate to return. When permission was not granted, he slipped out of Rome with the help of the historian Polybius.[81] He landed at Tripolis in 162 BCE (2 Macc 14:1-2). In Syria, he apparently won the support of the army and settlers as a legitimate member of the Seleucid family over Lysias, regent to the young Antiochus V. The Roman senate did not at first recognize Demetrius, and it kept up contact with rebellious elements in the Seleucid Empire. Timarchus, the satrap of Babylonia, and his brother Heraclides, satrap of Media, did not recognize Demetrius; Ptolemaus, satrap of Commegene, also led a revolt. Timarchus was not defeated until late 161 or early 160 BCE. It is within this context of Demetrius's attempt to gain control over a fragmenting Seleucid Empire that one must place the events of chapter 7.

7:2-4. Having taken control of the country, Demetrius marches on the royal palace at Antioch, 170 miles north of Tripolis. By executing Antiochus and Lysias, Demetrius consolidated his position, as Solomon had done when he came to power and had a rival son of David executed (1 Kgs 2:12-46).

7:5. As frequently in 1 Maccabees, trouble comes to the Jews from within their own ranks (1:1; 6:21; 9:23, 38), although later on these groups have no effect on the king (10:61; 11:21-25). So far in the narrative, the role of the high priest has not been an issue (as it will be in 2 Maccabees 4–5), although we have learned that Mattathias and his family are priests (2:1), that some priests fought unwisely (5:67), and that Judas chose blameless priests who cleansed the sanctuary and restored sacrifice (4:42-53). According to the narrative, proper temple worship had been in place since then; therefore, there must have been a high priest in place to celebrate the annual feast of Yom Kippur, although that high priest is not named. According to 1 Maccabees, Alcimus is appointed high priest by Demetrius I; at his death in 159 BCE, no mention is made of his replacement until the appointment of Jonathan in 152 BCE. Many more high priests are named in 2 Maccabees: Jason, 175–172 BCE; Menelaus, 172–163 BCE; Alcimus, possibly from 163 BCE. The writer of 2 Maccabees also reports that Alcimus was already high priest before the time of De-

81. Polybius 31.11-15.

metrius I Soter (2 Macc 14:3), whereas the writer of 1 Maccabees claims that Alcimus went to Demetrius requesting to be high priest (1 Macc 7:5). As the high priest seems to have been appointed by the king and required reappointment by a new king (2 Macc 4:7-10, 24), the contradiction may be more apparent than real. However, the question remains as to who

carried out the duties of high priest in the Temple restored by Judas.

7:6-7. The delegation's complaint is similar to the one voiced to Antiochus earlier (6:22-27). The word used here for "ruin" ($\dot{\epsilon}\xi o\lambda\epsilon\theta\rho\epsilon\acute{u}\omega$ *exolethreuō*) is from the same root used at 3:8 to describe how Judas had "destroyed" the ungodly out of the land.

1 Maccabees 7:8-20, The Incursion of Bacchides

NAB

⁸ Then the king chose Bacchides, one of the King's Friends, governor of West-of-Euphrates, a great man in the kingdom, and faithful to the king. ⁹ He sent him and the impious Alcimus, to whom he granted the high priesthood, with orders to take revenge on the Israelites. ¹⁰ They set out and, on arriving in the land of Judah with a great army, sent messengers who spoke deceitfully to Judas and his brothers in peaceful terms. ¹¹ But these paid no attention to their words, seeing that they had come with a great army. ¹² A group of scribes, however, gathered about Alcimus and Bacchides to ask for a just agreement. ¹³ The Hasideans were the first among the Israelites to seek peace with them, ¹⁴ for they said, "A priest of the line of Aaron has come with the army, and he will not do us any wrong." ¹⁵ He spoke with them peacefully and swore to them, "We will not try to injure you or your friends." ¹⁶ So they trusted him. But he arrested sixty of them and killed them in one day, according to the text of Scripture:

¹⁷ "The flesh of your saints they have strewn,
   and their blood they have shed round about Jerusalem,
   and there was no one to bury them.

¹⁸ Then fear and dread of them came upon all the people, who said: "There is no truth or justice among them; they violated the agreement and the oath that they swore."

¹⁹ Bacchides withdrew from Jerusalem and pitched his camp in Beth-zaith. He had many of the men arrested who deserted to him, throwing them into the great pit. ²⁰ He handed the province over to Alcimus, leaving troops to help him, while he himself returned to the king.

NRSV

⁸So the king chose Bacchides, one of the king's Friends, governor of the province Beyond the River; he was a great man in the kingdom and was faithful to the king. ⁹He sent him, and with him he sent the ungodly Alcimus, whom he made high priest; and he commanded him to take vengeance on the Israelites. ¹⁰So they marched away and came with a large force into the land of Judah; and he sent messengers to Judas and his brothers with peaceable but treacherous words. ¹¹But they paid no attention to their words, for they saw that they had come with a large force.

¹²Then a group of scribes appeared in a body before Alcimus and Bacchides to ask for just terms. ¹³The Hasideans were first among the Israelites to seek peace from them, ¹⁴for they said, "A priest of the line of Aaron has come with the army, and he will not harm us." ¹⁵Alcimus[a] spoke peaceable words to them and swore this oath to them, "We will not seek to injure you or your friends." ¹⁶So they trusted him; but he seized sixty of them and killed them in one day, in accordance with the word that was written,

¹⁷ "The flesh of your faithful ones and their blood
   they poured out all around Jerusalem,
   and there was no one to bury them."

¹⁸Then the fear and dread of them fell on all the people, for they said, "There is no truth or justice in them, for they have violated the agreement and the oath that they swore."

¹⁹Then Bacchides withdrew from Jerusalem and encamped in Beth-zaith. And he sent and seized many of the men who had deserted to him,[b] and some of the people, and killed them

[a] Gk *He*   [b] Or *many of his men who had deserted*

NRSV

and threw them into a great pit. ²⁰He placed Alcimus in charge of the country and left with him a force to help him; then Bacchides went back to the king.

COMMENTARY

7:8-11. Just as Lysias chose Ptolemy to lead an expedition against Judas (3:38), so also Demetrius chooses Bacchides, governor of the Trans-Euphrates province, between the Euphrates and Egypt. It is not clear whether this expedition was prior to or concomitant with Demetrius's move against Timarchus, who invaded Mesopotamia and planned to cross the Euphrates and invade Syria. The text as it stands suggests that Alcimus is commanded to take vengeance. The primary purpose of the expedition, however, seems to be to establish Alcimus's religious and political authority as high priest (v. 20). The action seems to take place in Jerusalem (see 7:19).

Like the chief of the Mysians (1:29-30), Bacchides speaks deceitfully, but Judas is wary of capture (7:10-11).

7:12-18, The Hasideans. 7:12. Unlike Judas, some Israelites are convinced by Bacchides's overtures. The term translated "scribe" (γραμματεῖς grammateis) is found only once elsewhere in 1 Maccabees (5:42) and is there translated "officers," following the usage of the Pentateuch when referring to commanders of the army and public officials (see Num 11:16; Deut 20:5, 8-9; Josh 1:2; 8:33; 23:2; 24:1). In this context of negotia tions for just terms, this is probably the proper nuance here as well. As opposed to its English denotation of a scribe's being a writer or intellectual, the term "scribe" used in this context should be seen as connoting a leader of the community, a role that would not exclude fighting..

7:13-14. The translation of v. 13 should read: "The Hasideans were the first [or leaders] among the sons of Israel, and they were seeking peace from them." The Hasideans are described in 2:42 as mighty warriors and a group who gathered with Judas, using language similar to that describing the group of scribes/officers who gathered with Alcimus and Bacchides. The Hasideans are leading members of the Israelite community who trust the words of Alcimus. There is thus presented a difference of opinion between Judas and the Hasideans over what strategy to employ. Judas's stance, for the author of 1 Maccabees, is one of uncompromising hostility toward the Seleucids, whereas the Hasideans believe that accommodation can be made. What exactly were the terms the Hasideans were proposing? Given that Judas does not trust Bacchides and Alcimus because they have come with a large force (7:11), perhaps Judas and the Hasideans differed over whether an occupation army should be in the land. The Hasideans feel they can trust the peaceful words this time (in contrast to what happened in 1:30), because an Aaronide priest is negotiating with them. The author of 1 Maccabees suggests that not everyone who says he or she is a Jew, even if a priest, is to be believed, but only those who adhere to the party of Judas and his followers. The thrust of the passage, then, is less against the Hasideans than it is against Jews like Alcimus.

7:15. Alcimus speaks "peaceable words" and promises no harm to the Hasideans. Peaceable words and oaths, however, have led to trouble before. The chief of the Mysians had spoken peaceable words to the residents of Jerusalem and had then attacked them (1:30). Antiochus V had negotiated a peace treaty with the Judeans, but had then broken his oath (6:61-62).

7:16. As the reader might expect from earlier examples, Alcimus goes back on his oath, seizing and killing sixty of the Hasideans. A similar execution of Jewish leaders was carried out by the Babylonians at the fall of Jerusalem in 586 BCE (2 Kgs 25:18-21; Jer 52:24-27).

7:17. The fate of the Hasideans is said to fulfill Ps 79:2-3. Note that "faithful ones" (חסידים ḥăsîdîm) is the same word that the NRSV translates as "your faithful" in Ps 79:2, and so a linguistic connection is being made between the people who have been killed and the words of the psalm. The author of 1 Maccabees has therefore related the text of the Hebrew Scriptures to a contemporary event. He saw his own times as being under the guidance of God, and in this his reading of the Hebrew Scriptures is formally similar to that of the Qumran covenanters, but without a sense that he is living in the end times. Note also the similarity to the lament sung after the citadel was built in Jerusalem (1:37).

7:18. The people "fear and dread." In the book of Judith, fear and dread of Holofernes fall upon the people of the cities on the coastlands when they hear how he has destroyed the cities of Syria (Jdt 2:28). In contradistinction to God, who does all things in faithfulness and justice (Ps 111:7; Prayer of Azariah 5 [Dan 3:28 LXX]), Alcimus acts wrongly and breaks the ordinance and the oath (6:62).

7:19-20. Beth-zaith lay south between Jerusalem and Beth-zur. What Bacchides did at Beth-zaith is told very cryptically. Instead of "deserted," the Greek used here (αὐτομολέω *automoleō*; see also v. 24) should be translated, "those who made peace with him" (cf. Josh 10:1-4; 2 Sam 3:8 LXX; 2 Sam 10:19). The action of Bacchides thus duplicates that of Alcimus in breaking agreements made, as Bacchides kills those who had made peace with him. Bacchides no doubt thought that he was executing justice on war criminals, whereas the author of 1 Maccabees stresses the act's perfidy. The expression "he slaughtered them into a great pit" pre-supposes some action of throwing the corpses into a pit (cf. Jer 41:7). His job of pacification done and Alcimus installed as high priest and dependent on the king's support, Bacchides returned to the king.

REFLECTIONS

The narrative here centers on the question of trust. Whom can one trust? When does trust move over into gullibility? The Hasideans trusted the Aaronide high priest Alcimus to their doom. But their trust was misplaced; they should have learned to be more suspicious as we readers have learned to be from the author's depictions of the actions of the chief of the Mysians (1:30) and Antiochus V (6:61-62). In the United States, for instance, people have become increasingly suspicious and cynical toward their leaders, both religious and political. The exposés of the excesses of televangelists and the prosecution of some pastors and priests for sexual abuse have forced us to be more concerned and alert to signs of abuse of power. Within the political realm, the ramifications of Watergate still linger. Yet the paranoia of paramilitary groups who see their government as evil reminds us that a society cannot survive without some degree of trust among its citizens. We must be "wise as serpents and innocent as doves" (Matt 10:16 NRSV), trusting yet wary.

1 Maccabees 7:21-25, The Inability of Alcimus to Rule

NAB	NRSV
21 Alcimus spared no pains to maintain his high priesthood, 22 and all those who were disturbing their people gathered about him. They took possession of the land of Judah and caused great distress in Israel. 23 When Judas saw all the evils that Alcimus and his men were bringing upon the Israelites, more than even the Gentiles had done, 24 he went about all the borders of Judea and took revenge on the men who had deserted, preventing them from going out into the country. 25 But	21Alcimus struggled to maintain his high priesthood, 22and all who were troubling their people joined him. They gained control of the land of Judah and did great damage in Israel. 23And Judas saw all the wrongs that Alcimus and those with him had done among the Israelites; it was more than the Gentiles had done. 24So Judas^a went out into all the surrounding parts of Judea, taking vengeance on
	a Gk he

NAB

when Alcimus saw that Judas and his followers were gaining strength and realized that he could not oppose them, he returned to the king and accused them of grave crimes.

NRSV

those who had deserted and preventing those in the city[a] from going out into the country. 25When Alcimus saw that Judas and those with him had grown strong, and realized that he could not withstand them, he returned to the king and brought malicious charges against them.

[a] Gk *and they were prevented*

COMMENTARY

7:21-23. To say that Alcimus "struggled" (ἀγωνίζομαι *agōnizomai*) to hold the high priesthood conveys the wrong nuance. It might be better to say that Alcimus fought or strove for the high priesthood. Here one begins to sense that the struggle has now become over who will have the political authority of the high priest as chief of state. The breakthrough will come when Jonathan achieves a modicum of independence (10:15-21). Alcimus is joined by "troublers of the people." In the opening hymn of praise to Judas, he is said to have burned those who troubled the people (3:5). Exactly what they did to the people is unspecified. Earlier, apostates had done evil in the land (1:52) in the context of religious persecution, but that is not mentioned here. The author tells us only that the damage done was great, using language previously applied to the captain of the Mysians (1:30), and that it exceeded the damage done by the Gentiles. The hatred characteristic of civil war can be seen here, as parties engaged in a civil war often resort to dehuman-izing their opponents more than they would strangers.

7:24. The destructiveness of civil war continues as Judas now attacks those who had made peace with Bacchides and Alcimus. This group has been caught in the middle; some of its members were seen by Bacchides as war criminals, while Judas sees them as traitors to "the cause." One can perhaps sense that this group who had accepted Alcimus and submitted to the Seleucids was quite large, as Judas is reduced to guerrilla tactics and acts as Mattathias had done by going around within the borders of Judea (2:45), avoiding the cities.

7:25. As a wrestler tests the opponent's strength, so Alcimus and Judas strive with each other. The author suggests that Alcimus was losing. Although Alcimus is said to bring "malicious charges" against Judas and his followers, it is more likely that Alcimus called for reinforcements to stamp out harassment from Judas's band.

1 MACCABEES 7:26-50, THE RULE OF NICANOR

1 Maccabees 7:26-32, The Treachery of Nicanor

NAB

26 Then the king sent Nicanor, one of his famous officers, who was a bitter enemy of Israel, with orders to destroy the people. 27 Nicanor came to Jerusalem with a large force and deceitfully sent to Judas and his brothers this peaceable message:

NRSV

26Then the king sent Nicanor, one of his honored princes, who hated and detested Israel, and he commanded him to destroy the people. 27So Nicanor came to Jerusalem with a large force, and treacherously sent to Judas and his brothers

NAB

28 "Let there be no fight between me and you. I will come with a few men to meet you peaceably."

29 So he came to Judas, and they greeted one another peaceably. But Judas' enemies were prepared to seize him. 30 When he became aware that Nicanor had come to him with treachery in mind, Judas was afraid and would not meet him again. 31 When Nicanor saw that his plan had been discovered, he went out to fight Judas near Caphar-salama. 32 About five hundred men of Nicanor's army fell; the rest fled to the City of David.

NRSV

this peaceable message, 28"Let there be no fighting between you and me; I shall come with a few men to see you face to face in peace."

29So he came to Judas, and they greeted one another peaceably; but the enemy were preparing to kidnap Judas. 30It became known to Judas that Nicanor[a] had come to him with treacherous intent, and he was afraid of him and would not meet him again. 31When Nicanor learned that his plan had been disclosed, he went out to meet Judas in battle near Caphar-salama. 32About five hundred of the army of Nicanor fell, and the rest[b] fled into the city of David.

a Gk *he*   *b* Gk *they*

COMMENTARY

"Nicanor" was a fairly common name, and so this is unlikely to be the same Nicanor mentioned in 3:38, or the Nicanor who helped Demetrius flee from Rome.[82] The author of 2 Maccabees states that this Nicanor had been in charge of the Seleucid elephant force (2 Macc 14:12) and repeats the charge that Nicanor hated the Jews (14:39; however, the account in 2 Macc 14:11-36 is quite different). Nicanor's mission, "to destroy the people," is the same command given to Lysias (3:35, 39). Like Bacchides and Alcimus (7:10), Nicanor is described as having a larger force and

yet first trying deceit (v. 27-28). The attempt to capture Judas is described very sensationally; Judas almost succumbs to Nicanor's treachery, but somehow learns of his plan (vv. 29-31). When the ruse fails, Nicanor tries an open assault (v. 31). The exact location of Caphar-salama is unknown, but it probably lies between Jerusalem and the Gophna Hills. Nicanor suffers a minor setback and retires to the citadel in Jerusalem (v. 32). No description of the battle is given, nor is there any indication of losses on Judas's side.

82. See Polybius 31.114.4; Josephus *Antiquities of the Jews* 12.402.

1 Maccabees 7:33-38, Nicanor Threatens the Temple

NAB

33 After this, Nicanor went up to Mount Zion. Some of the priests from the sanctuary and some of the elders of the people came out to greet him peaceably and to show him the holocaust that was being offered for the king. 34 But he mocked and ridiculed them, defiled them, and spoke disdainfully. 35 In a rage he swore: "If Judas and his army are not delivered to me at once, when I return victorious I will burn this temple down." He went

NRSV

33After these events Nicanor went up to Mount Zion. Some of the priests from the sanctuary and some of the elders of the people came out to greet him peaceably and to show him the burnt offering that was being offered for the king. 34But he mocked them and derided them and defiled them and spoke arrogantly, 35and in anger he swore this oath, "Unless Judas and his army are delivered into my hands this time, then if I

NAB

away in great anger. [36] The priests, however, went in and stood before the altar and the sanctuary. They wept and said: [37] "You have chosen this house to bear your name, to be a house of prayer and petition for your people. [38] Take revenge on this man and his army, and let them fall by the sword. Remember their blasphemies, and do not let them continue."

NRSV

return safely I will burn up this house." And he went out in great anger. [36]At this the priests went in and stood before the altar and the temple; they wept and said,

[37] "You chose this house to be called by your name,
> and to be for your people a house of prayer and supplication.
[38] Take vengeance on this man and on his army,
> and let them fall by the sword;
remember their blasphemies,
> and let them live no longer."

COMMENTARY

7:33. Nicanor now devises a new strategy and goes up to the Temple. The priests and elders come out from the temple court (which Nicanor could not enter) to greet the Seleucid commander peaceably (cf. v. 29), with no deceit in mind. Alcimus presumably was still with the king. The temple worship had included sacrifices on behalf of the ruling king from early Second Temple times (Ezra 6:10).

7:34-35. Nicanor openly shows his hostility by acting arrogantly as Antiochus IV had done on entering the sanctuary (1:21-24). The author uses the language of the psalms (Ps 44:13; 80:6) to describe how Nicanor mocks the priests, and he also notes that Nicanor defiles the priests, as Antiochus IV had ordered the sanctuary to be defiled (1:46). Nicanor's threat to destroy the Temple echoes the destruction of the First Temple (2 Kgs 25:9; 2 Chr 36:19; 1 Esdr 1:55; 4:45; 6:16).

7:36-38. The undefiled priests go into the inner court of the priests and pray. Their prayer recalls those of earlier times. When he dedicated the First Temple, Solomon had prayed that God would listen to the people whenever they turned to God (1 Kgs 8:22-53). When Jerusalem and its God were mocked by the Assyrian commander, King Hezekiah of Judea rent his clothes and sent his priests to Isaiah the prophet to ask him to pray for the people (2 Kgs 19:1-7; see also Isa 10:7-19). The author of 1 Maccabees has placed this assault of Nicanor in the context of an attack against God's Temple. As such, one knows the outcome: He will be destroyed.

1 Maccabees 7:39-50, The Death of Nicanor

NAB

[39] Nicanor left Jerusalem and pitched his camp at Beth-horon, where the Syrian army joined him. [40] But Judas camped in Adasa with three thousand men. Here Judas uttered this prayer: [41] "When they who were sent by the king blasphemed, your angel went out and killed a hundred and eighty-five thousand of them. [42] In the same way, crush this army before us today, and let the rest know that Nicanor spoke wickedly against your sanctuary; judge him according to his wickedness."

NRSV

[39]Now Nicanor went out from Jerusalem and encamped in Beth-horon, and the Syrian army joined him. [40]Judas encamped in Adasa with three thousand men. Then Judas prayed and said, [41]"When the messengers from the king spoke blasphemy, your angel went out and struck down one hundred eighty-five thousand of the Assyrians.[a] [42]So also crush this army before us today; let the rest learn that Nicanor[b] has spoken

[a] Gk of them   [b] Gk he

NAB

⁴³ The armies met in battle on the thirteenth day of the month Adar. Nicanor's army was crushed, and he himself was the first to fall in the battle. ⁴⁴ When his army saw that Nicanor was dead, they threw down their arms and fled. ⁴⁵ The Jews pursued them a day's journey, from Adasa to near Gazara, blowing the trumpets behind them as signals. ⁴⁶ From all the surrounding villages of Judea people came out and closed in on them. They hemmed them in, and all the enemies fell by the sword; not a single one escaped.

⁴⁷ Then the Jews collected the spoils and the booty; they cut off Nicanor's head and his right arm, which he had lifted up so arrogantly. These they brought to Jerusalem and displayed there. ⁴⁸ The people rejoiced greatly, and observed that day as a great festival. ⁴⁹ They decreed that it should be observed every year on the thirteenth of Adar. ⁵⁰ And for a short time the land of Judah was quiet.

NRSV

wickedly against the sanctuary, and judge him according to this wickedness."

⁴³So the armies met in battle on the thirteenth day of the month of Adar. The army of Nicanor was crushed, and he himself was the first to fall in the battle. ⁴⁴When his army saw that Nicanor had fallen, they threw down their arms and fled. ⁴⁵The Jews*ᵃ* pursued them a day's journey, from Adasa as far as Gazara, and as they followed they kept sounding the battle call on the trumpets. ⁴⁶People came out of all the surrounding villages of Judea, and they outflanked the enemy*ᵇ* and drove them back to their pursuers,*ᶜ* so that they all fell by the sword; not even one of them was left. ⁴⁷Then the Jews*ᵃ* seized the spoils and the plunder; they cut off Nicanor's head and the right hand that he had so arrogantly stretched out, and brought them and displayed them just outside Jerusalem. ⁴⁸The people rejoiced greatly and celebrated that day as a day of great gladness. ⁴⁹They decreed that this day should be celebrated each year on the thirteenth day of Adar. ⁵⁰So the land of Judah had rest for a few days.

ᵃ Gk *they*   ᵇ Gk *them*   ᶜ Gk *these*

COMMENTARY

7:39-40. Nicanor seems to have requested reinforcements, possibly from some troops on the coastal plain, like those of Seron (3:13). Nicanor went to meet them at the ascent of Beth-horon, the route Seron had taken to Jerusalem (3:16). Judas has 3,000 men, the same number who fought with him at the battle of Emmaus (4:6), which also took place near the Beth-horon ascent; however, this number was considerably fewer than the forces he had mustered in other campaigns (see 5:20). The exact location of Adasa is unknown, but it seems to lie near the top of the Beth-horon ascent.

7:41-42. The prayer before battle, which is ascribed to Judas, picks up on the reference in the priest's prayer to the blasphemies of Nicanor by remembering how Sennacherib's army had uttered similar blasphemies when the Assyrians besieged Jerusalem in 701 BCE (2 Kgs 18:14-35). In that encounter, the angel of the Lord is said

to have struck down the Assyrians, and the king of the Assyrians, Sennacherib, is said to have died soon after (2 Kgs 19:35-37). Judas asks for the same result to be meted out to Nicanor. The author of 2 Maccabees refers to the same biblical precedent when recounting the two battles against the two Nicanors (2 Macc 8:19; 15:22).

7:43-46. The battle is not described in great detail, specifying only the date, the defeat of Nicanor's army, and the fact that the divine vengeance falls first on the blasphemer. The Seleucid soldiers fled to Gazara (cf. 4:15), the closest Seleucid fort to the west. The trumpets alerted the men in the nearby villages to block the paths of the retreating army down the steep Beth-horon descent (cf. Num 10:6; Judg 3:27). Just as the entire army of Sennacherib had been destroyed (2 Kgs 19:35; Isa 37:36), so also all of Nicanor's army is killed.

7:47. Nicanor's body is dismembered in retaliation for this blasphemy (note the more colorful description at 2 Macc 15:30-35). One might compare the treatment of the bodies of the Athenian commanders Nicias and Demosthenes. The general assembly of the Syracusans condemned them to death, and their bodies were thrown out before the gates of the city and offered for a public spectacle.[83] The treatment of this slain king recalls such incidents from Israel's past: King Saul's body was fastened to the wall of Beth-shan (1 Sam 31:10); David brought Goliath's head to Jerusalem (1 Sam 17:54); Holofernes' head was hung from the parapet of Bethulia (Jdt 14:1, 11); and seven descendants of Saul were impaled at Gibeon on the mountain before the Lord (2 Sam 21:6, 9). The author of 1 Maccabees specifies that Nicanor's body is kept outside Jerusalem, so as not to defile the city.

7:48-50. The joy and festivity following the victory are similar to those at the dedication of the Temple (4:58-59). Surprisingly, the author does not mention that the Feast of Purim falls on 14 Adar. Since Adar falls around March, the battle took place either in March 161 or March 160. The account concludes with a formula known well from Judges (3:11, 30; 5:31; 8:28), which will be used again (9:57; 11:38, 52; 14:4). Although in Judges the formula speaks of the rest having lasted for many years, here it is only for a few days, because the Seleucid threat remained.

83. See Plutarch *Nicias* 27-28.

REFLECTIONS

This narrative shows how the Seleucids with their underling Alcimus tried to impose their rule by using scare tactics in killing former opponents and by threatening to wipe out the most sacred Jewish institution: the Temple in Jerusalem. Yet the narrative also shows how such methods were ineffective. When given the chance, the people rose up from their villages and pursued the enemy (7:46). When a people are determined to resist, no amount of coercion can overcome them. They may be cowed for a while, but eventually they will rise up. The collapse of the Soviet Union is a contemporary illustration of this fact. For so long, it appeared that the peoples of the Soviet Union would always be under the thumb of the Soviets. Yet, given the chance for freedom, the people took it. Times of transition are also times of uncertainty, and there have been excesses in the attempts of the former Soviet states to forge independent nations, just as one might deplore the vengeance wreaked on Nicanor by dismembering him. But this narrative reminds us that might does not make right, and until a group can be led to see that what is being proposed for them is for the good of them all there will be resistance. A minority, no matter how well-intentioned and how confirmed in their own belief that what they are doing is God's will, should not attempt to force through legislation with which the majority is not in agreement. Rather, they must debate their ideas in the open forum, in order to explain and attempt to persuade others to their views. Coercion never pays in the end.

1 MACCABEES 8:1-32, THE RELATIONSHIP WITH ROME

OVERVIEW

The formulaic phrase at the end of chapter 7 allows the author space before discussing the reaction of Demetrius to the news of Nicanor's defeat; note how 8:1 and 9:1 both begin with

"And Judas/Demetrius heard. . . . " The author describes here the delegation Judas sent to the Romans and draws a utopian picture of the Roman state. Josephus preserves the text of a letter of the consul Gaius Fannius (Roman consul in 161 BCE) on behalf of the Jewish envoys to the officials of the island of Cos.[84] Whatever the questions surrounding the exact tenor, language, and status of the letter preserved at 1 Macc 8:23-32 (Was it a treaty between equal nations, or was it diplomatic recognition by Rome of Judas and his supporters?), the author of 1 Maccabees sees it as a significant document to which he constantly refers (12:1-4; 14:16-19, 24; 15:15-24). Judea is seen as an independent nation among other nations. In this connection, it is interesting to note how the Jewish historian Eupolemus, who may be identical with the ambassador Judas sent to Rome (8:15), records letters of friendship from King Solomon to Vaphres, to the kings of Egypt, and to Souron, king of Tyre and Sidon and Phoenicia.[85] In this way, Solomon's status as equal to that of the Tyrians and the Egyptians is proclaimed. Here in 1 Maccabees, the independent status of Judea is evidenced by its ability to interact on an equal plane with other nations; one can see how the goal of the author of 1 Maccabees is the independence of Judea.

What is also striking about this discussion of the Romans is its utopian picture of them; they are generous to their friends, devastating to their foes. The Romans have been exalted, yet they are not proud (8:13-14). Their constitution is a mixture of egalitarian, aristocratic, and monarchic features. While the description of the Roman constitution in 1 Maccabees is not as detailed as that of Polybius,[86] it does contain a hint of a suggestion as to what is the best kind of government. A utopian description is, of course, also a critique of other systems. First of all, it is a critique of a monarchic form of government, such as that of the Seleucids, the inherent instability of which is shown in the dynastic infighting after the death of Antiochus IV. The description of the Romans, victorious in all their battles as was Alexander the Great, also contrasts with the puffed-up arrogance of Alexander (1:3) and Antiochus IV (1:22-24). But does this utopian description also critique the later Hasmonean rulers? Jonathan and Simon both wear purple and crowns (10:20; 14:43) and Simon is to be leader and priest forever, until a trustworthy prophet should arise (14:41), not a ruler for one year only. Simon appoints all the officials (14:42); there appears to be no group, like the Roman senate, to balance his power.

84. Josephus *Antiquities of the Jews* 14.233.
85. See Alexander Polyhistor "On the Jews," in Eusebius of Caesarea · *Praeparatio Evangelica* 9:31–34.1.

86. Polybius 6.11-18.

1 Maccabees 8:1-16, An Idealized Description of the Romans

NAB

8 Judas had heard of the reputation of the Romans. They were valiant fighters and acted amiably to all who took their side. They established a friendly alliance with all who applied to them. [2] He was also told of their battles and the brave deeds that they had performed against the Gauls, conquering them and forcing them to pay tribute. [3] They had gotten possession of the silver and gold mines in Spain, [4] and by planning and persistence had conquered the whole country, although it was very remote from their own. They had crushed the kings who had come against them from the far corners of the earth and had

8, 2: Omit *kai ʼoti eisi dynatoi ischyi:* dittog from v 1.

NRSV

8 Now Judas heard of the fame of the Romans, that they were very strong and were well-disposed toward all who made an alliance with them, that they pledged friendship to those who came to them, [2]and that they were very strong. He had been told of their wars and of the brave deeds that they were doing among the Gauls, how they had defeated them and forced them to pay tribute, [3]and what they had done in the land of Spain to get control of the silver and gold mines there, [4]and how they had gained control of the whole region by their planning and patience, even though the place was far distant from them. They also subdued the kings who

NAB

inflicted on them severe defeat, and the rest paid tribute to them every year. ⁵ Philip and Perseus, king of the Macedonians, and the others who opposed them in battle had been overwhelmed and subjugated. ⁶ Antiochus the Great, king of Asia, who had fought against them with a hundred and twenty elephants and with cavalry and chariots and a very great army, had been defeated by them. ⁷ They had taken him alive and obliged him and the kings who succeeded him to pay a heavy tribute, to give hostages and a section of ⁸ Lycia, Mysia, and Lydia from among their best provinces. The Romans took these from him and gave them to King Eumenes. ⁹ When the men of Greece had planned to come and destroy them, ¹⁰ the Romans discovered it, and sent against the Greeks a single general who made war on them. Many were wounded and fell, and the Romans took their wives and children captive. They plundered them, took possession of their land, tore down their strongholds and reduced them to slavery even to this day. ¹¹ All the other kingdoms and islands that had ever opposed them they destroyed and enslaved; ¹² with their friends, however, and those who relied on them, they maintained friendship. They had conquered kings both far and near, and all who heard of their fame were afraid of them. ¹³ In truth, those whom they desired to help to a kingdom became kings, and those whom they wished to depose they deposed; and they were greatly exalted. ¹⁴ Yet with all this, none of them put on a crown or wore purple as a display of grandeur. ¹⁵ They had made for themselves a senate house, and every day three hundred and twenty men took counsel, deliberating on all that concerned the people and their well-being. ¹⁶ They entrusted their government to one man every year, to rule over their entire country, and they all obeyed that one, and there was no envy or jealousy among them.

8, 8: (chōran tēn) Lykian (kai) Mysian (kai Lydian): conj.

NRSV

came against them from the ends of the earth, until they crushed them and inflicted great disaster on them; the rest paid them tribute every year. ⁵They had crushed in battle and conquered Philip, and King Perseus of the Macedonians,ᵃ and the others who rose up against them. ⁶They also had defeated Antiochus the Great, king of Asia, who went to fight against them with one hundred twenty elephants and with cavalry and chariots and a very large army. He was crushed by them; ⁷they took him alive and decreed that he and those who would reign after him should pay a heavy tribute and give hostages and surrender some of their best provinces, ⁸the countries of India, Media, and Lydia. These they took from him and gave to King Eumenes. ⁹The Greeks planned to come and destroy them, ¹⁰but this became known to them, and they sent a general against the Greeksᵇ and attacked them. Many of them were wounded and fell, and the Romansᶜ took captive their wives and children; they plundered them, conquered the land, tore down their strongholds, and enslaved them to this day. ¹¹The remaining kingdoms and islands, as many as ever opposed them, they destroyed and enslaved; ¹²but with their friends and those who rely on them they have kept friendship. They have subdued kings far and near, and as many as have heard of their fame have feared them. ¹³Those whom they wish to help and to make kings, they make kings, and those whom they wish they depose; and they have been greatly exalted. ¹⁴Yet for all this not one of them has put on a crown or worn purple as a mark of pride, ¹⁵but they have built for themselves a senate chamber, and every day three hundred twenty senators constantly deliberate concerning the people, to govern them well. ¹⁶They trust one man each year to rule over them and to control all their land; they all heed the one man, and there is no envy or jealousy among them.

ᵃ Or Kittim   ᵇ Gk them   ᶜ Gk they

COMMENTARY

8:1-2a. As mentioned earlier, Timarchus, the rebel satrap of Media, had obtained a decree from the senate, recognizing him as king, by which the Romans sought to undermine the position of Demetrius I.[87] Judas is thus acting very shrewdly. One would like to know exactly how Judas came to know about the Romans—through Jews who had visited them? Through mercenaries? The book of Daniel (11:18, 29-30) shows knowledge of Roman intervention in Seleucid affairs, but 1 Maccabees mentions nothing of Antiochus IV's humiliation in 168 BCE at the hands of the Roman legate C. Popillius Laenas, who forced Antiochus to leave Egypt.

The Romans are described in terms of their integrity, strength, and "brave deeds." The same phrase is used to describe the actions of Judas, Jonathan, and Simon (5:56), forging a link between the Hasmoneans and the Romans.

8:2b-4a. The author puts forward first a list of the victories of the Romans, starting from the far west to the east. "The Gauls" is most probably a reference to the tribes of Cisalpine Gaul who lived in what is today northern Italy and who were subdued by Rome over a period from 200 to 180 or possibly 175 BCE. These wars against the Gauls and the Ligurians were the first major step toward the Romanization of a sizeable piece of the Italian peninsula. The Carthaginian general Hamilcar Barca had conquered much of southern and southeastern Spain in 237–229 BCE, and so Spain was to become the scene for battles between Carthage and Rome in the Punic Wars. The victory under Scipio Africanus in 206 led to the annexation of two provinces soon after. These provinces proved turbulent, but Rome continually expanded its position. War erupted again in the 150s, and resistance finally was quelled in 133 BCE. It is noteworthy that the author of 1 Maccabees says that the Romans' goal in subduing Spain was to get control of the gold and silver (v. 3); the silver mines in Spain, particularly those near Cartagena and in the Sierra Morena, made possession of this territory extremely profitable.

8:4b. The reference to kings who came against the Romans may be an imprecise description of the great Carthaginian generals Hamilcar, Hasdrubal, and Hannibal, or it may introduce the following list of rulers to the east of Rome. The Romans had imposed indemnity payments (yearly tribute) on Philip V of Macedonia, one thousand talents to be paid over ten years and of fifteen thousand talents on Antiochus III.

8:5. The Romans are said to have been attacked by aggressive kings, a statement that does not adequately account for Roman ambition and expansion.

King Philip V of Macedon (238–179 BCE) was defeated after the Second Macedonian War (200–197 BCE) by the Roman consul Flaminius at Cynoscephalae in Thessaly. Perseus, son of Philip and king of Macedonia (179–168 BCE), fought the Third Macedonian War (171–168 BCE) but was defeated by the Roman consul Aemilius Paullus at Pydna in 168 BCE. The author of 1 Maccabees magnifies the exploits of the Romans by suggesting that other rulers on the same scale as Philip and Perseus had come against Rome in the past and had been defeated as well.

8:6-8. The author next moves closer to home by recounting the Romans' victory over Antiochus III, father of Antiochus IV, whose Seleucid kingdom was called Asia. Named "the Great" because, like Alexander, he had made incursions into India and Arabia, Antiochus III recovered the coastal territories of Asia Minor in 197/96 BCE. In 196 BCE, he crossed over to Thrace, bringing him into conflict with the Romans. In the ensuing war, he was defeated in 190 BCE at Magnesia ad Sipylum, just north of Smyrna in Asia Minor. The Romans did not take Antiochus III prisoner; instead by the Treaty of Apamea in 188 BCE he had to pay a high indemnity and evacuate all territory north and west of the Taurus Mountains. Much of this territory was incorporated into the kingdom of Eumenes II of Pergamum. The treaty required twenty hostages between the ages of eighteen and forty-five, and the future Antiochus IV was one of them. After the peace of Apamea, the Seleucids no longer had the possibility of acquiring major influence in western Asia Minor or in Europe. Their empire still stretched from the Taurus Mountains to eastern Iran, but they no longer had control in India or in the Greek state of Bactria. In his expedition to the east (212–208 BCE), Antiochus III regained the formal recognition of Seleucid supremacy by the Parthian ruler Arsaces II,[88] but Parthia remained fairly independent. Antiochus III also seems to have restored Seleucid

---

87. Diodorus Siculus 31.27a.

88. See Polybius 10.27-31.

administration in Media. The author of 1 Maccabees is, therefore, incorrect in speaking of Antiochus III's giving up of India, Media, and Lydia; in fact, he gave up all pretensions to Lydia. As to all western Asia Minor, India was not his to give, and he maintained control of Media. Perhaps the author is referring to the general fact that the enormous Seleucid Empire was difficult to control and frequently on the verge of losing territory.

8:9-10. The war of the Achaean league with Sparta in 146 led to war with Rome; the Achaeans were defeated by the Roman consul Lucius Mummius that same year, and democracy ceased to be the accepted form of government. In particular, Corinth was completely destroyed, and Mummius auctioned the women and children into slavery, broke down the walls, and confiscated the armaments of any city that had fought against Rome. Pausanias, writing in the second century CE, mentions that even in his day the Romans still sent out a governor of Achaia.[89] Thus the description by the author of 1 Maccabees is generally correct, but quite anachronistic for the time of Judas.

8:11-13. The author here gives a summary statement concerning the Romans: Those who oppose them are defeated; those who are friends are protected. As such, the reference could be to Carthage and the islands taken from it as well as to the Greek islands. The universal scope of Rome's domination is emphasized.

8:14-15. In Rome during this period, only victorious generals were allowed to wear a diadem and purple-colored clothing, which were royal prerogatives, during triumphal celebrations. Senators wore a broad purple upright stripe stitched to or woven into the fabric of their tunics.

The number of senators was about 300 until Sulla in 81 BCE doubled the number. It is not known where the author got the number 320—by adding the magistrates to the 300 senators, or possibly an analogy to the Jewish Sanhedrin.[90] The senate did not meet daily but only when summoned by the magistrates.

8:16. Usually, there were two consuls, and only in an emergency would a single dictator be appointed. It has been suggested that the author of 1 Maccabees concluded that there was only one consul because sometimes only one magistrate's name was mentioned in documents (see, e.g., 1 Macc 15:16). The author has put forward an idealized mixed blend of aristocracy and monarchy. The claim that there was no envy or jealousy among the Romans neglects the competition among leading families, the legislation passed in 181 BCE against bribery in elections, and the numerous prosecutions of leading figures.

---

89. Pausanias 7.16.5-6.

90. See *t. Sanh.* 7:1; *Sanh.* 88b. Little is known about the second-century BCE Sanhedrin, except that it existed. See 2 Macc 1:10; 4:44; 11:27. See also Josephus *Antiquities of the Jews* 12.138.

1 Maccabees 8:17-32, The Exchange of Letters

NAB

[17] So Judas chose Eupolemus, son of John, son of Accos, and Jason, son of Eleazar, and sent them to Rome to establish an alliance of friendship with them. [18] He did this to get rid of the yoke, for it was obvious that the kingdom of the Greeks was subjecting Israel to slavery. [19] After making a very long journey to Rome, the envoys entered the senate and spoke as follows: [20] "Judas, called Maccabeus, and his brothers, with the Jewish people, have sent us to you to make a peaceful alliance with you, and to enroll ourselves among your allies and friends." [21] The proposal pleased the Romans, [22] and this is a copy of the reply they

NRSV

[17] So Judas chose Eupolemus son of John son of Accos, and Jason son of Eleazar, and sent them to Rome to establish friendship and alliance, [18] and to free themselves from the yoke; for they saw that the kingdom of the Greeks was enslaving Israel completely. [19] They went to Rome, a very long journey; and they entered the senate chamber and spoke as follows: [20] "Judas, who is also called Maccabeus, and his brothers and the people of the Jews have sent us to you to establish alliance and peace with you, so that we may be enrolled as your allies and friends." [21] The proposal pleased them, [22] and this is a copy of the letter

NAB

inscribed on bronze tablets and sent to Jerusalem, to remain there with the Jews as a record of peace and alliance:

23 "May it be well with the Romans and the Jewish nation at sea and on land forever; may sword and enemy be far from them. 24 But if war is first made on Rome, or any of its allies in any of their dominions, 25 the Jewish nation will help them wholeheartedly, as the occasion shall demand; 26 and to those who wage war they shall not give nor provide grain, arms, money, or ships; this is Rome's decision. They shall fulfill their obligations without receiving any recompense. 27 In the same way, if war is made first on the Jewish nation, the Romans will help them willingly, as the occasion shall demand, 28 and to those who are attacking them there shall not be given grain, arms, money, or ships; this is Rome's decision. They shall fulfill their obligations without deception. 29 On these terms the Romans have made an agreement with the Jewish people. 30 But if both parties hereafter decide to add or take away anything, they shall do as they choose, and whatever they shall add or take away shall be valid.

31 "Moreover, concerning the wrongs that King Demetrius has done to them, we have written to him thus: 'Why have you made your yoke heavy upon our friends and allies the Jews? 32 If they complain about you again, we will do them justice and make war on you by land and sea.' "

NRSV

that they wrote in reply, on bronze tablets, and sent to Jerusalem to remain with them there as a memorial of peace and alliance:

23"May all go well with the Romans and with the nation of the Jews at sea and on land forever, and may sword and enemy be far from them. 24If war comes first to Rome or to any of their allies in all their dominion, 25the nation of the Jews shall act as their allies wholeheartedly, as the occasion may indicate to them. 26To the enemy that makes war they shall not give or supply grain, arms, money, or ships, just as Rome has decided; and they shall keep their obligations without receiving any return. 27In the same way, if war comes first to the nation of the Jews, the Romans shall willingly act as their allies, as the occasion may indicate to them. 28And to their enemies there shall not be given grain, arms, money, or ships, just as Rome has decided; and they shall keep these obligations and do so without deceit. 29Thus on these terms the Romans make a treaty with the Jewish people. 30If after these terms are in effect both parties shall determine to add or delete anything, they shall do so at their discretion, and any addition or deletion that they may make shall be valid.

31"Concerning the wrongs that King Demetrius is doing to them, we have written to him as follows, 'Why have you made your yoke heavy on our friends and allies the Jews? 32If now they appeal again for help against you, we will defend their rights and fight you on sea and on land.' "

COMMENTARY

8:17-20. As he had done before (4:42), Judas takes the initiative. Eupolemus, from the priestly clan of Hakkoz (1 Chr 24:10), was the son of the man who had won concessions from Antiochus III (2 Macc 4:10); it is possible to identify him with the Eupolemus who wrote in Greek "On the Kings of Judea," fragments of which survive. Nothing is known about Jason, son of Eleazar. It is noteworthy that both have Greek names.

"The yoke" (ζυγός zygos) was a frequent metaphor for servitude and slavery (see Gen 27:40; Lev 26:13; Isa 9:4; 10:27; 14:5, 25, 29; Ezek

34:27). In the ceremony of the red heifer, the heifer must never have been used for profane work—i.e., have been under a master—before being used in the ritual (Num 19:2). Thus Judas asks not to be enslaved but to be a friend of the Romans (8:11-12). The Roman historian Livy recounts that at the end of Rome's war with Perseus "the Macedonians and Illyrians were to be free, so that it might appear to all peoples that the arms of the Roman people do not bring servitude to freemen but rather freedom to slaves."[91]

91. Livy 45.18.1.

The ambassadors open their address by referring to the "people" (πλῆθος *plēthos*) of the Jews, rather than to the "nation" (ἔθνος *ethnos*; cf. 8:23; 12:3) or "people" (δῆμος *dēmos*; see 1 Macc 8:29). *Plēthos* sometimes translates the Hebrew "congregation" (קהל *qāhāl*; see Exod 12:6; 2 Chr 31:18), but one should note how it had just been used in 8:15 to refer to the Roman people.

8:21-22. The Romans had not yet recognized Demetrius I as king and may have been glad to further embarrass him. Only a very general statement of Roman agreement is made. There is no mention of an execration or oath, which would have been a necessary part of a formal treaty. No doubt the original document was inscribed on bronze tablets and kept at Rome. Verses 31-32 suggest that this is a letter that is being copied, although the full form of a letter is not present. The copy was presumably written in Latin or Greek, translated into Hebrew in the first edition of 1 Maccabees, and then translated into Greek for the extant text of 1 Maccabees. One should not expect to be able to reconstruct the exact wording of the document.

8:23-30. After the introductory wish for well-being come parallel clauses requiring that each come to the aid of the other, although the clause "as the occasion may indicate" (vv. 25, 27) allows for a wide range of interpretation. The phrase "without receiving any return" (v. 26; lit., "taking nothing") parallels "without deceit" (v. 28) and probably should be understood to mean "not accepting any bribes." Any changes had to have the consent of both parties.

8:31-32. The letter concludes by quoting another letter of the Romans to Demetrius I; the imagery is similar to that of 2 Chr 10:10-14. The Romans never followed up on the threat. Did events move too rapidly for them? Or did they use the loophole provided by the condition "as the occasion may indicate"? Whenever the senate decided that Rome could exploit a situation to its own advantage, the senate would act. Roman policy was guided by political considerations, rather than by questions of law and morality, as, for example, the Seleucids found out when the Romans unilaterally added to the Treaty of Apamea that the Seleucids could not make war on Egypt. Finally, whatever the Maccabees might have thought, the relationship they had forged with the Romans was most probably not a treaty between equals.[92] After defeating the king of Macedonia and the Seleucid king, the Romans became the dominant power in the world. Rome most likely granted the Maccabees a friendship pact, which gave Judah the appearance of being protected by Rome but did not necessarily mean that the Romans would indeed intervene to protect nations subject to other kings—although such a pact could provide the pretext for going to war with those kings. In fact, such a friendship pact was *de facto* an acknowledgment of Roman suzerainty.

Nevertheless, the author of 1 Maccabees sees this document as a major step toward independence from the Seleucids and keeps referring to it (12:1, 3-4; 14:18, 24).

---

92. S. Mandell, "Did the Maccabees Believe That They Had a Valid Treaty with Rome?" *CBQ* 53 (1991) 202-20.

REFLECTIONS

To someone who knows the future relations between Rome and Judea, this chapter is particularly poignant and ironic. That reader knows that the Romans took control of Judea under Pompey the Great in 63 BCE and—after the failure of Herod the Great's son Archelaus in 6 CE—ruled Judea as a province. The Jews revolted against the Romans twice, first in the great revolt of 66–73 CE and then in the revolt of Bar Kochba in 132–135 CE. Both times they were defeated and crushed. In the first revolt, the Temple in Jerusalem was burned and destroyed and not rebuilt. This destruction of the Temple led to a major restructuring of Jewish life and traditions, for the Temple had been where God had met the people and where the sacrifices commanded in Leviticus had been performed. No longer would those sacrifices be offered to God.

No doubt the Roman juggernaut would eventually have taken control of the Near East. One can see in the subsequent history of the Seleucid monarchs how Rome meddled in order to gain advantage. This early attempt by the Jews to gain the support of this powerful backer was advantageous in the short term, but disastrous for the long haul. If one allies oneself with a stronger partner, will such a move eventually lead to some loss of one's own independence? What compromises and concessions might one have to make in order to stay in union with such a partner? But if one does not have powerful allies, will one's independence be lost anyway? These questions beset the countries of Europe as they inched their way toward the creation of the European Economic Community, but they are also part and parcel of ordinary federal and local economic issues. Will a merger of school districts mean the loss of control over curricular issues? Will a business merger take someone out of the decision-making process? Yet, if one does not merge, can one have a viable school offering a sophisticated curriculum, or a business that can really compete? The old adage that there is unity in diversity should be kept in mind. Strength comes through acknowledging the diverse talents that each person, each community, and each nation brings. It is when unity means conformity that strength fails.

1 MACCABEES 9:1-22, THE DEATH OF JUDAS

NAB

9 When Demetrius heard that Nicanor and his army had fallen in battle, he again sent Bacchides and Alcimus into the land of Judah, along with the right wing of his army. ² They took the road to Galilee, and camping opposite the ascent at Arbela, they captured it and killed many people. ³ In the first month of the year one hundred and fifty-two, they encamped against Jerusalem. ⁴ Then they set out for Berea with twenty thousand men and two thousand cavalry. ⁵ Judas, with three thousand picked men, had camped at Elasa. ⁶ When his men saw the great number of the troops, they were very much afraid, and many slipped away from the camp, until only eight hundred men remained.

⁷ As Judas saw that his army was melting away just when the battle was imminent, he was panic-stricken, because he had no time to gather them together. ⁸ But in spite of his discouragement, he said to those who remained: "Let us go forward to meet our enemies; perhaps we can put up a good fight against them." ⁹ They tried to dissuade him, saying: "We certainly cannot. Let us save our lives now, and come back with our kinsmen,

9, 2: (*hodon tēn eis*) *Galilaian:* conj; cf LXX^MSS. The Greek translator had *mslwt*, which he took for a place name (LXX^MSS: *Maisalōth, Mesalōth, Masaloth,* etc.), instead of *m·lwt,* "ascent."
9, 4: (*eporeuthēsan eis*) *Berean:* so LXX^A,S,V,MSS.

NRSV

9 When Demetrius heard that Nicanor and his army had fallen in battle, he sent Bacchides and Alcimus into the land of Judah a second time, and with them the right wing of the army. ²They went by the road that leads to Gilgal and encamped against Mesaloth in Arbela, and they took it and killed many people. ³In the first month of the one hundred fifty-second year[a] they encamped against Jerusalem; ⁴then they marched off and went to Berea with twenty thousand foot soldiers and two thousand cavalry.

5Now Judas was encamped in Elasa, and with him were three thousand picked men. ⁶When they saw the huge number of the enemy forces, they were greatly frightened, and many slipped away from the camp, until no more than eight hundred of them were left.

7When Judas saw that his army had slipped away and the battle was imminent, he was crushed in spirit, for he had no time to assemble them. ⁸He became faint, but he said to those who were left, "Let us get up and go against our enemies. We may have the strength to fight them." ⁹But they tried to dissuade him, saying, "We do not have the strength. Let us rather save our own lives now, and let us come back with our kindred and fight them; we are too few."

a 160 B.C.

NAB

and then fight against them. Now we are too few." [10] But Judas said: "Far be it from me to do such a thing as to flee from them! If our time has come, let us die bravely for our kinsmen and not leave a stain upon our glory!" [11] Then the army of Bacchides moved out of camp and took its position for combat. The cavalry were divided into two squadrons, and the slingers and the archers came on ahead of the army, and all the valiant men were in the front line. [12] Bacchides was on the right wing. Flanked by the two squadrons, the phalanx attacked as they blew their trumpets. Those who were on Judas' side also blew their trumpets. [13] The earth shook with the noise of the armies, and the battle raged from morning until evening. [14] Seeing that Bacchides was on the right, with the main force of his army, Judas, with all the most stouthearted rallying to him, [15] drove back the right wing and pursued them as far as the mountain slopes. [16] But when the men on the left wing saw that the right wing was driven back, they turned and followed Judas and his men, taking them in the rear. [17] The battle was fought desperately, and many on both sides fell wounded. [18] Then Judas fell, and the rest fled.

[19] Jonathan and Simon took their brother Judas and buried him in the tomb of their fathers at Modein. [20] All Israel bewailed him in great grief. They mourned for him many days, and they said, [21] "How the mighty one has fallen, the savior of Israel!" [22] The other acts of Judas, his battles, the brave deeds he performed, and his greatness have not been recorded; but they were very many.

9, 15: Greek translator read Hebrew 'asdôd (Azotus) instead of 'asēdôt ("slopes"): conj.

NRSV

[10] But Judas said, "Far be it from us to do such a thing as to flee from them. If our time has come, let us die bravely for our kindred, and leave no cause to question our honor."

[11] Then the army of Bacchides[a] marched out from the camp and took its stand for the encounter. The cavalry was divided into two companies, and the slingers and the archers went ahead of the army, as did all the chief warriors. [12] Bacchides was on the right wing. Flanked by the two companies, the phalanx advanced to the sound of the trumpets; and the men with Judas also blew their trumpets. [13] The earth was shaken by the noise of the armies, and the battle raged from morning until evening.

[14] Judas saw that Bacchides and the strength of his army were on the right; then all the stouthearted men went with him, [15] and they crushed the right wing, and he pursued them as far as Mount Azotus. [16] When those on the left wing saw that the right wing was crushed, they turned and followed close behind Judas and his men. [17] The battle became desperate, and many on both sides were wounded and fell. [18] Judas also fell, and the rest fled.

[19] Then Jonathan and Simon took their brother Judas and buried him in the tomb of their ancestors at Modein, [20] and wept for him. All Israel made great lamentation for him; they mourned many days and said,

[21] "How is the mighty fallen,
    the savior of Israel!"

[22] Now the rest of the acts of Judas, and his wars and the brave deeds that he did, and his greatness, have not been recorded, but they were very many.

a Gk lacks of Bacchides

COMMENTARY

Chapter 9 centers on the second expedition of Bacchides to Judea. It opens with Demetrius sending Bacchides and Alcimus a second time, and ends with Bacchides deciding not to come again (v. 72). In between come the deaths of Judas and Alcimus and the rise of Jonathan, who will combine in himself their positions as leader and high priest. At the beginning of the chapter, Judas and his followers are in control of Jerusalem, except for the citadel; at the end, Jonathan is in Michmash.

9:1. Bacchides and Alcimus were first sent to Judah shortly after Demetrius had come to power (1 Macc 7:5-25). Alcimus must have remained at the court of Demetrius during the governorship of Nicanor.

"The right wing" (δεξιὸν κέρας *dexion keras*; lit., "the right horn") in battle formation refers to the right flank of the army (9:12). We cannot be exactly sure what it refers to here. Metaphorically, it could mean the strongest part of the army. In 161 or 160 BCE, Demetrius had defeated Timarchus, the rebellious satrap of Media, and so was free to move against Judas.

9:2. The geography of this verse is difficult to reconstruct. As written, the Seleucid army is encamped at a town called Mesaloth in Arbela, but scholars have suggested that "Mesaloth" is a misunderstanding of the Hebrew word for "public roads" (מסלות *mĕsillôt*). Bacchides would thus have camped at a crossroad. Arbela was identified by Josephus with Arbela in Galilee, and some scholars have followed him and consequently emended "Gilgal" to "Galilee."[93] Other scholars have wondered why Bacchides would carry out a campaign in Galilee, from which the Jews had been evacuated (5:23), when his object was Judas and his force in the Judean hills. Thus Bar-Kochva has suggested that "Arbela" should be corrected to "Mount Beth El" (הר בית־אל *har bêt-'ēl*), the high plateau north of Ramallah, and the "Gilgal" refers to the road that ran from the ancient Gilgal near Jericho to a small village, Beth ha-Gilgal, on the mountain plateau.[94] Bacchides would thus have tried a new tactical approach, coming neither from the west as Seron (3:16), Ptolemy, Nicanor, and Gorgias had done (3:40), nor from the south like Lysias (4:29; 6:31), but from the east.

9:3-4. On the Seleucid Babylonian calendar, the date of this campaign would be April/May 160 BCE. Bacchides is advancing from the north toward Jerusalem. Berea is most likely to be identified with a small town about ten miles north of Jerusalem, near Ramallah.

9:5-6. Elasa most probably should be identified with Il'asa, southwest of Al Bira and about half a mile distant from it. Three thousand is the number of men Judas had against Gorgias (4:6) and Nicanor (7:40). Those who were too frightened to go into battle were supposed to have left the army already, according to regulations (see Deut 20:8), but these soldiers are terrified by the "huge number of the enemy forces," and they desert the camp, dropping off like leaves. The same verb, "drop," is

used at Isa 64:5 in a confession of sin: "We have all withered like leaves,/ and our guilt carries us away like the wind" (NAB). It is also used at Deut 28:40 as an image of what will happen to an unfaithful people: "You shall have olive trees throughout all your territory, but you shall not anoint yourself with the oil, for your olives shall drop off" (NRSV). Judas's army was reduced to the number of men that he had had in the battle against Seron (3:24): eight hundred men.

9:7-10. The author of 1 Maccabees begins to forecast the outcome of the battle. The word so often used in 1 Maccabees to depict the defeat of enemies (3:23; 4:14, 36; 5:7, 21, 43; 7:43) is now used to say that Judas is "crushed" (συντρίβω *syntribō*) in his heart, and the language of exhortation, "Do not lose heart" (Deut 20:3 NRSV), is reversed here as Judas is feeling shaken (v. 8). It is interesting to compare the confident tone of Judas's earlier speeches. In earlier battles, his supporters had also complained of the scarcity of soldiers, but Judas had stressed that size had nothing to do with victory (3:17-22). Judas also had insisted it was better to die than to see misfortune, but that everything depended on God's will (3:59-60). Even though he had retreated before, as after the battle of Beth-zechariah (6:47, 54), now Judas follows the heroic ideal: death with glory rather than life without it. The phrase "if our time has come" resonates with the lament of someone feeling without hope: "Our time has come, our days are filled up, our time is at hand" (Lam 4:18 LXX). It also is attuned with Gen 6:13 LXX: "The time of every human has come before me, for the earth is filled with injustice by them, and behold, I will destroy them and the earth." Thus the phrase foretells the end; no mention of help from heaven is made, for the author knows none will come.

9:11-13. The cavalry takes position on the two wings, while the "slingers and archers" skirmish ahead of the phalanx formation in two parts. The author mentions the length of the battle to stress the bravery of the doomed Israelites.

9:14-18. The Seleucid phalanx had moved forward first to engage the Jewish infantry and would have carried the day, so Judas was forced to attempt an assault on the position where he assumed Bacchides would be and perhaps win the day by killing the enemy commander. The author of 1 Maccabees states that the right wing of the Seleucid army is crushed, but Bacchides seems to

---

93. Josephus *Antiquities of the Jews* 12.421.
94. Bezalel Bar-Kochva, *Judas Maccabeus* (Cambridge: Cambridge University Press, 1988) 382-84. His suggestion seems more likely than others.

have strategically withdrawn so that Judas and his cavalry could be caught in the pincer movement. They retreat as far as "Mount Azotus." Mount Azotus is unknown, and the city of Azotos/Ashdod is in the coastal plain. Scholars have suggested that the Greek translator read אשדוד (ʾašdôd) rather than אשדות (ʾăšēdôt), meaning "slopes." The slopes of the mountain could then refer to the area around Beth El. The Seleucid left wing follows after Judas. No explicit mention is made of Bacchides and the right wing's turning about, but Judas now seems to be caught in between. The author notes how, after desperate fighting, Judas himself falls, as befits a warrior. At the loss of their commander, the rest of the Jewish army flee.

9:19-22. Since the Jews had dismembered Nicanor's body (7:47), it is unlikely the Seleucid forces would have magnanimously allowed Judas's brothers to collect his body. However, the author provides no details of a fight over his body. Josephus speaks of a truce, but this does not seem based on reliable information.[95] It is also unclear how Jonathan and Simon would have been able to provide a proper burial without any interference from the now victorious Seleucid forces. The author, however, stresses the continuity of generations: Jonathan and Simon, Judas's successors, are described burying him using a phrase similar to that which was used when Mattathias was buried (2:70) and which will be used of Jonathan

95. Josephus *Antiquities of the Jews* 12.432.

(13:25-27). "Buried in the tomb of one's ancestors" is a phrase similar to ones used of Jacob (Gen 47:30), of Gideon (Judg 8:32), and of Samson (Judg 16:31). Judas is shown not to have been dishonored, as Saul had been (1 Sam 31:8-10), for to be buried away from one's ancestral land was a cause for shame (1 Kgs 13:22). Just as Mattathias had been mourned (2:70), so also is his son. The dirge to Judas resembles the one intoned over Saul and his son Jonathan (2 Sam 1:19, 25, 27), and resonates with the paean to Judas at the beginning of his career, where it is said that deliverance prospered through him (3:6). All Israel is said to grieve, emphasizing the significance of Judas's role for the nation, although not all Jews mourned his passing. On v. 22, scholars have pointed to the formula found often in the books of Kings: "Now the rest of the acts of Solomon, all that he did as well as his wisdom, are they not written in the Book of the Acts of Solomon?" (1 Kgs 11:41 NRSV). Scholars have debated whether the author implies that he based his work on written or oral sources. One should note a significant difference, however, between this verse and the formula in the books of Kings: The acts of the various kings have been written down. This confession of being unable to record all the deeds of heroes at their death was a common classical literary device. The author of 1 Maccabees thus does not seem to refer to ancient records, as in the books of Kings, but rather glorifies the magnitude of Judas's exploits.

REFLECTIONS

What had Judas actually accomplished? At his death, he was not in control of Jerusalem, his forces had been drastically reduced, and the early story of Jonathan (9:33-49) shows him, despite the author's best efforts, to be nothing but a guerrilla on the run, desperately seeking to avoid capture. Yet Judas's fame lives on despite his failures. One might compare the end of his life to that of King Saul in 1 Samuel 31. Saul, too, saw his bid for independence from the Philistines end in disaster. Saul, too, is lamented by David in "The Song of the Bow" (2 Sam 1:19-27), which is cited by the author of 1 Maccabees with reference to Judas. Yet Saul's failures are emphasized, while Judas's victories are stressed. History, of course, is written by the victors. The dynasty of David continued, while Saul's line failed. Judas's brothers continued after him and founded the Hasmonean dynasty. Their struggle for independence against all odds was rewarded, and it is perhaps the hope of ultimate victory that is so important a part of the story of Judas: He began something that did not die with him. The early Zionists would look back to Judas and the Hasmoneans as their heroes, for they had fought on, and when one died, another was there to take his or her place. Judas's was a movement that could not fail, for it depended not on him alone but on the vision that his father had sparked in many minds.

JONATHAN

OVERVIEW

Jonathan is an enigmatic yet crucial figure in the Maccabean revolt. Leader of the rebel groups for seventeen or eighteen years, twice as long as Judas, he became high priest and a figure to be reckoned with in Seleucid dynastic politics. Yet, unlike Judas and Simon, he is not mentioned in Mattathias's last will (2:65-66), nor does he receive a poem to laud or lament him.

1 MACCABEES 9:23-73, JONATHAN'S RISE TO POWER

1 Maccabees 9:23-31, The Succession of Jonathan

NAB	NRSV
23 After the death of Judas, the transgressors of the law raised their heads in every part of Israel, and all kinds of evildoers appeared. 24 In those days there was a very great famine, and the country deserted to them. 25 Bacchides chose impious men and made them masters of the country. 26 These sought out and hunted down the friends of Judas and brought them to Bacchides, who punished and derided them. 27 There had not been such great distress in Israel since the time prophets ceased to appear among the people. 28 Then all the friends of Judas came together and said to Jonathan: 29 "Since your brother Judas died, there has been no one like him to oppose our enemies, Bacchides and those who are hostile to our nation. 30 Now therefore we have chosen you today to be our ruler and leader in his place, and to fight our battle." 31 From that moment Jonathan accepted the leadership, and took the place of Judas his brother.	23After the death of Judas, the renegades emerged in all parts of Israel; all the wrongdoers reappeared. 24In those days a very great famine occurred, and the country went over to their side. 25Bacchides chose the godless and put them in charge of the country. 26They made inquiry and searched for the friends of Judas, and brought them to Bacchides, who took vengeance on them and made sport of them. 27So there was great distress in Israel, such as had not been since the time that prophets ceased to appear among them. 28Then all the friends of Judas assembled and said to Jonathan, 29"Since the death of your brother Judas there has been no one like him to go against our enemies and Bacchides, and to deal with those of our nation who hate us. 30Now therefore we have chosen you today to take his place as our ruler and leader, to fight our battle." 31So Jonathan accepted the leadership at that time in place of his brother Judas.

COMMENTARY

9:23. As in Judges, 1 Maccabees envisions a pattern whereby once a judge dies, Israel sins, is punished, and then another judge is raised up (Judg 2:11-23). In 1 Maccabees, whenever there is a break in the action, the lawless and renegades stir things up again (7:5; 9:58; the language here resembles that of Ps 92:7). When Mattathias first rose up, the surviving renegades had fled to the Gentiles, and Mattathias had free rein within the borders of Israel (2:44-46). Judas is praised for confounding lawless evildoers and destroying the ungodly out of the land (3:6-8). Now, at the death of Judas, the sinners come forward again in the borders of Israel.

9:24. This verse is frequently used as an argument that most Jews deserted Jonathan's cause, because the government controlled the food supply and thus could entice people to its side. Given, however, the unusual meaning this would give to "country" (χώρα *chōra*) as well as the penalty of sterility of the land as punishment for sin in the OT (Deut 11:16-17; 1 Kgs 8:35-40; Jer 12:4; Sir 39:29), one should not exclude the possibility of the author's suggesting that the famine symbolizes the rule of the godless over the land.

9:25-27. Bacchides keeps up the pressure against Judas's followers. Note how the author maintains the anonymity of Bacchides' lieutenants and simply classifies them as godless. There is a connection between Bacchides' making sport of/scoffing at the friends of Judas and the treatment of the prophets, who were scoffed at by the unfaithful "until the wrath of the LORD against his people became so great that there was no remedy" (2 Chr 36:16 NRSV). The author of 1 Maccabees sees his time as an era without prophets (4:46; 14:41). Did he envision his era as extending from the time of Haggai and Zechariah or Malachi? "Prophet," of course, encompasses much more than foretelling the future. A prophet is the interpreter of God's law (4:46), but Moses, Joshua, and the judges were also called prophets (Sir 46:1; Prologue to Sirach). The trouble is not as magnified as at Dan 12:1 or Mark 13:19 in speaking of the tribulation before the end of the world.

9:28-31. Unlike Judas, who was appointed by his father (2:66), Jonathan is elected to the post of ruler (cf. Judg 10:18; 11:6-11). But the same formula of succession that was used for Judas (3:1) is used for Jonathan.

1 Maccabees 9:32-49, Early Campaigns of Jonathan

NAB

32 When Bacchides learned of it, he sought to kill him. 33 But Jonathan and his brother Simon and all the men with him discovered this, and they fled to the desert of Tekoa and camped by the waters of the pool of Asphar.

35 Jonathan sent his brother as leader of the convoy to ask permission of his friends, the Nabateans, to deposit with them their great quantity of baggage. 36 But the sons of Jambri from Medaba made a raid and seized and carried off John and everything he had. 37 After this, word was brought to Jonathan and his brother Simon: "The sons of Jambri are celebrating a great wedding, and with a large escort they are bringing

9, 34: Omit the whole verse: dittog of v 43.

NRSV

32When Bacchides learned of this, he tried to kill him. 33But Jonathan and his brother Simon and all who were with him heard of it, and they fled into the wilderness of Tekoa and camped by the water of the pool of Asphar. 34Bacchides found this out on the sabbath day, and he with all his army crossed the Jordan.

35So Jonathan[a] sent his brother as leader of the multitude and begged the Nabateans, who were his friends, for permission to store with them the great amount of baggage that they had. 36But the family of Jambri from Medeba came out and seized John and all that he had, and left with it.

37After these things it was reported to Jonathan

[a] Gk *he*

NAB

the bride, the daughter of one of the great princes of Canaan, from Nadabath." [38] Remembering the blood of John their brother, they went up and hid themselves under cover of the mountain. [39] They watched, and suddenly saw a noisy crowd with baggage; the bridegroom and his friends and kinsmen had come out to meet the bride's party with tambourines and musicians and much equipment. [40] The Jews rose up against them from their ambush and killed them. Many fell wounded, and after the survivors fled toward the mountain, all their spoils were taken. [41] Thus the wedding was turned into mourning, and the sound of music into lamentation. [42] Having taken their revenge for the blood of their brother, the Jews returned to the marshes of the Jordan.

[43] When Bacchides heard of it, he came on the sabbath to the banks of the Jordan with a large force. [44] Then Jonathan said to his companions, "Let us get up now and fight for our lives, for today is not like yesterday and the day before. [45] The battle is before us, and behind us are the waters of the Jordan on one side, marsh and thickets on the other, and there is no way of escape. [46] Cry out now to Heaven for deliverance from our enemies." [47] When they joined battle, Jonathan raised his arm to strike Bacchides, but Bacchides backed away from him. [48] Jonathan and his men jumped into the Jordan and swam across to the other side, but the enemy did not pursue them across the Jordan. [49] A thousand men on Bacchides' side fell that day.

NRSV

and his brother Simon, "The family of Jambri are celebrating a great wedding, and are conducting the bride, a daughter of one of the great nobles of Canaan, from Nadabath with a large escort." [38]Remembering how their brother John had been killed, they went up and hid under cover of the mountain. [39]They looked out and saw a tumultuous procession with a great amount of baggage; and the bridegroom came out with his friends and his brothers to meet them with tambourines and musicians and many weapons. [40]Then they rushed on them from the ambush and began killing them. Many were wounded and fell, and the rest fled to the mountain; and the Jews[a] took all their goods. [41]So the wedding was turned into mourning and the voice of their musicians into a funeral dirge. [42]After they had fully avenged the blood of their brother, they returned to the marshes of the Jordan.

[43]When Bacchides heard of this, he came with a large force on the sabbath day to the banks of the Jordan. [44]And Jonathan said to those with him, "Let us get up now and fight for our lives, for today things are not as they were before. [45]For look! the battle is in front of us and behind us; the water of the Jordan is on this side and on that, with marsh and thicket; there is no place to turn. [46]Cry out now to Heaven that you may be delivered from the hands of our enemies." [47]So the battle began, and Jonathan stretched out his hand to strike Bacchides, but he eluded him and went to the rear. [48]Then Jonathan and the men with him leaped into the Jordan and swam across to the other side, and the enemy[a] did not cross the Jordan to attack them. [49]And about one thousand of Bacchides' men fell that day.

[a] Gk they

COMMENTARY

This period, from the death of Judas to the death of Alcimus, which is said to be thirteen months long (9:3, 54), is one of acute distress for Jonathan and his small band. They are forced to hide near a waterhole in the wilderness of Tekoa, about fifteen miles southeast of Jerusalem. The chronology of the following events is not very exact. The attack on the Jambrites is framed by two references to Bacchides (vv. 34, 43) that are very similar. The first serves to locate Bacchides on the east bank of the Jordan, where he and his army can entrap Jonathan in Transjordan on his way back from Medeba to Judea (vv. 43-49).

9:35-42. The situation had become so desperate that Jonathan sent away his brother and, presumably under the heading "the multitude," all those not able to fight, like women, children, and the elderly (v. 35). They are to travel with all their baggage (cf. 1 Macc 5:13, 45) across the Jordan to their friends, the Nabateans (1 Macc 5:25). The wagon train was intercepted and Jonathan's brother John was killed (v. 38) by a tribal group, the Jambrites, from the area around Medeba, a town near the northeastern tip of the Dead Sea (v. 36). We do not know whether this action was in concert with Bacchides, or just another tribal raid. No connection is made between this group and the Nabateans. When a wedding is arranged between the Jambrites and some other tribal group (v. 37)—exactly what "Canaan" and "Nadabath" refer to is uncertain—Jonathan and his group ambush the wedding party and kill many of the Jambrites to avenge the death of John; they also regain much baggage (vv. 38-40) the Jambrites had taken from them. Jonathan

and his group then slink back to the safety of the marshes of the Jordan valley (v. 42). The reader gains a sense from this narrative of the shrinking size of the followers of Jonathan. Even toward the end, Judas had been followed by three thousand men (9:5), but Jonathan's group can win a victory only by ambushing a wedding party, not a terribly noble feat.

9:43-49. Moving on the sabbath, either to catch the Jews off guard or to take advantage of their piety (cf. 2:29-41), Bacchides sets out to trap Jonathan's guerrilla band on the banks of the Jordan, between the river and the marshes of the Dead Sea (v. 45). The author tries to make the most of this sorry engagement by giving Jonathan a pre-battle speech (vv. 44-46) similar to that of Judas at 3:18-22. Jonathan tries to embolden his men by stating that Bacchides acted in a cowardly way and by exaggerating the number of Seleucid dead (vv. 47, 49). Jonathan, in fact, was lucky to escape alive.

1 Maccabees 9:50-53, The Strategy of Bacchides

NAB

50 On returning to Jerusalem, Bacchides built strongholds in Judea: the Jericho fortress, as well as Emmaus, Beth-horon, Bethel, Timnath, Pharathon, and Tephon, with high walls and gates and bars. 51 In each he put a garrison to oppose Israel. 52 He fortified the city of Beth-zur, Gazara and the citadel, and put soldiers in them and stores of provisions. 53 He took as hostages the sons of the leaders of the country and put them in custody in the citadel at Jerusalem.

NRSV

50Then Bacchides[a] returned to Jerusalem and built strong cities in Judea: the fortress in Jericho, and Emmaus, and Beth-horon, and Bethel, and Timnath, and[b] Pharathon, and Tephon, with high walls and gates and bars. 51And he placed garrisons in them to harass Israel. 52He also fortified the town of Beth-zur, and Gazara, and the citadel, and in them he put troops and stores of food. 53And he took the sons of the leading men of the land as hostages and put them under guard in the citadel at Jerusalem.

[a] Gk *he* [b] Some authorities omit *and*

COMMENTARY

After his return to Jerusalem, Bacchides strengthens key areas. Jericho would control the Jordan valley and Emmaus the way to the plain. Beth-zur, Gazara, and the citadel (v. 52) were already fortified. The other cities lay north of Jerusalem in northern Judea and southern Samaria, as if to deny the rebels access to those

parts of Judea where Judas had been so successful. Bacchides' strategy seems to have been to control those areas with several garrisons and to force the cooperation of leading citizens through taking their sons as hostages. Since Bacchides' attempt is to harass "Israel" (the author's term for true believers), these leading citizens were no doubt different from the "godless" who had been put in charge of the country (9:25), and the fortifications would have been used to strengthen the latter's position.

1 Maccabees 9:54-57, The Death of Alcimus

NAB

54 In the year one hundred and fifty-three, in the second month, Alcimus ordered the wall of the inner court of the sanctuary to be torn down, thus destroying the work of the prophets. But he only began to tear it down. 55 Just at that time he had a stroke, and his work was interrupted; his mouth was closed and he was paralyzed, so that he could no longer utter a word to give orders concerning his house. 56 Finally he died in great agony. 57 Seeing that Alcimus was dead, Bacchides returned to the king, and the land of Judah was quiet for two years.

NRSV

54In the one hundred and fifty-third year,[a] in the second month, Alcimus gave orders to tear down the wall of the inner court of the sanctuary. He tore down the work of the prophets! 55But he only began to tear it down, for at that time Alcimus was stricken and his work was hindered; his mouth was stopped and he was paralyzed, so that he could no longer say a word or give commands concerning his house. 56And Alcimus died at that time in great agony. 57When Bacchides saw that Alcimus was dead, he returned to the king, and the land of Judah had rest for two years.

a 159 B.C.

COMMENTARY

9:54-56. In 159 BCE, Alcimus, the high priest appointed by Demetrius, died. The Temple area had been rebuilt quickly under Judas (4:43-49), and Alcimus was probably doing some renovations and upscaling the repairs begun by Judas. Such building activity suggests that the activity of Jonathan had been severely curtailed and that the decline in warfare had led to an economic upswing. During this work, Alcimus died. The author of 1 Maccabees attributes the cause of his death to the action of God, as the passive verb "was stricken" implies. The sense of just deserts is shown as Alcimus, who had given orders that something be done to God's house, now cannot set his own house in order. The author gives the worst spin on what Alcimus was intending: Instead of renovation, Alcimus was breaking down the wall that separated the court of the priests from the rest of the Israelites, breaking laws of separation between the sacred and the profane (Ezek 42:13-14; 44:4-27). By mentioning the work of the prophets, the author may be referring to the work of the prophets Haggai and Zechariah in rebuilding the Temple (Ezra 5:1; 6:14). It is also noteworthy that the Jewish writer Eupolemus has Solomon build the Temple according to the command of Nathan the prohet.[96]

9:57. This verse shows how little we know of what was going on in Judea. On Alcimus's death, Bacchides went back to the king. Surely Bacchides would have left someone in charge of the now fairly pacified country. But no mention is made of any such ruler, nor are we told who became high priest until Jonathan's appointment in 152 BCE (1 Macc 10:21). Josephus holds that no one was high priest after Alcimus.[97] Such a length of time with no high priest to officiate Yom Kippur seems quite unusual, even if, for example, the high priest Menelaus was probably unable to perform the ritual while Judas controlled the Temple in 163 BCE (1 Macc 4:42). The author of 1 Maccabees gives us no information about the high priestly office before Alcimus (a proper anti-hero for him) or until Jonathan's appointment, so there

96. See Eusebius *Preparation for the Gospel* 9.34.2.
97. See Josephus *Antiquities of the Jews* 20.237, a lapse of seven years; *Antiquities of the Jews* 12.414, 419, 434; 13.46, a lapse of four years.

likely may have been a high priest about whom we know nothing.

The reason why Bacchides left the country may have had nothing to do with the death of Alcimus. Demetrius I was involved in 159/58 in an attempt to oust Ariarathes IV from Cappadocia and support his rival, Oropherenes. So Bacchides' main force may have been needed back in Antioch.

After his departure from Judea, the pressure against Jonathan eased (cf. 7:50). Even with the garrisons still in place (vv. 25, 50), the author sees the absence of the Seleucid forces under Bacchides as bringing rest to the land (v. 57). This period must have been extremely important for Jonathan and his followers, for this respite of two years seems to have allowed them to regroup.

1 Maccabees 9:58-73, The Last Expedition of Bacchides

NAB

58 Then all the transgressors of the law held a council and said: "Jonathan and his companions are living in peace and security. Now then, let us have Bacchides return, and he will capture all of them in a single night." 59 So they went and took counsel with him. 60 When Bacchides was setting out with a large force, he sent letters secretly to all his allies in Judea, telling them to seize Jonathan and his companions. They were not able to do this, however, because their plot became known. 61 In fact, Jonathan's men seized about fifty of the men of the country who were ring-leaders in the mischief and put them to death. 62 Then Jonathan and Simon and their companions withdrew to Bethbasi in the desert; they rebuilt and strengthened its fortifications that had been demolished. 63 When Bacchides learned of this, he gathered together his whole force and sent word to those who were in Judea. 64 He came and pitched his camp before Bethbasi, and constructing siege-machines, he fought against it for many days.

65 Leaving his brother Simon in the city, Jonathan, accompanied by a small group of men, went out into the field. 66 He struck down Odomera and his kinsmen and the sons of Phasiron in their encampment; these men had set out to go up to the siege with their forces. 67 Simon and his men then sallied forth from the city and set fire to the machines. 68 They fought against Bacchides, and he was beaten. This caused him great distress. Because the enterprise he had planned came to naught, 69 he was angry with the lawless men who had advised him to invade the province. He killed many of them and resolved to return to his own country.

9, 69: (kai) ebouleusato (tou apelthein): so LXXMSS, PMSS, V.

NRSV

58Then all the lawless plotted and said, "See! Jonathan and his men are living in quiet and confidence. So now let us bring Bacchides back, and he will capture them all in one night." 59And they went and consulted with him. 60He started to come with a large force, and secretly sent letters to all his allies in Judea, telling them to seize Jonathan and his men; but they were unable to do it, because their plan became known. 61And Jonathan's men[a] seized about fifty of the men of the country who were leaders in this treachery, and killed them.

62Then Jonathan with his men, and Simon, withdrew to Bethbasi in the wilderness; he rebuilt the parts of it that had been demolished, and they fortified it. 63When Bacchides learned of this, he assembled all his forces, and sent orders to the men of Judea. 64Then he came and encamped against Bethbasi; he fought against it for many days and made machines of war.

65But Jonathan left his brother Simon in the town, while he went out into the country; and he went with only a few men. 66He struck down Odomera and his kindred and the people of Phasiron in their tents. 67Then he[b] began to attack and went into battle with his forces; and Simon and his men sallied out from the town and set fire to the machines of war. 68They fought with Bacchides, and he was crushed by them. They pressed him very hard, for his plan and his expedition had been in vain. 69So he was very angry at the renegades who had counseled him to come into the country, and he killed many of them. Then he decided to go back to his own land.

70When Jonathan learned of this, he sent am-

a Gk they   b Other ancient authorities read they

NAB

⁷⁰ Jonathan learned of this and sent ambassadors to make peace with him and to obtain the release of the prisoners. ⁷¹ He agreed to do as Jonathan had asked. He swore an oath to him that he would never try to injure him for the rest of his life; ⁷² and he released the prisoners he had previously taken from the land of Judah. He returned to his own country and never came into their territory again.

⁷³ Then the sword ceased in Israel. Jonathan settled in Michmash; he began to judge the people, and he destroyed the impious in Israel.

NRSV

bassadors to him to make peace with him and obtain release of the captives. ⁷¹He agreed, and did as he said; and he swore to Jonathanᵃ that he would not try to harm him as long as he lived. ⁷²He restored to him the captives whom he had taken previously from the land of Judah; then he turned and went back to his own land, and did not come again into their territory. ⁷³Thus the sword ceased from Israel. Jonathan settled in Michmash and began to judge the people; and he destroyed the godless out of Israel.

ᵃ Gk him

COMMENTARY

As earlier (7:5-7), the peace is disrupted by the lawless, who conspire to bring Bacchides back to capture Jonathan and his followers. The Greek has a play on words in vv. 57-58: The land was "quiet" (ἡσύχασεν *hēsychasen*), and Jonathan was living in "quiet" (ἡσυχία *hēsychia*). Throughout this section, in fact, the author repeats similar words: "plan" (βουλή *boulē*, vv. 60, 68); "plotted," "counseled" (βουλεύομαι *bouleuomai*, vv. 58, 69); "consulted," "counseled" (συμβουλεύομαι *symbouleuomai*, vv. 59, 69); "capture," "seize" (συλλαμβάνω *syllambanō*, vv. 58, 60-61).

9:60-61. Although Bacchides is said to have come with a large force, it is clear from his later failure to capture Bethbasi that it was not the force with which he first came to Judea (7:10). This is also evident from the way he tries to get Jonathan first through allies who were already in place in Judea. The sequence of events is difficult to reconstruct. The NRSV has Jonathan's men kill fifty leaders of this "treachery" (lit., "evil"). This translation presumably understands the last phrase as referring to those who had tried to capture Jonathan. But the Greek has no change in subject from v. 60, where Bacchides' allies are told to seize Jonathan, and v. 61, where the same verb is used to describe the seizure of the fifty leaders; Jonathan is not mentioned until v. 62. Therefore, the reader may presume that Bacchides' allies tried to seize Jonathan, but when they couldn't, they seized instead fifty men from the countryside whom they credited with being associated in

some way with the damage Jonathan was doing (cf. 7:6-7). These fifty might then be compared to the sixty Hasideans who had sought to make peace with Bacchides and Alcimus (7:12-18).

9:62-64. Bacchides had made the country north of Jerusalem too difficult for Jonathan to pass through because of the garrisons stationed there, so Jonathan retreated south as he had done before (9:33), although not as far. Bethbasi lay about a mile and a quarter southeast of Bethlehem, on the way to Tekoa and the Jordan valley. The author tries to magnify the strength of Bacchides' forces, but Bacchides needed to supplement his detachment with his allies in Judea.

9:65-68. The course of the siege is confused. The NRSV suggests that Jonathan leaves Bethbasi with a small force, fights against some otherwise unknown nomadic tribes, and then turns back to attack Bacchides—a rather circuitous route to raise the siege. The text is difficult to reconstruct; one is not sure whether to read singular or plural verbs. The main problem lies in the verb "struck down" (ἐπάταξεν *epataxen*, v. 66). The sense of the passage would seem to be that Jonathan slipped away from the siege to gain allies, as those in the citadel had done against Judas's siege (6:18-27). Jonathan had friends among the Nabateans, if not among the Jambrites (9:35), as had Judas before him (5:25), and so he may have gone for reinforcements to Odomera and the people of Phasiron, and "placed" them beside him (ἐπέταξεν *epetaxen*), a verb attested by some

Greek manuscripts. At v. 67, then, Jonathan's small group, plus his reinforcements (not "he" as in the NRSV), begins to attack Bacchides' forces from the rear while Simon sallies out from the town and crushes Bacchides' group. Bacchides had relied on his allies in Judea, but they had been no help. The ability of Jonathan and Simon to mount such a counteroffensive shows their use of the two years to increase in numbers and their fighting ability; it also brings into view Jonathan's diplomatic skills.

9:69-72. Bacchides' reaction to defeat is anger. Is it a blind rage? Or has Bacchides become aware that it is not Jonathan who is disturbing the peace in Judea, but these "lawless" ones? Is it, in fact, a signal of peace toward Jonathan? That is how Jonathan understands it, and his penchant for making agreements is made apparent. Whereas Judas had refused the offers of peace made by Bacchides (7:10-11) and Nicanor (7:27-30), Jonathan now takes the initiative. The returned captives are not the hostages in the citadel (9:53; 10:6) but others possibly taken during this last campaign. The words of Bacchides in v. 71 echo the words of Alcimus to the Hasideans (7:15).

9:73. In almost idyllic terms, the author depicts the period after Bacchides' departure. It recalls Isa 2:4: "He shall judge between the nations,/ and shall arbitrate for many peoples;/ they shall beat their swords into plowshares,/ and their spears into pruning hooks" (NRSV). Jonathan returns to settle at Michmash in the rugged hills about seven miles north of Jerusalem, where King Saul had settled (1 Sam 13:2) and that was settled at the time of Ezra and Nehemiah (see Ezra 2:27; Neh 7:31; 11:31). Like the judges and the kings, Jonathan governs the people ideally by rooting out the godless. Of course, the citadel and the other garrisons were still in power and Jonathan probably did not undertake any more military activity lest the Seleucid forces return. What one would like to know is what Jonathan was doing from 157 BCE to 152 BCE, when 1 Maccabees resumes the narrative. When Jonathan is next heard of, Demetrius wishes him to become his ally—that is, he considers Jonathan able to supply him with auxiliary forces. When Bacchides had used his allies in Judea (9:60, 63), they had been bested by Jonathan's forces, and the reader should not forget that Judas's forces had faced a Seleucid phalanx and fought them all day long (9:12-13). Jonathan probably kept this reserve of battle-hardened troops battle trim, ready for any developments. Neither are we told anything about how Jonathan actually lived. We do not know whether he or his men took part in the temple liturgy, although when Jonathan becomes high priest no mention is made of sweeping changes in the way the ritual was carried out. How would one have distinguished between followers of Jonathan and other Jews? Was the distinction based more on allegiance to certain patrons, but raised to the level of theological absolutes to maintain loyalty and the ability to fight a civil war?

REFLECTIONS

The narrative reinforces the sense that the only factor capable of holding the country together was the movement under Jonathan. No matter how hard the Seleucid forces pressed Jonathan, no matter what harassment Bacchides inflicted on the people, no matter how many fortresses were erected to control the people, Jonathan's opponents had no effective leadership. Alcimus could have been a rallying point for the opposition; he clearly was energetic and pushed a program of restoration after the devastations of the war. Yet he died too early to be of any real use to them. His death is seen by the author of 1 Maccabees as divine retribution, as evidence once again that God was on the side of the Maccabees. When Bacchides tried to raise a force from those opposed to Jonathan, he found they were ineffective. Here again one sees the importance of dedicated single-mindedness on behalf of one's cause. Jonathan won out because he was willing to stay longer, endure longer, and put his life on the line. When a local population stiffly resists foreign oppression and seeks to maintain its own way and culture, its stubborn resistance will win out and it likely will not be defeated in the end.

1 MACCABEES 10:1–12:53, JONATHAN'S RULE

1 Maccabees 10:1-14, Jonathan and Demetrius I

NAB

10 In the year one hundred and sixty, Alexander, who was called Epiphanes, son of Antiochus, came up and took Ptolemais. He was accepted and began to reign there. ² When King Demetrius heard of it, he mustered a very large army and marched out to engage him in combat. ³ Demetrius sent a letter to Jonathan written in peaceful terms, to pay him honor; ⁴ for he said: "Let us be the first to make peace with him, before he makes peace with Alexander against us, ⁵ since he will remember all the wrongs we have done to him, his brothers, and his nation."

⁶ So Demetrius authorized Jonathan, as his ally, to gather an army and procure arms; and he ordered that the hostages in the citadel be released to him. ⁷ Accordingly Jonathan went up to Jerusalem and read the letter to all the people. The men in the citadel ⁸ were struck with fear when they heard that the king had given him authority to gather an army. ⁹ They released the hostages to Jonathan, and he gave them back to their parents. ¹⁰ Thereafter Jonathan dwelt in Jerusalem, and began to build and restore the city. ¹¹ He ordered the workmen to build the walls and encircle Mount Zion with square stones for its fortification, which they did. ¹² The foreigners in the strongholds that Bacchides had built, took flight; ¹³ each one of them left his place and returned to his own country. ¹⁴ Only in Beth-zur did some remain of those who had abandoned the law and the commandments, for they used it as a place of refuge.

10, 4: (*met'*) *autou* (*prin*): so LXX^MSS, P^MSS, V.
10, 11: (*ek lithōn*) *tetrapedōn*: so LXX^MSS.

NRSV

10 In the one hundred sixtieth year[a] Alexander Epiphanes, son of Antiochus, landed and occupied Ptolemais. They welcomed him, and there he began to reign. ²When King Demetrius heard of it, he assembled a very large army and marched out to meet him in battle. ³Demetrius sent Jonathan a letter in peaceable words to honor him; ⁴for he said to himself, "Let us act first to make peace with him[b] before he makes peace with Alexander against us, ⁵for he will remember all the wrongs that we did to him and to his brothers and his nation." ⁶So Demetrius[c] gave him authority to recruit troops, to equip them with arms, and to become his ally; and he commanded that the hostages in the citadel should be released to him.

⁷Then Jonathan came to Jerusalem and read the letter in the hearing of all the people and of those in the citadel. ⁸They were greatly alarmed when they heard that the king had given him authority to recruit troops. ⁹But those in the citadel released the hostages to Jonathan, and he returned them to their parents.

¹⁰And Jonathan took up residence in Jerusalem and began to rebuild and restore the city. ¹¹He directed those who were doing the work to build the walls and encircle Mount Zion with squared stones, for better fortification; and they did so. ¹²Then the foreigners who were in the strongholds that Bacchides had built fled; ¹³all of them left their places and went back to their own lands. ¹⁴Only in Beth-zur did some remain who had forsaken the law and the commandments, for it served as a place of refuge.

a 152 B.C.   b Gk them   c Gk he

COMMENTARY

10:1-2. After five years of relative stability, external factors once again threaten the land. Demetrius I had not made many friends; his failure in Cappadocia (157–154 BCE) had won him enemies in Asia Minor, his harsh treatment of his subjects led Antioch to revolt (which he suppressed with even harsher measures), and he had made an enemy of Ptolemy Philometor by trying to gain control of Cyprus in 155/54 BCE. A pretender to the Seleucid throne, Alexander Balas, who claimed to be the son of Antiochus IV, went to Rome and in 152 BCE gained permission from the senate to claim the throne of his ancestors.[98] Before October 152 BCE, Alexander arrived in Ptolemais, where the garrison went over to his side. One is not sure whether there were several battles between the two or only one before Demetrius's defeat and death in the summer of 150 BCE. In 1 Maccabees the contest between the two kings is taken up again at 10:48, and only one battle is described. In between is collected a series of documents from Demetrius and Alexander Balas, bidding for the services of Jonathan. Questions have been raised about the authenticity of these documents, particularly whether they are exact reproductions of the contents. One can wonder where the letters would have been kept, and how the author of 1 Maccabees could retrieve them from archives, which most likely did not have the same degree of organization as today's libraries. On the other hand, we do have from the ancient world collections of documents, such as the Zenon papyri, that have been preserved and have come down to us.

10:3-6. As Ptolemais lay south of Antioch but north of Jerusalem, Demetrius may have hoped to harass Alexander from the rear. The author of 1 Maccabees portrays Demetrius as conscious of the wrongs he has done against the Jews, just as Antiochus IV had been (6:12), and willing to do anything to save his throne. Jonathan's military

accomplishments are well-known, even after a lapse of five years. Jonathan is here raised to the position of leader of a vassal state, ally of the Seleucid throne and with the authority to raise and equip an army. It is a remarkable achievement to rise from a rebel in hiding to head of the nation in seven years. The hostages had been taken to keep the countryside from helping Jonathan (9:53). Now that Jonathan is to be an ally of the Seleucids, there is no need to keep them.

10:7-9. Jonathan makes the most of the occasion by having Demetrius's letter (which is not extant) read aloud publicly in Jerusalem; one wonders how the listeners knew the letter was genuine. Jonathan's authority to muster troops would have affected the citadel, as Judas had already shown a desire to attack it (6:19-20). Nevertheless, in spite of their misgivings, the troops in the citadel respect the king's wishes, even though Jonathan has shrewdly not yet formally responded to Demetrius's offer.

10:10-14. Like Judas, who had restored the Temple (4:47-51), Jonathan sets out to restore and refortify Jerusalem, which had been decimated by Lysias. He uses the kind of stone King Josiah is said to have used to rebuild the Temple (2 Chr 34:11). Jonathan is now so powerful that the Gentile garrisons Bacchides had established (9:50-52) flee, except for some apostates left in Beth-zur. Their plight, however—holed up in Beth-zur—is the reverse of what they had done to the Israelites when they were in power (1:52-53). In fact, the citadel remained intact, and the garrisons seem to have remained (11:41; 12:45). Perhaps some deserted or were recalled to help Demetrius against Alexander Balas.

---

98. Polybius 33.18.12.

1 Maccabees 10:15-21, Jonathan and Alexander Epiphanes

NAB

15 King Alexander heard of the promises that Demetrius had made to Jonathan; he was also told of the battles and valiant deeds of Jonathan and his brothers and the troubles that they had endured. 16 He said, "Shall we ever find another man like him? Let us now make him our friend and ally." 17 So he sent Jonathan a letter written in these terms: 18 "King Alexander sends greetings

NRSV

15Now King Alexander heard of all the promises that Demetrius had sent to Jonathan, and he heard of the battles that Jonathan[a] and his brothers had fought, of the brave deeds that they had done, and of the troubles that they had endured. 16So he said, "Shall we find another such man? Come now, we will make him our friend and ally."

a Gk he

NAB

to his brother Jonathan. ¹⁹ We have heard of you, that you are a mighty warrior and worthy to be our friend. ²⁰ We have therefore appointed you today to be high priest of your nation; you are to be called the King's Friend, and you are to look after our interests and preserve amity with us." He also sent him a purple robe and a crown of gold.

²¹ Jonathan put on the sacred vestments in the seventh month of the year one hundred and sixty at the feast of Booths, and he gathered an army and procured many arms.

NRSV

¹⁷And he wrote a letter and sent it to him, in the following words:

18"King Alexander to his brother Jonathan, greetings. ¹⁹We have heard about you, that you are a mighty warrior and worthy to be our friend. ²⁰And so we have appointed you today to be the high priest of your nation; you are to be called the king's Friend and you are to take our side and keep friendship with us." He also sent him a purple robe and a golden crown.

21So Jonathan put on the sacred vestments in the seventh month of the one hundred sixtieth year,ᵃ at the festival of booths,ᵇ and he recruited troops and equipped them with arms in abundance.

ᵃ 152 B.C.   ᵇ Or tabernacles

COMMENTARY

10:15-16. The bidding war for Jonathan's services begins. As a new player on the block, Alexander has to learn about Jonathan; one wonders from whom he had heard that Jonathan was such a valiant warrior in such glowing terms. "Friend of the king" was not the highest-ranking title in the Seleucid hierarchy. Mattathias had been asked to be one (2:18), and the author of 1 Maccabees seems to feel that it is an important title (3:38; 6:14, 28; 7:8).

10:17-20. The flattering letter that Alexander writes Jonathan, calling him "brother" (ἀδελφός adelphos), a title reserved for the highest dignitaries, is not written in good Greek. The phrase "man of valor" (ἀνὴρ δυνατός anēr dynatos, v. 19) is used frequently in the LXX (see Ruth 2:1; 2 Kgs 5:1; 15:20; 24:14; 1 Chr 5:2; 12:21). The letter does contain evidence that the Seleucid ruler, even if at that point a pretender to the throne, appointed Jonathan to the high priesthood. Jonathan's appointment is thus legitimate, and he becomes the official political and religious leader of Judea. Along with the letter, Alexander sends Jonathan "a purple robe and a golden crown." Friends of the king customarily wore a purple robe, and priests in the Hellenistic period wore purple robes and gold crowns.

10:21. Jonathan dons the sacred vestments

(Exod 28:1-5) on the fifteenth day of the seventh month (October), 152 BCE, during the Festival of Booths (Lev 23:33-36, 39-42; Deut 16:13-15). It is interesting that this occurs just five days after the celebration of Yom Kippur, when the high priest's presence was most required for the ritual atonement of the people (Leviticus 16). However, Jonathan may be playing on the symbolism of the festival whereby the people of Israel are reminded how God brought them out of the land of Egypt (Lev 23:43), and during which the law is to be read aloud every seventh year (Deut 31:10-13). The Festival of Booths was the first festival celebrated on the return from exile (Ezra 3:1-5), and it was the festival celebrated by Ezra (Neh 8:13-18). According to 2 Maccabees, the festival of Hanukkah at Judas's purification of the Temple was associated with the Festival of Booths (2 Macc 1:9; 10:6).

What is perhaps most striking is the very brevity with which this important event is recounted; the narrator immediately proceeds to describe the recruiting of troops and the securing of arms. The only religious act attributed to Jonathan is a prayer in battle (11:71), not a specifically high-priestly deed. Could this lack of emphasis be due to opposition to Jonathan's being high priest? Some scholars have suggested that the wicked priest of the Qumran documents is Jonathan, but such specificity is hard to obtain from these texts. What v. 21 does suggest is that Jonathan has taken the proposals from both Demetrius and Alexander without allying himself with either.

1 Maccabees 10:22-45, The Reaction of Demetrius I

NAB

22 When Demetrius heard of these things, he was distressed and said: 23 "Why have we allowed Alexander to get ahead of us by gaining the friendship of the Jews and thus strengthening himself? 24 I too will write them conciliatory words and offer dignities and gifts, so that they may be an aid to me."

25 So he sent them this message: "King Demetrius sends greetings to the Jewish nation. 26 We have heard how you have kept the treaty with us and continued in our friendship and not gone over to our enemies, and we are glad. 27 Continue, therefore, to keep faith with us, and we will reward you with favors in return for what you do in our behalf. 28 We will grant you many exemptions and will bestow gifts on you.

29 "I now free you, as I also exempt all the Jews, from the tribute, the salt tax, and the crown levies. 30 Instead of collecting the third of the grain and the half of the fruit of the trees that should be my share, I renounce the right from this day forward. Neither now nor in the future will I collect them from the land of Judah or from the three districts annexed from Samaria. 31 Let Jerusalem and her territory, her tithes and her tolls, be sacred and free from tax. 32 I also yield my authority over the citadel in Jerusalem, and I transfer it to the high priest, that he may put in it such men as he shall choose to guard it. 33 Every one of the Jews who has been carried into captivity from the land of Judah into any part of my kingdom I set at liberty without ransom; and let all their taxes, even those on their cattle, be canceled. 34 Let all feast days, sabbaths, new moon festivals, appointed days, and the three days that precede each feast day, and the three days that follow, be days of immunity and exemption for every Jew in my kingdom. 35 Let no man have authority to exact payment from them or to molest any of them in any matter.

10, 30: Omit *kai Galilaias:* conj: 10, 38; 11, 28.34.

NRSV

22When Demetrius heard of these things he was distressed and said, 23"What is this that we have done? Alexander has gotten ahead of us in forming a friendship with the Jews to strengthen himself. 24I also will write them words of encouragement and promise them honor and gifts, so that I may have their help." 25So he sent a message to them in the following words:

"King Demetrius to the nation of the Jews, greetings. 26Since you have kept your agreement with us and have continued your friendship with us, and have not sided with our enemies, we have heard of it and rejoiced. 27Now continue still to keep faith with us, and we will repay you with good for what you do for us. 28We will grant you many immunities and give you gifts.

29"I now free you and exempt all the Jews from payment of tribute and salt tax and crown levies, 30and instead of collecting the third of the grain and the half of the fruit of the trees that I should receive, I release them from this day and henceforth. I will not collect them from the land of Judah or from the three districts added to it from Samaria and Galilee, from this day and for all time. 31Jerusalem and its environs, its tithes and its revenues, shall be holy and free from tax. 32I release also my control of the citadel in Jerusalem and give it to the high priest, so that he may station in it men of his own choice to guard it. 33And everyone of the Jews taken as a captive from the land of Judah into any part of my kingdom, I set free without payment; and let all officials cancel also the taxes on their livestock.

34"All the festivals and sabbaths and new moons and appointed days, and the three days before a festival and the three after a festival—let them all be days of immunity and release for all the Jews who are in my kingdom. 35No one shall have authority to exact anything from them or annoy any of them about any matter.

36"Let Jews be enrolled in the king's forces to the number of thirty thousand men, and let the

NAB

[36] "Let thirty thousand Jews be enrolled in the king's army and allowances be given them, as is due to all the king's soldiers. [37] Let some of them be stationed in the king's principal strongholds, and of these let some be given positions of trust in the affairs of the kingdom. Let their superiors and their rulers be taken from among them, and let them follow their own laws, as the king has commanded in the land of Judah.

[38] "Let the three districts that have been added to Judea from the province of Samaria be incorporated with Judea so that they may be under one man and obey no other authority than the high priest. [39] Ptolemais and its confines I give as a present to the sanctuary in Jerusalem for the necessary expenses of the sanctuary. [40] I make a yearly personal grant of fifteen thousand silver shekels out of the royal revenues, from appropriate places. [41] All the additional funds that the officials did not hand over as they had done in the first years, shall henceforth be handed over for the services of the temple. [42] Moreover, the dues of five thousand silver shekels that used to be taken from the revenue of the sanctuary every year shall be canceled, since these funds belong to the priests who perform the services. [43] Whoever takes refuge in the temple of Jerusalem or in any of its precincts, because of money he owes the king, or because of any other debt, shall be released, together with all the goods he possesses in my kingdom. [44] The cost of rebuilding and restoring the structures of the sanctuary shall be covered out of the royal revenue. [45] Likewise the cost of building the walls of Jerusalem and fortifying it all around, and of building walls in Judea, shall be donated from the royal revenue."

10, 41: (*en tois prōtois*) *etesin:* so LXX[A,V,MSS], p[MSS], V.

NRSV

maintenance be given them that is due to all the forces of the king. [37]Let some of them be stationed in the great strongholds of the king, and let some of them be put in positions of trust in the kingdom. Let their officers and leaders be of their own number, and let them live by their own laws, just as the king has commanded in the land of Judah.

[38]"As for the three districts that have been added to Judea from the country of Samaria, let them be annexed to Judea so that they may be considered to be under one ruler and obey no other authority than the high priest. [39]Ptolemais and the land adjoining it I have given as a gift to the sanctuary in Jerusalem, to meet the necessary expenses of the sanctuary. [40]I also grant fifteen thousand shekels of silver yearly out of the king's revenues from appropriate places. [41]And all the additional funds that the government officials have not paid as they did in the first years,[a] they shall give from now on for the service of the temple.[b] [42]Moreover, the five thousand shekels of silver that my officials[c] have received every year from the income of the services of the temple, this too is canceled, because it belongs to the priests who minister there. [43]And all who take refuge at the temple in Jerusalem, or in any of its precincts, because they owe money to the king or are in debt, let them be released and receive back all their property in my kingdom.

[44]"Let the cost of rebuilding and restoring the structures of the sanctuary be paid from the revenues of the king. [45]And let the cost of rebuilding the walls of Jerusalem and fortifying it all around, and the cost of rebuilding the walls in Judea, also be paid from the revenues of the king."

[a] Meaning of Gk uncertain   [b] Gk *house*   [c] Gk *they*

COMMENTARY

10:22-24. Demetrius acts as if he has not already written to Jonathan (10:3-6). Demetrius's style reflects Hebrew syntax: "they may be with me to a help" (v. 24 author's trans.).

10:25-45. In contrast to the previous two letters (10:3, 18), Demetrius now addresses one "to the nation of the Jews." While it does mention

the high priesthood (v. 32), it does not name Jonathan at all. This had led some scholars to hold either that the letter does not belong in its present context, or that in fact Demetrius thought that he could gain the allegiance of Jews who may have been opposed to Jonathan and his supporters.

10:26-28. Demetrius claims that the Jews

have remained loyal to their treaty with him. Is this a rhetorical ploy, or does the letter belong in another context? Does the treaty refer to Bacchides' agreement (9:71) or to the general framework of a suzerain-vassal treaty? A treaty bound both parties. In its present context, the term "enemies" (ἐχθροί exthroi) refers to Alexander, but one should recall that there were frequent uprisings against Demetrius. Does this offer of immunities and gifts betray a note of desperation?

10:29-33. Comparison with a similar letter of Antiochus III indicates that the phrase "payment of tribute" probably should be understood as a head tax or a poll tax.[99] The mention of a "salt tax" (v. 29) may indicate that the Jews originally delivered to the king a quantity of salt, for which later a payment in cash was substituted. Note, however, that Demetrius II later relinquishes claims to the salt pits (1 Macc 11:35). "Crown levies" were at first presents to the king from his subjects, but later became compulsory upon his accession—and whenever he required them. A tax rate of one-third to one-half of a crop was extremely high and would have been very oppressive to the local economy. Would the Seleucids have so punished their supporters among the Jews? The three districts (v. 30) are named in the letter of Demetrius II (11:34). Verse 31 is difficult, but probably should read that Jerusalem was to be exempted from tithes and revenues, rather than that Jerusalem's tithes and revenues were to be free from taxation. Relinquishing control of the citadel (v. 32) was a major concession by Demetrius. No wonder the inhabitants of the citadel had earlier been afraid, as Jonathan now has a legitimate claim on the citadel. The release of all Jewish slaves throughout the entire Seleucid kingdom without compensation (v. 33) and cancellation of all customs and tolls on their way back to Judea are highly magnanimous and highly improbable.[100]

10:34-35. Demetrius further proclaims that, before and after holy days, Jews are to be exempted from customs and tolls and that they are not to be involved in legal affairs, in order to enable them to go to Jerusalem to celebrate their festivals (cf. v. 63). The list of festivals is similar to that at Ezek 45:17; thus it suggests Jewish

input into the content of the letter. The limit of three days refers to a journey of three days, and thus may specify the distance within which one was required to bring the actual tithes in the form of crops or animals, and not to turn it into money. It would thus be interpreting Deut 14:24, a specification also found at Qumran in the *Temple Scroll*.[101]

10:36-37. Jews served under both the Ptolemies (e.g., the Jewish generals Onias and Dositheus)[102] and the Seleucids.[103] The Jews in the army are presumably to be kept in special detachments in which they could follow Torah regulations. Would this include keeping the sabbath? The end of v. 37 suggests that Jews had been able to follow their ancestral traditions in Judea since the beginning of the reign of Demetrius I.

10:38-43. The three nomes lay near the area that had been the stronghold of Maccabean opposition. The high priest is recognized, as in v. 32, as the political leader of the Jewish nation. According to v. 1, Ptolemais was currently under the control of Alexander Balas. What exactly is being referred to in vv. 41-42 is difficult to reconstruct. One cannot be sure whether government officials have been withholding payments (so NRSV), or whether the priests have been using money given for sacrifices to fund other activities. What is clear is that Demetrius is being quite generous to the Temple. Again, in v. 43, what the king is actually allowing is hard to piece together. He seems to be granting to the Jerusalem Temple and its precincts the right of asylum for debtors, although the term for "asylum" is not used. The NRSV translation suggests that such refugees are to be forgiven their debts and get off scot-free. The Greek text is difficult, and perhaps what is being allowed is that the property of the refugees is not to be confiscated, rather than that their debts are forgiven.

10:44-45. The king further promises to pay out of his own budget the cost of rebuilding the Temple, the walls around Jerusalem, and all the walls of towns in Judea. Darius had agreed to shoulder the cost of rebuilding the Temple (Ezra 8), but Demetrius goes beyond that. The usual conclusion to a letter is missing.

99. See Josephus *Antiquities of the Jews* 12.142.
100. Cf. *Letter of Aristeas* 12-27; Josephus *Antiquities of the Jews* 12.144.

101. See 11QTemple 43.12-13; 52.13-14.
102. Josephus *Against Apion* 2.49-52.
103. Josephus *Antiquities of the Jews* 12.147-153.

1 Maccabees 10:46-66, Jonathan and Alexander

NAB

⁴⁶ When Jonathan and the people heard these words, they neither believed nor accepted them, for they remembered the great evil that Demetrius had done in Israel, and how sorely he had afflicted them. ⁴⁷ They therefore decided in favor of Alexander, for he had been the first to address them peaceably, and they remained his allies for the rest of his life.

⁴⁸ King Alexander gathered together a large army and encamped opposite Demetrius. ⁴⁹ The two kings joined battle, and when the army of Demetrius fled, Alexander pursued him, and overpowered his soldiers. ⁵⁰ He pressed the battle hard until sunset, and Demetrius fell that day. ⁵¹ Alexander sent ambassadors to Ptolemy, king of Egypt, with this message: ⁵² "Now that I have returned to my realm, taken my seat on the throne of my fathers, and established my rule by crushing Demetrius and gaining control of my country— ⁵³ for I engaged him in battle, defeated him and his army, and recovered the royal throne— ⁵⁴ let us now establish friendship with each other. Give me your daughter for my wife; and as your son-in-law, I will give to you and to her gifts worthy of you."

⁵⁵ King Ptolemy answered in these words: "Happy the day on which you returned to the land of your fathers and took your seat on their royal throne! ⁵⁶ I will do for you what you have written; but meet me in Ptolemais, so that we may see each other, and I will become your father-in-law as you have proposed."

⁵⁷ So Ptolemy with his daughter Cleopatra set out from Egypt and came to Ptolemais in the year one hundred and sixty-two. ⁵⁸ There King Alexander met him, and Ptolemy gave him his daughter Cleopatra in marriage. Their wedding was celebrated at Ptolemais with great splendor according to the custom of kings.

⁵⁹ King Alexander also wrote to Jonathan to come and meet him. ⁶⁰ So he went with pomp to Ptolemais, where he met the two kings and gave them and their friends silver and gold and many gifts and thus won their favor. ⁶¹ Some

NRSV

⁴⁶When Jonathan and the people heard these words, they did not believe or accept them, because they remembered the great wrongs that Demetrius[a] had done in Israel and how much he had oppressed them. ⁴⁷They favored Alexander, because he had been the first to speak peaceable words to them, and they remained his allies all his days.

⁴⁸Now King Alexander assembled large forces and encamped opposite Demetrius. ⁴⁹The two kings met in battle, and the army of Demetrius fled, and Alexander[b] pursued him and defeated them. ⁵⁰He pressed the battle strongly until the sun set, and on that day Demetrius fell.

⁵¹Then Alexander sent ambassadors to Ptolemy king of Egypt with the following message: ⁵²"Since I have returned to my kingdom and have taken my seat on the throne of my ancestors, and established my rule—for I crushed Demetrius and gained control of our country; ⁵³I met him in battle, and he and his army were crushed by us, and we have taken our seat on the throne of his kingdom— ⁵⁴now therefore let us establish friendship with one another; give me now your daughter as my wife, and I will become your son-in-law, and will make gifts to you and to her in keeping with your position."

⁵⁵Ptolemy the king replied and said, "Happy was the day on which you returned to the land of your ancestors and took your seat on the throne of their kingdom. ⁵⁶And now I will do for you as you wrote, but meet me at Ptolemais, so that we may see one another, and I will become your father-in-law, as you have said."

⁵⁷So Ptolemy set out from Egypt, he and his daughter Cleopatra, and came to Ptolemais in the one hundred sixty-second year.[c] ⁵⁸King Alexander met him, and Ptolemy[a] gave him his daughter Cleopatra in marriage, and celebrated her wedding at Ptolemais with great pomp, as kings do.

⁵⁹Then King Alexander wrote to Jonathan to come and meet him. ⁶⁰So he went with pomp to Ptolemais and met the two kings; he gave them and their Friends silver and gold and many gifts,

10, 49: (ephygen'e parembolē) Dēmētriou (kai ediōxen auton 'o) Alexandros: so LXX^{S,V,MSS}, P^{MSS}, Vet Lat, V.

a Gk he   b Other ancient authorities read *Alexander fled, and Demetrius*   c 150 B.C.

NAB

pestilent Israelites, transgressors of the law, united against him to accuse him, but the king paid no heed to them. ⁶² He ordered Jonathan to be divested of his ordinary garments and to be clothed in royal purple; and so it was done. ⁶³ The king also had him seated at his side. He said to his magistrates: "Go with him to the center of the city and make a proclamation that no one is to bring charges against him on any grounds or be troublesome to him in any way."

⁶⁴ When his accusers saw the honor paid to him in the proclamation, and the purple with which he was clothed, they all fled. ⁶⁵ The king also honored him by numbering him among his Chief Friends and made him military commander and governor of the province. ⁶⁶ So Jonathan returned in peace and happiness to Jerusalem.

NRSV

and found favor with them. ⁶¹A group of malcontents from Israel, renegades, gathered together against him to accuse him; but the king paid no attention to them. ⁶²The king gave orders to take off Jonathan's garments and to clothe him in purple, and they did so. ⁶³The king also seated him at his side; and he said to his officers, "Go out with him into the middle of the city and proclaim that no one is to bring charges against him about any matter, and let no one annoy him for any reason." ⁶⁴When his accusers saw the honor that was paid him, in accord with the proclamation, and saw him clothed in purple, they all fled. ⁶⁵Thus the king honored him and enrolled him among his chiefᵃ Friends, and made him general and governor of the province. ⁶⁶And Jonathan returned to Jerusalem in peace and gladness.

ᵃ Gk first

COMMENTARY

10:46-47. As Demetrius had worried, the Jews remember the wrongs done by him (v. 5) and do not trust his words; they are unlike the Hasideans, who had trusted Alcimus, sent by Demetrius (7:16). Again, the first offer of Demetrius (10:3-9) is ignored.

10:48-50. The sequence of events here is difficult to reconstruct. The NRSV follows one group of manuscripts that suggest that there was one decisive battle in which Alexander's army prevails and Demetrius dies. In another group of manuscripts, Alexander's army is routed, and Demetrius pursues and prevails, only to fall in battle.[104] This final battle took place sometime in the summer of 150 BCE.

10:51-58. The author of 1 Maccabees seems not to know that Ptolemy had helped Alexander in his bid for power in order to avenge himself on Demetrius for attacking Cyprus (see Commentary on 10:1-14). The syntax of Alexander's letter (vv. 52-54) follows Hebrew structure; it contains no flowery phrases and gets right to the heart of the matter. Ptolemy's daughter, Cleopatra Thea, is presented as the medium through which rela-

tions between two males take place when Ptolemy offers her in marriage to Alexander (v. 54). Ptolemy's response uses basically the same words (vv. 55-56). Neither letter has the opening greeting formula or the closing date. Ptolemais, on the seacoast, was easily reached from Egypt. The wedding took place in late summer 150 BCE.

10:59-60. Jonathan is invited to Ptolemais to meet Alexander. One can perhaps see why the author of 1 Maccabees gives the correspondence between Alexander and Ptolemy such prominence, for now the author, by having Alexander write to Jonathan to meet him, as Ptolemy had written to Alexander to meet him, puts Jonathan on the same playing ground as the Ptolemaic and Seleucid monarchs. Jonathan is also equated with the two kings as he travels "with pomp" (v. 60; cf. v. 58). One wonders how they communicated. Did Jonathan know some Greek, or did they use interpreters?

10:61-66. This time the scoundrels from Israel do not succeed in turning the king against Jonathan, as they had in the past (6:21-27; 7:5-7). Jonathan is granted immunity and is raised from the rank of friend to that of a "first friend." He becomes the military and political ruler in Judea.

104. See Justin *Epitome* 35.1.10-11.

1 Maccabees 10:67-89, The Uprising of Demetrius II

NAB

67 In the year one hundred and sixty-five, Demetrius, son of Demetrius, came from Crete to the land of his fathers. 68 When King Alexander heard of it he was greatly troubled, and returned to Antioch. 69 Demetrius appointed Apollonius governor of Coelesyria. Having gathered a large army, Apollonius pitched his camp at Jamnia. From there he sent this message to Jonathan the high priest:

70 "You are the only one who resists us. I am laughed at and put to shame on your account. Why are you displaying power against us in the mountains? 71 If you have confidence in your forces, come down now to us in the plain, and let us test each other's strength there; the city forces are on my side. 72 Inquire and learn who I am and who the others are who are helping me. Men say that you cannot make a stand against us because your fathers were twice put to flight in their own land. 73 Now you too will be unable to withstand our cavalry and such a force as this in the plain, where there is not a stone or a pebble or a place to flee."

74 When Jonathan heard the message of Apollonius, he was roused. Choosing ten thousand men, he set out from Jerusalem, and Simon his brother joined him to help him. 75 He pitched camp near Joppa, but the men in the city shut him out because Apollonius had a garrison there. When the Jews besieged it, 76 the men of the city became afraid and opened the gates, and so Jonathan took possession of Joppa.

77 When Apollonius heard of it, he drew up three thousand horsemen and an innumerable infantry. He marched on Azotus as though he were going on through the country, but at the same time he advanced into the plain, because he had such a large number of horsemen to rely on. 78 Jonathan followed him to Azotus, and they engaged in battle. 79 Apollonius, however, had left a thousand cavalry in hiding behind them. 80 When Jonathan discovered that there was an ambush behind him, his army was surrounded. From morning until evening they showered his men with arrows. 81 But his men held their ground, as Jonathan had commanded, whereas the

NRSV

67In the one hundred sixty-fifth year[a] Demetrius son of Demetrius came from Crete to the land of his ancestors. 68When King Alexander heard of it, he was greatly distressed and returned to Antioch. 69And Demetrius appointed Apollonius the governor of Coelesyria, and he assembled a large force and encamped against Jamnia. Then he sent the following message to the high priest Jonathan:

70"You are the only one to rise up against us, and I have fallen into ridicule and disgrace because of you. Why do you assume authority against us in the hill country? 71If you now have confidence in your forces, come down to the plain to meet us, and let us match strength with each other there, for I have with me the power of the cities. 72Ask and learn who I am and who the others are that are helping us. People will tell you that you cannot stand before us, for your ancestors were twice put to flight in their own land. 73And now you will not be able to withstand my cavalry and such an army in the plain, where there is no stone or pebble, or place to flee."

74When Jonathan heard the words of Apollonius, his spirit was aroused. He chose ten thousand men and set out from Jerusalem, and his brother Simon met him to help him. 75He encamped before Joppa, but the people of the city closed its gates, for Apollonius had a garrison in Joppa. 76So they fought against it, and the people of the city became afraid and opened the gates, and Jonathan gained possession of Joppa.

77When Apollonius heard of it, he mustered three thousand cavalry and a large army, and went to Azotus as though he were going farther. At the same time he advanced into the plain, for he had a large troop of cavalry and put confidence in it. 78Jonathan[b] pursued him to Azotus, and the armies engaged in battle. 79Now Apollonius had secretly left a thousand cavalry behind them. 80Jonathan learned that there was an ambush behind him, for they surrounded his army and shot arrows at his men from early morning until late afternoon. 81But his men stood fast, as Jonathan had commanded, and the enemy's[c] horses grew tired.

a 147 B.C.   b Gk he   c Gk their

NAB

enemy's horses became tired out. ⁸² When the horsemen were exhausted, Simon attacked the phalanx, overwhelmed it and put it to flight. ⁸³ The horsemen too were scattered over the plain. The enemy fled to Azotus and entered Beth-dagon, the temple of their idol, to save themselves. ⁸⁴ But Jonathan burned and plundered Azotus with its neighboring towns, and destroyed by fire both the temple of Dagon and the men who had taken refuge in it. ⁸⁵ Those who fell by the sword, together with those who were burned alive, came to about eight thousand men. ⁸⁶ Then Jonathan left there and pitched his camp at Ashkalon, and the people of that city came out to meet him with great pomp. ⁸⁷ He and his men then returned to Jerusalem, laden with much booty. ⁸⁸ When King Alexander heard of these events, he accorded new honors to Jonathan. ⁸⁹ He sent him a gold buckle, such as is usually given to King's Kinsmen; he also gave him Ekron and all its territory as a possession.

NRSV

82Then Simon brought forward his force and engaged the phalanx in battle (for the cavalry was exhausted); they were overwhelmed by him and fled, 83and the cavalry was dispersed in the plain. They fled to Azotus and entered Beth-dagon, the temple of their idol, for safety. 84But Jonathan burned Azotus and the surrounding towns and plundered them; and the temple of Dagon, and those who had taken refuge in it, he burned with fire. 85The number of those who fell by the sword, with those burned alive, came to eight thousand.

86Then Jonathan left there and encamped against Askalon, and the people of the city came out to meet him with great pomp.

87He and those with him then returned to Jerusalem with a large amount of booty. 88When King Alexander heard of these things, he honored Jonathan still more; 89and he sent to him a golden buckle, such as it is the custom to give to the King's Kinsmen. He also gave him Ekron and all its environs as his possession.

COMMENTARY

10:67-68. Demetrius I, before he finally engaged Alexander in battle, had sent his two sons, Demetrius and Antiochus, to Asia Minor. Alexander, after some initial popularity, had proved to be an inept ruler with little control over his empire. Around 148/47 BCE, he lost the two important satrapies of Media and Susiane. In 147 BCE, Demetrius, little more than thirteen years old, landed in Phoenicia with an army of mercenaries. Alexander, who had resided at Ptolemais, moved to Antioch, perhaps to check any attempt by Demetrius II to gain the capital.

10:69-73. Not much is known of what exactly transpired after Demetrius's arrival in "the land of his ancestors" (v. 67) except what is told here. The governor of Coelesyria, Apollonius, goes over to Demetrius's side and is confirmed in his position. Jonathan, however, remains loyal to Alexander (see v. 47). Apollonius takes up position on the coastal plain at Jamnia. Technically Apollonius is Jonathan's superior, and the reference to Jonathan as high priest (v. 69) underlies this difference in status. The Hebrew syntax of the message he sends to Jonathan (vv. 70-73) and the way it is tied in to the battle description suggest that the author of 1 Maccabees wrote what he thought Apollonius should have said. Apollonius sends a warrior's taunt and boast to Jonathan, emphasizing that it would be a disgrace for him to fight such a puny adversary, recalling how Goliath had mocked David (1 Sam 17:42-44) and how the experienced fighter Abner does not wish to fight his less experienced foe Asahel, but when forced to kills him (2 Sam 2:18-23). Apollonius contrasts Jonathan, a hill-person, with his own city forces on the plain. It is a taunt that was made earlier by the Arameans against Israel (1 Kgs 20:23-30). The statement that there would be "no stone or pebble" (v. 73) recalls the David and Goliath episode as well (1 Sam 17:40-49). The reference to ancestral defeats may allude to Judas's defeats at Beth-zechariah (6:47) and Elasa (9:18), but the use of "ancestral" (πατήρ *patēr*) suggests rather the Philistine defeat of the Israelites (1 Sam 4:1-11) and the defeat of Saul (1 Sam 31:1-7). One should also note the contrast between Apollonius's cavalry and Jonathan's forces, which are predicted to be unable to withstand such a mobile force. The battle description will maintain this contrast between cavalry and infantry.

10:74-76. Upon receiving this message, Jonathan first moves to secure Joppa, on the edge of his territory. It was strategically important to secure as a buffer to prevent attack from the rear on his way toward Apollonius.

10:77-85. Apollonius, knowing that Jonathan has responded to his taunt and that Apollonius is cut off from Demetrius's forces by Jonathan's capture of Joppa, seeks out the more advantageous position around Azotus than the rougher country of Jamnia (v. 77). He sets a trap so that Jonathan's flanks and rear will be vulnerable (v. 79), but Jonathan's skirmishers uncover them (v. 80). The battle is described: Jonathan's infantry are encircled and Apollonius's cavalry shoot arrows at them. In this description, Jonathan's infantry stands fast (v. 81) while the cavalry grows tired, the exact opposite of Apollonius's taunt. Note that the word translated "his men" is literally "people" (λαός *laos,* vv. 80-81), perhaps to emphasize the national quality of Jonathan's group.

Several details are missing from this picture. Where is Jonathan's cavalry (cf. Judas in 9:11-17)? It would be very foolish for a commander not to have cavalry to protect the flanks and rear of his infantry. Nor are we told what kind of cavalry Apollonius had. Did he deploy super-heavy cavalry, the cataphracts, which were heavily armed, as well as skirmishing mounted archers? The archers would try to make breaks in the infantry formation; the cataphracts would attack infantry but were not too effective against a fully defensive phalanx and because of their heavy armor would tire easily. It appears that Jonathan and Simon kept up a circular defensive posture with their shields up and their long pikes extended, so that the heavy cavalry troops could not penetrate and the arrows could be deflected. By afternoon the cavalry, both heavy and light, were tired (v. 81). Simon then drew out his infantry from the defensive into an offensive line (v. 82). They attacked Apollonius's phalanx and crushed it (v. 83). The cavalry could not stand in the plain and scattered and fled to Azotus (Ashdod). But Jonathan and his forces followed and plundered and burned Azotus and the surrounding towns; he also burned the temple of Dagon "and those who had taken refuge in it" (this temple is known from 1 Sam 5:1-5).

10:86. No mention is made of Apollonius's fate, but with his support for Demetrius II gone, the town of Askalon supports Alexander's cause and welcomes Jonathan with great pomp (cf. vv. 58-60).

10:87-89. Alexander had now been relieved of a threat to his south and, realizing the importance of Jonathan's support, raises his status still higher; "King's Kinsman" is a higher rank than first friend (v. 65). Jonathan can now fasten his purple cloak with a golden buckle. Ekron lay on the road from Jerusalem to the coast and was a clear extension of Jonathan's sphere of influence.

REFLECTIONS

The dynastic rivalry between different claimants to the Seleucid throne gave Jonathan the opportunity he needed. Only when the Seleucids were weak could the small state of Judea hope to gain its independence. Jonathan, with a battle-hardened following, was a strong man whom neither side could ignore. He was able to play hard-nosed politics as he strove to gain every advantage from his position. Playing both ends against the middle is a dangerous game, however. One has to make sure that one knows with whom one is dealing and not rely on anyone too much.

Jonathan's wheelings and dealings in international politics raise the issue of what role moral issues should play in such affairs. Jonathan was out for all he could get, although he did harbor resentment against Demetrius I for his early treatment of Jonathan (10:46). But is this a model for the way individuals or states should behave? Should one be concerned only for what one can get? Should one not be concerned also for what is happening to others or to other states? Is national interest to be defined only in terms of what is good for one's own nation? Are there not some issues that transcend narrow boundaries? Certainly we should be concerned about human rights, about genocide, about the starvation of millions. Yet implementing such policies is extremely difficult and must be carefully considered. Issues of morality should be aired and raised in policy discussions, not treated as naive and out of place.

Thinking only of one's own national gain in such circumstances as Jonathan found himself in can bring short-term benefits, but long-term loss. When one of the parties wins control, then the victor may not look so kindly on promises extracted under duress.

1 Maccabees 11:1-19, The Coming of Ptolemy VI

NAB

11 The king of Egypt gathered his forces, as numerous as the sands of the seashore, and many ships; and he sought by deceit to take Alexander's kingdom and add it to his own. ² He entered Syria with peaceful words, and the people in the cities opened their gates to welcome him, as King Alexander had ordered them to do, since Ptolemy was his father-in-law. ³ But when Ptolemy entered the cities, he stationed garrison troops in each one. ⁴ When he reached Azotus, he was shown the temple of Dagon destroyed by fire, Azotus and its suburbs demolished, corpses lying about, and the charred bodies of those burned by Jonathan in the war and stacked up along his route. ⁵ To prejudice the king against Jonathan, he was told what the latter had done; but the king said nothing. ⁶ Jonathan met the king with pomp at Joppa, and they greeted each other and spent the night there. ⁷ Jonathan accompanied the king as far as the river called Eleutherus and then returned to Jerusalem.

⁸ Plotting evil against Alexander, King Ptolemy took possession of the cities along the seacoast as far as Seleucia-by-the-Sea. ⁹ He sent ambassadors to King Demetrius, saying: "Come, let us make a pact with each other; I will give you my daughter whom Alexander has married, and you shall reign over your father's kingdom. ¹⁰ I regret that I gave him my daughter, for he has sought to kill me." ¹¹ His real reason for accusing Alexander, however, was that he coveted Alexander's kingdom. ¹² After taking his daughter away and giving her to Demetrius, Ptolemy broke with Alexander; their enmity became open. ¹³ Then Ptolemy entered Antioch and assumed the crown of Asia; he thus wore two crowns on his head, that of Egypt and that of Asia.

NRSV

11 Then the king of Egypt gathered great forces, like the sand by the seashore, and many ships; and he tried to get possession of Alexander's kingdom by trickery and add it to his own kingdom. ²He set out for Syria with peaceable words, and the people of the towns opened their gates to him and went to meet him, for King Alexander had commanded them to meet him, since he was Alexander's[a] father-in-law. ³But when Ptolemy entered the towns he stationed forces as a garrison in each town.

⁴When he[b] approached Azotus, they showed him the burnt-out temple of Dagon, and Azotus and its suburbs destroyed, and the corpses lying about, and the charred bodies of those whom Jonathan[c] had burned in the war, for they had piled them in heaps along his route. ⁵They also told the king what Jonathan had done, to throw blame on him; but the king kept silent. ⁶Jonathan met the king at Joppa with pomp, and they greeted one another and spent the night there. ⁷And Jonathan went with the king as far as the river called Eleutherus; then he returned to Jerusalem.

⁸So King Ptolemy gained control of the coastal cities as far as Seleucia by the sea, and he kept devising wicked designs against Alexander. ⁹He sent envoys to King Demetrius, saying, "Come, let us make a covenant with each other, and I will give you in marriage my daughter who was Alexander's wife, and you shall reign over your father's kingdom. ¹⁰I now regret that I gave him my daughter, for he has tried to kill me." ¹¹He threw blame on Alexander[d] because he coveted his kingdom. ¹²So he took his daughter away from him and gave her to Demetrius. He was estranged from Alexander, and their enmity became manifest.

a Gk *his*   *b* Other ancient authorities read *they*   *c* Gk *he*
d Gk *him*

NAB

¹⁴ King Alexander was in Cilicia at that time, because the people of that region had revolted. ¹⁵ When Alexander heard the news, he came to challenge Ptolemy in battle. Ptolemy marched out and met him with a strong force and put him to flight. ¹⁶ Alexander fled to Arabia to seek protection. King Ptolemy's triumph was complete ¹⁷ when the Arab Zabdiel cut off Alexander's head and sent it to Ptolemy. ¹⁸ But three days later King Ptolemy himself died, and his men in the fortified cities were killed by the inhabitants of the strongholds. ¹⁹ Thus Demetrius became king in the year one hundred and sixty-seven.

NRSV

13Then Ptolemy entered Antioch and put on the crown of Asia. Thus he put two crowns on his head, the crown of Egypt and that of Asia. ¹⁴Now King Alexander was in Cilicia at that time, because the people of that region were in revolt. ¹⁵When Alexander heard of it, he came against him in battle. Ptolemy marched out and met him with a strong force, and put him to flight. ¹⁶So Alexander fled into Arabia to find protection there, and King Ptolemy was triumphant. ¹⁷Zabdiel the Arab cut off the head of Alexander and sent it to Ptolemy. ¹⁸But King Ptolemy died three days later, and his troops in the strongholds were killed by the inhabitants of the strongholds. ¹⁹So Demetrius became king in the one hundred sixty-seventh year.ᵃ

ᵃ 145 B.C.

COMMENTARY

Chapter 11 continues the account of Jonathan's exploits outside the borders of Judea, as well as his attempts to oust the final Seleucid garrisons from within Judea. Jonathan's prominent position among the various Seleucid claimants to the throne is again emphasized, as is his trustworthiness compared to that of both the Ptolemies and the Seleucids.

11:1-3. Ptolemy VI Philometer, father-in-law of Alexander Epiphanes, intervened in the dynastic struggle, probably early in 145 BCE, since the final decisive battle and Ptolemy's subsequent death occurred in midsummer 145 BCE. The image of his troops being as numerous as sand on the seashore is a familiar one (Gen 22:17; Josh 11:4; Dan 3:36 LXX). The author of 1 Maccabees, who favors Alexander Epiphanes because of Jonathan's alliance with him, portrays Ptolemy as a treacherous land-grabber. Other historians state that Ptolemy really came to help Alexander, but turned against him either because he saw Alexander's incompetence or because of an attempt on Ptolemy's life by Alexander's minister Ammonius (see v. 10).¹⁰⁵ The author describes Ptolemy as

105. See Diodorus Siculus 32.9c; Josephus *Antiquities of the Jews* 13.106-107.

being deceitful, like the Seleucids before him (see 1:30; 7:10). Some of the southern coastal towns may have been friendly toward Demetrius II, as Jamnia, Joppa, and Azotus had been (10:69, 75, 83), and so Ptolemy's garrisoning of them may have been a prudent action. The author of 1 Maccabees interprets the action as a sinister move against the trusting Alexander.

11:4-7. Earlier, people had tried unsuccessfully to persuade a king to turn against Jonathan (10:61), and the same happens here. Despite the people's attempt to disparage Jonathan for the damage he had wrought in Azotus, Ptolemy greets Jonathan "with pomp." Since the destruction of Azotus had been the result of a battle with the forces of Demetrius II (10:83-85), Ptolemy could not openly break with Jonathan without seeming to side against Alexander. The river Eleutherus lay two hundred miles north of Joppa, far north from Judea.

11:8-12. Seleucia by the sea was the port of Antioch. Here Ptolemy's break with Alexander is made clear. The author of 1 Maccabees puts all the blame on Ptolemy VI for now, using his daughter as barter with Demetrius II, just as he had offered her to Alexander (10:54-56). We are not sure where Demetrius and Alexander were.

Josephus records that Demetrius landed in Cilicia,[106] and 1 Maccabees places Alexander there also (11:14), whereas Diodorus Siculus locates Alexander in Antioch at the time of Ptolemy's about-face.[107]

11:13. After he had made an alliance with Demetrius II, which promised him the rule of his father's kingdom (11:9), it seems unlikely that Ptolemy would actually seize control. According to Diodorus Siculus, Antioch was in an uproar at Ptolemy's turnaround.[108] The people revolted against Alexander's supporters, but did not want Demetrius II, and so they offered the crown to Ptolemy, which he declined. Rome had rejected Antiochus IV's attempt in 168 BCE to unite the Seleucid Empire and Egypt, and the author of

1 Maccabees had earlier stated that Antiochus IV wished to be king of Egypt (1:16). Now that the Achaean League had been defeated in 146 BCE, Rome was dominant in the region, and so Ptolemy may have been satisfied with the ceding of Coelesyria and Palestine by Demetrius.[109]

11:14-19. Ptolemy and Alexander join in battle near Antioch at the river Oenoparas. Alexander is defeated and forced to flee; Arabia here would refer to the northern desert, east of Damascus. Ptolemy is severely wounded in the battle, and dies soon after, leaving Demetrius the sole victor. Yet he cannot stop Ptolemy's army from returning to Egypt, so he seizes Ptolemy's war elephants, orders the garrisons in the coastal cities exterminated, and refuses to cede Coelesyria and Palestine. He became king in 145 BCE.

106. Josephus *Antiquities of the Jews* 13.86.
107. Diodorus Siculus 32.9c.
108. Ibid.

109. Ibid.

1 Maccabees 11:20-53, Demetrius II

1 Maccabees 11:20-37, Demetrius's Rise to Power

NAB	NRSV
20 At that time Jonathan gathered together the men of Judea to attack the citadel in Jerusalem, and they set up many machines against it. 21 Some transgressors of the law, enemies of their own nation, went to the king and informed him that Jonathan was besieging the citadel. 22 When Demetrius heard this, he was furious, and set out immediately for Ptolemais. He wrote to Jonathan to discontinue the siege and to meet him for a conference at Ptolemais as soon as possible.	20In those days Jonathan assembled the Judeans to attack the citadel in Jerusalem, and he built many engines of war to use against it. 21But certain renegades who hated their nation went to the king and reported to him that Jonathan was besieging the citadel. 22When he heard this he was angry, and as soon as he heard it he set out and came to Ptolemais; and he wrote Jonathan not to continue the siege, but to meet him for a conference at Ptolemais as quickly as possible.
23 On hearing this, Jonathan ordered the siege to continue. He selected some elders and priests of Israel and exposed himself to danger 24 by going to the king at Ptolemais. He brought with him silver, gold apparel, and many other presents, and found favor with the king. 25 Although some impious men of his own nation brought charges against him, 26 the king treated him just as his predecessors had done and showed him great honor in the presence of all his Friends. 27 He confirmed him in the high priesthood and in all	23When Jonathan heard this, he gave orders to continue the siege. He chose some of the elders of Israel and some of the priests, and put himself in danger, 24for he went to the king at Ptolemais, taking silver and gold and clothing and numerous other gifts. And he won his favor. 25Although certain renegades of his nation kept making complaints against him, 26the king treated him as his predecessors had treated him; he exalted him in the presence of all his Friends. 27He confirmed him in the high priesthood and in as many other honors as he had formerly had, and caused him

NAB

the honors he had previously held, and had him enrolled among his Chief Friends.

²⁸ Jonathan asked the king to exempt Judea and the three districts of Samaria from tribute, promising him in return three hundred talents. ²⁹ The king agreed and wrote the following letter to Jonathan about all these matters:

³⁰ "King Demetrius sends greetings to his brother Jonathan and to the Jewish nation. ³¹ We are sending you, for your information, a copy of the letter that we wrote to Lasthenes our kinsman concerning you. ³² 'King Demetrius sends greetings to his father Lasthenes. ³³ Because of the good will they show us, we have decided to bestow benefits on the Jewish nation, who are our friends and who observe their obligations to us. ³⁴ Therefore we confirm their possession, not only of the territory of Judea, but also of the three districts of Aphairema, Lydda, and Ramathaim. These districts, together with all their dependencies, were transferred from Samaria to Judea in favor of all those who offer sacrifices for us in Jerusalem instead of paying the royal taxes that formerly the king received from them each year from the produce of the soil and the fruit of the trees. ³⁵ From this day on we grant them release from payment of all other things that would henceforth be due to us, that is, of tithes and tribute and of the tax on the salt pans and the crown tax. ³⁶ Henceforth none of these provisions shall ever be revoked. ³⁷ Be sure, therefore, to have a copy of these instructions made and given to Jonathan, that it may be displayed in a conspicuous place on the holy hill.' "

11, 28: (*tas treis toparchias*) *tēs Samaritidos*: conj; cf 10, 30.38; 11, 34.

NRSV

to be reckoned among his chiefᵃ Friends. ²⁸Then Jonathan asked the king to free Judea and the three districts of Samariaᵇ from tribute, and promised him three hundred talents. ²⁹The king consented, and wrote a letter to Jonathan about all these things; its contents were as follows:

30"King Demetrius to his brother Jonathan and to the nation of the Jews, greetings. ³¹This copy of the letter that we wrote concerning you to our kinsman Lasthenes we have written to you also, so that you may know what it says. ³²'King Demetrius to his father Lasthenes, greetings. ³³We have determined to do good to the nation of the Jews, who are our friends and fulfill their obligations to us, because of the goodwill they show toward us. ³⁴We have confirmed as their possession both the territory of Judea and the three districts of Aphairema and Lydda and Rathamin; the latter, with all the region bordering them, were added to Judea from Samaria. To all those who offer sacrifice in Jerusalem we have granted release fromᶜ the royal taxes that the king formerly received from them each year, from the crops of the land and the fruit of the trees. ³⁵And the other payments henceforth due to us of the tithes, and the taxes due to us, and the salt pits and the crown taxes due to us—from all these we shall grant them release. ³⁶And not one of these grants shall be canceled from this time on forever. ³⁷Now therefore take care to make a copy of this, and let it be given to Jonathan and put up in a conspicuous place on the holy mountain.' "

ᵃ Gk *first*   ᵇ Cn: Gk *the three districts and Samaria*
ᶜ Or *Samaria, for all those who offer sacrifice in Jerusalem, in place of*

COMMENTARY

11:20-22. Jonathan takes advantage of the struggles in Syria to mount an attack on the citadel, as Judas had done at the death of Antiochus IV Epiphanes (6:18-20). Once again, as always at the beginning of each new king's reign (1:11; 10:61; see also 6:21-27; 7:5-7), opponents, labeled as lawless renegades, rise up to cause trouble. Demetrius II's response is the same as

that of earlier monarchs (3:27; 6:38). He moves south to Ptolemais, the former stronghold of Alexander, where Jonathan had met Alexander (10:60). Whereas previous monarchs had straightaway sent an army to enforce their will, Demetrius II's insecure hold of the throne is shown by his writing a letter to request that Jonathan stop the siege and to ask for a meeting. The word

Figure 3: Seleucid and Jewish Leaders in 1 and 2 Maccabees

Seleucid Rulers	Maccabean Leaders	Jewish High Priests
Antiochus III (223–187)		**Onias III** (196?–175)
Seleucus IV Philopator (187–175) (son of Antiochus III)		
Antiochus IV Epiphanes (175–164) (brother of Seleucus; originally regent for Seleucus's son)		**Jason** (175–172) **Menelaus** (172–162)
Antiochus V Eupator (164–162) (son of Antiochus IV; regent Lysias)	**Mattathias** (began revolt, 167) **Judas Maccabeus** (166–160)	
Demetrius I Soter (161–150) (son of Seleucus IV)		**Alcimus** (161–159) **no high priest** (159–152)
	Jonathan (160–143) (high priest 152–143)	
Alexander [Balas] V Epiphanes (150–145) (claimed to be son of Antiochus IV)		
Demetrius II Nicator (145–138; 129–125) (son of Demetrius I) **Antiochus VI Epiphanes** (145–142) (son of Alexander Balas)	**Simon** (143–134) (high priest 140–134)	
Antiochus VII Sidetes (138–129) (younger brother of Demetrius II)		**John Hyrcanus** (134–104)

for "meeting" (ἀπάντησις *apantēsis*) can have both a positive and a negative (i.e., "battle") connotation, so Jonathan's decision to go is risky.

11:23-24. Wisely, Jonathan keeps in play the bargaining chip of the siege of the citadel and goes to meet the king, surrounded by leaders of the nation, to show that he has strong national support. He is armed with gifts, which the king could well use. Jonathan's tactics prevail.

11:25-27. Just as Alexander had not listened to complaints against Jonathan (10:61-65), so too neither does Demetrius II. He confirms Jonathan in the high priesthood (cf. 10:20) as one of the king's chief friends (cf. 10:65), and possibly with the privilege of levying troops (10:6) and the offices of general and governor of the province (10:65).

11:28-29. Jonathan and Demetrius work out a deal. No mention is made of lifting the siege of the citadel, but this too must have been part of the bargain (see 11:41). Judea will not be completely free from paying tribute (cf. 13:39), but only from the levies specified in the appended letter.

11:30-32. The opening greeting of Demetrius's letter to Lasthenes links Jonathan with the nation of the Jews (cf. 10:18.25). According to Josephus, Lasthenes, from Crete, was the leader of a mercenary army that Demetrius had engaged in his attempt to take the throne.[110] The honorific title "Father" may signify that Lasthenes was a high-ranking minister in the royal court.

11:33-36. Demetrius's relationship with the nation of the Jews is depicted in terms of treaty

110. Josephus *Antiquities of the Jews* 13.86.

obligations. The Jews have kept their obligations, and now Demetrius is conferring his benefits. Jonathan keeps control of "the three districts," an area outside the borders of Judea (see 10:38). The exemptions Demetrius II allows are similar to those that Demetrius I is said to have allowed (10:30-32). What is interesting is the way recipients of the exemptions are described: "all those who offer sacrifice in Jerusalem" (v. 34). Is this similar to the release from tolls (10:34-35) and to the tax-free status of Jerusalem (10:31)? Or is the nation of the Jews now being defined as those who sacrifice in Jerusalem? Demetrius promises that these grants shall last forever (v. 36), a promise he will soon revoke.

11:37. This verse seems to return from the letter to Lasthenes to the one to Jonathan and the nation of the Jews. The grant is to be set up in a conspicuous place as a memorial. (Cf. the setting up of the stone of witness by Joshua after the people complete their covenant with God [Josh 24:24-27].) Demetrius I had already been said to have declared Jerusalem holy (10:31).

1 Maccabees 11:38-53, The Rule of Demetrius II

NAB

38 When King Demetrius saw that the land was peaceful under his rule and that he had no opposition, he dismissed his entire army, every man to his home, except the foreign troops which he had hired from the islands of the nations. So all the soldiers who had served under his predecessors hated him. 39 When a certain Trypho, who had previously belonged to Alexander's party, saw that all the troops were grumbling at Demetrius, he went to Imalkue the Arab, who was bringing up Alexander's young son Antiochus. 40 Trypho kept urging Imalkue to hand over the boy to him, that he might make him king in his father's place. During his stay there of many days, he told him of all that Demetrius had done and of the hatred that his soldiers had for him.

41 Meanwhile Jonathan sent the request to King Demetrius to withdraw his troops from the citadel of Jerusalem and from the other strongholds, for they were constantly hostile to Israel. 42 Demetrius, in turn, sent this word to Jonathan: "I will not only do this for you and your nation, but I will greatly honor you and your nation when I find the opportunity. 43 Do me the favor, therefore, of sending men to fight for me, because all my troops have revolted."

44 So Jonathan sent three thousand good fighting men to him at Antioch. When they came to the king, he was delighted over their arrival, 45 for the populace, one hundred and twenty thousand strong, had massed in the center of the city in an

NRSV

38When King Demetrius saw that the land was quiet before him and that there was no opposition to him, he dismissed all his troops, all of them to their own homes, except the foreign troops that he had recruited from the islands of the nations. So all the troops who had served under his predecessors hated him. 39A certain Trypho had formerly been one of Alexander's supporters; he saw that all the troops were grumbling against Demetrius. So he went to Imalkue the Arab, who was bringing up Antiochus, the young son of Alexander, 40and insistently urged him to hand Antiochus[a] over to him, to become king in place of his father. He also reported to Imalkue[b] what Demetrius had done and told of the hatred that the troops of Demetrius[a] had for him; and he stayed there many days.

41Now Jonathan sent to King Demetrius the request that he remove the troops of the citadel from Jerusalem, and the troops in the strongholds; for they kept fighting against Israel. 42And Demetrius sent this message back to Jonathan: "Not only will I do these things for you and your nation, but I will confer great honor on you and your nation, if I find an opportunity. 43Now then you will do well to send me men who will help me, for all my troops have revolted." 44So Jonathan sent three thousand stalwart men to him at Antioch, and when they came to the king, the king rejoiced at their arrival.

45Then the people of the city assembled within

a Gk *him*   *b* Gk *his troops*

NAB

attempt to kill him. ⁴⁶ But he took refuge in the palace, while the populace gained control of the main streets and began to fight. ⁴⁷ So the king called the Jews to his aid. They all rallied around him and spread out through the city. On that day they killed about a hundred thousand men in the city, ⁴⁸ which, at the same time, they set on fire and plundered on a large scale. Thus they saved the king's life. ⁴⁹ When the populace saw that the Jews held the city at their mercy, they lost courage and cried out to the king in supplication, ⁵⁰ "Give us your terms and let the Jews stop attacking us and our city." So they threw down their arms and made peace. ⁵¹ The Jews thus gained glory in the eyes of the king and all his subjects, and they became renowned throughout his kingdom. Finally they returned to Jerusalem with much spoil.

⁵² But when King Demetrius was sure of his royal throne, and the land was peaceful under his rule, ⁵³ he broke all his promises and became estranged from Jonathan. Instead of rewarding Jonathan for all the favors he had received from him, he caused him much trouble.

NRSV

the city, to the number of a hundred and twenty thousand, and they wanted to kill the king. ⁴⁶But the king fled into the palace. Then the people of the city seized the main streets of the city and began to fight. ⁴⁷So the king called the Jews to his aid, and they all rallied around him and then spread out through the city; and they killed on that day about one hundred thousand. ⁴⁸They set fire to the city and seized a large amount of spoil on that day, and saved the king. ⁴⁹When the people of the city saw that the Jews had gained control of the city as they pleased, their courage failed and they cried out to the king with this entreaty: ⁵⁰"Grant us peace, and make the Jews stop fighting against us and our city." ⁵¹And they threw down their arms and made peace. So the Jews gained glory in the sight of the king and of all the people in his kingdom, and they returned to Jerusalem with a large amount of spoil.

⁵²So King Demetrius sat on the throne of his kingdom, and the land was quiet before him. ⁵³But he broke his word about all that he had promised; he became estranged from Jonathan and did not repay the favors that Jonathan[a] had done him, but treated him very harshly.

a Gk *he*

COMMENTARY

11:38. This section is framed by the refrain "the land was quiet before him" (11:38, 52), but the appearance of that phrase almost guarantees something is going to disturb the peace. Historians report that Demetrius or his chancellor was cruel to the citizens of Antioch.[111] When Demetrius dismisses the regular troops, but keeps the mercenaries, he finds himself embattled on two fronts—from the unemployed soldiers and the harassed citizens of Antioch, and from supporters of another pretender to the throne, the son of Alexander.

11:39-40. Originally, Trypho's name was "Diodotus." "Trypho" means "magnificent," "luxurious." He is probably to be identified with the Diodotus who was a former general of Alex-

ander and who, together with Hierax, attempted to crown Ptolemy VI as king (cf. 1 Macc 11:13) rather than have Demetrius II rule.[112] Since coins with the image of Antiochus VI date from the year 167 of the Seleucid era (or 145 BCE), these events must have taken place soon after Alexander's death in midsummer of that year. As reported in 11:16, Alexander had fled after his defeat to the desert east of Damascus. Although he was killed, his young son Antiochus was not; he is in the guardianship of Imalkue the Arab (v. 39).[113] Trypho reports "what Demetrius had done" and urges Imalkue to relinquish Antiochus to him so that he might be set up as king in his father's place.

111. See Diodorus Siculus 33.4; Livy Summary of Book 52.

112. See Diodorus Siculus 32.9c; 33.3; Josephus *Antiquities of the Jews* 13.131.
113. Diodorus Siculus gives this Arab chieftain the name "Iamblichos," which is found in Emesa and in inscriptions from Palmyra. See Diodorus Siculus 33.4a.

11:41-51. Jonathan, always the opportunist, saw in Demetrius's difficulties a chance to gain back what he had just bargained away: control of the citadel, as well as the removal of all Syrian garrisons (v. 41). Demetrius, in no position to haggle, yields, promising greater blessings. In return, Demetrius requests Jewish troops, which Jonathan quickly sends (vv. 43-44), to help counteract the unrest in Antioch. These troops prove invaluable to Demetrius. In vicious street fighting, the Jewish soldiers pacify the city of Antioch (vv. 45-48). While 1 Maccabees does not mention the action of the king's mercenaries in these events, the Greco-Roman historian Diodorus Siculus does not mention the Jews, and so one can sense the nationalistic flavor of the accounts.[114] The author of 1 Maccabees extols the glory of the victory— the Jews have won wealth and a name for themselves by defeating civilians (v. 51).

11:52-53. The Jews had saved Demetrius II from one threat, but another, in the form of an army led by Trypho, is about to appear. This time, the Jews will not help. While Jonathan and the Jews have kept their goodwill toward Demetrius, he has not kept his word to them. Demetrius follows in the tradition of the Seleucids (6:62; 7:27-29) and the Ptolemies (11:1, 12), who could not be trusted. We cannot be sure of exactly what way Demetrius treated Jonathan harshly. Josephus states that Demetrius demanded taxes from Judeans going back to the time of the "first kings,"[115] but the phrase in 1 Maccabees usually refers to hardships in battle (9:7, 68; 10:46; 15:14). Given the short time frame in which these events happened, the phrase may signal that Demetrius II is acting like his father, Demetrius I (10:46).

114. Ibid., 33.4.2-3.

115. Josephus *Antiquities of the Jews* 13.143.

REFLECTIONS

The people of Antioch had genuine grievances against Demetrius II—he had treated them very harshly—but the author of 1 Maccabees makes no mention of it and rather has Jonathan act as Demetrius's enforcer to crush any resistance to his rule. The author is only too eager to tell of the Jewish people's misfortunes, but those of other nations do not concern him. Rather, he glories in the triumph of Jonathan's army over civilian fighters.

While it is important to be proud of one's religious and ancestral traditions, one must never lost sight of the basic humanity that unites us all. Does the advancement of one's own national interests above all other concerns ultimately benefit one's own nation? Moral factors must also be brought into play. In fact, one can see how none of Jonathan's manipulations won him respect. As soon as Demetrius had no use for Jonathan, Demetrius rejected him. A policy based solely on what is good for you, and not on what is best for others as well, is bound to fail.

These same concerns apply in the area of social policy. One should seek social justice, not simply what is best for oneself. We must not forget that tax codes, with their economic implications, also make moral statements about the kind of people we want to be thought of as. Our education and health policies reflect how we treat people, how we would want to be treated if we were they. As the great Rabbi Hillel said, "If I am not for myself, who am I? But if I am only for myself, what am I? And if not now, when?"[116] Thus individualism, who am I, must be balanced by concern for others; we must not be only for ourselves. And we should start behaving that way now, not at some distant time.

116. *Pirke Aboth* 1.14.

1 Maccabees 11:54-74, Jonathan and Antiochus VI

NAB

54 After this, Trypho returned and brought with him the young boy Antiochus, who became king and wore the royal crown. 55 All the soldiers whom Demetrius had discharged rallied around Antiochus and fought against Demetrius, who was routed and fled. 56 Trypho captured the elephants and occupied Antioch. 57 Then young Antiochus wrote to Jonathan: "I confirm you in the high priesthood and appoint you ruler over the four districts and wish you to be one of the King's Friends." 58 He also sent him gold dishes and a dinner service, gave him the right to drink from gold cups, to dress in royal purple, and to wear a gold buckle. 59 Likewise, he made Jonathan's brother Simon governor of the region from the Ladder of Tyre to the frontier of Egypt.

60 Jonathan set out and traveled through West-of-Euphrates and its cities, and all the forces of Syria espoused his cause as allies. When he arrived at Ashkalon, the citizens welcomed him with pomp. 61 But when he set out for Gaza, the people of Gaza locked their gates against him. So he besieged it and burned and plundered its suburbs. 62 Then the people of Gaza appealed to him for mercy, and he granted them peace. He took the sons of their chief men as hostages and sent them to Jerusalem. He then traveled on through the province as far as Damascus.

63 Jonathan heard that the generals of Demetrius had come with a strong force to Kadesh in Galilee, intending to remove him from office. 64 So he went to meet them, leaving his brother Simon in the province. 65 Simon besieged Beth-zur, attacked it for many days, and blockaded the inhabitants. 66 When they sued for peace, he granted it to them. He expelled them from the city, took possession of it, and put a garrison there.

67 Meanwhile, Jonathan and his army pitched their camp near the waters of Gennesaret, and at daybreak they went to the plain of Hazor. 68 There, in front of him on the plain, was the army of the foreigners. This army attacked him in the open, having first detached an ambush against him in the mountains. 69 Then the men in ambush rose out of their places and joined in the battle. 70 All

NRSV

54After this Trypho returned, and with him the young boy Antiochus who began to reign and put on the crown. 55All the troops that Demetrius had discharged gathered around him; they fought against Demetrius,[a] and he fled and was routed. 56Trypho captured the elephants[b] and gained control of Antioch. 57Then the young Antiochus wrote to Jonathan, saying, "I confirm you in the high priesthood and set you over the four districts and make you one of the king's Friends." 58He also sent him gold plate and a table service, and granted him the right to drink from gold cups and dress in purple and wear a gold buckle. 59He appointed Jonathan's[c] brother Simon governor from the Ladder of Tyre to the borders of Egypt.

60Then Jonathan set out and traveled beyond the river and among the towns, and all the army of Syria gathered to him as allies. When he came to Askalon, the people of the city met him and paid him honor. 61From there he went to Gaza, but the people of Gaza shut him out. So he besieged it and burned its suburbs with fire and plundered them. 62Then the people of Gaza pleaded with Jonathan, and he made peace with them, and took the sons of their rulers as hostages and sent them to Jerusalem. And he passed through the country as far as Damascus.

63Then Jonathan heard that the officers of Demetrius had come to Kadesh in Galilee with a large army, intending to remove him from office. 64He went to meet them, but left his brother Simon in the country. 65Simon encamped before Beth-zur and fought against it for many days and hemmed it in. 66Then they asked him to grant them terms of peace, and he did so. He removed them from there, took possession of the town, and set a garrison over it.

67Jonathan and his army encamped by the waters of Gennesaret. Early in the morning they marched to the plain of Hazor, 68and there in the plain the army of the foreigners met him; they had set an ambush against him in the mountains, but they themselves met him face to face. 69Then the men in ambush emerged from their places

a Gk him   b Gk animals   c Gk his

NAB

of Jonathan's men fled; no one stayed except the army commanders Mattathias, son of Absalom, and Judas, son of Chalphi. [71] Jonathan tore his clothes, threw earth on his head, and prayed. [72] Then he went back to the combat and so overwhelmed the enemy that they took to flight. [73] Those of his men who were running away saw it and returned to him; and with him they pursued the enemy as far as their camp in Kadesh, where they pitched their own camp. [74] Three thousand of the foreign troops fell on that day. Then Jonathan returned to Jerusalem.

NRSV

and joined battle. [70]All the men with Jonathan fled; not one of them was left except Mattathias son of Absalom and Judas son of Chalphi, commanders of the forces of the army. [71]Jonathan tore his clothes, put dust on his head, and prayed. [72]Then he turned back to the battle against the enemy[a] and routed them, and they fled. [73]When his men who were fleeing saw this, they returned to him and joined him in the pursuit as far as Kadesh, to their camp, and there they encamped. [74]As many as three thousand of the foreigners fell that day. And Jonathan returned to Jerusalem.

[a] Gk them

COMMENTARY

11:54-56. The first army Demetrius sends against Trypho is defeated. Gaining strength, Trypho wins control of Chalcis and then, in 145/44, forces Demetrius to leave Antioch and move to Seleucia or Cilicia.[117] The author of 1 Maccabees reports a single battle in which Demetrius is defeated and forced to flee, making no mention of his destination (v. 55).

11:57-59. Antiochus VI, son of Alexander Balas and Cleopatra Thea, is only two years old, but official letters must be sent in his name. As at the accession of a new king, Jonathan's position as high priest needs to be reconfirmed, as does his control over the four districts that Alexander had given to him (the three of 11:34 plus possibly Akrabattene on the eastern boundary of Judea and Samaria or maybe Ekron [10:89]). Jonathan is enrolled as a Friend of the new king with the prerogatives of a Kinsman (10:89). Jonathan's brother Simon is made a Seleucid appointee, as governor of the coastal area from Syria to Egypt. The Hasmoneans thus become integrated into the Seleucid administration, ironically fulfilling what the "renegades" had sought to do. One wonders if the author of 1 Maccabees was aware of the irony.

11:60-62. Jonathan loses no time in using his position and Simon's position to traverse the

province of Trans-Euphrates—the province west of the Euphrates—both gaining the allegiance of the cities to Antiochus VI and consolidating his own power. Askalon had received him beforehand (10:86), but Gaza has to be subdued (v. 61). Jonathan acts in a way similar to the way Bacchides, the earlier Seleucid general, had acted in Judea (9:53); he takes hostages to ensure the people's compliance. He ranges from Gaza in the southern coastal area to Damascus, well north and to the east of the Ladder of Tyre.

11:63. Demetrius II still controls the coastal region north of Tyre, and some of his forces come into Galilee while Jonathan is north in Damascus. Their mission was probably not, as the NRSV translates the end of v. 63, "to remove him from office," but to turn him away from his mission of consolidating the hold of Antiochus VI in the area from Gaza to Damascus.

11:64-66. Jonathan, last mentioned as being in Damascus (v. 62), marches south to meet Demetrius's army (v. 64). The easiest way to Kadesh was to travel south to Lake Gennesaret and then north through the plain of Hazor to Kadesh (see v. 67). Either Simon had been left behind in Judea, or he was now left behind while Jonathan marched north from the lake. Bacchides, deputy of Demetrius I, had fortified Beth-zur with troops and stores of food (9:52). Simon's successful siege of Beth-zur anticipates his siege of the

---

117. For Seleucia, see Livy Summary of Book 52; for Cilicia, see Josephus *Antiquities of the Jews* 13.145.

citadel (13:49-40). Capture of the town prevents it from becoming a base of attack from the rear.

11:67-74. The enemy forces have time to prepare for the battle, and so they choose a site that allows them to set an ambush. As Jonathan's troops march out, they are caught in the trap, which, except for the bravery of a few, would have succeeded (v. 71). Nothing more is known about the family of Chalphi than that Judas son of Chalphi was one of the two men who did not desert Jonathan. Mattathias son of Absalom was

the other; this may be the Absalom who was one of the ambassadors sent to Lysias (2 Macc 11:17). Jonathan, in the midst of the battle, performs the ritual of mourning (cf. Josh 7:6-9)—tearing his clothes, putting dust on his head, and praying—before returning to the fray. This time, he is successful and overruns the enemy's camp. Jonathan has fulfilled his mission of securing the area for Antiochus VI, and so he returns to Jerusalem.

REFLECTIONS

The price for advancement in the Seleucid power structure now appears. Jonathan has to behave as Bacchides had done by taking hostages to maintain order. He has to continue fighting so as to maintain his position and Simon's status as governor. In some ways, we become what we do. Jonathan had set out to gain respect within the Seleucid power structure, and in so doing he became a Seleucid functionary. When planning what we are to do, we should, like chess players, look ahead to see the consequences of our choices.

1 Maccabees 12:1-23, The Relationship with Rome

NAB

12 When Jonathan saw that the times favored him, he sent selected men to Rome to confirm and renew his friendship with the Romans. ² He also sent letters to Sparta and other places for the same purpose.

³ After reaching Rome, the men entered the senate chamber and said, "The high priest Jonathan and the Jewish people have sent us to renew the earlier friendship and alliance between you and them." ⁴ The Romans gave them letters addressed to the authorities in the various places, requesting them to provide the envoys with safe conduct to the land of Judah.

⁵ This is a copy of the letter that Jonathan wrote to the Spartans: ⁶ "Jonathan the high priest, the senate of the nation, the priests, and the rest of the Jewish people send greetings to their brothers the Spartans. ⁷ Long ago a letter was sent to the high priest Onias from Arius, who then reigned over you, stating that you are our brothers, as the attached copy shows. ⁸ Onias welcomed the envoy with honor and received the letter, which clearly referred to alliance and friendship. ⁹ Though we have no need of these things, since we have

NRSV

12 Now when Jonathan saw that the time was favorable for him, he chose men and sent them to Rome to confirm and renew the friendship with them. ²He also sent letters to the same effect to the Spartans and to other places. ³So they went to Rome and entered the senate chamber and said, "The high priest Jonathan and the Jewish nation have sent us to renew the former friendship and alliance with them." ⁴And the Romans[a] gave them letters to the people in every place, asking them to provide for the envoys[b] safe conduct to the land of Judah.

5This is a copy of the letter that Jonathan wrote to the Spartans: ⁶"The high priest Jonathan, the senate of the nation, the priests, and the rest of the Jewish people to their brothers the Spartans, greetings. ⁷Already in time past a letter was sent to the high priest Onias from Arius,[c] who was king among you, stating that you are our brothers, as the appended copy shows. ⁸Onias welcomed the envoy with honor, and received the letter, which contained a clear declaration of alliance and

a Gk *they*   *b* Gk *them*   *c* Vg Compare verse 20: Gk *Darius*

NAB

for our encouragement the sacred books that are in our possession, ¹⁰ we have ventured to send word to you for the renewal of brotherhood and friendship, so as not to become strangers to you altogether; a long time has passed since your mission to us. ¹¹ We, on our part, have never ceased to remember you in the sacrifices and prayers that we offer on our feasts and other appropriate days, as it is right and proper to remember brothers. ¹² We likewise rejoice in your renown. ¹³ But many hardships and wars have beset us, and the kings around us have attacked us. ¹⁴ We did not wish to be troublesome to you and to the rest of our allies and friends in these wars; ¹⁵ with the help of Heaven for our support, we have been saved from our enemies, and they have been humbled. ¹⁶ So we have chosen Numenius, son of Antiochus, and Antipater, son of Jason, and we have sent them to the Romans to renew our former friendship and alliance with them. ¹⁷ We have also ordered them to come to you and greet you, and to deliver to you our letter about the renewal of our brotherhood. ¹⁸ Therefore kindly send us an answer on this matter."

¹⁹ This is a copy of the letter that was sent to Onias: ²⁰ "Arius, king of the Spartans, sends greetings to Onias the high priest. ²¹ A document has been found stating that the Spartans and the Jews are brothers; both nations descended from Abraham. ²² Now that we have learned this, kindly write to us about your welfare. ²³ We, on our part, are informing you that your cattle and your possessions are ours, and ours are yours. We have, therefore, given orders that you should be told of this."

NRSV

friendship. ⁹Therefore, though we have no need of these things, since we have as encouragement the holy books that are in our hands, ¹⁰we have undertaken to send to renew our family ties and friendship with you, so that we may not become estranged from you, for considerable time has passed since you sent your letter to us. ¹¹We therefore remember you constantly on every occasion, both at our festivals and on other appropriate days, at the sacrifices that we offer and in our prayers, as it is right and proper to remember brothers. ¹²And we rejoice in your glory. ¹³But as for ourselves, many trials and many wars have encircled us; the kings around us have waged war against us. ¹⁴We were unwilling to annoy you and our other allies and friends with these wars, ¹⁵for we have the help that comes from Heaven for our aid, and so we were delivered from our enemies, and our enemies were humbled. ¹⁶We therefore have chosen Numenius son of Antiochus and Antipater son of Jason, and have sent them to Rome to renew our former friendship and alliance with them. ¹⁷We have commanded them to go also to you and greet you and deliver to you this letter from us concerning the renewal of our family ties. ¹⁸And now please send us a reply to this."

19This is a copy of the letter that they sent to Onias: ²⁰"King Arius of the Spartans, to the high priest Onias, greetings. ²¹It has been found in writing concerning the Spartans and the Jews that they are brothers and are of the family of Abraham. ²²And now that we have learned this, please write us concerning your welfare; ²³we on our part write to you that your livestock and your property belong to us, and ours belong to you. We therefore command that our envoys[a] report to you accordingly."

[a] Gk *they*

COMMENTARY

Just as Judas is said to have used the respite after his victory over Nicanor to contact the Romans (1 Maccabees 8), so also Jonathan, now that the southern coastal area has been subdued, renews diplomatic relationships with Rome and in-

itiates contacts with other nations. Serious questions have been raised about the authenticity of the Spartan correspondence, though some scholars maintain that it is genuine. What is interesting to note is the very different circumstances under which Judas and Jonathan wrote. In Judas's time, the Seleucid kingdom was united under Demetrius I, while during Jonathan's career Demetrius II and Antiochus VI were fighting for the throne. Judas operated within Judea, while Jonathan had a well-equipped army traversing the province of Trans-Euphrates. Judas was a rebel from the Seleucid king; Jonathan was his kinsman and Simon one of his governors. Jonathan is depicted as a respected member of the club, meeting with kings (10:60; 11:6) and forming alliances with them. The author of 1 Maccabees wants to put Jonathan on the world stage, and thus heighten the importance of Jonathan and the Jewish nation.

12:1-4. This section is enclosed between two encounters with commanders of Demetrius (11:63; 12:24). The friendship with Rome is a reference to Judas's earlier agreement (see 8:17-32). As noted in the Commentary on 8:17-32, such a friendship pact did not oblige the Romans to intervene but did give them an excuse to do so and might make a Seleucid king hesitate before acting, although Demetrius I had not done so. The brevity of the description of the Roman mission has led some scholars to suggest that it is simply a doublet of Simon's later embassy (15:15-24).

One wonders what "other places" the author of 1 Maccabees had in mind in v. 2. The very vagueness suggests that he had no information but the letter to Sparta to go on, but that he wishes to place Judea on a level with other nations. The Spartans had left the Achaean League and so had not been party to its defeat but had remained on good terms with Rome. Perhaps Sparta's relationship with Rome is the reason behind the attempt of the Jews to forge a kinship relationship with the Spartans, who would then speak to Rome on their behalf. However, the text of 1 Maccabees says nothing of this and simply speaks of Jonathan's wishing to become an ally and friend with other nations. Such a move seems to imply more than a hope for deterrence against any future Seleucid monarch; rather, it seems to be part of a strategy for complete independence. It should also be considered in the light of the "creative" history whereby many nations sought to enhance their prestige by connecting their heroes to the mythical heroes of Greece. Within the Jewish tradition, for example, Cleodemus Mal-

chus has the sons of Abraham accompany Heracles to Africa,[118] and Tacitus reports that the name "Jew" derives from Mt. Ida in Crete, thus forging a Cretan origin for the Jews.[119]

12:5-18. 12:5-6. Jonathan's letter to the Spartans follows. The Jewish senate was mentioned in a letter of Antiochus III,[120] but precisely what its membership was is unknown. Most probably it was composed of priests and leading members of the local aristocracy.

12:7-8. Jonathan reminds the Spartans of a letter that was sent from Onias to Arius. The Greek manuscripts give the name of the Spartan king as "Darius," while v. 20 names him Arius. The king referred to is probably Areus I (c. 312–265 BCE), rather than Areus II (262–254 BCE), who died as a child. Onias is probably the Jewish high priest Onias I (c. 320–290 BCE). Areus I had his hands full in combatting the encroachments of Macedonia, and the reader may wonder why he would seek an alliance with Judea. The letter quoted in vv. 20-23 does not explicitly speak of the formation of such an alliance. It is concerned, rather, with kinship and so with hospitality and diplomatic support. Such concerns could be the basis for forging an alliance.

12:9-10. Without the usual epistolary well-wishing, Jonathan gets to the reason for sending the letter: "to renew our family ties and friendship with you" (v. 10). The phrasing of these verses seems to present a backhanded compliment—i.e., "We don't really need you, but let's not become estranged." This may be an apologia against those who do not think Judea should become entangled in foreign alliances.

12:11-12. The wording of these verses is what is normally found at the beginning of letters, as the letter writer expresses care and concern for the addressees. The phrasing is similar, for example, to the opening well wishes of letters of Paul: "I thank my God every time I remember you, constantly praying with joy in every one of my prayers for all of you" (Phil 1:3-4 NRSV; cf. Rom 1:9).

12:13-15. Jonathan alludes to the "many trials and many wars" the Jews have faced. It is unclear who the "other allies and friends" he refers to were (v. 14). Again, these verses seem like a backhanded compliment—i.e., "We don't really

118. Josephus *Antiquities of the Jews* 1.239-241.
119. Tacitus *Histories* 5.2.
120. Josephus *Antiquities of the Jews* 12.142.

need allies." As such, it seems directed more at a Jewish than a Spartan audience. The role of prayer recalls 3:18-23, 53; 9:46.

12:16-18. These verses introduce the two ambassadors who deliver the letter to the Spartans: Numenius and Antipater. Their trip to Sparta is described later (14:22); in addition, Numenius will be sent to Rome by Simon (14:24). Jonathan requests a reply to his letter.

12:19-23. Jonathan includes here a copy of the letter that was sent to Onias. In the letter, Arius alludes to a writing that suggests that the Spartans and the Jews "are brothers and are of the family of Abraham" (v. 21). Scholars would dearly love to have the writing to which Arius refers. It is interesting that the Greek historian Herodotus states that the progenitors of the Spartan royal house came from Egypt,[121] and Hecataeus of Abdera holds that the Greek hero Danaos, whose descendants populated the Peloponnese, and Kadmos, the founder of Thebes, left Egypt when Moses led the Israelites out.[122] As mentioned earlier, Cleodemus Malchus had linked the descendants of Abraham with Heracles, and the Spartan kings were said to be descendants of Heracles. However the connection was made, it most probably would have been through figures of primeval history. The reference to livestock and property (v. 23) seems more appropriate to groups living alongside one another (cf. Gen 34:23). It may be a concretely phrased formula to express kinship and friendship through the fact that both parties hold something in common, even though neither would use the other's possessions without consent.

---

121. Herodotus 6.53.

122. See Diodorus Siculus 40.3.2.

1 Maccabees 12:24-38, Further Campaigns for Antiochus VI

NAB

24 Jonathan heard that the generals of Demetrius had returned to attack him with a stronger army than before. 25 He set out from Jerusalem and went into the country of Hamath to meet them, giving them no time to enter his province. 26 The spies he had sent into their camp came back and reported that the enemy had made ready to attack the Jews that very night. 27 Therefore, when the sun set, Jonathan ordered his men to be on guard and to remain armed, ready for combat, throughout the night. He also set outposts all around the camp. 28 When the enemy heard that Jonathan and his men were ready for battle, their hearts sank with fear and dread. They lighted fires and then withdrew. 29 But because Jonathan and his men were watching the lights burning, they did not know what had happened until morning. 30 Then Jonathan pursued them, but he could not overtake them, for they had crossed the river Eleutherus. 31 So Jonathan turned aside against the Arabs who are called Zabadeans, overwhelming and plundering them. 32 Then he marched on to Damascus and traversed that whole region.

12, 28: (*en tē parembolē autōn*) *kai anechōrēsan:* so LXXMSS; PMSS.

NRSV

24Now Jonathan heard that the commanders of Demetrius had returned, with a larger force than before, to wage war against him. 25So he marched away from Jerusalem and met them in the region of Hamath, for he gave them no opportunity to invade his own country. 26He sent spies to their camp, and they returned and reported to him that the enemy[a] were being drawn up in formation to attack the Jews[b] by night. 27So when the sun had set, Jonathan commanded his troops to be alert and to keep their arms at hand so as to be ready all night for battle, and he stationed outposts around the camp. 28When the enemy heard that Jonathan and his troops were prepared for battle, they were afraid and were terrified at heart; so they kindled fires in their camp and withdrew.[c] 29But Jonathan and his troops did not know it until morning, for they saw the fires burning. 30Then Jonathan pursued them, but he did not overtake them, for they had crossed the Eleutherus river. 31So Jonathan turned aside against the Arabs who are called Zabadeans, and he crushed them and plundered them. 32Then

a Gk *they*   *b* Gk *them*   *c* Other ancient authorities omit *and withdrew*

NAB

³³ Simon also set out and went as far as Ashkalon and its neighboring strongholds. He then turned to Joppa and occupied it, ³⁴ for he heard that its men had intended to hand over this stronghold to the supporters of Demetrius. He left a garrison there to guard it.

³⁵ When Jonathan returned, he assembled the elders of the people, and with them he made plans for building strongholds in Judea, ³⁶ for making the walls of Jerusalem still higher, and for erecting a high barrier between the citadel and the city, that would isolate the citadel and so prevent its garrison from commerce with the city. ³⁷ The people therefore worked together on building up the city, for part of the east wall above the ravine had collapsed. The quarter called Chaphenatha was also repaired. ³⁸ Simon likewise built up Adida in the Shephelah, and strengthened its fortifications by providing them with gates and bars.

NRSV

he broke camp and went to Damascus, and marched through all that region.

33Simon also went out and marched through the country as far as Askalon and the neighboring strongholds. He turned aside to Joppa and took it by surprise, ³⁴for he had heard that they were ready to hand over the stronghold to those whom Demetrius had sent. And he stationed a garrison there to guard it.

35When Jonathan returned he convened the elders of the people and planned with them to build strongholds in Judea, ³⁶to build the walls of Jerusalem still higher, and to erect a high barrier between the citadel and the city to separate it from the city, in order to isolate it so that its garrison[a] could neither buy nor sell. ³⁷So they gathered together to rebuild the city; part of the wall on the valley to the east had fallen, and he repaired the section called Chaphenatha. ³⁸Simon also built Adida in the Shephelah; he fortified it and installed gates with bolts.

a Gk *they*

COMMENTARY

12:24-32. 12:24-25. The commanders of Demetrius's armies return, a "larger force than before," to launch a second campaign. Their first campaign against Jonathan had ended in defeat (11:63-74). Previously the commanders had advanced south as far as Kadesh in Galilee. This time, Jonathan marches north before they can enter Judean territory (v. 25). Hamath was in the Orontes valley, well north of Jerusalem. This would seem a long way for Jonathan to go to make sure that his opponents did not enter Judea. Since he had not gone beyond the Eleutherus River earlier (11:7), since Simon's rule was over the Ladder of Tyre (also south of the Eleutherus), and since the enemy is said to flee across the Eleutherus River (v. 30), the reader should therefore see the confrontation as having taken place at the southern border of the region of Hamath, near the traditional northern limit of Israel's territory (see Num 34:8; Josh 13:5; 1 Kgs 8:65; 2 Kgs 14:25; Ezek 47:15).

12:26-32. Just as Gorgias had prepared a night

assault on Judas (4:1), so also the commanders of Demetrius plan a night raid on Jonathan's army. Their planned surprise attack, as well as their tricky retreat with no fighting, reinforces the sense that Jonathan's force is invincible.

Jonathan pursues them, but they elude him and cross the Eleutherus. So Jonathan turns "aside against the Arabs who are called Zabadeans" and conquers and plunders them (v. 31). The Zabadeans lived about thirty miles northwest of Damascus. Perhaps there is a connection between these people and the Zabdiel who murdered Alexander Balas (11:17). Jonathan is once again in control of the whole region of Coelesyria.

12:33-38. While Jonathan controls the north, Simon makes sure the southern coastal area remains quiet. Jonathan assembles the elders as Judas had assembled the people (6:19). Jonathan's military preparations, therefore, are seen as not arbitrary but the result of common consent. Jonathan's fortification of strategic areas in Judea, as well as Simon's installation of garrisons at

Beth-zur (11:65-66), at Joppa, and at Adida, near Lydda between the coastal plain and the hill country of Judea, seems to be part of a well-orchestrated plan to secure, perhaps to enlarge, the territory of Judea against all comers. Secure in his control of the area of Coelesyria, Jonathan once again tackles the problem of the citadel in Jerusalem, the remaining vestige of Seleucid authority over Judea (11:20-21, 41).

He strengthens Jerusalem's walls and repairs "the section called Chaphenatha" (v. 37) and seeks to starve out the inhabitants of the citadel, as Bacchides had successfully done to the sanctuary (6:51-54).[123] The eastern valley referred to is the Kidron Valley.

123. "Chaphenatha," an Aramaic word, is unknown outside of 1 Macc 12:37. Some scholars identify it with the "Second Quarter" (2 Kgs 22:14) at the northwest of the temple area.

1 Maccabees 12:39-53, The Capture of Jonathan

NAB

39 Trypho was determined to become king of Asia, assume the crown, and do away with King Antiochus. 40 But he was afraid that Jonathan would not permit him; but would fight against him. Looking for a way to seize and kill him, he set out and reached Beth-shan. 41 Jonathan marched out against him with forty thousand picked fighting men and came to Beth-shan. 42 But when Trypho saw that Jonathan had arrived with a large army, he was afraid to offer him violence. 43 Instead, he received him with honor, introduced him to all his friends, and gave him presents. He also ordered his friends and soldiers to obey him as they would himself. 44 Then he said to Jonathan: "Why have you put all your soldiers to so much trouble when we are not at war? 45 Pick out a few men to stay with you, send the rest back home, and then come with me to Ptolemais. I will hand it over to you together with other strongholds and their garrisons, as well as the officials, then I will leave and go home. That is why I came here."

46 Jonathan believed him and did as he said. He dismissed his troops, and they returned to the land of Judah. 47 But he kept with him three thousand men, of whom he sent two thousand to Galilee while one thousand accompanied him. 48 Then as soon as Jonathan had entered Ptolemais, the men of the city closed the gates and seized him; all who had entered with him, they killed with the sword.

49 Trypho sent soldiers and cavalry to Galilee and the Great Plain to destroy all Jonathan's men. 50 These, upon learning that Jonathan had been

12, 50: (synelēmphthē kai) apolēsan (hoi met' autou): conj; omit kai before met' autou: dittog.

NRSV

39 Then Trypho attempted to become king in Asia and put on the crown, and to raise his hand against King Antiochus. 40 He feared that Jonathan might not permit him to do so, but might make war on him, so he kept seeking to seize and kill him, and he marched out and came to Beth-shan. 41 Jonathan went out to meet him with forty thousand picked warriors, and he came to Beth-shan. 42 When Trypho saw that he had come with a large army, he was afraid to raise his hand against him. 43 So he received him with honor and commended him to all his Friends, and he gave him gifts and commanded his Friends and his troops to obey him as they would himself. 44 Then he said to Jonathan, "Why have you put all these people to so much trouble when we are not at war? 45 Dismiss them now to their homes and choose for yourself a few men to stay with you, and come with me to Ptolemais. I will hand it over to you as well as the other strongholds and the remaining troops and all the officials, and will turn around and go home. For that is why I am here."

46 Jonathan[a] trusted him and did as he said; he sent away the troops, and they returned to the land of Judah. 47 He kept with himself three thousand men, two thousand of whom he left in Galilee, while one thousand accompanied him. 48 But when Jonathan entered Ptolemais, the people of Ptolemais closed the gates and seized him, and they killed with the sword all who had entered with him.

49 Then Trypho sent troops and cavalry into Galilee and the Great Plain to destroy all Jonathan's soldiers. 50 But they realized that Jonathan

a Gk he

NAB

captured and his companions killed, encouraged one another and went out in compact body ready to fight. ⁵¹ As their pursuers saw that they were ready to fight for their lives, they turned back. ⁵² Thus all these men of Jonathan came safely into the land of Judah. They mourned over Jonathan and his men, and were in great fear, and all Israel fell into deep mourning.

⁵³ All the nations round about sought to destroy them. They said, "Now that they have no leader to help them, let us make war on them and wipe out their memory from among men."

NRSV

had been seized and had perished along with his men, and they encouraged one another and kept marching in close formation, ready for battle. ⁵¹When their pursuers saw that they would fight for their lives, they turned back. ⁵²So they all reached the land of Judah safely, and they mourned for Jonathan and his companions and were in great fear; and all Israel mourned deeply. ⁵³All the nations around them tried to destroy them, for they said, "They have no leader or helper. Now therefore let us make war on them and blot out the memory of them from human-kind."

COMMENTARY

12:39-40. Jonathan has aimed at securing Jerusalem and Judea from all attack, and a further goal seemed the complete independence of Judea from Seleucid control. While Jonathan is carrying out these operations, Trypho has been busy in northern Syria. He controls Antioch and most of its hinterlands, and the coastal cities of Aradus, Orthosia, Byblus, Berytus, Ptolemais, and Dora. Demetrius II retained Seleucia, Sidon, and Tyre. With Demetrius so contained, Trypho feels he needs to curtail Jonathan's power. The author of 1 Maccabees, however, implies that the reason for Trypho's treacherous attack is his ambition to be king in Antiochus's place and that Jonathan, as a loyal subject of Antiochus VI, would not allow this (v. 39). Beth-shan (i.e., Scythopolis) is strategically placed in the Jordan valley. It appears as if Trypho was coming through the Plain of Esdraelon from Ptolemais, as that is where Trypho takes Jonathan (12:45, 48). Trypho may have known that the western and southern approaches—Joppa, Adida, Beth-zur—were well fortified.

12:41-48. The author plays on the double meaning of "to meet" (ἀπαντάω *apantaō*), which can imply a meeting either in war or in friendship. When Jonathan comes to meet Trypho with a large, experienced force (v. 41), Trypho is forced to meet him in feigned friendship (vv. 42-45). Jonathan is used to being courted with gifts and promises (see chap. 10), so Trypho's actions

would seem legitimate. Jonathan is already a Friend and Kinsman of Antiochus VI (11:57-58), and Trypho cunningly lets him think he is on the same level as Trypho. Jonathan should have been suspicious of Trypho's offer to hand Ptolemais over to him, since the people of that city had been hostile to the Jews (5:15, 22). But Jonathan had once before been honorably received in Ptolemais by Alexander Balas, father of Antiochus VI (10:59-65), and even when threatened by Demetrius II there Jonathan had been able to emerge unscathed (11:22-28). One is not sure what the other strongholds mentioned were, but Trypho's offer of these cities and troops proved too tempting. When he enters the town, the people close the gates, seize him, and kill all the men with him. The reader of 1 Maccabees knows by now that one should never trust a Seleucid official (1:30; 7:16).

12:49-52. The two thousand troops left in Galilee, presumably in the Plain of Esdraelon through which one would travel from Ptolemais to Beth-shan and which separated Galilee from Samaria, successfully deter the forces Trypho has sent to capture them, and they return to Judea. Realizing that Jonathan has been captured, they conclude that he is dead along with his companions; they do not know that Trypho has captured him alive. As all Israel mourned at the deaths of Mattathias (2:70) and Judas (9:20), so now Jonathan is mourned. Great distress came upon

Israel after Judas's death (9:27); now fear comes to Israel at what might happen.

12:53. The nations surrounding Judea react to news that the Jews' leader and helper (cf. 9:30) is gone by trying to "destroy them." The message once again is driven home that one should be suspicious of one's neighbors and of the Seleucid Empire.

REFLECTIONS

Jonathan is a fascinating character. He was much more successful than Judas in gaining effective control of Judea and in widening its borders. He rose from being a rebel on the run to a high-ranking official in the Seleucid bureaucracy, and his army was feared by his enemies. Yet for some reason he got no respect. His name is omitted when Mattathias entrusts the fight to his sons (2:65-66), and he is not given a hymn of praise as Judas and Simon are (3:3-9; 14:4-15). Much of his activity in rallying and organizing the people is passed over, and yet the years he spent judging the people (9:73) must have been crucial for the success of the revolt. Jonathan remains a shadowy figure, even though he brings Israel into the arena of international politics. Perhaps there is too much of the diplomat about Jonathan and not enough of the dashing warrior for the author. Yet it is precisely that ability to negotiate a settlement that brings such success and prosperity to Israel. One of our great temptations is to romanticize war. But war destroys and maims and kills and embitters lives. War must be the last resort after all attempts to arrive at a peaceful solution have failed. Jonathan, in this light, might be someone to emulate.

Yet he also is a figure to warn us how not to behave. When he does use force, he uses it to compel submission (11:61), as an instrument of repression. Jonathan's ambition, his desire to wear purple and the gold buckle, to be on speaking terms with Rome and Sparta, to extend the territory of Judea beyond its borders, is what we must be wary of. That ambition is what brought Jonathan down. Trypho saw that Jonathan was greedy for power, and so he tempted him with the offer of more to make Jonathan let down his guard. Then he pounced and caught Jonathan in his trap. That longing for more has started so many wars and led to the downfall of so many people. "For the love of money is a root of all kinds of evil" (1 Tim 6:10 NRSV). To resist seeking more at the expense of others is a hard lesson to learn.

SIMON

1 MACCABEES 13:1-30, SIMON REPLACES JONATHAN

OVERVIEW

This section deals with the replacement of Jonathan by the last surviving Maccabean brother, Simon. Simon has been associated with Jonathan since the death of Judas (9:19, 32, 37, 62-67; 10:82; 11:59, 64-66; 12:33, 38), sharing in his exploits. Now he is to fulfill the prophecy of his father Mattathias (2:65) and become a father to Israel. But first Jonathan has to die, and so this section describes the treachery of Trypho, his murder of Jonathan, and Jonathan's burial.

1 Maccabees 13:1-11, Simon Takes Command

NAB

13 When Simon heard that Trypho was gathering a large army to invade and ravage the land of Judah, ² and saw that the people were in dread and terror, he went up to Jerusalem. There he assembled the people ³ and exhorted them in these words: "You know what I, my brothers, and my father's house have done for the laws and the sanctuary; what battles and disasters we have been through. ⁴ It was for the sake of these, for the sake of Israel, that all my brothers have perished, and I alone am left. ⁵ Far be it from me, then, to save my own life in any time of distress, for I am not better than my brothers. ⁶ Rather will I avenge my nation and the sanctuary, as well as your wives and children, for all the nations out of hatred have united to destroy us."

⁷ As the people heard these words, their spirit was rekindled. ⁸ They shouted in reply: "You are our leader in place of your brothers Judas and Jonathan. ⁹ Fight our battles, and we will do everything that you tell us." ¹⁰ So Simon mustered all the men able to fight, and quickly completing the walls of Jerusalem, fortified it on every side.

NRSV

13 Simon heard that Trypho had assembled a large army to invade the land of Judah and destroy it, ²and he saw that the people were trembling with fear. So he went up to Jerusalem, and gathering the people together ³he encouraged them, saying to them, "You yourselves know what great things my brothers and I and the house of my father have done for the laws and the sanctuary; you know also the wars and the difficulties that my brothers and I have seen. ⁴By reason of this all my brothers have perished for the sake of Israel, and I alone am left. ⁵And now, far be it from me to spare my life in any time of distress, for I am not better than my brothers. ⁶But I will avenge my nation and the sanctuary and your wives and children, for all the nations have gathered together out of hatred to destroy us."

⁷The spirit of the people was rekindled when they heard these words, ⁸and they answered in a loud voice, "You are our leader in place of Judas and your brother Jonathan. ⁹Fight our battles, and all that you say to us we will do." ¹⁰So he assembled all the warriors and hurried to complete the walls of Jerusalem, and he fortified it on

NAB

[11] He sent Jonathan, son of Absalom, to Joppa with a large force; Jonathan drove out the occupants and remained there.

NRSV

every side. [11]He sent Jonathan son of Absalom to Joppa, and with him a considerable army; he drove out its occupants and remained there.

COMMENTARY

13:1-3a. Ever since Bacchides had gone back to his own land (9:69), Jonathan had been able to secure Judea and fight outside the land. Now, as before (3:10, 13, 35-36; 5:1-2; 6:27; 7:8, 26; 9:1), forces are massed to invade Judea. As before, the people are afraid as they see all the promises of Seleucid kings broken. It is not clear whether Simon had been at Adida (12:38) all this time, or with the troops that Jonathan had sent back (12:56). Frequently Jonathan and Simon had divided the operations between them (11:65; 12:32-33), and this had strategically been an important division of labor. The author emphasizes, as earlier with Judas (3:3) and Jonathan (9:73), that the people are with Simon.

13:3b-6. Simon exhorts the people by recalling the past and making that the basis for his future actions, as Mattathias had recalled the deeds of the ancestors in times of distress (2:51-64; cf. the speeches of Mattathias [2:19-22] and Judas [3:58-60]). Simon at this point thinks his brother Jonathan is dead. The reasoning behind v. 5 seems to assume the deuteronomic theory

that death is punishment for sin. But if such good men as his father and brother died, then it must not have been because of their sin; times of distress had come upon Israel, and no one could be good enough to escape death.

13:7-11. Simon's speech is effective, and he is unanimously chosen leader in place of Jonathan. Simon knows that Trypho will attack, and so he completes the fortification of Jerusalem that Jonathan had begun (12:35-37). He already has a garrison in Joppa (12:33-34) but now decides to make sure that no uprising against it will take place, and the inhabitants are summarily thrown out of their city. As Joppa lay on the coast to the west of Adida (12:38) and the Beth-horon ascent (3:16), Simon was strengthening the western approach to Judea. Jonathan son of Absalom, who leads the troops to Joppa, is the brother of Mattathias, who stood by Jonathan when he was caught by an ambush (11:70). This may be the same Absalom who served as one of the ambassadors sent earlier to negotiate peaceful terms with Lysias (2 Macc 11:17).

1 Maccabees 13:12-24, Trypho's Invasion

NAB

[12] Then Trypho moved from Ptolemais with a large army to invade the land of Judah, bringing Jonathan with him as prisoner. [13] But Simon pitched his camp at Adida, facing the plain. [14] When Trypho learned that Simon had succeeded his brother Jonathan, and that he intended to fight him, he sent envoys to him with this message: [15] "We have detained your brother Jonathan on account of the money that he owed the royal treasury in connection with the offices that he held. [16] Therefore, if you send us a hundred

NRSV

[12]Then Trypho left Ptolemais with a large army to invade the land of Judah, and Jonathan was with him under guard. [13]Simon encamped in Adida, facing the plain. [14]Trypho learned that Simon had risen up in place of his brother Jonathan, and that he was about to join battle with him, so he sent envoys to him and said, [15]"It is for the money that your brother Jonathan owed the royal treasury, in connection with the offices he held, that we are detaining him. [16]Send now one hundred talents of silver and two of his sons

NAB

talents of silver, and two of his sons as hostages to guarantee that when he is set free he will not revolt against us, we will release him."

17 Although Simon knew that they were speaking deceitfully to him, he gave orders to get the money and the boys, for fear of provoking much hostility among the people, who might say 18 that Jonathan perished because Simon would not send Trypho the money and the boys. 19 So he sent the boys and the hundred talents; but Trypho broke his promise and would not let Jonathan go. 20 Next he began to invade and ravage the country. His troops went around by the road that leads to Adora, but Simon and his army moved along opposite him everywhere he went. 21 The men in the citadel sent messengers to Trypho, urging him to come to them by way of the desert, and to send them provisions. 22 Although Trypho got all his cavalry ready to go, there was a heavy fall of snow that night, and he could not go. So he left for Gilead. 23 When he was approaching Baskama, he had Jonathan killed and buried there. 24 Then Trypho returned to his own country.

NRSV

as hostages, so that when released he will not revolt against us, and we will release him."

17Simon knew that they were speaking deceitfully to him, but he sent to get the money and the sons, so that he would not arouse great hostility among the people, who might say, 18"It was because Simon[a] did not send him the money and the sons, that Jonathan[b] perished." 19So he sent the sons and the hundred talents, but Trypho[b] broke his word and did not release Jonathan.

20After this Trypho came to invade the country and destroy it, and he circled around by the way to Adora. But Simon and his army kept marching along opposite him to every place he went. 21Now the men in the citadel kept sending envoys to Trypho urging him to come to them by way of the wilderness and to send them food. 22So Trypho got all his cavalry ready to go, but that night a very heavy snow fell, and he did not go because of the snow. He marched off and went into the land of Gilead. 23When he approached Baskama, he killed Jonathan, and he was buried there. 24Then Trypho turned and went back to his own land.

[a] Gk *I*   [b] Gk *he*

COMMENTARY

This section is bounded by Trypho's entering (v. 12) and leaving the land (v. 24). For the first time we learn that Jonathan is still alive, and the drama arises as to what his fate will be.

13:12-13. Rather than approach Judea from the north through the Plain of Esdraelon, Trypho chooses to take the coastal route but does not first attempt to take Joppa. Jonathan is not dead but is being held prisoner by Trypho. Simon's army encamps at Adida.

13:14-16. With that force at Joppa behind him and Simon's army in front, Trypho decides to try deceit, a typical Seleucid trick, according to the author (e.g., 1:30; 7:10, 27). Trypho claims that Jonathan owes money, perhaps taxes that the high priest should have collected or a fee for being granted the high priesthood (cf. 2 Macc 4:7, 24).

Trypho also asks for two of Jonathan's sons as hostages. Hostage taking was a typical tactic: Antiochus IV (1:10; 8:7) had been a hostage in Rome, and Bacchides (9:53) and Jonathan (11:62) had taken hostages also. This is the first time we know that Jonathan was married.

13:17-19. The author of 1 Maccabees states that Simon recognizes that Trypho's request is a ploy. Yet he consents to pay lest, according to the author, he be seen as conniving at Jonathan's death and so gaining the leadership of Israel. The author does not mention that the sons of Jonathan might have been a potential source of opposition to Simon as leader and that, in agreeing to Trypho's demands, Simon might not have been too unhappy to have them out of the way. We do not know how old the two boys were, nor are we told what subsequently happened to them. Perhaps Trypho killed them when he killed Jonathan (v. 23). As expected, Trypho breaks his word (v. 19), just as Bacchides (7:18) and Demetrius II had done before him (11:53).

13:20-24. Trypho now attempts to invade the land. Simon keeps his army between the coastal plain and the hill country, and so forces Trypho to go south through Idumea to try a southern assault, as Lysias had done (4:29; 6:31). Adora was about five miles southwest of Hebron. Since to get to Jerusalem from there Trypho would have had to pass Beth-zur (where Simon had stationed a garrison [11:65-66]), the men of the citadel,

isolated and in need of provisions (12:36), may have offered to act as guides for Trypho, as they had for Gorgias and his cavalry (4:2). The wilderness referred to may be the wilderness of Tekoa (9:32). When the weather prevents Trypho's surprise attack, he moves across the Jordan to Gilead, thus making a circular tour of the land of Judea. The snowfall suggests winter, so, given the date in 13:41, this must have taken place during the winter of 143/42 BCE. The location of Baskama (v. 23) is unknown. Trypho's invasion has been frustrated, and he, like Bacchides (9:69), leaves Judea, which would now be at peace under Simon as it had been previously under Jonathan (9:73).

1 Maccabees 13:25-30, Jonathan's Tomb

NAB

25 Simon sent for the remains of his brother Jonathan, and buried him in Modein, the city of his fathers. 26 All Israel bewailed him with solemn lamentation, mourning over him for many days. 27 Then Simon erected over the tomb of his father and his brothers a monument of stones, polished front and back, and raised high enough to be seen at a distance. 28 He set up seven pyramids facing one another for his father and his mother and his four brothers. 29 For the pyramids he devised a setting of big columns, on which he carved suits of armor as a perpetual memorial, and next to the armor he placed carved ships, which could be seen by all who sailed the sea. 30 This tomb which he built at Modein is there to the present day.

NRSV

25Simon sent and took the bones of his brother Jonathan, and buried him in Modein, the city of his ancestors. 26All Israel bewailed him with great lamentation, and mourned for him many days. 27And Simon built a monument over the tomb of his father and his brothers; he made it high so that it might be seen, with polished stone at the front and back. 28He also erected seven pyramids, opposite one another, for his father and mother and four brothers. 29For the pyramids[a] he devised an elaborate setting, erecting about them great columns, and on the columns he put suits of armor for a permanent memorial, and beside the suits of armor he carved ships, so that they could be seen by all who sail the sea. 30This is the tomb that he built in Modein; it remains to this day.

[a] Gk *For these*

COMMENTARY

Simon buries Jonathan, and "all Israel" mourned his death (v. 26). The monument Simon erected over the family tomb was large, showy, and presumably quite expensive. Eusebius of Caesarea, in his *Onomasticon* (under the entry for Modein) of the early fourth century CE, wrote that it was still standing in his time. It has not survived, and its description in 1 Maccabees is not detailed enough so that one can reconstruct it.

On a platform of hewn stones, Simon placed a row of seven pyramids ("alongside" [κατέναντι *katenanti*], rather than "opposite" one another as in the NRSV, v. 28)—one each for his parents and four brothers and possibly one for himself; or perhaps seven is seen as a particularly potent number. Surrounding the pyramids were huge columns bearing trophies of arms and carved ships. Pyramids are usually associated with Egypt, but they were found in Italy and later in Jerusalem. Trophies of suits of armor were common among the Greeks, and the Romans adopted the custom by the mid-second century BCE. In Jerusalem, the so-called tomb of Jason has graffiti seemingly representing a naval battle. No one is sure why the non-seafaring Jews would put carved ships on a monument for the Maccabees. Was it part of regular decorative practice? Or does it suggest that the control of the seaport Joppa now gave the Jews access to the sea? What the monument clearly attests is the pretension of the Hasmoneans to display their wealth and power.

1 MACCABEES 13:31–14:3, JUDEA GAINS INDEPENDENCE

1 Maccabees 13:31-42, The Removal of Tribute

NAB

31 Trypho dealt treacherously with the young King Antiochus. He killed him 32 and assumed the kingship in his place, putting on the crown of Asia. Thus he brought much evil on the land. 33 Simon, on his part, built up the strongholds of Judea, strengthening their fortifications with high towers, thick walls, and gates with bars, and he stored up provisions in the fortresses. 34 Simon also sent chosen men to King Demetrius with the request that he grant the land a release from taxation, for all that Trypho did was to plunder the land. 35 In reply, King Demetrius sent him the following letter:

36 "King Demetrius sends greetings to Simon the high priest, the friend of kings, and to the elders and the Jewish people. 37 We have received the gold crown and the palm branch that you sent. We are willing to be on most peaceful terms with you and to write to our official to grant you release from tribute. 38 Whatever we have guaranteed to you remains in force, and the strongholds that you have built shall remain yours. 39 We remit any oversights and defaults incurred up to now, as well as the crown tax that you owe. Any other tax that may have been collected in Jerusalem shall no longer be collected there. 40 If any of you are qualified for enrollment in our service, let them be enrolled. Let there be peace between us."

41 Thus in the year one hundred and seventy, the yoke of the Gentiles was removed from Israel,

NRSV

31 Trypho dealt treacherously with the young King Antiochus; he killed him 32and became king in his place, putting on the crown of Asia; and he brought great calamity on the land. 33But Simon built up the strongholds of Judea and walled them all around, with high towers and great walls and gates and bolts, and he stored food in the strongholds. 34Simon also chose emissaries and sent them to King Demetrius with a request to grant relief to the country, for all that Trypho did was to plunder. 35King Demetrius sent him a favorable reply to this request, and wrote him a letter as follows, 36"King Demetrius to Simon, the high priest and friend of kings, and to the elders and nation of the Jews, greetings. 37We have received the gold crown and the palm branch that you[a] sent, and we are ready to make a general peace with you and to write to our officials to grant you release from tribute. 38All the grants that we have made to you remain valid, and let the strongholds that you have built be your possession. 39We pardon any errors and offenses committed to this day, and cancel the crown tax that you owe; and whatever other tax has been collected in Jerusalem shall be collected no longer. 40And if any of you are qualified to be enrolled in our bodyguard,[b] let them be enrolled, and let there be peace between us."

41In the one hundred seventieth year[c] the yoke of the Gentiles was removed from Israel, 42and

[a] The word *you* in verses 37-40 is plural   [b] Or *court*   [c] 142 B.C.

⁴² and the people began to write in their records and contracts, "In the first year of Simon, high priest, governor, and leader of the Jews."

the people began to write in their documents and contracts, "In the first year of Simon the great high priest and commander and leader of the Jews."

COMMENTARY

13:31-32. Exactly when Trypho came to the throne and had Antiochus VI murdered is a vexed question. The last coins of Antiochus are dated 142/41, which seems to be closest to the time line of 1 Maccabees (13:41 refers to 170 Sel Bab, or 142–141 BCE). Other ancient authorities, however, date Antiochus's murder to 139 BCE.[124] Trypho assumed the title Autokrator, and dated his coins not by the Seleucid era but by his own regnal years. Since Trypho was not descended from the Seleucids, he wanted to show his break with Seleucid tradition. His accession to the throne increased the chaos in the Seleucid realm.[125] "Asia" refers to the Seleucid Empire (8:6; 12:39).

13:33-38. Simon kept increasing the defenses of Judea begun under Jonathan and decided to reconcile with Demetrius II. However, there is no explicit request for reconciliation, and the wording of these verses implies that Simon has been on Demetrius's side all along and is asking for relief (cf. 7:6-7). The term for "relief" (ἄφεμα *aphema*) covers both tax relief (v. 37) and pardon (v. 39). The appended letter from Demetrius, however, speaks of Simon's having sent a gold crown and a palm branch to Demetrius (vv. 36-37), a clear recognition of kingship (cf. 2 Macc 14:4), as well as a peace offering, but the author of 1 Maccabees does not portray Simon as asking for peace with Demetrius II.

As before (11:23-37), Demetrius II shows a willingness to use tax concessions to win friends. He was, in fact, not in control of the southern part of his empire, and so could afford to be generous.

The greeting (v. 36) is different from that of Demetrius's previous letter (11:30), mentioning

"the priests" and ranking Simon as a "friend of kings" (cf. 11:20; 11:27, 54).

Simon had formally recognized Demetrius II as king, as Jonathan had done (11:24). This is the first indication that Simon had also succeeded Jonathan as high priest. There is no mention here of Demetrius's confirming Simon as high priest, except in the greeting of the letter. Demetrius's previous concessions (11:34-36) had been canceled (11:53). Although Demetrius II in fact would not have been able to destroy the strongholds Simon had built (v. 38), given that he was still at war with Trypho, this concession is a legal victory for Simon.

13:39. The verb translated "pardon" (ἀφίημι *aphiēmi*) is the same root as the words "release from tribute" in v. 37. Demetrius neatly glosses over Simon's and Jonathan's support of Antiochus VI. One is not sure whether the taxes mentioned here are more general than the ones remitted earlier (10:34; 11:35) or whether Jerusalem served as the place where all the taxes in Judea were collected.

13:40. Demetrius's request for Jews to join his bodyguard is not surprising. Jews are well-known for their military prowess, and Demetrius I had recruited Jewish soldiers for his army and allowed them to follow their own laws (10:36-37). In addition, troops sent by Jonathan had been instrumental in saving Demetrius II earlier (11:45-51).

13:41-42. Scholars debate exactly when the events in these verses took place, some placing them before 170 Sel Bab (i.e., before June 142), while others place it later. Clearly, the people (and the author) view Demetrius's concessions as the equivalent of granting them independence. The phrase "the yoke of the Gentiles" is a familiar image of the punishment that Israel would suffer if it disobeyed God's laws (Deut 28:48; Lam

124. Livy says that Antiochus VI was murdered by surgeons in league with Trypho (Summary of Book 54).
125. See Diodorus Siculus 33:28.

1:14). The prophets had foretold that God would remove the yoke of their oppressors (Isa 9:4; 10:27; 14:25; Jer 30:8; Ezek 34:27). Within 1 Maccabees, the yoke is the oppression of the Greeks (i.e., the Seleucids [8:18]), begun when the renegades yoked themselves to the Gentiles (1:15). Simon, who had already been named a commander by Antiochus VI (11:59) and leader by the people (13:7), is now officially recognized as high priest. Although the narrative refers to "the first year of Simon," the Seleucid dating system continues to be used (13:51; 14:1, 27; 16:14).

1 Maccabees 13:43-53, Further Acquisitions by Simon

NAB

43 In those days Simon besieged Gazara and surrounded it with troops. He made a siege machine, pushed it up against the city, and attacked and captured one of the towers. 44 The men who had been on the siege machine jumped down into the city and caused a great tumult there. 45 The men of the city, joined by their wives and children, went up on the wall, with their garments rent, and cried out in loud voices, begging Simon to grant them peace. 46 "Do not treat us according to our evil deeds," they said, "but according to your mercy."

47 So Simon came to terms with them and did not destroy them. He made them leave the city, however, and he purified the houses in which there were idols. Then he entered the city with hymns and songs of praise. 48 After removing from it everything that was impure, he settled there men who observed the law. He improved its fortifications and built himself a residence.

49 The men in the citadel in Jerusalem were prevented from going out into the country and back for the purchase of food; they suffered greatly from hunger, and many of them died of starvation. 50 They finally cried out to Simon for peace, and he gave them peace. He expelled them from the citadel and cleansed it of impurities. 51 On the twenty-third day of the second month, in the year one hundred and seventy-one, the Jews entered the citadel with shouts of jubilation, waving of palm branches, the music of harps and cymbals and lyres, and the singing of hymns and canticles, because a great enemy of Israel had been destroyed. 52 Simon decreed that this day should be celebrated every year with rejoicing. He also strengthened the fortifications of the temple hill alongside the citadel, and he and his companions

NRSV

43 In those days Simon[a] encamped against Gazara[b] and surrounded it with troops. He made a siege engine, brought it up to the city, and battered and captured one tower. 44 The men in the siege engine leaped out into the city, and a great tumult arose in the city. 45 The men in the city, with their wives and children, went up on the wall with their clothes torn, and they cried out with a loud voice, asking Simon to make peace with them; 46 they said, "Do not treat us according to our wicked acts but according to your mercy." 47 So Simon reached an agreement with them and stopped fighting against them. But he expelled them from the city and cleansed the houses in which the idols were located, and then entered it with hymns and praise. 48 He removed all uncleanness from it, and settled in it those who observed the law. He also strengthened its fortifications and built in it a house for himself.

49 Those who were in the citadel at Jerusalem were prevented from going in and out to buy and sell in the country. So they were very hungry, and many of them perished from famine. 50 Then they cried to Simon to make peace with them, and he did so. But he expelled them from there and cleansed the citadel from its pollutions. 51 On the twenty-third day of the second month, in the one hundred seventy-first year,[c] the Jews[d] entered it with praise and palm branches, and with harps and cymbals and stringed instruments, and with hymns and songs, because a great enemy had been crushed and removed from Israel. 52 Simon[e] decreed that every year they should celebrate this day with rejoicing. He strengthened the fortifications of the temple hill alongside the citadel, and

a Gk he b Cn: Gk Gaza c 141 B.C. d Gk they
e Gk He

NAB	NRSV
dwelt there. ⁵³ Seeing that his son John was now a grown man, Simon made him commander of all his soldiers, with his residence in Gazara.	he and his men lived there. ⁵³Simon saw that his son John had reached manhood, and so he made him commander of all the forces; and he lived at Gazara.

COMMENTARY

Simon continues the policy of extending his control. Bacchides had fortified Beth-zur, Gazara, and the citadel (9:52). With Beth-zur already taken (11:65-66), Simon now turns his attention to the two others.

13:43-48. Gazara (Gezer), an important site on the road from Jerusalem to Joppa, had a Seleucid garrison (4:15; 9:52) and was strategically situated on a hill surveying the coastal plain. Although Judas had already constructed "siege engines" (μηχανή *mēchanē*, 6:20), the weapon now used by Simon is an advanced Hellenistic siege device (ἐλεόπολις *heleopolis*). As earlier at Beth-zur (11:65-66), Simon allows the inhabitants to live while turning them into war refugees (v. 47). Simon does not engage in the practice of the ban as Judas had done (e.g., 5:28, 35) but contents himself with cleansing the city and repopulating it with devout Jews (v. 47), just as Josiah had cleansed the land and the Temple (2 Chr 34:3-8). Gazara had a good water supply and fertile land, so Simon was able to reward his supporters, as well as gain a base for operations in the coastal plain. Archaeologists have uncovered an elaborate system of cisterns in Gazara, suggested to be Jewish ritual bathing "pools" (מקואות *miqwā'ôt*), but the suggestion is far from certain. A Greek inscription found at Gazara reads: "Says Pampras: may fire pursue Simon's palace." Although the date and exact reference of the inscription are unsure, if dated to Simon's time, this curse may have been written by one of Simon's prisoners of war (cf. 14:7).

13:49-53. The citadel at Jerusalem, originally built by Antiochus VI in 169/68 (1:33), had housed a Seleucid garrison and served as a haven for Jews opposed to the Maccabees. Those trapped there, who had been under siege since Jonathan's time (almost two years, 143 to 141 BCE; see 12:36), now sue for peace. Almost exactly the same words are used to describe the outcome of this siege as the one at Gazara (cf. vv. 45-48 with v. 50), but the celebration is described more fully (v. 51). The author also parallels the capture of the citadel by Simon to the capture of the sanctuary by Judas (cf. 4:41-61; cf. also 4:36 with 13:51), and both events are to be celebrated yearly (v. 52). With the threat of foreign troops gone, the southern fortifications of the Temple can be repaired, and Jewish troops can occupy the citadel. We learn that Simon has a son who (literally) was a man (v. 53), i.e., not simply come of age, but someone who had reached warrior status (cf. 5:63). While Simon lives in Jerusalem, his son, commander of the army, lives at Gazara (Gezer), watching the coastal plain and guarding the western entrance to Judea.

REFLECTIONS

The author captures the mood of the followers of Simon at the recapture of the citadel. Here is proof positive that the yoke of the Gentiles had been removed, that Israel had gained its independence. This was a time to remember and to celebrate, just as the Fourth of July is a day for all U.S. citizens to rejoice in the gaining of their independence. Yet independence brings with it consequences for others. The joy of the Israelites contrasts starkly with what must have been the despair of those evicted from their homes in Gazara and their forced relocation. The cleansing of Beth-zur, Gazara, and the citadel and their repopulation by those who observed the law echo the injunctions to Joshua to clear the promised land of its former inhabitants and the call of Ezekiel to cleanse the land of uncleanness.

Should injunctions for ethnic cleansing be followed? Humans in conflict situations feel a need to draw sharp boundaries between themselves and other groups. We are the pure ones; we must have no part with you. In times of insecurity, communities pull the wagons into a circle to defend their own group, however defined, against all others. The only way to stop this only too human reaction is to somehow build each group's sense of security and well-being so that no one will react defensively but all will realize that problems can be worked out through mediation rather than by recourse to violence. Humans must learn to cooperate and respect each other's cultural and religious differences. Otherwise, there will be no end to conflict. Such attempts at reconciliation will be extremely difficult, as often atrocities are committed by both sides. To forgive is hard to accomplish when one cannot forget the past. Perhaps one way to do so is to think of the future, of the children who will come after us. Do we want them to continue the feuding? Or do we want them to learn to live in peace?

1 Maccabees 14:1-3, The Capture of Demetrius

NAB

14 In the year one hundred and seventy-two, King Demetrius assembled his army and marched into Media to obtain help so that he could fight Trypho. [2] When Arsaces, king of Persia and Media, heard that Demetrius had invaded his territory, he sent one of his generals to take him alive. [3] The general went forth and defeated the army of Demetrius; he captured him and brought him to Arsaces, who put him in prison.

NRSV

14 In the one hundred seventy-second year[a] King Demetrius assembled his forces and marched into Media to obtain help, so that he could make war against Trypho. [2] When King Arsaces of Persia and Media heard that Demetrius had invaded his territory, he sent one of his generals to take him alive. [3] The general[b] went and defeated the army of Demetrius, and seized him and took him to Arsaces, who put him under guard.

[a] 140 B.C.   [b] Gk *He*

COMMENTARY

The situation in the Seleucid Empire was at a stalemate, with Demetrius II, Trypho, and Simon each controlling his own area. Trypho had sought Roman support, but the Romans, while accepting his gifts, had them inscribed with the name of Antiochus VI, whom Trypho had murdered.[126] According to the author of 1 Maccabees, Demetrius tries to break the deadlock by going to Mesopotamia, which had remained loyal, to secure help. Demetrius's action was more likely an attempt to push back the Parthian forces that had invaded Seleucid territory (according to cuneiform tablets, Mithradates I [Arsaces] ruled in Babylon and Seleucia on the Tigris in July 141 and in Uruk by October 141). Demetrius left in autumn 141/40 BCE (172, according to the Seleucid Macedonian calendar), and was at first successful, since Persis, Elymais, and Bactria helped his effort. However, in Media he was defeated and captured in 140/39 BCE. His bold hope not only to help the eastern provinces but also to create an army strong enough to come back and defeat Trypho failed. Mithradates treated Demetrius honorably, settling him in Hyrcania and marrying him to one of his daughters.[127]

126. Diodorus Siculus 33:28a.

127. See Diodorus Siculus 33.28; 34.15; Appian *Syriaca* 67-68; Justin *Epitome* 36.1.2-6; 38.9.2-3.

1 MACCABEES 14:4-49, THE PRAISE OF SIMON

OVERVIEW

The rest of chapter 14 is given over to the praise of Simon. First comes a eulogy (vv. 4-15), comparable to that at the beginning of Judas's rule (3:3-9), followed by praise of Simon by Rome and the Spartans (vv. 16-24), and finally the decree of the people in honor of Simon (vv. 25-49).

1 Maccabees 14:4-15, Hymn of Praise

NAB

4 The land was at rest all the days of Simon,
   who sought the good of his nation.
His people were delighted with his power
   and his magnificence throughout his reign.
5 As his crowning glory he captured the port of Joppa
   and made it a gateway to the isles of the sea.
6 He enlarged the borders of his nation
   and gained control of the country.
7 He took many enemies prisoners of war
   and made himself master of Gazara, Beth-zur, and the citadel.

He cleansed the citadel of its impurities;
   there was no one to withstand him.
8 The people cultivated their land in peace;
   the land yielded its produce
   and the trees of the field their fruit.
9 Old men sat in the squares,
   all talking about the good times,
   while the young men wore the glorious apparel of war.
10 He supplied the cities with food
   and equipped them with means of defense,
   till his glorious name reached the ends of the earth.
11 He brought peace to the land,
   and Israel was filled with happiness.
12 Every man sat under his vine and his fig tree,
   with no one to disturb him.
13 No one was left to attack them in their land;
   the kings in those days were crushed.
14 He strengthened all the lowly among his people
   and was zealous for the law;
   he suppressed all the lawless and the wicked.

NRSV

4 The land[a] had rest all the days of Simon.
   He sought the good of his nation;
his rule was pleasing to them,
   as was the honor shown him, all his days.
5 To crown all his honors he took Joppa for a harbor,
   and opened a way to the isles of the sea.
6 He extended the borders of his nation,
   and gained full control of the country.
7 He gathered a host of captives;
   he ruled over Gazara and Beth-zur and the citadel,
and he removed its uncleanness from it;
   and there was none to oppose him.
8 They tilled their land in peace;
   the ground gave its increase,
   and the trees of the plains their fruit.
9 Old men sat in the streets;
   they all talked together of good things,
   and the youths put on splendid military attire.
10 He supplied the towns with food,
   and furnished them with the means of defense,
   until his renown spread to the ends of the earth.
11 He established peace in the land,
   and Israel rejoiced with great joy.
12 All the people sat under their own vines and fig trees,
   and there was none to make them afraid.
13 No one was left in the land to fight them,
   and the kings were crushed in those days.

a Other ancient authorities add of Judah

NAB	NRSV
15 He made the temple splendid and enriched its equipment.	14 He gave help to all the humble among his people; he sought out the law, and did away with all the renegades and outlaws. 15 He made the sanctuary glorious, and added to the vessels of the sanctuary.

COMMENTARY

The rule of Simon is described idyllistically and abounds in allusions to Hebrew Scriptures.

14:4. Like Judas (7:50) and Jonathan (9:57), Simon provides rest to the land, just as the judges had (Judg 3:11, 30; 5:31). Whereas those in the citadel had sought evil against the people (6:18), Simon seeks the good of the nation.

14:5-7. Simon's wartime exploits are celebrated, starting with his capture of Joppa during Jonathan's reign (12:33). The phrase "to crown all his honors he took Joppa for a harbor," literally "with all his glory," should be understood from the context as referring to Simon's troops (cf. Isa. 8:7, where the king of Assyria and all his glory are to come against Israel). Promises of enlarged territory in response to Torah obedience (v. 6) are found in Exodus (34:24) and Deuteronomy (19:8-9). Verse 7 highlights Simon's victories over the three main fortresses (11:65-66; 13:43-50) as well as the campaigns in which he must have gathered many captives. His Torah faithfulness is again stressed (v. 7*b*; cf. 11:66; 13:48, 50), and so he finds that no one resists him (cf. Deut 7:17-26; 11:25; Josh 1:5).

14:8-15. Once Simon's exploits in war have been praised, affairs in Judea are described in idyllic terms; these verses echo other descriptions of peace in the OT. The elderly can sit in the streets, reminiscing (v. 9; cf. Zech 8:4-5). The people are free to farm their land without fear of enemy attack or looting, and without having to pay oppressive taxes to outsiders (v. 8; 13:41-42), and the land's productivity flourishes (vv. 8, 10; Lev 26:3-5; Zech 8:12-13; cf. Ezek 34:25-31). The mourning and lamentation, such as followed Antiochus IV's sacking of Jerusalem (1:25-28), where the elders groaned and the young men became faint, are reversed. Just as Judas's renown went to the ends of the earth (3:9), so too does Simon's as his actions of defense and provisioning (13:33) are recalled. Just as Solomon brought safety to the land (1 Kgs 4:25), so too does Simon (v. 11). As the prophets Micah (4:4) and Zechariah (3:10) had foreseen, people sit under their own vines and fig trees (v. 12). Simon is the perfect picture of a just ruler (v. 14*a*), as envisioned by Ps 72:4 and Isa 11:3-4. Simon's destruction of the ungodly (v. 14*b*) again mirrors Judas (3:8). In particular, Simon adds to the work of Judas by restoring the sanctuary (4:49), as he wipes out the wrongs done against it under Antiochus IV, who had dishonored the Temple and taken away its glorious vessels (2:8-13).

1 Maccabees 14:16-24, Diplomacy with Rome and Sparta

NAB	NRSV
16 When people heard in Rome and even in Sparta that Jonathan had died, they were deeply grieved. 17 But when the Romans heard that his brother Simon had been made high priest in his place and was master of the country and the cities, 18 they	16It was heard in Rome, and as far away as Sparta, that Jonathan had died, and they were deeply grieved. 17When they heard that his brother Simon had become high priest in his stead, and that he was ruling over the country

NAB

sent him inscribed tablets of bronze to renew with him the friendship and alliance that they had established with his brothers Judas and Jonathan. ¹⁹ These were read before the assembly in Jerusalem.

²⁰ This is a copy of the letter that the Spartans sent: "The rulers and the citizens of Sparta send greetings to Simon the high priest, the elders, the priests, and the rest of the Jewish people, our brothers. ²¹ The envoys you sent to our people have informed us of your glory and fame, and we were happy that they came. ²² In accordance with what they said we have recorded the following in the public decrees: Since Numenius, son of Antiochus, and Antipater, son of Jason, envoys of the Jews, have come to us to renew their friendship with us, ²³ the people have voted to receive the men with honor, and to deposit a copy of their words in the public archives, so that the people of Sparta may have a record of them. A copy of this decree has been made for Simon the high priest."

²⁴ After this, Simon sent Numenius to Rome with a great gold shield weighing a thousand minas, to confirm the alliance with the Romans.

NRSV

and the towns in it, ¹⁸they wrote to him on bronze tablets to renew with him the friendship and alliance that they had established with his brothers Judas and Jonathan. ¹⁹And these were read before the assembly in Jerusalem.

20This is a copy of the letter that the Spartans sent:

"The rulers and the city of the Spartans to the high priest Simon and to the elders and the priests and the rest of the Jewish people, our brothers, greetings. ²¹The envoys who were sent to our people have told us about your glory and honor, and we rejoiced at their coming. ²²We have recorded what they said in our public decrees, as follows, 'Numenius son of Antiochus and Antipater son of Jason, envoys of the Jews, have come to us to renew their friendship with us. ²³It has pleased our people to receive these men with honor and to put a copy of their words in the public archives, so that the people of the Spartans may have a record of them. And they have sent a copy of this to the high priest Simon.'"

24After this Simon sent Numenius to Rome with a large gold shield weighing one thousand minas, to confirm the alliance with the Romans.ᵃ

ᵃ Gk *them*

COMMENTARY

14:16-19. The authenticity, chronology, and meaning of the events in these verses pose great difficulty. The author's Judeocentrism is evident in his claim that Rome and Sparta were deeply grieved at Jonathan's death. It is unlikely, however, that the Romans would take the initiative to write to a client state, such as Judea, without the formality of an embassy; the text of a letter from the Romans is not given, although they are said to have renewed their alliance with Judea (14:18). The reference to bronze tablets recalls those sent in Judas's time (8:22). As a result, Simon sends an ambassador to Rome with a gift to confirm the alliance (14:24), a Roman answer is received (15:15-21), and Demetrius II is said to confirm Simon in the high priesthood, because the Romans had received the envoys of Simon with honor (14:38-40). It

seems more likely that Simon did follow in the steps of Judas and Jonathan in seeking an alliance with Rome; the letter of 15:15-21 is probably the result of that embassy. Demetrius has already recognized Simon as high priest in an earlier letter written sometime in 142 BCE (13:36-40). Simon would not have had time to send an embassy to Rome after Jonathan's death (probably in the winter of 143/142 BCE, when no sailing could take place) and receive a reply before Demetrius wrote that letter preserved in 13:36-40. Perhaps Demetrius only needed to know that Simon had sent ambassadors to Rome.

14:20-23. As at 12:5, 16-17, the Spartan correspondence is linked with an embassy to Rome. "Rulers" (ἄρχοντες *archontes*) is a very generic title and does not suggest which specific officials are in view. Jonathan's letter to the Spartans had mentioned a council of the Jews in its address (12:6), but it is not mentioned here. The ambassadors (v. 22) are the same as those sent by Jonathan (12:16). Verses 22-23 seem to indicate that this letter was in response to an embassy sent by Simon.

14:24. As noted above, this embassy of Numenius was probably prior to the renewal of friendship by both Romans and Spartans. A mina weighs 431 grams, so the shield would have weighed 431 kilograms, approximately 862 pounds, a significant gift.

1 Maccabees 14:25-49, "The Great Assembly"

NAB

25 When the people heard of these things, they said, "How can we thank Simon and his sons? 26 He and his brothers and his father's house have stood firm and repulsed Israel's enemies. They have thus preserved its liberty." So they made an inscription on bronze tablets, which they affixed to pillars on Mount Zion. 27 The following is a copy of the inscription:

"On the eighteenth day of Elul, in the year one hundred and seventy-two, that is, the third year under Simon the high priest in Asaramel, 28 in a great assembly of priests, people, rulers of the nation, and elders of the country, the following proclamation was made:

29 " 'Since there have often been wars in our country, Simon, son of the priest Mattathias, descendant of Joarib, and his brothers have put themselves in danger and resisted the enemies of their nation, so that their sanctuary and law might be maintained, and they have thus brought great glory to their nation. 30 After Jonathan had rallied his nation and become their high priest, he was gathered to his kinsmen. 31 When the enemies of the Jews sought to invade and devastate their country and to lay hands on their temple, 32 Simon rose up and fought for his nation, spending large sums of his own money to equip the men of his nation's armed forces and giving them their pay. 33 He fortified the cities of Judea, especially the frontier city of Beth-zur, where he stationed a garrison of Jewish soldiers, and where previously the enemy's arms had been stored. 34 He also fortified Joppa by the sea and Gazara on the border of Azotus, a place previously occupied by the enemy; these cities he resettled with Jews, and furnished them with all that was necessary for their restoration. 35 When the Jewish people saw Simon's loyalty and the glory

NRSV

25When the people heard these things they said, "How shall we thank Simon and his sons? 26For he and his brothers and the house of his father have stood firm; they have fought and repulsed Israel's enemies and established its freedom." 27So they made a record on bronze tablets and put it on pillars on Mount Zion.

This is a copy of what they wrote: "On the eighteenth day of Elul, in the one hundred seventy-second year,[a] which is the third year of the great high priest Simon, 28in Asaramel,[b] in the great assembly of the priests and the people and the rulers of the nation and the elders of the country, the following was proclaimed to us:

29"Since wars often occurred in the country, Simon son of Mattathias, a priest of the sons[c] of Joarib, and his brothers, exposed themselves to danger and resisted the enemies of their nation, in order that their sanctuary and the law might be preserved; and they brought great glory to their nation. 30Jonathan rallied the[d] nation, became their high priest, and was gathered to his people. 31When their enemies decided to invade their country and lay hands on their sanctuary, 32then Simon rose up and fought for his nation. He spent great sums of his own money; he armed the soldiers of his nation and paid them wages. 33He fortified the towns of Judea, and Beth-zur on the borders of Judea, where formerly the arms of the enemy had been stored, and he placed there a garrison of Jews. 34He also fortified Joppa, which is by the sea, and Gazara, which is on the borders of Azotus, where the enemy formerly lived. He settled Jews there, and provided in those towns[e] whatever was necessary for their restoration.

a 140 B.C.   *b* This word resembles the Hebrew words for *the court of the people of God* or *the prince of the people of God*
c Meaning of Gk uncertain   *d* Gk *their*   *e* Gk *them*

he planned to bring to his nation, they made him their leader and high priest because of all he had accomplished and the loyalty and justice he had shown his nation. In every way he sought to exalt his people.

36 " 'In his time and under his guidance they succeeded in driving the Gentiles out of their country, especially those in the City of David in Jerusalem, who had built for themselves a citadel from which they used to sally forth to defile the environs of the temple and inflict grave injury on its purity. 37 In this citadel he stationed Jewish soldiers, and he strengthened its fortifications for the defense of the land and the city, while he also raised the wall of Jerusalem to a greater height. 38 Consequently, King Demetrius confirmed him in the high priesthood, 39 made him one of his Friends, and conferred the highest honors on him. 40 He had indeed heard that the Romans had addressed the Jews as friends, allies, and brothers and that they had received Simon's envoys with honor.

41 " 'The Jewish people and their priest have, therefore, made the following decisions. Simon shall be their permanent leader and high priest until a true prophet arises. 42 He shall act as governor general over them, and shall have charge of the temple, to make regulations concerning its functions and concerning the country, its weapons and strongholds; 43 he shall be obeyed by all. All contracts made in the country shall be dated by his name. He shall have the right to wear royal purple and gold ornaments. 44 It shall not be lawful for any of the people or priests to nullify any of these decisions, or to contradict the orders given by him, or to convene an assembly in the country without his consent, to be clothed in royal purple or wear an official gold brooch. 45 Whoever acts otherwise or violates any of these prescriptions shall be liable to punishment.

46 " 'All the people approved of granting Simon the right to act in accord with these decisions, 47 and Simon accepted and agreed to act as high priest, governor general, and ethnarch of the Jewish people and priests and to exercise supreme authority over all.' "

14, 41: Omit *hoti:* so 1 MSS; dittog from v 40.
14, 43: Omit *kai hopōs melē auto peri tōn hagiōn:* so a few MSS; dittog from v 42.

35"The people saw Simon's faithfulness[a] and the glory that he had resolved to win for his nation, and they made him their leader and high priest, because he had done all these things and because of the justice and loyalty that he had maintained toward his nation. He sought in every way to exalt his people. 36In his days things prospered in his hands, so that the Gentiles were put out of the[b] country, as were also those in the city of David in Jerusalem, who had built themselves a citadel from which they used to sally forth and defile the environs of the sanctuary, doing great damage to its purity. 37He settled Jews in it and fortified it for the safety of the country and of the city, and built the walls of Jerusalem higher.

38"In view of these things King Demetrius confirmed him in the high priesthood, 39made him one of his Friends, and paid him high honors. 40For he had heard that the Jews were addressed by the Romans as friends and allies and brothers, and that the Romans[c] had received the envoys of Simon with honor.

41"The Jews and their priests have resolved that Simon should be their leader and high priest forever, until a trustworthy prophet should arise, 42and that he should be governor over them and that he should take charge of the sanctuary and appoint officials over its tasks and over the country and the weapons and the strongholds, and that he should take charge of the sanctuary, 43and that he should be obeyed by all, and that all contracts in the country should be written in his name, and that he should be clothed in purple and wear gold.

44"None of the people or priests shall be permitted to nullify any of these decisions or to oppose what he says, or to convene an assembly in the country without his permission, or to be clothed in purple or put on a gold buckle. 45Whoever acts contrary to these decisions or rejects any of them shall be liable to punishment."

46All the people agreed to grant Simon the right to act in accordance with these decisions. 47So Simon accepted and agreed to be high priest, to be commander and ethnarch of the Jews and priests, and to be protector of them all.[d] 48And they gave orders to inscribe this decree on bronze

a Other ancient authorities read *conduct*   *b* Gk *their*
c Gk *they*   *d* Or *to preside over them all*

⁴⁸ It was decreed that this inscription should be engraved on bronze tablets, to be set up in a conspicuous place in the precincts of the temple, ⁴⁹ and that copies of it should be deposited in the treasury, where they would be available to Simon and his sons.

tablets, to put them up in a conspicuous place in the precincts of the sanctuary, ⁴⁹and to deposit copies of them in the treasury, so that Simon and his sons might have them.

COMMENTARY

The decree to memorialize the Maccabees by recording their deeds on bronze tablets to be put on "pillars on Mount Zion" (v. 27) is depicted as a spontaneous outpouring of thanks by the people. Its preface (vv. 27-28) and its concluding arrangements concerning publication follow the basic usage in contemporary honorific inscriptions. After the preface comes a historical rundown of the achievements of the Hasmoneans (vv. 29-30)—particularly Simon (vv. 31-40)—and this is followed by the resolution of the people (vv. 41-43), which was binding on them all (vv. 44-45).

14:25-26. The people's response seems to refer to v. 19, or may simply be a response to all that Simon achieved in chapter 13. The word used for "people" here (δῆμος *dēmos*) reflects official inscriptional usage (cf. its usage in the correspondence with Rome and Sparta [8:29; 12:6; 14:20-23; 15:18]). Throughout the decree, the usual term for "people" (λάος *laos*) is used. In his lament over what was happening to Israel, Mattathias had said that Jerusalem was "no longer free, she has become a slave" (1 Macc 2:11 NRSV). The people now recognize that Mattathias's descendants have redressed that lament and that they have given back to Israel its freedom.

14:27-28, The Preface. The date is September 140 BCE. The first year of Simon's high priesthood was 170 Sel Bab (142/41), so the third would be 172 Sel Bab (140/39 BCE).

Why the translator did not translate *Saramel* or *Asaramel* is unknown. The text has been interpreted both as a place name, "the court of the people of God" (reflecting Hebrew חצר עם־אל [ḥàṣar 'am²ēl]), or as a title for Simon, "prince of the people of God" (שׂר עם־אל *śar 'am 'ēl*). Both have difficulties; the place name is not usually

given after the date in such documents; one does not know how the preposition "in" (ἐν *en*) could be placed before a title.

The opening words of the decree (v. 28) make a distinction between various groups. Throughout the decree itself the basic grouping is "the Jews and their priests" (v. 41) or "the people and priests" (v. 44). The opening words mention also "the rulers of the nation and the elders of the country" (v. 28). The book of Ezra distinguishes between rulers and elders, reflecting a distinction between Jerusalem and the rest of the country (Ezra 10:8, 14). The wording of the decree, then, emphasizes that all important groups were included (as at Ezra 10:1). The decree was probably drafted by the nation's leaders and then read aloud to the people.

14:29-40, The Exploits of the Hasmoneans. 14:29-30. The author gives a very bland description of the tumultuous events under Antiochus IV with no specific mention of the actions of Mattathias or Judas; recall Judas's speeches (3:20-21, 58-59) as well as Mattathias's last will (2:49-50). Verse 29 recalls that Judas and his brothers were honored in Israel and among the Gentiles (5:63). Jonathan (v. 30) is mentioned as immediate predecessor of Simon in the high priesthood (10:20). His murder by Trypho is glossed over by the biblical expression "[he] was gathered to his people" (v. 30; cf. Gen 25:8, 17; 49:33; 2 Kgs 22:20).

14:31-34. Recorded on the bronze tablets is the invasion of Trypho (13:1-20). No mention had previously been made of Simon's using his own money either as ransom for Jonathan (13:15-19) or for the gold shield sent to Rome (14:24), but no doubt the booty taken in various campaigns had increased his wealth. Certainly the monument to his family at Modein (13:25-30) attests to his fortune. It is almost *de rigueur* in honorific texts to tell of personal wealth spent on public benefactions. Verses 33-34 provide a summary of Simon's build-up of Judea's defenses and fortification of towns of Judea (13:33), and of Beth-zur (11:65-66), Joppa (12:33-34; 13:11), and Gazara (13:43-48).

14:35. The people's response to Simon's actions is recorded. In the narrative of 1 Maccabees, the people had made Simon their leader (13:7-9) before Jonathan's death and before the events listed above, except for capturing Beth-zur and Joppa. The decree may suggest that there was another public assembly after Jonathan's death at which Simon was appointed high priest as well. Normally, as with Jonathan (10:20-21), the high priest was appointed by the Seleucid king. Simon is praised for his righteousness and faithfulness (cf. 1 Sam 26:23; 1 Macc 2:52).

14:36-37. The author concludes this list of Simon's achievements by mentioning, in the place of emphasis, the capture of the citadel (13:49-52). The descriptions of the actions of those in the citadel reflect 1:34-37; 6:18.

14:38-40. In the narrative of 1 Maccabees, Demetrius II writes to Simon as high priest (13:36) and is portrayed as being only too happy to have an ally against Rome, with no mention of a threat from the Romans. Had Simon sent an embassy to Rome after Jonathan's death in the winter of 143 BCE and before Demetrius's letter in 142 BCE? The Jews were called friends and allies by the Romans (8:31), but not brothers, as they had been by the Spartans (12:7; 14:20).

14:41-49, The Offices of Simon. This section is framed by two occurrences of the verb "to be pleased," "to agree," "to resolve" (εὐδοκέω *eudokeō*): (1) at v. 41, the Jews and the priests "agreed"/"resolved" and (2) at v. 46, all the people "agreed"/"resolved." The verb is also found at v. 47, where Simon agrees to be high priest, commander, ethnarch, and protector. Some scholars think that the decree ends in v. 45, while others see the provisions for publication in v. 48 as showing that the decree runs through v. 49. It has even been suggested that v. 41 refers to a different, more restricted group of leaders than all the people of v. 46; if that is the case, one would then have an approval of Simon by influential leaders distinct from his final approval by the

people. What one has in vv. 42*b*-43 is a specification of what it means for Simon to be leader, high priest, and commander, and v. 46 resumes what was said in vv. 41-45. At v. 42*b* begins a string of five clauses all beginning with "in order that," "for the purpose that" (ὅπως *hopōs*).

14:41-42a. "High priest" and "leader" are the same titles given to Simon in 13:42. The grouping "the Jews and their priests" reflects the use of "Jews" in v. 40 and the fact that the following offices Simon holds are related to the sanctuary and so affect the priests in a particular way. The twofold grouping reflects the dual role of Simon as high priest and commander. "Forever" (αἰών *aiōn*) certainly means that Simon will be high priest for his lifetime (the same expression is used in Exod 21:6 to describe how a slave who prefers to stay with his slave wife rather than go free will have his ear pierced and then serve his master "for ever," i.e., for life). The expression may suggest hereditary holding of the position, but not necessarily. Simon's descendants are not mentioned, whereas Aaron's are when the priesthood is given to them as a perpetual ordinance (Exod 29:9). The promise of the land made to Abraham, Isaac, and Israel was explicitly enjoined to their descendants forever (Exod 32:13), and God promised David that his dynasty would rule forever (2 Sam 7:12-13). The condition "until a trustworthy prophet should arise" was mentioned earlier in connection with what to do with the polluted stones of the altar (4:47). The author is aware that the events recounted occurred after the prophets ceased to appear (9:27), and so may reflect less an opposition to Simon than a hope for further restoration. The role of the "trustworthy prophet" has been variously interpreted: (1) The prophet is to replace Simon. (2) The prophet is to decide whether Simon is fit to be ruler. (3) Only a prophet, not an assembly of people and priests, has the right to appoint a ruler, as the trustworthy prophet Samuel (1 Sam 3:20) had anointed Saul and David (1 Sam 10:1; 16:13). Most scholars seem to agree that the prophet will decide whether Simon is fit to be a ruler, but the recognition by the priests and the people of their own limitations may be more likely. (See Commentary on 4:46.)

14:42b-43. The specification of what the titles "leader" and "high priest" entail is given in a string of purpose clauses that outline Simon's rights; as high priest and governor, he is the one in charge of the sanctuary and the one who controls appointments. He has the power to break any opposition to him by appointing his own men to important positions. What goes for the sanctuary applies also to Simon's power to have his own appointees in defense and administration. After this first clause comes a repetition of the opening words of the clause, which probably should be omitted as a simple reduplication. Second, Simon is to be obeyed by everyone, so that any opposition to his will would be seen as illegal. Third, Simon's authority extends to all aspects of civil and criminal law, since his name is required on every contract. Fourth, purple dress and a gold buckle were noble prerogatives (10:89; 11:58).

14:44-45. These verses spell out Simon's powers in negative terms. Not only can no one oppose Simon's decrees, but also the right of assembly is taken away. The word for "convene" (ἐπισυστρέψαι *episystrepsai*) here has a pejorative connotation at Num 16:42 (17:7 LXX), where it refers to the rebellious assembly of the congregation against Moses and Aaron; at 2 Kgs 15:15, the noun form is used to describe the conspiracy of Shallum against King Zechariah; at Ps 64:2 (Ps 63:2 LXX), the noun form is used to describe the plots of the wicked against the pious. The phrase "liable to punishment" means the death penalty at Lev 20:9, 11-13, 16, 27.

14:46-49. Just as the people had made Simon leader and high priest (v. 35), so also now they agree to hand over to Simon the just-mentioned rights (v. 46). Simon agrees to the job under the conditions outlined (v. 47). Jonathan had been "ruler" (ἄρχων *archōn*) of the people (9:30; 12:53), but now Simon is "ruler" (ἐθνάρχης *ethnarchēs*) of the nation (cf. Esth 3:12), which comprises all Jews, people and priests (cf. v. 41). No mention is made of putting the bronze tablets on pillars (vv. 48-49). They are simply to be made conspicuous. The treasury here refers to the temple treasury (see 2 Macc 3:6). God thus becomes a witness to this bargain between the people and Simon. Similar provisions are found in inscriptions for copies of the document to be displayed publicly and for a copy to be sent to the honoree.

Some scholars have suggested that the public statement of the unlimited powers given to Simon suggests that in fact Simon did not really have such unopposed power and that he had to face opposition in trying to place his own followers in power in the sanctuary and throughout the country from those already entrenched in those positions. No doubt there was opposition to Simon's rise to such heights of power. However, to see hints of opposition in this document requires that one assume that the condition of waiting for a trustworthy prophet is a limitation of Simon's power, not that of the Jews and their priests, and also that one argue from the document's silence whereby Simon is not declared king and no reference is given to his freeing Judea from taxation. Arguments from silence are not particularly convincing, however, especially since there is no hint in 1 Maccabees that Simon wants to be king. Some scholars have also worried as to why Simon waited until his third year before having such a decree drawn up. The author of 1 Maccabees, however, places the decree after the removal of Demetrius II from power (14:1-3) and suggests by this arrangement that it was only then that Simon could so publicly proclaim his quasi-independent position of ethnarch.

With this decree in honor of Simon, the book of 1 Maccabees seems to reach a climax. The wrongs of chapters 1 and 2 have been righted, and Judea is free from the yoke of the Gentiles and under its own ethnarch. The paeans to Judas (3:3-9) and Simon (14:4-15) round out the grand exploits of the Hasmoneans. Antiochus IV had polluted the Temple, outlawed Jewish religion, and installed a citadel in Jerusalem. In contrast, Judas had cleansed the Temple and restored ancestral religion, and Simon had rid Jerusalem of the citadel. Both of these deeds were celebrated with songs and music (4:52-59; 13:51-52). The testamentary hymn of Mattathias (2:49-68) had foretold the pre-eminence of these two men.

REFLECTIONS

1. The description of life under Simon is utopian and idyllic, fulfilling the prophets' promises of the good life to come. The land is at peace, each person under his or her own vines and fig trees. The law is observed. But this harmonious picture in the hymn of praise hides some problems. Those who disagree with Simon's notion of what Torah observance means are characterized as renegades and outlaws. The extension of the borders of Judea brings with it the expulsion of non-Jews from their homes and property. Success in war means the capture and enslavement of enemies. Thus success for some means loss for others. Behind the glory of empire lies the misery of slaves. The division of society into the haves and the have-nots is a critical issue.

When we read this picture of an ideal society, we must look at our own societies and ask whether each citizen has what he or she needs to live a full and prosperous life. Our concern must be that each citizen be given the opportunity to use the talents given to him or her to the best advantage. We must not rest until the inadequacies due to poor housing, insufficient health care, and lack of proper educational opportunities are done away with. We must strive to see that all people can have productive, fulfilling jobs that provide a decent wage to support their families. Our societies must not consist of two tiers of citizens, with the poor and unfortunate neglected. The ideal society must be one in which social justice reigns, in which we shall all be brothers and sisters, no matter what our racial or ethnic heritage or income level.

2. The second reflection that this chapter awakens is the contrast between the utopian picture of the hymn and the political structure envisioned by the decree. The decree makes clear the authoritarian nature of Simon's rule. He accumulates all positions of power to himself, and his edicts are to be obeyed. If it is true that he supplied the towns with food (14:10), it was at the cost of the people's independence. He controlled the legal apparatus as well as the police force (14:42-43). The reader may be reminded of some contemporary governments that promise food and jobs for everyone—but the promise carries also the heavy hand of the authoritarian police that went with it. What must be sought is a way to keep such promises without imposing a stifling governmental structure. What is first needed, of course, is a division of powers. The separation of the legislative from the executive and the judiciary branches of government is crucial. But one must also be concerned about the freedom of the press, a freedom to investigate unhindered. Such a freedom must not be compromised by the organs of the press being under the control of a few wealthy people who might wish to propagate a particular point of view. So, as always, we must be vigilant to see that our freedoms are preserved. But freedom brings a responsibility to work to make a better, more just society.

1 MACCABEES 15:1–16:10, FURTHER SELEUCID THREATS

1 Maccabees 15:1-14, The Rise of Antiochus VII Sidetes

NAB	NRSV
15 Antiochus, son of King Demetrius, sent a letter from the islands of the sea to Simon, the priest and ethnarch of the Jews, and to all the nation, ² which read as follows: "King Antiochus sends greetings to Simon, the priest and ethnarch, and to the Jewish nation.	**15** Antiochus, son of King Demetrius, sent a letter from the islands of the sea to Simon, the priest and ethnarch of the Jews, and to all the nation; ²its contents were as follows: "King Antiochus to Simon the high priest and ethnarch and to the nation of the Jews, greetings. ³Whereas

NAB

3 Whereas certain villains have gained control of the kingdom of my ancestors, I intend to reclaim it, that I may restore it to its former state. I have recruited a large number of mercenary troops and equipped warships 4 to make a landing in my country and take revenge on those who have ruined it and laid waste many cities in my realm.

5 "Now, therefore, I confirm to you all the tax exemptions that the kings before me granted you and whatever other privileges they conferred on you. 6 I authorize you to coin your own money, as legal tender in your country. 7 Jerusalem and its temple shall be free. All the weapons you have prepared and all the strongholds you have built and now occupy shall remain in your possession. 8 All debts, present or future, due to the royal treasury shall be canceled for you, now and for all time. 9 When we recover our kingdom, we will greatly honor you and your nation and the temple, so that your glory will be manifest in all the earth."

10 In the year one hundred and seventy-four, Antiochus invaded the land of his ancestors, and all the troops rallied to him, so that few were left with Trypho. 11 Pursued by Antiochus, Trypho fled to Dor, by the sea, 12 realizing what a mass of troubles had come upon him now that his soldiers had deserted him. 13 Antiochus encamped before Dor with a hundred and twenty thousand infantry and eight thousand horsemen. 14 While he invested the city, his ships closed in along the coast, so that he blockaded it by land and sea and let no one go in or out.

15, 5: (panta ta) aphemata (ha aphēkan): so LXX[S,V]; cf. 10. 28.

NRSV

certain scoundrels have gained control of the kingdom of our ancestors, and I intend to lay claim to the kingdom so that I may restore it as it formerly was, and have recruited a host of mercenary troops and have equipped warships, 4and intend to make a landing in the country so that I may proceed against those who have destroyed our country and those who have devastated many cities in my kingdom, 5now therefore I confirm to you all the tax remissions that the kings before me have granted you, and a release from all the other payments from which they have released you. 6I permit you to mint your own coinage as money for your country, 7and I grant freedom to Jerusalem and the sanctuary. All the weapons that you have prepared and the strongholds that you have built and now hold shall remain yours. 8Every debt you owe to the royal treasury and any such future debts shall be canceled for you from henceforth and for all time. 9When we gain control of our kingdom, we will bestow great honor on you and your nation and the temple, so that your glory will become manifest in all the earth."

10In the one hundred seventy-fourth year[a] Antiochus set out and invaded the land of his ancestors. All the troops rallied to him, so that there were only a few with Trypho. 11Antiochus pursued him, and Trypho[b] came in his flight to Dor, which is by the sea; 12for he knew that troubles had converged on him, and his troops had deserted him. 13So Antiochus encamped against Dor, and with him were one hundred twenty thousand warriors and eight thousand cavalry. 14He surrounded the town, and the ships joined battle from the sea; he pressed the town hard from land and sea, and permitted no one to leave or enter it.

a 138 B.C.   b Gk he

COMMENTARY

As the narrative is framed in 1 Maccabees, the reader might think that Antiochus VII was the son of Demetrius II, who was defeated and captured by Trypho (14:3). Rather, he is the son of Demetrius I and the brother of Demetrius II. Antiochus, surnamed Sidetes because he had been raised in Side in Pamphylia, determines again to take up the fight against Trypho. At the time Antiochus had been living in Rhodes. His letter to Simon (15:2-9) is probably one of many such letters sent to local leaders for support of his cause against Trypho.

15:1-2. The term "priest" could mean priest *par excellence,* i.e., high priest as in the following verse. The title "ethnarch" picks up on the title used at 14:47 and recognizes the quasi-independent status of Judea. Antiochus already claims the title "king" in his greeting.

15:3-5. The term "scoundrels" (λοιμοί *loimoi,* v. 3) literally means "plague" but is applied in Greek literature to subversive persons (it is used earlier at 10:61 and also at 15:21). Does it refer only to Trypho or also to Antiochus VI and Alexander Epiphanes? Antiochus blames all the troubles of the Seleucid Empire on Trypho (cf. the complaint against Judas at 7:7). It is not known from where he got the money to recruit "a host of mercenary troops" and to equip warships. To encourage Simon's help, Antiochus confirms the tax exemptions and gifts (v. 5) granted by Demetrius I (10:38-43) and by Demetrius II (13:37-40).

15:6. Antiochus grants Simon the right to mint his own coinage in Judea. Other cities in the Seleucid Empire could issue coinage, but being granted the privilege evidenced the increased status of Judea. No coins from Simon's time are extant, so we do not know whether he actually exercised this privilege.

15:7. Exactly what "freedom" Antiochus means to grant Jerusalem is vague. At 10:31, Demetrius I had made Jerusalem holy and free from taxation. Perhaps the same is meant here. Demetrius I had given Jonathan the right to prepare weapons (10:6), and Demetrius II had granted permission to gain control of the strongholds (11:42).

15:8-9. Demetrius II had also promised that the grants would not be cancelled from this time on (11:36), and he promised glory (11:42), but then had reneged (11:53).

15:10-14. Since Trypho controlled much of the coastline, Antiochus found it difficult to enter the kingdom. However, Demetrius II's wife, Cleopatra Thea, who was besieged by Trypho at Seleucia, let Antiochus land. She also married him, since Demetrius II had since married a Parthian princess. The year 174 (v. 10) in the Seleucid Macedonian calendar system was 139/38 BCE. Antiochus was proclaimed king and defeated Trypho in northern Syria. Trypho withdrew to Dor, a powerful fortress on the Phoenician coast, where Antiochus besieged him (vv. 11-13). The phrase "not to go out or go in" (v. 14) is repeated at 15:25, when the siege of Dor is picked up again.

1 Maccabees 15:15-24, Continued Roman Support

NAB	NRSV
15 Meanwhile, Numenius and his companions left Rome with letters such as this addressed to various kings and countries:	15Then Numenius and his companions arrived from Rome, with letters to the kings and countries, in which the following was written: 16"Lucius, consul of the Romans, to King Ptolemy, greetings. 17The envoys of the Jews have come to us as our friends and allies to renew our ancient friendship and alliance. They had been sent by the high priest Simon and by the Jewish people 18and have brought a gold shield weighing one thousand minas. 19We therefore have decided to write to the kings and countries that they should not seek their harm or make war against them and their cities and their country, or make alliance with those who war against them. 20And it has seemed good to us to accept the shield from them. 21Therefore if any scoundrels have fled to you from their country, hand them over to the high priest
16 "Lucius, Consul of the Romans, sends greetings to King Ptolemy. 17 Certain envoys of the Jews, our friends and allies, have come to us to renew their earlier alliance of friendship. They had been sent by Simon the high priest and the Jewish people, 18 and they brought with them a gold shield worth a thousand minas. 19 Therefore we have decided to write to various kings and countries, that they are not to harm them, or wage war against them or their cities or their country, and are not to assist those who fight against them. 20 We have also decided to accept the shield from them. 21 If, then, any troublemakers from their country take refuge with you, hand them over to	

NAB

Simon the high priest, so that he may punish them according to their law."

²² The consul sent similar letters to Kings Demetrius, Attalus, Ariarthes and Arsaces; ²³ to all the countries—Sampsames, Sparta, Delos, Myndos, Sicyon, Caria, Samos, Pamphylia, Lycia, Halicarnassus, Rhodes, Phaselis, Cos, Side, Aradus, Gortyna, Cnidus, Cyprus, and Cyrene. ²⁴ A copy of the letter was also sent to Simon the high priest.

15, 23: (kai) Sampsamē (kai Spartiatais): so LXX^{S,V,MSS}.

NRSV

Simon, so that he may punish them according to their law."

22The consul^a wrote the same thing to King Demetrius and to Attalus and Ariarathes and Arsaces, ²³and to all the countries, and to Sampsames,^b and to the Spartans, and to Delos, and to Myndos, and to Sicyon, and to Caria, and to Samos, and to Pamphylia, and to Lycia, and to Halicarnassus, and to Rhodes, and to Phaselis, and to Cos, and to Side, and to Aradus and Gortyna and Cnidus and Cyprus and Cyrene. ²⁴They also sent a copy of these things to the high priest Simon.

^a Gk *He*   ^b The name is uncertain

COMMENTARY

The author of 1 Maccabees tends to interpolate some events within others, often using frame language to connect the narrative; e.g., Antiochus's actions (3:37) are recounted (6:1); the defeat of Nicanor (7:43-49) is repeated (9:1) and frames Judas's embassy to Rome; Jonathan's battles against the commanders of Demetrius II (11:63-74; 12:24-32) frame Jonathan's embassy to Rome. So here Antiochus's siege of Dor (15:14, 25) frames the Romans' letter of alliance to Simon. The people's decree stated that Demetrius II had heard that the envoys of the Jews had been accepted with honor (14:40), so Simon's delegation probably was sent soon after Jonathan's death. In fact, Lucius, the consul, wrote the same letters to King Demetrius, which must have been before the failure of Demetrius II's campaign against Parthia became known. The only consul named Lucius between 142 and 137 BCE was Lucius Caecilius Metellus Calvus, consul of 142 BCE. It seems, then, as if this letter should be dated earlier than the time of Antiochus VII Sidetes. However, the author of 1 Maccabees, by positioning the response of the Romans here, concludes the list of honors accorded to Simon that began with a letter from Rome (14:16-18). The author also provides a break between the positive attitude of Antiochus VII toward the Jews and the negative one he adopts from v. 27 on.

15:15. Numenius was last mentioned at 14:24 as being on his way to Rome. It was common practice to send a copy of a letter to a person mentioned in the letter.

15:16. The common Roman practice for letter writing was for the writer to fully identify himself or herself, using not only the family name but also any official title he or she held. The addressee is Ptolemy VIII Euergetes (146–116 BCE), whom a Roman commission headed by Scipio Aemilianus had visited in 140/39 BCE.[128] Polybius, the Greek historian who probably accompanied Scipio, found the Greek and Jewish population of Alexandria virtually wiped out by Ptolemy's purges after his return to power.[129]

15:17-21. "Friends and allies" was the same phrase used when Judas set up an alliance with Rome (8:20); Jonathan is said to have renewed these ties (12:3). Verse 19 repeats much of what had been set out in the letter the Romans had sent in reply to the embassy that Judas had sent to them (8:24-28). The gold shield mentioned (v. 18) is the one described earlier (14:24). By accepting the shield (v. 20), the Romans signify the renewal of the relationship. Note that the Jews present a gift to the Romans but that none is given in return, so the relationship is not that of equals. The request that Rome's allies hand over "fugitives" (λοιμοί *loimoi*, v. 21; see "scoundrels," 10:61) is similar to the requirement of Antiochus III

128. Diodorus Siculus 33.28b.1-3.
129. Polybius 34.14.1-7.

by the Treaty of Apamea to deliver up to Rome's allies any of their deserters.[130] Augustus later gave the same privilege to Herod.[131]

15:22-24. The list of recipients first names kings (v. 22) and then countries (v. 23; cf. 15:15). The mention of Demetrius II indicates that the letter must have been written before news of his capture by the Parthians; Attalus II was king of Pergamum (159–138 BCE); Ariarathes V, king of Cappadocia (163–130 BCE); Arsaces (i.e., Mithradates I), king of Parthia (c. 171–138/37 BCE). "The Sampsames," most probably to be identified with Samsun on the Black Sea, was called "Amisos" by the Greeks. Myndos was near Halicarnassus

on the southwest coast of Asia Minor. Sicyon was a city near Corinth. Caria and Lycia lay in the mountainous region of southwest Asia Minor, and Pamphylia lay in the middle of the southern coast of Asia Minor. Samos, Rhodes, and Cos are islands off the southwest coast of Asia Minor. Halicarnassus was a city lying within Caria; Phaselis, a city within Lycia; Side, a city within Pampylia. Aradus, the main city of north Phoenicia, was situated on an island off the coast. Gortyna was an important city in southern Crete. Cnidus, a city, lay on a long peninsula at the southwest corner of Asia Minor. The island Cyprus at this time was under Ptolemaic control, as was the great North African city of Cyrene, to the west of the Egyptian delta.

130. Polybius 21.42.10; Livy 38.38.7.
131. Josephus *The Jewish War* 1.474.

1 Maccabees 15:25-36, Antiochus's Change of Heart

NAB

25 When King Antiochus was encamped before Dor, he assaulted it continuously both with troops and with the siege machines he had made. He blockaded Trypho by preventing anyone from going in or out. 26 Simon sent to Antiochus' support two thousand elite troops, together with gold and silver and much equipment. 27 But he refused to accept the aid; in fact, he broke all the agreements he had previously made with Simon and became hostile toward him.

28 He sent Athenobius, one of his Friends, to confer with Simon and say: "You are occupying Joppa and Gazara and the citadel of Jerusalem; these are cities of my kingdom. 29 You have laid waste their territories, done great harm to the land, and taken possession of many districts in my realm. 30 Therefore, give up the cities you have seized and the tribute money of the districts outside the territory of Judea of which you have taken possession; 31 or instead, pay me five hundred talents of silver for the devastation you have caused and five hundred talents more for the tribute money of the cities. If you do not do this, we will come and make war on you."

32 So Athenobius, the king's Friend, came to Jerusalem, and on seeing the splendor of Simon's

15, 25: Omit *en tȩ deuterą:* gloss.

NRSV

25King Antiochus besieged Dor for the second time, continually throwing his forces against it and making engines of war; and he shut Trypho up and kept him from going out or in. 26And Simon sent to Antiochus[a] two thousand picked troops, to fight for him, and silver and gold and a large amount of military equipment. 27But he refused to receive them, and broke all the agreements he formerly had made with Simon, and became estranged from him. 28He sent to him Athenobius, one of his Friends, to confer with him, saying, "You hold control of Joppa and Gazara and the citadel in Jerusalem; they are cities of my kingdom. 29You have devastated their territory, you have done great damage in the land, and you have taken possession of many places in my kingdom. 30Now then, hand over the cities that you have seized and the tribute money of the places that you have conquered outside the borders of Judea; 31or else pay me five hundred talents of silver for the destruction that you have caused and five hundred talents more for the tribute money of the cities. Otherwise we will come and make war on you."

32So Athenobius, the king's Friend, came to Jerusalem, and when he saw the splendor of Simon, and the sideboard with its gold and silver

a Gk *him*

NAB

court, the gold and silver plate on the sideboard, and the rest of his rich display, he was amazed. When he gave him the king's message, [33] Simon said to him in reply:

"We have not seized any foreign land; what we took is not the property of others, but our ancestral heritage which for a time had been unjustly held by our enemies. [34] Now that we have the opportunity, we are holding on to the heritage of our ancestors. [35] As for Joppa and Gazara, which you demand, the men of these cities were doing great harm to our people and laying waste our country; however, we are willing to pay you a hundred talents for these cities."

[36] Athenobius made no reply, but returned to the king in anger. When he told him of Simon's words, of his splendor, and of all he had seen, the king fell into a violent rage.

15, 35: (*kai tēn chōran*) *erēmon:* conj.

NRSV

plate, and his great magnificence, he was amazed. When he reported to him the king's message, [33]Simon said to him in reply: "We have neither taken foreign land nor seized foreign property, but only the inheritance of our ancestors, which at one time had been unjustly taken by our enemies. [34]Now that we have the opportunity, we are firmly holding the inheritance of our ancestors. [35]As for Joppa and Gazara, which you demand, they were causing great damage among the people and to our land; for them we will give you one hundred talents."

Athenobius[a] did not answer him a word, [36]but returned in wrath to the king and reported to him these words, and also the splendor of Simon and all that he had seen. And the king was very angry.

[a] Gk *He*

COMMENTARY

15:25-27. The narrative picks up where it ended before the report of the embassy to Rome (v. 14). But whereas before Antiochus VII had been so friendly to Simon, now his attitude has changed. Simon sent reinforcements as well as money to help the king defray his expenses (v. 26), but such gifts also signified the recognition of Antiochus VII as king. However, Antiochus insults Simon by not accepting (v. 27) his gifts, in contrast to Rome's acceptance of the golden shield (15:20). Since the troops of the Seleucid Empire had rallied to Antiochus (15:10) and his main enemy Trypho was trapped, Antiochus no longer had need of Simon's friendship. Just as Demetrius II had changed his attitude when his troubles disappeared (11:52-53), so also now Antiochus changes his, continuing the Seleucids' record of deception.

15:28-31. Athenobius, "the king's Friend" (v. 28), is unknown outside of 1 Maccabees. Simon is not invited to talk with Antiochus, but to a lower level delegation. The message contains no courteous address, but starts right away with claims. Two main points of honor for Simon had

been his control over Joppa as an opening to the sea (14:5, 34) and his cleansing of Gazara (13:43-48; 14:7, 34) and of the citadel (13:49-52; 14:7, 36-37). It is interesting that the citadel is here called a "city"; at 1:33 it encompassed the city of David, distinct from Jerusalem. In addition to the three cities mentioned, Simon also held Ekron (10:89), Adida (12:38; 13:13), and four other districts (11:34, 57). Whereas earlier the author of 1 Maccabees states that the citadel (14:36), Seleucid forces (1:30), and Jewish renegades (7:22) did great damage in Jerusalem and Israel, he now reports that Antiochus claims that Simon has done so to Seleucid territory (v. 29). Simon thus is classified with those forces against whom Antiochus VII intended to fight (15:4). A single indemnity of one thousand talents (v. 31) was high, but not beyond the reach of the Hasmoneans. Jonathan had promised three hundred for the districts of Samaria (11:28), and the golden shield sent to Rome would have cost a small fortune.

15:32a. Antiochus VII had promised to increase Simon's glory (15:9), but when Athenobius saw Simon's present glory, he was amazed. One might compare his reaction to that of the Queen of Sheba to Solomon's magnificence (1 Kgs 10:4-5), or to the incident in which King Hezekiah displayed Jerusalem's wealth to Babylonian envoys (2 Kgs 20:12-19).

15:32b-35. Antiochus VII had claimed that he was acting to regain control of the kingdom of his ancestors (15:3-4), and likewise now Simon reacts to Antiochus by claiming that he also only took back control of the inheritance of his ancestors (v. 33). He replies only to the charge about the citadel, and not to Antiochus's vague mention of many places (v. 29). Simon does not attempt to argue that Joppa and Gazara lie within the ancestral inheritance, but reports that they cause great damage to Judea, not Judea to them (15:29), and offers a tenth of the king's demand.

15:36. Athenobius returned "in wrath" to Antiochus to report Simon's reply. The anger of the king usually means trouble (3:27; 6:28)—and an expedition against Judea.

REFLECTIONS

What is interesting in this narrative is how Simon seems to go against basic rules of behavior of a subordinate to a superior. The wisdom teacher Sirach admonished his pupils, "Among the great do not act as their equal" (Sir 32:9 NRSV; cf. 13:11). The book of Proverbs recommends: "Do not put yourself forward in the king's presence/ or stand in the place of the great;/ for it is better to be told, 'Come up here,'/ than to be put lower in the presence of a noble" (Prov 25:6-7 NRSV). Simon's action in voluntarily sending men and abundant supplies to Antiochus VII in his siege of Dor could be taken as his acting as an equal to the king. Yet Simon's ostentatious display of wealth to the king's representative and then his refusal to pay what the king demanded only served to infuriate his superior. Simon acted unwisely and seems to have had the same weakness for gaining respect that Jonathan had had. The same ostentation had led Simon earlier to erect an enormous monument to his family. Simon had "made it"; he had risen from being the third son in a family from the outskirts of Judea to being the ruler of Judea, and he wanted everyone to acknowledge his success. He wanted respect. The lesson we have to learn from his actions is that we need to instill such self-confidence in all of our children that they will not need the outward trappings of success, but will be happy and content in being who they are. On the level of foreign affairs, strong nations must learn to be indulgent to smaller nations who are so concerned about their status and honor. The stronger nation must shows its strength, not by saber rattling, but by granting the proper respect that all nations should expect from one another.

1 Maccabees 15:37–16:10, The Expedition of Cendebeus

NAB

37 Trypho had gotten aboard a ship and escaped to Orthosia. 38 Then the king appointed Cendebeus commander in chief of the seacoast, and gave him infantry and cavalry forces. 39 He ordered him to move his troops against Judea and to fortify Kedron and strengthen its gates, so that he could launch attacks against the Jewish people. Meanwhile the king went in pursuit of Trypho. 40 When Cendebeus came to Jamnia, he began to harass the people and to make incursions into Judea, where he took people captive or massacred them.

NRSV

37Meanwhile Trypho embarked on a ship and escaped to Orthosia. 38Then the king made Cendebeus commander-in-chief of the coastal country, and gave him troops of infantry and cavalry. 39He commanded him to encamp against Judea, to build up Kedron and fortify its gates, and to make war on the people; but the king pursued Trypho. 40So Cendebeus came to Jamnia and began to provoke the people and invade Judea and take the people captive and kill them. 41He built up Kedron and stationed horsemen and troops there, so that

NAB

⁴¹ As the king ordered, he fortified Kedron and stationed horsemen and infantry there, so that they could go out and patrol the roads of Judea. **16** John then went up from Gazara and told his father Simon what Cendebeus was doing. ² Simon called his two oldest sons, Judas and John, and said to them: "I and my brothers and my father's house have fought the battles of Israel from our youth until today, and many times we succeeded in saving Israel. ³ I have now grown old, but you, by the mercy of Heaven, have come to man's estate. Take my place and my brother's, and go out and fight for our nation; and may the help of Heaven be with you!"

⁴ John then mustered in the land twenty thousand warriors and horsemen. Setting out against Cendebeus, they spent the night at Modein, ⁵ rose early, and marched into the plain. There, facing them, was an immense army of foot soldiers and horsemen, and between the two armies was a stream. ⁶ John and his men took their position against the enemy. Seeing that his men were afraid to cross the stream, John crossed first. When his men saw this, they crossed over after him. ⁷ Then he divided his infantry into two corps and put his cavalry between them, for the enemy's horsemen were very numerous. ⁸ They blew the trumpets, and Cendebeus and his army were put to flight; many of them fell wounded, and the rest fled toward the stronghold. ⁹ It was then that John's brother Judas fell wounded; but John pursued them until Cendebeus reached Kidron, which he had fortified. ¹⁰ Some took refuge in the towers on the plain of Azotus, but John set fire to these, and about two thousand of the enemy perished. He then returned to Judea in peace.

16, 10: (*kai enepyrisen*) *autous* (*en pyri*): so V.

NRSV

they might go out and make raids along the highways of Judea, as the king had ordered him. **16** John went up from Gazara and reported to his father Simon what Cendebeus had done. ²And Simon called in his two eldest sons Judas and John, and said to them: "My brothers and I and my father's house have fought the wars of Israel from our youth until this day, and things have prospered in our hands so that we have delivered Israel many times. ³But now I have grown old, and you by Heaven's[a] mercy are mature in years. Take my place and my brother's, and go out and fight for our nation, and may the help that comes from Heaven be with you."

4So John[b] chose out of the country twenty thousand warriors and cavalry, and they marched against Cendebeus and camped for the night in Modein. ⁵Early in the morning they started out and marched into the plain, where a large force of infantry and cavalry was coming to meet them; and a stream lay between them. ⁶Then he and his army lined up against them. He saw that the soldiers were afraid to cross the stream, so he crossed over first; and when his troops saw him, they crossed over after him. ⁷Then he divided the army and placed the cavalry in the center of the infantry, for the cavalry of the enemy were very numerous. ⁸They sounded the trumpets, and Cendebeus and his army were put to flight; many of them fell wounded and the rest fled into the stronghold. ⁹At that time Judas the brother of John was wounded, but John pursued them until Cendebeus[c] reached Kedron, which he had built. ¹⁰They also fled into the towers that were in the fields of Azotus, and John[c] burned it with fire, and about two thousand of them fell. He then returned to Judea safely.

a Gk *his*   *b* Other ancient authorities read *he*   *c* Gk *he*

COMMENTARY

15:37. Trypho managed to escape the noose around Dora and flee to Apamea, his hometown, by way of Ptolemais and Orthosia, a port north of Tripolis. There, besieged once more, he took his life. It is to be noted that 1 Maccabees leaves Trypho at Orthosia and does not record his death.

15:38-41. While Antiochus VII goes north in pursuit of Trypho, he arranges to gain control of the southern coast. He, like Demetrius I (7:8-9), Demetrius II (10:69; 11:63; 12:24), and Trypho (12:40), knows that the power of the Jews must be curtailed. Cendebeus is given the office that

Simon had held (11:59). Cendebeus was to fortify Kedron (v. 39), about four miles southeast of Jamnia and about eight or nine miles southwest of Gazara; it has also been identified by some scholars with Nihson, just over two miles southeast of Gezer, but such a base would be close to the mountains and almost twelve miles from Jamnia. With this fortified base, Cendebeus could sally out to attack the western routes to Jerusalem.

Cendebeus first invades Jamnia (v. 40), as Apollonius had done (10:69). From there he provokes Israel by raiding the land, taking captives, and murdering. His forces must not have been large enough to mount a full-scale assault in the now well-fortified Judea, but he concentrated on drawing the Jewish forces into the plain, as Apollonius had done (10:71-73). Kedron provided a base closer to the areas occupied by the Jews for quick, harassing incursions (v. 41). The continuing raids produce their desired effect and provoke the Hasmoneans to venture onto the plain.

16:1. John is in command of Gazara, which overlooks the plain. His garrison may not have been strong enough on its own to take on Cendebeus's forces, but he was aware of what Cendebeus "kept doing" (συνετέλεσεν *synetelesen*), not "had done," as in the NRSV, because the verb is in the imperfect. (The same verb is used elsewhere in 1 Maccabees to describe complaints; e.g., 8:31; 10:5; 11:40.)

16:2-3. Here the reader learns that Simon had another son besides John: Judas.[132] Nothing is known of the mother as, in this warrior book, family life is not considered. Simon's opening words recall earlier statements about him and Judas (3:6; 13:3; 14:26, 36), as well as the claim that deliverance was given to Israel exclusively through this family (5:62). The statement "I have grown old" (v. 3) usually comes before the last testament and blessing (Isaac, Gen 27:1-2; Joshua, Josh 23:2; Samuel, 1 Sam 12:2; Tobit, Tob 14:3). The Greek "Heaven's mercy" (ἔλεος *eleos,* lit., "the mercy") is a substitute for naming God (3:44; 4:24), just as "heaven" is substituted for God (3:19, 50; 4:24). Just as Jonathan had replaced Judas (9:30) and Simon had replaced Jonathan (13:8), so also Simon's sons will replace him. The text has the singular "my brother," which seems

to be a translation mistake; the Hebrew word אחי (*'ḥy*) without vowels can be read either "my brother" or "my brothers" (the same mistake seems to be present at 13:8). However, the reader might recall how Mattathias, in his dying speech, mentioned only Judas and Simon (2:65-66) and that now two young men, Judas and John, replace the two old men, Judas and Simon. Help from heaven has been a constant theme in 1 Maccabees (see 3:19, 50, 53, 60; 4:24; 12:15).

16:4. The Greek reads "he picked" (ἐπέλεξεν *epelexen*), but the subject here is most likely John, as in v. 1. Jonathan had also had 40,000 hand-picked warriors (12:41) when he went to meet Trypho. Cendebeus's strategy suggests that his was not a force of the full strength of the Seleucid army. Cavalry is mentioned for the first time on the Jewish side, perhaps in response to the description of Cendebeus's force, but earlier battles such as that at Elasa presuppose the use of cavalry (9:11-17). John and Judas do not take the direct route back to Gazara, but first go north to Modein. We are not told why. Perhaps he wished to avoid Seleucid raiding parties or to have Adida and Modein behind him and Gazara to his left as he went down the plain. To start marching from so far to the north seems to preclude choosing the route as a surprise tactic. The appearance of Modein here makes a nice reprise to the opening days of the Maccabean revolt (2:1).

16:5-8a. The description of the battle leaves much to be desired. As written, it seems as if the Seleucid forces were apprised of their movements and that the two forces met in the plain not far from Modein. In that case, the stream would most likely by the Wadi Aijalon, rather than the Sorek near Kedron, which would have required the Israelites to have marched about fourteen miles before arriving at the battle scene. John, as Judas had done before him (5:41-43), fearlessly leads his soldiers across a stream. The Greek literally says "he divided the people" (διεῖλεν τὸν λάον *dieilen ton laon,* v. 7), so that the sense of the engagement of the whole community is conveyed. John's tactics are determined by the size of the enemy's cavalry. Usually the cavalry units were on the wings of the infantry, but John must have realized that his cavalry was no match for cavalry that was either too numerous or too well armed. He decides to place his cavalry among, not "in

---

132. At 16:14, another son is named, Mattathias, and Josephus mentions another. See Josephus *Antiquities of the Jews* 13.228.

the center of," the infantry. Perhaps his plan was to divide his forces into several mobile units to attack the more massed phalanx of the Seleucids; perhaps he had noted that the enemy's phalanx was stretched wide because of the plain, and he used the cavalry within the infantry to force gaps in the enemy's phalanx. One does not know what the enemy's cavalry was doing. The author says only that the trumpets were sounded (1 Macc 5:33 [Num 10:8]) and that the enemy was routed, almost as though the trumpets decided the battle, as at Jericho (Joshua 6).

16:8b-10. The grammar of these verses is a little confused, as subjects of verbs are left out. It seems as if the Seleucid forces fled to the fortress, i.e., Kedron, which Cendebeus had been ordered to fortify (15:39). But during the pursuit Judas is wounded, and so John pursues alone until Cendebeus reaches Kedron. Others keep going until they reach the watchtowers positioned within the limits of Azotus (Ashdod). In the mosaic map of Judea found at Madeba, towers are depicted in the open country between Azotus and Jamnia.

What John burned is unclear: Was it Azotus, the last-mentioned city, which previously Jonathan had burned (10:84)? Or does "it" really refer to "the towers"? Or does "it" refer to Kedron? The author does not say that John pursued to Azotus or that the escapees fled to Azotus, but only to the towers within the limits of Azotus, whose borders reached to Gazara (14:34). As for "it" being a mistake for an original "them," one can more easily explain why a later copyist would have corrected the text from an unusual "it" to "them" rather than the other way around. One would then need to suppose that a translator mistook the original שׂרפה (*yiśrĕpehā,* "he burned it") and read ישׂרפם (*yiśrĕpēm,* "he burned them"). If "it" does refer to Kedron, it is likely that the author meant that John destroyed Cendebeus and those who took refuge in the fortress. Whatever the case, John followed the usual Maccabean practice of burning the town before returning to Judea. Later, John is said to be in Gazara (v. 19), so it is not clear whether he went back to Jerusalem before disbanding the army.

1 MACCABEES 16:11-22, THE DEATH OF SIMON

NAB

[11] Ptolemy, son of Abubus, had been appointed governor of the plain of Jericho, and he had much silver and gold, [12] being the son-in-law of the high priest. [13] But he became ambitious and sought to get control of the country. So he made treacherous plans to do away with Simon and his sons. [14] As Simon was inspecting the cities of the country and providing for their needs, he and his sons Mattathias and Judas went down to Jericho in the year one hundred and seventy-seven, in the eleventh month (that is, the month Shebat). [15] The son of Abubus gave them a deceitful welcome in the little stronghold called Dok which he had built. While serving them a sumptuous banquet, he had his men hidden there. [16] Then, when Simon and his sons had drunk freely, Ptolemy and his men sprang up, weapons in hand, rushed upon Simon in the banquet hall, and killed him, his two sons, and some of his servants. [17] By this vicious act of treason he repaid good with evil.

NRSV

[11] Now Ptolemy son of Abubus had been appointed governor over the plain of Jericho; he had a large store of silver and gold, [12] for he was son-in-law of the high priest. [13] His heart was lifted up; he determined to get control of the country, and made treacherous plans against Simon and his sons, to do away with them. [14] Now Simon was visiting the towns of the country and attending to their needs, and he went down to Jericho with his sons Mattathias and Judas, in the one hundred seventy-seventh year,[a] in the eleventh month, which is the month of Shebat. [15] The son of Abubus received them treacherously in the little stronghold called Dok, which he had built; he gave them a great banquet, and hid men there. [16] When Simon and his sons were drunk, Ptolemy and his men rose up, took their weapons, rushed in against Simon in the banquet hall and killed

[a] 134 B.C.

NAB

18 Then Ptolemy wrote an account of this and sent it to the king, asking that troops be sent to help him and that the country be turned over to him. 19 He sent other men to Gazara to do away with John. To the army officers he sent letters inviting them to come to him so that he might present them with silver, gold, and gifts. 20 He also sent others to seize Jerusalem and the mount of the temple. 21 But someone ran ahead and brought word to John at Gazara that his father and his brothers had perished, and that Ptolemy had sent men to kill him also. 22 On hearing this, John was utterly astounded. When the men came to kill him, he had them arrested and put to death, for he knew what they meant to do.

NRSV

him and his two sons, as well as some of his servants. 17So he committed an act of great treachery and returned evil for good.

18Then Ptolemy wrote a report about these things and sent it to the king, asking him to send troops to aid him and to turn over to him the towns and the country. 19He sent other troops to Gazara to do away with John; he sent letters to the captains asking them to come to him so that he might give them silver and gold and gifts; 20and he sent other troops to take possession of Jerusalem and the temple hill. 21But someone ran ahead and reported to John at Gazara that his father and brothers had perished, and that "he has sent men to kill you also." 22When he heard this, he was greatly shocked; he seized the men who came to destroy him and killed them, for he had found out that they were seeking to destroy him.

COMMENTARY

After an interval of three years, in the winter of 134 BCE, Simon's son-in-law, Ptolemy, son of Abubus, attempted a coup. He knew that Antiochus VII was opposed to Simon (15:27, 36, 38-39) and perhaps that Antiochus was preparing to invade Judea, which he did a few months later, when he ultimately captured Jerusalem. This victory of Antiochus VII is not mentioned in 1 Maccabees, a loose end left untied.

16:11-12. The fertile plain of Jericho is now securely in Hasmonean hands. One should note how Simon had kept powerful positions within the family. We learn here that Simon had at least one daughter besides his four sons; the author also indicates that Ptolemy was related by marriage to the family through whom deliverance was given to Israel (5:62). The wealth of Simon has already been indicated (15:32).

16:13. As Alexander's heart had been lifted up (1:3), so now is Ptolemy's. He wishes to control the country, as Simon had done. And like Nicanor, who had sought to take Judas and his brothers deceitfully and so destroy the people (7:26-27), and typical of the Seleucids, Ptolemy uses deceit "against Simon and his sons, to do away with them." In particular,

note how Ptolemy VI sought to get control of the Seleucid kingdom by treachery (11:1).

16:14. On a tour of inspection to determine how the country was being administered, Simon visits Jericho. The eleventh month of the Sel Bab year 177 would have fallen in January/February of 134 BCE. Winter would have been a good time to visit the warm area of Jericho, as summer is much too hot there.

16:15-17. Dok was a small fortress near Jericho that some scholars have identified with the top of the Mount of Temptation. Ptolemy commits one of the cardinal sins in the Greco-Roman world by breaking the law of hospitality. Once one had eaten or drunk with a guest, one was bound to treat that guest properly. On the contrary, Ptolemy prepares an ambush and kills the drunken Simon and his sons, repaying good with evil (cf. Ps 7:4). According to Josephus, Ptolemy did not immediately kill Simon's sons and wife but waited until later, when besieged by John.[133] We cannot be sure which version is true, although Josephus's account is highly emotional

133. Josephus *Antiquities of the Jews* 13.228-235.

and sensational. This discrepancy alerts us to the fact that ancient historians differed in their accounts of how leaders died—Alexander the Great was variously depicted as killed by poisoning, by carousing, or by a fever (see Commentary on 1:5-9). Given this tendency of ancient historians to create a death that they thought was appropriate, it is interesting that the author of 1 Maccabees reports that Simon and his sons get drunk at a great carousal and then are killed. Josephus, more discreetly, writes that Simon dies at a banquet, which a discerning reader would know included heavy drinking.[134] Did the author of 1 Maccabees feel obliged to tell the truth no matter what? He did not feel so obliged in describing the death of Antiochus IV because of disappointment and regret over what Antiochus had done in Judea (6:8-13). How would the author of 1 Maccabees have come by his knowledge of Simon's death?

The motif of being killed by one's enemies while one is drunk is found elsewhere in the Hebrew Scriptures. In 1 Kgs 16:8-10 it is used to describe the death of Elah, king of Israel. In Judith (12:10–13:10), Holofernes gets drunk at his own banquet, with dire results. The wisdom tradition in Judaism is against drunkenness:

> It is not for kings, O Lemuel,
>   it is not for kings to drink wine,
>   or for rulers to desire strong drink;
> or else they will drink and forget
>   what has been decreed,
> and will pervert the rights of all
>   the afflicted.
>   (Prov 31:4-5; cf. 23:29-35 NRSV)

134. Ibid.

Why would the author of 1 Maccabees insist, then, that Simon was drunk? Does he feel that this is the only way Simon could be overcome? But even this answer gives the picture of an old man taking part in the all-male ritual of drinking to excess, possibly with courtesans available. Such a picture of excess reinforces the image of magnificent extravagance conveyed in the "splendor of Simon" (15:32). The family of Mattathias is shown as indulging in the luxuries and extravagances of the wealthy.

16:18-22. Just as Alcimus had needed help from the Seleucids to control the country (7:20), so also Ptolemy now seeks help. "To turn over to him the towns and the country" resonates with what Antiochus VII had demanded (15:28-31). However, "country" in this context would refer to the territory of Judea (7:7, 20; 11:64; 12:25; 13:34; 14:6), just as the phrase "the country and the towns in it" (14:17) clearly refers to Judea. So Ptolemy had more in mind than placating Antiochus's demands; he intended to submit Judea again to Seleucid control. With such a goal, Ptolemy seems to bring the reader back to the beginning of the narrative, when renegades from Israel wanted to make a covenant with the Gentiles (1:11).

Ptolemy acts quickly to control the land. He needs to control Jerusalem and the temple mount, which Simon had fortified and where he had lived (13:52). Ptolemy also needs to win over the army leaders by bribes (16:11); most important, he needs to do away with John to complete his plan (16:13). The author emphasizes that John acts in self-defense, as opposed to Ptolemy's treachery.

1 MACCABEES 16:23-24, CONCLUSION

NAB	NRSV
23 Now the rest of the history of John, his wars and the brave deeds he performed, his rebuilding of the walls, and his other achievements— 24 these things are recorded in the chronicle of his pontificate, from the time that he succeeded his father as high priest.	23The rest of the acts of John and his wars and the brave deeds that he did, and the building of the walls that he completed, and his achievements, 24are written in the annals of his high priesthood, from the time that he became high priest after his father.

COMMENTARY

The ending tells us that John ruled successfully, so Ptolemy's rebellion did not last long. According to Josephus, John reached Jerusalem ahead of Ptolemy's men and gained control of the city. At that, Ptolemy retreated to Dok, where John besieged him. John is said to have abandoned the siege because a sabbatical year was coming on. Ptolemy fled to Zenon, the ruler of Philadelphia (Amman) in Transjordan.[135] That same year, Antiochus VII invaded Judea and besieged John in Jerusalem. After a lengthy siege marked by surprisingly indulgent behavior from Antiochus, who allowed a truce so that the Feast of Tabernacles could be celebrated, John and Antiochus VII reached a settlement in Jerusalem. The walls of Jerusalem were demolished and coins of Antiochus were minted. Later John accompanied Antiochus on his expedition against the Parthians (130/29 BCE).[136] Only after Antiochus's death on this campaign could John exert his own power. The independence of Judea depended on Seleucid weakness. None of this, however, is reported by the author of 1 Maccabees. He leaves Jerusalem free and independent.

Many questions remain unanswered in this narrative: How will Antiochus VII react to the death of his general Cendebeus? What will happen to the treacherous son-in-law? Does the author presuppose that the reader knows what happens? Why does he end at this point and choose this ending? No mention is made, as had been for Mattathias (2:70), Judas (9:20-21), and Jonathan (12:52; 13:26), that all Israel bewailed Simon's death. Rather, the author ends with a formula, so different from that at Judas's death (9:22) but so similar to that found throughout the books of Kings (e.g., 1 Kgs 14:29; 16:27; 2 Kgs 14:15, 18, 28; 20:20) and used of all rulers, both good and bad. One suspects that the author is hinting that the Hasmoneans have become a ruling family with all that it entails—wealth, a bureaucracy (responsible for writing the high priest's annals), and family intrigue. The heady days of the opening revolt against the Seleucids have been replaced by Hasmonean institutionalization.

135. Ibid., 13.230-235.
136. Ibid., 13.249-251.

REFLECTIONS

The narrative of 1 Maccabees seems to end where it had begun. As the "lawless renegades" had sought Seleucid intervention at the beginning of the story to bring about their control of Judea, so now within the Hasmonean family there are strife and fighting for control of Judea, and one side seeks the support of the Seleucids to gain control. Is the teaching of Ecclesiastes right? Is all vanity? And is there nothing new under the sun (Eccles 1:2, 10)? Perhaps. The author certainly reminds us that nations rise and fall, that rulers come and go, that "uneasy lies the head that wears a crown."

But that is not the total message of the book, for the author also acknowledges that the Maccabees had been the family through whom God had wrought deliverance in Israel. He emphasizes that God does act faithfully to the people if they attempt to follow God's commandments. Torah faithfulness, a longing to serve God at the Temple and at the place God has chosen, vibrates throughout the book. One may question whether today one should follow the same war tactics as Judas and his brothers did; one may be dismayed at the open acceptance of ethnic cleansing as a means to follow God's commandments. But one cannot question whether the Maccabees fought according to their own convictions to keep alive the worship of the God of Israel. For that, their name will be remembered.

THE SECOND BOOK OF MACCABEES

INTRODUCTION, COMMENTARY, AND REFLECTIONS
BY
ROBERT DORAN

THE SECOND BOOK OF
MACCABEES

INTRODUCTION

THE EPITOME, 2 MACCABEES 2:19–15:39

The Second Book of Maccabees is not a continuation of the First Book of Maccabees, but a completely independent work. It covers some of the same material as 1 Maccabees, but in a very different fashion. The story starts during the reign of Seleucus IV Philopator (187–175 BCE) and ends with the defeat of Nicanor in 161 BCE, providing much more detail than 1 Maccabees does about the parties and factions in Jerusalem prior to the persecution by Antiochus VI Epiphanes. The letters preserved in 2 Maccabees 11 are particularly important in reconstructing the events of this period. The book has a formal prologue and epilogue and is structured around three attacks on the Jerusalem Temple: (1) by Heliodorus under Seleucus IV (3:1-39); (2) under Antiochus IV Epiphanes (3:40–10:8); and (3) the final assault by Nicanor under Demetrius I (10:9–15:37).

Style. In contrast to 1 Maccabees, which was originally written in Hebrew and then translated into Greek, the bulk of 2 Maccabees (2:19–15:39, often referred to as the epitome) was written in the typical Greek style of the day. The prologue evidences knowledge of Hellenistic historiographical conventions, as do the reflections that the author (commonly called the epitomist) inserts into the narrative at 4:16-17; 5:17-20; 6:12-17. The narrative reveals an author who loves to indulge in metaphors and word play. The author also strives to heighten the emotional effect of the narrative on his readers or listeners, as in the scene of distress at Heliodorus's approach to the Temple (3:15-22), the attention given to the mother and her seven sons (chap. 7), the emotional turnaround of

Antiochus IV (chap. 9), and the distress of the priests at the insults of Nicanor (14:13-36). This emotional heightening is helped by the author's focusing on individual confrontations—Heliodorus and the high priest, and Nicanor and Judas in the first battle (chap. 8).

The narrative also abounds in tales of the miraculous, as in the graphic descriptions of the epiphanies of God's deliverance of the people at 3:24-28; 5:2-4; 10:29-30; 11:8-11. The presentation of these angelic helpers parallels the stories about divine helpers that one finds in Greco-Roman literature and is further evidence of the author's acquaintance with Greek literature. One could argue, in fact, that the narrative of the epitome falls within the Greek literary genre of epiphanic collections, which tell of the way a god defends his or her temple.

Worldview. While the narrative shows the influence of Greco-Roman literary conventions, the author has used these conventions to portray a confrontation between Judaism (2:21; 8:1; 14:38) and Hellenism (4:13). As far as we know, this is the first appearance of the term "Judaism." For this author, the Jews are the civilized norm, whereas the Greeks are barbarians (2:21; 10:4). The Jewish scribe Eleazar, and not his opponents, is the one who acts nobly (6:18-31). This attitude of separation of Jews from non-Jews is particularly evident in the author's discussion of the gymnasium in Jerusalem. For him, this change in educational system symbolizes the destruction of the Jewish ancestral religion, and he is particularly violent toward Jews participating in the gymnasium.

Although the author stresses that it is always non-Jews who instigate troubles against the Jews, who only defend themselves and their ancestral religion (10:12-14; 12:1-2), he goes out of his way to show that Jews and Gentiles can get along harmoniously. Non-Jews protest the execution of Onias (4:35) and the members of the Jewish council (4:49); the people of Scythopolis treat the Jews kindly during bad times (12:30-31). Even Antiochus IV claims that the Jews are good citizens and asks them to maintain their goodwill toward him and his son and heir (9:19-20, 26). Alcimus accuses the Jews under Judas of not being loyal citizens (14:6-10), but events prove him wrong as Judas makes an agreement with Nicanor and settles down to married life (14:20-25). What is striking about this narrative, in fact, is that the Jews are not portrayed as seeking to set up an independent realm. Rather, the story ends with the Jews able to celebrate their religion in peace, not with political independence. Judas seems quite happy to live a settled life under the Seleucids. This is in sharp contrast to the outlook of the author of 1 Maccabees, who views all Seleucids with suspicion.

The theology of the author has a distinctly deuteronomistic flavor about it. As long as the Jews obey the laws, God keeps them in peace, and they flourish. When they disobey, punishment comes (3:1; 4:16-17; 6:12-17). The author, therefore, shows Judas and his followers as strict observers of the sabbath (8:27) and other festivals (12:31) and links the Festival of Hanukkah to the older Feast of Tabernacles (10:6). The author is a strong believer in punishment fitting the crime, as seen in the fates of Jason and Menelaus, in the execution of Andronicus on the same spot where he had killed Onias (4:38), in the dismemberment of Nicanor (15:32-33), and in the providential care of God, who restores temple worship on the anniversary of the day that it had been profaned (10:5-6).

Date. The epitome of 2 Maccabees (2:19–15:39) is a shortened version of a no longer extant five-volume work by Jason of Cyrene. Scholars have speculated on how to reconstruct Jason's work and when he might have written it. At present, no sure answers to these questions can be given because all we have is the work of the epitomist. Scholars have also tried to reconstruct a "life of Judas" from the events common to both 1 and 2 Maccabees. One can certainly plot out from both books a sequence of battles in which Judas had engaged. But each book has its distinctive way of describing events. The fact that one account is a Greek translation of an original Hebrew text, whereas the other was written originally in Greek, is further reason to make one feel less than sanguine that any source document, in a meaningful sense of the term, can be recovered.

Who, then, was the epitomist of 2 Maccabees, and when and where did he write? We have even fewer clues to go on than with 1 Maccabees. Dates range from the second century BCE to the first century CE. Perhaps, since the text shows a friendly attitude toward the Romans, it might have been written before Pompey's entry into Jerusalem in 63 BCE. Momigliano has suggested that the epitome was written to accompany the first prefixed letter; therefore, the epitome would have been written in 124 BCE.[1] Yet, although one can make connections between the prefixed letters and the epitome, the author of the epitome makes no mention in his prologue that he was writing it to accompany a letter.

If there are no indications as to the date of the epitome, can one then suggest where it might have been written? Scholars have suggested, because it was written in Greek, that it must have come out of the diaspora, possibly from Alexandria, (given the great deal of literary activity by Jews there) or Antioch (since the Maccabean martyrs were celebrated there). The author's knowledge of events affecting Jews in Babylonia (8:20) and the author's polemic against Jews attending a gymnasium lend support to such a theory. Later inscriptional evidence from Cyrene shows that Jews did attend the gymnasium there. Therefore, one might conclude that the work was written by someone in the diaspora who was concerned that young Jewish men were beginning to attend the local gymnasium. The author wanted to write against that practice and yet still insist that Jews can be good and loyal residents wherever they live. But there is no reason why someone living in Jerusalem who was fluent in Greek could not have written it. The temptation to attend a gymnasium could be present anywhere in the Hellenistic world.

THE PREFIXED LETTERS, 1:1–2:18

The position of the two letters at the beginning of 2 Maccabees is quite perplexing. What is their connection to the epitome? Why were they added? From where do they come? Since the two letters are addressed to Alexandrian Jews, were they part of some

1. Momigliano, "The Second Book of Maccabees," *CP* 70 (1975) 83-84.

letter archive in Alexandria? Each letter is quite different from the other. Most scholars would see the first letter as authentic but have serious questions regarding the authenticity of the second one. While the first letter follows the conventions of letters written in Aramaic/Hebrew, the second does not and yet abounds in Semitisms. As mentioned above, Momigliano suggested that the epitome was written to accompany the first letter, but there is no explicit mention of this in either the letter or the prologue to the epitome. Also, the account of the death of Antiochus IV in the epitome cannot be reconciled with the account of his death in the second letter.

Yet connections can be seen between the letters and the epitome. While in 1 Maccabees Judas and his followers celebrate the purification of the Temple for eight days (1 Macc 5:56), only in the epitome and in the prefixed letters of 2 Maccabees is the festival explicitly connected with the Feast of Tabernacles (2 Macc 1:10, 18; 10:6). One might also note how both the first prefixed letter and the epitome use a Greek form—"to reconcile," "reconciliation" (καταλλάσσω *katallassō*; καταλλαγή *katallagē*)—which is very unusual in the LXX (2 Macc 1:5; 5:20; 7:33; 8:29). Finally, at the climactic battle against Nicanor, Judas's mission is divinely sanctioned and approved through the figure of the prophet Jeremiah (15:14-16), and Jeremiah figures prominently in the second letter (2:1-8). One should note, of course, that in the epitome the figure of Jeremiah is used to connect Judas with Israel's past, whereas in the letter Jeremiah's hiding of the temple vessels speaks of a discontinuity with the First Temple.

What binds the letters to the epitome most strongly is the connection between the Festival of Hanukkah and the Feast of Tabernacles in Kislev. The second letter dates itself to the lifetime of Judas (between 164 and 160 BCE), the first to 124 BCE. Perhaps the letters were added to the epitome sometime after 124 BCE, but exactly when is unknown. The most likely location of the writing, given the addressees of the letters, is Alexandria.

Finally, it is interesting to speculate whether the letters affect the message of the epitome. The addition of the first letter does not change the message much. The second letter, however, adds to the message of the epitome in several ways. Its emphasis on the continuity between the First and Second Temples and the connections it forges between Judas and Nehemiah underline God's concern with the covenant people and for their following covenant laws. In addition, the second letter concludes with a prayer for the ingathering of God's holy people (2 Macc 2:18). This prayer, which resonates with that of the priests at the miraculous rekindling of the temple fire (1:26-29), has eschatological overtones, especially given the concern that the Jews of the diaspora return to the holy land. The writer of the epitome, however, shows no concern for eschatology.

❖   ❖   ❖   ❖   ❖

For more discussion of the historical background of 1 and 2 Maccabees, of the ethics of violence in both books, and of the place of 1 and 2 Maccabees in Jewish and Christian tradition, see the Introduction to 1 Maccabees. See also the annotated bibliography located there.

OUTLINE OF 2 MACCABEES

I. 2 Maccabees 1:1–2:18, The Prefixed Letters

    A. 1:1-9, The First Letter

    B. 1:10–2:18, The Second Letter
        1:10-17, The Letter to Aristobulus
        1:18–2:18, The Holiness of the Second Temple

II. 2 Maccabees 2:19-32, The Prologue

III. 2 Maccabees 3:1-40, The First Crisis

    A. 3:1-8, The Problem

    B. 3:9-14*a*, The Attack on the Temple

    C. 3:14*b*-21, The Cry for Help

    D. 3:22-30, The Lord Defends His Temple

    E. 3:31-40, The Effect on Heliodorus

IV. 2 Maccabees 4:1–10:8, The Second Attack on the Temple

    A. 4:1–6:17, The Attack on the Traditional Way of Life
        4:1-6, The Removal of Onias
        4:7-22, The High Priesthood of Jason
        4:23-50, Menelaus in Control
        5:1-27, Antiochus Takes Control of Jerusalem
        6:1-11, The Pagan Cult Imposed in Jerusalem
        6:12-17, Punishment Seen as Discipline

    B. 6:18–7:42, The Reaction to the Persecutions
        6:18-31, Eleazar
        7:1-42, The Mother and Her Seven Sons

    C. 8:1–10:8, God's Defense of the People
        8:1-36, The First Victory
        9:1-29, The Death of Antiochus IV
        10:1-8, The Purification of the Temple

THE PREFIXED LETTERS

OVERVIEW

As mentioned in the Introduction, the epitome of events surrounding the successful rebellion of the Jews under Judas Maccabeus against their Seleucid overlords is preceded by two letters, 1:1-9 and 1:10–2:18. It is not known when or by whom these letters were prefixed, and so it is difficult to evaluate exactly what is the relationship between the letters and between the letters and the epitome. Some scholars have argued that the epitome was written to accompany the first letter; the Introduction suggests ways in which connections may be made between the language and themes of the letters and the epitome. But no explicit connection is made in the documents themselves, thus one could argue that the letters and the epitome circulated independently and that no intrinsic connection between the letters and the narrative should be sought.

2 MACCABEES 1:1-9, THE FIRST LETTER

NAB

1 The Jews in Jerusalem and in the land of Judea send greetings to their brethren, the Jews in Egypt, and wish them true peace! ² May God bless you and remember his covenant with his faithful servants, Abraham, Isaac and Jacob. ³ May he give to all of you a heart to worship him and to do his will readily and generously. ⁴ May he open your heart to his law and his commandments and grant you peace. ⁵ May he hear your prayers, and be reconciled to you, and never forsake you in time of adversity. ⁶ Even now we are praying for you here.

⁷ In the reign of Demetrius, the year one hundred and sixty-nine, we Jews wrote to you during the trouble and violence that overtook us in those years after Jason and his followers had revolted against the holy land and the kingdom, ⁸ setting fire to the gatehouse and shedding innocent blood. But we prayed to the LORD, and our prayer was heard; we offered sacrifices and fine flour; we lighted the lamps and set out the loaves

NRSV

1 The Jews in Jerusalem and those in the land of Judea,
To their Jewish kindred in Egypt,
Greetings and true peace.

2May God do good to you, and may he remember his covenant with Abraham and Isaac and Jacob, his faithful servants. ³May he give you all a heart to worship him and to do his will with a strong heart and a willing spirit. ⁴May he open your heart to his law and his commandments, and may he bring peace. ⁵May he hear your prayers and be reconciled to you, and may he not forsake you in time of evil. ⁶We are now praying for you here.

7In the reign of Demetrius, in the one hundred sixty-ninth year,ᵃ we Jews wrote to you, in the critical distress that came upon us in those years after Jason and his company revolted from the holy land and the kingdom ⁸and burned the gate and shed innocent blood. We prayed to the Lord and were heard, and we offered sacrifice and grain

ᵃ 143 B.C.

NAB

of bread. ⁹ We are now reminding you to cele-brate the feast of Booths in the month of Chislev.

NRSV

offering, and we lit the lamps and set out the loaves. ⁹And now see that you keep the festival of booths in the month of Chislev, in the one hundred eighty-eighth year.ᵃ

ᵃ 124 B.C.

COMMENTARY

1:1-6, Initial Greetings and Well Wishes. The first letter contains an initial indication of the addressees and the senders of the letter and greet-ings (v. 1), the well wishes (vv. 2-6), the body of the letter (vv. 7-9), and the concluding date (v. 10*a*), thus following the normal structure of a letter. The letter can be dated to the year 124 BCE (v. 9), which had seen in Egypt an uneasy end to the bitter civil war between Ptolemy VIII Euergetes II and his sister/wife Cleopatra II.

1:1. Cleopatra may have been helped in her struggle by Jewish generals, as they played a role in earlier and later debates.[2] But no mention is made of specific leaders in the letter, however, as the emphasis lies on strengthening the ties that bind all the Jews together; note in the initial greeting the repetition of "brothers" and "Jews," as the Jews in Egypt and in Judea are placed on an equal footing. The initial greeting formula "To X, Y," is often found in Aramaic letters. The present text of v. 1 has a double greeting—"greetings and true peace." The first is what one normally finds in Greek letters; the second is more Jewish.

1:2-6. Following this initial greeting is a long prayer of well wishing for the Egyptian Jews, similar to prayers in the openings of Pauline letters (see, e.g., Phil 1:9-11). The prayer is full of general wishes and hopes. The writers stress the covenant of God with the patriarchs as the common ground of their faith (v. 2). Just as God had heard the groaning of the Israelites while they were slaves in Egypt and had "remembered his covenant with Abraham, Isaac, and Jacob" and looked upon them to take notice of them (Exod 2:24-25 NRSV), so also the writers of this letter ask that God remember the covenant with the Egyptian

Jews, a resonance no doubt that the Egyptian readers would have picked up on (cf. Exod 6:4-5; Lev 26:42; Ps 105:8-10; see also Deut 4:31). They ask that God give their brethren a "heart" (v. 3), i.e., understanding; the letter resonates with the language of Ezek 36:26-27 where God promises that, at the renewal of Israel, God will give the Israelites a new heart and spirit so that they will walk in God's statutes and observe God's ordi-nances (cf. Jer 31:33-34; Ezek 18:31). The Egyp-tian Jews are to serve God, whose will is known through Moses' law (cf. Ps 103:7), wholeheart-edly and willingly, a phrase similar to that in 1 Chr 28:9, where David instructs his son Solo-mon to serve God. In contrast to that passage, however, the emphasis in the prayer before us is all on God's action. Verse 4 gives the same message as v. 3 but makes explicit the connection with the Torah and its ordinances; instead of God's giving them a heart, God will open their hearts/minds, a phrase in Acts, when God "opened the heart" of Lydia to listen to what Paul had to say (Acts 16:14) and in Luke, when the risen Jesus is said to appear to his disciples and to open their minds to understand the scriptures (Luke 24:45). God is the one who grants peace.

The verb for "be reconciled" (καταλλάσσω *katallassō*, v. 5) is unusual in the rest of the LXX, but is used at 2 Macc 7:33 and 8:29 as God's response to prayers. The same notion is found when Solomon, at the dedication of the Temple, prays that God will listen to the people's prayers and forgive them (2 Chr 6:19). As in Ps 20:1-4, God is asked to answer on the day of trouble and to grant the heart's desire and the plans of the one who prays. Sirach 51:10-12 states that Sirach himself prayed so that the Lord would not forsake him in his days of trouble; Sirach's prayer was heard, and he was delivered from an evil time.

2. Josephus *Against Apion* 2.49-52; *Antiquities of the Jews* 13.284-287, 348-355.

Some scholars have seen in this verse an allusion to specific events in Egypt: the civil war between Ptolemy VIII Euergetes and Cleopatra II. Some have also proposed that the reference to reconciliation is an oblique reference to the Egyptians' need for reconciliation because of the sin that Onias IV had committed in building a temple to Yahweh at Leontopolis in Egypt. Josephus, the Jewish historian of the first century CE, records that Onias IV, the son of Onias III, fled to Ptolemy Philometer for refuge after his uncle, the high priest Menelaus, was murdered. In Egypt Onias IV had requested permission from Ptolemy to build a temple in Egypt similar to that in Jerusalem, perhaps to fulfill the prophecy of Isa 19:19: "On that day there will be an altar to the LORD in the center of the land of Egypt" (NRSV). This temple, however, was set up for the Jewish military colony at Leontopolis under Onias IV.[3] It is not likely that it was set up as a temple for Egyptian Jews to rival that in Jerusalem, as it has such a remote location and receives no attention in other writings of Egyptian Jews. Rather than an oblique reference to Onias's temple the prayer should be viewed as expressing general wishes for the well-being of the Jews in Egypt. Nevertheless, general expressions could be given a specific meaning depending on the reader's own life situation. What is particularly striking in this prayer is the sense of God as the primary agent. The Egyptian Jews are not asked to open their hearts; rather, God is the one who opens hearts. At v. 6, a well-known formula in Aramaic letters, "and now," is used to show the end of this prayer for well-being. The unity of brethren is especially evidenced in the unity of prayer.

1:7-9, The Body of the Letter. 1:7-8a.
The body of the letter contains a quotation from a previous letter (v. 7). This letter had been written in the 169th year, according to the Seleucid Babylonian calendar—i.e., between spring 143 and spring 142 BCE. According to 1 Maccabees, the Judean Jews had a checkered relationship with Demetrius II (145–140). After Demetrius came to power, Jonathan the Hasmonean was at first in alliance with him, but later was estranged from him and became a supporter of the young Antiochus VI (145–142). After the treachery of Antio-

chus's general Trypho, Simon made peace with Demetrius (1 Macc 10:67–13:40). First Maccabees also states that in 170 by the Seleucid Babylonian calendar, Jews in Judea gave the date according to the year of Simon (1 Macc 13:42). The earlier letter, therefore, presumably preceded this lifting of the yoke of the Gentiles. But the text as we now have it is extremely difficult to translate. For example, it is not clear to what event the phrase "critical distress" refers. Since the letter was written in 143–142 BCE, it may refer to the fact that Jonathan had been captured (1 Macc 12:48; 13:23). After the opening well wishes, then, the authors may immediately quote from another letter, with no indication that they were so doing. The NRSV translation, on the other hand, suggests that an introductory statement is made: "In the reign of Demetrius . . . we Jews wrote to you." But the question still remains as to when the quotation begins, since there are no quotation marks in Greek. The sentence may mean either "During the reign of Demetrius we wrote in the great distress," or "During the reign of Demetrius we wrote, 'In the great distress that came upon us. . . . '" If the distress had been caused by Jonathan's death, why did the authors refer instead to Jason's withdrawal, which had occurred more than twenty years earlier? Thus, along with the NRSV, the quotation begins "In the great distress. . . ."

Even after settling this issue, problems remain: Who had set fire to the gates and shed innocent blood (v. 8)? Commentators have normally seen the subject as Jason and his followers, since Jason is described in 2 Macc 4:10 as leading Jews away from their ancestral customs. The end of v. 7, therefore, is translated as referring to Jason's revolt from the holy land and the kingdom (of God), with cross-reference to Jason's attack on Menelaus, when Jason slaughtered his fellow citizens relentlessly (2 Macc 5:6). There are some problems with this interpretation, however, both historically and grammatically. The author of 2 Maccabees reports that the gates of Jerusalem were burned by someone other than Jason (2 Macc 8:33; cf. 1 Macc 1:31; 4:38). It is also difficult to say that someone "revolted from" a land and a kingdom; one usually revolts from a person. One of these difficulties would be solved if we under-

---

3. Josephus *Antiquities of the Jews* 12.387; 13.62-73; *The Jewish War* 7.420-432.

stood the Greek verb ἀφίστημι (*aphistēmi*) not as "revolt," but with its basic geographical meaning "to withdraw from." While in the narrative of 2 Maccabees Jason institutes Greek customs, it is only after his withdrawal that Antiochus IV plunders the Temple and attempts to crush Jewish practices in Judea (2 Macc 5:7; 6:1-6). It is probably better, therefore, to understand the third-person plural verbs (ἐνεπύριοαν *enepyrisan*; ἐξεχεαν *exechean*), as frequently in Hellenistic Greek, in an impersonal sense: "the gate was burned and innocent blood shed." The reference would then be to the events of Antiochus IV's persecution. Burnt gates traditionally indicate a defenseless, plundered city. However one translates the verse, it is striking that the writers of the letter presuppose that their addressees know who Jason was, a figure who had left the scene over twenty-five years before the letter was sent, and also that there is no need to mention the name of Antiochus IV. One could contrast this shorthand version of events with those in 1 Maccabees, where Jason is not named and Antiochus IV is the evil force behind the persecution.

1:8b. The tumultuous events of the Hasmonean revolt and the rededication of the Temple in Jerusalem are summed up in this verse: We prayed. We were heard. We offered sacrifices. Once again the emphasis falls on God's action. Later in the narrative, emphasis will be placed on the martyrdoms as bringing about God's mercy. Here it is simply stated, "We prayed." The ritual actions referred to are the daily burnt offering (Exod 29:38-42), the continuously burning lamps (Exod 27:20-21), and the showbread, which was to be on the table before the Lord always (Exod 25:30; Lev 24:5-9). It is interesting that no mention is made of the daily offering of incense (Exod 30:7-8), whereas it is mentioned at the rededication of the Temple in 1 Macc 4:50 and 2 Macc 10:3 (Dan 11:31 mentions the suppression of the daily burnt offering by Antiochus IV).

1:9. The formula "and now" is used as at v. 6 as a dividing marker, here indicating the end of the quotation. The Feast of Booths (Sukkot) was celebrated in the seventh month of Tishri, not the ninth month of Chislev, as the author here states. Only here and at 2 Macc 1:18 and 10:6 is a connection made between the Feast of Booths and Hanukkah, the festival in Chislev to celebrate the rededication of the Temple. Hanukkah is said to last for eight days (2 Macc 10:6; cf. Lev 23:36; Num 29:35). According to 2 Chr 7:8-9, the dedication of Solomon's Temple, celebrated in conjunction with Booths, followed this model (although in 1 Kgs 8:65-66 Solomon sends the people away on the eighth day). The returning exiles followed it also when they celebrated Booths (Neh 8:18). Sukkot reminds the people of the Israelites who lived in the wilderness during the exodus from Egypt (Lev 23:42-43), and likewise the festival in Chislev recalls how Judas and his followers lived away from civilization (2 Macc 10:6). All of these connotations combine to allow the feast in the ninth month (Chislev) to be called the Feast of Sukkot. The date is given at the end of the letter: 124 BCE.

REFLECTIONS

This letter as it now stands has a very cryptic quality. If we did not possess the narrative of 2 Maccabees, we would not know who Jason was, or what was meant by celebrating the Feast of Tabernacles in the ninth month. Would the addressees of this letter, written over forty years after Jason's tenure as high priest, have had a clear grasp of what the letter was referring to? If they did, then we must presuppose a strongly held cultural tradition whereby the events of the Maccabean revolt were transmitted and kept alive. One can surmise that it was during the eight-day celebration of Hanukkah that the stories and traditions would have been related and retold. This context of community celebration and storytelling is not mentioned in our sources, but if we are to realize what life must have been like in the second century BCE, we have to use our imaginations to reconstruct the scene. Parents must have told the traditional stories to their children time and again; the children must have heard and seen them reenacted at liturgical celebrations, and so it must have penetrated into their consciousness.

This living reality of how traditions and cultures are transmitted often eludes us, but it is going on day after day in the stories we tell to our children, in the way our children see us behave toward others. We must learn to value and to recognize the importance of this teaching and transmission of values, a family- and community-based teaching that takes place not in the classroom, but in daily living. We must also recognize that there are other means by which values are being imparted to our children and must strive to filter out what is good from what is bad.

The letter also forces us to reflect on how important liturgical activity is to preserving a sense of community between geographically distant groups. It is central to the forging of familial relations. Can one hope that different religious communities would learn to celebrate together? Would this not help to strengthen bonds across communities and to dispel prejudice? At the same time, the letter stresses that this liturgical activity is dependent on God's action in moving human hearts and minds to action. This emphasis on God's grace, on God's being present in human affairs, is precious testimony to the strong belief of second-century BCE Judaism in God's gracious action. It should counterbalance any claim that Judaism before the time of Jesus was legalistic and barren. The belief in God's grace and in God's graciously covenanting with the Jews was still alive and strong.

2 MACCABEES 1:10–2:18, THE SECOND LETTER

OVERVIEW

While the length of the first letter is known from the initial greetings and the concluding date in 1:9, the extent of the second letter is quite problematic. At 1:18 the letter seems about to end with an exhortation to the addressees to celebrate the purification of the Temple on the twenty-fifth day of the month Chislev, but it then suddenly launches into an extended apologetic on the holiness of the Second Temple; at 2:16 one finds almost exactly the same phrase as at 1:18: "we shall celebrate the purification." No concluding date is given to the letter there. Should one consider the section 1:18–2:15 a digression or an insertion? Problems also arise concerning the authenticity of this letter. If it was written at the time of Judas Maccabeus and after the death of Antiochus IV, it must be dated between 164 BCE (Antiochus's death) and 160 BCE (Judas's death). Why, then, is no mention made of this letter by the writers of the first letter, written in 124 BCE, who quote an otherwise unknown letter from 143 BCE? More difficult to solve would be the chro-

nology involved. If Antiochus IV died between November 20 and December 18, 164, near Isfahan, how could the news of his death have reached Jerusalem in time for the council to convene a meeting, draft this letter, and then send it to Egypt so that it would reach there before mid-December 164 (25 Chislev)? Even if one dates the events to 165 BCE, the problem still remains. Scholars have attempted to solve this difficulty by suggesting that the letter was written so that the Egyptian Jews would celebrate the anniversary of the first feast of purification, but the language of 1:18, following on the account of Antiochus's death, suggests rather a first celebration. The most likely solution is that this letter was not written by Judas and his followers, but is an attempt by some later writer to show that two well-known Jewish contemporaries, Judas Maccabeus and Aristobulus, had dealings with each other.

2 Maccabees 1:10-17, The Letter to Aristobulus

NAB

[10] Dated in the year one hundred and eighty-eight.

The people of Jerusalem and Judea, the senate, and Judas send greetings and good wishes to Aristobulus, counselor of King Ptolemy and member of the family of the anointed priests, and to the Jews in Egypt. [11] Since we have been saved by God from grave dangers, we give him great thanks for having fought on our side against the king; [12] it was he who drove out those who fought against the holy city. [13] When their leader arrived in Persia with his seemingly irresistible army, they were cut to pieces in the temple of the goddess Nanea through a deceitful stratagem employed by Nanea's priests. [14] On the pretext of marrying the goddess, Antiochus with his Friends had come to the place to get its great treasures by way of dowry. [15] When the priests of the Nanaeon had displayed the treasures, Antiochus with a few attendants came to the temple precincts. As soon as he entered the temple, the priests locked the doors. [16] Then they opened a hidden trapdoor in the ceiling, hurled stones at the leader and his companions and struck them down. They dismembered the bodies, cut off their heads and tossed them to the people outside. [17] Forever blessed be our God, who has thus punished the wicked!

1, 11: (*hōs an pros*) tom (*basilea*) *parataxamenō:* conj; cf LXX[V].

NRSV

[10] The people of Jerusalem and of Judea and the senate and Judas,

To Aristobulus, who is of the family of the anointed priests, teacher of King Ptolemy, and to the Jews in Egypt,

Greetings and good health.

[11] Having been saved by God out of grave dangers we thank him greatly for taking our side against the king,[a] [12] for he drove out those who fought against the holy city. [13] When the leader reached Persia with a force that seemed irresistible, they were cut to pieces in the temple of Nanea by a deception employed by the priests of the goddess[b] Nanea. [14] On the pretext of intending to marry her, Antiochus came to the place together with his Friends, to secure most of its treasures as a dowry. [15] When the priests of the temple of Nanea had set out the treasures and Antiochus had come with a few men inside the wall of the sacred precinct, they closed the temple as soon as he entered it. [16] Opening a secret door in the ceiling, they threw stones and struck down the leader and his men; they dismembered them and cut off their heads and threw them to the people outside. [17] Blessed in every way be our God, who has brought judgment on those who have behaved impiously.

[a] Cn: Gk *as those who array themselves against a king*
[b] Gk lacks *the goddess*

COMMENTARY

1:10. The initial greeting has the form: X to Y. In contrast to the first letter, the addressees are not called "brothers." A senate in Jerusalem is first mentioned during the time of Antiochus III.[4] The chiastic structure of the greeting places Judas in contact with Aristobulus, the only person about whom further information is given. Fragments of the works of a Jewish author named Aristobulus, who presented a work to Ptolemy VI Philometer (180–145 BCE), are known from the later Christian writer Eusebius.[5] Aristobulus argued that Greek authors, like Homer and Hesiod, were dependent on the wisdom contained in the Torah. The author of this letter calls Aristobulus a tutor of the Ptolemaic king and an Aaronide (Exod 29:7, 29). The prestige of Judas is thus enhanced by connecting him with such a respected figure.

This formula "greetings and good health" is unusual. It appears in a letter from the fourth century BCE and then disappears until the middle

4. Josephus *Antiquities of the Jews* 12:142.

5. Eusebius *Preparation for the Gospel* 7.32.16-18; 8.9.28–8.10.17; 13.12.1-16.

of the first century BCE, and is then used only infrequently. This epigraphic silence, however, is not conclusive for dating the letter.

1:11-12. The account of the death of Antiochus is prefaced by a general statement about God's care for Jerusalem; God is the one who always expels those who attack the holy city (cf. 2 Macc 3:39). Here as elsewhere in the Hebrew Scriptures, God fights for Israel as a divine warrior (see, e.g., Exod 14:25; Deut 3:22).

1:13-16. This account of the death of Antiochus IV differs from that found in other contemporary sources (and 1 Macc 6:16; 2 Maccabees 9) in that they all agree that Antiochus did not die at the temple of Nanea.[6] The divergence here is similar to that of accounts of the death of Antiochus III. According to Diodorus Siculus, Antiochus III plundered a temple at Elymais and was later punished by the gods;[7] Justin, however, reports that Antiochus III died with his whole army in his attack on the temple.[8] The author of this account mentions the temple is that of Nanea, a goddess of fertility, which is similar to Polybius's account. In Polybius's version, Antiochus makes an expedition against the temple of Artemis in Elymais, but is foiled by the local tribes and dies while retreating. Polybius states that some say Antiochus was smitten with madness and that there were manifestations of divine displeasure at his attempt on the sanctuary.[9] What is interesting is how different the account in this letter is from that in 2 Macc 9:19-27. In that chapter, the author describes Antiochus's attempt to rob the temples in Persepolis. The people resist, and Antiochus retreats. At Ecbatana, Antiochus learns of Judas's success, rushes to return to defeat the Jews, but dies on the journey when he is smitten by an incurable disease. One cannot reconcile these accounts. The places are different, the manner of death is different. One must conclude,

therefore, that this letter and the epitome were produced independently of each other. This does not mean, however, that they do not have common themes which connect them as we shall see below.

Antiochus came to the temple of Nanea on the pretext of marrying the goddess. The marriage of a king to a goddess (v. 14) was an ancient ritual. Antiochus IV is elsewhere reported to have married Atargatis of Hierapolis-Bambyke in Syria and to have claimed as dowry the temple treasury. The priests of Nanea are portrayed as being particularly deceptive (vv. 15-16; cf. the hidden doors in Bel and the Dragon 21; Dan 14:21 LXX). The author seems to suggest ironically that the priests kill Antiochus IV with thunderbolts à la Zeus through a hidden door in the ceiling (the word translated "struck down" [συνεκεραύνωσαν *sunekeraunōsan*] literally means "strike with a thunderbolt"), and he enjoys recounting the grisly details. The author of the epitome will recount how Nicanor's head was cut off and hung up on the citadel in Jerusalem (2 Macc 15:30-35). In a similar way, Judith is said to have cut off the head of the invading general Holofernes and had his head hung up on the wall of the city (Judith 13–14), and the people of Abel of Beth-maacah cut off the head of Sheba, son of Bichri, who rebelled against David, and tossed his head out to Joab (2 Sam 20:22). In the book of Daniel, King Nebuchadnezzar threatens dismemberment to any of his dream interpreters who cannot tell the king what he had dreamed and its interpretation (Dan 2:5).

1:17. This verse recalls Ahimaz's report that the revolt of Absalom against David has been defeated (2 Sam 18:28). Does the impiety refer only to Antiochus's attack on Israel and Jerusalem (1:11-12), or does it include his attack on other temples as well? Given the context, it seems that the author sees the attack on other temples as improper behavior.

---

6. See Polybius 31:9; Appian *Syriaca* 66.
7. Diodorus Siculus 29.15.
8. Justin *Epitome* 32.2.1-2.
9. Polybius 31:9.

2 Maccabees 1:18–2:18, The Holiness of the Second Temple

NAB

18 We shall be celebrating the purification of the temple on the twenty-fifth day of the month Chislev, so we thought it right to inform you that you too may celebrate the feast of Booths and of the fire that appeared when Nehemiah, the re-builder of the temple and the altar, offered sacrifices. 19 When our fathers were being exiled to Persia, devout priests of the time took some of the fire from the altar and hid it secretly in the hollow of a dry cistern, making sure that the place would be unknown to anyone. 20 Many years later, when it so pleased God, Nehemiah, commissioned by the king of Persia, sent the descendants of the priests who had hidden the fire to look for it. 21 When they informed us that they could not find any fire, but only muddy water, he ordered them to scoop some out and bring it. After the material for the sacrifices had been prepared, Nehemiah ordered the priests to sprinkle with the water the wood and what lay on it. 22 When this was done and in time the sun, which had been clouded over, began to shine, a great fire blazed up, so that everyone marveled. 23 While the sacrifice was being burned, the priests recited a prayer, and all present joined in with them, Jonathan leading and the rest responding with Nehemiah.

24 The prayer was as follows: "LORD, LORD God, creator of all things, awesome and strong, just and merciful, the only king and benefactor, 25 who alone are gracious, just, almighty, and eternal, Israel's savior from all evil, who chose our forefathers and sanctified them: 26 accept this sacrifice on behalf of all your people Israel and guard and sanctify your heritage. 27 Gather together our scattered people, free those who are the slaves of the Gentiles, look kindly on those who are despised and detested, and let the Gentiles know that you are our God. 28 Punish those who tyrannize over us and arrogantly mistreat us. 29 Plant your people in your holy place, as Moses promised."

30 Then the priests began to sing hymns. 31 After the sacrifice was burned, Nehemiah ordered the rest of the liquid to be poured upon large stones. 32 As soon as this was done, a flame blazed up,

NRSV

18Since on the twenty-fifth day of Chislev we shall celebrate the purification of the temple, we thought it necessary to notify you, in order that you also may celebrate the festival of booths and the festival of the fire given when Nehemiah, who built the temple and the altar, offered sacrifices. 19For when our ancestors were being led captive to Persia, the pious priests of that time took some of the fire of the altar and secretly hid it in the hollow of a dry cistern, where they took such precautions that the place was unknown to anyone. 20But after many years had passed, when it pleased God, Nehemiah, having been commissioned by the king of Persia, sent the descendants of the priests who had hidden the fire to get it. And when they reported to us that they had not found fire but only a thick liquid, he ordered them to dip it out and bring it. 21When the materials for the sacrifices were presented, Nehemiah ordered the priests to sprinkle the liquid on the wood and on the things laid upon it. 22When this had been done and some time had passed, and when the sun, which had been clouded over, shone out, a great fire blazed up, so that all marveled. 23And while the sacrifice was being consumed, the priests offered prayer—the priests and everyone. Jonathan led, and the rest responded, as did Nehemiah. 24The prayer was to this effect:

"O Lord, Lord God, Creator of all things, you are awe-inspiring and strong and just and merciful, you alone are king and are kind, 25you alone are bountiful, you alone are just and almighty and eternal. You rescue Israel from every evil; you chose the ancestors and consecrated them. 26Accept this sacrifice on behalf of all your people Israel and preserve your portion and make it holy. 27Gather together our scattered people, set free those who are slaves among the Gentiles, look on those who are rejected and despised, and let the Gentiles know that you are our God. 28Punish those who oppress and are insolent with pride. 29Plant your people in your holy place, as Moses promised."

30Then the priests sang the hymns. 31After the materials of the sacrifice had been consumed,

NAB

but its light was lost in the brilliance cast from a light on the altar. [33] When the event became known and the king of the Persians was told that, in the very place where the exiled priests had hidden the fire, a liquid was found with which Nehemiah and his people had burned the sacrifices, [34] the king, after verifying the fact, fenced the place off and declared it sacred. [35] To those on whom the king wished to bestow favors he distributed the large revenues he received there. [36] Nehemiah and his companions called the liquid nephthar, meaning purification, but most people name it naphtha.

2 You will find in the records, not only that Jeremiah the prophet ordered the deportees to take some of the aforementioned fire with them, [2] but also that the prophet, in giving them the law, admonished them not to forget the commandments of the LORD or be led astray in their thoughts, when seeing the gold and silver idols and their ornaments. [3] With other similar words he urged them not to let the law depart from their hearts. [4] The same document also tells how the prophet, following a divine revelation, ordered that the tent and the ark should accompany him and how he went off to the mountain which Moses climbed to see God's inheritance. [5] When Jeremiah arrived there, he found a room in a cave in which he put the tent, the ark, and the altar of incense; then he blocked up the entrance. [6] Some of those who followed him came up intending to mark the path, but they could not find it. [7] When Jeremiah heard of this, he reproved them: "The place is to remain unknown until God gathers his people together again and shows them mercy. [8] Then the LORD will disclose these things, and the glory of the LORD will be seen in the cloud, just as it appeared in the time of Moses and when Solomon prayed that the Place might be gloriously sanctified."

[9] It is also related how Solomon in his wisdom offered a sacrifice at the dedication and the completion of the temple. [10] Just as Moses prayed to the LORD and fire descended from the sky and consumed the sacrifices, so Solomon also prayed and fire came down and burned up the holocausts. [11] Moses had said, "Because it had not been eaten, the sin offering was burned up." [12] Solomon also

NRSV

Nehemiah ordered that the liquid that was left should be poured on large stones. [32] When this was done, a flame blazed up; but when the light from the altar shone back, it went out. [33] When this matter became known, and it was reported to the king of the Persians that, in the place where the exiled priests had hidden the fire, the liquid had appeared with which Nehemiah and his associates had burned the materials of the sacrifice, [34] the king investigated the matter, and enclosed the place and made it sacred. [35] And with those persons whom the king favored he exchanged many excellent gifts. [36] Nehemiah and his associates called this "nephthar," which means purification, but by most people it is called naphtha.[a]

2 One finds in the records that the prophet Jeremiah ordered those who were being deported to take some of the fire, as has been mentioned, [2] and that the prophet, after giving them the law, instructed those who were being deported not to forget the commandments of the Lord, or to be led astray in their thoughts on seeing the gold and silver statues and their adornment. [3] And with other similar words he exhorted them that the law should not depart from their hearts.

[4] It was also in the same document that the prophet, having received an oracle, ordered that the tent and the ark should follow with him, and that he went out to the mountain where Moses had gone up and had seen the inheritance of God. [5] Jeremiah came and found a cave-dwelling, and he brought there the tent and the ark and the altar of incense; then he sealed up the entrance. [6] Some of those who followed him came up intending to mark the way, but could not find it. [7] When Jeremiah learned of it, he rebuked them and declared: "The place shall remain unknown until God gathers his people together again and shows his mercy. [8] Then the Lord will disclose these things, and the glory of the Lord and the cloud will appear, as they were shown in the case of Moses, and as Solomon asked that the place should be specially consecrated."

[9] It was also made clear that being possessed of wisdom Solomon[b] offered sacrifice for the dedication and completion of the temple. [10] Just as Moses

a Gk *nephthai*   b Gk *he*

NAB

celebrated the feast in the same way for eight days.

13 Besides these things, it is also told in the records and in Nehemiah's Memoirs how he collected the books about the kings, the writings of the prophets and of David, and the royal letters about sacred offerings. 14 In like manner Judas also collected for us the books that had been scattered because of the war, and we now have them in our possession. 15 If you need them, send messengers to get them for you.

16 As we are about to celebrate the feast of the purification of the temple, we are writing to you requesting you also to please celebrate the feast. 17 It is God who has saved all his people and has restored to all of them their heritage, the kingdom, the priesthood, and the sacred rites, 18 as he promised through the law. We trust in God, that he will soon have mercy on us and gather us together from everywhere under the heavens to his holy Place, for he has rescued us from great perils and has purified his Place.

NRSV

prayed to the Lord, and fire came down from heaven and consumed the sacrifices, so also Solomon prayed, and the fire came down and consumed the whole burnt offerings. 11And Moses said, "They were consumed because the sin offering had not been eaten." 12Likewise Solomon also kept the eight days.

13The same things are reported in the records and in the memoirs of Nehemiah, and also that he founded a library and collected the books about the kings and prophets, and the writings of David, and letters of kings about votive offerings. 14In the same way Judas also collected all the books that had been lost on account of the war that had come upon us, and they are in our possession. 15So if you have need of them, send people to get them for you.

16Since, therefore, we are about to celebrate the purification, we write to you. Will you therefore please keep the days? 17It is God who has saved all his people, and has returned the inheritance to all, and the kingship and the priesthood and the consecration, 18as he promised through the law. We have hope in God that he will soon have mercy on us and will gather us from everywhere under heaven into his holy place, for he has rescued us from great evils and has purified the place.

COMMENTARY

There are several components in this section: a discussion of fire at the time of Nehemiah (1:18-36); a section on Jeremiah (2:1-8); a comparison of Moses and Solomon (2:9-12); the founding of a library by Nehemiah and Judas's imitation of this (2:13-15); and a conclusion (2:16-18).

1:18-36. The first section is concerned to show the continuity between the Temple of Nehemiah with that of Solomon. Verse 18 is very difficult to translate, as the Greek is very elliptical and requires that something be added to the text to make it intelligible. The author attempts to provide precedents for celebrating the purification of the Temple under Judas Maccabeus, and therefore connects it both to the Feast of Booths/Suk-

kot, during which Solomon dedicated the Temple (1 Kgs 8:1-2; cf. 2 Macc 1:9; 10:6), and to Nehemiah, during whose reign the festival was reinstituted (Neh 8:13-18). Three Nehemiahs are found in the Bible: (1) a leader of the Jewish community who returned to Judea with Zerubbabel at the end of the Babylonian exile, shortly after 538 BCE (Ezra 2:2; Neh 7:7; 1 Esd 5:8); (2) a ruler around Beth-zur (Neh 3:16); and (3) Nehemiah, son of Hacaliah, the central figure in the book of Nehemiah, who began his reform activity in Jerusalem in 445 BCE (Neh 1:1; 2:1-11) and who rebuilt the walls of Jerusalem. The reference here is to the person last mentioned, as 2 Macc 1:20 refers to his being commissioned by the king of the Persians (cf. Neh 2:6-8). However, this figure is to be conflated with the first Nehemiah, as 2 Macc 1:20 presumes the condition of the first exile. This conflation was probably helped by the opening scene in Neh 1:1-3 which, set in the month of Chislev, describes a destruction of Jerusalem. Noteworthy is the fact that Nehemiah is credited with restoring temple worship, and not Jeshua or Zerubbabel (Ezra 3-6; cf. Sir 49:12-13). The author of 2 Maccabees may have identified Nehemiah with Zerubbabel, who is said in 1 Esd 4:47 to be commissioned to build the Temple, but such motifs can easily cluster around important individuals. It is interesting that Nehemiah is stressed as well in 2 Macc 2:13-14. One might suggest that Nehemiah, as governor of Judea (Neh 5:14), provided a model for Judas.

1:19-23. Fire is an important symbol of God's power. God led the Israelites out of Egypt as a pillar of fire by night (Exod 13:21-22). When God acts as divine warrior and thunders from the heavens, God sends through the clouds hailstones and coals of fire (Ps 18:11-12) and flashes forth flames of fire (Ps 29:7). In Elijah's competition with the priests of Baal, the god of fertility and rain, Elijah's sacrifice is consumed by God's fire from heaven, which shows that it is God who brings fertility to the land (1 Kings 18). The fire on God's altar was never to go out (Lev 6:12-13), and the sacrifices offered at the inauguration of the public ritual were miraculously consumed by fire that "came out from the LORD" (Lev 9:24 NRSV). So to establish the holiness of the Second Temple, which some disputed (Ezra 3:12; *1 Enoch* 89:73; *2 Bar* 68:5-6; and frequently in the Qumran literature), it was important to establish the continuity of the eternal fire. The author uses the motif of the finding of a hidden sacred object, as in the story of the finding of the book of the law (2 Kgs 22:8). The author stresses that the exact place where the fire was hidden was unknown, so as to bring out the miraculous aspect of the event. The place of exile was Babylonia, not Persia (v. 19), but Babylon had later become part of the Persian Empire. The "thick liquid" (or naphtha; see 1:36), a kind of petroleum, was well known to Hellenistic scientists and geographers.[10] A plausible etymology shows that the word de-

rives from the Persian *naft*; "nephthar" (2 Macc 1:36) is an adaptation of the Hebrew word טהרה (*ṭohŏrâ*; cf. Lev 14:11). The ancients saw the nature of naphtha as to draw fire to itself. Plutarch, in his *Life of Alexander the Great,* tells the story of the boy Stephanus, who smeared himself with naphtha, caught fire, and barely escaped with his life. Plutarch comments: "This naphtha . . . is so liable to catch fire, that before it touches the flame it will kindle at the very light that surrounds it, and often inflame the intermediate air also."[11] Naphtha is said to be able to draw fire from a distance as well.[12] So in this story, the naphtha blazes from the very light at the sudden appearance of the previously hidden sun. The effect of this miraculous sprinkling of the thick liquid resonates with the story of Elijah, in which the wood was wet so that it would seem impossible to catch fire (1 Kgs 18:33-38); here the liquid used draws the fire of the sun to itself. This power to catch on fire is also noted in 2 Macc 1:32, where the light from the blazing altar causes the naphtha on the rocks to be consumed.

The reference to Jonathan (v. 23) may be to either the high priest named Jonathan mentioned at Neh 12:11 or to Mattaniah, "who was the leader to begin the thanksgiving in prayer" (Neh 11:17 NRSV), since both names mean "God's gift" in Hebrew. But one cannot be certain about which Jonathan is intended.

1:24-29. Jonathan leads the people in a prayer that emphasizes God's power and mercy (cf. Neh 9:31-32). Its repetition of "alone . . . alone . . . alone" highlights God's singularity as creator. Its stress on God's election of Israel (cf. Deut 14:2; Sir 36:13-19; *Ps Sol* 8:28), leads into a plea that the people, who are God's own possession or "portion" (Deut 9:26; 32:9; 1 Kgs 8:53) might be consecrated and might return to the land (Deut 30:1-10; Isa 41:8-20; 49:7-26). They are to be replanted as God had first planted them on Mt. Zion (see Exod 15:17; 2 Sam 7:10; Amos 9:15), and the taunts of their enemies (Ps 42:3, 10; 79:10; 115:2; Joel 2:17; Mic 7:10) are to be answered. The image of God as the divine warrior runs throughout this prayer, as do the motifs of victory for the people and defeat of their enemies.

1:30-32. As when Zerubbabel and Jeshua laid

---

10. Dioscorides *De materia medica* 1.73; Strabo *Geog* 15.3.15; 16.1.15 (quoting Eratosthenes); Plutarch *The Life of Alexander* 35.

11. Plutarch *The Life of Alexander* 35.
12. Dioscorides *De materia medica* 1.73.

the foundation of the Temple (Ezra 3:10-11), so now hymns are sung. The Greek of vv. 31-32 is difficult, but the meaning seems to be that, with the sacrifices resumed and the eternal fire burning again, the naphtha has served its purpose and is consumed.

1:33-36. The miracle is proclaimed, and the Persian king verifies and acknowledges its truth. Nehemiah then gives the liquid a name: "nephthar." Nehemiah is thus shown to be the discoverer of naphtha, and so the story must be classed with other stories of inventors of things beneficial to humans.[13] It would be going too far to say that Nehemiah is described here as the founder of Persian religion, with its reverence for fire, but there is a hint of the derivation of Persian religion from Jewish temple worship.

2:1-8. Other stories are clustered around this one in an associative fashion. Verses 1-3 specify that Jeremiah had ordered that some of the fire be taken into exile by the priests and had admonished them not to forget the law. The exhortations against idolatry are similar to those found in the Letter of Jeremiah. A second story about Jeremiah (vv. 4-8) recounts how he saved the tabernacle and the ark from being captured. Eupolemus, a Jewish writer possibly sent on an embassy to Rome by Judas Maccabeus (1 Macc 8:17-18; 2 Macc 4:11), also states that Jeremiah preserved the ark and the tablets in it from being taken by the Babylonians.[14] The mountain mentioned in v. 4 is Mt. Nebo. The tent and ark recall the whole exodus story as the ark and the tent of meeting are described and outfitted at Sinai (Exodus 36–40) and go before the Israelites on their journey through the desert (Num 10:33-36). Just as Moses never entered the promised land but could only see it from Mt. Nebo (Deut 32:48-52; 34:1-6), so also in this story these ritual items are returned to the desert wandering state, away from the land of Israel. In the wilderness of Moab, at Mt. Nebo, the author of this letter reports, the tent and the ark and the altar of incense have been placed in hiding until God gathers in the people and again sends the glory and the cloud (other constant

components of the desert wandering [Exod 40:34-38]) to bring them back to the Temple when God restores the land fully (v. 8).[15] Verse 5 mentions the incense altar for the first time. Since it stood in the holy place and was most holy to the Lord (Exod 30:1-10), it too must not be despoiled, and so it is taken back to the desert. The secrecy of the hiding place is emphasized (vv. 6-8). Just as the place where Moses was buried is unknown (Deut 34:6), so also now these ritual vessels are to be kept in an unknown place until there is a new entry into the promised land. The ingathering of the people repeats the prayer of 1:27. "The glory and the cloud" refer to the exodus story also, as at Exod 40:34-38, where God's glory fills the tabernacle and the cloud leads the Israelites on their journey. When the priests brought the ark and its tablets into the Temple that Solomon built, a cloud filled the house of the Lord (1 Kgs 8:10). This story then stresses the continuity between the worship of Moses and that of the First Temple, but maintains a discontinuity between them; the tablets were not found. This story thus is in contrast with the previous story that emphasized the continuity between Solomon's Temple and the Second Temple.

2:9-12. These verses further develop the continuity between Moses and Solomon. First it is recalled (v. 9) how Solomon was granted wisdom (1 Kgs 3:5-15) and how he sacrificed before and after the ark was taken into the Temple (1 Kgs 8:5, 62). When Aaron was being inaugurated into the priesthood, he laid out the purification offering for himself and for the people, the burnt offering and the sacrifice for well-being (Lev 9:1-22). Moses is not said to have prayed, but both he and Aaron entered the tent of meeting; when they came out, they blessed the people, and "fire came out from the LORD and consumed the burnt offering and the fat on the altar" (Lev 9:24 NRSV). Thus the priesthood of Aaron was legitimized, and proper sacrifice commenced. At 2 Chr 7:1, fire is said to come down after Solomon's prayer and consume the burnt offering and the sacrifices. In this way, the chronicler legitimates sacrifice at

---

13. Among Jewish authors, Pseudo-Eupolemus claims Abraham as the inventor of astrology and mathematics. (Eusebius *Preparation for the Gospel* 9.17.3.) Artapanus suggests that Moses invented ships, earth-moving equipment, and military weapons and portrays him as the founder of Egyptian religion. (Eusebius *Preparation for the Gospel* 9.27.4-6.)

14. Eusebius *Preparation for the Gospel* 9.39.5.

15. At 2 Baruch 6, angels are said to take the veil, the holy ephod, the mercy seat, the two tables, the holy raiment of the priests, the altar of incense, the forty-eight precious stones with which the priests were clothed, and all the holy vessels of the tabernacle and to consign them to the earth, which swallows them up, until the time of its restoration. See also the *Lives of the Prophets* 2:11-19.

Solomon's Temple. The saying of Moses (v. 11) is not found elsewhere in the Hebrew Scriptures, but seems to derive from the scene in Lev 10:16-20, where Moses agrees that it was all right for Aaron not to eat the sin offering that time. After this saying, a reference to the command given to Moses at Lev 23:33-36 concerning the celebration of the Feast of Tabernacles for eight days may be missing. Solomon celebrated the dedication of the old Temple for eight days at this feast, according to 2 Chr 7:8-9, although the writer of 1 Kgs 8:65-66 states that Solomon sent the people away on the eighth day.

2:13-15. The mention of Solomon's celebration leads back to the story of Nehemiah (1:18-32). The mention of the consumption of Solomon's sacrifice (2:11) resonates with the account given earlier (1:31). In addition, Solomon's celebration of the eight days (2:12) leads the author to allude again to a similar celebration by Nehemiah (v. 14; see 1:31), although no such celebration has been recorded. These references most likely refer to the celebration of the Feast of Booths under Jeshua and Zerubbabel (Ezra 3:1-4) or Ezra (Neh 8:13-18). The phrase "memoirs of Nehemiah" refers to Nehemiah 1–7; 11–13; these memoirs, however, do not refer to some of the events mentioned or alluded to in 2 Maccabees 1–2, such as the building of the Temple, the finding of the fire, or the construction of a library.

After Seleucus I founded the great library at Alexandria, other kings, particularly the Attalids at Pergamon, followed suit. The author is thus attributing to Nehemiah what one expected a ruler to do in Hellenistic times. The author places in Nehemiah's library books about the kings and prophets, David's works, and letters of kings about votive offerings. There has been much discussion about the precise reference here. Do books about the kings refer to 1 Samuel through 2 Kings, the prophets from Isaiah to Malachi (with the possible exception of Daniel), David's works to the psalms, and the king's letters to those contained in Ezra and Nehemiah? The finds at Qumran have shown us that such equations are not so neat and that many works were available in the second century

about which we know little today. For example, Eupolemus tells us that Moses and Joshua were prophets and provides letters exchanged between Solomon and the king of Tyre and Sidon about supplies for building the Temple.[16] Non-canonical psalms have been found at Qumran as well. So it is best not to make too precise an identification of what Nehemiah's library contained. It is interesting to note that in 4 Ezra 14, Ezra is inspired to write the twenty-four public books, as well as seventy books that were to be shown only to the wise. A comparison of these accounts shows an emphasis on Nehemiah as ruler in the line of David, whereas Ezra's role is placed among the wise teachers.

In 1 Macc 1:56-57, the author describes how books of the law were torn to pieces and burned if found, whereas here the author notes how some had been hidden away from the persecutors. Judas, therefore, is cast as restoring the work of Nehemiah, and so with the connection between Judas and Nehemiah we return to the theme started at 1:18. Does the author hint in v. 15 that the books in Jerusalem are in better shape than those in Alexandria? (*Epistle of Aristeas* 30 seems to refer to unreliable Hebrew manuscripts in Egypt. The prologue to Sirach also stresses the superiority of knowing the works in the original Hebrew language as opposed to translations.)

2:16-18. The author returns to his request of 1:18. God again is addressed as the savior of the people, as at 1:25, to whom God gave the land of Israel as an inheritance (Exod 15:17; Deut 2:12; 1 Kgs 8:36). The people also are God's inheritance (Deut 9:26; 32:9; 1 Kgs 8:51-53). Once again the theme of ingathering appears (cf. 1:27-29; 2:7, following Deut 30:3-5). The repeated reference to all the people suggests hope for an end to the diaspora.

The end of v. 18 takes one back to the opening of this letter; recalling that God has rescued the people from great dangers (1:11) and has purified the Temple (1:18). No conclusion is given to the letter.

16. Eusebius *Preparation for the Gospel* 9:30.1-34.18.

REFLECTIONS

Throughout these two letters we see references to liturgical actions and, in particular, to prayers, hymns, and sacrifices. In the prayers, God's gracious choosing of the people and care for them are stressed. What these letters bring before us is the vibrant faith and belief of their authors. The second letter shows that part of that faith was a keen hope that God would bring about a new beginning, a new return to the promised land when all would be well, an ingathering of all the Jewish people scattered over the world. This utopian desire was animated by a sense that life could be made better, and this hope should be ours as we fight to make living conditions for all better and more humane.

What is especially noteworthy in the second letter is the way the author is so concerned to relate present actions to earlier traditions. What is happening now continues on the line of tradition from Moses through Solomon and Nehemiah to Judas. We need to reflect on how our present religious and cultural communities maintain and cherish their own traditional values. Here the role of a vibrant community and family setting in which children are told the stories of their past is vital. We should encourage parents to talk to their children and grandparents to their grandchildren about their lives when they were young to keep alive an oral history so that each child can see and learn his or her roots. As a country built on immigration, the United States often saw the children of first-generation immigrants discarding their cultural traditions as inappropriate in their new homeland. How can we foster the maintenance of cultural traditions different from our own, and yet not fragment into a splintered society?

The debate over whether one language should be declared official is a classic case where proponents of both sides of the issue need to be sensitive to the proposals of the other side. It is important for children to learn, and that may require schooling in languages other than the one used by the majority. But if the ultimate goal of education is for a person to become a functioning member of society, then each student has to be able to communicate clearly and well in the nation's predominant language. So the problem is to maintain traditions, and yet balance the claims of different traditions harmoniously within a single society.

Yet we also must be cautious, for sometimes traditions can become set in concrete. Traditions, if they are living, must grow. We also need to be alert to when traditions must be discarded. Traditions, like habits, can be good or bad. The authors of these letters, for example, maintain the image of the divine warrior, and so one sees the author caught in a war metaphor in which his side, to be victorious, must defeat and crush its enemies. Can we find another image to replace that of God the Warrior? Should we not ask for mutual understanding, instead of the annihilation of our enemies? Traditions should not close us in and keep others out, but we must learn to cherish traditions that are not exclusive.

THE PROLOGUE

NAB

[19] This is the story of Judas Maccabeus and his brothers, of the purification of the great temple, the dedication of the altar, [20] the campaigns against Antiochus Epiphanes and his son Eupator, [21] and of the heavenly manifestations accorded to the heroes who fought bravely for Judaism, so that, few as they were, they seized the whole land, put to flight the barbarian hordes, [22] regained possession of the world-famous temple, liberated the city, and reestablished the laws that were in danger of being abolished, while the LORD favored them with all his generous assistance. [23] All this, which Jason of Cyrene set forth in detail in five volumes, we will try to condense into a single book.

[24] In view of the flood of statistics, and the difficulties encountered by those who wish to plunge into historical narratives where the material is abundant, [25] we have aimed to please those who prefer simple reading, as well as to make it easy for the studious who wish to commit things to memory, and to be helpful to all. [26] For us who have taken upon ourselves the labor of making this digest, the task, far from being easy, is one of sweat and of sleepless nights, [27] just as the preparation of a festive banquet is no light matter for one who thus seeks to give enjoyment to others. Similarly, to win the gratitude of many we will gladly endure these inconveniences, [28] while we leave the responsibility for exact details to the original author, and confine our efforts to giving only a summary outline. [29] As the architect of a new house must give his attention to the whole structure, while the man who undertakes the decoration and the frescoes has only to concern himself with what is needed for ornamentation, so I think it is with us. [30] To enter into questions and examine them thoroughly from all sides is the task of the professional historian; [31] but the man who is making an adaptation should be allowed to aim at brevity of expression and to

NRSV

19The story of Judas Maccabeus and his brothers, and the purification of the great temple, and the dedication of the altar, 20and further the wars against Antiochus Epiphanes and his son Eupator, 21and the appearances that came from heaven to those who fought bravely for Judaism, so that though few in number they seized the whole land and pursued the barbarian hordes, 22and regained possession of the temple famous throughout the world, and liberated the city, and re-established the laws that were about to be abolished, while the Lord with great kindness became gracious to them— 23all this, which has been set forth by Jason of Cyrene in five volumes, we shall attempt to condense into a single book. 24For considering the flood of statistics involved and the difficulty there is for those who wish to enter upon the narratives of history because of the mass of material, 25we have aimed to please those who wish to read, to make it easy for those who are inclined to memorize, and to profit all readers. 26For us who have undertaken the toil of abbreviating, it is no light matter but calls for sweat and loss of sleep, 27just as it is not easy for one who prepares a banquet and seeks the benefit of others. Nevertheless, to secure the gratitude of many we will gladly endure the uncomfortable toil, 28leaving the responsibility for exact details to the compiler, while devoting our effort to arriving at the outlines of the condensation. 29For as the master builder of a new house must be concerned with the whole construction, while the one who undertakes its painting and decoration has to consider only what is suitable for its adornment, such in my judgment is the case with us. 30It is the duty of the original historian to occupy the ground, to discuss matters from every side, and to take trouble with details, 31but the one who recasts the narrative should be allowed to strive for brevity of expression and to forego exhaustive treatment. 32At this point therefore let us begin

NAB

NRSV

omit detailed treatment of the matter. [32] Here, then, we shall begin our account without further ado; it would be nonsense to write a long preface to a story and then abbreviate the story itself.

our narrative, without adding any more to what has already been said; for it would be foolish to lengthen the preface while cutting short the history itself.

COMMENTARY

The author writes an elegant prologue to his work in which he states his source (v. 23), the contents (vv. 19-22), his aims (vv. 24-25), and his methods (vv. 26-31). He states that he is condensing into one volume the five-volume work of Jason of Cyrene (v. 23), of whom nothing else is known. A group of Jews was said to have been settled on the North African coast in Cyrenaica by Ptolemy I Lagus,[17] and a large number of Jewish inscriptions, from a later date, have been found there. Josephus quotes Strabo as saying that at the time of Sulla (around 85 BCE), the city of Cyrene had four components: citizens, farmers, resident aliens, and Jews.[18] Jason would thus have been a Greek-speaking Jew from Cyrenaica, which was ruled by the Ptolemies.

Curiously the prologue does not mention Seleucus IV (2 Maccabees 3) or Demetrius I (2 Maccabees 14–15), both of whom are included in the later narrative. The word "appearance" (ἐπιφάνεια *epiphaneia*, v. 21) occurs, however, at 3:24; 14:15; and 15:27 and is a theme throughout the work. The author, who enjoys word plays, thus may have highlighted Antiochus *Epiphanes* in opposition to the *epiphanies* God had performed on behalf of the Jews. The author further contrasts Judaism with barbarism (v. 21). "Barbarian" (βάρβαρος *barbaros*) was the word Greeks used for non-Greeks; here the author turns the usage topsy-turvy and portrays the Greek Seleucids as barbarians. This is the first known occurrence of the word "Judaism," perhaps coined in opposition to Hellenism (2 Macc 4:13) and allophylism—foreign ways (2 Macc 4:13; 6:25). At 15:37, the author states that he ends his story where he does as the city has been in possession of the Hebrews since the defeat of Nicanor. The graciousness of the Lord is particularly shown at the turning point in the story, when the prayer for God's graciousness/mercy by the youngest martyr (7:37) is answered by God's turning from wrath to mercy (8:5).

The author describes his aims as pleasure and profit and ease for those who wish to memorize (v. 25). Memory is helped by clear organization, and so the history is structured around three important epiphanies. These aims are all rhetorical topoi for Hellenistic historians, and the author places himself squarely within this historiographical tradition. Sirach notes that the master of a feast should first take care of the guests before sitting down. "When you have fulfilled all your duties, take your place,/ so that you may be merry along with them/ and receive a wreath for your excellent leadership" (Sir 32:2 NRSV).

To achieve his aims, the author is going to epitomize the five books of Jason of Cyrene (v. 23). The motif of hard work willingly undertaken for one's readers' benefit (vv. 25-26) is a standard ploy to gain the readers' sympathetic hearing. "Flood of statistics" (τὸ χύμα τῶν ἀριθμῶν *to chyma tōn arithmōn*, v. 24) should be translated "large number of lines." The length of books was counted in terms of written lines, and the number of written lines given at the end of the papyrus roll as a comprehensive number. The author is saying that Jason's book had too many pages. Hellenistic historians tried various analogies to explain how their work differed from other writings. Lucian of Samosata, a writer of the second century CE, held that the historian works like a sculptor on raw material; a bare record of events was not enough, but one had to write them up in as fine a style as possible.[19] The Greek historian Timaeus (c. 356–260 BCE), to show that collecting the data required for writing history was a more serious task than

---

17. Josephus *Against Apion* 2.44.
18. Josephus *Antiquities of the Jews* 14.115.

19. Lucian of Samosata *On How to Write History* 16. 50-51.

declamatory writing, used the analogy of the difference between real buildings or furniture and the views seen in scene paintings.[20] Polybius (c. 200–after 188 BCE) states that "the difference between real buildings and scene paintings or between history and declamatory speech-making is not so great as is, in the case of all works, the difference between an account founded on participation, active or passive, in the occurrences and one composed from report and the narratives of others."[21] The author of 2 Maccabees, however, is not contrasting two different crafts—for example, unfinished and finished products—but rather contrasts two functions within the same craft—one that deals with the whole project and one that is more specialized, contrasting a full exposition versus a selective presentation. Plutarch had also used the image of a portrait painter capturing a subject's character through few select strokes versus an exhaustive model.[22]

20. Polybius 12.28a.1-2.
21. Ibid., 12.28a.6.
22. Plutarch *Alexander* I.

2 MACCABEES 3:1-40

THE FIRST CRISIS

OVERVIEW

This scene is complete in itself as shown by v. 40. It describes the first attack on the Temple during the time of Seleucus IV Philopator, who succeeded Antiochus III and ruled from 187–175 BCE. This is the first of the epiphanies of God related in the epitome. It is placed as an anti-type to what is to happen under Antiochus IV, when the high priests and the people are entangled in sin (5:18). The story has all the characteristics of accounts written in praise of a deity who defends his or her temple: attackers approach, the defenders ask for help from the deity, the deity responds, the attackers are repulsed, and the defenders rejoice. Within the biblical tradition, one has the repulsion of Sennacherib from Jerusalem (2 Chr 32:1-22; 2 Kgs 18:17–19:36). In 701 BCE, King Sennacherib of Assyria invaded Judea in retaliation for the revolt of King Hezekiah against him. Hezekiah set about strengthening the walls, but the chronicler also portrays him as exhorting the people to trust in God, who would defend them. Envoys from Sennacherib came to Jerusalem and taunted the king, saying, "Who among all the gods of those nations that my ancestors utterly destroyed was able to save his people from my hand, that your God should be able to save you from my hand?" (2 Chr 32:14 NRSV). Such contempt of God, speaking as if the God of Israel were like other gods, brought swift retribution as the Lord sent an angel into the Assyrians' camp to destroy the mighty warriors of the Assyrians; the king has to return to Assyria in disgrace, where he is then assassinated. The God of Israel has defended the Temple and Jerusalem, God's city, from the boastful attack of its adversaries. Within the Greek tradition, Herodotus describes how the temple of Apollo was preserved from the army of Xerxes in 480 BCE,[23] while Apollo is celebrated for repulsing the Gauls from Delphi in 179 BCE.[24] At Nippur, around the sixth century BCE, Enlil and the other gods saved the Ekur temple from Kuturnahhunte, king of Elam. The general pattern is widespread.

23. Herodotus 8.37-39.
24. Pausanias 10.23.2.

2 MACCABEES 3:1-8, THE PROBLEM

NAB

3 While the holy city lived in perfect peace and the laws were strictly observed because of the piety of the high priest Onias and his hatred of evil, [2] the kings themselves honored the Place and glorified the temple with the most magnificent gifts. [3] Thus Seleucus, king of Asia, defrayed from his own revenues all the expenses necessary for the sacrificial services. [4] But a certain Simon, of the priestly course of Bilgah, who had

NRSV

3 While the holy city was inhabited in unbroken peace and the laws were strictly observed because of the piety of the high priest Onias and his hatred of wickedness, [2]it came about that the kings themselves honored the place and glorified the temple with the finest presents, [3]even to the extent that King Seleucus of Asia defrayed from his own revenues all the expenses connected with the service of the sacrifices.

NAB

been appointed superintendent of the temple, had a quarrel with the high priest about the supervision of the city market. 5 Since he could not prevail against Onias, he went to Apollonius of Tarsus, who at that time was governor of Coelesyria and Phoenicia, 6 and reported to him that the treasury in Jerusalem was so full of untold riches that the total sum of money was incalculable and out of all proportion to the cost of the sacrifices, and that it would be possible to bring it all under the control of the king.

7 When Apollonius had an audience with the king, he informed him about the riches that had been reported to him. The king chose his minister Heliodorus and sent him with instructions to expropriate the aforesaid wealth. 8 So Heliodorus immediately set out on his journey, ostensibly to visit the cities of Coelesyria and Phoenicia, but in reality to carry out the king's purpose.

3, 5: (*pros Apollōnion*) *Tarsou:* conj; cf 4, 4.

NRSV

4But a man named Simon, of the tribe of Benjamin, who had been made captain of the temple, had a disagreement with the high priest about the administration of the city market. 5Since he could not prevail over Onias, he went to Apollonius of Tarsus,*a* who at that time was governor of Coelesyria and Phoenicia, 6and reported to him that the treasury in Jerusalem was full of untold sums of money, so that the amount of the funds could not be reckoned, and that they did not belong to the account of the sacrifices, but that it was possible for them to fall under the control of the king. 7When Apollonius met the king, he told him of the money about which he had been informed. The king*b* chose Heliodorus, who was in charge of his affairs, and sent him with commands to effect the removal of the reported wealth. 8Heliodorus at once set out on his journey, ostensibly to make a tour of inspection of the cities of Coelesyria and Phoenicia, but in fact to carry out the king's purpose.

a Gk *Apollonius son of Tharseas*   *b* Gk *He*

COMMENTARY

3:1-3. The author portrays the city as being idyllically at peace (v. 1). Such a utopian picture is credited by the author to the piety and hatred of wickedness of the high priest, Onias III, son of the high priest Simon. Note that the peace of the land depends on the leader, a theme that is found earlier in God's warning to Solomon to follow God's commandments. If Solomon and his descendants did not keep God's statutes, God would cast the Temple down (1 Kgs 9:1-9). The thrust ultimately becomes the explanation for the destruction of the northern kingdom (2 Kgs 17:7-8), the fall of Jerusalem, and the exile (2 Kgs 21:11-15). The piety of Onias will contrast sharply with that of his rivals and successors—Jason, Menelaus, and Alcimus—who all bring ruin upon the Temple. The author states his belief clearly at 5:19: The Lord did not choose the nation for the sake of the holy place, but the holy place for the sake of the nation. The well-being of the Temple depends on the holiness of the people, as stated so forcibly by the prophets (e.g., Jeremiah 19). The utopian

quality of the description is at variance with the description of conflict and division that one finds in *1 Enoch* 1–11 and in the history of the Qumran covenanters (CD 1). In these works, Israel is described as being divided between the elect and the ungodly, between the faithful remnant and those who forsake the covenant.

The idyllic picture is enhanced by the author's recounting the preferable treatment and lavish gifts that Jerusalem and the Temple had received (vv. 2-3). Antiochus III, when he had recaptured Judea and Coelesyria from the Ptolemies (198 BCE), had bestowed tax exemptions and privileges on Jerusalem. In this action, he was following what the Ptolemies had done.[25] Before that, the Persian kings had provided for the sacrificial cult (Ezra 6:9-10; 7:20-23). Antiochus's generosity is said by the author to have continued under his son Seleucus IV Philopator. Note that Seleucus

25. Josephus *Antiquities of the Jews* 12.50, 58, 138-144; *Against Apion* 2.48.

205

defrays expenses for the sacrifices; this will be the bone of contention in the following verse.

3:4-8. Just as Satan enters to destroy the pretty picture in Job 1:6, so also here a troublemaker comes on the scene. Simon probably belonged to one of the priestly families in Jerusalem, from the clan of Bilgah (Neh 12:5, 18; 1 Chr 24:14), following the Latin and Armenian translations, not of the tribe of Benjamin (so the Greek). His brothers were Menelaus and Lysimachus. Simon's exact position is not known, as the term for "captain" (προστάτις *prostatis*) can encompass civil and military as well as religious affairs. Nor do we know by whom he was appointed—whether by the high priest or by the Seleucid governor. He was certainly an important person.

The author does not specify what caused the disagreement between Simon and Onias. Perhaps Simon wanted to install one of his own followers as clerk of the city market to supervise all aspects of buying and selling. Perhaps Onias disagreed with Simon as to what precisely the duties of the market supervisor should be. Or perhaps it involved the interpretation of purity rules for the market. The *Temple Scroll* stipulates that the only animal hides allowed in Jerusalem were those from animals sacrificed in Jerusalem,[26] a much tighter restriction than that found in the decree of Antiochus III, where only the skins of unclean animals were forbidden.[27] Such a restriction obviously had economic repercussions. More likely, the disagreement reflected a power play between two factions in the small city-state. The historical

romance of the Tobiads suggests that earlier in the Ptolemaic period there had been a division of powers among important families in Jerusalem.[28] In any case, Simon went over Onias's head to the governor of Coelesyria and Phoenicia (vv. 5-6), the region between the Euphrates and Egypt (see 1 Macc 7:8). The governor, Apollonius son of Tharseas, was most likely a brother or relative of the holder of the same office from 201 to 195 BCE under Antiochus III.[29] Since the Seleucids had capitulated to the Romans and a huge indemnity had been placed on them at the Peace of Apamea in 188 BCE, they had been short of funds. Simon, therefore, cleverly plays on their need by telling Apollonius about the large sums of money available that the king could seize (v. 6). Simon clearly does not want to infringe on the sacrificial cult in Jerusalem, but simply to undermine the position of Onias III. Apollonius was not about to interfere in temple affairs on his own initiative, and so he relayed the information to the king (v. 7). Seleucus approved of the suggestion, since it did not involve any sacrilege as the money dedicated to the temple cult was not involved. He appoints Heliodorus to seize the money. Heliodorus, brought up with the king, was chancellor of the realm. Later he had the king assassinated on September 3, 175.

The author sees all events as revolving around the Temple, so while Heliodorus may have been inspecting the province, this inspection is simply seen as subterfuge.

26. See 11QTemple 47:7-18.
27. Josephus *Antiquities of the Jews* 12.146.
28. Ibid., 12.154-236.
29. See ibid., 12.138-144, in which Antiochus addresses a letter to Ptolemy, son of Thraseas.

2 MACCABEES 3:9-14a, THE ATTACK ON THE TEMPLE

NAB

⁹ When he arrived in Jerusalem and had been graciously received by the high priest of the city, he told him about the information that had been given, and explained the reason for his presence, and he asked if these things were really true. ¹⁰ The high priest explained that part of the money was

NRSV

9When he had arrived at Jerusalem and had been kindly welcomed by the high priest of[a] the city, he told about the disclosure that had been made and stated why he had come, and he inquired whether this really was the situation.

[a] Other ancient authorities read *and*

NAB

a care fund for widows and orphans, [11] and a part was the property of Hyrcanus, son of Tobias, a man who occupied a very high position. Contrary to the calumnies of the impious Simon, the total amounted to four hundred talents of silver and two hundred of gold. [12] He added that it was utterly unthinkable to defraud those who had placed their trust in the sanctity of the Place and in the sacred inviolability of a temple venerated all over the world. [13] But because of the orders he had from the king, Heliodorus said that in any case the money must be confiscated for the royal treasury. [14] So on the day he had set he went in to take an inventory of the funds.

NRSV

[10]The high priest explained that there were some deposits belonging to widows and orphans, [11]and also some money of Hyrcanus son of Tobias, a man of very prominent position, and that it totaled in all four hundred talents of silver and two hundred of gold. To such an extent the impious Simon had misrepresented the facts. [12]And he said that it was utterly impossible that wrong should be done to those people who had trusted in the holiness of the place and in the sanctity and inviolability of the temple that is honored throughout the whole world.

13But Heliodorus, because of the orders he had from the king, said that this money must in any case be confiscated for the king's treasury. [14]So he set a day and went in to direct the inspection of these funds.

COMMENTARY

3:9-10. The author insists on the friendly attitude of the high priest and the whole city toward the Seleucid minister. The attack on the Temple, therefore, is something quite unexpected. The author has the high priest cleverly respond to Heliodorus by showing how heinous it would be to take the money of the most defenseless in the kingdom: widows and orphans, who are especially protected by God (Ps 146:9); whoever attacks them is cursed and will be punished (Deut 27:19; Isa 1:23; Ezek 22:7). Deposits in temples should not be violated. The combination "widows and orphans" may suggest that the author is referring here to the tithes set aside for them (Deut 14:28-29; 16:11-14; cf. Tob 1:8).

3:11. The mention of Hyrcanus, son of Tobias, has raised many questions. Josephus relates the history of the family of the Tobiads that shows them as closely allied with the Ptolemies.[30] The youngest son, Hyrcanus, son of Joseph, son of Tobias, was forced by his brothers to flee Jerusalem; he escaped to the Transjordan, where he is said to have committed suicide when he realized he could not escape the clutches of Antiochus IV. Many scholars believe that the fact that Onias III

has deposits in his temple of a pro-Ptolemaic, anti-Seleucid Hyrcanus shows the pro-Ptolemaic leanings of the high priest and thus that the debate between Onias and Simon was really between parties sympathetic to the Ptolemies and the Seleucids respectively. Such an analysis reads a great deal into one brief mention in a dramatically composed speech. Thucydides (c. 460–400 BCE), the great historian of the Peloponnesian war, laid down the rule that, as it was difficult to remember the exact words a speaker used, the writer should make the speakers say what was appropriate for each occasion.[31] It seems totally out of place that the high priest, when wanting to appease the Seleucids so the temple treasury would not be confiscated, would suddenly flaunt his anti-Seleucid leanings to the Seleucid chancellor. More likely, Hyrcanus, a Tobiad, is mentioned simply as an important person. The reader should not too hastily identify him with the romantic brigand of the Tobiad romance.

3:12. On the general rule for deposits, see Exod 22:7-15. Deposits at the Lord's Temple are doubly inviolate.

---

30. Josephus *Antiquities of the Jews* 12.154-236.

31. Thucydides *The Peloponnesian War* 1.22.

2 MACCABEES 3:14b-21, THE CRY FOR HELP

NAB

There was great distress throughout the city. [15] Priests prostrated themselves in their priestly robes before the altar, and loudly begged him in heaven who had given the law about deposits to keep the deposits safe for those who had made them. [16] Whoever saw the appearance of the high priest was pierced to the heart, for the changed color of his face manifested the anguish of his soul. [17] The terror and bodily trembling that had come over the man clearly showed those who saw him the pain that lodged in his heart. [18] People rushed out of their houses in crowds to make public supplication, because the Place was in danger of being profaned. [19] Women, girded with sackcloth below their breasts, filled the streets; maidens secluded indoors ran together, some to the gates, some to the walls, others peered through the windows, [20] all of them with hands raised toward heaven, making supplication. [21] It was pitiful to see the populace variously prostrated in prayer and the high priest full of dread and anguish.

NRSV

There was no little distress throughout the whole city. [15] The priests prostrated themselves before the altar in their priestly vestments and called toward heaven upon him who had given the law about deposits, that he should keep them safe for those who had deposited them. [16] To see the appearance of the high priest was to be wounded at heart, for his face and the change in his color disclosed the anguish of his soul. [17] For terror and bodily trembling had come over the man, which plainly showed to those who looked at him the pain lodged in his heart. [18] People also hurried out of their houses in crowds to make a general supplication because the holy place was about to be brought into dishonor. [19] Women, girded with sackcloth under their breasts, thronged the streets. Some of the young women who were kept indoors ran together to the gates, and some to the walls, while others peered out of the windows. [20] And holding up their hands to heaven, they all made supplication. [21] There was something pitiable in the prostration of the whole populace and the anxiety of the high priest in his great anguish.

COMMENTARY

The author uses highly emotional language to describe the reaction to Heliodorus's decision to carry on with the confiscation. The taking of the deposits would not profane the Temple, but it would be an insult—a dishonor (3:18). The word for "distress" ($\dot{\alpha}\gamma\omega\nu\dot{\iota}\alpha$ *agōnia,* v. 14b) is repeated as "anguish" at v. 16 (it can also mean "pain"), and the verb form is found at v. 21: "in great anguish." The emphasis throughout is focused on the way the agony of the high priest mirrors that of the whole populace. Even married women, who are normally excluded from public affairs and restricted to the household, now appear in the streets in mourning. Sackcloth, from which shrouds were made, is the classic symbol of mourning (Neh 9:1; Jonah 3:6; Esth 4:1). Even the unmarried women, kept hidden in the household, are mentioned to show how all the people were involved.

2 MACCABEES 3:22-30, THE LORD DEFENDS HIS TEMPLE

NAB

22 While they were imploring the almighty LORD to keep the deposits safe and secure for those who had placed them in trust, 23 Heliodorus went on with his plan. 24 But just as he was approaching the treasury with his bodyguards, the LORD of spirits who holds all power manifested himself in so striking a way that those who had been bold enough to follow Heliodorus were panic-stricken at God's power and fainted away in terror. 25 There appeared to them a richly caparisoned horse, mounted by a dreadful rider. Charging furiously, the horse attacked Heliodorus with its front hoofs. The rider was seen to be wearing golden armor. 26 Then two other young men, remarkably strong, strikingly beautiful, and splendidly attired, appeared before him. Standing on each side of him, they flogged him unceasingly until they had given him innumerable blows. 27 Suddenly he fell to the ground, enveloped in great darkness. Men picked him up and laid him on a stretcher. 28 The man who a moment before had entered that treasury with a great retinue and his whole bodyguard was carried away helpless, having dearly experienced the sovereign power of God. 29 While he lay speechless and deprived of all hope of aid, due to an act of God's power, 30 the Jews praised the LORD who had marvelously glorified his holy Place; and the temple, charged so shortly before with fear and commotion, was filled with joy and gladness, now that the almighty LORD had manifested himself.

NRSV

22While they were calling upon the Almighty Lord that he would keep what had been entrusted safe and secure for those who had entrusted it, 23Heliodorus went on with what had been decided. 24But when he arrived at the treasury with his bodyguard, then and there the Sovereign of spirits and of all authority caused so great a manifestation that all who had been so bold as to accompany him were astounded by the power of God, and became faint with terror. 25For there appeared to them a magnificently caparisoned horse, with a rider of frightening mien; it rushed furiously at Heliodorus and struck at him with its front hoofs. Its rider was seen to have armor and weapons of gold. 26Two young men also appeared to him, remarkably strong, gloriously beautiful and splendidly dressed, who stood on either side of him and flogged him continuously, inflicting many blows on him. 27When he suddenly fell to the ground and deep darkness came over him, his men took him up, put him on a stretcher, 28and carried him away—this man who had just entered the aforesaid treasury with a great retinue and all his bodyguard but was now unable to help himself. They recognized clearly the sovereign power of God.

29While he lay prostrate, speechless because of the divine intervention and deprived of any hope of recovery, 30they praised the Lord who had acted marvelously for his own place. And the temple, which a little while before was full of fear and disturbance, was filled with joy and gladness, now that the Almighty Lord had appeared.

COMMENTARY

Verses 22-23 recapitulate vv. 12-14 and set off the description of the people's distress. The author employs a wide variety of words to describe God—the word "Sovereign" (δυνάστης *dynastēs,* v. 24) is used also at 12:15, 28; 15:4-5, 23, 29; and is picked up at v. 28 in "the sovereign power."

(It is found also in 3 Macc 2:3; 6:39; 1 Tim 6:15 and in the context of an epiphany in 1 Tim 6:14.) In Greek, the same word means both "spirit" and "wind" (πνεῦμα *pneuma*). The title "Sovereign of spirits" is similar to the way Heb 1:7, interpreting Ps 104:4, states that God makes angels winds/spirits, and the Wisdom of Solomon says that God knows the powers of spirits/winds (7:20).

This is the first epiphany in the narrative. Some scholars have divided the narrative into two accounts, one with a horseman (vv. 24-25, 27-28, 30) and the other with two young men (vv. 26, 29, 31-34). But the author may also be displaying the power of God through various agents. The description of the avenging figures has all the usual traits of divine interventions in Hellenistic literature: golden armor, handsome young men (see the description in 5:2-3; 10:29; 11:8). To be flogged was humiliating. As the book of Proverbs states, "A whip for the horse, a bridle for the donkey,/ and a rod for the back of fools" (Prov 26:3 NRSV). Flogging was a punishment for wrongdoing, and Jewish law stipulated that no more than forty lashes should be given, for otherwise the person flogged would be degraded (Deut 25:1-3). This punishment could be administered more "mildly," as when the authorities in

Caesarea tried to stifle the fights between the Jews and the Greeks in the town by the use of scourges and imprisonment.[32] Paul underwent such punishment at the hands of Jewish and Roman authorities (Acts 16:22-25; 21:24; 2 Cor 11:24-25). A more severe beating could be administered for other crimes, and could sometimes lead to the death of the condemned person. Heliodorus is said to have been flogged continually until he fainted, which suggests the more severe punishment. That someone of his high rank should be subjected to the punishment for criminals would be seen as especially degrading to him. Darkness is often a sign of destruction, as in the ninth plague (Exod 10:21) and for Saul as he was dying (2 Sam 1:9 LXX). The day of the Lord is to be a day of darkness (Amos 5:18; Joel 2:2, 31). The contrast of vv. 22-23 is now reversed in the contrast of vv. 29-30.

32. Josephus *The Jewish War* 2.266-270.

2 MACCABEES 3:31-40, THE EFFECT ON HELIODORUS

NAB

31 Soon some of the companions of Heliodorus begged Onias to invoke the Most High, praying that the life of the man who was about to expire might be spared. 32 Fearing that the king might think that Heliodorus had suffered some foul play at the hands of the Jews, the high priest offered a sacrifice for the man's recovery. 33 While the high priest was offering the sacrifice of atonement, the same young men in the same clothing again appeared and stood before Heliodorus. "Be very grateful to the high priest Onias," they told him. "It is for his sake that the LORD has spared your life. 34 Since you have been scourged by Heaven, proclaim to all men the majesty of God's power." When they had said this, they disappeared.

35 After Heliodorus had offered a sacrifice to the LORD and made most solemn vows to him who had spared his life, he bade Onias farewell, and

NRSV

31Some of Heliodorus's friends quickly begged Onias to call upon the Most High to grant life to one who was lying quite at his last breath. 32So the high priest, fearing that the king might get the notion that some foul play had been perpetrated by the Jews with regard to Heliodorus, offered sacrifice for the man's recovery. 33While the high priest was making an atonement, the same young men appeared again to Heliodorus dressed in the same clothing, and they stood and said, "Be very grateful to the high priest Onias, since for his sake the Lord has granted you your life. 34And see that you, who have been flogged by heaven, report to all people the majestic power of God." Having said this they vanished.

35Then Heliodorus offered sacrifice to the Lord and made very great vows to the Savior of his life, and having bidden Onias farewell, he marched off with his forces to the king. 36He bore

returned with his soldiers to the king. [36] Before all men he gave witness to the deeds of the most high God that he had seen with his own eyes. [37] When the king asked Heliodorus who would be a suitable man to be sent to Jerusalem next, he answered: [38] "If you have an enemy or a plotter against the government, send him there, and you will receive him back well-flogged, if indeed he survives at all; for there is certainly some special divine power about the Place. [39] He who has his dwelling in heaven watches over that Place and protects it, and he strikes down and destroys those who come to harm it." [40] This was how the matter concerning Heliodorus and the preservation of the treasury turned out.

testimony to all concerning the deeds of the supreme God, which he had seen with his own eyes. [37] When the king asked Heliodorus what sort of person would be suitable to send on another mission to Jerusalem, he replied, [38] "If you have any enemy or plotter against your government, send him there, for you will get him back thoroughly flogged, if he survives at all; for there is certainly some power of God about the place. [39] For he who has his dwelling in heaven watches over that place himself and brings it aid, and he strikes and destroys those who come to do it injury." [40] This was the outcome of the episode of Heliodorus and the protection of the treasury.

COMMENTARY

In contrast to the story in 3 Maccabees 1–2, where Ptolemy IV Philopator attempts to enter the holy of holies and is punished but does not repent, here Heliodorus recognizes the power of the deity. Such recognition of divine power by a former enemy is also found in Greek literature as, for example, in the Lindos Chronicle, which portrays how, before the battle of Marathon, the Persian commander Dates was forced to proclaim the greatness of the goddess Athena through a miraculous thirst she sent on his forces as they besieged the isle of Lindos.

The author emphasizes that this miracle was no tricky ambush played on Heliodorus but the work of God by asserting that the high priest prayed for Heliodorus to assure that the king would not get the wrong impression about what had happened. The text does not specify what kind of sacrifice was offered, but possibly it was an offering concerning deposits (Lev 6:1-7; Num 5:5-10). The importance of the sacrificial cult is underscored as bringing forgiveness to a Gentile and the holiness of the high priest is stressed. Gentiles were healed by Moses (Exod 8:28-29) and Elisha (2 Kgs 5:1-19), and Josephus reports that later sacrifices were offered daily for the emperors.[33] Heliodorus in his turn offered sacrifice, presumably a sacrifice of well-being (Lev 7:11-18; 22:21-25). This witness of Heliodorus to the power of God does not mean that Heliodorus has converted, but that he recognizes the power of the deity who resides in Jerusalem. The confession emphasizes the supreme position of the God of Israel. One important theme of the epitome is that Jews and Gentiles can live on good terms with one another (see Introduction); this theme is shown here in the healing of Heliodorus and in his respect for the Jews.

33. Josephus *Against Apion* 2.77.

REFLECTIONS

This narrative recalls that the relationship between God and the people is a reciprocal relationship. If the people obey God's laws, God will help them; but if they disobey, God will punish them. Such a relationship demands that each person in the community strive to his or her utmost. The narrative also stresses how one is to combat attacks on the community: The whole community is to be united in its steadfastness. The attack from outside only occurs because of an internal breakdown, a power struggle between community leaders. Envy is a tumor that can eat away, and the desire for personal status must be resisted.

In the political realm, we often see the struggle between what one should do as a partisan politician and what one should do for the well-being of the nation. So it is in the sphere of organized religion as well. Responsible leaders will always opt for what is best for the community. One recalls the response of Jesus to debates among his followers; the true leader is the one who serves (Mark 10:41-45). Paul shamed Corinthian Christians who were so concerned about their status that they began to take one another to court (1 Cor 6:1-11). Placing self before the welfare of the community must be resisted.

What is also striking about the resistance of the community to Heliodorus is that it is a passive resistance, with no attempt to take up arms. Later in the narrative, the author will argue that the Macceabeans' success came through the martyrdoms of Eleazar and the mother and her seven sons. Such a position recalls that of the chronicler as outlined by Susan Niditch.[34] She notes how the authors of 1 and 2 Chronicles are especially fond of having weak and humbled Israelites call upon God for help (e.g., 2 Chr 14:9-15). This theme, as Niditch points out, is at the heart of the exodus tradition. In Chronicles, this theme reemerges in full force alongside a stress on the power of God and the helplessness of human fighters, particularly in the narrative of 2 Chronicles 20. When a great multitude is about to attack Judea, King Jehoshaphat prays, "We are powerless before this vast multitude that comes against us. We are at a loss what to do, hence our eyes are turned toward you" (2 Chr 20:12 NAB). Without any fighting, God delivers the people. The chronicler certainly revels in the death of Israel's enemies, but there are hints that he does not want the Israelites to take part in war but to leave it all up to God. The book of Daniel also stresses the defeat of oppressors by supernatural means. In Daniel 2, the great statue that represents various kingdoms is broken into pieces by a stone not cut by human hands (Dan 2:34). The arrogant beast of Daniel 7 falls under divine judgment and is put to death (Dan 7:11), and the king of Daniel 8 is broken, but not by human hands (Dan 8:25). In Daniel 11, the king simply comes to an end, with no one to help him (Dan 11:45).

This same idea of divine intervention is present in this narrative in 2 Maccabees 3. It is also reminiscent of Paul's advice to never avenge oneself, but to leave room for the wrath of God (Rom 12:19). This ideology of non-participation, to use Niditch's phrase, gives the narrative of 2 Maccabees a pacifist tinge unlike 1 Maccabees. The emphasis on confronting evil with defiant passivity rather than with arms, an emphasis that people like Gandhi and Martin Luther King, Jr., evidenced in their lives, is important. Recourse to violence should always be the last resort after all else has failed. We, too, must be willing to follow humbly but persistently what we hold to be right. We will not expect angels to come to our aid, but we must believe that right will win out in the end if we pursue our goals with integrity.

34. Susan Niditch, *War in the Hebrew Scriptures: A Study of the Ethics of Violence* (New York: Oxford, 1993) 139-49.

2 MACCABEES 4:1–10:8

THE SECOND ATTACK ON THE TEMPLE

OVERVIEW

The second attack on the Temple in Jerusalem follows the same basic pattern as the attack described in 3:1-40: the attack against Jerusalem and the people's traditional way of life (4:6–6:17); the cry for help (6:18–7:42); God's response (chaps. 8–9); the purification of the Temple (10:1-8).

2 MACCABEES 4:1–6:17, THE ATTACK ON THE TRADITIONAL WAY OF LIFE

OVERVIEW

The attack on Jerusalem comes from both internal and external forces. The internal forces were the removal of Onias from Jerusalem (4:16), which brought changes under the new high priest, Jason (4:7-22), and the events under his replacement, Menelaus (4:23–5:10). The external attack came from Antiochus IV (5:11–6:11). Throughout this section the author reflects on the significance of these events (4:16-17; 5:17-20; 6:12-17). These reflections are important indicators of the worldview of the author—his belief in the election of Israel by God and the necessity that Jews live according to God's covenantal laws.

2 Maccabees 4:1-6, The Removal of Onias

NAB

4 The Simon mentioned above as the informer about the funds against his own country, made false accusations that it was Onias who threatened Heliodorus and instigated the whole miserable affair. ² He dared to brand as a plotter against the government the man who was a benefactor of the city, a protector of his compatriots, and a zealous defender of the laws. ³ When Simon's hostility reached such a point that murders were being committed by one of his henchmen, ⁴ Onias saw that the opposition was serious and that Apollonius, son of Menestheus, the governor of Coelesyria and Phoenicia, was abetting

NRSV

4 The previously mentioned Simon, who had informed about the money against[a] his own country, slandered Onias, saying that it was he who had incited Heliodorus and had been the real cause of the misfortune. ²He dared to designate as a plotter against the government the man who was the benefactor of the city, the protector of his compatriots, and a zealot for the laws. ³When his hatred progressed to such a degree that even murders were committed by one of Simon's approved agents, ⁴Onias recognized that the rivalry

a Gk and

213

NAB

Simon's wickedness. ⁵ So he had recourse to the king, not as an accuser of his countrymen, but as a man looking to the general and particular good of all the people. ⁶ He saw that, unless the king intervened, it would be impossible to have a peaceful government, and that Simon would not desist from his folly.

NRSV

was serious and that Apollonius son of Menes-theus,ᵃ and governor of Coelesyria and Phoenicia, was intensifying the malice of Simon. ⁵So he appealed to the king, not accusing his compatriots but having in view the welfare, both public and private, of all the people. ⁶For he saw that without the king's attention public affairs could not again reach a peaceful settlement, and that Simon would not stop his folly.

ᵃ Vg Compare verse 21: Meaning of Gk uncertain

COMMENTARY

The author had insisted that the piety of the high priest Onias was the reason for the well-being of the holy city (3:1), and so, it is an ominous sign if, because of slander, Onias has to leave Jerusalem. In 2 Baruch, a pseudepigraphical work usually dated to around the beginning of the second century CE, Baruch is told by God to tell Jeremiah and all like-minded people to leave Jerusalem, for their works had become a firm pillar for the city and their prayers a strong wall (2 Baruch 2).³⁵ Then the city will be handed over to be captured. One might also note how the prophet Ezekiel witnesses the departure of the glory of the Lord from Jerusalem before its destruction (Ezekiel 10).

There are close grammatical links between 3:39 and 4:1; 3:39 sums up the events in chapter 3, but 4:1 shows how the underlying problem in chapter 3, the rivalry among the families of the ruling elite, still continues. The concern of Onias that Seleucus not get the wrong idea that the Jews had committed "foul play" (3:32) is shown to be justified as Simon slanders the high priest about this event. The breakdown of civility in the city

is dramatically shown by the increase of violence. Simon is shown to be the opposite of Onias, as he instigates murder (v. 3), which goes against the commands of God (Exod 20:13; 21:12; Num 35:30-34). The local rivalry takes on larger dimensions, however, as the Seleucid authorities become involved. The new governor of Coelesyria and Phoenicia does not assume the passive attitude of the previous governor (3:7) but actively supports Simon (4:4). It is not known why, or what benefit a governor might gain from fomenting civil unrest. Whatever the reason, the high priest decides to go over the governor's authority by petitioning the king to decide the case at the royal court at Antioch (v. 5; see also v. 33). Such an appeal could be construed as playing party politics. The author of 2 Maccabees instead insists on Simon's selfishness and on Onias's selflessness. Such concern on Onias's part, not for his own good but for that of the nation, also contrasts with the power-hungry desire the author says drove Menelaus (13:3) and Alcimus (14:3). The section ends with Onias seeking to restore the peace (vv. 5-6) with which the narrative began (3:1).

35. A similar account may be found in *Paraleipomena Jeremiou* 1.1-2.

2 Maccabees 4:7-22, The High Priesthood of Jason

NAB

⁷ But Seleucus died, and when Antiochus surnamed Epiphanes succeeded him on the throne,

NRSV

7When Seleucus died and Antiochus, who was called Epiphanes, succeeded to the kingdom,

NAB

Onias' brother Jason obtained the high priesthood by corrupt means: [8] in an interview, he promised the king three hundred and sixty talents of silver, as well as eighty talents from another source of income. [9] Besides this he agreed to pay a hundred and fifty more, if he were given authority to establish a gymnasium and a youth club for it and to enroll men in Jerusalem as Antiochians.

[10] When Jason received the king's approval and came into office, he immediately initiated his countrymen into the Greek way of life. [11] He set aside the royal concessions granted to the Jews through the mediation of John, father of Eupolemus (that Eupolemus who would later go on an embassy to the Romans to establish a treaty of friendship with them); he abrogated the lawful institutions and introduced customs contrary to the law. [12] He quickly established a gymnasium at the very foot of the acropolis, where he induced the noblest young men to wear the Greek hat. [13] The craze for Hellenism and foreign customs reached such a pitch, through the outrageous wickedness of the ungodly pseudo-high-priest Jason, [14] that the priests no longer cared about the service of the altar. Disdaining the temple and neglecting the sacrifices, they hastened, at the signal for the discus-throwing, to take part in the unlawful exercises on the athletic field. [15] They despised what their ancestors had regarded as honors, while they highly prized what the Greeks esteemed as glory. [16] Precisely because of this, they found themselves in serious trouble: the very people whose manner of life they emulated, and whom they desired to imitate in everything, became their enemies and oppressors. [17] It is no light matter to flout the laws of God, as the following period will show.

[18] When the quinquennial games were held at Tyre in the presence of the king, [19] the vile Jason sent envoys as representatives of the Antiochians of Jerusalem, to bring there three hundred silver drachmas for the sacrifice to Hercules. But the bearers themselves decided that the money should not be spent on a sacrifice, as that was not right, but should be used for some other purpose. [20] So the contribution destined by the sender for the

4. 8: (peri poleōs kai) dēmou (kai): so LXX[V, MSS], Vet Lat, P, V.

NRSV

Jason the brother of Onias obtained the high priesthood by corruption, [8]promising the king at an interview[a] three hundred sixty talents of silver, and from another source of revenue eighty talents. [9]In addition to this he promised to pay one hundred fifty more if permission were given to establish by his authority a gymnasium and a body of youth for it, and to enroll the people of Jerusalem as citizens of Antioch. [10]When the king assented and Jason[b] came to office, he at once shifted his compatriots over to the Greek way of life.

[11]He set aside the existing royal concessions to the Jews, secured through John the father of Eupolemus, who went on the mission to establish friendship and alliance with the Romans; and he destroyed the lawful ways of living and introduced new customs contrary to the law. [12]He took delight in establishing a gymnasium right under the citadel, and he induced the noblest of the young men to wear the Greek hat. [13]There was such an extreme of Hellenization and increase in the adoption of foreign ways because of the surpassing wickedness of Jason, who was ungodly and no true[c] high priest, [14]that the priests were no longer intent upon their service at the altar. Despising the sanctuary and neglecting the sacrifices, they hurried to take part in the unlawful proceedings in the wrestling arena after the signal for the discus-throwing, [15]disdaining the honors prized by their ancestors and putting the highest value upon Greek forms of prestige. [16]For this reason heavy disaster overtook them, and those whose ways of living they admired and wished to imitate completely became their enemies and punished them. [17]It is no light thing to show irreverence to the divine laws—a fact that later events will make clear.

[18]When the quadrennial games were being held at Tyre and the king was present, [19]the vile Jason sent envoys, chosen as being Antiochian citizens from Jerusalem, to carry three hundred silver drachmas for the sacrifice to Hercules. Those who carried the money, however, thought best not to use it for sacrifice, because that was inappropriate, but to expend it for another purpose. [20]So this money was intended by the

a Or by a petition   b Gk he   c Gk lacks true

NAB

sacrifice to Hercules was in fact applied, by those who brought it, to the construction of triremes.

²¹ When Apollonius, son of Menestheus, was sent to Egypt for the coronation of King Philometor, Antiochus learned that the king was opposed to his policies; so he took measures for his own security. ²² After going to Joppa, he proceeded to Jerusalem. There he was received with great pomp by Jason and the people of the city, who escorted him with torchlights and acclamations; following this, he led his army into Phoenicia.

NRSV

sender for the sacrifice to Hercules, but by the decision of its carriers it was applied to the construction of triremes.

21When Apollonius son of Menestheus was sent to Egypt for the coronation*a* of Philometor as king, Antiochus learned that Philometor*b* had become hostile to his government, and he took measures for his own security. Therefore upon arriving at Joppa he proceeded to Jerusalem. ²²He was welcomed magnificently by Jason and the city, and ushered in with a blaze of torches and with shouts. Then he marched his army into Phoenicia.

a Meaning of Gk uncertain   *b* Gk *he*

COMMENTARY

4:7-17, Jason's Rise to Power. The author quickly passes over the events of the end of Seleucus's reign on September 3, 175—his assassination by Heliodorus, the installation of Seleucus's young son, and the usurpation of the throne by Seleucus's brother, Antiochus IV Epiphanes, who returned from being held hostage in Rome (cf. Dan 11:20-21; Appian *Syriaca* 45). The author uses a standard formula to describe Seleucus's death (cf. 11:23). At his or her accession a new monarch would appoint or confirm rulers in their position (cf. 1 Macc 11:24-27, 57-58). Jason seizes the opportunity afforded by Antiochus's accession to seek the position of high priest by playing on the need of the Seleucids for money to pay the indemnity to Rome. All in all, Jason promises 590 talents of silver, quite a sizable amount for a small country like Judea. The annual payment imposed by the Romans as a heavy indemnity on the Seleucids was 1,000 talents of silver, and so this extra money is a significant amount. The last installment of the indemnity was to be paid in 173 BCE.

Besides becoming high priest, what Jason asked for in exchange for the money has been the subject of long scholarly debate. The gymnasium was a unique feature of Greek life. Originally designed for athletic activity, it usually consisted of a running track and a wrestling area with perhaps jumping pits and areas for throwing the javelin or discus. Adjacent would be buildings for dressing, bathing, storing oil, etc. Later, gymnasia became centers of both physical and intellectual training, with halls for lectures on music, literature, and philosophy. The exact chronology of this development, however, is unclear, and it is unknown how much of such intellectual training would have been connected with a gymnasium in a city like Jerusalem in the early second century BCE. The same uncertainty surrounds the word translated "body of youth" in the NRSV (ἐφηβεῖον *ephēbeion*). These were boys who had reached the age of puberty. At Athens, for a short period of time in the late fourth century, all young men aged eighteen to twenty, the ephebes, underwent a two-year compulsory military training. Such military exercises as archery and the use of siege engines were still being done by ephebes in the late second century. But few families could afford their sons' not working for two years, so this training period, like most education, was primarily for the sons of rich families. The ephebes, through their training, became involved in the public life of a city, its religious festivals and processions. The reader needs to keep in mind that there was no core curriculum for education in the Hellenistic world, and education was primarily preparation to be a citizen of a particular city with all its particular religious and community responsibilities. The physical exercises, of course, would be common to all, and so cities could compete against each other in games (see 4:18-20). While we cannot be sure what intellectual training took place at the gymnasium in Jerusalem, except no doubt that Greek was taught, the physical training already showed that the people desired to be part of a wider world. Outfitting and maintaining such an athletic facility would have been expensive, and thus one gets a sense of the wealth of the high priestly families. The exact location of the gymnasium is unknown. According to 4:12, the gymnasium lay right under the citadel. If one locates the citadel on the southeastern hill, then the gymnasium would have been either between the city of David and the Temple or in a broad ravine, the Tyropoion, which separated the Lower City from the Upper City.[36]

Besides a gymnasium, Jason also asked for some sort of concession for citizens of Jerusalem (4:9*b*). The verse has been variously translated: to enroll the people of Jerusalem as Antiochians, i.e., citizens of Antioch; to enroll the Antiochenes in Jerusalem. Who and what are these Antiochenes? Four possibilities have been suggested: that the Hellenized Jews would be made citizens of Antioch in Syria; that Antiochus IV had set up a new republic like the Roman one and that its citizens were to be called Antiochenes;[37] that a Hellenistic corporation would have been set up within Jerusalem and its members called Antiochenes;[38] that Jerusalem itself would now be called Antioch-in-Jerusalem and its citizens called Antiochenes.[39] The first three are unlikely. As regards the first proposition, even the king could not force a city to give citizenship en bloc to citizens of another city. As for the second option, the evidence we do have suggests that Antiochus IV supported local traditions and not that he sought to make a republic. Against the third position, "Antiochene" never refers to a corporation, but to citizenship. Even the last suggestion has its problems; 1 Maccabees does not mention such a change in name and status, nor does the author of 2 Maccabees,

even though he knows how to protest a name change (6:2-3), complain openly about it. Nevertheless, many ancient cities received new Greek names, and this seems to be the best explanation of this verse. Did this name change have juridical or constitutional implications? Tcherikover argues that only those who received ephebic training could become citizens and that since Jason controlled the enrollment of the gymnasium, he would now be able to decide who became a citizen of his city. Yet we have no evidence that in the Hellenistic period a city's name change meant constitutional change as well, or that undergoing ephebic training was the only way to become a citizen. Perhaps all one should say is that "to enroll the people of Jerusalem as Antiochenes" means simply that the name of the city was henceforth to be Antioch-in-Jerusalem, and that this does not imply either Jason's control of who was a citizen or a constitutional change in Jerusalem.

However, it is likely that Jason controlled who was enrolled in the gymnasium. And since this educational training would have tracked its students for entrance into higher governmental and diplomatic posts, Jason would have been able to manipulate who would receive this favored treatment as well. This was patronage with a vengeance.

The change of Jerusalem into a Greek city also implies that Jason wanted to integrate Jerusalem into the Seleucid Empire, particularly since his position depended on Antiochus IV's favor. Why would Antiochus have so readily granted the request? He always needed the money for lavish expenditures, but, perhaps just as important, it strengthened his southern region near the border with Egypt at a time of increasing tension.

The author of 2 Maccabees sees what Jason did as the abandonment of traditional Jewish religion (vv. 11, 17). He refers in particular to the privileges bestowed by Antiochus III through the father of Eupolemus, the Jewish ambassador to Rome under Judas Maccabeus (1 Macc 8:17). The author contrasts what is lawful with what is unlawful and uses the word "Hellenization" (v. 13), which formerly meant the use of a pure Greek style of speech, in a new way as the opposite of Judaism (see also 2:21; 8:1; 14:38). The author mocks those concerned with physical

36. Josephus *The Jewish War* 5.40.
37. See Jonathan A. Goldstein, *2 Maccabees*, AB 41A (Garden City, N.Y.: Doubleday, 1983).
38. See Elias Bickerman, *The God of the Maccabees: Studies on the Meaning and Origin of the Maccabean Revolt*, SJLA 32 (Leiden: Brill, 1979).
39. See V. Tcherikover, *Hellenistic Civilization and the Jews* (Philadelphia: Jewish Publication Society, 1961).

exercises rather than spiritual pursuits. Since education in the ancient world was so intimately tied to training for citizenship, one can see how the author understands Jason's educational reforms as a denial of Jewish traditions. The athletes wore the Greek-style hat (v. 12), which was a broad-brimmed hat worn to protect them from the sun; it was said to have been similar to the hat worn by Hermes, the god of athletics. The signal (v. 14) was typically to start activity in the gymnasium, not specifically for discus throwing. At vv. 16-17, the author reflects on what was taking place and points forward to the persecutions that will soon happen. The author also introduces his motif of just deserts—punishment meted out is appropriate to the crime committed (see 4:26, 32-33, 38; 5:9-10; 13:8).

4:18-22, Jason's Further Tenure. Every four years games were held at Tyre in honor of the God Melgart/Heracles.[40] Following his capture of Tyre after a long siege in 332 BCE, Alexander celebrated games to Heracles in the spring of 331 BCE.[41] These quadrennial games may have followed that precedent. Antiochus IV, as a supporter of local traditions, was present at these games (v. 18). The envoys sent by Jason (v. 19) were official representatives at another city's festivals. The corollary of Jason's founding a gymnasium is clearly seen here as Antioch-in-Jerusalem now interacts openly with other cities. At the festivals, "sacred envoys" (θεωροί theōroi) normally offered sacrifices in the name of their cities. The author sees Jason, the "vile" Jason, as again apostatizing when he sends envoys with three hundred silver drachmas, the price of a sacrificial ox, to offer in sacrifice to the Greek god. Those envoys, however, "thought best not to use it for sacrifice" (v. 19), but use the money to pay for the outfitting of triremes, Greek ships with three rows of oars on each side.

Here again surfaces the issue of self-definition: How were Jews who lived in Greek cities and who interacted with the citizens of these cities to behave toward the deities of those cities? How was Jason, as the leader of the Greek city Antioch-at-Jerusalem, to behave toward his counterparts? Would Jason have insulted other leaders by not recognizing in some way the fact that they paid homage to their patron deity? Jason presumably thought it consistent with Judaism as he understood it to offer such a sacrifice, but his envoys did not.

A similar divergence of opinion emerges in the fragments attributed to the Jewish author Eupolemus, usually identified with the ambassador of Judas Maccabeus to Rome (1 Macc 8:17; 2 Macc 4:11), who wrote that Solomon sent to Souron (i.e., Hiram), king of Tyre, as a gift for his help in building the Temple in Jerusalem "the golden column, which is set up in Tyre in the temple of Zeus."[42] Eupolemus attempted to identify Solomon as the origin of the well-known pillar in Tyre, mentioned by the Greek historian Herodotus as being in a temple to Heracles.[43] Eupolemus thus connects Solomon with votive offerings in a temple of Zeus. Immediately following this fragment of Eupolemus's work in Eusebius is a fragment from another Jewish author, Theophilus, who insists that Solomon simply sent the remaining gold back to Souron. Souron then commissioned a full-length gold statue of his daughter and placed the golden pillar near it as a covering for the statue.[44] We know nothing about Theophilus except that he wrote this fragment. We do not know when or where Theophilus wrote, or whether he wrote in conscious opposition to Eupolemus. We do see him, however, as trying to distance Solomon from any connection with a foreign cult, while that is less of a problem for Eupolemus.

It is also interesting to note how the LXX translates Exod 22:28 as "You shall not revile God." The Hebrew term for "God" (אלהים 'elōhîm) is a plural noun, and the Greek translator has translated it as plural: "You shall not revile the gods." Does this translation imply that the gods of other nations could be honored, but only as subordinate to the supreme God, the God of Israel?

We do not know for precisely what action Apollonius son of Menestheus (4:4) went to Egypt as an envoy of the Seleucids (v. 21). Perhaps it was the first time the young king had presided at a state banquet. Ptolemy VI Philometor, after the death of his father, Ptolemy V Epiphanes, in

---

40. The Tyrian god Melgart came to be regarded as an alias for the Greek deity Heracles.
   41. Arrian *Anabasis* 3.6.1.

42. Eusebius *Preparation for the Gospel* 9.34.18.
43. Herodotus 2:44.
44. Eusebius *Preparation for the Gospel* 9.34.19.

181/180, had been under the control first of his mother, Cleopatra I, who died in 176, and then of guardians; he proclaimed himself to be of age in 170. The event recorded here seems to take place around 172 BCE, and tension had been building for a long time. Ptolemy V Epiphanes might possibly have gone to war with the Seleucids if he had not been assassinated. Antiochus IV, to forestall any invasion, made a tour of his southern areas. Joppa (v. 21) lay on the coast to the northwest of Jerusalem. The language used to describe Antiochus's welcome to Jerusalem (v. 22) is that of the ceremonial reception for Hellenistic kings. One might compare it with the narrative of the arrival of Alexander the Great in Jerusalem, a narrative that also emphasizes the friendly relations between Jews and the Greek rulers.[45]

45. See Josephus *Antiquities of the Jews* 11.329-339.

REFLECTIONS

This section raises in heightened fashion the question of how a religious community is to identify itself and maintain that identity. What boundaries must one not cross if one is to remain part of that community and true to its traditions? The author of the epitome clearly sees Jason as overstepping the boundaries of Jewish identity as the author defines it. Jews, for him, should not participate in the education in gymnasia or have anything to do with the religious activities associated with Greek festivals. Jason thought differently.

We face similar questions about identity and boundaries in contemporary society. Should Christians send their children to public schools, or should they have their own schools to instill their own sense of Christian values? How much television should we expose our children to? Should one study Scripture only within the confines of one's own religious tradition, or does one need to be open to the insights of scholars from differing religious traditions who read it from a very different perspective? How is one to respect other religious traditions, to show respect for the festivals of Islam, of Hinduism, of Buddhism, of Native American religious traditions? How do we maintain our belief in the privileged position of our own religious tradition when we are faced with the idea that people do not come to the knowledge of God by one way alone? These questions come to the surface as we see the Jews of the second century BCE struggling with diverse cultural values. If a multi-cultural society is to survive, the various subgroups that populate it must learn to respect one another's traditions and cultures. This is easy to say, but hard to do. If religion is thought of as something individual, private, that each person has the right to do in his or her own private way, then a simple solution seems attainable. Everyone will be able to worship in his or her own way, but the individual's religion will not impinge on society as a whole. But religious beliefs do have social consequences. The debate over abortion has clearly shown that. The late nineteenth and early twentieth centuries also saw surface a conflict between those who held that following the gospel precepts would bring prosperity and that the poor were therefore lazy sinners, and those who held that the gospel required concern and help for the poor. Religious beliefs *do* have social consequences, and so the task of forming a viable society out of many belief systems requires all of us to work hard at empathizing with those of other faiths.

2 Maccabees 4:23-50, Menelaus in Control

NAB	NRSV
23 Three years later Jason sent Menelaus, brother of the aforementioned Simon, to deliver the money to the king, and to obtain decisions on	23After a period of three years Jason sent Menelaus, the brother of the previously mentioned Simon, to carry the money to the king and

some important matters. 24 When he had been introduced to the king, he flattered him with such an air of authority that he secured the high priesthood for himself, outbidding Jason by three hundred talents of silver. 25 He returned with the royal commission, but with nothing that made him worthy of the high priesthood; he had the temper of a cruel tyrant and the rage of a wild beast. 26 Then Jason, who had cheated his own brother and now saw himself cheated by another man, was driven out as a fugitive to the country of the Ammonites.

27 Although Menelaus had obtained the office, he did not make any payments of the money he had promised to the king, 28 in spite of the demand of Sostratus, the commandant of the citadel, whose duty it was to collect the taxes. For this reason, both were summoned before the king. 29 Menelaus left his brother Lysimachus as his substitute in the high priesthood, while Sostratus left Crates, commander of the Cypriots, as his substitute.

30 While these things were taking place, the people of Tarsus and Mallus rose in revolt, because their cities had been given as a gift to Antiochis, the king's mistress. 31 The king, therefore, went off in haste to settle the affair, leaving Andronicus, one of his nobles, as his deputy. 32 Then Menelaus, thinking this a good opportunity, stole some gold vessels from the temple and presented them to Andronicus; he had already sold some other vessels in Tyre and in the neighboring cities. 33 When Onias had clear evidence of the facts, he made a public protest, after withdrawing to the inviolable sanctuary at Daphne, near Antioch. 34 Thereupon Menelaus approached Andronicus privately and asked him to lay hands on Onias. So Andronicus went to Onias, and by treacherously reassuring him through sworn pledges with right hands joined, persuaded him, in spite of his suspicions, to leave the sanctuary. Then, without any regard for justice, he immediately put him to death.

35 As a result, not only the Jews, but many people of other nations as well, were indignant and angry over the unjust murder of the man. 36 When the king returned from the region of Cilicia, the Jews of the city, together with the

to complete the records of essential business. 24But he, when presented to the king, extolled him with an air of authority, and secured the high priesthood for himself, outbidding Jason by three hundred talents of silver. 25After receiving the king's orders he returned, possessing no qualification for the high priesthood, but having the hot temper of a cruel tyrant and the rage of a savage wild beast. 26So Jason, who after supplanting his own brother was supplanted by another man, was driven as a fugitive into the land of Ammon. 27Although Menelaus continued to hold the office, he did not pay regularly any of the money promised to the king. 28When Sostratus the captain of the citadel kept requesting payment—for the collection of the revenue was his responsibility—the two of them were summoned by the king on account of this issue. 29Menelaus left his own brother Lysimachus as deputy in the high priesthood, while Sostratus left Crates, the commander of the Cyprian troops.

30While such was the state of affairs, it happened that the people of Tarsus and of Mallus revolted because their cities had been given as a present to Antiochis, the king's concubine. 31So the king went hurriedly to settle the trouble, leaving Andronicus, a man of high rank, to act as his deputy. 32But Menelaus, thinking he had obtained a suitable opportunity, stole some of the gold vessels of the temple and gave them to Andronicus; other vessels, as it happened, he had sold to Tyre and the neighboring cities. 33When Onias became fully aware of these acts, he publicly exposed them, having first withdrawn to a place of sanctuary at Daphne near Antioch. 34Therefore Menelaus, taking Andronicus aside, urged him to kill Onias. Andronicus[a] came to Onias, and resorting to treachery, offered him sworn pledges and gave him his right hand; he persuaded him, though still suspicious, to come out from the place of sanctuary; then, with no regard for justice, he immediately put him out of the way.

35For this reason not only Jews, but many also of other nations, were grieved and displeased at the unjust murder of the man. 36When the king returned from the region of Cilicia, the Jews in

a Gk He

Greeks who detested the crime, went to see him about the murder of Onias. ³⁷ Antiochus was deeply grieved and full of pity; he wept as he recalled the prudence and noble conduct of the deceased. ³⁸ Inflamed with anger, he immediately stripped Andronicus of his purple robe, tore off his other garments, and had him led through the whole city to the very place where he had committed the outrage against Onias; and there he put the murderer to death. Thus the LORD rendered him the punishment he deserved.

³⁹ Many sacrilegious thefts had been committed by Lysimachus in the city with the connivance of Menelaus. When word was spread that a large number of gold vessels had been stolen, the people assembled in protest against Lysimachus. ⁴⁰ As the crowds, now thoroughly enraged, began to riot, Lysimachus launched an unjustified attack against them with about three thousand armed men under the leadership of Auranus, a man as advanced in folly as he was in years. ⁴¹ Reacting against Lysimachus' attack, the people picked up stones or pieces of wood or handfuls of the ashes lying there and threw them in wild confusion at Lysimachus and his men. ⁴² As a result, they wounded many of them and even killed a few, while they put all the rest to flight. The sacrilegious thief himself they slew near the treasury.

⁴³ Charges about this affair were brought against Menelaus. ⁴⁴ When the king came to Tyre, three men sent by the senate presented to him the justice of their cause. ⁴⁵ But Menelaus, seeing himself on the losing side, promised Ptolemy, son of Dorymenes, a substantial sum of money if he would win the king over. ⁴⁶ So Ptolemy retired with the king under a colonnade, as if to get some fresh air, and persuaded him to change his mind. ⁴⁷ Menelaus, who was the cause of all the trouble, the king acquitted of the charges, while he condemned to death those poor men who would have been declared innocent even if they had pleaded their case before Scythians. ⁴⁸ Thus, those who had prosecuted the case for the city, for the people, and for the sacred vessels, quickly suffered unjust punishment. ⁴⁹ For this reason, even some Tyrians were indignant over the crime and provided sumptuously for their burial. ⁵⁰ But Men-

the city^a appealed to him with regard to the unreasonable murder of Onias, and the Greeks shared their hatred of the crime. ³⁷Therefore Antiochus was grieved at heart and filled with pity, and wept because of the moderation and good conduct of the deceased. ³⁸Inflamed with anger, he immediately stripped off the purple robe from Andronicus, tore off his clothes, and led him around the whole city to that very place where he had committed the outrage against Onias, and there he dispatched the bloodthirsty fellow. The Lord thus repaid him with the punishment he deserved.

³⁹When many acts of sacrilege had been committed in the city by Lysimachus with the connivance of Menelaus, and when report of them had spread abroad, the populace gathered against Lysimachus, because many of the gold vessels had already been stolen. ⁴⁰Since the crowds were becoming aroused and filled with anger, Lysimachus armed about three thousand men and launched an unjust attack, under the leadership of a certain Auranus, a man advanced in years and no less advanced in folly. ⁴¹But when the Jews^b became aware that Lysimachus was attacking them, some picked up stones, some blocks of wood, and others took handfuls of the ashes that were lying around, and threw them in wild confusion at Lysimachus and his men. ⁴²As a result, they wounded many of them, and killed some, and put all the rest to flight; the temple robber himself they killed close by the treasury.

⁴³Charges were brought against Menelaus about this incident. ⁴⁴When the king came to Tyre, three men sent by the senate presented the case before him. ⁴⁵But Menelaus, already as good as beaten, promised a substantial bribe to Ptolemy son of Dorymenes to win over the king. ⁴⁶Therefore Ptolemy, taking the king aside into a colonnade as if for refreshment, induced the king to change his mind. ⁴⁷Menelaus, the cause of all the trouble, he acquitted of the charges against him, while he sentenced to death those unfortunate men, who would have been freed uncondemned if they had pleaded even before Scythians. ⁴⁸And so those who had spoken for the city and the villages^c and the holy vessels quickly suffered the

a Or in each city   b Gk they   c Other ancient authorities read the people

NAB	NRSV
elaus, thanks to the covetousness of the men in power, remained in office, where he grew in wickedness and became the chief plotter against his fellow citizens.	unjust penalty. [49]Therefore even the Tyrians, showing their hatred of the crime, provided magnificently for their funeral. [50]But Menelaus, because of the greed of those in power, remained in office, growing in wickedness, having become the chief plotter against his compatriots.

COMMENTARY

4:23-29, Menelaus Gains the High Priesthood. Jason, although a usurper, was of the Oniad family and thus a Zadokite. He is replaced by Menelaus, a brother of Simon and member of the clan of Bilgah (3:4), and thus not a member of the priestly family. Just as Jason had gained the high priesthood by offering money, so also Menelaus, while delivering the annual tribute, promises an annual tribute of six hundred talents of silver (v. 24), which he is unable to deliver (v. 27). The author dehumanizes Menelaus and suggests by the use of the term "orders," or "instructions" (ἐντολή *entolē*), that Menelaus is but a puppet of the king (v. 25). Jason flees across the Jordan (v. 26); the Tobiad Hyrcanus had previously fled there to Araq-el-Emir, about twelve miles east of the Jordan and ten miles northwest of Heshbon.[46]

The author now informs us that there was a Seleucid garrison in the city (v. 28; according to 1 Maccabees, the citadel had not yet been built). Antiochus III had spoken of the expulsion of a Ptolemaic garrison from the citadel in Jerusalem,[47] but this is the first time the reader learns of a Seleucid garrison in Jerusalem. Perhaps it was stationed there in response to the Ptolemaic threat. Since one of Sostratus's duties was to collect revenues, there must have been some division of authority within Jerusalem, with a regular royal functionary operating within and above the city's political structure. Sostratus and Menelaus are summoned by the king to Antioch to resolve the matter (v. 28). Cyprus was at this time a Ptolemaic possession, so Cyprian troops (v. 29) must have been mercenaries.

4:30-38, The Murder of Onias. When Sostratus and Menelaus arrive in Antioch, Antiochus IV is away from Antioch, settling an uprising in the Cilician towns of Tarsus and Mallus caused by an affront to their standing as independent cities (v. 30). The authority of the king in Greek cities, particularly those in strategic Asia Minor, varied from city to city, but in general the Seleucids showed a certain respect for the independence of these cities. For Antiochus to summarily hand them over to his concubine would have been seen as disrespectful.

In the king's absence, Menelaus gives some golden vessels stolen from the Temple to Andronichus, Antiochus's deputy, either as payment of the overdue tribute or as a bribe to have Onias murdered (v. 32). This narrative is quite intriguing. Menelaus, we learn, has been selling temple vessels in Tyre and neighboring cities, perhaps due to his need for cash (v. 27). One might recall how the pious king Hezekiah had paid off Sennacherib with temple silver and gold (2 Kgs 18:13-16; an incident not repeated in the parallel account in 2 Chronicles 32). Menelaus, therefore, may have thought it proper to use the temple furnishings as payment to the king, although he could not have thought that it was right to use the temple treasures to bribe Andronicus. Clearly Onias III, as well as the author, thought Menelaus did not have the authority to sell temple vessels (v. 33). What is intriguing is that, once he has exposed Menelaus's actions, the pious Onias III (3:1) is pictured as taking asylum in the famous temple of Apollo and Artemis in Daphne. What, then, is Onias's view of the power of the Greek gods? Here surfaces another of the motifs of 2 Maccabees: Jews and Gentiles can live in peace together (12:30-31). Andronicus, by murdering Onias (v. 34), is shown as utterly treacherous, a treachery resented even

---

46. Josephus *Antiquities of the Jews* 12.229-233.
47. Ibid., 12.138.

by non-Jews (v. 35). Someone named Andronicus is said by Hellenistic historians to have murdered the son of Seleucus IV, who seems to have been co-regent with Antiochus IV prior to Antiochus's rise to power.[48] (The death of Seleucus's son is dated to July/August 170 BCE from the Babylonian kinglist.) It seems likely that the same Andronicus is meant in both cases. Perhaps Antiochus IV took the opportunity of Onias's murder to do away with an embarrassing accomplice, although Antiochus IV is shown by the author as being concerned only with the death of Onias, and as extremely moved by it (v. 37). Andronicus is stripped of the purple robe, symbol of the order of the Friends of the King (v. 38; see 1 Macc 10:20), and is publicly humiliated. The motif of one's getting one's just deserts thus appears again, while the king does not take action with regard to Menelaus's role in the death.

4:39-50, Further Charges Against Menelaus. The sacrilegious actions of the Bilgah clan result in rioting against Lysimachus. The attack against Lysimachus, Menelaus's brother (vv. 39-42), seems to take place while Menelaus is at Antioch and Lysimachus is in charge in Jerusalem (v. 29). The events narrated here stand in sharp contrast to what occurred earlier (2 Maccabees 3). Onias had protected the money deposited in the Temple, but Lysimachus sells the temple vessels. The people had gathered around the high priest Onias in sympathy; here they accuse Lysimachus. Earlier the action was against outsiders; now it is an internal conflict. Lysimachus resorts to violence (v. 40), just as his brother Simon had done (4:3). The reader may wonder what the Seleucid garrison (4:29) was doing during this confrontation and how Lysimachus could so easily procure arms for three thousand men, a small militia in itself. Lysimachus is supported by an otherwise unknown figure, Auranus, whose description contrasts markedly with that of a later, older man, Eleazar, who suffers martyrdom rather than breach the law (6:18). The author intimates divine help in that an unarmed group puts the three thousand armed men to flight and that Lysimachus dies at the very place he was robbing (v. 42), just as Andronicus was killed on the very spot where he had killed Onias (v. 38).

We do not know how the report about the selling of the temple vessels spread (v. 39), but we can see how the factions mentioned in 4:1-6 still exist. Now, as Onias III had done, the three members of the Jerusalem council (v. 44), a body known from a letter of Antiochus III but whose exact function and responsibilities are unknown,[49] go to the king for justice. We are not told who is in charge of Jerusalem or the outcome of the uprising against Lysimachus. The author insists that the uprising was blamed on Menelaus (c. 43 BCE), but the three high-ranking councilors may have been called to answer questions about the incident. Ptolemy, son of Dorymenes, may already have held the office of governor of Coelesyria and Phoenicia (1 Macc 3:38; 2 Macc 8:8) and may have been present there for the trial. As the previous governor had favored Simon, Menelaus's brother (4:4), and as bribery had won the day before (4:32), so now the author shows the same factors at work. Justice, in the opinion of the author of 1 Maccabees, is perverted (vv. 45-48). The Scythians were a byword for irrational cruelty.[50] As at the murder of Onias, the author depicts here some non-Jews sympathetic to the fate of the executed councilors (v. 49). Once again the contrast with Onias III stands out: Whereas Onias was not an accuser of his compatriots but only sought their welfare, Menelaus is the chief plotter against his compatriots.

---

48. Diodorus Siculus 30.7.2.

49. Josephus *Antiquities of the Jews* 12.142.
50. Herodotus 4.64-75; Polybius 9.34.11.

REFLECTIONS

This section details the intrigues and plots and the breakdown of civility within the Jewish polity. Menelaus uses every means in his power to remain in power: illicitly drawing upon funds that do not belong to him; resorting to violence to quell discontent; silencing the opposition by murder. The story reads almost like the plot for a movie: a politician who steals public monies and then uses his position of power to threaten and get rid of opponents in whatever way is necessary. Unfortunately, art sometimes copies life, and the number of politicians and religious leaders who have been indicted for abuse of trust seems to grow every year. The public figure who can be bribed, like Andronicus, also stands as a warning. Politicians need to be extremely sensitive to even the appearance of a conflict of interest. It does not seem right, for instance, that a senator or member of Congress who owns stocks and shares in oil or gas companies should sit on the committees determining energy policy.

The contrast between the desire for private, short-term gain at the expense of the long-term common welfare of the community is striking in this narrative. It is a contrast each society and each community knows and must deal with. The narrative reminds us of the truth of the maxim cited in 1 Tim 6:10: "The love of money is a root of all kinds of evil" (NRSV). Money donated to charitable works and missions needs to be carefully administered and not squandered on personal affairs or self-aggrandizement. Religious leaders should lead lives of simplicity, and not lord it over their flock. As Jesus said, "You know that among the Gentiles those whom they recognize as their rulers lord it over them, and their great ones are tyrants over them. But it is not so among you; but whoever wishes to become great among you must be your servant" (Mark 10:42-43 NRSV). We should not muzzle the ox while it is treading out the grain (1 Cor 9:8-12), but the ox should not become fat either.

2 Maccabees 5:1-27, Antiochus Takes Control of Jerusalem

NAB

5 About this time Antiochus sent his second expedition into Egypt. ² It then happened that all over the city, for nearly forty days, there appeared horsemen charging in midair, clad in garments interwoven with gold—companies fully armed with lances ³ and drawn swords; squadrons of cavalry in battle array, charges and counter-charges on this side and that, with brandished shields and bristling spears, flights of arrows and flashes of gold ornaments, together with armor of every sort. ⁴ Therefore all prayed that this vision might be a good omen.

⁵ But when a false rumor circulated that Antiochus was dead, Jason gathered fully a thousand men and suddenly attacked the city. As the defenders on the walls were forced back and the city was finally being taken, Menelaus took refuge in the citadel. ⁶ Jason then slaughtered his fellow citizens without mercy, not realizing that triumph over one's own kindred was the greatest failure, but imagining that he was winning a victory over his enemies, not his fellow countrymen. ⁷ Even so, he did not gain control of the government, but in the end received only disgrace for his treachery, and once again took refuge in the country of the Ammonites. ⁸ At length he met a

NRSV

5 About this time Antiochus made his second invasion of Egypt. ²And it happened that, for almost forty days, there appeared over all the city golden-clad cavalry charging through the air, in companies fully armed with lances and drawn swords— ³troops of cavalry drawn up, attacks and counterattacks made on this side and on that, brandishing of shields, massing of spears, hurling of missiles, the flash of golden trappings, and armor of all kinds. ⁴Therefore everyone prayed that the apparition might prove to have been a good omen.

5When a false rumor arose that Antiochus was dead, Jason took no fewer than a thousand men and suddenly made an assault on the city. When the troops on the wall had been forced back and at last the city was being taken, Menelaus took refuge in the citadel. ⁶But Jason kept relentlessly slaughtering his compatriots, not realizing that success at the cost of one's kindred is the greatest misfortune, but imagining that he was setting up trophies of victory over enemies and not over compatriots. ⁷He did not, however, gain control of the government; in the end he got only disgrace from his conspiracy, and fled again into the country of the Ammonites. ⁸Finally he met a miserable

NAB

miserable end. Called to account before Aretas, king of the Arabs, he fled from city to city, hunted by all men, hated as a transgressor of the laws, abhorred as the butcher of his country and his countrymen. After being driven into Egypt, [9] he crossed the sea to the Spartans, among whom he hoped to find protection because of his relations with them. There he who had exiled so many from their country perished in exile; [10] and he who had cast out so many to lie unburied went unmourned himself with no funeral of any kind or any place in the tomb of his ancestors.

[11] When these happenings were reported to the king, he thought that Judea was in revolt. Raging like a wild animal, he set out from Egypt and took Jerusalem by storm. [12] He ordered his soldiers to cut down without mercy those whom they met and to slay those who took refuge in their houses. [13] There was a massacre of young and old, a killing of women and children, a slaughter of virgins and infants. [14] In the space of three days, eighty thousand were lost, forty thousand meeting a violent death, and the same number being sold into slavery. [15] Not satisfied with this, the king dared to enter the holiest temple in the world; Menelaus, that traitor both to the laws and to his country, served as guide. [16] He laid his impure hands on the sacred vessels and gathered up with profane hands the votive offerings made by other kings for the advancement, the glory, and the honor of the Place. [17] Puffed up in spirit, Antiochus did not realize that it was because of the sins of the city's inhabitants that the LORD was angry for a little while and hence disregarded the holy Place. [18] If they had not become entangled in so many sins, this man, like Heliodorus, who was sent by King Seleucus to inspect the treasury, would have been flogged and turned back from his presumptuous action as soon as he approached. [19] The LORD, however, had not chosen the people for the sake of the Place, but the Place for the sake of the people. [20] Therefore, the Place itself, having shared in the people's misfortunes, afterward participated in their good fortune; and what the Almighty had forsaken in his anger was

5, 8: egklētheis (pros Aretan): conj.

NRSV

end. Accused[a] before Aretas the ruler of the Arabs, fleeing from city to city, pursued by everyone, hated as a rebel against the laws, and abhorred as the executioner of his country and his compatriots, he was cast ashore in Egypt. [9]There he who had driven many from their own country into exile died in exile, having embarked to go to the Lacedaemonians in hope of finding protection because of their kinship. [10]He who had cast out many to lie unburied had no one to mourn for him; he had no funeral of any sort and no place in the tomb of his ancestors.

[11]When news of what had happened reached the king, he took it to mean that Judea was in revolt. So, raging inwardly, he left Egypt and took the city by storm. [12]He commanded his soldiers to cut down relentlessly everyone they met and to kill those who went into their houses. [13]Then there was massacre of young and old, destruction of boys, women, and children, and slaughter of young girls and infants. [14]Within the total of three days eighty thousand were destroyed, forty thousand in hand-to-hand fighting, and as many were sold into slavery as were killed.

[15]Not content with this, Antiochus[b] dared to enter the most holy temple in all the world, guided by Menelaus, who had become a traitor both to the laws and to his country. [16]He took the holy vessels with his polluted hands, and swept away with profane hands the votive offerings that other kings had made to enhance the glory and honor of the place. [17]Antiochus was elated in spirit, and did not perceive that the Lord was angered for a little while because of the sins of those who lived in the city, and that this was the reason he was disregarding the holy place. [18]But if it had not happened that they were involved in many sins, this man would have been flogged and turned back from his rash act as soon as he came forward, just as Heliodorus had been, whom King Seleucus sent to inspect the treasury. [19]But the Lord did not choose the nation for the sake of the holy place, but the place for the sake of the nation. [20]Therefore the place itself shared in the misfortunes that befell the nation and afterward participated in its benefits; and what was forsaken in the wrath of the Almighty was

a Cn: Gk Imprisoned   b Gk he

restored in all its glory, once the great Sovereign became reconciled.

²¹ Antiochus carried off eighteen hundred talents from the temple, and hurried back to Antioch. In his arrogance he planned to make the land navigable and the sea passable on foot, so carried away was he with pride. ²² But he left governors to harass the nation: at Jerusalem, Philip, a Phrygian by birth, and in character more cruel than the man who appointed him; ²³ at Mount Gerizim, Andronicus; and besides these, Menelaus, who lorded it over his fellow citizens worse than the others did. Out of hatred for the Jewish citizens, ²⁴ the king sent Apollonius, commander of the Mysians, at the head of an army of twenty-two thousand men, with orders to kill all the grown men and sell the women and young men into slavery. ²⁵ When this man arrived in Jerusalem, he pretended to be peacefully disposed and waited until the holy day of the sabbath; then, finding the Jews refraining from work, he ordered his men to parade fully armed. ²⁶ All those who came out to watch, he massacred, and running through the city with armed men, he cut down a large number of people.

²⁷ But Judas Maccabeus with about nine others withdrew to the wilderness where he and his companions lived like wild animals in the hills, continuing to eat what grew wild to avoid sharing the defilement.

5, 23: (*en de*) *Garizein* (*Andronikon*): so LXX^{MSS}; cf Vet Lat^{MSS}, V. Join *apechthē . . . diathesin* to the following words, and omit *de* in v 24: so LXX^{V MSS}, Vet Lat, V, P.

restored again in all its glory when the great Lord became reconciled.

21So Antiochus carried off eighteen hundred talents from the temple, and hurried away to Antioch, thinking in his arrogance that he could sail on the land and walk on the sea, because his mind was elated. ²²He left governors to oppress the people: at Jerusalem, Philip, by birth a Phrygian and in character more barbarous than the man who appointed him; ²³and at Gerizim, Andronicus; and besides these Menelaus, who lorded it over his compatriots worse than the others did. In his malice toward the Jewish citizens,^a ²⁴Antiochus^b sent Apollonius, the captain of the Mysians, with an army of twenty-two thousand, and commanded him to kill all the grown men and to sell the women and boys as slaves. ²⁵When this man arrived in Jerusalem, he pretended to be peaceably disposed and waited until the holy sabbath day; then, finding the Jews not at work, he ordered his troops to parade under arms. ²⁶He put to the sword all those who came out to see them, then rushed into the city with his armed warriors and killed great numbers of people.

27But Judas Maccabeus, with about nine others, got away to the wilderness, and kept himself and his companions alive in the mountains as wild animals do; they continued to live on what grew wild, so that they might not share in the defilement.

^a Or *worse than the others did in his malice toward the Jewish citizens*
^b Gk *he*

COMMENTARY

5:1-10, The Occasion for the Attack on the Temple. The author of 1 Maccabees locates Antiochus IV's attack on the Temple after his second invasion of Egypt (168 BCE), while 2 Maccabees places it after his first invasion of Egypt (170–169 BCE). Daniel 11:28-30 speaks of two invasions of Egypt and two attacks against the Temple, but does not explicitly imply that Antiochus IV entered Jerusalem in person on the second attack. In this case, the chronology of 1 Maccabees is to be preferred (1 Macc 1:20-35).

Most likely the epitomist has conflated the pillaging of the Temple after the first invasion of Egypt with an armed attack on Jerusalem by the Seleucid Apollonius, captain of the Mysians (1 Macc 1:29; 2 Macc 5:24; note how 1 Maccabees gives a precise date for this attack, "two years later," while 2 Maccabees does not).

5:1-4. Portents or signs in the heavens before a momentous event are frequently reported in Jewish and non-Jewish literature (see esp. Tacitus, the Roman historian [c. 56–115 CE], Pliny the

Elder, a Roman writer of the first century CE, and Josephus, the first-century CE Jewish historian).[51] Such portents could, of course, be variously interpreted, and they heightened the narrative tension as to what is in fact to happen (v. 4).

5:5-10. The outcome of battles was always questionable, and so rumors of defeats could easily circulate. The rebuff of Antiochus IV by the Romans after his second invasion of Egypt in 168 BCE would be an appropriate occasion for the rise of such a rumor (v. 5). Lysimachus had been able to muster three thousand men (4:40), but now Jason, with only a thousand men, successfully makes an unexpected attack on Jerusalem and forces Menelaus to take refuge in the citadel, presumably with the Seleucid garrison. Jason must have hoped that, with Menelaus defeated, the successor of Antiochus IV would see him as the strong man of Judea, just as Menelaus had gained the high priesthood by presenting himself as powerful (v. 24). Jason, like Menelaus, attacks his compatriots (v. 6). The author does not tell us why Jason failed in his attempt to gain control (v. 7). Some scholars have suggested that a third force, neither Jason nor Menelaus, but the crowds (see 4:40), rose up in a popular uprising. It is more likely, however, that the citadel was well stocked and ably defended by the Seleucid garrison and could hold out against Jason while waiting for reinforcements. Possibly Jason fled in the face of a Seleucid force sent to reestablish order. The author is only concerned to draw out the moral of the story, and not to provide the details. Jason is forced to return to Ammon (4:26). That Jason fled to Egypt presumes that Egypt was no longer under Seleucid control, but these events may have taken place either just before or after Antiochus IV's second invasion of Egypt. The author indulges in a series of contrasts to show how God brings just deserts upon sinners.

The fictive kinship of the Jews with the Lacedaemonians, or Spartans (v. 9), found also in the exchange of letters cited at 1 Macc 12:6, 18, 20-23, parallels the attempt of many Hellenistic cities to attach themselves to famous events and cities from the Golden Age of Greece (e.g., the Romans traced their origins to Aeneas the Trojan). The Spartans were legendary for their austere way of life and for their military prowess, particularly as exhibited in the wars against the invading Persian army of Xerxes in 480 BCE. The Spartan way of life and educational system were quite different from that of other Greek cities, particularly Athens. Hecataeus of Abdera, a Greek historian (c. 300 BCE), wrote that in ancient times foreigners dwelling among the Egyptians were driven out because it was thought that the strangers had disrupted the traditional services to the Egyptian gods. Among those driven out, some went to Greece, while most went to Judea under Moses.[52] So some connection was being made between the Greeks and the Jews—although very slight. A more direct connection between the Jews and the Spartans may be through the legendary hero Heracles, to whom Spartan kings traced their ancestry. The Hellenistic-Jewish writer Cleodemus Malchus stated that Afera and Iafra, sons of Abraham through Keturah (Gen 25:4, Ephah and Epher), fought alongside Heracles in his campaign against Antaios and that Africa was named after them. Heracles is said to have married one of the daughters of Afera.[53] This makes a closer connection between the Spartans and the Jews, but does not explain why the Jews and the Spartans were thought to be kin. Perhaps the separation of the Spartans from the rest of the Greeks in their way of life and educational system allowed for a similarity to be drawn between them and the Jews, who were also distinctive in their way of life.

To die far from one's ancestral tomb (v. 10) was a heavy punishment. When a prophet was tricked into disobeying the command that God had laid on him not to eat or drink, he was told that he would not come to his ancestral tomb (1 Kgs 13:22). When Saul's and his sons' bodies were ignominiously displayed on the walls of Beth-shan, the people of Jabesh-Gilead took them down (1 Sam 31:10-13), and later David transferred the bones of Saul and his son Jonathan back to Saul's father's tomb in the land of Benjamin (2 Sam 21:10-14).

5:11-16, The Attack. The narrative parallels 1 Macc 1:20-24. Here, in contrast to 1 Maccabees, Antiochus acts to suppress a revolt. As mentioned earlier, according to 1 Macc 1:20, Antiochus plundered the Temple in Jerusalem

---

51. Tacitus *Histories* 2.50.2; 2.78.2; cf. Pliny *Natural History* 2.148. Josephus *The Jewish War* 6.288-309.

52. See Diodorus Siculus 40.3.1-3.
53. See Josephus *Antiquities of the Jews* 1.239-41.

after his first invasion of Egypt. The author of 2 Maccabees, however, places the plunder of the Temple after the second invasion in 168 BCE, when Antiochus was forced to leave Egypt at the intervention of the Romans. In addition, the author of 2 Maccabees makes no mention of the reversal Antiochus had suffered at the hands of the Romans, but implies that the only reason why Antiochus left Egypt was to put down the revolt in Jerusalem. The problem of determining in exactly what order the events occurred is further complicated by the version in Dan 11:28-31:

> "He [Antiochus IV] shall return to his land with great wealth, but his heart shall be set against the holy covenant. He shall work his will, and return to his own land. At the time appointed he shall return and come into the south, but this time it shall not be as it was before. For ships of Kittim shall come against him, and he shall lose heart and withdraw. He shall be enraged and take action against the holy covenant. He shall turn back and pay heed to those who forsake the holy covenant. Forces sent by him shall occupy and profane the temple and fortress." (NRSV)

Here in cryptic form are outlined the first and second invasions of Antiochus IV against Egypt. That he "works his will" seems to refer to the plundering of the Temple. After his aborted second invasion, Antiochus is enraged and sends forces to despoil the Temple. This chronology seems to be the same as that of 1 Macc 1:20-35, which speaks of the plunder of the Temple after the first invasion of Egypt in 169 BCE and then reports that two years later, in 167, Antiochus sent forces against Jerusalem, although 1 Maccabees does not speak of the second invasion of Egypt by Antiochus or of his rebuff by the Romans (i.e., the Kittim). The author of 2 Maccabees thus seems to have run together two events: the plunder of the Temple after the first invasion and the second Syrian attack on the Temple.

There is also a problem with the first invasion of Egypt. We do not know why Antiochus IV withdrew from Egypt. He had not captured Alexandria, but had set up a protectorate of sorts with himself as guardian of his nephew, Ptolemy VI Philometor. Some scholars have suggested that

Antiochus withdrew to garner more forces, but a Babylonian text records that he celebrated his victory in Egypt with a great festival in August/September 169 BCE. Here again a chronological problem surfaces. The Greek historian Polybius speaks of a great festival held by Antiochus IV, the Festival of Daphnae, but this is usually dated to 166 BCE.[54] The problem arises as to whether Antiochus would have celebrated two festivals for his victories in Egypt. The triumphal festival recorded in the Babylonian diaries appears to be the act of someone satisfied with the results of his invasion, or at least of someone who wants to appear satisfied with the results, since we do not know why he left Egypt. Perhaps Antiochus left because he had settled for a divided, and therefore weakened, Ptolemaic Empire.

The account in 2 Maccabees suggests that the only reason why Antiochus IV left Egypt was to put down the revolt in Jerusalem (v. 11). He is portrayed as being furious that someone should revolt against him. Once again the author of 2 Maccabees dehumanizes the enemy of the Jews by using bestial descriptions—"inwardly raging" is literally "wild beast-like in soul" (τεθηριωμένος τῇ ψυχῇ tetheriōmenos tē psychē). Such descriptions show that Antiochus is not in control of himself, not properly human. The author is not concerned with exact chronology so much as with rhetorical flourish. The numbers of those slaughtered and enslaved are exaggerated (v. 14). The text of Dan 11:30 also describes Antiochus as enraged, but there his rage seems rather the result of being humiliated by the Romans. Scholars sometimes explain the harsh treatment of Jerusalem at the hands of Antiochus as a response to his humiliation by the Romans in Egypt in 168 BCE and his wanting to show that he was still a force to be reckoned with. The same motivation would lie behind his ostentatious festival of Daphnae if it is dated to 166 BCE. But Antiochus did not plunder the Temple out of rage after the success of his first invasion of Egypt. Rather, at about the same time in 169 BCE, he was forcibly extracting treasures from the temple in Babylon, so his plunder of the Jerusalem Temple should not be seen as a special case. If his rage at his humiliation by the Romans is seen as a motivating

54. Polybius 30.25-26.

factor for his subsequent actions, it is a rather delayed reaction for the festival—which, if dated to 166 BCE, took place two years later—and also for the persecution of the Jews, which occurred almost a year after Antiochus's rebuff by the Romans. No doubt Antiochus smarted at the humiliation, but this still does not seem a sufficient reason for the slow buildup of measures against the Jews, which culminated in the attempted suppression of their cultural and religious traditions.

After plundering Egypt (1 Macc 1:19),[55] Antiochus must have thought Jerusalem was small pickings. Antiochus's liberal gifts to Greek cities, particularly Athens, where he wished to complete the magnificent temple of Olympian Zeus, made him always glad of further revenue. In contrast to Onias III, whose piety brought it about that kings honored and glorified the Temple (3:1-2), Menelaus now helps Antiochus despoil the Temple. The role of Menelaus is not mentioned in the parallel account in 1 Maccabees.

5:17-20, The Author's Reflections. At this disastrous turn of events the author feels compelled to comment. He stresses the dichotomy between what Antiochus thinks and what God proposes. Antiochus is "puffed up in spirit," an attitude against which he will be warned in 7:34, and thinks he is special (cf. 5:21; 9:8, 10), whereas God is using Antiochus as the instrument of God's anger. This misperception of one's role is also ascribed to the king of Assyria at Isa 10:5-15. In addition, the author has the same theology that is found in Deuteronomy, where, if the people disobey God's laws, they will be punished (Deut 11:13-17, 28; cf. 2 Macc 6:12-17). The author stresses that the welfare of Jerusalem, the place God chose (Deut 12:5-7), depends on the people's keeping the covenant with its blessings and curses. The author, in v. 20, looks forward to the turnaround of the misfortune of the people, which will take place in chapter 8, and reflects on the prayer of Solomon at the dedication of the Temple (1 Kgs 8:46-53; 2 Chr 7:12-22; see also Isa 54:7-8; Jer 7:3-15; Zech 1:12-17 for examples of God's anger turning to compassion).

5:21-26, Antiochus's Measures in Jerusalem. In his arrogance (stressed in 1 Maccabees

also; see 1 Macc 1:21), Antiochus carries off 1,800 talents from the Temple, quite a large sum. The way the king is described calls to mind the Persian king Xerxes, who dared to bridge the Hellespont and cut a canal through Mt. Athos.[56] Antiochus is being depicted as someone who fights against God (see 7:19).

Philip (who appears again in 6:11 and 8:8), a Phrygian (in Asia Minor), possibly was in charge of the Seleucid garrison in Jerusalem, from which he could make forays into the countryside. Again, note how this enemy of the Jews is described: "more barbarous than the man who appointed him" (v. 22). The Greek official is termed a barbarian, the exact reversal of normal Greek usage, in which non-Greeks are the barbarians (cf. 2:21). Andronicus was left in charge of Gerizim, the center of Samaria. Note how the Samaritans are included in "the race"/"people" (v. 22; 6:2). The author does not see any conflict between the Jews and the Samaritans.[57] Andronicus, a Mysian (in northwestern Asia Minor), was perhaps the predecessor of Apollonius in Samaria (1 Macc 3:10). Menelaus remains high priest and is described as being even worse than these non-Jewish officials. The description of Apollonius's attack parallels that of 1 Macc 1:29-40, although the author here states that the attack took place on the sabbath, thereby heightening the offense.[58] An army of 22,000 seems much too large for an attack force against unarmed Jerusalem. The purpose of the attack, to kill all the men and sell the women and children as slaves, appears to replicate what Antiochus had already done (5:13-14). The attack of Apollonius, as narrated by the epitomist, appears completely unprovoked and a senseless act of cruelty. The parallel account in 1 Maccabees provides the purpose for Apollonius's attack: to install and fortify a strong Seleucid garrison in the city. As the author of 1 Maccabees dates the event to two years after Antiochus's first invasion of Egypt (i.e., 167 BCE), he thus locates it not long after Antiochus's humiliation at the hands of the Romans in Egypt. So the reader might see these reinforced fortifications as part of an attempt to strengthen the Seleucid Empire's southern border.

55. See also Polybius 30.26.9.

56. See Herodotus 7:22-24, 34-37; Aeschylus *Persians* 69-72, 744-51.
57. Josephus records a letter from some Samaritans arguing against classifying them with the Jews. See *Antiquities of the Jews* 5.260-61.
58. Cf. Josephus *Against Apion* 1:209-11.

Throughout all this activity, where was Menelaus? Was he away from the city at Antioch, or was he a witness to the power of the Seleucid army?

5:27. In the midst of this destruction, the author again sounds a hopeful note: Judas Maccabeus appears on the scene (v. 27). The author of 2 Maccabees makes no mention of Mattathias, although, like the author of 1 Maccabees, he has the Hasmoneans first living in Jerusalem (1 Macc 2:1). The author of 1 Maccabees has placed the exit from Jerusalem of Mattathias and his family after the narrative of the religious persecution (1 Macc 1:41-62), whereas the author of 2 Maccabees places Judas's exit before the persecution (2 Macc 6:1-11). However, these differences can perhaps be accounted for by the goals of the two authors. The author of 1 Maccabees introduces his account with the vague phrase "in those days," so an exact chronology cannot be determined. Since the purpose of this author is to concentrate

on the reaction to the persecution in Mattathias and his sons, he accentuates Mattathias's grief by including a lament (2:7-13), while giving little space to the martyrdoms (1 Macc 1:60-63). The author of 2 Maccabees, on the other hand, emphasizes martyrdom as the appropriate reaction to persecution (6:10–7:42), and for him it is the martyrdoms that bring God's mercy (7:38; 8:5). Therefore, he places the story of Judas's exit from Jerusalem so as to offer the reader a glimpse of hope. The wilderness was a traditional place of refuge, where Moses had fled from Pharaoh (Exod 3:1), David had fled from Saul (1 Sam 23:14), and Elijah had fled from Jezebel (1 Kgs 19:1-9). Judas escapes from the pollution of the city life into the more natural life in the mountains (cf. Hos 2:14-15; Mark 1:12). The final clause of v. 27, "so that they might not share in the defilement," qualifies their living apart from the city as escaping evil influences and not simply eating "what grew wild."

REFLECTIONS

The author of 2 Maccabees, as noted, provides his own comments on what was happening in Jerusalem (5:17-20) and in the way he portrays the just deserts meted out to Jason. What the reader might ponder here is that so often we are caught up in the leading personalities of the conflict. How terrible were Jason and Menelaus? How arrogant was Antiochus? What we sometimes forget is the fate of those slaughtered and enslaved, however inaccurate the figures might be (80,000, 5:14; "great numbers," 5:26). These are the ordinary people who so often bear the brunt of their leaders' pride and ambition. Even in an age when missiles can be targeted with pinpoint accuracy, it is still so often the civilian population that suffers. Here the problem of what constitutes a just war arises again. Can the slaughter of civilians ever be tolerated, however accidental? What level of killing can be tolerated in the prosecution of a war? Can there ever be a just nuclear war? These horrific war stories from the second century BCE should make us reflect on the equally horrible atrocities of our age.

2 Maccabees 6:1-11, The Pagan Cult Imposed in Jerusalem

NAB

6 Not long after this the king sent an Athenian senator to force the Jews to abandon the customs of their ancestors and live no longer by the laws of God; [2] also to profane the temple in Jerusalem and dedicate it to Olympian Zeus,

6, 2: (*ton en*) *Garizein:* so LXX[MSS]; cf Vet Lat[MSS], V. (*kathōs*) *ētēkesan* (*hoi ton topon oikountes*): conj.

NRSV

6 Not long after this, the king sent an Athenian[a] senator[b] to compel the Jews to forsake the laws of their ancestors and no longer to live by the laws of God; [2]also to pollute the temple in Jerusalem and to call it the temple of Olympian Zeus, and to call the one in Gerizim the temple

[a] Other ancient authorities read *Antiochian*   [b] Or *Geron an Athenian*

NAB

and that on Mount Gerizim to Zeus the Hospitable, as the inhabitants of the place requested. ³ This intensified the evil in an intolerable and utterly disgusting way. ⁴ The Gentiles filled the temple with debauchery and revelry; they amused themselves with prostitutes and had intercourse with women even in the sacred court. They also brought into the temple things that were forbidden, ⁵ so that the altar was covered with abominable offerings prohibited by the laws.

⁶ A man could not keep the sabbath or celebrate the traditional feasts, nor even admit that he was a Jew. ⁷ Moreover, at the monthly celebration of the king's birthday the Jews had, from bitter necessity, to partake of the sacrifices, and when the festival of Dionysus was celebrated, they were compelled to march in his procession, wearing wreaths of ivy.

⁸ At the suggestion of the citizens of Ptolemais, a decree was issued ordering the neighboring Greek cities to act in the same way against the Jews: oblige them to partake of the sacrifices, ⁹ and put to death those who would not consent to adopt the customs of the Greeks. It was obvious, therefore, that disaster was impended. ¹⁰ Thus, two women who were arrested for having circumcised their children were publicly paraded about the city with their babies hanging at their breasts and then thrown down from the top of the city wall. ¹¹ Others, who had assembled in nearby caves to observe the sabbath in secret, were betrayed to Philip and all burned to death. In their respect for the holiness of that day, they had scruples about defending themselves.

6, 8: (*poleis*) *Ptolemaiōn hypothemenōn* (*tēn autēn*): so LXX^MSS, Vet Lat^MSS, V.

NRSV

of Zeus-the-Friend-of-Strangers, as did the people who lived in that place.

3Harsh and utterly grievous was the onslaught of evil. ⁴For the temple was filled with debauchery and reveling by the Gentiles, who dallied with prostitutes and had intercourse with women within the sacred precincts, and besides brought in things for sacrifice that were unfit. ⁵The altar was covered with abominable offerings that were forbidden by the laws. ⁶People could neither keep the sabbath, nor observe the festivals of their ancestors, nor so much as confess themselves to be Jews.

7On the monthly celebration of the king's birthday, the Jews^c were taken, under bitter constraint, to partake of the sacrifices; and when a festival of Dionysus was celebrated, they were compelled to wear wreaths of ivy and to walk in the procession in honor of Dionysus. ⁸At the suggestion of the people of Ptolemais^d a decree was issued to the neighboring Greek cities that they should adopt the same policy toward the Jews and make them partake of the sacrifices, ⁹and should kill those who did not choose to change over to Greek customs. One could see, therefore, the misery that had come upon them. ¹⁰For example, two women were brought in for having circumcised their children. They publicly paraded them around the city, with their babies hanging at their breasts, and then hurled them down headlong from the wall. ¹¹Others who had assembled in the caves nearby, in order to observe the seventh day secretly, were betrayed to Philip and were all burned together, because their piety kept them from defending themselves, in view of their regard for that most holy day.

a Gk *they*   *b* Cn: Gk *suggestion of the Ptolemies* (or *of Ptolemy*)

COMMENTARY

Antiochus IV now takes further measures against the Jews in Jerusalem. As noted in the Introduction, the motives behind this action remain unknown, although many theories abound. What one notes is that these measures are the

final step in a process of attempting to control what was going on in Jerusalem and presumably to stabilize conditions in this southern region of the kingdom. The measures against Judaism were directed at Jews in Judea, and not empire-wide.

For some reason, Antiochus must have considered the Jewish cult in Judea, centered around the Temple, to be a focal point of resistance to the smooth running of the Seleucid administration of the city, even though his friend Menelaus was high priest. Were opposition and resistance to the Seleucid government and the regime of Menelaus already growing before the rise of the Maccabees? The parallel account in 1 Macc 1:41-64 stresses the megalomania of the king, but, since the decree mentioned at 1 Macc 1:41 is not confirmed by other evidence, one should try to find an explanation that fits the particular situation in Judea. What is intriguing is the silence about the role of Menelaus. Some scholars have suggested that he instigated the persecution. As will be noted later on, the reference to Menelaus in the letter of Antiochus IV, which repeals the persecution (11:27-33), could be taken to mean that Menelaus was instrumental in the repeal of the persecution. He, therefore, may have been overruled when the king decided, for whatever reasons and prompted by whatever advisers, to suppress Judaism in Judea and install paganism. (See also Commentary on 2 Maccabees 11.)

6:1-2. The king's agent is named Geron the Athenian. The Jews are no longer to follow the religious customs of their ancestors. Such a decree might indicate that the Jews could not follow them in public but possibly could in private. However, the instances of people's ignoring the ban show that private observance was also forbidden. The first change is one of nomenclature: the temples in Jerusalem and Gerizim are given new names, Zeus Olympios and Zeus Xenios respectively (i.e., friend of strangers). Olympios and Xenios were both common epithets for Zeus (Antiochus IV had undertaken to complete the temple in Athens dedicated to Zeus Olympios). The author gives a reason for the change to Zeus Xenios at Gerizim, but the meaning is uncertain. Scholars frequently emend the text to bring it into line with a petition from some Samaritans to Antiochus IV requesting that their temple be renamed Zeus Hellenios and translate v. 2*b* as in the NAB: "as the inhabitants of the place requested."[59] However, since the author has previously linked what happens at Jerusalem with what happens at

Gerizim (5:22-23) and seems to hold no antipathy to the Samaritans, one might keep the text as is and translate "as those who live there are, i.e., hospitable." A Hellenistic-Jewish writer, in retelling Genesis 14, describes how Abraham was "hospitably received" ($\xi\epsilon\nu\iota\zeta\omega$ *xenizō*) by the city at the temple of Gerizim,[60] and this may reflect a positive view of the Samaritans.

6:3-6. The author offers a description of the imposed cult that is not found in other contemporary sources. Cult prostitution was prohibited in Israelite religion (Deut 23:17), and various kings were praised for ridding the land of cult prostitutes (1 Kgs 15:12; 22:46; 2 Kgs 23:7), and the presence of cult prostitutes is a sign of the evil reign of Rehoboam (1 Kgs 14:24). The author of 2 Maccabees is using stereotypical accusations to show that what the Gentiles were doing was barbaric. While Antiochus III had issued a proclamation forbidding improper sacrificial animals to be brought to the city and allowed only the sacrificial animals known to their ancestors,[61] now unfit sacrificial offerings are introduced. What is noteworthy is that the author does not mention the desolating sacrilege of Dan 11:31; 1 Macc 1:54. Also, it is unclear what exactly is meant by "nor even admit that he was a Jew" (v. 6). Does the term "Jew" here have simply a geographical designation so that people who used to live in or originate from Judea were called Jews, but now were going to be called after the new name for the area, a name derived from the name change of Jerusalem to Antioch-in-Jerusalem (2 Macc 4:9, 19)? Would such a geographical name change be applied even to those people originally from Judea who were living outside Judea, or only to those living in Judea? Or does "Jew" here mean more than a geographical designation—i.e., one who follows the Torah? Given the context of the suppression of distinctive religious and cultural traditions derived from the Torah, probably it means the latter. When discussing Exod 20:6, which speaks of those who love God and keep the commandments, a rabbinic commentator writes: "Rabbi Nathan says: 'Of them that love me and keep my commandments' refers to those who dwell

---

59. Josephus *Antiquities of the Jews* 12.261.

60. Eusebius *Preparation for the Gospel* 9.17.5.
61. Josephus *Antiquities of the Jews* 12.145-146.

in the land of Israel and risk their lives for the sake of the commandments."[62]

6:7-9. The cult imposed was not for one particular divinity, but responded to paganism in general, here to the cult of the king and to the cult of Dionysus, the Greek god of wine and harvest. The author insists that the Jews were forced to take part in these festivals, but 1 Macc 1:52 suggests that many were eager to follow the new practices. The monthly celebration of Antiochus IV's birthday, was on the twenty-fifth of the month (1 Macc 1:58-59). The persecution, or attempt to force neighboring Jews to follow Greek ways, is extended to neighboring cities, most probably those immediately bordering on Judea so that the Judeans could not easily cross the border to practice their religion. The translation of v. 8 is difficult; the verb can mean either "suggest" or, more strongly, "enjoin," and the manuscripts read both "of Ptolemy" (i.e., Ptolemy son of Dorymenes the governor of Coelesyria and Phoenicia; 4:45; 8:8) and "of Ptolemais" (i.e., the coastal city in Phoenicia also known as Acco). Ptolemais seems a good distance from the borders of Judea, as it lies near Galilee. However, 1 Macc 5:15 reports that the people of Ptolemais and Tyre and Sidon and all Galilee of the Gentiles had gathered together against the Jews. Only one decree is said to be issued, whereas each Greek city should pass its own vote. We must imagine, therefore, either that Ptolemy, hostile to the Jews in 2 Macc 4:45; 8:8, strongly recommended to the cities around Judea that they persecute the Jews, or that the citizens of Ptolemais so acted on their own accord and induced other cities to follow their lead. The latter reading makes the persecution a more "grassroots" movement than does the former.

6:10-11. Two examples of the suffering imposed are then adduced (cf. 1 Macc 1:60-61; 2:31-38). Note the use of political language: the women are led publicly through the "city" (πόλις *polis*) and thrown down from the wall (which protects the city). The victims are described as women with babies at their breasts—here women and their babies, the basis for the continued growth and prosperity of any city, are paraded as antithetical to the city values Antiochus IV is espousing.

Immediately following the execution of the women and their babies is an account of some men who were meeting outside the city, out of sight, to "observe the sabbath day" (v. 11). Yet they are betrayed to Philip and are burned to death.[63] Their actions are depicted as anti-social and anti-*polis*. Plato had argued that no one should possess shrines in private houses and that anyone who disobeyed was to be executed.[64] The rites of Dionysus were suppressed in Rome in 186 BCE because, as the Roman historian Livy states, they are secret/hidden rites performed at night. They are alien rites.[65] So here the rituals of the Jews are attacked as anti-*polis,* as a threat to the state and as if they were foreign, and yet the reader knows that the observance of the sabbath, the most holy day, is part and parcel of ancestral Jewish tradition and that Philip, a Phrygian (2 Macc 5:22), is the foreigner.

---

62. Mekilta de Rabbi Ishmael. *Tractate Bahodesh* 6.

63. *Assumption of Moses* 8; Josephus *The Jewish War* 1.312-313.
64. Plato *Laws* 10.909-910D.
65. Livy 39.14.8.

2 Maccabees 6:12-17, Punishment Seen as Discipline

NAB	NRSV
[12] Now I beg those who read this book not to be disheartened by these misfortunes, but to consider that these chastisements were meant not for the ruin but for the correction of our nation. [13] It is, in fact, a sign of great kindness to punish sinners promptly instead of letting them go for long. [14] Thus, in dealing with other nations, the LORD patiently waits until they reach the full measure	[12] Now I urge those who read this book not to be depressed by such calamities, but to recognize that these punishments were designed not to destroy but to discipline our people. [13] In fact, it is a sign of great kindness not to let the impious alone for long, but to punish them immediately. [14] For in the case of the other nations the Lord waits patiently to punish them until they have

of their sins before he punishes them; but with us he has decided to deal differently, [15] in order that he may not have to punish us more severely later, when our sins have reached their fullness. [16] He never withdraws his mercy from us. Although he disciplines us with misfortunes, he does not abandon his own people. [17] Let these words suffice for recalling this truth. Without further ado we must go on with our story.

reached the full measure of their sins; but he does not deal in this way with us, [15]in order that he may not take vengeance on us afterward when our sins have reached their height. [16]Therefore he never withdraws his mercy from us. Although he disciplines us with calamities, he does not forsake his own people. [17]Let what we have said serve as a reminder; we must go on briefly with the story.

COMMENTARY

The author interprets the persecution against the Jews as God's training/education of the people. As a parent disciplines a child, so God disciplines Israel (Deut 8:5). God regards Israel as a mother nursing her child (Isa 49:14-16); God may be angry, but God's love is everlasting (Isa 54:7-8). Israel is God's chosen people, treated differently from the way other nations are treated.

Such a reflection is in line with later rabbinic teaching on the goodness of suffering.

Rabbi Akiba says: "You shall not do with me" (Exod 20:20). You shall not behave towards Me in the manner in which others behave towards their deities. When good comes to them they honor their gods, as it is said: "Therefore they sacrifice unto their net," etc. (Hab 1:16). But when evil comes to them they curse their gods, as it is said: "And it shall come to pass that when they shall be hungry they shall fret themselves and curse their king and their god" (Isa 8:21). But you, if I bring good upon you, give thanks, and when I bring suffering upon you, give thanks. . . . Furthermore, a man should even rejoice when in adversity more than when in prosperity. For even if a man lives in prosperity all his life, it does not mean that his sins have been forgiven him. But what is it that does bring a man forgiveness? You must say, suffering. Rabbi Eliezer the son of Jacob says: Behold it says: "My son, despise not the chastening of the Lord" (Prov 3:11). Why? "For whom the Lord loves He corrects," etc. You must reason: Go out and see what was it that made this son a delight to his father? You must say, suffering . . . Rabbi Jose the son of Rabbi Judah says: Precious are chastisements, for the name of God rests upon him to whom chastisements come.[66]

In some ways the teaching here differs from that in Sirach, which emphasizes how slow to anger the Lord is and warns against counting on God's indulgence (Sir 5:4-9; cf. 18:10-14). The Wisdom of Solomon also teaches that the righteous receive benefit through punishments (Wis 11:1-14), but it also speaks of God's allowing other nations time to repent: "Though you were not unable to/ give the ungodly into the/ hands of the righteous in battle,/ or to destroy them at one blow by/ dread wild animals or your stern word,/ But judging them little by little/ you gave them an/ opportunity to repent" (Wis 12:9-10 NRSV; cf. 12:20).

66. Mekilta de Rabbi Ishmael *Tractate Baḥodesh* 10.

2 MACCABEES 6:18–7:42, THE REACTION TO THE PERSECUTIONS

2 Maccabees 6:18-31, Eleazar

NAB

18 Eleazar, one of the foremost scribes, a man of advanced age and noble appearance, was being forced to open his mouth to eat pork. 19 But preferring a glorious death to a life of defilement, he spat out the meat, and went forward of his own accord to the instrument of torture, 20 as men ought to do who have the courage to reject the food which it is unlawful to taste even for love of life. 21 Those in charge of that unlawful ritual meal took the man aside privately, because of their long acquaintance with him, and urged him to bring meat of his own providing, such as he could legitimately eat, and to pretend to be eating some of the meat of the sacrifice prescribed by the king; 22 in this way he would escape the death penalty, and be treated kindly because of their old friendship with him. 23 But he made up his mind in a noble manner, worthy of his years, the dignity of his advanced age, the merited distinction of his gray hair, and of the admirable life he had lived from childhood; and so he declared that above all he would be loyal to the holy laws given by God.

He told them to send him at once to the abode of the dead, explaining: 24 "At our age it would be unbecoming to make such a pretense; many young men would think the ninety-year-old Eleazar had gone over to an alien religion. 25 Should I thus dissimulate for the sake of a brief moment of life, they would be led astray by me, while I would bring shame and dishonor on my old age. 26 Even if, for the time being, I avoid the punishment of men, I shall never, whether alive or dead, escape the hands of the Almighty. 27 Therefore, by manfully giving up my life now, I will prove myself worthy of my old age, 28 and I will leave to the young a noble example of how to die willingly and generously for the revered and holy laws."

He spoke thus, and went immediately to the instrument of torture. 29 Those who shortly before had been kindly disposed, now became hostile

NRSV

18Eleazar, one of the scribes in high position, a man now advanced in age and of noble presence, was being forced to open his mouth to eat swine's flesh. 19But he, welcoming death with honor rather than life with pollution, went up to the rack of his own accord, spitting out the flesh, 20as all ought to go who have the courage to refuse things that it is not right to taste, even for the natural love of life.

21Those who were in charge of that unlawful sacrifice took the man aside because of their long acquaintance with him, and privately urged him to bring meat of his own providing, proper for him to use, and to pretend that he was eating the flesh of the sacrificial meal that had been commanded by the king, 22so that by doing this he might be saved from death, and be treated kindly on account of his old friendship with them. 23But making a high resolve, worthy of his years and the dignity of his old age and the gray hairs that he had reached with distinction and his excellent life even from childhood, and moreover according to the holy God-given law, he declared himself quickly, telling them to send him to Hades.

24"Such pretense is not worthy of our time of life," he said, "for many of the young might suppose that Eleazar in his ninetieth year had gone over to an alien religion, 25and through my pretense, for the sake of living a brief moment longer, they would be led astray because of me, while I defile and disgrace my old age. 26Even if for the present I would avoid the punishment of mortals, yet whether I live or die I will not escape the hands of the Almighty. 27Therefore, by bravely giving up my life now, I will show myself worthy of my old age 28and leave to the young a noble example of how to die a good death willingly and nobly for the revered and holy laws."

When he had said this, he went[a] at once to the rack. 29Those who a little before had acted

[a] Other ancient authorities read *was dragged*

NAB	NRSV
toward him because what he had said seemed to them utter madness. ³⁰ When he was about to die under the blows, he groaned and said: "The LORD in his holy knowledge knows full well that, although I could have escaped death, I am not only enduring terrible pain in my body from this scourging, but also suffering it with joy in my soul because of my devotion to him." ³¹ This is how he died, leaving in his death a model of courage and an unforgettable example of virtue not only for the young but for the whole nation.	toward him with goodwill now changed to ill will, because the words he had uttered were in their opinion sheer madness.ᵃ ³⁰When he was about to die under the blows, he groaned aloud and said: "It is clear to the Lord in his holy knowledge that, though I might have been saved from death, I am enduring terrible sufferings in my body under this beating, but in my soul I am glad to suffer these things because I fear him."
	31So in this way he died, leaving in his death an example of nobility and a memorial of courage, not only to the young but to the great body of his nation.
	ᵃ Meaning of Gk uncertain

COMMENTARY

The story of Eleazar is retold in greater detail in 4 Maccabees 5–7, where he is called a priest (4 Macc 5:4). The word translated "scribe" (γραμματεύς *grammateus*) often in the OT refers to officers of the people (e.g., Num 11:16; Josh 8:33; 23:2; 24:1; 1 Chr 23:4 LXX), so one should see him as a leading official. Since he is said to be well known to those in charge of the unlawful sacrifice, are these officials Jews or non-Jews? Like all heroes, Eleazar is described as being handsome. He is also dignified and from a noble family (v. 23). The author relates that Eleazar was forced to violate the Torah prohibition of eating pork (Lev 11:7-8; Deut 14:8; cf. 1 Macc 1:47, 62-63). But when he refuses to eat the pork, "welcoming death with honor rather than life with pollution" (v. 19), he is sentenced to be tortured on the rack (so the NRSV). Exactly what the torture was is unclear; the Greek word (τύμπανον *tympanon*, v. 19) can be translated "drum," "stick," or "wagon wheel," and so it connotes something

turning around—i.e., a rack. Eleazar refuses to act ignobly, for he knows that God knows all things (v. 30). The narrative, in fact, is full of fine rhetorical passages that are common in Greek literature, in which the person's last words before dying bravely are designed to arouse emotion in the reader. But the narrative also resonates with the contrasts, also common in Greek literature, of honor and dishonor (vv. 19, 25). Eleazar eschews any contradiction between his private and his public behavior. His life is to be marked with consistency, not hypocrisy, an example of nobility, a memorial or ἀρετή (*aretē*, "virtue"/"valor"/"excellence"). To die well is the better part of *aretē*. This classical virtue is found in this narrative in a Jew rather than in the officials who counsel pretense to prolong life. Eleazar is not victimized; rather he willingly chooses honor. There is no mention of restoration to life, only to the bleak world of Hades/Sheol. Eleazar, however, is not seeking a reward, only to live nobly.

2 Maccabees 7:1-42, The Mother and Her Seven Sons

NAB	NRSV
7 It also happened that seven brothers with their mother were arrested and tortured with whips and scourges by the king, to force	**7** It happened also that seven brothers and their mother were arrested and were being compelled by the king, under torture with whips

NAB

them to eat pork in violation of God's law. ² One of the brothers, speaking for the others, said: "What do you expect to achieve by questioning us? We are ready to die rather than transgress the laws of our ancestors." ³ At that the king, in a fury, gave orders to have pans and caldrons heated. ⁴ While they were being quickly heated, he commanded his executioners to cut out the tongue of the one who had spoken for the others, to scalp him and cut off his hands and feet, while the rest of his brothers and his mother looked on. ⁵ When he was completely maimed but still breathing, the king ordered them to carry him to the fire and fry him. As a cloud of smoke spread from the pan, the brothers and their mother encouraged one another to die bravely, saying such words as these: ⁶ "The LORD God is looking on, and he truly has compassion on us, as Moses declared in his canticle, when he protested openly with the words, 'And he will have pity on his servants.'"

⁷ When the first brother had died in this manner, they brought the second to be made sport of. After tearing off the skin and hair of his head, they asked him, "Will you eat the pork rather than have your body tortured limb by limb?" ⁸ Answering in the language of his forefathers, he said, "Never!" So he too in turn suffered the same tortures as the first. ⁹ At the point of death he said: "You accursed fiend, you are depriving us of this present life, but the King of the world will raise us up to live again forever. It is for his laws that we are dying."

¹⁰ After him the third suffered their cruel sport. He put out his tongue at once when told to do so, and bravely held out his hands, ¹¹ as he spoke these noble words: "It was from Heaven that I received these; for the sake of his laws I disdain them; from him I hope to receive them again." ¹² Even the king and his attendants marveled at the young man's courage, because he regarded his sufferings as nothing.

¹³ After he had died, they tortured and maltreated the fourth brother in the same way. ¹⁴ When he was near death, he said, "It is my choice to die at the hands of men with the God-given hope of being restored to life by him; but for you, there will be no resurrection to life."

NRSV

and thongs, to partake of unlawful swine's flesh. ²One of them, acting as their spokesman, said, "What do you intend to ask and learn from us? For we are ready to die rather than transgress the laws of our ancestors."

3The king fell into a rage, and gave orders to have pans and caldrons heated. ⁴These were heated immediately, and he commanded that the tongue of their spokesman be cut out and that they scalp him and cut off his hands and feet, while the rest of the brothers and the mother looked on. ⁵When he was utterly helpless, the king*a* ordered them to take him to the fire, still breathing, and to fry him in a pan. The smoke from the pan spread widely, but the brothers*b* and their mother encouraged one another to die nobly, saying, ⁶"The Lord God is watching over us and in truth has compassion on us, as Moses declared in his song that bore witness against the people to their faces, when he said, 'And he will have compassion on his servants.'"*c*

7After the first brother had died in this way, they brought forward the second for their sport. They tore off the skin of his head with the hair, and asked him, "Will you eat rather than have your body punished limb by limb?" ⁸He replied in the language of his ancestors and said to them, "No." Therefore he in turn underwent tortures as the first brother had done. ⁹And when he was at his last breath, he said, "You accursed wretch, you dismiss us from this present life, but the King of the universe will raise us up to an everlasting renewal of life, because we have died for his laws."

10After him, the third was the victim of their sport. When it was demanded, he quickly put out his tongue and courageously stretched forth his hands, ¹¹and said nobly, "I got these from Heaven, and because of his laws I disdain them, and from him I hope to get them back again." ¹²As a result the king himself and those with him were astonished at the young man's spirit, for he regarded his sufferings as nothing.

13After he too had died, they maltreated and tortured the fourth in the same way. ¹⁴When he was near death, he said, "One cannot but choose to die at the hands of mortals and to cherish the

a Gk he   *b* Gk they   *c* Gk slaves

NAB

¹⁵ They next brought forward the fifth brother and maltreated him. ¹⁶ Looking at the king, he said: "Since you have power among men, mortal though you are, do what you please. But do not think that our nation is forsaken by God. ¹⁷ Only wait, and you will see how his great power will torment you and your descendants."

¹⁸ After him they brought the sixth brother. When he was about to die, he said: "Have no vain illusions. We suffer these things on our own account, because we have sinned against our God; that is why such astonishing things have happened to us. ¹⁹ Do not think, then, that you will go unpunished for having dared to fight against God."

²⁰ Most admirable and worthy of everlasting remembrance was the mother, who saw her seven sons perish in a single day, yet bore it courageously because of her hope in the LORD. ²¹ Filled with a noble spirit that stirred her womanly heart with manly courage, she exhorted each of them in the language of their forefathers with these words: ²² "I do not know how you came into existence in my womb; it was not I who gave you the breath of life, nor was it I who set in order the elements of which each of you is composed. ²³ Therefore, since it is the Creator of the universe who shapes each man's beginning, as he brings about the origin of everything, he, in his mercy, will give you back both breath and life, because you now disregard yourselves for the sake of his law."

²⁴ Antiochus, suspecting insult in her words, thought he was being ridiculed. As the youngest brother was still alive, the king appealed to him, not with mere words, but with promises on oath, to make him rich and happy if he would abandon his ancestral customs: he would make him his Friend and entrust him with high office. ²⁵ When the youth paid no attention to him at all, the king appealed to the mother, urging her to advise her boy to save his life. ²⁶ After he had urged her for a long time, she went through the motions of persuading her son. ²⁷ In derision of the cruel tyrant, she leaned over close to her son and said in their native language: "Son, have pity on me,

7, 18: *dio* (*axia thaumasmou*) so LXX^MSS, P.
7, 23: (*palin*) *apodōsei:* so LXX^MSS.

NRSV

hope God gives of being raised again by him. But for you there will be no resurrection to life!"

15Next they brought forward the fifth and maltreated him. 16But he looked at the king,[a] and said, "Because you have authority among mortals, though you also are mortal, you do what you please. But do not think that God has forsaken our people. 17Keep on, and see how his mighty power will torture you and your descendants!"

18After him they brought forward the sixth. And when he was about to die, he said, "Do not deceive yourself in vain. For we are suffering these things on our own account, because of our sins against our own God. Therefore[b] astounding things have happened. 19But do not think that you will go unpunished for having tried to fight against God!"

20The mother was especially admirable and worthy of honorable memory. Although she saw her seven sons perish within a single day, she bore it with good courage because of her hope in the Lord. 21She encouraged each of them in the language of their ancestors. Filled with a noble spirit, she reinforced her woman's reasoning with a man's courage, and said to them, 22"I do not know how you came into being in my womb. It was not I who gave you life and breath, nor I who set in order the elements within each of you. 23Therefore the Creator of the world, who shaped the beginning of humankind and devised the origin of all things, will in his mercy give life and breath back to you again, since you now forget yourselves for the sake of his laws."

24Antiochus felt that he was being treated with contempt, and he was suspicious of her reproachful tone. The youngest brother being still alive, Antiochus[c] not only appealed to him in words, but promised with oaths that he would make him rich and enviable if he would turn from the ways of his ancestors, and that he would take him for his Friend and entrust him with public affairs. 25Since the young man would not listen to him at all, the king called the mother to him and urged her to advise the youth to save himself. 26After much urging on his part, she undertook to persuade her son. 27But, leaning close to him, she

a Gk *at him*   b Lat: Other ancient authorities lack *Therefore*
c Gk *he*

NAB

who carried you in my womb for nine months, nursed you for three years, brought you up, educated and supported you to your present age. ²⁸ I beg you, child, to look at the heavens and the earth and see all that is in them; then you will know that God did not make them out of existing things; and in the same way the human race came into existence. ²⁹ Do not be afraid of this executioner, but be worthy of your brothers and accept death, so that in the time of mercy I may receive you again with them."

³⁰ She had scarcely finished speaking when the youth said: "What are you waiting for? I will not obey the king's command. I obey the command of the law given to our forefathers through Moses. ³¹ But you, who have contrived every kind of affliction for the Hebrews, will not escape the hands of God. ³² We, indeed, are suffering because of our sins. ³³ Though our living LORD treats us harshly for a little while to correct us with chastisements, he will again be reconciled with his servants. ³⁴ But you, wretch, vilest of all men! do not, in your insolence, concern yourself with unfounded hopes, as you raise your hand against the children of Heaven. ³⁵ You have not yet escaped the judgment of the almighty and all-seeing God. ³⁶ My brothers, after enduring brief pain, have drunk of never-failing life, under God's covenant, but you, by the judgment of God, shall receive just punishments for your arrogance. ³⁷ Like my brothers, I offer up my body and my life for our ancestral laws, imploring God to show mercy soon to our nation, and by afflictions and blows to make you confess that he alone is God. ³⁸ Through me and my brothers, may there be an end to the wrath of the Almighty that has justly fallen on our whole nation." ³⁹ At that, the king became enraged and treated him even worse than the others, since he bitterly resented the boy's contempt. ⁴⁰ Thus he too died undefiled, putting all his trust in the LORD. ⁴¹ The mother was last to die, after her sons.

⁴² Enough has been said about the sacrificial meals and the excessive cruelties.

7, 36: (*theou*) *pepōkasi:* conj.

NRSV

spoke in their native language as follows, deriding the cruel tyrant: "My son, have pity on me. I carried you nine months in my womb, and nursed you for three years, and have reared you and brought you up to this point in your life, and have taken care of you.^a ²⁸I beg you, my child, to look at the heaven and the earth and see everything that is in them, and recognize that God did not make them out of things that existed.^b And in the same way the human race came into being. ²⁹Do not fear this butcher, but prove worthy of your brothers. Accept death, so that in God's mercy I may get you back again along with your brothers."

³⁰While she was still speaking, the young man said, "What are you^c waiting for? I will not obey the king's command, but I obey the command of the law that was given to our ancestors through Moses. ³¹But you,^d who have contrived all sorts of evil against the Hebrews, will certainly not escape the hands of God. ³²For we are suffering because of our own sins. ³³And if our living Lord is angry for a little while, to rebuke and discipline us, he will again be reconciled with his own servants.^e ³⁴But you, unholy wretch, you most defiled of all mortals, do not be elated in vain and puffed up by uncertain hopes, when you raise your hand against the children of heaven. ³⁵You have not yet escaped the judgment of the almighty, all-seeing God. ³⁶For our brothers after enduring a brief suffering have drunk^f of ever-flowing life, under God's covenant; but you, by the judgment of God, will receive just punishment for your arrogance. ³⁷I, like my brothers, give up body and life for the laws of our ancestors, appealing to God to show mercy soon to our nation and by trials and plagues to make you confess that he alone is God, ³⁸and through me and my brothers to bring to an end the wrath of the Almighty that has justly fallen on our whole nation."

³⁹The king fell into a rage, and handled him worse than the others, being exasperated at his scorn. ⁴⁰So he died in his integrity, putting his whole trust in the Lord.

⁴¹Last of all, the mother died, after her sons.

⁴²Let this be enough, then, about the eating of sacrifices and the extreme tortures.

^a Or *have borne the burden of your education*   ^b Or *God made them out of things that did not exist*   ^c The Gk here for *you* is plural   ^d The Gk here for *you* is singular   ^e Gk *slaves*   ^f Cn: Gk *fallen*

COMMENTARY

After the noble death of an honorable man comes the emotionally charged story of a mother and her seven sons who are martyred for their faith. Such stories of whole families perishing under attack are found both in Jewish and Greek literature.[67] The particular motif of a mother's dying with her seven sons was a favorite one in later Jewish literature, where the event takes place either before a Roman emperor[68] or "in the days of persecution."[69] The folktale motif of the youngest son's being the most important is also present, as we see the tortures crescendo until finally the seventh son gives the longest and most effective speech and undergoes the worst torture. This suggests a more popular type of narrative. Some scholars have suggested that the story originally circulated independent of 2 Maccabees and was inserted into the narrative. However, the closing sentence of the chapter (7:42) links the stories of Eleazar and the mother under the rubrics of "eating of sacrifices" (6:18) and extreme tortures (7:1, 13, 15). The pattern of a mother and her seven sons dying may be traditional and have existed independently, but the author of 2 Maccabees has skillfully woven it into his narrative.

Although there is no indication of a change of scene from the previous story, scholars have speculated as to where these events took place. Later tradition, both Christian and Jewish, located them at Antioch, where Antiochus would have held court, since there is no indication that Antiochus ever visited Jerusalem again. The traditional folktale, in which a ruler is bested by a wiser subject, seems to spotlight the evil character of Antiochus. Throughout the scene, the martyrs respond calmly while the king loses control (7:3, 39).

7:1-6. Like Eleazar, the mother and her sons are arrested and ordered to eat pork (v. 1). The first son, who expresses the family's willingness to suffer martyrdom rather than disobey the law

(v. 2), is forced to suffer dehumanizing torture by order of the king (vv. 3-5). His tongue, the instrument of speech and of human communication, his hands, and his feet are cut off, and he is scalped. Pans and caldrons are heated, and he is placed inside one to fry as one would cook animal flesh. Thus he is completely dehumanized. Each son, in turn, will suffer the same fate.

As they look on, the mother and the other sons confess that God also is watching (v. 6), and that God "has compassion" (παρακαλέω *parakaleō*). They allude to Moses' declaration that his song will comfort the people as a witness when terrible troubles come upon them (Deut 32:21). The quotation is from the Song of Moses (Deut 32:36), in which God, after chastising the people for their apostasy, begins to take vengeance on his instruments of anger who overstep the mark.

7:7-9. The second son is even more painfully scalped. The contrast between the torturers and the tortured person is further brought out by his responding to the torturers in Hebrew, the ancestral language (v. 8; see also vv. 21-27). He tells them that God will "raise us up to an everlasting renewal of life, because we have died for his laws" (v. 9) The title he uses for God, "King of the universe," clearly contrasts with the limited power of the earthly king Antiochus.

The confident reliance upon God demonstrated by this son evidences that the persecution of Antiochus Epiphanes gave impetus to the development of a belief in resurrection and judgment after death. The story of Eleazar reflected the traditional belief in a shade-like existence in Sheol/Hades (v. 23; see Pss 6:5; 30:9; 88:11-12; 115:16-17; Eccl 3:21; Sir 17:27-28; 41:4). In that story, the author had been concerned to emphasize the nobility and dignity of Eleazar as he underwent torture, so there is no discussion of afterlife. In the story of the mother and her seven sons, however, the author concentrates on contrasting the fate of the martyrs with the eventual fate of the king. Drawing on the notion of a life for the righteous after this life, the author highlights the paradox that the dying martyrs are in fact happier than the supposedly successful king.

There are passages in the OT, particularly in

---

67. Examples from Jewish literature: the story of Taxo and his seven sons (*Assumption of Moses* 9), and the account of the Galilean martyrs (Josephus *The Jewish War* 1.312-313; *Antiquities of the Jews* 14.429-430). Examples from Greek literature: the deaths of Theoxena and her sister's children under Philip V of Macedon (Polybius 23.10; Livy 40.4).

68. See *b. Git* 57*b*; m.Lam 1:16.

69. See *Pesiq. R.* 43.

Psalms (Pss 16:9-11; 73:23-26; 84:10), in which the faithful practically long for a continued enjoyment of God, and passages that speak of resurrection in the context of national restoration (Isa 26:19; Ezekiel 37; Hos 6:2). The first Jewish discussion of an after-death judgment is found in the earliest parts of *1 Enoch* (*1 Enoch* 22:27; 90:33; 91:10; 93:2; 104:1-6). And Dan 12:2-3 is a clear expression of a belief in resurrection. One should also note how the Greek translators of passages like Isa 26:19; Job 19:24-26, and Job 14:14 had great difficulty and seem to move toward a sense of individual renewal. So the belief in resurrection pre-dates the persecution of Antiochus. The author of 2 Maccabees, with his threefold repetition of the first-person plural in v. 9, shows that he is speaking of individual resurrection. The language is similar to, though not identical with, Dan 12:2.

The belief portrayed in 2 Maccabees 7 should be distinguished from the earlier tradition about the shades in Sheol, of which a hint is preserved in Isa 14:9-22. The burial customs unearthed by archaeologists suggest a widespread cult of the dead. It was thought that sometimes these shades could be brought back from Sheol, where they may be called divine beings, but they do not like to be disturbed (1 Sam 28:8-19). It is a different kind of existence from this present life, however, and the shades do not return (Job 14:7-22). What v. 9 asserts is that the dead will be given life again, presumably life on this earth as it is described at v. 23 in language resonating with the creation of the first human (Gen 2:7). This hope of the return of a bodily existence should be distinguished from the hope expressed by an author like that of the Wisdom of Solomon. For that author, in human existence "a perishable body weighs down the soul, and this earthly tent burdens the thoughtful mind" (Wis 9:14-15). The author of the Wisdom of Solomon betrays here how he has been influenced by Platonic philosophy with its distinction between the body and the soul. For such an author, "the souls of the righteous are in the hand of God, and no torment will ever touch them" (Wis 3:1). The author is looking forward to a renewed bodily existence, not the continued existence of an immortal soul.

7:10-12. The third son also meets his fate courageously, again expressing a belief in bodily resurrection. "Heaven" here is an epithet for God.

The amazement of onlookers at the endurance of suffering was a common topos in Hellenistic literature.[70] Hecataeus of Abdera stated that the Jews deserve admiration because of their willingness to undergo any torture rather than transgress their ancestral laws,[71] and in the story of Aristeas the Exegete, God is amazed at Job's courage.[72] Recall also the amazement of kings at the suffering servant (Isa 52:15).

7:13-14. The fourth son's dying words deny Antiochus the opportunity of resurrection. For the first time, Antiochus is threatened with punishment. Given the belief in the divinity of kings, this statement is quite radical (cf. the end of the ungodly in Wis 3:10-13, 16-19).

7:15-17. The fifth son warns Antiochus that his authority and power are not due to the abandonment of Israel by God. Punishment is now threatened not only on Antiochus but on his descendants as well.

7:18-19. The sixth son warns Antiochus that, even though God is using Antiochus to punish the people, Antiochus should not be arrogant. Israel's sins have brought this punishment. The Lord promised Solomon that if the people did not keep the commandments, Israel would become a taunt among the nations, and they would conclude that Judea was ruined because the people had forsaken the Lord (1 Kgs 9:6-9). Deutero-Isaiah promised that Zion would no longer be called "Forsaken" (Isa 62:4, 12; cf. Isa 49:14-15; 54:5-6; 60:14-15). Anyone who fights against God is sure to lose.

7:20-23. This story of the mother, as noted above, was retold in rabbinic literature. In Midrash Lamentations 1:16, the mother of seven tells her youngest son to tell Abraham not to be proud because he had offered only one son as a test while she offered her seven sons indeed. Here her attachment to ancestral traditions is stressed through her use of the ancestral language, Hebrew. In a patriarchal culture, her nobility is shown through her possessing "a man's courage" (v. 21). The origin of human life is unknown (Ps 139:13-16; Eccl 11:5), but the author plays on the language of Gen 2:7 to explain how God will recreate her sons: God, the creator of the world,

---

70. E.g., the death of Calanus, the Indian gymnosophist. See Aelian *Varia Historia* 5.6; Arrian *Anabasis* 7.2.
71. Josephus *Against Apion* 1.190-193.
72. Eusebius *Preparation for the Gospel* 9.25.4.

forms humans by breathing into their nostrils the breath of life.

7:24-29. Often in traditional literature, when dealing with a powerful opponent the hero or heroine resorts to trickery to outsmart the official. Antiochus does not know what the mother says in Hebrew, but he catches the tone (v. 24). He resorts to bribing the youngest son to change his mind, even offering to make him a Friend, the official title of the king's advisers (1 Maccabees records that such an offer was made to Mattathias [1 Macc 2:18]). The young man's refusal is symbolized by his not even listening to the king (v. 25). The king tries to make the mother act as his advocate, but she cleverly agrees to persuade her son, but does not specify what she will persuade him to do (v. 26). Her "manly" courage (vv. 20-21) is shown as she asks her son to show her pity, not by sparing himself, but by suffering cruel torments and death. The mother refers, as before (vv. 22-23), to God's creating power (v. 28). She states that God did not create from what previously existed—i.e., as properly formed—but that God shaped the unformed world (see Gen 1:2, especially in the LXX). Christian writers and the Latin translator of 2 Maccabees took this to mean that God had created everything out of nothing (*ex nihilo*).[73] The mother further insults the king by calling him a public executioner (v. 29), a job usually performed by slaves.

7:30-38. The last and most impressive speech is given to the youngest son; in traditional literature, the youngest son is always the most important. His speech rehearses the themes met before: The Hebrews suffer because of their sins, as God disciplines them (vv. 32-33; see 5:17-20; 6:12-17); the king should not be elated or arrogant (v. 34; see 4:17, 21; 7:15); God will surely punish Antiochus (vv. 31, 35; see 7:14-19). The sons'

discipline at the hands of Antiochus is short, but Antiochus's punishment will be long (v. 36; see 6:12-17). Note how the Jews are called "the heavenly children" (v. 34; "heaven" was used as an epithet for God at v. 11), and so Antiochus is again accused of fighting against God (v. 19). The text of v. 36 is difficult to translate; it may be read either as "endured a brief suffering in exchange for everlasting life and have fallen under God's covenant" or "endured a brief suffering and have fallen to everlasting life under God's covenant." The meaning reflects their earlier statements that God will renew their life because they have followed God's laws (7:9, 23). The youngest son ends his speech by foretelling what the following narrative will show (vv. 37-38): God's just anger does turn to mercy (8:5, 27; cf. 2:22). Antiochus will learn through sickness to confess the power of God (9:5-18).

7:39-41. The king again rages as he had done at the beginning of the chapter. The last son is said to die "pure" (καθαρός *katharos*), perhaps suggesting not only the separation from the unclean Gentiles, but also the purification of the Temple, which will occur soon (10:3-7). Here the mother is said to die, but we are not told how—a classic example of patriarchal neglect. Throughout the story, the reader may wonder where the woman's husband is, but the author omits all reference to him to focus the reader's attention on the maternal role of the woman.

7:42. This verse sums up the martyrdoms of both Eleazar and the seven sons by the use of the phrase "eating of sacrifices" (σπλαγχνισμός *splagchnismos*), a term found only in the account of Eleazar's martyrdom (6:7-8, 21), and "tortures" (αἰκίαι *aikiai*), a word whose root is found in the account of the mother and her seven sons (7:1, 13, 15).

73. See, e.g., Origen *On First Principles* 2.1.5.

REFLECTIONS

Martyr stories are filled with highly charged emotional rhetoric in which the opposition between the martyrs and their opponents is driven home again and again. The author presents the reader with a public, well-born official and a private family forced into the spotlight. All sectors of society are represented and thus symbolize the attempted destruction of the city and its culture. Eleazar presents the picture of a person choosing death because it is the right and honorable thing to do; the family chooses death because God will reward them with life. But God will also have compassion on the nation because of its suffering. The motif of suffering's bringing salvation has a long history. In Judges 11, Jepthah vows that, if the Lord would give the enemy into his hands, he would offer up as a burnt offering to the Lord whoever came out of the doors of his house to meet him (Judg 11:30-31). Jepthah is victorious, but it is his daughter who first greets him and whom Jepthah has to sacrifice. Victory came at the price of her suffering. In the Suffering Servant song of Isa 52:13–53:12, the suffering servant "was wounded for our transgressions,/ crushed for our iniquities;/ upon him was the punishment that made us whole,/ and by his bruises we are healed" (Isa 53:5 NRSV). In the Council of the Community at Qumran there were to be twelve men and three priests who would atone for sin by practicing justice and by suffering the sorrows of affliction.[74] Similarly, when the Moabites were being defeated by the Israelites, the king of Moab "took his firstborn son who was to succeed him, and offered him as a burnt offering on the wall. And great wrath came upon Israel, so they withdrew from him and returned to their own land" (2 Kgs 3:27 NRSV). The same motif is found in Greek literature also, for example, in the story of Iphigenia in Aeschylus's tragedy *Agamemnon.* In this drama, Agamemnon angers the goddess Artemis, who delays the sailing of the Greek fleet against Troy until his daughter Iphigenia is sacrificed. Such stories, of course, have disturbing overtones, for they carry the notion of the efficacy of human sacrifice in appeasing an angry God. Is that an image of God we can be comfortable with today?

Yet these stories of heroic endurance and constancy of faith were extremely influential in Christian tradition. The author of the pseudepigraphical book of 4 Maccabees, writing possibly in the first century CE, uses the martyrdoms as prime examples of how devout reason can master the passions. A tradition grew that the martyrdoms occurred in the city of Antioch, and already in pre-Constantinian times there was a grave associated with the martyrs near the synagogue in a suburb of Antioch. Sometime before 386 CE this synagogue had been taken over by Christians, for John Chrysostom preached four homilies on the Maccabean martyrs and implied Christian possession of their relics. Ambrose and Augustine both record the influence of the stories of the Maccabean martyrs. Bishop Gregory of Nazianzos (c. 329–390), in his 26th Oration "On the Maccabees," defends their veneration against some members of his congregation who opposed it because the Maccabees were not Christians. Gregory argued that those who gained perfection before the coming of Christ did so through faith in Christ. Within Syrian Christianity, the mother was called "Shmuni," first attested in the Christian writer Aphrahat in his Fifth Demonstration, while a fresco (c. 650 CE) in the church of Santa Maria Antiqua in Rome gives her name as "Salomone." Their festival was celebrated usually on August 1.

The stories also stress the clash of traditions. All of us hope that if we were placed in a situation as unambiguous as these martyrs were, we would choose death rather than capitulation. We, too, are confronted not only with the question of what we would be willing to die for but also with what we consider so central to our own religious tradition and culture that to do away with it would be to lose our self-identity. Living in a multi-cultural society, we have to decide when to draw the line. Most likely, the decision will be in a situation not quite so unambiguous as eating pork sacrificed to idols. What is also interesting about these stories is that both Eleazar and the family do not come forward on their own accord but that the confrontation is forced upon them. In early Christianity, church leaders often had to warn against Christians' volunteering for martyrdom and asking Roman governors to kill them.[75] Can we maintain our traditions and values without forcing a confrontation?

74. 1QS 8:1-3.
75. See, e.g., *Martyrdom of Polycarp;* Tertullian *To Scapula* 5.1.

2 MACCABEES 8:1–10:8, GOD'S DEFENSE OF THE PEOPLE

OVERVIEW

After describing the disasters that came upon the people after they abandoned their ancestral laws (chaps. 4–7), the author now describes how, following the covenantal obedience of the mar-tyrs, God helps the people (chap. 8), afflicts the archenemy Antiochus IV (chap. 9), and regains and purifies the Temple (10:1-8).

2 Maccabees 8:1-36, The First Victory

NAB

8 Judas Maccabeus and his companions en-tered the villages secretly, summoned their kinsmen, and by also enlisting others who re-mained faithful to Judaism, assembled about six thousand men. ² They implored the LORD to look kindly upon his people, who were being op-pressed on all sides; to have pity on the temple, which was profaned by godless men; ³ to have mercy on the city, which was being destroyed and about to be leveled to the ground; to hearken to the blood that cried out to him; ⁴ to remember the criminal slaughter of innocent children and the blasphemies uttered against his name; and to manifest his hatred of evil. ⁵ Once Maccabeus got his men organized, the Gentiles could not with-stand him, for the LORD's wrath had now changed to mercy. ⁶ Coming unexpectedly upon towns and villages, he would set them on fire. He captured strategic positions, and put to flight a large num-ber of the enemy. ⁷ He preferred the nights as being especially helpful for such attacks. Soon the fame of his valor spread everywhere.

⁸ When Philip saw that Judas was gaining ground little by little and that his successful advances were becoming more frequent, he wrote to Ptolemy, governor of Coelesyria and Phoenicia, to come to the aid of the king's government. ⁹ Ptolemy promptly selected Nicanor, son of Pa-troclus, one of the Chief Friends, and sent him at the head of at least twenty thousand armed men of various nations to wipe out the entire Jewish race. With him he associated Gorgias, a pro-

NRSV

8 Meanwhile Judas, who was also called Maccabeus, and his companions secretly entered the villages and summoned their kindred and enlisted those who had continued in the Jewish faith, and so they gathered about six thou-sand. ²They implored the Lord to look upon the people who were oppressed by all; and to have pity on the temple that had been profaned by the godless; ³to have mercy on the city that was being destroyed and about to be leveled to the ground; to hearken to the blood that cried out to him; ⁴to remember also the lawless destruction of the innocent babies and the blasphemies committed against his name; and to show his hatred of evil.

5As soon as Maccabeus got his army organized, the Gentiles could not withstand him, for the wrath of the Lord had turned to mercy. ⁶Coming without warning, he would set fire to towns and villages. He captured strategic positions and put to flight not a few of the enemy. ⁷He found the nights most advantageous for such attacks. And talk of his valor spread everywhere.

8When Philip saw that the man was gaining ground little by little, and that he was pushing ahead with more frequent successes, he wrote to Ptolemy, the governor of Coelesyria and Phoeni-cia, to come to the aid of the king's government. ⁹Then Ptolemyᵃ promptly appointed Nicanor son of Patroclus, one of the king's chiefᵇ Friends, and sent him, in command of no fewer than twenty thousand Gentiles of all nations, to wipe out the whole race of Judea. He associated with him

ᵃ Gk *he*   ᵇ Gk *one of the first*

fessional military commander, well-versed in the art of war. [10] Nicanor planned to raise the two thousand talents of tribute owed by the king to the Romans by selling captured Jews into slavery. [11] So he immediately sent word to the coastal cities, inviting them to buy Jewish slaves and promising to deliver ninety slaves for a talent— little did he dream of the punishment that was to fall upon him from the Almighty.

[12] When Judas learned of Nicanor's advance and informed his companions about the approach of the army, [13] the cowardly and those who lacked faith in God's justice deserted and got away. [14] But the others sold everything they had left, and at the same time besought the LORD to deliver those whom the ungodly Nicanor had sold before even meeting them. [15] They begged the LORD to do this, if not for their sake, at least for the sake of the covenants made with their forefathers, and because they themselves bore his holy, glorious name. [16] Maccabeus assembled his men, six thousand strong, and exhorted them not to be panic-stricken before the enemy, nor to fear the large number of the Gentiles attacking them unjustly, but to fight courageously, [17] keeping before their eyes the lawless outrage perpetrated by the Gentiles against the holy Place and the affliction of the humiliated city, as well as the subversion of their ancestral way of life. [18] "They trust in weapons and acts of daring," he said, "but we trust in almighty God, who can by a mere nod destroy not only those who attack us, but the whole world." [19] He went on to tell them of the times when help had been given their ancestors: both the time of Sennacherib, when a hundred and eighty-five thousand of his men were destroyed, [20] and the time of the battle in Babylonia against the Galatians, when only eight thousand Jews fought along with four thousand Macedonians; yet when the Macedonians were hard pressed, the eight thousand routed one hundred and twenty thousand and took a great quantity of booty, because of the help they received from Heaven. [21] With such words he encouraged them and made them ready to die for their laws and their country.

Then Judas divided his army into four, [22] placing his brothers, Simon, Joseph, and Jonathan,

Gorgias, a general and a man of experience in military service. [10]Nicanor determined to make up for the king the tribute due to the Romans, two thousand talents, by selling the captured Jews into slavery. [11]So he immediately sent to the towns on the seacoast, inviting them to buy Jewish slaves and promising to hand over ninety slaves for a talent, not expecting the judgment from the Almighty that was about to overtake him.

[12]Word came to Judas concerning Nicanor's invasion; and when he told his companions of the arrival of the army, [13]those who were cowardly and distrustful of God's justice ran off and got away. [14]Others sold all their remaining property, and at the same time implored the Lord to rescue those who had been sold by the ungodly Nicanor before he ever met them, [15]if not for their own sake, then for the sake of the covenants[b] made with their ancestors, and because he had called them by his holy and glorious name. [16]But Maccabeus gathered his forces together, to the number six thousand, and exhorted them not to be frightened by the enemy and not to fear the great multitude of Gentiles who were wickedly coming against them, but to fight nobly, [17]keeping before their eyes the lawless outrage that the Gentiles[a] had committed against the holy place, and the torture of the derided city, and besides, the overthrow of their ancestral way of life. [18]"For they trust to arms and acts of daring," he said, "but we trust in the Almighty God, who is able with a single nod to strike down those who are coming against us, and even, if necessary, the whole world."

[19]Moreover, he told them of the occasions when help came to their ancestors; how, in the time of Sennacherib, when one hundred eighty-five thousand perished, [20]and the time of the battle against the Galatians that took place in Babylonia, when eight thousand Jews[b] fought along with four thousand Macedonians; yet when the Macedonians were hard pressed, the eight thousand, by the help that came to them from heaven, destroyed one hundred twenty thousand Galatians[c] and took a great amount of booty.

[21]With these words he filled them with courage and made them ready to die for their laws

a Gk they   b Gk lacks Jews   c Gk lacks Galatians

NAB

each over a division, assigning to each fifteen hundred men. ²³ (There was also Eleazar.) After reading to them from the holy book and giving them the watchword, "The Help of God," he himself took charge of the first division and joined in battle with Nicanor. ²⁴ With the Almighty as their ally, they killed more than nine thousand of the enemy, wounded and disabled the greater part of Nicanor's army, and put all of them to flight. ²⁵ They also seized the money of those who had come to buy them as slaves. When they had pursued the enemy for some time, ²⁶ they were obliged to return by reason of the late hour. It was the day before the sabbath, and for that reason they could not continue the pursuit. ²⁷ They collected the enemy's arms and stripped them of their spoils, and then observed the sabbath with fervent praise and thanks to the LORD who kept them safe for that day on which he let descend on them the first dew of his mercy. ²⁸ After the sabbath, they gave a share of the booty to the persecuted and to widows and orphans; the rest they divided among themselves and their children. ²⁹ When this was done, they made supplication in common, imploring the merciful LORD to be completely reconciled with his servants.

³⁰ They also challenged the forces of Timothy and Bacchides, killed more than twenty thousand of them, and captured some very high fortresses. They divided the enormous plunder, allotting half to themselves and the rest to the persecuted, to orphans, widows, and the aged. ³¹ They collected the enemies' weapons and carefully stored them in suitable places; the rest of the spoils they carried to Jerusalem. ³² They also killed the commander of Timothy's forces, a most wicked man, who had done great harm to the Jews. ³³ While celebrating the victory in their ancestral city, they burned both those who had set fire to the sacred gates and Callisthenes, who had taken refuge in a little house; so he received the reward his wicked deeds deserved.

³⁴ The accursed Nicanor, who had brought the thousand slave dealers to buy the Jews, ³⁵ after

8, 23: (eti de kai) Eleazar: so 1 LXXᴹˢˢ; cf 1 Mc 2, 5.
8, 27: (archēn eleous) staxantos (autois): so a few LXXᴹˢˢ, Vet Lat, V; haplog.

NRSV

and their country; then he divided his army into four parts. ²²He appointed his brothers also, Simon and Joseph and Jonathan, each to command a division, putting fifteen hundred men under each. ²³Besides, he appointed Eleazar to read aloud[a] from the holy book, and gave the watchword, "The help of God"; then, leading the first division himself, he joined battle with Nicanor.

²⁴With the Almighty as their ally, they killed more than nine thousand of the enemy, and wounded and disabled most of Nicanor's army, and forced them all to flee. ²⁵They captured the money of those who had come to buy them as slaves. After pursuing them for some distance, they were obliged to return because the hour was late. ²⁶It was the day before the sabbath, and for that reason they did not continue their pursuit. ²⁷When they had collected the arms of the enemy and stripped them of their spoils, they kept the sabbath, giving great praise and thanks to the Lord, who had preserved them for that day and allotted it to them as the beginning of mercy. ²⁸After the sabbath they gave some of the spoils to those who had been tortured and to the widows and orphans, and distributed the rest among themselves and their children. ²⁹When they had done this, they made common supplication and implored the merciful Lord to be wholly reconciled with his servants.[b]

³⁰In encounters with the forces of Timothy and Bacchides they killed more than twenty thousand of them and got possession of some exceedingly high strongholds, and they divided a very large amount of plunder, giving to those who had been tortured and to the orphans and widows, and also to the aged, shares equal to their own. ³¹They collected the arms of the enemy,[c] and carefully stored all of them in strategic places; the rest of the spoils they carried to Jerusalem. ³²They killed the commander of Timothy's forces, a most wicked man, and one who had greatly troubled the Jews. ³³While they were celebrating the victory in the city of their ancestors, they burned those who had set fire to the sacred gates, Callisthenes and some others, who had fled into one little house; so these received the proper reward for their impiety.[a]

a Meaning of Gk uncertain   b Gk slaves   c Gk their arms

NAB

being humbled through the Lord's help by those whom he had thought of no account, laid aside his fine clothes and fled alone across country like a runaway slave, until he reached Antioch. He was eminently successful in destroying his own army. [36] So he who had promised to provide tribute for the Romans by the capture of the people of Jerusalem testified that the Jews had a champion, and that they were invulnerable for the very reason that they followed the laws laid down by him.

NRSV

[34]The thrice-accursed Nicanor, who had brought the thousand merchants to buy the Jews, [35]having been humbled with the help of the Lord by opponents whom he regarded as of the least account, took off his splendid uniform and made his way alone like a runaway slave across the country until he reached Antioch, having succeeded chiefly in the destruction of his own army! [36]So he who had undertaken to secure tribute for the Romans by the capture of the people of Jerusalem proclaimed that the Jews had a Defender, and that therefore the Jews were invulnerable, because they followed the laws ordained by him.

COMMENTARY

To present dramatically how God's anger has changed to mercy, the author singles out one battle and one opponent. The dramatization can easily be seen by comparing this account with that in 1 Maccabees. After describing the onset of Judas's guerrilla tactics, 1 Maccabees describes two battles, one against Apollonius (1 Macc 3:10-12) and one against Seron (1 Macc 3:13-26), before the account most like that of 2 Maccabees 8 (cf. 1 Macc 3:38–4:25). In particular, 1 Maccabees emphasizes the tactical maneuvers: a surprise attack by Gorgias, Judas's escape and his surprise attack on Gorgias's camp, and the subsequent flight of Gorgias (1 Macc 4:1-25). In 2 Maccabees, there are no such maneuvers, but one pitched battle decides all. The battles with Apollonius and Seron receive only the vaguest mention; Judas "captured strategic positions and put to flight not a few of the enemy" (8:6). In addition, although 1 Maccabees reports that Lysias sent Ptolemy, Nicanor, and Gorgias (1 Macc 3:38), with the main villain being Gorgias, in 2 Maccabees Ptolemy sends Nicanor and Gorgias, and Nicanor is the main villain. The author may have highlighted this name to balance and reflect the Nicanor in chaps. 14–15, as both are called thrice-wretched (8:34; 15:3). The account then is highly stylized.

8:1-7, The Rise of Judas. Last mentioned as being in the desert (5:27), Judas and his companions now begin to gather their kindred, most likely referring not to near relatives but to Israelites of the same persuasion. Once again the author uses the term "Judaism" (2:21; 14:38) as opposed to "Jewish faith." The number 6,000, the total of people gathered (v. 1), is later repeated (8:16), although some of Judas's force is said to have left (see 1 Macc 4:6, where Judas marches against Gorgias with 3,000 men). The group appeals to the Lord as the last of the martyred sons had done (7:37). The prayer employs traditional language. The blood crying out from the ground (v. 3) recalls the blood of the innocent Abel (Gen 4:10; cf. Deut 32:43; Heb 12:24). The reference to the imminent leveling of the city looks forward to Antiochus's vow (9:13). Once God is with Judas, he is unstoppable (v. 5), although his activity probably consisted of surprise raids and ambushes by night, nuisance raids as the "little by little" of v. 8 suggests.

8:8-11, The Response of the Seleucids. Philip the Phrygian, the governor of Jerusalem (5:22; 6:11), alerts Ptolemy, the son of Dorymenes (4:45), to Judas's success. Ptolemy appoints Nicanor and Gorgias to deal with these guerrillas. First Maccabees reports that Antiochus was informed of the matter (1 Macc 3:27), but the account in 2 Maccabees, which restricts handling of the insurrection to lower echelon officials and subordinates Nicanor and Gorgias to Ptolemy, seems more likely. Someone named Nicanor is mentioned in the letter of the Sidonians in Shechem to Antiochus IV as a royal agent.[76] Later, another Nicanor was in Rome with Demetrius, son of Seleucus IV, and was one of the closest of his friends when he became Demetrius I in 161 BCE,[77] and there was also a Nicanor the Cyprian (2 Macc 12:2). "Nicanor" was thus a common name, and it is unlikely that all these references are to the same person. Gorgias was later governor of Idumea (2 Macc 10:14; 12:32), and it seems prudent that Nicanor would be joined by someone with local experience.

The author notes the ethnic mix of the army (v. 9). His estimate of the size (20,000) is half that of 1 Macc 3:38, but still high. The aim, payment of the tribute to Rome (v. 10), is the same as stated in 1 Macc 3:35, 52, 58. By 165 BCE, the time of Antiochus's march on Persia, the Seleucid indemnity to Rome had already been paid, but Antiochus was well-known as desiring money to pay for his extravagant generosity. In order to raise money, Nicanor intends to sell the captured Jews into slavery. Ninety slaves per talent (v. 11) was a low price, perhaps expressing contempt for the Jews. At that rate, Nicanor would need to sell 180,000 slaves to pay the tribute, many more than those already taken from Jerusalem (5:41). In 1 Macc 3:41, the traders come of their own free will, whereas here Nicanor is the instigator of the plan for slavery. Nicanor is thus seen in 2 Maccabees as the source of all evil designs against the Jews. Such a portrayal prepares the way for the dénouement of the story, as Nicanor has to flee like a runaway slave (8:35). This reversal of affairs fits in with the author's desire to make the punishment fit the crime.

8:12-20, Judas's Preparation. The author, in order to magnify Judas's courage, emphasizes the fear of the Jews, outnumbered more than three to one. One wonders why those around Judas sold all they had (v. 14)—in order to run away? They pray for God to remember the covenants with the ancestors (v. 15; note the list in Sir 44:16–45:25), as God has promised (Lev 26:42; cf. Wis 18:22), for they are a people called by God's name (1 Sam 12:22; Dan 9:19; cf. Deut 28:10). Judas, by contrast, is not afraid (v. 16).

The Gentiles act with hubris, reflecting the arrogance of Antiochus (5:17-21). The phrase "torture of the derided city" (v. 17) reflects the language used about the martyrs (7:1, 7, 10, 13, 15, 42), while the overthrow of the ancestral way of life recalls what was said about Jason (4:11). The overwhelming power of God is captured in the image of "one nod" (v. 18). As any good speechmaker, Judas proffers examples of God's help. The first is the defeat of Sennacherib in 701 BCE (2 Kgs 19:35-36; Isa 37:36; see also 1 Macc 7:41; 2 Macc 15:22). The second example (vv. 19-20) is taken from more recent history, but the precise reference is unknown. The "Galatians" were the Celts, who, due to unrest in western and central Europe, were forced to migrate to the east and southeast. In 280/79, some Celts marched through Macedonia and Thrace and invaded Greece, while others, complete tribal groups, went to Asia Minor in 278/77 and overran many Greek cities. After a long struggle, they were confined to an area north of Phrygia, later called Galatia. Scholars have suggested that the incident in 2 Maccabees may refer to the battle of Antiochus I against the Celts in the 270s (although this took place in Asia Minor, which would cause the text of 2 Maccabees to be emended from *Babulonia* to *Bagadaonia*), near the Taurus mountains in Cilicia; to an incident in the suppression of the rebellion of Molon, governor-general of the eastern satrapies, by Antiochus III in 220 BCE; or to the rebellion in 227–26 of Antiochus Hierax, who used Galatian mercenaries, in the east against his brother Seleucus III. The latter seems the most likely scenario. The Galatian invasion made a lasting impression on the cities of Asia Minor. What this passage shows is that Jewish soldiers served under the Seleucids, and it supports the report of Josephus that Antiochus III transferred Jewish soldiers from Babylonia to Phrygia and Lydia.[78]

8:21-29, The Defeat of Nicanor. Judas is the counterpart to Menelaus, who was a traitor to laws and country. The division of troops described here (v. 22) is different from that of 1 Macc 3:55. The text (vv. 22-23) is very difficult to translate. Major manuscripts read as if Judas appointed his four brothers, Simon, Joseph,

---

76. Josephus *Antiquities of the Jews* 12.257-264.
77. Polybius 31.14.4; Josephus *Antiquities of the Jews* 12.402.
78. Josephus *Antiquities of the Jews* 12:147-153.

Jonathan, and Eleazar, to lead the four 1,500-man units and that Judas read to them from the Scriptures. In this case, it is unclear whether the first division (σπεῖρα *speira*) refers to a phalanx of 256 men) was part of one of these four 1,500-man units. Other manuscripts suggest, and are followed by the NRSV, that Eleazar read aloud from the Scriptures (the Latin manuscripts read Ezra instead of Eleazar). The names of Judas's brothers in 1 Macc 2:3-5 are John, Simon, Eleazar, and Jonathan. But this account lists Joseph instead of John; some scholars have suggested that this is a reference to the envious couple Joseph and Azariah of 1 Macc 5:18, 55-62, but there Joseph is called "son of Zechariah." Eleazar seems to play the role of priest (Deut 20:2); it is interesting that "Eleazar," in Hebrew, means "help of God" (אלעזר *'elʿāzār*). On the reading of the Scriptures, see the parallel statement at 1 Macc 3:48. The *War Scroll* from Qumran indicates that "God's help" was one of the insignia on the standards of God's army,[79] and such watchwords were common in the Hellenistic world.[80] Whatever the intended meaning for vv. 22-23, the author insists that Judas calls on God for aid and that Judas's whole family is involved in the enterprise. To this end, he divides the forces based on the number of brothers in a way that has no parallel in Jewish or Hellenistic tactical tradition. The concern of the author is clearly not about tactical maneuvers, for the description of the battle takes up only one verse (v. 24). What is important is that God is their ally. That connection with God is reinforced by the description of the Jews' observance of the sabbath (vv. 26-27). The last two verses (vv. 28-29) refer to the story of the martyrs; the spoils are to be distributed not only to widows and orphans but also to the tortured (2 Macc 7:1, 42). Here not only the fighters benefit from their victory but so also do those whose prayer for them has great efficacy—i.e., widows and orphans (Deut 14:29; 26:12-15) and those who have been persecuted (2 Macc 7:37-38; 8:3). The language of v. 29 reflects that of the prayer of the seventh son in the martyrdom stories (7:33).

8:30-33, The Defeat of Timothy and Bacchides. The nature of 2 Maccabees as an epitome

is evident in this section. People and events are mentioned without any preparation, and these accounts of other campaigns disrupt the focus on Nicanor, whose story is picked up in v. 34.

In 1 Maccabees, Bacchides is a much more important figure than the quick mention at 2 Macc 8:30 would suggest. He was the governor of the province Beyond the River, i.e., between the Euphrates and Egypt. He is sent by Demetrius I to subdue Judea, which he does (1 Macc 7:8-20). After the later defeat of Nicanor, he returns again and defeats Judas, who dies in the battle. Then Bacchides pursues Judas's brother Jonathan but finally comes to terms with him (1 Macc 9:1-70). His activity is completely absent from the corresponding narrative in 2 Maccabees. It is unlikely that such a high-ranking personage would be listed after the middle-level commander Timothy, and so one wonders whether another Bacchides is meant here.

The death of Timothy is recorded at 2 Macc 9:3 and 10:24-38, but 2 Macc 12:10-25 records Timothy's escape; so there seems to be two Timothys involved in 2 Maccabees. However, in 1 Maccabees there is only one Timothy who fights with Judas's forces on three occasions: (1) when Judas defeats Timothy, captures Iazer, and returns to Judea (1 Macc 5:6-8); (2) when Timothy's men are surprised by Judas (1 Macc 5:28-34); and (3) when Timothy, having regrouped his forces, challenges Judas again and is defeated near Carnaim (1 Macc 5:37-44). All three meetings in 1 Maccabees occur after the purification of the Temple. One will note the specific parallels between the accounts of 1 and 2 Maccabees, if the accounts in 2 Maccabees are accepted as being out of order. If one accepts as more historically reliable the outline of events in 1 Maccabees, then the author of 2 Maccabees has misplaced events. Most scholars agree that 2 Macc 12:1-25 parallels the battles in Gilead recounted in 1 Macc 5:28-44. There are also parallels between 2 Macc 10:24-38 and the account in 1 Macc 5:6-8, although 2 Maccabees records that Timothy dies in that battle, whereas 1 Maccabees does not. The events in 2 Macc 8:30-33 also seem out of order: Judas seems to be in control of Jerusalem (v. 31) even though the Jews do not recapture the city until 10:1-8; mention of strongholds (v. 30) reflects the account of 2 Macc 12:10-25. It would thus seem as if vv.

79. 1QM 4.15.
80. See, e.g., Vegetius 3.5; Xenophon *Anabasis* 1.8.16; *Cyropaedia* 3.3.58.

30-32 summarize the Gilead campaign told later in 2 Maccabees 12.

This summary, however, has been well woven into the context. The author refers to the same groups—the tortured, the widows, and the orphans—in vv. 28 and 30. The same word is used for collecting the arms of the enemy at vv. 27 and 31. Just as the author uses the theme of appropriate retribution for Nicanor when he is forced to flee as a slave, so also in this section the burners are burned. The author of 2 Maccabees narrates these events possibly to suggest that there were other campaigns before the purification of the Temple or to note how Judas's men behave after victories and also to heighten the dramatic tension as one wonders what happened to Nicanor. The spoil taken to Jerusalem (v. 31) is probably God's portion (Num 31:28). The word for "commander" (φύλαρχος *phylarchos*, v. 32) is sometimes taken as a proper name, Phylarchos.

The Greek word does not refer to the city, Jerusalem, but to the "fatherland" (πατρίς *patris*; see 4:1; 5:8, 9, 15; 8:21; 13:3, 11, 14; 14:18). Nothing else is known about Callisthenes (v. 33).

8:34-36, The Fate of Nicanor. The epithet "thrice accursed" will be used again of the Nicanor in the last battle in 2 Maccabees (15:13). His plan (v. 11) backfires, and he receives the appropriate punishment (v. 35). The author sarcastically contrasts his "success" (v. 35) with that of Judas's (8:8). The help of the Lord (v. 35) resonates with the watchword given to the army (8:23), and the word for "defender" (ὑπέρμαχος *hypermachos*, v. 36) is related to the word for "ally" (σύμμαχος *symmachos*, v. 24). The author returns to the theme enunciated at 3:1: The Jews are invincible once they follow God's law. Nicanor, as Heliodorus had done before him (3:35-39), proclaims the power of God.

REFLECTIONS

Throughout this chapter, the author emphasizes the power of prayer and the need to keep God's covenant; these are the sure ways to victory. His emphasis on fidelity to one's religious convictions and traditions needs to be repeated. But one must also be careful, for in this war context, the stress on standing by one's own traditions, on knowing who one is, at times results in denigrating the opponent. Throughout this chapter, the author seeks to dramatize his story by contrasting the two foes, Judas and Nicanor, almost as light and darkness, but this rhetorical presentation at times obscures what actually happened. So we must not let our rhetoric lead us to paint those who disagree with us as "the enemy," "godless" people.

2 Maccabees 9:1-29, The Death of Antiochus IV

NAB

9 About that time Antiochus retreated in disgrace from the region of Persia. ² He had entered the city called Persepolis and attempted to rob the temple and gain control of the city. Thereupon the people had swift recourse to arms, and Antiochus' men were routed, so that in the end Antiochus was put to flight by the natives and forced to beat a shameful retreat. ³ On his arrival in Ecbatana, he learned what had happened to Nicanor and to Timothy's forces. ⁴ Overcome with anger, he planned to make the Jews suffer for the injury done by those who had put him to flight. Therefore he ordered his

NRSV

9 About that time, as it happened, Antiochus had retreated in disorder from the region of Persia. ²He had entered the city called Persepolis and attempted to rob the temples and control the city. Therefore the people rushed to the rescue with arms, and Antiochus and his army were defeated,ª with the result that Antiochus was put to flight by the inhabitants and beat a shameful retreat. ³While he was in Ecbatana, news came to him of what had happened to Nicanor and the forces of Timothy. ⁴Transported with rage, he conceived the idea of turning upon the Jews the

ª Gk *they were defeated*

NAB

charioteer to drive without stopping until he finished the journey.

Yet the condemnation of Heaven rode with him, since he said in his arrogance, "I will make Jerusalem the common graveyard of the Jews as soon as I arrive there." [5] So the all-seeing LORD, the God of Israel, struck him down with an unseen but incurable blow; for scarcely had he uttered those words when he was seized with excruciating pains in his bowels and sharp internal torment, [6] a fit punishment for him who had tortured the bowels of others with many barbarous torments. [7] Far from giving up his insolence, he was all the more filled with arrogance. Breathing fire in his rage against the Jews, he gave orders to drive even faster. As a result he hurtled from the dashing chariot, and every part of his body was racked by the violent fall. [8] Thus he who previously, in his superhuman presumption, thought he could command the waves of the sea, and imagined he could weigh the mountaintops in his scales, was now thrown to the ground and had to be carried on a litter, clearly manifesting to all the power of God. [9] The body of this impious man swarmed with worms, and while he was still alive in hideous torments, his flesh rotted off, so that the entire army was sickened by the stench of his corruption. [10] Shortly before, he had thought that he could reach the stars of heaven, and now, no one could endure to transport the man because of this intolerable stench.

[11] At last, broken in spirit, he began to give up his excessive arrogance, and to gain some understanding, under the scourge of God, for he was racked with pain unceasingly. [12] When he could no longer bear his own stench, he said, "It is right to be subject to God, and not to think one's mortal self divine." [13] Then this vile man vowed to the LORD, who would no longer have mercy on him, [14] that he would set free the holy city, toward which he had been hurrying with the intention of leveling it to the ground and making it a common graveyard; [15] he would put on perfect equality with the Athenians all the Jews, whom he had judged not even worthy of burial, but fit only to be thrown out with their children to be

9, 9: (hō̆ste kai ek) tou sō̆matos (tou dyssebous): so almost all LXX[MSS], V, P.

NRSV

injury done by those who had put him to flight; so he ordered his charioteer to drive without stopping until he completed the journey. But the judgment of heaven rode with him! For in his arrogance he said, "When I get there I will make Jerusalem a cemetery of Jews."

5But the all-seeing Lord, the God of Israel, struck him with an incurable and invisible blow. As soon as he stopped speaking he was seized with a pain in his bowels, for which there was no relief, and with sharp internal tortures— 6and that very justly, for he had tortured the bowels of others with many and strange inflictions. 7Yet he did not in any way stop his insolence, but was even more filled with arrogance, breathing fire in his rage against the Jews, and giving orders to drive even faster. And so it came about that he fell out of his chariot as it was rushing along, and the fall was so hard as to torture every limb of his body. 8Thus he who only a little while before had thought in his superhuman arrogance that he could command the waves of the sea, and had imagined that he could weigh the high mountains in a balance, was brought down to earth and carried in a litter, making the power of God manifest to all. 9And so the ungodly man's body swarmed with worms, and while he was still living in anguish and pain, his flesh rotted away, and because of the stench the whole army felt revulsion at his decay. 10Because of his intolerable stench no one was able to carry the man who a little while before had thought that he could touch the stars of heaven. 11Then it was that, broken in spirit, he began to lose much of his arrogance and to come to his senses under the scourge of God, for he was tortured with pain every moment. 12And when he could not endure his own stench, he uttered these words, "It is right to be subject to God; mortals should not think that they are equal to God."[a]

13Then the abominable fellow made a vow to the Lord, who would no longer have mercy on him, stating 14that the holy city, which he was hurrying to level to the ground and to make a cemetery, he was now declaring to be free; 15and the Jews, whom he had not considered worth burying but had planned to throw out with their

[a] Or not think thoughts proper only to God

NAB

eaten by vultures and wild animals; [16] he would adorn with the finest offerings the holy temple which he had previously despoiled; he would restore all the sacred vessels many times over; and would provide from his own revenues the expenses required for the sacrifices. [17] Besides all this, he would become a Jew himself and visit every inhabited place to proclaim there the power of God. [18] But since God's punishment had justly come upon him, his sufferings were not lessened, so he lost hope for himself and wrote the following letter to the Jews in the form of a supplication. It read thus:

[19] "To my esteemed Jewish citizens, Antiochus, their king and general, sends hearty greetings and best wishes for their health and happiness. [20] If you and your children are well and your affairs are going as you wish, I thank God very much, for my hopes are in heaven. [21] Now that I am ill, I recall with affection the esteem and good will you bear me. On returning from the regions of Persia, I fell victim to a troublesome illness; so I thought it necessary to form plans for the general welfare of all. [22] Actually, I do not despair about my health, since I have great hopes of recovering from my illness. [23] Nevertheless, I know that my father, whenever he went on campaigns in the hinterland, would name his successor, [24] so that, if anything unexpected happened or any unwelcome news came, the people throughout the realm would know to whom the government had been entrusted, and so not be disturbed. [25] I am also bearing in mind that the neighboring rulers, especially those on the borders of our kingdom, are on the watch for opportunities and waiting to see what will happen. I have therefore appointed as king my son Antiochus, whom I have often before entrusted and commended to most of you, when I made hurried visits to the outlying provinces. I have written to him the letter copied below. [26] Therefore I beg and entreat each of you to remember the general and individual benefits you have received, and to continue to show good will toward me and my son. [27] I am confident that, following my policy, he will treat you with mildness and kindness in his relations with you."

[28] So this murderer and blasphemer, after extreme sufferings, such as he had inflicted on

NRSV

children for the wild animals and for the birds to eat, he would make, all of them, equal to citizens of Athens; [16]and the holy sanctuary, which he had formerly plundered, he would adorn with the finest offerings; and all the holy vessels he would give back, many times over; and the expenses incurred for the sacrifices he would provide from his own revenues; [17]and in addition to all this he also would become a Jew and would visit every inhabited place to proclaim the power of God. [18]But when his sufferings did not in any way abate, for the judgment of God had justly come upon him, he gave up all hope for himself and wrote to the Jews the following letter, in the form of a supplication. This was its content:

[19]"To his worthy Jewish citizens, Antiochus their king and general sends hearty greetings and good wishes for their health and prosperity. [20]If you and your children are well and your affairs are as you wish, I am glad. As my hope is in heaven, [21]I remember with affection your esteem and goodwill. On my way back from the region of Persia I suffered an annoying illness, and I have deemed it necessary to take thought for the general security of all. [22]I do not despair of my condition, for I have good hope of recovering from my illness, [23]but I observed that my father, on the occasions when he made expeditions into the upper country, appointed his successor, [24]so that, if anything unexpected happened or any unwelcome news came, the people throughout the realm would not be troubled, for they would know to whom the government was left. [25]Moreover, I understand how the princes along the borders and the neighbors of my kingdom keep watching for opportunities and waiting to see what will happen. So I have appointed my son Antiochus to be king, whom I have often entrusted and commended to most of you when I hurried off to the upper provinces; and I have written to him what is written here. [26]I therefore urge and beg you to remember the public and private services rendered to you and to maintain your present goodwill, each of you, toward me and my son. [27]For I am sure that he will follow my policy and will treat you with moderation and kindness."

[28]So the murderer and blasphemer, having

NAB	NRSV
others, died a miserable death in the mountains of a foreign land. 29 His foster brother Philip brought the body home; but fearing Antiochus' son, he later withdrew into Egypt, to Ptolemy Philometor.	endured the more intense suffering, such as he had inflicted on others, came to the end of his life by a most pitiable fate, among the mountains in a strange land. 29And Philip, one of his courtiers, took his body home; then, fearing the son of Antiochus, he withdrew to Ptolemy Philometor in Egypt.

COMMENTARY

Following the defeat of Nicanor and Timothy, the gruesome death of Antiochus IV is described. This arrangement ignores the more complex order of events as they can be pieced together. In 1 Maccabees, after the defeat of the expedition of Nicanor and Gorgias, Judea is invaded by Lysias, the regent left behind in charge of affairs by Antiochus IV while he went on campaign in the eastern part of his empire (1 Macc 5:26-35). There also seems to have been an attempt to negotiate a peaceable settlement of the rebellion as seen in the letter of Antiochus IV (2 Macc 11:27-33), which 2 Maccabees has put out of order, and possibly in the replacement of Ptolemy son of Dorymenes, an enemy of the Jews, by Ptolemy Macron, who was more friendly to the Jews (2 Macc 10:12-13). The author of 2 Maccabees has arranged events for the best dramatic effect. He wants to show no change of heart in the archenemy Antiochus IV until he is humiliated by God's power. His humiliation brings about his regret at his actions against the Jews and the Temple. He then dies, and only after his death is the Temple purified. Dramatically speaking, the death of the one who brought on the initial misfortune has to occur before things can be put right again and the Temple purified. According to 1 Maccabees, Antiochus IV dies after the purification of the Temple (1 Macc 6:5-7). According to a Babylonian chronicle, news of Antiochus IV's death reached Babylonia in the month Kislev in the year 148 according to the Babylonian calendar (between November 20 and December 18 165 BCE). It thus seems that the sequence in 2 Maccabees, where the king dies before the purification of the Temple, is correct, although some scholars still dispute this, suggesting that chapter 9 has been inserted

into the narrative and that 10:1-8 should be placed before chapter 9. The connections between 2 Macc 9:3 and the events in chapter 8, as well as the similar threat mentioned at 8:3 and 9:14, suggests that the two chapters work together dramatically. A major threat to the Temple is averted, and then the purification of the Temple can be accomplished.

9:1-4, Antiochus IV Receives News of the Defeat of Nicanor. The geographical and historical data provided in these verses are confusing and conflict with other sources. Persepolis was the old capital of the Persian Empire, while Ecbatana lies in Media, hundreds of miles away to the northwest. According to other sources, Antiochus attempted to rob the temple of Nanaia in Eylmais, to the south of Ecbatana (see 1 Macc 6:1; 2 Macc 1:13-15).[81] Here, however, Antiochus attempts to gain control of Persepolis and to plunder its temples. In addition, this chapter contains only one of several ancient versions of the death of Antiochus IV (see, e.g., 1 Macc 6:1-16; 2 Macc 1:13-14).

Antiochus IV had set out in mid to late 165 BCE to consolidate his rule in the eastern satrapies. A local dynasty of priests and princes had risen to power around Persepolis and Istakhr and had won their independence in the early years of Antiochus IV. Antiochus's reputation for plundering temples is at play here, and he no doubt would have welcomed the money to finance his campaign to regain control of the eastern satrapies. In this temple attack, in contrast to the attack on the Temple at Jerusalem, no divine epiphany is described. Verse 3 links this story to chapter 8,

81. See also Polybius 31.9.

including the out-of-place reference to Timothy. The last time the king appeared in the narrative, he was in a rage (7:39). Here his rage continues, and he is portrayed as a bully wanting to show how tough he is to those weaker than he. The seventh son had prayed that the arrogance of Antiochus would be justly punished (7:36; cf. 5:21), and it begins to happen. The irony of Antiochus's threat to turn Jerusalem into a cemetery (v. 4) is revealed in v. 14.

9:5-12, The Punishment of Antiochus. As so often in 2 Maccabees, the punishment fits the crime (vv. 5-6). Yet Antiochus remains arrogant in spite of his illness, and his mad rage is the cause of his downfall (v. 7). The description of his arrogant self-importance (v. 8; see also 5:21) reflects feats that only God can accomplish (Isa 40:12). The cruel punishment he suffers of death by putrefaction is found in Greek writings as well;[82] the mention of worms recalls Isa 66:24 and Jdt 16:17. The author relishes relating the gruesome torments and accords well with other stories of the deaths of scoffers against the gods. Verse 10 captures marvelously the foolishness of humans thinking they are gods and not mortals (cf. the hymns against proud kings in Isa 14:4-21, particularly the boast of the king of Babylon in vv. 13-14; Ezek 28:12-19). Antiochus, under the flogging of God, comes to knowledge (v. 11). His confession is almost proverbial. One must not fight against God (2 Macc 7:19).

9:13-27, The Repentance of Antiochus. **9:13-17.** Although Antiochus makes a vow to the Lord, his prayer will no longer be heard (v. 13). Although Jason (4:18) and Nicanor (15:32) were also said to be "abominable," Antiochus is the worst of all (7:34). The word translated "abominable" (μιαρός *miaros*) also has the connotation of "polluted," "defiled with blood," and thus raises the issue of blood guilt as the reason why God refuses to have mercy on Antiochus (see Isa 1:15). The phrases "level to the ground" (as in 8:3) and "make a cemetery" (as at 9:4) recall Antiochus's earlier misdeeds against Jerusalem and heighten the irony of his current condition (v. 14). Antiochus's earlier threat not to allow the burial of corpses (v. 15) was a great anti-social, dehumanizing action as well (cf. David's boast to

Goliath that David will give "the dead bodies of the Philistine army this very day to the birds of the air and to the wild animals of the earth" [1 Sam 17:46 NRSV]; see also Isa 56:9-11; Jer 7:33; 12:9; 15:3; 16:4; 19:7; 34:20; Ezek 29:5; 39:4, 17). It is not sure exactly what declaring Jerusalem "free" means in this context. It seems to imply more than freedom from taxes (1 Macc 10:31). Freedom in the sense of autonomy was always a slogan of great appeal in any propaganda war (as, for example, the counterclaims of Antigonus Gonatas and Ptolemy I to set all Greek cities free and the declaration by the Roman Senate in 196 BCE that all Greeks were to be free). But the relationship between the monarch and each "free" city, which had its own traditions and system of government, was a special one. It is not clear exactly what is meant by making the Jews equal to the Athenians. Athens was considered the guardian of classical culture, and during the second century the Parthenon was restored and the Agora reconstructed. In 174 BCE, Antiochus IV had promised to finish the unfinished temple of Olympia Zeus. Similarly, Antiochus vows to restore the Temple in Jerusalem to even more grandeur than at the time of Onias III (v. 16; see 2 Macc 3:1). Antiochus's promise to proclaim the power of God worldwide (v. 17) exceeds what Heliodorus had done (3:34, 36). Antiochus even promises to become a Jew. What exactly this means is unclear, although it probably did not mean becoming a Judean (a citizen of Judea). The word "Jew" here is not a geographical designation, but a religious one. What would be required in the second century BCE to become a Jew? Would it mean more than did the worship of Naaman (2 Kgs 5:15-18) or the confession of Nebuchadnezzar (Dan 4:34-37)? Does the author of 2 Maccabees envisage that Antiochus would be circumcised and follow all the laws of the Torah? We do not know. Josephus, the first-century CE Jewish historian, recounts a story in which Izates, the king of Adiabene, wishes to convert to Judaism and thus to be circumcised. However, his mother, who had earlier converted to Judaism, and the Jew who had converted her, Ananias, dissuade him. Later, Eleazar, another Jew, comes to Adiabene and insists that he be circumcised. Izates follows Eleazar's advice.[83]

---

82. See Herodotus 3.66; Diodorus Siculus 21.16.4-5.

83. Josephus *Antiquities of the Jews* 20.34-48.

9:18-27. The author reemphasizes that Antiochus will not escape God's judgment (v. 18), and thus the king, although in such pain, pens a letter. Since the writing of a deathbed testament was a well-known literary device in Hellenistic literature, the authenticity of the letter that follows has been greatly debated. Those who affirm its authenticity agree that the original letter has been added to; those who deny its authenticity agree that it is modeled on a genuine letter, possibly to the army, whose support would have been crucial in any change of leadership. Whatever its origins, the letter has been adapted so as to further the rhetorical aims of the author. This is most easily seen in the way the addressees of the letter, the Jewish citizens, are mentioned before the king and are addressed as "esteemed" or "worthy" (v. 19). It is not specified to whom the term "citizens" refers, whether to the people of Antioch-in-Jerusalem or to those Jews who were citizens of various cities throughout the Seleucid Empire. Since the Jews as a whole were never given citizen rights in any community in which they lived (see, e.g., 2 Macc 12:3, where the citizens of Joppa are distinguished from the Jews living among them), the letter is most likely addressed to the former. The phrasing, however, if imprecise, suits the aim of the author: to show that the Jews can be good citizens, that they are not anti-social. The greeting formula is quite extravagant with its threefold wish of hearty greetings, health, and prosperity (more so than the greeting in 1:10*b*). The addition of the term "general" (στρατηγός *strategos*) supports the suggestion that the letter may have been, or was modeled on, a letter to the army. At vv. 20-21 come the usual well wishes for the recipient's health, although the text itself is variously transmitted in the manuscripts. Note how the king remembers with affection the esteem and goodwill of the Jews (v. 21)! Given that this letter comes after the events narrated in 9:1-12, to describe the king's condition as an annoying illness is a marvelous understatement and shows that this letter, authentic or not, does not really belong with the situation of 9:1-8. Rather, vv. 23-25 make clear that the letter originally concerned the orderly transfer of power. Antiochus IV's father, Antiochus III the Great, had appointed his son Seleucus IV as his successor. Following Antiochus III's death, while attempting to raise money in the east after his defeat by Rome, Seleucus took the throne. Following this precedent, Antiochus IV names his own son, Antiochus V Eupator (who was still a young boy and needed a regent; see 1 Macc 3:33; 6:14-15), as heir to the throne. What is astonishing is that in this context, Antiochus places his trust in the Jews for the success of this transfer of power and the stability of the realm (v. 25). The Jews are asked to continue their goodwill toward Antiochus and his son (9:26). Verse 27 is also incongruous in the context, as Antiochus IV was in no way moderate and kind to the Jews. Needless to say, the advice will not be followed. The thrust of this letter in this context is to argue that the Jews are not anti-social, as so many stories circulating in the Hellenistic world suggested.

9:28-29, The Death of Antiochus. Antiochus dies in a strange land (see 5:9-10, the death of Jason). Philip, who has the title σύντροφος (*syntrophos*), meaning "brought up with"—but in the Seleucid hierarchy has the meaning "intimate friend"—takes Antiochus's body home. In contrast to 1 Maccabees, in the account in 2 Maccabees, Philip flees to Egypt because he fears Antiochus V, not Lysias. According to 1 Maccabees, the dying Antiochus IV replaces Lysias by Philip as guardian of Antiochus V (3:32-33; 6:14-15). When Philip returns from the east, he takes control of Antioch, but Lysias forces him out (6:55-56, 63). Philip's unsuccessful attempt is mentioned at 2 Macc 13:23, although, since the author of 2 Maccabees has the Philip who was with the dying Antiochus IV flee to Egypt, he seems to distinguish him from the Philip of the coup attempt in 13:23. Ptolemy VI Philomotor, to whom Philip is said to flee, had been driven out of Alexandria to Rome in October 164, just before Antiochus IV's death, and did not return until the middle of 163. The conflict between Philip and Lysias, therefore, must have taken place in the first half of 163. According to Josephus, Lysias had Philip murdered before he could reach Egypt.[84]

---

84. Josephus *Antiquities of the Jews* 12.386.

REFLECTIONS

The account of the punishment of Antiochus IV draws on a well-attested theme in the Bible: the sharp distinction between humans and God. The serpent had tempted Eve in the Garden of Eden to eat of the fruit of the forbidden tree (Gen 3:5). So the prohibition was broken, and the humans were expelled from the garden for trying to be like God. In the story of the tower of Babel, humans had thought to breach the distance separating them from the heavens and for their pains had been scattered over the face of the earth, speaking different languages (Gen 11:1-9). The hymns of Isaiah against the hubris of the kings of Babylon and how it would result in their humiliation (Isa 14:47) and the sayings of Ezekiel over the king of Tyre (Ezek 28:2) are eloquent testimony to the need to maintain this high, exalted notion of God. The story in Daniel 4 tells how King Nebuchadnezzar fell from his place of honor and dignity and was driven away from human society to become like an animal, eating grass like oxen and having hair as long as eagle feathers and fingernails like bird claws. Humans are shown to be stupid if they try to "play God."

These stories raise important issues for our own time. We have had enormous advances in medicine, science, and technology. Yet we have not yet grasped the ethical implications of these advances, especially in the area of human biology. For instance, how are we to use responsibly the technology for gene manipulation in medicine? Clearly it will be a great advantage if doctors are someday able to eradicate genetic disorders, like muscular dystrophy. But what limits should be put on the use of these techniques? Will parents want to manipulate what kind of child they will have, what sex, hair or eye color, body size? Religious communities will need to pay careful attention to such issues. With all of our advances, we still need to recognize our limitations and weaknesses. We must not try to play God.

2 Maccabees 10:1-8, The Purification of the Temple

<table>
<tr><td>NAB</td><td>NRSV</td></tr>
<tr><td>

10 When Maccabeus and his companions, under the LORD's leadership, had recovered the temple and the city, ² they destroyed the altars erected by the Gentiles in the marketplace and the sacred enclosures. ³ After purifying the temple, they made a new altar. Then, with fire struck from flint, they offered sacrifice for the first time in two years, burned incense, and lighted lamps. They also set out the showbread. ⁴ When they had done this, they prostrated themselves and begged the LORD that they might never again fall into such misfortunes, and that if they should sin at any time, he might chastise them with moderation and not hand them over to blasphemous and barbarous Gentiles. ⁵ On the anniversary of the day on which the temple had been profaned by the Gentiles, that is, the twenty-fifth of the same month Chislev, the purification of the temple took place. ⁶ The Jews celebrated joyfully for eight days as on the feast of Booths, remembering

</td><td>

10 Now Maccabeus and his followers, the Lord leading them on, recovered the temple and the city; ²they tore down the altars that had been built in the public square by the foreigners, and also destroyed the sacred precincts. ³They purified the sanctuary, and made another altar of sacrifice; then, striking fire out of flint, they offered sacrifices, after a lapse of two years, and they offered incense and lighted lamps and set out the bread of the Presence. ⁴When they had done this, they fell prostrate and implored the Lord that they might never again fall into such misfortunes, but that, if they should ever sin, they might be disciplined by him with forbearance and not be handed over to blasphemous and barbarous nations. ⁵It happened that on the same day on which the sanctuary had been profaned by the foreigners, the purification of the sanctuary took place, that is, on the twenty-fifth day of the same month, which was Chislev. ⁶They celebrated it

</td></tr>
</table>

NAB

how, a little while before, they had spent the feast of Booths living like wild animals in caves on the mountains. [7] Carrying rods entwined with leaves, green branches and palms, they sang hymns of grateful praise to him who had brought about the purification of his own Place. [8] By public edict and decree they prescribed that the whole Jewish nation should celebrate these days every year.

NRSV

for eight days with rejoicing, in the manner of the festival of booths, remembering how not long before, during the festival of booths, they had been wandering in the mountains and caves like wild animals. [7]Therefore, carrying ivy-wreathed wands and beautiful branches and also fronds of palm, they offered hymns of thanksgiving to him who had given success to the purifying of his own holy place. [8]They decreed by public edict, ratified by vote, that the whole nation of the Jews should observe these days every year.

COMMENTARY

After the elimination of the prime antagonist against the Temple, Antiochus IV, the author now describes the people's joy at righting the wrong Antiochus had done. As mentioned in the Commentary on chap. 9, some scholars suggest that this section has been misplaced from going before chapter 9, but the joy belongs after the death of the enemy (as in the victory-enthronement pattern in Exodus 15). In contrast to the blasphemer Antiochus IV, whose body is "brought back" (παρεκομίζετο parekomizeto) to Antioch (9:29), Judas and his companions "bring back" for themselves—i.e., "recover" (ἐκομίσαντο ekomisanto, v. 1)—the Temple and the city. The parallel passage in 1 Macc 4:36-59 puts emphasis not only on the purification of the sanctuary, but also on its dedication (as in 1 Kgs 8:63; 2 Chr 7:5; Ezra 6:16-17). The author of 2 Maccabees also recognizes the action as a dedication (2:19), but as he has stressed that the Temple was overthrown because of the sins of the people (5:17-20; 6:12-17), he now stresses the purification of the Temple and the sin of the people. No mention is made of the priests who performed the sacrifices, whereas 1 Macc 4:42 stresses the choice of blameless priests.

The author makes no mention of the citadel (2 Macc 4:28), although it is mentioned later (15:31). In contrast, 1 Maccabees stresses the need to defend the Temple from the troops at the citadel (1 Macc 4:41, 60). The description of altars around the agora (v. 2) reflects Greek custom and supports the notion that Antiochus IV had simply instituted pagan worship practices in Jerusalem rather than one particular cult. The sacrifices (v. 3) most probably refer to the contin-

ual daily sacrifice (see Exod 29:38-42; Num 28:3-8). The incense offering (Exod 30:7-8), the lighting of lamps (Exod 27:20-21; Lev 24:2-3), and the setting out of the showbread (Exod 25:30; Lev 24:5-9) show the concern of the author to portray Judas as following the Torah (2 Chr 13:11; 1 Macc 4:50-51). In contrast to the two-year lapse in Jewish sacrifices in the Temple (2 Macc 10:3), 1 Maccabees has an interval of three years (1 Macc 1:54; 4:52), while Dan 12:7 has three and a half years. Most likely 1 Maccabees is correct. The language of v. 4 is similar to that of 6:12-17. Once again the nations are described as barbarous (2:21). The prayer recalls that of Solomon at the dedication of the Temple, where he also prays for mercy for the people's sin (1 Kgs 8:46-50).

To show the providential care of God, the author emphasizes that the renewed sacrifice took place on the anniversary of the day of the defilement (v. 5; see also 2 Macc 6:7; cf. 1 Macc 4:52). The author then refers to Judas's flight to the mountains (v. 6; 5:27). The connection with the Feast of Tabernacles (vv. 6-7) is found in the prefixed letters (1:9, 18), but is not made in 1 Maccabees. The carrying of branches, signifying fertility, is commanded at Lev 23:40. The word translated "ivy-wreathed wands" (θύρσοι thyrsoi, v. 7) was also used for what was carried in processions of Dionysus, and the author may be showing once again the reversal from the persecution when the Jews were forced in procession to Dionysus (2 Macc 6:7). The language at v. 8 is repeated almost word for word at 15:36, and so binds the two festivals together.

REFLECTIONS

The second act of this story finishes as the first had done, with the Jews celebrating the power of God in their Temple. Two major opponents of "proper" Jewish behavior have been defeated, the high priest Jason and the Seleucid king Antiochus IV. The reader can anticipate that any further attack on the Temple in Jerusalem will also be unsuccessful, and can also expect that there will be such an attack, since one opponent, the high priest Menelaus, still remains. This has been a much more serious attack on the Temple than that of Heliodorus in 2 Maccabees 3. The first attack had been on the Jewish educational system because Jason had built a gymnasium, thereby attempting to erase any distinction between the Jews and their neighbors. Menelaus had also despoiled the Temple for his own private gain. Finally, Antiochus IV had attempted to wipe out the very practice of Judaism within Judea. The author of 2 Maccabees shows how these attempts had been foiled by God after the martyrs had offered up their lives rather than transgress God's commandments.

The story stresses the need for covenantal loyalty on the part of the Jews. Because they aped Greek ways, disaster had befallen them. Because the martyrs showed their faithfulness to God, God had come to Israel's aid. The martyrs provide a striking example of how death can be fruitful, whereas Antiochus IV dies without accomplishing anything.

The story is one of great heroism, but it is one in which it is easy to tell who are the villains. As in western movies where the bad guys wear black hats and the good guys wear white hats, the author of this narrative shows clearly who he thinks the bad guys are. Where one group is trying to oppress another and suppress their right to worship, it is a pretty clear call. When religion was outlawed, or at least put under very tight rein, in the Soviet Union and in China, it was easy to see that the authorities were in the wrong. Opposition and oppression have a way of helping us to define what we stand for. They have a way of demarcating a believing community from those who wish to suppress or curtail its activities. The blood of martyrs is said to have watered the seeds of Christianity. We all hope that if we were put in such a position we would have the courage and conviction to stand up for our beliefs.

But how are we to keep a sense of community when we are not under attack? When Judea's national symbol, the Temple, was polluted, when the distinctive markers of Judaism—the Torah scrolls, circumcision, the Jewish festivals—were forbidden, it was clear that those who wished to maintain their religious practices had to take a stand. But once the threat has passed, how will a community maintain its sense of identity? The history of sectarian strife within Christianity suggests that the answer may not lie in the direction of trying to define who is and who is not a "proper" member of the community. We can see the beginning of this problem in the attitude of the author of 2 Maccabees. It would appear that, for him, a "true" Jew did not attend a gymnasium. When a community tries to make these kinds of distinctions, problems will always arise, for all of us are different with different backgrounds and different educational and life experiences. When a community is not under threat or attack, perhaps the best solution to maintaining it is to celebrate the various gifts that each member of the community brings to it, to revel in the "rainbow" quality of our community. The apostle Paul speaks to all of our communities when he says, "Love is patient; love is kind; love is not envious or boastful or arrogant or rude. It does not insist on its own way" (1 Cor 13:4-5 NRSV). The moral character of the high priests Jason and Menelaus, as portrayed in this narrative, is shown to be such that they sought only their own aggrandizement, sought ways that they could keep their positions of power and important status. They insisted on their own way to the detriment of the community. They are the anti-type of the high priest Onias, who sought only what was good for the community.

The Third Act: Further Defense of the Temple

Overview

This third section of the epitome deals with further attacks on the Temple under the successors of Antiochus IV. There is a marked contrast between the rather condensed account of many campaigns in 10:14–13:26 and the more expansive account of Nicanor's expedition in chaps. 14–15.

2 MACCABEES 10:9–13:26, THE ATTACKS UNDER ANTIOCHUS V

Overview

This section of 2 Maccabees seems to be structured around a pattern whereby first attacks by local leaders occur (10:14-38; 12:3-45), then come a major expedition and peace (2 Maccabees 11; 13).

2 Maccabees 10:9-13, Dynastic Changes

NAB	NRSV
9 Such was the end of Antiochus surnamed Epiphanes. 10 Now we shall relate what happened under Antiochus Eupator, the son of that godless man, and shall give a summary of the chief evils caused by the wars. 11 When Eupator succeeded to the kingdom, he put a certain Lysias in charge of the government as commander in chief of Coelesyria and Phoenicia. 12 Ptolemy, surnamed Macron, had taken the lead in treating the Jews fairly because of the previous injustice that had been done them, and he endeavored to have peaceful relations with them. 13 As a result, he was accused before Eupator by the King's Friends. In fact, on all sides he heard himself called a traitor for having abandoned Cyprus, which	9Such then was the end of Antiochus, who was called Epiphanes. 10Now we will tell what took place under Antiochus Eupator, who was the son of that ungodly man, and will give a brief summary of the principal calamities of the wars. 11This man, when he succeeded to the kingdom, appointed one Lysias to have charge of the government and to be chief governor of Coelesyria and Phoenicia. 12Ptolemy, who was called Macron, took the lead in showing justice to the Jews because of the wrong that had been done to them, and attempted to maintain peaceful relations with them. 13As a result he was accused before Eupator by the king's

NAB

Philometor had entrusted to him, and for having gone over to Antiochus Epiphanes. Since he could not command the respect due to his high office, he ended his life by taking poison.

NRSV

Friends. He heard himself called a traitor at every turn, because he had abandoned Cyprus, which Philometor had entrusted to him, and had gone over to Antiochus Epiphanes. Unable to command the respect due his office,[a] he took poison and ended his life.

a Cn: Meaning of Gk uncertain

COMMENTARY

10:9-11. As at 3:40–4:1, the author provides a transitional sentence to the next episode, the reign of Antiochus V Eupator. Antiochus V was only nine years old and was, in fact, under the guardianship of Lysias (1 Macc 3:33).[85] Lysias had been placed in charge of the area from the Euphrates to the border of Egypt by Antiochus IV (1 Macc 3:32). In contrast to the NRSV translation, v. 11 should be translated "appointed one Lysias to have charge of the government, and Protarchos as governor of Coelesyria and Phoenicia," since the offices of chief minister of the empire and governor of Coelesyria did not overlap.

10:12-13. The situation described in these verses is similar to that at 13:24. Ptolemy Macron, as governor of Cyprus, had been loyal to Ptolemy VI Philometor of Egypt, but the botched maneuverings of the Ptolemaic court and the subsequent loss of the Ptolemies to Antiochus IV in the war of 170/169 had led him to go over to the Seleucid side (c. 168 BCE) when Antiochus IV's fleet invaded Cyprus. The description of Ptolemy Macron

85. See Appian *Syriaca* 46.66.

as being friendly towards the Jews should not be seen as simply a peaceful disposition. As previous governors of Coelesyria and Phoenicia had been hostile to the pious Jews (Apollonius son of Menestheus, 4:4; Ptolemy son of Dorymenes, 4:45; 8:8) and their stance seems to reflect court policy, this change in attitude should be seen as reflecting the policy of the governor's superiors. Since such a change in attitude would probably have occurred after the peace negotiations following the first expedition of Lysias (2 Macc 11:14, 16-21), which actually took place during the reign of Antiochus IV (1 Macc 4:28-29; 2 Macc 11:27-33), these events have been misplaced by the author of 2 Maccabees in order to portray Antiochus IV as the evil opponent of the Jews, and not as someone who entered into peace negotiations with them. The court gossip mentioned at 2 Macc 10:13 no doubt reflects the intrigues at court following the restoration of the Temple and preceding Lysias's second expedition (1 Macc 6:21-28). The last part of v. 13 is very corrupt; the conjecture of the NRSV translation is as good as any.

2 Maccabees 10:14-23, Campaigns in Idumea

NAB

[14] When Gorgias became governor of the region, he employed foreign troops and used every opportunity to attack the Jews. [15] At the same time the Idumeans, who held some important strongholds, were harassing the Jews; they welcomed fugitives from Jerusalem and endeavored to continue the war. [16] Maccabeus and his companions,

NRSV

14When Gorgias became governor of the region, he maintained a force of mercenaries, and at every turn kept attacking the Jews. 15Besides this, the Idumeans, who had control of important strongholds, were harassing the Jews; they received those who were banished from Jerusalem, and endeavored to keep up the war. 16But Mac-

after public prayers asking God to be their ally, moved quickly against the strongholds of the Idumeans. [17] Attacking vigorously, they gained control of the places, drove back all who manned the walls, and cut down those who opposed them, killing as many as twenty thousand men. [18] When at least nine thousand took refuge in two very strong towers, containing everything necessary to sustain a siege, [19] Maccabeus left Simon and Joseph, along with Zacchaeus and his men, in sufficient numbers to besiege them, while he himself went off to places where he was more urgently needed. [20] But some of the men in Simon's force who were money lovers let themselves be bribed by some of the men in the towers; on receiving seventy thousand drachmas, they allowed a number of them to escape. [21] When Maccabeus was told what had happened, he assembled the rulers of the people and accused those men of having sold their kinsmen for money by setting their enemies free to fight against them. [22] So he put them to death as traitors, and without delay captured the two towers. [23] As he was successful at arms in all his undertakings, he destroyed more than twenty thousand men in the two strongholds.

cabeus and his forces, after making solemn supplication and imploring God to fight on their side, rushed to the strongholds of the Idumeans. [17]Attacking them vigorously, they gained possession of the places, and beat off all who fought upon the wall, and slaughtered those whom they encountered, killing no fewer than twenty thousand.

[18]When at least nine thousand took refuge in two very strong towers well equipped to withstand a siege, [19]Maccabeus left Simon and Joseph, and also Zacchaeus and his troops, a force sufficient to besiege them; and he himself set off for places where he was more urgently needed. [20]But those with Simon, who were money-hungry, were bribed by some of those who were in the towers, and on receiving seventy thousand drachmas let some of them slip away. [21]When word of what had happened came to Maccabeus, he gathered the leaders of the people, and accused these men of having sold their kindred for money by setting their enemies free to fight against them. [22]Then he killed these men who had turned traitor, and immediately captured the two towers. [23]Having success at arms in everything he undertook, he destroyed more than twenty thousand in the two strongholds.

COMMENTARY

10:14-17. Gorgias was governor of Idumea (2 Macc 12:32) and seems also to have been in control of Jamnia (1 Macc 5:59). He is characterized as being experienced in military affairs and had already taken part in an attack on the Jews (2 Macc 8:9). The author makes sure to mention that it was not the Jews who initiated the attacks, but the Seleucid forces (1 Macc 5:3-5 also has the Idumeans as hostile to Judas and his forces). The Jews who have been banned from Jerusalem (v. 15) are presumably followers of Menelaus, although the author does not explicitly say so and does not mention the garrison in the citadel or use the term "ungodly Israelites" (1 Macc 6:18-27). In fact, the whole account is very sparse on geographical details, not specifying which Idumean strongholds were attacked and captured (vv. 16-17). The author's main concern is not in

those details but in stressing that the Jews pray to God to be their ally (v. 16; see 2 Macc 8:24). The figure of 20,000 dead (v. 17) is high, as are the figures 9,000 for those who "took refuge" in the towers (v. 18) and 20,000 for those whom Judas is said to have killed "in the two strongholds" (v. 23; cf. the numbers at 2 Macc 8:30).

10:18-23. The three commanders left in charge of the siege (v. 19) are most likely two brothers of Judas, Simon and Joseph (8:22), and an otherwise unknown Zacchaeus. Scholars have suggested that this episode is a doublet of 1 Macc 5:18, 55-61, where two commanders—Joseph son of Zechariah and Azariah—became jealous of the successes of Judas and Simon and attempted to capture Jamnia but were defeated. The siege fails because of the treachery of some of Simon's men, who are described as "lovers of money" (v.

20; cf. Luke 16:14), a common accusation against opponents. Since Simon is glorified in the account of 1 Maccabees, but not here, some scholars have further concluded that the author is anti-Hasmonean in bent. The author of 2 Maccabees, however, includes many stories of deception (2 Macc 13:21), compromise (12:24-25), and backsliding (12:39-40), so this episode need not be taken as anti-Hasmonean propaganda. What it

does is show the faithfulness and incorruptibility of Judas. He summons the leaders of the people (v. 21), perhaps the commanders of the army (following Deut 1:15). The men are accused of treachery (similarly to Menelaus, 2 Macc 5:15) and are executed (v. 22). With that transgression done away with, Judas quickly captures the two towers.

2 Maccabees 10:24-38, The Defeat of Timothy

NAB

24 Timothy, who had previously been defeated by the Jews, gathered a tremendous force of foreign troops and collected a large number of cavalry from Asia; then he appeared in Judea, ready to conquer it by force. 25 At his approach, Maccabeus and his men made supplication to God, sprinkling earth upon their heads and girding their loins in sackcloth. 26 Lying prostrate at the foot of the altar, they begged him to be gracious to them, and to be an enemy to their enemies, and a foe to their foes, as the law declares.

27 After the prayer, they took up their arms and advanced a considerable distance from the city, halting when they were close to the enemy. 28 As soon as dawn broke, the armies joined battle, the one having as pledge of success and victory not only their valor but also their reliance on the LORD, and the other taking fury as their leader in the fight.

29 In the midst of the fierce battle, there appeared to the enemy from the heavens five majestic men riding on golden-bridled horses, who led the Jews on. 30 They surrounded Maccabeus, and shielding him with their own armor, kept him from being wounded. They shot arrows and hurled thunderbolts at the enemy, who were bewildered and blinded, thrown into confusion and routed. 31 Twenty-five hundred of their foot soldiers and six hundred of their horsemen were slain. 32 Timothy, however, fled to a well-fortified stronghold called Gazara, where Chaereas was in command. 33 For four days Maccabeus and his men eagerly besieged the fortress. 34 Those inside, relying on the strength of the place, kept repeating outrageous blasphemies and uttering abominable

10, 30: Omit *dyo:* so LXX^V,MSS; gloss.

NRSV

24Now Timothy, who had been defeated by the Jews before, gathered a tremendous force of mercenaries and collected the cavalry from Asia in no small number. He came on, intending to take Judea by storm. 25As he drew near, Maccabeus and his men sprinkled dust on their heads and girded their loins with sackcloth, in supplication to God. 26Falling upon the steps before the altar, they implored him to be gracious to them and to be an enemy to their enemies and an adversary to their adversaries, as the law declares. 27And rising from their prayer they took up their arms and advanced a considerable distance from the city; and when they came near the enemy they halted. 28Just as dawn was breaking, the two armies joined battle, the one having as pledge of success and victory not only their valor but also their reliance on the Lord, while the other made rage their leader in the fight.

29When the battle became fierce, there appeared to the enemy from heaven five resplendent men on horses with golden bridles, and they were leading the Jews. 30Two of them took Maccabeus between them, and shielding him with their own armor and weapons, they kept him from being wounded. They showered arrows and thunderbolts on the enemy, so that, confused and blinded, they were thrown into disorder and cut to pieces. 31Twenty thousand five hundred were slaughtered, besides six hundred cavalry.

32Timothy himself fled to a stronghold called Gazara, especially well garrisoned, where Chaereas was commander. 33Then Maccabeus and his men were glad, and they besieged the fort for four days. 34The men within, relying on the

NAB

words. [35] When the fifth day dawned, twenty young men in the army of Maccabeus, angered over such blasphemies, bravely stormed the wall and with savage fury cut down everyone they encountered. [36] Others who climbed up the same way swung around on the defenders, taking the besieged in the rear; they put the towers to the torch, spread the fire and burned the blasphemers alive. Still others broke down the gates and let in the rest of the troops, who took possession of the city. [37] Timothy had hidden in a cistern, but they killed him, along with his brother Chaereas, and Apollophanes. [38] On completing these exploits, they blessed, with hymns of grateful praise, the LORD who shows great kindness to Israel and grants them victory.

NRSV

strength of the place, kept blaspheming terribly and uttering wicked words. [35]But at dawn of the fifth day, twenty young men in the army of Maccabeus, fired with anger because of the blasphemies, bravely stormed the wall and with savage fury cut down everyone they met. [36]Others who came up in the same way wheeled around against the defenders and set fire to the towers; they kindled fires and burned the blasphemers alive. Others broke open the gates and let in the rest of the force, and they occupied the city. [37]They killed Timothy, who was hiding in a cistern, and his brother Chaereas, and Apollophanes. [38]When they had accomplished these things, with hymns and thanksgivings they blessed the Lord who shows great kindness to Israel and gives them the victory.

COMMENTARY

This campaign, also sparse in chronological and geographical details, is often seen as reporting the same events as 1 Macc 5:6-8, an even sparser description of a campaign into Ammonite territory. But there are major differences in this passage: Timothy's death, not mentioned in 1 Maccabees, is described with considerable detail (10:37). Here Timothy invades Judea (vv. 24-25), whereas in 1 Maccabees Judas crosses over the Jordan to attack the Ammonites (1 Macc 5:6). Second Maccabees describes a single battle that seems to take place in Judea (although Judas and his forces go out "a considerable distance" from the city to engage Timothy [10:27]), whereas 1 Macc 5:7 mentions "many battles" with the Ammonites. And the account in 2 Maccabees describes in detail the siege and capture of Gazara (Gezer), whereas 1 Maccabees recounts only the capture of Jazer, in the Transjordan (5:8; according to 1 Maccabees, Gazara was not conquered until the reign of Simon [1 Macc 13:43-48]).

10:24. As mentioned previously, the author of 2 Maccabees must have thought that there were two Timothys, the one here and at 8:30-33, the other at 12:17-25. Whether there were two or whether one should follow the order of 1 Maccabees and only have one Timothy is disputed,

but most likely there was only one. The author does not specify the number of mercenaries but, since over 21,000 die in the battle (v. 31), the author means the numbers to be frightening.

10:25-28. The Jews in their distress turn to supplicate God (v. 25; cf. 10:4), using the traditional signs of national mourning by putting earth on their heads as if they were buried and wearing sackcloth, from which shrouds are cut (Neh 9:1; Esth 4:1-3; Jer 6:26; Dan 9:3). Gathered around the new altar, they ask for God's mercy (v. 26; Joel 2:17). The reference to the law is from Exod 23:22, which specifies that God will act this way if the people obey the commandments (cf. 1 Kgs 8:37-39). The calm confidence of the Jews (v. 28) is contrasted with the animal rage of their opponents.

10:29-31. The epiphany to defend Judas and to scatter the enemy has many Greek elements. Often in the *Iliad,* for example, a hero is protected by a god. When Delphi was defended against the Persians and the Gauls, gigantic figures pursued the fleeing attackers while thunderbolts crashed down on them.[86] Zeus is pre-eminently Zeus Keraunos who hurls thunderbolts at his enemies.[87]

---

86. See Herodotus 8.36-39; Pausanias 1.4.4; 10.23.1-6.
87. See Homer *Odyssey* 23.330; Hesiod *Theogony* 854.

No one has satisfactorily explained the number five for the supernatural figures (v. 29). One might note how the following siege lasts five days (v. 35).

10:32-38. According to 1 Macc 5:8, the defeat of the army led by Timothy took place in Jazer in Transjordan, not Gazara on the border of Judea to the west of Jerusalem. The motif of the taunting defenders (v. 34), found again at 12:14-16, mirrors the taunts of the Jebusites during David's siege of Jerusalem (2 Sam 5:6-9). A cistern (v. 37), a large pit with plastered walls for storing water, was a perfect hiding place. The victory hymn (v. 38) may be compared to the song of Miriam after the defeat of Pharaoh (Exod 15:20-21), or to the song after David's defeat of Goliath (1 Sam 18:6-7).

REFLECTIONS

Throughout this narrative, the opponents of the Jews are shown to instigate the problems. While the Jews wish to be left alone to follow their own ancestral customs, the non-Jews will not let them. When someone does try to help them, as in the case of Ptolemy Macron, he is dismissed. The local governors, Gorgias and Timothy, constantly seek to attack the forces of Judas Maccabeus. Here again we see the Maccabees behaving in line with just-war principles, acting only out of self-defense. The reader may be particularly intrigued as to what Ptolemy Macron's peace proposals would have been, but the story reminds us that the peacemakers are often the first casualties of war as more extreme voices for violence drown out the calls for peace.

Yet even while the Maccabees are only acting in self-defense, there are also uglier overtones in these stories. Simon's followers, who let enemy forces go (2 Macc 10:20-21), are portrayed as mercenaries, money-lovers, as not looking for the welfare of the community but only for their self-interest. The assumption behind this telling, however, seems to be that the only good enemy is a dead enemy, for Judas immediately sets out to destroy all those who were left besieged. Such an attitude of taking no hostages, of accepting no ransom for prisoners, is disturbing. It violates the later-formulated principles of just war. These stories are told by someone who definitely thinks that God is on the Maccabees' side, and that their enemies are to be destroyed. Such a cavalier attitude toward human life and its dignity is one that we must seriously question. Even in battle, the object should be not to kill, but to render harmless.

2 Maccabees 11:1-12, The Campaign of Lysias

NAB

11 Very soon afterward, Lysias, guardian and kinsman of the king and head of the government, being greatly displeased at what had happened, [2] mustered about eighty thousand infantry and all his cavalry and marched against the Jews. His plan was to make Jerusalem a Greek settlement; [3] to levy tribute on the temple, as he did on the sanctuaries of the other nations; and to put the high priesthood up for sale every year. [4] He did not take God's power into account at all, but felt exultant confidence in his myriads of foot soldiers, his thousands of horsemen, and his eighty elephants. [5] So he invaded Judea, and when

NRSV

11 Very soon after this, Lysias, the king's guardian and kinsman, who was in charge of the government, being vexed at what had happened, [2] gathered about eighty thousand infantry and all his cavalry and came against the Jews. He intended to make the city a home for Greeks, [3] and to levy tribute on the temple as he did on the sacred places of the other nations, and to put up the high priesthood for sale every year. [4] He took no account whatever of the power of God, but was elated with his ten thousands of infantry, and his thousands of cavalry, and his eighty elephants. [5] Invading Judea, he approached Beth-zur,

NAB

he reached Beth-zur, a fortified place about twenty miles from Jerusalem, launched a strong attack against it. ⁶ When Maccabeus and his men learned that Lysias was besieging the strongholds, they and all the people begged the LORD with lamentations and tears to send a good angel to save Israel. ⁷ Maccabeus himself was the first to take up arms, and he exhorted the others to join him in risking their lives to help their kinsmen. Then they resolutely set out together. ⁸ Suddenly, while they were still near Jerusalem, a horseman appeared at their head, clothed in white garments and brandishing gold weapons. ⁹ Then all of them together thanked God for his mercy, and their hearts were filled with such courage that they were ready to assault not only men, but the most savage beasts, yes, even walls of iron. ¹⁰ Now that the LORD had shown his mercy toward them, they advanced in battle order with the aid of their heavenly ally. ¹¹ Hurling themselves upon the enemy like lions, they laid low eleven thousand foot soldiers and sixteen hundred horsemen, and put all the rest to flight. ¹² Most of those who got away were wounded and stripped of their arms, while Lysias himself escaped only by shameful flight.

NRSV

which was a fortified place about five stadia*a* from Jerusalem, and pressed it hard.

6When Maccabeus and his men got word that Lysias*b* was besieging the strongholds, they and all the people, with lamentations and tears, prayed the Lord to send a good angel to save Israel. ⁷Maccabeus himself was the first to take up arms, and he urged the others to risk their lives with him to aid their kindred. Then they eagerly rushed off together. ⁸And there, while they were still near Jerusalem, a horseman appeared at their head, clothed in white and brandishing weapons of gold. ⁹And together they all praised the merciful God, and were strengthened in heart, ready to assail not only humans but the wildest animals or walls of iron. ¹⁰They advanced in battle order, having their heavenly ally, for the Lord had mercy on them. ¹¹They hurled themselves like lions against the enemy, and laid low eleven thousand of them and sixteen hundred cavalry, and forced all the rest to flee. ¹²Most of them got away stripped and wounded, and Lysias himself escaped by disgraceful flight.

a Meaning of Gk uncertain   *b* Gk *he*

COMMENTARY

The story of the first expedition of Lysias is told here as having occurred during the reign of Antiochus V (who was only nine years old at this time). It actually occurred, however, under Antiochus IV. As mentioned before, the author did not wish to shift focus away from Antiochus IV as the main and constant antagonist of the Jews, and the author narrated one major battle (chap. 8) before the death of Antiochus IV. First Maccabees reports that Lysias, as chancellor of Antiochus IV, sent out the expedition of Nicanor (1 Macc 3:32, 38) before himself invading (4:24-35).

11:1-3. For the first time, Lysias is described as the guardian of Antiochus V (v. 1; see 1 Macc 3:33). He is also described as being "in charge of the government," a position he held under Antiochus IV (1 Macc 3:32), and is given the high

title "kinsman" (Lysias is said to be of royal lineage, probably a reference to this title; see 1 Macc 3:32). Jonathan, Judas's brother, was later given the same title (1 Macc 10:89). The full description of Lysias here, after the brief mention at 2 Macc 10:10, suggests some misplaced order. The figure of 80,000 infantry and "all the cavalry" (v. 2) exceeds the numbers at 1 Macc 4:28. The author of 1 Maccabees reports that Lysias sent the expedition of Nicanor to destroy the people (1 Macc 3:38, 42), as Antiochus IV had commanded him, which contrasts with the description of Lysias's intentions here. The events described here—enforced Hellenization, taxing the temple revenue, and selling the high priesthood (vv. 2-3)—seem closer to what happened during the high priesthood of Jason (2 Macc 4:11-15), who purchased the office (2 Macc 4:7-9). Lysias's actions also seem to presuppose that the Temple and the city were controlled by Judas, and not by the followers of Menelaus.

11:4-5. The author enjoys contrasting the might of humans with the power of God (v. 4; 3:34; 10:28). Here, he states that Lysias "did not take God's power into account at all, but felt exultant confidence" in his own troops (v. 4). The treaty of Apamea with the Romans in 188 had forbidden the Seleucids to use elephants in future battles, but Lysias has eighty; elephants could be quite successful against peoples who had no experience of them. As in 1 Macc 4:29, Lysias approaches Jerusalem from the south (v. 5); 2 Maccabees describes Beth-zur as being five *schoinoi* (σχονοί), *not stadia* (στάδια), as the NRSV translates, from Jerusalem. The *schoinos,* a Persian measure, could equal thirty, forty, or sixty *stadia.* Since a *stadium* is about one-fifth of a kilometer, five *schoinoi* of thirty *stadia* would locate Beth-zur about 30 kms south of Jerusalem (it is actually 28.5 kms south).

11:6-12. Once again, prayer precedes the battle (v. 6), and Judas sets the example (v. 7). As

God had sent an angel before the Israelites in the past (Exod 23:20; 33:2; Josh 5:13-15; 2 Kgs 19:35), so now they pray for God to do likewise for them. The closest parallels to this scene, however, are from nonbiblical accounts: the battle between the Romans and the Latins, when the Dioscuri, the twin gods, charged at the head of the Roman force and forced the Latins to flee;[88] Athena's help to the citizens of Cyzicus;[89] and Theseus, who at Marathon rushed before the Greeks at the barbarians.[90] In this account, the role of the divine heroes of the Greeks has been taken over by an angel of the Lord. God's mercy is again praised (2 Macc 8:3, 5; 10:26), and God is described as Israel's ally (v. 10; 8:24; 10:16), giving them the courage to win a convincing victory (v. 11). Lysias saves himself by a disgraceful flight, as had Nicanor (2 Macc 8:34-35). According to 1 Maccabees, the numbers of those killed are much smaller (1 Macc 4:34), and Lysias made an orderly retreat.

88. Dionysius of Holicarnassus *Roman Antiquities* 6.13.
89. Plutarch *Lucillus* 10.3.
90. Plutarch *Theseus* 35.

2 Maccabees 11:13-38, Peace Negotiations

NAB

[13] But Lysias was not a stupid man. He reflected on the defeat he had suffered, and came to realize that the Hebrews were invincible because the mighty God was their ally. He therefore sent a message [14] persuading them to settle everything on just terms, and promising to persuade the king also, and to induce him to become their friend. [15] Maccabeus, solicitous for the common good, agreed to all that Lysias proposed; and the king, on his part, granted in behalf of the Jews all the written requests of Maccabeus to Lysias.

[16] These are the terms of the letter which Lysias wrote to the Jews: "Lysias sends greetings to the Jewish people. [17] John and Absalom, your envoys, have presented your signed communication and asked about the matters contained in it. [18] Whatever had to be referred to the king I called to his attention, and the things that were acceptable he has granted. [19] If you maintain your loyalty to the

NRSV

13As he was not without intelligence, he pondered over the defeat that had befallen him, and realized that the Hebrews were invincible because the mighty God fought on their side. So he sent to them [14]and persuaded them to settle everything on just terms, promising that he would persuade the king, constraining him to be their friend.[a] [15]Maccabeus, having regard for the common good, agreed to all that Lysias urged. For the king granted every request in behalf of the Jews which Maccabeus delivered to Lysias in writing.

16The letter written to the Jews by Lysias was to this effect:

"Lysias to the people of the Jews, greetings. [17]John and Absalom, who were sent by you, have delivered your signed communication and have asked about the matters indicated in it. [18]I have informed the king of everything that needed to be brought before him, and he has agreed to what

[a] Meaning of Gk uncertain

government, I will endeavor to further your interests in the future. ²⁰ On the details of these matters I have authorized my representatives, as well as your envoys, to confer with you. ²¹ Farewell." The year one hundred and forty-eight, the twenty-fourth of Dioscorinthius.

²² The king's letter read thus: "King Antiochus sends greetings to his brother Lysias. ²³ Now that our father has taken his place among the gods, we wish the subjects of our kingdom to be undisturbed in conducting their own affairs. ²⁴ We understand that the Jews do not agree with our father's policy concerning Greek customs but prefer their own way of life. They are petitioning us to let them retain their own customs. ²⁵ Since we desire that this people too should be undisturbed, our decision is that their temple be restored to them and that they live in keeping with the customs of their ancestors. ²⁶ Accordingly, please send them messengers to give them our assurances of friendship, so that, when they learn of our decision, they may have nothing to worry about but may contentedly go about their own business."

²⁷ The king's letter to the people was as follows: "King Antiochus sends greetings to the Jewish senate and to the rest of the Jews. ²⁸ If you are well, it is what we desire. We too are in good health. ²⁹ Menelaus has told us of your wish to return home and attend to your own affairs. ³⁰ Therefore, those who return by the thirtieth of Xanthicus will have our assurance of full permission ³¹ to observe their dietary laws and other laws, just as before, and none of the Jews shall be molested in any way for faults committed through ignorance. ³² I have also sent Menelaus to reassure you. ³³ Farewell." In the year one hundred and forty-eight, the fifteenth of Xanthicus.

³⁴ The Romans also sent them a letter as follows: "Quintus Memmius and Titus Manius, legates of the Romans, send greetings to the Jewish people. ³⁵ Whatever Lysias, kinsman of the king, has granted you, we also approve. ³⁶ But the matters on which he passed judgment should be submitted to the king. As soon as you have considered them, send someone to us with your decisions so that we may present them to your

was possible. ¹⁹If you will maintain your goodwill toward the government, I will endeavor in the future to help promote your welfare. ²⁰And concerning such matters and their details, I have ordered these men and my representatives to confer with you. ²¹Farewell. The one hundred forty-eighth year,ᵃ Dioscorinthius twenty-fourth."

²²The king's letter ran thus:

"King Antiochus to his brother Lysias, greetings. ²³Now that our father has gone on to the gods, we desire that the subjects of the kingdom be undisturbed in caring for their own affairs. ²⁴We have heard that the Jews do not consent to our father's change to Greek customs, but prefer their own way of living and ask that their own customs be allowed them. ²⁵Accordingly, since we choose that this nation also should be free from disturbance, our decision is that their temple be restored to them and that they shall live according to the customs of their ancestors. ²⁶You will do well, therefore, to send word to them and give them pledges of friendship, so that they may know our policy and be of good cheer and go on happily in the conduct of their own affairs."

²⁷To the nation the king's letter was as follows:

"King Antiochus to the senate of the Jews and to the other Jews, greetings. ²⁸If you are well, it is as we desire. We also are in good health. ²⁹Menelaus has informed us that you wish to return home and look after your own affairs. ³⁰Therefore those who go home by the thirtieth of Xanthicus will have our pledge of friendship and full permission ³¹for the Jews to enjoy their own food and laws, just as formerly, and none of them shall be molested in any way for what may have been done in ignorance. ³²And I have also sent Menelaus to encourage you. ³³Farewell. The one hundred forty-eighth year,ᵃ Xanthicus fifteenth."

³⁴The Romans also sent them a letter, which read thus:

"Quintus Memmius and Titus Manius, envoys of the Romans, to the people of the Jews, greetings. ³⁵With regard to what Lysias the kinsman of the king has granted you, we also give consent. ³⁶But as to the matters that he decided are to be referred to the king, as soon as you have consi-

ᵃ 164 B.C.

advantage, for we are on our way to Antioch. [37] Make haste, then, to send us those who can inform us of your intentions. [38] Farewell." In the year one hundred and forty-eight, the fifteenth of Xanthicus.

dered them, send some one promptly so that we may make proposals appropriate for you. For we are on our way to Antioch. [37]Therefore make haste and send messengers so that we may have your judgment. [38]Farewell. The one hundred forty-eighth year,[a] Xanthicus fifteenth."

[a] 164 B.C.

COMMENTARY

While Lysias is said in 1 Maccabees to retreat to Antioch in order to regroup and gather an even larger force (1 Macc 4:35), here, continuing under the assumption that these events occurred during the reign of Antiochus V, Lysias recognizes, even as Heliodorus had done (2 Macc 3:38-39), that the Hebrews were invincible while God was their ally (v. 13). Such a realization leads Lysias to negotiate for peace (v. 14; cf. the request of the Hasideans at 1 Macc 7:12, where the same phrase "just terms" [δίκαιοι *dikaioi*] is used). The end of v. 14 is difficult, as two verbs "persuade" (πείθω *peithō*) and "compel" (ἀναγκάζω *anagkazō*) are found. The verse should be translated: "promising that he would compel the king to be their friend." Most likely scribes found it doubtful that a minister could compel a king to do anything and so inserted the verb for "to persuade." Just as Onias III had the people's welfare in view (2 Macc 4:6), so too does Judas (v. 15), who sets down the terms in writing.

The context allows the author to insert four documents, the dating, content, and order of which have been much discussed. Three of the letters, the first (vv. 16-21), the third (vv. 27-33), and the fourth (vv. 34-38), are dated to the 148th year, which precedes the death of Antiochus IV. The second letter (vv. 22-26) is undated. The dates given in the documents also represent problems. The month mentioned in the first letter, Dioscorinthius (v. 21), is otherwise unknown in the Macedonian calendar. In addition, both the third and the fourth letters are dated 15 Xanthicus (vv. 33, 38), although their respective contents make it improbable that they were written on the same day. According to the third letter, it was Menelaus and not Judas who conducted the ne-

gotiations with Lysias (v. 32), whereas the first and fourth letters seem unlikely to have originated from Menelaus's followers. The order of the letters does not seem correct, as the fourth letter precedes the decision of the king, while the second and third are decisions of a king.

Accordingly, scholars have sought the correct dating and occasion for these letters. Such a search, however, depends on the way one reconstructs the sequence of events. According to C. Habicht's reconstruction, letter three reflects a mission of peace by Menelaus to Antiochus IV before setting out on his eastern expedition.[91] When this mission failed, Lysias made his first attack on Judea, but when it in turn failed, he entered into negotiations with the rebels. The negotiations broke down when Antiochus IV died, thus letter two grants amnesty to the rebels on Antiochus V's accession to the throne. According to Bar-Kochva's reconstruction, after the defeat of Nicanor and Gorgias, Ptolemy son of Dorymenes, an enemy of the Jews, was replaced by Ptolemy Macron, friendly to the Jews (2 Macc 10:12), and negotiations with the rebels began.[92] The first letter thus represents an interim report on the negotiations, and letter four a sign of Roman willingness to help negotiate. According to Bar-Kochva, Antiochus IV refused to negotiate, but Menelaus's request for conditional amnesty was allowed (letter three). Letter two is the official reprieve of the persecution by Antiochus V. In general, the arguments of Bar-Kochva are very plausible, although letter three should probably be

91. C. Habicht, "Royal Documents in Maccabees II," *Harvard Studies in Classical Philology* 80 (1976) 1-18.
92. B. Bar-Kochva, *Judas Maccabeus* (Cambridge: Cambridge University Press, 1989) 516-42.

placed earlier. After the failure of local initiatives against the rebels in 166/165 BCE (1 Macc 3:10-26; 2 Maccabees 8), Menelaus saw the opportunity to convince Antiochus IV that his measures in Jerusalem were ill-conceived and that a conditional amnesty and the end of the religious persecutions should take place. Antiochus IV agreed while on his expedition to the eastern satrapies (March 164 BCE; letter three). For some unknown reason, possibly because of the popular hatred of Menelaus and the belief that he was a traitor (2 Macc 4:39-50; 5:15), the amnesty offer was rejected. Lysias took up peace negotiations again after his first expedition (letter one), and the Roman emissaries asked Judas's group for a report on the negotiations (letter four). Either at the death of Antiochus IV or at the end of Lysias's second expedition, after the Seleucids had recaptured Jerusalem (1 Macc 6:48-59), letter two returned to the Jews the Temple and the repeal of the edicts against the ancestral religion.

11:16-21, The First Letter. Lysias chooses a neutral term, πλῆθος (*plēthos,* which may mean "multitude" or "mass," sometimes "people"; cf. 1 Macc 8:20), to refer to the addressees (v. 16), rather than the formal "nation" (ἔθνος *ethnos*), "senate" (γερουσία *gerousia*), or "people" (δῆμος *dēmos*). Such a neutral address suggests that the letter was not written to a formally recognized group within the Seleucid Empire. The envoys of this group, John and Absalom (v. 17), are otherwise unknown, but it is interesting that they bear Hebrew, not Greek, names. Two sons of an Absalom, Mattathias (1 Macc 11:70) and Jonathan (1 Macc 13:11), fight alongside Judas's successors, Jonathan and Simon. The document referred to in v. 17 is said to be "appended below" (ἐπιδόντες *epidontes*) to this letter, not "delivered" (NRSV) or "presented" (NAB). Verse 18 distinguishes between those issues that had to be referred to the king and those that Lysias felt competent to grant. The verse should not be translated "he has agreed to what was possible" (NRSV) but rather "what lies within my competence, I have agreed to" (author's trans.). Lysias leaves the working out of further specifics to his subordinates (v. 20). "Goodwill" (εὔνοια *eunoia,* v. 19) is the same word used in the letter of Antiochus IV (2 Macc 9:21, 26). The year 148 in the Macedonian Seleucid calendar (v. 21) would lie between Oc-

tober 165 and September 164 BCE. Dioscorinthius has been interpreted as Dios, the first month in the Macedonian calendar, or Dystros, the fifth month, or Daisios, the eight month.

11:22-26, The Second Letter. This letter is undated. Verse 23 uses a phrase that was customarily used at the death of a king (cf. 2 Macc 4:7) and would suggest a time near the accession of Antiochus V. As such, the letter would be a granting of amnesty at the start of a reign. Yet Bar-Kochva suggests that the writer uses vague, "diplomatic" wording to cover recent negative actions and to point to a new start; thus he dates the letter after the second campaign of Lysias (the negotiations mentioned at 1 Macc 6:59).[93]

Antiochus's addressing Lysias as "brother" is normal court language, and does not infer a close relationship between them; Lysias held the rank of kinsman (2 Macc 11:1). The desire for one's kingdom to be undisturbed is found also in the Greek Esth 3:13, but there it is given as a reason for destroying the disturbing Jews. Although the author of 2 Maccabees saw the reforms initiated by Jason as the adoption of Greek customs (2 Macc 4:10-11), the letter here (v. 24) refers most probably to the decrees of Antiochus IV (1 Macc 1:41-59; 2 Macc 6:1 uses the same verb "conduct their lives," "live" [πολιτεύομαι *politeuomai*] found in v. 25). The language in v. 25 is very similar to that of the letter of Antiochus III, when the king declared that the Jews should live by their ancestral religion.[94] According to v. 25, the letter also stipulates the restoration of the Temple. However, if this letter is dated to the beginning of Antiochus V's reign, the Temple already was under Judas's control, and this is simply a diplomatic recognition of the status quo. If the letter is dated to the end of the second expedition (1 Macc 6:55-62), it is a real concession.

11:27-33, The Third Letter. The "senate" (*gerousia,* v. 27) is known from the same letter of Antiochus III (see above) and was the official municipal body in Jerusalem (2 Macc 4:44). The mention of Menelaus (v. 29) raises the question of whether the letter was addressed only to his supporters. The accompanying phrase, "to other Jews," seems to be quite general. As at v. 23, the

93. B. Bar-Kochva, *Judas Maccabeus* (Cambridge: Cambridge University Press, 1989) 523-25.
94. See Josephus *Antiquities of the Jews* 12.142.

Jews are said to wish to return to normality (vv. 29, 31). The letter mentions two dates, 30 Xanthicus (i.e., the end of March 164 BCE), and 15 Xanthicus, the middle of March 164 BCE. In the later *Megillat Ta'anit*, the *Scroll of Fasting*, an entry dated 28 Adar (February/March) states that the good news reached the Jews that they did not have to depart from the Torah. Given that the date of this entry is March 164, then the king must be Antiochus IV, as it seems unlikely that his nine-year-old son would have written such a letter, even at the direction of Lysias. Since Antiochus IV had left for the eastern campaign in late 165 BCE, Menelaus must have accompanied him or perhaps visited him during his first stop in Greater Armenia, to the northeast of Syria. Fifteen days to deliver this document from Greater Armenia (or from Media) to Jerusalem and to announce the amnesty would be cutting it very close. Perhaps Antiochus agreed to Menelaus's request in principle and the letter was dated from the chancery at Antioch. Nevertheless, the amnesty ends the persecution, allowing the Jews to follow their own customs (vv. 30-31; emending the text to διαιτήματα [*diaitēmata*], rather than to δαπανήματα [*dapanēmata*], as the Kosher laws would have been included in the reference to the Torah). But amnesty is conditional upon the cessation of hostilities and the return home of the rebels. If this condition was not met, hostility would break out again.

This letter is very important and intriguing for the role it gives to Menelaus. Since the rest of 2 Maccabees portrays Menelaus as a traitor to Judaism, it is difficult to determine what role he is playing. Perhaps he supported Antiochus's suppression of Judaism in the beginning but later saw that policy as losing ground. Or perhaps he recognized that if he was to remain as civil as well as religious leader of Judea, he would have to switch position and try reconciliation before things got too out of hand in Judea. Or does this letter reveal him as someone who, a little over two years after Antiochus IV had forcibly attempted to suppress Judaism in Judea, succeeded in showing him the stupidity of these measures and convinced him to allow the Jews in Judea to follow their ancestral customs? Does Menelaus comes across, not as a traitor to Judaism, but as an advocate for his people who tries to change the monarch's will not by armed confrontation but by slowly working on him diplomatically? Was it his diplomacy combined with the Maccabean successes that won the day?

11:34-38, The Fourth Letter. After the Romans had forced Antiochus IV from Egypt in 168, they had kept a wary eye on Antiochus IV and his ambitions and did not want him cooperating with Eumenes II of Pergamum. An embassy had been sent to Antioch in 166 BCE, led by T. Sempronius Gracchus. A third embassy would be sent in 163/62, during which the Roman ambassador Octavius would be killed after ordering the Seleucid fleet burned and the Seleucid war elephants hamstrung, since they had contravened the peace treaty of Apamea. The embassy referred to in this letter probably took place in autumn 164, so the date appended to the letter should be disregarded as having been copied from the third letter. The embassy contacted the Jewish forces under Judas, addressing them as "a people" (δῆμος *dēmos*) rather than "a multitude" (*plēthos*; the same term is found in official correspondence in 1 Macc 8:29; 12:6; 14:20, 23; 15:17). Such a recognition was tacit support of the rebels. Rome enjoyed putting a cat among the chickens; also in 164 the Roman commissioner G. Sulpicius Gallus publicly invited accusations against Eumenes II of Pergamum in his own capital at Sardis.[95]

95. Polybius 31.6

REFLECTIONS

This chapter raises interesting questions about how one is to confront aggression. It is noteworthy that 1 Maccabees is completely silent about these first peace negotiations of Menelaus and Lysias; when the author does mention peace attempts after Lysias's second expedition, it is only to point out that one cannot trust the Seleucids, since they always break their word (1 Macc 6:55-63). In fact, the author of 1 Maccabees shows distinct reserve about relations with the Seleucids and seems always to argue that Judea was able to defend itself independently against its neighbors, who were always suspect. On the other hand, 2 Maccabees is open to negotiations with the Seleucid central government, but argues that these always fail because of jealous minor officials (2 Macc 12:2; 14:26). It also denigrates the memory of Menelaus, who attempted to restore the ancestral customs. What one has to ponder again is when and if one has to resort to armed resistance to counter naked aggression. Under what conditions does non-violent resistance work, and when will it only lead to annihilation of the people and its culture? The third letter suggests that a balanced combination of diplomacy and show of force may be the most pragmatic approach in an armed world for nations to settle disputes.

The fourth letter suggests that the intervention of an outside force may be required to get negotiations going. Such intervention usually does not work, however, if the parties do not want to negotiate. If people want to kill one another, it is exceedingly difficult to stop them. The Romans were not at all altruistic in their intervention. They were seeking to extend their power base. But an organization such as the United Nations can be helpful in bringing opposing parties to the bargaining table and in helping to limit disputes. Its power is limited, however, by the will of the parties involved in the conflict. When all sides have become sickened by the killing, then a mediator like the U.N. can be of most assistance—not when warring factions insist on continuing the conflict.

2 Maccabees 12:1-45, Further Local Hostilities

NAB

12 After these agreements were made, Lysias returned to the king, and the Jews went about their farming. ² But some of the local governors, Timothy and Apollonius, son of Gennaeus, as also Hieronymus and Demophon, to say nothing of Nicanor, the commander of the Cyprians, would not allow them to live in peace.

³ Some people of Joppa also committed this outrage: they invited the Jews who lived among them, together with their wives and children, to embark on boats which they had provided. There was no hint of enmity toward them: ⁴ this was done by public vote of the city. When the Jews, not suspecting treachery and wishing to live on friendly terms, accepted the invitation, the people of Joppa took them out to sea and drowned at least two hundred of them.

⁵ As soon as Judas heard of the barbarous deed perpetrated against his countrymen, he summoned his men; ⁶ and after calling upon God, the just judge, he marched against the murderers of his kinsmen. In a night attack he set the harbor on fire, burnt the boats, and put to the sword those who had taken refuge there. ⁷ When the gates of the town were shut, he withdrew, in-

NRSV

12 When this agreement had been reached, Lysias returned to the king, and the Jews went about their farming.

2But some of the governors in various places, Timothy and Apollonius son of Gennaeus, as well as Hieronymus and Demophon, and in addition to these Nicanor the governor of Cyprus, would not let them live quietly and in peace. ³And the people of Joppa did so ungodly a deed as this: they invited the Jews who lived among them to embark, with their wives and children, on boats that they had provided, as though there were no ill will to the Jews;ᵃ ⁴and this was done by public vote of the city. When they accepted, because they wished to live peaceably and suspected nothing, the people of Joppaᵇ took them out to sea and drowned them, at least two hundred. ⁵When Judas heard of the cruelty visited on his compatriots, he gave orders to his men ⁶and, calling upon God, the righteous judge, attacked the murderers of his kindred. He set fire to the harbor by night, burned the boats, and massacred those who had taken refuge there. ⁷Then, because the city's gates were closed, he withdrew, intending to come again and root out the whole community

ᵃ Gk *to them*   ᵇ Gk *they*

tending to come back later and wipe out the entire population of Joppa.

⁸ On hearing that the men of Jamnia planned to give like treatment to the Jews who lived among them, ⁹ he attacked the Jamnian populace by night, setting fire to the harbor and the fleet, so that the glow of the flames was visible as far as Jerusalem, thirty miles away.

¹⁰ When the Jews had gone about a mile from there in the campaign against Timothy, they were attacked by Arabs numbering at least five thousand foot soldiers, and five hundred horsemen. ¹¹ After a hard fight, Judas and his companions, with God's help, were victorious. The defeated nomads begged Judas to make friends with them and promised to supply the Jews with cattle and to help them in every other way. ¹² Realizing that they could indeed be useful in many respects, Judas agreed to make peace with them. After the pledge of friendship had been exchanged, the Arabs withdrew to their tents.

¹³ He also attacked a certain city called Caspin, fortified with earthworks and ramparts and inhabited by a mixed population of Gentiles. ¹⁴ Relying on the strength of their walls and their supply of provisions, the besieged treated Judas and his men with contempt, insulting them and even uttering blasphemies and profanity. ¹⁵ But Judas and his men invoked the aid of the great Sovereign of the world, who, in the day of Joshua, overthrew Jericho without battering-ram or siege machine; then they furiously stormed the ramparts. ¹⁶ Capturing the city by the will of God, they inflicted such indescribable slaughter on it that the adjacent pool, which was about a quarter of a mile wide, seemed to be filled with the blood that flowed into it.

¹⁷ When they had gone on some ninety miles, they reached Charax, where there were certain Jews known as Toubiani. ¹⁸ But they did not find Timothy in that region, for he had already departed from there without having done anything except to leave behind in one place a very strong garrison. ¹⁹ But Dositheus and Sosipater, two of Maccabeus' captains, marched out and destroyed the force of more than ten thousand men that Timothy had left in the stronghold. ²⁰ Meanwhile, Maccabeus divided his army into cohorts, with a

of Joppa. ⁸But learning that the people in Jamnia meant in the same way to wipe out the Jews who were living among them, ⁹he attacked the Jamnites by night and set fire to the harbor and the fleet, so that the glow of the light was seen in Jerusalem, thirty milesᵃ distant.

10When they had gone more than a mileᵇ from there, on their march against Timothy, at least five thousand Arabs with five hundred cavalry attacked them. ¹¹After a hard fight, Judas and his companions, with God's help, were victorious. The defeated nomads begged Judas to grant them pledges of friendship, promising to give him livestock and to help his peopleᶜ in all other ways. ¹²Judas, realizing that they might indeed be useful in many ways, agreed to make peace with them; and after receiving his pledges they went back to their tents.

13He also attacked a certain town that was strongly fortified with earthworksᵈ and walls, and inhabited by all sorts of Gentiles. Its name was Caspin. ¹⁴Those who were within, relying on the strength of the walls and on their supply of provisions, behaved most insolently toward Judas and his men, railing at them and even blaspheming and saying unholy things. ¹⁵But Judas and his men, calling upon the great Sovereign of the world, who without battering rams or engines of war overthrew Jericho in the days of Joshua, rushed furiously upon the walls. ¹⁶They took the town by the will of God, and slaughtered untold numbers, so that the adjoining lake, a quarter of a mileᵉ wide, appeared to be running over with blood.

17When they had gone ninety-five milesᶠ from there, they came to Charax, to the Jews who are called Toubiani. ¹⁸They did not find Timothy in that region, for he had by then left there without accomplishing anything, though in one place he had left a very strong garrison. ¹⁹Dositheus and Sosipater, who were captains under Maccabeus, marched out and destroyed those whom Timothy had left in the stronghold, more than ten thousand men. ²⁰But Maccabeus arranged his army in divisions, set menᶜ in command of the divisions, and hurried after Timothy, who had with him one

ᵃ Gk *two hundred forty stadia*   ᵇ Gk *nine stadia*
ᶜ Gk *them*   ᵈ Meaning of Gk uncertain   ᵉ Gk *two stadia*
ᶠ Gk *seven hundred fifty stadiaⁱ*

NAB

commander over each cohort, and went in pursuit of Timothy, who had a force of a hundred and twenty thousand foot soldiers and twenty-five hundred horsemen. [21] When Timothy learned of the approach of Judas, he sent on ahead of him the women and children, as well as the baggage, to a place called Karnion, which was hard to besiege and even hard to reach because of the difficult terrain of that region. [22] But when Judas' first cohort appeared, the enemy was overwhelmed with fear and terror at the manifestation of the All-seeing. Scattering in every direction, they rushed away in such headlong flight that in many cases they wounded one another, pierced by the swords of their own men. [23] Judas pressed the pursuit vigorously, putting the sinners to the sword and destroying as many as thirty thousand men.

[24] Timothy himself fell into the hands of the men under Dositheus and Sosipater; but with great cunning, he asked them to spare his life and let him go, because he had in his power the parents and relatives of many of them, and could make these suffer. [25] When he had fully confirmed his solemn pledge to restore them unharmed, they let him go for the sake of saving their brethren.

[26] Judas then marched to Karnion and the shrine of Atargatis, where he killed twenty-five thousand people. [27] After the defeat and destruction of these, he moved his army to Ephron, a fortified city inhabited by people of many nationalities. Robust young men took up their posts in defense of the walls, from which they fought valiantly; inside were large supplies of machines and missiles. [28] But the Jews, invoking the Sovereign who forcibly shatters the might of his enemies, got possession of the city and slaughtered twenty-five thousand of the people in it. [29] Then they set out from there and hastened on to Scythopolis, seventy-five miles from Jerusalem. [30] But when the Jews who lived there testified to the good will shown by the Scythopolitans and to their kind treatment even in times of adversity, [31] Judas and his men thanked them and exhorted them to be well disposed to their race in the future also. Finally they arrived in Jerusalem, shortly before the feast of Weeks.

NRSV

hundred twenty thousand infantry and two thousand five hundred cavalry. [21] When Timothy learned of the approach of Judas, he sent off the women and the children and also the baggage to a place called Carnaim; for that place was hard to besiege and difficult of access because of the narrowness of all the approaches. [22] But when Judas's first division appeared, terror and fear came over the enemy at the manifestation to them of him who sees all things. In their flight they rushed headlong in every direction, so that often they were injured by their own men and pierced by the points of their own swords. [23] Judas pressed the pursuit with the utmost vigor, putting the sinners to the sword, and destroyed as many as thirty thousand.

[24] Timothy himself fell into the hands of Dositheus and Sosipater and their men. With great guile he begged them to let him go in safety, because he held the parents of most of them, and the brothers of some, to whom no consideration would be shown. [25] And when with many words he had confirmed his solemn promise to restore them unharmed, they let him go, for the sake of saving their kindred.

[26] Then Judas[a] marched against Carnaim and the temple of Atargatis, and slaughtered twenty-five thousand people. [27] After the rout and destruction of these, he marched also against Ephron, a fortified town where Lysias lived with multitudes of people of all nationalities.[b] Stalwart young men took their stand before the walls and made a vigorous defense; and great stores of war engines and missiles were there. [28] But the Jews[c] called upon the Sovereign who with power shatters the might of his enemies, and they got the town into their hands, and killed as many as twenty-five thousand of those who were in it.

[29] Setting out from there, they hastened to Scythopolis, which is seventy-five miles[d] from Jerusalem. [30] But when the Jews who lived there bore witness to the goodwill that the people of Scythopolis had shown them and their kind treatment of them in times of misfortune, [31] they thanked them and exhorted them to be well disposed to their race in the future also. Then they

a Gk *he*   b Meaning of Gk uncertain   c Gk *they*
d Gk *six hundred stadia*

NAB

³² After this feast called Pentecost, they lost no time in marching against Gorgias, governor of Idumea, ³³ who opposed them with three thousand foot soldiers and four hundred horsemen. ³⁴ In the ensuing battle, a few of the Jews were slain. ³⁵ A man called Dositheus, a powerful horseman and one of Bacenor's men, caught hold of Gorgias, grasped his military cloak and dragged him along by main strength, intending to capture the vile wretch alive, when a Thracian horseman attacked Dositheus and cut off his arm at the shoulder. Then Gorgias fled to Marisa. ³⁶ After Esdris and his men had been fighting for a long time and were weary, Judas called upon the LORD to show himself their ally and leader in the battle. ³⁷ Then, raising a battle cry in his ancestral language, and with songs, he charged Gorgias' men when they were not expecting it and put them to flight.

³⁸ Judas rallied his army and went to the city of Adullam. As the week was ending, they purified themselves according to custom and kept the sabbath there. ³⁹ On the following day, since the task had now become urgent, Judas and his men went to gather up the bodies of the slain and bury them with their kinsmen in their ancestral tombs. ⁴⁰ But under the tunic of each of the dead they found amulets sacred to the idols of Jamnia, which the law forbids the Jews to wear. So it was clear to all that this was why these men had been slain. ⁴¹ They all therefore praised the ways of the LORD, the just judge who brings to light the things that are hidden. ⁴² Turning to supplication, they prayed that the sinful deed might be fully blotted out. The noble Judas warned the soldiers to keep themselves free from sin, for they had seen with their own eyes what had happened because of the sin of those who had fallen. ⁴³ He then took up a collection among all his soldiers, amounting to two thousand silver drachmas, which he sent to Jerusalem to provide for an expiatory sacrifice. In doing this he acted in a very excellent and noble way, inasmuch as he had the resurrection of the dead in view; ⁴⁴ for if he were not expecting the fallen to rise again, it would have been useless and foolish to pray for them in death. ⁴⁵ But if he did this with a view to the splendid reward that

NRSV

went up to Jerusalem, as the festival of weeks was close at hand.

³²After the festival called Pentecost, they hurried against Gorgias, the governor of Idumea, ³³who came out with three thousand infantry and four hundred cavalry. ³⁴When they joined battle, it happened that a few of the Jews fell. ³⁵But a certain Dositheus, one of Bacenor's men, who was on horseback and was a strong man, caught hold of Gorgias, and grasping his cloak was dragging him off by main strength, wishing to take the accursed man alive, when one of the Thracian cavalry bore down on him and cut off his arm; so Gorgias escaped and reached Marisa.

³⁶As Esdris and his men had been fighting for a long time and were weary, Judas called upon the Lord to show himself their ally and leader in the battle. ³⁷In the language of their ancestors he raised the battle cry, with hymns; then he charged against Gorgias's troops when they were not expecting it, and put them to flight.

³⁸Then Judas assembled his army and went to the city of Adullam. As the seventh day was coming on, they purified themselves according to the custom, and kept the sabbath there.

³⁹On the next day, as had now become necessary, Judas and his men went to take up the bodies of the fallen and to bring them back to lie with their kindred in the sepulchres of their ancestors. ⁴⁰Then under the tunic of each one of the dead they found sacred tokens of the idols of Jamnia, which the law forbids the Jews to wear. And it became clear to all that this was the reason these men had fallen. ⁴¹So they all blessed the ways of the Lord, the righteous judge, who reveals the things that are hidden; ⁴²and they turned to supplication, praying that the sin that had been committed might be wholly blotted out. The noble Judas exhorted the people to keep themselves free from sin, for they had seen with their own eyes what had happened as the result of the sin of those who had fallen. ⁴³He also took up a collection, man by man, to the amount of two thousand drachmas of silver, and sent it to Jerusalem to provide for a sin offering. In doing this he acted very well and honorably, taking account of the resurrection. ⁴⁴For if he were not expecting that those who had fallen would rise again, it

awaits those who had gone to rest in godliness, it was a holy and pious thought. Thus he made atonement for the dead that they might be freed from this sin.

would have been superfluous and foolish to pray for the dead. [45]But if he was looking to the splendid reward that is laid up for those who fall asleep in godliness, it was a holy and pious thought. Therefore he made atonement for the dead, so that they might be delivered from their sin.

COMMENTARY

12:1-2. This chapter details hostilities with local officials. The author insists, as he often does, that the Jews are peaceful (10:14-15; 14:25), only desirous of following their own customs undisturbed (v. 1). However, their enemies will not leave them alone (v. 2). The author of 2 Maccabees regards the Timothy in these verses as distinct from the Timothy who earlier invaded Judea and whose death is recorded in 10:37, but most likely the author is mistaken. The Apollonius mentioned here is distinguished from others of the same name (Apollonius captain of the Mysians [2 Macc 5:24] and Apollonius from Samaria [1 Macc 3:10-11]). Hieronymus and Demophon are otherwise unknown. Nicanor was not "governor of Cyprus," which was then part of the Ptolemaic Empire, but was the commander of Cypriot troops, like Crates (2 Macc 4:29), and thus of quite a lower rank from the Nicanor mentioned in chaps. 8 and 14–15.

12:3-9. The incident of the drowning of the Jews of Joppa is not found in 1 Maccabees. Joppa was an important coastal harbor town, about thirty-two miles from Jerusalem (see 4:21). The Jews were not citizens, but lived in the town. Perhaps the Jews thought they were being given a pleasure cruise; v. 4 seems to suggest that they did not know the reason for the voyage, but obeyed simply to keep the peace, since the whole citizen body had voted in favor of it. Would a non-citizen minority group have had any say in the matter? Once again, in response to this tragedy, Judas and his forces call on God (cf. Ps 7:6-11). Judas is unable to take full revenge, however. Later his brother Simon will drive out the inhabitants of Joppa and settle there (1 Macc 13:11; 14:5). Jamnia lay about twelve miles south of Joppa, about thirty-four miles in a straight line from Jerusalem, but much farther by road. Thus it

is doubtful that a fire in Jamnia could actually have been seen in Jerusalem, but it is a nice hyperbole.

12:10-12. From this point on, the events in this chapter loosely parallel the account of Judas's campaign in Gilead as recorded in 1 Macc 5:9-36. This section begins awkwardly: A mile away from Jamnia and the west coast, the Israelites begin to march against Timothy in Transjordan (1 Macc 5:24), when they are attacked by Arabs (1 Macc 5:39 reports that Arabs served as mercenaries in Timothy's forces, but records that the first encounter with the Nabateans was a peaceful one [1 Macc 5:24-25]). The author of 2 Maccabees stresses God's help in the battle (v. 11). Judas again shows a willingness to negotiate peace (vv. 11-12). Later, Judas's brother Jonathan will draw on this friendship (1 Macc 9:35).

12:13-16. Although a town named Chaspho is mentioned at 1 Macc 5:36 as one of several cities captured by Judas in Gilead, here the author provides a more elaborate story of the capture of Caspin, which is probably the same city. The strength of the city is stressed as the basis for the inhabitants' arrogance (v. 14). As usual, the author contrasts the blasphemous behavior of the Gentiles with Judas's piety (v. 15; see also 10:34; 15:4-5). The reference to Joshua's attack on Jericho (Josh 6:1-21) provides a biblical example for the following destruction and slaughter. The gruesome image of the blood-filled lake (v. 16) is emotionally powerful and is similar to the image of how, in the war against Syracuse, the defeated Athenians were drinking the river stained with their own blood (cf. 2 Kgs 3:22-23).[96]

96. Thucydides 7.84.

12:17-26. Judas and his men travel about ninety miles south to the area around Araq-el-Emir, where Hyrcanus the Tobiad had built a fort (see 3:11). Since the battle with Timothy occurs at Carnaim, near Caspin, this account seems to have been misplaced. According to 1 Macc 5:13, all the male Jews in the "land of Tobiani" (ἐν τοῖς Τουβίου *en tois Toubiou*) had been killed as part of the persecution of the Jews that had prompted Judas's expedition into Gilead. The author of 2 Maccabees, to the contrary, insists that Timothy had not accomplished anything except to leave a garrison behind (v. 18), perhaps at one of the deserted strongholds of the Toubiani. At this point in the narrative of 1 Maccabees, Judas divides his forces into three parts, one under Simon to go to Galilee, another under himself and Jonathan to go into Gilead, the third under Joseph and Azariah to be left in Judah (1 Macc 5:17-18). The author of 2 Maccabees may allude to this in v. 20. The parallel account of the battle with Timothy (vv. 20-26) is found at 1 Macc 5:37-43. Although both engagements take place around Carnaim, the two accounts vary greatly. The size of Timothy's forces is greatly exaggerated (v. 20; see 1 Macc 5:38). According to the author, another epiphany of God takes place (v. 22). Timothy's army reacts in terror and fear (cf. Exod 15:16; Deut 2:25; 11:25) and flees in panic (cf. Josh 10:10; 1 Sam 7:10; 2 Kgs 7:6-7; the description of God as "the one who sees all things" is also found at 2 Macc 15:2; see also Exod 2:25; 2 Macc 7:6). Judas's victory (v. 23) is not complete, since Dositheus and Sosipater, who had successfully destroyed Timothy's garrison (v. 19) are deceived by Timothy (vv. 24-25). Their motive, however, is praiseworthy in contrast to that of the troops under Simon, who had accepted bribes to allow their enemies to escape (2 Macc 10:20).

Judas now destroys Carnaim, where the women and children of Timothy's camp had taken refuge (v. 21), and the temple of Atargatis (v. 26). Atargatis, the Syrian goddess and consort of Hadad, was identified with the Canaanite goddess Astarte. The meaning of "Carnaim" is "two horns," which may reflect the iconography of the goddess, where the horns symbolize power (cf. 1 Kgs 22:11; Zech 1:18-21).

12:27-28. According to 1 Macc 5:45-51, Judas escorted all the Jews in Gilead back to Judea.

In these verses, he marches toward Ephron, which lay on the road back to Judea. The townspeople, however, will not let the army through, whereupon Judas besieges and destroys the city. This account suggests that Lysias, the chancellor of Syria, had a residence in this Transjordanian town (v. 27), which prompts the attack. The story seems typecast like that of the siege of Caspin (12:13-16): a mixed multitude in a well-defended town (v. 27), the prayer of the Jews (v. 28), the sovereign who shatters the enemy (cf. Exod 15:3, 7; Josh 10:10). The number killed is the same as at Carnaim, 25,000 (vv. 26, 28).

12:29-31. Scythopolis, or Beth-shean, is mentioned at 1 Macc 5:52 as a place the refugees from Gilead simply pass by. Here, no reason is given for Judas's "hastening" there (v. 29). Perhaps the reason is that the author of 2 Maccabees enjoys recounting the goodwill between Gentiles and Jews (vv. 30-31; 2 Macc 9:21, 26). The Festival of Weeks, or Shabuot, was a harvest celebration (Exod 23:16; Lev 23:15-22) called Pentecost in Greek—i.e., the fifty days after Passover. The author stresses the piety of Judas's forces in that they break off their campaigning to celebrate the festival.

12:32-42a. The emphasis on the piety of Judas's forces (v. 31) is balanced by a story highlighting what happens to those who are not pious. Compare this passage with 1 Macc 5:55-68, which recounts an encounter with Gorgias near Jamnia in which Joseph and Azariah join battle with Gorgias on their own initiative and are defeated. The author of 1 Maccabees used the story as propaganda for the Hasmonean family.

12:32-37. After recounting battles to the east, the author now turns to activities in the south. Gorgias was already mentioned as harassing the Jews (10:14). The actual size of the battle is not given. The battle starts out poorly for the Jews (v. 34), until the heroic actions of Dositheus (v. 35), a cavalryman who should not be identified with the commander mentioned earlier (12:19, 24; the NRSV identifies him as one of Bacenor's men, but the better reading would have him as one of the Toubiani). The story here belongs to a bardic tradition of hero stories, like the roster of David's warriors in 2 Samuel 23. Whereas in the encounter in 1 Macc 5:55-61 Gorgias is victorious, here the author has him fleeing from the battle scene

(v. 35) like Nicanor (8:34-35) and Lysias (1:12), to Marisa, one of the major cities in Idumea. The commander Esdris is mentioned without any preparation (v. 36), another sign of the shorthand nature of the work. Some scholars have suggested that he should be identified with the Eleazar of 8:23. As he and his men tire, Judas calls on the Lord to be their ally and leader. The author again stresses the piety of Judas by noting his use of the ancestral language (v. 37), as had the martyred mother and her seven sons (7:21-27). The sudden frenzied onrush catches Gorgias's troops unawares. Some part of the battle description seems to have been left out, since it is unlikely that Gorgias's troops would have remained fighting after Gorgias had fled (v. 35).

12:38-42a. Judas, ever observant, goes to Adullam, about eight miles northeast of Marisa, and he and his soldiers purify themselves and keep the sabbath (v. 38). Since there is no specific need to purify oneself, to become ritually clean so that one can participate in temple service, before honoring the sabbath so far from the Temple, their purification seems, therefore, to refer to purifying oneself after coming into contact with a dead body (Num 19:10-22; 31:24).[97] As opposed to Jason (2 Macc 5:10), these fallen Israelite soldiers are to be buried in their ancestral tomb (v. 39)—not to be so buried was a punishment (1 Kgs 13:22). While 1 Maccabees explains the death of some of Judas's forces as being due to their jealousy of Judas and his brothers (1 Macc 5:56-62, 67), the author of 2 Maccabees explains it as their lack of Torah observance (v. 40). Under the tunic of each dead man was found "sacred tokens of the idols of Jamnia." These sacred objects may have been taken during the raid on Jamnia (12:8-9); such objects were forbidden to Jews (Deut 7:25-26). Greek inscriptions from Delos set up by people from Jamnia honor Heracles and Horon, two Phoenician deities. Would the soldiers have car-

ried booty into battle with them? More likely what they had were amulets used to protect the wearer. The proverbial wisdom that God sees all things is applied here (v. 41; see also 12:22; cf. Prov 15:11; 16:2; 24:12; Mark 4:22).

12:42b-45. These verses are difficult textually and also difficult to translate. Verse 42b seems to reflect a sacrifice for the reparation of the community, whose sin has come to light, similar to the reparation offering (Lev 4:13-35; the language of Lev 4:26, 35 is similar to that of 2 Macc 12:45). The community aspect of the sacrifice is shown by each man's contributing to the sacrifice (v. 43). The phrase "taking account of the resurrection" is a comment by the author that interprets Judas's action. As seen in chap. 7, the author believes in the resurrection. The language there (particularly 7:23) evokes the language of creation. The hope of the brothers (7:11, 14) is that they will live again in a newly created world. In this passage, vv. 44-45 offer two alternatives: *either* Judas does not think that the dead rise and believes that it is foolish to pray for them, *or* he believes that a reward awaits those who die piously, a holy and pious thought. Some scholars have suggested that the expressions "superfluous and foolish to pray for the dead" and "holy and pious thought" are later insertions. However, in the light of recent research on rituals for the dead in Israel (e.g., those rites underlying Isaiah 57), "to pray for the dead" may in fact reflect a custom of which only traces can be discerned. The Israelites clearly believed that the dead had another existence (see, e.g., Deut 18:11-12, which forbids seeking oracles from the dead; 1 Sam 28:14-19; Isa 65:4, which rails against those "who sit inside tombs,/ and spend the night in secret places" [NRSV]). The customs and rituals surrounding the dead suggest the belief that there is a community that stretches beyond death. The author argues that these customs and rituals mean that one can make atonement for those who have died; such practices presuppose a resurrection of the dead.

97. In the *War Scroll* from Qumran, the soldiers, after having left their dead enemies, all sing the Psalm of Return and, the morning after, wash their garments and cleanse themselves of the blood of the bodies of the ungodly. See 1QM 14:1-2.

REFLECTIONS

The story of the complicity of the citizens of Joppa in the murder of the Jews living among them has fearful resonances for us who live with the memories of the Holocaust of World

War II, the ethnic cleansing in Bosnia, and the genocide in Rwanda. We are not told in 2 Maccabees why the peoples round about took offensive action against the Jews. What we are forced to consider is how prejudice can grow and be present in traditional stories about the relations of peoples and how this prejudice can be kindled into active hatred by unscrupulous leaders. One way to prevent that might be to examine what stories we tell our children and whether they may contain unsympathetic portraits of other groups. Are ethnic jokes really all that funny? Should statements demeaning women or minority groups be tolerated?

One particular area in which this problem surfaces is the way the term οἱ Ἰουδαῖοι *hoi Ioudaioi* should be translated in the New Testament. The literal translation, "the Jews," most frequently occurs in the Gospel of John and the Acts of the Apostles, and in these two books it is regularly used to characterize those who oppose Jesus or the early movement of Jesus' followers after his death. The result is that "the Jews" appear as the villains in these books. An unsophisticated reader might even get the impression that Jesus and his followers were not even Jews. Such a reader would not grasp that not all Jews in the first century opposed Jesus' movement, and that often the people who did oppose Jesus were simply other Jews who did not accept Jesus as Messiah. Not all Jews were involved in the death of Jesus; the responsibility for Jesus' crucifixion falls on the Roman officials in Judea, as well as on some Jewish leaders at that time. Certainly "the Jews" as a blanket group are not Christ-killers, as the second-century Christian polemic against them would state and as they would be labeled throughout the medieval period. How, then, are we to translate *hoi Ioudaioi?* If we are to translate the term as "the Jews," we must be sure to point out that this term does not refer to all Jews, not even all Jews in the first century CE.

2 Maccabees 13:1-26, The Second Expedition of Lysias

NAB

13 In the year one hundred and forty-nine, Judas and his men learned that Antiochus Eupator was invading Judea with a large force, [2] and that with him was Lysias, his guardian, who was in charge of the government. They led a Greek army of one hundred and ten thousand foot soldiers, fifty-three hundred horsemen, twenty-two elephants, and three hundred chariots armed with scythes.

[3] Menelaus also joined them, and with great duplicity kept urging Antiochus on, not for the welfare of his country, but in the hope of being established in office. [4] But the King of kings aroused the anger of Antiochus against the scoundrel. When the king was shown by Lysias that Menelaus was to blame for all the trouble, he ordered him to be taken to Beroea and executed there in the customary local method. [5] There is at that place a tower seventy-five feet high, full of ashes, with a circular rim sloping down steeply on all sides toward the ashes. [6] A man guilty of

NRSV

13 In the one hundred forty-ninth year[a] word came to Judas and his men that Antiochus Eupator was coming with a great army against Judea, [2]and with him Lysias, his guardian, who had charge of the government. Each of them had a Greek force of one hundred ten thousand infantry, five thousand three hundred cavalry, twenty-two elephants, and three hundred chariots armed with scythes.

[3]Menelaus also joined them and with utter hypocrisy urged Antiochus on, not for the sake of his country's welfare, but because he thought that he would be established in office. [4]But the King of kings aroused the anger of Antiochus against the scoundrel; and when Lysias informed him that this man was to blame for all the trouble, he ordered them to take him to Beroea and to put him to death by the method that is customary in that place. [5]For there is a tower there, fifty cubits high, full of ashes, and it has a rim running around it that on all sides inclines precipitously into the

13, 6: *(pepoiēmenon) harpasantes (prosōthousin)*: conj.

a 163 B.C.

NAB

sacrilege or notorious for certain other crimes is brought up there and then hurled down to destruction. ⁷ In such a manner was Menelaus, the transgressor of the law, fated to die; he was deprived even of decent burial. ⁸ It was altogether just that he who had committed so many sins against the altar with its pure fire and ashes should meet his death in ashes.

⁹ The king was advancing, his mind full of savage plans for inflicting on the Jews worse things than those they suffered in his father's time. ¹⁰ When Judas learned of this, he urged the people to call upon the LORD night and day, to help them now, if ever, ¹¹ when they were about to be deprived of their law, their country, and their holy temple; and not to allow this nation, which had just begun to revive, to be subjected again to blasphemous Gentiles. ¹² When they had all joined in doing this, and had implored the merciful LORD continuously with weeping and fasting and prostrations for three days, Judas encouraged them and told them to stand ready. ¹³ After a private meeting with the elders, he decided that, before the king's army could invade Judea and take possession of the city, the Jews should march out and settle the matter with God's help. ¹⁴ Leaving the outcome to the Creator of the world, and exhorting his followers to fight nobly to death for the laws, the temple, the city, the country, and the government, he pitched his camp near Modein. ¹⁵ Giving his men the battle cry "God's Victory," he made a night attack on the king's pavilion with a picked force of the bravest young men and killed about two thousand in the camp. They also slew the lead elephant and its rider. ¹⁶ Finally they withdrew in triumph, having filled the camp with terror and confusion. ¹⁷ Day was just breaking when this was accomplished with the help and protection of the LORD.

¹⁸ The king, having had a taste of the Jews' daring, tried to take their positions by a stratagem. ¹⁹ So he marched against Beth-zur, a strong fortress of the Jews; but he was driven back, checked, and defeated. ²⁰ Judas then sent supplies to the men inside, ²¹ but Rhodocus, of the Jewish army, betrayed military secrets to the enemy. He was

13, 15: (*kat oikan onti*) *synekentēse*: conj; cf 1 Mc 6, 46.

NRSV

ashes. ⁶There they all push to destruction anyone guilty of sacrilege or notorious for other crimes. ⁷By such a fate it came about that Menelaus the lawbreaker died, without even burial in the earth. ⁸And this was eminently just; because he had committed many sins against the altar whose fire and ashes were holy, he met his death in ashes.

9The king with barbarous arrogance was coming to show the Jews things far worse than those that had been done*ᵃ* in his father's time. ¹⁰But when Judas heard of this, he ordered the people to call upon the Lord day and night, now if ever to help those who were on the point of being deprived of the law and their country and the holy temple, ¹¹and not to let the people who had just begun to revive fall into the hands of the blasphemous Gentiles. ¹²When they had all joined in the same petition and had implored the merciful Lord with weeping and fasting and lying prostrate for three days without ceasing, Judas exhorted them and ordered them to stand ready.

13After consulting privately with the elders, he determined to march out and decide the matter by the help of God before the king's army could enter Judea and get possession of the city. ¹⁴So, committing the decision to the Creator of the world and exhorting his troops to fight bravely to the death for the laws, temple, city, country, and commonwealth, he pitched his camp near Modein. ¹⁵He gave his troops the watchword, "God's victory," and with a picked force of the bravest young men, he attacked the king's pavilion at night and killed as many as two thousand men in the camp. He stabbed*ᵇ* the leading elephant and its rider. ¹⁶In the end they filled the camp with terror and confusion and withdrew in triumph. ¹⁷This happened, just as day was dawning, because the Lord's help protected him.

18The king, having had a taste of the daring of the Jews, tried strategy in attacking their positions. ¹⁹He advanced against Beth-zur, a strong fortress of the Jews, was turned back, attacked again,*ᶜ* and was defeated. ²⁰Judas sent in to the garrison whatever was necessary. ²¹But Rhodocus, a man from the ranks of the Jews, gave secret information to the enemy; he was sought for,

ᵃ Or *the worst of the things that had been done*   *ᵇ* Meaning of Gk uncertain   *ᶜ* Or *faltered*

NAB

found out, arrested, and imprisoned. ²² The king made a second attempt by negotiating with the men of Beth-zur. After giving them his pledge and receiving theirs, he withdrew ²³ and attacked Judas and his men. But he was defeated. Next he heard that Philip, who was left in charge of the government in Antioch, had rebelled. Dismayed, he parleyed with the Jews, submitted to their terms, and swore to observe their rights. Having come to this agreement, he offered a sacrifice, and honored the temple with a generous donation. ²⁴ He approved of Maccabeus and left him as military and civil governor of the territory from Ptolemais to the region of the Gerrenes. ²⁵ When he came to Ptolemais, the people of that city were angered by the peace treaty; in fact they were so indignant that they wanted to annul its provisions. ²⁶ But Lysias took the platform, defended the treaty as well as he could, and won them over by persuasion. After calming them and gaining their good will, he returned to Antioch.

That is how the king's attack and withdrawal went.

13, 24: *hēgemonidēn = hēgemona.*

NRSV

caught, and put in prison. ²²The king negotiated a second time with the people in Beth-zur, gave pledges, received theirs, withdrew, attacked Judas and his men, was defeated; ²³he got word that Philip, who had been left in charge of the government, had revolted in Antioch; he was dismayed, called in the Jews, yielded and swore to observe all their rights, settled with them and offered sacrifice, honored the sanctuary and showed generosity to the holy place. ²⁴He received Maccabeus, left Hegemonides as governor from Ptolemais to Gerar, ²⁵and went to Ptolemais. The people of Ptolemais were indignant over the treaty; in fact they were so angry that they wanted to annul its terms.^a ²⁶Lysias took the public platform, made the best possible defense, convinced them, appeased them, gained their goodwill, and set out for Antioch. This is how the king's attack and withdrawal turned out.

^a Meaning of Gk uncertain

COMMENTARY

The author of 2 Maccabees, like the author of 1 Maccabees, records two expeditions of Lysias against the Jews. The account in 2 Maccabees 13 parallels the one in 1 Macc 6:28-63, which dates the invasion to the 150th year in the Seleucid Babylonian calendar, or 162 BCE (1 Macc 6:20). Second Maccabees, however, which seems to use the Seleucid Macedonian calendar, places this invasion in 149, or between September 164 and October 163 BCE. The epitome in 2 Maccabees gives only two dates aside from those in the letters in chap. 11. Some scholars prefer the dating in 2 Maccabees, while others follow 1 Maccabees and propose that, since the letters in chap. 11 all carry the date of 148 Seleucid era, either Jason or the epitomist placed the second expedition a year later.

13:1-2. No explanation is given for the change of attitude toward the Jews after the supposed agreements in chap. 11, except that the young king wanted to do worse things than his father had done

(13:9). As the expedition comes after the events of chap. 12, these Seleucid setbacks must have been thought by the author sufficient reason. The force assembled is enormous and exaggerated, and the text followed by the NRSV should be emended. It is unreasonable that both Antiochus and Lysias would each have his own force, particularly since Antiochus V was a minor. Instead of reading "each of them" (ἕκαστος *hekastos*), the text should preferably be read as "besides" or "as well" (ἐκτός *ektos*), and thus translated "coming with Lysias, his guardian and chancellor, and he had as well a Greek force. . . . " It is also unlikely that scythed chariots would have been used, as they would have been useless in the hilly terrain of Judea.

13:3-8. Menelaus, who has not been mentioned for some time, now reappears. His role in attempting peace negotiations (11:29, 32) is completely reversed here: Menelaus now "encourages" Antiochus V in his invasion (v. 3; see 11:32)

as he had helped his father (5:15). He resumes the role he had played before, a plotter against his fellow citizens (4:50; 5:23). He is the opposite of the good high priest Onias III, who only had in mind the welfare of all the people (4:5). The author stresses that God rules all events and so uses the epithet "King of kings" for God (v. 4; see *1 Enoch* 9:4), an epithet used of Persian kings (Ezra 7:12; Dan 2:37) and of Nebuchadnezzar (Ezek 26:7). Since it seems unlikely that Lysias and his charge would have executed Menelaus before an expedition to regain control of Judea, it has been suggested that this description of Menelaus's death (vv. 5-6) may belong after the expedition of Lysias. The author has placed the account here, just as Jason's death is told at the time of his attack on Jerusalem (5:5-10), even though it took place later. Josephus places Menelaus's death after the expedition.[98] The failure of Menelaus's peace overtures (11:29, 32) may have convinced Lysias that Menelaus, who had been supported by Antiochus IV, was now a liability and could be removed. Beroea (v. 4) was the name given to Aleppo in Syria by Seleucus I. Death by ashes was a Persian punishment. If the ashes were cold, the criminal would be suffocated; if they were hot, he would burn to death. Menelaus had been accused of sacrilege earlier (vv. 7-8; see 4:39). The author's motif of appropriate retribution surfaces again (see 4:26; 5:9-10; 9:6, 28), as does the cruel fate of no burial. The holiness of the altar fire was illustrated in the punishment of Aaron's two sons, Nadab and Abihu (Lev 10:1-5). There was a special dump for the sacrificial ashes in Jerusalem (Lev 4:12; Jer 31:40).

13:9-17, The Engagement with Lysias at Modein. 13:9-12. The depiction of Antiochus V as being worse than his father recalls Rehoboam's statements (1 Kgs 12:13-14). Antiochus's intent is the opposite of the desire stated in his letter that the Jews be undisturbed and live according to their customs (11:25). Once again, the Seleucid king is said to be barbarous (2:21; 4:25). The response of Judas is, as expected, ceaseless prayer (v. 10). Judas had earlier exhorted his followers to be ready to die for their laws and their country (8:21). Here is added the holy Temple, and the prayer in v. 11 echoes the supplication at the purification of the Temple

(10:4). The emphasis on the whole community at prayer (v. 12) recalls the community response before the entrance of Heliodorus to the Temple (3:14-22). Fasting and weeping and mourning are the classical ritual acts of repentance to ask the Lord's mercy (e.g., Jer 36:9; Joel 2:12-17; Dan 9:3).

13:13. The elders with whom Judas consults (v. 13) are either members of a council or senate (4:44; 11:27) or some consultative body. According to the *Temple Scroll* from Qumran, the king should always have with him twelve princes of his people, twelve priests, and twelve Levites, without whom he should make no decision; before going to war, he should have the high priest consult the Urim and Tummim.[99] At Qumran the role of the priest was stressed, but the thrust was to limit the power of the king. Judas in 2 Maccabees is also portrayed as not acting arrogantly, as opposed to his enemies.

13:14-17. The account of the engagement with Lysias is colored by the theological stance of the author. With God on their side, the Jews are invincible and Judea cannot be overrun. So what was really a defeat for the Jews at Beth-zechariah (1 Macc 6:32-47), resulting in the Seleucids regaining control of Jerusalem (1 Macc 6:48-62), is depicted as a victory for the Jews instead. With the addition of the term "commonwealth," or "way of life" (πολιτεία *politeia*), to the list of what the Jews are fighting for (v. 14), the crisis is placed in the same category as when Jason overthrew their way of life (4:11) and when Antiochus IV sent Geron to compel the Jews to live no longer by the laws of God (6:1). Modein, which in 1 Maccabees is the hometown of the Maccabees (1 Macc 2:1), is mentioned only here in 2 Maccabees. Modein is seven miles east of Lydda, seventeen miles northwest of Jerusalem, and lies at the northeastern end of the Low Shephela, the hilly region between the Judean hills and the coastal plain. It is not far from the Gophna Hills and the ascent of Beth-horon to the mountain plateau near Jerusalem. The author seems to suggest that Judas made a surprise attack on the Seleucid forces as they marched down the coastal plain to enter Judea from the south (1 Macc 6:31; cf. the movement of John Hyrcanus in 1 Macc 16:4-5 to Modein from where he could march into the plain). The author of 1 Maccabees depicts no such surprise attack on Lysias's forces.

Judas gives a watchword (v. 15), just as he had before the battle with Nicanor (8:23). "God's victory" is what the Sons of Light are to write on their standards when they return from battle.[100] The author of 2 Maccabees delights in tales of heroic achievements. Here Judas, with "a picked force," kills more than 2,000 of the enemy; he also kills the leading elephant and fills the camp with confusion (v. 15) and retires safely (v. 16). Judas's feat parallels that of Eleazar (1 Macc 6:43-46), but Eleazar's occurred in the midst of a disastrous battle during which he lost his life. Verse 17 contains the poetic image of Judas under God's shelter (cf. Pss 91:1; 121:5; Isa 25:4; as well as in the phrase "under the shelter of God's wings," Pss 17:8; 36:7; 61:4; 63:7).

13:18-26, Antiochus V's Treaty. The king, recognizing the strength of the Jewish troops (as had Lysias in his first expedition [11:13]), now tries deceit (v. 18). According to 1 Maccabees, the Jews at Beth-zur fought courageously but eventually capitulated through lack of provisions (1 Macc 6:31, 49-50). Here the king's forces are defeated (v. 19), the defenders of Beth-zur get whatever provisions are necessary from Judas (v. 20), and the king eventually withdraws after making a separate peace treaty with the people of Beth-zur (v. 22; did the people of Beth-zur agree not to attack the king's forces from behind?). In the middle of this account of what occurred at Beth-zur is another exciting tale of deception by a Jew that failed (v. 21). In 1 Macc 6:32-47, the battle of Beth-zechariah is described in detail, and the defeat of the Jews is noted. In 2 Maccabees, Beth-zechariah is not mentioned by name, and it is only briefly stated that when the king attacked Judas's forces he was defeated (v. 21b). This may be an inversion of what really happened, or it could refer to the fact that Lysias and the king were unsuccessful in their siege of the Temple and thus decided to make peace (1 Macc 6:51-61). Second Maccabees shows the invasion of the king and Lysias to be unsuccessful and the Jews undefeated. Both 1 and 2 Maccabees agree that Lysias and the king break off their attack because

of an attempt by Philip to seize control of the government. However, in 1 Maccabees, Antiochus IV appoints Philip to be in charge of the kingdom and guardian of Antiochus V Eupator (1 Macc 6:14-15). Since 2 Maccabees has reported that this Philip fled to Egypt following Antiochus IV's death (9:29), in the condensed statement of 2 Macc 13:23, one might suppose that someone else named Philip had been left in charge of affairs in Antioch by Antiochus V and was now leading a revolt.

According to 2 Maccabees, Antiochus V behaves honorably, agrees to just terms, honors the Temple, and gives gifts to it (v. 23). In doing so, Antiochus is acting as kings had done before him (3:1). He also sacrifices in the Temple, as had Alexander the Great and Ptolemy IV Philopator.[101] In 1 Maccabees, the king breaks his oath and has the walls of Jerusalem torn down (1 Macc 6:62). Most interestingly, here Antiochus meets Judas graciously (v. 24), whereas in 1 Maccabees Judas does not seem to be anywhere near Jerusalem. The author seems to continue the theme of the Jews' being willing to act as good citizens and be on good terms with Gentiles if they are allowed to do so (12:29-31; 14:24-25). A new governor is installed for the region of Ptolemais to the land of the Gerrenians. The location of land of the Gerrenians is uncertain; some scholars place it southward from Gaza and west of Beersheba, others as far south as Lake Sirbonis, near Pelusium (even though this area was then under Ptolemaic control); still others suggest that it be placed north of Ptolemais at Gerrha, southeast of Beirut. The change of administrators perhaps reflects a more sympathetic policy toward the Jews, as earlier with Ptolemy Macron (10:12), and in opposition to the role local governors had taken (12:2). If the area covered by Hegemonides lay south of Ptolemais, he would have controlled Jamnia, Joppa, and possibly part of Idumea; he may have replaced Gorgias (12:32-37). If the area of his control lay northward, Hegemonides would have controlled Ptolemais, Tyre, and Sidon (1 Macc 5:15). The citizens of Ptolemais, possibly already described as instigators of anti-Jewish decrees (1 Macc 5:15; 2 Macc 6:8), do not like the agreement, as later Alcimus does not like the peaceful

100. See 1QM 4:13.

101. For Alexander, see Josephus *Antiquities of the Jews* 11.336; for Ptolemy IV Philopator, see 3 Macc 1:9.

arrangements between Nicanor and Judas (14:20, 26). With Philip in revolt, Lysias had to appease the citizens of Ptolemais so that his rear guard would be secure.

REFLECTIONS

This chapter shows again the power of a historian to determine the way history is written. Guided by his worldview that Torah-observant Jews could not be defeated by any enemy, the author of 2 Maccabees has selected his facts, embellished them, and distorted what actually happened. The narrative surely is a warning to us to examine the assumptions we bring to any discussion as well as the ways we have told our cultural histories. Have we looked at our religion's past through rose-colored spectacles and not attempted to see what drove our opponents or to empathize with their views? If we begin every discussion with the entrenched view that we are right and our opponents are wrong, how can we ever advance beyond conflict? It is easy to see the speck in our neighbor's eye and not notice the log in our own (Matt 7:3-5), but we must learn to examine ourselves and our traditions with clear vision.

2 MACCABEES 14:1–15:36, THE INVASION BY NICANOR

2 Maccabees 14:1-2, Demetrius Becomes King

NAB

14 Three years later, Judas and his men learned that Demetrius, son of Seleucus, had sailed into the port of Tripolis with a powerful army and a fleet, ² and that he had occupied the country, after doing away with Antiochus and his guardian Lysias.

NRSV

14 Three years later, word came to Judas and his men that Demetrius son of Seleucus had sailed into the harbor of Tripolis with a strong army and a fleet, ²and had taken possession of the country, having made away with Antiochus and his guardian Lysias.

COMMENTARY

The last two chapters of 2 Maccabees parallel 1 Maccabees 7. The author swiftly shifts to the new ruler, Demetrius I. Demetrius, son of Seleucus IV and nephew of Antiochus IV, had been held hostage in Rome in accordance with the Treaty of Apamea. He had replaced Antiochus IV in 178 on the latter's succession to the throne and had been kept in Rome even after the indemnity had been paid off in 173. On the death of Antiochus IV, Demetrius had argued it was useless to keep him a hostage and requested permission to leave, but the Roman senate had refused, no doubt preferring to deal with an underage king like Antiochus V. After the murder of the Roman envoy in Laodicea in 163 BCE, Demetrius applied again for permission to leave, was again refused, and then slipped away to wrest control of the kingdom. The author of 2 Maccabees specifies that he landed in Tripolis and was acclaimed king by the end of 162 BCE (the "three years" of v. 1 means within the third year). The last date given in 2 Maccabees (13:1) was the 149th year; the next date is the 151st year (14:4), so the events of vv. 1-2 come within that span. According to both 1 Macc 7:1 and Polybius,[102] Demetrius arrived in Tripolis with only a handful of supporters.

102. See Polybius 31.14.8-13.

2 Maccabees 14:3-25, Nicanor's Expedition

NAB

3 A certain Alcimus, a former high priest, who had willfully incurred defilement at the time of the revolt, realized that there was no way for him to salvage his position and regain access to the holy altar. 4 So he went to King Demetrius in the year one hundred and fifty-one and presented him with a gold crown and a palm branch, as well as some of the customary olive branches from the temple. On that occasion he kept quiet. 5 But he found an opportunity to further his mad scheme when he was invited to the council by Demetrius and questioned about the dispositions and intentions of the Jews. He replied: 6 "Those Jews called Hasideans, led by Judas Maccabeus, are warmongers, who stir up sedition and keep the kingdom from enjoying peace and quiet. 7 For this reason, now that I am deprived of my ancestral dignity, that is to say, the high priesthood, I have come here— 8 first, out of my genuine concern for the king's interests, and secondly, out of consideration for my own countrymen, since our entire nation is suffering great affliction from the unreasonable conduct of the people just mentioned. 9 When you have informed yourself in detail on these matters, O king, act in the interest of our country and its hard-pressed people with the same gracious consideration that you show toward all. 10 As long as Judas is around, it is impossible for the state to enjoy peace." 11 When he had said this, the other Friends who were hostile to Judas quickly added fuel to Demetrius' indignation.

12 The king immediately chose Nicanor, who had been in command of the elephants, and appointed him governor of Judea. He sent him off 13 with orders to put Judas to death, to disperse his followers, and to set up Alcimus as high priest of the great temple. 14 The Gentiles from Judea, who would have banished Judas, came flocking to Nicanor, thinking that the misfortunes and calamities of the Jews would mean prosperity for themselves. 15 When the Jews heard of Nicanor's coming, and that the Gentiles were rallying to him, they sprinkled themselves with earth and prayed to him who established his people forever, and who always comes to the aid of his heritage.

NRSV

3Now a certain Alcimus, who had formerly been high priest but had willfully defiled himself in the times of separation,[a] realized that there was no way for him to be safe or to have access again to the holy altar, 4and went to King Demetrius in about the one hundred fifty-first year,[b] presenting to him a crown of gold and a palm, and besides these some of the customary olive branches from the temple. During that day he kept quiet. 5But he found an opportunity that furthered his mad purpose when he was invited by Demetrius to a meeting of the council and was asked about the attitude and intentions of the Jews. He answered:

6"Those of the Jews who are called Hasideans, whose leader is Judas Maccabeus, are keeping up war and stirring up sedition, and will not let the kingdom attain tranquility. 7Therefore I have laid aside my ancestral glory—I mean the high priesthood—and have now come here, 8first because I am genuinely concerned for the interests of the king, and second because I have regard also for my compatriots. For through the folly of those whom I have mentioned our whole nation is now in no small misfortune. 9Since you are acquainted, O king, with the details of this matter, may it please you to take thought for our country and our hard-pressed nation with the gracious kindness that you show to all. 10For as long as Judas lives, it is impossible for the government to find peace." 11When he had said this, the rest of the king's Friends,[c] who were hostile to Judas, quickly inflamed Demetrius still more. 12He immediately chose Nicanor, who had been in command of the elephants, appointed him governor of Judea, and sent him off 13with orders to kill Judas and scatter his troops, and to install Alcimus as high priest of the great[d] temple. 14And the Gentiles throughout Judea, who had fled before[e] Judas, flocked to join Nicanor, thinking that the misfortunes and calamities of the Jews would mean prosperity for themselves.

15When the Jews[f] heard of Nicanor's coming and the gathering of the Gentiles, they sprinkled

a Other ancient authorities read *of mixing*   b 161 B.C
c Gk *of the Friends*   d Gk *greatest*   e Meaning of Gk uncertain
f Gk *they*

NAB

16 At their leader's command, they set out at once and came upon the enemy at the village of Adasa. 17 Judas' brother Simon had engaged Nicanor, but because of the sudden appearance of the enemy suffered a slight repulse. 18 However, when Nicanor heard of the valor of Judas and his men, and the great courage with which they fought for their country, he shrank from deciding the issue by bloodshed. 19 So he sent Posidonius, Theodotus and Mattathias to arrange an agreement. 20 After a long discussion of the terms, each leader communicated them to his troops; and when general agreement was expressed, they assented to the treaty. 21 A day was set on which the leaders would meet by themselves. From each side a chariot came forward and thrones were set in place. 22 Judas had posted armed men in readiness at suitable points for fear that the enemy might suddenly carry out some treacherous plan. But the conference was held in the proper way. 23 Nicanor stayed on in Jerusalem, where he did nothing out of place. He got rid of the throngs of ordinary people who gathered around him; 24 but he always kept Judas in his company, for he had a cordial affection for the man. 25 He urged him to marry and have children; so Judas married, settled down, and shared the common life.

14, 16: (epi kōmēn) Adasa: conj; cf 1 Mc 7, 40
14, 17: bracheōs (de dia ten aiphnidion tōn antipalōn) epiphaneia (eptaikōs): cf LXX[MSS].

NRSV

dust on their heads and prayed to him who established his own people forever and always upholds his own heritage by manifesting himself. 16At the command of the leader, they[a] set out from there immediately and engaged them in battle at a village called Dessau.[b] 17Simon, the brother of Judas, had encountered Nicanor, but had been temporarily[c] checked because of the sudden consternation created by the enemy.

18Nevertheless Nicanor, hearing of the valor of Judas and his troops and their courage in battle for their country, shrank from deciding the issue by bloodshed. 19Therefore he sent Posidonius, Theodotus, and Mattathias to give and receive pledges of friendship. 20When the terms had been fully considered, and the leader had informed the people, and it had appeared that they were of one mind, they agreed to the covenant. 21The leaders[d] set a day on which to meet by themselves. A chariot came forward from each army; seats of honor were set in place; 22Judas posted armed men in readiness at key places to prevent sudden treachery on the part of the enemy; so they duly held the consultation.

23Nicanor stayed on in Jerusalem and did nothing out of the way, but dismissed the flocks of people that had gathered. 24And he kept Judas always in his presence; he was warmly attached to the man. 25He urged him to marry and have children; so Judas[a] married, settled down, and shared the common life.

[a] Gk he   [b] Meaning of Gk uncertain   [c] Other ancient authorities read slowly   [d] Gk The

COMMENTARY

14:3-5. The peace gained at the end of chap. 13 is now to be broken, just as the peace at the end of chap. 11 had been. Alcimus, also called Yakim, had been appointed high priest after Menelaus.[103] Alcimus is said to have "defiled" himself in the "times of separation" (ἀμειξίας χρόνοις ameixias chronois, v. 3). Scholars have puzzled over this characterization. Some have noted that, since Alcimus was initially acceptable to the

Hasidim (1 Macc 7:12-18), he could not have defiled himself the way Menelaus had done and, therefore, that his defilement resulted from the incident in which sixty Hasidim were executed (1 Macc 7:12-18). Some have further suggested that "the time of separation" mentioned here thus refers to the disagreement between the Hasidim and Judas over Alcimus. Other scholars accept that the massacre is the incident referred to by 2 Maccabees, but follow a different manuscript reading and translate "in times of peace" (ἐπιμιξία

103. See Josephus Antiquities of the Jews 12.385-87.

epimixia), that is, in the time following the treaty with Antiochus V. The execution of the sixty Hasidim, however, occurs in 1 Maccabees after Alcimus's installation by Demetrius I, and so after the events being reported here. But describing Alcimus as "defiled" does not necessarily indicate ritual defilement; the term translated "defile" (μολύνω *molynō*) can have the general meaning of "disgrace": "A whisperer degrades himself/ and is hated in his neighborhood" (Sir 21:28 NRSV). The term may be used here in a general way to contrast Alcimus's behavior to that of Judas, who left Jerusalem so as not to share in the defilement (2 Macc 5:27), and with that of Razis, who had risked his life by remaining obedient to the law during the persecution (14:38). The description of Alcimus thus is the author's character assassination, since Alcimus was not one of Judas's followers and had not (like Razis) risked body and soul for Judaism. We should perhaps not look for a more specific way in which Alcimus had defiled himself—e.g., by eating non-kosher food or by persecuting those who did not obey the emperor's orders. The statement that Alcimus could not be safe suggests that he had been forced out of Jerusalem (cf. 1 Macc 7:6). At the installation of a new king, he had come for confirmation in his office (v. 4; 1 Macc 10:60-64; 11:23-27) and brought the requisite gifts: a gold crown, a palm, and olive branches from the Temple (cf. 1 Macc 13:36-37; "olive branches" [θαλλοί *thalloi*] may be translated by the more general "gifts"). Alcimus, although his folly is like Simon's (4:6), cunningly bides his time. When the king seeks the advice of those Friends of his at hand, it is natural for him to include the high priest in the discussions on Judea (v. 5).

14:6-10. The author provides Alcimus with an appropriate speech for the circumstances. He first answers the king's questions (v. 6), then claims to have the king's and his own country's best interests at heart (vv. 7-8) and requests help (v. 9). In 1 Macc 2:42 and 7:13, the Hasideans are distinguished from the Maccabeans. Here Judas is portrayed as their leader, and the group is distinguished from the rest of the nation (v. 8). The accusation against Judas and his followers is exactly the opposite of what the reader knows to be true from the narrative: It is not Judas and his followers but Gorgias and those who were ban- ished from Jerusalem who keep up the war (10:14-15); it is the local military commanders who will not let the Jews live in peace (12:2). Judas, in fact, will make peace with Nicanor (vv. 18-25) and settle down, the opposite of what Alcimus charges (v. 6). The charge that the state will never enjoy peace (v. 10) parallels the charge made by Onias III against the original trouble- maker Simon (2 Macc 4:6). In several late Jewish narratives we find the pattern whereby the accu- sation is made that Jews are disturbers of the realm, and this accusation is later disproved (Esth 3:13; 3 Macc 3:26; 6:28; 7:4-7 LXX).

Verse 7 has been interpreted to mean that Al- cimus has had the high priesthood taken away from him. That the phrase would have this meaning where Alcimus is presenting himself as humbly seeking the best interests of his people seems out of context. Since the verb ἀθαιρέω (*aphaireō*) can mean "take off a garment" (Esth 4:4; Esth 4:17k LXX), it might suggest that Alcimus is claiming that, because of his concern for his people, he has left behind his high priestly duties to come to the king (cf. Onias III at 4:5-6). The glory here would refer to the glorious robe of the high priesthood (Sir 45:8; 50:5-11). The motives Alcimus gives for coming to the king resemble those of Onias III (4:5-6).

14:11-14. The king's Friends instigate action against Judas (cf. 10:13). The Nicanor involved here is unlikely to have been the same Nicanor mentioned earlier (8:9; 12:2), but the author assimilates the two by giving the same epithet to both (8:34; 15:3). The author of 2 Maccabees makes no mention of the expedition of Bacchides and Alcimus or of Alcimus's tenure as high priest (1 Macc 7:8-25). Such an imposition of Seleucid control would have spoiled his depiction of Judea and Judas as invincible. Since the Roman ambas- sador C. Octavius had had the Seleucid elephants hamstrung in early 162 BCE, perhaps Nicanor was out of a job. Only here, when Nicanor is ap- pointed, is mention made of a governor of Judea (v. 12). The same rank was used earlier to de- scribe local military commanders (12:2), which is probably what is meant here. Nicanor's orders are to do away with Judas (v. 13), as Antiochus V and Lysias had been done away with, to "scatter" his forces (at 1 Macc 7:6, Judas's opponents claim that he had "scattered" them out of the land),

and to install Alcimus as high priest. At v. 14, one should probably delete "Gentiles," since the group the author intends seems to be the Israelites who opposed Judas and had been driven out of Judea (10:15). The contrast of prosperity and calamities resembles that made by the author regarding Jason's slaughter of his fellow Israelites (5:6).

14:15-25. As customary, before going into the battle the Jews pray to God (v. 15; see 10:25), who "established his own people forever" by awesome deeds, who "upholds his own heritage by manifesting himself" (cf. Deut 9:26-29; 2 Macc 1:26; literally "with an epiphany"; see 2:21). The place at which the Jews pray and from which they set out (v. 16) seems to be presupposed by the author to be Jerusalem. The location of Dessau, at which the battle takes place, is unknown, but it seems to have been within Judea. Simon, one of the commanders (8:22; 10:19), receives a slight check (v. 17), but Nicanor decides to negotiate (v. 18; there is no mention in 1 Maccabees of an engagement at Dessau or of any contact before Nicanor opens peace negotiations). In 1 Maccabees 7:27, the Seleucid commander from the beginning planned treachery (a motif that occurs frequently in 1 Maccabees [1:30; 7:10-18], as the author is suspicious of any peace settlement with

the Seleucids). Here a different picture is given, much like the description of Antiochus V's dealings with Jerusalem (13:23-24): Nicanor acts honorably (vv. 19-20), and Judas acts with commendable caution (v. 22), although no specific reason is given for it. It is also noteworthy how Judas consults with the people before agreeing to the treaty (v. 20). The ambassadors mentioned in v. 19 are otherwise unknown. The scene for the signing of the agreement is vividly drawn (v. 21), with the two chariots coming toward each other and the two leaders sitting on facing chairs. The description of Nicanor given here, that he becomes a friend of Judas and stays on in Jerusalem, completely contradicts that of 1 Maccabees. Nicanor dismissed the group of enemies of Judas (v. 23; note the play between "flocked" [ἀγεληδόν *ageledon*], v. 14, and "flocks" [ἀγελαίους *agelaious*], v. 23). One might suspect that Nicanor kept Judas near him (v. 24) so that Judas could not get up to any mischief, but the author insists on the warm attachment of Nicanor to Judas. Verse 25 shows signs of having been shortened, as three verbs follow one after another (see also 13:19, 22-23, 26). No better peace could be imagined than the fiery soldier Judas married with children and taking part in normal community life.

REFLECTIONS

Judas is shown here as the model citizen. He is not aggressive against the Seleucids, as Alcimus had suggested. When honorable peace conditions can be achieved, he agrees to them and then retires to private life. He does not try to usurp Alcimus's position, but is content with the restoration of peace under the Seleucid government. He is not ambitious and does not seek to use his armed backers as a tool for advancement. He makes the transition from soldier to civilian with apparent ease. There are two lessons for us here. One is again the counsel against ambition. The ambition of Jason and Menelaus had rent apart the social fabric earlier, and Alcimus was about to do it again. In a free-market economy, such as that of the United States, competitiveness is instilled in children from the very first days at school. It is good to be competitive, to be as good as one can be, to excel in intellectual pursuits and in sports. But we do well to remind ourselves and our children that we should not try to win at all costs, that ambition should not make us trample down others.

We should also be reminded as we read about Judas's return to private life how difficult such a transition can be. In today's world, a soldier who returns to civilian life after having fought in a war requires all the support and help he or she can get to move back to normal family life. The horrors of war can be imprinted on the subconscious, and we have to show ourselves as caring for those who have defended our homes and way of life.

Finally, 1 and 2 Maccabees give two very different accounts of Nicanor's behavior, and we should reflect on what that signifies for our appreciation of biblical literature. In 1 Maccabees, Nicanor is treacherous from the start, and Judas is rightly seen to be suspicious of him and his intentions. The mistrust grows and hostilities ensue. The endemic mistrust that the author of 1 Maccabees depicts between the Maccabees and the Seleucids seems as if it could only be resolved by the independence of Judea. In 2 Maccabees, however, Nicanor is depicted as an admirer of Judas. Judas is properly cautious in meeting with him, but the two are said to strike up a friendship. The Jew and the Gentile live on good terms. Proper worship is being performed at the Temple, since its purification and restoration. Judas seems content that normalcy has returned, a normalcy that includes Judea's being part of the Seleucid Empire. Judas does not seek independence for Judea, but appears satisfied with the situation.

Such a strong difference between the two accounts should not be explained away by claiming that one is more accurate than the other, that one deserves to be believed more than the other. Rather, the two accounts remind us of how the same event can be retold in completely different ways even by eyewitnesses of the event. The telling depends on the perspective of the account. This sense of different perspective is one that we should be sensitive to in our reading of the Scriptures. The two accounts of God's creation of the universe in Genesis 1 and Genesis 2–3 show us two different perspectives on the origins of humanity. The four different Gospels allow us to see how different communities at the beginning of the Jesus movement viewed him and his teaching in diverse ways. Difference does not mean contradiction; it simply means diversity of viewpoint.

2 Maccabees 14:26-36, The Change in Nicanor

NAB	NRSV
26 When Alcimus saw their friendship for each other, he took the treaty that had been made, went to Demetrius, and said that Nicanor was plotting against the state, and that he had appointed Judas, the conspirator against the kingdom, to be his successor. 27 Stirred up by the villain's calumnies, the king became enraged. He wrote to Nicanor, stating that he was displeased with the treaty, and ordering him to send Maccabeus as a prisoner to Antioch without delay. 28 When this message reached Nicanor he was dismayed, for he hated to break his agreement with a man who had done no wrong. 29 However, there was no way of opposing the king, so he watched for an opportunity to carry out this order by a stratagem. 30 But Maccabeus noticed that Nicanor was becoming cool in his dealings with him, and acting with unaccustomed rudeness when they met; he concluded that this coldness betokened no good. So he gathered together a large number of his men, and went into hiding from Nicanor. 31 When Nicanor realized that he had been disgracefully outwitted by the man, he went to the great and holy temple, at a time when the	26But when Alcimus noticed their goodwill for one another, he took the covenant that had been made and went to Demetrius. He told him that Nicanor was disloyal to the government, since he had appointed that conspirator against the kingdom, Judas, to be his successor. 27The king became excited and, provoked by the false accusations of that depraved man, wrote to Nicanor, stating that he was displeased with the covenant and commanding him to send Maccabeus to Antioch as a prisoner without delay. 28When this message came to Nicanor, he was troubled and grieved that he had to annul their agreement when the man had done no wrong. 29Since it was not possible to oppose the king, he watched for an opportunity to accomplish this by a stratagem. 30But Maccabeus, noticing that Nicanor was more austere in his dealings with him and was meeting him more rudely than had been his custom, concluded that this austerity did not spring from the best motives. So he gathered not a few of his men, and went into hiding from Nicanor. 31When the latter became aware that he had been cleverly outwitted by the

priests were offering the customary sacrifices, and ordered them to surrender Judas. [32] As they declared under oath that they did not know where the wanted man was, [33] he raised his right hand toward the temple and swore this oath: "If you do not hand Judas over to me as prisoner, I will level this shrine of God to the ground; I will tear down the altar, and erect here a splendid temple to Dionysus." [34] With these words he went away. The priests stretched out their hands toward heaven, calling upon the unfailing defender of our nation in these words: [35] "LORD of all, though you are in need of nothing, you have approved of a temple for your dwelling place among us. [36] Therefore, O holy One, LORD of all holiness, preserve forever undefiled this house, which has been so recently purified."

man, he went to the great[a] and holy temple while the priests were offering the customary sacrifices, and commanded them to hand the man over. [32]When they declared on oath that they did not know where the man was whom he wanted, [33]he stretched out his right hand toward the sanctuary, and swore this oath: "If you do not hand Judas over to me as a prisoner, I will level this shrine of God to the ground and tear down the altar, and build here a splendid temple to Dionysus."

[34]Having said this, he went away. Then the priests stretched out their hands toward heaven and called upon the constant Defender of our nation, in these words: [35]"O Lord of all, though you have need of nothing, you were pleased that there should be a temple for your habitation among us; [36]so now, O holy One, Lord of all holiness, keep undefiled forever this house that has been so recently purified."

[a] Gk greatest

COMMENTARY

The relations between Nicanor and Judas are characterized as ideal ("goodwill," v. 26; see 9:21, 26; 11:19), but Alcimus intervenes to ruin the peace, as had been done earlier against Ptolemy Macron (10:13). The account presupposes that Alcimus is in Jerusalem, so he must have been installed as high priest as part of the negotiations. He accuses Nicanor with the same accusation Simon had made against Onias III (4:2). Nicanor had appointed Judas as his "deputy," or "substitute" (διάδοχος *diadochos;* see 4:29), rather than successor, for only the king could nominate the governor of an area. If this is not a trumped-up charge on the part of Alcimus, it implies that Judas had become a part of the normal bureaucracy of Jerusalem. Just as the false accusations of the wicked Simon had caused Seleucus IV to send Heliodorus to remove funds from the Jerusalem treasury (3:7), so also false accusations work their evil now. The king acts unwisely, as his anger shows (cf. 7:3, 39) and he annuls the terms of the agreement (v. 27; cf. 13:25). The author notes the distress of Nicanor, an honorable man, at having to break covenant when Judas was inno-

cent, but he obeys orders (v. 28). The author of 1 Maccabees simply states that Judas came to know of Nicanor's treachery (1 Macc 7:30). Here, in vv. 29-30, a whole scene is played out, as Judas is shown to be observant in outwitting Nicanor (v. 30). In the narrative at 1 Maccabees, Judas's escape is followed by his victory over Nicanor at Caphar-salama (1 Macc 7:31-32). The author of 2 Maccabees makes no mention of this battle, but moves directly to Nicanor's attack on the Temple (v. 31). Why would Nicanor think that the priests would know where Judas had hidden? Does he think they will follow the principle that it is better for one man to die than for the nation to be destroyed (2 Sam 20:14-22; John 11:50)? At this point, Nicanor's character changes; by obeying the king's unjust orders, he turns into someone who fights against God. The author deliberately and effectively contrasts Nicanor's stretching out his right hand toward the Temple (v. 33) and the priests' stretching out their hands in prayer (v. 34). As Antiochus had threatened to level the holy city (9:13; 8:3), so Nicanor threatens to level the shrine to the ground (14:33; the altars of the Lord had been thrown down in King Ahab's time [1 Kgs 18:31], and the reader might recall the taunt of Gideon after he pulled down the altar of Baal [Judg 6:28-32]). If Judas is not handed over to him, Nicanor threatens, he will build a "splendid" (ἐπιφανές *epiphanes*) temple to Dionysus, foreshadowing ironically God's "manifestation" (ἐπιφανεία *epiphaneia*) in defeating Nicanor (15:27). The priests in their prayer call on God as the defender of the nation (8:36); Jerusalem is the place that God chose (Deut 12:5-11). The author

has chosen the Greek term σκηνόω (*skēnoō*, lit., "tenting") to describe God's presence, reflecting the term for God's tent of meeting in the wilderness (Exod 25:8-9), which was placed in Solomon's Temple (1 Kgs 8:4; Pss 15:1; 43:3; 61:4; 74:7; 84:1; see also 1 Kgs 6:1; 7:51; 8:16-21, 41-43; Ps 26:8; Sir 24:8). The prayer of the priests, which refers to the purification (10:1-4), will be fulfilled; the blessing at 15:34 will repeat the language of 14:36.

REFLECTIONS

The slander of Alcimus and its acceptance by the king remind us that we must never believe everything we hear, particularly bad news. If we need to know what happened, we should check out all parties to hear every side of the story. But we are also confronted in this narrative with a more serious issue: the question of obedience to authority. The chapter is fascinating in its development of Nicanor's character. First he is portrayed as a soldier who, on seeing the commitment and readiness to die on the part of Judas and his forces, has the wisdom to settle the dispute and gain the main objective of the king, Alcimus's installation as high priest, through a negotiated settlement. Nicanor is not a stubborn, stupid man who can settle things only by violence. But then occurs a moral crisis for Nicanor: Should he obey the unjust decision of the king? He is troubled, but eventually decides that he must obey the king. One would not want to be in his shoes, for what were his alternatives? Could he try to reason with the king, who already had shown signs of anger? If he disobeyed, he would no doubt have been executed, and someone else would have been sent to carry out the king's wishes. So Nicanor obeyed an order he knew was unjust. From that point on his character changes for the worse, and he is shown as fighting against God. His excuse echoes throughout history: He was only following orders. It was heard at the Nuremberg trials after World War II. It was given for what occurred at My Lai during the Vietnam war. And it will always be the excuse for not exercising moral autonomy, for thinking that we are not responsible if we can blame someone else. The ethical issue posed by Nicanor's problem is far-reaching: How can one tell if the order of a superior is "unjust"? Yet how can we "train" people to be morally autonomous and to have the courage to blow the whistle on moral violations they witness in the companies they work for? How can an army operate if every soldier has to decide that the action is morally justified? Lurking under the narrative of Nicanor's actions is the whole issue of conscience and authority, an issue that will always keep surfacing.

2 Maccabees 14:37-46, The Razis Affair

NAB

37 A certain Razis, one of the elders of Jerusalem, was denounced to Nicanor as a patriot. A man highly regarded, he was called a father of the Jews because of his love for them. 38 In the early days of the revolt, he had been convicted of Judaism, and had risked body and life in his ardent zeal

NRSV

37A certain Razis, one of the elders of Jerusalem, was denounced to Nicanor as a man who loved his compatriots and was very well thought of and for his goodwill was called father of the Jews. 38In former times, when there was no mingling with the Gentiles, he had been accused of

NAB

for it. ³⁹ Nicanor, to show his detestation of the Jews, sent more than five hundred soldiers to arrest him. ⁴⁰ He thought that by arresting such a man he would deal the Jews a hard blow. ⁴¹ But when these troops, on the point of capturing the tower, were forcing the outer gate and calling for fire to set the door ablaze, Razis, now caught on all sides, turned his sword against himself, ⁴² preferring to die nobly rather than fall into the hands of vile men and suffer outrages unworthy of his noble birth. ⁴³ In the excitement of the struggle he failed to strike exactly. So while the troops rushed in through the doors, he gallantly ran up to the top of the wall and with manly courage threw himself down into the crowd. ⁴⁴ But as they quickly drew back and left an opening, he fell into the middle of the empty space. ⁴⁵ Still breathing, and inflamed with anger, he got up and ran through the crowd, with blood gushing from his frightful wounds. ⁴⁶ Then, standing on a steep rock, as he lost the last of his blood, he tore out his entrails and flung them with both hands into the crowd, calling upon the LORD of life and of spirit to give these back to him again. Such was the manner of his death.

NRSV

Judaism, and he had most zealously risked body and life for Judaism. ³⁹Nicanor, wishing to exhibit the enmity that he had for the Jews, sent more than five hundred soldiers to arrest him; ⁴⁰for he thought that by arresting[a] him he would do them an injury. ⁴¹When the troops were about to capture the tower and were forcing the door of the courtyard, they ordered that fire be brought and the doors burned. Being surrounded, Razis[b] fell upon his own sword, ⁴²preferring to die nobly rather than to fall into the hands of sinners and suffer outrages unworthy of his noble birth. ⁴³But in the heat of the struggle he did not hit exactly, and the crowd was now rushing in through the doors. He courageously ran up on the wall, and bravely threw himself down into the crowd. ⁴⁴But as they quickly drew back, a space opened and he fell in the middle of the empty space. ⁴⁵Still alive and aflame with anger, he rose, and though his blood gushed forth and his wounds were severe he ran through the crowd; and standing upon a steep rock, ⁴⁶with his blood now completely drained from him, he tore out his entrails, took them in both hands and hurled them at the crowd, calling upon the Lord of life and spirit to give them back to him again. This was the manner of his death.

a Meaning of Gk uncertain   b Gk he

COMMENTARY

The episode of Razis' martyrdom interrupts the focus on Nicanor and Judas. Just as the martyrdom accounts in 6:17–7:42 were placed after the desecration of the Temple and brought about God's mercy, so also the author places Razis' death after Nicanor's threat against the Temple. After Razis' willing death comes the removal of the threat.

14:37-40. Razis, an unusual name, is an elder, perhaps one of those consulted earlier by Judas (13:13). He is a lover of his compatriots, quite the opposite of Alcimus, who claims to be looking out for his compatriots (14:8), but he is not. The title "father of the Jews" is unexpected, but it may be a position similar to benefactor of the city, held by Onias III (4:2). No reason is given for why Razis was denounced to Nicanor. Was he one of those who had gone into hiding with Judas (14:30) because of his former zeal for Judaism at the time of persecution (v. 38)? Nicanor is now said to hate the Jews (v. 39). This is in accordance with the way 1 Macc 7:26 characterizes Nicanor from the first. Sending 500 soldiers to arrest one man seems a bit exaggerated; the author stresses by this figure the importance of Razis.

14:41-42. This scene seems to take place in a private house in which there was a tower overlooking a courtyard. Presumably Razis has been betrayed and surprised in someone's house. Surrounded on all sides, Razis attempts to kill himself. Like Eleazar (6:23), he prefers to die "nobly" (εὐγενῶς eugenōs) rather than be insulted "unworthily" (ἀναξίως anaxiōs) of his proper ability. The Mediterranean code of honor and disgrace is strongly at play here. Plato, in the ninth book of his *Laws,* states that suicide is allowable under judicial constraint, under the constraint of unavoidable misfortune, and to avoid participating in a dishonorable deed. In 2 Maccabees 8, Nicanor had been defeated and had run away under the guise of a slave. He chose to act dishonorably, fleeing like a slave, when he might have committed suicide under the third condition of the code. Razis does choose to kill himself under the second condition of the code; he has

no means of escape from his enemies, who are rushing to take him.

14:43-46. The suicide act is stretched out to draw the reader in with its vivid description; the sword doesn't do the trick, Razis' throwing himself off a wall doesn't, so he tears out his entrails and throws them on the troops—his blood is literally upon them. The intensity of his commitment is clear in this last grisly act. His last prayer (v. 46) recalls the prayers of the martyrs (7:11, 22-23).

REFLECTIONS

Once again the narrative forces us to confront a contemporary ethical issue: the right to die. Within first-century Judaism, "honorable" suicide was debated. After the town of Jotapata had fallen, Josephus's men urged suicide while he opposed it, although Josephus praised Phasael, who committed suicide rather than be in the power of his enemy Antigonus.[104] Philo of Alexandria supported those Jews who were willing to kill themselves rather than see the statue of Emperor Caligula placed in the Temple.[105] According to 4 Maccabees, the mother of the seven martyred sons committed suicide rather than let the king's men touch her.[106] Within fourth-century Christianity, as well, there was a great debate between Donatist Christians, who advocated suicide, and their opponents who did not.[107] These debates over suicide raise the question of whether a believer in God, who gives life, can honestly take his or her life. Must one endure unbearable suffering or the certainty of a painful death through an incurable disease or can one muster moral arguments in support of suicide? It is a vital question in medical ethics today, and one about which we must all inform ourselves.

104. See Josephus *The Jewish War* 1.271-272; 3.355-391; *Antiquities of the Jews* 13.367-369; 15.13. See also the account of the suicides at Masada, in Josephus *The Jewish War* 7.320-401.
105. Philo *Embassy to Gaius* 228-242, 308.
106. See 4 Macc 17:1.
107. See Augustine *Against Gaudentius* 1.28-32 (PL 43.725-732); Letter 204.

2 Maccabees 15:1-36, The Victory over Nicanor

NAB

15 When Nicanor learned that Judas and his companions were in the territory of Samaria, he decided to attack them in all safety on the day of rest. **2** The Jews who were forced to follow him pleaded, "Do not massacre them in that way, like a savage barbarian, but show respect for the day which the All-seeing has exalted with holiness above all other days." **3** At this the thrice-sinful wretch asked if there was a ruler in heaven who prescribed the keeping of the sabbath day. **4** When they replied that there was indeed such a ruler in heaven, the living LORD himself,

NRSV

15 When Nicanor heard that Judas and his troops were in the region of Samaria, he made plans to attack them with complete safety on the day of rest. **2** When the Jews who were compelled to follow him said, "Do not destroy so savagely and barbarously, but show respect for the day that he who sees all things has honored and hallowed above other days," **3** the thrice-accursed wretch asked if there were a sovereign in heaven who had commanded the keeping of the sabbath day. **4** When they declared, "It is the living Lord himself, the Sovereign in heaven, who ordered us

NAB

who commanded the observance of the sabbath day, [5] he said, "I, on my part, am ruler on earth, and my orders are that you take up arms and carry out the king's business." Nevertheless he did not succeed in carrying out his cruel plan.

[6] In his utter boastfulness and arrogance Nicanor had determined to erect a public monument of victory over Judas and his men. [7] But Maccabeus remained confident, fully convinced that he would receive help from the LORD. [8] He urged his men not to fear the enemy, but mindful of the help they had received from Heaven in the past, to expect that now, too, victory would be given them by the Almighty. [9] By encouraging them with words from the law and the prophets, and by reminding them of the battles they had already won, he filled them with fresh enthusiasm. [10] Having stirred up their courage, he gave his orders and pointed out at the same time the perfidy of the Gentiles and their violation of oaths. [11] When he had armed each of them, not so much with the safety of shield and spear as with the encouragement of noble words, he cheered them all by relating a dream, a kind of vision, worthy of belief.

[12] What he saw was this: Onias, the former high priest, a good and virtuous man, modest in appearance, gentle in manners, distinguished in speech, and trained from childhood in every virtuous practice, was praying with outstretched arms for the whole Jewish community. [13] Then in the same way another man appeared, distinguished by his white hair and dignity, and with an air about him of extraordinary, majestic authority. [14] Onias then said of him, "This is God's prophet Jeremiah, who loves his brethren and fervently prays for his people and their holy city." [15] Stretching out his right hand, Jeremiah presented a gold sword to Judas. As he gave it to him he said, [16] "Accept this holy sword as a gift from God; with it you shall crush your adversaries."

[17] Encouraged by Judas' noble words, which had power to instill valor and stir young hearts to courage, the Jews determined not to delay, but to charge gallantly and decide the issue by hand-to-hand combat with the utmost courage, since

15, 11: (oneiron axiopiston) hypar (ti): so LXX^MSS.

NRSV

to observe the seventh day," [5] he replied, "But I am a sovereign also, on earth, and I command you to take up arms and finish the king's business." Nevertheless, he did not succeed in carrying out his abominable design.

[6] This Nicanor in his utter boastfulness and arrogance had determined to erect a public monument of victory over Judas and his forces. [7] But Maccabeus did not cease to trust with all confidence that he would get help from the Lord. [8] He exhorted his troops not to fear the attack of the Gentiles, but to keep in mind the former times when help had come to them from heaven, and so to look for the victory that the Almighty would give them. [9] Encouraging them from the law and the prophets, and reminding them also of the struggles they had won, he made them the more eager. [10] When he had aroused their courage, he issued his orders, at the same time pointing out the perfidy of the Gentiles and their violation of oaths. [11] He armed each of them not so much with confidence in shields and spears as with the inspiration of brave words, and he cheered them all by relating a dream, a sort of vision,[a] which was worthy of belief.

[12] What he saw was this: Onias, who had been high priest, a noble and good man, of modest bearing and gentle manner, one who spoke fittingly and had been trained from childhood in all that belongs to excellence, was praying with outstretched hands for the whole body of the Jews. [13] Then in the same fashion another appeared, distinguished by his gray hair and dignity, and of marvelous majesty and authority. [14] And Onias spoke, saying, "This is a man who loves the family of Israel and prays much for the people and the holy city—Jeremiah, the prophet of God." [15] Jeremiah stretched out his right hand and gave to Judas a golden sword, and as he gave it he addressed him thus: [16] "Take this holy sword, a gift from God, with which you will strike down your adversaries."

[17] Encouraged by the words of Judas, so noble and so effective in arousing valor and awaking courage in the souls of the young, they determined not to carry on a campaign[b] but to attack bravely, and to decide the matter by fighting hand

[a] Meaning of Gk uncertain   [b] Or to remain in camp

NAB

their city and its temple with the sacred vessels were in danger. [18] They were not so much con cerned about their wives and children or their brothers and kinsmen; their first and foremost fear was for the consecrated sanctuary. [19] Those who remained in the city suffered a like agony, anxious as they were about the battle in the open country.

[20] Everyone now awaited the decisive moment. The enemy were already drawing near with their troops drawn up in battle line, their elephants placed in strategic positions, and their cavalry stationed on the flanks. [21] Maccabeus, contemplating the hosts before him, their elaborate equipment, and the fierceness of their elephants, stretched out his hands toward heaven and called upon the LORD who works miracles; for he knew that it is not through arms but through the LORD's decision that victory is won by those who deserve it. [22] He prayed to him thus: "You, O LORD, sent your angel in the days of King Hezekiah of Judea, and he slew a hundred and eighty-five thousand men of Sennacherib's army. [23] Sovereign of the heavens, send a good angel now to spread fear and dread before us. [24] By the might of your arm may those be struck down who have blasphemously come against your holy people!" With this he ended his prayer.

[25] Nicanor and his men advanced to the sound of trumpets and battle songs. [26] But Judas and his men met the army with supplication and prayers. [27] Fighting with their hands and praying to God with their hearts, they laid low at least thirty-five thousand, and rejoiced greatly over this manifestation of God's power. [28] When the battle was over and they were joyfully departing, they discovered Nicanor lying there in all his armor; [29] so they raised tumultuous shouts in their native tongue in praise of the divine Sovereign.

[30] Then Judas, who was ever in body and soul the chief defender of his fellow citizens, and had maintained from youth his affection for his countrymen, ordered Nicanor's head and whole right arm to be cut off and taken to Jerusalem. [31] When he arrived there, he assembled his countrymen, stationed the priests before the altar, and sent for those in the citadel. [32] He showed them the vile Nicanor's head and the wretched blasphemer's arm that had been boastfully stretched out against

NRSV

to hand with all courage, because the city and the sanctuary and the temple were in danger. [18]Their concern for wives and children, and also for brothers and sisters[a] and relatives, lay upon them less heavily; their greatest and first fear was for the consecrated sanctuary. [19]And those who had to remain in the city were in no little distress, being anxious over the encounter in the open country.

[20]When all were now looking forward to the coming issue, and the enemy was already close at hand with their army drawn up for battle, the elephants[b] strategically stationed and the cavalry deployed on the flanks, [21]Maccabeus, observing the masses that were in front of him and the varied supply of arms and the savagery of the elephants, stretched out his hands toward heaven and called upon the Lord who works wonders; for he knew that it is not by arms, but as the Lord[c] decides, that he gains the victory for those who deserve it. [22]He called upon him in these words: "O Lord, you sent your angel in the time of King Hezekiah of Judea, and he killed fully one hundred eighty-five thousand in the camp of Sennacherib. [23]So now, O Sovereign of the heavens, send a good angel to spread terror and trembling before us. [24]By the might of your arm may these blasphemers who come against your holy people be struck down." With these words he ended his prayer.

[25]Nicanor and his troops advanced with trumpets and battle songs, [26]but Judas and his troops met the enemy in battle with invocations to God and prayers. [27]So, fighting with their hands and praying to God in their hearts, they laid low at least thirty-five thousand, and were greatly gladdened by God's manifestation.

[28]When the action was over and they were returning with joy, they recognized Nicanor, lying dead, in full armor. [29]Then there was shouting and tumult, and they blessed the Sovereign Lord in the language of their ancestors. [30]Then the man who was ever in body and soul the defender of his people, the man who maintained his youthful goodwill toward his compatriots, ordered them to cut off Nicanor's head and arm and carry them to Jerusalem. [31]When he arrived there and had

a Gk *for brothers*   b Gk *animals*   c Gk *he*

NAB

the holy dwelling of the Almighty. [33] He cut out the tongue of the godless Nicanor, saying he would feed it piecemeal to the birds and would hang up the other wages of his folly opposite the temple. [34] At this, everyone looked toward heaven and praised the LORD who manifests his divine power, saying, "Blessed be he who has kept his own Place undefiled!"

[35] Judas hung up Nicanor's head on the wall of the citadel, a clear and evident proof to all of the Lord's help. [36] By public vote it was unanimously decreed never to let this day pass unobserved, but to celebrate it on the thirteenth day of the twelfth month, called Adar in Aramaic, the eve of Mordecai's Day.

NRSV

called his compatriots together and stationed the priests before the altar, he sent for those who were in the citadel. [32]He showed them the vile Nicanor's head and that profane man's arm, which had been boastfully stretched out against the holy house of the Almighty. [33]He cut out the tongue of the ungodly Nicanor and said that he would feed it piecemeal to the birds and would hang up these rewards of his folly opposite the sanctuary. [34]And they all, looking to heaven, blessed the Lord who had manifested himself, saying, "Blessed is he who has kept his own place undefiled!" [35]Judas[a] hung Nicanor's head from the citadel, a clear and conspicuous sign to everyone of the help of the Lord. [36]And they all decreed by public vote never to let this day go unobserved, but to celebrate the thirteenth day of the twelfth month—which is called Adar in the Aramaic language—the day before Mordecai's day.

[a] Gk *He*

COMMENTARY

15:1-5, Nicanor's Arrogance. The narrative of Nicanor's search for Judas continues. Nicanor hears that Judas is in the region around Samaria (v. 1), possibly referring to the Gophna hills just northeast of Modein and bordering Samaria, where Mattathias and his sons had fled in the first stages of the revolt (1 Macc 2:28). There is no specific mention of this search in 1 Maccabees, but 1 Macc 7:39 has Nicanor encamping in Bethhoron, just south of the Gophna hills. Taking advantage of the sabbath rest to attack the Jews had been a tactic used by the enemy in the early days of the revolt (1 Macc 2:29-38), so the Hasmoneans and their supporters had decided that they would defend themselves even if attacked on the sabbath (1 Macc 2:4-41). The Jewish observance of the sabbath was well known to non-Jews, and was portrayed as a superstition that allowed them to be taken unawares. The author of 2 Maccabees has stressed the observance of the sabbath by Judas and his followers (2 Macc 8:26-27). The incident reported here is designed to stress Nicanor's battle against God. The Jews in Nicanor's company (v. 2) may refer

to those mentioned earlier who opposed Judas (10:15; 14:14), but the author, in characterizing them as forced to be with Nicanor, seems to introduce them as a foil to point out Nicanor's arrogance. As often with non-Jews, Nicanor's attitude is characterized as barbarous (2:21; 4:25; 10:4; 11:9). God is described as the all-seeing one (12:22; cf. 7:35; 9:5). Nicanor, the thrice-accursed wretch (v. 3; see 8:34), now taunts/challenges God, as Goliath taunted the Israelites (1 Sam 17:8-10, 26) and as Pharaoh's army had boasted in pursuing Moses and the Israelites (Exod 15:9; at Exod 20:8-11, the observance of the sabbath is grounded in God's creating heaven and earth). Nicanor's strategy does not work.

15:6-10, The Battle Preparations. The arrogance of Nicanor resembles that of Antiochus IV (9:8). As so often (12:14-15, 27-28), the author contrasts the two sides (cf. 15:20-26). Judas, like Moses (Exod 14:13) and Joshua (Josh 10:25; cf. Josh 8:1), exhorts his men not to fear and follows the speech proposed at Deut 20:1-4. Judas cites victories from the Torah and the Prophets, but also reminds his troops of their own prowess and skill. The perfidy of the Gentiles refers to Nicanor's violation of the covenant he had made (14:20-22, 28). In any competition, after all the training has been done, it is mental toughness that counts, and this is what Judas is instilling in his men (v. 11).

15:11-16, Judas's Vision. In antiquity, dreams were believed to be a means by which humans kept company with the gods. People were aware that not all dreams were heaven sent, but rather were a way the gods visited humans. Dreams are reported frequently in the narrative of Genesis as a way of learning God's will (e.g., Gen 15:12; 20:3; 40–41), whereas Jeremiah polemizes against the lying dreams of prophets (Jer 23:23-32). Daniel is both a dream interpreter (Daniel 2; 4) and a dreamer himself (Dan 7:1). The author of 2 Maccabees characterizes Judas's dream as "a certain waking reality" (v. 11; reading ὕπαρ τι [hypar ti] instead of ὕπερ τι [hyper ti], "beyond measure"). Such a term was as old as Homer[108] and applies either to the fact that the figures in the dream are so realistic or to the significance of the details that will come to pass. The detailed description of the dream suggests the first possibility here: The elements in the dream are so realistic that Judas thinks he is awake.

The characters in the dream are significant. Onias III (v. 12) takes the reader back to the beginning of the narrative (3–4:6); he is described using the expression to denote a perfect Greek gentleman, one trained in "all that belongs to excellence" (ἀρετή aretē; see also the lists describing Eleazar [6:18, 23] and Razis [14:37-38, 42]). Just as the priests had stretched out their hands (14:34), so also does Onias. The author stresses Onias's concern for the whole community. Whereas in 12:42-45 the living pray for the dead, here the dead Onias prays for the living. There is thus a continuance of existence beyond the grave. A second person of even more majestic mien appears but does not speak (v. 13). He is identified by Onias as Jeremiah (v. 14). Jeremiah's message was often one of doom and destruction to Judah, but he was also sent to build and to plant (Jer 1:10). Although commanded at one stage of his ministry not to pray for the people (Jer 7:16; 11:14; 14:11), once his prediction of

destruction had come true (Jeremiah 42) Jeremiah was asked to pray for the remnant of the people. At 2 Macc 2:1-8, he is portrayed as hiding the temple vessels until God discloses their whereabouts. Here he gives Judas a golden sword (v. 15; see 3:25; 5:2), the giving of which reflects that this is a battle against one who fights against God, and thus it is divine assurance of victory.[109]

15:17-19. The forces determine either "not to encamp" or "not merely to march" (v. 17). In either case, the effect of Judas's dream is shown as arousing the adrenalin of the soldiers. The author strives for emotional effect by picturing the anxiety of those in the city, but insisting that the main concern was for the Temple, and not the relatives (v. 18). The image almost suggests that those inside the city could see what was happening out in the open (v. 19), but that would be impossible for a battle at Adasa (see 1 Macc 7:40; the location of the battle is not given in 2 Maccabees). Earlier the author had claimed that the fires in Jamnia could be seen in Jerusalem (12:9).

15:20-27, The Battle. The tactics of this battle are not described in detail in 1 Maccabees. The deployment of the Seleucid army, described here, seems based on standard practice in Hellenistic armies (v. 20). It is unlikely the elephants were employed, as Octavius had had the Seleucid war elephants hamstrung in 162 BCE, before Demetrius ascended as king. The two sides are contrasted. While the Seleucid force draws on battle array (15:20), Judas prays for help (15:21-24), stretching out his hands to heaven (cf. 14:34), reciting Scripture (v. 21). In his prayer, Judas mentions the defeat of Sennacherib (v. 22; 2 Kgs 18:13–19:35; Isaiah 36–37), to which the author already alluded during the battle against the first Nicanor (8:19; cf. 1 Macc 7:41-42). Judas addresses God as "Sovereign of the heavens" (v. 23), playing off the boast of Nicanor (15:4-5). Judas asks that God send an angel (see 11:6) and that God send fear and trembling on the enemy (see Exod 23:20; 2 Kgs 19:35). The reference to "God's mighty arm" (v. 24) recalls the victory hymn at Exod 15:16, which recounts God's triumph over those who attack the people. The

---

108. See Homer *Odyssey* 19.547; 20.90.

109. The giving of special weapons to a hero is found widely in traditional literature. In the *Enuma Elish,* the Babylonian creation epic, Marduk is given special magic to subdue Tiamat. In the *Iliad,* Achilles is given special weapons to fight Hector. In Egyptian accounts, a god often gives a sword to Pharaoh to defeat his enemy.

battle songs of the Seleucids (v. 25; παιάνων *paianōn,* "paeans") were often addressed to Apollo as soldiers went into battle; these songs are contrasted here with the prayers of Judas's forces (v. 26; see 12:37). God once again is manifested (v. 26; see 2:21) in helping the people. The numbers killed are exaggerated.

15:28-36, The Dismemberment of Nicanor. The success of the Sovereign (15:4-5, 23), who is God of the Jews, is again signaled through the use of the ancestral language, Hebrew (v. 29; see 7:8, 12, 27; 12:37). The army returns from the battlefield toward Jerusalem (v. 28), recalling the victory procession of the divine Warrior to God's abode (Exod 15:17). Judas is described in glowing terms (v. 30), reminiscent of Onias III's concern for his compatriots (4:2, 5).

Judas orders his men to "cut off Nicanor's head and arm and carry them to Jerusalem" (v. 30). Decapitation and cutting off the right hand, the sword hand, was a custom found among the Persians,[110] but dismemberment is also found among the Greeks[111] and the Romans.[112] In Jewish tradition, David had brought the head of Goliath into Jerusalem (1 Sam 17:54), Judith displayed the head of Holofernes on the walls of Bethulia (Jdt 14:1, 11), and the Philistines cut off Saul's head and fastened his body to the wall of Bethshan (1 Sam 31:9-10). The details of the narrative here may have been influenced by heroic tales like these. Certainly the punishment is seen to fit the crime (vv. 32, 34; see 14:33, 36). While the author distinguishes those in the citadel from Judas's compatriots (v. 31), he has all the groups

blessing the Lord (v. 34). The fact that Judas can hang Nicanor's head from the citadel (v. 35) suggests that it is in Judas's control. All this is effective literarily, but probably incorrect historically, since the citadel remained under the control of the enemies of the Hasmoneans (1 Macc 9:53; 10:9); although Jonathan tried to gain control of it, he could not (1 Macc 11:20, 41), and it was not until 141 BCE that Simon conquered it (1 Macc 13:49-52). According to the author of 1 Maccabees, the Jews displayed Nicanor's head and right hand just outside Jerusalem (1 Macc 7:47). It seems unlikely that the corpse of an unclean Gentile could be brought into the view of the priests around the altar; if a Gentile was not to enter the Temple, and the skins of unclean animals were forbidden in Jerusalem, how much more so would a dead Gentile render the Temple unclean?[113]

The wording of v. 36 is exceedingly similar to that of 10:8, suggesting how the book was structured. The Jewish calendar begins at Nisan (March/April), and the last month, Adar, falls in February/March. It is interesting that the author of 2 Maccabees helps to identify the feast day by reference to Mordecai's day, known from the book of Esther (Esth 3:7; 9:20-23). The feast of Mordecai is thus acknowledged as well-established for the author of 2 Maccabees. Since the author of 2 Maccabees shows knowledge of otherwise unknown events in Babylonia (8:20), he may also have known about this popular celebration.

---

110. See, e.g., Xenophon *Anabasis* 1.10.1; 3.1.17; Plutarch *Aratus* 13.2.

111. See, e.g., Plutarch *Nicias* 27-28; Cleomenes 38.

112. See, e.g., Plutarch *Cicero* 48-49.

113. There is a debate among scholars as to whether some later rabbinic texts would allow a corpse into the court of women, although *Mishnah Kelim* 1.7 explicitly forbids burial within towns.

REFLECTIONS

The author himself drives home the point remorselessly that Torah obedience brings God's salvation. This last battle of the war books of 1 and 2 Maccabees brings us back, however, to reflect on how one can wage war justly. The dehumanizing treatment of Nicanor—cutting out his tongue, his right hand, leaving only the decapitated torso—recalls what the first of the seven martyrs underwent (7:4). The author revels in the maltreatment of Nicanor, but can we? Will such enjoyment not make us like our enemies? The difficult question is always, How do we resist the temptation to turn our enemy into a non-human, a monster, a tool of Satan? As we end the reading of these wars, let us take that problem with us.

2 MACCABEES 15:37-39

THE EPILOGUE

NAB

³⁷ Since Nicanor's doings ended in this way, with the city remaining in possession of the Hebrews from that time on, I will bring my own story to an end here too. ³⁸ If it is well written and to the point, that is what I wanted; if it is poorly done and mediocre, that is the best I could do. ³⁹ Just as it is harmful to drink wine alone or water alone, whereas mixing wine with water makes a more pleasant drink that increases delight, so a skillfully composed story delights the ears of those who read the work. Let this, then, be the end.

NRSV

37This, then, is how matters turned out with Nicanor, and from that time the city has been in the possession of the Hebrews. So I will here end my story.

38If it is well told and to the point, that is what I myself desired; if it is poorly done and mediocre, that was the best I could do. ³⁹For just as it is harmful to drink wine alone, or, again, to drink water alone, while wine mixed with water is sweet and delicious and enhances one's enjoyment, so also the style of the story delights the ears of those who read the work. And here will be the end.

COMMENTARY

The author chooses to end his account here, even though in his narrative he seems to at least mention events that occurred after Judas's defeat of Nicanor in March 161 BCE. For example, the author seems to know of the embassy of Eupolemus to Rome after this victory (2 Macc 4:11; cf. 1 Macc 8:17), although this is not certain, as there may have been earlier contacts with Rome that prompted the letter in 2 Macc 11:34-38. It is hard to reconcile the epitomist's statement that from the defeat of Nicanor the city was in the possession of the Hebrews (v. 37). Only a year after the defeat of Nicanor, Bacchides came back to Judea and conquered it, defeating and killing Judas and reinstalling Alcimus (1 Macc 9:1-57). The absence of any reference to Bacchides' first expedition (1 Macc 7:8-20) in 2 Maccabees supports the notion that the epitomist suppressed what did not fit into his program of profiting his readers. This book is propaganda history, and it should not be judged by any other criteria. It is a tightly structured story to praise the God of the Hebrews, who defends the Temple.

The last verses recall the different images the epitomist had used in his prologue (2:29-31) and his humble posture (2:26-27). Wines in the ancient world were so strong that they were usually mixed with water.

REFLECTIONS

One wonders at the end of the book whether it has been a bit too sweet a drink. It is patently a laudatory work, a work of aggrandizement. To the victor belong the spoils, and the historian of the victor helps to perpetuate the victor's point of view. But sometimes truth is despoiled as well. Yet the author of 2 Maccabees was following the conventions of Hellenistic historiography. The author of 2 Maccabees has centered his narrative around the Jerusalem Temple, the attempts to despoil it and the heroic deeds to save it. He may have been a trifle enthusiastic, however, in describing the valorous actions of Judas and his men.

The enduring contribution of 2 Maccabees lies in its affirmation of the ability of humans to have moral autonomy, to say no to oppression even at the cost of one's life, to hold to God's covenant even in the bleakest moments. The narratives of the martyrs are paradoxical, for these most gruesome descriptions of hideous deaths bring forth life and hope. Razis' exuberant tearing out of his entrails leads into the story of Nicanor's defeat and the safety of the Temple. Judas, against more numerous foes, risks all for God's glory. In this willingness to risk all, heroism shines forth, for God backs up the gamble.

The narrative is about events in history, but it is a history wherein God is the principal operator. The covenant faithfulness of the Jews brings God's defense of the Temple; their waywardness brings God's wrath. In the brokenness of this existence, God guides the people. This message of the presence of God within the events of human history, with all its suffering and toil, is one we must listen to. We do not expect to see men on horses with golden bridles fighting to protect us, but we do know that whatever our pain and travail, God is present in this world.

INTRODUCTION TO HEBREW POETRY

ADELE BERLIN

I t has been recognized since ancient times that the Hebrew Bible contains poetry, but the definition of what constitutes biblical poetry, the description of poetic features, and the identification of poetic passages have varied greatly over the centuries. This article will present a summary of the poetic features considered most relevant by contemporary biblical scholars, and will show how an understanding of them may lead to better interpretations of biblical poetry.

INTERNAL EVIDENCE FOR THE DEFINITION OF POETRY

A good starting place would seem to be the Bible's own terminology. Certain terms occur in superscriptions or within passages that may indicate poetic genres. The broadest of these is *šîr* (שיר) or *šîrâ* (שירה), meaning "song" or "poem." *Šîr* may stand alone, as in Judg 5:12 and Ps 65:1, or it may be qualified, as in *šîr hammaʿălôt* (שיר המעלות, "pilgrimage song"; Psalms 120–134), *šîr ṣiyyôn* (שיר ציון, "Zion song"; Ps 137:3), *šîr ḥādāš* (שיר חדש, "new song"; Pss 96:1; 98:1; 149:1). For other types of *šîr*, see Pss 30:1; 45:1; 137:4. The "feminine" form, *šîrâ,* is found, e.g., in Exod 15:1; Deut 31:30; Num 21:17. Another frequent term is *mizmôr* (מזמור, "song," "psalm"), which appears in numerous psalms, sometimes in combination with *šîr* (e.g., Pss 67:1; 68:1). A third term, *qînâ* (קינה, "lament"), is known from 2 Sam 1:17; Amos 8:10. While these terms provide a useful entrée into ancient notions of literary, or perhaps musical, genres, they do not encompass every passage that a modern reader would consider poetry.

Likewise, the ancient scribal tradition, practiced from rabbinic times, of writing certain sections of the Hebrew Bible stichographically (i.e., with space left between lines of a poem; see, e.g., Exodus 15; Deuteronomy 32; Judges 5) is suggestive of what may have been perceived as poems. Yet it is not a sufficient criterion by today's standards because, like the term *šîr,* stichographic writing was not used for all poetic passages and is occasionally used for nonpoetic lists (Josh 12:9-24; Esth 9:7-9).

The internal features of the biblical text neither adequately define nor identify poetry. Moreover, no ancient Israelite or ancient Near Eastern treatises on poetry or poetics have been found. Hence, scholars in each time and place, beginning with the Greco-Roman period, have applied to the biblical text definitions of poetry from their own literary tradition. Early Christian scholars discussed biblical poetry in terms of classical metrical systems, medieval Jewish scholars searched the Bible for the types of rhyme and metrical patterns found in medieval Hebrew poetry, and English Renaissance scholars sought the attributes of their style of poetry in the Bible. We do the same today, applying all we know of systems of versification, poetic syntax and vocabulary, symbolic and metaphoric representation—in short, all the ways in which language may be distinguished as poetic (as opposed to non-poetic)—to the study of biblical poetry. The result is an increasingly complex and sophisticated view of the Hebrew Bible's poetry and, by extension, all biblical language, as well as an ever-deepening aesthetic appreciation for it.

VERSE OR POETRY?

When we speak of verse we mean a type of discourse with formal properties, generally quantifiable, such as meter or rhyme, that distinguish it from other types of discourse. The search for such properties in biblical poetry has a long and largely unsuccessful history. For most of this history, attempts were made to uncover the Bible's metrical system. Biblical verse has been, at various times and places, described as quantitative, syllabic, or accentual. But despite much effort, no one has been able to demonstrate convincingly the existence of a consistently occurring metrical system. (See the section "Meter and Rhythm," below.)

M. O'Connor has suggested that instead of looking for formal arrangements built on the recurrence of phonological units (which is what most metrical systems are), we will find the formal properties of biblical verse in the arrangement of syntactic units. O'Connor proposed a system of syntactic constraints to define a line of verse.[1] The terms that he employs are *clause,* a verbal clause or a verbless clause; *constituent,* each verb and nominal phrase and the particles dependent on it; and *unit,* the independent verb or noun along with the particles dependent on it (generally equivalent to a word). According to this system, a line of biblical verse may contain no more than three clauses; it may contain between one and four constituents; and it may contain between two and five units. The dominant line form, according to O'Connor's description, contains one clause and either two or three constituents of two or three units. For example, Exod 15:7 may be analyzed as

7a.	וברב גאונך תהרס קמיך	*ûběrō b gě'ôněkā tahărōs qāmêkā*
7b.	תשלח חרנך	*těšallaḥ ḥărōněkā*
7c.	יאכלמו כקש	*yō'kělē mô kaqqaš*

In your great majesty, you smash your foes,
You send forth your anger,
It consumes them like stubble.[2]

Line 7*a* contains one clause of three constituents, 7*b* contains one clause of two constituents, and 7*c* contains one clause of two constituents. While O'Connor's work is frequently cited, and is generally recognized as an innovative description grounded on a sound linguistic basis, it has rarely been applied to analyses of biblical poetry. Perhaps his description has not replaced the older types of search for meter because it is technical and complex, or because it is difficult to imagine that a native poet would have thought in these syntactic categories.

Other scholars, including myself, feel that the quest for a formal system of versification should be abandoned because it does not exist. It is preferable, therefore, to speak of "poetry" rather than "verse." By "poetry" I mean a type of discourse that employs a high degree of the tropes and figures that are described below. Poetry can be distinguished from non-poetic discourse (historical narrative, legal discourse) by the comparatively high density of these tropes and by the structuring of some of them into recurring patterns. Poetry also employs sound and joins it to meaning in interesting ways. In stating this, I espouse a Jakobsonian view, which sees poetry as focusing on the message for its own sake. A poem conveys thought, and, moreover, it conveys that thought in a self-conscious manner, through a special structuring of language that calls attention to the "how" of the message as well as to the "what." At the same time, the "how" and the "what" become indistinguishable. Robert Alter, taking his approach from New Criticism, puts it slightly differently: "Poetry . . . is not just a set of techniques for saying impressively what could be said otherwise. Rather, it is a particular way of imagining the world."[3]

GENRES OF BIBLICAL POETRY

There does not seem to have been a formal or structural distinction between different kinds of poems. Hebrew poetry has no fixed number of lines or type of patterning that is characteristic of a par-

---

1. M. O'Connor, *Hebrew Verse Structure* (Winona Lake, Ind.: Eisenbrauns, 1980).

2. Unless otherwise specified, translations of the biblical text are the author's.
3. Robert Alter, *The Art of Biblical Poetry* (New York: Basic Books, 1985) 151.

ticular genre. If the ancient Israelites did make genre distinctions, those genres are largely lost to us. (They are presumably similar to the genres of other ancient Near Eastern literatures.)[4]

As one might have expected, form-critical studies have discovered genres or subtypes of poetry, especially as they can be related to a specific *Sitz im Leben,* such as victory songs or communal laments. Hermann Gunkel's work remains the classic source on form-critical types of psalms.[5] Following Gunkel, most scholars find the following genres in the book of Psalms: individual and communal laments, hymns of praise, thanksgiving songs, royal psalms, songs of Zion, and wisdom psalms.

Modern scholars tend to impose their own notions of genre, based for the most part on analogy with the tone and contents of genres in other literatures, when they divide up the poetic territory in the Bible. This division corresponds to a large degree with the biblical books in which the poems are found; thus Proverbs and Job are wisdom literature; Psalms contains praise (or lyric) or perhaps liturgy; Lamentations has laments; Song of Songs is love poetry (or perhaps wedding songs). In other books, one may find victory songs (Exodus 15; Judges 5; Num 21:28) or elegies (2 Sam 1:19-27; 3:33-34). Prophetic writing makes an interesting test case, as Robert Alter has observed, for some prophetic speeches are written as poetry and others as prose. Alter has suggested that the vocative (addressing the reader in the second person) and monitory (admonishing) nature of prophetic poetry distinguishes it from other poetic genres.

Actually, most studies of biblical poetry are not concerned with genre per se, but concentrate on the common features of all biblical poetry. These are presented in the following sections.

TERSENESS

Scholars of comparative literature who have searched for a universal definition of poetry have noticed that poetic lines tend to be shorter and terser than lines of prose. This feature seems to occur whether or not there are metrical constraints on the length of lines. Whatever the reason, poetry has a tendency to be more terse, more concise, than non-poetic discourse, both within a single line and, in the case of biblical poetry, over the discourse as a whole. Biblical poems are relatively short, usually thirty verses or less; there are no epic poems in the Bible. Lines are short, and the relationships or transitions between lines are often unexpressed. This gives the impression that in poetry each word or phrase is more loaded with meaning, since fewer words must bear the burden of the message. In biblical poetry, terseness within lines is achieved largely by the omission of the definite article (ה *ha*), the accusative marker (את *ʾēt*), and the relative pronoun (אשׁר *ʾăšer*). The decreased usage of these particles has been documented in computerized counts.[6] The relationship between lines is frequently not made explicit, but is implied by the parallelism that compels the reader to construe some type of relationship.

We can see some of the terseness and the effect of parallelism in a comparison of Judg 4:19 and 5:25, a poetic and a prose version of the same incident:

Then he said to her, "Please give me a little water to drink; for I am thirsty." So she opened a skin of milk and gave him a drink and covered him.
> (Judg 4:19 NRSV)

He asked water and she gave him milk,
 she brought him curds in a lordly bowl.
> (Judg 5:25 NRSV)

The poetic version is both more concise and more redundant. The parallelism in 5:25 sets up an exact equivalence, a reciprocity, which brings into focus the contrast between what was requested and what was served. The addition of "she brought him curds in a lordly bowl" does not add to the sequence of actions but doubles back upon the milk, stressing once more its "dairiness" (as opposed to water) and the noble flourish with which it was offered. The prose version carries the reader step by step along the narrative sequence, giving more information but not highlighting any part of it as the poetic version does.

PARALLELISM

Since the work of Robert Lowth, parallelism has come to be viewed as one of the two identifying

---

4. For biblical terms that may possibly indicate different genres see above, "Internal Evidence for the Definition of Poetry."

5. Hermann Gunkel, *Einleitung in die Psalmen. Die Gattingen der religiösen Lyrik Israels* (Göttingen, 1933).

6. See F. I. Andersen and A. D. Forbes, " 'Prose Particle' Counts of the Hebrew Bible," in *The Word of the Lord Shall Go Forth,* ed. C. Meyers and M. O'Connor (Winona Lake: Eisenbrauns, 1983) 165-83.

markers of poetry.[7] And since the other marker, meter, is notoriously resistant to analysis, parallelism, which is relatively easy to perceive (at least since Lowth called attention to it), has emerged as the predominant feature of biblical poetry. We should note at the outset, however, that parallelism is also present in non-poetic discourse, albeit to a more limited extent. So the mere existence of parallelism is not a sufficient indication of poetry, although a high frequency of parallelism in adjacent lines or verses has a high correlation with what we consider poetic discourse.

Parallelism may be defined as the repetition of similar or related semantic content or grammatical structure in adjacent lines or verses. The repetition is rarely identical, and it is the precise nature of the relationship between the two lines that has been the focus of most discussion. Indeed, the flexibility of this relationship, its capacity for variation, makes parallelism rhetorically interesting.

The Semantic Relationship. There have been two schools of thought on how to describe the semantic relationship between parallel lines. The first, introduced by Lowth and followed until recently, emphasizes the sameness of the relationship and the types and degree of correspondence between the lines. Lowth's classic definition is

> The correspondence of one Verse, or Line, with another I call Parallelism. When a proposition is delivered, and a second subjoined to it, or drawn under it, equivalent, or contrasted with it, in Sense; or similar to it in the form of Grammatical Construction; these I call Parallel Lines; and the words or phrases answering one to another in the corresponding Lines Parallel Terms.[8]

Lowth advanced his description by proposing discrete categories into which parallelisms could fit, depending on the nature of the correspondence of the lines. His categories are synonymous, antithetic, and synthetic. In synonymous parallelism, the same thought is expressed in different words, as in Ps 117:1:

Praise the LORD, all you nations!
    Extol him, all you peoples! (NRSV)

7. Robert Lowth, *De sacra poesi Hebraeorum* (*Lectures on the Sacred Poetry of the Hebrews*), 1753; *Isaiah: A New Translation with a Preliminary Dissertation and Notes Critical, Philological, and Explanatory,* 1778.
8. Lowth, *Isaiah,* 10-11.

In antithetic parallelism, the second line contradicts, or is opposed to, the first line, as in Prov 10:1:

"A wise child makes a glad father,
    but a foolish child is a mother's grief" (NRSV).

Synthetic parallelism, a much looser designation, accounts for parallelisms that lack exact correspondence between their parts but show a more diffuse correspondence between the lines as a whole. An example is Cant 2:4:

"He brought me to the banqueting house,
    and his intention toward me was love" (NRSV).

This tripartite system of categorization of types of parallelisms gained wide popularity, for it accounted for large numbers of parallel lines.

As scholars continued to study parallelism, they refined Lowth's original categories, furthering his typological approach by adding subcategories, such as staircase parallelism, in which the second line repeats part of the first but moves beyond it, as in Jer 31:21:

"Return, O virgin Israel,
    return to these your cities" (NRSV)

and janus parallelism, hinging on the use of a single word with two different meanings, one relating to what precedes it and one to what follows, as in Cant 2:12:

"The flowers appear on the earth;
    the time of singing [הַזָּמִיר *hazzāmîr;* or "pruning"]) has come
    and the voice of the turtledove/ is heard in our land."

In such an approach, the weak link was synthetic parallelism, because at best it appeared to be nothing more than a catchall of undefined categories or, at worst, a grouping of lines containing no parallelism. But the weakness of synthetic parallelism began to spread, as it was observed that no set of parallel lines is exactly synonymous or antithetic.

A major turning point came in the 1980s with the work of Robert Alter and James Kugel. Whereas Lowth's approach emphasized the similarity between parallel lines, Alter and Kugel emphasized their differences. Kugel rejected the notion of the synonymity of parallel lines and substituted the notion of continuity, phrasing his definition of parallelism as "A, what's more, B." Alter, moving independently in the same direction, spoke of the "consequentiality" of parallel lines. He saw the relationship between the lines as one of progression or intensification.

Indeed, both approaches contain elements of truth, for parallelism contains relationships of both similarity and difference. Take, for example, Ps 18:9 (Eng. 18:8 = 2 Sam 22:9):

> Smoke went up from his nostrils,
>   and devouring fire from his mouth;
>   glowing coals flamed forth from him. (NRSV)

There is a grammatical and semantic similarity among the three lines: *smoke/fire/coals* coming forth from his *nostrils/mouth*. But at the same time, within the general sameness there is an intensification, an escalation of the sense of burning. A clearer example is Lam 5:11:

> They raped women in Zion,
> Virgins in the Judean towns.

At first glance, these lines are synonymous, but on further reflection one sees intensification as one moves from *women* to *virgins* and progresses from *Zion* to *the Judean towns.*

Parallel Word Pairs. Lowth's definition had called attention to "parallel terms"—that is, "words or phrases answering one to another in corresponding lines"—but it was only with the discovery of Ugaritic poetry and the widespread acceptance of the theory of oral composition that efforts to analyze parallelism focused on parallel word pairs, or, as they came to be called, "fixed word pairs." Scholars noticed that certain sets of terms regularly recurred in parallel lines, such as *day/night* (e.g., Ps 121:6: "The sun shall not strike you by day,/ nor the moon by night" [NRSV]) and *heaven/earth* (e.g., Isa 1:2: "Hear, O heavens, and listen, O earth" [NRSV]). Such pairs were taken to have been the functional equivalents of the formulas in Greek and Yugoslavian poetry that enabled the poet to compose orally. The pairs were thought to have been fixed—i.e., they were stock pairs of words learned by poets who would then use them as the building blocks around which a parallelism could be constructed. Much research concentrated on discovering and listing these pairs (which were often the same in Hebrew

and Ugaritic) and charting their frequency, the order in which the members of a set occurred, their grammatical form, and the semantic relationship between them. This last element led to categories not unlike those elicited by Lowth: synonyms and antonyms. But new categories were also noted, such as a whole and a part, abstract and concrete, common term and archaic term, and the breakup of stereotyped phrases. Examples of recurring word pairs abound: *Jerusalem/Judah* (Isa 3:8; Jer 9:10); *father/mother* (Ezek 16:3; Prov 1:8); *right/left* (Gen 13:9; Ezek 16:46; Cant 2:6).

Research on word pairs advanced the scholarly understanding of the components of parallel lines and the lexical and poetic similarities between Hebrew and Ugaritic. But because the study was largely based on an unproven hypothesis about the oral composition of Greek poetry and a tenuous analogy between Greek formulas and Hebrew word pairs, it misconstrued the nature of word pairs. They are not "fixed," and they do not drive the composition of parallel lines. Rather, the process of composing parallel lines calls forth word pairs, which are nothing more than commonly associated terms that can be elicited by any speaker of the language (as word association games have shown). In fact, many of the same pairs occur together in non-parallel discourse (e.g., right/left, Num 20:17; 22:26).

Linguistic Models. In the 1970s and 1980s the focus of research on parallelism began to move away from word pairs and back to the lines as a whole. By then, however, there were new theories and models from the field of linguistics that offered new and better possibilities for understanding parallelism. Among the scholars employing linguistic models were A. Berlin, T. Collins, S. Geller, E. Greenstein, D. Pardee, and W. G. E. Watson. They drew on structural linguistics and transformational grammar for a grammatical analysis of parallelism. The major influence came from the work of Roman Jakobson, whose most famous dictum on parallelism was

> Pervasive parallelism inevitably activates all the levels of language—the distinctive features, inherent and prosodic, the morphological and syntactic categories and forms, the lexical units and their semantic classes in both their convergences and divergences acquire an autonomous poetic value.[9]

9. Roman Jakobson, "Grammatical Parallelism and Its Russian Facet," *Language* 42 (1966) 423.

This statement suggests that not only lexical units (word pairs) or semantic relationships, but all linguistic features as well come into play in parallelism.

Parallelism can be viewed as a phenomenon involving linguistic equivalences or contrasts that may occur on the level of the word, the line, or across larger expanses of text. (However, the analysis of parallelism generally operates at the level of the line.) Linguistic equivalence not only means identity, but also refers to a term or construction that belongs to the same category or paradigm, or to the same sequence or syntagm. This kind of equivalence can easily be seen in word pairs. Pairs like day and night or father and mother belong to the same grammatical paradigm (nouns) and might be said to belong to the same semantic paradigm ("time" and "family members").

Similarly, entire lines can be grammatically equivalent—that is, contain the same grammatical deep structure (and perhaps surface structure). I call this the *grammatical aspect.* In fact, Lowth had called attention to lines with similar grammatical construction in his definition of parallelism, but this feature had never been carefully analyzed before. With the advent of transformational grammar, it began to receive major attention.

For example, Ps 103:10:

Not according to our sins did he deal with us,
And not according to our transgressions did he
    requite us.

These lines have the same surface structure as well as the same deep structure. More often, though, the surface structure varies in some way, while the deep structure remains the same. For instance, in Mic 6:2*b* a nominal clause is paired with a verbal clause:

For the Lord has a quarrel with his people,
And with Israel will he dispute.

In Prov 6:20, a positive clause is paired with a negative clause:

Guard, my son, the commandments of your father,
And do not forsake the teaching of your mother.

The subject of one clause may become the object in the parallel clause, as in Gen 27:29:

Be lord over your brothers,
    and may the sons of your mother bow down to you.
(NIV)

Parallelism may pair lines of different grammatical mood, as in Ps 6:6 (Eng. 6:5) where a negative indicative clause parallels an interrogative one.

For in death there is no mention of you,
In Sheol, who can acclaim you?

All parallelism involves the pairing of terms, the *lexical aspect*; as already suggested, the process whereby specific terms are paired is similar to the process that generates associations in psycholinguistic word association games. Linguists have discovered rules that account for the kinds of associations made, much as biblical scholars had tried to discover the principles at work in "fixed word pairs." They have noted that in word association games a word may elicit itself; so, too, in parallelism a word may parallel itself or another word from the same root— e.g., 2 Sam 22:7: *I called//I called*; Job 6:15: *stream//bed of streams.* Linguists have also noted that a word may have a number of different associates and that some are likely to be generated more often than are others, thereby giving rise to the perception that some associations are "fixed."

The rules for word association are categorized by linguists as paradigmatic and syntagmatic (like the rules for the grammatical, and other, aspects of parallelism). Paradigmatic pairing involves the selection of a word from the same class as a previous word. The most common type of paradigmatic pairing is one with minimal contrast, which produces an "opposite," such as *good/bad* or *man/woman.* Other linguistic rules explain other paradigmatic choices.

Syntagmatic responses involve the choice of an associate from the same sequence rather than from the same class. This is often realized in the completion of idiomatic phrases or conventional coordinates, like *horses/chariots* or *loyalty/truth.* (This phenomenon is similar to what had been called the breakup of stereotyped phrases.) Another type of syntagmatic pairing involves the splitting of the components of personal or geographic names; e.g., *Balak//king of Moab* (Num 23:7) and *Ephrathah//Bethlehem* (Ruth 4:11).

While this lexical aspect of parallelism generally accompanies the grammatical aspect (the pairing of lines with equivalent syntax), it may occur in the absence of grammatical parallelism (strictly speaking, lines with paradigmatic grammatical equivalence). An example is Ps 111:6:

The power of his deeds he told to his *people,*
In giving to them the inheritance of *nations.*

The grammatical relationship of the lines is not paradigmatically equivalent. Moreover, *people* and *nations* do not refer to the same entity in this verse (*people* refers to Israel, and *nations* refers to non-Israelite nations). But the pair *people/nation* is a known association that occurs frequently, usually referring to the same entity. The manner in which this pair is used is somewhat novel, but the use of a common pair helps to draw the two lines together, making them appear more parallel.

Even in the presence of grammatical equivalence, word pairs may run counter to this equivalence instead of reinforcing it, as is more usual. An example is Job 5:14:

By day they encounter darkness,
And as at night they grope at noon.

Both lines express a similar thought (semantic content); during the daytime it will seem like nighttime. The semantic and syntactic equivalent terms here are *day/noon* and *darkness/night.* But the poet has employed a common word association, *day/night,* and has placed these terms in the same position in each line. In this case, the lexical pairing is at odds with the semantic and syntactic pairing, creating a tension between the two, which in turn sets up a competing relationship between the lines, thereby binding them even more closely together.

This illustration reminds us that the sense of the entire verse comes into play in the selection of word pairs, for words are chosen to express or emphasize a particular message. Just as the selection of parallel words is not totally random, so also it is not totally fixed. Through linguistics, we have come to understand better the process of word selection, and so to understand better the workings of parallelism and the effect of a particular word choice. Another illustration will demonstrate the subtle difference that the choice of a word pair can make. Compare, for example, Ps 102:13 [Eng. 102:12] with Lam 5:19:

But you, O LORD, are enthroned forever;
your *name* endures to all generations.
(NRSV, italics added)
But you, O LORD, reign forever;
your *throne* endures to all generations.
(NRSV, italics added)

The difference in the choice of one word underscores the difference in the messages of these two passages. Psalm 102 contrasts the weakness and fleetingness of a human being with the permanence of God. God's name—that is, God's existence—lasts forever. The author of Lamentations, on the other hand, laments the destruction of the Temple, the locus of God's throne. Despite its physical destruction, he maintains that God's throne—the metaphoric seat of God's rulership—will remain intact.

I have made reference to the *semantic aspect* of parallelism, which pertains to the relationship between the meaning of the parallel lines. Lowth characterized this relationship as synonymous, antithetic, or synthetic, and Kugel called it "A, what's more, B." From a linguistic perspective, the semantic relationship between lines (like the lexical and grammatical relationships) can be described as either paradigmatic or syntagmatic. It is not always easy, however, to decide specific cases, for often one reader sees similarity where another sees sequential development (see above the discussion on Lowth vs. Alter and Kugel.) Part of the confusion arises because both paradigmatic and syntagmatic elements may be present.

Ascend a high hill, Herald (to) Zion,
Lift your voice aloud, herald (to) Jerusalem. (Isa 40:9)

The actions of the herald are sequential (syntagmatic), but the vocatives, "herald (to) Zion/ Jerusalem," are paradigmatic. It seems to be the nature of parallelism to combine syntagmatic and paradigmatic relationships on different levels or in different aspects. The effect is to advance the thought, while at the same time creating a close relationship between the parallelism's constituent parts.

Another linguistic aspect that may come into play in parallelism is phonology. Equivalences in sound may be activated in parallelism just as equivalences in grammar are. This is the *phonological aspect,* which often takes the form of pairing words with similar consonants. These pairs may also be semantic or lexical pairs, such as שלום (*šālôm*) // שלוה (*šalvâ*), "peace" // "tranquility" (Ps 122:7); or they may be unrelated, as in Ps 104:19:

He made the moon for time-markers [מועדים *mô'ădîm*],
The sun knows its setting [ידע מבואו *yāda' měbô'ô*].

Sound pairs reinforce the bond between lines created by grammatical and lexical pairings, providing an additional type of linguistic equivalence in the parallelism. The more linguistic equivalences there are, the stronger is the sense of correspondence between one line and the next. Such similarity, in turn, promotes the sense of semantic unity.

There are infinite ways to activate linguistic equivalences, and hence there are infinite ways to construct a parallelism. No one type is "better" or "worse" than another. Each is designed for its own context and purpose.

METER AND RHYTHM

Although I earlier rejected meter as a demonstrably formal requirement of biblical verse, it is appropriate to summarize some of the modern analyses of meter because they are so pervasive in discussions of biblical poetry, and because they raise important questions about the nature of that poetry. Moreover, it is practically impossible for someone raised in a modern North American or European tradition to imagine poetry without meter.

Strictly speaking, meter requires the recurrence of an element or group of elements with mathematical regularity. The element to be measured may be the syllable (or a certain type or length of syllable), the accent or stress, or the word. (M. O'Connor's system of syntactic constraints is a substitute for meter, or a metrical system of a different order.) There have been various metrical theories of biblical poetry involving one or more of these elements. The theory of word meter assumes that there is a fixed number of word units in each line of verse. Related to word meter is the theory of thought meter, in which the thought unit (usually one or two words receiving one major stress) constitutes the basic unit of measurement. A third theory counts the number of syllables (without respect to whether they are open or closed, or stressed or unstressed). While technically not a metrical theory, syllable counting is related to discussions of syllabic meter. The most

popular theory of biblical meter is accentual, which counts the number of accents or stresses per line. This approach is sometimes combined with the counting of the number of words or syllables.

All of these metrical theories suffer from several deficits. First, none has gained sufficient acceptance among scholars to place it clearly above its competitors. Second, all have had problems defining precisely the unit to be counted. For instance, what constitutes a "word"? Does it include affixed prepositions? Is a construct noun (a noun linked grammatically to an adjacent noun, as in "mountain top") a separate word? Finally, when the counting is done, the pattern of recurrence of the unit does not appear with sufficient regularity, even within a few lines, not to mention throughout an entire poem. While there are certain parameters for the number of words or syllables that may occur in a line, these parameters do not appear to result in a metrical system. They are, rather, a factor of the biblical Hebrew language, the terseness of poetic lines, and parallelistic construction. It seems best, therefore, to abandon the quest for meter in the poetry of the Bible.

The absence of a real metrical system notwithstanding, sounds do seem to recur with some regularity in biblical poetry, and this recurrence can be differentiated from non-poetic discourse. I prefer to use the term *rhythm* rather than *meter* for this type of recurrence because *rhythm* conveys the notion of the recurrence of sound, or the patterning of sound, without the requirement of measured regularity.

The rhythm of biblical poetry results from terse parallel lines. The number of thoughts and, therefore, of words and of stresses in each line of a parallelism tends to be about the same—not necessarily precisely the same, but about the same. Benjamin Hrushovski has described this as "semantic-syntactic-accentual free parallelism,"[10] which, as far as the recurrence of sound is concerned, produces "free accentual meter." In this system, most lines have between two and four stresses. More important, the lines within a parallelism tend to have the same number of stresses. Thus parallel lines are rhythmically balanced. Lines throughout a poem may vary in number of stresses (within linguistic constraints), but sets of parallel lines tend to be of the same "length." An exception is the so-called *qinah* meter, the rhythm found in

10. "Note on the Systems of Hebrew Versification," in *The Penguin Book of Hebrew Verse*, ed. T. Carmi (New York: Penguin, 1981) 58.

laments, which has an unbalanced 3-2 stress pattern. Many lines in the Songs of Ascent collection (Psalms 120–134) have similarly unbalanced lines, but the pattern is not consistent. On the whole, though, a rhythmic balance within a parallelism, and sometimes over larger textual expanses, seems to be present, no matter what elements are counted. This rhythm, a by-product of parallelism, may be viewed as the "metrical" aspect of biblical poetry.

REPETITION AND PATTERNING

All discourse entails repetition, but we have come to expect more of it in poetry because we expect poetry to be more formally organized around certain structures and patterns. Patterning depends on repetition. We have already seen that parallelism, the most dominant characteristic of biblical poetry, involves many types of linguistic repetition or equivalences—grammatical structures, semantic terms, words, and sounds. While much of the repetition described in this section occurs in parallelism, and some is a direct result of parallel structuring, other forms of repetition occur independently of parallelism. Whether or not they are found in discourse formally designated as poetic, they add to the poetic nature of the discourse because they encourage the reader to focus on the message for its own sake; in Jakobsonian terms, they contribute to the poetic function.

The repetition described below involves repeating the same word or triliteral Hebrew root, or the same or closely related basic sounds. The repetition may occur in various combinations or patterns. Sometimes it seems designed to emphasize the message or to focus attention on only a part of that message. At other times, the effect is less discernible, but nevertheless creates an agreeable impression.

Key Words. The same word or root may occur numerous times throughout a passage. For example, the root שמר (šāmar, "guard") occurs six times in the eight verses of Psalm 121. In Psalm 137 (nine verses) the root זכר (zākar, "remember") occurs three times, and the root שיר (šîr, "sing/song") occurs five times. In both cases, the key words point to the essence of the psalm's message. Psalm 121 assures us that God is the guardian who never sleeps, and Psalm 137 struggles with the conflict between remembering Zion and singing Zion-songs—that is, between the

need to remember the Temple and the impossibility of performing the temple worship.

Anaphora. Several consecutive lines may begin with the same word or phrase. An excellent example is Psalm 150, in which every line begins with "praise him." Compare also Eccl 3:2-8: "a time to . . . and a time to. . . . " More often, the repetition occurs within just a few lines, as in Ps 13:2-3: "How long" (four times).

Cataphora (Epiphora). Consecutive lines end with the same word or phrase. This is rare in the Hebrew Bible and may be considered incidental. An example is Isa 40:13-14; both of these verses end with "instructed him."

Anadiplosis. In this type of repetition, the last word or phrase of a line is repeated at the beginning of the next line. Examples are Ps 96:13:

> before the LORD; for he is coming,
> for he is coming to judge the earth.
> He will judge the world with righteousness. (NRSV)

and Ps 98:4b-5:

> break forth into joyous song and sing praises.
> Sing praises to the LORD with the lyre,
> with the lyre and the sound of melody. (NRSV)

Side-by-side Repetition. This is the immediate repetition of the same word (a device used also in prose); for example, "Comfort, O comfort my people" (Isa 40:1 NRSV); "Awake, awake,/ put on your strength" (Isa 52:1 NRSV). Isaiah 28:10 (NRSV) makes extensive use of this form:

> "For it is precept upon precept,
> precept upon precept,
> line upon line, line upon line,
> here a little, there a little."

Refrain. A refrain is a phrase that is repeated after every verse or at major subdivisions of the poem. The refrain may have been chanted by a chorus in liturgical poems, such as Psalm 136, in which every verse contains the refrain "for his steadfast love endures forever" (cf. Ps 107:1, 8, 15, 21, 31). An example of a refrain in a non-liturgical poem occurs in David's lament over the death of Saul and Jonathan: "How the mighty have fallen!" (2 Sam 1:19, 25, 27 NRSV).

Inclusio (Envelope Figure, Frame). In this figure, the passage or poem begins and ends with the same word or phrase. The inclusio in Psalm 8 is

"O LORD, our Sovereign,/ how majestic is your name in all the earth!" (NRSV). In Psalm 103 it is "Bless the LORD, O my soul" (NRSV). The framing of a poem gives a sense of closure and completeness.

Chiasm (ABBA Word Patterning). There are many types of chiasm, or reverse patterning, ranging from within one verse to entire books. The figure has been widely documented. I cite here only two examples of the ABBA patterning of words in one verse or two.

Ah, you who call evil good and good evil,
who put darkness for light
and light for darkness,
who put bitter for sweet
and sweet for bitter! (Isa 5:20 NRSV)

Even youths will *faint* and be *weary,*
and the young will fall exhausted;
but those who wait for the LORD
shall renew their strength,
they shall mount up with wings like eagles,
they shall run and not be *weary,*
they shall walk and not *faint.*
(Isa 40:30-31 NRSV, italics added; this is part of a larger patterning of these words)

ABAB Word Patterning. Isaiah 54:7-8:

For a brief *moment* I abandoned you,
But with great *compassion* I will gather you.
In overflowing wrath for a *moment* I hid my face from you,
But with everlasting love I will have *compassion* on you.

Notice that the patterned words in Isa 54:7-8 are not semantically related, as they are in Isa 51:6:

Lift up your eyes to the *heavens,*
And look at the *earth* beneath.
For the *heavens* will vanish like smoke,
And the *earth* will wear out like a garment.

Sound Patterning. Various types of sound patterning are possible in poetry. I have already mentioned the use of sound pairs, terms in parallel lines that share the same or similar phonemes (see the section "Parallelism," above). The most common type of sound patterning that one might expect is rhyme, but such rhyme as can be found in the Bible is incidental. There are many examples of alliteration, the repetition of the same sound or sounds (or more precisely, consonance, the repetition of con-

sonant sounds). For example, Isa 1:2 contains what may be viewed as consonance in an AABB pattern: שמעו שמים והאזיני ארץ (*šim'û šāmayim wĕha'ăzînî 'ereṣ*; cf. also Ps 46:10; Job 5:8).

Closely related to consonance and to parallel sound pairs is paronomasia, or word play—the use of words with different meanings but similar sounds. This is a favorite technique in the Hebrew Bible, and it occurs in prose as well as in poetry. A classic example is in Isa 5:7:

ויקו למשפט והנה משפח   *wayĕqav lĕmišpāṭ*
                                              wĕhinnēh miśpāḥ
לצדקה והנה צעקה   *liṣdāqâ wĕhinnēh ṣĕʿāqâ*

This play on words is rendered in the Tanakh translation as:

"And He hoped for justice,
But behold, injustice;
For equity,
But behold, iniquity! (See also Isa 61:3; Zeph 2:4.)

The discussion thus far has focused on repetition and patterning within small passages of text, usually a line or two. Many more possibilities may occur in an entire poem. Of course, the most obvious structuring device is the alphabetic acrostic (Psalms 9–10; 25; 34; 37; 111; 112; 119; 145; Prov 31:10-31; Lamentations 1–4). Daniel Grossberg has analyzed centripetal and centrifugal structures. An adequate appreciation of the ways in which poems may be structured requires a separate study. I cite here only an example of the manner in which the various types of repetition presented above may intertwine and interact in one poem, Psalm 122.[11]

The key words of the psalm are *Jerusalem* (3 times) and *peace* (3 times), and they are good pointers to the message. The phonemes of *Jerusalem* echo in the word *peace* (שלום *šālôm*) and in several other words throughout the poem, so the entire poem reverberates with the sound of the city's name. *House of the Lord* (Temple) forms an inclusio, and at the midpoint, in verse 5, is *House of David.* Anadiplosis occurs in vv. 2-3 in the repetition of *Jerusalem,* and in two lines in v. 4: "To it the tribes go up,/ the tribes of the LORD" (NRSV). There is anaphora in the repetition of *there* in vv. 4-5 and *for*

---

11. See also Grossberg's analysis of this poem in Daniel Grossberg, *Centripetal and Centrifugal Structures in Biblical Poetry* (Atlanta: Scholars Press, 1989).

the sake of in vv. 8-9. The words שָׁלוֹם (*šālôm,* "peace") and שָׁלֵו/שָׁלָה (*šālâ/ šalvâ,* "have peace"/ "ease") alternate in an ABAB pattern in vv. 6-7; v. 6 has a high degree of consonance. Moving away from the repetition of words and sounds, we might note that the poem employs five verbs of speaking (*say, praise, ask, speak, request*) and four verbs of motion (*walk/go, stand, ascend, sit*). All of these forms of repetition help to bind the poem into a tight unity of sound and meaning.

IMAGERY

Metaphor and simile are hallmarks of poetry in all languages, to the extent that some theorists would define poetry in terms of the presence or dominance of metaphor rather than in terms of formal linguistic structures, like meter or parallelism. While biblical scholars generally do not view metaphor as the *sine qua non* of poetry, there is widespread acknowledgment that metaphor abounds in the Bible's poetic discourse. At the same time, there is widespread ignorance of how metaphor operates in biblical poetry, both from a theoretical point of view and on the practical level of how it affects the message of the poem.[12] An introductory article such as this one does not permit a full treatment of the theory of metaphor, or of the wealth of biblical examples, but a few observations on the use and effect of metaphor may be offered.

Imagery involves more than a simple comparison of one object to another. By placing the two objects in juxtaposition, a relationship between them is established such that their qualities become interchanged. This can be seen in Ps 42:2-3 [Eng. 42:1-2]:

As a deer longs for flowing streams, [אָפִיק *'āpîq*]
  so my soul longs for you, O God.
My soul thirsts for God. (NRSV)

Water, the life-sustaining element, is equated with God; and the psalmist's thirst for God is like the deer's thirst for water. It is a natural, intuitive thirst for a basic substance. Thus the qualities of the deer image are transposed to the psalmist. But "longing" is not an emotion usually associated with a deer. It is a human emotion, transposed from the psalmist's longing for God onto the deer. The verb that one would expect in v. 1 in connection with the deer, "to thirst," is used for the psalmist in v. 2. There is a crossover effect: The deer longs (like a human) for water, and the human thirsts (like a deer) for God. (The psalm continues in v. 4 with "My tears have been my food day and night" [NIV]—continuing the parallelism between "water" and "food/bread" and doing so through another metaphor, equating "tears" [water, non-food, a symbol of despair] with "food.")

Even stock images like water can be used creatively. Let us see how the same term found in Ps 42:2, "stream" (*'āpîq*), is used in two other passages.

My brothers are treacherous like a wadi,
Like a wadi-stream ['*āpîq*] that runs dry. (Job 6:15)

Restore our fortunes, O LORD,
like streams ['*āpîq*] in the Negev. (Ps 126:4 NIV)

The image in both verses is taken from nature: the wadis that flow with water in the winter and dry up in the summer. The primary transfer of qualities in Job 6:15 is from the water to the friends. They are treacherously inconsistent like the wadis; they are unreliable, changing with the seasons. The choice of water imagery may also suggest that, like water, the friends should be life-giving and that, therefore, their betrayal is all the more disappointing. But there is also a transfer in the other direction. One does not normally think of wadis as traitors; yet that is what is suggested here in a hint of personification of the wadis. (The root "to betray, be treacherous" [בגד *bāgad*] is never used of inanimate objects.)

The same natural reference serves a more optimistic purpose in Ps 126:4, where the return of the streams in the rainy season forms the basis of the image. Is the restoration of fortunes, like the streams in their cyclical return, a certainty? Or is it unpredictable (as in the Job verse), and therefore an act of grace?

Sometimes multiple metaphors are linked to one subject, generally to clarify or to reinforce the thought. The metaphors derive from different images and are linked only in that they convey a shared idea.

---

12. One of the few volumes devoted to this topic, G. B. Caird, *The Language and Imagery of the Bible* (London: 1980), is not helpful except as a catalogue of common images. The interpretations of Harold Fisch and Meir Weiss on specific passages are much more successful in explaining the workings of metaphor. See Harold Fisch, *Poetry with a Purpose* (Bloomington: Indiana University Press, 1988); Meir Weiss, *The Bible from Within* (Jerusalem: Magnes, 1984).

[two different images for speed]:
They go by like skiffs of reed,
    like an eagle swooping on the prey. (Job 9:26 NRSV)

And it [the sun] is like a bridegroom coming out
    from his wedding canopy,
It rejoices like a strong man in running his/its
    course. (Ps 19:6 [Eng. 19:5])

In the example from Psalm 19, which I have translated literally, it is not clear whether both images have the same sense—eagerness—or whether the first represents happiness/brightness and the second eagerness/strength. Again there is a crossover, this time between the two images, for "rejoices" (שׂושׂ *śûś*) is a verb more aptly used for a bridegroom than for a runner. The NRSV has neatly bound the two images together:

which comes out like a bridegroom from his wedding
    canopy,
and like a strong man runs its course with joy.[13]

There may also be a series of metaphors deriving from a central image—a conceit—as in Eccl 12:1-7; or a series of different metaphors for different parts of the subject, like the *wasfs* in Song of Songs 4–7.

When the Bible talks about God, it must speak, by necessity, metaphorically. God is *sui generis* and abstract, having no form, shape, color, or size. The deity is not like anything else, hence the only way to picture God is to compare God to other things. The most commonly used metaphor is that of a human, which results in anthropomorphisms, but aspects of God may also be compared to natural phenomena (Deut 32:11; Ps 36:5-7) or to the works God created (Ps 48:13-15).

On occasion, the same image may recur in close proximity with a new twist that gives a jarring effect, thereby reinforcing the power of the image, as in Isa 1:9-10:

If the LORD of hosts
    had not left us a few survivors,
we would have been *like Sodom*,
    and become *like Gomorrah*.
Hear the word of the LORD,
    you rulers of *Sodom!*
Listen to the teaching of our God,
    you people of *Gomorrah*. (NRSV, italics added)

---

13. But the NRSV may have gone astray here. The word occurs in Job 39:21 in connection with strength or eagerness. It may well be that the image in Psalm 19 is not one of joy, but of virility. See my article "On Reading Biblical Poetry: The Role of Metaphor" forthcoming in *VT*.

Because the Sodom-and-Gomorrah image has two different connotations, Isaiah is able to use it for two different effects. He first invokes the association of Sodom and Gomorrah with total destruction, suggesting that the destruction that he describes might have been, but for the grace of God, just as catastrophic. But then, in an arresting reversal, he calls upon the association of Sodom and Gomorrah with total corruption, equating his present audience with the wickedness of Sodom and Gomorrah, which must inevitably lead them to a similarly catastrophic end:

Raise your eyes to the heavens,
And look upon the earth beneath.
Though the heavens should evaporate like smoke,
And the earth wear out *like a garment,*
And its inhabitants in like manner die out,
My salvation shall stand forever.
My deliverance shall not cease.
Listen to me, you who know the right,
You people with my teaching in its heart.
Fear not human insults,
And be not dismayed at their jeers.
For the moth shall eat them up *like a garment,*
The caterpillar shall eat them like wool.
But my deliverance shall endure forever,
My salvation through the ages. (Isa 51:6-8)

The image of the earth's wearing out like a garment makes the earth, which does not wear out nearly so quickly, seem ephemeral compared to the permanence of God's victory. Then, in v. 8, the jeering enemy will be eaten as a garment eaten by a moth, making the enemy not only ephemeral but also powerless before the attack of a small insect that will come to punish it. While the single use of "Sodom and Gomorrah" and "being eaten like a garment" would be effective, the reuse of these images strengthens the rhetoric by forcing the audience to give deeper thought to the image and its range of associations.

Finally, when reading the Bible, especially Hebrew poetry, it is not always easy to know when to read the text figuratively and when literally. What are we to make of Ps 114:3-4?

The sea looked and fled;
    Jordan turned back.
The mountains skipped like rams,
    the hills like lambs. (NRSV)

It seems clear that the personification of the sea and the Jordan refers to a "literal" event, the crossing of the Reed Sea and the crossing of the Jordan, which form a frame around the wandering in the wilderness at the time of the exodus. But what of the animation of the mountains and hills? Was this earth imagery made up to match the water imagery, to provide a kind of figurative background? Or does it, perhaps, also refer to a "literal" event, the theophany at Sinai?

Psalm 133:1 presents a different case:

How very good and pleasant it is
   when kindred live together in unity! (NRSV)

Most modern scholars interpret this verse literally as a reference to family harmony. They perceive the entire psalm as a practical teaching on correct conduct. But, as I have shown elsewhere, this verse is both more concrete and more metaphoric than is generally understood. The phrase "live together in unity" is a technical legal term for joint tenancy (cf. Gen 13:6; 36:7; Deut 25:5), but the psalm uses the phrase metaphorically. The joint tenancy refers to the united monarchy. The psalm is expressing an idealistic hope for the reunification of Judah and Israel, with Zion as the capital and focal point.

FIGURES OF SPEECH

The notion of "figures of speech" is a Greek invention, as is much of the terminology used to describe poetic diction, but many of the phenomena that the Greeks identified in their own poetry and rhetoric may be found in other literatures as well. There is no clear consensus among modern scholars as to the figures of speech used in biblical poetry.[14] Among the figures of speech usually cited are allusion, apostrophe, hendiadys, hyperbole and litotes, irony, merismus, oxymoron, personification, and rhetorical questions. It should be noted that these figures also appear in the non-poetic sections of the Hebrew Bible, with the same rhetorical force. They are rhetorical figures, not poetic figures per se. These figures are not critical to the structuring of the poetry, nor do they dominate the poetic landscape like repetition or parallelism. They are merely deco-

rative, enhancing the rhetorical effect of the message.

For example, in Ps 107:26 sailors tossed about in a storm are described through hyperbole (extravagant exaggeration) and merismus (the expression of a totality through mention of its representative components) as: " . . . mounted up to the heavens and went down to the depths" (NIV). Often hyperbole is conveyed through metaphor or simile, as in Obadiah 4: "If she [Edom] soars aloft like an eagle; if she places her nest among the stars."

Personification of death can be seen in Isa 28:15 and Ps 49:15; and wisdom is personified as a woman in Prov 1:20-33 and Proverbs 8.

Rhetorical questions may occur in series (Job 38; Amos 3) or singly. The effect can be as varied as the message in which the question is contained: anguish in Lam 5:21; sarcasm in Job 8:12 and Zeph 2:15; instruction in Prov 31:10; amazement in Ps 8:5. A rhetorical question is a good way to draw the listener into the argument, and it is effectively employed by the prophets, as in Isa 5:4 and Jer 5:7, 9.

MOTIFS AND THEMES

A number of motifs or themes recur throughout or are specific to certain types of biblical poetry. These devices, no less than parallelism and repetition, are part of the forms of poetic expression. The recognition of motifs and themes allows the reader to understand them as overarching cultural references or metaphors and to compare their use in different contexts. They may be taken from the natural world, from human relationships, or from historical or mythical references.

Some themes are well-known, but even these have rarely been studied systematically. Among these are the prophetic use of familial relationships—i.e., husband-wife, father-child—to represent the relationship between God and Israel. Familial imagery is found throughout prophetic writing and reaches its height in the book of Hosea. Brief examples are:

I accounted to your favor
The devotion of your youth,
Your love as a bride. (Jer 2:2)

For I am ever a father to Israel,
Ephraim is my firstborn. (Jer 31:9)

14. The standard reference is W. Bühlmann and K. Scherer, *Stilfiguren der Bibel* (Fribourg: 1973), but compare, for example, the list of "Figures of Speech" in L. Alonso Schökel, *A Manual of Hebrew Poetics* (Rome: Pontificio Istituto Biblico, 1988), and the list of "Poetic Devices" in W. G. E. Watson, *Classical Hebrew Poetry* (Sheffield: JSOT, 1986).

Another pervasive theme is creation, which may be used to demonstrate God's infinite power over the enemy (Isaiah 40); God's benevolence to the natural world (Psalm 104); the awe and mystery of God's deeds (Job 38); the appreciation of the place of humans in the cosmos (Psalm 8); or the venerability of wisdom (Proverbs 8). Each iteration of the creation theme is different—in the wording used, in the items enumerated, in the aspects omitted or emphasized—so that the effect in each instance is tailored to the specific tone and message of the poem in which it is located.[15]

Other common motifs include God as a shepherd (Ps 23:1; Isa 40:11) and water as a metaphor for the life-sustaining nature of God (Ps 1:3; Jer 2:13). Less commonly recognized as a motif, but used frequently in the psalms, is the enemy or foe. This may be taken literally, but it is just as likely that it is intended to be an image for a more generalized type of danger or distress, physical or psychological.

O LORD, how many are my foes!
Many are rising against me. (Ps 3:1 NRSV)

O LORD my God, I take refuge in you;
save and deliver me from all who pursue me.
(Ps 7:1 NIV)
Lest my enemy say, "I have overcome him,"
My foes exult when I totter. (Ps 13:5)

An individual poet or prophet may have his own motifs or refrains, as Jeremiah does with "to uproot and tear down, to destroy and overthrow, to build and to plant" (Jer 1:10 NIV; 18:7-9 and passim) and Ezekiel does with "O, human being" (12:2, 9 and passim).

READING A POEM

Most scholarly analysis of biblical poetry has concentrated on its measurable features, such as formal structuring devices, repetition, parallelism, meter, and the like. Commentaries generally offer line-by-line interpretations focusing on difficult words and constructions or unusual references. Occasionally provided by the exegete, but often left to the reader, has been the actual reading of the poem—the making of sense and beauty from its sounds, words, and structures, the perception that it is a unified entity with a distinctive message. This,

after all, is the raison d'etre for all the analysis, but because it requires more art than science, there has been some reluctance to engage in it. But there are ways to approach the reading of poetry and some guidelines to direct the reading process. One might look for the movement within the poem, the repeated words or phrases, unexpected expressions or images, and the general tone and the effect that it produces. It is also useful to compare similar passages, with an eye to their differences. (Meir Weiss does this with great skill and insight.) An introductory article does not permit a full-blown discussion of these points, but a few examples may be offered.

Movement in Psalm 13. The psalm begins at the depths of despair: "How long, O LORD? Will you forget me forever?" (v. 1 NRSV). It slowly moves toward the possibility of hope: "Look at me, answer me, O Lord, my God" (v. 3). Then it reaches its climax in hope and exultation: "But I trust in your faithfulness . . . I will sing to the Lord for he has been good to me." The reader of this psalm, if identifying with the speaker, traverses the same emotional path from despair to hope.

Repetition in Job 38. Job 38 contains numerous rhetorical questions that involve first- and second-person pronouns: "Where were you when I laid the earth's foundation?" (v. 4 NIV); "Do you know who fixed its dimensions?" (v. 5); "Who closed the sea behind doors . . . when I clothed it in clouds?" (vv. 8-9); "Have you ever commanded the day to break?" (v. 12); "Have you penetrated the vaults of snow . . . which I have put aside for a time of adversity?" (v. 22). The effect of these pronouns is to create an opposition between the "you" and the "I"—Job and God—and the answers to the rhetorical questions prove that Job lacks even a fraction of God's knowledge and power. The combined effect is to show that Job is no match for God.

BIBLIOGRAPHY

The bibliography on biblical poetry is extensive, and much of it is extremely technical. It includes monographs and articles on specific features of poetry as well as explanations of poetic verses and sections in the Hebrew Bible. I have listed here only the most broad-based studies. References to more narrowly focused studies were made in the body of the discussion when appropriate. For additional bibliography, see Berlin,

15 See A. Berlin, "Motif and Creativity in Biblical Poetry," *Prooftexts* 3 (1983) 231-41.

The Dynamics of Biblical Parallelism; O'Connor, *Hebrew Verse Structure*; and Watson, *Classical Hebrew Poetry* (all cited below).

Alonso Schökel, L. *A Manual of Hebrew Poetics.* Rome: Pontificio Istituto Biblico, 1988.

Alter, R. *The Art of Biblical Poetry.* New York: Basic Books, 1985.

Berlin, A. *Biblical Poetry Through Medieval Jewish Eyes.* Bloomington: Indiana University Press, 1991.

———. *The Dynamics of Biblical Parallelism.* Bloomington: Indiana University Press, 1985.

———. "Parallelism." *Anchor Bible Dictionary.* New York: Doubleday, 1992. 5:155-62.

Fisch, H. *Poetry with a Purpose.* Bloomington: Indiana University Press, 1988.

Freedman, D. N. "Pottery." In *Poetry and Prophecy: Collected Essays on Hebrew Poetry.* Winona Lake, Ind.: Eisenbrauns, 1980.

Garr, W. "The Qinah: A Study of Poetic Meter, Syntax and Style," *ZAW* 95 (1983) 54-75.

Grossberg, D. *Centripetal and Centrifugal Structures in Biblical Poetry.* Atlanta: Scholars Press, 1989.

Hrushovski, B. "Prosody, Hebrew." In *EncJud.* 13:1195-1203.

Kugel, J. *The Idea of Biblical Poetry: Parallelism and Its History.* New Haven: Yale University Press, 1981.

Kuntz, J. K. "Recent Perspectives on Biblical Poetry," *RelSRev* 19, 4 (1993) 321-27.

O'Connor, M. *Hebrew Verse Structure.* Winona Lake, Ind.: Eisenbrauns, 1980.

Petersen, D., and K. Richards. *Interpreting Hebrew Poetry.* Minneapolis: Fortress, 1992.

Watson, W. G. E. *Classical Hebrew Poetry.* Sheffield: JSOT, 1986.

Weiss, M. *The Bible from Within.* Jerusalem: Magnes, 1984.

THE BOOK OF JOB

INTRODUCTION, COMMENTARY, AND REFLECTIONS
BY
CAROL A. NEWSOM

THE BOOK OF
JOB

INTRODUCTION

There was once a man in the land of Uz whose name was Job." With these words, the Bible introduces one of its most memorable characters. In the popular imagination Job is an icon, emblematic of the sufferer who endures the unendurable without complaint. Yet what many generations have tended to remember about Job is only one aspect of his story. The "patience of Job" has become a cliché that obscures the much more complex figure who appears in the biblical book. Although the book of Job begins with just such a depiction of Job the pious, patiently enduring calamity, that initial image serves as a foil for the contrasting representation of Job that follows: Job the rebel, who debunks the piety of his friends and boldly accuses God of injustice. In contrast to the majority of Jewish and Christian interpreters over the centuries, who have often seemed somewhat embarrassed by Job's unrestrained blasphemies, many twentieth-century readers, reeling from a century of unparalleled horror, have been drawn to Job's anger as a voice of moral outrage against a God who could permit such atrocities. The attempt to claim Job as the patron saint of religious rebellion, however, also encounters embarrassment, for at the end of the book, after God's speech from the whirlwind, Job withdraws his words against God. Neither the character nor the book of Job yields to an easy appropriation. To the reader who is willing to forgo simplistic answers, however, the book offers a challenging exploration of religious issues of fundamental importance: the motivation for piety, the meaning of suffering, the nature of God, the place of justice in the world, and the relationship of order and chaos in God's design of creation.

READING THE BOOK OF JOB: ISSUES OF STRUCTURE AND UNITY

Job is a challenging book to read, not only because of the theological issues it treats but also because of the form in which it is written. It begins with a simple prose story (1:1–2:13) describing Job's piety, the conversation between God and the *satan,* which leads to a decision to test Job, and the disasters that befall Job as the test of his piety. Abruptly, the style of the book changes in chap. 3, as Job and the friends who have gathered to comfort him begin to debate the meaning of what has befallen him and the proper posture Job should assume toward God. In contrast to the simple prose of the first two chapters, this dialogue is composed in elegant, sophisticated poetry, full of rare words and striking images. The climax of this section is the long speech of God from the whirlwind and Job's brief reply (38:1–42:6). At that point, just as abruptly, the style again shifts back to simple prose for the conclusion, as Job's well-being is restored and the remainder of his long life is briefly described (42:7-17). The changes between the beginning, middle, and end of the book are not merely stylistic, but also correspond to changes in the representation of characters and in the nature of the religious issues under consideration.

Although the relationship between the prose and the poetic sections poses the most intriguing questions about how one is to read the book of Job, the form of the central poetic dialogue also presents issues that affect one's understanding of the book. The dialogue takes shape initially as an exchange between Job and the three friends who have come to comfort him. Following Job's initial speech (chap. 3), this exchange exhibits a regular and symmetrical pattern throughout two cycles, but appears to break down in the third (see Fig. 4, "Dialogue Between Job and the Three Friends," below). In this third cycle, Bildad's speech is only six verses long (25:1-6), and Zophar has no speech at all. Even more perplexing, what Job says in parts of chaps. 24, 26, and 27 seems to contradict his own previous words and to assert views like those of the friends.

		Eliphaz	Job	Bildad	Job	Zophar	Job
First cycle:	chaps.	4–5	6–7	8	9–10	11	12–14
Second cycle:	chaps.	15	16–17	18	19	20	21
Third cycle:	chaps.	22	23–24	25	26	——	27

Figure 4. Dialogue Between Job and the Three Friends

Between the end of the third cycle and Job's long speech in chaps. 29–31 comes a poem on the elusiveness of wisdom (chap. 28). No heading introduces the chapter, yet its style and content are so different from the surrounding speeches that it is difficult to imagine its being spoken by any of the characters. Job's long closing speech in chaps. 29–31 is no longer addressed to the friends as part of the dialogue but contains a challenge to God (31:35-37). Yet instead of God's reply, the following chapters introduce a new character, Elihu, whose speech is uninterrupted for six chapters (chaps. 32–37). Only then does the divine speech occur, bringing an end to the poetic section of the book.

In scholarly discussions of the past century, these various elements have usually been interpreted as evidence that the book of Job grew by stages, the various parts attributable to different authors working at different times. Although there are many different versions of this hypothesis,[1] it usually includes at least the following claims.

Stage 1. The oldest form of the book would have been the prose tale, an ancient story, originally told orally, about Job the pious. This stage is represented by chaps. 1–2 and 42:7-17. The middle part of this form of the story is no longer extant, but would have included some sort of brief dialogue between Job and his friends in which they spoke disparagingly of God, while Job steadfastly refused to curse God.

Stage 2. An Israelite author who considered the old story inadequate and in need of critique decided to use it as the framework for a much more ambitious, sophisticated retelling of the story in which the figure of Job does not remain the patiently enduring character of the traditional tale, but challenges God's treatment of him. According to this hypothesis, the author substituted a new poetic dialogue between Job and his friends (3:1–31:37) in place of the discussion in which they engaged in the older story and added a long speech by God as the climax (38:1–42:6). The author used the conclusion of the old story (42:7-17) as the conclusion of his thoroughly transformed new version of the book. The poem on wisdom in chap. 28 may be a composition by this author, who used it as a transition between Job's dialogue with his friends and Job's dialogue with God, or it may be an addition by a later hand.

Stage 3. Another author, writing sometime later, considered the new version of the book of Job unsatisfactory, because he perceived that Job had gotten the better of his three friends in their argument, and because he did not find the divine speeches to be an entirely adequate answer to Job. Consequently, he created a new character, Elihu, and inserted his long speech into the book in order to provide what seemed to him a decisive refutation of Job's arguments.

Stage 4. Sometime during the transmission of the book, copyists who were shocked by Job's blasphemous words attempted to soften their impact by rearranging the third cycle of speeches, putting some of Bildad's and Zophar's speeches into Job's mouth.

Perhaps the least persuasive part of the hypothesis is the supposed rearrangement of the third cycle of speeches. Although some disruption may have occurred, the final result suggests incoherence more than a depiction of Job in the process of rethinking his views. Much more persuasive is the claim that the Elihu speeches are a secondary intrusion. The removal of his speeches would create no disruption in the rest of the book, for Elihu is not mentioned outside of chaps. 32–37, either in the frame story or in the dialogues. The absence of Elihu from the conclusion of the story is difficult to explain if he were an original part of the composition of either the prose frame story or the poetic dialogue. Also pointing to the secondary nature of the Elihu material is the fact that Elihu's speeches stand apart

---

1. See the discussions in H. H. Rowley, "The Book of Job and Its Meaning," in *From Moses to Qumran* (London: Lutterworth, 1963) 151-61; M. Pope, *Job*, 3rd ed., AB 15 (Garden City, N.Y.: Doubleday, 1979) xxiii-xxx; J. E. Hartley, *The Book of Job*, NICOT (Grand Rapids: Eerdmans, 1988) 20-33.

as a long monologue, unlike the speeches of Job's three friends, which are interspersed more or less regularly with Job's replies in the body of the dialogue. Elihu's discourse is also written differently, as he is the only character who explicitly cites other characters' words, a feature that suggests that the author of this section had the book of Job before him as he composed Elihu's speech. Since Elihu is the only character who bears a Hebrew name, it is possible, although quite speculative, that Elihu is actually the name of the writer who added these chapters—i.e., that he is a disgruntled reader who quite literally wrote himself into the book.

The hypothesis of growth by stages also provides a plausible account of the relationship between the prose tale and the poetic dialogue, and it offers an explanation for the incongruity that exists between the end of the poetic section and the final prose conclusion. In 42:7-9, God rebukes the friends for not having spoken correctly about God, as Job has done. This comment is difficult to reconcile with the book as we know it, but it seems to point back to a different form of the story, the "missing middle" that was displaced to make room for the poetic dialogues. No direct evidence for the independent existence of the old prose tale exists, but there is indirect testimony. Bishop Theodore of Mopsuestia (c. 350–428 CE) was familiar with an oral version of the story of the pious Job that did not contain the angry speeches of the canonical book and that was popular among both Jews and others. Indeed, Bishop Theodore considered the oral story to be the true story of Job, considering the biblical version as a literary production composed to show off the learning and poetic skill of its author.[2]

Critics who argue that the book of Job developed in this way rarely address the question of how one is supposed to read the book as it now exists. Indeed, one of the unfortunate consequences of this hypothesis about the composition of Job is that it has often led to interpretations of the book that fail to take its final or canonical form seriously. In recent years there has been a reaction against this tendency to treat the book as an assortment of parts rather than a single whole. Increasingly, even commentators who consider that the book may well have undergone some form of growth and redaction have nevertheless argued that one should read the book "as if" it were the product of a single author.[3] Occasionally, the claim is made that the book possesses a literary, thematic, and even stylistic unity best accounted for as the work of a single author.[4] Supporting the argument in favor of a single author is the contention that the prose tale in chapters 1–2 and 42 cannot be understood as more or less a transcription of an oral folktale but is a highly sophisticated piece of narrative art written

2. See the report of Isho'dad of Merv, the ninth-century CE author who summarizes Bishop Theodore's views, cited in D. Zaharopoulos, *Theodore of Mopsuestia on the Bible: A Study of His Old Testament Exegesis* (New York: Paulist, 1989) 45-48. B. Zuckerman has suggested that the epistle of James alludes to the familiar oral tale rather than to the canonical book of Job when it says, "You have *heard* of the patience of Job" (James 5:11) rather than "you have *read* [in the Bible] of the patience of Job" (Zuckerman, *Job the Silent: A Study in Historical Counterpoint* [New York: Oxford University Press, 1991] 13-14).

3. E.g., F. Andersen, *Job: An Introduction and Commentary,* Tyndale Old Testament Commentaries (Downers Grove, Ill.: Inter-Varsity, 1976) 55; J. G. Janzen, *Job,* Interpretation (Atlanta: John Knox, 1985).

4. N. Habel, *The Book of Job,* OTL (Philadelphia: Westminster, 1985) 35-40. Cf. Hartley, *The Book of Job,* 20.

in a deliberately "pseudo-naive" style.[5] To make that claim is not to reject the evidence for the existence of oral tales and traditions about Job, but only to recognize that the form of the story as we have it in Job 1–2; 42 is the product of a skilled author who has written an artistic imitation of such a popular story as the framework for his retelling of the story of Job.

Apart from the Elihu speeches, which seem quite clearly to be a later addition to the book, I confess to being an agnostic on the question of whether the book of Job grew by stages or was written by a single author, although I incline to the latter view. Interpretively, the important issue is not how the book attained its present form but how the shape of the book contributes to its meaning. In this regard, the presence of Elihu, the incoherence of the third cycle, and the role of the poem on wisdom raise interesting but relatively minor interpretive issues. The vital question is how one understands the significance of the abrupt juxtaposition of the two very different ways of telling the story of Job one finds in the prose and poetic parts of the book. The position taken in this commentary is that the incongruities produced by the transition to the prose conclusion in 42:7-9 are intentionally designed to call attention to these differences and to frustrate attempts to read the book as a single coherent narrative.[6] Whether this structure was produced by an editor who chose to let the discrepancies stand when the prose tale was adopted as a framing device, or whether it was produced by a single author who composed both prose and poetry, cleverly planning the incongruities, the effect is of a book "at odds with itself."[7]

Far from being an embarrassment, recognition that the book is at odds with itself is key to understanding its meaning and purpose. Dialogue is at the heart of the book of Job. The clash of divergent perspectives is represented in the three cycles of disputation between Job and his friends (chaps. 3–27). Job's final speech of self-justification (chaps. 29–31) stands over against God's answer from the whirlwind (chaps. 38–41) in dialogical relationship. By means of the cleverness of editor or author, the book as a whole is also structured as a dialogue of two very different prose and poetic voices, two very different ways of telling the same story that cannot be harmonized into a single perspective.

Representing two different ways of telling the same story within a single composition presents an artistic challenge. One could, of course, tell one version of the story in its entirety and then tell the other. The dialogic relationship is enhanced, however, by having one way of telling the story interrupt the other, as happens in the book of Job. This structure of two intersecting ways of telling the story may be visualized as follows:

5. D. Clines, "False Naivete in the Prologue to Job," HAR 9 (1985) 127-36. The extensive and symmetrical repetition, highly stylized characters, and studied aura of remote antiquity imitate but exaggerate features of folktale style. Alongside these features are subtle word plays and verbal ambiguities that suggest an ironic distance from the aesthetic of simple naivete.

6. See C. Newsom, "Cultural Politics in the Book of Job," *Biblical Interpretation* 1 (1993) 119-34. In contrast, cf. the interpretive position taken by N. Habel, *The Book of Job*, 25-35.

7. Zuckerman, *Job the Silent*, 14.

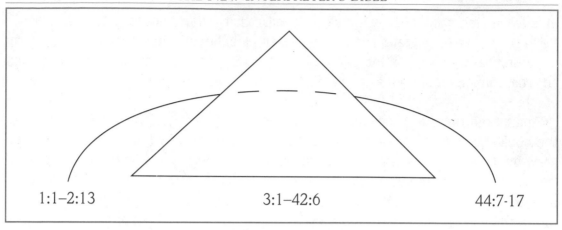

Figure 5: The Narrative Structure of Job

1:1–2:13   3:1–42:6   44:7-17

This design works artistically because the frame story, whether considered as a naive popular tale or a "pseudo-naive" tale, invokes certain narrative conventions belonging to traditional storytelling that give such stories a high degree of predictability. As surely as a story that begins "Once upon a time . . . " must end with " . . . and they all lived happily ever after," readers know almost immediately what kind of story is being told in Job 1–2, how it will develop, and how it must end. One can plot the trajectory of the story line on the basis of these conventions. After God and the narrator have vouched for Job's character against the detractions of the *satan,* there can be no doubt about how Job will conduct himself. Since significant features often cluster in sequences of three in traditional storytelling, one expects three trials of Job's piety, before the obligatory happy ending. Thus, when the author of Job interrupts the frame story with the very different material in 3:1–42:6, a dialogical relationship is set up between what one knows is "supposed" to happen in this sort of a tale and what is actually happening in the story.

The tension set up by this structure is not only an aesthetic one. Social, moral, and religious values and assumptions are always embedded in particular modes of telling a story. By disrupting the prose tale, the poetic section of Job also challenges its assumptions about the nature of piety, the grounds of the relationship between humans and God, the proper stance toward suffering, etc.

If the book of Job had ended with a smooth transition from the poetic section to the concluding prose, then perhaps a synthesis of perspectives might have been fashioned. In the book as we have it, however, the transition to the prose tale is both abrupt and incongruous. The prose conclusion takes no account of the poetic dialogue but gestures back to the missing middle of the traditional tale, to what was "supposed" to happen according to its conventions. Moreover, as the Commentary on 42:7-17 will discuss, the presence of the prose conclusion following the dialogue and divine speeches actually creates both dissonance and irony, which threaten to unravel the sense of closure created by God's speech and Job's reply at the end of the poetic section. The book of Job thus presents the reader with unresolved perspectives. The theological implications of this structure are considered below.

DATE AND PROVENANCE

When, by whom, and for whom a book is written are important in understanding its meaning and significance. As the preceding discussion already suggests, those are difficult questions to answer with respect to Job, since different parts of the book may have been composed at different times for different audiences. Estimates for the date of the book as a whole (excepting the Elihu speeches), have ranged from the tenth century to the second century BCE, with most scholars opting for dates between the seventh and fifth centuries BCE.[8] Part of the difficulty in establishing a date for the book is that it contains no references to historical events or persons. Attempts to date the book according to its themes or place within the history of the religion of Israel are precarious, since it is difficult to demonstrate that the issues and religious values of the book of Job would be at home in only one era. More persuasive is the argument that certain motifs, such as the representation of the *satan* in chaps. 1–2, have their closest parallels in literature from the early post-exilic period (cf. 1 Chr 21:1; Zech 3:1-2).

Linguistic evidence has also been used to date the book; yet even here one encounters ambiguity. The poetic dialogues contain linguistic forms that one would expect to find in archaic Hebrew, from approximately the tenth century BCE.[9] Since these speeches appear to be written in a deliberately archaizing style and lack other poetic features one associates with very ancient Hebrew poetry, the argument for such an early date has not been generally accepted. The prose tale also contains narrative and stylistic details that suggest great antiquity.[10] Yet here, too, one must distinguish between what is genuinely archaic from an artistic imitation of archaic style. The most careful linguistic study has argued that the prose tale in its present form is no older than the sixth century BCE.[11] If that is the case, the book of Job as a whole is best taken as a composition of the early post-exilic period (sixth–fifth centuries BCE), whether one considers the book to have been composed by a single author, writing in two different styles, or by an author who appropriated an existing prose tale as the framework for a new composition.[12]

The Elihu speeches are difficult to date for many of the same reasons. The latest date for their composition is determined by their presence in the Aramaic translation of Job found in the Dead Sea Scrolls. Although that manuscript dates from the first century CE, the translation may have taken place as early as the second century BCE.[13] The only other

8. See J. Roberts, "Job and the Israelite Religious Tradition," *ZAW* 89 (1977) 107-14.

9. D. Robertson, *Linguistic Evidence in Dating Early Hebrew Poetry,* SBLDS 3 (Missoula, Mont.: SBL, 1972) 153-56.

10. N. Sarna, "Epic Substratum in the Prose of Job," *JBL* 76 (1957) 13-25.

11. A. Hurvitz, "The Date of the Prose Tale of Job Linguistically Reconsidered," *HTR* 67 (1974) 17-34.

12. B. Zuckerman, *Job the Silent: A Study in Historical Counterpoint* (New York: Oxford University Press, 1991) 26, however, argues that the linguistic evidence as a whole indicates that the dialogues are chronologically older than the prose tale.

13. Here, too, the basis for that date is linguistic. See J. P. M. van der Ploeg and A. S. van der Woude, *Le Targum de Job de la Grotte XI de Qumran* (Leiden: Brill, 1972) 4.

basis upon which to date the Elihu speeches is the similarity of their ideas and expressions to other literature. While such evidence is not decisive, recent scholarship on the Elihu speeches has tended to place them in the third century BCE.[14]

Arguably more important than date is the question of by whom and for whom the book was written. Since no independent evidence exists, this question has to be posed in terms of the assumptions and values embodied in the book. Although much remains elusive, there are certain clues to its intellectual context and social class perspectives.

The book of Job is an immensely learned and cosmopolitan work. One recognizes this quality in the texture of the language itself, which is full of rare vocabulary and archaic verbal forms. The complex and beautiful poetry contains numerous mythological allusions, some of which appear to be based on Egyptian and Mesopotamian traditions. Furthermore, the poetic dialogue presents Job in terms of a sophisticated reworking of the Mesopotamian tradition of "the righteous sufferer" (see "The Book of Job and Ancient Near Eastern Tradition," 328-34). This same command of cultural and literary forms is evident in the author's treatment of genres and stylistic features drawn from Israelite tradition. The speeches of Job and his friends are largely shaped as disputations and make use of a rich variety of rhetorical devices one finds in wisdom, prophetic, and legal argumentation (e.g., rhetorical questions, wisdom sayings, appeals to ancient tradition). The author also displays a similar command of the genres of Israelite piety, in particular the hymn, the psalm of praise, and the complaint psalm. Not only are these forms cited in their traditional modes, but in the speeches of Job they are also rendered as exquisite parodies. Legal vocabulary, categories, and practices are similarly drawn upon for the development of a forensic metaphor through which to explore Job's relationship with God. The overall impression is of an author who has a remarkable command of the religious literature and traditions of Israel and its neighbors.

Although the author of Job orchestrates motifs, genres, and themes from a variety of different discourses in a way that is not characteristic of the books of Proverbs and Ecclesiastes, one should identify the book of Job primarily with the wisdom tradition. The very subject matter of the book suggests as much. Wisdom literature is centrally concerned with the nature of the proper moral and religious conduct of an individual and with the relation of such conduct to personal and communal well-being. Moreover, wisdom tends to pursue such questions in ways that do not make use of distinctively national religious traditions so much as they employ the conventions, styles, and language of an international discourse of wisdom. This orientation characterizes the book of Job, in which traditions about the non-Israelite Job are used to develop a critical reflection on the assumption that good conduct and well-being are related. More specifically, the theme of "fearing God," which is programmatic for the book of Proverbs (Prov 1:7; 9:10), also occurs in significant places in the framing of the book of Job, not only in the prose tale but also in the poem that concludes the dialogue between Job and his friends (1:1, 8; 2:3; 28:28). The friends'

14. H.-M. Wahl, *Der Gerechte Schoepfer,* BZAW 207 (Berlin and New York: Walter de Gruyter, 1993) 182-87. Cf. T. Mende, *Durch Leiden zur Vollendung,* Trierer Theologische Studien 49 (Trier: Paulinus-Verlag, 1990) 419-27.

speeches, too, contain the sort of advice and admonition that has been described as "sapiential counselling."[15] The theme of wisdom is most explicit in the poem in chap. 28, in the refrain, " 'But where shall wisdom be found?' " (28:12, 20 NRSV). The prominence of creation motifs, both in chap. 28 and especially in the divine speeches, is also characteristic of wisdom, which often sets the question of the moral order of the world in terms of the structures of creation (e.g., Proverbs 3; 8; Ecclesiastes 1; Sirach 24). Finally, the wisdom tradition as a whole is typified both by conventional voices, which one largely hears in Proverbs, and skeptical, subversive voices, such as Ecclesiastes. In Job these two voices are joined in dialogue, not only in the dialogue between Job and his friends but also in the very form of the book, as discussed above. Thus the book of Job, although unique in many respects, is best understood as a part of the intellectual and cultural world of wisdom.

There is little consensus about the social identity of Israel's sages.[16] Although the sources of wisdom thought may lie in the social structures of families and tribes, wisdom *books* like Job are likely to emerge from a different institutional setting. Analogies with Egyptian wisdom literature suggest that such works were the product of a scribal class, the members of which served as administrators in the court or temple. Alternatively, it has been suggested that schools for the education of upper-class youths provided the social context for the composition of wisdom books. But the existence of such institutions is speculative. Although it is clear that Job is the product of an intellectual milieu, the exact nature of the social context in which it was produced and read cannot be known.

The issue of social class perspectives in the book of Job is complicated by the fictional setting of the book. Simply because the characters are depicted as wealthy aristocrats, one cannot necessarily assume that the author and audience are of that class. The more appropriate question to ask is what ethos is reflected in the book; when the issue is framed in those terms it is easy to agree that, whatever the actual social class of the author, the book addresses issues through the perspective of aristocratic sensibilities and values. In particular, Job's final speech (chaps. 29–31) provides an extended statement of the moral values of an aristocratic and patriarchal culture.[17] Attempts have been made to locate the social context of Job more specifically within the socioeconomic changes of the Persian period, when disruptions in traditional economic and social relations threatened to displace many old aristocratic families and brought increased suffering to the very poor, while the *nouveau riche,* who lacked traditional aristocratic religious and social values, exploited the new possibilities for their own benefit (cf. Nehemiah 5).[18]

15. N. Habel, *The Book of Job,* OTL (Philadelphia: Westminster, 1985) 118.

16. See, e.g., R. N. Whybray, "The Social World of the Wisdom Writers," in R. E. Clements, *The World of Ancient Israel* (Cambridge: Cambridge University Press, 1989) 227-50; M. B. Dick, "Job 31, the Oath of Innocence, and the Sage," ZAW 95 (1983) 31-53.

17. C. Newsom, "Job," in *The Women's Bible Commentary,* ed. C. Newsom and S. Ringe (Philadelphia: Westminster/John Knox Press; London: SPCK, 1992) 133-35; M. B. Dick, "Job 31, the Oath of Innocence, and the Sage," ZAW 95 (1983) 31-53.

18. See F. Cruesemann, "Hiob und Kohelet: Ein Beitrag zum Verstaendnis des Hiobbuches," *Werden und Wirken des Alten Testaments* (Westermann Festschrift), ed. R. Albertz et al. (Goettingen and Neukirchen: Vandenhoeck & Ruprecht and Neukirchener Verlag, 1980) 373-93; R. Albertz, "Der sozialgeschichtliche Hintergrund des Hiobbuches und der 'Babylonischen Theodizee,' " *Die Botschaft und die Boten* (Wolff Festschrift), ed. J. Jeremias and L. Perlitt (Neukirchen: Neukirchen Verlag, 1981) 349-72.

Although it is plausible to consider the author of the Joban dialogues as representing the perspectives of the old aristocratic culture in the context of the economic upheavals of the Persian period, it would be difficult to claim that the social conflicts presupposed by Job and his friends were unique to that period.

THE BOOK OF JOB AND ANCIENT NEAR EASTERN TRADITION

Scholars agree that neither the character Job nor the story about his misfortunes originated in Israel. The name "Job" is not a typically Israelite name, although forms of the name are attested in Syria-Palestine in the second millennium BCE.[19] Moreover, the story itself associates Job with the land of Uz, a place that is to be located either in Edomite or Aramean territory. Job's three friends—Eliphaz the Temanite, Bildad the Shuhite, and Zophar the Naamathite—also come from non-Israelite locales. (See Commentary on Job 1:1; 2:11). The story as we have it in the Bible has been adapted for an Israelite religious context, however, so that Yahweh is assumed to be the God whom Job serves.

Although no trace of a pre-Israelite Job story exists in sources yet discovered from the ancient Near East, there is one biblical text that associates Job with two other non-Israelite characters whose stories had been incorporated into Israelite tradition. The prophet Ezekiel refers to Job in the context of an oracle from God concerning judgment against Jerusalem:

> "Mortal, when a land sins against me by acting faithlessly, and I stretch out my hand against it, and break its staff of bread and send famine upon it, and cut off from it human beings and animals, even if Noah, Daniel, and Job, these three, were in it, they would save only their own lives by their righteousness, says the Lord [Yahweh] . . . as I live, says the Lord [Yahweh], they would save neither son nor daughter; they would save only their own lives by their righteousness." (14:13, 20 NRSV)

Noah, the hero of the flood story, is a non-Israelite (or pre-Israelite) character whose story is told in Genesis 6–9. Although the name "Noah" is known only from biblical tradition, the character and his story originate in Mesopotamia, where he is variously known as Utnapishtim and Atrahasis.[20] Dan'el is not the Judean exile, hero of the book of Daniel, but a legendary Canaanite king. Although he is otherwise mentioned in the Bible only in Ezek 28:3, his story is told in the Ugaritic epic of Aqhat, the text of which was found in the second millennium BCE tablets excavated at Ras Shamra.[21]

Ezekiel's brief allusion takes for granted that his audience knows the stories of all these ancient paragons of righteousness. Yet it is difficult to say in detail exactly what stories about these figures Ezekiel and his audience know, whether they are the same ones preserved in the written accounts or from different oral traditions. The reference in Ezek 14:20 appears to suggest that all three somehow save their children from danger by means

19. M. Pope, *Job,* 3rd ed., AB 15 (Garden City, N.Y.: Doubleday, 1979) 5-6.
20. For the Mesopotamian versions of the flood story, see James B. Pritchard, ed., *Ancient Near Eastern Texts Relating to the Old Testament* (*ANET*), 3rd ed. with supplement (Princeton: Princeton University Press, 1969) 93-95, 104-6.
21. Ibid., 149-55.

of their own righteousness. In Genesis 6–9, Noah's righteousness saves not only his own life but also those of his children when he takes them aboard the ark. Dan'el's story from the Ugaritic tablets is unfortunately broken off at a critical place, but it does involve the death of his son at the hand of the goddess Anat, the recovery of his body, and Dan'el's seven years of mourning for Aqhat. Whether the story told of Aqhat's restoration to life because of Dan'el's righteousness, as Ezekiel's allusion might suggest, is not known. With respect to Job, Ezekiel's allusion may refer to Job's attempting to protect his children by sacrificing on their behalf, in case "my children have sinned, and cursed God in their hearts" (Job 1:5 NRSV). In the canonical story of Job, the children are eventually killed as a part of the test of Job's righteousness. Ezekiel, however, may have known versions of the stories different from the ones preserved in written sources. Like Noah and Dan'el, Job appears to have been an ancient non-Israelite or pre-Israelite whose story, originally developed in other parts of the ancient Near East, had been incorporated into Israelite religious culture by the sixth century BCE.

In contrast to the prose tale, for which there are only tantalizing hints but no clear ancient Near Eastern parallels, the poetic dialogue in the book of Job has been compared to a variety of ancient Near Eastern texts from Egypt, Mesopotamia, and Ugarit.[22] For the most part, however, the similarities are much too general to be significant and do little to illumine the specific literary tradition to which the poetic dialogue of Job belongs. Only two categories of texts warrant discussion. The first is the tradition of Mesopotamian liturgical texts from the second millennium BCE in which a sufferer praises his god for deliverance from suffering. Among these are the Sumerian composition known as "Man and His God: A Sumerian Variation on the 'Job' Motif"[23] and the Babylonian text "I Will Praise the Lord of Wisdom," often called the "Babylonian Job."[24] Although these texts offer some parallels to the description of suffering one finds in Job, their importance for understanding the literary tradition to which Job belongs has been overrated. They are much closer in form and function to biblical psalms of thanksgiving than to the book of Job.[25] At most they provide background for the general ancient Near Eastern conventions for describing physical suffering and social ostracism.[26]

Much more significant is the striking similarity of form and content between Job and the text known as the Babylonian Theodicy. In contrast to the liturgical poems discussed above, the Babylonian Theodicy is a wisdom text.[27] Written c. 1000 BCE, the text was

22. See, e.g., J. Gray, "The Book of Job in the Context of Near Eastern Literature," *ZAW* 82 (1970) 251-69; J. Leveque, *Job et son Dieu* (Paris: J. Gabalda, 1970) 13-90; Pope, *Job,* lvi-lxxi.

23. *ANET,* 589-91.

24. Ibid., 596-600.

25. M. Weinfeld, "Job and Its Mesopotamian Parallels—A Typological Analysis," in W. Claassen, ed., *Text and Context: Old Testament and Semitic Studies for F. C. Fensham* (Sheffield: Sheffield Academic Press, 1988) 217-26; Gray, "The Book of Job in the Context of Near Eastern Literature," 256.

26. But see Zuckerman, *Job the Silent,* 93-103, who suggests a larger role for this genre in the development of the book of Job.

27. Gray, "The Book of Job in the Context of Near Eastern Literature," 267-68; S. Denning-Bolle, *Wisdom in Akkadian Literature* (Leiden: Ex Oriente Lux, 1992) 136-58.

apparently quite popular even in the Hellenistic period, when a commentary on it was written by a Mesopotamian scribe from Sippar.[28] The Babylonian Theodicy consists of a dialogue between a sufferer and his friend and is composed as an acrostic poem of twenty-seven stanzas of eleven lines each, with a strict alternation of stanzas between the two characters. This formal design is quite similar to the dialogue in Job, although in Job the role of the friend is divided among three characters: Eliphaz, Bildad, and Zophar. Equally striking is the similarity in the way the individual speeches begin. In the Babylonian Theodicy, most of the stanzas begin with a compliment to the general intelligence of the other party. When the friend speaks, this general compliment is followed by a criticism that in this particular case the sufferer has said something irrational, erroneous, or blasphemous. For example:

"Respected friend, what you say is gloomy.
You let your mind dwell on evil, my dear fellow.
You make your fine discretion like an imbecile's" (ll. 12-14)
"My reliable fellow, holder of knowledge, your thoughts are perverse.
You have forsaken right and blaspheme against your god's designs." (ll. 78-79)[29]

Similarly, when the sufferer speaks, his opening compliment is followed by a request that his friend truly listen to what he has to say:

"My friend, your mind is a river whose spring never fails,
The accumulated mass of the sea, which knows no decrease.
I will ask you a question; listen to what I say.
Pay attention for a moment; hear my words" (ll. 23-26).

In Job many of the speeches begin with a similar characterization of the previous speaker's words and wisdom, although the tone is generally sarcastic rather than the polite-but-frank tone that typifies the Babylonian Theodicy. As Job says:

"Doubtless you are the people,
    and wisdom will die with you!
But I have a mind as well as you;
    I am not inferior to you.
Who does not know all these things?" (12:2-3 NIV)

Similarly, Eliphaz replies:

"Would a wise man answer with empty notions
or fill his belly with the hot east wind?

. . . . .

28. W. G. Lambert, *Babylonian Wisdom Literature* (Oxford: Clarendon, 1960) 63.
29. Translation according to ibid., 71-89.

But you even undermine piety
    and hinder devotion to God." (15:2, 4 NIV)

Like the sufferer of the Babylonian Theodicy, Job asks that his words be heard, yet Job spoke without the confidence that his friends are capable of true understanding: " 'Listen carefully to my words,/ and let this be your consolation./ Bear with me, and I will speak;/ then after I have spoken, mock on' " (21:2-3 NRSV).

The content of the "Babylonian Theodicy" and of the Joban dialogues contains close parallels. In each of his speeches, the Babylonian sufferer complains about either personal misfortune or his perception that the world itself is morally disordered, with the unworthy and the criminal prospering while the deserving and the pious languish in misery.

"My body is a wreck, emaciation darkens [me,]
My success has vanished, my stability has gone.
My strength is enfeebled, my prosperity has ended,
Moaning and grief have blackened my features."

Compare Job:

"My skin grows black and peels;
    my body burns with fever.
My harp is tuned to mourning,
    and my flute to the sound of wailing." (30:30-31 NRSV)

The Babylonian sufferer complains that the impious flourish:

"[...]the nouveau riche who has multiplied his wealth,
Did he weigh out precious gold for the goddess Mami?" (ll. 52-53).
"Those who neglect the god go the way of prosperity,
While those who pray to the goddess are impoverished and dispossessed" (ll. 70-71).

Similarly, Job:

"Why do the wicked live on,
    reach old age, and grow mighty in power?

. . . . .

They say to God, 'Leave us alone!
    We do not desire to know your ways.' " (21:7, 14 NRSV)

Like Job's friends, the friend in the Babylonian Theodicy argues that retribution will come eventually to the wicked, whereas the pious one who bears temporary distress patiently will have his prosperity returned to him:

"The godless cheat who has wealth,
A death-dealing weapon pursues him.
Unless you seek the will of the god, what luck have you?
He that bears his god's yoke never lacks food, though it be sparse.
Seek the kindly wind of the god,
What you have lost over a year you will make up in a moment" (ll. 237-42).

Compare Eliphaz's words:

"Consider now: Who, being innocent, has ever perished?
    Where were the upright ever destroyed?
As I have observed, those who plow evil
    and those who sow trouble reap it." (4:7-8 NIV; cf. 5:17-26).

Similarly, just as the Babylonian friend argues that "the divine mind, like the centre of the heavens, is remote; Knowledge of it is difficult; the masses do not know it" (ll. 256-57), so also Zophar asks Job:

"Can you fathom the mysteries of God?
    Can you probe the limits of the Almighty?
They are higher than the
        heavens—what can you do?
    They are deeper than the depths of
        the grave—what can you know?
Their measure is longer than the earth
    and wider than the sea." (11:7-8 NIV)

Despite the striking similarities between particular arguments, the dialogues end quite differently. In the Babylonian Theodicy, when the sufferer complains that people praise the wicked and abuse the honest person, his friend not only agrees with him but also attributes this sad state of affairs to the gods, who "gave perverse speech to the human race. With lies, and not truth, they endowed them for ever" (ll. 279-80). Apparently satisfied that he has been heard, the sufferer thanks his friend, repeats his claim that he has suffered even though he has behaved properly, and concludes with an appeal to the mercy of the gods:

"May the god who has thrown me off give help,
May the goddess who has [abandoned me] show mercy,
For the shepherd Shamash guides the peoples like a god" (295-97).

By contrast, there is no rapprochement between Job and his friends. Following Job's lengthy concluding defense of his conduct, he does not appeal for God's mercy but wishes for a legal confrontation with his divine adversary (31:35-37). The Babylonian Theodicy contains nothing like the speech from the whirlwind, which forms the climax of the book of Job.

Although it is possible that the author of Job knew and drew upon the Babylonian Theodicy itself, it is more likely that the relationship is indirect and that there was a larger tradition of wisdom dialogues about the problem of the righteous sufferer and the general issue of moral disorder in a world supposedly governed by divine justice.[30] If that is so, then the similarities between Job and the Babylonian Theodicy, coming from different times and different national and religious contexts, allow one at least to identify the contours of that genre: the formal structuring of the dialogue, the rhetorical acknowledgment by speakers of each other, the characteristic arguments for and against the just ordering of the world. The lack of a narrative framework, as in the Babylonian Theodicy, is probably also a characteristic of the genre. Even if one assumes that the dialogue in Job was written explicitly with the frame tale in mind, it is striking that, except for the names of the characters, the dialogue makes no reference whatsoever to the particulars of the frame story. The dialogue appears to have been left intentionally unintegrated. As compared to the Babylonian Theodicy, the Joban dialogue is a much more sophisticated literary work. Without other examples, however, one cannot say whether the more ambitious scope and daring tone of the Joban dialogues mark a radical departure from the tradition or build on examples more fully developed than the Babylonian Theodicy.

Having traced what can be known of the ancient Near Eastern background to the prose and poetic parts of the book of Job, it is possible to venture a suggestion about the composition of the biblical book. All suggestions are necessarily speculative. They amount to claims that the shape of the book and its component parts make the most sense if one assumes that it arose in such and such a fashion. They are in that sense suggestions about how one should read the book. With that caution in mind, I suggest that one read the book "as if" it came into existence in the following fashion. One might assume that an Israelite sage from the sixth or fifth century knew various oral traditions about the legendary Job and also knew the literary wisdom tradition of the dialogue of a righteous sufferer and his friend. Since Job was such an archetypal righteous sufferer, it is possible that the name "Job" had already been attached to versions of such dialogues. The religious perspectives of the two traditions, however, would have been sharply different, the tale of Job stressing a model of righteousness that takes the form of legendary endurance of extraordinary misfortune without protest, and the dialogue tradition casting Job in the role of skeptical protester against unwarranted personal misfortune and general moral disorder. How might one bring these traditions together so that they may both assert their claims and be challenged by the other's vision of reality? The solution devised by this clever Israelite sage was the artistic device of inter-cutting, beginning the book with a version of the traditional story, then sharply interrupting the telling of the tale with a version of the

---

30. W. G. Lambert, *Babylonian Wisdom Literature* (Oxford: Oxford University Press, 1960) 90-91, suggests that another very fragmentary text may be a second example of such a dialogue.

skeptical dialogue of the righteous sufferer, abruptly followed by the resumption of the traditional tale. Although it is possible that the speech from the whirlwind has antecedents in some other literary tradition, one might be inclined to think that the divine speech is the author's innovation, a reinterpretation of wisdom traditions about creation that serves to set the entire conversation about the experience of suffering in a quite different context than that envisioned either by the old tale or by the conventions of the dialogue of the righteous sufferer.

THEOLOGICAL ISSUES

However the book of Job achieved its present form, it presents a series of thought-provoking theological issues. The initial theological question of the book is framed in the prose tale by the *satan,* who asks about the motives of piety (1:9-11). Why does Job, and by extension any person, reverence God? Is it an implicit bargain for security and well-being, or is the relationship independent of circumstances? Traditional religion often talks about the blessings that come from piety and obedience to God, and the *satan*'s probing question asks whether such expectations subtly corrupt the relationship between human beings and God. The prose story, taken by itself, describes Job's piety as unshaken by extreme and inexplicable misfortune, and so affirms the possibility of wholly unconditional love of God. As important as such a question is, the way in which it is treated in the prose tale leaves a great deal unexplored. *Should* one serve God unconditionally and without question? What *is* the nature of the relationship between God and human beings? What is the character of God, and how does one have knowledge of that character? The dialogue and the divine speeches serve as a vehicle for considering these further questions, as well as other religious issues as they emerge from the experience of suffering.

Perhaps the most prominent issue in the dialogues is that of the proper conduct of a person in suffering. For the friends, suffering is an occasion for moral and religious self-examination and reflection. Although there is no single "meaning" for suffering, it is to be understood in some way as a communication from God. For the wicked, it is judgment (15:20-35); for the ethically unsteady, it is a warning (33:14-30); for the morally immature, it is a form of educational discipline (5:17-19); and for the righteous, it is simply something to be borne with the confidence that God will eventually restore well-being (4:4-7; 8:20-21). In every case the proper response is to turn to God in humility, trust, and prayer (5:8; 8:5; 11:13-19; 22:21-30). Implicit in the friends' view is the assumption that God is always right and that it is the human being who must make use of the experience to learn what God is trying to communicate. Although Job does not engage the friends' arguments explicitly, his own stance toward God implies a very different understanding of the divine-human relationship. Rather than turning inward in self-examination, Job demands an explanation from God (7:20; 10:2; 13:23; 23:5; 31:35). For Job, God has no right to cause suffering to come upon a person unless that person deserves punishment.

The proper response where suffering appears to be undeserved is not humble prayer but confrontation of God. Thus Job rejects the notion of unconditional piety, at least insofar as it would mean submission to a God who acts without regard to what is just.

The differences between Job and the friends on the matter of proper conduct in suffering also bring into focus the issue of the character of God and God's governance of the world. In contrast to the conventional views of the friends, which take God's goodness and justice to be axiomatic (8:3; 34:12), Job often depicts God as a violator of justice (27:2) who acts out of obsessive and malicious curiosity (7:17-20; 10:8-14) or in a spirit of sadistic rage (16:9-14). The world over which God exercises supposed "moral" governance is characterized by anarchic destruction (12:14-25), the prosperity of the wicked (21:30-33), and the pervasive abuse of the poor (24:1-12). If Job is correct when he depicts God in these ways, then the very possibility of reverence for God is at an end, for God is a monster of cruelty. Job's speeches set up the theological issue in a more complex fashion, however, for Job's view of God's character is contradictory. He cannot give up the idea that, despite the evidence of his experience and his observations, God will ultimately be revealed as a God of justice (13:15-22; 23:3-7). The theological and emotional power of the book is due in large measure to the apparently insoluble nature of this contradictory experience. Job is not unique in raising the problem of a just God and the existence of injustice in the world (cf. Psalm 73). What is unusual about Job is the way in which he attempts to pursue and ultimately resolve this excruciating dilemma.

Some of the most intriguing theological issues in the book are never raised to the level of explicit debate between Job and his friends but can be teased out by attentive readers. One of these is the way claims to knowledge are authorized. Job and his friends not only hold different positions about the nature of God, the moral order of the world, and the meaning of what has befallen Job, but they also authorize their claims on very different grounds. The friends appeal to common sense, what "everybody" knows (4:7). Consequently, they assume that Job, too, will share their perceptions (5:27). Sometimes they argue deductively from what they consider to be universally agreed principles (34:10-12). At other times they cite anecdotal evidence (4:8; 5:3) or even the transcendent authority of private revelation (4:13-16). Most important of all, however, is their reliance on the authority of tradition. Not only do they appeal explicitly to ancestral tradition (8:8-10), but by filling their speeches with the forms of traditional religious language (e.g., sayings, didactic examples, doxologies), they also embody that authority. Job opposes this arsenal of common sense, rational argument, revelation, and tradition because he knows that what the friends claim is inconsistent with his own experience. Job often expresses the vivid immediacy of this experience and the claims to knowledge that it warrants in terms of the body's organs of perception (tongue, eyes, ears; 6:30; 13:1). Thus the book stages a conflict between different ways of grounding and authorizing knowledge.

Related to the conflict over the grounds for knowledge of truth is the book's exploration of the adequacy and limits of various kinds of religious language. Job's parodies of traditional psalmic and hymnic forms (7:17-19; 12:13-25) expose what appears to him to be their pervasive hypocrisy about the real nature of the divine-human relationship. Such forms of religious speech allow one to speak only of the goodness of God's transforming power, care for human beings, etc., but exclude from view the terrible experiences that give rise to the crisis of religious doubt about the nature of God. Traditional prayer also, which the friends keep urging upon him, is inadequate for the kind of conversation Job seeks to have with God, because it has no means of imposing accountability on God. Rejecting the conventional alternatives, Job's speeches gradually explore the possibilities of a new religious language based on a radically different underlying metaphor of the divine-human relationship. Job reimagines the relationship in legal categories, most concretely in terms of the possibility of a trial with God. This idea occurs first as parody (9:2-4) but eventually develops into a serious model for engaging God (23:3-7; 31:35-37). It serves Job's purposes well, for the model envisions a relationship of mutual accountability, undistorted by discrepancies of power, in which both parties acknowledge common standards of justice as binding. Such a way of talking about God and with God would have radical implications for the nature of religion. The book never fully develops these implications but leaves them as a provocative possibility.

Throughout the long dialogues between Job and his friends, theological issues and options are set up as alternatives between the traditional positions championed by the friends and the radical challenges posed by Job. The friends argue for the goodness of God, the moral order of the world, the purposiveness of suffering, and the importance of humble submission to God. Job questions the justice of God, describes the world as a moral chaos, depicts suffering in terms of victimization, and stakes his life on the possibility of legal confrontation with God. What goes largely unnoticed is the extent to which both positions depend on the same paradigm of understanding. They both take as unquestionable the assumption that justice, specifically retributive justice, should be the central principle of reality. They disagree only as to whether such justice is operative in the world or whether God should be called to account for failing to enforce such justice. The speeches of God from the whirlwind, however, challenge the paradigm that both Job and the friends have taken for granted. When God speaks of the "design" of the cosmos, which Job has obscured (38:2), the categories that underlie God's descriptions are not categories of justice/injustice but order/chaos.

The divine speeches do not explicitly engage the particular arguments Job had made but implicitly call into question their fundamental assumptions. As the juxtaposition of Job's final speech (chaps. 29–31) and the divine speeches (chaps. 38–41) shows, Job's theological categories had been derived from the social and moral assumptions that structured community life and social roles in his own experience. From these assumptions Job had extrapolated his expectations concerning God and the world. God's speeches, by beginning with the great structures of creation and speaking scarcely at all of the place of human beings in the cosmos, expose the limits of Job's anthropocentric categories.

Similarly, Job's legal model for understanding divine-human relationships is also implicitly challenged. In Job's understanding, the fundamental categories are "right and wrong." No place exists in such a schema for the chaotic. Yet in God's speeches, the play between fundamental order and the restricted but still powerful forces of the chaotic is crucial for understanding the nature of reality. Through images of the sea (38:8-11), the criminal (38:12-15), the anarchic wild animals (38:39–39:30), and finally the legendary beasts Behemoth and Leviathan (40:15–41:34[41:26]), God confronts Job with things that his legal categories cannot possibly comprehend. The evocative but elusive language of the divine speeches provides resources for the reconstruction of theological language of a very different sort than that employed by Job and his friends, but the divine speeches do not do that work themselves. Theological construction properly remains a human task.

The provocative challenge of the divine speeches, which incorporate an image of God and the world quite different from that embodied in either the prose tale or the dialogues, brings one back to the original theological issue of the book: Why does one reverence God? What had been a question about the nature of human piety in the prose tale was transformed in the dialogues into a question about the character of God. Job's reply suggests that the divine speeches have provided him with a transformed vision of God and thus a very different basis for reverence (42:5); but his brief and enigmatic words (42:1-6) do not make clear exactly how his understanding has changed. If the author had made Job's interpretation of the divine speeches more explicit, then the reader would have been left with little to do beyond approving or disapproving of Job's response. By making Job's response so elusive, however, the author forces the reader to grapple more directly with the meaning of the divine speeches and so enter into the work of theological reconstruction that they invite.

One final theological issue remains to be considered, an issue that arises from the overall structure of the book, as discussed above. This issue might be stated in language taken from the book of Job itself: "Where can wisdom be found?" (28:12 NIV)—i.e., to which of the many voices in the book should one listen for the word of truth? One might reasonably assume that the divine speeches contain the essential truth of the book of Job. Not only does the voice of God carry transcendent authority, but the structure of the book up to that point seems to encourage such a judgment as well. The book appears to have been directing the reader from less to more adequate perspectives. The naive prose tale presents a moral perspective that is made to appear inadequate by the more literarily and theologically sophisticated dialogues. Within the dialogues, the friends' moral perspectives are shown to be inadequate by the compelling power of Job's words. The inadequacy of Job's perspective, however, is disclosed by the extraordinary speeches of God from the whirlwind. Surely one is supposed to adopt and endorse the perspective articulated by none other than God. Yet the book gives the last word to the prose tale. Moreover, the transition to the prose conclusion creates ironies that undermine the conviction that the book as a whole endorses the perspective of the divine speeches as the one true point of view. By having God declare that *Job* has spoken rightly (42:7), and by having events turn out just as the *friends* had predicted, the book wryly affirms perspectives that had appeared to be superseded and rejected.

What gets challenged in this process is the very notion that discerning truth is a matter of choosing one perspective and rejecting all others, that the truth about a complex question can be contained in a single perspective. Each perspective in the book of Job, taken by itself, contains valid insights. Yet each one, by virtue of its distinctive angle of vision, is of necessity oblivious to other dimensions of the question. When one looks back at the various views articulated by the different voices in the text, one finds that they are not so much contradictory as incommensurable.

It may be that the truth about a complex question can only be spoken by a plurality of voices that can never be merged into one, because they speak from different experiences and different perspectives. This is not to suggest that every position has equal validity or that with enough conversation consensus will be reached. As the book of Job illustrates, serious theological conversation places different voices in relationship precisely so that their limitations as well as their insights may be clearly identified. The dialogic truth that emerges from such a conversation is not to be found either in the triumph of one voice over the others or in an emerging consensus. It is to be found in the intersection of the various voices in their mutual interrogation. Such a perspective does not mean that one never gets beyond talk to decision. On the contrary, every person must choose how to live. In terms of the issues posed by the book of Job, choosing how to live involves deciding about the character of God, the structure of creation, the place of suffering in the world, and the significance of the moral and pious life. What the structure of the book challenges, however, is the assumption that such a decision, once made, accounts for everything and resolves every question. Instead, the significance of a choice can be appreciated only when it is questioned from other perspectives and by persons who have made different choices. The book of Job models a kind of theological inquiry in which multiple perspectives are not merely helpful but essential. By closing in a manner that frustrates closure, the book signals that the conversation it has begun about the nature of divine-human relations is not finished but requires to be continued by new communities of voices.

BIBLIOGRAPHY

1. Commentaries

Andersen, F. I. *Job: An Introduction and Commentary.* Tyndale Old Testament Commentaries. Downers Grove, Ill.: Inter-Varsity, 1976. An exceptionally good short commentary, written from an evangelical perspective.

Clines, David J. A. *Job 1–20.* WBC 17. Dallas: Word, 1989. A superb exegetical commentary with many original insights into Job.

Good, Edwin M. *In Turns of Tempest: A Reading of Job with a Translation.* Stanford, Calif.: Stanford University Press, 1990. A somewhat idiosyncratic but often provocative commentary, informed by contemporary literary approaches to the Bible. The translation is noteworthy for its attempt to render the Masoretic Text without emendation.

Habel, Norman C. C. *The Book of Job*. OTL. Philadelphia: Westminster, 1985. One of the best commentaries on Job, especially valuable for its sensitivity to literary dimensions of the book.

Hartley, John E. *The Book of Job*. NICOT. Grand Rapids, Mich.: Eerdmans, 1988. A thorough, helpful, and well-balanced commentary.

Janzen, J. Gerald. *Job*. Interpretation. Atlanta: John Knox, 1985. An accessible and thoughtful commentary that makes the existential questions raised by Job central to the theological interpretation of the book.

Pope, Marvin H. *Job*. 3rd ed. AB 15. Garden City, N.Y.: Doubleday, 1979. A classic commentary with excellent linguistic notes and comparisons with other ancient literature. The introduction is particularly valuable.

2. The following books and collections of essays by biblical scholars and theologians are particularly recommended.

Duquoc, Christian, and Casiano Floristan, eds. *Job and the Silence of God*. New York: Seabury, 1983.

Gordis, R. *The Book of God and Man: A Study of Job*. Chicago: The University of Chicago Press, 1965.

Gutiérrez, Gustavo. *On Job: God-Talk and the Suffering of the Innocent*. Translated by M. J. O'Connell. Maryknoll, N.Y.: Orbis, 1987.

Perdue, Leo G. *Wisdom in Revolt: Metaphorical Theology in the Book of Job*. JSOTSup 112. Sheffield: JSOT Press, 1991.

Perdue, Leo G., and W. Clark Gilpin, eds. *The Voice from the Whirlwind: Interpreting the Book of Job*. Nashville: Abingdon, 1992.

Zuckerman, Bruce. *Job the Silent: A Study in Historical Counterpoint*. New York: Oxford University Press, 1991.

3. Job's status as literary classic as well as sacred Scripture for both Judaism and Christianity has encouraged many who are neither biblical scholars nor theologians to write about the book. The following are particularly engaging recent examples of such work.

Bloom, Harold, ed. *The Book of Job*. New York: Chelsea House, 1988. Essays by philosophers and literary critics.

Girard, Rene. *Job: The Victim of His People*. Translated by Yvonne Freccero. Stanford, Calif.: Stanford University Press, 1987. An interpretation that considers Job in the light of the author's understanding of sacred violence and the phenomenon of the scapegoat.

Mitchell, Stephen. *The Book of Job*. San Francisco: North Point, 1987. A translation of Job by a poet who takes a poet's liberties with the text. The result is one of the most powerful artistic renderings of Job available.

Wiesel, Elie. *The Trial of God: A Play in Three Acts*. Translated by M. Wiesel. New York: Schocken, 1979. Set in the anti-Jewish pogroms of seventeenth-century Russia, the play engages issues raised by the book of Job by means of characters who correspond to Job, his friends, and the *satan*.

Wilcox, J. T. *The Bitterness of Job: A Philosophical Reading*. Ann Arbor: University of Michigan Press, 1989. An exploration of the necessity of affirmation in a world that cannot be adequately comprehended in moral categories.

OUTLINE OF JOB

I. Job 1:2–2:13, The Prose Narrative: Introduction

  A. 1:1-22, The First Test
    1:1-5, Scene 1: Introduction to Job
    1:6-12, Scene 2: A Dialogue About Job
    1:13-22, Scene 3: The Test–Destruction of "All That He Has"

  B. 2:1-10, The Second Test
    2:1-6, Scene 4: A Second Dialogue About Job
    2:7-10, Scene 5: The Test–Disease

  C. 2:11-13, Scene 6: The Three Friends

II. Job 3:1–31:40, The Poetic Dialogue Between Job and His Friends

  A. 3:1–14:22, The First Cycle
    3:1-26, Job Curses the Day of His Birth
    4:1–5:27, Traditional Understandings of Misfortune
    6:1–7:21, Job Defends the Vehemence of His Words
      6:1-30, Anguish Made Worse by the Failure of Friendship
      7:1-21, Job Confronts God
    8:1-22, A Metaphor of Two Plants
    9:1–10:22, Job Imagines a Trial with God
    11:1-20, Zophar Defends God's Wisdom
    12:1–14:22, Job Burlesques the Wisdom of God and Struggles with Mortality
      12:1–13:2, Job Parodies Traditional Praise of God
      13:3-19, Job Criticizes Deceitful Speech
      13:20–14:22, Job Experiences the Destruction of Hope

  B. 15:1–21:34, The Second Cycle
    15:1-35, Eliphaz Describes the Fate of the Wicked
    16:1–17:16, Job Complains of God's Criminal Violence
    18:1-21, Bildad Describes the Fate of the Wicked
    19:1-29, Job Denounces God's Injustice
    20:1-29, Zophar Describes the Fate of the Wicked
    21:1-34, The Fate of the Wicked Is Prosperity and Honor

  C. 22:1–27:23, The Third Cycle
    22:1-30, Eliphaz Urges Job to Repent
    23:1–24:25, Divine Justice Is Elusive
    25:1–26:14, Bildad and Job Argue About the Power of God
    27:1-23, Job Defends His Integrity

  D. 28:1-28, Interlude: Where Can Wisdom Be Found?

JOB 1:2–2:13

The Prose Narrative: Introduction
Overview

The story of Job has often been called a folktale, and there are certain elements of the folktale in Job 1–2. The main character is a traditional figure, one whose story was apparently told not only in Israel but also among other peoples (see Introduction). The style of chaps. 1–2 has many of the marks of traditional folklore: repetition, economy of plot, characters who are types rather than complex figures.[31] Moreover, the central plot device, the testing of a character who does not know that he or she is being tested, recurs not only in the Old Testament (the testing of Abraham in Genesis 22) but also in many other cultures.

Although the term *folktale* is somewhat helpful in describing what kind of a story Job 1–2 is, it is not specific enough to account for the more distinctive features of the story and the way it is told. Compared with other biblical narratives containing elements of traditional or folk style (e.g., the wife-sister stories of Genesis 12; 20; and 26 or the wise courtier stories of Joseph in Genesis 41 and Daniel in Daniel 2), the story of Job is told in an exaggeratedly schematized style. The design of the story is symmetrically structured, organized around pairs of complementary scenes. Also notable is the extensive repetition of key words, phrases, sentences, and even whole passages. Schematic and symbolic numbers abound, both explicitly and in the structuring of scenes. Characters and events are described in exaggerated and hyperbolic terms, and the characters exemplify traits rather than undergo development. Also distinctive is the syntax of the opening line, literally, "a man there was . . . " rather than the more common "there was a man." The narrator is explicitly evaluative, both at the beginning of

the story and at crucial points within it. Although some of these features can be found in traditional folk narratives, taken together they point to a different genre.

In terms of both its style and its function, the story of Job is best understood as a didactic story, very much like the story that Nathan tells to David about a rich man and a poor man (2 Sam 12:1-4). There, too, the story opens with the same unusual subject-verb word order ("two men there were"). The setting of the story is similarly vague ("in a certain city"). Most important, the narrative style is characterized by highly schematic, parallel, and exaggerated descriptions of characters and events, as well as by extensive verbal repetition. The plot of the story is simple in the extreme, serving, as in Job, to disclose the character of the rich man. The comparison of Job with Nathan's story also suggests something of the function of this type of storytelling. Corresponding to the narrative schematization of the story is a moral schematization. In Nathan's story there are no shades of gray; right and wrong are unmistakable. It is a didactic story used to orient its audience (in this case David) to clear moral values. David responds to the story appropriately by voicing his outrage at the rich man's behavior. That judgment is just what the story is designed to provoke, although David does not foresee that he will be identified with the rich man.

Like Nathan's story, the tale of Job uses its schematic style to orient its audience to certain judgments about the existence and nature of true piety. Very frequently, such didactic stories serve to explore and resolve apparent contradictions in the values or beliefs of a community. That is clearly how the story of Job 1–2 is structured. The *satan* is given the role of casting doubt. The plot of the story shows such doubt to have been wrong, and in so doing reaffirms the belief of the

31. S. Niditch, *Folklore and the Hebrew Bible* (Minneapolis: Fortress, 1993) 6.

community in the possibility of disinterested piety. The simplicity of that story and its moral views will be challenged in the poetic dialogue that begins in chap. 3. In order for that challenge to have its full effect, however, one must first appreciate the didactic tale on its own terms.

The story of Job 1–2 is composed of a series of six distinct scenes (1:1-5; 1:6-12; 1:13-21; 2:1-7*a*; 2:7*b*-10; 2:11-13), the first five of which alternate between earth and heaven. Scenes 2 and 3 and scenes 4 and 5 form symmetrical pairs, each consisting of a dialogue in heaven about Job and a test of Job on earth. With the arrival of the friends after the conclusion of the second test, the symmetry of alternation between earth and heaven is broken, and the story prepares for the beginning of the dialogue between Job and his friends. The anticipated seventh scene, in which Job is restored, occurs in 42:7-17.

JOB 1:1-22, THE FIRST TEST

Job 1:1-5, Scene 1: Introduction to Job

NIV

1 In the land of Uz there lived a man whose name was Job. This man was blameless and upright; he feared God and shunned evil. ²He had seven sons and three daughters, ³and he owned seven thousand sheep, three thousand camels, five hundred yoke of oxen and five hundred donkeys, and had a large number of servants. He was the greatest man among all the people of the East.

⁴His sons used to take turns holding feasts in their homes, and they would invite their three sisters to eat and drink with them. ⁵When a period of feasting had run its course, Job would send and have them purified. Early in the morning he would sacrifice a burnt offering for each of them, thinking, "Perhaps my children have sinned and cursed God in their hearts." This was Job's regular custom.

NRSV

1 There was once a man in the land of Uz whose name was Job. That man was blameless and upright, one who feared God and turned away from evil. ²There were born to him seven sons and three daughters. ³He had seven thousand sheep, three thousand camels, five hundred yoke of oxen, five hundred donkeys, and very many servants; so that this man was the greatest of all the people of the east. ⁴His sons used to go and hold feasts in one another's houses in turn; and they would send and invite their three sisters to eat and drink with them. ⁵And when the feast days had run their course, Job would send and sanctify them, and he would rise early in the morning and offer burnt offerings according to the number of them all; for Job said, "It may be that my children have sinned, and cursed God in their hearts." This is what Job always did.

COMMENTARY

1:1. The character of Job is the pivot upon which the entire book turns. In the first verse the reader is told three things about Job: his homeland, his name, and the qualities of his character. The location of the land of Uz is not entirely certain; probably it refers to an area south of Israel in Edomite territory (Jer 25:20; Lam 4:21; cf. Gen 36:28), although some traditions associate the name with the Arameans, who lived northeast of Israel (Gen 10:23; 22:21). In any event it is not an Israelite location. Similarly, the name "Job" would have had a foreign and archaic ring to it. It was not a name used in Israel, but similar names are known from ancient Near Eastern texts of the second millennium BCE.[32] Although later Jewish and Christian interpreters were concerned with whether Job was an Israelite or a Gentile,[33] his ethnicity plays no role in the story itself. Whatever the origins of the figure of Job, his story has been naturalized into Israelite religious culture, so that Job is presented unself-consciously as a worshiper of Yahweh (1:21). Job's archaic name and foreign homeland help to establish a sense of narrative distance, which facilitates the presentation of Job as a paradigmatic figure.

The crucial information about Job is the description of his character: "blameless and upright, one who feared God and turned away from evil." These are all very general moral and religious terms, particularly frequent in the wisdom literature and the book of Psalms (see, e.g., Pss 25:21; 37:37; Prov 3:7; 14:16; 16:6, 17). Although their content is important, the form of their presentation is also meaningful: two pairs of parallel terms. There is something hyperbolic in this piling up of adjectives. Even Noah, that other legendary righteous man (see Ezek 14:14), is described with only two (Gen 6:9).[34] More significant, the use of the numerical schema of four qualities, neatly paired, suggests completeness and perfection (cf. below on the fourfold destruction of "all that he has"). The leading term of the sequence, "blameless" (תם *tām*), carries connotations of wholeness and is often translated "integrity." This term becomes central to the story, as both God and Job's wife characterize him as one who "persists in his integrity" (תמה *tummâ*, 2:3, 9). The first term of the second pair, "one who fears God," is also echoed in a thematically crucial verse (1:9). "Fearing God" is a traditional Hebrew term for respectful and unsentimental piety.

1:2-3. The description of Job continues with an account of his children, his property, his household, and his status. Although it is not often reflected in the translations, the first word of v. 2 is "And" (ו *wě*). It is grammatically possible to translate it simply as "and," a word that coordinates two independent observations, or it could be translated "and so," indicating a causal rela-

tionship. Does Job just happen to be rich and have a large family, or does he have these things because he is a man of exemplary piety? Although the narrator does not say explicitly, the very description of Job's family and wealth suggests a connection. All the numbers used are symbolic, suggesting completeness and perfection: seven sons and three daughters, for a total of ten children; sheep and camels in the same ratio of seven thousand and three thousand; and agricultural animals in a balanced distribution of five hundred plus five hundred. Just as Job's piety is complete and perfect, so also his family and property are complete and perfect. The reader is encouraged to see these as two things that fit naturally together. What binds them is the religious notion of blessing. Although the word "blessing" is not yet used, the picture the narrator draws of Job is easily recognized as the image of the righteous person blessed by God (cf. Pss 112:1-3; 128:1-4; Prov 3:33; 10:22). As with Isaac (Gen 26:12-14) Job's greatness (v. 3), i.e., his wealth and the status that accompanies it, can also be seen as a mark of divine blessing.

1:4-5. These verses illustrate the untroubled happiness of Job's family and the extraordinary piety of Job himself. Directing the reader's attention to the children foreshadows their crucial place in the destruction that follows (vv. 13, 18-19). Job's sons live like a king's sons, each in his own home (cf. 2 Sam 13:7; 14:31). Some interpreters see the series of banquets that the sons host "each on his day" as nonstop partying every day of the week,[35] but that interpretation seems unlikely. Since the brothers formally invite their sisters to each banquet and Job conducts sacrifices on their behalf "when the feast days had run their course," it is more likely that what is referred to here is a cycle of banquets lasting several days, hosted by each son on the occasion of his birthday (cf. 3:1, where "his day" refers to Job's birthday). In contrast to the frequent OT narrative theme of conflict between brothers (e.g., Cain and Abel in Genesis 4; Absalom and Amnon in 2 Samuel 13), Job's sons live harmoniously and honor their sisters with particular attention. Nothing seems amiss in this picture.

32. M. Pope, *Job*, 3rd ed., AB 15 (Garden City, N.Y.: Doubleday, 1979) 5-6.

33. J. Baskin, *Pharaoh's Counsellors*, BJS 47 (Chico, Calif.: Scholars Press, 1983) 8-26.

34. A. Brenner, "Job the Pious? The Characterization of Job in the Narrative Framework of the Book," *JSOT* 43 (1989) 41.

35. E. Dhorme, *A Commentary on the Book of Job*, trans. H. Knight (London: Nelson, 1967) 4; G. Fohrer, *Das Buch Hiob*, KAT xvi (Guetersloh: Gerd Mohn, 1963) 77; H. Rowley, *The Book of Job*, rev. ed., NCB (Grand Rapids, Mich.: Eerdmans, 1976; original ed., 1970) 29.

Job's action, however, is the focal point of the passage. "To send and sanctify" suggests that Job summons his children to a solemn occasion at the conclusion of each banquet in order to offer sacrifice on their behalf (cf. Exod 19:10, 14; Lev 25:10; Joel 1:14; 2:15).[36] The sin that Job fears, cursing God, is a serious one, punishable by death (Exod 22:28 [27]; Lev 24:14-16; 1 Kgs 21:10). Job, however, does not even imagine that his children have cursed God aloud, but only "in their hearts." Moreover, the children may not be guilty of any misdeed at all. Job offers the sacrifice just in case his children have sinned. As with almost every other detail in this story, there is something a little exaggerated in the description of his careful intercession. The image of Job, protectively sacrificing on behalf of his children, recalls Ezekiel's allusion to Job (Ezek 14:14-20) as a legendary figure whose own righteousness sufficed to save the lives of sons and daughters. The irony of this scene is that it is precisely Job's righteousness that will set in motion events leading to the deaths of his children.

The English reader often misses a peculiarity of the text that is present in the Hebrew. Where the

translations render "cursed God" in v. 5, the Hebrew text actually reads, "perhaps my children have sinned and *blessed* God in their hearts." The translators correctly recognize that "blessed" (ברך *bārak*) is used euphemistically here in place of "curse" (קלל *qll*), as in 1 Kgs 21:13. This euphemism is probably not a later substitution of the scribes who transmitted the biblical text; if it were, one would expect the euphemism to be standard throughout the Bible. There are, however, passages in which the literal words "curse God" (יקלל אלהיו *yĕqallēl ʾĕlōhāw*) appear (Lev 24:15; see Exod 22:28 [27]). Instead, this rather prim euphemism is a matter of the stylistic preference of the author. It may even be a part of the artistry of the story. Each of the seven times the word occurs in the prose tale (1:5, 10, 11, 21; 2:5, 9; 42:12), the reader must negotiate its meaning. Does it mean "bless" or "curse"? Even though most of the instances are easily enough resolved, the antithetical use of the word "bless" draws attention to itself. The word is thematically crucial. Just as "blessing" is used in a self-contradictory way, the story will explore a contradiction deeply hidden in the dynamic of blessing itself. (See Reflections at 2:11-13.)

36. Dhorme, *A Commentary on the Book of Job*, 4.

Job 1:6-12, Scene 2: A Dialogue About Job

NIV

[6]One day the angels[a] came to present themselves before the LORD, and Satan[b] also came with them. [7]The LORD said to Satan, "Where have you come from?"

Satan answered the LORD, "From roaming through the earth and going back and forth in it."

[8]Then the LORD said to Satan, "Have you considered my servant Job? There is no one on earth like him; he is blameless and upright, a man who fears God and shuns evil."

[9]"Does Job fear God for nothing?" Satan replied. [10]"Have you not put a hedge around him and his household and everything he has? You have blessed the work of his hands, so that his flocks and herds are spread throughout the land.

a6 Hebrew the sons of God   b6 Satan means accuser.

NRSV

[6]One day the heavenly beings[a] came to present themselves before the LORD, and Satan[b] also came among them. [7]The LORD said to Satan,[b] "Where have you come from?" Satan[b] answered the LORD, "From going to and fro on the earth, and from walking up and down on it." [8]The LORD said to Satan,[b] "Have you considered my servant Job? There is no one like him on the earth, a blameless and upright man who fears God and turns away from evil." [9]Then Satan[b] answered the LORD, "Does Job fear God for nothing? [10]Have you not put a fence around him and his house and all that he has, on every side? You have blessed the work of his hands, and his possessions have increased in the land. [11]But stretch out your hand now, and touch all that he has, and he will curse you to

a Heb sons of God   b Or the Accuser; Heb ha-satan

NIV

[11]But stretch out your hand and strike everything he has, and he will surely curse you to your face."

[12]The LORD said to Satan, "Very well, then, everything he has is in your hands, but on the man himself do not lay a finger."

Then Satan went out from the presence of the LORD.

NRSV

your face." [12]The LORD said to Satan,[a] "Very well, all that he has is in your power; only do not stretch out your hand against him!" So Satan[a] went out from the presence of the LORD.

[a] Or the Accuser, Heb ha-satan

COMMENTARY

1:6. The first scene closed with the observation that "this is what Job *always* did," literally, "all the days." Scene 2 opens with the contrasting punctual phrase, "One day...." The divine council is the setting of scene 2. Like its neighbors in the ancient Near East, Israel often imagined God as a king holding court, taking counsel, and rendering judgments about various matters (see 1 Kgs 22:19-23; Psalm 82; Isa 6:1-8; Dan 7:9-14).[37] The divine court consists of heavenly beings who are generally presented as an anonymous group, rarely distinguished by title or function. In Hebrew they are called the "sons of God." The term does not refer to a family relationship but is a Hebrew idiom for specifying the group to which an individual belongs. Thus "sons of cattle" means "cattle," "sons of Israel" means "Israelites," and "sons of God" means "divine beings" (see Gen 6:2, 4). Here the divine beings "present themselves before Yahweh," a formal gesture (see Deut 31:14;

Judg 20:2). The image is one of divine beings reporting to God, receiving commissions to execute, and reporting back from their missions. The most suggestive parallel to Job 1:6 is Zech 6:5, where the chariots of the four winds/spirits of heaven are described as setting out to patrol the earth after having "presented themselves before Yahweh."

It is unfortunate that so many translations, including the NRSV and the NIV, render the Hebrew הַשָּׂטָן (*haśśāṭān*) in Job 1 2 as "Satan," which is linguistically inaccurate and highly misleading. The word *satan* is a common noun, meaning "accuser," "adversary," and is related to a verb meaning "to accuse," "to oppose." Here, where the noun is accompanied by the definite article, it cannot be understood as a personal name but simply as "the accuser." To read back into Job 1–2 the much later notions of Satan-the-devil is seriously to misunderstand the story of Job.

37. E. T. Mullen, "Divine Assembly," in *The Anchor Bible Dictionary*, ed. D. N. Freedman (New York: Doubleday, 1992) 2:214-17.

❖　　❖　　❖　　❖

EXCURSUS: THE ROLE OF SATAN IN THE OLD TESTAMENT

Elsewhere in the OT the word *satan* is used to describe both human (1 Sam 29:4; 1 Kgs 5:4 [18]; Ps 109:6) and heavenly beings (Num 22:22; Zech 3:1), who act as adversaries or accusers. The context may be personal, legal, or political, but in each case the noun simply defines a function. It is likely that by the early post-exilic period, when the book of Job was probably written, the expression "the satan" had come to designate a particular divine being in the heavenly court, one whose specialized function was to seek out and accuse persons disloyal to God. The chief evidence for this is Zech 3:1, which describes the heavenly trial of the high priest Joshua, who is "standing before the angel of Yahweh, with the accuser [*ha-satan*] standing at his right hand to accuse [*satan*] him" (author's trans.). Some scholars have speculated that the figure of the accuser in Zechariah and Job may be modeled on officials in the Persian court who served as informers ("the eyes and ears of the king" [cf. Zech 4:2, 10*b*]) and even as *agents provocateurs*,[38] although this is less certain.

There is an ambivalence in the relation between Yahweh and the accusing angel that is important for understanding the development of this figure. The accusing angel is a subordinate of God, a member of the divine court who defends God's honor by exposing those who pose a threat to it. In that sense he is not *God's* adversary but the adversary of sinful or corrupt human beings. Yet in Zech 3:2, Yahweh rejects the accuser's indictment of the high priest and rebukes the accuser instead. In Job 1–2, Yahweh and the accuser take opposing views of the character of Job. As one who embodies and perfects the function of opposition, the *satan* is depicted in these texts as one who accuses precisely those whom God is inclined to favor. In this way the ostensible defender of God subtly becomes God's adversary.

Many scholars have seen in the development of the *satan* a process whereby ambivalent characteristics of God are externalized as a subordinate divine character. The *satan*'s actions are therefore not directly attributable to God and may even be rejected. The story of David's census of Israel is often cited as evidence of this process. In 2 Sam 24:1, the narrative says that "the anger of Yahweh was kindled against Israel" (author's trans.) and that Yahweh incited David to sinful behavior in conducting the census. In the later, parallel story in 1 Chr 21:1, however, the verse says, "Satan stood up against Israel, and incited David to count the people of Israel" (NRSV). In 1 Chronicles 21 the term *satan* is apparently used as a proper name for the first time,[39] and Satan represents an externalization, or hypostasis, of divine anger. In Zech 3:1, the accusing angel is the externalizing of the divine function of strict judgment in contrast to divine graciousness, which is then exercised by God (Zech 3:2).[40] In Job 1–2, the accuser is the externalizing of divine doubt about the human heart, which allows God to voice confident approval of Job's character.

In later centuries the figure of Satan develops into the dualistic opponent of God.[41] This hostile image of Satan is presumed by the New Testament (see, e.g., Mark 3:22-30; Luke 22:31; John 13:27; Rev 20:1-10). In the story of Job, however, that later development has not yet taken place. The accuser is simply the wily spirit who embodies his given function to perfection. In Goethe's famous phrase, he is *der Geist der stets verneint*, "the spirit who always negates."

38. N. H. Tur-Sinai, *The Book of Job: A New Commentary* (Jerusalem: Kiryath Sepher, 1957) 41; Pope, *Job*, 9-11.
39. But cf. P. Day, *An Adversary in Heaven: Satan in the Hebrew Bible*, HSM 43 (Atlanta: Scholars Press, 1988) 141-42.
40. Ibid., 117.
41. V. P. Hamilton, "Satan," *ABD*, 5:985-89.

❖ ❖ ❖ ❖

1:7. There is a formal, almost ritual quality to the initial exchange between Yahweh and the *satan*. As a sovereign receiving a subordinate returned from his mission, Yahweh inquires whence he has come, and the *satan* replies (v. 7). His answer is neither evasive nor disrespectful.[42] The verbs are the same ones used in Zechariah

42. Contra R. Gordis, *The Book of Job: Commentary, New Translation, and Special Studies* (New York: Jewish Theological Seminary, 5738/1978) 15; F. Andersen, *Job: An Introduction and Commentary,* Tyndale Old Testament Commentaries (Downers Grove, Ill.: Inter-Varsity, 1976) 83.

of the "eyes of Yahweh who range [שׁוּט *šûṭ*] through the earth" (Zech 4:10) and of the "divine horsemen and chariots who patrol [הלך *hālak*] it" (Zech 1:11; 6:5). At the same time, the *satan*'s reply presents him as a figure of wit and intelligence. His words are cast in poetic parallelism (AB//A′ B′) and contain a visual pun on his own title. The first verb, "to rove," "to go to and fro," is spelled *šûṭ*; and *satan* is *śāṭān*.

1:8. From his title one can assume that the

satan has been patrolling the earth looking for disloyalty or sinful behavior to indict before Yahweh. Before the *satan* can give his report, however, Yahweh challenges him with a pre-emptive question. This is not a request for information. Narratively, Yahweh's challenging question suggests an ongoing rivalry with the *satan*. The grounds for such an edgy relationship are implicit in the *satan*'s function. One who defends a king's honor by zealously ferreting out hidden disloyalty simultaneously exposes the king to dishonor by showing that he is disrespected. Here, Yahweh pre-empts such activity and in effect defends his own honor by directing attention to "my servant Job" (cf. Gen 26:24; Exod 14:31; 2 Sam 7:5), the one person whose perfect loyalty and regard for God cannot be doubted. Yahweh's words in v. 8*b* are precisely those by which the narrator introduced Job in v. 1*b*, but God's praise is even more hyperbolic than the narrator's. Job is not merely the "greatest of all the people of the east" (v. 3); in God's judgment, "there is none like him on the earth."[43]

1:9-10. One of the conventions of Hebrew narrative is that the narrator can be trusted. When God confirms what the narrator says, the structures of narrative authority are doubly reinforced. Job's perfect character would seem to leave no crack for the accuser's doubt to penetrate. But as an accuser the *satan* must be true to type. The *satan*'s strategy is to shift the grounds of the debate. He meets God's rhetorical question with a rhetorical question of his own. "Is it for nothing [חנם *hinnām*] that Job fears God?" (v. 9, author's trans.). The *satan* shifts the focus to the question of what motivates Job's behavior. This is not necessarily, as it first appears, merely a questioning of Job's sincerity. The following rhetorical question is directed at God's activity in protecting and blessing Job. It is blessing itself that casts doubt on the very possibility of disinterested piety, even in such a paragon as Job. The *satan*'s insinuation suggests the symbolic image used by Henry James in *The Golden Bowl,* a vessel gleaming and perfect on the surface, but flawed by a hidden crack within. The crack in the golden bowl that the accuser claims to see is the subtly corrupting

influence of blessing on piety, which then becomes a tool of manipulation.

The *satan*'s language in v. 10 is vivid. As an image of God's protection, the hedge is an agricultural metaphor. The well-tended vineyard protected by a thorn hedge is safe from the destructive trampling of wild animals and theft by passers by (Ps 80:8-13 [9-14]; Isa 5:1-7). What is thus protected for Job is described in a three-part sequence that proceeds from the most intimate to the most distant: himself, his house (i.e., family), his possessions. While protection is described with a metaphor of containment (the hedge [שׂוך *śûk*]), Job's blessing is depicted as a "bursting forth" of flocks and herds (פרץ *pāraṣ*; see Gen 30:30).

1:11-12. The words that the *satan* utters in v. 11 are no wager but a challenge to a test. Job and God are mutually self-deceived in thinking that piety can ever be freely offered when it is routinely met with blessing. Breaking the nexus will prove the accuser right. If God breaches the protective hedge and destroys what Job has, Job will openly repudiate God. The language of the challenge requires comment. Literally translated, the sentence reads, "but stretch out your hand and touch all that he has—if he doesn't 'bless' you to your face." The euphemistic substitution of "bless" for "curse" is recognizable here, as in v. 5. The clause beginning with "if" is a form of self-curse. The full form contains both a protasis (an "if" statement) and an apodosis (a "then" statement), as in Ps 7:4-5 [5-6] ("If I have repaid my ally with harm/ or plundered my foe without cause,/ then let the enemy pursue and overtake me,/ trample my life to the ground,/ and lay my soul in the dust" [NRSV]). Commonly, a shortened form of the self-curse, without the apodosis, functions as an exclamation (Gen 14:23; 1 Sam 3:14; 14:45). Although occasionally an interpreter will argue that the accuser's exclamation is a seriously intended self-curse,[44] most recognize the conventional nature of the expression. Both the form and the nuance of the *satan*'s statement can be colloquially but aptly rendered as "stretch forth your hand and strike all that he has, and I'll be damned if he doesn't curse you to your face!" The *satan*'s challenge makes Job's *speech* about God the decisive factor in the

43. For a somewhat different understanding of the dynamics of the exchange, see J. G. Janzen, *Job,* Interpretation (Atlanta: John Knox, 1985) 39; D. Clines, *Job 1–20,* WBC 17 (Dallas: Word, 1989) 23-25.

44. E. Good, *In Turns of Tempest* (Stanford, Calif.: Stanford University Press, 1990) 194-95.

drama. As Gutiérrez astutely observes, how to talk about God becomes the central issue in the whole book.[45]

The concluding words of v. 11 echo and contrast with v. 5. Where Job sacrificed on behalf of his children because he feared they might have cursed God in their hearts, the accuser challenges God to sacrifice Job's well-being to see if he will curse God to God's face. God consents and sets the terms. For the third time in as many verses, the phrase "all that he has" is repeated. The

protective hedge is removed; God reserves for protection only the person of Job. Note that the threefold distinction of v. 10 has now become a twofold distinction. Job's family is incorporated into the category of "all that he has."

Yahweh will not personally "stretch forth his hand" against Job, as the *satan* suggested, but the difference is not significant. Yahweh and the *satan* have, metaphorically, joined hands to destroy Job. The scene ends dramatically: The accuser, having received a new commission, goes out from Yahweh's presence (v. 12; cf. 1 Kgs 22:22; Zech 6:5). (See Reflections at 2:11-13.)

45. G. Gutiérrez, *On Job: God-Talk and the Suffering of the Innocent,* trans. M. O'Connell (Maryknoll, N.Y.: Orbis, 1987) 3.

Job 1:13-22, Scene 3: The Test—Destruction of "All That He Has"

NIV

[13]One day when Job's sons and daughters were feasting and drinking wine at the oldest brother's house, [14]a messenger came to Job and said, "The oxen were plowing and the donkeys were grazing nearby, [15]and the Sabeans attacked and carried them off. They put the servants to the sword, and I am the only one who has escaped to tell you!"

[16]While he was still speaking, another messenger came and said, "The fire of God fell from the sky and burned up the sheep and the servants, and I am the only one who has escaped to tell you!"

[17]While he was still speaking, another messenger came and said, "The Chaldeans formed three raiding parties and swept down on your camels and carried them off. They put the servants to the sword, and I am the only one who has escaped to tell you!"

[18]While he was still speaking, yet another messenger came and said, "Your sons and daughters were feasting and drinking wine at the oldest brother's house, [19]when suddenly a mighty wind swept in from the desert and struck the four corners of the house. It collapsed on them and they are dead, and I am the only one who has escaped to tell you!"

[20]At this, Job got up and tore his robe and shaved his head. Then he fell to the ground in worship [21]and said:

"Naked I came from my mother's womb,

NRSV

13One day when his sons and daughters were eating and drinking wine in the eldest brother's house, [14]a messenger came to Job and said, "The oxen were plowing and the donkeys were feeding beside them, [15]and the Sabeans fell on them and carried them off, and killed the servants with the edge of the sword; I alone have escaped to tell you." [16]While he was still speaking, another came and said, "The fire of God fell from heaven and burned up the sheep and the servants, and consumed them; I alone have escaped to tell you." [17]While he was still speaking, another came and said, "The Chaldeans formed three columns, made a raid on the camels and carried them off, and killed the servants with the edge of the sword; I alone have escaped to tell you." [18]While he was still speaking, another came and said, "Your sons and daughters were eating and drinking wine in their eldest brother's house, [19]and suddenly a great wind came across the desert, struck the four corners of the house, and it fell on the young people, and they are dead; I alone have escaped to tell you."

20Then Job arose, tore his robe, shaved his head, and fell on the ground and worshiped. [21]He said, "Naked I came from my mother's womb, and naked shall I return there; the LORD gave, and the LORD has taken away; blessed be the name of the LORD."

NIV

and naked I will depart.[a]
The LORD gave and the LORD has taken away;
    may the name of the LORD be praised."
[22]In all this, Job did not sin by charging God with wrongdoing.

[a]21 Or *will return there*

NRSV

[22]In all this Job did not sin or charge God with wrong-doing.

COMMENTARY

1:13. This scene opens with two verbal echoes that set an ominous tone. Its first words, "one day . . . ," are the same as those that opened the preceding scene of the heavenly council at which the destruction was decreed. The description of the sons and daughters "eating and drinking wine" echoes v. 4. Although ostensibly the verse serves only to set the scene, it foreshadows the transformation of celebration into destruction and grief. There is also an ironic echo of the divine council. Just as emissaries come to Yahweh to report, so also messengers come to Job with reports. But Job is not sovereign over the events that befall him.

1:14-19. The account of the four messengers in vv. 14-19 is an astonishing piece of verbal art, using symmetrical structures and closely patterned repetition and variation. In vv. 2-3 Job's blessings were enumerated in the sequence of (1) sons and daughters, (2) herds of sheep and camels, (3) agricultural animals (oxen and asses), and (4) servants. In the reports of the messengers, the sequence is presented in almost the reverse order. The destruction of the servants, however, is distributed throughout the four reports. To keep the numerical total of four, the accounts of the destruction of the camels and sheep are separate events. Thus the disasters are reported in the order: (1) oxen and asses, (2) sheep, (3) camels, (4) children. Other symmetries are present as well. The first and the fourth reports (vv. 14-15, 18-19) are longer and begin with a description of the peaceful scene before the destruction. The second and the third reports begin with an immediate identification of the agent of destruction (vv. 16-17). The agents of destruction alternate between human predators (Sabeans, Chaldeans) in the first and third reports and natural forces (lightning and a storm wind) in the second and fourth.

It becomes clear in the fourth messenger's report why the author has chosen to distribute the death of the servants throughout the account. A different term is used for the servants in vv. 14-19, not '*ăbûdâ* (עבדה) as in v. 3, but *nĕ'ārîm* (נערים). Although *nĕ'ārîm* is often used to mean "servants," its primary meaning is "boys," "young people." This strategic shift on the author's part allows a momentary ambiguity when the fourth messenger, reporting on the destruction of the eldest brother's house, says that it "fell on the *nĕ'ārîm* and they are dead." But Job and the reader know that this time the term includes both the servants and the children. For the reader, too, another echo is recognizable. In the fourth messenger's description of the situation before the disaster, he repeats word for word the narrator's scene-setting description in v. 13. The ominous anticipation has been fulfilled; the destruction is complete.

What is one to make of the narrative art of this description? At one level it is simply part of a schematic and hyperbolic style. But form always has meaning, although it may be elusive. Clearest is the use of the number four to suggest totality.[46] The interlinking of the four distinct reports in the various ways described underscores the fact that they are aspects of a single event. At a more comprehensive level of analysis, the totality is part of the story's structure. The completeness of Job's piety (v. 1) and the completeness of his blessing (vv. 2-3) are answered by the completeness of his destruction (vv. 14-19).

46. G. Fohrer, *Das Buch Hiob,* KAT 16 (Guetersloh: Gerd Mohn, 1963) 88-89. Fohrer notes the use of fourfold destruction in Ezek 14:12-23; Zech 2:3; and in ancient Near Eastern literature in the story of Gilgamesh, 11:177-85.

The interlocking of the four messenger reports, the formulaic repetition of the way the narrator introduces each ("while this one was speaking, another came and said," vv. 16-18), and the way each messenger ends his speech ("and I alone have escaped to tell you," vv. 15-17, 19) contribute not only to the scene's unity but also to its emotional impact. No time has been allowed for Job to respond to each individual destruction. The terms of the test were that "all that he has" be destroyed. Only now is it time for Job's response.

In contrast to the nonstop, overlapping words of the messengers, Job's response is initially nonverbal. He expresses himself in the ancient gestures of mourning, which the narrator enumerates in a series of brief clauses (v. 20). Tearing the robe in grief (see Gen 37:34; Josh 7:6; 2 Sam 1:11; 3:31; 13:31; Ezra 9:3, 5; Esth 4:1) and shaving the head (see Ezra 9:3; Isa 22:12; Jer 7:29; Ezek 7:18; Mic 1:16) are customary responses to catastrophe. Falling to the ground may also be (see Josh 7:6; cf. 2 Sam 13:31). The last verb in the sequence (lit., "to prostrate oneself" [השתחוה *hištaḥăwâ*]) is not otherwise used in a context of grieving. It is distinctly a gesture of worship (1 Sam 1:3; Ps 95:6; Ezek 46:9). This is the decisive moment of Job's response. Why Job understands it to be an appropriate sequel to his gestures of grief is disclosed in his words.

1:20-21. Contrary to what one might expect, Job does not use the language of the funeral song or the lament. Those genres guide the grieving to experience and to express loss by contrasting what was with what is ("How the mighty have fallen" [2 Sam 1:25*a* NRSV]; "She that was a princess . . . has become a vassal" [Lam 1:1*c* NRSV]). Job also reaches for traditional words to orient himself in the face of shattering loss, but the words he chooses are proverbial ones from the wisdom tradition (v. 21). Variants of the saying about the mother's womb occur in Eccl 5:15 and Sir 40:1. Differences in form and context suggest that those later authors are not borrowing directly from Job. More likely the saying in Job 1:21*a* was traditional. Unlike the contrastive structure of the lament, the wisdom saying Job repeats is shaped according to a structure of equivalence. The governing image is that of the naked body, glimpsed as just-birthed infant and as corpse. The image is even more apt if one recalls that in the ancient

Near East bodies were often arranged in the fetal position for burial. Thus the womb of the mother becomes the metaphor for the grave, and indeed for the earth, from which one comes and to which one returns (cf. Gen 3:19*b*; Ps 139:13-15). If the privileged image is that of the naked body at birth and death, then all else—not only possessions but also human relationships—is implicitly likened to the clothes one wears. However much clothes may feel like a second skin, they are put on and eventually must be put off. By means of the proverbial saying, Job is orienting himself to the hard but necessary reality of relinquishing what cannot be held on to.

The proverbial saying in v. 21*a* is followed by a specifically religious one in which the orientation is no longer to the experience of the human individual but to the activity of Yahweh. Fohrer is probably correct that the saying presumes an ancient idea that possessions are a loan from God, who may require them back at any time (cf. the notion of the present moment as a gift in Ecclesiastes).[47] But how would such a notion and such a statement lead to the final benediction, "blessed be the name of Yahweh"? First one must notice that the word order of the saying places the emphasis not on the verbs but on the subject. "It is *Yahweh* who has given and *Yahweh* who has taken away." The parallelism between the first saying and the second one is also important. In the first saying, the terror of birth and death, the vulnerability of nakedness, is contained through the image of the mother. It is she who sends and she who receives back again. In the second saying, Yahweh occupies the same place as the mother and is to be understood in the light of that image. The fragility of the gift and the desolation of the loss are endurable only if it is Yahweh who gives and Yahweh who takes (cf. Ps 104:27-30). Human words of blessing addressed to God are an act of worship that reaffirms relationship with God. It is not in spite of his loss but precisely because of its overwhelming dimensions that Job moves from the ritual of grief to words of blessing, which echo the liturgical formula in Ps 113:2.

1:22. In the Hebrew text the crucial word "blessed" (מברך *měbôrāk*) comes last in Job's speech. Its occurrence reminds the reader of what is at stake in Job's response. What Job has said

47. Ibid., 93.

contradicts the accuser's prediction that Job would curse God openly. Rather, in the light of the euphemism in 1:11, Job ironically says precisely what the *satan* predicted: He blesses God. The narrator sums up Job's response in v. 22. The word תפלה (*tiplâ*), which the NRSV and the NIV translate as "wrongdoing," is obscure. It is related to a word that means "insipid," "without taste" (Job 6:6; Lam 2:14), but the precise nuance of *tiplâ* remains uncertain. According to Clines, the context suggests that attributing *tiplâ* to God must be the most modest form of cursing God.[48] Job does not do even this. Thus Job's words are judged to have been absolutely blameless. The

narrator's comment serves as a guide to what issues are central and how the reader is supposed to respond. Job's words demonstrate that piety can be disinterested, that it is not necessarily corrupted by divine blessing or destroyed by loss. There is no hidden crack in the golden bowl after all. The narrator's summing up also has a restrictive function. Other issues and questions that the reader might wish to raise about the characters, their actions, and their values are subtly discouraged as beside the point. Perhaps the author of Job has emphasized this stylistic trait of narrative control in order to make Job's outburst in chapter 3 all the more powerful. (See Reflections at 2:11-13.)

---

48. D. Clines, *Job 1–20*, WBC 17 (Dallas: Word, 1989) 40.

JOB 2:1-10, THE SECOND TEST

Job 2:1-6, Scene 4: A Second Dialogue About Job

NIV

2 On another day the angels[a] came to present themselves before the LORD, and Satan also came with them to present himself before him. [2]And the LORD said to Satan, "Where have you come from?"

Satan answered the LORD, "From roaming through the earth and going back and forth in it."

[3]Then the LORD said to Satan, "Have you considered my servant Job? There is no one on earth like him; he is blameless and upright, a man who fears God and shuns evil. And he still maintains his integrity, though you incited me against him to ruin him without any reason."

[4]"Skin for skin!" Satan replied. "A man will give all he has for his own life. [5]But stretch out your hand and strike his flesh and bones, and he will surely curse you to your face."

[6]The LORD said to Satan, "Very well, then, he is in your hands; but you must spare his life."

a1 Hebrew the sons of God

NRSV

2 One day the heavenly beings[a] came to present themselves before the LORD, and Satan[b] also came among them to present himself before the LORD. [2]The LORD said to Satan,[b] "Where have you come from?" Satan[b] answered the LORD, "From going to and fro on the earth, and from walking up and down on it." [3]The LORD said to Satan,[b] "Have you considered my servant Job? There is no one like him on the earth, a blameless and upright man who fears God and turns away from evil. He still persists in his integrity, although you incited me against him, to destroy him for no reason." [4]Then Satan[b] answered the LORD, "Skin for skin! All that people have they will give to save their lives.[c] [5]But stretch out your hand now and touch his bone and his flesh, and he will curse you to your face." [6]The LORD said to Satan,[b] "Very well, he is in your power; only spare his life."

a Heb sons of God   b Or the Accuser, Heb ha-satan
c Or All that the man has he will give for his life

COMMENTARY

2:1-3. The fourth scene begins in a way virtually identical to the second (1:6-12). The addition of the phrase "to present [himself] before Yahweh" at the end of v. 1 points to the *satan's* report as the one that matters for this story.[49] God initiates the dialogue as before, and the *satan* replies in the same way. Such repetition has several functions. It reinforces the stylized quality of the narrative. Repetition also increases the reader's sense of participation, as well as the sense of familiarity. Moreover, repetition increases anticipation. Whatever words break the repetition become the focus of attention. These crucial words occur in v. 3*b*. In the first part of that statement God echoes the narrator's positive judgment about Job, using the key term "integrity" (תמה *tûmmâ*). The following part of God's statement requires more reflection, however: "although you incited me against him, to destroy him for no reason." The wording shifts the focus momentarily from Job's character to the actions of God and the *satan.* Consider the difference if the storyteller had written, "He still holds fast to his integrity, even when the hedge around him is removed." The momentary loss of focus on Job runs counter to the highly controlled style of the didactic tale. It serves the design of the book as a whole, however. In the poetic dialogues God's character will become one of the main issues.

The author signals the thematic importance of this brief line more directly. The last word of Yahweh's statement ("without cause" [חנם *hinnām*]) is in Hebrew the same as the first word of the *satan's* crucial question in 1:9 ("for nothing"). The Hebrew term *hinnām* has a range of meanings: "without compensation," "in vain," "without cause," or "undeservedly." It is possible to translate the line *"in vain* you incited me to destroy him," the point being that the test did not work as the *satan* predicted.[50] The word order, however, makes it more likely that the phrase is to be translated "to destroy him for no reason"—i.e., undeservedly. Something of the play on words can

be suggested in English by the related words *gratis* and *gratuitously.* The use of the same word with different nuances in 1:9 and 2:3 suggests that the issues of the story are more complex than first envisioned. The didactic tale has been guiding the reader to affirm that disinterested piety, a fully unconditional love of God, is both possible and commendable. Yahweh's echo of the term *hinnām* in the context of "gratuitous destruction," however, suggests the dark possibilities inherent in a relationship that is radically unconditional.

2:4-6. The *satan* is a formidable adversary. Unwilling to concede defeat, he shifts ground again. The proverbial saying that the *satan* cites is obscure.[51] It probably derives from a marketplace setting and has to do with comparative values. As Good argues, it should not be translated "skin for skin," which would be expressed in Hebrew with a different preposition. Rather, it is better translated "skin up to skin."[52] A person trying to trade for a skin would be willing to offer anything of value, up to an equivalent skin. But if the cost of a skin is another skin, then the deal is off, because there is no advantage in it. So the *satan* argues in the following line, which uses the same preposition, "All that a man has he will give, *up to* [בעד *bĕ'ad*] his life."

The *satan's* rhetoric is persuasive because it builds on Job's own images. Job used the image of the naked body as the essential self. So the *satan* turns to the image of skin, the reality of bone and flesh. The expression "bone and flesh" is an idiom elsewhere used to describe the identity of kinship, as in Laban's greeting of Jacob in Gen 29:14. Following the same wording as in the previous challenge (1:11), the *satan* now predicts that if God strikes Job's body, Job will openly curse God. As before, God places Job under the power of the accuser, this time preserving only his life (v. 6). Parallel to 1:12, the *satan* departs from the presence of God (1:7*a*). (See Reflections at 2:11-13.)

---

49. Contra R. Gordis, *The Book of Job: Commentary, New Translation, and Special Studies* (New York: Jewish Theological Seminary, 5738/1978) 19.

50. F. Andersen, *Job: An Introduction and Commentary,* Tyndale Old Testament Commentaries (Downers Grove, Ill.: Inter-Varsity, 1976) 90.

51. See Clines, *Job 1–20,* 43-46, for a survey of various interpretations.

52. E. Good, *In Turns of Tempest* (Stanford, Calif.: Stanford University Press, 1990) 52, 198.

Job 2:7-10, Scene 5: The Test—Disease

NIV

7So Satan went out from the presence of the LORD and afflicted Job with painful sores from the soles of his feet to the top of his head. 8Then Job took a piece of broken pottery and scraped himself with it as he sat among the ashes.

9His wife said to him, "Are you still holding on to your integrity? Curse God and die!"

10He replied, "You are talking like a foolish[a] woman. Shall we accept good from God, and not trouble?"

In all this, Job did not sin in what he said.

a10 The Hebrew word rendered foolish denotes moral deficiency.

NRSV

7So Satan[a] went out from the presence of the LORD, and inflicted loathsome sores on Job from the sole of his foot to the crown of his head. 8Job[b] took a potsherd with which to scrape himself, and sat among the ashes.

9Then his wife said to him, "Do you still persist in your integrity? Curse[c] God, and die." 10But he said to her, "You speak as any foolish woman would speak. Shall we receive the good at the hand of God, and not receive the bad?" In all this Job did not sin with his lips.

a Or the Accuser, Heb ha-satan   b Heb He   c Heb Bless

COMMENTARY

2:7. Since the second test is an attack on Job's body, there is no place for a scene such as 1:14-19. Instead, the destruction is briefly described in a narrative summary (2:7b). Here, too, however, there is a symbolic representation of the totality of Job's affliction, as he is struck with skin sores "from the soles of his feet to the top of his head." The identity of Job's disease has long intrigued interpreters; attempts at diagnosis are beside the point, however. It is significant that it is a disease of the skin. Perhaps because so much of a person's identity is invested in the skin and because at least hands and face are involved in the public presentation of the self, diseases of the skin often evoke social revulsion. In the ancient Near East, where disease in general was often seen as a sign of divine displeasure, serious and intractable skin disease was particularly likely to be so interpreted.[53] There is, for instance, a strong echo between the description of Job's disease and the disease threatened as one of the curses for disobedience to the covenant in Deut 28:35. Similarly, in the Prayer of Nabonidus, a fragmentary Aramaic narrative from Qumran, a Babylonian king is stricken with "painful sores" (the same phrase as in Job 2:7). He recovers only when a "Jewish exorcist" pardons his sins and teaches him to worship the Most High God. Thus the disease with which the *satan* afflicts Job is one that would easily lend itself to interpretation as a mark of divine displeasure.

2:8. Job's response to this new disaster is described in quite different terms from the parallel scene. Job engages in no new acts of mourning. The NIV translation, "as he sat among the ashes," reflects well the syntax of the Hebrew. The clause identifies existing circumstances, not new action. As Clines observes, the implication is that Job has been sitting in the ashes as part of his mourning for his previous losses (cf. Jer 6:26; Ezek 27:30).[54] Now Job's only response to this new, terrible suffering is a purely physical one: He picks up a piece of a broken pot and scratches himself with it. The gesture communicates nothing explicit about Job's inner state, although its very noncommunicativeness has a somewhat ominous quality.

2:9. The silence is broken by Job's wife. For a character with only one line to speak, she has made an indelible impression on interpreters of the book of Job. The ancient tradition, reflected in Augustine, Chrysostom, Calvin, and many others, that she is an aide to the *satan* underestimates the complexity of her role. Verbally, her speech echoes both God's evaluation of Job (2:3) and the

53. See K. van der Toorn, *Sin and Sanction in Israel and Mesopotamia,* SSN 22 (Assen and Maastricht: Van Gorcum, 1985) 72-75.

54. Clines, *Job 1–20,* 5, 49.

satan's prediction of what Job will eventually say (1:11; 2:5; she, too, employs the euphemistic "blessed" [ברך *brk*]). Her words contain an ambiguity seldom recognized, one having to do with the thematically important word "integrity" (*tûmmā*).[55] That word and its cognates denote a person whose conduct is completely in accord with moral and religious norms and whose character is one of utter honesty, without guile. (In Psalm 101, for instance, integrity of heart and conduct is contrasted with images of a twisted heart, secret slander, deceit, and lies.) Ordinarily, it would be unthinkable that a conflict would exist between the social and personal dimensions of the word. Just such a tension, however, is implicit in the words of Job's wife. One could hear her question as a frustrated, alienated cry of bitterness stemming from immeasurable loss and pity, the equivalent of "Give up your integrity! Curse God, and in so doing, put yourself out of your misery!" More hauntingly, one could hear her words as recognition of a conflict between integrity as guileless honesty and integrity as conformity to religious norms. If Job holds on to integrity in the sense of conformity to religious norm and blesses God as he did before, she senses that he will be committing an act of deceit. If he holds on to integrity in the sense of honesty, then he must curse God and violate social integrity, which forbids such cursing.

2:10. However Job hears the words of his wife, he rejects them with strong language of his own, characterizing her as talking like one of the נבלות (*něbālōt*). Often translated "foolish women," this term has both moral and social connotations.[56] In English, one could capture something of the nuance by saying that she "talks like trash." Job's reply may also contain an element of social disdain for the outspoken woman (cf. Prov 21:9, 19; 25:24; 27:15-16). Although Job's criticism of his wife has largely set the tone for her evaluation by interpreters, there are more sympathetic interpretations of her character. The Septuagint gives her a longer speech, allowing her to talk about Job's sufferings and her own. In the *Testament of Job,* a Jewish retelling of the story of Job from the first century BCE, she is a character of pathos, whose

suffering as she tries to care for her husband is vividly described. In both of these accounts, however, Job is the morally superior character who corrects her understanding. The sympathetic interpretation, as much as the hostile interpretation, obscures the role of Job's wife in articulating the moral and theological dilemma of his situation. Significantly, Job's rebuke of his wife is the last thing that he says for some time. When he speaks again in chap. 3, his words bear traces of hers. Although he does not curse God, he curses the day of his birth. Although he does not die, he talks longingly of death. In subsequent chapters, his persistence in his integrity—both in the sense of his moral conduct and in the sense of his absolute honesty—motivates his own angry speech. His wife's troubling question will have become his own.[57]

Those developments lie in the future, however. In the present scene Job responds to his wife's question with another rhetorical question. Although it is not otherwise attested in wisdom literature, the rhythmic balance of the saying suggests that here, too, Job turns to tradition for words to orient himself and his wife to a proper response. The notion that both "weal and woe" come from God is a conventional way of acknowledging God's sovereignty (Isa 45:7; cf. Deut 32:39).

The artistic use of parallel scenes in the story directs the reader back to the equivalent scene and words in 1:20-21. There are contrasts: Job's words here are much less personal; there is no concluding blessing. At the same time, nothing in Job's words can be construed as cursing God. The comparison of the narrator's concluding evaluation is even more striking. The first words are the same: "In all this Job did not sin." But whereas the narrator in 1:22 went on to add "or charge God with wrongdoing" (NRSV), the narrator now adds only the phrase "with his lips." That phrase could with equal legitimacy be construed in two contradictory ways. It could be taken to mean that Job, like the ideal righteous person, was in control of himself from the inside out (cf. Ps 39:2; Prov 13:3; 18:4; 21:23).[58] Alternatively,

---

55. See J. G. Janzen, *Job,* Interpretation (Atlanta: John Knox, 1985) 50, for a similar interpretation.

56. Van der Toorn, *Sin and Sanction in Israel and Mesopotamia,* 107.

57. C. Newsom, "Job," *The Women's Bible Commentary,* ed. C. Newsom and S. Ringe (Philadelphia: Westminster/John Knox Press, 1992) 131-32.

58. So Gordis, *The Book of Job,* 22; G. Fohrer, *Das Buch Hiob,* KAT xvi (Guetersloh: Gerd Mohn, 1963) 103; Andersen, *Job,* 94.

it could suggest, as the Talmud says, that "Job did not sin with his lips; but in his heart he did."[59] That, after all, was what Job imagined his children might do, simply in the careless spirits of a feast (1:5). Of course, even if one conceded what the Talmud suggests, the terms of the test were about cursing God to God's face. Nevertheless, a merely technical victory is not a very satisfying outcome. This entire scene has suggested increasing strain on Job, and the ambiguous concluding verse raises the level of narrative tension. That tension must be resolved in a third and decisive scene.

It is almost disingenuous to talk about narrative tension, however, in this sort of story. The reader has been told by the authoritative narrator and by God that Job is "blameless and upright," etc. The situation is similar to that in a melodrama, where the audience knows that the hero will triumph over the villain and so can enjoy the pseudo-anxiety of the conflict. So here, the reader of the tale can enjoy the pseudo-anxiety that the hero will fall from perfection, knowing that in the third and decisive test the hero will triumphantly dispel all doubt about his character. Or so one could expect if the whole book of Job were told as a traditional tale. (See Reflections at 2:11-13.)

59. *b. B. Bat.* 16a. See M. Weiss, *The Story of Job's Beginning* (Jerusalem: Magnes, 1983) 71-74

JOB 2:11-13, SCENE 6: THE THREE FRIENDS

NIV

[11]When Job's three friends, Eliphaz the Temanite, Bildad the Shuhite and Zophar the Naamathite, heard about all the troubles that had come upon him, they set out from their homes and met together by agreement to go and sympathize with him and comfort him. [12]When they saw him from a distance, they could hardly recognize him; they began to weep aloud, and they tore their robes and sprinkled dust on their heads. [13]Then they sat on the ground with him for seven days and seven nights. No one said a word to him, because they saw how great his suffering was.

NRSV

[11]Now when Job's three friends heard of all these troubles that had come upon him, each of them set out from his home—Eliphaz the Temanite, Bildad the Shuhite, and Zophar the Naamathite. They met together to go and console and comfort him. [12]When they saw him from a distance, they did not recognize him, and they raised their voices and wept aloud; they tore their robes and threw dust in the air upon their heads. [13]They sat with him on the ground seven days and seven nights, and no one spoke a word to him, for they saw that his suffering was very great.

COMMENTARY

The alternation of scenes between earth and heaven breaks off as the perspective shifts to another location on earth. The reader first sees the three friends of Job come together with the intention of visiting him in his grief (v. 11), and then sees Job through the eyes of the friends as they approach (v. 12).

Like Job in 1:1, the three friends are identified by name and place. The significance of the names and locations is no longer entirely clear, although the likelihood is that the three are presented as Edomites and, therefore, countrymen of Job.[60]

The friends' action, going to Job "to console and comfort" him, is a traditional expression of solidarity in grief. To be deprived of this gesture of friendship made suffering even more difficult to endure (cf. Ps 69:20[21]; Isa 51:19; Nah 3:7,

60. So E. Dhorme, *A Commentary on the Book of Job,* trans. H. Knight (London: Nelson, 1967) xxvi-xxvii; Gordis, *The Book of Job,* 23; D. Clines, *Job 1–20,* WBC 17 (Dallas: Word, 1989) 57. For a different opinion, see Fohrer, *Das Buch Hiob,* 105-6.

where the same pair of words occurs). Although the text says that the friends did not recognize Job, they clearly do, for it is the sight of him, changed *almost* beyond recognition, that provokes their gestures and cries of grief (cf. Isa 52:14). Weeping and tearing one's robe are both conventional expressions of mourning and distress, as is the use of dust. The precise nature and significance of "sprinkling dust in the air upon their heads" is obscure. The particular verb (זרק *zāraq*) and direction (lit., "heavenward" [השמימה *haśśāmāymâ*]) recall how Moses flung soot into the air (Exod 9:10) to bring on the plague of "boils" (שחין *šĕḥîn,* the same word as in Job 2:7). The meaning and purpose of the actions, however, seem quite different.[61] Perhaps the word "heavenward" was not originally part of the text (cf. LXX) but was added as a gloss by a scribe who noted other similarities with Exod 9:10. Others suggest that the word may be an error for a similarly written word, "appalled" (השמם *hašamēm*; cf. Ezek 3:15; Ezra 9:3).[62]

61. But see Gordis, *The Book of Job,* 24; M. Weiss, *The Story of Job's Beginning* (Jerusalem: Magnes, 1983) 76; N. Habel, *The Book of Job,* OTL (Philadelphia: Westminster, 1985) 97, who all argue that it is some form of magical gesture, though they disagree as to whether the intent is to express empathy or to ward off a similar fate.

62. So N. H. Tur-Sinai, *The Book of Job: A New Commentary* (Jerusalem: Kiryath Sepher, 1957) 30; J. G. Janzen, *Job,* Interpretation (Atlanta: John Knox, 1985) 58.

Symbols of completeness and "perfection" are present in this scene, as in every other: the numerical symbols of three friends and seven days; the complementary images of seven days and seven nights. (Elsewhere periods of grief or silent distress may be described as seven days [Gen 50:10; 1 Sam 31:13; Ezek 3:15] but never as seven days and seven nights.)[63] The final words in 2:13 about the greatness of Job's suffering ironically echo the introduction of Job in 1:3 as the greatest among the peoples of the east. He has now exceeded all in suffering as he had in good fortune.

The picture of Job's friends sitting in silence on the ground is a conventional image of grieving, recalling Lam 2:10. The narrator focuses the scene through their eyes ("for they saw that his suffering was very great"). The friends' silence is respectful, even awed. In their silence they present a contrast to Job's wife, who, whatever her motives and meaning, sought to bring an end to Job's suffering by urging him to curse God. Ironically, the space created by the friends' silent presence is what finally provokes Job to a curse, moving the story out of the safe confines of the simple tale.

63. Clines, *Job 1–20,* 63.

REFLECTIONS

This seemingly simple story presents any number of issues for reflection. Three of them will be examined: (1) the relation of blessing and self-interested religion; (2) attachment, loss, and grief; (3) the disturbing image of God in Job 1–2 and the cultural context it assumes.

In the OT blessing is primarily an expression of a close relationship or bond between God and an individual or a people. Divine blessing makes people flourish, and that flourishing is often talked about in very concrete terms: a large family, material prosperity, social power and status (e.g., Psalms 112; 128). Moreover, often one finds the promise of blessing offered as motivation for good conduct (Gen 17:1-2; Deuteronomy 28). That is the problem addressed by the *satan*'s cynical question: Hasn't the way people understand divine blessing slipped into essentially a barter religion? "If you will do this for me, I will do that for you." "If you will guarantee me this, then I will agree to do that." It does not take long, listening to religious talk shows or browsing through religious book stores, to feel the force of the *satan*'s question. Explicitly or implicitly, much of religion seems preoccupied with striking a bargain with God.

It is easy enough to deplore crude expressions of self-interested religion. The *satan*'s challenge goes deeper, however, suggesting that the distortion in the religious relationship is so deeply ingrained that people are not even aware of its presence until something happens to upset their assumptions. One finds out what people really believe when they face a crisis. The baby lies gravely ill, and the father rejects God in rage. The question that Job 1–2 poses to such a situation is not about the proper pastoral response or even about whether it is emotionally and religiously healthy to express the anger one feels. The story's question is about the theology implied by that rage, a theology that contains the unspoken assumption of a contract with God: God is bound to protect me from tragedy because I have been good or simply because I belong to God. Such a brittle faith will not sustain a person in crisis; yet it is often taught subliminally in the way religious communities talk about God. (There is, of course, much more to be said about the relation between anger and faith; later parts of the book will provide opportunity to reflect on different dimensions of that issue.)

It can be difficult to make the distinction between the appropriate human desire to protect what is precious and the inappropriate belief that one can strike a bargain with God. The story in Job 1–2 explores this subtle distinction by showing the reader a character who is fully aware of the human fears that drive so many to try to bargain with God but who does not understand his own piety and religious acts as a guarantee of security. The story engages readers by drawing them into emotions that readers have themselves experienced, as well as drawing them into situations and feelings that seem foreign or strange. Job's gathering his children and offering sacrifice for them "just in case" is the representative of every parent who has sat looking at his or her children around the dinner table, knowing that there is so much danger in the world and longing to protect them from it. The very exuberance and high spirits that make young people so dear is one of the things that produces anxiety in a parent's heart. Job knows this, like any parent, and evidently worries that his children would not think through the consequences of their actions, would get caught up in the partying and do something foolish, or in the process of trying to impress one another would make a bad judgment with possibly fatal consequences. It is a rare parent who has not, like Job, offered up a prayer to God on behalf of her or his children.

Such prayers are not necessarily attempts to strike a bargain with God, although the temptation is always there. Praying on behalf of another is an act of caring. When that prayer concerns a sin that the other person is unable or unwilling to bring before God, then it can be an act of reconciliation. Only when such prayer is assumed to have struck a deal is the proper function of prayer abused. Job's response to the sudden loss of children, property, and health shows that his piety was not the sort corrupted by the assumption of an implicit bargain. To understand the religious perspective that grounds piety like that of Job, it is necessary to look at the issues of attachment, loss, and grief, and at the way in which they are illustrated by Job.

The agony of love is that it cannot ensure the safety of the one we love so deeply. All the prayers, all the good advice, all the superstitious rituals ("if I imagine all the bad things that could happen, then they won't happen") cannot guarantee it. Loving is risky business; there is no way to bargain with God about that. Vulnerability is a condition of our being finite and mortal creatures. The greater evil would be to fear loss too much to risk loving at all. Mary Oliver says it well:

> To live in this world
>
> you must be able
> to do three things:
> to love what is mortal;
> to hold it
>
> against your bones knowing
> your own life depends on it;
> and, when the time comes to let it go,
> to let it go.[64]

---

64. Mary Oliver, "In Blackwater Woods," in *American Primitive*, by Mary Oliver. (Boston: Little, Brown, 1983) 83. Copyright © 1983 by Mary Oliver. First appeared in *Yankee*. Used by permission of Little, Brown and Company (Inc.).

Job's blessings, especially as they are manifested in his children, but also in his prosperity and in his health, may appear to the *satan* as a hedge of security, but they can be seen equally well as a measure of Job's vulnerability. Health, financial security, family—these things matter. There is nothing venal or sinful or wrong in caring about them very much. It is because they are so important that the story insists that it is also important to think about the experience of losing them, and about the related but distinct experience of letting them go. Losing something one cares about deeply is a devastating experience. Numbness, disorientation, anger, an overwhelming sense of helplessness—all of these emotions and more wash over a person in waves. This is the first part of grieving, but the work of grief requires something more. Finally, one has to let go of what has been lost. This does not mean forgetting or no longer feeling the aching absence. Letting it go does mean recognizing the reality of loss and accepting its finality. Both aspects of this process are reflected in Job's response, the first in the silent gestures of grief, the second in the words that he utters.

There are many ways to accept the finality of loss, because people bring different understandings of the world and of God to that process. For Job, letting go is made possible precisely because all things—both good and bad—ultimately come from God. To many readers, this is a baffling, if not an outrageous, position. There is a wisdom in Job's words, however, that is deep and powerful. Job's words are not about causality in the narrow sense. They do not deny the reality of tornadoes or bandits. Especially in the case of human violence it is right to be angry, to seek justice, to prevent such violence from occurring again. Energies directed in those directions are important, but they do not finish the work of grieving. One also has to come to grips with the terrible fragility of human life itself, the vulnerability that attends all of existence. It is God the creator who has made us as we are, capable of love and attachment, but also susceptible to disease, accidents, violence. In this sense, it is God who gives and takes away, from whom we receive both what we yearn for and what we dread. There is a tendency to want to associate God with only what is good. If one does that, however, then when trouble comes it is easy to feel that one has fallen into a godforsaken place. At the time, when one most needs the presence of God, there is only the experience of absence. The wisdom of Job's stance is that it allows him to recognize the presence of God even in the most desolate of experiences. Job blesses God in response to that presence.

This kind of reflection, which focuses on the religious values of Job and views God only through Job's statements about God, does not get at all of the difficult issues raised by this story. After all, the reader knows what Job does not—namely, what has gone on in heaven. No reflection on this story can be complete that has not wrestled with the difficult question of what to do with the image of God presented by the narrative itself. Some readers are so outraged by God's treatment of Job that they can hardly focus on any other aspect of the story. Others do not see this as an important issue at all. After all, they would say, this is not "really" God but a fictional story in which God is represented as a character. The whole business of testing Job is necessary to the plot, and without it there would be no story. Both of these responses have merit. It is important to be attuned to the genre and style of the story—to its playfulness and freedom of the imagination. Like some parables, it adopts a frankly outrageous premise to enable its readers to see something important. On the other hand, it would be a mistake to set Job 1–2 aside as "just a story," as though other speech about God could be literally descriptive. That is not so. *All* speech about God is the making of an image of God. All verbal or visual images of God are attempts to make a claim about who God is and what God is like. These images are suggestive, of course, rather than literal. Taking the genre of Job 1–2 fully into account, it remains necessary to reflect on the story's claim about who God is.

The representation of God as king of the universe in Job 1–2 is quite familiar from other biblical imagery and serves as a graphic way of attributing authority and sovereignty to God.

The way the story represents God's motives in the actions that constitute the plot, however, puzzles many modern readers. What is God doing in bringing up Job's name, almost as a provocation, and then responding to the *satan*'s counterprovocation? To many readers, the exchange seems childish and quite unworthy as a representation of God.[65] Why the characters act as they do can be understood only when one recognizes that they represent the values of a culture of honor. When the *satan* casts doubt on Job's motives, he also besmirches God's honor by suggesting that even the best humans do not love God for God's own sake, but simply for what they can get out of it. Since God has just praised Job, God appears as a dupe. In cultures in which honor is a paramount value and losing face is a matter of shame, such a challenge cannot be ignored. Not only God's dignity but also God's authority would be compromised if the issue remained unaddressed. Readers who share those assumptions are not likely to consider God's response as "just showing off" but as something much more serious.

The narrative of Job 1–2 makes a radical case for the religious values accompanying a culture of honor. In doing so, it also exposes the limits of those religious values. Most readers of this commentary probably belong to communities in which honor, although important, is not such a central moral value as it appears in the narrative of Job 1–2. It takes a stretch of the imagination to enter into its worldview and theological values. Only after one has made the effort to appreciate those values, however, is criticism of their limitations legitimate.

God's honor and Job's freely given piety are two sides of the same religious values. Giving such devotion to God not only honors God but also provides the source of Job's own identity and self-worth. He is not a mercantile, self-oriented person, but one whose values are emphatically non-materialistic. That is what the story honors in Job and holds up as an ideal value. It is because of the integrity of his own devotion that Job can experience God's blessing as free grace. He places absolutely no conditions on his loyalty to God, and so does not feel forsaken by God even in the midst of his loss. Søren Kierkegaard praised Abraham as a "knight of faith." Yet Job excels Abraham.

The analogy with Abraham, however, raises questions about the intent of the Job narrative. In a sense, it radicalizes the story of Abraham. God tested Abraham, apparently uncertain of whether Abraham would sacrifice Isaac. When Abraham made it clear that he would, God spared Isaac—and Abraham. God has no doubts about Job. Yet neither Job's children nor Job is spared. It is as though the narrative asks the reader to look at values believed to be true—God's honor and Job's unconditional piety—and then forces the reader to evaluate those values under the most extreme circumstances. Can either value stand when weighed against the death of ten children and the torment of a loyal servant? The narrative appears to ask the reader to say yes by presenting Job's response as a sublime example of selfless piety. But is Job's response an example of sublime faith or of religious masochism? If the honor of God is absolutized, then nothing is too precious to be sacrificed to it—not the lives of children, not the body of a devoted worshiper. Job's own self-worth has been invested in his integrity as one who "fears God for nothing." But has his integrity itself become such a fetish that he cannot recognize the perversity of blessing the one who destroys him for no reason?

The literary genius of the prose tale is that one genuinely cannot say whether it intends to be a straightforward didactic tale that represents the sublime expression of a true knight of faith who loves God unconditionally, or whether it is a subversive didactic tale that exaggerates the traditional style just sufficiently to reveal the obscenity lurking behind the values of God's honor and the integrity of disinterested piety.

---

65. Cf. Robert Frost's humorous lines in "A Masque of Reason," when God confesses to Job: "I was just showing off to the Devil, Job,/ As is set forth in Chapters One and Two" (*The Poetry of Robert Frost*, ed. Edward Connery Latham [New York: Holt, Rinehart and Winston, 1969] 484-85, ll. 327-28).

JOB 3:1–31:40

THE POETIC DIALOGUE BETWEEN JOB AND HIS FRIENDS

OVERVIEW

The narrative of chaps. 1–2 has created the expectation that Job will speak one final time, the conflict will be resolved, and the story will move on to its happy ending. Job speaks in chap. 3, but in a way that confounds narrative expectations and makes immediate resolution impossible. His long, highly developed poetic speech in chap. 3 belongs to a very different literary style from that of the prose tale. Biblical critics have generally assumed that this sharp contrast preserves the literary seam where a sophisticated poetic dialogue was inserted into a pre-existing traditional tale. Perhaps this is so, but it is also possible to understand the sharp change in literary styles as an intentional strategy on the part of a single author (see the Introduction).

Job's bitter outburst, so different in style and tone from his previous remarks, provides the occasion for the friends who have come to comfort him to speak. The dialogue through which this takes place, however, has a highly formal, stylized structure. Each friend speaks to Job in a set order, and Job replies to each, giving the sequence Eliphaz-Job; Bildad-Job; Zophar-Job. This sequence is followed for two complete cycles (first cycle, chaps. 4–14; second cycle, chaps. 15–21). In the third cycle (chaps. 22–27) the sequence breaks down, and it is not clear whether this disruption is due to mistakes made in the long history of the text's transmission or whether it is a literary representation of the breakdown of the dialogue itself.

The word *dialogue* may be misleading if the reader thinks of speakers who reply directly to each other's specific arguments. Although there are occasional instances in which one speaker appears to allude intentionally to what another has said, for the most part this is not so. More-

over, virtually none of the concrete details of Job's situation, as developed in the prose tale, are referred to in the dialogue, while many topics not seemingly germane to Job's particular case are discussed at length. To a great extent, the dialogue is best thought of as a disputation concerning traditional religious ideology and its ability to make sense of misfortune. Job, the archetypal righteous sufferer, provides the occasion for the debate, but the scope of the disputation is not limited to his case.

It is not evident why there should be three friends instead of one, as in the Babylonian Theodicy, or why the dialogue should be structured in three cycles. Presumably the three friends are a traditional feature of the Job legend and not a detail that the author of the book of Job was free to alter. A more perplexing question is whether any significant differentiation exists in the characterization or in the content of the three friends' arguments.[66] Interpreters frequently attempt to distinguish the three as having different styles. Eliphaz is often described as a character of great dignity and urbanity, primarily on the basis of his first speech, which is carefully solicitous of Job.[67] Bildad and Zophar are by contrast dogmatic

---

66. The most developed argument for a clear differentiation in character and argument of the three friends is that of D. Clines, "The Arguments of Job's Three Friends," in *Art and Meaning: Rhetoric in Biblical Literature,* ed. D. Clines, D. Gunn, A. Hauser, JSOTSup 19 (Sheffield: JSOT, 1982) 199-214.

67. E.g., R. Gordis, *The Book of God and Man: A Study of Job* (Chicago: University of Chicago Press, 1965) 77-78. Some, however, consider Eliphaz to be sarcastic, e.g., J. C. Holbert, "The Function and Significance of the 'Klage' in the Book of 'Job,' with Special Reference to the Incidence of Formal and Verbal Irony" (Ph.D. diss., Southern Methodist University, 1975) 123. A much more subtle reading is that of K. Fullerton, who suggests that Eliphaz "is simply a rather stupid good person, blundering into words that would cut Job to the quick because he did not have a sufficiently sympathetic imagination to realize what impression he was likely to make by them." See Fullerton, "Double Entendre in the First Speech of Eliphaz," *JBL* 49 (1930) 340.

and mean-spirited. Differences between the styles of Bildad and Zophar, however, are much more difficult to establish. The whole question of character differences may well be the wrong one to ask. If it were a stylistic feature of the book, one would expect Bildad and Zophar to be more clearly distinguished. Moreover, the distinctions that one can make in the first cycle appear to evaporate in the second cycle, where the three friends all say essentially the same thing in essentially the same way. Throughout the dialogue the crucial contrast is between the three friends on the one hand and Job on the other. In this regard, they function as a collective character, similar to the way Shadrach, Meshach, and Abed-nego in Daniel 3 serve collectively as a contrast to Nebuchadnezzar. If Job's three friends have slightly different roles in the first cycle, it may be more a function of the sequence in which they speak rather than a character type that they represent.

The issue of the differentiation (or lack thereof) among the friends cannot be separated from the issue of the relation between the different cycles of speeches and between the friends' speeches and those of Job. In his first speech in chaps. 4–5, Eliphaz actually presents the whole repertoire of arguments that the friends will employ in all three cycles. There is, however, a clear progression in the perception of Job in the friends' first three speeches, from Eliphaz's assertion of Job's blamelessness (4:6), through Bildad's conditional language about Job's purity and uprightness (8:6), to Zophar's assumption that Job is guilty of something (11:6). Also characteristic of the first cycle is the friends' use of a number of different arguments and illustrations. In the second cycle there is only one issue: the retribution that befalls the wicked. This narrowing of focus implies that defense of this belief is central to the defense of the whole religious tradition represented by the friends. The relation between Job's situation and the fate of the wicked is left ambiguous. In the second cycle none of the friends identifies Job with the wicked person they describe. Only in the first speech of the third cycle does Eliphaz explicitly accuse Job of great wickedness and identify his evildoing as the cause of his suffering. Unfortunately, the disarray of the third cycle makes it impossible to know if there was a par-ticular focus to the friends' speeches beyond the indictment made by Eliphaz.

Taken as a set, Job's speeches do not show a simple developmental pattern. Themes are repeated throughout, and Job's mood vacillates from beginning to end. Various features, however, give his speeches a certain dynamic movement. One such feature is the theme of death. In chaps. 3 and 6–7, death is depicted as a refuge from God, a desirable alternative to the suffering of life. In chap. 10, even though life is something Job would rather not have experienced, death is no longer presented as a desirable state. Chapter 14 presents death as a terrible fate that destroys hope. By chaps. 16 and 19, death is an obstacle threatening what Job seeks from God, so that Job attempts to imagine a way around that obstacle.

To understand the changing role that death plays in Job's imagination, one has to note the emergence of another theme in Job's speeches, the lawsuit with God. In the early speeches (chaps. 3; 6–7), Job has rejected traditional approaches to suffering offered by religious convention. He has no reason to live. In chaps. 9–10, however, Job begins to toy with the notion, absurd on the face of it, of meeting God in a court trial (9:2-4, 14-24, 28-35; 10:1-2). As that model of engaging God begins to take shape in Job's mind, he gradually loses his desire to die. Even if it is a chimerical hope, the notion of a trial organizes his energy. The lawsuit metaphor appears in only a limited number of verses, yet it occupies an increasingly important place in Job's imagination (13:3, 17-19; 16:18-21; 19:23-29), until it becomes the mode by which Job attempts to force a confrontation with God (chap. 31).

A connection also exists between the development of Job's thought and the change in the way his friends respond to him. In the first cycle the vehement and even sarcastic tone of Job's replies in chaps. 6–7 and 9–10 is directly related to the hardening of the friends' responses to him. Job's final speech in the first cycle, however, shifts the focus of his attack (chaps. 12–14). He speaks less about his own distress and turns his attack more generally to the inadequate and deceptive modes of speaking about God and the world that characterize the friends' traditional religion. Apparently, this general attack on religious ideology provokes Eliphaz's direct accusation that Job's speech is sinful (15:2-16) and calls forth the friends' defensive demonstration of the reality of retributive justice in the speeches concerning the fate of the wicked. In the second cycle of speeches, when the friends reiterate their defense of retributive justice (chaps. 15; 18; 20), Job does not reply directly to their words in his first two speeches. In chap. 21, however, he refutes their depiction by a counterspeech concerning the good fortune of the wicked. Immediately following Job's direct repudiation of this most cherished notion of the friends, Eliphaz explicitly accuses Job of wickedness (chap. 22).

Unfortunately, the structure of the third cycle is too uncertain to make it clear how it relates to the preceding speeches. The disarray of the third cycle is followed, however, by the interlude of the poem on wisdom in chap. 28. This poem provides important connections to the major parts of the book. Its claim that wisdom cannot be found by mortals, but only by God, serves as a critique of the preceding dialogue and an anticipation of the voice from the whirlwind. The echo of the prose tale in 28:28 (cf. 1:1) reminds the reader of the alternative moral vision of the tra-

ditional story with its veneration of unconditional piety. As an interlude, however, the poem does not serve to resolve the book's conflicts so much as it provides an opportunity for the reader to detach from the intensity of the dialogue.

The final part of the dialogue is Job's concluding speech (chaps. 29–31), which corresponds structurally to his opening speech in chap. 3. This speech is quite different from what has preceded and serves as an important indication of how Job understands that his conflict with God can be resolved. Somewhat nostalgically, he describes his place in society before disaster overtook him (chap. 29). In so doing, he articulates a moral vision of the good society as he understands it. Job contrasts that vision with a detailed description of the social misery of his current plight (chap. 30). Finally, he challenges God with a great oath to present the charges against him (chap. 31). Implicitly, Job's assurance and his challenge are grounded in his assumption that God's relation to him is analogous to Job's relation to those in society dependent upon him, that God's values are analogous to Job's values. With Job's bold challenge to God, the dialogue ends.

JOB 3:1–14:22, THE FIRST CYCLE

Job 3:1-26, Job Curses the Day of His Birth

NIV	NRSV
3 After this, Job opened his mouth and cursed the day of his birth. ²He said:	**3** After this Job opened his mouth and cursed the day of his birth. ²Job said:
³"May the day of my birth perish, and the night it was said, 'A boy is born!'	³ "Let the day perish in which I was born, and the night that said, 'A man-child is conceived.'
⁴That day—may it turn to darkness; may God above not care about it; may no light shine upon it.	⁴ Let that day be darkness! May God above not seek it, or light shine on it.
⁵May darkness and deep shadowᵃ claim it once more; may a cloud settle over it; may blackness overwhelm its light.	⁵ Let gloom and deep darkness claim it. Let clouds settle upon it; let the blackness of the day terrify it.
⁶That night—may thick darkness seize it;	⁶ That night—let thick darkness seize it! let it not rejoice among the days of the year;

ᵃ5 Or *and the shadow of death*

NIV

may it not be included among the days of the year
nor be entered in any of the months.
[7]May that night be barren;
may no shout of joy be heard in it.
[8]May those who curse days[b] curse that day,
those who are ready to rouse Leviathan.
[9]May its morning stars become dark;
may it wait for daylight in vain
and not see the first rays of dawn,
[10]for it did not shut the doors of the womb on me
to hide trouble from my eyes.

[11]"Why did I not perish at birth,
and die as I came from the womb?
[12]Why were there knees to receive me
and breasts that I might be nursed?
[13]For now I would be lying down in peace;
I would be asleep and at rest
[14]with kings and counselors of the earth,
who built for themselves places now lying in ruins,
[15]with rulers who had gold,
who filled their houses with silver.
[16]Or why was I not hidden in the ground like a stillborn child,
like an infant who never saw the light of day?
[17]There the wicked cease from turmoil,
and there the weary are at rest.
[18]Captives also enjoy their ease;
they no longer hear the slave driver's shout.
[19]The small and the great are there,
and the slave is freed from his master.
[20]"Why is light given to those in misery,
and life to the bitter of soul,
[21]to those who long for death that does not come,
who search for it more than for hidden treasure,
[22]who are filled with gladness
and rejoice when they reach the grave?
[23]Why is life given to a man
whose way is hidden,
whom God has hedged in?
[24]For sighing comes to me instead of food;
my groans pour out like water.
[25]What I feared has come upon me;
what I dreaded has happened to me.
[26]I have no peace, no quietness;
I have no rest, but only turmoil."

[b]8 Or the sea

NRSV

let it not come into the number of the months.
[7] Yes, let that night be barren;
let no joyful cry be heard[a] in it.
[8] Let those curse it who curse the Sea,[b]
those who are skilled to rouse up Leviathan.
[9] Let the stars of its dawn be dark;
let it hope for light, but have none;
may it not see the eyelids of the morning—
[10] because it did not shut the doors of my mother's womb,
and hide trouble from my eyes.

[11] "Why did I not die at birth,
come forth from the womb and expire?
[12] Why were there knees to receive me,
or breasts for me to suck?
[13] Now I would be lying down and quiet;
I would be asleep; then I would be at rest
[14] with kings and counselors of the earth
who rebuild ruins for themselves,
[15] or with princes who have gold,
who fill their houses with silver.
[16] Or why was I not buried like a stillborn child,
like an infant that never sees the light?
[17] There the wicked cease from troubling,
and there the weary are at rest.
[18] There the prisoners are at ease together;
they do not hear the voice of the taskmaster.
[19] The small and the great are there,
and the slaves are free from their masters.

[20] "Why is light given to one in misery,
and life to the bitter in soul,
[21] who long for death, but it does not come,
and dig for it more than for hidden treasures;
[22] who rejoice exceedingly,
and are glad when they find the grave?
[23] Why is light given to one who cannot see the way,
whom God has fenced in?
[24] For my sighing comes like[c] my bread,
and my groanings are poured out like water.
[25] Truly the thing that I fear comes upon me,
and what I dread befalls me.
[26] I am not at ease, nor am I quiet;
I have no rest; but trouble comes."

COMMENTARY

3:1-2. Chapter 3 begins with two introductory sentences, one in the style of the prose tale (v. 1), the other in the style of the dialogue that follows (v. 2). The opening phrase ("after this") establishes continuity with the seven days and seven nights of silence during which Job's friends have sat with him. This period of silence occupies the narrative place of a third test of Job. Just as the other two tests hinged on whether Job would "curse God," so also here Job's speech is critical, solemnly introduced by the statement "he opened his mouth." According to the conventions of traditional storytelling, which often use patterns of three, the third repetition should provide both heightened tension and definitive resolution. Just at the critical moment, the narrator says he "opened his mouth and cursed." The word is not the euphemistic "blessed" (ברך *bērēk,* as in 1:5, 11; 2:5, 9), but the word it has masked in chaps. 1–2, "cursed" (קלל *qillēl*). Only with the last word of the sentence does the narrator apparently resolve the tension: "he opened his mouth and cursed *his day*" (i.e., the day of his birth; see. v. 3).

What does it signify to curse the day of one's birth? In antiquity curses and blessings were understood to be acts that had real effect under the proper conditions. Although some interpreters assume that Job is attempting an effective curse,[68] other references in the Bible to cursing the day of one's birth suggest that it is a rhetorical gesture. Most obviously, it is a highly charged way of expressing the wish that one had never been born (Sir 23:14[19]). The curse takes the energy of self-directed aggression and transfers it to an external object, the day of one's birth. Apart from Job 3 there is only one other preserved example of such a curse, Jer 20:14-18. Like Job 3, it contains four elements: a curse on the day of birth itself (Jer 20:14; Job 3:3*a,* 4-5), a curse on the messenger who brought the news (Jer 20:15-16; Job 3:3*b,* 6–9), the reason for the curse (Jer 20:17; Jer 3:10), and a lament for having been born (Jer 20:18; Job 3:11-16). In the case of Jeremiah, even though the words are framed as a curse, one can argue that Jeremiah intends them

as an implicit appeal to God, what Zuckerman calls "a lament-of-final-resort," the function of which was "to portray a sufferer's distress in the most nihilistic terms possible for the purpose of attracting God's attention and thus leading to the rescue of the sufferer from affliction."[69] As an implicit appeal, it is an act of faith.

Understood in this context, the announcement in Job 3:1 is perfectly in keeping with the dynamics of the prose story and with the image of Job created there. Even in extremis he will curse the day of his birth rather than God, his words of despair a tacit plea for deliverance. If that is what the friends and the reader expect, however, the actual words Job uses overturn those expectations and decisively break open the closed world of the prose tale. Job subverts the conventions of the birthday curse through his radical use of (anti-) creation imagery, his inversion of divine speech, and his bitterly ironic description of life as oppression and death as a valuable treasure. Whatever this is, it is not a tacit appeal for deliverance.

3:3-10. Job's speech divides into two major sections: the curse proper (vv. 3-10) and the lament over having been born (vv. 11-26). The former begins in v. 3 with a curse on the day of birth and on the night of conception. First, day is cursed with a deprivation of light (vv. 4-5). Then night is cursed with a deprivation of fellowship and frustration of desire (vv. 6-9). Finally, the reason for the curse is given: the failure of that day to prevent Job's birth (v. 10).

The object of the curse, identified generally as "his day" in v. 1, is divided into two distinct times, the day of birth and the night of conception (v. 3). In Jeremiah, not only is the day cursed but also the messenger who brought the news to the father (Jer 20:15-16). Job's curse personifies the night as announcing the news of the conception. Since ordinarily birth is announced rather than conception, some interpreters rationalize the image by translating the Hebrew word as "born" instead of "conceived" (on the basis of 1 Chr 4:17; see the NIV) or by assuming a textual error

68. M. Fishbane, "Jeremiah iv 23-26 and Job iii 3-13: A Recovered Use of the Creation Pattern," *VT* 21 (1971) 153-55.

69. B. Zuckerman, *Job the Silent: A Study in Historical Counterpoint* (New York: Oxford University Press, 1991) 125-26.

and reading "behold!"[70] In so doing they underestimate the extravagant quality of Job's language.

"Day of birth" and "night of conception" are complementary terms in that conception and birth mark the beginning and end of gestation. "Night" and "day" are also complementary terms that designate the corresponding parts of a single day (cf. "evening and morning" in Genesis 1). The double resonance of these terms creates a poetically condensed image of Job's coming into being. It also allows Job to exploit the ambiguities of the term "day."

The day of one's birth might be understood to refer either to a unique historical day or to a calendar day that occurs once each year. Although the limited amount of evidence concerning such curses makes it difficult to know what was customary, the references in Sirach and in Jeremiah focus on the unique historical day. Jeremiah, for instance, draws attention to the events and persons attending his birth. Clines declares such curses to be rhetorical rather than magical acts, because a day that is already passed cannot be affected.[71] In sharp contrast to Jeremiah, however, Job develops his curse through images that minimize the sense of the historical particularity of the day and instead focus on the calendrical and cosmic aspects of day/night. Job may well be breaking with traditional expectations here and exceeding the bounds of what was "appropriate" in such a rhetorical gesture. Certainly the images give his curse a disturbing quality.

Unlike Jeremiah, who begins his curse with a technical formula ("cursed be the day. . . ," Jer 20:14), Job begins with a specific word of destruction ("let the day . . . the night perish," v. 3; cf. Ps 109:6-19). But how does one imagine the perishing of a day or a night? What is a suitable fate to wish upon them? The dominant motif in his curse on "that day" is the reversal of light into darkness. To deprive day of light is to deprive it of its essential characteristic, but it is also a punishment that fits the crime. Because that day allowed Job to "see light" (cf. v. 16), Job deprives that day of light. Six different expressions for darkness appear in vv. 4-5, but its most powerful formulation is the opening phrase "that day—let

it be darkness!" (חשׁך יהי *yĕhî ḥōšek*). As is often noted, this phrase is an allusion to and reversal of God's words of creation in Gen 1:3, "let there be light" (אור יהי *yĕhî ʾôr*). A secondary motif, having to do with abandonment/possession, is introduced in the following phrase, "Let Eloah above not seek it." Perhaps this is a mythic allusion that we can no longer recognize, but "seeking" is elsewhere used of God's protective relation (Deut 11:12; Isa 62:12); not to be sought is to be an outcast (Jer 30:17). The third image ("let light not shine upon it") assumes that light is not an intrinsic quality of day but something that must be given to it. Taken together, the two sentences suggest that Job would thwart a divine creation of day.

Verse 5 complements the image of God's abandonment of day with the image of hostile possession by others. The word translated "claim" is the same word elsewhere rendered "redeem" (גאל *gāʾal*). It is from the language of family law relating to the responsibility of the next-of-kin to buy back the family's mortgaged property or family members sold into slavery (Lev 25:25-55). Here gloom and deep darkness (lit., "the shadow of death") are cast as the next of kin who "buy back" that day, a shrewd image, since in cosmogonic terms day is the offspring of night.[72] This is no true redemptive moment, as the following images indicate. There is something claustrophobic in the image of the cloud bank settling on the day. Even more ominous is the hostility expressed in the image of the "blackness of the day" (כמרירי יום *kimrîrê yôm*), presumably an eclipse, terrifying that day. This expression is actually vocalized to read "like the bitternesses of the day." Most interpreters, however, assume that a rare word meaning "blackness" is the original reading.[73] Gordis and Habel translate "demons of the day," following a medieval Jewish interpretation.[74]

The curse on "that night" is pronounced in vv. 6-9. Continuity with vv. 2-5 is provided through the opening image of ominous "thick darkness," but the dominant motif of these curses is the denial of joy in relationships. Here, too, the curse

70. So de Wilde, following the LXX. See A. de Wilde, *Das Buch Hiob*, OTS xxii (Leiden: Brill, 1981) 97.

71. D. Clines, *Job 1–20*, WBC 17 (Dallas: Word, 1989) 79.

72. Ibid., 84.

73. See M. Pope, *Job*, 3rd ed., AB 15 (Garden City, N.Y.: Doubleday, 1979) 29.

74. R. Gordis, *The Book of Job: Commentary, New Translation, and Special Studies* (New York: Jewish Theological Seminary, 5738/1978) 33; N. Habel, *The Book of Job*, OTL (Philadelphia: Westminster, 1985) 100.

corresponds to the offense. Because the night presided over the sexual union of Job's parents and announced his conception, night will be punished by exclusion from joy and fellowship and by a frustration of desire.

Where day was grotesquely "redeemed," night is "seized," "taken away" (v. 6). Like a captive, it can no longer enjoy the company of its fellows. The difference between the NIV and the NRSV in the translation of v. 6*b* points to a play on words. Literally, the text reads "let it not rejoice" (אל־יחד 'al-yiḥad). But the parallelism with "come into," "enter" in the next line suggests that one read instead the similar sounding "not be included" (אל־יחד 'al-yēḥad; cf. also Gen 49:6, where the parallelism is "enter"//"be included"). Poetic speech often exploits echoes between two similar sounding words with different meanings. Since both deprivation of joy and exclusion from fellowship are thematic, one should read "let it not rejoice" and hear the echo of "let it not be included."

That Job should curse the night of his conception with "barrenness" (גלמוד galmûd, a rare word otherwise used only in Isa 49:21) is not surprising, but he intensifies the punishment by excluding also the cry of joy. In context, this would refer to the exclamations of sexual pleasure. What Job envisions is that on this night of the year, sexual union will mysteriously produce neither pleasure nor conception.

In v. 8 the imagery shifts toward the cosmic plane. As in v. 6, an unexpected word, "day" (יום yôm), occurs where the parallelism with Leviathan leads one to expect "Sea" (ים yām; cf. NIV, NRSV). Leviathan is the name of the primordial dragon-like creature associated with the mythic Sea (Ps 74:14; Isa 27:1; cf. Isa 51:9; Hab 3:8; it is to be equated with Lotan in Ugaritic mythology). As symbols of chaos, Leviathan and Sea are often depicted as opponents whom God overcomes in the cosmogonic battle.[75] Some interpreters assume that a mistake has been made in the text and that v. 8 originally read "Sea."[76] Supporting that suggestion is the fact that there is no

evidence of persons in ancient Israel who were expert in "cursing day," but there are later Jewish magical texts that invoke Sea and Leviathan as a parallel pair: "I enchant you with the adjuration of Sea, and the spell of Leviathan the serpent."[77] Nevertheless, the substitution of "sea" for "day" in v. 8, although initially appealing, will not work. In contrast to the Jewish magical text, Job is not appealing to a spell that binds Leviathan but to a spell that rouses Leviathan. Similarly, he does not wish to curse Sea, i.e., the forces of chaos.[78] As vv. 4-5 indicate, Job seeks to let loose the chaotic forces of darkness (see Gen 1:2) to attack his "day." The shock effect of v. 8 is precisely in its calculated misuse of the formulae of "white magic."

In v. 9, Job curses night precisely by breaking the bond that joins night to day: the time of dawn, when dark mingles with first light. Night is personified in ways that suggest a lover, one who waits expectantly, desiring to look upon the eyes of its partner, dawn. Job's curse would deny that union. The cosmic horror lurking in Job's curse is that it would break the dependable alternation of opposites upon which creation is established. God's promise to humankind after the flood was that "As long as the earth endures,/ seedtime and harvest, cold and heat,/ summer and winter, day and night,/ shall not cease" (Gen 8:22 NRSV).

The reason for Job's curse finally appears in v. 10: "because it did not shut the doors of my mother's womb,/ and hide trouble from my eyes." The expression "opening/closing the womb" is an idiom for the ability to conceive (Gen 29:31; 1 Sam 1:5). Thus v. 10 appears to be tied most closely to the curse on night and only secondarily to the curse on the day of birth. In Israelite thought, of course, it is not night but God who opens or closes the womb. Job's poetic displacement of this function may indicate that the object of his anger is God, although he does not acknowledge this, perhaps even to himself. His feelings are revealed, however, by his choice of images. The second part of Job's reason in v. 10 is also closely related to v. 9*b*. Because night did not prevent Job from seeing what he did not

75. J. Day, *God's Conflict with the Dragon and the Sea,* University of Cambridge Oriental Publications 35 (Cambridge: Cambridge University Press, 1985).

76. So Pope, *Job,* 30, following H. Gunkel, *Schoepfung und Chaos in Urzeit und Endzeit* (Göttingen: Vandenhoeck und Ruprecht, 1895) 59n. 1; L. Perdue, *Wisdom in Revolt: Metaphorical Theology in the Book of Job,* Bible and Literature Series 29 (Sheffield: JSOT, 1991) 92.

77. C. D. Isbell, *Corpus of the Aramaic Incantation Bowls,* SBLDS 17 (Missoula, Mont.: Scholars Press, 1975) 19.

78. Gordis, *The Book of Job,* 34.

wish to see, Job's curse will prevent night from seeing what it most desires.

3:11-26. This section is often called a lament. That label can be misleading if one thinks in terms of the psalms of lament, where the individual addresses God directly and seeks relief. Here, even though some terms and images from the lament tradition are used, Job does not address his words to anyone in particular.[79] What Job says is not a lament in the classic sense but the rhetorical wish that one had never been born, which formally belongs to the curse on the day of one's birth (Jer 20:18; Sir 23:14b [19b]). This wish never to have been born is not the same as the wish to die, which a number of characters in the Bible express (Rebekah, Gen 27:46; Elijah, 1 Kgs 19:4; Jonah, Jonah 4:3; Tobit and Sarah, Tob 3:6, 10, 13, 15; Mattathias, 1 Macc 2:6, 13). Except for 1 Macc 2:6, these are requests that the person should no longer continue to live, rather than the specific desire that one had never lived or had died at birth.

Job transforms what is a briefly expressed wish in Jeremiah into a baroque fantasy of death. The death wish is expressed in vv. 11-12 as the desire to have died as a newborn and in v. 16 as the desire to have been stillborn. In vv. 13-15 and 17-10, Job describes the advantages of such death without life. He expands the wish for death with a reflection on the irony that life is given to those who crave death (vv. 20-24). Finally, Job concludes by stating the reason for his vehement curse (vv. 25-26).

Job begins this section with rhetorical questions expressing the desire to have died during birth (v. 11) or, if not, then to have been refused the life-sustaining nurture an infant requires. Why? If he had not been held and suckled, Job says, now he would be lying down, quiet and asleep (v. 13). With bitter irony Job takes the image of the child who sleeps after feeding and applies it to himself as a child fortunately dead from lack of nurture.

The images that follow are more perplexing, for it is not immediately clear why Job would speak of the company of rulers and wealthy princes as a particular feature of death (vv. 14-15). As "the greatest of all the people of the east" (1:3), Job certainly enjoyed their company in life.

The meaning of the image is to be sought in the contrasts and similarities that the passage sets up between the lives and deaths of infants and magnates. Unlike the infant, the rulers engaged in intensive activity. This contrast is expressed most ironically in v. 14b, where the text says literally that they "built ruins for themselves." The phrase captures the ambiguity of such activity. Ancient Near Eastern kings took great pride in rebuilding ancient ruins of cities and temples (Ezra 6:1-5; Isa 44:26-28);[80] yet whatever was built eventually would fall into ruin again. Similarly, the silver and gold that princes amassed (v. 15) remained in their houses at death. What the infant and the magnates share in death is rest, the one desirable thing in Job's view. The infant who died at birth, however, received this good without either "toil" or "trouble" (v. 10; עמל ['āmāl] has both meanings).

Verse 16 resumes the rhetorical question of v. 11. Job's desire for death is expressed in an image even more extreme. Here he envisions not the brief life of the infant but the stillborn child who "never saw the light." Parallel to the account of kings and princes now at rest, vv. 17-19 also describe the quietness that comes in death to various social groups who had been bound together in oppressive relationships, characterized by agitation and exhaustion. "Wicked" (רשעים rĕšā'îm) in v. 17 is a term that, as Clines has shown, has not only moral but also specifically antisocial overtones.[81] Thus those "exhausted by power" (v. 17b) are victims of the wicked, just as the captive corresponds to the taskmaster and the slave to the master.[82] Common to all of these relations is a disproportion of power and an inability of the weaker member to resist the will and violent energy ("turmoil, troubling") of the stronger.

These are not idly chosen images; yet they seem initially incongruous for Job. He has said nothing about his particular suffering, the loss of possessions, servants, children, and health, even though that is what motivates his words. Somehow those specific losses have been transmuted

79. C. Westermann, *The Structure of the Book of Job,* trans. C. A. Muenchow (Philadelphia: Fortress, 1981) 37-38.

80. Cf. the reports of rebuilding by Cyrus and Antiochus Soter in *ANET,* 315, 317.
81. Clines, *Job 1–20,* 96; F. Horst, *Hiob,* Biblischer Kommentar xvi (Neukirchen-Vlun: Neukirchener Verlag, 1960) 53.
82. E. Good, *In Turns of Tempest* (Stanford, Calif.: Stanford University Press, 1990) 56.

during seven days of silence (2:13) into these defining images of death and life. Perhaps these images indicate that Job's fundamental perception of the world has changed. A person can survive devastating losses if the sense of the world as a fundamentally trustworthy place is still intact, as Job's words in 1:21 were meant to suggest. Now his images suggest that he perceives the world as crushing and inescapable bondage, from which death is the only release. It is tempting to interpret Job's use of the images of social oppression as an indication that his sufferings have caused him to identify with the oppressed of the earth.[83] As later chapters will show, however, Job's social perceptions, even as they are shaped by his suffering, are complex (cf. Job 24 and 30).

A second rhetorical question, which begins in v. 20 and is resumed in v. 23, explores the irony of unwelcome life. Literally, the sentence begins "why does he give light to one in misery . . . ?" Hebrew often uses such a construction as the equivalent of a passive (i.e., "Why is light given . . . ?"), but the words could also be understood as a reference to God as the one who gives, echoing 1:21 and more faintly 2:10.[84] Job often responds to the bitter ironies he perceives by exposing them through parody. He develops the image of the embittered sufferer, first as one whose expectant waiting for death is disappointed (v. 21a). Then the passivity changes to activity as Job employs the image of the treasure hunter, with death as the prize (v. 21b). That is an ideal image for Job's purposes, since as Clines observes, most buried treasure in the ancient world consisted of valuables placed with the dead in tombs.[85] Thus Job invokes the familiar picture of the grave robber. The graverobbers' eagerness and exultant delight at the discovery of a rich grave grotesquely becomes the image of the one for whom the grave itself is the treasure (v. 22).

The resumption of the rhetorical question in v. 23 provides insight into the way Job experiences his situation. His images are those of restricted movement: one whose way is hidden, whom Eloah has hedged in. "Way" (דרך *derek*) is a frequent and important image in Israelite moral discourse. Based on the concrete image of the

path along which one walks, it refers to a course of conduct, the knowledge of how to proceed (1 Kgs 2:4; 2 Chr 13:22; Ps 1:6).[86] The image of the hedge was used by the *satan* as a metaphor of God's protection of Job in 1:10 (a slightly different verb). Here, however, it has an obstructive, hostile sense, as in Hos 2:6 (2:8). Job is trapped in a perverse, unintelligible world. Under such circumstances life is, quite literally, meaningless; hence his ironic rhetorical question about the pointlessness of light and life.

Verse 24 provides a transition. Using images familiar from traditional psalms of lament (cf. Ps 102:4-5, 9[5-6, 10]), Job again speaks in the first person. The following words of v. 25 are elliptical: "What I feared has come upon me;/ what I dreaded has happened to me." To what does Job refer? The character of Job in the prose tale had seemed a rather transparent figure, and the only anxiety he expressed was concern about the careless thoughts of his children (1:5). With these words, however, the author has created a character of depth and complexity who is not immediately accessible to the reader. What has Job feared? A clue appears in v. 26. The poetic construction of the line is powerful. Even readers who do not know Hebrew can appreciate the effect:

לא שלותי ולא שקטתי   *lō' šālawtî wĕlō' šāqattî*
ולא־נחתי ויבא רגז   *wĕlō'-nāḥĕtî wayyābō' rōgez*

("I have no ease, no quiet, no rest—what comes is turmoil"). Here, a threefold repetition of the same grammatical construction produces a repetition of sounds, almost like the tolling of a bell. Each phrase is also synonymous. The fourth element contrasts grammatically, as well as in meaning. The verb that introduces the last word is "come" (בוא *bô'*), the same verb used in v. 25 ("what I dreaded has come to me"). The parallel points to רגז (*rōgez*, "turmoil") as the word that Job chooses to identify his dread. The reliability of his world, the quality of existence that had allowed Job to experience the quietness of trust, has been shattered.

83. Clines, *Job 1–20*, 93.
84. J. G. Janzen, *Job*, Interpretation (Atlanta: John Knox, 1985) 65.
85. Clines, *Job 1–20*, 100.

86. See N. Habel, "The Symbolism of Wisdom in Proverbs 1–9," *Int.* 26 (1972) 131-57.

REFLECTIONS

The nihilism of Job's words is frightening. Like Samson, pulling down the pillars of the temple of Dagon, Job seems intent on pulling down the pillars of the cosmos itself. The pain that produces such words is like a black hole, the enormous gravitational force of which draws everything into itself. As unsettling as Job's words are, there is one thing that would be even more disturbing. Imagine how vastly different the book of Job would be if the seven days and seven nights of silence were never broken. The withdrawal into permanent silence would have been a withdrawal into despair and apathy. The fact that Job *can* speak of a despair so profound that it threatens to consume the cosmos is vital.

Theologian Dorothee Soelle has examined what she describes as necessary phases of suffering.[87] First of all comes mute suffering. It is a time of numbness and disorientation, in which the person experiences an acute sense of helplessness. Extreme suffering turns a person inward, making communication almost impossible and intensifying a sense of isolation. In this phase nothing can be done. Suffering has to find a voice before it can be worked on. That process is not an easy one, nor does it take place in the same way for every person. The first two chapters of Job show him attempting to make use of inherited words of proverbial wisdom to find a resolution for his grief. Perhaps because Job tries to resolve his suffering before he has adequately given voice to its enormity, his attempts fail, and he sinks into a prolonged period of mute suffering.

In some way the friends' presence facilitates Job's speaking in chap. 3. Even though he does not address them, the fact that they sit before him and with him is instrumental in bringing forth his cry. Certainly what Job says is not what they would have anticipated, yet it moves Job into the second phase of suffering in which he finds a language of pain and lament.

One of the things that makes this stage of suffering so difficult to enter into or even to witness is that it initially intensifies suffering. The anesthesia of numbness is gone, as is any attempt to deny the reality and severity of what has happened. To speak, however, is to begin to emerge from passivity and utter helplessness. The one who speaks names what is wrong or broken and so begins to organize the experience. Perhaps most important, speaking begins to break down the isolation that is so much a part of the devastation of acute suffering. Although a sympathetic listener may be the most helpful in enabling a sufferer to speak, it is also possible for some of this process to take place through writing down one's words when there is no one to whom they can be spoken. The page itself can become the image of the one who would know how to listen.

One should not think that the words a suffering person first finds will necessarily be "constructive" words. Certainly Job's are not. Gustavo Gutiérrez gives insight into the nature of the first language of suffering when he compares Job's words in chap. 3 with a poem by César Vallejo.[88] Vallejo's poem is an unrelenting cry of pain. Paradoxically, as Gutiérrez observes, the poem is entitled "I Am Going to Talk about Hope." Vallejo does not explain the title, nor is there anything in the content of the poem that looks remotely like what one ordinarily thinks of as hope. The title can refer only to the act of speaking itself. That startling dissonance between title and content provokes one into a new way of listening to words of pain, words of anger, and even words of nihilistic despair. Job cannot remain forever in his nihilism any more than the speaker in Vallejo's poem can remain forever in a cry of pain. In both cases, however, nothing can be done until suffering has been given a voice. In that sense even a cry of pain or an angry curse on the day of one's birth is also a token of hope.

A sufferer's friends and community often find it difficult to accept anger such as Job utters as a legitimate way of finding a voice for suffering. Anger is a very common element in the

---

87. D. Soelle, *Suffering,* trans. E. Kalin (Philadelphia: Fortress, 1975) 68-74.
88. G. Gutiérrez, *On Job: God-Talk and the Suffering of the Innocent,* trans. M. O'Connell (Maryknoll, N.Y.: Orbis, 1987) 9-10, 111-12n. 8.

experience of suffering and grief, yet the expression of anger is one of the most frequently discouraged actions in many religious communities. The reason why is not difficult to understand. Anger claims not only that the situation is painful but also that something is fundamentally not right about the situation, that what has happened *should not* have happened. Anger is frightening because it often exposes contradictions in the community or points to a scandal in the belief system. It claims to disclose a disturbing reality that others are covering over with self-deceiving illusions. Anger directed at other members of the community is difficult because it requires facing up to responsibility and admitting and assessing guilt. Anger directed at God or, as in Job's words, at life itself is disturbing because it questions fundamental beliefs of the culture. If a religious community is supple and resilient, it is easier for it to allow and even encourage the expression of anger in connection with suffering. If a community and its beliefs are fragile or brittle, however, the reaction to anger is more likely to be defensive and repressive. One cannot minimize what is at stake. As the book of Job shows, once the contradictions are pursued, an entire belief system may be shattered. Yet that may be the only way forward to a more mature and adequate faith.

Israelite religion is often admired for making a place for anger within religious language. The psalms of lament are particularly noted for allowing the speaker to articulate anger. Although this is true, it is often overlooked that even there expressions of anger are strictly circumscribed by the form of the lament, which begins and ends with expressions of trust. If the response of the friends to Job can be taken as indicative, exceeding the appropriate bounds for the expression of anger created anxiety and the need to contain such expressions in ancient Israel as it does in many other cultures. One should remember, however, that even though God criticizes Job's words, it is Job who is commended for "speaking rightly" of God (42:7). The book of Job validates the legitimacy of anger arising out of the experience of suffering, even when that anger makes others uncomfortable, and even when that anger is directed at God. Anger that settles into bitterness is not the final resting place, but often the anger of suffering has to be expressed and explored in all its dimensions before it can be transmuted into something else.

As discussed above, Job's curse on the day of his birth is a token of hope because it marks his ability to enter into the phase of suffering in which muteness is replaced by speaking. There is also a third phase of suffering, one that is enabled in part by the process of finding a voice. Soelle calls this phase "changing" and characterizes it as a phase in which active behavior is possible, objectives can be identified, and solidarity with other persons forms new community. Although she is thinking largely in terms of the suffering produced by social oppression, what Soelle says about this phase of suffering also applies to other forms of grief and loss. The young woman paralyzed from a car accident who has found the language in which to express her anger and to grieve her loss is better able to organize her energies for learning a new way of living. Sometimes, as in Job's case, this phase of changing is first of all a matter of changing one's own perspectives, no longer being willing to accept what everyone else says is so. In such circumstances, solidarity may not be so easy to find, as Job discovers; yet the energy that comes from engaging in this change is an important part of overcoming the power of suffering.

Job 4:1–5:27, Traditional Understandings of Misfortune

NIV	NRSV
4 Then Eliphaz the Temanite replied:	**4** Then Eliphaz the Temanite answered:
² "If someone ventures a word with you, will you be impatient?	² "If one ventures a word with you, will you be offended?

NIV

But who can keep from speaking?
³Think how you have instructed many,
how you have strengthened feeble hands.
⁴Your words have supported those who stumbled;
you have strengthened faltering knees.
⁵But now trouble comes to you, and you are discouraged;
it strikes you, and you are dismayed.
⁶Should not your piety be your confidence
and your blameless ways your hope?

⁷"Consider now: Who, being innocent, has ever perished?
Where were the upright ever destroyed?
⁸As I have observed, those who plow evil
and those who sow trouble reap it.
⁹At the breath of God they are destroyed;
at the blast of his anger they perish.
¹⁰The lions may roar and growl,
yet the teeth of the great lions are broken.
¹¹The lion perishes for lack of prey,
and the cubs of the lioness are scattered.

¹²"A word was secretly brought to me,
my ears caught a whisper of it.
¹³Amid disquieting dreams in the night,
when deep sleep falls on men,
¹⁴fear and trembling seized me
and made all my bones shake.
¹⁵A spirit glided past my face,
and the hair on my body stood on end.
¹⁶It stopped,
but I could not tell what it was.
A form stood before my eyes,
and I heard a hushed voice:
¹⁷'Can a mortal be more righteous than God?
Can a man be more pure than his Maker?
¹⁸If God places no trust in his servants,
if he charges his angels with error,
¹⁹how much more those who live in houses of clay,
whose foundations are in the dust,
who are crushed more readily than a moth!
²⁰Between dawn and dusk they are broken to pieces;
unnoticed, they perish forever.
²¹Are not the cords of their tent pulled up,
so that they die without wisdom?'ᵃ

ᵃ21 Some interpreters end the quotation after verse 17.

NRSV

But who can keep from speaking?
³ See, you have instructed many;
you have strengthened the weak hands.
⁴ Your words have supported those who were stumbling,
and you have made firm the feeble knees.
⁵ But now it has come to you, and you are impatient;
it touches you, and you are dismayed.
⁶ Is not your fear of God your confidence,
and the integrity of your ways your hope?

⁷ "Think now, who that was innocent ever perished?
Or where were the upright cut off?
⁸ As I have seen, those who plow iniquity
and sow trouble reap the same.
⁹ By the breath of God they perish,
and by the blast of his anger they are consumed.
¹⁰ The roar of the lion, the voice of the fierce lion,
and the teeth of the young lions are broken.
¹¹ The strong lion perishes for lack of prey,
and the whelps of the lioness are scattered.

¹² "Now a word came stealing to me,
my ear received the whisper of it.
¹³ Amid thoughts from visions of the night,
when deep sleep falls on mortals,
¹⁴ dread came upon me, and trembling,
which made all my bones shake.
¹⁵ A spirit glided past my face;
the hair of my flesh bristled.
¹⁶ It stood still,
but I could not discern its appearance.
A form was before my eyes;
there was silence, then I heard a voice:
¹⁷ 'Can mortals be righteous beforeᵃ God?
Can human beings be pure beforeᵃ their Maker?
¹⁸ Even in his servants he puts no trust,
and his angels he charges with error;
¹⁹ how much more those who live in houses of clay,
whose foundation is in the dust,
who are crushed like a moth.
²⁰ Between morning and evening they are destroyed;

ᵃ Or more than

NIV

5 "Call if you will, but who will answer you?
To which of the holy ones will you turn?
[2]Resentment kills a fool,
and envy slays the simple.
[3]I myself have seen a fool taking root,
but suddenly his house was cursed.
[4]His children are far from safety,
crushed in court without a defender.
[5]The hungry consume his harvest,
taking it even from among thorns,
and the thirsty pant after his wealth.
[6]For hardship does not spring from the soil,
nor does trouble sprout from the ground.
[7]Yet man is born to trouble
as surely as sparks fly upward.

[8]"But if it were I, I would appeal to God;
I would lay my cause before him.
[9]He performs wonders that cannot be fathomed,
miracles that cannot be counted.
[10]He bestows rain on the earth;
he sends water upon the countryside.
[11]The lowly he sets on high,
and those who mourn are lifted to safety.
[12]He thwarts the plans of the crafty,
so that their hands achieve no success.
[13]He catches the wise in their craftiness,
and the schemes of the wily are swept away.
[14]Darkness comes upon them in the daytime;
at noon they grope as in the night.
[15]He saves the needy from the sword in their mouth;
he saves them from the clutches of the powerful.
[16]So the poor have hope,
and injustice shuts its mouth.

[17]"Blessed is the man whom God corrects;
so do not despise the discipline of the Almighty.[a]
[18]For he wounds, but he also binds up;
he injures, but his hands also heal.
[19]From six calamities he will rescue you;
in seven no harm will befall you.
[20]In famine he will ransom you from death,
and in battle from the stroke of the sword.
[21]You will be protected from the lash of the tongue,

[a]17 Hebrew *Shaddai*; here and throughout Job

NRSV

they perish forever without any regarding it.
[21]Their tent-cord is plucked up within them,
and they die devoid of wisdom.'

5 "Call now; is there anyone who will answer you?
To which of the holy ones will you turn?
[2]Surely vexation kills the fool,
and jealousy slays the simple.
[3]I have seen fools taking root,
but suddenly I cursed their dwelling.
[4]Their children are far from safety,
they are crushed in the gate,
and there is no one to deliver them.
[5]The hungry eat their harvest,
and they take it even out of the thorns;[a]
and the thirsty[b] pant after their wealth.
[6]For misery does not come from the earth,
nor does trouble sprout from the ground;
[7]but human beings are born to trouble
just as sparks[c] fly upward.

[8]"As for me, I would seek God,
and to God I would commit my cause.
[9]He does great things and unsearchable,
marvelous things without number.
[10]He gives rain on the earth
and sends waters on the fields;
[11]he sets on high those who are lowly,
and those who mourn are lifted to safety.
[12]He frustrates the devices of the crafty,
so that their hands achieve no success.
[13]He takes the wise in their own craftiness;
and the schemes of the wily are brought to a quick end.
[14]They meet with darkness in the daytime,
and grope at noonday as in the night.
[15]But he saves the needy from the sword of their mouth,
from the hand of the mighty.
[16]So the poor have hope,
and injustice shuts its mouth.

[17]"How happy is the one whom God reproves;
therefore do not despise the discipline of the Almighty.[d]

[a]Meaning of Heb uncertain   [b]Aquila Symmachus Syr Vg: Heb *snare*   [c]Or *birds*; Heb *sons of Resheph*   [d]Traditional rendering of Heb *Shaddai*

NIV

and need not fear when destruction comes.
²²You will laugh at destruction and famine,
and need not fear the beasts of the earth.
²³For you will have a covenant with the stones of
the field,
and the wild animals will be at peace with
you.
²⁴You will know that your tent is secure;
you will take stock of your property and find
nothing missing.
²⁵You will know that your children will be many,
and your descendants like the grass of the
earth.
²⁶You will come to the grave in full vigor,
like sheaves gathered in season.

²⁷"We have examined this, and it is true.
So hear it and apply it to yourself."

NRSV

¹⁸ For he wounds, but he binds up;
he strikes, but his hands heal.
¹⁹ He will deliver you from six troubles;
in seven no harm shall touch you.
²⁰ In famine he will redeem you from death,
and in war from the power of the sword.
²¹ You shall be hidden from the scourge of the
tongue,
and shall not fear destruction when it
comes.
²² At destruction and famine you shall laugh,
and shall not fear the wild animals of the
earth.
²³ For you shall be in league with the stones of
the field,
and the wild animals shall be at peace with
you.
²⁴ You shall know that your tent is safe,
you shall inspect your fold and miss nothing.
²⁵ You shall know that your descendants will be
many,
and your offspring like the grass of the earth.
²⁶ You shall come to your grave in ripe old age,
as a shock of grain comes up to the
threshing floor in its season.
²⁷ See, we have searched this out; it is true.
Hear, and know it for yourself."

COMMENTARY

Eliphaz's speech is composed of several distinct parts. After the narrator's introduction (4:1), Eliphaz acknowledges Job's vulnerability and explains his own need to speak (4:2). He reminds Job of how he had previously sustained others who were distraught and encourages him to find confidence in the very fact of his piety and uprightness (4:3-6). Eliphaz supports his claim by reminding Job of the beliefs they have shared concerning the moral structure of the world (4:7-11). In the following passage, Eliphaz tells Job of a visionary experience that bears on the moral implications of human frailty (4:12-21). What Eliphaz says next is difficult to interpret, but has to do with the consequences of foolish behavior (5:1-5) and the source of evil and trouble (5:6-7). Encouraging Job to turn to God, Eliphaz grounds

his advice by reciting a hymn in praise of God's power to transform (5:8-16). Finally, Eliphaz interprets suffering as a form of correction. If embraced, this hard pedagogy results in security and blessedness (5:17-26). A final call for Job to hear and acknowledge the truth of Eliphaz's words concludes his speech (5:27).

4:1-6. The solicitude in Eliphaz's opening words indicates his concern for Job. The nuance of the first part of v. 2 is difficult to render in English, but the Tanakh captures it better than either the NRSV or the NIV: "If one ventures a word with you, will it be too much?" (v. 2 TNK). A sage does not rush to speak prematurely (Prov 15:14), and one shows respect by listening in silence (Job 29:9). Only Job's evident distress as manifested in his terrible curse overcomes Eliphaz's reluctance to speak (v. 2b).

Eliphaz's admonition is designed to show Job how he has lost perspective, unable to appropriate for his own situation the very instruction he had given to others (vv. 3-5). In Eliphaz's view, Job has lost sight of who he is and consequently of the stability that comes from such knowledge. The metaphors that describe the person overcome with affliction are those of weakness in the limbs and joints, an apt metaphor for the emotional and psychic prostration that accompanies traumatic experiences and profound fear (2 Sam 4:1; Ps 109:24; Isa 13:7; Ezek 7:17). Correspondingly, the sage's words are intended to provide the stiffening to put someone "back on his feet," as we might say. The term translated "instruct" (יסר yissar, v. 3) identifies the type of assistance Eliphaz is attempting to render. The word is capable of a variety of nuances, ranging from instruction to warning to discipline to punishment. At the heart of its meaning is the idea of correction.[89] This activity is different from the support rendered simply by a sympathetic presence. Instruction refers to the support, both sympathetic and confrontational, that has as its goal keeping a person oriented to the life-giving beliefs, values, and behaviors of the community.

The reorientation Eliphaz attempts to effect is succinctly stated in the rhetorical question of v. 6: "Is not your piety (the grounds of) your confidence, your hope the integrity of your conduct?" Unknowingly, the qualities that Eliphaz attributes to Job, piety (lit., fear [of God]) and integrity of way, are the same words used by the narrator and God to characterize Job (1:1, 8; 2:3). This echo serves first of all to make clear that Eliphaz does not assume Job is sinful. It also reminds the reader that questions raised in the prose tale about the relationship between well-being and moral character are also going to play an important but different role in the dialogue.

The surface simplicity of v. 6 conceals a complex set of assumptions about God, the world, and how one chooses to talk about suffering. Note how Eliphaz's question frames the issues. His words do not address what has happened to Job or his present distress but are oriented wholly to the future. Job should concentrate on hope, which Habel eloquently describes as "the hidden source of new life and purpose in the face of death and disaster."[90] That is no small thing. Eliphaz's words are based on an assumption, axiomatic for much of Israel's piety, that a person's moral character and ultimate well-being are inherently linked (Pss 18:20[21]; 112:1-10; Prov 11:8; 23:18; 24:14). Thus because Job knows that he is a person of piety and integrity, he can have confidence in his future. If the assumption is correct, then the conclusion must follow. The book of Job is going to subject that assumption to a rigorous scrutiny, however.

4:7-11. These verses serve as a more detailed argument in support of the assumption that moral character and ultimate fate are organically related. The rhetorical features of these verses are just as important as the content. Eliphaz begins with an imperative, "recall, now," followed by a rhetorical question. Asking Job to remember shifts the claim from something for which Eliphaz can vouch to something Job himself can authenticate on the authority of his own knowledge. Similarly, a rhetorical question presumes that the answer is so self-evident that everyone must agree. Eliphaz's claim, however, is problematic on its very face: "who that was innocent ever perished?/ Or where were the upright cut off?" (cf. Ps 37:25[24]). Yet Ps 10:8; Jer 22:17; and 2 Kgs 21:16 all refer to the murder of the innocent. Eliphaz, of course, does not mean that such things never happen. His words are a rhetorical exaggeration. Eliphaz would not be swayed by a counterexample, however, because he is not interested in "isolated cases" but in the fundamental regularities of the world that he perceives and that he is certain Job also perceives. Eliphaz's call for Job to "remember" suggests something important about the way perception and memory and meaning are related. Human perceptions of the world are necessarily based on selective memory. Myriad facts and events exist, but not all are treated as interpretively significant. Ordinarily, those events that confirm the worldview one already holds have greater significance; those that contradict it appear as mere anomalies. Hence Eliphaz's confidence in v. 7. The same process underlies Eliphaz's claim

89. E. Dhorme, *A Commentary on the Book of Job,* trans. H. Knight (London: Nelson, 1967) 43.

90. N. Habel, *The Book of Job,* OTL (Philadelphia: Westminster, 1985) 125.

that *"as I have seen,* those who plough mischief and sow trouble reap it" (v. 7). He sees clearly only what the screen of his worldview allows him to see. His belief in the intrinsic relation of act and consequence, a fundamental tenet of wisdom thinking, is evident also in his choice of the agricultural metaphor of sowing and reaping (cf. Prov 14:22; 22:8; also Hos 10:13). The book of Job can be understood as a crisis in moral perception, which emerges when the organizing schemata are challenged as radically distorting (see Reflections).

Eliphaz pairs his statement about the organic relationship of evil and its consequences with a claim about divine punishment, phrased in the image of the breath of God and wind of God's anger (v. 9). These are simply alternative ways of expressing the same reality as v. 8. The catchword "perish" serves as a link with the concluding saying (vv. 10-11), a verbally sophisticated proverb that uses five different terms for "lion." Here, as often, the lion is a symbol for the wicked (Ps 17:12; Prov 28:15; Nah 2:11-12[12-13]).

It is evident why Eliphaz would speak about the fate of the innocent and upright person, but why does he devote most of this section to the issue of the fate of the wicked? Eliphaz is not subtly insinuating that Job is one of the wicked, as v. 6 makes clear. Since the appropriate fates of the upright and the wicked are complementary aspects of the same moral order, these comments can serve to reassure Job. Nevertheless, as will become evident, Eliphaz and his friends do talk much more extensively about the fate of the wicked than about the hope of the righteous (15:20-35; 18:5-21; 20:4-29; 22:5-20; see the Commentary and Reflections on chap. 18.).

Although Eliphaz does not intend to imply that Job is among the wicked, his actual words come disconcertingly close to describing the fate that has actually befallen Job. The punishing wind that Eliphaz alludes to in v. 9 recalls the "great wind" (1:19) that crushed Job's children. The "irony and innuendo" of these words is not, as Fullerton properly observes, "the irony and innuendo of Eliphaz at the expense of Job but the irony and innuendo of the author at the expense of Eliphaz and of the orthodox reader whose position he represents."[91] That the classic description of the

fate of the wicked should match the situation of one who is righteous undermines the cogency of Eliphaz's moral language, even if he is not aware of it.

4:12-21. While dreams and visions are not usually associated with the wisdom tradition as represented by Proverbs, Ecclesiastes, and Sirach, another tradition, sometimes called mantic wisdom, does include revelatory dreams and visions among the sources of the sage's wisdom. In the biblical tradition, Daniel is an example of this type of sage (Dan 1:17; 2:19-23). More generally, dreams and night visions are associated with a variety of biblical characters, including patriarchs, kings, prophets, and ordinary individuals (e.g., Gen 15:12-17; 28:10-15; 37:5-11; 40:8-19; 41:1-7; 1 Sam 3:1-14; 2 Sam 7:17; 1 Kgs 3:5; Zech 1:8). Although dreams and visions could be deceptive (Zech 13:4), they are accepted as legitimate channels of divine revelation.

Eliphaz spends almost half of his account describing the experience, turning to its content only in v. 17. That description is not unrelated to the content but prepares for it. A person who experiences a revelatory dream or vision enters into a liminal state, "betwixt and between" ordinary states of being, where the divine and human meet. It is a space of numinous power, hence the seer's ability to receive a revelation, but it is also a space of intense vulnerability and danger. Isaiah implicitly likens the danger to that of an unclean person entering the zone of holiness in the Temple (Isa 6:5). Daniel experiences weakness and helplessness, including prostration, during the vision (Dan 10:8), exhaustion, and illness afterward (Dan 8:27). Since the two themes of human uncleanness/unrighteousness and physical human frailty are the subject of the revelation Eliphaz receives, the experience of the vision underscores the message and may account for the lengthy description.

4:12-14. The elusiveness of the experience is well expressed in Eliphaz's opening description of the word approaching him with stealth (NIV: "secretly"; NRSV more literally, "stealing"). The word translated "whisper" (שֶׁמֶץ *šēmeṣ*) is obscure but more likely means "a small piece," "fragment" (Sir 10:10; 18:32).[92] Thus "my ear seized only a

---

91. K. Fullerton, "Double Entendre in the First Speech of Eliphaz," *JBL* 49 (1930) 340.

92. So R. Gordis, *The Book of Job: Commentary, New Translation, and Special Studies* (New York: Jewish Theological Seminary, 5738/1978) 48; D. Clines, *Job 1–20*, WBC 17 (Dallas: Word, 1989) 111; contra A. de Wilde, *Das Buch Hiob, OTS* xxii (Leiden: Brill, 1981) 107.

fragment of it." From the first Eliphaz is in the presence of something that eludes his grasp. Verse 13 does not describe the vision itself but the temporal and psychological context. Although the term "deep sleep" (תרדמה *tardēmâ*) can refer to a trance-like state, such as Abraham experiences (Gen 15:12; cf. 1 Sam 26:12), it can also describe ordinary deep sleep (Prov 19:15; cf. Jonah 1:5).[93] Eliphaz uses the term to describe what we know as that part of the sleep cycle associated with dreaming. Moreover, Eliphaz is already experiencing anxiety from vaguely identified "disquieting dreams" when a more intense terror seizes him (v. 14). This scene setting is not only evocative but also significant for the content. The middle of the night is the time when persons are most isolated from their fellows, when they feel most vulnerable, most aware of their own fragility.

4:15. Eliphaz's words in v. 15 are more ambiguous than the NIV and the NRSV indicate. Although רוח (*rûaḥ*) is once used in the Bible to mean a heavenly being (1 Kgs 22:21//2 Chr 18:20) and becomes a common term for angels in post-biblical literature, it most frequently means "wind." (Cf. Hab 1:11, where the same noun and verb are used: "they sweep past like the wind" [NIV].) The most natural understanding of Eliphaz's words is that he is describing a physical phenomenon, an eerie movement of air across his face, which increases his terror. A number of commentators, including Gordis, Habel, and Clines, render the parallel line as "a whirlwind made my flesh shiver"[94] rather than "the hair of my flesh bristled." The words for "hair" (שערה *śaʿărâ*) and "whirlwind" (שערה *śěʿ ārâ*) are very similar. Bristling hair is a common reaction to the uncanny in ancient Near Eastern literature, however, and there is no need to emend the text.[95]

4:16. Verse 16 begins abruptly with a verb that has only an indefinite subject ("it stood still"). Eliphaz underscores the eerie sense of amorphous presence by saying that he could not recognize what it was. Similarly, the ancient Mesopotamian king Gudea said of a mysterious being who appeared to him in a dream, "I could not recognize

him."[96] Eliphaz's choice of terms in the last part of the verse thus intimates but never explicitly claims that the apparition is a manifestation of God. "Form" (תמונה *těmûnâ*) is elsewhere used of God (Num 12:8; Deut 4:12, 17; Ps 17:15). The words "silence" (דממה *děmāmâ*) and "voice" (קול *qôl*) echo the terms describing the theophany to Elijah (1 Kgs 19:12).

4:17. The KJV and many older translations render v. 17 as a question of whether mortals can be "more righteous" and "more pure" than God. Although that translation is grammatically possible, the context makes it unlikely. Most modern translations render righteous or pure "before" God (cf. Num 32:22). Even that does not quite get the nuance right. The entrance liturgies in the psalms indicate that moral purity and righteousness are expected of one who comes before God in the sanctuary (Psalms 15; 24), yet the rhetorical question of v. 17 points to something obviously impossible. What is at stake is a comparison between the very being of God and mortals, and so one should translate "in relation to" or "as against" God (so the NAB).[97]

4:18-21. The comparative nature of the claim is evident in the following verses (vv. 18-19), which argue from the greater to the lesser, from the angelic to the human. There appears to be a shift in categories, however, from morality to mortality as the focus turns to human beings. The physicality of human existence (the metaphor of the body as a house of clay; see Wis Sol 9:15; cf. Gen 3:19) and the susceptibility to sudden death are introduced to substantiate the claim of v. 17. The apparent illogicality of the connection irritates some,[98] but the connection is a symbolic, not a logical, one. The same process is reflected in the development of our word *corrupt*. Although now used primarily as a moral term, it derives from a Latin word meaning "broken in pieces." This link between mortality and moral culpability is unusual in the Hebrew Bible, although it occurs twice more in Job (15:14-16; 25:4-6). Some Mesopotamian texts have a similarly negative view of human moral capacity,[99] but the closest ancient

93. D. Clines, "Job 4,13: A Byronic Suggestion," *ZAW* 92 (1980) 289-91.

94. Gordis, *The Book of Job*, 42; Habel, *The Book of Job*, 113; Clines, *Job 1–20*, 107.

95. S. Paul, "Job 4,15—A Hair Raising Encounter," *ZAW* 95 (1983) 119-21.

96. Cited by Dhorme, *A Commentary on the Book of Job*, 51.

97. See B. Waltke and M. O'Connor, *An Introduction to Biblical Hebrew Syntax* (Winona Lake, Ind.: Eisenbrauns, 1990) 11.2.11e[3] and 14.4e.

98. See Clines, *Job 1–20*, 133.

99. De Wilde, *Das Buch Hiob*, 108; L. Perdue, *Wisdom in Revolt: Metaphorical Theology in the Book of Job*, Bible and Literature Series 29 (Sheffield: JSOT, 1991) 118.

parallel comes from the texts of the Dead Sea Scrolls. Although written much later, these passages do not appear to be based on Job but reflect an independent development of the same idea. For example, "and I am a creature of clay and a thing kneaded with water, a foundation of shame and a well of impurity, a furnace of iniquity and an edifice of sin, a spirit of error, perverted, without understanding, and terrified by righteous judgments."[100]

There are several obscure words and phrases in vv. 19-21, although they do not greatly affect the overall meaning. Since "moths" (עָשׁ 'āš) are otherwise used as images of destructiveness rather than of vulnerability (Isa 50:9; 51:8), some read the quite similar word "birdnest" (so the NEB).[101] In v. 20 it is not clear whether the sentence intends to say that people may die without anyone else noticing or that people are taken by death unawares.[102] In either case, the end is the same: People die without wisdom (v. 21). The relevance of Eliphaz's message to Job's situation and its relation to theodicy in general are discussed below in the Reflections.

5:1-7. This passage is the most difficult part of Eliphaz's speech to understand. First, the text is garbled in v. 5; second, it is not clear how the verses fit together; third, vv. 6-7 can be interpreted in contradictory ways. Any interpretation must therefore be tentative.

5:1-2. The sense of the inevitability of the human condition, with which the previous section concluded, is echoed in the opening rhetorical question in 5:1, which insists on the futility of appealing to angelic beings for help. The proverb that follows (v. 2) appears to be logically disconnected, although it should probably be viewed as Eliphaz's rebuke of Job's violent outburst in chap. 3.[103] The Hebrew terms are difficult to render in English, because they are capable of a variety of nuances. "Vexation" and "jealousy" are not appropriate for this context. "Resentment" and "anger" are closer. The wisdom ethos Eliphaz represents considered extreme anger and its unregulated expression as not just unwise (Prov 12:16) but dangerous, since uncontrolled anger

has the power to consume a person's very essence (Prov 14:30). Since human beings are inescapably subject to sudden death, railing against the inevitability of the human condition is just such a dangerously foolish obsession in Eliphaz's view.

5:3-5. Eliphaz's proverb used the term "fool" (אֱוִיל 'ĕwîl) for the person who gives in to angry resentment. To illustrate the fatal danger Eliphaz employs a little set piece about the fool. It does not have to do specifically with anger and so is not entirely germane to the point Eliphaz is making. But that is the nature of Eliphaz's way of thinking and speaking; he joins together pieces of received wisdom as though that would do his thinking for him. Just how problematic this can be is evident in the ghastly inappropriateness of this set piece to Job's situation. The text appears garbled in several places, but its basic meaning is clear. The contrast expressed in v. 3 is between the fool seeming to be secure ("taking root") and "suddenly" encountering disaster. The Hebrew text of v. 3b literally says "and suddenly I cursed their dwelling." Many interpreters plausibly emend the text to a passive, "and suddenly his house was cursed," since it is not evident why Eliphaz would be doing the cursing. Moreover, the fundamental contrast of the fool's security/sudden disaster is weakened if attention shifts to the onlooker and his act of cursing. Verse 4 refers to the helplessness of the fool's children against those who would oppress them in business and legal dealings. "The gate" is the place of such activities, where the poor were often subject to abuse if they lacked a more powerful advocate (29:7; 31:21; Prov 22:22; Amos 5:12). Although the text of v. 5 is obscure, the basic image is of the greedy (lit., "hungry" and "thirsty") consuming all of the fool's possessions. If this is indeed meant to serve as a warning to Job of the dangers of persisting in the folly of anger, it could scarcely be more grotesque, for Job has already lost his children and his possessions. As one with literally nothing left to lose (since he does not even wish to keep his life), why should Job not persist in the "folly" of his rage? But Eliphaz apparently does not notice the irony of his own words.

5:6-7. Following the digression of vv. 3-5, the main line of thought is completed with the explanation of why Job's anger is misplaced, and he cannot reasonably expect assistance from the holy

100. 1QH 1.21-23.
101. Gordis, *The Book of Job*, 50.
102. Ibid., 51.
103. G. Fohrer, *Das Buch Hiob*, KAT xvi (Guetersloh: Gerd Mohn, 1963) 146.

ones. The clearest part of the statement is v. 7*a* with its statement that mortals "are born to trouble." The second part of the verse supplies an analogy ("as sparks fly upward"), which underscores the fatalism. Verse 6 is open to two possible interpretations. Both the NIV and the NRSV render it as a contrasting statement—i.e., misery and trouble do not come from nature but from human nature.[104] In Hebrew, however, questions are sometimes not expressly marked as such, so that it would also be possible to translate the verse as a claim that trouble is inherent in nature, and hence in human nature: "Does not misery come from the dust and trouble spring from the soil?"[105] Many commentators resolve the tension between vv. 6 and 7 in a different way, emending the text of v. 7 to read "human beings *give birth to* trouble."[106] This emendation is prompted by a desire to make Eliphaz's statement consistent with his argument in 4:7-11 that people create their own trouble. The more immediate context, however, is Eliphaz's reflections on the intrinsic moral and physical frailty of human nature as such (4:12-21). A fatalistic reading of 5:6-7 ("Does not misery come from the dust and trouble spring from the soil?") seems the most appropriate.

Whether or not there is an intentional allusion to Gen 3:17-19 in vv. 6-7, it is striking that four of the same terms are used in discussing a similar theme, the genesis of the hardship that is the heritage of all human existence. Both passages contain a play on words between "human beings" (אדם *'ādām*) and "soil" (אדמה *'ădāmâ*), as well as references to things that "sprout" (צמח *ṣāmaḥ*; thorns and thistles in Gen 3:18; misery in Job 5:6). In Gen 3:19, humans come from and return to the "dust" (עפר *'āpār*), while in Job 5:6 it is a question of whether trouble comes from that source.

5:8-16. Eliphaz shifts the focus from human nature to divine nature and from the inappropriate stance of uncontrolled anger to what he urges as the proper stance: committing the situation to God. The introductory verse is poetically striking.

Of the nine words in the verse, all but the last begin with the same letter, א (*'aleph*). Form embodies content also in that the phrases that occupy the center of the verse, concluding the first half-line and beginning the second, are "to El, to Elohim" (see the NRSV). Eliphaz urges Job to orient himself to God.

Eliphaz supports this advice by reciting a doxology in praise of God as one who transforms situations (vv. 9-16). Here traditional language, images, and forms function in their most sympathetic role in Eliphaz's speech. Although Eliphaz may be composing the doxology for the occasion, it is constructed almost wholly out of phrases and images that are a familiar part of the repertoire of worship and wisdom. The power of such familiar words and forms at a time of chaos resides in their ability to reconnect a disoriented person with a reality once experienced as reliable and trustworthy, and that has not ceased to exist despite the present collapse of the individual's world. Such, at least, is Eliphaz's belief.

The doxology begins with a summary acknowledgment of the "great" and "wonderful things" that God does (cf., e.g., Pss 26:7; 40:5[6]; 105:5; 106:21-22). The first substantiation of this general praise is the giving of rain (v. 10). As Clines notes, in the Near Eastern desert climate the rain that marks the change of seasons transforms the appearance of the land with great suddenness from dry and brown to green and colorful with flowers.[107] The doxology's most important image, God's transforming the situation of the lowly and grieving (v. 11), is a central motif in Israelite religious language (cf. 1 Sam 2:7-8; Pss 113:7-8; 147:6). The passage will return to a closely related image in its concluding verses (vv. 15-16). Linking these two crucial parts, vv. 12-14 present a complementary image, God's transforming into harmlessness the power of those who scheme. The vocabulary of vv. 12-13 is more characteristic of wisdom than of psalms, but the general idea often appears both in Proverbs and in Psalms (e.g., Pss 7:15-16; 9:16; 35:8; 57:6[7]; Prov 26:27; 28:10). Whereas vv. 11 and 12-14 dealt with the lowly and the powerful separately, v. 15 brings the two together in an image of deliverance. Incidentally, v. 13 is the only verse from Job cited in the New Testament (1 Cor 3:19).

---

104. Similarly, ibid., 128.

105. See M. Pope, *Job,* 3rd ed., AB 15 (Garden City, N.Y.: Doubleday, 1979) 42; Habel, *The Book of Job,* 117; and Perdue, *Wisdom in Revolt,* 120, for a similar interpretation on different grammatical grounds.

106. So Clines, *Job 1–20,* 116; Gordis, *The Book of Job,* 55; H. Rowley, *The Book of Job,* rev. ed., NCB (Grand Rapids, Mich.: Eerdmans, 1976; original ed., 1970) 53.

107. Clines, *Job 1–20,* 144-45.

Note that Eliphaz does not deny the existence of drought, oppression, grief, scheming villains, or poverty. But by making the image of transformation central to his language, he strategically shifts the focus from situation to process. Implicitly, Eliphaz claims that the crucial aspect of reality is that it is always open. The final verse of the doxology contains the word that is thematically central for Eliphaz: "hope" (תקוה *tiqwâ*; see also 4:6). This word is important because hope contains an ineradicable element of the future (cf. Jer 29:11). Job's preoccupation with death in chap. 3 had closed off both hope and the possibility of a future. In his recourse to the traditional language of God as transformer of situations, Eliphaz attempts to restore that possibility to Job.

5:17-27. The concluding part of Eliphaz's long speech begins with what is known as a macarism, a statement in the form "happy is X." Such sayings are frequent in Proverbs and Psalms, but what is striking in Eliphaz's macarism is his use of the form in connection with something painful. The general notion that misfortune could be "correction" or "discipline" from God is very much a part of the moral thinking of the ancient Near East. In Psalms 6 and 38 the psalmists, using the same terminology, acknowledge their sufferings as divine discipline, but pray that God not discipline them in anger. The particular understanding that lies behind Eliphaz's bold macarism is that expressed in Prov 3:11-12, where divine discipline is understood as being motivated by love, such as a father has for a son. The general statement is illustrated in v. 18 with the imagery of wounding and healing, striking and binding up. As shocking as such images may be to modern readers, the use of beatings in education was considered appropriate and compatible with a loving relationship (cf. Prov 20:30; 22:15; 23:13-14).

Although introduced by the macarism about discipline, vv. 19-26 actually shift the focus to the sustaining protection of God in occasions of distress that are more collective than personal in nature. Verse 19 also uses a traditional sayings pattern, the ascending numerical form ("six . . . seven"; cf., e.g., Ps 62:11-12[12-13]; Prov 6:16; 30:15-16; Amos 1:3-15). That the following list exceeds seven is not atypical of the form.[108] But what is Eliphaz's point? The rhetorical exaggeration in Eliphaz's words in vv. 19-22 makes them easy to dismiss. The imagery moves from mere survival in v. 20 (not dying from famine, not being killed in war) to secure protection in v. 21 (being hidden from slander and its destructive power) to active confidence in v. 22 (the ability to laugh fearlessly at the disasters of famine and predatory animals). Read literally, Eliphaz's speech seems to be promising the magical protection of a lucky charm. Read more sympathetically, and with more appreciation of the nature of poetic language, Eliphaz's imagery evokes something of the life-giving power of God, which sustains a person even in calamity, the inextinguishable source of strength that prevents a person who is gravely suffering from shattering entirely and even enables that person to flourish again.

Eliphaz's final set of images describes just such flourishing after great suffering. Here, too, the images are extravagant but evocative. The notion of a covenant with the stones of the field is not otherwise attested, but clearly suggests the reversal of the ancient conflict between human cultivation and the earth's resistance, described in somewhat different images in Gen 3:17b-18. Moreover, peace with the wild animals is an image associated with eschatological blessedness (cf. Isa 11:6-9). The general images in vv. 24-25 of security in the house and field, coupled with abundant descendants, are evocative of the types of blessings enumerated in more concrete detail in the covenant blessings of Lev 26:3-13 and Deut 28:1-14. The concluding verse describes death under the figure of the harvest of a sheaf of grain. In contrast to the debility that can make old age fearful (Eccl 12:1-7), Eliphaz describes death in the fullness of one's powers, a death like that granted to Moses (Deut 34:7).[109]

The reader who finds Eliphaz's words in vv. 19-26 trite should compare them with Psalm 23. If Eliphaz's words are to be dismissed, so too is much that religious people are accustomed to affirming. At the same time, how can one hear Eliphaz's words about a safe home and a fold with nothing missing and not think of Job's flocks decimated and his children crushed? The book of Job forces one to listen to traditional religious

---

108. Cf. W. M. W. Roth, *Numerical Sayings in the Old Testament: A Form-Critical Study*, VTSup 13 (Leiden: Brill, 1965) 68n. 2.

109. Clines, *Job 1–20*, 153.

language in a much more complex way than one is accustomed to, experiencing its truth and its falsity in uncomfortable ways. This unease is not part of Eliphaz's experience, however. In v. 27, he again asks Job to acknowledge for himself the traditional insights that the community has examined and found true.

REFLECTIONS

Even if one takes account of cultural differences and listens to Eliphaz as one who speaks from a somewhat different moral world than one's own, and even if one gives Eliphaz full credit for consciously good intentions, his speech remains deeply disturbing. Although Eliphaz speaks out of genuine concern for Job, at the heart of his speech lies fear. He is afraid because of what has happened to Job, but he is also afraid of Job. In part, what makes Eliphaz's speech troubling is the ambiguity about whose needs he is tending. Eliphaz's situation is not an unusual one. Anyone who has confronted another whose suffering is great and irremediable knows the fear and the temptation. The cry of despair is so terrible, opening onto a seeming abyss, that one desires to make it stop, to muffle it, to silence it. At such moments it is very easy to confuse the needs of the sufferer with the impulses of one's own anxiety. The silence that comes when a suffering voice is repressed, however, is not the quiet of true consolation.

One way of reflecting on what Eliphaz does is to consider whether he aids Job in finding a voice or whether he acts to silence Job. Eliphaz, one can be certain, would understand himself as restoring Job's true voice to him. After all, he is reminding Job of how Job used to talk to others (4:3-4). That, however, is an evasion and a self-deception. Eliphaz attempts to speak *in place of* Job, saying what he thinks Job should have said, and that is the antithesis of helping Job find his voice. However kindly the intention, the person who says to a grieving widow, "It was God's will," or who says to a father whose child has died, "God needed your baby in heaven," or who says to a terminal cancer patient, "God works miracles," is signaling to that person what the acceptable limits of speech are. Perhaps those words coincide with the suffering person's own speech, but if they do not, they serve as a means of silencing a grief that needs to find its own expression.

It would be a mistake to understand Eliphaz's response to Job as a purely individual shortcoming. Although suffering is a radically individual experience, it is also a culturally shaped experience. The inbreaking of great suffering, like a flood or an earthquake, threatens to overwhelm the structures that give life order and direction. At such a time, both sufferers and comforters tend to reach for the traditional rituals and formulas their culture has developed to shape the experience and guide the persons through it. Particular cultures and subcultures vary enormously in what they encourage and discourage. Some cultures disapprove of any but the most minimal display of emotion. Others encourage extravagant gestures of grief. Whatever the prevailing expectations within a particular culture, however, very little deviation from the norm is usually tolerated. The person who behaves "inappropriately" or who rejects the traditional formulas is seen as a threat to the community's worldview, even if no one would be comfortable in admitting it. As discussed in the Reflections on chap. 3, Job transgresses the cultural assumptions about the ways in which anger arising from suffering may be expressed. This is what makes Eliphaz afraid of Job, and his fear gives an edge of aggressiveness to the words he intends kindly.

The tension between Job and Eliphaz cannot be resolved simply by declaring that Job is right and Eliphaz is wrong. It would be inappropriate to suggest that anger is the only appropriate response to suffering or that there is something misguided in the attempt to try to place an experience of suffering in a context of meaning. On the contrary, in some way, integrating the disrupting and disorienting experiences of suffering into a larger understanding of life and world is essential. That effort to find meaning may be as simple as a belief that the power of a person's life transcends death through the impact that person had on the lives of others. Or meaning may be found in a community's resolve to remedy an unjust situation so that a victim's suffering "will not have been in vain." Meaning may be a matter of recognizing that God's love is powerful even in the midst of suffering. Other more rationalistic approaches will attempt to give reasons for the occurrence of suffering. What is common to all these efforts is the impulse to deny the last word to suffering, to refuse to let it be the ultimate reality. There is a fine line to be walked, however, between denying ultimacy to suffering and simply engaging in denial.

What makes chaps. 4–5 so deeply offensive is not that they attempt to integrate suffering into a context of meaning but that they are the attempt of someone who is not suffering to silence the "unacceptable" words of one who is. Chapters 4–5 would have a very different resonance if they were Job's own words. Readers might argue about whether the individual passages represented good or bad ways of grappling with the disorientation of radical suffering, but they could be seen as authentic attempts to use traditional beliefs to incorporate the suffering into a structure of meaning capable of sustaining a future.

Since statements of the type present in chaps. 4–5 are often made by sufferers struggling to come to terms with their own situations, it is important to reflect on the nature of these arguments and the reasons why people are drawn to them. There are two distinct impulses in the material in chaps. 4–5. One, which is not very strongly developed in these chapters, is to attempt to justify suffering by endowing it with an intrinsic logic and purpose. The other, much more pronounced impulse is to bypass questions of cause and to focus instead on the grounds for hope beyond suffering.

The approach that attempts to justify suffering is represented by Eliphaz's statements about suffering as divine discipline (5:17-19) and hinted at in his observations about the wicked, who reap what they sow (4:8-9). The idea of suffering as disciplinary has been a persistent notion in Judaism and Christianity from antiquity to the present. As problematic as such an idea is, it has a strong appeal because it brings terrifying and chaotic events into a structure of meaning and purpose. Suffering understood that way can be incorporated into the context of a personal relationship with a deity in whom love predominates over anger. Although there is never any explicit criticism of this view in the book of Job (Job himself never answers it directly), the book exposes the lurking obscenity in this perspective simply by the disproportionate way it is applied. The suffering that Eliphaz identifies as divine "correction" includes the deaths of ten children.

Eliphaz makes one other extended attempt to justify suffering: his contrast between the nature of divine and human being (4:17-21). Many readers find this argument bizarre, and yet it is a type of argument that recurs in various forms in biblically based religion. Eliphaz places Job's catastrophe in the context of all human vulnerability to sudden death. In so doing, he attempts to take away the terror of a unique and incomprehensible suffering. That is not the main point, however. By stressing the enormous gulf between human and divine nature, Eliphaz makes human perishing seem not simply inevitable but intrinsic to the affirmation that all values, meaning, and being itself are located in God. God and humanity are posited as opposites. By this logic, the more one affirms the presence of certain values in God, the more one must negate them in human beings. In his study of how religious meaning is developed and sustained, Peter Berger refers to this type of thinking as a "masochistic theodicy."[110] God is absolute being; the human over against God is absolute nothingness. Out of this dynamic arises a kind of ecstasy. It is not comfort in the traditional sense but ecstatic transcendence through self-negation that the sufferer receives.

110. P. Berger, *The Sacred Canopy* (Garden City, N.Y.: Doubleday, 1967) 73-76.

The psychological cost of this type of theodicy is evident. Its theological problems are just as grave, however. The goodness of creation, a fundamental tenet of biblical religion, has to be ignored. Moreover, the richly nuanced biblical understanding of divine holiness as not only dangerous but also life-giving is reduced to an image of all-consuming sterility.

For the most part, however, chaps. 4–5 are not concerned with arguments that attempt to justify suffering in general or Job's situation in particular. Rather, they are concerned with establishing hope. Over and over again, the ultimacy of suffering is denied. "Lions" are real, but their power to destroy is checked (4:10). Human beings are "born to trouble" (5:7), but God can transform situations (5:8-16). Disasters abound, but the power of God sustains even in the face of destruction (5:19-26). These types of statements are more frequently in the mouths of sufferers than are rationalizations and justifications; they have a legitimacy that rationalizations do not. What is characteristic of this way of talking is its narrative quality. Suffering becomes an episode in a larger story. As important as that way of understanding can be for someone attempting to live through a crisis, it also has its dangers. Not all stories have happy endings. A way of talking about suffering that can describe meaning only in terms of happy endings is defective. Although the way Eliphaz talks about suffering is not without value, his speech is ultimately flawed by denial. Even if these were Job's own words, they would not suffice.

Job 6:1–7:21, Job Defends the Vehemence of His Words

OVERVIEW

Job is not silenced by Eliphaz's words. In chaps. 6–7, Job replies with a spirited defense of his own speech, a sharp indictment of the friends' failure, and a bold accusation against God. Although the two chapters are linked by the themes of rash speech and human frailty, they have different emphases and serve different purposes in Job's reply. Chapter 6 is primarily concerned with a justification of Job's way of speaking and his insistence on what is necessary for a true dialogue with his friends. The chapter begins (vv. 2-3) and ends (vv. 28-30) with Job's defense of both the vehemence and the truth of his words. The long section in which Job criticizes his friends (vv. 14-27) focuses specifically on the failure of the friends to take Job's words seriously and to respond to him with the same degree of integrity that he exhibits. A second topic, developed in vv. 4-13, concerns Job's rejection of life. It continues the death-wish theme of chap. 3, using language and images from the lament tradition.

Although briefly treated, the theme of unrestrained speaking plays a crucial role in chap. 7, occurring in the central verse of the chapter (v. 11). In the verses leading up to this declaration, Job justifies his need to speak without restraint through a reflection on the misery of the human condition in general (vv. 1-2) and of his own condition in particular (vv. 3-6). Directly addressing God (v. 7), he meditates on the ephemeral quality of human life (vv. 7-10). Impelled by misery and mortality to speak without restraint (v. 11), Job addresses God in words utterly without parallel in the Bible. The content of his accusation (vv. 12-21) is that God has a misplaced and inappropriate obsession with inspecting and punishing human behavior. What makes Job's words both powerful and shocking, however, is his use of sarcasm and parody. Unlike the expression of simple anger, sarcasm and parody do not have a recognized place in the language of Israel's religious traditions. When Job introduces them into his speech, he defies all the conventions of piety.

Job 6:1-30, Anguish Made Worse by the Failure of Friendship

NIV

6 Then Job replied:

2"If only my anguish could be weighed
and all my misery be placed on the scales!
3It would surely outweigh the sand of the seas—
no wonder my words have been impetuous.
4The arrows of the Almighty are in me,
my spirit drinks in their poison;
God's terrors are marshaled against me.
5Does a wild donkey bray when it has grass,
or an ox bellow when it has fodder?
6Is tasteless food eaten without salt,
or is there flavor in the white of an egg*a*?
7I refuse to touch it;
such food makes me ill.

8"Oh, that I might have my request,
that God would grant what I hope for,
9that God would be willing to crush me,
to let loose his hand and cut me off!
10Then I would still have this consolation—
my joy in unrelenting pain—
that I had not denied the words of the Holy
One.

11"What strength do I have, that I should still
hope?
What prospects, that I should be patient?
12Do I have the strength of stone?
Is my flesh bronze?
13Do I have any power to help myself,
now that success has been driven from me?

14"A despairing man should have the devotion of
his friends,
even though he forsakes the fear of the
Almighty.
15But my brothers are as undependable as
intermittent streams,
as the streams that overflow
16when darkened by thawing ice
and swollen with melting snow,
17but that cease to flow in the dry season,
and in the heat vanish from their channels.
18Caravans turn aside from their routes;
they go up into the wasteland and perish.

a6 The meaning of the Hebrew for this phrase is uncertain.

NRSV

6 Then Job answered:
2 "O that my vexation were weighed,
and all my calamity laid in the balances!
3 For then it would be heavier than the sand of
the sea;
therefore my words have been rash.
4 For the arrows of the Almighty*a* are in me;
my spirit drinks their poison;
the terrors of God are arrayed against me.
5 Does the wild ass bray over its grass,
or the ox low over its fodder?
6 Can that which is tasteless be eaten without
salt,
or is there any flavor in the juice of
mallows?*b*
7 My appetite refuses to touch them;
they are like food that is loathsome to me.*b*

8 "O that I might have my request,
and that God would grant my desire;
9 that it would please God to crush me,
that he would let loose his hand and cut
me off!
10 This would be my consolation;
I would even exult*b* in unrelenting pain;
for I have not denied the words of the Holy
One.
11 What is my strength, that I should wait?
And what is my end, that I should be
patient?
12 Is my strength the strength of stones,
or is my flesh bronze?
13 In truth I have no help in me,
and any resource is driven from me.

14 "Those who withhold*c* kindness from a friend
forsake the fear of the Almighty.*d*
15 My companions are treacherous like a
torrent-bed,
like freshets that pass away,
16 that run dark with ice,
turbid with melting snow.
17 In time of heat they disappear;

a Traditional rendering of Heb Shaddai   b Meaning of Heb uncertain   c Syr Vg Compare Tg: Meaning of Heb uncertain   d Traditional rendering of Heb Shaddai

NIV

¹⁹The caravans of Tema look for water,
    the traveling merchants of Sheba look in
        hope.
²⁰They are distressed, because they had been
        confident;
    they arrive there, only to be disappointed.
²¹Now you too have proved to be of no help;
    you see something dreadful and are afraid.
²²Have I ever said, 'Give something on my behalf,
    pay a ransom for me from your wealth,
²³deliver me from the hand of the enemy,
    ransom me from the clutches of the ruthless'?

²⁴"Teach me, and I will be quiet;
    show me where I have been wrong.
²⁵How painful are honest words!
    But what do your arguments prove?
²⁶Do you mean to correct what I say,
    and treat the words of a despairing man as
        wind?
²⁷You would even cast lots for the fatherless
    and barter away your friend.

²⁸"But now be so kind as to look at me.
    Would I lie to your face?
²⁹Relent, do not be unjust;
    reconsider, for my integrity is at stake.ᵃ
³⁰Is there any wickedness on my lips?
    Can my mouth not discern malice?"

ᵃ29 Or *my righteousness still stands*

NRSV

    when it is hot, they vanish from their place.
¹⁸ The caravans turn aside from their course;
    they go up into the waste, and perish.
¹⁹ The caravans of Tema look,
    the travelers of Sheba hope.
²⁰ They are disappointed because they were
        confident;
    they come there and are confounded.
²¹ Such you have now become to me;ᵃ
    you see my calamity, and are afraid.
²² Have I said, 'Make me a gift'?
    Or, 'From your wealth offer a bribe for me'?
²³ Or, 'Save me from an opponent's hand'?
    Or, 'Ransom me from the hand of
        oppressors'?

²⁴ "Teach me, and I will be silent;
    make me understand how I have gone
        wrong.
²⁵ How forceful are honest words!
    But your reproof, what does it reprove?
²⁶ Do you think that you can reprove words,
    as if the speech of the desperate were wind?
²⁷ You would even cast lots over the orphan,
    and bargain over your friend.

²⁸ "But now, be pleased to look at me;
    for I will not lie to your face.
²⁹ Turn, I pray, let no wrong be done.
    Turn now, my vindication is at stake.
³⁰ Is there any wrong on my tongue?
    Cannot my taste discern calamity?"

ᵃ Cn Compare Gk Syr: Meaning of Heb uncertain

COMMENTARY

6:1-7. 6:1-2. Throughout his speech, Job echoes a number of words previously used by Eliphaz.[111] Such repetition of words used by the previous speaker is a fairly frequent device in the dialogue. Whether or not the characters are to be understood as replying explicitly to each other's arguments, the struggle over the meaning of certain words is an important part of the conflict. In 5:2, Eliphaz chided Job for his outburst with a

_____

111. N. Habel, *The Book of Job,* OTL (Philadelphia: Westminster, 1985) 141.

proverb concerning anger. Here, Job picks up that same word (כעש *ka'aś*), now used with the nuance of "anguish," and incorporates it into an image of weight and measure, part of his defense of the way he is speaking (v. 2). Heaviness is a common metaphor in many cultures for the oppressiveness of suffering. In Job's extravagant image the weight of anguish bearing down on him is imaginarily objectified and displaced from his own body to a set of giant scales. Scales belong to the cultural sphere of the public market, where they serve to establish agreement between parties who are by the nature of things inclined to mistrust each other's valuations. Job's use of the image implies that Eliphaz has underestimated the weight of his suffering.

6:3. The specific comparison establishes the magnitude of Job's anguish as something that wholly transcends human scale, since the sand of the sea was itself proverbial for its weight (Prov 27:3; Sir 22:15) and for its numberless grains (Gen 22:17; cf. Isa 48:19; Jer 15:8). Thus the image serves as a justification for Job's speaking rashly. Although rash speech was understood in the wisdom tradition as something that one later regretted (Prov 20:25), the rest of the chapter makes clear that Job is by no means apologizing for what he has said.

6:4. Job identifies the source of his calamity through images of divine violence, specifically, images of God as warrior (cf. Deut 32:23-24; Lam 2:4; Hab 3:3-12). This is conventional language, and Job simply states the obvious. According to his worldview, so much devastation was almost certainly the result of divine anger (cf. Pss 38:1-3[1-4]; 90:7-8; Lam 3:1, 12-13). In the biblical tradition, God's dangerousness can express itself in sudden violence, as in the stories about the incineration of Nadab and Abihu (Lev 10:1-7), Miriam's leprosy (Numbers 12), and the striking down of Uzzah (2 Sam 6:6-11). In every case it was assumed that God's anger was not arbitrary but was provoked by something that the individual had done. Divine compassion, however, was understood to be more profound than anger, so that an afflicted person could turn in yearning to God, who was always inclined to respond by turning anger into compassion. Psalm 38 is an excellent example of just the sort of response that a person in Job's situation might be expected to make. Job, however, resolutely rejects that expected response. Just how "rash" Job's words are can be better appreciated if one first reads Psalm 38 and then reads the rest of chap. 6.

6:5-7. Job continues with two proverbial sayings in the form of rhetorical questions (vv. 5-6). Following after vv. 3-4, v. 5 initially serves as a further defense of Job's outcry, using the images of animals who do not bray or bellow when they have food. The second saying does not continue the focus on noisy complaint, however, but shifts to the food itself. The last phrase in v. 6 is quite obscure, as the divergent translations of the NRSV and the NIV suggest.[112] The general image is clear, however: Food that has no taste does not appeal. Verse 7, also obscure at the end, strengthens the image, with its suggestion of revulsion at such food. The embedded metaphor is that of life as food, and the will to live as the appetite. Job's situation differs from that of the wild ass or ox in an essential way. Their food is appropriate and appealing.[113] Job's food (= life) is so disgusting that he has no attachment to it and certainly will not cry out for more of it, as Job makes clear in what follows.[114]

6:8-13. 6:8-9. In the following verses, Job does not actually pray.[115] As will become increasingly evident, the fundamental trust governing the relationship between the person and God in Israelite prayer traditions has been shattered for Job. He is left with only the fragments of a language of prayer, which he employs in parodistic fashion. Traditionally, those who prayed psalms of lament begged God for life because they were in danger of being swallowed up by death (Pss 22:12-21[13-22]; 143:7-12). Job's wish for death (v. 9) turns the language of prayer upside down. It is not just death but specifically death by divine violence that Job desires, parodying other psalmists who pray for God's hand to be lifted from them (Pss 32:4; 39:10[11]), who pray not to be cut off (Ps 88:5; Isa 38:12), and who pray for relief from being crushed by God (Ps 38:2, 8[3, 9]). Job's identification of this as his "hope" (v. 8) mocks Eliphaz's use of the word (4:6; 5:16). In Eliphaz's moral world, hope is the openness of life to a future; Job's only "hope" is to close off the future through a quick death.

6:10. Disagreement over the translation of v. 10 leads to sharply differing interpretations. It is quite unclear whether Job refers to "exulting" in unrelenting pain (so NRSV and NIV) or whether he speaks of "recoiling" in unrelenting pain (so TNK). The evidence does not allow a certain decision. More important is the translation of the

---

112. See D. Clines, *Job 1–20*, WBC 17 (Dallas: Word, 1989) 158.
113. Cf. G. Fohrer, *Das Buch Hiob*, KAT xvi (Guetersloh: Gerd Mohn, 1963) 169.
114. For a different understanding of these verses, see Habel, *The Book of Job*, 145-46.
115. Contra F. Andersen, *Job: An Introduction and Commentary*, Tyndale Old Testament Commentaries (Downers Grove, Ill.: Inter-Varsity, 1976) 128.

last phrase. Most translations render something like "for I have not denied the words of the Holy One." The interpretation lying behind this translation is exemplified by Clines, who likens Job to a prisoner under torture, longing for death to come before he breaks down and curses God.[116] In this way, Job still "holds fast to his integrity." Although this interpretation offers a fascinating psychological portrait of Job, it runs into trouble on the grounds that the verb כחד (kāḥad) does not really mean "deny." The literal meaning is much closer to "hide," "conceal" and always has to do with the control of information.[117] This is clear from other instances in which the verb occurs, as when Eli tells Samuel not to conceal anything that God has told Samuel (1 Sam 3:17-18; cf. 2 Sam 14:18; Jer 38:14, 25). "Hide" or "conceal" is also the meaning of the verb elsewhere in Job (15:18; 27:11). The phrase "words of the Holy One" need not refer only to the teachings of God in general but can also refer to divine decisions,[118] in this case God's decision to attack Job (v. 4). Thus Job would find ironic "comfort," even in the midst of unrelenting pain, in that he had not hidden the fact that it is God who has decreed his affliction.[119] Although it is uncertain whether Psalm 119 was extant when Job was written, an ironic echo exists between Job 6:10 and Ps 119:50, which reads: "This is my comfort in affliction: that your word gives me life." Life, as he has just made clear, is the last thing Job wants.

6:11-13. Waiting with hope and expectation is the traditional stance of the psalmists (e.g., Pss 33:18, 22; 71:14; 147:11). In vv. 11-13, Job explains why he cannot take up the stance of hopeful waiting. That reason is his body. The contrast with stones and bronze underscores the limits set by the fragility of flesh. The psalmists, too, often invoke the body's weakness as part of their rhetoric, urging God to come quickly because they are in distress (Pss 22:12-21[13-22]); 38:3-8, 22[4-9, 23]; 69:1-3, 16-18[2-4, 17-19]). The psalms of lament frame a moment when the situation is urgent but open to transformation. They never look at the eventuality in which help comes too late. Job exposes the blindness of traditional piety to the real limits of human endurance. To wait for God's help (e.g., Ps 33:20), Job would have to have help and resources within himself; yet that has been driven out of him (v. 13). Neither can he find the strength he needs in the support of his friends, as the next section makes clear.

6:14-21. Another fragment from the language of psalms of lament is the motif of being abandoned by one's friends (Pss 31:11[12]; 38:11[12]; 88:8[9], 18[19]). Echoing that tradition, Job transforms it into an accusation and the basis for a direct appeal to the friends, rather than using the motif as part of a plea to God. The text of v. 14 is difficult and possibly corrupt. The divergent translations of the NRSV and the NIV reflect the two main options.[120] "Loyalty" (a better translation in this context for חסד [ḥesed] than "kindness" or "devotion") was prized in ancient Israel as the primary quality of friendship (1 Sam 18:1; 20:14-15; Prov 17:17; 18:24). According to the NIV, Job radicalizes the claims of such loyalty so that they must be honored even toward a person who has rejected God.[121] Yet when Job makes explicit what he asks of his friends (vv. 24-30), it is nothing so heroic. More likely, v. 14 should be construed as in the NRSV, equating failure to meet the claims of friendship with a failure of piety.

Job characterizes the failure of the friends in a strikingly developed metaphor, comparing them with the "treachery" of a Near Eastern wadi, a stream bed that alternates between torrential flow and dryness (vv. 14-17; cf. Jer 15:18). Although translation difficulties occur, they do not obscure the basic image of a stream that has abundant water when it is least needed but dries up during the heat of summer. In an expansion of the metaphor (vv. 18-20), Job implicitly likens himself to desperate caravaneers who futilely relied upon the presence of water in the streams. How seriously Job takes the failure of the friends is suggested by the comparison; it is a matter of life and death (v. 18). The intermingling of the metaphorical imagery with the psychological and social reality it describes is evident in the verbs of vv. 19-20. The expectant looking of v. 19 is appropriate to the image of the caravaneers, but the

---

116. Clines, *Job 1–20*, 174.

117. See E. Dhorme, *A Commentary on the Book of Job*, trans. H. Knight (London: Nelson, 1967) 82; Habel, *The Book of Job*, 140.

118. Dhorme, *A Commentary on the Book of Job*, 82; Perdue, 42-46.

119. Similarly, Habel, *The Book of Job*, 147.

120. Cf. Clines, *Job 1–20*, 176-78.

121. See N. Habel, " 'Only the Jackal Is My Friend': On Friends and Redeemers in Job," *Int.* 31 (1977) 230.

verbs of v. 20 ("be ashamed," "be confounded" [בוש *bôš*]) come from the language of social relations. They connote the shame experienced by those who have lost status or the respect with which they were formerly treated (Isa 24:23; Jer 15:9; Mic 3:7). In Job's world, the failure of his friends' loyalty itself undercuts his standing and leaves him publicly shamed, a theme to which he will return in chaps. 19 and 30.

Another textual problem obscures the first half of v. 21, but the main point is clear. Job uses a play on words between "you see" (תראו *tir'û*) and "you are afraid" (תיראו *tîrā'û*) to explain the metaphorical drying up of his friends' loyalty. *That* Job believes his friends have failed him and *why* he thinks they have are explicitly stated. But Job has not yet said *how* his friends have fallen short or what he expects of them.

6:22-30. 6:22-24. Through a series of rhetorical questions, Job lists several substantial claims that one friend might make on another, all of which involve money or an element of danger (vv. 22-23); yet Job has asked nothing like this from his friends. What he does want is described in vv. 24-26. The reader should be careful not to assume that Job wants what the reader might want in a friend. Job expresses himself in the categories of sapiential friendship. He needs his friends to help him understand the truth about his situation. The "error" to which he refers (v. 24*b*) could be either some fault that has led to the divine anger, or an error of understanding that has led him to misconstrue the significance of his experience. In either case, Job's plea, "Teach me, and I will be silent," echoes the beginning of the chapter, where Job acknowledged the rashness of his own words. Only understanding will bring Job genuine quietness. His words underscore a major theme of the rest of the book. The subsequent failure of the friends to meet Job's need for understanding will serve to expose the inadequacies of the traditional discourse of wisdom and piety. Job will become silent after the divine speeches (chaps. 38–41), and the reader will have to decide whether the divine speeches have finally given Job the understanding that he craves or whether he has merely been silenced by divine might.

6:25. One can imagine Eliphaz's surprise at Job's words. Has he not tried to show Job where

he has erred? Why is Job unsatisfied with his efforts? Just where Job faults Eliphaz is evident in v. 25, as he refers to the painfulness of straight talk. Translations that emend the expression to "how pleasant" (cf. NAB)[122] or that soften the expression to "how forceful" (NRSV) miss the point. Job knows that only painful words could do justice to his deeply painful situation. Eliphaz's words were full of hope for a bright future. He deftly avoided laying blame for the situation with either Job or God, except in broad generalizations about the universal human condition. Eliphaz's words lack the relentless honesty that Job demands of himself and of his friends, an honesty that will not conceal (v. 10). In an alliterative phrase that mocks the surface prettiness of Eliphaz's words, Job dismisses Eliphaz's arguments as meaningless (v. 25*b*).

6:26-27. Job carries the issue further in v. 26. To reprove or correct "words" is a fundamental task of the sage. But Job resents that his words are treated as so much "wind"—i.e., trivialized—precisely because he is desperate. Job would not think kindly of the statement made concerning him in the Talmud: "a person is not held responsible for what he says while in distress."[123] Although Job had earlier characterized his own words as rash (v. 3), he insisted that they were motivated by his circumstances. Now he makes a much bolder defense of his own ability to discern the truth, not in spite of but because of the fact that he has been driven to the margins of life itself. In v. 27, Job boldly asserts that refusing to take seriously the words of a sufferer is the moral equivalent of casting lots for an orphan or selling out a friend. These words, too, strike some commentators as rash overstatement,[124] but Job's comparison requires that one consider what unites these cases. In each instance one who is vulnerable is devalued and treated as less than a person.

6:28. In vv. 28-30, Job attempts to set the conditions for a true dialogue about his situation. The image dominating v. 28 is that of the face. The phrase translated "look at me" is literally

122. M. Pope, *Job,* 3rd ed., AB 15 (Garden City, N.Y.: Doubleday, 1979) 55.
123. *b. B. Bat.* 16b.
124. F. Andersen, *Job,* 133.

"face me" (פְנוּ־בִי‬ *pĕnû-bî*). In the following half-line Job uses a solemn oath formula to declare to his friends that he will not lie "to your face" (עַל־פְּנֵיכֶם‬ *'al-pĕnêkem*). The image of the face is a profound symbol of human identity. Faces are what an infant first learns to recognize visually as it establishes a sense of social relationship. A face always makes a moral claim on another face.

6:29. The imperatives with which Job addresses his friends can be translated conceptually, as in the NIV's "relent . . . reconsider." After the vividness of "face me," however, the underlying physical nuance of these verbs is better expressed by "turn" or "turn back." The two terms that Job contrasts in v. 29 (עוֹלָה‬ *'awlâ*; צֶדֶק‬ *ṣedeq*) have a range of meanings. They could be translated as "injustice" and "vindication" respectively, anticipating the legal language that will occupy so much of Job's thinking.[125] As Habel observes, however, *'awlâ* is often associated in the book of Job with speech, so that it takes on the nuance of "deceit,"[126] contrasting with the "rightness" (*ṣedeq*) or integrity that Job claims is at stake for him.

6:30. In the final verse, Job brings together images of the body (tongue, palate) with the metaphor of taste as discernment, recalling the similar images of vv. 4-7. What does Job claim to be able to discern? The two words used have double meanings, both of which should be heard. As noted above, *'awlâ* means both "injustice" and "deceit." Similarly, the very last word of the line can mean "calamity," as it does in v. 2, yet it can also carry the meaning of "deceit," "falsehood" (Ps 5:9[10]; Mic 7:3).[127] Thus Job is making two claims, which, significantly, he does not distinguish. Through these words he asserts that he is not lying to his friends, since his own tongue can detect deceit and falsehood. At the same time he claims that he is able to tell the objective truth about his situation, since his own tongue is able to discern injustice and calamity when he tastes it. These are, in fact, claims of a quite different nature. Whether Job is aware of the difference is difficult to say but of great importance.

125. See E. Good, *In Turns of Tempest* (Stanford, Calif.: Stanford University Press, 1990) 214-15.
126. Habel, *The Book of Job,* 150.

127. R. Gordis, *The Book of Job: Commentary, New Translation, and Special Studies* (New York: Jewish Theological Seminary, 5738/1978) 78.

REFLECTIONS

Job's speeches are highly imagistic, inviting the reader to search for meaning among the images as well as in the explicit claims he makes. The reader who expects to find a transparent, consistently worked out system of metaphors and symbols is often frustrated, however, discovering instead a hodgepodge of apparently "ill-connected images."[128] Yet what is ill-connected on one level may prove quite coherent on another. It is always worth investigating when a person shows a preference for certain types of images or for words from a particular semantic field, even if these images and words are used in superficially disparate contexts. The individual may not be aware of it, but in such imagistic play the symbolic processes of speech itself are at work, exploring and attempting to resolve some fundamental dilemma that hovers on the edges of conscious discourse. So it is with Job's speech.

The body in all its physicality serves as a point of reference for Job. He thinks by means of the body in several ways. First, Job makes use of the image of the body as limit (see Commentary on Job 7). Even the relationship with God must take account of the finitude of the human body. It is surprisingly easy for moral and religious language to become abstract, to fail to take the body into account or to represent the body in unrealistic ways. Job uses a variety of images that insist on the vulnerability of the body. He graphically portrays his affliction in terms of arrows that have penetrated his body (v. 4), twice uses words for pain (vv. 10, 25), and explicitly contrasts the limited strength of flesh with that of the unfeeling, invulnerable strength of stones and bronze (v. 12). In this way Job's speech sharply contrasts with Eliphaz's

128. Good, *In Turns of Tempest,* 214.

sanitized references to binding up wounds and healing bruises (5:18) and to the swords and famines that in Eliphaz's miraculous world leave no scars or ravages (5:19-22). A religious language that cannot be realistic about the body is suspect, and Job calls into question the traditional language of prayer, because it does not acknowledge the limits of the body as one waits for God's deliverance (see Commentary above).

Second, the image of the body as the organ of perception dominates chap. 6. Almost all of Job's language about perception, judgment, and discrimination is developed in terms of body imagery, most important the bodily function of eating and drinking. He perceives his affliction in terms of his spirit's "drinking" poison (v. 4). He compares his outburst to animals who bray or bellow when deprived of food (v. 5). He describes his life in terms of insipid, tasteless food (v. 6). Even the image of nauseated revulsion is a bodily image (v. 7; the word for "appetite" [נֶפֶשׁ *nepeš*] concretely means "throat," "gullet"). Job images loyalty in terms of water and himself as one who dies of thirst when he fails to find it in his friends (v. 18). At the end of the chapter, Job refers to the tongue and palate, which are both the organs of speech and of taste, as he makes a claim about his ability to judge and discriminate (v. 30).

Third, for Job the question of how one knows something has to be referred to the body's experience. The body's knowledge is immediate and direct. What is significant about such images is that they depict a kind of knowledge that is at the same time indisputable and radically subjective. No one else can tell me whether I am hungry or thirsty or nauseated. Only I can know. Moreover, these are not things about which I am likely to be confused or in doubt. I know such things with the immediacy and certainty of the body's knowledge. By using such imagery, Job makes a very powerful claim for the authority of what he knows. There is, however, something troubling and problematic about that imagery when it is used to authenticate knowledge about the world. Nothing is more subjective than taste. We use the phrase "a matter of taste" when we want to say that there are no objective standards to which one can appeal. Yet Job represents the tongue and the palate as the privileged organs of discrimination and judgment. The problem that lurks in the appeal and the limit of these images is the problem of how to make a subjective claim valid intersubjectively. How can I make what seems as clear to me as the taste of salt equally clear to you?

Job struggles with this problem through his use of images. His opening image of transferring his inner anguish onto a set of scales is just such an attempt. He recognizes the need for a way of perceiving that can be shared between persons who do not have the same immediacy of experience. The problem, of course, is that this is a fantasy image. Anguish cannot be made as tangible as the weight of sand. At the end of the chapter Job tries again for an image that will be faithful to his primary commitment to the body as the privileged organ of perception and yet adequate to the reality of intersubjective distance. He finds what he is seeking in the image of the face (v. 28). Such an image is faithful to Job's concern for the body, because there is no other part of one's physical self in which identity is invested more than in the face. The face is also that part of the body that is the primary means of establishing connection with another person, through the expression of the eyes and the mouth. The mutual scrutiny of face meeting face creates an environment that discourages a lie (v. 28*b*). Yet for all his concern to acknowledge the claims of intersubjective distance, Job returns in the end to claim for himself the final authority in adjudicating the truth of his own speech and the judgment on his own situation (v. 30).

The issue lying behind Job's images of the body as the organ of perception remains quite lively in contemporary theological discussion—namely, the issue of the role of experience in establishing knowledge about the world and about God. Increasingly, persons whose experience has not traditionally been taken into account insist that they be heard. Often this experience is understood quite specifically in terms of the body—the body that is female rather than male, the body whose skin is not white, the disabled body, the body crushed by poverty. As with

Job, there is an immediacy and authenticity in such experience that commands respect. As with Job, there is also the difficulty of translating what is a wholly convincing subjective experience into a mode of communication that is genuinely dialogical. The danger is that the gap will not be bridged and that competing subjectivities will find no common ground.

Job 7:1-21, Job Confronts God

<table>
<tr><th>NIV</th><th>NRSV</th></tr>
<tr><td>

7 "Does not man have hard service on earth?
    Are not his days like those of a hired man?
²Like a slave longing for the evening shadows,
    or a hired man waiting eagerly for his wages,
³so I have been allotted months of futility,
    and nights of misery have been assigned to me.
⁴When I lie down I think, 'How long before I get up?'
    The night drags on, and I toss till dawn.
⁵My body is clothed with worms and scabs,
    my skin is broken and festering.

⁶"My days are swifter than a weaver's shuttle,
    and they come to an end without hope.
⁷Remember, O God, that my life is but a breath;
    my eyes will never see happiness again.
⁸The eye that now sees me will see me no longer;
    you will look for me, but I will be no more.
⁹As a cloud vanishes and is gone,
    so he who goes down to the grave*a* does not return.
¹⁰He will never come to his house again;
    his place will know him no more.

¹¹"Therefore I will not keep silent;
    I will speak out in the anguish of my spirit,
    I will complain in the bitterness of my soul.
¹²Am I the sea, or the monster of the deep,
    that you put me under guard?
¹³When I think my bed will comfort me
    and my couch will ease my complaint,
¹⁴even then you frighten me with dreams
    and terrify me with visions,
¹⁵so that I prefer strangling and death,
    rather than this body of mine.
¹⁶I despise my life; I would not live forever.
    Let me alone; my days have no meaning.
¹⁷"What is man that you make so much of him,

a9 Hebrew Sheol

</td><td>

7 "Do not human beings have a hard service on earth,
    and are not their days like the days of a laborer?
² Like a slave who longs for the shadow,
    and like laborers who look for their wages,
³ so I am allotted months of emptiness,
    and nights of misery are apportioned to me.
⁴ When I lie down I say, 'When shall I rise?'
    But the night is long,
    and I am full of tossing until dawn.
⁵ My flesh is clothed with worms and dirt;
    my skin hardens, then breaks out again.
⁶ My days are swifter than a weaver's shuttle,
    and come to their end without hope.*a*

⁷ "Remember that my life is a breath;
    my eye will never again see good.
⁸ The eye that beholds me will see me no more;
    while your eyes are upon me, I shall be gone.
⁹ As the cloud fades and vanishes,
    so those who go down to Sheol do not come up;
¹⁰ they return no more to their houses,
    nor do their places know them any more.

¹¹ "Therefore I will not restrain my mouth;
    I will speak in the anguish of my spirit;
    I will complain in the bitterness of my soul.
¹² Am I the Sea, or the Dragon,
    that you set a guard over me?
¹³ When I say, 'My bed will comfort me,
    my couch will ease my complaint,'
¹⁴ then you scare me with dreams
    and terrify me with visions,
¹⁵ so that I would choose strangling
    and death rather than this body.
¹⁶ I loathe my life; I would not live forever.

a Or as the thread runs out

</td></tr>
</table>

NIV

that you give him so much attention,
[18] that you examine him every morning
and test him every moment?
[19] Will you never look away from me,
or let me alone even for an instant?
[20] If I have sinned, what have I done to you,
O watcher of men?
Why have you made me your target?
Have I become a burden to you?[a]
[21] Why do you not pardon my offenses
and forgive my sins?
For I will soon lie down in the dust;
you will search for me, but I will be no
more."

[a]20 A few manuscripts of the Masoretic Text, an ancient Hebrew scribal tradition and Septuagint; most manuscripts of the Masoretic Text *I have become a burden to myself.*

NRSV

Let me alone, for my days are a breath.
[17] What are human beings, that you make so
much of them,
that you set your mind on them,
[18] visit them every morning,
test them every moment?
[19] Will you not look away from me for a while,
let me alone until I swallow my spittle?
[20] If I sin, what do I do to you, you watcher of
humanity?
Why have you made me your target?
Why have I become a burden to you?
[21] Why do you not pardon my transgression
and take away my iniquity?
For now I shall lie in the earth;
you will seek me, but I shall not be."

COMMENTARY

7:1-10. Having made the solemn claim that he would speak the truth, Job begins to describe the human condition. Although he ostensibly continues to address his friends in vv. 1-6, Job is primarily concerned to speak to God. Job first addresses God directly in v. 7 and continues to do so for the rest of the chapter. The unifying topic of the chapter is the nature of human existence, which Job invokes both to justify his own behavior and to bring God's into question.

7:1-2. As in chap. 6, Job's argument is developed through a grim play with several clusters of interrelated images. In the opening verses these include metaphors of work, payment, rest, and time. The three governing images for life in vv. 1-2—forced labor, day-labor, and slavery—are all characterized by subjection to someone else's power and will. Job's focus is more precise, however. As indicated by the clause "like the *days* of a day-laborer are his *days*," Job draws attention specifically to the way such conditions affect the experience of time. For such workers, the horizon of expectation is severely limited. The slave's sense of time is governed by the coming of evening shade (v. 2*a*), when the slave might cease work for the day. The day-laborer's expectation is also focused on the end of the day, when the worker was supposed to be paid (Deut 24:15), an arrangement often abused (Jer 22:13; Mal 3:5). Implicitly, the only satisfaction was in cessation of work and in meager reward, not in the work itself. As metaphors, these images create a relentlessly negative depiction of human existence.

7:3-5. In v. 3, Job applies the image to his own condition, which fails even to offer the meager rewards of the day-laborer. The theme of time is emphasized, as Job describes himself as being paid in the coin of time—months and nights. It is a defective payment, however, as the qualifying words "emptiness" (שוא *šāw'*) and "trouble" (עמל *'āmāl*) make clear. The phrase "nights of trouble" provides the transition to Job's examination of the other image, the slave who seeks rest in the shadows of evening. For Job there is no rest. What is striking about v. 4 is its rendering of the reality of time as experienced by one who cannot rest. Expected values are reversed. The night that should be desirable is treated with impatience. Time that should seem all too short is experienced as frustratingly prolonged. Verse 5 interrupts the sequence of images having to do with work and time. In one of the most graphically physical descriptions in the book, it describes Job's ravaged skin. Following v. 4, the description serves to explain why Job can get no rest. The reference to worms, which are part of the traditional imagery of death and decay (17:14; 21:26; 24:20; Isa 14:11), suggests how close to the border between death and life Job is.

7:6. The sense of contradictoriness in the experience of time, which was developed in v. 4, is renewed in v. 6 by the image of days moving quickly. The image of life as a cloth woven of a person's days is a common one in many cultures. Hezekiah speaks of his death in a similar image: "like a weaver I have rolled up my life;/ he cuts me off from the loom" (Isa 38:12 NRSV). The medieval Jewish writer Ibn Ezra invokes the image when he says "man in the world weaves like a weaver, and certainly his days are the thread."[129] Job's use of the image is characteristically subversive. He does not take the product of weaving— the cloth—as the image of life, as do Hezekiah and Ibn Ezra. Rather, the metaphor is the shuttle itself, specifically its repetitive back-and-forth movement. Job makes the same point with this image as he did with the image of the slave and the day-laborer. There is no accomplishment in Job's image of the shuttle. What makes the metaphor so devastating, however, is the play on words Job makes between the words "thread" and "hope" (both תקוה *tiqwâ*). The shuttle's incessant, repetitious movement simply stops abruptly "when the thread [*tiqwâ*] runs out," just as life abruptly stops "without hope [*tiqwâ*]."

7:7a. The sense of the tenuousness of life, developed in vv. 5-6, motivates Job's direct appeal to God in v. 7. Calling upon God to remember is a traditional motif of prayer. God may be asked to remember many things: the individual who prays (Judg 16:28), particular deeds or sufferings of the individual (2 Kgs 20:3; Ps 89:50[51]), or God's own mercy (Ps 25:6). When the psalmists say that God remembers that humans are mortal beings, creatures of dust (Ps 103:14) like a passing wind (Ps 78:39), the context has to do with God's compassionate restraint. Job, too, will ask for God's restraint, but in a way quite different from the psalmists.

7:7b-10. In v. 7*b*, Job introduces an image that will become increasingly important in the book, the image of the eye that gazes and the object of its gaze. In keeping with his theme of the transitoriness of human existence, in vv. 7-10

Job primarily uses the image to talk about what the eye cannot hold and fix. His own eye will not again "see happiness." More important is Job's association of the image of the gazing eye with God (vv. 8, 19). The association of God with sight is frequently made in the OT. Hagar calls God *El-roi,* "God of seeing" (Gen 16:13), and the psalmists often refer to God's attentive vision (Pss 11:4; 33:18; 34:15[16]; 139:16). Job's use of the motif, however, stresses the limits of that seeing, in particular the powerlessness of even God's gaze to hold its object in the face of the dissolution of death (v. 8*b*). Death is depicted as a kind of vanishing, compared with the way a cloud simply vanishes (v. 9*a*). Although Job invokes the traditional motif of death as a journey without return (v. 9*b*-10*a*),[130] he ties this motif to the imagery of vision in the last line of this series. The term rendered "know" is more properly a perceptual verb, "recognize" (נכר *nākar*), often associated with seeing (Gen 42:7; Ruth 3:14).[131] Although the connection is not made explicitly, this section is also about time. The limit of mortality on human time must always be considered. Moreover, the transition between life and death is a matter of an instant; it happens "in the blink of an eye," as we say.

7:11-21. 7:11. The misery of human life (vv. 1-6), which deprives experienced time of satisfaction, and the limits and suddenness of mortality (vv. 7-10) combine to create an urgent need to speak (v. 11). Cultural inhibitions against unrestrained speech were considerable. The wisdom tradition valued control of speech highly (Prov 10:19; 17:27). Job's situation, however, might better be compared with the psalmists'. They, too, recommended restraint of rash speech and trust in God (Ps 4:4[5]). Psalm 39 offers the closest comparison with Job 7, since in that psalm a sufferer struggles to keep silent but finally must speak out. There are even a number of motifs shared by the psalm and Job's words (cf. Ps 39:5[6] with Job 7:16*b*; Ps 39:11[12] with Job 7:18, 20; Ps 39:13[14] with Job 7:19); yet the difference in tone could not be more marked. The psalmist manages to shape the words forced

---

129. Cited in E. Dhorme, *A Commentary on the Book of Job,* trans. H. Knight (London: Nelson, 1967) 101.

130. N. Tromp, *Primitive Conceptions of Death and the Nether World in the Old Testament,* BibOr 21 (Rome: Pontifical Biblical Institute, 1969) 189-90.

131. Dhorme, *A Commentary on the Book of Job,* 103, translates "see again."

out by burning anguish into the forms and sentiments sanctioned by tradition (Ps 39:2-3[3-4]). Job, however, will deliberately savage traditional forms (vv. 17-18). Job describes his speech as being characterized by "anguish of spirit" and "bitterness of soul" (v. 11). Although these can be conventional terms for someone deeply grieved (Ps 4:1[2]; Isa 38:15; Ezek 27:31), "bitterness of soul" can also describe those who are so alienated that they defy social conventions and can even be dangerous (Judg 18:25; 1 Sam 22:2). Such alienation distinguishes Job's ironic and parodying speech from that of the psalmist.

7:12. Job begins his complaint with an ironic rhetorical question based on a mythological allusion (v. 12). Throughout the ancient Near East there were stories about the conflict between the deities who create and govern and the forces of chaos represented by the sea or sea monsters. In Mesopotamia, conflict between the god Marduk and the primordial sea Tiamat forms the central plot of the creation epic, the *Enuma Elish*.[132] In Ugarit, Baal's kingship is secured by his victory over Yam, the sea. The goddess Anat also fights Yam and muzzles the dragon Tannin.[133] Israel, too, recounted Yahweh's victory over Yam the sea and Tannin the dragon as part of the creation and governance of the world (Ps 74:13; cf. Isa 27:1; 51:9).[134]

The ironic contrast in v. 12 between Job, a person of fleeting days, and the great cosmic opponents of God serves as an accusation that God is treating Job with an intensity wholly disproportionate to his significance, a point that Job will make more explicitly in vv. 17-19 and v. 20. What is less transparent is the way in which Job characterizes this divine treatment. Unlike 6:4, where he used the image of an attack, Job here speaks of God's putting a "guard" or a "watch" on him. Although it has been suggested that Job is making an allusion to a specific mythic motif, such as Marduk's posting a guard to keep the waters of the sky in place, the analogy is not that close.[135] Job's image of a "guard" appears not to be drawn specifically from a myth but represents

132. James B. Pritchard, ed., *Ancient Near Eastern Texts Relating to the Old Testament* (*ANET*), 3rd ed. with supplement (Princeton: Princeton University Press, 1969) 60-72.

133. Ibid., 129-42.

134. See D. A. Diewert, "Job 7:12: Yam, Tannin and the Surveillance of Job," *JBL* 106 (1987) 203-15, for a thorough review of the ancient Near Eastern and biblical parallels.

135. Ibid., 204.

his interpretation of his own situation. Although the Hebrew term involved (שמר *šāmar*) is not semantically related to words for seeing, as the English word *watch* is, the aspect of surveillance is very much a part of the concept of "setting a guard against" someone (see Neh 4:22-23[4:16-17]). Job will develop this notion of surveillance in the following verses.

7:13-16. In v. 13, Job turns to a traditional psalmic motif: the sufferer in the privacy of the sickbed. In the psalms, the bed is the place of quiet introspection (Ps 4:4[5]), or the place of weeping, to which God hears and responds (Ps 6:6[7]), healing the sick (Ps 41:3[4]). Job, however, undercuts that traditional motif by charging that instead of finding comfort and relief in his bed, he is subjected by God to terrifying dreams and visions (v. 14). The image is an aggressive, invasive one, a psychic counterpart to the physical image of piercing arrows in 6:4. Dreams and visions are a type of forced seeing and serve here as a counterpart to God's surveillance of Job; God watches Job, but Job's vision is filled with horrors. The notion of dreams as a means of divine aggression is unusual, although it may be what Eliphaz and Bildad refer to as the nameless terrors that pursue the wicked (15:21; 18:11; cf. Sir 40:6).

In Job's case, such divine aggression reinforces his desire to die (v. 15). As in chap. 6, Job's language for himself is graphically physical, much more so than the translations usually suggest. The word translated simply as "I" is נפש (*nepeš*), which literally designates the air passage in the throat. The word rendered "body" is literally "bones" (עצם *'eṣem*). Thus "my throat would choose strangling, [and I would choose] death rather than my own bones." Job concludes this section with the image of his life's being as transient as a puff of air (v. 16*b*), echoing his appeal to God in v. 7.

7:17-21. The last section of the chapter opens with Job's bitter parody of Psalm 8:4[5]. In the psalm, humankind's confessed insignificance vis-à-vis the moon and the stars serves as a foil for grateful acknowledgment that God has given humans an exalted place of dominion over creation (cf. Ps 144:3). Job draws the image into the themes of divine surveillance and of God's absurd exaggeration of danger, already introduced in v.

12. Thus the first verb, "make great," "magnify" (גדל *gādal*), echoes the descriptions of exaltation in Ps 8:5-6[6-7]; here, however, the sarcastic intent is unmistakable, as Job questions God's sense of proportion. Where the psalmist marveled at God's mindfulness of human beings and care for them, Job reinterprets this divine attentiveness as unwelcome scrutiny (v. 17*b*). Hebrew allows a particularly clever word play, since the same verb that the psalmist uses to mean "care for" (פקד *pāqad*) can also mean "inspect" or even "call to account" (v. 18*a*).

The paradoxes of time, which were explored at the beginning of the chapter, return in v. 16 and in vv. 17-19. As a human being, Job's days are as transient as a breath of air (v. 16*a*). Yet he would not choose to live forever (v. 16*b*), because of God's unrelenting presence, which is expressed in successively smaller units of time—every morning, every moment (v. 18). When Job speaks of a period of relief, he does so characteristically in terms of time as measured by the body, long enough to "swallow my spit" (v. 19*b*). This image, like those of v. 14-15, also suggests the invasive quality of divine scrutiny, which interferes with even the most intimate of bodily functions.

Job's alienation from the traditional language of prayer is underscored when one compares vv. 19-21 with Psalm 39. As in Job 7:19, the psalmist also makes the unusual plea that God turn away God's gaze (Ps 39:13[14]). The accompanying reflection on sin, however, is quite different. The psalmist pleads with God to "deliver me from all my [transgressions]" (Ps 39:8[9] NRSV), acknowledging the legitimacy of divine anger but pleading for relief because human existence is "mere breath" (Ps 39:11[12]; cf. Job 7:16) and the psalmist will soon "be no more" (Ps 39:13[14]; cf. Job 7:21). Whether one takes Job's opening words in v. 20 to be hypothetical, as most do, or confessional,[136] what Job says is no prayer. Pursuing the logic of his meditation on human transiency and

insignificance, Job insists that he cannot have harmed God, a calculation that would be utterly alien to the psalmist. This assertion motivates his question of why God does not simply pardon whatever offenses Job has committed. Neither sin nor the forgiveness of sin would be of much consequence to God. This is not the thinking of traditional piety, in which the seriousness of sin and the generosity of God's compassion are taken with utmost seriousness (e.g., Psalm 32).

That Job's mode is parody rather than prayer is evident also from the epithet "watcher of humans" (v. 20). The related verb (נצר *nāṣar*) is often used in the psalms to describe God as protector (e.g., Pss 12:7[8]; 32:7; 40:11[12]; 140:1, 4[2, 5]). Job's development of the theme of divine surveillance, however, gives this epithet a wholly different and more threatening character.

It is more difficult to determine Job's tone in the last half-verse of the chapter (v. 21*b*). At issue is how one takes the introductory words. They can be translated "for now"/"for soon," as in the NRSV and the NIV, indicating that God must act quickly, since Job will soon be dead. If God then seeks Job out in order to restore him, it will be too late. In this interpretation, Job ends his speech on a pleading note, not unlike the ending of Psalm 39. Given what has preceded, it seems likely that Job is imitating the words of a plea but subverting the meaning. One can also take the first two words as introducing a consequence, "for then" (i.e., "If you forgive me, then thus and so will happen").[137] In this reading, Job says in essence that the consequence of divine forgiveness will be that he is allowed to die.[138] And when God searches for him in renewed surveillance, Job will be safely beyond God's power, for he "will be no more" (cf. v. 8).[139] Such a sentiment would provide a fitting conclusion for Job's anti-psalm.

136. So F. Andersen, *Job: An Introduction and Commentary,* Tyndale Old Testament Commentaries (Downers Grove, Ill.: Inter-Varsity, 1976) 132.

137. Cf. G. Fohrer, *Das Buch Hiob,* KAT xvi (Guetersloh: Gerd Mohn, 1963) 164.
138. R. Gordis, *The Book of Job: Commentary, New Translation, and Special Studies* (New York: Jewish Theological Seminary, 5738/1978) 68, 83.
139. N. Habel, *The Book of Job,* OTL (Philadelphia: Westminster, 1985) 167.

REFLECTIONS

The bitterness Job expresses through his savage parody of the language of psalms arises from his sense of contradiction between the image of God as it has been traditionally rendered in psalms and the image of God that seems necessary to account for Job's recent experiences. Job takes over unchallenged from his culture the assumption that extraordinary suffering is to be understood as the action of God, specifically a response to sin (vv. 20-21). The lack of proportion between whatever sin he might have committed and the extent of his devastation is incomprehensible to him, however, and in order to make it comprehensible, he must imagine the type of God capable of acting in such a fashion. The disparity of his experience leads him to conclude that only a God madly obsessed with scrutinizing and punishing human behavior could act this way.

The assumptions of Job and his friends about suffering as punishment for sin is not entirely a relic of the past. It crops up from time to time in religious polemics, almost always in a mean-spirited way. It also emerges, sometimes to the surprise of the individual in question, in the instinctive response to misfortune: "What have I done to deserve this?" One of the distinctive features of contemporary religious thinking, however, is a tendency to reject the notion that God intentionally inflicts suffering on people as punishment. One might think, therefore, that people who do not share the assumptions of Job concerning sin and punishment would read chap. 7 with a sense of detachment. Yet often, even people who do not in any way share that perspective are nevertheless deeply drawn into Job's anger. What makes Job's outcry so compelling even to persons who do not share his theological assumptions? It may be because Job speaks so powerfully about the fragility of human life and its propensity to misery. For many human beings there is no escape from harassing powers and oppressive structures. As in Job's description, their lives are deprived of even the most limited autonomy as they struggle from day to day, all dignity denied by incessant oppression. For those who suffer unrelentingly, there is no luxury of unlimited time. As Job observes, human life is bounded inexorably by death. This is the reservoir of outrage that Job's words open.

Modern reflection on human suffering often focuses on the role of the immediate causes of misery: political oppression, economic exploitation, the destruction of family and social structures, the deadly combination of ethnic prejudice and power. For the religious, however, Job's question about the nature of the God who presides over a world in which such things happen is finally inescapable. In his speech, Job models a kind of theological reflection that insists on beginning with the concrete realities of life. What image of God makes sense in the context of undeniable, incessant, unending misery? Job's answer is that it is a God who gazes, like a child poking an anthill, entranced by the spectacle of brokenness and confusion. The temptation, when one is confronted with such a radical claim, is to reject and dismiss it as the raving of someone whose misfortunes have caused him to lose perspective (6:26). It may be the case, however, that those who are pushed to the limits of endurance are precisely the ones who no longer deceive themselves with the platitudes that blind the comfortable with an easy self-deception.

How does someone who is that angry and that alienated speak about God or to God? Anyone who has experienced such intense alienation knows how infuriating much conventional religious language can be. The cheerful hymns of assurance and the bland responsive readings appear intentionally blind to all the pain in the world. The benign image of God they project seems disconcertingly like the packaged images of politicians running for office and deflects serious questioning in much the same way. At such times, it is not surprising that one wants to tear apart conventional religious language that seems intent on denying the spiritual agony of religious persons struggling with the hard realities of life. Taking the words of easy assurance and placing them in a context in which their shallowness is exposed, as Job does in chap. 7, is not only satisfying but also an important step toward making a more honest and adequate religious language possible.

Although exposing the inadequacy of much conventional religious language is part of what is involved in the "anti-psalms" Job utters, there is another dimension that should not be overlooked. The poignancy of these words arises from the sense of betrayal that echoes through them. Savaging the words of a traditional prayer or hymn can often be a way of expressing the painful sense that God has betrayed the relationship. The old familiar words expressed who one had understood God to be; they were the promises of God's love and presence. Now it is God who seems to make a mockery of everything upon which one had relied. Like a betrayed lover, one feels a fool for having been taken in. Flinging the shreds of that language of prayer and praise back at God is a way of protesting such treatment. The Bible does not shy away from this way of talking to God. Although Job's speeches are the most sustained words of protest, Jeremiah also voiced the sense of having been betrayed by God, when he said:

> O LORD, you deceived me, and I was deceived;
> you overpowered me and prevailed.
> I am ridiculed all day long;
> everyone mocks me. (Jer 20:7 NIV)

The Commentary argued that Job's words are not prayer. This is certainly true in the sense that Job does not use conventional forms of prayer or compose his emotions into those traditionally shaped by psalmic prayers. But in the more profound sense, is it prayer? One should not answer that question too quickly. Not all angry language addressed to God is prayer. It may make a pastor or a spiritual adviser more comfortable to think so, but one should probably make distinctions. Such discrimination requires careful listening. There are some angry words that are a prelude to the indifference that comes from the death of a relationship. Yet other angry words, no matter how laced with the protective rhetoric of sarcasm, do not have the mark of finality about them. In subtle ways they seek a response. So it is with Job's speech, above all in the ambiguity with which he uses the expression "you will search for me" in his concluding words (v. 21). Job's words are the prayer of a person who cannot "pray," but whose conversation with God is far from over.

Job 8:1-22, A Metaphor of Two Plants

NIV	NRSV
8 Then Bildad the Shuhite replied:	**8** Then Bildad the Shuhite answered:
2"How long will you say such things? Your words are a blustering wind.	2 "How long will you say these things, and the words of your mouth be a great wind?
3Does God pervert justice? Does the Almighty pervert what is right?	3 Does God pervert justice? Or does the Almighty[a] pervert the right?
4When your children sinned against him, he gave them over to the penalty of their sin.	4 If your children sinned against him, he delivered them into the power of their transgression.
5But if you will look to God and plead with the Almighty,	5 If you will seek God and make supplication to the Almighty,[a]
6if you are pure and upright, even now he will rouse himself on your behalf and restore you to your rightful place.	6 if you are pure and upright,

a Traditional rendering of Heb *Shaddai*

NIV

[7]Your beginnings will seem humble,
so prosperous will your future be.

[8]"Ask the former generations
and find out what their fathers learned,
[9]for we were born only yesterday and know
nothing,
and our days on earth are but a shadow.
[10]Will they not instruct you and tell you?
Will they not bring forth words from their
understanding?
[11]Can papyrus grow tall where there is no marsh?
Can reeds thrive without water?
[12]While still growing and uncut,
they wither more quickly than grass.
[13]Such is the destiny of all who forget God;
so perishes the hope of the godless.
[14]What he trusts in is fragile[a];
what he relies on is a spider's web.
[15]He leans on his web, but it gives way;
he clings to it, but it does not hold.
[16]He is like a well-watered plant in the sunshine,
spreading its shoots over the garden;
[17]it entwines its roots around a pile of rocks
and looks for a place among the stones.
[18]But when it is torn from its spot,
that place disowns it and says, 'I never saw
you.'
[19]Surely its life withers away,
and[b] from the soil other plants grow.

[20]"Surely God does not reject a blameless man
or strengthen the hands of evildoers.
[21]He will yet fill your mouth with laughter
and your lips with shouts of joy.
[22]Your enemies will be clothed in shame,
and the tents of the wicked will be no more."

a14 The meaning of the Hebrew for this word is uncertain.
b19 Or Surely all the joy it has / is that

NRSV

surely then he will rouse himself for you
and restore to you your rightful place.
[7] Though your beginning was small,
your latter days will be very great.

[8] "For inquire now of bygone generations,
and consider what their ancestors have
found;
[9] for we are but of yesterday, and we know
nothing,
for our days on earth are but a shadow.
[10] Will they not teach you and tell you
and utter words out of their understanding?

[11] "Can papyrus grow where there is no marsh?
Can reeds flourish where there is no water?
[12] While yet in flower and not cut down,
they wither before any other plant.
[13] Such are the paths of all who forget God;
the hope of the godless shall perish.
[14] Their confidence is gossamer,
a spider's house their trust.
[15] If one leans against its house, it will not stand;
if one lays hold of it, it will not endure.
[16] The wicked thrive[a] before the sun,
and their shoots spread over the garden.
[17] Their roots twine around the stoneheap;
they live among the rocks.[b]
[18] If they are destroyed from their place,
then it will deny them, saying, 'I have never
seen you.'
[19] See, these are their happy ways,[c]
and out of the earth still others will spring.

[20] "See, God will not reject a blameless person,
nor take the hand of evildoers.
[21] He will yet fill your mouth with laughter,
and your lips with shouts of joy.
[22] Those who hate you will be clothed with
shame,
and the tent of the wicked will be no more."

a Heb He thrives   b Gk Vg: Meaning of Heb uncertain
c Meaning of Heb uncertain

COMMENTARY

In chap. 6, Job complained about the failure of his friends to respond to him as they should (see 6:24, 26, 30). Bildad attempts to address Job's challenge, at least according to his own understanding of it. Job's invitation to "teach me" is certainly congenial to Bildad, whose speech has a distinctly didactic flavor. How one understands the structure of Bildad's speech depends on the resolution of difficult interpretive problems in vv. 16-19 (see below). The speech is best understood as organized throughout according to a set of contrasts. After a verse referring to the nature of Job's words (v. 2), Bildad begins the first part of his speech with the general principle that governs his whole understanding (v. 3). Following from this general principle, Bildad contrasts the fate of Job's children (v. 4) with Job's own prospects (vv. 5-7). The second part of the speech is introduced by an appeal to the authority of ancient tradition (vv. 8-10). Two contrasting metaphorical descriptions compare the fate of the godless (vv. 11-15) with that of the blameless person (vv. 16-19). The point of this metaphorical comparison is made explicit in v. 20, which contrasts God's relation to the blameless and the evildoer. The speech comes to an end with a prediction of the very different futures in store for Job (v. 21) and his enemies (v. 22).

8:1-2. Bildad begins, as will most of the speakers, with a criticism of the previous speaker's words (cf. 11:2-3; 12:2-3; 15:2-6; 16:2-3; 18:2-3; 19:2-3; 20:2-3; 21:2-3; 26:2-4). This technique is a familiar part of a disputation, not only in Israel but also in Mesopotamian wisdom literature. In the Babylonian Theodicy, for instance, one of the characters says to the other, "My reliable fellow, holder of knowledge, your thoughts are perverse, you have forsaken right and blaspheme against your God's designs."[140] The frequency of such remarks in Job is unusual, however. It draws attention to the crisis of human words and human wisdom that is thematic in the book of Job.

The way Bildad formulates his criticism echoes Job's complaint in 6:26 that the friends treat his words as so much "wind." Most commonly, "wind" (רוח *rûaḥ*) connotes something insubstantial and empty (cf. Job 15:2; 16:3; Isa 41:29; Jer 5:13; Mic 2:11). Bildad, however, changes the traditional image by referring to Job's words as a "mighty wind" (רוח כביר *rûaḥ kabbîr*). Something that is *kabbîr* is the very opposite of insubstantial;

it must be reckoned with, like the "mighty waters" of Isa 28:2 (cf. Job 15:10; 34:17, 24; Isa 17:12). Calling Job's words a "mighty wind" draws attention not only to their emptiness but also and almost paradoxically to the destructiveness inherent in their emptiness (cf. the "great wind" that destroyed the house of Job's eldest son, 1:19).[141]

8:3-7. To refute Job's unsatisfactory words, Bildad produces an axiom in the form of a rhetorical question. The word order puts the emphasis on "El" (אל *ʾēl*) and "Shaddai" (שדי *šadday*), the terms for God. Thus Bildad makes God's character the issue. The values Bildad specifies, "justice" (משפט *mišpāṭ*) and "the right" (צדק *ṣedeq*), are frequently used in combination to describe the just order of the world established and commanded by God.[142] According to tradition, nothing could be more intrinsic to God's nature than *mišpāṭ* and *ṣedeq*. They are the foundation of God's throne (Ps 97:2), what God loves (Ps 33:5), God's gift to the king (Ps 72:1-2), what God expects of Israel (Isa 5:7), and what God will give to Zion (Isa 33:5). *Mišpāṭ* and *ṣedeq* are the basis of the covenant in Hosea (2:19 [21]) and God's demand in Amos (5:24). The notion that God would pervert them is, according to tradition, simply unthinkable. Bildad's faith in the axioms of tradition may be unshakable, but for Job the question Bildad poses in v. 3 is not rhetorical but painfully real.[143]

For Bildad, the axiom about God serves as the fixed point from which Job's situation can be properly understood. In Hebrew, vv. 4, 5, and 6 all begin with the same word, "if" (אם *ʾim*). As the NIV recognizes, however, v. 4, concerning the sin of Job's children, is not hypothetical for Bildad, but a deduction from the fact of their violent and unexpected deaths and the axiom that God does not pervert the right.[144] Unbeknownst to Bildad, Job, too, had entertained concerns about the possible sins of his children, but had

140. W. G. Lambert, *Babylonian Wisdom Literature* (Oxford: Oxford University Press, 1960) 77. This and other examples are cited in Habel, *The Book of Job,* 173.

141. D. Clines, *Job 1–20,* WBC 17 (Dallas: Word, 1989) 202; contra Fohrer, *Das Buch Hiob,* 188.

142. J. J. Scullion, "Righteousness (OT)," *Anchor Bible Dictionary,* ed. D. N. Freedman (New York: Doubleday, 1992) V:727, 731.

143. J. G. Janzen, *Job,* Interpretation (Atlanta: John Knox, 1985) 87-88.

144. So Gordis, *The Book of Job,* 88; M. Pope, *Job,* 3rd ed., AB 15 (Garden City, N.Y.: Doubleday, 1979) 64; Habel, *The Book of Job,* 169; Clines, *Job 1–20,* 198; contra Dhorme, *A Commentary on the Book of Job,* 113; E. Good, *In Turns of Tempest* (Stanford, Calif.: Stanford University Press, 1990) 68.

assumed that his actions on their behalf would protect them (1:5; cf. Ezek 14:20). Bildad's words seem grossly insensitive, and it may well be that he is presented as the type of the rigid, doctrinaire moralist who loses his humanity in his desire to perceive the world according to a set of rules. His certitude is implicitly ridiculed by the author, who has let the reader know that the deaths of Job's children have nothing to do with any sin at all. It will not do simply to dismiss Bildad as a caricature, however, for he articulates one side of a complex moral problematic in ancient Israel concerning sin and its consequences. The larger context of Bildad's position is discussed in the Reflections below.

Bildad does not explicitly say whether he thinks Job has sinned. Given Bildad's views, he must assume so, else how could he account for Job's other catastrophic losses and his ominous skin disease? The critical difference is that God has not taken Job's life, perhaps indicating that Job's sin was not as serious as that of his children.[145] In any event, that is not Bildad's main concern. Like Eliphaz, he is primarily concerned to reassure Job about the prospects for his future restoration. Bildad's advice in v. 5 echoes that of Eliphaz in 5:8. In contrast to Eliphaz's advice, however, Bildad's words in vv. 5-6 are true conditionals. Job must do two things. First, he must approach God in the spirit of true piety, seeking God (cf. Ps 63:1[2]; Isa 26:9; Hos 5:15) and imploring God's favor (cf. Pss 30:8[9]; 142:1[2]). Second, Job must be morally "pure and upright." The image of restoration at the end of v. 6 may be understood in more than one way. Some translate "restore your righteous abode"[146] or "safeguard your righteous dwelling."[147] The interpretation reflected in the NRSV and the NIV, however, better reflects Bildad's understanding of how God acts. The verb translated "restore" (שלם *šillam*) is often used in legal contexts for restitution, or in contexts of payment of debt or other settling of accounts. Frequently, it serves an image of divine judgment, in which God "pays back" a person for deeds committed, both negatively (e.g., Deut 32:

41; 2 Sam 3:39; Jer 51:56) and positively (e.g., Ruth 2:12; 1 Sam 24:19[20]). Similarly, the translation "rightful place" captures Bildad's belief that a person's outward circumstances should correspond to that person's character, and he believes in Job's fundamentally good character (vv. 20-21).

Bildad concludes his description of Job's restoration with a rhetorical flourish, contrasting past and future (v. 7). Like Eliphaz in 5:17-26, Bildad avoids talking about Job's present sufferings, preferring to focus on the future. Bildad's schematic terms for time contrast sharply with Job's perception of time as constricted by suffering (7:1-3) and measured by the body's experience (7:4-6).

Throughout this section the reader's knowledge of the real cause of Job's misfortunes creates irony at Bildad's expense. His pompous certainty is exposed as false and his ideas discredited. The chapter lays the groundwork for a more difficult irony, however. What Bildad predicts in v. 7 is close to what actually happens. There is even a verbal echo when it is said in 42:12 that "Yahweh blessed the *latter* days of Job more than his *former* days," describing how Job's possessions were restored to him twofold (42:10).

8:8-10. Bildad invokes the authority of ancestral tradition to introduce his comparison of the fate of the wicked and the fate of the righteous (vv. 11-19). The appeal to ancient tradition is a familiar motif in biblical rhetoric (cf. Deut 4:32-35; 32:7-9; Isa 40:21-24; 46:8-11).[148] Here, Bildad creates a sense of the chain of tradition by referring first to a former generation and then to the ancestors who preceded them (cf. Sir 8:9). Although some argue that Bildad is referring to "the previous generations in the more recent past,"[149] similar appeals stress the primordial nature of tradition (cf. Deut 4:32; Isa 40:21).[150] Both in Mesopotamia and in Israel there was a belief that the antediluvian generations possessed special knowledge. One of the oldest existing wisdom texts, The Instructions of Shuruppak, is presented as the instructions of the survivor of the flood to

145. Fohrer, *Das Buch Hiob,* 189-90; D. Clines, "The Arguments of Job's Three Friends," in *Art and Meaning: Rhetoric in Biblical Literature,* ed. D. Clines, D. Gunn, A. Hauser, *JSOTSup* 19 (Sheffield: JSOT, 1982) 206.

146. Habel, *The Book of Job,* 167; Clines, *Job 1-20,* 197.

147. Gordis, *The Book of Job,* 86.

148. The classic study is that of N. Habel, "Appeal to Ancient Tradition as a Literary Form," *ZAW* 88 (1976) 253-72.

149. Dhorme, *A Commentary on the Book of Job,* 116; similarly Gordis, *The Book of Job,* 89.

150. Habel, "Appeal to Ancient Tradition as a Literary Form," 255.

his son.[151] In post-exilic Israel, too, traditions developed about the wisdom of the long-lived, antediluvian patriarchs, especially Enoch.[152] Wisdom itself is personified as a primordial figure (Prov 8:22-31).

The crucial role that antiquity plays in authenticating and discrediting claims to wisdom is embodied in the contrast between the vista of generations receding into antiquity in v. 8 and the abrupt metaphor in v. 9a ("we are but of yesterday, and we know nothing"). In v. 9b, Bildad echoes ideas and words Job had used in his speech ("shadow," 7:2; "days," 7:1, 6, 16; "upon the earth," 7:1). The notion of the ephemerality of human life is a common motif, especially in the psalms (e.g., Pss 90:5-6; 102:11[12]; 103:14-16; 109:23). There, however, it is used, as Job employs it, to establish a contrast between the nature of divine and human existence, not as Bildad uses it, to discredit knowledge based on an individual's experience.

Job had asked his friends to teach him and show him where he had been wrong (6:24). Bildad both demurs and accepts this invitation. *He* cannot teach Job, for Bildad includes himself in the category of those who "know nothing" (v. 9). It is the ancestors who must teach Job (v. 10). Although he does not say so explicitly, Bildad presents himself as a conduit through which tradition passes, pure and undistorted.

8:11-15. Bildad's teaching is traditional. First, he cites a proverb (v. 11), which might be used in any of a number of contexts to make various points. Next, he develops the proverb in a mini-narrative. Staying within the metaphorical world of the proverb, he unfolds the features of the saying that are relevant to the situation he addresses (v. 12). Finally, he makes explicit application to human experience (v. 13). A second comparison with an image from nature underscores the moral (vv. 14-15).

The saying in v. 11 is a nature proverb concerning the relation of cause and effect. Such proverbs are to be found in every culture. Compare the Mesopotamian proverb, "The mother brew is bitter. How is the beer sweet?"[153] Or the

Israelite proverb, "For lack of wood the fire goes out" (Prov 26:20a NRSV). Bildad develops the relevant aspects of the proverb by describing how an apparently flourishing and green plant withers before its time (v. 12). The cause: no water; the effect: premature death. Proverbs work by establishing analogies. Thus in the application in v. 13 God is implicitly compared to the water essential for life, whereas "those who forget God" and "the godless" correspond to the plants. The analogy with Job's children is unmistakable (v. 4).

In v. 13a, the NRSV follows the MT, "the *paths* of all who forget God" (ארחות *ʾorḥôt*), while the NIV follows the LXX, "the *destiny*" (τὰ ἔσχατα *ta eschata* = אחרית *ʾaḥărît*). The parallelism with the future-oriented word "hope" (תקוה *tiqwâ*) in v. 13b might favor reading "destiny," but perhaps the author is playing with the similar sounds and appearance in Hebrew of the two words "paths"/"destiny" to suggest the close connection between chronic behavior and ultimate consequences (cf. Prov 1:19).

The smooth translations of v. 14a in the NRSV and the NIV mask difficult textual problems.[154] The basic meaning is clear, however, from the parallel in v. 14b, where what the godless person relies upon is compared with a spider's web, literally, a spider's "house," which cannot support the weight of one who leans upon it (v. 15).

8:16-19. 8:16. These verses pose the most difficult exegetical problem of chap. 8. Do they provide a second comparison of the godless to a plant that first thrives and then dies?[155] Or do they provide a contrasting comparison of the blameless person who endures despite harsh conditions and thrives after apparent disaster?[156] The latter interpretation, already suggested by the medieval Jewish commentator Saadiah,[157] appears the more likely. It fits well with Bildad's preference for contrasting fates in vv. 4-7 and 20-22. Moreover, the comparison of the righteous and the wicked under the image of two plants is a rhetorical device that also occurs in Jer 17:5-8 and

151. *ANET,* 594-96.

152. J. Collins, "The Sage in Apocalyptic and Pseudepigraphic Literature," in *The Sage in Israel and the Ancient Near East,* ed. J. Gammie and L. Perdue (Winona Lake, Ind.: Eisenbrauns, 1990) 344-47.

153. W. G. Lambert, *Babylonian Wisdom Literature* (Oxford: Oxford University Press, 1960) 271.

154. See Pope, *Job,* 66-67; and Clines, *Job 1–20,* 199-200.

155. So F. Horst, *Hiob,* Biblischer Kommentar xvi (Neukirchen-Vlun: Neukirchener Verlag, 1960) 133-34; Fohrer, *Das Buch Hiob,* 193; Clines, *Job 1–20,* 209-10; Good, *In Turns of Tempest,* 219-20.

156. So Gordis, *The Book of Job,* 521, followed by Habel, *The Book of Job,* 177-78; J. E. Hartley, *The Book of Job,* NICOT (Grand Rapids, Mich.: Eerdmans, 1988) 161-63; J. G. Janzen, *Job,* 85-86.

157. Saadiah ben Joseph al-Fayyumi, *The Book of Theodicy,* trans. by L. E. Goodman (New Haven: Yale University Press, 1988) 217, 220.

Psalm 1. Although no transitional phrase in v. 16 signals a change in topic, the contrast is established by the first word in the verse. Whereas vv. 11-12 were concerned with the plant that lacked water, the first word of v. 16 is "the well-watered (plant)." (The NRSV, misleadingly, supplies the phrase "the wicked" and translates the adjective "well-watered" as a verb.)

8:17. Like the tree planted by water in Jer 17:8, which stays green even during the hottest times, the well-watered plant in v. 16 grows healthily even under the hot sun. The growth of the shoots in v. 16*b* finds its counterpart in the growth of the plant's roots in v. 17*a*. The notion of a plant "looking for" or "gazing at" a house of stones (v. 17*b*; יחזה *yeḥĕzeh*) strikes some interpreters as so odd that they prefer to emend the text to "live" (יחיה *yiḥyeh,* following the LXX; so the NRSV) or to "grasp" (יאחזו *y'ōḥĕzû*).[158] Whatever the verb, the image of the house of stones, with its suggestion of strength, contrasts with the insubstantial spider's house of v. 14. A plant that winds its roots around rocks is solidly grounded.

8:18. Surprisingly, however, v. 18 describes the plant being torn from its place. The contrast between two symbolic plants does not ordinarily contain such a detail (cf. Jer 17:5-8; Psalm 1). Bildad, however, is applying the traditional motif to Job's situation. Just as his earlier proverb corresponded to the premature deaths of Job's children (v. 12), so also the traditional motif of the well-watered plant is adapted to correspond to the situation of Job, a basically good person who has experienced an unexpected disaster. There is even an echo of Job's own rhetoric in the personification of the place that does not recognize (7:10) or denies having seen (8:18) its former occupant.

8:19. Unfortunately, v. 19 is difficult to interpret. The first part of the verse reads, "See, such is the joy of his way" (cf. NRSV). Those who understand the passage as applying to the wicked must either take the phrase ironically or emend the text, as the NIV does (reading "withers" [מסוס

mĕsôs] instead of "joy" [משוש *māśôś*]). More naturally, the phrase seems to introduce the good news of the plant's revival. The last part of the verse can be translated in ways that complement either interpretation. The ambiguity is that one word (אחר *'aḥēr*) may be read as a noun ("another"), as an adjective ("other soil"), or as an adverb ("later," perhaps emending to *'aḥar*). In keeping with their interpretation of the plant as a symbol of the wicked, the NRSV and the NIV adopt the first alternative. Those who understand the passage as referring to the righteous translate either "such is the joy of its way, that from other soil it sprouts forth"[159] or "such is the joy of its way, that from the soil later it sprouts forth."[160] The latter translation seems better. The "later" (*'aḥēr/'aḥar*) return of the plant echoes the restoration in the "latter days" (*'aḥarît*) that Bildad foresees for Job in v. 7.[161]

8:20-22. Verse 20, with its contrast between the blameless and the evildoers, serves as a summary of the preceding teaching, as well as a reaffirmation of Bildad's initial axiom about God's justice (v. 3). The term "blameless" (תם *tām*) was used to describe Job by the narrator (1:1) and by God (1:8). In the last two verses, Bildad again addresses Job in the second person. The image of a mouth filled with laughter and exuberant shouts is elsewhere associated with restoration from calamity (Job 33:26; Ps 126:2; cf. Ps 27:6). In making reference to God's shaming Job's enemies (v. 22), Bildad simply draws on the traditional language of the psalmists. Ironically, in Psalms these enemies are sometimes described as persons who turn against the one who suffers, because they take such suffering as proof of sin (cf. Ps 35:11-15; 109:29).[162] By the end of the dialogue, Job's friends will have become just such enemies.

---

158. E.g., M. Pope, *Job,* 3rd ed., AB 15 (Garden City, N.Y.: Doubleday, 1979) 67.

159. Similarly, R. Gordis, *The Book of Job: Commentary, New Translation, and Special Studies* (New York: Jewish Theological Seminary, 5738/1978) 93; cf. N. Habel, *The Book of Job,* OTL (Philadelphia: Westminster, 1985) 168.

160. Similarly, J. G. Janzen, *Job,* Interpretation (Atlanta: John Knox, 1985) 86.

161. Ibid., 86.

162. G. Fohrer, *Das Buch Hiob,* KAT xvi (Guetersloh: Gerd Mohn, 1963) 194.

REFLECTIONS

It is all too easy to dismiss Bildad as boorish and insensitive to Job's suffering. To judge him simply according to the standards of pastoral care, ancient or modern, is to overlook the fact that the book of Job is a drama of ideas as much as it is a drama of human suffering. The moral position Bildad represents was an important part of a long and never fully resolved deliberation in ancient Israel concerning the moral consequences of deeds and the relation between the individual and the community. It is not possible to do justice to the complexity of the issue in this brief reflection. At its most basic level, however, the issue concerns whether the responsibility and consequences for sin were understood to be corporate (whether within a family or settlement, or extending between generations, or between ruler and people) or limited to the individual. Intergenerational inheritance of the consequences of sin is reflected in the popular proverb cited by both Jeremiah and Ezekiel, "The fathers have eaten sour grapes,/ and the children's teeth are set on edge" (Jer 31:29 NIV; Ezek 18:2; cf. also Joshua 7; 2 Sam 13:13-14; 21:1-9). Both Jeremiah and Ezekiel, however, repudiate the popular proverb (Jer 31:27-30; Ezekiel 18; cf. Deut 24:16; 2 Kgs 14:5-6). Ezekiel's long treatment of individual responsibility is particularly important for understanding Bildad's moral stance. Although Ezekiel was addressing the problem that the generation of the Babylonian exile had with accepting responsibility for its own situation, he formulates his teaching in terms of case examples concerning a father, a son, and a grandson. Ezekiel's conclusion in every case is that each one bears the responsibility for and the consequences of his own actions: "The person who sins shall die" (Ezek 18:20a NRSV). Even in the course of an individual life, the sinner who repents will live and not die (Ezek 18:21-23). This is precisely the stance that Bildad embodies in his reply to Job (vv. 3-7). Job's children were their own moral agents, not extensions of Job's moral identity. Job's fate remains in his own hands. It is critical to recognize the context that shapes Bildad's thinking and hence the way in which a longstanding moral controversy is introduced into the book of Job.

It is difficult for a modern person to take Bildad seriously because he does not question two crucial assumptions. First, Bildad does not question the assumption that he can deduce the cause (sin) from the effect (death); second, neither he nor Job questions the theological assumption that God uses illness, destruction, and death as punishment for individual sins. If, however, one takes the issue of individual vs. corporate moral responsibility out of the limits of Bildad's frame of reference and places it in a more general framework, then one suddenly discovers that far from being an obvious question that was settled long ago, the question of who bears the moral responsibility for sin is a very lively question in our own time. The consequences of one person's sin often do fall upon another. Justice may demand that one generation make right the wrongs of a previous generation, even at great cost to itself. And yet there is something compelling in the insistence that morally no person can be treated as simply an extension of another. These are the complex issues that the post–World War II generation in Germany has struggled with. Although these persons were not responsible for the Holocaust, they have largely acknowledged that they have a moral duty to make reparations, to uncover the truth, to warn others. Americans have been much more conflicted about acknowledging intergenerational responsibility for the consequences of the sin of slavery. The complex question of individual vs. corporate responsibility is also present in smaller contexts in the events of everyday life. Especially in fairly small, closed communities, it is easy for the sins of the parents to be unfairly visited on the children, at least in terms of reputation and public opinion.

There are times, however, when it is appropriate for an individual to take responsibility for the misdeeds of others. It is disappointing to see a person who has taken on a position of leadership and oversight in a business, church, or civic group respond to the exposure of wrongdoing in the organization by hurrying to say, "It's not *my* fault," instead of acknowledging the corporate responsibility that comes with leadership. These diverse examples are simply intended to indicate that, even though one may find Bildad's remarks about Job's children not worth taking seriously, the larger context out of which he speaks remains an area of moral and pastoral concern.

The other significant issue raised by Bildad concerns the sources of trustworthy moral knowledge. By and large, Israelite wisdom understood tradition and individual experience to be complementary sources of knowledge. Job and Bildad, however, polarize the issue. Job's championing of subjective experience was discussed in the Reflections on chap. 6. But what is implied by Bildad's insistence that only ancestral tradition is valid? He clearly believes that insight into the moral structures of the world can be obtained through observing the regular patterns that emerge only over long periods of time. That, in and of itself, is a valid insight.

What is troubling about Bildad's position is not his championing of tradition, but his understanding of tradition as a closed body of knowledge. He does not see tradition as being continually modified by the incorporation of new observations and experiences. If he did, he could not speak of the present generation as one that "knows nothing" (v. 9). For Bildad, the ancestors discovered truths that were valid for all time. Individual experience that contradicts those truths has to be wrong. Anyone who has ever lived through a time of change knows that it is not that simple.

A community's social relations are strongly shaped by inherited traditions, "the way we do things around here." Individual experience that does not fit those traditional ways poses a challenge. The proper roles of women and men, the nature and structure of families, acceptable modes of sexuality—many of the currently contested social issues involve a tension between the claims of tradition and the claims of experience. The same is true of many volatile issues in the church concerning how to understand and talk about God. The way forward is not found by polarizing the claims of tradition and experience and arguing about which has the superior claim, but by realizing that experience and tradition are part of a continuum. Tradition, after all, is the deposit of experience in the past; present experience may be tradition in the making. Once that is recognized, then it is possible to ask about the presuppositions, assumptions, and values that shape both tradition and present experience in order to see what is valuable and should be retained, and what should be modified in the light of new perspectives and changed circumstances.

An important part of the reflection on tradition always needs to be an examination of *whose* experience has contributed to the formation of tradition. One of the misunderstandings about the nature of tradition that Bildad makes is overestimating the objectivity of this process. Bildad does not appreciate the way in which the perspectives of observers shape what they see. The conclusion that people get what they deserve and deserve what they get is more likely to be reached by the comfortable than by the miserable. A tradition that does not incorporate the perspectives of persons from various parts of the social order confuses the self-interest of a few with truth itself. Many of the most vehemently contested issues of the present involve the complaint that people whose experience should have been incorporated had no part in shaping the traditions that they are now expected to uphold. In Bildad, one sees not the failure of tradition as such, but the ease with which tradition can be distorted both by the temptation to make it a closed body of knowledge and by the temptation to absolutize its insights.

Job 9:1–10:22, Job Imagines a Trial with God

NIV

9 Then Job replied:

2 "Indeed, I know that this is true.
But how can a mortal be righteous before God?
3 Though one wished to dispute with him,
he could not answer him one time out of a thousand.
4 His wisdom is profound, his power is vast.
Who has resisted him and come out unscathed?
5 He moves mountains without their knowing it
and overturns them in his anger.
6 He shakes the earth from its place
and makes its pillars tremble.
7 He speaks to the sun and it does not shine;
he seals off the light of the stars.
8 He alone stretches out the heavens
and treads on the waves of the sea.
9 He is the Maker of the Bear and Orion,
the Pleiades and the constellations of the south.
10 He performs wonders that cannot be fathomed,
miracles that cannot be counted.
11 When he passes me, I cannot see him;
when he goes by, I cannot perceive him.
12 If he snatches away, who can stop him?
Who can say to him, 'What are you doing?'
13 God does not restrain his anger;
even the cohorts of Rahab cowered at his feet.

14 "How then can I dispute with him?
How can I find words to argue with him?
15 Though I were innocent, I could not answer him;
I could only plead with my Judge for mercy.
16 Even if I summoned him and he responded,
I do not believe he would give me a hearing.
17 He would crush me with a storm
and multiply my wounds for no reason.
18 He would not let me regain my breath
but would overwhelm me with misery.
19 If it is a matter of strength, he is mighty!
And if it is a matter of justice, who will summon him[a]?

[a]19 See Septuagint; Hebrew *me.*

NRSV

9 Then Job answered:
2 "Indeed I know that this is so;
but how can a mortal be just before God?
3 If one wished to contend with him,
one could not answer him once in a thousand.
4 He is wise in heart, and mighty in strength
—who has resisted him, and succeeded?—
5 he who removes mountains, and they do not know it,
when he overturns them in his anger;
6 who shakes the earth out of its place,
and its pillars tremble;
7 who commands the sun, and it does not rise;
who seals up the stars;
8 who alone stretched out the heavens
and trampled the waves of the Sea;[a]
9 who made the Bear and Orion,
the Pleiades and the chambers of the south;
10 who does great things beyond understanding,
and marvelous things without number.
11 Look, he passes by me, and I do not see him;
he moves on, but I do not perceive him.
12 He snatches away; who can stop him?
Who will say to him, 'What are you doing?'

13 "God will not turn back his anger;
the helpers of Rahab bowed beneath him.
14 How then can I answer him,
choosing my words with him?
15 Though I am innocent, I cannot answer him;
I must appeal for mercy to my accuser.[b]
16 If I summoned him and he answered me,
I do not believe that he would listen to my voice.
17 For he crushes me with a tempest,
and multiplies my wounds without cause;
18 he will not let me get my breath,
but fills me with bitterness.
19 If it is a contest of strength, he is the strong one!
If it is a matter of justice, who can summon him?[c]

[a] Or *trampled the back of the sea dragon*   [b] Or *for my right*
[c] Compare Gk: Heb *me*

NIV

²⁰Even if I were innocent, my mouth would
condemn me;
if I were blameless, it would pronounce me
guilty.
²¹"Although I am blameless,
I have no concern for myself;
I despise my own life.
²²It is all the same; that is why I say,
'He destroys both the blameless and the
wicked.'
²³When a scourge brings sudden death,
he mocks the despair of the innocent.
²⁴When a land falls into the hands of the wicked,
he blindfolds its judges.
If it is not he, then who is it?

²⁵"My days are swifter than a runner;
they fly away without a glimpse of joy.
²⁶They skim past like boats of papyrus,
like eagles swooping down on their prey.
²⁷If I say, 'I will forget my complaint,
I will change my expression, and smile,'
²⁸I still dread all my sufferings,
for I know you will not hold me innocent.
²⁹Since I am already found guilty,
why should I struggle in vain?
³⁰Even if I washed myself with soap[a]
and my hands with washing soda,
³¹you would plunge me into a slime pit
so that even my clothes would detest me.

³²"He is not a man like me that I might answer
him,
that we might confront each other in court.
³³If only there were someone to arbitrate between
us,
to lay his hand upon us both,
³⁴someone to remove God's rod from me,
so that his terror would frighten me no more.
³⁵Then I would speak up without fear of him,
but as it now stands with me, I cannot.

10 "I loathe my very life;
therefore I will give free rein to my
complaint
and speak out in the bitterness of my soul.
²I will say to God: Do not condemn me,
but tell me what charges you have against
me.

a30 Or *snow*

NRSV

²⁰ Though I am innocent, my own mouth would
condemn me;
though I am blameless, he would prove me
perverse.
²¹ I am blameless; I do not know myself;
I loathe my life.
²² It is all one; therefore I say,
he destroys both the blameless and the
wicked.
²³ When disaster brings sudden death,
he mocks at the calamity[a] of the innocent.
²⁴ The earth is given into the hand of the wicked;
he covers the eyes of its judges—
if it is not he, who then is it?

²⁵ "My days are swifter than a runner;
they flee away, they see no good.
²⁶ They go by like skiffs of reed,
like an eagle swooping on the prey.
²⁷ If I say, 'I will forget my complaint;
I will put off my sad countenance and be
of good cheer,'
²⁸ I become afraid of all my suffering,
for I know you will not hold me innocent.
²⁹ I shall be condemned;
why then do I labor in vain?
³⁰ If I wash myself with soap
and cleanse my hands with lye,
³¹ yet you will plunge me into filth,
and my own clothes will abhor me.

³² For he is not a mortal, as I am, that I might
answer him,
that we should come to trial together.
³³ There is no umpire[b] between us,
who might lay his hand on us both.
³⁴ If he would take his rod away from me,
and not let dread of him terrify me,
³⁵ then I would speak without fear of him,
for I know I am not what I am thought to
be.[c]

10 "I loathe my life;
I will give free utterance to my complaint;
I will speak in the bitterness of my soul.
² I will say to God, Do not condemn me;
let me know why you contend against me.
³ Does it seem good to you to oppress,

a Meaning of Heb uncertain   b Another reading is *Would that there
were an umpire*   c Cn: Heb *for I am not so in myself*

NIV

³Does it please you to oppress me,
  to spurn the work of your hands,
    while you smile on the schemes of the
      wicked?
⁴Do you have eyes of flesh?
  Do you see as a mortal sees?
⁵Are your days like those of a mortal
  or your years like those of a man,
⁶that you must search out my faults
  and probe after my sin—
⁷though you know that I am not guilty
  and that no one can rescue me from your
    hand?

⁸"Your hands shaped me and made me.
  Will you now turn and destroy me?
⁹Remember that you molded me like clay.
  Will you now turn me to dust again?
¹⁰Did you not pour me out like milk
  and curdle me like cheese,
¹¹clothe me with skin and flesh
  and knit me together with bones and sinews?
¹²You gave me life and showed me kindness,
  and in your providence watched over my
    spirit.

¹³"But this is what you concealed in your heart,
  and I know that this was in your mind:
¹⁴If I sinned, you would be watching me
  and would not let my offense go unpunished.
¹⁵If I am guilty—woe to me!
  Even if I am innocent, I cannot lift my head,
  for I am full of shame
    and drowned in*a* my affliction.
¹⁶If I hold my head high, you stalk me like a lion
  and again display your awesome power
    against me.
¹⁷You bring new witnesses against me
  and increase your anger toward me;
    your forces come against me wave upon
      wave.

¹⁸"Why then did you bring me out of the
    womb?
  I wish I had died before any eye saw me.
¹⁹If only I had never come into being,
  or had been carried straight from the womb
    to the grave!
²⁰Are not my few days almost over?

a15 Or *and aware of*

NRSV

  to despise the work of your hands
    and favor the schemes of the wicked?
⁴ Do you have eyes of flesh?
  Do you see as humans see?
⁵ Are your days like the days of mortals,
  or your years like human years,
⁶ that you seek out my iniquity
  and search for my sin,
⁷ although you know that I am not guilty,
  and there is no one to deliver out of your hand?
⁸ Your hands fashioned and made me;
  and now you turn and destroy me.*a*
⁹ Remember that you fashioned me like clay;
  and will you turn me to dust again?
¹⁰ Did you not pour me out like milk
  and curdle me like cheese?
¹¹ You clothed me with skin and flesh,
  and knit me together with bones and sinews.
¹² You have granted me life and steadfast love,
  and your care has preserved my spirit.
¹³ Yet these things you hid in your heart;
  I know that this was your purpose.
¹⁴ If I sin, you watch me,
  and do not acquit me of my iniquity.
¹⁵ If I am wicked, woe to me!
  If I am righteous, I cannot lift up my head,
  for I am filled with disgrace
    and look upon my affliction.
¹⁶ Bold as a lion you hunt me;
  you repeat your exploits against me.
¹⁷ You renew your witnesses against me,
  and increase your vexation toward me;
    you bring fresh troops against me.*b*

¹⁸ "Why did you bring me forth from the womb?
  Would that I had died before any eye had
    seen me,
¹⁹ and were as though I had not been,
  carried from the womb to the grave.
²⁰ Are not the days of my life few?*c*
  Let me alone, that I may find a little comfort*d*
²¹ before I go, never to return,
  to the land of gloom and deep darkness,
²² the land of gloom*e* and chaos,
  where light is like darkness."

a Cn Compare Gk Syr: Heb *made me together all around, and you
destroy me*   *b* Cn Compare Gk: Heb *toward me; changes and a
troop are with me*   *c* Cn Compare Gk Syr: Heb *Are not my days
few? Let him cease!*   *d* Heb *that I may brighten up a little*
e Heb *gloom as darkness, deep darkness*

NIV

Turn away from me so I can have a moment's
    joy
[21]before I go to the place of no return,
    to the land of gloom and deep shadow,[a]
[22]to the land of deepest night,
    of deep shadow and disorder,
    where even the light is like darkness."

[a]21 Or *and the shadow of death*; also in verse 22

COMMENTARY

Job's speech begins with an ironic rhetorical question about the possibility of being "in the right" with God (9:2). The question leads Job to the image that will dominate not only this speech but also his whole understanding of his situation: the notion of a lawsuit with God (9:2-4). Such a lawsuit is transparently impossible to Job because of the enormous disparity between God's power and his own (9:5-13); yet Job cannot leave off his exploration of the idea. Convinced that God's overwhelming power would prevent a just outcome (9:14-21), Job's conclusions about God become increasingly negative (9:22-24). Lamenting the brevity of his life (9:25-26), Job tries three times to imagine a resolution to his situation (9:27-28, 29-32, 33-35). The extent to which the image of a lawsuit has taken hold of his imagination is evident from the fact that the impossibility of a resolution is expressed each time in legal language (9:28b, 32-33).

Job imagines the kind of speech he would make if he could engage God in a trial (10:1-7). His imaginary speech slips gradually into speculation about God's intentions toward him, a reflection that combines pathos and bitter accusation (10:8-17). Job concludes bleakly, with an appeal for a moment's respite before the unrelenting darkness of death (10:18-22).

9:1-4. As v. 2 is translated in the NRSV and the NIV, Job appears to agree with what Bildad has just said. If so, Job is being ironic. More likely, the "truth" to which Job assents is contained in the rhetorical question in v. 2b: "Truly, I know that this is so: how can . . . " (see REB, TNK).[163]

That rhetorical question contains a crucial play on different nuances of the Hebrew verb צדק (*ṣādaq*), which an English translation cannot capture. The verb can have a general moral meaning, "to be righteous," but it can also have a distinctly forensic connotation, "to be [legally] in the right" (see Exod 23:7; Deut 25:1). Initially, Job appears simply to be agreeing with Eliphaz's words in 4:17a ("Can mortals be righteous before God?"). The next verse, however, changes the context. The words "contend"/"dispute" and "answer" are often used specifically for legal disputes (Exod 23:2-3; Deut 19:16-19; Prov 18:17). In that context it becomes apparent that underlying Job's ostensible agreement with Eliphaz is a very different question: "How could a mortal be legally vindicated against God?"

The ambiguity of the Hebrew pronouns in v. 3 makes it grammatically possible to understand Job's words in three different ways: (1) "if [God] wished to dispute with one, one could not answer him one in a thousand"; (2) "if [one] wished to dispute with [God], one could not answer him" (cf. NRSV); (3) "if [one] wished to dispute with him, [God] would not answer" (cf. 33:13).[164] For the most part, Job's use of the legal metaphor in chaps. 9–10 casts God as the one bringing charges and Job as the one accused (e.g., 9:15, 20; 10:2). Consequently, I am inclined to translate v. 3 according to the first alternative.

A more important issue than ambiguous syntax, however, is the question of the image's background. Legal metaphors occur in Israelite religion, most frequently in the context of the relation

163. A. B. Davidson, *The Book of Job*, Cambridge Bible for Schools and Colleges 15 (Cambridge: Cambridge University Press, 1891) 66; D. Clines, *Job 1–20*, WBC 17 (Dallas: Word, 1989) 227.

164. Habel, *The Book of Job*, 189.

of God and the people as a whole (entering into litigation with the people, as in Isa 3:13-14; Mic 6:1-2, or arguing the case of the people, as in Isa 49:25b; Jer 50:34). Although less common, there are some instances of legal imagery in personal piety. God is said to "enter into judgment with" a person in Ps 143:2 and Eccl 11:9, and in Ps 119:154a God is asked to "argue the case" of the psalmist. In none of these instances, however, is a person represented as a plaintiff against God. Only in the prophetic rhetoric of Jeremiah does one find such a boldly imagined use of the metaphor: "You will win, O LORD, if I make claim against You,/ Yet I shall present charges against You" (Jer 12:1 TNK). For Jeremiah, the metaphor is merely a rhetorical flourish. For Job, however, the metaphor gradually moves from being a bold piece of rhetoric to becoming the organizing model for his relationship with God.[165]

Job explores the contradictoriness of the notion of a trial with God. The qualities that make someone successful in arguing a case, cleverness and forcefulness, belong overwhelmingly to God (v. 4; cf. Isa 40:26). Job could not answer God in a lawsuit (v. 14). Before he states that conclusion, however, Job takes time to substantiate his statement about God's power and cleverness by reciting fragments of language traditionally used to praise God.

9:5-13. Job links together two doxologies (vv. 5-7, 8-10), followed by two conditional statements (vv. 11-12) and a simple concluding sentence (v. 13). Traditional doxological style is formally indicated in Hebrew by the use of introductory participles (with the article in vv. 5-7, without it in vv. 8-10). The NRSV suggests this style through its use of clauses introduced by "who."

9:5-7. Although many commentators claim that Job is parodying traditional doxologies by presenting God's power as violent and destructive (vv. 5-7),[166] the content of Job's words has parallels elsewhere in biblical praise of God. The appearance of God, the divine warrior, is often described

in terms of the quaking of the earth, the disruption of the mountains, and the general disturbance of nature (Pss 18:7-15 [8-16]; 97:1-5; 114:1-8; Nah 1:1-6; Hab 3:3-13). The darkening of the light of the sun and the stars is part of the divine warrior's struggle against the dragon Egypt in Ezek 32:7-8. This is not violence directed at nature per se. When God appears to fight against God's enemies, however, the effects of the struggle are felt by the entire cosmos. This representation of God is traditionally a positive one, since divine violence is associated with God as mythic victor over chaos (Psalm 29), as champion of Israel against its oppressors (Nah 1:1-6; Hab 3:3-13), and as deliverer from distress (Psalm 18). Even where the anger is directed against Israel, it is set in the context of God's righteous judgment (Isa 5:25; Jer 4:23-26). Job, however, has contextualized the images of divine violence differently. What is reassuring when imagined as the champion who rescues one from danger (e.g., Psalm 18) becomes terrifying when imagined as one's opponent in court.

9:8-11. The second doxology in vv. 8-10 substantiates God's power and wisdom by describing God's creative acts. Stretching out the heavens (v. 8a) is a common motif (Ps 104:2; Zech 12:1), occurring most frequently in Second Isaiah (40:22; 42:5; 44:24; 45:12). In Jer 10:12, it is associated explicitly with divine wisdom. The NRSV and the NIV translations of v. 8b obscure the mythological allusion to God's trampling the "back of Sea" (NRSV mg), a reference to the cosmogonic battle by which God secures the order of creation against the forces of chaos.[167] The ordering of the heavens and the subduing of Sea are complemented by the creation of constellations. It is no longer possible to identify with certainty which constellations are intended,[168] but the making of constellations and control over the stars are motifs used in other doxologies to praise God's effective power (Isa 40:26; Amos 5:9). Moreover, God will refer to the motif in the speeches from the whirlwind (38:31-33). Even more clearly than in vv.

---

165. Cf. J. J. M. Roberts, "Job's Summons to Yahweh: The Exploitation of a Legal Metaphor," *ResQ* 16 (1973) 161-62. Because the legal metaphor plays such a prominent role in Job's thought, it is unfortunate that we know so little about trial procedure. The only narrative account of a trial in the OT concerns the blasphemy charges brought against Jeremiah (Jer 26:7-19).

166. E.g., Gordis, *The Book of Job*, 522; C. Westermann, *The Structure of the Book of Job*, trans. C. A. Muenchow (Philadelphia: Fortress, 1981) 73-74; Janzen, *Job*, 90-91; K. Dell, *The Book of Job as Sceptical Literature*, BZAW 197 (Berlin and New York: de Gruyter, 1991) 148.

167. F. M. Cross and D. N. Freedman, "The Blessing of Moses," *JBL* 67 (1948) 196, 210.

168. See A. de Wilde, *Das Buch Hiob*, OTS xxii (Leiden: Brill, 1981) 142-47; G. Schiaparelli, *Astronomy in the Old Testament* (Oxford: Clarendon, 1905).

5-7, the second doxology contains only traditional words of praise of God. There is no overt parody, yet Job will set the traditional words in a context in which they become troubling rather than comforting.

The key to this reversal is the summary verse of the doxology (v. 10), which is virtually identical to the line Eliphaz used to introduce his praise of God in 5:9. For Eliphaz, the key words in the line are "great things" and "wonders," by which he means God's actions in transforming situations. For Job, the key words are the modifiers, "beyond understanding," "without number." What troubles Job is the way God eludes human understanding. Job's own words immediately following the doxology have to do with his incapacity to "see" or to "perceive" God. The NIV suggests the close relation between these verses through its fourfold repetition of the word "cannot" (לֹא . . . לֹא . . . אֵין . . . אֵין 'ên . . . 'ên . . . lō' . . . lō'). In v. 11, the verbs "pass by" (עבר 'ābar) and "move on" (חלף ḥālap) recall God's elusive manifestation to Moses (Exod 33:18-23) and to Elijah (1 Kgs 19:11-12). Those episodes, however, were occasions of revelation, even as they preserved the awful transcendence of God. For Job, there is no such revelatory disclosure, only the sense of divine hiddenness.

9:12-13. Similarly, in v. 12 Job invokes traditional expressions for the autonomy of God's power (cf. Job 11:10; Isa 43:13; 45:9; Dan 4:35[32]). Although God's willingness to revoke anger is often affirmed in tradition (Deut 13:17; Ps 78:38), in v. 13a Job draws attention to the countertheme of the relentlessness of divine anger (cf. 2 Kgs 23:26; Isa 9:12[11], 17[16], 21[20]; 10:4). Job's final image (v. 13b) is drawn from the mythic tradition. Rahab is the name of a chaos monster, similar to Leviathan. Like the Mesopotamian chaos monster Tiamat, Rahab is depicted as having allies.[169] In Ps 89:10-14[11-15] the violent defeat of Rahab is connected with the creation of the world and of a just order. That is not, however, the way Job's following words contextualize the allusion.

9:14-24. 9:14-16. Job creates a sense of estrangement from traditional words of praise of God's power and wisdom by juxtaposing them to

legal imagery (vv. 14-16). The direct consequence of God's superiority in strength and cleverness is that Job would be unable to answer charges brought against him (v. 14). Verse 15 provides a succinct example of how Job's legal metaphor transforms the significance of a traditional word of piety. Bildad had urged Job to "make supplication" (חנן ḥānan) to God (8:5), a stance frequently taken by psalmists, regardless of whether they have sinned against God (Pss 45:5; 51:3) or not (Pss 6:2[3]; 26:11; 119:132; ḥānan trans. as "be gracious"). Having to "plead for mercy" (ḥānan) with an adversary when one is in the right is an intolerable perversion of what should be (Deut 16:18-20). Similarly, Job cannot imagine God respecting the solemn injunction that a full hearing be given to every party without partiality (Deut 1:17) in his case (v. 16).

9:17-18. These verses may be either Job's imagination of the violence that would disrupt his lawsuit (so NIV)[170] or a reference to his experience, which makes him doubt God's capacity for restraint (so NRSV).[171] Although v. 17 reads "crush me with a *tempest*" (שערה śĕ'ārâ), many commentators emend to "crush me for a *hair*" (שערה śa'ărâ), i.e., a trifle.[172] The emendation improves the parallelism with "for no reason" in 17b. Yet as the rabbis recognized (b. B. Bat. 16a), there may be an ironic foreshadowing here, since God will speak to Job "from a tempest" in 38:1. Similarly, Job's complaint that God increases his wounds "for no reason" (חנם ḥinnām) repeats the thematically significant word from 1:9 and 2:3.

9:19-21. In v. 19, Job contrasts two forms of resolution: a trial of strength and a trial at law. Both are impossible for Job because of God's superior power. The devastating effects of this power are explored in vv. 20-21. In his earlier words to his friends, Job had expressed great confidence in his own ability to speak the truth in a face-to-face encounter (6:28). His tongue would be free of deceit, and his palate would discern falsehood (6:30). Now, as he contemplates a trial with God, Job envisions his own mouth speaking a lie. Horrifyingly, it is a lie against his own innocence (v. 20; the NRSV's "though" is to

---

169. *ANET,* 67.

170. Habel, *The Book of Job,* 193.
171. D. Clines, *Job 1–20,* WBC 17 (Dallas: Word, 1989) 235.
172. E.g., E. Dhorme, *A Commentary on the Book of Job,* trans. H. Knight (London: Nelson, 1967) 136; Pope, *Job,* 72; Clines, *Job 1–20,* 214.

be preferred to the NIV's "even if"). What Job envisions as the effect of a trial with God is not the recovery of truth but the loss of the integrity that has characterized his very essence. Significantly, the thematically crucial word "blameless" (םת *tām*; cf. 1:1, 8; 2:3, 9) occurs twice, as the self-affirmation that Job knows his own mouth will repudiate (vv. 20*b*, 21*a*). The statement that follows, "I do not know myself" (NRSV), is sometimes taken as an idiom (NIV),[173] but its literal meaning is preferable here. To be forced to confess a lie about oneself is to risk a dissolution of the self. When that occurs, the will to live also disintegrates (v. 21*b*).

9:22. The collapse of the essential moral distinction between innocence and guilt in his own case leads Job to generalize about God's governance of the world (v. 22-24). Although one can find a number of statements acknowledging that God is the source of both good and bad fortune (as Job himself says in 2:10), weal and woe (Isa 45:7), life and death (Deut 32:39), stating that God destroys the blameless and the wicked alike (v. 22) makes a claim of a different sort. The fundamental distinction between the righteous and the wicked was the foundation of moral thought in the ancient Near East, including Israel (see Pss 1:6; 7:8-9[9-10]; 9:4-5[5-6]). The role of the gods as ultimate authority for and upholders of the moral order was axiomatic (Ps 89:14[15]).[174] Job's assertion that God makes no such distinction is a radical denial of the basis of the moral order.[175]

9:23-24. Job inverts the traditional moral thought represented by Bildad in two ways. First, in 8:21-22 Bildad claims that God would fill Job's mouth with laughter, the laughter of the triumph of good and the end of evil. The laughter that Job describes, however, is quite different. The book of Proverbs warns that "those who mock the poor insult their Maker;/ those who are glad at calamity

will not go unpunished" (Prov 17:5 NRSV). Yet in the topsy-turvy moral world of Job's perception, God's derisive laughter mocks the death of the innocent in their catastrophe (v. 23). Second, God's justice and righteousness (8:3) were understood to be the source of the justice exercised by human rulers (e.g., Ps 72:1-2). So, Job argues, a God whose own ways are corrupt must be the source of abuse and judicial corruption on earth (v. 24).

9:25-35. 9:25-28. Job abruptly shifts from his parody of divine morality to a lament about the brevity of his own life (vv. 25-26). The images—drawn from land, water, and air—depict movements of increasing swiftness.[176] As in 7:16, Job's sense of limited life adds urgency to the need for resolution and relief. Yet each movement of his imagination encounters the limits that render such hope futile. First, Job imagines a change in his own expression and response (v. 27). Such a gesture would be a claim of personal autonomy, the ability to exercise a measure of control over his situation. The dread that prevents such a course is not fear of physical pain but fear of what that pain means (v. 28). God, not Job, controls the situation, refusing to declare Job innocent. Note that Job addresses God directly here for the first time in this speech.

9:29-31. Job's second attempt to imagine resolution is introduced by a statement of futility, also phrased in legal language (v. 29). Although echoes of a legal ritual may be present in the washing of hands (v. 30; cf. Deut 21:1-9), Job's vividly imagined scene reaches back to the symbolic power of cleanness and filth. The metaphorical connection between dirt and guilt, cleanness and innocence, is deeply embedded in the human psyche (Deut 21:6-7; Pss 26:6; 51:2[4]; 73:13; Isa 1:18).[177] Job's image, however, is not a static contrast between clean and dirty, but between the actions of making clean and making filthy. Job's inability to control his own body lies at the heart of the image. He powerfully expresses his dehumanization at the hands of God in the final image, "my clothes will abhor me." This image reverses a person's actual revulsion at wet and

---

173. S. M. Paul, "An Unrecognized Medical Idiom in Canticles 6,12 and Job 9,21," *Bib* 59 (1978) 545-47; Clines, *Job 1–20*, 237.

174. B. Zuckerman, *Job the Silent: A Study in Historical Counterpoint* (New York: Oxford University Press, 1991) 109; K. van der Toorn, *Sin and Sanction in Israel and Mesopotamia*, SSN 22 (Assen and Maastricht: Van Gorcum, 1985) 45.

175. There is one known parallel to Job's words. In the Babylonian poem, the Erra Epic, the pestilence god Erra confesses that "the righteous and the wicked, I did not distinguish, I felled." Quoted in P. Dion, "Formulaic Language in the Book of Job," *SR* 16 (1987) 189. The Erra Epic, however, is precisely a story about the collapse of the moral order and its restoration.

176. G. Fohrer, *Das Buch Hiob*, KAT xvi (Guetersloh: Gerd Mohn, 1963) 210; Gordis, *The Book of Job*, 109.

177. P. Ricoeur, *The Symbolism of Evil*, trans. E. Buchanan (Boston: Beacon, 1967) 25-46.

dirty clothes.[178] Personifying the clothes makes Job himself into the object of disgust (cf. 30:19).

9:32-35. In v. 32, Job again negates his final image of resolution in advance, by stating the condition that renders it impossible. God is not a human being. What would be an obvious and wholly unproblematic theological statement in many other contexts here becomes the essence of the problem. The legal metaphor upon which Job builds assumes a rough equality of power between the parties, if justice is to be done. As Job has argued (vv. 2-14), this condition does not obtain between himself and God. Therefore, he can have no justice. Grammatically, it is not clear whether Job continues in the indicative ("There is no umpire" [v. 33 NRSV]) or states a condition contrary to fact ("If only there were someone to arbitrate" [v. 33 NIV]). The meaning is much the same. What is significant, however, is the extent to which Job's imagination draws him into the details of this impossible desire, so that it momentarily takes on the concreteness of reality.

The figure Job refers to as an "umpire" or "arbitrator" (מוכיח *môkîaḥ*) is a recognized part of Israelite legal procedure, although the precise nature and extent of the *môkîaḥ*'s role is not well understood (hence the variety of translations).[179] The basic function of the *môkîaḥ* seems to have been that of deciding between two parties (Gen 31:37) or alternatives (1 Chr 12:17[18]). Two texts locate the *môkîaḥ* "in the gate," the setting of civil lawsuits, and underscore the necessity for the independence and impartiality of the *môkîaḥ* if justice was to be done (Isa 29:21; Amos 5:10). Job's words stress the mediating, restraining role of the *môkîaḥ* (v. 33). Most likely, the *môkîaḥ* should be taken as the subject of the first verb in v. 34 (so NIV), as the one who restrains God's rod. The absurd contradictoriness of Job's fantasy is transparent. Traditionally, the image of *môkîaḥ* was applied to God, as one who judged persons and nations (1 Chr 12:17[18]; Isa 2:4; Mic 4:3). To imagine a *môkîaḥ* who decides between God and Job is to envision a legal authority superior to the very God who was traditionally understood as the ultimate source of law and authority.[180]

The final half verse of chap. 9 is grammatically obscure (lit., "for not thus am I with myself"). Probably, it represents Job's recognition that the conditions necessary for speaking to God in a trial do not exist (so NIV).[181] The NRSV follows an interpretive tradition stemming from the medieval Jewish commentator Ibn Ezra, taking the line to refer to Job's defense of what he knows about himself against God's misapprehension of him.

10:1-2. As in chap. 7, Job's sense of the brevity of his life and the futility of his situation, which he has explored in 9:25-35, leads him to speak boldly (v. 1). Even though Job had denied that the conditions exist that would allow him to speak without fear before God (9:32-35), nevertheless he can imagine what he would say if he could confront God (v. 2). The metaphor of affliction as legal action by God against a person is not original with Job. It is probably already present in Ps 143:2 and is explicit in a Mesopotamian prayer to the God Shamash: "In the (legal) cause of the illness which has seized me, I am lying on my knees for judgment. Judge my cause, give a decision for me."[182] In contrast to the psalm and the Mesopotamian prayer, however, Job asks neither for a judgment nor to be spared a judgment. He asks for a statement of the charges, which he is prepared to refute. By treating a conventional metaphor as a creative one, Job turns it to his advantage.

10:3-17. Job continues to imagine how he would press God concerning the irrationality of God's actions toward him. The argument Job makes can be understood on its own terms but is better grasped against the background of a prayer like Psalm 139. That psalm begins and ends with images of God "searching" the psalmist, examining the speaker's moral condition. There is even an element of aggression in the way this is described (Ps 139:5), and yet the overall impression is one of complete solidarity between the speaker and God. In particular, the themes of God's knowledge of the psalmist and of God's intimate creation of him in the womb are closely connected. The psalmist describes himself as com-

---

178. N. Habel, *The Book of Job*, OTL (Philadelphia: Westminster, 1985) 196.

179. M. B. Dick, "The Legal Metaphor in Job 31," *CBQ* 41 (1979) 46.

180. Zuckerman, *Job the Silent*, 111.

181. But cf. D. Clines, *Job 1–20*, WBC 17 (Dallas: Word, 1989) 244.

182. Cited in Dick, "The Legal Metaphor in Job 31," 39-40.

pletely united with God in sharing the same enemies and prays that God will destroy the wicked. It is unlikely that Job is parodying Psalm 139 itself but the complex of religious themes to which Psalm 139 gives expression.

10:3. The phrase "work of your hands" (יגיע כפיך *yĕgîaʿ kappekā*) employs a word that connotes actual toil rather than the more common, bland words for making or forming (עשה *ʿāśâ,* כון *kûn;* e.g., Ps 119:73). In vv. 8-12, the image is developed in quite specific terms. Comparison with Psalm 139 helps to illumine the otherwise odd contrast in v. 3 between "the work of your hands" and "the wicked." As in the psalm, divine toil in creating the individual should serve as a symbol of the special bond between the individual and God. Thus the wicked would be the mutual enemies of God and the speaker. For Job, however, this relationship has been reversed.

10:4-7. In these verses, Job parodies the theme of God's complete and effortless knowledge of the individual (cf. Ps 139:2-6). The difference between divine and human sight was proverbial (1 Sam 16:7; see also Ps 139:12, 16), yet Job complains that God is acting like a human who cannot readily see what is in the heart of another (v. 4). Similarly, the urgency of mortality that motivates Job's words could hardly be a consideration for God (v. 5), whose transcendence of the ages is often noted (Ps 90:4; Isa 48:12). The contradiction for Job is that God seems to be searching obsessively for something that God already knows does not exist (vv. 6-7*a*).[183] The unit concludes with an expression ordinarily used in praise of God's power ("there is no one to deliver out of your hand"; cf. Deut 32:39; Isa 43:13), but here ironically indicating Job's entrapment (cf. Ps 139:5).

10:8-12. Job now returns to the theme of himself as the work of God's hands. In v. 8, the general contrast is between making and destroying, the latter word being the same one used in 2:3. Verses 9-12 develop the image of Job as the work of God's hands in concrete, sensuous terms. As anyone who has made a craft object knows, a piece has value not only for its intrinsic usefulness but also because the intimacy of its crafting creates a bond between creator and creation. Hence the pathos of v. 9, which envisages the creator as destroyer. The image of God as potter is familiar (Gen 2:7; Isa 64:8[7]; Jer 18:5). Less common is the image of God the creator as cheesemaker. The metaphor of gestation as a "curdling" of the father's semen and the mother's blood in Wis 7:2 suggests that the comparison of cheesemaking to the formation of the embryo may be implicit in v. 10.[184] The development of the fetus as a divine crafting is more explicit in v. 11, where weaving and sewing are images for the development of the skeletal structure, soft tissues, and skin. Job extends the imagery beyond physical creation to the gift of life and nurture (v. 12). The parallel between vv. 9-12 and Ps 139:13-18 is particularly close. But whereas the motif in Psalm 139 connects the intimate knowledge God has of the psalmist with God's providential care (Ps 139:16), in Job's case the divine intention is more sinister.

10:13-14. With most commentators, I take v. 13 as introducing v. 14 (so NIV).[185] What appeared to be loving creation was only a cover for God's true intention of inspecting for sin. Nor would this searching out and testing lead to a reformed life, such as the psalmist prays for (Ps 139:23-24), but rather a judgmental inspection with neither justice nor mercy (vv. 14-15). Job returns in these verses to judicial language ("acquit," "guilty," "innocent").

10:15-17. A series of images of Job's affliction and God's implacable aggression complete this section. Several textual and grammatical problems stand behind the different translations in the NIV and the NRSV. In v. 15*c*, the word translated "look upon" (ראה *rāʾâ*) is probably only a variant spelling of the word for "drenched" (רוה *rāwâ*),[186] which is preferable on the basis of parallelism. The subject of the first word in v. 16 is uncertain,

---

183. See A. C. M. Blommerde, *Northwest Semitic Grammar and Job,* BibOr 22 (Rome: Pontifical Biblical Institute, 1969) 59-60; M. Pope, *Job,* 3rd ed., AB 15 (Garden City, N.Y.: Doubleday, 1979) 80; Clines, *Job 1–20,* 246-47, for a different understanding of the grammar of v. 7.

184. E. Dhorme, *A Commentary on the Book of Job,* trans. H. Knight (London: Nelson, 1967) 149-50, lists parallels from later literature.

185. R. Gordis, *The Book of Job: Commentary, New Translation, and Special Studies* (New York: Jewish Theological Seminary, 5738/1978) 114; and F. Andersen, *Job: An Introduction and Commentary,* Tyndale Old Testament Commentaries (Downers Grove, Ill.: Inter-Varsity, 1976) 154, assume that v. 13 points back to the images of intimate creation in vv. 9-12. Thus God's intentions were originally benevolent but have somehow become mysteriously hidden away in God's mind. As Andersen notes, however, this interpretation makes the transition to v. 14 quite abrupt.

186. Clines, *Job 1–20,* 222.

and one must assume either that "my head" (v. 15) is the subject ("if my head is high"; cf. NIV) or that the text should be changed to "if I raise up" (ואגאה *wĕ'eg'eh* in place of ויגאה *wĕyig'eh*). The NRSV's adverb "boldly" is the product of a similar emendation (to וגאה *wĕge'eh*). The more interesting question is whether God or Job is portrayed as a lion. Grammatically, either is possible. The tradition of royal lion hunts in the ancient Near East as manifestations of the king's prowess suggests that God is here depicted as the hunter of Job, the lion.[187] The last verse appears to mix judicial and military imagery ("witnesses . . . troops"), although it is possible that the word translated "witnesses" (עדיך *'ēdeykā*) is a rare word meaning "military forces."[188] Throughout his speeches, Job will alternate between judicial imagery and imagery of divine violence. Both are ways of depicting God's aggression. The image of a trial at least permits a way of imagining the containment of such aggression through legal procedures, even though at this point Job can only imagine such constraints being overrun by uncontrollable divine power and anger. The images of the hunt and of the battle, on the other hand, are figures in which uncontrolled violence is of the essence. From these images, Job turns to a concluding lament and complaint in vv. 18-22.

10:18-22. The final verses of the chapter echo motifs from Job's earlier speeches in chaps. 3 and 7, although there are subtle but significant differences. Job's wish to have died at birth (v. 18) is similar to 3:11. In chap. 3, however, Job simply lamented the conditions of his birth. Now,

following chapters in which he has begun to reflect on God's actions toward him, Job decries his birth in terms of God's active role. Whereas earlier Job spoke of the advantage of never having seen the light (3:16b), here he speaks of the advantage of not having been seen by any eye (cf. 7:8, 12). Although Job still considers nonexistence preferable to life (v. 19; cf. 3:16a), and failing that seeks respite from God's oppressive presence (v. 20; cf. 7:16b, 19), his attitude toward death seems to have changed. In 3:17-18, 21-22, Job described death in highly desirable terms, something to be actively sought. Even in chap. 7, Job spoke of death as a form of protection from the relentlessness of God (7:21). Now, however, Job's description of death is decidedly negative. The irreversibility of death confronts Job (v. 21a), and his dread is communicated through the piling up of images of darkness (vv. 21b-22). Although these are traditional ways of describing Sheol (cf. Ps 88:7, 13; Isa 45:18-19),[189] Job intensifies them. He invokes images that suggest the chaos prevailing before creation, particularly through the phrase "darkness without order" and the paradoxical statement that the land of death "shines like darkness."[190] In Gen 1:2, darkness is the primordial characteristic of chaos. Even after the creation of light, light and darkness are mingled and must be separated and given structure for day and night to appear (Gen 1:3-4). In contrast to chap. 3, where Job seemed to relish the idea of invoking chaos, now he dreads it.

187. Cf. James B. Pritchard, ed., *The Ancient Near East in Pictures Related to the Old Testament* (*ANEP*) (Princeton: Princeton University Press, 1954) 56-57, pls. 182-84.

188. W. G. E. Watson, "The Metaphor in Job 10,17," *Bib* 63 (1982) 255-57.

189. See N. Tromp, *Primitive Conceptions of Death and the Nether World in the Old Testament,* BibOr 21 (Rome: Pontifical Biblical Institute, 1969) 95-98.

190. So Pope, *Job,* 79. Pope aptly cites Milton's description from *Paradise Lost* I.63: "No light, but rather darkness visible."

REFLECTIONS

What has changed Job, causing him to move from asking for death (6:8-9) to at least a subjective resistance of death (10:18-22)? Nothing has changed in his circumstances; no acceptable response has come from his friends; nor has he received any word from God. The change has to be sought in Job's own words. Although his words in chaps. 3 and 6–7 were remarkable for their expressiveness and imaginative power, they were primarily reactive, without an organizing center. In chaps. 9–10, however, Job finds such a center in the metaphor of a trial with God. Even though Job happens upon the metaphor almost by accident in the course of a satire of Eliphaz (9:2-4), and even though Job repeatedly denies that the metaphor can correspond with reality, the very act of engaging in such an imaginative exploration of his situation vis-à-vis God gives Job a desire to live, however tenuous at this point. Metaphor is a creative act, a reorganizing of perception. Ricoeur calls it a redescription of reality.[191] As such, it gives to the one using it a measure of power in relation to a situation. For this reason, writing, and poetry in particular, has always been a strategy of resistance and a source of strength for political prisoners, for the chronically ill, and for others who must endure situations in which much of their power is taken away.

One can think about metaphor's ability to empower in relation to Soelle's three phases of suffering (see Reflections on Job 3). Soelle identified these phases as mute suffering, lamenting, and changing. In lamenting, a person begins to describe what the oppressive situation is like. Many of the initial metaphors and similes that a person uses may simply serve to confirm the awfulness of the situation, expressing self-pity and even despair. The man who is blinded in an accident may lament that he is like a child lost in the woods at night, vulnerable and terrified, afraid to move. Playing with such images in order to give suffering a voice may be grim play, but it is play nonetheless, and play is an intrinsically creative activity. Different images begin to overlap and compete with the initial ones. One can imagine others besides lost children who may find themselves alone in the woods, such as explorers in a strange land. Explorers are wary and cautious, knowing that danger can come unexpectedly; but they are also courageous, knowing how to acknowledge their fear without being paralyzed by it. With the shift in metaphor, the nature of the situation is changed, at least in the realm of the imagination. That "redescription of reality" makes it significantly easier to change one's way of acting and so make some significant changes in the situation itself. As the man who is blind discovers the undeveloped capacities of his senses of hearing, touch, and smell to orient him in the world, the metaphor of the explorer may be transformed into the metaphor of the forest dweller. To such a person the forest itself speaks in many ways that are unrecognizable to those who do not live there or know its language.

The use of metaphor to open up new ways of perceiving is one of the important ways that a person moves from the phase of lamenting to the phase of changing. Job first uses the legal metaphor to depict himself as one who could not possibly hope for justice in a trial with an opponent as powerful as God. In his grim play with the image, however, the metaphor allows Job to see himself as a person with rights, no matter how badly abused those rights are. The ability to imagine a trial, even if it seems a practical impossibility, is enough to make Job no longer desire death.

The role of metaphor in the process of suffering is related to the role of metaphor in theology. It is not too bold to say that metaphor is at the heart of theology. One cannot speak literally of God, because God is transcendent and human language is finite. Consequently, all of our affirmations of God partake of metaphor. Calling God Father or Mother, saying that God is love, or speaking of God as judge uses categories from human experience to speak of what transcends. All theological metaphors organize experience of God into images that can be grasped. But not all metaphors have the same scope and interpretive capacity. To speak of God as "the rock that shelters me" is an evocative image of security, but one with little capacity for organizing other aspects of experience. The more significant metaphors for God tend to be drawn from the realms of human social organization: the family, political community, etc. Speaking of God as parent leads naturally to a richly developed theological vocabulary based on that governing metaphor. Speaking of God as ruler leads to an equally rich, but quite different, theological vocabulary. Both the power and the limit of metaphors are found in their selectivity. Metaphors bring certain aspects of experience into clear focus by obscuring others. In order to be adequate to the complexity of experience, religious language uses a variety of

191. P. Ricoeur, *The Rule of Metaphor,* trans. R. Czerny, University of Toronto Romance Series 37 (Toronto: University of Toronto Press, 1977) 229-39.

overlapping metaphors. Even so, experiences often occur for which there is no adequate language, or even more critically, experiences occur that are contradicted by traditional religious language.

Job's response to his experience reveals much about the way in which theological language changes. He does not set to work systematically but responds to an acute, specific problem: his need to articulate his inchoate sense of being treated wrongly. Legal language seems most adequate for this purpose. Once the legal metaphor is introduced into Job's speech, however, it takes on a life of its own. Indeed, part of metaphor's power is its ability to do its work beneath the surface of consciousness. Once one accepts the power of a metaphor to disclose the truth about one aspect of a situation, it is easy to accept the application of other aspects of the metaphor to other dimensions of reality. The legal metaphor will thus come to dominate Job's thinking about God, the world, and himself. Although there is little explicit critique of Job's legal metaphor (the friends, except Elihu, simply ignore it), the book itself reveals the problems with Job's metaphor by showing how its logic finally leads to a set of untenable alternatives (see Reflections on Job 31). It can be hard to give up a religious metaphor that has shaped one's understanding in important ways. In Job's case, one could even say that the legal metaphor saved his life. Eventually, however, the legal metaphor comes to be more of an obstacle than a help in understanding the nature of God, the world, and Job's relationship to both. Wisely, Job will let it go.

Job makes it easier to see why and how metaphors matter, how powerfully they can remake theological understanding, and how they sometimes need to be given up when they have served their purpose or when they have been shown to be less useful than they first appeared. There is, however, no simple "lesson" from Job to apply to contemporary debates about the adequacy of traditional theological language and the viability of new metaphors. One who reads Job attentively, however, begins to listen differently to the metaphors in religious discourse and to understand their powers and their limitations.

Job 11:1-20, Zophar Defends God's Wisdom

NIV

11 Then Zophar the Naamathite replied:
2 "Are all these words to go unanswered?
Is this talker to be vindicated?
3 Will your idle talk reduce men to silence?
Will no one rebuke you when you mock?
4 You say to God, 'My beliefs are flawless
and I am pure in your sight.'
5 Oh, how I wish that God would speak,
that he would open his lips against you
6 and disclose to you the secrets of wisdom,
for true wisdom has two sides.
Know this: God has even forgotten some of
your sin.
7 "Can you fathom the mysteries of God?
Can you probe the limits of the Almighty?
8 They are higher than the heavens—what can
you do?

NRSV

11 Then Zophar the Naamathite answered:
2 "Should a multitude of words go
unanswered,
and should one full of talk be
vindicated?
3 Should your babble put others to silence,
and when you mock, shall no one shame
you?
4 For you say, 'My conduct[a] is pure,
and I am clean in God's[b] sight.'
5 But O that God would speak,
and open his lips to you,
6 and that he would tell you the secrets of wisdom!
For wisdom is many-sided.[c]
Know then that God exacts of you less than
your guilt deserves.

[a] Gk: Heb *teaching*   [b] Heb *your*   [c] Meaning of Heb uncertain

NIV

They are deeper than the depths of the
grave[a]—what can you know?
[9]Their measure is longer than the earth
and wider than the sea.

[10]"If he comes along and confines you in prison
and convenes a court, who can oppose him?
[11]Surely he recognizes deceitful men;
and when he sees evil, does he not take note?
[12]But a witless man can no more become wise
than a wild donkey's colt can be born a man.[b]

[13]"Yet if you devote your heart to him
and stretch out your hands to him,
[14]if you put away the sin that is in your hand
and allow no evil to dwell in your tent,
[15]then you will lift up your face without shame;
you will stand firm and without fear.
[16]You will surely forget your trouble,
recalling it only as waters gone by.
[17]Life will be brighter than noonday,
and darkness will become like morning.
[18]You will be secure, because there is hope;
you will look about you and take your rest
in safety.
[19]You will lie down, with no one to make you
afraid,
and many will court your favor.
[20]But the eyes of the wicked will fail,
and escape will elude them;
their hope will become a dying gasp."

[a]8 Hebrew *than Sheol*   [b]12 Or *wild donkey can be born tame*

NRSV

[7] "Can you find out the deep things of God?
Can you find out the limit of the Almighty?[a]
[8] It is higher than heaven[b]—what can you do?
Deeper than Sheol—what can you know?
[9] Its measure is longer than the earth,
and broader than the sea.
[10] If he passes through, and imprisons,
and assembles for judgment, who can hinder
him?
[11] For he knows those who are worthless;
when he sees iniquity, will he not consider it?
[12] But a stupid person will get understanding,
when a wild ass is born human.[c]

[13] "If you direct your heart rightly,
you will stretch out your hands toward him.
[14] If iniquity is in your hand, put it far away,
and do not let wickedness reside in your tents.
[15] Surely then you will lift up your face without
blemish;
you will be secure, and will not fear.
[16] You will forget your misery;
you will remember it as waters that have
passed away.
[17] And your life will be brighter than the
noonday;
its darkness will be like the morning.
[18] And you will have confidence, because there
is hope;
you will be protected[d] and take your rest in
safety.
[19] You will lie down, and no one will make you
afraid;
many will entreat your favor.
[20] But the eyes of the wicked will fail;
all way of escape will be lost to them,
and their hope is to breathe their last."

[a] Traditional rendering of Heb *Shaddai*   [b] Heb *The heights of heaven*   [c] Meaning of Heb uncertain   [d] Or *you will look around*

COMMENTARY

Zophar is the last of Job's friends to reply. Although his speech is the shortest of the three, it crystallizes the terms on which the conflict between Job and his friends will be carried out. Unlike Eliphaz, who stressed Job's blamelessness as the grounds for his hope, and unlike Bildad, who used the presumed sinfulness of Job's children to urge Job to seek God in purity and uprightness, Zophar bluntly accuses Job himself of sin (v. 6). Beginning with a sharp rebuke of Job's glib and hostile rhetoric (vv. 2-3), Zophar contrasts Job's false self-assessment with the profound knowledge God could reveal (vv. 4-6). Zophar uses a traditional figure of speech to reinforce his argument that God's wisdom far exceeds human abilities to understand (vv. 7-9). His specific point, however, is that God's superior knowledge reliably detects evil (vv. 10-11). Despite his exasperation at Job's empty-headedness, expressed in a clever proverb (v. 12), Zophar reassures Job that if he will reorient himself to God and reform his conduct (vv. 13-14), then the troubles he has endured will pass away, and he will experience a secure and blessed future (vv. 15-19). The wicked, however, will have neither security nor hope (v. 20).

11:1-3. The wisdom tradition had a deep suspicion of one who was too facile with words (Prov 10:8, 14). Job's dazzling but parodic way of speaking is itself an indication of falsehood to someone like Zophar, steeped in the sober and conservative values of the sages. Indeed, the first two words of Zophar's speech echo Prov 10:19, "In a multitude of words, sin is not lacking." Zophar attempts to rebut Job's whole way of understanding; in his first sentence, he uses the word Job made central to his last speech: "to be righteous," "in the right" (צדק ṣādaq). Following Job's use of the word in a forensic sense, one immediately hears a legal nuance, hence the translation "vindicated" in the NRSV and the NIV. Zophar, however, has no intention of accepting Job's way of setting the terms for debate. As his speech will make clear, Zophar is primarily interested in the sapiential and religious sense of ṣdq, the sense of the right order of the world established by God's wisdom and maintained by God's oversight of the world. Zophar will advise Job to internalize this right order. A "man of lips," the literal meaning of the phrase in v. 2b, is one who talks superficially (cf. the primordial elders who speak from the "heart," the center of the body, in 8:10). Job's wild and iconoclastic words mark him out as someone who is not "in right order."

Although Zophar pejoratively declares Job's words to be "babbling," he is concerned that they not go unrefuted (v. 3a). More specifically, Zophar characterizes Job's words as mockery, a form of verbal aggression (v. 3b). To mock is to treat with sarcastic disrespect something that others take quite seriously. This is precisely what Job's bitter parodies do. His words are his only weapons against a religious ideology that now seems monstrous to him. Zophar attempts to respond with a weapon from the same arsenal, "shaming" Job—i.e., depriving him of social respect in an effort to restore him to a sense of proper values. But Job is already far too alienated from his former world of values for Zophar's shaming to have the desired effect.

11:4-6. Zophar ostensibly cites Job's words. They are not literally Job's words, however, but a representation of what Zophar has heard Job say, filtered through his own understanding of what is at stake. This subtle distortion is most evident in the first half of the verse, lit., "you say, 'My teaching is pure.' " The phrase "my teaching" (לקחי liqḥî) seems so inapt that the NRSV emends it to "my conduct" (לכתי lēktî). But "teaching," a sapiential term, reflects well the way Zophar would have understood Job. Zophar is not prepared to hear in Job's words the agony of a person whose world has collapsed. All he can hear is the theology, and Zophar is prepared to argue theology. It is true, as suggested in the Reflections on chaps. 9–10, that there are implicit theological claims in Job's words. But what distinguishes Job and Zophar is that for Job theology emerges out of the concrete experience of his life, whereas Zophar thinks that theology is primarily a matter of doctrine. And doctrine is what Zophar hears in Job's words.

Job had insisted that he was "blameless" (9:21) and that God knew he was "not guilty" (10:7), so Zophar's second quotation in v. 4b is less interpretive than his first, although the terms "pure" and "clean" are not terms Job himself used. It is notable, however, that Zophar avoids the specifically forensic terminology Job made central to his speech. Zophar does not want to argue with Job on those terms.

The contrast between Job and Zophar is also evident in vv. 5-6. Job had wanted God to tell him something quite specific: "what charges you have against me" (10:2). Zophar wishes that God would talk to Job at a much higher level of abstraction (v. 6). The sapiential orientation of Zophar is disclosed in two key words: "wisdom" (חכמה ḥokmâ) and "efficacy" (תושיה tûšiyyâ; translated "true wisdom" in the NIV). "Efficacy" is awkward, but the Hebrew word refers to the practical knowledge that allows one to solve problems and act effectively.[192] In short, Zophar says that what Job needs to know is the hidden workings of God in ordering the world. Only from this overarching perspective can Job's particular situation be understood.

In the last part of v. 6, Zophar moves to his conclusion about Job's sin, which refutes the self-evaluation of Job quoted in v. 4. In 10:7, Job had claimed that God *knew* he was not guilty. Echoing that word, Zophar says, *"Know* this. . . . " The difference in the translations of the NRSV and the NIV in v. 6*b* reflects uncertainty about which of two similarly spelled Hebrew words is used here. The NIV is more likely.[193] Fohrer suggests that Zophar is alluding to Job's request in 7:21 that God forgive his sins rather than continue punishing him.[194] Zophar's retort is that God's justice has already been tempered with mercy in Job's case. There is a certain exasperated, rhetorical exaggeration in Zophar's words. Yet the question is irrepressible: How does he know? Zophar does not claim that he has access to the "secrets of wisdom," yet he is certain about Job's guilt. This is not an inconsistency on Zophar's part. He believes in God's wise and effective governance of the world; consequently, to borrow the words of Alexander Pope, Zophar believes that "whatever is, is right."[195] Because God governs wisely and with skill, Job's acute suffering can only be interpreted as punishment for his guilt. Therefore, Job must be guilty. Insofar as both mercy and justice are characteristic of God, God will have applied both qualities to Job's situation.[196]

11:7-12. 11:7. Zophar reiterates his argument in the following verses, using a traditional figure of speech. The metaphorical image underlying Zophar's beliefs is a spatial one: the smallness of the human being in a vast world, which itself only gestures toward the transcendent vastness of divine wisdom. The spatial quality of v. 7 is somewhat obscured in translation. The noun חקר (ḥēqer; lit., "the process or object of searching") can have the sense of uttermost limit, as in 38:16 ("the recesses of the deep"). The parallel word תכלית (taklît, "boundary," "limit") adds to the sense of physical distance, as does the verb מצא (māṣāʾ), which means not only "find out" in an intellectual sense but also "reach," "arrive." Thus one might translate, "Have you reached the uttermost limits of God, or have you arrived at the boundary of Shaddai?" There is an evocation here of the ancient Near Eastern motif of the heroic journey, as it appears in the story of Gilgamesh. In that narrative, the hero's journey to the uttermost limits ends in a confrontation with his human finiteness.[197]

11:8-9. Zophar contrasts transcendent divine wisdom and corresponding human incapacity by placing each in relation to his symbolic map of the cosmos (vv. 8-9). Based on the number four, a symbol of totality, Zophar's map identifies the four dimensions of height, depth, length, and breadth with the four regions of the cosmos: heaven, Sheol, land, and sea (cf. Pss 135:6; 139:8-9; Hag 2:6). A Mesopotamian text uses a similar motif to express human limitedness: "Who is tall enough to ascend to heaven? Who is broad enough to embrace the earth?"[198] The Mesopotamian saying expresses despair that human beings cannot attain the perspective that makes choosing the right course of action possible. In Zophar's speech, too, rhetorical questions that must be answered in the negative (vv. 7-8) reinforce the sense of human incapacity. For Zophar, however, the conclusion is not one of despair but of confidence in the wisdom of God, which is greater than the reaches of the cosmos.

11:10-11. The specific purpose of Zophar's comparison is expressed in these verses, in which he echoes and contests Job's complaint about God (9:10-12). There Job had objected that the "unsearchable" God (אין חקר ʾên ḥēqer) is one whom he cannot "see" (ראה rāʾâ) or "perceive" (בין bîn), who "passes by" (חלף ḥālap) and seizes, "unhindered" (מי ישיבנו mî yĕšîbennû). Having made the

---

192. M. Fox, "Words for Wisdom," *ZAH* 6 (1993) 163-65. The word translated "two sides" or "many-sided" (כפלים kiplayim) is peculiar in this context. It is often suggested that a similarly spelled word meaning "like wonders" (כפלאים kiplāʾîm) should be read here, parallel to "secrets" in the first half of the verse. See ibid., 164n. 44; similarly, Gordis, *The Book of Job*, 121.

193. See Clines, *Job 1–20*, 254-55; but cf. Habel, *The Book of Job*, 203.

194. G. Fohrer, *Das Buch Hiob*, KAT xvi (Guetersloh: Gerd Mohn, 1963) 226.

195. See Alexander Pope *An Essay on Man*.

196. As Fohrer, *Das Buch Hiob*, 226, observes, the emphasis on divine mercy is more characteristic of prophetic rather than wisdom traditions. Similarly, see Clines, *Job 1–20*, 261-62.

197. See James B. Pitchard, ed., *Ancient Near Eastern Texts Relating to the Old Testament (ANET)*, 3rd ed. with supplement (Princeton: Princeton University Press, 1969) 72-99.

198. Ibid., 438.

point that Job cannot search out God (v. 7), Zophar turns Job's words inside out. Using the same expressions Job had used, Zophar describes the God's passing through (חלף *ḥālap*) to inspect the earth (v. 10*a*). Where Job had referred to God's seizing or "snatching," a word with criminal implications, Zophar reverses the image, referring to God's imprisoning and convening a court, terms drawn from legal procedure (v. 10; cf. Lev 24:12; Num 15:34; Ezek 16:40; Neh 5:7). That no one can "hinder" God (v. 10*b*) is in Zophar's opinion not only true but proper as well. The issue is not, as Job had complained, whether Job can see and perceive God, but what God sees and considers (v. 11*b*). Although Zophar makes no explicit reference to Job in v. 11, there is no doubt that he considers God to have seen deceit and evil in Job (cf. v. 6*c*).

11:12. Here the author's irony at the expense of Zophar is palpable. Zophar's rhetorically and philosophically sophisticated arguments, which are genuinely powerful on their own terms, have led him to absolutely wrong conclusions. As the reader knows, what God has seen is that Job is a person unlike anyone else on earth, blameless and upright, one who fears God and turns from evil (1:8). Zophar's elegant *a priori* reasoning is false. Thus, when Zophar in exasperation applies the proverb about the unlikeliness of an empty-headed person getting understanding (v. 12), the reflective reader knows that the saying applies more readily to Zophar than to Job.

The proverb itself is clever. The first half of the line has a striking use of assonance (איש נבוב ילבב *ʾîš nābûb yillābēb*). Unfortunately, a syntactical problem in the second half makes the translation uncertain. There are two words for "ass" in the line, the first meaning "domesticated ass" (עיר *ʿayir*; not "colt," as in the NIV), the second meaning "wild ass" (פרא *pereʾ*). Probably these are variants and one of the terms should be deleted (so the NRSV).[199]

11:13-20. Having rebuked Job as a donkey-brain for not seeing what is so evident to himself, Zophar appeals to Job to take the steps that will restore hope and security to him (cf. 5:17-27; 8:5-7, 20-22). Zophar had described an orderly cosmos, in its fourfold divisions and dimensions.

The proper human stance within that cosmos is not a Promethean attempt to rival and challenge God's wisdom. For Zophar, destruction comes into people's lives precisely because they are "out of order" with the rightness of God's wisdom. The proper response to such a situation is to reorder one's life in harmony with the rightness (צדקה *ṣĕdāqâ*) of God's world. The reordering is first of all a matter of the body: heart, palms, hands, face (vv. 13-15). As Clines notes, "directing the heart" is an idiom used by the rabbis for the mindfulness that prepares one for prayer.[200] Here, too, it precedes the advice to spread out the palms in prayer. Throughout the ancient Near East, the posture of prayer was to stand with the palms raised, facing outward (Exod 9:29, 33; 1 Kgs 8:22, 38).[201] The sense of reordering of life is reinforced by the following images of separation from evil. To have wrongdoing in one's hand is a common idiom for guilt (cf. 1 Sam 24:12; 1 Chr 12:17[18]; Ps 7:3[4]). Putting iniquity away from one's hand implies that moral reordering is a matter of the will, since "hand" is a metaphor for power and control.[202] Like the hand, the tent is an image of what is closely associated with a person (18:6; 29:4), and Job is urged to distance deceit from the hospitality of his dwelling.

The result of this reordering is described first in terms of the body, the lifting up of the face, which Job said God denied to him (v. 15*a*; cf. 10:15). For Zophar, however, it is not a matter of the vindication of Job but of the healing of Job, as the accompanying phrase "without blemish" suggests. Although used in a moral sense, "blemish" (מום *mûm*) is primarily a term for physical disfiguration, which makes an animal unfit as an offering to God or a priest unfit to approach the altar (Lev 21:17; Deut 15:21). Thus, graphically, Zophar describes Job as lifting up a face no longer disfigured by sin.

Other striking images elaborate the transformation that comes from this reordering of the self.

---

199. Pope, *Job*, 86, discusses the grammatical basis for the reading given in the NIV.

200. Clines, *Job 1–20*, 267.
201. O. Keel, *The Symbolism of the Biblical World: Ancient Near Eastern Iconography and the Book of Psalms* (New York: Seabury, 1978) pls. 415, 416, 422.
202. Clines observes that Zophar's approach to sin is characteristic of wisdom thinking: "How does Zophar propose Job can get rid of his sin? Not by sacrifice or atonement, not even by repentance, but by . . . a distancing of himself from it, putting himself far from it . . . (cf. Ps 1:1; Prov 1:10-15; 4:14, 24; 5:8; 30:8)" (*Job 1–20*, 268).

In v. 15*b*, a Job who is "firm" (מֻצָק *muṣāq*; lit., "cast" like metal) is contrasted with troubles that flow away like water (v. 16*a*). Clines notes the striking synonymous use of "forget" and "remember" to describe the psychological reality of being able to recall a past trauma without its having power over one any longer.[203] In v. 17, Zophar also reverses Job's images of the fearful darkness of approaching death (10:21-22). In contrast to Job's image of light that is "like darkness" (10:22), Zophar says of Job's life that "its darkness will be like the morning" (v. 17*b*; cf. Isa 58:10*b*). Whereas Job lamented the brevity of his days (10:20), Zophar describes a "lifespan" (חֶלֶד *ḥeled*) that will rise higher than the sun at noon (v. 17*a*).

The concluding images in vv. 18-19 develop the theme of security and hope. Here Zophar is true to the moral imagination of the wisdom tradition, which understands such security as coming from conducting oneself in harmony with the wisdom and right order of God (cf. Prov 3:21-26). The two images of v. 19 are coordinate descrip-

203. Ibid., 269.

tions of the social dimensions of security: having no enemies but only those who seek one's favor. The image in v. 19*a* is concretely that of a flock, safe from predators (see Zeph 3:13, where it is also associated with moral wholeness). The final image of having one's favor courted (lit., "soften the face") may strike a jarring note with modern readers, but in highly communal, paternalistic cultures, it is a strong image of being embedded securely in the social networks that sustain the community.

Zophar's final word, which speaks of the loss of security and hope for the wicked, initially resembles Bildad's contrast between the blessed fate that awaits Job and the destruction of his enemies (8:21-22). But Zophar does not identify the wicked of v. 20 with Job's enemies. He switches from the "you" of direct address to Job (v. 19) to a third-person plural comment about the wicked in general (v. 20). Thus Zophar sets before Job a word of warning like that of Prov 10:28, for at this point Zophar considers Job to be at risk of experiencing the fate of the wicked.

REFLECTIONS

Job's speech in chaps. 9–10 and Zophar's in chap. 11 present the reader with a clash of certainties. Job is certain that he is innocent; Zophar is certain that he is guilty. Job is certain that he knows the truth about himself; Zophar is certain that only God can know such a thing. The clash between the two extends also to their favored images of truth. For Zophar, truth resides in the "hidden things" of knowledge, the mysteries of God's ways, which no human can grasp. It is not necessary for humans to know the details, only to trust in the wisdom of God. For Job, truth can—indeed, must—be open to scrutiny, as in a trial. A human being can know the truth about himself or herself, and, if not overpowered, can defend that truth before God. Resolution comes not from human submission to a mystery of divine knowledge, as for Zophar, but from mutual acknowledgment of the truth.

The fascinating thing about such contradictory positions is that they often point to a common assumption that neither party is capable of recognizing. Both Job and Zophar assume a world of complete rationality and tight causality, a world with no randomness in it, at least so far as acute human suffering is concerned. Zophar and Job are willing to pay a terrible price to avoid considering Job's suffering simply as part of the contingency of living. Zophar is willing to declare Job guilty; Job is willing to consider the criminality of God. Neither seems capable of seeing, let alone questioning, the assumption they share. It is so obvious to them both that it is invisible.

It is not just Job and his friends who are determined to find a unifying explanation for disturbing events. That impulse remains intensely strong in many people. The words that echo in the mind of a person to whom a catastrophe has occurred are frequently, "Why? Why did this happen?" Even those who do not want to claim that "sin" is always the cause of suffering nevertheless may be heard to say, "Everything happens for a reason."

Why is the impulse to deny the contingent quality of life so strong? Most likely, the answer lies in our fragility as human beings, our intense vulnerability. Part of the passion for discerning a reason behind distressing events has to do with a desire to have as much control as possible. If one can understand why something happens, then one can sometimes influence what will happen. The intense need for a reason, however, most often emerges after a catastrophe has taken place, when there is no chance of changing events. In those instances, the terrible experience to which the question "Why?" gives voice is the collapse of the world into chaos, where anything can happen and nothing is secure. Asking "Why?" is an attempt to gain some control over that horrifying sense that everything is falling into an abyss. Distinguishing between the ostensible question ("Why did *this* happen?") and the underlying request ("Please reassure me that the chaos I feel is not all there is") is critical. What is needed is not an explanation of the causes of an accident or an illness but words that communicate the sustaining structures of God's creation, which contain chaos, and the reliable presence of God's love even in the experiences of deep darkness. Israel recognized the connection between the disorienting experience of disaster and the power of creation traditions to provide a measure of reassurance. One often finds images of God's containment of chaos and establishment of orders of creation incorporated into psalms of lament (e.g., Psalms 74; 77).

The common human sense of vulnerability is not the only factor involved in the attempt to find a reason for catastrophes. Much traditional religious language about God contributes to the assumption that Job and Zophar take for granted that God is directly responsible for what happens to people. The biblical image of God as a ruler who governs the world, an image with which the book of Job itself begins, is often implicit in such thinking. If God is the one who runs things, then God must be responsible. As Job puts it, "If it is not he, who then is it"? (9:24).

In fact, biblical reflection on such matters is remarkably diverse. Especially in the narrative traditions, the unpredictability of the consequences of other people's choices and the simple contingency of existence are presented as part of the texture of human life. Hagar and Ishmael's suffering happened for no particular divine reason, but was the consequence of some poorly conceived decisions made by Sarah and Abraham and the social pressures that made Hagar and Sarah into rivals. Neither the famine that drove Naomi's family from Judah nor the premature death of her two sons is represented by the narrator as anything other than simple misfortune. And even though he is not happy about it, the author of Ecclesiastes acknowledges that "time and chance happen to them all" (Eccl 9:11 NRSV). The Bible simply does not speak with a single voice on the question of the causes of human suffering.

Zophar and Job are both so eloquent, however, that it is difficult not to get drawn into their vision of things and to assume that one must choose between the two positions they articulate, even though these are not the only ways of looking at what happens to people. That is not to suggest, however, that some obvious third alternative waits just offstage. What one can say is that both of their responses evade acknowledging the way radical suffering refuses to be confined and contained by rational explanations. Neither Zophar nor Job is willing to contemplate the tragic dimension of human life. Neither is willing to imagine suffering that cannot be reduced to fault, whether human or divine. To risk thinking along those lines will necessitate a very different image of God than that which exists in the mind of either Zophar or Job. There will be an opportunity to return to these questions in the Reflections on chaps. 38–41.

Job 12:1–14:22, Job Burlesques the Wisdom of God and Struggles with Mortality

OVERVIEW

Job's final speech in the first cycle is the longest and most complex. The traditional division into three chapters identifies important differences in tone and mode of speech, as well as in content. What is obscured by that structure, however, is the division of the speech into two parts, according to whom Job addresses. In 12:1–13:19, Job addresses his friends; in 13:20–14:22, he addresses God. Although Job's words are directed to all his friends in 12:1–13:9, he is most directly engaged with Zophar's claims about his asinine intelligence, the superiority of hidden wisdom, and God's careful supervision and right ordering of the world. Savage parody is Job's chosen weapon in this part of his speech, introduced by his mocking compliment to the friends' wisdom (vv. 2-3). A brief aside in which Job bitterly comments on the contradictoriness of his own fate as a righteous person and that of the wicked suggests Job's true feelings (vv. 4-6). When he resumes, however, Job gives a parodic imitation of a wisdom discourse, burlesquing Zophar's claims about the inaccessibility of wisdom (vv. 7-10) and "granting" the traditional belief that wisdom resides with the aged (vv. 11-12), only to turn that premise into the basis of a sarcastic doxology that parodies God's wisdom and counsel (vv. 13-25).

Chapter 13 is linked to chap. 12 by repetition of the claim that Job's knowledge is equal to that of the friends (12:2-3//13:1-3). This repetition marks a turning point in the speech, however, as Job abandons parody and sarcasm. The rest of his words consist of an earnest and passionate speech that is thoroughly shaped by the legal metaphor Job began to explore in chaps. 9–10. Job criticizes the friends as lying witnesses for God (vv. 4-12) and reflects on the urgency of bringing his case before God (vv. 13-19).

In 13:20, Job begins to address God directly, as though a trial were in fact beginning (vv. 20-28). The intensity of Job's imagination, as he is gripped by the vision of a lawsuit with God, leads him to a sense of confident strength and expectation unparalleled in his other speeches (vv. 16-19). Almost as soon as he has begun to speak to God, however, his confidence falters as he again confronts the reality of the overwhelming inequality of power (vv. 25-28).

Consequently, in chap. 14 Job abandons the language of legal disputation and instead takes up a meditative reflection on the ephemerality of human life (vv. 1-6). For the rest of the chapter, Job struggles with the tension between mortality and hope. A series of vivid images from nature in vv. 7-12 and 18-19 articulates the problem and frames Job's bold attempt to imagine a place for hope (vv. 13-17). In the end, however, death has the last word (vv. 20-22).

Job 12:1–13:2, Job Parodies Traditional Praise of God

NIV	NRSV

12 Then Job replied:
 	
2"Doubtless you are the people,
    and wisdom will die with you!
3But I have a mind as well as you;
    I am not inferior to you.
    Who does not know all these things?
 	
4"I have become a laughingstock to my friends,
	12 Then Job answered:
	2 "No doubt you are the people,
	    and wisdom will die with you.
	3 But I have understanding as well as you;
	    I am not inferior to you.
	    Who does not know such things as these?
	4 I am a laughingstock to my friends;
	    I, who called upon God and he answered me,

NIV

though I called upon God and he answered—
a mere laughingstock, though righteous and
blameless!
⁵Men at ease have contempt for misfortune
as the fate of those whose feet are slipping.
⁶The tents of marauders are undisturbed,
and those who provoke God are secure—
those who carry their god in their hands.^a

⁷"But ask the animals, and they will teach you,
or the birds of the air, and they will tell
you;
⁸or speak to the earth, and it will teach you,
or let the fish of the sea inform you.
⁹Which of all these does not know
that the hand of the LORD has done this?
¹⁰In his hand is the life of every creature
and the breath of all mankind.
¹¹Does not the ear test words
as the tongue tastes food?
¹²Is not wisdom found among the aged?
Does not long life bring understanding?

¹³"To God belong wisdom and power;
counsel and understanding are his.
¹⁴What he tears down cannot be rebuilt;
the man he imprisons cannot be released.
¹⁵If he holds back the waters, there is drought;
if he lets them loose, they devastate the land.
¹⁶To him belong strength and victory;
both deceived and deceiver are his.
¹⁷He leads counselors away stripped
and makes fools of judges.
¹⁸He takes off the shackles put on by kings
and ties a loincloth^b around their waist.
¹⁹He leads priests away stripped
and overthrows men long established.
²⁰He silences the lips of trusted advisers
and takes away the discernment of elders.
²¹He pours contempt on nobles
and disarms the mighty.
²²He reveals the deep things of darkness
and brings deep shadows into the light.
²³He makes nations great, and destroys them;
he enlarges nations, and disperses them.
²⁴He deprives the leaders of the earth of their reason;
he sends them wandering through a trackless
waste.

^a6 Or secure / in what God's hand brings them   ^b18 Or shackles
of kings / and ties a belt

NRSV

a just and blameless man, I am a
laughingstock.
⁵ Those at ease have contempt for misfortune,^a
but it is ready for those whose feet are
unstable.
⁶ The tents of robbers are at peace,
and those who provoke God are secure,
who bring their god in their hands.^b

⁷ "But ask the animals, and they will teach you;
the birds of the air, and they will tell you;
⁸ ask the plants of the earth,^c and they will teach
you;
and the fish of the sea will declare to you.
⁹ Who among all these does not know
that the hand of the LORD has done this?
¹⁰ In his hand is the life of every living thing
and the breath of every human being.
¹¹ Does not the ear test words
as the palate tastes food?
¹² Is wisdom with the aged,
and understanding in length of days?

¹³ "With God^d are wisdom and strength;
he has counsel and understanding.
¹⁴ If he tears down, no one can rebuild;
if he shuts someone in, no one can open
up.
¹⁵ If he withholds the waters, they dry up;
if he sends them out, they overwhelm the
land.
¹⁶ With him are strength and wisdom;
the deceived and the deceiver are his.
¹⁷ He leads counselors away stripped,
and makes fools of judges.
¹⁸ He looses the sash of kings,
and binds a waistcloth on their loins.
¹⁹ He leads priests away stripped,
and overthrows the mighty.
²⁰ He deprives of speech those who are trusted,
and takes away the discernment of the
elders.
²¹ He pours contempt on princes,
and looses the belt of the strong.
²² He uncovers the deeps out of darkness,
and brings deep darkness to light.

^a Meaning of Heb uncertain   ^b Or whom God brought forth by his
hand; Meaning of Heb uncertain   ^c Or speak to the earth
^d Heb him

NIV

25They grope in darkness with no light;
    he makes them stagger like drunkards.

13 "My eyes have seen all this,
    my ears have heard and understood it.
2What you know, I also know;
    I am not inferior to you."

NRSV

23 He makes nations great, then destroys them;
    he enlarges nations, then leads them away.
24 He strips understanding from the leaders[a] of
    the earth,
    and makes them wander in a pathless waste.
25 They grope in the dark without light;
    he makes them stagger like a drunkard.

13 "Look, my eye has seen all this,
    my ear has heard and understood it.
2 What you know, I also know;
    I am not inferior to you."

[a] Heb adds *of the people*

COMMENTARY

12:1-3. By this point in the dialogue, the reader expects each speech to begin with a sharp criticism of the previous speaker and/or a defense of the present speaker's words. Here, as Job concludes the first round of speeches, he offers a tongue-in-cheek compliment to his friends. The syntax of v. 2 is difficult, and it is not clear what Job means by referring to his friends as the "people." Suggestions that the phrase means something like "the gentry" lack supporting evidence.[204] It is better to translate "truly, you are the people with whom wisdom will die."[205] The exaggeration is Job's caricature of the way his friends have been presenting themselves as the ultimate representatives of wisdom. (The verse is also susceptible to the satirical reading that the friends are killing wisdom.)[206] Corresponding to the rhetorical exaggeration of v. 2 is the rhetorical modesty in what Job claims for himself (v. 3). He does not claim anything special, but only such things as everyone knows (v. 3c). In part, this may be a reply to Zophar's appeal for a revelation of hidden mysteries (11:5-6). That is not necessary, Job implies; all that it is necessary to know is common knowledge. These introductory verses set up the primary work of the chapter, which is

to subject such "common knowledge" to a critical scrutiny.

12:4-6. Although they seem to interrupt the logical flow of thought between v. 3 and v. 7, vv. 4-6 perform a very important role in the rhetoric of Job's speech. As in a play, they are an "aside," which discloses the speaker's mood and inner thoughts, giving a context within which to hear the speaker's following words.

In v. 4, the NRSV and the NIV insert the first-person pronoun in places where the Hebrew text has the third person. One can make sense of the literal words, however, if one reads them as Job's echoing of the way people have talked about him in the past and in his present distress. One needs to hear traces of quotation marks around these stock phrases. Thus "a 'laughingstock-to-his-friends' I have become. 'One-who-calls-on-God-and-he-answers-him,' 'a righteous-and-perfect person,' (I have become) a laughingstock." The phrase "righteous and perfect" (צדיק תמים *ṣaddîq tāmîm*) evokes the hyperbolic language of the narrator's description of Job in 1:1 (cf. Gen 6:9). To be known as "one who calls upon God and he answers him" is to be known as one in God's favor (see Ps 99:6). By contrast, a community tends to make a laughingstock out of someone who is deemed out of favor with God and thus a safe target. (For the special misery of being mocked by friends, see Ps 55:12-15[13-16].)

In v. 5, Job reflects briefly on the social dynam-

204. M. Pope, *Job*, 3rd ed., AB 15 (Garden City, N.Y.: Doubleday, 1979) 89; but cf. D. Clines, *Job 1–20*, WBC 17 (Dallas: Word, 1989) 278.
205. J. A. Davies, "A Note on Job XII 2," *VT* 25 (1975) 670-71.
206. E. Good, *In Turns of Tempest* (Stanford, Calif.: Stanford University Press, 1990) 234.

ics at work. It is a disturbing but well-recognized phenomenon that the precipitous misfortune of someone previously respected and successful sometimes evokes contempt rather than sympathy. Perhaps this is the reflex of a need to rationalize inexplicable misfortune, a need for those "at ease" to believe that it could not happen to them. The contradiction that Job experienced between his own "righteous and perfect" conduct and the way he has been treated as a laughingstock finds its counterpart in another contradiction described in v. 6, the peace and security of those who have been actively evil. Zophar had described such security as the blessing for those whose lives reflected the right order of God's world (11:13-19). What Job observes, however, is a world in which something is fundamentally not right. The issue of the fate of the wicked, introduced only briefly here, will become the primary topic of the friends' speeches in the second cycle (chaps. 15; 18; 20) and will dominate Job's final speech in that cycle (chap. 21).

The last clause in v. 6 is obscure. The words could be translated either "the one who brings God in his hand" or "the one(s) whom God brings into his hand." The sentence is generally taken, according to the first reading, to refer to the arrogance of the wicked, who trust in their own power. A somewhat similar idiom appears in Gen 31:29; Deut 28:32; Neh 5:5; Mic 2:1,[207] although the wording is not the same. Moreover, it is odd that the verb in v. 6c is singular, whereas the rest of v. 6 is cast in the plural. Clines, following the second alternative, translates "those whom God has in his own power."[208] Although it, too, has problems, that translation is probably to be preferred. It anticipates the reference in the last verse of the next unit, vv. 7-10, to what God has "in his hand."

12:7-10. Verse 7 resumes the line of thought in v. 3. Job will demonstrate that he is not less intelligent than his friends by giving a wisdom discourse in just their style. That this speech has something of the quality of a performance is suggested by Job's use of second-person singular verbs and pronouns in vv. 7-10, instead of the

plural forms Job used at the beginning of his speech (v. 2-3), a distinction that cannot be represented in English. Moreover, there is not a word from vv. 7-13 that could not have been said by the friends. Job is not *quoting* his friends,[209] however, but imitating the type of speech they use. Job's relationship to this manner of talking is complex. The dominant tone is one of parody. Job will show the bankruptcy of this platitudinous, cliché-ridden way of speaking. Yet there are genuinely "Joban" elements in what he says, especially in vv. 7-10. Perhaps these verses can be understood best as Job's forcing even a language of hypocrisy to bear witness to the truth. This double-voicing of Job's words is facilitated by vv. 4-6 immediately preceding, which indicate Job's passionate sense that the world is not rightly ordered.

12:7-8. Job opens his wisdom discourse with an appeal to authority that acknowledges and challenges the similar appeals made by his friends. The words "but ask . . . and they will teach you" echo Bildad's appeal to ancient generations in 8:8-10. Job also engages Zophar's reflections on knowledge in 11:5-9. Zophar attempted to persuade Job that he could not attain the boundary of God's knowledge, which transcends the four dimensions of the cosmos. Here Job shifts the issue away from what is not accessible to what is readily accessible to all the creatures who inhabit the land, the air, and the sea. One could make Job's figure parallel Zophar's more exactly by translating "earth" (ארץ 'ereṣ) as "underworld."[210] The underworld, however, was seldom treated as a source of knowledge in Hebrew wisdom,[211] so that "earth" is more likely. The NRSV and the NIV differ in translating v. 8, depending on whether the Hebrew word שׂיח (śîaḥ) is read as a verb ("speak") or as a noun ("plant"). The parallelism is better if one translates "plant" or "shrub," since then each line contains a reference to a creature.

Although Hebrew literature sometimes contrasts human intelligence with that of animals (Job 18:3; Dan 4:16[13]), nature is generally a positive

207. E. Dhorme, *A Commentary on the Book of Job,* trans. H. Knight (London: Nelson, 1967) 171; Pope, *Job,* 90; N. Habel, *The Book of Job,* OTL (Philadelphia: Westminster, 1985) 213.

208. D. Clines, *Job 1–20,* 3rd ed., AB 15 (Garden City, N.Y.: Doubleday, 1979) 275.

209. Cf. R. Gordis, "Quotations as a Literary Usage in Biblical, Oriental and Rabbinic Literature," *HUCA* 22 (1949) 157-219; R. Gordis, *The Book of Job: Commentary, New Translation, and Special Studies* (New York: Jewish Theological Seminary, 5738/1978) 523-24; Clines, *Job 1–20,* 292.

210. M. Dahood, *Proverbs and Northwest Semitic Philology* (Rome: Pontifical Biblical Institute, 1963) 58; followed by Pope, *Job,* 91.

211. L. Perdue, *Wisdom in Revolt: Metaphorical Theology in the Book of Job,* Bible and Literature Series 29 (Sheffield: JSOT, 1991) 152n. 1.

source of knowledge in the wisdom tradition (Prov 6:6; 30:24-28; see also 1 Kgs 4:33[5:13]). Job's point, however, is not a comparative one but a direct challenge to Zophar's wish that God would reveal to Job the "hidden things of wisdom" (11:6). To the contrary, Job says, all that it is necessary to know is readily available, anywhere in the cosmos.

12:9-10. What is the crucial knowledge that every creature understands? In keeping with his rhetorical strategy, Job states it in the form of a well-known saying: "that the hand of the Lord has done this" (v. 9). The exact words are also found in Isa 41:20b, and it is likely that both authors are simply using a familiar formula. In fact, the cliché quality of this statement is indicated by the presence of the divine name "Yahweh." Throughout the poetic section of Job, the divine name is otherwise never used by the author. Whether the poet used it intentionally to signal Job's citation of a common saying, or whether a scribe accidentally substituted the more familiar form of the saying, the "slip" is a telling one. This phrase is on everyone's lips.

The ambiguity of the word "this" in v. 9 is calculated. Does it point forward to the platitudinous statement in v. 10? Or does it point backward to what Job said in vv. 4-6 about the contradictions between what should be and what is? By allowing the ambiguity to remain unresolved, Job forces his audience to recognize that the clichés they thought protected their complacent view of the world can be turned against them. Even the platitude in v. 10 serves Job's purposes. None of the friends would contradict such a statement, and yet the phrase "in his hand" or "in his power" echoes Job's description of the rampant injustice he described in v. 6. All that one needs to know, Job suggests, is that God is ultimately responsible.

12:11–13:2. 12:11. Job is not finished with his parodic performance of a wisdom discourse. He introduces the second part in v. 11 with a traditional saying used to invite agreement with the speaker. Elihu will use the same saying in 34:3 at the beginning of his second discourse. The saying is based on the image of the discriminating palate as a metaphor of critical judgment. Here, too, Job chooses his platitude carefully. As Clines notes, the saying has a disingenuous quality to it.

Although it ostensibly honors the hearer's judgment, it is used as an assertion that the speaker is right and that the audience members naturally all share the same tastes.[212] Job's own testing of words, as the following verses will make abundantly clear, is a genuinely critical exercise. He takes seriously the individual, experiential basis of knowledge implicit in the words of the saying but largely ignores the way it is customarily employed (cf. 13:1-2).

12:12-13. The words that Job asks his audience to test belong to another clichéd sentiment—that wisdom and understanding are characteristic of age (v. 12). The issue that engages many commentators, whether Job could possibly believe such a claim himself,[213] is not entirely to the point. Job is playing a sophisticated game with his friends, and he first offers them a saying that they could certainly test and find sound. Following the traditional style of logic that argues from the lesser to the greater, Job goes on to assert that God (who, after all, is the ancient of days) possesses not only wisdom and understanding, but also power and counsel, qualities having to do with the ability to effect what one plans (v. 13). Again, the friends would certainly find this statement to their taste. As often noted, the four qualities attributed to God in v. 13 are also the God-given qualities of the ideal ruler (Isa 11:2). It is precisely these words—*wisdom, understanding, counsel, strength*—that Job wishes to test in order to determine their real meaning in relation to God's governance of the world, not the debased meaning they have in the platitudes of common speech.

Verse 13 is not just the second part of a lesser-to-greater argument. It also introduces the satirical doxology that occupies the rest of the chapter. Verses 13, 16, and 22 provide the general statements illustrated by the concrete examples in the following verses. Ostensibly serving to substantiate the divine qualities listed in v. 13, the examples actually destabilize their meaning.

12:14-25. Job's rhetorical strategy begins to change in vv. 14-25. Whereas previously he had used the very platitudes that characterized the

212. Clines, *Job 1–20*, 295.
213. E.g., Pope, *Job*, 92; H. Rowley, *The Book of Job*, rev. ed., NCB (Grand Rapids, Mich.: Eerdmans, 1976; original ed., 1970) 94; Clines, *Job 1–20*, 295.

friends' speech, now he uses traditional hymnic style but gives the content a decidedly negative cast. Even here, however, Job uses much of the phraseology and themes from familiar hymnic praise of God. Psalm 107 is particularly close and may even be specifically quoted by Job (Ps 107:40 = Job 12:21*a*, 24*b*). Isaiah 44:24-28 and Dan 2:20-23 also have striking similarities to this passage. The important issue is not whether Job alludes specifically to any of these passages. It is, rather, the way in which the common idioms of praise, which in Job's opinion have served as a kind of verbal fog, obscuring real knowledge of God, are now used by him in a subversive way to disclose the truth about God's governance of the world.

12:14-15. The subtlety of Job's inflections of traditional speech can be seen in vv. 14-15, which offer substantiations for v. 13. The pairs of verbs in v. 14 ("tears down . . . rebuild"; "shut in . . . open up") are conventional ones, elsewhere used in positive contexts to define power and authority (cf. Isa 22:22; Jer 1:10). In those contexts, however, the actions are complementary. In Jeremiah, reconstruction follows destruction; in Isaiah, opening and closing suggest proper regulation. By contrast, Job highlights only the destructive, restrictive element of each pair. More distantly, Job's words parody Eliphaz's hymn of God's transforming power (5:8-16). Here, however, constructive activity is precisely what is prevented.

In contrast to v. 14, where only one type of action was featured, v. 15 describes God's engaging in two complementary actions—but with similarly devastating results. The unmotivated, destructive manipulation of water in v. 15 contrasts with Ps 107:33-37, where water is dried up and released specifically as punishment and blessing.

12:16-21. These verses constitute the second part of the satirical doxology. The first line of v. 16 is closely parallel to v. 13, merely adding "strength" and "effectiveness" to the list of divine qualities. But the second line is startling. Job employs a merismus, a figure of speech that indicates totality by naming opposite categories, such as "bond and free" (Deut 32:36; 1 Kgs 14:10) or "great and small" (Esth 1:5). The categories Job chooses are not social ones, however, but "deceived and deceiver." For Job the heart of human experience is error and the cynical ma-

nipulation of truth, and it is God to whom this situation must be attributed. By placing these words at the end of the sequence of divine qualities in vv. 13 and 16, Job creates an utterance that is at the literal level contradictory. The God of wisdom and understanding is the God of error and manipulation.

The implicit contradiction is explored further in the substantiating examples in vv. 17-21. Here, as Habel notes, Job satirizes the claim made by passages such as Prov 8:14-16 that divine wisdom is the source of just and effective human government.[214] In Proverbs, personified wisdom claims: "to me belong *counsel* and *effectiveness*; I am *understanding*; to me belongs *strength.* By me *kings* govern and leaders decree what is right; by me rulers rule, and *nobles,* all who *judge* rightly" (words in common with Job 12:13-21 are italicized). In vv. 17-21, Job lists nine categories of persons who provide leadership for a community in its political, religious, and social life. In contrast to the claims of Proverbs 8, however, Job's doxology describes the activities of God that destroy just governance. One way is by insidiously depriving leaders of reason, so that they do not have the "counsel and understanding" of wisdom (vv. 17*b*, 20). God also causes leaders to be defeated and humiliated, that is, deprived of "strength and effectiveness" (vv. 17*a*, 18-19, 21). Several images refer to the practice of stripping, a symbolic act represented in ancient Near Eastern art.[215] Since the garments of leaders are often badges of office, the humiliation is not merely personal but also an act of violence against the community.

A discordant echo occurs in v. 21*a*, where Job incorporates the exact words of Ps 107:40*a*. In the psalm, God is praised for the action of "pouring contempt upon nobles," represented as God's intervention to save the poor from their oppressors and restore right order (Ps 107:39-42). Job, however, takes the same "snapshot" of divine intervention and sets it in a different context, giving it a wholly different and deeply disturbing meaning.

12:22-25. Verse 22 introduces the final strophe

214. N. Habel, *The Book of Job,* OTL (Philadelphia: Westminster, 1985) 216.
215. James B. Pritchard, ed., *The Ancient Near East in Pictures Related to the Old Testament* (*ANEP*) (Princeton: Princeton University Press, 1954), 98-99, 111; pls. 305, 332.

of the doxology. Although the verse shares some vocabulary with Ps 107:10, 14, its celebration of God's knowledge of things "deep and dark" is closer to the language of the doxology in Dan 2:20-23, in which Daniel celebrates God as a revealer of mysteries. Job 12:22a is almost identical to Dan 2:22a. Job's deviation from standard, orthodox language in v. 22 is very slight but highly significant. The only word that is out of place is צלמות (ṣalmāwet), literally, "shadow of death" (NRSV, "deep darkness"; NIV, "deep shadows"). This word is not part of the semantics of mystery, as simple "darkness" is (חשׁך ḥōšek; as in Dan 2:22), but always connotes danger and evil. When Job uses both words together, he intends them to signify something sinister (3:5; 10:21). Now the allusion to Ps 107:10, 14 can be properly understood. The psalmist describes prisoners who sit in "darkness and the shadow of death," prisoners whom God "brings forth." Job, however, metaphorically treats this menacing shadow of death as itself the prisoner whom God brings forth and sets free.

The fruits of this divine activity are described in the examples of vv. 23-25. These verses are also best understood against the background of Psalm 107. The image with which Psalm 107 begins and ends is that of a scattered and directionless people being brought together and settled in an orderly and prosperous land (Ps 107:2-9, 33-41). Their oppressors were the ones whom God caused to wander, lost in the wilderness (Ps 107:40b). But here God's action has a disturbing quality of purposelessness. Nations are apparently made great only to be destroyed (v. 23). Citing Ps 107:40b, Job depicts God's power to disorient as directed not at oppressors but at those whose responsibility it is to lead (v. 24). The final verse (v. 25) departs from the participial style of the doxology (represented in the NRSV and the NIV by the initial "he" in vv. 17-24). The focus shifts from inexplicable divine activity to the pathos of disoriented leaders, groping and staggering like drunks.

13:1-2. Although the chapter division segments Job's speech here, these verses correspond in form and content to the words with which Job opened his speech in 12:3, reasserting his claim to be equal to his friends in knowledge. Job's knowledge is grounded differently than that of the friends, however. Zophar had argued in an *a priori* fashion from the premise of the superior wisdom of God. Bildad had insisted upon the authority of ancestral tradition. Eliphaz had grounded his teachings on a revelatory encounter. But Job insists on the authority of experience: what his own eye has seen, what his own ear has heard (13:2).

REFLECTIONS

There is a great deal to think about in this part of Job's speech, but one issue seems particularly important: Job's devastating critique of a theological language constructed of clichés and platitudes. Job's parody of such language hits close to home. Although the problem is not unique to religious discourse, one cannot help remembering the sermons, Sunday school lessons, funeral homilies, and words of appreciation for volunteers that seemingly consist of nothing but a string of platitudes. More alarmingly, one hears one's own voice mouthing those tired phrases and trite words.

What is wrong with platitudes? If the issue were simply one of style or a lack of sophistication, then very little would be at stake. Job, however, is talking about something much more serious. The issue is how language serves or fails to serve truth. In Job's view, a language riddled with platitudes is a diseased language that can no longer serve this essential function. Platitudes are ready-made, standard-issue speech, and they suffer from the problem that besets other one-size-fits-all products: They seldom fit. The richness, complexity, and ambiguity of situations are lost when a speaker attempts to force them into the simplistic patterns of perception provided by a language of clichés.

Even in the most innocuous cases, one senses what is wrong with such language. Think of a typically trite appreciation speech. Even if the words are truly applied and the person being honored is in fact "generous to a fault," "a pillar of the community," "always ready to lend a helping hand," "the backbone of the church," "beloved by his/her children," etc., saying such words drains the person of individuality. It reduces the person to a monochromatic blandness, and so ends up being false.

The emptiness of such speech makes it easy to use in a more perniciously false way, by misapplying the platitudes. When words have been debased, one does not treat them with value and care. They become pretend words that describe the way one wants a situation to be, even if it is actually the opposite. So one introduces the new chair of the board as a "devoted family man," even if it is known that he is abusive to his children. One refers to the mayor who lined her pockets while in office as a "dedicated public servant." Such a language of collective self-deception is the verbal equivalent of the emperor's new clothes. It is not just the language of personal evaluation that is corrupted by cliché and platitude. Social and moral problems also are reduced to formulas by such speech. It becomes impossible to see what the problems actually are because the platitude substitutes for discriminating judgment. Once the label is applied, no further thought is needed.

People succumb to the temptations of clichéd speech for many reasons, including simple laziness. Social insecurity, too, leads people to say words they have heard before, words that they hope will make them fit in. More disturbingly, people are drawn to platitudinous language when they are uneasy in the presence of something they do not understand and fear to examine. Religious leaders in particular often assume that they are supposed to have answers for every human dilemma. How much easier it is to speak in an authoritative voice of "the wisdom of God which we cannot comprehend" or "the plan of God for your life" than to admit that there is no simple answer for the pain, confusion, and devastation that erupt unexpectedly in people's lives. How much easier it is to mouth the conventional words of comfort than to find words for the unspeakable contradiction between a God of love and a world of cruelty and broken bodies.

Job will not stand for this. He knows that his friends are frightened by the anomaly he represents and that they use language to defend themselves against having to look into the truth of his devastation. In their response to him, they reveal how debased their religious language has become. It provides them with only so many pigeonholes, and they are determined to make Job's situation fit one of them: "Think now, who that was innocent ever perished?" (4:7 NRSV). "Happy is the one whom God reproves" (5:17 NRSV). "Does God pervert justice?" (8:3 NRSV). "If you will seek God . . . [God will] restore to you your rightful place" (8:5-6 NRSV). "Know then that God exacts of you less than your guilt deserves" (11:6 NRSV).

Even worse, in Job's view, they misapply words until such words literally have no meaning. His friends are ready to speak of God's "wisdom and understanding." But the reality Job experiences cannot be appropriately described as the result of God's wisdom and understanding. When words no longer refer to some reality, then they are simply nonsense syllables that can be used in any way at all. Perhaps the worst result of the friends' corrupt language is that they have allowed it to become a substitute for seeing and hearing. Their platitudes persuade them that they already know, without needing to look or listen, what the world is like and why things happen as they do.

A language so debased and corrupted as the one the friends speak is almost impervious to criticism. How does one break in and interrupt its self-satisfied noise? One effective strategy is parody—mimicking the tone and favored vocabulary of debased speech, exaggerating its characteristic features, and bringing into full view the ugly things such speech tries so hard to hide. That, of course, is precisely what Job does in chap. 12. He mimics the way the friends talk, exaggerating the use of wisdom figures, proverbs, traditional sayings, and hymnic forms. In doing so, he draws attention to the problems inherent in using language worn too smooth by too many mouths. The most important part of Job's parody, however, is the way he creates a thoroughly incoherent speech to show just how the friends' words have lost their meaning. Job aggressively juxtaposes the words *wisdom* and *understanding* with concrete examples that cannot possibly be included in anybody's definition of them. Job forces the contradiction between words and reality, which the friends have ignored, into his own parodic speech, where the contradiction between one word and another cannot be missed.

After one has heard an effective parody, after it has disrupted the smoothness of familiar forms of speech, it becomes hard to hear the traditional speech without also hearing an echo of the parody. The mocking voice, the dissenting opinion, is always there like a whisper. Parody of the sort Job uses disrupts the universalizing claims made by "straight" speech by posing an undeniable counterexample. After Job has spoken, one cannot hear Psalm 107 and its confident claims about God's leading a people to a settled and orderly life without also hearing the echo of Job's counterexample of a whole leadership class destroyed and the senseless destruction of a nation. One hears religious leaders claiming to recognize God's power in the movements toward democracy in the modern world; the Joban parodist would mimic their speech, saying that one has only to look at the increasing number of genocidal conflicts in the world to see evidence of God's power.

As much as such language needs to be questioned, there are limits to what parody can accomplish. Parody is a critical, but not constructive, tool. It can expose the inadequacies of someone's speech, but it cannot by itself provide an alternative way to talk about reality. Moreover, parody has its own dangerous seductions. There is great energy in its negative power. Without equal commitment to a constructive alternative, the negativity of parody can become a cynical nihilism. Job seems to recognize this danger. In chap. 13, he will turn from his scathing critique of the way the friends talk about God to explore an alternative way of talking about God and with God that he finds more adequate to the rigorous demands of speaking the truth.

Job 13:3-19, Job Criticizes Deceitful Speech

NIV

3"But I desire to speak to the Almighty
    and to argue my case with God.
4You, however, smear me with lies;
    you are worthless physicians, all of you!
5If only you would be altogether silent!
    For you, that would be wisdom.
6Hear now my argument;
    listen to the plea of my lips.
7Will you speak wickedly on God's behalf?
    Will you speak deceitfully for him?
8Will you show him partiality?
    Will you argue the case for God?
9Would it turn out well if he examined you?
    Could you deceive him as you might deceive
        men?
10He would surely rebuke you
    if you secretly showed partiality.
11Would not his splendor terrify you?
    Would not the dread of him fall on you?

NRSV

3 "But I would speak to the Almighty,[a]
    and I desire to argue my case with God.
4 As for you, you whitewash with lies;
    all of you are worthless physicians.
5 If you would only keep silent,
    that would be your wisdom!
6 Hear now my reasoning,
    and listen to the pleadings of my lips.
7 Will you speak falsely for God,
    and speak deceitfully for him?
8 Will you show partiality toward him,
    will you plead the case for God?
9 Will it be well with you when he searches you
        out?
    Or can you deceive him, as one person
        deceives another?
10 He will surely rebuke you
    if in secret you show partiality.

a Traditional rendering of Heb *Shaddai*

NIV

12Your maxims are proverbs of ashes;
    your defenses are defenses of clay.

13"Keep silent and let me speak;
    then let come to me what may.

14Why do I put myself in jeopardy
    and take my life in my hands?

15Though he slay me, yet will I hope in him;
    I will surely*a* defend my ways to his face.

16Indeed, this will turn out for my deliverance,
    for no godless man would dare come before
        him!

17Listen carefully to my words;
    let your ears take in what I say.

18Now that I have prepared my case,
    I know I will be vindicated.

19Can anyone bring charges against me?
    If so, I will be silent and die."

a15 Or He will surely slay me; I have no hope — / yet I will

NRSV

11 Will not his majesty terrify you,
    and the dread of him fall upon you?

12 Your maxims are proverbs of ashes,
    your defenses are defenses of clay.

13 "Let me have silence, and I will speak,
    and let come on me what may.

14 I will take my flesh in my teeth,
    and put my life in my hand.*a*

15 See, he will kill me; I have no hope;*b*
    but I will defend my ways to his face.

16 This will be my salvation,
    that the godless shall not come before him.

17 Listen carefully to my words,
    and let my declaration be in your ears.

18 I have indeed prepared my case;
    I know that I shall be vindicated.

19 Who is there that will contend with me?
    For then I would be silent and die."

b Gk: Heb Why should I take . . . in my hand?
c Or Though he kill me, yet I will trust in him

COMMENTARY

13:3-12. Despite his expressed intention to speak with God (v. 3), Job has not finished his critique of the friends' speech. Although the expression "smear with lies" (v. 4) is a traditional phrase for slander (Ps 119:69; Sir 51:5), the context suggests that Job uses it in a different way. As the following verses indicate, what bothers Job is not lies about himself but misrepresentations of the nature of God (v. 7). Verse 4 makes most sense if one assumes that both lines are part of a medical image.[216] The friends are "worthless physicians" because the salves or plasters with which they have tried to heal Job are but lies they have spoken about God.

Job's sarcastic comment that the friends could best show their wisdom by remaining silent (cf. Prov 17:28) is perhaps an ironic allusion to Zophar's claim that Job's babblings have silenced others (11:2). If only it were so! The call to be silent and listen (vv. 5-6) here introduces Job's

criticism of the friends (vv. 7-12), but is repeated in vv. 13 and 17, as Job introduces his address to God. In both places Job uses legal terminology to characterize his words, in v. 6 as "pleadings" (רבות *ribôt*; cf. Deut 17:8) and in v. 18 as a "case" (משפט *mišpāṭ*).

Having framed his remarks in legal terminology, Job's accusation that the friends have spoken "falsely" and "deceitfully" for God (v. 7) amounts to a charge that they have borne "false witness." Job reinforces the legal metaphor by describing the friends as "showing partiality" to God in arguing God's case (v. 8). The friends, of course, have not thought of themselves as participating in a trial. They are simply counseling a friend about the proper religious understanding of his situation. By insisting on viewing their words through the lens of legal categories, however, Job is demanding that theological language be held to the same strict standards of truth required of participants in a trial. The severe penalties prescribed for those who give false witness (Deut 19:16-19; cf. Exod 20:16; Deut 5:20) and the stringent prohibition

216. So the LXX; cf. G. Fohrer, *Das Buch Hiob,* KAT xvi (Guetersloh: Gerd Mohn, 1963) 247; and D. Clines, *Job 1–20,* WBC 17 (Dallas: Word, 1989) 306.

of partiality (Exod 23:2-3, 6-8) indicate how seriously such matters were taken.

There is an irony in Job's imagining God examining and rebuking the friends (vv. 9-10). Although Job will be examined in God's searching speeches at the end of the book, the friends will be rebuked because they "have not spoken of me what is right" (42:7 NRSV). In v. 10, Job speaks of the friends "showing partiality in secret." From their own perspective, the accusation is wrong on both counts. Their defense of God is not partiality, and they have been quite open in their views. Job's words are psychologically acute, however. The friends' motives and the character of their words are hidden, even from themselves. Their lack of perception is evident in the glibness with which they speak deceit, without a sense of the awfulness of an angry God (v. 11). Job knows of what he speaks, for he has experienced the terror of the divine presence, even though he is blameless (6:4; 7:14; 9:34-35).

Job's passionate depiction of a God enraged by false witness and partiality contrasts sharply with his earlier depiction of a God whose power overrides justice (9:14-20; 10:15) and who even corrupts judges (9:24). Both images appear true to Job, and yet they are contradictory.

The terms Job uses in v. 12 to summarize his dismissal of the friends' speech as worthless are quite comprehensive. "Maxims" (זכרון *zikkārôn*, lit. "something remembered") alludes to tradition.[217] "Proverbs" (משל *māšāl*) are the commonplaces of speech by which people order their thinking. The final term is actually a play on words, for it means both "replies" and "defenses" (גב *gab*),[218] suggesting the friends' rhetorical argumentation. In the wisdom tradition, wise and appropriate words are compared to precious and desirable objects (choice silver, honeycomb, apples of gold in a setting of silver; see Prov 10:20; 16:24; 25:11) because they have the capacity to save and to give life (Prov 10:11; 11:14; 12:6; 15:4). By contrast, all of the resources of language at the friends' disposal are "clay" and "ashes," images of what crumbles into nothingness (Job 4:4-19; Ezek 28:18; Mal 4:3[3:21]).

13:13-16. Since the friends' speech is worthless, they should be silent (v. 13*a*). In contrast to the friends, who seem to be oblivious to the danger of speaking falsely about God, Job assesses the risk he takes in speaking honestly before God (vv. 13*b*-16). Formally, this passage is like the statements in 7:11 and 10:1 with which Job introduced his earlier address to God. There Job referred to the "bitterness of spirit" forcing him to speak. Here the urgency is expressed somewhat differently.

As often happens, ambiguities in the text allow for more than one translation and somewhat different depictions of Job's state of mind. The NRSV and the NIV make quite different interpretive choices, and the issues deserve careful attention. In v. 14, the phrase meaning "why" (על־מה *'al-mâ*) is probably an accidental recopying of the last letters in v. 13 ("upon me what may" [עלי מה *ālay mâ*]). The NIV retains the phrase and takes v. 14 as a rhetorical question answered in vv. 15-16. The NRSV, following the LXX, omits the phrase and takes v. 14 as a statement of determination, further developed in v. 15 and qualified in v. 16. Although the image of taking one's life into one's hands is attested elsewhere (Judg 12:3; 1 Sam 19:5; 28:21), the parallel image of taking one's flesh into one's teeth is not.

The most famous textual problem in the book of Job occurs in v. 15. There are several ambiguities. The first word (הן *hēn*) may be translated either as "behold," "see" (so NRSV) or as the word that means "if," "even if" (so NIV). The second verb (יחל *yiḥēl*) means "to wait" and, since it can suggest expectant waiting, is sometimes translated "to hope." The crux of the textual problem is reflected in the difference between the NRSV ("I have no hope") and the NIV ("yet will I hope in him"). The Hebrew Bible preserves both traditions in the marginal notation known as *Ketib/Qere,* which means "what is written"/"what is read." While the body of the text clearly contains the negative (לא *lō'*; hence, "I cannot wait" or "I have no hope"), the marginal note records an ancient alternative reading "to/for him" (לו *lô*; hence, "I will wait for him" or "I will hope in him"). Both traditions were known to the rabbis, as *Mishnah Sota* 5.5 indicates in its discussion of Job: "The matter is undecided—do I hope in him [*lô*] or not hope [*lō'*]?"[219]

217. Cf. R. Gordis, *The Book of Job: Commentary, New Translation, and Special Studies* (New York: Jewish Theological Seminary, 5738/1978) 143, who associates the term with Bildad's appeal to ancient authority.

218. L. Koehler and W. Baumgartner, *Hebräisches und Aramäisches Lexicon,* 3rd ed. (Leiden: Brill, 1967) 170.

219. Gordis, *The Book of Job,* 144. B. Zuckerman, *Job the Silent: A Study in Historical Counterpoint* (New York: Oxford University Press, 1991) 170, discusses the evidence for the antiquity of the variant reading.

How one resolves these ambiguities is as much a matter of context as text. The NIV presents Job as still entangled in the paradox of a God whose irrational violence is real but whose commitment to truth is just as real. There is genuine danger that if Job presses his case, God will kill him (cf. 9:17-18). The "hope" (v. 15) and the "deliverance" (v. 16) of which Job speaks are not that he will escape death but that he will be vindicated, since his integrity will be attested by the very fact of his daring to come before God (v. 16b). Such an interpretation is both textually and contextually defensible. Only when v. 15 is taken out of context and made into a slogan of masochistic piety is the authenticity of this reading abused.

The NRSV interpretation, equally defensible, presents Job in a more defiant mode. Job does not pose a rhetorical question about why he is willing to risk death, but makes a statement (v. 14), intensified into a certainty (v. 15), that God will kill him. Such a dramatic claim sets off Job's determination to speak in defiance of all the power of God. One could also stress the note of urgency rather than defiance with a slightly different translation: "See, he may kill me; I cannot wait, but I must argue my ways to his face."[220] Such a translation would parallel the reference to the urgency of impending death with which Job introduces his address to God in 7:7-11. The textual ambiguities in 13:14-16 are not mere annoyances but occasions for pondering the image of Job: Is he a figure pressed by the urgency of death, a Promethean rebel, or a person wracked by the paradoxes of God? Meditating on alternative interpretations is more valuable than choosing one too quickly.

13:17-19. Although Job is primarily concerned to address God, he cares that his friends hear and understand what he says (v. 17). As his language in vv. 18-19 makes clear, Job continues to think of his encounter with God in terms of a court case. An interpretive choice must be made here, too. If one translates v. 18b as "I know I shall be vindicated," then Job appears to be expressing a confidence in God's justice that contradicts his earlier feelings (9:15, 29). Such an interpretation gives Job a certain psychological complexity, although Habel prefers to translate Job's words as conditional: "I should be vindicated."[221] The line, however, need not refer to what God will do at all, but to Job's own certainty about himself: "I know that I am innocent."[222] (Cf. 9:20-21, where Job's self-knowledge threatened to disintegrate under the pressure of God's overwhelming power.) This interpretation fits well with the following line (v. 19a), in which Job asks rhetorically who could bring charges against him (cf. Isa 50:8, where the same expression is used in a similar expression of confidence). There is no real doubt in Job's mind about his own innocence when he says, "For then I would be silent and die" (v. 19). What the line reveals is how closely linked speech and life are for Job. In chap. 3, Job did not want to live. Even in chaps. 6–7 death was as much desired as feared. Beginning in chap. 9, however, the image of a trial with God has given Job a conceptually powerful way to articulate his sense of grievance. Now, the desire to state his case has given Job the will to live. If, to his surprise, a case were proven against him, then his ability both to speak and to live would evaporate together.

---

220. Similarly E. Good, *In Turns of Tempest* (Stanford, Calif.: Stanford University Press, 1990) 85.

221. N. Habel, *The Book of Job,* OTL (Philadelphia: Westminster, 1985) 224, 231. Cf. Gordis, *The Book of Job,* 130.

222. So Clines, *Job 1–20,* 277; and Good, *In Turns of Tempest,* 85.

REFLECTIONS

Job is the representative of those whose resistance to suffering takes the form of a determination to bring truth to light. From the perpetrators of genocide who attempt to destroy all witnesses to their crime to the incest survivor who is threatened so that she or he will never tell anyone, silence continues the violence against the abused. Bearing witness is both a means of survival and an act of defiance. The passion to speak is the power to live.

Speaking out can be especially difficult where society's uneasiness about a problem takes the form of blaming the victim, as has often been the case with survivors of sexual crimes, such as rape and incest. Undeserved shame serves as a strong deterrent to their publicly disclosing what happened to them. Even close friends and family members who are otherwise supportive may become uneasy and even embarrassed if a survivor insists on speaking out. Job's situation is strikingly similar, which makes his struggle particularly instructive. As discussed in the Commentary to chaps. 1–2, overwhelming catastrophes in general and skin diseases in particular carried with them the suggestion that the victim had perhaps done something wrong and was being punished for it. Such suffering was associated with a taint of shamefulness, as the description of the suffering servant suggests: "He was despised and rejected by others;/ a man of suffering and acquainted with infirmity;/ and as one from whom others hide their faces,/ he was despised, and we held him of no account" (Isa 53:3 NRSV). For Job to demand a trial in which he could be vindicated and God's wrongful action exposed is to reject the implication that he should feel shame for what has happened to him. One wishes that such courage always brought forth support from others. Often it does not, and speaking out can be lonely. As the example of Job shows, however, the very act of speaking can become a source of energy, confidence, and the will to live.

Bearing witness is also an act of faith. It testifies to the belief that if people only knew the truth, they would do something to change the situation, because they desire justice. The Chinese dissident who smuggles out an account of forced labor camps, the Central American widow who publishes the names of the army officers who tortured and murdered her husband, the small-town newspaper reporter who writes about the conditions of migrant workers—such people bear witness not only to the existence of evil but also to the possibility of good. Sometimes their faith is rewarded; other times, it is disappointed, when their testimony is met with chilling indifference. That such people continue to call upon others to hear is an act of faith that the community has more goodness and power than it has yet acknowledged. This dynamic sheds light on the apparent contradictoriness of Job's appeal for justice to a God he has accused of corrupting justice. Unlike the friends, Job does not flinch from the realities that appear to show God's indifference, if not cruelty. Nevertheless, Job's act of faith is that God is fundamentally a God of justice who will yet respond, if only God will listen.

In one important respect, Job's situation is different from that of persons bearing witness against human abuse and oppression. In those instances, the criminal nature of the acts themselves is clear. Job's life, however, has been devastated by a series of catastrophes, the origin and significance of which are not at all clear. He knows that the traditional explanations provided by the friends are unsatisfactory, but he is groping to find a way of talking about what has happened that will be more adequate to his experience. His characterization of what has happened and what it implies about God and his relation to God has an exploratory quality. Only after Job has taken up the legal metaphor does the notion of bearing witness become essential. One is still left with the question, however, of whether the metaphor of a trial is the appropriate one for Job's situation. In the end, it may not be, a possibility that will raise its own issues for reflection. At this point, however, it is the most compelling model available to Job for understanding his situation, and he is prepared to follow what it requires of him, courageously bearing witness to the truth, even if it means risking his life in a confrontation with God.

Job 13:20–14:22, Job Experiences the Destruction of Hope

NIV

20"Only grant me these two things, O God,
    and then I will not hide from you:
21Withdraw your hand far from me,
    and stop frightening me with your terrors.
22Then summon me and I will answer,
    or let me speak, and you reply.
23How many wrongs and sins have I committed?
    Show me my offense and my sin.
24Why do you hide your face
    and consider me your enemy?
25Will you torment a windblown leaf?
    Will you chase after dry chaff?
26For you write down bitter things against me
    and make me inherit the sins of my youth.
27You fasten my feet in shackles;
    you keep close watch on all my paths
    by putting marks on the soles of my feet.

28"So man wastes away like something rotten,
    like a garment eaten by moths.

14 "Man born of woman
    is of few days and full of trouble.
2He springs up like a flower and withers away;
    like a fleeting shadow, he does not endure.
3Do you fix your eye on such a one?
    Will you bring him*a* before you for judgment?
4Who can bring what is pure from the impure?
    No one!
5Man's days are determined;
    you have decreed the number of his months
    and have set limits he cannot exceed.
6So look away from him and let him alone,
    till he has put in his time like a hired man.

7"At least there is hope for a tree:
    If it is cut down, it will sprout again,
    and its new shoots will not fail.
8Its roots may grow old in the ground
    and its stump die in the soil,
9yet at the scent of water it will bud
    and put forth shoots like a plant.
10But man dies and is laid low;
    he breathes his last and is no more.
11As water disappears from the sea
    or a riverbed becomes parched and dry,
12so man lies down and does not rise;

a3 Septuagint, Vulgate and Syriac; Hebrew me

NRSV

20 Only grant two things to me,
    then I will not hide myself from your face:
21 withdraw your hand far from me,
    and do not let dread of you terrify me.
22 Then call, and I will answer;
    or let me speak, and you reply to me.
23 How many are my iniquities and my sins?
    Make me know my transgression and my
        sin.
24 Why do you hide your face,
    and count me as your enemy?
25 Will you frighten a windblown leaf
    and pursue dry chaff?
26 For you write bitter things against me,
    and make me reap*a* the iniquities of my
        youth.
27 You put my feet in the stocks,
    and watch all my paths;
    you set a bound to the soles of my feet.
28 One wastes away like a rotten thing,
    like a garment that is moth-eaten.

14 "A mortal, born of woman, few of days
    and full of trouble,
2 comes up like a flower and withers,
    flees like a shadow and does not last.
3 Do you fix your eyes on such a one?
    Do you bring me into judgment with you?
4 Who can bring a clean thing out of an unclean?
    No one can.
5 Since their days are determined,
    and the number of their months is known
        to you,
    and you have appointed the bounds that
        they cannot pass,
6 look away from them, and desist,*b*
    that they may enjoy, like laborers, their
        days.

7 "For there is hope for a tree,
    if it is cut down, that it will sprout again,
    and that its shoots will not cease.
8 Though its root grows old in the earth,
    and its stump dies in the ground,
9 yet at the scent of water it will bud

a Heb inherit   b Cn: Heb that they may desist

NIV

till the heavens are no more, men will not
awake
or be roused from their sleep.

¹³"If only you would hide me in the grave*ᵃ*
and conceal me till your anger has passed!
If only you would set me a time
and then remember me!
¹⁴If a man dies, will he live again?
All the days of my hard service
I will wait for my renewal*ᵇ* to come.
¹⁵You will call and I will answer you;
you will long for the creature your hands have
made.
¹⁶Surely then you will count my steps
but not keep track of my sin.
¹⁷My offenses will be sealed up in a bag;
you will cover over my sin.

¹⁸"But as a mountain erodes and crumbles
and as a rock is moved from its place,
¹⁹as water wears away stones
and torrents wash away the soil,
so you destroy man's hope.
²⁰You overpower him once for all, and he is gone;
you change his countenance and send him
away.
²¹If his sons are honored, he does not know it;
if they are brought low, he does not see it.
²²He feels but the pain of his own body
and mourns only for himself."

ᵃ13 Hebrew *Sheol*   *ᵇ14* Or *release*

NRSV

and put forth branches like a young plant.
¹⁰ But mortals die, and are laid low;
humans expire, and where are they?
¹¹ As waters fail from a lake,
and a river wastes away and dries up,
¹² so mortals lie down and do not rise again;
until the heavens are no more, they will not
awake
or be roused out of their sleep.
¹³ O that you would hide me in Sheol,
that you would conceal me until your wrath
is past,
that you would appoint me a set time, and
remember me!
¹⁴ If mortals die, will they live again?
All the days of my service I would wait
until my release should come.
¹⁵ You would call, and I would answer you;
you would long for the work of your hands.
¹⁶ For then you would not*ᵃ* number my steps,
you would not keep watch over my sin;
¹⁷ my transgression would be sealed up in a bag,
and you would cover over my iniquity.

¹⁸ "But the mountain falls and crumbles away,
and the rock is removed from its place;
¹⁹ the waters wear away the stones;
the torrents wash away the soil of the earth;
so you destroy the hope of mortals.
²⁰ You prevail forever against them, and they pass
away;
you change their countenance, and send
them away.
²¹ Their children come to honor, and they do not
know it;
they are brought low, and it goes unnoticed.
²² They feel only the pain of their own bodies,
and mourn only for themselves."

ᵃ Syr: Heb lacks *not*

COMMENTARY

Since the friends lack the wisdom necessary to help him (cf. 6:24), Job desires to speak directly to God (v. 3), which he now does. The pattern of Job's direct speech to God is perplexing. In the speech with which he broke his silence (chap. 3), Job did not address God at all. Each of his three speeches in the first cycle concludes with an extended address to God (7:7-21; 10:2-22; 13:20–14:22). After the first cycle, however, Job does not address God again in any extended fashion.

Two verses in 17:3-4, perhaps two in 16:7-8, and a brief passage in 30:20-23 are the only words Job addresses directly to God before he replies to God's own speech in 40:3-5 and 42:1-6. What role this use and avoidance of direct address to God plays in the dramatic structure of the book and in the development of Job's character is not immediately self-evident. It can best be understood by recalling that the traditional language for direct address to God is the language of prayer, and Job does not wish to pray. In his three addresses to God, he attempts to find an alternative language. In chap. 7, Job burlesques the language of lament and praise, the traditional language of prayer. In chap. 10, he attempts to cast his words not as prayer but as a legal speech, and a hypothetical one at that. The motifs and language of prayer seep into his speech, however, especially in evocations of the creator/creature relationship in 10:8-12, although Job bitterly repudiates the possibility that such language could provide the basis for an appeal to God, and reasserts the categories of legal language (10:13-17). In chaps. 13–14, too, Job introduces his words as legal speech (13:17-22). In the latter part of this speech, however, Job starts to be drawn into the language of prayer (14:13-17). Nowhere else is his yearning for God expressed in such a direct way. At the last moment, however, Job turns away from prayer's traditional words of appeal (14:18-22). The language of prayer is still too powerful and too seductive for Job to trust himself to speak in its accents. After this, he will talk about God, but not to God, and the legal metaphor will increasingly direct his speech.

13:20-28. As in chaps. 9–10, Job recognizes that the imbalance of power between himself and God is a barrier to a fair trial. In contrast to 9:32-35, however, Job addresses God directly (v. 20). A lawsuit with God is not impossible—*if* God voluntarily removes the fearsomeness and the oppressive peremptory punishment that leave Job scarcely able to breathe (v. 21; cf. 7:13-16). Job imagines the encounter as a structured dialogue with either party taking the initiative. The wrong impression may be created by commentators who interpret v. 22 as offering God the position of either plaintiff or defendant.[223] The roles of parties

in legal disputes in the ancient Near East were not differentiated in quite the same way as in modern systems and could be quite fluid.[224] Moreover, in Job the metaphor of a trial as the way in which speech with God can be envisioned remains a suggestive metaphor rather than a literal event.

Job's rhetorical demand to know the number and nature of his iniquities, sins, and offenses is modeled after similar expressions often used in legal disputes to assert innocence. (Cf. Gen 31:36, where Jacob says to Laban, "What is my offense? What is my sin?" [NRSV], as he calls upon those present to act as judges in the dispute.)[225] A number of commentators are at pains to argue that Job does not claim never to have sinned, as though he were in danger of saying something "religiously incorrect."[226] That is not the issue, for Job's complete innocence is the narrative premise on which the story is built.[227] What is important here is the way in which the introduction of legal language changes the way Job talks about sin before God. No parallel exists for this kind of challenging question in the traditional language of Israelite prayer or in the cultic laws that govern relations between individuals and God. By transferring the patterns and idioms of language used to talk about the legal resolution of disputes between persons, Job begins to remap the territory of divine-human relations.

Although the image of God's hiding God's face (v. 24) is a familiar motif in psalms (Pss 27:9; 30:7[8]; 104:29), the rhetoric of vv. 24-25 is quite similar to that used by David in his dispute with Saul (1 Samuel 24). There, too, the issue is why Saul unjustly considered David an enemy (v. 24*b*; cf. 1 Sam 24:9, 19). Just as David asks rhetorically why Saul pursues "a dead dog? A single flea?" (1 Sam 24:14), so also Job chides God for pursuing "a windblown leaf . . . dry chaff" (v. 25). Job's accusations continue in v. 26. Exactly what it means to "write bitter things against" a person is

---

223. So M. Pope, *Job,* 3rd ed., AB 15 (Garden City, N.Y.: Doubleday, 1979) 101; Habel, *The Book of Job,* 231.

224. H. J. Boecker, *Law and the Administration of Justice in the Old Testament and Ancient East,* trans. J. Moiser (Minneapolis: Augsburg, 1980) 23; M. B. Dick, "The Legal Metaphor in Job 31," *CBQ* 41 (1979) 38.

225. Dick, "The Legal Metaphor in Job 31," 38n. 10, cites a similar example from a Babylonian letter of a man accused by his superior. He defends his innocence by saying, "What offense have I committed against my lord?"

226. Ibid., 167-68; Gordis, *The Book of Job,* 146; J. E. Hartley, *The Book of Job,* NICOT (Grand Rapids, Mich.: Eerdmans, 1988) 226-27.

227. Clines, *Job 1–20,* 318.

---

not clear. The verb can refer to the writing out of an indictment (cf. 31:35), but since Job complains that he has not been told what he is charged with, the phrase is better taken as the writing of a decree allotting bitter things to Job (cf. Isa 10:1).[228] The harsh nature of God's treatment is suggested also by the reference to "the sins of my youth" in v. 26*b*. Children were assumed to have a less fully formed moral understanding than adults (Deut 1:39; cf. Jonah 4:11). Even though a child was culpable for sins committed, God's mercy could be invoked to overlook the sins of youth (Ps 25:7). For such to be charged against Job implies a merciless harshness on God's part. The theme of obsessive divine scrutiny, raised by Job in 7:17-20 and 10:14-17, is repeated in v. 27. Although the verse is grammatically difficult, the images all have to do with circumscribed movement. The NIV interprets the last image according to a fanciful hypothesis about an ancient custom of inscribing an owner's name on the soles of the feet of slaves.[229] The NRSV more plausibly understands the verb to refer to inscribing a boundary to restrict movement.[230]

Verse 28 interrupts syntactically (lit., "and he . . . ") and is thematically more closely related to what follows than to the preceding lines. Many commentators suggest moving the verse to follow 14:2.[231] Although the image of decay and disintegration would not be inappropriate as a transition between chaps. 13 and 14, translations such as those of the NIV and the NRSV, which attempt this reading, have to paraphrase in order to minimize the syntactical problem.

14:1-6. The vocabulary and tone of legal challenge are abandoned in chap. 14, as Job turns instead to contemplate the ephemerality of human existence. The first six verses of chap. 14 divide into three groups, with the main point expressed in the middle pair. An initial comment on the transient quality of human life (vv. 1-2) leads to the central objection that God's bringing Job into judgment is cruelly absurd (vv. 3-4). The power that God has over the human lifespan becomes an argument for a brief respite (vv. 5-6).

14:1-2. Job's reflections, although prompted by his own experience, are expressed in universal terms. Commentators who see in the phrase "born of woman" (v. 1) an allusion to female weakness or impurity disclose their own misogyny, not that of the text.[232] The phrase simply means "every person," since there is no one who is not born of a woman (cf. 15:14; 25:4; Sir 10:18; 1QS 13.14; 1QH 18.12-13). The phrase may also contain the suggestion of inescapable mortality.[233] In the narratives of Genesis 3–4, birth takes place only outside the garden, when death has been sealed as humanity's fate. Birth is inextricably linked with death.

Job laments not only mortality but also the fleeting quality of life. The images of v. 2 are traditional (Job 8:6; Pss 37:2; 90:5-6; 103:15; 144:4; Eccl 6:12; Isa 40:6-8). The similes work by making phenomena that even human beings experience as ephemeral—flowers and shadows—into the symbols of human life itself. Job's bitterness is evident in the way his phrase "few of days and full of trouble" (v. 1*b*) reverses the traditional phrase "old and full of days" (Gen 25:8; 35:29; 1 Chr 29:28).

14:3-4. God's seemingly absurd determination to treat Job as a powerful adversary is a theme Job has broached before (7:12, 17-18). Here he casts it in terms of God's legal aggression against him (v. 3; whether one follows the MT in reading a first-person reference to Job [so NRSV] or the ancient versions in seeing a general reference to humanity [so NIV] makes little difference.). Commentators are often perplexed by v. 4 because they fail to recognize it as a figure of speech expressing an impossible transformation. It has the same general structure as the saying that one cannot "make a silk purse out of a sow's ear" or that one cannot "spin straw into gold." The comparison is even sharper, however, because "clean and unclean," categories drawn from the sphere of cultic practice, are logical opposites. The saying

228. F. Andersen, *Job: An Introduction and Commentary,* Tyndale Old Testament Commentaries (Downers Grove, Ill.: Inter-Varsity, 1976) 168.

229. N. H. Tur-Sinai, *The Book of Job: A New Commentary* (Jerusalem: Kiryath Sepher, 1957) 230; Gordis, *The Book of Job,* 146; cf. the critique of Clines, *Job 1–20,* 322.

230. A. B. Davidson, *The Book of Job,* The Cambridge Bible for Schools and Colleges 15 (Cambridge: Cambridge University Press, 1891) 101; A. S. Peake, *Job,* NCB (London: T.C. & E.C. Jack, 1904) 145; so Tanakh.

231. E. Dhorme, *A Commentary on the Book of Job,* trans. H. Knight (London: Nelson, 1967) 193; Pope, *Job,* 106; F. Horst, *Hiob,* Biblischer Kommentar xvi (Neukirchen-Vlun: Neukirchener Verlag, 1960) 206.

232. Peake, *Job,* 145; Dhorme, *A Commentary on the Book of Job,* 194; H. Rowley, *The Book of Job,* rev. ed., NCB (Grand Rapids, Mich.: Eerdmans, 1976; original ed., 1970) 103.

233. A. de Wilde, *Das Buch Hiob,* OTS xxii (Leiden: Brill, 1981) 172.

as a whole, not the individual terms, is to be applied to the situation at hand. God and Job cannot be appropriate adversaries at law because God and human beings are logical opposites, like clean and unclean, whereas parties at law must share a common legal status. Job is facing the same dilemma that he articulated in 9:32: "For he is not a mortal, as I am . . . that we should come to trial together."

14:5-6. The notion of a rivalry between humans and God and God's decision to limit the human lifespan or otherwise restrict human power are common mythic motifs throughout the ancient Near East. In the Bible, they are featured in the expulsion from the garden. After the humans eat the fruit that makes them "like God," they must be excluded from the tree of life, which would allow them to live forever (Gen 3:22). A similar divine restriction on human life follows the intermarriage of divine beings and human women in Gen 6:3. Job alludes to these traditions in v. 5. God has nothing to fear from human beings, since God has already set limits to human life. Consequently, God might drop the obsessive scrutiny (v. 6a). The NRSV and the NIV differ in their translations of v. 6b depending on which of two Hebrew homonyms (רצה rāṣâ) each translates; the NIV ("put in his time") is preferable (cf. Lev 26:34).[234]

14:7-12. The consequences of "the bounds that [humans] cannot pass" are worked out in a series of striking comparisons and contrasts with natural phenomena. Descriptive images in Hebrew poetry are generally brief and undeveloped. Job's vivid and extensively developed image of the tree (vv. 7-9) draws part of its power from its contrast with ordinary style. More important, however, is the complex pattern of cross-identification that the image creates. The expression "there is hope for a tree" has become so familiar that one seldom notices the figure of personification. Hope is an emotion, a characteristic of human beings. One does not ordinarily attribute hope to trees. Such personification, however, establishes a point of contact between the nature of the tree and of human experience. What "hope" means will be defined metaphorically by what

the poet says about the tree. The images of vulnerability, too, invite metaphorical appropriation. The felling of a tree in its prime (v. 7) and the aging and death of roots in dry ground (v. 8) are evocative of human susceptibility to violence and to loss of vitality in old age. Hope is concretely imaged in the growth of new shoots from a cut-off trunk (v. 7) and in the green response of dry roots to water (v. 9). Hope is the power of regeneration.

There is bitter irony in the complex figure. Although the poet "inappropriately" transfers the human emotion of hope to the tree at the beginning, the pursuit of the metaphor discloses that it is only the tree, and not human beings, who can truly lay claim to hope, for only the tree has the power of regeneration (v. 10).

The use of the tree for this metaphorical exploration needs to be understood in the context of the ambivalence of tree symbolism in the ancient Near East. Very commonly the tree is a symbol of life, longevity, and the power of renewal available to the righteous (Pss 1:3; 92:12-14[13-15]. The life-giving power of wisdom (Prov 3:18; Sir 24:13-17), of the king (Dan 4:10-12[7-9]), and of God (Hos 14:5-8[6-9]) are all expressed by the symbolism of the tree.[235] Over against all of the images that stress identification with the tree and its life-giving powers, however, must be set the image of the cherubim with the flaming sword who forever bar the way to the tree of life (Gen 3:24). Although expressed in poetic and not mythic terms, the tree in Job 14 represents that capacity for regenerative life from which humans are definitively excluded.

The second image from nature that Job chooses to represent the human situation, the vanishing of water from lakes and rivers, is unexpected but perceptive (v. 11). There are plenty of examples in the Near East of seasonal wadis and other bodies of water that might give rise to an image of regeneration, but seasonal dryness is not what Job is talking about. His image is that of the irreversible loss of water that occurs, for instance, when an earthquake cuts off the spring that feeds a stream or a lake. In ancient cosmology, this process was envisioned as the sealing up of a fountain of the great underground freshwater sea

---

234. Dhorme, *A Commentary on the Book of Job,* 198; L. Perdue, *Wisdom in Revolt: Metaphorical Theology in the Book of Job,* Bible and Literature Series 29 (Sheffield: JSOT, 1991) 157.

235. Perdue, *Wisdom in Revolt,* 158-60; O. Keel, *The Symbolism of the Biblical World* (New York: Seabury, 1978), figs. 46, 47, 48, 479, 480.

that was thought to lie beneath the earth (cf. Gen 2:6; 8:2). One expects lakes and rivers to be permanent features, and human beings, despite knowing that they will die, persist in an irrational but deeply held conviction of their own permanence; yet the death of each is irreversible.

Job subtly attacks another human evasion in his play with the image of death as sleep (v. 12). That image, common in many cultures, attempts to obscure death's finality, since sleep and waking are logically coordinate terms. Job insists, however, that there is no rising from this lying down, no rousing from this sleep. The phrase "until the heavens are no more" is an idiom meaning "forever."

14:13-17. Trapped between the anger of God and the inexorability of death, Job's imagination attempts to secure a place for hope. Even though Job speaks of Sheol in v. 13, he does not see death as a refuge from God, as he did in 3:13-19 and 7:8-10, 21. Death has become part of the problem, because Job's desire has changed. He wishes to have the mutuality of his relation with God restored. This longing is expressed poignantly in v. 15. The words "you would call, and I would answer you" echo those of 13:22 and by so doing underscore how torn Job is. In 13:22, the words are part of the adversarial vocabulary of legal challenge and reply; in 14:15, they are part of a vocabulary of piety expressed in the most personal terms. Job's imagining God "longing for the work of your hands" also contradicts his earlier sense of God's despising the "work of [God's] hands" (10:3). The very verb Job uses ("to long for" כסף *kāsap*) has connotations of the most instinctive, elemental urges: the hunger of a lion for prey (Ps 17:12), the desire of a bird to nest (Ps 84:2[3]), the homesickness of a person in a faraway land (Gen 31:30). Such is the bond that connects God and the creature God has made. Death threatens the restoration of this bond, since death in ancient Israelite thought is a realm cut off from God's presence. As the psalmist laments, "I am set apart with the dead,/ like the slain who lie in the grave,/ whom you remember no more,/ who are cut off from your care" (Ps 88:5[6] NIV).

This very idea, however, becomes the seed of Job's imaginary solution. If Sheol could become his temporary refuge, he could be protected from God's anger until it had passed (v. 13), in much

the same way that Israel traditionally spoke of God hiding people from their enemies (Ps 27:5; 31:20[21]; Isa 49:2; cf., however, Amos 9:2-4). But as a living human being, Job cannot enter Sheol on his own; that act would have to be God's. The contradictions in Job's image of God are here projected into God's very will; God would hide Job from God's own anger, which seeks to destroy Job.

That Job is not talking about death and resurrection is made clear by the rhetorical question of v. 14.[236] He imagines the time in Sheol as a kind of "pressed service" (צבא *ṣābā'*), as in a labor gang or an army, with a set time and an occasion for release. The same image is used in Isa 40:2 for the exile in Babylon. Here, too, Job inverts his previous words. Whereas in 13:15 he declared "I have no hope," now he says that "all the days of my service I would wait[/hope]."

Job also has to imagine how his relationship with God could be resumed without a renewal of God's obsession to find fault, which has led to his suffering (vv. 16-17). As earlier, Job must project a contradiction into God's behavior, a simultaneous seeing and not seeing. God would count Job's steps but not observe his sin. As Fohrer notes, counting the steps is never an image of providential care, but scrutiny of conduct (cf. 31:4; 34:21; Lam 4:18).[237] How could God scrutinize yet not see? This could happen only by a kind of divine self-interference analogous to what Job imagined in v. 13, God's sealing up offenses in a bag or painting over iniquities, so that God does not see them. When Job thought in legal terms, he demanded disclosure of his alleged sins, offenses, and iniquities, so that he could refute them (13:23). When he thinks in the relational terms of personal religion, images of concealment provide the resolution (14:16-17). Two rival ways of thinking about his relationship with God compete in Job's imagination, each with its own set of images and metaphors that organize his thinking about how to speak with God (13:22// 14:15), whether or not hope is possible (13:15// 14:14), and how to deal with sin (13:23//14:16-17).

14:18-22. Abruptly, the imaginary vision is displaced by another scene. In Hebrew the change

236. G. Fohrer, *Das Buch Hiob*, KAT xvi (Guetersloh: Gerd Mohn, 1963) 257-58.
237. Ibid., 259.

is marked by an introductory disjunctive word, "but" (ואולם *wĕʾûlām*). With exceptional artistry, the poet delays explicit interpretation of the figure (v. 19*b*), but form and meaning are closely interrelated. As erosion is the governing metaphor, so the images move sequentially from mountain to crag to stones to dust (vv. 18-19*a*). Grammatically, the first two scenes are described in the passive voice, with no agent mentioned. In the second two, however, the eroding agents, water and torrents, are the subjects of active verbs. In the final line, which identifies God as the agent, the verb is causative (lit., "cause to perish" [האבדת *heʾĕbadtā*]).

Most extraordinary is Job's choice of the mountain as an image of human hope. In contrast to fragile, transient flowers and shadows, which Job used to describe the fleetingness of life (v. 2), hope is as strong and resistant as a mountain. It can be destroyed only by relentless and inexorable abrasion of almost unimaginable duration; but it can be destroyed. As opposites, water and stone are natural enemies, joined in a struggle in which water will always eventually triumph. To employ this metaphor for the relationship between God and human beings is to suggest that their opposite natures make them inevitable opponents, with the slow destruction of what is human a foregone conclusion.

The fundamental opposition underlying Job's metaphor is that of life, which belongs to God, and death, which is the lot of human beings. This sense of the fundamental chasm between the divine and human haunted ancient Near Eastern reflections. It permeates the book of Ecclesiastes and lies also at the heart of the ancient Babylonian poem of Gilgamesh ("Gilgamesh, whither rovest thou? The life thou pursuest thou shalt not find.

When the gods created mankind, death for mankind they set aside, life in their own hands retaining").[238] For Job, this difference is experienced not simply as a difference of nature but as active antagonism. Like water against stone, God "prevails against" (v. 20) human beings.

Job's concluding images of death are governed by the figure of separation. The notion, alluded to earlier, that death is the realm where one is cut off from God, is echoed in Job's use of verbs of movement: "he is gone"; "you send him away" (v. 20). Job also notes that death is a separation from the bonds of kinship. In a culture that had no belief in immortality, descendants formed a link between the dead and the living community. The childless Absalom poignantly set up a memorial stone, "for he said, 'I have no son to keep my name in remembrance'" (2 Sam 18:18 NRSV). Job, however, reverses the ordinary perspective. He considers not what the living remember of the dead but what the dead can know about the living—which is nothing, neither their good fortune nor their bad (v. 21; cf. Eccl 9:5-6, 10). The final verse does not describe a postmortem pain, but moves back to the process of dying.[239] As so often, Job's perception is acute. There comes a stage when the dying person becomes wholly concentrated on the business of dying. This turning inward, which separates the dying from their community even before the last breath is taken, becomes for Job the symbol of death as utter isolation.

238. James B. Pritchard, ed. *Ancient Near Eastern Texts Relating to the Old Testament* (*ANET*), 3rd ed. with supplement (Princeton: Princeton University Press, 1969) 90.

239. So D. Clines, *Job 1–20*, WBC 17 (Dallas: Word, 1989) 336; Fohrer, *Das Buch Hiob*, KAT xvi (Guetersloh: Gerd Mohn, 1963) 261; contra M. Pope, *Job*, 3rd ed., AB 15 (Garden City, N.Y.: Doubleday, 1979) 111; H. Rowley, *The Book of Job*, rev. ed., NCB (Grand Rapids, Mich.: Eerdmans, 1976; original ed., 1970) 107.

REFLECTIONS

Hope is one of the most fundamental experiences of human life; yet it is not easy to describe. Anyone who has ever looked at a beloved child or started a new business or sat beside a hospital bed listening to quiet breathing knows what hope feels like, including the way in which hope and fear shadow each other. Most people know, too, what loss of hope feels like—the sensation that accompanies the rejection letter, the foreclosure notice, or the results of the medical test confirming the worst. Recovering hope can be difficult, and for those who have repeatedly had their hopes crushed, despair may seem more attractive. Despair at least does not tantalize, then disappoint. The problem of hope and despair is one to which Job and his friends repeatedly return in the course of their dialogue. Their different perspectives illumine some of the complexities of hope and suggest what is needed in order to resist the suicide of the spirit that is despair.

Eliphaz understands hope as the horizon of a future open to change, the prospect that things may yet be other than they are (5:8-16). The transforming power of God to open such a future is grounds for "the poor [to] have hope" (5:16 NRSV). Unquestionably, Eliphaz is correct in linking the sustaining power of hope with a sense of an open future. Perhaps that connection sheds light on one of the perplexing aspects of hope and despair among young people. Teenagers often lack a realistic sense of the future: Everything is possible; nothing can change. This tendency to see the future in such radically different and equally unrealistic ways is not a defect but an ordinary part of the process of maturation. The ability to dream a bright future gives some young people the resiliency to endure hardships and deprivations that would crush a more "realistic" adult. The other side of this phenomenon, however, is despair that comes from believing that nothing can ever change. Consequently, problems that do not seem so severe to an adult—the breakup of a relationship, being teased or ridiculed by others at school—can seem overwhelming to a young person who cannot imagine that someone else will love him or that she could ever be admired.

Eliphaz's extravagant language of a future completely turned around raises other questions. When does hope become false hope? Can such language be not only insensitive but even dangerous? Assurances that everything will turn out for the best are especially offensive when they are offered as a rote response. Even in the mouth of the sufferer, extravagant hope may be simply a form of denial that interferes with the person's ability to address the realities of a situation. Yet one should be cautious in assessing the meaning and function of the language of hope, especially in communities whose culture is different from one's own. Communities in which hard living and recurrent tragedy are all too familiar often have a more vivid language of hope than do communities in which tragedy is an infrequent visitor. Where people are not accustomed to *needing* hope, such language can be looked at with suspicion, dismissed as mere "pie in the sky" talk. Distinguishing between language that sustains and language that deceives is in part a matter of knowing the individual and the traditions of the community.

In any cultural context, cultivating a language of hope that does justice to the reality of loss as well as to the possibility of renewal requires appropriate images. The contrast between Zophar's image of hope and Job's is instructive. For Zophar, the fulfillment of hope means that "you will forget your misery;/ you will remember it as waters that have passed away" (11:16 NRSV). Perhaps that is true for some situations, but Job has lost his children as well as his possessions and his health. Any way of talking about hope for someone like Job has to acknowledge the emptiness that will always remain. Even though Job invokes the tree as a symbol of hope, only to reject it (14:7-9), it is worth looking more closely at that image. As a figure of the power of regeneration, the tree that is cut down but sprouts again incorporates a sense of the future as essential to the meaning of hope. The regenerative new growth of the tree, however, does not abolish the cut stump. In Job's way of envisioning hope, its fulfillment does not negate pain and loss but incorporates it into new being. Even in the tree's renewed life, the stump gestures to the now invisible outlines of the tree that once was but is no more.

The most difficult issue still remains. Throughout the book, Job repeatedly raises the objection that death puts an end to hope and so renders talk about hope empty. This association is present in the word play and metaphor of 7:6, in which life is likened to the rapid movement of a shuttle that ceases abruptly, without "thread," or "hope" (תקוה *tiqwâ*). The drained sea and dried-up river of 14:11, the eroded mountain of 14:18-19, and the uprooted tree of 19:10 are all images of the destruction of hope by death. In 17:15-16, Job asks rhetorically whether his hope will accompany him into Sheol. In this way, he exposes the evasion contained in the speech of the friends. In the friends' representation there is always time, always a limitless future to which hope can attach itself; but there is not. To talk of hope without facing the limit of death is dishonest.

In part, the issue is a matter of what one hopes for. The person with an incurable disease needs to give up unrealistic hopes, but that is not the same as giving up hope. Rather, hope is allowed to find its appropriate objects. Such a person's hope may be for the chance to put affairs in order, to seek reconciliation with an estranged loved one, to revisit a place that was important, or simply to find peace. Pursuing those hopes gives meaning to a life that is drawing to a close.

This discussion, however, does not quite get to the issue that Job is raising. Death as a temporal limit is not the whole point, and perhaps not even the main problem for him. Even if Job could be assured of limitless years, that would not necessarily provide him with the power of regeneration. Death is a threat not merely because it cuts off the future, but also because it would make permanent Job's condition of isolation, evocatively described in 14:20-22. At the heart of Job's struggle with despair is the sense of utter isolation. Like the psalmist in Psalm 88, he is as one already dead.

Hope as the power for regeneration, even from moment to moment, is nurtured by the sense of another's presence, communion, and fellowship. That presence is the water that stirs response in dry roots. No one can sustain hope in utter isolation. To that extent, hope is as much a gift of grace as it is an act of courage. The presence of the other sustains and makes possible the energy and even pain involved in regeneration. Despite the implications of Eliphaz's initial comment (4:6), hope is not a facile confidence in full recovery. The content of hope varies and often takes surprising forms, but it is always a green presence. Where there is hope, there is life.

Job's sense that death is the enemy of hope has often led Christian interpreters to see the problem of Job as being solved by resurrection. One must be very careful in thinking about these issues, however, for the notion of resurrection is one that is easily abused. The book of Job itself addresses the problem of Job's hopelessness without recourse to any notion of resurrection, which was not a part of Israel's religious thinking before the Hellenistic period. Thus to see the book as presenting a problem that can only be addressed by resurrection is simply false. Moreover, Job's challenge to the justice of God certainly cannot be addressed by any idea of resurrection and reward. Doing so would be to treat resurrection as religious hush money, used to cover over a moral scandal at the heart of faith.

Christian thinking about resurrection nevertheless does have a place in the dialogue initiated by Job. Resurrection, rooted in the religious imagination of Jewish apocalyptic, represents the inbreaking of the kingdom of God even into the realm of death. No more can death be thought of as a place cut off from the power and presence of God, a place of isolation. As Paul says, "Who will separate us from the love of Christ? Will hardship, or distress, or persecution, or famine, or nakedness, or peril, or sword? . . . I am convinced that neither death, nor life, nor angels, nor rulers, nor things present, nor things to come, nor powers, nor height, nor depth, nor anything else in all creation, will be able to separate us from the love of God in Christ Jesus our Lord" (Rom 8:35, 38 NRSV). In that assurance of ineradicable presence is the ground of hope.

Job 15:1–21:34, The Second Cycle

OVERVIEW

With chap. 15, the second cycle of speeches begins. In each cycle, Eliphaz's initial speech plays a key role in setting the theme and tone. The sympathetic concern and didactic content of his speech in chaps. 4–5 established the model of sapiential counseling prominent in the first cycle. In the second cycle, Eliphaz shifts emphasis. The key to this difference lies in Eliphaz's accusation that Job's words are undermining religion (15:4). For the friends the issue becomes defending religious ideology against a blasphemer. What must be defended at all costs is the doctrine of retribution. The importance of this belief can be gauged by the fact that it is the only topic addressed by the friends in the second cycle. Moreover, they each use the same form to do so: a vivid poetic description of the fate of the wicked (15:17-35; 18:5-21; 20:4-29). More than anywhere else in the book, the friends speak here with one voice.

Commentators usually assume that the friends are using the topos of the fate of the wicked to accuse Job of wickedness, even though none of the friends specifically relates his description to Job's case. Although the similarity between Job's own situation and what the friends say about the wicked raises an important question, the structure of the second cycle suggests that at this point the issue is more a struggle over religious ideology than an accusation against Job. During his first two speeches in this cycle (chaps. 16–17 and 19), Job does not directly engage the fate of the wicked, preferring instead to focus on the issue of divine violence. In his third and final speech, however, Job explicitly addresses the matter, directly contradicting all that the friends have said (chap. 21) and prompting the accusations of heinous sin with which Eliphaz will begin the third cycle of speeches.

Job 15:1-35, Eliphaz Describes the Fate of the Wicked

NIV

15 Then Eliphaz the Temanite replied:

2"Would a wise man answer with empty notions
  or fill his belly with the hot east wind?
3Would he argue with useless words,
  with speeches that have no value?
4But you even undermine piety
  and hinder devotion to God.
5Your sin prompts your mouth;
  you adopt the tongue of the crafty.
6Your own mouth condemns you, not mine;
  your own lips testify against you.

7"Are you the first man ever born?
  Were you brought forth before the hills?
8Do you listen in on God's council?
  Do you limit wisdom to yourself?
9What do you know that we do not know?
  What insights do you have that we do not have?

NRSV

15 Then Eliphaz the Temanite answered:
2 "Should the wise answer with windy knowledge,
  and fill themselves with the east wind?
3 Should they argue in unprofitable talk,
  or in words with which they can do no good?
4 But you are doing away with the fear of God,
  and hindering meditation before God.
5 For your iniquity teaches your mouth,
  and you choose the tongue of the crafty.
6 Your own mouth condemns you, and not I;
  your own lips testify against you.

7 "Are you the firstborn of the human race?
  Were you brought forth before the hills?
8 Have you listened in the council of God?
  And do you limit wisdom to yourself?
9 What do you know that we do not know?

NIV

¹⁰The gray-haired and the aged are on our side,
    men even older than your father.
¹¹Are God's consolations not enough for you,
    words spoken gently to you?
¹²Why has your heart carried you away,
    and why do your eyes flash,
¹³so that you vent your rage against God
    and pour out such words from your mouth?

¹⁴"What is man, that he could be pure,
    or one born of woman, that he could be
        righteous?
¹⁵If God places no trust in his holy ones,
    if even the heavens are not pure in his eyes,
¹⁶how much less man, who is vile and corrupt,
    who drinks up evil like water!

¹⁷"Listen to me and I will explain to you;
    let me tell you what I have seen,
¹⁸what wise men have declared,
    hiding nothing received from their fathers
¹⁹(to whom alone the land was given
    when no alien passed among them):
²⁰All his days the wicked man suffers torment,
    the ruthless through all the years stored up
        for him.
²¹Terrifying sounds fill his ears;
    when all seems well, marauders attack him.
²²He despairs of escaping the darkness;
    he is marked for the sword.
²³He wanders about—food for vultures*ᵃ*;
    he knows the day of darkness is at hand.
²⁴Distress and anguish fill him with terror;
    they overwhelm him, like a king poised to
        attack,
²⁵because he shakes his fist at God
    and vaunts himself against the Almighty,
²⁶defiantly charging against him
    with a thick, strong shield.

²⁷"Though his face is covered with fat
    and his waist bulges with flesh,
²⁸he will inhabit ruined towns
    and houses where no one lives,
    houses crumbling to rubble.
²⁹He will no longer be rich and his wealth will
        not endure,
    nor will his possessions spread over the land.
³⁰He will not escape the darkness;

ᵃ23 Or about, looking for food

NRSV

    What do you understand that is not clear
        to us?
¹⁰ The gray-haired and the aged are on our side,
    those older than your father.
¹¹ Are the consolations of God too small for you,
    or the word that deals gently with you?
¹² Why does your heart carry you away,
    and why do your eyes flash,*ᵃ*
¹³ so that you turn your spirit against God,
    and let such words go out of your mouth?
¹⁴ What are mortals, that they can be clean?
    Or those born of woman, that they can be
        righteous?
¹⁵ God puts no trust even in his holy ones,
    and the heavens are not clean in his sight;
¹⁶ how much less one who is abominable and
        corrupt,
    one who drinks iniquity like water!

¹⁷ "I will show you; listen to me;
    what I have seen I will declare—
¹⁸ what sages have told,
    and their ancestors have not hidden,
¹⁹ to whom alone the land was given,
    and no stranger passed among them.
²⁰ The wicked writhe in pain all their days,
    through all the years that are laid up for the
        ruthless.
²¹ Terrifying sounds are in their ears;
    in prosperity the destroyer will come upon
        them.
²² They despair of returning from darkness,
    and they are destined for the sword.
²³ They wander abroad for bread, saying, 'Where
        is it?'
    They know that a day of darkness is ready
        at hand;
²⁴ distress and anguish terrify them;
    they prevail against them, like a king
        prepared for battle.
²⁵ Because they stretched out their hands against
        God,
    and bid defiance to the Almighty,*ᵇ*
²⁶ running stubbornly against him
    with a thick-bossed shield;
²⁷ because they have covered their faces with
        their fat,

ᵃ Meaning of Heb uncertain   ᵇ Traditional rendering of Heb Shaddai

NIV

a flame will wither his shoots,
and the breath of God's mouth will carry him
away.

[31] Let him not deceive himself by trusting what is
worthless,
for he will get nothing in return.

[32] Before his time he will be paid in full,
and his branches will not flourish.

[33] He will be like a vine stripped of its unripe
grapes,
like an olive tree shedding its blossoms.

[34] For the company of the godless will be barren,
and fire will consume the tents of those who
love bribes.

[35] They conceive trouble and give birth to evil;
their womb fashions deceit."

NRSV

and gathered fat upon their loins,

[28] they will live in desolate cities,
in houses that no one should inhabit,
houses destined to become heaps of ruins;

[29] they will not be rich, and their wealth will not
endure,
nor will they strike root in the earth;[a]

[30] they will not escape from darkness;
the flame will dry up their shoots,
and their blossom[b] will be swept away[c] by
the wind.

[31] Let them not trust in emptiness, deceiving
themselves;
for emptiness will be their recompense.

[32] It will be paid in full before their time,
and their branch will not be green.

[33] They will shake off their unripe grape, like the
vine,
and cast off their blossoms, like the olive
tree.

[34] For the company of the godless is barren,
and fire consumes the tents of bribery.

[35] They conceive mischief and bring forth evil
and their heart prepares deceit."

[a] Vg: Meaning of Heb uncertain   [b] Gk: Heb *mouth*
[c] Cn: Heb *will depart*

COMMENTARY

Chapter 15 divides into two distinct parts. The first (vv. 2-16) corresponds formally to the introductory remarks by which a speaker justifies his own words or denigrates those of the previous speaker. What has been a brief rhetorical introduction in previous instances (4:2; 6:2-3; 8:2; 9:2*a*; 11:2-3; 12:2-3), however, occupies fully half of Eliphaz's entire speech, suggesting that it has a thematic as well as a rhetorical function. The issue Eliphaz engages is religious epistemology—the sources, nature, methods, and limits of knowledge about God and the moral order of the world. Eliphaz begins by discrediting Job's claims to speak as a sage (vv. 2-6), contrasting them with the reliable authority on which the friends' speech is based (vv. 7-10). Eliphaz shames Job for his rash words (vv. 11-13), reminding him of the basic truth about human nature, its inherent corruptness in the eyes of God (vv. 14-16).

In contrast to Job's defective knowledge, Eliphaz sets out reliable knowledge (vv. 17-19). His words are not a rebuttal to a specific argument made by Job but an attempt to refute Job's basic claim: that God's world is morally incoherent. As evidence for the moral order of the world, Eliphaz chooses the traditional topos of the fate of the wicked, who becomes a prey to terrifying anxiety (vv. 20-24) because of his moral hubris (vv. 25-26). Despite initial appearances, the wicked person's fate is dispossession and futility (vv. 27-30), described further in images of profitless commerce, unfruitful vegetation, and barrenness (vv. 31-34). The underlying moral order of the world is evident. It is the wicked who give birth to wickedness (v. 35)—not, as Job has implied, an amoral and irrational God.

15:1-16. 15:1-6. Eliphaz's initial rebuke of Job's words in vv. 2-6 has a chiastic structure. Verses 2-3 claim that Job does not speak as a wise person speaks; vv. 5-6 make the contrasting claim that iniquity directs his mouth. At the center of the passage (v. 4) is the scandal itself: What Job is saying destroys religion. Although some commentators suggest that Eliphaz is concerned about Job's destroying his own faith,[240] v. 4 does not support such a limited application of Eliphaz's words. If Job is correct, then God is not worthy of worship.

The term that Eliphaz uses, "fear" (יראה *yir'â*) is an abbreviation of the phrase "fear of God" (יראת אלהים *yir'at 'ēlōhîm*; cf. 1:1, 8). Especially in the wisdom literature, it is the comprehensive term for that orientation to God that organizes a person's understanding and conduct (Ps 111:10; Prov 9:10). "Meditation before God," as Pope observes, has the nuance of the English word *devotion,* in the sense of a religious exercise (see Ps 119:23, 27, 48, 78, 97, 99).[241] From Eliphaz's conventional perspective the trusting, submissive relationship necessary for such piety is destroyed by the way Job speaks. It would be completely alien to Eliphaz's understanding that Job's words could be a terrible but faithful meditation before God.

Eliphaz's values are also implicit in the way he says that a wise person should speak. Such words should be "useful" and "profitable" (v. 3), or as one might say today, constructive rather than negative. Characterizing Job's words as "wind" (v. 2) marks them as empty (cf. Isa 41:29; Eccl 1:14, 17) and perhaps also as destructive (cf. 1:19; Hos 12:1[2]). Eliphaz's defensiveness is such that he cannot entertain the question of whether critical speech directed toward God (or toward traditional beliefs about God) is true or false. By its very nature, it must be false; therefore, it serves to indict the one who speaks it (v. 6). Moreover, one can deduce from such speech the motives giving rise to it, motives that cannot be noble but must be of the same nature as the speech itself

(v. 5). To one not sharing his perspective, Eliphaz's logic is hopelessly circular. From his own perspective, however, his certainty is a legitimate deduction from the unquestionable truth that God is just.

There is no doubt that Eliphaz here accuses Job of sin, specifically the sin of speaking blasphemously and destructively. Possibly, Eliphaz's words in vv. 5-6 also mean that he now believes Job to be a "hardened sinner and rebel against God."[242] More likely, Eliphaz is himself caught in a contradiction of perception that he does not know how to resolve. He believes that Job is fundamentally a person of integrity who fears God, as he said in 4:6. Yet now Job is destroying "fear of God" by speaking in the rash and angry way Eliphaz warned against in 5:2. Not until chap. 22 will Eliphaz resolve the contradiction by concluding that Job is, and has long been, an evil person. Even then Eliphaz will hold out the possibility of redemption to Job. The way he resolves the cognitive dissonance, however, reveals much about Eliphaz. Faced with a contradiction between his personal knowledge of the goodness of his friend and that friend's rejection of the religious ideology by which they both had lived, Eliphaz chooses faithfulness to ideology over faithfulness to his friend.

15:7-10. In vv. 2-6, Eliphaz attacked Job's words on the basis of their destructive effect. In vv. 7-10, he takes on the issue of authority. Job had claimed authority on the basis of what "my eye has seen . . . my ear has heard" (13:1 NRSV). In vv. 7-8, Eliphaz attacks the individualism implicit in Job's assertion. The only *individual* who could claim authentic knowledge superior to the communal knowledge of the elders would be the "firstborn of the human race" (v. 7). Here Eliphaz invokes an old creation tradition, different from the canonical story of Genesis 2–3, but one that has left its traces in Ezekiel 28. Later Jewish tradition combined this myth with the Genesis account to produce a portrait of primordial Adam, perfect in wisdom and beauty.[243] Not only in Israel, but also in Mesopotamia, the earliest inhabitants of the earth, especially those from "be-

---

240. See F. Andersen, *Job: An Introduction and Commentary,* Tyndale Old Testament Commentaries (Downers Grove, Ill.: Inter-Varsity, 1976) 175; J. E. Hartley, *The Book of Job,* NICOT (Grand Rapids, Mich.: Eerdmans, 1988) 245; Clines, *Job 1–20,* 348.
241. Pope, *Job,* 114.

242. Ibid., 114. Clines, *Job 1–20,* 346-54, overstates the case for Eliphaz as a sympathetic voice in chap. 15, but his remarks are a good counter to the prevailing opinion.
243. See R. Gordis, "The Significance of the Paradise Myth," *AJSL* 52 (1936) 86-94.

fore the flood," were believed to possess exceptional knowledge, because the lines separating the divine and human realms were not so sharply drawn. Eliphaz's words describe the firstborn human as birthed "before the hills" and as one who listens in the "council of God," the assembly of divine beings who consult with God (cf. 1 Kgs 22:19-22; Ps 82; Jer 23:18). In the wisdom tradition, these characteristics of the firstborn human were applied to personified wisdom itself (Prov 8:22-31; Sir 24:1-12). Thus Eliphaz mocks what appears to him as Job's arrogance and pretense to superior knowledge, citing Job's own words (13:1) in v. 9.

How does one establish a claim to superior knowledge? In Eliphaz's opinion, two criteria authenticate wisdom: age and consensus. Both of these criteria are invoked in v. 10, where Eliphaz refers to the "gray-haired and the aged," who are in agreement with what the friends have been saying. Job had dismissed both age and consensus in his parody of the wisdom of the aged in chap. 12 and in his championing of individual judgment (13:2). In Eliphaz's opinion, since no ordinary person can claim the superior knowledge of the firstborn human (vv. 7-8), the surest source of reliable wisdom is that preserved in the communal tradition of the elders, passed down from generation to generation (cf. Ps 78:1-4).

15:11-13. There is poignancy in Eliphaz's words about the "consolations of God" and the "word that deals gently" (v. 11), by which he refers to his own attempt to counsel Job according to ancestral traditions (chaps. 4–5). Eliphaz knows that every person and every society must face painful and perplexing aspects of life and attempt to integrate them into some structure of meaning.[244] Although Eliphaz might not agree, there is always an element of denial, a compromise with reality, in such attempts. Nevertheless, some such peacemaking with the pain of existence is necessary if one is to continue to live. What Eliphaz sees clearly is the price one pays for rejecting such "consolations": alienation from God expressed in just such angry words as Job has used (v. 13). What Eliphaz cannot fathom is the turn of mind (v. 12; in Hebrew, the heart [לב *lēb*] is the organ

of reason) that leads Job to choose alienation over consolation.

15:14-16. The teaching that Eliphaz chooses to restate from his previous speech (cf. 4:17-19) is not randomly chosen, but shows that Eliphaz has heard Job clearly. Job's resistance to traditional wisdom is grounded in his insistence that he is innocent (9:15, 21; 10:23-24). Eliphaz argues that such a claim is literally nonsensical, since no human being is innocent before God (v. 14). He even uses the comprehensive "born of woman," which Job himself had employed (14:1). As in chap. 4, Eliphaz invokes the comparison with heavenly beings to argue from the greater to the lesser (v. 15). The terms Eliphaz uses to characterize human nature, "abhorrent" (נתעב *nit'ab*) and "corrupt" (נאלח *ne'ĕlāḥ*) are strongly emotive words, suggesting the almost visceral revulsion he imagines God to feel. The image of human beings "drinking iniquity like water" is a vivid and economical representation of the idea that sin is both intentional (since drinking, unlike breathing, is a conscious act) and unavoidable (since one must drink water to live). In this way of thinking, Job's claim to innocence is meaningless.

By themselves, Eliphaz's words do not look much like consolation to modern readers. One must place them in the context of ancient Near Eastern religious assumptions and practices. In Israel, as in Mesopotamia, it was assumed that God related to human beings in a number of different ways. From the perspective of justice, God distinguished between the righteous and the wicked. From the perspective of loving creator, God's mercy was like that of a parent for a child. From the perspective of transcendent purity, however, divine revulsion at human iniquity could cause God to turn away God's protecting presence from an individual, or even to unleash divine wrath. Eliphaz seems to suspect that, for unknown reasons, Job has somehow become the object of such divine revulsion at corrupt human nature. If Job leaves this possibility out of consideration, he cannot make sense of his situation. By attending to Eliphaz's counsel, Job can not only understand his situation, but also act to change it. Ancient traditions of prayer recognize the great gulf between divine being and human being and God's wrath at corrupt human nature (e.g., Ps 90:1-12), but they also appeal to God to set aside

---

244. Cf. P. Berger, *The Sacred Canopy: Elements of a Sociological Theory of Religion* (Garden City, N.Y.: Doubleday, 1990) 53-80.

this way of perceiving human existence and to draw instead on divine mercy (e.g., Ps 90:13-17; cf. also Psalm 25). Ultimately, God's love proves more profound than God's revulsion at inherent human sinfulness. Prayer is answered, and the relationship is restored. These are the consolations of God, traditional religion's way of coping with the inexplicable sorrows of life.[245]

15:17-35. 15:17-19. Eliphaz introduces the second part of his speech with an instruction formula (v. 17). Like Job, he refers to "what he has seen," but Eliphaz does not privilege individual experience as such. For him there can be no contradiction between individual experience and the teaching of the sages, which goes back to ancestral tradition (v. 18). As Clines puts it, Eliphaz "has sold his soul to tradition, and has so ensured that he will never have any experience that runs counter to it."[246] Eliphaz's statement that this tradition comes from a time when there was no alien in the land is not well understood but appears to suggest the unadulterated origin of the tradition to which he is heir.

15:20-24. Eliphaz wants Job to accept the fact, articulated in vv. 14-16, that all human beings are vile before God, so that Job can understand how he, a basically righteous person, has nevertheless been subject to such suffering. Although that insight is necessary for accounting for certain apparent anomalies, it is not the central fact about the world. Eliphaz and his friends believe deeply that the moral order of the world nurtures good and rejects evil. This is the conviction that Eliphaz expressed at the beginning of his first speech (4:7-8) and of which Job appears to be losing sight (cf. 12:4-6).

One common way of dealing with the apparent contradiction that the wicked prosper is to argue that their retribution is only delayed (e.g., Psalms 37; 73). Eliphaz, however, makes the more sophisticated argument that the wicked are already in torment ("all the days" of the wicked, "all the years" in store for the ruthless, v. 20). He takes the traditional belief that the wicked have no security (cf. 8:13; 11:20; Ps 73:18; Prov 12:3) and reflects on the psychological implications of knowing that destruction is certain to occur (vv.

22b, 23b), but at an unknown time (v. 21b). The anticipation of disaster creates present terror. Verse 21 is best understood as depicting the subjective state of the wicked person, in which every sound is interpreted as a harbinger of destruction that could erupt even in the midst of apparent peace. Such insecurity leads to loss of confidence (v. 22a). The same Hebrew letters in v. 23a can be read one way to state that the wicked person wanders about searching for food (so NRSV, following MT) or in another way to say that the wicked wanders about as food for vultures (so NIV, following LXX). The clustering of images of violence and destruction ("sword" in v. 22b and "day of darkness" in v. 23b; cf. Amos 5:18-20) makes the image of the wicked as carrion quite apt. Being eaten by birds and animals is the fate of those defeated in battle (cf. Ezek 32:4-6; 39:5); the wicked, however, experience themselves as carrion even though they are not yet slain. The psychic insecurity that terrifies the wicked finally takes shape as the image of an attacking king (v. 24).

15:25-26. The wisdom tradition was quite taken by the notion that actions rebound on their perpetrators with a kind of poetic justice (e.g., Prov 26:27). So here, there is an ironic appropriateness that the wicked person's terrors take the shape of a warrior, since his own sin was to "play the hero" against God (vv. 25-26). Note that the NRSV breaks the passage differently, reading vv. 25-27 as reasons for the consequences described in vv. 28-30. In the NIV, vv. 25-26 give the cause for the psychological terror of vv. 20-24. Verse 27 introduces a separate section that is organized around another motif: the inability of the wicked person to retain the good fortune that is briefly and tantalizingly his.

15:27-30. Commentators are quite divided about the moral significance of the wicked person's fat (v. 27),[247] in part because the OT itself reflects an ambivalent attitude toward fatness. On one occasion, obesity figures as a crucial detail in a satirical story (Judges 3), but obesity is generally

---

245. See further T. Jacobsen, "Personal Religion," in *Treasures of Darkness* (New Haven: Yale University Press, 1976) 147-64.

246. Clines, *Job 1–20*, 355.

247. For negative views, see M. Pope, *Job*, 3rd ed., AB 15 (Garden City, N.Y.: Doubleday, 1979) 118; N. Habel, *The Book of Job*, OTL (Philadelphia: Westminster, 1985) 259; E. Dhorme, *A Commentary on the Book of Job*, trans. H. Knight (London: Nelson, 1967) 221; F. Andersen, *Job: An Introduction and Commentary*, Tyndale Old Testament Commentaries (Downers Grove, Ill.: Inter-Varsity, 1976) 178. For positive views, see G. Fohrer, *Das Buch Hiob*, KAT xvi (Guetersloh: Gerd Mohn, 1963) 275; D. Clines, *Job 1–20*, WBC 17 (Dallas: Word, 1989) 360.

not what the biblical text has in mind when it refers to fatness. In an agricultural economy in which famine and scarcity are recurrent problems (see, e.g., Gen 12:10; 26:1; 41:25-32; Ruth 1:1), fatness is positively associated with adequate food, good health, strength, and security (2 Sam 1:22; Neh 9:25). Negative associations arise when security becomes complacency and satiety becomes self-satisfaction (Deut 32:15; Ps 119:70; Jer 5:28). If one takes v. 27 as introducing the following verses (so NIV), then fatness represents the material good fortune that fails to provide security for the wicked.

To dwell in uninhabited ruins (v. 28) is to be dispossessed from human society. Such places were deeply dreaded as the haunt of hostile animals and demons (Isa 13:19-22; 34:8-15; Jer 50:39-40; 51:37-44).[248] In the poetic tradition they are often described as godforsaken, compared with Sodom and Gomorrah. Such lands are the opposite of the rich, settled agricultural land such as Israel was promised, where "you shall eat your fill and bless the LORD your God for the good land" (Deut 8:10 NRSV; see Deut 8:7-10).

The motif of the instability of the wicked person's good fortune continues in v. 29. As Gordis argues, the point is not whether the wicked person can become rich, but that he or she cannot remain rich (cf. Prov 13:11).[249] Although the last part of the verse is obscure (the meaning of מִנְלָם [minlām] is not certain), the general point is clear.

Verse 30 summarizes the fate of the wicked. The first line echoes v. 22*a,* with the emphasis now on external event rather than internal fear. As in Bildad's allegory of the withering plant (8:11-13), Eliphaz uses the image of a sun-blasted sprout to suggest the insubstantiality of the wicked person's flourishing. Once again the end of the line is obscure. A slight emendation produces a continuation of the plant metaphor (so NRSV).[250] Others read the MT's "the breath of his mouth"

as a reference to God's action (so NIV) or to that of personified death.[251]

15:31-35. The admonition in v. 31 gives the principle that explains the fate of the wicked: Relying on nothingness provides nothing on which to rely. The examples that illustrate the results of such behavior are somewhat akin to futility curses in which a person's actions fail to produce normal consequences (see Deut 28:30, 38-41). Some commentators object to the introduction of a commercial metaphor in vv. 31*b*-32, emending the text to produce a consistent plant metaphor.[252] Quickly changing metaphors are not alien to Hebrew poetry, however, and the notion of being paid back emptiness in full, even before the due date, is a striking image of an ironically futile commercial transaction. The images of the vine that casts its grapes prematurely and of olive fruit that fails to set are related to traditional images of divine curse and punishment (cf. Deut 28:40; Isa 18:5). Here they are simply the outward manifestation of the emptiness on which the wicked person is established. Similarly, barrenness and the loss of one's tent, conventional images of the family (29:4-5), reinforce the motif of the inability of the wicked to be established (v. 34).

Although the last verse is related to v. 34 through its use of birth imagery, its point is quite different. Verse 35 focuses not on the self-depleting and self-destroying nature of the wicked but on the way the wicked bring trouble and deceit into being. On its own terms it is an example of the traditional wisdom claim that like begets like. In the context of the dialogues, however, it responds to Job's claim that God produces social futility and destruction (12:14-25). On the contrary, Eliphaz argues that the world is morally coherent. The wicked generate trouble, but because they derive their being from nothingness, that nothingness ultimately claims them.

---

248. O. Keel, *Jahwes Entgegnung an Ijob,* FRLANT 121 (Goettingen: Vandenhoeck & Ruprecht, 1978) 64-65.

249. R. Gordis, *The Book of Job: Commentary, New Translation, and Special Studies* (New York: Jewish Theological Seminary, 5738/1978) 165.

250. Dhorme, *A Commentary on the Book of Job,* 223; Clines, *Job 1–20,* 344.

251. Habel, *The Book of Job,* 248.

252. N. H. Tur-Sinai, *The Book of Job: A New Commentary* (Jerusalem: Kiryath Sepher, 1957) 259; Habel, *The Book of Job,* 248; Clines, *Job 1–20,* 344; J. E. Hartley, *The Book of Job,* NICOT (Grand Rapids, Mich.: Eerdmans, 1988) 250; Pope, *Job,* 119.

REFLECTIONS

The intensity of Eliphaz's attack on Job's claims and his defensiveness about his own words indicate the presence of a crisis in religious knowledge. The particular issue of whether Eliphaz or Job is right is in many respects less significant than the broader questions. What makes a claim about the world trustworthy and reliable? What is the authority for believing anything? What makes such claims and beliefs persuasive—to oneself as well as to others?

The crisis in knowledge in the book of Job does not concern simple facts: whether it was Sabeans or Edomites who made off with Job's cattle, or whether Job's disease is leprosy or something else. The question that triggers the crisis is, What does it all mean? How is one to make sense of what has happened? What can one know about how the world works, so that one knows its moral foundation—or whether there *is* a moral foundation to the world? How does one know where to place one's trust, what to value, how to choose what to do or what stance to take? These are the perennial questions of religion, of philosophy, of ethics, and of politics. Although they may become quite abstract, such questions most often arise out of dilemmas posed by very concrete situations, as in Job.

The book of Job is not a treatise on religious epistemology. It does, however, offer an opportunity to experience characters attempting to state their beliefs persuasively and to defend them authoritatively. How they go about this business is actually quite similar to the way people today talk about the bases for their beliefs. Although the friends make many different arguments and appeals in the course of their speeches, these can be roughly grouped into three types, depending on the nature of the authority the friends invoke. First is the appeal to external (i.e., non-human) authority. Second is the appeal to consensus within the human community. Third is the appeal to individual experience. Although some of these appeals are explicit and self-conscious, in many instances the friends may not be aware that they are making such claims. Rather, authenticating words and phrases are woven into speech as a natural part of talking. Once one begins to listen for such attempts to underwrite the truth, one discovers that they are a constant presence, in both the friends' speech and one's own.

The appeal to external authority in the friends' speeches takes two forms. One is the claim of direct divine revelation (e.g., 4:17-19; cf. 11:5-6). This kind of an appeal to authority is fairly rare in modern religious language, but it does occur. The televangelist may say that God has revealed to him God's plans for a mighty, new ministry, for which he is now soliciting funds. In a more subtle form, one also hears people speak of God's guidance in a difficult decision or God's showing them the truth about themselves, which they had not wanted to see. Whatever one thinks about the content of the claim, the appeal to authority is similar. The insight is claimed to be reliable because it comes from God.

The other appeal to external authority is the appeal to nature. Analogies with nature are virtually universal in the moral language of human cultures[253] and are very common in the friends' speeches (e.g., 4:10-11, 19; 5:6-7; 8:10-19). Their persuasive force seems to reside in the assumption that the same structure underlies all of creation. Significant patterns that are more easily identified in the plant or animal world can be transferred to illumine the truth about human experience. For example, talking about the "seasons" of a person's life authenticates the claim that certain tasks or experiences are characteristic of different ages by invoking the analogy of the very different activities that occur in nature in spring, summer, autumn, and winter.

The second category, the appeal to the authority of consensus, is perhaps the most pervasive. When everyone else believes something to be so, it is extremely difficult to believe otherwise. People seldom explicitly say that they believe something just because everybody else does, but the appeal to the authority of consensus is reflected in the way

---

253. M. Douglas, *How Institutions Think* (Syracuse, N.Y.: Syracuse University Press, 1986) 45-53.

people use certain catch-words and slogans that are on everyone's lips. These words seem true because others use them, and no one challenges them. The rhetoric of biblical inerrancy sounds self-evidently true in a fundamentalist church; the rhetoric of historical criticism sounds self-evidently true in a modernist church. Similarly, in Job, the friends' astonishment that Job does not agree with what seems so obvious to them is manifested in every speech they make. Consensus among the contemporary community is a weighty claim, but it is made even stronger when it is connected with the authority of tradition, which is a consensus that spans generations.

In the third category, claims to truth are grounded in an appeal to individual experience. The claim "this happened to me" or "I saw this myself" (5:3) is powerful. More generally, anecdotes of various kinds are persuasive not only because they "actually happened," but also because they cast complex issues in personal terms. The personal dimension makes them seem more immediate and emotionally involving. In contemporary political rhetoric, the anecdote is one of the most frequently used persuasive devices, as anecdotes about the abuse of a government program serve to arouse public sentiment against the program, or anecdotes about the violation of human rights in a foreign country garner support for sanctions against that country.

The problem with all of these appeals to authority, of course, is that they prove nothing. The ancient world, no less than the modern, was aware of the difficulty of distinguishing true from false revelation. Analogies from nature can be used to support contradictory propositions, and Job is as adept at invoking nature as are his friends. Consensus is vulnerable to the weakness of collective opinion. As an ancient Egyptian proverb puts it, "one who raves with the crowd is not counted a fool." Nor is tradition a guarantee. There are old lies, as well as old truths. Even experience is no guarantee of truth. For every anecdote there is one that points in the opposite direction. Not every event has genuine explanatory power. Some things may be true in the sense that they actually happened but may be quite false if taken as indicative of underlying reality.

But where does this leave us? Cynicism is no resting place. Every human society must have a broadly shared commitment to certain basic beliefs and values if it is to be a moral community. As much as people would like to have a simple and definitive way of establishing those truths, however, there is no shortcut. The work of establishing moral values requires a great deal of listening to many voices—voices of tradition, voices of dissent. The moral understandings of a community must always be under negotiation, as aspects of that community's beliefs are reexamined, challenged, overturned, or reaffirmed. The reader is given access to one such negotiation in the book of Job. This process can be painful, and it is easy to understand the appeal of simplistic alternatives, such as one finds in the bumper-sticker assertion: "God said it. I believe it. That settles it." Such a comment is both deceptive and evasive, however. It is deceptive because it pretends that one does not have to be an active listener to the word of God, which must be taken into ever-changing situations. It is evasive because it seeks to avoid moral responsibility for interpreting what it means to be faithful to God in the face of unanticipated circumstances.

There is no escape from the hard work of moral dialogue, no escape from trying to give an account of one's values and commitments and the bases for them, no escape from listening to a person whose experience runs counter to one's own. Such a process does not mean embracing a lazy relativism or an abandonment of judgment. On the contrary, when one realizes that there is no simple appeal to the answer book, the act of moral judgment takes on a weighty seriousness. Nor does it mean disregarding the authority of divine disclosure, the teachings of nature, tradition, the prevailing consensus of the community, or personal experience. Each of these is a resource for the work of moral reflection, but none of them alone suffices. God has made humans as moral beings and entrusted us with the work of creating communities of value in an ever-changing world. Fidelity to God lies in the honesty and openness with which we take up the task, as it also lies in the concrete commitments we make.

Job 16:1–17:16, Job Complains of God's Criminal Violence

NIV

16 Then Job replied:

2"I have heard many things like these;
   miserable comforters are you all!
3Will your long-winded speeches never end?
   What ails you that you keep on arguing?
4I also could speak like you,
   if you were in my place;
 I could make fine speeches against you
   and shake my head at you.
5But my mouth would encourage you;
   comfort from my lips would bring you relief.

6"Yet if I speak, my pain is not relieved;
   and if I refrain, it does not go away.
7Surely, O God, you have worn me out;
   you have devastated my entire household.
8You have bound me—and it has become a
      witness;
   my gauntness rises up and testifies against me.
9God assails me and tears me in his anger
   and gnashes his teeth at me;
   my opponent fastens on me his piercing eyes.
10Men open their mouths to jeer at me;
   they strike my cheek in scorn
   and unite together against me.
11God has turned me over to evil men
   and thrown me into the clutches of the
      wicked.
12All was well with me, but he shattered me;
   he seized me by the neck and crushed me.
 He has made me his target;
13   his archers surround me.
 Without pity, he pierces my kidneys
   and spills my gall on the ground.
14Again and again he bursts upon me;
   he rushes at me like a warrior.

15"I have sewed sackcloth over my skin
   and buried my brow in the dust.
16My face is red with weeping,
   deep shadows ring my eyes;
17yet my hands have been free of violence

NRSV

16 Then Job answered:
2 "I have heard many such things;
   miserable comforters are you all.
3 Have windy words no limit?
   Or what provokes you that you keep on
      talking?
4 I also could talk as you do,
   if you were in my place;
 I could join words together against you,
   and shake my head at you.
5 I could encourage you with my mouth,
   and the solace of my lips would assuage
      your pain.

6 "If I speak, my pain is not assuaged,
   and if I forbear, how much of it leaves me?
7 Surely now God has worn me out;
   he has*a* made desolate all my company.
8 And he has*a* shriveled me up,
   which is a witness against me;
 my leanness has risen up against me,
   and it testifies to my face.
9 He has torn me in his wrath, and hated me;
   he has gnashed his teeth at me;
   my adversary sharpens his eyes against me.
10 They have gaped at me with their mouths;
   they have struck me insolently on the
      cheek;
   they mass themselves together against me.
11 God gives me up to the ungodly,
   and casts me into the hands of the wicked.
12 I was at ease, and he broke me in two;
   he seized me by the neck and dashed me
      to pieces;
 he set me up as his target;
13   his archers surround me.
 He slashes open my kidneys, and shows no
      mercy;
   he pours out my gall on the ground.
14 He bursts upon me again and again;

a Heb *you have*

455

NIV

and my prayer is pure.

18"O earth, do not cover my blood;
    may my cry never be laid to rest!
19Even now my witness is in heaven;
    my advocate is on high.
20My intercessor is my friend[a]
    as my eyes pour out tears to God;
21on behalf of a man he pleads with God
    as a man pleads for his friend.

22"Only a few years will pass
    before I go on the journey of no return.

17 My spirit is broken,
    my days are cut short,
    the grave awaits me.
2Surely mockers surround me;
    my eyes must dwell on their hostility.

3"Give me, O God, the pledge you demand.
    Who else will put up security for me?
4You have closed their minds to understanding;
    therefore you will not let them triumph.
5If a man denounces his friends for reward,
    the eyes of his children will fail.

6"God has made me a byword to everyone,
    a man in whose face people spit.
7My eyes have grown dim with grief;
    my whole frame is but a shadow.
8Upright men are appalled at this;
    the innocent are aroused against the ungodly.
9Nevertheless, the righteous will hold to their ways,
    and those with clean hands will grow stronger.

10"But come on, all of you, try again!
    I will not find a wise man among you.
11My days have passed, my plans are shattered,
    and so are the desires of my heart.
12These men turn night into day;
    in the face of darkness they say, 'Light is near.'
13If the only home I hope for is the grave,[b]
    if I spread out my bed in darkness,
14if I say to corruption, 'You are my father,'
    and to the worm, 'My mother' or 'My sister,'
15where then is my hope?
    Who can see any hope for me?
16Will it go down to the gates of death[b]?
    Will we descend together into the dust?"

a20 Or My friends treat me with scorn   b13, 16 Hebrew Sheol

NRSV

he rushes at me like a warrior.
15 I have sewed sackcloth upon my skin,
    and have laid my strength in the dust.
16 My face is red with weeping,
    and deep darkness is on my eyelids,
17 though there is no violence in my hands,
    and my prayer is pure.

18 "O earth, do not cover my blood;
    let my outcry find no resting place.
19 Even now, in fact, my witness is in heaven,
    and he that vouches for me is on high.
20 My friends scorn me;
    my eye pours out tears to God,
21 that he would maintain the right of a mortal with God,
    as[c] one does for a neighbor.
22 For when a few years have come,
    I shall go the way from which I shall not return.

17 My spirit is broken, my days are extinct,
    the grave is ready for me.
2 Surely there are mockers around me,
    and my eye dwells on their provocation.

3 "Lay down a pledge for me with yourself;
    who is there that will give surety for me?
4 Since you have closed their minds to understanding,
    therefore you will not let them triumph.
5 Those who denounce friends for reward—
    the eyes of their children will fail.

6 "He has made me a byword of the peoples,
    and I am one before whom people spit.
7 My eye has grown dim from grief,
    and all my members are like a shadow.
8 The upright are appalled at this,
    and the innocent stir themselves up against the godless.
9 Yet the righteous hold to their way,
    and they that have clean hands grow stronger and stronger.
10 But you, come back now, all of you,
    and I shall not find a sensible person among you.
11 My days are past, my plans are broken off,
    the desires of my heart.

c Syr Vg Tg: Heb and

NRSV

12 They make night into day;
    'The light,' they say, 'is near to the
        darkness.'ᵃ
13 If I look for Sheol as my house,
    if I spread my couch in darkness,
14 if I say to the Pit, 'You are my father,'
    and to the worm, 'My mother,' or 'My
        sister,'
15 where then is my hope?
    Who will see my hope?
16 Will it go down to the bars of Sheol?
    Shall we descend together into the dust?"

ᵃ Meaning of Heb uncertain

COMMENTARY

In the opening speech of the second cycle, Eliphaz had bitterly criticized Job for undermining piety (15:4), amazed at Job's disdain for the traditional consolations of religion (15:11). Job's reply ridicules the inadequacy of conventional responses (16:1-6). Job's alienation from traditional religious language becomes evident as he takes up one form of traditional lament language that would seem adequate to his situation: the depiction of God as adversary (16:7-17; cf. Lam 3:1-20). Just at the point at which the traditional form would lead to acceptance and prayerful turning to God (cf. Lam 3:21), Job disrupts the form, calling out in legal language for the avenging of his blood and an advocate who will vindicate his name (16:18-21).

The impending death, which lends urgency to his words (16:22), also undermines his hope. Job is exhausted by the mockery to which God has exposed him (17:1-7). Ironically, Job has become an object lesson that reinforces the complacent certainties of the "upright" (17:8-10). Even the reassurances of his friends (17:11-12) are fatuous because they fail to deal seriously with the power of death to destroy hope (17:13-16).

16:1-6. As usual, Job's speech begins with criticism of the friends' words. The structure of the passage is obscured by the inability of English translations to distinguish between "you" (plural) and "you" (singular). In vv. 2 and 4-5, Job uses the plural. In v. 3, he uses the singular. Since Job

does not ordinarily address the friends individually, it is more likely that v. 3 represents Job's quotation of what the friends have said to him (cf. 15:2).²⁵⁴

Job's characterization of the friends in v. 2b exploits an ambiguity in Hebrew syntax. The phrase is literally "comforters of misery," and that is undoubtedly how the friends see themselves. In Hebrew, however, the prepositional phrase "of misery" can also be the equivalent of an adjective, hence "miserable comforters." The quotation in v. 3 illustrates how the friends increase rather than comfort Job's misery. Job represents them as asking what ails him to make him keep arguing (v. 3b). They should not need to ask. What ails Job physically is apparent to the eye. What ails him emotionally is what he has been trying to say. The friends refuse to see or to hear him as he really is, and this is what makes them miserable comforters.

Job criticizes the conventional, ready-made quality of traditional consolation. Already in v. 2a he devalues it by saying that he has heard "many things like these." As in chap. 12, where Job gave an imitation of a wisdom speech, so here, Job says that he, too, knows how to console (vv. 4-5). The nuance of these verses can be taken in various

254. D. Clines, *Job 1–20*, WBC 17 (Dallas: Word, 1989) 378-79. Other commentators understand Job to be addressing Eliphaz in v. 3. E.g., J. E. Hartley, *The Book of Job*, NICOT (Grand Rapids, Mich.: Eerdmans, 1988) 257; G. Fohrer, *Das Buch Hiob*, KAT xvi (Guetersloh: Gerd Mohn, 1963) 284; N. Habel, *The Book of Job*, OTL (Philadelphia: Westminster, 1985) 271.

ways. Many understand Job to be saying that he would know how to be unsympathetic but would choose instead to be a genuine comforter (NIV).[255] More plausibly, Job may be saying that he, too, is master of all the various strategies of conventional consolation. He knows how to be critical (v. 4a) or to nod in sympathy (v. 4b; to "shake the head" can be a positive as well as a negative gesture). He knows how to speak strengthening words (v. 5a) or how to be silent (v. 5b; the line can be translated "sympathy would restrain my lips").[256] He is as well-trained a sapiential counselor as any of them (cf. 4:3-4) and could perform as well, if the roles were reversed. Job's suffering has taught him the hollowness of the wisdom he had shared with the friends. It has not, however, given him words that will assuage such affliction. Nothing, neither speech nor silence, lessens the pain (v. 6).

16:7-17. Job does not speak in order to ease his pain; he speaks in order to discover the truth about his situation. In vv. 7-17, Job speaks vividly of God as his adversary. Many readers are shocked by the descriptions of divine violence. In order to understand this passage, however, one must recognize that Job speaks in thoroughly traditional terms. The biblical lament tradition includes a way of speaking about affliction that understands some suffering as direct divine violence. Elements of this language occur in the psalms (e.g., Pss 32:4; 38:2[3]; 39:10b[11b]), but it is most clearly represented in Lamentations 3. Even though the book of Lamentations responds to the national catastrophe of Zion's destruction, chap. 3 takes the form of an individual lament. Lamentations 3 and Job 16:7-17 share so many similarities, both general and particular, that it is possible Job alludes specifically to that lament. If not, he certainly engages this type of lament.

16:7-8. These verses introduce the lament. Oddly, the verbs switch from third person in v. 7a to second person in vv. 7b and 8a, and back to third person in vv. 9-14. Although some scholars defend the alternation as consistent with Hebrew poetic style,[257] it is more likely that the

passage, as description, should be in the third person throughout.[258] Themes of personal exhaustion and isolation from a community of support, introduced in v. 7, will be developed in chap. 17 (vv. 1-2, 7-9, 11-14). Verse 8 is more closely related to the imagery of the rest of chap. 16, specifically that of the body (prominent in vv. 9-17) and forensic imagery (developed in vv. 18-21). At one level, Job's comment simply alludes to the common assumption that emaciation resulting from illness is a sign of divine punishment for sin.[259] By invoking the image of his own body as a hostile witness, however, Job indicates the way this religious belief results in an inescapable self-alienation (cf. 9:20, where Job imagines his own mouth betraying him).

16:9-14. Divine violence is more directly depicted through a series of increasingly intense images. The sequence begins in v. 9 with a personification of God's anger (lit., "his anger tore me and hated me"). Through the verb "to tear" (טרף *ṭārap*), God is implicitly visualized as an animal attacking prey. Such a comparison is quite rare, but significantly occurs in Lam 3:10-11 (see also Hos 5:14; 6:1). The image is concretely developed through reference to the parts of the face that convey focused rage: gnashing teeth and "sharpened" eyes. Even the word for "anger" is an old facial metaphor, literally, "nose" (אף *'ap*). For Job, this savage malice is the face of God.

In strictly logical terms, one might expect v. 11, which describes how God has given Job over into the power of the wicked, to precede v. 10, which describes their assault on Job. The transition, however, is more cinematic than logical. The visual focus on the threatening face of God in v. 9 bleeds into the image of the gaping mouths of the crowd. The devouring God is merged with the jeering crowd. Such overlap is not incidental. In laments, the aggression of a human mob is often taken as a sign that God has forsaken or is punishing the speaker (e.g., Pss 22:12-13[13-14]; Lam 3:30).

Military images dominate the second part of the description (vv. 12-14). In Job's words, the violence is presented as personal physical assault

255. E.g., Clines, *Job 1–20,* 379-80; Habel, *The Book of Job,* 271; Hartley, *The Book of Job,* 257.

256. R. Gordis, *The Book of Job: Commentary, New Translation, and Special Studies* (New York: Jewish Theological Seminary, 5738/1978) 175.

257. Ibid., 175.

258. Clines, *Job 1–20,* 381 (so NRSV). The NIV makes all verbs in vv. 7-8 second person, adding "O God" to the text for clarity.

259. For "shrivel" (NRSV) instead of "bound" (NIV) see S. R. Driver and G. B. Gray, *A Critical and Exegetical Commentary on the Book of Job,* ICC (Edinburgh: T. & T. Clark, 1921) Part II, 105; Gordis, *The Book of Job,* 176.

(seizing by the neck; cf. Gen 49:8). Its annihilating character is suggested by the choice of verbs, which not only denote a shattering into pieces but also are employed elsewhere to describe God as a divine warrior "breaking open" (פרר *pārar*; see Ps 74:13) the chaotic sea and "shattering" (פצץ *pāṣaṣ*; see Hab 3:6) the mountains. What the English reader misses, however, is the powerful effect generated by the repetition of sounds in v. 12, which suggests the relentlessly repeated assaults of God (ויפרפרני . . . ויפצפצני *wayparpĕrēnî . . . waypaṣpĕṣēnî*). A similar device is used in v. 14, where the breaking of Job is expressed in Hebrew as יפרצני פרץ על־פני־פרץ (*yipṛĕṣēnî pereṣ 'al-pĕnê-pāreṣ*; lit., "he breaches me breach upon breach").

In vv. 12c-13, the assault is reimaged as an arrow attack against Job as the target. As in vv. 9-11, the agency of the attack is fluid, alternately God and the archers whom God directs. The image of being helpless, surrounded, and attacked appears frequently in the lament tradition (Pss 22:12-13[13-14]; 3121b[22b]; 35:15). Here, however, the image culminates in the fatal penetration of Job's body by God's arrows (cf. 6:4; Ps 38:2[3]; and esp. Lam 3:12-13). To the modern reader, the kidneys are simply internal organs particularly susceptible to pain and essential to life. To the ancient reader, however, the kidneys were not only a part of the physical body but also a central part of the emotional being. We often speak in symbolic terms about a person's heart as the emotional center, and the Hebrew word for "kidneys" (כליה *kilyâ*) is often translated as "heart" to capture that nuance. In describing the intimacy of divine creation, the psalmist says "you formed my kidneys" (Ps 139:13). Here that symbol of intimacy becomes the site of violent assault. Job's pairing of the image of the assaulted kidneys with that of gall spilled upon the ground is evocative. Similar to the way the English word *gall* has an emotional as well as a physical nuance, the Hebrew for "gall" (מררה *mĕrērâ*) is related to the word meaning "bitter" (מרר *mārōr*). As Clines remarks, "If the affections and sympathies are assaulted, it is bitterness that spills out."[260]

In the final image of violence, Job represents himself as a besieged city (v. 14; cf. Lam 3:5-9, where the speaker is besieged and imprisoned by

God). Job does not develop the image as one of constriction, as Lamentations does. Instead, Job exploits the image of the breaching of the city wall. Like the preceding figure of an arrow that tears the kidneys, the breaching is an image of forced penetration, not just once but "breach upon breach." Attributing this violence to God the warrior sets up various echoes. In contrast to Eliphaz, who represented the wicked as one who charges against God like a warrior (15:25-27), Job claims that it is God who attacks him. More disturbingly, the image of God as warrior was traditionally a positive image of the one who fights for Israel (Exod 15:3-4; Ps 24:8; Isa 42:13) and for the suffering psalmist (Pss 7:12[13]; 64:7[8]).[261] Here, as in Lamentations 3, God the warrior's violence is turned against the one who laments.

16:15-16. Throughout this section, the image of violence against the body has become increasingly savage and invasive, from the insult of having one's cheek slapped (v. 10), to being seized by the neck (v. 12), to having one's kidneys pierced (v. 13), to having one's body broken open like a breached city invaded by hostile warriors (v. 14). In vv. 15-16, Job describes the effects of such violence. Although sackcloth is a familiar image of mourning (Gen 37:34; 2 Kgs 6:30; Ps 35:13), there is no other reference to sewing it upon oneself. Perhaps Job suggests that his grief is so profound that he will never be able to leave off mourning, and so the symbolic garments may be permanently sewn in place as a second skin (cf. Ps 30:11[12]). The paired image, literally, "I have thrust my horn in the dust," connotes abject humiliation, a reversal of the uplifted bull's horn, commonly used as a metaphor of strength (1 Sam 2:1; Pss 75:4-5[5-6]; 92:10[11]). Dust itself is symbolic both of the humiliation of one defeated and of the abjection of one who grieves (cf. Lam 3:16, 29). Finally, the furious face of God, who savages Job (v. 9), which introduced this description of violence, contrasts with the closing image of Job's face (v. 16), reddened by weeping (cf. Lam 2:11) and marked not just with darkness but with the dark "shadow of death" (צלמות *ṣalmāwet*).

---

260. Clines, *Job 1–20*, 385.

261. For a discussion of the motif of God as divine warrior, see F. M. Cross, *Canaanite Myth and Hebrew Epic* (Cambridge, Mass.: Harvard University Press, 1973) 91-111; P. D. Miller, *The Divine Warrior in Early Israel*, HSM 5 (Cambridge, Mass.: Harvard University Press, 1973).

16:17. At this point, the comparison with Lamentations 3 is crucial for understanding Job 16. In Lamentations 3, the transition between the recital of divine violence and the rest of the poem begins with the comment, "But this I call to mind,/ and therefore I have hope:/ the mercies of God do not end" (Lam 3:20). In the following verses, the speaker reflects on God's goodness (Lam 3:21-24) and the appropriateness of accepting affliction quietly (Lam 3:25-30), because it comes reluctantly from God, as punishment for sin (Lam 3:31-39). Consequently, one should confess and turn to God (Lam 3:40-42), portraying to God vividly the suffering God has inflicted (Lam 3:43-48). The pattern of plea to God and description of suffering recurs throughout the rest of the chapter (Lam 3:49-66).

Job has imitated the pattern of the lament in vv. 7-16 in order to portray God's violence against him. At the point where the traditional form would direct Job to accept his suffering and confess his guilt, however, he ruptures the form by asserting his innocence. Some have suggested that Job is here echoing another cultic form of speech, the declaration of righteousness (cf. Pss 17:1; 24:4).[262] Habel argues that the terminology has a legal resonance.[263] In either case, Job breaks the cultural form and the way it seeks to direct and control the experience of affliction. One cannot go on with the lament after v. 17.

16:18-22. Unlike Job's use of parody to disrupt traditional forms of speech in 7:17-18 and 12:13-25, here Job uses the technique of juxtaposing the discourse of the lament with discourse of a very different type: legal speech. Whether or not Habel is correct about v. 17, the legal language in vv. 18-21 is explicit. Job invokes the ancient principle that shed blood must be avenged (Gen 9:5-6; cf. Num 35:16-21). If blood was covered over and not perceived, then the crime might not be avenged (Isa 26:21; Ezek 24:7-8). Calling upon the earth not to cover his blood (v. 18a), Job invokes the image of the murdered Abel (Gen 4:10). The parallel line in v. 18b is part of the same image, since Abel's blood, too, is per-

sonified as "crying out from the earth." By invoking this tradition, Job names God's violence against him as murder, not justified punishment, as the lament tradition would interpret it.

Even before his death, Job seeks legal vindication for the injustice done to him. Corresponding to the help he pleads for from the earth, Job also looks for help from heaven in the form of a witness who will advocate for him (v. 19). Widespread attempts to interpret the heavenly witness as none other than God[264] are not grounded in the text but result from an anachronistic imposition of monotheistic categories.[265] As v. 21 makes clear, Job speaks of someone who will argue his case *with God.* The type of figure Job envisions is one like the angel of Yahweh in Zechariah 3, who defends the high priest against the accusations of the *satan.* Such a figure is mentioned by other characters in the book of Job itself, both by Eliphaz, who doubts the willingness of the "holy ones" to answer Job's call (5:1), and by Elihu, who is confident that an angel will intercede with God on behalf of an essentially upright person who has fallen into sin and is punished by God (33:23-26).[266] Although Job had earlier rejected as impossible the notion of a mediator who could adjudicate between himself and God (9:33), here he speaks not of a judge but of an advocate, similar to the redeemer/avenger to whom he will refer in 19:25.

Unfortunately, the text of v. 20 is obscure and ambiguous. Pope outlines the alternative readings of v. 20a succinctly: "My interpreter[s]/scorner[s] [is/are] my friend[s]/thought[s]/shepherd[s]."[267] These alternatives are not all equally plausible, however. The NIV's translation of v. 20a is more likely than that of the NRSV, since the Hebrew word מליץ (*mēlîṣ*) elsewhere refers to an inter-

---

262. Hartley, *The Book of Job,* 262; similarly Fohrer, *Das Buch Hiob,* 290, citing Isa 53:9 and 1 Chr 12:18.

263. Habel, *The Book of Job,* 265, following S. Scholnick, "Lawsuit Drama in the Book of Job" (Ph.D. diss., Brandeis University, 1975) 27n. 37.

264. E. Dhorme, *A Commentary on the Book of Job,* trans. H. Knight (London: Nelson, 1967) 239; H. Rowley, *The Book of Job,* rev. ed., NCB (Grand Rapids, Mich.: Eerdmans; London: Marshall, Morgan & Scott, 1976; original ed., 1970) 121; Fohrer, *Das Buch Hiob,* 292; F. Andersen, *Job: An Introduction and Commentary,* Tyndale Old Testament Commentaries (Downers Grove, Ill.: Inter-Varsity, 1976) 183.

265. Contra Gordis, *The Book of Job,* 527.

266. Clines (*Job 1–20,* 390) interprets the witness as a personification of Job's own outcry (v. 18). B. Zuckerman, *Job the Silent: A Study in Historical Counterpoint* (New York: Oxford University Press, 1991) 115, understands the figure as an imaginary divine figure, a countergod conjured out of the traditional imagery of God as champion of the oppressed.

267. M. Pope, *Job,* 3rd ed., AB 15 (Garden City, N.Y.: Doubleday, 1979) 125.

mediary of some sort, a translator (Gen 43:23), advocate (Job 33:23), envoy (2 Chr 32:31), spokesperson (Isa 43:27), or minister of a ruler (Sir 10:2), but does not otherwise mean "scorner," which is expressed by the Hebrew word ליץ (lēṣ). Since the word translated "friend" (רע rēaʿ) is spelled the same as that meaning "thoughts," it is possible to translate "interpreter of my thoughts."[268] Yet Job does not need someone to explain his thoughts to God, a task he handles quite well on his own. What he needs is a member of the heavenly council who can intervene on his behalf with God.[269] How Job would conduct himself while his advocate speaks for him is obscured by a difficult word (v. 20b). Hebrew דלף (dālap) may mean "drip" (hence, "my eyes pour out tears"), or it may mean "be sleepless" (hence, "my eyes look sleeplessly to God").[270] What is most important, however, is not Job's weeping or sleeplessness, but the way Job imagines the heavenly figure advocating his case, as a person does for a friend (v. 21; cf. Judah's interceeding for Benjamin in Gen 44:18-34). The idea of a heavenly advocate also appears in Mesopotamian religion.[271]

The last verse of the chapter (v. 22) expresses Job's urgency for vindication in the face of impending death and provides a transition to the lament over his loneliness and hopelessness in chap. 17. Job's reference to death as "the way of no return" expresses both the separation and the finality that death imposes (cf. 2 Sam 12:23).[272]

17:1-5. Unlike some of Job's other speeches, chap. 17 does not have a clear structure. What unifies it is the theme of isolation. The hostility of mockers, the inability of his friends to understand and support him, and the complicity of God in his humiliation leave Job with no companion but death. His allusion to the grave in v. 1 anticipates his bitterly ironic description of Sheol, which concludes the chapter in vv. 13-16.

The role of mockery and social ostracism in Job's suffering (v. 2) is a topic that he first broached in chap. 16, but which becomes increasingly important, not only in this chapter (vv. 6, 8) but also in later speeches (19:13-19; 30:1-15). Honor and shame, incorporation and exclusion from human fellowship are powerful modes of social control. Although such behavior may serve to establish the moral boundaries of a community, it may just as easily express jealousy, rivalry, and resentment. In the book of Psalms and other literature related to the lament, as in the book of Job, one hears the voice of persons who experience social humiliation (Pss 22:6-8[7-9]; 31:11-13[12-14]; Isa 50:6). No matter how confident one may be of one's own uprightness, rejection by one's community is devastating. As the psalmists' words make evident, an assurance of God's solidarity with the rejected person is absolutely crucial (Pss 22:9-11[10-12]; 31:14-18[15-19]; Isa 50:7).

Given this cultural pattern of seeking support from God in the face of social ostracism, it is not surprising that Job addresses God directly in vv. 3-4. Job's sense of God's enmity, however, precludes his confident reliance on God's solidarity. Unfortunately, as so often, obscurity in the text prevents certainty about what Job says. The motif Job uses is that of "surety," a pledge given to ensure the performance of some act or to support a claim. Property, or even a life, might be pledged (Gen 43:9; 44:32; Prov 11:15). One person might pledge on behalf of another, or one might pledge for oneself (Jer 30:21). Some interpreters understand Job to be asking God to "go surety for him" as an act of solidarity (so NRSV, NIV). Such an expression does occur in other laments and psalms (Ps 119:122; Isa 38:14). In such a reading, Job speaks much like the psalmists, contrasting God's support with his inability to find support anywhere among his own community. What Job says is slightly different, however, from what one finds in Isaiah 38 or Psalm 119. In Job 17:3, God *receives* the pledge.

Job's statement is best understood as a claim that he is willing to place his own life in pledge in order to come before God and clear his name: "Put my pledge by you" (i.e., "accept my pledge"; cf. Jer 30:21).[273] Such an interpretation is similar

268. So ibid., 125-26.

269. L. Perdue, *Wisdom in Revolt: Metaphorical Theology in the Book of Job*, Bible and Literature Series 29 (Sheffield: JSOT, 1991) 172.

270. G. Fohrer, *Das Buch Hiob*, KAT xvi (Guetersloh: Gerd Mohn, 1963) 281; Clines, *Job 1–20*, 372; E. Good, *In Turns of Tempest* (Stanford, Calif.: Stanford University Press, 1990) 95.

271. T. Jacobsen, "Personal Religion," in *Treasures of Darkness* (New Haven: Yale University Press, 1976) 159-60.

272. Fohrer, *Das Buch Hiob*, 294, notes similar expressions in Babylonian literature. See *ANET*, 106.

273. Habel, *The Book of Job*, 266; Clines, *Job 1–20*, 393-4.

to Job's earlier statement in 13:14-16. Thus, unlike the psalmists who turn from human mockers to seek support from God, Job believes that God is actually behind the mockers (v. 6) and that God's actions have caused the failure of his friends to support him (vv. 3*b*-4*a*). Job must be his own surety.

Grammatical obscurity also plagues 17:4. The verb in v. 4*b* does not make sense as written, and every translation requires some modest emendation. The NRSV and the NIV add an object for the verb ("them"), but the resulting sentence is very strange, even on the assumption that God is of two minds about Job. The reading of the verb as a passive is much more plausible: "Since you have closed their minds to understanding, therefore you will not be exalted."

Verse 5 is even more problematic. It is apparently a traditional saying, but the words are susceptible of quite different translations. The interpretation represented by the NRSV and the NIV understands it as a saying that rebukes the friends for betraying the obligations of friendship.[274] Alternatively, one can translate the proverb as "a person invites his friends to share his bounty, while the eyes of his own children grow faint (with hunger)."[275] So translated, the proverb might be an ironic criticism of the friends for inviting Job to share the "bounty" of their wisdom, when in fact it is too meager even to feed their own children. Fohrer, however, suggests that the saying applies to the relation between God and Job, by comparing God with one who favors outsiders while his own child (i.e., Job) is starved.[276] That interpretation fits well with the complaint against God in v. 6 and with Job's use of the image of failing eyes to describe himself in v. 7.

17:6-9. Verses 6-7 mirror vv. 1-2 as they repeat the themes of mockery (cf. Deut 25:9; Pss 44:14[15]; 69:11-12[13-14]) and physical exhaustion (cf. Pss 6:7[8]; 31:9-10[10-11]. The following verses are best taken ironically, representing the self-understanding of those who mock and spit at Job (cf. TNK). They perceive themselves as up right persons, shocked at the ungodliness of Job now revealed through his punishment (v. 8). As

a consequence of this object lesson, the "righteous" hold more firmly than ever to their way of life (v. 9; the first word of the Hebrew text may be read either as "and" or "but").[277] Like the cathartic effect of a Greek tragedy, the spectacle of Job's fate purges and purifies those who witness it.[278] All of this from Job's mouth, of course, is a parody of self-righteous judgment.

17:10-16. It seems improbable that Job is inviting his friends to change their minds and take a more sympathetic approach to him.[279] More likely, he is mockingly inviting them to try once more to present their positions. Job exposes the fatuous quality of what they say by contrasting the reality of his situation (v. 11) with the false comfort that the friends give (v. 12).[280] Especially in the first cycle of speeches, each of the friends suggested to Job the prospects of a reversal of fortune (5:19-26; 8:21; 11:15-19), even using the image of darkness that "will be like the morning" (11:17). Job seeks to contest the friends' insistence on the power of hope. As discussed in the Reflections on chap. 14, hope cannot endure without the presence of fellowship. For Job, death renders such fellowship impossible. His community, destroyed by the suffering God has imposed on him (16:7), can only be reconstituted as a community of nothingness in Sheol. Job's sardonic wit in describing Sheol as the only "house" he can hope to occupy (v. 13) perhaps alludes to the practice in the ancient Near East of making ossuaries in the shape of houses. Similarly, the bier on which a corpse was laid (2 Chr 16:14) is imagined as a bed in Sheol (Isa 14:11; Ezek 32:25). Job elaborates on the reconstitution of this nihilistic household, using the recognition formulas ("my mother," "my sister"; v. 14) that acknowledge close relationships (cf. Pss 2:7; 89:26[27]; Prov 7:4; Jer 2:27). The rhetorical questions of vv. 15-16 assume a negative answer

---

274. Similarly, Habel, *The Book of Job,* 277; Hartley, *The Book of Job,* 269; Andersen, *Job,* 184.

275. A. S. Peake, *Job,* NCB (London: T.C. & E.C. Jack, 1904) 173; Gordis, *The Book of Job,* 181-82; Clines, *Job 1–20,* 395.

276. Fohrer, *Das Buch Hiob,* 294; Clines, *Job 1–20,* 395.

277. See J. G. Janzen, *Job,* Interpretation (Atlanta: John Knox, 1985) 126, for an interpretation along the lines of the NRSV and the NIV translations.

278. Rene Girard, *Job: The Victim of His People,* trans. Y. Freccero (Stanford: Stanford University Press, 1987) 71.

279. Hartley, *The Book of Job,* 270; cf. Habel, *The Book of Job,* 278.

280. For a very different interpretation, reading vv. 11-12 as a statement of pathos on the loss of the heart's desires, see Gordis, *The Book of Job,* 184; Habel, *The Book of Job,* 278; Clines, *Job 1–20,* 398.

(cf. Ps 49:17[18]).[281] As in his previous speeches, the reflection on death brings his words to an end

(7:21; 10:21-22; 14:18-22). Job 16–17 are, however, the last of the speeches to conclude in this fashion.

281. So Fohrer, *Das Buch Hiob,* 295-96; Clines, *Job 1–20,* 400; contra Habel, *The Book of Job,* 279.

REFLECTIONS

The book of Job presents no more difficult issue for reflection than that of divine violence. Although readers rightly associate Job with the theme, it is actually Eliphaz who introduces it: God "wounds, but he binds up;/ he strikes, but his hands heal" (5:18). The very casualness with which Eliphaz describes God's violence should be more disturbing than Job's painfully graphic description. Eliphaz's remark is an index of the extent to which the violence of God is so much woven into the language of piety as to have become almost invisible: "Day and night your hand was heavy upon me;/ my strength was dried up as by the heat of summer" (Ps 32:4 NRSV); "Your arrows have sunk into me,/ and your hand has come down on me" (Ps 38:2[3] NRSV); "I am worn down by the blows of your hand" (Ps 39:10*b*[11*b*] NRSV); "let the bones that you have crushed rejoice" (Ps 51:8*b*[10*b*] NRSV); "You have put me in the depths of the Pit,/ in the regions dark and deep" (Ps 88:6[7] NRSV); "you have lifted me up and thrown me aside" (Ps 102:10*b*[11*b*] NRSV); "The Lord has punished me severely,/ but he did not give me over to death" (Ps 118:18 NRSV); "He has made my teeth grind on gravel,/ and made me cower in ashes" (Lam 3:16 NRSV).

Christians cannot escape from a confrontation with the issue of the violence of God by disingenuously asserting that such violence is a characteristic of the OT but not the NT. Divine violence is present in the NT (one has only to think of Heb 12:5-11 or the book of Revelation). Moreover, Christian prayer and piety have also been traditionally influenced by images of divine violence. The poet John Donne wrote:

Batter my heart, three-personed God, for you
As yet but knock, breathe, shine, and seek to mend;
That I may rise and stand, o'erthrow me; and bend
Your force to breake, blow, burn, and make me new.
("Holy Sonnets," 10.1-4)

The issue of divine violence cannot be understood in isolation from other related language about God. In the psalms from which the statements above are excerpted, it is evident that the words about the anger, rejection, and violence of God are part of a broader and more complex way of talking about God, in which God is experienced as personal and emotive. The angry emotions, however, are only a part of the picture. The relation between God and person is intimate and mutual, founded on a deep and primary bond of love. The individual offers love and obedience to God. Utterly dependent on God for all, the individual expects compassion and active protection from enemies, but also expects correction and punishment in cases of disobedience. The relationship is a deeply personal one, and the sense of closeness and trust is one of the most profound needs and satisfactions expressed in the psalms. The origins of this language of piety in the older religious literature of Mesopotamia have been traced. The root metaphor that generates this way of talking about God is that of parent and child.[282] In Israelite psalms, even though other social relationships (e.g., king and people) influence the religious language, the relation between parent and child is the hidden "deep structure," shaping the way in which God is experienced and talked about.

The relationship between parent and child, the most primary of human relationships, provides

282. T. Jacobsen, "Personal Religion," in *Treasures of Darkness* (New Haven: Yale University Press, 1976) 157-60.

a religious metaphor of immense power, resonance, and richness, one capable of nurturing a complex and nuanced religious life. Like all root metaphors, however, the analogies it makes available for understanding experience may create as well as resolve problems. Nowhere is this clearer than in the problem of understanding acute suffering. The image of God as an all-powerful parent virtually requires the understanding that God must be responsible for an individual's suffering, either by directly causing it or by neglecting to protect that person. Although the psalms primarily address suffering in terms of urging God to save and protect the psalmist from the aggression of enemies, they also speak of God as the source of violence, as in the citations above. In such instances, when the logic of the metaphor is fully developed, what emerges is the image of God as abusive parent. Because the underlying parental metaphor is so deeply a part of religious language, however, the image of God as abusive is difficult to resist or critique. Instead, the one who prays may be drawn into the pathological thought patterns of the cycle of abuse.

One can see this happening in Lamentations 3, the text that so engages Job. The violence inflicted on the speaker is represented as being for his own good. Indeed, the one who is subjected to violence has to internalize this message ("It is good for a person to bear a yoke when he is young, to sit alone in silence when [God] has imposed it, to put his mouth in the dust [Lam 3:27-29a]). There is no question of proportionality. Whatever the punishment (Lam 3:1-20), it must be accepted as such ("Why should any person who lives complain when punished for his sin?" [Lam 3:39]). There can be no question of resistance (It is appropriate "to give one's cheek to the smiter, and be filled with insults" [Lam 3:30]). The relationship is not simply one of absolute dependency on a God experienced as all powerful (Lam 3:27) and as the source of good as well as of pain (Lam 3:38). There is also the memory of a relation that includes tenderness and affection ("The Lord is good to one who waits on him, to the soul that seeks him" [Lam 3:25]; "you came near when I called on you; you said, 'Do not be afraid'" [Lam 3:57]). Consequently, the one who is hurt attempts not only to justify the abuse but also to excuse the abuser ("Although [God] causes grief, he will have compassion . . . for he does not willingly afflict or grieve anyone" [Lam 3:32a-33 NRSV]). The one who is abused thus takes responsibility for the abuse ("Let us test and examine our ways,/ and return to the LORD. . . . We have transgressed and rebelled" [Lam 3:40, 42 NRSV]).

There are, to be sure, differences between Lamentations 3 and the thought processes of an abused child, which would require a much longer reflection to explore. An ancient Israelite lament cannot be read as the transcript of a modern counseling session. Nevertheless, the similarities in the modes of thinking and perceiving are striking enough to be deeply disturbing. There is something grotesquely wrong with a religious language that deals with suffering as justified abuse, whether the individual is guilty or innocent of wrongdoing. Job's speech in chap. 16 recognizes, exposes, and challenges the pathology embedded in the lament tradition. Job's description of God's violence against him differs in no essential way from the description in Lam 3:1-20. At the point at which tradition calls upon him to justify the punishment and to speak words of confidence in God's compassion, however, Job refuses. When Job says, "O earth, do not cover my blood," he renames this violence as abuse, as murder. With these words, Job delegitimizes the language of divine violence that the lament tradition had represented as natural. He takes the language of violence out of the context of prayer and insists that one consider it in the context of criminality.

What is one to do with Job's exposure of the scandal that lies in this traditional language of lament? One alternative has been to understand Job's words as a fatal critique of the religious imagination that bases itself on the metaphor of a personal God and to seek a radically different language about God based on a different root metaphor. It is possible to read the divine speeches in chaps. 38–41 as an attempt to do just that, depicting a God whose image is to be found not so much in human parents as in the rhythms of nature, the balance of light and darkness, life and death.[283] A religious language constructed upon such an image would deal with the issue of suffering quite differently than do the psalms. Suffering would not be seen as implying either the violence of God or divine neglect, for the image of God would not be that of a passionate, acting, and reacting being, but an image of the creator and sustainer of a world in which the destructive energies of chaos are contained but not eliminated. Whether or not this is the intent of the divine speeches will be considered later, but in either case, this position is a possible response to the crisis exposed by Job's recognition that traditional language about God can lead to the sanctification of a model of abuse.

Another alternative, perhaps even more radical, is championed by those who wish to claim that the personal, parental root metaphor provides the most adequate model for experiencing God, and who are also persuaded that Job's dilemma is not merely a problem of language.[284] This alternative requires the recognition that God *is* abusive. It is not just a matter of how God is portrayed but a matter of how God acts. Like human parents who physically abuse their children, however, God is not always abusive but may also be loving, nurturing, and responsive. As moral agents who answer to God for their own behavior, humans have the right to call God to answer for what God does or fails to do, when it results in abusive violence. As outrageous, even blasphemous, as such a position may sound, it has a biblical pedigree. Abraham confronts God with the immoral implications of God's intentions in Gen 18:23-25. In Psalm 44, the nation accuses God of a neglect that amounts to abuse. Job's critique is the most direct and sustained confrontation of God for abuse of the innocent, but it is not an isolated one. Jewish writers have long maintained the tradition of moral argument with God,[285] but it is the attempt to think about God in the wake of the Holocaust that has produced the most systematic exploration of divine violence and human response. For some, confrontation of God, like that in Job 16, is psychologically, morally, and religiously necessary. It is God and not Job who should repent. It is God who must confess to having remained a bystander while God's chosen people were slaughtered.[286]

For many people wrestling with the issue of suffering and the traditional language of divine violence, which Job has so powerfully exposed in chaps. 16–17, these two alternatives may seem to polarize the issues in an unacceptable way. Only if one takes the language about God as parent or ruler in a naively literal fashion, describing a being who regularly intervenes directly in the affairs of the world, does it seem necessary to take up the stance of confronting God as abusive parent. Giving up personal language about God entirely, however, would impoverish the richness of traditional imagery for God, changing Judeo-Christian religion beyond recognition. The middle ground is not easy to stake out. The contradiction between a God of love and a world in which pain is so much a presence defies resolution. Perhaps the only way of addressing such a paradox is the one that the Bible follows. Instead of attempting to define a single true image that resolves all contradictions, the Bible works instead with the complexities of human experience. In some circumstances, God's presence *feels* violently oppressive. At other times, God's presence *feels* like the love of a mother. In still other contexts, God may be experienced as the foundation that restrains chaos but does not protect individuals from the risks that are intrinsic to creation. Religious language can speak only in fragments. That limitation may frustrate human desire for a clearer understanding of issues that have a burning urgency, but what it is possible to say within the contradictory but honest language of religious experience can produce a tradition capable of addressing the complexity of emotions faced by those who bring their suffering before God.

283. Cf. N. Habel, "In Defense of God the Sage," in *The Voice from the Whirlwind*, ed. L. G. Perdue and W. Clark Gilpin (Nashville: Abingdon, 1992), 35.

284. See D. R. Blumenthal, *Facing the Abusing God: A Theology of Protest* (Louisville: Westminster/John Knox Press, 1993).

285. See A. Laytner, *Arguing with God: A Jewish Tradition* (Northvale, N.J.: Jason Aronson, 1990).

286. See, e.g., the character of Michael in Elie Wiesel's *The Town Beyond the Wall* (New York: Holt, Reinhart and Winston, 1964) 52-53.

Job 18:1-21, Bildad Describes the Fate of the Wicked

NIV

18 Then Bildad the Shuhite replied:

2"When will you end these speeches?
　Be sensible, and then we can talk.
3Why are we regarded as cattle
　and considered stupid in your sight?
4You who tear yourself to pieces in your anger,
　is the earth to be abandoned for your sake?
　Or must the rocks be moved from their place?

5"The lamp of the wicked is snuffed out;
　the flame of his fire stops burning.
6The light in his tent becomes dark;
　the lamp beside him goes out.
7The vigor of his step is weakened;
　his own schemes throw him down.
8His feet thrust him into a net
　and he wanders into its mesh.
9A trap seizes him by the heel;
　a snare holds him fast.
10A noose is hidden for him on the ground;
　a trap lies in his path.
11Terrors startle him on every side
　and dog his every step.
12Calamity is hungry for him;
　disaster is ready for him when he falls.
13It eats away parts of his skin;
　death's firstborn devours his limbs.
14He is torn from the security of his tent
　and marched off to the king of terrors.
15Fire resides*a* in his tent;
　burning sulfur is scattered over his dwelling.
16His roots dry up below
　and his branches wither above.
17The memory of him perishes from the earth;
　he has no name in the land.
18He is driven from light into darkness
　and is banished from the world.
19He has no offspring or descendants among his
　　people,
　no survivor where once he lived.
20Men of the west are appalled at his fate;
　men of the east are seized with horror.
21Surely such is the dwelling of an evil man;
　such is the place of one who knows not God."

a15 Or *Nothing he had remains*

NRSV

18 Then Bildad the Shuhite answered:
2 "How long will you hunt for words?
　Consider, and then we shall speak.
3 Why are we counted as cattle?
　Why are we stupid in your sight?
4 You who tear yourself in your anger—
　shall the earth be forsaken because of you,
　or the rock be removed out of its place?

5 "Surely the light of the wicked is put out,
　and the flame of their fire does not shine.
6 The light is dark in their tent,
　and the lamp above them is put out.
7 Their strong steps are shortened,
　and their own schemes throw them down.
8 For they are thrust into a net by their own
　　feet,
　and they walk into a pitfall.
9 A trap seizes them by the heel;
　a snare lays hold of them.
10 A rope is hid for them in the ground,
　a trap for them in the path.
11 Terrors frighten them on every side,
　and chase them at their heels.
12 Their strength is consumed by hunger,*a*
　and calamity is ready for their stumbling.
13 By disease their skin is consumed,*b*
　the firstborn of Death consumes their limbs.
14 They are torn from the tent in which they
　　trusted,
　and are brought to the king of terrors.
15 In their tents nothing remains;
　sulfur is scattered upon their habitations.
16 Their roots dry up beneath,
　and their branches wither above.
17 Their memory perishes from the earth,
　and they have no name in the street.
18 They are thrust from light into darkness,
　and driven out of the world.
19 They have no offspring or descendant among
　　their people,
　and no survivor where they used to live.
20 They of the west are appalled at their fate,
　and horror seizes those of the east.

a Or *Disaster is hungry for them*　　*b* Cn: Heb *It consumes the limbs of his skin*

NRSV

²¹ Surely such are the dwellings of the ungodly,
    such is the place of those who do not know
    God."

COMMENTARY

Bildad's reply begins with the typical objection to the previous speaker's words and attitudes (vv. 2-3), although, curiously, he uses second-person plural forms. In v. 4, he identifies the scandal he hears in Job's words, which motivates his own reply. The rest of his speech is devoted to a descriptive account of the fate of the wicked (vv. 5-21), developed through images of extinguished light (vv. 5-6), loss of vigorous movement (v. 7), entrapment like a hunted animal (vv. 8-10), predation by the forces of destruction (vv. 11-13), seizure and arraignment by death's servants (v. 14), and the annihilation of all traces of existence, including place, progeny, and memorial (vv. 15-19). The description concludes with a universal reaction of horror (v. 20) and Bildad's summary appraisal (v. 21). What makes the passage difficult to interpret is that Bildad never explicitly indicates the purpose of his speech or how he intends his words to be taken.

18:2-4. Although the problem is not evident in an English translation, Bildad's words in vv. 2-3 are couched in the second-person plural. Occasional attempts have been made to understand these verses as being addressed to Eliphaz and Zophar rather than to Job,[287] but this suggestion is not persuasive. It is easier to assume a textual error and to read these verses as being directed at Job. Whether Bildad is irritated by Job's "hunting for words" or impatient for him to "end these speeches" depends on the interpretation of a rare Hebrew word (קִנְצֵי *qēneṣ*). The Aramaic targum of Job from Qumran supports the NIV.

As so often, the first issue in the speech deals with what is preventing genuine dialogue. In Bildad's view, such conversation can take place only within a framework of essential, shared presuppositions and in an atmosphere of respect. For Bildad, dialogue is not simply a matter of

exchanging words. Indeed, Job's words are making serious discussion impossible. Bildad wants Job to stop talking and "recognize" certain essential things (בִּין *bîn*; NRSV, "consider"; NIV, "be sensible"; the Hebrew word has connotations of both perception and understanding). Only then can useful dialogue take place (v. 2*b*). Bildad's concern for the foundations of moral discourse is also reflected in the images of v. 4, where "the earth" and "the rock" are symbols of the encompassing structures and secure bases on which all else rests. He rightly perceives that Job's words in such passages as 12:13-25 are a challenge to the very foundations of the world.

Bildad's objection that Job considers the friends to be "like cattle" (v. 3) is acute. Even though Job has not used such a term, he has ridiculed the herd mentality embedded in the clichéd and platitudinous language of the friends (see Reflections on Job 13). Bildad's request for respect seems innocuous enough. Sometimes, however, insistence on civility can be a means of control by those who do not want a discussion to disturb the foundations of things in which their security and their very identities are invested. A comparable rhetorical strategy is evident in Bildad's characterization of Job as one who "tears" himself "in his anger" (v. 4*a*). Bildad recasts Job's serious attack on the foundations as mere self-destructive behavior. His words have subtle overtones of animality ("tear" [טֹרֵף *ṭārap*] is used of animals attacking prey) and of madness, since only if he were insane would Job mutilate himself in his anger. By these means, he belittles Job's words and patronizes him.

18:5-21. At this point Bildad introduces his description of the fate of the wicked. The context of the preceding verses gives some clue as to the description's function. This vision is what Bildad wants Job to perceive, a precondition for further dialogue. Bildad presents this description as the

287. E. Dhorme, *A Commentary on the Book of Job*, trans. H. Knight (London: Nelson, 1967) 257, noting Elihu's rebuke of the friends in 32:3.

rock that cannot be moved from its place without endangering the whole superstructure of piety and morality (cf. 15:4). That the wicked come to a bad end is a commonplace in the wisdom literature (cf. the numerous sayings in Proverbs 11–13). In these proverbs the fate of the wicked is usually presented in a binary saying, in which the complementary half of the verse describes the good fortune of the righteous. What is at stake in such proverbs is the claim that the world is founded on a just moral order. A developed description of the fate of the wicked also occurs in a number of psalms. In Ps 7:14-16[15-17], it is part of the prayer of an innocent person who is reassured about the moral order of the world by envisioning the recoil of evil upon the wicked (cf. also Ps 49:13-20[14-21], where the issue is the power of wealth). In Psalm 64, the description serves to resolve the psalmist's complaint about the predations of the wicked. In Ps 73:17-28, it explicitly answers the psalmist's question of theodicy.

The apparent good fortune of the wicked seems to have been a much more problematic issue than the misfortune of the righteous. Perhaps this is because there were so many possible explanations for the temporary distress of the righteous, many of them catalogued in Eliphaz's speech in chaps. 4–5. Moreover, religious practice always provided something for the righteous sufferer to do about the situation: pray to an ever compassionate God. But if, as Van der Toorn has suggested, the fundamental conviction throughout the ancient Near East was that "nothing happens on earth unless it is decreed in heaven,"[288] then the good fortune of the wicked was a theological scandal, a contradiction of the moral order of the world. Moreover, there was no religious practice comparable to a prayer of lament by which one could reverse the good fortune of the wicked and so restore coherency to the world. It remained a scandal. The vividness of the descriptions of Eliphaz, Bildad, and Zophar are in part attempts to create a virtual reality in which the ultimate downfall of the wicked can be experienced. One might object that the friends are answering a question Job has not asked. As elsewhere, they are responding with prefabricated replies. Never-

theless, they are right to recognize in Job's words an attack on the plausibility of the belief that the world has a moral structure. Their replies reiterate that moral structure at the place where they feel it to be most vulnerable.

Those who interpret Bildad's words as an identification of Job as one of the wicked and an announcement of his fate are not entirely wrong,[289] but they collapse a more complex process that takes place over several chapters. Bildad is not yet ready to declare Job wicked. The moral order Bildad reaffirms, however, has no place for an anomaly such as Job represents. Almost inevitably, the resolution of that intolerable contradiction will be made by declaring Job to be one of the wicked, which Eliphaz will say in chap. 22. Since the reader knows what none of the characters do, that all this disaster has in fact happened to a person who is "blameless and upright, one who feared God and turned away from evil" (1:1 NRSV), the reader's confidence in the religious ideology that results in such a false accusation is seriously undermined.

18:5-6. The images Bildad invokes throughout his description are primarily those of disintegration.[290] The first of these is the image of a light going out (vv. 5-6). In Hebrew, none of the verbs used denotes an active agent. Rather, the light simply "goes out" (דעך *dāʿak*) and "grows dark" (חשׁך *ḥāšak*); the flame "does not shine" (לא־יגה *lōʾ-yiggah*), and the lamp "goes out" (*dāʿak*). As in Bildad's previous image of a plant that withers for lack of life-giving water (8:11-13), the life and power of the wicked are self-limited because they are cut off from the source of all life. The symbolic association of light/darkness with life/death is common in the OT and particularly frequent in Job (e.g., 3:20; 10:21-22; 15:22; 17:13). The lamp in the tent is more specifically an image of security and protection, as in Job's evocative use in 29:3.

The saying "the lamp of the wicked goes out" is a traditional one (Prov 13:9; 24:20; cf. Prov 20:20). Throughout the description, Bildad shows

288. K. van der Toorn, *Sin and Sanction in Israel and Mesopotamia,* SSN 22 (Assen and Maastricht: Van Gorcum, 1985) 56.

289. E.g., F. Andersen, *Job: An Introduction and Commentary,* Tyndale Old Testament Commentaries (Downers Grove, Ill.: Inter-Varsity, 1976) 190; M. Pope, *Job,* 3rd ed., AB 15 (Garden City, N.Y.: Doubleday, 1979) 137; N. Habel, *The Book of Job,* OTL (Philadelphia: Westminster, 1985) 282; J. G. Janzen, *Job,* Interpretation (Atlanta: John Knox, 1985) 128. Contrast D. Clines, *Job 1–20,* WBC 17 (Dallas: Word, 1989) 409.

290. E. Good, *In Turns of Tempest* (Stanford, Calif.: Stanford University Press, 1990) 253.

a particular fondness for familiar images and phrases. In his earlier speech, he had insisted on the reliability of ancestral words as bearers of truth. By populating his speech with traditional figures, Bildad makes his own words a conduit of that authoritative, ancestral voice.

18:7-10. In this section, Bildad's images have to do with arrested movement. Shortening steps (v. 7) are an evocative image of diminishing vitality, a contrasting image to the broad strides that the books of Psalms and Proverbs use as an image of the vigor that comes from divine support (Ps 18:36[37]; Prov 4:12). In those passages, the parallel image of walking without stumbling also contrasts with Bildad's description of the wicked being cast down by their own schemes. The notion that the evil planned by the wicked eventually causes their own ruin is a very common motif in wisdom thought (e.g., Prov 11:3*b*, 5*b*, 6*b*; 26:27). Behind this notion lies the belief that the world is structured to respond supportively to good and to resist evil. Thus the plans of the wicked, no matter how clever, are doomed to failure because they are contradictory to the fundamental moral order of the world.

Bildad's description of traps in vv. 8 10 is a tour de force of imagery. Unfortunately, it is not possible to identify the particular types of traps, snares, nets, and other devices referred to by the six different words he uses. What they all have in common is that they work because the victim cannot perceive them and so blunders into destruction. For Bildad, what is morally significant is not that wicked people exist but that their existence is tenuous, because the world for them is a field baited with snares that they cannot see and so cannot escape. Imagery of the snare and trap appears in many contexts to express anxiety about a hostile and uncontrollable situation (Pss 9:16; 124:7; 140:5[6]; 142:3*b*[4*b*]; Jer 18:22*b*; 48:44).

18:11-14. The imagery now shifts from hidden menace to the aggression of death's forces, represented as a pack of hunting predators. Verse 11 describes the chase, v. 12 the cornering of the prey, and v. 13 the devouring. The agents are variously described but are all traditional designations for the servants of death. The word "terrors," (בלהות *ballāhôt*) for instance, does not primarily refer to subjective psychological reac-

tions but to the servants of personified Death who cause terror (v. 11).[291] Similarly, "calamity" (אָוֶן *'ôn*) and "disaster" (אֵיד *'êd*) are agents of death (v. 12). The graphic image of death's firstborn consuming the skin and limbs brings the image of predation to its logical conclusion, but it also alludes to the specific effects of deadly diseases that eat away flesh (v. 13). This is probably an allusion to plague as the personified firstborn of Death, as in Mesopotamian mythology the plague god Namtar is the vizier and apparently the firstborn of Erishkigal, queen of the underworld.[292]

Textual problems and grammatical ambiguities in vv. 12-13 permit an alternative interpretation in which death itself is described, personified as the "Hungry One" (v. 12), and named with the honorific title "First-Born Death" (v. 13),[293] as in Habel's translation: "The Hungry One will be his strength,/ Calamity ready as his escort./ He consumes his skin with both hands;/ Firstborn Death consumes with both hands."[294] The god Mot (Death) is an important figure in Ugaritic mythology, and death is often represented in mythic terms in the OT. Death is also associated with an insatiable hunger (Isa 5:14; Hab 2:5). In Ugaritic myth, Mot is described as having "one lip to earth and one to heaven, [he stretches his to]ngue to the stars. Baal enters his mouth, descends into him like an olive-cake."[295] As that image suggests, however, personified Death is not characteristically represented as roaming the earth in search of victims but as the king of the underworld to whom all come. Thus it seems less likely that vv. 12-13 refer to personified Death. Dramatically, Death appears only at the climax of Bildad's description. In v. 14, the imagery of the "hounds of Hell" modulates into that of sudden arrest by unnamed agents who march the victim off to the presence of Death, the "king of terrors."

18:15-19. A series of images of annihilation follows. Textual problems obscure the first line. The initial words can be translated "nothing of

---

291. N. Tromp, *Primitive Conceptions of Death and the Nether World in the Old Testament,* BibOr 21 (Rome: Pontifical Biblical Institute, 1969) 74; Pope, *Job,* 134; Clines, *Job 1–20,* 416.

292. Dhorme, *A Commentary on the Book of Job,* 265; J. B. Burns, "The Identity of Death's First-Born (Job xviii 13)," *VT* 37 (1987) 363; cf. N. Sarna, "The Mythological Background of Job 18," *JBL* 82 (1963) 315-17.

293. Pope, *Job,* 135; Habel, *The Book of Job,* 287.

294. Habel, *The Book of Job,* 280.

295. James B. Pritchard, ed., *Ancient Near Eastern Texts Relating to the Old Testament* (*ANET*), 3rd ed. with supplement (Princeton: Princeton University Press, 1969) 138.

---

his dwells in his tent" (see NRSV), although it is very awkwardly expressed in Hebrew. It is also possible to emend the text slightly and read "fire" as a parallel to "sulfur" (NIV).[296] Fire and sulfur, traditionally "fire and brimstone," are associated as agents of destruction (Gen 19:24; Ps 11:6; Ezek 38:22). The sprinkling of land with sulfur, as with salt (Judg 9:45), renders it unfruitful and unfit for habitation (Deut 29:23[22]). In Greek tradition, sprinkling sulfur served as a disinfectant for corpse contamination.[297] Either connotation would fit the context.

In the following verses, Bildad uses merismus, the rhetorical device of expressing totality by naming paired opposites: root and branch in v. 16, farmlands and grazing lands in v. 17,[298] one's own kin and place of sojourn in v. 19, and westerners and easterners in v. 20. Note also the use of polar terms in the phrase "from light to darkness" (v. 18) and the synonymous terms "offspring or descendants" (v. 19). Although Bildad's speech is not, properly speaking, magical, he empowers his words by imitating the reality he wishes to evoke in the texture of his language, the totality of the annihilation of the wicked.

In v. 16, the withering of "root and branch" (Mal 4:1[3:19]; Sir 23:25), like that of "root and fruit" (Ezek 17:9; Hos 9:16; Amos 2:9),[299] expresses the failure of possessions and progeny, those things that the individual has "put forth" like a tree.[300] Verse 17 makes the same point more directly by referring to the cessation of the mention of the deceased person's name, which is connected less with reputation than with the children who carry the name into succeeding generations (cf. 2 Sam 14:7; 18:18; Ps 109:13). In v. 19, the extinction of the entire line is explicitly stated, not even excepting a survivor dwelling in a foreign land. In a culture that did not believe in immortality or continued existence after death except through one's progeny, the protection of that continuity was a matter of anxiety and considerable creativity. The problem of childlessness is a recurrent one in ancient Israelite and Canaanite literature (cf. the stories of Abraham in Genesis 16–22 and of Keret and Dan'el Ugaritic literature),[301] and the variety of social practices designed to ensure offspring (polygamy, concubinage, adoption, Levirate marriage) attests to the importance of progeny.[302] The horror of such an end is captured in Bildad's image that such a person is "driven out of the world" (v. 18).

18:20-21. The description concludes by evoking the horrified reaction of the whole world to the spectacle of the annihilation of the wicked and his line (v. 20). Picking up the references to habitation (v. 15) and tent (vv. 6, 14-15), Bildad uses the terms "dwelling" (משכן *miškan*) and "place" (מקום *māqôm*) as metaphors for the existence of the "one who knows not God" (v. 21). The term "place" also echoes v. 4, where Bildad asked rhetorically if the rock should be moved from its place. Bildad's summary appraisal in v. 21 thus frames the vivid immediacy of the poem and succinctly states his didactic theme.

---

296. M. Dahood, "Some Northwest-Semitic Words in Job," *Biblica* 38 (1957), 312-14, followed by Pope, *Job,* 136; Habel, *The Book of Job,* 282; Clines, *Job 1–20,* 407.

297. See Homer *Odyssey* 22.480-81.

298. Translation following Clines, *Job 1–20,* 404; cf. Dhorme, *A Commentary on the Book of Job,* 267.

299. See Eshumunazar Inscription in *ANET,* 662.

300. Clines, *Job 1–20,* 420.

301. *ANET,* 142-55.

302. Pope, *Job,* 136-37. Perpetuation of the "name" is the issue associated with male childlessness. In narratives about childless women, social status is the problem.

REFLECTIONS

As dramatic poetry, the three speeches on the fate of the wicked (chaps. 15; 18; 20) are among the most compelling in the book of Job. They also model a provocative way of imagining evil and the people who embody it. Many readers may feel that the moral imagination evoked by these poems is strange and alien to modern sensibilities. As one explores them more closely, however, one may recognize some familiar and disturbing modes of thinking.

To understand this way of thinking about evil, it is necessary to look briefly at the way good and evil were envisioned in Israel's wisdom tradition. Ancient Israelite wisdom tended to think of good and evil as active forces in a world composed of active forces.[303] Good and

303. This analysis is based on G. von Rad, *Wisdom in Israel,* trans. J. D. Martin (Nashville: Abingdon, 1972) 77-81.

evil are not merely matters of the disposition of the human heart, but forces that have the power to create or destroy things of value: contentment, reputation, possessions, a life, a family, a community. As active qualities, good produces good and evil produces evil, for self and for others. The created order, however, has a bias toward life and thus toward the good. The world responds favorably to good but resists and rejects evil. Evil can be described as participation in the realm of death. An evil person spreads death among the community, but in the end is claimed by the same power of death. This understanding is illustrated in Prov 1:10-19, where violent persons use the imagery of death to describe their own activity (Prov 1:12a), yet in the end destroy themselves (Prov 1:18). By identifying their violence with death, they give death a claim over them. So, too, in Bildad's speech, the forces of life reject the wicked person (vv. 5-7), who is claimed by death (vv. 11-14).

Similar ideas inform the understanding of the curse that falls on a people because they have done evil or repudiated the covenant. The curse also often takes the form of unleashing the enmity of the powers of life itself against the ones who are cursed. In Deuteronomy 28, for instance, one section of the covenant curse describes the refusal of sky and earth to open themselves to the accursed. Vividly stated, the sky becomes bronze and the earth iron; the rain that falls turns into dust, until all perish (Deut 28:23-24). Similarly, the fundamental trustworthiness of the world, which allows one to act and accomplish the basic functions of life, does not hold for the one accursed. In the so-called futility curses, actions no longer produce dependable results, whether in the production of food, in the establishment of a family, or in social and community relations (Deut 28:30-32, 38-44). These curses create the image of someone's being rejected by the powers of life, subjected to terror and confusion because that person no longer has a place in the domain of life. As in Bildad's account (18:20), the cursed person becomes an object of horror (Deut 28:37). This reaction is not simple moral disapproval but a much more visceral reaction against someone whom life itself seems to have rejected.

Just as the natural world expelled evil that was identified as accursed by God, so also the human community's reaction might take a similar shape, as in the story of Achan in Joshua 7. After an unexpected defeat, oracular inquiry reveals that the defeat was caused by a person's having violated the principles of holy war. When the guilty party is identified, the entire community participates in the destruction of Achan, together with "his sons and daughters, with his oxen, donkeys, and sheep, and his tent and all that he had. . . . And all Israel stoned him to death; they burned them with fire, cast stones on them, and raised over him a great heap of stones that remains to this day" (Josh 7:24b-25a, 26a NRSV). Like the wicked person described by Bildad, Achan is "driven out of the world," annihilated "root and branch" as his possessions and his progeny are destroyed along with his own life (cf. Job 18:15-19).

The understanding of good and evil as active forces bearing life and bearing death is a powerful model that envisions the world as a holistic environment in which what is good is nurtured and what is evil is isolated and expelled. Nevertheless, this way of imagining evil and the world's response to it is deeply disturbing. Most obviously, it becomes very easy to identify suffering itself as a sign of rejection by the life-giving forces of the world, and thus as a sign that the person who suffers is in some way evil. That elements of this perception are present in modern culture is evident from the common reactions of fear, disgust, and even hatred that people sometimes experience when confronted by a person whose body is deformed or disfigured by illness and suffering. These reactions are residual elements of a subconscious, subrational chain of association: a horribly suffering body, which death is so visibly claiming, is seen as a body rejected by life and all the goodness associated with life. It is seen as a body cursed and, therefore, a presence of evil. Healthy persons, anxious to associate themselves with the powers of life and dissociate themselves from death, react by driving the suffering one away, either literally or figuratively.

A number of diseases have particularly evoked such a response. There is a trace of it in one of the synonyms for *cancer*: *malignancy,* a malign or evil thing. Not too many years ago, cancer was spoken of in whispers; a vague sense of shame was attached to it, and people often attempted to conceal the nature of their disease. More dramatic has been the response to leprosy. Even though the disease is not highly contagious, it evoked such horror that sufferers were expelled from the community and forced to live as outcasts. Most recently, AIDS sufferers have encountered similar reactions. Despite the fact that the mechanisms of the disease's transmission are well understood and controllable, the announcement of plans for an AIDS hospice is likely to produce a nearly hysterical reaction from neighbors. In each of these diseases, the powers of life and health, which normally protect the body, fail spectacularly, leaving the body open to the ravages of disease and death, which attack with virulence. For people who are influenced by the type of thinking reflected in Bildad's speech, the rejection of the body by the forces that normally protect it appears as a rejection of the person by God. This symbolic association, which may take place on a subconscious level, encourages the communal response of expulsion and annihilation, all in a spirit of great self-righteousness. The cruel injustice of this reaction, a form of blaming the victim, is obvious once it is exposed. Because such associations tend to be rooted deep in the psyche, however, they are often difficult to bring to surface where they may be examined and corrected.

To be fair to Bildad, one could say that the confusion of the physical with the moral is a *mis*application of his understanding of how the world expels evil from its midst. What he is trying to talk about is moral evil, not physical suffering. Yet there are reasons to be uneasy about Bildad's vision of things even when it is applied to the case of a person who is truly and deeply evil. Janzen expresses the concern well in his recollection of the crowds that savaged the lifeless body of Mussolini, "dragging it through the streets, hanging it heels-up against the wall, then pelting it with stones and spitting at it. In viewing the scene, one was drawn into the moral energy of the action; yet more deeply, one felt a pathos of horror that any human being, no matter in what moral state, could be so driven out of the world."[304] Bildad's vision dehumanizes the wicked. The wicked become objectified, something wholly other than "good people"; they become monsters against whom any violence is legitimate. Such dichotomizing between the wicked and the righteous leads to a deceptively dangerous misapprehension of the nature of evil. In fact, no one is completely free of the taint of evil. The crowds who attacked the body of Mussolini were not themselves wholly innocent of complicity in evil. Indeed, the knowledge of that complicity may have been the source of some of their fury. The understanding of evil articulated by Bildad and his friends and enacted by avenging mobs encourages the hypocrisy of pretending that evil is something we can expel from ourselves (individually or communally) by exterminating one whom we have judged to be radically evil.

304. Janzen, *Job,* 130.

Job 19:1-29, Job Denounces God's Injustice

19 Then Job replied:

2"How long will you torment me
    and crush me with words?
3Ten times now you have reproached me;
    shamelessly you attack me.
4If it is true that I have gone astray,

19 Then Job answered:
2 "How long will you torment me,
    and break me in pieces with words?
3 These ten times you have cast reproach upon
    me;
    are you not ashamed to wrong me?
4 And even if it is true that I have erred,

NIV

my error remains my concern alone.
⁵If indeed you would exalt yourselves above me
  and use my humiliation against me,
⁶then know that God has wronged me
  and drawn his net around me.

⁷"Though I cry, 'I've been wronged!' I get no
    response;
  though I call for help, there is no justice.
⁸He has blocked my way so I cannot pass;
  he has shrouded my paths in darkness.
⁹He has stripped me of my honor
  and removed the crown from my head.
¹⁰He tears me down on every side till I am gone;
  he uproots my hope like a tree.
¹¹His anger burns against me;
  he counts me among his enemies.
¹²His troops advance in force;
  they build a siege ramp against me
  and encamp around my tent.

¹³"He has alienated my brothers from me;
  my acquaintances are completely estranged
    from me.
¹⁴My kinsmen have gone away;
  my friends have forgotten me.
¹⁵My guests and my maidservants count me a
    stranger;
  they look upon me as an alien.
¹⁶I summon my servant, but he does not answer,
  though I beg him with my own mouth.
¹⁷My breath is offensive to my wife;
  I am loathsome to my own brothers.
¹⁸Even the little boys scorn me;
  when I appear, they ridicule me.
¹⁹All my intimate friends detest me;
  those I love have turned against me.
²⁰I am nothing but skin and bones;
  I have escaped with only the skin of my
    teeth.ᵃ

²¹"Have pity on me, my friends, have pity,
  for the hand of God has struck me.
²²Why do you pursue me as God does?
  Will you never get enough of my flesh?

²³"Oh, that my words were recorded,
  that they were written on a scroll,
²⁴that they were inscribed with an iron tool onᵇ
    lead,

ᵃ20 Or only my gums   ᵇ24 Or and

NRSV

my error remains with me.
⁵ If indeed you magnify yourselves against me,
  and make my humiliation an argument
    against me,
⁶ know then that God has put me in the wrong,
  and closed his net around me.
⁷ Even when I cry out, 'Violence!' I am not
    answered;
  I call aloud, but there is no justice.
⁸ He has walled up my way so that I cannot
    pass,
  and he has set darkness upon my paths.
⁹ He has stripped my glory from me,
  and taken the crown from my head.
¹⁰ He breaks me down on every side, and I am
    gone,
  he has uprooted my hope like a tree.
¹¹ He has kindled his wrath against me,
  and counts me as his adversary.
¹² His troops come on together;
  they have thrown up siegeworksᵃ against
    me,
  and encamp around my tent.

¹³ "He has put my family far from me,
  and my acquaintances are wholly estranged
    from me.
¹⁴ My relatives and my close friends have failed
    me;
¹⁵ the guests in my house have forgotten me;
  my serving girls count me as a stranger;
  I have become an alien in their eyes.
¹⁶ I call to my servant, but he gives me no
    answer;
  I must myself plead with him.
¹⁷ My breath is repulsive to my wife;
  I am loathsome to my own family.
¹⁸ Even young children despise me;
  when I rise, they talk against me.
¹⁹ All my intimate friends abhor me,
  and those whom I loved have turned against
    me.
²⁰ My bones cling to my skin and to my flesh,
  and I have escaped by the skin of my teeth.
²¹ Have pity on me, have pity on me, O you my
    friends,
  for the hand of God has touched me!

ᵃ Cn: Heb their way

NIV

or engraved in rock forever!
[25]I know that my Redeemer[a] lives,
    and that in the end he will stand upon the
        earth.[b]
[26]And after my skin has been destroyed,
    yet[c] in[d] my flesh I will see God;
[27]I myself will see him
    with my own eyes—I, and not another.
        How my heart yearns within me!

[28]"If you say, 'How we will hound him,
    since the root of the trouble lies in him,[e] '
[29]you should fear the sword yourselves;
    for wrath will bring punishment by the sword,
    and then you will know that there is
        judgment.'"

[a]25 Or *defender*   [b]25 Or *upon my grave*   [c]26 Or *And after
I awake, / though this ⌊body⌋ has been destroyed, / then*   [d]26 Or
/ apart from   [e]28 Many Hebrew manuscripts, Septuagint and
Vulgate; most Hebrew manuscripts *me*   [f]29 Or */ that you may come
to know the Almighty*

NRSV

[22] Why do you, like God, pursue me,
    never satisfied with my flesh?

[23] "O that my words were written down!
    O that they were inscribed in a book!
[24] O that with an iron pen and with lead
    they were engraved on a rock forever!
[25] For I know that my Redeemer[a] lives,
    and that at the last he[b] will stand upon the
        earth;[c]
[26] and after my skin has been thus destroyed,
    then in[d] my flesh I shall see God,[e]
[27] whom I shall see on my side,[f]
    and my eyes shall behold, and not another.
        My heart faints within me!
[28] If you say, 'How we will persecute him!'
    and, 'The root of the matter is found in
        him';
[29] be afraid of the sword,
    for wrath brings the punishment of the
        sword,
    so that you may know there is a judgment."

[a] Or *Vindicator*   [b] Or *that he the Last*   [c] Heb *dust*
[d] Or *without*   [e] Meaning of Heb of this verse uncertain
[f] Or *for myself*

COMMENTARY

Although Job echoes Bildad's opening words (cf. 18:2 and 19:2), his speech is not so much a reply to Bildad as a further investigation of the themes and issues of his previous speech in chap. 16. Following a reproach to the friends for their aggressive and misplaced attacks on him (vv. 2-6), Job uses traditional lament motifs to describe his suffering at God's hand. Job describes both God's violent aggression against him (vv. 7-12) and his alienation from friends and family (vv. 13-19), concluding with a description of his own body's deterioration (v. 20). Whereas the tradition of psalmic laments would direct Job to plead to God for mercy, Job makes an ironic appeal to the friends instead (vv. 21-22). Rather than prayer, he thinks in terms of legal confrontation with God, expressing the wish that his words could be permanently preserved (vv. 23-24). Although Job expresses certainty that a defender will arise to

take up his case after he is dead (vv. 25-26a), what he most wants is to confront God before his death (vv. 26b-27). For the first time in the dialogue, Job does not close his speech with a meditation on death but with a final rebuke and warning addressed to the friends who persecute him.

19:1-6. In his previous opening comments, Job parodied the words of the friends (9:2-3), made fun of their pretense to knowledge (12:2), and criticized them as "miserable comforters" whose talk is both empty and destructive (16:2-3). Here, however, Job's reproach is more severe, as he accuses them of acts of verbal violence (v. 2). In vv. 21-22 and 28-29 as well, Job will explicitly accuse the friends of a kind of obsessive aggression manifested in their slanders. Job does not distinguish among his friends or between their first and second speeches but lumps all that they have said together ("ten times," v. 3, is a round number; cf. Gen 31:7; Num 14:22). Whatever the friends' intentions, Job has heard their words as impugning his integrity. He casts the issue in terms of honor and shame. By attempting to expose him to shame, they have actually exposed their own shameful conduct (v. 3; "cast reproach" does not capture the nuance of the Hebrew [כלם *kālam*]; "insult" or "humiliate" is closer to the meaning). Job's sense of the social dimension of well-being and suffering is acute, as vv. 13-19 illustrate. He will return to the theme in chaps. 29–30.

The same theme of agonistic social relations appears in v. 5, as Job depicts the friends' "making themselves big" by using Job's humiliation against him. Their attitude would be improper under any circumstance (cf. 31:29), but it is particularly abhorrent because it is not Job who has done wrong but God who has wronged Job (v. 6). The word Job uses in v. 6*a* is the same one Bildad employed in 8:3 in his rhetorical question "does God *pervert* (עות *'iwwēt*) justice?" Note also Job's echo of the word "justice" (משפט *mišpāṭ*) in v. 7*b*.

The enigmatic v. 4 is best understood in the context of vv. 5-6. The NRSV gives a fairly literal translation of the verse, although the verb translated "remains" is, more concretely, "lodges" (לון *lîn*). The conduct referred to is inadvertent sin, i.e., sin committed in ignorance or without intent.[305] Although real sin with real consequences, it was not considered to be as serious as intentional, willful sin. In this verse, Job is not admitting that he has committed this less serious type of sin, but is stating a conditional proposition: "If it were true that I had inadvertently sinned. . . ." But what does Job mean by saying that "my inadvertent sin would lodge with me"? The NIV understands Job to say that such sin is his business alone. Sin was not so clearly a purely private matter in ancient Israel, however. In the wisdom tradition in particular, public reproach for behavior that "departs from the way" was necessary and expected (e.g., Prov 12:1; 13:1; 15:5). More plausibly, Job acknowledges that if he had sinned, even inadvertently, then that sin and its consequences would indeed lodge with him. In such a case, the friends would have grounds to reproach

him (v. 5). But the true state of affairs is that the wrongdoing is God's, not Job's (v. 6).

19:7-12. In another context there would be little in these verses, or in vv. 13-20, that would strike one as untraditional. Job uses conventional lament vocabulary, imagery, and motifs. Following Job's statement in v. 6 that God has wronged him (lit., "twisted"), however, these verses take on the connotation of an accusation rather than a proper lament. This rhetorical strategy is similar to what Job uses in 9:2-14 and 16:9-21, where he recontextualizes a doxology and a lament, respectively. As in chap. 16, there are many similarities between vv. 7-12 and Lamentations (esp. Lam 3:5-9).

Although Job uses a variety of images in vv. 7-12, most have overtones of violent aggression and evoke a sense of powerlessness. It has been suggested that the cry "Violence!" (v. 7) is the equivalent of the English plea "Help!"—a cry of alarm that should bring aid.[306] In Lam 3:8 and Hab 1:2, such cries are addressed to God, who, however, refuses to hear or delays action. Following v. 6*b*, which describes God as casting a net (or possibly a siegework)[307] against Job, he vainly cries out against God's violence. What Job seeks is not rescue, but justice; yet that is precisely what is absent (v. 7*b*; cf. Hab 1:2-4).

As in Lam 3:8-9, the image of futile outcry is followed by that of a blocked way. Blocking a road or obscuring a path (v. 8) controls a person's movement and options, depriving him or her of self-determination (cf. Hos 2:6[8]). The emotional overtone of being in someone else's power is also present in the image of being stripped of dignity and crown (v. 9; cf. Lam 5:16). The social background for such an image is the humiliation of a captive, as in 12:17-19, where Job described the stripping of leaders by God. Verse 10 intensifies the sense of powerlessness. In 14:7-9, Job had evocatively described hope as the power of regeneration, likening it to the ability of a hewn tree's roots to put forth new growth. Here, however, Job describes his hope as being torn up by the roots, so that the capacity for self-regeneration is utterly destroyed.

The concluding set of images reinforces the

---

305. J. Milgrom, "The Cultic Segaga and Its Influence in Psalms and Job," *JQR* 58 (1967) 73-79.

306. H. Haag, "chamas," G. Johannes Botterweck and Helmer Ringgren, eds., *Theological Dictionary of the Old Testament* (*TDOT*), 5 vols. (Grand Rapids: Eerdmans, 1974–86) 4:484.

307. R. Gordis, *The Book of Job: Commentary, New Translation, and Special Studies* (New York: Jewish Theological Seminary, 5738/1978) 201; N. Habel, *The Book of Job*, OTL (Philadelphia: Westminster, 1985) 291; D. Clines, *Job 1–20*, WBC 17 (Dallas: Word, 1989) 428.

theme of powerlessness. Job attributes his destruction to God's having intentionally increased his anger against Job, treating him as an enemy (cf. Lam 2:5). The outcome of such hostility is expressed in the image of a military operation: the gathering of troops, the building of a siege ramp, and the final besieging of Job's tent (cf. Lam 3:5, 7). As often noted, a disproportion exists between the description of preparations, which would suffice for an attack on a city, and the object of the operation, which is merely a tent.[308] Here perhaps is a trace of Job's ironic, subtly mocking voice, as in 7:17-18.

19:13-20. There is no irony in the following section, however. In these verses, Job also employs a traditional lament motif, the alienation of the speaker from family and friends (cf. Pss 31:11-13[12-14]; 38:11[12]; 41:9[10]; 55:12-14[13-15]; 69:8[9], 18[19]. In contrast to the psalms, Job's account is much longer and more detailed. Verses 13-19 contain some twelve different terms for social and kinship categories. Unfortunately, the precise meaning of many of them is unknown or disputed. Even without such knowledge, however, one has the impression that Job is giving a detailed map of the relational world from which he is now excluded. The account begins (vv. 13-14) and ends (vv. 18-19) with the broader social contexts, placing the intimate domestic sphere at the center (vv. 15-17). The verbs used trace a different pattern, a crescendo of repudiation. The sequence begins with passively expressed alienation (distancing, estrangement, forgetting; see vv. 13-14), then records the changed attitudes of others, which result in the refusal of customary relations (vv. 15-16). A description of visceral repulsion follows (v. 17), concluding with active rejection and antagonism (vv. 18-19). The very first verb in the series stands out for another reason as well. While the passage is primarily descriptive, the first clause speaks of causation: God is responsible for the terrible isolation Job experiences (v. 13a).

In vv. 13-14, paired terms identify the extended family and friends in general. The NIV's "brothers" (אחים 'aḥîm) in v. 13, although literal, obscures that word's broader nuance, "kin." The parallel term in v. 14 (קרוב qārôb) refers to the closer family circle (cf. Lev 21:2-3; Num 27:11).

Probably, the two terms for friends (ידע yōdēa' and מידע mĕyūdā') also designate "friends" and "familiar friends," respectively,[309] although the evidence is less clear (cf. 2 Kgs 10:11; Ps 55:13[14]).

The NRSV and the NIV divide the lines differently in vv. 14 and 15, with the NRSV following the opinion of most commentators. The precise meaning of the phrase translated "guests in my house" (גרי ביתי gārê bêtî) is uncertain. Since גר (gēr) refers to resident aliens, the phrase means something like "retainers," persons not related by blood to the community but who are protected by the patronage of a householder (cf. Exod 3:22, where the phrase means "tenant").[310] Such a person would ordinarily be bound by the strongest motives of loyalty to the one who had given the outsider a place in the social order.

Verses 15-16 describe a social world turned upside down. Maidservants were not only low-ranking members of a household but were also often ethnic foreigners, captured in war or sold into slavery (Lev 25:44-46; 2 Kgs 5:2). For the maidservants to treat the master of the house as the "stranger" and the "foreigner" reverses the relationship. Similarly, the manservant was expected to attend to the needs of the master, taking his cue from the master's gestures as well as words (cf. Ps 123:2). For Job not only to have to verbalize his request ("with my mouth" is emphatic in v. 16b) but even to beg, and still to get no response (NIV) is to experience the collapse of a social relationship previously taken for granted.

The dissolution of the most intimate relationships is described in v. 17. Word play in the initial phrase (רוחי זרה rûḥî zārâ) allows it to be read both "my spirit is alien" and "my breath is repulsive" to my wife. Whether or not the pun is intentional, it captures the way in which revulsion at a previously insignificant physical characteristic often serves as the focus for and symbol of the alienation between two persons. Another pun occurs in the second half of the verse. In context the verb must mean "be loathsome"; yet it is spelled the same as the verb "to seek favor" (חנתי ḥannōtî). Opinion is divided as to whether those who find Job repellent (בני בטני bĕnê bitnî; lit.,

308. J. E. Hartley, *The Book of Job*, NICOT (Grand Rapids, Mich.: Eerdmans, 1988) 286; Habel, *The Book of Job*, 301.

309. S. R. Driver and G. B. Gray, *A Critical and Exegetical Commentary on the Book of Job*, ICC (Edinburgh: T. & T. Clark, 1921) Part I, 167.
310. Clines, *Job 1–20*, 446-47.

"sons of my belly") are his own children (i.e., those whom his loins have engendered) or his uterine brothers (i.e., sons of the same womb from which he came). The objection to the first alternative is that Job's children are dead (1:19). In this passage, however, Job is using a conventional form of lament, which might well be employed as a traditional topos, whether or not the details fit the narrative framework. Parallelism favors "wife and children" here. Whichever interpretation is elected, the painful sense of intimacy turned to repulsion is clear.

In vv. 18-19, the description turns again to the larger social world but also to more marked expressions of rejection. The collapse of two very different kinds of social relations are depicted. In the first it is the respect of children for elders, which was taken with great seriousness in the ancient world (cf. 2 Kgs 2:23-24). In the second, it is the solidarity of persons who belong to a circle of friends bound by mutuality. The intensity of such relationships and the particular pain when they turned to enmity is expressed also in the poignancy of Ps 55:12-14[13-15].

A single verse describes Job's physical disintegration (v. 20). Such descriptions are not uncommon in laments, but the precise meaning of this verse is unusually obscure. Clines's suggestion for v. 20 is the best.[311] Flesh and skin are ordinarily supported by the structure of the bones. When the bones "cling to" or are supported by soft tissues, then the normal relationships of the healthy body are reversed. Although there is a close parallel to v. 20a in Ps 102:5[6], v. 20b is unique. The KJV's literal translation, "and I am escaped with the skin of my teeth," has provided the English language a memorable proverb, but Job is not talking about a narrow escape here, as the adage has come to mean. Teeth, of course, have no skin, so that the expression is a paradoxical way of saying "nothing." Thus "and I have escaped with [or am left with] nothing."

19:21-22. In the preceding verses Job has used a conventional topos from the lament tradition to describe his radical isolation. As in chap. 16, however, he rejects the stance of humble appeal to God to which the lament form would direct him. His subversion of the form is ironic. The imperative "have pity on me" is ordinarily

addressed by the sufferer to God (occurring some eighteen times in Psalms; e.g., 4:1[2]; 6:2[3]; 41:10[11]; 57:1[2]). In Ps 41:9-10[10-11], for instance, the psalmist recounts the betrayal by his trusted friend as a reason for God to take pity on him. But Job has no intention of appealing to God for mercy. Rather, he parodies this convention of traditional piety. Inverting the relationships, he calls on the *friends* to have pity because *God* has struck him. A second level of irony in Job's appeal can be gauged by the fact that he has already criticized his cautious friends' readiness to take God's side, even if it means acting as false witnesses (13:7-8). They are certainly not going to take pity on one whom God has struck.[312] The subversion of traditional religious categories is also present in v. 22. Even though ostensibly addressed to the friends as a criticism of their persecution and insatiable appetite for Job's flesh, the sting in v. 22 is the phrase "like God" (כמו־אל *kĕmô'ēl*). In contrast to the conventions of psalmic piety in which God is deliverer, Job identifies God's role as like that of the wicked who pursue the psalmist (e.g., Ps 7:1[2]; 31:15[16]; 71:11).

19:23-27. In addition to the serious textual problems in this section, the most difficult exegetical challenge of these verses may be their excessive familiarity. Only the rare individual can read v. 25a without hearing the strains of Handel's *Messiah* in the background. The very term "redeemer" (גאל *gō'ēl*) has been so Christianized that the use of that word in translations tends to distort the contextual meaning of the underlying Hebrew. Unfortunately, both the NRSV and the NIV improperly capitalize the word "redeemer," as though it were a title rather than a simple noun. In addition to christological interpretation of v. 25a, early Christian tradition also found in vv. 25-27 a proof text for bodily resurrection. Although that position is rarely advanced in scholarship today, the issue still draws a disproportionate amount of attention to these verses. To understand this passage in terms of its original context and significance, one must set aside the later history of its appropriation in Christianity.

Since Job has parodied and rejected the language of prayer (vv. 21-22) and realized that his

---

311. Clines, *Job 1–20,* 450-52.

312. See Hartley, *The Book of Job,* 290, for a contrasting interpretation.

outcry brings no response or justice (v. 7), there appears to be no way for him to bring his words before God. Already in 16:18-22, Job struggled to find a way to keep his cry for justice alive after his own death. Now, in 19:23-26a, he returns to that problem. Initially his imagination turns to the distant future, as the words "forever" (לעד *lā'ad*, v. 24) and "at the last" (אחרון *'aḥărôn*, v. 25) indicate. The first part of his reflection is distinctly marked as an impossible wish ("Oh that . . . " [מי־יתן *mî yittēn*]), as Job fantasizes the preservation of his words as a future testimony (vv. 23-24). Although there is some uncertainty about the interpretation of the imagery, it appears that Job describes three materials on which his words might be recorded—scroll, lead tablet, engraved rock—each more enduring than the last (so NIV).[313] Alternatively, it is possible to interpret all three lines as describing the inscription of words on stone, as in Habel's translation: "Oh, if only it were inscribed on a stela/ With iron stylus and lead,/ Carved on rock forever!"[314]

Just as in 16:18-19, where the cry of Job's blood was paired with his assurance that a witness on high would take his part, so also here Job's words of testimony are paired with his certainty that he has a kinsman-defender (*gō'ēl,* v. 25). The term *gō'ēl* comes from the field of family law. It designates the nearest male relative, who was responsible for protecting a person's interests when that individual was unable to do so. The *gō'ēl* would buy back family property sold in distress (Lev 25:25; Ruth 4:4-6; Jer 32:6-7), recover what had been stolen (Num 5:8), redeem a kinsman sold into slavery (Lev 25:28), or avenge a murdered kinsman's blood (Deut 19:6-12; 2 Sam 14:11). The *gō'ēl* is the embodiment of family solidarity. There is perhaps a note of defiance in Job's confidence that his *"gō'ēl* lives," following his account of how God has alienated all his friends and relatives. In Israelite tradition, God is sometimes referred to as the *gō'ēl* of the orphan and the widow (Prov 23:11; Jer 50:34) and of others who experienced helplessness (Ps 119:154; Lam 3:58), yet Job is clearly seeking a *gō'ēl* to defend his interests against

God.[315] Indeed, there may be reproach in his very choice of that term.

To whom does Job refer? The close similarity between 16:18-21 and 19:23-26 suggests that the *gō'ēl,* like the witness, is a heavenly figure, similar to the intercessory angel to whom Elihu refers in 33:23-24.[316] Or it has been argued that the *gō'ēl* is simply the personified figure of Job's own cry for justice.[317] The issue of the identity of the *gō'ēl,* however, is less important than the function this figure plays in Job's thought. For Job, the notion of the *gō'ēl* supplies the certainty that there is someone with the power and the presence to take up his case with God (the verb "arise" [קום *qûm*] can have a forensic connotation, as in Deut 19:16). It is also clear that Job envisions this as taking place sometime in the future. That this is understood to be after Job's death is likely from the general context, even if the phrase "upon the dust" more likely means "upon the earth" (cf. 41:33[25]) than referring to Job's grave.[318] Unfortunately, v. 26a is linguistically obscure but is generally taken also as referring to a time after Job's death. Although the verb is unusual in this context, it is possible to achieve a plausible meaning with only a modest emendation ("thus" [כזאת *kězō't*], instead of "this" [זאת *zō't*]), so that the text reads "and after my skin has been stripped off thus."

Additional confusion has been introduced into the interpretation of this passage by the assumption that vv. 26b-27 refer to the same scene that Job envisions in vv. 25-26a. If read all together, then Job sees his vindication by God after his death. This is a most unlikely notion to ancient Israelites, who did not believe in a bodily resurrection and assumed that the dead know nothing, as Eccl 9:5 succinctly puts it (cf. Job 14:12, 21). Commentators who attempt to read all of these verses together are consequently forced into assuming that a religious leap toward the notion of resurrection is being squeezed out of Job's agony,[319] or that Job as a disembodied shade will

313. Driver and Gray, *A Critical and Exegetical Commentary on the Book of Job,* 171.
314. Habel, *The Book of Job,* 290, 292.

315. Ibid., 305-6, and S. Terrien, "Job" *The Interpreter's Bible,* ed. G. Buttrick (Nashville: Abingdon, 1954) 3:1052, provide detailed refutations of the arguments of those who have suggested that the redeemer is God.
316. S. Mowinckel, "Hiob's go'el und Zeuge im Himmel," BZAW 41 (1925), 207-12; M. Pope, *Job,* 3rd ed., AB 15 (Garden City, N.Y.: Doubleday, 1979) 146; Terrien, "Job," 1052.
317. Clines, *Job 1–20,* 459.
318. E. Dhorme, *A Commentary on the Book of Job,* trans. H. Knight (London: Nelson, 1967) 283.
319. J. G. Janzen, *Job,* Interpretation (Atlanta: John Knox, 1985) 144.

be granted a special vision of his vindication by God (NRSV).[320] Neither approach is persuasive.

A much simpler solution has been suggested by Clines, anticipated to a degree by Habel.[321] The key to this interpretation is the recognition that vv. 25-26a and 26b-27 do not refer to the same scene. In vv. 25-26a, Job describes his certainty that a redeemer will arise and vindicate him after his death. As important as that certainty is to Job, it is not what he most desires. What he desires is expressed in vv. 26b-27, not a postmortem vindication but a vindication that he can experience before he dies, in his flesh and with his own eyes. This interpretation requires no emendation, only a recognition that the conjunction in v. 26b can be read as "but," and that the following verbs are not to be translated as simple futures but as modal imperfects expressing a wish. Thus "I know that my defender lives, and that at the last he will arise upon the earth—after my skin has been stripped off! But I would see God from my flesh, whom I would see for myself; my eyes would see, and not a stranger." Although it is linguistically possible to translate v. 27a "whom I shall see *on my side,*" as the NRSV does, the interpretation proposed here makes it more likely that Job is emphasizing his desire to see for himself (so NIV).

This understanding of vv. 25-27 fits well with the development of Job's thought. As Job has

explored the legal metaphor as a model for his confrontation with God, he has imagined various heavenly figures who might assist him: an arbitrator (9:33), a witness (16:18), and a defender (19:25). The necessity of these figures has been forced on him by the increasing certainty of his impending death. Yet just as Job's confidence in the presence of such a figure reaches its climax, he realizes that such a solution would not truly satisfy him. He desires what he described in 13:13-22, a direct presentation of his case to God and God's reply. After 19:25, Job says no more about heavenly intermediaries; rather, in chaps. 23 and 31 he pursues his determination to carry his case to God's presence. Whether Job experiences yearning or fear (v. 27c), there is no doubt about the enormity of what he desires.

19:28-29. At least for the present Job is certain about finding vindication, as his final words to his friends indicate. In v. 22, Job had spoken of the friends persecuting him like God; now he threatens them with judgment. Although Job does not mention God explicitly, his belief in his own vindication is closely connected with his sense that the moral order of the world will be reaffirmed and that the friends will receive judgment for their behavior toward Job (vv. 28-29) and toward God (13:7-11). Just where one expects a despairing meditation on death, Job instead speaks boldly of judgment against his accusers. After chap. 19, Job does not again speak of death, either in longing or in despair.

320. G. Hoelscher, "Hiob 19, 25-27 und Jubil 23, 30-31," *ZAW* 53 (1935) 277-83.

321. Clines, *Job 1–20,* 457-8, 461-62; Habel, *The Book of Job,* 290-91, 308-9.

REFLECTIONS

No one could have anticipated, when this story began as a simple narrative about the nature of true piety, that it would come to this. Even Job was uncertain for a long time about the nature and meaning of his story. His first reaction was to understand it as a story of immense, boundless, and irresistible suffering, the only response to which was bitterness and a desire to die (chaps. 3; 6–7). Gradually, however, Job has recast the nature of his story. By the time one reaches chap. 19, it is no longer the story of a suffering man but that of a man unjustly accused.

The story of the unjustly accused is a paradigmatic one in our own culture, a story that we tell over and over, with different characters, exploring different dimensions of its significance. It is the story told in the novels *The Ox-Bow Incident* and *To Kill a Mockingbird,* in the film *In the Name of the Father,* in the documentary *The Thin Blue Line,* and in countless other works. Whenever a community tells the same story over and over, it signals that the problem presented goes to the foundations of that community. These repeated stories tell of an anxiety that will not go away, even as they reaffirm a truth that is necessary for existence. The story of the unjustly accused emerges as a paradigmatic story only in cultures that organize themselves upon the basis of law and justice. In ancient Israel, justice was such a foundational value. "Righteousness and justice are the foundation of your throne," says the psalmist (Ps 89:14a[15a] NRSV), and "O God, give your justice to the king and your righteousness to the king's son; may he judge your people with righteousness, and your poor with justice" (Ps 72:1-2). In ways that combine both religious and secular traditions, American culture is also deeply committed to the "self-evident truths" that make justice the essential foundation of society.

Justice does not always prevail, even in societies in which justice is a basic value. The people who exercise responsibility for justice are fallible and sometimes corrupt. Systems designed to serve justice do not always do so. Anxieties and fears having nothing to do with justice cloud vision. Only a blind dogmatist could insist that nothing ever goes wrong. Telling the story of the miscarriage of justice is a way of exploring the moral significance of such failures, reflecting on the qualities of character necessary to maintain a society based on justice, and ultimately determining whether the underlying structure can still be trusted and affirmed. Where God's character and governance of the world are understood in large part through the category of justice, telling such a story also becomes an important exercise in the testing and reformation of religious beliefs.

There are many ways to organize a story of the unjustly accused. One can place the focus on the community and its complicity in a desire not to know the truth. Or the focus can fall on the tireless defender who brings truth to light. The most compelling stories, however, are those that focus on the person of the unjustly accused, as in Job. It is remarkable how many of the dramatic elements that one would find in a contemporary narrative of the unjustly accused occur in Job 19: the unheeded cry for justice (v. 7); the sense of powerlessness (vv. 8-12); the gradual withdrawal of social support and the resultant isolation (vv. 13-19); the sense of having been left with absolutely nothing (v. 20). What is perhaps most unendurable is having to hear one's story unrecognizably and falsely told by others who are certain that they recognize the pattern of the criminal or the terrorist or the sinner in one's own case—"broken in pieces by words" is how Job puts it (vv. 2-3). Society is made uncomfortable by an accused person who will not confess, for that raises anxiety about the reliability of the system of justice. It is not "satisfied with the flesh" of the unjustly accused (v. 22) but seeks the victim's own complicity.

In the paradigmatic story, a moment arrives when the unjustly accused must make a fundamental decision: whether to give in to overwhelming pressures and sink into passivity and disintegration or to find the will to fight. Job exemplifies this transition. As angry as his words were in chap. 3, they were essentially the words of a defeated person seeking nothing more than oblivion. His sharp wit and capacity for parody gave him some energy (chaps 7; 9; 12), but they could not keep him from sinking into despair, as the recurrent concluding reflections on death indicate (10:18-22; 14:18-22; 17:13-16). Even though the strength of character of the unjustly accused person is a crucial element, that person cannot succeed alone. The ability to resist is catalyzed by the presence of someone who will stand in solidarity and publicly defend the innocence of the accused. For Job, that crucial assurance comes in 16:18 and in 19:25 with his certainty that a witness and a defender will stand up for him. Even as Job determines to pursue his case himself, he is strengthened by the vision of his witness and his defender.

The unjustly accused persons who seek justice accomplish more than simply personal vindication. They also redeem a compromised system. Their determination to right the wrong done to them is a commitment to the belief that the system of justice is not wholly corrupt, but that through the exposure of its own failures it can be called back to its true nature. That is why Job has become such a compelling figure by chap. 19, and why the narrative of the unjustly accused is such a crucial story in our own culture. It is possible for such stories to be misleading, if they convey the impression that *all* miscarriages of justice are eventually corrected. At their best, however, such stories provide a nuanced and complex way of exploring the elements that lead to a failure of justice. They allow for an honest confrontation of the corruption that besets even the best systems of law. Such stories also serve as models of the moral character and kind of social commitment that is essential for the hard work of maintaining justice. By doing so, they provide an alternative to the complacency of those who refuse to see evil and the cynicism of those who refuse to believe that anything can be done about it.

Job 20:1-29, Zophar Describes the Fate of the Wicked

NIV

20 Then Zophar the Naamathite replied:
²"My troubled thoughts prompt me to answer
because I am greatly disturbed.
³I hear a rebuke that dishonors me,
and my understanding inspires me to reply.

⁴"Surely you know how it has been from of old,
ever since man*ᵃ* was placed on the earth,
⁵that the mirth of the wicked is brief,
the joy of the godless lasts but a moment.
⁶Though his pride reaches to the heavens
and his head touches the clouds,
⁷he will perish forever, like his own dung;
those who have seen him will say, 'Where is he?'
⁸Like a dream he flies away, no more to be found,
banished like a vision of the night.
⁹The eye that saw him will not see him again;
his place will look on him no more.
¹⁰His children must make amends to the poor;
his own hands must give back his wealth.
¹¹The youthful vigor that fills his bones
will lie with him in the dust.

¹²"Though evil is sweet in his mouth
and he hides it under his tongue,
¹³though he cannot bear to let it go
and keeps it in his mouth,
¹⁴yet his food will turn sour in his stomach;
it will become the venom of serpents within him.
¹⁵He will spit out the riches he swallowed;
God will make his stomach vomit them up.
¹⁶He will suck the poison of serpents;
the fangs of an adder will kill him.
¹⁷He will not enjoy the streams,
the rivers flowing with honey and cream.
¹⁸What he toiled for he must give back uneaten;

ᵃ4 Or Adam

NRSV

20 Then Zophar the Naamathite answered:
² "Pay attention! My thoughts urge me to answer,
because of the agitation within me.
³ I hear censure that insults me,
and a spirit beyond my understanding answers me.
⁴ Do you not know this from of old,
ever since mortals were placed on earth,
⁵ that the exulting of the wicked is short,
and the joy of the godless is but for a moment?
⁶ Even though they mount up high as the heavens,
and their head reaches to the clouds,
⁷ they will perish forever like their own dung;
those who have seen them will say, 'Where are they?'
⁸ They will fly away like a dream, and not be found;
they will be chased away like a vision of the night.
⁹ The eye that saw them will see them no more,
nor will their place behold them any longer.
¹⁰ Their children will seek the favor of the poor,
and their hands will give back their wealth.
¹¹ Their bodies, once full of youth,
will lie down in the dust with them.

¹² "Though wickedness is sweet in their mouth,
though they hide it under their tongues,
¹³ though they are loath to let it go,
and hold it in their mouths,
¹⁴ yet their food is turned in their stomachs;
it is the venom of asps within them.
¹⁵ They swallow down riches and vomit them up again;
God casts them out of their bellies.
¹⁶ They will suck the poison of asps;

NIV

he will not enjoy the profit from his trading.
^{19}For he has oppressed the poor and left them destitute;
he has seized houses he did not build.
^{20}"Surely he will have no respite from his craving;
he cannot save himself by his treasure.
^{21}Nothing is left for him to devour;
his prosperity will not endure.
^{22}In the midst of his plenty, distress will overtake him;
the full force of misery will come upon him.
^{23}When he has filled his belly,
God will vent his burning anger against him
and rain down his blows upon him.
^{24}Though he flees from an iron weapon,
a bronze-tipped arrow pierces him.
^{25}He pulls it out of his back,
the gleaming point out of his liver.
Terrors will come over him;
^{26} total darkness lies in wait for his treasures.
A fire unfanned will consume him
and devour what is left in his tent.
^{27}The heavens will expose his guilt;
the earth will rise up against him.
^{28}A flood will carry off his house,
rushing waters^a on the day of God's wrath.
^{29}Such is the fate God allots the wicked,
the heritage appointed for them by God."

^{a}28 Or *The possessions in his house will be carried off, / washed away*

NRSV

the tongue of a viper will kill them.
^{17} They will not look on the rivers,
the streams flowing with honey and curds.
^{18} They will give back the fruit of their toil,
and will not swallow it down;
from the profit of their trading
they will get no enjoyment.
^{19} For they have crushed and abandoned the poor,
they have seized a house that they did not build.

^{20} "They knew no quiet in their bellies;
in their greed they let nothing escape.
^{21} There was nothing left after they had eaten;
therefore their prosperity will not endure.
^{22} In full sufficiency they will be in distress;
all the force of misery will come upon them.
^{23} To fill their belly to the full
God^a will send his fierce anger into them,
and rain it upon them as their food.^{b}
^{24} They will flee from an iron weapon;
a bronze arrow will strike them through.
^{25} It is drawn forth and comes out of their body,
and the glittering point comes out of their gall;
terrors come upon them.
^{26} Utter darkness is laid up for their treasures;
a fire fanned by no one will devour them;
what is left in their tent will be consumed.
^{27} The heavens will reveal their iniquity,
and the earth will rise up against them.
^{28} The possessions of their house will be carried away,
dragged off in the day of God's^c wrath.
^{29} This is the portion of the wicked from God,
the heritage decreed for them by God."

^{a} Heb *he* ^{b} Cn: Meaning of Heb uncertain ^{c} Heb *his*

COMMENTARY

Like Eliphaz and Bildad before him, Zophar's speech in the second cycle consists almost wholly of a conventional poem on the fate of the wicked. After the typical introduction to the disputation, in which he characterizes Job's words as offensive and explains his own need to reply (vv. 2-3), Zophar appeals to ancient authority (v. 4) for the truth of the proposition he wishes to illustrate:

that the joy of the wicked is short-lived (v. 5). Zophar first describes the insubstantial nature of the wicked person and his complete destruction (vv. 6-11). The second part of the poem explores the self-destructive nature of evil through a striking series of metaphors pertaining to eating (vv. 12-23). In the third part, Zophar describes the inescapable destruction of the wicked by all the elements of the earth and the heavens (vv. 24-28). A concluding summary underscores that this destruction is God's decree (v. 29).

What Job has said about his own innocence and the wrong done him by God threatens Zophar at a basic level. As Clines puts it, "If Job is right everything Zophar stands for is wrong."[322] Zophar's speech should not be interpreted as an intentional but indirect accusation that Job is one of the wicked who perish so miserably. Like Eliphaz and Bildad, Zophar reasserts the foundations of his moral world in the face of the implications of Job's claims. That foundation is his conviction that evil does not have the same grounding in reality that good has, and that, consequently, its flourishing is ephemeral. This is the fate God has apportioned and decreed for the wicked. That Job hears Zophar's speech (and, indeed, those of Eliphaz and Bildad) as a general claim about the moral order of the world rather than as a personal attack is indicated by the nature of Job's reply in chap. 21, where he refutes the general proposition that the wicked come to an early, miserable end. Only after Job explicitly refutes the moral foundation of their world will Eliphaz resolve the intolerable contradiction by declaring Job guilty of great wickedness and thus an example of precisely the dynamics the friends have been describing as a general proposition (chap. 22).

20:1-3. Most of the opening statements have been directed at the content of the previous speaker's words (8:2-3; 9:2*a*; 11:2-3; 12:2-3; 15:2-3; 18:2-4), although Job has also referred to the social dynamics of the exchange, describing the friends as "comforters" who increase misery (16:2-3), and charging them with using words as weapons to crush him (19:2-3). Zophar opens with words that show that he, too, is upset by the dynamics of the disputation. His agitation and emotional disturbance (v. 2) are caused by the fact that Job has insulted the friends. In a culture strongly oriented to the values of honor and shame, insults are taken seriously. From the friends' perspective, they are warranted in giving Job the kind of tough-minded counsel that characterized wisdom instruction, even if it involves confronting Job with prima facie evidence of his sin (11:6*b*) or with evidence of a sinful disposition expressed in his very words (15:4-6). For Job to

characterize their intentions and actions as vicious aggression and as shameful conduct (19:2-3), deserving "punishment by the sword" (19:29), is in Zophar's view an intolerable smear on their character. Job, of course, sees things very differently. Knowing himself to be innocent of any wrongdoing, he hears all of the friends' direct rebukes and their teachings about the fate of the wicked as an intolerable insult to his own character (19:3). Given the different assumptions that each side brings to the dialogue, this impasse was inevitable. Now that Job and Zophar have cast the dispute in terms of personal insult, the dialogue is doomed.

20:4-5. The foundational nature of what Zophar will say is already implicit in his appeal to ancient authority (v. 4). The moral order was established with the placing of human beings upon the earth (cf. Deut 4:32). Zophar articulates that moral order in terms of the fleeting nature of the joy of the wicked, an idea expressed in similar terms in Ps 37:2, 10. To modern minds, that notion may seem like a peculiar choice for a fundamental insight into the structure of the world. In the moral imagination of ancient wisdom, however, the contrast between the enduring and the ephemeral was of greatest importance. This is not simply a contrast of chronological duration; the difference has ontological significance—that is, it has to do with the nature of reality. A teaching from the Egyptian wisdom text "The Instruction of Ptahhotep" makes this point in describing *maat,* a concept that has connotations of order, justice, and integrity, somewhat similar to the Hebrew word for "righteousness" (צדק *ṣedeq*). The text says, "Great is justice [*maat*], lasting in effect,/ Unchallenged since the time of [the god] Osiris. . . . Baseness may seize riches,/ Yet crime never lands its wares;/ In the end it is justice [*maat*] that lasts."[323] Both evil and good, criminality and justice exist in the world. No one would deny that. The saying insists, however, that, by the nature of things, justice is grounded in the foundations of reality in a way that criminality is not, so that justice eventually reasserts itself, and evil loses its hold. In Hebrew thought, too, God is עולם (*'ôlām*),

322. D. Clines, *Job 1–20*, WBC 17 (Dallas: Word, 1989) 482.

323. Translation adapted from M. Lichtheim, *Ancient Egyptian Literature: A Book of Readings,* vol. 1 (Berkeley: University of California Press, 1973) 64.

the lasting one. Divine wisdom, the foundation of justice, is likewise "from eternity" (see Prov 8:23). Those persons and actions that are grounded in wisdom and partake of God's nature participate in that reality and stability in a way that evil does not. The imagery of Psalm 1 is illustrative. The righteous are like durable live trees with deep roots fed by streams of water; by contrast, the wicked are ephemeral dry chaff, material no longer rooted or living but subject to being blown off by the wind (Ps 1:3-4). Although Israelite thought is expressed in concrete rather than ab-stract terms, these images make a fundamental philosophical claim about the nature of reality and the difference between good and evil.

20:6-11. Zophar substantiates his claim about the fleeting nature of the joy of the wicked with a series of images. Although varied, all illustrate the inability of the wicked to secure a hold either on the objects of their ambition or, indeed, on existence itself. The image of reaching to the clouds and the heavens (v. 6) echoes mythic stories about human ambition, such as the tower of Babel (Gen 11:4). In that story, the purpose of building the tower was to secure the builders' reputation and to protect against being scattered and dispersed. Just as the activity of the builders of the tower brought about the very thing they most feared, so also the wicked person's ambition to transcend earthly limits results in a most earthy fate: perishing like his or her own excrement (v. 7a). Although it is possible that the image here is of animal dung destroyed by being burned for fuel (cf. 1 Kgs 14:10), the suffixed expression *"his* excrement" more likely refers to the practice of discarding human excrement like dirt (cf. Zeph 1:17). In either case, the wicked person is no longer to be seen (v. 7b; cf. Ps 37:10, 20).

Verses 8-9 continue the imagery of seeing, begun in v. 7b. Dreams seem quite vivid while they occur, but they have no reality in the external world (cf. Isa 29:8), and so they "fly off" or are "chased away" by the act of waking. In Zophar's view, this is also the nature of the wicked (v. 8). Lacking reality, the wicked are subject to the same sudden dispersal into nothingness. Verse 9 shifts the perspective to that of an observer who looks at an object that is suddenly no longer there. Job had used similar imagery to speak of the vanishing of a person in death (7:8-10), but for Zophar the disappearance of

the wicked has a significance different from that of general human transiency (e.g., Ps 103:15-16).

The final two verses in this section seem quite different, and some commentators move v. 10 to another place,[324] or simply delete it (so NAB),[325] because of its reference to the children of the wicked person. The verses are, however, consis-tent with the underlying theme that the wicked, because they lack "reality," are unable to secure their hold on what is desirable. Neither the NRSV nor the NIV gives an adequate translation. Better is the TNK, "His sons ingratiate themselves with the poor;/ His own hands must give back his wealth." The possession of secure wealth, which could be left to one's children as a heritage, was an important value in ancient society (cf. Ruth 4:6; Prov 19:14). Because the wicked cannot secure anything (cf. Prov 11:18; 20:21; 28:8, 22), they have nothing to pass on to their children, who are then so destitute that they must beg even from those who are poor.[326] The last verse de-scribes the inability of the wicked to hold on to life itself. As Clines notes, the first clause is concessive, "though his bones are full of vigor."[327] (For the premature death of the wicked, see Ps 55:23[24].)

20:12-23. In this central section of the speech, Zophar explores the self-destructive nature of the wicked person's obsession with evil through a brilliant succession of metaphors, all related to eating. This life-giving and sustaining activity, which is ordinarily the source of pleasure as well as nourishment, becomes an occasion of pain and death for the wicked.

20:12-15. The first image developed is that of evil as a delicious morsel of food, held in the mouth and savored for all its sweetness. The wicked person's sensuous pleasure in evil is sug-gested by the threefold description of hiding under the tongue, reluctance to let go of the pleasure, and holding on to the food (vv. 12b-13). Evil is by nature deceptive, however, attractive on the surface but deadly in its essence. Zophar's image captures this quality by the contrast of "sweet"/

324. E. Dhorme, *A Commentary on the Book of Job,* trans. H. Knight (London: Nelson, 1967) 299.

325. Clines, *Job 1–20,* 472, 487, marks it as "unsuitable."

326. Similarly, G. Fohrer, *Das Buch Hiob,* KAT xvi (Guetersloh: Gerd Mohn, 1963) 329; F. Andersen, *Job: An Introduction and Commentary,* Tyndale Old Testament Commentaries (Downers Grove, Ill.: Inter-Varsity, 1976) 196.

327. Clines, *Job 1–20,* 488.

"bitter poison" and "in the mouth"/"in the belly." The same dynamic is expressed in Proverbs not only through images of food (Prov 9:17; 20:17; 26:22) but also through images of evil as illicit sexual pleasure, seductive but ultimately deadly (Prov 7:6-27). Zophar relentlessly follows the logic of his metaphor. Just as poison often induces vomiting, so also the wicked person vomits up what he or she has swallowed (v. 15). In this verse, however, Zophar breaks out of metaphorical speech to identify the evil of v. 12 specifically as economic crime, for what the wicked swallows is property ("riches"). That the wicked cannot keep food down, as we would say, is a representation of the same inability to secure possession that was addressed in vv. 6-11.

20:16. This verse takes up a term from v. 14 and restates the preceding description in terms of the image of snake venom. The term for "bitter poison" in v. 14 is literally "the gall of asps." It was believed in antiquity that the venom of snakes was actually their bitter gall, released through the tongue.[328] In v. 16, the wicked persons' activity is redescribed, not through their own self-deception that evil is sweet, but in the light of its actual nature. When they thought they were savoring delicious food, they were actually sucking on snake venom, which will kill them.

20:17-19. Whereas vv. 14-16 describe the effect of the wicked person's ingesting fatal poison, vv. 17-19 describe the inability of the wicked to ingest truly desirable food. Honey and milk curds (v. 17) are traditional images of plenty, often associated with the land of Canaan (Exod 3:8, 17). In 29:6, Job refers to milk and streams of oil as symbols of his blessedness (cf. the similar description in the Ugaritic Baal epic, "the heavens rain oil, the wadis flow with honey").[329] The wicked are excluded not only from these manifestations of divine blessing, but even from the enjoyment of the fruit of their own toil and trade as well (v. 18). This verse underscores once again the motif that the wicked cannot secure their hold on anything.

Finally, Zophar identifies the crimes of the wicked, which are the reason for the futility of their efforts. As in v. 15, they are economic and social offenses, neglect and oppression of the poor, and the seizure of houses built by others. To a certain extent, these are stereotypical images of evil. Treatment of the poor is a measure of righteousness and wickedness in the book of Job (22:5-9; 29:12-17; 31:13-23), as in Proverbs (Prov 14:31; 19:17; 22:23; 29:7), and in the prophetic tradition (Isa 10:1-4; 58:6-10; Jer 22:13-17; Amos 5:11-12; 8:4-8). It is also possible, however, that something more specific lies behind the prominence of economic and social themes in the book of Job. If the book of Job was composed in the fifth century, then it may be that the social and economic issues addressed in Nehemiah 5 lie behind the repeated references to economic crimes and the plight of the poor in the book of Job.[330]

20:20-23. The final image in this series is the uncontrollable appetite of the wicked, which leads to punishment by God. These verses are somewhat difficult to translate, but the development of the theme is clearer in the NRSV translation than in the NIV. Zophar's imagery is graphic, as he describes the incessant, restless craving of the belly, which leads the wicked to consume everything. There is perhaps a trace of grotesque personification in v. 21, where the term "nothing left" ordinarily designates a human survivor (שָׂרִיד *śārîd*). The wicked person's appetite is like a destroying army that lets none escape. There is a certain fascinating energy in phenomena that do not know the regulating limits of satiety, as in the saying of Prov 30:15b-16: "Three things are never satisfied;/ four never say, 'Enough':/ Sheol, the barren womb,/ the earth ever thirsty for water,/ and the fire that never says, 'Enough' " (NRSV). As the proverb suggests, however, the paradox of such insatiability is that such forces consume incessantly, yet have nothing to show for all that effort. This, too, is the paradox of the wicked. For all their greed, they cannot establish lasting prosperity (v. 21b).

The punishment that Zophar describes for the wicked is ironically fitting. The moment of greatest fullness is at the same time the moment when distress (lit., "narrowness" [צַר *ṣar*]) comes upon

---

328. D. Pardee, "*mĕrorat-pĕtanim* 'Venom' in Job 20.14," *ZAW* 91 (1979) 401-16.

329. James B. Pritchard, ed., *Ancient Near Eastern Texts Relating to the Old Testament* (*ANET*), 3rd ed. with supplement (Princeton: Princeton University Press, 1969) 140.

330. The most sustained attempt to provide such a social context for the book of Job is the work of Ranier Albertz, "Der sozialgeschichtliche Hintergrund des Hiob-buches und der 'Babylonischen Theodizee'," in J. Jeremias and L. Perlitt, eds., *Die Botschaft und die Boten: Festschrift fuer Hans Walter Wolff zum 70. Geburtstag* (Neukirchen-Vluyn: Neukirchener Verlag) 349-72.

him (v. 22*a*). The mode of his punishment, which corresponds to the insatiable appetite of the wicked, echoes the description of God raining manna upon the hungry Israelites in the wilderness (Exod 16:4). Here, however, God's anger rains upon the wicked as food, which he must unwillingly now consume (v. 23).

20:24-29. The final section recounts the rejection and utter extermination of the wicked by all the forces of the world (cf. 18:5-21). Verses 24-25 use the imagery of deadly wounds in a context of battle, whereas vv. 26-28 describe the enmity of darkness, fire, heaven, earth, and flood. The motif of escaping one peril only to fall victim to another (vv. 24-25) is conventional (cf. Isa 24:18; Amos 5:19). Here, poetically, the wicked person flees from personified weapons, rather than from the warriors who wield them. In many cultures weapons are symbolically represented as having personal qualities or even wills of their own. In Ugaritic myth, Baal's two clubs are named Chaser and Driver and are directly exhorted to chase and drive away Baal's enemy Yam.[331] Elsewhere in the OT swords are personified as thirsting for and drinking blood (e.g., Isa 34:5-6). Verse 24 mentions two weapons, one of iron, the other of bronze (lit., a "bronze bow," although often translated as "bronze arrow"). Perhaps the metals iron and bronze are specifically mentioned to form a link with the other natural phenomena listed in vv. 26-28 (darkness, fire, heaven, earth, flood) as seeking out the wicked person for destruction.

331. *ANET,* 131.

Verse 26*a* contains a more clever image than comes across in English translation. The word for "treasures" is literally "things hidden away" (צפונים *ṣĕpûnîm*) so that Zophar describes darkness as concealing itself in order to seize what the wicked person has concealed. An "unfanned fire" (v. 26*b*) is not necessarily a divine fire.[332] In the context of the poetic imagination in this section, it is simply one of the active forces of nature intent on destroying the wicked person.

Analogously, heaven and earth take on the role of witnesses and accusers against the wicked (v. 27; cf. Deut 32:1; Isa 1:2; Mic 6:1-2; and cf. Job 16:18). Textual and grammatical problems obscure v. 28. The difficult word יבול (*yĕbûl*) is best taken as "flood" rather than "produce" (so NIV), in keeping with the parallel term נגרות (*niggārôt*) in v. 28*b,* which means "torrents."[333] Thus, after the heavens and the earth have borne witness against the wicked, the floods carry out the sentence. Although the elements act directly, they all act as agents of divine anger (v. 28*b*).

Zophar concludes his speech with a summary evaluation emphasizing the role of God. Ironically, in view of the futile efforts of the wicked to lay secure hold of any of the objects of their desire, his utter destruction is the one thing that can be called their "portion" and their "inheritance" (v. 29).

332. Contra R. Gordis, *The Book of Job: Commentary, New Translation, and Special Studies* (New York: Jewish Theological Seminary, 5738/1978) 221; M. Pope, *Job,* 3rd ed., AB 15 (Garden City, N.Y.: Doubleday, 1979) 153; Fohrer, *Das Buch Hiob,* 333.

333. So Dhorme, *A Commentary on the Book of Job,* 306; Gordis, *The Book of Job,* 221; Pope, *Job,* 153.

REFLECTIONS

Is Zophar right? The modern reader's strong identification with Job often means that what the friends say is dismissed simply because they say it. Yet Zophar's underlying claim, that good and evil have a different relation to fundamental reality, deserves more thoughtful consideration. Part of the difficulty in giving Zophar a hearing lies with the way he develops the argument in terms of the fate of individual persons. Job will make short work of that form of the argument in chap. 22. Nevertheless, there is something provocative about the notion that good and evil are different in nature—that there is a resilient, lasting quality to good that derives from its participation in the fundamental structures of God's creation, and that evil, no matter how large it looms, is nevertheless fragile and subject to sudden collapse precisely because it is not part of that creation but a distortion of it.

The claim made by Zophar and by ancient wisdom in general cannot be confirmed or refuted simply by citing examples and counterexamples. It is not so much a conviction deduced from observation as it is a claim of faith, which in turn shapes perception. Even those who are initially skeptical about its validity, however, may be more willing to consider its merits when the question is phrased in terms of what gives persons the strength to oppose massive evil. A long struggle can be sustained only if a deeply held conviction exists that evil is inherently unstable and must eventually break apart. The opponents of official racial segregation in the United States and of apartheid in South Africa were sustained by the conviction that such injustice simply could not preserve itself in the face of the claims of simple human justice. The dissidents in the Soviet Union and Eastern Europe resisted in the knowledge that the massive structures of oppression would eventually show themselves to be hollow. The democracy movement in China is supported by the certainty that such repressive power will one day crumble. At its most profound, Zophar's perception offers not a denial of evil, but a bulwark against despair.

Criticisms can be brought against the position Zophar articulates, however. It does not seem able to account for the insidious persistence of evil. A cruel system of repression may vanish like a dream or die suddenly, poisoned by its own appetite for evil. In the aftermath, however, new evil often seems to sprout as vigorously as good. The claims of Zophar and the wisdom tradition in general about the lasting nature of good and the ephemeral nature of evil have little explanatory power in those situations.

Rather than simply deciding for or against the understanding of good and evil represented by Zophar, one might do better to reflect on the variety of ways in which the Bible talks about good and evil and how they differ from Zophar's perspective. Although there is not space here to explore them in detail, three models in particular suggest something of the range of thinking found in the OT. Drawing on ancient Near Eastern mythic traditions, biblical accounts of the struggle between Yahweh and the primordial chaos monster represent evil as something that is contained and restrained by God but never fully eliminated from the world (Job 38:8-11; Psalms 74; 114). Although the great victory that occurred in connection with the establishment of the created world was decisive, elements of the chaotic continue to break forth. In quelling them, God reenacts the great cosmogonic victory (Isa 51:9-11). This is a very insightful way of thinking about evil, one that deserves greater presence in contemporary theological reflections. In its own mythic language, this perspective acknowledges that disruptive and painful elements are and always have been part of the world. In contrast to Zophar's view of evil as ephemeral, such an understanding has no difficulty in accounting for the persistence of evil, for the very nature of the chaotic is to break out suddenly and unexpectedly. The psalmists often used the image of the surging waters of chaos to evoke the personal sense of being overwhelmed by illness, danger, and death. It is equally evocative of the disasters that overtake whole communities and threaten their existence.

For Zophar, hope is mostly a matter of waiting. One need do nothing if evil will self-destruct. The mythic tradition of God's battle with chaos suggests a different stance. Hope is assured because the decisive victory is already won, and the power of the creating God is now present in every struggle, sustaining and restoring the community of life. Such a perspective leads to a less passive stance than Zophar's, for it is in one's own struggles against the inbreaking of chaos that one experiences the power of God the creator. Finally, one possible misapprehension should be addressed. The mythic account is not a dualistic model, and it is perhaps somewhat misleading to talk about it primarily in terms of good and evil. It is a more comprehensive vision of the tensions that exist within creation between order and disorder, chaos and cosmos, death and regeneration, as well as good and evil.

The apocalyptic tradition, by contrast, does develop a model of good and evil that becomes increasingly dualistic. The struggle between good and evil on earth mirrors a struggle between good and evil heavenly forces (Daniel 7; 10–12). Although the OT does not speak of a chief of heavenly forces of evil, other non-canonical Jewish literature and certain books of the NT do present a malign angelic being—variously called Mastema, Satan, Belial, or Beelzebub—who is the source of evil and God's opponent. In sharp contrast to Zophar's view, apocalyptic stresses the reality of evil. Evil does not self-destruct, but has to be violently overcome. The apocalyptic perspective accounts for the persistence of evil, as cycles of evil and its defeat recur in the history of the world until eventually God triumphs decisively over all evil (e.g., *1 Enoch* 85–90).

One of the most serious problems with apocalyptic approaches to evil, however, is that they tend to overschematize the problem. Simple human stupidity, venality, insecurity, and alienation are responsible for a great deal of the woe in the world, and it is implausible to see much of this as part of a great cosmic drama. In this respect, Zophar's images of individual ambition, greed, and self-absorption are much more apt. Apocalyptic can also be a very dangerous model of evil, because its black-and-white scenario allows for no shades of gray. It becomes all too easy to demonize one's opponents and to fail to see the evil that may lodge in one's own self and community. This tendency to divide the world into two categories is not limited to apocalyptic. Zophar, too, thinks in terms of righteous and wicked *people* rather than in terms of people who are variously capable of doing righteous and wicked deeds.

In this respect, the understanding of good and evil presented in Genesis 2—3 is a refreshing alternative. One must be careful not to import into this story later Christian reinterpretation, which tends to read it through the lens of apocalyptic. On its own terms, Genesis 2—3 is the one account that chooses not to locate good and evil in relation to cosmic structures but in relation to the complexities of being human. This subtle story locates the issue in the human desire to imitate God's ability to choose for oneself between what is desirable and undesirable, good and bad. The problem is that such choices are always made with respect to a center of value. When that center of value becomes the human self, then the way is open both to great creativity and to great destructiveness. The consequences of this divine prerogative, now lodged in human beings with limited wisdom, are evident in the stories that follow Genesis 2–3: fratricidal murder (4:8) but also the founding of civic culture (4:17); the development of the arts of civilization, including animal husbandry, music, and metalworking (4:20-22), but also the impulse to revenge (4:23-24). Good and evil are inextricably mixed in the restless human heart, which is always engaged in exercising power for which it lacks adequate wisdom. Such a vision of good and evil is much more radically open than the others described; there is no guarantee that goodness will triumph. Indeed, the opposite is most likely, as the human descent into almost universal corruption suggests (Gen 6:1-4). From this perspective, the grace of God, not the fundamental structures of reality, ensures the continuation of life and goodness (Gen 8:21-22).

The challenge presented by Job's account of his situation and his radical reinterpretation of the nature of the world has forced Zophar to articulate his fundamental understanding of the world's moral structure. Readers who take these issues seriously are similarly forced to consider how they understand the nature of the world, the structure of good and evil, and God's role. What is evil like? Is it mostly an illusion, something that lacks the grounding in reality that good possesses? Or is it very much a part of the structure of the world, always threatening, but ultimately limited in its power to destroy? Is it a malign will that seeks out and tries to annihilate every good thing? Or is it largely the side effect of human self-centeredness and lack of understanding? It is not easy to decide what one thinks about these questions, and perhaps no one of these perspectives is adequate by itself. How one understands the nature of evil, however, plays a very important role in the way a person responds to the crises of life and community.

Job 21:1-34, The Fate of the Wicked Is Prosperity and Honor

NIV

21 Then Job replied:

2"Listen carefully to my words;
    let this be the consolation you give me.
3Bear with me while I speak,
    and after I have spoken, mock on.

4"Is my complaint directed to man?
    Why should I not be impatient?
5Look at me and be astonished;
    clap your hand over your mouth.
6When I think about this, I am terrified;
    trembling seizes my body.
7Why do the wicked live on,
    growing old and increasing in power?
8They see their children established around them,
    their offspring before their eyes.
9Their homes are safe and free from fear;
    the rod of God is not upon them.
10Their bulls never fail to breed;
    their cows calve and do not miscarry.
11They send forth their children as a flock;
    their little ones dance about.
12They sing to the music of tambourine and harp;
    they make merry to the sound of the flute.
13They spend their years in prosperity
    and go down to the grave*a* in peace.*b*
14Yet they say to God, 'Leave us alone!
    We have no desire to know your ways.
15Who is the Almighty, that we should serve him?
    What would we gain by praying to him?'
16But their prosperity is not in their own hands,
    so I stand aloof from the counsel of the
        wicked.

17"Yet how often is the lamp of the wicked snuffed
        out?
    How often does calamity come upon them,
    the fate God allots in his anger?
18How often are they like straw before the wind,
    like chaff swept away by a gale?
19It is said, 'God stores up a man's punishment
        for his sons.'
    Let him repay the man himself, so that he
        will know it!
20Let his own eyes see his destruction;

a13 Hebrew *Sheol*   *b13* Or *in an instant*

NRSV

21 Then Job answered:
2 "Listen carefully to my words,
    and let this be your consolation.
3 Bear with me, and I will speak;
    then after I have spoken, mock on.
4 As for me, is my complaint addressed to
        mortals?
    Why should I not be impatient?
5 Look at me, and be appalled,
    and lay your hand upon your mouth.
6 When I think of it I am dismayed,
    and shuddering seizes my flesh.
7 Why do the wicked live on,
    reach old age, and grow mighty in power?
8 Their children are established in their
        presence,
    and their offspring before their eyes.
9 Their houses are safe from fear,
    and no rod of God is upon them.
10 Their bull breeds without fail;
    their cow calves and never miscarries.
11 They send out their little ones like a flock,
    and their children dance around.
12 They sing to the tambourine and the lyre,
    and rejoice to the sound of the pipe.
13 They spend their days in prosperity,
    and in peace they go down to Sheol.
14 They say to God, 'Leave us alone!
    We do not desire to know your ways.
15 What is the Almighty,*a* that we should serve
        him?
    And what profit do we get if we pray to
        him?'
16 Is not their prosperity indeed their own
        achievement?*b*
    The plans of the wicked are repugnant to me.
17 "How often is the lamp of the wicked put
        out?
    How often does calamity come upon them?
    How often does God*c* distribute pains in his
        anger?
18 How often are they like straw before the
        wind,
    and like chaff that the storm carries away?

a Traditional rendering of Heb *Shaddai*   *b* Heb *in their hand*
c Heb *he*

NIV

let him drink of the wrath of the Almighty.[a]
²¹For what does he care about the family he leaves
behind
when his allotted months come to an end?

²²"Can anyone teach knowledge to God,
since he judges even the highest?
²³One man dies in full vigor,
completely secure and at ease,
²⁴his body[b] well nourished,
his bones rich with marrow.
²⁵Another man dies in bitterness of soul,
never having enjoyed anything good.
²⁶Side by side they lie in the dust,
and worms cover them both.

²⁷"I know full well what you are thinking,
the schemes by which you would wrong me.
²⁸You say, 'Where now is the great man's house,
the tents where wicked men lived?'
²⁹Have you never questioned those who travel?
Have you paid no regard to their accounts—
³⁰that the evil man is spared from the day of
calamity,
that he is delivered from[c] the day of wrath?
³¹Who denounces his conduct to his face?
Who repays him for what he has done?
³²He is carried to the grave,
and watch is kept over his tomb.
³³The soil in the valley is sweet to him;
all men follow after him,
and a countless throng goes[d] before him.

³⁴"So how can you console me with your
nonsense?
Nothing is left of your answers but
falsehood!"

a17-20 Verses 17 and 18 may be taken as exclamations and 19 and
20 as declarations.   b24 The meaning of the Hebrew for this word
is uncertain.   c30 Or man is reserved for the day of calamity, /
that he is brought forth to   d33 Or / as a countless throng went

NRSV

¹⁹ You say, 'God stores up their iniquity for their
children.'
Let it be paid back to them, so that they
may know it.
²⁰ Let their own eyes see their destruction,
and let them drink of the wrath of the
Almighty.[b]
²¹ For what do they care for their household after
them,
when the number of their months is cut off?
²² Will any teach God knowledge,
seeing that he judges those that are on high?
²³ One dies in full prosperity,
being wholly at ease and secure,
²⁴ his loins full of milk
and the marrow of his bones moist.
²⁵ Another dies in bitterness of soul,
never having tasted of good.
²⁶ They lie down alike in the dust,
and the worms cover them.

²⁷ "Oh, I know your thoughts,
and your schemes to wrong me.
²⁸ For you say, 'Where is the house of the
prince?
Where is the tent in which the wicked
lived?'
²⁹ Have you not asked those who travel the roads,
and do you not accept their testimony,
³⁰ that the wicked are spared in the day of
calamity,
and are rescued in the day of wrath?
³¹ Who declares their way to their face,
and who repays them for what they have
done?
³² When they are carried to the grave,
a watch is kept over their tomb.
³³ The clods of the valley are sweet to them;
everyone will follow after,
and those who went before are
innumerable.
³⁴ How then will you comfort me with empty
nothings?
There is nothing left of your answers but
falsehood."

a Traditional rendering of Heb Shaddai

COMMENTARY

Throughout the second cycle of speeches, the friends have focused on one theme only: the fate of the wicked (chaps. 15; 18; 20). In his first two speeches, Job did not reply directly to their claims but pursued the theme of God's violence against him, using legal imagery to explore a way of securing his vindication (chaps. 16–17; 19). Now, however, in his final speech in this cycle, Job addresses the cumulative arguments of the friends concerning the fate of the wicked. Job's speech is a simple one. He introduces his words by asking for a hearing, sarcastically granting the friends permission to mock him when he is finished (vv. 2-3). Job recognizes the radical nature of what he is about to say. Not only will it shock his friends, but the thought of it is also enough to terrify Job himself (vv. 4-6). Modern readers may miss the horror implicit in Job's words. In the ancient wisdom tradition, however, the notion of the punishment of the wicked was the fulcrum of the entire moral order. By denying that the wicked are regularly punished, Job in effect denies the moral order of the world. He develops his claim in four parts. First, he describes the actual fate of the wicked in terms that orthodox thought would use to describe those blessed by God (vv. 7-16). In the second section, Job argues that disaster seldom overtakes the wicked and that a punishment visited upon the wicked person's descendants is no punishment at all (vv. 17-21). Next, Job points out the apparent randomness of fate and the common end awaiting all persons (vv. 22-26). Finally, Job engages the anecdotal claims of the friends concerning the destruction of the wicked by appealing to an equally familiar scene: the wicked person who escapes judgment in life and is honored in death with a splendid funeral and memorial (vv. 27-33). Job concludes by judging the friends' words to be not only empty but also a betrayal of the truth (v. 34).

21:1-6. The ironic use of the motif of consolation opens and closes Job's speech (vv. 2, 34). In the first speech of this cycle, Eliphaz used the phrase "the consolations of God" to refer to the teachings through which a person could be reassured about the nature of God and the world. Job has had more than enough of such teachings, however. The only consolation the friends could give him is to listen to what he has to say. This is not unlike the appeal Job made in 6:24-30. Then, however, Job still considered it possible for a genuine exchange of truth to take place. Now, after having heard what the friends have to say, Job no longer expects them to listen with understanding, but only asks them to hold their mockery until the end of his speech (v. 3).

As Job indicates through a rhetorical question, the issue at stake is not a mere dispute with another human being, but something much more fundamental (v. 4a). The term translated "impatient" (קָצַר qāṣar), however, does not quite capture the nuance of his words, which literally mean "my spirit is short" (v. 4b). Elsewhere, this and similar phrases designate the psychological state of a person immediately before some decisive word is spoken or action is taken (Num 21:4; Judg 10:16; 16:16; Zech 11:8). The pent-up tension can no longer be held in; what is said or done will change the course of events.

It is not his appalling physical condition to which Job directs the attention of his friends (v. 5); they have seen that before. Rather, it is what he is about to say. The expression "look at me" is the same one Job used in 6:28 when he asked the friends to attend to the truthfulness of his words. The gesture of placing the hand to the mouth indicates silence (Judg 18:19), although it may be silence induced by respect (29:9), shame (Prov 30:32; Mic 7:16; cf. 40:4), or shock, as here. Despite the boldness of Job's words, he, too, is aware that what he is about to say will destroy the foundations of the moral world in which he, as well as his friends, have lived. It is not the audacity of his saying it that makes him tremble, however, but the terrifying nature of what confronts him as simple truth (v. 6).

21:7-16. Job announces the topic of his complaint in v. 7. Contrary to what should be, the wicked actually live long and prosperous lives. In the following verses, he gives a detailed description of their experience. If encountered out of context, vv. 8-13 would appear to be a description of God's blessings upon the righteous. Job recounts the security of descendants (v. 8; cf. Pss

112:2; 128:3, 6; 144:12), a peaceful household, free from fear or divine punishment (v. 9; cf. Ps 112:7-8; Prov 1:33), multiplication of herds (v. 10; cf. Gen 30:29-30; Ps 144:13; also note Deut 28:4, 18), the carefree frolicking of children and general festivity (vv. 11-12; cf. Ps 21:6[7]; Prov 10:28; Jer 31:4; Zech 8:5), and a life of unbroken prosperity concluding in a peaceful death (v. 13; cf. Gen 25:8). The description is quite similar to Eliphaz's account of the fate of the righteous (5:23-26), which includes peace, security, prosperity, descendants, and a long life ending in a good death. Job's account completely contradicts the traditional claims, repeated by the friends, about the fate of the wicked, that their offspring are cut off (18:19; 20:10; Ps 37:28*b*, 38*b*), that their households are destroyed (18:14-15; 20:28; Prov 14:11; 21:12), that their wealth dissipates (15:29; 20:10, 15; Prov 11:18; 13:22; 28:22), that they are subject to terrors (15:21), and that they experience violent and premature death (15:30; 18:13-14; 20:23-25; Pss 37:20; 55:23[24]; Prov 11:19, 23; 14:32; 21:7).

Those who have experienced the goodness that Job describes are not the righteous, however, but those who have repudiated God. Job dramatizes their attitude by quoting the words that they might have said, a device often used in depicting the wicked (see Pss 10:4, 6, 11; 12:4[5]; 14:1; 53:1[2]; 94:7). In this case, the wicked are portrayed as not desiring to know the ways of God (v. 14), the very opposite stance from the righteous, who ask for such knowledge (e.g., Ps 25:4-5). The wicked calculate the possible benefits and decide that righteousness is not worthwhile (v. 15). Job is perhaps slyly mocking the tendency of traditional religious discourse to stress the material benefits of righteousness as a motive for obedience to God (Deut 28:1-2; Psalm 128; Prov 13:21-22, 25). As Fohrer notes, the entire plot of Job begins with the question of whether the benefits of piety corrupt its purity.[334]

The translation and interpretation of the final verse of this section (v. 16) is disputed.[335] The NRSV takes 16*a* as an implicit rhetorical question, to the effect that the wicked are indeed respon-

sible for their own prosperity. This interpretation fits well with vv. 14-15, but it leaves unexplained why Job would rather primly distance himself from "the plans of the wicked" (v. 16*b*). The NIV takes v. 16*a* as a simple statement that the prosperity of the wicked is *not* in their own control. This judgment, contradicting vv. 14-15, does not seem consistent with Job's other statements in this chapter. The problem of interpretation disappears if one understands this verse as Job's mimicking of a typical pious platitude. This statement, as the NIV translates it, is just the sort of thing that the friends would say; indeed, it is the theme of Zophar's last speech. Thus conventional wisdom responds to the claims of the wicked (vv. 14-15) by saying that they are not really in control of their fleeting prosperity; God is (v. 16*a*). Consequently, the pious distance themselves from the way the wicked think (v. 16*b*). But Job will refute such conventional wisdom by pointing out that God seldom seems to do anything about the prosperity of the wicked (vv. 17-21).

Job is not the first person to have noticed and been troubled by the apparent contradiction between the claims of religious ideology and the evidence of experience. This problem was addressed in a number of writings in the ancient Near East, particularly in Mesopotamia and in Israel. The Mesopotamian text most closely resembling Job, the Babylonian Theodicy, is also framed as a dialogue between a sufferer, who is innocent of wrongdoing, and his friend. In his complaints, the sufferer observes that the moral order seems to be the reverse of what it should be. "Those who do not seek the god go the way of prosperity, While those who pray to the goddess become destitute and impoverished" (ll. 70-71).[336] In Israelite tradition, Psalms 10; 37; and 73 are sustained examinations of this problem and the threat it posed to faith. In Psalm 73, the psalmist's description of the good fortune of the wicked (Ps 73:4-11) is as long and as vivid as Job's. The difference, however, is that in all of these instances the problem is expressed in a context that contains and finally defeats the threat to orthodox faith. In the Babylonian Theodicy, the friend's replies are appreciatively accepted and finally seem to overcome the sufferer's alienation, for he ends with a humble plea for mercy (ll. 295-97).[337]

334. G. Fohrer, *Das Buch Hiob*, KAT xvi (Guetersloh: Gerd Mohn, 1963) 343.

335. Gordis, *The Book of Job*, 230, and N. Habel, *The Book of Job*, OTL (Philadelphia: Westminster, 1985) 322, emend the text. Pope, *Job*, 159, suggests that the verse is misplaced or is a pious gloss.

336. *ANET*, 602.
337. Ibid., 604.

The tone of Psalm 37 is consistently one of assurance that the wicked will be quickly cut off. Even Psalm 73 represents its anxiety about the good fortune of the wicked as a danger to faith that troubled the psalmist in the past but was later overcome through the psalmist's experience of God's presence. These texts operate as safety valves, allowing the pressure of perceived contradictions to be expressed in a controlled manner, without doing harm to the basic structure of belief. Job, by contrast, can no longer be satisfied with such measures. He is determined to expose the radical nature of the contradiction between what orthodoxy claims and what experience knows to be the case.

21:17-21. Job refutes two arguments in this section. The first is the claim that the wicked have a tenuous existence and are quickly destroyed (cf. v. 16a NIV). In vv. 17-18, Job alludes to several popular images by which this idea was expressed, that the lamp of the wicked is extinguished (cf. 18:5; Prov 13:9; 24:20), that the wicked are like chaff blown off by the wind (cf. Pss 1:4; 35:5), that God's anger apportions destruction to the wicked (cf. 20:28-29), and that calamity overtakes them (cf. 18:12; Prov 6:15). To all of this Job simply asks, "How often?" To claim that a pattern of events is part of a true moral order, one must be able to show that the events occur in a regular and predictable way. It is not enough to say that sometimes the wicked are cut off, but sometimes they are not.

In v. 19a, Job cites a possible objection, that even if a wicked person is not punished, it is because God has stored up the punishment for the wicked person's children. (The phrase "you say" or "it is said" is not explicit in the text but added for clarity in the translations.) The notion that God might punish a later generation for the sin of a former generation was common in ancient Israel (Exod 20:5; Deut 5:9; 2 Sam 12:13-14; Lam 5:7), but was also contested (Jer 31:29-30; Ezek 18:1-4). Curiously, however, it is not used elsewhere in the context of theodicy, as Job uses it here. When the friends speak of the fate of the children of the wicked, it is as an extension of their punishment, not as a substitute for it (5:4; 18:19; 20:10).[338] Perhaps the idea was more com-

mon than the surviving literature suggests, or perhaps Job, like a confident debater, is adding an argument to the friends' repertoire, only to dismantle it. In either case, Job's reply to this hypothetical objection is of a piece with his previous reflection on the limit imposed by death (14:21-22). In death all knowledge and all concern for one's descendants are cut off (v. 21). Thus only direct recompense during the individual's life suffices. Job's imagery is highly sensory: seeing and drinking (v. 20). This kind of immediacy is necessary for one to *know* a moral order, to understand a correlation between evil and punishment (v. 19b). Although he does not draw the conclusion, what Job has been doing in this section is to establish the conditions necessary for a principle to be recognized as part of a moral order. Such a principle must be direct enough to be perceived as a response to one's actions (vv. 19-21), and it must be regular enough to be perceived as a structure rather than as an accident of existence (vv. 17-18). The claim about the punishment of the wicked meets neither criterion.

21:22-26. In contrast to the implicit conditions for a moral order Job has just articulated, he now demonstrates that existence is actually characterized by a lack of rational discrimination between one person's fate and another's. Job introduces his argument with a citation of a common cliché: No one can teach God understanding, since God is the judge of the highest (v. 22; cf. Isa 40:13-14). The ability to make discriminating judgments is, after all, the distinguishing characteristic of divinity (Gen 3:5). Yet Job follows this cliché with the claim that two persons, otherwise indistinguishable ("one . . . another . . . " [זה . . . זה, *zeh . . . zeh*], NRSV), suffer diametrically opposite fates (vv. 23-25). To look at the situation from another perspective, no matter how deserving of different fates they were, in death they experience the same end (v. 26). Whichever way one looks at it, the world is characterized more by randomness than by discriminating moral judgment exercised by a powerful God. Job's critique is also developed in Ecclesiastes, where the inability to discern a moral order leads to the judgment that existence itself is absurd (Eccl 2:14-15; 9:1-3).

21:27-34. Most commentators think that v. 27 is Job's barbed reply to the friends' attempt to identify him indirectly as one of the wicked (i.e.,

338. G. Fohrer, *Das Buch Hiob,* KAT xvi (Guetersloh: Gerd Mohn, 1963) 344.

the wicked are destroyed; Job has been destroyed; therefore, Job is one of the wicked).[339] Certainly the phrasing "the schemes by which you would wrong me" fits this interpretation. The problem, however, is that what follows this statement has nothing to do with Job personally but is his reply to another typical argument of theodicy. The entire attempt to interpret the friends' arguments in the second cycle as veiled accusations against Job stresses the personal dimension too much and ignores the more general argument about the moral structure of the world, which is what Job actually engages. The terminology of v. 27 is probably to be understood in relation to the disputation ("I know the devices by which you plan to attack me," i.e., my arguments) rather than as Job's reply to subtle personal accusations.

The sudden disappearance of the establishments of the wicked (v. 28) is one of the most pervasive moral themes in biblical piety. It is a claim made by each of the three friends (8:14-15; 15:34; 18:15-21; 20:26-28), and it is prominent in Proverbs (Prov 6:15; 10:30; 14:11) and Psalms (Pss 37:10, 20, 35-36; 52:7[9]; 73:18-20; 112:10). Such a claim is essentially anecdotal. Job, in reply, appeals to those who have access to a wide range of anecdotal information, those who travel the roads (v. 29), whether as vagabonds, itinerant laborers, or traders (cf. Pss 80:13; 89:42; Prov

9:15; Lam 1:12; 2:15). Such people, Job claims, will be able to give accounts that directly contradict prevailing orthodoxies, accounts of how the evil person was spared in the day of calamity (v. 30; cf. 20:28; Prov 11:4; Zeph 1:18).

Even more strongly, Job insists that such persons are never confronted with their conduct or paid back for what they have done in life (v. 31; cf. Prov 11:31). The dishonoring of the corpse was the final way in which such a wicked person might be repaid (e.g., Jer 22:18-19). Job, however, recounts the irony of the wicked person's being given a distinguished burial. Far from having memory of that person perish (Prov 10:7), a watch will be kept over the tomb (v. 32b), and a great funeral procession will accompany the interment (v. 33; cf. Eccl 8:10).

In the final verse of his speech, Job returns to the motif of consolation. What the friends have offered him is "emptiness" (הבל *hebel*), the same word that serves as the theme of Ecclesiastes. Even more strongly, Job identifies their consolation as fraudulent (מעל *ma'al*). As Gordis observes, in priestly contexts the term designates the violation of something sacred, an act of faithlessness or treachery.[340] In using this word, Job implies that the friends' attempt to answer him with empty platitudes is a violation of truth, which is itself sacred (cf. Prov 16:10).

---

339. F. Andersen, *Job: An Introduction and Commentary,* Tyndale Old Testament Commentaries (Downers Grove, Ill.: Inter-Varsity, 1976) 201; N. Habel, *The Book of Job,* OTL (Philadelphia: Westminster, 1985) 329.

340. R. Gordis, *The Book of Job: Commentary, New Translation, and Special Studies* (New York: Jewish Theological Seminary, 5738/1978) 236.

REFLECTIONS

Does the world possess a fundamental moral order, or are events and fates merely random? We are accustomed to assume that such radical questions, which go to the heart of traditional religious belief, only emerged in the modern period. Not so. These honest questions are embedded within the Bible itself. In the psalms there may be a certain nervousness about raising such questions and a too hasty attempt to put the lid back on. But in Job and in Ecclesiastes questions about whether a moral order exists in the world are asked with all the freedom and passion imaginable. In these books, the doubts that are raised are not introduced in order to be triumphantly refuted. In Ecclesiastes, Qoheleth works out the nature of a faith that remains deeply skeptical about the accessibility of a clear moral order. In Job, even though God will reject Job's arguments as "words without knowledge" (38:2), God's own words about the nature of the world are as much a challenge to the orthodoxies of the friends as are Job's questions. Far from closing off the discussion, the book as a whole invites it to continue.

Too often religious people repress hard questions and expressions of doubt, embarrassed that they cannot simply accept what others seem to believe so easily. In many Sunday school classes, Bible studies, and discussion groups anyone attempting to voice such doubts might be criticized and made to feel "unchristian" for having said so. Many leave, concluding that their questions have no place within the church. One should remember, however, that at the end of the book, Job—not the friends—is commended for "speaking rightly." Those who are hostile to doubt fail to understand that doubt is not merely compatible with faith but also essential to it. Mature and resilient faith is nurtured by the honest exploration of all the questions arising from experience. Fearful, unexamined faith is brittle and unsustaining, as the contrast between Job and his friends shows. By placing the radical questions of Job and Ecclesiastes squarely within its bounds, the Bible models the confidence of a mature community of faith for whom these questions are a natural part of religious life.

It is one thing to celebrate the freedom to ask hard questions; it is quite another to grapple with the content of Job's challenge. Does the world have a moral order or not? Job's insistence on looking at what actually happens in the world leads to skepticism if not outright rejection of the notion that people regularly get what they deserve and deserve what they get. Although people sometimes do bring trouble upon themselves, just as often it seems to be a random fate or victimization by others. Taken on his own terms, Job is right; there is no discernible moral order in the world. But Job and his friends have all been assuming that a moral order somehow operates (or should operate) automatically, like a cosmic "happy-ending machine," producing the proper pattern of outcomes for everyone. Perhaps that is not the appropriate way to think about the moral order of the world.

A moral order is something that has to be created, or more properly, co-created. It comes into being and continues to exist through the actions of individual moral agents. This notion is easier to grasp if one thinks in terms of moral order in relation to an actual community, such as the community formed by people who work together in a business. Everyone knows the content of a moral order in such a community. It means fairness in dealing with others, respectful treatment, honesty, diligent work, etc. Under such conditions, everyone flourishes. That moral order does not happen automatically, but comes into existence through the actions of the people who make up the community. Those who violate the moral order can cause great damage, both to individuals and to the community. An employee who spreads malicious gossip or a supervisor who abuses power threatens the moral order that has been created. Restoring the health of the organization requires the hard work of those who understand the importance of the moral order and are willing to take risks in order to support it. In the world at large, the moral order is more complex but not fundamentally different in nature.

What is the role of God in the moral order? It is clear to Job and to anyone who observes the gross injustices occurring every day that God is not a heavenly "enforcer" who guarantees that everyone acts properly, meting out rewards and punishments to make certain that they do. Some might say that God commands persons to live morally but leaves humans free to obey or disobey. That perspective is partially correct but overlooks an important way in which God is also related to the moral order through creation. Every moral order must be grounded on a notion of value. God brings the moral order into being through God's judgment that each created being is "good" (Gen 1:10, 12, 18, 21, 26, 31). Thus each being is a center of value that must be treated with respect. In addition to value, a moral order requires relationships of "rightness." These relationships are in part a matter of mutual limits that secure a place for each being. They are also a matter of cooperative behavior that ensures mutual flourishing. Such an order of harmony and flourishing is described in Genesis 1, where each aspect of creation must respect the limits proper to it to make room for its opposite, and where cooperative interaction between these different creatures makes possible the flourishing of all. These orders of rightness, experienced in the rhythms and structures of nature, are the pattern for the moral order. As creatures endowed with freedom, human beings have to choose to perceive and embody such an order of rightness and respect in community. To covet, to steal, to commit adultery, to bear false witness, to kill—all such actions violate the integrity of a fellow human. To honor one's parents and to respect God enhance the cooperative bonds that form community. To keep the sabbath, the sign of God's creation, is to recognize the close relationship between the order of rightness embodied in creation and the order of rightness embodied in the moral law.

Israel's wisdom tradition offers ways of thinking about the moral order that are congenial to this understanding. According to the wisdom tradition, animals are wise by nature (Prov 30:24-28), living "rightly" in harmony with the order of creation. But for human beings, living rightly is not so simple. It requires above all the cultivation of insight, the perception of the wisdom that lies at the heart of creation (Prov 3:19-20), the righteousness and justice that are the foundations of God's throne (Ps 89:14[15]). Such insight is not easy to achieve, since it is always tempting to confuse one's personal interest with transcendent values. Yet it is possible to know what is right. Understanding is the first act, but it is also necessary not just to know what is right but, as the biblical idiom puts it, to "do righteousness" as well. Doing righteousness is a cosmos-creating activity, an activity that brings into being the very values that direct it. The moral order is a co-creative activity of God and human beings as moral agents.

Thinking of the moral order in these dynamic terms also requires that one acknowledge the possibility of cosmos-destroying activities. The wisdom tradition names this folly. It is primarily a failure of understanding (Prov 28:5). Without insight into the moral order, persons do destructive things with devastating consequences. By asserting that wisdom is part of the fabric of creation itself, however, the wisdom tradition does not leave the moral order as a merely contingent phenomenon dependent on the weak minds and wills of individual human beings. No matter how destructive the folly and malice of those who lack insight, the grounding of the moral order in creation provides it with a resiliency and vitality that cannot be ultimately destroyed.[341]

341. For a philosophical development of the idea of the relation between the moral order and the order of nature, see Erazim Kohak, *The Embers and the Stars: A Philosophical Inquiry into the Moral Sense of Nature* (Chicago: The University of Chicago Press, 1984).

JOB 22:1–27:23, THE THIRD CYCLE

OVERVIEW

In the first two cycles of speeches the sequence of speakers has been regular and symetrical: Eliphaz-Job; Bildad-Job; Zophar-Job. Although the third cycle begins in a similar manner with speeches by Eliphaz and Job, the expected sequence soon begins to break down. Bildad's speech in chap. 25 is only 6 verses long. Although Job replies to Bildad in chap. 26, chap. 27 begins with the unusual heading "And Job again took up his discourse and said . . . " (27:1), as though Job's speech had been interrupted. In the third cycle there is no speech attributed to Zophar. The content of the speeches presents difficulties. Each of the speeches attributed to Job contains material that sounds more like the opinions and style of the friends, especially in 24:18-25; 26:5-14; 27:13-23. Since the poem on wisdom in chap. 28 contains no separate heading, it is occasionally taken as a continuation of Job's speech,[342] but most recognize it as a separate composition placed after the dialogue, which concludes with chap. 27. Its independence from both what precedes and what follows is suggested by the fact that 29:1 begins with the heading "and Job again took up his discourse and said . . . " (cf. 27:1).

The majority of modern scholars have made the assumption that the third cycle originally con-

342. E.g., J. G. Janzen, *Job*, Interpretation (Atlanta: John Knox, 1985) 187-201.

tained the same sequence of speakers as the first two cycles. The present state of disarray is presumed to be the result either of unintentional scribal error or a deliberate attempt by a concerned copyist to put some traditionally pious words into the mouth of Job, borrowing them from the speeches of Bildad and Zophar. Although it is quite possible that some such disturbance of the text occurred, there is no independent evidence of it. The earliest translations, the targum of Job from Qumran and the Septuagint, exhibit the same distribution of speeches that one finds in the MT. Those who assume that the third cycle has been disturbed have made a bewildering variety of proposals for reconstructing the original cycle.[343] Gordis serves as a good example of the most modest rearrangement. In his view the third cycle had the following original structure: Eliphaz, 22:1-30; Job 23:1–24:25; Bildad, 25:1-6 + 26:5-14; Job 26:1-4 + 27:1-12; Zophar, 27:13-23.[344] Others typically add all or part of 24:18-25 to Zophar's or, more rarely, to Bildad's speech.[345] The problem with this approach is that such rearrangement creates a text that may never have existed except in the scholarly reconstruction.

There are good reasons for being cautious about resorting to textual surgery. The assumption that the third cycle must be structured like the first two overlooks the fact that the dialogue has broken down. It is entirely possible that the disarray of the third cycle is an artistic representation of the impasse that Job and his friends have reached in their attempt to persuade each other. Giving Bildad a short speech and having Zophar fail to speak at all are apt ways of suggesting that the friends have nothing more to say or see no point in saying it again.[346] The apparent contradictoriness in what Job says in chaps. 24, 26, and 27 is a more difficult matter. Nevertheless, it is quite possible to read and interpret those speeches as belonging entirely to Job, if, for instance, one assumes that Job is citing the friends in order to refute them (24:18-25) or sarcastically mimicking their predictable ways of speaking (26:5-14; 27:13-23). This approach is not without its own difficulties, however, for it depends on recognizing literary techniques that are somewhat different from those used in earlier parts of the dialogue.

Neither approach to the third cycle solves all the interpretive problems. In the commentary to the third cycle, I attempt to read the text without rearrangement, although I think that a case can be made for taking 26:5-14 as part of Bildad's speech (see Commentary on Job 25–26).

The beginning of the third cycle is closely related to the end of the second cycle of speeches. In chap. 21 Job attacked the central element of the friends' moral imagination, their belief in divine retribution as reflected in the miserable fate of the wicked. At the beginning of the third cycle in chap. 22 Eliphaz responds by accusing Job of being one of the wicked, even as he holds out the continuing possibility of repentance and restoration. Job, alienated from the entire tradition of religiosity represented by Eliphaz, seeks a vindication of his integrity not through prayer but through a legal hearing (chap. 23). The questions that trouble him, however, do not just concern the chances for his vindication by God but also the failure of God to ensure a moral order in the world (chap. 24). Bildad's reply to Job (25:1-6; 26:5-14), sarcastically interrupted by Job (26:1-4), attempts to shift the focus of the conversation away from Job's personal situation and even from the fate of the wicked. He wishes to speak of the wholly otherness of the cosmic creator and the comparative nothingness of all human existence. But Job refuses to be swayed from his determination to confront the God "who has taken away my right" (27:2), and in chap. 27 swears an oath defending his integrity. His mocking imitation of the friends' platitudes in the second half of the chapter pre-empts Zophar's reply and brings the dialogue to an end.

343. J. Leveque, *Job et son dieu* (Paris: Gabalda, 1970) 217n. 1, contains a long list.

344. Gordis, *The Book of Job*, 534-35. Gordis thinks that some original material is now missing, however.

345. See, e.g., E. Dorme, *A Commentary on the Book of Job*, trans. H. Knight (London: Nelson, 1967) 386; M. Pope, *Job*, 3rd ed., AB 15 (Garden City, N.Y.: Doubleday, 1979) 188-89.

346. A. B. Davidson, *The Book of Job*, Cambridge Bible for Schools and Colleges 15 (Cambridge: Cambridge University Press, 1891) 180, 186; Andersen, *Job*, 214; Janzen, *Job*, 171-86.

Job 22:1-30, Eliphaz Urges Job to Repent

NIV

22 Then Eliphaz the Temanite replied:

2"Can a man be of benefit to God?
Can even a wise man benefit him?
3What pleasure would it give the Almighty if you
were righteous?
What would he gain if your ways were
blameless?
4"Is it for your piety that he rebukes you
and brings charges against you?
5Is not your wickedness great?
Are not your sins endless?
6You demanded security from your brothers for
no reason;
you stripped men of their clothing, leaving
them naked.
7You gave no water to the weary
and you withheld food from the hungry,
8though you were a powerful man, owning
land—
an honored man, living on it.
9And you sent widows away empty-handed
and broke the strength of the fatherless.
10That is why snares are all around you,
why sudden peril terrifies you,
11why it is so dark you cannot see,
and why a flood of water covers you.
12"Is not God in the heights of heaven?
And see how lofty are the highest stars!
13Yet you say, 'What does God know?
Does he judge through such darkness?
14Thick clouds veil him, so he does not see us
as he goes about in the vaulted heavens.'
15Will you keep to the old path
that evil men have trod?
16They were carried off before their time,
their foundations washed away by a flood.
17They said to God, 'Leave us alone!
What can the Almighty do to us?'
18Yet it was he who filled their houses with good
things,
so I stand aloof from the counsel of the
wicked.
19"The righteous see their ruin and rejoice;
the innocent mock them, saying,

NRSV

22 Then Eliphaz the Temanite answered:
2 "Can a mortal be of use to God?
Can even the wisest be of service to him?
3 Is it any pleasure to the Almighty[a] if you are
righteous,
or is it gain to him if you make your ways
blameless?
4 Is it for your piety that he reproves you,
and enters into judgment with you?
5 Is not your wickedness great?
There is no end to your iniquities.
6 For you have exacted pledges from your family
for no reason,
and stripped the naked of their clothing.
7 You have given no water to the weary to drink,
and you have withheld bread from the
hungry.
8 The powerful possess the land,
and the favored live in it.
9 You have sent widows away empty-handed,
and the arms of the orphans you have
crushed.[b]
10 Therefore snares are around you,
and sudden terror overwhelms you,
11 or darkness so that you cannot see;
a flood of water covers you.

12 "Is not God high in the heavens?
See the highest stars, how lofty they are!
13 Therefore you say, 'What does God know?
Can he judge through the deep darkness?
14 Thick clouds enwrap him, so that he does not
see,
and he walks on the dome of heaven.'
15 Will you keep to the old way
that the wicked have trod?
16 They were snatched away before their time;
their foundation was washed away by a flood.
17 They said to God, 'Leave us alone,'
and 'What can the Almighty[a] do to us?'[c]
18 Yet he filled their houses with good things—
but the plans of the wicked are repugnant
to me.
19 The righteous see it and are glad;

a Traditional rendering of Heb Shaddai   b Gk Syr Tg Vg: Heb were
crushed   c Gk Syr: Heb them

NIV

20'Surely our foes are destroyed,
and fire devours their wealth.'

21"Submit to God and be at peace with him;
in this way prosperity will come to you.
22Accept instruction from his mouth
and lay up his words in your heart.
23If you return to the Almighty, you will be
restored:
If you remove wickedness far from your tent
24and assign your nuggets to the dust,
your gold of Ophir to the rocks in the ravines,
25then the Almighty will be your gold,
the choicest silver for you.
26Surely then you will find delight in the Almighty
and will lift up your face to God.
27You will pray to him, and he will hear you,
and you will fulfill your vows.
28What you decide on will be done,
and light will shine on your ways.
29When men are brought low and you say, 'Lift
them up!'
then he will save the downcast.
30He will deliver even one who is not innocent,
who will be delivered through the cleanness
of your hands."

NRSV

the innocent laugh them to scorn,
20 saying, 'Surely our adversaries are cut off,
and what they left, the fire has consumed.'

21 "Agree with God,a and be at peace;
in this way good will come to you.
22 Receive instruction from his mouth,
and lay up his words in your heart.
23 If you return to the Almighty,b you will be
restored,
if you remove unrighteousness from your
tents,
24 if you treat gold like dust,
and gold of Ophir like the stones of the
torrent-bed,
25 and if the Almightya is your gold
and your precious silver,
26 then you will delight yourself in the Almighty,b
and lift up your face to God.
27 You will pray to him, and he will hear you,
and you will pay your vows.
28 You will decide on a matter, and it will be
established for you,
and light will shine on your ways.
29 When others are humiliated, you say it is pride;
for he saves the humble.
30 He will deliver even those who are guilty;
they will escape because of the cleanness of
your hands."c

a Heb him   b Traditional rendering of Heb *Shaddai*   c Meaning
of Heb uncertain

COMMENTARY

Throughout their responses to Job, the three friends have never yet identified Job with the wicked. In the first cycle, Eliphaz spoke of him as a pious person who only needs to wait for restoration (4:6), whose misfortunes are a form of divine discipline leading to a secure future (5:17-26), and who is part of sinful humanity and so shares in its fate (4:17-21; cf. 15:14-16). Bildad argued that Job's children were the sinners (8:4). Zophar assumed that Job must have sinned in some fashion, but perhaps in a way that Job himself was not conscious of, since he lacks divine wisdom (11:4-6). Such inadvertent sin, although

punishable, did not carry with it the stigma of much more serious willful and blatant sin. In the opening speech of the second cycle, Eliphaz warned that the destructive words Job now speaks are prompted by a sinful disposition (15:5-6), but he made no judgment on Job's previous life. In the course of the second cycle, the friends reaffirmed the foundation of their moral world: the order of retribution as it is evident in the horrifying fate of the wicked (chaps. 15; 18; 20). Even here, none claims that Job is one of the wicked. Job's last speech in the second cycle, however, in which he flatly denies the principle of retribution, pushed Eliphaz to the inevitable conclusion that the friends have resisted until this moment: Job must be a blatant, willful sinner.

Eliphaz begins without the customary introductory complaint about windy words, lack of wisdom, or insulting speech. Instead, he launches directly into his argument that since God derives no benefit from human righteousness, Job's punishment must recompense for his wickedness (vv. 2-5). In support of this insight, Eliphaz details the sins Job must have committed, concluding that he has been punished for just this conduct (vv. 6-11). In a second argument, Eliphaz accuses Job of denying God's knowledge and judgment, conduct that since ancient times leads to certain ruin (vv. 12-20). Despite his conviction that Job's behavior is characterized by great evil, Eliphaz does not conclude his speech with judgment, but with an appeal. If Job returns to God and reforms his conduct under God's instruction, then not only will he be restored, but also his favor with God will be so great that he can even intercede on behalf of others (vv. 21-30). For Eliphaz, the resources of traditional religion are always sufficient. All that he asks of Job is that he acknowledge his sin. What Eliphaz asks, however, is the one thing that Job's integrity will not allow him to do.

22:1-11. 22:1-3. In 21:15, Job had represented the wicked as dismissing piety because there was no benefit in it. Eliphaz begins his reply with a series of rhetorical questions denying that God receives any benefit from human righteousness (vv. 2-3). At the end of his speech, he will return to this theme, arguing that humans benefit from piety, for turning to God brings complete well-being (vv. 21-30).

22:4-5. Eliphaz's words assert the impartiality of God (cf. 35:6-8). Consequently, Job's claim of complete innocence (9:21; 16:17) is implausible to Eliphaz. Since he believes with Bildad that God does not pervert justice, Eliphaz's rhetorical questions in v. 4 have a tone of exasperated incredulity about them. Ironically, it is precisely Job's piety (lit., "fear [יראה *yir'â*] of God") that has resulted in his devastation, even though that devastation is neither rebuke nor judgment, as Eliphaz assumes. Eliphaz's moral imagination encompasses only certain possibilities. Having interpreted Job's suffering as divine judgment, and knowing that God does not punish piety, he inevitably concludes that Job must be a wicked person (v. 5).

22:6. Eliphaz supports his claim with a detailed accusation. The form of this section is evocative of prophetic judgment speeches, with the accusations introduced by "because" (כי *kî*, v. 6; NRSV, "for"), and the judgment introduced by "therefore" (על-כן *'al-kēn*; v. 10).[347] As in the poems on the fate of the wicked, the crimes are specifically abuses of social and economic power. The seizing of pledges for repayment of debt (v. 6) was strictly regulated in Israel, precisely because the poor, who had little with which to secure a debt, were so vulnerable. If the tools by which they made their living or the cloak in which they slept were taken, then their very lives were at risk (Exod 22:25-26; Deut 24:6, 17). If v. 6*b* is intended to specify the nature of the pledge taken, then Eliphaz clearly refers to someone who possesses nothing of value except the clothes they wear. To seize a pledge "for no reason" suggests a particular hardness; extracting it from one's family, toward whom one had a special obligation, is heinous.

22:7-9. Callous disregard for elemental human solidarity is reflected in the accusation that Job refused water to the thirsty or bread to the hungry (v. 7). Response to or rejection of these basic needs was the touchstone of human decency and faithfulness to the creator of all (Isa 58:7; Ezek 18:7, 16; Matt 25:34-45). Similarly, protection of the widow and the orphan (v. 9) was one of the most fundamental obligations of those possessing power and position within ancient society. This theme occurs in the Code of Hammurapi[348] and in the Ugaritic epics of Keret and Aqhat,[349] as well as in the Bible (Exod 22:22[21]; Deut 10:18; 24:17; Isa 1:17; Jer 22:3; Zech 7:10). The widow and the orphan were especially under God's protection (Exod 22:22-23[21-22]; Pss 10:14; 68:5[6]; 146:9). To show cruelty toward the widow and the orphan was to show contempt for the moral foundation of the social order. It is difficult to imagine a more serious accusation.

In the midst of these accusations, v. 8 stands out. Some interpret this verse as an accusation that Job has favored the powerful,[350] or as a

347. E. Good, *In Turns of Tempest* (Stanford, Calif.: Stanford University Press, 1990) 273. See C. Westermann, *Basic Forms of Prophetic Speech*, trans. H. C. White (Lousiville: Westminster/John Knox, 1991) 137-68.

348. James B. Pritchard, ed., *Ancient Near Eastern Texts Relating to the Old Testament (ANET)*, 3rd ed. with supplement (Princeton: Princeton University Press, 1969) 178.

349. Ibid., 149, 151.

350. Dhorme, *A Commentary on the Book of Job*, 329.

reference to Job himself as a land-grabber who dispossessed neighbors.[351] The Aramaic translation of the book of Job found at Qumran introduces this verse with the phrase "and you say," as though the words were Job's self-satisfied justification for selfishness.[352] Verse 8, however, contains no moral condemnation in itself. It is rather like certain proverbs that simply make observations about the world. The powerful and influential in a very real sense do "possess the land." For Eliphaz and the social ethic he advocates, such power entails corresponding responsibilities. Job, as just such a powerful person, has betrayed the social contract by the crimes against the poor detailed in vv. 6-7, 9 (so NIV).[353] There is no disagreement between Eliphaz and Job on the nature of the social ethic, only about whether Job has violated it. Job will defend himself as a righteous person precisely by referring to these values (chaps. 29; 31).

22:10-11. Having laid out the accusation, Eliphaz delivers the judgment in vv. 10-11. The imagery of snares and terror (v. 10) evokes Bildad's description of the fate of the wicked (18:8-11). Darkness and flood are also part of the repertoire of those accounts (18:5-6; 20:28).

22:12-20. In 21:22, Job used a pious cliché about God's knowledge and judgment in a sarcastic manner to introduce his claim that experience shows no rational discrimination between the fates of people. Here Eliphaz attempts to reclaim the truth of that traditional belief in the face of Job's cynical denial and to warn Job against the consequences of the beliefs he seems to be embracing.

22:12-14. For Eliphaz, the loftiness ascribed to God is an index of God's ability to see and know all things (v. 12; cf. Ps 33:13-14; Isa 40:22, 26-27). The contrasting position, which he attributes to Job (vv. 13-14), is traditionally associated with sinners, a claim that God's transcendence is such that God cannot see or is not interested in what people do on earth (e.g., Pss 10:11; 73:11; Isa 29:15; Jer 23:23-24; Ezek 8:12). The impious, as Eliphaz represents them, cleverly employ the very images used to praise God: the shielding dark cloud associated with theophanies (ערפל *'ărāpel*;

cf. Exod 20:21; 1 Kgs 8:12: Ps 18:11[12]), the clouds signifying the presence of the divine warrior (cf. Judg 5:4; Ps 18:12[13]), and the heavenly dome formed by God (cf. Prov 8:27; Isa 40:22). Yet the impious exploit different nuances of these images: connotations of obscurity and distance. That has not been the burden of Job's accusations against God. When Job has used the imagery of sight, it has been in the context of a complaint of incessant divine scrutiny (e.g., 7:17-20; 10:4-6). Eliphaz, however, is not concerned to answer Job's particular claims. Having concluded that Job is a sinner, Eliphaz can only see him in the stereotyped image of the sinner that tradition describes.

22:15-20. Here Eliphaz begins the first of two appeals to Job. Verses 15-20 consist of negative examples of the destruction of the wicked; in vv. 21-30, the motivation for repentance is developed through images of a close relationship with God. The metaphor of a path, representing habitual conduct (v. 15), is an important part of wisdom imagery.[354] It implies that moral conduct is not simply a series of particular choices but a commitment to a pattern of behavior leading in a particular direction. Jeremiah develops the image vividly, describing his audience as standing at a crossroad, faced concretely with the dilemma of discerning and choosing "the good way" (Jer 6:16). The expression "ancient paths" (נתבות עולם *nĕtibôt 'ôlām*; cf. Jer 6:16; 18:15) even suggests that alternative patterns of conduct were established in antiquity, so that in choosing between them one participates in a community of moral conduct rooted in ancient times. In early Jewish moral instruction, examples of the "two ways" drawn from remote antiquity were particularly popular.[355]

Eliphaz contrasts the actual destruction that befalls the wicked (v. 16) with their own self-deceiving perception (v. 17), dramatizing the supposed words of the wicked (cf. Ps 10:4, 6, 11; 94:7). These lines are quite close to Job's representation of the wicked in 21:14-16. Both Eliphaz and Job agree that the wicked contemptuously dismiss God. Job represents them as denying that God can do anything *for* them, and Eliphaz rep-

---

351. Pope, *Job*, 165.
352. Similarly, Gordis, *The Book of Job*, 246.
353. See ibid., 245, for the justification of such a translation.

354. See N. Habel, "The Symbolism of Wisdom in Proverbs 1–8," *Int.* 26 (1962) 131-57.
355. E.g., T. Asher; *Damascus Document* 2:14–3:12.

resents them as denying that God can do anything *to* them. But Eliphaz directly engages Job's sarcastic citation of the pious cliché " 'their prosperity is not in their own hands,/ so I stand aloof from the counsel of the wicked' " (21:16 NIV). To Job's mind, the cliché, which supposedly denied the autonomy of the wicked, actually served as evidence that God favors the wicked. Eliphaz surprisingly agrees with Job that the prosperity of the wicked does come from God (18*a*); yet in the context of Eliphaz's speech that claim serves to show up the ingratitude of the wicked, who accept the gracious bounty but reject the one who gives it. Thus when Eliphaz restates the line "the counsel of the wicked is far from me," he restores it to its non-ironic, non-sarcastic meaning. Eliphaz concludes this section with a motif familiar from the psalms: the rejoicing of the righteous over the destruction of the wicked (vv. 19-20; see Pss 52:6-7[8-9]; 58:10-11[11-12]; 107:42).

22:21-30. 22:21-22. A second and much more developed appeal concludes Eliphaz's speech. In vv. 21-22, he uses imperative sentences to establish what Job must do. A word play in v. 21 cannot be represented in English. The same verb meaning "benefit" in v. 2 (סכן *sākan*) has a related form that means "accustom oneself to," "submit to" in v. 21*a* (הסכן *hasken*). The relationship between God and humanity is not symmetrical. Although a person cannot benefit (*sākan*) God through any conduct, submitting (*hasken*) to God is the source of all that is good for a person. A textual problem obscures v. 21*b* and leads to disagreement about the tenor of Eliphaz's claim. A garbled word (תבואתך *tĕbô'ātĕkā*) might be corrected either to a noun ("your yield" [תבואתך *tĕbû'ātkā*]) or a verb ("will come to you" [תבואך *tĕbô'ākā*]). The first alternative ("by this means your yield will be good") would give Eliphaz's advice a rather materialistic overtone.[356] Eliphaz, however, defines the benefits of being at peace with God in the following verses, and they are decidedly not materialistic.[357] In this context the NIV's "prosperity" is too narrow for the sense of holistic well-being that the Hebrew word טוב (*tôb*) signifies. The wisdom background for Eliphaz's

advice is evident in his choice of words in v. 22, not only "instruction" (תורה *tôrâ*; cf. Prov 4:2; 13:14) and "word" (Prov 4:5; 5:7; 7:24), but also the imagery of mouth and heart (e.g., Ps 119:11; Prov 10:11).

22:23-25. The motivation for Eliphaz's appeal to Job is developed in a series of conditional sentences (see Isa 58:13-14 for a very similar appeal). It is possible to divide the sentences differently (cf. v. 25 NRSV and NIV), although the NRSV probably reflects the grammatical structure of the Hebrew text better. Eliphaz begins in v. 23*a* with a simple statement that summarizes all that he will say: "if you return to Shaddai, you will be restored." Eliphaz's vision is of a gracious God, always ready to receive the repentant. In v. 23*b,* he begins to specify the nature of repentance (cf. 11:14). Reordering the self according to God's teaching (v. 22) leads to reordering commitments (what is "in one's tent," v. 23) and values (vv. 24-25). The contrast between those who put their trust in material things and those who put their trust in God is a staple of psalmic and wisdom piety (31:24-25; Ps 119:36; Prov 11:4; Sir 5:7-8). Eliphaz vividly develops the theme by depicting Job as actually returning gold to the places from which it was dug (the NIV's "assign," not the NRSV's "treat") and taking God as his gold and silver instead (v. 25; in Proverbs, wisdom is often compared favorably to gold and silver; e.g., Prov 3:14-15; 8:10-11, 19). Returning gold to the far away and legendary land of Ophir (28:16; 1 Kgs 9:28; Ps 45:9[10]; Isa 13:12) would be a gesture of extravagant proportions. Yet Job would receive something more valuable than what he parted with, which would more than repay his efforts.

22:26-28. The first result of Job's reformation of self, commitments, and values is the transformation of his desire. Now God becomes the source of his pleasure (v. 26*a;* cf. Ps 37:4). Moreover, Job's relationship with God is transformed from alienation to intimacy and trust. The imagery of lifting up the face (v. 26*b*) can describe the trust required for individuals to look at each other directly (cf. Gen 4:6; 2 Sam 2:22). Just as sin makes a person ashamed to lift the face to God in prayer (Ezra 9:6), so also repentance restores that intimacy. The context of prayer is explicit in v. 27, as Eliphaz assures Job that God will hear his prayers. Vows (v. 27*b*) were often

---

356. So Dhorme, *A Commentary on the Book of Job,* 336; Pope, *Job,* 167; J. E. Hartley, *The Book of Job,* NICOT (Grand Rapids, Mich.: Eerdmans, 1988) 331.

357. Contra Dhorme, *A Commentary on the Book of Job,* 336.

made in the course of petitionary prayer, so that the fulfillment of a vow is another indication that prayer has been answered (cf. 1 Sam 1:10-11; Pss 22:25[26]; 61:5-8[6-9]; 65:1-2[2-3]; Jonah 2). The ability to determine a course of action and to see where one is going (v. 28) connotes someone whose will is in harmony with God's (e.g., Deut 28:29; Prov 4:18-19), the opposite of the condition described in futility curses (e.g., Deut 28:38-44).

22:29-30. Eliphaz's culminating image of well-being, the ability to intervene on behalf of sinners, is obscured in the NRSV. The difficulty comes from confusion about how to translate the Hebrew word גוה (*gēwâ*, v. 29*a*). It is one of a family of words that connote height, and so often have come to represent pride or arrogance. Here, however, the contrast with "brought low" suggests that it is used as an exhortation—"be lifted up."[358] That word of encouragement is grounded on Job's ability to draw from his own uprightness to save the guilty (v. 30).[359] In this way, Job would be like Abraham interceding for Sodom (Gen 18:21-33) or Moses for the people of Israel (Exod 32:9-14). The prophet Ezekiel remembered Job, together with Noah and the Canaanite king Dan'el, as persons whose righteousness was popularly thought to be sufficient to save others (Ezek 14:14, 20). The irony in Eliphaz's depiction of Job's restoration as an intercessor is that it truly comes to pass, when Job intercedes with God to spare Eliphaz and his two friends from God's anger (42:8).

358. Similarly, Gordis, *The Book of Job*, 252; Habel, *The Book of Job*, 333.

359. See R. Gordis, "Corporate Personality in the Book of Job," *JNES* 4 (1945), 54-55, for a brief survey of the theme of intercession in biblical and rabbinic thought, what Gordis calls "horizontal corporate responsibility."

REFLECTIONS

Eliphaz's speech is a masterpiece of prophetic and pastoral counseling. Now, at last, he thinks he understands Job's situation and knows the right words to speak. Eliphaz's speech is a powerful evocation of the fundamental religious theme of sin and redemption. The parallels between Eliphaz's depiction and the story of Daniel and King Nebuchadnezzar in Daniel 4 are striking. Both Eliphaz and Daniel perceive themselves to be faced with a person who is a great sinner, a person whose true humanity has been distorted by arrogance, but who can be redeemed by repentance and by turning in humility toward God (cf. Dan 4:27[24], 33-34[30-31]).

The story of the redeemed sinner is a popular one that has great power in Judeo-Christian tradition. Second Chronicles 33 turns the story of the reign of the evil King Manasseh into an edifying narrative about his suffering, repentance, and reformation (2 Chr 33:10-17; cf. 2 Kings 21). The canon of the Orthodox Church even includes the text of his prayer of repentance (Prayer of Manasseh). In the NT book of Acts, the story of Paul, the persecutor who becomes an apostle (Acts 8–9), draws its narrative power in part from this paradigm of the transformed sinner. Popular moral literature also makes use of this theme. The figure of Ebenezer Scrooge in Charles Dickens' *A Christmas Carol* has become an icon of the hard and selfish miser transformed into a person of true humanity and generosity. These stories and the religious paradigm they embody provide an alternative to the harsh "fate of the wicked" vision of judgment. They appeal to us because they allow us to envision good overcoming evil in a redemptive rather than a judgmental manner.

Eliphaz thinks that the paradigm of the repentant sinner can resolve the problem of Job. He had initially been faced with an apparent contradiction: why a good person would experience the fate normally associated with divine punishment. That contradiction is resolved as soon as Eliphaz concludes that Job must be a great sinner. Yet Eliphaz does not mean to abandon his friend. Instead, he holds out to Job the promise of redemption, the transformation of Job the oppressor of the widow and the orphan into Job the intercessor. Job need only accept this portrait of himself and act according to the paradigm. The problem, of course, is that Eliphaz's depiction of Job has nothing to do with the reality of Job's situation or the truth about Job's character.

This sobering observation leads one back to the most scandalous aspect of this chapter: Eliphaz's denunciation of Job in vv. 6-11. There is no doubting Eliphaz's sincerity at this point. But how could he do this? How could he throw such accusations against someone he has known so well? It is tempting to be smug and dismissive of Eliphaz, but the phenomenon he represents is more common than it is comfortable to admit. The bizarre allegations of anti-Semitic propaganda from the Middle Ages to the present have often found a large audience willing to believe them. Christians who defended their Jewish neighbors against such egregious slanders were all too rare. In seventeenth-century Salem, accusations of witchcraft against well-known and respected persons were widely credited as true. Few who experienced the "red scare" of the 1950s and 1960s can forget how easily the claim that someone was a communist agent could be believed, even when the accused was wholly innocent. Another manifestation of this phenomenon takes the form of allegations of systematic child abuse, often linked with satanic cult practices. In all of these cases there is an element of hysteria that obliterates a community's ability to distinguish between actual problems (communist agents did exist; child abuse does occur) and wild accusations that are only the concrete manifestations of a community's anxiety about many things over which it has no control. Although it is disturbing enough to observe how such allegations can be believed about strangers, it is truly frightening that people can be willing to believe the most heinous accusations about neighbors and friends whom they have known well for many years.

What is common to all of these situations is an unacknowledged sense of the fragility of the social order. Life together requires a fundamental trust in other people. That trust is sometimes broken, even in shocking ways. In a healthy society, those betrayals can be acknowledged and confronted while still leaving intact the grounding faith in the trustworthiness of the members of the community. Faith is not easy, however, and the fear that such faith may be misplaced is always present. All too quickly a community can give in to the anxiety that the bland surface of normality is only a thin cover over something horribly and dangerously wrong, an unseen threat that will seize from below. A breakdown of fundamental social trust is replaced with a belief that deception may be the rule, not the exception. If that is so, then it is entirely possible to believe that one's next-door neighbor, who has always seemed a friendly and kind person, is actually a monster of evil. Sometimes even the victims of false accusations are so swept up in the hysteria that they, too, believe the whole scenario and, no longer trusting their own sense of themselves, confess to crimes they never committed.

This type of social paranoia is most common where religious or political beliefs are highly dualistic, conceived of as a battle between good and evil. In such a context, it takes enormous courage to say no to collective hysteria. It also requires a deep faith in the goodness of God's creation and in the persons whom God has created in God's image. It requires a belief that truth is more fundamental than deception and, therefore, that it is possible to distinguish the evil that actually exists from the fantasies created by anxiety.

Job 23:1–24:25, Divine Justice Is Elusive

NIV

23 Then Job replied:

2"Even today my complaint is bitter;
his hand[a] is heavy in spite of[b] my groaning.
3If only I knew where to find him;
if only I could go to his dwelling!

a2 Septuagint and Syriac; Hebrew / the hand on me   b2 Or heavy on me in

NRSV

23 Then Job answered:

2 "Today also my complaint is bitter;[a]
his[b] hand is heavy despite my groaning.
3 Oh, that I knew where I might find him,
that I might come even to his dwelling!
4 I would lay my case before him,

a Syr Vg Tg: Heb rebellious   b Gk Syr: Heb my

NIV

⁴I would state my case before him
　and fill my mouth with arguments.
⁵I would find out what he would answer me,
　and consider what he would say.
⁶Would he oppose me with great power?
　No, he would not press charges against me.
⁷There an upright man could present his case
　　before him,
　and I would be delivered forever from my
　　judge.

⁸"But if I go to the east, he is not there;
　if I go to the west, I do not find him.
⁹When he is at work in the north, I do not see
　　him;
　when he turns to the south, I catch no
　　glimpse of him.
¹⁰But he knows the way that I take;
　when he has tested me, I will come forth as
　　gold.
¹¹My feet have closely followed his steps;
　I have kept to his way without turning aside.
¹²I have not departed from the commands of his
　　lips;
　I have treasured the words of his mouth more
　　than my daily bread.

¹³"But he stands alone, and who can oppose him?
　He does whatever he pleases.
¹⁴He carries out his decree against me,
　and many such plans he still has in store.
¹⁵That is why I am terrified before him;
　when I think of all this, I fear him.
¹⁶God has made my heart faint;
　the Almighty has terrified me.
¹⁷Yet I am not silenced by the darkness,
　by the thick darkness that covers my face.

24 "Why does the Almighty not set times for
　judgment?
　Why must those who know him look in vain
　　for such days?
²Men move boundary stones;
　they pasture flocks they have stolen.
³They drive away the orphan's donkey
　and take the widow's ox in pledge.
⁴They thrust the needy from the path
　and force all the poor of the land into hiding.
⁵Like wild donkeys in the desert,
　the poor go about their labor of foraging food;

NRSV

and fill my mouth with arguments.
⁵ I would learn what he would answer me,
　and understand what he would say to me.
⁶ Would he contend with me in the greatness
　　of his power?
　No; but he would give heed to me.
⁷ There an upright person could reason with
　　him,
　and I should be acquitted forever by my judge.

⁸ "If I go forward, he is not there;
　or backward, I cannot perceive him;
⁹ on the left he hides, and I cannot behold him;
　I turn[a] to the right, but I cannot see him.
¹⁰ But he knows the way that I take;
　when he has tested me, I shall come out
　　like gold.
¹¹ My foot has held fast to his steps;
　I have kept his way and have not turned
　　aside.
¹² I have not departed from the commandment
　　of his lips;
　I have treasured in[b] my bosom the words
　　of his mouth.
¹³ But he stands alone and who can dissuade
　　him?
　What he desires, that he does.
¹⁴ For he will complete what he appoints for me;
　and many such things are in his mind.
¹⁵ Therefore I am terrified at his presence;
　when I consider, I am in dread of him.
¹⁶ God has made my heart faint;
　the Almighty[c] has terrified me;
¹⁷ If only I could vanish in darkness,
　and thick darkness would cover my face![d]

24 "Why are times not kept by the
　Almighty,[c]
　and why do those who know him never see
　　his days?
² The wicked[e] remove landmarks;
　they seize flocks and pasture them.
³ They drive away the donkey of the orphan;
　they take the widow's ox for a pledge.
⁴ They thrust the needy off the road;

---

[a] Syr Vg: Heb *he turns*　　[b] Gk Vg: Heb *from*
[c] Traditional rendering of Heb Shaddai　　[d] Or *But I am not de-*
stroyed by the darkness; he has concealed the thick darkness from
me　　[e] Gk: Heb *they*

NIV

the wasteland provides food for their children.
⁶They gather fodder in the fields
and glean in the vineyards of the wicked.
⁷Lacking clothes, they spend the night naked;
they have nothing to cover themselves in the
cold.
⁸They are drenched by mountain rains
and hug the rocks for lack of shelter.
⁹The fatherless child is snatched from the breast;
the infant of the poor is seized for a debt.
¹⁰Lacking clothes, they go about naked;
they carry the sheaves, but still go hungry.
¹¹They crush olives among the terraces*a*;
they tread the winepresses, yet suffer thirst.
¹²The groans of the dying rise from the city,
and the souls of the wounded cry out for help.
But God charges no one with wrongdoing.

¹³"There are those who rebel against the light,
who do not know its ways
or stay in its paths.
¹⁴When daylight is gone, the murderer rises up
and kills the poor and needy;
in the night he steals forth like a thief.
¹⁵The eye of the adulterer watches for dusk;
he thinks, 'No eye will see me,'
and he keeps his face concealed.
¹⁶In the dark, men break into houses,
but by day they shut themselves in;
they want nothing to do with the light.
¹⁷For all of them, deep darkness is their morning*b*;
they make friends with the terrors of darkness.*c*

¹⁸"Yet they are foam on the surface of the water;
their portion of the land is cursed,
so that no one goes to the vineyards.
¹⁹As heat and drought snatch away the melted
snow,
so the grave*d* snatches away those who have
sinned.
²⁰The womb forgets them,
the worm feasts on them;
evil men are no longer remembered
but are broken like a tree.
²¹They prey on the barren and childless woman,
and to the widow show no kindness.
²²But God drags away the mighty by his power;

*a11 Or olives between the millstones; the meaning of the Hebrew for this
word is uncertain.   b17 Or them, their morning is like the shadow of
death   c17 Or of the shadow of death   d19 Hebrew Sheol*

NRSV

the poor of the earth all hide themselves.
⁵ Like wild asses in the desert
they go out to their toil,
scavenging in the wasteland
food for their young.
⁶ They reap in a field not their own
and they glean in the vineyard of the
wicked.
⁷ They lie all night naked, without clothing,
and have no covering in the cold.
⁸ They are wet with the rain of the mountains,
and cling to the rock for want of shelter.

⁹ 'There are those who snatch the orphan child
from the breast,
and take as a pledge the infant of the poor.
¹⁰ They go about naked, without clothing;
though hungry, they carry the sheaves;
¹¹ between their terraces*a* they press out oil;
they tread the wine presses, but suffer thirst.
¹² From the city the dying groan,
and the throat of the wounded cries for
help;
yet God pays no attention to their prayer.

¹³ "There are those who rebel against the light,
who are not acquainted with its ways,
and do not stay in its paths.
¹⁴ The murderer rises at dusk
to kill the poor and needy,
and in the night is like a thief.
¹⁵ The eye of the adulterer also waits for the
twilight,
saying, 'No eye will see me';
and he disguises his face.
¹⁶ In the dark they dig through houses;
by day they shut themselves up;
they do not know the light.
¹⁷ For deep darkness is morning to all of them;
for they are friends with the terrors of deep
darkness.

¹⁸ "Swift are they on the face of the waters;
their portion in the land is cursed;
no treader turns toward their vineyards.
¹⁹ Drought and heat snatch away the snow
waters;
so does Sheol those who have sinned.

a Meaning of Heb uncertain

NIV

though they become established, they have
    no assurance of life.

²³He may let them rest in a feeling of security,
    but his eyes are on their ways.

²⁴For a little while they are exalted, and then they
    are gone;
    they are brought low and gathered up like all
        others;
    they are cut off like heads of grain.

²⁵"If this is not so, who can prove me false
    and reduce my words to nothing?"

NRSV

²⁰ The womb forgets them;
    the worm finds them sweet;
    they are no longer remembered;
    so wickedness is broken like a tree.

²¹ "They harm[a] the childless woman,
    and do no good to the widow.

²² Yet God[b] prolongs the life of the mighty by his
    power;
    they rise up when they despair of life.

²³ He gives them security, and they are
    supported;
    his eyes are upon their ways.

²⁴ They are exalted a little while, and then are
    gone;
    they wither and fade like the mallow;[c]
    they are cut off like the heads of grain.

²⁵ If it is not so, who will prove me a liar,
    and show that there is nothing in what I
      say?"

[a] Gk Tg: Heb *feed on* or *associate with*   [b] Heb *he*   [c] Gk: Heb *like all others*

COMMENTARY

Job's first speech in the third cycle presents some of the most difficult exegetical problems in the entire book. Not only are there many grammatical problems and obscurities in the individual verses, but also the ending of the speech (24:18-24) sounds in some ways more like the words of one of Job's friends than Job's own words. The interpretation taken here, however, is that the entire speech belongs to Job and that the difficult last part of the speech is to be understood as Job's provocative demand that God act to bring judgment against the wicked and so resolve the intolerable contradiction between a God of justice and a world of unpunished criminality.

Job's speech begins on a note of bitter defiance (23:2). After Eliphaz's last speech, one might have imagined that the model of the repentant sinner would have been an appealing one for Job to adopt, for it would have put a shattered world together again. For Job, however, integrity is everything. He has not betrayed his community or his God, and he will not betray himself. Al-though he does not reply directly to Eliphaz's accusations that he is wicked, Job repeats his assertions of innocence and integrity. Whereas Eliphaz had advised Job to seek God through prayer, repentance, and submission (22:21-30), Job seeks the resolution of a trial, in which he is certain God will give him a hearing, and he will be vindicated (23:3-7). Job's confidence is checked by his inability to find God (23:8-9), but it returns as he considers that God knows his integrity (23:10). In striking contrast to his earlier imaginings (e.g., 9:20, 28), Job is persuaded that God's judgment of him and his own testimony to his uprightness will be the same (23:10*b*-12). At the peak of his confidence, Job's dread returns, grounded in the overwhelming power of a God who completes what has been decreed (23:13-16). At the very end, however, the grim determination with which he began reappears, as Job refuses to be silenced (23:17).

The second part of the speech in chap. 24 returns to the problem that Job addressed in chap.

21: the absence of moral order in the world. He begins with a question that governs the rest of the chapter: Why does God not set times of judgment that are discernible to the faithful (24:1)? Job describes the world as he knows it, a world in which the most heinous types of oppression regularly occur (24:2-4) and the destitute suffer unspeakably (24:5-12b). In the absence of divine judgment, however, Job concludes that apparently God sees nothing amiss (24:12c). Job resumes with an account of the criminal violence that is a nightly occurrence (24:13-17). Challenging God's failure, Job invokes judgment on these wicked persons in almost curse-like language (24:18-20). Again, Job describes God's indulgence of the mighty who prey on the most defenseless in society (24:21-23) and demands that the retribution they deserve finally come upon them (24:24). He concludes his speech with a challenge to anyone to refute him (24:25).

23:1-7. Job's opening words echo 21:4, where he also spoke of his "complaint" against God and the urgency that gripped him. Neither Eliphaz's accusations against him nor his plea for Job to submit to God has changed anything. Now Job characterizes his complaint as "defiant" (מרי *měrî*). The LXX, followed by the NRSV and the NIV, reads instead the similar Hebrew word "bitter" (מר *mar*). It is likely that there is a play on words and that the word "bitter" brings the echo of the similar-sounding "defiant" in its wake. Job has earlier spoken of the bitterness of his soul (7:11; 10:1). Job correlates his own bitter defiance with the unrelenting pressure of God's hand.[360]

Job's defiance consists precisely of his insistence on seeking resolution for his complaint through a legal hearing rather than through the traditional religious practices of prayer and lament. As in his previous speeches, the notion of a trial with God remains in the realm of the imagination, for Job does not know how to find his way into God's presence (23:3). This time his words are altogether more confident than before. In chaps.

9–10, when the notion of a trial first occurred to him, he treated it as a subject for satire, although he could not help imagining what he would say if there were a way to restrain the overwhelming power of God. When he considered the idea again in chap. 13, Job fluctuated between confidence that he could defend himself before God and be vindicated, and fear that God's power would annihilate him. Nevertheless, he rehearsed the arguments that he would bring before God. In chap. 16, Job seemed to have given up the notion of defending himself, but envisioned an advocate who would argue his case even after his death. His thoughts began much the same way in chap. 19, envisioning a heavenly defender (גאל *gōʾēl*) who would advocate for him (19:25-26a). In the end, however, Job reasserted his ardent desire to see God for himself (19:26b-27).

Now he returns to imagining this direct encounter with God. In contrast to the earlier chapters in which Job rehearsed particular arguments (e.g., 10:2-7; 13:23-28), here he focuses on the respectful attention of the parties, as Job imagines first stating his case and supporting arguments (23:4) and then considering what God would say in reply (23:5; cf. 13:22b). Previously, the issue of God's overwhelming power blocked Job from envisioning a trial (9:32-35; 13:20-21), but now he can imagine God's restraint (23:6). The elliptical syntax of the Hebrew in 23:6b (lit., "he would fix upon me") gives rise to both the NRSV's "give heed to" and the NIV's "press charges." What makes it possible for Job to imagine a fair trial before God is Job's affirmation (23:7) that in such a setting one could reason with God and depend upon God for a just verdict. Despite the injustice of his own situation, Job cannot let go of the fundamental belief, rooted in everything that has shaped him, that God is a god of justice.

23:8-12. Job's desire for a trial, however, is blocked by the elusiveness of God. In 23:8-9, Job names the four directions of bodily orientation (NRSV), which are the same in Hebrew as the four compass directions (NIV; cf. Gen 14:15; 1 Sam 23:19; Isa 9:12[11]). Like Zophar's listing of the four components of the cosmos (heaven, Sheol, earth, sea; 11:8-9), it is an image of totality. In 23:9, the presence of possible homonyms (עשה *ʿāśâ*, "to act" or "to hide"; עטף *ʿāṭap*, "to turn" or "to cover oneself") and certain differences in the

---

360. Accepting a slight emendation of the text and reading "his hand" (ידו *yādô*) instead of "my hand" (ידי *yādî*), with the LXX. Dhorme and Good retain the MT, interpreting the line as describing suppression of grief (E. Dhorme, *A Commentary on the Book of Job,* trans. H. Knight [London: Nelson, 1967] 343) or the discouragement that comes from grief (E. Good, *In Turns of Tempest* [Stanford, Calif.: Stanford University Press, 1990] 112). Cf. the similar expression in the Babylonian poem of the righteous sufferer, *Ludlul bel nemeqi:* "His hand was heavy [upon me]. I could not bear it" (W. G. Lambert, *Babylonian Wisdom Literature* [Oxford: Clarendon, 1960] 49).

versions lead to a variety of translations. Each half line of these two verses, however, ends by reiterating the crucial point: "he is not there"; "I cannot perceive him"; "I cannot see him"; "I cannot glimpse him" (cf. 9:11). Job's frustrated search is an ironic contrast to the psalmist's imaginary flight from God in Ps 139:7-12.

Job's unwillingness to let go of the vision of vindication glimpsed in 23:4-7 leads him to attempt to overcome the problematic realization that he cannot search out the elusive God. He does this by returning to a theme that he had introduced in earlier speeches: God's scrutiny of his way (23:10; cf. 7:17-19; 10:4-7). Even if he cannot see God, God can perceive Job (cf. Ps 139:1-4). In the earlier passages, God's scrutiny and testing were experienced as hostile and unwelcome. Now, however, Job invokes the notion with the assurance that God's knowledge of him will ensure his vindication. He will be like an unknown metal that is tested and proves to be gold (v. 10b; cf. Ps 17:3). Ironically, Job has unwittingly described the scenario of the prose tale in which God's knowledge of Job's way is coupled with God's assurance that Job will prove as good as gold when tested. As Prov 17:3 notes, gold is tested in a crucible. Job, however, does not pursue the possible connection between suffering and testing.

In 23:11-12, Job comes closest to speaking in the accents of traditional prayer and wisdom. His "way" (23: 10) is defined metaphorically as walking in the steps of God, without turning aside (23:11; cf. Pss 17:5; 44:18[19]; 119:3, 59; Prov 4:27). Job describes his piety in terms of the sapiential orientation to "the precepts of his lips" and "the words of his mouth" (23:12; cf. Ps 119:13, 72, 88; Prov 2:1). Although the NIV attempts to render the MT in 23:12b ("more than my daily bread" [מחקי mēḥuqqî]),[361] most translations follow the LXX in reading "in my bosom" (בחקי bĕḥēqî). The heart or bosom is often used to suggest the integral and intimate relationship between the pious and God's word (22:22; cf. Deut 6:6; 30:14; Ps 119:11; Jer 31:33). For one brief moment, Job is once again at home with his inherited religious language and can use it to express his unity with God. That moment is fleeting, however, as Job recalls an aspect of God's character that fills him with dread.

23:13-17. Although the expression Job uses at the beginning of v. 13 is somewhat peculiar (lit., "but he is as one"), it is probably either an idiom for "unchangeable"[362] or an expression of divine sovereignty.[363] Its meaning is best judged by the rest of the verse, which describes an unopposable God who does what he pleases (cf. 9:12; 11:10). There are strong similarities between this verse and the language of Second Isaiah (e.g., Isa 43:13). What would be words of praise in Second Isaiah have a very different meaning in Job's mouth, however. The decree that God will complete concerning Job (23:14a) is God's inexplicable determination to destroy him.

The outcome of Job's meditation is a return of the terror and dread that has plagued him every time he has attempted to consider what confrontation with God really means (23:15; cf. 3:25-26; 9:34-35; 13:21). The difficult exegetical issue is how to translate 23:17 and understand its relationship to 23:16. That terror has made his heart faint (23:16) is clear, but does Job succumb to his discouragement with a return of the death wish that concluded his earlier speeches (23:17 NRSV; cf. 3:11-24; 7:21; 10:18-22)? Or does Job resist the terror and recover the note of defiant complaint with which he began (23:17 NIV)? Unfortunately, the crucial verb (צמת ṣāmat,) is not well attested in Hebrew. Etymologically, it could mean either "be destroyed" or "be silenced." In fact, it is possible that both meanings were current in Hebrew.[364] The second half of the verse can be translated grammatically either with the NRSV or the NIV. Those who favor the NRSV reading, however, must change the initial negative word "not" (לא lōʾ) to the similar-sounding word "if only" (לו lû). The context also favors a reading like that of the NIV. Job's following words in chap. 24 are more consistent with a recovered determination to resist than with a desire for oblivion. The better reading is "Yet I am not

361. Since the word means "prescription" or "rule," as well as "portion," N. Habel, *The Book of Job*, OTL (Philadelphia: Westminster, 1985) 344, translates the same term as "beyond that required of me."

362. R. Gordis, *The Book of Job: Commentary, New Translation, and Special Studies* (New York: Jewish Theological Seminary, 5738/1978) 262.

363. F. Andersen, *Job: An Introduction and Commentary,* Tyndale Old Testament Commentaries (Downers Grove, Ill.: Inter-Varsity, 1976) 210.

364. See the discussion in L. Koehler and W. Baumgartner, *Hebräisches und Aramäisches Lexikon*, 3rd ed. (Leiden: Brill, 1983) fasicle III, 970.

silenced by the darkness, or by the thick darkness that covers my face."[365]

24:1-4. Job's complaint in chap. 24 is that, in opposition to all that traditional religion has claimed, oppression and criminality flourish on the earth without any discernible sign of God's judgment. It is, nonetheless, grammatically questionable to translate the first line with either the NRSV or the NIV.[366] Gordis provides a more grammatically defensible translation: "Why, since times of judgment are not hidden from Shaddai, do His Friends not see His day (of judgment)?"[367] Following Gordis's translation, Job first cites a theological commonplace: God knows the days of judgment. Then he pointedly asks why that day never seems to arrive. After all, psalms such as Ps 37:34 promise that the pious will "inherit the land" and "look on the destruction of the wicked." Yet the friends of God see a world in which basic moral constraints are violated with impunity.

Land for agriculture and herds for pasturing were the bases of ancient Israelite economy. Moreover, land was a family heritage, so that the theft of land by moving boundary markers was an assault on the social stability of the community (24:2*a*). The seriousness of this crime is suggested by the frequency with which it is mentioned in laws (Deut 19:14), covenant curses (Deut 27:17), prophetic denunciations (Hos 5:10), and wisdom teachings (Prov 22:28; 23:10). Laws concerning animals underscore the social solidarity of the community. Not only was animal theft prohibited, but a person was also required to go after and return a neighbor's straying animal, even if that meant caring for it until it could be returned (Deut 22:1-3). Theft of entire flocks (24:2*b*) implied the utter absence of social bonds, as between warring nations (Jer 51:23) or bandits and their victims (Job 1:14, 17).

In the moral world of ancient Israel, treatment of the orphan and the widow (24:3) was the most fundamental measure of a society's moral status.

As vulnerable members of the community, they were under the special protection of God and the king (Deut 10;18; Ps 72: 12-14; Prov 23:11; Isa 1:23). Laws specifically restricted what could be taken in pledge from such persons (Deut 24:17). To take an ox or ass, essential for subsistence farming, was reprehensible (1 Sam 12:3). The vivid image of the powerful forcing the needy off the road and into hiding (24:4) concludes the listing of abuses and introduces Job's more detailed description of the wretchedness of the destitute in the following verses.

24:5-12. Job's metaphor of the destitute as wild asses that are not fed, as domestic animals are, but must forage in the dry land (24:5), captures the social and economic exclusion of the poor. The term "fodder" (בליל *bĕlîl*) in 24:6 strikes some as odd. The NRSV redivides the word and translates "not their own" (בלי לו *bĕlî lô*); others emend slightly and translate "at night" (בליל *bĕlayil*)[368] or "in the field of the villain [בליעל *bĕliyya'al*]."[369] The use of the word "fodder," however, provides a link with the animal imagery of 24:5 and suggests that the two verses be interpreted in the light of each other. The fields and vineyards where the poor scavenge are like the sparse vegetation of the wasteland. Israelite law specifically forbade the owner to go back over fields, orchards, and vineyards a second time to collect the overlooked crops; those were to be left for the poor (Lev 19:10; Deut 24:19-22). A generous owner, like Boaz in the story of Ruth, made certain that plenty was left (Ruth 2:15-16). By contrast, the owner here is described as "evil." Moreover, the word translated "glean" (לקש *liqqēš*) is not the usual one but may refer to picking the fruit that ripens only after the main harvest.[370] If so, then the food available is extremely scanty.[371]

The destitution of these wretched of the earth is absolute (24:7-8). They are without adequate clothes against the cold, without shelter from the driving rain. Homeless, they huddle against a rock for protection. The "rock" is a traditional image of God as protector (Pss 18:2[3]; 62:2[3], 6-7[7-8];

---

365. Similarly, Dhorme, *A Commentary on the Book of Job,* 352; contra M. Pope, *Job,* 3rd ed., AB 15 (Garden City, N.Y.: Doubleday, 1979)173; cf. Gordis, *The Book of Job,* 263; Habel, *The Book of Job,* 346.

366. The expression מן נצפנו (*nispĕnû min*) means "hidden from" or possibly "stored up by," but scarcely "kept by" or "set." Moreover, judging from the context, Job does not seem to be asking why God does not *delay* retribution, as the translation "why are times (of judgment) not stored up by Shaddai" would suggest (cf. 21:19-20, where Job rejects delayed retribution as morally worthless).

367. Gordis, *The Book of Job,* 264.

368. Dhorme, *A Commentary on the Book of Job,* 358.

369. Pope, *Job,* 176.

370. S. R. Driver and G. B. Gray, *A Critical and Exegetical Commentary on the Book of Job,* ICC (Edinburgh: T. & T. Clark, 1921) Part II, 166-67.

371. See Dhorme, *A Commentary on the Book of Job,* 356-58, for a different interpretation of these verses.

71:3; 94:22). Use of that word here gives Job's words an added sting. Job's language also echoes the imagery of passages like Isa 25:4, which says of God: "you have been a stronghold for the poor, a stronghold for the needy in their distress; a shelter from the driving rain, shade from the heat" (author's trans.).

The indigent are also vulnerable to the cruelty of their creditors (24: 9). Second Kings 4:1-7 tells the story of a widow whose children had been taken as slaves because she could not pay her debt. In that story, the prophet of God works a miracle of abundance that redeems the children and provides for their future security; Job draws attention to the vast majority for whom there is no wonder-working prophet.

Without resources of their own, the poor must work as day laborers in the fields of those who have much (24:10-11). The scandal of the hungry carrying grain and the thirsty treading the wine grapes is enhanced by the echo of Deut 25:4, which prohibits a farmer from muzzling an ox as it treads out the grain. The exploited laborer lacks even the consideration afforded the ox.

This grim panorama of wretchedness ends, appropriately, with a scene of the wounded and dying who groan and cry out vainly for help (24:12ab). The shock comes as Job suddenly shifts perspective from human misery to divine perception (24:12c). In the face of misery and oppression that contradicts all that covenant law tries to establish, Job observes that "God charges no one with wrongdoing." The NRSV's translation, "yet God pays no attention to their prayer," depends on a slight emendation of the Hebrew text (from תפלה [tiplâ, "wrongdoing"] to תפלה [těpillâ, "prayer"]). Although there is no sufficient reason to change the Hebrew text, poetic language often exploits the relationship between the word actually written and the echo of similar words with different meanings. Both translations are required for one to hear the text in all the fullness of its meaning, the NIV representing the primary tone, the NRSV a poetic overtone. God's responses of judgment and salvation alike depend on God's hearing the cry of the oppressed and taking note of the crimes of the oppressor (cf. Exod 2:21-25).

In 24:12, Job's initial question about why the friends of God do not see God's day of judgment (24:1) finds an ironic answer: God does not per-

ceive anything wrong with the world. The word "wrongdoing" (tiplâ) has another significant echo. It is the same word used in 1:22, where after the loss of his wealth, servants, and children, "Job did not sin by charging God with wrongdoing" (NIV).

24:13-17. In these verses, Job evokes the moral chaos of criminality. The term *chaos* is particularly apt, since Job uses the image of the reversal of the values of light and darkness, the primordial structures of creation (Gen 1:3-5), to suggest the destructiveness that results when fundamental prohibitions are violated. The three types of criminals whom Job names—the murderer, the adulterer, and the house-breaker (cf. Hos 4:2; Jer 7:9)—respectively threaten the life of the individual, the integrity of the marital bond, and the security of the household. These are the elements upon which the social life of the entire community depends. Thus it is appropriate that Job calls the criminals "rebels against the light" (24:13). In contrast to his own close adherence to the "steps" and "way" of God (23:11), the threatening, chaotic nature of criminals is suggested by their alienation from the established ways and paths of light (24:13).

In successive verses, Job describes the inverted worlds of the three types of criminals. Reversing the normal order, the murderer rises at dusk to do his work in the night (24:14). Job's critique of criminality is related to his social critique in 24:2-12, for he observes that the victims tend to be precisely the vulnerable "poor and needy." The adulterer is described through a poetic play with the image of the "eye," a part of the body closely associated with illicit desire (cf. 31:1; Prov 6:25). The adulterer's eye watches for dusk (cf. Prov 7:8), when there is insufficient light for another eye to discern him (24:15). Similarly, the house-breaker digs at night (24:16; cf. Exod 22:2) when others do not work, and seals himself up during the day when others go out to work (Ps 104:23). Job concludes his account of this counterworld of the criminal in 24:17 with an ironic comment. Traditionally, morning is the time of security and returning hope, and deep darkness (lit., "shadow of death") the time of fearfulness; but for these perverted beings the values are reversed.

24:18-25. If these verses are taken as simple declarative sentences, as in most translations, then the whole section is completely incongruous in

Job's mouth, for it would be a statement about the certainty of God's judgment against the wicked. This incongruity leads many commentators to assume that these verses are part of the missing speech of Zophar or Bildad, somehow erroneously attached to Job's speech (see Overview above). The early versions—the LXX, the Vulgate, and the Peshitta—point to a better understanding of these verses, however. They translate them as optatives—that is, as Job's wish for what should happen. This interpretation is not without its own grammatical problems.[372] Nevertheless, this approach offers an interpretation that does justice to the tensions with which Job is struggling in chaps. 23–24 and is consistent with rhetorical techniques he has already used in chap. 21. Of the current translations, the Tanakh, which translates these verses as Job's curse upon the criminal, comes closest to the interpretation proposed here.[373]

Job believes passionately and fervently in justice. Moreover, he cannot abandon the belief that God is a god of justice. That is why the legal metaphor is so important to Job's thinking and why he begins his speech in chap. 23 with a vivid evocation of a trial in which God appears as the just and reasonable judge. When Job says in 24:1, "why, since times of judgment are not hidden from God, do his friends not see his days?" it is partly a rhetorical question, but partly a genuine one. Verses 2-17 express Job's angry conviction that there are in fact no days of judgment. Verses 18-25 express Job's anguished demand that his belief in God's justice not turn out to be a lie. The rhetorical form in which this urgent plea is expressed is not unlike 21:17-21, where Job's struggle with the absence of evident judgment leads him to a demand: Let it be done.

24:18-20. This section begins with a peculiar statement: "קַל [qal] is he upon the face of the water" (24:18). Job is presumably speaking of the criminal, whose perverted values he has just finished describing. The Hebrew word qal can mean "swift" (NRSV) or "light," "insignificant," hence the NIV's "foam." Since there is a close similarity with the word "cursed" (קִלֵּל qillēl), which appears in the second half of the verse, one suspects

that qal is pejorative. Although it is not certain, the REB may have the right nuance, "Such men are scum [qal] on the surface of the water." Job's evaluative description provides the transition from his account of the criminals to his wish/curse/demand for their punishment: "let their portion of the land be cursed [תְּקֻלַּל tĕqullal], so that no one goes to the vineyards."

In an earlier speech, Job used the image of a wadi that dries up in the heat as a symbol of something disastrously changed from what one expects (6:15-17). Here Job invokes the image as a metaphor for the power of Sheol over the sinner: "let dryness and heat consume snow waters, Sheol those who have sinned" (24:19; cf. Ps 49:14[15]). The imagery of life and death, initiated in 24:19, is developed in 24:20 with the contrasting reactions of the womb, a symbol of life, and the worm, a symbol of death. Since a person who died continued to be part of the community through the memory of others, the motif of forgetting contributes to the picture of the sinner's utter annihilation: "let the womb forget him, the worm find him sweet, until he is no longer remembered." The final image, "and let iniquity be broken like a stick," recalls the type of symbolic images of destruction often included in treaty curses.[374] In Ezek 37:15-23, the joining of two sticks is a symbol of reunification.

24:21-25. Grammatical ambiguities and words with a wide range of possible meanings permit a bewildering variety of translations for these verses (e.g., NRSV, NIV, TNK). None of these translations is without difficulties, but neither is any so arbitrary as to be impossible. I am inclined to follow the NRSV's translation of 24:21-23 as both defensible in its grammatical interpretations and consistent with the overall content of the chapter. The cruelty of the wicked toward the defenseless is the central feature of Job's description of the world, and no one represents such defenselessness more than the widow without children (24:21). The contradiction tormenting Job is that God, who is supposed to defend just such persons (Deut 10:18; cf. Isa 54:1), instead appears to favor the powerful oppressor of the weak (24:22-23). As Job said earlier in a similar context, "If it is not he, who then is it?" (9:24

---

372. Driver-Gray, *A Critical and Exegetical Commentary on the Book of Job*, 211; but see J. E. Hartley, *The Book of Job*, NICOT (Grand Rapids, Mich.: Eerdmans, 1988) 350-51.

373. See also Hartley, *The Book of Job*, 350-54.

374. *ANET*, 539.

NRSV). The burden of this chapter is Job's urgent need to resolve the contradiction and to see clearly the days of judgment supposedly known to God. Thus in 24:24 he returns to his demand that what tradition has claimed should be done. One may translate: "Exalted for a little while, let them be no more. Let them be brought low and shriveled up like grass; and like the heads of grain let them be cut off."

Job ends in a defiant mood. At the conclusion of his previous speech, he had rejected the friends' arguments as worthless and false. Correspondingly, he now defends the truth and significance of his own words with an angry challenge (24:25).

REFLECTIONS

There is no stronger indictment of God in the book of Job than the depiction in chap. 24 of divine indifference in the face of the pervasive misery, abuse, and injustice endured by the most vulnerable of people. We tend to think of the twentieth century as unique in its experience of evil so enormous that it makes the very idea of God a scandal. It is not just because of the Holocaust, although that event remains the most numbing of horrors. There is also the experience of wars of unparalleled destruction, oppression on a previously unimaginable scale, and crushing poverty created by the very forces that brought unprecedented wealth to a minority of the world's population. The book of Job reminds us that others have also struggled with the theological scandal presented by a world where injustice is rampant.

For those nurtured in the religious traditions of the Bible, belief in God and belief in God as a champion of justice and a protector of the vulnerable are inseparable ideas. The central event in the faith of Israel is the exodus, portrayed as God's response to the suffering of God's people: " 'I have observed the misery of my people who are in Egypt; I have heard their cry on account of their taskmasters. Indeed, I know their sufferings, and I have come down to deliver them from the Egyptians' " (Exod 3:7-8a NRSV). This is the God who says, "You shall not wrong or oppress a resident alien. . . . You shall not abuse any widow or orphan. If you do abuse them, when they cry out to me, I will surely heed their cry" (Exod 22:21-23 NRSV). This is the God whom the psalmist calls "lover of justice" who establishes equity (Ps 99:4). This is the God whom Amos represents as "roaring" in anger at the war crimes, social abuses, and lawlessness of many nations (Amos 1–2). Taking the Bible seriously requires that one take seriously its claims about God's active role in establishing and preserving justice. But how can one say those words over the body of an abandoned child who starved to death or speak those words to a peasant woman raped and tortured by soldiers? How can one say those words in the shadow of Auschwitz?

It is hard to stay with this contradiction between what the Bible affirms about God and the atrocities that speak of God's absence. One is tempted to speak instead about human evil and the need for human resistance to evil, or to change the focus and talk about God's sustaining presence with the victim, or to reinterpret God's power in terms of non-coercive love. These are not irrelevant matters—they have their place—but they must not be engaged too quickly or used as a means of evading the painful contradiction itself. Martin Buber aptly calls this contradiction "the rent in the heart of the world."[375]

In a paradoxical way, one often comes to know the meaning of a thing through its absence rather than its presence. An illustration, which originally derives from the philosopher Heidegger, makes this point. It speaks of a carpenter who goes into his well-furnished workshop, with its stacks of wood, containers of nails, and racks of tools. Intent on the activity of the project, the carpenter pays little attention to the individual items. The wood, the nails, the hammer are simply taken for granted as part of the whole of the carpenter's activity. But suddenly, the hammer breaks, the shaft snapping off at the head. For the first time the carpenter

375. M. Buber, *The Prophetic Faith* (New York: Harper and Bros., 1949) 191.

becomes genuinely aware of the hammer. It has never been so vivid in its wholeness as it has become in its brokenness. The image of the hammer, what it does, how essential it is to the task of carpentry, are all inescapably present to the carpenter precisely because of its absence. So it is with Job. One can imagine Job before his catastrophe speaking fluently about God, justice, and the moral order of the world. In a certain sense, he would have understood what he was talking about, but only in a way comparable to the carpenter who, as he walked into the workshop, could have described the wood, the nails, and the hammer. Only now that Job has experienced the brokenness of justice and the absence of the God of justice does he possess the urgent, existential knowledge of justice and of God.

This illustration also suggests why Job and so many others who have experienced the unendurable do not simply dismiss God as an illusion. It would seem so much easier to do so, yet for these persons God's love and passion for justice are no more an illusion than the hammer is for the carpenter. They have known it and experienced it and can doubt its existence no more than their own reality. What is unbearable is the equally undeniable experience of its brokenness and its absence, just where it should be most present. This is the unresolved contradiction in Job's speech (chaps. 23–24), which contains his passionate belief in a God of justice and his devastating expose of a God indifferent to a world of injustice.

What kind of faith is possible for a person who refuses to let go of either reality? Martin Buber says of Job that in spite of all that he experienced, "Job's faith in justice is not broken down. But he is no longer able to have a *single faith* in God and in justice. . . . He believes now in justice in spite of believing in God, and he believes in God in spite of believing in justice. But he cannot forego his claim that they will again be united somewhere, sometime, although he has no idea in his mind how this will be achieved."[376]

The faith of Job, as expressed in chaps. 23–24, is the prototype of the defiant post-Holocaust faith of many of the characters in the books and plays of Elie Wiesel. In *The Trial,* a play with many similarities to the book of Job, the character Berish is just such a Job-like figure. A survivor of a pogrom in which virtually the entire Jewish community of the village of Shamgorod was destroyed, Berish engages a troupe of Purim actors to stage a "trial" of God, with Berish acting as the prosecutor. He speaks as witness for all the slaughtered: "Let their premature, unjust deaths turn into an outcry so forceful that it will make the universe tremble with fear and remorse!"[377] The trial is interrupted by the news that a second pogrom is about to occur. Berish refuses to save himself by accepting a priest's offer to baptize him, saying, "My sons and my fathers perished without betraying their faith; I can do no less."[378] He denies, however, that this decision suggests a reconciliation with God. "I lived as a Jew, and it is as a Jew that I shall die—and it is as a Jew that, with my last breath, I shall shout my protest to God! And because the end is near, I shall shout louder! Because the end is near, I'll tell Him that He's more guilty than ever!"[379] Berish's decision is to live and die in faithful defiance/defiant faithfulness. As difficult as that may be, for many it is the only authentic response to the biblical God.

376. Ibid., 192.
377. E. Wiesel, *The Trial* (New York: Schocken Books, 1979), 130.
378. Ibid., 154.
379. Ibid., 156.

Job 25:1–26:14, Bildad and Job Argue About the Power of God

NIV

25 Then Bildad the Shuhite replied:

2"Dominion and awe belong to God;
    he establishes order in the heights of heaven.

NRSV

25 Then Bildad the Shuhite answered:
2 "Dominion and fear are with God;[a]
    he makes peace in his high heaven.

a Heb *him*

NIV

3Can his forces be numbered?
Upon whom does his light not rise?
4How then can a man be righteous before God?
How can one born of woman be pure?
5If even the moon is not bright
and the stars are not pure in his eyes,
6how much less man, who is but a maggot—
a son of man, who is only a worm!"

26 Then Job replied:

2"How you have helped the powerless!
How you have saved the arm that is feeble!
3What advice you have offered to one without wisdom!
And what great insight you have displayed!
4Who has helped you utter these words?
And whose spirit spoke from your mouth?

5"The dead are in deep anguish,
those beneath the waters and all that live in them.
6Death^a is naked before God;
Destruction^b lies uncovered.
7He spreads out the northern ⌊skies⌋ over empty space;
he suspends the earth over nothing.
8He wraps up the waters in his clouds,
yet the clouds do not burst under their weight.
9He covers the face of the full moon,
spreading his clouds over it.
10He marks out the horizon on the face of the waters
for a boundary between light and darkness.
11The pillars of the heavens quake,
aghast at his rebuke.
12By his power he churned up the sea;
by his wisdom he cut Rahab to pieces.
13By his breath the skies became fair;
his hand pierced the gliding serpent.
14And these are but the outer fringe of his works;
how faint the whisper we hear of him!
Who then can understand the thunder of his power?"

a6 Hebrew *Sheol*   b6 Hebrew *Abaddon*

NRSV

3 Is there any number to his armies?
Upon whom does his light not arise?
4 How then can a mortal be righteous before God?
How can one born of woman be pure?
5 If even the moon is not bright
and the stars are not pure in his sight,
6 how much less a mortal, who is a maggot,
and a human being, who is a worm!"

26 Then Job answered:
2 "How you have helped one who has no power!
How you have assisted the arm that has no strength!
3 How you have counseled one who has no wisdom,
and given much good advice!
4 With whose help have you uttered words,
and whose spirit has come forth from you?
5 The shades below tremble,
the waters and their inhabitants.
6 Sheol is naked before God,
and Abaddon has no covering.
7 He stretches out Zaphon^a over the void,
and hangs the earth upon nothing.
8 He binds up the waters in his thick clouds,
and the cloud is not torn open by them.
9 He covers the face of the full moon,
and spreads over it his cloud.
10 He has described a circle on the face of the waters,
at the boundary between light and darkness.
11 The pillars of heaven tremble,
and are astounded at his rebuke.
12 By his power he stilled the Sea;
by his understanding he struck down Rahab.
13 By his wind the heavens were made fair;
his hand pierced the fleeing serpent.
14 These are indeed but the outskirts of his ways;
and how small a whisper do we hear of him!
But the thunder of his power who can understand?"

a Or *the North*

COMMENTARY

Chapters 25–26 pose difficult interpretive questions. As the text stands, Bildad's speech in chap. 25 is only six verses long. Job begins his speech in chap. 26 with sarcastic remarks of the sort that have opened several of his other speeches. The body of the speech in 26:5-15, however, a description of God's creative power, lacks the ironic touches that characterize Job's previous use of that theme (e.g., 9:2-10; 12:13-25) and is not what one expects to hear from Job. No speech by Zophar follows chap. 26. Instead, chap. 27 begins with the unusual notice "Job again took up his discourse and said . . . " (27:1). That same notice is used to introduce Job's speech in chaps. 29–31, following the poem on wisdom in chap. 28.

Although the third cycle of speeches may have been damaged and garbled in the copying of the text, one should be cautious in attempting to reconstruct what may never have existed. The text itself gives certain clues as to how the speeches are to be sorted out, although these clues are not unambiguous. The starting place is the unique introductory formula that occurs in 27:1 and 29:1. To say that Job "again" took up his discourse suggests that it has been interrupted. Most scholars regard chap. 28 as an independent poem separating Job's final speech in the dialogue (chap. 27) from his summation and challenge to God (chaps. 29–31). Thus, even though chap. 28 is not marked at the beginning as an independent poem, the notice in 29:1 is an *ex post facto* acknowledgment that it should be read as such. The relationship of chaps. 28 and 29 provides an analogy for understanding the significance of 27:1. There, too, the notice that Job "again" took up his discourse suggests that it had been interrupted by the immediately preceding material. As with chap. 28, the beginning of that interruption is not marked in the text, but the change in style and content suggests that the interruption consists of 26:5-14.[380]

If this is the case, then whose words are 26:5-14? Although it is possible to understand

them as an independent poem, like chap. 28,[381] most scholars regard them as the second part of Bildad's speech.[382] What happens in these chapters represents the deterioration of the dialogue. Bildad begins to speak in 25:1-6, but is interrupted by Job, who sarcastically mocks what Bildad has said (26:1-4). Undeterred, Bildad completes his speech (26:5-14), at which point Job resumes his discourse. Such a structure may be the author's attempt to represent the interruptive and even overlapping speech of the parties to a conversation that has irretrievably broken down.

25:1-6. Like Eliphaz in 22:2, Bildad begins abruptly, without the introductory remarks that have characterized his previous speeches (8:2-4; 18:2-4). His theme is announced in the first words he speaks: the dominion and awesomeness of God (25:2*a*). Throughout his speech, this theme will be developed by reference to the mythic acts of God as creator and governor of the cosmos. Although many details of his description are distinctive, it has been suggested that his account employs a sequence of themes similar to the creation poem in Psalm 104.[383]

Bildad's statement that God "makes peace" ("establishes order" [NIV]) in the heights of heaven alludes to traditions about conflict among the gods or a rebellion in heaven. The OT itself contains only a few allusions to these myths (e.g., Isa 14:12-15). The narratives lying behind these allusions, however, seem to have influenced later apocalyptic traditions of a revolt of the angels and war in heaven (cf. Daniel 10; *1 Enoch* 6–11; 1QM). The troops of God the divine warrior, to which Bildad refers in 25:3*a,* are a frequent motif in epic poetry (Deut 33:2-3; Judg 5:20), in

---

380. Alternatively, A. B. Davidson, *The Book of Job,* Cambridge Bible for Schools and Colleges 15 (Cambridge: Cambridge University Press, 1891) 186; and E. Good, *In Turns of Tempest* (Stanford, Calif.: Stanford University Press, 1990) 286, suggest that the notice in 27:1 does not reflect an interruption but Job's pause, as he waits in vain for Zophar to speak. See also J. E. Hartley, *The Book of Job,* NICOT (Grand Rapids, Mich.: Eerdmans, 1988) 368.

381. So G. Fohrer, *Das Buch Hiob,* KAT xvi (Guetersloh: Gerd Mohn, 1963) 381-85.

382. E.g., R. Gordis, *The Book of Job: Commentary, New Translation, and Special Studies* (New York: Jewish Theological Seminary, 5738/1978) 534-35; M. Pope, *Job,* 3rd ed., AB 15 (Garden City, N.Y.: Doubleday, 1979) 180-86; N. Habel, *The Book of Job,* OTL (Philadelphia: Westminster, 1985) 366-68. Janzen assumes that Job is the speaker, but that in these verses Job "finishes Bildad's speech for him . . . with an angry sureness of eloquence and tone" (J. G. Janzen, *Job,* Interpretation [Atlanta: John Knox, 1985] 173). Janzen's suggestion is a very appealing one, although it does not entirely account for the unique form of the introduction in 27:1.

383. R. J. Clifford, *Creation Accounts in the Ancient Near East and in the Bible.* CBQMS 26 (Washington: Catholic Biblical Association, 1994) 190.

psalms (Ps 68:17[18]), and in prophetic poetry (Isa 40:26; Hab 3:5). Similarly, the shining of God's light in 25:3*b* is also associated with the appearance of the divine warrior, much as Deut 33:2-3 speaks of God "dawning" from Seir and "shining forth" from Mount Paran, as God approaches with the heavenly army.

In terms of poetic imagery, the continuation of Bildad's description appears in 26:5, where the trembling of the "shades" is described. Bildad, however, inserts a parenthetical observation into his description of the divine warrior's might, indicating the significance of his words for the issue at hand (25:4-6). Taking up the theme introduced by Eliphaz twice before (4:17-19; 15:14-16), Bildad asks rhetorically whether a mere human being can be righteous or pure before God (25:4). The first line of Bildad's question is also a literal citation of Job's words in 9:2*b*. Whereas Job framed the question in legal terms, Bildad develops the line in a way that makes it clear he understands the issue to pertain to human existence itself.

Like Eliphaz, Bildad refers to the human as one "born of woman" (25:4*b*), a phrase that connotes mortality. That which is born also must die. In 25:6, Bildad makes this point in a striking figure of speech. Calling a human being "worm" and "maggot" draws attention to the brutal fact that bodies decay; where flesh was, worms will be. Throughout Job's speeches the worm is a symbol of death and Sheol (7:5; 17:14; 21:26; 24:20). Bildad juxtaposes this earthy image to that of the moon and the stars, heavenly entities characterized by light rather than mortal flesh (Gen 1:14-16; Isa 60:20; Jer 31:35). These are creatures of God that stand high in the hierarchy of the cosmos (Pss 8:3[4]; 148:3), entrusted with responsibility (Ps 136:9), symbols of what is not mortal (Ps 72:7). The moon is even designated a "faithful witness" (Ps 89:37[38]). Bildad uses a pun to make his point. The word that means "morally pure" (זכה *zākâ*, 25:4*b*) is related to a word that means both "morally pure" and "bright" (זכך *zākak*, 25:5). If even the heavenly luminaries are not "bright"/"pure" before God, how could what is characterized by dark, wormy decay be so? The implicit logic in Bildad's comparison is that physical corruption and moral corruption are two aspects of the same reality.

26:1-4. Job interrupts Bildad at this point (26:1). In contrast to most of Job's opening words, these are not addressed to the friends as a group, but to Bildad alone (cf. 21:3*b*). Since Bildad has characterized human existence in terms of its physical and moral inferiority, Job makes this the starting point of his remarks. He sardonically refers to himself, the recipient of Bildad's help, rescue, and counsel, as one "without power . . . without strength . . . without wisdom" (26:2-3*a*). There is a subtle linguistic play, however. The words that at first glance appear to describe Job could also be taken as phrases describing Bildad's advice. "How you have helped, without strength! How you have rescued, with a powerless arm! How you have counseled, without wisdom! And you have given your advice so abundantly!"[384] Job's rhetorical question in 26:4 concerning the source of Bildad's remarkable words hovers between personal insult and blasphemy. It suggests on the one hand that Bildad needed assistance even to mouth such banalities. On the other hand, if Bildad is understood to speak divine truths, then Job's contempt for those words extends to their divine source as well.

26:5-14. As suggested above, Bildad's and Job's speeches are interwoven. Ignoring Job's interruption, Bildad continues with his invocation of God's majesty. Job will resume his own interrupted words in 27:1.

26:5-6. In 25:2-3, Bildad described God the divine warrior. Now in vv. 5-6 he describes the terror with which the underworld responds to God's appearance. The "shades" (רפאים *rĕpāʾîm*) are the dead who persist in shadowy form in Sheol (see Ps 88:10[11]; Prov 2:18; 9:18; 21:16). In Isaiah 14:9, there is a trace of the old mythological tradition that the *rĕpāʾîm* are the spirits of dead heroes and kings. As in several other places in the OT, the presumption that the underworld is situated at the bottom of the sea (26:5*b*; cf. 2 Sam 22:5-6; Pss 18:4-5[5-6]; 88:6-7[7-8]; Jonah 2:2-6). The motif of the exposure of the channels of the sea by the divine warrior's gusty breath (cf. Ps 18:15[16]) and the motif of the visibility of Sheol and Abaddon to God's eye (Prov 15:11) may be merged in Bildad's image (26:6). Bildad, however, adds a vivid note of personification in his use of

---

384. Translated similarly by the NEB, the TNK, and Habel, *The Book of Job*, 375.

the terms "naked" (ערום 'ārôm) and "without covering" (אין כסות 'ên kĕsût; cf. 24:7). The term "Abaddon" is a synonym for "Sheol," derived from the Hebrew verb "to perish" (אבד 'ābad).

26:7-9. Bildad changes both the focus of his description and the literary form. Here his gaze moves from the underworld to the cosmic mountain of God, and his style becomes hymnic (in Hebrew vv. 7-9 all begin with participles; cf. the style of 5:9-13). Instead of the expected poetic image of stretching out the heavens (cf. 9:8; Ps 104:2; Isa 40:22), Bildad refers to God stretching out "the north" (26:7). The north (צפון ṣāpôn) is the designation of the mythic mountain that is the site of the divine assembly, Mount Zaphon (see Isa 14:13; Mount Zaphon has the same function in Ugaritic mythology). In this way, Bildad's image of the establishment of the cosmos incorporates an image of divine governance. The striking imagery of 26:7 uses "chaos" (תהו tōhû; cf. Gen 1:2, "formless and empty" [תהו ובהו tōhû wābōhû]) and "nothing" (בלי־מה bĕlî-mâ, lit., "without-what") as contrasting parallels to the heavenly mount of assembly and the earth. The figure of the void provides a vivid contrast for the creative power of God in stretching out the celestial north and suspending the earth from it. Because of the poetic nature of the language, it is difficult to say whether Bildad's description represents a significant departure from traditional Israelite cosmology,[385] or whether it is simply an alternative way of speaking of the tripartite structure of heavens, earth, and chaotic waters.[386]

Control over rain is a divine power (5:10; 36:27-29; Deut 28:12; 1 Kgs 18:1; Ps 65:9-10[10-11]; Prov 30:4), and rain is often represented as being held in celestial storehouses (Jer 10:13; Sir 43:14). Here the clouds are depicted as the storage containers (cf. 38:37). The use of the verb "split" (בקע bāqaʿ) in 26:8b suggests the concrete image of the clouds as waterskins. The concluding image of this section of Bildad's poem in 26:9 is connected to the preceding by the focus on clouds. Because of an ambiguous word, it is not clear whether Bildad refers to God covering "the full moon" (כסה keseh)[387] with a screen of clouds

or covering his "throne" (כסא kissēʾ; cf. 22:14; Ps 97:2).[388] Given the immediate context, "full moon" seems more appropriate.

26:10. The horizon has always held a strong fascination for the human imagination, because it is such a visible marker of the structure of the cosmos. As in Prov 8:27, Bildad understands it to be a circle inscribed on the cosmic waters, a boundary marker dividing the light from the darkness (26:10; cf. Isa 40:22). In the Mesopotamian story of Gilgamesh, the Mashu mountains are a similar cosmic boundary marker, the very place where the sun moves from the upper world to the nether world.[389]

26:11-14. The concluding verses of Bildad's description return to the dynamic myth of the creation of the cosmos in the divine warrior's battle with the watery chaos monster. As in other accounts, the appearance of the divine warrior with his thunderous battle cry causes shaking and fear among the mountains, here described as the "pillars of the sky" (26:11; cf. Pss 18:7[8]; 29:3-9; 114:3-7). Verse 12 describes the cosmic battle with the Sea/Rahab. Yahweh's battle with the sea is of the same type and has the same significance as Baal's battle with Yam in Ugaritic mythology[390] and Marduk's battle with Tiamat in Mesopotamian religion.[391] The name "Rahab," which is frequently used in biblical texts for the sea monster, means something like "the boisterous" or "stormy one" (see 9:13; Pss 89:10[11]; Isa 51:9). Only with the subjugation of chaotic forces, so aptly represented in the shapeless but powerful waters of the sea, can the structures necessary to support life be established.

Bildad names both "power" and "wisdom" as the means by which God's victory is achieved (see also Jer 10:12). As Pope observes, cleverness or the assistance of a clever helper is a characteristic in Mesopotamian and Ugaritic myths as well.[392] Curiously, the verb in 26:12a (רגע rāgaʿ) can mean either "stir up" (NIV, "churned up") or "still" (NRSV). Since the Sea rather than the divine warrior is typically depicted as the aggressor

385. So Habel, *The Book of Job*, 371.
386. So Hartley, *The Book of Job*, 366.
387. See Fohrer, *Das Buch Hiob*, 382; Pope, *Job*, 184. The suggestion goes back to the medieval Jewish scholar Ibn Ezra.

388. So Gordis, *The Book of Job*, 279; Habel, *The Book of Job*, 365.
389. *ANET*, 88.
390. Ibid., 130-31.
391. Ibid., 66-67. For a broad overview, see R. J. Clifford, *Creation Accounts in the Ancient Near East and in the Bible*; J. Day, *God's Conflict with the Dragon and the Sea* (Cambridge: Cambridge University Press, 1985).
392. Pope, *Job*, 185.

in the cosmogonic battle, "stilled" is preferable here, signifying the subjugation of the chaotic forces. Although wind or breath is a characteristic weapon of the divine warrior against the sea (26:13a; e.g., Exod 15:8; Ps 18:15[16]), a reference to the sky's becoming fair is not otherwise associated with such accounts. Attempts to emend the text have produced some intriguing suggestions, but none is entirely persuasive.[393] Piercing the fleeing serpent, however, is a familiar

image, both from Ugaritic mythology[394] and from Israelite accounts (see Isa 27:1; 51:9).

Bildad concludes his account of God's dominion and awesomeness in a rhetorically effective manner (26:14). Having given a remarkably vivid account of the cosmogonic battle and the structures of the cosmos, he minimizes what he has said, declaring that all of this is only the "outskirts," a "whisper." The full force of the powerful thunder of God's majesty is beyond human comprehension.

393. Pope (ibid., 181), suggests "By his wind he bagged the Sea," an image that evokes the strategy used by Marduk to subdue Tiamat.

394. *ANET,* 137.

REFLECTIONS

The clash in perspective between Job's speech in chaps. 23–24 and Bildad's in chaps. 25–26 could not be more profound. Job's religious imagination is deeply grounded in the ethical and the personal (see Commentary on Job 23; 24). By contrast, Bildad's religious imagination is grounded in a profound sense of the holy and of the "wholly otherness" of God. He is drawn to the experience of the transcendent, as his imagery reflects. In Bildad's speech, one encounters absolute heights and depths, immense voids, distant horizons, mythic conflicts. Both Job's perspective and that of Bildad have deep roots in Israelite religion. Yet juxtaposed as they are here, one is aware of their radical differences and not surprised that these two individuals cannot communicate with each other.

One can deduce what Bildad finds unacceptable in Job's speech. From his perspective, Job has let the "personal" quality of God become an intimacy that destroys the necessary and proper sense of awe that should be present in religious experience. Job has made God accountable to Job himself and talks as though they were two neighbors with a quarrel. Anyone who has listened closely to Job knows, of course, that his language about God is more complex than that. Nevertheless, the general point is worth thinking about. The Judeo-Christian tradition uses personal and intimate language about God with a striking boldness, especially in traditions of prayer and psalmody. To speak of God, the creator of the universe, in parental images or to pour out one's innermost pains in the confidence that God will listen is an extraordinary claim to make. If the necessary tension between the augustness of God and intimacy with God is lost, however, personal language becomes a shallow sentimentality. One sees this in certain traditional hymns, as well as in much contemporary Christian music. Or it may find expression in the general domestication of the image of God, so that God becomes an amiable caregiver, rather like the congregation's image of the ideal pastor. Bildad may be shocked at Job's language about God; he would be absolutely appalled if he listened to the language about God that flows freely at Sunday morning services in many contemporary churches.

Bildad champions a very different kind of experience of God and language about God. It is very close to what historian of religion Rudolf Otto wrote about in his classic study *The Idea of the Holy.* Otto stressed what he called a quality of "wholly otherness," which cannot be evoked by personal imagery. Its characteristics are an awefulness that produces a profound dread, an overpowering sense of majesty, a forceful energy, and yet an element of fascination. The great theophanic images of Yahweh in the Bible use imagery that attempts to communicate such an experience: the imagery of whirlwind, of fire, of the numinous cloud that glows from within and yet shields the divine presence from view. Bildad's language, although it is more graphically mythic, has many of these same qualities of the *mysterium tremendum et fascinans* that Otto describes.

In another respect, too, Bildad draws out an implication similar to what Otto discusses. An encounter with the holy, Otto noted, produces an experience of "creature-consciousness," which he describes as "the emotion of a creature, submerged and overwhelmed by its own nothingness in contrast to that which is supreme above all creatures."[395] It is an experience of the "annihilation of the self" that comes with contemplation of that which is absolute being. This is the experience to which Bildad refers in 25:4-6, when he contrasts the exalted being of God, before whom even the moon and stars are not bright, with the nothingness of mortal decay, which is human existence. Such an experience is far from a negative one, for it is accompanied by a sense of participating in that transcendent reality.[396] In mystical encounter, the structures of the individual ego are broken down and one's identity is taken up into the holy itself. Otto cites the experience recounted by William James: "The perfect stillness of the night was thrilled by a more solemn silence. The darkness held a presence that was all the more felt because it was not seen. I could not any more have doubted that *He* was there than that I was. Indeed, I felt myself to be, if possible, the less real of the two."[397] Although Bildad is not so explicit, he renders this experience poetically by drawing the reader so much into the transcendent description of God's majesty that it comes almost as a shock when he shifts the perspective back to that of the finite mortal in 26:14, declaring that all this majesty is but a whisper of the ineffable thunder of the divine reality.

Although Bildad may simply be reacting to what he considers the blasphemous familiarity and lack of respect in Job's way of talking about God, one needs to ask how the language of "the holy" would address the experience of suffering and whether it possesses resources for consolation. In at least one important respect it does. One of the characteristics of acute suffering is its tendency to obliterate all other experience. It can become almost impossible to see, hear, or feel anything beyond one's own suffering, as though that suffering were all that existed in the world. In such a situation, images of God that stress the intimate, personal quality of God, likening God to one who suffers with the grieving, may not be what is needed. What one craves is reassurance that one's own suffering is *not* the whole of reality. The religious experience of the holiness of God, of God as wholly otherness, is capable of providing such reassurance. As Bildad's speech suggests, religious language that speaks of the transcendence of God often does so in terms of creation. God's power in overcoming chaos and establishing the reliable structures of the cosmos can be an important support for one whose own experience is a wilderness of pain and anxiety. Thus one should not assume that only the religious traditions that speak of God in personal and intimate terms are of importance to one who suffers. There is also solace to be found in the language of God's majesty and transcendence.

395. R. Otto, *The Idea of the Holy*, 2nd ed., trans. J. W. Harvey (London: Oxford University Press, 1958; 1st ed. 1923) 10.
396. Ibid., 21-22.
397. Ibid., 22-23.

Job 27:1-23, Job Defends His Integrity

NIV	NRSV
27 And Job continued his discourse:	**27** Job again took up his discourse and said:
2"As surely as God lives, who has denied me justice, the Almighty, who has made me taste bitterness of soul,	2 "As God lives, who has taken away my right, and the Almighty,[a] who has made my soul bitter,
	a Traditional rendering of Heb *Shaddai*

NIV

³as long as I have life within me,
    the breath of God in my nostrils,
⁴my lips will not speak wickedness,
    and my tongue will utter no deceit.
⁵I will never admit you are in the right;
    till I die, I will not deny my integrity.
⁶I will maintain my righteousness and never let
        go of it;
    my conscience will not reproach me as long
        as I live.

⁷"May my enemies be like the wicked,
    my adversaries like the unjust!
⁸For what hope has the godless when he is cut
        off,
    when God takes away his life?
⁹Does God listen to his cry
    when distress comes upon him?
¹⁰Will he find delight in the Almighty?
    Will he call upon God at all times?

¹¹"I will teach you about the power of God;
    the ways of the Almighty I will not conceal.
¹²You have all seen this yourselves.
    Why then this meaningless talk?

¹³"Here is the fate God allots to the wicked,
    the heritage a ruthless man receives from the
        Almighty:
¹⁴However many his children, their fate is the
        sword;
    his offspring will never have enough to eat.
¹⁵The plague will bury those who survive him,
    and their widows will not weep for them.
¹⁶Though he heaps up silver like dust
    and clothes like piles of clay,
¹⁷what he lays up the righteous will wear,
    and the innocent will divide his silver.
¹⁸The house he builds is like a moth's cocoon,
    like a hut made by a watchman.
¹⁹He lies down wealthy, but will do so no more;
    when he opens his eyes, all is gone.
²⁰Terrors overtake him like a flood;
    a tempest snatches him away in the night.
²¹The east wind carries him off, and he is gone;
    it sweeps him out of his place.
²²It hurls itself against him without mercy
    as he flees headlong from its power.
²³It claps its hands in derision
    and hisses him out of his place."

NRSV

³ as long as my breath is in me
    and the spirit of God is in my nostrils,
⁴ my lips will not speak falsehood,
    and my tongue will not utter deceit.
⁵ Far be it from me to say that you are right;
    until I die I will not put away my integrity
        from me.
⁶ I hold fast my righteousness, and will not let
        it go;
    my heart does not reproach me for any of
        my days.

⁷ "May my enemy be like the wicked,
    and may my opponent be like the
        unrighteous.
⁸ For what is the hope of the godless when God
        cuts them off,
    when God takes away their lives?
⁹ Will God hear their cry
    when trouble comes upon them?
¹⁰ Will they take delight in the Almighty?ᵃ
    Will they call upon God at all times?
¹¹ I will teach you concerning the hand of God;
    that which is with the Almightyᵃ I will not
        conceal.
¹² All of you have seen it yourselves;
    why then have you become altogether vain?

¹³ "This is the portion of the wicked with God,
    and the heritage that oppressors receive
        from the Almighty:ᵃ
¹⁴ If their children are multiplied, it is for the sword;
    and their offspring have not enough to eat.
¹⁵ Those who survive them the pestilence buries,
    and their widows make no lamentation.
¹⁶ Though they heap up silver like dust,
    and pile up clothing like clay—
¹⁷ they may pile it up, but the just will wear it,
    and the innocent will divide the silver.
¹⁸ They build their houses like nests,
    like booths made by sentinels of the vineyard.
¹⁹ They go to bed with wealth, but will do so no
        more;
    they open their eyes, and it is gone.
²⁰ Terrors overtake them like a flood;
    in the night a whirlwind carries them off.
²¹ The east wind lifts them up and they are gone;

ᵃ Or He (that is God)

NRSV

it sweeps them out of their place.
[22] It[a] hurls at them without pity;
    they flee from its[b] power in headlong flight.
[23] It[a] claps its[b] hands at them,
    and hisses at them from its[b] place."

[a] Or *He* (that is God)   [b] Or *his*

COMMENTARY

Chapter 27, the final chapter in the third cycle of speeches, poses many of the same interpretive difficulties as chaps. 23–24 and 25–26. The perspectives that were clearly separated into coherent, contrasting points of view in the earlier parts of the dialogue, seem jumbled together in a bewildering manner in these speeches. As in the case of chaps. 23–24 and 25–26, scholars have tended to resolve the problem by dividing up the material, assigning part of chap. 27 to Job (usually vv. 1-12) and part to Zophar (usually vv. 13-23).[398] Such a solution does not solve all the problems, however. One is left with two fragments instead of two complete speeches, and even that surgical separation does not remove all of the seeming inconsistencies from Job's speech. It is more appropriate to struggle with the text as it stands. The third cycle's difficulties, incoherencies, and tensions are an apt representation of a disintegrating dialogue. Although begun in classical symmetry, it ends incomplete and without clarity. These are persons who finally have no more to say to one another and no desire to hear one another any longer.

It is possible to read chap. 27 without reassigning the verses. By this point in the book, Job has emerged as a very complex character who has an extremely complicated relationship to the traditional moral language that had once seemed so uncomplicated to him. There is more than one legitimate way a reader might understand how the words of chap. 27 are used by Job and what

they mean coming from his mouth.[399] The interpretation offered here is only one of those possibilities.

After the heading (v. 1), Job begins with a series of oaths in which he defends the honesty of his speech, his integrity, and his determination not to declare his friends right (vv. 2-6). Following these oaths, Job utters a curse on any enemy who would rise up against him (vv. 8-10). In vv. 11-12, Job declares his intention to instruct the friends in the true nature of God's power and criticizes them for merely "blowing wind." In vv. 13-23, Job satirically and dismissively imitates just such drivel as the friends have been speaking. By doing so, Job in effect preempts Zophar, who never speaks in the third cycle. Job's promise to disclose the nature of God's power is fulfilled in his final oration in chaps. 29–31, where he recalls the God who once protected but now persecutes him and challenges the God who has "taken away my right" (27:2).

27:1-6. As noted in the Overview to chaps. 25–26, the unusual heading in 27:1 and 29:1 ("Job again took up his discourse") implies that his discourse has been interrupted. Thus 26:5-14 may be taken as the conclusion of Bildad's speech, begun in 25:1-4.

In 26:2-4, Job had already dismissed the sort of speech Bildad was making. Now he moves directly to his own statement. Job begins by swearing on the life of God (cf., e.g., Judg 8:19; 1 Sam 14:45; 2 Sam 2:27). Frequently, such an oath formula is expanded with an epithet for God,

398. E.g., E. Dhorme, *A Commentary on the Book of Job,* trans. H. Knight (London: Nelson, 1967) xlvii-l; Habel, *The Book of Job,* 37, II. Rowley, *The Book of Job,* rev. ed., NCB (Grand Rapids, Mich.: Eerdmans, 1976; original ed., 1970) 174-78.

399. Contrast, e.g., the interpretations of F. Andersen, *Job: An Introduction and Commentary,* Tyndale Old Testament Commentaries (Downers Grove, Ill.: Inter-Varsity, 1976) 219-22; Janzen, *Job,* 172-74; and Good, *In Turns of Tempest,* 286-90, all of whom attribute chap. 27 in its entirety to Job.

as when Saul says, "As Yahweh lives, who saves Israel . . . " (1 Sam 14:39; cf. 1 Kgs 2:24; Jer 16:14; 23:7). The use of God's name in an oath was intended to invoke God as a witness and guarantor of the oath, and the epithet served to remind the oath taker and the ones before whom the oath was taken of the power and effectiveness of the God in whose name the oath is made.[400] Job's formula, however, is paradoxical to the point of contradiction, for he swears by the life of the God who has "taken away my right" and "embittered my soul" (v. 2). This contradiction is the unavoidable consequence of the legal metaphor Job has invoked. His integrity has been called into question not only by what his friends have said, but also by God's actions. In this manner, "his right" to be treated as an innocent person has been violated. In the context of the legal metaphor, the resolution of his situation is understood in terms of vindication. Job's vindication requires two things: that his own word about himself be acknowledged as true and that he receive divine affirmation of his innocence. By means of his oath in 27:2-4, Job attempts to establish the veracity of his word. The great oath in chap. 31 will constitute his demand for vindication from God. In both cases, Job is staking everything on his belief that, despite all that he has experienced, God is ultimately a God of justice and will vindicate him.

The expressions Job uses in v. 3 to set the duration of the oath also point to the irony of his situation and to the ground of his paradoxical hope. The commonplace expression, "while my breath is still in me," generally warrants no particular notice. It simply means "while I am still alive" (cf. 2 Sam 1:9). Job, however, scrutinizes the term "breath" (נשמה *něšāmâ*) and turns the cliché into a provocative claim. "Breath" is not some autonomous possession of human existence. It is a gift of God (Gen 2:7; Ps 104:29-30; Isa 42:5). Indeed, God's own breath or spirit enlivens a person (v. 3*b*). Just as Job speaks with God's own breath, he makes his claim against God with God's own passion for justice.

In v. 4, Job states the content of his oath; he will speak neither falsehood nor deceit. (The NIV's "wickedness" is too general. When עולה

['awlâ] is used with verbs of speaking, it refers specifically to lies; cf. Isa 59:3; Zeph 3:13.) Job made a similar claim in his first reply to Eliphaz (6:30), bitterly condemning his friends for speaking "falsehood" and "deceit" about God (13:7). At this point, speaking the truth means that Job can never declare the friends to be right, for that would be a betrayal of his own integrity (v. 5). Consequently, the resolution they had hoped to achieve by dialogue with Job is absolutely impossible. The dialogue is at an end.

In v. 6, Job describes the determination that has been the central feature of his character throughout the dialogues: to hold fast to his righteousness and to know that his own conscience (lit., "heart") will never have anything for which to reproach him. Here, too, there are echoes of the prose tale in the terms "integrity" (תמה *tummâ*) in v. 5 and "hold fast" or "persist" (החזיק *heḥĕzîq*) in v. 6. After the first test, when Job spoke words of acceptance, God said to the *satan,* "He still persists in his integrity" (2:3*a* NRSV). Later in that same chapter, Job's wife urged him to a different course of action, saying, " 'Do you still persist in your integrity? Curse God and die!' " (2:9 NRSV).

27:7-10. Job completes the section of his speech containing his oath by invoking a curse against his "enemy" (v. 7). In this context, the enemy is not God, as some have suggested.[401] The content of the curse makes no sense on that supposition. Although it is possible that Job refers specifically to his friends, it seems more likely that the curse is generic. Dhorme is probably correct in suggesting that it is a rhetorical form of speech. "Instead of saying: 'May I not suffer the fate of the wicked!' he says: 'May my enemy suffer the fate of the wicked.' "[402] The central enigma for Job has been that he, a righteous person, has experienced what tradition said is the fate of the wicked. It is his opposite, the one who rises up against him with malice, who deserves such a fate.

The tension between what should be and what

---

400. M. Pope, "Oaths," IDBSup, 577; H. Ringgren, "chayah," *TDOT* IV, 339-40.

401. So Habel, *The Book of Job,* 381-82, and Good, *In Turns of Tempest,* 287-88.

402. E. Dhorme, *A Commentary on the Book of Job,* trans. H. Knight (London: Nelson, 1967) 382. In Dan 4:19*b* (16*b*), Daniel uses a similar expression when he is reluctant to interpret Nebuchadnezzar's dream: " 'My lord, may the dream be for those who hate you, and its interpretation for your enemies' " (NRSV).

Job has experienced lends an ironic element to his description of the wicked person's situation. Job phrases the question in terms of "hope," a word that resonates with Job's previous words about the destruction of his own hope (cf. 14:7, 19; 17:15; 19:10). Here, he specifically identifies hope with God's willingness to hear a person in distress (v. 9a). Verse 10 is better taken, not as a second set of questions following v. 9a (as in NIV and NRSV), but as further development of the situation in v. 9b, as in the TNK's translation: "Will God hear his cry/ When trouble comes upon him,/ When he seeks the favor of Shaddai,/ Calls upon God at all times?" The wicked person has no such hope, but can Job hope for God to hear him, a righteous person? That remains the unresolved question that Job will put to the test in the great oath that constitutes his challenge to God (chap. 31).

27:11-12. With v. 11, the style changes, as Job addresses the friends directly, adopting a didactic manner of speaking. He is perhaps mocking them, as in chap. 12, when he imitated a typical wisdom discourse. In v. 11, Job offers to teach them concerning God's power, but in v. 12 he alters his focus, drawing attention to the inanity of what the friends have said. For Job, the direct evidence of eyes and ears is the basis for speaking truth (see 13:1). Since the friends can see (v. 12a), it is incomprehensible that they speak nonsense (v. 12b). More literally, Job says that they "blow wind," using the noun הבל (hebel), a word that concretely means "puff of wind," and the related verb (hābal; cf. 21:34).

27:13-23. These verses are best understood as Job's imitation of just such empty words as he has been hearing from his friends. As an example of prefabricated tradition, they will contrast with the testimony of his own experience in chaps. 29–31. That these are not Job's own words but an imitation of the friends' speech is indicated by the way the introductory verse 13 mimics the last verse of Zophar's speech from the second cycle (20:29). As Janzen suggests, Job is in essence giving Zophar's speech for him.[403]

Traditional elements abound in Job's version of the fate of the wicked. In describing the destruction of the wicked person's offspring in vv. 14-15

(cf. 18:19), Job invokes a version of the traditional threefold disaster: war, famine, and pestilence (cf. Ezek 6:11-12). Here, as in Jeremiah, the term "death" serves as an epithet for plague (Jer 15:2; 43:11; cf. Job 18:13, where "death's firstborn" is a plague-like disease). Verse 14 evokes the so-called futility curses, in which what appears to be good fortune only prepares for disaster (cf. Deut 28:41). To be "buried by death" (v. 15) implies having no proper burial at all, a fate greatly dreaded in the ancient world (see Isa 14:18-20; Jer 22:18-19). For widows not to lament suggests a destruction so overwhelming that the most elemental obligations to the dead are no longer honored (see Ps 78:64).

Verses 16-19 describe the ephemeral nature of the wealth of the wicked. In the first example, vv. 16-17, Job pairs "silver" with "clothing" rather than the more common "silver and gold" (cf. Zech 9:3, which also uses the comparison with dust/dirt). The impending loss is already implied in the very terms used to describe the wicked person's abundance. Dust functions as a symbol both of abundance (Gen 13:16; 28:14) and of decay (17:16).[404] That the righteous enjoy the wealth that the wicked have gathered is a cliché of wisdom literature (Prov 13:22b; 28:8; cf. Eccl 2:26). The second example, the insubstantiality of the wicked person's house, is a theme already canvassed by Eliphaz (5:3-5) and Bildad (18:15). The imagery of v. 18a is obscured by uncertainty about the meaning of the word עשׁ ('āš). In addition to "moth" and "bird's nest," it has been suggested that the word means "guard."[405] If so, then the two parts of the verse are more nearly parallel, and the point is that the house of the wicked is like the flimsy shelters put up by guards and sentinels (cf. Isa 1:8; 24:20). The third example, of wealth that vanishes between sleeping and waking (v. 19; cf. Prov 23:4-5), completes the series.[406]

The culmination of the destruction of the wicked is depicted in ways that suggest expulsion from the world. The "terrors" of v. 20a are not subjective fears, but as in Bildad's speech (18:11,

403. J. G. Janzen, *Job*, Interpretation (Atlanta: John Knox, 1985) 174.

404. N. Habel, *The Book of Job*, OTL (Philadelphia: Westminster, 1985) 386.

405. M. Pope, *Job*, 3rd ed., AB 15 (Garden City, N.Y.: Doubleday, 1979) 193.

406. Habel, *The Book of Job*, 387, suggests that the verse refers to the wicked person's life rather than to wealth.

14), objective forces of death unleashed into the world. These terrors are compared to the mighty flood waters that figure frequently as a symbol of death and destruction (Pss 18:16[17]; 32:6; Isa 28:17). Similarly, the storm (v. 20 b) and east wind (v. 21 a) that carry off the wicked are traditional symbols of disaster and punishment (Prov 1:27; 10:25; Jer 18:17; Hos 13:15). The clapping and whistling in v. 23 are gestures of contempt and scorn (Jer 49:17; Lam 2:15; Zeph 2:15), ways of punishing by shame. Since the subject of a verb need not be separately expressed in Hebrew, it is not clear who or what is the subject of the verbs in vv. 22-23. Perhaps the ambiguity is deliberate. Certainly, it adds to the eerie quality of the description that one cannot quite be certain whether it is the personified east wind that hurls itself against the wicked, clapping and whistling, or the generic "people" who do this,[407] or perhaps God (NRSV mg). Reality dissolves, as divine judgment and human contempt are made present in the incessant whistling and snapping of the wind that pursues the wicked.

407. Dhorme, *A Commentary on the Book of Job,* 397.

REFLECTIONS

Job's words in 27:2-6 offer an opportunity to reflect on some of the painful ironies that may confront a person who is determined to speak without falsehood or deceit about an experience of betrayal. Telling the truth about his situation as he understands it has required Job to say things he previously could not have imagined himself saying. Job's words against God have been so bitter that one can seriously ask whether Job has cursed God.[408] Although Job has not used a technical curse formula, there is no doubt that he has spoken blasphemy—i.e., reviling words against God. Alleging that God has given the earth into the hands of the wicked and even corrupted judges (9:24) is blasphemy. So is Job's depiction of God as one who acts destructively in apparent random fashion against whole peoples (12:13-25). One could add many such statements. One rather cynical comment in the rabbinic discussion of Job in *b. Bat.* 15 b says, "There was a certain pious man among the heathen named Job, but he [thought that he had] come into the world only to receive [here] his reward, and when the Holy One, blessed be He, brought chastisements upon him, he began to curse and blaspheme, so the Holy One, blessed be He, doubled his reward in this world so as to expel him from the world to come."[409]

That judgment is too hard on Job and misconstrues the nature of his words. An important distinction needs to be made between Job's blasphemy and what the *satan* had in mind when he said that Job would "curse God." The *satan* assumed that Job would repudiate God. It is certainly true that one may speak bitterly and disparagingly of a person one has repudiated, with whom there can be no further relationship; but not all bitter and abusive words are acts of repudiation. Sometimes they are acts of a harrowing intimacy. Job's blasphemous words are not a farewell to God but a searing truth-telling to the God he will not leave. In a paradoxical way that completely escapes the friends, Job's "holding fast to his integrity," even though it means speaking blasphemy, is the only way he can hold fast to God. It is doubtful that Job could sustain indefinitely the moral energy required to support this position, but at this point Job has not cursed God.

One of the ironic truths of life is that in certain circumstances loyalty and fidelity can only be expressed in opposition. Perhaps the most familiar instance of this paradoxical loyalty through opposition is to be found in the figure of the political dissident. For the dissident, love of country does not mean blind endorsement of whatever policies are developed by its leaders.

408. J. T. Wilcox, *The Bitterness of Job: A Philosophical Reading* (Ann Arbor: University of Michigan Press, 1989) 51-70.

409. I. Epstein, ed., *The Babylonian Talmud: Seder Nezikin: Baba Bathra,* vol. 1, trans. M. Simon (New Work: Rebecca Bennet Publications, 1959) 75.

Love of country means deep and abiding commitment to the values that make it worthy of love. When those values are betrayed, then love expresses itself in opposition and in an attempt to recall the country to its true identity. In ancient Israel, the role of the dissident was often borne by the prophet. Jeremiah is the most poignant example, as one sees how painful it was for Jeremiah to confront Judah with its fatal inability to be faithful, how excruciating it was to be hated by former friends and by relatives for speaking the truth given to him by God. Jeremiah also reflects the desire often expressed by dissidents who would keep silent if only they could, and yet who know that the word of protest is a fire shut up in their bones (see Jer 20:9). In the contemporary church, this role of reluctant dissident has come to many women whose denominations refuse to acknowledge the legitimacy of the ministries to which they have been called. To outsiders it appears a simple matter for such women to leave and take their gifts where they would be welcomed. But the true dissident has a deep identity with the object of her protest and is bound by love for the institution she seeks to call to repentance. This sense of identity is what Job alludes to when he refers to speaking against God by means of the breath of God and when he swears in the name of the very God who has deprived him of his right (vv. 2-3).

Confronting a person or an institution with the contradiction between what is and what should be is painful beyond all reckoning. To attack what one loves in the name of that love forces one into a bewildering confusion of emotions. It is morally dangerous, too, for it is but a small step into self-righteousness. Being the object of such anger and accusation is equally wrenching. As individuals and as members of institutions, there is always the temptation to resort to defensiveness, seeing the accuser as merely destructive, motivated by resentment rather than love. It is a difficult encounter to negotiate to the end, unpredictable in its outcome, but it is often the only alternative to ending things with a curse.

JOB 28:1-28, INTERLUDE: WHERE CAN WISDOM BE FOUND?

NIV

28 "There is a mine for silver
and a place where gold is refined.
[2] Iron is taken from the earth,
and copper is smelted from ore.
[3] Man puts an end to the darkness;
he searches the farthest recesses
for ore in the blackest darkness.
[4] Far from where people dwell he cuts a shaft,
in places forgotten by the foot of man;
far from men he dangles and sways.
[5] The earth, from which food comes,
is transformed below as by fire;
[6] sapphires[a] come from its rocks,
and its dust contains nuggets of gold.
[7] No bird of prey knows that hidden path,
no falcon's eye has seen it.

[a]6 Or *lapis lazuli*; also in verse 16

NRSV

28 "Surely there is a mine for silver,
and a place for gold to be refined.
[2] Iron is taken out of the earth,
and copper is smelted from ore.
[3] Miners put[a] an end to darkness,
and search out to the farthest bound
the ore in gloom and deep darkness.
[4] They open shafts in a valley away from human habitation;
they are forgotten by travelers,
they sway suspended, remote from people.
[5] As for the earth, out of it comes bread;
but underneath it is turned up as by fire.
[6] Its stones are the place of sapphires,[b]
and its dust contains gold.

[7] "That path no bird of prey knows,

[a] Heb *He puts*   [b] Or *lapis lazuli*

NIV

⁸Proud beasts do not set foot on it,
and no lion prowls there.
⁹Man's hand assaults the flinty rock
and lays bare the roots of the mountains.
¹⁰He tunnels through the rock;
his eyes see all its treasures.
¹¹He searchesᵃ the sources of the rivers
and brings hidden things to light.

¹²"But where can wisdom be found?
Where does understanding dwell?
¹³Man does not comprehend its worth;
it cannot be found in the land of the living.
¹⁴The deep says, 'It is not in me';
the sea says, 'It is not with me.'
¹⁵It cannot be bought with the finest gold,
nor can its price be weighed in silver.
¹⁶It cannot be bought with the gold of Ophir,
with precious onyx or sapphires.
¹⁷Neither gold nor crystal can compare with it,
nor can it be had for jewels of gold.
¹⁸Coral and jasper are not worthy of mention;
the price of wisdom is beyond rubies.
¹⁹The topaz of Cush cannot compare with it;
it cannot be bought with pure gold.

²⁰"Where then does wisdom come from?
Where does understanding dwell?
²¹It is hidden from the eyes of every living thing,
concealed even from the birds of the air.
²²Destructionᵇ and Death say,
'Only a rumor of it has reached our ears.'
²³God understands the way to it
and he alone knows where it dwells,
²⁴for he views the ends of the earth
and sees everything under the heavens.
²⁵When he established the force of the wind
and measured out the waters,
²⁶when he made a decree for the rain
and a path for the thunderstorm,
²⁷then he looked at wisdom and appraised it;
he confirmed it and tested it.
²⁸And he said to man,
'The fear of the Lord—that is wisdom,
and to shun evil is understanding.'"

ᵃ11 Septuagint, Aquila and Vulgate; Hebrew *He dams up*   ᵇ22 Hebrew
Abaddon

NRSV

and the falcon's eye has not seen it.
⁸ The proud wild animals have not trodden it;
the lion has not passed over it.

⁹ "They put their hand to the flinty rock,
and overturn mountains by the roots.
¹⁰ They cut out channels in the rocks,
and their eyes see every precious thing.
¹¹ The sources of the rivers they probe;ᵃ
hidden things they bring to light.

¹² "But where shall wisdom be found?
And where is the place of understanding?
¹³ Mortals do not know the way to it,ᵇ
and it is not found in the land of the living.
¹⁴ The deep says, 'It is not in me,'
and the sea says, 'It is not with me.'
¹⁵ It cannot be gotten for gold,
and silver cannot be weighed out as its price.
¹⁶ It cannot be valued in the gold of Ophir,
in precious onyx or sapphire.ᶜ
¹⁷ Gold and glass cannot equal it,
nor can it be exchanged for jewels of fine
gold.
¹⁸ No mention shall be made of coral or of crystal;
the price of wisdom is above pearls.
¹⁹ The chrysolite of Ethiopiaᵈ cannot compare
with it,
nor can it be valued in pure gold.

²⁰ "Where then does wisdom come from?
And where is the place of understanding?
²¹ It is hidden from the eyes of all living,
and concealed from the birds of the air.
²² Abaddon and Death say,
'We have heard a rumor of it with our ears.'

²³ "God understands the way to it,
and he knows its place.
²⁴ For he looks to the ends of the earth,
and sees everything under the heavens.
²⁵ When he gave to the wind its weight,
and apportioned out the waters by measure;
²⁶ when he made a decree for the rain,
and a way for the thunderbolt;
²⁷ then he saw it and declared it;
he established it, and searched it out.

ᵃ Gk Vg: Heb *bind*   ᵇ Gk: Heb *its price*   ᶜ Or *lapis lazuli*
ᵈ Or *Nubia*; Heb *Cush*

28 And he said to humankind,
'Truly, the fear of the Lord, that is wisdom;
and to depart from evil is understanding.'"

COMMENTARY

The poem on wisdom in chap. 28 is one of the most exquisite poetic compositions of the entire Bible. Precious jewels serve as an important image within the poem and might also serve as an image for the poem itself. Like a gemstone, this poem is beautifully crafted, clear and luminous, yet full of mysterious depths. Its unique literary form and meditative tone have led many commentators to conclude that it must be a late addition to the book, rather than an integral part of its composition; but that view betrays a rather wooden notion of the book's composition. Moreover, it overlooks the fact that the diction, grammar, and style of chap. 28 are quite similar to other passages in the dialogues and the divine speeches. The similarities between chaps. 28 and 38 are especially close.[410] The important issue is not whether chap. 28 belongs where it is placed, but what role it plays.

The first issue to be resolved is the speaker's identity. Since no heading separates chap. 28 from chap. 27, it would initially appear that it is a continuation of Job's speech. The abrupt change of tone, topic, and imagery, however, makes a distinct break from the preceding material. Similarly, the heading introducing chap. 29, which indicates that Job is "resuming" his discourse, implies that chap. 28 is not Job's speech. Moreover, the contrast between the content and the perspective of chaps. 28 and 29–31 is so striking that it is virtually impossible to imagine chap. 28 as Job's words at this point in the story.[411] It is equally unlikely that chap. 28 contains the "missing" speech of Zophar for the third cycle. Even though the theme of the poem bears some resem-

blance to Zophar's comments in 11:7-12, the style and mood of chap. 28 are completely different from any of the speeches in the dialogue. Both those who consider the speech to be original and those who consider it to be a later addition agree that it serves as a sort of meditative interlude, reflecting on the dialogue that precedes it, and preparing for the final section of the book, which will reach its climax in the divine speeches in chaps. 38–41.[412]

The structure of the poem is clearly marked. The first section of the poem (vv. 1-11) describes the place of precious metals in the world and the heroic human search to find and obtain them. These verses serve as a foil to the second section of the poem (vv. 12-27), which describes the inability of humans, in contrast to God, to find or obtain wisdom. This second section is divided into two parts both by the repetition of the thematic rhetorical question concerning the source and place of wisdom (vv. 12, 20) and by the repetition of the statement that neither living beings nor the personified cosmic realms of Sea and Death are able to locate and so gain access to wisdom (vv. 13-14, 21-22). Thus the structure of the poem draws attention to the contrast between the inability of humankind to obtain wisdom, even in exchange for all the riches procured by mining (vv. 15-19), and God's knowledge of the way and place of wisdom in the cosmos, expressed most fully in God's encounter with wisdom in the act of creation (vv. 23-27).

The final verse of the poem (v. 28) stands apart from the comprehensive structure and provides an unexpected conclusion to the poem. In contrast to the contention that humans cannot obtain wisdom, v. 28 presents God as saying that, for

410. See the list compiled by S. A. Geller, " 'Where Is Wisdom?' A Literary Study of Job 28 in Its Settings," in *Judaic Perspectives on Ancient Israel*, eds. J. Neusner, B. Levine, and E. S. Frerichs (Philadelphia: Fortress, 1987) 177n. 1. See also Habel, *The Book of Job*, 392.

411. Janzen, *Job*, 187-201, is the only recent commentator to defend the speech as Job's. E. Good, *In Turns of Tempest* (Stanford, Calif.: Stanford University Press, 1990) 290-93, concludes that it was not originally composed as a speech of Job, but that its insertion within the book has made it appear to be Job's, and so he attempts to interpret it as such.

412. E.g., F. Andersen, *Job: An Introduction and Commentary,* Tyndale Old Testament Commentaries (Downers Grove, Ill.: Inter-Varsity, 1976) 222-24; J. E. Hartley, *The Book of Job,* NICOT (Grand Rapids, Mich.: Eerdmans, 1988) 26-27; Habel, *The Book of Job,* 391-94.

humans, piety ("fear of the LORD") is the equivalent of wisdom, and morality ("turning from evil") the equivalent of understanding. Stylistically, the verse echoes the prose narrative with which the book began, as well as presenting its point of view. Interpreters who judge every deviation in style or perspective to be a sign of later editorial tampering with the text tend to treat v. 28 as an intrusion. One should remember, however, that the entire book of Job is structured dialogically, setting one perspective over against another. Not only is this true of the dialogue between Job and his friends or between Job and God, but it is also true of the way that the prose narratives at the beginning and end of the book are set over against the poetic material in the middle. Verse 28 should be taken as an integral part of the chapter. It imitates in miniature the structure of the end of the book in which the long poetic speeches about creation are followed by a return to the voice of the prose narrative. The interpretive problem of understanding v. 28 in relation to the preceding poem anticipates the similar interpretive problem of understanding the narrative conclusion of the book in relation to the divine speeches.

28:1-11. The first part of the poem, concerning the godlike power of human beings to search out and mine precious minerals, is divided into a series of small strophes. In the first (vv. 1-2), the topic is announced. Verses 3-4 recount the search for minerals in a distant and inaccessible land. Verses 5-6 describe the land and its subterranean riches. The extraordinary human achievement in locating the source of such riches is underscored by contrasting the animals' ignorance concerning its location (vv. 7-8). The climax comes in the account of the mining operation itself and the successful bringing to light of hidden treasures (vv. 9-11).

Verse 1 has a double function in the chapter. In its immediate context, it is paired with v. 2 and introduces the list of precious minerals (silver, gold, iron, copper), together with the places in which they are found and the material from which they are derived. But v. 1 is also the first part of a parallel that is not completed until v. 12. The verbal similarities between the two verses are obscured in English translation, but the two key words in v. 1 are "mine" (מוצא *môṣāʾ*; lit., "place of coming forth") and "place" (מקום *māqôm*). In

v. 12*b, māqôm* is also used; and in v. 12*a* the verb "be found" (מצא *māṣāʾ*), although from a different Hebrew root than *môṣāʾ*, has a similar sound. Thus the contrast is established. There is a site where silver can be *found* and a *place* for gold, but where can wisdom be *found,* or where is the *place* of understanding?

Verses 3-4 are quite difficult to translate and to interpret. Although individual words are problematic, the main question is whether the verses refer to prospecting or to mining. (The NRSV's "miners" is interpretive; the Hebrew text simply has "he" or "one.") Although these verses have generally been interpreted to refer to the act of mining, a good case can be made that the mining and extraction procedures are not described until vv. 9-11.[413] Verse 3 summarizes the entire process and its goal. Specifically, the allusion to "putting an end to darkness" anticipates the result that is not made explicit until v. 11*b*, in which the "hidden things" of the earth are "brought to light." One should not miss the overtones of godlike activity in this phrase (cf. Gen 1:2-3); themes of power and creation are used in complex ways in this chapter. That prospecting is in view seems especially clear from the phrase "searching to the farthest limit." In 26:10 the same word (תכלית *taklît*) was used to identify the horizon as the boundary between darkness and light. Zophar used the phrase "the limit of Shaddai" to talk about divine wisdom in 11:7*b*, employing the four cosmic dimensions as comparison. In v. 3 the sense of the direction of this search to the limits of the cosmos is suggested by the description of the ore that is sought as the "stone of gloom and the shadow of death." These phrases are used elsewhere to describe the darkness of Sheol (10:21-22). The enterprise of prospecting and mining leads to the far reaches of the world and from thence into the depths of the earth, where the boundary between the land of life and the land of death is easily crossed. Such a quest is fraught with both power and danger.

As Andersen says, "Everyone is reduced to despair by v. 4, and, comparing several versions . . . it is hard to believe that they all had the same Hebrew text in front of them."[414] There are two problems with the translations of the NRSV and

413. Cf. Geller, " 'Where Is Wisdom?' " 158-59.
414. Andersen, *Job,* 225.

the NIV. First, the term translated "shafts" (נחל *naḥal*) is nowhere else attested with that meaning, but is the ordinary word for "wadi," the dry river bed that crosses the desert landscape. Second, the expression "dangles and sways" or "sway suspended" is based on a very problematic interpretation of the Hebrew verb דלל (*dālal*). With minimal emendation, Geller tentatively proposes a much more likely translation, which I would adapt as follows: "They spread out through wadis far from habitation, they wandered through (wadis) forgotten by travelers, poor in population."[415] However one translates v. 4, its contribution to the imagery is captured in its threefold repetition of the expression "far from," followed by some expression that suggests human presence. Whether the text refers to prospecting or mining, the one who seeks out precious minerals journeys deep into utter isolation.

Verses 5-6 describe this remote region where precious minerals are found (cf. Deut 8:9). The contrast in v. 5 is between the surface and the depths.[416] Volcanic activity was recognized as an indication of fire under the earth. It is possible that the expression "stones of fire," used as a term for gemstones in Ezek 28:14, suggests a belief that precious stones were formed in such environments.[417] In any event the fiery depths of this region are associated with lapis lazuli and with gold.[418]

The references to not knowing the path, not seeing, and not traversing the area all indicate that vv. 7-8 refer to the hidden and inaccessible location of the land that is so rich in minerals. Birds of prey are used as an example because of their extraordinary eyesight and ability to look over large territories from great heights (cf. 39:29). The significance of lions and the other wild animals referred to in Hebrew as "children of pride" is less clear. An ingenious case has been made that the word translated "lion" (שחל *šaḥal*) should be rendered "snake," which would give a fitting parallelism between creatures of the air and crea-

tures of the dust. The "children of pride" are elsewhere mentioned only in Job 41:34[26], in connection with the reptilian Leviathan, and so might designate lizards, which, as Prov 30:29 notes, find their way into unlikely places.[419] The problem with this otherwise appealing suggestion is that *šaḥal* is clearly used with the meaning "lion" in Eliphaz's list of five different terms for lions (4:10-11).

Verses 9-11 form the climax of this section of the poem, describing the technical power by which human beings delve into the earth. Here, as in the search for mineral lands, there are overtones of godlike ability. "Overturning the roots of the mountains" evokes the similar image of God's power in 9:5 (cf. Hab 3:6). Not only mountains but also waters are controlled, as vv. 10*a* and 11*a* contrast "forcing open" (בקע *biqqēaʿ*) channels and binding the sources of rivers. There is no reason to emend the text of v. 11*a* to "search," as the NRSV and the NIV do. It destroys the parallelism and does not improve the sense. Although one can imagine the sort of mining techniques that would involve the control of water, the godlike qualities of the acts are equally important for the symbolism of the poem. Habakkuk 3:9 refers to God "splitting" (*bāqaʿ*) the earth with rivers. Similarly, in a description of creation, Ps 74:15 contrasts God's "forcing open" springs and channels with God's drying up of rivers. The cosmic overtones of the scene in Job 28 are underscored by the term used for "sources of the rivers" (מבכי נהרות *mibkî nĕhārôt*, v. 11), for it is the same term used in Ugaritic mythology to describe the abode of the god El, "at the sources of the two rivers, in the midst of the channels of the two seas."[420] Human activity extends to the very doorstep of the gods. The success of the enterprise in seeing the precious things (v. 10*b*) and bringing "the hidden things to light" (v. 11*b*) also echoes the divine ability to bring the things of darkness to light (12:22; cf. Dan 2:22).

One should note that these divine overtones are not used in a critical fashion to condemn human technological power. To the contrary, they celebrate it as the means by which human beings

---

415. Geller, " 'Where Is Wisdom?' " 178n. 9.

416. An alternative interpretation, which takes this verse to refer to mining operations, suggests that a technique of heating rocks to make them crack is what is described here. See Pope, *Job*, 201.

417. Habel, *The Book of Job*, 396.

418. The translation "sapphire," instead of "lapis lazuli" is anachronistic. That gem was not known until Roman times, as H. Rowley notes, *The Book of Job*, rev. ed., NCB (Grand Rapids, Mich.: Eerdmans, 1976; original ed., 1970) 181.

419. See S. Mowinckel, *"shahal,"* in *Hebrew and Semitic Studies Presented to Godfrey Rolles Driver*, ed. D. Winton Thomas and W. D. McHardy (Oxford: Clarendon, 1963) 95-103. His suggestion is adopted by Geller, " 'Where Is Wisdom?' " 179-80.

420. James B. Pritchard, ed., *Ancient Near Eastern Texts Relating to the Old Testament (ANET)* 3rd ed. with supplement (Princeton: Princeton University Press, 1969) 133.

approximate the extraordinary powers of God. In the overall strategy of the poem, however, the pinnacle of power and achievement that mining represents is used as a foil for the utter inability of human striving to find and secure something much more precious: wisdom.

28:12-19. Only now, approximately 40 percent of the way through the poem, is its true theme announced. Although one usually speaks of "wisdom" as the subject of the poem, actually two words are used, "wisdom" (חכמה *ḥokmâ*) and "understanding" (בינה *bînâ*; cf. Prov 1:2; 4:5, 7; 9:10; 16:16). *Ḥokmâ* is a very general term, the precise meaning of which depends on the context in which it is used. *Bînâ*, by contrast, has a somewhat more restricted meaning, referring to intellectual discernment, both as a capacity that an individual might possess and as the knowledge produced by such discernment.[421] By pairing these terms and setting them in the context of imagery that has already established the whole cosmos as its frame of reference, the poet is apparently asking about the kind of understanding that would provide insight into the nature and meaning of the entire cosmos. There are several examples within wisdom literature of this type of poem, which reflect on wisdom as the organizing principle of the cosmos (Prov 8:22-31; Wis 7:15-30; Sir 1:1-10; 24:1-29; Bar 3:9-4:4). In contrast to Proverbs 8 and Sirach 24, however, wisdom is not personified in Job 28.[422]

As noted above, v. 12 complements v. 1. The use of similar terminology of place establishes a metaphorical relationship between precious minerals and wisdom. But the "place" of wisdom is precisely what is problematic about it. Verse 13 bluntly states that human beings do not know the way to the place of wisdom (NRSV, following LXX; the NIV's "value," following MT, is apparently influenced by the topic of comparative value introduced in vv. 15-19). Verse 13*b* denies that wisdom can be found in the entire "land of the living," a term used in contrast to the pit and the watery depths that are the realm of death (Ezek 26:19-20; cf. Isa 38:10-11). But wisdom is not to be found in those watery depths either, as the personified cosmic deep testifies in v. 14 (cf. vv.

421. M. Fox, "Words for Wisdom," *ZAH* 6 (1993) 154.
422. Contra Habel, *The Book of Job*, 394.

21-22, which similarly pair the realms of the living and the dead).

The next section, vv. 15-19, transforms certain commonplaces of wisdom teaching. In the book of Proverbs one frequently encounters the admonition to "acquire" wisdom (e.g., Prov 4:5, 7), an expression whose commercial overtones are playfully exploited (Prov 23:23). The value of wisdom is also compared with that of silver, gold, and jewels (Prov 3:13-15), and the two themes are combined in the advice that one "buy" wisdom rather than gold (Prov 16:16). Here, however, the poet reverses the traditional imagery. One cannot buy wisdom for all the precious metals and jewels in the world.

The entire passage has a list-like quality, as the same point is made in subtly varying sentences. One notes this in the long list of precious gems and metals named. In addition to silver, there are five different expressions for "gold," impossible to render in English, but suggesting a connoisseur's familiarity with rarities among rarities. Seven different gemstones are named. Although it is not always possible to be certain which particular gems are intended, the very enumeration has a sensuous quality that suggests all the fabled riches coming from widely differing places in the world. As the products of mining, they represent not only wealth but also evidence of the technological power of mining celebrated in vv. 1-11. There is also a list-like quality in the synonymous verbs for exchange or value: "given," "weighed out" (v. 15); "be paid for" (v. 16); "valued" (v. 17). The sequence is interrupted in v. 18 with the humorous phrase "don't even mention . . . " and completed in v. 19 with a repetition of the verbs "valued" and "be paid for." The governing repetition, however, which is not varied but tolls like a bell, is the negative particle "not" (לא *lō'*). It begins each verse, except the next to last (v. 18), where it is the third word.

28:20-27. The final section of the poem opens with a repetition of the rhetorical question of v. 12, differing only in the use of the verb "come" (בוא *bô'*) rather than "be found" (מצא *māṣā'*). Verses 21-22 parallel vv. 13-14, excluding the notion that wisdom can be found either among the living or in the realm of the dead. In terms of scope, the phrase "all living" includes not only humans (v. 13) but also animals (cf. Gen 6:19;

8:21) and is complemented by mention of the "birds of the heavens." Verse 21 teases the reader with the notion that wisdom has a place, albeit elusively hidden. Analogously, the words of personified Abaddon and Death in v. 22 have a teasing quality when compared with v. 14. In contrast to the simple negative of the Deep and Sea, these regions report having heard a rumor of the place of wisdom. At the same time, such statements underscore how far removed from human reach such a place must be.

These tantalizing words prepare for the climactic statement in v. 23: "God understands the way to it." Both the word "God" (אלהים 'ĕlōhîm) and the pronoun "he" (הוא hû') are in emphatic positions in the sentences, marking the contrast between God and humanity. Verse 24 continues to tease the reader with the notion of wisdom's place, as it seems to connect God's knowledge of wisdom's place with God's ability to see to the ends of the earth and everything under heaven.

It is thus somewhat surprising that the text shifts from spatial language to temporal language with v. 25. Grammatically, both v. 25 and v. 26 are subordinate clauses that introduce the main clause in v. 27. Thus, literally and somewhat woodenly, one might translate "at (the time of) the setting of weight for the wind . . . in the setting of a limit for the rain . . . then he saw it." Or, more fluidly, "when . . . when . . . then." This grammatical structure is important because it is typical of the way in which many stories and poems about creation are told. The Babylonian creation myth, the Enuma Elish, begins: "When on high the heaven had not been named. . . . When no gods whatever had been brought into being. . . . Then it was that the gods were formed within [the waters of Apsu and Tiamat]."[423] There is a similar grammatical structure in the Israelite creation story in Gen 2:4b-7: "In the day that the LORD God made the earth and the heavens, when no plant of the field was yet in the earth . . . then the LORD God formed man from the dust of the ground" (NRSV). In the wisdom poem of Prov 8:22-31 the same grammatical structure appears: "When there were no depths I was brought forth. . . . Before the mountains had been shaped. . . . When he assigned to the sea its limit . . . when

he marked out the foundations of the earth, then I was beside him" (NRSV). In each case the main clause, the one introduced by "then," contains the crucial element.

There is a subtle difference between the creation accounts just mentioned and the creation language of vv. 25-27. In the Enuma Elish and Genesis 2, the "when" clauses establish conditions that exist before the crucial event. Proverbs 8 plays with this tradition by reversing it. Wisdom exists prior to all the things named in the "when" clauses. Job 28:25-27 does something slightly different. Instead of setting up a before and after relationship, the "when" clauses establish a relationship of simultaneity. It was "in the act of" (לעשות la'ăśôt, בעשתו ba'ăśōtô, vv. 25a, 26a) creating the world that God perceived wisdom. Now the poet's teasing references about wisdom's "place" appear in a new light. Wisdom's place is not a location; wisdom is found in an act of creativity.[424] The particular acts that vv. 25-26 recount all have to do with bringing order to things that have a certain formlessness about them: wind, water, rain, thunderstorms (cf. 36:27-33; 38:4-38; Isa 40:12). Weight and measure (v. 25) are purely physical terms, but the corresponding terms in v. 26, "limit" (חק hōq; lit., "groove," by extension "decree" or "rule")[425] and "way" or "path" (דרך derek) have both physical and moral connotations, depending on context. In the activity of making order, of giving substance to creatures and of simultaneously setting limits for them, God perceives wisdom.

The specific verbs used in v. 27 are difficult to translate appropriately, as a comparison of various translations shows. The first verb phrase, "he saw it," is simple enough (cf. v. 24). But what is one to make of the other verbs? The NIV translation attempts to bring out nuances of the verbs that would support the metaphor of wisdom as a jewel, tested and confirmed as without flaws.[426] Although an appealing interpretation, it is not clear that the Hebrew words have those precise connotations. Certainly the point could have been made more explicitly. Gordis suggests a more likely explanation in noting that the Hebrew words "innumerable" (אין מספר 'ên mispār) and

423. ANET, 61.

424. Similarly, Janzen, Job, 197.
425. Pope, Job, 205.
426. Similarly, Habel, The Book of Job, 400.

"unsearchable" (חקר אין 'ên ḥēqer), elsewhere used of divine wisdom (Ps 147:5; Isa 40:28), are related to the verbs used here, "declared" or "appraised" (ספר sippēr) and "searched" (חקר ḥāqar).[427] These verbs suggest the complete and thorough knowledge of wisdom that God obtains. Although some would emend the verb "confirmed" or "established" (כון kûn) to "discerned" (בין bîn) in order to make it parallel to "saw,"[428] the meaning of the verse does not require it.

What has the poem asserted about wisdom and its place in the world? Wisdom cannot be found by mining, because it is not a thing deposited somewhere in the world and waiting to be dug up. Searching for it as though it were is an act of futility doomed to failure. Similarly, wisdom is not a commodity that can be possessed. Even God's relation to wisdom is described in ways that challenge notions of wisdom as some objectified thing. Wisdom is perceived and known fully only in the act of creation itself. What the poet describes is rather like what an artisan experiences. The wisdom that makes the crafting possible is known only in the exercise of that skill. It is a faculty of the maker, and yet that wisdom is also worked into every aspect of the thing that is made. If that is what the poem says, then wisdom is in the world, worked into its very fabric (cf. Prov 3:19-20), yet not in a way that allows it to be extracted. The poem has not yet said, however, whether and how human beings can experience wisdom, once its true nature is recognized.

28:28. One expects some sort of summary or conclusion after v. 27, but not the one that actually appears. The introductory words of v. 28, "and he said to humankind," have the syntax of prose, not poetry, and consequently draw attention to themselves as interruptive. The allusion to 1:1 in the phrases "fear of the Lord" (יראת אדני yir'at 'ădōnāy; cf. "fears God" [וירא אלהים wîrē' 'ĕlōhîm] in 1:1) and "turning from evil" (סור מרע sûr mērā') give this interrupting voice the tone of the narrator of the prose tale.[429] The use of the word "Lord"

('ădōnāy), otherwise unattested in the book of Job, leads some commentators to regard v. 28 as a later addition to the text. Whether secondary or original, however, v. 28 does provide an interpretive conclusion to the poem by means of a voice that distinguishes itself from the voice of the poem and so sets up a dialogue with it.

There is something shocking and outrageous about coming to the end of such a profound poem and being met by a cliché. These are the shopworn phrases of conventional instruction found in Prov 1:7; 3:7; 9:10; and in Ps 111:10. Moreover, hearing these phrases in the accents of the prose narrator gives them an unbearable smugness, as though chaps. 3–27 have meant nothing. But perhaps the affront is part of the artistic design and pedagogical strategy. Readers are accustomed to finding the meaning of a work at the end. The process is not unlike mining, where the precious thing one wishes to extract lies at the bottom of the pit or the far end of the tunnel. So here, even though the poem has been at pains to tell us that wisdom is not a thing to be located and extracted, we have still been expecting to find the extractable nugget at the end. To be met with dross instead of gold is disconcerting.

Disorientation can be a useful pedagogical tool, however, for it often makes one look at the familiar in new ways. Only if the proverbial saying is taken in isolation is it something that the reader already knows. Here it is set in a context that permits it to disclose something previously unperceived. The interpretive v. 28 sets up a parallel with vv. 25-27. "Fear of the LORD" and "turning from evil" play the same role in relation to humans that "giving weight to the wind" and "setting a limit for the rain" play in relation to God. God's acts are cosmos-creating acts, and God perceives and establishes wisdom in the midst of that activity. The human actions of true piety—fearing God and turning from evil—those too are acts of creation. They are cosmos-creating acts, not as acts of physical creation but as acts of moral creation. Humankind cannot find wisdom by searching for it as though it could be mined or purchased. One cannot possess wisdom; one can only embody it.

427. R. Gordis, *The Book of Job: Commentary, New Translation, and Special Studies* (New York: Jewish Theological Seminary, 5738/1978) 311.
428. See Dhorme, *A Commentary on the Book of Job*; Pope, *Job,* 206; Geller, " 'Where Is Wisdom?' " A few manuscripts actually read "discerned it."
429. So Dhorme, *A Commentary on the Book of Job,* 414; Pope, *Job,* 206; G. Fohrer, *Das Buch Hiob,* KAV xvi (Guetersloh: Gerd Mohn, 1963) 392.

REFLECTIONS

Chapter 28 speaks of a paradox, of something that cannot be found because it is everywhere, of a quest whose end is the same as its beginning. To understand this paradox, one needs to think more about the nature of wisdom. Habel calls wisdom that which integrates the phenomena of the cosmos.[430] One might rephrase that definition by saying that wisdom is the point of coherence of the universe, the point from which the integrity of creation can be perceived, the point from which the interrelatedness of things can be understood. Wisdom of that sort brings both profound peace and profound security. There is no one who does not yearn for that, and yet it seems so elusive.

Job and his friends have been seeking wisdom in terms of an explanatory principle that will make sense of everything. Their efforts have failed and are doomed to fail, although they are not yet ready to acknowledge this. Wisdom is not a principle of explanation. Chapter 28 talks of it instead as a means of participation in the world. In identifying that mode of participation, v. 28 uses the two phrases "fear of the LORD" and "turning from evil."

The notion of "fear of the LORD," a general term for piety, is not so different from what is sometimes called mindfulness. It is an orientation to God developed and nurtured by the disciplines of piety: prayer, meditation, and other religious observances that serve to remind one of God's continual presence. The forms that such disciplines of piety take vary from one religious tradition to another and from one individual to another. In the monastic tradition, for instance, it is the daily observance of the divine liturgy. For others it may be silent meditation. In the tradition of Psalm 119, it is reflection on the beauty of Torah. Whatever form it takes, the function of such practices is to integrate the individual into the same realities that are expressed by the reference to God's "setting a weight for the wind and establishing the waters by measure, establishing a limit for the rain, and a way for the thunderstorm" (vv. 25-26, author's trans.).

"Turning from evil" is a condensed expression for the moral capacity of human beings. That, too, is a form of participation in divine creativity. Love does not exist without someone who will love. Justice does not come into being without someone to do justice. This notion is embedded in the Hebrew phrase to *do* righteousness," a phrase used of humans as well as of God (see, e.g., Ps 106:3; Prov 21:3; Isa 56:1; 58:2; Jer 9:23; Ezek 18:21). To do righteousness and to turn from evil are acts of moral creation. The philosopher Erazim Kohak puts it this way: "There is an order, a rightness as well as a rhythm of time. The generations of the porcupines, the phases of the forest, even the death of the chipmunk, all attest to a rightness of time. The glory of being human is the ability to recognize the pattern of rightness and to honor it as a moral law. The horror of being human is the ability to violate that rightness, living out of season—doing violence to the other, perverting the most sacred human relationships, devastating the world in greed, overriding its rhythm, not in the name of necessity and charity, but in the compulsion of coveting."[431]

In the disciplines of piety and of moral order, human beings may also perceive and participate in wisdom, experiencing in mindfulness and in moral action the integrity of creation. Through this participation in wisdom comes a peace and security that are not a denial of the tragic dimension of life, but an ability to be sustained in tragedy by experiencing the creating, sustaining presence of God. This is what is portrayed by the Job of the prose tale.

The story has shown, however, that Job did not, after all, "fear God for naught." Like his friends, Job had tacitly assumed that by embodying wisdom he somehow secured himself and

---

430. N. Habel, *The Book of Job*, OTL (Philadelphia: Westminster, 1985) 397.
431. E. Kohak, *The Embers and the Stars: A Philosophical Inquiry into the Moral Sense of Nature* (Chicago: University of Chicago Press, 1984) 84.

---

his household from tragedy. If not, he would not be so furious at his "unjust" treatment. By the end of chap. 28, however, the reader knows that the world is not as Job wishes it were. Job has shown, not only from his own story but also from the experiences of others, that suffering comes even to those who fear God and turn from evil. If one believes Job, and if one also believes the poet of chap. 28, then one has to believe that it is possible through a life of true piety to experience something of the coherency of the universe, to experience something of the wisdom embodied in divine creative activity through one's own participation in that creation. In such participation there is real presence and strength. But one also has to recognize that such participation will not make one secure from suffering. In that sense, there is no choice about it; one *must* "fear God for naught," for God does not offer insurance against all harm.

As Job discovers, giving up such a claim upon God is harder than one would expect, even for those who think that they have made no such claims. That is not to say that one must give up anger at the fact of a life cut short by death or outrage at the callous violation of life by those who engage in the cosmos-destroying activity of violence. The absence of those emotions in Job's initial responses to loss (1:21; 2:10) suggests that there was something incomplete and truncated in his reaction. But now that Job has explored the depths of his anger, there is a danger that he will remain mired in what Wilcox calls "moral bitterness."[432] If he is to avoid this, Job must find his way back to what was true about his original stance. Yet there is no simple going back into naiveté. The quest may end where it began, but the hero will have been transformed.

The provocative echo of the first verse of the book in the last verse of chap. 28 suggests that the resolution of Job's anguish must somehow be made in terms of where he began. Just how that might happen is not spelled out. This process is not restricted to the particulars of Job's story, of course. It is a familiar part of human experience, in the lives of individuals and institutions. The structures of meaning that once seemed so necessary and that later come to seem so hollow and even oppressive may yet be encountered in a way that renews and transforms them. The following lines from T. S. Eliot's "Little Gidding" might well serve as a gloss on Job 28:

> We shall not cease from exploration
> And the end of all our exploring
> Will be to arrive where we started
> And know the place for the first time.[433]

432. J. Wilcox, *The Bitterness of Job: A Philosophical Reading* (Ann Arbor: University of Michigan Press, 1989) 100-17.
433. T. S. Eliot, *Collected Poems 1909–1962* (New York: Harcourt, Brace & World, 1963) 208.

JOB 29:1–31:40, JOB'S CONCLUDING SPEECH

Job 29:1-25, Job Recalls an Idyllic Past

NIV	NRSV

29 Job continued his discourse:
 ²"How I long for the months gone by,
     for the days when God watched over me,
 ³when his lamp shone upon my head
     and by his light I walked through darkness!
	29 Job again took up his discourse and said:
	 ² "O that I were as in the months of old,
	     as in the days when God watched over me;
	 ³ when his lamp shone over my head,
	     and by his light I walked through darkness;
	 ⁴ when I was in my prime,

NIV

⁴Oh, for the days when I was in my prime,
  when God's intimate friendship blessed my
    house,
⁵when the Almighty was still with me
  and my children were around me,
⁶when my path was drenched with cream
  and the rock poured out for me streams of
    olive oil.

⁷"When I went to the gate of the city
  and took my seat in the public square,
⁸the young men saw me and stepped aside
  and the old men rose to their feet;
⁹the chief men refrained from speaking
  and covered their mouths with their hands;
¹⁰the voices of the nobles were hushed,
  and their tongues stuck to the roof of their
    mouths.
¹¹Whoever heard me spoke well of me,
  and those who saw me commended me,
¹²because I rescued the poor who cried for help,
  and the fatherless who had none to assist him.
¹³The man who was dying blessed me;
  I made the widow's heart sing.
¹⁴I put on righteousness as my clothing;
  justice was my robe and my turban.
¹⁵I was eyes to the blind
  and feet to the lame.
¹⁶I was a father to the needy;
  I took up the case of the stranger.
¹⁷I broke the fangs of the wicked
  and snatched the victims from their teeth.

¹⁸"I thought, 'I will die in my own house,
  my days as numerous as the grains of sand.
¹⁹My roots will reach to the water,
  and the dew will lie all night on my branches.
²⁰My glory will remain fresh in me,
  the bow ever new in my hand.'

²¹"Men listened to me expectantly,
  waiting in silence for my counsel.
²²After I had spoken, they spoke no more;
  my words fell gently on their ears.
²³They waited for me as for showers
  and drank in my words as the spring rain.
²⁴When I smiled at them, they scarcely believed
    it;
  the light of my face was precious to them.ᵃ

ᵃ24 The meaning of the Hebrew for this clause is uncertain.

NRSV

  when the friendship of God was upon my
    tent;
⁵ when the Almightyᵃ was still with me,
  when my children were around me;
⁶ when my steps were washed with milk,
  and the rock poured out for me streams of
    oil!
⁷ When I went out to the gate of the city,
  when I took my seat in the square,
⁸ the young men saw me and withdrew,
  and the aged rose up and stood;
⁹ the nobles refrained from talking,
  and laid their hands on their mouths;
¹⁰ the voices of princes were hushed,
  and their tongues stuck to the roof of their
    mouths.
¹¹ When the ear heard, it commended me,
  and when the eye saw, it approved;
¹² because I delivered the poor who cried,
  and the orphan who had no helper.
¹³ The blessing of the wretched came upon me,
  and I caused the widow's heart to sing for
    joy.
¹⁴ I put on righteousness, and it clothed me;
  my justice was like a robe and a turban.
¹⁵ I was eyes to the blind,
  and feet to the lame.
¹⁶ I was a father to the needy,
  and I championed the cause of the stranger.
¹⁷ I broke the fangs of the unrighteous,
  and made them drop their prey from their
    teeth.
¹⁸ Then I thought, 'I shall die in my nest,
  and I shall multiply my days like the
    phoenix;ᵇ
¹⁹ my roots spread out to the waters,
  with the dew all night on my branches;
²⁰ my glory was fresh with me,
  and my bow ever new in my hand.'

²¹ "They listened to me, and waited,
  and kept silence for my counsel.
²² After I spoke they did not speak again,
  and my word dropped upon them like dew.ᶜ
²³ They waited for me as for the rain;
  they opened their mouths as for the spring
    rain.

ᵃ Traditional rendering of Heb Shaddai   ᵇ Or like sand   ᶜ Heb
lacks like dew

NIV

²⁵I chose the way for them and sat as their chief;
    I dwelt as a king among his troops;
    I was like one who comforts mourners."

NRSV

²⁴ I smiled on them when they had no confidence;
    and the light of my countenance they did
      not extinguish.^a
²⁵ I chose their way, and sat as chief,
    and I lived like a king among his troops,
    like one who comforts mourners."

^a Meaning of Heb uncertain

COMMENTARY

Job begins his final speech in chap. 29 with a retrospective reflection on the conditions that gave his life meaning and value before disaster shook him to the foundations. By speaking in this way, Job gives the reader insight into his moral world. Only in the light of this description can one understand the full nature of Job's suffering and loss. Since Job's image of God is shaped so strongly by his understanding of his own place in this moral world, one also learns a great deal about the sources and nature of Job's theology. Job's description of "the good life," in the sense of moral goodness as well as of deep satisfaction, is noteworthy first of all for its deeply social orientation. As Job describes the various categories of persons with whom he interacts, he virtually draws a map of his social world. There is, indeed, a spatial quality to his account, which moves from the household to the city gate. This sense of a social map will continue in the following chapter, as Job describes the boundary of his social world and his own sense of having been cast out from it.

The ethical sense that pervades Job's moral world is a paternalistic one, in which the most important ethical actions are those involving the protection of the powerless against exploitation. The deepest satisfactions for a person like Job in this society are the gratitude of those he has aided and the respect of his peers. Both gratitude and respect are important measures of honor, the preeminent value in a moral world such as Job inhabited. Job begins his account with the image of God's protective presence, expressed in terms of personal relationship, and with the image of the household and its well-being, expressed in terms of progeny and abundance (vv. 2-6). Next

the horizon moves outward to encompass Job's interaction with his peers in social rituals of honor at the city gate (vv. 7-10). The longest part of the description is given over to Job's paternal care for marginalized members of society (vv. 11-17). The mutually life-giving nature of Job's relation with his community is evoked first in images of Job's anticipated long life, nurtured by resources that would sustain and renew him (vv. 18-20). Job's description of his expectations for himself are matched by his final word concerning the way in which his leadership gave life, direction, and comfort to his community (vv. 21-25).

29:1. As in 27:1, Job's speech opens with the observation that he "again" took up his discourse, implying that it has been interrupted. In this case, the poem on wisdom separates Job's reply to Bildad in chap. 27 from this, his final speech.

29:2-6. In describing the wholeness and meaningfulness of the life he has lost, Job first recounts his sense of God's protective presence (vv. 2-4). His language is personal, relational, and richly emotive. For God to "watch over" (v. 2*b*) someone connotes a deep sense of security (cf. Psalm 121, where the sixfold repetition of the same verb creates a sense of protection). In keeping with the general spatial organization of the speech, Job begins with the most intimate horizon, depicting God as light in relation to his own body and movement (v. 3). The imagery is traditional (cf. Pss 18:28[29]; 36:9[10]; Mic 7:8; cf. Job 18:5-6). The imagery of light connotes security, as suggested by the reference to walking through darkness. Darkness represents unseen dangers that cannot be eliminated from the world. But the one who is illumined by God's light may see and avoid them, in contrast to the one whose light is extinguished and so blunders helplessly into danger (18:7-10).

In the next verses, the horizon moves slightly outward to the "tent" or household under the protection of God's friendship (v. 4*b*; cf. Ps 25:14). This relationship is visualized in terms of the patriarch's relation to his children gathered round about him. The fundamental relationship in this social and moral world, and the one with the strongest emotional meaning, is the relationship between parents and children (cf. Gen 15:2; Ps 127:3). The patriarch also provides for his household. Job had spoken of the horror of the destitute who are not able to provide for their children (24:5, 9). The contrasting blessing is overflowing abundance (v. 6). The word translated "cream" or "milk" (חמה *ḥēmâ*) denotes a yogurt-like food, often associated with gestures of hospitality (Gen 18:8; Judg 5:25). Olive oil, too, is an evocative symbol, not only of the goodness of food, but also of the pleasures of the body. Deuteronomy 32:13 describes Asher's blessing in terms of bathing his feet in oil, and Psalm 133 likens the joy of brotherly unity to the pleasure of oil poured on the head and dripping into the beard. For such richness to come from the very rocks is a traditional image of abundance (Deut 32:12; cf. Ps 81:16).

29:7-10. In the next section the horizon moves outward to the city gate and the plaza, where prominent men of the community met to take counsel, resolve disputes, and conduct business (cf. Deut 21:19; Ruth 4:1; 2 Chr 32:6). God's presence with Job finds expression in the respect and honor accorded to him by his peers. Spatial imagery is important here, too. Much as his children were depicted as gathered round about him in v. 5, so here, when Job goes out to the plaza to take his seat (v. 7), he becomes the center around which others station themselves. Young men "hide themselves," withdrawing to the margins (v. 8*a*), but even the elders, who had previously been seated as centers of attention, now arise and stand, acknowledging Job's place (v. 8*b*; cf. Lev 19:32; Isa 49:7). The same social rearrangement that took place in terms of physical position also occurs with respect to speech. Even princes and nobles, who would normally give counsel, fall silent when Job appears, waiting respectfully for him to speak (vv. 9-10). Job's

understanding of what brings satisfaction finds its symbolic form in images of center and periphery. To be the dynamic center that reorganizes social space is an expression of what is highly valued.

29:11-17. It would be a mistake to understand Job's pleasure in the honor paid to him simply in terms of ego satisfaction. As this section of the speech makes clear, Job receives honor because he embodies the values of the community. In vv. 9-10, Job spoke of the respectful silence with which his presence was greeted. That does not mean that his peers did not evaluate him, however. What Job said and did was continuously judged by the ear and eye of the community (v. 11). There are few experiences so gratifying as to receive the approbation of one's peers for having embodied the shared values of the group.

What those values are can be judged from the following verses (vv. 12-17). Here the focus shifts from the inner circle of Job's peers to persons occupying a more marginal place in the social map: the poor, the orphan, the wretched, the widow, the blind, the lame, the needy, the stranger. The responsibility of the leaders of a community for its weakest members is one of the foundations of the ancient Near Eastern moral world (see Ps 72:1-4, 12-14).[434] It is easy to see how these persons depend upon Job, but one should not overlook the fact that Job also depends on them in certain significant ways. The powerful one gives protection and intervention; in return, he receives gratitude, described in v. 13 as the blessing of the wretched and the widow's song. This recognition by the powerless is as important in establishing the patriarch's social identity as is the respect and approbation of his peers. Job identifies his intervention on behalf of the powerless as "righteousness" and "justice." How essential these aspects are to his sense of identity is indicated through his use of clothing imagery in v. 14, for clothes are one's "public skin."

Job's language of aid is personal and intimate. In v. 16, he uses paternal imagery, and in v. 15 he even identifies his assistance in terms corresponding to the damaged bodies of the needy. Job's championing of the poor is not merely a matter of largess, however, but a protective rage against their victimi-

---

434. See also the Epilogue to Hammurapi's Law, *ANET*, 178; the inscription of Kilamuwa, *ANET*, 654-55.

zation. His metaphor in v. 17 is implicitly that of the shepherd, someone like David, who would risk his own life to rescue a sheep carried off by a predator (cf. 1 Sam 17:34-35). The poor are Job's flock, and his sense of responsibility for them in large measure defines his identity.

The values and identity that Job articulates for himself are very similar to those Israel attributed to God. God, too, is a champion of the oppressed (Deut 24:17-22; Prov 23:10-11), a father to the orphan and a protector of widows (Ps 68:5[6]), closely identified with righteousness and justice (Ps 89:14[15]), a shepherd (Ps 23:1) who delivers victims from the jaws of the wicked (Ps 3:7[8]).

29:18-20. As in Eliphaz's description of the righteous person in 5:17-26, Job describes a good death as the culmination of a meaningful life (v. 18). The verse is susceptible of two quite different translations, reflected in the NRSV and the NIV. At issue is the translation of the word חול (ḥôl) in v. 18b. Ordinarily, the word means "sand" (NIV),[435] and the image of sand traditionally represents a vast number (Gen 32:12; 41:49; Ps 139:18; Isa 48:19). The image in the first line of the verse, however, "Then I thought, 'I shall die in my nest'" (NRSV; NIV paraphrases), suggests translating ḥôl as "phoenix," the mythical bird that lived for a vast number of years and then renewed its life by rising from the ashes of its burned nest.[436] This interpretation is already attested in the Talmud,[437] and is supported by certain evidence from Ugaritic texts.[438] Ironically, this *will* be Job's fate. He will experience renewed life that arises out of the ashes of his previous existence and will die in the midst of his family at a very advanced age, "old and full of days" (42:12-17).

Additional images of sustaining strength and renewal occur in vv. 19-20. Job implicitly compares himself to a tree (v. 19), whose roots are fed by underground water (cf. Ps 1:3; Jer 17:8; Ezek 31:7) and whose leaves are refreshed by dew (Deut 33:28; Ps 133:3; Zech 8:12). Renewal of "glory" in v. 20a may be a more physical image than first appears, since the same word can occasionally mean "liver" (cf. Ps 7:5[6]; 16:9).[439] Analogously, the "bow" in 20b is a familiar symbol for masculine prowess (Gen 49:24; 1 Sam 2:4; Ps 37:15[16]).

29:21-25. The final section of the chapter turns from the sustaining strength Job received to the way he sustained his community. Job's leadership was expressed first of all through his role as counselor (vv. 21-23). The great respect with which a wise counselor was held is suggested by the reputation of Ahitophel, of whom it was said that it was "as if one consulted the oracle of God" (2 Sam 16:23 NRSV). Similarly, Job's advice was literally the last word to his fellows. The metaphor of life-giving rain in v. 23 echoes the water imagery of v. 19. Just as Job was sustained by transcendent sources of strength represented as water, so also he became a transcendent source of strength for his community (cf. Deut 11:14; Jer 5:24; Hos 6:3). Although v. 24 can be legitimately translated in more than one way (cf. NRSV and NIV), the basic sense is clear. The expressions of goodwill communicated by Job's face were themselves enough to sustain those who depended on him.

The final cluster of images in v. 25 surprises some readers. The first three all have to do with leadership in terms of royal authority and the ability to make decisions on behalf of the entire community. The final image, however, is that of "one who comforts mourners." A few commentators, seeking consistency, emend the last words to read "where I led them, they were willing to go."[440] Leadership in ancient Israel, however, was understood to be personal and nurturing, as well as a matter of decisive action. The image of the king as shepherd, and of God as shepherd, reflects well the combination of these qualities (e.g., Isa 40:10-11; Ezekiel 34). That Job should make the role of comforting mourners the final word of his description of leadership is significant. This is the task the friends undertook and failed to perform

435. S. R. Driver and G. B. Gray, *A Critical and Exegetical Commentary on the Book of Job*, ICC (Edinburgh: T. & T. Clark, 1921) Part I, 249; Part II, 201-4; M. Pope, *Job*, 3rd ed., AB 15 (Garden City, N.Y.: Doubleday, 1979) 208, 213-16; J. E. Hartley, *The Book of Job*, NICOT (Grand Rapids, Mich.: Eerdmans, 1988) 392.

436. See R. van den Broek, *The Myth of the Phoenix According to Classical and Early Christian Traditions*, EPRO 24 (Leiden: Brill, 1972).

437. See b. Sanh. 108b.

438. M. Dahood, "*Ḥôl* 'Phoenix' in Job 29:18 and in Ugaritic," *CBQ* 36 (1974) 85-8; L. Grabbe, *Comparative Philology and the Text of Job: A Study in Methodology*, SBLDS 34 (Missoula, Mont.: Scholars Press, 1977) 98-101; R. Gordis, *The Book of Job: Commentary, New Translation, and Special Studies* (New York: Jewish Theological Seminary, 5738/1978) 321-22; but see Pope, *Job*, 213-16.

439. Habel, *The Book of Job*, 411.

440. E. Dhorme, *A Commentary on the Book of Job*, trans. H. Knight (London: Nelson, 1967) 422; similarly, Pope, *Job*, 212.

for Job. One senses from chap. 29 why Job would have been a better comforter. Comfort is not a matter of supplying reasons but of providing a sense of supportive community in a time when chaos threatens to overwhelm.

It is striking how many of Job's images for himself in chap. 29 are elsewhere applied to kings and even to God. Proverbs 16:15 refers to the life-giving quality of the "light of a king's face" and even compares the king's favor to the clouds bringing spring rain. Similarly, the king is compared to rain in Ps 72:6. Wise counsel is a quality of the ideal ruler in Isa 9:6. The protection of the powerless, a function Job claims in vv. 11-17, is also that of the king in Ps 72:12-14, and the association of the king with righteousness and justice is a commonplace (e.g., Isa 9:7). Perhaps more striking is the parallel between Job's self-description and traditional images of God. God brings life-giving rains (Deut 11:14; Jer 5:4; Hos 6:3). Most strikingly, "the light of your face" is a phrase most often associated with God's presence (Num 6:25; Pss 4:6[7]; 44:3[4]; 89:15[16]). Readers who take these similarities as evidence of Job's arrogance misunderstand their function.[441] Job uses these images because they characterize the ideals of leadership in his community, whether that is the leadership of the patriarch, of the king, or of God. Indeed, to a very large extent the image of God is shaped according to the ideal model of a patriarch or king. The expressions that echo traditional language about God are also the poet's way of reminding the reader that Job's expectations of God are similar to what he expects of himself (see Commentary on Job 31).

---

441. Habel suggests that "Job virtually usurps the functions of God" (*The Book of Job*, 406), and Perdue says that "the language of this chapter borders on self-idolatry" (L. Perdue, *Wisdom in Revolt: Metaphorical Theology in the Book of Job*, JSOTSup 112 [Sheffield: JSOT, 1991] 192).

REFLECTIONS

Job's long speech about his past and present experience is both appealing and disturbing. Readers often wonder, however, whether it is appropriate to make judgments about the moral values presented by figures from another culture and another time. There is certainly a danger that one will either romanticize the past or dismiss it simply because it is different from one's own set of values. It is both appropriate and necessary, however, to take seriously the claims about the nature of the moral life as they are made in a text like Job 29. Because modern readers stand largely outside that cultural world, it is easier to see some of the limitations and problems with its vision of character and culture than it would have been for contemporaries. The judgment does not proceed in one direction only, however. Reflecting on the moral vision that informs Job's sense of himself can also lead to a clearer vision of the limitations and problems in one's own moral world.

Perhaps the most striking feature of Job's moral sense is its deeply relational character. In his world, persons are not autonomous individuals so much as they are persons in relation. Job locates himself in relation to God, to his children, to his peers, to those who need his protection, to those who need his leadership. These sets of relationships are what feed and refresh him, root and branch. His is a world in which community has an organic quality. Both the best and the most troubling aspects of Job's moral world concern his relationship with the marginal and vulnerable members of his community. That his own worth should be so connected with his role as their defender and helper is admirable, but what Job cannot see is the limitations of an essentially paternalistic relationship. Such a relationship is necessarily tied to the logic of inequality. The binary relationship of dominant/subordinate or donor/recipient undergirds the sense of moral obligation. The limitation of such a structure is that it can embrace amelioration of suffering on an individual basis, but it cannot comprehend the transformation of the very structures that generate the inequalities that produce suffering. The social rewards that such a system offers to its leading members are based on the gratitude of the poor and the respect of one's peers—in short, the reward of honor. Such a social system requires a measure of inequality and even a vulnerable, marginal class in order to function.

Using Job's speech as a model, it is worth thinking how a modern citizen of the United States might look over his or her life and talk about what elements gave it meaning and value. The modern culture is much more complex than the world of ancient Israel, of course, and so there would undoubtedly be many different accounts. Nevertheless, a number of the elements would be fairly common to our stories of what matters in life. Undoubtedly, relationships would have a prominent place, but they would be quite different in nature and scope from Job's account. Most citizens of the U.S. would speak of the importance of family, much as Job did. On closer investigation, however, the scope of "family" would be quite different. For modern Americans, the nuclear family is what is primarily meant, not the extended kinship group that had so much greater importance in traditional societies like that of ancient Israel. A modern person would also be very likely to mention a romantic relationship as central to well-being, something completely absent from Job's account. Perhaps the most striking difference would be the modern individual's references to personal autonomy. The word *choice* shows up frequently in people's accounts of their lives: choosing a mate, choosing a career, choosing a church, choosing a life-style, choosing values for oneself. Such a language and its implications for the nature of the individual would be absolutely incomprehensible to someone like Job. Although it is often difficult to get enough distance to reflect on it, the immense value placed on personal autonomy points to some of the limitations of our own moral world. It can easily become a kind of moral consumerism, in which there is no common good, only personal preference.

The other striking difference between Job's moral world and that of the modern world concerns the public or civic sphere. Modern persons also seek the respect of their peers. Most often, however, the context for this social validation is the workplace. That is where, at least in good situations, persons experience the satisfaction of teamwork and the commendation of a job well done. In our society, self-worth is deeply tied up with having a job in the first place and in being respected for the work one does. It is not so closely tied to one's efforts on behalf of the poor. Whereas for Job such care for the socially vulnerable was at the very core of his identity, in modern society such matters are generally considered admirable, but optional. Civic work, charity, and social justice involvements are things that one does as a volunteer, an indication of their marginal status. This is not to say that such work might not be of central importance for a particular individual, but that the culture in general does not consider it to be an essential measure of a person's worth.

Finally, the place of religion would be a great variable. For some it would be the starting point, as it is in Job's narration. For others, including some readers of this commentary, it would be an element that has a place in the story of what is meaningful, but not the obvious starting place. And for many, it would not appear at all. The fact of such variability is itself an indication of the great distance between Job's cultural world and our own.

Such reflections do not lead to simple conclusions. The point is not to judge one vision of moral community better or worse than another so much as it is to underscore the importance of learning how to articulate one's understanding of what constitutes the life worth living and to develop the critical distance necessary for perceiving both its limitations and its strengths. In a recent study of American moral self-understanding, the authors of *Habits of the Heart* noted the great difficulty many persons had in being able to explain the foundation for the values they held and the vision of moral worth and community implied by them. The language in which most persons attempted to articulate their moral sense was a language of radical individualism. Quite apart from the limitations such a moral vision might entail in itself, the authors also noted that such language simply failed to describe adequately the much richer lives that most of the persons interviewed actually lived.[442] The church is the bearer of a long

---

442. R. Bellah et al., *Habits of the Heart: Individualism and Commitment in American Life* (Berkeley: University of California Press, 1985), esp. 81-83.

tradition of moral discourse that can provide alternatives and correctives to the prevailing language of individualism. It is, of course, neither possible nor desirable simply to take up a biblical model, such as the one Job gives voice to. Our world is not his world and never can be; nor is it clear that one would want to return to such a world even if it were possible. What engagement with a text like Job can do is to challenge some of our assumptions and lead us into a much richer sense of how we might rethink the meaning of moral community.

Job 30:1-31, Job Laments His Present Humiliation

NIV

30 "But now they mock me,
men younger than I,
whose fathers I would have disdained
to put with my sheep dogs.
²Of what use was the strength of their hands to me,
since their vigor had gone from them?
³Haggard from want and hunger,
they roamed[a] the parched land
in desolate wastelands at night.
⁴In the brush they gathered salt herbs,
and their food[b] was the root of the broom tree.
⁵They were banished from their fellow men,
shouted at as if they were thieves.
⁶They were forced to live in the dry stream beds,
among the rocks and in holes in the ground.
⁷They brayed among the bushes
and huddled in the undergrowth.
⁸A base and nameless brood,
they were driven out of the land.

⁹"And now their sons mock me in song;
I have become a byword among them.
¹⁰They detest me and keep their distance;
they do not hesitate to spit in my face.
¹¹Now that God has unstrung my bow and afflicted me,
they throw off restraint in my presence.
¹²On my right the tribe[c] attacks;
they lay snares for my feet,
they build their siege ramps against me.
¹³They break up my road;
they succeed in destroying me—
without anyone's helping them.[d]
¹⁴They advance as through a gaping breach;

a3 Or gnawed   b4 Or fuel   c12 The meaning of the Hebrew for this word is uncertain.   d13 Or me. / 'No one can help him,'ᵢthey sayᵢ.

NRSV

30 "But now they make sport of me,
those who are younger than I,
whose fathers I would have disdained
to set with the dogs of my flock.
² What could I gain from the strength of their hands?
All their vigor is gone.
³ Through want and hard hunger
they gnaw the dry and desolate ground,
⁴ they pick mallow and the leaves of bushes,
and to warm themselves the roots of broom.
⁵ They are driven out from society;
people shout after them as after a thief.
⁶ In the gullies of wadis they must live,
in holes in the ground, and in the rocks.
⁷ Among the bushes they bray;
under the nettles they huddle together.
⁸ A senseless, disreputable brood,
they have been whipped out of the land.

⁹ "And now they mock me in song;
I am a byword to them.
¹⁰ They abhor me, they keep aloof from me;
they do not hesitate to spit at the sight of me.
¹¹ Because God has loosed my bowstring and humbled me,
they have cast off restraint in my presence.
¹² On my right hand the rabble rise up;
they send me sprawling,
and build roads for my ruin.
¹³ They break up my path,
they promote my calamity;
no one restrains[a] them.
¹⁴ As through a wide breach they come;
amid the crash they roll on.

a Cn: Heb helps

NIV

amid the ruins they come rolling in.
15Terrors overwhelm me;
my dignity is driven away as by the wind,
my safety vanishes like a cloud.

16"And now my life ebbs away;
days of suffering grip me.
17Night pierces my bones;
my gnawing pains never rest.
18In his great power ⌐God⌐ becomes like clothing
to me*e*;
he binds me like the neck of my garment.
19He throws me into the mud,
and I am reduced to dust and ashes.

20"I cry out to you, O God, but you do not
answer;
I stand up, but you merely look at me.
21You turn on me ruthlessly;
with the might of your hand you attack me.
22You snatch me up and drive me before the wind;
you toss me about in the storm.
23I know you will bring me down to death,
to the place appointed for all the living.

24"Surely no one lays a hand on a broken man
when he cries for help in his distress.
25Have I not wept for those in trouble?
Has not my soul grieved for the poor?
26Yet when I hoped for good, evil came;
when I looked for light, then came darkness.
27The churning inside me never stops;
days of suffering confront me.
28I go about blackened, but not by the sun;
I stand up in the assembly and cry for help.
29I have become a brother of jackals,
a companion of owls.
30My skin grows black and peels;
my body burns with fever.
31My harp is tuned to mourning,
and my flute to the sound of wailing."

a18 Hebrew; Septuagint ⌐God⌐ grasps my clothing

NRSV

15 Terrors are turned upon me;
my honor is pursued as by the wind,
and my prosperity has passed away like a
cloud.

16 "And now my soul is poured out within me;
days of affliction have taken hold of me.
17 The night racks my bones,
and the pain that gnaws me takes no rest.
18 With violence he seizes my garment;*a*
he grasps me by*b* the collar of my tunic.
19 He has cast me into the mire,
and I have become like dust and ashes.
20 I cry to you and you do not answer me;
I stand, and you merely look at me.
21 You have turned cruel to me;
with the might of your hand you persecute
me.
22 You lift me up on the wind, you make me ride
on it,
and you toss me about in the roar of the
storm.
23 I know that you will bring me to death,
and to the house appointed for all living.

24 "Surely one does not turn against the needy,*c*
when in disaster they cry for help.*d*
25 Did I not weep for those whose day was hard?
Was not my soul grieved for the poor?
26 But when I looked for good, evil came;
and when I waited for light, darkness came.
27 My inward parts are in turmoil, and are never
still;
days of affliction come to meet me.
28 I go about in sunless gloom;
I stand up in the assembly and cry for help.
29 I am a brother of jackals,
and a companion of ostriches.
30 My skin turns black and falls from me,
and my bones burn with heat.
31 My lyre is turned to mourning,
and my pipe to the voice of those who weep."

*a Gk: Heb my garment is disfigured   b Heb like   c Heb ruin
d Cn: Meaning of Heb uncertain*

COMMENTARY

Idyllic recollections of a world that was satisfying and meaningful are shattered as Job turns his attention to his present situation. Three times Job punctuates his account with the introductory phrase "but now . . ." as he describes a world turned upside down. The particular quality of Job's suffering is closely linked to the features that made his previous life so fulfilling. Just as he derived his sense of identity from being a person of honor, honored by others, so also he experiences his devastation most acutely in terms of being an object of contempt, even to the contemptible. As he describes his anger and sense of betrayal at what has happened to him, Job reveals certain disturbing features of his moral world that were only barely visible in chap. 29. Job's baffled disappointment in what he took to be the moral structures of his world, however, lends a note of poignancy to his speech.

The chapter divides into four major sections, the first three marked by the repeated phrase "but now" (עתה 'atâ, vv. 1, 9, 16), and the last introduced by the word "surely" (אך 'ak, v. 24). In vv. 1-8, Job begins to describe the mockery to which he is subjected (v. 1), but interrupts himself to utter his own contemptuous description of those who treat him with such disrespect (vv. 2-8). Resuming his account of the scorn with which he is regarded, Job shows how such contempt can quickly become savage maltreatment by those whose resentment is unleashed (vv. 9-15). The third section (vv. 16-23) turns from an account of the social dimensions of Job's suffering to an account of physical and psychic suffering. As Job talks about God's enmity, he addresses God directly (vv. 20-23). In the final section of the chapter (vv. 24-31), Job expresses his outraged sense of having received evil in the place of good and concludes with striking images of his alienation from a world that has no place for him.

30:1-8. The phrase "but now" introduces the contrast with the ideal lost world of "months of old" (29:2). Where Job had been the object of respect even by those older than he (29:8b), now he is the object of mockery by those who are younger (v. 1). Although public mockery is painful in any society, there are certain cultures in which it is particularly devastating. Where group ties are especially strong and identity is fixed by one's place in the group, rather than by achievements as an autonomous individual, the shame of public ridicule is one of the most excruciating experiences imaginable. Only in this context can one understand the social dimensions of Job's suffering. Cultures in which the values of honor and shame are central are also often organized by a strong sense of social hierarchy.[443] Job's first words here reflect the values of a hierarchy of age, in which youth respects age. Thus an insult that would be hard enough to bear from a contemporary is even more painful when it comes from someone who is younger.

Youth and age are not the only aspects of the social hierarchy of Job's moral world. Social stigma may be passed from generation to generation, and so Job expresses his own contempt for his mockers by insulting their fathers (v. 1b). Job is a master of the insult. The ostensible point of his comment is that he would not even have hired these men to be his shepherds; but that is not the way Job phrases it. He says instead that he would not have "put them with the dogs of [his] flock," thus insinuating that these men were not worthy even to be associated with his dogs. Since the term "dog" (כלב keleb) was itself a serious insult if applied to others and a term of deep self-abasement if used of oneself (cf. 1 Sam 24:14; 2 Sam 9:8; 2 Kgs 8:13), Job could scarcely have said anything more contemptuous.

Opinion is divided as to whether vv. 2-8 describe the young men who insult Job (so NRSV) or their fathers (so NIV; "their sons" in v. 9 is not in the Hebrew text but is added by the translators). Although either interpretation is possible, the continuity of imagery is clearer if one understands Job to be talking primarily about the young men. In truth, there is little distinction between them, since they share each other's characteristics. What makes these people so contemptible is their abject poverty. In v. 2, Job comments on their lack of strength. In vv. 3-4, it becomes obvious why they have lost their vigor: They have

---

443. See, e.g., J. Pitt-Rivers, *The Fate of Shechem,* Cambridge Studies in Social Anthropology 19 (Cambridge: Cambridge University Press, 1977); B. Malina, *The New Testament World: Insights from Cultural Anthropology,* rev. ed. (Louisville: Westminster/John Knox, 1983).

nothing to eat. Job represents them as scavengers who live off the meager foods that can be gathered in wastelands not fit for cultivation. The location that Job assigns them is symbolically significant. Traditionally, the unsown land beyond the cities and their surrounding fields was associated with dangerous and hostile forces. Beyond the boundaries of ordered and civilized society, wild animals and even demonic beings lurked.[444] The destitute may roam the wastelands out of necessity, but their association with that eerie place makes it easy to treat them as dangerous and alien, and so to exclude them from a place in the social order. This is precisely what is reflected in v. 5. Note that Job does not say that they *are* thieves, but that people drive them out from society, shouting at them *as if* they were thieves. Simply by being who they are, these people evoke the fear and rejection appropriate to criminals.

Verses 6-8 largely recapitulate the previous description in vv. 3-5. Here, however, the contrast between these alien outsiders and the people of the town is not made in terms of food, as in vv. 3-4, but in terms of their dwellings. They are homeless. They do not live in houses like everyone else, but in makeshift dwellings: caves, rock shelters, and gullies (cf. 1 Sam 14:11). The fact that they live in the scrubland, outside the normal place for human beings, makes it easy to compare them with the wild animals whose land they share, as Job implicitly does by referring to their "braying" among the bushes (v. 7), a term elsewhere used of the wild ass (6:5). In such subtle symbolic ways these marginal figures are dehumanized. Corresponding to v. 5, Job again underscores the judgment that these people have no place in human society (v. 8), but are "whipped out of the land." It is difficult to render Job's terms for them in colloquial English. He calls them "sons of a fool" and "sons of a 'no-name.'" Although the term "fool" (נבל *nābāl*) can have a general sense, it originates as a social term, designating the poverty, but even more, the lack of proper values to be found in the lower classes.[445] Thus

when Job told his wife that she spoke as "one of the foolish women" (2:10a), one might get the gist by saying that she "talks like trash." The social dimensions of the insult are explicit in Job's designation of his tormentors as "sons of a 'no-name.'" In Job's world, an important part of a person's dignity and honor comes from having a distinguished lineage. These persons are by birth destined for low status and are despised for it.

One of the interpretive problems posed by this section is its striking contrast with Job's sympathetic description of the destitute in 24:3-8. It will not do to attempt to evade the contradiction by supposing that Job is talking about two different groups, the deserving poor vs. the rabble.[446] Both accounts use the same imagery: exclusion from the public sphere, scavenging for food, lack of shelter, and even comparison with the wild asses. What is different is Job's point of view. The collapse of Job's world, and with it the collapse of his complacency, had given him a certain ability to look at his world through the eyes of those who have nothing and who are rejected by others. This he expresses clearly in 24:3-8. There are barriers to any true solidarity between Job and the wretched of the earth, however. For all the insight that his recent experience has brought him, Job was not born destitute; rather, he was born to privilege. The social resentment that lurks in strongly hierarchical societies often finds intense expression when a high-ranking member of society falls from his or her position.[447] Consequently, Job is not welcomed by the outcasts as someone who has become one of them, but becomes the object for their pent up rage. Not surprising, Job reacts to this hostility by taking refuge in his own social class perceptions and values, lashing out with words that reinscribe the distinctions between "those people" and Job himself. In these two passages, the author of Job has given a dismal but acutely observed depiction of an all too familiar social drama.

30:9-15. Repeating the phrase "and/but now," Job returns to his main topic, a description of his mockery and ill-treatment by this rabble. There is a crescendo pattern in Job's account,

444. See A. Haldar, *The Notion of the Desert in Sumero-Accadian and West-Semitic Religions* (Uppsala: A.-B. Lundequistska Bokhandeln, 1950).
445. K. van der Toorn, *Sin and Sanction in Israel and Mesopotamia,* SSN 22 (Assen and Maastricht: Van Gorcum, 1985) 107; R. Gordis, *The Book of Job: Commentary, New Translation, and Special Studies* (New York: Jewish Theological Seminary, 5738/1978) 332. The social dimensions of the term can be seen in Prov 30:21-23.

446. Contra N. Habel, *The Book of Job,* OTL (Philadelphia: Westminster, 1985) 419.
447. See Rene Girard, *Job: The Victim of His People,* trans. Y. Freccero (Stanford: Stanford University Press, 1987) 51-52.

beginning with verbal aggression in v. 9, proceeding to insulting gestures in v. 10, and culminating in images of physical violence in vv. 12-14. In a society in which dignity and reputation are highly valued, having satirical songs made up about one and one's name used as a byword is devastating (v. 9; cf. Lam 3:14). Although in modern cultures persons are expected to develop a measure of indifference to such talk, most readers can sense the dynamics by remembering the terrible power of taunts and jokes in the different social world of the playground and the school. Gestures of shunning and spitting have a more aggressive edge to them, since they are enacted in the despised person's presence. (For spitting, see 17:6 and Isa 50:6*b*.)

In v. 11, Job reflects on how it is that these "nobodies" have gained the nerve to attack one who was once so powerful and high ranking. Both Job and the rabble understand the catastrophe that has overtaken him as God's own aggression against and humiliation of Job. As such, it gives permission for anyone else to treat Job similarly. The image of the loosening of the bowstring is a telling one, for it suggests that God has deprived Job of the ability to defend himself. By contrast, Ps 18:34[35] describes divine protection as bringing with it the ability to bend a bow of bronze.

A number of obscurities in the Hebrew text lead to slightly different translations of vv. 12-14 in the NRSV and the NIV. The overall imagery of military aggression is somewhat clearer in the NIV. The roadworks (or seige ramps) of the aggressors are built up, while those of Job are torn down (vv. 12-13; cf. 19:12). As in 16:14, Job describes his destruction in terms of soldiers breaching the walls of a beseiged city (v. 14).

Despite the very physical imagery, Job makes it clear that what these people have succeeded in destroying is his dignity (v. 15). The word that Job uses is נדיבה (*nĕdîbâ*), an abstract term related to the noun meaning "a noble" (נדיב *nādîb*). The parallel term is translated in the NRSV as "prosperity" and in the NIV as "safety," but the TNK is probably correct in understanding the word to be related to שוע (*šôaʿ*), "noble." It is Job's honor (ישעתי *yĕšūʿātî*) that has been assaulted.

30:16-23. In this section, Job turns from the social dimensions of his degradation to its physical and psychic counterpart. Here again, the phrase "and/but now" serves to contrast his description of the "days of affliction" (v. 16) with the "days when God watched over me" (29:2). Job begins with an account of physical pain that is especially acute at night, similar to 7:4-5. As in his previous references to physical distress, Job experiences it as direct divine violence (cf. 7:13-16; 10:16-17; 16:9, 12-14). Unfortunately, the Hebrew text of v. 18 is so difficult that it is simply not possible to be certain what image Job uses to describe God's action against him. In v. 19, however, Job echoes an image he had used earlier, of God's forcing him into filth (cf. 9:30-31). Such a gesture is intended to be symbolic, and Job acknowledges its effect on his identity; he is made to feel like dirt (lit., "dust and ashes"). Given Job's symbolic universe, it is very difficult for acute and prolonged suffering not to feel like degradation. It is experienced as God's rejection of and contempt for a person (v. 11), echoed in the social contempt expressed by others (v. 9-10).

For the first time since chap. 16, Job addresses God directly in vv. 20-23. His words recall earlier accusations about God's silence and Job's unanswered cry (v. 20*a*; cf. 19:7), the obsessive but uncommunicative scrutiny to which God subjects him (v. 20*b*; cf. 7:17-19), and God's enmity toward him (v. 21; cf. 16:9, where the same verb is used). Although the NIV takes v. 22 simply as a negative image of God's buffeting Job like a storm wind (cf. 27:20-21), it is possible to take the first part of the verse in a positive sense. God is often represented as "riding the wind" (see Ps 18:10[11]); 104:3), and this verse may assert that God has first lifted Job up to an almost divine status, only to bring him down.[448] Such a contrast would echo the larger structure of chaps. 29–30. Although the notion has been implicit in much that Job has said, here he states explicitly that that God is seeking his death (v. 23; cf. 10:8-9).

30:24-31. Unfortunately, the verse that introduces the final section of the chapter is extremely obscure. Literally, it reads, "surely one does not stretch out a hand against a ruin, if in his calamity therefore a cry." Modest emendations produce a variety of plausible translations, although none of them is certain. Given the context of what fol-

448. Similarly, Habel, *The Book of Job*, 421. Textual problems allow for additional ways of interpreting this verse. Compare Gordis, *The Book of Job*, 336, and Habel, *The Book of Job*, 416.

lows, it appears that Job states a general moral principle that one does not answer a person in distress with violence. This has been the rule of his own conduct (cf. 29:12a, which is similar in wording, if one emends "ruin" [עי 'î] to "poor" [עני 'ānî] in 30:24). Inexplicably, God has behaved in just the opposite way to Job.

Verses 25-26 express Job's bafflement at the incoherence of the moral world he now experiences. Wisdom traditions insisted that good produced good and evil produced evil, both for others and for oneself (11:17, 24-25, 31; 13:2; 14:14; 15:27; 26:27). Yet Job's compassion for others has not resulted in compassion for himself. Rather, his expectations have been met by their opposites (for this figure of speech, see Isa 5:7b; Jer 8:15). These verses stand in considerable tension with Job's words in 2:10b, "Shall we receive the good at the hand of God, and not receive the bad?" (NRSV). At least in some sense the *satan* appears to have been right; Job did not "fear God for nothing" (1:9). Job assumed, much as his friends did, that the principle of moral retribution was an essential part of the relationship between God and human beings. Upon this basis, he formed his expectations (cf. 29:18-20), and he is now outraged at God's injustice.

Job's description of his present situation is an inversion of his past. Whereas he previously experienced physical vigor and the renewal of inner strength (29:19-20), now he experiences inner turmoil (v. 27a; cf. Lam 1:20; 2:11). The respectful reception by his peers (29:10) is parodied in the greeting he receives from personified "days of affliction" (v. 27b). The darkness to which Job refers in v. 28a is probably not the discoloration of his skin by disease (so NIV) but Job's sense that he now walks in gloom (so NRSV), in contrast to the light of God, which previously illumined his way (29:3). Whereas Job used to preside in the assemblies at the gate (29:7), now his role is that of suppliant (v. 28b), like the poor who once cried out to him (29:12). The kin and friendship relations who provided his social identity (29:5) now take the grotesque form of a kinship with the animals of the wasteland, the jackel and the ostrich (v. 29; the NIV's "owl" is less likely). Like the wild ass, the jackel and the ostrich are associated with desolate land (cf. Ps 44:19[20]; Jer 9:10-11),[449] the place of exclusion where Job located the despised "sons of a 'no-name.'" Job recognizes that his calamity has turned him into a figure who instills fear and rejection by those belonging to the protecting world of the town. In vv. 30-31, Job concludes with references to his physical and psychic suffering, much as he had described them in vv. 16-17. His concluding reference in v. 31 to his own songs of mourning recalls the mocking songs others sing about him (v. 9). More poignantly, Job's isolation in his mourning contrasts with the culminating line of Job's own self-description in 29:25 as "one who comforts mourners."

449. O. Keel, *Jahwes Entgegnung an Ijob*, FRLANT 121 (Goettingen: Vandenhoeck und Ruprecht, 1978) 83-84.

REFLECTIONS

Despite the poignancy of Job's words, one cannot help being shocked by the way he expresses his contempt for the outcasts who now mock him. This is not to criticize Job as a person but to recognize that, given his moral world, such language and views are inevitable. Job's world is a highly stratified one that makes sharp distinctions. It distinguishes "vertically" between the nobles and the lowly who depend on them (29:11-17), and it distinguishes "horizontally" between the grateful poor and the mocking rabble (30:1-10). This social stratification is also related to the moral and social values of honor and shame. Although the sense of what is honorable and what is shameful is intended to apply to conduct, it often gets drawn into distinctions of social class and wealth. Society is predisposed to assume that a person of high birth and wealth is a good person, and that a person who is poor and a "nobody" is also likely to have bad morals. From there it is only a short step to associating poverty itself with what is contemptible.

Even though the ancient Near East, including ancient Israel, was a culture deeply invested in the values of honor and shame, Israelite religion often provided a critical judgment against the tendency to associate these values with differences in wealth and status. Israel reminded itself often of its own lowly origins, that its ancestors had been slaves (Exod 20:2; Deut 5:15). The Israelites' obligation not to reject or oppress the alien does not arise out of a sense of *noblesse oblige* (as it may for Job), but is mandated because Israelites, too, knew what it meant to be alien (Exod 22:21). The prophets criticize the arrogance of "all that is lifted up and high" (Isa 2:12 NRSV), recognizing that wealth and status could lead to greediness and cruelty as easily as to social responsibility. Eventually, terms such as "poor" and "lowly" came to be associated not with moral laxity but with righteousness and piety (e.g., Zeph 3:12-13; Luke 1:46-55). In the NT, too, Jesus showed acceptance of "shameful" people, of prostitutes (Luke 7:36-50), of tax collectors (Matt 9:9-12), of beggars (Luke 18:35-42), even of despised Samaritans (John 4:4-42).

We would like to think that our culture, and in particular our churches, has learned these lessons and that we do not treat the marginal, the destitute, and the outsider with contempt. Unfortunately, those attitudes are very deeply ingrained. It is the rare middle-class parent who lets her child play with a friend who lives in the trailer park. It is the rare storeowner who does not watch the migrant worker with a careful eye, because everyone "knows" that "those people steal." Even in churches with night shelters, it is rare that homeless persons feel welcome at worship. To a disturbing extent, we still make unconscious judgments about moral character on the basis of social and economic class, and those judgments communicate themselves not only through words but also through gestures and glances. The poor know when they are regarded with fear and contempt. It is not necessary to "shout" (v. 5).

In Job's world, the two categories of the poor show very clearly where the boundaries of community lie. Even though the "deserving poor" may occupy the fringes of society, their claim on the attention of the nobles marks their place within the protecting boundaries of the social structure. By contrast, the outer boundary of community is marked by the exclusion of the rabble, whose place is literally outside the city walls in the wilderness. That social boundary marking function of an excluded group is a disturbingly recognizable feature. In our own society, that excluded group may be sociocultural, such as the distinction between "poor white trash" and the deserving poor. Much more often, however, those boundaries have been marked along racial and ethnic lines. It is an all too familiar story how the exclusion and dehumanization of blacks has been used to form a secure boundary, a sense of community identity, for a white society.

This tendency to define a community by who is excluded from it is quite pervasive. In some instances it may be innocuous, but more often it is used as an instrument of social power. Women may be kept out of particular occupations or organizations in order to reassure men of their superiority. Recent immigrants may be kept out of certain jobs or housing in order to reassure the grandchildren and great-grandchildren of earlier immigrants that they are truly Americans. Anxiety about identity, however, cannot be assuaged by excluding others. Yet expecially when an individual or a community feels vulnerable, as Job so clearly does in chapter 30, it is easy to translate that sense of vulnerability into social polarization.

Job 31:1-40, Job's Oath of Innocence

NIV

31 "I made a covenant with my eyes not to look lustfully at a girl.
²For what is man's lot from God above,

NRSV

31 "I have made a covenant with my eyes; how then could I look upon a virgin?
² What would be my portion from God above,

NIV

his heritage from the Almighty on high?
³Is it not ruin for the wicked,
disaster for those who do wrong?
⁴Does he not see my ways
and count my every step?

⁵"If I have walked in falsehood
or my foot has hurried after deceit—
⁶let God weigh me in honest scales
and he will know that I am blameless—
⁷if my steps have turned from the path,
if my heart has been led by my eyes,
or if my hands have been defiled,
⁸then may others eat what I have sown,
and may my crops be uprooted.

⁹"If my heart has been enticed by a woman,
or if I have lurked at my neighbor's door,
¹⁰then may my wife grind another man's grain,
and may other men sleep with her.
¹¹For that would have been shameful,
a sin to be judged.
¹²It is a fire that burns to Destruction*ᵃ*;
it would have uprooted my harvest.

¹³"If I have denied justice to my menservants and
maidservants
when they had a grievance against me,
¹⁴what will I do when God confronts me?
What will I answer when called to account?
¹⁵Did not he who made me in the womb make
them?
Did not the same one form us both within
our mothers?

¹⁶"If I have denied the desires of the poor
or let the eyes of the widow grow weary,
¹⁷if I have kept my bread to myself,
not sharing it with the fatherless—
¹⁸but from my youth I reared him as would a
father,
and from my birth I guided the widow—
¹⁹if I have seen anyone perishing for lack of
clothing,
or a needy man without a garment,
²⁰and his heart did not bless me
for warming him with the fleece from my
sheep,
²¹if I have raised my hand against the fatherless,
knowing that I had influence in court,

ᵃ12 Hebrew *Abaddon*

NRSV

and my heritage from the Almighty*ᵃ* on
high?
³ Does not calamity befall the unrighteous,
and disaster the workers of iniquity?
⁴ Does he not see my ways,
and number all my steps?

⁵ "If I have walked with falsehood,
and my foot has hurried to deceit—
⁶ let me be weighed in a just balance,
and let God know my integrity!—
⁷ if my step has turned aside from the way,
and my heart has followed my eyes,
and if any spot has clung to my hands;
⁸ then let me sow, and another eat;
and let what grows for me be rooted out.

⁹ "If my heart has been enticed by a woman,
and I have lain in wait at my neighbor's
door;
¹⁰ then let my wife grind for another,
and let other men kneel over her.
¹¹ For that would be a heinous crime;
that would be a criminal offense;
¹² for that would be a fire consuming down to
Abaddon,
and it would burn to the root all my
harvest.

¹³ "If I have rejected the cause of my male or
female slaves,
when they brought a complaint against
me;
¹⁴ what then shall I do when God rises up?
When he makes inquiry, what shall I answer
him?
¹⁵ Did not he who made me in the womb make
them?
And did not one fashion us in the womb?

¹⁶ "If I have withheld anything that the poor
desired,
or have caused the eyes of the widow to
fail,
¹⁷ or have eaten my morsel alone,
and the orphan has not eaten from it—
¹⁸ for from my youth I reared the orphan*ᵇ* like a
father,

ᵃ Traditional rendering of Heb *Shaddai*   ᵇ Heb *him*

NIV

22then let my arm fall from the shoulder,
   let it be broken off at the joint.
23For I dreaded destruction from God,
   and for fear of his splendor I could not do
      such things.

24"If I have put my trust in gold
   or said to pure gold, 'You are my security,'
25if I have rejoiced over my great wealth,
   the fortune my hands had gained,
26if I have regarded the sun in its radiance
   or the moon moving in splendor,
27so that my heart was secretly enticed
   and my hand offered them a kiss of homage,
28then these also would be sins to be judged,
   for I would have been unfaithful to God on high.

29"If I have rejoiced at my enemy's misfortune
   or gloated over the trouble that came to
      him—
30I have not allowed my mouth to sin
   by invoking a curse against his life—
31if the men of my household have never said,
   'Who has not had his fill of Job's meat?'—
32but no stranger had to spend the night in the street,
   for my door was always open to the
      traveler—
33if I have concealed my sin as men do,a
   by hiding my guilt in my heart
34because I so feared the crowd
   and so dreaded the contempt of the clans
   that I kept silent and would not go outside

35("Oh, that I had someone to hear me!
   I sign now my defense—let the Almighty
      answer me;
   let my accuser put his indictment in writing.
36Surely I would wear it on my shoulder,
   I would put it on like a crown.
37I would give him an account of my every step;
   like a prince I would approach him.)—

38"if my land cries out against me
   and all its furrows are wet with tears,
39If I have devoured its yield without payment
   or broken the spirit of its tenants,
40then let briers come up instead of wheat
   and weeds instead of barley."

The words of Job are ended.

a33 Or as Adam did

NRSV

and from my mother's womb I guided the
      widowa—
19 if I have seen anyone perish for lack of clothing,
   or a poor person without covering,
20 whose loins have not blessed me,
   and who was not warmed with the fleece
      of my sheep;
21 if I have raised my hand against the orphan,
   because I saw I had supporters at the gate;
22 then let my shoulder blade fall from my
      shoulder,
   and let my arm be broken from its socket.
23 For I was in terror of calamity from God,
   and I could not have faced his majesty.

24 "If I have made gold my trust,
   or called fine gold my confidence;
25 if I have rejoiced because my wealth was great,
   or because my hand had gotten much;
26 if I have looked at the sunb when it shone,
   or the moon moving in splendor,
27 and my heart has been secretly enticed,
   and my mouth has kissed my hand;
28 this also would be an iniquity to be punished
      by the judges,
   for I should have been false to God above.

29 "If I have rejoiced at the ruin of those who
      hated me,
   or exulted when evil overtook them—
30 I have not let my mouth sin
   by asking for their lives with a curse—
31 if those of my tent ever said,
   'O that we might be sated with his flesh!'c—
32 the stranger has not lodged in the street;
   I have opened my doors to the traveler—
33 if I have concealed my transgressions as others do,d
   by hiding my iniquity in my bosom,
34 because I stood in great fear of the multitude,
   and the contempt of families terrified me,
   so that I kept silence, and did not go out of
      doors—
35 O that I had one to hear me!
   (Here is my signature! Let the Almightye
      answer me!)
   O that I had the indictment written by my
      adversary!

aHeb her   bHeb the light   cMeaning of Heb uncertain
dOr as Adam did   eTraditional rendering of Heb Shaddai

NRSV

³⁶ Surely I would carry it on my shoulder;
　　I would bind it on me like a crown;
³⁷ I would give him an account of all my steps;
　　like a prince I would approach him.

³⁸ "If my land has cried out against me,
　　and its furrows have wept together;
³⁹ if I have eaten its yield without payment,
　　and caused the death of its owners;
⁴⁰ let thorns grow instead of wheat,
　　and foul weeds instead of barley."

The words of Job are ended.

COMMENTARY

The final chapter in Job's last speech begins abruptly. It is immediately clear, however, that the tone is different from the words of lament with which chap. 30 ended. In a manner similar to the rhetorical strategy of chaps. 16 and 19, lament language is interrupted by legal language. Job's words in chap. 31 are cast in the form of an elaborate oath, by means of which he attempts to establish his innocence of any wrongdoing (cf. 1 Sam 24:10-16; 1 Kgs 8:31-32). His speech has been compared to the process by which an accused person whose opponent refuses to produce evidence compels his accuser to come to court.[450] This is a suggestive analogy, although Job's reference to a hearing in vv. 35-37 appears as something of an afterthought and an impossible desire. Moreover, it should be remembered that Job uses the oath in an adapted, rhetorical manner, not as an actual legal proceeding. The rhetorical adaptation is apparent in that the behaviors of which Job claims to be innocent are largely matters that the law does not cover. Rather, they are elements of what Gordis calls Job's "code of honor,"[451] the revered moral values of his culture by which he has defined himself.[452]

The chapter has several functions. For Job, it serves to support his claim that he is indeed a person of honor, much as he described himself in chap. 29, not deserving of the contempt and humiliation to which he has been subjected by others and even by God. For the reader, Job's words reaffirm and give specific content to the narrator's original description of Job as a person of integrity and uprightness, who fears God and turns from evil. Not only Job's values are in evidence here, however. At several points, Job refers to God's passion for these values as the basis for his own moral seriousness. In this way the reader again sees the extent to which Job assumes a continuity between his own moral being and that of God. This assumption provides the basis for a possible resolution of the conflict between Job and God and a resolution of the issues of the book. That approach to a resolution is not one that God chooses, however; hence the book challenges many of Job's assumptions about God and the relationship between God and the world.

The structure of the chapter can be perceived if one examines the oath forms that are used and attends to the way they are grouped by topic. Two forms of the oath appear here. The complete oath has the form, "If I have done X, may Y happen to me" (vv. 7-10, 21-22, 38-40). An abbreviated oath has the form, "If I have done X . . ." with the consequences left unspecified. In effect, it serves as an assertion of innocence: "I

---

450. M. B. Dick, "The Legal Metaphor in Job 31," *CBQ* 41 (1979) 42.
451. Gordis, *The Book of Job,* 339.
452. G. Fohrer, "The Righteous Man in Job 31," in *Studien zum Buch Hiob,* 2nd ed., BZAW 159 (Berlin: Walter de Gruyter, 1983) 78-93; and M. B. Dick, "Job 31, the Oath of Innocence, and the Sage," *ZAW* 95 (1983) 31-53, discuss various genres to which Job 31 bears a resemblance.

have not done X." There are some ten examples of the abbreviated oath in chap. 31 (vv. 5, 13, 16, 19, 24, 25, 26, 29, 31, 33). Only the first claim of innocence is expressed in a non-oath form (v. 1). The topical structure of the chapter has largely escaped notice, and yet it seems quite straightforward. There are five groups of oaths, interrupted by Job's wish for a hearing in vv. 35-37. The general issues covered are (1) sexual and general morality (vv. 1-12), (2) justice and social obligation (vv. 13-23), (3) proper allegiance (vv. 24-28), (4) social relations (vv. 29-34), and (5) land ethics (vv. 38-40). Within several groups the structure is chiastic (i.e., having an ABBA or an ABA pattern; see below). The inclination of many commentators to see Job's desire for a hearing as the climax of the passage (to the extent that some even rearrange the text)[453] imposes the commentators' own sense of how the speech "should" have been composed. The oath of clearance is itself the point of the speech. The NIV correctly places all of vv. 35-37 in parentheses to indicate that these words are an aside by Job, not the goal of his speech.

31:1-12. The first group of four oaths begins and ends with sexual ethics, specifically, conduct toward a virgin (vv. 1-4) and toward the wife of another man (vv. 9-12). The two oaths in the middle address ethical conduct in general (vv. 5-8).[454] There is greater unity to the section than might first appear. Imagery in v. 4 concerning ways and steps anticipates the imagery of walking that introduces the second oath in v. 5, and reference to the heart toward the end of the third oath in v. 8 is echoed by the use of the same word at the beginning of the fourth oath in v. 9. Moreover, advice about sexual ethics in the wisdom tradition often had more than a literal application. It was the favorite image for proper conduct in general and was often used to introduce ethical admonitions of various sorts.[455]

In a strongly patriarchal society, sexual restrictions are important in both social and symbolic ways as a means of articulating the order of the social world.[456] Thus the combination of topics is quite in keeping with literary conventions in wisdom literature and an appropriate starting point for a comprehensive oath of innocence. These verses also employ a rhetorical device familiar from Proverbs, the use of particular parts of the body as images of the moral will (e.g., feet, heart, eyes, hands; see Prov 4:20-27).

31:1-4. The seduction or rape of an unmarried woman was a serious offense primarily because it threatened the rights of the father and thus undermined the social organization of the community (Exod 22:16-17[15-16]; Deut 22:23-29). Job, however, asserts that he has controlled not just his behavior but even his desire (v. 1). The eye often symbolizes desire (Ps 119:37; Isa 33:15), especially in sexual matters (Sir 9:5, 8). Job's image of making a covenant with his eyes is an unusual one, and the syntax of v. 1*a* is that of the imposition of a covenant by a superior on an inferior party.[457] Job claims to be master of his passions.

Verses 2-4 give the reasons why Job takes this commitment so seriously. His moral language is quite close to that of the friends, as he talks of the "portion" and "heritage" God allots to persons according to their conduct (v. 2; cf. Zophar in 20:20), the disaster that overtakes the evildoer (v. 3; cf. Bildad in 18:12), and God's scrutiny of an individual's behavior (v. 4; cf. Zophar in 11:11). Like that of the friends, Job's entire moral world and the motives for his own conduct have been shaped by the conviction that God directly rewards and punishes moral and immoral behavior. Precisely because what has happened to him threatens the meaningfulness of this fundamental belief, Job is determined to put this structure of meaning back together again. His words here indicate that he can conceive of no alternative to the beliefs by which he has lived.

31:5-8. The second oath in this series (vv. 5-6) uses the common wisdom metaphor of "walking" for behavior (cf. Ps 1:1; Prov 2:13), as well as the general moral terminology of falsehood and deceit,

453. E.G., E. Dhorme, *A Commentary on the Book of Job*, trans. H. Knight (London: Nelson, 1967) liii; Gordis, *The Book of Job*, 545; M. Pope, *Job*, 3rd ed., AB 15 (Garden City, N.Y.: Doubleday, 1979) 230; J. E. Hartley, *The Book of Job*, NICOT (Grand Rapids, Mich.: Eerdmans, 1988) 422; but see Habel, *The Book of Job*, 427-31; and E. Good, *In Turns of Tempest* (Stanford, Calif.: Stanford University Press, 1990) 312, who retain the order of the biblical text.

454. Gordis's suggestion, *The Book of Job*, 345, that these verses concern specifically business ethics is not persuasive.

455. Dick, "Job 31, the Oath of Innocence, and the Sage," 46. The attempt by Pope, *Job*, 229, to understand "virgin" as a reference to the Canaanite goddess Anat overlooks this traditional function of sexual topics in ethical discourse.

456. C. Newsom, "Woman and the Discourse of Patriarchal Wisdom: A Study of Proverbs 1-9," in P. Day, ed., *Gender and Difference in Ancient Israel* (Philadelphia: Fortress, 1989) 142-60.

457. Pope, *Job*, 228.

contrasted with integrity (cf. Ps 24:4). The image of God as one who "weighs" the hearts of persons is traditional (Prov 16:2; 24:12), but Job's use of the phrase "honest scales" also echoes legal and moral traditions in which God commands that honest scales be used among persons engaged in trade (Lev 19:35-36; Prov 20:10, 23; Ezek 45:10). Job assumes that the same morality governing relations between persons, according to God's command, will also govern his relation with God.

The first complete oath formula appears in vv. 7-8. The various parts of the body named (feet [lit. "steps"], eyes, heart, hands) suggest the totality of an individual's will and action (cf. Prov 4:25-27). There is no particular relation between the conduct described and the content of the curse in v. 8.[458] For someone to eat what another has sown, however, is a frequent image of divine punishment (Lev 26:16; Mic 6:15; cf. Isa 65:22).

31:9-12. Job rounds off the first series of oaths with the fundamental principle of Israelite ethics, sexual avoidance of a neighbor's wife (Exod 20:17; Deut 5:21; Prov 6:24-35; 7:6-27; Sir 23:18-27). "Door" is a double entendre, suggesting both the doorway of the neighbor's house and the sexual "doors of the womb" (3:10; cf. Cant 4:12). Although legal tradition treats adultery as a crime against the community and against God,[459] the sense that the husband is the injured party also appears in biblical literature (e.g., Prov 6:34-35). This perception underlies Job's oath that if he has violated the wife of another man, his own wife should be violated in return (cf. Deut 28:30; 2 Sam 12:11). The imagery in v. 10 ("grind," "kneel") has sexual connotations, as traditional Jewish interpretation recognized.[460] The vulnerability of servant women to sexual exploitation is perhaps alluded to in the play of literal and figurative meanings of the expression "may my wife grind for another" in v. 10*a*. The seriousness with which Job considers adultery is explicit in vv. 11-12. Fire is also used as a metaphor of the destructiveness of adultery in Prov 6:27-29, although here its terrible effect is virtually cosmic.

31:13-23. The second group of four oaths is

concerned with the topics of justice and social obligation. As in the preceding series, there is a chiastic structure. In the first and fourth oaths Job denies depriving the weak of justice (vv. 13-15, 21-23), and in the second and third he denies ever having refused food and clothing to the needy (vv. 16-20). All of these oaths concern the ethics of power in a relationship of inequality.

31:13-15. First, Job asserts that he has never denied justice to his male or female slaves when they have had a grievance (רִיב *rîb*) against him (v. 13). Although various laws governed the limited rights of slaves (e.g., Exod 21:1-11, 20-21; Lev 25:39-55; Deut 5:14; 15:12-18; 23:15-16; cf. Jer 34:8-22), Job's language suggests a more general concern for fairness, the basis for which is given in v. 15: God is the maker of both master and servant (cf. Prov 14:31; 22:2). Job clearly assumes that he will be answerable to God for anything less than justice toward his slaves (v. 14). Although this section does not receive particular emphasis within the chapter, it contains the implicit analogy that grounds Job's conviction that his complaint (*rîb*) against God can be resolved fairly. Just as God demands justice *of* him, so also God will show justice *to* him, despite the difference in power, if Job can gain a hearing (cf. 23:2-7).

31:16-20. The central two oaths of this series concern the essential ancient Near Eastern moral value of generosity to the poor. When Eliphaz attempted to depict Job as wicked, abuse of the orphan, the widow, and the poor was precisely the example he chose (22:7-9). Here, as in 29:12-17, Job refutes those accusations. The sharing of food and clothes, basic necessities of existence, is often mentioned in admonitions (Prov 22:9; Isa 58:7; Tob 4:6-11, 16-17; cf. Ezek 18:7). Job's familial imagery in v. 18 reflects the analogy that undergirded the sense of moral obligation to vulnerable members of society. The ancient Syrian king Kilamuwa recounts his care for the poor in these terms: "to some I was a father. To some I was a mother. To some I was a brother."[461]

31:21-23. The final oath in the series contains the complete formula. Job recognizes the truth of the proverb that "the poor are shunned even by their neighbors,/ but the rich have many friends"

458. Contra F. Andersen, *Job: An Introduction and Commentary,* Tyndale Old Testament Commentaries (Downers Grove, Ill.: Inter-Varsity, 1976) 241.

459. T. Frymer-Kensky, "Deuteronomy," in C. Newsom and S. Ringe, *The Women's Bible Commentary* (Louisville: Westminster/John Knox, 1992) 58.

460. Gordis, *The Book of Job,* 346.

461. James B. Pritchard, ed., *Ancient Near Eastern Texts Relating to the Old Testament (ANET),* 3rd ed. with supplement (Princeton: Princeton University Press, 1969) 654.

(Prov 14:20 NIV). Here he asserts that he never abused his influence to exploit the powerless in legal affairs. The hand (v. 21) is a symbol of power and perhaps more specifically of condemnation and judgment (cf. Isa 19:16; Zech 2:9).[462] In this instance, Job envisions a form of poetic justice for the abuse of such power: the breaking of his arm. Similarly, he knows that he would have to answer to one wielding even greater power (v. 22). Once again, the relation between Job and a more vulnerable member of the community is mirrored by Job's relation to God.

31:24-28. The third series of oaths concerns ultimate allegiance, the first two oaths involving wealth and the third other deities. Wealth brings with it a measure of security and confidence (Sir 40:26); for that very reason, it is morally ambiguous. "Trust," "confidence," and "joy" (vv. 24-25) define attitudes properly directed to God, not to wealth (cf. Pss 40:4[5]; 49:6[7]; 52: 7[9]; 62:10[11]; 71:5; Prov 11:28; Jer 17:7; Sir 5:1-3; 31:5-11). Like shining gold, the luminous sun and moon have a seductive appeal (v. 26-27a). The Deuteronomic tradition is particularly concerned to warn against worship of the sun and the moon (see Deut 4:19; 17:2-3; 2 Kgs 21:3-5; 23:5; Jer 8:1-2). Although the gesture described in v. 27b is not entirely clear, it is probably similar to what we describe as "blowing a kiss."[463] Job is clear about the moral significance of such compromised allegiance. It is a betrayal of God and so deserving of punishment (cf. Josh 24:27; Deut 17:2-7).

31:29-34. The three oaths making up the fourth series appear to be the most diverse, although they all have to do with situations in which the bonds of social solidarity are threatened.

31:31-32. The central oath of this series treats the exercise of hospitality to strangers. As outsiders not covered by the moral obligations that members of a clan or village have to each other, traveling strangers were particularly vulnerable to abuse, often expressed as sexual violence. The episodes at Sodom (Genesis 19) and Gibeah (Judges 19) are illustrative. In such cases, hospitality was more than a gracious gesture. It offered

protection and a social bond where none existed before. Although there are difficulties with the translation of v. 31, the clear reference of v. 32 to the plight of the stranger makes the NRSV's v. 31 preferable. In that verse, Job denies that any members of his household ever expressed the desire to abuse the stranger sexually; on the contrary, Job's house was a place of refuge (v. 32).[464] The NIV takes v. 31 to refer to Job's generosity with food as part of his hospitality.[465]

31:29-30, 33-34. The first and third oaths of this series (vv. 29-30, 33-34) correspond. In societies in which the dynamics of honor and shame are strong, social relations are often highly competitive. Concern for who is higher and lower in public esteem, for flaunting good fortune and hiding what would bring one into disrepute are very strong pressures. The book of Psalms, with its frequent references to enemies who taunt and boast, and with its heartfelt curses against such enemies, gives a sense of the dynamics of such a society (see, e.g., Psalms 52; 59; 64; 69; 109). Jeremiah, who in so many other instances is similar to Job, called down God's wrath upon his enemies in traditional terms (Jer 11:20; 12:3). When Job swears that he has neither rejoiced in the ruin of his enemies nor sought to curse them, he lays claim to the most difficult ideals of moral behavior (cf. Prov 17:5b; 24:17-18). In vv. 33-34, Job refers to the corresponding moral issue, the proper conduct of a person who has done wrong, or who at least has done something of which the community would disapprove. For certain categories of infractions, the legal literature assumes that a person who has incurred guilt must make it right in a fairly public way, through an offering and restitution (e.g., Lev 4:1-6:7). Although the way in which psalms were used is not known, it is possible that psalms of confession were also used in public confessions (e.g., Psalm 51). Whatever the expectations, in a society in which shame was a primary sanction, the temptation to conceal sins would have been intense. Job indicates as much in his vivid depiction of the contempt to which such a person would be exposed (v. 34). Although the phrase at the end of v. 33a can be translated "as others do," it may also be rendered "as Adam did," invoking the primordial story of the

462. N. Habel, *The Book of Job,* OTL (Philadelphia: Westminster, 1985) 436.
463. See M. Pope, *Job,* 3rd ed., AB 15 (Garden City, N.Y.: Doubleday, 1979) 235, for an extended discussion. A possible illustration of this religious gesture is found in James B. Pritchard, ed., *The Ancient Near East in Pictures Related to the Old Testament (ANEP)* (Princeton: Princeton University Press, 1954) pls. 204, 622.

464. See Pope, *Job,* 236-37, for a defense of the interpretation of v. 31 as pertaining to sexual abuse.
465. Similarly, J. E. Hartley, *The Book of Job,* NICOT (Grand Rapids, Mich.: Eerdmans, 1988) 420.

one whose reluctance to have his failure exposed led to concealment and thus a breaking of the social bond (Gen 3:8-13). Significantly, Job does not claim that he has never done anything wrong. His honor consists in having always been willing to take responsibility for his actions, even when it would have been possible to conceal them.

31:35-37. It is not accidental that Job interrupts the oath of clearance at this juncture with his ardent desire that someone give him a legal hearing. He knows that in this instance he has done nothing wrong and has nothing to hide; the moral outrage is that he is being treated as guilty without having been charged with any wrongdoing. Although Job's oath by itself need not have legal significance, his words have a distinct legal nuance and so give the entire chapter a more forensic connotation. (An oath of clearance was often part of a demand for a trial.)[466]

The Hebrew word for "mark" (תו *tāw,* v. 35*b*) designates the last letter of the Hebrew alphabet and was formed like an *x*. In Ezek 9:4, 6 it is used to identify those who are to be spared God's judgment. Here it apparently indicates Job's signature. The legal response that Job expects in return is an "indictment in writing," indicated in the Hebrew by the term "document" (ספר *sēper*). That term is used to designate a variety of legal documents, including divorce decrees (Deut 24:1; Isa 50:1) and deeds (Jer 32:11-12). In the context of the expression "adversary at law" (איש ריב *îš rîb*) the meaning "charge" or "indictment" is likely, although it is also possible that the document might be a decree of release or acquittal.[467] The reference in v. 37 to approaching the adversary to give an account of conduct makes the interpretation of a written indictment the most probable.

The image in v. 36 is somewhat obscure, for there are no clear parallels for someone wearing a legal document; perhaps the image was more apparent to its original audience. Persons did wear stamp and cylinder seals, which were used to authenticate transactions. Isaiah 22:22 refers to the official Eliakim ben Hilkiah wearing a key on his shoulder as a sign of his authority. The instruction in Deut 6:8; 11:18 to bind the commands of God upon the wrist and forehead gave rise to the practice in Judaism of wearing phylacteries (cf. Exod 13:16). Whatever the precise meaning, it is clear that far from facing shame, Job regards the occasion as an opportunity for displaying his dignity and honor (v. 37).

31:38-40. Job's words in vv. 35-37 constitute an aside, although an important one for understanding the intent of his oath. With vv. 38-40, he returns to complete his oath of clearance with a final double oath concerning land ethics. In v. 38, the land is personified as crying out and its furrows weeping. Although Job does not specify the reasons for which land might protest, a number of laws in Israelite tradition served to protect the land.[468] It was to remain fallow during sabbath and jubilee years (Exod 23:10-11; Lev 25:1-22), and regulations forbade the mixing of different types of seeds (Lev 19:19; Deut 22:9), as well as eating the produce of newly bearing trees for three years (Lev 19:23-25). More broadly, certain kinds of sin were considered to pollute the land (Deut 24:3). The book of Chronicles interprets the exile as a time of rest for the land to compensate for the sabbaths that were not observed (2 Chr 36:21; cf. Lev 26:34-35, 43).

The corresponding oath in v. 39 concerns ethical obligations to those who own and/or work the land. The judicial murder of Naboth and the seizure of his land by Ahab and Jezebel (1 Kings 21) are the most notorious examples of what was a recurrent issue of social justice (Isa 5:8; Neh 5:1-13; cf. Lev 25:23-38). Workers on the land were often at the mercy of owners for payment of the meager wages to which they were entitled (24:10-11; Lev 19:13; Deut 24:14-15; Mal 3:5). The curse Job invokes for such behavior is a fitting one, the growth of weeds instead of grain (cf. Gen 3:17-18; Jer 12:13).

The chapter concludes with the narrator's comment that "the words of Job are ended" (cf. Ps 72:20; Jer 51:64), signaling the end of the dialogue.

466. M. B. Dick, "The Legal Metaphor in Job 31," *CBQ* 41 (1979) 42.
467. See Habel, *The Book of Job,* 439. For an example from the Jewish colony of Elephantine in Egypt, see *ANET,* 491.

468. L. Perdue, *Wisdom in Revolt: Metaphorical Theology in the Book of Job,* JSOTSup 112 (Sheffield: JSOT, 1991) 187-88.

REFLECTIONS

Throughout his final speech in chaps. 29–31, Job presents himself as a man of honor and gives a fairly full account of the values entailed by that identity. Particularly in the long oath of clearance in chap. 31, Job often invokes God as the source and guarantor of the values constituting his sense of self. Clearly, Job assumes that the values that give content to his own character also define the character of God. The values that structure his relations with others are the values he assumes should structure God's relation with him. Job's image of God is developed out of the highest and best values of his society, values that Job has always tried to embody.

This implicit analogy provides Job with the possibility of a resolution of the inexplicable events that have cast doubt on his integrity. Among the affirmations Job makes of himself in chap. 31 is the claim that he never rejected the grievance of his own slaves when they brought a just complaint against him. That is how a man of honor behaves. One can think of the patriarch Judah, who was ready to have his daughter-in-law Tamar killed for adultery. Yet when she showed him evidence that he was the father of her child, Judah recognized his own failure to sustain the rights of his daughter-in-law and confessed, "She is more in the right than I." King Saul groundlessly believed that David was his enemy and tried on numerous occasions to kill him. When David finally managed to confront Saul with the unmistakable evidence that David was not his enemy, however, Saul acknowledged it with the statement, "You are more in the right than I." The words that Job wants to hear from God are the same words: "You are more in the right than I." By configuring his claim in terms of the code of honor, Job provides for a resolution that would confer dignity on both parties. Like a person of honor, God will hear Job's complaint and judge justly, vindicating Job's innocence. Far from demeaning God, such an action will show God's honor, just as Job claimed that hearing the complaints of his own slaves was a demonstration of his honor.

The book could find its resolution on the terms Job has laid out. Many wish that it did. The task for reflection, however, is to think carefully about both the theological method implicit in the workings of Job's imagination and the content of the image of God he generates. These questions are scarcely separable. The workings of Job's theological imagination are very much in keeping with the larger Judeo-Christian tradition, which encourages thinking about God by means of metaphors drawn largely from the realm of human relations. The Bible speaks of God's emotions (e.g., love, anger, regret, forgiveness), as well as of God's intentions and actions. This language is so ubiquitous in the traditional way of thinking about God that one tends to forget that it is metaphorical, a way of talking about God in terms drawn from the model of human nature and expression. More easily recognized as metaphors are representations of God in terms of human relations (e.g., God as parent, king, kin-redeemer). The conviction that such metaphors provide knowledge of God is based on the belief that one can in some way know the creator through the creation. Even though metaphors based on human existence are not the only ones used of God, they are particularly important in the light of the Bible's claim that humans are made in the image and likeness of God. In some significant, but not fully articulated way, a continuity exists between human nature and divine nature. Job has good warrant for trying to know God by knowing what is best about himself.

One danger of theological metaphors is that one forgets that they are metaphors and treats them as literal statements. Unconsciously, one comes to think of God as a sort of ideal person who feels, thinks, and behaves (or ought to) according to the highest human standards. What gets lost in such a literalizing of language is the sense of God as "wholly other," to use Rudolph Otto's phrase.[469] Certain religious experiences disclose where metaphors drawn from human experience meet their limits and, indeed, are revealed as simply incapable of rendering God's nature. To a great extent, Job has become so caught up by the power of his generative metaphor for God that he has lost sight of its limits and inadequacies.

469. See R. Otto, *The Idea of the Holy,* 2nd ed., trans. J. W. Harvey (London: Oxford University Press, 1958; 1st ed. 1923).

The temptation to literalize metaphor is not the only problem. A related problem concerning the metaphorical language that informs Job's thinking, and indeed much of Judeo-Christian theology, involves the scope of the dominant metaphors. To put it concretely, Job has attempted to understand the nature of the cosmos on the basis of his understanding of the social world of village patriarchy. Metaphors drawn from primary human relationships such as Job describes (e.g., parent-child, patron-dependent, leader-community) are powerful because they are so richly endowed with meaning for human beings and are so accessible. Meaning is readily given when one starts from one's embeddedness in a particular social context. But metaphors based on such local relationships may not be comprehensive enough for understanding the fundamental nature of reality. The most serious problem is the ease with which certain parochial social arrangements can become "sacralized" when used as religious metaphors. Despite the genuine power of Job's use of his own social reality to gain insight into God's nature, modern readers are likely to have some reservations about the analogy Job seems to imply between his own social values and God's just order. Job's assumption that a fitting punishment if he committed adultery would be the sexual abuse of his own wife strikes most people today as utterly abhorrent. Nor would one like to see the paternalism and contempt for outcasts that are such an unself-conscious part of Job's moral vocabulary inform understandings of God's righteousness.

Many of these problems with the use of human metaphors to understand God can be addressed by critical reflection and self-consciousness about the nature of religious language. But a more intractable dilemma lurks in the analogy Job establishes between his values and God's, one that remains a deeply troubling problem for all people of faith. As Job's words in chaps. 29–31 make clear, he believes that his own passion for justice and rage against victimization of the weak by the strong are grounded in a similar passion of God. The whole of the Judeo-Christian tradition affirms with Job that this is so. Moreover, only metaphors drawn from human experience are capable of expressing this aspect of the divine nature, for only human beings possess the distinctive traits that make us "like God," the reflective knowledge of good and evil and the will to choose. The painful contradiction embedded in Job's anger against God is the recognition that no human parent filled with love for a child, no redeemer bound by ties of kinship, no king committed to the protection of the vulnerable would stand by in the face of abuse, murder, and genocide. Yet these things happen in God's world. One cannot evade the contradiction by talking about human responsibility for human deeds. Nature, too, is constructed with violence as an essential part of its order, a food chain that requires the painful death of some creatures as the price of life for others. Language about God that is based solely on metaphors of human beings and human relationships is simply not adequate to comprehend the presence of so much pain, violence, and oppression in God's world. To a certain extent, the divine speeches will address this issue, representing God and creation by means of images quite different from those that have informed Job's own theological imagination. Although the divine speeches will provide new resources for thinking about the presence of pain and disorder in a world created by a good God, the book as a whole will not attempt to resolve the matter in any simple way. It is an issue with which Judaism and Christianity must always struggle.

THE SPEECHES OF ELIHU

OVERVIEW

hatever one expects to follow Job's oath of clearance, it is not Elihu. The appearance of this new character, with his long, uninterrupted discourse poses two distinct but related questions. First, are the Elihu speeches part of the original composition of the book, or a later addition to it? Second, what is their purpose in the book as it now stands?

There are very strong reasons for recognizing the Elihu speeches as a later addition. Elihu is not mentioned in the prose tale that begins the book, where all other characters are introduced, and he does not appear in the epilogue. When God rebukes Job's friends by name in 42:7-9, Elihu is not mentioned. This omission is inexplicable if Elihu were one of the original characters but makes more sense if his speeches were added by a later writer who valued the ideas put into Elihu's mouth and did not want him included in the divine rebuke of the friends. Many compositional and stylistic features also suggest a different author. Elihu is the only character bearing an Israelite name. The prose by which he is introduced in 32:1-5 differs in tone and style from the spare, pseudo-naive style of the prologue and epilogue. In the speeches themselves, certain linguistic traits give Elihu a distinctive profile—e.g., preference for the divine name El and for the short form of the first-person pronoun (אֲנִי 'ǎnî rather than אָנֹכִי 'ānōkî), use of a word for "knowledge" (דֵּעַ dēa') not found elsewhere in the book, the presence of more Aramaisms than in the other speeches.[470]

Much more significant, however, is the distinctive way in which Elihu calls Job by name (32:12;

33:1, 31; 34:5, 7, 35, 36; 35:16; 37:14) and quotes fragments of Job's speeches (see 33:8-13; 34:5-6; 35:2-3). Since this trait is not characteristic of the original dialogue, it strongly suggests the work of an author who knows the written text and is intent on refuting specific statements. More generally, Elihu appears to engage in "correcting" the entire book. Not only does he refute Job explicitly, but also he criticizes the arguments of the friends as inadequate, indicating his intention to use arguments different from theirs (32:10-14). Although he does not criticize God explicitly, Elihu's speech in 36:22–37:24 anticipates elements of the divine speeches, while at the same time altering their nature so as to engage issues raised by Job more explicitly. The overall impression is that chaps. 32–37 derive from a later writer, dissatisfied with the failure of a powerful book and confident of his ability to supply the voice it lacks.

In recent years, perhaps in reaction to the excesses of historical-critical disassembly of the book of Job, some commentators have argued that the Elihu speeches are an integral part of the original composition of the book.[471] Their arguments, however, are more ingenious than persuasive. It is certainly true that the original author could have given Elihu a different style and diction in an effort to distinguish him from the other characters; yet such an explanation begs the question of why the three friends are not so clearly

---

470. This is difficult evidence to evaluate. See the discussions in S. R. Driver and G. B. Gray, *A Critical and Exegetical Commentary on the Book of Job,* ICC (Edinburgh: T. & T. Clark, 1921) xlii-xlviii; E. Dhorme, *A Commentary on the Book of Job,* trans. H. Knight (London: Nelson, 1967) civ-cv; R. Gordis, *The Book of Job: Commentary, New Translation, and Special Studies* (New York: Jewish Theological Seminary, 5738/1978) 547-48.

471. Cf. esp. Habel, "The Role of Elihu in the Design of the Book of Job," in *In the Shelter of Elyon: Essays on Palestinian Life and Literature in Honor of G. W. Ahlstrom,* JSOTSup 31, ed. W. B. Barrick and J. S. Spencer (Sheffield: JSOT, 1984) 81-88; Habel, *The Book of Job,* 36-37, 443-47; J. G. Janzen, *Job,* Interpretation (Atlanta: John Knox, 1985) 217-18, 221-25. See also F. Andersen, *Job: An Introduction and Commentary,* Tyndale Old Testament Commentaries (Downers Grove, Ill.: Inter-Varsity, 1976) 49-52. R. Gordis, *The Book of God and Man: A Study of Job* (Chicago: University of Chicago Press, 1965) 104-16, argues that the Elihu speeches are a later addition, but written by the author of the rest of the book of Job. Cf. D. N. Freedman, "The Elihu Speeches in the Book of Job," *HTR* 61 (1968) 51-59.

distinguished from one another in their speech and style. Those who argue for the orginality of Elihu sometimes explain his absence from the prologue by making him a bystander who takes up the role of adjudicator. If so, it is odd that the prose tale gives the impression that Job and his three friends are the only actors on the scene, with no bystanders around. The assumption that an author with a controlling design wrote the Elihu speeches as part of an original composition virtually requires the conclusion that Elihu be understood as a self-destructing character, a self-parody undermined by his own words and by the rest of the book. Perhaps this interpretation derives much of its appeal from the fact that Elihu's style and argumentation are so little to the taste of modern readers. That modern readers have difficulty taking Elihu seriously, however, does not necessarily mean that his speech was intentionally composed to be unpersuasive. In short, arguments for the Elihu speeches as original to the book do not account for features of the speeches and their relation to the rest of the book as persuasively as does the hypothesis that they are the work of a somewhat later author who was dissatisfied with the book as it existed.

Assuming that the Elihu speeches were later additions to the book of Job, it is not clear when they were composed. They are present in the first century CE targum of Job from the Dead Sea Scrolls, but more precise evidence is elusive. Certain ideas in the Elihu speeches bear an intriguing resemblance to notions current in Jewish literature from the Hellenistic period, leading some to suggest a third century BCE date for their composition.[472] Although far from certain, the date is plausible. Modes of thinking about moral and religious issues underwent considerable development during the Hellenistic period, so that an intellectual of that age might well judge the book of Job unsatisfactory in not setting the religious issues in terms that had recently become influential and persuasive. Zuckerman suggests that this "generation gap" between the original book and the author of Elihu is symbolized in the repre-

sentation of Elihu as a younger character.[473] Thus the conflict of the author's desire to correct the book, coupled with a reluctance to tamper with it, are given expression in the long self-justification with which Elihu begins his speech.

The Elihu speeches are best understood as disputations, as the narrative introduction and Elihu's own self-introduction make clear. While the speeches of the friends are at least somewhat embedded in the dramatic setting of the book and reflect the pastoral dimensions of sapiential friendship, Elihu's speeches are more exclusively engaged in a battle of ideas.[474] Elihu's primary idiom is that of wisdom, although he does engage Job's legal language more than the other friends have. His speeches, however, should not be understood as an attempt to make a legal case against Job in the strict sense.[475]

After a prose paragraph introducing Elihu (32:1-5), narrative headings divide Elihu's words into four speeches: 32:6–33:33; 34:1-37; 35:1-16; 36:1–37:24. The first speech begins with a long self-justification for speaking (32:7-22). In the main body of the speech, Elihu addresses Job, explaining ways in which, contrary to Job's assertion, God does "speak" to persons through dreams and through illness, in order to lead them to moral insight and so preserve them from destruction (33:1-33). Elihu concludes that speech with an offer to teach Job wisdom, an offer that is fulfilled in the following discourse. In 34:1-37, Elihu's style imitates a general wisdom discourse, addressed to an audience of "sages" and "men of reason" who are invited to judge Job's words. Contrary to Job's accusations, Elihu argues for the righteousness of God's character, exhibited in just governance and in judgment executed against abusive rulers. In the following speech (35:1-16), Elihu again directly challenges Job concerning the validity of his words about himself and about God. Elihu explains the implications of divine transcendence and the reasons why certain protests against oppression, including Job's, do not seem to receive divine response. Elihu's long final discourse divides into two parts. In 36:1-21, Elihu recapitu-

472. H.-M. Wahl, *Der Gerechte Schoepfer*, BZAW 207 (Berlin: Walter de Gruyter, 1993) 182-87. Cf. T. Mende, *Durch Leiden zur Vollendung*, Trierer Theologische Studien 49 (Trier: Paulinus-Verlag, 1990) 419-27.

473. B. Zuckerman, *Job the Silent: A Study in Historical Counterpoint* (New York: Oxford University Press, 1991) 148, 153.

474. C. Westermann, *The Structure of the Book of Job*, trans. C. A. Muenchow (Philadelphia: Fortress, 1981) 146.

475. Contra Habel, *The Book of Job*, 445-47, 452; and, rather differently, Zuckerman, *Job the Silent*, 151-53.

lates many of the themes previously addressed. With 36:22–37:24, he begins to anticipate the divine speeches, describing the wonders of God as Lord of the weather and reminding Job of his comparative powerlessness and ignorance. In Elihu's account, the wonders of God testify to God's righteous providence, before which the only possible response is awe and praise. A concluding description of a theophany leads directly to the speeches of God from the stormwind, which follow in chap. 38.

JOB 32:1–33:33, ELIHU ATTEMPTS TO ANSWER JOB

Job 32:1-22, Elihu's Compulsion to Speak

NIV

32 So these three men stopped answering Job, because he was righteous in his own eyes. [2]But Elihu son of Barakel the Buzite, of the family of Ram, became very angry with Job for justifying himself rather than God. [3]He was also angry with the three friends, because they had found no way to refute Job, and yet had condemned him.[a] [4]Now Elihu had waited before speaking to Job because they were older than he. [5]But when he saw that the three men had nothing more to say, his anger was aroused.

[6]So Elihu son of Barakel the Buzite said:

"I am young in years,
    and you are old;
that is why I was fearful,
    not daring to tell you what I know.
[7]I thought, 'Age should speak;
    advanced years should teach wisdom.'
[8]But it is the spirit[b] in a man,
    the breath of the Almighty, that gives him
        understanding.
[9]It is not only the old[c] who are wise,
    not only the aged who understand what is
        right.
[10]"Therefore I say: Listen to me;
    I too will tell you what I know.
[11]I waited while you spoke,
    I listened to your reasoning;
while you were searching for words,
[12]   I gave you my full attention.
But not one of you has proved Job wrong;
    none of you has answered his arguments.

---

[a]3 Masoretic Text; an ancient Hebrew scribal tradition *Job, and so had condemned God*   [b]8 Or *Spirit*; also in verse 18   [c]9 Or *many; or great*

NRSV

32 So these three men ceased to answer Job, because he was righteous in his own eyes. [2]Then Elihu son of Barachel the Buzite, of the family of Ram, became angry. He was angry at Job because he justified himself rather than God; [3]he was angry also at Job's three friends because they had found no answer, though they had declared Job to be in the wrong.[a] [4]Now Elihu had waited to speak to Job, because they were older than he. [5]But when Elihu saw that there was no answer in the mouths of these three men, he became angry.

6Elihu son of Barachel the Buzite answered:

"I am young in years,
    and you are aged;
therefore I was timid and afraid
    to declare my opinion to you.
[7] I said, 'Let days speak,
    and many years teach wisdom.'
[8] But truly it is the spirit in a mortal,
    the breath of the Almighty,[b] that makes for
        understanding.
[9] It is not the old[c] that are wise,
    nor the aged that understand what is right.
[10] Therefore I say, 'Listen to me;
    let me also declare my opinion.'

[11] "See, I waited for your words,
    I listened for your wise sayings,
        while you searched out what to say.
[12] I gave you my attention,
    but there was in fact no one that confuted
        Job,

---

[a]Another ancient tradition reads *answer, and had put God in the wrong*   [b]Traditional rendering of Heb *Shaddai*   [c]Gk Syr Vg: Heb *many*

NIV

[13] Do not say, 'We have found wisdom;
    let God refute him, not man.'
[14] But Job has not marshaled his words against me,
    and I will not answer him with your
        arguments.

[15] "They are dismayed and have no more to say;
    words have failed them.
[16] Must I wait, now that they are silent,
    now that they stand there with no reply?
[17] I too will have my say;
    I too will tell what I know.
[18] For I am full of words,
    and the spirit within me compels me;
[19] inside I am like bottled-up wine,
    like new wineskins ready to burst.
[20] I must speak and find relief;
    I must open my lips and reply.
[21] I will show partiality to no one,
    nor will I flatter any man;
[22] for if I were skilled in flattery,
    my Maker would soon take me away."

NRSV

    no one among you that answered his words.
[13] Yet do not say, 'We have found wisdom;
    God may vanquish him, not a human.'
[14] He has not directed his words against me,
    and I will not answer him with your
        speeches.

[15] "They are dismayed, they answer no more;
    they have not a word to say.
[16] And am I to wait, because they do not speak,
    because they stand there, and answer no
        more?
[17] I also will give my answer;
    I also will declare my opinion.
[18] For I am full of words;
    the spirit within me constrains me.
[19] My heart is indeed like wine that has no vent;
    like new wineskins, it is ready to burst.
[20] I must speak, so that I may find relief;
    I must open my lips and answer.
[21] I will not show partiality to any person
    or use flattery toward anyone.
[22] For I do not know how to flatter—
    or my Maker would soon put an end to
        me!"

COMMENTARY

Chapter 32 introduces Elihu, first through narrative (vv. 1-5) and then through self-presentation (vv. 6-22). Both introductions are concerned primarily with establishing the motivation for Elihu's intervention. The *leitmotif* of the narrative introduction is Elihu's anger, which is mentioned four times. In the self-presentation Elihu establishes three things: that he will speak (vv. 6-10), that he can speak (vv. 11-14), and that he must speak (vv. 15-22).[476]

32:1-5. Although good reasons exist for regarding chaps. 32–37 as the work of a later author, nonetheless the chapters have been artfully crafted to fit into the book. By explaining why the three friends cease to answer Job, the author of the Elihu speeches provides closure for the friends' role in the dialogue. As in 2:11-13, a

shocking perception leads to silence. In 2:12, the friends "lift up their eyes" to see Job, transformed by illness almost beyond recognition. As a consequence they sit before him for seven days and nights in silence (2:13). Now the friends, here called "these three men," are again silenced by the perception of a Job who is morally transformed almost beyond recognition. They now see Job as he sees himself, "righteous in his own eyes" (v. 1). In one sense, that is simply the literal truth; Job does consider himself innocent, in the right (cf. 27:1-6). But the idiom ("X in his own eyes") is a pejorative one that in wisdom discourse describes a fatuous and complacent person, a fool or worse (cf. Prov 12:15; 26:5, 12, 16; 28:11; 30:12). The friends have no more to say to such a person.

Elihu is introduced in v. 2. The narrator gives his name (Elihu), his father's name (Barakel), the

476. G. Fohrer, "Die Weisheit des Elihu (Hi 32-37)," *Studien zum Buche Hiob (1956–1979),* 2nd ed. (Berlin: Walter de Gruyter, 1983) 95.

city or territory from whence he comes (Buz), and his clan affiliation (Ram). The name "Elihu," which belongs to several minor biblical characters (1 Sam 1:1; 1 Chr 12:20[21]; 26:7; 27:18), means "He is my God," a variant of the name "Elijah," "Yahweh is my God." Although the name "Barakel" ("God has blessed") is not known from biblical sources, it was borne by certain diaspora Jews from Nippur.[477] The territory of Buz is mentioned in Jer 25:23, along with Dedan and Tema, cities located in northwest Arabia. The name "Ram" is not otherwise known as a clan designation, although it occurs as the name of one of David's ancestors (Ruth 4:19; 1 Chr 2:9-10, 25, 27).

Two things are puzzling about Elihu's designation: why his identification is so much longer than those of the other characters, and why he alone bears an Israelite name. Some have suggested that the names are semantically significant,[478] but the meanings do not seem especially crafted to describe his role. Moreover, whereas Ram would have positive significance ("lofty" [רם *rām*]), the name "Buz" (בוז *bûz*) puns on a negative word ("shame" [בוש *bôš*]). One can only speculate, but Elihu may simply be the name of the author of chapters 32–37, an angry reader who literally wrote himself into the book. If it is the case that the Elihu speeches come from the third or early second century BCE, then a precedent exists for a wisdom writer's using his own name in his composition. In the epilogue of Sirach, the author writes, "Instruction in understanding and knowledge/ I have written in this book,/ Jesus son of Eleazar son of Sirach of Jerusalem,/ whose mind poured forth wisdom" (Sir 50:27 NRSV).

Whether or not Elihu is the name of an actual person who has fictionalized himself as a character in the book of Job, the representation of Elihu in vv. 2-5 is an artful psychological portrait. First his anger is described in absolute terms (v. 2*a*). Next his anger against Job and the reason for it (v. 2*b*), and his anger against the friends and the reason for it (v. 3), are recounted in parallel clauses. Elihu is angry at Job for much the same reason that the friends cease to speak: because of Job's opinion

that he, and not God, is in the right (the same Hebrew root [צדק *ṣādaq*], appears in vv. 1 and 2*b*). His anger at the three friends is more intriguing; Elihu thinks they have failed in their responsibility to overcome Job's disturbing claims. Thus his anger is evidence that ancient readers, not just modern ones, consider Job to have gotten the better of the friends in the dialogue.

Ancient Masoretic tradition identifies the end of v. 3 as one of the "corrections of the scribes" (*tiqqune sopherim*), a correction of the text made in the interests of piety.[479] Accordingly, the original text would have read "and so put God in the wrong," a perception that would fit well with Elihu's anger against the friends.

The syntax of v. 4 is awkward. Although it probably means that Elihu had been waiting during the entire dialogue (cf. v. 11), Gordis suggests that it be read "Elihu waited with Job for them to speak,"[480] drawing attention to the silence that signals the friends' refusal to argue further with Job (v. 5; cf. v. 13). In either case, Elihu's reticence is motivated by the strong cultural value of respect for elders (cf. 15:10; 30:1; Sir 32:7-9). Their inability to answer Job sets up a conflict of values for Elihu: respect for elders vs. the need to defend God, a conflict that expresses itself emotionally as anger (v. 5).

32:6-10. Although Elihu is often faulted for being long-winded and overly self-conscious,[481] he must overcome the strong prohibition against putting himself forward in the presence of elders. Elihu's reference to his own youth as a reason for holding back (v. 6) is a traditional self-deprecating remark, part of the rhetoric of politeness. Such a statement often occurs, however, in stories of remarkable leaders singled out by God for special service, such as Gideon (Judg 6:15), Saul (1 Sam 9:21), and Jeremiah (Jer 1:6). Elihu may wish for his politeness to intimate similar moral leadership.

An inclusio marks the limits of the first argument, as Elihu transforms the statement "I was afraid to tell you what I know" (v. 6*b*, author's trans.) into the assertion "I myself will tell you what I know" (v. 10*b*, author's trans.). Elihu presents the transformation as one taking place

477. See M. Coogan, *West Semitic Personal Names in the Murashu Documents* (Cambridge, Mass.: Harvard Semitic Museum, 1975) 16-17.

478. E.g., Gordis, *The Book of God and Man,* 115; J. E. Hartley, *The Book of Job,* 429; and rather differently, E. Good, *In Turns of Tempest* (Stanford, Calif.: Stanford University Press, 1990) 320.

479. Gordis, *The Book of Job,* 366.

480. Ibid., 367.

481. E.g., Habel, *The Book of Job,* 444; H. Rowley, *The Book of Job,* rev. ed., NCB (Grand Rapids, Mich.: Eerdmans, 1976; original ed., 1970) 207; Good, *In Turns of Tempest,* 321.

within himself, although his goal is to make it plausible to his audience, so that they will be willing to listen to him despite his youth. He presents as his own initial belief the traditional axiom that age should speak, because age possesses wisdom (v. 7; cf. 8:8-10; 15:10). Next he confronts it with a different axiom, but one that was also traditional and widely shared: the Spirit of God gives understanding (v. 8; cf. Exod 31:3; Num 11:26-30; 27:18). Implicitly assuming that the second axiom takes precedence over the first, Elihu concludes that age (alone) does not provide insight (v. 9). Thus he can move from his initial assumption ("I said, 'Let age speak' " [v. 7a, author's trans.]) to his new conclusion ("Therefore I say, 'Listen to me' " [v. 10a]).

Whether Elihu refers in v. 8 to a special inspiration[482] or to a general knowledge available to all is disputed.[483] The terms "spirit"/"breath" (רוח *rûaḥ* / נשׁמה *něšāmâ*) can refer to that which gives life to all (cf. 27:3; 33:4; Gen 2:7), or to that which gives wisdom to a select few (Gen 41:38; Judg 6:34; Isa 11:2). Only the context can determine the appropriate meaning; in this case, Elihu clearly is talking about an unusual quality that overrides the presumptive association of wisdom with age. He is attempting to present himself according to the model of the young man whose God-given wisdom allows him to surpass those older and more experienced than he (cf. Joseph in Genesis 41 or Daniel and his three friends in Dan 1:17-20). In the LXX version of Susanna, the contrast between youth and age is drawn very sharply, with the clever youth Daniel foiling the plot of the wicked elders. The LXX draws the moral of that story as follows: "Wherefore the youths are the beloved of Jacob because of their integrity. . . . For if the youths live reverently, a spirit of understanding and insight will be in them for ever."[484] A similar, rather pointed claim appears in Ps 119:99-100 that meditation on and obedience to Torah gives the speaker "more insight than all my teachers . . . more understanding than the elders." These various passages from the literature of the late Persian and Hellenistic

periods suggest that the challenge to the dominance of elders was part of a broader intellectual and social phenomenon.

32:11-14. In this second section of his self-introduction, Elihu establishes his ability to contribute to the dialogue. He underscores his attentiveness to the friends' words, thus rhetorically establishing both his own proper behavior and his authority as one who knows and thus can judge what they have said (v. 11). The failure with which Elihu charges the friends is the same one that vv. 1-5 indicated as the source of Elihu's anger: their failure to refute Job (v. 12). In v. 12, Elihu echoes a term Job had used earlier, "confuted" (מוכיח *môkîaḥ,* NRSV). Whereas Job used the term to refer to one who would arbitrate between oneself and God (9:33), Elihu uses it in its more general sense of "one who corrects, rebukes" (NIV, "proved Job wrong"; NRSV, "confuted Job").[485] Elihu interprets the friends' silence as their conclusion that no one but God can successfully answer Job (v. 13), perhaps a sly acknowledgment that the author of the Elihu speeches knows the structure of the whole book. For Elihu to make a place for himself, he has to claim that his arguments will be different from those of the friends (v. 14). A number of commentators scoff at his claims, insisting that he brings little new to the conversation,[486] but Elihu's arguments differ significantly from those of the friends, as the discussion of succeeding chapters will show.

32:15-22. Elihu ends with a vivid representation of his urgent need to speak. Like an actor addressing an aside to the audience, Elihu describes the defeated silence of the friends (v. 15) and rhetorically asks if he need wait any longer to speak, when they clearly have no more to say (v. 16). Answering his own rhetorical question with a bold announcement that he will speak (v. 17), Elihu repeats the concluding words of v. 10b. The phrase "I also," which Elihu uses three times in vv. 10 and 17, is artful, for the Hebrew words "also" and "anger" are homonyms (אף *'ap*). Even as Elihu presents his words within the discipline of sapiential politeness and careful

482. So Janzen, *Job,* 218; A. de Wilde, *Das Buch Hiob, OTS* xxii (Leiden: Brill, 1981) 311; J. W. McKay, "Elihu—A Proto-Charismatic?" *ExpTim* 90 (1979) 168.

483. Habel, *The Book of Job,* 451; Perdue, *Wisdom in Revolt,* 248.

484. R. Doran, "The Additions to Daniel," *HBC,* ed. J. L. Mays et al. (San Francisco: Harper & Row, 1988) 865.

485. Contra Habel, *The Book of Job,* 452, who assumes that Elihu also uses the term in a forensic context.

486. E.g., Driver and Gray, *A Critical and Exegetical Commentary on the Book of Job,* xli; Pope, *Job,* xxvii-xxviii.

argumentation, his anger is underscored, as his self-asserting words "I also" echo the claim "I am angry."

It is almost impossible for a modern reader to listen with a straight face as Elihu describes himself as having a belly full of words like a wineskin full of fermenting wine (v. 19). Those who view Elihu as a parody created by the author of the rest of the book of Job make much of this passage.[487] What is humorous in one culture, however, is no reliable guide to what is humorous in another. Within the context of ancient values and metaphors, Elihu says nothing absurd. Because discipline in speech was so highly valued, words that might sound excessive required justification. For example, Eliphaz acknowledged the boldness of his own first reply to Job with the rhetorical question, "but who can keep from speaking?" (4:2b NRSV). Job also justified his "speaking rashly" by making a reference to the immensity

of his anguish (6:2-3), and Zophar spoke of the "agitation" impelling him to speak (20:2). More graphically, the prophet Jeremiah likened God's word within him to "fire shut up in my bones" (Jer 20:9 NRSV). The wineskin bursting from the pressure of fermentation would have been a vivid and appropriate image (cf. Matt 9:17).

Elihu concludes by insisting that he will not abuse the authority of speech by showing partiality or using flattery (vv. 21-22). Since he has made it clear that he intends to be critical both of Job and of the friends, partiality is not likely to be a problem. Ironically, Elihu notes that God would carry him away if he did flatter or show partiality. It does not occur to Elihu that his judgments are uncritically partial to God. This is precisely the blindness of piety that Job has attempted to expose but that Elihu cannot begin to accept as a legitimate issue for discussion. Thus Elihu cannot engage Job in a significant way, because their presuppositions about the way one must talk about God are so radically different.

487. E.g., Habel, "The Role of Elihu in the Design of the Book of Job," in *In the Shelter of Elyon: Essays on Palestinian Life and Literature in Honor of G. W. Ahlstrom,* JSOTSup 31, ed. W. B. Barrick and J. S. Spencer (Sheffield: JSOT, 1984) 91.

REFLECTIONS

Why do people loathe Elihu? The strong identification of modern readers with Job tends to generate criticism of all his opponents, but no one comes in for such vituperative comments as Elihu: "a pompous, insensitive bore,"[488] "a fanatic and a bigot,"[489] and "ridiculous"[490] are typical judgments. Perhaps one reason for the intense reactions Elihu generates is hinted at in the title Gordis gives him, "Elihu the Intruder."[491] Elihu intrudes into an intense moment, not just among the characters in the book, but also between the reader and the book. He breaks the dramatic spell and spoils the integrity of an aesthetic, emotional, and religious encounter at the climax of the book. The author of the Elihu speeches chooses a strategic location in which to insert his words. His location allows him a privileged position from which to interpret the dialogues. They are now completed, so that his voice is not simply one among others, but one that looks back over the whole and declares what the critical issues are. As much as a reader may recognize the distortions Elihu introduces, it is difficult to prevent them from having their effect. By the end of chap. 37, Elihu has distanced the reader from the immediacy of Job's passion and has changed the nature of the reader's experience of the book, so that ideas dominate over passions. Elihu also changes the experience of the divine speeches that follow. In everyday life one can recognize the need to control that is manifested when a friend insists on giving a strongly evaluative description of a person whom one is soon to meet. Similarly, Elihu's need to control—to control the reader's perception of God and perhaps even

488. E. Good, *In Turns of Tempest* (Stanford, Calif.: Stanford University Press, 1990) 321.
489. J. B. Curtis, "Why Were the Elihu Speeches Added to the Book of Job?" *Proceedings of the Eastern Great Lakes and Midwest Biblical Societies* 8 (1988) 93.
490. H. Rowley, *The Book of Job,* rev. ed., NCB (Grand Rapids, Mich.: Eerdmans, 1976; original ed., 1970) 209.
491. R. Gordis, *The Book of God and Man: A Study of Job* (Chicago: University of Chicago Press, 1965) 104-16.

to control God—is amply on display when he speaks. This dynamic, coupled with Elihu's unconcealed conviction that he alone understands what is said and can point out and remedy its defects is what earns Elihu the undying resentment of generations of readers.

One can reflect on Elihu, or perhaps one should say on the author of the Elihu speeches, as a cautionary example of the temptations that beset all interpreters. Whether one is preaching a sermon, teaching a Bible study, or writing a commentary, there is often a temptation to use one's authoritative role in an improperly controlling fashion. By selecting some issues and passing over others in silence, by subtle distortions of what the text says, or by caricaturing and ridiculing other interpretations, one can make it appear that there is no other way to understand the text and the issues it presents. This temptation is particularly acute when texts bear on controversial issues. In our own day biblical texts concerning matters of sexuality or the role of women are often subjected to such tendentious interpretations by people on both sides of the issue. It can be very difficult to allow a text to speak in its own voice, especially when one thinks that the text is wrong. Like Elihu, we experience the impulse to argue the text into silence or to put a "spin" on it so that it will be read in a way that we approve.

This is not to say that an interpreter can be utterly objective or should be wholly dispassionate. All interpretation is interpretation from a particular, and limited, perspective. Many factors, including the interpreter's age, gender, ethnicity, social class, denomination, and particular life experience, will shape what a person is able to see in a text. The author of the Elihu speeches, for instance, is able to see omissions in the discussion of suffering (see chap. 33) because he comes from a later age that reflected on such issues differently. Nor is anger at a text necessarily a bad thing. A text that offends can be a stimulus to think about issues in a way that one otherwise would not have to. It is not Elihu's anger that sets a bad example, but what he does with it.

Part of what is troubling about the role of the Elihu speeches in the book of Job is the way in which they change the nature of the discourse. The preceding speeches, and indeed the book as a whole, are structured as a dialogue between very different points of view. The Elihu speeches, however, do not integrate themselves into this dialogical structure but privilege themselves as a long monologue. They do not allow another voice to answer back. In certain settings of interpretation, for instance in Bible studies, it is comparatively easy to set interpretation in the context of a dialogue of voices. Other interpretive genres, such as sermons and commentaries, have the form of a monologue. Even in such forms of speech, however, it is often possible to acknowledge and sometimes even incorporate other voices with their differing interpretive possibilities. It is always possible to speak and write in a way that recognizes that one's interpretation is only *an* interpretation, not *the* interpretation. Such a stance should not be a wishy-washy claim that one interpretation is as good as another but rather a recognition of the inexhaustible richness of texts that require many different voices to engage in the work of interpretation.

Job 33:1-33, God Uses Suffering to Warn and Redeem

NIV

33 "But now, Job, listen to my words; pay attention to everything I say.
²I am about to open my mouth;
  my words are on the tip of my tongue.
³My words come from an upright heart;

NRSV

33 "But now, hear my speech, O Job, and listen to all my words.
² See, I open my mouth;
  the tongue in my mouth speaks.
³ My words declare the uprightness of my heart,

NIV

my lips sincerely speak what I know.
⁴The Spirit of God has made me;
   the breath of the Almighty gives me life.
⁵Answer me then, if you can;
   prepare yourself and confront me.
⁶I am just like you before God;
   I too have been taken from clay.
⁷No fear of me should alarm you,
   nor should my hand be heavy upon you.

⁸"But you have said in my hearing—
   I heard the very words—
⁹'I am pure and without sin;
   I am clean and free from guilt.
¹⁰Yet God has found fault with me;
   he considers me his enemy.
¹¹He fastens my feet in shackles;
   he keeps close watch on all my paths.'

¹²"But I tell you, in this you are not right,
   for God is greater than man.
¹³Why do you complain to him
   that he answers none of man's words^a?
¹⁴For God does speak—now one way, now
      another—
   though man may not perceive it.
¹⁵In a dream, in a vision of the night,
   when deep sleep falls on men
   as they slumber in their beds,
¹⁶he may speak in their ears
   and terrify them with warnings,
¹⁷to turn man from wrongdoing
   and keep him from pride,
¹⁸to preserve his soul from the pit,^{b}
   his life from perishing by the sword.^{c}
¹⁹Or a man may be chastened on a bed of pain
   with constant distress in his bones,
²⁰so that his very being finds food repulsive
   and his soul loathes the choicest meal.
²¹His flesh wastes away to nothing,
   and his bones, once hidden, now stick out.
²²His soul draws near to the pit,^{d}
   and his life to the messengers of death.^{e}

²³"Yet if there is an angel on his side
   as a mediator, one out of a thousand,
   to tell a man what is right for him,
²⁴to be gracious to him and say,

^{a}13 Or that he does not answer for any of his actions ^{b}18 Or preserve him from the grave ^{c}18 Or from crossing the River
^{d}22 Or He draws near to the grave ^{e}22 Or to the dead

NRSV

and what my lips know they speak sincerely.
⁴ The spirit of God has made me,
   and the breath of the Almighty^a gives me
      life.
⁵ Answer me, if you can;
   set your words in order before me; take your
      stand.
⁶ See, before God I am as you are;
   I too was formed from a piece of clay.
⁷ No fear of me need terrify you;
   my pressure will not be heavy on you.

⁸ "Surely, you have spoken in my hearing,
   and I have heard the sound of your words.
⁹ You say, 'I am clean, without transgression;
   I am pure, and there is no iniquity in me.
¹⁰ Look, he finds occasions against me,
   he counts me as his enemy;
¹¹ he puts my feet in the stocks,
   and watches all my paths.'

¹² "But in this you are not right. I will answer
      you:
   God is greater than any mortal.
¹³ Why do you contend against him,
   saying, 'He will answer none of my^b words'?
¹⁴ For God speaks in one way,
   and in two, though people do not perceive
      it.
¹⁵ In a dream, in a vision of the night,
   when deep sleep falls on mortals,
   while they slumber on their beds,
¹⁶ then he opens their ears,
   and terrifies them with warnings,
¹⁷ that he may turn them aside from their deeds,
   and keep them from pride,
¹⁸ to spare their souls from the Pit,
   their lives from traversing the River.
¹⁹ They are also chastened with pain upon their
      beds,
   and with continual strife in their bones,
²⁰ so that their lives loathe bread,
   and their appetites dainty food.
²¹ Their flesh is so wasted away that it cannot be
      seen;
   and their bones, once invisible, now stick
      out.

^{a} Traditional rendering of Heb Shaddai ^{b} Compare Gk: Heb his

NIV

'Spare him from going down to the pit[a];
    I have found a ransom for him'—
25then his flesh is renewed like a child's;
    it is restored as in the days of his youth.
26He prays to God and finds favor with him,
    he sees God's face and shouts for joy;
    he is restored by God to his righteous state.
27Then he comes to men and says,
    'I sinned, and perverted what was right,
    but I did not get what I deserved.
28He redeemed my soul from going down to the
        pit,[b]
    and I will live to enjoy the light.'

29"God does all these things to a man—
    twice, even three times—
30to turn back his soul from the pit,[c]
    that the light of life may shine on him.

31"Pay attention, Job, and listen to me;
    be silent, and I will speak.
32If you have anything to say, answer me;
    speak up, for I want you to be cleared.
33But if not, then listen to me;
    be silent, and I will teach you wisdom."

a24 Or grave   b28 Or redeemed me from going down to the grave
c30 Or turn him back from the grave

NRSV

22 Their souls draw near the Pit,
    and their lives to those who bring death.
23 Then, if there should be for one of them an
        angel,
    a mediator, one of a thousand,
    one who declares a person upright,
24 and he is gracious to that person, and says,
    'Deliver him from going down into the Pit;
    I have found a ransom;
25 let his flesh become fresh with youth;
    let him return to the days of his youthful
        vigor';
26 then he prays to God, and is accepted by him,
    he comes into his presence with joy,
  and God[a] repays him for his righteousness.
27   That person sings to others and says,
    'I sinned, and perverted what was right,
    and it was not paid back to me.
28 He has redeemed my soul from going down
        to the Pit,
    and my life shall see the light.'

29 "God indeed does all these things,
    twice, three times, with mortals,
30 to bring back their souls from the Pit,
    so that they may see the light of life.[b]
31 Pay heed, Job, listen to me;
    be silent, and I will speak.
32 If you have anything to say, answer me;
    speak, for I desire to justify you.
33 If not, listen to me;
    be silent, and I will teach you wisdom."

a Heb he   d Syr: Heb to be lighted with the light of life

COMMENTARY

With chap. 33 Elihu begins the task of answering Job. He introduces his discourse in vv. 1-7 with a call to hear (v. 1) and a self-recommendation of what he has to say (vv. 2-3), along with a claim that, as a fellow human, he speaks to Job as an equal (vv. 4-7). He summarizes Job's complaint (vv. 8-11) by drawing primarily on Job's speeches in chaps. 9 and 13. The gist of Job's complaint, as Elihu interprets it, is that even though Job is innocent, God has treated him as an enemy and punished him. Elihu sets up his refutation of Job by citing one of the specific complaints Job had made: that God refuses to reply to a person's words (vv. 12-13).

The main body of Elihu's speech is set off by the inclusio in vv. 14 and 29-30 ("once, twice . . . two times, thrice" [author's trans.]), referring to God's attempts to communicate with a person and to turn the person back from death. Although Elihu draws in various ways on what the friends have said, the distinctive quality of his argument is the account of God's comprehensive concern to warn and correct humans and so to save them from destruction. Elihu describes a three-stage process, involving dreams (vv. 15-18), illness (vv. 19-22), and the intervention of an angelic mediator (vv. 23-28), who finally effects the recognition of wrongdoing, restoration, and reconciliation. A concluding call to Job to hear and reply (vv. 31-33), if he has anything to say, brings this part of Elihu's speech to a conclusion and provides for the transition to chap. 34.

Elihu's preoccupation with the process of moral regeneration is distinct from the arguments of the friends. Although the date of composition of the Elihu speeches is not certain (see Overview of Job 32:1–37:24), there was a growing interest in Jewish moral literature of the Persian and Hellenistic periods in issues of character, and particularly in the acknowledgment of sin and repentance. The chronicler provides an account of the repentance of King Manasseh, for instance (2 Chr 30:10-20), and later tradition even supplied the text of his penitential prayer (Prayer of Manasseh). The stories of King Nebuchadnezzar in Daniel 2–4 show how a proud king is warned by dreams (Daniel 2; 4) and by suffering (Daniel 4) to humble himself and confess the Most High God. Similarities between these narratives and the account Elihu gives of the process of moral regeneration suggest that the author of the Elihu speeches comes from a generation in which this topic was central to any understanding of the meaning of suffering.

33:1-7. The first three verses of Elihu's introduction are a fairly typical piece of didactic rhetoric, consisting of a call to hear addressed explicitly to Job (v. 1; cf. Deut 5:1; Prov 1:8; Isa 1:10) and a self-recommendation of what he has to say (vv. 2-3; cf. Prov 8:6-8). Verses 4-7, however, specifically engage the concerns Job had expressed in chap. 13, that the unrestrained power of God makes dialogue impossible. Here Elihu presents himself as one who, as a mere human like Job, can engage him in dialogue without intimidation. The argument is organized in an ABAB pattern, v. 4 corresponding to v. 6 and v. 5 to v. 7. In vv. 4 and 6, human nature is described in terms of the breath of God (v. 4) and clay (v. 6), as in Gen 2:7. The motif of being snipped off from clay was also known in Mesopotamian[492] and Egyp-

tian[493] literature. Elihu invites Job to "answer" and "prepare" his words in terms evocative of Job's own challenge to God (13:18a, 22b). The phrase "if you are able" (v. 5) has a double nuance. When Job considered confronting God, Job's ability to answer was put in question by the inequality of power. But here, as Elihu's words suggest, Job's ability to reply depends on the intrinsic strength of his arguments, which, Elihu subtly suggests, are inadequate. Elihu closes his argument with a pointed allusion to Job's words in 13:21b, where Job asked God not to allow God's fearfulness to terrify him when they spoke together (cf. also 9:34). If one follows the NIV in taking the word אכפי (’akpî) as a variant form of כפי (kapî, "my hand"),[494] then Elihu also echoes 13:21a.

33:8-18. Elihu summarizes what he considers to be the essence of Job's complaint, making use of explicit citations as well as more general summaries. As Habel notes, these verses pair four claims to innocence (v. 9) with four complaints against God (vv. 10-11).[495] Although v. 9 does not use Job's exact words, Job had claimed to be innocent of serious wrongdoing (9:20-21; 27:4-6; 31:1-40). Verses 10-11 contain a nearly verbatim quotation of Job's words in 13:24b and 27a.

Having set forth a summary of Job's arguments, Elihu announces his judgment and his intent to refute (v. 12a), stating the principle that grounds all the arguments he will make: God is greater than humankind.[496] In Elihu's opinion, Job's entire understanding of God is wrong, but he introduces his own interpretation of God's motives and methods by means of another specific complaint Job has made about God: that one could not "contend" with God (13a: cf. 9:3a) because God would not "answer" (13b; cf. 9:3b). In fact, the pronouns in 9:3b are ambiguous, and it is not clear whether Job is saying that a person *could not* answer God or that God *would not* answer a person (see Commentary on Job 9:2-4). Elihu

---

492. E.g., the *Gilgamesh Epic* (*ANET*, 74).

493. E.g., in the Instructions of Anememopet, (*ANET*, 424).

494. M. Dahood, "Hebrew-Ugaritic Lexicography I," *Biblica* 44 (1963), 293.

495. N. Habel, *The Book of Job*, OTL (Philadelphia: Westminster, 1985) 465.

496. R. Gordis, *The Book of Job: Commentary, New Translation, and Special Studies* (New York: Jewish Theological Seminary, 5738/1978) 374; and Habel, *The Book of Job*, 467, take v. 12b as part of Elihu's citation of Job's arguments. As Habel translates: "Well, in this you are not in the right. I will answer you./ If 'Eloah is greater than humans,'/ Then why do you bring a suit against him,/ Since (as you claim), 'He answers none of my charges' " (Habel, *The Book of Job*, 455).

has taken it in the latter sense, and it is certainly the case that Job complains about the elusive, non-responsiveness of God (23:8-9).

In singling out 9:2-4 and 13:18-27, Elihu draws attention to the legal metaphor that has been important in shaping Job's complaint, but that the other three friends have not acknowledged in their replies. Some commentators think that Elihu's engagement of the legal metaphor constitutes his distinctive contribution to the book,[497] but that does not seem to be borne out by the way Elihu engages Job's legal language. Elihu does not point Job toward a solution by using legal categories but by showing how they have confused and misled Job. Job had complained that God would not answer his words in the context of a legal case; Elihu points out that God often speaks, but in ways that go unnoticed by people like Job (v. 14).

God's mode of communication is not a trial but dreams and night visions that carry warnings (vv. 15-16). Job had complained that God terrified him with dreams and visions (7:14), implying an obsessive and sadistic character for God. Elihu reinterprets these phenomena as attempts by God to turn a person away from wrongful deeds or pridefulness (v. 17). Far from being acts of hostility, they are attempts by God to save a person's life. (Parallelism makes the NRSV's "traversing the River [of death]," more likely than the NIV's "perishing by the sword," although both are linguistically possible.) In general, dreams and visions are recognized in the Bible as means of divine revelation (see Gen 15:1; 28:10-17; 31:10-13, 24; 40:8-18; 41:1-32). Similar to Elihu's description, God sends Abimelech a dream, warning him against unintentionally committing the serious sin of sexual intercourse with Sarah, wife of Abraham (Gen 20:3-7).

Elihu identifies two objects of divine warning: an "act" that might be committed and a disposition, "pride," the character flaw that leads to wrongful deeds (cf. the dream of Nebuchadnezzar in Dan 4:10-11[7-8], where the lofty tree whose top "touched the heavens" symbolizes pride). The choice of this characteristic is significant, since, as Gordis notes, hubris is the flaw to which good

people are particularly susceptible,[498] and Job's insistence on his own rightness over against God would seem to Elihu evidence of just such arrogance.

33:19-22. A second and more emphatic form of divine communication is illness, which Elihu characterizes as a kind of reproof or chastening (v. 19). Eliphaz had briefly mentioned such divine correction in 5:17, using the same term. He focused on the objective outcome of such divine correction, however, whereas Elihu is more concerned with the process itself and the moral regeneration of the individual. The psalms, too, sometimes interpret illness in terms of divine reproof (cf. Pss 6:1[2]; 38:1[2]). Yet they associate divine reproof with anger, whereas Elihu assumes that the divine intent is not punitive but salvific (v. 30). Although Elihu's words engage those of Eliphaz and the psalmists, they are most specifically directed at Job's interpretation of his illness as a sign of God's enmity and desire to humiliate him (19:20; 30:16-19, 30-31). This section reaches its climax at the point where the sufferer approaches death itself (v. 22). In the psalms the approach to death is often the moment of appeal to God and of God's deliverance (Pss 18:4-6[5-7]; 30:1-3[2-4]; cf. Isa 38:9-20; Jonah 2:2-9).

33:23-28. Although Elihu generally follows the scenarios of the lament and thanksgiving psalms in vv. 19-22, his imagination differs from those scenarios in that the psalms simply depict the person in trouble calling out to God and being delivered. They seldom if ever attempt to explore what makes that appeal to God possible. For Elihu that process, which the psalms pass over in silence, is of utmost importance. How is it that repentance, restoration, and reconciliation become possible for a person who is blind and deaf to God's warnings (cf. Isa 42:18-25)? The impasse, Elihu claims, is broken by an angelic mediator (מליץ *mēlîṣ*). The term refers primarily to an interpreter (e.g., Gen 42:23), but also comes to have a broader meaning of "intermediary," "advocate." Job used the term in 16:20 in the sense of a legal advocate who would argue his case with God. In later Judaism, the notion of an angelic defense attorney became part of traditions concerning the high holy days, when each person

497. Habel, *The Book of Job* 56, 445; B. Zuckerman, *Job the Silent: A Study in Historical Counterpoint* (New York: Oxford University Press, 1991) 150-53.

498. Gordis, *The Book of Job,* 375.

would be judged by the heavenly court.[499] Intercessory angels are already attested in *1 Enoch* 9:3; 15:2 and in the *Testaments of the Twelve Patriarchs*.[500]

What Elihu says must be interpreted on its own terms and in its own context, however, and does not necessarily imply later ideas about angels and their functions. It is not clear, for instance, whether the phrase "one of a thousand" (v. 23) is intended to suggest the rarity of such an angelic mediator or its ready availability. Equally ambiguous is the following phrase, which could be translated either "to declare a person upright" (see NRSV),[501] or "to tell a person what is right for him," i.e., his duty (see NIV).[502] Although the later tradition of the intercessory angel would support the translation "to declare a person upright," the case that Elihu has been building about the inability of a person to perceive the divine message would support the translation "to tell a person what is right for him." The angelic interpreter translates the "language" of suffering into words that a person can understand. Perhaps the ambiguity is intentional. Elihu is both appropriating and correcting the idea that Job advanced in chap. 16. The angelic mediator's speech expresses belief in the sufferer's essential uprightness; yet the sufferer's life is endangered by a moral flaw to which he remains oblivious. In that sense, Elihu claims that the angel speaks both *for* and *to* the sufferer.

The results of this activity are seen in the words of the angel to God (vv. 24-25) and in the transformed understanding and words of the sufferer (vv. 27-28). Although it has been objected that God should be understood as the subject of the verbs in v. 24, because an angel does not possess the authority to redeem (cf. v. 24 TNK),[503] the words "deliver him from the Pit" are not a command but an urgent plea to God. The nature of the "ransom" (כפר *kōper*) is ambiguous. In the legal literature, *kōper* designates the compensation paid by an injuring party to the injured party (e.g., Exod 21:30; Num 35:31-32). Correspondingly, here the ransom would be the repentance

of the sinner.[504] A ransom may be paid by another (cf. Isa 43:3), however, and so this may be the angel's pledge to stand surety for the person.[505]

Verse 26 is a highly condensed account of the cultic process of prayer and reconciliation that forms the setting for psalms of lament and thanksgiving. In contrast to the person's failure to perceive and respond to God's "speaking" (v. 14) through dreams and illness, God accepts the person's prayerful entreaty (v. 26). The joy of God's life-giving presence (cf. Num 6:24-26; Pss 4:7; 17:15; 31:16[17]) contrasts with the previous pain, depression, and emaciation (vv. 19-21). God's concluding and most significant act is ambiguously phrased, as the contrasting translations of v. 26*b* in the NRSV and the NIV suggest. As in v. 23*b*, the ambiguity may be strategic. Corresponding to the person's essential righteousness, "God repays him for his righteousness" (NRSV), but through the difficult process of turning the person from wrongful deeds and suppressing pride, he has been "restored by God to his righteous state" (NIV).

Until this point the individual has been talked about, but the individual's own understanding of events has not been described. Elihu brings together the theme of the transformation of moral self-understanding with the theme of cultic reconciliation as he dramatizes the individual's own words in the performance of the vow of praise. (The vow of praise is a frequent feature in psalms of lament; cf. Ps 22:22-31[23-32]). In v. 27, the individual confesses sin and perversion of "what is right" (ישר *yāšār*; cf. ישר *yōšer* in v. 23*b*), presumably the pride that distorted the person's understanding of God's message, but also acknowledges God's essential graciousness ("it was not paid back to me"). Elihu shifts the focus away from suffering as retributive, seeing it rather as redemptive, a notion expressed in images of redemption from the Pit and restoration to the light in v. 28.

33:29-30. Elihu summarizes in vv. 29-30, using inclusio to indicate the completion of the argument. The numerical figure of speech in v.

499. See ibid., 377.
500. *T. Levi* 3:5-6; *T. Dan* 6:2-6.
501. See ibid., 377; Habel, *The Book of Job*, 470.
502. J. F. Ross, "Job 33:14-30: The Phenomenology of Lament," *JBL* 94 (1975) 40.
503. Gordis, *The Book of Job*, 377.

504. G. Fohrer, "Die Weisheit des Elihu (Hi 32-37)," *Studien zum Buche Hiob (1956–1979)*, 2nd ed. (Berlin: Walter de Gruyter, 1983) 97; H.-M. Wahl, *Der Gerechte Schoepfer*, BZAW 207 (Berlin: Walter de Gruyter, 1993) 67.
505. Habel, *The Book of Job*, 470, thinks that it is a combination of the person's past behavior and surety by the angel.

14 ("once, twice") is echoed in v. 29 ("two times, thrice"), and images used in the thanksgiving in v. 28 are echoed in v. 30. It is no accident that the grammatical construction in v. 30 is a purpose clause, for Elihu's point throughout has been to stress the redemptive purposefulness of what appears to Job to be God's arbitrary or hostile action.

33:31-33. The final three verses renew the call to hear with which Elihu began his speech (v. 1//v. 33) and the invitation for Job to speak (v. 5//v. 32*a*). One should look at these words not so much in terms of Elihu's rhetoric but in terms of the strategic role of these words in the work of the *author* of the Elihu speeches. That author has no intention of letting Job reply and so turn Elihu's monologue into a dialogue. Rhetorically, having Elihu invite Job to speak and yet having Job remain silent make it appear that Elihu's speeches are more persuasive to Job than those of the friends had been. Verse 33, which presumes Job's silence, provides the transition to Elihu's further words in the following chapters.

REFLECTIONS

Elihu is a formidable thinker—and a dangerous one. In this chapter he articulates a powerful idea: God intentionally sends suffering to people in order to make them better—indeed, to save them. There is so much that is repugnant in this idea that it can be difficult to understand why it has had such a persistent grip on the moral imagination of countless generations of Jews and Christians. Yet it has been extremely influential, both in popular piety and in learned reflection.[506] In an almost uncanny echo of Elihu, the Christian scholar and novelist C. S. Lewis wrote the following in his book *The Problem of Pain:*

> Now God, who has made us, knows what we are and that our happiness lies in Him. Yet we will not seek it in Him as long as He leaves us any other resort where it can even plausibly be looked for. While what we call "our own life" remains agreeable we will not surrender it to Him. What then can God do in our interests but make "our own life" less agreeable to us, and take away the plausible sources of false happiness? . . . We are perplexed to see misfortune falling upon decent, inoffensive, worthy people—on capable, hard-working mothers of families or diligent, thrifty, little trades-people, on those who have worked so hard, and so honestly, for their modest stock of happiness and now seem to be entering on the enjoyment of it with the fullest right. . . . Let me implore the reader to try to believe, if only for the moment, that God, who made these deserving people, may really be right when He thinks that their modest prosperity and the happiness of their children are not enough to make them blessed: that all this must fall from them in the end, and that if they have not learned to know Him they will be wretched. And therefore He troubles them, warning them in advance of an insufficiency that one day they will have to discover.[507]

Lewis captures not only the essence of Elihu's argument but also the smugness of tone and the abstract quality of his reasoning. One might think that these are the arguments of someone who has never suffered, but that is not the case. Lewis's mother died when he was a child. It appears, however, that through ideas such as these he attempted to deal with his grief through a rationalization that seemed to give meaning and purpose even to such a terrible event.

That is apparently why the idea of suffering as divine pedagogy has such a strong appeal. Like the notion of suffering as punishment for sin, it organizes the disorienting chaos of suffering into a meaningful pattern. Fearing meaninglessness almost above all else, people are willing to pay a great deal to restore a meaningful structure to experiences over which they have no control. Moreover, the explanation of suffering as a warning is superior to the idea of suffering as punishment in that it provides not only reason but also purpose. What was evil from one

---

506. See J. A. Sanders, *Suffering as Divine Discipline in the Old Testament and Post-Biblical Judaism* (Rochester, N.Y.: Colgate Rochester Divinity School, 1955).
507. C. S. Lewis, *The Problem of Pain* (New York: Macmillan, 1940) 84-85.

perspective can be seen as positively good from another, and people are extremely reluctant to admit the reality of things that are simply and truly evil. The belief that God has a purpose in bringing suffering enlists the energies of the one who suffers to discern that purpose and to work toward fulfilling it. Suffering as redemptive discipline may also seem more appealing than retribution in its image of God. Instead of an angry God, it offers the image of a caring God who desires a person to live and be whole and uses pain only as a last resort.

When one begins to examine these ideas, however, their grotesque nature becomes apparent. A parent who would break a child's arm or kill a child's dog to draw the child's attention to some moral lesson or to remind the child of its absolute dependence is no loving parent but a sadist who takes a perverted pleasure in cruelty. No ultimate good for the child, even if it were the parent's sincere purpose, could make those actions anything other than evil. This is too high a price to pay for meaning. Yet this is essentially the image of God offered by Elihu and by Lewis in *The Problem of Pain.*

It should not be surprising that a belief in suffering as divine pedagogy often leaves the one who believes it terribly vulnerable when tragedy occurs. The brittleness of the explanation is swept away by the reality of grief. We do not know what might have happened to the character Elihu in later life, but C. S. Lewis was overtaken by a second terrible loss when his wife died of cancer. In his response to that grief, he leaves behind all his Elihu-like complacent rationalizations. Instead, his voice echoes the pain, rage, and sense of betrayal that one hears in Job:

> Meanwhile, where is God? . . . When you are happy, so happy that you have no sense of needing Him, so happy that you are tempted to feel His claims upon you as an interruption, if you remember yourself and turn to Him with gratitude and praise, you will be—or so it feels—welcomed with open arms. But go to Him when your need is desperate, when all other help is vain, and what do you find? A door slammed in your face. . . . After that, silence. . . . Not that I am (I think) in much danger of ceasing to believe in God. The real danger is of coming to believe such dreadful things about Him. The conclusion I dread is not "So there's no God after all," but "So this is what God's really like. Deceive yourself no longer."[508]

Lewis's honest grappling with his pain and bewilderment is, like Job's, the voice of a deep faith. Like Job, he does not find a simple answer.

Part of the problem with attempts to grapple with the meaning of suffering is that suffering does not a have a single cause or a single shape, and so it cannot have a single meaning. It may arise out of human cruelty, out of self-inflicted folly, out of the inescapable reality of finitude, or any number of things. The notion that God wills particular suffering in order to teach something, however, can lead only to the conclusion that God is a monster of cruelty. It is a false belief that should be rejected.

The connection between suffering and learning is an important one, however, once it is detached from the notion that learning is the *purpose* of suffering. Suffering is not meaningful or purposeful in and of itself. Some kinds of suffering can never be anything but meaningless, but that is not always the case. One of the dehumanizing aspects of suffering is that it tends to make persons experience themselves as powerless and passive. Suffering takes away so much. The determination to learn from suffering, to wrest something back from it, can be a powerful means of resisting its soul-destroying force. One sees this in the struggles of the abused and the oppressed who are able to learn how to transmute suffering into solidarity. But one also sees this in the bereaved, whose suffering arises from the natural event of death, when they take back from the experience of immeasurable loss the capacity for a new compassion. Suffering is not sent, nor does it *have* meaning and purpose. Rather, the ability to take its emptiness and to put it to the service of meaning and purpose is the power to

508. C. S. Lewis, *A Grief Observed* (San Francisco: Harper, 1989) 17-19.

resist the evil in suffering. In that experience, one discovers the power and presence of God in suffering.

JOB 34:1-37, GOD, THE ABSOLUTE SOVEREIGN, ALWAYS ACTS JUSTLY

NIV

34 Then Elihu said:

²"Hear my words, you wise men;
    listen to me, you men of learning.
³For the ear tests words
    as the tongue tastes food.
⁴Let us discern for ourselves what is right;
    let us learn together what is good.

⁵"Job says, 'I am innocent,
    but God denies me justice.
⁶Although I am right,
    I am considered a liar;
although I am guiltless,
    his arrow inflicts an incurable wound.'
⁷What man is like Job,
    who drinks scorn like water?
⁸He keeps company with evildoers;
    he associates with wicked men.
⁹For he says, 'It profits a man nothing
    when he tries to please God.'

¹⁰"So listen to me, you men of understanding.
    Far be it from God to do evil,
    from the Almighty to do wrong.
¹¹He repays a man for what he has done;
    he brings upon him what his conduct
        deserves.
¹²It is unthinkable that God would do wrong,
    that the Almighty would pervert justice.
¹³Who appointed him over the earth?
    Who put him in charge of the whole world?
¹⁴If it were his intention
    and he withdrew his spirit[a] and breath,
¹⁵all mankind would perish together
    and man would return to the dust.

¹⁶"If you have understanding, hear this;
    listen to what I say.
¹⁷Can he who hates justice govern?
    Will you condemn the just and mighty One?

a14 Or Spirit

NRSV

34 Then Elihu continued and said:
² "Hear my words, you wise men,
    and give ear to me, you who know;
³ for the ear tests words
    as the palate tastes food.
⁴ Let us choose what is right;
    let us determine among ourselves what is
        good.
⁵ For Job has said, 'I am innocent,
    and God has taken away my right;
⁶ in spite of being right I am counted a liar;
    my wound is incurable, though I am
        without transgression.'
⁷ Who is there like Job,
    who drinks up scoffing like water,
⁸ who goes in company with evildoers
    and walks with the wicked?
⁹ For he has said, 'It profits one nothing
    to take delight in God.'

¹⁰ "Therefore, hear me, you who have sense,
    far be it from God that he should do
        wickedness,
    and from the Almighty[a] that he should do
        wrong.
¹¹ For according to their deeds he will repay them,
    and according to their ways he will make it
        befall them.
¹² Of a truth, God will not do wickedly,
    and the Almighty[a] will not pervert justice.
¹³ Who gave him charge over the earth
    and who laid on him[b] the whole world?
¹⁴ If he should take back his spirit[c] to himself,
    and gather to himself his breath,
¹⁵ all flesh would perish together,
    and all mortals return to dust.

¹⁶ "If you have understanding, hear this;
    listen to what I say.

a Traditional rendering of Heb Shaddai   b Heb lacks on him
c Heb his heart his spirit

NIV

¹⁸Is he not the One who says to kings, 'You are worthless,'
and to nobles, 'You are wicked,'
¹⁹who shows no partiality to princes
and does not favor the rich over the poor,
for they are all the work of his hands?
²⁰They die in an instant, in the middle of the night;
the people are shaken and they pass away;
the mighty are removed without human hand.

²¹"His eyes are on the ways of men;
he sees their every step.
²²There is no dark place, no deep shadow,
where evildoers can hide.
²³God has no need to examine men further,
that they should come before him for judgment.
²⁴Without inquiry he shatters the mighty
and sets up others in their place.
²⁵Because he takes note of their deeds,
he overthrows them in the night and they are crushed.
²⁶He punishes them for their wickedness
where everyone can see them,
²⁷because they turned from following him
and had no regard for any of his ways.
²⁸They caused the cry of the poor to come before him,
so that he heard the cry of the needy.
²⁹But if he remains silent, who can condemn him?
If he hides his face, who can see him?
Yet he is over man and nation alike,
³⁰ to keep a godless man from ruling,
from laying snares for the people.

³¹"Suppose a man says to God,
'I am guilty but will offend no more.
³²Teach me what I cannot see;
if I have done wrong, I will not do so again.'
³³Should God then reward you on your terms,
when you refuse to repent?
You must decide, not I;
so tell me what you know.

³⁴"Men of understanding declare,
wise men who hear me say to me,
³⁵'Job speaks without knowledge;
his words lack insight.'

NRSV

¹⁷ Shall one who hates justice govern?
Will you condemn one who is righteous and mighty,
¹⁸ who says to a king, 'You scoundrel!'
and to princes, 'You wicked men!';
¹⁹ who shows no partiality to nobles,
nor regards the rich more than the poor,
for they are all the work of his hands?
²⁰ In a moment they die;
at midnight the people are shaken and pass away,
and the mighty are taken away by no human hand.

²¹ "For his eyes are upon the ways of mortals,
and he sees all their steps.
²² There is no gloom or deep darkness
where evildoers may hide themselves.
²³ For he has not appointed a time^a for anyone
to go before God in judgment.
²⁴ He shatters the mighty without investigation,
and sets others in their place.
²⁵ Thus, knowing their works,
he overturns them in the night, and they are crushed.
²⁶ He strikes them for their wickedness
while others look on,
²⁷ because they turned aside from following him,
and had no regard for any of his ways,
²⁸ so that they caused the cry of the poor to come to him,
and he heard the cry of the afflicted—
²⁹ When he is quiet, who can condemn?
When he hides his face, who can behold him,
whether it be a nation or an individual?—
³⁰ so that the godless should not reign,
or those who ensnare the people.

³¹ "For has anyone said to God,
'I have endured punishment; I will not offend any more;
³² teach me what I do not see;
if I have done iniquity, I will do it no more'?
³³ Will he then pay back to suit you,
because you reject it?
For you must choose, and not I;
therefore declare what you know.^b

^a Cn: Heb *yet*   ^b Meaning of Heb of verses 29-33 uncertain

NIV

³⁶Oh, that Job might be tested to the utmost
    for answering like a wicked man!
³⁷To his sin he adds rebellion;
    scornfully he claps his hands among us
    and multiplies his words against God."

NRSV

³⁴ Those who have sense will say to me,
    and the wise who hear me will say,
³⁵ 'Job speaks without knowledge,
    his words are without insight.'
³⁶ Would that Job were tried to the limit,
    because his answers are those of the wicked.
³⁷ For he adds rebellion to his sin;
    he claps his hands among us,
    and multiplies his words against God."

COMMENTARY

Chapter 34 is a very different kind of speech from chap. 33. Whereas chap. 33 is addressed specifically to Job and concerned with the very personal process of moral regeneration, chap. 34 is addressed to a general audience of the wise and presents an almost philosophical reflection on God's nature and governance of the world. As in chap. 33, however, Elihu is concerned to refute a specific claim made by Job that God has "taken away Job's right." Although there is only one explicit citation of Job's words (v. 5*b*, citing 27:2*a*), Elihu refutes the attacks Job has made on God's governance in the world in chaps. 12; 21; and 24.

The speech has a fairly clear structure. Following the introductory heading (v. 1), Elihu begins with a developed rhetorical appeal to his audience to listen and judge with him the words of Job (vv. 2-9). A similar, briefer appeal and judgment closes the speech (vv. 34-37). The body of the speech is developed in a series of related arguments. Elihu defends the just governance of God by appealing to God's absolute sovereignty (vv. 10-15) and character as a disinterested lover of justice (vv. 16-20). In response to Job's complaint that times for judgment are not evident, Elihu describes the sudden and surprising ways in which God overturns the wicked (vv. 21-30). Satirizing Job's insistence on being restored on his own terms while refusing to admit guilt (vv. 31-33), Elihu renews his call for the judgment of all right-thinking people against Job's rebellious and ignorant words (vv. 34-37).

34:1-9. Three times in the course of his speech Elihu addresses his audience as "wise men," "people of learning," and "men of reason"

(vv. 2, 10, 34). According to the narrative context, the only people present are Job and his three friends, none of whom Elihu considers wise. Elihu is rhetorically addressing an imaginary audience, the truly wise, for whom Elihu is the spokesperson. This device serves as an appeal to readers who may assume the title of wise by agreeing with Elihu's judgment.

The introductory appeal is tightly structured. Following the call to hear (v. 2; cf. Deut 5:1; Prov 1:8; Isa 1:10), Elihu cites a proverb (v. 3), which authorizes his appeal for the audience to exercise discriminating judgment (v. 4). Next, he cites the words of Job, which are to be judged (vv. 5-6), makes his own judgment about Job's character as reflected in his words (vv. 7-8), and reinforces his conclusion by adding another citation of Job's obviously impious words (v. 9).

The proverb Elihu cites in v. 3 is the same one Job used in 12:11 to introduce his satirical doxology of God's governance in 12:13-25, and the echo suggests something of Elihu's attempt to turn Job's words to his own purposes. The theme of the chapter is introduced in Elihu's invitation to determine "what is right" (משפט *mišpāṭ*). The term *mišpāṭ* occurs six times in the course of the speech, although with varying nuances. Here, as in v. 6*a*, it means the determination of what is correct in a particular case, as the parallel line in v. 4*b* confirms. To "know what is good" is to be able to make discriminating judgments between good and bad, sound and unsound (cf. Gen 3:22; 2 Sam 14:20). Elsewhere in the chapter, *mišpāṭ* designates a legal right or judgment (vv. 5, 12, 23), on the one hand, and the broader principle of just governance (v. 17) on the other. For Elihu, as for Job, these various dimensions of meaning are related. Job has argued inductively from the sense of injustice done to him to a critique of divine governance in general. Elihu will argue deductively from a conviction of God's righteous governance to the conclusion that God could not have acted unjustly in Job's case. Both assume that only one view can be judged correct.

The words of Job that Elihu cites are a pastiche of 27:2*a* ("As God lives, who has taken away my right" [NRSV]), 9:20 ("Though I am innocent, my own mouth would condemn me" [NRSV]), and 6:4 ("the arrows of the Almighty" [NRSV]). Elihu's composite citation is a fair representation of Job's views. For the moment Elihu does not seek to refute them so much as to disqualify them by characterizing them as "scorn," the sort of mockery associated with the impious (cf. Ps 1:1; Prov 1:22). By using the idiom "to drink X like water" (cf. 15:16), Elihu implies that such derisive speech is habitual with Job. With his rhetoric, Elihu shifts the focus away from the content of Job's words in order to make Job's character the issue. Similarly, without explicitly saying that Job is a bad person, Elihu accuses him of being a "fellow-traveler" of the wicked (v. 8), because Job says the same sort of things they say (v. 9). In reality, Job had attributed words like those in v. 9 to the wicked, from whom he certainly distinguished himself (21:15). Elihu, however, implies that Job's complaints (e.g., that God destroys both blameless and wicked persons [9:22], that the wicked prosper [21:7-17], and that, despite his own upright behavior, he has received evil instead of good [30:26]), all amount to much the same thing as the wicked say.

34:10-15. Repeating his summons to "men of reason" (v. 10*a*), Elihu introduces the first of his arguments in support of God's righteous governance. His initial statements are not so much arguments as assertions (vv. 10*b*-12). The oath formula in v. 10*b* ("far be it from . . .") and the emphatic exclamation in v. 11*a* ("of a truth") establish a rhetorical stance that the NIV captures well in its rendering of v. 11. Elihu presents it as literally unthinkable that God could do evil or pervert justice. It is a logical contradiction. The grounds for Elihu's claims are articulated in vv. 13-15; yet their obliqueness requires the reader

to work out the connection. When Elihu asks rhetorically who appointed God over the earth (v. 13), he draws attention to God's absolute sovereignty. God has no superiors, only creatures who depend on God for every breath they draw (vv. 14-15). Here Elihu echoes Job's similar assertion in 12:10 that in God's "hand is the life of every living thing/ and the breath of every human being" (NRSV). Whereas Job used this observation to introduce his complaint about God's mismanagement of the world, Elihu's words point to the question of motive. Why would one who is absolutely sovereign do evil or pervert the right? Those are rather the actions of individuals who are insecure and have something to gain by doing evil.

34:16-20. What was only obliquely indicated in vv. 10-15 becomes explicit in the following argument. Elihu's call to hear is expressed in the singular in v. 16. Although he addresses Job directly in v. 33, here it is more likely that Elihu is addressing each member of the audience who "has understanding." Modern readers, skeptical and suspicious of official power, may be inclined to answer in the affirmative Elihu's rhetorical question, "Can one who hates justice govern?" Tyranny provides ample evidence. But that misses Eliphaz's subtle, philosophical point about the relationship between the character and action of God. Elihu has already established that God's authority over the world is freely chosen, neither derivative nor imposed. The two nuances of *mišpāṭ,* "governance" and "justice," assist Elihu in making his point. If God chooses to govern, it must be because it is in the nature of God to love justice. It would be self-contradictory for God to choose to do what God hates. Elihu makes the same point even more sharply in v. 17*b.* "Righteousness" (צדקה *ṣĕdāqâ*) and "wickedness" (רשע *rāšā'*) are logically contradictory terms. Given that God is not only the "righteous one" (צדיק *ṣadîq*) but also the "(all-)powerful one" (כביר *kabbîr*), it is logically contradictory that God would do evil.

Elihu substantiates his claims with illustrations of God's behavior toward human rulers, whom God judges according to the standards of righteousness and good governance (v. 18; the NRSV and the NIV follow the LXX; cf. the TNK). Divine judgment against unjust rulers is commonplace in prophetic literature (e.g., Isa 10:1-4; Jer 22; Amos

7:10-17) and in the historical books (e.g., 1 Kgs 15:1-5; 2 Kgs 16:1-4; 21:1-26). God's impartiality toward nobles and the poor (v. 19; cf. Deut 10:17) is also required by God of human judges (Deut 16:18-20).

The mysterious suddenness with which the powerful die and are swept away (v. 20) is taken by Elihu as evidence of God's judgment. Here, as elsewhere (see Overview of Job 33), similarities exist between Elihu's words and the stories in Daniel 1–6. The story of Belshazzar (Daniel 5) illustrates sudden and mysterious divine judgment against a prideful king at the very height of his glory, one who is killed "in the very night" that judgment is decreed (Dan 5:30). Like the powerful one removed "without human hand" in Job 34:20, the statue symbolizing imperial rule in Dan 2:34 is shattered by a rock cut "without human hand" (cf. Dan 8:25).

34:21-30. Elihu's third argument addresses several charges raised by Job in 24:1-17. In 24:13-17, Job had described the way in which criminals take advantage of the dark to carry out their crimes, because "no eye will see me." Furthermore, Job had complained that the times of judgment are not seen by God's friends (24:1; see comm.). In his description of the misery of the destitute, Job had also observed that while the murdered cry out, God seems to notice nothing wrong (24:12). Elihu attempts to address each of these issues.

Using several of the same words that Job used in 24:13-17, Elihu insists that God's eyes *do* see human deeds and that even deep darkness provides no cover for evildoers (vv. 21-22). In v. 23, he responds to Job's complaint about times of judgment. There are various ways of understanding the grammar and text of v. 23. The translations of both the NRSV and the NIV can be defended, although the NIV requires a fairly tortuous understanding of the syntax, and the meaning of the NRSV is not entirely clear. The simplest reading is that suggested by Gordis, "It is not for man to set the times to go to God for judgment."[509] Elihu is also implicitly challenging Job's obsession with a legal hearing, although the

focus here remains on the judgment of the wicked. Elihu's argument is that since God knows all that the wicked do, no investigation and no set time for judgment are needed. God simply acts suddenly and decisively to overthrow the mighty and put others in their place (vv. 24-27; cf. Dan 2:21). This overthrow of the wicked also serves as Elihu's evidence that the cry of the oppressed comes before God and is acted upon (vv. 28, 30). The NRSV cleverly interprets v. 30 as the completion of the sentence, with v. 29 as an interjection, but the grammatical construction of the Hebrew makes this interpretation unlikely. Although not without its own problems, the NIV is to be preferred.

The conclusion that Elihu draws from his reflection on God's preferred way of dealing with oppressive rulers is twofold. First, God's silence cannot be judged (v. 29*a*; cf. v. 24), nor can God's seeming absence from human history be made transparent to human inquiry (v. 29*b*). At the same time, God's sovereignty is the warrant that the godless will not triumph (v. 30). The issues with which Elihu struggles are similar to those found in apocalyptic literature, although his solution is somewhat different. As in apocalyptic, Elihu tends to set the issue of theodicy in terms of kings and nations. God's sovereignty is a similarly important theme (cf. Dan 2:44; 4:34-35[31-32]). Both Elihu and apocalyptic texts conceive of God's power as sudden and mysterious, expressed in the dramatic overturning of established rulers (Dan 2:21; 8:8, 25). But whereas Elihu accepted the inability of humans to know the times of judgment, apocalyptic writers, appealing to mysterious divine revelation, came to believe that it was possible to know the plan of God (Dan 7:15-28) and even the times of judgment (Dan 9:24-27; 12:7-12) and so endure the dissonance produced by the presence of evil in a world where God is sovereign.

34:31-37. These verses are extremely difficult to interpret. By means of a modest emendation of v. 31, they can be read as Elihu's advice to Job, "But say instead to God, 'I have borne my punishment, I will offend no more.' "[510] Others suggest, with somewhat different emendations, that Elihu is sarcastically describing the kind of

---

509. R. Gordis, *The Book of Job: Commentary, New Translation, and Special Studies* (New York: Jewish Theological Seminary, 5738/1978) 390; cf. also N. Habel, *The Book of Job,* OTL (Philadelphia: Westminster, 1985) 474, 484; Guillaume, *Studies in the Book of Job* (Leiden: E. J. Brill, 1968) 120.

510. Gordis, *The Book of Job,* 393; similarly Habel, *The Book of Job,* 476.

divine apology Job expects from God, "Should God say to you, 'I have erred, I will offend no more'?"[511] The NIV, however, proposes a translation that involves minimal emendation, yet makes good sense of the lines. In its interpretation, Elihu contrasts a properly repentant and teachable person (cf. 33:26-28) with the obdurate Job, who appears to Elihu to expect restoration even though he refuses to repent. (The verb translated "refuse" or "reject" [מאס *māʾas*] in v. 33 has no expressed object in the Hebrew text; the NIV supplies "to repent" according to its understanding of the passage.) The NIV translation of vv. 31-33 also allows for a smooth transition to the final verses in the chapter, which again call upon the "men of reason" to judge Job's words as ignorant and

obtuse (vv. 34-35). This judgment anticipates Elihu's words at the conclusion of his next speech (35:16).

In v. 35, the author of the Elihu speeches appropriates the similar criticism of Job's words by God in 38:2. Whether God's objection is actually the same as Elihu's is a different question, but by creating an anticipatory echo of the divine words, the author of these chapters sets up what appears to be an endorsement of his insight. There is a similarly opportunistic quality to Elihu's wish that Job be "tested to the limit" (v. 36). That, after all, has been agreed to in the prologue (1:12; 2:6), although none of the original parties to the dialogue know it. Elihu's call for such testing, however, does not concern Job's character before disaster struck him, but the quality of his words in response to that calamity (v. 37).

511. G. Fohrer, *Das Buch Hiob*, KAT xvi (Guetersloh: Gerd Mohn, 1963) 465; H.-M. Wahl, *Der Gerechte Schoepfer*, BZAW 207 (Berlin: Walter de Gruyter, 1993) 89-91.

REFLECTIONS

Elihu's speech provides an opportunity to reflect on the way in which rigidly dogmatic religion attempts to use rationalistic argument to avoid the discomforting claims of individual experience. Job, as Elihu represents him, speaks out of the immediacy of his experience. He knows himself to be innocent, yet experiences violence from God, and so concludes that God is acting unjustly toward him (vv. 4-6). From Elihu's point of view, Job's experience cannot be trusted as a reliable source of knowledge about God for the simple reason that it contradicts propositions about the nature of God that are part of accepted tradition ("it is unthinkable . . . that the Almighty would pervert justice," v. 12; cf. vv. 10, 17). In effect, Elihu argues deductively. Since God could not act inconsistently with God's nature, it is impossible that God could act unjustly. Therefore, Job must not know what he is talking about.

What is disturbing about the type of argument in which Elihu engages is not the use of rational argument itself, or even of deductive reasoning. The ability to reflect clearly and systematically about the nature of religious experience and the primary metaphors that speak of God is essential to theology. But Elihu attempts to use deductive arguments to exclude the very possibility that an individual's experience might put in question his or her propositions about God. In Elihu's hands, rational argument serves to defend a closed dogmatism.

One often encounters a kind of pseudo-rationalistic theology in fundamentalist churches, although it can appear in other religious traditions as well. Propositions are lined up and conclusions drawn to "prove" the various claims that the preacher or evangelist wishes to make. It does not matter that the logic of the arguments would generally not stand up to scrutiny. What is being offered in this type of religious ethos is the appearance of certainty. Even those who are not drawn to such religious cultures can recognize their appeal. It is difficult to live in a world that often seems to make no sense at all, and the desire for certainty is an understandable response to a disturbingly confusing world. The offer of absolute clarity and certainty is a strong part of the appeal of fundamentalism and other dogmatic approaches to faith. One can memorize the arguments and so have a ready answer for every doubting thought, whether it comes from others or from one's own heart.

The problem, of course, is that the alluring simplicity and certainty offered by dogmatic religion is often too rigid to stand up to the complexities of real life. People faced with tragedies may find themselves led to question the goodness of God. Or they may be caught in moral dilemmas, torn between the claims of conflicting values. A theology that rejects the legitimacy of such questioning leaves people without the resources to sustain faith, for they must either deny their own experience or risk rejection by their religious community. Not everyone has the courage of Job and is willing to endure the criticism that outspokenness in a dogmatic community entails. Some people hide their doubts, blaming themselves for a failure of faith, and so bear the double burden of the doubt itself and of the guilt for having been prey to doubt.

A mature and resiliant faith requires a willingness to let go of the need for absolute certainty. It requires the ability to trust, even when one does not know where questions may lead. Much as a human relationship develops in richness as persons become increasingly free to be honest with each other, the relationship that is faith in God draws strength from the ability to bring all experiences and all questions before God.

JOB 35:1-16, GOD DOES NOT ANSWER THE PRIDEFUL

NIV

35 Then Elihu said:

2"Do you think this is just?
    You say, 'I will be cleared by God.ᵃ'
3Yet you ask him, 'What profit is it to me,ᵇ
    and what do I gain by not sinning?'

4"I would like to reply to you
    and to your friends with you.
5Look up at the heavens and see;
    gaze at the clouds so high above you.
6If you sin, how does that affect him?
    If your sins are many, what does that do to him?
7If you are righteous, what do you give to him,
    or what does he receive from your hand?
8Your wickedness affects only a man like yourself,
    and your righteousness only the sons of men.

9"Men cry out under a load of oppression;
    they plead for relief from the arm of the powerful.
10But no one says, 'Where is God my Maker,
    who gives songs in the night,
11who teaches more to us than toᶜ the beasts of the earth
    and makes us wiser thanᵈ the birds of the air?'

a2 Or *My righteousness is more than God's*   b3 Or *you*   c11 Or *teaches us by*   d11 Or *us wise by*

NRSV

35 Elihu continued and said:
2 "Do you think this to be just?
    You say, 'I am in the right before God.'
3 If you ask, 'What advantage have I?
    How am I better off than if I had sinned?'
4 I will answer you
    and your friends with you.
5 Look at the heavens and see;
    observe the clouds, which are higher than you.
6 If you have sinned, what do you accomplish against him?
    And if your transgressions are multiplied, what do you do to him?
7 If you are righteous, what do you give to him;
    or what does he receive from your hand?
8 Your wickedness affects others like you,
    and your righteousness, other human beings.

9 "Because of the multitude of oppressions people cry out;
    they call for help because of the arm of the mighty.
10 But no one says, 'Where is God my Maker,
    who gives strength in the night,

NIV

¹²He does not answer when men cry out
  because of the arrogance of the wicked.
¹³Indeed, God does not listen to their empty plea;
  the Almighty pays no attention to it.
¹⁴How much less, then, will he listen
  when you say that you do not see him,
that your case is before him
  and you must wait for him,
¹⁵and further, that his anger never punishes
  and he does not take the least notice of
    wickedness.ᵃ
¹⁶So Job opens his mouth with empty talk;
  without knowledge he multiplies words."

a15 Symmachus, Theodotion and Vulgate; the meaning of the Hebrew for this word is uncertain.

NRSV

¹¹ who teaches us more than the animals of the
    earth,
  and makes us wiser than the birds of the
    air?'
¹² There they cry out, but he does not answer,
  because of the pride of evildoers.
¹³ Surely God does not hear an empty cry,
  nor does the Almightyᵃ regard it.
¹⁴ How much less when you say that you do not
    see him,
  that the case is before him, and you are
    waiting for him!
¹⁵ And now, because his anger does not punish,
  and he does not greatly heed transgression,ᵇ
¹⁶ Job opens his mouth in empty talk,
  he multiplies words without knowledge."

a Traditional rendering of Heb Shaddai   b Theodotion Symmachus Compare Vg: Meaning of Heb uncertain

COMMENTARY

In this address Elihu takes up two of Job's complaints and attempts to set them in a larger religious context: the complaint that no benefit accrues from refraining from sin (v. 3) and the complaint that God takes no notice of his case (v. 14). The body of the speech is enclosed by a rhetorical question at the beginning, which asks whether Job's evaluation of himself is correct (v. 2), and by a statement of judgment at the end, which declares Job's words to be empty and ignorant (v. 16). Elihu introduces the first issue with an alleged quotation of Job's words (v. 3) and an announcement of his intent to reply to them (v. 4). The substance of his argument appears in vv. 5-8. The second issue is structured in reverse fashion. Elihu begins to explain in general why the cries of some oppressed people go unanswered (vv. 9-12) and then relates the general theme to Job's particular case (v. 13), concluding with a quotation of Job's words (vv. 14-15). The summary judgment in v. 16 brings the speech to an end.

35:1-8. At the beginning of his last speech Elihu invited the "wise" to judge for themselves what was "right" (משפט *mišpāṭ*, 34:4), following that invitation with a citation of Job's words, "For

Job says, 'I am in the right [צדקתי *ṣādaqtî*].' " Eliphaz now poses the same challenge to Job (v. 2), and the words of Job that he quotes are a variation of those in 34:4. The word צדק (*ṣādēq*) has both a general moral sense and a legal one (cf. 4:17; 9:2), so one might translate either "I am more righteous than God" (cf. NIV mg) or "I am more in the right than God." Both nuances are relevant to Elihu's speech. Curiously, both the NRSV and the NIV soften the statement by eliminating the comparative force of the preposition מן (*min*), which can mean "more than." The stronger claim seems more in keeping with Elihu's representation of Job.

In v. 3, Elihu cites another alleged statement of Job, that there is neither advantage nor profit in refraining from sin. This statement is similar to the citation of Job's supposed words in 34:9. As noted there, Job has not said anything quite like this, although Elihu is confident that this is the implication of Job's general position. Although no verbal similarity exists, the theme is related to the question posed by the prologue, whether Job is pious only because there is an advantage in being so. Why Elihu should address his refutation not only to Job but also to "your friends with you" is not clear, since Eliphaz has already made an argument similar to the one Elihu will propose (22:2-3).

The heavens and the high clouds (v. 5), which in a pre-industrial age seemed untouchable by human activity, serve Elihu as a metaphor for the relationship between God and humans. Elihu organizes his argument systematically, considering first the effect of human sin (v. 6) and then the effect of human righteousness (v. 7) on God, concluding that human good and evil affect only other humans (v. 8). Job had used a similar argument ironically (7:20) to suggest that since his sins did not affect God, God should not act so obsessively and violently toward him. But Elihu is not much given to irony when talking about God.

The content of Elihu's refutation does not exactly match the alleged quotation from Job. Job had supposedly asked how it profited *him* to refrain from sin, and Elihu replies that Job can neither harm nor benefit *God* by his sin or by his righteousness. The difference between their two arguments, as Elihu would presumably see it, is that Job's thinking is self-centered, whereas his own is God-centered.

35:9-16. A new argument begins with v. 9. Elihu describes a situation like that Job described in 24:12, in which people in distress cry out and yet do not seem to be heard by God. Elihu explains this apparent anomaly. The people may "cry out," but they do not cry out *in prayer.* The words "where is God my creator" are not words of alienation but the traditionally sanctioned words of faithful appeal to God for deliverance. The same argument appears in Jer 2:5-6, where God rebukes the people for abandoning God and failing to say, "Where is Yahweh who brought us up out of Egypt?" Analogous to the way God is addressed in terms of saving deeds in Jer 2:6, Elihu represents the proper prayer as addressing God as the one "who gives strength in the night" (v. 10; cf. Exod 15:2). The word translated "strength" (זמרות *zĕmirôt*) has a homonym that means "songs." Either meaning is plausible here. It seems odd, however, that persons suffering from oppression would congratulate themselves that God has made them wiser than animals and birds (v. 11). A more plausible translation is "who teaches us *by means of* the animals and makes us wise *by means of* the birds of the air" (cf. NIV

mg). Elihu is echoing Job's satiric invitation to "ask the animals, and they will teach you, or the birds of the air, and they will tell you . . . that the hand of Yahweh has done this" (12:7, author's trans.). Here, as in vv. 5-8, Elihu attempts to reclaim a traditional saying from Job's ironic subversion. Elihu does believe that the hand of God is at work even when oppression seems to go unchecked (cf. 34:24-28). That is the wisdom that the pious learn from the animals.

In vv. 9-16, however, Elihu is concerned with those who do not address their cries to God in prayer. People who merely cry aloud receive no answer (v. 12*a*). Opinion is divided as to whether the phrase "because of the pride of evildoers" modifies "cry out" (so NIV) or "does not answer" (so NRSV). The word order of the Hebrew favors the NRSV. Although it might seem odd that Elihu would describe oppressed persons as themselves "evil," pride is the particular flaw to which he draws attention in his account of the person brought to the brink of death (33:17). A prideful person who does not turn to God in suffering is evil in Elihu's eyes.[512] He concludes his general description by characterizing the outcry not addressed to God as "empty" (v. 13).[513] That Job is the object of his description is fairly obvious, for Job has continually rejected the friends' advice to turn to God in prayer (5:8; 8:5; 11:13; 22:17) and has cast his own cries in terms of legal accusations (19:7). In v. 14, Elihu makes this point explicitly, casting his words in the form of an indirect quotation of Job, echoing the sentiments of Job expressed in 23:8-9. The NIV is probably correct in taking v. 15 as a continuation of Elihu's quotation, with "you say" in v. 14 governing both verses. Here, too, although the exact words are not Job's, they reflect his complaints in chaps. 21 and 24.

In the concluding v. 16, Elihu himself answers the question he posed to Job in v. 2 and declares Job's words to be empty and ignorant. The phrase "words without knowledge" is the same one God will use in 38:2, creating the impression that God is endorsing Elihu's judgment. It apparently does not occur to Elihu that he is afflicted by the sin of pride.

512. H. Rowley, *The Book of Job,* rev. ed., NCB (Grand Rapids, Mich.: Eerdmans, 1976; original ed., 1970) 226.
513. For an alternative translation and interpretation of this verse, see Gordis, *The Book of Job,* 402.

REFLECTIONS

There is no doubt that Job's speeches have produced considerable anxiety in the author of the Elihu speeches. One of the consequences of the anxiety that can arise in the course of religious debate is the tendency of those who feel threatened to become narrow and rigid, taking refuge in carefully controlled behaviors and words. Anything that does not fit one's model of proper religious values can be judged illegitimate and forced out. This tendency is evident in Elihu's response to Job. Job has refused to make use of the traditionally validated language of prayer, because his experience has made it impossible for him to use that language with integrity. That the only language he can now use in order to voice his outcry is structured largely by legal imagery does not mean that he is not faithful, as Elihu seems to suppose (vv. 14-16). Job's cries of outrage are a dark and anguished form of prayer, but one that Elihu cannot recognize (see Reflections on Job 7). Job's words, provoked by extreme suffering, are not without their own problems. Nevertheless, it is essential for Job to explore the alternative language that he creates, searching out its potential to deal more adequately with his experience. But because Job's radical departure from the language of tradition frightens Elihu, he hurries to declare it illegitimate and to suggest that God only hears cries when they are addressed in the traditionally approved form (vv.12-13).

Elihu is on shakier ground than he might wish to acknowledge. The Bible as a whole does not make the distinction that Elihu tries to make. Although it assumes that people who cry out generally address their cries in prayer to God, it recognizes other types of expression as well. In the exodus story, for instance, it is said that "the Israelites groaned in their slavery and cried out, and their cry for help because of their slavery went up to God. God heard their groaning and he remembered his covenant with Abraham, with Isaac and with Jacob. So God looked on the Israelites and was concerned about them" (Exod 2:23*b*-35 NIV). The text leaves it quite uncertain whether the Israelites "pray" in the sense that Elihu would recognize or simply "groan" and "cry out." Even the words "for help" are not in the Hebrew text, so there is no indication that the Israelites' cry is specifically addressed to anyone at all. It may simply be a cry of anguish that cannot be contained. But the cry itself "goes up" to God and evokes a response, not because it is addressed in the proper form, but because the covenant people are in need.

The positions represented by Job and Elihu have echoes in many contemporary churches, where arguments about the "idolatry" of traditional religious language and the "heresy" of alternative religious language threaten to tear communities apart. Perhaps both sides of this often acrimonious debate might reflect on the confrontation of Job and Elihu. Job witnesses to the fact that experience may make it necessary to challenge traditional ways of speaking about God and to God. He also witnesses to the fact that searching for an alternative way of speaking is a groping, exploratory process, as new metaphors are tested for their possibilities. Driven by its own pressing need, such a search may produce new and valid religious insight, but it also has its own blindness. As the character of Job illustrates, it can be arrogant. Job is no role model for civil debate. However justified by the extremity of his own pain, his sarcasm and contemptuous dismissal of the friends' traditional language ignores much that remains powerful and valid in that tradition. Protest movements are inherently susceptible to the sin of smug superiority, because they are filled with the conviction of having perceived something to which others are blind. The protestors often do not realize that singleminded focus on one aspect of an issue may also make them blind to other important values embedded in the tradition they would so easily dismiss. Such an attitude undermines the possibility of community and of transformative dialogue.

Although a challenge like Job's may be disturbing and disruptive, a vibrant and healthy religious community is invigorated by the presence of a Joban voice, faithful in its protest, even if irritating in its manner of speaking. Elihu is potentially the more dangerous to faith, because he secures his own voice by silencing others. Although sincerely believing himself to serve God, Elihu arrogantly attempts to usurp God's role, declaring what language God finds acceptable. The danger that religious people like Elihu pose is that they will succeed in preserving the form but lose the substance of faith, standing guard over an empty shrine. If Elihu's were the last voice to answer Job, no doubt Job would turn away in utter alienation. Certainly many in the church would be relieved if all those who were unhappy with traditional language and practices would just go away. But complex problems of faith, practice, and belief are never resolved by recourse to a simplistic "love it or leave it" stance.

The book of Job recognizes that arguments sometimes reach an impasse. The voice from the whirlwind surprises us by undercutting the assumptions and arguments of all the parties, enabling a new vision that neither side could accomplish while stuck in the polarization of endless debate. Although the mechanism may not be quite so dramatic as in the book of Job, divine disclosure that has the power to transform understanding and reconcile opponents occurs more often than many people realize.

JOB 36:1–37:24, ELIHU DESCRIBES THE CHARACTER OF GOD

OVERVIEW

Elihu's final speech faces in two directions. In the first part (36:1-21), he remains concerned with correcting the views Job and his friends have advanced in the dialogues. The second part of the speech (36:22–37:24), however, anticipates the divine speeches. That chaps. 36–37 function as a conclusion is indicated by the fact that Elihu no longer explicitly quotes and refutes Job. Instead, in introducing the speech Elihu again commends his own words (36:1-4), as he did in his first address (32:6-22). In the first part of the body of the speech (36:5-15), Elihu reprises several of his themes: God's superiority, divine justice, God's redemptive concern for those who err, expressed through the disciplines of affliction. An admonition and warning to Job concludes the first part of the speech (36:16-21). A very different kind of discourse begins in 36:22. In this part of the speech, the author of the Elihu speeches attempts to shape the reader's understanding of the speeches from the whirlwind by drafting a poem that uses several of the motifs of chap. 38 but incorporates them into Elihu's own understanding

of God. Thus Elihu is positioned to stage manage the introduction of God. In 36:22-33, Elihu both introduces and summarizes the rest of his speech. The structure of this section is indicated by the threefold repetition of the introductory exclamation "behold" or "see" (הן *hēn*) in vv. 22, 26, and 30 (not clearly reflected in the NRSV and the NIV). The first part (36:22-25) praises the irreproachable greatness of God and exhorts Job to join in praise; the second (36:26-29) praises God as Lord of the rain, and the third (36:30-33) describes God's control of lightning. Elihu's personal exclamation in 37:1 marks a new section in which he first expounds the theme of lightning as the voice of God (37:1-5), followed by a celebration of the power of God manifested in winter storms (37:6-13). A series of rhetorical questions that imitate the style of the divine speeches serve as an admonition to Job (37:14-20), while a brief description of a theophany (37:21-24) provides the segue to God's appearance in the stormwind in the next chapter.

Job 36:1-21, God Redeems by Affliction

36 Elihu continued:

² "Bear with me a little longer and I will show you
that there is more to be said in God's behalf.
³ I get my knowledge from afar;
I will ascribe justice to my Maker.
⁴ Be assured that my words are not false;
one perfect in knowledge is with you.

⁵ "God is mighty, but does not despise men;
he is mighty, and firm in his purpose.
⁶ He does not keep the wicked alive
but gives the afflicted their rights.
⁷ He does not take his eyes off the righteous;
he enthrones them with kings
and exalts them forever.
⁸ But if men are bound in chains,
held fast by cords of affliction,
⁹ he tells them what they have done—
that they have sinned arrogantly.
¹⁰ He makes them listen to correction
and commands them to repent of their evil.
¹¹ If they obey and serve him,
they will spend the rest of their days in prosperity
and their years in contentment.
¹² But if they do not listen,
they will perish by the sword*a*
and die without knowledge.

¹³ "The godless in heart harbor resentment;
even when he fetters them, they do not cry for help.
¹⁴ They die in their youth,
among male prostitutes of the shrines.
¹⁵ But those who suffer he delivers in their suffering;
he speaks to them in their affliction.

¹⁶ "He is wooing you from the jaws of distress
to a spacious place free from restriction,
to the comfort of your table laden with choice food.
¹⁷ But now you are laden with the judgment due the wicked;
judgment and justice have taken hold of you.

a12 Or will cross the River

36 Elihu continued and said:

² "Bear with me a little, and I will show you,
for I have yet something to say on God's behalf.
³ I will bring my knowledge from far away,
and ascribe righteousness to my Maker.
⁴ For truly my words are not false;
one who is perfect in knowledge is with you.

⁵ "Surely God is mighty and does not despise any;
he is mighty in strength of understanding.
⁶ He does not keep the wicked alive,
but gives the afflicted their right.
⁷ He does not withdraw his eyes from the righteous,
but with kings on the throne
he sets them forever, and they are exalted.
⁸ And if they are bound in fetters
and caught in the cords of affliction,
⁹ then he declares to them their work
and their transgressions, that they are behaving arrogantly.
¹⁰ He opens their ears to instruction,
and commands that they return from iniquity.
¹¹ If they listen, and serve him,
they complete their days in prosperity,
and their years in pleasantness.
¹² But if they do not listen, they shall perish by the sword,
and die without knowledge.

¹³ "The godless in heart cherish anger;
they do not cry for help when he binds them.
¹⁴ They die in their youth,
and their life ends in shame.*a*
¹⁵ He delivers the afflicted by their affliction,
and opens their ear by adversity.
¹⁶ He also allured you out of distress
into a broad place where there was no constraint,

a Heb ends among the temple prostitutes

NIV

¹⁸Be careful that no one entices you by riches;
   do not let a large bribe turn you aside.
¹⁹Would your wealth
   or even all your mighty efforts
   sustain you so you would not be in distress?
²⁰Do not long for the night,
   to drag people away from their homes.^a
²¹Beware of turning to evil,
   which you seem to prefer to affliction."

a20 The meaning of the Hebrew for verses 18-20 is uncertain.

NRSV

and what was set on your table was full of
   fatness.

¹⁷ "But you are obsessed with the case of the
   wicked;
   judgment and justice seize you.
¹⁸ Beware that wrath does not entice you into
   scoffing,
   and do not let the greatness of the ransom
   turn you aside.
¹⁹ Will your cry avail to keep you from distress,
   or will all the force of your strength?
²⁰ Do not long for the night,
   when peoples are cut off in their place.
²¹ Beware! Do not turn to iniquity;
   because of that you have been tried by
   affliction."

COMMENTARY

36:1-4. The beginning of Elihu's final speech differs from earlier ones in that no words of Job are cited (cf. 33:8-11; 34:5-6; 35:3). Instead, Elihu turns attention to his own speech, rhetorically appealing for patience for the rest of what he has to say about God (v. 2) and commending the soundness of his knowledge (vv. 3*a*, 4). Elihu also gives a succinct summary of the purpose of his speech: to ascribe righteousness to God (v. 3*b*; cf. 35:2*b*). The expression "perfect in knowledge" leads many to comment about Elihu's arrogance,[514] but in fairness to him the Hebrew word (תמים *tāmîm*), the same word used of Job's integrity, is merely a claim to "sound," "whole-some" knowledge.

36:5-15. Verse 5 introduces Elihu's first major argument concerning the character and acts of God. In this brief statement Elihu makes three claims, which echo what he has said in his previous speeches and anticipate what he will say in the remainder of this speech. First, Elihu stresses God's sovereign power through his twofold repetition of the word "mighty" (כביר *kabbîr*; cf. 34:17). Next he alludes to God's receptiveness (lit, "he does not despise"; the verb is without an

object, which the NRSV and the NIV supply according to sense; cf. 33:26). Finally, he appeals to God's powerful mind (cf. 36:22).

Elihu sets up his argument more specifically by means of an axiom asserting God's just retribution to the wicked and the afflicted alike (v. 6). The common term of contrast for "the wicked" (רשע *rāšā*ʿ) in wisdom writings is not "the afflicted" (עניים *ʿăniyyîm*) but "the righteous" (צדיק *ṣaddîq*), an expression Elihu uses in v. 7, apparently as a further designation of the afflicted (cf. Ps 14:6). In the psalms, however, and particularly in psalms of lament, the "wicked" and the "afflicted" are often used as contrasting types, the wicked preying on the poor (cf. Psalm 10).[515] Elihu appears to be influenced by the lament tradition, which he combines in his distinctive way with a concern for moral pedagogy.

In vv. 7-12, Elihu develops the theme of the afflicted and in vv. 13-14 that of the wicked. God's exaltation of the righteous (v. 7) is a familiar motif, present in Eliphaz's hymn in 5:11 and in thanksgiving psalms such as 1 Sam 2:8 and Ps 113:7-8. But Elihu's understanding of God's care for the afflicted righteous is more complex than

514. E.g., E. Good, *In Turns of Tempest* (Stanford, Calif.: Stanford University Press, 1990) 331.

515. D. Pleins, "Poor, Poverty," *ABD* 5:409-10.

that of the traditional thanksgiving psalm, since it also involves redemption by means of affliction. Complementing his description of illness as a means of moral redemption (33:19-22), Elihu mentions the social misery of imprisonment in fetters and ropes (v. 8). Although this language may be figurative, it is grounded in an all too familiar social reality (cf. 2 Kgs 25:7; 2 Chr 33:11; Nah 3:10). As in chap. 33, Elihu interprets such a time of affliction as an occasion for God to disclose to persons their sins and to provide an opportunity for repentance (vv. 9-10; cf. 2 Chr 33:10-17). Characteristically for Elihu, arrogance is the distinguishing feature of the sinner's wrongdoing (cf. 33:17). In an artful conclusion, Elihu contrasts the consequences of the person's fateful choice: "if he listens . . . if he does not listen . . . " (vv. 11-12). A word play not visible in translation but present in the Hebrew text enhances the contrast, as "serve" (עבד 'ābad) is echoed by "perish" (עבר 'ābar). The representation of the moral life as a decisive choice between two antithetical modes of being is common in Israelite thought, as in early Jewish and Christian writings (cf. Deut 30:15-20; Jer 21:8-9; Sir 15:14-17; *T. Asher* 1:3-9; Matt 7:12-14; *Didache* 1).

The reference to the one who chooses not to listen provides the transition to the case of the utterly godless (vv. 13-14; cf. v. 6*b*). Elihu's characterization of their anger and refusal to cry for help suggests the kind of pridefulness he finds so offensive. It may well be an indirect characterization of Job. Like those who refused to listen to God's word in affliction (v. 12), the fate of the godless is death, and an early death at that. Elihu parallels the term "youth" (נער *nō'ar*) with the word קדשים (*qĕdēšîm*), usually rendered "male temple prostitutes." Although little is known about this phenomenon, apparently both men and women were at times employed as temple prostitutes, their wages going to the temple treasury. The Deuteronomic tradition was violently opposed to this practice (Deut 23:17-18[18-19]; 2 Kgs 23:7).[516] Elihu concludes by restating his primary point concerning the redemptive use God makes of affliction (v. 15).

36:16-21. This text is extremely difficult and obscure, leading to significantly different transla-

tions. There are a few clues to its structure and meaning, however. Clearly, Elihu attempts to apply to Job's specific situation the general message he has articulated in vv. 5-15. This much is indicated by the introductory words "and also" in v. 16 and by the similar summary references to purposive affliction in vv. 15 and 21. The repetition of the two key words סות (*sût*, "woo," "allure," "entice") and צר (*ṣar*, "narrow straits," "distress") in v. 16 and vv. 18-19 suggest that Elihu structures his argument by contrasting what God has done for Job with the destructive dangers posed by anger (NRSV) or wealth (NIV). The images of spaciousness and abundance in v. 16 are typical images of salvation (cf. Pss 18:19[20]; 23:5; 31:8[9]). The NRSV and the NIV differ as to whether v. 17 describes objective conditions of judgment that have befallen Job (NIV)[517] or Job's own obsession with a legal resolution of his case and of all such instances of injustice (NRSV).[518] Although certainty is not possible, the interpretation of the NRSV fits with Elihu's contrast between the proper language of prayer and the improper pursuit of a legal case in 35:14.

About all that is clear in vv. 18-19 is that Elihu describes the enticement of a dangerous alternative that will lead to distress rather than away from it. Although the majority of commentators follow the line of interpretation presupposed by the NIV,[519] it is not clear why Elihu would warn Job about the dangers of wealth. To be sure, the prologue had explored whether wealth as a divine "hedge" corrupted piety, but that has not been a concern of Elihu. Although not without its own grammatical difficulties, the translation of the NRSV is consistent with Elihu's themes.[520] The warning against "wrath" recalls the "anger" of the godless in v. 13. Similarly, the noun translated

516. K. van der Toorn, "Prostitution (Cultic)," *ABD* 5:511-12.

517. J. E. Hartley, *The Book of Job,* NICOT (Grand Rapids, Mich.: Eerdmans, 1988) 472.

518. N. Habel, *The Book of Job,* OTL (Philadelphia: Westminster, 1985) 495. M. Pope, *Job,* 3rd ed., AB 15 (Garden City, N.Y.: Doubleday, 1979) 270; and R. Gordis, *The Book of Job: Commentary, New Translation, and Special Studies* (New York: Jewish Theological Seminary, 5738/1978) 416, following N. H. Tur-Sinai, *The Book of Job: A New Commentary* (Jerusalem: Kiryath Sepher, 1957) 499, redivide the consonants of the text to produce a different reading: "But you did not plead the cause of the poor, nor the suit of the orphan" (Gordis, *The Book of Job,* 416).

519. See Habel, *The Book of Job,* 498-99; Pope, *Job,* 271; and H.-M. Wahl, *Der Gerechte Schoepfer,* BZAW 207 (Berlin: Walter de Gruyter, 1993) 111, for the grammatical issues involved.

520. See also G. Fohrer, *Das Buch Hiob,* KAT xvi (Guetersloh: Gerd Mohn, 1963) 477; A. de Wilde, *Das Buch Hiob,* OTS xxii (Leiden: Brill, 1981) 337-38.

"scoffing" (סֶפֶק *sepeq*) is related to the verb Elihu uses to characterize Job in 34:37 ("He claps his hands [in mockery]"). The "great ransom" that might turn Job aside is the necessary acceptance of affliction and humble repentance that allows the mediating angel to say "I have found a ransom" (33:24). Verse 19 also refers to one of Elihu's themes, the destruction of sinners that takes place suddenly in the night (34:20-22).

The translation of v. 21*b* in the NRSV requires a very modest emendation (revocalizing the verb from active to passive) and is more in keeping with Elihu's themes than that of the NIV. Although the referent of "this" is rather vague, Elihu is the only character who points to the actual reason for Job's affliction: God's decision to allow Job's piety to be tested.

Job 36:22–37:24, God Manifest in the Thunderstorm

NIV

22"God is exalted in his power.
　　Who is a teacher like him?
23Who has prescribed his ways for him,
　　or said to him, 'You have done wrong'?
24Remember to extol his work,
　　which men have praised in song.
25All mankind has seen it;
　　men gaze on it from afar.
26How great is God—beyond our understanding!
　　The number of his years is past finding out.

27"He draws up the drops of water,
　　which distill as rain to the streams*a*;
28the clouds pour down their moisture
　　and abundant showers fall on mankind.
29Who can understand how he spreads out the
　　　clouds,
　　how he thunders from his pavilion?
30See how he scatters his lightning about him,
　　bathing the depths of the sea.
31This is the way he governs*b* the nations
　　and provides food in abundance.
32He fills his hands with lightning
　　and commands it to strike its mark.
33His thunder announces the coming storm;
　　even the cattle make known its approach.*c*

37 "At this my heart pounds
　　and leaps from its place.
2Listen! Listen to the roar of his voice,
　　to the rumbling that comes from his mouth.
3He unleashes his lightning beneath the whole
　　　heaven
　　and sends it to the ends of the earth.
4After that comes the sound of his roar;

a27 Or distill from the mist as rain   b31 Or nourishes
announces his coming— / the One zealous against evil
c33 Or

NRSV

22 See, God is exalted in his power;
　　who is a teacher like him?
23 Who has prescribed for him his way,
　　or who can say, 'You have done wrong'?

24 "Remember to extol his work,
　　of which mortals have sung.
25 All people have looked on it;
　　everyone watches it from far away.
26 Surely God is great, and we do not know him;
　　the number of his years is unsearchable.
27 For he draws up the drops of water;
　　he distills*a* his mist in rain,
28 which the skies pour down
　　and drop upon mortals abundantly.
29 Can anyone understand the spreading of the
　　　clouds,
　　the thunderings of his pavilion?
30 See, he scatters his lightning around him
　　and covers the roots of the sea.
31 For by these he governs peoples;
　　he gives food in abundance.
32 He covers his hands with the lightning,
　　and commands it to strike the mark.
33 Its crashing*b* tells about him;
　　he is jealous*c* with anger against iniquity.

37　"At this also my heart trembles,
　　and leaps out of its place.
2 Listen, listen to the thunder of his voice
　　and the rumbling that comes from his
　　　mouth.
3 Under the whole heaven he lets it loose,
　　and his lightning to the corners of the earth.
4 After it his voice roars;

a Cn: Heb they distill   b Meaning of Heb uncertain

NIV

he thunders with his majestic voice.
When his voice resounds,
   he holds nothing back.
⁵God's voice thunders in marvelous ways;
   he does great things beyond our
      understanding.
⁶He says to the snow, 'Fall on the earth,'
   and to the rain shower, 'Be a mighty
      downpour.'
⁷So that all men he has made may know his
      work,
   he stops every man from his labor.ᵃ
⁸The animals take cover;
   they remain in their dens.
⁹The tempest comes out from its chamber,
   the cold from the driving winds.
¹⁰The breath of God produces ice,
   and the broad waters become frozen.
¹¹He loads the clouds with moisture;
   he scatters his lightning through them.
¹²At his direction they swirl around
   over the face of the whole earth
   to do whatever he commands them.
¹³He brings the clouds to punish men,
   or to water his earthᵇ and show his love.

¹⁴"Listen to this, Job;
   stop and consider God's wonders.
¹⁵Do you know how God controls the clouds
   and makes his lightning flash?
¹⁶Do you know how the clouds hang poised,
   those wonders of him who is perfect in
      knowledge?
¹⁷You who swelter in your clothes
   when the land lies hushed under the south
      wind,
¹⁸can you join him in spreading out the skies,
   hard as a mirror of cast bronze?

¹⁹"Tell us what we should say to him;
   we cannot draw up our case because of our
      darkness.
²⁰Should he be told that I want to speak?
   Would any man ask to be swallowed up?
²¹Now no one can look at the sun,
   bright as it is in the skies
   after the wind has swept them clean.
²²Out of the north he comes in golden splendor;

*a7 Or / he fills all men with fear by his power   b13 Or to favor
them*

NRSV

he thunders with his majestic voice
   and he does not restrain the lightningsᵃ
      when his voice is heard.
⁵ God thunders wondrously with his voice;
   he does great things that we cannot
      comprehend.
⁶ For to the snow he says, 'Fall on the earth';
   and the shower of rain, his heavy shower
      of rain,
⁷ serves as a sign on everyone's hand,
   so that all whom he has made may know
      it.ᵇ
⁸ Then the animals go into their lairs
   and remain in their dens.
⁹ From its chamber comes the whirlwind,
   and cold from the scattering winds.
¹⁰ By the breath of God ice is given,
   and the broad waters are frozen fast.
¹¹ He loads the thick cloud with moisture;
   the clouds scatter his lightning.
¹² They turn round and round by his guidance,
   to accomplish all that he commands them
   on the face of the habitable world.
¹³ Whether for correction, or for his land,
   or for love, he causes it to happen.

¹⁴ "Hear this, O Job;
   stop and consider the wondrous works of
      God.
¹⁵ Do you know how God lays his command
      upon them,
   and causes the lightning of his cloud to
      shine?
¹⁶ Do you know the balancings of the clouds,
   the wondrous works of the one whose
      knowledge is perfect,
¹⁷ you whose garments are hot
   when the earth is still because of the south
      wind?
¹⁸ Can you, like him, spread out the skies,
   hard as a molten mirror?
¹⁹ Teach us what we shall say to him;
   we cannot draw up our case because of
      darkness.
²⁰ Should he be told that I want to speak?
   Did anyone ever wish to be swallowed up?
²¹ Now, no one can look on the light

a Heb them   b Meaning of Heb of verse 7 uncertain

NIV

God comes in awesome majesty.
²³The Almighty is beyond our reach and exalted
    in power;
    in his justice and great righteousness, he does
      not oppress.
²⁴Therefore, men revere him,
    for does he not have regard for all the wise
      in heart?ᵃ"

ª24 Or for he does not have regard for any who think they are wise.

NRSV

when it is bright in the skies,
    when the wind has passed and cleared
      them.
²² Out of the north comes golden splendor;
    around God is awesome majesty.
²³ The Almightyᵃ—we cannot find him;
    he is great in power and justice,
    and abundant righteousness he will not
      violate.
²⁴ Therefore mortals fear him;
    he does not regard any who are wise in
      their own conceit."

ª Traditional rendering of Heb Shaddai

COMMENTARY

36:22-25. In praising God as powerful and an incomparable teacher, Elihu brings together two traditional themes. The closest parallel to Elihu's words in vv. 22-23 is Isa 40:12-14. There, using the same type of rhetorical questions, Second Isaiah praises God as the incomparable creator who needed no counselor (cf. Isa 40:14, "Whom did the LORD consult to enlighten him,/ and who taught him the right way?" [NIV]). Although Elihu's point is similar in v. 23, he reaccents this motif by describing God not only as one who is not taught, but also as the supreme teacher (v. 22*b*). The theme of God as moral teacher is an important one for Elihu (33:14-22; 34:32; 35:11). In chaps. 33–35 he develops this theme in ways similar to the psalms (cf. Pss 25:8-14; 94:12). Although Elihu's description of storms and lightning mostly exalt God's power, he interprets God's presence in the storms as having a moral purpose (36:31-32; 37:13, 23-24), thus uniting the themes of God as Lord of creation and as moral teacher. Whether consciously or not, the author of the Elihu speeches appears to be remedying what must have seemed to him a defect in the divine speeches of chaps. 38–41: the lack of any apparent connection between God as creator and the moral dimensions of creation.

The form of Elihu's rhetorical questions in vv. 22*b*-23 presumes not only a negative answer but also the very absurdity of anything but a negative answer. Yet Job *has* in essence said to God, "You

have done wrong" (v. 23*b*; cf. 19:7; 24:12; 27:2). By characterizing such a charge as absurd and urging Job instead to speak the words of praise that all people sing (v. 24), Elihu attempts to silence Job's alienated voice and reintegrate him into the collective voice of universal praise. Elihu describes this communal praise as a response to *seeing* (v. 25), and in what follows Elihu attempts to provide such an experience of seeing through the highly visual quality of the poetic imagery. It may be that Elihu is attempting to anticipate (and take a measure of credit for) Job's confession of the decisive significance of "seeing" God (42:5).

36:26-29. Elihu introduces his celebration of the wonders of God with a statement of praise (v. 26) similar in form to v. 22. Here, however, the emphasis is not on God's greatness per se but on the inability of human understanding to grasp it (cf. 5:9; Eccl 8:17; Sir 43:27-33). Thus, like Bildad, he characterizes his own description as no more than a "whisper" of divine thunder (26:14).

The cycle of rain is the topic of vv. 27-29. As Wahl observes, Elihu's description uses less of the mythic language that characterizes the motif of rain in the divine speeches (cf. 38:22-30).[521] The precise mechanism Elihu describes is not entirely clear, however. Most translations assume that

---

521. H.-M. Wahl, *Der Gerechte Schoepfer,* BZAW 207 (Berlin: Walter de Gruyter, 1993) 120.

Elihu refers to the evaporation cycle in vv. 27-28. The NRSV retains the translation "mist" for אד (*'ēd*), even though it is now generally agreed that the word refers to the primordial underground reservoir from which rivers emerge (cf. Gen 2:5-6).[522] The image of the spreading clouds with their attendant thunder (v. 29) provides the transition to the next topic, God's control of lightning (vv. 30-33; note the repetition of "spread out," "scatter" [פרש *pāraś*] in vv. 29-30).

36:30-33. The imagery of v. 30*b* is somewhat obscure. The NRSV renders the Hebrew literally as "and covers the roots of the sea." Some translate it as *"un*cover the roots of the sea," either by emending the verb or by arguing that it means both "covers" and "uncovers," or that to cover something with light is to uncover it.[523] A modest emendation produces the reading "the roots of the sea are his throne."[524] Such imagery would be similar to that of Psalm 29, which celebrates the thundering of God's voice and speaks of God's being "enthroned over the flood" (Ps 29:10 NRSV). It is also possible that the verse simply presents a contrast between the illumination of God's pavilion in the heavens and the covered depths of the sea below.

For Elihu, appreciation of God's majesty reflected in the grandeur of storms is not the whole point. Storms also have purposes related to God's governance of the world. Although some argue that poetic parallelism requires the verb "nourish" in v. 31*a*,[525] there is no reason to reject the ordinary meaning "judges" (or "governs"). The thunder, lightning, clouds, and rain of storms are frequently associated with the activities of God the divine warrior (cf. Pss 18:7-15[8-16]; 97:1-9). Whereas v. 31*a* points forward to God's use of lightning as a weapon in judgment (v. 32), v. 31*b*, with its reference to food, points back to the rain of vv. 27-28 and the nurture of God (cf. the relation between water, God's providence, and food in Ps 104:10-16).

Obscurity plagues the final verse of the chapter. The first half can be fairly literally translated "his roar announces him," referring to the approaching thunder. The second half of the verse reads "the

cattle also [announce] the one who comes up." Although it is not impossible that the text refers to a presentiment of storms by cattle, the words can be revocalized to render a more likely meaning. Gordis suggests that originally the word for "storm" (עלעולה *'il'ôlâ*) was misread as "concerning the one who comes up" (על-עולה *al-'ôleh*) and that "[his] indignant wrath" (מקנה אף [from מקנא *miqnēh 'ap*) was misread as "the cattle also" (מקנה אף *miqneh 'ap*). Thus without changing the consonantal text one can read with Gordis: "His thunderclap proclaims His presence; His mighty wrath, the storm."[526] The emendation underlying the NRSV is similar in its interpretation of *miqneh 'ap*. It differs from Gordis in reading "concerning iniquity" (על-עולה *'al-'awlâ*).

37:1-5. Elihu develops the themes of lightning in these verses. A new section is marked first by his reference to his own emotional reaction to the dramatic scene he has just described (v. 1) and by his call to others to listen (v. 2). Here, even more explicitly, thunder is described as the voice of God in a manner reminiscent of Psalm 29. The function of this passage is sensuous, inviting the reader to "listen, listen" (v. 2). In v. 5*b*, Elihu returns to the theme he announced in 36:26, the inability of humans to comprehend God and God's works (cf. 5:9).

37:6-13. In this section, Elihu describes the particular qualities of winter storms (cf. Sir 43:13-20). Snow occurs occasionally in Israel, especially in the northern areas, but cold rain is the distinctive feature of winter weather (v. 6).[527] As so often, v. 7 is obscure. The key to understanding, however, is in its parallel with v. 8. Just as animals go into their dens to avoid the winter storms, so also people stay indoors. With two small emendations (reading the preposition בעד [*bĕ'ad*] in place of the phrase ביד [*bĕyad*], "on the hand" and adding one letter (אנשים *'ănāšîm* ["people"] instead of אנשי *'anšê* ["people of"] one can translate "he shuts in every person, so that all people may know his work" (author's trans.).[528]

The image of humans and animals shut up tight in their dwellings is complemented by that of the cold stormwind emerging from its chamber (v. 9;

522. Pope, *Job*, 273.
523. Gordis, *The Book of Job*, 422; Habel, *The Book of Job*, 499; Hartley, *The Book of Job*, 476.
524. Pope, *Job*, 267.
525. Ibid., 274.

526. Gordis, *The Book of Job*, 424.
527. Wahl, *Der Gerechte Schoepfer*, 122.
528. For similar translations, see Pope, *Job*, 281; Fohrer, *Das Buch Hiob*, 481.

cf. 38:22-24; Ps 135:7; Jer 10:13; 51:16; Sir 43:14). Elihu juxtaposes two different poetic images for the wind. One is of wind stored away and called out at God's command (v. 9); the other is of wind as the breath of God (v. 10 cf. Exod 14:21; 15:8, 10; Ps 18:15[16]; the closest parallel to Elihu's image is Ps 147:16-18). Returning to the two images that have governed his poem, Elihu speaks again of rain and lightning (v. 11). In vv. 12-13, he brings this section of the poem to a close with an observation about the moral purposes of such natural phenomena. The language of command and guidance (v. 12) is similar to that of the divine speeches (e.g., 38:10-12), although in Elihu's speech it is given a climactic prominence that quite alters its significance. Nowhere in the divine speeches is the moral intent of God's control of nature as pronounced as in Elihu's summary that God uses weather "for punishment or for acceptance or for love" (37:13, author's trans.; cf. *1 Enoch* 59:1). The interpretation of the phrase here translated "for acceptance" is contested. The Hebrew text reads "for his land" (cf. NRSV), but a geographical expression fits awkwardly between "punishment" and "love." The NIV attempts to join the phrases with the following words, but the translation eases over very difficult syntactical problems. It is possible that the middle phrase does not have to do with the word for "land" (ארץ *'ereṣ*) but with the word for "pleasure" or "acceptance" (רצה *rāṣâ*). Thus the three terms could describe a range of divine purposes: punishment, acceptance, love.[529]

37:14-20. Elihu's direct summons to Job to "hear this" (v. 14) marks the final part of his speech (cf. 33:1, 31). The theme of general human inability to comprehend the ways of God is applied specifically to Job's case as a way of mocking his pretensions. Here, more explicitly than before, Elihu mimics the style of the divine speeches, with their series of rhetorical questions designed to contrast God's power and wisdom with Job's ignorance and lack of control. By imitating the style Elihu also attempts to appropriate the authority of the divine speeches, as though he and God think and speak alike. The examples Elihu uses are largely those already addressed in his celebration of God as lord of the weather, although the reference to the cosmogonic act of stretching out the sky introduces a new element (v. 18; cf. Isa 40:22; Sir 43:12; for mirrors of bronze, see Exod 38:8). In contrast to God's control of all the earth's weather, Job is powerless to keep himself cool when the hot south wind casts a pall upon all activity (v. 17).

Elihu's sarcastic appeal to Job to "teach us what we should say to him" contrasts with both his designation of God as teacher (36:22) and his own attempts to instruct Job and the three friends. The "darkness" (v. 19*b*) that characterizes human ignorance contrasts with the brightness of God's appearance, which Elihu will describe in vv. 21-22. Elihu apparently mocks Job's eagerness to speak with God (9:35; 13:22; 23:4-5; 31:35-37) by rejecting with horror the notion that God should be informed that Elihu wished to speak with God, for that would be tantamount to a death wish (v. 20).

37:21-24. The final verses serve both to sum up Elihu's main points and to prepare the way for the theophany. The impossibility of looking upon the sun (אור *'ôr*; lit., "light") in a clear sky is implicitly compared with the impossibility of confronting God (v. 21; cf. Sir 43:1-5). In almost cinematic fashion Elihu invites the reader to imagine the brilliance of the sun, only to overlay that image with one of surpassing brilliance, the theophany of God appearing in golden splendor. Although much less elaborate, Elihu's description shares several features with the divine vision Ezekiel describes. In both instances the divine appearance comes "from the north," the mythic home of the deity (Ezek 1:4; cf. Ps 48:2[3]; Isa 14:13). The appearance is characterized by movement ("coming"; cf. Ezek 1:4). Although "gold" is not ordinarily associated with theophanies, Ezekiel describes the radiance of the divine vision as like חשמל (*ḥašmal*), an enigmatic term often translated "electrum" (NIV, "glowing metal"). The "fearful majesty" surrounding God (v. 22*b*) is a frequent description of the numinous splendor of the divine presence (Ps 104:1-2; Hab 3:3-4). One feature of Ezekiel's description that is absent from Elihu's is that of the stormy wind (סערה *sĕ'ārâ*), but that is precisely the element that will be mentioned in

529. Cf. F. Andersen, *Job: An Introduction and Commentary,* Tyndale Old Testament Commentaries (Downers Grove, Ill.: Inter-Varsity, 1976) 266.

the narrative heading to the divine speeches in 38:1.

Elihu cannot conclude without an explicitly moral comment. As he has been at pains to argue throughout his speech, God's power is coordinate with justice and righteousness (v. 23). As is too often the case, the last verse is textually obscure. The first line is clear enough, and it draws a conclusion concerning human response: "therefore people revere him" (lit., "fear"). The parallel line should not be translated as the NRSV does, however, since "wise of heart" is a positive and not a pejorative designation.[530] Following the LXX,

some take "all the wise of heart" as the subject and render "indeed, all the wise of heart see him."[531] But Andersen makes a more intriguing suggestion. The verb that means "regard" (ראה rā'â) is quite similar to that meaning "to fear" (ירא yārē'), and Andersen suggests that one repoint the verb and read "surely all wise of heart fear him." The use of the same verb in both lines of a verse is common in the poetry of Job. With such a reading, as Andersen observes, "we have come full circle to Job 28:28."[532]

530. Gordis, *The Book of Job,* 434.

531. E.g., Hartley, *The Book of Job,* 483.
532. Andersen, *Job,* 268.

REFLECTIONS

In the second part of his speech, Elihu uses a description of nature, specifically of the processes of weather, for two purposes: to instill a sense of wonder and to show how God's presence in the order of nature has a moral purposiveness that points to the moral character of God. In this way, Job's challenge to God's righteousness can be answered. Elihu's attempt to relate the realm of nature to the realm of moral order warrants a closer look. It is a persistent but quite perplexing issue that has preoccupied religious thinkers from ancient times until the present.

Elihu has a distinctive way of talking about the function of weather. The manipulation of rain and lightning, he says, is the way that God "judges the nations" (36:31a). More specifically, he refers to the provision of food (36:32b) and to God's commanding the lightning to strike its target (36:32). Later, Elihu says that God uses the clouds, loaded with moisture and filled with lightning, in order to punish or to show God's love (37:13). The thunder, as the voice of God, expresses God's anger (36:33b). In Elihu's perception, nature is filled with specific divine intentionality. Weather is understood in instrumental terms, as the means by which God expresses emotions and judgments.

Elihu's perspective reflects a quite traditional notion. Exodus 14:21-22; 15:8-10 speak of God's intentional use of wind and water to achieve the rescue of the Israelites and the destruction of Pharaoh's army. In Judg 5:20-21 the stars and the rivers engage in battle with the Canaanite armies. Heat, drought, blight, and even mildew are instruments of God's punishment for covenant disobedience, according to Deut 28:22-24. A three-year long drought is announced by Elijah and ended dramatically as part of his struggle against Ahab and his support of the worship of Baal (1 Kings 17–18). The control of rain as warning and punishment, along with the use of crop blight and devouring locusts, is described vividly by Amos (Amos 4:7-9). Although the counter observation that the rain falls upon the just and the unjust also appears (Matt 5:45), the image of weather as a direct instrument of God's judgment is the prevalent one.

This way of representing the forces of nature is, of course, part of a pre-scientific under-standing of the natural world. One occasionally still hears these views. When earthquakes or extraordinary floods devastate an area or prolonged drought causes famine, there are always those who will identify them as divine judgments, even though it is difficult to see why the residents of Missouri or of Bangladesh are more culpable than the rest of the human race. These arguments are less and less common, however, in part because of increasing knowledge about how natural processes work and in part because of changing notions about God's relationship with the world. One can, of course, continue to use the old language in an extended sense, talking about the judgment of earthquakes on the folly of humans who persist in building rigid buildings on known fault lines, or about devastating floods as judgment against deforestation. As valid as these observations may be on their own terms, this is not what Elihu has in mind when he talks about divine judgment exercised through rain, storm, and lightning.

It is tempting simply to declare Elihu's language out of date and no longer useful. As post-Enlightenment people, moderns tend to draw a sharp distinction between the natural order and the moral order. In certain circles any comment about the moral sense of nature suffices to bring on the criticism that one is talking nonsense. But even if one cannot (and would not want to) speak like Elihu, with his image of God hurling lightning bolts at unsuspecting sinners, the larger question of whether one can speak of a relationship between the order of nature and the moral order is an extremely important one. The ancient religious perception that a relationship exists should not be facilely dismissed.

Part of the problem with Elihu's way of talking is that he has a very restricted, even impoverished sense of the moral. For him, the justice of God visible in the natural order can only be understood in terms of intentional acts of reward and punishment. The role of nature in disclosing the character of God as moral "teacher" (36:22) is to communicate these specific judgments. This narrow view must be abandoned as false. Lightning may be attracted to metal, but it is not attracted to evil.

There are other ways of thinking about the relationship between the natural order and the moral order, however. As was suggested in the Reflections on Job 21, the place to start is not with the question of retribution but with the question of value. What gives value to a being, and so makes it a proper object of moral concern, is the status of that being as God's creation. The goodness of a thing—the earth, the seas, the plants, the animals, and human beings—is established, not by means of a utilitarian calculation of worth, but absolutely by virtue of being a creature of God (cf. Genesis 1). When a being has intrinsic value, it must be treated with respect. Thus the moral obligation to do justice is indeed part of the structure of creation.

Elihu touches on another aspect of the moral sense of nature when he draws attention to seasonality in the way animals and humans alike withdraw to their shelters during cold and rainy winter. Contemplation of nature leads inevitably to the perception of the order it embodies: the alternation of night and day, of seasons, of activity and rest, of birth and death. These are not random or discordant orders but coordinate ones that nurture life. There is a rightness in them, what in Hebrew could be called *ṣĕdāqâ*, a rightness that is disturbed only at a terrible price. Human beings are part of this order of rightness. Our bodies are attuned to the rhythms of the physical order of being. But humans are not simply like other creatures who are attuned to the natural order of rightness by instinct. For humans, the understanding and the will are involved in responding to and extending the order of rightness in creation to the order of rightness in social community. As the wisdom poem cited in Ecclesiastes puts it, "For everything there is a season, and a time for every matter under heaven" (Eccl 3:1 NRSV). Taking that insight further, a modern philosopher has said, "the glory of being human is the ability to recognize the pattern of rightness and to honor it as a moral law. The horror of being human is the ability to violate that rightness, living out of season—doing violence to the other, perverting the most sacred human relationships, devastating the world in greed, overriding its rhythm, not in the name of necessity and charity, but in the compulsion of coveting."[533]

Elihu wants to believe that the horror of being human is closely circumscribed by a God who pours out grain for proper behavior and delivers electric shocks for improper behavior

---

533. E. Kohak, *The Embers and the Stars: A Philosophical Inquiry into the Moral Sense of Nature* (Chicago: University of Chicago Press, 1984) 84.

(36:31-32). He wants to believe that the world operates as a giant "Skinner box," such as those used to induce learning in laboratory rats. The world is not like that, of course. Human beings do, by and large, "love righteousness," as the wisdom tradition would put it. A sense of peace and joy comes from experiencing life in harmony. One who has known it yearns for it and seeks to embody it. But if that is the case, why do human individuals and communities so often act in disorder and in violation of the order of rightness? Israel's wisdom tradition sometimes spoke of an unruly will or of undisciplined appetites as destructive forces, but for the most part the wisdom tradition regards the problem as a failure of understanding. "The evil do not understand justice,/ but those who seek the LORD understand it completely" (Prov 28:5 NRSV). "A ruler who lacks understanding is a cruel oppressor" (Prov 28:16a NRSV). "The righteous know the rights of the poor;/ the wicked have no such understanding" (Prov 29:7 NRSV). For the wisdom tradition, to *know* the good was to do the good. One who had truly understood the order of creation would embody its order of rightness in the moral will. Thus the contemplation of nature is no irrelevancy or merely the source of casual illustrations but the essential place in which moral understanding is grounded.

Elihu is right in intuiting that God's speaking to Job in terms of creation and the orders of nature had something to do with answering Job's questions about the moral order of the world. But Elihu seriously misunderstands the import of God's speech from the storm.

JOB 38:1–42:6

GOD'S SPEECHES FROM THE WHIRLWIND AND JOB'S REPLIES

OVERVIEW

There is no more dramatic moment in the book of Job than that signaled by the words "then [Yahweh] answered Job out of the whirlwind" (38:1). Job has both sought and dreaded a confrontation with God (9:14-20, 32-35; 13:3, 15-24; 23:3-7, 15-17; 31:35-37). For the reader, too, this is a moment of high anticipation. Job's words have exposed the inadequacies of the traditional "consolations of religion" articulated by the friends. His characterization of God as unjust, capricious, and savagely violent has cast doubt on the very basis for religious trust. Job has refused, however, to abandon completely his belief that God will ultimately turn out to be a God of justice who acknowledges Job's claim of right. He has initiated a way of speaking about his relationship with God based on a legal metaphor and developed by means of reflection on his own moral identity as a person of honor. The presence of the Elihu speeches, which attempt to reinterpret Job's situation along other lines, merely adds to a sense of frustration. Job has so dominated the dialogue that no other way of talking seems credible. Consequently, expectations for what God will say are shaped by the deep investment that both Job and the reader have in the assumptions and moral claims embedded in Job's way of perceiving the issues.

God's answer comes as a complete overturning of these expectations and a frustration of the desire for an explicit reply to Job's own words. That Job is rebuked and confronted with his limits is clear (38:2; 40:2, 8-14). But the bulk of what God has to say seems to concern cosmology, meteorology, and zoology, rather than the specific issues of justice Job had raised. Not surprisingly, readers' reactions vary considerably. Some may be angry and disappointed; others, intrigued. It is generally recognized that God's

frustration of expectations is strategic. The very obliqueness of the speeches is part of the way they function as an answer. Having recognized that, most commentators develop interpretations that incorporate the disorienting quality of the divine speeches into an interpretation of the way by which the speeches serve to reorient Job. Yet interpreters come to strikingly different conclusions about the meaning of the divine speeches and thus the nature of that reorientation.[534]

These differences are not necessarily the product of good vs. bad exegesis. Instead, they point to the way in which certain irreducible ambiguities embedded in the divine speeches legitimately permit more than one interpretation of their meaning and significance. The most important ambiguity is the oblique relationship of the divine speeches to Job's complaints, since neither God nor the narrator ever says explicitly how the divine speeches pertain to Job's quite different questions. But there are others. The tone of the speeches, for example, could be interpreted as one of dominating power, playful mockery, or slightly exasperated instruction. The richly visual quality of the speeches also contributes to the surplus of meaning, since visual imagery tends to be more polyvalent than conceptual language, more evocative and saturated with subtle emotional dimensions that resist reduction to simple propositions. Most important, in the course of the speeches God draws upon language and imagery from many different discourses: wisdom discourse, mythic discourses of creation and of the divine warrior, legal discourse, the discourse of honor and shame, royal

---

534. See, for example, the side-by-side interpretations of "God the sage" (N. Habel) and "God the victor" (T. Mettinger) in *The Voice from the Whirlwind*, ed. L. G. Perdue and W. Clark Gilpin (Nashville: Abingdon, 1992) 21-49.

discourse, etc. As each type of language is invoked, the values, meanings, and images of God connected with it are evoked. Yet the various ways of talking do not all fit together smoothly; indeed, they may not be entirely compatible. Many of the different interpretations arise as readers make one of these discourses the interpretive key to the divine speeches as a whole, muting or repressing the significance of the other discourses.

This teasing ability of the divine speeches to evade a single definitive interpretation is not mere evasion. Like the juxtaposition of different styles, genres, and perspectives in the structure of the book as a whole, the elusiveness of the divine speeches requires the reader to assume a more active role in making meaning than does a text in which the "message" is simple and transparent. Since no single interpretation can adequately incorporate all elements of the text, every interpretation remains to a degree unsatisfactory and unstable, as what it has left out demands to be taken into account. The interpretation of the divine speeches given here is only one possibility. It should serve primarily as a stimulus to the reader's own wrestling with the evocative but elusive divine disclosure.

Not all is puzzlement. The outline of the divine speeches is quite clear.[535] Each of the two speeches (38:1–39:30; 40:1–41:34[26]) begins with an identical narrative introduction (38:1; 40:6). Challenges to Job follow (38:2-3; 40:7-14), each of which contains the identical demand for Job to gird up his loins and to answer God's questions (38:3; 40:7). These challenges articulate important themes that the body of the speeches are designed to address. In the first speech, the theme is divine "counsel" or "plan" (עצה '*ēṣâ*; 38:2); in the second it is משפט (*mišpāṭ*, 40:7), a word that may have legal connotations ("judgment," "justice," "right") or administrative ones ("governance" or "sovereignty").[536] The body of the speech follows (38:4–39:30; 40:15–41:34[26]). Each speech divides into two main parts, according to its content. In the first speech, God talks first about cosmological and meteorological phenomena (38:4-38), then about five pairs of animals (38:39–39:30). The second speech concerns a single pair of animals, Behemoth (40:15-24) and Leviathan (41:1-34[40:25–41:26]). After each speech Job responds. Following the first speech, God specifically asks for a response (40:1-2), and Job replies by declining to speak (40:3-5). Following the second speech, Job replies without a specific divine request (42:1-6).

In terms of both form and function the divine speeches are best understood as disputations. Like many of the speeches of Job and his friends, they begin with challenges and satirical characterizations of the inadequacies of the opponent's speech and ability. The rhetorical questions and imperatives, along with the descriptive passages, are typical devices of disputations. Although the divine speeches do not address the issues Job raised in the terms in which Job and the friends argued, they are designed to change Job's mind and to cause him to withdraw his charges, which in fact happens. With respect to form and function the closest parallel to the divine speeches is found in the disputation speech of Isa 40:12-31. As Isa 40:27-31 shows, that disputation is intended to refute the complaint of the people that " 'My way is hidden from [Yahweh];/ and my right is disregarded by my God' " (Isa 40:27 NRSV). In order to do this, the prophet uses many of the same rhetorical devices one finds in Job 38–41: rhetorical questions, imperatives, and descriptive passages that challenge the inadequate perception of the people and assert God's sovereignty, primarily through images of God as creator.[537]

Disputations often incorporate and make allusion to other genres as a means of shaping their own arguments. The genre upon which the disputation in Job 38–41 primarily draws is the hymn of God the creator, especially as it is represented in Psalm 104. Both the similarities and the differences in the way motifs are presented in that psalm are important for understanding the divine speeches. The sequence of topics is generally similar between the two compositions, with the description of the foundation of cosmic structures (Ps 104:1-9; cf. Job 38:4-38) preceding the account of care for the animals (Ps 104:10-23; cf. Job 38:39–39:30). The final descriptive passage of the psalm, marked as a separate section by the

535. Cf. V. Kubina, *Die Gottesreden im Buche Hiob*, FThSt (Freiburg: Herder, 1979) 121.

536. S. Scholnick, "The Meaning of Mispat in the Book of Job," *JBL* 101 (1982) 521-29.

537. Cf. Kubina, *Die Gottesreden im Buche Hiob*, 131-42; H. Rowold, "Yahweh's Challenge to Rival: The Form and Function of the Yahweh-Speech in Job 38–39," *CBQ* 47 (1985) 207-9.

introductory word of praise, concerns the sea creatures, Leviathan in particular (Ps 104:24-26; cf. Job 41:1-35[40:25–41:26]). There are also several points of similarity in details. The long list of particular animals in the psalm (wild ass, stork, mountain goat, rock badger, lion, Leviathan) is unusual in a hymn, and four of the six also occur in the divine speeches in Job. The motif of lions seeking food from God is unique to Psalm 104 and Job 38. Moreover, the function of the sun in setting a limit to the predation of the lions is analogous to the function of dawn setting a limit to the activity of the wicked in Job 38:12-15. There are, of course, many differences between the two compositions, but two particular ones suggest the way in which the Job poet is intentionally transgressing the motifs of the psalm. First, the harmonious alternation between descriptions of animals and humans in Psalm 104 contrasts with the utter absence of reference to humans in the divine speeches. Second, the peaceful image of Leviathan playing in the sea where ships sail contrasts with the prolonged description of Leviathan as a creature of terror in Job 41. The use the divine speeches make of this tradition of creation hymns is a complex but essential part of the way they construct their meaning.

As helpful as similarities with other texts and genres are, the most important clue to the way the divine speeches attempt to change Job's perception is found in the sequence of themes and images in the speeches themselves. The first part of the first speech (38:4-38), which concerns the structures of creation, makes use of images of boundary, path, way, and place to create the sense of a secure and well-ordered cosmos. The second part of that speech, with its focus on the five pairs of animals (38:39–39:30), invokes themes of providential care, especially through its images of food, birth, and freedom. But the animals chosen as examples almost all belong to the hostile and alien realm of the wild, lying outside the boundaries of cultivated land. Thus the animals evoke emotions of ambivalence, if not threat. When Job's answer to the first divine speech proves equivocal and unsatisfactory, God uses an extended description of a single pair of animals as the sole subject of the second speech. What was subtly present in the previous descriptions comes to the fore here. Behemoth and Leviathan are not ordinary animals but legendary creatures with mythic overtones. Leviathan in particular is a creature of utter terror whose associations with primeval chaos make it the ultimate symbol of the alien and threatening other. Leviathan is at the heart of God's answer to Job, and Job gives his definitive reply immediately following the account of Leviathan.

As this brief summary suggests, the divine speeches move Job, imaginatively, from places of secure boundaries to places where boundaries are threatened. In narrative sequence, they run counter to the traditional mythic schema in which the creator god's defeat of the chaos monster precedes the creation of the structures of the cosmos (as in the Enuma Elish; cf. Ps 74:12-17; Isa 51:9-11).[538] An element of "uncreation" takes place in the experience provided by means of the divine speeches, as Job is led to a sustained and intimate encounter with the symbol of the chaotic.

538. James B. Pritchard, ed., *Ancient Near Eastern Texts Relating to the Old Testament (ANET)*, 3rd ed. with supplement (Princeton: Princeton University Press, 1969) 66-68.

JOB 38:1–40:5, UNDERSTANDING THE DIVINE PLAN IN THE WORLD

OVERVIEW

One does not envy the Job poet the task of writing the speech from the whirlwind. The literary and dramatic problems are nearly as daunting as the theological ones. In a book already flooded with words, how does one make space for God's words? How is it possible to imagine God's speech so that the divine words engage what has gone before without sounding merely like one of the previous characters? In no other speech are rhetorical issues so closely related to the meaning and function of the speech itself.

Several features give the first divine speech its distinctive quality. First is the unrelenting use of rhetorical questions: "Who?" "Where?" "How?" "What . . . can you . . . have you . . . do you know . . . ?" These questions focus attention in three directions: Job, God, and creation itself. Second is the intensely visual quality of the divine speech. Other speakers have used striking images, but only incidentally. Here pictorial imagery is primary. Third is the highly structured form of the divine speech, which sets it apart from the speeches of the other characters. Following the narrative introduction (38:1) and the challenge to Job (38:2-3), the first part of the divine speech concerns itself with cosmology and meteorology:

the structuring of the earth (38:4-7); the control of the sea (38:8-11); the functions of the dawn (38:12-15); the place of the abysses of sea and death (38:16-18); the dwellings of light and darkness (38:19-21); the storehouses of snow, hail, lightning, and wind (38:22-24); the course of rain for the desert (38:25-27); the origin of rain, dew, ice, and frost (38:28-30); the movement of constellations (38:31-33); the control of clouds and rain (38:34-38). After cosmology and meteorology come the five pairs of animals: (1) the lions and ravens (38:39-41); (2) the mountain goats and deer (39:1-4); (3) the onager and wild ox (39:5-12); (4) the ostrich and the war horse (39:13-25); (5) the hawk and the vulture (39:26-30). What unifies form and content is the theme announced in the challenge to Job: the "design" of God (עצה 'ēṣâ).

Job 38:1-38, The Cosmic Structures

NIV	NRSV
38 Then the LORD answered Job out of the storm. He said:	**38** Then the LORD answered Job out of the whirlwind:

2"Who is this that darkens my counsel
  with words without knowledge?
	2 "Who is this that darkens counsel by words
	    without knowledge?

3Brace yourself like a man;
  I will question you,
  and you shall answer me.
	3 Gird up your loins like a man,
	  I will question you, and you shall declare to
	    me.

4"Where were you when I laid the earth's
    foundation?
  Tell me, if you understand.
	4 "Where were you when I laid the foundation
	    of the earth?
	  Tell me, if you have understanding.

5Who marked off its dimensions? Surely you know!
  Who stretched a measuring line across it?
	5 Who determined its measurements—surely
	    you know!
	  Or who stretched the line upon it?

6On what were its footings set,
  or who laid its cornerstone—
	6 On what were its bases sunk,
	  or who laid its cornerstone

7while the morning stars sang together
  and all the angels[a] shouted for joy?
	7 when the morning stars sang together
	  and all the heavenly beings[a] shouted for joy?

8"Who shut up the sea behind doors
  when it burst forth from the womb,
	8 "Or who shut in the sea with doors
	  when it burst out from the womb?—

9when I made the clouds its garment
  and wrapped it in thick darkness,
	9 when I made the clouds its garment,
	  and thick darkness its swaddling band,

10when I fixed limits for it
  and set its doors and bars in place,
	10 and prescribed bounds for it,
	  and set bars and doors,

11when I said, 'This far you may come and no farther;	

^a7 Hebrew *the sons of God*

a Heb *sons of God*

NIV

here is where your proud waves halt'?

12"Have you ever given orders to the morning,
or shown the dawn its place,
13that it might take the earth by the edges
and shake the wicked out of it?
14The earth takes shape like clay under a seal;
its features stand out like those of a garment.
15The wicked are denied their light,
and their upraised arm is broken.

16"Have you journeyed to the springs of the sea
or walked in the recesses of the deep?
17Have the gates of death been shown to you?
Have you seen the gates of the shadow of
death*?
18Have you comprehended the vast expanses of
the earth?
Tell me, if you know all this.

19"What is the way to the abode of light?
And where does darkness reside?
20Can you take them to their places?
Do you know the paths to their dwellings?
21Surely you know, for you were already born!
You have lived so many years!

22"Have you entered the storehouses of the snow
or seen the storehouses of the hail,
23which I reserve for times of trouble,
for days of war and battle?
24What is the way to the place where the lightning
is dispersed,
or the place where the east winds are
scattered over the earth?
25Who cuts a channel for the torrents of rain,
and a path for the thunderstorm,
26to water a land where no man lives,
a desert with no one in it,
27to satisfy a desolate wasteland
and make it sprout with grass?
28Does the rain have a father?
Who fathers the drops of dew?
29From whose womb comes the ice?
Who gives birth to the frost from the heavens
30when the waters become hard as stone,
when the surface of the deep is frozen?

31"Can you bind the beautiful*b* Pleiades?
Can you loose the cords of Orion?

a17 Or gates of deep shadows   *b31 Or the twinkling; or the chains of the*

NRSV

11 and said, 'Thus far shall you come, and no
farther,
and here shall your proud waves be
stopped'?

12 "Have you commanded the morning since
your days began,
and caused the dawn to know its place,
13 so that it might take hold of the skirts of the
earth,
and the wicked be shaken out of it?
14 It is changed like clay under the seal,
and it is dyed*a* like a garment.
15 Light is withheld from the wicked,
and their uplifted arm is broken.

16 "Have you entered into the springs of the sea,
or walked in the recesses of the deep?
17 Have the gates of death been revealed to you,
or have you seen the gates of deep darkness?
18 Have you comprehended the expanse of the
earth?
Declare, if you know all this.

19 "Where is the way to the dwelling of light,
and where is the place of darkness,
20 that you may take it to its territory
and that you may discern the paths to its
home?
21 Surely you know, for you were born then,
and the number of your days is great!

22 "Have you entered the storehouses of the snow,
or have you seen the storehouses of the hail,
23 which I have reserved for the time of trouble,
for the day of battle and war?
24 What is the way to the place where the light
is distributed,
or where the east wind is scattered upon
the earth?

25 "Who has cut a channel for the torrents of
rain,
and a way for the thunderbolt,
26 to bring rain on a land where no one lives,
on the desert, which is empty of human life,
27 to satisfy the waste and desolate land,
and to make the ground put forth grass?

a Cn: Heb and they stand forth

NIV

³²Can you bring forth the constellations in their
seasons*a*
or lead out the Bear*b* with its cubs?
³³Do you know the laws of the heavens?
Can you set up ⌊God's*c*⌋ dominion over the
earth?

³⁴"Can you raise your voice to the clouds
and cover yourself with a flood of water?
³⁵Do you send the lightning bolts on their way?
Do they report to you, 'Here we are'?
³⁶Who endowed the heart*d* with wisdom
or gave understanding to the mind*d*?
³⁷Who has the wisdom to count the clouds?
Who can tip over the water jars of the
heavens
³⁸when the dust becomes hard
and the clods of earth stick together?"

*a32 Or the morning star in its season   b32 Or out Leo   c33 Or
his; or their   d36 The meaning of the Hebrew for this word is
uncertain.*

NRSV

²⁸ "Has the rain a father,
or who has begotten the drops of dew?
²⁹ From whose womb did the ice come forth,
and who has given birth to the hoarfrost of
heaven?
³⁰ The waters become hard like stone,
and the face of the deep is frozen.

³¹ "Can you bind the chains of the Pleiades,
or loose the cords of Orion?
³² Can you lead forth the Mazzaroth in their season,
or can you guide the Bear with its children?
³³ Do you know the ordinances of the heavens?
Can you establish their rule on the earth?

³⁴ "Can you lift up your voice to the clouds,
so that a flood of waters may cover you?
³⁵ Can you send forth lightnings, so that they
may go
and say to you, 'Here we are'?
³⁶ Who has put wisdom in the inward parts,*a*
or given understanding to the mind?*a*
³⁷ Who has the wisdom to number the clouds?
Or who can tilt the waterskins of the
heavens,
³⁸ when the dust runs into a mass
and the clods cling together?"

a Meaning of Heb uncertain

COMMENTARY

38:1. A storm often accompanies a divine appearance in biblical tradition (Pss 18:7-15[8-16]; 50:3; 68:8[9]; Ezek 1:4; Nah 1:3; Zech 9:14). The particular term used here, סערה (*sĕ'ārâ*), can refer specifically to a whirlwind (2 Kgs 2:11), although in other instances it seems to refer more generally to a violent storm (e.g., Ps 107:29; Ezek 13:11, 13). The same term is used to describe the theophany in Ezek 1:4.

More difficult to determine is the significance of the use of the divine name Yahweh in this verse. Although the name "Yahweh" is associated with theophanies elsewhere in the Bible,[539] the distribution of divine names within the book of

Job itself is more directly pertinent. The name "Yahweh" otherwise occurs only in the prose narration (1:1–2:13; 42:7-17).[540] In the dialogues only the names "El," "Eloah," "Elohim," and "Shaddai" appear. The use of the name "Yahweh" in the headings to the divine speeches thus reasserts the voice of the narrator as the one who frames the entire book.

The reappearance of this name from the narrative world of the prose tale provides an occasion for thinking about the issue that occasioned the events of the story. The *satan* had alleged that Job's respect for God was based only on the "hedge" of blessing and that, if everything were

539. J. E. Hartley, *The Book of Job,* NICOT (Grand Rapids, Mich.: Eerdmans, 1988) 491.

540. The occurrence of "Yahweh" in 12:9 is either a scribal error or occurs because the verse contains the quotation of a popular proverb.

lost, Job would curse God to God's face. Now there is to be a face to face encounter, and the decisive word has yet to be spoken. But the dialogues have changed the nature of what is at stake. No longer is the question simply whether unconditional piety exists; one needs to know how such a stance could be meaningful. From the perspective of Job, who makes justice the central value, the notion of radically unconditional piety is at best meaningless and at worst monstrous, for it would appear to sanction divine arbitrariness and cruelty. The task God faces is to articulate a theological vision that will make such a stance not only meaningful but also profound. It is a high-stakes gamble.

38:2-3. The very first words of God's speech ("Who is this . . . ?") set both tone and theme. The question raises the issue of Job's standing to challenge God's counsel. It is not Job's humanity per se that disqualifies his challenge, but that he speaks "words without knowledge." One might object that God is being evasive in not replying to Job's explicit demand that God "tell me what charges you have against me" (10:2*b*, author's trans.), and declare "how many wrongs and sins have I committed? Show me my offense and my sin" (13:23, author's trans.). The problem, however, is that those demands make sense only within the context of a certain paradigm of understanding, a paradigm that God is contesting. God makes an ironic allusion to Job's demands and the legal context in which he had placed them by echoing Job's words from 13:22, "Then call, and I will answer;/ or let me speak, and you reply" (NRSV). That Job's challenge to God is accepted, although not in the way Job anticipated, is reflected in God's command that Job gird his loins, a preparation for action (Jer 1:17) that may refer to tucking the ends of one's robe into a belt, so that movement will be unimpeded (Exod 12:11; 1 Kgs 18:46). In this case, Job will need unimpeded intellectual agility.

The use of the vocabulary of "counsel" and "knowledge" in v. 2 sets the divine speeches within the context of wisdom traditions.[541] The theological assumptions and presuppositions of wisdom tradition are particularly evident in the importance the divine speeches place on insight into the primordial structures of creation as a means of understanding God and the world (cf. Job 28; Proverb 8; Sirach 24).

The translation of עצה (*'ēṣâ*) as "counsel" is less than clear. The word refers to careful thinking and planning and to the capacity to do such planning.[542] "Plan" or "design" is better, so long as those words are understood in the active sense. In chap. 12, Job had mocked the "wisdom and power . . . counsel and understanding" of God, as Job described an irrational world of destructive forces, confusion, and the contemptuous undermining of human attempts to construct wise social order (12:13-25). What God's design "brought to light," Job contended, was deep darkness, "the shadow of death" (12:22). It is appropriate that God chooses this ground on which to engage Job, for all of Job's specific accusations are ultimately rooted in his challenge to God's design.

38:4-7. The rhetorical questions of the divine speech manage to do several things at once. While they confront Job with the limits of his knowledge and capacity, and contrast it with the wisdom and resourcefulness of God, they also create vivid pictorial images of the cosmos. In 38:4-7, the earth is imaged as a great building that God, as architect and builder, constructs. The general notion is quite traditional (cf. Pss 24:2; 89:11[12]; 102:25[26]; 104:5; Prov 3:19; Isa 48:13; 51:13; Zech 12:1), although nowhere else is it developed with so many concrete details. The combination of planning activities (making measurements, stretching out the line) and the accomplishment of structurally crucial physical activities (sinking footings, laying foundations) makes the image a particularly apt illustration of divine *'ēṣâ* as planning and design.[543] The concluding image of the morning stars and heavenly beings singing and shouting for joy is not simply a festive grace note but serves to interpret the creation of the earth as the building of God's temple (cf. Isa 66:1-2*a*).

---

541. Cf. N. Habel, "In Defense of God the Sage," in *The Voice from the Whirlwind*, ed. Perdue and Gilpin, 21-38.

542. M. Fox, "Words for Wisdom," *ZAH* 6 (1993) 160. The term *'ēṣâ* does not necessarily have connotations of God's action *in history*, as J. Lévêque, *Job et son Dieu* (Paris: Gabalda, 1970) 511, has argued. Attempts to load this term with connotations of historical providence (e.g., Kubina, *Die Gottesreden im Buche Hiob*, 122-23; G. Gutiérrez, *On Job: God-Talk and the Suffering of the Innocent*, trans. M. O'Connell [Maryknoll, N.Y.: Orbis, 1987] 69) run counter to the content of the divine speeches.

543. Various passages in other contexts refer to details of building, including the use of measuring and plumb lines (2 Kgs 21:13; Isa 34:11; Jer 31:39; Zech 1:16), foundation or capstones (Ps 118:22; Isa 28:16; Jer 51:26), and footings for pillars (Exod 26:19; Cant 5:15).

The laying of a temple's foundations and the placing of the capstone were liturgical occasions when musicians and singers praised God, and the people joined in shouts of blessing and praise (Ezra 3:10-11; Zech 4:7; cf. 2 Chr 5:11-14).[544] The motif may be more distantly echoed in personified wisdom's joyful response to God's creation of the cosmos (Prov 8:30-31).

38:8-11. The sea, the traditional symbol of primordial chaos, is a frequent image in creation accounts. In mythic tradition, the sea is often represented as a hostile force, subdued in battle by the creator god (e.g., Ps 74:13-14; 89:9-13[10-14]; Isa 51:9-10).[545] A somewhat different tradition speaks of the establishment of boundaries for the sea in the process of creation (Ps 104:5-9; Prov 8:29; Jer 5:22). The waves of the sea, which restlessly lap at the shore and which, during storms, reach aggressively across the boundary separating land from sea, suggest a force that would break out if it were not contained. For these reasons the sea became a potent image by which to describe personal or national distress that threatened to overwhelm and from which only God could rescue (Pss 18:4-10[5-20]; 77:16-20[17-21]; 144:7; Isa 17:12-14).

The divine speeches both adapt and transform these traditions. The language of boundaries, bars, and doors as well as of verbal command (38:10-11) is all in keeping with the tradition of restricting the aggressive sea to its appointed place. Here that aggressiveness is depicted in the image of "proud waves," anticipating the theme of pride, which is of such importance in the second divine speech. In striking contrast to the motif of battle between God and the sea, however, God here appears as the midwife who births the sea and wraps it in the swaddling bands of cloud and darkness. Whether this image is a creation of the Job poet or the appropriation of an otherwise unknown tradition cannot be determined. The metaphorical connections between this image of birthing and the more traditional language can be traced, however. Birth is an event in which an irrepressible force breaks through containment and transgresses boundaries. Specifically, the

breaking through of water from the womb signals the onset of the process. Swaddling bands in which babies were wrapped were restraints to prevent the baby's arms and legs from moving about and were believed to calm the child. Thus both the aggressive force of the sea and the restraints placed upon it are taken up into this new image. The image of the baby in turn transforms the emotional resonance of the image of the sea. Far from being a hostile, alien power it is associated with the vigor of new life, and the restraints placed upon it are associated with nurture and protection. In Job 38:8-11, this new imagery does not displace the more traditional language; rather, it stands side by side with it. The chaotic waters have a place in God's design of the cosmos, yet one that is clearly circumscribed. They are the object not only of divine restriction but also of divine care.

38:12-15. Ironic echoes of Job's opening speech occur in God's words. God asks rhetorically if Job has ever commanded the morning and shown dawn its place (38:12). Job had in fact attempted to command dawn through a curse (3:9). In God's design the coming of the light of dawn has a different task. The imagery suggests that the darkness of the earth at night is like the cloak with which sleepers cover themselves. The term "skirts" (כנפות *kĕnāpôt*) is a standard figure of speech for the edges of the earth (37:3; Isa 11:12 ; 24:16; cf. its literal use in Ruth 3:9). For dawn to take the "skirts" of the earth and shake the wicked out of them (38:13) implicitly likens the wicked to vermin, which are attracted to the warmth and darkness of such a cover.[546]

It is easy for modern readers to be amused at the image of shaking out the cosmic bedbugs and to miss the more profound dimensions of this section. In the ancient Near East, each morning was considered a recapitulation of creation, or perhaps better, each morning was part of the continuing work of creation.[547] In a pair of striking images, the poet describes the power of dawn's light to "create" the earth by bringing it from

---

544. Cf. also the celebration that accompanies the building of Babylon as the gods' sanctuary in Enuma Elish (*ANET*, 68-72) and the building of Baal's house/temple in the Baal cycle (*ANET*, 134).

545. See also Enuma Elish IV (*ANET*, 66-67).

546. See, e.g., the Egyptian Hymn to the Aton (*ANET*, 370). In Ps 104:19-23, night is the time when lions prowl, seeking prey, and humans sleep. When dawn comes, the lions sleep, and humans go out to work. Symbolically, lions represent danger and are sometimes used as symbols of the wicked (cf. 4:10-11).

547. B. Janowski, *Rettungsgewissheit und Epiphanie des Heils*, WMANT 59, Bd. I, 1989, 183-84.

undifferentiated formlessness into the order that is creation (cf. Genesis 1). Just as precise images are stamped onto clay by a seal, so also light brings forth the distinct shapes of the earth's features. Similarly, colors, which merge into indistinguishable gray in darkness, are brought back into being by light.[548]

The final verse returns to the topic of the wicked. To say that the coming of dawn deprives the wicked of their "light" is to draw on the same motif that Job used in 24:13-17, that for criminals day and night are inverted, and "deep darkness is morning to all of them" (24:17a NRSV). In Job's mouth, the words were a criticism of God's order. Here, however, containment of the violence of the wicked is set in the context of the work of creation, which is renewed each day. Like the hedging in of the sea with bars and doors, the light of day contains and limits but does not eliminate the wicked from the world.

38:16-21. In these sections, God questions Job about his experience of the four dimensions of the world: the great deep (38:16), the underworld (38:17), the expanse of the earth (38:18), and the heavens (38:19-21; cf. 11:7-9; 28:14, 22). The vocabulary evokes a journey: enter, walk, see, gaze upon; recesses, gates, way, place, territory, paths. One could compare the epic journey of the Mesopotamian hero Gilgamesh, who sought to evade the inevitability of death. In his journey he roamed the steppe, came to the mountains that are the gates of sunrise and sunset, ventured through the dark underworld passage where the sun travels at night, and even crossed the waters of death.[549] For this he was called "he who saw everything to the ends of the land, who all things experienced, considered all."[550] As God's rhetorical question makes clear, Job cannot claim such a heroic journey, although in a certain way the divine speeches with their vivid descriptive imagery evoke the sense of a virtual journey to these hidden places. The outcome for Job will be like that for Gilgamesh: a recognition of the necessity to renounce a deeply held but ultimately impos-

sible desire (42:6). Yet that renunciation makes reintegration into community and return to the activities of life possible.

The cosmic geography in vv. 16-17 is thematically more closely related to the preceding sections than might first appear. The springs of the sea and the great deep refer to the primordial waters, which were divided and contained by God at creation (Gen 1:6; cf. Ps 33:6-7). Although they are the sources of oceans and of fresh waters that well up from the earth, their sudden release can return the world to its chaotic, pre-creation state. In the Priestly account of the deluge, the opening of the springs of the great deep and of the floodgates of the heavens destroys the earth and its inhabitants (Gen 7:11). Similarly, the gates of death designate the boundary between the realms of life and death (Pss 9:13[14]; 107:18; Isa 38:10; Jonah 2:6[7]). The Mesopotamian myth of the Descent of Ishtar to the netherworld contains a graphic description of the progress of the goddess through seven gates, as she is progressively stripped of all the attributes of life.[551] In Israel, the image of the gates of death primarily figures as a symbol of the fact that one who goes down to Sheol cannot return (Jonah 2:6[7] speaks of the bars of the underworld). Gates also mark the limit of death's domain. Although the servants of death may carry off persons to the King of Terrors (18:14), the realm of death may no more burst through its gates to devour all life than the sea may break through its restraining doors.

Verses 18-19 refer to the most primordial of all the acts of creation (cf. the sarcastic comment in v. 21 that Job must know, since he was born then, as though he were as primordial as wisdom itself; cf. 15:7-8; Prov 8:22-31). In Gen 1:3, the creation of light and the separation of light from darkness is the first of God's acts, a separation that makes possible the alternation of day and night. In Gen 8:22, the assurance that "as long as the earth endures,/ seedtime and harvest, cold and heat,/ summer and winter, day and night,/ shall not cease" (NRSV) is the divine promise that the fundamental structures of creation, which make life possible, will not be destroyed. The Bible does not otherwise speak of the dwelling places of light and darkness (38:20; cf. Ps 19:4-6[5-7]);

548. Since the expression "they stand forth like a garment" makes little sense, most emend the Hebrew verb יצב (yāsab) to the similar verb צבע (sābā', "to dye"; so NRSV). See E. Dhorme, *A Commentary on the Book of Job,* trans. H. Knight (London: Nelson, 1967) 581; M. Pope, *Job,* 3rd ed., AB 15 (Garden City, N.Y.: Doubleday, 1979) 295.

549. *ANET,* 88-91.

550. Ibid., 73.

551. Ibid., 107.

the Greek poet Hesiod refers to a house at the edge of the world, where Atlas lifts up the heavens. There night and day dwell alternately, each entering when the other leaves.[552]

38:22-24. With v. 22 the poem turns from the great cosmogonic structures of creation to meteorological phenomena (vv. 22-38), things that are closer and more accessible to humans than the primordial structures of creation. Yet in each sphere Job's ignorance and inability to control are complete.

The image of storehouses for the various phenomena of weather is common (37:9; Deut 28:12; Jer 10:13; Sir 39:29; 43:14). Because knowledge of such matters was regarded as utterly beyond the reach of human ability, it later becomes part of the esoteric mysteries revealed to the apocalyptic seer. Enoch's heavenly journey, for instance, includes a detailed examination of the cosmic storehouses (*1 Enoch* 41:4; 60:11-21). Hail frequently appears as a weapon of God (Exod 9:22-26; Josh 10:11; Isa 28:17; 30:30; Ezek 13:11, 13; Hag 2:17; Sir 39:29), along with other things that may fall from the sky. Since it would seem odd for "light" (38:24*a*) to be included in this sequence, the word should be understood as a synonym for "lightening" (so NIV), as in 37:11. The east wind is, with perhaps one exception (Ps 78:26), always associated with destruction (e.g., Gen 41:6; Exod 10:13; Jer 18:17; Ezek 27:26; Jonah 4:8). Thus three of the four elements mentioned do damage on earth. They are associated here, however, with words of regulation and control: storehouses, proper times, way, place, reserve, distribute, disperse.

38:25-27. In contrast to the east wind, which destroys vegetation in cultivated lands (Gen 41:6; Ezek 19:12; Jonah 4:8), the rains bring forth grass in the desolate wasteland. The imagery is provocative. Constructing water channels was one of the defining acts of human civilization in the ancient Near East. Although more characteristic of Mesopotamia and Egypt, artificial canals were also known in Israel. God uses the language paradoxically, to talk of the channeling of rain onto desert lands, which are, it is twice emphasized, "empty of human life." Some commentators interpret this section as a repudiation of the idea of God's use

of rain as reward or punishment (e.g., 37:13; Jer 3:3; Hos 6:3),[553] but that does not seem to be quite the point. The contrast challenged in these verses is between the sown and the unsown, between cultivated land, which is associated with order and creation, and desolate land, which is associated with chaos.[554] Although the term "desert" (מדבר *midbār*) may have many connotations, the characterization of this land as "waste and desolate" (שאה ומשאה *šōʾâ ûměšōʾâ*) gives it strongly negative associations. *Š* is a term often associated with the desolation that accompanies destruction (Ps 35:8; Isa 10:3; 47:11; Ezek 38:9). Job himself made use of the negative connotations of the phrase *šōʾâ ûměšōʾâ* when he described the outcast and despised "persons of no name" as grubbing out their meager existence in the "waste and desolate" land (30:3). In Job's view, such a place is both dehumanized and godforsaken. Yet this is precisely the place that God "satisfies" with rain and causes to bring forth grass, an image associated with creation (Gen 1:11; 2:5-6). This is not to say that the dry land is permanently transformed into a paradise, as may be the implication of certain eschatological passages (e.g., Isaiah 35). Rather, in the same way that each morning partakes in the work of creation, when the occasional heavy rains come, the land that is ordinarily desolate and hostile becomes for a while a place of lushness and beauty.

38:28-30. The theme of water continues in these verses. Since the questions are rhetorical and not requests for information, it is unlikely that one should search for mythological identities for a father of rain or a mother of ice. The questions identify wondrous and mysterious phenomena, like the listing of "three things [that] are too wonderful for me;/ four I do not understand" in Prov 30:18-19 (NRSV). Imagery of begetting and birth directs attention to the mysterious way in which various forms of water come into being or are transformed from one to another. What makes some clouds produce rain and not others? Dew seemingly appears from nowhere. Ice and frost are absent one cold day but present the next. The reference to ice, in particular, points to the odd

---

552. Hesiod *Theogony* 745-57. See also G. Fuchs, *Mythos and Hiobdichtung* (Stuttgart: Kohlhammer, 1993) 207.

553. M. Tsevat, "The Meaning of the Book of Job," *HUCA* 37 (1966) 99-100.

554. O. Keel, *Jahwehs Entgegnung an Ijob* (Goettingen: Vandenhoeck und Ruprecht, 1978) 58.

transformation of which water is capable. Job 38:30*a* literally reads, "water hides itself like a rock." Ice is water in hiding.

38:31-33. The section concerning the constellations is the only one in the second half of the chapter that does not deal with water. Perhaps it has been misplaced from an earlier part of the chapter, although there is no evidence in the texts and translations. It may be, however, that the changing visibility and times of rising and setting of the constellations were signs associated with seasonal changes in rainfall, so that their mention here would seem thematically appropriate to an audience familiar with those traditions.[555] If so, then the references to binding and loosing would refer to the ability to control not only the movement of the stars but also the rainy and dry seasons associated with them. Some connection between what happens in the heavens and what happens on earth is presupposed in the question to Job about knowing the ordinances of the heavens and establishing their rule on earth (38:33). As in several other sections of this chapter, the vocabulary of order is prominent.

Where possible, English translations use familiar names derived from Greek to specify the constellations. In Hebrew, the Pleides were called "the herd" (כימה *kîmâ*) and Orion "the fool" (כסיל *kĕsîl*). Mazzaroth (מזרות) cannot be identified with certainty; possibly it is a form of the word that means constellations in general (see NIV; cf. 2 Kgs 23:5). A. de Wilde argues that it refers to Sirius, the dog star, whose appearance was associated with the rising of the Nile.[556] The bear and its children are commonly taken as Ursa Major, although de Wilde argues for Aldebaran and the Hyades. As he notes, Orion, Sirius, and Aldebaran appear together at the time when the Pleiades would be "bound," i.e., not visible.[557]

38:34-38. Anyone who has endured long days of drought knows the longing to command the clouds to pour out rain or to summon the lightning of the thunderstorm (38:34-35). Such power does not belong to humankind, nor does the wisdom to know when rain will fall. It was popularly believed, however, that certain birds had such knowledge. In 38:36 the translation of the Hebrew words טחות (*ṭūḥôt*) and שכוי (*śekwî*) is probably not "mind" and "heart," but rather "the ibis" and "the cock."[558] The ibis was believed to announce the rising of the Nile, and the cock the coming of rain.[559] The concluding image (38:37-38) is one of stewardship. Here the clouds are metaphorically represented as waterskins or jars (cf. Sir 43:8). Since water is a precious commodity, it requires the wisdom of a careful steward to know the number of containers and determine how many may be poured out upon the dry ground. (See Reflections on 38:39–40:5.)

555. See A. de Wilde, *Das Buch Hiob,* OTS xxii (Leiden: Brill, 1981) 142-47, 366-37.

556. Ibid., 367.

557. Ibid., 144.

558. E. Dhorme, *A Commentary on the Book of Job,* trans. H. Knight (London: Nelson, 1967) 593; R. Gordis, *The Book of Job: Commentary, New Translation, and Special Studies* (New York: Jewish Theological Seminary, 5738/1978) 452-53; G. Fohrer, *Das Buch Hiob,* KAT xvi (Guetersloh: Gerd Mohn, 1963) 508-9; but see M. Pope, *Job,* 3rd ed., AB 15 (Garden City, N.Y.: Doubleday, 1979) 302.

559. Jussen, "Le Coq et la pluie," *RB* (1924) 574-82. In classical sources, see Virgil *Georgics* I.374ff.

Job 38:39–39:30, The World of Wild Animals

NIV	NRSV
39"Do you hunt the prey for the lioness / and satisfy the hunger of the lions / 40when they crouch in their dens / or lie in wait in a thicket? / 41Who provides food for the raven / when its young cry out to God / and wander about for lack of food?	39 "Can you hunt the prey for the lion, / or satisfy the appetite of the young lions, / 40 when they crouch in their dens, / or lie in wait in their covert? / 41 Who provides for the raven its prey, / when its young ones cry to God, / and wander about for lack of food?

NIV

39 "Do you know when the mountain goats
give birth?
    Do you watch when the doe bears her fawn?
²Do you count the months till they bear?
    Do you know the time they give birth?
³They crouch down and bring forth their young;
    their labor pains are ended.
⁴Their young thrive and grow strong in the wilds;
    they leave and do not return.

⁵"Who let the wild donkey go free?
    Who untied his ropes?
⁶I gave him the wasteland as his home,
    the salt flats as his habitat.
⁷He laughs at the commotion in the town;
    he does not hear a driver's shout.
⁸He ranges the hills for his pasture
    and searches for any green thing.

⁹"Will the wild ox consent to serve you?
    Will he stay by your manger at night?
¹⁰Can you hold him to the furrow with a harness?
    Will he till the valleys behind you?
¹¹Will you rely on him for his great strength?
    Will you leave your heavy work to him?
¹²Can you trust him to bring in your grain
    and gather it to your threshing floor?

¹³"The wings of the ostrich flap joyfully,
    but they cannot compare with the pinions and
        feathers of the stork.
¹⁴She lays her eggs on the ground
    and lets them warm in the sand,
¹⁵unmindful that a foot may crush them,
    that some wild animal may trample them.
¹⁶She treats her young harshly, as if they were
        not hers;
    she cares not that her labor was in vain,
¹⁷for God did not endow her with wisdom
    or give her a share of good sense.
¹⁸Yet when she spreads her feathers to run,
    she laughs at horse and rider.

¹⁹"Do you give the horse his strength
    or clothe his neck with a flowing mane?
²⁰Do you make him leap like a locust,
    striking terror with his proud snorting?
²¹He paws fiercely, rejoicing in his strength,
    and charges into the fray.
²²He laughs at fear, afraid of nothing;
    he does not shy away from the sword.

NRSV

39 "Do you know when the mountain goats
        give birth?
    Do you observe the calving of the deer?
² Can you number the months that they fulfill,
    and do you know the time when they give
        birth,
³ when they crouch to give birth to their
        offspring,
    and are delivered of their young?
⁴ Their young ones become strong, they grow
        up in the open;
    they go forth, and do not return to them.

⁵ "Who has let the wild ass go free?
    Who has loosed the bonds of the swift ass,
⁶ to which I have given the steppe for its home,
    the salt land for its dwelling place?
⁷ It scorns the tumult of the city;
    it does not hear the shouts of the driver.
⁸ It ranges the mountains as its pasture,
    and it searches after every green thing.

⁹ "Is the wild ox willing to serve you?
    Will it spend the night at your crib?
¹⁰ Can you tie it in the furrow with ropes,
    or will it harrow the valleys after you?
¹¹ Will you depend on it because its strength is
        great,
    and will you hand over your labor to it?
¹² Do you have faith in it that it will return,
    and bring your grain to your threshing
        floor?ᵃ

¹³ "The ostrich's wings flap wildly,
    though its pinions lack plumage.ᵇ
¹⁴ For it leaves its eggs to the earth,
    and lets them be warmed on the ground,
¹⁵ forgetting that a foot may crush them,
    and that a wild animal may trample them.
¹⁶ It deals cruelly with its young, as if they were
        not its own;
    though its labor should be in vain, yet it has
        no fear;
¹⁷ because God has made it forget wisdom,
    and given it no share in understanding.
¹⁸ When it spreads its plumes aloft,ᵇ
    it laughs at the horse and its rider.

ᵃ Heb *your grain and your threshing floor*   ᵇ Meaning of Heb
uncertain

NIV

23The quiver rattles against his side,
along with the flashing spear and lance.
24In frenzied excitement he eats up the ground;
he cannot stand still when the trumpet sounds.
25At the blast of the trumpet he snorts, 'Aha!'
He catches the scent of battle from afar,
the shout of commanders and the battle cry.

26"Does the hawk take flight by your wisdom
and spread his wings toward the south?
27Does the eagle soar at your command
and build his nest on high?
28He dwells on a cliff and stays there at night;
a rocky crag is his stronghold.
29From there he seeks out his food;
his eyes detect it from afar.
30His young ones feast on blood,
and where the slain are, there is he."

NRSV

19 "Do you give the horse its might?
Do you clothe its neck with mane?
20 Do you make it leap like the locust?
Its majestic snorting is terrible.
21 It paws[a] violently, exults mightily;
it goes out to meet the weapons.
22 It laughs at fear, and is not dismayed;
it does not turn back from the sword.
23 Upon it rattle the quiver,
the flashing spear, and the javelin.
24 With fierceness and rage it swallows the ground;
it cannot stand still at the sound of the trumpet.
25 When the trumpet sounds, it says 'Aha!'
From a distance it smells the battle,
the thunder of the captains, and the shouting.

26 "Is it by your wisdom that the hawk soars,
and spreads its wings toward the south?
27 Is it at your command that the eagle mounts up
and makes its nest on high?
28 It lives on the rock and makes its home
in the fastness of the rocky crag.
29 From there it spies the prey;
its eyes see it from far away.
30 Its young ones suck up blood;
and where the slain are, there it is."

a Gk Syr Vg: Heb *they dig*

COMMENTARY

The transition to the second part of the divine speech is marked simply by an abrupt change of topic, from the phenomena of weather to the lives of animals. Animals are powerful symbols in all human cultures, although their emotive and symbolic significance varies greatly from one culture to the next. Consequently, one must be careful not to assume that the values a modern reader would automatically associate with the animals named are the same as those in an ancient text like Job. In the religious and cultural contexts of the ancient world, the sphere of the wild is the Other against which human society defines itself.

Consequently, attitudes toward it are ambivalent but largely negative. The desert waste in particular is contrasted with inhabited land as a hostile and dangerous place (Deut 32:10; Ps 107:4-7). Since the desert is a symbol of chaos, divine punishment often takes the form of making a city into just such an uninhabited wilderness (Ps 107:33-38; Isa 34:8-15; Hos 2:3b[5b], 12[14]). The punished city, which had been structured and ordered like creation itself, now partakes of the disorder and confusion of chaos (cf. Isa 34:11-12, echoing Gen 1:2). Wild animals are also part of this pattern of opposition and enmity. Those that lived in the desolate places and ruined cities took on the aura of those places (Isa 13:19-21; 34:8-15; Jer 50:39-40; Zeph 2:13-15; animals mentioned in those contexts include several described in the divine speech: the lion, the raven, the wild ass, and the ostrich). Divine punishment was often depicted as letting wild animals savage a land, predators attacking persons and livestock (Lev 26:22; Ezek 5:17; Isa 56:9), and other animals trampling and eating crops (Ps 80:13[14]; Isa 5:5-6; Hos 2:12[14]). This deep divide between humans and animals goes back to the re-creation of the world after the deluge, when God declared to Noah that all living creatures would be in "fear and dread of you" (Gen 9:2 NIV). The ideal of a "covenant" with the animals of the earth (Job 5:23; Hos 2:18[20]) and of an eschatological transformation in which wild animals "will neither harm nor destroy" (see Isa 11:6-9) only underscores the enmity that was understood to define the relationship between wild animals and humans in the present.

Two motifs in ancient Near Eastern art illustrate this perception of animals. One is the motif of the royal hunt. Both Egyptian and Mesopotamian kings are depicted as hunting a variety of animals, including lions, mountain goats, deer, wild asses, wild oxen, ostriches, and birds of prey of all kinds—virtually all of the animals listed in Job 39. The king's hunt was not simply a recreational activity, but a symbolic act. Just as the king protected the integrity of the land against hostile human enemies by going out to war, so also he enacted his role as protector of the land against the hostile forces represented by animals by engaging in the hunt.[560] The other motif is that of the "Lord of the animals." Mesopotamian art has numerous representations of a divine figure flanked by wild animals, which he holds in each hand. The gesture is clearly one of control. Again, although there are variations according to region and date, most of the animals represented in the king's hunt and in Job 39 are also represented in the "Lord of the animals" motif.[561] It is always difficult to interpret pictorial symbolism without an accompanying text, but it appears that control of the animals by a divine figure is analogous to the mythic motif of the restriction of the chaotic

sea. A wild force that is part of the world is limited by a divine power as part of an orderly creation. Although no exact counterpart to these representations appears in biblical literature, a similar idea is expressed in Jer 27:5-7, where God grants sovereignty to Nebuchadnezzar, including the promise that even the beasts of the field will serve him.

These are not the only ways in which animals were represented. The wisdom tradition regarded particular animals as examples of wise behavior (Prov 6:6-8; 30:24-28; cf. 1 Kgs 4:32-33) and of wondrous ways that eluded human comprehension (Prov 30:18-19). Certain psalms that praise God as creator include references to wild animals and the provision God has made for them in creation, alongside human beings (Pss 104:10-30; 147:8-9, 12-14; cf. Ps 148:7-12. As noted above in the overview to the divine speeches, Psalm 104 is particularly important as a background for God's words.) These psalms may be compared with the motif of the "world tree" in Mesopotamian art. There a stylized tree or a divine figure with tree motifs is represented as providing food for animals.[562] In the Bible the motif is also used as a royal symbol. Daniel 4:12[9] describes the tree that represents Nebuchadnezzar: "Its foliage was beautiful,/ its fruit abundant,/ and it provided food for all./ The animals of the field found shade under it,/ the birds of the air nested in its branches,/ and from it all living beings were fed" (NRSV; cf. Ezek 31:1-9). In Mesopotamian art, the motif of the "Lord of the animals" is sometimes combined with that of the "world tree," so that the animals turn their heads to eat from the tree while also being restrained by the divine figure. In this way the themes of abundance and control of the wild are brought together.

All of these traditions provide important background, but the meaning of the divine speech depends on the particular way in which traditions are put to use. First, as in 38:4-38, all but one of the individual sections in 38:39–39:30 are introduced by the familiar rhetorical questions that serve to point out the limits of Job's knowledge and ability, while underscoring God's power and wisdom. Second, each section also includes a closely observed description of the animal in a

---

560. Keel, *Jahwehs Entgegnung an Ijob,* 71.
561. Ibid., 87.

562. *ANEP,* pl. 464.

characteristic activity. Elsewhere in the Bible references to animals are brief and incidental. Only here is sustained attention given to the simple description of animals. The animals are presented, not as they were traditionally perceived in human perspective, but in ways that challenge human perspective. Thus, in interpreting the significance of the passage one must attend to the background of the various traditions, the rhetorical setting, and the unprecedented focus on animal activity.

38:39-41. It is no accident that the sequence should begin with the image of the lion, which was *the* wild animal in the imagination of ancient Israel. The detail that most engaged attention was the lion's prowess as a predator, a feature that occurs in the vast majority of references to the lion in the Bible (e.g., Gen 49:9; Num 23:29; Ps 17:2; Isa 5:29; Amos 3:4; Nah 2:12). As noted above, this passage has particularly close connections with Ps 104:21. There the lion's roar is interpreted as its request to God for food. Here the imagery is even bolder. The rhetorical questions posed to Job point out something he cannot do, but that God can do. Asking Job if he can "hunt" on behalf of the lions depicts him, and by extension God, as a lioness who brings down prey to satisfy the hunger of members of the pride. The implications of this image of God are important. Although lions hunt many different kinds of prey, the Bible often refers to the lions' attack on flocks of sheep and the consequent enmity between lions and shepherds (1 Sam 17:34-37; Isa 31:4; Jer 25:38; Mic 5:8). Like the image of God's treating the sea with protective care, hunting on behalf of the lions is an image of nurture toward an element of creation perceived as hostile by humans.

Why the raven is grouped with the lion is not certain.[563] As with the lion, the feeding of the raven figures in a creation psalm (Ps 147:9). The Job poet appears to have combined two traditional motifs in such hymnody. The image in Ps 147:9 is quite similar to that of 38:41, as both refer to the raven's offspring and to the sound of their crying out for food. The symbolic significance of the raven is more elusive, however. It is one of the unclean birds (Lev 11:15; Deut 14:14), a scavenger (Prov 30:17) associated with desolate places (Isa 34:11). Yet ravens fed Elijah when the

prophet hid in a wadi east of the Jordan (1 Kgs 17:4-6).

There is perhaps an oblique parody of Job in these verses. Job had represented himself as a provider, one who heard the cries of the poor (29:12; the same verb as in 38:41), and before whom others opened their mouths as if to receive rain (29:23). But Job's vision of society has no place for literal or metaphorical lions and ravens. His world is sharply delineated between the village and the wasteland, the latter symbolic of all that was feared and rejected. Lions appear in Job's speech only as an image of the wicked (29:17), to be dealt with violently.

39:1-4. Although the mountain goat and the deer are objects of the king's hunt in Mesopotamian and Egyptian art and are frequently represented as animals controlled by the "Lord of the animals,"[564] they do not bear connotations of threat in Israelite literature. Instead, they are noted for their agility (2 Sam 22:34; Isa 35:6) and beauty (Gen 49:21; Prov 5:19), and even appear in love poetry (Cant 2:7, 9, 17; 3:5); one song was entitled "The Doe of the Dawn" (Ps 22:1). Deer also appear in Israelite poetry as images of suffering, since they are vulnerable to hunger and thirst during times of drought (Ps 42:1[2]; Jer 14:5; Lam 1:6).

Mountain goats and deer, as browsing animals, are similar to domestic sheep and goats. The questions God poses to Job imply just such a comparison, as a means of underscoring how different are the relations of domestic and wild animals to human beings. Knowledge of the seasons of birth and of the precise gestation periods of domestic sheep and goats was essential if the flocks were to increase. Although the Bible does not provide much detail about actual practices, the story of Jacob's clever breeding suggests a strong preoccupation with all aspects of the reproduction of the flocks (Gen 30:31-43). Yet Job knows nothing of the reproduction of these wild creatures. Similarly, lambing season is a time of intense activity for the shepherd, who must not only protect the safety of vulnerable ewes and lambs but also assist with difficult births. Translations often miss the proper nuance of the verb rendered "watch" and "observe" (שמר *šāmar*) in

563. J. E. Hartley, *The Book of Job*, NICOT (Grand Rapids, Mich.: Eerdmans, 1988) 505n. 4, notes the word play between "ambush" (ארב *'ārab*) and "raven" (ערב *'ōrēb*), in vv. 40-41.

564. Keel, *Jahwehs Entgegnung an Ijob*, 72-75, 87-94.

39:1*b*. It should be translated by its meaning of "watch over," "guard." What the passage implies is that these animals are alien to the protective relation between shepherd and sheep, which was important not only to the economic but also to the symbolic life of ancient Israel. These animals need no shepherd, nor are they considered to form a flock. Instead, they are represented as reaching maturity and leaving, not to return (39:4). Job's symbolic world, which has been structured primarily in terms of dependence and protection, cannot comprehend such beings within its categories.

39:5-12. The resistance of the sphere of the wild to incorporation within Job's organizing categories, implicit in the description of the mountain goat and deer, becomes explicit in the representation of the wild ass and the wild ox. These animals have exact counterparts within the domestic world, and the contrast with those domestic animals forms the focus of these sections. The wild ox, perhaps the now extinct aurochs, is mentioned elsewhere in the Bible primarily in connection with its remarkable strength (Num 23:22; 34:8; Deut 33:17; Pss 22:22; 92:11). Here, however, emphasis falls on the absolute impossibility of domesticating this wild creature. The hallmark of domestication is the exchange of food in return for service (Isa 1:3), yet that is what 39:9 treats as an absurdity. Domestication involves domination (39:10), but also a relationship of trust (39:11-12). These categories, so evocative of Job's hierarchical and paternalistic moral world, break down when confronted with the wild ox. The aurochs's utter alienness confounds Job's customary ways of thinking.

The wild ass, or onager, is an even more evocative subject, for it holds a more developed position in Israel's symbolic world, and in Job's. Throughout the Bible the wild ass stands for everything opposed to the world of human order and culture. Ishmael is called "a wild ass of a man" precisely because "his hand will be against everyone and everyone's hand against him, and he will live in hostility toward all his brothers" (see Gen 16:12). The wild ass is associated with ruined and deserted cities destroyed by the judgment of God (Isa 32:14). Thus they are evocative of the resurgence of the chaotic into what had once been the sphere of creation. Job twice draws on the connection between the wild ass and the

barren wasteland it inhabits (24:5; 30:7; cf. Jer 14:6). He uses the wild ass as a symbol for a certain social category, the destitute and outcast. Given the symbolic function of the wild ass as defining what is opposed to the sphere of the human, there can be few more powerful symbols of rejection and dehumanization.

The divine description draws on traditional depictions in associating the wild ass with the barren salt flats (39:6) and with rugged areas where vegetation is scarce (39:8). From the human perspective such places are the opposite of fruitful, habitable land. They are, rather, a place of punishment (Ps 107:34; Jer 17:6). Yet for the wild ass they are home. As in Ps 104:11, the wild ass is an object of divine care. The divine speeches exploit the traditional contrast between the human and the wild ass, but in a way that reverses the values. The city, the emblem of human culture, is represented as a place of noise and oppression (39:7), a place of bondage from which God has set the wild ass free (39:5). When Job had looked on the wasteland and its inhabitants, whether in sympathy or in contempt, all that he could see was a place of rejection. God's presence in such a place had utterly eluded him.

39:13-25. 13:13-18. The ostrich and the war horse (39:19-25) are both uncanny animals, associated here because of their speed, their exuberance, and their disdain for fear. The passage concerning the ostrich does not begin with the characteristic rhetorical questions and refers to God in the third person (39:17). Possibly, it is a set piece incorporated from another context. Be that as it may, its imagery and themes fit well into the divine speech.

Identifying symbolic associations with the ostrich is unfortunately complicated by a disagreement concerning names. In 39:13 the unique term "screechers" (רנגים *rěnānîm*) is used, instead of the ordinary term for "ostrich" (יען *yāʿēn*; see Lam 4:3, which also mentions its alleged cruelty to its offspring). The dispute is whether the related term יענה (*yaʿănâ*), which occurs frequently in the Bible, should be understood as referring to ostriches (so NRSV) or to owls (so NIV). What makes this rather technical issue important is that the *yaʿănâ* bird is frequently associated with uninhabited places, especially ruins of cities destroyed by God. There it keeps company with other eerie and ominous animals, including jackals, hyenas, buzzards, owls, the demon Lilith, and other creatures often associated with the demonic, including wild cats and feral goats (Isa 13:21; 34:13; 43:20; Jer 50:30). Most important, in describing his own sense of ruin and exclusion, Job had called himself "a brother of jackals,/ and a companion of ostriches [ya'ănâ]" (30:29 NRSV). The argument in favor of owls is that they do have a fondness for living in ruins. As Keel has argued, however, one should not confuse naturalistic observation with symbolic language. Destruction transfers a city from the sphere of the inhabited to the sphere of the wasteland, and the ostrich is one of the characteristic animals of uninhabited wasteland.[565] The clear pairing of the jackal and the ostrich (yā'ēn) in Lam 4:3 suggests that the fixed pair of the jackal and the ya 'ănâ bird in Isa 34:13; 43:20; Mic 1:8; and in Job 30:29 also refers to the jackal and the ostrich. These observations, together with the evidence of the versions and cognate languages, suggest that the NRSV is correct in translating ya'ănâ as "ostrich."

This detour into bird names allows one to consider the symbolic evocations of the ostrich and the way in which this passage both alludes to and overturns them. In 39:13-18, Job is confronted with an animal with which he had claimed companionship (30:29) in order to evoke a sense of isolation from human society and perhaps also the mourning with which the ostrich's sound was associated (30:31; cf. Mic 1:8). Here in radical contrast the ostrich appears as an image of pure heedless joy. Its shrill sound becomes the basis for its name, rěnānîm, but that word means "cry of joy," not mourning. Moreover, the verb translated "flap wildly" literally means "to be glad," "rejoice" (עלס 'ālas). The second half of 39:13 is corrupt, although it clearly has something to do with the feathers of the bird's wings. More likely than either the NRSV or the NIV is the suggestion of Gordis, "is her wing that of the stork or the falcon?"[566] The ostrich's joyous wings are not for flight, as are those of other birds; yet the ostrich is not put at a disadvantage. As the concluding v. 18 notes, the ostrich, spreading its plumes, laughs at the pursuit of horse and rider.

This image is particularly important in relation to the symbolic significance of the hunt, which, as discussed above, represents the opposition between culture and nature and the defense of order against the chaotic.[567] The laughter of the ostrich echoes that of the wild ass (39:7), which similarly evades human control.

The central part of the description (39:14-17) concerns the strange lack of parental concern displayed by ostriches. That ostriches do not in fact abandon their eggs is beside the point. Such was the belief not only in ancient Israel, but also in Egypt.[568] That supposed behavior was so alien to the nurture of the young characteristic of animals and humans alike that Lam 4:3 uses it as a symbol of the collapse of elemental social bonds in a destroyed community. What is most remarkable in this passage, however, is that God explicitly takes credit for the arrangement, having deprived the ostrich of the wisdom and understanding by which other animals care for their young. Whatever the "design" of God signifies (38:3), it is not something that one could comprehend simply from the imagery of lamplight and the family circle (29:3-5). The harshness and joy of the ostrich's character are also part of that design.

39:19-25. The reference to horse and rider in v. 18 provides a transition to the section on the horse. The horse is an apparent anomaly in the series, since it is the only domesticated animal, but that is precisely the point of departure for the passage. In domesticating a horse one can make it tractable, but one cannot give it the wild lust for battle described here. That character comes from another source. In participating in battle, the horse is no more a "servant" of humans than is the wild ass.

Translators attempt to "domesticate" the text by rendering רעמה (ra'mâ) in 39:19 as "mane."[569] Yet the word means "thunder," and the striking image should not be obscured. As Habel observes, the horse is presented with the same terminology used of a warrior god.[570] "Might" (12:13), "thunder," (40:9), "majesty" (37:22), and "terror" (9:34; 13:21) are all characteristic terms for the appearance of God in glory. The comparison of the horse to the leaping locust is part of the same

565. Ibid., 67-68n. 232.
566. Gordis, The Book of Job, 459; similarly, Fohrer, Das Buch Hiob, 514. Alternatively, Dhorme, A Commentary on the Book of Job, 603, suggests "she possesses a gracious plumage and pinions." See also N. Habel, The Book of Job, OTL (Philadelphia: Westminster, 1985) 525.

567. For a depiction of Pharaoh Tutankhamen hunting ostriches, see Keel, Jahwehs Entgegnung an Ijob, 72.
568. Pope, Job, 309.
569. E.g., ibid., 311.
570. Habel, The Book of Job, 547.

complex of imagery by which the prophet Joel compares the sight of a locust plague to an approaching army of horses, the army of God on the day of Yahweh (Joel 2:1-11).

The war horse is like the ostrich in its lack of concern for consequences. As the ostrich feels no "anxiety" (פחד *paḥad*) for eggs that might be crushed and "laughs" (שׂחק *śāḥaq*) at the pursuit of the hunt, so the horse laughs at fear (ישׂחק לפחד *yiśḥaq lĕpaḥad*) as it charges into the midst of flailing weapons. The image is not exactly one of courage, however, but of something more radical, as the image of unrestrained eagerness at the smell of battle and the sound of the trumpet suggests (39:25). Animals ordinarily are drawn by the smell of water when thirsty or by the hormonal smells and characteristic cries that signal the time for breeding (Jer 2:24; 14:6). For the war horse, however, the desire for battle is as compelling as the drive for water or sex.

39:26-30. The final vignette will conclude with one of the most disturbing images in the entire series, yet it is introduced with an allusion to one of the wisdom tradition's more beautiful themes, the mystery of the flight of birds (cf. Prov 30:18-19). What is "too wonderful" for the sage and beyond Job's insight and power of command is nevertheless part of God's design. The flight of the hawk to the south (39:26) perhaps alludes to the annual migration of hundreds of thousands of raptors from eastern Europe to their wintering territory in Africa.[571] The horizontal imagery of great distance

in v. 26 is paired with vertical imagery of great heights in vv. 27-28. A natural association leads from the theme of secure nests to the provision of food for the nestlings and occasions the observation about the extraordinary vision of raptors (39:29). Only in the final verse does the grim object of the bird's sight come into view for the reader: the corpses of those slain in battle. Here is the blood that the brood will drink. This detail makes it clear that most translations err in rendering "eagle" instead of "vulture." Although נשׁר (*nešer*) can refer to either bird, it is evident that this bird is a carrion eater, not a predator (cf. Ezek 32:4; 39:4-5; Matt 24:28; Luke 17:37). Nor can one think of the vulture's food as simply another dead animal. The term "slain" (חלל *ḥālāl*) is used almost exclusively of humans in biblical Hebrew.[572] Literally, it means "pierced" and is the common term used for those killed in battle, pierced by the sword (see, e.g., Judg 9:40; 1 Sam 17:52; Jer 14:18; Ezek 31:17).

In the most disconcerting way, the divine speech asks Job and the reader to look at battle not from the human perspective of victory or punishment, liberation or oppression, but through the eyes of the horse, who finds it exhilarating, and through the eyes of the vulture, who finds it nourishing. The end of the series is marked by an inclusio. The feeding of the vulture's brood (39:29-30) corresponds to the provision of prey for the raven and its hungry fledglings (38:41). (See Reflections at 40:1-5.)

571. E. Firmage, "Zoology (Animal Profiles)," *ABD* 4:1144.

572. Dhorme, *A Commentary on the Book of Job,* 613.

Job 40:1-5, Job's Response

NIV	NRSV

40 The LORD said to Job:
 	
2"Will the one who contends with the Almighty
    correct him?
  Let him who accuses God answer him!"
3Then Job answered the LORD:
4"I am unworthy—how can I reply to you?
  I put my hand over my mouth.
5I spoke once, but I have no answer—
  twice, but I will say no more."
	40 And the LORD said to Job:
	2 "Shall a faultfinder contend with the
	    Almighty?[a]
	  Anyone who argues with God must
	    respond."
	
	3 Then Job answered the LORD:
	4 "See, I am of small account; what shall I
	    answer you?
	  I lay my hand on my mouth.
	
	a Traditional rendering of Heb *Shaddai*

NRSV

[5] I have spoken once, and I will not answer;
twice, but will proceed no further."

COMMENTARY

God's first words to Job had announced God's intention to question Job and receive an answer (38:2-3). Now following the questions of the first divine speech, God demands that answer. Although the NRSV and the NIV disagree as to which word should be the subject and which the verb in 40:2*a,* it is clear that God casts the relationship with Job in terms of a disputation. Job has reproached God publicly; God has responded. Now Job must answer. One might assume at this point that there will be a resumption of the type of disputation Job engaged in with the friends. Those disputation speeches often began with words characterizing and criticizing the opponent's speech (e.g., 8:2; 11:2-3; 12:2-3; 15:2-3; 16:2-3; 18:2-3; 19:2-3; 21:2-3; 38:2-3). Job's first words, however, characterize himself and signal his withdrawal from the disputation (40:4-5). The language and images he uses belong to the discourse of honor.[573] The NIV paraphrases the Hebrew, but what Job says literally is, "I am small" or "light" (קלל *qālal*). "Small" is the opposite of the word "honor" (כבד *kābēd*; lit., "heavy"), as is clear from the way both terms are used in 2 Sam 6:22, where Michal and David argue about his conduct. It is difficult to determine the precise nuance in 40:3. Although the word "small" can be used to signify shame and contempt (Gen 16:4-5; 2 Sam 6:22), that nuance comes to the fore when the issue is how one appears in the eyes of others. But "small" and "heavy" are also words of status and hierarchy. By applying the term to himself, Job acknowledges the difference in status between God and himself. The accompanying gesture, placing the hand over the mouth (40:4*b*), is the same gesture of deference and respect that Job's own presence evoked among even high-ranking members of his own community when he appeared among them (29:9). They refrained from speaking in his presence (29:9-10) in much the same way that Job indicates that he will no longer speak before God (40:5). The significance of what Job says and does, however, has to be seen in terms of what he had previously said about his honor and status. In 31:35-37, in the context of his long oath of clearance, Job had challenged God to answer him, declaring that he would approach God "like a prince." From that perspective, Job here does engage in an act of self-humiliation, as he implicitly acknowledges the gross impropriety of having ventured to rebuke God.

573. See C. Muenchow, "Dust and Dirt in Job 42:6," *JBL* 108 (1989) 608.

REFLECTIONS

Why does the enounter with God not end here? Why is this not enough? By word and gesture Job has indicated his intention to discontinue his argument and his acknowledgment of God's superiority in power, status, and honor. The issue of divine honor is an important one for the book of Job, but it is not the only issue. God has addressed Job concerning the way Job's words have obscured the design of God (38:2). Nothing in Job's reply indicates that he has yet perceived and understood the nature of that design and its significance for his own situation. Until he does, the encounter with God cannot find closure.

Everything that God has to say to Job is contained in this first speech. Like many people who have experienced catastrophe, Job's world had been shattered, and along with it his ability to trust. Job would draw into the abyss of his own pain the very creation that had brought him into being only to expose him to such suffering (chap. 3). For such a person, recovery of trust in the fundamental structures of existence is essential. The situation is like that of a clergy couple who undertook to foster three children whose lives had been devastated by tragedy, witnessing their mother kill their father and then be arrested. On the first night the children were in the clergy couple's care, the family gathered and read together the creation account in Genesis 1. As the husband later explained, the children had experienced the sudden and violent loss of so much that they needed to know there was something upon which they could still rely. To hear the measured and ordered words of God's creation of a good world in the presence of adults who would stand by them was a first step to restoring a sense of trust to these children. God's words of creation have something of this function for Job, although Job does not seem capable of hearing and responding to them.

God's task in responding to Job is rather more complicated than that of the foster parents caring for the devastated children, since God not only has to persuade Job of the fundamental reliability of the structures of creation but also simultaneously has to persuade him to recognize the presence of the chaotic as a part of the design of creation. As noted in the Commentary, God incorporates this theme in various ways throughout the first divine speech, in the representation of the sea (38:8-11), in the remarks about the persistence of the wicked (38:12-15), and above all in the long description of animals who are associated with the anarchic and chaotic forces in the world (38:39–39:30). Yet Job seems equally incapable of hearing and responding to this part of the divine speech.

Fundamental changes of perception do not happen easily, whether in the realm of therapeutic understanding, political commitment, or spiritual transformation. For the longest time one may hear the arguments that are supposed to persuade one or lead one to insight and yet be completely baffled by them. One may even, like Job, shrug in resignation, willing to concede without ever having understood. What blocks understanding is not an intellectual inability to comprehend. One must be ready to understand. Sometimes, too, people protect themselves, consciously or unconsciously, from having to examine the one thing they fear confronting, because that is precisely where their carefully built edifices of belief are vulnerable. By announcing one's intention to say no more, one can continue to protect from scrutiny whatever it is that one fears to examine. It takes a shrewd partner in dialogue to recognize what that protected area is and to know how to require a person to confront a reality that he or she must face if life is to be transformed. In the book of Job, God recognizes Job's inability to confront the existence of the chaotic as the source of his entrapment in a system of beliefs that can lead only to isolation and moral bitterness. Thus God's second speech to Job is one that makes confrontation with the chaotic inescapable.

JOB 40:6–42:6, UNDERSTANDING THE NATURE OF DIVINE GOVERNANCE

OVERVIEW

Compared with the long series of brief but vivid descriptions of the cosmos and its creatures that give the first divine speech its panoramic character, the focus of the second speech is tight and intense. If the rhetorical strategy of the first speech was enumeration and repetition, here it is close encounter, mediated by vivid poetry. After a brief thematic introduction (40:6-14), Job is directed to "look at Behemoth," the description of whom continues for some ten verses (40:15-24). Without transition, the focus shifts to Leviathan, who is described in a poem of thirty-four verses (41:1-34[40:25–41:26]). In the course of this poem, Job is brought, figuratively speaking, face to face with Leviathan. Immediately after the description of Leviathan, Job utters his second response, reflecting the changed understanding that leads to his withdrawing the challenge (42:1-6). Both conceptual language and poetic language play an important role in constructing the meaning of this speech. If conceptual language alone were sufficient, the speech could be much briefer; the introductory section would suffice. But the meaning of the speech is also constructed and communicated as experience. For that, the primary images and their power to evoke emotional response and recognition are also essential.

The old dispute about whether Behemoth and Leviathan are animals (e.g., the hippopotamus and the crocodile) or mythical monsters engages in a false dichotomy. They are animals in the sense that they are creatures of God. That much is said explicitly about Behemoth (40:15), and Leviathan also is best understood, as in Ps 104:26, as a creature made by God (41:33[25]; cf. Gen 1:21). Although the description of these creatures may well draw details from the hippopotamus and the crocodile, they are not "mere" animals. There is a suggestion of the primordial about Behemoth (40:15), and Leviathan is described in terms that clearly evoke the mythic traditions associated with its name (41:18-21[10-13]). These are liminal creatures, betwixt and between the categories of ordinary animal and mythic being. As with medieval maps in which the outer oceans bear the inscription "Here be dragons," Behemoth and Leviathan are creatures that mark the limits of the symbolic map of the world. Even more than the wild animals of chaps. 38–39, they represent the frightening and alien "other," bearing the terror of the chaotic in their very being. The subtler articulation of this theme in both parts of the first divine speech evoked no response from Job. Now it is amplified in a way that permits no evasion.

Job 40:6-14, The Challenge

NIV	NRSV

⁶Then the LORD spoke to Job out of the storm:
⁷"Brace yourself like a man;
  I will question you,
  and you shall answer me.
 	
⁸"Would you discredit my justice?
  Would you condemn me to justify yourself?
⁹Do you have an arm like God's,
  and can your voice thunder like his?
¹⁰Then adorn yourself with glory and splendor,
  and clothe yourself in honor and majesty.
¹¹Unleash the fury of your wrath,
  look at every proud man and bring him low,
¹²look at every proud man and humble him,
  crush the wicked where they stand.
¹³Bury them all in the dust together;
  shroud their faces in the grave.
¹⁴Then I myself will admit to you
  that your own right hand can save you."
	6Then the LORD answered Job out of the whirlwind:
	⁷ "Gird up your loins like a man;
	  I will question you, and you declare to me.
	⁸ Will you even put me in the wrong?
	  Will you condemn me that you may be justified?
	⁹ Have you an arm like God,
	  and can you thunder with a voice like his?
	
	¹⁰ "Deck yourself with majesty and dignity;
	  clothe yourself with glory and splendor.
	¹¹ Pour out the overflowings of your anger,
	  and look on all who are proud, and abase them.
	¹² Look on all who are proud, and bring them low;
	  tread down the wicked where they stand.
	¹³ Hide them all in the dust together;
	  bind their faces in the world below.^a
	¹⁴ Then I will also acknowledge to you
	  that your own right hand can give you victory."

a Heb *the hidden place*

COMMENTARY

40:6-8. The beginning of the second divine speech in v. 6 is marked by the same narrative introduction as in 38:1, and the challenge statement of 38:3 is repeated in 40:7. The thematic question corresponding to 38:2 is announced in v. 8 and elaborated in vv. 9-14. In v. 8, God uses three words that have been of key importance for Job. In Job's mouth they have had legal connotations: "a claim of right" (משפט *mišpāṭ*; 9:15; 27:2), "declare guilty" (רשע *rāšaʿ*; 9:20; 10:2), "declare innocent" (צדק *ṣādēq*; 9:15, 20). But *mišpāṭ* has other connotations as well. It belongs to the language of governance, as well as to the language of judging.[574] In the question of v. 8, the double resonance of *mišpāṭ* points to unexamined problems inherent in Job's paradigm of understanding. Job's legal paradigm is a system of simple oppositions: For one party to be right, the other must be wrong; for one to be innocent, the other must be guilty. If *mišpāṭ* is simply about judicial decisions, then the choice is between God's taking away Job's right (27:2), and Job's discrediting God's justice (40:8). But the *mišpāṭ* that is God's governance of the world cannot be reduced to legal categories. In attempting to do so, Job has fundamentally misconstrued the nature of the world and God's role. Thus the thematic question about governance in 40:8 is analogous to the question about the design of creation in 38:2.

40:9-14. These verses introduce a shift in language and imagery. Here the topics are power and pride, anticipating the imagery associated with Behemoth and Leviathan in the body of the speech. Reduced to its barest outlines, this section rhetorically asks Job if he has power comparable to God's and the ability to bring down the proud. If so, then God will recognize Job's ability to win his own victory. Behemoth and Leviathan thus serve as examples of creatures of power and pride whom Job could not possibly overcome. That much is clear. The more difficult question is what this speech says about the nature of the world and divine governance. As in the first speech, one must carefully note not only how traditional speech and images are invoked but also how they may be used differently than in other settings, in order to determine what they mean in this particular context.

The challenge to Job in vv. 9-14 is constructed out of traditional, almost clichéd language about God. The arm (Exod 15:16; Pss 77:15[16]; 89:13[14]; Isa 63:5) and thundering voice (37:4; Pss 18:13[14]; 77:18[19]; 104:7) are typical attributes of the divine warrior. Similarly, the abstract terms of v. 10—"majesty," "dignity," "glory," and "splendor"—all connote the awe-inspiring quality of divinity (Exod 15:7; Pss 96:6; 104:1; 138:5; Isa 2:10, 19, 21; 24:14).

This description of God introduces the vocabulary of pride that is thematically important throughout the second speech. Terms for "pride" in Hebrew are frequently derived from words referring to height. For instance, the waves of the sea in 38:11 are described literally as "high" (גאון *gāʾôn*), metaphorically as "proud." Similarly, here in v. 10 the words translated "majesty" and "dignity" ("glory" and "splendor") literally have to do with height (*gāʾôn* and גבה *gōbah*). A related word (גאה *gēʾeh*) is the negative term for "pride" in vv. 11*b* and 12*a*. As these examples already suggest, "height" is a complex category in biblical imagery. In its associations with God it is wholly positive. But precisely because it is godlike, it provokes ambivalence as a human characteristic. As "majesty," it is tolerated and in certain contexts even encouraged, unless it becomes excessive "pride." Then what has grown too high is "brought low" and "abased" (40:11*b*, 12*a*).[575] In the allegories of Ezekiel 31 and Daniel 4 the goodness of the trees that nurture all the creatures of the world is in part a virtue of their height; yet height as arrogance is the fatal flaw that finally requires that they be cut down (Ezek 31:10-12; Dan 4:30[27]). One cannot say of *gāʾôn* that it is either good or bad, right or wrong. The issue is one of appropriate limits. Thus the symbolic system associated with *gāʾôn* and related words is one of regulation and containment. Such a way of imagining the world and its governance belongs to an entirely different paradigm from Job's legal categories.

---

574. S. H. Scholnick, "The Meaning of Mishpat in the Book of Job," *JBL* 101 (1983) 522.

575. In apocalyptic literature, this symbolic system is turned into a veritable philosophy of history. See Daniel 8; 10–12.

The only power capable of this kind of regulation, the reversal of high into low, arrogance into abasement, is God. Thus the transcendent height of God in 40:10 parallels images of depth in 40:13 (dust and the hidden place—i.e., the underworld). Echoing the image of the "arm of God" with which the passage began, God says that if Job can abase the proud, then God will acknowledge that Job's "own right hand" can give him victory (40:14), for he will be like God.

The ambivalence surrounding the category of pride is in large part what makes the interpretation of the figures of Behemoth and Leviathan so difficult. Following vv. 9-14, they are clearly examples of the proud, whom Job is challenged to "bring low." Leviathan, in particular, is traditionally associated with the chaos monster, whom God defeats in battle. Yet in chaps. 40–41 they are not presented as enemies of God. Although God's capacity to overcome them is acknowledged, hostility between God and these creatures plays no role in the description. Rather, they appear as magnificent creatures whose pride is appropriate to their place in creation. One should not attempt to resolve the ambiguity in their representation. It is an irreducible part of the role they play in the divine speeches. (See Reflections at 41:1-34.)

Job 40:15-24, Behemoth

NIV	NRSV

[15]"Look at the behemoth,[a]
    which I made along with you
    and which feeds on grass like an ox.
[16]What strength he has in his loins,
    what power in the muscles of his belly!
[17]His tail[b] sways like a cedar;
    the sinews of his thighs are close-knit.
[18]His bones are tubes of bronze,
    his limbs like rods of iron.
[19]He ranks first among the works of God,
    yet his Maker can approach him with his
       sword.
[20]The hills bring him their produce,
    and all the wild animals play nearby.
[21]Under the lotus plants he lies,
    hidden among the reeds in the marsh.
[22]The lotuses conceal him in their shadow;
    the poplars by the stream surround him.
[23]When the river rages, he is not alarmed;
    he is secure, though the Jordan should surge
       against his mouth.
[24]Can anyone capture him by the eyes,[c]
    or trap him and pierce his nose?"
	[15] "Look at Behemoth,
	    which I made just as I made you;
	    it eats grass like an ox.
	[16] Its strength is in its loins,
	    and its power in the muscles of its belly.
	[17] It makes its tail stiff like a cedar;
	    the sinews of its thighs are knit together.
	[18] Its bones are tubes of bronze,
	    its limbs like bars of iron.
	
	[19] "It is the first of the great acts of God—
	    only its Maker can approach it with the sword.
	[20] For the mountains yield food for it
	    where all the wild animals play.
	[21] Under the lotus plants it lies,
	    in the covert of the reeds and in the marsh.
	[22] The lotus trees cover it for shade;
	    the willows of the wadi surround it.
	[23] Even if the river is turbulent, it is not
	       frightened;
	    it is confident though Jordan rushes against
	       its mouth.
	[24] Can one take it with hooks[a]
	    or pierce its nose with a snare?"

[a]15 Possibly the hippopotamus or the elephant [b]17 Possibly trunk [c]24 Or *by a water hole*	[a] Cn: Heb *in his eyes*

COMMENTARY

The name "Behemoth" is simply the "plural of majesty" of the ordinary word for "animal" or "cattle."[576] Thus it is the animal *par excellence*. Unlike Leviathan, a name attested in several other places in biblical and non-biblical sources, there are no earlier instances of the name "Behemoth." Possibly, it is a creation of the Job poet, who needed a land animal to pair with the sea creature Leviathan, or it may be the poet's rendering of an older tradition otherwise unattested.

What sort of animal is the model for Behemoth? Its habitat is described as a marshy place where reeds, wadi poplars, and the thorny lotus grow (40:21-22). It is closely associated with rivers, in particular the Jordan, although its food is said to come from the mountains (40:20, 23). Its fondness for water suggests to many that Behemoth is modeled after the hippopotamus, although the mention of mountains is something of an embarrassment for this interpretation. That there were no hippopotamuses in the Jordan in antiquity is no fatal objection, since a legendary creature may live where a poet wishes to place it. In Egyptian mythology, the hippopotamus was an ominous creature, associated with the god Seth, the opponent of Horus. The temple of Edfu, for example, contains illustrations of the god Horus hunting Seth in the form of a hippopotamus.[577] Such a background would provide Behemoth with an aura comparable to that of Leviathan. It is also possible, however, that the primary animal imagery from which Behemoth is shaped is that of the water buffalo, which also enjoys submerging itself in rivers and marshy areas and inhabited the Lake Huleh region in northern Palestine in antiquity. Behemoth is said to "eat grass like an ox," and numerous bull-like monsters appear in Ugaritic and Mesopotamian mythology.[578] The terrifying "Bull of Heaven" let loose by the goddess Ishtar and killed by Gilgamesh and Enkidu is the best-known example.[579] Later apocalyptic literature speculated on the nature of Behemoth and Leviathan. According to 2 Esdras 6:49-52, they were formed on the fifth day of creation. Because the sea was not large enough to hold both of them, Behemoth was given a part of the dry land where a thousand mountains stood, and Leviathan was left in the sea (cf. Apoc. Bar. 29:4; *1 Enoch* 60:7-9).

The passage about Behemoth divides into two parts, vv. 15-19 and vv. 20-24. The first section begins and ends with references to Behemoth's creation (40:15, 19) and contains a description of its extraordinary strength.

40:15-19. Earlier in the chapter God had rhetorically asked if Job could compare with God in power (v. 9). Here Job's attention is directed to Behemoth, a creature that, God says, "I made along with you." Yet even this fellow creature's power greatly exceeds Job's. The focus on the loins and belly in v. 16 and the thighs in v. 17*b* makes it quite likely that the word "tail" (זנב *zānāb*) in v. 17 is a euphemism for "penis," as is often suggested.[580] Although it is not at all clear why a literal tail would be a symbol of strength or be compared to a cedar tree, the masculine association of a large erection with power fits the context well. Bulls often symbolize sexual potency, another reason for thinking of Behemoth as a bovine creature rather than as one modeled after the hippopotamus. Corresponding to the impressive sinews in v. 17, the bones are described in v. 18 as being made of bronze and iron. In summarizing, God praises the powerful Behemoth as "the first" or "the best" of God's works (v. 19*a*; the word ראשית [*rē 'šît*] can have either or both senses). What exactly is meant by this claim? The same phrase is used to describe primordial wisdom in Prov 8:22, where it clearly has a temporal meaning. Behemoth is possibly being depicted as the most ancient of all creatures,[581] but the focus on Behemoth's extraordinary power suggests that its superiority is praised (so NIV). Such a claim parallels the presentation of Levia-

576. The earlier attempt to relate Behemoth to a supposed Egyptian term for "hippopotamus" is now recognized as erroneous. See E. Dhorme, *A Commentary on the Book of Job,* trans. H. Knight (London: Nelson, 1967) 618.

577. O. Keel, *Jahwehs Entgegnung an Ijob* (Goettingen: Vandenhoeck & Ruprecht, 1978) 138-39; V. Kubina, *Die Gottesreden im Buche Hiob,* FThSt (Freiburg: Herder, 1979) 71.

578. M. Pope, *Job,* 3rd ed., AB 15 (Garden City, N.Y.: Doubleday, 1979) 321-22.

579. James B. Pritchard, ed., *Ancient Near Eastern Texts Relating to the Old Testament* (*ANET*), 3rd ed. with supplement (Princeton: Princeton University Press, 1969) 83-85.

580. E.g., Pope, *Job,* 324; N. Habel, *The Book of Job,* OTL (Philadelphia: Westminster, 1985) 553.

581. G. Fuchs, *Mythos und Hiobdichtung* (Stuttgart: Kohlhammer, 1993) 238.

than, too, as a creature "without equal," a king over all the proud (41:33-34[25-26]).

Often, an obscure line can become the basis for an interpretation of the whole passage. The sentence "only its Maker can approach it with the sword" (v. 19*b*) is just such a case. The text and grammar of v. 19*b* are much more ambiguous than the NRSV and the NIV suggest. There are no words in the Hebrew for "only" or "yet" or "with." The verse literally reads: "He is the first of the ways of God; his maker brings near his sword." As the NRSV and the NIV render the line, the verse implies that God does, or at least could do, battle with Behemoth. Basing their ideas on such a translation, some commentators attempt to understand the divine speeches as an allusion to the old *Chaoskampf* myth, the ancient battle between the creator god and the chaos monster.[582] A translation of v. 19*b* that implies a confrontation between God and Behemoth is not impossible in the larger context of the chapter, especially in the light of the reference to "bringing low the proud" as a godlike act (40:9), but it does not fit the immediate context well. The force of the descriptions of both Behemoth and Leviathan is not containment of their power but the vivid representation of the immensity of their prowess.

Alternatively, some have argued that the sword

in question is Behemoth's[583] and that Yahweh brings the sword to Behemoth as a token of his lordship over other animals (40:20). The word translated "his maker" (העשׂו *hā'ōśô*) is grammatically anomalous, however, and the Hebrew consonants suggest that it is actually the word "made" (*he'āśû*), the same word that occurs in the description of Leviathan as "made without fear" (41:33[25]). Without changing the consonantal text of v. 19*b*, the line could be revocalized to read: "He is the first of the ways of God, made to dominate his companions."[584] Such a translation fits smoothly into the context. But the point is not so much to recommend this emendation as to caution against reading into this passage a version of the *Chaoskampf* on a shaky textual basis. Violence is not what the passage associates with Behemoth.

40:20-24. The second part of the description concerns Behemoth's idyllic life. The mountains provide food (v. 20*a*; cf. Ezek 36:8) in a setting of peace where animals frolic (v. 20*b*), while the marshlands provide a shady resting place (vv. 21-22). Far from being an aggressive creature, Behemoth is associated with security. The very Jordan at flood (Josh 3:15) does not cause him to flee (v. 23). Even less need Behemoth fear capture by humans (v. 24). (See Reflections at 41:1-34.)

582. E.g., T. Mettinger, "God the Victor," in *The Voice from the Whirlwind*, ed. L. Perdue and C. Gilpin (Nashville: Abingdon, 1992) 45-46; J. C. L. Gibson, "On Evil in the Book of Job," *Biblical and Other Studies in Memory of P. C. Craigie*, JSOTSup 67 (Sheffield: JSOT Press, 1988) 399-419.

583. H. Rowley, *The Book of Job*, rev. ed., NCB (Grand Rapids, Mich.: Eerdmans, 1976; original ed., 1970) 257.

584. See the discussion in ibid., 256. Similarly, Dhorme, *A Commentary on the Book of Job*, 621; G. Fohrer, *Das Buch Hiob*, KAT xvi (Guetersloh: Gerd Mohn, 1963) 522.

Job 41:1-34, Leviathan

NIV

41 "Can you pull in the leviathan[a] with a fishhook
> or tie down his tongue with a rope?
2Can you put a cord through his nose
> or pierce his jaw with a hook?
3Will he keep begging you for mercy?
> Will he speak to you with gentle words?
4Will he make an agreement with you
> for you to take him as your slave for life?
5Can you make a pet of him like a bird

a1 Possibly the crocodile

NRSV

41[a] "Can you draw out Leviathan[b] with a fishhook,
> or press down its tongue with a cord?
2 Can you put a rope in its nose,
> or pierce its jaw with a hook?
3 Will it make many supplications to you?
> Will it speak soft words to you?
4 Will it make a covenant with you
> to be taken as your servant forever?
5 Will you play with it as with a bird,

a Ch 40.25 in Heb   b Or the crocodile

NIV

or put him on a leash for your girls?
⁶Will traders barter for him?
    Will they divide him up among the merchants?
⁷Can you fill his hide with harpoons
    or his head with fishing spears?
⁸If you lay a hand on him,
    you will remember the struggle and never do
        it again!
⁹Any hope of subduing him is false;
    the mere sight of him is overpowering.
¹⁰No one is fierce enough to rouse him.
    Who then is able to stand against me?
¹¹Who has a claim against me that I must pay?
    Everything under heaven belongs to me.

¹²"I will not fail to speak of his limbs,
    his strength and his graceful form.
¹³Who can strip off his outer coat?
    Who would approach him with a bridle?
¹⁴Who dares open the doors of his mouth,
    ringed about with his fearsome teeth?
¹⁵His back hasᵃ rows of shields
    tightly sealed together;
¹⁶each is so close to the next
    that no air can pass between.
¹⁷They are joined fast to one another;
    they cling together and cannot be parted.
¹⁸His snorting throws out flashes of light;
    his eyes are like the rays of dawn.
¹⁹Firebrands stream from his mouth;
    sparks of fire shoot out.
²⁰Smoke pours from his nostrils
    as from a boiling pot over a fire of reeds.
²¹His breath sets coals ablaze,
    and flames dart from his mouth.
²²Strength resides in his neck;
    dismay goes before him.
²³The folds of his flesh are tightly joined;
    they are firm and immovable.
²⁴His chest is hard as rock,
    hard as a lower millstone.
²⁵When he rises up, the mighty are terrified;
    they retreat before his thrashing.
²⁶The sword that reaches him has no effect,
    nor does the spear or the dart or the javelin.
²⁷Iron he treats like straw
    and bronze like rotten wood.

ᵃ15 Or *His pride is his*

NRSV

or will you put it on leash for your girls?
⁶ Will traders bargain over it?
    Will they divide it up among the merchants?
⁷ Can you fill its skin with harpoons,
    or its head with fishing spears?
⁸ Lay hands on it;
    think of the battle; you will not do it again!
⁹ᵃ Any hope of capturing itᵇ will be
        disappointed;
    were not even the godsᶜ overwhelmed at
        the sight of it?
¹⁰ No one is so fierce as to dare to stir it up.
    Who can stand before it?ᵈ
¹¹ Who can confront itᵈ and be safe?ᵉ
    —under the whole heaven, who?ᶠ

¹² "I will not keep silence concerning its limbs,
    or its mighty strength, or its splendid frame.
¹³ Who can strip off its outer garment?
    Who can penetrate its double coat of mail?ᵍ
¹⁴ Who can open the doors of its face?
    There is terror all around its teeth.
¹⁵ Its backʰ is made of shields in rows,
    shut up closely as with a seal.
¹⁶ One is so near to another
    that no air can come between them.
¹⁷ They are joined one to another;
    they clasp each other and cannot be
        separated.
¹⁸ Its sneezes flash forth light,
    and its eyes are like the eyelids of the dawn.
¹⁹ From its mouth go flaming torches;
    sparks of fire leap out.
²⁰ Out of its nostrils comes smoke,
    as from a boiling pot and burning rushes.
²¹ Its breath kindles coals,
    and a flame comes out of its mouth.
²² In its neck abides strength,
    and terror dances before it.
²³ The folds of its flesh cling together;
    it is firmly cast and immovable.
²⁴ Its heart is as hard as stone,
    as hard as the lower millstone.
²⁵ When it raises itself up the gods are afraid;
    at the crashing they are beside themselves.
²⁶ Though the sword reaches it, it does not avail,

ᵃCh 41.1 in Heb   ᵇHeb *of it*   ᶜCn Compare Symmachus Syr:
Heb *one is*   ᵈHeb *me*   ᵉGk:Heb *that I shall repay*   ᶠHeb *to
me*   ᵍGk: Heb *bridle*   ʰCn Compare Gk Vg: Heb *pride*

NIV

28Arrows do not make him flee;
   slingstones are like chaff to him.
29A club seems to him but a piece of straw;
   he laughs at the rattling of the lance.
30His undersides are jagged potsherds,
   leaving a trail in the mud like a threshing
      sledge.
31He makes the depths churn like a boiling caldron
   and stirs up the sea like a pot of ointment.
32Behind him he leaves a glistening wake;
   one would think the deep had white hair.
33Nothing on earth is his equal—
   a creature without fear.
34He looks down on all that are haughty;
   he is king over all that are proud."

NRSV

   nor does the spear, the dart, or the javelin.
27 It counts iron as straw,
   and bronze as rotten wood.
28 The arrow cannot make it flee;
   slingstones, for it, are turned to chaff.
29 Clubs are counted as chaff;
   it laughs at the rattle of javelins.
30 Its underparts are like sharp potsherds;
   it spreads itself like a threshing sledge on
      the mire.
31 It makes the deep boil like a pot;
   it makes the sea like a pot of ointment.
32 It leaves a shining wake behind it;
   one would think the deep to be
      white-haired.
33 On earth it has no equal,
   a creature without fear.
34 It surveys everything that is lofty;
   it is king over all that are proud."

COMMENTARY

Whereas Behemoth's extraordinary power finds its artistic representation in images of repose and security, Leviathan is rendered in images of violence, fire, and turmoil. The segue between the two poems is hunting imagery, which closes the poem on Behemoth (40:24) and opens the one on Leviathan (41:1[40:25]). As a motif, hunting is much more extensively developed in the Leviathan section, since it provides a way to talk about Leviathan's dangerous violence.

Unlike "Behemoth," the name "Leviathan" brings with it a well-developed set of symbolic associations. Both in Ugaritic mythology and in the Bible, "Leviathan" (or "Lotan") is the name of a sea monster with which Yahweh, Baal, and Anat do battle. In the Baal epic, the god Mot refers to a victory of Baal, "when you killed Lotan, the Fleeing Serpent, finished off the Twisting Serpent, the seven-headed monster." Elsewhere, the goddess Anat says, "Didn't I demolish El's Darling, Sea? didn't I finish off the divine river, Rabbim? didn't I snare the Dragon? I enveloped him, I demolished the Twisting Serpent, the seven-headed monster."[585] In the Bible, the psalmist praises Yahweh, saying, "It was you who split open the sea by your power;/ you broke the heads of the monster in the waters./ It was you who crushed the heads of Leviathan/ and gave him as food to the creatures of the desert" (Ps 74:13-14 NIV). Establishment of the orders of creation follows this victory. Isaiah 27:1 describes the eschatological future as involving the same act: "In that day Yahweh will punish with his sword, his fierce, great and powerful sword, Leviathan the gliding serpent, Leviathan the coiling serpent; he will slay the monster of the sea" (author's trans.). Similar associations are in Job's mind when he refers to those prepared to "rouse up Leviathan" in a curse (3:8). As the Ugaritic quotations suggest, Leviathan is one of a group of closely related figures, all of whom are associated with the sea in its symbolic value as chaotic power, represented in the Bible by Rahab the dragon (9:13; 26:12; Ps 89:10[11]; Isa 51:9) and the sea monster תנין (tannîn; 7:12; Ps 74:13; Isa 27:1; Ezek 29:3; 32:2).

The fluid boundary between the mythical and the nonmythical, as well as the ambivalent status of the chaotic in relation to creation, is suggested by texts in which tannîn and Leviathan are crea-

585. M. Coogan, *Stories from Ancient Canaan* (Philadelphia: Westminster, 1978) 92, 106.

tures formed by God and not at all hostile. In Gen 1:21, the *tannînim* are sea animals created as part of the work of the fifth day of creation, concerning which God said that "it was good." In Ps 148:7, the *tannînim* are called upon to praise God as part of universal praise. Similarly, Leviathan in Ps 104:26 is an animal that God has formed to play in the sea. The representation of Leviathan in chap. 41 [chaps. 40–41] draws associations from both the mythic tradition and the tradition represented in Genesis and the book of Psalms.

The passage on Leviathan can be divided into three parts: (1) 41:1-12[40:25–41:4], which consists of rhetorical questions about hunting Leviathan and God's comments upon such an enterprise; (2) 41:13-24[5-16], the physical description of Leviathan; and (3) 41:25-32[17-24], Leviathan's defiance of attack and movement out to sea. A concluding description of Leviathan as king over all the proud concludes the poem (41:33-34[25-26]).

41:1-12. 41:1-8. The barrage of rhetorical questions in 41:1-7[40:25-31] is predicated upon absurdity. Images of capture begin and end the series. So little is known about the technologies of ancient hunting and fishing that it is not entirely clear whether an ancient audience would have recognized the use of hook and cord, harpoon and spear as specific to a particular kind of hunting.[586] In any case, these would be ludicrously inadequate for Leviathan. The practice of controlling captives with a rope passed through a hole in the nose or cheek is well attested (2 Kgs 19:28; Isa 37:29; Ezek 29:4; 38:4),[587] but creates an absurd image when applied to Leviathan. In Egyptian myth, Isis warns Horus not to listen to the crocodile if it speaks sweetly to him.[588] The image in vv. 3-4 (40:29-30) is of Leviathan begging not to be killed and offering perpetual servitude as an alternative. The height of domestication is the image of Leviathan as a child's pet (41:5[40:30]). In 41:6[40:31], the rhetorical question imagines the dead Leviathan cut up and sold as meat (41:6[40:31]), so huge that it has to be divided among many traders. That image provides a transition back to the topic of hunting, which

brings the series of rhetorical questions to a close (41:7[40:31]), rounded off by the comment that the memory of one encounter would be enough to prevent one's ever attempting another (41:8[40:32]).

41:9-12. The following four verses provide a transition between the rhetorical questions and the description of Leviathan's appearance and behavior. Escalating the imagery from that of 41:8[40:32], which spoke of laying hands on Leviathan, 41:9[1] insists that the mere sight of it is enough to cast one down. The syntax of the line is awkward, and some translators follow the Greek text of Symmachus and the Syriac in reading "the gods were cast down at the sight of him" (so NRSV), which would require only a modest emendation of the Hebrew. The fear of the gods is a frequent motif in both Ugaritic and Mesopotamian myth. The threatening message that Yam (Sea) sends Baal causes the assembled gods to drop their heads onto their knees in fear.[589] In the Enuma Elish, after the first unsuccessful confrontation with the chaos monster Tiamat, the gods are of the opinion, "No god can go [to battle and], facing Tiamat, escape [with his life]."[590] Following the NRSV, the text alludes to the mythic character of Leviathan.

Textual problems and ambiguous references make the next three verses susceptible to more than one interpretation, leading to radically different interpretations of the meaning of the entire speech. Since so much hangs on the issue, it is necessary to explain the alternatives. The first half of 41:10[2] is clear, echoing 3:8. In the second half of the verse, however, the Hebrew manuscripts are divided between "who is able to stand against him" (so NRSV) and "who is able to stand against me" (so NIV). One cannot decide between the two alternatives until the problems of the following verse are resolved.

The text of 41:11[3] is clearly first-person speech. Some interpreters consider this first-person reference out of place and change it to third-person speech, so that the passage is understood as God's describing the inability of anyone to confront the powerful Leviathan.[591] Those inter-

586. These are considered not to be the weapons of crocodile hunting in any case. E. Ruprecht, "Das Nilpferd im Hiobbuch. Beobachtungen zu der sogennanten zweiten Gottesrede," *VT* 21 (1971) 221-22; Kubina, *Die Gottesreden im Buche Hiob*, 91.

587. See also James B. Pritchard, ed., *The Ancient Near East in Pictures Related to the Old Testament* (*ANEP*) (Princeton: Princeton University Press, 1954) pls. 296, 447.

588. Kubina, *Die Gottesreden im Buche Hiob*, 74.

589. *ANET*, 130.

590. Ibid., 64.

591. E.g., Dhorme, *A Commentary on the Book of Job*, 631; H. Rowley, *The Book of Job*, rev. ed., NCB (Grand Rapids, Mich.: Eerdmans, 1976; original ed., 1970) 261; Fohrer, *Das Buch Hiob*, 527; R. Gordis, *The Book of Job: Commentary, New Translation, and Special Studies* (New York: Jewish Theological Seminary, 5738/1978) 483; A. de Wilde, *Das Buch Hiob*, OTS xxii (Leiden: Brill, 1981) 387-99.

preters also read 41:10[2] as third-person. The advantage of this interpretation is that it preserves the consistency of the references. Accordingly, a new section begins in 41:12[4] with God declaring the intention to describe Leviathan's appearance.

Other interpreters keep the first-person references in 41:11[3] and interpret them as referring to God (so NIV).[592] They generally also choose the first-person pronoun in 41:10[2]. In this way, Leviathan serves as a point of comparison for God. If Job (or anyone else) cannot confront Leviathan, how much less could Job confront God? This is not an impossible interpretation, since God has mockingly challenged Job to gird his loins (40:7) and has rhetorically asked if he has an arm and a voice like God's (40:9). Nevertheless, the appearance of this topic in the midst of the description of Leviathan seems abrupt. Those who take 41:10b-11[2b-3] as referring to God are divided on their interpretation of 41:12[4]. Some take it as beginning a new section in which God will describe Leviathan's appearance (so NIV). Others, however, translate 41:12[4] very differently: "Did I not silence his boasting, his mighty word and his persuasive case?"[593] The difficult question is whether this translation fits the context. In 40:12, God had challenged Job to humble the proud. Accordingly, 41:12[4] would be an example of God's humbling Leviathan's proud boasting. The problem is that confrontation between God and Leviathan does not seem to be the point of the speech. What follows does not describe God's victory over the chaos monster but a celebration of the awesome and terrifying power of Leviathan, culminating in the declaration that he is unequalled on earth, king over all the children of pride (41:33-34[25-26]). Moreover, the interpretation of 41:12[4] as God's silencing Leviathan's boasting does not fit well with the problem Job presents. Job has not questioned God's power, but he has been unable to recognize the presence of the chaotic within God's design and governance of the world.

Consequently, the translations and interpretations of 41:10-12[2-4] that take these verses as referring simply to the power and dangerousness of Leviathan are to be preferred (e.g. NRSV). The linguistic arguments of Habel, Rowold, and Mettinger, however, suggest an even more provocative possibility. One might take 40:10[2] as God's speech to the effect that no one can stand against Leviathan, 40:11[3] as a quotation of Leviathan's boast, and 40:12[4] as God's statement that God will *not* silence Leviathan's boast.[594] Thus:

God: Who is so fierce as to rouse him up? Who is there who could stand against him?

Leviathan: Whoever confronts me, I will repay. Under all the heavens, he is mine!

God: I will not silence his boasting, his mighty word, and his persuasive case.

Leviathan's claim to repay any who confront it simply repeats what God has already said (41:8[40:32]) and will shortly describe in more detail (41:25-29[17-21]). Significantly, Leviathan describes the sphere of its dominion as "under all the heavens." Leviathan does not challenge heaven itself. Its boasting is confined to the domain appropriate to its status. Moreover, God seems to endorse just this claim, since God will end the poem by declaring, "on earth it has no equal" or, as the words might also be translated, "on earth there is no one who can dominate it" (41:33[25]). Because it says only what it is entitled to say, God shocks Job by refusing to silence Leviathan's boasting. The description of Leviathan that follows in 41:13-32[5-24] is thus designed not only to make the validity of Leviathan's claim indisputable but also to provide an experience of this chaotic force whose place in the world cannot be ignored.

41:13-24. 41:13-17. As Perdue notes, beauty as well as power characterizes Leviathan in Yahweh's description of this extraordinary creature.[595] Armored like a warrior, its head is wreathed about with fire and smoke, impervious to any form of weapon, its thrashing is capable of transforming

592. E.g., Habel, *The Book of Job*, 555; J. E. Hartley, *The Book of Job*, NICOT (Grand Rapids, Mich.: Eerdmans, 1988) 531-32; Perdue, 227.

593. Mettinger, "God the Victor," 235n. 34. Similarly, Habel, *The Book of Job*, 551; H. Rowold, "Mi hu? Li hu!" *JBL* 105 (1986) 104-9. The verse is not marked as a question in the text but is taken as an implicit question by these scholars.

594. Although talking animals are not common in the Bible (see only the snake in Genesis 2–3 and Balaam's ass in Numbers 22), the motif of Leviathan's speech has already been introduced in the poem in 41:3[40:27]. In contrast to those imagined "soft words," Leviathan's boast is proud and defiant.

595. L. Perdue, *Wisdom in Revolt: Metaphorical Theology in the Book of Job*, JSOTSup 112 (Sheffield: JSOT, 1991) 230n. 7.

the appearance of the sea itself. The description of Leviathan begins by visualizing its skin as a coat of impenetrable mail (41:13[5] NRSV, reading with the LXX; cf. the description of Goliath's armor in 1 Sam 17:5). Leviathan's terrifying face is the next focus of attention. Its jaws, poetically described as "the doors of its face," are the setting for its fearsome teeth, similar perhaps to the "sharp-toothed" dragons created by Tiamat for her battle with the gods in the Enuma Elish.[596]

The common practice of emending "pride" to "back" in 41:15[7] and interpreting vv. 16-17[8-9] as referring to Leviathan's scales is questionable. Words for "pride" are of such thematic importance in this speech (40:10, 12; 41:34[26]) that one should hesitate to emend. It is perfectly meaningful to translate "his rows of shields are his pride" (cf. TNK). Moreover, the emendation also obscures the focus on the description of the face. The rows of shields are Leviathan's teeth, set so close that there is no space between them.[597]

41:18-21. The description next moves to the fiery phenomena that stream from Leviathan's mouth, eyes, and nose. Fieriness is a characteristic of divine beings, both gods and monsters. In Ugaritic myth, when the messengers of Sea deliver their words to the gods, "fire, burning fire doth flash; a whetted sword [are their e]yes."[598] When the god Marduk speaks, he blazes forth fire.[599] Yahweh's face, too, is a source of fire, as Ps 18:8[9] indicates: "Smoke went up from his nostrils,/ and devouring fire from his mouth;/ glowing coals flamed forth from [it]" (NRSV; cf. Ps 29:7). In the context of so much terror the image of "eyes like the rays of the dawn" disorients by its beauty. As the NIV's translation suggests, the word does not refer to a physical part of the eye (NRSV, "eyelids") but to the glance coming from the eye, imaged as a beam of light. Dawn's light has a reddish glow to it, as the German word *morgenrot* (lit., "the red of morning") and the Homeric formula "rosy-fingered dawn" reflect. Here the inner fire that

burns in Leviathan is projected out through its glance, as dawn sends out its reddish rays.[600]

41:22-24. Moving on from the face, the poet traces Leviathan's neck, the folds of flesh below the neck, and the chest. The artistry in the sequence of this description is subtle, for one would see those features only if Leviathan raised itself up, which is precisely what is described in the following verse (41:25[17]). It is as though the visual description itself introduces motion into the picture. The images of 41:22-24[14-16] are mostly of hardness and impenetrability, culminating in the description of Leviathan's chest (lit., "heart") as like a lower millstone.

41:25-32. The raising up of Leviathan (41:25[17]) should present an adversary with the opportunity to strike it. Yet even the gods are terrified of Leviathan because it is invulnerable to any weapon. The catalogue of weaponry in 41:26-29[18-21]—sword, spear, dart, javelin, iron, bronze, arrow, slingstone, club, lance—freezes the moment when Leviathan lifts itself up and allows the eye to contemplate its invincibility. In the final line of the sequence the motif of the wild animal's laughter is again introduced. Just as the wild ass laughs at the noisy town (39:7), the ostrich laughs at the pursuing horse and rider (39:18), the war horse laughs at fear (39:22), and the animals of the field frolic (lit., "laugh") in the company of Behemoth (40:20), so also Leviathan laughs at the rattling lance (41:29[21]). These creatures and the anarchistic, chaotic element of creation that they represent are utterly beyond the control of the human will.

The physical description of Leviathan, interrupted by the catalogue of weapons, resumes in 41:30[22], with a comparison of its rough and scaly belly to jagged potsherds. But the focus is on the transformation of shore and sea as Leviathan moves over them. Habel is probably right that "mire" (טיט *ṭîṭ*; cf. Isa 57:20), "the depths" (מצולה *měṣûlâ*; cf. Jonah 2:4), and "the deep" (תהום *těhôm*; cf. 28:14; 38:16) are evocative of the chaotic, as is the image of churning water.[601] Yet the three images used are progressively less violent and increasingly beautiful. The image of

596. *ANET,* 62.

597. So N. H. Tur-Sinai, *The Book of Job: A New Commentary* (Jerusalem: Kiryath Sepher, 1957) 569; Kubina, 99.

598. *ANET,* 130.

599. Ibid., 62.

600. Hartley, *The Book of Job,* 532n. 42, notes that in ancient Egyptian hieroglyphs the eyes of the crocodile stand for the red morning light.

601. N. Habel, *The Book of Job,* OTL (Philadelphia: Westminster, 1985) 573.

the threshing sledge is elsewhere associated with violence (e.g., Amos 3:1; Isa 41:15). A pot of boiling ointment is also an image of agitation, yet is one not associated with danger. The small size of such a pot subtly introduces an element of visual distance into the picture, as though one were watching the sea from far away. The sense of distance is further enhanced in the last verse of the series, as one looks not at Leviathan, but at its wake as it swims away. The image with which the wake is visualized is no longer one of agitation, but a calm image of the deep as white-haired.

41:33-34. As God declared Behemoth's status as "first in rank among the works of God," so Leviathan's place is proclaimed. Leviathan is no threat to God, but upon earth it is supreme. As noted above, the word for "without equal" is spelled the same way as the phrase "none can dominate him" (אין משלו; *'ên mošlô*; 41:33[40:25]); both meanings are probably intended here. The preceding poem is ample testimony to that claim and to the statement that he is "made without fear." As in chap. 39, the conclusion of the poem is marked by an inclusio, as 41:34[26] echoes 40:11*b*. There Job was challenged to "look on every proud one and bring him low." Here it is said that Leviathan "looks on all that are haughty." Far from being brought low, Leviathan is their king.

REFLECTIONS

At the end of the dialogue, as Job prepared to make his decisive challenge to God, he gave a lengthy account of his moral world and the basis upon which he was confronting God and seeking vindication. Job's moral thinking, both its admirable qualities and its disturbing elements, have been considered in the Reflections to Job 29–31. Here one may simply note that it was a fairly rigid moral perspective, quite without resources for dealing with the ineradicable presence of the chaotic as a part of the natural or the social world. What Job has been confronted with in the divine speeches will have rendered his old moral categories no longer adequate to his new perception. Indeed, anyone who approaches the divine speeches with a dogmatic, legally oriented moral system is likely to feel a similar disorientation. How is one to rebuild a coherent moral perspective after the experience of the voice from the whirlwind?

The divine speeches do not contain an explicit moral teaching that can be simply summarized. Indeed, they do not seem to employ much explicitly "moral" language at all. God does not remake Job's moral world for him; that remains properly a human task. But God does provide Job and the reader with the resources for that undertaking. The divine speeches contain the lumber from which a new house of meaning can be built. The resources God offers to Job and to each reader include provocative questions about identity, new ways of perceiving the world, patterns and structures of thought different from accustomed ones, and, above all, images that can become generative metaphors for a renewed moral imagination.

As Janzen has noted, the rhetorical questions God addresses to Job (Who is this? Where were you? Are you able?) are not merely rhetorical questions, but in an ironic sense real, existential questions about identity and vocation.[602] Questions of identity and vocation are fundamentally moral questions. The way a person answers such questions is in large part a matter of the horizon of meaning within which a person thinks. The contrast between the horizon within which Job presents himself in chaps. 29–31 and the horizon within which God asks Job to locate himself could not be sharper. Job's primary horizon of meaning was the village and the family. God challenges the parochialism of Job's moral imagination by making the starting point nothing less than the whole of creation. We, too, often tend to think of the moral world as having to do simply with the relation of humans to other humans. Yet human abuse of creation in the wanton destruction of the environment should make modern readers

---

602. J. G. Janzen, *Job,* Interpretation (Atlanta: John Knox, 1985) 225-28.

particularly alert to the significance of God's insistence that the questions of human identity and vocation must first be answered in the context of the whole of creation. Not only does such a horizon of meaning alter one's relation to non-human creation, but it also causes one to understand human relations differently. By the choice of their starting place, the divine speeches suggest that one understand human identity and human community in the light of creation, rather than attempting to understand God and the cosmos on the basis of particular human social arrangements.

Not only the scope of the horizon but also the disciplines of attention that God requires of Job and the reader contribute to the remaking of the moral sense. Readers may be impatient for explicit moral discourse, but the divine speeches require a prolonged and disciplined act of contemplation as the first task. There are probably not many ethics courses in colleges or seminaries that spend the first three days in silence—one day in the forest, one day at the shore of the sea, one night in a field gazing at the stars. Yet something like that is what God requires of Job as the starting point for a new moral understanding. As was discussed in the Reflections to Job 36–37, the "moral sense of nature" is above all an affirmation that the natural world has intrinsic value. The morning stars' cry of joy (38:7) is the recognition of the intrinsic value that God speaks of as "goodness" in Genesis 1. The starting point for the development of the moral sense in the divine speeches is a contemplation of the goodness of the natural world: earth and rain and raven.

The account of creation in the divine speeches contains metaphors that are strongly suggestive of the formation of a moral order. The imagery of place, limit, and nonencroachment recurs frequently. Most explicitly, it occurs in the account of the sea, which is told that it may come so far and not farther (38:11). Such imagery is also present in the pervasive language of gates, paths, ways, storage chambers, channels. The language of place, limit, and nonencroachment is a language of balance, what we would speak of today as an ecological language. What kind of an ethic might emerge from meditation on these formative images? If one realizes that each thing, each person has place, purpose, and limit, then there are places where I must not tread, places where the energy and vitality, indeed, the violence of my being must meet its limit. Correspondingly, I do have a place, which none must violate.[603]

Where the language of limit challenges much customary moral thinking is in its application to the case of the wicked. God's description of the coming of dawn as setting a limit to the activity of the wicked (38:12-15) is quite different from Job's description of breaking the jaws of the wrongdoer and wresting the prey from his teeth (29:17). Neither image can be taken out of context and used, for example, as a proof text in an argument over the proper response to the problem of violent crime in modern society. Each image, however, can be a starting place for reflection on the very different visions of moral thinking and social order it implies. The heroism and decisiveness of Job's image are immensely appealing. Yet it is an image of meeting violence with violence that in no way transcends the cycle of violence. Job's figure of speech contains an implicit analogy that compares the criminal with the lion that raids the flock. The implication is that the criminal is not a member of the community who has done evil but one who is wholly an enemy, to be driven out and if necessary annihilated. The dehumanization of the criminal is inscribed in the image. Such an understanding of the criminal is very much a part of moral thinking that draws sharp lines between insiders and outsiders. God's image of setting limits to criminal activity emerges out of a different vision of social relations. It implicitly acknowledges that the antisocial impulse is always present in human communities and that, while it may be restrained, it will certainly return. The divine speeches do not develop the image, but certain implications might be traced out. Once a community has recognized that it cannot deal with the criminal by expulsion or annihilation, then it has

---

603. C Newsom, "The Moral Sense of Nature: Ethics in the Light of God's Speech to Job," *The Princeton Seminary Bulletin* 15 New Series (1994) 9-27.

also acknowledged the criminal as a part of the community, however disruptive a presence. Only on the basis of that recognition is redemption possible.

It is important to remember that the divine speeches do not primarily serve to lay out a moral teaching about the world. They serve, rather, as a revelatory experience. Such moments of revelation always have an elusive, enigmatic quality that escapes reduction to a "message." This is true not only of the stories of revelatory disclosure in the Bible but also in the epiphanies that occur in every person's life. Yet a person is repeatedly drawn to remember those moments out of a recognition that they contain the generative seed of a wholly new way of understanding God, the world, and oneself. Teasing out the possibilities of such a moment may require a lifetime, but in that process one engages the existential questions of identity and vocation that God poses to each person.

Job 42:1-6, Job's Response

NIV

42 Then Job replied to the LORD:

2 "I know that you can do all things;
   no plan of yours can be thwarted.
3 You asked, 'Who is this that obscures my
   counsel without knowledge?'
   Surely I spoke of things I did not understand,
   things too wonderful for me to know.
4 "You said, 'Listen now, and I will speak;
   I will question you,
   and you shall answer me.'
5 My ears had heard of you
   but now my eyes have seen you.
6 Therefore I despise myself
   and repent in dust and ashes."

NRSV

42 Then Job answered the LORD:

2 "I know that you can do all things,
   and that no purpose of yours can be
   thwarted.
3 'Who is this that hides counsel without
   knowledge?'
   Therefore I have uttered what I did not
   understand,
   things too wonderful for me, which I did
   not know.
4 'Hear, and I will speak;
   I will question you, and you declare to me.'
5 I had heard of you by the hearing of the ear,
   but now my eye sees you;
6 therefore I despise myself,
   and repent in dust and ashes."

COMMENTARY

Immediately following God's speech concerning Behemoth and Leviathan, Job replies. As the decisive word that Job speaks in God's presence, this reply provides the dramatic climax anticipated since the *satan*'s prediction that, once deprived of his family, possessions, and health, Job would curse God to God's face (1:11; 2:5). Job's words are not a curse, but the significance of what he says is not easily discerned. His words are elusive and enigmatic. That Job will no longer attempt to argue with God is clear, but his state of mind and the reasons for his withdrawal can be understood in more than one way. The ambiguity is perhaps strategic. By making Job's reply enigmatic, the poet requires readers to assume a more active role in construing the meaning and significance of the divine speeches and how they might resolve the conflict between Job and God.

The outline of Job's brief response is clear. He begins with a confession of God's effective power (42:2). Two quotations from God's speech (42:3*a*, 4; the NIV supplies "You asked . . . you said") introduce Job's two conclusions, each marked with a form of the word "therefore" (לכן *lākēn*, 42:3*b*, 5-6). The meaning of his reply is more difficult to judge. Although he uses somewhat different terminology from that employed by God, Job's confession (42:2) acknowledges God's power (cf. 40:9) and ability to implement plans (cf. 38:2; 40:8). In 42:3*a*, Job echoes God's words from 38:2 in a slightly altered form. By incorporating God's words into his own speech, Job suggests that he now views himself from God's perspective. More explicitly, with his following words (42:3*b*) Job accepts God's judgment that he has spoken without knowledge and understanding (38:2). Those words do not make clear, however, how Job has understood the substantive meaning of the divine speeches.

In 42:4, Job again echoes God's words, as 42:4*b* ("I will question you,/ and you shall answer me") cites 38:3*b* and 40:7*b*. The beginning of the verse ("Hear, and I will speak") is not a direct quotation of God's words, but a poetic expansion of 42:4*b*. It allows Job to introduce the word "hear" (שמע *šāmaʿ*), which is significant for his own reply in v. 5. Most interpreters assume that in v. 5 Job is contrasting past hearing with present seeing.[604] The "hearing of the ear" can be used of rumors or secondhand reports (cf. 28:22*b*; Ps 18:44[45]). The theologies of Job and his friends would be just such secondhand constructions of God. By contrast, the immediacy of the divine revelation could be characterized as "seeing." Although this interpretation is entirely plausible, it overlooks the relationship between v. 4 and v. 5. Job characterizes God's command to him as a command to listen while God speaks. It would be odd if Job's next words were a denigration of "hearing." Instead, one should take 42:5*a* as Job's confirmation that he has indeed listened, as God has commanded him; the consequence of that hearing is that Job now "sees" God (i.e., "I have listened to you with my ears, and now my eye sees you" [author's trans.]).[605] The language of "seeing" God has a special place in Israelite religious tradition. Seeing God is rarely permitted and often associated with a momentous occasion in the life of an individual or a people (Gen 16:13; Exod 24:9-11; 33:20-23; Isa 6:1). Job had earlier expressed the fervent desire to see God with his own eyes

(19:26-27). The context in which that desire has been fulfilled, however, is quite different from what Job had anticipated. His words in 42:5 say nothing about the way in which his understanding of God has been changed by this new "seeing."

One expects the final verse of Job's reply in v. 6 to clarify matters. Instead, it is not only as terse and enigmatic as the preceding verses but also grammatically ambiguous.[606] Almost every word in v. 6 is susceptible of more than one interpretation, as a brief survey of the grammatical problems, followed by a sampling of alternative translations will illustrate. The word translated "despise" or "reject" (מאס *māʾas*) ordinarily requires an object, yet none is present in 42:6, and so it must be supplied by context. Hence, "I despise myself" or "I reject my words"— i.e., "I retract" or "I recant."[607] One could argue, however, that the object is present in the words "dust and ashes" (עפר ואפר *ʿāpār wāʾēper*).[608] Alternatively, it may be that the verb is a variant of another Hebrew verb meaning "to melt" (מסס *māsas*), and might be translated here as "I submit."[609]

Similar ambiguities affect the translation of the phrase ונחמתי על (*wĕniḥamtî ʿal*). It may be translated "I repent upon/on account of . . . " or "I am consoled concerning . . . " or "I have changed my mind concerning . . . " or "I forswear. . . . "[610] The translation of the phrase "dust and ashes" is straightforward enough, but the expression has two related yet different metaphorical meanings. It can refer to human mortality, especially the human condition as contrasted with divine being (cf. Gen 18:27; Sir 10:9). The phrase can also be used to describe particular humiliation or degradation (Job 30:19; Sir 40:3).[611] Other suggestions that the phrase refers to the ash heap upon which Job sits (2:8)[612] or to dust as a symbol of mourning (2:12)[613] are less likely, since they involve only

604. See E. Dhorme, *A Commentary on the Book of Job,* trans. H. Knight (London: Nelson, 1967) 646; R. Gordis, *The Book of Job: Commentary, New Translation, and Special Studies* (New York: Jewish Theological Seminary, 5738/1978) 492; M. Pope, *Job,* 3rd ed., AB 15 (Garden City, N.Y.: Doubleday, 1979) 347.

605. See E. Good, *In Turns of Tempest* (Stanford, Calif.: Stanford University Press, 1990) 373-75.

606. See W. Morrow, "Consolation, Rejection, and Repentance in Job 42:6," *JBL* 105 (1986) 211-25, for a thorough discussion of the grammatical issues.

607. L. Kuyper, "The Repentance of Job," *VT* 9 (1959) 91-94; Fohrer, *Das Buch Hiob,* 536; N. Habel, *The Book of Job,* OTL (Philadelphia: Westminster, 1985) 582.

608. D. Patrick, "The Translation of Job 42.6," *VT* 26 (1976) 369-71.

609. Dhorme, *A Commentary on the Book of Job,* 646-47.

610. Morrow, "Consolation, Rejection, and Repentance in Job 42:6," 215-17.

611. Ibid., 216-17.

612. E.g., Dhorme, *A Commentary on the Book of Job,* 646-47; Pope, *Job,* 349.

613. Cf. Habel, *The Book of Job,* 583.

one term of what is clearly a set phrase; but they are not impossible.

Taking account of these various possibilities, one could legitimately translate v. 6 in any of the following ways:

(1) "Therefore I despise myself and repent upon dust and ashes" (i.e., in humiliation; cf. NRSV; NIV);

(2) "Therefore I retract my words and repent of dust and ashes" (i.e., the symbols of mourning);[614]

(3) "Therefore I reject and forswear dust and ashes" (i.e., the symbols of mourning);[615]

(4) "Therefore I retract my words and have changed my mind concerning dust and ashes" (i.e., the human condition);[616]

(5) "Therefore I retract my words, and I am comforted concerning dust and ashes" (i.e., the human condition).[617]

With a slightly different understanding of the grammar, the TNK translates, "Therefore, I recant and relent,/ Being but dust and ashes." These examples do not exhaust the various nuances that might be heard in the ambiguity of the Hebrew of 42:6, but they suggest something of the possible range of meaning.

Asking which possibility is correct misses the interpretive significance of the ambiguity of Job's reply, which corresponds to the ambiguity that is also part of the divine speeches. A reader who has interpreted the divine speeches as a defense of God's honor and a rebuke to the audacity of a mere human in challenging God will tend to hear Job's words more or less according to the first alternative suggested above, or as the TNK renders the line. A reader who understands the book largely in terms of the legal metaphor and takes God's speeches as a rebuttal of Job's lawsuit might be inclined to hear Job's words in terms of

the second alternative. One who emphasizes the celebratory tone of the divine speeches might hear Job's words according to the third alternative. In the interpretation of the divine speeches proposed here, which understands them as challenging Job's legal paradigm and placing the question of human existence in terms of a world in which the chaotic must be acknowledged, either the fourth or the fifth alternative appears fitting. The ambiguities inherent in the divine speeches and Job's reply resist every attempt to reduce them to a single, definitive interpretation. That ambiguity does not mean that a reader should refrain from arguing for a particular interpretation of the divine speeches and Job's reply, but only that a reader must recognize that more than one legitimate interpretation is possible. Here, it is appropriate to consider how one should understand Job's reply in the light of the interpetation of the divine speeches developed in this commentary.

In v. 3, Job repudiated his previous words as having been spoken without understanding. He had attempted to speak of "wonderful things" (נפלאות *niplāʾôt*), i.e., God's design (38:2), without realizing that such knowledge was beyond his scope. Thus it is appropriate to assume that in v. 6 Job rejects or retracts his previous words. He also refers to what he has heard about God (v. 5a), a hearing that has led to a new way of perceiving God (v. 5b). Job had earlier been caught in a dilemma. He could attribute the wretchedness of the human condition to only the arbitrariness and perhaps the hostility of God. Now, given what has been disclosed to him in the divine speeches, Job is able to perceive a world in which the vulnerability of human existence can be understood, not in terms of divine enmity, but in terms of a creation within which the chaotic is restrained but never fully eliminated. Thus it is fitting that Job should speak of a change of mind and perhaps of a consolation concerning the human condition. His final words signal his appropriation of the vision of reality and the nature of God disclosed in the divine speeches.

614. Cf. ibid., 575.

615. Cf. Patrick, "The Translation of Job 42.6," 369-70.

616. Cf. Janzen, *Job,* 6-57.

617. Cf. L. Perdue, *Wisdom in Revolt: Metaphorical Theology in the Book of Job*, JSOTSup 112 (Sheffield: JSOT, 1991) 232.

REFLECTIONS

1. Job's observation that he now "sees" (42:5b) is the key to the significance of his reply to God. However one chooses to translate 42:6, Job confesses that he now perceives God in a way that transforms his understanding of himself and his situation. As Job's reply suggests, "seeing" is a complex business, involving much more than simply having one's eyes physically open. An old proverb makes the point nicely: "Ninety percent of what a person sees lies behind the eyes." Even at the literal level, this proverb is true, for the brain structures visual stimuli into meaningful patterns. By means of these patterns, some features are made to appear prominent and others are virtually screened out, so that the visual stimulus may be recognized as a meaningful thing—e.g., an apple, a knife, a face. Without the templates that organize raw perception, a person could not see in any real sense. The proverb is even more true at the level of moral perception. What a person is able to see in a situation depends a great deal on the organizing and interpretive frameworks that person brings to it. Some aspects of an experience will be made to appear significant and others will be relegated to the periphery or not perceived at all, so that the experience may be interpreted—e.g., as a situation of injustice, an act of caring, a show of indifference. Most of the time we are not aware of these frameworks, because they lie "behind the eyes," at the level of subconscious presuppositions, but they very directly influence what we are capable of seeing. So it was with Job. He could see only injustice in his situation, because his interpretive paradigm, based on a legal metaphor, organized his experience in terms of rights and wrongs.

As Job discovered, events do occur that challenge and sometimes overturn the paradigms that have shaped one's perceptions. Yet people do not readily let go of the frameworks that have shaped their vision of reality. Often, it is when we have already begun to suspect that something is wrong with our paradigms that we become most resistant to allowing them to be challenged. It is not just that we *cannot* see something, but that we are *afraid* of looking squarely at what we can glimpse just at the periphery of our vision. Like the characters in the book of Job, many people are reluctant to confront the reality that human beings cannot secure their lives and their families against harm. We do not want to see that bad things happen to good people. Yet horrible things can happen, without apparent rhyme or reason. Premature death, accidents, violence, and illness can happen to anyone at any time. We all know that to be true, and yet we resist it with all our being. Drunk drivers exist, but why must one kill *my* child? Cancer is a reality, but why must it strike *my* spouse? The seeming randomness of such events is terrifying, and so we cling to interpretive paradigms of experience that will mask the reality, organize it in a way that makes it appear to be something else. Job's friends employed a number of such frameworks, which allowed disaster to be seen as moral discipline, punishment, etc. Job rejected those frameworks but embraced an alternative, legal paradigm that allowed him to declare the disasters morally wrong and to have someone to blame. All of these paradigms allowed them not to see what they were afraid to see—that the chaotic is an irreducible aspect of creation that must be taken into account in any adequate understanding of experience. To that extent, their moral paradigms served them as a means of denial.

The reality that Job has to confront in the divine speeches is the ineradicable presence of the chaotic in existence. God's speeches do not invite speculation as to *why* the chaotic is a part of creation. They are not a theodicy in the sense that a theodicy attempts to explain or to justify the presence in God's creation of those things that render human existence fragile and vulnerable. Theodicies, too, are explanatory frameworks that often serve to mask or obscure something that is difficult to acknowledge. When, in their attempts to justify death, pain, or suffering, theodicies speak of such things as only "appearing" to be evils but "really" being for some greater good, then they are forms of denial. Job's friends had attempted just such justifications (see Reflections on Job 4; 5), as they suggested that suffering was divine discipline, but the divine speeches make no such claims. They insist that the presence of the chaotic be acknowledged as part of the design of creation, but they never attempt to justify it. The pain caused by the eruption of the chaotic into human life must be recognized as such.

Sometimes a dramatic confrontation is required to overcome the resistance people often experience in acknowledging the reality of something they have tried hard not to see. Leviathan plays that role in God's speech to Job. Job had concluded his first speech in chap. 3, which was filled with the imagery of chaos, with the words, "the dread which I dreaded has come upon me" (3:25b, author's trans.). Like many people, Job intuited but was not yet willing to face what he most feared. Job's quarrel with God has been a long attempt to keep that dread at bay by trying to engage God in a very different kind of argument. God's wisdom, however, is to know that Job can neither make his decision about God (1:1; 2:5) nor continue with his life until he has acknowledged the reality of what he fears. Finally, in the divine speeches Job encounters the very image of his dread in the face of Leviathan. When that happens, it is as though a spell is broken. Job is released from his obsession with justice and can begin the process of living beyond tragedy. Putting one's life together again is not easy. For most people, the "happy ending" does not come in the quick and apparently simple resolution that the book of Job describes in 42:7-17. But the book of Job is wise in its recognition that false or distorting frameworks to which people cling in an attempt to defend themselves against what they dread may prevent them from seeing what they need to acknowledge, if they are to get on with their lives.

2. Confronting the reality of the presence of the chaotic in the design of the world is essential, but if the divine speeches had nothing to say to Job except that pain is part of life, then they would hardly be worth reading. One has to ask how they comfort and strengthen. It is essential to remember that Leviathan is not the only topic in the divine speeches. Before God speaks of that emblem of the chaotic, God has already described a world in which the chaotic, although present, is contained within the secure boundaries of a created order that is also rich with goodness. The power of these speeches to comfort was powerfully articulated by a mother whose teenage son had been killed in an automobile accident. She described how, on the morning of his funeral, she rose early and reached for her Bible, reading to herself the speeches of God from the whirlwind. When asked why she chose those chapters, she said, "I needed to know that my pain was not all there was in the world." Her anguish was like that of Job's in chap. 3, an inward spiral of pain that threatened to swallow all of creation. What she needed was the reassurance of a God whose power of creation and re-creation is stronger than the power of the chaotic. Job had been ready in his pain to give in to the overwhelming sense of despair, to use a curse to destroy the structures of creation that had led to his unbearable existence (3:3-10). God cannot now take away the defenses that Job has erected in the succeeding chapters without addressing that original cry of despair. The first divine speech in chaps. 38–39 acknowledges Job's sense of a fall into the abyss. With its orderly pattern of visually powerful images, this divine speech is a verbal re-creation of the world. Hearing the words of the establishment of the earth on secure foundations, the reliable return of the dawn each day, the regulation of life-giving water, and the nurture of the animals is a reassurance that in spite of the reality of pain and loss, God's creation supports and sustains.s

The divine speeches offer comfort in another way, too. A person who has suffered a great loss or who has finally faced up to a painful reality long denied often experiences an overwhelming sense of isolation, alienation, and godforsakenness. There is a need to share the burden, and yet such sharing may be difficult. Cultures often make sharing more difficult than it need be, for instance, by placing too much value on stoic endurance or, as in Job's culture, by treating suffering as somehow a sign of divine rejection. The result is to increase the burden of isolation. The divine speeches address this issue by means of the creation imagery they employ. Speaking of the relation of the created world to issues of pain and grief, Kohak talks explicitly about the book of Job:

A human alone, surrounded by the gleaming surfaces of his artifacts, cannot bear the pain. He can do that only when the grief can disperse, radiate out and be absorbed. [Even] fellow humans and their works, bearing the same burden, cannot absorb it. . . . To reconcile, that is what the forest does, silent and accepting, as if God were present therein, taking the grief unto Himself. When humans no longer think themselves alone, masters of all they survey, when they discern the humility of their place in the vastness of God's creation, then that creation and its God can share the pain. . . . That is the age-old wisdom of the book of Job. . . . When God speaks . . . [God] speaks not of pain but of the vastness of the creation, of the gazelle in her mountain fastness and the mighty creatures of the deep sea. God is not avoiding the issue. [God] is teaching Job the wisdom of bearing the pain that can neither be avoided nor abolished but can be shared when there is a whole living creation to absorb it. . . . When the human, in the solitude of dusk, surrenders his pride of place and learns to bear the shared pain, he can begin to understand the pain that cannot be avoided as a gift which teaches compassion and opens understanding. . . . It opens him to receive, in empathy, the gift of the other, not in censure but in gratitude and love.[618]

Kohak's words explain why the divine speeches enable Job to take up his life again. The acknowledgment of the reality of "pain that can neither be avoided nor abolished" may have broken the spell of denial, but living beyond tragedy requires the ability to receive and to give within community.

3. The divine speeches also challenge Job's understanding of where the presence of God may be found. Like many who suffer, Job experienced himself as godforsaken. In his way of thinking, God's presence was to be found in the peace and fulfillment of the family circle and the satisfaction of doing good within the community (chap. 29). To a certain extent, Job was not wrong, for God is to be found there. Job found it impossible, however, to experience the presence of God in desolation (chap. 30). As a symbol of his outcast condition, Job described himself as "a brother of jackals,/ a companion of ostriches" (30:29 NRSV), identifying in his misery with the creatures who inhabit desolate places. God's view of such creatures and their world is quite different from Job's. The vivid image of God's "satisfying the desolate wasteland" with rain, symbol of divine blessing, strongly suggests that Job is wrong in thinking that there is any place or any condition beyond the sustaining power of God's presence.

God's nurture of and pleasure in the animals of the wasteland is a provocative image. As noted in the Commentary, these animals were symbolic of the hostile and alien "other." In Job's imagination, they provided an image for describing the rejected and despised human "beasts" cast out of society (30:5-8). It is worth pursuing that connection. In our own society, many groups of people cluster at the margins of society; the mentally ill and the homeless are those we think of first. But one should also think of the biker culture, petty criminals, and others who live on the fringes of the law. The lives of such people often seem to be desolate wastelands, and the emotions they provoke in others are often a mixture of pity and fear. They seem so alien, so far outside the bounds of the ordinary social life that most people take as normative. But that is to view them from Job's perspective. From God's perspective, there is no alien outsider; there are only children of God. It can be difficult for "good Christian people" to imagine, but the destitute may know more of the grace of God than do the comfortable, and the petty criminal's life may be touched by the love of God in ways that the "respectable" person can scarcely imagine. God's revivifying rain continues to satisfy the desolate places. Indeed, those places are the ones most likely to respond with exuberant flowering, even though that beauty may go unseen by most of the world.

618. E. Kohak, *The Embers and the Stars: A Philosophical Inquiry into the Moral Sense of Nature* (Chicago: University of Chicago Press, 1984) 45-46.

The Prose Narrative: Conclusion

NIV

7After the LORD had said these things to Job, he said to Eliphaz the Temanite, "I am angry with you and your two friends, because you have not spoken of me what is right, as my servant Job has. 8So now take seven bulls and seven rams and go to my servant Job and sacrifice a burnt offering for yourselves. My servant Job will pray for you, and I will accept his prayer and not deal with you according to your folly. You have not spoken of me what is right, as my servant Job has." 9So Eliphaz the Temanite, Bildad the Shuhite and Zophar the Naamathite did what the LORD told them; and the LORD accepted Job's prayer.

10After Job had prayed for his friends, the LORD made him prosperous again and gave him twice as much as he had before. 11All his brothers and sisters and everyone who had known him before came and ate with him in his house. They comforted and consoled him over all the trouble the LORD had brought upon him, and each one gave him a piece of silver[a] and a gold ring.

12The LORD blessed the latter part of Job's life more than the first. He had fourteen thousand sheep, six thousand camels, a thousand yoke of oxen and a thousand donkeys. 13And he also had seven sons and three daughters. 14The first daughter he named Jemimah, the second Keziah and the third Keren-Happuch. 15Nowhere in all the land were there found women as beautiful as Job's daughters, and their father granted them an inheritance along with their brothers.

16After this, Job lived a hundred and forty years; he saw his children and their children to the fourth generation. 17And so he died, old and full of years.

a11 Hebrew *him a kesitah*; a kesitah was a unit of money of unknown weight and value.

NRSV

7After the LORD had spoken these words to Job, the LORD said to Eliphaz the Temanite: "My wrath is kindled against you and against your two friends; for you have not spoken of me what is right, as my servant Job has. 8Now therefore take seven bulls and seven rams, and go to my servant Job, and offer up for yourselves a burnt offering; and my servant Job shall pray for you, for I will accept his prayer not to deal with you according to your folly; for you have not spoken of me what is right, as my servant Job has done." 9So Eliphaz the Temanite and Bildad the Shuhite and Zophar the Naamathite went and did what the LORD had told them; and the LORD accepted Job's prayer.

10And the LORD restored the fortunes of Job when he had prayed for his friends; and the LORD gave Job twice as much as he had before. 11Then there came to him all his brothers and sisters and all who had known him before, and they ate bread with him in his house; they showed him sympathy and comforted him for all the evil that the LORD had brought upon him; and each of them gave him a piece of money[a] and a gold ring. 12The LORD blessed the latter days of Job more than his beginning; and he had fourteen thousand sheep, six thousand camels, a thousand yoke of oxen, and a thousand donkeys. 13He also had seven sons and three daughters. 14He named the first Jemimah, the second Keziah, and the third Keren-happuch. 15In all the land there were no women so beautiful as Job's daughters; and their father gave them an inheritance along with their brothers. 16After this Job lived one hundred and forty years, and saw his children, and his children's children, four generations. 17And Job died, old and full of days.

a Heb *a qesitah*

COMMENTARY

I mmediately following Job's reply to God, the voice of the prose narrator takes up the story and brings it to a conclusion. This shift is more than a change in style, for the prose conclusion seems to presume a significantly different story line from the one that has just been enacted in the dialogues and divine speeches. First, Yahweh's rebuke of the friends, that they "have not spoken of me what is right, as my servant Job has" (vv. 7-8), is difficult to square with the iconoclasm of Job's words in the dialogue and God's rebuke of Job as having spoken "words without knowledge" (38:2*b*). Second, the resolution of the story by means of the restoration of Job's wealth and the birth of a new family, which fits with the narrative and moral world of the didactic story in chaps. 1–2 (see Commentary on Job 1; 2), clashes with the moral complexity of the dialogue and the divine speeches.

As discussed in the Introduction, some commentators have attributed the discrepancy between the frame story and the poetic material to an editor who combined the beginning and end of an old traditional tale with a long poetic dialogue from a different author, not bothering to smooth out the inconsistencies created by joining the two. Yet it is also possible that a single author wrote the entire book, artfully using contrasting styles and sharply disjunctive transitions between the frame story and the dialogue to create the illusion of two different compositions joined together. Whichever way the book of Job achieved its present shape, that shape gives 42:7-17 two different functions. It serves as the conclusion to the simple, didactic prose story, and it serves as the conclusion to the book of Job as a whole. When considered as the conclusion to the didactic tale, the happy ending provides a smooth and satisfying conclusion. When considered as the conclusion to the book as a whole, the ending creates dissonance and disruption. Commentators who attempt to read the entire book as a unity often soften these discrepancies. Thus attempts are made to interpret Job's "speaking rightly" in terms of sincerity, i.e., his avoidance of "dissembling and

flattery." [619] The happy ending is read as an act of the free grace of God[620] or as a narrative symbol of Job's putting aside moral bitterness and experiencing reconciliation with God and community.[621] Such interpretive moves evade rather than engage the dissonance of the ending of the book of Job. The position taken in this commentary is that the dissonance is part of the narrative strategy of the book (see Introduction). By leaving the tension between the two parts unresolved, the book as a whole allows the frame story and the dialogue to explore different dimensions of the complex question of the moral basis for divine-human relations. That dissonance both recognizes and refuses the reader's desire for closure to the story and a definitive resolution of the issues it has raised.

The prose conclusion divides into two parts: vv. 7-9 concern God's rebuke of Job's three friends and Job's role as intercessor for them; vv. 10-17 describes the restoration of Job's wealth, family, and well-being, concluding with an account of his long life.

42:7-9. The impossibility of harmonizing v. 7 with the preceding material in chaps. 3:1–42:6 is clearly indicated in the connotation of the word "right" (נכונה *nĕkônâ*). As Pope argues, it does not have the nuance of "sincerity." Instead, its basic meaning is "correct" (cf. 1 Sam 23:23).[622] Job cannot be both praised for speaking "correctly" (42:7) and rebuked for speaking "words without knowledge" that obscure the design of God (38:2). Verse 7 thus gestures back to the story line begun by the didactic prose tale in chaps. 1–2, in which Job is the model of piety and his friends warrant rebuke.

In the didactic story itself, without 3:1–42:6, Job is the hero of unconditional piety who never wavers in his commitment, despite extraordinary and inexplicable adversity (1:21-22; 2:10). The

619. N. Habel, *The Book of Job*, OTL (Philadelphia: Westminster, 1985) 583.

620. Ibid., 584; J. G. Janzen, *Job*, Interpretation (Atlanta: John Knox, 1985) 267; J. E. Hartley, *The Book of Job*, NICOT (Grand Rapids, Mich.: Eerdmans, 1988) 540.

621. J. Wilcox, *The Bitterness of Job: A Philosophical Reading* (Ann Arbor: University of Michigan Press, 1989) 209.

622. M. Pope, *Job*, 3rd ed., AB 15 (Garden City, N.Y.: Doubleday, 1979) 350.

test of fidelity having been completed, restoration of the hero's fortunes is the ending that this sort of narrative requires. Generously, the story even includes the rebuked friends in its happy ending. The sacrifice of vv. 8-9, commanded by Yahweh, reaffirms Job's role as intercessor (cf. 1:5) and serves as the mechanism for the reconciliation of God and the friends. The extravagant offering of seven bulls and rams is in keeping with the exaggerated style and use of symbolic numbers characteristic of the prose tale (see Commentary on Job 1; cf. also the folkloristic Balaam story, in which seven bulls and seven rams are sacrificed on seven altars [Num 23:1, 4, 14, 29-30]).

42:10-17. Following the reconciliation between God and Job's three friends, the story describes the restoration of Job's fortunes. That Job should receive twice as much as before (v. 10) is an appropriate feature in this type of story (cf. the restoration of good fortune that comes to the pious and long-suffering Tobit and Sarah in the book of Tobit). Rather than taking the visit of Job's family and friends as subsequent to the restoration of his fortunes,[623] one should interpret v. 11-12 as describing the *way* in which God restored the fortunes of Job. That is, even before Job's fortunes are restored, his family and friends come to share a meal and offer gestures of comfort. The solidarity of Job's family in sorrow echoes the family solidarity of the joyful birthday celebrations shared by the brothers and sisters in 1:4. Job's family and friends all give him gifts, a piece of money (קְשִׂיטָה *qĕśîṭâ*) and a gold ring. The value of a *qesita* is not known, but it was apparently a modest but not insignificant gift (see Gen 33:19; Josh 24:32). From these shared gifts, God's blessing would create the enormous fortune Job enjoyed in the latter part of his life (v. 12; cf. Gen 30:30).

A new family is also born as part of Job's restoration, seven sons and three daughters (v. 13). An unusual form of the word for "seven" is used here (שִׁבְעָנָה *šib'ānâ*), leading some to interpret it as a dual form, indicating that Job's second family included fourteen sons (cf. 1 Chr 25:5, where a family of fourteen sons and three daughters are given to Heman the seer "through the

promises of God to exalt him").[624] If that is the correct interpretation, then the extraordinary number of Job's sons would be matched by the extraordinary beauty of Job's daughters (v. 15a). The narrator lingers on the daughters, giving their names. The first is named Jemimah, which means "dove"; the second is named Keziah, which means fragrant "cinnamon" (cf. Ps 45:8); the third is named Keren-Happuch, which means "cosmetics box" (lit., "Horn of Eyeshadow"; cf. 2 Kgs 9:30; Jer 4:30). The image of a joyful and harmonious society is underscored by the note that Job gave his daughters an inheritance along with their brothers (v. 15b). That this detail should receive special mention apparently indicates that it was not the normal state of affairs (cf. Num 27:3-4).

It may seem shocking that the story seems to overlook that beloved children cannot be replaced by new ones, as wealth may be replaced. Without knowing more about the conventions of storytelling in ancient Israel, it is difficult to say whether such "outrageous" features are supposed to be accepted simply as part of the way one tells a story like this, or whether the author is subtly using this detail to make readers uncomfortable with a story that they would otherwise accept without question. The narrator makes no evaluative comment but continues with the account of Job's restoration.

The final indication of Job's blessedness lies in the length of life granted to him (v. 16a). As his fortunes and the number of his sons were doubled, so the years of his life after his calamity (140 years) are the equivalent of two normal lifetimes (cf. Ps 19:10). An ordinarily blessed life includes seeing one's children's children, two generations (Ps 128:6); thus Job's doubly blessed life allows him to see four generations of his descendants (v. 16b). Echoing the language used of Israel's patriarchs, the final verse of the story describes Job's death as occurring when he was "old and full of days" (v. 17; cf. Gen 25:8; 35:29; 1 Chr 29:28).

When vv. 7-17 are read as the conclusion to the didactic tale, every detail contributes to the coherency of the story. In the book as we have it, however, the conclusion follows the dialogue

623. So, e.g., E. Dhorme, *A Commentary on the Book of Job,* trans. H. Knight (London: Nelson, 1967) 651; Pope, *Job,* 351.

624. So the Targum to Job. See Dhorme, *A Commentary on the Book of Job,* 651-52; R. Gordis, *The Book of Job: Commentary, New Translation, and Special Studies* (New York: Jewish Theological Seminary, 5738/1978) 498. See also N. Sarna, "Epic Substratum in the Prose of Job," *JBL* 76 (1957) 18.

and divine speeches, not the didactic tale. In this actual context, the conclusion produces ironic dissonance rather than coherency. The effect is to reawaken questions that had ostensibly been resolved. This ironic affirmation that Job has spoken "correctly" of God directs the reader's attention back to what Job has in fact said: that God has treated him with cruel injustice and has abdicated proper governance of the world. A reader who has too quickly put aside Job's passionate argument with God in the face of the divine speeches' alternative paradigm is given a chance to reconsider. Can God be the ultimate source of the moral order without behaving as a moral being toward Job or acting responsibly toward the world? Is not Job's challenge to God concerning the misery of the destitute still valid, and still awaiting an answer? The narrative compounds the irony through its depiction of the twofold restoration of Job's fortunes. A reader who knows Israelite legal tradition may recall that a thief or a negligent trustee of another's property was required to pay double to the injured party (Exod 22:4, 7, 9[3, 6, 8]). Thus in the light of Job's accusations against God in the dialogue, the restoration in vv. 10-12 seems to be a piece of narrative irony at God's expense, as God performs the act of restitution expected of a criminal. Yet a person persuaded by the justice of Job's accusations is not likely to be satisfied that the fundamental issues are resolved by such restitution.

Just as the affirmation of Job's words in vv. 7-8 produces ironic dissonance, so too does the rebuke of the friends' words. The friends repeatedly urged Job to endorse the wisdom of traditional piety, turning to God in prayer and humble self-examination, trusting that God would restore him to peace and security (e.g., 11:13-19). In fact, when Job does confess humbly before God, his arrogance in speaking rashly about "what I did not understand" (v. 3), events turn out just as the friends said they would. The statement that God "blessed the latter days" (אחרית *'aḥărît*) of Job more than his beginning (ראשית *rēʾšît*, v. 12) is a verbal echo of what Bildad had said in 8:7: "Though your beginning [*rēʾšît*] was small,/ your latter days [*'aḥărît*] will be very great" NRSV). Moreover, Eliphaz's description of God as one who "wounds, but binds up" is an apt account of Job's experience of God. Just as Eliphaz had anticipated, God does preserve Job from absolute destruction even in the midst of calamity, and then restores him to a blessed old age (cf. 5:19-26), culminating in a peaceful death (v. 17) in which Job might be said to "come to [his] grave in ripe old age,/ as a shock of grain comes up to the threshing floor in its season" (5:26 NRSV). Despite God's rebuke of the friends, the ironic structure of the narrative as a whole seems to ratify this dimension of the friends' understanding of the divine-human relationship.

REFLECTIONS

The prose conclusion in 42:7-17, which ostensibly serves to give closure to the book of Job, in fact does just the opposite. Throughout the course of the book, four different perspectives have been presented: that of the didactic prose tale, that of the friends, that of Job, and that of the divine speeches. Although initially the structure of the book appeared to be leading to a progressive rejection of the first three perspectives, the device of giving the last word to the prose tale undercuts this seeming momentum toward closure. Through its ironic dissonance with what has gone before, the prose conclusion makes it less clear which voice, if any, holds the key to the troubling issues raised by the book of Job. Just where one expects resolution, the book offers frustration instead. One could easily be angry at the book for having asked its readers to work hard at difficult moral and religious questions and then ended with a tease instead of an answer.

This sense of betrayal can be especially acute since the book of Job is part of Scripture. People want answers to difficult questions, and many people assume that the Bible is the place to find them. The teasing quality of the book of Job is actually more characteristic of biblical teaching than one might think. For example, Jesus' parables have a similar frustrating elusiveness for those who look to them for simple moral directions. Rather than merely being irritated at the ending of Job, one might reflect on what the book is trying to teach us by refusing to give the clear answers we crave.

Especially in our modern culture, there is a tendency to assume that every issue has a single answer; every problem has a single solution. If one works hard at it, then the answer will appear, the problem will be resolved, and one can move on. In religious terms, this assumption expresses itself in the expectation that study, prayer, and instruction will result in knowing the answers to the questions of life. The structure of the book of Job draws our attention to the fallacy in this assumption. Not all the things that trouble us are issues that can be resolved; instead, some of them are dilemmas with which we must continue to live. As the book of Job demonstrates, the anguish that wells up in the question, "Why?" is one such dilemma. There is no single answer that can put an end to that question once and for all.

To deny that there is a single definitive answer is not to say that one cannot gain insight into the problem of suffering in a world created by a loving God. What the book of Job models is a community of voices struggling to articulate a range of perspectives, each one of which contains valid insights as well as blindness to other dimensions of the problem. At different times and in different circumstances, one or another of the voices may seem more powerful, may be the word we need to hear in order to work our way through a particular experience. By refusing to give the book a neat resolution and declare one of the perspectives to be *the* solution, the book of Job draws us toward a recognition that our craving for an answer is an attempt to evade what we know to be true. Especially in times of religious crisis, richness of meaning and even a sense of peace are not to be found in a pre-packaged answer but emerge from the experience of wrestling with God.

Nevertheless, one must reflect on the author's choice to conclude the book of Job not merely with a "happy ending" but with one that takes the reader back to the beginning of the book. The presence of the happy ending is provocative. As much as it may remind readers of unfinished questions, it also poses a new issue that must be reckoned with. Readers must decide whether such an ending "fits." Is the image of reconciliation and flourishing new life an appropriate ending, or is it a betrayal of what has gone before? When people compare their opinions about the fittingness of 42:7-17 as a conclusion for the book of Job, differences of opinion about the book's ending often turn out to be related to differences of opinion about the nature of life itself, whether existence has a fundamentally tragic structure or a comedic structure.

Finally, one needs to consider the significance of a return at the end of the book to the same narrative style with which the book began. As in chap. 28, which also echoed the prose of 1:1 in its concluding verse, one is invited to consider Job's experience as a journey that ends where it began; and yet neither Job nor those who have accompanied him vicariously as readers can experience that place in the same way. It is possible, I think, to imagine Job again uttering the words of 1:21 ("Yahweh has given and Yahweh has taken away; may the name of Yahweh be blessed") and 2:10 ("Shall we accept good from God, and not trouble?" [NIV]). What those words mean, or are capable of meaning, is quite different after one has encountered the voice from the whirlwind from what they meant when one first read them.

THE BOOK OF PSALMS

INTRODUCTION, COMMENTARY, AND REFLECTIONS
BY
J. CLINTON McCANN, JR.

THE BOOK OF
PSALMS

INTRODUCTION

O ne of the most outstanding and highly respected international leaders of the twentieth century was Sweden's Dag Hammarskjöld. As Secretary-General of the United Nations, he devoted the final years of his life to pursuing the principles espoused in the United Nations Charter—international cooperation and reconciliation toward a peaceful world. As Dorothy V. Jones points out, Hammarskjöld viewed his work not simply as a political role but as a religious calling. Jones reports:

> On his travels around the world Hammarskjöld always took three items with him. These items were found in his briefcase that was recovered after the plane crash that took his life in September 1961: a copy of the New Testament, a copy of the Psalms and a copy of the United Nations Charter.[1]

Hammarskjöld apparently understood—quite correctly—that the book of Psalms presents nothing short of God's claim upon the whole world and that it articulates God's will for justice, righteousness, and peace among all peoples and all nations. It is the purpose of this commentary to elucidate that claim and to enable the reader to hear the Word of God as it comes to us in the psalms. I write as a Christian biblical scholar and theologian, and, like Hammarskjöld, I consciously and constantly hold side by side the psalms and the New Testament. A careful reading of each reveals that the psalms anticipate Jesus' bold presentation of God's claim upon the whole world ("the kingdom of God has come near"

1. Dorothy V. Jones, "The Example of Dag Hammarskjöld: Style and Effectiveness at the UN," *The Christian Century* 111, 32 (Nov. 9, 1994) 1050.

[Mark 1:15 NRSV]) and that Jesus embodied the psalter's articulation of God's will for justice, righteousness, and peace among all peoples and all nations. In other words, the approach to the psalms in this commentary is explicitly *theological,* and it takes seriously the canonical shape of the book of Psalms itself as well as the psalter's place in the larger canon of Scripture.

To be sure, this approach differs from the predominant scholarly approach to the psalms in the twentieth century. For the most part, Psalms scholarship has been explicitly *historical.* Undoubtedly, the historical-critical method has produced exciting, enduring, and important results. For instance, when scholars asked historical questions that were informed by sociological analysis (see below on form criticism), they arrived at the understanding that the psalms are not just the products of pious individuals in ancient Israel and Judah but that they are the liturgical materials used in ancient Israelite and Judean worship. In short, the psalter represents the hymnbook or the prayer book of the Second (and perhaps the First) Temple. This conclusion is not incorrect, but it is only partially correct. When scholars began to ask historical questions that were informed by literary sensitivity (see below on rhetorical criticism), they arrived at a new appreciation of the psalmists as highly skilled and sophisticated poets and of each psalm as a unique poetic creation. This conclusion is not incorrect either, but it too is only partially correct.

As important as it is to view the psalms as the sacred poetry that was used in ancient Israelite and Judean worship, this conclusion fails to do justice to another crucial dimension of the psalms: It fails to deal with the fact that the psalms were appropriated, preserved, and transmitted not only as records of human response to God but also as God's word to humanity. As Brevard Childs puts it:

> I would argue that the need for taking seriously the canonical form of the Psalter would greatly aid in making use of the Psalms in the life of the Christian Church. Such a move would not disregard the historical dimensions of the Psalter, but would attempt to profit from the shaping which the final redactors gave the older material in order to transform traditional poetry into Sacred Scripture for the later generations of the faithful.[2]

In short, the book of Psalms has been preserved and transmitted as Scripture, a dimension that is more evident when the final shape of the book of Psalms is taken seriously and when the psalms are heard in conversation with the whole canon of Scripture.

It is my intent in the following commentary to interpret the psalms both as humanity's words to God and as God's word to humanity. Underlying this intent is a very *incarnational* view of Scripture, but the origin and transmission of the psalms in this regard is really no different from other parts of the canon. *All* Scripture originated as the record of humanity's encounter with and response to God, a record that generations of God's people judged to

---

2. Brevard Childs, "Reflections on the Modern Study of the Psalms" in *Magnalia Dei, the Mighty Acts of God: Essays in Memory of G. Ernest Wright,* eds. F. M. Cross, W. E. Lemke, P. D. Miller, Jr. (Garden City, N.Y.: Doubleday, 1976) 385.

be authentic and true; thus it was preserved and transmitted as the Word of God. To be sure, such an incarnational view of Scripture is scandalously particularistic, but no more so than the fundamental Jewish and Christian convictions that God chose Israel or that God is fully known finally in one Jesus of Nazareth, who was "fully human"—"the Word became flesh and lived among us" (John 1:14 NRSV).

To interpret the psalms both as human words to God and as God's word to humans means that a multiplicity of methods is necessary. To appreciate the psalms as humanity's response to God—as sacred poetry as well as songs and prayers used in worship—it is necessary to employ form criticism and rhetorical criticism. To be sure, these methods may yield insights that lead to fruitful theological reflection; however, as Childs suggests, to appreciate the psalms more fully as God's word to humanity—as Scripture—it is helpful to consider the canonical shape of the psalter itself. Thus the following commentary consciously employs a multiplicity of methods in an attempt to interpret the psalms both historically and theologically. To illustrate what this means in practice, it is helpful to consider the history of the critical study of the psalms in the twentieth century.

CRITICAL STUDY OF THE BOOK OF PSALMS

For centuries, interpreters of the psalms assumed that they were written by the persons whose names appear in the superscriptions. Since David's name appears in the superscriptions of seventy-three psalms, interpreters often have assumed by generalization that David must have written most of the untitled psalms as well. With the emergence of critical scholarship in the nineteenth century, these assumptions began to be questioned. Even so, at the beginning of the twentieth century, the psalms were still understood primarily as the work of pious individuals (although not necessarily the persons whose names appear in the superscriptions) who composed prayers and songs either for their private devotional use or in response to particular historical events. Thus scholars were intent upon determining and attempting to describe the authors of the psalms, to discern the historical circumstances of their composition, and to date each psalm as specifically as possible. The tendency was to date most of the psalms very late (third to second century BCE) and to view them as evidence of an individualized spirituality that was superior to the corporate worship of earlier centuries of Israelite and Judean history.

This approach has been characterized by W. H. Bellinger, Jr., as "the personal/historical method."[3] It is still being practiced in some circles, not only by interpreters who tend to read the Bible literally, but also by critical scholars. Michael Goulder, for instance, has recently proposed that Psalms 51–72, a collection attributed to David, actually date from David's time, that they were probably written by one of David's sons, and that they are in chronological order, with Psalm 51 deriving from the events of the David/Bathsheba episode in 2 Samuel 11–12 and subsequent psalms reflecting the succeeding events

3. W. H. Bellinger, Jr., *Psalms: Reading and Studying the Book of Praises* (Peabody, Mass.: Hendrickson, 1990) 15.

narrated in the rest of 2 Samuel through 1 Kings 1. Thus 1 Kings 1, which narrates Solomon's accession to the throne, corresponds to Psalm 72, which is attributed to Solomon.[4] A major weakness in Goulder's proposal is that the historical superscriptions of Psalms 52; 54; 56; 57; 59; 60; and 63 do not fit the scheme, since they allude to events much earlier in David's life. Thus most scholars remain unconvinced by Goulder's proposal, which, although ingenious and skillfully argued, contains a high degree of speculation. Nevertheless, Goulder's work illustrates well the variety of possible approaches to the psalms; and the personal/historical method at least reminds us that the psalms grew out of concrete historical situations in which real people sought to live their lives under God. While this reminder is valuable, most scholars agree that dating the psalms with any degree of precision or certainty is virtually impossible. To be sure, there are a few exceptions (see Psalm 137), and it often makes sense to relate certain psalms or groups of psalms to broad historical eras (see below on the shaping of the psalter in response to the exile). By and large, however, scholars have abandoned the personal/historical method in favor of a method that has dominated the study of Psalms in the twentieth century: form criticism.

Form Criticism. Early in the twentieth century, German scholar Hermann Gunkel became convinced of the inadequacy of the personal/historical method. He noted the many references in the psalter to liturgical activities (singing, dancing, shouting, sacrifice, prayer, etc.) and places (the Temple, the house of the Lord, gates, courts, etc.); he concluded that the psalms were as much or more related to the corporate worship of ancient Israel and Judah than to the meditation of pious persons. Gunkel pioneered a method known as form criticism. He classified the psalms as various forms or types or genres, and then sought to determine where each type would have fit into the worship of ancient Israel or Judah—its "setting in life."[5] Although Gunkel's work has been modified, extended, and refined (see below), it remains the foundation of a method that dominated psalms scholarship for much of the century and that still remains a viable and vital approach. Gunkel's types are described in the following sections, which also include observations concerning how subsequent scholars have responded to Gunkel's work and how the following commentary generally deals with the issues.

Lament of an Individual. The lament of an individual, which some scholars prefer to call the complaint or prayer for help, is the most frequent type in the psalter. Characteristic elements include:

- Opening address, often including a vocative, such as, "O LORD"
- Description of the trouble or distress (the lament or complaint proper)
- Plea or petition for God's response (the prayer for help), often accompanied by reasons for God to hear and act

4. Michael Goulder, *The Prayers of David (Psalms 51–72): Studies in the Psalter II,* JSOTSup 102 (Sheffield: JSOT, 1990) 24-30.
5. See Hermann Gunkel, *The Psalms: A Form-Critical Introduction,* trans. T. M. Horner, FBBS 19 (Philadelphia: Fortress, 1967).

❖ Profession of trust or confidence in God (Gunkel's "certainty of being heard")
❖ Promise or vow to praise God or to offer a sacrifice

Not all of the typical elements appear in every prayer. Furthermore, the order of the elements varies from psalm to psalm, and the elements vary considerably in length and intensity among the prayers. This means that each lament has some degree of uniqueness, an observation that is especially important to rhetorical critics (see below).

When it came to the question of the setting in life for the laments of an individual, Gunkel did not break completely with the older personal/historical approach. He still maintained that the prayers were late spiritual compositions by individuals, but he claimed that the authors based their creations upon prototypes that had originated in the worship of an earlier period. In Gunkel's view, the cultic prototypes arose out of a situation in which a sick person came to the Temple to pray for God's help. Recurring features of the prayers were explained in relation to this basic situation. For instance, the dramatic turn from complaint and petition to trust and praise is explained as the psalmist's response to a priestly salvation oracle, which is not preserved in the text. The wicked or enemies are those who slandered or sought to take advantage of the psalmist's distress. Some prayers include the psalmist's plea for revenge against the enemies (Gunkel's Imprecatory Psalms). In some prayers, as a way of asserting that the distress is undeserved, the psalmist explicitly defends his or her behavior (Gunkel's Protestations of Innocence). In other prayers, the psalmist admits her or his guilt and is content to leave the situation with God (Gunkel's Penitential Psalms).

Needless to say, subsequent scholarship has not been entirely content with Gunkel's conclusions. In particular, the question of the setting in life of the laments has been and still is much debated. While it is true that the language and imagery of several of the laments of an individual clearly suggest an original situation of sickness (see Psalms 6; 38; 41; 88), such is not the case with many others. Rather than sickness, the primary distress in some cases seems to be persecution by ruthless opponents. Consequently, several scholars have suggested that some of the prayers have arisen out of a situation in which the psalmist was falsely accused of some offense (see Psalms 5; 7; 11; 17; 26; 59; 109). According to this view, the psalmist has come to the Temple—perhaps has even taken up residence there—to seek asylum and to request redress from God (see 1 Kgs 1:50-53). This situation explains the protestations of innocence and the need to request revenge against the enemies, or in short, to ask that justice be done. The existence of praise following the complaint and petition is explained as a portion of the psalm that was added later, when the psalmist had been exonerated.

Still other laments of an individual seem to have arisen from circumstances involving neither sickness nor false accusation. The imagery is primarily military (see Psalms 3; 35; 56–57). This has led some scholars to identify the speaker in these psalms as the king, the military leader of the people. In the absence of any explicit indications in this regard, however, it is more likely that the military imagery is metaphorical. Indeed, the imagery of sickness and accusation may also be metaphorical. If this is the case, then the attempt to specify precisely the original circumstances of these prayers is finally futile and unnecessary. The work of Erhard Gerstenberger points to this conclusion. Maintaining that scholars "know little about the exact use of individual complaint psalms," Gerstenberger concludes that they "belonged to the realm of special offices for suffering people who, probably assisted by their kinfolk, participated in a service of supplication and curing under the guidance of a ritual expert."[6] While Gerstenberger's work is clearly historical and form critical, it is to be noted that his conclusions are fairly modest in comparison to earlier attempts and that his focus is on primary social groups, like the family, rather than on the Temple and its rituals.

In the following commentary, scholarly proposals concerning the possible origins of the laments will be regularly noted. The emphasis, however, will lie elsewhere, for this reason: Regardless of the circumstances out of which the prayers arose, the language and imagery were eventually heard and appropriated metaphorically (and perhaps were even *intended* to function metaphorically from the beginning). This means that the language and imagery are symbolic and stereotypical enough to be applicable to a variety of situations. While this may be a frustration to scholars who are attempting to pin down precisely the historical circumstances of a psalm's origin, it is a distinct advantage to faithful communities and people who actually pray the prayers and look to them for a word about God and their own lives under God. As Patrick D. Miller, Jr., suggests:

> The search for a readily identifiable situation as the context for understanding the laments may, however, be illusory or unnecessary. The language of these psalms with its stereotypical, generalizing, and figurative style is so open-ended that later readers, on the one hand are stopped from peering behind them to one or more clearly definable sets of circumstances or settings in life, and on the other hand, are intentionally set free to adapt them to varying circumstances and settings.[7]

In other words, the really pertinent questions in approaching the laments are *not,* What was wrong with the psalmist? Who were her or his enemies? Rather, the crucial interpretive questions are these: What is wrong *with us?* Who or what are *our* enemies? This approach opens the way for an explicitly *theological,* as well as historical, understanding of the laments of an individual. For instance, rather than approaching the transition from complaint/petition to trust/praise chronologically or liturgically, the interpreter can take the simultaneity of complaint and praise as an expression of the perennial reality of the life of faith. Such an approach has profound implications for understanding human suffering and the suffering of God (see below on "The Theology of the Psalms" as well as Commentary and Reflections on Psalms 3; 13; 22; 31; 51; 69; 88; 109; 130).

6. Erhard S. Gerstenberger, *Psalms: Part 1, with an Introduction to Cultic Poetry,* Forms of the OT Literature 14 (Grand Rapids: Eerdmans, 1988) 13-14.
7. Patrick D. Miller, Jr., *Interpreting the Psalms* (Philadelphia: Fortress, 1986) 8; see also 48-52.

Thanksgiving Song of an Individual. The thanksgiving song of an individual can be thought of as the offering of the praise that is regularly promised in the concluding sections of the laments (see above). It may have originally accompanied a sacrifice offered in the Temple, including perhaps a sacrificial meal. Typical elements include:

❖ expressions of praise and gratitude to God
❖ description of the trouble or distress from which the psalmist has been delivered
❖ testimony to others concerning God's saving deeds
❖ exhortation to others to join in praising God and acknowledging God's ways

Because the thanksgiving songs seem to look back on the kinds of distressing situations described in the laments, the same basic interpretive issues come into play (see above). In fact, because of the difficulty of translating Hebrew verb tenses, scholars sometimes disagree on whether a psalm should be classified as a lament or a thanksgiving song (see Psalms 28; 56; 57). From a theological perspective, the difference is not crucial, since the larger context of the book of Psalms suggests that deliverance is finally experienced not beyond but in the midst of suffering. In the following commentary, historical matters will not be ignored, but the emphasis will fall on the consideration of what it means to make gratitude one's fundamental posture toward God (see Commentary and Reflections on Psalms 30; 34; 92; 107; 116).

Lament of the Community. The characteristic elements of the lament of the community are essentially the same as those of the lament of the individual (see above), but the prayer is offered in the first-person plural. In addition, the communal prayers frequently include a reminder to God of the history of God's relationship with the people and of God's mighty deeds on behalf of the people. The communal prayers are less likely to include the turn from complaint and petition to trust and praise. Like the laments of an individual, however, each communal prayer is unique.

The communal prayers obviously originated amid situations of communal distress, and scholars offer a range of proposals for each psalm. The most dramatic communal setback in the biblical period was the destruction of Jerusalem in 587 BCE and the subsequent exile. While it is not clear that all of the communal laments arose in response to this crisis, it is likely that several of them did; it is even more likely that all of them were eventually read and heard in view of this crisis. In the following commentary, the possible historical origins of the communal prayers will be noted. More attention will be given, however, to the apparently intentional attempt to place strategically the communal laments in the final form of the psalter. The second psalms in Books II and III are communal laments (Psalms 44; 74), and several more communal prayers appear in Book III (Psalms 79; 80; 83; and perhaps 77; 85; and 89; see "The Shape and Shaping of the Psalter"). The placement of these prayers encourages a theological as well as a historical approach to them, and it gives them a significance greater than their relative paucity might indicate. In particular, the communal laments encourage reflection on what it means to continue to profess faith in God's sovereignty in situations of severe extremity (see "The Theology of the Book of Psalms" as well as the Commentary and Reflections on Psalms 44; 74; 79; 80).

Hymn or Song of Praise. Whereas there are elements of praise in the above-mentioned types, the hymn or song of praise is oriented exclusively in this direction. The basic form is very simple:

❖ Opening invitation to praise
❖ Reasons for praise, often introduced by the Hebrew particle translated "for" (כִּי *kî*)
❖ Recapitulation of invitation to praise

As with the other types, these elements may vary in length and arrangement, thus giving each song of praise a certain individuality. For instance, in some hymns, the invitation is greatly extended and occupies most or all of the psalm (see Psalms 100; 148; 150). Then, too, the reasons for praise cite a variety of events, themes, and characteristics of God, and they employ a variety of vocabulary and imagery.

The songs of praise ordinarily refer to God in the third person rather than addressing God directly, as in the prayers, but there are exceptions (see Psalm 8). While it is clear that the communal laments are the corporate correlate of the laments of individuals, it seems to be that the hymns or songs of praise serve as the corporate correlate of the thanksgiving songs of individuals. In several cases where God is addressed directly in praise, however, some scholars prefer to categorize the psalm as a thanksgiving song of the community (see Psalms 65–67). In the final analysis, though, precision of categorization is not crucial. Claus Westermann, for instance, has chosen not to use "song of thanksgiving" at all in categorizing the psalms. Rather, he prefers to distinguish between descriptive praise, which celebrates God's general character and activity, and declarative praise, which celebrates God's deliverance in a specific situation of distress.[8]

Usually treated as sub-categories of the songs of praise are two more groupings customarily known as the enthronement psalms and the songs of Zion. The enthronement psalms are those that explicitly proclaim the reign of God (see Psalms 29; 47; 93; 95–99), and the songs of Zion are poems that focus praise on the city of Jerusalem (see Psalms 46; 48; 76; 84; 87; 122). While Gunkel was inclined to treat these psalms as "Eschatological Hymns" directed toward a vision of the end of time, his form-critical successors sought a liturgical setting for these psalms. For instance, Sigmund Mowinckel began by criticizing Gunkel's view that cultic prototypes had been spiritualized. Mowinckel characterized his own approach as the cult-functional method, and he made the enthronement psalms the foundation for an overarching proposal for a liturgical setting in life of many psalms. In particular, Mowinckel suggested that the enthronement psalms can be taken as evidence

---

8. Claus Westermann, *Praise and Lament in the Psalms,* trans. K. R. Crim and R. N. Soulen (Atlanta: John Knox, 1981) 30-35.

that Israel, like certain other ancient Near Eastern peoples, celebrated annually the enthronement or re-enthronement of their deity, Yahweh, as king of the universe.[9] According to Mowinckel, this New Year Festival formed the setting in life of not just the enthronement psalms but many others as well. In a similar move, but one that went in a different direction, Hans-Joachim Kraus focused on the songs of Zion and the royal psalms (see below) in his proposal that many of the psalms were used liturgically in an annual Royal Zion Festival, which celebrated God's choice of Jerusalem and the Davidic dynasty. The basic problem with these two proposals, as well as with Artur Weiser's attempt to relate many psalms to a Covenant Renewal Festival, is that there is simply no solid biblical evidence for such festivals.[10]

Because of the lack of biblical evidence, subsequent scholarship has generally abandoned the proposals of Mowinckel, Kraus, and Weiser. Even so, they were not totally misguided. They had the value of emphasizing the liturgical origins and use of the psalms, and they served to highlight crucial themes in the psalter, especially the reign of God and the centrality of Zion. While the proposals of Mowinckel and Kraus may have gone beyond the confines of the evidence, it can hardly be doubted that the kingship of God and God's choice of Zion were celebrated cultically in some manner in ancient Israel or Judah. Neither can it be doubted that the songs of praise played a major role in such celebrations and more generally in worship at the major pilgrimage festivals (see the festal calendars in Exod 23:14-17; Lev 23:3-44; Deut 16:1-17).

In the following commentary, possible liturgical origins and uses of the songs of praise will be noted; however, in keeping with the shape of the psalter itself (see below, "The Shape and Shaping of the Psalter"), the emphasis will fall on hearing the hymns as proclamations of the reign of God. Not only do the enthronement psalms proclaim God's reign (see Psalms 29; 47; 96), but so also do the other songs of praise (see Psalms 8; 33; 100; 103; 104; 113), including the songs of Zion (see Psalms 46; 48; 122).

Royal Psalms. The royal psalms are actually not a form-critical category but rather a grouping based on a particular *content.* In this category, Gunkel included all the psalms that deal primarily with the Israelite or Judean king or the monarchy. For instance, Psalm 2 seems to be a portion of a coronation ritual; Psalm 45 celebrates a royal wedding; Psalm 72 is a prayer for the king, perhaps originally upon his coronation day (see also Psalms 18; 20; 21; 89; 101; 110; 132; 144).

Form-critical appropriation of the royal psalms involves the attempt to determine a precise setting for each psalm; such attempts will be noted in the following commentary. More emphasis will be given, however, to the function of the royal psalms in the final form of the psalter. Gerald Wilson has noted that royal psalms occur at the "seams" of

9. Sigmund Mowinckel, *The Psalms in Israel's Worship,* 2 vols., trans. D. R. Ap-Thomas (Nashville: Abingdon, 1962) 1:106-92.

10. See H.-J. Kraus, *Psalms 1–59: A Commentary,* trans. H. C. Oswald (Minneapolis: Augsburg, 1988) 56-58; Artur Weiser, *The Psalms,* OTL, trans. H. Hartwell (Philadelphia: Westminster, 1962) 23-52.

Books I–III.[11] It may also be important, as Childs suggests, that the royal psalms are generally scattered throughout the psalter (see below "The Shape and Shaping of the Psalter").[12] The effect is to give these psalms themselves and the psalter as a whole a messianic orientation; that is to say, the royal psalms are not only poetic relics from the days of the Davidic dynasty but are also expressions of the ongoing hope that God will continue to manifest God's sovereignty in concrete ways in the life of God's people and in the life of the world. Such an appropriation of the royal psalms takes seriously the historical fact that they were preserved and were found meaningful long after the disappearance of the monarchy (see below on "The Theology of the Book of Psalms" and the Commentary and Reflections on Psalms 2; 18; 89; 101; 110; 132; 144).

Wisdom/Torah Psalms. Gunkel suggested that certain psalms should be identified as wisdom poetry (see Psalms 1; 37; 73; 128). Like the royal psalms, wisdom poetry is not strictly a form-critical category. Rather, for Gunkel, wisdom psalms "consist entirely of pious reflections."[13] Mowinckel also distinguished certain psalms as wisdom poetry, and he suggested that these poems were the only non-cultic material in the psalter.[14] Subsequent scholars have debated these conclusions, sometimes trying to identify various characteristics or themes as constitutive of wisdom psalmody and sometimes seeking a cultic setting for the wisdom psalms.[15]

In the following commentary, it will be noted when a psalm shares characteristics and themes with the wisdom literature. More important, however, is the fact that one of the wisdom psalms opens the psalter and serves as a kind of preface. Psalm 1, along with Psalms 19 and 119, is often identified as a torah psalm (NIV and NRSV "law" in Ps 1:2 translates the Hebrew word תורה [tôrâ]; see also Ps 19:7; 119). As James L. Mays points out, these three psalms, along with numerous other expressions throughout the psalter of a didactic intent (see Psalms 18; 25; 33; 78; 89; 93; 94; 99; 103; 105; 111; 112; 147; 148), serve to give the whole psalter an instructional orientation. The effect, according to Mays, is this: "Form-critical and cult-functional questions are subordinated and questions of *content and theology* become more important."[16] In short, the existence of the wisdom/torah psalms is finally a stimulus to interpret the psalms theologically as well as historically (see below on "The Shape and Shaping of the Psalter").

Entrance Liturgies. Although a relatively minor category, since it contains only Psalms 15 and 24, the psalms that Gunkel called entrance liturgies have commanded a good deal of scholarly attention. The similarity between the two psalms is evident:

11. Gerald H. Wilson, *The Editing of the Hebrew Psalter,* SBLDS 76 (Chico, Calif.: Scholars Press, 1985) 207-8.
12. Brevard Childs, *Introduction to the Old Testament as Scripture* (Philadelphia: Fortress, 1979) 515-16.
13. Gunkel, *The Psalms,* 38.
14. Mowinckel, *Psalms in Israel's Worship,* II:104-25.
15. See Roland E. Murphy, "A Consideration of the Classification 'Wisdom Psalms'," VTSup 9 (1962) 156-67; J. K. Kuntz, "The Canonical Wisdom Psalms of Ancient Israel—Their Rhetorical, Thematic, and Formal Dimensions," in *Rhetorical Criticism: Essays in Honor of J. Muilenburg,* eds. J. J. Jackson and M. Kessler (Pittsburgh: Pickwick, 1994) 186-22; L. Perdue, *Wisdom and Cult: A Critical Analysis of the View of Cult in the Wisdom Literature of Israel and the Ancient Near East,* SBLDS 30 (Missoula, Mont.: Scholars Press, 1977).
16. James L. Mays, "The Place of the Torah-Psalms in the Psalter," *JBL* 106 (1987) 12; italics added.

❖ The question apparently asked by those approaching the Temple or sanctuary
❖ The answer, perhaps delivered by a priestly voice, involving standards of admission
❖ Concluding blessing or affirmation

While the liturgical origin and use of Psalms 15 and 24 are perhaps more evident than with any other genre, the following commentary will move beyond an investigation of historical matters. In particular, the entrance liturgies invite theological reflection on what it means to enter God's reign and to submit to God's sovereign claim upon the life of God's people and the world.

Prophetic Exhortation. Gunkel noticed prophetic sayings or oracles in several psalms, an insight developed by Mowinckel and subsequent scholars to the point that Psalms 50, 81, and 95 are often called prophetic exhortations. More recently, Gerstenberger has suggested that these psalms may represent what he calls a "liturgical sermon."[17] In any case, as with the wisdom/torah psalms, the instructional intent is evident. These psalms challenge the reader to make a decision regarding God's sovereign claim, and thus they will be treated in the following commentary as a further indication of a theological appropriation of the psalms.

Psalms of Confidence/Trust. According to Gunkel, the psalms of confidence are to be explained as derivatives of the lament of an individual; that is, when the "certainty of being heard" (see above) became detached from the elements of complaint and petition, the result was psalms like Psalms 16, 23, and 91. It is not at all clear that this explanation is correct; however, it has been largely adopted by subsequent scholars, and it does make sense to categorize certain psalms under the rubric of confidence or trust. In the following commentary, a consideration of the historical or liturgical origin of these psalms is subordinated to the theologically significant fact that these psalms offer eloquent professions of faith in God's protective presence and power amid threatening circumstances. In short, these psalms assert God's sovereignty, despite appearances to the contrary.

Mixed Types and the Move Beyond Form Criticism. Even though his methodological emphasis would seem to belie it, Gunkel was well aware of the individuality of each psalm. When psalms were especially unique, and thus resistant to easy categorization, Gunkel resorted to a category that he called "mixed types."[18] In retrospect, it is clear that the very existence of this category would eventually undermine the basic goals of the form-critical and cult-functional approaches. Gunkel, Mowinckel, and their successors sought first of all to discern what was *typical* about particular psalms. Thus practitioners of the form-critical and cult-functional methods tended to overlook the *individuality* of each psalm. This neglect opened the way for James Muilenburg and others to issue the call for scholars to supplement form criticism with rhetorical criticism in an attempt to appreciate the unique literary features of each psalm. It is to rhetorical criticism, the

17. Gerstenberger, *Psalms,* 210.
18. Gunkel, *The Psalms,* 36-39.

immediate successor of form criticism, that we now turn. But first, it should be noted that Gunkel's explanation of the existence of mixed types also anticipates a further scholarly move beyond form criticism. In Gunkel's words: "Mixtures or inner transformations occur with great frequency when the literature we are discussing becomes old, especially when the original setting of the literary types has been forgotten or is no longer clear."[19]

In short, Gunkel recognizes that discernment of the types and liturgical origins of the psalms is not sufficient for understanding them in their final form and literary setting. It is precisely this recognition that eventually invited the movement beyond a method that aims at appreciating the *typical* and the *original* to methods that aim at appreciating the *individual* and the *final*. In other words, the limited aims of form criticism invited the movement first toward rhetorical criticism and then toward a consideration of the importance of the shape and the shaping of the book of Psalms as a literary context for interpreting the individual psalms.

Rhetorical Criticism. In 1968, James Muilenburg issued his widely heeded call for biblical scholarship "to venture beyond the confines of form criticism into an inquiry into other literary features which are all too often ignored today."[20] Muilenburg did not advocate the abandonment of form criticism, but rather suggested that it be supplemented by what he called rhetorical criticism. As applied to the book of Psalms, rhetorical criticism has meant an attention to literary features that leads to an appreciation of each psalm as a unique poetic creation.

Just as the following commentary will attend to the possible liturgical origins and uses of the psalms, so it will also attend to the literary features that make the psalms good poetry. The more prominent of these features are described below, including an indication of how these features will be treated in the commentary.

Parallelism. Perhaps the most persistent poetic feature of the psalms is parallelism. While several of the psalms' poetic features cannot readily be captured in translation, parallelism can be, and even a casual reader is likely to notice that the second half of a typical poetic line is often related somehow to the first half of the line. Earlier generations of scholars categorized parallelism as either synonymous (the second part of the line echoes the first), antithetical (the second part of the line states opposition to the first), or synthetic (which is a catch-all category and often really meant that no parallelism could be detected). In these terms, the most frequent type of parallelism is synonymous; however, recent scholars have pointed out that the echoing involved is only rarely precisely synonymous. Rather, the second part of the poetic line usually has the effect of intensifying or specifying or concretizing the thought expressed in the first part of the line.[21] While there are far too many instances of parallelism for it to be noted regularly, the commentary will point out

19. Ibid., 36.
20. James Muilenburg, "Form Criticism and Beyond," *JBL* 88 (1969) 4.
21. See James L. Kugel, *The Idea of Biblical Poetry* (New Haven: Yale University Press, 1981); Robert Alter, *The Art of Biblical Poetry* (New York: Basic Books, 1985). For a more technical discussion that proposes a broader understanding of parallelism, see Adele Berlin, *The Dynamics of Biblical Parallelism* (Bloomington: Indiana University Press, 1985).

particularly striking instances of parallelism (see Commentary on Psalms 1; 3; 13; 90; see also the article entitled "Introduction to Hebrew Poetry," 301-15).

Repetition. Another very common, and probably the most important, poetic feature of the psalms is repetition. While it is often considered bad writing style to use the same word repeatedly, such apparently was not the case in Hebrew. Consequently, repetition occurs frequently in a variety of patterns and for a variety of purposes. For instance, the same word will occur several times in a psalm in order to draw the reader's attention to a key word or concept, such as salvation/deliverance (Psalm 3), righteousness (Psalms 71; 85), justice/judgment (Psalm 82), or steadfast love (Psalms 103; 109; 136). Unfortunately, both the NIV and the NRSV sometimes obscure the Hebrew repetition by choosing different English words to translate the same Hebrew word. In the commentary, such instances will be identified, and such instances will often serve as a primary clue to the theological significance of the psalm.

When a word, phrase, or poetic line occurs in both the opening and the closing line of a psalm or section of a psalm, the repetition is called an *inclusio*, or envelope structure. This framing technique again often identifies a crucial theological theme or concept (see Psalms 8; 21; 67; 73; 103; 107; 118). The same effect is frequently achieved by the use of a refrain, a poetic line that occurs in exactly or essentially the same form two or more times in the psalm (see Psalms 8; 42–43; 46; 49; 56; 57; 59; 62; 80; 99; 107; 116; 136). Still another form of repetition is known as step-like or stair-like repetition, since it involves repeating a word either in both parts of the same line or in juxtaposed lines. Not coincidentally, it occurs most frequently in the Songs of Ascents or Songs of the Steps (Psalms 120–134; see Commentary on Psalms 120–122 and others in the collection). While it is not necessary to categorize every instance of repetition, and while some instances are clearly more noticeable and significant than others, this commentary will regularly call attention to cases of repetition and will take them as a primary stylistic clue to discern the theological message and significance of the psalms.

Chiasm. A special form of repetition is known as a chiasm. *Chiasm* is a word derived from the Greek letter *chi* (X), and it denotes the arrangement of elements in an ABBA or ABCBA pattern. The number of elements in a chiasm may vary, but the effect is to provide a sort of multiple envelope structure that focuses attention on the center of the chiasm. Chiasm occurs frequently, and on various scales, in the psalms. It may involve the arrangement of words in a single poetic line (see Pss 3:7; 6:10; 25:9; 83:1; 100:3; 142:2); it may involve the arrangement of corresponding words or phrases in several poetic lines (see Pss 1:5-6; 3:1-2; 36:6-7, 10-11; 56:3-4; 72:1-2; 87:3-7; 90:1-2, 5-6; 97:6-7; 101:3-7; 137:5-6); or it may involve the arrangement of the poetic lines or sections of a psalm with the effect of focusing attention on a central panel or pivotal verse (see Psalms 1; 5; 11; 12; 17; 26; 67; 86; 92). In the commentary, chiasm will be treated not only as an important literary device but also as a clue to appropriate directions for theological reflection and appropriation.

Structure. Whereas form critics are interested in the structure of a psalm in order to discern characteristic elements and their typical arrangement, rhetorical critics are more interested in what is unique about the way a psalm is structured. In this commentary, an attempt is made to treat the structure of a psalm not only as a literary issue but also as a clue to theological significance and appropriation. To be sure, some psalms are more amenable to such analysis than others (e.g., Psalms 8; 73; 122). In many cases, it seems fairly clear that a poem falls into distinct sections, sometimes even into formal stanzas or strophes (although I have avoided these terms because such formal regularity is rare). In several cases, however, the structure of a psalm can justifiably be perceived in several ways, depending upon which structural clues one chooses to focus. In this case, it is not necessary to declare one structural proposal correct to the exclusion of others. Rather, it is proper to conclude that the structure or movement of the psalm occurs at more than one level (see Psalms 62; 77; 87; 94; 101; 113; 122; 128; 129; 136; 140; 142; 145; 146).

Other Figurative Uses of Language. The literary features described above can be captured in English translation, at least to a certain extent. Nevertheless, other figurative uses of language in the psalms are virtually impossible to render recognizably into English. For instance, although there is disagreement over how to define it and even over whether it exists, most scholars are willing to speak of the meter of Hebrew poetry. There is no really satisfactory way to capture the rhythmical quality of psalms, except perhaps to render the psalms in poetic lines rather than as continuous prose; and both the NIV and the NRSV do this. Also difficult to capture in English are instances in which Hebrew syntax or word order is unique or striking; however, in the commentary, the more prominent of such cases will be mentioned and described (see Pss 3:1-2, 6-7; 5:1; 22:9-10; 31:15; 36:5-6; 38:15; 62:7; 90:4; 93:2; 114:7; 123:3). So will other figures of speech that cannot be readily rendered into English, such as alliteration (see Pss 54:3-4; 63:1, 11; 122:6-8), onomatopoeia (see Pss 29:3-7; 140:3), and plays on words (see Pss 28:5; 39:4-5; 48:4; 146:3-4).

Another literary feature of the psalms that cannot be captured in English is the apparently intentional ambiguity of some Hebrew words, phrases, and grammatical constructions. Although an English translation cannot preserve the ambiguity, it will be pointed out in the commentary (see Pss 1:3; 25:12; 40:9; 51:14; 71:7; 87:4-5; 96:13; 100:3; 122:3; 127:3; 135:3; 147:1).

Aside from specific instances of intentional ambiguity, however, there is a sense in which all poetry is inevitably ambiguous. That is, poetry aims not so much at describing things objectively as it does at evoking the reader's imagination. As Thomas G. Long puts it, "Psalms operate at the level of the imagination, often swiveling the universe on the hinges of a single image."[22] This means that the psalms put the reader in touch with a source of mystery that cannot be precisely defined, objectively described, or even fully comprehended. As S. E. Gillingham says of biblical poetry, including the book of Psalms:

22. Thomas G. Long, *Preaching and the Literary Forms of the Bible* (Philadelphia: Fortress, 1989) 47.

Its diction is full of ambiguity of meaning. As with all poetry, but perhaps especially in this case, the concealing/revealing aspect of biblical verse means that any interpretation involves as much the power of imaginative insight as any so-called "objective" analysis. . . .

. . . The language of theology needs the poetic medium for much of its expression, for poetry, with its power of allusion, reminds us of the more hidden and mysterious truths which theology seeks to express. Poetry is a form which illustrates our need for a sense of balance in our study of theology. On the one hand, good poetry still testifies to the need to be properly analytical in our pursuit of knowledge, but on the other, it illustrates the importance of being open to the possibility of mystery and ambiguity in our pursuit of meaning.[23]

In keeping with the direction Gillingham suggests, the following commentary will attend analytically to the literary and stylistic devices that make the psalms good poetry, but it will always do so with an eye toward theology—that is, to the way the psalms encounter the reader with the majesty of God and with the mystery of God's involvement with the world.

The Shape and Shaping of the Psalter. As already suggested, Hermann Gunkel's own conclusions about the psalms left the way open for the emergence of rhetorical criticism and for the scholarly consideration of individual psalms in the context of their final *literary* setting within the book of Psalms. It is in the latter direction that Psalms scholarship has moved in the past fifteen years. Although they did not make much of them, scholars have long been aware of various features that pointed to a process involving the gradual collection of individual psalms and groups of psalms into what we now have as the book of Psalms. Such features are described below, including an indication of their significance for the following commentary.

Superscriptions. Of the 150 psalms, 117 have a superscription, ranging from a single phrase (see Psalms 25–28) to several lines (see Psalms 18; 60; 88). The superscriptions contain three kinds of information:

(1) *Personal Names.* The superscriptions of seventy-three psalms mention David; others mention Jeduthun (Psalms 39; 62; 77; see 1 Chr 16:41-42; 25:1-8), Heman (Psalm 88; see 1 Kgs 4:31; 1 Chr 2:6; 6:17; 16:41-42; 25:1-8), Ethan (Psalm 89; see 1 Kgs 4:31; 1 Chr 2:6), Solomon (Psalms 72; 127), Moses (Psalm 90), the Korahites (Psalms 42; 44–49; 84–85; 87–88), and the Asaphites (Psalms 50; 73–83). While it is possible in some cases that these names indicate authorship (see above on the personal/historical method), it is more likely that they originated in the process of collection. David, for instance, was remembered as the initiator of psalmody in worship (see 1 Chr 16:7-43). To be sure, the chronicler wrote hundreds of years after the actual time of David, but the memory may be an ancient one. In any case, it is more likely that many psalms were attributed to David as a result of this memory rather than as a result of Davidic authorship. Similarly, the process of collection accounts for the association of thirteen psalms with specific moments

23. S. E. Gillingham, *The Poems and Psalms of the Hebrew Bible,* Oxford Bible Series (Oxford: Oxford University Press, 1994) 277-78.

in David's life (see Psalms 3; 7; 18; 34; 51; 52; 54; 56; 57; 59; 60; 63; 142). These references should not be construed as historically accurate, but neither should they be dismissed as irrelevant. Rather, they provide an illustrative narrative context for hearing and interpreting particular psalms as well as a clue to the appropriateness of imagining narrative contexts for other psalms that do not contain superscriptions.

Not surprisingly, several of the other names found in the superscriptions are also associated with David's establishment of worship—Jeduthun, Heman, Korah (see 1 Chr 6:22, 37; 9:19), and Asaph (1 Chr 6:39; 9:15; 16:5, 7; 37; 25:1-8). The significant Korahite and Asaphite collections probably point to a process of both authorship and collection of psalms within Levitical guilds. It is not clear how well these collections reflect the actual work of these guilds, and this issue remains the subject of scholarly debate.[24] Of more relevance for the consideration of the shape and shaping of the psalter is the appearance of those collections at the beginning of Books II and III. Interestingly, too, the name Solomon occurs at the end of Book II and the name Moses at the beginning of Book IV. This pattern seems more than coincidental, and I shall return to these observations later.

(2) *Liturgical Instructions.* Fifty-five superscriptions contain the phrase "to the leader" (למנצח *lamnaṣṣēaḥ* ; see NRSV). As the NIV suggests with its translation, "for the director of music," this phrase is probably some sort of liturgical instruction (see NIV "directing" and NRSV "lead" in 1 Chr 15:21, where the Hebrew word occurs as a verb). Its precise significance is unknown, as is that of other words and phrases that probably indicate moods, modes, or even melodies accompanying the original singing of certain psalms (see *sheminith* [השמינית *haśśĕmînît*] in Psalms 6; 12; and 1 Chr 15:21; *gittith* [הגתית *haggittît*] in Psalms 8; 81; 84; NRSV, *Muth-labben* [עלמות לבן *ʿalmût labbēn*]; NIV, "the tune of 'The Death of the Son' " in Psalm 9; NRSV, "The Deer of the Dawn"; NIV, "the tune of 'The Doe of the Morning' " in Psalm 22 [אילת השחר *ʾayyelet haśśaḥar*]; "Lilies" [ששנים *šōš annîm*] in Psalms 45 and 69; "Lily of the Covenant" [שושן עדות *šûšan ʿēdût*] in Psalm 60; NRSV, "Lilies, a Covenant"; NIV, "the tune of 'The Lilies of the Covenant' " in Psalm 80 [שושנים *šōšannîm ʿēdût*]; *alamoth* [עלמות *ʿālāmôt*] in Psalm 46 and 1 Chr 15:20; *mahalath* [מחלת *māḥălat*] in Psalm 53; *mahalath leannoth* [מחלת לענות *māḥălat lĕ ʾāmôt*] in Psalm 88; NRSV, "Dove on Far-off Terebinths"; NIV, "to the tune of 'A Dove on Distant Oaks' " in Psalm 56 [יונת אלם רחקים *yônat ʾēlem rĕḥōqîm*]; and "Do Not Destroy" in Psalms 57–59; 75 [אל־תשחת *ʾal-tašḥēt*]). According to some scholars, however, these mysterious terms may designate musical instruments or the original liturgical settings of certain psalms, as is more clearly the case with other words and phrases. For instance, musical instruments are mentioned in the superscriptions of Psalms 4; 5; 6; 54; 55; 61; 67; 76, and several superscriptions indicate a particular setting or use for their psalms. Psalms 30 and 92 are the most specific in this regard, but the superscriptions of Psalms 38; 45; 70; and 100 may also point to cultic occasions. The liturgical instructions in the superscriptions clearly suggest that many

---

24. See M. D. Goulder, *The Psalms of the Sons of Korah,* JSOTSup 20 (Sheffield: JSOT, 1982); H. D. Nasuti, *Tradition History and the Psalms of Asaph,* SBLDS 88 (Atlanta: Scholars Press, 1988).

of the psalms were meant to be sung, but we know very little about actual performance. Consequently, little attention will be devoted to the liturgical instructions in the following commentary. The same applies to the term *selah,* which occurs in the body of several psalms. While it almost certainly represents a liturgical instruction of some kind—perhaps a signal to the musical director or levitical choir—its precise meaning and significance are not known.

(3) *Genre Designations.* The term "Genre designation" may be misleading, since it is clear that the ancient authors and performers of the psalms were not form critics in the contemporary sense (see above). For instance, while the most important contemporary rubrics are "prayer" and "praise," these terms occur infrequently in the superscriptions— "praise" only in Psalm 145 and "prayer" only in Psalms 17; 86; 90; and 102 (and only in Psalm 102 does the superscription further identify the prayer as a "lament"; see the NIV). Even so, the ancient collectors did apparently distinguish among types of poems. The most frequent designation in the superscriptions is the Hebrew word מזמור (*mizmôr*; 57 times), which is traditionally rendered "psalm," an English transliteration of the Greek translation (ψαλμός *psalmos*) of *mizmôr* and the term that has provided the Greek and English names for the entire collection (the Hebrew title of the book is תהלים [*tĕhillîm,* "Praises"]). The Hebrew root occurs frequently in the Psalms as a verb, and it describes both singing and the musical accompaniment to singing. Aside from "psalm," the most frequent designation in the superscriptions is "song" (שיר *šîr*), and it too points to the musical performance of the poems. What difference the ancient authors and collectors perceived between a "psalm" and a "song" is not clear, especially in view of the fact that thirteen psalms are identified as both and that both labels are applied to psalms that contemporary form critics categorize in a variety of ways. Psalm 88 is even triply identified as a "song," a "psalm," and a "maskil" (משכיל *maśkîl*). This term, which occurs in the superscriptions of thirteen psalms as well as in Ps 47:7 (see NIV and NRSV notes), appears to derive from a root that means "be attentive, prudent, wise." Thus it may mean something like "contemplative poem" or "didactic poem." Certainty of meaning is impossible, however, and the term is best left untranslated. The same conclusion applies to the terms מכתם (*miktām,* Psalms 16; 56–60) and שגיון (*šiggāyôn,* Psalm 7; see the similar term in Hab 3:1), which are even more obscure. Since the origin, meaning, and significance of the ancient genre designations are so elusive, little further is said of them in the commentary.

Collections. The existence of collections within the Psalter has long been obvious, but the exact process behind the compilation of these collections to form the book of Psalms remains unknown. While the superscriptions of many psalms may not be original, they do offer a clue as to which psalms were perceived as somehow belonging together. For instance, psalms with the same ancient genre designation often occur in sequence (see Psalms 42–45; 52–55; 56–60), but more important, the personal names mentioned in the superscriptions indicate the existence of a collection. With the exception of Psalms 1–2; 10; and 33, the superscription of every psalm in Book I mentions David. Another

Davidic collection is formed by Psalms 51–72. While Psalms 66–67 and 71–72 do not mention David, the notice in 72:20 suggests the ancient editors' awareness of a collection. Interestingly, most of the psalms in the two Davidic collections are laments of an individual, although the ancient genre designations vary. Between the two Davidic collections that form the bulk of Books I–II are a Korahite collection (Psalms 42–49) and a single Asaph psalm (Psalm 50) that anticipates the Asaphite collection (Psalms 73–83), which forms the bulk of Book III.

A mysterious feature of Books II–III is the existence of another kind of collection, the so-called Elohistic psalter (Psalms 42–83), a grouping in which the divine name *Elohim* occurs far more frequently than it does in Psalms 1–41 or 84–150 (*Elohim* occurs 244 times in Psalms 42–83 as opposed to only 49 times in Psalms 1–41 and 70 times in Psalms 84–150). For years, scholars have usually concluded that the Elohistic psalter is the result of the work of a redactor who changed many of the occurrences of *Yahweh* to *Elohim*; however, this conclusion is questionable. For instance, it does not satisfactorily explain why 44 occurrences of *Yahweh* remain in Psalms 42–83 or why the redactor would have stopped with Psalm 83 rather than continuing through Psalm 89, the end of Book III. Thus it appears likely that the occurrences of *Elohim* are original to the composition of Psalms 42–83 and that these psalms originated and existed independently. Only later, it seems, were they joined to Psalms 3–41 (or 1–41) and only later were Psalms 84–89 attached as a sort of appendix to form Books I–III.[25]

It appears that Books I–III were in place prior to Books IV–V. Indications to this effect include the facts that 28 of the 33 untitled psalms occur in Books IV–V and that the psalters found at Qumran show a great deal more variation from the MT in Books IV–V than they do in Books I–III.[26] In short, it is likely that a different and later process of collection was operative for Books IV–V. For instance, the name of David is not nearly so prominent (see only Psalms 101; 103; 108–110; 122; 124; 131; and the Davidic collection, Psalms 138–145). At the same time, the laments of an individual are far less prominent and songs of praise become predominant (see below). Collections are marked more by the theme of praise, as with Psalms 93–99 (the reign of God) and Psalms 113–118 (or 111–118). More formally, Psalms 146–150 all begin and end with the imperative "Praise the LORD!" Book V contains what is clearly a discrete collection, the Songs of Ascents (Psalms 120–134; see Commentary on Psalm 120).

While scholars have long noticed the existence of various collections, only recently have they begun to try to discern the significance of the shape of the whole book of Psalms. While much about the process of collection remains and will undoubtedly always remain unknown, certain directions can be detected and will be discussed under the heading "The Editorial Purpose of the Psalter."

The Five-Book Arrangement. As both the NIV and the NRSV suggest, the doxologies

25. Beth L. Tanner, " 'Where Is Your God?' The Shape of the Elohistic Psalter," unpublished paper delivered at the Annual Meeting of the SBL, Nov. 20, 1994, Chicago, Illinois.

26. Gerald H. Wilson, "Shaping the Psalter: A Consideration of Editorial Linkage in the Book of Psalms" in *The Shape and Shaping of the Psalter,* ed. J. C. McCann, Jr., JSOTSup 159 (Sheffield: JSOT, 1993) 73-74.

in Pss 41:13; 72:19; 89:52; and 106:48 have the effect of dividing the psalter into five books:

Book I	Psalms 1–41
Book II	Psalms 42–72
Book III	Psalms 73–89
Book IV	Psalms 90–106
Book V	Psalms 107–150

This is not a new observation. Indeed, the *Midrash Tehillim* states, "As Moses gave five books of laws to Israel, so David gave five books of Psalms to Israel."[27] Despite this ancient tradition, some scholars conclude that the five-book arrangement is coincidental rather than intentional; that is, the doxologies are simply original parts of Psalms 41; 72; 89; and 106 and were never meant to serve any editorial function. This conclusion has recently been definitively refuted by Gerald H. Wilson, who points out that the movements from Psalms 41 to 42, 72 to 73, and 89 to 90 are marked not only by doxologies but also by shifts in the ancient genre designation and in the personal names mentioned in the superscriptions.[28] Thus, while a five-book arrangement may not have been the original goal of the earliest editors or collectors, it did become a goal of those who put the psalter in its final form. Wilson's work has been a major stimulus in moving Psalms scholarship in the direction of attempting to discern the editorial purpose of the psalter, and it is to this issue that we now turn.

The Editorial Purpose of the Psalter. The detection and description of an editorial purpose for the psalter does not involve the attempt to explain how each individual psalm reached its current literary placement. The following commentary will point out relationships between adjacent psalms and among several psalms that seem to form a coherent sequence or pattern, and it will take these literary relationships seriously as a context for theological interpretation. At the same time, however, the commentary reflects the attempt not to force relationships or to read too much into patterns that may simply be coincidental. It by no means assumes that every psalm can be tied to an overarching editorial purpose, but rather that the psalter in its final form often reflects the earlier shape of the smaller collections of which it is composed. Following Wilson's lead, the commentary's governing assumption is that editorial activity most likely took place at the "seams" of the psalter—that is, at the beginning or conclusion of the whole or of the various books.[29] Proceeding on this assumption, the interpreter of the whole psalter notices several patterns that seem too striking to be coincidental.

Books I–III (Psalms 1–89). The most striking observation about Books I–III is that royal psalms occur near the beginning of Book I (Psalm 2) and at the conclusion of Books II

---

27. William G. Braude, *The Midrash on Psalms* (New Haven: Yale University Press, 1954) 1:5.
28. Gerald H. Wilson, *The Editing of the Hebrew Psalter*, SBLDS 76 (Chico, Calif.: Scholars Press, 1985) 139-97.
29. See ibid., 207-8; see also G. H. Wilson, "The Use of Royal Psalms at the 'Seams' of the Hebrew Psalter," *JSOT* 35 (1986) 85-94. For a survey, see David M. Howard, Jr., "Editorial Activity in the Psalter: A State-of-the-Field Survey," in *The Shape and Shaping of the Psalter*, 52-70.

(Psalm 72) and III (Psalm 89). To be sure, the pattern would be even more striking if Psalm 41 were a royal psalm; but even so, it is impressive enough as Psalm 2 forms with Psalm 72 an envelope structure for Books I–II and with Psalm 89 an envelope structure for Books I–III. As Wilson points out, the progression from Psalms 2 to 72 to 89 is revealing. Psalm 2 establishes the intimate relationship between God and the Davidic king; Psalm 72 reinforces this relationship; and while Psalm 89 begins as a comprehensive rehearsal of all the features of this relationship (vv. 1-37), it concludes with a wrenching description of God's rejection of the covenant with David (vv. 38-45) and with the pained, poignant prayer of the spurned anointed one (vv. 45-51). As Wilson concludes concerning the effect of this progression, "The Davidic covenant introduced in Psalm 2 has come to nothing and the combination of these books concludes with the anguished cry of the Davidic descendants."[30] In other words, Books I–III document the failure of the Davidic covenant—at least as traditionally understood—that was made evident by the destruction of Jerusalem in 587 BCE and the subsequent exile. Thus Books I–III call out for a response, and, according to Wilson, this response is offered by the proclamation of God's reign, which is prominent in Books IV–V.

Before considering Books IV–V in detail, however, it should be noted that the opening psalms of Books II–III already begin both to anticipate the crisis of exile that is fully articulated in Psalm 89 and to point toward a constructive response. Again, a strikingly similar pattern exists between Books II and III. Not only does each of these books conclude with royal psalms, but also each begins with psalms in which an individual voice expresses deep alienation from God and God's place (Psalms 42–43; 73). In each case, these opening psalms are followed by communal laments that are strongly reminiscent of the destruction of Jerusalem and the exile (Psalms 44; 74). Furthermore, impressive verbal links exist between Psalms 42–43 and 44 and between Psalms 73 and 74 (see the Commentary there). The effect is to provide a corporate orientation and context for hearing Psalms 42–43; 73 as well as other individual expressions of opposition and defeat in Books II–III. Such expressions predominate in Book II (see Psalms 51–71). They occur also in Book III (see Psalms 86; 88), although Book III is actually pervaded by communal laments (Psalms 74; 79; 80; 83; 89:38-51), which suggests that the whole book may have been decisively shaped by the experience of exile. In any case, the opening psalms of Books II–III effectively instruct the community to face exile (Psalms 44; 74) with "Hope in God" (Pss 42:5, 11; 43:5) and with the assurance that "God is the strength of my heart and my portion forever" (Ps 73:26 NRSV).[31]

Although not exactly the same as the opening of Books II and III, a similar pattern creates the same effect at the beginning of Book I. Psalm 1 states the problem of the wicked and the righteous in individual terms, and then Psalm 2 states the same problem in corporate terms. Like Psalms 42–44 and 73–74, Psalms 1 and 2 are connected by significant verbal links (see Commentary on Psalms 1 and 2). Although, unlike Psalms 44 and 74, Psalm 2

30. Wilson, *The Editing of the Hebrew Psalter,* 213.

31. See J. C. McCann, Jr., "Books I–III and the Editorial Purpose of the Hebrew Psalter" in *The Shape and Shaping of the Psalter,* 93-107.

is a royal psalm, it does feature a problem that was preeminent in the exilic and postexilic eras: the reality and continuing threat of the domination of Israel by the nations. By portraying God as judge of the wicked (Ps 1:4-6) and ruler of the nations (Psalm 2), Psalms 1–2 affirm the possibility of hope amid the hard realities of the exilic and postexilic eras. By standing at the head of Book I (and the whole psalter; see further below), Psalms 1 and 2 provide a literary context for hearing Psalms 3–41. As in the case of Book II, the shape of Book I suggests that the laments of an individual, which heavily dominate Book I, may be heard also as expressions of communal plight. In short, the final form serves to instruct the community to face crises in the same manner as the "I" of the laments, who always accompanies the articulation of distress with expressions of trust and praise (see above on the laments of an individual).

Because the laments of an individual are so numerous in Book I, psalms of other types are quite noticeable (see Psalms 8; 15; 19; 24; 29; 33; 37). It may be that these other psalms have been placed intentionally between small collections of laments.[32] In any case, however, the juxtaposition of complaint and praise both within a single psalm and between psalms is theologically significant, and it will serve as a basis for theological reflection in the commentary.

In view of the foregoing discussion of Books I–III and in anticipation of the consideration of Books IV–V, it is necessary to define further what is meant here and throughout the following commentary by reference to the exile. To be sure, the exile was a historical event that began with the deportation of Judeans to Babylon in 597 BCE, continued with the destruction of Jerusalem in 587 by the Babylonians, and lasted until 539 when Cyrus permitted the Judean exiles in Babylon to return to Palestine. But in a broader sense, the exile was a theological problem, and it represented an ongoing theological crisis well beyond 539. The destruction of Jerusalem and the deportation to Babylon meant that the people of God lost their three most fundamental and cherished religious institutions: the Temple, the land, and the monarchy. To say that this loss precipitated a crisis is an understatement. Although some of the exiles returned to Palestine after 539, and although the Temple was rebuilt by 515, things were never really the same as before. National autonomy was never achieved again except briefly in the second century BCE. Furthermore, the Davidic monarchy was never reestablished. The Davidic king had been viewed as nothing less than God's own adopted son (see Ps 2:7), and the monarchy represented theologically the concrete embodiment of God's purposes on earth (see Psalm 72). The loss of the monarchy was thus an ongoing theological crisis that made it necessary for the people of God to come to a new understanding of God and of their existence under God. When the commentary refers to the exile, it means primarily not the historical event but the ongoing theological crisis.[33] Because this theological crisis persisted for centuries, the fact that we cannot precisely date the final formation of the psalter is not of crucial

32. See Lawrence Boadt and William J. Urbrock, "Book I of the Psalter: Unity, Direction, and Development," unpublished paper delivered at the Annual Meeting of the SBL, Nov. 20, 1994, Chicago, Illinois.

33. See Ralph W. Klein, *Israel in Exile: A Theological Interpretation* (Philadelphia: Fortress, 1979) 1-8.

significance. The Hebrew psalter may have taken final form in the fourth to third centuries BCE, as many scholars suggest; however, the manuscript evidence from Qumran complicates this conclusion, since it suggests the fluidity of Books IV–V into the second century BCE or beyond.[34] But even if the psalter did not take final form until the first century CE, its shape can still be understood as a response to the exile in the sense of an ongoing theological crisis. This crisis called for new understandings of God and of human faithfulness to God. The shape of the psalter indicates that its editors intended the psalms to participate in the theological dialogue that resulted in new perspectives on both divine and human sovereignty and suffering (see further below on "The Theology of the Psalms").

Books IV–V (Psalms 90–150). The anguished questions of the Davidic descendants (Ps 89:46; 49) cry out for a response, and a fitting answer is provided by Psalm 90 and the subsequent psalms in Book IV—namely, Israel's true home is, always has been, and always will be God alone (Ps 90:1-2). There is, of course, no better voice to deliver this assurance than that of Moses, whose intimate experience of God and leadership of the people occurred before there ever was a temple or a monarchy and before entry into the land! Not coincidentally, the superscription of Psalm 90 is the only one to bear the name of Moses, and seven of the eight references to Moses in Psalms occur in Book IV.[35]

Furthermore, Book IV affirms that Israel's true monarch is not the Davidic king but Yahweh—again, the way it was in Moses' time (see Exod 15:18) and before the monarchy (see 1 Samuel 8). This affirmation is found explicitly in Book IV in the so-called enthronement psalms (Psalms 93; 95–99), a collection that dominates Book IV and that Wilson properly called "the theological 'heart' " of the psalter.[36] While it appears at first sight that Psalm 94 is an intrusion into this collection, it has significant thematic parallels with the enthronement psalms. This fact, plus the verbal links between Psalms 92 and 94, suggest that the placement of Psalm 94 may be intended to bind the enthronement collection more closely to Psalms 90–92, which also share significant verbal links (see Commentary on Psalms 90–92; 94).[37] It may also be more than coincidental that Psalms 95 and 100 are similar (cf. 95:7 and 100:3) and that they form a frame around Psalms 96–99. Furthermore, Psalm 100 recalls Psalm 2, since 2:11 and 100:2 are the only two occurrences in the psalter of the imperative, "Serve the LORD" (NIV and NRSV "Worship" in 100:2). That the theological heart of the psalter recalls its beginning may be a coincidence, but if so, it is an auspicious one that reinforces the psalter's pervasive proclamation of God's sovereignty (see further on "The Theology of the Psalms").

The intent of Book IV to address the crisis of exile helps to explain the placement of

34. G. H. Wilson, "A First Century CE Date for the Closing of the Hebrew Psalter?" in *Haim M. I. Geraryahu Memorial Volume* (Jerusalem: World Jewish Bible Center, 1990) 136-43.

35. See Marvin E. Tate, *Psalms 51–100,* WBC 20 (Dallas: Word, 1990) xxvi. Tate characterizes Book IV as a "Moses-book."

36. Wilson, "The Use of Royal Psalms," 92. See also James L. Mays, *The Lord Reigns: A Theological Handbook to the Psalms* (Louisville: Westminster John Knox, 1994) 12-22.

37. Wilson, "Shaping the Psalter," 75-76. See also David M. Howard, "A Contextual Reading of Psalms 90–94," in *The Shape and Shaping of the Psalter,* 114-22.

Psalms 101–102, which have proven extremely enigmatic in the light of earlier approaches. If Psalm 89 has documented the failure of the Davidic monarchy, for instance, why is a royal psalm like Psalm 101 in Book IV at all? While absolute certainty is elusive, it is crucial to note that when 101:2 is not emended (cf. the NIV with the NRSV), Psalm 101 can be reasonably read as a royal lament. In view of the concluding verses of Psalm 89 (see above), the placement of this royal complaint makes perfect sense. As a lament out of the experience of exile, Psalm 101 also anticipates Psalm 102, vv. 12-17 of which have baffled commentators, since these verses represent a corporate profession out of exile following an apparently individual prayer in vv. 1-11. But together, Psalms 101–102 rehearse the three crucial elements of the crisis of exile: loss of monarchy, Zion/Temple, and land. Fittingly, and congruent with the move from Psalms 89 to 90, Psalm 103 returns the reader to a Mosaic perspective, even though it is labeled "Of David." Not surprisingly, Book IV ends with a historical review, which concludes with the exile (Ps 106:40-46) and the people's plea to be gathered "from among the nations" (Ps 106:47).

In view of the sevenfold occurrence of the Hebrew word for "steadfast love" (חסד *ḥesed,* NRSV) in Psalm 89, culminating in the question of v. 49 ("Lord, where is your steadfast love of old . . . ?" [NRSV]), it is significant that Ps 90:14 prays for God's steadfast love and that Psalm 106 features this word as well (see vv. 1, 7, 45). Furthermore, Psalm 103, which follows immediately the two psalms in Book IV that most clearly articulate the pain of exile (see above on Psalms 101–102), contains four occurrences of the word (vv. 4, 8, 11, 17; see also Pss 92:2; 94:18; 98:3; 100:5). What is more, the six occurrences of the word in Psalm 107, the opening psalm of Book V, suggest that Book V picks up where Book IV left off—that is, it continues the response to the crisis of exile (cf. also Pss 106:47 and 107:2-3). Indeed, Psalm 107 can properly be considered a sermon on God's steadfast love that sounds as if it could have been written in response to Ps 89:49 (see Commentary on Psalm 107). Psalms 108 (v. 3) and 109 (vv. 21, 26) continue the focus on God's steadfast love, and the opening verse of Psalm 107 reappears as the first and last verses of Psalm 118. While Psalms 113–118 are a traditional liturgical unit within Judaism, the literary connections between Psalms 107 and 118 (107:1; 118:1, 29) suggest that Psalms 107–118 may form a redactional unit within Book V. Psalms 107 and 118 both recall the exodus, but the language is also appropriate for describing the return from exile. Significant in this regard, however, Psalm 118 moves toward a petition for continuing help (see v. 25). In short, even after the historical return from exile (see Pss 107:2-3; 118:21-24), the crisis persisted, and the shape of Book V continues the psalter's response.

The imposing Psalm 119, for instance, whenever it may have originated, admirably articulates the experience of the post-exilic generations. While the psalmist is faithful to God and God's instruction, he or she nonetheless is scorned and persecuted and so must live in waiting as a suffering servant—just like the post-exilic generations. This perspective is what the following commentary regularly calls "eschatological," since it involves the proclamation of God's reign amid circumstances that seem to deny and belie it—that is, it leaves the people simultaneously celebrating and awaiting God's reign (see below on "The Theology of the Psalms").

This same eschatological perspective characterizes the movement of the Songs of Ascents (Psalms 120–134) and is particularly evident in Psalm 126. Not surprisingly, the final three psalms (135–137), which form a sort of appendix to the Songs of Ascents, are the most explicit statement in the psalter of the pain of exile (see Commentary on Psalm 137). Psalms 135–137 are the prelude to a final Davidic collection, the first and last psalms of which return to the theme of God's steadfast love, which is prominent at key points in Books IV–V (see Pss 138:2, 8; 145:8; see above on Psalms 89; 90; 106; 107; 118). The core of this collection consists of psalms of lament, culminating in Psalm 144, which is a royal lament. Thus, near the end of both Books IV and V, there are royal laments (see above on Psalm 101) that effectively call to mind the ongoing theological crisis of exile. Significantly, Psalm 145 responds to Psalm 144 by affirming God's steadfast love, just as Psalm 103 had responded to Psalms 101–102 (see Pss 103:8; 145:8). Of further significance, Psalm 145 begins by addressing God as "King," thus also recalling Psalms 93; 95–99, the dominant collection of Book IV and the theological heart of the psalter.

Actually, Psalm 145 proves to be transitional. Not only does it conclude the Davidic collection, forming with Psalm 138 an envelope of praise around a core of laments, but it also anticipates Psalms 146–150. Each psalm in this concluding collection is bounded by "Praise the LORD [הללו־יה hallelu-yah]!" The psalter's final invitation to praise (150:6) has been anticipated by 145:21. Furthermore, the explicit proclamation of God's sovereignty, reintroduced in Ps 145:1, recurs in Pss 146:10 and 149:2, thus recalling the theological heart of the psalter and its beginning as well. More particularly, Ps 149:6-9 features the same cast of characters present in Psalm 2: the rebellious "nations" and "peoples" and "kings." In contrast to Psalm 2, however, Psalm 149 assigns to the "faithful" (see vv. 1, 5, 9)—not to the Davidic king as in Psalm 2—the task of concretely implementing God's reign in the world. Thus Psalm 149 completes a direction that was initiated earlier in Books IV–V and that is another piece of the psalter's response to the crisis of exile—namely, the transfer to the whole people of claims and promises formerly attached to the Davidic monarchy (see the Commentary on Psalms 105; 110; 132; 144; 149). The literary and conceptual links and contrasts between Psalms 2 and 149 are another reminder of the crucial significance of Psalms 1–2, and further consideration of their role is necessary.

Psalms 1–2 as an Introduction to the Psalter. As already suggested, Psalms 1–2 are a fitting introduction to Books I and to Books I–III as a unit. As the psalter progresses, however, it becomes increasingly clear that Psalms 1–2 have set the interpretive agenda and provided an orientation for reading the whole book of Psalms. Scholars have traditionally concluded that Psalm 1 represents an intentional preface or introduction to the psalter, but the introductory function clearly belongs to Psalms 1 and 2 together. Neither psalm has a superscription, and they are bound by several literary links, including the crucial word translated "happy" (אשׁרי *'ašrê*), which forms an envelope structure (Pss 1:1; 2:12).

Psalm 1 portrays happiness as constant openness to God's "instruction" (v. 2; NIV and NRSV "law"), the fundamental orientation of life to God. The repetition of "instruction" (תורה *tôrâ*) is emphatic and suggests that the book of Psalms itself will serve as a source of divine instruction. While Psalm 1 counsels the reader to be open to God's instruction, including the subsequent psalms, Psalm 2 introduces the basic content of that instruction—namely, that God rules the world. Although the role of the Davidic monarch as an agent of God's rule will change as the psalter proceeds (see above), nothing will alter the pervasive proclamation of God's reign, which is first articulated in Ps 2:11-12. Thus happiness essentially belongs to those who "take refuge in" *God* (Ps 2:12), *not* in the Davidic monarch! In short, happiness is essentially trusting God, living in dependence upon God, an affirmation to which the conclusion of the psalter will return (see Ps 146:5). As Psalms 1 and 2 already make clear, and as subsequent psalms will clarify even further, the rule of God is persistently opposed. Thus the perspective of the psalter from the beginning is eschatological—that is, God's reign is proclaimed as a present reality, but it is always experienced by the faithful amid opposition. In this sense, the faithful live both with fulfillment and in waiting (see below, "The Theology of the Psalms").

Beyond Psalms 1 and 2, the rest of the psalter will portray the shape of the faithful life—including what it looks like and feels like and leads people to say and do—and it will reveal how the faithful life constitutes happiness. The portrayal of the faithful life is congruent with the portrayal of the character of God in Psalms, and both portrayals constitute a profoundly important revelation about the nature of divine sovereignty. In other words, while the book of Psalms originated as liturgical responses to God, it has been preserved and transmitted as God's word to humanity. As such, it not only represents a theological resource for dealing with the crisis of exile, but is also a theological resource for the people of God in every generation.

Methodological Conclusion. As suggested at the beginning of this Introduction, the approach to the psalms in the commentary that follows is explicitly theological. To be sure, it is theologically significant that Israel sang songs of praise to God, addressed honest and heartfelt prayers to God, and composed sacred poetry either addressed to or devoted to God. Thus the methods of form criticism and rhetorical criticism will be employed regularly. As traditionally practiced, however, form criticism and rhetorical criticism have not yielded theological conclusions. It is sustained attention to the shaping and final form of the psalter that pushes the interpreter toward theological interpretation. Klaus Seybold summarizes well the purpose of the psalter in its final form:

With the new preface ([Psalm] 1) and the weight of the reflexive proverbial poem ([Psalm] 119), which in terms of its range is effectively a small collection in itself, the existing Psalter now takes on the character of a documentation of divine revelation, to be used in a way analogous to the *Torah,* the first part of the canon, and becomes an instruction manual for the theological study of the divine order of salvation, and for meditation.[38]

As a theological instruction manual that aims at nothing less than the "documentation of divine revelation," the psalter in its final form demands to be interpreted theologically. Thus, while form criticism and rhetorical criticism will regularly be employed to arrive at historical, sociological, and literary conclusions, the ultimate purpose in the commentary is "to compose a commentary based on the book itself as the interpretive context of the psalms."[39] In short, I shall attempt to discern how the psalter was for Israel and is for us "an instruction manual for the theological study of the divine order of salvation"—in other words, what the psalter reveals about the life of God and the life God intends for humankind and for the world.

THE THEOLOGY OF THE PSALMS

Given the importance of the final form of the psalter, it is necessary to begin a consideration of the theology of the psalms with Psalms 1–2; even more specifically, with the very first word of the psalter: "Happy" (NRSV). In a real sense, the rest of the psalter will portray the shape of human happiness, and it is clear from the beginning and throughout Psalms that the definition of human happiness is thoroughly God-centered. The "happy" are those who constantly delight in God's "instruction" (תורה *tôrâ,* Ps 1:2; NIV and NRSV, "law"). In short, happiness derives from the complete orientation of life to God, including perpetual openness to God's instruction. Not only does Ps 1:2 have the effect of orienting the reader to approach the rest of the psalter as Scripture, as "an instruction manual for the theological study of the divine order of salvation" (see Seybold quotation above), but it also introduces a key concept—happiness—and begins to give it a thoroughly theocentric definition. Not surprisingly, the word for "happy" (אשרי *ašrê*) will occur throughout Book I and the rest of the psalter, including as soon as the conclusion of Psalm 2 (see also Pss 32:1-2; 33:12; 34:8; 40:4; 41:4; 65:4; 84:4-5, 12; 89:15; 94:12; 106:3; 112:1; 119:1-2; 127:5; 128:1; 137:8-9; 144:15; 146:5).

Psalm 2:12 begins to fill out the portrait of the happy person, and it does so by introducing another key word that will also occur throughout Book I and the rest of the psalter: "refuge" (חסה *ḥāsâ;* see Pss 5:11; 7:1; 11:1; 14:6; 16:1; 18:30; 25:20; 31:1, 19; 34:8, 22; 36:7; 37:40; 46:1; 57:1; 61:3-4; 62:7-8; 64:10; 71:1, 17; 73:28; 91:2, 4, 9; 94:22; 118:8-9; 141:8; 142:5; 144:2). The happy are those who "take refuge in" God. In short, happiness derives from living in complete dependence upon God rather than upon the self. The word *ḥāsâ* has several synonyms that also occur frequently throughout the psalms (variously translated as "refuge," "fortress," "stronghold"), the most important of which is "trust"

---

38. Klaus Seybold, *Introducing the Psalms,* trans. R. G. Dunphy (Edinburgh: T. & T. Clark, 1990) 24. See also Harvey H. Guthrie, Jr., *Israel's Sacred Songs: A Study of Dominant Themes* (New York: Seabury, 1966) 188-93; J. Clinton McCann, Jr., "The Psalms as Instruction," *Int.* 46 (1992) 117 28.

39. James L. Mays, *Psalms,* Interpretation (Louisville: John Knox, 1994) 19.

(see Pss 4:5; 9:10; 13:5; 21:7; 22:4-6; 25:2; 26:1; 28:7; 31:6, 14; 32:10; 37:3, 5; 40:3; 52:8; 55:23; 56:3-4, 11; 62:8; 84:12; 86:2; 91:2; 115:9-11; 125:1; 143:8). To be happy is to entrust one's whole self, existence, and future to God. As one would expect, there are several instances in which the words for "refuge" and "trust" occur in the same context (see Pss 31:1, 4, 6, 14, 19; 52:7-8; 62:7-8; 71:1, 3, 5; 91:2, 4, 9; 143:8-9); in addition to 2:12, the word "happy" is associated with either "refuge" or "trust" in Pss 34:8; 84:12; and 146:3, 5. Not surprisingly too, several of the occurrences of ḥāsâ or related words occur at key places in the psalter (see Pss 2:12; 91:2, 4, 9; 146:3, 5). Indeed, Jerome F. D. Creach argues that the editors of the psalter intended by the placement of certain psalms to call particular attention to the word ḥāsâ and related words.[40] In any case, whether intentional or not, the sheer repetition of "refuge," "trust," and several other synonyms effectively portrays the happy, faithful life as one characterized by complete dependence upon God (see Commentary and Reflections on Psalms 1; 2).

This fundamental dependence upon God for life and future defines another key word in Psalms, at least insofar as it applies to human beings: "righteousness" (צדק ṣĕdeq) or "the righteous" (צדיק ṣaddîq). "Righteousness" is not primarily a moral category but a relational term. To be sure, behavior follows from one's commitments, but the righteous in the psalms should not be seen as morally superior persons whose good behavior lays an obligation on God to reward them. Rather, the righteous are persons who acknowledge their fundamental dependence upon God for life and future. Their happiness derives ultimately from God's forgiveness (see Ps 32:1-2) and the gift of God's faithful love (see Ps 32:10-11). In short, the happy, the righteous, are those who live by grace. As is evident from Psalm 1 onward, the righteous live constantly in the presence of the wicked, who are also called "scoffers," "sinners," "enemies," "foes," "adversaries," etc. As follows from the above definition of the righteous, the wicked are not outrageously or even obviously bad people, but are persons who live in fundamental dependence upon the self rather than upon God. In short, the wicked are persons who consider themselves to be autonomous, which means literally "a law unto oneself." Self-centered, self-directed, and self-ruled, the wicked see no need for dependence upon God or for consideration of others. The really frightening thing about this conclusion is that the essence of wickedness in the psalms—autonomy—is often what North American culture promotes as the highest virtue (see Commentary and Reflections on Psalm 1).

The definitions of "happiness" and "righteousness" in terms of refuge, the fundamental dependence upon God for life and future, makes sense only in the light of the affirmation that lies at what has been identified as the theological heart of the psalter: the Lord reigns (Psalms 93–99)! Indeed, this affirmation pervades the psalter. God is frequently addressed as "King" (see Pss 5:2; 10:16; 24:7-10; 29:10; 44:4; 47:2, 7; 48:2; 68:24; 74:12; 84:3; 95:3; 98:6; 145:1; 149:2), but even when the language of kingship and reigning is not

40. See Jerome F. D. Creach, *The Choice of YHWH as Refuge and the Editing of the Hebrew Psalter,* JSOTSup (Sheffield: JSOT, forthcoming).

explicitly present, God's rule is articulated by means of other words and concepts. For instance, God's role as universal judge is a function of God's cosmic sovereignty (see Pss 7:7-11; 9:7-8), as is God's role as the divine warrior who enacts the divine will for the world (see Pss 24:8; 68:1-3; 89:5-18).

Furthermore, the royal psalms, which are scattered throughout the psalter, located in strategic places (see above, "Royal Psalms"), serve to articulate God's sovereignty. To be sure, these psalms focus directly on the earthly kings of Israel and Judah, but the earthly kings are presented as agents of God's rule. Psalm 2, for instance, culminates not in an invitation to serve the earthly king but to "Serve the LORD" (v. 11 NRSV). God's reign involves the enactment of justice and righteousness among all people (see Pss 96:10-13; 97:1-2; 98:4-9), and it is precisely the mission of the earthly king as God's agent to embody justice and righteousness on a cosmic scale (see Psalm 72). In this way, too, the royal psalms articulate God's sovereign claim on the whole world.

Even the songs of Zion, although they focus on a very particular place, are finally affirmations of God's universal reign. Psalms 46 and 48, for instance, surround Psalm 47, which explicitly celebrates God's kingship. Not surprisingly, both Psalms 46 and 48 portray God in the role of a warrior who wages peace (see also Ps 76:4-9), and Psalm 48 addresses God as "King" and describes the effect of God's worldwide involvement as "righteousness" (v. 10 NIV) and justice (v. 11; cf. "judgments" in NIV and NRSV; see Ps 122:5). In short, a particular place, Jerusalem, has become a concrete symbol of the extension of God's rule in all places and times. God claims the whole world and all its peoples (see Psalm 87).

At the same time that they affirm God's cosmic reign, however, the royal psalms and songs of Zion also make it clear that God's rule is constantly and pervasively opposed. As the psalter begins, the nations and peoples are aligned against God and God's chosen king (Ps 2:1-3). Jerusalem is regularly the target of attack (see Pss 46:6; 48:5; 76:3-6). This apparent anomaly—constant and powerful opposition to the cosmic rule of God—calls attention to a crucial characteristic of the psalter that I frequently refer to in the commentary as its *eschatological* perspective. Because this word may be subject to misunderstanding, it needs to be carefully defined. By *eschatological,* I mean the proclamation of God's universal reign amid circumstances that seem to deny it and belie it. The word *eschatological* literally means "a word about last things," and it is popularly perceived as having to do primarily with the future. But in the commentary, the word focuses attention on the *present.* That is, the psalms regularly affirm God's reign as a *present* reality. To be sure, the reality of opposition implies the future consummation of God's reign, but the emphasis in the psalms is clearly on the presence of God's reign as the only true source of refuge, happiness, and, indeed, life.

While the eschatological perspective of the psalter is clear enough from Psalm 2, the movement from Psalm 2 to Psalm 3 makes it clear that not only are God's chosen king and God's chosen place constantly opposed, but so also are God's people. In other words, happiness (Pss 1:1; 2:12), prosperity (Ps 1:3), and refuge (Ps 2:12) exist not beyond but rather in the midst of opposition and suffering. Consequently, in addition to "the righteous" and synonyms such as "the upright," the most frequent designations the psalmists use for themselves include "the poor," "the afflicted," "the meek," "the humble," "the needy," "the helpless," and "the oppressed" (see Psalms 9–10). Not surprisingly, therefore, the dominant voice in the psalter is that of prayer. Indeed, prayer is a way of life for those who entrust themselves fully to God's care. Prayer is the offering of the whole self to God, including pain, grief, fear, loneliness, and sinfulness as well as expressions of innocence and desire for vengeance (which in the final form of the psalter are to be understood as pleas for justice; see Psalms 58; 109; 137).

Although prayer and praise are usually treated as separate voices involving distinct categories of psalms (that is, laments/complaints and songs of praise; see above on form criticism), it is of crucial theological significance to notice that prayer and praise are finally inseparable. Almost without exception, each prayer for help moves toward expressions of trust and praise. Furthermore, Books I–III, the portions of the psalter dominated by laments, include songs of praise at regular intervals, that are often linked verbally to the preceding prayer (see below Commentary on Psalms 7; 8; 32; 33) as if to remind the reader of the inseparability of prayer and praise. Thus, while laments and songs of praise may have represented in ancient Israel separate liturgical movements or moments, their regular juxtaposition within the same psalm and in the final arrangement of the psalter suggests theological connections. The juxtaposition prevents the conclusion that the songs of praise represent merely the ideology of the rich and powerful that is used to celebrate the status quo.[41] To state it positively, the juxtaposition means that for the faithful, suffering and glory are inseparable. In explicitly Christian terms, the people of God are inevitably and always identified by *both* the cross and the resurrection (see Reflections on Psalms 13; 22; 31; 69).

When construed as ultimately inseparable voices, both prayer and praise are means of expressing complete dependence upon God. While prayer is the offering of the whole self to God by way of direct address to God involving bitter complaint, brutally honest confession of sin or innocence, and poignant petition and intercession, praise is the offering of the whole self to God by way of joyful affirmation of God's sovereignty, enthusiastic celebration of God's character and activity, and direct address to others to invite them to join in the song. Praise affirms a simple but profound good news—namely, that the whole cosmos and all its peoples, creatures, and things belong to God. This good news has extraordinary political, socioeconomic, and ecological implications.

Because our lives belong to God, we are not our own. Thus the autonomy that much of North American culture promotes is a dead end; it will lead only to a society of isolated selves rather than to the community of justice and righteousness that God wills among all people (see Commentary on Psalms 1; 100).

Because our lives belong to God, and because God wills life for all people, "justice for

41. See Walter Brueggemann, *Israel's Praise: Doxology Against Idolatry and Ideology* (Philadelphia: Fortress, 1988).

all" becomes far more than a phrase out of a pledge or a matter of democratic fairness. Rather, "justice for all" means that God wills political and economic systems that exclude *no one* from access to provision for life and future; God will be content with nothing less than peace on earth (see Commentary on Psalms 29; 46; 68; 72; 82). Because God wills life for the whole creation as well as for all people, ecological awareness becomes not simply a matter of preserving limited natural resources in order to maintain for ourselves and our children the standard of living to which we have grown accustomed. Rather, ecology and theology are inseparable. To live under God's rule is to live in partnership with all other species of creature and in partnership with the earth itself (see Commentary on Psalms 8; 19; 29; 104; 147; 148).

The psalter's eschatological character has profound significance for understanding the fundamental identity of both humanity and God. As for humanity, the psalms teach us that human happiness—indeed, authentic human life—exists only when people acknowledge God's reign and respond by taking refuge in God. Because God's reign is constantly opposed by humans, however, happiness and life inevitably involve suffering. Therefore, the faithful, righteous life consists of suffering servanthood.

As for God, the reality of constant opposition to God's reign calls for an understanding of divine sovereignty that differs from the usual view of sovereignty. Sovereignty is ordinarily thought of as the power to enforce one's will. But God simply does not do this. Rather, God invites, encourages, and empowers people to do God's will. But from the very beginning of the biblical story, people have chosen *not* to do God's will (see Genesis 3). God's only choice is either to enforce the divine will, which will mean the destruction of humanity, or to suffer the consequences of human disobedience (see Genesis 6–9). God chooses the latter, and it is a monumentally important choice, for it means that God willingly becomes vulnerable for the sake of relating genuinely to humankind. Terence Fretheim calls God's choice "a divine *kenosis,* a self-emptying, an act of self-sacrifice," and he concludes, "The very act of creation thus might be called the beginning of the passion of God."[42] In other words, God suffers, too, and it is necessary to conclude that divine sovereignty consists not of sheer force but of sheer love. The eschatological perspective of the psalter—the proclamation of God's reign amid persistent opposition—reinforces the conclusion that God's power is essentially that of pure, unbounded love. God's life, too, consists of suffering servanthood!

This being the case, it is not an exaggeration to say that the most important theological concept in the book of Psalms is represented by the Hebrew word חסד (*ḥesed*), which the NIV often translates as "unfailing love" and the NRSV regularly translates as "steadfast love." It occurs as early as Ps 5:7 and frequently thereafter in all five books of the psalter, often in crucially placed psalms (see Psalms 42; 89; 90; 106; 107; 118; 138; 145). Its range is not restricted to a particular type. Rather, Israel appeals to God's *ḥesed* in prayer (see Commentary on Psalms 6; 13; 31; 44; 51; 63), and Israel celebrates God's *ḥesed* in

---

42. Terence Fretheim, *The Suffering of God: An Old Testament Perspective* (Philadelphia: Fortress, 1984) 58.

songs of praise (see Psalms 33; 100; 103; 136; 145; 147). Indeed, the opening line of several psalms constitutes a brief hymn in itself as it celebrates God's *ḥesed* (see Pss 107:1; 118:1; 136:1; cf. 100:5; 113:2), and this formulation appears to have functioned as a sort of "favorite hymn," which also has the character of a basic profession of faith (see 2 Chr 5:13; 7:3; 20:21; Ezra 3:11).

Given that the final form of the psalter has the character of "instruction" (*tôrâ*; see above), it is not surprising that the importance of *ḥesed* in the psalms matches its importance in the Pentateuch, the Torah. At a crucial turning point when the future of Israel hangs in the balance, God reveals Godself to be "merciful and gracious, slow to anger, and abounding in steadfast love and faithfulness" (Exod 34:6 NRSV). In fact, this or a very similar formulation occurs several more times in the Pentateuch and beyond; it seems to constitute a basic profession of Israel's faith (see Num 14:18; Neh 9:17; Joel 2:13; Jonah 4:2). Not unexpectedly, it also occurs in the psalms (see Pss 86:15; 103:8; 145:8). The other terms in the formulation of Exod 34:6 are also important in the psalms. The NRSV's "merciful" (רחום *raḥûm*) is from the same root as a noun that means "womb" (רחם *rḥm*); thus it conveys God's motherly compassion (see also Pss 25:6; 40:11; 51:1; 69:16; 79:8; 106:45; 111:4). The word "gracious" (חנון *ḥanûn*) is regularly paired with "merciful" (*raḥûm*), and another form of the root indicates that God's grace is the basis for appeals to God for help (e.g., see "Be gracious" in Pss 4:1; 6:2). The words "faithfulness" (אמת *'ĕmet*) and "steadfast love" (*ḥesed*) are paired frequently in the psalms as in Exod 34:6 (see Pss 25:10; 36:5; 40:10-11; 57:3; 61:7; 85:10; 89:14; 117:2). The word "faithfulness" occurs alone as well (see Pss 54:5; 71:22; 91:4; 143:1), but the word *ḥesed* appears more frequently and serves virtually as a one-word summary of Israel's understanding of the character of God.

That God is fundamentally compassionate, gracious, faithful, and loving does not mean that anything goes with God. From the beginning, the psalter recognizes the wrath of God (see Ps 2:5, 12). The psalmists appeal to God's wrath against their enemies (Pss 56:7; 59:13), and they are aware of experiencing God's wrath (Pss 6:1; 38:1; 78:59, 62; 88:7, 16; 89:38, 46; 90:7, 9, 11). Again, this picture is consistent with Exodus 34, where God's self-revelation as *ḥesed* (v. 6) is followed closely by the statement that God "does not leave the guilty unpunished" (v. 7 NIV). But how can God be both loving and wrathful, gracious and just, forgiving and punishing? The question is not easily answered for us—or for God! Indeed, this very dilemma is the inevitable result of God's choice to love a sinful humanity, and it bespeaks God's willingness to be vulnerable and to suffer for love's sake. What we can say is that retribution is clearly not operative as a mechanistic scheme. Rather, reward is the experience of authentic life in dependence upon God, and punishment is the inevitable outcome of the choice not to be related to God. The book of Psalms affirms that evil will not endure (see Psalm 1). But given Israel's awareness of its own sinfulness (see Psalms 32; 51; 78; 106; 130) and the sinfulness of all humanity (see Psalms 1–2; 14; 143), one must finally conclude that God's justice is ultimately manifest as love. For Christian readers, the psalter's presentation of the mystery of sovereignty made perfect in steadfast love comes into sharpest focus on the cross of Jesus Christ.

THE PSALMS AND THE NEW TESTAMENT

The early church's use of the psalms was in keeping with both major directions suggested by recent scholarly study of the book of Psalms—that is, the church used the psalms both as liturgical materials in early Christian worship and as a theological resource. Evidence for the first use is found in Paul's advice to the Colossians to "sing psalms, hymns, and spiritual songs to God" (3:16 NRSV; see also Eph 5:19). Although it is not clear precisely what each of these three terms designates, it is almost certain that "psalms" (and perhaps "hymns") refers to material from the book of Psalms. After all, the earliest followers of Jesus were Jews, so it only makes sense that they would continue to use in worship some of the same materials they had always used. To be sure, new materials were used in Christian worship as well, and it is likely that "spiritual songs" refers explicitly to Christian material that may have been created with inspiration from the psalms. For instance, Mary's Song (Luke 1:46-55) contains echoes of Psalms 98 and 113, and the Song of Simeon (Luke 2:28-32) echoes Ps 119:123.

While it is likely that the early Christians prayed and sang the psalms, it is absolutely clear that they used the psalms as a theological resource. The book of Psalms is quoted and alluded to in the NT more than any other OT book. This is not at all surprising in view of the fact that the theology of the psalms is congruent with the core of Jesus' preaching and teaching. What was identified earlier as the theological heart of the psalter—God reigns—is precisely the fundamental good news that Jesus announced from the beginning of his public ministry (see Mark 1:14-15). Jesus proclaimed the reign of God as a present reality, and he invited people to enter it and experience it immediately. Thus Jesus' preaching was eschatological in the sense in which this term was defined—that is, he proclaimed the reign of God amid constant opposition. This persistent opposition meant that Jesus' own life, as well as the lives of his followers and of those to whom his ministry was most often directed, may be characterized in the same terms that regularly describe the psalmists: *afflicted, oppressed, poor, needy, weak, meek,* and *persecuted.* But like the psalms, it is precisely the afflicted whom Jesus pronounces "Happy" or "Blessed" (see Matt 5:1-11; Luke 6:20-23).

In short, like the psalms, Jesus' ministry of suffering servanthood pushes toward a radical redefinition of the usual understanding of sovereignty. Sovereignty is not the demonstration of sheer power but the embodiment of sheer love, which ultimately is revealed to be the most powerful reality of all. The gracious, incarnational involvement of God with humanity, already evident in the psalms (and elsewhere in the OT), is, from the Christian perspective, completed in Jesus' ministry of suffering servanthood. Thus, in reflecting on Jesus' identity, the early Christians concluded that Jesus was nothing less than God incarnate, "the Word became flesh and lived among us" (John 1:14 NRSV). Because Jesus had fully revealed what God is like, thus fulfilling the role of the ancient kings of Judah and Israel to enact God's justice and righteousness, the early church saw in Jesus the culmination of the monarchical ideal. Thus they accorded Jesus the royal titles "anointed" (משיח *māšîaḥ*; Χριστός *Christos*; see Ps 2:4; Mark 1:1) and Son of God (see Mark 1:1; Ps 2:7). The cross, far from being a sign of defeat, was the clearest demonstration of God's character and sovereignty. The resurrection did not remove the scandal of the cross but instead validated its revelation that the power of sheer love is the only authentic source of life. Thus Jesus' invitation to discipleship is essentially an invitation for people to share his ministry of suffering servanthood: "let them deny themselves and take up their cross and follow me" (Mark 8:34 NRSV). The lives of Jesus' followers, like Jesus' own life, will replicate the lives of the psalmists, who are pronounced "happy" not beyond but in the midst of their constant affliction.

Given the congruence between the portrayal of God and the faithful life in the psalms and by Jesus, it is not surprising that the Gospel writers cannot tell the story of Jesus without frequently referring or alluding to a psalm. For instance, the words of the heavenly beings in Luke's account of Jesus' birth recall the content and movement of Psalm 29, thus suggesting that Jesus' birth signals the presence of God's reign (see Luke 2:13-14 and Commentary on Psalm 29). The heavenly voice at Jesus' baptism quotes a portion of Ps 2:7, thus introducing Jesus as the one who would ultimately embody God's will and finally fulfill the purpose of the monarchy (see Matt 3:17; Mark 1:11; Luke 3:22). Psalm 2:7 is cited again at Jesus' transfiguration, immediately after the first prediction of his passion in the synoptic Gospels (see Matt 17:5; Mark 9:7; Luke 9:35). The effect is to reinforce the message that Jesus will embody God's character and will do so precisely by way of his suffering servanthood.

This message is, of course, regularly reinforced as well by Jesus' ministry of compassion and his teaching (see Commentary on Psalms 24; 37; and 73, which are specifically recalled by Jesus' Beatitudes; see also Psalms 41; 126). But it is seen most clearly in Jesus' passion, and in telling this part of Jesus' story, the Gospel writers rely most heavily on the psalms. Jesus' entry into Jerusalem is narrated with reference to Psalm 118, thus suggesting that Jesus' upcoming passion is to be viewed in sequence with the exodus and return from exile, God's saving deeds of old (see Matt 21:9; Mark 11:9-10; Luke 19:38; John 12:12). The account of the crucifixion in all four Gospels has been shaped by Psalm 22, and in Matt 27:46 and Mark 15:34, the words Jesus speaks from the cross are a quotation of Ps 22:1. These words are not present in Luke and John, but Jesus' final words in Luke are a quotation of Ps 31:5 (Luke 23:46), and Jesus' final words in John seem also to allude to Ps 31:5 and perhaps to Ps 22:31 (John 19:30). The passion accounts have also been influenced by Psalm 69 (cf. Matt 27:48; Mark 15:36; John 19:28-29 with Ps 69:21; and Ps 69:4 with John 15:25). In short, the Gospel writers drew upon the three longest and most impressive of the laments of an individual in order to relate the story of Jesus' suffering (see also Psalms 38; 41). In other words, Jesus is presented as the ultimate paradigm of the faithful sufferer. What is more, it is precisely Jesus' faithful suffering on behalf of others that reveals what God is like. Thus, as suggested already, the cross is for Christians the ultimate revelation of the mystery the Psalms present—that is, divine sovereignty manifested as perfect love.

The paradox of strength made perfect in weakness (see 2 Cor 12:9), although "a stumbling block to Jews and foolishness to Gentiles" (1 Cor 1:23 NRSV), should not be misunderstood. God's strength—the power of sheer love—is *real* strength. As William Placher, citing Jürgen Moltmann's *The Crucified God,* puts it: "It would be a weak, poor God . . . who could not love or suffer. Such a God would be caught in a prison of impassability."[43] It is precisely the God revealed in Psalms and in Jesus Christ that is strong enough to be vulnerable. This apparent weakness turns out to be the greatest strength of all, as the resurrection of Jesus demonstrated. For us to understand properly the paradox of divine sovereignty, the cross and the resurrection must be inseparable, and the NT always presents them this way.[44] Indeed, the inseparability of cross and resurrection is analogous to the way in which lament and praise are finally inseparable in the psalms (see above). Given this analogy, it is appropriate that the resurrection as well as the crucifixion is proclaimed in the NT by way of the psalms. The first recorded Christian sermon—Peter's sermon on the Day of Pentecost—is based primarily on Pss 16:8-11; 110:1; and 132:11 (see Acts 8:25-34); Psalm 110 is often quoted or alluded to in articulating the glory of the crucified one (see 1 Cor 15:25; Eph 1:20; Col 3:1; Heb 1:3; 8:1; 10:12-13; 12:2).

The radical implications of Jesus' embodiment of God's sovereignty in suffering love were not lost on the apostle Paul. As Elsa Tamez points out, Jesus' proclamation of the reign of God becomes, in Pauline terms, justification by grace—or better yet, "the revelation of the justice of God."[45] As Jesus revealed and as Paul clearly understood, God's justice is ultimately manifested as grace. The traditional exposition of justification by faith as the forgiveness of sins is not incorrect, but it is not broad enough. The revelation of God's justice involves fundamentally the good news that God's gracious love extends to *all* people. God's justice means the affirmation of life for all people, not based on any system of human merit but as a result of God's loving gift. The message is again congruent with that of the psalms, and Paul appeals to the psalms to support his case. No human being can deserve God's gift of life (see Rom 3:9-20, where Paul cites several psalms, including 14:1-3; 143:2). The gift of divine forgiveness (see Rom 4:7-8, which cites Ps 32:1-2) means the leveling of all distinctions and human systems that exclude. This theology of divine justice revealed as gracious love—which Paul found in the psalms and which Jesus had embodied—led Paul to the radical step of casting aside sacred but exclusivistic symbols,

43. William C. Placher, *Narratives of a Vulnerable God: Christ, Theology, and Scripture* (Louisville: Westminster John Knox, 1994) 19.

44. See Charles B. Cousar, *A Theology of the Cross: The Death of Jesus in the Pauline Letters* (Philadelphia: Fortress, 1990) 103-8.

45. Elsa Tamez, *The Amnesty of Grace: Justification by Faith from a Latin American Perspective,* trans. Sharon H. Ringe (Nashville: Abingdon, 1993) 157.

such as circumcision and dietary regulations, in order to open the church to all people. It is appropriate that Paul found warrant for this step in the psalms (see Rom 15:9-11, which quotes Pss 89:49; 117:1).

It is appropriate that a final word about the psalms and the NT come from the Revelation to John. While direct quotation of the psalms is rare (see only Rev 2:26-27, which cites Ps 2:8-9), the Revelation is full of singing and songs that could well have been inspired by the psalter. The Revelation shares the psalter's fundamental conviction that God rules the world (see Rev 11:15; 12:10; 15:3), and the mention of "a new song" (Rev 5:9; 14:3) explicitly recalls Psalms 96; 98; and 149, all of which assert God's reign. It is particularly interesting that the Revelation, like Psalm 149, envisions God's people reigning with God in a redeemed world that includes "the healing of the nations" (Rev 22:1-5 NRSV; see also 2:26-27; 5:10; and cf. Ps 149:5-9). While the Revelation is usually classified as apocalyptic literature, it should not be construed as a timetable for the chronological end of the world. Rather, it portrays the future that God wills, which is possible because God rules the world, and which, indeed, becomes a present reality for those who acknowledge God's claim and enter God's realm of life. Insofar as it depicts the "end" or destiny of the world, it portrays the faithful gathered to God and singing a song that recalls Pss 86:9-10 and 145:17 (see Rev 15:3-4). As a vision of the "end," it might be beneficial for contemporary folk to hold this scenario alongside secular apocalyptic scenarios like nuclear winter, nuclear holocaust, or an earth laid waste by the radiation that enters through an atmosphere depleted of ozone. To be sure, such warnings should not be dismissed, although it is unlikely that we shall be frightened into reform. What will go further than anything else to prevent such catastrophes will be living toward a different vision, the biblical vision of faithful folk from all times and places, gathered, as the psalmists of old, to acknowledge God's reign by singing a new song.

BIBLIOGRAPHY

Commentaries:

Allen, Leslie C. *Psalms 101–150*. WBC 21. Waco: Word, 1983. Contains the author's translation, a survey of scholarly treatment, and theological reflection. Especially rich in structural and stylistic analysis.

Bratcher, Robert G., and William D. Reyburn. *A Translator's Handbook on the Book of Psalms*. New York: United Bible Societies, 1991. Provides analysis of many recent translations with a focus on the RSV and the GNB. Also provides many helpful structural and stylistic insights.

Brueggemann, Walter. *The Message of the Psalms: A Theological Commentary*. Minneapolis: Augsburg, 1984. Organized according to a contemporary typology (orientation, disorientation, new orientation), this treatment of fifty-eight psalms is rich in literary insights and theological appropriation.

Craigie, Peter. *Psalms 1–50*. WBC 19. Waco: Word, 1983. Contains the author's translation, a survey of scholarly treatment, and theological reflection. Heavily oriented to form criticism with attention to ancient Near Eastern backgrounds.

Gerstenberger, Erhard S. *Psalms: Part 1, with an Introduction to Cultic Poetry*. Forms of the OT Literature 14. Grand Rapids: Eerdmans, 1988. Although thoroughly form critical, this volume proposes that psalms should be understood as rituals originally set in small primary groups, such as the family or the local synagogue. Contains commentary on Psalms 1–60.

Kraus, Hans-Joachim. *Psalms 1–59* and *Psalms 60–150.* Translated by H. C. Oswald. Minneapolis: Augsburg, 1988 and 1989. Although still primarily form critical, Kraus has modified his earlier stance. His work is full of sensitive theological insights and references to classical sources, especially Luther and Calvin.

Mays, James L. *Psalms.* Interpretation. Louisville: John Knox, 1994. Excellent commentary for preachers and teachers. Reflects the best of all recent methods with results that are theologically profound, relevant to pastors, and shaped with an eye toward the church's liturgical calendar.

Stulmueller, Carroll. *Psalms 1* and *Psalms 2.* OT Message 21 and 22. Wilmington, Del.: Michael Glazier, 1983. Employs a variety of approaches to interpret the psalms in their original contexts but always with an eye toward NT use and contemporary appropriation.

Tate, Marvin E. *Psalms 51–100.* WBC 20. Dallas: Word, 1990. Contains the author's translation, a survey of scholarly treatment, and very helpful theological reflection. Reflects judicious use of all methods, including attention to the shape and shaping of the psalter.

Weiser, Artur. *The Psalms.* Translated by H. Hartwell. OTL. Philadelphia: Westminster, 1962. The theory of a Covenant Renewal Festival is pervasively evident, but this volume contains many keen theological insights and illustrates them with frequent references to classical Lutheran sources and hymnody.

Westermann, Claus. *The Living Psalms.* Translated by J. R. Porter. Grand Rapids: Eerdmans, 1989. Organized according to form-critical categories, this volume contains commentary on forty-six psalms by a sensitive exegete and theologian.

Other Studies:

Bellinger, W. H., Jr. *Psalms: Reading and Studying the Book of Praises.* Peabody, Mass.: Hendrickson, 1990. A brief introduction that aims at preparing persons to engage in their own informed study of Psalms.

Brueggemann, Walter. *Praying the Psalms.* Winona, Minn.: St. Mary's, 1982. A sensitive treatment of the theological issues involved in reading and praying the psalms.

Gillingham, S. E. *The Poems and Psalms of the Hebrew Bible.* Oxford Bible Series. Oxford: Oxford University Press, 1994. Accessible, helpful introduction to Hebrew poetry and to what it means to read the psalms as poems.

Gunkel, Hermann. *The Psalms: A Form-Critical Introduction.* Translated by T. M. Horner. FBBS 19. Philadelphia: Fortress, 1967. Makes available in English the basis of Gunkel's classical work on Psalms.

Guthrie, Harvey H. *Israel's Sacred Songs: A Study of Dominant Themes.* New York: Seabury, 1966. Departs from form-critical insights but is constantly concerned with how and why the psalms continue to be spoken and to speak to contemporary persons.

Holladay, William L. *The Psalms Through Three Thousand Years: Prayerbook of a Cloud of Witnesses.* Minneapolis: Fortress, 1993. Illustrates how the psalms have functioned throughout history and also addresses contemporary theological issues in interpreting and using the psalms. Good companion to Prothero's work (see below).

Kraus, Hans-Joachim. *Theology of the Psalms.* Translated by Keith Crim. Minneapolis: Augsburg, 1986. Illumines basic topics in their ancient setting— God, people, Zion, the king, the enemies, the individual— and concludes with a consideration of the use of the psalms in the NT.

Levine, Herbert J. *Sing Unto God a New Song: A Contemporary Reading of the Psalms.* Bloomington: Indiana University Press, 1995. A sensitive discussion of the psalms and their use in view of the conflict between faith and experience and the consequent issue of theodicy, concluding with a chapter on Jewish interpretation of the psalms after the Holocaust.

Limburg, James. *Psalms for Sojourners.* Minneapolis: Augsburg, 1986. Brief essays on psalms of various types with constant concern to address their meaning for today. Very useful for preachers and teachers.

McCann, J. Clinton, Jr. *A Theological Introduction to the Book of Psalms: The Psalms as Torah.* Nashville: Abingdon, 1993. Focuses on hearing the psalms in the contemporary context as Scripture—as instruction about God, humanity, and the faithful life.

Mays, James L. *The Lord Reigns: A Theological Handbook to the Psalms.* Louisville: Westminster John Knox, 1994. A series of essays on the theological issues involved in the ongoing use of the psalms as both Scripture and liturgy. Excellent companion to Mays's Psalms commentary (see above).

Miller, Patrick D., Jr. *Interpreting the Psalms.* Philadelphia: Fortress, 1986. Introductory essays on contemporary issues in Psalms interpretation are followed by excellent expository essays on ten psalms.

Mowinckel, Sigmund. *The Psalms in Israel's Worship.* Translated by D. R. Ap-Thomas. Nashville: Abingdon, 1962. Presents Mowinckel's influential cult-functional approach and his conclusions concerning the use and setting of the various types, several of which are involved in his theoretical Enthronement Festival of Yahweh.

Nowell, Irene. *Sing a New Song: The Psalms in the Sunday Lectionary.* Collegeville, Minn.: Liturgical Press, 1993. Organized by form-critical type, this volume relates the psalms lection to the other readings in the Roman Catholic lectionary and makes a plea for the use of the psalms in the Sunday service.

Peterson, Eugene H. *Answering God: The Psalms as Tools for Prayer.* San Francisco: Harper & Row, 1989. An accessible rationale for and guide to the use of the psalms in contemporary prayer.

Pleins, J. David. *The Psalms: Songs of Tragedy, Hope, and Justice.* Maryknoll, N.Y.: Orbis, 1993. Takes seriously the contemporary realities of socioeconomic oppression as a point of departure for hearing the psalms as "poetry of justice" and for considering their theological implications for worship and work.

Prothero, Rowland E. *The Psalms in Human Life and Experience.* New York: E. P. Dutton, 1903. Illustrates the use of Psalms in Christian history through the nineteenth century. A good companion to Holladay's work (see above).

Sarna, Nahum M. *Songs of the Heart: An Introduction to the Book of Psalms.* New York: Schocken, 1993. Introduces Psalms primarily by way of nine essays on individual psalms of various types. Especially useful for treating the psalms in their ancient Near Eastern context and for relating them to rabbinic sources as well as to medieval and contemporary Jewish commentators.

Smith, Mark S. *Psalms: The Divine Journey.* New York: Paulist, 1987. Drawing on ancient Near Eastern solar imagery, this volume treats Psalms primarily from the perspective of the psalmists' experience of God in the Temple.

Wilson, Gerald H. *The Editing of the Hebrew Psalter.* SBLDS 76. Chico, Calif.: Scholars Press, 1985. Ground-breaking study of the shape and shaping of the psalter that is responsible for much of the impetus to interpret the book of Psalms in its final literary context.

Zenger, Erich. *A God of Vengeance? Understanding the Psalms of Enmity.* Translated by Linda M. Maloney. Louisville: Westminster John Knox, 1995. A comprehensive rationale and plea for the use of the psalms of enmity in Christian worship so as to be liturgically sound, theologically faithful, and not Marcionite or anti-Jewish.

OUTLINE OF PSALMS

I. Psalms 1–41, Book I

    A. 1:1-6, Delight in God's Teaching

    B. 2:1-12, The Reign of God

    C. 3:1-8, God Helps Those Who Cannot Help Themselves

    D. 4:1-8, You Alone, O Lord

    E. 5:1-12, Lead Me, O Lord

    F. 6:1-10, O Lord—How Long?

    G. 7:1-17, O Righteous God!

    H. 8:1-9, The Majesty of God and the Glory of Humanity

    I. 9:1–10:18, The Needy Shall Not Always Be Forgotten

    J. 11:1-7, The Upright Shall Behold God's Face

    K. 12:1-8, I Will Now Arise

    L. 13:1-6, But I Trust in Your Steadfast Love

    M. 14:1-7, No One Does Good

    N. 15:1-5, They Shall Not Be Moved

    O. 16:1-11, I Keep the Lord Always Before Me

    P. 17:1-15, Beholding Your Likeness

    Q. 18:1-50, Steadfast Love to the Anointed

    R. 19:1-14, God's Instruction Is All-Encompassing

    S. 20:1-9, We Trust in the Name of the Lord Our God

    T. 21:1-13, The King Trusts in the Lord

    U. 22:1-31, My God, My God, Why Have You Forsaken Me?

    V. 23:1-6, Like a Child at Home

    W. 24:1-10, The Earth Is the Lord's

    X. 25:1-22, To You, O Lord, I Offer My Life

    Y. 26:1-12, Establish Justice for Me, O Lord

    Z. 27:1-14, Your Face, Lord, Do I Seek

    AA. 28:1-9, The Lord Is My Strength

    BB. 29:1-11, Glory to God!

    CC. 30:1-12, So That My Soul May Praise You

    DD. 31:1-24, My Life and Future Are in Your Hand

    EE. 32:1-11, You Forgave the Guilt of My Sin

PSALMS 1–41

BOOK I

PSALM 1:1-6, DELIGHT IN GOD'S TEACHING

NIV

BOOK I

Psalms 1–41

Psalm 1

¹Blessed is the man
who does not walk in the counsel of the
wicked
or stand in the way of sinners
or sit in the seat of mockers.
²But his delight is in the law of the LORD,
and on his law he meditates day and night.
³He is like a tree planted by streams of water,
which yields its fruit in season
and whose leaf does not wither.
Whatever he does prospers.

⁴Not so the wicked!
They are like chaff
that the wind blows away.
⁵Therefore the wicked will not stand in the
judgment,
nor sinners in the assembly of the
righteous.
⁶For the LORD watches over the way of the righteous,
but the way of the wicked will perish.

NRSV

BOOK I

(Psalms 1–41)

Psalm 1

¹ Happy are those
who do not follow the advice of the wicked,
or take the path that sinners tread,
or sit in the seat of scoffers;
² but their delight is in the law of the LORD,
and on his law they meditate day and night.
³ They are like trees
planted by streams of water,
which yield their fruit in its season,
and their leaves do not wither.
In all that they do, they prosper.

⁴ The wicked are not so,
but are like chaff that the wind drives away.
⁵ Therefore the wicked will not stand in the
judgment,
nor sinners in the congregation of the
righteous;
⁶ for the LORD watches over the way of the
righteous,
but the way of the wicked will perish.

COMMENTARY

1:1. The book of Psalms begins with a beatitude, a form usually associated with wisdom literature but that occurs most frequently in Psalms (see e.g., Pss 2:12; 32:1-2; 33:12; 34:8; 40:4; 41:1; 106:3; 112:1; 119:1-2; "blessed" or "happy" [אשרי *ašrê*] occurs 25 times in the Psalms

and 8 times in Proverbs). Because the opening phrase stands outside the parallel structure of the remainder of the verse, and because Psalm 1 is a preface or introduction to the psalter (see the Introduction), the effect is to offer the exclamation, "Happy are those . . ." as an interpretative clue both to this particular psalm and to the whole psalter. In some sense, *all* of the psalms will involve a portrayal of what it means to be "happy" or "blessed."

The remainder of v. 1 describes the happy person over against the "wicked" (רשעים *rĕšā'îm*), "sinners" (חטאים *ḥaṭṭā'îm*), and "scoffers" (לצים *lēṣîm*). The effect of defining the happy person initially in negative terms is to sharpen the contrast between what will in v. 6 be called "the way of the righteous" and the "way of the wicked." The two occurrences of "way" (דרך *derek*) in v. 6, along with the occurrence in v. 1 in the phrase "way of sinners" (דרך חטאים *derek ḥaṭṭā'îm*; NRSV "path"), suggest that this psalm and the entire psalter will offer a choice between two fundamentally different ways of life or life-styles. The outcomes of one's choice of ways are described by the first and last words of the psalm. That choice will either make one "happy" or will lead one to "perish." In short, the way one chooses is a matter of life and death. The comprehensiveness of this choice is probably reinforced poetically by the fact that "happy" (*'ašrê*) begins with the first letter of the Hebrew alphabet, and "perish" (תאבד *tō'bēd*) begins with the last letter—that is, Psalm 1 is an all-embracing presentation of what it means to be "happy."

As the only three-part line in the psalm, v. 1 effectively emphasizes that the way of the wicked is to be studiously avoided. The vocabulary of this verse also begins to suggest what Psalm 1 and the psalter mean by wickedness and righteousness. As is often the case, the parallelism in v. 1 is not precisely synonymous. The general term "wicked" is followed by a more specific term, "sinners," suggesting those who miss the mark or choose the wrong way. The most specific term is "scoffers," which elsewhere connotes persons who are arrogantly unwilling to accept instruction (see Prov 1:22; 9:7-8; 13:1; 14:6; 15:12). This specific term prepares for the positive presentation of the happy person as one whose "delight is in the *instruction* [תורה *tôrâ*] of the LORD" (see v. 2).

The three verbs in v. 1 are important: "walk" (הלך *hālak*; NRSV "follow"), "stand" (עמד *'āmad*; NRSV, "take"), "sit" (ישב *yāšab*). The variety of postures covered by these verbs not only reinforces the importance of how one positions oneself, but also has the effect of associating motion

and thus instability with the wicked. Insofar as the wicked do achieve stability—the verb for "to sit" also means "to dwell"—it is in the wrong place. Like the nouns in v. 1, the verbs prepare for the positive presentation of the happy person, whose fruitfulness is made possible by a stable rootedness in a favorable location (v. 3).

1:2. The negative characterization of v. 1 is followed by a strong adversative particle ("but" [כי אם *kî 'im*]) at the beginning of v. 2, which introduces the positive portrayal of happy persons. While the NRSV and the NIV regularly translate the Hebrew word *tôrâ* as "law," this translation is misleading. Many interpreters have understood "the law" in v. 2 to mean the Deuteronomistic code, and they have taken Psalm 1 as recommending a rigid legalism that is accompanied by a mechanistic system of reward and punishment for obedience or disobedience. Consequently, Psalm 1 has often been dismissed as simplistic and naive. Such a conclusion is not necessary. The word *tôrâ* fundamentally means "instruction." In contrast to scoffers who arrogantly refuse all instruction, happy persons delight in God's instruction, having it always before them. What is commended, therefore, is not a close-minded legalism, but a posture of constant openness to God's instruction. That this openness to God's instruction was not a burden but a source of delight is indicated by Psalms 19 and 119, which along with Psalm 1 are often categorized by scholars as torah psalms (see Introduction).

Verse 2*b* is reminiscent of Josh 1:8. As Joshua succeeds Moses, he is told by God that "this book of the law" is something he is to "meditate on . . . day and night" in order to "make your way prosperous" (NRSV; cf. "prospers" in Ps 1:3). The king of Israel also is to have "a copy of this law" and is to "read . . . it all the days of his life" (Deut 17:18-19 NRSV). It is likely that "law" in these two texts does, indeed, designate the Deuteronomistic code; however, such need not be the case in Ps 1:2. There is no mention of a book or a copy of the law. "Instruction" here refers not to a particular corpus of stipulations, but more broadly to the whole sacred tradition of God's revelation. It is helpful to recall that the Torah for Judaism—the Pentateuch—contains both stipulations and identity-forming stories of God's dealings with the world and God's people. But even the

Pentateuch is too narrow a referent for the "instruction" of v. 2. The two occurrences of *torah* here, especially in conjunction with the division of the psalter into five books, suggests that the psalms are to be received in a manner analogous to the Pentateuch—that is, as an identity-forming, life-shaping source of God's instruction. What Psalm 1 commends, therefore, is a devotion that looks to tradition, to Scripture, and to contemporary words and events as sources of God's revelation (see Commentary on Psalm 119). What the righteous, "happy" life involves is constant openness to God's teaching.

1:3-4. These verses lie at the center of the psalm, and each contains a simile. Persons who are open to God's instruction are like trees transplanted beside a source of water; they are never without a resource to sustain their lives—namely, God's life-giving instruction (see Ps 19:7). What the tree imagery highlights is not primarily the aspect of fruitfulness but the importance of a stable rootedness. The root is in precisely the proper place—beside water, which represents God's life-giving instruction (see the importance of water in Job 14:7-9). The identical image appears also in Jer 17:8, which specifically mentions the tree's roots. It is deep rootedness in the proper ground that allows the tree to withstand drought and to always bear fruit. As Jer 17:7 suggests, when read along with Ps 1:1-3, to be open to God's teaching is to trust God and to entrust one's life to God. Those who do so always have a resource to sustain their lives. This understanding of the simile illumines the meaning of the final line of v. 3, which has often been interpreted to mean that obedience is materially rewarded. Instead, to "prosper" in "all that they do" should be understood as an affirmation that persons who trust God have a resource for sustaining their lives under any circumstance. As James L. Mays puts it, the way of the righteous is "not so much a reward as a result of life's connection with the source of life."[46]

Verse 4 is introduced by an emphatic form of the negative particle, which has already occurred three times in v. 1 and once in v. 3 and will occur again in v. 5. This sixfold repetition sharpens the contrast between the righteous and the wicked. The second simile (v. 4*b*) is preceded by the same adversative particle ("but") that introduced v. 2 and that reinforces the contrast. The similarity of the Hebrew words for "tree" (עֵץ *'ēṣ*) and "chaff" (מֹץ *mōṣ*)—both are two-letter nouns ending in the same letter—also serves to highlight the contrasting sense of the two similes. While the righteous are like a well-placed tree whose stability allows it to live and bear fruit, the wicked are like chaff, which is the insubstantial waste product that "the wind blows away" while the heavier fruit of the grain falls back to the threshing floor. The wicked have no stability, no rootedness, no place to stand. As suggested already by v. 1, the wicked are always in motion. The instability or "lightness" of the wicked is represented by the relatively brief amount of space accorded to the second simile. The simile of the tree occupies three poetic lines, while the simile of the chaff occupies only one.

1:5. The instability and uselessness of the chaff prepare for the description of the wicked in v. 5. The wicked "will not stand in the judgment." The Hebrew word used here for "stand" (קוּם *qûm*) is different from the one translated "stand" in v. 1 (עמד *'āmad*), but the effect of each is to communicate that the wicked have no foundation, no connection with the source of life. The meaning of v. 5 is disputed. It may mean that the wicked will not endure when the judgment of God occurs. Dahood, for instance, finds here a description of "the final judgment," and concludes that Psalm 1 offers "a rather advanced concept of resurrection and immortality."[47] Most scholars disagree. Craigie, for instance, understands v. 5 to assert that "the wicked hold no weight or influence in the important areas of human society."[48] When persons meet to determine matters of "judgment" (or "justice" [מִשְׁפָּט *mišpāṭ*], as the word may be translated), the wicked will have no influence, no place in "the assembly of the righteous." Insofar as vv. 5 and 6*b* do suggest a kind of judgment, it need not be understood mechanistically as punishment (see below on v. 6).

What is clearer about v. 5 is its literary correspondence with v. 1. The same characters are involved—the "wicked" and "sinners"—and the

---

46. James L. Mays, *Psalms*, Interpretation (Louisville: John Knox, 1994) 43-44.

47. Mitchell Dahood, *Psalms I (1–50)*, AB 16 (Garden City, N.Y.: Doubleday, 1966) 4.

48. Peter C. Craigie, *Psalms 1–50*, WBC 19 (Waco: Word, 1983) 61.

similarity of the Hebrew words for "counsel" (עצה '*ēṣâ*) and "assembly" (עדה '*ēdâ*) also suggests a correspondence. Petersen and Richards take this correspondence as one piece of a larger chiastic structure (see Introduction) of vv. 1-5, which they outline as follows:

A Description of the righteous (vv. 1*b*-2)
  B Simile (v. 3*a-b*)
    C Objectifying conclusion (v. 3*c*)
    C' Objectifying introduction (v. 4*a*)
  B' Simile (v. 4*b*)
A' Description of the wicked (v. 5)

This analysis identifies "a hinge" (C/C') consisting of the following two lines (vv. 3*c*-4*a*):

> And (in) everything which he(it) does, he(it)
>   prospers.
> Not so the wicked!

Verse 3*c* may be understood as the continuation of the tree simile if the subject of the verbs is taken as "it," or the verse may be understood as an "objectifying conclusion" to the simile if the subject is taken as "he" (i.e., the person open to God's instruction). The Hebrew permits either construal, and the ambiguity is probably intentional. Since v. 4*a* precedes the simile, it can more clearly be taken as an "objectifying introduction." The effect is to create a "hinge" that demonstrates again that the whole psalm turns on the crucial contrast between the wicked and the righteous.[49]

1:6. The concluding verse of Psalm 1 stands outside the chiastic structure outlined above, thus effectively emphasizing again the contrast between "the way of the righteous" and "the way

of the wicked." The conjunctive particle at the beginning of v. 6 suggests, however, that it should not be totally isolated from v. 5. Furthermore, the repetition of "righteous" and "wicked" links v. 6 to v. 5; not surprisingly, the pattern of the repetition is chiastic: "wicked . . . righteous . . . righteous . . . wicked." The effect is to present the righteous as central and preeminent, both literarily and theologically. In vv. 5-6, the wicked perish on the periphery (note "judgment" in v. 5*a* and "perish" in v. 6*b*), while the righteous are at the center of God's attention. Indeed, for the first time in the psalm, the Lord is the subject of a verb. The Lord "knows" (ידע *yāda'*, RSV; NIV and NRSV, "watches over"), which in other contexts suggests a relation as intimate as sexual intercourse. The happy or righteous persons are those who are constantly open to God's teaching, thus always connected to God, who is the source of life.

The wicked, on the other hand, are those who refuse to attend to God's teaching, thus cutting themselves off from the source of life. That they "perish" is not so much a punishment, but the inevitable outcome of their own choice not to be related to God. In short, wickedness in Psalms is fundamentally to be self-centered rather than God-centered. It is autonomy, which literally means to be a "law unto oneself," or in terms of my translation of *torah*, to be wicked is to be self-instructed rather than open to God's instruction.

By offering the sharpest possible contrast between "the way of the righteous" and "the way of the wicked," Psalm 1 prepares the reader to hear the rest of the psalter. These two "ways" and their results will be in view again and again, and the reader will be challenged to choose the way of openness to God's instruction, the way that leads to happiness and life.

49. D. L. Petersen and K. H. Richards, *Interpreting Hebrew Poetry* (Minneapolis: Fortress, 1992) 95-96.

REFLECTIONS

Psalm 1 offers an understanding of happiness, life, prosperity, and righteousness/wickedness that differs profoundly from the way these things are ordinarily understood. The understanding of reality in Psalm 1 is thoroughly God-centered; the perception of reality among contemporary persons is almost inevitably self-centered. This means that happiness tends to be understood essentially as enjoying oneself; one's life goal is understood in terms of self-actualization or self-fulfillment; prosperity becomes a matter of attaining what one wants; and righteousness and wickedness become moral categories that are measured among some by the ability or inability of persons to obey a set of rules and among others by the ability or inability to enact particular programs and policies. In either case, righteousness is measured in terms of a capacity of the self; it is essentially self-righteousness.

For Psalm 1 (and the rest of the psalter), happiness involves not enjoying oneself but delight in the teaching of God. The goal of life is to be found not in self-fulfillment but in praising God (see the Introduction concerning the songs of praise). Prosperity does not involve getting what one wants; rather, it comes from being connected to the source of life—God. The righteous are not primarily persons who make the proper choices or implement the proper policies (although some psalms include the psalmist's affirmation of innocence), but those who know that their lives belong to God and that their futures are secured by God (see Ps 2:12). In the book of Psalms, the righteous are constantly assailed, persecuted, and threatened (Pss 3:1; 34:19), while the wicked visibly prosper (Pss 37:7; 73:3). The prosperity of the righteous is real but hidden. It is an openness to and connectedness with God that sustains life amid all threats. It is real, but not "as the world gives" (John 14:27 NRSV).

What is so unsettling about all of this is that what Psalm 1 and the rest of the psalter call "wickedness" is perhaps what North American culture promotes as the highest virtue—autonomy. What generally marks maturity among contemporary North Americans is self-sufficiency. Wanting or needing help, whether from others or from God, is taken as a sign of weakness or instability. The effect is to produce a society of isolated selves. The irony is tragic—the pursuit of self-fulfillment yields self-alienation (see Mark 8:35).

In her story "A Good Man Is Hard to Find," Flannery O'Connor strikingly portrays "the way of the wicked." When a character called the Misfit is asked why he does not pray, he replies: " 'I don't want no hep,' he said, 'I'm doing all right by myself.' "

The Misfit represents what Psalm 1 and the rest of the psalter call wickedness—the conviction that we are doing all right by ourselves, that we need no help. It is not surprising that the Misfit's words conclude the story: " 'It's no real pleasure in life.' "[50] He is telling the truth. Failing to trust God and to make connection with God as the source of life, persons cannot be "happy." It is not surprising that contemporary societies of isolated selves consistently fail to produce people who are "happy," even though these societies are among the wealthiest, healthiest, and most educated in human history. In biblical terms, to be autonomous, to be alienated from God and other people, is to "perish."

The choice presented by Psalm 1 is always contemporary. We may choose to be self-instructed and self-directed, or we may choose to open ourselves to God's teaching and to God's direction. In a real sense, what Psalm 1 commends is what John Calvin described as "a teachable frame."[51] This "teachable frame" means a reverence for Scripture, God's written "instruction" (see Luke 11:28), as well as an openness to new ways in which God continues to act and be revealed in the lives of persons and the life of the world. Or, as Calvin insisted, the written Word must be read under the inspiration of the Holy Spirit.

What is commended, therefore, is not a self-righteous legalism but a commitment of the whole self to God. The call to decision presented by Psalm 1 is not unlike Jesus' call to repent and to enter the reign of God (Mark 1:14-15)—that is, to give up self-sovereignty to live under the sovereignty of God (see Mark 8:34). Like Psalm 1, Jesus also promised that his followers would be "blessed" or "happy" (Matt 5:3-11). As in the psalms, this happiness is not incompatible with persecution and suffering (Matt 5:10-11); as in the book of Psalms, the way Jesus commends constitutes a righteousness that fulfills the law (Matt 5:17-20) without being a self-justifying legalism (see Matt 5:21, which initiates a series of new teachings introduced by, "But I say to you . . . "). As an introduction, Psalm 1 not only orients us to read and hear the psalms as Scripture or "instruction," but it also prepares us to hear the affirmation of God's sovereignty, which is explicit in Psalm 2 and which pervades the psalter.

50. Flannery O'Connor, *The Complete Stories* (New York: Farrar, Straus, and Giroux, 1971) 130, 133.
51. John Calvin, *Commentary on the Book of Psalms*, Calvin Translation Society, 5 vols. (Grand Rapids: Baker, 1981) IV:1:xl.

PSALM 2:1-12, THE REIGN OF GOD

NIV	NRSV
Psalm 2	**Psalm 2**

NIV

¹Why do the nations conspire[a]
   and the peoples plot in vain?
²The kings of the earth take their stand
   and the rulers gather together
against the LORD
   and against his Anointed One.[b]
³"Let us break their chains," they say,
   "and throw off their fetters."

⁴The One enthroned in heaven laughs;
   the Lord scoffs at them.
⁵Then he rebukes them in his anger
   and terrifies them in his wrath, saying,
⁶"I have installed my King[c]
   on Zion, my holy hill."
   ⁷I will proclaim the decree of the LORD:
He said to me, "You are my Son[d];
   today I have become your Father.[e]
⁸Ask of me,
   and I will make the nations your inheritance,
   the ends of the earth your possession.
⁹You will rule them with an iron scepter[f];
   you will dash them to pieces like pottery."

¹⁰Therefore, you kings, be wise;
   be warned, you rulers of the earth.
¹¹Serve the LORD with fear
   and rejoice with trembling.
¹²Kiss the Son, lest he be angry
   and you be destroyed in your way,
for his wrath can flare up in a moment.
   Blessed are all who take refuge in him.

[a]1 Hebrew; Septuagint *rage*   [b]2 Or *anointed one*   [c]6 Or *king*
[d]7 Or *son*; also in verse 12   [e]7 Or *have begotten you*   [f]9 Or
will break them with a rod of iron

NRSV

¹ Why do the nations conspire,
   and the peoples plot in vain?
² The kings of the earth set themselves,
   and the rulers take counsel together,
   against the LORD and his anointed, saying,
³ "Let us burst their bonds asunder,
   and cast their cords from us."

⁴ He who sits in the heavens laughs;
   the LORD has them in derision.
⁵ Then he will speak to them in his wrath,
   and terrify them in his fury, saying,
⁶ "I have set my king on Zion, my holy hill."

⁷ I will tell of the decree of the LORD:
He said to me, "You are my son;
   today I have begotten you.
⁸ Ask of me, and I will make the nations
      your heritage,
   and the ends of the earth your possession.
⁹ You shall break them with a rod of iron,
   and dash them in pieces like a potter's
      vessel."

¹⁰ Now therefore, O kings, be wise;
   be warned, O rulers of the earth.
¹¹ Serve the LORD with fear,
   with trembling ¹²kiss his feet,[a]
or he will be angry, and you will perish in
      the way;
   for his wrath is quickly kindled.

Happy are all who take refuge in him.

[a]Cn: Meaning of Heb of verses 11b and 12a is uncertain

COMMENTARY

Psalm 2 joins Psalm 1 as a paired introduction to the book of Psalms. It makes even more explicit what Psalm 1 has already clearly suggested by its sharply drawn contrast between the righteous and the wicked—namely, "happy" persons are those who know that their lives depend on God (2:12). While Psalm 1 orients the reader to receive the whole collection as instruction, Psalm 2 makes explicit the essential content of that instruction— the Lord reigns! The entire psalter will be about the "happy"/"blessed" life, and it will affirm throughout that this life derives fundamentally from the conviction that God rules the world.

That Psalms 1 and 2 are meant to be read together is indicated by the literary links between them. Most significant is the repetition of "happy"/"blessed" at the beginning of Psalm 1 and the end of Psalm 2, forming an envelope structure that holds the two together. To delight in and to be constantly open to God's instruction (1:2) means that one will "take refuge in" God (2:12). Both psalms commend a dependence upon God that is the antithesis of autonomy.

2:1-3. Another impressive literary link between Psalms 1 and 2 is the Hebrew repetition represented by "plot" (הגה *hāgâ*) in 2:1 and "meditate" (*hāgâ*) in 1:2. The repetition creates a contrast between persons who meditate on God's instruction and those whose thinking is vain, empty, purposeless. The effect is to identify "the nations," "the peoples," "the kings," and "the rulers" of 2:1-2 with the wicked of Psalm 1. Therefore, it is not surprising that their destiny, if they persist in opposing God, is described the same way as in Psalm 1: "you will *perish* in the *way*" (2:12, italics added; see "perish" [אבד *'ābad*] and "way" [דרך *derek*] in 1:6). In effect, Psalm 2 portrays in corporate terms what Psalm 1 depicts in individual terms: the contrast between the righteous, who are open to God's teaching and God's rule, and the wicked, who assert themselves and make their own plans in opposition to the reign of God.

Twentieth-century scholarship has focused attention more on the theology of the Davidic monarchy than on the reign of God. Psalm 2 is ordinarily classified as a royal psalm that was used either upon the coronation of a new king or at a yearly celebration of God's choosing Jerusalem and the Davidic house. Indeed, it is not difficult to imagine Psalm 2 as a coronation liturgy. Verses 1-3 focus on the desire of the nations to rebel, a desire that would have been heightened by the relative instability during a change of administrations. "Bonds" and "cords" (v. 3) elsewhere indicate servanthood (Jer 2:20; 30:8) as well as knowledge of and obedience to the "way of the LORD" (Jer 5:5). But the kings and rulers have no intention of recognizing God's sovereignty, which v. 2 suggests is exercised through God's "anointed," or messiah—the king.

2:4-6. God's response to the rebellious kings and rulers is given in these verses. The NIV's "enthroned" is better than the NRSV's "sits." Because God is the real ruler, God can laugh at the opponents (see Pss 37:13; 59:9; cf. 52:6 where the righteous "laugh" at the defeat of "the evildoer"). In another key text, the Song of Moses (Exod 15:1-18), God's "fury" (Exod 15:7) and ability to "terrify" (Exod 15:15) God's opponents are associated with God's everlasting reign (Exod 15:18). As in vv. 1-3, v. 6 suggests that God's sovereignty is exercised through a chosen agent—"my king," as opposed to the other "kings of the earth" (v. 2; see v. 10). The pronoun "I" in v. 6 is emphatic; God is the primary actor. It is God's king who occupies God's chosen place—"my holy hill" (see Pss 3:4; 15:1; 43:3; 48:2)—elsewhere a designation of Mount Zion. Verse 6 may have been spoken by a priest or prophet at the climactic moment in a coronation ceremony.

2:7-9. If v. 6 was used during a coronation, then the speaker changes in v. 7. The first "I" of v. 7 is the king, and the king's speech in vv. 7-9 describes the relationship God has established with him and rehearses the accompanying promises. The declaration of the king's sonship in v. 7 recalls Nathan's oracle to David (esp. 2 Sam 7:14; see also 1 Chr 28:6; Ps 89:26-27). Other ancient Near Eastern cultures also viewed their kings as sons of the divinity. Several Egyptian texts suggest a physical relationship between the king and the god, whereas the Mesopotamian conception involved adoption of the king. The Israelite conception is closer to the Mesopotamian. By "decree" (see Ps 105:10 where "decree" is virtually synonymous with "covenant"), God gives birth to a new agent of God's rule. The "today" of v. 7 thus refers to the day of enthronement.[52] The second "I" in v. 7, like the "I" of v. 6, is emphatic; God's initiative and activity are crucial. The promises in vv. 8-9 are also part of the ancient Near Eastern ideology of kingship. The king has the prerogative to request the benefit of God's power (see Pss 20:2; 21:4). The rebellious nations (see v. 1) will be subject to God, and the king will share God's universal sovereignty (see Ps 72:8). The difference between the NRSV's "break" and the NIV's "rule"

---

52. For details, including citing of Egyptian and Mesopotamian texts, see H.-J. Kraus, *Psalms 1–59: A Commentary,* trans. H. C. Oswald (Minneapolis: Augsburg, 1988) 129-32.

in v. 9a may reflect an original play on words. The Hebrew verbs for "to break" (רעע rā'a') and "to shepherd, rule" (רעה rā'â) are very similar. The Hebrew text supports the NRSV, while the LXX supports the NIV. Either meaning is appropriate, and the noun in v. 9a can designate a shepherd's implement (Ps 23:4; Ezek 20:37), a ruler's scepter (Gen 49:10; Ps 45:6), or an implement for inflicting blows (2 Sam 7:14; Ps 89:32; Mic 5:1). Throughout the ancient Near East, kings were perceived as shepherds of the people (see Ezek 34:1-10). While the parallelism of v. 9a with v. 9b suggests that the NRSV meaning is primary; the ambiguity is appropriate.

2:10-12. The psalm concludes with a warning to the rebellious leaders who had spoken in v. 3. Being "wise" is defined elsewhere for Israel as meditating day and night on God's instruction (see "successful" in Josh 1:8 [NRSV]; cf. Ps 1:2), and being "warned" or "disciplined" elsewhere consists of being taught God's instruction (Ps 94:12). In other words, the kings and rulers are invited to be like the "happy"/"righteous" persons of Psalm 1—open to God's instruction, God-directed rather than self-assertive. Verse 11a puts it even more explicitly: To "serve the LORD" means to live under the rule of God, to depend on God for life. The only other invitation in the psalms to "serve the LORD" occurs in 100:2 (NIV and NRSV "worship"), a psalm that immediately follows a group of psalms that proclaim the Lord's reign (Psalms 93; 95–99). It is significant that the introduction to the psalter and the theological heart of the psalter (see Introduction) make the same proclamation: The Lord reigns! This is the essential claim underlying and pervading the book of Psalms. The final line of v. 12 both reinforces this claim and suggests the proper response to God's rule. To "take refuge" (חסה ḥāsâ) in God means to depend on God, to trust God, to entrust one's life and future to God. Like the proclamation of God's rule, the theme of refuge is pervasive (see, e.g., 5:11; 7:1; 11:1; 16:1; 25:20; and Introduction).

The end of v. 11 and the beginning of v. 12 are probably also meant to exhort the leaders of the earth to acknowledge God's rule (see "trembling" in Exod 15:15; Ps 48:6; both contexts affirm God's kingship); however, the meaning is uncertain, as shown by a comparison of the NIV with the NRSV. The NIV attempts to follow the Hebrew word order more closely; however, "Kiss

the Son" is doubly problematic. First, the Hebrew underlying "Son" is actually the Aramaic word for "son" (בר bar; the Hebrew word for "son" [בן bēn] occurs in v. 7), so the text seems to be corrupt. Second, the NIV has capitalized the word "son" (see v. 7 as well), thus strongly implying a christological meaning that is foreign to the original. On the assumption that the text is corrupt, the NRSV has followed a widely adopted scholarly emendation. The safest route is to admit that the meaning of vv. 11b-12a "is difficult if not impossible to understand."[53]

The disparity between the affirmations of vv. 8-9 and historical accuracy is very evident. At no time did an Israelite or Judean king possess "the ends of the earth" (v. 8); neither was any king able to dominate opponents the way v. 9 promises. To be sure, Psalm 2 can be treated simply as an example of ancient Near Eastern royal ideology with its characteristic tendency toward hyperbole. But Psalm 2 was preserved by the community of faith as something more than a historical artifact of the Davidic dynasty. In periods of monarchical weakness and even after the disappearance of the monarchy, Psalm 2 was preserved and treasured as Israel's poetic answer to the fundamental question, Who rules the world? And the answer is clear: The Lord reigns! When it appeared otherwise, as it always does, Psalm 2 thus served as a powerful affirmation of faith and hope. In short, this psalm functioned eschatologically (see Introduction).[54] It enabled its readers and hearers to perceive amid contrary indications the reality of God's reign and to hope for the consummation of God's rule. That hope took different forms. Some in the post-exilic era may have hoped for a literal restoration of the Davidic dynasty and the political independence of bygone days.[55] Others saw their hope fulfilled in Jesus of Nazareth, who proclaimed and embodied the fundamental affirmation of Psalm 2 and the psalter: God rules the world (see Mark 1:14-15).

53. R. G. Bratcher and W. D. Reyburn, *A Translator's Handbook on the Book of Psalms* (New York: United Bible Societies, 1991) 32.

54. See J. W. Watts, "Psalm 2 in the Context of Biblical Theology," *HBT* 12 (1990) 79-80.

55. See Erhard S. Gerstenberger, *Psalms, Part 1, With an Introduction to Cultic Poetry,* Forms of the OT Literature 14 (Grand Rapids: Eerdmans, 1988) 48. Gerstenberger suggests that Psalm 2 originated in the exilic or post-exilic eras as an expression of the hope for a Davidic savior who would liberate the people "by overthrowing the world powers that held Israel captive."

REFLECTIONS

1. The crucial questions Psalm 2 addresses are always contemporary: Who rules the world? Who is in control? Verses 1-2 are as timely as today's headlines—nations conspiring, peoples plotting, world leaders posturing to be as powerful as possible. Conditions in our cities—not to mention our schools and homes and churches—seem out of control. Just as it must have seemed to ancient Israelites and Judeans during a variety of monarchical crises, and just as it must have seemed to a restored but embattled post-exilic community, so also it seems to us: It does *not* appear that God rules the world.

But it is precisely the disparity between the proclamations and promises of Psalm 2 and historical actualities that presents us with the crucial interpretive issue. This disparity reveals the strange way that God exercises sovereignty. The power of God is not the absolute power of a dictator but the power of committed love. In worldly terms, might makes right. But on God's terms, right makes might. The righteous—those who live under God's sovereignty—will be vulnerable to the powers of the world (Ps 3:1-2), but they will never be without help (3:8). The striking claim of Psalm 2 is that true happiness is found by those "who take refuge in" God (2:12).

Thus, like Psalm 1, Psalm 2 calls for a decision: Who rules the world? Whom shall we trust? Will we trust the apparent power of the kings and rulers of the earth—the wicked? Or will we trust God? The "happy," the righteous, are those who, amid competing claims and powers, put their trust in God. In the eyes of the world, this decision makes no sense.

2. Given the choice presented by the disparity in Psalm 2, it is not surprising that the church would later identify God's "anointed" (v. 2), God's "son" (v. 7), with the suffering Jesus. At Jesus' baptism, the heavenly voice declares, "You are my son" (Mark 1:11 NRSV; cf. Ps 2:7; Matt 3:17; Luke 3:22). The declaration continues with an apparent allusion to Isa 42:1, one of the suffering servant songs in Isaiah 40–55. Jesus is thus portrayed from the beginning as God's suffering messiah. At the transfiguration, the heavenly voice again alludes to Ps 2:7 and adds "listen to him" (Mark 9:7 NRSV; cf. Matt 17:5; Luke 9:35). What Jesus had been saying, and would say again, is that he must suffer and die (Mark 8:31-33; 9:30-32; 10:32-34). The opposition to Jesus can be seen as analogous to the opposition of the nations, peoples, kings, and rulers to God's reign (see Ps 2:1-2, which is quoted in Acts 4:25-26). To the world, Jesus' proclamation of the reign of God, and his embodiment of it in suffering, made no sense (see 1 Cor 1:23).

The relationship between Psalm 2 and Jesus is highlighted by Flannery O'Connor in a story entitled "Why Do the Heathen Rage?" (Ps 2:1 KJV). In this story, a dominating mother laments the fact that her grown son will not take over the responsibilities of running the family farm after her husband has had an incapacitating stroke. Instead of attending to practical matters, the son "read books that had nothing to do with anything that mattered now." One day the mother picked up one of the books and was struck by a passage her son had underlined. It was from a letter of St. Jerome to Heliodorus, who had abandoned his avowed calling:

> "Listen! The battle trumpet blares from heaven and see how our General marches fully armed, coming amid the clouds to conquer the whole world. Out of the mouth of our King emerges a double-edged sword that cuts down everything in the way. Arising finally from your nap, do you come to the battlefield! Abandon the shade and seek the sun."

The final lines of the story record the mother's reaction: "This was the kind of thing he read—something that made no sense for now. Then it came to her, with an unpleasant little jolt, that the General with the sword in his mouth, marching to do violence, was Jesus."[56]

---

56. O'Connor, *The Complete Stories,* 486-87.

As O'Connor suggests, King Jesus—although he conquers by the power of love, and although his crown is a cross—is content with nothing less than claiming the whole world for God. Psalm 2, like Jesus, calls us to affirm the jolting good news that God rules the world, and it calls us to live under God's reign. To the world, that decision will make no sense for now. But to the psalmist and to Jesus, that decision is the source of happiness beyond all the world can give and the promise of a future of incomparable glory (see the citing of Ps 2:8-9 in Rev 2:26-27; see also Rev 11:15; 22:5).

PSALM 3:1-8, GOD HELPS THOSE WHO CANNOT HELP THEMSELVES

NIV

Psalm 3

A psalm of David. When he fled from his son Absalom.

[1] O LORD, how many are my foes!
How many rise up against me!
[2] Many are saying of me,
"God will not deliver him."   *Selah[a]*

[3] But you are a shield around me, O LORD;
you bestow glory on me and lift[b] up my head.
[4] To the LORD I cry aloud,
and he answers me from his holy hill. *Selah*

[5] I lie down and sleep;
I wake again, because the LORD sustains me.
[6] I will not fear the tens of thousands
drawn up against me on every side.

[7] Arise, O LORD!
Deliver me, O my God!
Strike all my enemies on the jaw;
break the teeth of the wicked.

[8] From the LORD comes deliverance.
May your blessing be on your people. *Selah*

a2 A word of uncertain meaning, occurring frequently in the Psalms; possibly a musical term   b3 Or LORD, / my Glorious One, who lifts

NRSV

Psalm 3

A Psalm of David, when he fled from his son Absalom.

[1] O LORD, how many are my foes!
Many are rising against me;
[2] many are saying to me,
"There is no help for you[a] in God."   *Selah*

[3] But you, O LORD, are a shield around me,
my glory, and the one who lifts up my head.
[4] I cry aloud to the LORD,
and he answers me from his holy hill.   *Selah*

[5] I lie down and sleep;
I wake again, for the LORD sustains me.
[6] I am not afraid of ten thousands of people
who have set themselves against me all around.

[7] Rise up, O LORD!
Deliver me, O my God!
For you strike all my enemies on the cheek;
you break the teeth of the wicked.

[8] Deliverance belongs to the LORD;
may your blessing be on your people!
Selah

a Syr: Heb him

COMMENTARY

The plight of the psalmist (vv. 1-2) and the faith he or she displays in the midst of threat (vv. 3, 5-6, 8) illustrate the truth of Ps 2:12: The psalmist finds a "refuge" in God. The movement from Psalms 1–2 to Psalm 3 also effectively demonstrates that to "prosper" (1:3) or to be "happy" (1:1; 2:12) does not mean to live without struggle or opposition. As the first actual prayer for help in the psalter (although the prayer is accompanied by professions of faith in vv. 4-6, 8), Psalm 3 dramatically introduces the situation and the faith that is evident in all the prayers: "Many are the afflictions of the righteous,/ but the LORD rescues them from them all" (Ps 34:19 NRSV).

3:1-2. The most evident stylistic feature of the psalm is the threefold repetition of "many" (רב *rab*) in these verses. Each occurrence intensifies the threat. While the foes are simply present in v. 1*a,* they actively oppose the psalmist in v. 1*b* (see the verb "rise" [קוּם *qûm*] in 54:3; 86:14), and they directly address the psalmist in v. 2*a* with a statement that flatly contradicts 2:12*b.* Their words reveal them to be opponents not only of the psalmist but also of God. Like the peoples and leaders in 2:1-2 and the wicked in Psalm 1, the foes embody autonomy. They trust no one but themselves and recognize no rule other than their own.

The plight of the psalmist is highlighted by the syntax of v. 1. The first word is "LORD" and the last is "me"; thus the word order represents what the foes are attempting to do—to stand between the psalmist and God.[57] Their words also reveal this intent: "Don't look to God for help." Interestingly, the foes introduce the concept to which the psalmist will return in his or her own plea (v. 7) and profession (v. 8): "help" (ישע *yš'*; NIV, "deliver"; the NIV helpfully uses the same English word in vv. 2, 7, 8 to capture the effect of the Hebrew repetition). While the syntax of v. 1 underscores the psalmist's dilemma, the syntax of vv. 1-2 together offers a clue to the psalmist's hope. The last word in v. 2 is "God" (אלהים *'ĕlōhîm*). Thus the two references to Lord/God open and close this section. God has the enemies surrounded.

3:3-4. God also surrounds the psalmist. In the battle against the foes, the Lord is the psalmist's shield (see Pss 7:10; 18:2; 28:7; 33:20; 59:11; 84:9, 11; 115:9-11; 119:114; see esp. 18:30; 144:2, where "shield" is associated with taking "refuge" in God, as in 2:12). The phrase "my glory" (כבודי *kĕbôdî*) may refer to the Lord, but the NIV probably has captured the proper sense. In Ps 4:2, "my glory" is threatened by others; whereas in 62:7; 84:11, "my glory" (NIV and NRSV, "my honor") depends on God as in Psalm 3. The vocabulary of Psalm 3 is also present in both contexts—"deliverance" in 62:7 and "shield" in 84:11. The lifting up of the head also signifies deliverance or preeminence (see Pss 27:6; 110:7; 140:9). Verse 4 seems to suggest that the deliverance still lies in the future (see v. 7), but the psalmist is confident that God will respond (see v. 8).

3:5-6. Thus in vv. 5-6, the psalmist can rest assured. The pronoun "I," which begins v. 5, is emphatic, recalling the pronoun "you," which began v. 3, and providing a link between the two sections. Because the "you" is "a shield around [בעדי *ba'ădî*] me" (v. 3), the "I" can sleep and awake normally (v. 5), unafraid of "ten thousands . . . all around" (סביב *sābîb,* v. 6; the prepositions differ in Hebrew, but convey the same idea). The word translated "ten thousands" (רבבה *rĕbābâ*) is related to the word "many" in vv. 1-2. The opposition is real, but the governing reality of the psalmist's life is his or her relatedness to God. While the foes presume to stand between the psalmist and God (vv. 1-2), the psalmist knows better. As if to signify the inseparability of the psalmist and God, the syntax has changed in vv. 3-4 and vv. 5-6. Noting phrases such as the Lord "answers me" (v. 4) and "the LORD sustains me" (v. 5), John Kselman suggests, "Yahweh and the psalmist are in constant interaction."[58] The psalmist trusts that no amount of opposition will separate her or him from God (see Rom 8:38-39).

The above discussion has assumed the NIV and NRSV division of the psalm into vv. 1-2, 3-4, 5-6,

---

57. See John S. Kselman, "Psalm 3: A Structural and Literary Study," *CBQ* 49 (1987) 574-75.

58. Ibid., 573-80.

7-8; but several scholars propose a division as follows: vv. 1-3 (the foes and God's response), vv. 4-6 (the psalmist and God), vv. 7-8 (petition and profession).[59] The effect of this alternate proposal is to focus attention on v. 5 as the center of the psalm. In fact, the tradition apparently has focused on v. 5 in designating Psalm 3 for use as a morning prayer. A focus on v. 5 also suggests a conceptual parallel between the psalmist and the "happy" person, who is open to God's instruction "day and night" (Ps 1:1-2). Constant dependence on God rather than on self has the very practical effect of making rest and refreshment a daily possibility (see 4:8). Given the psalmist's circumstances (vv. 1-3), this is not an inconsiderable achievement. The daily equilibrium of life is possible, because God "sustains" (סמך *sāmak*; see "upholds"/"upholder" in Pss 37:17, 24; 54:4; 145:14).

3:7-8. The final section contains petition (vv. 7*a*, 8*b*) and profession (vv. 7*b*-8*a*). The opening imperatives clearly recall vv. 1-2. While the foes are "rising against me" (v. 1), the psalmist appeals in faith for God to "Rise up" (see Pss 7:6; 9:19; 10:12; 17:13; 44:26; 74:22). Then the psalmist appeals to God to do precisely what the foes had said God could not do: "Deliver me" (cf. v. 2). The autonomous foes trust only themselves. The psalmist trusts the one to whom he or she is inseparably related: "my God!" The verbs in v. 7*b* are not grammatical imperatives, despite the NIV's rendering. Verse 7*b* probably should be understood as the beginning of the psalmist's profession of faith, as the NRSV suggests. The NRSV does not preserve the chiastic structure (see Introduction), however. The verbs "strike" (נכה *nkh*) and "break" (שבר *šābar*) begin and end the poetic line. Again, the enemies are surrounded (see Commentary on vv. 1-2). Fittingly, God's activity strikes at the organs of speech, which uttered the presumptuous words of v. 2 (see Ps 58:6).

In v. 8*a*, the psalmist directly contradicts the words of the foes (v. 2): God does help those who cannot help themselves! The affirmation of God's "deliverance"/"help"/"salvation" pervades the psalter (see "deliverance" in 14:7 and "salvation" in 35:3; 62:1; 69:29; 70:4; 91:16; 96:2; 118:14, 21; see also Exod 15:2 and Introduction). Verse 8*b* introduces the concept of "blessing" (see Pss 5:12; 28:9; 29:11; 67:1, 6, 7; 115:12-13; 133:3; 134:3; 147:13). Biblical theologians often distinguish between God's saving—deliverance from particular crises—and God's blessing—the sustenance of life on an ongoing, daily basis. The psalmist had experienced both—the actual or assured anticipation of rescue from foes (vv. 3-4), which led to the ongoing possibility of normal life on a daily basis (v. 5). The psalmist concludes with a prayer that all God's people would share this experience.

The superscription assigns the psalm to David and specifies a setting (see 2 Samuel 15–18). This should not be taken as a historically accurate remembrance, but some scholars do conclude from the superscription that the person praying was a king and that Psalm 3 is a royal psalm. The juxtaposition with Psalm 2 and the shared phrase "holy hill" (2:6; 3:4) may provide support for this conclusion; however, it is by no means necessary, nor is it the majority view. It is more likely that the superscription is intended to encourage the reader to imagine a situation like that of David's during Absalom's revolt. In this episode, David appeared as anything but kingly. His family—indeed, his life—was a wreck. Absalom had killed his brother Amnon for raping his sister Tamar (2 Samuel 13). David forgave Absalom (2 Samuel 14), but Absalom rebelled against his father and drove him from Jerusalem (2 Samuel 15). The whole sorry situation is illustrative of the messy situations we regularly experience—violence, turmoil, rebellion, threats to job and even to life itself. Following Psalms 1–2, Psalm 3 proclaims that "happiness"/"blessedness" consists of the good news that God's help (v. 8) is forthcoming precisely in the midst of such threats in order to make life possible (vv. 3-4) and to offer us a peace (v. 5) that the world says is not possible (v. 2).

59. Ibid., 573-80.

REFLECTIONS

1. The good news the psalmist affirms—that God helps those who cannot help themselves—is not the prevailing profession of contemporary society. In fact, it is the *foes* who express what functions as a credo for a secular world: "There is no help for you in God" (v. 2). To put it in the form we usually hear it: "God helps those who help *themselves.*" Interestingly and tellingly, many people assume that this cultural creed is in the Bible! As suggested above (see Commentary on Psalm 1), autonomy, or *self*-sufficiency, is often promoted as the highest virtue.

It is ironic that even our best intentions are frequently motivated by, and thus promote, the persuasive notion that God helps those who help themselves. Speaking of the church's ministry and mission, Stanley Hauerwas and William H. Willimon observe:

> Most of our social activism is formed on the presumption that God is superfluous to the formation of a world of peace with justice. Fortunately, we are powerful people who, because we live in a democracy, are free to use our power. *It is all up to us.*
>
> The moment that life is formed on the presumption that we are not participants in *God's* continuing history of creation and redemption, we are acting on unbelief rather than faith.[60]

In directly contradicting the foes' assertion, the psalmist affirms that human identity and destiny are shaped ultimately by the reality of God. The psalmist thus proclaims the paradoxical good news that full human selfhood is experienced in the yielding of oneself to God (see Mark 8:35).

2. The psalmist's thoroughly theological comprehension of reality is a challenge to us who live in a world where the human self is preeminent, a world that promotes self-fulfillment, self-reliance, self-help. As did Psalms 1 and 2, Psalm 3 calls for a decision. Concerning the foes' assertion in 3:2, Mays comments:

> One can either believe it or believe in God. The psalm is composed to encourage faith and to give it language. . . . It recites the doctrine that "salvation belongs to the LORD" to remind the distressed that no trouble is beyond help and no human hostility can limit God's help. In all these ways the psalm encourages and supports faith and invites the distressed to pray, the ultimate act of faith in the face of the assault on the soul.[61]

In other words, prayer is for those who know they are *not* self-sufficient; it is for those who know they need help. It is both word and act, language and life-style. As Eugene Peterson puts it, "Prayer is the language of people who are in trouble and know it, and who believe or hope that God can get them out." Peterson goes on to quote Isaac Bashevis Singer, "I only pray when I'm in trouble, but I'm in trouble all the time."[62] Prayer is both the language and the life-style of persons who know that their lives, their futures, and the destiny of the world depend on God (3:8; see 1:1-2; 2:12). To pray subverts the prevailing worldly wisdom that God helps those who help themselves. Therefore, to pray in our kind of world is a revolutionary act, but it is one that may yield indirectly the same practical consequence for us as it did for the psalmist—a good night's sleep (vv. 4-5).

60. Stanley Hauerwas and William H. Willimon, *Resident Aliens: Life in the Christian Colony* (Nashville: Abingdon, 1989) 36-37, italics added.
61. James L. Mays, *Psalms,* Interpretation (Louisville: John Knox, 1994) 53.
62. Eugene A. Peterson, *Answering God: The Psalms as Tools for Prayer* (San Francisco: Harper & Row, 1989) 36.

PSALM 4:1-8, YOU ALONE, O LORD

NIV

Psalm 4

For the director of music. With stringed instruments. A psalm of David.

[1]Answer me when I call to you,
  O my righteous God.
Give me relief from my distress;
  be merciful to me and hear my prayer.

[2]How long, O men, will you turn my glory
    into shame[a]?
How long will you love delusions and seek
    false gods[b]?   *Selah*
[3]Know that the LORD has set apart the godly
    for himself;
  the LORD will hear when I call to him.

[4]In your anger do not sin;
  when you are on your beds,
  search your hearts and be silent.   *Selah*
[5]Offer right sacrifices
  and trust in the LORD.

[6]Many are asking, "Who can show us any
    good?"
Let the light of your face shine upon us,
    O LORD.
[7]You have filled my heart with greater joy
    than when their grain and new wine
    abound.
[8]I will lie down and sleep in peace,
    for you alone, O LORD,
    make me dwell in safety.

a2 Or you dishonor my Glorious One   b2 Or seek lies

NRSV

Psalm 4

To the leader: with stringed instruments. A Psalm of David.

[1] Answer me when I call, O God of my right!
    You gave me room when I was in distress.
    Be gracious to me, and hear my prayer.

[2] How long, you people, shall my honor
      suffer shame?
  How long will you love vain words, and
      seek after lies?   *Selah*
[3] But know that the LORD has set apart the
      faithful for himself;
    the LORD hears when I call to him.

[4] When you are disturbed,[a] do not sin;
    ponder it on your beds, and be silent. *Selah*
[5] Offer right sacrifices,
    and put your trust in the LORD.

[6] There are many who say, "O that we might
      see some good!
  Let the light of your face shine on us,
      O LORD!"
[7] You have put gladness in my heart
    more than when their grain and wine
    abound.

[8] I will both lie down and sleep in peace;
    for you alone, O LORD, make me lie
      down in safety.

a Or are angry

COMMENTARY

The similarities between Psalms 3 and 4 have led a few scholars to suggest their original unity, and even more propose that the confident conclusion in 3:8 is the point of departure for Psalm 4 (see "answer" [ענה *ʿānâ*] in 3:4; 4:1; "glory" [כבוד *kābôd*] in 3:3; 4:2 [NRSV, "honor"]; "cry aloud" [קרא *qārāʾ*] in 3:4 = "call" in 4:1, 3; "lie down and sleep" [שכב *šākab* and ישן *yāšēn*] in 3:5; 4:8).

In any case, both psalms clearly identify God as the source of "deliverance" (3:8) and its results, "peace" and "safety" (4:8; note too the confident conclusions in 1:6; 2:12). Like Psalm 3, Psalm 4 is basically a prayer for help, but one in which the psalmist also addresses other people with questions and exhortations that function as professions of faith (4:2-5; cf. 3:4-6, 8).

After an initial plea and acknowledgment of past help, the psalmist addresses others in vv. 2-5. The opponents seem clearly in view in vv. 2-3, but vv. 4-5 could be addressed to the faithful congregation as well. Thus the NRSV and the NIV propose a break between vv. 3 and 4. In v. 6*a* the psalmist quotes what others say, and then gives a response in vv. 6*b*-7. Verse 8 may be understood as a continuation of v. 7 (NIV) or as a sort of independent concluding prayer (NRSV). A division into vv. 1, 2-3, 4-5, 6-7, 8 focuses attention on vv. 4-5 as a central panel surrounded by a pair of contrasts in vv. 2-3 and 6-7. Verses 2-3 contrast those who pursue vanity or "false gods" with the faithful, who belong to the Lord. Verses 6-7 contrast those who always want more with the psalmist, who is content with God's provision.[63]

4:1. "Answer me" is a frequent petition (see Pss 13:3; 55:2; 69:13, 16, 17; 86:1; 108:6; 143:7; see esp. 27:7; 143:1). It is addressed to "O God of my right." "Righteousness" is both an attribute of God and a characteristic of God's reign (see, e.g., 9:8; 96:13; 97:2, 6). God's ability to set things right is the foundation of the psalmist's advice to "trust in the LORD" (v. 5). The petition is followed by an example of God's past righteousness (following the NRSV). The verb (רחב *rāḥab*) in "gave me room" literally means "wide," and the noun translated "distress" (צר *ṣār*) means "narrow." In a contemporary idiom, the psalmist says, "You gave me some space when I was in a tight spot." But now the psalmist is needy again, and the petition continues with two characteristic pleas (see "be gracious" in Pss 6:2; 9:13; 25:16; 26:11; 27:7; 30:10; 31:9; and "hear my prayer" in 39:12; 54:2; 84:8; 102:1; 143:1). Like the appeal to God's righteousness, the prayer that God "be gracious" is an appeal to God's character (see Exod 34:6, God's self-revelation to Moses as "gracious").

4:2-3. In v. 2, the question "How long?" (often addressed to God; see Ps 13:1-2) is addressed to the psalmist's opponents. They are apparently responsible for injuring the psalmist's reputation (see "shame" in Ps 69:7) with their "vain words." The word "vain" (ריק *rîq*) recalls Ps 2:1 and thus suggests that the psalmist's opponents are oppo-

nents of God as well. This lends plausibility to the NIV's translation, "seek false gods" (see Ps 40:4; Amos 2:4 NIV); however, the Hebrew word elsewhere designates the false and damaging speech of the wicked, as the NRSV suggests (Pss 5:6; 58:3; 62:4). In contrast to the opponents, the psalmist belongs to God (v. 3; see Exod 33:16, where "be distinct" [פלה *pālâ*] is the same as "set apart" here). The designation "faithful" (חסיד *ḥāsîd*) is a form of the noun that the NRSV ordinarily translates as "steadfast love" and that, like righteousness and grace (v. 1), is a fundamental attribute of God (see Exod 34:6-7; see "faithful" in Pss 12:2; 30:5; 31:24; 32:6; 37:28; 85:9; 86:2; 97:10, and see the Introduction). Persons who belong to God are those whose identity has been formed by God's character. Their opponents may slander them and question their reputation, but the "glory" or "honor" of the faithful is secure because it derives from God (see Pss 3:3; 62:6). Thus "the faithful" can be confident that God "hears" when they "call" (see both verbs in v. 1).

Verses 2-3 may offer a clue to the original setting of Psalm 4. It is possible that the falsely accused psalmist has been vindicated in a ritual court proceeding held in the Temple.[64] If so, then the advice in vv. 4-5 may be offered not only to the opponents but also to anyone who was present to hear it, including the contemporary reader.

4:4-5. Verse 4 is usually understood as the psalmist's command to the opponents to refrain from their harmful speech; however, it can be heard also as advice to the faithful. In 1 Sam 7:10, being "disturbed" is a state caused by enemies. Thus v. 4 may exhort the faithful to stand firm in their identity and not be led into temptation by their opponents. In this case, "be silent" (דמם *dāmam*) would better be translated "be quieted" and would advise composure and peace of mind (see v. 8, which has to do with nighttime activity). The NIV's "anger" derives from the LXX and perhaps was chosen because v. 4 is quoted in this form in Eph 4:26—where, by the way, it is advice to the faithful.

The exhortation in v. 5 would be appropriate for either the foes or the faithful. In Ps 51:19, "right sacrifices" are apparently a possibility for those who have first been reconciled to God and have offered their whole selves to God (see vv.

---

63. See ibid., 63.

64. See H.-J. Kraus, *Psalms 1—59: A Commentary,* trans. H. C. Oswald (Minneapolis: Augsburg, 1988) 146-47.

16-17). To "trust in the LORD" also involves yielding the whole self to God. It is essentially synonymous with taking refuge in God (Ps 2:12); like the theme of refuge, the theme of trust is pervasive in Psalms (see, e.g., 9:10; 21:7; 22:4-5; 25:2; 26:1; 28:7; 32:10; 37:3; 40:4; 55:23; 56:3, 11; 84:12; 115:9-11; 125:1; 143:8; see esp. 62:8; 91:2, where "refuge" occurs with "trust" in the same verse; see also the Introduction).

4:6-7. In v. 6, the psalmist quotes what others say, although the NIV and the NRSV disagree on the extent of the quotation; the NIV seems preferable. When vv. 6-7 are read as a unit, it appears that the "many" were praying for material prosperity, whereas the psalmist desires a different kind of fulfillment—the light of God's face (see Num 6:25; Pss 31:16; 67:1; 80:3, 7, 19). In

contrast to the "many" and their "restless dissatisfaction with what they have," the psalmist "has been given more joy by the sign of God's acceptance [see v. 3] than would be gained from an abundance of meat and drink. The gift of trusting God transcends the value of any material good."[65] Again, the psalmist's identity is secured by her or his relationship to God.

4:8. This relationship to God, this gift of trusting God, dispels anxiety (see Ps 3:5) and makes for genuine "peace" (*shalom*) and "safety" (בֶּטַח *betaḥ*; the Hebrew word is related to "trust" in v. 5). Neither the "vain words" nor the material prosperity of others can direct the psalmist's attention from what is truly essential for life—namely, "You alone, O LORD" (v. 8).

65. Mays, *Psalms,* 56.

REFLECTIONS

The psalmist apparently was tempted by two things that still have a way of keeping us from appreciating what life is truly all about: (1) concern over reputation—what other people think and say about us (vv. 2-3)—and (2) concern over material possessions, particularly the fact that others may have more than we do (vv. 6-7). To be sure, these may be legitimate concerns, especially when persons are impugned unjustifiably, as the psalmist apparently was. The point, however, is that not even this kind of pressure could shake the psalmist's conviction that his or her life was of inestimable value because it belonged to God. Belonging to God changes everything—values, priorities, life-style. The "faithful"—those whose identity is shaped by experience of God's "steadfast love"—are different, "set apart" (v. 3). So the psalmist can advise others, to paraphrase vv. 4-5: "When things work against you, don't let it throw you off [the root sense of "sin" is "to miss the mark"]. Don't lose any sleep over it. Keep your composure. Offer your entire self to God. Entrust your life to God." Mays suggests: "The psalmist has a basis of identity that transcends the judgments of others—the relation to God."[66] As the apostle Paul put it, "If God is for us, who is against us?" (Rom 8:31 NRSV; see also Isa 50:7-9). In the topsy-turvy world where God reigns and everything is different, it is even possible to say, as Jesus did, "Blessed are you when people revile you and persecute you and utter all kinds of evil against you falsely on my account" (Matt 5:11 NRSV).

Those who belong to God know, too, that material possessions can be of only relative importance. Jesus said, "One does not live by bread alone, but by every word that comes from the mouth of God" (Matt 4:4 NRSV; cf. Deut 8:3), and "One's life does not consist in the abundance of possessions" (Luke 12:15 NRSV). The psalmist knew this good news, and so he or she could sleep without anxiety (v. 8; see Matt 6:25-33) in the enjoyment of that "peace of God, which surpasses all understanding" (Phil 4:7 NRSV). In our media culture, which leads us daily to believe that life does consist in the abundance of possessions, and in which presenting the proper self-image is paramount, the psalmist has a powerful lesson to teach us and a timely challenge to offer us. God alone is the guarantor of ultimate security (v. 8), so "put your trust in the LORD" (v. 5).

66. Ibid., 55.

PSALM 5:1-12, LEAD ME, O LORD

NIV

NRSV

Psalm 5

For the director of music. For flutes. A psalm of David.

¹Give ear to my words, O LORD,
consider my sighing.
²Listen to my cry for help,
my King and my God,
for to you I pray.
³In the morning, O LORD, you hear my voice;
in the morning I lay my requests before you
and wait in expectation.

⁴You are not a God who takes pleasure in evil;
with you the wicked cannot dwell.
⁵The arrogant cannot stand in your presence;
you hate all who do wrong.
⁶You destroy those who tell lies;
bloodthirsty and deceitful men
the LORD abhors.

⁷But I, by your great mercy,
will come into your house;
in reverence will I bow down
toward your holy temple.
⁸Lead me, O LORD, in your righteousness
because of my enemies—
make straight your way before me.

⁹Not a word from their mouth can be trusted;
their heart is filled with destruction.
Their throat is an open grave;
with their tongue they speak deceit.
¹⁰Declare them guilty, O God!
Let their intrigues be their downfall.
Banish them for their many sins,
for they have rebelled against you.
¹¹But let all who take refuge in you be glad;
let them ever sing for joy.
Spread your protection over them,
that those who love your name may
rejoice in you.
¹²For surely, O LORD, you bless the righteous;
you surround them with your favor as
with a shield.

Psalm 5

To the leader: for the flutes. A Psalm of David.

¹ Give ear to my words, O LORD;
give heed to my sighing.
² Listen to the sound of my cry,
my King and my God,
for to you I pray.
³ O LORD, in the morning you hear my voice;
in the morning I plead my case to you,
and watch.

⁴ For you are not a God who delights in
wickedness;
evil will not sojourn with you.
⁵ The boastful will not stand before your eyes;
you hate all evildoers.
⁶ You destroy those who speak lies;
the LORD abhors the bloodthirsty and
deceitful.

⁷ But I, through the abundance of your
steadfast love,
will enter your house,
I will bow down toward your holy temple
in awe of you.
⁸ Lead me, O LORD, in your righteousness
because of my enemies;
make your way straight before me.

⁹ For there is no truth in their mouths;
their hearts are destruction;
their throats are open graves;
they flatter with their tongues.
¹⁰ Make them bear their guilt, O God;
let them fall by their own counsels;
because of their many transgressions cast
them out,
for they have rebelled against you.

¹¹ But let all who take refuge in you rejoice;
let them ever sing for joy.
Spread your protection over them,
so that those who love your name may
exult in you.

NIV

12 For you bless the righteous, O LORD;
 you cover them with favor as with a
 shield.

COMMENTARY

Like Psalms 3 and 4, this prayer for help illustrates that righteousness does not go unopposed (see v. 8). The psalmist is apparently threatened by violent schemes and is already the victim of deceit and lies (vv. 6, 9-10). The psalm may have originally been prayed in the Temple by a person who had been slandered or falsely accused, perhaps of idolatry (vv. 1-3, 7; see Psalms 7; 17; the Introduction). The psalmist's final appeal rests with God, perhaps in a ritual involving a priestly oracle or sign. Be that as it may, the psalm was and is appropriate for wider use. For instance, it is an appropriate prayer for persecuted individuals, like Jeremiah or Jesus or contemporary political prisoners, or for persecuted communities like postexilic Israel or the early church or Christian communities today who live under repressive regimes.[67]

The structural divisions in the NIV and the NRSV are helpful: vv. 1-3, 4-6, 7-8, 9-10, 11-12. The psalm consists of sections that alternate between a focus on the psalmist's appeal and approach to God (vv. 1-3, 7-8) and on the wicked and God's dealing with them (vv. 4-6, 9-10; note that both vv. 4 and 9 begin with "For" in the NRSV). A final section (vv. 11-12) also involves appeal and approach to God, but now all the righteous are involved. The alternation focuses attention on vv. 7-8 as a structural and theological center.

5:1-3. The Hebrew word order in v. 1 is significant; "my words" is the first and "my sighing" the last element of the line, and the middle word is "LORD." In effect, the psalmist surrounds God with petitions (see "give ear" in Pss 17:1; 39:12; 54:2; 55:1; 80:1; 84:8; 86:6; 140:6; 141:1; 143:1). The plea continues in v. 2 (see "listen" or "attend" in Pss 17:1; 55:2; 61:1; 86:6) where the NIV's "cry for help" is a more accurate

translation (see Pss 18:6, 41; 22:24; 28:2; 30:2; 31:22; 88:13, and a different form of the word in Exod 2:23). The address of God as "my King" represents the first occurrence in the psalter of the Hebrew root מלך (*mālak,* "to reign," "to be king"), and it serves to connect Psalm 5 and similar prayers for help to the affirmation that pervades and forms the theological heart of the psalter: The Lord reigns (see Psalm 2 and the Introduction). Here, as in Psalm 2 and throughout Psalms, the affirmation of God's kingship is made in the presence of the competing claims of evildoers and enemies (vv. 5-6, 8). In short, it is eschatological. It articulates the psalmist's conviction that God rules, but it also anticipates a future consummation of that reign. Trust in the present reality of God's rule explains why the psalmist continues to pray and appeal his or her case to God (see Job 23:4) with confidence that God hears (v. 3; morning seems to have been a set time for prayer and praise, as in Pss 55:17; 58:16; 88:13; 92:2). That God's reign is yet to be fully manifested explains why the psalmist continues to "wait in expectation" (see Mic 7:7; Hab 2:1).

5:4-6. As one of "the righteous" (v. 12), the psalmist appeals to a king whose righteous royal policy (see v. 8) is to oppose "wickedness" (v. 4; note that the two contrasting ways of Ps 1:6 are present here). To "sojourn" or "dwell" with God (Ps 15:1) involved being a "doer of righteousness" and a "speaker of truth" (15:2); it meant controlling the tongue, avoiding evil and opposing the wicked, and protecting the neighbor and the innocent (15:3-5). Thus "evil" and "the wicked" cannot "sojourn" or "dwell" with God (v. 4). The wicked are "doers of iniquity" (v. 5), who "speak lies" (v. 6; see 4:2; cf. v. 9); they are "deceitful" (see Pss 10:7; 24:4; 52:4; 35:20; 34:13; 36:3; 43:1) and prey on others (see "bloodthirsty" in Pss 20:9; 55:23; 59:2; 139:19; Prov 29:10). There are seven words for "evil" in vv. 4-6, perhaps

67. Mays, *Psalms,* 58.

suggesting the completeness of God's opposition, which is stated in the strongest possible terms—"hate" (שנא śānē'; see Ps 11:5) and "abhors" (תעב tāʿab; see Ps 106:40; the noun form of this word is usually translated "abomination" [תועבה tôʿēbâ] and covers a variety of evils; see, e.g., Jer 6:15; 8:12). The word for "destroy" (אבד ʾābad) in v. 6 means literally "cause to perish," recalling Pss 1:6 and 2:12. Those who oppose God's sovereignty will ultimately perish, because they cut themselves off from the giver of life.

5:7-8. In contrast to the "boastful" or "arrogant" (see Pss 73:3; 75:4), who will not stand before God, the psalmist will enter God's house. The psalmist humbly attributes this, not to personal worthiness but to God's merciful love (v. 7). This is the first occurrence in Psalms of the word חסד ḥesed, which the NRSV ordinarily translates as "steadfast love" and the NIV as "unfailing love." If any one Hebrew word serves to describe the character of God, it probably is this one (see Exod 34:6-7). It is difficult to translate because it rolls into one the concepts of God's grace, mercy, compassion, patience, faithfulness, loyalty, and love. It is frequently celebrated in Israel's songs of praise and is appealed to in the prayers for help (see, e.g., Pss 23:6; 31:7, 16, 21; 32:10; 33:5, 18, 22; 100:5; 103:4, 8, 11, 17; 130:7; and the Introduction). The psalmist makes the proper response to such grace. "Bow down" (שחה šḥh) indicates what subjects do in the presence of a monarch (see 1 Sam 24:8; 2 Sam 14:4). Thus the psalmist takes the position of a loyal servant before "my King" (see "bow down" or "worship" in Pss 29:2; 95:6; 96:9; 99:9, all in the context of God's kingship; see also Exod 34:8, and note that "awe" or "fear" is also associated with the recognition of God's sovereignty in Ps 2:11). Psalm 5 represents the strange notion of sovereignty that is present throughout the Bible. God's sovereignty is exercised not as absolute power but as committed love. A royal policy of committed love is true "righteousness" (see Commentary on Ps 4:1 and the Introduction), and the psalmist humbly requests to be led in this way (see "lead" in Pss 23:2; 26:11; 31:3; 61:2; 72:21; 139:10, 24; 143:10). This petition at the center of the psalm indicates a relinquishing of self-reliance in dependence upon God and anticipates the celebration of refuge and protection in vv. 11-12. The mention of "my enemies" (שוררי šôrĕray) links the central section with vv. 4-6 and 9-10. The particular word used here means more literally "those watching for me" (see Pss 27:11; 54:5; 56:2; 59:10; 92:11).

5:9-10. Verse 9 is dominated by anatomy, as if to say that the wicked are evil through and through. Actually, three of the four parts mentioned are organs of speech, which is appropriate in view of vv. 5-6. Similar descriptions of the wicked are found elsewhere. Their character or speech amounts to "destruction" (cf. Pss 38:12; 52:2; 91:3; 94:20). Their flattering tongues are deadly (see Pss 12:3-4; 52:2; 57:4; 64:2-3; 140:3). In v. 10 the psalmist prays that the deadly threats of the wicked may fall back upon themselves (see vv. 4-6). The word "transgressions" connotes willful rebellion against God, and the final line of v. 10 completes the portrait of the wicked as those who reject the Lord's sovereignty. "Counsels" is the same word as "advice" in Ps 1:1. As suggested there and reinforced here, the righteous (see v. 12) are those open to God's instruction (1:2), whereas the wicked live only for themselves.

5:11-12. One of the responsibilities of a king was to provide for and protect his people, and the psalmist appeals in vv. 11-12 for the fulfillment of that role. These are the things for which the psalmist waits "in expectation" (v. 3)—joy (see 4:7), blessing (see 3:8), favor. The verbs could be translated as future indicatives—"will rejoice" and so on. The psalmist is certain that the future holds security and joy for those whose refuge is in God (see Ps 2:12). As in Pss 1:1-2; 2:12; 3:5; 4:8, this conviction enables the psalmist, amid persistent opposition (vv. 4-6, 9-10), to live with reverent purpose (v. 7), unshakable hope (v. 3), and enduring joy (v. 11).

REFLECTIONS

1. Because it affirms the sovereignty of God (v. 2) amid continuing opposition from the wicked and evil (vv. 4-6, 8-10), Psalm 5 is an eloquent profession of the faith that underlies

all the prayers for help. Indeed, bold affirmation of God's reign while simultaneously waiting patiently (vv. 2-3) is the perennially appropriate posture for the people of God. Jesus invited persons to enter and live under the rule of God, but he made it clear that the life of disciples involves bearing a cross. Thus Jesus taught his disciples to pray, "Thine is the kingdom," and simultaneously, "Thy kingdom come."

2.   The apostle Paul quoted Ps 5:9 in Rom 3:13 as part of his argument that all people "are under the power of sin" (Rom 3:9 NRSV). Paul seems unconcerned by the fact that v. 9 functions within the psalm as an indictment of particular enemies (see v. 8) rather than a characterization of all humanity. Even so, Paul's use of Psalm 5 and the psalmist's life of humble reliance upon God challenge the contemporary reader to make a decision. Are we among the boastful, who rely essentially on their own resources and live for themselves at the expense of others? Or do we take refuge in God? Do we seek first our own wills and our own way? Or do we pray with the psalmist, "Lead me, O Lord, in your righteousness" (5:8 NRSV), or in effect, "Thy will be done"? As Craigie suggests, Psalm 5 can be for us "a prayer of self-examination and a request for forgiveness and deliverance."[68]

3.   Psalm 5 can also serve to remind us of the power of human speech and of its importance in standing with or against God. Walter Brueggemann suggests that human beings are "the speech creature *par excellence.*"[69] It matters what we say. Words can give life, and, as the psalmist testifies, words can kill (vv. 6, 9). As the Letter of James recognizes, "no one can tame the tongue—a restless evil, full of deadly poison. With it we bless the Lord and Father, and with it we curse those who are made in the likeness of God" (James 3:8-9 NRSV; see vv. 5-12). The psalmist was the victim of such a curse, and his or her plight instructs us that destructive speech does violence to other people and fails to conform to God's will. The righteous rule of God requires the truth to be told for God's sake and the sake of others. Thus Psalm 5 reinforces the importance of the ninth commandment, "You shall not bear false witness against your neighbor" (Exod 20:16 NRSV). Mays concludes: "So this psalm asks us whether we take the opposition between truth and lie seriously enough as a matter of faith, whether we are ready to stand with those damaged by falsehood and propaganda, and whether we are alert to the lies to us and about us told by the powers and opinions of our culture."[70] The conventional wisdom is that "talk is cheap," but, as the psalmist reveals, the effects of human speech can be terribly costly.

68. Peter C. Craigie, *Psalms 1–50,* WBC 19 (Waco: Word, 1983) 89.
69. Walter Brueggemann, *The Book of Genesis,* Interpretation (Atlanta: John Knox, 1982) 31.
70. Mays, *Psalms,* 58.

PSALM 6:1-10, O LORD—HOW LONG?

NIV	NRSV
Psalm 6	Psalm 6
For the director of music. With stringed instruments. According to *sheminith.*[a] A psalm of David.	To the leader: with stringed instruments; according to The Sheminith. A Psalm of David.
¹O Lord, do not rebuke me in your anger	¹ O Lord, do not rebuke me in your anger, or discipline me in your wrath.

aTitle: Probably a musical term

NIV

or discipline me in your wrath.
²Be merciful to me, Lord, for I am faint;
    O Lord, heal me, for my bones are in
      agony.
³My soul is in anguish.
    How long, O Lord, how long?

⁴Turn, O Lord, and deliver me;
    save me because of your unfailing love.
⁵No one remembers you when he is dead.
    Who praises you from the grave*ᵃ*?

⁶I am worn out from groaning;
    all night long I flood my bed with weeping
    and drench my couch with tears.
⁷My eyes grow weak with sorrow;
    they fail because of all my foes.

⁸Away from me, all you who do evil,
    for the Lord has heard my weeping.
⁹The Lord has heard my cry for mercy;
    the Lord accepts my prayer.
¹⁰All my enemies will be ashamed and
      dismayed;
    they will turn back in sudden disgrace.

ᵃ5 Hebrew Sheol

NRSV

² Be gracious to me, O Lord, for I am
    languishing;
    O Lord, heal me, for my bones are
      shaking with terror.
³ My soul also is struck with terror,
    while you, O Lord—how long?

⁴ Turn, O Lord, save my life;
    deliver me for the sake of your steadfast
      love.
⁵ For in death there is no remembrance of you;
    in Sheol who can give you praise?

⁶ I am weary with my moaning;
    every night I flood my bed with tears;
    I drench my couch with my weeping.
⁷ My eyes waste away because of grief;
    they grow weak because of all my foes.

⁸ Depart from me, all you workers of evil,
    for the Lord has heard the sound of my
      weeping.
⁹ The Lord has heard my supplication;
    the Lord accepts my prayer.
¹⁰ All my enemies shall be ashamed and
      struck with terror;
    they shall turn back, and in a moment be
      put to shame.

COMMENTARY

Like Psalms 3–5, Psalm 6 is a prayer for help. As in the preceding psalms, foes are present (vv. 7-8, 10); however, these foes are not the psalmist's main problem. Rather, the real problem is God! The language and imagery suggest that Psalm 6 was originally composed by a sick person as a prayer for healing (cf. Psalms 38; 41; see also the Introduction), and the psalmist begins by attributing the sickness to the wrath of God (v. 1). But if God is the problem, God is also the solution. So the psalmist appeals immediately for God's mercy and God's healing action (v. 2). This thoroughly theocentric understanding of reality presents both interpretive problems and possibilities (see Reflections).

While Psalm 6 seems to describe a physical illness that threatens the psalmist with death, it is also possible that the language functions metaphorically. In short, the psalm need not be heard exclusively as a prayer for healing from physical illness. The expressions of terror (vv. 2-3) and grief (vv. 6-7) may arise from a variety of circumstances. For instance, several scholars have suggested that Psalm 6 reflects threatening circumstances in the life of Jeremiah; Patrick D. Miller has suggested the appropriateness of reading Psalm 6 against the narrative background of Hannah's plight in 1 Samuel 1.[71] That the language and imagery of Psalm 6 are capable of being heard on several levels is indicated by the fact

71. Patrick D. Miller, Jr., *Interpreting the Psalms* (Philadelphia: Fortress, 1986) 56-57.

that Psalm 6 became by the fifth century one of the church's seven penitential psalms (see also Psalms 32; 38; 51; 102; 130; 143), even though it has no explicit confession of sin and only the mildest implication of sinfulness in vv. 1-2. Nevertheless, the psalm's articulation of disease, mortality, and grief serves as a reminder of human finitude and fallibility, which impel persons to confront their essential neediness and to depend ultimately for life on the grace of God. This humble dependence on God for life is the essence of penitence.

As the NIV and the NRSV suggest, the psalm is best understood in four sections: vv. 1-3, 4-5, 6-7, 8-10. Verses 1-3 and 4-5 consist of petition and supporting reasons. Verses 6-7 focus on the psalmist's sorrowful present, while vv. 8-10 focus on the psalmist's hopeful future. Verse 6 is the only three-part line in the psalm. The way the editors of a recent Hebrew Bible have arranged the poetry serves to isolate v. 6a as a kind of hinge that functions as the culmination of vv. 1-5 and the introduction of vv. 6b-10.

6:1-3. The key to understanding v. 1 is the use of the words "anger" (אף 'ap) and "wrath" (חמה ḥēmâ). The Lord's "rebuke" and "discipline" are seen elsewhere as signs of God's loving guidance (see Prov 3:11-12), but the psalmist can see nothing educational about the present experience—be it sickness or otherwise—because it threatens his or her very life (see Ps 38:1). The psalmist knows God to be a God of grace (see Exod 34:6; Ps 4:1) and of healing (see Exod 15:26; Pss 30:2; 41:4; 103:3; 147:3; Isa 57:18-19; Jer 3:22; 33:6; Hos 7:1; 14:4), and so can interpret the present experience only as an indication of God's wrath. Psalm 6 may testify to the ancient belief that sin caused sickness (see Ps 41:4; Mark 2:1-12); however, because it lacks an explicit confession of sin, the psalm testifies even more strongly to the psalmist's conviction that every experience of life is somehow an experience of God (see Deut 32:39). "Terror" (or "dismay" [בהל bhl], vv. 2-3) is associated elsewhere with the experience of God's presence as judgment or wrath (Pss 2:5; 48:5 [NIV]; 83:15; 90:7 [NIV]; see also Exod 15:15) or with the experience of God's absence (Pss 30:7; 104:29). It is often the wicked whom God terrifies. In effect, the psalmist concludes that he or she is being treated by God as

an *enemy,* and this conclusion shakes the psalmist's whole being (see Pss 31:9-10; 35:9-10, where "bones" and "soul" appear in the same context to describe the pervasive effect of grief or joy). But firm in the conviction that God is the only hope, the psalmist can only ask, "How long?" (v. 3; see Pss 13:1-2; 35:17; 74:10; 79:5; 80:4; 89:46; 90:13; 94:3; 119:84).

6:4-5. As in Ps 90:13-14, here the question "How long?" is juxtaposed with the plea that God "turn" or "repent" and with an appeal to God's "steadfast love." The request is also reminiscent of Exod 32:12-14, where Moses intercedes for the people with the plea, "Turn from your fierce wrath" (32:12 NRSV; cf. Ps 6:2). The problem in Exod 32:1-14 was the people's sinfulness, and it is possible that this fundamental story from the Pentateuch influenced the appropriation of Psalm 6 as a penitential psalm. The outcome of the episode in Exod 32:1-14 is the revelation of God as a God of "steadfast love" (Exod 34:6-7)—precisely the basis of the appeal in Ps 6:4 (see Ps 5:7 and the Introduction). At issue in Exodus 32–34 was the very life of the people, and the very life of the psalmist also hangs on the plea in 6:4. The psalmist appeals to the grace and love that God had historically shown to the chosen people. The pronoun "me" is a translation of the same Hebrew word rendered "my soul" in v. 3 (נפש nepeš). The psalmist's whole being, terrified at experiencing God as an enemy, depends ultimately on God's steadfast love (on "deliver," see Ps 3:2, 7-8).

Verse 5 and similar expressions throughout Psalms are often viewed as attempts to appeal to God's self-interest (see 30:9; 88:10-12); that is, since the dead went to Sheol, and since Sheol was ordinarily understood to be beyond even God's reach, God would have one less worshiper if the psalmist died. While this approach is plausible, it is also possible to hear v. 5 as the psalmist's affirmation of God's good gift of life. Consider the words of Jürgen Moltmann: "In this world, with its modern 'sickness unto death,' true spirituality will be the restoration of the love of life—that is to say, *vitality.* The full and unreserved 'yes' to life, and the full and unreserved love for the living are the first experiences of God's spirit."[72] If this be the case, then v. 5 can

---

72. Jürgen Moltmann, *The Spirit of Life: A Universal Affirmation* (Minneapolis: Fortress, 1992) 97.

be heard as the psalmist's " 'yes' to life" and an affirmation of "love for the living." To make such an affirmation is, in essence, to praise God. Thus the question in v. 5b is itself an act of praise, and, as is regularly the case in the psalms, praise is offered amid difficult circumstances (see the Introduction).

6:6-7. Although perhaps surprising to contemporary folk, it is not unusual in Psalms that the psalmist's praise—the love of life and desire to live—occurs in the midst of an experience summarized by a poetic line that stands at the very center of the psalm (v. 6a): weariness (see Ps 69:3). This weariness is manifested and compounded by incessant weeping (vv. 6bc-7; cf. Ps 31:9). The foes (v. 7) apparently are not the direct cause of the psalmist's plight but are persons who fail to support the psalmist and thereby exacerbate the suffering. Verse 6a is duplicated exactly in Baruch's lament in Jer 45:3, to which God responds with the promise, "I will give you your life . . . in every place to which you may go" (Jer 45:5 NRSV). While no such divine promise is recorded here, a similar conviction on the psalmist's part seems to underlie the expression of confidence in vv. 8-10.

6:8-10. In any case, vv. 8-10 are remarkably different in tone from vv. 1-7. The psalmist trusts that he or she has been "heard" (vv. 8-9). The repetition of vocabulary from vv. 1-4 marks the reversal. "Be merciful" was the plea in v. 2, and now the psalmist is sure that the "cry for mercy" (v. 9; "supplication" [NRSV]) has been heard. Whereas "terror" had pervaded the psalmist's being (vv. 2-3), now the enemies will be "struck with terror" (v. 10). The psalmist trusts that God will heed the plea to "turn" (v. 4), and the result is that enemies shall "turn back" (v. 10). The chiastic structure (see Introduction) of v. 10 is significant. The verb "be ashamed" (בוש bôš) is the first and the penultimate word in the line, suggesting that the enemies (see vv. 7-8) will be surrounded by shame.

Scholars continue to debate the cause and significance of the transition from vv. 1-7 to vv. 8-10 (see Introduction). Perhaps the psalmist is responding to a priestly oracle or a promise that the text no longer records. Perhaps the psalmist has recovered from illness. But there is no solid evidence for either of these proposals. As the psalm now stands, the psalmist's physical condition and circumstances remain unchanged. Thus vv. 8-10 represent a profession of the trust that God makes life and hope possible even amid the stark daily realities of terror, disease, weariness, and grief. Praise and complaint remain inseparable realities (see Psalms 13; 22; Introduction).

REFLECTIONS

The thoroughly theocentric understanding of reality that characterizes the book of Psalms is thrown into particularly sharp relief by Psalm 6. God is both the problem and the solution. On the one hand, God is responsible for the psalmist's plight; on the other hand, God is the psalmist's only hope. If physical illness lies behind the origin of the prayer, as seems likely, then we are presented with troubling interpretive issues. In our world, we have other explanations for sickness and suffering—germs, viruses, chemical pollutants, improper diet, abuse of our own bodies. To suggest that God's wrath causes sickness and suffering seems to be dangerous reinforcement for a cruel doctrine of retribution that enables us to conclude that the prosperous must deserve God's favor and the afflicted must deserve God's wrath. Indeed, this is precisely what Job's friends unjustifiably concluded about Job (see, e.g., Job 11:2-6; 22:4-11).

Nevertheless, the psalmist's insistence that his or her plight be understood in relation to God may be instructive for contemporary readers. If all we can talk about in regard to sickness and suffering is viruses or germs, then we are in danger of removing God from the whole realm of the human experience of sickness, suffering, and death. Psalm 6 resists such a move. On the basis of Psalm 6, we need not make the mistake Job's friends made by adopting a doctrine of retribution that would interpret all sickness and suffering as God's direct action to punish particular sins. Rather, Psalm 6 encourages us to understand sickness, suffering, and death as the conditions of creatureliness that should make it obvious to us that the ability to secure our lives lies ultimately beyond our control. This relinquishment of self-control in dependence upon the grace and love of God has the liberating effect of allowing us to accept sickness, suffering, and death as inevitable realities of being mortal, finite, fallible. Like the psalmist, we live daily with the stark realities of terror, disease, weariness, grief, and the awareness of our mortality. The good news the psalmist offers is that none of these realities is sufficiently powerful to separate us from the love of God (see Rom 8:31-39). Amid them all, it is possible to live with integrity, purpose, and hope—by the grace of God. Without minimizing the difficulties of life, Psalm 6 offers a resounding " 'yes' to life," grounded not in self-confidence but in the steadfast love of God (v. 4). Thus, while this first penitential psalm does not even mention sin, it articulates the essence of penitence: humble reliance on the grace of God.

PSALM 7:1-17, O RIGHTEOUS GOD!

NIV

Psalm 7

A *shiggaion*[a] of David, which he sang to the Lord concerning Cush, a Benjamite.

[1]O Lord my God, I take refuge in you;
    save and deliver me from all who pursue
        me,
[2]or they will tear me like a lion
    and rip me to pieces with no one to
        rescue me.

[3]O Lord my God, if I have done this
    and there is guilt on my hands—
[4]if I have done evil to him who is at peace
        with me
    or without cause have robbed my foe—
[5]then let my enemy pursue and overtake me;
    let him trample my life to the ground
    and make me sleep in the dust.   *Selah*

[6]Arise, O Lord, in your anger;
    rise up against the rage of my enemies.
    Awake, my God; decree justice.
[7]Let the assembled peoples gather around you.
    Rule over them from on high;
[8] let the Lord judge the peoples.
Judge me, O Lord, according to my
        righteousness,
    according to my integrity, O Most High.
[9]O righteous God,

aTitle: Probably a literary or musical term

NRSV

Psalm 7

A Shiggaion of David, which he sang to the Lord concerning Cush, a Benjaminite.

[1] O Lord my God, in you I take refuge;
    save me from all my pursuers, and
        deliver me,
[2] or like a lion they will tear me apart;
    they will drag me away, with no one to
        rescue.

[3] O Lord my God, if I have done this,
    if there is wrong in my hands,
[4] if I have repaid my ally with harm
    or plundered my foe without cause,
[5] then let the enemy pursue and overtake
        me,
    trample my life to the ground,
    and lay my soul in the dust.   *Selah*

[6] Rise up, O Lord, in your anger;
    lift yourself up against the fury of my
        enemies;
    awake, O my God;[a] you have appointed
        a judgment.
[7] Let the assembly of the peoples be gathered
        around you,
    and over it take your seat[b] on high.
[8] The Lord judges the peoples;

aOr awake for me   bCn: Heb return

NIV

who searches minds and hearts,
bring to an end the violence of the wicked
and make the righteous secure.
[10]My shield[a] is God Most High,
who saves the upright in heart.
[11]God is a righteous judge,
a God who expresses his wrath every day.
[12]If he does not relent,
he[b] will sharpen his sword;
he will bend and string his bow.
[13]He has prepared his deadly weapons;
he makes ready his flaming arrows.

[14]He who is pregnant with evil
and conceives trouble gives birth to
disillusionment.
[15]He who digs a hole and scoops it out
falls into the pit he has made.
[16]The trouble he causes recoils on himself;
his violence comes down on his own head.

[17]I will give thanks to the LORD because of his
righteousness
and will sing praise to the name of the
LORD Most High.

a10 Or sovereign   b12 Or If a man does not repent, / God

NRSV

judge me, O LORD, according to my
righteousness
and according to the integrity that is in me.

[9] O let the evil of the wicked come to an end,
but establish the righteous,
you who test the minds and hearts,
O righteous God.
[10] God is my shield,
who saves the upright in heart.
[11] God is a righteous judge,
and a God who has indignation every day.

[12] If one does not repent, God[a] will whet
his sword;
he has bent and strung his bow;
[13] he has prepared his deadly weapons,
making his arrows fiery shafts.
[14] See how they conceive evil,
and are pregnant with mischief,
and bring forth lies.
[15] They make a pit, digging it out,
and fall into the hole that they have made.
[16] Their mischief returns upon their own heads,
and on their own heads their violence
descends.

[17] I will give to the LORD the thanks due to
his righteousness,
and sing praise to the name of the LORD,
the Most High.

a Heb he

COMMENTARY

Psalm 7 is a prayer for help from a person whose enemies are bearing down. It is likely that the psalmist had been falsely accused by opponents and appealed to God for help, perhaps in a judicial proceeding in the Temple (see Psalms 5; 17; Introduction). The psalm is sometimes labeled a protestation of innocence, since the psalmist makes the appeal on the basis of "my righteousness" (v. 8; cf. vv. 3-5 and Psalms 17; 26). The historical note in the superscription is enigmatic, since no Cush appears in the Davidic narratives.

A comparison of the NIV with the NRSV reveals different ways of understanding the structure and movement of the psalm; the NIV translation is preferable. An opening affirmation and a petition (vv. 1-2) are followed by an oath of innocence (vv. 3-5). Petition is resumed in vv. 6-9, and it is followed by sections of affirmation. Verses 10-13 affirm God's protection and righteous judgment, while vv. 14-16 affirm that the evil of the wicked will eventually fall back upon them. Verse 17 is a concluding promise to praise God.

7:1-2. The opening affirmation in v. 1 recalls Pss 2:12 and 5:11. Both psalms proclaim God's sovereignty, which the psalmist here recognizes. Thus he or she entrusts life, including the present crisis, to God. As in Psalm 3, the psalmist recognizes that "deliverance belongs to the LORD" (3:8). The plea, "Save me," translates the same Hebrew word as "deliver"/"deliverance" (ישע *yš'*) in 3:2, 7-8. The opposition is real and strong (v. 2; see "pursue"/"persecute" in Pss 31:15; 35:3; 69:26; 109:26; 142:6; 143:3; see similar animal imagery in Pss 10:9; 17:12; 22:13, 21), but not as strong as God.

7:3-5. Here the psalmist proclaims innocence with an oath formula—in effect, "Let me be cursed if I'm in the wrong." The "wrong" (v. 3) or "harm" (v. 4) that the psalmist is apparently accused of is not specified. The word "soul" in v. 5 is more literally "glory" (כבוד *kābôd*; see Pss 3:3; 4:2). The psalmist would be willing to be dishonored and humiliated if such was deserved, but it is not. The closest biblical parallel to vv. 3-5 is Job 31, where Job uses the same formula to affirm his innocence as he rests his case with God. Indeed, Psalm 7 as a whole is reminiscent of Job, whose friends end up finally pursuing him (Job 19:22, 25) with false accusations (see Job 11:2-6; 22:4-11; 42:7). Verses 3-5 anticipate the petition of v. 8.

7:6-9. In v. 6, God is summoned to action against the enemies (see "rise up" in Ps 3:7; "awake"/"rouse" in Pss 44:23; 59:4). The divine "anger" that the psalmist hoped to avoid in Ps 6:1 is appropriate for the enemies, because they are in the wrong. The psalmist is certain that God has "appointed a judgment," or more literally, "ordained justice." Verse 7 affirms the worldwide sovereignty over "the peoples" (see Ps 2:1) that gives God the prerogative to judge. Both the NIV and the NRSV understand the disputed verb (שובה *šûbâ*) in v. 7*b* to be the same verb translated as "enthroned" in 2:4, and God's position "on high" is associated with God's kingship in Ps 93:1, 4. Using a different verb, the psalmist again affirms God's role as judge (v. 8*a*; see Ps 96:10, which also affirms God's kingship); the psalmist does not hesitate to request that the cosmic judge of the world "judge me" (the same root [שפט *šāpaṭ*] as "judgment" in v. 6). The basis for the appeal is "my

righteousness" and "integrity" (see Pss 25:21; 26:1; 41:12). Verse 8 is again reminiscent of Job, who declares his own righteousness (see Job 29:14) and integrity (31:6; and see the NRSV's "blameless" in Job 1:1, 8; 2:3; 8:20; 9:20-22). Verse 9 can be translated in a jussive (NRSV), an imperative (NIV), or an indicative sense. In any case, it articulates the policy of the cosmic judge—to oppose the wicked and establish the righteous (see Ps 1:6). As cosmic judge, God operates with the most personal information (see "test"/"try" [בחן *bāḥan*] in Pss 11:5; 17:3; 26:2; 139:23; Jer 11:20; 17:10; 20:12).

7:10-13. Because God's knowledge and sphere of influence are both cosmic and personal, the psalmist in v. 10*a* can claim "God Most High" as "my shield" (cf. Ps 3:3). In v. 10*b*, the psalmist, who is among "the upright in heart" (cf. Pss 11:2; 32:11; 36:10; 64:10; 94:15; 97:11), affirms what he or she had prayed for in v. 1: God saves. The protection God offers grows out of God's role as "righteous judge" (v. 11). The word "righteous" (צדק *sedeq*; צדיק *saddîq*) occurs five times in this psalm (vv. 8, 9 [twice], 11, 17), and the word "judge" (שפט *šāpaṭ*; משפט *mišpāṭ*) occurs three times (vv. 6, 8, 11). These key words emphasize that it is God's will to enact justice and righteousness on a daily basis and a cosmic scale.

In vv. 12-13, the subject of the verbs is not specified. The NRSV suggests that the wicked should be understood as the subject of the first verb and that God be understood as subject of the remaining verbs, whereas the NIV suggests that God is the subject of all the verbs. Some interpreters suggest that the wicked be understood as subject of all the verbs, in which case, anticipating vv. 15-16, the military preparations of v. 12 must be understood as backfiring in v. 13 so that the wicked themselves are destroyed. Certainty is elusive, but the immediate antecedent of the pronouns in vv. 12-13 is "God," so the NIV translation seems preferable. Elsewhere, God is portrayed as executing judgment as a warrior (see Deut 32:41-42; Pss 38:3; 64:7; Lam 2:4; 3:12).

7:14-17. The subject of the verbs in these verses remains unspecified, but is clearly the wicked. The procreation imagery in v. 14 is striking; the whole process is perverse (see Job 15:35; Isa 59:4). The words "evil" (און *'āwen*) and "mischief" (עמל 'āmāl) are also paired elsewhere (cf. Ps 55:10: "iniquity and trouble"; Job 4:8; 15:35). These verses affirm the faith that the wicked will ultimately destroy themselves (see Pss 9:16; 35:7-8; 57:6; 141:10; Prov 26:27). "Violence" (חמס ḥāmās) characterizes the wicked (see Pss 27:12; 25:19; 58:2; 73:6), and God opposes it (Pss 11:5; 18:48; 55:9; 140:1, 4, 11). The juxtaposition of vv. 16 and 17 suggests that the destruction of the wicked is ultimately the working out of God's "righteousness" (see vv. 9, 11), for which God is to be praised.

REFLECTIONS

Like the preceding psalms, Psalm 7 affirms that the sovereign God will ultimately secure the lives of the righteous and the downfall of the wicked (see Pss 1:6; 2:12; 3:7-8; 5:4-6, 11-12; 6:8-10; see also Reflections on Psalm 6). The affirmation is eschatological, reflecting hope in God's future victory, for wickedness persists in the present; however, God's work is *already* effective, and the psalmists already experience God as a "shield" (3:3; 5:12; 7:10) and a "refuge" (2:12; 5:11; 7:1).

The problematic aspect of Psalm 7 is that the prayer for help in this case appears to be based on the psalmist's own righteousness and integrity (v. 8). This problem, however, is more apparent than real. The psalm is not a profession of general perfection or sinlessness but of the psalmist's innocence or rightness in a *particular* case that the enemies are pressing (vv. 1-2). This psalm's similarities with the book of Job are instructive at this point. Job also defended his own righteousness and integrity (see 29:14; 31:6) against his friends' accusations, and God declared that Job spoke "what is right" (42:7). Neither the book of Job nor Psalm 7 is about *self*-righteousness. Rather, both are fundamentally about the righteousness of God. Like Job, the psalmist rests the case with God, trusting God to be a "righteous judge" (v. 11; see also v. 9) and celebrating finally God's "righteousness" (v. 17), not the psalmist's own. If anyone is self-righteous in Psalm 7, it is the enemies who presumptuously usurp the prerogative of God by condemning the psalmist.

What the enemies need to hear is "Do not judge, so that you may not be judged" (Matt 7:1 NRSV). As for the psalmist, to defend righteousness and integrity against the enemies is, in effect, to profess trust in God and loyalty to God's ways (see Ps 26:1-3). In his interpretation of Psalm 7, Luther cites Paul's submission to the judgment of God (1 Cor 4:1-6) and issues a call for Christians to stand for justice and truth:

> Thus we see that it is not enough that if someone suffers for a just cause or for the truth, he commits the matter to God and is ready to yield and to be turned to dust together with his glory, but he should diligently pray that God judge and justify the cause of the truth, not for the petitioner's own advantage, but for the service of God and the salvation of the people. . . . We must pray that the truth may triumph.[73]

In Psalm 7, the psalmist prayed for the triumph of truth. In doing so, like Jesus, the psalmist "entrusted himself to the one who judges justly" (1 Pet 2:23 NRSV).

---

73. Quoted in H.-J. Kraus, *Psalms 1–59: A Commentary,* trans. H. C. Oswald (Minneapolis: Augsburg, 1988) 176.

PSALM 8:1-9, THE MAJESTY OF GOD AND THE GLORY OF HUMANITY

NIV

Psalm 8

For the director of music. According to *gittith.*[a]
A psalm of David.

[1]O LORD, our Lord,
how majestic is your name in all the earth!

You have set your glory
above the heavens.
[2]From the lips of children and infants
you have ordained praise[b]
because of your enemies,
to silence the foe and the avenger.

[3]When I consider your heavens,
the work of your fingers,
the moon and the stars,
which you have set in place,
[4]what is man that you are mindful of him,
the son of man that you care for him?
[5]You made him a little lower than the
heavenly beings[c]
and crowned him with glory and honor.

[6]You made him ruler over the works of your
hands;
you put everything under his feet:
[7]all flocks and herds,
and the beasts of the field,
[8]the birds of the air,
and the fish of the sea,
all that swim the paths of the seas.

[9]O LORD, our Lord,
how majestic is your name in all the earth!

[a]*Title: Probably a musical term*   [b]*2 Or strength*   [c]*5 Or than God*

NRSV

Psalm 8

To the leader: according to The Gittith. A
Psalm of David.

[1] O LORD, our Sovereign,
how majestic is your name in all the earth!

You have set your glory above the heavens.
[2]   Out of the mouths of babes and infants
you have founded a bulwark because of
your foes,
to silence the enemy and the avenger.

[3] When I look at your heavens, the work of
your fingers,
the moon and the stars that you have
established;
[4] what are human beings that you are
mindful of them,
mortals[a] that you care for them?

[5] Yet you have made them a little lower than
God,[b]
and crowned them with glory and honor.
[6] You have given them dominion over the
works of your hands;
you have put all things under their feet,
[7] all sheep and oxen,
and also the beasts of the field,
[8] the birds of the air, and the fish of the sea,
whatever passes along the paths of the seas.

[9] O LORD, our Sovereign,
how majestic is your name in all the earth!

[a]*Heb ben adam, lit. son of man*   [b]*Or than the divine beings or
angels: Heb elohim*

COMMENTARY

Psalm 8 has several distinctions. It is the first hymn or song of praise in the psalter. Unlike other hymns that consist of an invitation to and reasons for praise, Psalm 8 is unique in addressing God throughout in the second person. In a different sphere, Psalm 8 had the distinction of being the first biblical text to reach the moon, when the Apollo 11 mission left a silicon disc containing messages from seventy-three nations, including the Vatican, which contributed the text of this psalm.[74] Psalm 8 was clearly an appropriate choice for this cosmic journey, for it is both an eloquent proclamation of the cosmic sovereignty of God and a remarkable affirmation of the exalted status and vocation of the human creature.

8:1a, 9. The most obvious stylistic feature of Psalm 8 is the refrain in vv. 1a, 9. As if to fulfill the promise in Ps 7:17 that "I will . . . sing praise to the *name* of the LORD," vv. 1a, 9 enthusiastically proclaim the majesty of God's "*name* in all the earth!" The word "name" (שֵׁם *šēm*) connotes character and essence; everything in the world gives evidence of God's sovereign activity. The title "our Lord" or "our Sovereign" is used elsewhere to address a king (see 1 Kgs 1:11, 43, 47), and the adjective "majestic" (אַדִּיר *'addîr*) is used of kings in Ps 136:18 (NIV, "mighty"; NRSV, "famous") and of God in Ps 93:4 in the context of the proclamation that "the LORD is king" (Ps 93:1). In short, the proclamation of God's reign frames the psalm. The subsequent affirmation of humanity's royal status and dominion must be understood within the context of God's reign.

8:1b-2. Before the focus shifts to humanity, however, vv. 1b-2 explicitly extend the reach of God's sovereignty beyond "all the earth" to "above the heavens." The word "glory" (הוֹד *hôd*) is also used of earthly kings (Ps 45:3; see also "splendor," Ps 21:5) and of God to support the proclamation of God's reign (see also Pss 96:6 [NIV, "splendor"; NRSV, "honor"]; 145:5, "majesty"). The text of v. 1b is difficult, and there are numerous proposals for translating it and relating it to the beginning of v. 2. The NIV and the NRSV agree in construing the Hebrew as literally as possible and in taking v. 1b as a self-contained thought; however, many translations render v. 1b differently and take v. 2a as a continuation of v. 1b: "Thou whose glory above the heavens is chanted/ by the mouth of babes and infants" (RSV). In this reading, the idea is that even babies recognize God's cosmic sovereignty. The NIV's rendering of v. 2, following the LXX, would

support this idea. The NRSV's translation of v. 2, however, seems to assert that God can use even the speech of vulnerable, helpless infants as a power to oppose God's foes. The "foes"/"enemy"/"avenger" are probably the chaotic forces that God conquered and ordered in the sovereign act of creation. Understood this way, v. 2 anticipates the assertion of vv. 3-8 that God uses the weak and seemingly insignificant human creature as a partner in caring for a creation that is constantly threatened by its enemy, chaos (see Gen 1:1–2:4, to which Ps 8:6-8 is obviously related; see also Job 38:8-11; Pss 29:10; 74:12-17; 89:9-11; 104:5-9).

8:3-4. In v. 3, the focus shifts to humanity, but even in vv. 3-8, the primary actor is God. The only time a human is the subject of a verb is in v. 3, and the action of looking is very passive. When looking into the night sky, the psalmist is struck by the vastness of God's "work" (see Ps 102:25). How does the God who is responsible for the creation and care of such an immense universe have time to attend to the tiny human creature? This question lies at the structural and thematic center of the psalm (v. 4). Whereas the boundaries of the psalm deal with the issue of God's "name" or identity, the heart of the psalm raises the issue of the identity of humanity. The two issues are inseparable. Indeed, vv. 1a, 9 and 4 are verbally linked by the Hebrew particle מה (*mâ*), translated "how" in vv. 1a, 9 and "what" in v. 4. In short, the character of God's sovereignty cannot be understood apart from the knowledge that God *does* choose to be "mindful" and to "care for" humanity; the identity of humanity cannot be understood apart from this relationship with God.

8:5-8. The identity of both God and humans is addressed even more explicitly in these verses. That God rules the world has already been proclaimed (vv. 1-2), but now it is affirmed that humanity has royal status, too—indeed, "a little lower than God" (v. 5; the Hebrew word translated "God" [אֱלֹהִים *'ĕlōhîm*] may also be translated "heavenly beings" as in the NIV and as the NRSV note suggests). The attributes with which humans are "crowned" (see 2 Sam 12:30; Ps 21:3; Jer 13:18; Ezek 21:26) are royal ones. Both human kings and God as king possess "glory" (see Pss 21:5; 24:7-10; 29:1-3, 9; cf. 145:5, 12, "glori-

---

74. See James Limburg, "Who Cares for the Earth? Psalm 8 and the Environment," *Word and World Supplement Series* 1 (1992) 43. Limburg's source is NASA News Release No. 69-83F (July 1969).

ous"; the Hebrew word differs here from the one translated "glory" in v. 1) and "honor" (cf. Pss 21:5, "majesty"; 145:5-12, "splendor"). The sovereign God has bestowed sovereignty upon the human creature. This remarkable affirmation is described in different terms in vv. 6-8. The human exercises the kingly function of "dominion" (see NRSV "rule"/"ruler"/"sovereign" in Gen 45:8, 26; Judg 8:22-23; 9:2; 2 Sam 23:3; 1 Kgs 4:21) over "all things" (v. 6). Although the Hebrew words translated "dominion" differ in v. 6 (משל *māšal*) and Gen 1:26-28 (רדה *rādâ*), Psalm 8 clearly recalls Genesis 1. The phrase "image of God" does not occur in Psalm 8, but the language and movement of Psalm 8 suggest that humans represent God in the world. This, of course, has profound implications for understanding both God and humanity. God and humans are partners in the care of creation, because God has made the risky choice to share God's power!

8:9. This conclusion is reinforced by the second occurrence of the refrain. Verse 9 is an exact verbal repetition of v. 1*a*, but the second occurrence has a fuller sense that is achieved primarily by repetition of the word "all" (כל *kōl*, vv. 1*a*, 6-7, 9). When the refrain occurs the second time, it is clear that the majesty of God's name, which is known "in all the earth," includes the dominion of humanity, for God has given them dominion over God's "works" (v. 6; cf. v. 4) by putting "all things under their feet" (v. 6; see v. 7).[75] God's "name" or reputation is bound up with the human performance of dominion, and human dominion is a responsibility that is to be bounded by God's ultimate sovereignty (see Reflections). The identity and destiny of God, of humanity, and of the creation are inextricably intertwined. Theology, anthropology, and ecology are inseparable.

75. See Robert Alter, *The Art of Biblical Poetry* (New York: Basic Books, 1985) 119.

REFLECTIONS

For Psalm 8, structural and canonical observations are starting points for theological reflection.

1. As suggested above, the psalm is framed by proclamation of God's sovereignty, and at the center of the psalm (v. 4) is the question that leads to the proclamation of God-given human sovereignty (vv. 5-8). Walter Brueggemann suggests that the crucial interpretative move is to hold the boundaries and the center together.[76] To fail to take seriously the central importance of humanity in God's plan for the creation is to abdicate the God-given responsibility to be partners with God in caring for the earth (see Ps 115:16). At the same time, it is necessary to recognize that the proclamation of human sovereignty is bounded, both structurally and theologically, by the proclamation of God's sovereignty. In other words, human sovereignty is derivative. Apart from the limits of God's sovereign will, the exercise of dominion is in danger of becoming simply human autonomy, or self-rule. As suggested above (see Commentary on Psalms 1; 2), the attempt to live beyond the claim of God is the essence of wickedness. In other words, dominion without the recognition of God's claim on us and on the earth becomes domination. To leave God out of the partnership invites disaster; indeed, frightening signs of ecological disaster are all around us, from eroding soil to polluted streams to the possible depletion of the ozone layer. Psalm 8 is thus a reminder "that the God-praising and the earth-caring community are one."[77]

2. The canonical placement of Psalm 8 also invites theological reflection. The juxtaposition of Psalms 3-7 and Psalm 8 suggests another crucial interpretative question: What should we conclude about the human creature who both suffers miserably (Psalms 3-7) and is "little lower than God" and "crowned . . . with glory and honor" (v. 5)? The movement from Psalms 3-7 to Psalm 8 suggests at least that the royal status and vocation of humanity are not

76. Walter Brueggemann, *The Message of the Psalms* (Minneapolis: Augsburg, 1984) 37-38.
77. Limburg, "Who Cares for the Earth?" 51.

diminished by suffering. In fact, as regards the human, we may conclude that to be created in the "image of God" inevitably means that we will suffer. As regards God, we may conclude that divine partnership with humanity inevitably involves God in suffering. These same conclusions are articulated in the book of Job. Given that Psalm 7 recalled the book of Job at several points (see above), it is not surprising that Psalm 8 figures prominently in Job. In the beginning, Job's suffering leads him to deny the royal status and vocation of humanity that is voiced by Ps 8:4-5 (cf. Job 7:17 with Ps 8:4; Job 19:9 with Ps 8:5). Job eventually moves toward reclaiming the vision of Psalm 8 (see the royal imagery in Job 31:36-37), and God's challenge at the end of the book (40:10) leads Job to change his mind. Job finally concludes: "I . . . change my mind about dust and ashes [vulnerable humanity]" (Job 42:6; see Gen 18:27; Job 30:19).[78] What Job has learned is that the royal status and vocation of humanity involves suffering as well as glory. The clear implication of Job's conclusion is that God suffers too and that human suffering should be understood ultimately as part of the experience of sharing in partnership with God a burden of responsibility in caring for the earth.

The juxtaposition of Psalms 3–7 and Psalm 8, along with the use of Psalm 8 in the book of Job, anticipate the NT understanding of the identity of God and humanity. Hebrews 2:6-8 quotes Ps 8:4-5, 6b, and Heb 2:9 applies Ps 8:5 to Jesus (see also 1 Cor 15:27; Eph 1:22). It appears on the surface that the author of Hebrews has simply understood the phrase "son of man" in Ps 8:5 as a christological title. This may be the case; however, it is also the case that Hebrews 2 as a whole points in the same direction as Psalm 8—namely, the inseparability of suffering and glory for both God and humanity. It is Jesus—"the reflection of God's glory" (Heb 1:3) and the complete embodiment of authentic humanity (see Heb 2:14, 17; 4:15)—who conclusively reveals that God's glory is not incompatible with suffering and thus that the suffering of human beings does not preclude their sharing in the glory of God (Heb 2:10-18; see esp. "glory" in 1:3 and 2:10). Finally, then, the use of Psalm 8 in Hebrews 2 is faithful to the message of the original. Psalm 8, Hebrews 2, and the NT as a whole call human beings to live under God's rule and to exercise "dominion over . . . all things" in the same way that God exercises dominion: as a suffering servant (see Mark 10:41-45; Phil 2:5-11).[79]

78. For an explanation, see J. Gerald Janzen, *Job,* Interpretation (Atlanta: John Knox, 1985) 254-59. This translation differs significantly from the NIV and the NRSV.

79. Portions of the treatment of this and several other psalms in this commentary are similar to the author's comments in C. B. Cousar, B. R. Gaventa, J. C. McCann, Jr., J. D. Newsome, *Texts for Preaching: A Lectionary Commentary Based on the NRSV—Year C* (Louisville: Westminster John Knox, 1994).

PSALMS 9:1–10:18, THE NEEDY SHALL NOT ALWAYS BE FORGOTTEN

NIV	NRSV
Psalm 9[a]	Psalm 9
For the director of music. To ⌐the tune of⌐ "The Death of the Son." A psalm of David.	To the leader: according to Muth-labben. A Psalm of David.
[1] I will praise you, O LORD, with all my heart;	[1] I will give thanks to the LORD with my whole heart; I will tell of all your wonderful deeds.
[a] Psalms 9 and 10 may have been originally a single acrostic poem, the stanzas of which begin with the successive letters of the Hebrew alphabet. In the Septuagint they constitute one psalm.	[2] I will be glad and exult in you;

I will tell of all your wonders.
²I will be glad and rejoice in you;
   I will sing praise to your name, O Most
      High.

³My enemies turn back;
   they stumble and perish before you.
⁴For you have upheld my right and my cause;
   you have sat on your throne, judging
      righteously.
⁵You have rebuked the nations and destroyed
      the wicked;
   you have blotted out their name for ever
      and ever.
⁶Endless ruin has overtaken the enemy,
   you have uprooted their cities;
   even the memory of them has perished.

⁷The Lord reigns forever;
   he has established his throne for judgment.
⁸He will judge the world in righteousness;
   he will govern the peoples with justice.
⁹The Lord is a refuge for the oppressed,
   a stronghold in times of trouble.
¹⁰Those who know your name will trust in you,
   for you, Lord, have never forsaken those
      who seek you.

¹¹Sing praises to the Lord, enthroned in Zion;
   proclaim among the nations what he has
      done.
¹²For he who avenges blood remembers;
   he does not ignore the cry of the afflicted.

¹³O Lord, see how my enemies persecute me!
   Have mercy and lift me up from the gates
      of death,
¹⁴that I may declare your praises
   in the gates of the Daughter of Zion
   and there rejoice in your salvation.
¹⁵The nations have fallen into the pit they have
      dug;
   their feet are caught in the net they have
      hidden.
¹⁶The Lord is known by his justice;
   the wicked are ensnared by the work of
      their hands.   *Higgaion.ᵃ Selah*
¹⁷The wicked return to the grave,ᵇ
   all the nations that forget God.
¹⁸But the needy will not always be forgotten,

ᵃ16 Or *Meditation*; possibly a musical notation   ᵇ17 Hebrew *Sheol*

I will sing praise to your name, O Most
   High.

³ When my enemies turned back,
   they stumbled and perished before you.
⁴ For you have maintained my just cause;
   you have sat on the throne giving
      righteous judgment.

⁵ You have rebuked the nations, you have
      destroyed the wicked;
   you have blotted out their name forever
      and ever.
⁶ The enemies have vanished in everlasting
      ruins;
   their cities you have rooted out;
   the very memory of them has perished.

⁷ But the Lord sits enthroned forever,
   he has established his throne for
      judgment.
⁸ He judges the world with righteousness;
   he judges the peoples with equity.

⁹ The Lord is a stronghold for the oppressed,
   a stronghold in times of trouble.
¹⁰ And those who know your name put their
      trust in you,
   for you, O Lord, have not forsaken those
      who seek you.

¹¹ Sing praises to the Lord, who dwells in Zion.
   Declare his deeds among the peoples.
¹² For he who avenges blood is mindful of
      them;
   he does not forget the cry of the afflicted.

¹³ Be gracious to me, O Lord.
   See what I suffer from those who hate me;
   you are the one who lifts me up from
      the gates of death,
¹⁴ so that I may recount all your praises,
   and, in the gates of daughter Zion,
   rejoice in your deliverance.

¹⁵ The nations have sunk in the pit that they
      made;
   in the net that they hid has their own
      foot been caught.

NIV

nor the hope of the afflicted ever perish.

19Arise, O LORD, let not man triumph;
    let the nations be judged in your presence.
20Strike them with terror, O LORD;
    let the nations know they are
        but men.   *Selah*

Psalm 10ᵃ

1Why, O LORD, do you stand far off?
    Why do you hide yourself in times of
        trouble?
2In his arrogance the wicked man hunts down
        the weak,
    who are caught in the schemes he devises.
3He boasts of the cravings of his heart;
    he blesses the greedy and reviles the LORD.
4In his pride the wicked does not seek him;
    in all his thoughts there is no room for
        God.
5His ways are always prosperous;
    he is haughty and your laws are far from
        him;
    he sneers at all his enemies.
6He says to himself, "Nothing will shake me;
    I'll always be happy and never have
        trouble."
7His mouth is full of curses and lies and threats;
    trouble and evil are under his tongue.
8He lies in wait near the villages;
    from ambush he murders the innocent,
    watching in secret for his victims.
9He lies in wait like a lion in cover;
    he lies in wait to catch the helpless;
    he catches the helpless and drags them off
        in his net.
10His victims are crushed, they collapse;
    they fall under his strength.
11He says to himself, "God has forgotten;
    he covers his face and never sees."

12Arise, LORD! Lift up your hand, O God.
    Do not forget the helpless.
13Why does the wicked man revile God?
    Why does he say to himself,
    "He won't call me to account"?

ᵃPsalms 9 and 10 may have been originally a single acrostic poem,
the stanzas of which begin with the successive letters of the Hebrew
alphabet. In the Septuagint they constitute one psalm.

NRSV

16 The LORD has made himself known, he has
    executed judgment;
    the wicked are snared in the work of
        their own hands.   *Higgaion. Selah*

17 The wicked shall depart to Sheol,
    all the nations that forget God.

18 For the needy shall not always be forgotten,
    nor the hope of the poor perish forever.

19 Rise up, O LORD! Do not let mortals prevail;
    let the nations be judged before you.
20 Put them in fear, O LORD;
    let the nations know that they are only
        human.   *Selah*

Psalm 10

1 Why, O LORD, do you stand far off?
    Why do you hide yourself in times of
        trouble?
2 In arrogance the wicked persecute the
        poor—
    let them be caught in the schemes they
        have devised.

3 For the wicked boast of the desires of their
        heart,
    those greedy for gain curse and renounce
        the LORD.
4 In the pride of their countenance the
        wicked say, "God will not seek it
        out";
    all their thoughts are, "There is no God."

5 Their ways prosper at all times;
    your judgments are on high, out of their
        sight;
    as for their foes, they scoff at them.
6 They think in their heart, "We shall not be
        moved;
    throughout all generations we shall not
        meet adversity."

7 Their mouths are filled with cursing and
        deceit and oppression;
    under their tongues are mischief and
        iniquity.

NIV

[14]But you, O God, do see trouble and grief;
    you consider it to take it in hand.
The victim commits himself to you;
    you are the helper of the fatherless.
[15]Break the arm of the wicked and evil man;
    call him to account for his wickedness
    that would not be found out.

[16]The LORD is King for ever and ever;
    the nations will perish from his land.
[17]You hear, O LORD, the desire of the afflicted;
    you encourage them, and you listen to
        their cry,
[18]defending the fatherless and the oppressed,
    in order that man, who is of the earth,
        may terrify no more.

NRSV

[8] They sit in ambush in the villages;
    in hiding places they murder the innocent.

Their eyes stealthily watch for the helpless;
[9] they lurk in secret like a lion in its covert;
they lurk that they may seize the poor;
    they seize the poor and drag them off in
        their net.

[10] They stoop, they crouch,
    and the helpless fall by their might.
[11] They think in their heart, "God has
        forgotten,
    he has hidden his face, he will never see
        it."

[12] Rise up, O LORD; O God, lift up your hand;
    do not forget the oppressed.
[13] Why do the wicked renounce God,
    and say in their hearts, "You will not call
        us to account"?

[14] But you do see! Indeed you note trouble
        and grief,
    that you may take it into your hands;
the helpless commit themselves to you;
    you have been the helper of the orphan.

[15] Break the arm of the wicked and evildoers;
    seek out their wickedness until you find
        none.
[16] The LORD is king forever and ever;
    the nations shall perish from his land.

[17] O LORD, you will hear the desire of the
        meek;
    you will strengthen their heart, you will
        incline your ear
[18] to do justice for the orphan and the
        oppressed,
    so that those from earth may strike terror
        no more.[a]

[a] Meaning of Heb uncertain

COMMENTARY

As the NIV note indicates, it is likely that Psalms 9 and 10 were originally a single acrostic poem with every other line beginning with a successive letter of the alphabet. The pattern remains largely intact, and there are further indications of unity, including the fact that the LXX treats Psalms 9–10 as a single psalm and that Psalm 10 is one of only four psalms in Book I without a superscription (see Psalms 1; 2; 33). In addition, a shared vocabulary links the two psalms, especially the designations of the major human characters—the wicked (9:5, 16-17; 10:2-4, 13, 15) and the "afflicted"/"poor"/"oppressed"/"meek" (9:12, 18; 10:2, 9, 12, 17; additional links are noted below).

Psalms 9 and 10 seem to have no discernible structural regularity, perhaps due to the acrostic pattern. This does not mean, however, that the progression of thought is simply random. Psalm 9 begins like a psalm of thanksgiving and retains this basic character throughout. After an initial announcement of thanks (vv. 1-2) and account of deliverance (vv. 3-4), the psalmist generalizes from his or her experience to God's treatment of "the nations" and "the wicked" (v. 5). The nations remain particularly in view in Psalm 9 (see vv. 15, 17, 19-20), while the wicked will be especially prominent in Psalm 10 (see above). Verses 5-8 contrast the disappearance of the wicked (vv. 5-6) with the permanent enthronement of God (vv. 7-8). This leads to an affirmation of God's protection (vv. 9-10), invitation to praise (vv. 11-12), petition (vv. 13-14), assessment of the contrasting fates of the wicked and the poor (vv. 15-18), and renewed petition (vv. 19-20). The two sections of petition in Psalm 9 anticipate the character of Psalm 10, which in contrast to Psalm 9 is primarily a prayer for help. This is evident from the complaint in vv. 1-2, which is followed by an extended description of the wicked (vv. 3-11) and by alternating petitions (vv. 12-13, 15) and affirmations of trust (vv. 14, 16-18).

The original setting of Psalms 9–10 is unclear (see the Introduction), but there are indications that these psalms would have been especially appropriate for post-exilic worship. The post-exilic community was subject to domination by the nations, yet in the midst of such oppression, the community affirmed the rule of God (see 9:4, 7, 11; 10:16; Introduction). The post-exilic situation evoked both complaint and confidence, which may explain the juxtaposition of thanksgiving (Psalm 9) and prayer for help (Psalm 10) as well as the alternating expressions of petition and confidence within both psalms.

9:1-8. Perhaps not coincidentally, vv. 1-2 recall Ps 7:17. The "righteousness" mentioned there, and thematic in Psalm 7, will also be thematic in Psalms 9–10 (cf. 9:4 with 7:11). The thanksgiving the psalmist intends to offer seems to consist not simply of sacrifice but of proclamation (see v. 15; Ps 26:7). God's "wonderful deeds" could include historic events like the exodus (see Exod 3:20; 15:11; see also Pss 77:11, 14; 78:12) or personal experiences of deliverance (see Ps 88:10, 12). In fact, the psalmist cites a personal episode in vv. 3-4. The enemies have "perished," an outcome that recalls the destiny of the wicked (and the nations) in Pss 1:6 and 2:12, and that signals a thematic word in Psalms 9–10 (see 9:5, "destroyed"; 9:6, 18; 10:16). Verse 4 also introduces key themes of Psalms 9–10—God rules (see 9:7, 11, where "enthroned" and "dwells" translate the same word rendered in v. 4 as "sat" [יָשַׁב yāšab]; see also "king" in 10:16), and God's royal policy is to enact justice (see "just"/"judgment"/"judge"/"justice" here and in 9:7-8, 16, 19; 10:5, 18; see also 89:14; 97:2).

The psalmist apparently sees his or her experience as paradigmatic. What happened to the psalmist's enemies has happened to "the nations" and "the wicked" as well—God has "destroyed" (v. 5; lit., "caused to perish"). Indeed, even their "memory . . . has perished" (v. 6; see also Ps 34:16). The destruction of the nations and the wicked is also testimony to God's reign and to the goal of God's royal policy—justice, righteousness, and equity (vv. 7-8; see v. 4; Pss 96:10, 13; 98:9; 99:4).

9:9-12. Because of God's commitment to justice and righteousness, there is hope for the "oppressed" (see 10:18). God is their "stronghold" (see "refuge"/"fortress"/"sure defense" in Pss 18:2; 46:7, 11; 48:4; 59:9, 16-17; 62:2, 6; 94:22; 144:2). Those who "know" God's character and reputation know that God stands for justice (see 9:16), and their response is well-founded trust (see Ps 4:5; Introduction). Thus the psalmist invites others to do what he or she will do: "sing praises" (v. 11; see also v. 2) and proclaim God's deeds (v. 11; see also v. 1). Verse 12, like v. 10, emphasizes the reliability of God. One "who avenges blood" means one who values human life

Figure 6: The Hebrew Alphabet

א	ʼāleph	ט	ṭêt	פ	pē ʼ
ב	bêt	י	yôd	צ	ṣādê
ג	gîmel	כ	kaph	ק	qôph
ד	dālet	ל	lāmed	ר	rêš
ה	hē ʼ	מ	mēm	שׂ	śîn
ו	wāw	נ	nûn	שׁ	šîn
ז	zayin	ס	sāmek	ת	tāw
ח	ḥêt	ע	ʻayin		

(In alphabetic acrostics, the letters śîn and šîn are treated as a single letter.)

(see Gen 9:5; Ezek 33:6). Because God values life, God "remembers" those who entrust themselves to God and who cry for help. This dynamic was operative in the historic deliverance of the people (see "cry" in Exod 3:7, 9; 14:10; Deut 26:7; Josh 24:7) and in a variety of other crises, both corporate and personal (Pss 34:17; 77:1; 88:1; 107:6, 28). Verse 12 contains the first occurrence of a Hebrew root (עַנָה ʻānâ) that appears in two similar forms in Psalms 9–10 and is translated by the NRSV as "afflicted" (9:12), "poor" (9:18; 10:2, 9), "oppressed" (10:12), and "meek" (10:17). This sevenfold repetition is part of a cluster of words that designate those who belong to God—the "oppressed" (9:9; 10:18), the "needy" (9:18), the "innocent" (10:8), and the "helpless" (10:8, 10, 14). The "afflicted" are those who know they are not self-sufficient. They know they need help (see Psalm 3), and so entrust their lives and future to God. Elsewhere, these people are called "the righteous" (see Pss 1:5-6; 5:12).

9:13-18. While the psalm began by celebrating deliverance, it seems that not all is settled. Verse 13 consists of petition (v. 13a; see Ps 4:2) and complaint (v. 13b), but there is also confidence (v. 13c; see Job 38:17; Ps 107:18), which enables the psalmist to envision again declaring (the NRSV's "recount" is the same Hebrew word [ספר sāpar] as "tell" in v. 1) God's "praise" (see Pss

22:4; 34:2; 51:15; 71:6; 100:4; 102:21; 106:2, 12). Those who cannot help themselves will rejoice in God's help (NRSV, "deliverance"; NIV, "salvation"; see also Ps 3:2, 7-8). The expression of confidence continues in vv. 15-18. As the working out of God's justice is revealed, the nations and the wicked will be victims of their own designs (see Ps 7:15-16), and death is their destiny (see "Sheol" in Ps 6:5 and the description of the results of forgetting God in Deut 8:17-20). Verse 18 reinforces v. 12: God will not forget the helpless. In contrast to the enemies who perish (9:3, 5-6), the "hope of the poor" (see Pss 62:5; 71:5) will not perish.

9:19-20. The focus on the nations continues in these verses and the petition is another link with Psalm 10 (see 10:12; see also 3:7; 7:6). The Hebrew word for "mortals"/"human" (אֱנוֹשׁ ʼĕnôš) seems to have the connotation of weakness. The strength of the nations is no match for God's sovereignty. The parallelism of "judge" (v. 19b) and "know" (v. 20b) recalls v. 16. Unlike the power of mortals, God's power is always exercised for justice. The word translated as "mortals"/"human" (ʼĕnôš) in vv. 19-20 occurs also in the final verse of Psalm 10 in the NRSV's phrase "those from earth." There, too, their defeat means "justice" for those who need help (10:18).

10:1-11. The petitions in vv. 13, 19-20 have

anticipated the change of tone marked by the complaint of 10:1-2 (see Ps 22:1). That things remain unsettled for the psalmist is indicated by the fact that 10:1 contradicts 9:9, and 10:2*b* prays for what 9:15-16 has already celebrated. Clearly, the poor are still being persecuted by the arrogant wicked (see Ps 30:11), who become the focus of Psalm 10 (see vv. 2-4, 13, 15). In fact, an extended description of the wicked follows in vv. 3-11 (see Ps 73:3-12). The wicked "boast" (v. 3; see Pss 5:5; 73:3, "arrogant"; 75:4) of their selfishness. Unlike the afflicted, the wicked see themselves as self-sufficient, so they "renounce" God (v. 3; see v. 13) and see themselves accountable to no one (v. 4; see Psalm 14). Even so, the wicked seem to prosper with impunity (v. 5); with apparent justification, they consider themselves untouchable. To not be "moved" or "shaken" (v. 6) is elsewhere supposed to be the result of righteousness (see Pss 15:5; 16:8; 62:2, 6). Here, however, the wicked perceive themselves to be secure, despite their deceitful, violent treatment of the helpless, the poor, and the innocent (vv. 7-10; see 5:6, 9; 7:2, 14; 17:10-12; 22:13; 55:10-11; 140:1-5). In v. 11, the wicked arrogantly contradict the faith of the psalmist: God "has forgotten" (cf. 9:12, 18). The wicked cruelly attempt to deepen the doubt expressed in 10:1: God "has hidden." According to the wicked, there will be no help from God (see Ps 3:2).

10:12-14. The petition in v. 12 responds directly to v. 11 as it asks God not to forget, and v. 13 quotes the wicked again so as to remind God directly of their arrogant assertions. The expression of confidence in v. 14 also responds directly to v. 11. The wicked say that God does not "see," but the helpless know better: "You do see!" The "you" here and in the final line of v. 14 is an emphatic use of the Hebrew pronoun (אתה *'attâ*). The word "trouble" (עמל *'āmāl*) here is the same as "mischief" in v. 7. God sees both the "mischief" of the wicked and the "trouble" and "grief" (see Ps 6:7) it causes the helpless, and God responds as "helper" (see Pss 33:20; 70:5; 115:9-11; 146:5) of the "orphan" (see v. 18; Exod 22:22-23; Deut 24:17-20; Pss 68:5; 94:6; 146:9).

10:15-18. This expression of trust is followed by further petition, which includes the request that God do precisely what the wicked said God could not do: "call . . . to account" (v. 15; see v. 13 NIV). The psalm ends in trusting affirmation. Verse 16 recalls the affirmation of God's reign that followed the descriptions of the enemies' demise in 9:3-4, 5-8. The psalmist's confidence is ultimately founded on the conviction that God rules the world and that God will enact the royal policy of justice (v. 18). While the wicked boast of the "desires of their heart" (10:3), God hears the "desire of the meek," and it is "their heart" that God "will strengthen" (v. 17). Because God rules the world, the meek will ultimately inherit the earth (see Ps 37:11; Matt 5:5).

REFLECTIONS

In a sense, Psalms 9–10 are a mirror image of Psalms 1–2. Psalm 1 framed the problem of rebellion against God in terms of the wicked (vv. 1, 5-6), whereas Psalm 2 put the problem in terms of peoples and nations (vv. 1, 8). Conversely, Psalm 9 focuses attention primarily on the rebellion of the nations, while Psalm 10 speaks mainly in terms of wicked persons. Both Psalms 1–2 and 9–10 affirm that, appearances to the contrary, God rules the world.

A crucial clue to recognizing the eschatological orientation of Psalms 9–10 is the apparent contradiction between 9:9 and 10:1, as well as the juxtaposition of thanksgiving (Psalm 9) and complaint (Psalm 10). Kraus writes:

> Godforsakenness and triumph are juxtaposed in one and the same psalm, and that quite abruptly. Jubilation and lament permeate the song. Two experiences lie adjacent to each other, just as they are met with under the world reign of God on Zion: wondrous rescue and incomprehensible delay.[80]

In other words, Psalms 9–10 leave the faithful where Jesus' proclamation of the reign of God

---

80. H.-J. Kraus, *Psalms 1–59: A Commentary,* trans. H. C. Oswald (Minneapolis: Augsburg, 1988) 199.

leaves them. We are invited both to enter the reign of God as a present reality (Mark 1:14-15; Luke 17:20-21) and to await its consummation (Mark 13:23, 28-31; Luke 21:29-36).

As we wait, we pray as the psalmist prayed in Psalms 9–10—as one of the "poor" and the "helpless." Mays suggests that the prayer is for all the poor: "It is, so to say, a class action appeal. 'Blessed are you poor, for yours is the kingdom of God' (Luke 6:20); it is the lowly who by dependence and anticipation already live in the rule of God."[81] To be sure, we live in the rule of God amid competing rules and claims from wicked persons and nations, among whom we must certainly at times count ourselves and our nation. North American culture trains people to be self-centered, and it encourages us to be accountable to no one but ourselves. Whatever nation we live in, we can be sure it pursues above all its own national security with little or no consideration of the impact on others and even less for something as elusive as the will of God. Yet, despite the wickedness in ourselves, in others, and in society, we dare to trust with the psalmist that the "LORD is king forever and ever" (10:16) and that justice will prevail. This conviction and hope impels us into the struggle to join God at God's work in the world.

81. James L. Mays, *Psalms,* Interpretation (Louisville: John Knox, 1994) 73.

PSALM 11:1-7, THE UPRIGHT SHALL BEHOLD GOD'S FACE

NIV

Psalm 11

For the director of music. Of David.

[1] In the LORD I take refuge.
How then can you say to me:
"Flee like a bird to your mountain.
[2] For look, the wicked bend their bows;
they set their arrows against the strings
to shoot from the shadows
at the upright in heart.
[3] When the foundations are being destroyed,
what can the righteous do[a]?"

[4] The LORD is in his holy temple;
the LORD is on his heavenly throne.
He observes the sons of men;
his eyes examine them.
[5] The LORD examines the righteous,
but the wicked[b] and those who love violence
his soul hates.
[6] On the wicked he will rain
fiery coals and burning sulfur;
a scorching wind will be their lot.

[a]3 Or *what is the Righteous One doing* [b]5 Or *The LORD, the Righteous One, examines the wicked, /*

NRSV

Psalm 11

To the leader. Of David.

[1] In the LORD I take refuge; how can you say to me,
"Flee like a bird to the mountains;[a]
[2] for look, the wicked bend the bow,
they have fitted their arrow to the string,
to shoot in the dark at the upright in heart.
[3] If the foundations are destroyed,
what can the righteous do?"

[4] The LORD is in his holy temple;
the LORD's throne is in heaven.
His eyes behold, his gaze examines humankind.
[5] The LORD tests the righteous and the wicked,
and his soul hates the lover of violence.
[6] On the wicked he will rain coals of fire and sulfur;
a scorching wind shall be the portion of their cup.
[7] For the LORD is righteous;

[a]Gk Syr Jerome Tg: Heb *flee to your mountain, O bird*

NIV

⁷For the LORD is righteous,
   he loves justice;
      upright men will see his face.

NRSV

he loves righteous deeds;
   the upright shall behold his face.

COMMENTARY

Because of its uniqueness, Psalm 11 is difficult to categorize. It is usually classified as a song of trust, but if the verbs in vv. 6-7 are understood as jussives ("let [God] rain coals . . ."), then vv. 6-7 can be construed as petition, and the psalm may be heard as an individual complaint or prayer for help. Gerstenberger suggests that Psalm 11 is a unique sort of complaint that he calls a Psalm of Contest, and he suggests that an accused person is given a chance in the context of a worship service to confront his or her opponents and offer a defense.[82] Other scholars suggest that the psalmist has found asylum in the Temple and is awaiting a ritual judicial proceeding that will result in vindication (see Psalms 5; 7; 17; Introduction). While the advisers recommend flight (v. 1), apparently due to the degree of opposition and the hopelessness of the case (vv. 2-3), the psalmist expresses confidence in God's sovereign righteousness and entrusts his or her destiny to God (vv. 4-7).

The above proposals support the NIV and the NRSV divisions of the psalm into two major sections: vv. 1-3, 4-7. It often makes sense to view the structure or movement of a psalm on more than one level, and an alternative perspective in this case involves a chiastic arrangement (see the Introduction), as follows:

A   v. 1 the security of the psalmist (the righteous)

   B   vv. 2-3 the threat of the wicked

      C   v. 4 the sovereignty of God

   B′   vv. 5-6 the destiny (punishment) of the wicked

A′   v. 7 the destiny (security) of the righteous

82. Erhard S. Gerstenberger, *Psalms, Part 1, with an Introduction to Cultic Poetry,* Forms of the OT Literature 14 (Grand Rapids: Eerdmans, 1988) 77, 79; he cites Psalms 4; 52; 62; Jer 11:18-23; 18:18-23; 20:7-13 as similar texts.

This proposal highlights v. 4, which, like several of the preceding psalms, affirms that God rules the world and enacts a royal policy of setting things right (see Psalms 1–2; 5; 7:7-11; 9:7-8; 10:15-18; Introduction).

11:1-3. Regardless of the accuracy of the proposals for a cultic setting, it is clear that Psalm 11 poses two alternatives for the faithful when confronted by the wicked and their threats—the faithful can either flee or stand firm in their profession of trust in the righteous rule of God. The psalm begins by stating the alternative that the psalmist has chosen: to trust God (see "refuge" in Pss 2:12; 5:11; 7:1; see also Isa 28:16; Introduction). Thus the psalmist categorically rejects the advice of those who say to "flee" like a bird to a mountain hideaway (see Pss 102:7; 124:7, where the psalmist is portrayed as a bird). Instead, the psalmist will find a home with God, as do the birds in Ps 84:3. It is not clear how far to extend the quote of the advisers. Some commentators conclude it with v. 1 or v. 2, but the NIV and the NRSV seem justified in carrying the quote through v. 3. In any case, whether the words of the advisers or the psalmist's own assessment, vv. 2-3 describe the desperate situation the psalmist faces. The wicked are a deadly threat (v. 2; see similar imagery in Pss 7:12-13; 37:14; 57:4; 64:2-4; 91:5). The situation appears hopeless (v. 3). The Hebrew word translated "foundations" (שׁת *šāt*) is rare, but it seems to refer to the basic structures of society. Thus v. 3 asks, in effect, "What can be done when things are falling apart?" The question opens the way for the psalmist to elaborate upon the chosen alternative; vv. 4-7 tell what it means to "take refuge" in God.

11:4-7. To trust God means fundamentally to affirm, despite appearances (vv. 2-3), that God is in control. God is properly positioned on earth—in the "holy temple" (v. 4; see Ps 5:7)—and "in heaven," where God's "throne" is located (see Ps

9:4, 7). God sees what is going on, and God is involved. As the NIV suggests, the same Hebrew word (בחן *bāḥan,* "examines,") occurs in v. 4*b* and v. 5*a.* This same activity is associated in Ps 7:9 (NRSV, "test"; NIV, "search") with God's judgment of the wicked and establishment of the righteous. The same parties are involved in Ps 11:5. As in Psalm 7, God's royal policy stands in opposition to the "violence" of the wicked (see 7:16); the wicked will be judged. Verse 6 recalls Gen 19:24, the judgment upon Sodom and Gomorrah, and the image of a "cup" of judgment occurs in Ps 75:9; Isa 51:17; Jer 25:15. The judgment occurs because God "is righteous" (v. 7*a*). God's righteousness is both the assurance of the downfall of the wicked and the hope of the righteous. Whereas the wicked are "lover[s] of

violence" (v. 5), God "loves righteous deeds" (v. 7*b*). This phrase contains the fourth occurrence in this psalm of the Hebrew root meaning "righteous" (צדק *ṣdq,* vv. 3, 5, 7*a*, 7*b*). Righteous persons derive their identity and hope from God. Because the "eyes" of the righteous judge "behold" what is going on among the wicked and the righteous (vv. 4-5), the righteous shall "behold" God's "face" (v. 7). God's vision of humanity leads ultimately to humanity's vision of God. To "behold" God's face may suggest an original setting in the Temple (see Ps 24:3-6, esp. v. 6); however, more generally, to behold God's face means that the "upright" (v. 7; see v. 2) take their stand with God in the assurance that God stands with them. When things seem to be falling apart, this is what the righteous can do (v. 3).

REFLECTIONS

The message of Psalm 11 can be effectively summarized in the words of a familiar hymn: "Though the wrong seems oft so strong, God is the ruler yet." Faced by hostile powers that made the situation seem utterly hopeless (vv. 2-3), the psalmist professes faith in God's rule (v. 4) and lives out of the hope that God's rule will be fully manifested (vv. 5-7). In short, Psalm 11 is eschatological; when it least appears that God rules, the psalmist proclaims God's reign. Faced with a choice, the psalmist chooses not flight but faith. The choice, in effect, is the relinquishing of self-sufficiency in dependence upon God (see Commentary on Psalms 1–3). As Kraus puts it, "This trust is a confession to God's ability to protect and a rejection of all self-help."[83]

Like the psalmist, we live in a world whose "foundations" seem to be "destroyed" (v. 3). Things seem to be falling apart around us. Basic social structures and institutions are threatened—family, school, neighborhood, city, church. We often find ourselves asking essentially the same question raised by the psalmist's advisers (or perhaps by the psalmist) in v. 3: What can we do? The overwhelming temptation is to do what the psalmist was advised to do—give up. We may not literally be tempted to flee, but we are tempted to seek refuge in sheltered enclaves—perhaps in the latest home-security system or in the comfort of insulated congregations that convince us that things are not really as bad as they seem. Seldom does it occur to us even to consider what it might mean to reject self-help and to take refuge in God.

For us to take refuge in God may mean, as for the psalmist, for us to reject flight in order to fight—that is, to stand firm in contesting the forces of hostility and violence, which God hates. The final verse of Psalm 11 suggests that to take refuge in God, in the face of seemingly overwhelming opposition, means to be motivated by hope to do the "righteous deeds" that God loves. A contemporary confession of faith says it well:

> We know that we cannot bring in God's kingdom.
> But hope plunges us into the struggle
>   for victories over evil that are possible now in
>   the world, in the church, and our individual
>   lives.

83. Kraus, *Psalms 1–59,* 203.

Hope gives us courage and energy
to contend against all opposition,
however invincible it may seem,
for the new world and the new humanity
that are surely coming.[84]

Psalm 11 is, indeed, a Psalm of Contest, a psalm that calls for the confrontation of God's enemies. It impels us into the contest for righteousness, upheld by a righteous God whose face we behold precisely in the midst of the struggle.

84. "A Declaration of Faith" (10.5) in *The Proposed Book of Confessions of the Presbyterian Church in the U.S.* (Atlanta: Materials Distribution Service, 1976) 172.

PSALM 12:1-8, I WILL NOW ARISE

NIV

Psalm 12

For the director of music. According to *sheminith.*[a] A psalm of David.

[1]Help, LORD, for the godly are no more;
    the faithful have vanished from among men.
[2]Everyone lies to his neighbor;
    their flattering lips speak with deception.

[3]May the LORD cut off all flattering lips
    and every boastful tongue
[4]that says, "We will triumph with our tongues;
    we own our lips[b]—who is our master?"

[5]"Because of the oppression of the weak
    and the groaning of the needy,
I will now arise," says the LORD.
    "I will protect them from those who
        malign them."
[6]And the words of the LORD are flawless,
    like silver refined in a furnace of clay,
    purified seven times.

[7]O LORD, you will keep us safe
    and protect us from such people forever.
[8]The wicked freely strut about
    when what is vile is honored among men.

aTitle: Probably a musical term   b4 Or   / our lips are our plowshares

NRSV

Psalm 12

To the leader: according to The Sheminith. A Psalm of David.

[1] Help, O LORD, for there is no longer anyone
        who is godly;
    the faithful have disappeared from
        humankind.
[2] They utter lies to each other;
    with flattering lips and a double heart
        they speak.

[3] May the LORD cut off all flattering lips,
    the tongue that makes great boasts,
[4] those who say, "With our tongues we will
        prevail;
    our lips are our own—who is our master?"

[5] "Because the poor are despoiled, because
        the needy groan,
    I will now rise up," says the LORD;
    "I will place them in the safety for which
        they long."
[6] The promises of the LORD are promises that
        are pure,
    silver refined in a furnace on the ground,
    purified seven times.

[7] You, O LORD, will protect us;
    you will guard us from this generation
        forever.
[8] On every side the wicked prowl,
    as vileness is exalted among humankind.

COMMENTARY

Psalm 12 is a prayer that would be particularly appropriate in the circumstances described in Psalm 11—that is, when "the foundations are destroyed" (Ps 11:3). As in Psalms 9–11, the problem is the wicked (v. 8; see 11:2, 6; 9:5, 16-17; 10:2-4, 13, 15). The Lord's response to the wicked in 12:5 recalls especially Pss 9:18-19 and 10:12-13, for God promises to "rise up" on behalf of the "poor" and "needy," as requested in Psalms 9–10.

Psalm 12 may be the prayer of an individual or that of the community.[85] Because of the word from the Lord in v. 5, many commentators suggest that this psalm was originally spoken by a cultic prophet. The lament over the prevalence of wickedness may also suggest a prophetic character (see Isa 57:1-13; 59:1-21; Jer 5:1-3; Hos 4:1-3; Mic 7:1-7).

Both the NIV and the NRSV divide the psalm into four two-verse sections. The repetition of "lips" (vv. 2-4) and the focus on speech suggest that vv. 1-4 belong together as a larger unit of plea and complaint. Verses 5-8 then offer God's response and express confidence in divine protection by contrasting the reliability of God's speech with the empty, deceitful speech of the wicked. Just as with Psalm 11, so also it is possible to detect a chiastic structuring (see the Introduction) of Psalm 12. This alternative proposal serves especially well to emphasize the contrast:

A v. 1 plea amid human corruption
  B v. 2 empty, deceptive speech of the wicked
    C vv. 3-4 plea for the Lord to cut off
      boasters
    C′ v. 5 the Lord's response
  B′ v. 6 the reliable speech of the Lord
A′ vv. 7-8 the Lord's protection amid human corruption[86]

12:1-4. The psalm begins with perhaps the most basic human prayer: "Help!" (see "deliver" in Pss 3:7; 6:4 and "save" in 7:1). The "godly" are identified in Ps 4:3 (see NIV) as persons who belong to God, but they, not the wicked, have come to an end (see Ps 7:9). The faithful individual or community seems to be alone in the world (see 1 Kgs 19:10), surrounded by those whose speech is characterized by deception and hypocrisy (v. 2; see similar descriptions of speech in Pss 5:9; 41:6; 144:8, 11; Isa 59:4; Ezek 13:8). Verses 3-4 suggest that the speech of the wicked is indicative of their character. They boast in their own strength. Verse 4b is literally "our lips are with us," perhaps a play on what would be the proper profession, "God is with us." But the wicked do not recognize God's sovereignty. In their minds, they are accountable to no one but themselves (see Pss 10:4, 6; 73:8-9). Such autonomy is the essence of wickedness (see Psalms 1–2; Introduction).

12:5-8. The wicked apparently intend their question in v. 4b to be rhetorical. They expect no response, least of all from God. This makes the divine speech in v. 5 all the more effective. The true word exposes the wicked and their illusions of grandeur. Because God is sovereign, God has not only seen the behavior of the wicked (see Ps 11:4) and heard their boasting, but also has seen the despoiling of "the poor" (v. 5a; the Hebrew word translated "despoiled" [שֹׁד šōd] occurs elsewhere almost exclusively in prophetic books; see, e.g., "violence" in Jer 6:7; 20:8; Ezek 45:9; Hos 12:1; Amos 3:10; Hab 1:3; "desolation" in Isa 59:7; "devastation" in Isa 60:18) and heard their groaning (see Pss 79:11; 102:20). Just as the speech of the wicked reveals their character, so also God's speech reveals the divine character. God acts (see "rise up" in 3:7; 9:19; 10:12) to help the poor and needy (see Exod 22:21-24; 1 Sam 2:8-9; Pss 3:8; 10:17-18). The NRSV's "safety" is from the same Hebrew root as the opening plea for help. The prayer will be answered; God helps those who cannot help themselves (cf. Psalm 3). This good news lies at the heart of Psalm 12. The chiastic structure emphasizes its centrality, and even commentators with differing structural proposals recognize v. 5 as the "focal point."[87] The final phrase in v. 5 is difficult, but the basic sense of the verse is clear.

85. See Gerstenberger, *Psalms,* 80. He categorizes Psalm 12 as both a "Complaint of the Individual" and a "Congregational Lament."
86. See Robert G. Bratcher and William D. Reyburn, *A Translator's Handbook on the Book of Psalms* (New York. United Bible Societies, 1991) 115.
87. Kraus, *Psalms 1–59,* 209.

The "words" or "promises" in v. 5 can be relied on (v. 6), in contrast to the deceptive words of the wicked (v. 2). This reliability grounds the expression of confidence in v. 7. Both the NRSV and the NIV follow the LXX in rendering the objects of both verbs as "us" rather than "them" and "him," as in the Hebrew. The initial "You" is emphatic. God will assure the future of God's people. This assurance derives ultimately from God's word in v. 5. Verse 8 recalls v. 1, and the effect is a reminder that the promises of God are always surrounded by the apparent triumph of the wicked. In short, Psalm 12, like the preceding psalms, is eschatological (see Commentary on Psalms 2; 5; 7; 9–11; Introduction). Trust in God's word and character is indeed a blessed assurance in the present, but it also leaves the faithful awaiting the fuller experience of this foretaste of glory divine (see Ps 31:23-24).

REFLECTIONS

While the assessment in vv. 1, 8 of the pervasiveness of the wicked among humankind may be hyperbolic, it is not too much of an exaggeration to say that the church exists now, as it always has, as a beleaguered minority. In a thoroughly secularized society, it is almost impossible not to buy in to the credo of the wicked in v. 4—that is, we are masters of our own destiny, and we are accountable to no one but ourselves. Nevertheless, as the people of God, we profess that we live not by these selfish, sinful words but by the Word of God. We profess that our security lies in God's activity, not our own. We profess that God is our master, which positions us as servants whose lives are not our own. This radical departure from the secular norm means nothing less than that, in effect, we live as "resident aliens," as a distinctive colony in a prevailing culture dedicated to self-sufficiency and self-fulfillment.[88] In Jesus' words, we have been sent "into the world," but we "do not belong to the world" (John 17:16, 18). In the final analysis, Psalm 12 can be heard as a challenge to the church to claim its distinctiveness. Charles B. Cousar suggests, "The issue that confronts the church, then, is one of identity, of understanding and articulating who it is, of claiming its distinctiveness."[89] It is revealing that in John 17, Jesus prayed for precisely the same thing the psalmist prays for and celebrates in this psalm: God's protection (vv. 1, 7; cf. John 17:11, 15).

88. See Stanley Hauerwas and William H. Willimon, *Resident Aliens: Life in the Christian Colony* (Nashville: Abingdon, 1989) 92.
89. See Charles B. Cousar, *A Theology of the Cross: The Death of Jesus in the Pauline Letters* (Philadelphia: Fortress, 1990) 176.

PSALM 13:1-6, BUT I TRUST IN YOUR STEADFAST LOVE

NIV	NRSV
Psalm 13	Psalm 13
For the director of music. A psalm of David.	To the leader. A Psalm of David.
[1] How long, O LORD? Will you forget me forever? How long will you hide your face from me? [2] How long must I wrestle with my thoughts and every day have sorrow in my heart? How long will my enemy triumph over me?	[1] How long, O LORD? Will you forget me forever? How long will you hide your face from me? [2] How long must I bear pain[a] in my soul,
	[a] Syr: Heb *hold counsels*

NIV

³Look on me and answer, O LORD my God.
　　Give light to my eyes, or I will sleep in
　　　death;
⁴my enemy will say, "I have overcome him,"
　　and my foes will rejoice when I fall.

⁵But I trust in your unfailing love;
　　my heart rejoices in your salvation.
⁶I will sing to the LORD,
　　for he has been good to me.

NRSV

and have sorrow in my heart all day long?
　　How long shall my enemy be exalted over
　　　me?

³ Consider and answer me, O LORD my God!
　　Give light to my eyes, or I will sleep the
　　　sleep of death,
⁴ and my enemy will say, "I have prevailed";
　　my foes will rejoice because I am shaken.

⁵ But I trusted in your steadfast love;
　　my heart shall rejoice in your salvation.
⁶ I will sing to the LORD,
　　because he has dealt bountifully with me.

COMMENTARY

Because it is the shortest and simplest of the prayers for help, Psalm 13 is often cited by commentators as the textbook example of an individual lament or complaint. The complaint appears in vv. 1-2, petition in vv. 3-4, and expression of trust and praise in vv. 5-6.

13:1-2. Both the impatience and the desperation of the psalmist are emphasized by the fourfold occurrence of "How long . . . ?" in vv. 1-2. Robert Alter points out that each occurrence introduces a question that "reflects an ascent on a scale of intensity, the note of desperate urgency pitched slightly higher with each repetition."[90] It seems at first that God may simply have forgotten (see Pss 9:12, 10:12). But no, it is worse than that. God has intentionally turned away, an action often indicative of God's wrath (see Deut 31:17; 32:20; Pss 22:24; 27:8-9; 30:7; 69:17; 88:14; 102:2; 143:7; Isa 8:17; 54:8; Jer 33:5; Mic 3:4). God's apparent apathy or anger is a source of anxiety for the psalmist. The NIV translation of v. 2*a* is preferable; it suggests the psalmist's inner agitation and turmoil. The NRSV note indicates that the translators have followed the Syriac, although some scholars claim that the Hebrew word in question (עצה *'ēṣâ*) can mean "pain" as well as "counsels" or "thoughts." The word "sorrow" (יגון *yāgôn*) in v. 2*b* indicates the urgency

of the situation; it is used elsewhere in the context of the death of individuals (Gen 42:38; 44:31) or of the nation (Jer 8:18). Thus v. 2 implies what vv. 3-4 will make explicit: The crisis at hand is a matter of life and death. Verse 2 is a three-part poetic line; it serves to isolate and emphasize the climactic element, v. 2*c*. In the psalms, it is supposed to be God who is "exalted" (see 18:46; 21:13; 46:11; 57:5, 11; 108:5). In short, it seems to the psalmist that God has been displaced. The place to which one looks for help is occupied by the enemy. This is the worst possible news.

It has traditionally been suggested on the basis of vv. 1-2 that the psalmist was seriously ill and facing imminent death. A related notion is that the enemy in v. 2*c* should be understood as death. These proposals make some sense, but the precise nature of the problem and the identity of the enemy are by no means certain. It is more likely that the language and imagery are intended to be stereotypical and open-ended (see Introduction). What is more clear is that vv. 1-2 portray the interrelation of the three major "characters" in Psalms: the psalmist, the enemy, and God. The psalms consistently hold together the three corresponding realms of experience that we contemporary people are inclined to separate—the psychological, the sociological, and the theological. For the psalmist, every experience of the self or the other is also an experience of God. While

90. Robert Alter, *The Art of Biblical Poetry* (New York: Basic Books, 1985) 65.

this view of reality may be problematic—leading, for instance, to the conclusion that God causes sickness and suffering—it does at least affirm God's intimate involvement in the world. The value of the psalmist's view of reality is that it can remind us of the marvelous complexity and ambiguity of human life, amid which God is somehow present. Thus, even while the psalmist complains of God's absence (v. 1), the psalmist addresses the complaint and the subsequent petition precisely to "my God" (v. 3; see Ps 22:1).

13:3-4. In these verses a threefold petition is supported by three reasons why God should act. The NIV's "Look" is more accurate than the NRSV's "Consider"; the request calls for God to reverse the action of hiding God's face (v. 1; see Ps 10:14: NRSV, "note"; NIV, "consider"). The request that God "answer" is also particularly appropriate, since the complaint in vv. 1-2 was framed as a series of questions (on the plea "answer," see Ps 4:1). The final petition may also recall v. 1, since God's face is often described as a source of light (see Num 6:25; Pss 4:6; 31:16; 67:1; 80:3, 7, 19; 119:135). In any case, the request is for strength (see 1 Sam 14:27, 29; Pss 6:6; 38:10; Lam 5:17). Without renewed strength, the psalmist will die (see Dan 12:2). As in v. 2, the "enemy" in v. 4a could be death, but the plural "foes" in v. 4b suggest human enemies who will rejoice over the psalmist's defeat or demise (see "shake"/"shaken" in Pss 10:6; 15:5; 16:8; 21:7; 30:6; 62:2, 6; 112:6 NIV).

13:5-6. The movement from complaint to petition seems logical, but the transition from vv. 1-4 to vv. 5-6 is more of a surprise. To be sure, the prayers for help regularly become expressions of trust and praise, but the transition here seems unusually abrupt. The NIV's translation of the verb (בטח *bāṭaḥ*) in v. 5a in the present tense is preferable. The psalmist's trust is ongoing (see "trust" in Pss 4:5; 9:10; see also the Introduction); trust is properly directed to the fundamental attribute of God's character: "steadfast love" (see Pss 5:7; 21:7; Introduction). Trust is accompanied by rejoicing in God's "salvation" (see Commentary on Ps 3:2, 7-8). The transition is brought into even sharper focus by the repetition of several words from vv. 1-4. The "sorrow in my heart" (v. 2) has been replaced by a "heart" that "shall rejoice" (v. 5). Only a verse earlier, the enemies were the ones who would "rejoice" (v. 4). The last words of the psalm, "with me" (עלי *ʿālāy*), are a repetition of the last words of v. 2, "over me." Whereas the enemy had been "exalted over me," now God has "dealt bounty over me." The psalmist seems now to be unshakable.

Scholars disagree concerning both the nature and the explanation of the remarkable transition between vv. 1-4 and vv. 5-6 (see Introduction). Some scholars suggest that vv. 5-6 reflect a materially changed situation; that is, the psalmist has been cured, the enemies have been defeated, or some other problem has been solved. In this case, vv. 5-6 must have been written after vv. 1-4 and added to the complaint and petition. A more frequent conclusion is that the change reflected in vv. 5-6 involves not the psalmist's situation or condition but the psalmist. In this view, vv. 5-6 constitute an affirmation of faith that anticipates future deliverance, perhaps made in response to a promise of salvation delivered by a priest or some other religious functionary in the context of a temple or synagogue ritual or house prayer service.

To be sure, it is possible that the psalmist either looks back in gratitude or forward in trust, but the text remains ambiguous. This very ambiguity, however, is a theological gain, for it invites the interpreter to view complaint and praise as simultaneous rather than separate moments. Thus the ambiguity and complexity of the psalm accurately represent the ambiguity and complexity of the life of faith. As people of faith, we will always find it necessary to pray, "How long, O LORD?" even as we simultaneously profess that the Lord "has been good to me."

REFLECTIONS

1. The juxtaposition of complaint and praise in Psalm 13 bears reflection. According to Mays:

Luther in his exposition of the Psalm calls the mood of the prayer the "state in which hope despairs, and yet despair hopes at the same time. . . ."

> There is a coherence which holds the apparently separate moments together. . . . This is the deep radical knowledge of faith which cannot separate God from any experience of life and perseveres in construing all, even life's worst, in terms of relation to God. . . .
>
> . . . The Psalm is not given to us to use on the rare occasions when some trouble seems to make it appropriate. It is forever appropriate as long as life shall last. We do not begin at one end and come out at the other. The agony and the ecstasy belong together as the secret of our identity.[91]

In other words, by holding together complaint and praise, we are taught about both God and ourselves. God is involved in all of life—even life at its worst. Such a conviction opens the way to see God's involvement even in such an apparently God-forsaken event as the crucifixion (see Commentary on Psalm 22).

As for us, we are simultaneously confronted with our own perpetual neediness and comforted by the proclamation of God's unfailing love. The agony and the ecstasy belong together. In Christian terms, we are simultaneously people of the cross and people of the resurrection. Thus Psalm 13 anticipates the message of the Gospels and the letters of Paul. In effect, Psalm 13 reminds us both that there is no following Jesus without bearing a cross (Mark 8:34) and that those who lose their life for Jesus' "sake, and for the sake of the gospel, will save it" (Mark 8:35 NRSV). In his discussion of Phil 3:2-11 and the way Paul's theology of the cross and resurrection affects the Christian life, Charles B. Cousar writes: "Instead of discovering that sufferings may be endured for a time because the sufferers will ultimately be vindicated, we find in the text that the resurrection-power comes to expression in the very midst of the tribulations."[92] Here, too, as in Psalm 13, "the agony and the ecstasy belong together as the secret of our identity."

2. Because it is such a succinct example, Psalm 13 also serves to teach us about prayer. It involves not only the nice, positive expressions of vv. 5-6, but also the bold, brutally honest complaints and accusations of vv. 1-2 and the urgent petitions of vv. 3-4. This kind of prayer challenges us to locate and articulate both our pain and the suffering of others in a way that we often hesitate to do out of fear of offending God, shocking others, or embarrassing ourselves. Psalm 13 gives voice to things we often do not talk about—forsakeness, abandonment, anxiety and inner turmoil, defeat, the fear of death. As Walter Brueggemann suggests of these kinds of prayers, "How wondrous that these Psalms make it clear that precisely such dimensions of our life are the stuff of prayer."[93]

91. J. L. Mays, "Psalm 13," *Int.* 37 (1983) 281-82.
92. Cousar, *A Theology of the Cross*, 161.
93. Walter Brueggemann, *Praying the Psalms* (Winona, Minn.: St. Mary's Press, 1988) 31.

PSALM 14:1-7, NO ONE DOES GOOD

NIV	NRSV
Psalm 14	Psalm 14
For the director of music. Of David.	To the leader. Of David.
[1]The fool[a] says in his heart, "There is no God."	[1] Fools say in their hearts, "There is no God." They are corrupt, they do abominable deeds; there is no one who does good.
a1 The Hebrew words rendered *fool* in Psalms denote one who is morally deficient.	

NIV

They are corrupt, their deeds are vile;
    there is no one who does good.

²The LORD looks down from heaven
    on the sons of men
to see if there are any who understand,
    any who seek God.
³All have turned aside,
    they have together become corrupt;
there is no one who does good,
    not even one.

⁴Will evildoers never learn—
    those who devour my people as men eat bread
    and who do not call on the LORD?
⁵There they are, overwhelmed with dread,
    for God is present in the company of the
    righteous.
⁶You evildoers frustrate the plans of the poor,
    but the LORD is their refuge.

⁷Oh, that salvation for Israel would come out
    of Zion!
When the LORD restores the fortunes of his
    people,
    let Jacob rejoice and Israel be glad!

NRSV

² The LORD looks down from heaven on
    humankind
    to see if there are any who are wise,
    who seek after God.

³ They have all gone astray, they are all alike
    perverse;
    there is no one who does good,
    no, not one.

⁴ Have they no knowledge, all the evildoers
    who eat up my people as they eat bread,
    and do not call upon the LORD?

⁵ There they shall be in great terror,
    for God is with the company of the righteous.
⁶ You would confound the plans of the poor,
    but the LORD is their refuge.

⁷ O that deliverance for Israel would come
    from Zion!
When the LORD restores the fortunes of
    his people,
    Jacob will rejoice; Israel will be glad.

COMMENTARY

Like Psalm 12, Psalm 14 has a prophetic character. The psalmist's observations in vv. 1-3 serve as an indictment that apparently targets all humanity (see Ps 12:1, 8). Verses 1-3 are perhaps hyperbolic, for v. 4 narrows the indictment to "all the evildoers" (see below on the tension between vv. 1-3 and vv. 4-6). These persons victimize God's people (v. 4). Verses 5-6 function as an announcement of judgment upon the evildoers and as an oracle of salvation for the righteous. Verse 7 expresses the conviction that God will help the victimized people, and it celebrates the anticipated deliverance. Psalm 14 appears in a slightly different version as Psalm 53 (see Commentary on Psalm 53).

Because of its prophetic character, and because it is neither prayer nor praise, Psalm 14 is often categorized as a prophetic exhortation. Pointing to the mention of "fools" in v. 1 as well as the words "wise" (v. 2) and "knowledge" (v. 4), some scholars also detect an affinity with wisdom literature. In any case, Psalm 14 does have an instructional intent.

14:1. The NIV note suggests that the term "fool" (נבל *nābāl*) is more a moral assessment than an intellectual one. As the second half of v. 1 suggests, foolishness is not a lack of knowledge in general but the failure to acknowledge God in trustful obedience (see v. 4; see also Deut 32:6; 2 Sam 13:13; Ps 74:18, 22; Jer 17:11). The failure to acknowledge God will inevitably mean misplaced priorities and misguided behavior. What the fools say to themselves in v. 1a should not be understood as a statement of philosophical atheism. Rather, the issue is a much more subtle and widespread practical atheism—that is, acting as if there is no God to whom one is accountable in any way. Thus foolishness turns out to be synonymous with wickedness—that is, autonomy, being a "law unto oneself" (see Commentary on

Psalm 1). Indeed, the wicked in Ps 10:4 say precisely what the fools say in Ps 14:1 (see also Pss 10:5-6, 13; 73:11).

14:2. This verse asserts precisely what the wicked and the foolish ignore—namely, God's sovereignty. God is positioned *over* humankind. In Psalm 102:18-22, God's looking down from heaven occurs in the same context with peoples and kingdoms gathering to serve the Lord. The Hebrew word translated "serve" means essentially "to be subject," "to live under the sovereignty of another." In Ps 14:2, God is looking for those who are "wise," which Psalm 2 earlier defined precisely in terms of serving when it exhorted the kings of the earth to "be wise" (2:10) and to "Serve the LORD" (2:11). To seek God also suggests recognizing God's rule. Seeking God means trusting God (9:10), worshiping God (22:6-7), taking refuge in God (34:8-10; see 14:6).

14:3. This verse is clearly similar to v. 1. The verbs that describe human behavior in vv. 1 and 3 recall two key events in the Pentateuch: the flood story (see "corrupt"/"corrupted" in v. 1 and Gen 6:12) and Israel's worship of the golden calf (see Exod 32:7, where the verb here translated "corrupt" in v. 1 appears as "acted perversely" in the NRSV; and Exod 32:8, where "gone astray" in v. 3 appears as "turn aside"). Both of these episodes prove to be paradigmatic. The history of both Israel and humankind reveals that the repeated assessment in vv. 1 and 3 is not much of an exaggeration: "there is no one who does good." The added "no, not one" in v. 3 emphasizes the point. This phrase represents the fourth occurrence of a Hebrew negative particle (אֵין 'ên), and the effect is to reinforce the negative assessment of humankind. This message of universal human perversity is used by the apostle Paul in Rom 3:10-18, where he quotes portions of Ps 14:1, 3 as well as several additional verses of a longer version of Psalm 14 that is found in the Greek Old Testament (see below).

14:4-6. These verses seem to contradict vv. 1-3, since vv. 4-6 distinguish between "the evildoers" and those identified as "my people" (v. 4), "the righteous" (v. 5), and "the poor" (v. 6). These verses may reflect a divided society in which a strong upper class oppressed the majority of the people. Such a situation is suggested, for instance, in Mic 3:1-4, which also uses the image of some people's being fed upon by others (Ps 14:4, Mic 3:3). As in Pss 9:17-18; 10:17-18; and 12:5-7, God will act on behalf of the poor. The oppressors will be terrified (see Exod 15:16), for God is on the side of the righteous; and the poor will find their refuge in God (see Pss 2:12; 5:11; 7:1; 11:1; Introduction). The word "there" (שָׁם šām) in v. 5 is difficult, but it may suggest that the evildoers will be terrified somehow precisely in the midst of their attempts to oppress others.

14:7. Many scholars consider v. 7 to be a post-exilic addition to the psalm in order to make it especially applicable to a situation in which Israel was dominated by other nations. This is certainly possible and may find support in the appearance of the phrase "restore the fortunes," which often specifically indicates return from exile and always suggests restoration from a major setback, such as the exile and its aftermath (see Deut 30:3; Jer 29:14; 30:3, 18; 31:23; 32:44; 33:7, 11; Pss 85:2; 126:1). Verse 7a is actually stated in the form of a question, "Who will give from Zion help for Israel?" The answer is God. Despite what the foolish or the wicked may say (Pss 3:2; 10:4; 14:1), God is the help of God's people, individual persons or the body as a whole (Pss 3:8; 10:14; 14:5-7).

REFLECTIONS

Reflection on Psalm 14 must begin with the apparent contradiction between vv. 1-3 and vv. 4-6. It is possible in the light of vv. 4-6 to conclude that the seemingly universal indictment of humanity in vv. 1-3 is hyperbole; however, as Mays suggests, "theologically we would do well to let the tensions stand unresolved."[94] When we allow vv. 1-3 to speak apart from vv. 4-6, they assert that all humans are sinful, a lesson that should not be ignored (see Luke 18:9-14). Indeed, this is precisely the message that Paul derived from Ps 14:1, 3 and used to

---

94. James L. Mays, *Psalms,* Interpretation (Louisville: John Knox, 1994) 83.

---

argue that all people "are under the power of sin" (Rom 3:9 NRSV). As Kraus puts it, we "must come to realize how shocking the assertions of Psalm 14 actually are."[95] He is right. What is truly shocking is that what Psalm 14 calls foolishness, and what other psalms call wickedness, is essentially what our culture teaches people to be—autonomous, self-directed, self-sufficient. Of course, such cultural wisdom makes some sense psychologically, but we often unconsciously translate the message into theological conclusions: We don't need other people, and we don't need God! While philosophical atheism is relatively rare, this kind of practical atheism is rampant. For us, in effect, "there is no God." Lest we think that our advanced, sophisticated era has left corruption and perversity behind, all we need do is remind ourselves of the persistent, daily realities of our world—poverty, hunger, homelessness, political corruption, violence in our homes and cities as well as throughout the world. Although our rugged individualism (that is, our autonomy) may lead us to deny it, not one of us is uninvolved in or unaffected by these realities—"no, not one."

While vv. 1-3 remind us of the pervasive sinfulness of humanity, vv. 4-6 proclaim that sin does not have the final word. The good news is that God is able to gather sinners into "the company of the righteous"—Israel, the church. Paul knew this too. After arguing on the basis of Ps 14:1, 3 that all "are under the power of sin" (Rom 3:9 NRSV), he goes on to proclaim the good news that all people "are now justified by his grace as a gift, through the redemption that is in Christ Jesus" (Rom 3:23-24). As Paul makes clear, this justification or righteousness is not a human achievement but a gift. We remain sinners and victims of sin; however, we know that our inability to do good is not the final word. This is true "knowledge" (v. 4), the wisdom for which God is looking (v. 2), for it amounts to dependence upon God rather than upon self. In short, the Lord is our refuge (v. 6).

Of course, this kind of wisdom—dependence upon God rather than self—may appear foolish to the world. But Paul also proclaims, "God chose what is foolish in the world to shame the wise" (1 Cor 1:27 NRSV). According to Paul, the wisdom for which God is looking ultimately takes the shape of a cross (1 Cor 1:24-25). Indeed, the cross reveals clearly the two realities with which Psalm 14 confronts us: the reality of human sin (vv. 1-3) and the reality of God's grace (vv. 5-6). To live among "the company of the righteous" is to trust that the reality of God's grace is the ultimate reality, the final word about our sinful human existence. Thus we are to live not by what we see so pervasively around us (vv. 1, 3) but by what we believe and what we hope for (see v. 7).

95. H.-J. Kraus, *Psalms 1–59: A Commentary,* trans. H. C. Oswald (Minneapolis: Augsburg, 1988) 223-24.

PSALM 15:1-5, THEY SHALL NOT BE MOVED

NIV	NRSV
Psalm 15	Psalm 15
A psalm of David.	A Psalm of David.

¹Lord, who may dwell in your sanctuary?
    Who may live on your holy hill?
	¹ O Lord, who may abide in your tent?
	    Who may dwell on your holy hill?

²He whose walk is blameless
    and who does what is righteous,
who speaks the truth from his heart
	² Those who walk blamelessly, and do what
	    is right,

NIV

3   and has no slander on his tongue,
who does his neighbor no wrong
and casts no slur on his fellowman,
4who despises a vile man
but honors those who fear the LORD,
who keeps his oath
even when it hurts,
5who lends his money without usury
and does not accept a bribe against the
innocent.

He who does these things
will never be shaken.

NRSV

and speak the truth from their heart;
3 who do not slander with their tongue,
and do no evil to their friends,
nor take up a reproach against their
neighbors;
4 in whose eyes the wicked are despised,
but who honor those who fear the LORD;
who stand by their oath even to their hurt;
5 who do not lend money at interest,
and do not take a bribe against the
innocent.

Those who do these things shall never be
moved.

COMMENTARY

Along with Psalm 24, Psalm 15 is ordinarily classified as an entrance liturgy (see also Isa 33:13-16; Mic 6:6-8), a question-and-answer ritual enacted as persons prepared to enter the temple gates. There is evidence from Israel and other ancient Near Eastern sources that there were requirements for entering a holy place (see Deut 23:1-8; 2 Chr 23:19); however, Psalm 15 concludes not with a judgment about admission but with an observation that has the character of a promise. While perhaps modeled on an entrance liturgy, Psalm 15 in its present form has more the tone of liturgical instruction. In its present literary context, it serves to portray the shape of the lives of those who have been mentioned frequently in preceding psalms—those who take refuge in God (Pss 2:12; 5:11; 7:1; 11:1; 14:6), the poor/oppressed/afflicted/meek (Pss 9:9, 12, 18; 10:2, 9, 12, 17-18; 12:5; 14:6), the righteous or "company of the righteous" (Pss 1:5-6; 5:12; 7:9; 11:3, 5; 14:5). In fact, there is a revealing progression from Psalm 13 to Psalm 15. The movement is from the threat of being "shaken" (13:6) to the affirmation that "God is with the company of the righteous" (14:5) to the portrayal of the righteous dwelling with God, the result being that they "shall never be moved" (15:5c; "moved" here is the same Hebrew word [מוט *môṭ*] as "shaken" in 13:4 NRSV).

The questions in v. 1 are followed by a series of answers in vv. 2-5ab, the origin and organization of which are variously understood. Many scholars suggest that the answers have been shaped by the influence of the Ten Commandments, but it is not clear that there are actually ten items. The organization of the items is also debated. Bratcher and Reyburn detect twelve items, arranged in an alternating pattern of three positive statements (vv. 2, 4abc) and three negative statements (vv. 3, 4d-5b; the last line of v. 4 actually contains a positive and a negative that are obscured by the NRSV and the NIV—lit., "he swears to his hurt and he will *not* change"). In their view, "the contrast of plusses and minuses . . . serves the purpose of focusing attention upon the exemplary conduct of those who would enter the Temple for worship."[96] A different (or perhaps complementary) proposal construes v. 2 as an answer to v. 1 in general terms, while vv. 3-5ab offer specific illustrations in the realms of dealing with neighbors (v. 3), with the religious community (v. 4ab), and with people and practices in society at large (vv. 4c-5b).[97] Support for this view may be derived from the fact that each item in v. 2 is introduced by an active participle, whereas the other items use finite verb forms

96. Robert G. Bratcher and William D. Reyburn, *A Translator's Handbook on the Book of Psalms* (New York: United Bible Societies, 1991) 133.
97. Mays, *Psalms*, 84.

(with the exception of v. 4a, where the NRSV's "the wicked" is the subject and is accompanied by a passive participle). Complicating this proposal is the observation that each item in v. 2 is paralleled in v. 3—that is, vv. 2a and 3a have to do with walking (the word "slander" [רגל rāgal] in v. 3a is more literally "tread" or "foot it"); vv. 2b and 3b have to do with acting (see "do" in both cases, although the Hebrew differs [פעל pāʿal in v. 2b and עשה ʿāśâ in v. 3b]); and vv. 2c and 3c have to do with speech. It is possible that several structural patterns are operating simultaneously.

15:1. The word "tent" (see Exod 33:7-11; Num 12:5, 10; Pss 27:5-6; 61:5) and the phrase "holy hill" (Pss 2:6; 3:4; 43:3) may certainly refer to the Temple on Mount Zion, God's chosen dwelling place on earth (see Pss 24:3; 46:4-5; 48:1-3; 132:13-14; 1 Kgs 8:1-11). The Temple symbolized God's presence. Thus, in effect, v. 1 inquires about the identity or life-position of those who belong to God (see Ps 1:1, 5). The first verb in v. 1 (גור gûr) means literally "sojourn, be a resident alien." It suggests that no one can *deserve* to reside in God's presence. Rather, persons dwell with God only because of God's gracious permission (see Ps 5:7).

15:2-5b. God's gracious acceptance of persons into the divine presence has an important implication for understanding the answers in vv. 2-5ab. These answers should not be understood as requirements; rather, they portray the character of persons whose lives have been shaped in conformity with God's character. Mays suggests of vv. 2-5ab, "It is a picture, not prescription."[98] Not surprisingly, the words that describe the deeds and speech of those who belong to God are used elsewhere to describe God's own character, work, or word. For instance, God is "blameless" or "perfect" in God's way (Ps 18:30), work (Deut 32:4), and instruction (Ps 19:7). Those who belong to God mirror God's character. This is not to say that they are absolutely sinless (see Commentary on Ps 14:1-3) but that their lives are completely oriented to and dependent upon God (the Hebrew root of "blameless[ly]" [תמים tāmîm] means essentially "to be complete"; see Deut 18:13 NRSV, where this word is translated as

"completely loyal"). Persons identified elsewhere as blameless include Noah (Gen 6:9), Abraham (Gen 17:1), David (1 Kgs 9:4; NRSV, "integrity"), Job (Job 1:1, 8; 2:3), and the psalmist (Pss 18:23; 26:1, 11; NRSV, "integrity"; see also Ps 119:1). Psalm 101 is particularly reminiscent of Psalm 15, for here the psalmist, probably the king, studies "the way that is blameless" (101:2), walks "with blameless heart" (101:2), and admits into his presence those "whose walk is blameless" (101:6; cf. Ps 101:4-5 with 15:3 and 101:7 with 15:2).

Those who belong to God also mirror God's character as they "do what is right," for God is righteous (see Pss 5:8; 7:9, 11; 9:4, 8; see esp. 11:7). God is also characterized by "faithfulness" (see Exod 34:6), and those who speak faithfulness or truth mirror God's character and embody God's will (see Jer 9:5; Zech 8:16; cf. Ps 5:6; Amos 5:10). As God's character is manifested in concrete actions, the character of those who belong to God will be manifested as well. Their tongues will not be instruments of deceit or oppression (v. 3; see Pss 5:9; 12:4). They will bring no harm upon their neighbor by speech or action (v. 3; see Exod 20:16-17; Lev 19:18; Pss 28:3; 101:5). They will oppose those who oppose God, and honor those who honor God (v. 4ab; see Ps 1:1). They will keep their word even when they suffer for it (see Ps 24:4; Matt 5:33-37). Just as God acts on behalf of the poor and oppressed (see Pss 9:18; 10:17-18; 12:5), so also the business practices of those who belong to God will benefit the poor (v. 5a; see Exod 22:25; Lev 25:36-37, where the refusal to exact interest is to protect the poor; see also Deut 23:20; Ezek 18:8, 13, 17). As God avoids bribery to enact justice (Deut 10:17-18; Ps 9:4), those who belong to God will do the same (v. 5b; see Exod 23:7-8; Deut 16:19-20; 1 Kgs 8:3; cf. Ps 10:8).

15:5c. This verse concludes the psalm with a statement that is both an affirmation and a promise. Just as God has established the earth (Pss 93:1; 96:10; 104:5) and Zion (Pss 46:5; 125:1) so that they cannot be "moved" or "shaken" by chaotic forces, so also God secures the lives of those who belong to God. In view of the rest of the book of Psalms, this clearly does not mean that the righteous will live unopposed (see Pss 3:1-2; 5:7-8; 7:6; 9:13-14; 10:1-2; 12:1-4; 13:1-4; 14:4; 34:19). Rather, in even the worst of circum-

98. Ibid., 84.

stances, the righteous will have in God's presence and power a resource to sustain their lives. That promise is equivalent to the promise of happiness to those who take refuge in God (Ps 2:12) and of prosperity for the righteous in all they do (Ps 1:3). That is to say, those who trust God will always have a solid foundation for facing the world; they will not be moved (see Pss 10:6; 13:4; 16:8; 17:5; 21:7; 30:6; 62:2, 6; 112:6).

REFLECTIONS

The refrain of a well-known African American spiritual consists of references to both Ps 1:3 and Ps 15:5c: "Like a tree that's planted by the water, we shall not be moved."[99] The juxtaposition reveals a profound understanding of both psalms. While Psalm 15 may be modeled on an entrance liturgy, its present form and context suggest that its primary purpose is to portray what it means to be constantly open to God's instruction (Ps 1:2), to take refuge in God (Pss 2:12, 5:11, 7:1, 11:1, 14:6, 16:1, 17:7), to live under God's rule (Pss 2:11, 5:2, 7:7-8; 8:1, 9; 9:7-8, 10:16, 11:4, 14:2).

The answers to the questions in v. 1, therefore, are not requirements or prescriptions. Rather, like the content of the Sermon on the Mount in Matthew 5–7, vv. 2-5b portray what life is like when it is lived under God's reign instead of in reliance upon oneself (see Commentary on Psalm 24). While the answers in vv. 2-5b and the teachings in the Sermon on the Mount are not requirements, both do suggest that the lives of those who are loyal and faithful to God will look different from the lives of the wicked and foolish, who autonomously deny God's claim (see Pss 10:3-4; 14:1; see also Matt 7:21-23). The character and behavior of the righteous will inevitably mirror God's character and God's values. Recipients of grace (see Commentary on v. 1) will inevitably be gracious.

Consideration of Psalm 15 in terms of entry into the Temple, or simply in terms of preparation for or participation in worship, raises the question, What does God desire from the worshiper? A traditional answer was that God desires sacrificial offerings; however, the prophets proclaimed that sacrifice was not sufficient. God desires justice, righteousness, knowledge, goodness, and love (see Isa 1:12-17; Hos 6:6; Amos 5:21-24; Mic 6:6-8). Psalm 15 is consistent with these prophetic texts. In short, God desires the loyalty of the whole self—lifestyle (see "walk" in v. 2), action (see "do" in v. 2), and speech (see "speak" in v. 2). The proper gift to bring into God's presence is the gift of one's life (see Pss 25:1; 50:12-15, 23; 51:15-17; 86:4; 143:8). Psalm 15 calls for "a living sacrifice, holy and acceptable to God, which is your spiritual worship" (Rom 12:1 NRSV). As Paul recognized, such a gift involves being transformed rather than "conformed to this world" (Rom 12:2 NRSV). In other words, those who live under God's rule rather than the rule of self will be different (see Reflections on Psalm 12). Such faithfulness will invite opposition, as the life of Jesus reveals, but God's promise to the faithful is a peace greater than the world can give (see John 14:27). Indeed, persons who entrust themselves to God "shall never be moved" (v. 5c).

99. See, e.g., *The United Methodist Hymnal* (Nashville: United Methodist Publishing House, 1989) 738.

PSALM 16:1-11, I KEEP THE LORD ALWAYS BEFORE ME

NIV

Psalm 16

A miktam[a] of David.

[1]Keep me safe, O God,
  for in you I take refuge.

[2]I said to the LORD, "You are my Lord;
  apart from you I have no good thing."

[3]As for the saints who are in the land,
  they are the glorious ones in whom is all
    my delight.[b]

[4]The sorrows of those will increase
  who run after other gods.
 I will not pour out their libations of blood
  or take up their names on my lips.

[5]LORD, you have assigned me my portion and
    my cup;
  you have made my lot secure.

[6]The boundary lines have fallen for me in
    pleasant places;
  surely I have a delightful inheritance.

[7]I will praise the LORD, who counsels me;
  even at night my heart instructs me.

[8]I have set the LORD always before me.
  Because he is at my right hand,
  I will not be shaken.

[9]Therefore my heart is glad and my tongue
    rejoices;
  my body also will rest secure,

[10]because you will not abandon me to the
    grave,[c]
  nor will you let your Holy One[d] see decay.

[11]You have made[e] known to me the path of life;
  you will fill me with joy in your presence,
  with eternal pleasures at your right hand.

[a]Title: Probably a literary or musical term   [b]3 Or *As for the pagan priests who are in the land / and the nobles in whom all delight, I said:*   [c]10 Hebrew *Sheol*   [d]10 Or *your faithful one*   [e]11 Or *You will make*

NRSV

Psalm 16

A Miktam of David.

[1] Protect me, O God, for in you I take refuge.
[2] I say to the LORD, "You are my Lord;
  I have no good apart from you."[a]

[3] As for the holy ones in the land, they are
    the noble,
  in whom is all my delight.

[4] Those who choose another god multiply
    their sorrows;[b]
  their drink offerings of blood I will not
    pour out
  or take their names upon my lips.

[5] The LORD is my chosen portion and my cup;
  you hold my lot.
[6] The boundary lines have fallen for me in
    pleasant places;
  I have a goodly heritage.

[7] I bless the LORD who gives me counsel;
  in the night also my heart instructs me.
[8] I keep the LORD always before me;
  because he is at my right hand, I shall
    not be moved.

[9] Therefore my heart is glad, and my soul
    rejoices;
  my body also rests secure.
[10] For you do not give me up to Sheol,
  or let your faithful one see the Pit.

[11] You show me the path of life.
  In your presence there is fullness of joy;
  in your right hand are pleasures
    forevermore.

[a]Jerome Tg: Meaning of Heb uncertain   [b]Cn: Meaning of Heb uncertain

COMMENTARY

After a brief opening petition, the rest of v. 1 "strikes the main theme of the prayer"—refuge or trust.[100] Accordingly, Psalm 16 is usually classified as a psalm of confidence/trust. There is a meaningful progression from Psalm 13 to Psalm 15 (see Commentary on Psalm 15), and Psalm 16 fits well with this sequence. Psalm 15 portrayed the identity of those who enter God's presence and dwell with God; the focus there was on deeds. Psalm 16 also portrays the identity of those who abide in God's presence (see esp. vv. 8, 11; cf. v. 8 with Pss 13:6; 15:5*c*), but the focus here is on the psalmist's joyful attitude (vv. 8-9, 11; cf. v. 9 with Ps 14:7) and speech (v. 2). Indeed, Gerstenberger aptly labels Psalm 16 a "Confession of Faith" as well as a "Song of Confidence," and he concludes, "The psalm can be compared in its function with the Apostles' Creed in Christian worship."[101]

16:1. The opening petition of Psalm 16 occurs also in Pss 17:8; 25:20; 86:2; 140:5; 141:9 (NRSV, "guard," "keep," or "preserve"; see also Psalm 121 and the sixfold repetition of "keep[s]"/ "keeper"). It is followed immediately by a supporting rationale that ties the psalm to a pervasive theme in the psalter, especially in Psalms 1–72: refuge (see 2:12; 5:11; 7:1; 11:1; 14:6; 17:7; Introduction). Some scholars give a geographical interpretation to the act of taking refuge; that is, the psalmist flees to the Temple to gain asylum from persecutors or visits the Temple to seek healing or social restoration. More broadly, however, to take refuge in God means to trust God, to recognize God's sovereignty, to live in dependence upon God rather than on self.

16:2. As in Psalm 2, the concepts of sovereignty and refuge are explicitly linked. In v. 2*a,* the psalmist addresses God as "master" or "Lord," thus accepting the role of God's servant. The Hebrew of v. 2*b* is uncertain. Most translators agree essentially with the NIV and the NRSV translations, which suggest the psalmist's dependence on God. Dahood seeks to make sense of the Hebrew, suggesting a translation that highlights

God's sovereignty: " 'You are my Lord, my Good,/ there is none above you.' "[102]

16:3-4. These verses are even more uncertain than v. 2*b.* Both the NIV and the NRSV construe the "saints"/"holy ones" and the "glorious ones"/"noble" to be other members of God's people. Thus an affirmation of loyalty to the people of God (v. 3) accompanies a profession of loyalty to God alone in keeping with the first commandment (v. 4). Many scholars suggest, however, that the terms in v. 3 refer to other gods, and many translations of v. 3 differ significantly from the NIV and the NRSV (see the NIV note). The New American Bible, for instance, reads: "Worthless are all the false gods of the land./ Accursed are all who delight in them." In any case, vv. 3-4 are almost certainly the psalmist's assertion that he or she will have no other gods. There will be no participation in idolatrous sacrifices or worship.

16:5-6. As if to emphasize as sharply as possible the contrast between loyalty to other gods and loyalty to the true God, v. 5 begins with the most personal of the divine names: "LORD." Doubly emphatic is the appearance of the Hebrew pronoun "you" (אתה *'attâ*) in v. 5*b.* Indeed, it recalls the appearance of the pronoun in v. 2 in the phrase, "You are my Lord." In short, there is no doubt that the psalmist belongs to God. And in a sense, God belongs to the psalmist as well— not in the sense of ownership but in the sense of relatedness. The word "portion" (חלק *ḥēleq*) is used in the book of Joshua to designate every Israelite's share in the land (see Josh 19:9). Thus it represented the possibility of sustenance, life, future. For the psalmist, God is the source of all these good things (see v. 2). To call God "my cup" suggests the same idea (see Pss 23:6; 116:13). The word "lot" (גורל *gôrāl*) recalls both the method and the results of apportioning the land in the book of Joshua (18:6, 8, 10; 19:51); the lot was also a method for determining duty or function (see 1 Chr 24:5, 7). The final line of v. 5 thus affirms again that the psalmist's life and future lie with God and that the psalmist is willing

100. Erhard S. Gerstenberger, *Psalms, Part 1, with an Introduction to Cultic Poetry,* Forms of the OT Literature 14 (Grand Rapids: Eerdmans, 1988) 90.

101. Ibid., 92.

102. Mitchell Dahood, *Psalms I (1–50),* AB 16 (Garden City, N.Y.: Doubleday, 1966) 86.

to be used by God for God's purposes. Since the priests and the Levites had no portion in the land and were specifically told that God was their portion (see Num 18:20; Deut 10:9; 12:12), some scholars conclude that the psalmist was a priest or Levite serving in the Temple. While this is possible, it is more likely that the language and conceptuality of the book of Joshua are being used symbolically and poetically (see Pss 73:26; 119:57; 142:6; Lam 3:24). More language from Joshua occurs in v. 6: "boundary lines" (see 17:5: NIV, "share," NRSV, "portions") and "inheritance"/"heritage" (see 14:3; 17:6). The images effectively communicate the psalmist's affirmation that entrusting one's life to God has favorable consequences. God has provided (see v. 2).

16:7-8. This verse develops further an idea found in v. 5: the psalmist's willingness to be used by and for God. The word "bless" (ברך *bārak*) in its root sense means "to kneel," as in paying homage to a superior (see Pss 26:12; 34:1; 63:4; 103:20-22; 104:1, 35). As suggested earlier by the word "refuge" (v. 1), the psalmist recognizes God's sovereignty. And as one who subjects oneself to God, the psalmist is open to God's instruction or "counsel" (v. 7*a*; see Commentary on Psalm 1, esp. v. 2; see also Ps 32:8). Verse 7*b* implies that the psalmist may be involved in self-instruction, but that is not necessarily so, since the heart (lit., "kidneys") was especially accessible to God's examination and influence (see Pss 7:9; 26:2; Jer 11:20; 20:12). The verb "instructs" (יסר *yāsar*) recalls Ps 2:10, where it is rendered "be warned" and parallels the command to "Serve the LORD" (2:11). Thus, even v. 7*b* represents the psalmist's intention to be subject to God in every way. Verse 8 conveys the same idea; for the psalmist, God is "always before me," the constant center of attention. Somehow—whether it be the psalmist's entry into the Temple or a keen awareness of God's pervasive presence (see Ps 139:1-12)—the psalmist finds that God is always accessible and available (see "right hand" in Pss 73:23; 109:31). In apparent contrast to Psalm 13, in which the psalmist's perception of God's absence led to the fear of being "shaken" (see 13:4), here the psalmist's perception of God's presence

provides an unshakable foundation (see Commentary on Pss 13:4; 15:5*c*; see also Psalm 1).

16:9-11. The trust expressed in v. 8 is a source of joy. In v. 9, the psalmist is and does precisely what Ps 14:7 says Israel will be and do when it experiences God's help. The psalmist's whole being is involved—"heart," "soul" (lit., "glory"; see Pss 3:3; 4:2; 7:5: NRSV, "soul"; NIV, "me"), and "body." The word "secure" (בטח *betaḥ*) is from a Hebrew root that means "trust." Security for the psalmist is not an achievement but a result of a life entrusted to God (see Pss 4:5; 9:10; Introduction). As vv. 10-11 suggest, God is the guarantor of life and life's constant guide. What vv. 10-11 affirm precisely remains unclear. Perhaps it is the psalmist's profession of faith that death—Sheol or the Pit—will be averted when the prayer for healing is answered in the Temple. Dahood even suggests that vv. 10-11 articulate the psalmist's belief "that he will be granted the same privilege accorded Enoch and Elijah; he is convinced that God will assume him to himself, without suffering the pains of death."[103] While this may be possible (see also Pss 49:15; 73:24), it is unlikely. Mays suggests a more likely approach for understanding the conclusion of Psalm 16:

> It can be read as the general prayer of the faithful who, without any doctrine of resurrection or eternal life to explain just how, nonetheless trust the LORD to keep them with such total confidence that they cannot imagine a future apart from life in God's presence. The language of the psalm presses toward an unbroken relation between LORD and life.[104]

In the vision of poetic outreach, the psalmist is convinced "that neither death, nor life . . . will be able to separate us from the love of God" (Rom 8:38-39 NRSV; see also Commentary on Psalm 22, esp. v. 27). The psalmist's "pleasant" lot in the present (v. 6) becomes a promise of a presence that yields "pleasures forevermore" (v. 11). The present joy (v. 9) will be complete (v. 11).

103. Ibid., 91.
104. James L. Mays, *Psalms,* Interpretation (Louisville: John Knox, 1994) 88.

REFLECTIONS

1. One can detect a sort of progression from Psalm 13 to Psalm 16. Actually, the apparent movement from complaint (Psalm 13) to trust (Psalm 16) is already present within Psalm 13 in the movement from vv. 1-4 to vv. 5-6. In a sense, Psalm 16 is a kind of elaboration upon 13:5-6, articulating more fully the trust and joy and experience of bounty mentioned there. Psalm 16 should not be understood as a better profession of faith than Psalm 13. Rather, just as vv. 1-4 and vv. 5-6 of Psalm 13 should be understood as simultaneous moments (see Commentary on Psalm 13), so also should Psalms 13 and 16 be understood as equally legitimate and simultaneous professions. Indeed, only one who is facing the full force of death's assaults (13:1-4) need pray, "Protect me" (16:1), and is in a position to utter the assurance of v. 10. Thus Psalm 16 articulates the experience of life and joy, not apart from suffering, but in the midst of it. For those who entrust their lives and futures completely to God, suffering and glory are inseparable. To be sure, this was Jesus' experience, but it is also the experience of his followers—from bold first-century martyrs, like Peter and Paul, to courageous twentieth-century martyrs, like Martin Luther King, Jr.

2. While the psalmist probably did not possess a doctrine of resurrection, it is theologically appropriate that 16:8-11 is one of the texts Peter used on the Day of Pentecost to proclaim the resurrection of Jesus (Acts 2:25-28; see also 13:35). Faced with the full force of death's assault, Jesus both complained (Mark 15:34; see Ps 22:1) and petitioned for the removal of the cup of suffering (Mark 14:36); yet, at the same time he completely entrusted his life and future to God (Mark 14:36). Jesus' life, death, and resurrection are testimony to the truth that Psalm 16 already articulates: Suffering and glory are inseparable. Indeed, the author of Hebrews can even speak of Jesus' enduring the cross "for the sake of the joy that was set before him" (Heb 12:2 NRSV).

3. Those who entrust their lives to God experience a depth of stability (v. 8) and joy (v. 9a) and security (v. 9b) that not even death can undermine. In the contemporary world, where the fear of death often motivates frantic attempts to achieve our own security and joy, frequently through material abundance, Psalm 16 points us in an entirely different direction. Abundant life will not be something we achieve but something we receive. We begin to experience this gift when we say with the psalmist, "You are my Lord" (v. 2). This act of humility promises exaltation. Psalm 16 is thus both a challenge to keep the Lord always before us and a promise that the experience of God's presence is its own reward: abundant life and fullness of joy (see John 10:1-11; 16:16-24; see also Commentary on Psalm 73).

PSALM 17:1-15, BEHOLDING YOUR LIKENESS

NIV	NRSV
Psalm 17	Psalm 17
A prayer of David.	A Prayer of David.

¹Hear, O LORD, my righteous plea;
    listen to my cry.
Give ear to my prayer
    it does not rise from deceitful lips.
	¹ Hear a just cause, O LORD; attend to my cry;
	    give ear to my prayer from lips free of
	        deceit.
	² From you let my vindication come;

NIV

²May my vindication come from you;
   may your eyes see what is right.

³Though you probe my heart and examine me
      at night,
   though you test me, you will find nothing;
   I have resolved that my mouth will not sin.
⁴As for the deeds of men—
   by the word of your lips
 I have kept myself
   from the ways of the violent.
⁵My steps have held to your paths;
   my feet have not slipped.

⁶I call on you, O God, for you will answer me;
   give ear to me and hear my prayer.
⁷Show the wonder of your great love,
   you who save by your right hand
   those who take refuge in you from their
      foes.
⁸Keep me as the apple of your eye;
   hide me in the shadow of your wings
⁹from the wicked who assail me,
   from my mortal enemies who surround me.

¹⁰They close up their callous hearts,
   and their mouths speak with arrogance.
¹¹They have tracked me down, they now
     surround me,
   with eyes alert, to throw me to the ground.
¹²They are like a lion hungry for prey,
   like a great lion crouching in cover.

¹³Rise up, O LORD, confront them, bring them
     down;
   rescue me from the wicked by your sword.
¹⁴O LORD, by your hand save me from such
     men,
   from men of this world whose reward is in
     this life.

You still the hunger of those you cherish;
   their sons have plenty,
   and they store up wealth for their children.
¹⁵And I—in righteousness I will see your face;
   when I awake, I will be satisfied with
     seeing your likeness.

NRSV

   let your eyes see the right.

³ If you try my heart, if you visit me by night,
   if you test me, you will find no
     wickedness in me;
   my mouth does not transgress.
⁴ As for what others do, by the word of your
     lips
   I have avoided the ways of the violent.
⁵ My steps have held fast to your paths;
   my feet have not slipped.

⁶ I call upon you, for you will answer me,
     O God;
   incline your ear to me, hear my words.
⁷ Wondrously show your steadfast love,
   O savior of those who seek refuge
   from their adversaries at your right hand.

⁸ Guard me as the apple of the eye;
   hide me in the shadow of your wings,
⁹ from the wicked who despoil me,
   my deadly enemies who surround me.
¹⁰ They close their hearts to pity;
   with their mouths they speak arrogantly.
¹¹ They track me down;[a] now they surround me;
   they set their eyes to cast me to the ground.
¹² They are like a lion eager to tear,
   like a young lion lurking in ambush.

¹³ Rise up, O LORD, confront them, overthrow
     them!
   By your sword deliver my life from the
     wicked,
¹⁴ from mortals—by your hand, O LORD—
   from mortals whose portion in life is in
     this world.
   May their bellies be filled with what you
     have stored up for them;
   may their children have more than enough;
   may they leave something over to their
     little ones.

¹⁵ As for me, I shall behold your face in
     righteousness;
   when I awake I shall be satisfied,
     beholding your likeness.

aOne Ms Compare Syr: MT *Our steps*

COMMENTARY

Psalm 17 is a prayer for help that contains near its beginning a protestation of innocence (vv. 3-5; see Pss 7:3-5; 26:1-7; Introduction) and concludes with a striking expression of trust (v. 15). Structural division of the psalm varies. A focus on form and content units yields the following: opening petition (vv. 1-2), protestation of innocence (vv. 3-5), petition (vv. 6-9), complaint (vv. 10-12), petition (vv. 13-14), affirmation of trust/confidence (v. 15). An eye to poetic symmetry, however, suggests an alternative: opening petition (God and the psalmist) and trust (vv. 1-3), description of the psalmist (vv. 4-6), central petition (vv. 7-9), description of the wicked (vv. 10-12), concluding petition (God and the wicked) and trust (vv. 13-15). Verses 4-6 and 10-12 also display a chiastic arrangement (see Introduction):

A v. 4 the psalmist's non-violence
  B v. 5 the psalmist's stability
    C v. 6 the psalmist's humble speech
      D vv. 7-9 central petition
    C' v. 10 the wicked's arrogant speech
  B' v. 11 the wicked's attempt to destabilize
A' v. 12 the wicked's violence

The chiasm effectively focuses attention on the central petition (vv. 7-9), including the exact structural center of the psalm (v. 8). Not surprisingly, in terms of poetic symmetry, v. 8 is linked conceptually to the beginning and end of the psalm. The request to be "the apple [lit., "pupil"] of the eye" highlights the function of seeing and calls to mind God's face. The request thus recalls v. 2, which reads literally, "From your *face* let my justification come; let your *eye see* the right." The request also anticipates v. 15, in which the psalmist "will *see* your *face.*" Because God sees (vv. 2, 8), the psalmist too will see (v. 15). God and the psalmist stand face to face.

It may be more than coincidental that the conclusion of Psalm 17 locates the psalmist in the very same place that the end of Psalm 16 does. Psalm 16:11a reads literally, "Fullness of joy [is] with your *face.*" As in Psalm 16, the sight of God's face in 17:15 yields the experience of fullness: "I shall be satisfied" ("satisfied" [שׂבע *śābaʿ*] is the same Hebrew root as "fullness" in 16:11). Like Psalm 16, Psalm 17 may have originally been set

in the Temple, where perhaps the psalmist sought refuge (v. 7; see Ps 16:1) and vindication (v. 2) from enemies who had made false accusations (see Psalms 5; 7; 26; Introduction). The mention of night in 16:7 and 17:3 (see also "awake" in 17:15) suggests the possibility that the original use of these psalms involved the psalmist's spending the night in the Temple. Further links between the two psalms include the mention of God's "right hand" (16:11; 17:7), the identical plea to "keep" (16:1; 17:8), and the affirmation of not being "moved" (16:8; 17:5).

17:1-3. The opening plea already suggests that the psalmist is on the defensive; it reads literally, "Hear a righteousness" (see v. 15; cf. Ps 7:8). The word "cry" (רנה *rinnâ*) usually indicates a joyful exclamation, but here it indicates petition (see Pss 61:2; 88:2; 142:6). The psalmist's description of her or his lips as "free of deceit" suggests both that the psalmist has been falsely accused and that she or he is prepared to face God (see Ps 24:4c; see also Pss 10:7; 34:13; 35:20; 36:3). Indeed, it is "from your face" (v. 2) that justice will come for the psalmist. God will see that the psalmist is in the "right," because God judges with "right" (or "equity"; see Pss 9:8; 96:10; 98:9; 99:4). The psalmist is sure that she or he can stand God's most careful examination (v. 3; see Pss 7:9; 11:4-5; 26:2; 66:10). The last line of v. 3 recalls the final line of v. 1.

17:4-6, 10-12. Verse 4 is difficult, and Bratcher and Reyburn point out, "There are almost as many different renditions of these lines as there are commentaries and translations."[105] The Hebrew appears to read literally, "As for the deeds of others, by the word of your lips I have kept the paths of the violent." The NIV supplies the preposition "from" to give the verse the opposite sense, and the NRSV seems to have achieved the same effect with a paraphrase. It is possible to construe the verb in the sense of "observe" rather than "keep," thus mitigating the problem (cf. NIV). Perhaps the best alternative is offered by *Biblica Hebraica Stuttgartensia,* which

105. Robert G. Bratcher and William D. Reyburn, *A Translator's Handbook on the Book of Psalms* (New York: United Bible Societies, 1991) 152.

suggests reading the last portion of v. 3 with v. 4, and the last portion of v. 4 with v. 5. The result is:

> My mouth has not crossed over into the deeds
>   of others,
> The word of your lips, I have kept.
> (On) the violent way, my steps hold fast.
> On your paths, my feet are not moved.
> (vv. 3c-5, author's trans.)

In any case, the intent seems to be to contrast the psalmist and the wicked (see Pss 7:9-11; 11:4-5; 12:1-2, 7-8). The chiastic arrangement of vv. 4-6, 10-12 reinforces the contrast, as do the two first-person pronouns in vv. 4, 6, which emphasize that the psalmist's action and speech are directed to God. While the psalmist lives by God's word (v. 4), the wicked prey on others (v. 12; see Pss 7:2; 10:9; 22:13, 21; 58:6). The wicked seek to bring down the psalmist (v. 11), but the psalmist is not moved (v. 5; see Pss 13:4; 15:5; 16:8). The psalmist directs her or his words to God (v. 6), while the wicked "speak arrogantly" (v. 10). Verse 6b returns to the imperative, and the plea "hear" is repeated, recalling v. 1. The psalmist wants God to hear the "words" (v. 6), since they issue from "lips free of deceit" (v. 1) and a "mouth [that] does not transgress" (v. 3).

17:7-9. While vv. 1-6 have dealt almost exclusively with the psalmist, vv. 7-9 specifically introduce the "adversaries"/"foes" (v. 7) and "the wicked" (v. 9), who are the primary subject of vv. 10-14. In the midst of arrogant and violent opponents, the psalmist humbly requests God's "steadfast love" (v. 7; see Pss 5:7; 13:5; Introduction). Aware of personal need, the psalmist looks to God as "savior" (see "deliver"/"deliverance" in Ps 3:2, 7, 8 NIV). Life is entrusted to God's care (see "refuge" in Pss 2:12; 5:11; 7:1; 11:1; 14:6; 16:1; Introduction). The "right hand" of God symbolizes both presence and power. The psalmist stakes her or his life on both (see vv. 13, 15). Craigie points out that v. 7 is reminiscent of Exod 15:11-13, where the words "wonders" (v. 11), "right hand" (v. 12), and "steadfast love" (v. 13) also occur. The psalmist's recollection of the exodus is a source of strength, and he or she envisions a sort of "personal 'exodus.'" [106]

106. Peter C. Craigie, *Psalms 1–50,* WBC 19 (Waco, Tex.: Word, 1983) 163.

Verse 8 is also reminiscent of God's care for all Israel (see Deut 32:10-11). To be hidden in the shadow of God's wings may originally have had a geographical referent; that is, the wings may be those of the seraphs that were associated with the ark in the Temple. The phrase is associated with "refuge" in Pss 36:7 and 57:1. In Pss 36:7 and 63:7, God's house or sanctuary is the apparent setting for this experience of protection. It is also possible that the imagery of God's wings derives from the observation of a mother bird protecting her young (see Matt 23:37); such feminine imagery for God occurs elsewhere in Psalms (see Psalm 131) and the OT (see Isa 66:13). In any case, the imagery was eventually understood metaphorically.

17:13-15. The word "adversaries"/"foes" in v. 7 is literally "risers"; in v. 13, the psalmist requests God to "rise" (see Pss 3:7; 9:19; 10:12) against the wicked and, literally, "meet their face." The psalmist desires to see God face to face and wants the same experience for the wicked, for the psalmist is confident that God's "eyes see the right" (v. 2). Verse 14 is difficult. The first part may be construed as a continuation of v. 13 that further defines the wicked. In contrast to those whose portion is God (Ps 16:5), the wicked are those who look for security in worldly things and accomplishments. The remainder of v. 14, according to the NRSV, says, in effect, "If that's what they want, let them have it." The tone should be understood as sarcastic (see Num 11:19-20 and Matt 6:2, 16 concerning "reward"). In contrast to those who can "be filled" (מלא *mālā'*) by stuffing "their bellies," the psalmist will "be satisfied" (*śāba'*, the same word as "have more than enough" in v. 14) only by the higher good of seeing God's face (v. 15; see Pss 11:7; 24:6) and "likeness." In short, the psalmist will be privileged to see God face to face, as Moses did (see Num 12:8, where "form" is the same word as "likeness" [תמונה *těmûnâ*] here). This interpretation of v. 14b and its relationship to v. 15, however, is by no means certain. The NIV, for instance, construes v. 14b in a good sense as an articulation of God's provision for the psalmist and others who seek refuge in God.

REFLECTIONS

The psalmist's certainty of the rightness of his or her cause (vv. 1-2) and the protestation of innocence (vv. 3-5) seem problematic; they may suggest that the psalmist is proud or self-righteous. But as suggested in the Reflections on Psalm 7, the psalmist asserts not sinlessness in general but rightness in a particular case involving false accusation by opponents. In this sense, Psalm 17, like Psalm 7, is reminiscent of the book of Job. If anyone is arrogant in Psalm 17, it is the psalmist's opponents, who have apparently condemned the psalmist and do not hesitate to exact punishment. The psalmist actually displays humble trust in God's steadfast love and willingness to save (v. 7). The protestation of innocence is essentially an expression of the psalmist's willingness to be completely open and honest to God. In sharp contrast to the adversaries, the psalmist professes to live by God's word (v. 4).

We are not told the outcome of the psalmist's appeal for righteousness and justice (vv. 1-2); however, in view of v. 15, this issue becomes irrelevant. The assurance that the psalmist will somehow see God's face and likeness puts the opposition of enemies in a new perspective. The psalmist now knows that nothing will be able to separate her or him from God's protecting love (see v. 8; see also Ps 16:8-11; Rom 8:38-39). We are not told how the psalmist will see God. Israel was prohibited from making any likeness of God (Exod 20:4); yet, there is testimony that people "saw the God of Israel" (Exod 24:10; see Num 12:8; Isa 6:1-8; Pss 11:7; 24:6; 42:2; 63:2). Perhaps this experience involved worshiping in the Temple (see Isa 6:1-8; Psalms 24; 42; 63). Christians profess to see God in worship, and that experience is celebrated in prayer and song (e.g., the communion hymn "Here, O My Lord, I See Thee Face to Face"). There may be other ways that Israel and we see God—in momentous historical events, like the exodus or the dismantling of apartheid in South Africa, or in daily rituals that sustain and nourish, or in the faces of friends and loved ones, or in the faces of strangers, who may be among the least of our sisters and brothers. In any case, the psalmist is convinced of and apparently transformed by the possibility of experiencing unbroken communion with God. The psalmist anticipates the experience that Jesus proclaimed: "Blessed are the pure in heart, for they will see God" (Matt 5:8 NRSV). Christian tradition has interpreted v. 15 as a reference to the resurrection. While the psalmist probably had no doctrine of resurrection, her or his language pushes toward the notion of a communion with God that nothing—not even death—can interrupt (see Commentary on Pss 16:10-11; 22:27; see also Rom 8:38-39). It is thus appropriate that Christians hear in v. 15 an added dimension.

The final two verses of Psalm 17 leave modern believers with the challenge of considering what it is that truly satisfies. Shall we be content with a "portion in life" that consists only of what the world can cram into our greedy stomachs and minds? One of the real dangers of a culture of affluence is the boredom that results from satiation. We have our reward, but it does not truly satisfy. Luxuriance does not constitute life (see Luke 12:15). We hunger for a higher good. Psalm 17 promises a satisfaction that does not fade, for it involves nothing less than seeing God's likeness—unbroken communion with God, whose "eyes see the right" (v. 2). Again, the psalmist anticipates the experience Jesus proclaimed: "Blessed are those who hunger and thirst for righteousness, for they will be filled" (Matt 5:6 NRSV; see also John 4:13-14; 6:27, 35).

PSALM 18:1-50, STEADFAST LOVE TO THE ANOINTED

NIV

NRSV

Psalm 18

For the director of music. Of David the servant of the LORD. He sang to the LORD the words of this song when the LORD delivered him from the hand of all his enemies and from the hand of Saul. He said:

¹I love you, O LORD, my strength.

²The LORD is my rock, my fortress and my
    deliverer;
  my God is my rock, in whom I take refuge.
  He is my shield and the horn[a] of my
    salvation, my stronghold.
³I call to the LORD, who is worthy of praise,
  and I am saved from my enemies.

⁴The cords of death entangled me;
  the torrents of destruction overwhelmed me.
⁵The cords of the grave[b] coiled around me;
  the snares of death confronted me.
⁶In my distress I called to the LORD;
  I cried to my God for help.
From his temple he heard my voice;
  my cry came before him, into his ears.

⁷The earth trembled and quaked,
  and the foundations of the mountains shook;
  they trembled because he was angry.
⁸Smoke rose from his nostrils;
  consuming fire came from his mouth,
  burning coals blazed out of it.
⁹He parted the heavens and came down;
  dark clouds were under his feet.
¹⁰He mounted the cherubim and flew;
  he soared on the wings of the wind.
¹¹He made darkness his covering, his canopy
    around him—
  the dark rain clouds of the sky.
¹²Out of the brightness of his presence clouds
    advanced,
  with hailstones and bolts of lightning.
¹³The LORD thundered from heaven;

[a]2 *Horn* here symbolizes strength.   [b]5 Hebrew *Sheol*

Psalm 18

To the leader. A Psalm of David the servant of the LORD, who addressed the words of this song to the LORD on the day when the LORD delivered him from the hand of all his enemies, and from the hand of Saul. He said:

¹ I love you, O LORD, my strength.
² The LORD is my rock, my fortress, and my
    deliverer,
  my God, my rock in whom I take refuge,
  my shield, and the horn of my salvation,
    my stronghold.
³ I call upon the LORD, who is worthy to be
    praised,
  so I shall be saved from my enemies.

⁴ The cords of death encompassed me;
  the torrents of perdition assailed me;
⁵ the cords of Sheol entangled me;
  the snares of death confronted me.

⁶ In my distress I called upon the LORD;
  to my God I cried for help.
From his temple he heard my voice,
  and my cry to him reached his ears.

⁷ Then the earth reeled and rocked;
  the foundations also of the mountains
    trembled
  and quaked, because he was angry.
⁸ Smoke went up from his nostrils,
  and devouring fire from his mouth;
  glowing coals flamed forth from him.
⁹ He bowed the heavens, and came down;
  thick darkness was under his feet.
¹⁰ He rode on a cherub, and flew;
  he came swiftly upon the wings of the
    wind.
¹¹ He made darkness his covering around him,
  his canopy thick clouds dark with water.
¹² Out of the brightness before him
  there broke through his clouds

NIV

the voice of the Most High resounded.[a]
14He shot his arrows and scattered ⌐the
enemies⌐,
great bolts of lightning and routed them.
15The valleys of the sea were exposed
and the foundations of the earth laid bare
at your rebuke, O LORD,
at the blast of breath from your nostrils.

16He reached down from on high and took
hold of me;
he drew me out of deep waters.
17He rescued me from my powerful enemy,
from my foes, who were too strong for me.
18They confronted me in the day of my disaster,
but the LORD was my support.
19He brought me out into a spacious place;
he rescued me because he delighted in me.

20The LORD has dealt with me according to my
righteousness;
according to the cleanness of my hands he
has rewarded me.
21For I have kept the ways of the LORD;
I have not done evil by turning from my
God.
22All his laws are before me;
I have not turned away from his decrees.
23I have been blameless before him
and have kept myself from sin.
24The LORD has rewarded me according to my
righteousness,
according to the cleanness of my hands in
his sight.

25To the faithful you show yourself faithful,
to the blameless you show yourself
blameless,
26to the pure you show yourself pure,
but to the crooked you show yourself
shrewd.
27You save the humble
but bring low those whose eyes are
haughty.
28You, O LORD, keep my lamp burning;
my God turns my darkness into light.
29With your help I can advance against a troop[b];
with my God I can scale a wall.

a13 Some Hebrew manuscripts and Septuagint (see also 2 Samuel
22:14); most Hebrew manuscripts resounded, / amid hailstones and
bolts of lightning   b29 Or can run through a barricade

NRSV

hailstones and coals of fire.
13 The LORD also thundered in the heavens,
and the Most High uttered his voice.[a]
14 And he sent out his arrows, and scattered
them;
he flashed forth lightnings, and routed
them.
15 Then the channels of the sea were seen,
and the foundations of the world were
laid bare
at your rebuke, O LORD,
at the blast of the breath of your nostrils.

16 He reached down from on high, he took me;
he drew me out of mighty waters.
17 He delivered me from my strong enemy,
and from those who hated me;
for they were too mighty for me.
18 They confronted me in the day of my
calamity;
but the LORD was my support.
19 He brought me out into a broad place;
he delivered me, because he delighted in
me.

20 The LORD rewarded me according to my
righteousness;
according to the cleanness of my hands
he recompensed me.
21 For I have kept the ways of the LORD,
and have not wickedly departed from my
God.
22 For all his ordinances were before me,
and his statutes I did not put away from
me.
23 I was blameless before him,
and I kept myself from guilt.
24 Therefore the LORD has recompensed me
according to my righteousness,
according to the cleanness of my hands
in his sight.

25 With the loyal you show yourself loyal;
with the blameless you show yourself
blameless;
26 with the pure you show yourself pure;
and with the crooked you show yourself
perverse.

a Gk See 2 Sam 22.14: Heb adds hailstones and coals of fire

NIV

30As for God, his way is perfect;
  the word of the LORD is flawless.
 He is a shield
  for all who take refuge in him.
31For who is God besides the LORD?
  And who is the Rock except our God?
32It is God who arms me with strength
  and makes my way perfect.
33He makes my feet like the feet of a deer;
  he enables me to stand on the heights.
34He trains my hands for battle;
  my arms can bend a bow of bronze.
35You give me your shield of victory,
  and your right hand sustains me;
  you stoop down to make me great.
36You broaden the path beneath me,
  so that my ankles do not turn.

37I pursued my enemies and overtook them;
  I did not turn back till they were destroyed.
38I crushed them so that they could not rise;
  they fell beneath my feet.
39You armed me with strength for battle;
  you made my adversaries bow at my feet.
40You made my enemies turn their backs in
    flight,
  and I destroyed my foes.
41They cried for help, but there was no one to
    save them—
  to the LORD, but he did not answer.
42I beat them as fine as dust borne on the
    wind;
  I poured them out like mud in the streets.

43You have delivered me from the attacks of
    the people;
  you have made me the head of nations;
  people I did not know are subject to me.
44As soon as they hear me, they obey me;
  foreigners cringe before me.
45They all lose heart;
  they come trembling from their strongholds.

46The LORD lives! Praise be to my Rock!
  Exalted be God my Savior!
47He is the God who avenges me,
  who subdues nations under me,
48 who saves me from my enemies.
 You exalted me above my foes;
  from violent men you rescued me.

NRSV

27 For you deliver a humble people,
  but the haughty eyes you bring down.
28 It is you who light my lamp;
  the LORD, my God, lights up my darkness.
29 By you I can crush a troop,
  and by my God I can leap over a wall.
30 This God—his way is perfect;
  the promise of the LORD proves true;
  he is a shield for all who take refuge in
    him.

31 For who is God except the LORD?
  And who is a rock besides our God?—
32 the God who girded me with strength,
  and made my way safe.
33 He made my feet like the feet of a deer,
  and set me secure on the heights.
34 He trains my hands for war,
  so that my arms can bend a bow of bronze.
35 You have given me the shield of your
    salvation,
  and your right hand has supported me;
  your help[a] has made me great.
36 You gave me a wide place for my steps
    under me,
  and my feet did not slip.
37 I pursued my enemies and overtook them;
  and did not turn back until they were
    consumed.
38 I struck them down, so that they were not
    able to rise;
  they fell under my feet.
39 For you girded me with strength for the
    battle;
  you made my assailants sink under me.
40 You made my enemies turn their backs to me,
  and those who hated me I destroyed.
41 They cried for help, but there was no one
    to save them;
  they cried to the LORD, but he did not
    answer them.
42 I beat them fine, like dust before the wind;
  I cast them out like the mire of the
    streets.

43 You delivered me from strife with the
    peoples;[b]

a Or gentleness   b Gk Tg: Heb people

NIV

⁴⁹Therefore I will praise you among the
    nations, O LORD;
  I will sing praises to your name.
⁵⁰He gives his king great victories;
  he shows unfailing kindness to his anointed,
  to David and his descendants forever.

NRSV

  you made me head of the nations;
    people whom I had not known served
      me.
⁴⁴ As soon as they heard of me they obeyed
      me;
    foreigners came cringing to me.
⁴⁵ Foreigners lost heart,
    and came trembling out of their
      strongholds.

⁴⁶ The LORD lives! Blessed be my rock,
    and exalted be the God of my salvation,
⁴⁷ the God who gave me vengeance
    and subdued peoples under me;
⁴⁸ who delivered me from my enemies;
    indeed, you exalted me above my
      adversaries;
    you delivered me from the violent.

⁴⁹ For this I will extol you, O LORD, among
    the nations,
    and sing praises to your name.
⁵⁰ Great triumphs he gives to his king,
    and shows steadfast love to his anointed,
    to David and his descendants forever.

COMMENTARY

Psalm 18 is one of the longest and most literarily complex in the psalter. Since David is mentioned in v. 50, and since David recites in 2 Samuel 22 a song that is virtually identical to Psalm 18, scholars have traditionally categorized Psalm 18 as a royal psalm. It rehearses and celebrates God's deliverance of the king from some dire threat; thus, more specifically, it seems to be a royal song of thanksgiving.

Partly because of the link to 2 Samuel 22, and partly because of the nature of its language and syntax, Psalm 18 is traditionally understood as having originated in David's time and used by him and his descendants, perhaps upon occasions of victorious military battles. While this view may not be ruled out, it is by no means certain. Gerstenberger, for instance, concludes that Psalm 18 originated in the post-exilic era. Using older theophanic (see vv. 7-15) and monarchical tradi-

tions, the early Jewish community created "a messianic thanksgiving song" for use in synagogal worship. According to Gerstenberger, the intent of Psalm 18 is: "The psalmist sought to keep hope alive in hard-pressed Jewish communities. As Yahweh had always intervened for Israel—in mighty theophanies, in individual acts of redemption, in special aid to the kings of old—he would thus always take the side of his struggling faithful and lead them toward a bright future."[107]

The disparity between the traditional dating of Psalm 18 and Gerstenberger's date is approximately 500 years! While historical certainty is impossible, Gerstenberger's proposed date does greater justice to the message of Psalm 18 in its placement within the psalter. The psalter in its

107. Erhard S. Gerstenberger, *Psalms, Part 1, with an Introduction to Cultic Poetry,* Forms of the OT Literature 14 (Grand Rapids: Eerdmans, 1988) 100.

final form has an eschatological orientation; that is, it proclaims the reign of God amid circumstances that suggest God does *not* reign (see the Introduction). Even if Psalm 18 originated very early, it would have taken its place in the collected psalter at a time when the monarchy had disappeared (see the Introduction; see also Commentary on Psalm 144, which appears to be a post-exilic re-reading of Psalm 18). Thus its function, as Gerstenberger suggests, was to keep hope alive by proclaiming God's sovereignty over the nations. In this regard, Psalm 18 is like Psalm 2; Mays even suggests that "Psalm 18 is a sequel to Psalm 2."[108]

The structure of Psalm 18 is complicated enough that some scholars contend that it should be viewed as two separate psalms (1) vv. 1-30 and (2) vv. 31-50; however, there is a unifying plot. Out of his distress, the king calls upon God (vv. 1-6), and God comes down to rescue him (vv. 16-19), an action that is introduced as a dramatic theophany (vv. 7-15). The praise that is expected following the account of deliverance is postponed until vv. 31-50, being preceded by descriptions of the king's righteousness (vv. 20-24) and God's faithfulness (vv. 25-30). Thus, in terms of its basic structure and movement, Psalm 18 does have the form of a royal song of thanksgiving for God's deliverance from distress. The fact that it functions eschatologically is suggested by the observation that each part of the psalm contains universalistic, cosmic language and imagery. The king's plight involves "torrents" (v. 4) and "mighty waters" (v. 16), which are reminiscent of the watery chaos that God commands to become an orderly cosmos. God's arrival has cosmic effects—the earth shakes, the heavens part, and there is participation by mountains, clouds, wind, lightning, and hail (vv. 7-15). The rescue also has universal proportions; the king becomes "head of the nations" (v. 43) and praises God "among the nations" (v. 49). This hyperbolic description is congruent with those in other royal psalms. In Psalm 2, God is sovereign over peoples and nations (vv. 4, 10-12), and in Psalm 72, the king's righteous rule is to be recognized and reinforced by hills and mountains (v. 3) as well as by kings and "all nations" (vv. 11, 17). These

hyperbolic descriptions obviously exceed the reality that any Israelite or Judean king actually experienced. In short, the descriptions affirm Israel's faith in God's rule amid circumstances that seem to deny it. Psalm 18, as the other royal psalms, functions eschatologically.

Even the superscription reinforces the eschatological dimension. There never was really a day when David was delivered from *all* of his enemies. Even 2 Samuel 22, where David sings this song near the end of his career, is followed by further threats to David and to the kingdom. And if the use of David's name in the superscription is meant to allude to the Davidic house (see v. 50), it reinforces even more strongly the eschatological dimension.

18:1-6, Invocation and Distress. The opening "I love you" is unusual, and it is not in 2 Sam 22:2. The text can be emended slightly to read "I exalt you," which seems more fitting here. There follows an impressive series of metaphors in v. 2 indicating effectively that God is the source of the king's life and "strength" (v. 1; see vv. 32, 39, where the Hebrew word [חיל *ḥayil*] differs from the one here [חזק *ḥēzeq*]). Metaphors for God occur throughout the psalter—"rock" (סלע *sela'*, Pss 31:3; 42:9; 71:3), "fortress" (מצודה *mĕṣûdâ*, Pss 31:2-3; 71:3; 91:2; 144:2); "rock" (צור *ṣûr*; see vv. 31, 46; Pss 19:14; 28:1; 31:2; 62:2, 6-7; 73:26 NIV and NRSV, "strength"; 78:35; 89:26; 92:15; 95:1; 144:1; see also Deut 32:4, 18); "refuge" (חסה *ḥāsâ*, Ps 2:12; see the Introduction); "shield" (מגן *māgēn*, Ps 3:4); "stronghold" (משגב *miśgāb*, Ps 9:10). The words "salvation" (v. 2) and "saved" (v. 3) are from the same Hebrew root (ישע *yš'*), which is a key word throughout the psalm (see vv. 27, 35, 41, 46). It emphasizes that the king owes his life to God. The repetition of the root underlying "deliver" (פלט *pālaṭ*) has the same effect (see vv. 43, 48).

Whoever or whatever the enemies (v. 3) may be, the threat is urgent. Indeed, the king is already in the clutches of death (vv. 4-5) and Sheol (see Ps 6:5; see also Jonah 2:1-9 for similar language and imagery). Verse 6 repeats the verb "call" from v. 3, and there are also two occurrences of the root that means "cry for help" (v. 6b, 6d; see also Pss 5:3; 22:24; 28:2; 30:2; 31:22; 34:15; 39:12; 72:12; 88:13; 145:19; Exod 2:23; Jonah 2:2). The repetition emphasizes the urgency of the situation,

108. James L. Mays, *Psalms* Interpretation (Louisville: John Knox, 1994) 90.

but God has heard. God's "temple" probably indicates God's heavenly abode, but the Jerusalem Temple symbolized the point where heaven touched earth, so it too may be implied here (see Ps 28:1-2).

18:7-19, God's Response. Preceding the actual account of deliverance (vv. 16-19) is an extended account of a theophany (vv. 7-15). God "was angry" (v. 7), because God's chosen agent was being threatened, and so God "came down" (v. 9). The language of theophany is generally expressive of God's presence and power (see Pss 50:2-3; 68:7-8). It occurs elsewhere in contexts that specifically assert God's sovereignty (see Pss 29:3-9; 97:1-5; 99:1; see also Psalm 144, which is reminiscent of Psalm 18 and where the plea for a theophany in vv. 5-8 accompanies in vv. 9-11 an appeal for deliverance and a celebration of the God who "rescues his servant David"). It occurs also in passages that celebrate God's historic deliverance of the people—exodus and entry into the land (cf. Ps 18:7, 15 with Exod 15:8, 10, 14-16 and Judg 5:4-5). The cosmic effects of God's coming down are emphasized by the repetition of "foundations" in vv. 7, 15. The cosmic dimension is also evident in the description of the threat—"mighty waters" (v. 16) and the phrase "confronted me" (v. 18), which recalls v. 5 and the deadly power of Sheol. The cosmic language is a reminder that the one threatened is the king, the earthly representative and sign of God's universal claim. To oppose God's anointed is to oppose God. At issue ultimately is God's sovereignty, and the deliverance of the king asserts God's rule. The deliverance is described in spatial terms (v. 19; see NRSV's "broad place" in Pss 31:8 and 118:5; the verb is used as a figure for deliverance in v. 36 and Ps 4:1; see also Exod 3:8, where an adjectival form of the root describes the promised land as "broad"). The rationale for the deliverance provides a transition to vv. 20-30 (see 1 Kgs 10:9; Pss 22:8; 41:11).

18:20-30, Character of the King and God. Just as the presence of the cosmic dimension in vv. 7-19 is attributable to the psalm's royal subject matter, so also is its presence in vv. 20-30. Verses 20-24 sound like the self-righteous boasting of the king, but the chiastic structure (see Introduction) of vv. 20-24 focuses attention on v. 22. That is, God's "ordinances" (more literally, "jus-

tices") and "statutes" are the source of the king's "righteousness" and "cleanness" (vv. 20, 24; see Pss 24:4; 73:1). In short, the king is simply saying that he has been what God has intended and enabled him to be (see Deut 17:18-10; Ps 72:1-7). In fact, v. 22 is reminiscent of Ps 1:1-2; the king is constantly open to God's instruction.

The king's dependence on God is reiterated in vv. 25-30, which are linked to vv. 20-24 by repetition of the words "blameless" (תמים tāmîm, vv. 23, 25; "perfect" in v. 30 is also the same Hebrew word) and "cleanness"/"pure" (vv. 20, 24, 26). This section ends by affirming God as "refuge," recalling not only v. 2 but also Ps 2:12. David was known as the "lamp of Israel" (2 Sam 21:17), and here the king says to God, "You light my lamp" (v. 28). The initial pronoun "you" in vv. 27-28 is emphatic, reinforcing God's initiative and the conclusion that the king's righteousness is but a reflection of God's own character. Verses 25-26 suggest even more strongly that the "loyal," "blameless," and "pure" are mirroring God's own character. Blamelessness means essentially completeness or reliability (see Ps 15:2). God's complete reliability (vv. 25, 30) enables the king to be "blameless" (v. 23)—to depend utterly on God (see also Ps 19:13, which clearly suggests that "blamelessness" does not mean sinlessness). Loyalty to or trust in God is well placed, for God is trustworthy and loyal (v. 25a). Not coincidentally, these crucial affirmations about God lie "at the psalm's midpoint" and perform the "pivotal function" of proclaiming why God delivers the king—namely, because God is steadfast in love.[109] The verb in "show yourself loyal" (חסד ḥsd, v. 25a) is the same root as the noun "steadfast love" (ḥesed, see v. 50), which more than any other word serves to describe what God is like (see Exod 34:6-7; Pss 5:7; 6:4; 13:5; Introduction). The word "shield" in v. 30, along with the word "refuge," recalls v. 2 and the series of metaphors for God.

18:31-50, The King's Response of Praise. The genre of vv. 31-50 may be a victory hymn, but the function is to articulate the king's praise for deliverance. There are clear lines of continuity with vv. 1-30. As in v. 1, God is the source of the psalmist's strength (vv. 32, 39). This affirma-

109. J. Kenneth Kuntz, "Psalm 18: A Rhetorical-Critical Analysis," *JSOT* 26 (1983) 19; see also 18.

tion is reinforced by repetition of the rock metaphor (vv. 2, 31, 46) as well as by the assertion that God "makes my way perfect" (v. 32), which corresponds to v. 30. In short, God protects the life and future of the king. God equips and prepares the king (vv. 33-36), enabling him to defeat his enemies (vv. 37-48). While the king shares in the action (vv. 37-38, 42), his victory is God's victory (vv. 40-41, 43-48, 50). It is evidence of God's sovereignty over peoples (v. 47) and nations (vv. 43, 49; see also Psalm 2), and it is testimony to God's steadfast love (v. 50; see also v. 25; 2 Sam 7:15).

REFLECTIONS

If Psalm 18 is viewed simply as a royal psalm of thanksgiving used by David or one of his descendants upon the occasion of a military victory, then it must be viewed essentially as a literary artifact—an interesting museum piece, but not something for contemporary handling and use. Taking a clue from Gerstenberger, however, the interpreter may move in a different direction. Gerstenberger's proposal that Psalm 18 was intended "to keep hope alive in hard-pressed Jewish communities" is all the more likely when we consider that, in some post-exilic circles, the promises originally attached to the Davidic monarchy were applied to the whole community (see, e.g., Isa 55:3-5, in which v. 5 even seems to echo Ps 18:43; see also Pss 105:15; 144; Introduction). In essence, then, Psalm 18 was and is a profession of faith in God's will and ability to reverse the fortunes of the humble and the oppressed (see v. 27). The focus is on God, as suggested from the beginning of the psalm with its impressive series of metaphors for God (v. 2). Donald K. Berry says of v. 2, "The effect is to focus acute attention upon Yahweh himself, a feature which flavors the reading of the entire poem."[110] In other words, Psalm 18 is more about God than about David; insofar as it is about David and his descendants, they represent persons who were chosen as agents of *God's* rule. Psalm 18, therefore, is a powerful affirmation of the cosmic, universal reign of God, and it is upon this foundation of faith that hope is built.

In the post-exilic era—indeed, always—the assertion of God's sovereignty is made amid circumstances and powers that deny it (see vv. 4-5). Psalm 18, therefore, like Psalm 2, is eschatological (see Commentary on Psalm 2; Introduction). It is no more evident in our day than it was in the post-exilic era that God rules the world. Yet that is exactly what Jesus preached (Mark 1:14-15) and what the church continues to proclaim as the basis of its hope.

This apparent disparity between what we proclaim and what is reality—evil, sin, violence, destruction—is precisely what calls us to a decision. It is the same decision with which Jesus confronted his hearers. Shall we enter the hidden reign of God, where strength is made perfect in weakness? Shall we trust that "this God" shows us the "way" that "is perfect," and thus is indeed a reliable "refuge" (v. 30)? If we decide to trust the righteous and steadfastly loving God rather than the forces of hatred and greed that are so evidently at work in the world, then we will find that we are in for a fight—like the king in Psalm 18 (vv. 33-42) and like King Jesus. Our fight, however, involves not waging war but waging peace. It will be no less a struggle, and, like the king in Psalm 18, we will need God's strength—indeed, the "whole armor of God" (Eph 6:11, 13; cf. Eph 6:10-17 with Ps 18:33-42; in Eph 6:10-17 as in Psalm 18, the battle has cosmic dimensions). At issue is nothing less than the ultimate question of who rules the world.

The circumstances and faith of the psalmist, as well the intent of Psalm 18 to keep hope alive, are captured in Jesus' parting words to his disciples: "Peace I leave with you; my peace I give to you. I do not give to you as the world gives. Do not let your hearts be troubled, and do not let them be afraid. . . . I have said this to you, so that in me you may have peace. In the world you face persecution. But take courage; I have conquered the world!" (John 14:27; 16:33 NRSV). Our hope is built on nothing less than the conviction that pervades Psalm

110. Donald K. Berry, *The Psalms and Their Readers: Interpretive Strategies for Psalm 18*, JSOTSup 153 (Sheffield: JSOT, 1993) 115.

18: God will ultimately fulfill God's steadfastly loving purposes for the world and for all its peoples (Ps 18:43-50; see John 3:16-17).

PSALM 19:1-14, GOD'S INSTRUCTION IS ALL-ENCOMPASSING

<table>
<tr><td>

NIV

Psalm 19

For the director of music. A psalm of David.

¹The heavens declare the glory of God;
  the skies proclaim the work of his hands.
²Day after day they pour forth speech;
  night after night they display knowledge.
³There is no speech or language
  where their voice is not heard.ᵃ
⁴Their voiceᵇ goes out into all the earth,
  their words to the ends of the world.

In the heavens he has pitched a tent for the sun,
⁵ which is like a bridegroom coming forth
      from his pavilion,
  like a champion rejoicing to run his course.
⁶It rises at one end of the heavens
  and makes its circuit to the other;
  nothing is hidden from its heat.

⁷The law of the LORD is perfect,
  reviving the soul.
 The statutes of the LORD are trustworthy,
  making wise the simple.
⁸The precepts of the LORD are right,
  giving joy to the heart.
 The commands of the LORD are radiant,
  giving light to the eyes.
⁹The fear of the LORD is pure,
  enduring forever.
 The ordinances of the LORD are sure
  and altogether righteous.
¹⁰They are more precious than gold,
  than much pure gold;
 they are sweeter than honey,
  than honey from the comb.
¹¹By them is your servant warned;
  in keeping them there is great reward.

ᵃ3 Or They have no speech, there are no words; / no sound is heard from them   *ᵇ4 Septuagint, Jerome and Syriac; Hebrew line*

</td><td>

NRSV

Psalm 19

To the leader. A Psalm of David.

¹ The heavens are telling the glory of God;
  and the firmamentᵃ proclaims his
    handiwork.
² Day to day pours forth speech,
  and night to night declares knowledge.
³ There is no speech, nor are there words;
  their voice is not heard;
⁴ yet their voiceᵇ goes out through all the
    earth,
  and their words to the end of the world.

In the heavensᶜ he has set a tent for the
    sun,
⁵ which comes out like a bridegroom from
    his wedding canopy,
  and like a strong man runs its course
    with joy.
⁶ Its rising is from the end of the heavens,
  and its circuit to the end of them;
  and nothing is hid from its heat.

⁷ The law of the LORD is perfect,
  reviving the soul;
 the decrees of the LORD are sure,
  making wise the simple;
⁸ the precepts of the LORD are right,
  rejoicing the heart;
 the commandment of the LORD is clear,
  enlightening the eyes;
⁹ the fear of the LORD is pure,
  enduring forever;
 the ordinances of the LORD are true
  and righteous altogether.
¹⁰ More to be desired are they than gold,
  even much fine gold;

ᵃOr dome   *ᵇGk Jerome Compare Syr: Hcb line*   *ᶜHeb In them*

</td></tr>
</table>

NIV

12Who can discern his errors?
    Forgive my hidden faults.
13Keep your servant also from willful sins;
    may they not rule over me.
Then will I be blameless,
    innocent of great transgression.

14May the words of my mouth and the
        meditation of my heart
    be pleasing in your sight,
    O LORD, my Rock and my Redeemer.

NRSV

sweeter also than honey,
    and drippings of the honeycomb.

11 Moreover by them is your servant warned;
    in keeping them there is great reward.
12 But who can detect their errors?
    Clear me from hidden faults.
13 Keep back your servant also from the
        insolent;a
    do not let them have dominion over me.
Then I shall be blameless,
    and innocent of great transgression.

14 Let the words of my mouth and the
        meditation of my heart
    be acceptable to you,
    O LORD, my rock and my redeemer.

aOr from proud thoughts

COMMENTARY

Like Psalms 1 and 119, Psalm 19 highlights the importance of God's *torah,* "instruction" (v. 7, "law"). Despite the fact that Psalm 19 can be understood as an artistic unity, scholars have often divided it into two separate poems: Psalm 19A (vv. 1-6), which deals with creation, and Psalm 19B (vv. 7-14), which deals with *torah.* This approach, however, failed to detect that there are actually three separate sections to the psalm: (1) vv. 1-6, (2) vv. 7-10, (3) vv. 11-14. While vv. 1-6 do focus on creation and vv. 7-10 on *torah,* vv. 11-14 focus on the psalmist, "your servant" (vv. 11, 13), and the words and thoughts the psalmist offers to God (v. 14).

The traditional approach also failed to detect unifying features of the psalm. For instance, "speech" (vv. 2-3) and "words" (v. 14) are the same Hebrew word (אמר *'ōmer*), thus linking vv. 11-14 to vv. 1-6. And "perfect" (v. 7) is the same Hebrew word as "blameless" (v. 13), linking vv. 11-14 to vv. 7-10. On a conceptual level, the theme of the rising and setting of the "sun" unifies the three parts. The sun is explicitly mentioned in v. 4, and language that describes the effects of the sun is applied to *torah* in vv. 7-10 and 11-14—"giving light" (v. 8) and "illuminated" (v.

11; the NIV and the NRSV prefer another sense of the word with their translation "warned"). Nahum M. Sarna even suggests that each of the attributes and actions of *torah* in vv. 7-10 is applied to the sun god in various ancient Near Eastern texts. He proposes that Psalm 19 was composed as "a tacit polemic" in the time of Josiah to oppose the Assyrian-influenced worship of astral deities, including the sun.[111] In any case, to hear Psalm 19 as a unity is to appreciate its bold and sweeping claims about God's *torah,* "instruction." In short, Psalm 19 intends to teach. Its instructional intent may be emphasized by its placement within a series of royal psalms (Psalms 18, 20–21); that is, Psalm 19, especially vv. 7-14, describes the orientation to life that faithful kings were supposed to embody and model for the people (see Pss 18:20-30; 21:7; note especially the repetition of "blameless" in 18:23, 25 and 19:13).[112]

19:1-6. As traditional commentary has recognized, vv. 1-6 focus on creation. The sun was an object of worship in the ancient Near East, and it is likely that an original hymn to the sun lies

111. Nahum M. Sarna, *Songs of the Heart* (New York: Schocken, 1993) 74.
112. See Leslie C. Allen, "David as Exemplar of Spirituality: The Redactional Function of Psalm 19," *Biblica* 67 (1986) 544-46.

behind vv. 1-6. But here the sun is not a god. Rather, along with the heavens, the firmament, and day and night (see Genesis 1), the sun is a created object that testifies to the sovereignty of its creator. The testimony is characterized first as "glory," a word that often appears in contexts that explicitly affirm that God reigns (see Pss 24:7-10; 29:1-3, 9; 145:5, 12). Without actually speaking, the universe itself instructs humanity (see "knowledge," v. 2) about God's rule. No corner of the cosmos is unreached. The "words" of day and night reach "to the end of the world" (the word for "world" here often occurs in contexts that celebrate God's reign; see Pss 93:1; 96:10; 97:4; 98:7, 9), and the course of the sun reaches to "the end of the heavens" (v. 6). The heat of the sun, from which nothing is hidden, suggests the sun's pervasive, energizing, life-giving power.

19:7-10. As suggested above, the movement from vv. 1-6 to v. 7 has caused problems for many commentators, but the transition is really not so abrupt. In vv. 1-6, the created order has proclaimed God's sovereignty, and it is the privilege and responsibility of a sovereign to provide life-sustaining guidance and instruction for the servants (see vv. 11, 13; see also Ps 93:1, 5, where the assertion of God's reign culminates in an assessment of God's decrees that is similar to Ps 19:7b). This *torah,* "instruction," is the focus of vv. 7-10. Verse 7a would be translated better as: "The instruction of the LORD is all-encompassing, restoring life." As vv. 4b-6 describe the all-encompassing circuit of the sun, so v. 7a asserts that God's *torah* is all-encompassing. Because "nothing is hidden from its heat" (v. 6b), the sun constantly energizes the earth and makes life possible. So it is, the psalmist claims, with God's *torah*; it makes life possible. In short, when vv. 7-10 are heard following vv. 1-6, they present *torah* on a cosmic scale. God's instruction is built into the very structure of the universe, and life depends on *torah* as much as it depends on the daily rising of the sun.

Following the mention of *torah* in v. 7a are five more words that describe God's revelation, each of which is accompanied by a phrase that either indicates the effect of God's word on humanity (vv. 7b-8) or further elaborates the nature of God's word (v. 9). God's *torah* accomplishes what God intends for human life: wisdom (see

Deut 4:6; Ps 2:10), joy (see Ps 4:8), enlightenment (see Ps 36:9). The "fear of the LORD" in v. 9a actually describes not God's revelation but the human response of conformity to God's word. Living by God's word makes one pure. The word for "pure" (טהורה *ṭĕhôrâ*) elsewhere indicates ritual cleanness, which could be conditional and temporary (see Lev 7:19; 13:13, 17, 37; 15:8). Living by *torah,* however, constitutes a cleanness that endures. The word "ordinances" (משפטים *mišpāṭîm*) in v. 9b is literally "judgments"/"justices"; the Hebrew root is often paired with the word "righteous," as here (see also Amos 5:24). In short, living by *torah* constitutes righteousness—life as God intends it. Neither wealth nor the richest food can make life possible the way that God's instruction does (v. 10), because God's *torah* makes accessible to humanity the "speech" and "knowledge" of the cosmos. It is revealing that the personal name for God, Yahweh ("LORD"), occurs six times in vv. 7-9, whereas it does not occur at all in vv. 1-6. What makes life possible is relatedness to God, and this personal relatedness is mediated by *torah.* The creation speaks (vv. 1-6), but more important, God has spoken a personal word to humanity that enables the human creature to live in harmony with God and with the whole creation (vv. 7-10).

Indeed, this is the "great reward" of v. 11. The phrase would be better translated "great consequence" in order to avoid the implication that God's *torah* represents a mechanistic system of reward and punishment for obedience and disobedience. God's *torah* does not consist of a static body of revelation but a dynamic, living relationship. The great consequence of keeping God's *torah* is fundamentally the same thing that Ps 1:3 means when it says that those who meditate constantly on God's *torah* "prosper." The prosperity or reward consists of connection to the true source of life: God (see Commentary on Psalm 1).

19:11-14. That the psalmist means by *torah* something other than a static system of reward/punishment is further indicated by vv. 12-14. In the final analysis, even God's personal instruction to humanity is not sufficient to ensure that human behavior will be in harmony with God and God's ordering of the world. Verse 12 indicates that inevitably there will be "errors" and "hidden faults." Verses 12b-13b are essentially a petition for forgiveness, and v. 13c suggests that the psalmist will be "blameless" (see "perfect" in v. 7a; see also Pss 15:2; 18:23, 25, 30, 32) and "innocent" (the word is from the same root [נקה nqh] as "forgive" in v. 12b) as a result of God's grace. To be "blameless" is not to be sinless but to live in dependence upon God (see Commentary on Psalms 15; 18). This dependence upon God for forgiveness and for life itself is what makes one's words and thoughts "acceptable" to God (v. 14). By the grace of God, the psalmist's words are in harmony with the "speech" (vv. 2-3) of the cosmos. In other contexts, "acceptable" designates a worthy sacrifice (see Exod 28:38; Lev 22:19-20). Thus Ps 19:14 suggests that the kind of sacrifice God ultimately desires consists of human lives that are lived in humble dependence upon God (see Pss 50:22-23; 51:15-17; Rom 12:1-2).

The psalmist's address of God as "my rock" reinforces this conclusion; the psalmist's strength is from God (see Ps 18:2, 31, 46). The address of God as "my redeemer" suggests that this strength is experienced very personally. The term derives from the realm of family relationships, where it was the responsibility of family members to buy back, or "redeem," relatives who had fallen into slavery (see Lev 25:47-49). Thus "redeemer" connotes intimacy; the NRSV sometimes translates גאל (gōʾēl) as "next of kin" (see Ruth 4:1, 3). Considering the way Psalm 19 begins, the implications of this address are astounding: The God who set the sun on its course is the same God the psalmist has experienced personally as "my next of kin"!

REFLECTIONS

C. S. Lewis considered Psalm 19 to be "the greatest poem in the Psalter and one of the greatest lyrics in the world."[113] As remarkable as the lyrical quality of Psalm 19, however, is its extraordinary theological claim. In essence, Psalm 19 affirms that love *is* the basic reality. According to the psalmist, the God whose sovereignty is proclaimed by cosmic voices is the God who has addressed a personal word to humankind—God's *torah*. Furthermore, this God is experienced ultimately by humankind not as a cosmic enforcer but as a forgiving next of kin! God is love, and love is the force that drives the cosmos. This is, indeed, an extraordinary thought!

This extraordinary thought has radical implications for a scientifically oriented, secular culture. Psalm 19 is not anti-science, but it does offer a view of the universe as something more than an object to be studied and controlled. To be sure, nature is not divine, but it is incomprehensible apart from God. In some sense, nature "knows" God (v. 2), and thus it can proclaim God's sovereignty. In short, like the human who addresses God as "next of kin" (see v. 14), the creation is related to God. On some level, we are *all* part of the same family. The Hebrew language itself recognizes the family resemblance—the word for "humanity" is אדם (ʾādām), and the word for "earth"/"ground" is אדמה (ʾădāmâ). The ecological implications of this view of the world are astounding. In God's ordering of the cosmos, the future of the creature is linked inextricably to the future of the creation.

None of this implies that Psalm 19 offers simply a natural theology. The creation does offer knowledge (v. 2), but God has also addressed a personal word to humanity: God's *torah,* which makes human life possible (v. 7a) and orders it rightly (v. 9b). Again, the implications are radical. Human life can be adequately understood only in relationship to God. This is the antithesis of secularity and its creed of autonomy (see Commentary on Psalm 1). According to the psalmist, humans live not by our ability to earn, achieve, or possess (see v. 10, which suggests the insufficiency of money and the finest food), but by "every word that comes from the mouth of God" (Matt 4:4 NRSV; see Deut 8:3).

113. C. S. Lewis, *Reflections on the Psalms* (New York: Harcourt, Brace, and Company, 1986) 63.

The juxtaposition of creation and *torah,* then, is theologically significant. Not surprisingly, the same juxtaposition characterizes the Pentateuch, where the story of creation (the book of Genesis) precedes the story of redemption from bondage and revelation at Sinai (the book of Exodus). What this movement suggests is that creation is not secondary. God's instruction to humanity works toward the fulfillment of God's creational purposes (see Commentary on Psalms 33; 65–66). The love that motivated God to create humankind and bear the burden of human disobedience (Genesis 1–11) is the same love manifested in the story of Israel (see esp. Exodus 32–34), in the life of the psalmist (vv. 11-14), and, as Christians profess, in the life, death, and resurrection of Jesus. Love is the basic reality of the universe.

PSALM 20:1-9, WE TRUST IN THE NAME OF THE LORD OUR GOD

NIV	NRSV
Psalm 20	Psalm 20
For the director of music. A psalm of David.	To the leader. A Psalm of David.

NIV

Psalm 20

For the director of music. A psalm of David.

¹May the LORD answer you when you are in
distress;
  may the name of the God of Jacob protect
  you.
²May he send you help from the sanctuary
  and grant you support from Zion.
³May he remember all your sacrifices
  and accept your burnt offerings.   *Selah*
⁴May he give you the desire of your heart
  and make all your plans succeed.
⁵We will shout for joy when you are victorious
  and will lift up our banners in the name of
  our God.
May the LORD grant all your requests.

⁶Now I know that the LORD saves his anointed;
  he answers him from his holy heaven
  with the saving power of his right hand.
⁷Some trust in chariots and some in horses,
  but we trust in the name of the LORD our
  God.
⁸They are brought to their knees and fall,
  but we rise up and stand firm.

⁹O LORD, save the king!
  Answer[a] us when we call!

[a]9 Or *save! / O King, answer*

NRSV

Psalm 20

To the leader. A Psalm of David.

¹ The LORD answer you in the day of trouble!
  The name of the God of Jacob protect you!
² May he send you help from the sanctuary,
  and give you support from Zion.
³ May he remember all your offerings,
  and regard with favor your burnt
  sacrifices.   *Selah*

⁴ May he grant you your heart's desire,
  and fulfill all your plans.
⁵ May we shout for joy over your victory,
  and in the name of our God set up our
  banners.
May the LORD fulfill all your petitions.

⁶ Now I know that the LORD will help his
  anointed;
  he will answer him from his holy heaven
  with mighty victories by his right hand.
⁷ Some take pride in chariots, and some in
  horses,
  but our pride is in the name of the LORD
  our God.
⁸ They will collapse and fall,
  but we shall rise and stand upright.

⁹ Give victory to the king, O LORD;
  answer us when we call.[a]

[a] Gk: Heb *give victory, O LORD; let the King answer us when we call*

COMMENTARY

Psalm 20 is almost unanimously classified as a royal psalm, due to the mention of the "anointed" (v. 6) and "the king" (v. 9). The uniqueness of the psalm lies in the fact that only v. 9 is an actual prayer. This peculiarity raises the question of its origin and setting. Several features point to a liturgical ceremony in the Temple: the mention of "sanctuary" and Zion in v. 2 and sacrifices in v. 3, as well as the public character of the psalm and the king's need to pray for help (vv. 1, 4-5). The traditional conclusion is that Psalm 20 was performed originally in the Temple as a king prepared to go into battle. The king was there to pray for help (see 1 Sam 7:7-11; 13:9-12; 1 Kgs 8:44-45), and the people wished him well in the name of God (vv. 1-5), professed their faith in God's help for king and nation (vv. 6-8), and prayed directly for the king and themselves (v. 9).

This proposal may well account for the original use of Psalm 20; however, it may also be insufficient for understanding how the psalm was finally heard and how it functions in the psalter as a literary collection. As suggested about Psalm 18, another royal psalm that has to do with the king in battle (see esp. vv. 31-50), the psalm is really more about God than it is about the king. The same is true about Psalm 20. While the king is not unimportant, the primary actor in the psalm is God. The post-exilic and subsequent generations of God's people would have preserved and transmitted the psalm not so much as a historical recollection of a long-lost monarchy but as testimony to God's continuing ability to save the people. This is especially likely when one considers that the promises attached to the monarchy seem to have been applied to the people as a whole (see Psalms 18; 144; 149; Isa 55:3-5; Introduction).

The three key words in Psalm 20 emphasize the role of God. The word "answer" (ענה 'ānâ) occurs three times, including the first and last verses (vv. 1, 6, 9). God must answer if there is going to be "help"/"victory"/"victories" (ישע yš'). This word occurs four times (vv. 5, 6, 9; see NIV, "save," "saving power"). Psalm 20 illustrates the affirmation of the concluding verse of Psalm 3: "From the LORD comes deliverance" (Ps 3:8; the Hebrew root is again yš'). The threefold occur-rence of "name" (vv. 1, 5, 7) also emphasizes God's primacy. The "name" of God not only is synonymous with God's presence and power, but also suggests the importance of identity and character. It is to God's character that the people appeal, and God's character will assure the future of king and people.

20:1-5. The wishes expressed in vv. 1-5 are for the protection and welfare of the king, but the subject of each verb is God (with the exception of v. 5a). In the light of the mention of the "God of Jacob" in v. 1b, it is perhaps not surprising that v. 1a recalls Jacob's words in Gen 35:3 (see "answer" also in Pss 3:4; 4:1). As here, God's protection is associated with God's name in Ps 91:14. Verses 1-2 are reminiscent of Ps 18:6, where help for the king also comes from God's dwelling in a time of distress. As suggested above, vv. 3-5 seem to indicate an original liturgical setting. Sacrifices regularly accompanied prayers for help, and help is precisely what the king needs (vv. 4, 5b). As reflected in vv. 4, 5b, it was the prerogative of the king to make requests of God (see Commentary on Ps 2:8-9; see also 1 Kgs 3:5-14; Ps 21:4). Verse 5a indicates that the welfare and future of the people are bound up with that of the king.

20:6-8. The same reality is evident in these verses. Help from God for the "anointed" (v. 6; see Pss 2:2; 18:50; 28:8; 89:38, 51; 132:10, 17) accompanies the deliverance of the people. In contrast to those who "trust" in the instruments of warfare, the people of God trust God (v. 7; see Ps 33:16-17). The verb that the NIV translates as "trust" (זכר zākar) more literally means "to cause to remember." Thus persons who cause God's name to be remembered will live (v. 8). Memory leads to hope.

20:9. Verse 9 can be construed in several ways, as the NRSV note suggests. Both the NRSV and the NIV have chosen to follow the LXX, which seems to make more sense than the Hebrew. As these translations construe v. 9, it is a prayer for both king and people. This is particularly appropriate in the light of vv. 6-8, and it also made and makes the psalm more appropriate for the generations of God's people that came after the disappearance of the monarchy.

REFLECTIONS

1. On one level, it is possible to hear Psalm 20 as nothing more than a piece of ancient Judean political propaganda—that is, God is on our side, and God will give us the victory. It seems to be an ancient example of the kind of thinking that is so dangerous and frightening in our day, thinking that leads people to conclude that God sanctions whatever our nation does and to label our opponents as evil empires.

On the other hand, it is possible to hear Psalm 20 quite differently, building upon the insight that the primary actor in the psalm is God, not the king or the people. Keeping this in mind, we can hear in Psalm 20 the lesson that the people of any nation in some sense depend on their leaders, as well as the admonition that both the people and their leaders are to depend on God. Mays concludes:

> As Scripture the psalm teaches the church to pray for those who hold the power of office, because they, like us, are dependent on the LORD. It warns against ever letting our dependence on their service turn into the trust we owe to God alone. It warns against allowing their fascination with military strength to make us support policies based on trust in military might.[114]

In other words, Psalm 20 is actually anti-militaristic. It exhorts us to submit our will to God's will rather than pretend that our will is God's will. It is another invitation to live under God's reign (see Introduction): "Thy kingdom come, thy will be done."

2. The Christian tradition has often read Psalm 20 christologically, especially on the basis of v. 6. If this approach is followed, one should not hear v. 6 as a prediction of Jesus' coming. Rather, Christians may see in Jesus the "anointed one" (*messiah*) who really did submit himself fully to God's will (see Mark 14:36), who did not resort to violence on account of his complete trust in God, and who gathered around himself a community of people who also professed to find life as "we trust in the name of the LORD our God" (v. 7).

114. James L. Mays, *Psalms,* Interpretation (Louisville: John Knox, 1994) 103.

PSALM 21:1-13, THE KING TRUSTS IN THE LORD

NIV

Psalm 21

For the director of music. A psalm of David.

[1]O LORD, the king rejoices in your strength.
  How great is his joy in the victories you
    give!
[2]You have granted him the desire of his heart
  and have not withheld the request of his
    lips. *Selah*
[3]You welcomed him with rich blessings
  and placed a crown of pure gold on his
    head.
[4]He asked you for life, and you gave it to
    him—

NRSV

Psalm 21

To the leader. A Psalm of David.

[1] In your strength the king rejoices, O LORD,
  and in your help how greatly he exults!
[2] You have given him his heart's desire,
  and have not withheld the request of his
    lips. *Selah*
[3] For you meet him with rich blessings;
  you set a crown of fine gold on his head.
[4] He asked you for life; you gave it to him—
  length of days forever and ever.
[5] His glory is great through your help;
  splendor and majesty you bestow on him.

NIV

length of days, for ever and ever.
[5]Through the victories you gave, his glory is
    great;
    you have bestowed on him splendor and
    majesty.
[6]Surely you have granted him eternal blessings
    and made him glad with the joy of your
    presence.
[7]For the king trusts in the LORD;
    through the unfailing love of the Most High
    he will not be shaken.

[8]Your hand will lay hold on all your enemies;
    your right hand will seize your foes.
[9]At the time of your appearing
    you will make them like a fiery furnace.
In his wrath the LORD will swallow them up,
    and his fire will consume them.
[10]You will destroy their descendants from the
    earth,
    their posterity from mankind.
[11]Though they plot evil against you
    and devise wicked schemes, they cannot
    succeed;
[12]for you will make them turn their backs
    when you aim at them with drawn bow.

[13]Be exalted, O LORD, in your strength;
    we will sing and praise your might.

NRSV

[6]You bestow on him blessings forever;
    you make him glad with the joy of your
    presence.
[7]For the king trusts in the LORD,
    and through the steadfast love of the
    Most High he shall not be moved.

[8]Your hand will find out all your enemies;
    your right hand will find out those who
    hate you.
[9]You will make them like a fiery furnace
    when you appear.
The LORD will swallow them up in his
    wrath,
    and fire will consume them.
[10]You will destroy their offspring from the
    earth,
    and their children from among
    humankind.
[11]If they plan evil against you,
    if they devise mischief, they will not
    succeed.
[12]For you will put them to flight;
    you will aim at their faces with your
    bows.

[13]Be exalted, O LORD, in your strength!
    We will sing and praise your power.

COMMENTARY

Like Psalm 20, to which it is closely linked, Psalm 21 is a royal psalm. Verses 1-6 are a thankful celebration of the fulfillment of the wishes expressed for the king in Ps 20:1-5 (cf. 20:4 and 21:2) and of the arrival of the anticipated "victory"/"help" from God in Ps 20:5-9 (see the Hebrew root for "help"/"victories" [ישע *yšʿ*] in 20:5, 6, 9; 21:1, 5).

Verse 7 is the structural center of the psalm and also its theological heart. This verse makes it clear that Psalm 21, like other royal psalms (see 2; 18; 20; Introduction), is really more about God than about the king. The king lives in dependence upon God and God's loving purposes, as vv. 1-6 have already described. As the midpoint of the psalm, v. 7 is transitional. Whereas vv. 1-6 ad-dressed God directly, vv. 8-12 address the king (although there is some ambiguity here), antici-pating future victories. Verse 13 again focuses attention directly on God and on God's "strength," recalling the mention of God's "strength" in v. 1 and forming an envelope struc-ture. In other words, everything that can be said about the king begins and ends with God's strength.

Like Psalm 20, Psalm 21 may have been used originally in a military context, either upon the king's departure for or return from battle. Several scholars suggest that it may have been used as a coronation ritual (see v. 3; Psalm 2) or as a liturgy for the anniversary of a king's coronation. In any case, it is clear that the psalm must have functioned differently in the post-exilic era and that it functions differently in its current literary setting. Gerstenberger concludes: "As a possible synagogal prayer—which it became in any case, earlier or later—it would have implored the protection and help of Yahweh for the local congregation, which still existed in the traditions of the past."[115] Because the real subject of Psalm 21 is God's sovereignty, the psalm can continue to serve for every generation of God's people as an affirmation of trust in God and in God's commitment to the people and their future (see esp. v. 7).

21:1-6. The focus on God's sovereignty is evident in v. 1. God's strength is elsewhere explicitly associated with God's reign (Pss 29:1; 93:1; 96:6-7; 99:4; see also Exod 15:13, 18). God's "strength" and "help" are determinative, not the king's. As suggested above, vv. 1-2 recall Psalm 20. Verse 1 repeats the key word "help" (יְשׁוּעָה *yĕšûʿâ*; see Ps 20:5, 6, 9), and v. 2 asserts that the wish of 20:4 has been answered. In fact, every good thing the king enjoys has come from God—the king's office (v. 3b; see Ps 2:6-7) and the eminence associated with royalty (v. 5), abundant daily provision (see "blessings" in vv. 3, 7; see also Pss 45:2; 72:15), indeed, life itself (v. 4; see 1 Kgs 3:11). The gift of life and the attendant blessings are to endure "forever" (vv. 4, 6; see Ps 72:17). Such language should probably be understood as poetic hyperbole rather than an indication of the king's divinity, although some ancient Near Eastern cultures did view the king as divine. Although different Hebrew words are used, the concept of joy (vv. 1, 6) envelopes the first section. Again, the source is God's character and activity—indeed, God's very "presence" (v. 6; lit., "your face").

21:7. Considering the list of benefits the king has experienced from God (vv. 1-6), it appears that the king's trust in God is well-founded. In any case, it is significant that the king is to relate

115. Erhard S. Gerstenberger, *Psalms, Part 1, with an Introduction to Cultic Poetry,* Forms of the OT Literature 14 (Grand Rapids: Eerdmans, 1988) 108.

to God just as any faithful Israelite should: by trusting God (see Pss 4:5; 9:10; 22:4-5; 31:6; 32:10; see also 2 Kgs 18:5) and by depending on God's steadfast love (see Pss 5:7; 31:7, 16, 21; 32:10; Introduction; note that "trust" and "steadfast love" are associated in Pss 31:6-7; 32:10; see also 2 Sam 7:15; 1 Kgs 3:6). Like other psalmists, the king "shall not be moved" (see Pss 15:5; 16:8; 62:2, 6; note the occurrence of "trust" in 62:8 and "steadfast love" in 62:12). The reason why is God.

21:8-12. Most commentators understand vv. 8-12 as being addressed to the king. Several commentators, however, construe the addressee as God. The ambiguity is theologically appropriate. The king's victories, described in vv. 8-12, are God's doing, as v. 9b makes explicit. In any case, whereas God's blessing (that is, daily provision) of the king is elaborated in vv. 1-6, God's saving help (vv. 1, 5) is described in detail in vv. 8-12. Verse 10 seems particularly brutal, but such rhetoric was standard ancient Near Eastern fare for communicating victory (see 2 Kgs 8:12; Ps 137:8-9; Isa 13:16; Hos 10:14; 13:16; Nah 3:10). Other descriptions in the royal psalms of the king's relationship to the nations are more uplifting (see, e.g., Ps 72:17b).

21:13. This verse clearly addresses God directly. The imperative "Be exalted" may have been intended as an ascription of praise, as v. 13b seems to suggest (see Pss 46:11; 99:2). Given the military context of vv. 8-12, it could be understood as a request for God to arise—namely, in preparation for battle, as in the holy war traditions. Strength is exerted elsewhere by God against enemies (see Exod 15:13; Pss 66:3; 68:28; 77:15), and "power" occurs often in military contexts (see Ps 20:6). In either case, by referring again to God's strength (see v. 1), v. 13 reinforces the conclusion that both the king and the people depend for their lives and futures on the presence and power of God, which is experienced as steadfast love.

REFLECTIONS

As was the case with Psalm 20, it is possible to see in Psalm 21 a literary artifact of the monarchical period; however, it can be more. Like Psalms 2; 18; 20 and other royal psalms,

Psalm 21 is ultimately testimony to God's sovereignty, not the king's sovereignty. Corresponding to Psalm 20, in which the people profess, "We trust in the name of the LORD our God" (v. 7), is the assertion in Psalm 21 that "the king trusts in the LORD" (the Hebrew words translated "trust" differ; see Commentary on Ps 20:7). In essence, the king is portrayed in Psalm 21 as the model of faith, one who lives not in dependence upon self but in dependence upon God. The king thus demonstrates what Psalm 1 means by happiness and prosperity (see vv. 1, 3) and what Psalm 2 means by taking refuge in God (see v. 12). The king may be surrounded by foes (21:8-12), but he knows that there is "help . . . in God" (Ps 3:2; see "deliver"/"deliverance" in 3:7-8; cf. 21:1, 5).

While the king is presented here as the model of faith (see Deut 17:14-20), and while a few kings actually embodied this model (see 2 Kgs 18:5-7), the monarchy for the most part modeled self-assertion and self-reliance. Even Solomon, who asked God for understanding and discernment (1 Kgs 3:3-14) rather than for more material things (cf. 1 Kgs 3:11 with Ps 21:2-6), could not manage finally to control his desire for riches, power, and fame (see 1 Kgs 5:13-14; 6:38–7:1; 11:1-13). King Ahaz, invited by the prophet Isaiah to trust God's ability to deliver, appealed instead to Assyrian military might for security (Isa 7:1-17). Even Hezekiah, who is commended for his trust in 2 Kgs 18:5, lapsed in his later years (Isaiah 39). In actuality, the king often did not trust God; neither did the people, and neither do we.

It would fall to Jesus to model authentic kingship and authentic humanity. The ancient kings were known as sons of God (see Ps 2:7) and were viewed in some sense as sharing God's sovereignty and even God's attributes (see Ps 21:5). Christians profess Jesus Messiah as Son of God, sharing God's sovereignty and attributes to the point of being fully divine as well as fully human. King Jesus "did not regard equality with God as something to be exploited, but emptied himself, taking the form of a slave" (Phil 2:6-7 NRSV). Jesus "humbled himself" (Phil 2:8) in the way that kings, living in dependence upon God, were supposed to do (Ps 21:7). He served as kings were supposed to do (see Psalm 72), and he called his followers to do the same (Mark 8:34-35). The basics of faithfulness are present in Psalms 20–21: trusting God and living in dependence on God's steadfast love (20:7; 21:7)—even if leaders and people, then and now, fail to measure up.

PSALM 22:1-31, MY GOD, MY GOD, WHY HAVE YOU FORSAKEN ME?

NIV	NRSV
Psalm 22	Psalm 22
For the director of music. To ˌthe tune ofˌ "The Doe of the Morning." A psalm of David.	To the leader: according to The Deer of the Dawn. A Psalm of David.
¹My God, my God, why have you forsaken me? Why are you so far from saving me, so far from the words of my groaning? ²O my God, I cry out by day, but you do not answer, by night, and am not silent. ³Yet you are enthroned as the Holy One;	¹ My God, my God, why have you forsaken me? Why are you so far from helping me, from the words of my groaning? ² O my God, I cry by day, but you do not answer; and by night, but find no rest.

NIV

you are the praise of Israel.[a]
⁴In you our fathers put their trust;
    they trusted and you delivered them.
⁵They cried to you and were saved;
    in you they trusted and were not
        disappointed.

⁶But I am a worm and not a man,
    scorned by men and despised by the
        people.
⁷All who see me mock me;
    they hurl insults, shaking their heads:
⁸"He trusts in the LORD;
    let the LORD rescue him.
 Let him deliver him,
    since he delights in him."

⁹Yet you brought me out of the womb;
    you made me trust in you
        even at my mother's breast.
¹⁰From birth I was cast upon you;
    from my mother's womb you have been
        my God.
¹¹Do not be far from me,
    for trouble is near
    and there is no one to help.

¹²Many bulls surround me;
    strong bulls of Bashan encircle me.
¹³Roaring lions tearing their prey
    open their mouths wide against me.
¹⁴I am poured out like water,
    and all my bones are out of joint.
 My heart has turned to wax;
    it has melted away within me.
¹⁵My strength is dried up like a potsherd,
    and my tongue sticks to the roof of my
        mouth;
    you lay me[b] in the dust of death.
¹⁶Dogs have surrounded me;
    a band of evil men has encircled me,
    they have pierced[c] my hands and my feet.
¹⁷I can count all my bones;
    people stare and gloat over me.
¹⁸They divide my garments among them
    and cast lots for my clothing.

¹⁹But you, O LORD, be not far off;
    O my Strength, come quickly to help me.

a3 Or *Yet you are holy, / enthroned on the praises of Israel*   b15 Or
/ *I am laid*   c16 Some Hebrew manuscripts, Septuagint and Syriac;
most Hebrew manuscripts / *like the lion,*

NRSV

³ Yet you are holy,
    enthroned on the praises of Israel.
⁴ In you our ancestors trusted;
    they trusted, and you delivered them.
⁵ To you they cried, and were saved;
    in you they trusted, and were not put to
        shame.

⁶ But I am a worm, and not human;
    scorned by others, and despised by the
        people.
⁷ All who see me mock at me;
    they make mouths at me, they shake
        their heads;
⁸ "Commit your cause to the LORD; let him
        deliver—
    let him rescue the one in whom he
        delights!"

⁹ Yet it was you who took me from the
        womb;
    you kept me safe on my mother's breast.
¹⁰ On you I was cast from my birth,
    and since my mother bore me you have
        been my God.
¹¹ Do not be far from me,
    for trouble is near
    and there is no one to help.

¹² Many bulls encircle me,
    strong bulls of Bashan surround me;
¹³ they open wide their mouths at me,
    like a ravening and roaring lion.

¹⁴ I am poured out like water,
    and all my bones are out of joint;
 my heart is like wax;
    it is melted within my breast;
¹⁵ my mouth[a] is dried up like a potsherd,
    and my tongue sticks to my jaws;
    you lay me in the dust of death.

¹⁶ For dogs are all around me;
    a company of evildoers encircles me.
 My hands and feet have shriveled;[b]
¹⁷ I can count all my bones.
 They stare and gloat over me;
¹⁸ they divide my clothes among themselves,

a Cn: Heb *strength*   b Meaning of Heb uncertain

NIV

^{20}Deliver my life from the sword,
my precious life from the power of the
dogs.
^{21}Rescue me from the mouth of the lions;
save^a me from the horns of the wild oxen.

^{22}I will declare your name to my brothers;
in the congregation I will praise you.
^{23}You who fear the LORD, praise him!
All you descendants of Jacob, honor him!
Revere him, all you descendants of Israel!
^{24}For he has not despised or disdained
the suffering of the afflicted one;
he has not hidden his face from him
but has listened to his cry for help.

^{25}From you comes the theme of my praise in
the great assembly;
before those who fear you^b will I fulfill my
vows.
^{26}The poor will eat and be satisfied;
they who seek the LORD will praise him—
may your hearts live forever!
^{27}All the ends of the earth
will remember and turn to the LORD,
and all the families of the nations
will bow down before him,
^{28}for dominion belongs to the LORD
and he rules over the nations.

^{29}All the rich of the earth will feast and
worship;
all who go down to the dust will kneel
before him—
those who cannot keep themselves alive.
^{30}Posterity will serve him;
future generations will be told about the
Lord.
^{31}They will proclaim his righteousness
to a people yet unborn—
for he has done it.

^{a}21 Or / you have heard ^{b}25 Hebrew *him*

NRSV

and for my clothing they cast lots.

^{19} But you, O LORD, do not be far away!
O my help, come quickly to my aid!
^{20} Deliver my soul from the sword,
my life^a from the power of the dog!
^{21} Save me from the mouth of the lion!

From the horns of the wild oxen you have
rescued^b me.
^{22} I will tell of your name to my brothers and sisters;^{c}
in the midst of the congregation I will
praise you:
^{23} You who fear the LORD, praise him!
All you offspring of Jacob, glorify him;
stand in awe of him, all you offspring of Israel!
^{24} For he did not despise or abhor
the affliction of the afflicted;
he did not hide his face from me,^{d}
but heard when I^e cried to him.

^{25} From you comes my praise in the great
congregation;
my vows I will pay before those who
fear him.
^{26} The poor^f shall eat and be satisfied;
those who seek him shall praise the LORD.
May your hearts live forever!

^{27} All the ends of the earth shall remember
and turn to the LORD;
and all the families of the nations
shall worship before him.^{g}
^{28} For dominion belongs to the LORD,
and he rules over the nations.

^{29} To him,^{h} indeed, shall all who sleep in^i the
earth bow down;
before him shall bow all who go down to
the dust,
and I shall live for him.^{j}
^{30} Posterity will serve him;
future generations will be told about the Lord,
^{31} and^k proclaim his deliverance to a people
yet unborn,
saying that he has done it.

^{a}Heb *my only one* ^{b}Heb *answered* ^{c}Or *kindred* ^{d}Heb *him*
^{e}Heb *he* ^{f}Or *afflicted* ^{g}Gk Syr Jerome: Heb *you*
^{h}Cn: Heb *They have eaten and* ^{i}Cn: Heb *all the fat ones*
^{j}Compare Gk Syr Vg: Heb *and he who cannot keep himself alive*
^{k}Compare Gk: Heb *it will be told about the Lord to the genera-
tion,* ^{31}*they will come and*

COMMENTARY

The haunting words that open Psalm 22 anticipate the alternation of complaint and trust/praise that characterizes the psalm. The psalmist complains of being forsaken, yet still addresses God as "my God." To be sure, the presence of both complaint and trust/praise is typical of the prayers for help, as is the element of petition. In a sense, then, Psalm 22 is a typical prayer for help; however, commentators have long suggested that Psalm 22 is unique. Of course, one may suspect that Psalm 22 is singled out because v. 1a is quoted by Jesus from the cross (Matt 27:46; Mark 15:34) and because Psalm 22 figures prominently in the passion story (see the use of v. 7 in Matt 27:34 and Mark 15:29; v. 8 in Matt 27:43; v. 15 in John 19:28; v. 18 in Matt 27:35; Mark 15:24; Luke 23:34; John 15:24).

But there is more to this psalm's uniqueness than that. There is an intensity and inclusiveness that sets Psalm 22 apart. While recognizing that it is composed of the typical elements, Mays suggests that this psalm represents "a development of the type that raises it to its very limits and begins to transcend them."[116] For instance, the complaint is extended, consisting of two major parts (vv. 1-11, 12-21), which in turn consist of two parts (vv. 1-5, 6-11 and vv. 12-15, 16-21). The praise section of the psalm (vv. 22-31) is also extended. It consists of two parts (vv. 22-26, 27-31), the second of which draws everyone—living and dead alike—into the sphere of God's reign. This elaborate construction and elevated conceptuality led Ellen F. Davis to speak of the "balanced extravagances of the lament and the vow or call to praise." Davis noted that it is the "poet's extravagance of expression" and the "exuberance of the poetic vision that explodes the limits" both of the typical form and of "Israel's traditional understandings" of God, of the world, of life, and of death.[117] In short, the expansiveness—indeed, explosiveness—of Psalm 22 makes it unique and made it particularly suitable for use in recounting the revolutionary story of Jesus' suffering and death. Psalm 22 is not unique because it is used in the NT; rather, it is used in the NT because it is unique.

116. James L. Mays, "Prayer and Christology: Psalm 22 as a Perspective on the Passion," *TToday* 42 (1985) 322.
117. Ellen F. Davis, "Exploding the Limits: Form and Function in Psalm 22," *JSOT* 53 (1992) 97, 103.

22:1-11. These verses consist of two complaints (vv. 1-2, 6-8), each of which is followed by an expression of trust that looks back to a better time, either in the life of the whole people (vv. 3-5) or in the psalmist's own life (vv. 9-10). A petition closes the unit (v. 11). The poignant alternation of complaint and trust serves only to make the psalmist's current distress seem all the more bitter. Actually, the effect is already achieved in the opening line. The particular form of the address, "my God," is rare and seems to represent an especially intimate form of address based on close personal attachment (see also v. 10; Exod 15:2; Pss 63:1; 68:14; 89:26; 102:24; 118:28; 140:6; Isa 44:17). If this is indeed the case, the subsequent question is all the more urgent: Why? Why has God "forsaken" God's own? The verb means more literally "to leave" (עזב *'āzab*). God, who had been experienced personally and closely, is now "far" (v. 2). The word "far" (רחוק *rāhôq*) recurs in the two petitions as the psalmist asks for a reversal (vv. 11, 19).

The memorable v. 3 is difficult to translate; the NIV and the NRSV give two major options. In either case, v. 3 asserts God's sovereignty (see vv. 27-31) and suggests that in the past God had given Israel reason to praise: the deliverance and salvation mentioned in vv. 4-5. The verb "trusted" (בטח *bātaḥ*) occurs three times in vv. 4-5 (see Pss 4:5; 9:10; 21:7; Introduction). The ancestors trusted and were delivered when "they cried," which is supposed to be the case (see Ps 9:10). The psalmist has also cried to God (v. 2; the Hebrew words differ in vv. 2, 5), and vv. 1-2 imply that the psalmist has also trusted God (see v. 10 NIV), but finds no help. Thus the affirmation of trust in vv. 3-5 actually communicates the psalmist's despair. It may be coincidental, but three key words from Psalms 20–21 recur in vv. 1-5: "helping" (ישע *yš'*, v. 1; see Pss 20:5-6, 9; 21:1, 5), "answer" (ענה *'ānâ*, v. 2; see Ps 20:1, 6, 9), and "trust" (*bātaḥ*, vv. 4-5; see Ps 21:7). In Psalms 20–21, there is the certainty that the sovereign God will answer and help the king, who lives by his trust in God. Thus the canonical sequence emphasizes the sharp contrast; there is no help and no answer for the psalmist.

Complaint resumes in vv. 6-8. While the deliverance experienced by earlier generations led them to enthrone God on their praises (v. 3), the psalmist's experience is utterly dehumanizing (see "worm" in Job 25:6; Isa 41:14). Apparent rejection by God leads to the psalmist's being "scorned by others" as well (see Pss 31:11; 69:7; 69:19-20; Psalms 31 and 69 also figure prominently in the story of Jesus' passion). Their words are biting and cruel. The word "deliver" in v. 8 recalls "delivered" in v. 4, thus reminding the psalmist of past glories that contrast with current pain. The words of the mockers imply that the psalmist must have been mistaken about the closeness of his or her relationship with God (cf. v. 8 with Ps 18:20).

The mocking words move the psalmist to recall not just the past of the whole people but his or her own past with God (vv. 9-10). The "you" in v. 9a is emphatic—"it was *you.*" The same Hebrew pronoun concludes v. 10, thus reinforcing literarily the closeness to God that the psalmist claimed with the address "my God," which is repeated in v. 10—namely, his or her life from the beginning was surrounded by "you," God. The psalmist was not mistaken; he or she and God go way back together. The NIV translation of v. 9b is more literal: "you made me trust." Thus v. 9 recalls vv. 4-5. Like the ancestors, the psalmist has trusted God, but apparently to no avail. God is now "far" (see v. 1); only "trouble is near."

22:12-21. The imagery shifts in vv. 12-21 to provide a terrifying description of the trouble. Like vv. 1-11, this section is composed of two complaints (vv. 12-15, 16-18), each with two elements, followed by a petition (vv. 19-21). The first element in each case employs animal imagery (vv. 12-13, 16ab). In both cases, the psalmist is surrounded (vv. 12, 16; see NIV), by either bulls (see Deut 32:14; Amos 4:1) or dogs. The animal imagery is apparently used to represent powerful and rapacious people (see Pss 7:2; 10:9; 27:2; 68:30; Isa 10:13; Jer 4:7; 5:6). In some ancient Near Eastern texts, however, animals are used to represent demonic forces; this dimension of the metaphor should be considered here as well. In other words, the powers of evil are unleashed against the psalmist so as to make it appear that the only possible consequence is death.

This leads to the second element of each com-

plaint: descriptions employing anatomical terms to indicate the nearness of death (vv. 14-15, 16c-18). The first bodily part mentioned in vv. 14-15 and the last in vv. 16c-18 is "bones," but also involved are the heart, breast, mouth, tongue, jaws, hands, and feet. The text is unclear at v. 16c (the NIV retains the more familiar reading; see the NIV's note); more generally, the precise nature of the affliction remains unclear. What the imagery does clearly communicate is that the psalmist is as good as dead. Indeed, he or she says to God that "you lay me in the dust of death" (v. 15), while the enemies also assume that death is imminent and so begin to appropriate the psalmist's possessions (v. 18).

Like the first larger complaint (vv. 1-11), the second ends with petition (vv. 19-21), which features animal characters from the previous complaints and is linked to the previous petition by the repetition of "far" and "help" (v. 19; see v. 11). The recurrence of the animal imagery indicates that the psalmist's plight continues, but something is changing. Whereas the psalmist had concluded that there was no one to help (v. 11), here the psalmist addresses God as "my help" or "my strength" (v. 19). This is the first clue that vv. 19-21 are transitional. Further evidence is provided by the three verbs in vv. 20-21: "deliver," "save" (NIV, "rescue") and "answer" (NRSV, "rescued"; NIV, "save"). Each of these verbs occurs in vv. 1-11 with a negative sense. The taunts of the enemy imply that God cannot deliver (v. 8; NRSV, "rescue" [נצל *nṣl*]). The psalmist complains that God is "so far from saving me" (v. 1; or "helping") and that God does "not answer" (v. 2). But the addressing of God as "my help," as well as the continuing plea for God to deliver and to save, indicates a remarkable depth of faith in an apparently hopeless, deathful situation.

The final line of vv. 19-21 is particularly important, and it completes the transition as it moves beyond petition to affirmation. A comparison of the NIV with the NRSV reveals that v. 21b can be translated variously (see the RSV and the NAB for another frequent reading that is based on the LXX, Syriac, and the work of Jerome). The Hebrew text, however, is readable and should be translated literally here: "from the horns of the wild oxen you have answered me." In short, the opening complaint has been reversed (see "answer" in v. 2). God has answered! The answer comes, not beyond the suffering, however, but precisely in the midst of and even from the suffering! God is somehow present in the depths and even amid death (v. 15; see vv. 17-18).

22:22-31. As suggested above, the extravagant affirmation of v. 21*b* prepares for the praise section of Psalm 22; the NRSV even includes v. 21*b* with vv. 22-26. It is characteristic of the prayers for help that they end with either praise or expressions of trust (see Commentary on Psalm 13, esp. vv. 5-6; Introduction). Even so, the exuberance and extent of the praise here are surprising. Earlier in the psalm, the memory of the whole community had only increased the psalmist's despair (vv. 3-5), but here the psalmist becomes a witness to the congregation (v. 22). The psalmist's invitation for others to "glorify" God (v. 23) indicates renewed recognition of God's sovereignty (see Isa 24:15 and 25:3, where glorifying God occurs in the context of the affirmation of God's reign in 24:23; see also Isa 43:20; 23 in the context of 43:15).

The congregation is also invited to join the psalmist in praising God (vv. 22-23). Indeed, the Hebrew root for "praise" occurs in every verse of vv. 22-26 except the middle verse (v. 24), which gives the reason for praise: God "did not despise or abhor the affliction of the afflicted." This reason sounds quite unbelievable in view of vv. 1-21, but something has changed! The affliction is still very real, but the affliction itself has somehow become an answer (v. 21*b*). What the psalmist now affirms is that God is present with the afflicted (see also Pss 9:12; 34:6; 35:10; 40:17; 140:12, where God is with or for the afflicted; the Hebrew word here translated "afflicted" [עָנִי *ʿānî*] occurs elsewhere in the NRSV as "weak," "poor [soul]," "needy"). The praise the psalmist offers (v. 22) and invites the congregation to offer (v. 23) comes out of the depths in the midst of suffering. The four occurrences of *hll* in vv. 22-26 recall v. 3, "enthroned on the praises of Israel" and removes the bitterness of that phrase. Now the psalmist also enthrones God on praise, but for God still to be enthroned on Israel's praises in vv. 22-26 must mean that God is "enthroned" or "dwells" (the Hebrew word [יָשַׁב *yāšab*] can mean either one) in the depths. In short, God is positioned among the afflicted. God is not hiding God's face, and

God can hear the psalmist's cry (v. 24; see v. 2), because God is present. God does not despise the suffering of the afflicted. God shares it! The forsakenness of the psalmist (v. 1) is the forsakenness of God. If God is the source of the psalmist's death (v. 15), God is also the source of the psalmist's praise (v. 25*a*). To praise God is to live, and so v. 26*b* forms an appropriate conclusion to the first unit of the praise section: "May your hearts live forever!" In the face of the traditional Israelite understanding that death constantly encroaches upon life, the psalmist affirms that life encroaches upon death! Traditional boundaries are transcended.

The payment of vows is a typical element of the prayers for help and songs of thanksgiving (v. 25; see Pss 56:12; 61:8; 65:1; 66:13; 116:14, 18), and such payment apparently involved a thank offering and the sharing of a sacrificial meal. The participants, those who "fear" God (vv. 23, 25), are the "poor" (v. 26), a word that derives from the same root as "afflicted" in v. 24. They "shall eat and be satisfied" (v. 26). In short, the afflicted psalmist, having been assured of God's presence in his or her affliction, becomes a source of life for other sufferers. Life defies death.

Traditional boundaries and borders are obliterated even more completely in vv. 27-31. The testimony and praise offered by and on behalf of the afflicted in vv. 22-26 have universal effects. "All the ends of the earth" and "all the families of the nations" will recognize God's reign (vv. 27-28; the word translated here as "dominion" [מְלוּכָה *mĕlûkâ*] occurs in Pss 103:19; 145:11-13 ["kingdom"]; it derives from the Hebrew root for "to reign" [מָלַךְ *mālak*]). Ethnic and national boundaries are superseded; God's people include the whole world (see Gen 12:1-3). God's rule is extended not only in space but also in time. There will be an unbroken communion of God's servants, because "future generations will be told" (v. 30), and they in turn will proclaim God's "righteousness to a people yet unborn" (v. 31). Even more remarkably, the dying and even those already dead will worship God (v. 29). To be sure, this affirmation is not the traditional Israelite view of life and death, and v. 29 is difficult to translate. The middle portion of v. 29, however, is clear and is translated literally by both the NIV and the NRSV. The phrase "go down to the dust" indicates that death is almost a certainty in view of v. 15, which mentions "the dust of death." Davis offers a cogent analysis of the psalmist's remarkable affirmation:

> Emerging suddenly out of a deathlike loss of meaning, the psalmist's joyful confidence that God is responsive to his plea demands that the dead above all may not be excluded from celebration and worship. It is the exuberance of the poetic vision that explodes the limits of Israel's traditional understandings. The shift in thought occurs first within the linguistic sphere, when a poet's productive imagination glimpses a possibility that only later (perhaps even centuries later) will receive doctrinal formulation as the resurrection of the dead.[118]

Thus Psalm 22 anticipates Paul's affirmation that "whether we live or whether we die, we are the Lord's" (Rom 14:8 NRSV), as well as the Christian doctrine of the communion of saints.

118. Ibid., 102-3.

REFLECTIONS

The communal dimension of Psalm 22 is particularly worthy of note. It is present from almost the beginning of the psalm (vv. 3-5), even when it seems to be a meager source of comfort and hope. But immediately upon being answered by God (v. 21b), the psalmist turns to the congregation, praising God and inviting their participation (vv. 22-23). Then the psalmist gathers a table-sharing community consisting of "the afflicted" (v. 24) and "the poor" (v. 26), who will "be satisfied" and join the chorus of praise—indeed, who will experience life in all its fullness (v. 26). Even more remarkable, this community of afflicted ones will be the stimulus for the formation of a community that knows no bounds, consisting of people from all nations—living, dead, and yet unborn! God's reign will be universally acclaimed.

We might cynically conclude that the poet's exuberance has gotten out of control or that the poetic imagination has gone wild. This community of the faithful from all times and places sounds like neither Israel nor the church, both of which could and can be terribly parochial and exclusivistic. But if the psalmist was not merely misguided or mistaken, what do we make of this remarkable psalm? To state it positively, we must conclude that Psalm 22, like the psalter as a whole, has an eschatological character (see Introduction). It portrays what God intends for the world. It affirms God's reign over all peoples and nations in all times and places, despite appearances to the contrary. The poet's exuberant vision is not a mistake but a challenge, a call to enter the reign of God.

Mays points out that throughout the OT God deals with the nations through the agency of the whole people, Israel, or of a unique individual, the Davidic king (the messiah, "anointed one"; see Psalms 20–21, which may be juxtaposed intentionally with Psalm 22, and see above concerning the linguistic links between Psalms 20–21 and 22:1-5). Thus Mays concludes concerning Psalm 22 and its speaker:

> Psalm 22 cannot be the prayer of just any afflicted Israelite. Though we cannot know for certain for whom it was written and through what revisions it may have passed in the history of its use, in its present form the figure in the psalm shares in the corporate vocation of Israel and the messianic role of David.[119]

For the Gospel writers, who saw in Jesus the fulfillment of Israel's history and the arrival of the Messiah, Psalm 22 thus represented an ideal resource. The effect of their use of Psalm 22 is in keeping with the central thrust of Jesus' proclamation, for as a commentary on Jesus' death and resurrection, Psalm 22 "interprets Jesus' passion and resurrection as a summons to the world (in the most inclusive sense of that term) to believe in the reign of the Lord."[120]

The inclusiveness of Psalm 22 touches on another aspect that made it an ideal resource for

119. James L. Mays, "Prayer and Christology: Psalm 22 as a Perspective on the Passion," *TToday* 42 (1985) 329.
120. Ibid., 330.

articulating the story of Jesus—namely, its poetic explosion of limits, which resulted in a new and expanded vision of God, of human life and vocation, and of death. By telling the story of Jesus using Psalm 22, the Gospel writers affirm that in Jesus' faithful suffering, as in the psalmist's faithful suffering, God was present. God's presence with the afflicted and dying opens up new possibilities for understanding and living human life, as well as for understanding and accepting death. Because of these new possibilities, the Gospel writers saw in Psalm 22 a source for articulating the meaning of both the cross and the resurrection. Thus Jesus' cry from the cross (Matt 27:46; Mark 15:34; cf. Ps 22:1) is not simply a cry of dereliction; it is an affirmation of faith in a God who, as the psalmist comes to understand and articulate, shares human affliction and enables even the dead to praise God.

Entrusting one's life to this kind of God, as the psalmist did and as Jesus did, changes everything. For instance, life can be understood not as a frantic search for self-satisfaction and self-security, but as a matter of dependence upon God (see Matt 6:25-33). Suffering can be understood not as something to be avoided at all costs, but as something to be accepted—even embraced on behalf of others—with the knowledge that God shares the suffering of the afflicted (see Heb 2:14-18). Death can be understood not as the ultimate insult to human sovereignty, but as something to be entrusted to God with the assurance that nothing in all creation can separate us from God (see Rom 8:31-39).

It is not surprising that Jesus embodied these transformed perspectives. He lived in humble dependence on God. He did not welcome suffering, but embraced it on behalf of others. He faced death with the conviction that God's power is greater than death's power. All of this may be summarized in Jesus' words, "Not what I want, but what you want" (Mark 14:36 NRSV). In short, Jesus lived, like the psalmist, as one of the afflicted, but in the knowledge that God does not despise the afflicted (Ps 22:24). Rather, God loves the afflicted, and God shares their suffering. So Jesus, like the psalmist, gathered around himself a community of the afflicted, the poor, the outcast. He sat at table with them, and he still invites to his table those who profess to live in humble dependence upon God rather than self.

In essence, the Gospel writers recognized that Psalm 22 affirms what the life, death, and resurrection of Jesus affirm. Suffering and glory are inseparable, both for the people of God and for God's own self![121]

121. Portions of the treatment of this and several other psalms in this commentary are similiar to the author's comments in J. Clinton McCann, *A Theological Introduction to the Book of Psalms* (Nashville: Abingdon, 1993).

PSALM 23:1-6, LIKE A CHILD AT HOME

NIV

Psalm 23

A psalm of David.

[1]The LORD is my shepherd, I shall not be in want.
[2] He makes me lie down in green pastures, he leads me beside quiet waters,
[3] he restores my soul.
He guides me in paths of righteousness for his name's sake.
[4]Even though I walk

NRSV

Psalm 23

A Psalm of David.

[1] The LORD is my shepherd, I shall not want.
[2] He makes me lie down in green pastures; he leads me beside still waters;[a]
[3] he restores my soul.[b]
He leads me in right paths[c] for his name's sake.

[a] Heb *waters of rest*   [b] Or *life*   [c] Or *paths of righteousness*

NIV

through the valley of the shadow of death,[a]
I will fear no evil,
    for you are with me;
your rod and your staff,
    they comfort me.

[5]You prepare a table before me
    in the presence of my enemies.
You anoint my head with oil;
    my cup overflows.
[6]Surely goodness and love will follow me
    all the days of my life,
and I will dwell in the house of the LORD
    forever.

[a]4 Or *through the darkest valley*

NRSV

[4] Even though I walk through
        the darkest valley,[a]
    I fear no evil;
for you are with me;
    your rod and your staff—
    they comfort me.

[5] You prepare a table before me
    in the presence of my enemies;
you anoint my head with oil;
    my cup overflows.
[6] Surely[b] goodness and mercy[c] shall follow me
    all the days of my life,
and I shall dwell in the house of the LORD
    my whole life long.[d]

[a]Or *the valley of the shadow of death*   [b]Or *Only*   [c]Or *kindness*   [d]Heb *for length of days*

COMMENTARY

Certainly the most familiar psalm, and perhaps the most familiar passage in the whole Bible, Psalm 23 is a challenge for the interpreter. On the one hand, its familiarity and obvious power seem to make commentary superfluous. On the other hand, its very familiarity invites the attempt to hear it in a fresh way. The challenge in this regard is the fact that Psalm 23 has become what William L. Holladay calls "an American Secular Icon,"[122] and it is almost exclusively associated with a particular contemporary setting: the funeral service. To be sure, it is appropriate that Psalm 23 be read and heard in the midst of death and dying. It may be more important, however, that this psalm be read and heard as a psalm about living, for it puts daily activities, such as eating, drinking, and seeking security, in a radically God-centered perspective that challenges our usual way of thinking. Furthermore, it calls us not simply to claim individual assurance but also to take our place with others in the household of God.

23:1-3. The psalm begins with a simple profession. In the ancient world, kings were known as shepherds of their people. Thus to profess "The LORD is my shepherd" is to declare one's loyalty to God and intention to live under God's reign. It was the responsibility of kings to provide for and protect the people, but they frequently failed to do so (see Jer 23:1-4; Ezek 34:1-10). In contrast to the failure of earthly kings, God does what a shepherd is supposed to do: provide life and security for the people (see Ezek 34:11-16). Thus the psalmist affirms, "I shall lack nothing," as v. 1*b* is better translated (see Deut 2:7; Neh 9:21). The rest of the psalm explains how God fulfills the role of a good shepherd (see also Gen 49:24; Pss 28:9; 74:1; 79:13; 80:1; 95:7; 100:3; Isa 40:11; Jer 31:10; Mic 7:14).

Contrary to the usual understanding, the imagery in vv. 2-3 is not aimed primarily at communicating a sense of peace and tranquility. It does this, to be sure, but its primary intent is to say that God keeps the psalmist alive. For a sheep, to be able to "lie down in green pastures" means to have food; to be led "beside still waters" means to have something to drink; to be led "in right paths" means that danger is avoided and proper shelter is attained (see Pss 5:8; 27:11). In short, God "restores my soul," or, better translated, God "keeps me alive." The sheep lack nothing, be-

122. William L. Holladay, *The Psalms Through Three Thousand Years: Prayerbook of a Cloud of Witnesses* (Minneapolis: Fortress, 1993) 359; see also 359-71.

cause the shepherd provides the basic necessities of life—food, drink, shelter. Thus the psalmist professes that his or her life depends solely on God and that God keeps the psalmist alive "for his name's sake" (v. 3b)—that is, in keeping with God's fundamental character.

By alluding to God's character, v. 3b anticipates the mention of "goodness and mercy," two fundamental attributes of God (see below on v. 6). Not surprisingly, the vocabulary of vv. 2-3 occurs elsewhere in relation to key events that reveal God's character. For instance, the two Hebrew verbs translated "leads" in vv. 2-3 occur together in Exod 15:13 in the song that celebrates the exodus. The verb in v. 2 also occurs in Isa 40:11, where God is also portrayed as a shepherd who leads the people home from exile (see also Isa 49:10-11). Although the psalmist's personal address to God as "my shepherd" is unique, the way the psalmist experiences God is entirely in keeping with God's character and historic deeds.

23:4. This is the structural and theological center of Psalm 23. Even in the most life-threatening situation, God's provision is sufficient. The word that the NIV translates "the shadow of death" elsewhere seems to mean simply "darkness" or "deep darkness" (see Job 3:5; 10:22; 12:22; 16:16; Pss 44:19; 107:10; Amos 5:8). The word, however, is unusual. It appears to be a compounding of words meaning "shadow" and "death," and in Job 10:22 it describes the realm of the dead. Thus the traditional translation seems appropriate (see v. 4 NIV). The similarity between the Hebrew words for "evil" (רע *ra'*) and "my shepherd" (רעי *rō'î*) is striking, and the effect is to pit dramatically the shepherd against the threatening evil. The threat is real, but it is not to be feared, for the shepherd's provision is sufficient. The expression "fear no evil" is reminiscent of the central feature of the prophetic salvation oracle, which is particularly prominent in Isaiah 40–55 (see Isa 41:11-13, 14-16; 43:1-7; 44:6-8; 54:4-8). The word "comfort" (נחם *nhm*) is also thematic in Isaiah 40–55 (see Isa 40:1-2; 49:13; 51:3, 12, 19; 52:9). The historical setting of Isaiah 40–55 is that of exile, Israel's "darkest valley." The message of the prophet is that even in exile, God will provide. Indeed, the introductory oracle concludes that God "will feed his flock like a shepherd" (Isa 40:11 NRSV).

The central affirmation, "you are with me," is made even more emphatic by the shift from third to second person in referring to God and by presence of the Hebrew pronoun for "you." The direct address heightens the expression of the intimacy of God's presence. As Brueggemann points out, the only two occurrences of the personal name for God, Yahweh (LORD), occur in vv. 1 and 6, as if to indicate that Yahweh's presence is all-surrounding.[123]

The "rod" in v. 4 makes sense as a shepherd's implement; however, the word even more frequently signifies royal authority and rule (see "scepter" in Gen 49:10; Ps 45:6; Isa 14:5). What is ultimately comforting is the assurance that God is sovereign and that God's powerful presence provides for our lives.

23:5-6. While some interpreters discern the sheep/shepherd imagery in these verses, it is more likely that God is here portrayed as a gracious host. In any case, whether the metaphor shifts is not crucial. The gracious host does for the guest exactly what the shepherd did for the sheep—provides food ("You prepare a table"), drink ("my cup overflows"), and shelter/protection (v. 6).

Like vv. 1-4, vv. 5-6 suggest that it is God's very character to provide for God's people. The clue in vv. 1-4 is the phrase "for his name's sake." The primary indication in vv. 5-6 is the Hebrew word חסד (*hesed*), which the NRSV translates as "mercy" and the NIV as "love." God's *hesed* lies at the very heart of God's character, as suggested by the fact that the word occurs twice in God's self-revelation to Moses in Exod 34:6-7 (see the Introduction). The word "goodness" (טוב *tôb*) is also reminiscent of God's self-revelation to Moses, for God's "goodness" passes before Moses in Exod 33:19 (see Pss 100:5; 106:1; 107:1; 118:1, where "goodness" and *hesed* are paired as reasons for praising God).

Most translations suggest that God's goodness and *hesed* will "follow" the psalmist, but the Hebrew verb (רדף *rādap*) has the more active sense of "pursue." God is in active pursuit of the psalmist! This affirmation is particularly noteworthy in view of "the presence of my enemies." Ordinarily in the psalms, it is precisely the enemies who "pursue" the psalmist (see 7:5; 71:11; 109:16). Here the enemies are present but

123. Walter Brueggemann, *The Message of the Psalms: A Theological Commentary* (Minneapolis: Augsburg, 1984) 154-55.

have been rendered harmless, while God is in active pursuit.

The mention of "the house of the LORD" in v. 6 may indicate the Temple and, along with the mention of "a table" in v. 5, may be a clue to the psalm's original cultic setting. It is possible that the psalm was used at a meal sponsored by a worshiper as part of his or her thanksgiving offering (see Commentary on Ps 22:22-26), perhaps in gratitude for deliverance from enemies (v. 5). Other scholars take v. 6b very literally and conclude that the psalmist was one of the temple personnel or that she or he spent the night in the Temple during a distressing time to await a reassuring oracle. It is more likely, however, that the "stay in the sanctuary is probably metaphorical for keeping close contact with the personal God."[124]

124. Erhard S. Gerstenberger, *Psalms, Part 1, with an Introduction to Cultic Poetry*, Forms of the OT Literature 14 (Grand Rapids: Eerdmans, 1988) 115.

In any case, the mention of "the house of the LORD" is significant. To be in "the house of the LORD," literally or metaphorically, provides a communal dimension to this psalm that is usually heard exclusively individualistically. This communal dimension is reinforced when Psalm 23 is heard in conjunction with Psalm 22, as the editors of the psalter may have intended. Not only can the depth of trust expressed in Psalm 23 be appreciated more fully after reading Psalm 22, but also the conclusion of Psalm 22 (vv. 22-31) seems to anticipate the ending of Psalm 23 (vv. 5-6). Psalm 22 ends with the psalmist in the "congregation" (vv. 22, 25), which would have been found in the house of the Lord (23:6). Thus the personal assurance articulated by the psalmist is finally experienced in the community of God's people.

REFLECTIONS

1. In a consumer-oriented society, it is extremely difficult to hear the simple but radical message of Psalm 23: God is the only necessity of life! While v. 1 is best translated "I shall lack nothing," the traditional translation preserved by the NIV and the NRSV is particularly appropriate in a culture that teaches people to want everything. Driven by greed rather than need, we can hardly imagine having only the necessities of life—food, drink, shelter/protection. Clever advertisers have succeeded in convincing us that what former generations considered incredible luxuries are now basic necessities. To say in our prosperous context that God is the only necessity of life sounds hopelessly quaint and naive. Then again, the words of Jesus also strike us as naive:

> "Therefore I tell you, do not worry about your life, what you will eat or what you will drink, or about your body, what you will wear. . . . But strive first for the kingdom of God and his righteousness, and all these things will be given to you as well." (Matt 6:25, 33 NRSV)

In effect, to make Psalm 23 our words is to affirm that we do not need to worry about our lives (or our deaths). God will provide, and God's provision is grounded in the reality of God's reign. The proper response to the simple good news of Psalm 23 and Jesus Christ is to trust God. But this is precisely the rub. In a secular society, we are encouraged to trust first ourselves and to work first to secure our own lives and futures. Psalm 23 thus challenges us to affirm with the psalmist: "The LORD is my shepherd, I shall not want." To say that means to live humbly and gratefully as a child of God.

The third stanza of Isaac Watts's beautiful metrical version of Psalm 23 expresses eloquently the simple trust that Psalm 23 communicates and commends to us:

> The sure provisions of my God
> Attend me all my days;
> O may Your House be my abode,
> And all my work be praise.
> There would I find a settled rest,

While others go and come;
No more a stranger or a guest,
But like a child at home.[125]

Not only does Watts's paraphrase capture the childlike trust articulated by Psalm 23, recalling Jesus' words about entering the reign of God "like a little child" (Mark 10:15 NIV), but also it calls to our attention the communal dimension of Psalm 23.

To be a child at home means inevitably to be part of a family, to share community around a table (see v. 5). Thus we are led to reflect on what it means to be a part of God's household (see v. 6). The implications are profound and radical: We are not our own! We belong to God and to one another! In his book *God the Economist,* M. Douglas Meeks recognizes the radical implications of Psalm 23. He quotes Aubrey R. Johnson's rendering of Psalm 23:6:

Yea, I shall be pursued in unfailing kindness every day of my life,
finding a home in the Household of Yahweh for many a long year.

Meeks understands Psalm 23 to be an articulation of the same message ultimately embodied in the Lord's Supper, which also has to do with God's gracious provision of food, drink, and security within God's household. Meeks puts it as follows:

The celebration of the Lord's Supper is under orders from God the Economist and is a concrete instance of God's providential *oikonomia* [the Greek word from which our word *economy* is derived; it means literally "law of the household"] with implications for all eating and drinking everywhere. For this reason, the disciples of Jesus should pray boldly for daily bread (Luke 11:3). They should keep the command to eat and drink, recognizing that it includes the command that they should share daily bread with all of God's people.
. . . Psalm 23 depicts the work of God's economy overcoming scarcity in God's household.[126]

Because, as Psalm 23 affirms, God is the source of all food and drink and security, because we belong first and forever to God's household, our lives are transformed. Daily realities are not to be taken for granted and certainly not to be treated as rewards we have earned. Psalm 23, like the Lord's Supper, becomes finally an invitation to live under God's rule and in solidarity with all God's children. Thus to make Psalm 23 our own is a profoundly radical affirmation of faith that transforms our lives and our world. To be sure, Psalm 23 is to be heard in the midst of death and dying, but it is also to be heard amid the ordinary daily activities of living. And it gives these daily activities an extraordinary significance, for it invites us to share daily bread with all of God's people.

2. It is inevitable that Christians hear in Psalm 23 testimony to Jesus Christ. Jesus became the gracious host who prepares a table that reconciles enemies and offers life (see Mark 14:22-25; interestingly, Mark 14:27 alludes to Zech 13:7, a passage about sheep and shepherds). In a story with obvious eucharistic overtones (Mark 6:30-44, esp. vv. 41-42), Jesus feeds people. The crowd is to "sit down . . . on the green grass" (Mark 6:39 NRSV), a detail that recalls Ps 23:2. That the allusion is not coincidental is suggested by Mark's description of Jesus' motivation for having compassion on the crowd: "they were like sheep without a shepherd" (Mark 6:34 NRSV). Jesus serves as both host and shepherd, acting out the two metaphors of Psalm 23.

Jesus is cast even more clearly in the role of shepherd in John 10:1-17. As in Psalm 23, the shepherd leads the sheep (John 10:3), providing food (John 10:9) and protection (John 10:12-13) for the purpose of sustaining life itself (John 10:10). And Jesus says specifically, "I am the good shepherd" (John 10:11, 14 NRSV). Interesting too in John 10 is the enigmatic

---

125. Isaac Watts, 1719, altered 1972, in *Hymns, Psalms, and Spiritual Songs* (Louisville: Westminster/John Knox, 1990) no. 172.
126. M. Douglas Meeks, *God the Economist: The Doctrine of God and Political Economy* (Minneapolis: Fortress, 1989) 180.

---

mention of "other sheep that do not belong to this fold" (v. 16 NRSV). Does this refer to Christians beyond the Johannine community? Does this refer more broadly to adherents of other world religions? The solution is unclear, but in the light of the communal conclusion to Psalm 23 (especially in view of the conclusion of Psalm 22, where "all the ends of the earth" and "all the families of the nations" are to "turn to the LORD" and "worship before him" [22:27]); it is worthy of note that John 10 envisions God's household in very open terms, with room perhaps for "enemies" (Ps 23:5) and even for "all the families of the nations" (Ps 22:27).

This thrust toward universality is present too in the relationship between Jesus and Ps 23:4, "you are with me." According to Matthew, Jesus is to be named "Emmanuel . . . 'God is with us' " (Matt 1:23 NRSV). This affirmation provides a frame for the Gospel, the final words of which are "I am with you always, to the end of the age" (Matt 28:20 NRSV). This final affirmation of Emmanuel is in the context of Jesus' commission to "make disciples of all nations" (Matt 28:19 NRSV). God intends for God's household to include "the ends of the earth" (Ps 22:27).

In short, in NT terms, Jesus is shepherd, host, Emmanuel. When Psalm 23 is heard in the context of Psalm 22 and of Jesus Christ, its profoundly radical implications are even clearer: God is with us, but God is not ours to own; the God who shepherds us to life also gives life to the world; the table at which we are hosted is one to which the whole world is invited.

PSALM 24:1-10, THE EARTH IS THE LORD'S

NIV

Psalm 24

Of David. A psalm.

[1]The earth is the LORD's, and everything in it,
 the world, and all who live in it;
[2]for he founded it upon the seas
 and established it upon the waters.

[3]Who may ascend the hill of the LORD?
 Who may stand in his holy place?
[4]He who has clean hands and a pure heart,
 who does not lift up his soul to an idol
 or swear by what is false.[a]
[5]He will receive blessing from the LORD
 and vindication from God his Savior.
[6]Such is the generation of those who seek him,
 who seek your face, O God of Jacob.[b] *Selah*

[7]Lift up your heads, O you gates;
 be lifted up, you ancient doors,
 that the King of glory may come in.
[8]Who is this King of glory?

a4 Or *swear falsely*   b6 Two Hebrew manuscripts and Syriac (see also Septuagint); most Hebrew manuscripts *face, Jacob*

NRSV

Psalm 24

Of David. A Psalm.

[1] The earth is the LORD's and all that is in it,
 the world, and those who live in it;
[2] for he has founded it on the seas,
 and established it on the rivers.

[3] Who shall ascend the hill of the LORD?
 And who shall stand in his holy place?
[4] Those who have clean hands and pure
 hearts,
 who do not lift up their souls to what is
 false,
 and do not swear deceitfully.
[5] They will receive blessing from the LORD,
 and vindication from the God of their
 salvation.
[6] Such is the company of those who seek him,
 who seek the face of the God
 of Jacob.[a]   *Selah*
 and be lifted up, O ancient doors!

a Gk Syr: Heb *your face, O Jacob*

NIV

The LORD strong and mighty,
    the LORD mighty in battle.
⁹Lift up your heads, O you gates;
    lift them up, you ancient doors,
    that the King of glory may come in.
¹⁰Who is he, this King of glory?
    The LORD Almighty—
    he is the King of glory.   *Selah*

NRSV

⁷ Lift up your heads, O gates!
    that the King of glory may come in.
⁸ Who is the King of glory?
    The LORD, strong and mighty,
    the LORD, mighty in battle.
⁹ Lift up your heads, O gates!
    and be lifted up, O ancient doors!
    that the King of glory may come in.
¹⁰ Who is this King of glory?
    The LORD of hosts,
    he is the King of glory.   *Selah*

COMMENTARY

Perhaps more than any other psalm, Psalm 24 allows the interpreter to imagine a liturgical ceremony in which it may have been used. Like Psalm 15, it is usually classified as an entrance liturgy (see also Isa 33:13-16; Mic 6:6-8). Verses 1-2 consist of an opening profession of faith by the worshipers; vv. 3-6 offer an exchange between worshipers (v. 3) and priests (vv. 4-6) concerning entrance into the sanctuary; and vv. 7-10 consist of a responsorial liturgy that takes place as the processional prepares to enter the temple gates. It is very possible that the procession accompanied the bringing of the ark into the sanctuary (see 2 Samuel 6; Ps 132:8-10). Earlier generations of scholars associated Psalm 24 with an annual enthronement of the Lord or celebration of Zion and the Davidic dynasty; however, Gerstenberger has suggested more modestly that "Psalm 24 has to do with some ritual celebrated at the Second Temple (see Ezekiel 43–44), the coming of Yahweh into his sanctuary, and his passing through heavily guarded temple gates," or perhaps an "even more symbolic enactment of such a coming in a templeless, synagogal environment."[127]

While the identification of Psalm 24 as an entrance liturgy is reasonable and the attempts to describe its liturgical setting are plausible, they do not necessarily do justice to the psalm as a literary product in its final form. Whatever may have been its original setting and use, Psalm 24 in its current form is a powerful affirmation of the sovereignty

of God, the identity of humankind, and the relationship between humanity and God.

24:1-2. While the reign of God is not explicitly proclaimed in vv. 1-2, and neither is God called "King" as in vv. 7-10, the sovereignty of God is clear enough. The whole world belongs to God, including all its people! The reason is simple: God created it. The "seas" and "rivers" are symbolic of the chaos that God has ordered into a cosmos, a world. God has "founded" it (see Pss 78:69; 89:11; 102:25; 104:5; Isa 48:13; 51:13, 16). The words translated here as "world" (תבל *tēbēl*) and "established" (יסד *yāsad*) also occur together in Pss 93:1 and 96:10, both of which explicitly affirm, "The LORD reigns." Thus vv. 1-2 anticipate vv. 7-10, where God is addressed five times as "the King of glory."

24:7-10. In addition to the word "king," other elements of the vocabulary of vv. 7-10 also focus attention on God's reign. The adjective "strong" (עזוז *'izzûz*, v. 8) occurs elsewhere only in Isa 43:17, almost immediately following an affirmation of God's kingship in Isa 43:15. A related noun, "strength" (עז *'ōz*), is prominent in the psalms that explicitly proclaim God's reign (see 29:1; 93:1; 96:6-7; 99:4). The same can be said of the noun "glory" (כבוד *kābôd*, vv. 7-10). Although the phrase "King of glory" is unique to Psalm 24, the concept of "glory" is frequently associated with God's reign (see Pss 29:1, 3, 9; 96:3, 7-8; 97:6; 145:11-12). The phrase "mighty in battle" (v. 8) recalls the description of the Lord as a "man of war" near the beginning of the Song

127. Gerstenberger, *Psalms,* 119.

of the Sea (Exod 15:3), a song that concludes with the affirmation "The LORD will reign forever and ever" (Exod 15:18 NRSV).

The portrayal of God as a warrior provides another link between vv. 1-2 and 7-10, for creation was often viewed in the ancient Near East as a battle. God has won the battle against chaos, thus demonstrating sovereignty. The title "LORD of hosts" may also be a military term, since the word "host" (צבא *ṣābā'*) can designate an army. This title also occurs in Pss 46:7, 11 and 48:8, psalms that celebrate God's protection of Zion in apparent military confrontations with hostile kings and nations. The word "hosts" may also refer to the assembly of heavenly beings that form God's heavenly court (see Pss 29:1-2; 82:1; 89:6-8). In any case, the phrase "LORD of hosts" appears immediately following the title "King" in Isa 6:5, as if it were God's throne name. It points to God's sovereignty and is also associated with the ark, God's earthly throne (see 1 Sam 4:3-4). If vv. 7-10 were a liturgy of entrance for the ark, the ritual would have been a visible enactment of God's sovereignty. "The entrance liturgy of verses 7-10 is the dramatic version of the confession of verses 1-2."[128]

24:3-6. Verse 3 recalls Ps 15:1 and refers to the Temple on Mount Zion, symbolic of God's earthly dwelling place (see Isa 2:3; 30:29; Mic 4:2 for occurrences of the phrase "mountain of the LORD," which the NIV and the NRSV translate here as "hill of the LORD"). God's place is "holy" (see Pss 2:6; 3:4; 15:1; 43:3; 48:1), and those entering God's presence should be holy as well. It should be recalled that the two affirmations of God's sovereignty frame vv. 3-6. Thus, when the questions of v. 3 and responses of vv. 4-6 are heard in the context of vv. 1-2, 7-10, the issue becomes larger than entrance into the Temple. Rather, the questions in v. 3 ask, in effect, Who will live under God's sovereignty? Who will enter the reign of God?

This concern is addressed in v. 4. That v. 4*a* should not be interpreted simply as requirements for entering the Temple is indicated by the lack of specificity in the response to the questions of v. 3. "Clean hands" and "pure hearts" may be intended to indicate outward behavior and inward motivation respectively; however, these phrases

do not designate ritual holiness or preparation that could easily be measured. Rather, they seem to indicate proper relatedness to God and neighbor in every aspect. The phrase "pure of heart" occurs elsewhere only in Ps 73:1, where the parallel is "Israel." Perhaps not coincidentally, the psalmist also says in Ps 73:13, "I have . . . washed my hands in innocence" (NRSV); and the word "innocence" (נקי *nāqî*) is from the same Hebrew root as "clean" in Ps 24:3. While Psalm 73 offers no more indication than Psalm 24 of the specific behavior involved, the psalmist does suggest that if she or he did not wash the "hands in innocence," the psalmist would be forsaking the "generation of your [God's] children" (Ps 73:15 NRSV). Psalm 24:6 also concludes that "those who have clean hands and pure hearts" constitute "the generation of those who seek" God. Thus v. 4*a* serves more as an invitation than an examination. Those who will stand in God's presence are persons whom God has claimed as God's own and whose lives reflect the intention to live together under God's rule.

Verse 4*bc* reinforces this conclusion. Verse 4*b* recalls the third commandment of the Decalogue (Exod 20:7), which could be translated literally: "You shall not *lift up* the name of the LORD your God to *nothingness* [the same Hebrew word (שוא *šāwě'*) as "what is false," NRSV], for the LORD will not *hold clean* [the same Hebrew root (*nāqî*) as "clean" in v. 4*a*] the one who *lifts up* his name to *nothingness."*

As the NIV suggests, the noun "nothingness" can have the sense of "idol" (see Ps 31:7; Jer 18:5). Thus both Exod 20:7 and Ps 24:4 affirm that cleanness results from nothing less than trusting God completely and unreservedly. It is significant that the idiom "to lift up the soul" occurs again in Ps 25:1. In this case, and the two other cases where the psalmist lifts her or his soul to God, the word "trust" occurs in the immediate context (see Pss 25:1-2; 86:2, 4; 143:8). While v. 4*b* describes proper relation to God, v. 4*c* communicates solidarity with neighbor. Although the vocabulary differs, v. 4*c* recalls the ninth commandment: "You shall not bear false witness against your neighbor" (Exod 20:16 NRSV). In short, persons who will enter God's reign are those whose lives are shaped by complete loyalty to God and love of neighbor. It is not a matter

128. James L. Mays, *Psalms,* Interpretation (Louisville: John Knox, 1994) 123.

of earning entrance by displaying this behavior but of being shaped by the claim of the sovereign God upon the world and all its people (vv. 1-2).

Those who entrust their lives to God receive blessing (v. 5); that is, their daily needs are provided for. Thus, like Psalm 23, Psalm 24 affirms that the sovereign God provides for God's people (see esp. 23:1). They also receive "righteousness" (or "vindication"). "Righteousness" (צדקה *ṣĕdāqâ*) is a term that can describe an attribute of the sovereign God (see Pss 36:7; 71:19), proper relatedness among human beings (in which case, it is often parallel to "justice" [משפט *mišpāṭ*]; see Amos 5:24), and even proper relatedness between humanity and the created order (in which case, it is often parallel to "salvation" [ישע *yēša'*]; see Isa 45:8). In other words, those who enter God's reign—those who know that "the earth is the LORD's" (v. 1)—will discover what it means to live in harmony with God, with other people, and with the whole creation. This is the ultimate blessing for those "who seek the face of the God of Jacob" (v. 6; see Ps 11:7).

REFLECTIONS

The Commentary suggests that Ps 24:4 recalls the Ten Commandments, the first in a series of commandments given at Sinai. The Ten Commandments are not rules for earning God's favor; rather, they are given only *after* God has already shown favor and after God's reign has been proclaimed (Exod 15:18). In short, they are instruction for those who are committed to live under God's sovereignty. Given the points of contact between Psalm 24 and the Ten Commandments, the OT instruction *par excellence,* it is not surprising that there are also points of contact between Psalm 24 and the NT instruction *par excellence,* the Sermon on the Mount (Matthew 5–7). The same proclamation found in Ps 24:1-2, 7-10 lies at the heart of the Sermon on the Mount: God reigns. In Matthew's terms, "the kingdom of heaven has come near" (Matt 4:17 NRSV), the announcement that inaugurates Jesus' public ministry and the concept that pervades the Sermon on the Mount. For instance, the first and last of what appear to be the original eight Beatitudes (Matt 5:3, 10; vv. 11-12 seem to be an expansion of v. 10) mention the kingdom of heaven, thus providing an envelope for the series. That is to say, the proclamation of God's reign surrounds the Beatitudes, both structurally and theologically (see also Matt 5:19-20; 6:33; 7:21).

Furthermore, just as Psalm 24 features the concepts of blessing and righteousness (v. 5), so also does the Sermon on the Mount. Each of the Beatitudes begins with "Blessed," and the concept of righteousness is central to the Beatitudes and to the entire sermon (see Matt 5:6, 10, 20; 6:33; see also Matt 3:15). Just as in Psalm 24, so also it is clear that righteousness is not simply a matter of meeting a list of requirements (see Matt 5:21-22, 27-28, 33-34, 38-39, 43-44) but of yielding one's whole life to God's claim. It is interesting, too, that one of the Beatitudes speaks in terms of seeing God: "Blessed are the pure in heart, for they will see God" (Matt 5:8 NRSV). The similarity to Ps 24:4-6 is clear; persons with "pure hearts" (v. 4) constitute "the company of those . . . who seek the face of the God of Jacob" (v. 6). In Exod 33:17-23, seeing God's face is prohibited; even Moses can see only God's back. Thus it is rather extraordinary for Ps 24:6 to speak of seeking God's face and for Matt 5:8 to speak of those who will see God (see Pss 11:7; 17:15). What a monumental experience is in view—indeed, nothing short of the creation of a new world that turns the current world upside down (see Acts 17:6). Such is the import of Psalm 24 and the Sermon on the Mount as they invite persons to enter the extraordinary new world of God's reign.

As for Matthew, the determining factor for Psalm 24 is the reality of God's universal claim (see esp. vv. 1-2, 7-10). Like Matthew 5–7, Psalm 24 is eschatological; it proclaims God's reign amid the reality of sin and amid the reality of opposition, which God must fight (see

Psalm 2; Introduction). When read and heard in its final literary form and setting, it calls for a decision: Who is sovereign? Who rules the world? Who will enter the reign of God (v. 3)?

The Sermon on the Mount is often considered under the rubric of ethics. So is Psalm 24, especially vv. 4-6. Verses 4-6 do not reduce ethical activity to following a specific set of rules and regulations. This same position is argued forcefully by Stanley Hauerwas and William H. Willimon: "So the primary ethical question is not, What ought I now to do? but rather, How does the world really look? . . . Our ethics derive from what we have seen of God."[129]

This is precisely the theological point of Psalm 24. Indeed, v. 1 gives a very clear and specific answer to "the primary ethical question": "The earth is the LORD's." For those who see the world first and foremost as the sphere of God's reign, every human activity and ethical decision—personal, political, ecological, and otherwise—will be grounded in and result from unreserved trust in God and the desire to embody God's loving, life-giving purposes for "the world, and all who live in it" (v. 1).

129. Stanley Hauerwas and William H. Willimon, *Resident Aliens: Life in the Christian Colony* (Nashville: Abingdon, 1989) 88, 90.

PSALM 25:1-22, TO YOU, O LORD, I OFFER MY LIFE

NIV	NRSV
Psalm 25[a]	**Psalm 25**
Of David.	Of David.
[1]To you, O LORD, I lift up my soul;	[1] To you, O LORD, I lift up my soul.
[2] in you I trust, O my God.	[2] O my God, in you I trust;
Do not let me be put to shame,	do not let me be put to shame;
nor let my enemies triumph over me.	do not let my enemies exult over me.
[3]No one whose hope is in you	[3] Do not let those who wait for you be put to shame;
will ever be put to shame,	let them be ashamed who are wantonly treacherous.
but they will be put to shame	
who are treacherous without excuse.	
[4]Show me your ways, O LORD,	[4] Make me to know your ways, O LORD;
teach me your paths;	teach me your paths.
[5]guide me in your truth and teach me,	[5] Lead me in your truth, and teach me,
for you are God my Savior,	for you are the God of my salvation;
and my hope is in you all day long.	for you I wait all day long.
[6]Remember, O LORD, your great mercy and love,	[6] Be mindful of your mercy, O LORD, and of your steadfast love,
for they are from of old.	for they have been from of old.
[7]Remember not the sins of my youth	[7] Do not remember the sins of my youth or my transgressions;
and my rebellious ways;	according to your steadfast love remember me,
according to your love remember me,	for your goodness' sake, O LORD!
for you are good, O LORD.	

[a]This psalm is an acrostic poem, the verses of which begin with the successive letters of the Hebrew alphabet.

NIV

[8] Good and upright is the LORD;
    therefore he instructs sinners in his ways.
[9] He guides the humble in what is right
    and teaches them his way.
[10] All the ways of the LORD are loving and
        faithful
    for those who keep the demands of his
        covenant.
[11] For the sake of your name, O LORD,
    forgive my iniquity, though it is great.
[12] Who, then, is the man that fears the LORD?
    He will instruct him in the way chosen for
        him.
[13] He will spend his days in prosperity,
    and his descendants will inherit the land.
[14] The LORD confides in those who fear him;
    he makes his covenant known to them.
[15] My eyes are ever on the LORD,
    for only he will release my feet from the
        snare.

[16] Turn to me and be gracious to me,
    for I am lonely and afflicted.
[17] The troubles of my heart have multiplied;
    free me from my anguish.
[18] Look upon my affliction and my distress
    and take away all my sins.
[19] See how my enemies have increased
    and how fiercely they hate me!
[20] Guard my life and rescue me;
    let me not be put to shame,
    for I take refuge in you.
[21] May integrity and uprightness protect me,
    because my hope is in you.

[22] Redeem Israel, O God,
    from all their troubles!

NRSV

[8] Good and upright is the LORD;
    therefore he instructs sinners in the way.
[9] He leads the humble in what is right,
    and teaches the humble his way.
[10] All the paths of the LORD are steadfast love
        and faithfulness,
    for those who keep his covenant and his
        decrees.

[11] For your name's sake, O LORD,
    pardon my guilt, for it is great.
[12] Who are they that fear the LORD?
    He will teach them the way that they
        should choose.

[13] They will abide in prosperity,
    and their children shall possess the land.
[14] The friendship of the LORD is for those who
        fear him,
    and he makes his covenant known to them.
[15] My eyes are ever toward the LORD,
    for he will pluck my feet out of the net.

[16] Turn to me and be gracious to me,
    for I am lonely and afflicted.
[17] Relieve the troubles of my heart,
    and bring me[a] out of my distress.
[18] Consider my affliction and my trouble,
    and forgive all my sins.

[19] Consider how many are my foes,
    and with what violent hatred they hate
        me.
[20] O guard my life, and deliver me;
    do not let me be put to shame, for I take
        refuge in you.
[21] May integrity and uprightness preserve me,
    for I wait for you.

[22] Redeem Israel, O God,
    out of all its troubles.

[a] Or The troubles of my heart are enlarged; bring me

COMMENTARY

As the NIV note indicates, Psalm 25 is an acrostic poem. This form, in which each verse begins with a successive letter of the Hebrew alphabet, may account for the frequent scholarly perception that Psalm 25 lacks a clear structure and organization; however, some scholars do detect a degree of regularity. Bratcher and Reyburn, for instance, identify a series of five petitions (vv. 2b-3, 4-7, 11, 16-18, 19-22) following an opening address (vv. 1-2a). The middle petition (v. 11) is set off from the others by a section of praise (vv. 8-10) and assurance (vv. 12-15).[130]

There are other indications that the psalmist intended to focus attention on the center of the psalm. For instance, the words "shame" (vv. 2-3) and "wait" (vv. 3, 5, 21) occur only near the beginning and end of the psalm, thus directing attention to the center. The same effect is achieved by the change in person. Verses 1-7 are in the first person (except v. 3), as are vv. 15-21. In contrast, vv. 8-14 are in the third person, with the exception of v. 11. Again, attention is focused on v. 11, which is also the middle line in the psalm. Furthermore, if the first letters of vv. 1, 11, and 22 (which actually lies outside the acrostic structure) are taken in order, they spell out the word אלף (ʾālep), the first letter of the alphabet.

To be sure, all of the above may be simply coincidental; yet, the evidence does suggest that there are structural and stylistic regularities in Psalm 25 that focus attention on v. 11. At the same time, there is a compelling reason not to draw too sharp a distinction between v. 10 and v. 11—namely, a cluster of vocabulary in these two verses that clearly recalls Exod 34:6-10: "steadfast love" (v. 10; cf. Exod 34:6); "faithfulness" (v. 10; cf. Exod 34:6); "covenant" (v. 10; cf. Exod 34:10); "pardon" (v. 11; cf. Exod 34:9); "guilt"/"iniquity" (v. 11; cf. Exod 34:7, 9). Thus it seems that vv. 10-11 function as a kind of theological center for Psalm 25, the effect of which is to focus attention on the character of God and to offer a narrative background (Exodus 32–34) for hearing and understanding major words and concepts throughout the psalm.

In form, Psalm 25 is a prayer for help—for deliverance from enemies (vv. 2-3, 19-21), for relief from distress (vv. 16-18, 22), for forgiveness (vv. 6-7, 11, 18b), for guidance and instruction (vv. 4-5). It is voiced mainly in the first-person singular, but it seems appropriate also for corpo-

rate use, especially in the light of v. 22. On account of the acrostic form and didactic interests (see esp. vv. 4-5, 8-9, 12), some scholars conclude that Psalm 25 would not have been used in congregational worship, but this conclusion is not compelling. On the other hand, it is clear that the psalm is a prayer that serves the purpose of instruction or catechesis; that is, it teaches about the character of God, the identity of humankind, and the relationship between God and people. There is no reason why such a purpose would have disqualified Psalm 25 from liturgical use.

Using the same idiom found in Ps 24:4 (see Commentary on Psalm 24), the opening line of Psalm 25 anticipates the central affirmation and plea of vv. 10-11. Because God is loving and faithful, the psalmist entrusts her or his life to God. The verse could also be translated, "To you, O LORD, I offer my life" (see Ps 96:8; Ezek 20:32, where the verb translated "lift up" also means "to bring an offering"). To offer one's life to God means to trust God amid threatening circumstances (v. 2; see Pss 4:5; 9:10; 21:7; 22:5-6; 26:1; Introduction). As is always the case, faith and hope are inseparable (see Heb 11:1). Thus to offer one's life to God means also to wait for God, to live with hope (v. 3; see vv. 5, 21; see also Pss 27:14; 37:34; 39:7; 40:2; 130:5). In God is the psalmist's only hope of not being defeated or destroyed by enemies or circumstances (that is, "put to shame," v. 2; see vv. 3, 20 and Pss 35:4; 26; 40:14; 69:6; 71:24).

In two other psalms, the psalmist also says, "I lift up my soul" to God (86:4; 143:8). In both of these contexts, as in Psalm 25, the psalmist affirms trust in God (86:2; 143:8) and appeals to God's steadfast love as the basis for trust (86:5, 13, 15; 143:8, 12). As in Ps 25:4-5, the offering of the self to God is accompanied by the request that God teach the psalmist God's way (86:11; 143:8, 10). Verse 5a could also be translated, "Lead me by your faithfulness" (see v. 10). Thus faith and hope in God are characterized by openness to God's instruction and God's faithful leading. The word "way[s]" (דרך derek) occurs four times (vv. 4, 8, 9, 12), and the same Hebrew root underlies the translation "lead[s]" (or "guide[s]") in vv. 5, 9. The word connotes "way of life" or "life-style," and in this regard, v. 9 is particularly interesting. Its chiastic structure ("leads . . . hum-

130. See Robert G. Bratcher and William D. Reyburn, A Translator's Handbook on the Book of Psalms (New York: United Bible Societies, 1991) 244.

ble . . . humble . . . way") has the visual effect of surrounding the humble with God's way or leading. The life-style of those who trust God will be characterized by humility—openness to God's teaching and reliance not on the self but on God (see Commentary on Psalms 1; 2). The result will be "justice" (or "what is right"). In short, by way of God's instruction, God justifies sinners.

The psalmist is confident that God does teach and lead (vv. 8-9, 12), but is also very much aware of failing to follow God (vv. 7, 11, 18). Thus the basis of the offering of self to God (v. 1) is not one's own worthiness, but the need for forgiveness. In vv. 6-7, the psalmist appeals to God's "mercy" (better translated, "motherly compassion" [רחמים raḥămîm]; the word is related to the Hebrew word that means "womb"; see Exod 33:19; 34:6) and steadfast love (see Introduction). The word "remember" (זכר zākar) occurs three times in vv. 6-7 (see NIV). What the psalmist requests is that God remember God's own character—the way that God has revealed God's own self to be "from of old" (v. 6).

The mention of "mercy," "steadfast love," "sins," and "transgressions" in vv. 6-7 anticipates the theological center in vv. 10-11. The vocabulary of these four verses is strongly reminiscent of Exod 34:6-10; the revelation "from of old" of God's self to Moses and Moses' response at the conclusion of the golden calf episode, which begins in Exod 32:1 (see above on vv. 10-11 and Exod 34:6-10; note that the adjectival form of "mercy" occurs in Exod 34:6 and that "sins" and "transgressions" occur in Exod 34:7). Especially when heard against the narrative background of Exodus 32–34, Psalm 25 is eloquent testimony to the character of God, whose commitment to sinful people requires that God's fundamental attributes, all of which occur in Psalm 25, be those rehearsed in Exod 34:6-7—"steadfast love" (vv. 6-7, 10), "faithfulness" (v. 10; the word also occurs in v. 5 as "truth"), "mercy" (v. 6), and "grace" (see "gracious" in v. 16). These attributes take concrete form in God's willingness to "pardon" (v. 11; see Exod 34:9) and to "forgive" (v. 18; see Exod 34:7), which is the good news that enables the psalmist to offer her or his life to God (v. 1).

As for vv. 10-11, there is the same inevitable tension that is present in Exod 34:6-9, where God forgives iniquity but without "clearing the guilty"

(34:7 NRSV). Psalm 25 implies that the steadfast love and faithfulness of God are reserved for those who obey God, but the psalmist has *not* obeyed, as v. 11 makes clear. The psalmist's ultimate appeal is to God's character, God's "name's sake" (v. 11), which the psalmist trusts will ultimately manifest itself in forgiveness (see Commentary on Psalms 99; 103).

Verse 12 returns to the theme of instruction, which pervades Psalm 25. The psalmist has already asked God to teach her or him (vv. 4-5) and has affirmed that God does teach and guide (vv. 8-9). Three different verbs meaning "teach" are used in vv. 4-5, 8-9, 12. The one that the NIV translates as "instruct(s)" in vv. 8, 12 represents the same root as the noun *torah,* "instruction," which is fundamental in approaching the psalter (see Ps 1:2; Introduction). In short, v. 12 functions as the psalmist's exhortation to others to posture themselves as the psalmist has, trusting God and being open to God's instruction (see Psalms 1–2). Verse 12*b* is grammatically ambiguous. In contrast to the NRSV and the NIV, it could be translated: "He [God] will teach them the way that he [God] chooses." This translation would make v. 12 more congruent with vv. 8-9.

Verses 13-15 describe the lives of persons who offer themselves to God. The translation of טוב (*ṭôb*) as "prosperity" in v. 13*a* is probably misleading, because contemporary persons tend to hear it exclusively in material terms. The Hebrew word is the same one translated as "good" in v. 8 ("goodness" in v. 7 is a very similar word from the same Hebrew root). In other words, those open to God's instruction will share in the "goodness" that characterizes God. As was the case with Ps 1:3 (where the word "prosper" is a different Hebrew word), the reward is that one's life is connected with the source of life: God. It was God who had given the land to Israel as a source of livelihood, so v. 13*b* suggests too that those who entrust themselves to God will experience life in all its fullness (see Ps 37:11; Matt 5:5). Verse 14 reinforces the conclusion that the real issue is relatedness to God. "Covenant" is obviously a relational word, and God is the initiator (see "Make me . . . know" in v. 4 NRSV). The NIV and the NRSV differ in translating v. 14*a,* but each translation suggests intimacy with God. The Hebrew word סוד (*sôd*) elsewhere describes the place or process whereby prophets receive revelation from God (see "council" in Jer 23:18, 22; see also Amos 3:7). As an example to others, the psalmist affirms that her or his life is safe from the traps of opponents (see "net" in Pss 9:15; 10:9; 31:4; 35:7; 140:5).

The final two petitions occur in vv. 16-18 and 19-21. Verse 16 may be a standard petition (see Pss 86:16; 119:132), but it appeals to God's character (see "gracious" in Exod 34:6) and activity "from of old" on behalf of the afflicted (see "affliction" also in v. 18; see also Deut 26:7, where the word also occurs; the word "toil" in Deut 26:7 is also the same as "trouble" in Ps 25:18). Verses 19-21 recall the opening address and first petition with its mention of foes, as well as the repetition of "soul" (cf. "life" in v. 1), "shame" (see vv. 2-3), and "wait" (see vv. 3, 5). To take refuge in God is synonymous with trusting, hoping, offering one's life to God (see Pss 2:12; 5:11; Introduction). This utter dependence on God constitutes "integrity" or wholeness (see Pss 7:8; 26:1, 11; 41:12).

Verse 22 stands outside the acrostic structure and may have been appended to an original version of Psalm 25 to give it a more specifically corporate application; however, it is a thoroughly appropriate theological conclusion. Although the psalm appears to articulate primarily the prayer of an individual, the identity and speech of this individual are incomprehensible apart from Israel's basic understanding of the character and historic activity of God in dealing with God's people (see above on Exodus 32–34). To pray "deliver me" (v. 20) and "Redeem Israel" (v. 22) is finally, in the psalmist's view, to pray the same thing. The psalmist's faith and hope derive from and represent the faith and hope of Israel in a God who teaches the people the way that God chooses (vv. 8-9, 12) and yet who persistently forgives them for failing to follow (vv. 11, 18).

REFLECTIONS

1. Psalm 25 offers a model of prayer and a model of living that are increasingly difficult to appreciate or even to comprehend in the midst of a secular culture that promotes self-actualization, self-sufficiency, and instant gratification. Instead of living for self, the psalmist prays, and that prayer is an offering of his or her life to God (v. 1; see Rom 12:1-2). Instead of depending on self and personal resources, the psalmist depends on God in trust, finding security or refuge in God (vv. 2, 20). Instead of seeking instant gratification, the psalmist is content to wait for God (vv. 3, 5, 20) in the confidence that being related to God is the essence of fullness of life (vv. 5, 12-15, 21). For the psalmist, prayer is not a way to pursue what one wants. Rather, it is a means to seek God's ways (vv. 4-5, 8-9, 12): "Thy will be done."

Although apparently persecuted (vv. 2, 19), "lonely and afflicted" (v. 16), troubled and distressed (vv. 17-18), the psalmist nonetheless models what Psalms 1–2 call "happiness"— openness to God's instruction (1:1-2) and dependence upon God (2:12). The psalmist's awareness of personal shortcomings (vv. 7, 11), accompanied by humbly seeking God's direction (vv. 4-5, 8-9, 12), offers an example to every generation of God's people. This example may be especially timely as the church faces new and controversial issues that call for discernment of the will of God for our place and time. For many of the issues we confront, there are no clear, unambiguous biblical answers. Thus these questions generate strong differences of opinion. In such circumstances, humility is called for, as is the conviction that God really does continue to teach us God's ways. In essence, the psalmist's openness to God's instruction seems to be an example of what the Reformers called for when they insisted that the Bible must be read under the direction of the Spirit. As Mays concludes, Psalm 25 "teaches the church to pray for the Spirit to bring into our lives not only the power and mercy of God but as well a being-taught the way we are to live through the knowledge of God's ways with us."[131]

131. James L. Mays, *Psalms,* Interpretation (Louisville: John Knox, 1994) 127.

2. Worthy of reflection, too, is the psalmist's awareness of the faith stories of Israel. As Mays suggests, the psalmist seeks new insight into God's ways, but out of awareness of God's character and activity "from of old" (v. 6). This is why the psalmist's petitions and affirmations clearly recall Exodus 32–34, for instance, and why the psalm is both a prayer and an eloquent testimony to the essential character of God. There are lessons here for us. Tradition is crucial and needs to be taken seriously, but not simply for tradition's sake. Rather, awareness of the tradition becomes the foundation for openness to further instruction from God. This ongoing revelation will be consistent with God's character and the motivation for God's historic activity—"merciful and gracious, slow to anger, and abounding in steadfast love and faithfulness" (Exod 34:6 NRSV; cf. Ps 25:6-7, 10, 16)—but it will also be genuinely new and will call for openness on our part.

3. Psalm 25 is traditionally used during both Advent and Lent. The psalmist's posture of humble penitence is clearly appropriate for the season of Lent. The trust that yields both present assurance and hope is obviously appropriate for Advent, a season that both celebrates God's coming in Jesus Christ and anticipates the consummation of God's rule. Indeed, the psalmist's dependence on God is appropriate for all seasons.

PSALM 26:1-12, ESTABLISH JUSTICE FOR ME, O LORD

NIV

Psalm 26

Of David.

[1] Vindicate me, O LORD,
    for I have led a blameless life;
I have trusted in the LORD
    without wavering.
[2] Test me, O LORD, and try me,
    examine my heart and my mind;
[3] for your love is ever before me,
    and I walk continually in your truth.
[4] I do not sit with deceitful men,
    nor do I consort with hypocrites;
[5] I abhor the assembly of evildoers
    and refuse to sit with the wicked.
[6] I wash my hands in innocence,
    and go about your altar, O LORD,
[7] proclaiming aloud your praise
    and telling of all your wonderful deeds.
[8] I love the house where you live, O LORD,
    the place where your glory dwells.
[9] Do not take away my soul along with sinners,
    my life with bloodthirsty men,
[10] in whose hands are wicked schemes,

NRSV

Psalm 26

Of David.

[1] Vindicate me, O LORD,
    for I have walked in my integrity,
    and I have trusted in the LORD without
      wavering.
[2] Prove me, O LORD, and try me;
    test my heart and mind.
[3] For your steadfast love is before my eyes,
    and I walk in faithfulness to you.[a]

[4] I do not sit with the worthless,
    nor do I consort with hypocrites;
[5] I hate the company of evildoers,
    and will not sit with the wicked.

[6] I wash my hands in innocence,
    and go around your altar, O LORD,
[7] singing aloud a song of thanksgiving,
    and telling all your wondrous deeds.

[8] O LORD, I love the house in which you dwell,

[a] Or *in your faithfulness*

NIV

whose right hands are full of bribes.
¹¹But I lead a blameless life;
redeem me and be merciful to me.

¹²My feet stand on level ground;
in the great assembly I will praise the LORD.

NRSV

and the place where your glory abides.
⁹ Do not sweep me away with sinners,
nor my life with the bloodthirsty,
¹⁰ those in whose hands are evil devices,
and whose right hands are full of bribes.

¹¹ But as for me, I walk in my integrity;
redeem me, and be gracious to me.
¹² My foot stands on level ground;
in the great congregation I will bless the LORD.

COMMENTARY

Psalm 26 has affinities with several psalms that precede it in the psalter. It is most often classified with Psalms 7 and 17. In all three psalms, the psalmist requests that justice be done (7:8; 17:1-2; 26:1a) and accompanies this plea with the invitation for God to test him or her (7:9; 17:3; 26:2) and with a so-called protestation of innocence (7:3-5; 17:4-5; 26:1b, 3-5, 11a; see Introduction). It is usually assumed that Psalms 7; 17; and 26 reflect a setting in which the psalmist has been falsely accused by enemies and visits the Temple to appeal to God for justice (see Psalm 5; Introduction; see also Exod 22:7-8; Deut 17:8-9; 1 Kgs 8:31-32).

Psalm 26 is also occasionally classified with Psalms 15 and 24 as an entrance liturgy, since vv. 1-5 seem to anticipate and perhaps prepare for activities that would be carried out in the Temple (vv. 6-8, 12). Furthermore, the words "blameless" in v. 1 and "truth" in v. 3 recall Ps 15:2, and the phrase "in innocence" in v. 6 corresponds in Hebrew to "clean" in Ps 24:4. It is used of hands in both instances and may reflect ritual preparation for entering the Temple.

The protestation of innocence in Ps 26:4-5 also recalls Ps 1:1. In both cases, the psalmist defines herself or himself over against "the wicked." Thus the implication is that the psalmist in Psalm 26 is among the happy or the righteous who live in dependence upon God and in openness to God's instruction (see Commentary on Psalm 1). In this regard, Psalm 26 is akin also to Psalm 25; it is not surprising that several key words link the two psalms. For instance, Ps 25:9 affirmed that "God

leads the humble into justice" (author's trans.), and Ps 26:1 opens with the plea, "Establish justice for me" (author's trans.). The basis for this plea involves the psalmist's "integrity" (v. 1; see 25:21) as well as the fact that the psalmist has trusted God (26:1; see 25:2) and has been guided by God's steadfast love and faithfulness (26:3; see 25:10). Both psalms include near their end the petition that God "be gracious" (25:16; 26:11) and "redeem" (25:22; 26:11). Thus, in both psalms, the psalmist recognizes that life and future ultimately depend on the grace of God.

While the affinities between Psalm 26 and Psalms 1; 7; 15; 17; 24; and 25 are interesting, they are not conclusive, and the issue of genre and setting remains elusive. Paul Mosca has recently criticized the standard proposals and has sought to determine a setting based not on the usual categories but on the content of the psalm itself. Pointing out the likelihood that only priests could "go around your altar" (v. 6b) and that priests were required to wash their hands and feet before approaching the altar lest they die (see Exod 30:17-21), Mosca concludes that Psalm 26 originated as the private prayer of a priest for approval to serve at the temple altar.[132] While Mosca may be correct about the origin of Psalm 26, his proposal does not account for its continued use. In short, we must consider the possibility that v. 6 was meant to be understood figuratively rather than literally or that it came to be understood figuratively so as to make the psalm suitable

---

132. Paul Mosca, "Psalm 26: Poetic Structure and the Form-Critical Task," *CBQ* 47 (1985) 212-37.

for broader use. In its current literary form and setting, there is no explicit indication of exclusively priestly use. Thus Psalm 26 functions as both a prayer for justice and a profession of loyalty to God, to God's ways, and to God's people.

There is a variety of ways to understand the structure and movement of Psalm 26. The NRSV's divisions are convincing, except that v. 8 belongs with vv. 6-7 rather than with vv. 9-10. The psalm is organized chiastically (see Introduction). Verses 1-3 and 11-12 focus on the psalmist and God, and they are linked by repetition of the verb "walk" and the noun "integrity." Verses 4-5 and 9-10 focus on the psalmist and the wicked, sharply contrasting them and their ways. The central section, vv. 6-8, again focuses on God and the psalmist; but it is distinctive in that no petition is present and in that it gives prominence to a particular place: the Temple.[133]

26:1-3. Verses 1 and 2-3 show a similar structure: an imperative (v. 1) or imperatives (v. 2) followed by a profession of loyalty or trust. The opening imperative would be translated better as "Judge me" or "Establish justice for me" (see Pss 7:8; 9:4; 10:18; 43:1; 96:13; 98:9). It is the prerogative and responsibility of a sovereign to judge or establish justice. Thus the psalmist recognizes God's sovereignty and appropriately expresses loyalty to God. The word translated "my integrity"/"blameless life" (תמ *tōm*) does not indicate personal achievement or sinlessness. The Hebrew root has the sense of completeness or wholeness, and its use here indicates complete devotion or total orientation of one's life to God (see Gen 17:1; 1 Kgs 9:4; Job 1:1, 8; 2:3; Pss 7:8; 15:2; 18:23; 25:21; 41:12; see also Commentary on Psalms 15; 18). As vv. 2-3 suggest, integrity in this sense derives from trusting God (see Pss 4:5; 9:10; 21:7; 22:5-6; Introduction) and from being led by God's steadfast love (see Pss 5:7; 21:7; 25:10; Introduction) and faithfulness (see Ps 25:5a, which could be translated, "Lead me by your faithfulness"). As a means of expressing complete devotion to God, the psalmist invites God's examination (see similar requests or statements, including use of the same vocabulary in Pss 7:9; 11:4-5; 17:3; 66:10; 139:23). The repetition of "walk" (הלך *hālak*) in vv. 1, 3 binds this

section together. The verb "walk" connotes "walk of life" or "life-style." Again, the psalmist's whole life is oriented to God. As a poetic means of expressing this reality, "heart and mind" are mentioned in v. 2, to be followed by "eyes" (v. 3), "hands" (v. 6), and "foot" (v. 12). In short, from the core of the being to the tips of the bodily extremities, the psalmist's whole self belongs to God (see "my soul" in v. 9 NIV).

26:4-5. Continuing the protestation of innocence, but now in the negative, vv. 4-5 shift the focus to the psalmist and "the wicked." Occurrences of the verb for "to sit" (ישב *yāšab*) at the beginning of v. 4 and the end of v. 5 recall the occurrences of this root in Ps 1:1, as does the mention of the wicked (see Ps 1:1, 4-6) and the three accompanying synonyms. The NRSV's "worthless men" is more literally "men of emptiness" (see "false" in Job 11:11; Pss 24:4; 31:6 NRSV; as Ps 31:6 and the NIV of 24:4 suggest, the word is sometimes associated with idolatry), and the word "hypocrites" (נעלמים *na 'ălāmîm*) is more literally "those who conceal themselves." As the NIV suggests, the word "assembly" (מקהלים *maqhēlîm*) is repeated in v. 12 (see v. 5 NIV) to designate God's worshiping community, to which the psalmist belongs. The effect is to contrast sharply the psalmist and the wicked, as in Psalm 1. The assertion "I hate" (v. 5) emphasizes the contrast as well. It should be understood not as an emotional reaction but as an expression of resolute opposition. God opposes evil (see Ps 5:5), and so does the psalmist.

26:6-8. The central section, vv. 6-8, returns the focus to God and the psalmist with an added spatial dimension: the Temple. As suggested above, it is possible to interpret literally the activities in v. 6; however, this is by no means necessary. Verse 6a is identical in Hebrew to Ps 73:13b, and the phrase "clean hands" in Ps 24:4 is essentially the same. Neither Psalm 24 nor Psalm 73 seems to deal exclusively with priests. If the imagery originated in priestly experience, it came to be understood more broadly. In effect, the psalmist continues to profess loyalty to God. His or her faithful life-style (vv. 1-5) is accompanied by faithful worship in the Temple, including joyful expression of gratitude (perhaps accompanied by the bringing of a thank offering) and witness to God's activity (v. 7; see Pss 9:1; 73:28).

133. Ibid., 220-29.

While hating evil, the psalmist loves the Temple (v. 8a), because there God's presence is experienced (v. 8b; see "glory" in Exod 16:7, 10; Pss 24:7-10; 63:3; Isa 60:1-2; Ezek 43:4-5).

26:9-10. Although the terms for the wicked differ, vv. 9-10 correspond in the chiastic structure to vv. 4-5 and seem to sharpen the contrast between the psalmist and the wicked. Unlike the "bloodthirsty" (see Pss 5:6; 55:23; 59:2; 139:19), whose hands are polluted by destructive plans (which elsewhere include murder, sexual misconduct, idolatry) and dishonest gain (see "bribe" in Exod 23:8; 1 Sam 8:3; Isa 1:23; Mic 3:11), the psalmist's hands are clean (see v. 6). The petition in v. 9 is essentially the equivalent of v. 1a.

26:11-12. Verse 11a forms with v. 1 an envelope structure. That the psalmist's "integrity" does not mean absolute sinlessness is indicated by the petitions in v. 11b. The essence of wickedness is dependence on self (see Psalm 1); the psalmist lives in dependence on the grace of God. The psalmist does not "stand in the way of sinners" (Ps 1:1) but on "level ground," a phrase that could be understood in view of v. 12b to mean the safety of the Temple floor or to designate the life-style of the psalmist. In a final act of submission to God, the psalmist takes his or her place in the congregation, blessing God, kneeling in homage to the one upon whom life depends (see Pss 16:7; 34:1; 63:4; 103:20-22; 104:1, 35; 135:19-20; esp. 145:2, following the address of God as "King" in 145:1).

REFLECTIONS

Two aspects of Psalm 26 may prove bothersome. First, it may seem that the psalmist bases this appeal for justice on self-righteousness—"my integrity" (vv. 1, 11). Second, the psalmist seems rather elitist in separating from the wicked to the point of even hating them. Christians may wonder about all this. The psalmist may sound like the Pharisee whom Jesus criticizes for exalting himself, thanking God that he was "not like other people" (Luke 18:11 NRSV). And did not Jesus regularly mingle with sinners and tax collectors, loving and forgiving rather than hating and condemning?

These problems, however, are more apparent than real. As was the case with Psalms 7 and 17, it is likely that the psalmist defends his or her innocence in a specific case in which the psalmist has been falsely accused by the wicked. At any rate, the psalmist's integrity or wholeness derives not from self-achievement but from entrusting life to God and attempting to follow God's direction in matters of life-style (vv. 1-5), worship (vv. 6-7), and witness (vv. 7, 12b). The final petition is "be gracious" (v. 11).

As for the apparent separatism, the psalmist's positioning of self over against the wicked is actually an act of humility rather than one of arrogance. In the psalter, wickedness is fundamentally self-rule (see Commentary on Psalm 1), so the stand against the wicked is equivalent to yielding oneself to God's rule. It is helpful at this point to remind ourselves that while Jesus did love and forgive sinners and tax collectors, he also had some pointed and condemning words for persons who failed to yield to God's sovereignty: "Hypocrites!" (Matt 23:13-36; see Ps 26:4).

Psalm 26 reminds us, then, that there is a legitimate form of separatism. Not anything goes! God opposes evil. Those who submit their lives to God's sovereignty will be different from those who follow only the direction of the self. There is a particular shape to the faithful life. It involves daily "walk" (vv. 1, 3). It involves participation in worship, where unlike "those who conceal themselves" (v. 4), the faithful publicly proclaim their gratitude to God and testify to the source of their wholeness and life (vv. 6-8). It involves taking one's place in the proper assembly (vv. 5, 12)—the worshiping community of persons who deny themselves in recognition of God's sovereign claim upon their lives. W. H. Bellinger concludes, "Participation in the worshiping community brings renewal for the significant life of trust and integrity."[134]

In short, Psalm 26 offers a challenge: "Choose this day whom you will serve" (Josh 24:15

---

134. W. H. Bellinger, Jr., "Psalm XXVI: A Test of Method," *VT* 43 (1993) 458.

NRSV), the challenge to recognize the truth of Jesus' claim, "No one can serve two masters. . . . You cannot serve God and mammon" (Matt 6:24 RSV).

PSALM 27:1-14, YOUR FACE, LORD, DO I SEEK

NIV

Psalm 27

Of David.

[1]The LORD is my light and my salvation—
   whom shall I fear?
The LORD is the stronghold of my life—
   of whom shall I be afraid?
[2]When evil men advance against me
   to devour my flesh,[a]
when my enemies and my foes attack me,
   they will stumble and fall.
[3]Though an army besiege me,
   my heart will not fear;
though war break out against me,
   even then will I be confident.

[4]One thing I ask of the LORD,
   this is what I seek:
that I may dwell in the house of the LORD
   all the days of my life,
to gaze upon the beauty of the LORD
   and to seek him in his temple.
[5]For in the day of trouble
   he will keep me safe in his dwelling;
he will hide me in the shelter of his
      tabernacle
   and set me high upon a rock.
[6]Then my head will be exalted
   above the enemies who surround me;
at his tabernacle will I sacrifice with shouts
      of joy;
   I will sing and make music to the LORD.

[7]Hear my voice when I call, O LORD;
   be merciful to me and answer me.
[8]My heart says of you, "Seek his[b] face!"
   Your face, LORD, I will seek.
[9]Do not hide your face from me,
   do not turn your servant away in anger;

[a]2 Or *to slander me*   [b]8 Or *To you, O my heart, he has said, "Seek my*

NRSV

Psalm 27

Of David.

[1] The LORD is my light and my salvation;
   whom shall I fear?
The LORD is the stronghold[a] of my life;
   of whom shall I be afraid?

[2] When evildoers assail me
   to devour my flesh—
my adversaries and foes—
   they shall stumble and fall.

[3] Though an army encamp against me,
   my heart shall not fear;
though war rise up against me,
   yet I will be confident.

[4] One thing I asked of the LORD,
   that will I seek after:
to live in the house of the LORD
   all the days of my life,
to behold the beauty of the LORD,
   and to inquire in his temple.

[5] For he will hide me in his shelter
   in the day of trouble;
he will conceal me under the cover of his tent;
   he will set me high on a rock.

[6] Now my head is lifted up
   above my enemies all around me,
and I will offer in his tent
   sacrifices with shouts of joy;
I will sing and make melody to the LORD.

[7] Hear, O LORD, when I cry aloud,
   be gracious to me and answer me!
[8] "Come," my heart says, "seek his face!"

[a] Or *refuge*

NIV

you have been my helper.
Do not reject me or forsake me,
    O God my Savior.
[10]Though my father and mother forsake me,
    the LORD will receive me.
[11]Teach me your way, O LORD;
    lead me in a straight path
    because of my oppressors.
[12]Do not turn me over to the desire of my foes,
    for false witnesses rise up against me,
    breathing out violence.

[13]I am still confident of this:
    I will see the goodness of the LORD
    in the land of the living.
[14]Wait for the LORD;
    be strong and take heart
    and wait for the LORD.

NRSV

    Your face, LORD, do I seek.
[9] Do not hide your face from me.

    Do not turn your servant away in anger,
        you who have been my help.
    Do not cast me off, do not forsake me,
        O God of my salvation!
[10] If my father and mother forsake me,
        the LORD will take me up.

[11] Teach me your way, O LORD,
        and lead me on a level path
        because of my enemies.
[12] Do not give me up to the will of
            my adversaries,
        for false witnesses have risen against me,
        and they are breathing out violence.

[13] I believe that I shall see the goodness of
            the LORD
        in the land of the living.
[14] Wait for the LORD;
        be strong, and let your heart take courage;
        wait for the LORD!

COMMENTARY

The first six verses of Psalm 27 are a remarkable profession of faith in God. The shift to direct address of God in v. 7 marks the beginning of a prayer for help that extends through v. 12. Verse 13 returns to profession, and v. 14 is an exhortation to the congregation or readers. Because of the shift between vv. 6 and 7, Psalm 27 has often been treated as two separate psalms. The verbal links between vv. 1-6 and 7-14, however, support the unity of the psalm (see "my salvation" in vv. 1, 9; "adversaries" in vv. 2, 12; "heart" in vv. 3, 8, 14; "rise up"/"risen against" in vv. 3, 12; "seek" in vv. 4, 8; "life"/"living" in vv. 1, 4, 13). There is a conceptual unity, too. The profession of faith serves as the basis for the prayer (vv. 7-12) as well as the concluding testimony and exhortation (vv. 13-14). The sequence conveys an important point. Faith in God does not spare God's servants from difficulties. But it equips them (v.

9) to live with courage and hope despite difficulties (vv. 13-14).

27:1-6. The opening line of the psalm summarizes its entire message. The Hebrew words translated "light" (אוֹר 'ôr) and "fear" (ירא yārē') are similar, and the word play highlights the available alternatives—fear or faith (see Mark 5:36). Elsewhere, the blessing or saving presence and activity of God are associated with light (see Isa 9:2; 51:4; John 1:4-5; 8:12; 12:46; see also Isa 42:6; 49:6). The addressing of God as "my light" also anticipates vv. 8-9, since God's "face" appears as light or "shines" upon people (see Num 6:25; Pss 4:6; 31:16; 44:3; 67:1; 80:3, 7, 19; 89:15; 119:135). Thus, in both profession and prayer, the psalmist affirms the desire and intention to live in God's presence. The address of God as "my salvation" (see Exod 15:2; Pss 18:3; 24:5; 25:5; 95:1) and "my stronghold" (see "refuge" in Pss 28:8; 31:2,

4; 37:39; 43:2) reinforces the psalmist's conviction that God is the source and sustainer of life.

This faith casts out fear, even amid the dire threats to life described in vv. 2-3 (cf. v. 2 to Ps 14:4). The same alternatives are evident again in v. 3. The psalmist "shall not fear" (see v. 1) but "will be confident," which represents the Hebrew root that the NRSV and the NIV usually translate as "trust" (בטח *bāṭaḥ*; see Pss 4:5; 9:10; Introduction). While the military language need not be taken literally, vv. 2-3, along with v. 12, may indicate the psalmist's problem: persecution by enemies. Likewise, vv. 4-6 may indicate that the psalmist sought asylum in the Temple. But again, the language may well have been intended metaphorically; it certainly came to function that way eventually. In short, what the psalmist singlemindedly seeks is the experience of God's presence (v. 4; see "seek" in v. 8; see also Ps 23:6). It is not clear what specific activities are described in v. 4c. To "behold the beauty of" may mean something like to "experience the favor of" (see Ps 90:17, where the word translated "beauty" [נעם *nō'am*] here appears as "favor"). If "inquire" or "seek" originally indicated a specific ritual, it is not clear what—perhaps awaiting an answer to prayer (see Ps 5:3).

The psalmist is convinced that God will be his or her protection and deliverance (vv. 5-6a). As in v. 4, it is possible to read literally and interpret the Temple as the place of shelter (v. 5a; see Pss 31:20; 76:2 [NRSV, "abode"]; Lam 2:6 [NRSV, "booth"]). Recalling Israel's early history, the psalmists sometimes refer to the Temple as God's "tent" (v. 5b; see Pss 15:1; 61:4; see also 2 Sam 7:2). The Temple mount was a "rock" (see Isa 30:29), and perhaps by extension, God too is often the psalmist's "rock" (Pss 31:3; 61:2; 62:7; 71:3). The NRSV's "set me high" (v. 5) and "lifted up" (v. 6a; see Pss 3:3; 110:7) are the same Hebrew word (רום *rûm*). The humbled one will be exalted and will respond with gratitude, joy, and praise (v. 6bc; see Exod 15:1; Pss 9:11; 89:15-16; 107:22).

27:7-12. The prayer for help that begins with the petitions in v. 7 is clearly linked to vv. 1-6 by the occurrences of "my heart" (v. 8; see v. 3) and "seek" (v. 8; see v. 4). As vv. 1-6 have already suggested, the psalmist seeks God's presence, which is symbolized by the three occurrences of

"face" in vv. 8-9. The psalmists are convinced elsewhere of the benefits of seeing God's face (see Pss 11:7; 17:15; 24:6; 42:2; 102:2; the word "presence" [פנים *pānîm*] in Pss 16:11; 21:6; 140:13 is literally "face"). This is striking, given the tradition that one could not see God's face and live (see Exod 33:20), but it powerfully articulates the intimacy of communion with God that the psalmist seeks.

Verse 9 begins a series of seven imperatives that ask God to be present and involved in the psalmist's life. Expressions of assurance accompany the petitions, recalling vv. 1-6: God is "my help" (v. 9; see Pss 22:19; 40:17; 46:1; 63:7; 115:9-11) and "my salvation" (v. 9; see v. 1). The assurance in v. 10 picks up the verb "forsake" (עזב *'āzab*) in v. 9 (see Pss 22:1; 38:21). Even when forsaken by family, a serious threat to life in ancient cultures, the psalmist can depend on God to "take me up" (see Isa 40:11 [NRSV, "gather"]). The request in v. 11 is reminiscent of the claim in Psalm 1 (see also Pss 25:8, 12; 86:11) that those who are continually open to God's instruction (1:2 [NRSV, "law"]; the noun in 1:2 and the verb "teach" in 27:11 are from the same Hebrew root) are truly happy. Such happiness is not freedom from trouble and threat (see vv. 2-3, 12), but a solid grounding of faith that enables one to endure trouble and threat. The word "level" (מישור *mîšôr*) in v. 11 is the same as "level ground" in 26:12, where the context suggests a location in the Temple—that is, in God's presence (see also Ps 5:7-8). God's presence sustains the solid foundation on which the psalmist stands.

27:13-14. These verses conclude the psalm with another expression of the psalmist's faith (v. 13, "I believe"), and its inseparable companion, hope (v. 14; see Ps 37:34; Rom 8:24-25; Heb 11:1). Verse 13 recalls Ps 25:13, where God's "goodness" is also mentioned in the context of a plea for instruction (see 25:4-5, 12). It also recalls Exod 33:19-20, where Moses is prohibited from seeing God's face but is shown God's "goodness." Thus the psalmist trusts that he or she will be privileged to share the same experience as Moses. God will reveal God's own self to the psalmist. As an exhortation to others, v. 14 has the character of a public witness. The psalmist had earlier declared in v. 3 that "my heart shall not fear" and had been exhorted by his or her own heart

(v. 8). Now the psalmist exhorts others to "let your heart take courage" (see Ps 31:24; Deut 31:7-8). This exhortation is surrounded by "Wait for the LORD," suggesting that strength and courage begin and end with hope. Thus vv. 13-14 invite others, including contemporary readers, to join the psalmist in a community of faith, hope, and courage.

REFLECTIONS

1. When Jesus overheard people tell Jairus that his daughter was dead, Jesus exhorted Jairus: "Do not fear, only believe" (Mark 5:36 NRSV). Jesus' words effectively summarize the message of Psalm 27. In the presence of dire threat to life (vv. 2-3, 12), the psalmist dares to believe: "even then will I be confident" (v. 3*d,* which could also be translated, "through this I am trusting") and "I believe" (v. 13). Twice the psalmist uses "my salvation" to refer to God (vv. 1, 9). In biblical terms, salvation means life, especially life made possible when death is threatening (see Exod 15:2). Threatened by deadly forces, the psalmist lives by faith.

As both Mark 5:36 and Psalm 27 suggest, the opposite of faith is not so much doubt as it is fear. For the psalmist to say, "My heart shall not fear" (v. 3*b*; see v. 1), is to say, "I believe" (v. 13; see v. 3*d*). Psalm 27:3 recalls Ps 23:4. There, too, the psalmist is threatened by deadly forces but is able to say, "I fear no evil." The determining factor is trust in God's presence— "you are with me"—and it is precisely God's presence that the psalmist both affirms and continues to seek in Psalm 27 (see vv. 1, 4-5, 8-11; cf. v. 4 with Ps 23:6).

Our era has been called the Age of Anxiety, which makes the psalmist's example of faith all the more important. Kraus suggests that the psalmist is an example of one who "has anchored his life entirely in Yahweh."[135] How difficult this is in our secular world! The real measure of the difficulty is not outright doubt—still relatively few people profess to be atheists or agnostics—but the pervasive anxiety that characterizes contemporary existence. This anxiety is often interpreted as a failure of nerve, but Psalm 27 suggests that it is a failure to trust. Left to depend on ourselves instead of on God, we fail to experience joy (v. 6) and life in all its fullness (v. 13).

2. Verse 14 is a call to anchor our lives entirely in God. As the psalmist's address to others, v. 14 envisions a community of people who will "wait for the LORD"—an eschatological community. We wait for the Lord, but, like the psalmist, our waiting contains already (see "Now" in v. 6) the possibility of joy, strength, and courage. It should be noted that waiting for God is active rather than passive. The psalmist, for instance, resolutely seeks God through active involvement in worship, in the Temple or elsewhere (vv. 4-6). Mays states that "trust is nurtured and strengthened by the exercise and discipline of religion. . . . Trust needs the stimulus and renewal that come from confronting and contemplating religion's representation of the revelation of God in liturgy, architecture, and proclamation."[136]

3. In several ways, Psalm 27 is reminiscent of the final chapter of the book of Micah. Violence and oppression surround the prophet. He cannot trust even the closest of kin (Mic 7:1-6; cf. Ps 27:10). His response is to "wait for the God of my salvation" (Mic 7:7 NRSV; cf. Ps 27:9, 14), who is "a light to me" (Mic 7:8 NRSV; cf. Ps 27:1). Amid the anxiety, inhumanity, brutality, and greed of our world, Micah 7 joins Psalm 27 and Jesus in inviting us to trust rather than fear— to seek light, life, strength, courage, and direction in God. When the church located the presence of God in the Word that became flesh, the accompanying good news is the same as Psalm 27: "The light shines in the darkness, and the darkness did not overcome it" (John 1:5 NRSV). Such is the faith and hope that give us life and peace (see John 8:12; 14:27).

---

135. H.-J. Kraus, *Psalms 1–59: A Commentary,* trans. H. C. Oswald (Minneapolis: Augsburg, 1988) 337.
136. James L. Mays, *Psalms,* Interpretation (Louisville: John Knox, 1994) 133.

PSALM 28:1-9, THE LORD IS MY STRENGTH

NIV

Psalm 28

Of David.

¹To you I call, O LORD my Rock;
    do not turn a deaf ear to me.
For if you remain silent,
    I will be like those who have gone down
        to the pit.
²Hear my cry for mercy
    as I call to you for help,
as I lift up my hands
    toward your Most Holy Place.

³Do not drag me away with the wicked,
    with those who do evil,
who speak cordially with their neighbors
    but harbor malice in their hearts.
⁴Repay them for their deeds
    and for their evil work;
repay them for what their hands have done
    and bring back upon them what they
        deserve.
⁵Since they show no regard for the works of
        the LORD
    and what his hands have done,
he will tear them down
    and never build them up again.

⁶Praise be to the LORD,
    for he has heard my cry for mercy.
⁷The LORD is my strength and my shield;
    my heart trusts in him, and I am helped.
My heart leaps for joy
    and I will give thanks to him in song.

⁸The LORD is the strength of his people,
    a fortress of salvation for his anointed one.
⁹Save your people and bless your inheritance;
    be their shepherd and carry them forever.

NRSV

Psalm 28

Of David.

¹ To you, O LORD, I call;
    my rock, do not refuse to hear me,
for if you are silent to me,
    I shall be like those who go down to the Pit.
² Hear the voice of my supplication,
    as I cry to you for help,
as I lift up my hands
    toward your most holy sanctuary.ᵃ

³ Do not drag me away with the wicked,
    with those who are workers of evil,
who speak peace with their neighbors,
    while mischief is in their hearts.
⁴ Repay them according to their work,
    and according to the evil of their deeds;
repay them according to the work of their
        hands;
    render them their due reward.
⁵ Because they do not regard the works of
        the LORD,
    or the work of his hands,
he will break them down and build them
        up no more.

⁶ Blessed be the LORD,
    for he has heard the sound of my pleadings.
⁷ The LORD is my strength and my shield;
    in him my heart trusts;
so I am helped, and my heart exults,
    and with my song I give thanks to him.

⁸ The LORD is the strength of his people;
    he is the saving refuge of his anointed.
⁹ O save your people, and bless your heritage;
    be their shepherd, and carry them forever.

ᵃ Heb *your innermost sanctuary*

COMMENTARY

Psalm 28 begins as a prayer for help, including the psalmist's plea to be heard (vv. 1-2) and the petition that the wicked get what they deserve (vv. 3-4). Verse 5 is transitional. It expresses the confidence that God will deal with the wicked; thus it prepares for the praise, profession of faith, and thanksgiving of vv. 6-7. Verse 8 broadens the profession to include the whole people and the king, and v. 9 closes the psalm with renewed petition.

Because of its variety of component parts, Psalm 28 is difficult to categorize. Most scholars conclude that vv. 6-7 indicate that the petitions of vv. 1-4 have been answered, in which case it makes sense to label Psalm 28 a song of thanksgiving. Gerstenberger, however, concludes that vv. 6-7 anticipate deliverance, suggesting that v. 7cd is a vow that could be translated, " 'If helped, I will rejoice and give thanks.' "[137] He classifies the psalm as an individual complaint. Because of the mention of the "anointed" in v. 8, others view Psalm 28 as a royal psalm; however, there is nothing that would have prevented an individual from praying for the king, especially in the context of praying for the whole people, as here.

28:1-2. The psalm opens with the prepositional phrase "To you," suggesting immediately the urgency of the call that the rest of the verse reinforces. If God is "silent" (see Pss 35:22; 39:12; 83:1; 109:1; Isa 64:11; 65:6), the psalmist will be as good as dead. The "pit" is synonymous with Sheol, the realm of the dead (see Pss 6:5; 30:3; 88:4; 143:7; Isa 14:19). At the same time, the address of God as "my rock" implies confidence in God's ability to help (see Pss 18:2, 31, 46; 19:14; 31:22; 62:2, 6-7; 73:26). The plea continues in v. 2. The NIV's "cry for mercy" better captures the sense of the Hebrew root (חנן ḥānan; see Pss 31:23; 86:6; 130:2; 140:6; 143:1). It and the word translated "cry . . . for help" (שוע šwʿ; see Pss 18:6, 41; 30:2; 31:22) effectively communicate the psalmist's need without specifically identifying what it is. The psalmist's words are accompanied by the proper posture of prayer: hands lifted (see Pss 63:4; 134:2; 141:2), perhaps toward the holy of holies where God was symbolically enthroned (see 1 Kgs 6:5; 8:6, 8).

28:3-5. The substance of the psalmist's prayer is contained in these verses. Although the vocabulary differs, the essence of the request in v. 3 is the same as in Ps 26:9-10. If the behavior of the

wicked is an indication of what the psalmist has personally experienced (v. 3bc; see Pss 5:9; 7:14), then the psalmist may have been slandered or falsely accused. At any rate, the prayer is an implicit protestation of innocence (see Psalms 7; 17; 26; Introduction). Jeremiah 9:8-9 promises retribution for those who speak peacefully but act violently, and it is this sort of promise to which the psalmist appeals. The prayer that the wicked get what they deserve is not a matter of personal revenge but a matter of divine justice (see Ps 94:2). A comparison of vv. 4 and 5 makes this clear. The same Hebrew root (פעל pʿl) occurs in v. 4 in the phrase "their work" and in v. 5 in the phrase "works of the LORD." Similarly, a different but synonymous Hebrew word (מעשה maʿăśeh) occurs in v. 4 in the phrase "work of their hands" and in v. 5 in the phrase "work of his [God's] hands." The effect of the repetition is to say that the wicked are completely self-absorbed. Their deeds show no comprehension of or participation in the goodness and order that God wills for creation and humanity. In effect, the behavior of the wicked sows the seeds of its own destruction. They leave God nothing with which to work. As a just and righteous God, God has no choice but to "break them down and build them up no more" (see Pss 10:3-4; 54:5; 73:18-20). This conclusion is reinforced by a play on words in v. 5. Because the wicked do not "regard" (יבינו yābînû), God will not "build them" (יבנם yibnēm).

28:6-7. These verses apparently assume that the petitions of vv. 1-4 have been answered and that the promise of v. 5 has been effected (see esp. v. 6b, which the NIV correctly suggests is a direct response to v. 2a). God has proven to be the psalmist's strength (see Exod 15:2; Pss 46:1; 59:1). "Strength" is elsewhere associated with God's sovereignty (see Pss 29:1, 10-11; 93:1; 96:7), and the word occurs again in v. 8 in relation to the whole people (see Ps 29:11). The psalmist and the whole people live as a result of God's claim on them and on their world. The word "shield" (מגן māgēn) also communicates empowerment as well as protection (see Pss 3:4; 7:10). Recognizing God's sovereignty, the "heart" of the psalmist "trusts" (see Pss 4:5; Introduction) and rejoices (v. 7), whereas the "hearts" of the wicked were filled with "mischief" (רעה rāʿâ, v.

---

137. Erhard S. Gerstenberger, *Psalms, Part 1, with an Introduction to Cultic Poetry,* Forms of the OT Literature 14 (Grand Rapids: Eerdmans, 1988) 129.

3). This word is often translated elsewhere as "evil," as in Ps 15:3, which suggests that those who recognize God's claim on their lives "do no evil to their friends." As suggested throughout the Psalms (see Commentary on Psalm 1), wickedness is essentially dependence on self. In contrast, the psalmist entrusts life to God—God is "my strength"—and responds to God's help (see Pss 10:14; 22:19; 37:40; 46:1) with gratitude (see Pss 7:17; 9:1).

28:8-9. The psalm concludes with a communal affirmation (v. 8) and a prayer for the community (v. 9). What God is for individuals, God is also for the entire people and the king, who embodies the life of the community: "strength" (עֹז *'ōz*, vv. 7-8) and "refuge" (מָעוֹז *mā'ôz*, v. 8; the Hebrew word used here is the same as "stronghold" in Ps 27:1). The words "strength" and "salvation" (יְשׁוּעָה *yĕšû'â*, see v. 8 NIV) also occur together in Exod 15:2 at the beginning of the Song of the Sea, which concludes with an affirmation of God's reign (Exod 15:18). Again, God's claim upon the world and its people is the source of empowerment and protection. While "salvation" is claimed in v. 8, it is nonetheless prayed for in v. 9. "Save" (see "deliver"/"deliverance" in Pss 3:7-8; 6:4; 7:1) and "bless" (see Gen 12:1-3; Pss 3:8; 5:12; 29:11) suggest respectively rescue from distress and daily provision for needs. The plea "be their shepherd" could more literally be translated, "feed them," which is what shepherds did for their flocks (see Ps 23:1-3). The term "shepherd" again calls to mind the reality of God's sovereignty, since kings were often designated as shepherds in the ancient Near East (see Ezek 34:1-16). Whereas the language of v. 8 alluded to the exodus (Exod 15:2), the language of v. 9 alludes to return from exile (see Isa 40:11). These two great saving events are recalled as the psalmist prays for the people. Communal conclusions to predominantly individual psalms are also found in Pss 3:8; 5:11-12; 14:7; 25:22; 31:23-24; 51:18-19; and 130:7-8.

REFLECTIONS

1. The communal conclusion of Psalm 28 is instructive. While the psalms speak frequently of individuals' being saved or helped (see 28:7), Ps 28:8-9 reminds us that ultimately there is no such thing as individual salvation. To live under God's claim, to live as God intends, is to live as part of God's people. To belong to God means also to belong to others. Artur Weiser concludes that the psalmist lives "*in* the fellowship of faith and *from* that fellowship."[138]

2. It is instructive, too, that the psalm claims both strength and salvation for the people (v. 8) and yet still prays for saving and blessing (v. 9). In short, the perspective is eschatological. The psalmist and the people already experience the benefits of God's reign—"strength" (vv. 7-8), "help" (v. 7), "salvation" (v. 8)—yet not completely. As is always the case, the reign of God is proclaimed amid circumstances and powers that seem to deny it (see Psalm 2; Introduction).

In effect, the psalmist's perspective in prayer is the one articulated by Jesus when he taught his disciples to pray both "thine is the kingdom" and "thy kingdom come." The particular petitions in Psalm 28 also bring to mind the Lord's prayer. The prayer for justice in vv. 3-4 could well be paraphrased, "Thy will be done . . . deliver us from evil." And the petition "be their shepherd," or literally, "feed them," could well be paraphrased, "Give us this day our daily bread." Psalm 28, like the Lord's prayer, affirms that God's people live in dependence upon God rather than upon self. Indeed, the poignant words of v. 1 suggest that the psalmist will live ultimately "by every word that comes from the mouth of God" (Matt 4:4 NRSV; see Deut 8:3).

3. The lives of those who recognize God's claim will have a particular character that begins with trust (v. 8). Psalm 2:12 claims that happiness belongs to "all who take refuge in" God, and Psalm 28 also represents this claim. The trusting heart is the joyful, singing heart (v. 7).

138. Artur Weiser, *The Psalms*, OTL, trans. H. Hartwell (Philadelphia: Westminster, 1962) 258.

Those who attempt to make their way by "the work of their hands" (v. 4)—who live in dependence upon self—will be characterized by pride that is ultimately destructive of community (see v. 3). Those who attend to the work of God's hands (v. 5)—who receive life as a gift to be lived in dependence upon God—will be characterized by gratitude (v. 7) that impels them into the community of God's people (vv. 8-9).

PSALM 29:1-11, GLORY TO GOD!

NIV	NRSV
Psalm 29	**Psalm 29**
A psalm of David.	A Psalm of David.
¹Ascribe to the LORD, O mighty ones, ascribe to the LORD glory and strength.	¹ Ascribe to the LORD, O heavenly beings,ᵃ ascribe to the LORD glory and strength.
²Ascribe to the LORD the glory due his name; worship the LORD in the splendor of hisᵃ holiness.	² Ascribe to the LORD the glory of his name; worship the LORD in holy splendor.
³The voice of the LORD is over the waters; the God of glory thunders, the LORD thunders over the mighty waters.	³ The voice of the LORD is over the waters; the God of glory thunders, the LORD, over mighty waters.
⁴The voice of the LORD is powerful; the voice of the LORD is majestic.	⁴ The voice of the LORD is powerful; the voice of the LORD is full of majesty.
⁵The voice of the LORD breaks the cedars; the LORD breaks in pieces the cedars of Lebanon.	⁵ The voice of the LORD breaks the cedars; the LORD breaks the cedars of Lebanon.
⁶He makes Lebanon skip like a calf, Sirionᵇ like a young wild ox.	⁶ He makes Lebanon skip like a calf, and Sirion like a young wild ox.
⁷The voice of the LORD strikes with flashes of lightning.	⁷ The voice of the LORD flashes forth flames of fire.
⁸The voice of the LORD shakes the desert; the LORD shakes the Desert of Kadesh.	⁸ The voice of the LORD shakes the wilderness; the LORD shakes the wilderness of Kadesh.
⁹The voice of the LORD twists the oaksᶜ and strips the forests bare. And in his temple all cry, "Glory!"	⁹ The voice of the LORD causes the oaks to whirl,ᵇ and strips the forest bare; and in his temple all say, "Glory!"
¹⁰The LORD sitsᵈ enthroned over the flood; the LORD is enthroned as King forever.	¹⁰ The LORD sits enthroned over the flood; the LORD sits enthroned as king forever.
¹¹The LORD gives strength to his people; the LORD blesses his people with peace.	¹¹ May the LORD give strength to his people! May the LORD bless his people with peace!

ᵃ2 Or LORD with the splendor of   ᵇ6 That is, Mount Hermon
ᶜ9 Or LORD makes the deer give birth   ᵈ10 Or sat

ᵃHeb sons of gods   ᵇOr causes the deer to calve

COMMENTARY

Psalm 29 is often considered to be the oldest of the psalms, due in part to what seems to be an archaic pattern of repetition (see vv. 1-2), but due primarily to the observation that it seems to be an Israelite adaptation of an ancient Canaanite hymn to Baal, a god of weather and fertility. Following the opening invitation to praise (vv. 1-2), vv. 3-9 consist of a poetic description of a thunderstorm, responsibility for which the Canaanites attributed to Baal. Psalm 29 is fundamentally polemical, for it clearly attributes all power to Yahweh (LORD), who is enthroned in v. 9 with the exclamation, "Glory!" That enthronement is indeed the effect of v. 9 is indicated by the affirmation of Yahweh's kingship in v. 10, followed by the appeal for Yahweh to fulfill the royal role of blessing the people.

While Psalm 29 is traditionally categorized as an enthronement psalm (see also Psalms 47; 93; 95–99; Introduction) and shares several typical features of such psalms, much about it is unique. For instance, in vv. 1-2, the invitation to praise is addressed not to any earthly congregation but to "heavenly beings" (cf. Ps. 96:7-8, where the same invitation is addressed to "families of the peoples"). Although these beings could be understood as angels, more likely they should be viewed as the deposed gods of the Canaanite pantheon—another indication of the psalm's polemical thrust. In any case, Psalm 29 preserves the ancient conception of a divine council (see Gen 1:26; 1 Kgs 22:19; Pss 58:1; 82:1; 89:7; 103:19-21; 148:1-2), whose members are invited to acknowledge (which is the sense of "ascribe to") Yahweh's glory and strength, in other words Yahweh's absolute sovereignty. Both of these attributes are associated frequently with God's reign (see "glory" in Pss 24:7-10; 96:3, 7-8; 145:5, 11-12; Isa 6:3; and "strength" in Exod 15:2, 13; Pss 93:1; 96:6-7; 99:4 [NRSV, "Mighty"]). "Glory" (כבוד *kābôd*) recurs in v. 2, not surprisingly in an invitation involving God's "name." The personal name "Yahweh" occurs eighteen times in Psalm 29 so as to emphasize the exclusiveness of Yahweh's claim. God's "glory," which becomes the key word in the psalm (see vv. 1-3, 9), consists of the strength mentioned in v. 1, described in

detail in vv. 3-9 and exercised on behalf of God's people in v. 11. The imperative "worship" (השתחוו *hištaḥăwû*) also bespeaks God's sovereignty; it means literally "to bow down" before a monarch (see 1 Sam 24:8; 1 Kgs 1:31 of earthly kings; and Pss 95:6; 96:9; 99:5, 9 in the context of God's kingship). It is not clear exactly what "holy splendor" (הדרת-קדש *hadrat-qōdeš*) indicates. It may refer to the appropriate attitude or even the proper attire of those called upon to glorify Yahweh (see 1 Chr 16:29; 2 Chr 20:21; Ps 96:9).

The polemical thrust of Psalm 29 is also clear in vv. 3-9. In these verses, the phrase "the voice of the LORD" occurs seven times, with the number 7 symbolizing fullness or completion. Yahweh's strength, which is represented by the sevenfold mention of the voice, is all-powerful. Yahweh's sovereignty—not Baal's—is absolute. As the verb in v. 3b suggests, the "voice of the LORD" is thunder (see 1 Sam 2:10; Job 37:4-5; Ps 18:13). The noun here translated "voice" (קול *qôl*) is sometimes translated "thunder" by the NRSV (see Exod 19:19). The repetition may be intended to be onomatopoeic. The "waters" in v. 3 could be a reference to the Mediterranean Sea, over which the thunderstorm gathers force before crashing into the coast of Palestine. It is likely, too, that we should hear an allusion to the cosmic waters above and below the earth (see v. 10; Gen 6:17; 7:6, 7, 10; see also Psalm 93). In other words, the effects of the storm are to be understood as testimony to Yahweh's sovereignty over all creation. The two adjectives that describe the voice in v. 4 also connote sovereignty, occurring elsewhere in contexts that affirm earthly or divine kingship (see "power" in Exod 15:6; 1 Chr 22:12; 2 Chr 20:6; "majesty" in Ps 21:5; "splendor" in Ps 145:5).

Verses 5-9 offer a poetic description of the effect of a violent thunderstorm. Trees are uprooted and ripped apart (vv. 5, 9ab; see Exod 9:25); lightning flashes (see Exod 9:24; Pss 83:14; 97:3-4; Rev 4:5); the earth itself seems to shake (vv. 6, 8; see Pss 97:5; 114:4, 6). The described effects are similar to those generally found in theophanies, portrayals of appearances of God (see Pss 18:7-15; 68:4, 8, 33; 77:16-18; 97:1-5; 104:3-

4). In the ancient Near East, thunder would have been the loudest sound known. Not surprisingly, thunderstorms were associated with divine appearances, especially manifestations of the Canaanite god Baal, whose voice was supposed to be the thunder. But here the heavenly beings interpret this powerful display as testimony to Yahweh's sovereignty over all, which they affirm in v. 9c (see vv. 1-3). The temple in v. 9c seems to designate God's heavenly abode, where the divine council would have gathered (see Pss 11:4; 18:6; Isa 63:15); however, the reference is ambiguous. In all likelihood, human worshipers who would have gathered in the Jerusalem Temple are also invited to join in acknowledging Yahweh's reign.

This likelihood is supported by the first explicit mention of human beings, which comes in the conclusion of the psalm (vv. 10-11). As the eternal ruler of all creation (the word "flood" [מבול mabbûl] occurs only here and in Genesis 6–11; see Gen 6:17; 7:6-7; 9:11, 15), God is in a position to provide strength (see v. 1; see also Exod 15:2; Pss 28:7-8; 46:1; 38:35; 84:5; 86:16; 138:3) and the blessing (see Ps 28:9) of *shalom* (see Num 6:26). Just as it was the role of the earthly king to provide peace for his people (see Ps 72:1-7, esp. vv. 3, 7; *shalom* is translated "prosperity" in v. 3), so also it is the duty of Yahweh, the heavenly king, to provide peace for all creation.

REFLECTIONS

1. Psalm 29 is a marvelous profession of the message that lies at the heart of the psalter and the gospel: The Lord reigns! It speaks eloquently what Christians affirm regularly in the conclusion to the Lord's prayer: "for thine is the kingdom, and the power, and the glory forever." This message had a polemical thrust in the ancient Near Eastern context as well as in the time of Jesus—and it does still today. To be sure, contemporary persons are not tempted to worship Baal as such, but what the Baalistic cult represented is a major temptation to us. H. D. Beeby states, "This religion was for the Canaanites (and for most of the Israelites) what scientific humanism and technology are for people of the 20th century: essential to the means of production and for ensuring regular increase of the Gross National Product."[139] In short, the religion of Baal asserted what humans are all too inclined to believe in any era, that ultimately *we* are in control and that *our* efforts can ensure security. While Psalm 29 is not necessarily anti-science or anti-technology, it does suggest definite limits to both. The universe is the sphere of God's reign. It derived from and belongs to God and thus is not simply an object for our study, much less for our manipulation and control. Similarly, our strength (v. 11)—including our scientific knowledge and technological capabilities—are gifts from God, not simply results of human inquiry and ingenuity. Thus *shalom*—peace, well-being, security—does not begin with our efforts but with our openness to God's claim upon us and the ways God has gifted us.

2. Needless to say, to view the world as the sphere of God's sovereignty rather than the arena of human progress would have profound ecological and economic implications. Creation does not exist simply for the sake of humanity. When we act as if it does, the results are disastrous—dirty water, polluted air, soil erosion, and perhaps even depletion of the ozone layer. Inequitable distribution of land and resources threatens life in our cities and destabilizes delicate international relations. Ironically, the more we seek to secure our own future, the less secure we become. Psalm 29 becomes a call to yield control to the sovereignty of God. Enduring strength and *shalom* will derive from joining the heavenly beings in their cry, "Glory!" (v. 9c). To paraphrase the first answer in the Westminster Shorter Catechism, the chief end of humankind is to glorify God and enjoy God forever. Obviously, this assertion is a monumental

---

139. H. E. Beeby, *Grace Abounding: A Commentary on the Book of Hosea*, International Theological Commentary (Grand Rapids: Eerdmans, 1989) 2.

challenge in the midst of a culture that teaches us that our chief end is to enjoy ourselves—another indication of the polemical thrust of Psalm 29.

3. The use of Psalm 29 on the First Sunday After the Epiphany is particularly appropriate. Epiphany follows Christmas; Psalm 29 spans the two seasons. The movement of Psalm 29 from proclaiming God's glory (v. 9c) to peace on earth (v. 11) recalls the account of Jesus' birth in Luke (Luke 2:14). The birth of Jesus is the event by which God's universal reign became manifest. In addition, the cosmic proclamation of God's reign in Psalm 29 is appropriate for the season of Epiphany (which means "manifestation"), because Jesus' baptism is celebrated on the First Sunday After the Epiphany (Luke 3:15-22). Immediately following his baptism, a heavenly voice proclaims Jesus "my Son" (Luke 3:22), publicly manifesting Jesus as the one who would soon proclaim and enact "the good news of the kingdom of God" (Luke 4:43-44 NRSV). Mays's conclusion about the pairing of Psalm 29 and the baptism of Jesus applies as well to the similarity between Psalm 29 and Luke 2: "The Christology is not adequate unless its setting in cosmology is maintained. The Old Testament doxology is necessary to the gospel."[140] For the NT, Jesus becomes the ultimate embodiment of God's kingdom, power, and glory (see John 1:14; 1 Cor 2:8; 2 Cor 4:6).

140. Mays, *Psalms*, 138.

PSALM 30:1-12, SO THAT MY SOUL MAY PRAISE YOU

NIV	NRSV
Psalm 30	**Psalm 30**
A psalm. A song. For the dedication of the temple.[a] Of David.	A Psalm. A Song at the dedication of the temple. Of David.
[1]I will exalt you, O LORD, for you lifted me out of the depths and did not let my enemies gloat over me.	[1] I will extol you, O LORD, for you have drawn me up, and did not let my foes rejoice over me.
[2]O LORD my God, I called to you for help and you healed me.	[2] O LORD my God, I cried to you for help, and you have healed me.
[3]O LORD, you brought me up from the grave[b]; you spared me from going down into the pit.	[3] O LORD, you brought up my soul from Sheol, restored me to life from among those gone down to the Pit.[a]
[4]Sing to the LORD, you saints of his; praise his holy name.	[4] Sing praises to the LORD, O you his faithful ones, and give thanks to his holy name.
[5]For his anger lasts only a moment, but his favor lasts a lifetime; weeping may remain for a night, but rejoicing comes in the morning.	[5] For his anger is but for a moment; his favor is for a lifetime. Weeping may linger for the night, but joy comes with the morning.
[6]When I felt secure, I said, "I will never be shaken."	

aTitle: Or *palace* b3 Hebrew *Sheol*

aOr *that I should not go down to the Pit*

NIV

⁷O Lord, when you favored me,
    you made my mountain*ᵃ* stand firm;
but when you hid your face,
    I was dismayed.

⁸To you, O Lord, I called;
    to the Lord I cried for mercy:
⁹"What gain is there in my destruction,*ᵇ*
    in my going down into the pit?
Will the dust praise you?
    Will it proclaim your faithfulness?
¹⁰Hear, O Lord, and be merciful to me;
    O Lord, be my help."

¹¹You turned my wailing into dancing;
    you removed my sackcloth and clothed me
        with joy,
¹²that my heart may sing to you and not be
        silent.
    O Lord my God, I will give you thanks
        forever.

ᵃ7 Or hill country   *ᵇ9 Or there if I am silenced*

NRSV

⁶ As for me, I said in my prosperity,
    "I shall never be moved."
⁷ By your favor, O Lord,
    you had established me as a strong
        mountain;
you hid your face;
    I was dismayed.

⁸ To you, O Lord, I cried,
    and to the Lord I made supplication:
⁹ "What profit is there in my death,
    if I go down to the Pit?
Will the dust praise you?
    Will it tell of your faithfulness?
¹⁰ Hear, O Lord, and be gracious to me!
    O Lord, be my helper!"

¹¹ You have turned my mourning into dancing;
    you have taken off my sackcloth
    and clothed me with joy,
¹² so that my soul*ᵃ* may praise you and not be
        silent.
    O Lord my God, I will give thanks to
        you forever.

ᵃHeb that glory

COMMENTARY

The superscription makes Psalm 30 one of few psalms associated with a specific occasion. Rabbinic sources identify Psalm 30 with the Feast of Dedication (Hanukkah), which originated as a celebration of the restoration of proper worship under the Maccabees in 165 BCE after the desecration of the Temple by Antiochus IV Epiphanes (see 2 Maccabees 10). Most scholars conclude that the association of Psalm 30 with Hanukkah is secondary, since the psalm is likely to be much older than the second century BCE, since it appears to have no specific relevance for a dedication, and since the prayer is offered in the first-person singular. For the latter reason as well, Psalm 30 is usually categorized as an individual song of thanksgiving.

Even so, it would not be entirely exceptional to articulate in the first-person singular the experience of a communal deliverance. Psalm 118, for instance, which is also regularly categorized as an individual thanksgiving, clearly recalls the exodus and was (and is) traditionally used at Passover. Thus the expression of thanksgiving and joy in Psalm 30 would have made it quite appropriate for use in celebrating Hanukkah (see 2 Macc 10:7: "they offered hymns of thanksgiving" [RSV]), or perhaps even the return from exile, which led to the construction and dedication of the Second Temple in 515 BCE. Of course, Psalm 30 is appropriate for individual use as well, and most scholars identify it as the celebratory prayer of a person who has recovered from sickness (see v. 2). In short, regardless of how it originated, Psalm 30 may well have functioned in a variety of settings. Of enduring theological significance is the fact that while the psalm is predominantly a prayer, the substance of the prayer is praise.

30:1-3. The psalmist's praise in prayer is

voiced in the opening words using the verb "extol" (רום *rûm*). God is extolled elsewhere simply because God is king (see Pss 99:5, 9; 145:1) or because God has demonstrated sovereignty by delivering the people from their enemies (cf. Exod 15:2; Ps 118:28) or other distress (cf. Pss 34:3; 107:32). The word "extol" more literally means "to lift up"; it is an appropriate choice here, since God has "lifted . . . out" the psalmist (v. 1b; see Exod 2:16, 19, where the verb is used of drawing water from a well). The imagery anticipates v. 3, where God has "brought up" those who have "gone down." Sheol (see Ps 6:5) and the Pit (see Ps 28:1) are designations for the realm of the dead (see Ps 88:3-4 and Isa 38:18, where the terms occur together). In other words, the distress, which the foes (v. 1) have either caused or seek to take advantage of, is life-threatening. The different imagery in v. 2 suggests a sickness from which the psalmist had been "healed" when he or she "called . . . for help" (see Pss 5:2; 18:41). It is possible that Psalm 30 originated as a prayer to celebrate deliverance from a serious illness (see Psalm 6 and Isa 38:9-20, each of which shares vocabulary and conceptuality with Psalm 30). The verb "to heal" (רפא *rāpā'*), however, can be used metaphorically (see Ps 147:3; Hos 6:1; 11:3; 14:4; Jer 3:22; 33:6); as Kraus suggests of vv. 2-3, "In this formulary, room could be found for many of the misfortunes of life."[141]

30:4-5. These verses interrupt the prayer as the psalmist invites the congregation (see Ps 4:3) to join in the praise and thanksgiving. The two verbs in v. 4 recur in v. 12, where the psalmist makes a lifetime commitment to these activities. The word "name" (זכר *zēker*) in v. 4 is more literally "remembrance" (see Ps 97:12). As Ps 6:5 suggests, there is no "remembrance" or praise of God in Sheol (see below on v. 9). Praise and thanksgiving are the vocation of the living (Isa 38:19). Indeed, as Kraus concludes, what the psalmist has learned from the whole experience is that "the purpose of his existence is to praise God."[142] This new understanding of life motivates the psalmist to be a witness to others concerning

the character of God (v. 5a; see "favor" in v. 7 and Pss 5:12; 89:17; 106:4). It also prompts a reevaluation of suffering (v. 5b). God's commitment to life (v. 3) and lifetime commitment of favor mean that the ultimate end of human suffering is not "weeping" but "rejoicing" (see Ps 6:8; Isa 65:19; Jer 31:16). Thus v. 5 anticipates v. 11, just as v. 4 anticipates v. 12.

30:6-12. The reevaluation continues in v. 6 as the prayer resumes. Verses 6-12 seem to be a sort of flashback in which the psalmist reviews the former distress (vv. 6-10) and deliverance (vv. 11-12), even quoting a portion of the prayer for help mentioned in v. 2 (vv. 9-10). The psalmist's former approach to life apparently involved a false sense of security (v. 6). Even though there is something compelling about attributing prosperity to God's favor and misfortune or "dismay" to God's absence, as the psalmist does in v. 7 (see Ps 104:29; see also Ps 6:2-3, where the same root is rendered by the NRSV as "shaking with terror" and "struck with terror"), this theology is ultimately not profound enough. Although the psalmist says in v. 6, "I shall not be shaken forever" (author's trans.; see Pss 10:6; 15:5; 16:8), the psalmist *was* shaken by the experience of misfortune. This experience leads the psalmist, however, to plead for the mercy of God (see vv. 8, 10). The two pleas for mercy frame the questions of v. 9, which are often interpreted as the psalmist's attempt to appeal to God's self-interest (see the similar question or assertions in Pss 6:5; 88:10-12; Isa 38:18), but which may more positively be heard as the psalmist's affirmation of the desire to live, despite suffering. Indeed, the psalmist's question about praise is a question about life, since for the psalmists to live is to praise God and to praise God is to live (see Reflections).

By v. 12, the psalmist is committed to being thankful "forever," in contrast to the false confidence that was presumed to be "forever" in v. 6. To be sure, it seems that the psalmist's situation has improved (v. 11), but one is left with the impression that when the next round of distress arrives, as it inevitably does, the psalmist will remain "forever" thankful even as she or he offers a new prayer for help. In short, the psalmist has arrived at a new awareness of God's presence, even amid suffering, when God appears to be absent (see Commentary on Psalm 22). And the psalmist will not be silent; that is, the psalmist

141. H.-J. Kraus, *Psalms 1-59: A Commentary,* trans. H. C. Oswald (Minneapolis: Augsburg, 1988) 355.

142. Ibid., 356.

will be a faithful witness to this new and deeper understanding of the availability of God's gracious presence and help. Now, in distress as well as in prosperity, the psalmist will live to praise God "forever."

REFLECTIONS

1. Mays speaks of the psalmist's experience as risky, since it is possible to hear Psalm 30 in a very simplistic way—that is, pray long enough and God will make everything all right.[143] But it is also possible to hear Psalm 30 differently. Kraus suggests that the psalmist's new orientation to life means a reevaluation of suffering and joy: "Suffering is fitted into the course of life in a comprehensive way . . . the new reality of the nearness of God and the help of God fills life and determines the understanding of existence."[144] In short, suffering need not be an indication of the absence of God for those who take refuge in God (Ps 2:12). The existence of suffering does not negate the good news that life is a gift from God.

But if this is the case, then joy is possible in the depths. And praise is not reserved for seasons of prosperity; rather, it becomes a constant way of life. As Mays concludes:

> The psalmist had made the loss of praise the very basis of his supplication and thereby dared to make one of the most important statements in the Bible about the theological value of praise. . . . Praise is the way the faithfulness of the LORD becomes word and is heard in the LORD's world (v. 9). For people, it is the language of joy and gladness that goes with life and is life in contrast to the silence of death (vv. 11-12). And salvation is here understood as reaching its goal, not just in the restoration of the needy, but finally in the praise of God.[145]

The psalmist prays to live and lives to praise.

2. Psalm 30 is traditionally used during the season of Easter. It is appropriate for Easter, because it is an affirmation of both God's life-giving power and life as God's good gift. In a real sense, the psalmist's deliverance is not so much from physical sickness to physical health as it is from a deadly misunderstanding of human security (vv. 6-7) to a lively awareness of God's presence in all of life (vv. 11-12). This awareness engenders thanks, praise, and dancing (vv. 4, 11-12; see Reflections on Psalm 6). In this light, as suggested above, v. 9 need not be understood as an appeal to God's self-interest, but may be heard as the psalmist's embrace of life as a God-given gift. Clothed with joy (v. 11) and giving thanks to God forever, the psalmist's whole life becomes praise (v. 12).

143. James L. Mays, *Psalms,* Interpretation (Louisville: John Knox, 1994) 142.
144. H.-J. Kraus, *Psalms 1–59,* 356-57.
145. Mays, *Psalms,* 141.

PSALM 31:1-24, MY LIFE AND FUTURE ARE IN YOUR HAND

NIV	NRSV
Psalm 31	Psalm 31
For the director of music. A psalm of David.	To the leader. A Psalm of David.
[1]In you, O LORD, I have taken refuge; let me never be put to shame;	[1] In you, O LORD, I seek refuge; do not let me ever be put to shame;

NIV

deliver me in your righteousness.
²Turn your ear to me,
  come quickly to my rescue;
 be my rock of refuge,
  a strong fortress to save me.
³Since you are my rock and my fortress,
  for the sake of your name lead and guide
    me.
⁴Free me from the trap that is set for me,
  for you are my refuge.
⁵Into your hands I commit my spirit;
  redeem me, O LORD, the God of truth.

⁶I hate those who cling to worthless idols;
  I trust in the LORD.
⁷I will be glad and rejoice in your love,
  for you saw my affliction
  and knew the anguish of my soul.
⁸You have not handed me over to the enemy
  but have set my feet in a spacious place.

⁹Be merciful to me, O LORD, for I am in
    distress;
  my eyes grow weak with sorrow,
  my soul and my body with grief.
¹⁰My life is consumed by anguish
  and my years by groaning;
 my strength fails because of my affliction,ᵃ
  and my bones grow weak.
¹¹Because of all my enemies,
  I am the utter contempt of my neighbors;
 I am a dread to my friends—
  those who see me on the street flee from
    me.
¹²I am forgotten by them as though I were
    dead;
  I have become like broken pottery.
¹³For I hear the slander of many;
  there is terror on every side;
 they conspire against me
  and plot to take my life.

¹⁴But I trust in you, O LORD;
  I say, "You are my God."
¹⁵My times are in your hands;
  deliver me from my enemies
  and from those who pursue me.
¹⁶Let your face shine on your servant;
  save me in your unfailing love.

ᵃ10 Or guilt

NRSV

in your righteousness deliver me.
² Incline your ear to me;
  rescue me speedily.
 Be a rock of refuge for me,
  a strong fortress to save me.

³ You are indeed my rock and my fortress;
  for your name's sake lead me and guide me,
⁴ take me out of the net that is hidden for me,
  for you are my refuge.
⁵ Into your hand I commit my spirit;
  you have redeemed me, O LORD, faithful
    God.

⁶ You hateᵃ those who pay regard to
        worthless idols,
  but I trust in the LORD.
⁷ I will exult and rejoice in your steadfast love,
  because you have seen my affliction;
  you have taken heed of my adversities,
⁸ and have not delivered me into the hand of
    the enemy;
  you have set my feet in a broad place.

⁹ Be gracious to me, O LORD, for I am in distress;
  my eye wastes away from grief,
  my soul and body also.
¹⁰ For my life is spent with sorrow,
  and my years with sighing;
 my strength fails because of my misery,ᵇ
  and my bones waste away.

¹¹ I am the scorn of all my adversaries,
  a horrorᶜ to my neighbors,
 an object of dread to my acquaintances;
  those who see me in the street flee from me.
¹² I have passed out of mind like one who is dead;
  I have become like a broken vessel.
¹³ For I hear the whispering of many—
  terror all around!—
 as they scheme together against me,
  as they plot to take my life.
¹⁴ But I trust in you, O LORD;
  I say, "You are my God."
¹⁵ My times are in your hand;
  deliver me from the hand of my enemies
  and persecutors.

ᵃOne Heb Ms Gk Syr Jerome: MT I hate   ᵇGk Syr: Heb my
iniquity   ᶜCn: Heb exceedingly

NIV

¹⁷Let me not be put to shame, O Lord,
    for I have cried out to you;
but let the wicked be put to shame
    and lie silent in the grave.ᵃ
¹⁸Let their lying lips be silenced,
    for with pride and contempt
    they speak arrogantly against the righteous.

¹⁹How great is your goodness,
    which you have stored up for those who
        fear you,
which you bestow in the sight of men
    on those who take refuge in you.
²⁰In the shelter of your presence you hide them
    from the intrigues of men;
in your dwelling you keep them safe
    from accusing tongues.

²¹Praise be to the Lord,
    for he showed his wonderful love to me
    when I was in a besieged city.
²²In my alarm I said,
    "I am cut off from your sight!"
Yet you heard my cry for mercy
    when I called to you for help.

²³Love the Lord, all his saints!
    The Lord preserves the faithful,
    but the proud he pays back in full.
²⁴Be strong and take heart,
    all you who hope in the Lord.

ᵃ17 Hebrew Sheol

NRSV

¹⁶ Let your face shine upon your servant;
    save me in your steadfast love.
¹⁷ Do not let me be put to shame, O Lord,
    for I call on you;
    let the wicked be put to shame;
    let them go dumbfounded to Sheol.
¹⁸ Let the lying lips be stilled
    that speak insolently against the righteous
        with pride and contempt.

¹⁹ O how abundant is your goodness
    that you have laid up for those who fear you,
    and accomplished for those who take refuge
        in you,
    in the sight of everyone!
²⁰ In the shelter of your presence you hide them
    from human plots;
    you hold them safe under your shelter
    from contentious tongues.

²¹ Blessed be the Lord,
    for he has wondrously shown his
        steadfast love to me
    when I was beset as a city under siege.
²² I had said in my alarm,
    "I am driven farᵃ from your sight."
But you heard my supplications
    when I cried out to you for help.

²³ Love the Lord, all you his saints.
    The Lord preserves the faithful,
    but abundantly repays the one who acts
        haughtily.
²⁴ Be strong, and let your heart take courage,
    all you who wait for the Lord.

ᵃ Another reading is cut off

COMMENTARY

This prayer for help is traditionally classified as an individual complaint, but Gerstenberger points out that it shows "neither logical nor literary order."[146] Perhaps its irregularity is an appropriate representation of the psalmist's chaotic life (see

vv. 9-13). In any case, it is clear that expressions of trust alternate with petitions accompanied by reasons that indicate the severity of the psalmist's plight. The effect is a psalm that begins (v. 1a), ends (vv. 19-24), and is pervaded by expressions of trust in God (vv. 3a, 4b-8, 14-15a). While it is possible to divide the psalm into two (vv. 1-8, 9-24) or three parts (vv. 1-8, 9-18, 19-24), its

146. Erhard S. Gerstenberger, *Psalms, Part 1, with an Introduction to Cultic Poetry,* Forms of the OT Literature 14 (Grand Rapids: Eerdmans, 1988) 137.

most prominent feature is the frequent alternation between petition and trust.

31:1-2. The opening line, which the NIV translates better than the NRSV does, effectively summarizes the message of the whole psalm and much of the psalter. In entrusting his or her life to God, the psalmist arrives at what the introduction to the psalter calls "happy" (Ps 2:12; see "refuge" also in Pss 5:11; 7:1; 11:1; 14:6; 16:1; 31:19; and esp. 71:1-3, which is almost identical to 31:1-3; see Introduction). The initial expression of trust is followed by a series of petitions in vv. 1b-2 that make it clear that the psalmist depends on God. The psalmist's integrity depends on God (v. 1b; see "shame" in v. 17 and Pss 25:2-3, 20; Ps 25:20 specifically associates not being ashamed with taking refuge in God). Indeed, the psalmist's life depends on God as the three nearly synonymous verbs suggest: "deliver" (פלט *pālaṭ*; see Ps 22:5, 9), "rescue" (נצל *nṣl*; see Ps 7:2), and "save" (ישע *yš'*; see Pss 3:2 [NIV, "deliver"; NRSV, "help"]; 6:4; 7:1). The variety of nouns also emphasizes the psalmist's dependence upon God—"rock" (see Pss 18:2, 31, 46; 19:14; 28:1), "refuge" (a different Hebrew word than in v. 1; cf. "stronghold" in Ps 27:1), "fortress" (see Pss 18:2). By appealing to God's righteousness, vv. 1b-2 anticipate vv. 3-8. The psalmist affirms that it is God's character to set things right. Subsequent verses will also highlight two of God's fundamental characteristics: faithfulness (v. 5) and steadfast love (vv. 7, 16, 21).

31:3. The psalmist returns briefly to another expression of trust in v. 3a, repeating "fortress" from v. 2 and using a different Hebrew word for "rock" (see Pss 18:2; 42:9). The piling up of synonyms for the original "refuge" in v. 1 makes the point emphatically: the psalmist's life depends on God. The syntax of v. 3a reinforces the point. The line contains no verb, thus necessitating the use of the personal pronoun "You," which emphasizes God's role in the psalmist's life. The return to petition in v. 3b is marked by the phrase "for your name's sake," which again directs attention to God's character. The two verbs in v. 3b also occur together in Ps 23:2-3 (see NIV). There, too, the provision God makes for the psalmist's need is "for his [God's] name's sake" (see also Ps 25:11). The two verbs also occur in Exod 15:13, where Moses and the Israelites celebrate the exo-

dus and guidance effected by God's steadfast love. In Psalm 31 as well, the psalmist will rejoice and appeal to God's steadfast love (vv. 7, 16, 21).

31:4-5. The prayer for God to "take me out" (v. 4a) is also reminiscent of the exodus, which is often described with the same verb (see Exod 13:9, 14, 16; 18:1; 20:2). The psalmist requests a sort of personal exodus, based on his or her awareness that God's past activity has revealed God to be one who sees affliction (Ps 31:7; see Exod 3:7, 17) and liberates captives. It is not clear exactly what type of affliction is indicated in v. 4a (see "net" in Pss 10:9; 25:15; 35:7; 57:6; 140:6). The imagery in vv. 4, 9-13 is sufficiently graphic to suggest real affliction, but it is open-ended enough to apply to a variety of circumstances. Obviously, the psalmist is being persecuted somehow; he or she is suffering precisely on account of faith in God.

Verse 4b contains another emphatic personal pronoun—"*you* are my refuge" (the same word as in v. 2)—and introduces another expression of trust that extends through v. 8. The most direct affirmation of the psalmist's dependence on God is v. 5a, which is quoted by Jesus from the cross in Luke 23:46. In Jesus' case, this affirmation comes at the moment of death, which is certainly appropriate; but for the psalmist, this affirmation is as much for living as for dying. The word "spirit" (רוח *rûaḥ*) can also mean "breath," and it is virtually synonymous with "life" (see Job 34:14-15; Ps 104:29-30). The psalmist says, in effect, "I put my life in your hand," or "I turn my life over to you." The psalmist's confidence is obviously not *self*-confidence; it is grounded in God's activity ("you have redeemed"; see Pss 25:22; 26:11) and God's character ("faithful God"; see Exod 34:6, where God's self-revelation includes faithfulness).

31:6-8. As the NIV suggests, v. 6 should begin with "I hate." Thus the psalmist expresses loyalty to God by affirming opposition to those who oppose God (see Pss 5:5; 26:5). It is another way of saying what the psalmist has affirmed all along and says explicitly in v. 6b: "I trust in the LORD" (see Pss 4:5; 9:10; Introduction). The "I" is emphatic, effectively contrasting the psalmist and those who are loyal to "worthless idols" (see Jonah 2:8; for the word here translated "worthless," see "false" in Ps 24:4; see also Jer 18:15).

The progression in vv. 5-6 from "into your hand" to "I trust" anticipates vv. 14-15*a,* the next expression of trust, where the sequence is reversed. The psalmist's trust in God allows the psalmist to "exult and rejoice" (v. 7). Again, the goal for rejoicing is God-centered rather than self-centered—"in your steadfast love" (see vv. 16, 21). Like the word "faithful" in v. 5, the word "steadfast love" occurs in Exod 34:6-7 in God's self-revelation (see Pss 5:7; 6:4; Introduction). The psalmist depends on God to do what God had done in the book of Exodus—namely, to see affliction (v. 7; Exod 3:7, 17) and to break the power of the enemy for the sake of the life of God's people. "Broad place" in v. 8 connotes safety and security or, in a more contemporary idiom, "You have given me some space." Given the recollections of the exodus noted above, it is perhaps not coincidental that the same Hebrew root (רחב *rḥb*) is used in Exod 3:8 to designate the land of promise as a "broad" land (see also Pss 4:1; 18:19; 118:5).

31:9-13. Whereas vv. 7-8 make one think that deliverance has already occurred (see also vv. 19-22), vv. 9-13 return to a petition ("Be merciful" [חנן *ḥānan*]; see Pss 4:1; 6:2) followed by an extended description of the psalmist's "distress" (צר *ṣar,* see the same Hebrew root in v. 7 [NRSV, "adversities"; NIV, "anguish"]). The language is open-ended; it seems to suggest simultaneously grief, sickness, depression, and persecution. Not surprisingly, several of the formulations are echoed in other complaints. For instance, v. 9*b* recalls Ps 6:7*a* (the verb "waste[s] away" [עשש *'āšēš*] occurs only in Pss 6:7 and 31:9-10); and the vocabulary of v. 10 appears elsewhere—"sorrow" (v. 10*a*; see Pss 13:2*b*; Jer 20:18); "groaning"/"sighing" (v. 10*b*; see Pss 6:6; 38:9; 102:5); "strength" (v. 10*c*; see Pss 38:10; 71:9; 102:23); "bones" (v. 10*d*; see Pss 6:2; 22:14, 17; 102:3). Elsewhere, too, the psalmist is an object of "scorn" or "contempt" (v. 11; see Pss 22:6; 39:8; 69:7, 9-10 [NRSV, "reproach" and "insult(s)"]; see also Jer 20:8 [NRSV, "reproach"]). The image of a "broken vessel" in v. 12 is particularly graphic and poignant (see Jer 22:28). The phrase is more literally "perishing vessel," thus suggesting that despite, or perhaps because of, his or her trust in God, the psalmist is experiencing what is supposed to be reserved for the wicked (see "perish"

in Pss 1:6; 2:12). Support for the latter option is found in the similarity between Psalm 31 and the book of Jeremiah, which is particularly evident in v. 13 (see Jeremiah 20; see esp. "terror all around" in Ps 31:13 and Jer 20:3, 10; note also "sorrow" in Ps 31:10 and Jer 20:18; "scorn"/"reproach" in Ps 31:11 and Jer 20:8; and "shame" in Ps 31:1, 17 and Jer 17:18; 20:18). Jeremiah suffers *because of* his trust and his faithfulness in proclaiming the word of God (see Jer 20:8). Like the psalmist, Jeremiah's very life was threatened by his persecutors (see Jer 38:4-6).

31:14-24. Like the psalmist, too, Jeremiah alternates between petition/complaint and trust, ultimately turning his case over to God (Jer 20:10-12). The psalmist returns emphatically to trust in vv. 14-15*a,* which, as suggested above, reverses the sequence of affirmations in vv. 5-6. Here *"I trust"* (v. 14; as in v. 6, the "I" is emphatic) leads to "My times are in your hand" (v. 15), or better translated, "in your hand is my *future."* In vv. 5-6, 14-15, the psalmist entrusts life and future to God. The word "hand" (יד *yād*) connotes "grasp" or "power." Thus the psalmist affirms that the operative power in his or her life is ultimately God and not the enemy (see "hand" in association with enemies in vv. 8, 15). The syntax of v. 15 is revealing; the first word is the emphatic pronoun "I," and the last word is the pronoun "you." The effect is to highlight the intimacy of relation on which the psalmist stakes his or her life and future.

Verses 15*b*-18 renew the petition, repeating earlier pleas ("deliver" in v. 15*b* is the same as "rescue" in v. 2; see "save" in vv. 2, 16*b* and "shame" in vv. 1, 17) and adding a new one in v. 16*a*: "Let your face shine" (see Num 6:25; Pss 4:6; 67:1; 80:3, 7, 19; see "face" in Pss 11:7; 17:15; 27:8-9). God's "face" symbolizes God's presence, and as is often the case, the request seems to correlate good fortune with God's presence and suffering with God's absence. This correlation is understandable and even helpful to the extent that it attempts to relate all of life to God; however, it also represents a limited understanding of God, and the psalmists regularly push beyond it. Psalm 31:20 moves in this direction; that is, "the shelter of God's face" (author's trans.) is available to the persecuted. And v. 22 goes further, as the psalmist suggests that he or she was mistaken in the earlier conclusion that suffering had completely separated her or him from God. This is certainly the faith that Luke articulates as Jesus quotes Ps 31:5a from the cross (Luke 23:46; see Introduction and Commentary on Psalms 13; 22; 30).

In addition to recalling the petition with which the psalm began (see v. 1), vv. 17-18 juxtapose the contrasting alternatives that are present in Psalm 1 and throughout the psalter: "the wicked" (v. 17) and "the righteous" (v. 18). As vv. 19-20 make clear, Psalm 31 affirms, as do Psalms 1 and 2, that there is much to be gained—"abundant . . . goodness"—from being open to God's instruction (Ps 1:1-3) and taking refuge in God (v. 19; see Ps 2:12). This "reward" is clearly not material prosperity or an easy life (see vv. 4, 9-13, 15b-18) but the conviction that one's life and future really are in God's hand. This conviction issues in praise that celebrates God's fundamental character— steadfast love (v. 21). For the psalmist, to praise God is to live abundantly, regardless of outward circumstances. Interestingly, the psalmist envisions the future of the wicked as lying "silent" (v. 17), whereas Ps 30:12 had concluded with the affirmation that the psalmist would "not be silent"

as a result of God's life-giving power. The psalmist's "unsilence" consists of unending praise—the offering of the self to God—which constitutes life as God intends.

Meanwhile, of course, all is not as God intends. The psalmist is opposed (vv. 7, 11, 13, 15, 18), and so is God. Thus Psalm 31, like Psalms 1 and 2 and the psalter as a whole, is eschatological (see Introduction). God's goodness is simultaneously something to be experienced in the present and something to be awaited, hoped for (v. 24; see Ps 27:14). Thus the psalmist both celebrates deliverance as already having occurred (vv. 5b, 7-8, 21-22) and continues to pray for it (vv. 1b-2, 3b-4a, 9-13, 15b-18). This tension is the persistent reality of the life of faith. As we wait, there is the possibility of strength and courage, because we wait as God's "saints . . . the faithful" (v. 23). These two words are related to the two fundamental attributes of God celebrated in Psalm 31: steadfast love (vv. 7, 16, 21; "saints" [חסידים ḥāsîdîm] could be translated "steadfastly loving ones" or "steadfastly loved ones") and faithfulness (v. 5). In short, the people of God derive their identity from God's identity, and therein lies genuine hope (v. 24) and the possibility of love (v. 23).

REFLECTIONS

Scholars regularly observe that the frequent expressions of trust in Psalm 31 give it a creedal character or even a didactic thrust. What John Calvin said about v. 5 applies to the whole psalm, "This is one of the principle places of Scripture which are most suitable for correcting distrust."[147] In short, Psalm 31 is a prayer that teaches us about trusting God, both in dying and in living.

As suggested above, Psalm 31 became a resource for the gospel writers in understanding and relating the passion and death of Jesus (see also Psalms 22; 41; 69; Introduction). Jesus' quotation of v. 5a makes the final act of his earthly life an affirmation of trust in God that anticipates the resurrection. God's power to redeem will not be thwarted even by death (see also Rom 14:8). Following the example of Jesus, several great saints of the church—Jerome, Martin Luther, John Knox—died with the words of Ps 31:5 on their lips (see also Acts 7:59).[148] Psalm 31 can teach us how to die.

But just as important, Psalm 31 teaches us how to live. Jesus' words from the cross are not simply an interpretation of how Jesus died but also an interpretation of how Jesus lived his whole life—trusting God, proclaiming and embodying the reign of God in word and deed. The affirmations in vv. 5, 15 are for living, but this is precisely the difficulty we have with Psalm 31. What does it mean for us to turn our lives and futures over to God? What does it mean to live as a "servant" (v. 16) under God's sovereignty? The difficulty of answering these

147. John Calvin, *Commentary on the Book of Psalms,* Calvin Translation Society, 5 vols. (Grand Rapids: Baker, 1981) IV:1:503.
148. See Rowland E. Prothero, *The Psalms in Human Life and Experience* (New York: E. P. Dutton, 1903) 93, 199.

questions is indicated by the way contemporary people are inclined to hear vv. 4, 9-13, 15*b*. People tend to think the psalmist is paranoid. How can anybody be that threatened or persecuted? To be sure, it is a legitimate question for those of us who manage fairly well to order our lives satisfactorily most of the time. But that's also the real rub; *we* manage to order our lives. And that makes it very difficult to appreciate what Psalm 31 is fundamentally about: "the act of self-surrender to Yahweh."[149] Perhaps the most important thing Psalm 31 can teach us is that persons who trust God unreservedly should expect opposition from those who choose to trust themselves or any of the "worthless idols" (v. 6) that abound in our culture and in our churches.

In this regard, it is significant that much of the language of Psalm 31 is similar to the book of Jeremiah, especially those portions in which Jeremiah complains that his very faithfulness in proclaiming God's word has disrupted his life. Like Jeremiah, Jesus' very faithfulness to the reign of God engendered opposition, culminating in the cross, from which Jesus spoke the words of Ps 31:5. Those of us whom Jesus calls to "deny themselves and take up their cross and follow me" (Mark 8:34 NRSV) can also expect opposition. To surrender self in order to follow God is no more popular today than it was in the time of Jeremiah or Jesus. What Reinhold Niebuhr wrote in the 1920s is just as true today, and it is particularly pertinent to preachers:

> The real meaning of the gospel is in conflict with most of the customs and attitudes of our day at so many places that there is an adventure in the Christian message, even if you only play around with its ideas in a conventional world. . . .
>
> An astute pedagogy and a desire to speak the truth in love may greatly decrease opposition to a minister's message and persuade a difficult minority to entertain at least, and perhaps to profit by, his message; but if a gospel is preached without opposition it is simply not the gospel which resulted in the cross. It is not, in short, the gospel of love.[150]

The faithful psalmist knew in her or his life the kind of opposition that resulted in the cross. The psalmist also knew the paradoxical secret of what Scripture calls "happy": that to surrender one's life to God is truly to claim one's life (see Mark 8:35). Psalm 31 can teach us how to live.

To entrust our lives and futures to God, to belong to God in living and dying means ultimately that we derive our identity not from the worthless idols of our culture but from the character of God, to whom we entrust ourselves. The two fundamental characteristics of God that are emphasized in Psalm 31 are God's faithfulness (v. 5) and God's steadfast love (vv. 7, 16, 21), and the psalmist's closing admonition addresses the people of God as God's steadfastly loved (or loving) ones and "the faithful" (v. 23). God's faithfulness and love enable and empower the existence of a people who in turn can be faithful and loving to God and to each other. In our world—full of isolated selves and with "terror all around" (v. 13)—that good news invites a commitment to God and to the church that makes it possible to "be strong . . . take courage . . . wait for the LORD" (v. 24).[151]

149. Kraus, *Psalms 1–59,* 367.
150. Reinhold Niebuhr, *Leaves from the Notebook of a Tamed Cynic* (San Francisco: Harper & Row, 1980) 27, 140.
151. Portions of the above treatment of Psalm 31 appeared originally in substantially the same form in J. C. McCann, Jr., "Psalm 31:1-8: Psalm for the Fifth Sunday of Easter," *No Other Foundation* 13/2 (Winter 1992–93) 30-35.

PSALM 32:1-11, YOU FORGAVE THE GUILT OF MY SIN

NIV

Psalm 32

Of David. A *maskil.*[a]

[1]Blessed is he
    whose transgressions are forgiven,
    whose sins are covered.
[2]Blessed is the man
    whose sin the LORD does not count against
        him
    and in whose spirit is no deceit.
[3]When I kept silent,
    my bones wasted away
    through my groaning all day long.
[4]For day and night
    your hand was heavy upon me;
my strength was sapped
    as in the heat of summer.   *Selah*
[5]Then I acknowledged my sin to you
    and did not cover up my iniquity.
I said, "I will confess
    my transgressions to the LORD"—
and you forgave
    the guilt of my sin.   *Selah*

[6]Therefore let everyone who is godly pray to
        you
    while you may be found;
surely when the mighty waters rise,
    they will not reach him.
[7]You are my hiding place;
    you will protect me from trouble
    and surround me with songs
        of deliverance.   *Selah*

[8]I will instruct you and teach you in the way
        you should go;
    I will counsel you and watch over you.
[9]Do not be like the horse or the mule,
    which have no understanding
but must be controlled by bit and bridle
    or they will not come to you.
[10]Many are the woes of the wicked,

[a] Title: Probably a literary or musical term

NRSV

Psalm 32

Of David. A Maskil.

[1] Happy are those whose transgression is
    forgiven,
    whose sin is covered.
[2] Happy are those to whom the LORD imputes
    no iniquity,
    and in whose spirit there is no deceit.

[3] While I kept silence, my body wasted away
    through my groaning all day long.
[4] For day and night your hand was heavy
    upon me;
    my strength was dried up[a] as by the heat
    of summer.   *Selah*

[5] Then I acknowledged my sin to you,
    and I did not hide my iniquity;
I said, "I will confess my transgressions to
    the LORD,"
    and you forgave the guilt of my sin. *Selah*

[6] Therefore let all who are faithful
    offer prayer to you;
    at a time of distress,[b] the rush of mighty
    waters
    shall not reach them.
[7] You are a hiding place for me;
    you preserve me from trouble;
    you surround me with glad cries of
    deliverance.   *Selah*

[8] I will instruct you and teach you the way
    you should go;
    I will counsel you with my eye upon you.
[9] Do not be like a horse or a mule, without
    understanding,
    whose temper must be curbed with bit
    and bridle,
    else it will not stay near you.

[a] Meaning of Heb uncertain   [b] Cn: Heb *at a time of finding only*

NIV	NRSV

but the Lord's unfailing love
    surrounds the man who trusts in him.
 	
[11]Rejoice in the Lord and be glad, you
    righteous;
    sing, all you who are upright in heart!
	[10] Many are the torments of the wicked,
	    but steadfast love surrounds those who
	        trust in the Lord.
	[11] Be glad in the Lord and rejoice, O righteous,
	    and shout for joy, all you upright in heart.

COMMENTARY

On account of its description of deliverance from sin and its harmful effects (vv. 3-5), as well as the elements of testimony (vv. 6-7) and invitation (v. 11), Psalm 32 is often classified as a psalm of thanksgiving. Several scholars, however, categorize it as a wisdom psalm, because of the opening beatitudes (vv. 1-2) and the explicitly instructional intent (vv. 8-9). Drawing on both sets of observations, Gerstenberger suggests that Psalm 32 "comes very close to being a homily on penitence."[152] For this reason, church tradition has named Psalm 32 the second of the penitential psalms (see also Psalms 6; 38; 51; 102; 130; 143). While there is no actual confession of sin in the psalm, it does report the psalmist's experience of confessing sin and receiving forgiveness (vv. 3-5). Psalm 32 is thus instructive testimony as to the nature and benefits of confession, as well as to God's character as a gracious, forgiving God. The psalm may originally have been used in ceremonies of confession or cleansing in the Temple, although most scholars suggest a later date, associating its origin and use with the post-exilic synagogue (see Ezra 9; Nehemiah 9; Daniel 9). In any case, it continues to function as instruction for readers in any generation, and it continues to invite the people of God to confession of sin, to trust, and to joy (vv. 6-11).

Psalm 32 begins with two beatitudes that recall the beginning of the psalter (see 1:1; 2:12). Several other items of the vocabulary of Psalm 32 also recall Psalms 1-2: "sin" (vv. 1, 5; see "sinners" in 1:1, 5), "day and night" (v. 4; see 1:2), "teach" (v. 8; the root is the same as "law" or "instruction" in 1:2), "way" (v. 8; see 1:1, 6; 2:12), "wicked" (v. 10; see 1:1, 4-6), and "righ-

teous" (v. 11; see 1:6). By defining happiness in terms of forgiveness, Psalm 32 functions as an important check against any tendency to misunderstand Psalm 1. That is, to be righteous is not a matter of being sinless but a matter of being forgiven, of being open to God's instruction (Ps 1:2; see 32:8-9), and of trusting God rather than self (v. 10; see Ps 2:12). In fact, as Psalm 32 suggests, sin and its effects are pervasive in the life of the righteous. Verse 2c apparently anticipates v. 5 and the confession of sin described there; that is, confession of sin must be made honestly and humbly. The pervasiveness of sin is not an excuse for further sinning but an opportunity to seek forgiveness sincerely.

The pervasiveness of sin is represented literarily by the fact that three words for sin in vv. 1-2, 5 envelope the psalmist's self-description in vv. 3-4: "transgression(s)" (vv. 1, 5), "sin(s)" (vv. 1, 5), "iniquity"/"guilt" (עוֹן 'āwōn, vv. 2, 5). While there are other words for "sin," these words represent Israel's basic vocabulary (see Ps 51:1-5). The word "sin" (פשע peša') is the most general, meaning fundamentally "to miss the mark." "Transgression" connotes willful rebellion, and "iniquity"/"guilt" (חטאה ḥăṭā'â) suggests the enduring, destructive effects of disobedience. The psalmist's life is characterized by all three (v. 5), and the results are very real, even physical, causing the psalmist's "bones" (see Pss 22:14; 31:10; 38:3) to waste away (cf. Job 13:28) through "groaning" (cf. Job 3:24; Pss 22:1; 38:8). While the imagery of v. 4 suggests God's judgment (see 1 Sam 5:11; Ps 38:4), the impression left by vv. 3-4 is that the real problem is not God's wrath but the psalmist's silence. As v. 5c indicates, God is fully willing to forgive. But first the psalmist's

152. Erhard S. Gerstenberger, *Psalms, Part 1, with an Introduction to Cultic Poetry,* Forms of the OT Literature 14 (Grand Rapids: Eerdmans, 1988) 143.

805

silence must be broken, for "the silence is the rejection of grace."[153]

That the reality of divine forgiveness is even more encompassing than the reality of sin is also represented by the literary structure of the psalm. Whereas sin encompassed the description of the psalmist's life, God's forgiveness encompasses sin (see "forgiven"/"forgave" in vv. 1*a,* 5*c*). Those who do "not *cover up . . .* iniquity" (v. 5) will be the "happy" ones whose "sins are *covered"* (v. 1). Verse 5*c,* which marks the turning point of the psalm, is crucial. Its pronoun "you" is emphatic; it is nearly, perhaps exactly, the central poetic line. After the announcement of forgiveness in v. 5*c,* none of the words for "sin" occur again. The situation changes for persons who acknowledge their sin in reliance on God's grace.

While the psalmist focuses on himself or herself in vv. 3-5, the reality of forgiveness directs the psalmist outward. Attention is now focused on "the faithful" (v. 6), the Hebrew word for which (חסיד *ḥāsîd*) anticipates the occurrence of the related steadfast love in v. 10. The faithful derive their identity not from their own accomplishments but from *God's* faithfulness in forgiving and renewing them (see Ps 31:23). Prayer becomes a way of life for those who know that their own accomplishments, capabilities, and intentions are always inadequate. That is, it is a way of life for those "who trust in the LORD" (v. 10).

Attention is also focused on God. Prayer, of course, is directed "to you"—to God (v. 6), and the three affirmations in v. 7 focus directly on God as well. The first word in v. 7 is the emphatic pronoun "You," which recalls the emphatic "you" that began v. 5*c.* In each of the three affirmations in v. 7, God is the subject and the psalmist is the object of God's action. God's character and activity are determinative; God is a faithful protector (the word for "hiding place" [סתר *sēter*] also occurs as "cover" or "shelter" in Pss 27:5; 31:20; 61:4; 91:1). Robert Jenson points out that "the psalmist's own stance is that of *witness,* to his experience and to the grace of God."[154] The substance of the psalmist's witness in v. 7*c* anticipates vv. 10-11, which also underscore God's character and activity. The word "surround(s)"

recurs in v. 10 in connection with God's steadfast love, a fundamental divine attribute (see Exod 34:6-7, where the issue is also forgiveness; see also Introduction). The Hebrew root translated "songs of deliverance" (רנה *rinnâ*) in v. 7*c* underlies "sing" in v. 11. The psalmist can invite others to sing, because God has already surrounded the psalmist with "songs of deliverance." Verses 6-7 and 10-11 are also linked structurally in a chiastic pattern (see Introduction): "invitation" (v. 6), profession of faith (v. 7), profession of faith (v. 10), invitation (v. 11).

The chiastic pattern of these verses serves to emphasize vv. 8-9, which are probably another instance of the psalmist's witness. Several scholars understand the "I" of v. 8 to be God, and thus view vv. 8-9 to be a divine word delivered by a priest or prophet; however, in view of the psalmist's witness in vv. 6-7, 10-11, it is more likely that the psalmist is speaking in vv. 8-9 to offer instruction to others. As in Psalm 51, which is another penitential psalm, the forgiven sinner teaches God's ways to others (see 51:13). This educational ministry is not presumptuous, for the psalmist witnesses not to his or her own righteousness but to divine grace—God's willingness and God's ability to set things and persons right. Thus "the way you should go" (v. 8) points to the psalmist's example of breaking silence to confess sin (vv. 3, 5) and to his or her conviction of God's willingness to forgive and restore (vv. 7, 10). The psalmist's witness in vv. 6-11 is in essence an invitation to others, including the readers of Psalm 32, to confess their own sinfulness and to live in dependence upon the grace of God (see "trust" in Pss 4:5; 9:10; Introduction). The invitation is explicit in v. 11, which is a final reminder that the "righteous" (see Ps 1:5-6) and the "upright in heart" (see Pss 7:10; 11:2; 36:10; 64:10; 94:15; 97:11; 125:4) are not the sinless but the forgiven. Joy and happiness (vv. 1-2) derive not from human achievement but from God's gracious activity on behalf of sinners. Perhaps not coincidentally, Psalm 33 begins with essentially the same invitation that concludes Psalm 32; it is an extended celebration of the divine steadfast love (vv. 5, 18, 22; see 32:10), which surrounds the penitent (32:10) and, indeed, fills the earth (33:5; see Commentary on Psalms 19; 33).

153. James L. Mays, *Psalms,* Interpretation (Louisville: John Knox, 1994) 147.
154. Robert W. Jenson, "Psalm 32," *Int.* 33 (1979) 175.

REFLECTIONS

As the Commentary shows, Psalm 32 recalls Psalm 1 and reinforces the understanding of righteousness articulated on the basis of Psalm 1. That is to say, to be righteous is not to manage somehow to obey all the rules, to be sinless. Rather, as Psalm 32 suggests, the lives of the righteous are pervaded by sin and its consequences (vv. 3-5). To be righteous is to be forgiven (v. 5). To be righteous is to be a witness to God's grace (vv. 6-11).

Not surprisingly, one of the greatest witnesses to God's grace, the apostle Paul, knew Psalm 32 and cited vv. 1-2a in his own teaching in Rom 4:6-8. Paul did not invent the notion of justification by grace. He found it in the story of Abraham (see esp. Gen 15:6) and in psalms like Psalm 32 (see also Psalm 51). Another of the great witnesses to God's grace, Augustine, is said to have had the words of Psalm 32 inscribed above his bed so that they would be the first thing he saw upon awakening.[155]

The experience of being happy (vv. 1-2), of being forgiven (v. 5), of being in the right (v. 11), is an important dimension of human life in any era. Indeed, "facing up to one's errors and being pardoned are important modes of interaction even today, which go far beyond all the existing penitential rites of religious and ideological groups."[156] While Gerstenberger is undoubtedly correct, it is also true that we contemporary folk do not readily think of ourselves as being sinners; neither are we inclined to think in terms of sin as an explanation for our corporate ills. Karl Menninger pointed this out several years ago in a book entitled *Whatever Became of Sin?* After documenting the disappearance of sin, Menninger makes a simple proposal:

> My proposal is for the revival or reassertion of personal responsibility in all human acts, good and bad. Not total responsibility, but not zero either. I believe that all the evildoing in which we become involved to any degree tends to evoke guilt feelings and depression. These may or may not be clearly perceived, but they affect us. They may be reacted to and covered up by all kinds of escapism, rationalization, and reaction or symptom formation. To revive the half-submerged idea of personal responsibility and to seek appropriate measures of reparation might turn the tide of our aggressions and of the moral struggle in which most of the world population is engaged.[157]

Menninger recognizes what Ps 32:3-4 also recognizes: the devastating physical, emotional, and spiritual effects of failing to acknowledge our sinfulness. Like the psalmist, he calls on us to break our silence (v. 3). Menninger calls on everyone to contribute to the revival of the term *sin,* but he suggests that the clergy have a special responsibility: "It is their special prerogative to study sin—or whatever they call it—to identify it, to define it, to warn us about it, and to spur measures for combating and rectifying it."[158]

For clergy and laity alike, Psalm 32 is an impetus and a resource to study sin. It also suggests how to begin to combat it and rectify it: by forthright confession of sin, acceptance of the grace of God, and humble dependence on God's steadfast love rather than on human initiative and ingenuity.

155. See Rowland E. Prothero, *The Psalms in Human Life and Experience* (New York: E. P. Dutton, 1903) 29.
156. Gerstenberger, *Psalms,* 141.
157. Karl Menninger, *Whatever Became of Sin?* (New York: Hawthorn Books, 1973) 178.
158. Ibid., 192.

PSALM 33:1-22, THE EARTH IS FULL OF GOD'S UNFAILING LOVE

NIV

Psalm 33

¹Sing joyfully to the LORD, you righteous;
  it is fitting for the upright to praise him.
²Praise the LORD with the harp;
  make music to him on the ten-stringed lyre.
³Sing to him a new song;
  play skillfully, and shout for joy.

⁴For the word of the LORD is right and true;
  he is faithful in all he does.
⁵The LORD loves righteousness and justice;
  the earth is full of his unfailing love.

⁶By the word of the LORD were the heavens
    made,
  their starry host by the breath of his mouth.
⁷He gathers the waters of the sea into jarsª;
  he puts the deep into storehouses.
⁸Let all the earth fear the LORD;
  let all the people of the world revere
    him.
⁹For he spoke, and it came to be;
  he commanded, and it stood firm.
¹⁰The LORD foils the plans of the nations;
  he thwarts the purposes of the peoples.
¹¹But the plans of the LORD stand firm forever,
  the purposes of his heart through all
    generations.

¹²Blessed is the nation whose God is the LORD,
  the people he chose for his inheritance.
¹³From heaven the LORD looks down
  and sees all mankind;
¹⁴from his dwelling place he watches
  all who live on earth—
¹⁵he who forms the hearts of all,
  who considers everything they do.

¹⁶No king is saved by the size of his army;
  no warrior escapes by his great strength.
¹⁷A horse is a vain hope for deliverance;
  despite all its great strength it cannot save.
¹⁸But the eyes of the LORD are on those who
    fear him,

ª7 Or *sea as into a heap*

NRSV

Psalm 33

¹ Rejoice in the LORD, O you righteous.
  Praise befits the upright.
² Praise the LORD with the lyre;
  make melody to him with the harp of
    ten strings.
³ Sing to him a new song;
  play skillfully on the strings, with loud
    shouts.

⁴ For the word of the LORD is upright,
  and all his work is done in faithfulness.
⁵ He loves righteousness and justice;
  the earth is full of the steadfast love of
    the LORD.

⁶ By the word of the LORD the heavens were
    made,
  and all their host by the breath of his
    mouth.
⁷ He gathered the waters of the sea as in a
    bottle;
  he put the deeps in storehouses.

⁸ Let all the earth fear the LORD;
  let all the inhabitants of the world stand
    in awe of him.
⁹ For he spoke, and it came to be;
  he commanded, and it stood firm.

¹⁰ The LORD brings the counsel of the nations
    to nothing;
  he frustrates the plans of the peoples.
¹¹ The counsel of the LORD stands forever,
  the thoughts of his heart to all
    generations.
¹² Happy is the nation whose God is the LORD,
  the people whom he has chosen as his
    heritage.

¹³ The LORD looks down from heaven;
  he sees all humankind.
¹⁴ From where he sits enthroned he watches

NIV

on those whose hope is in his unfailing
love,
¹⁹to deliver them from death
and keep them alive in famine.
²⁰We wait in hope for the LORD;
he is our help and our shield.
²¹In him our hearts rejoice,
for we trust in his holy name.
²²May your unfailing love rest upon us, O LORD,
even as we put our hope in you.

NRSV

all the inhabitants of the earth—
¹⁵ he who fashions the hearts of them all,
and observes all their deeds.
¹⁶ A king is not saved by his great army;
a warrior is not delivered by his great
strength.
¹⁷ The war horse is a vain hope for victory,
and by its great might it cannot save.

¹⁸ Truly the eye of the LORD is on those who
fear him,
on those who hope in his steadfast love,
¹⁹ to deliver their soul from death,
and to keep them alive in famine.

²⁰ Our soul waits for the LORD;
he is our help and shield.
²¹ Our heart is glad in him,
because we trust in his holy name.
²² Let your steadfast love, O LORD, be upon us,
even as we hope in you.

COMMENTARY

One of the few songs of praise in Books I–II of the psalter, Psalm 33 seems to be a direct response to the invitation of Ps 32:11 (note the absence of a superscription for Psalm 33). Verse 1 addresses an invitation to the same parties addressed in 32:11—the "righteous" and the "upright"—and the NRSV's "shout for joy" (32:11) and "rejoice" (33:1) translate the same Hebrew verb. Furthermore, the culminating affirmation of Ps 32:11 highlighted the concepts of steadfast love and trust, both of which are also prominent in Psalm 33. The word "trust" (בטח *bāṭaḥ*) is featured in the culminating affirmation of Psalm 33 (v. 21), and v. 5*b* boldly proclaims that the steadfast love, which surrounds those who trust God (32:11), also fills the earth! This is the crucial verse in the psalm; everything that follows is essentially an explanation of it.[159] What is affirmed as the psalm unfolds is that God is sovereign over all (note the word "all" in vv. 6, 8, 13, 14, 15)—creation (vv. 6-9), the nations and peoples (vv. 10-12), humanity in general (vv. 13-15), human teachers and symbols of power (vv. 16-17), as well as those who explicitly acknowledge their hope in God's steadfast love (vv. 18-19).

The intent of Psalm 33 to acknowledge God's comprehensive sovereignty is reinforced by the fact that it consists of 22 lines—the same number of lines as the letters in the Hebrew alphabet. The psalm is not an acrostic, but its structure does bespeak completeness. When Psalms 32 and 33 are read in sequence, the striking claim is that the grace God shows in forgiving sinners (Psalm 32) is the force that accounts for the origin of the world (vv. 6-9), the unfolding of history (vv. 10-12), the care of individual persons (vv. 13-15), the real power behind human illusions of power (vv. 16-17), and the hope of God's own people (vv. 18-19). Appropriately, the psalm concludes with a joyful affirmation of faith in God's beneficence and power (vv. 20-21) and a prayer for what constitutes the fundamental reality of the universe: God's steadfast love (v. 22).

33:1-3. The invitation in v. 1 extends into vv.

159. See Mays, *Psalms,* 149.

2-3. Praise is appropriate to those who acknowledge their dependence on God (see Ps 147:1), for praise is essentially the offering of the self to God, including one's musical gifts. Verse 2 represents the first reference to musical instruments in the psalms (see the first word in Pss 43:4; 57:8; 71:22; 81:3; 92:3; 98:5; 108:2; 137:2; 147:7; 149:3; 150:3; see also 1 Sam 16:16; 2 Sam 6:5; 1 Chr 13:8; see also the second word in Pss 57:8; 71:22; 81:3; 92:4; 108:3; 144:9; 150:3; see also 2 Sam 6:5; 1 Chr 13:8). Verses 1-2 together suggest that what is important about praise is more the motive and the goal than the means. Instrumentation is appropriate, as is the human voice, singing or shouting (v. 3). The Hebrew root of "loud shouts" (תרועה *tĕrûʿâ*) occurs in verbal form in Pss 47:1; 95:1-2; 98:4 (see also Ps 100:2), all of which specifically celebrate God's reign. The motive for praise is the recognition of God's reign, and the goal is to offer oneself and one's best gifts to the source of one's existence. The singing of a "new song" is also associated elsewhere with the celebration of God's reign (see Pss 96:1; 98:1; 149:1; see also Pss 40:3; 144:9; Isa 42:10).

33:4-5. As is typical in the songs of praise, the invitation is followed by reasons for praise. God's "word" and "work" are manifestations of God's own self (v. 4); God is elsewhere described as "upright" (see Pss 25:8; 92:15; see also Ps 32:11; 33:1, which suggest that God's people derive their identity from God) and possessing "faithfulness" (see Pss 36:5; 88:12; 89:1-2, 5, 8, 33, 49; 92:2; 98:3; 100:5). Verse 5 describes the goal of God's speaking and acting in terms associated elsewhere with God's character and rule: "righteousness and justice" (see Pss 97:2; 99:4), manifested in steadfast love (Pss 98:3; 145:8; see also Exod 34:6-7; Pss 5:7; 119:64; Introduction). As suggested above, the rest of the psalm is an elaboration upon v. 5*b*, illustrating the full extent of the reach of God's loving purposes.

33:6-9. Verse 6*a* repeats the key terms from v. 4: "word" (דבר *dābār*) and the root "to do," "to make" (עשׂה *ʿāśâ*; "work" in v. 4 and "made" in v. 6). The focus is on God's Word, as suggested by the mention of "the breath" of God's "mouth" (v. 6*b*) and by the verbs in v. 9. God's Word effects God's work. Verses 6 and 9 especially recall the creation account in Genesis 1, and vv. 7-8 allude to the exodus, which, as Terence

Fretheim persuasively argues, represents the fulfillment of God's creational purposes.[160] Verse 7 clearly recalls Exod 15:8 (see "deeps" in both verses, as well as the word the NRSV renders as "heap"/"bottle"; see the NIV's note); and v. 8 describes precisely the response of the Israelites when they saw what God "did" (the same root as "work" in v. 4) against the Egyptians—they "feared the LORD" (Exod 14:31 NRSV).[161] The two occurrences of "he" in v. 9 represent the emphatic use of the pronoun—*God* is behind it all!

33:10-12. The focus shifts from God's word to God's will and from the sphere of creation to the sphere of history (insofar as the two can be separated). As the NIV suggests, the two key terms from v. 10 are repeated in v. 11, effectively contrasting God's enduring will with the transient human will (see Neh 4:15; Prov 19:21, 30-31; Isa 14:26-27; 25:1; 46:10-11). Contrary to a frequent appropriation of v. 12, it is *God* who chooses a nation and a people, not vice-versa. The unremitting focus in Psalm 33 is on God's sovereignty.

33:13-15. God's sovereignty is clearly in view in v. 14 (see "sits" or "enthroned" or both in Pss 2:4; 9:8; 29:10; 99:1). Because God rules over all, God sees everyone and everything (vv. 13-15; see Pss 11:4; 14:2; 102:19). The universality of vv. 13-14 recalls v. 8, but there is a particularity here as well. As creator or fashioner of every heart (see "formed" in Gen 2:7), God knows each person.

33:16-19. The greatest of human personages and their trappings of power are negated in vv. 16-17. Kings, of course, represent human sovereignty, and armies and horses are their means for enforcing their own will to power. Such apparent greatness (see "great" three times in vv. 16-17) is an illusion (see Prov 21:30-31). Salvation ("saved" in v. 16 and "victory" in v. 17 represent the same Hebrew root [ישׁע *yšʿ*]), or life, is God's gift, not a human achievement. Those who "fear" God (v. 18; cf. v. 8) know that God delivers them from death and keeps them alive (v. 19; see Ps 107:4-9, where sustenance and life result from God's steadfast love).

160. Terence Fretheim, *Exodus,* Interpretation (Louisville: Westminster/John Knox, 1991) 12-14.
161. See Peter C. Craigie, *Psalms 1–50,* WBC 19 (Waco, Tex.: Word, 1983) 273.

33:20-22. Thus, they "wait in hope" (v. 20). חכה (ḥākâ) is not a commonly used word for "hope" in the psalter (elsewhere only Ps 106:13), but it is essentially synonymous with the more frequently used words that occur here and elsewhere (see "hope" in vv. 18, 22; see also Pss 27:14; 31:24; 130:7; 131:3). Faith, hope, and joy characterize the lives of those who recognize God as a "help" (see Pss 22:19; 27:9; 40:17; 70:5; see esp. Ps 115:9-11, where the admonition to trust accompanies the same affirmation as here) and a "shield" (see Pss 3:3; 7:10; 28:7; 115:9-11). The psalm concludes with a prayer for what it earlier had affirmed fills the earth: God's steadfast love (v. 22; see also vv. 5b, 18). Like the psalter as a whole, Psalm 33 is eschatological. It proclaims God's reign amid persons and circumstances that deny it. Thus God's rule is something both to be celebrated with joyful praise (vv. 1-3; see v. 21) and to be awaited in fervent hope (vv. 20-22).

REFLECTIONS

As Peter Craigie suggests, Psalm 33 is a "timely reminder of the essence of biblical theology."[162] That is to say, Psalm 33 proclaims what lies at the heart of the good news of all of Scripture, including the psalter as a whole and the preaching of Jesus: God rules the world (see Psalm 2; Mark 1:14-15; Introduction). The reminder is timely, because the message is so difficult to believe in the context of contemporary, secularized culture. Seldom does it occur to us that life and the resources that sustain life (see vv. 18-19) are the provision of a gracious, steadfastly loving God! Instead, we view life simply as a biological fact, or perhaps as a "human right," and the resources that sustain life are seen as the product of our sophisticated educational and economic system, the benefits of which we attain personally by our own hard work. We earn it!

Likewise, seldom do we understand the world (vv. 6-9) in anything other than scientific terms; so creation becomes not a sacred trust but a realm to be explored and then exploited. Seldom, if ever, do we think of international politics in terms of God's will; we have made even human relatedness a "political science," the subject of which is exclusively "the counsel of the nations" and the "plans of the peoples" (v. 10). In fact, we do believe that nations are saved by their great armies and that security is found in the implements of war (vv. 16-17), and this faith has been and still is the cornerstone of the foreign policy of the United States and every other nation in the world. The great irony, as Reinhold Niebuhr pointed out years ago, is that the very efforts to secure our own destiny and future have rendered us even more insecure and vulnerable. To be sure, neither Niebuhr nor Psalm 33 calls us to passivity but to properly motivated activity. Niebuhr characterized the biblical view of human history: "The evil in human history is regarded as the consequence of man's wrong use of his unique capacities. The wrong use is always due to some failure to recognize the limits of his capacities of power, wisdom, and virtue. Man is an ironic creature because he forgets that he is not simply a creator but also a creature."[163]

We forget that God rules the world and we do not. Instead of praising God, our first inclination is to congratulate ourselves (see Commentary on Psalm 65). Psalm 33 is finally, then, a call to humility and to trust in God rather than in human power, wisdom, or virtue. To heed this call means nothing less than a revolutionary transmutation of values. The things and people that seem so obviously powerful—politicians, armies, weapons—are exposed in the light of God's sovereignty to be illusions. The real power behind the universe, human history, and personal existence is the steadfast love of God, which fills the earth (Ps 33:5b) and is revealed ultimately not by God's absolute enforcement of God's will but by God's forgiveness of sin (Psalm 32). The astounding good news is that the ultimate reality and power

162. Ibid., 275.
163. Reinhold Niebuhr, *The Irony of American History* (New York: Charles Scribner's Sons, 1952) 156.

in the universe is love (see Commentary on Psalm 19). This power, to be sure, is made perfect in weakness (see 2 Cor 12:9). Indeed, Christians profess to see it revealed most clearly in the cross of Jesus Christ.

PSALM 34:1-22, I WILL TEACH YOU THE FEAR OF THE LORD

<table>
<tr><td>

NIV

Psalm 34[a]

Of David. When he pretended to be insane before Abimelech, who drove him away, and he left.

[1]I will extol the LORD at all times;
  his praise will always be on my lips.
[2]My soul will boast in the LORD;
  let the afflicted hear and rejoice.
[3]Glorify the LORD with me;
  let us exalt his name together.

[4]I sought the LORD, and he answered me;
  he delivered me from all my fears.
[5]Those who look to him are radiant;
  their faces are never covered with shame.
[6]This poor man called, and the LORD heard him;
  he saved him out of all his troubles.
[7]The angel of the LORD encamps around those who fear him,
  and he delivers them.

[8]Taste and see that the LORD is good;
  blessed is the man who takes refuge in him.
[9]Fear the LORD, you his saints,
  for those who fear him lack nothing.
[10]The lions may grow weak and hungry,
  but those who seek the LORD lack no good thing.

[11]Come, my children, listen to me;
  I will teach you the fear of the LORD.
[12]Whoever of you loves life
  and desires to see many good days,
[13]keep your tongue from evil
  and your lips from speaking lies.

</td><td>

NRSV

Psalm 34

Of David, when he feigned madness before Abimelech, so that he drove him out, and he went away.

[1] I will bless the LORD at all times;
  his praise shall continually be in my mouth.
[2] My soul makes its boast in the LORD;
  let the humble hear and be glad.
[3] O magnify the LORD with me,
  and let us exalt his name together.

[4] I sought the LORD, and he answered me,
  and delivered me from all my fears.
[5] Look to him, and be radiant;
  so your[a] faces shall never be ashamed.
[6] This poor soul cried, and was heard by the LORD,
  and was saved from every trouble.
[7] The angel of the LORD encamps
  around those who fear him, and delivers them.
[8] O taste and see that the LORD is good;
  happy are those who take refuge in him.
[9] O fear the LORD, you his holy ones,
  for those who fear him have no want.
[10] The young lions suffer want and hunger,
  but those who seek the LORD lack no good thing.

[11] Come, O children, listen to me;
  I will teach you the fear of the LORD.
[12] Which of you desires life,
  and covets many days to enjoy good?
[13] Keep your tongue from evil,
  and your lips from speaking deceit.

</td></tr>
</table>

[a] This psalm is an acrostic poem, the verses of which begin with the successive letters of the Hebrew alphabet.

[a] Gk Syr Jerome: Heb *their*

NIV

¹⁴Turn from evil and do good;
    seek peace and pursue it.

¹⁵The eyes of the Lord are on the righteous
    and his ears are attentive to their cry;
¹⁶the face of the Lord is against those who do evil,
    to cut off the memory of them from the
        earth.

¹⁷The righteous cry out, and the Lord hears them;
    he delivers them from all their troubles.
¹⁸The Lord is close to the brokenhearted
    and saves those who are crushed in spirit.

¹⁹A righteous man may have many troubles,
    but the Lord delivers him from them all;
²⁰he protects all his bones,
    not one of them will be broken.

²¹Evil will slay the wicked;
    the foes of the righteous will be
        condemned.
²²The Lord redeems his servants;
    no one will be condemned who takes
        refuge in him.

NRSV

¹⁴ Depart from evil, and do good;
    seek peace, and pursue it.

¹⁵ The eyes of the Lord are on the righteous,
    and his ears are open to their cry.
¹⁶ The face of the Lord is against evildoers,
    to cut off the remembrance of them from
        the earth.

¹⁷ When the righteous cry for help, the Lord hears,
    and rescues them from all their troubles.
¹⁸ The Lord is near to the brokenhearted,
    and saves the crushed in spirit.

¹⁹ Many are the afflictions of the righteous,
    but the Lord rescues them from them all.
²⁰ He keeps all their bones;
    not one of them will be broken.

²¹ Evil brings death to the wicked,
    and those who hate the righteous will be
        condemned.
²² The Lord redeems the life of his servants;
    none of those who take refuge in him
        will be condemned.

COMMENTARY

Psalm 34 is an acrostic poem (see NIV note) that is similar in several ways to Psalm 25 (see above). For instance, as in Psalm 25, v. 22 lies outside the acrostic structure, and if the first letters of vv. 1, 11 (the central poetic line), and 22 are taken in order, they spell the word אלף ('ālep), the first letter of the alphabet. This apparently intentional literary cleverness is often associated with wisdom literature (see the acrostic poem in Prov 31:10-31), and Psalm 34 shares other characteristics with the wisdom literature as well. It explicitly intends to teach, as is clear in v. 11, which addresses "children" as in the book of Proverbs (see Prov 1:8; 3:1; 4:1). Furthermore, the topic of the teaching—"the fear of the Lord"—is a major theme in Proverbs (see Prov 1:7, 29; 2:5; 9:10; 15:33). And the goal of the teaching—to impart "life"—also is in keeping with Proverbs (see Prov 3:2, 16, 18; 4:22-23; 5:6; 10:17). So is the behavior involved in fearing God—proper speech (Prov 4:24, 27; 6:17, 19; 10:18), departure from evil and doing good (Prov 2:20; 3:7; 4:14), the pursuit of peace (Prov 3:17).

Psalm 34 is usually classified as a song of thanksgiving, due to the psalmist's expressed intent to praise God (vv. 1-3), as well as to the account of deliverance in v. 4, which is echoed in vv. 6, 15, 17-18. It is also possible that v. 8 alludes poetically to the sacrificial meal that accompanied a thank offering, but the language may be metaphorical (see below). In any case, it is not necessary to conclude, as most scholars have done, that Psalm 34 was a private composition intended for personal use. To be sure, it can be used for personal meditation, but Gerstenberger suggests that Psalm 34 was probably used originally in synagogue services where "the individual's anxieties and hopes, suffering and salvation were dealt with in meditation, adoration, and instruction."[164]

164. Gerstenberger, *Psalms,* 149.

The superscription is enigmatic. It is most closely related to 1 Sam 21:13, but the king in that story is named Achish, so what the editor may have intended is not clear. Within the overarching acrostic structure, it is possible to identify several divisions. The opening section expresses the psalmist's intent to praise God (vv. 1-2) and invites others to participate (v. 3). The next section is marked by the repetition of "sought"/"seek" (vv. 4-10). The psalmist narrates his or her own experience of deliverance (vv. 4, 6). This experience, as well as the generalizations the psalmist makes from this experience (vv. 7, 9b-10), serve as the basis for inviting others to turn to God (vv. 5, 8). Hence, even before v. 11, Psalm 34 is instructional; however, vv. 11-14 are more explicitly so. The instruction continues in vv. 15-22 by way of a series of affirmations that are united by their concern with how God relates to the righteous and the wicked.

34:1-3. The psalmist's opening statements make it clear that she or he lives in dependence upon God. To "bless" means essentially to kneel before a sovereign (see Pss 16:7; 26:12). The words "praise" and "boast" are derived from the same Hebrew root (הלל *hll*); praise involves the offering of the self to God (see Pss 22:22-23, 25-26; 33:1; Introduction). Interestingly, while the praise is directed to God, it is also intended to be overheard by the "humble" (cf. NRSV: Pss 9:12, "afflicted"; 10:12, "oppressed"; 22:26, "poor"; 25:9; 69:32, "oppressed"), who are immediately invited to join the psalmist in magnifying (see Ps 69:30) and exalting God (Exod 15:2; see "extol" in Pss 30:1; 99:5, 9; 145:1; note the connections with proclamations of God's reign). As in Ps 69:30-33, the psalmist here offers his or her own life and praise as an example to others who are oppressed, not in an arrogant way but as testimony to God's character (see Ps 20:7; 1 Cor 1:31; 2 Cor 1:12; 10:12-18; 12:1-10).

34:4-10. The psalmist's intent to be an example is clear in these verses. Following the recountings of his or her own experience (vv. 4, 6), the psalmist says to others, in effect, "Experience it for yourselves" (vv. 5, 8-9)! What has been experienced is deliverance (v. 4), salvation (v. 6)—in short, life (see v. 12). It is not something the psalmist has to offer, for he or she is one of the "poor" (v. 6; "poor" [עני *ʿānî*] is the same Hebrew

root as "humble"/"afflicted" in v. 2). Rather, life is something that *God* offers. The psalmist's advice is not, "Look to me," but, "Look to God" (v. 5)—or, as v. 8 puts it, "Taste and see." In other words, "Get a taste of it yourself, and you'll see" (see Prov 31:18, where the verb translated "taste" is used figuratively as "perceive" [NRSV]; see also Job 12:11; 34:3, where tasting suggests trying something out). What others will "see" is that God is "good"; that is, they will be put in touch with one of Israel's fundamental professions (see Pss 73:1; 86:5; 100:5; 106:1; 107:1; 118:1, 29; 136:1; see also Exod 33:19). Entrusting their lives to God, they will be "radiant" (see Isa 60:5), "happy" (v. 8; see Pss 1:1; 2:12; Introduction), and will be fully provided for (vv. 8-9; see Deut 2:7; 15:18; Ps 23:1).

The key word in vv. 4-10 is "fear" (ירא *yārēʾ*, vv. 7, 9; see Pss 22:25; 25:12, 14; 31:19; 33:8). While a few OT references to fearing God suggest actual fright (see 1 Sam 12:18; 2 Sam 6:9), fearing God usually connotes reverence for, trust in, and dependence upon God. In effect, it is synonymous with taking refuge in God (v. 8; see Pss 2:12; 5:11; 7:1; 11:1; Introduction) or seeking God (v. 10).

34:11-14. The three occurrences of "fear" in vv. 7, 9 anticipate v. 11, where "fear of the LORD" is the subject of the psalmist's instruction. The fear of God leads to life (v. 12), and, as vv. 13-14 suggest, obedience is involved as well. In the book of Deuteronomy, fearing God appears to be virtually synonymous with obeying God's commandments (see Deut 6:2, 24; 10:12-13). Evil (vv. 13-14; see also vv. 16, 21) and deceit (see Pss 10:7; 17:1; 24:4; 36:3) are to be avoided; good and peace are to be pursued (cf. Amos 5:14-15).

34:15-22. The movement from vv. 11-14 to vv. 15-16 seems to suggest that the righteous earn life (v. 12) by their good behavior while God punishes evildoers; however, the situation is more complex. The righteous have plenty of troubles about which to cry to God (vv. 15, 17; see also v. 6; the Hebrew words translated "cry"/"cried" differ in each case). Indeed, "Many are the afflictions of the righteous" (v. 19). Faithfulness to God will mean anything but a carefree life! As v. 18 suggests, the good news is that God is with "the brokenhearted" (see Ps 51:17; Isa 61:1) and the "crushed in spirit" (see Ps 51:17; Isa 57:15). In other words, "life" will be experienced in the midst of suffering, not beyond it. Indeed, God will be experienced in the midst of suffering (see Commentary on Psalms 13; 22; 31). Fear of God is rewarded not in a material, mechanistic sense but with the nearness of God (see Commentary on Psalm 1, where it is suggested that the prosperity of the righteous consists in their being connected to the source of life; see also Commentary on Psalm 73). To take refuge in God, to belong to God, is to live (v. 22). To separate oneself from God, which is the essence of wickedness (see Commentary on Psalm 1, esp. 1:6), is to die. To be a servant of God (v. 22) means to recognize God's sovereign claim on one's life. Thus to be a servant of God is to live in dependence on God, which is the essence of righteousness (see Commentary on Psalms 1; 2).

REFLECTIONS

Psalm 34 employs four different Hebrew roots to describe God's activity on behalf of persons who cry out to God in their affliction or trouble. Each word points to God's life-giving activity and serves to focus attention on the question that lies at the heart of Psalm 34 and that is as current as this morning's newspaper: "Which of you desires life?" (v. 12).

Of course, we all desire life. There are further questions, however, such as What is life? And how do we attain it? Psalm 34 offers some answers, but they are not ones we can easily comprehend, because they contradict what culture often teaches us about life. For instance, the culture of the United States would lead one to believe that life consists of driving the classiest car, being surrounded with the most beautiful people, carrying the proper credit card, drinking the right beverages, and generally enjoying oneself to the fullest every moment of the day and night. Millions of advertising dollars are spent every day to try to convince us that life *does* consist in the abundance of possessions (see Luke 12:15), and most of us believe it most of the time. We are good consumers.

In striking contrast to what our culture may teach us, Psalm 34 teaches us that life begins with fearing God—life is a gift from God for which God makes gracious provision (vv. 8-9). What culture teaches us fosters greed, whereas what Psalm 34 teaches us fosters gratitude (vv. 1-3). If life is defined the way our culture defines it, there is no allowance for suffering or for comprehension of the dilemma of the human condition—in short, no possibility for happiness or joy except in the most shallow of senses. Again, Psalm 34 offers a sharp contrast, as Peter Craigie points out:

> The fear of the Lord establishes joy and fulfillment in all of life's experiences. It may mend the broken heart, but it does not prevent the heart from being broken; it may restore the spiritually crushed, but it does not crush the forces that may create oppression. The psalm, if fully grasped, dispels the naiveté of that faith which does not contain within it the strength to stand against the onslaught of evil.[165]

The psalmist experiences life amid suffering, not beyond it. His or her faith is thus the kind that Jesus embodied and to which Jesus calls his disciples—faith that knows the paradoxical good news that to lose one's life for God's sake is truly to find it (see Mark 8:35). Thus it is easy to imagine the psalmist, like the apostle Paul, enumerating her or his "many afflictions" (Rom 8:31) and then concluding that nothing "will be able to separate us from the love of God" (Rom 8:38 NRSV; see also 2 Cor 4:7-12). Like Paul, too, the psalmist says to others, in effect, "be imitators of me" (1 Cor 4:16; 11:1; see also Phil 3:17). This is not arrogance but testimony to God's grace at work in one's life. The boast is in the Lord (v. 2; see 1 Cor 1:31).

Psalm 34 is traditionally associated with the Lord's supper, primarily because of the word

---

165. Peter C. Craigie, *Psalms 1–50,* WBC 19 (Waco, Tex.: Word, 1983) 282.

"taste" in v. 8. In a sense, this connection is superficial; however, as a whole, Psalm 34 is appropriately associated with the Lord's Supper. The Lord's Supper celebrates God's gracious provision for life, which is the good news proclaimed by Psalm 34. The proper response is gratitude (vv. 1-3)—eucharist!

PSALM 35:1-28, O LORD, WHO IS LIKE YOU?

NIV

Psalm 35

Of David.

¹Contend, O LORD, with those who contend
        with me;
    fight against those who fight against me.
²Take up shield and buckler;
    arise and come to my aid.
³Brandish spear and javelin*a*
    against those who pursue me.
Say to my soul,
    "I am your salvation."

⁴May those who seek my life
    be disgraced and put to shame;
may those who plot my ruin
    be turned back in dismay.
⁵May they be like chaff before the wind,
    with the angel of the LORD driving them
        away;
⁶may their path be dark and slippery,
    with the angel of the LORD pursuing them.
⁷Since they hid their net for me without
        cause
    and without cause dug a pit for me,
⁸may ruin overtake them by surprise—
    may the net they hid entangle them,
    may they fall into the pit, to their ruin.
⁹Then my soul will rejoice in the LORD
    and delight in his salvation.
¹⁰My whole being will exclaim,
    "Who is like you, O LORD?
You rescue the poor from those too strong
        for them,
    the poor and needy from those who rob
        them."

¹¹Ruthless witnesses come forward;

a3 Or and block the way

NRSV

Psalm 35

Of David.

¹ Contend, O LORD, with those who contend
        with me;
    fight against those who fight against me!
² Take hold of shield and buckler,
    and rise up to help me!
³ Draw the spear and javelin
    against my pursuers;
say to my soul,
    "I am your salvation."

⁴ Let them be put to shame and dishonor
    who seek after my life.
Let them be turned back and confounded
    who devise evil against me.
⁵ Let them be like chaff before the wind,
    with the angel of the LORD driving them
        on.
⁶ Let their way be dark and slippery,
    with the angel of the LORD pursuing
        them.

⁷ For without cause they hid their net*a* for me;
    without cause they dug a pit*b* for my life.
⁸ Let ruin come on them unawares.
And let the net that they hid ensnare them;
    let them fall in it—to their ruin.

⁹ Then my soul shall rejoice in the LORD,
    exulting in his deliverance.
¹⁰ All my bones shall say,
    "O LORD, who is like you?
You deliver the weak
    from those too strong for them,

a Heb a pit, their net   b The word pit is transposed from the preceding line

---

NIV

they question me on things I know
nothing about.
¹²They repay me evil for good
and leave my soul forlorn.
¹³Yet when they were ill, I put on sackcloth
and humbled myself with fasting.
When my prayers returned to me unanswered,
¹⁴ I went about mourning
as though for my friend or brother.
I bowed my head in grief
as though weeping for my mother.
¹⁵But when I stumbled, they gathered in glee;
attackers gathered against me when I was
unaware.
They slandered me without ceasing.
¹⁶Like the ungodly they maliciously mocked[a];
they gnashed their teeth at me.
¹⁷O Lord, how long will you look on?
Rescue my life from their ravages,
my precious life from these lions.
¹⁸I will give you thanks in the great assembly;
among throngs of people I will praise you.

¹⁹Let not those gloat over me
who are my enemies without cause;
let not those who hate me without reason
maliciously wink the eye.
²⁰They do not speak peaceably,
but devise false accusations
against those who live quietly in the land.
²¹They gape at me and say, "Aha! Aha!
With our own eyes we have seen it."

²²O Lord, you have seen this; be not silent.
Do not be far from me, O Lord.
²³Awake, and rise to my defense!
Contend for me, my God and Lord.
²⁴Vindicate me in your righteousness, O Lord
my God;
do not let them gloat over me.
²⁵Do not let them think, "Aha, just what we
wanted!"
or say, "We have swallowed him up."

²⁶May all who gloat over my distress
be put to shame and confusion;
may all who exalt themselves over me
be clothed with shame and disgrace.
²⁷May those who delight in my vindication

a16 Septuagint; Hebrew may mean *ungodly circle of mockers.*

NRSV

the weak and needy from those who
despoil them."

¹¹ Malicious witnesses rise up;
they ask me about things I do not know.
¹² They repay me evil for good;
my soul is forlorn.
¹³ But as for me, when they were sick,
I wore sackcloth;
I afflicted myself with fasting.
I prayed with head bowed[a] on my bosom,
¹⁴ as though I grieved for a friend or a
brother;
I went about as one who laments for a
mother,
bowed down and in mourning.

¹⁵ But at my stumbling they gathered in glee,
they gathered together against me;
ruffians whom I did not know
tore at me without ceasing;
¹⁶ they impiously mocked more and more,[b]
gnashing at me with their teeth.

¹⁷ How long, O Lord, will you look on?
Rescue me from their ravages,
my life from the lions!
¹⁸ Then I will thank you in the great
congregation;
in the mighty throng I will praise you.

¹⁹ Do not let my treacherous enemies rejoice
over me,
or those who hate me without cause
wink the eye.
²⁰ For they do not speak peace,
but they conceive deceitful words
against those who are quiet in the land.
²¹ They open wide their mouths against me;
they say, "Aha, Aha,
our eyes have seen it."

²² You have seen, O Lord; do not be silent!
O Lord, do not be far from me!
²³ Wake up! Bestir yourself for my defense,
for my cause, my God and my Lord!
²⁴ Vindicate me, O Lord, my God,

aOr *My prayer turned back*   bCn Compare Gk: Heb *like the pro-*
fanest of mockers of a cake

NIV

shout for joy and gladness;
may they always say, "The LORD be exalted,
who delights in the well-being of his
servant."
28My tongue will speak of your righteousness
and of your praises all day long.

NRSV

according to your righteousness,
and do not let them rejoice over me.
25 Do not let them say to themselves,
"Aha, we have our heart's desire."
Do not let them say, "We have swallowed
youa up."

26 Let all those who rejoice at my calamity
be put to shame and confusion;
let those who exalt themselves against me
be clothed with shame and dishonor.

27 Let those who desire my vindication
shout for joy and be glad,
and say evermore,
"Great is the LORD,
who delights in the welfare of his servant."
28 Then my tongue shall tell of your
righteousness
and of your praise all day long.

a Heb *him*

COMMENTARY

Psalm 35 is a prayer for help that is traditionally classified as an individual lament or complaint. The usual elements are present, but the psalm moves back and forth among them in a way that makes it difficult to identify neat structural divisions. There is petition for deliverance (vv. 1-3, 17, 22-25), petition for judgment upon enemies (vv. 4-6, 8, 19, 26), complaint (vv. 7, 11-12, 15-16, 20-21), vow to praise (vv. 9-10, 18, 28), an apparent expression of innocence (vv. 13-14), and even a brief petition for the supporters of the psalmist (v. 27). Some scholars suggest a division of the psalm into three major sections: (1) vv. 1-10, (2) vv. 11-18, (3) vv. 21-28—each of which concludes with a vow to praise. Perhaps it is best not to attempt to discern too much literary order in the psalm, but to interpret the apparent literary disarray as an appropriate indication of the chaotic conditions that prevailed in the life of the psalmist.

The attempt to identity precisely the nature of these conditions has led to strikingly divergent understandings of the origin and setting of Psalm 35. It is often viewed as the prayer of a falsely accused person (see Psalms 5; 7; 17; 26; Introduction), perhaps one who is sick (v. 13) and whose opponents interpret this sickness as a sign of wrongdoing that justifies persecution. This approach relies heavily on the legal imagery in the psalm (vv. 1a, 11, 23-24). Other scholars focus more on the military imagery (vv. 1b-3). Craigie, for instance, labels Psalm 35 as "A Royal Prayer for International Crisis," suggesting that it is similar to Psalm 20 in being the prayer of a king for God's help in dealing with national enemies.[166] Both of these approaches construe the legal and military language literally, but Gerstenberger is probably correct in proposing that the language is metaphorical. He concludes that the original setting of Psalm 35 was a "private cultic" ritual and that the psalm would have been used by a suffering individual "as a central part of the recitations that were obligatory for the sufferer who underwent such rehabilitating ritual in the circle of friends and family."[167]

166. Ibid., 282-86.
167. Erhard S. Gerstenberger, *Psalms, Part 1, with an Introduction to Cultic Poetry*, Forms of the OT Literature 14 (Grand Rapids: Eerdmans, 1988) 150, 153.

The very existence of such different proposals is sufficient indication that the language and imagery of Psalm 35 are open-ended enough to be applicable to a variety of circumstances. Thus Psalm 35 has remained a resource for sufferers throughout the generations, serving both as a prayer for help and as a testimony to God's character. In fact, this latter function is highlighted by a unique feature of this psalm: the psalmist's quoting of God (v. 3), of his or her own bones (v. 10), of enemies (vv. 21, 25), and of supporters (v. 27). Verses 3, 10, and 27 in particular offer instruction about God's character as one who helps, delivers, and provides for the weak, the needy, and the vulnerable.

35:1-3. The plea for God to "contend" (v. 1*a*) has a legal background, but it is usually used figuratively of God's calling oppressors to accountability (see v. 23, "my cause"; see also Ps 43:1; Isa 3:13; 49:25; Lam 3:58). Military imagery dominates the rest of vv. 1-3. The verb "fight" (לחם *lāham*) usually refers to battle, but it is used elsewhere of general opposition by enemies (see Pss 56:2; 109:3, where "attack" is accompanied by "without cause" as in 35:7, 19; Jer 1:19; 15:20). Elsewhere, God is addressed as "shield" (Pss 3:3; 7:10), and God's protection is described as covering with a buckler (a large shield; see Pss 5:12; 91:4). Likewise, the subsequent plea is frequent in Psalms: "rise" (Pss 3:7; 9:19; 10:12), and God is often seen as the psalmist's "help" (Pss 22:19; 30:10; 33:20; 54:4; 115:9-11). The "spear" is a weapon, of course, but it also symbolizes the presence and authority of a king (see 1 Sam 26:7-8, 11). In effect, the psalmist asks God to take charge of the situation, which means in this case to deal with the "pursuers" (cf. Pss 7:1; 31:15). Entrusting his or her life to God, the psalmist desires to hear God say precisely what the foes in Ps 3:2 deny—that is, that God is a source of "help"/"salvation" (ישועה *yěšû'â*; the Hebrew word is the same in 3:2; 35:3).

35:4-8. Verses 4-6 elaborate upon what it will mean when God rises against the enemies. For the psalmist to escape from those seeking his or her life (see Pss 38:12; 40:14; 54:3; 63:9; 70:2; 86:14; see also 1 Sam 23:15; 1 Kgs 19:10; Jer 38:16), the enemies must be stopped—"put to shame" (see v. 26; see also, e.g., Pss 6:10; 69:6) and "dishonored" (see Pss 40:14; 69:6; 70:2) and

"confounded" (see "confusion" in v. 26; see also Pss 71:24 [NRSV, "disgraced"]; 40:15 and 70:2 [NRSV, "confusion"]; 83:17 [NRSV, "dismayed"]). The psalmist's plea in v. 5*a* recalls Ps 1:4, implying the wickedness of the enemies. The root of the word "slippery" (חלקלקות *hălaqlaqqôt*, v. 6) is also used elsewhere to describe the destiny of the wicked (Ps 73:18). Verse 6 asks that the "pursuers" (v. 3) become the pursued (see "angel," or messenger, in Pss 34:7; 91:11). The effect of vv. 7-8 is the same: "ruin" (see Ps 63:10: "those who seek my life will come to ruin" [NAB]; 73:18)—that is, let them experience what they are attempting to perpetrate (see "net" in Pss 9:15; 10:9; "pit" in Pss 7:15; 9:15). The two occurrences of the phrase "without cause" in v. 7 (see v. 19) anticipate the psalmist's self-defense in vv. 13-14.

35:9-18. Verse 9 articulates the promise of joy when God effects "deliverance" (*yěšû'â*; the word is the same as "salvation" in v. 3). The psalmist anticipates too the role of witness. Quoting his or her "bones"—that is, whole being (see Ps 6:2)—the psalmist first asks a question focused on God's character, and then answers it. God acts on behalf of the "weak"/"afflicted"/"poor"/"oppressed," as the NRSV variously translates the word עני (*'ānî*; see Pss 9:12; 10:2, 9; 12:5; 14:6; 25:16; 37:14; 40:17; 70:6; 74:21; 82:3; 86:1; 109:16, 22). This affirmation lies at the heart of Israel's faith (see "misery" in Exod 3:7; 4:31; see also Deut 26:7). Suffering is not an indication of God's disfavor but an opportunity for God's presence and activity (see Commentary on Psalms 9–10; 13; 22; 31).

The psalmist's enemies clearly do not interpret the suffering this way. Just as Job's "friends" interpreted his suffering as evidence of his sinfulness, so apparently do the psalmist's associates as well. Thus, they think, the psalmist can justifiably be persecuted. The complaint in v. 11 returns to legal imagery; more literally, "witnesses of violence" oppose the psalmist (see Ps 27:12, where the same vocabulary is present). The opposition leaves the psalmist "forlorn" (שכול *šěkôl*); this word is often associated with the bereavement of childlessness or barrenness (see Isa 47:8). Thus it is a particularly poignant choice of words in view of the way the psalmist responded to the suffering of others—that is, as a family member. When others were afflicted, the psalmist joined them in their affliction (v. 13c; the root of "afflicted" is the same as "weak" in v. 10). Thus the psalmist's response contrasts sharply with that of the enemies, who "exalt themselves against me" (v. 26). This insensitive, self-centered manner is evident in vv. 15-16. Wild beasts, not other people, ordinarily tear at people (v. 15; see Hos 13:8), an action perhaps related to the image of gnashing teeth (v. 16; see Job 16:9; Pss 37:12; 112:10; Lam 2:16; Job 16:9). And the enemies are explicitly called "lions" in v. 7 (see Ps 58:6). Having been utterly dehumanized, the psalmist perceives that his or her life is in danger, and the psalmist again returns to petition (v. 17b), followed by the anticipation of deliverance in v. 18 (see vv. 9-10, 28; Pss 22:22-25; 26:12).

35:19-27. The petition in v. 19 employs another legal term; "treacherous" often describes false testimony in court (see "false" in Ps 27:12). The word also occurs in Ps 69:4, where the psalmist is again hated without cause (cf. John 15:25). By not speaking *shalom* (v. 20), the enemies reveal themselves to be opponents also of God, who does will *shalom* (cf. "welfare," v. 27) for God's servants. The opponents' self-centered arrogance is also revealed in their exclamation in v. 22 (see v. 25; Ps 40:15). What the opponents do not realize is that they are not the only ones who have "seen"; God has seen too (v.

22), and so the psalmist can confidently address a series of petitions to God in vv. 22-26. The enemies have spoken, and now the psalmist wants God to speak (v. 22a; see also Pss 83:1; 109:1). The enemies have been present, and now the psalmist wants God to be present (v. 22b; see also Pss 22:11, 19; 38:21; 71:12), even if it takes a wake-up call (v. 23a; see Ps 59:5). Legal terminology again dominates vv. 23-24. The phrase "my defense" (v. 23a) could be translated "my justice"; the same root in verbal form opens v. 24, where it could be translated, "Establish justice for me." As the rest of the verse makes clear, the appeal is to God's character as sovereign judge— that is, to God's righteousness (see Pss 7:17; 9:8; 96:13; 97:2), to which the psalmist promises to be a witness (v. 28; see above on v. 10). The psalmist also invites others—specifically, those who desire his or her "vindication" (צדק *sedeq*; the root is the same as "righteousness" in vv. 24, 28)—to join in the affirmation of what God is like. In contrast to the enemies, who "make themselves great" (or "exalt themselves," v. 26), the psalmist's supporters will proclaim God's greatness (v. 27; see also Ps 40:16), a greatness that consists of God's identification with and setting things right for the suffering and the vulnerable (vv. 1-3, 10, 23-24, 27).

REFLECTIONS

As Gerstenberger suggests, Psalm 35 is a particularly "aggressive and defensive" prayer for help.[168] For this reason, perhaps, contemporary readers may find various aspects of this psalm troubling—the military imagery (vv. 1-3), the psalmist's prayer for the punishment of enemies (vv. 4-6, 8, 26), the psalmist's self-commendation (vv. 13-14). However, the psalmist prays, in effect, exactly what Jesus taught his disciples to pray: "Deliver us from evil." The psalmist's self-commendation should not be a problem; it is simply a way of affirming loyalty to God and faithfulness to others. The psalmist's prayer against the enemies is not a selfish, vengeful prayer. Rather, it should be understood as a prayer for justice for the oppressed—"thy will be done on earth as it is in heaven." For justice to be done on earth, however, requires that evil oppressors be opposed. It is for God's opposition to oppressors that the psalmist prays. She or he recognizes, quite realistically, that oppressors do not give up without a fight. Thus God's opposition to oppression (v. 10), God's work of setting things right in the world (vv. 23-24, 27), will necessarily mean that God has to "fight" (v. 1b). In this sense, the military imagery is understandable and appropriate (see Eph 6:10-17).

To put it in different terms, the psalmist prays for the enactment of what Jesus expressed in his saying, "all who exalt themselves will be humbled, but all who humble themselves will

168. Ibid., 153.

be exalted" (Luke 18:14 NRSV). While the enemies "exalt themselves" (v. 26), the psalmist and his supporters humble themselves and exalt God (vv. 13, 27). The petitions for deliverance and the petitions against the enemies represent requests that God reveal God's character, for God is for the weak and the needy (v. 10). The petitions imply, of course, that persons who exalt themselves have not yet been humbled. Thus Psalm 35, like the psalter as a whole, is eschatological; it asserts God's sovereignty amid the existence of competing claims and powers (see Psalm 2; Introduction). The psalmist trusts God's sovereign will and ability to help (vv. 1-3, 10, 22-24, 27), and yet still prays for and awaits God's help.

While Psalm 35 is testimony to God's character and activity, it also teaches about suffering and the life of faith. It is easy to imagine Psalm 35 as the prayer of Elijah or Jeremiah or Job or Jesus (see John 15:25), all of whom were hated without cause, all of whom were pursued by their enemies, all of whom suffered on account of their righteousness and faithfulness to God. Clearly, suffering in these cases cannot be understood as punishment. If anything, suffering must be understood as the inevitable cost of discipleship. In this regard, then, Psalm 35 offers us a model of discipleship and invites our decision. Are we willing, like the psalmist and like Jesus, to humble ourselves in identification with the affliction of others (v. 13)? Are we willing, like the psalmist and like Jesus, to entrust our lives to God, praying all the while, "Thy will be done . . . deliver us from evil"?

PSALM 36:1-12, IN YOUR LIGHT

NIV

Psalm 36

For the director of music. Of David the servant of the LORD.

[1]An oracle is within my heart
concerning the sinfulness of the wicked:[a]
There is no fear of God
before his eyes.
[2]For in his own eyes he flatters himself
too much to detect or hate his sin.
[3]The words of his mouth are wicked and deceitful;
he has ceased to be wise and to do good.
[4]Even on his bed he plots evil;
he commits himself to a sinful course
and does not reject what is wrong.

[5]Your love, O LORD, reaches to the heavens,
your faithfulness to the skies.
[6]Your righteousness is like the mighty
mountains,
your justice like the great deep.
O LORD, you preserve both man and beast.
[7] How priceless is your unfailing love!

[a]1 Or heart: / Sin proceeds from the wicked.

NRSV

Psalm 36

To the leader. Of David, the servant of the LORD.

[1] Transgression speaks to the wicked
deep in their hearts;
there is no fear of God
before their eyes.
[2] For they flatter themselves in their own eyes
that their iniquity cannot be found out
and hated.
[3] The words of their mouths are mischief and
deceit;
they have ceased to act wisely and do
good.
[4] They plot mischief while on their beds;
they are set on a way that is not good;
they do not reject evil.

[5] Your steadfast love, O LORD, extends to the
heavens,
your faithfulness to the clouds.
[6] Your righteousness is like the mighty
mountains,

NIV

Both high and low among men
    find[a] refuge in the shadow of your wings.
[8]They feast on the abundance of your house;
    you give them drink from your river of
        delights.
[9]For with you is the fountain of life;
    in your light we see light.

[10]Continue your love to those who know you,
    your righteousness to the upright in heart.
[11]May the foot of the proud not come against
      me,
    nor the hand of the wicked drive me away.
[12]See how the evildoers lie fallen—
    thrown down, not able to rise!

a7 Or love, O God! / Men find; or love! / Both heavenly beings and men / find

NRSV

your judgments are like the great deep;
    you save humans and animals alike, O LORD.

[7] How precious is your steadfast love, O God!
    All people may take refuge in the shadow
        of your wings.
[8] They feast on the abundance of your house,
    and you give them drink from the river
        of your delights.
[9] For with you is the fountain of life;
    in your light we see light.

[10] O continue your steadfast love to those
        who know you,
    and your salvation to the upright of heart!
[11] Do not let the foot of the arrogant tread on me,
    or the hand of the wicked drive me away.
[12] There the evildoers lie prostrate;
    they are thrust down, unable to rise.

COMMENTARY

Although scholars generally agree in classifying Psalm 36 as an individual lament/complaint or prayer for help, only vv. 10-11 are petition. Verses 5-9, while addressed to God, have more the character of a profession of faith, and vv. 1-4, 12 consist of a description of the behavior and destiny of the wicked. The apparent discontinuity between vv. 1-4, 12 and vv. 5-11 has led numerous scholars to treat Psalm 36 as two separate psalms; however, it is preferable to treat the psalm as a unity (note the occurrence of "wicked" in vv. 1, 11 (רשע *rāšā'* in v. 1; רשעים *rĕšā'îm* in v. 11), linking the two supposedly separate sections). When the psalm is read as a unity, vv. 1-4, 12 provide a framework for hearing the words addressed to God in vv. 5-11. This framework suggests that the psalmist's praise (vv. 5-9) and prayer (vv. 10-11) arise not from untroubled circumstances, but from the midst of opposition and threat.

36:1-2. A comparison of the NIV and the NRSV discloses that the translation of v. 1a is a problem. The Hebrew reads literally, "utterance of rebellion to the wicked in the midst of my heart." The NIV's translation may be an attempt

to paraphrase this literal reading, but it misses the point that the oracle is *to* the wicked. Some Hebrew manuscripts and the Syriac version read "his heart," a reading on which the NRSV depends—and it is preferable. The intent seems to be sarcastic. The word "utterance" (נאם *nĕ'um*; or "speaks," "oracle") elsewhere is almost always followed by the divine name, and the resultant phrase—usually translated "says the LORD"—occurs almost exclusively in the prophetic books to indicate an oracle from God. Thus the psalmist says, in effect, that all the wicked hear is "says rebellion." In short, "rebellion" or "transgression" is their god. They perceive no reason whatsoever to be accountable to the true God, as v. 1b suggests. Together, v. 1a and v. 1b cover hearing and seeing. Verse 2 develops the latter; it repeats the word "eyes" (עינים *'ênayim*) from v. 1, linking the wicked's failure to honor God and their self-assertion. In other words, idolatry and selfishness are inseparable. The NIV and the NRSV construe v. 2b differently, but either reading suggests the arrogant autonomy of the wicked (see Commentary on Psalms 1; 2). Given the way the psalm begins, the unique superscription takes on even fuller significance. As opposed to the wicked, who serve only themselves, David is identified as "the servant of the LORD."

36:3-4. The arrogance of the wicked manifests itself in speech (v. 3a), in action (v. 3b), and in thought (v. 4a). As the NRSV suggests, the word "mischief" (אָוֶן 'āwen) occurs in vv. 3-4, although "mischief" probably does not communicate the seriousness of the behavior (cf. the NIV's "wicked" and "evil"; see also v. 12, where the term "evildoers" also contains the same Hebrew word). The word designates the destructive effects of evil, and, not surprisingly, it is elsewhere associated with idolatry (see "iniquity" in Hos 12:11 NRSV). The word "deceit(ful)" often characterizes the speech and thinking of the wicked (see Pss 5:6; 34:13; 35:20; 38:12 [NRSV, "treachery"]; 52:4; 109:2). Elsewhere, "to be wise" (v. 3b) is associated with serving God (Ps 2:10-11)—that is, acknowledging God's sovereignty. It is precisely this, of course, that the wicked do not do. Rather, their hearing, seeing, speaking, acting, and thinking (cf. v. 4a with Mic 2:1) are focused on themselves. Rejecting "good" (vv. 3-4), they embody "evil" (v. 4; see Ps 34:13-14).

36:5-6. While clearly aware of the reality of the wicked and their threatening thoughts and deeds, the psalmist perceives a more profound reality. His or her profession, praise, and prayer center on God's "steadfast love" (vv. 5, 7, 10); and there is no other word in the OT that serves so well to describe the character of God (see Exod 34:6-7; Pss 5:7; 6:4; 13:5; 33:5, 18, 22; Introduction). In vv. 5-6, it is joined by three other central aspects of God's character (see also Ps 89:14, where essentially the same four attributes are present). God's love is unbounded (v. 5a; see Pss 33:5; 57:10; 71:19). God is ultimately dependable (v. 5b, "faithfulness"; see Pss 89:24; 92:2; 98:3, where "steadfast love" and "faithfulness" are paired). In ancient Near Eastern cosmology, the mountains anchor the dry land, holding up the firmament and holding back the waters of the deep. Just as the life and future of the earth thus depend on the mountains, so also the world depends on God's "righteousness"—God's will and ability to set things right (v. 6a). As the "great deep" represents inexhaustible power, so it is with God's "justice" (v. 6b; see Pss 89:14; 97:2; 99:4). To be noted is that each attribute of God in vv.

5-6 is described in cosmic terms that are arranged in descending order according to the ancient view—"heavens" above all, "clouds" above the earth, "mighty mountains" as the highest earthly point, and "the great deep" below the earth. In short, God's character is built into the very structure of the universe. Everything and every creature—"humans and animals alike" (v. 6c)—depends on God for its existence and future. This affirmation is reinforced by the syntax of vv. 5-6. The first word in v. 5 and the last word in v. 6 is "Yahweh" ("LORD"). God surrounds it all!

36:7-8. The exclamation of v. 7a is founded on the conviction that the life of the whole world depends on God's love. To take refuge in God (see the same image in Pss 17:8; 57:1; 63:7) means simply to acknowledge dependence on God. This is the precise opposite of the wicked, who assert their self-sufficiency (vv. 1-2) and who pursue their own selfish ways (vv. 3-4). Psalm 36 ends by professing the faith that the way of the wicked will ultimately prove futile (v. 12), thus recalling the beginning of the psalter, which affirms that "the way of the wicked will perish" (1:6) and "happy are those who take refuge in [God]" (2:12 NRSV; see also 5:11; 7:1; 11:1; 16:1; Introduction).

Verse 8 portrays God's provision of life for people. They are fed and given drink. God's "house," as well as the "shadow of your wings" in v. 7c (see Commentary on Ps 17:8), may designate the Temple and indicate an original liturgical setting for the psalm, but the meaning need not be literal (after all, there is no river in the Temple). As Mays suggests, the language is symbolic and intends to express poetically the conviction that life is a gift received from and nurtured by God: "It is this receiving from God that occurs in complex and related ways—through common life, liturgy, and the inner world of the spirit—that the psalm seeks to describe."[169] The affirmation is similar to that of Ps 23:5-6 (see Isa 55:1-3).

36:9-12. The psalmist's profession culminates with the memorable v. 9, which sums up vv. 6c-8: God is the source of life (see Ps 68:27; Prov 14:27; Jer 2:13; 17:13). As elsewhere, God's presence itself is described poetically as "light" (אוֹר 'ôr, Pss 4:6; 44:3; 69:15; see "shine," the

---

169. James L. Mays, *Psalms*, Interpretation (Louisville: John Knox, 1994) 157.

verbal form of the Hebrew root, in Num 6:25; Pss 4:6; 31:16; 67:1; 80:3, 7, 19). Likewise, the experience of God's presence is described as light (see Pss 27:1; 97:11; 118:27; Isa 9:2; 10:17; Mic 7:8). Again, the language is richly symbolic. The same imagery is used by the Gospel of John, which locates God's presence in Jesus Christ, in whom "was life, and the life was the light of all people" (John 1:4 NRSV). The prologue of John goes on to acknowledge the presence of darkness but affirms that God's presence in Christ affords a light that cannot be overcome (John 1:5). In effect, Psalm 36 ends the same way; the psalmist prays in v. 10 for the continuation of God's steadfast love (see Jer 31:3) and "righteousness" (see v. 6) for the "upright in heart" (see Pss 7:10; 11:2; 32:11). The psalmist acknowledges the presence of evil (v. 11) but affirms that God's presence (see "there"—that is, wherever God is present— in v. 12; see also Ps 14:5) affords a power that the wicked cannot overcome.

REFLECTIONS

A consumer-oriented culture teaches people to view life as a reward to be earned; Psalm 36, however, is a radical profession of faith. It teaches us that life is not a reward to be earned but a gift to be received! God gives life (vv. 6c, 9), and God will provide for the life of the world and its people (vv. 7-8). This remarkable affirmation of faith lies at the heart of the book of Psalms and the entire Bible (see Psalms 23; 34, esp. v. 12; 73, esp. vv. 25-26).

It is not surprising that the NT employs the same imagery to affirm God's gracious gift of and provision for life. The Gospel of John, for instance, affirms that Jesus is the "living water" (John 4:10; cf. Ps 36:8b-9a), "the bread of life" (John 6:35; cf. Ps 36:8a), and "the light of the world" (John 8:12, see also 1:4; cf. Ps 36:9). Jesus says, "I come that they may have life, and have it abundantly" (John 10:10 NRSV), and the Gospel of John professes that those who believe in Jesus will have "eternal life" (3:16). Life in Christ is effective now, and the joy and peace are real (16:24, 33). But life is experienced amid persistent opposition from "the world," and so Jesus must pray for the ongoing protection of his followers (17:14-19). In the same way, Psalm 36 is eschatological; God's sovereignty is asserted amid persistent opposition (see Psalm 2; Introduction). Those who belong to God (see v. 10a, "those who know you") already experience refuge and abundant provision (vv. 5-9), but this gift of life (v. 9) is experienced amid persistent opposition from the wicked (vv. 1-4, 11-12), and so the psalmist must pray for the continuation of God's love and God's work of setting things right (v. 10).

The psalmist can be confident in praying for God's steadfast love and righteousness, because the psalmist trusts that God's love is the fundamental reality in the universe (v. 5; see Commentary on Psalms 19; 33) and that God's righteousness holds the world together (v. 6). Again, Psalm 36 is a radical profession of faith, since hatred and violence seem so prevalent among us, and, indeed, it often seems that the world is falling apart. Here again, Psalm 36 anticipates the NT affirmation that God is love (1 John 4:8, 16) and that God's love relates to, as Col 1:20 puts it, "all things, whether on earth or in heaven" (cf. Ps 36:5-6). Indeed, Col 1:17 attributes to Jesus what Psalm 36 attributes to God's righteousness: "in him all things hold together" (NRSV).

Obviously, this remarkable affirmation of faith has profound implications for the way we view the world and our place in it. This affirmation is simultaneously good news and a warning. Consider, for instance, the ecological implications. The good news is that there is hope for the world despite the fact that in caring for the earth we have acted the part of the wicked; we "have ceased to act wisely and do good" (v. 3b). The affirmation that God saves "humans and animals alike" (v. 6c) is good news as well, but it also functions as a warning that calls for a reverence for all creatures and their habitats that is seldom evidenced in our relentless desire for development and "progress." Our plans for the future (ecological and otherwise) often reveal a self-flattery that our "iniquity cannot be found out" (v. 2)—that is, that we are not accountable (see Commentary on Psalms 1; 2). God so loves the world, and God calls us to do the same.

PSALM 37:1-40, THE MEEK SHALL INHERIT THE LAND

NIV

Psalm 37[a]

Of David.

[1]Do not fret because of evil men
  or be envious of those who do wrong;
[2]for like the grass they will soon wither,
  like green plants they will soon die away.

[3]Trust in the LORD and do good;
  dwell in the land and enjoy safe pasture.
[4]Delight yourself in the LORD
  and he will give you the desires of your
    heart.

[5]Commit your way to the LORD;
  trust in him and he will do this:
[6]He will make your righteousness shine like
    the dawn,
  the justice of your cause like the noonday
    sun.

[7]Be still before the LORD and wait patiently for
    him;
  do not fret when men succeed in their
    ways,
  when they carry out their wicked schemes.

[8]Refrain from anger and turn from wrath;
  do not fret—it leads only to evil.
[9]For evil men will be cut off,
  but those who hope in the LORD will
    inherit the land.

[10]A little while, and the wicked will be no
    more;
  though you look for them, they will not be
    found.
[11]But the meek will inherit the land
  and enjoy great peace.

[a] This psalm is an acrostic poem, the stanzas of which begin with the successive letters of the Hebrew alphabet.

NRSV

Psalm 37

Of David.

[1] Do not fret because of the wicked;
  do not be envious of wrongdoers,
[2] for they will soon fade like the grass,
  and wither like the green herb.

[3] Trust in the LORD, and do good;
  so you will live in the land, and enjoy
    security.
[4] Take delight in the LORD,
  and he will give you the desires of your
    heart.

[5] Commit your way to the LORD;
  trust in him, and he will act.
[6] He will make your vindication shine like
    the light,
  and the justice of your cause like the noonday.

[7] Be still before the LORD, and wait patiently
    for him;
  do not fret over those who prosper in
    their way,
  over those who carry out evil devices.

[8] Refrain from anger, and forsake wrath.
  Do not fret—it leads only to evil.
[9] For the wicked shall be cut off,
  but those who wait for the LORD shall
    inherit the land.

[10] Yet a little while, and the wicked will be
    no more;
  though you look diligently for their place,
    they will not be there.
[11] But the meek shall inherit the land,

NIV

¹²The wicked plot against the righteous
and gnash their teeth at them;
¹³but the Lord laughs at the wicked,
for he knows their day is coming.

¹⁴The wicked draw the sword
and bend the bow
to bring down the poor and needy,
to slay those whose ways are upright.
¹⁵But their swords will pierce their own hearts,
and their bows will be broken.

¹⁶Better the little that the righteous have
than the wealth of many wicked;
¹⁷for the power of the wicked will be broken,
but the Lord upholds the righteous.

¹⁸The days of the blameless are known to the
Lord,
and their inheritance will endure forever.
¹⁹In times of disaster they will not wither;
in days of famine they will enjoy plenty.

²⁰But the wicked will perish:
The Lord's enemies will be like the beauty
of the fields,
they will vanish—vanish like smoke.

²¹The wicked borrow and do not repay,
but the righteous give generously;
²²those the Lord blesses will inherit the land,
but those he curses will be cut off.

²³If the Lord delights in a man's way,
he makes his steps firm;
²⁴though he stumble, he will not fall,
for the Lord upholds him with his hand.

²⁵I was young and now I am old,
yet I have never seen the righteous forsaken
or their children begging bread.
²⁶They are always generous and lend freely;
their children will be blessed.

²⁷Turn from evil and do good;
then you will dwell in the land forever.
²⁸For the Lord loves the just
and will not forsake his faithful ones.

They will be protected forever,
but the offspring of the wicked will be cut
off;
²⁹the righteous will inherit the land
and dwell in it forever.

NRSV

and delight themselves in abundant
prosperity.

¹² The wicked plot against the righteous,
and gnash their teeth at them;
¹³ but the Lord laughs at the wicked,
for he sees that their day is coming.

¹⁴ The wicked draw the sword and bend their
bows
to bring down the poor and needy,
to kill those who walk uprightly;
¹⁵ their sword shall enter their own heart,
and their bows shall be broken.

¹⁶ Better is a little that the righteous person has
than the abundance of many wicked.
¹⁷ For the arms of the wicked shall be broken,
but the Lord upholds the righteous.

¹⁸ The Lord knows the days of the blameless,
and their heritage will abide forever;
¹⁹ they are not put to shame in evil times,
in the days of famine they have
abundance.

²⁰ But the wicked perish,
and the enemies of the Lord are like the
glory of the pastures;
they vanish—like smoke they vanish
away.

²¹ The wicked borrow, and do not pay back,
but the righteous are generous and keep
giving;
²² for those blessed by the Lord shall inherit
the land,
but those cursed by him shall be cut off.

²³ Our steps[a] are made firm by the Lord,
when he delights in our[b] way;
²⁴ though we stumble,[c] we[d] shall not fall headlong,
for the Lord holds us[e] by the hand.

²⁵ I have been young, and now am old,
yet I have not seen the righteous forsaken
or their children begging bread.
²⁶ They are ever giving liberally and lending,

a Heb a man's steps   b Heb his   c Heb he stumbles   d Heb he
e Heb him

NIV

³⁰The mouth of the righteous man utters
> wisdom,
> and his tongue speaks what is just.
³¹The law of his God is in his heart;
> his feet do not slip.

³²The wicked lie in wait for the righteous,
> seeking their very lives;
³³but the LORD will not leave them in their
> power
> or let them be condemned when brought
> to trial.

³⁴Wait for the LORD
> and keep his way.
> He will exalt you to inherit the land; .
> when the wicked are cut off, you will see
> it.

³⁵I have seen a wicked and ruthless man
> flourishing like a green tree in its native
> soil,
³⁶but he soon passed away and was no more;
> though I looked for him, he could not be
> found.
³⁷Consider the blameless, observe the upright;
> there is a future*ª* for the man of peace.
³⁸But all sinners will be destroyed;
> the future*ᵇ* of the wicked will be cut off.

³⁹The salvation of the righteous comes from
> the LORD;
> he is their stronghold in time of trouble.
⁴⁰The LORD helps them and delivers them;
> he delivers them from the wicked and
> saves them,
> because they take refuge in him.

ª37 Or there will be posterity   ᵇ38 Or posterity

NRSV

and their children become a blessing.
²⁷ Depart from evil, and do good;
> so you shall abide forever.
²⁸ For the LORD loves justice;
> he will not forsake his faithful ones.

The righteous shall be kept safe forever,
> but the children of the wicked shall be
> cut off.
²⁹ The righteous shall inherit the land,
> and live in it forever.

³⁰ The mouths of the righteous utter wisdom,
> and their tongues speak justice.
³¹ The law of their God is in their hearts;
> their steps do not slip.

³² The wicked watch for the righteous,
> and seek to kill them.
³³ The LORD will not abandon them to their
> power,
> or let them be condemned when they
> are brought to trial.

³⁴ Wait for the LORD, and keep to his way,
> and he will exalt you to inherit the land;
> you will look on the destruction of the
> wicked.

³⁵ I have seen the wicked oppressing,
> and towering like a cedar of Lebanon.*ª*
³⁶ Again I*ᵇ* passed by, and they were no more;
> though I sought them, they could not be
> found.

³⁷ Mark the blameless, and behold the upright,
> for there is posterity for the peaceable.
³⁸ But transgressors shall be altogether destroyed;
> the posterity of the wicked shall be cut off.

³⁹ The salvation of the righteous is from the
> LORD;
> he is their refuge in the time of trouble.
⁴⁰ The LORD helps them and rescues them;
> he rescues them from the wicked, and
> saves them,
> because they take refuge in him.

ª Gk: Meaning of Heb uncertain   ᵇ Gk Syr Jerome: Heb he

COMMENTARY

Psalm 37, as Gerstenberger suggests, "can perhaps be called a homily."[170] It addresses a theological issue that is a perennial pastoral concern: the apparent prosperity of the wicked. Like any good sermon, Psalm 37 proclaims the faith, instructs the faithful, and calls for a decision. Because of its clearly instructional intent, Psalm 37 is generally classified as a wisdom psalm. This classification is adequate, as long as Psalm 37 is not understood simply as a private meditation. The central issue of Psalm 37 was a characteristic concern of the wisdom tradition (e.g., the book of Job). The psalm also contains sayings similar to those in the book of Proverbs (see vv. 8, 16, 21), and the contrast between the righteous and the wicked is also characteristic of wisdom literature.

To be sure, the contrast between the righteous and the wicked is also characteristic of the book of Psalms, beginning with Psalm 1. By sheer repetition, Psalm 37 raises the intensity of the contrast. The "righteous" (צדיק ṣaddîq) are mentioned nine times in Hebrew (vv. 12, 16, 17, 21, 25, 28, 29, 32, 39), and the "wicked" (רשע rāšāʿ) even more (vv. 10, 12, 14, 16, 17, 20, 21, 28, 32, 34, 35, 38, 40, plus vv. 1, 9, where a different Hebrew word [מרעים měrēʿîm] is used). As in Psalm 1, the righteous are those who are attentive to God's instruction (v. 31; cf. 1:2) and are known by God (v. 18; cf. 1:6 NIV). Thus they will "inherit the land" (see vv. 9, 11, 22, 29, 34; cf. v. 3). Although it is possible to understand this affirmation literally, it is better to approach it symbolically. Since possession of the land afforded access to the resources necessary to sustain life, the righteous "live," whereas the wicked "perish" (v. 20; see 1:6) and "shall be cut off" (vv. 9, 22, 28, 34, 38; cf. "destruction" in v. 34 NRSV).

This conclusion is based on the psalmist's conviction that God rules the world, a conviction that underlies everything in Psalm 37 and that is most explicit in the assertion that "the LORD laughs at the wicked" (v. 13). This assertion recalls Psalm 2 (see v. 4), which is fundamentally an affirmation of God's sovereignty over the nations and rulers of the earth (see 2:10-12). As in Psalm 2, so it is in Psalm 37 that the affirmation of God's rule is made in circumstances that seem to deny it. In short, Psalm 37 is eschatological. For *now,* the wicked *do* "prosper in their way" (v. 7; cf. 1:3). Thus the future tense of the two refrains is significant—"*shall* inherit" and "*shall be* cut off."

37:1-11. The contrast between what is (present) and what shall be (future) provides the context for understanding the imperative exhortations in vv. 1, 3-5, 7-8, as well as the attached promises in vv. 2, 6, 9-11. The righteous live their lives not on the basis of present appearances, but based on what they know is assured in the future. Thus, in the midst of the present prosperity of the wicked, the psalmist can say, "Do not fret" (vv. 1*a,* 7-8) and "do not be envious" (v. 1*b*; see also Ps 73:3), or, to state the same exhortation positively, "Trust in the LORD" (v. 3; see also v. 5; Pss 4:5; 9:10; Introduction). The verb "delight" (v. 4*a*; see v. 11) is associated elsewhere with God's provision of resources for life (see Isa 55:2; 58:14; 66:11). In other words, God's providence can be trusted, as v. 4*b* also suggests. The righteous will live by faith and by what is always inseparable from faith: hope (v. 7*a*; see vv. 9, 34, where a different Hebrew word from the one used in v. 7*a* is translated "wait" by the NRSV).

But to live eschatologically means not only to live *for* the future but also to live *by* the future. Living by faith and hope has a profound impact on the present, in terms of emotion and behavior. The verb in the phrase "do not fret" (חרה ḥārâ) and the noun "wrath" (חמה ḥēmâ, v. 8) have similar root meanings: "to be kindled" or "to be hot." Thus the psalmist's advice in vv. 1, 7-8, in modern parlance, is "Be cool." Trusting God enables one to live in the present with a certain serenity (see "be still" in v. 7; see also Ps 62:1, 5) and peace of heart and mind (vv. 1, 7-8). Trusting God also enables one to live constructively in the present, to continue to "do good" (vv. 3, 27) even when it appears that evil pays quite well.

The promises attached to the exhortations declare the transience of the wicked (v. 2; see also Ps 129:6) and their ultimate demise (vv. 9*a*, 10;

170. Erhard S. Gerstenberger, *Psalms, Part 1, with an Introduction to Cultic Poetry,* Forms of the OT Literature 14 (Grand Rapids: Eerdmans, 1988) 158.

the verb translated "cut off" [כרת *kārat*] refers in Gen 9:11 to the destruction of all humanity in the flood and elsewhere is used in association with the death penalty; see also Prov 2:22). On the other hand, things will be set right for those who trust God (v. 6*a*); "justice" will prevail (v. 6*b*; see also vv. 28, 30). Life belongs ultimately to those who "wait for" God (v. 9)—the "meek" (v. 11; see also Pss 10:27; 22:26; 25:9; 34:2; see also the closely related term usually translated "poor"/"afflicted"/"weak"/"oppressed" [עני *'ānî*] in Pss 9:12; 10:2, 9; 14:5; 35:10; see also Matt 5:5). It is they who enjoy *shalom* (v. 10; see v. 37), even if it is not "as the world gives" (John 14:27 NRSV).

37:12-20. The imperatives that predominate in vv. 1-11 are much less frequent in vv. 12-40 (only in vv. 27, 34), which consist primarily of observations about the righteous, the wicked, and their respective destinies. Verses 12-15 focus on the wicked. While they "plot" (see Ps 31:13) and "gnash their teeth" (see Pss 35:16; 112:10), God laughs. While they seek to live at the expense of others ("poor" ['*ānî*] in v. 14 is the same Hebrew root as "meek" in v. 11), they will not succeed. In effect, vv. 14-15 assert that those who live by the sword will die by the sword (see vv. 2, 10).

Verse 17 makes essentially the same observation (see "broken" in vv. 15, 17). It is paired with the proverbial saying in v. 16; because the wicked will disappear, their abundance is illusory. Contrary to worldly calculations, less can be better (see Prov 15:16; 16:8; 28:6). Verse 18 tells why. The "blameless" may have only a little, but it "will endure forever" (cf. Prov 28:10). As suggested above (see Psalms 15; 18; 19), blamelessness connotes not sinlessness but dependence on God. This mode of life is a form of wealth that retains its value in all seasons (v. 19; see also Matt 5:6). Recalling "perish" in Ps 1:6, v. 20 again affirms that the wicked will disappear.

37:21-26. Verses 21 and 26 are linked verbally by the words "borrow"/"lend" (the two English words translate the same Hebrew root) and "generous(ly)"; and vv. 21-26 illustrate what was affirmed in vv. 3-4. Those who trust in God are motivated and enabled to "do good" (v. 3). Even though they already have more, the wicked greedily seek more, while the righteous share their resources (see Ps 12:5; Prov 14:31; 19:17;

28:8, 17). The Hebrew word translated "generous(ly)" (חונן *ḥônēn*) is more literally "gracious," and it is one of God's essential characteristics (see Exod 34:6; Introduction). In short, the righteous are persons whose character has been shaped by God's character; having known grace, they can be gracious. Because they trust God to protect and provide (vv. 23-25; note the repetition of "upholds" in vv. 17, 24; see 54:4; 119:116; 145:14; see also "sustains" in Ps 3:5), the righteous are able to know the happiness of giving (see Acts 20:35). Having been blessed (v. 22), they become a blessing (v. 26; see also Gen 12:1-3).

37:27-29. Whereas vv. 21-26 recall vv. 3-4, v. 27 explicitly repeats the exhortation of v. 3, "do good." Not surprisingly, the motivation is explicitly linked to the way God is. The word "justice" (משפט *mišpāṭ*) in v. 28*a* recalls v. 6 and anticipates v. 30, where again the righteous reflect God's character by their own behavior. The designation "faithful ones" also moves in this direction; it could also be translated "steadfastly loved [or loving] ones," thus linking it as well to a primary characteristic of God (see Exod 34:6-7; Introduction).

37:30-40. The vocabulary of vv. 30-31 recalls Ps 1:2. The word translated "utter" (הגה *hāgâ*) here appears as "meditate" in 1:2, which also twice mentions God's "law" or "instruction" (see Commentary on Psalm 1). Here the righteous meditate on or utter "wisdom" (see Ps 49:3; Prov 31:26), but wisdom begins with fearing God (see Job 28:28; Ps 111:10; Prov 1:7; 9:10; 15:33). Thus, as in Psalm 1, the righteous are those who do not pursue their own ways but are open to God's instruction because they recognize God's sovereignty. God's instruction is the solid foundation on which their lives are built.

The word "abandon" (עזב *'āzab*, v. 33) represents the third occurrence of this Hebrew root in the psalm (see "forsaken"/"forsake" in vv. 25, 28). In the confidence that God will not forsake the righteous, the psalmist offers a final exhortation in v. 34, "Wait" (קוה *qāwâ*; see also v. 9, and a different Hebrew word translated "wait" in v. 7 [חול *ḥûl*]). The humble (see "meek" in v. 11 and "poor" in v. 14) *will be* exalted. Verses 35-36 articulate again the theme of the transience of the wicked (see vv. 2, 10, 13-15, 17, 20), as does v. 38. The word "posterity" (אחרית *'aḥărît*) in vv. 37-38 is better translated "future." In contrast to the wicked, the "blameless" (v. 37; see also v. 18) have a future! It is not due to their own efforts, of course, as the wicked would conclude; rather, it is "from the LORD" (v. 39). In biblical terms, salvation (v. 39; see "saves" in v. 40) means life in the fullest sense of the word. It is a gift from God. It does not mean a trouble-free existence (v. 39; see also vv. 19, 24) or the absence of opposition (v. 40; see also vv. 7, 12, 14, 32, 35), but it does mean God's availability as a source of help (see Pss 22:19; 30:10; 54:4) and a reliable "stronghold" (v. 39; see also Ps 27:1) and "refuge" (see Ps 2:12; Introduction).

REFLECTIONS

Psalm 37—along with Psalms 49; 73; and the book of Job—is often labeled a theodicy, because it implies the question, How can God be just while there is so much evil in the world? "Theodicy" means literally, "justice of God"; while this label may be too restrictive, there is some rationale for considering Psalm 37 to be a homiletical exploration of the issue of God's justice. The word "justice" (משפט *mišpāṭ*) occurs in vv. 6, 28, 30 (the phrase "when brought to trial" in v. 33 NIV also represents the same Hebrew root). If God "loves justice" (v. 28) and will bring justice to light (v. 6), then why are the wicked able to "prosper in their way" (v. 7)? To put the question from the human side: Why do the righteous suffer?

To be sure, Psalm 37 does not satisfactorily answer these questions, but it does as much as any sermon can do. As Thomas G. Long says in an article entitled "Preaching About Suffering": "We can only go so far down the path of theodicy. . . . We must admit that we have been placed in the middle of life and that, from our vantage point, suffering is an unsolvable mystery. We must affirm that the meaningful question is not 'Is theism unintelligible because I am suffering?' but 'Is God a God of salvation—is God one who can help?' "[171]

If this is the meaningful question, then Psalm 37 does offer an answer. Yes, salvation "is from the LORD. . . . The LORD helps them . . . and saves them" (vv. 39-40). And so Psalm 37 invites trust (vv. 3, 5) and hope (vv. 7, 9, 34) in God's will and ability to set things right.

Long goes on to say that for Christians, the response to the question above is finally "a story, *the* story of the love of God and the passion of Jesus Christ."[172] Of course, Psalm 37 does not tell the story of Jesus Christ, but it does proclaim God's love and thus anticipates the story of Jesus. For instance, Psalm 37 proclaims the sovereignty of God as the basis for trust and for doing good (vv. 3, 13, 27), and the same message forms the core of Jesus' preaching: "the kingdom of God has come near; repent, and believe in the good news" (Mark 1:15 NRSV). For Jesus, the reality of God's rule turned worldly values upside down. Because God rules the world, "the meek . . . will inherit the earth" (Matt 5:5 NRSV; see also Ps 37:11*a*). Because God rules the world, "those who hunger and thirst for righteousness . . . will be filled" (Matt 5:6 NRSV; see also Ps 37:19). Because God rules the world, there is a source of joy and an experience of peace greater than the world can give (see John 14:27; 16:24, 33; see also Ps 37:11*b*). Because God rules the world, "life does not consist in the abundance of possessions" (Luke 12:15 NRSV; see also Ps 37:16). Because God rules the world, " 'It is more blessed to give than to receive' " (Acts 20:35 NRSV; see also Ps 37:21, 26). Because God rules the world, there is no need to "worry about your life" (Matt 6:25 NRSV; see also Ps 37:4).

As Jesus' life showed, trusting God and doing good engender opposition, and the opposition to the righteous is very clear in Psalm 37 (see esp. vv. 14, 32). But as Jesus' life and death and resurrection demonstrated, and as Psalm 37 also proclaims, God "rescues them from the wicked" (v. 40) and creates a future "for the peaceable" (v. 37). Psalm 37 thus promises what

171. Thomas G. Long, "Preaching About Suffering," *Journal for Preachers* 15/2 (Lent 1992) 13.
172. Ibid., 13.

Jesus promised too: "all who exalt themselves will be humbled, but all who humble themselves will be exalted" (Luke 18:14 NRSV; see also Ps 37:34; Commentary on Psalm 35).

To be sure, all of these affirmations and promises are eschatological. There is no proving them to the wicked, except insofar as we embody them in our lives. The only proof we can offer that God rules the world is the tangible existence of a community that is shaped by the character of God and God's claim. We prove that God rules the world when we trust in God (vv. 3, 5), "do good" (vv. 3, 27), commit our way to God (v. 5), "give generously" (v. 21), "speak justice" (v. 30), open ourselves to God's instruction (v. 31), and "take refuge in" God (v. 40). Such humble dependence on God is, in effect, to "inherit the land"—it is life as God intends it, abundant and eternal.

PSALM 38:1-22, THERE IS NO SOUNDNESS IN MY FLESH

NIV

Psalm 38

A psalm of David. A petition.

¹O LORD, do not rebuke me in your anger
   or discipline me in your wrath.
²For your arrows have pierced me,
   and your hand has come down upon me.
³Because of your wrath there is no health in
      my body;
   my bones have no soundness because of
      my sin.
⁴My guilt has overwhelmed me
   like a burden too heavy to bear.

⁵My wounds fester and are loathsome
   because of my sinful folly.
⁶I am bowed down and brought very low;
   all day long I go about mourning.
⁷My back is filled with searing pain;
   there is no health in my body.
⁸I am feeble and utterly crushed;
   I groan in anguish of heart.

⁹All my longings lie open before you, O Lord;
   my sighing is not hidden from you.
¹⁰My heart pounds, my strength fails me;
   even the light has gone from my eyes.
¹¹My friends and companions avoid me because
      of my wounds;
   my neighbors stay far away.
¹²Those who seek my life set their traps,

NRSV

Psalm 38

A Psalm of David, for the memorial offering.

¹ O LORD, do not rebuke me in your anger,
   or discipline me in your wrath.
² For your arrows have sunk into me,
   and your hand has come down on me.

³ There is no soundness in my flesh
   because of your indignation;
there is no health in my bones
   because of my sin.
⁴ For my iniquities have gone over my head;
   they weigh like a burden too heavy for
      me.

⁵ My wounds grow foul and fester
   because of my foolishness;
⁶ I am utterly bowed down and prostrate;
   all day long I go around mourning.
⁷ For my loins are filled with burning,
   and there is no soundness in my flesh.
⁸ I am utterly spent and crushed;
   I groan because of the tumult of my
      heart.

⁹ O Lord, all my longing is known to you;
   my sighing is not hidden from you.
¹⁰ My heart throbs, my strength fails me;
   as for the light of my eyes—it also has
      gone from me.

NIV

those who would harm me talk of my ruin;
    all day long they plot deception.

¹³I am like a deaf man, who cannot hear,
    like a mute, who cannot open his mouth;
¹⁴I have become like a man who does not hear,
    whose mouth can offer no reply.
¹⁵I wait for you, O LORD;
    you will answer, O Lord my God.
¹⁶For I said, "Do not let them gloat
    or exalt themselves over me when my foot
        slips."

¹⁷For I am about to fall,
    and my pain is ever with me.
¹⁸I confess my iniquity;
    I am troubled by my sin.
¹⁹Many are those who are my vigorous enemies;
    those who hate me without reason are
        numerous.
²⁰Those who repay my good with evil
    slander me when I pursue what is good.

²¹O LORD, do not forsake me;
    be not far from me, O my God.
²²Come quickly to help me,
    O Lord my Savior.

NRSV

¹¹ My friends and companions stand aloof
        from my affliction,
    and my neighbors stand far off.

¹² Those who seek my life lay their snares;
    those who seek to hurt me speak of ruin,
    and meditate treachery all day long.

¹³ But I am like the deaf, I do not hear;
    like the mute, who cannot speak.
¹⁴ Truly, I am like one who does not hear,
    and in whose mouth is no retort.

¹⁵ But it is for you, O LORD, that I wait;
    it is you, O Lord my God, who will
        answer.
¹⁶ For I pray, "Only do not let them rejoice
        over me,
    those who boast against me when my
        foot slips."

¹⁷ For I am ready to fall,
    and my pain is ever with me.
¹⁸ I confess my iniquity;
    I am sorry for my sin.
¹⁹ Those who are my foes without cause[a] are
        mighty,
    and many are those who hate me
        wrongfully.
²⁰ Those who render me evil for good
    are my adversaries because I follow after
        good.

²¹ Do not forsake me, O LORD;
    O my God, do not be far from me;
²² make haste to help me,
    O Lord, my salvation.

[a] Q Ms: MT *my living foes*

COMMENTARY

Psalm 38 is, according to Gerstenberger, among "the most impressive individual laments."[173] Although not as familiar or widely used as the others, Psalm 38 is one of the church's seven penitential psalms (see also Psalms 6; 32; 51; 102; 130; 143). Like Psalm 6, the language and imagery of Psalm 38 suggest that it may have originally been used by sick persons as a prayer for help (see vv. 1, 21-22). Like Psalm 6, too, Psalm 38 begins with a petition that seems to indicate that the sickness

173. Gerstenberger, *Psalms*, 160.

is the result of God's wrath (vv. 1-2). More explicitly than Psalm 6, Psalm 38 suggests that God's wrath has been provoked by the psalmist's sinfulness (vv. 3-4; see also "foolishness" or "sinful folly" in v. 5; cf. v. 18).

Thus Psalm 38 is evidence of the ancient belief that sin causes sickness (see Pss 32:3-5; 39:10-11; 41:4; 88:7, 16; 107:17-18; Mark 2:1-12). This belief, which is also a contemporary one in some circles, is very problematic; but the association of sin and sickness holds interpretative possibilities, especially if the link is not viewed mechanistically or individualistically (see Reflections). Actually, the nature of the imagery and its extent discourage an individualistic or biographical interpretation of Psalm 38. Although several commentators conclude that the psalmist must have had leprosy (see Leviticus 13–14), the description of the disease is too stereotypical and hyperbolic to make such a specific diagnosis. As Craigie points out, if the description is taken clinically, it would appear that the psalmist "has almost every disease in the book."[174] But the description is poetic, and so the psalm could be and has been perceived to be applicable to a variety of persons and situations throughout the centuries.

After the initial petition and accompanying rationale (vv. 1-2), the psalmist describes his or her condition in vv. 3-10. The social effects of the disease and the psalmist's response are described in vv. 11-14, followed by an expression of trust in God in vv. 15-16. Verses 17-20 are a sort of review of the whole situation in preparation for the concluding petition in vv. 21-22.

A comparison of the NIV and the NRSV reveals that the meaning of the final phrase of the superscription is unclear (see the same phrase in Psalm 70). Translated literally, it means "to cause to remember." Whether this should be understood as a reference to "the memorial offering" (cf. Lev 2:2, 9, 16 NIV) is not clear. It is just as likely, as the NIV suggests, that the phrase refers to the purpose of the prayer—that is, to cause God to remember the psalmist's need or perhaps to remember God's own gracious character and promises (see Exod 2:24; 32:12).

38:1-4. Verse 1 is identical to Ps 6:1, except that different Hebrew words underlie the transla-

tion "anger" (קצף qeṣep, 38:1; אף ʾap, 6:1) in each verse. While "rebuke" (יכח ykḥ) and "discipline" (יסר yāsar) are elsewhere indications of God's guidance (see Prov 3:11-12), this is not the case when they are done in "anger" and "wrath." Instead of being experienced as guidance, they are experienced as punishment (v. 2), as "arrows" (see Pss 7:13; 64:7) and the blow of God's hand (see Pss 32:4; 39:10). The identical syntax of the two parts of v. 3 emphasizes the point: God's "indignation" (see Pss 69:24; 102:10) and the psalmist's "sin" are parallel. The result is "no soundness in my flesh" (cf. Isa 1:6). The phrase is repeated in v. 7b; between the two occurrences lies a chilling description of physical disease. While "flesh" suggests the bodily exterior, the interior body is indicated by "bones" (v. 3b; see also Job 30:17, 30; Pss 22:14; 31:10; 102:3). The NRSV's "health" in v. 3b translates the Hebrew *shalom*; the psalmist knows no "peace." The mention of "sin" (חטאה ḥaṭṭāʾt) in v. 3b is followed in v. 4a by the occurrence of "iniquities" (or "guilt" עון ʿāwôn]; see also Pss 32:1-2, 5; 51:2, 5). The two words also occur together in v. 18. The iniquities rise like flood waters (v. 4a), while at the same time they pull the psalmist down like a heavy weight (v. 4b). It appears that the psalmist will drown in his or her own guilt.

38:5-8. The seriousness of the situation is also clear in vv. 5-8. The verb translated "grow foul" (באש bāʾaš) is more literally rendered "stink." Both it and the verb "fester" or "rot" (מקק mqq) are used elsewhere of corpses (see "stench" in Isa 34:3 and "rot away" in Isa 34:4). Again, it appears that the psalmist is as good as dead. The cause was iniquities in v. 4; in v. 5, it is "foolishness" (אולת ʾiwwelet), a word that, as the NIV suggests, has more to do with morality than intelligence (see Ps 107:17 [see the NIV and NRSV notes]; Prov 1:7; 14:9; Jer 4:22). The words "prostrate" and "mourning" occur together in Ps 35:14 to indicate the psalmist's sympathy for those who are suffering. Here it is the psalmist who seems to be irreversibly "crushed" (see Ps 51:8).

38:9-10. But v. 9 interjects a glimmer of hope, anticipating vv. 15-16, 21-22. The psalmist's "longing(s)" (or "desire"; see Ps 10:17) are before God, as well as his or her "sighing" (cf. "moaning"/"groaning" in Job 3:24; Pss 6:6; 31:10; 102:5). Verse 10, however, returns to complaint,

174. Peter C. Craigie, *Psalms 1–50*, WBC 19 (Waco, Tex.: Word, 1983) 303.

repeating "heart" from v. 8. Verse 10 may indicate failing sight as the psalmist loses strength, but "light" may also be symbolic of life (see Job 33:30; Pss 13:3; 56:13).

38:11-14. These verses continue the complaint but with a shift of focus from the psalmist's condition to the social effects of the situation. The psalmist is abandoned by those who would be expected to provide support (see Job 19:13-19; Ps 88:8, 18). Verse 11*b* reads literally, "and my near ones stand far off." Thus it anticipates the petition in v. 21*b*, where the psalmist asks God to "not be far." The psalmist's friends have become enemies, seeking the psalmist's life (see Pss 35:4; 40:14). Their opposition is demonstrated by their actions (v. 12*a*), by their speech (v. 12*b*), and by their thoughts (v. 12*c*). As ones who meditate treachery or "deceit" (see Pss 10:7; 34:13; 36:3), the psalmist's opponents reveal themselves to be opponents of God as well. Those loyal to God are called to meditate on or utter something different—namely, God's instruction (Ps 1:2) or wisdom (Ps 37:30). Verses 13-14 seem to describe the psalmist's reaction to the opposition of former friends; the psalmist pretends not to hear and makes no response. In view of such treachery, there is nothing left to say (see Matt 26:63; 27:11-14).

38:15-16. Given the human response to his or her suffering, the psalmist's only possible appeal is to God. So the psalmist will "wait" for or hope in God (see Pss 31:24; 33:18, 22; 69:3; 71:14; 130:7; 131:3). The syntax of v. 15 emphasizes God's role. The poetic line starts with the prepositional phrase "for you" (כִּי־לְךָ *kî-lĕkā*), and the appearance of the personal pronoun "you" in v. 15*b* adds emphasis. *God* is the psalmist's only hope; God "will answer" (see Pss 3:4; 4:1; 22:21 NRSV note). God does not rejoice in the psalmist's suffering, and God is the only one who can prevent others from doing so (v. 16; see Pss 13:4; 35:24).

38:17-22. Verses 17-20 review the major aspects of the situation. Verse 17 summarizes the complaint and its urgency (see vv. 2-10). Using the two words from vv. 3*b*-4*a*, v. 18 rehearses the psalmist's confession. The verb in v. 18*b* means more literally "troubled"; however, the fact that the psalmist is troubled seems to indicate a penitent stance, as the NRSV suggests. Verse 19*a*, which the NIV translates more accurately, recalls vv. 11-12. Verses 13-14 have implied that the opposition to the psalmist is wrong, but v. 19*b* states this explicitly, and v. 20 reinforces this statement. Verse 20*b* seems to contradict what the psalmist had said earlier; that is, the psalmist had asserted his or her sinfulness (vv. 3-5, 18), but now says "I follow after good." But this need not be a contradiction; rather, it likely suggests that the psalmist, having been "troubled by" his or her sin (v. 18*b*) and having experienced the destructive effects of sinfulness (vv. 2-10), has repented.

Thus, even if the indignation of God may once have been deserved, such is the case no longer. In any case, the response of others to the psalmist's suffering is not justified. As Ps 35:13-14 suggested, the proper response to the suffering of others is sympathy and even participation in the suffering, not further accusation (see Ps 69:26). There has thus been some movement between vv. 1-10 and vv. 17-20. According to the psalmist, sin has produced pain (v. 17), but it is precisely pain that God sees (v. 9) and responds to compassionately (v. 15; see Exod 3:7, where the word "sufferings" [מכאוב *mak'ôb*] is the same as "pain" in Ps 38:17). The repentant, suffering psalmist thus has a solid foundation for the complaint against the opponents (v. 20) and for the final appeal in vv. 21-22. These verses are especially reminiscent of Psalm 22. The petition in v. 21*a* recalls Ps 22:1, and the pleas in vv. 21*b*-22 recall Ps 22:11, 19 (see also Ps 35:22*b*). While Psalm 38 does not make the dramatic turn to praise that is found in Psalm 22, the final petitions do indicate the psalmist's trust that neither one's own sinfulness, nor suffering (whatever the cause), nor the opposition of others will be able to separate one from the one properly addressed as "my salvation" (v. 22; see "salvation"/"deliverance" in Pss 3:8; 88:1; 118:14, 21; Exod 15:2).

REFLECTIONS

As suggested above, the ancient belief that sickness or suffering could be directly explained as the punishment of God is very problematic. Indeed, there is ample protest within Scripture against such a mechanistic doctrine of retribution that would lead one to conclude that the prosperous must have earned God's favor and suffering persons must be experiencing God's wrath. The book of Job, for instance, clearly demonstrates that Job's suffering is not punishment from God, and it severely criticizes Job's friends for accusing Job of deserving his plight (cf. Job 11:2-6 and 22:4-11 with 42:7).

At the same time, it may be proper to retain some association of sin and suffering, even of sin and sickness. Sin—the failure to honor God and the way God has ordered human life and the world—has destructive consequences, including physical consequences. For instance, abuse of one's body, including overwork and stress, can literally make one sick. This does not mean, however, that all sickness and suffering can be interpreted as God's punishment of particular sins on a one-to-one basis. This would be to make the mistake of Job's friends. Rather, like the book of Job, Psalm 38 invites us to view sickness, suffering, and death as inevitable realities of being mortal, finite, and fallible. To be sure, sin causes suffering, but the suffering we experience is not necessarily the result of our own particular sins. As a penitential psalm, Psalm 38 may serve as an invitation to personal confession and repentance, but it also serves as an invitation to live constantly in humble reliance upon God in a world where our sufferings may have much more to do with the sinfulness of others than with our personal misdeeds (see Reflections on Psalm 6).

While Psalm 38 has implications for understanding our own suffering, it is especially instructive in terms of how we are called to respond to the suffering of others. The "friends," "companions," and "neighbors" of v. 11 are clearly a negative example, as suggested by vv. 12 and 20 and by the literary context of Psalm 38 (see Ps 35:12-14). In short, it is not proper to treat those who are suffering as if they deserve their suffering (even if they might deserve it, as the psalmist suggests of himself or herself!). Rather, we are called to be forgiving and compassionate, as God is forgiving and compassionate. This lesson is easily forgotten. The inclination of many individual Christians and congregations is to *blame* those who suffer. We often conclude that if people are poor or homeless or carriers of HIV, they must have done something to deserve it. It is a convenient excuse for allowing ourselves to "stay far away" (v. 11) rather than to love those whom God loves. It is also a cruel and proudly self-deceptive response, since it involves our condemnation of others and our congratulation of ourselves.

Unlike several other of the more impressive individual laments (see Psalms 22; 31; 69), Psalm 38 does not figure prominently in the narrative of Jesus' suffering and death. The reason why almost certainly is that the psalmist attributes the suffering to sinfulness. Nevertheless, v. 11 anticipates Jesus' experience (see Matt 26:56; 27:55), and vv. 13-14 anticipate Jesus' response to the treachery committed against him (see Matt 26:63; 27:11-14). Jesus, though sinless, suffered, and other people were perfectly willing to interpret his suffering as God's punishment (see Matt 26:65-68; 27:20-23, 38-44). Thus the cross of Jesus constitutes the ultimate sign of the rejection of a doctrine of retribution that would interpret all suffering as the punishment of God. The cross too proclaims the good news that Psalm 38 affirms: God is a source, not of condemnation, but of hope (v. 15), and sinners may address God as "my God" (v. 21) and "my salvation" (v. 22).

PSALM 39:1-13, MY HOPE IS IN YOU

NIV

Psalm 39

For the director of music. For Jeduthun.*
A psalm of David.

¹I said, "I will watch my ways
    and keep my tongue from sin;
I will put a muzzle on my mouth
    as long as the wicked are in my presence."
²But when I was silent and still,
    not even saying anything good,
    my anguish increased.
³My heart grew hot within me,
    and as I meditated, the fire burned;
    then I spoke with my tongue:

⁴"Show me, O LORD, my life's end
    and the number of my days;
    let me know how fleeting is my life.
⁵You have made my days a mere handbreadth;
    the span of my years is as nothing before
        you.
    Each man's life is but a breath.   *Selah*
⁶Man is a mere phantom as he goes to and fro:
    He bustles about, but only in vain;
    he heaps up wealth, not knowing who will
        get it.

⁷"But now, Lord, what do I look for?
    My hope is in you.
⁸Save me from all my transgressions;
    do not make me the scorn of fools.
⁹I was silent; I would not open my mouth,
    for you are the one who has done this.
¹⁰Remove your scourge from me;
    I am overcome by the blow of your hand.
¹¹You rebuke and discipline men for their sin;
    you consume their wealth like a moth—
    each man is but a breath.   *Selah*

¹²"Hear my prayer, O LORD,
    listen to my cry for help;
    be not deaf to my weeping.
For I dwell with you as an alien,
    a stranger, as all my fathers were.
¹³Look away from me, that I may rejoice again
    before I depart and am no more."

NRSV

Psalm 39

To the leader: to Jeduthun. A Psalm of David.

¹ I said, "I will guard my ways
    that I may not sin with my tongue;
I will keep a muzzle on my mouth
    as long as the wicked are in my
        presence."
² I was silent and still;
    I held my peace to no avail;
my distress grew worse,
³   my heart became hot within me.
While I mused, the fire burned;
    then I spoke with my tongue:

⁴ "LORD, let me know my end,
    and what is the measure of my days;
    let me know how fleeting my life is.
⁵ You have made my days a few
        handbreadths,
    and my lifetime is as nothing in your
        sight.
Surely everyone stands as a mere
        breath.   *Selah*
⁶   Surely everyone goes about like a shadow.
Surely for nothing they are in turmoil;
    they heap up, and do not know who will
        gather.

⁷ "And now, O Lord, what do I wait for?
    My hope is in you.
⁸ Deliver me from all my transgressions.
    Do not make me the scorn of the fool.
⁹ I am silent; I do not open my mouth,
    for it is you who have done it.
¹⁰ Remove your stroke from me;
    I am worn down by the blowsª of your
        hand.

¹¹ "You chastise mortals
    in punishment for sin,
consuming like a moth what is dear to
        them;
    surely everyone is a mere breath.   *Selah*

ª Heb *hostility*

NRSV

12 "Hear my prayer, O LORD,
   and give ear to my cry;
   do not hold your peace at my tears.
For I am your passing guest,
   an alien, like all my forebears.
13 Turn your gaze away from me, that I may
      smile again,
   before I depart and am no more."

COMMENTARY

In some ways, Psalm 39 is like other prayers for help. Like Psalm 38, for instance, it could have originated from a person who was ill (see v. 10), and it implies a connection between sickness and sin (vv. 8, 10-11; the NRSV's "chastise" and "punishment" in v. 11 are from the same roots as the words "rebuke" and "discipline" in Ps 38:1 NRSV). Even the psalmist's opening resolve to be silent (vv. 1-2) has a possible parallel in Ps 38:13-14, and in both the psalmist places hope in God ("wait" in 38:15 and "hope" in 39:7 translate the same Hebrew root [יחל *yḥl*]). Despite these similarities, Psalm 39 is unique. Major commentators describe it using words like *enigma, unusual,* and *strange.* The extended opening meditation (vv. 1-3) is not typical, nor is the final petition that seems to ask for God's inattention (v. 13). Perhaps the most unique feature of Psalm 39, however, is the content of the complaint (vv. 4-6), which articulates not specific problems but the general condition of human transience.

The uniqueness of Psalm 39 has given rise to widely divergent understandings. Kraus, for instance, concludes that "the psalm breaks off in despair; it is plunged into darkness without parallel."[175] Craigie, on the other hand, suggests that Psalm 39 is the product of mature spiritual reflection; the psalmist "has regained his perspective on the transitory nature of human life and can face death with calmness."[176] These contradictory viewpoints suggest another possibility. As Robert Alter puts it, "the speaker flounders in a world of radical ambiguities."[177] In other words, Psalm 39

articulates despair and hope *simultaneously.* In so doing, it portrays the way life really is: terrifyingly short, yet awesomely wonderful. And it represents the tension inevitably involved in our response to life—that is, both hopeful awe and nearly unspeakable despair that finally cannot be silenced.

As both the NIV and the NRSV suggest, Psalm 39 falls into four sections. As important as these structural divisions, however, is Alter's observation that the movement of Psalm 39 involves the presentation and interweaving of three themes: silence (vv. 1-3, 9, 12c), human transience (vv. 4-6, 11c-12), and sin/suffering (vv. 8, 10-11b). The first two, which are more prominent, come together in the climactic v. 13, and v. 7, the exact middle line of the poem, functions as a turning point.[178] The existence of these themes and their complex interrelatedness contribute to the sense of ambiguity and tension mentioned above.

39:1-3. The psalm begins with the unusual, "I said." What is then stated is the psalmist's intention not to speak. Apparently, the psalmist wants to avoid the sin of accusing God of wrong doing (see Job 1:22; 2:10); furthermore, the psalmist does not want to provide the wicked with ammunition for their attacks. So the psalmist "was silent" (see Isa 53:7) and "still" (see "silence" in Ps 62:1, 5, where it seems to connote patience). Although v. 2b may be variously construed (cf. the NIV with the NRSV), the verb means "to keep silence" (חשה *ḥāšâ*; see Eccl 3:7). But silence does not work. The worsening "distress" (v. 2; cf. Job 2:6) has internal effects—heartburn, as it were (v. 3a; see Deut 19:6, where a similar phrase is translated "hot anger"), indicating an over-

175. H.-J. Kraus, *Psalms 1–59: A Commentary,* trans. H. C. Oswald (Minneapolis: Augsburg, 1988) 420.

176. Peter C. Craigie, *Psalms 1–50,* WBC 19 (Waco, Tex.: Word, 1983) 310.

177. Robert Alter, *The Art of Biblical Poetry* (New York: Basic Books, 1985) 69.

178. Ibid., 68-73.

whelming compulsion (see Jer 20:9). The phrase "I spoke" in v. 3 recalls v. 1a, and the repetition of "tongue" recalls v. 1b. Like Job, the psalmist moves from pious, resigned silence to speech (cf. Job 1–2 with Job 3).

39:4-6. The content of the speech that begins in v. 4, however, is surprising—no cursing the day of his or her birth (see Job 3:1), no accusing God or asking "how long?" (see Ps 13:1-2). Indeed, there seems nothing particularly sinful about what the psalmist says in vv. 4-6. Verse 4 is framed as a request for information about "my end" (see Job 6:11), although v. 4c suggests that the psalmist already knows about the transience of life. The Hebrew word translated "fleeting" (חדל ḥādēl) anticipates v. 5 by way of a play on words with the Hebrew word translated by the NRSV as "lifetime" (חלד ḥeled), and v. 5 confirms the knowledge that v. 4c implied. In v. 5ab, the psalmist focuses on his or her own life, concluding it is "as nothing" (כאין kĕʾayin; cf. Ps 103:16, "it is gone"). This word occurs again as the final word of the psalm ("no more," v. 13), and it is also the foundation for the following three generalizations about all human life (vv. 5c-6b), each of which is introduced by the particle "surely" (אך ʾak).

Two Hebrew words are used in vv. 5c-6 to describe the human situation (v. 5c), human vocation (v. 6a), and human aspiration (v. 6b). The word translated "shadow" or "phantom" (צלם ṣelem) more literally denotes a likeness or "image" (see Gen 1:26-27). Here it clearly implies an image devoid of actual reality; so the psalmist suggests that human life is really an illusion (see Ps 73:20, where the word is translated "phantoms" or "fantasies" and is used of the wicked). The words "breath" (v. 5c) and "for nothing" (v. 6b) translate the same Hebrew word (הבל hebel), which is related by alliteration to the nouns in vv. 4c, 5b. It indicates a vapor, a puff of wind, a breath—something insubstantial and fleeting (see Job 7:16; Pss 62:9; 94:11; 144:4; Isa 57:13). It is especially prominent in Ecclesiastes, where it occurs over thirty times (e.g., Eccl 1:2, 14; 2:1, 15; 12:8). By describing a situation that Ecclesiastes identifies as "vanity," v. 6c also recalls Eccl 2:18-21).

39:7-8. Just as the emphatic expression of the intent to be silent unexpectedly issued in speech (vv. 1-3), so also the psalmist's emphatic expression of human transience (vv. 4-6) unexpectedly issues in hope in v. 7. This verse uses both of the primary Hebrew roots for "hope" (for the word here translated "wait for" [qāwâ] , see Pss 25:5, 21; 27:14; 37:34; for the word here translated "hope" [תוחלת tôḥelet], see Pss 31:24; 33:18, 22; 38:15). The exact center of the psalm, v. 7 represents a turning point. It is followed immediately by the introduction of the third theme: sin/suffering. There is still no accusation or railing at God. Rather, the psalmist, implicitly confessing sin, makes a humble request for forgiveness. As in v. 1, the psalmist is again concerned about the response of the wicked or, as they are called here, fools (see Ps 14:1). Both petitions are much more typical of other prayers for help (see "scorn" in Ps 31:10) than were the opening meditation (vv. 1-3) and complaint (vv. 4-6).

39:9-11. Verse 9 returns to the theme of silence and makes better sense in the past tense, as in the NIV. The personal pronoun "you" in v. 9b is emphatic. In vv. 9b-11b, the psalmist seems to affirm the traditional connection between sin and sickness as God's punishment (see Commentary on Psalm 38; the Hebrew word translated "stroke" [נגע negaʿ] in 39:10a also underlies the NRSV's "affliction" in 38:11). Verse 11 again represents a generalization from the psalmist's own experience to all humanity (see vv. 5-6), and v. 11c links the themes of sin/suffering and transience by means of the repetition of "breath" from vv. 5-6. This linkage is reminiscent of Psalm 90.

39:12. The three petitions in v. 12 are the most traditional-sounding part of Psalm 39 (see also Ps 4:1). The third petition returns to the theme of silence with a twist, requesting that God *not* be silent at the psalmist's "tears" (see Pss 6:6; 56:8). The accompanying rationale involves the theme of transience again. The two terms elsewhere designate non-Israelite residents of the land, but Lev 25:23 suggests that in view of God's ownership of the land, all Israelites "are but aliens and tenants" (NRSV). David's final praise of God in 1 Chronicles cites this tradition, recognizing that it seems to imply hopelessness but that it actually serves to emphasize God's gracious provision (see 1 Chr 29:15). Thus v. 12de offers an appropriate basis for the petitions in v. 12abc by reminding God of how God has historically provided for the people.

39:13. This allusion to God's gracious provision makes v. 13 all the more surprising, even in a poem that is full of surprises. One might expect at this point something like, "Let the light of your face shine on us" (Ps 4:6*b*); however, v. 13*a* requests just the opposite! Like Job, the psalmist asks for God to "look away" (the verb also occurs in Job 7:19; cf. Job 7:17-21; 10:20-22; 14:1-6; the word the NRSV translates as "smile" [בְּלִי *blg*] in Ps 39:13 also appears in Job 10:20 as "comfort"). The apparent contradiction between v. 13 and v. 12 may be softened by assuming that the psalmist associates God's gaze with punishment, as Job seems to do in Job 7:20-21. However, this approach does not remove the tension between the psalmist's experience of God as "my hope" to whom appeal is made (v. 12) and the experience of God as an oppressive presence who is responsible for human transience (v. 11). The themes of silence and transience come together in the final word of the psalm: "no more," which anticipates the psalmist's death—the ultimate silence. The ambiguity is not resolved. Hope and despair stand side by side.

REFLECTIONS

The ambiguity or tension that characterizes Psalm 39 invites theological reflection. The place to begin is with the similar movement in vv. 1-3 and vv. 4-7. In vv. 1-3, the psalmist moves from silence to speech. In vv. 4-7, the articulation of despair moves toward hope. The movements are related; that is, the psalmist *speaks* his or her way to hope. In other words, the very existence of the psalmist as a speech partner with God belies the apparent insignificance of humanity. Walter Brueggemann says, "The Psalm evidences courage and ego strength before Yahweh which permits an act of hope, expectant imperatives, and an insistence that things be changed before it is too late."[179] In effect, the psalm suggests a paraphrase of Descartes: "I speak; therefore, I am."

A further clue in this direction is the repetition of "as nothing"/"no more" in vv. 5, 13. In the light of v. 13, in which the psalmist speaks about death, v. 5 implies that "my lifetime" is really no better than death. But again, the very act of speech subverts this implication. Any being that has the courage to tell God, "Look away" (v. 13), cannot be entirely insignificant, even if life is fleeting. In this sense, the fact that the psalmist speaks is of more importance than the content of the speech.

On the other hand, the content of the psalmist's speech is important as well. Particularly noteworthy is the ambiguity or tension already pointed out. In language reminiscent of Ecclesiastes and Job, the psalmist articulates the fleeting quality and apparent futility of life (vv. 4-6), even suggesting that God's presence is a hindrance (v. 13). At the same time, however, the psalmist expresses hope in God (v. 7), articulates in very traditional language a relationship between sin and suffering (vv. 10-11), and invokes God's forgiveness and help (vv. 8, 12). This juxtaposition may indicate, as Alter suggests, "a psychological dialectic in the speaker,"[180] but it has theological significance as well. It suggests that Psalm 39, like Job and Ecclesiastes, deals with the issue of theodicy, that it is an exploration of the issue of God's justice in view of sin and human suffering (see Reflections on Psalm 37). The simultaneous use of and subversion of traditional formulations is revealing. The psalmist does not give up on God or relinquish the conviction of God's governance of the world; rather, like Job and Ecclesiastes, the psalmist articulates hope in God on a new basis. The inability to keep silent and the honest articulation of the transience and futility of human life suggest that God's governance of the world cannot be reduced to a simple moral calculus, a mechanistic system of reward and punishment. In this sense, the psalmist's speech is fundamentally a protest, as was Job's speech, not so much against God as against a too simple understanding of God. As

179. Walter Brueggemann, "The Costly Loss of Lament," *JSOT* 36 (1980) 66.
180. Alter, *The Art of Biblical Poetry*, 70.

both Psalm 39 and the book of Job suggest, God is not a scorekeeper of human rights and wrongs but a partner with humanity in the complex matter of life. That humanity speaks and God listens is crucial. Not only is God made accessible to humanity, and hence vulnerable to human shortcoming, but also humanity is given the exalted status of partnership with God. Paradoxically, the psalmist's articulation of fleetingness and futility is eloquent testimony to the importance of humanity. To be sure, human transience is a reality, and life is uncertain and difficult. But the good news is that hope and joy are possible, because human beings live as partners of God.

Finally, then, Psalm 39 is not an affirmation of futility but a profession of faith. As the NT recognizes as well, to live as a "passing guest" is to entrust one's life and future to God amid all the uncertainties and ambiguities of the world (see Heb 11:13; 1 Pet 2:11). Like the psalmist, we must live with hope in an apparently hopeless world. In the face of discouragement and despair, we must dare to speak to God and thus claim our partnership with God. While it may be coincidental, it is interesting that the word "shadow" or "image" in v. 6 is used in Gen 1:26-27 to describe humankind's creation in the "image of God." It is a bold affirmation that our finite, creaturely status does not mean insignificance. It does not detract from the royal vocation of "dominion" (Gen 1:28)—in effect, the calling to participate with God as a partner in ruling the world! Just as God spoke humanity into being, so also humanity is called to continue the conversation, as the psalmist does so honestly and eloquently in Psalm 39.

PSALM 40:1-17, I DELIGHT TO DO YOUR WILL

NIV

Psalm 40

For the director of music. Of David. A psalm.

[1]I waited patiently for the LORD;
    he turned to me and heard my cry.
[2]He lifted me out of the slimy pit,
    out of the mud and mire;
he set my feet on a rock
    and gave me a firm place to stand.
[3]He put a new song in my mouth,
    a hymn of praise to our God.
Many will see and fear
    and put their trust in the LORD.

[4]Blessed is the man
    who makes the LORD his trust,
who does not look to the proud,
    to those who turn aside to false gods.[a]
[5]Many, O LORD my God,
    are the wonders you have done.
The things you planned for us
    no one can recount to you;
were I to speak and tell of them,

[a]4 Or to falsehood

NRSV

Psalm 40

To the leader. Of David. A Psalm.

[1] I waited patiently for the LORD;
    he inclined to me and heard my cry.
[2] He drew me up from the desolate pit,[a]
    out of the miry bog,
and set my feet upon a rock,
    making my steps secure.
[3] He put a new song in my mouth,
    a song of praise to our God.
Many will see and fear,
    and put their trust in the LORD.

[4] Happy are those who make
    the LORD their trust,
who do not turn to the proud,
    to those who go astray after false gods.
[5] You have multiplied, O LORD my God,
    your wondrous deeds and your thoughts
        toward us;
    none can compare with you.
Were I to proclaim and tell of them,

[a]Cn: Heb pit of tumult

NIV

they would be too many to declare.

⁶Sacrifice and offering you did not desire,
  but my ears you have pierced[a, b];
burnt offerings and sin offerings
  you did not require.
⁷Then I said, "Here I am, I have come—
  it is written about me in the scroll.[c]
⁸I desire to do your will, O my God;
  your law is within my heart."

⁹I proclaim righteousness in the great assembly;
  I do not seal my lips,
  as you know, O LORD.
¹⁰I do not hide your righteousness in my heart;
  I speak of your faithfulness and salvation.
I do not conceal your love and your truth
  from the great assembly.

¹¹Do not withhold your mercy from me,
  O LORD;
  may your love and your truth always
  protect me.
¹²For troubles without number surround me;
  my sins have overtaken me, and I cannot
  see.
They are more than the hairs of my head,
  and my heart fails within me.

¹³Be pleased, O LORD, to save me;
  O LORD, come quickly to help me.
¹⁴May all who seek to take my life
  be put to shame and confusion;
may all who desire my ruin
  be turned back in disgrace.
¹⁵May those who say to me, "Aha! Aha!"
  be appalled at their own shame.
¹⁶But may all who seek you
  rejoice and be glad in you;
may those who love your salvation always say,
  "The LORD be exalted!"

¹⁷Yet I am poor and needy;
  may the Lord think of me.
You are my help and my deliverer;
  O my God, do not delay.

a6 Hebrew; Septuagint but a body you have prepared for me (see also Symmachus and Theodotion)   b6 Or opened   c7 Or come / with the scroll written for me

NRSV

they would be more than can be
  counted.

⁶ Sacrifice and offering you do not desire,
  but you have given me an open ear.[a]
Burnt offering and sin offering
  you have not required.
⁷ Then I said, "Here I am;
  in the scroll of the book it is written of
  me.[b]
⁸ I delight to do your will, O my God;
  your law is within my heart."

⁹ I have told the glad news of deliverance
  in the great congregation;
see, I have not restrained my lips,
  as you know, O LORD.
¹⁰ I have not hidden your saving help within
  my heart,
  I have spoken of your faithfulness and
  your salvation;
I have not concealed your steadfast love
  and your faithfulness
from the great congregation.

¹¹ Do not, O LORD, withhold
  your mercy from me;
let your steadfast love and your faithfulness
  keep me safe forever.
¹² For evils have encompassed me
  without number;
my iniquities have overtaken me,
  until I cannot see;
they are more than the hairs of my head,
  and my heart fails me.

¹³ Be pleased, O LORD, to deliver me;
  O LORD, make haste to help me.
¹⁴ Let all those be put to shame and confusion
  who seek to snatch away my life;
let those be turned back and brought to
  dishonor
  who desire my hurt.
¹⁵ Let those be appalled because of their shame
  who say to me, "Aha, Aha!"

¹⁶ But may all who seek you
  rejoice and be glad in you;

a Heb ears you have dug for me   b Meaning of Heb uncertain

NRSV

> may those who love your salvation
> say continually, "Great is the LORD!"
> [17] As for me, I am poor and needy,
> but the Lord takes thought for me.
> You are my help and my deliverer;
> do not delay, O my God.

COMMENTARY

Because of the marked difference between vv. 1-10 and vv. 12-17, Psalm 40 is often treated as two separate psalms that have been placed together by an editor, who perhaps provided v. 11 as a transition. Recalling and celebrating a past deliverance, vv. 1-10 have the character of a song of thanksgiving. Verse 11 shifts to petition, however, and vv. 12-17 constitute a typical lament or complaint. Further impetus to treat the two sections as separate psalms is provided by the fact that vv. 13-17 are virtually identical to Psalm 70.

Even so, there are compelling reasons to treat Psalm 40 as a unity, regardless of its compositional history. For instance, several repeated words or roots bind the two sections ("see" in vv. 3, 12; "thought[s]" in vv. 5, 17; "more" in vv. 5, 12; "counted"/"number" in vv. 5, 12; "desire"/ "delight" in vv. 6, 8, 14; "will"/"be pleased" in vv. 8, 13; "salvation" in vv. 10, 16; plus the emphatic pronoun "you" in reference to God in vv. 5, 9, 11, 17, although the NIV and the NRSV obscure its appearance in v. 11). Furthermore, there is a coherence to Psalm 40 in its final form. This coherence may well be a "liturgical integrity," as Gerstenberger suggests.[181] In any case, it makes sense that a past deliverance would be recalled (vv. 1-10) as the basis for a prayer for help in a new situation of distress (vv. 11-17). While this sequence may not be typical, neither is it without parallel in the psalter (see Psalms 9–10; 27; 44; 89).

40:1-3. In v. 1, the psalmist affirms emphatically that she or he has done what several psalms exhort and encourage: waited for God (see Pss 25:3, 5, 21; 27:14; 37:34; 39:7). And the waiting

was not in vain. God's hearing the "cry" (שׁועה šawʿâ; see Pss 18:6; the word "cry" also occurs in Ps 39:12, which makes an interesting juxtaposition to Ps 40:1, especially in light of 39:13; see Commentary on Psalm 39) is accompanied by God's active response (v. 2). The poetic language of v. 2*ab* does not permit an exact determination of the distress but does indicate its life-threatening nature. The word "pit" (בור bôr) in v. 2*a* often occurs in parallel with "Sheol," the realm of the dead (see Pss 30:3; 88:3-4, 7; see "pit" alone in Pss 28:1; 143:7). In Ps 7:15, the enemies endanger the psalmist by digging a pit. Similarly, the same word designates the pit where Joseph's brothers threw him to be eaten by animals (Gen 37:20, 22, 24, 28) and the cistern where Jeremiah's enemies left him to die of hunger (see Jer 38:6). The parallel to "pit" in v. 2*b* would be more literally translated "mud of the mire" (טיט היון ṭîṭ hayāwen), again recalling Jer 38:6, where "mud" (ṭîṭ) appears twice (the same word also occurs in Pss 18:42; 69:14, where it is translated "mire" by the NRSV). Thus the Joseph and Jeremiah narratives illustrate literally what the psalmist here describes poetically, although the parallels suggest that enemies may have been involved in the former and current threat to the psalmist's life (see v. 14).

In any case, whatever brought the psalmist down, God brought the psalmist up, establishing a solid foundation for life (see "rocks" in Isa 33:17 and God as "rock" in Pss 18:2, 31:3). Elsewhere, God's "word" or "law" secures the psalmist's "steps" (v. 2; see also Pss 17:4-5; 37:31), suggesting that God is the real source of life; this conclusion is reinforced by v. 3. Even the response to deliverance—the "new song"—is something for which God is responsible. The new song

---

181. Erhard S. Gerstenberger, *Psalms, Part 1, with an Introduction to Cultic Poetry,* Forms of the OT Literature 14 (Grand Rapids: Eerdmans, 1988) 169.

elsewhere is explicitly associated with God's sovereignty (see Pss 96:1; 98:1; 149:1; see also 33:3; 144:9), the proper response to which is trust (see Pss 4:5; 9:10; Introduction). Thus, when others see the deliverance God has effected for the psalmist, they too will be led to fear, which is synonymous with trust ("see and fear" represent a play on two similar Hebrew words [ראה *rā'â* and ירא *yārā'*] see also Ps 52:6; for "fear" and "trust" used in the same context, see Ps 33:18, 21).

40:4-5. Repeating the word "trust" (מבטח *mibṭāḥ*), v. 4 recalls the beginning of the psalter, which suggests that happy persons are those who are open to God's instruction (1:2) and "who take refuge in" God (Ps 2:12). In short, happiness is derived from dependence on God, not from powerful humans or from other gods. To support the affirmation of v. 4, the psalmist in v. 5 breaks into praise addressed to God. Perhaps v. 5 is even the new song mentioned in v. 3a. In any case, the pronoun "you" in v. 5 emphasizes God's initiative in terms of God's activity (see Pss 9:1; 26:7) and God's will (see v. 7; Ps 92:5; Isa 55:8, 9). The effect of v. 5 is to place the psalmist's deliverance (vv. 2-3) in continuity with God's historic activity on behalf of the whole people (see "wonders" in Exod 3:20; 34:10 NIV). God's deeds are incomparable (see Isa 40:18) and incalculable. Verse 5 anticipates vv. 9-10, where the psalmist will serve as witness to God's activity and character, as well as v. 12, where the psalmist's troubles are described as incalculable.

40:6-8. These verses address the issue of response to God's activity (see Ps 116:12)—that is, what God may desire (v. 6) and thus what the psalmist will desire (v. 8). Ordinarily, response to God's activity would have included some form of sacrifice as well as a song of thanksgiving (see Pss 56:12; 107:22; 116:17), but, in words reminiscent of several prophetic texts, the psalmist concludes that God does not really—or at least primarily—want sacrifice (see 1 Sam 15:22; Isa 1:12-17; Hos 6:6; Amos 5:21-24). The four terms for various sacrifices surround a statement that reads literally, "ears you have dug for me" (v. 6b). This statement seems to suggest that what the psalmist can hear is more important than what he or she may do. And what the psalmist can hear and be open to is God's will (v. 8a; see Pss

103:21; 143:10) and God's instruction (v. 8b). Like v. 4, v. 8 recalls the beginning of the psalter; it contains two words from Ps 1:2 ("delight" and "law"). In short, what the psalmist presents to God is her or his own self (see v. 7a), open to God's instruction and committed to living in dependence upon God alone (see v. 4).

The nature and significance of the "scroll" (מגלה *měgillâ*) in v. 7b is unclear; this verse may be a way of supporting the "Here I am" of v. 7a. To be written about in God's book is to belong to God and to be fully known by God (see Pss 56:8; 69:28; 139:16), so perhaps the psalmist affirms that she or he offers God the whole self. Another plausible explanation is that the scroll contained written testimony to the psalmist's deliverance (all or part of vv. 1-5) and perhaps to the psalmist's resolve to do God's will (v. 8). If so, it may have been brought as an offering in place of a sacrifice. Thus it would have provided a material representation and witness to the psalmist's offering of her or his transformed, committed self to God. The scroll would have provided the visible evidence of the psalmist's profession that God's instruction is internalized "within my heart" (v. 8b; cf. Jer 31:31-34).

40:9-10. If the scroll was a witness of sorts, it was not the only witness. In vv. 9-10, the psalmist describes the public witness (see vv. 9b, 10c) that he or she has made, or perhaps continues to make (cf. the tenses in NRSV and NIV). The Hebrew verb "told the glad news" (בשר *bśr*) in v. 9a underlies the Greek word κήρυγμα (*kērygma*). The psalmist preaches the good news. The word *kērygma* occurs most frequently in Isaiah 40–55 to describe the prophetic proclamation of the good news of forgiveness, which led to the end of the exile (see Isa 40:9; 41:27; 52:7; Isa 60:6; 61:1). It also occurs in Ps 96:2, where to tell of God's salvation is accompanied by "a new song" (Ps 96:1; cf. 40:3) and leads ultimately to the proclamation of God's reign (96:10; cf. Isa 52:7). In short, the psalmist proclaims God's rule, which here and elsewhere is characterized by "righteousness" (צדק *ṣedeq*, v. 9a), God's setting things right (see Pss 96:13; 97:2; 99:4). It happened at the exodus; it happened with the return from exile; it happened in the psalmist's life—God sets things right. The word "righteousness" (in a slightly different Hebrew form) occurs again in v.

10a. While the psalmist had internalized God's will (v. 8), it does not remain "in my heart" (v. 10a; the Hebrew words translated "heart" differ in vv. 8b [מעה mē'eh] and 10a [לב lēb]). Supporting the proclamation of God's righteousness is the psalmist's reference to key words that describe the essence of God's character—"faithfulness" (vv. 10b, 10c; the Hebrew forms differ but are from the same root [אמן 'mn]) and "steadfast love" (חסד hesed, v. 10b; see Exod 34:6-7; Pss 5:7; 6:4; Introduction)—and God's purpose for humanity: salvation (see v. 16).

40:11-12. Verse 11 can be read as either a petition, as the NIV and the NRSV suggest, or a statement. The verb "withhold" (כלא kālā') is the same Hebrew word as "restrained" in v. 9. The psalmist has not withheld testimony to God and now either asks that God not withhold or affirms that God will not withhold mercy. Perhaps the ambiguity is intentional. In any case, the effect of v. 11 is to express confidence for the future on the basis of God's character, the description of which employs the vocabulary of v. 10 and adds "mercy" or "motherly compassion." (See "merciful" in Exod 34:6, which also contains "steadfast love" and "faithfulness"; see also Ps 25:6; Introduction.) Trust in God's character and recollection of past manifestations of it (vv. 5, 9-11) form the foundation for the complaint in v. 12 and the petition in vv. 13-15.

The complaint in v. 12 reveals the current distress but without real specificity. Several repetitions from earlier verses make the description all the more poignant. As God's wonderful deeds had been described as incalculable (v. 5), so now are the present troubles. While previously others could see the psalmist's example and be led to trust (v. 3), now the psalmist "cannot see." Although the psalmist's heart has been filled with knowledge of God's instruction and righteousness (vv. 8, 10), now the heart "fails." So the psalmist prays for help.

40:13-17. The opening petition (v. 13) is from the same Hebrew root as "will" in v. 8. In other words, "make my deliverance part of your will." Verse 13 indicates the urgency of the situation (see essentially the same plea in Pss 22:19b; 35:26). Verse 14 indicates that, as is often the case in the prayers for help, enemies are at least one aspect of the crisis. On the content of the petitions in vv. 14-15, see Pss 35:4, 21, 26; 71:13, 24. Verse 14b contains the third occurrence of "desire" (see vv. 6, 8). While the psalmist's desire is focused on God's will, the desire of the enemies involves the injury of others.

Similarly, the enemies and the faithful are contrasted by what they seek (vv. 14, 16) and by what they say (vv. 15-16). Again, the enemies seek the psalmist's life, and their speech is mocking. The faithful seek God and declare God's greatness; they recognize God's rule (see Pss 35:27; 47:2; 95:3; 96:4; 99:2-3, where God's greatness is recognized in the context of the proclamation of God's reign). The psalmist, too, concludes by aligning with God; the sight of the poor and the needy motivates God to action (see Pss 12:6; 86:1; 109:22, 31; see Commentary on Psalms 9–10). Verse 17cd indicates trust in God (see "help" in v. 13; Pss 32:19; 38:22), but the final petition also indicates the urgency of the current situation; it is especially noticeable in the light of the psalm's opening words. Patient waiting may not always be possible!

REFLECTIONS

The somewhat unusual movement of Psalm 40 from thanksgiving to complaint and urgent petition is significant and instructive. It suggests that, whether individually or corporately, we always pray out of need, at least in the sense that no deliverance is final in this mortal life. To be sure, we can testify to experiences of deliverance, to God's life-giving power at work in our lives and in our churches. But with each new deliverance comes a new threat, imposed perhaps by our own shortcomings (see v. 12) or by external sources. The story of Israel demonstrates this reality. The deliverance from Egypt led immediately to a new threat, precipitated by the people's own "iniquities"—their worship of the golden calf (Exodus 32–34). Delivered from themselves and from external enemies in the wilderness, the people entered the land, where new threats awaited them (the book of Judges narrates several cycles of deliverance/new threat). The monarchy was instituted as a means of deliverance from the Philistine threat, but it in turn threatened the life of the people from within, resulting in exile and eventual restoration. The story of the Christian church or of our individual lives is no different; we are perpetually needy. Mays concludes, "The psalm teaches that the *torah* in the heart does not prevent sin, nor does the experience of salvation spare us from the need of God's help."[182] Patient waiting for the Lord is a way of life for the people of God—we live eschatologically.

But to live eschatologically is to live in the paradox of being perpetually needy and experiencing new life simultaneously. Quite appropriately, then, Psalm 40 not only instructs us about our neediness but also offers in vv. 4-10 what Brueggemann calls "a comprehensive proposal for what the new life should look like."[183] The new life involves trust in God alone (v. 4), the offering of the whole self to God in openness to God's instruction (vv. 6-8), and the sharing with others of the good news of God's will and ability to set things right (vv. 5, 9-10). In effect, the psalmist fulfills Paul's injunction in Rom 12:1-2, offering the self as a living sacrifice (v. 7), committed to discerning the will of God (v. 8). The exhortation in Rom 12:1-2 is made to those who live in the midst of "the sufferings of this present time" (Rom 8:18 NRSV; cf. Ps 40:12) and those who live "in hope" (Rom 8:24) and who wait "with patience" (Rom 8:25 NRSV; cf. Ps 40:1, 13-17) for what they "do not see" (Rom 8:25 NRSV; cf. "see" in Ps 40:3, 12). As much in adversity as in security, the psalmist proves to be a faithful witness. In commenting on v. 11, which he suggests be read as a statement of trust rather than as a petition, Mays concludes: "The psalmist trusts himself to the gospel he has proclaimed in the situation in which he now is. He does what is usually so difficult to do—live by the gospel you preach."[184]

Psalm 40:6-8, in a form that differs from both the Hebrew text and the LXX, is quoted by the author of Hebrews in 10:5-7. The words of the psalm are attributed to Jesus and are interpreted by the author to support the abolition of the OT sacrificial system in view of Jesus' "once for all" offering of himself (Heb 10:10). While the attribution should not be taken literally, it is significant that the author of Hebrews viewed the psalmist as a type of Christ. As in Psalm 40, the proper sacrifice is the offering of the obedient self. Because Jesus invited his followers to pick up their crosses and follow him (Mark 8:34), the psalmist also becomes a type for all disciples. Psalm 40 and the gospel call us, in recognition of God's sovereign claim upon us (vv. 3-5, 16), to offer God our whole selves, our lives—open to God's instruction and delighting to do God's will (v. 8).

182. James L. Mays, *Psalms,* Interpretation (Louisville: John Knox, 1994) 169.
183. Walter Brueggemann, *The Message of the Psalms: A Theological Commentary* (Minneapolis: Augsburg, 1984) 130.
184. Mays, *Psalms,* 168-69.

PSALM 41:1-13, HAPPY ARE THOSE WHO CONSIDER THE POOR

NIV	NRSV
Psalm 41	Psalm 41
For the director of music. A psalm of David.	To the leader. A Psalm of David.
[1]Blessed is he who has regard for the weak; the LORD delivers him in times of trouble.	[1] Happy are those who consider the poor;[a]
	aOr *weak*

NIV

[2]The LORD will protect him and preserve his
    life;
    he will bless him in the land
    and not surrender him to the desire of his
        foes.
[3]The LORD will sustain him on his sickbed
    and restore him from his bed of illness.

[4]I said, "O LORD, have mercy on me;
    heal me, for I have sinned against you."
[5]My enemies say of me in malice,
    "When will he die and his name perish?"
[6]Whenever one comes to see me,
    he speaks falsely, while his heart gathers
        slander;
    then he goes out and spreads it abroad.

[7]All my enemies whisper together against me;
    they imagine the worst for me, saying,
[8]"A vile disease has beset him;
    he will never get up from the place where
        he lies."
[9]Even my close friend, whom I trusted,
    he who shared my bread,
    has lifted up his heel against me.

[10]But you, O LORD, have mercy on me;
    raise me up, that I may repay them.
[11]I know that you are pleased with me,
    for my enemy does not triumph over me.
[12]In my integrity you uphold me
    and set me in your presence forever.

[13]Praise be to the LORD, the God of Israel,
    from everlasting to everlasting.
        Amen and Amen.

NRSV

    the LORD delivers them in the day of trouble.
[2] The LORD protects them and keeps them alive;
    they are called happy in the land.
    You do not give them up to the will of
        their enemies.
[3] The LORD sustains them on their sickbed;
    in their illness you heal all their
        infirmities.[a]

[4] As for me, I said, "O LORD, be gracious to me;
    heal me, for I have sinned against you."
[5] My enemies wonder in malice
    when I will die, and my name perish.
[6] And when they come to see me, they utter
        empty words,
    while their hearts gather mischief;
    when they go out, they tell it abroad.
[7] All who hate me whisper together about me;
    they imagine the worst for me.

[8] They think that a deadly thing has fastened
        on me,
    that I will not rise again from where I lie.
[9] Even my bosom friend in whom I trusted,
    who ate of my bread, has lifted the heel
        against me.
[10] But you, O LORD, be gracious to me,
    and raise me up, that I may repay them.

[11] By this I know that you are pleased with me;
    because my enemy has not triumphed
        over me.
[12] But you have upheld me because of my
        integrity,
    and set me in your presence forever.

[13] Blessed be the LORD, the God of Israel,
    from everlasting to everlasting.
        Amen and Amen.

[a] Heb *you change all his bed*

COMMENTARY

At the heart of Psalm 41 (vv. 4-10) lies a prayer for help, which is framed by identical petitions in vv. 4 and 10 and contains in vv. 5-9 a fairly typical complaint against the enemies. What is unclear, however, is whether the complaint describes the psalmist's current situation or whether the psalmist is rehearsing what he or she had said during a past situation of distress. The introduction to v.

4 suggests the latter, as does the affirmation in vv. 11-12, which seems to indicate that the psalmist has already been delivered from the threats described in vv. 5-9 (note the repetition of "enemies"/"enemy" in vv. 5, 11). Thus most scholars suggest that Psalm 41 is an individual song of thanksgiving, and this seems to be the soundest conclusion. It is possible, though, to construe the verb tenses in vv. 11-12 as future and to conclude that the psalmist still awaits deliverance. In this case, priority is given to vv. 4-10, and Psalm 41 is understood as an individual lament or complaint.[185]

41:1-3. In any case, the psalm begins in a unique way—with a beatitude. Two other psalms in Book I begin with beatitudes (see Pss 1:1; 32:1-2), and there are four more beatitudes in Book I (see Pss 2:12; 33:12; 34:8; 40:4); but in each of these, happiness has to do with the psalmist in relationship to God. In Psalm 41, however, happiness belongs to "those who consider the poor" (v. 1a; cf. Prov 14:21), but this beatitude should not be understood as contradictory to the others. Rather, it follows from the others and from the character of God as it has been portrayed in the preceding psalms in Book I. Because Psalm 41 is the last psalm in Book I, the opening "happy" especially recalls Ps 1:1-2, where happiness involves openness to God's instruction, including the subsequent psalms themselves as sources of instruction (see Commentary on Psalm 1). If Psalms 2–40 have made anything clear, it is that God considers the oppressed (see Pss 9:9, 18; 10:17-18; 12:5; 14:6; 22:24; 34:19; 37:11; 40:17). Thus those who are open to God's instruction and God's leading, those who live under God's rule, will also "consider the poor." (The word translated "poor" [דל *dal*] occurs here for the first time in the psalter, but it is synonymous with other terms that have occurred frequently in Book I; the word occurs later in as "weak" in Pss 72:13; 82:3-4; in 113:7, it is parallel to several of the more frequently used terms.) In other words, the way one treats the poor follows from the way one relates to God.

We may reasonably conclude that the psalmist is among "those who consider the poor," since

vv. 1b-3 anticipate what apparently actually happens to the psalmist. That is, as vv. 11-12 suggest, the psalmist is delivered, kept alive, and not subdued by the enemies, all of which seems to involve recovery from sickness (see vv. 3-4). But even if one assumes that the psalmist still awaits healing, the affirmation of v. 1a is still effective. Happiness is not simply material good fortune. Rather, it involves the connectedness of one's life to the source of life; it means fundamentally dependence upon God (see Commentary on Psalms 1; 2). As v. 2a suggests, *God* "keeps them alive"; and v. 2b reinforces this conclusion. To be "in the land" need not be taken literally, since the land represented access to the God-given resources necessary to sustain life (see above on Ps 37:3, 9, 11, 22, 29, 34). Regardless of whether he or she has actually been healed or still awaits healing, the psalmist's opening affirmation (v. 1-3), prayer for help (vv. 4-10), and concluding assurance (vv. 11-12), indicate that the psalmist lives in dependence upon God.

41:4-9. The petition in v. 4a is used frequently (see Ps 4:1). Especially in the light of v. 3, v. 4b (see Ps 6:2) makes a connection between sickness and sin. As suggested above, however, the connection is a complex one (see Commentary on Psalms 6; 38). The sickness is an occasion for the psalmist to confess sin, but it does not justify the enemies' inconsiderate response, which is described in vv. 5-9. The enemies clearly do not show any awareness of the beatitude in v. 1a; they either do not know or do not care that God acts on behalf of the weak and the needy. Instead, they interpret the psalmist's need as punishment for sin and as license to inflict further punishment. Thus they attempt to capitalize on the psalmist's misfortune. Their speech is malicious (v. 5a), "empty" (v. 6a; see the NRSV "lies" in Pss 12:3; 144:8, 11), and slanderous (vv. 6c-7a). Their thoughts and intentions are characterized by "mischief" (און *'āwen*; v. 6b; see Ps 36:3-4) and "the worst" (lit., "evil" [רעה *rā'â*], 7b; the word is from the same root [רעע *r''*] as "malice" in v. 5 and "trouble" in v. 1). The phrase in v. 8a that the NRSV translates as "deadly thing" means more literally, "thing of worthlessness." As the NIV suggests, it may refer to the psalmist's sickness. The phrase also occurs in Deut 15:9 to describe the "wicked thought" of those who would greed-

185. See Erhard S. Gerstenberger, *Psalms, Part 1, with an Introduction to Cultic Poetry,* Forms of the OT Literature 14 (Grand Rapids: Eerdmans, 1988) 174-77.

ily take advantage of their needy neighbor. Thus, while the referent of the phrase differs in Deut 15:9 and Ps 41:8, the concern of Deut 15:9 is to prevent the kind of greed and exploitation that the enemies demonstrate in Psalm 41. Indeed, even the psalmist's "close friend" (v. 9*a*; lit., "person of my peace," suggesting those who had formerly worked for the psalmist's well-being) has become an opponent (see Pss 38:11; 88:8, 18; see also Job 29–30; John 13:18).

41:10-13. As already suggested, the setting of the petition and complaint (vv. 4-10) between the opening affirmation (vv. 1-3) and concluding assurance (vv. 11-12) suggests that the enemies' behavior is not justified (see Commentary on Psalm 38). The final petition in v. 10 reinforces this conclusion. While the enemies think that the psalmist "will not rise again" (v. 8*b*), the psalmist's petition indicates that she or he trusts God can "raise me up." The psalmist's expressed intent to repay them is not simply an expression of personal revenge. Rather, it may be interpreted as

a matter of justice (see Ps 31:23). Liberation for the oppressed means judgment upon oppressors. As v. 11 demonstrates, the failure of the enemies is not just the psalmist's will but God's will as well. The psalmist is "upheld" in his or her "integrity" (v. 12*a*; see Ps 63:8; Isa 42:1, where the mission of the servant in 42:6-8 clearly involves consideration of the poor, in keeping with Ps 41:1*a*). Integrity is not a matter of the psalmist's merit (as the NRSV seems to suggest) but indicates the psalmist's dependence upon God for life and future (see the discussion of "blameless"/"integrity" above in Pss 7:8; 15:2; 18:25; 19:13; 25:21; 26:1, 11). The phrase "in your presence" (לפניך *lĕpānēkā*; lit., "to your face") may indicate a liturgical setting in the Temple (see "face" in Pss 11:7; 17:15; 24:6; 27:8-9), but it more generally articulates symbolically the psalmist's assurance that God is with him or her. Verse 13 is a doxology that marks the end of Book I (see Pss 71:19; 89:52; 106:48; Introduction).

REFLECTIONS

As the conclusion of Book I, Psalm 41 forms with Psalm 1 an appropriate frame for the whole. Both psalms begin with a beatitude. While Psalm 1 commends openness to God's instruction, Psalm 41 commends openness to the needs of others. The two beatitudes are not contradictory but complementary. In effect, then, the framework of Book I portrays happy persons as those who love God and love neighbor.

A verbal link between Pss 1:2 and 41:11 offers another connection. The root (חפץ *ḥāpēṣ*) translated "delight" in 1:2 is translated "pleased with" in 41:11. Book I opens with a portrayal of those who delight in God, and it concludes with an affirmation of God's delighting in the psalmist. The effect is to articulate the mutuality of the relationship between God and humanity. From the human side, the essence of the relationship is trusting or taking refuge in God, which is the subject of the beatitudes in Pss 2:12; 34:8; 40:4 (see Introduction). From the divine side, the relationship is grounded in the way God is: fundamentally gracious (see vv. 4, 10) and steadfastly loving (see Pss 5:7; 40:10-11; Introduction). In particular, God is committed to those persons variously described in Book I as weak, poor, needy, afflicted, humble, meek, and oppressed. In short, God helps those who cannot help themselves (see Psalm 3). This conviction underlies both the appeal and the opening beatitude in Psalm 41. In essence, happiness belongs to those who are like God—those who consider the poor. As Jesus would say it, "Blessed are the merciful, for they will receive mercy" (Matt 5:7 NRSV).

This basic conviction that God helps the afflicted undercuts any mechanistic doctrine of retribution. The psalmist may be motivated by sickness to confess sins (v. 4), but there is no justification for us to conclude that the psalmist deserves the sickness as punishment for sin, and there is clearly no justification for us to reject the sufferer or take advantage of the suffering (see Commentary on Psalms 6; 38).

In John 13:18, Judas's betrayal of Jesus is interpreted as a fulfillment of Ps 41:9*b*. Thus, like other psalms (see esp. 22; 31; 69), Psalm 41 illuminated for the Gospel writers the suffering of Jesus. Judas's betrayal was motivated, in part at least, by greed, so that he became a representation of the enemies who throughout the psalms seek to take advantage of the humble and the afflicted. As Judas's destiny suggests, this way—the way of self-aggrandizement—is the way of death. The way Jesus walked—the way of suffering that led to a cross—is the way of life. Jesus becomes the ultimate paradigm of the faithful sufferer, who entrusts life and future to God and who likewise considers the poor. The good news of Psalm 41 is that the seemingly rejected one is the one who can finally say to God, "You . . . set me in your presence forever" (Ps 41:12 NRSV). This movement anticipates the NT. The humble are exalted. The crucified one is raised. Suffering and glory belong together as the secret of our identity and God's identity as well (see Commentary on Psalms 13; 22).

BOOK II

PSALMS 42:1–43:5, HOPE IN GOD

BOOK II

Psalms 42–72

Psalm 42[a]

For the director of music. A *maskil*[b] of the Sons of Korah.

[1]As the deer pants for streams of water,
    so my soul pants for you, O God.
[2]My soul thirsts for God, for the living God.
    When can I go and meet with God?
[3]My tears have been my food
    day and night,
while men say to me all day long,
    "Where is your God?"
[4]These things I remember
    as I pour out my soul:
how I used to go with the multitude,
    leading the procession to the house of God,
with shouts of joy and thanksgiving
    among the festive throng.

[5]Why are you downcast, O my soul?
    Why so disturbed within me?
Put your hope in God,
    for I will yet praise him,
    my Savior and [6]my God.

My[c] soul is downcast within me;
    therefore I will remember you
from the land of the Jordan,
    the heights of Hermon—from Mount Mizar.
[7]Deep calls to deep
    in the roar of your waterfalls;

---

a In many Hebrew manuscripts Psalms 42 and 43 constitute one psalm.
b Title: Probably a literary or musical term   c5,6 A few Hebrew manuscripts, Septuagint and Syriac; most Hebrew manuscripts *praise him for his saving help. / 6 my God, my*

BOOK II

(Psalms 42–72)

Psalm 42

To the leader. A Maskil of the Korahites.

[1] As a deer longs for flowing streams,
    so my soul longs for you, O God.
[2] My soul thirsts for God,
    for the living God.
When shall I come and behold
    the face of God?
[3] My tears have been my food
    day and night,
while people say to me continually,
    "Where is your God?"

[4] These things I remember,
    as I pour out my soul:
how I went with the throng,[a]
    and led them in procession to the house
        of God,
with glad shouts and songs of thanksgiving,
    a multitude keeping festival.
[5] Why are you cast down, O my soul,
    and why are you disquieted within me?
Hope in God; for I shall again praise him,
    my help [6]and my God.

My soul is cast down within me;
    therefore I remember you
from the land of Jordan and of Hermon,
    from Mount Mizar.
[7] Deep calls to deep
    at the thunder of your cataracts;

---

a Meaning of Heb uncertain

NIV

all your waves and breakers
> have swept over me.

⁸By day the LORD directs his love,
> at night his song is with me—
> a prayer to the God of my life.

⁹I say to God my Rock,
> "Why have you forgotten me?
Why must I go about mourning,
> oppressed by the enemy?"
¹⁰My bones suffer mortal agony
> as my foes taunt me,
saying to me all day long,
> "Where is your God?"

¹¹Why are you downcast, O my soul?
> Why so disturbed within me?
Put your hope in God,
> for I will yet praise him,
> my Savior and my God.

Psalm 43ᵃ

¹Vindicate me, O God,
> and plead my cause against an ungodly
> > nation;
> rescue me from deceitful and wicked men.
²You are God my stronghold.
> Why have you rejected me?
> Why must I go about mourning,
> oppressed by the enemy?
³Send forth your light and your truth,
> let them guide me;
> let them bring me to your holy mountain,
> to the place where you dwell.
⁴Then will I go to the altar of God,
> to God, my joy and my delight.
I will praise you with the harp,
> O God, my God.

⁵Why are you downcast, O my soul?
> Why so disturbed within me?
Put your hope in God,
> for I will yet praise him,
> my Savior and my God.

ᵃ In many Hebrew manuscripts Psalms 42 and 43 constitute one psalm.

NRSV

all your waves and your billows
> have gone over me.
⁸ By day the LORD commands his steadfast
> > love,
> and at night his song is with me,
> a prayer to the God of my life.

⁹ I say to God, my rock,
> "Why have you forgotten me?
Why must I walk about mournfully
> because the enemy oppresses me?"
¹⁰ As with a deadly wound in my body,
> my adversaries taunt me,
while they say to me continually,
> "Where is your God?"

¹¹ Why are you cast down, O my soul,
> and why are you disquieted within me?
Hope in God; for I shall again praise him,
> my help and my God.

Psalm 43

¹ Vindicate me, O God, and defend my cause
> against an ungodly people;
from those who are deceitful and unjust
> deliver me!
² For you are the God in whom I take refuge;
> why have you cast me off?
Why must I walk about mournfully
> because of the oppression of the enemy?

³ O send out your light and your truth;
> let them lead me;
let them bring me to your holy hill
> and to your dwelling.
⁴ Then I will go to the altar of God,
> to God my exceeding joy;
and I will praise you with the harp,
> O God, my God.

⁵ Why are you cast down, O my soul,
> and why are you disquieted within me?
Hope in God; for I shall again praise him,
> my help and my God.

COMMENTARY

Because of their shared vocabulary, themes, and refrain, Psalms 42–43 are a unit. They open a collection attributed to the Korahites (Psalms 42–49; see also Psalms 84–85; 87–88; Introduction), which in turn opens Book II. While Psalms 42–43 appear to be the prayer of an individual, the rest of the collection has a communal character. This fact, plus the linguistic links between Psalms 42–43 and 44 (see "taunt"/"taunters" in 42:10 and 44:13, 16; "oppress"/"oppression" in 42:9; 43:2; 44:24; "cast off"/"rejected" in 43:2; 44:10; "forgotten"/"forget" in 42:9; 44:24; "face" in 42:2; 44:24; "light" in 43:3; 44:3; "steadfast love" in 42:8; 44:26), suggests that the "I" of Psalms 42–43 speaks for the people (see Reflections below). Not coincidentally, perhaps, the speaker in Psalms 42–43 seems to be exiled from the Temple, and Psalm 44 is a communal lament that recalls the Babylonian exile and dispersion (see esp. 44:9-12). Interestingly, Book III begins in a similar way, with an "I" psalm (Psalm 73) followed by a communal lament (Psalm 74) as the first two psalms in the Asaph collection, which like the Korah collection, has a communal orientation. The pattern with which both books begin provides a context for reading subsequent psalms throughout the books—for instance, the Davidic collection of Psalms 51–72—with a communal orientation. This would have particularly suited both books for addressing the exilic and post-exilic eras (see Introduction).

Several scholars conclude that Psalms 42–43 in particular are suited for addressing concerns of the post-exilic era. Gerstenberger, for instance, places these psalms in "the synagogal worship of the Persian times," but he also recognizes that Psalms 42–43 speak "in very general terms of danger, threats, anxiety, trust, and hope."[186] This fact has made Psalms 42–43 adaptable to a variety of situations. Indeed, they express the fundamental biblical conviction that human life depends on relatedness to God.

The poem may be divided into three sections, each concluding with the refrain: (1) 42:1-5; (2) 42:6-11; (3) 43:1-5. The first two sections are primarily complaint. The final section is primarily

186. Gerstenberger, *Psalms,* 182.

petition, giving the whole the character of a prayer for help. Psalms 42–43 also share the spirit of the songs of Zion, in that the psalmist longs to return to Jerusalem and to enter the Temple again (see 43:3-4).

42:1-5. The opening verses articulate the psalmist's need for God with the image of thirst. The opening simile (see Joel 1:20) is followed by a direct statement of the psalmist's need. The two occurrences of "soul" (vv. 1*b*, 2*a*) anticipate the refrain. The psalmist's soul "thirsts for God" (v. 2*a*; see Pss 63:1; 143:6). Thirst is not just a desire, for the human body cannot live without water. For the psalmist, God is a necessity of life. Verse 2*b* begins to suggest that the psalmist is exiled or at least is prevented from making a pilgrimage to the Temple to "behold the face of God." More symbolically, the psalmist desires a communion with God that is not currently available. The mention of "the face of God" (v. 2) and "bread" (v. 3) reinforces the conclusion that the desire for communion with God is expressed as the wish to visit the Temple, which contained the "bread of the face" (or "bread of the Presence"; see Exod 25:30; 1 Sam 21:6; 1 Kgs 7:48). The psalmist is unable to visit the Temple, so his or her "bread" has been tears (see Ps 80:5). The grief of absence has been made worse by the question of others, "Where is your God?" (v. 3; see also v. 10; Pss 79:10; 115:2; Joel 2:17; Mic 7:10).

Unable to visit the Temple, all the psalmist can do is remember (v. 4; see also Ps 137:1, 6; Lam 1:7), so she or he recalls the joy of past visits. The poignancy of the scene is expressed by the expression "pour out my soul," for it continues the thirst imagery of vv. 1-2. God's absence means that there is no water to be poured to alleviate the psalmist's thirst; therefore, the psalmist must "pour out" her or his soul by praying (see 1 Sam 1:15; see Pss 62:8; 102:1; 142:2; Lam 2:19). The happy memories that accompany the prayer, however, exacerbate the present sense of despair, which is expressed in the refrain by the verbs "cast down" (חחש *šḥḥ,* which translates the same verb as "bowed down" in Ps 35:14 and "pros-

852

trate" in Ps 38:6) and "disquieted" (המה *hāmâ*, which translates the same verb as "moan" in Pss 55:17; 77:4). The refrain also articulates the possibility of hope (see Pss 31:24; 33:18, 22; 38:15) and help (more literally, with a slight emendation that makes the refrain here virtually identical to 42:11 and 43:5, "the salvation of my face"; see Exod 15:2; Pss 3:2; 22:1). Although the refrain remains the same, these hopeful notes will be heard more clearly by the conclusion of the poem, which provides the refrain with a different context.

42:6-11. The beginning of the second section echoes the first line of the refrain, thus emphasizing the note of despair. Again, the psalmist's response is to "remember you" (v. 6; see v. 4). The geographical terms in v. 6 are sometimes understood literally and are thus cited by those who want to locate the psalmist outside the land. The names seem to indicate the region where the Jordan River begins, and it is more likely that the psalmist refers to this region as a poetic way of introducing the water imagery of v. 7. Whereas scarcity of water had been the poetic image used to describe the psalmist's need in vv. 1-2, there is too much water in v. 7. The "deep" (תהום *tĕhôm*) represents the chaotic forces that plague (cf. Jonah 2:5) and threaten to overwhelm the psalmist (see Pss 69:1-2; 124:4-5; Jonah 2:3).

Verse 8 is unexpectedly hopeful, and commentators often treat it as the psalmist's recollection of a happier time (see 42:4). The reference to "day" and "night" recalls v. 3, and v. 8 even seems to answer the question raised in v. 3, affirming the presence of God's steadfast love (see Pss 5:7; 23:6; 31:7, 16, 21; 32:10; 33:5, 18, 22; Introduction). The refrain has already hinted at hope and help, and the psalm is moving in the direction of assurance (see 43:3-4), so perhaps the expression of confidence here should not be so surprising. After all, despair and hope may exist simultaneously (see Commentary on Psalm 13), and, again, the refrain clearly demonstrates this. In fact, v. 9 also points to the simultaneity of hope and despair. While addressing God as "my rock" (see Pss 18:2; 31:3), the psalmist also wonders why God has "forgotten me" (see Ps 13:1) and why mourning must continue (see Pss 35:14; 38:6) as "the enemies oppress me" (cf. Exod 3:9; Deut 26:7; Pss 56:1; 106:42). The enemies' haunting and taunting question is repeated from v. 3 (see "taunt"/"scorn" in Pss 22:6; 31:11; 55:12; 79:12 NRSV), leading to the second occurrence of the refrain.

43:1-5. The final section moves from complaint to petition. "Vindicate me" (שפטני *šō pṭēnî*) could also be translated "Establish justice for me" (v. 1; see also Pss 10:18; 26:1). The second petition in v. 1 is framed in legal terms (see Ps 119:154; Lam 3:58; cf. Ps 74:22). The enemies in the psalms are often described as "deceitful" (see Pss 5:6; 10:7; 36:3) and "unjust" (cf. Pss 37:1; 58:2). Verse 2 demonstrates again the simultaneity of hope and despair. While the psalmist still has questions (see 42:9), she or he is clearly moving toward a more hopeful conclusion as the visit to the Temple is envisioned. The psalmist anticipates being led (see Ps 31:3) to the "holy hill" (Pss 2:6; 3:4; 15:1; 48:2) by God's "light" (see Ps 27:1) and "faithfulness" (NIV and NRSV "truth"). Usually, "steadfast love" and "faithfulness" are paired in the psalms (see 57:3; 85:10; 89:14), and Ps 5:7 even affirms that God's steadfast love leads the psalmist to the Temple. Perhaps the normal pairing is altered to include "light" here, since light is often associated with God's "face," which the psalmist longs to see (see Ps 42:2; see also Ps 4:6). Psalm 43:4 articulates the joy of arriving at the Temple, where the psalmist will respond with praises on the harp (see Ps 33:2). The word "praise" (ידה *yādâ*) in v. 4 serves this time to emphasize the hopeful aspect of the refrain: "I shall again praise."

REFLECTIONS

1. The spirit of Psalms 42–43 pervades the opening paragraph of Augustine's *Confessions*: "The thought of [God] stirs [the human being] so deeply that he cannot be content unless he praises you, because you made us for yourself and our hearts find no peace until they rest in you."[187] The imagery of Psalms 42–43 was used by early Christians as symbols for baptism: "The hart [or "deer"; 42:1] . . . was the emblem of those thirsting souls who, in the cooling streams of the baptismal font, drank deeply of the fountain of eternal life."[188] This psalm was sung when Augustine was baptized on Easter Sunday 387 CE. Such use of this symbolism is appropriate, for Psalms 42–43 affirm what Christians profess in baptism: Each human life derives from and belongs to God, and life can be lived authentically only in relationship to God. In short, human life depends on God.

2. As memorable as the opening line of Psalm 42 is the threefold refrain. Although the refrain seems to be intensely personal, it may actually be more liturgical than autobiographical, as Mays suggests:

> In it the ego who speaks to the downcast soul is the liturgical and confessional ego speaking to the consciousness shaped by a society and circumstances that do not support faith. . . .
>
> . . . For Christians who live in a world that constantly raises the question, "Where is your God?" these psalms are indispensable liturgy and Scripture. They disclose the real nature of our souls' disquiet as thirst for God. They turn us toward the worship of praise, sacraments, and preaching in and through which our Lord wills to be present for the congregation.[189]

In other words, the refrain and Psalms 42–43 as a whole profess the faith of the people of God, the church. That they did so in a hostile environment makes them all the more timely. As Hauerwas and Willimon put it, the church is in a sort of permanent exile, at least in North America. Christians live as "resident aliens" in a culture that clearly does not support faith or affirm that human life derives from and depends on God. Instead, our culture teaches us that we are self-grounded and self-directed; "It is all up to us."[190] In this cultural context, the most important thing we can do is to hope in God and to claim God as our help (Pss 42:5, 11; 43:5).

3. To hope in God means that we live eschatologically, that we know and articulate hope and despair simultaneously (see Commentary on Psalm 2; Introduction). That we cannot escape this inevitable reality is demonstrated by Jesus, who echoes the refrain of Psalms 42–43 in his prayer in the Garden of Gethsemane (Matt 26:38; John 12:27). Even Jesus, who fully embodied dependence upon God, could not escape disquietude of soul. Neither shall we. The good news, however, is that neither shall we be able to escape the steadfast love and faithfulness of God, which are manifested in God's desire to lead us back to God's own self (see 42:8; 43:3). This is the source of our hope and, indeed, the hope of the world.

187. Augustine, *Confessions*, I.1, trans. R. S. Pine-Coffin (New York: Penguin Books, 1961) 21.
188. Rowland E. Prothero, *The Psalms in Human Life and Experience* (New York: E. P. Dutton, 1903) 9-10.
189. Mays, *Psalms*, 175-76.
190. Stanley Hauerwas and William H. Willimon, *Resident Aliens: Life in the Christian Colony* (Nashville: Abingdon, 1989) 36; see also Commentary on Psalm 3.

PSALM 44:1-26, LIKE SHEEP FOR SLAUGHTER

NIV	NRSV
Psalm 44	Psalm 44
For the director of music. Of the Sons of Korah. A *maskil.*[a]	To the leader. Of the Korahites. A Maskil.
[1]We have heard with our ears, O God;	[1] We have heard with our ears, O God, our ancestors have told us, what deeds you performed in their days,
[a] Title: Probably a literary or musical term	

NIV

our fathers have told us
what you did in their days,
in days long ago.
²With your hand you drove out the nations
and planted our fathers;
you crushed the peoples
and made our fathers flourish.
³It was not by their sword that they won the
land,
nor did their arm bring them victory;
it was your right hand, your arm,
and the light of your face, for you loved
them.

⁴You are my King and my God,
who decrees^a victories for Jacob.
⁵Through you we push back our enemies;
through your name we trample our foes.
⁶I do not trust in my bow,
my sword does not bring me victory;
⁷but you give us victory over our enemies,
you put our adversaries to shame.
⁸In God we make our boast all day long,
and we will praise your name forever. *Selah*

⁹But now you have rejected and humbled us;
you no longer go out with our armies.
¹⁰You made us retreat before the enemy,
and our adversaries have plundered us.
¹¹You gave us up to be devoured like sheep
and have scattered us among the nations.
¹²You sold your people for a pittance,
gaining nothing from their sale.

¹³You have made us a reproach to our
neighbors,
the scorn and derision of those around us.
¹⁴You have made us a byword among the
nations;
the peoples shake their heads at us.
¹⁵My disgrace is before me all day long,
and my face is covered with shame
¹⁶at the taunts of those who reproach and
revile me,
because of the enemy, who is bent on
revenge.

¹⁷All this happened to us,
though we had not forgotten you
or been false to your covenant.

^a4 Septuagint, Aquila and Syriac; Hebrew *King, O God; / command*

NRSV

in the days of old:
² you with your own hand drove out the
nations,
but them you planted;
you afflicted the peoples,
but them you set free;
³ for not by their own sword did they win
the land,
nor did their own arm give them victory;
but your right hand, and your arm,
and the light of your countenance,
for you delighted in them.

⁴ You are my King and my God;
you command^a victories for Jacob.
⁵ Through you we push down our foes;
through your name we tread down our
assailants.
⁶ For not in my bow do I trust,
nor can my sword save me.
⁷ But you have saved us from our foes,
and have put to confusion those who
hate us.
⁸ In God we have boasted continually,
and we will give thanks to your name
forever.   *Selah*

⁹ Yet you have rejected us and abased us,
and have not gone out with our armies.
¹⁰ You made us turn back from the foe,
and our enemies have gotten spoil.
¹¹ You have made us like sheep for slaughter,
and have scattered us among the nations.
¹² You have sold your people for a trifle,
demanding no high price for them.

¹³ You have made us the taunt of our
neighbors,
the derision and scorn of those around us.
¹⁴ You have made us a byword among the
nations,
a laughingstock^b among the peoples.
¹⁵ All day long my disgrace is before me,
and shame has covered my face
¹⁶ at the words of the taunters and revilers,
at the sight of the enemy and the
avenger.

^aGk Syr: Heb *You are my King, O God; command*   ^bHeb *a shaking of the head*

NIV

¹⁸Our hearts had not turned back;
    our feet had not strayed from your path.
¹⁹But you crushed us and made us a haunt for
      jackals
    and covered us over with deep darkness.

²⁰If we had forgotten the name of our God
    or spread out our hands to a foreign god,
²¹would not God have discovered it,
    since he knows the secrets of the heart?
²²Yet for your sake we face death all day long;
    we are considered as sheep to be
      slaughtered.

²³Awake, O Lord! Why do you sleep?
    Rouse yourself! Do not reject us forever.
²⁴Why do you hide your face
    and forget our misery and oppression?
²⁵We are brought down to the dust;
    our bodies cling to the ground.
²⁶Rise up and help us;
    redeem us because of your unfailing love.

NRSV

¹⁷ All this has come upon us,
    yet we have not forgotten you,
    or been false to your covenant.
¹⁸ Our heart has not turned back,
    nor have our steps departed from your
      way,
¹⁹ yet you have broken us in the haunt of
      jackals,
    and covered us with deep darkness.

²⁰ If we had forgotten the name of our God,
    or spread out our hands to a strange god,
²¹ would not God discover this?
    For he knows the secrets of the heart.
²² Because of you we are being killed all day
      long,
    and accounted as sheep for the slaughter.

²³ Rouse yourself! Why do you sleep, O Lord?
    Awake, do not cast us off forever!
²⁴ Why do you hide your face?
    Why do you forget our affliction and
      oppression?
²⁵ For we sink down to the dust;
    our bodies cling to the ground.
²⁶ Rise up, come to our help.
    Redeem us for the sake of your steadfast
      love.

COMMENTARY

Psalm 44 is the first communal lament or complaint in the psalter. Two major issues have dominated the scholarly discussion of the psalm: (1) the circumstances in which it arose, and (2) the identity of the speaker(s). As for the first issue, a wide variety of proposals has been offered. The origin of the psalm is sometimes placed during the monarchy (see 2 Chr 20:1-12) and is often associated with Sennacherib's campaign of 701 BCE (see 2 Kgs 18:13–19:37; Isa 36:1–37:37). Then, too, Psalm 44 is clearly reminiscent of the exile, which involved the scattering of the people (see v. 11). Since vv. 17-22 seem inconsistent with the dominant OT view that the exile was a deserved punishment (see 2 Kgs 17:19-20; 24:4-5), other dates have also been proposed, including the second-century BCE Maccabean period, when the Temple was desecrated by Antioches IV Epiphanes. The very fact that these proposals cover a range of over 500 years suggests the difficulty of dating the psalm. As John Calvin suggested long ago, almost any date after the exile would fit, "for after the return of the Jews from the captivity of Babylon, they were scarcely ever free from severe afflictions."[191]

The second issue is related to the first. Noting that vv. 4, 6, 15-16 depart from the predominant first-person plural, several scholars suggest that this speaker must be the king, who speaks as a representative of the nation during the crisis.

191. John Calvin, *Commentary on the Book of Psalms*, Calvin Translation Society, 5 vols. (Grand Rapids: Baker, 1981) V:2·148.

Obviously, this view necessitates a pre-exilic dating of the psalm. Craigie, for instance, argues that Psalm 44 originated during some unknown pre-exilic crisis and was used during subsequent crises throughout the history of the nation.[192] But as Gerstenberger points out, the alternating of plural and singular speakers can be attributed to the liturgical use of the psalm, and he suggests that the origin and use of Psalm 44 are to be associated with "Jewish worship in Persian times," the purpose of which in part was to encourage and strengthen congregations in a threatening environment.[193]

Perhaps more accessible than the question of the origin of Psalm 44 is the issue of its final placement. There are striking linguistic links between Psalms 42–43 and 44 (see Commentary on Psalms 42–43), which open Book II. While Psalms 42–43 seem to be the prayer of an exiled individual, Psalm 44 is the prayer of a scattered people. Together, they set the tone for hearing the rest of the psalms in Book II, and thus they reinforce the ability of the collection to address the perpetually threatened people of God (see Introduction). This recognition allows Psalm 44 to be heard not simply as a historical artifact but as an ongoing theological resource for the people of God as they confront their vocation and the suffering that it inevitably involves (see Reflections below).

Psalm 44 can be divided into four major sections. Verses 1-8 have the character of a profession of faith that is motivated by historical recollection. In view of v. 8*b*, the section of bitter complaint in vv. 9-16 is unexpected, thus increasing its rhetorical impact. The vehemence of the complaint is perhaps more understandable in the light of vv. 17-22, the people's protestation of innocence. The psalm culminates in the petition of vv. 23-26.

44:1-8. The book of Deuteronomy directs that children be told of God's deliverance of the people from Egypt and of God's gift of the land (Deut 6:20-25), and Psalm 44 begins by affirming that this has happened (see Judg 6:13; Ps 78:3-4). The "you" that begins v. 2 is emphatic. God's power—

symbolized by God's "hand" (v. 2), "right hand," (v. 3; see Exod 15:6, 13), and "arm" (v. 3; see Exod 15:16; Ps 77:15)—has been operative in the people's history. The latter is specifically contrasted in v. 3 with "their own arm." As in the exodus and holy war traditions (see Exodus 15; Joshua 8–12), God is portrayed as a warrior. The result is "victory" (ישועה *yĕšû'â,* v. 3; lit., "salvation"; see vv. 4, 6, 7; and Exod 15:2 NIV); the nations have been driven out (see Deut 7:17) and the people "planted" (see Exod 15:17; Jer 24:6; 32:41). Whereas in Ps 42:2, the psalmist could not see "the face of God," Ps 44:3 attributes victory to "the light of your face" (see also Ps 4:6). The section concludes with the observation that Israel's past has been evidence of God's love (see Deut 7:7-11, where the same observation is made with different vocabulary; see also Ps 149:4, where the NRSV's "takes pleasure" translates the same verb here translated "delighted" [רצה *rāṣâ*] and where it also accounts for the people's "victory").

The emphatic pronoun "you" opens v. 4 as it did v. 2, focusing attention on God. God's control of the destiny of nations and peoples—God's victory—is evidence of God's sovereignty; so God is addressed as "my King" (see Pss 5:2; 68:24; 74:12; 84:3; see also Exod 15:1-18; Pss 98:1-3; 149:1-7, where God's "victory"/"salvation," God's control of the nations, and God's reign are explicitly associated; see also Psalm 2; Introduction). In addition to the repetition of "victory," vv. 4-8 are linked to vv. 1-3 by the repetition of "sword" (vv. 3, 6). While the participation of the people is somewhat more evident in v. 5 than in vv. 2-3, the victory still belongs to God (the word translated "tread down" [בוס *bûs*] is used elsewhere of God as warrior; see Pss 60:12; 108:13; Isa 14:21; 63:6). The people's trust (v. 6; see Pss 4:5; 9:10; Introduction), boasting (v. 8; see Ps 34:2; cf. Pss 52:1; 97:7), and gratitude (see Pss 75:1; 79:13) are properly directed to God.

44:9-16. Nothing in vv. 1-8 has prepared for the complaint in vv. 9-16. Suddenly, delight has become rejection (v. 9; see v. 23 NIV; see also Pss 43:2; 60:1, 10; 74:1; 77:7; 88:14; 89:38; 108:11); victory has become retreat and defeat (v. 10). God is no longer the good shepherd of the "sheep" (see Pss 74:1; 79:13; 95:7; 100:3). Rather, the sheep are either being killed (v. 11*a*;

192. Peter C. Craigie, *Psalms 1–50,* WBC 19 (Waco, Tex.: Word, 1983) 331-33.

193. Erhard S. Gerstenberger, *Psalms, Part 1, with an Introduction to Cultic Poetry,* Forms of the OT Literature 14 (Grand Rapids: Eerdmans, 1988) 186.

see v. 22; Jer 12:3) or scattered (see Ezek 5:12; 12:14; 20:23). The word "sold" (מכר *mākar*, v. 12) recalls former times that were not so auspicious (see Judg 2:14; 3:8; 4:2). The language of vv. 13-16 is similar to that of other individual and communal complaints. The people are taunted (v. 16; see Ps 22:6), derided (see Ps 22:7), and scorned (see Ps 79:4, where all three words occur). The word "byword" (see Ps 69:11) occurs in Deut 28:37 as part of the curses for violating the covenant, thus preparing for the people's defense in vv. 17-22.

44:17-22. In vv. 20-21, the people suggest that they could accept their misfortune if they had worshiped a "strange god" (see Ps 81:9; Isa 43:12). But they have neither forgotten God (vv. 17, 20) nor violated the covenant (see Deut 4:23; 2 Kgs 17:15). They have not "turned back" (see Ps 78:57), yet they suffer (v. 19; on v. 19*a,* cf. Isa 34:13; Jer 9:11; 10:22; on v. 19*b,* cf. Pss 23:4; 107:10). Thus all they can conclude is that their suffering is "Because of you" (v. 22). Verse 22 recalls v. 11*a,* although the Hebrew words translated "slaughter" differ in the two verses (מאכל *ma'ăkāl,* v. 11*a*; טבחה *tibhâ,* v. 22). The one in v. 22 occurs also in Isa 53:7 (see Ps 69:7), which

is part of the climactic Suffering Servant song, another text that pushes toward new and deeper understandings of suffering (see Reflections below).

44:23-26. Given the people's conclusion in v. 22, all that they can do is desperately plead for God to wake up (see Pss 7:6; 35:23; 59:4-5) as they bombard God with questions. God is not supposed to sleep (see Ps 121:4); God is not supposed to hide God's face (see Pss 13:1; 22:24; 27:9); God is not supposed to forget affliction (see Pss 9:12, 18; 10:12; 42:9). A final complaint (v. 25; the NRSV's "sinks down" translates a verb [שחח *šāhâ*] that is very similar to "cast down" in Pss 42:5, 11; 43:5) precedes the threefold petition of the concluding verse: "Rise up" (see Pss 3:7; 74:22), "help" (see Pss 22:19; 38:22; 40:13), "redeem" (see Pss 25:22; 34:22). The appeal is to God's fundamental character: steadfast love (see Exod 34:6-7; Pss 5:7; 6:4; Introduction). While God is the problem, God is also the solution. As Mays suggests, "the last hope of a faithful people is the faithfulness of God."[194]

194. James L. Mays, *Psalms,* Interpretation (Louisville: John Knox, 1994) 178.

REFLECTIONS

The unexpected movement from vv. 1-8 to vv. 9-16 reveals the pathos of Psalm 44; God's faithful people suffer, even when they do not deserve it (vv. 17-22). Thus they are left to appeal for help (vv. 23-26) to the one who is apparently the source of the problem (vv. 11, 22). This is the paradox of the individual complaints and of the book of Job as well. For the psalmists and for Job, every experience of life is somehow an experience of God. Like Psalm 44, for instance, Psalm 13 moves from bitter complaint (cf. Ps 13:1 to 44:24) to petition and to the psalmist's taking a stand on God's steadfast love (cf. 13:5 to 44:26). The paradox of the complaints pushes toward a profound understanding of suffering (see Commentary on Psalms 13; 22).

Crucial in this regard in Psalm 44 are vv. 11 and 22. In commenting on v. 22, Mays concludes:

"For your sake" meant they could see no other meaning and purpose in their confession and trust [see vv. 1-8] than that they were accounted as sheep for slaughter. But that minimal and doleful interpretation of their suffering opens on the prospect of an understanding of suffering as a service to the kingdom of God. The prospect leads to the suffering servant of Isaiah 53, to Jewish martyrs, and to the cross of Calvary.[195]

For Israel, the experience of exile and the ongoing afflictions of the post-exilic era necessitated a reconsideration of suffering. While it is not clear that the origin of Psalm 44 can be related to the exile, it is certain that Psalm 44 and other complaints assisted Israel to reach in the

195. Ibid., 179.

post-exilic era a new and profound understanding of its suffering and its vocation. In this regard, the similarity to Isaiah 53 is not surprising (cf. Ps 44:11, 22 to Isa 53:7). Israel came to understand its mission to the world in terms of a suffering that is somehow redemptive.

This understanding of suffering, election, and vocation makes comprehensible the life and death of Jesus Christ. Jesus could even pronounce his followers blessed when they experienced the kind of rejection and derision described in Ps 44:13-16 (see Matt 5:10-11). In his consideration of "the sufferings of this present time" (Rom 8:18 NRSV) that are experienced by "God's elect" (Rom 8:33 NRSV), the apostle Paul quoted Ps 44:22 (see Rom 8:36) to illustrate the nature of the Christian life. Suffering is not a sign of separation from God or from God's love; rather, it marks those who have been chosen to follow Jesus Christ (see Mark 8:34-35).

PSALM 45:1-17, FOR THE CAUSE OF TRUTH, HUMILITY, AND RIGHTEOUSNESS

NIV

Psalm 45

For the director of music. To ⌐the tune of⌐ "Lilies." Of the Sons of Korah. A *maskil.*[a] A wedding song.

[1]My heart is stirred by a noble theme
    as I recite my verses for the king;
    my tongue is the pen of a skillful writer.

[2]You are the most excellent of men
    and your lips have been anointed with
        grace,
    since God has blessed you forever.
[3]Gird your sword upon your side, O mighty
        one;
    clothe yourself with splendor and majesty.
[4]In your majesty ride forth victoriously
    in behalf of truth, humility and
        righteousness;
    let your right hand display awesome
        deeds.
[5]Let your sharp arrows pierce the hearts of
        the king's enemies;
    let the nations fall beneath your feet.
[6]Your throne, O God, will last for ever and
        ever;
    a scepter of justice will be the scepter of
        your kingdom.
[7]You love righteousness and hate wickedness;

a Title: Probably a literary or musical term

NRSV

Psalm 45

To the leader: according to Lilies. Of the Korahites. A Maskil. A love song.

[1] My heart overflows with a goodly theme;
    I address my verses to the king;
    my tongue is like the pen of a ready
        scribe.

[2] You are the most handsome of men;
    grace is poured upon your lips;
    therefore God has blessed you forever.
[3] Gird your sword on your thigh, O mighty
        one,
    in your glory and majesty.

[4] In your majesty ride on victoriously
    for the cause of truth and to defend[a] the
        right;
    let your right hand teach you dread
        deeds.
[5] Your arrows are sharp
    in the heart of the king's enemies;
    the peoples fall under you.

[6] Your throne, O God,[b] endures forever and
        ever.
    Your royal scepter is a scepter of equity;

a Cn: Heb *and the meekness of*   b Or *Your throne is a throne of God, it*

NIV

therefore God, your God, has set you
    above your companions
by anointing you with the oil of joy.
[8]All your robes are fragrant with myrrh and
    aloes and cassia;
from palaces adorned with ivory
    the music of the strings makes you glad.
[9]Daughters of kings are among your honored
    women;
    at your right hand is the royal bride in
    gold of Ophir.

[10]Listen, O daughter, consider and give ear:
    Forget your people and your father's house.
[11]The king is enthralled by your beauty;
    honor him, for he is your lord.
[12]The Daughter of Tyre will come with a gift,[a]
    men of wealth will seek your favor.

[13]All glorious is the princess within her
    chamber;
    her gown is interwoven with gold.
[14]In embroidered garments she is led to the
    king;
    her virgin companions follow her
    and are brought to you.
[15]They are led in with joy and gladness;
    they enter the palace of the king.

[16]Your sons will take the place of your fathers;
    you will make them princes throughout
    the land.
[17]I will perpetuate your memory through all
    generations;
    therefore the nations will praise you for
    ever and ever.

[a]12 Or A Tyrian robe is among the gifts

NRSV

[7] you love righteousness and hate wickedness.
Therefore God, your God, has anointed you
    with the oil of gladness beyond your
    companions;
[8] your robes are all fragrant with myrrh and
    aloes and cassia.
From ivory palaces stringed instruments
    make you glad;
[9] daughters of kings are among your ladies
    of honor;
    at your right hand stands the queen in
    gold of Ophir.

[10] Hear, O daughter, consider and incline your
    ear;
    forget your people and your father's house,
[11] and the king will desire your beauty.
Since he is your lord, bow to him;
[12] the people[a] of Tyre will seek your favor
    with gifts,
    the richest of the people [13]with all kinds
    of wealth.

The princess is decked in her chamber with
    gold-woven robes;[b]
[14] in many-colored robes she is led to the king;
    behind her the virgins, her companions,
    follow.
[15] With joy and gladness they are led along
    as they enter the palace of the king.

[16] In the place of ancestors you, O king,[c] shall
    have sons;
    you will make them princes in all the earth.
[17] I will cause your name to be celebrated in
    all generations;
    therefore the peoples will praise you
    forever and ever.

[a]Heb daughter   [b]Or people. [13]All glorious is the princess within,
gold embroidery is her clothing   [c]Heb lacks O king

COMMENTARY

Unique in the book of Psalms and the entire OT, Psalm 45 is essentially a song of praise addressed to a human being: the king (see esp. vv. 1, 16-17). As the superscription suggests, it is a love song, or more specifically, a wedding song. Almost certainly this royal psalm was composed for use at the wedding of some Israelite or Judean king to a princess from another country. Scholars frequently suggest the wedding of Ahab to Jezebel, since v. 12 mentions the "Daughter of Tyre." But it is not clear that this title designates the new queen, nor is any certainty possible regarding the time and place of the origin of Psalm 45. All that can safely be said is that it originated during the existence of the monarchy and was probably used at several royal weddings.

A crucial question is, Why was this seemingly secular psalm included in the book of Psalms? After the disappearance of the monarchy, Psalm 45 came to be understood messianically by Jews as well as by Christians (see Heb 1:8-9, which quotes Ps 45:6-7), and this fact may account for its inclusion in the psalter. It is misleading, however, to view Psalm 45 simply as a secular psalm. The king was not just a secular ruler; rather, he represented God's own sovereignty, to the point that he was known as God's own son (see Commentary on Psalm 2). Verse 6 even seems to address the king with a term ordinarily reserved for divinity. Regardless of how v. 6 is interpreted, however, it is clear that God is intimately involved with the life and future of the king (see vv. 2, 7), and that the king is entrusted with the implementation of God's royal policy—that is, God's will (vv. 4, 6-7). An important event in the life of the king—such as a royal wedding—is thus an important event in the life of God's kingdom. Thus, even apart from a messianic interpretation, Psalm 45 would with reason have been preserved as part of the book of Psalms. And apart from a messianic interpretation, it still has an important message for contemporary readers (see Reflections below).

45:1. Unlike any other psalm, this one begins with the author's description of his or her task. The phrase "goodly theme" is more literally "good word." It is possible, as some have suggested, that the author was a cultic prophet; however, the matter is unclear. The psalmist may have been a court poet or "scribe" (see Ezra 7:6), although the latter is used in a simile and does not necessarily designate the author's position. As suggested above, the addressing of praise to a human being is also unique.

45:2-5. The judgment of v. 2a may be understood as part of the ancient Near Eastern ideology of kingship (see 1 Sam 16:12, where the narrator cannot help noting that David is handsome, even

though God has already announced through Samuel in 1 Sam 16:7 that outward appearance is unimportant; see also 1 Sam 9:2). While v. 2b is primarily intended to describe the king's speaking ability, it may be significant that "grace" (חן ḥēn) is an element of God's character and something God bestows (see Exod 34:6; Pss 4:1; 6:2). Thus v. 2b may anticipate v. 2c, where it is explicitly stated that "God has blessed you forever" (see 2 Sam 7:29; Pss 21:3, 6; 72:15). In other words, the king enjoys a special relationship with God that is elaborated on in the following verses.

The prerogatives of this relationship include military strength (v. 3a) and, more generally, the splendor of the royal office (v. 3b; the word the NIV translates "splendor" [הוד hôd] is also associated with the earthly king in Ps 21:6 and 1 Chr 29:25 and with God's kingship in Pss 96:6; 145:5; for the word the NIV and the NRSV translate "majesty" [הדר hādār] see Pss 21:6; 96:6; 145:5). But this power and majesty (vv. 3-4) are not intended for the king's personal benefit. Rather, they are to be directed toward the enactment of God's royal policy, beginning with "faithfulness." That is, as the sovereign God demonstrates faithfulness to God's people (see Exod 34:6; Pss 25:10; 54:5; 57:3; 71:22), so also should the king, the earthly agent of God's reign. As a comparison of the NIV with the NRSV indicates, the next phrase in v. 4 may be understood differently. It seems to mean, literally, "the oppression of righteousness." The word "righteousness" elsewhere appears in association with God's reign to designate God's will for the world (see Pss 9:8; 96:13; 97:2; 98:9). The phrase in question may indicate the suppression of God's policy, which the king is to address with the power and majesty that God has bestowed upon him (see "righteousness" also in v. 7 and Ps 72:1, 7; see the similar notion in Ps 101:1). The word "oppression" in this form, however, is unusual. The root of the word is the same as the word that occurs frequently in Psalms to designate persons whom God especially responds to—the afflicted/humble/poor/oppressed (see Pss 9:12; 10:2, 9; 14:6). As the NIV suggests, the phrase may suggest more specifically that the king is to join God as an advocate of the oppressed. The "awesome deeds" that the king is to learn are elsewhere what God performs (see Exod 34:10; Ps 66:3, 5), again suggesting that the king's power is to be directed to the fulfillment of God's will. The king's enemies in v. 5 are enemies of God as well (see Pss 2:1-3; 21:8-12; 72:8-11).

45:6-7. These verses reinforce the direction of vv. 4-5. The king, the one whom God has "anointed" (v. 7b; see also Ps 2:2), embodies God's values. The word "righteousness" recurs in v. 7 (see v. 4), and the contrast of "righteousness" and "wickedness" recalls Psalm 1. In contrast to the wicked, who pursue their own ends, the king pursues God's purposes. The king's "scepter," symbolic of his power and authority (see Ps 2:9), promotes equity, another of God's values, often parallel to righteousness (see Pss 9:8; 67:4; 96:10; 98:9; 99:4). In fact, the poet so identifies the king with God's purposes that the psalmist even addresses the king in v. 6a as "elohim" (אלהים ʾĕlōhîm). This name is most frequently used for God, as the NIV and the NRSV suggest; however, it occasionally designates human beings who exercise God-given authority over others (see Exod 4:16, where Moses is "God" for Aaron, and Exod 7:1, where Moses is "God" to Pharaoh; the same kind of usage may be intended in Exod 21:6; 22:8-9, as the NIV and NRSV notes suggest; see also Zech 12:8). This seems to be the case here. While other ancient Near Eastern cultures viewed the king as divine, and while Israel certainly accorded the king special relatedness to God (see Ps 2:7), it is not likely that Israelite or Judean kings were viewed as divine (see Isa 9:6, where the similar term "el" [אל ʾēl] is used at the birth of a royal child, but this term, too, can occasionally designate powerful human beings as well as

gods and God). Verse 7b clearly traces the king's authority to God.

45:8-9. These verses more clearly suggest the setting of a royal wedding. The king's garments exude sensuality. The setting is elegant (see "ivory" in Amos 3:15); the music contributes to the joyous mood; the prestigious attendants are in place and so is the queen (see Neh 2:6; the wedding setting prompts the NIV's "royal bride") in elegant attire (see 1 Chr 29:4; Job 28:16; Isa 13:12). The mention of the queen in v. 9 prepares for the next section of the poem.

45:10-17. Verses 10-15 focus on the queen, who is addressed in vv. 11-12 and described in vv. 13-15, especially as regards her participation in the wedding ceremony. The queen is encouraged to embrace the new relationship (v. 10), which will involve submission to the king (v. 11), but which will also bring recognition and honor to her (v. 12). Verses 16-17 seem to be addressed again to the king (see the NRSV note), anticipating the continuation of the dynasty (see 2 Sam 7:12-17, 29). The "I" in v. 17 may be the poet, whose poem will "perpetuate the king's memory." Or the "I" may be God, whose promise of sons will perpetuate the king's memory (see 2 Sam 18:18). The latter understanding would provide a more logical progression between vv. 16 and 17. The words "therefore" and "forever" in v. 17b recall the beginning of the poem (v. 2). God's blessing of the king will be matched by human recognition. Ordinarily, praise is reserved for God, but, as suggested above, to recognize the king's sovereignty is also to recognize the sovereignty of God.

REFLECTIONS

1. It would be possible to dismiss Psalm 45 as a relic of the ancient Near Eastern ideology of kingship or as a piece of Israelite or Judean political propaganda. Indeed, if its portrayal of women is taken as a criterion, Psalm 45 should be dismissed (see vv. 10-15). But it seems that the psalm was preserved as Scripture, because it has the potential to facilitate theological reflection about the nature of legitimate political authority. Such reflection is crucial, especially in the light of the apostle Paul's assertion that "those authorities that exist have been instituted by God" (Rom 13:1 NRSV), as well as in the light of the persistent human tendency to be fascinated with powerful people, be they royalty or politicians or even self-appointed dictators.

In fact, Psalm 45 may serve as testimony to the seemingly inevitable human tendency to glorify political leaders. Perhaps there is even a certain necessity in this tendency, for it helps to maintain the structure and stability of a society. However, Psalm 45 also warns us about this tendency. While the king could be lavishly honored and addressed, and while the events of his life could be opulently celebrated, it is clear that his power is finally derivative. Thus, while the poet praises the king and contributes material for the celebration, he or she also reminds the king of his responsibility to embody not his own will but the will of God—faithfulness, righteousness, equity (vv. 4-7). By implication, at least, the failure to enact God's will removes one's God-given authority, as indeed the prophets frequently reminded the kings.

2. As for the contemporary scene, perhaps Psalm 45 suggests that we can allow a degree of pageantry and splendor in our state houses and governors' mansions; however, it also reminds us that among the criteria for discerning which authorities are indeed "instituted by God" must be the question of whether our leaders get around to acting "in behalf of truth, humility and righteousness" (v. 4). If they do not, our fascination with them and loyalty to them are misdirected.

As suggested in the commentary, Psalm 45 came to be read messianically within Judaism; that is, given the failure of the monarchy, people longed for the arrival of one who would indeed rule as God intended. The early church identified this one—this Son of God (see Ps 2:7)—as Jesus of Nazareth, "the reflection of God's glory and the exact imprint of God's very being" (Heb 1:3 NRSV; see Heb 1:8-9). In short, as a king was supposed to do, Jesus embodied God's faithfulness, ministered to the humbled and afflicted, and enacted God's will for rightly ordering the world. In view of Jesus' person and work, as Mays points out, "Christians have traditionally understood the psalm as a song of the love between Christ and his church." This kind of allegorical interpretation is legitimate, at least insofar as it serves as "a safeguard against attributing the divine right of rule to any other save Christ, in whose hands it is utterly safe."[196] In short, Psalm 45 reminds us of what Jesus also proclaimed: that our ultimate political loyalty is to God's reign.

196. Ibid., 182.

PSALM 46:1-11, OUR REFUGE AND STRENGTH

NIV	NRSV
Psalm 46	Psalm 46
For the director of music. Of the Sons of Korah. According to *alamoth.*[a] A song.	To the leader. Of the Korahites. According to Alamoth. A Song.
¹God is our refuge and strength, an ever-present help in trouble. ²Therefore we will not fear, though the earth give way and the mountains fall into the heart of the sea, ³though its waters roar and foam and the mountains quake with their surging. *Selah* ⁴There is a river whose streams make glad the city of God,	¹ God is our refuge and strength, a very present[a] help in trouble. ² Therefore we will not fear, though the earth should change, though the mountains shake in the heart of the sea; ³ though its waters roar and foam, though the mountains tremble with its tumult. *Selah* ⁴ There is a river whose streams make glad the city of God,
a Title: Probably a musical term	*a* Or *well proved*

NIV

the holy place where the Most High dwells.
⁵God is within her, she will not fall;
    God will help her at break of day.
⁶Nations are in uproar, kingdoms fall;
    he lifts his voice, the earth melts.

⁷The LORD Almighty is with us;
    the God of Jacob is our fortress.   *Selah*

⁸Come and see the works of the LORD,
    the desolations he has brought on the earth.
⁹He makes wars cease to the ends of the earth;
    he breaks the bow and shatters the spear,
    he burns the shields*ᵃ* with fire.
¹⁰"Be still, and know that I am God;
    I will be exalted among the nations,
    I will be exalted in the earth."

¹¹The LORD Almighty is with us;
    the God of Jacob is our fortress.   *Selah*

ᵃ9 Or chariots

NRSV

the holy habitation of the Most High.
⁵ God is in the midst of the city;*ᵃ* it shall not
        be moved;
    God will help it when the morning
        dawns.
⁶ The nations are in an uproar, the kingdoms
        totter;
    he utters his voice, the earth melts.
⁷ The LORD of hosts is with us;
    the God of Jacob is our refuge.*ᵇ*   *Selah*

⁸ Come, behold the works of the LORD;
    see what desolations he has brought on
        the earth.
⁹ He makes wars cease to the end of the earth;
    he breaks the bow, and shatters the spear;
    he burns the shields with fire.
¹⁰ "Be still, and know that I am God!
    I am exalted among the nations,
    I am exalted in the earth."
¹¹ The LORD of hosts is with us;
    the God of Jacob is our refuge.*ᵇ*   *Selah*

ᵃ Heb of it   *ᵇ Or fortress*

COMMENTARY

"God is our refuge and strength." Whether in this traditional translation or in Martin Luther's paraphrase, "A mighty fortress is our God," the opening line of Psalm 46 is one of the most memorable and powerful in all the book of Psalms. After the opening affirmation of faith (vv. 1-3), vv. 4-6 shift the focus to the city of God and to God's activity on behalf of it. Following the first occurrence of the refrain (v. 7), the final section begins with an invitation to consider God's "works" (v. 8*a*), which are then described in vv. 8*b*-9. Another invitation is issued in v. 10, but this time it is in the divine first person. It effectively summarizes the message of the entire psalm in preparation for the final refrain (v. 11). Because of the focus on the city of God in vv. 4-6, Psalm 46 is usually classified as a song of Zion (see Psalms 48; 76; 84; 87; 122; Introduction); however, its significance is much broader than the focus on Zion. It is fundamentally an affirmation of faith—not in Zion, but in God. Thus it is often classified as a song of confidence or trust.

46:1. The psalm begins with a threefold description of God: "refuge," "strength," and "help." The word "refuge" (מחסה *maḥseh*) is one of the most important in the book of Psalms, especially in Books I–II (Psalms 1–72). It occurs for the first time in Psalm 2, which, along with Psalm 1, serves as an introduction to the book of Psalms: "Happy are all who take refuge in" God (2:12 NRSV). This beatitude sets the tone for what follows, and in Books I–II the word "refuge" becomes a sort of one-word refrain, occurring twenty-three more times (see Pss 5:11; 7:1; 11:1; 14:6; 16:1; 57:1; 61:3; 62:7-8; 71:7; Introduction). To "take refuge in" God means to trust God, and not surprisingly, trust is also a key theme in the psalms, especially in Books I–II (see Pss 4:5; 9:10; 22:4-5; 25:2; 26:1; 31:6, 14; 55:23; 56:3-4, 11; 62:8; Introduction). Thus Psalm 46 begins with the affirmation that God is a reliable refuge; God is worthy of trust.

Underlying this affirmation is the conviction that God rules the world; God's strength or power lies behind the origin and continuing life of the universe. In short, God is in control—*not* the wicked or the enemies or the nations that regularly threaten the life of the psalmist or the existence of God's people (see Pss 2:1-3, 11; 7:1; 11:1-2; 25:19-20; 31:19-20). The word "strength" (עז *'ōz*) points to this conviction of God's sovereignty. It occurs frequently in the psalms that explicitly announce God's reign (see 29:1; 93:1; 96:7; 99:4). God can be trusted, because God rules the world. Perhaps not coincidentally, the very next psalm explicitly refers to God as "a great king over all the earth" (47:2 NRSV).

Psalm 46 affirms that the strength behind the universe is not simply a neutral power. Rather, it is "for us" (v. 1*a* in Hebrew reads literally, "God is *for us* a refuge and strength"). Or, as v. 1*b* suggests, this power is inclined toward our "help" (see God as "help" or "helper" in Pss 10:14; 22:19; 28:7; 30:10; 33:20; 37:40; 40:17).

46:2-3. To illustrate how powerful a help God can be in trouble, these verses present the ultimate worst-case scenario. The "change" in the earth described in vv. 2-3 seems like a simultaneous 10.0 earthquake and class-five hurricane, but actually it is even worse! According to the ancient Near Eastern view of the universe, the mountains were both the foundations that anchored the dry land in the midst of a watery chaos and the pillars that held up the sky. Thus the worst thing that could happen would be for the mountains to shake (v. 2) or tremble (v. 3), for the earth would be threatened from below by water and from above by the sky's falling. Verses 2-3, then, may be thought of as an ancient version of the contemporary doomsday scenarios that are more familiar to us—nuclear winter or the depletion of the ozone layer and the rapid rise of the earth's temperature. To use the words of Luther's hymn, vv. 2-3 depict circumstances that "threaten to undo us." Even in this degree of trouble—when the very structures of the universe as we know it cannot be depended upon, when our world is falling apart—God is still a reliable refuge. God can be trusted. Therefore, the astounding affirmation in the face of the ultimate worst-case scenario is simply, "We will not fear" (v. 2; see Ps 23:4).

46:4-7, 11. The trouble, which is portrayed in cosmic terms in vv. 2-3, is described in human terms in vv. 4-6. The "nations are in an uproar" (v. 6; "uproar" translates the same Hebrew word as "roar" [המה *hāmâ*] in v. 3). The "kingdoms totter" (v. 6; "totter" translates the same Hebrew word as "shake" [מוט *môt*] in v. 2). As in vv. 2-3, and even using the same vocabulary, v. 6 suggests that everything is in motion. In the midst of the mayhem, there is one point of stability: "the city of God" (v. 4), in whose midst is God (v. 5), and "it shall not be moved" (v. 5). The verb translated "moved" is the same one translated "shake" in v. 2 and "totter" in v. 6 (the NIV translates the verb "fall" in each case). The pattern of repetition emphasizes the assurance; God's presence can be solidly depended upon.

The "city of God" is Jerusalem, in which is located the Temple, "the holy habitation of the Most High" (v. 4). Without intending to confine God to Zion or the Temple, the prevailing theology did view Zion as God's special place. In this and other Zion songs, "the city of God" is thus symbolic of God's presence. The refrain (vv. 7, 11) summarizes the assurance: God is "with us," "our refuge." The Hebrew word translated "refuge" in vv. 7, 11 differs from the one used in v. 1, but it is virtually synonymous (see the NRSV's "stronghold" in Pss 9:9; 18:2; 94:22; 144:2; "sure defense" in 48:3; and "fortress" in 59:9, 16-17; 62:2, 6). In the midst of international, and even cosmic, chaos, God can be trusted.

The title "LORD of hosts" is particularly appropriate following vv. 4-6. Verse 4 has referred to God's "habitation," and the title "LORD of hosts" is elsewhere associated with the ark, God's symbolic throne (see 1 Sam 4:3-4). The title also seems to have a military background, since "hosts" (צבאות *ṣĕbā'ôt*) can mean "armies" (see 1 Sam 17:45; see also Commentary on Psalm 24). The uproar in v. 6 apparently is meant to suggest an attack on Jerusalem. In this confrontation, the Lord of the armies is on Jerusalem's side—"with us." The word "refuge" also functions elsewhere as a military term (in addition to the occurrences and translations cited above, see Isa 25:12 where it is part of the phrase that the NRSV translates as "high fortifications"). Thus the vocabulary of the refrain anticipates vv. 8-10, where God is a warrior, but is one who wages peace.

The significance of the "river" in v. 4 is metaphorical rather than geographical. The threatening, chaotic waters of vv. 2-3 have become a life-giving stream. That there is actually no river flowing through Jerusalem is no problem. This river is symbolic, like the river in Ezek 47:1-12, which flows from the Temple, and like the river in Rev 22:1-12, which flows from the throne of God, which has replaced the Temple in the New Jerusalem. Both of these rivers yield sustenance for life (Ezek 47:9-12; Rev 22:2). In other words, the river in Ps 46:4 is another way of symbolizing the assurance of God's power and provision, even amid the worst imaginable trouble (v. 2). As v. 5 suggests, repeating a key word from v. 1, the presence of God means help when the world should threaten to undo us.

Verse 6b is another indication of God's sovereignty. God's voice is powerful. When the psalmist says, "the earth melts," it sounds as if God has taken over the role of destroyer; however, the word "melts" serves elsewhere to describe poetically the effects of God's appearing (see Amos 9:5; Nah 1:5), including God's melting human opposition in order to enact the divine will (see Exod 15:15; Josh 2:9, 24; Jer 49:23). This seems to be the meaning here, as the refrain suggests; God's presence ("with us") means protection for God's people.

46:8-10. Verses 8 and 10 begin with imperatives, between which lies a description of God's "works" (vv. 8b-9). The invitation to "Come and see" (v. 8) calls to mind Philip's similar invitation to Nathanael in John 1:46. When Nathanael saw Jesus' works, he hailed him as "the king of Israel"

(John 1:49). The same movement is intended in Psalm 46, which moves toward the explicit acknowledgment of God's sovereignty in v. 10b. The verb translated "exalted" (רום *rûm*) in v. 10b is used elsewhere in the context of kingship, both of earthly kings (Num 24:7; Ps 89:19) and of God as king (see Pss 99:5, 9; 145:1). Thus, in the climactic divine speech in v. 10, God proclaims sovereignty over the nations (see v. 6) and the earth (see vv. 2, 6). God rules the world!

In the ancient Near East, it was the particular responsibility of rulers to establish peace for their people. This is precisely what God's works involve, according to v. 9 (see Isa 2:4; Mic 4:3-4); v. 10a should be understood in close relationship to v. 9. The imperatives in v. 10a are explicitly instructional (see "know" in Ps 100:3). Although the NIV and the NRSV retain it because of its familiarity, "Be still" (רפה *rāpâ*) is not a good translation. Contemporary readers almost inevitably hear it as a call to meditation or relaxation, when it should be heard in the light of v. 9 as something like "Stop!" or "Throw down your weapons!" In other words, "Depend on God instead of yourselves."

In the light of the description of God's activity in v. 9, it seems that v. 8b may be sarcastic. The "desolations" that God brings, in contrast to human efforts, involve the cessation of war and the destruction of all human implements of destruction. In the light of v. 9, the military imagery of the refrain is given a new orientation. Whereas Israel often sought security in military might, v. 9 affirms that God the warrior fights for peace. The final occurrence of the refrain thus reinforces what v. 9 and the whole psalm have affirmed: Ultimate security derives from God alone.

REFLECTIONS

Although Christians do not view Jerusalem as the symbolic locus of God's presence and power as Psalm 46 does, that concrete and particularistic way of thinking is not entirely foreign to Christianity. For the early Christians, Jesus Christ became what the Temple had once represented. Indeed, Jesus became the new locus of God's presence and power to such a degree that the Gospel of John can say that "the Word became flesh" (1:14 NIV, NRSV). Jesus was God incarnate; Jesus was also known as Emmanuel, "God is with us" (Matt 1:23 NRSV; see "with us" in Ps 46:7, 11).

It should not be surprising, then, that the fundamental message Jesus proclaimed and embodied is essentially the same as that of Psalm 46: God rules the world (see Mark 1:14-15).

Like Jesus, too, Psalm 46 calls people to decision (vv. 8, 10); that is, it invites its hearers to enter the reign of God, to live in dependence upon God, to find ultimate security in God rather than in self or in any human systems or possessions. Because it eloquently affirms that the ruling power in the universe is for us (v. 1) and inclines toward our help (vv. 1, 5), Psalm 46 has been a source of strength, consolation, and hope to believers throughout the centuries in a variety of situations—in ancient Judah, in the Protestant Reformation, in the lives of countless Jews and Christians who humbly look to God for help in trouble (v. 1). Indeed, Psalm 46 suggests a spiritual exercise that might be thought of as the opposite of positive thinking. Perhaps we should regularly imagine, as the psalmist did (vv. 2-3, 6), the *worst* possible thing that could happen to us, as a way of preparing ourselves to say in the midst of the crises that will inevitably come, "We will not fear" (v. 2).

The affirmation in Psalm 46 of God's sovereignty and God's will for peace among nations and in the cosmos is eschatological, as was Jesus' proclamation of the reign of God, for it does not appear that God reigns or that peace prevails. But it is precisely this eschatological orientation that calls us to decision: Shall we see the world as the sphere of God's rule? In our day, as much as in the days of the psalmist and Jesus, the decision to recognize God's sovereignty is crucial. We are tempted more than ever to conclude that our security finally depends on ourselves or our possessions or our technology or our weapons. The governments of the world attempt to justify terribly repressive and destructive activities in the name of national security. And, of course, our implements of destruction are no longer just arrows and spears and shields. We have tanks and submarines and nuclear missiles, and more readily than any generation in history, we are able to picture a "worst-case scenario" resulting from our own actions. Faced with the temptation to self-assertion, yet aware of its frightening results, we hear in Psalm 46 the good news that our ultimate security lies not in our own strength or our own efforts or our own implements, but in the presence and power of God.[197]

197. Portions of the above treatment of Psalm 46 appear in substantially the same form in J. Clinton McCann, "Psalm 46: Psalm for the Third Sunday After Pentecost," *No Other Foundation* 14/2 (Winter 1993–94) 32-36.

PSALM 47:1-9, KING OF ALL THE EARTH

NIV

Psalm 47

For the director of music. Of the Sons of Korah. A psalm.

¹Clap your hands, all you nations;
  shout to God with cries of joy.
²How awesome is the Lord Most High,
  the great King over all the earth!
³He subdued nations under us,
  peoples under our feet.
⁴He chose our inheritance for us,
  the pride of Jacob, whom he loved.   *Selah*

⁵God has ascended amid shouts of joy,
  the Lord amid the sounding of trumpets.

NRSV

Psalm 47

To the leader. Of the Korahites. A Psalm.

¹ Clap your hands, all you peoples;
  shout to God with loud songs of joy.
² For the Lord, the Most High, is awesome,
  a great king over all the earth.
³ He subdued peoples under us,
  and nations under our feet.
⁴ He chose our heritage for us,
  the pride of Jacob whom he loves.   *Selah*

⁵ God has gone up with a shout,
  the Lord with the sound of a trumpet.
⁶ Sing praises to God, sing praises;

NIV

⁶Sing praises to God, sing praises;
   sing praises to our King, sing praises.

⁷For God is the King of all the earth;
   sing to him a psalm*ᵃ* of praise.

⁸God reigns over the nations;
   God is seated on his holy throne.

⁹The nobles of the nations assemble
   as the people of the God of Abraham,
for the kings*ᵇ* of the earth belong to God;
   he is greatly exalted.

ᵃ7 Or a maskil (probably a literary or musical term)   *ᵇ9 Or shields*

NRSV

   sing praises to our King, sing praises.

⁷ For God is the king of all the earth;
   sing praises with a psalm.*ᵃ*

⁸ God is king over the nations;
   God sits on his holy throne.

⁹ The princes of the peoples gather
   as the people of the God of Abraham.
For the shields of the earth belong to God;
   he is highly exalted.

ᵃ Heb Maskil

COMMENTARY

Along with Psalm 24, Psalm 47 offers perhaps the clearest view of a liturgical procession to celebrate the kingship of God. As if in response to the concluding imperatives of Psalm 46 (see vv. 8, 10), Psalm 47 begins by inviting everyone to acknowledge God's sovereignty (v. 1). The invitation to praise is renewed in v. 6. The fundamental reason for praise in each case is God's kingship over "all the earth" (vv. 2, 7). Evidence for and results of God's kingship are given in vv. 3-4 and vv. 8-9. In between these two hymnic forms stands v. 5, and this central verse seems to depict the liturgical enthronement of God. As Mowinckel suggested, v. 5 describes the "royal entry of Yahweh, at which he himself is present, symbolized by his holy 'ark.'" For Mowinckel, v. 5 portrayed "the preeminent visible center of the experiences connected with the enthronement festival."[198]

Mowinckel's theory of an annual celebration of God's enthronement at the New Year festival (as part of the Feast of Booths) is questionable; however, it cannot be doubted that the theological heart of the psalter—God reigns! (see Psalms 29; 93; 95–99; Introduction)—was celebrated liturgically upon some occasion, perhaps in a procession involving the ark (see 2 Samuel 6; Pss 24:7-10; 132:8). It is simply impossible to know whether such a liturgical enactment took place as part of a New Year festival, as part of one of the three pilgrimage feasts, or as Gerstenberger has

suggested, as a regular part "of early Jewish worship liturgy that jubilantly recalls the history of Israel's election by Yahweh (vv. 4-5) and glorifies his supreme, as yet unrealized, power over all the earth (vv. 3, 8, etc.)."[199] Given this uncertainty, one must conclude that more important than the original setting of Psalm 47 is the actual content of the psalm: God rules the earth!

47:1-2. Because God rules over all the earth, "all you peoples" are included in the invitation in v. 1. Hand clapping was apparently a gesture of celebration or triumph, as it still can be today (see Nah 3:19). Shouting sometimes served as a battle cry, but here it bespeaks joyful praise. The verb for "shout" (רוע *rûaʿ*) occurs in several other songs of praise as well, often in the context of the proclamation of God's reign (see Pss 66:1; 81:2; 95:1-2; 98:4, 6; 100:1; see also 1 Sam 10:24; Zech 9:9, where earthly kings are also greeted with a shout). The characterization of God as "awesome" in v. 2a recalls historic manifestations of the sovereignty that is explicitly affirmed in v. 2b (see "awesome" in Exod 15:11, the Song of the Sea, which culminates in Exod 15:18 with the proclamation of God's reign; cf. Ps 68:35 with 68:24, and 145:6 with 145:1). In addition to the enthronement psalms that explicitly affirm God's reign, several psalms scattered throughout the psalter describe or address God as "king" (see 5:2;

198. Sigmund Mowinckel, *The Psalms in Israel's Worship*, 2 vols., trans. D. R. Ap-Thomas (Nashville: Abingdon, 1962) 1:171.

199. Erhard S. Gerstenberger, *Psalms, Part 1, with an Introduction to Cultic Poetry,* Forms of the OT Literature 14 (Grand Rapids: Eerdmans, 1988) 198.

10:16; 44:4; 48:2; 68:24; 74:12; 84:3; 145:1; 149:2), and the adjective "great" is frequently associated with God's rule (see 95:3; 96:4; 99:2).

47:3-4. These verses offer a specific illustration of God's rule: the conquest and possession of the land. It is all God's doing. What preceding psalms have said that God did for the king, vv. 3-4 affirm that God the King has done for the whole people: God "subdued peoples" (see Ps 18:47) and provided a "heritage" (see Ps 2:8; see also Josh 11:23). The "pride of Jacob" seems to mean the land and its wealth and defenses (see Amos 6:8; 8:7). All of this God provided out of love (see Deut 7:8; Ps 78:68; Isa 43:4; Hos 11:1).

47:5. The *Selah* after v. 4 serves to set vv. 1-4 apart from v. 5. It is possible to construe v. 5 as the beginning of a new section that extends through v. 6 (NIV) or v. 7 (NRSV) or perhaps to the end of the psalm; however, since v. 6, like v. 1, is an invitation to praise, it is also possible to construe v. 5 as a central panel surrounded by two hymnic sections (vv. 1-4, 6-9). The vocabulary of v. 5 reinforces this conclusion. On the one hand, v. 5 recalls v. 1, repeating "shout" and the Hebrew word the NIV translates as "cries" in v. 1 and "sounding" in v. 5 (קול *qôl*). On the other hand, v. 5 anticipates v. 9 by way of repetition of the key root "gone up"/"ascended" (עלה *'ālâ*), which appears in v. 9 as "exalted." Thus both the pattern of repetition and the structure of the psalm serve to highlight the liturgical enactment of God's enthronement. To borrow Mowinckel's words, v. 5 itself is a "preeminent visible center." In contrast to Mowinckel, however, we may conclude that what is celebrated—God's reign—lay at the heart of *all* Israelite worship, just as the proclamation of God's reign lies at the theological heart of the psalter (see Introduction). Just as a trumpet blast accompanied the coronation of earthly kings (see 1 Kgs 1:34; 39), so also here

it accompanies the celebration of God's enthronement (see Ps 98:6).

47:6-9. In v. 6, four of the six Hebrew words are the verb "sing praises" (זמר *zimmēr*; cf. Pss 9:11; 68:32). Thus each half of the verse literally surrounds either God or "our King" with praise. The effect is appropriate, for "the king of all the earth" (v. 7; cf. v. 2) deserves no less. The word "king" occurs again in v. 8 (although in a verbal form in Hebrew), thus emphasizing God's sovereignty. References elsewhere to God's "throne" occur in the context of God's cosmic rule (see Pss 89:15; 93:2; 97:2; 113:19). Thus v. 8*a* proclaims God's rule over all persons, and v. 8*b* proclaims God's rule over all things. What was celebrated liturgically (v. 5) both derives from and shapes the Israelite view of the world; it and all of its people are subject to God (v. 8; cf. Ps 24:1-2, 7-10). Thus the congregation of God's people— "the people of the God of Abraham" (v. 9)—can include nothing less than the gathering of all the peoples (see v. 1) and their leaders. The word "shields" (מגן *māgēn*) probably is figurative for leaders (see the NIV; cf. Ps 89:18); they and their people belong to God. Verse 9 recalls Gen 12:1-3, where the promise of blessing to Abraham and his descendants is somehow to involve "all peoples on earth" (Gen 12:3 NIV; see also Isa 19:23-25).

By the end of Psalm 47, the word "earth" (ארץ *'ereṣ*) has occurred three times (vv. 2, 7, 9), recalling Psalm 46, where it occurred five times (vv. 2, 6, 8, 9, 10). Both psalms proclaim God's sovereignty over all the earth, concluding in each case with a proclamation that God is exalted (46:10; 47:9; the Hebrew words differ, however). When read together, they also offer a compelling rationale for God's opposition to all warfare (46:9)—namely, in any war, God is always the loser, because it is always God's people who are killed.

REFLECTIONS

It was a persistent temptation for the people of Israel, and it has been and is a persistent temptation for the church to make our God too small. We are quick to recall that God "chose our heritage for us" and loves us (v. 4), but we are quick to forget that God loves the world and that all the world's rulers and people "belong to God" (v. 9). The Christian practice of speaking about Jesus as a personal Savior may be symptomatic of our forgetfulness, for often we seem to mean that we own God rather than that God owns us. To worship the God of Abraham and the God revealed in Jesus Christ is to worship a universal sovereign, and it means claiming every other person in the world as a sister or brother. To acknowledge God's universal sovereignty might even mean that we give our assent and support to the simple proposal that we Christians take a first step toward world peace by refusing to kill each other!

By virtue of its structure as well as its content, Psalm 47 highlights the nature and importance of liturgy. In worship, we say and act out our conviction of who God is and of what the world is really like. In accordance with Psalm 47 and in accordance with the proclamation of Jesus (see Mark 1:14-15), we say that God rules over all and thus that the world is the sphere of God's sovereignty. Our profession is eschatological, because it does not appear that God rules, and the world is full of opposition to God's sovereignty (see Commentary on Psalm 2; Introduction). But our profession is thereby no less real. In liturgy, we say and act out the reality that our lives and our world have been shaped by God's loving rule. At the same time, our speaking and acting contribute to the further shaping of ourselves and of our world in conformity to God's claim. For us, the "real world" exists insofar as God's sovereignty is acknowledged in word and in deed. In short, liturgy is indispensable for both experiencing God's rule and expressing the reality of that experience.

Psalm 47 is traditionally used by the church on Ascension Day. The church thereby claims that the life, death, and resurrection of Jesus represent the essential claim of Psalm 47: that God rules the world and lovingly claims all the world's peoples.

PSALM 48:1-14, GREAT IS THE LORD

NIV

Psalm 48

A song. A psalm of the Sons of Korah.

[1]Great is the LORD, and most worthy of praise,
in the city of our God, his holy mountain.
[2]It is beautiful in its loftiness,
the joy of the whole earth.
Like the utmost heights of Zaphon[a] is Mount Zion,
the[b] city of the Great King.
[3]God is in her citadels;
he has shown himself to be her fortress.

[4]When the kings joined forces,
when they advanced together,
[5]they saw ⌐her⌐ and were astounded;
they fled in terror.
[6]Trembling seized them there,
pain like that of a woman in labor.
[7]You destroyed them like ships of Tarshish
shattered by an east wind.

[8]As we have heard,

a2 Zaphon can refer to a sacred mountain or the direction north.
b2 Or earth, / Mount Zion, on the northern side / of the

NRSV

Psalm 48

A Song. A Psalm of the Korahites.

[1] Great is the LORD and greatly to be praised
in the city of our God.
His holy mountain, [2]beautiful in elevation,
is the joy of all the earth,
Mount Zion, in the far north,
the city of the great King.
[3] Within its citadels God
has shown himself a sure defense.

[4] Then the kings assembled,
they came on together.
[5] As soon as they saw it, they were
astounded;
they were in panic, they took to flight;
[6] trembling took hold of them there,
pains as of a woman in labor,
[7] as when an east wind shatters
the ships of Tarshish.
[8] As we have heard, so have we seen

NIV

so have we seen
in the city of the LORD Almighty,
in the city of our God:
God makes her secure forever.   *Selah*

⁹Within your temple, O God,
we meditate on your unfailing love.
¹⁰Like your name, O God,
your praise reaches to the ends of the earth;
your right hand is filled with righteousness.
¹¹Mount Zion rejoices,
the villages of Judah are glad
because of your judgments.

¹²Walk about Zion, go around her,
count her towers,
¹³consider well her ramparts,
view her citadels,
that you may tell of them to the next
generation.
¹⁴For this God is our God for ever and ever;
he will be our guide even to the end.

NRSV

in the city of the LORD of hosts,
in the city of our God,
which God establishes forever.   *Selah*

⁹ We ponder your steadfast love, O God,
in the midst of your temple.
¹⁰ Your name, O God, like your praise,
reaches to the ends of the earth.
Your right hand is filled with victory.
¹¹   Let Mount Zion be glad,
let the towns[a] of Judah rejoice
because of your judgments.

¹² Walk about Zion, go all around it,
count its towers,
¹³ consider well its ramparts;
go through its citadels,
that you may tell the next generation
¹⁴   that this is God,
our God forever and ever.
He will be our guide forever.

[a] Heb *daughters*

COMMENTARY

The opening verse of Psalm 48 is a superbly appropriate response to Psalm 47, which has depicted God's enthronement (v. 5) and proclaimed God's universal sovereignty (vv. 2, 7-9). Without abandoning the universal perspective, Psalm 48 focuses on God's particular place, Mount Zion (v. 2). Like Psalm 46, this psalm is a song of Zion (see also Psalms 76; 84; 87; 122; Introduction). In fact, because of the similarities among Psalms 46; 47; and 48, these psalms can be viewed as a "trilogy . . . honoring Jerusalem."[200] More accurately, however, they could be called a trilogy *honoring God.* As Psalm 48 suggests, Jerusalem is important because it is God's place; thus it can serve as a witness to God's character. What Psalm 48 really celebrates is God's greatness (v. 1); God's protection (v. 3); God's steadfast love, righteousness, and justice (vv. 9-11); and God's enduring presence (vv. 13-14). Because the focus is

really more on God than on Zion, Psalm 48 has continued to be used throughout the centuries to express the faith of the people of God.

Psalm 48 may have served originally as a song to be used by pilgrims as they approached and entered Jerusalem. Verses 1-3 give the impression of viewing Zion from afar, a position that allows the visitor to imagine how Jerusalem may have appeared to invading kings (vv. 4-7). Verses 8-11 locate the pilgrim in the city, including the Temple (v. 9), which serves as testimony to God's character and activity throughout the world (vv. 10-11). Verses 12-14 suggest that every architectural feature of the city can serve a similar purpose. The city itself proclaims God's greatness.

48:1-3. The psalm begins with an affirmation of God's greatness, an attribute that is explicitly associated elsewhere with God's sovereignty (cf. Pss 95:3; 96:4; 99:2). The praise due the sovereign God is to take place "in the city of our God"; however, what follows in v. 2 appears to be not praise of God but praise of the city itself. The seven designations for Jerusalem in vv. 1*b*-2

200. Carroll Stuhlmueller, "Psalm 46 and the Prophecy of Isaiah Evolving into a Prophetic, Messianic Role," in *The Psalms and Other Studies on the Old Testament,* ed. J. C. Knight and L. A. Sinclair (Nashotah, Wis.: Nashotah House Seminary, 1990) 21.

clearly emphasize the importance of the city; however, even these designations suggest that the city derives its importance from God, and the dramatic element of the series even makes God's sovereignty explicit with the title "great King" (the Hebrew word translated "great" [רב *rab*] here differs from the one used in v. 1; in fact, the phrase occurs only here in the OT, although an analogous phrase occurs in other ancient Near Eastern literature to designate human or divine monarchs).

Several of the designations for Jerusalem occur elsewhere—for instance, "city of our God" (see Ps 46:4), "holy mountain" (see Pss 2:6; 3:4; 15:1), Mount Zion. Other terms are more distinctive. The phrase "in the far north" is puzzling. As the NIV suggests, the word translated "north" (צפון *ṣāpôn*) should probably be understood as "Zaphon," the name of the mountain that the Canaanites believed was the residence of the gods. Thus this designation seems to be a way of affirming that Yahweh has displaced the Canaanite deities; Yahweh is the true sovereign of the universe, the genuine "great King" (see Ps 82:1). In short, the designations in v. 2 are more symbolic than geopolitical. Jerusalem does occupy a mountain, but to affirm that it is "beautiful in elevation" is to say more about its significance to the eye of faith than about its actual altitude. Similarly, to say that Jerusalem is the "joy of all the earth" (cf. Isa 60:15; 65:18; Lam 2:15) is to make the confessional claim that Jerusalem is the indisputable capital of the world! In other words, God reigns, and Jerusalem is God's city, within which God has proven to be "a sure defense" (v. 3; the Hebrew word is the same one translated "refuge" in Ps 46:7, 11 NRSV). Verse 3 is apparent testimony to the belief in Zion's indestructibility, a conviction upon which Isaiah's advice to King Ahaz seems to be based (see Isa 7:1-16) and that Jeremiah later opposes (see Jer 7:1-15).

48:4-7. Of course, the claim of Jerusalem's centrality was regularly disputed, as these verses make clear. That is to say, God's sovereignty was disputed. In opposition to "the great King," other "kings joined forces." The Hebrew for "joined forces" (נועדו *nôʿădû*) recalls the claim of v. 3*b*, which could literally be translated, "God has made Godself known [נודע *nôdaʿ*] as a fortress." The play on words emphasizes the contrast. The kings'

joining of forces will be futile in the face of God's *revelation*. Indeed, as soon as the kings *saw* Jerusalem, they were as good as defeated. The description of their reaction recalls Exodus 15, the Song of the Sea following the deliverance from the Egyptian king and his forces. In Psalm 48, the kings "were in panic" (v. 5; see "dismayed" in Exod 15:15 NRSV; Ps 2:5); "trembling took hold of them" (v. 6; see "trembling seized" in Exod 15:15 NRSV) as did "pains" (v. 6; see "pangs" in Exod 15:14 NRSV). Furthermore, the "east wind" in v. 7 recalls the "east wind" of Exod 14:21, which drove back the sea for the Israelites' passage. The song in Exod 15:1-18 concludes with a reference to "the mountain," which is God's "own possession" (15:17 NRSV). This place is the one God has established (15:17) and presumably the place from which God "will reign forever and ever" (15:18 NRSV). This is precisely what Psalm 48 is about—the "great King" (v. 2) ruling from the city that God "establishes forever" (v. 8). The numerous allusions in Psalm 48 to the Song of the Sea also explain perhaps the curious circumstance that Jerusalem is depicted as the site of a sea battle (v. 7). The battle is more metaphorical than geographical.

48:8-11. The very sight of Jerusalem is overwhelming, not only to the invading kings but also to approaching pilgrims. What they have seen (v. 8; see v. 5) in Jerusalem has a profound effect on their perception of space and time. The sight of Jerusalem connects their current experience with the past deliverance from Egypt and with God's universal dominion "to the ends of the earth" (v. 10; see v. 2)—the spatial extension of God's reign. The present sight of Jerusalem takes the worshiper back in time to the exodus and forward in time to "forever" (v. 8; see vv. 13-14)—the temporal extension of God's reign. Robert Alter aptly sums up the perspective of Psalm 48: "Thus, the towering ramparts of the fortress-city become a nexus for all imagined time and space."[201]

One further link between Psalm 48 and Exodus 15 is the occurrence of the word translated "steadfast love" (חסד *ḥesed*, v. 9; Exod 15:13). In Exodus 15, God's guidance in "steadfast love" brings people to God's place (see Ps 5:7); and in Psalm 48, it is precisely "steadfast love" that the

---

201. Robert Alter, *The Art of Biblical Poetry* (New York: Basic Books, 1985) 124; I am indebted to several of Alter's insights found on pp. 121-29.

people think about in the Temple. The word *ḥesed* describes God's fundamental character (see Exod 34:6-7; Pss 13:5; 17:7; Introduction). As the exodus revealed God's fundamental character, so the present experience in Jerusalem puts the pilgrim in touch with God's historical (past) and enduring (future) essence. Not surprisingly, v. 10 mentions God's "name," a word expressive of reputation or character, as well as God's "righteousness," a word expressive of God's character in action (see Pss 7:17; 9:8; 96:13; 97:6). As is often the case, God's righteousness is mentioned in conjunction with God's "judgments" (v. 11; see Pss 9:4; 97:2). That is to say, God's implementation of justice is in keeping with God's character.

48:12-14. Just as the city of Jerusalem proclaims God's greatness (vv. 1-3), so also it proclaims God's character (vv. 8-11). This is the rationale for the invitation in vv. 12-14 to consider Jerusalem in all its concrete detail—towers, ramparts, citadels (see v. 4). The five imperatives in vv. 12-13 are thus not simply an invitation to take an architectural tour of the city. Much more is at stake, as is emphasized by the repetition of the Hebrew root ספר (*sāpar*), translated "count" in v. 12 and "tell" in v. 13. In the third and central of the five imperatives, worshipers are invited to "count" Jerusalem's towers so that they may "tell" future generations about God. Alter's translation captures the pun: *"count* its towers.... So that you may *recount* to the last generation:/ That this is God, our God,/ forever."[202] In short, observation of spatial detail leads to proclamation about God. God is "our God forever and ever" (v. 14)—the temporal extension of God's reign. God "will be our guide forever" (v. 14)—the spatial extension of God's reign as Israel is led from place to place. The movement in vv. 12-14, emphasized by the repetition of *sāpar,* is remarkable testimony to the power of sacred space. The seemingly simple matter of seeing a particular place—Jerusalem—leads to the powerful proclamation of God's reign in all times and places.

202. Ibid., 122, italics added.

REFLECTIONS

To contemporary readers, the claims made about Jerusalem are likely to seem highly exaggerated or perhaps even extremely parochial and dangerously wrong. To assert that Jerusalem is the indisputable and indestructible capital of the world was probably as inflammatory in ancient times as it would be today. Besides, we know that Jerusalem was not indestructible; hostile kings and their forces were not put to flight by the very sight of Jerusalem. Indeed, the city was destroyed in 587 BCE by the Babylonians and again in 70 CE by the Romans. Was the psalmist simply mistaken? Was his or her perception blurred by an overly zealous nationalism? Was the psalmist a political propagandist? So one might cynically conclude. But before dismissing the psalmist as a naive optimist or a misguided patriot or a clever politician, we must remember that the details of Psalm 48 are as much metaphorical as geopolitical. What Psalm 48 embodies is "poetic form used to reshape the world in the light of belief."[203] In this case, Jerusalem, a seemingly ordinary place, has become to the eye of faith "the city of the great King" (v. 2), a powerful symbol of God's reign in all places (vv. 2, 10) and in all times (vv. 8, 14). In effect, the psalmist has created in poetic form an alternative worldview, a new reality that for the faithful becomes the deepest and most profound reality of all: God rules the world, now and forever! Psalm 48 articulates the faith that no power on earth or the passing of any amount of time can ultimately thwart the just and righteous purposes of a steadfastly loving God (see vv. 9-11).

The spirit of Psalm 48 is captured eloquently in a novel by Elie Wiesel:

JERUSALEM: the face visible yet hidden, the sap and blood of all that makes us live or renounce life. The spark flashing in the darkness, the murmur rustling through shouts of happiness and

203. Ibid., 133.

joy. A name, a secret. For the exiled, a prayer. For all others, a promise. Jerusalem: seventeen times destroyed yet never erased. The symbol of survival. Jerusalem: the city which miraculously transforms man into pilgrim; no one can enter it and go away unchanged.[204]

The psalmist knew precisely this about Jerusalem: "no one can enter it and go away unchanged"—not because Jerusalem is indestructible or universally acclaimed. Rather, for believers, Jerusalem becomes a spatial, temporal symbol for the reality of God's rule in all times and in places. Thus the footsteps of pilgrims approaching this particular place at any particular moment "reverberate to infinity."[205]

If this sounds strange to Christian readers of Psalms, they need only consider how the same paradox, the same scandal of particularity, lies at the heart of Christianity. For Christians, a particular event in time (the crucifixion of Jesus) at a particular place (Golgotha) becomes the central event of history. What appeared to be an ordinary execution of a common criminal is for Christians the focal point of all space and time. In a way just as particularist and strange and scandalous as the Zion theology of Psalm 48, Christians profess the incarnation of God in Jesus, a first-century Jew from an out-of-the-way place called Nazareth. Essentially, what Christians proclaim is "Christ crucified, a stumbling block to Jews and foolishness to Gentiles, but to those who are called, both Jews and Greeks, Christ the power of God and the wisdom of God" (1 Cor 1:23-24 NRSV). What Psalm 48 and Elie Wiesel say about Jerusalem is what Christians profess about Jesus: No one can see him and go away unchanged. Indeed, the early followers of Jesus were known as ones "who have been turning the world upside down" (Acts 17:6 NRSV; see also Mark 13:1-2; 14:58; 15:29, where the Gospel writer suggests that Jesus has replaced the Temple, that Jesus is the new locus of God's revelation in space and time).

To be sure, neither the theology of Psalm 48 nor the Christian proclamation of Jesus is a facile utopianism. The psalmists knew, the apostles knew, and we still know that we live in time and space as part of a world that is fragile and troubled, terrified and terrifying. Yet, in the midst of it all, we join the psalmist in proclaiming a new reality: God rules the world! What's more, we claim to live by that reality above all others. For the psalmist, the vision of Jerusalem, the city of God, reshaped time and space. For Christians, the life, death, and resurrection of Jesus of Nazareth have reshaped the world, reshaped our time and space into a new reality. Thus, amid the same old realities of trouble and turmoil, we are changed and are able to discern by the eye of faith the dimensions of a new creation (see 2 Cor 5:17). In short, we live eschatologically. (See Commentary on Psalms 2; 46; Introduction.)

204. Elie Wiesel, *A Beggar in Jerusalem* (New York: Pocket Books, 1970) 19.
205. Ibid., 20.

PSALM 49:1-20, GOD WILL REDEEM MY LIFE

NIV	NRSV
Psalm 49	Psalm 49
For the director of music. Of the Sons of Korah. A psalm.	To the leader. Of the Korahites. A Psalm.
¹Hear this, all you peoples; listen, all who live in this world, ²both low and high, rich and poor alike:	¹ Hear this, all you peoples; give ear, all inhabitants of the world, ² both low and high, rich and poor together. ³ My mouth shall speak wisdom;

NIV

3My mouth will speak words of wisdom;
   the utterance from my heart will give
      understanding.
4I will turn my ear to a proverb;
   with the harp I will expound my riddle:

5Why should I fear when evil days come,
   when wicked deceivers surround me—
6those who trust in their wealth
   and boast of their great riches?
7No man can redeem the life of another
   or give to God a ransom for him—
8the ransom for a life is costly,
   no payment is ever enough—
9that he should live on forever
   and not see decay.

10For all can see that wise men die;
   the foolish and the senseless alike perish
   and leave their wealth to others.
11Their tombs will remain their houses[a] forever,
   their dwellings for endless generations,
   though they had[b] named lands after
      themselves.

12But man, despite his riches, does not endure;
   he is[c] like the beasts that perish.

13This is the fate of those who trust in
      themselves,
   and of their followers, who approve their
      sayings.   *Selah*
14Like sheep they are destined for the grave,[d]
   and death will feed on them.
The upright will rule over them in the
      morning;
   their forms will decay in the grave,[e]
   far from their princely mansions.
15But God will redeem my life[e] from the grave;
   he will surely take me to himself.   *Selah*

16Do not be overawed when a man grows rich,
   when the splendor of his house increases;
17for he will take nothing with him when he
      dies,
   his splendor will not descend with him.
18Though while he lived he counted himself
      blessed—
   and men praise you when you prosper—

a11 Septuagint and Syriac; Hebrew *In their thoughts their houses will remain*   b11 Or / *for they have*   c12 Hebrew; Septuagint and Syriac read verse 12 the same as verse 20.   d14 Hebrew *Sheol*; also in verse 15   e15 Or *soul*

NRSV

   the meditation of my heart shall be
      understanding.
4 I will incline my ear to a proverb;
   I will solve my riddle to the music of the
      harp.

5 Why should I fear in times of trouble,
   when the iniquity of my persecutors
      surrounds me,
6 those who trust in their wealth
   and boast of the abundance of their
      riches?
7 Truly, no ransom avails for one's life,[a]
   there is no price one can give to God for
      it.
8 For the ransom of life is costly,
   and can never suffice,
9 that one should live on forever
   and never see the grave.[b]

10 When we look at the wise, they die;
   fool and dolt perish together
   and leave their wealth to others.
11 Their graves[c] are their homes forever,
   their dwelling places to all generations,
   though they named lands their own.
12 Mortals cannot abide in their pomp;
   they are like the animals that perish.

13 Such is the fate of the foolhardy,
   the end of those[d] who are pleased with
      their lot.   *Selah*
14 Like sheep they are appointed for Sheol;
   Death shall be their shepherd;
straight to the grave they descend,[e]
   and their form shall waste away;
   Sheol shall be their home.[f]
15 But God will ransom my soul from the
      power of Sheol,
   for he will receive me.   *Selah*

16 Do not be afraid when some become rich,
   when the wealth of their houses increases.
17 For when they die they will carry nothing
      away;
   their wealth will not go down after them.

a Another reading is *no one can ransom a brother*   b Heb *the pit*   c Gk Syr Compare Tg: Heb *their inward* (thought)   d Tg: Heb *after them*   e Cn: Heb *the upright shall have dominion over them in the morning*   f Meaning of Heb uncertain

NIV	NRSV

¹⁹he will join the generation of his fathers,
    who will never see the light ⌐of life⌐.
 	
²⁰A man who has riches without understanding
    is like the beasts that perish.
	¹⁸ Though in their lifetime they count
	        themselves happy
	    —for you are praised when you do well
	        for yourself—
	¹⁹ they^a will go to the company of their
	        ancestors,
	    who will never again see the light.
	²⁰ Mortals cannot abide in their pomp;
	    they are like the animals that perish.

ᵃ Cn: Heb *you*

COMMENTARY

Psalm 49 is a wisdom psalm (see v. 3) or a didactic poem that functions as a profession of faith in God. If v. 4 is a reliable indication, apparently the psalm was presented as a song accompanied by the harp (see Ps 33:2). The introduction consists of an invitation for everyone in the world to hear (vv. 1-2) and a characterization of the subsequent song (vv. 3-4). The song itself can be divided into two major sections (vv. 5-12, 13-20), each ending with a similar refrain.

Since Psalms 46–48 form a coherent sequence (see Commentary on Psalm 48), it is natural to ask whether Psalm 49 is a part of that sequence. At first sight, it does not appear to be; yet, given the fact that Psalms 46–48 proclaim God's universal sovereignty, it is at least significant that Psalm 49 addresses "all you peoples" (see Ps 47:1). Furthermore, the message of Psalm 49 complements from the human side the message of Psalms 46–48: that rich and powerful human beings, despite their illusions of grandeur and the status accorded them by others (vv. 6, 18), are *not* really in control of the world, or even of their own lives and destinies (vv. 7-9). In short, only God rules the world and ultimately determines human destiny (v. 15). The fundamental message of Psalm 49 may have been particularly pertinent in the post-exilic era, when God's people were perennially subject to richer and more powerful peoples; however, the message of Psalm 49 is also eminently relevant in the contemporary era, when our abundance tempts us to trust in our wealth

and to overlook our finitude and fallibility (see Reflections below).

49:1-2. Although perhaps performed in the Temple or synagogue, the psalm intends to offer a message of universal significance (v. 1). Verse 2*a* reads literally, "also children of a human, also children of a man," but the idiom probably connotes high and low status (see Ps 62:9). The parallel in v. 2*b* reinforces this interpretation. The word "rich" (עשיר *'āšîr*) becomes a key word in the psalm (see vv. 6, 16), and the proper attitude to wealth lies at the heart of the psalm's message.

49:3-4. The psalmist's intent to "speak wisdom" (v. 3) indicates an educational purpose. Of course, the psalmist's interest is not primarily intellectual. Rather, wisdom and understanding have to do with God's instruction and thus with the orientation of one's life to God (see Pss 19:14; 37:30, where what one should speak and think has to do with God's "instruction" [תורה *tôrâ*, or "law"]; see also Deut 4:6; Ps 111:10; Prov 1:7; 3:13; 9:10; 15:33). The subsequent instruction will have to do with wealth, but it will also make very clear that one's stance on wealth is inseparable from one's stance on God. Verse 4 more specifically indicates the psalmist's educational approach or lesson plan. The message will be communicated by way of a "proverb." The Hebrew root of the noun translated "proverb" (משל *māšāl*) also occurs in the refrain as a verb, "are like" (vv. 12*b*, 20*b*). Thus the lesson will involve a comparison that takes the form of a riddle (see Ps 78:2 NIV "hidden things," NRSV, "dark sayings"; Ezek 17:2 NIV "allegory"; Prov 1:6). If the answer to the riddle is contained in the refrain, then we can state the riddle as follows: How are human beings and animals alike? The answer is basic to the psalmist's message about relating to wealth and to God.

49:5-12. The question raised in vv. 5-6 already implies an answer. The persecutors need not be feared, because, having cut themselves off from God, they have no future (see Ps 52:5-7). The only proper object of trust is God (see Pss 4:5; 9:10; 40:4; Introduction), but the persecutors trust their own resources. The only proper object of boasting is God (see Ps 34:2), but again the persecutors boast essentially in themselves. In short, they view themselves as sovereign and autonomous, denying God's claim on their lives and futures. Such self-centeredness, such dependence upon one's own resources, may give the appearance of success (see v. 18), but it is ultimately an illusion.

Verses 7-12 explain why. In a word, as vv. 7-8 suggest, life cannot be bought. Verses 7-8 seem to allude primarily to the provision made in Exod 13:11-16 for redemption of the firstborn; God will allow the sacrifice of an animal to take the place of the sacrifice of a firstborn male child. In this sense, a human life might be bought. Even so, as vv. 7-8 suggest, one should never conclude that the payment is adequate or that such a provision removes God's sovereign claim on human life. Verses 7-8 may also allude to the provisions made in some legal cases involving death; that is, the death of the victim might be redeemed by the payment of an appropriate ransom rather than by the death of the person responsible (see Exod 21:28-32). Here again, in a sense, life could be bought. But while payment may suffice in the realm of human relations (see also Prov 13:8), no payment will suffice to compensate God.

There is one unambiguous sign of the human inability to buy life: death (v. 9). Everybody dies, wise and foolish, rich and poor (vv. 10-11; see Ps 39:4-6; Eccl 2:12-26). Death thus exposes the illusion of human sovereignty. The sense of v. 12 is captured more accurately by the NIV. No amount of money will enable a person to escape death (the NIV's "riches" is from the same Hebrew root as "costly" in v. 8). In this sense, humans and animals are alike. Although humans were given dominion over the animals (Gen 1:28), this did not make humans into gods. Death is a reminder that human dominion is derivative of and not a replacement for God's sovereignty (see Commentary on Psalm 8). Therefore, those persons who would trust or boast in their own resources are not finally to be feared. Verse 12 thus answers the question of vv. 5-6 and anticipates the advice given in v. 16.

49:13-20. As the book of Ecclesiastes demonstrates (esp. 2:12-26), the realization of the universality of death is not necessarily comforting and encouraging. It can be, insofar as it serves to cut the wealthy and the powerful down to size, which is the intent of vv. 5-12. But what about those who have not trusted their own wealth and have not sought to buy life? Whereas vv. 5-12 have portrayed death as the great equalizer, vv. 13-20 move in a different direction by distinguishing between how death will affect the "foolhardy" (v. 13; see "fool" in v. 10) and the "upright" (v. 14). As a comparison of the NIV and the NRSV of vv. 13-14 indicates, the text is very difficult and is subject to several construals. Given the reference to sheep in v. 14a, the NRSV is probably correct to suggest that death is personified as shepherding the foolish to Sheol (see Pss 6:5; 9:17; 31:17), but the NIV is probably correct as well in reading the Hebrew more literally in v. 14b, thus preserving the reference to the upright and their ultimate dominion over powerful, wealthy persons. At any rate, v. 15 maintains a distinction between the future of the foolhardy, who are destined to Sheol (v. 14), and the psalmist's own future. The concept of ransom is reintroduced in v. 15. Whereas human beings cannot purchase ultimate security (vv. 7-8), God "will ransom." The enigmatic assertion that God "will receive me" is reminiscent of Enoch and Elijah (Gen 5:24; 2 Kgs 2:1-12; see also Ps 73:24). The affirmation that the power of God is finally greater than the power of Sheol is a departure from the usual Israelite view of life and death. While v. 15 probably does not represent a developed doctrine of resurrection or afterlife, it certainly does, like Psalm 22:29, push beyond the normal limits (see also Ps 16:10-11). The psalmist trusts that nothing, not even death, will finally be able to separate the faithful from God (see Rom 8:38-39; 14:7-8).

On the basis of this conviction, the psalmist can instruct others not to fear the rich (v. 16; see also vv. 5-6). Although they and their admirers may delude themselves into thinking they have it made (v. 18), they will soon discover that they cannot take it with them (v. 17; see also vv. 10-11, where the same thought precedes the first occurrence of the refrain). The second occurrence of the refrain highlights the difference between vv. 5-12 and 13-20. Although the NRSV translates v. 20 exactly the same as v. 12, the Hebrew in each verse is different, as the NIV recognizes. The word "understanding" (בִּין *bîn*) recalls v. 3. The answer to the riddle has been given a twist. To be like the animals finally means to fail to understand, and thus to die without hope. The wise, who know what the psalmist has affirmed (v. 15) and who entrust themselves to God, will die with the assurance that the power of God is greater than the power of death.

REFLECTIONS

We have all heard and probably said what vv. 10-11, 17 suggest: "You can't take it with you." We know this, of course, intellectually speaking. But existentially speaking, it is very difficult for us to believe this obvious assertion, because we live in a society that systematically teaches us to define ourselves in terms of our incomes, our bank accounts, our stock portfolios, and our possessions. Despite all the blessings and remarkable achievements of capitalistic economic systems, our economy has moved far beyond the simple principle of supply and demand—that is, the principle of providing what people *need* to live. Rather, our economy thrives on the creation of demand, and we are very good at it. Advertisers convince millions of people every day that they can neither be happy nor really have lives worth living unless they drive the right car, drink the proper beverage, roll on the most effective deodorant, choose the best pain remedy, or use the most widely accepted credit card. In short, our economy aims not to meet people's needs but to stimulate people's greed. As Reinhold Niebuhr put it, "Greed has thus become the besetting sin of a bourgeois culture."[206] In other words, the very success of our economic system subtly tempts us to seek security in our wealth; in effect, we become our own gods. With good reason as responsible spouses and parents, we purchase securities and life insurance, almost as if we believe that we really can buy life (see vv. 7-8)! In short, it is exceedingly difficult in our culture, if not impossible, to avoid the conclusion that life *does* consist in the abundance of possessions (see Luke 12:15). For this reason, Brueggemann concludes, "In the consumer capitalism of our society, this poem is important."[207]

To be sure, as the reference to Luke 12 suggests, greed has always been a problem. In fact, the philosophy of the rich fool in Jesus' parable could serve admirably as a statement of the American dream as well as a restatement of the description of the wealthy in Ps 49:6. Not surprisingly, Jesus says that God reminds the rich fool, in keeping with Psalm 49, that he cannot take it with him (Luke 12:20; see also Matt 6:19-21, 24). Psalm 49 is reminiscent, too, of the story of the rich man who refuses to follow Jesus because of his "great wealth" (Mark 10:17-22). Following this incident, Jesus tells his followers how difficult it is for the rich to enter the kingdom of God (Mark 10:25). Wealth inevitably tempts people to depend on themselves and to convince themselves that life can be bought. To the disciple's question, "Then who can be saved?" (Mark 10:26 NRSV), Jesus replies that "for God all things are possible" (Mark 10:27 NRSV). This is what the psalmist knew! What we humans cannot achieve or purchase, God can and does provide for those who are humbly willing to receive it: life (Ps 49:15).

Life is not a prize to be earned or another possession to be bought. Rather, it is a gift to be received (see Mark 8:36-37). The good news of Psalm 49 and the Gospel is that God wills that we live, so much so that Christians profess that God has paid the price by sending Jesus

206. Reinhold Niebuhr, *The Nature and Destiny of Man* (New York: Charles Scribner's Sons, 1964) 1:191; see also 139.
207. Walter Brueggemann, *The Message of the Psalms: A Theological Commentary* (Minneapolis: Augsburg, 1984) 110.

Christ "to give his life as a ransom for many" (Mark 10:45 NRSV; see 1 Tim 2:6). Those who enter the reign of God will live not by greed but by gratitude; they will live in the assurance that the exalted are humbled, and the humble are exalted (see Luke 18:14); they will see in the death and resurrection of Jesus Christ the ultimate embodiment of the affirmation of Ps 49:15 that the power of God is greater than the power of death. True wealth is the wisdom that understands that God is the only giver and ultimate guarantor of life.

PSALM 50:1-23, OFFER TO GOD A SACRIFICE OF THANKSGIVING

NIV

Psalm 50

A psalm of Asaph.

[1]The Mighty One, God, the LORD,
    speaks and summons the earth
    from the rising of the sun to the place
        where it sets.
[2]From Zion, perfect in beauty,
    God shines forth.
[3]Our God comes and will not be silent;
    a fire devours before him,
    and around him a tempest rages.
[4]He summons the heavens above,
    and the earth, that he may judge his
        people:
[5]"Gather to me my consecrated ones,
    who made a covenant with me by
        sacrifice."
[6]And the heavens proclaim his righteousness,
    for God himself is judge.   *Selah*

[7]"Hear, O my people, and I will speak,
    O Israel, and I will testify against you:
    I am God, your God.
[8]I do not rebuke you for your sacrifices
    or your burnt offerings, which are ever
        before me.
[9]I have no need of a bull from your stall
    or of goats from your pens,
[10]for every animal of the forest is mine,
    and the cattle on a thousand hills.
[11]I know every bird in the mountains,
    and the creatures of the field are mine.
[12]If I were hungry I would not tell you,
    for the world is mine, and all that is in it.

NRSV

Psalm 50

A Psalm of Asaph.

[1] The mighty one, God the LORD,
    speaks and summons the earth
    from the rising of the sun to its setting.
[2] Out of Zion, the perfection of beauty,
    God shines forth.

[3] Our God comes and does not keep silence,
    before him is a devouring fire,
    and a mighty tempest all around him.
[4] He calls to the heavens above
    and to the earth, that he may judge his
        people:
[5] "Gather to me my faithful ones,
    who made a covenant with me by
        sacrifice!"
[6] The heavens declare his righteousness,
    for God himself is judge.   *Selah*

[7] "Hear, O my people, and I will speak,
    O Israel, I will testify against you.
    I am God, your God.
[8] Not for your sacrifices do I rebuke you;
    your burnt offerings are continually before
        me.
[9] I will not accept a bull from your house,
    or goats from your folds.
[10] For every wild animal of the forest is mine,
    the cattle on a thousand hills.
[11] I know all the birds of the air,[a]
    and all that moves in the field is mine.

[a] Gk Syr Tg: Heb *mountains*

NIV

¹³Do I eat the flesh of bulls
    or drink the blood of goats?
¹⁴Sacrifice thank offerings to God,
    fulfill your vows to the Most High,
¹⁵and call upon me in the day of trouble;
    I will deliver you, and you will honor me."
    ¹⁶But to the wicked, God says:

    "What right have you to recite my laws
    or take my covenant on your lips?
¹⁷You hate my instruction
    and cast my words behind you.
¹⁸When you see a thief, you join with him;
    you throw in your lot with adulterers.
¹⁹You use your mouth for evil
    and harness your tongue to deceit.
²⁰You speak continually against your brother
    and slander your own mother's son.
²¹These things you have done and I kept silent;
    you thought I was altogether^a like you.
    But I will rebuke you
    and accuse you to your face.

²²"Consider this, you who forget God,
    or I will tear you to pieces, with none to
        rescue:
²³He who sacrifices thank offerings honors me,
    and he prepares the way
    so that I may show him^b the salvation of
        God."

^{a}21 Or thought the 'I AM' was ^{b}23 Or and to him who considers
his way / I will show

NRSV

¹² "If I were hungry, I would not tell you,
    for the world and all that is in it is mine.
¹³ Do I eat the flesh of bulls,
    or drink the blood of goats?
¹⁴ Offer to God a sacrifice of thanksgiving,^{a}
    and pay your vows to the Most High.
¹⁵ Call on me in the day of trouble;
    I will deliver you, and you shall glorify me."

¹⁶ But to the wicked God says:
    "What right have you to recite my
        statutes,
    or take my covenant on your lips?
¹⁷ For you hate discipline,
    and you cast my words behind you.
¹⁸ You make friends with a thief when you
        see one,
    and you keep company with adulterers.

¹⁹ "You give your mouth free rein for evil,
    and your tongue frames deceit.
²⁰ You sit and speak against your kin;
    you slander your own mother's child.
²¹ These things you have done and I have
        been silent;
    you thought that I was one just like
        yourself.
    But now I rebuke you, and lay the charge
        before you.

²² "Mark this, then, you who forget God,
    or I will tear you apart, and there will be
        no one to deliver.
²³ Those who bring thanksgiving as their
        sacrifice honor me;
    to those who go the right way^b
    I will show the salvation of God."

^{a}Or make thanksgiving your sacrifice to God ^{b}Heb who set a
way

COMMENTARY

Neither a song of praise nor a prayer, Psalm 50 is often labeled a prophetic exhortation (see also Psalms 81; 95), and many scholars have suggested that its original use was some form of covenant renewal ceremony. The mention of "covenant" (vv. 5, 16), however, does not necessarily imply a special covenant renewal ceremony. The proper relation to God is an appropriate concern for any worship service. Thus Gerstenberger more simply calls Psalm 50 a liturgical sermon, and he links its origin and use to the post-exilic synagogue, where instruction was a paramount concern and, in his view, a regular feature of liturgy.[208]

To be sure, the accusatory tone of Psalm 50 does not accord well with contemporary homiletical theory, but as Gerstenberger rightly points out, "Accusatory and threatening rhetoric still today is part and parcel of many a Christian sermon."[209] In any case, the function of the accusatory rhetoric is certainly legitimate: to call the people away from self-centeredness to proper relationship with God. In addition, Psalm 50 has much to commend it homiletically. For instance, it appears that the preacher has assessed the congregation well, identifying and addressing two problems in the two parts of the sermon: (1) a misunderstanding of sacrifice (vv. 7-15) and (2) the failure of congregational members to live lives consistent with the beliefs they profess (vv. 16-22). In short, the preacher criticizes the congregation's worship and its work. The two parts of the sermon are introduced by vv. 1-6, and v. 23 is a summary and conclusion. The superscription attributes the psalm to Asaph, the first such attribution in the psalter (see Psalms 73–83; Introduction). It is not clear why Psalm 50 is separated from the other Asaph psalms, unless perhaps the editors of the psalter wanted representatives of both Levitical collections (that is, Korah and Asaph) to introduce the Davidic collection (Psalms 51–72), since representatives of both Levitical collections follow the Davidic collection (see Psalms 73–83; 84–85; 87–88).[210]

50:1-6. The psalm begins by naming God three times, starting with the ancient Canaanite name for the supreme deity and concluding with Israel's personal name for God: "El, Elohim, Yahweh" (אל 'ēl; אלהים 'ĕlōhîm; יהוה yhwh). The effect is to emphasize Yahweh's authority to speak, since God speaks throughout most of the psalm. Yahweh's speech in the first instance is a summons (vv. 1, 4), first to the earth and then to the heavens and the earth. That God can summon, in effect, the whole creation is indicative

of God's sovereignty. The heavens and earth are to serve as court officials and perhaps witnesses in God's trial against the people (see Deut 32:1; Isa 1:2; Mic 6:1-2, where the heavens and earth also are called to witness to God's speaking or acting). They summon the people to court (v. 5). The mention of a covenant "by sacrifice" recalls the covenant ceremony following the giving of the Decalogue (Exod 24:1-8), where sacrifice accompanied the reading of "the book of the covenant" (Exod 24:7 NRSV). In that setting, the people promised, "We will obey" (Exod 24:7 NIV). Psalm 50 suggests that God's people have not obeyed; rather, they have violated the covenant. God may have kept silent (v. 21) in the past regarding the people's breach of the covenant, but God will keep silent no longer (v. 3). Therefore, God is coming to judge them (vv. 4, 6; the Hebrew words for "judge" דין dîn, v. 4; שפט šōpēṭ, v. 6] differ but are essentially synonymous).

As Mays suggests, it is a "trial whose proceedings can be seen only by the eye of faith."[211] In other words, the trial scenario serves as a rhetorical device for bringing the word of God to bear upon the congregation. As in v. 1, the theophany imagery in vv. 2-3 communicates God's authority to speak and judge. As in Deut 33:2, God "comes" from a mountain—although here it is Zion (see Amos 1:2)—and God "shines forth" (cf. Ps 18:7-15). The storm imagery in v. 3 continues the memory of Sinai, where God appeared in order to establish the covenant and to give the commandments, which the people disobeyed (see Exodus 19, esp. vv. 5-6, 8, 16, 18). The heavens, which God has summoned, "declare [God's] righteousness" (v. 6). The heavens do the same thing in Ps 97:6, again following the description of a theophany (97:2-5). Psalm 97 begins with the affirmation that "The LORD is king!" Psalm 50:5-6 also proclaims God's sovereignty as the basis for God's authority to speak and to act to set things right, beginning with God's own people.

50:7-15. With the exception of v. 14, vv. 7-15 are framed in the divine first person—that is, the prophet or preacher delivers the Word of God. Verse 7 recalls a key text from the book of Deuteronomy—the Shema, "Hear, O Israel" (Deut 6:4 NRSV), which follows immediately the

208. See Erhard S. Gerstenberger, *Psalms, Part 1, with an Introduction to Cultic Poetry,* Forms of the OT Literature 14 (Grand Rapids: Eerdmans, 1988) 210.

209. Ibid., 209.

210. See Gerald H. Wilson, "Shaping the Psalter: A Consideration of Editorial Linkage in the Book of Psalms," in *The Shape and Shaping of the Psalter,* ed. J. C. McCann, Jr., JSOTSup 159 (Sheffield: JSOT, 1993) 76-77.

211. James L. Mays, *Psalms,* Interpretation (Louisville: John Knox, 1994) 194.

repetition of the Decalogue. Just as the whole book of Deuteronomy serves as a covenant renewal as the people prepare to enter the land, so also Psalm 50 is a call for renewal. In this context, the issue of the misuse of the sacrificial system (see vv. 8-15) need not be viewed as a call to abolish the system. In fact, "a sacrifice of thanksgiving" (v. 14) still involved the slaughter of animals. Rather, the call is to put sacrifice in proper perspective (see Pss 40:6-8; 51:16-19; Isa 1:12-17; Hos 6:6; Amos 5:21-24). Instead of bringing their sacrificial offerings out of gratitude to God, the people were doing so as a means of asserting their own merit and self-sufficiency, as if God needed them instead of their needing God (see vv. 12-13). In response to this misunderstanding, God, through the preacher, proclaims divine ownership of all animals (v. 10; see also Ps 104:14-18, 24-25, 27-30). Thus the proper sacrifice is really the thanksgiving itself (v. 14; see the NRSV's note), which is often associated with the payment of vows (see Pss 22:25; 61:8; 65:1; 116:14, 17-18). In short, the proper approach to God begins with gratitude. Verse 15 reinforces the message of v. 14: What God asks is that the people seek their security not in themselves but in God. This will prevent self-glorification, for the people will honor God (see v. 23; see also Pss 22:23; 86:12).

50:16-22. The translations of v. 16a may be misleading, for they suggest that vv. 16-22 are addressed to a different group than are vv. 7-15. But it is precisely God's people who have become "the wicked." They apparently say the right things (v. 16) but fail to act in accordance with their covenant identity (v. 17). In short, they are hypocrites. The "you" that begins v. 17 is emphatic. The people actually "hate discipline" or "instruction" (cf. Deut 11:2; Jer 17:23), and they discard God's word (see Neh 9:26). Verses 18-20 illustrate how the people have violated the covenant. The preacher alludes to the Decalogue, specifically the commandments against stealing, adultery, and bearing false witness (see Exod 20:14-16; Jer 7:9-10; Hos 4:1-3; see also Mic 7:5-6, where kinship ties are disrupted by disobedience). Verse 21 returns to the legal imagery of vv. 1-6. As v. 3 has already suggested, God breaks the divine silence and indicts the people for their faithlessness. The fundamental problem is that the people have forgotten God, thus inviting destruction (v. 22; see also Deut 8:19; Hos 8:14; 13:6). The imperative that begins v. 22 is more literally, "Understand." It represents the same root that occurred in the closing verse of Psalm 49 (see the NIV's "understanding"). Thus Psalm 50 joins Psalm 49 in inviting an understanding that consists of gratefully entrusting one's life and future to God rather than trusting wealth (49:6) or even one's own religious behavior (50:7-16).

50:23. This verse concludes the sermon with a brief summary of the two sections and a declaration of good news. Verse 23a summarizes the critique of sacrifices (vv. 7-15; see esp. vv. 14-15), whereas v. 23b summarizes the people's failure to obey the covenant (vv. 16-22; "way" suggests behavior or life-style). God's will is to save, and God will "show . . . salvation" to those who can forget themselves long enough to understand their neediness and insufficiency.

REFLECTIONS

Like all good sermons, Psalm 50 challenges its hearers to make a decision. The basis for decision is, like Jesus' preaching, grounded in the reality of God's claim on the world (Ps 50:1-6). Lest the sermon sound simply judgmental, we should remember that God's purpose in judgment is to set right people and things—that is, to establish justice (vv. 4-6; see 1 Pet 4:17). We should recall, too, that Jesus in his preaching did not hesitate to identify hypocrisy, the discrepancy between profession and behavior (see Matt 9:10-13; 12:1-7; 23:1-36; cf. Ps 50:16-17). Indeed, in his Sermon on the Mount, Jesus recognized the insufficiency of simply going through the right motions or saying the right words. The same call to decision contained in Psalm 50 (esp. vv. 14-15, 22-23) is implicit in Jesus' words, "Not everyone who says to me, 'Lord, Lord,' will enter the kingdom of heaven, but only the one who does the will of my Father in heaven" (Matt 7:21 NRSV).

The apostle Paul articulated the same call to decision. His dual appeal to the Christian congregation in Rome parallels themes in Psalm 50: (1) "present your bodies as a living sacrifice, holy and acceptable to God, which is your spiritual worship" (Rom 12:1 NRSV), and (2) "Do not be conformed to this world, but be transformed by the renewing of your minds, so that you may discern what is the will of God" (Rom 12:2 NRSV).

The call to decision presented by Psalm 50, by Jesus, and by Paul is still a crucial one. Hypocrisy is a persistent temptation. Good faith is always in danger of becoming bad religion—a mechanistic system to put God at our disposal and to give us the illusion of merit and self-control. If we think that we are deserving, and if we think that we have things essentially under control, then there will be no need for us to call upon God or to live in dependence upon God. All that is left is to glorify ourselves (see v. 15). The issue, then, is this: Will we live to gratify ourselves? Or will we live in gratitude to God?

PSALM 51:1-19, ACCORDING TO YOUR STEADFAST LOVE

NIV

Psalm 51

For the director of music. A psalm of David. When the prophet Nathan came to him after David had committed adultery with Bathsheba.

¹Have mercy on me, O God,
    according to your unfailing love;
according to your great compassion
    blot out my transgressions.
²Wash away all my iniquity
    and cleanse me from my sin.

³For I know my transgressions,
    and my sin is always before me.
⁴Against you, you only, have I sinned
    and done what is evil in your sight,
so that you are proved right when you speak
    and justified when you judge.
⁵Surely I was sinful at birth,
    sinful from the time my mother conceived me.
⁶Surely you desire truth in the inner parts^a;
    you teach^b me wisdom in the inmost place.

⁷Cleanse me with hyssop, and I will be clean;
    wash me, and I will be whiter than snow.
⁸Let me hear joy and gladness;
    let the bones you have crushed rejoice.
⁹Hide your face from my sins

^{a}6 The meaning of the Hebrew for this phrase is uncertain. ^{b}6 Or
you desired . . . ; / you taught

NRSV

Psalm 51

To the leader. A Psalm of David, when the prophet Nathan came to him, after he had gone in to Bathsheba.

¹ Have mercy on me, O God,
    according to your steadfast love;
according to your abundant mercy
    blot out my transgressions.
² Wash me thoroughly from my iniquity,
    and cleanse me from my sin.

³ For I know my transgressions,
    and my sin is ever before me.
⁴ Against you, you alone, have I sinned,
    and done what is evil in your sight,
so that you are justified in your sentence
    and blameless when you pass judgment.
⁵ Indeed, I was born guilty,
    a sinner when my mother conceived me.

⁶ You desire truth in the inward being;^{a}
    therefore teach me wisdom in my secret
    heart.
⁷ Purge me with hyssop, and I shall be clean;
    wash me, and I shall be whiter than
    snow.
⁸ Let me hear joy and gladness;

^{a}Meaning of Heb uncertain

NIV

and blot out all my iniquity.

10Create in me a pure heart, O God,
and renew a steadfast spirit within me.
11Do not cast me from your presence
or take your Holy Spirit from me.
12Restore to me the joy of your salvation
and grant me a willing spirit, to sustain me.

13Then I will teach transgressors your ways,
and sinners will turn back to you.
14Save me from bloodguilt, O God,
the God who saves me,
and my tongue will sing of your
righteousness.
15O Lord, open my lips,
and my mouth will declare your praise.
16You do not delight in sacrifice, or I would
bring it;
you do not take pleasure in burnt offerings.
17The sacrifices of God are*a* a broken spirit;
a broken and contrite heart,
O God, you will not despise.

18In your good pleasure make Zion prosper;
build up the walls of Jerusalem.
19Then there will be righteous sacrifices,
whole burnt offerings to delight you;
then bulls will be offered on your altar.

a17 Or My sacrifice, O God, is

NRSV

let the bones that you have crushed
rejoice.
9 Hide your face from my sins,
and blot out all my iniquities.

10 Create in me a clean heart, O God,
and put a new and right*a* spirit within me.
11 Do not cast me away from your presence,
and do not take your holy spirit from me.
12 Restore to me the joy of your salvation,
and sustain in me a willing*b* spirit.

13 Then I will teach transgressors your ways,
and sinners will return to you.
14 Deliver me from bloodshed, O God,
O God of my salvation,
and my tongue will sing aloud of your
deliverance.

15 O Lord, open my lips,
and my mouth will declare your praise.
16 For you have no delight in sacrifice;
if I were to give a burnt offering, you
would not be pleased.
17 The sacrifice acceptable to God*c* is a broken
spirit;
a broken and contrite heart, O God, you
will not despise.

18 Do good to Zion in your good pleasure;
rebuild the walls of Jerusalem,
19 then you will delight in right sacrifices,
in burnt offerings and whole burnt
offerings;
then bulls will be offered on your altar.

a Or steadfast   b Or generous   c Or My sacrifice, O God,

COMMENTARY

Dominated by petition, Psalm 51 is ordinarily classified as a prayer for help or an individual lament/complaint. What sets it apart is that the psalmist's complaint involves his or her own sinfulness. Thus the church has with good reason included it among the seven penitential psalms (see also Psalms 6; 32; 38; 102; 130; 143). Indeed, with the possible exception of Psalm 130,

Psalm 51 is the most dramatic and familiar of the Penitential Psalms. As Kraus suggests, it "stands out in the Psalter. Its peak statements are unique. And its fullness of insight is incomprehensible."[212]

The superscription is the first clue to what Psalm 51 is about: sin and forgiveness. Although

212. H.-J. Kraus, *Psalms 1–59: A Commentary,* trans. H. C. Oswald (Minneapolis: Augsburg, 1988) 507.

it is possible to conclude that the superscription dates the psalm accurately,[213] it is much more likely that it was added later by the editors of the psalter to invite readers to hear Psalm 51 against the background of the story of David's taking of Bathsheba and murder of her husband Uriah (2 Samuel 11), as well as the subsequent confrontation between Nathan and David (2 Sam 12:1-14; cf. Ps 51:4 and 2 Sam 12:13). This story is as much or more about God's character than it is about human sinfulness, both of which are in view in Ps 51:1-6. The series of imperatives in vv. 7-12 petition God for forgiveness and re-creation. The series is broken by v. 13, and vv. 13-15 anticipate the psalmist's transformed existence. Verses 16-17 offer the psalmist's concluding observations about sin and sacrifice, while vv. 18-19 seem to be a second conclusion, perhaps an addition to an original vv. 1-17.

51:1-6. In the story of David and Bathsheba, what is finally determinative is not David's sinfulness but God's grace. To be sure, David's sin had grave consequences; the first child born to Bathsheba died (see 2 Sam 12:16-19), and David's family nearly fell apart (see 2 Samuel 13–1 Kings 1). Nevertheless, David's sin was forgiven; he was allowed to live and to remain king (2 Sam 12:13), despite having broken at least half of the Ten Commandments, including the ones prohibiting adultery and murder! Because God's amazing grace is the most outstanding feature of the story of David and Bathsheba, it is appropriate in view of its superscription that Psalm 51 begin with a focus on God. Before any mention of the vocabulary of sin that dominates vv. 1-5, the psalmist appeals to God's character using three key Hebrew words that communicate God's grace. The NIV and the NRSV usually translate the first, "mercy," as "gracious" (חנן *ḥānan*; see the frequent plea "be gracious" in Pss 4:1; 6:2). The second word, "steadfast love" (חסד *ḥesed*), is virtually a one-word summary of God's gracious, self-giving character (cf. Pss 5:7; 6:4; 13:5; 25:6-7, 10; 33:5, 18, 22; Introduction). The third, "compassion" (רחמים *raḥămîm*), which might more accurately be translated "motherly compassion" (see Commentary on Ps 25:6; Introduction), often ap-

pears in conjunction with "steadfast love." Indeed, because all three key words appear in Exod 34:6-7, along with three of the four terms for sin found in Ps 51:1-5 ("iniquity," "trangression," and "sin"), it is appropriate to read Psalm 51 against the narrative background of the golden calf episode of Exodus 32–34 as well as against the background of the story of David and Bathsheba. Both stories are about God's forgiveness of grievous sin. Just as in 2 Samuel 11–12, so also in Exodus 32–34, God's character is determinative and keeps relationship intact. Both Israel and David are justified, made right with God, by God's grace. So it is with the psalmist, who quite rightly admits that God is "proved right" in God's judgment (v. 4) but later affirms also that "my tongue will sing of your righteousness" (v. 14). The psalmist has been or anticipates being set right, being justified by God's grace.

After appealing to God's character, the psalmist turns to his or her own sinfulness. Israel's basic vocabulary of sin pervades vv. 1-5 (cf. Ps 32:1-5). In these verses, the most general Hebrew word for "sin" (חטא *ḥātā᾿*, vv. 2-4) appears with one of three more specialized words: "iniquity"/"guilty" (עון *᾿āwôn*, vv. 2, 5; see also v. 9) involves the personal guilt or culpability of the sinner; "transgressions" (פשע *peša᾿*, v. 3; see also v. 1) suggests willful rebellion; and "evil" (רע *ra᾿*) conveys the injurious effects of sinful behavior. The repetition drives home the point. Sin and its consequences are pervasive. The emphatic "you, you only" in v. 4 is not meant to indicate that the psalmist's sinful behavior did not have destructive consequences for other people; rather, it suggests that sin has its origin in the failure to honor God. The climactic v. 5 has traditionally been cited in discussions of "original sin," and rightfully so. It is not intended to suggest that sin is transmitted biologically or that sexuality is sinful by definition. Rather, it conveys the inevitability of human fallibility. In each human life, in the human situation, sin is pervasive. We are born into it, and we cannot escape it. While sin is a matter of individual decision, it also has a corporate dimension that affects us, despite our best intentions and decisions.

Three of the four terms for sin in vv. 1-5 also occur in Exod 34:7, recalling again the narrative context of Exodus 32–34. Furthermore, David's

213. See Michael Goulder, *The Prayers of David (Psalms 51–72): Studies in the Psalter II,* JSOTSup 102 (Sheffield: JSOT, 1990) 24-30, 51-69.

behavior is characterized in 2 Sam 12:9 as "evil" (cf. Ps 51:4; "evil" is the one term that does not appear in Exod 34:7), and David admits in 2 Sam 12:13, "I have sinned against the LORD" (NRSV). Again, the recalling of these narrative contexts suggests that the reality of God's steadfast love (see Exod 34:6-7; 2 Sam 7:15) is more fundamental than the reality of human sinfulness. In short, God forgives sinners. Appropriately, each of the repeated words for sin in vv. 1-5 appears as the object of an imperative addressed to God in vv. 1-2—"blot out" (v. 1*d*; see also v. 11; Isa 43:25; 44:22), "wash" (v. 2*a*; see also v. 7; Jer 2:22; 4:14), "cleanse" (v. 2*b*; see also vv. 7*a*, 10*a*; Lev 16:30; Jer 33:8; Ezek 36:25, 33; 37:23). Verse 6 also suggests that sin is not the final word about humanity. God desires not sinfulness but faithfulness (אמת *ĕmet*; NIV and NRSV, "truth"; see Pss 26:3; 45:4). The wisdom that the psalmist requests consists of openness to God and dependence upon God (see Pss 37:30; 49:3; 90:12; Prov 1:7; 9:10). While sin is inevitable and pervasive in the human situation, it is not ultimately the determining reality.

51:7-12. Thus in these verses the psalmist prays for forgiveness and re-creation. The imperative "purge" (v. 7) is from the same Hebrew root as the word "sin" in vv. 2-5, 9. It occurs elsewhere in this particular verbal form in conjunction with purifying rituals involving hyssop (see Lev 14:49, 52; Num 19:18-19). While it is clear that the psalmist alludes to ritual practices in vv. 1*d*-2, 7-9, the language is figurative. The real point is that by God's action, the psalmist has been or will be forgiven and transformed. Sin and guilt will not be the final words; they will give way to joy (vv. 8, 12).

The psalmist's faith in God's transforming power is particularly evident in vv. 10-12. The verb "create" (ברא *bārā'*) is used in the OT only of God's activity. It is particularly prominent in the opening chapters of Genesis (1:1, 21, 27; 2:3, 4) and in Isaiah 40–55, where God's creative activity involves the doing of a "new thing" (Isa 43:15-19; 48:6-7; see also Isa 41:20; 45:7-8). It is significant, too, that "create" is used in the context of God's self-revelation in Exodus 34. Immediately following God's words to Moses in Exod 34:6-7, Moses appeals to God that "the LORD go with us" and "pardon our iniquity and our sin"

(34:9 NRSV). God responds by making a covenant and by promising to "perform marvels, such as have not been performed [lit., "been created"] in all the earth or in any nation" (34:10 NRSV). In short, it is God's fundamental character to restore, rehabilitate, re-create sinners. In the context of Exodus 32–34, Israel's life depended on it; in the context of 2 Samuel 11–12, David's life depended on it; and in Psalm 51, the psalmist affirms that his or her life also depends on God's willingness to forgive and God's ability to re-create sinners.

The association of the terms "clean," "heart," "new," and "spirit" calls to mind Ezek 36:25-27, which also testifies to God's willingness to forgive and ability to re-create. The repetition of the word "spirit" (רוח *rûaḥ*) in vv. 10-12 reinforces this message. The mention of God's "holy spirit" is unusual (see elsewhere only Isa 63:10-11), but God's Spirit elsewhere is also suggestive of God's creative activity. In Gen 1:2, God's Spirit moves over the deep; God's Spirit is responsible for all life and its sustenance (Job 34:14-15). For the psalmist to receive a new spirit (v. 10) and to live in the presence of God's Spirit (v. 11) means nothing short of new life. In biblical terms, to be saved means to be restored to conditions that make life possible, and for the psalmist, forgiveness means salvation (v. 12; see also v. 14). What precisely is meant by "a willing spirit" is unclear, but it may connote generosity (see Exod 35:5, 22). In Isa 32:5, 8, the Hebrew word for "noble" (נדיב *nādîb*) is the opposite of "fool" (נבל *nābāl*; recall "wisdom" in Ps 51:6), and the noble are those who attend to the needs of others (see Isa 32:6).

51:13-17. The psalmist directs his or her thoughts to others in v. 13. Having been made new, the psalmist promises to share this experience with others. The vocabulary that dominates vv. 1-5 recurs in v. 13, but with a twist. The chief among transgressors and sinners will be the *teacher* of transgressors and sinners. The reconciled will bear the message of reconciliation (see Ps 32:8). Because sheer grace is always a scandal, those who faithfully witness to God's grace will always need to pray, "Deliver me from bloodshed" (v. 14). This may especially be the case for one who has been known previously as a notorious sinner. As a comparison of the NRSV with the NIV suggests, v. 14*a* can be interpreted differently. The Hebrew word in question (דמים *dāmîm*) can mean "bloodshed" or "violence," but it can also mean the guilt incurred from shedding blood. This meaning would also be suitable for one who has presented oneself as chief among sinners, especially if Psalm 51 is heard in the context of David's murder of Uriah. In this case, v. 14*a* continues the appeal for forgiveness in vv. 1-2, 6-12. Perhaps the ambiguity is intentional, but even if not, it is quite appropriate.

Despite opposition or anticipated opposition, the psalmist is committed to making a public witness. An inward transformation is not sufficient. The clean heart and new spirit will be accompanied by outwardly visible and audible proclamation. God's "new thing" must be declared (see Isa 48:6). Every organ of speech will participate—"my tongue," "my lips," "my mouth" (vv. 14-15). This outpouring of praise is apparently intended to replace what may customarily have been offered as a public witness—namely, a ritual sacrifice (v. 16). At this point, Psalm 51 recalls Ps 50:14, 23, where the proper sacrifice is identified as "thanksgiving"—that is, humble gratitude accompanied by faithful words and deeds (see Ps 50:17-21). Verse 16 also recalls the prophetic critiques of sacrifice that communicate God's desire that ritual actions be accompanied by personal commitment and transformation (see 1 Sam 15:22; Isa 1:12-17; Hos 6:6; Amos 5:21-24; Mic 6:6-8); in short, God desires the whole self.

And this is exactly what the forgiven, transformed psalmist affirms in v. 17 and, at least implicitly, offers to God (see NIV and NRSV notes). What God desires is "a broken spirit; a broken and contrite heart." The two occurrences of "broken" (נשבר *nišbār*) translate the Hebrew root very literally; and that translation may be misleading. Contemporary persons tend to hear "broken," when used in regard to people, as something like "dysfunctional." Even elsewhere in the OT, brokenheartedness is not a desirable condition but something from which God delivers

(see Ps 34:18, Isa 61:1). What brokenheartedness means in Ps 51:17, however, is captured by the word "contrite," which is a more interpretive translation of a word that literally means "crushed" (see v. 8). God does not want "broken" or "crushed" persons in the sense of "oppressed" or "dysfunctional." Rather, God desires humble, contrite persons who are willing to offer God their whole selves. If pride is the fundamental sin that leads to idolatry, then the transformed psalmist now evidences a humility that inevitably leads to praise. The psalmist's offering to God is the whole self. The psalmist has much to proclaim, but it is not about self. It is about God (vv. 14-15). The psalmist's public witness is directed in precisely the same direction as was the urgent appeal: at the character of God.

51:18-19. These verses may be a later addition to clarify the perspective on sacrifice in vv. 16-17. In any case, the effect of the final form is to give the intensely personal testimony of vv. 1-17 a corporate dimension, one that perhaps has been prepared for by the similarity in terminology between vv. 10-12 and prophetic texts like Ezek 36:16-36, which envisions the restoration of Israel after the exile. Because of the prayer for Zion and Jerusalem in v. 18, several scholars suggest that vv. 18-19 were added in the post-exilic period to make Psalm 51 more suited for corporate use in that era. (See the Introduction for a description of evidence that the psalter as a whole was shaped in response to the crisis of exile.) In any case, these verses are an apt reminder that sin is never simply a matter of individual decision; it is also a matter of corporate, institutionalized evil. They suggest also that the justification of the individual sinner does not obviate the need for participation in the worship of the community but enables proper participation. "Right sacrifices" will be offered by those who have first offered their whole selves to God. By the mercies of God, even the traditional rituals, the same old order of worship, will be transformed.

REFLECTIONS

1. Psalm 51 calls to our attention a perennial feature of the human situation: sin (see Commentary on Psalm 32). As A. Whitney Brown has said of human history, "Any good history book is mainly just a long list of mistakes, complete with names and dates. It's very embarrassing."[214] This characterization is preeminently true of the Bible. Israel's story is indeed a long list of mistakes. Claus Westermann pointed out that Exodus 32–34 proves to be paradigmatic of the whole history of Israel.[215] David's story and the history of the subsequent monarchy are indeed very embarrassing. So is the psalmist's story in Psalm 51. So is the behavior of the disciples in the Gospels (see Matt 26:56). So is the situation of the early church, revealed in the letters of Paul (see esp. 1 Corinthians). So is the history of the Christian church throughout the centuries. So are the denominational and congregational lives of the contemporary church. So are the details of our life stories, if we are honest enough to admit it. In short, Psalm 51 is not just about Israel or David or some unknown ancient psalmist; it is also about us! It is about who we are and how we are as individuals, families, churches—sin pervades our lives. It's very embarrassing.

That is the bad news. But the good news of Psalm 51 is even more prominent. Psalm 51 is not just about human nature; it is also about God's nature. And the good news is that God is willing to forgive sinners and is able to re-create people. Israel's corporate life is an example (see Ezek 36:16-36). David's life is an example. And the psalmist here offers his or her own life as an example as well. To be sure, sin is a powerful and persistent reality, but God's grace is a more powerful and enduring reality. By the grace of God, a persistently disobedient people become partners with God in "an everlasting covenant" (Isa 55:3 NRSV). By the grace of God, dull and disobedient disciples of Jesus become known as those "who have been turning the world upside down" (Acts 17:6 NRSV). By the grace of God, Saul, the former murderer, becomes Paul, ambassador for Christ. Grace is fundamental. That is the good news.

2. It should not surprise us that the apostle Paul knew Psalm 51. He quoted it in Rom 3:4 as part of his argument for the universality of human sinfulness. But this argument is the prelude to Paul's proclamation of justification of the sinful by God's grace (see Rom 3:21-31). Paul, of course, saw this reality revealed in Jesus Christ. What Paul proclaimed to the Corinthians (2 Cor 5:17-20) is reminiscent of Ps 51:10-13:

> So if anyone is in Christ, there is a new creation; everything old has passed away; see, everything has become new! All this is from God, who reconciled us to himself through Christ, and has given us the ministry of reconciliation; that is, in Christ God was reconciling the world to himself, not counting their trespasses against them, and entrusting the message of reconciliation to us. So we are ambassadors for Christ, since God is making his appeal through us; we entreat you on behalf of Christ, be reconciled to God. (NRSV)

Psalm 51 is also an invitation to "be reconciled to God." As Paul knew, reconciliation happens as a result of God's willingness to forgive; the result is a new creation (see Ps 51:10-12), and the reconciled are entrusted with the message of reconciliation (see Ps 51:13). Like the psalmist, too, Paul must have found it necessary to pray often, "Deliver me from bloodshed" (Ps 51:14; see 2 Cor 6:4-5). Jesus also, of course, experienced the violence of persons who opposed what they perceived to be the scandalous proclamation of God's grace.

In the final analysis, Psalm 51 is a proclamation of the good news of the justification of sinners by God's grace. As suggested above, Paul's fullest exposition of this good news is his letter to the Romans. Following the exposition in Romans 1–11, Paul laid out the implications for response in 12:1-2. His appeal is reminiscent of the point at which the psalmist arrives in 51:17 and the direction taken to get there (see Reflections on Psalm 50):

> I appeal to you therefore, brothers and sisters, by the mercies of God, to present your bodies as a living sacrifice, holy and acceptable to God, which is your spiritual worship. Do not be conformed to this world, but be transformed by the renewing of your minds, so that you may discern what is the will of God—what is good and acceptable and perfect. (NRSV)

214. A. Whitney Brown, *The Big Picture: An American Commentary* (New York: Harper Perennial, 1991) 12.
215. See Claus Westermann, *Elements of Old Testament Theology*, trans. D. W. Stott (Atlanta: John Knox, 1982) 50, 54.

The psalmist has anticipated Paul's advice. By the mercies of God (v. 1), the psalmist presents his or her whole self as a living sacrifice (51:17). The transformed psalmist (vv. 10-12) then is able to discern the will of God (v. 13*a*) and begins to participate with God in transforming the world (v. 13*b*). By the grace of God, amid the persistent reality of human sinfulness, there is a new creation.

3. As testimony to the pervasiveness of sin and as a call to be reconciled to God, Psalm 51 is clearly appropriate for its assigned use on Ash Wednesday and during the season of Lent. As a powerful proclamation of God's grace, this psalm is clearly also a psalm for all seasons, and it is appropriate that it is used often in worship. Paraphrases of Psalm 51, especially of vv. 1-5 and 10-12, are frequently used as confessions of sin. Many persons would recognize v. 15 as a call to worship, and perhaps they would appreciate it even more if they knew its source and context.

PSALM 52:1-9, I TRUST IN GOD'S UNFAILING LOVE

NIV

Psalm 52

For the director of music. A *maskil*[a] of David. When Doeg the Edomite had gone to Saul and told him: "David has gone to the house of Ahimelech."

[1]Why do you boast of evil, you mighty man?
  Why do you boast all day long,
  you who are a disgrace in the eyes of God?
[2]Your tongue plots destruction;
  it is like a sharpened razor,
  you who practice deceit.
[3]You love evil rather than good,
  falsehood rather than speaking the
    truth.   *Selah*
[4]You love every harmful word,
  O you deceitful tongue!

[5]Surely God will bring you down to
    everlasting ruin:
  He will snatch you up and tear you from
    your tent;
  he will uproot you from the land of the
    living.   *Selah*
[6]The righteous will see and fear;
  they will laugh at him, saying,
[7]"Here now is the man
  who did not make God his stronghold

[a] Title: Probably a literary or musical term

NRSV

Psalm 52

To the leader. A Maskil of David, when Doeg the Edomite came to Saul and said to him, "David has come to the house of Ahimelech."

[1] Why do you boast, O mighty one,
    of mischief done against the godly?[a]
    All day long [2]you are plotting destruction.
  Your tongue is like a sharp razor,
    you worker of treachery.
[3] You love evil more than good,
    and lying more than speaking the
      truth.   *Selah*
[4] You love all words that devour,
    O deceitful tongue.

[5] But God will break you down forever;
    he will snatch and tear you from your
      tent;
    he will uproot you from the land of the
      living.   *Selah*
[6] The righteous will see, and fear,
    and will laugh at the evildoer,[b] saying,
[7] "See the one who would not take
    refuge in God,
    but trusted in abundant riches,
    and sought refuge in wealth!"[c]

[a] Cn Compare Syr: Heb *the kindness of God*   [b] Heb *him*
[c] Syr Tg: Heb *in his destruction*

NIV

but trusted in his great wealth
and grew strong by destroying others!"

⁸But I am like an olive tree
flourishing in the house of God;
I trust in God's unfailing love
for ever and ever.
⁹I will praise you forever for what you have done;
in your name I will hope, for your name is
good.
I will praise you in the presence of your
saints.

NRSV

⁸ But I am like a green olive tree
in the house of God.
I trust in the steadfast love of God
forever and ever.
⁹ I will thank you forever,
because of what you have done.
In the presence of the faithful
I will proclaimᵃ your name, for it is good.

ᵃ Cn: Heb *wait for*

COMMENTARY

Like Psalm 50, Psalm 52 is neither prayer nor praise directed to God. Rather, vv. 1-5 are addressed to a "mighty one"—who appears to be a powerful person who intends to practice his or her wicked ways on the psalmist and perhaps others of "the righteous" (v. 6). The superscription identifies this "mighty one" as Doeg, one of Saul's servants, who informed Saul of David's locale and killed the priests of Nob at Saul's command (see 1 Samuel 21–22; 22:9 is quoted in the superscription). While Psalm 52 makes sense as the words of David in such a situation, it is much more likely that the superscription should be taken illustratively rather than historically. In short, Psalm 52 may have served and still can serve as the words of God's faithful but threatened people in a variety of times and places (see Reflections below).

Following the address to the "mighty one" in vv. 1-5 is an affirmation about the righteous (v. 6), a quotation of their words (v. 7), and the psalmist's profession of faith (v. 8). God is addressed directly only in v. 9. Because of its unique structure, Psalm 52 "resists form-critical analysis." It is sometimes categorized as a prophetic exhortation (see Psalms 50; 81; 95), although Gerstenberger suggests communal instruction, the use of which he locates in the post-exilic synagogue for the purpose of fortifying the community against threatening opponents.[216] Gerstenberger's pro-

posal offers further evidence of the suitability of this psalm to a variety of historical contexts.

52:1-5. The content of the psalm's exhortation or instruction involves the nature of true security, wealth, and power. Verse 1 clearly contrasts the alternatives for seeking security, although the NIV and the NRSV unnecessarily obscure the matter by failing to follow the Hebrew text (see the NRSV note). The Hebrew of v. 1 could be translated more literally, "Why do you boast about evil, you mighty one? The steadfast love of God lasts all the day." In other words, security can be sought either in doing evil or in God's love. Verses 2-4 explore the first alternative that the mighty one has clearly chosen—to pursue security by self-assertion at the expense of other persons. The mighty one has no qualms about perpetrating "destruction" (הוה *hawwâ*, v. 2; the Hebrew word recurs in v. 7, as the NIV suggests; see also Pss 5:9; 38:12; 55:12). Both v. 2 and v. 4 mention "tongue" and "deceit"/"deceitful" (cf. Pss 10:7; 35:20; 36:3; 38:12; 55:23). Verse 3 repeats the word "evil" from v. 1, and it also portrays the mighty one as a liar (see Pss 7:14; 31:18; 109:2). The mighty one has no love for doing "good" (v. 3; see also v. 11; Pss 34:15; 37:3, 27; Amos 5:14-15; Mic 3:2) or for speaking "righteousness" (v. 3). The mighty one is willing to use any means to get ahead, regardless of how destructive. In short, the mighty one represents the essence of wickedness in the Psalms: autonomy, self-rule (see Commentary on Psalm 1).

The psalmist affirms that the alternative to

216. Erhard S. Gerstenberger, *Psalms, Part 1, with an Introduction to Cultic Poetry,* Forms of the OT Literature 14 (Grand Rapids: Eerdmans, 1988) 216.

autonomy is dependence upon God and God's steadfast love. Verse 1 has indicated that this alternative is the only true and enduring one; v. 5 illustrates the reason why (see Ps 73:18-20). In contrast to the affirmation that God "will uproot" the wicked, the psalmist uses the self-portrait of a stable, fruitful tree in v. 8, which also contains the affirmation that the psalmist has chosen the proper alternative: God's steadfast love. The psalmist knows the nature of true security: Life ultimately depends on God rather than on ourselves or our possessions (see Luke 12:13-21, esp. v. 15).

52:6-7. The righteous will see the judgment announced in v. 5, and they will interpret it as confirmation of their choice to trust God (v. 6; see "see and fear" in Ps 40:3). Just as God laughs at those who oppose the divine will (see Pss 2:4; 37:13; 59:8; Prov 1:26), so also do the righteous. Their words indicate their understanding of the proper direction of trust (v. 7). As the NIV suggests, the Hebrew root that the NRSV translates "refuge" in v. 7 means basically "strength" (מעוז *mā'ôz*; see Ps 27:1). The so-called mighty ones seek their strength not in God but in destroying others. The psalmist recognizes that such a strategy is finally futile (see Pss 37:1-11, 37-40; 49:5-6; 62:10). Verses 5-7 do not describe a reward/punishment scheme that operates mechanistically. The punishment of the wicked is that by pursuing wealth they have cut themselves off from God, who is the source of life. Conversely, the reward of the righteous is that they are grounded in God

and thus connected to life's source and destiny (see Commentary on Psalm 1).

52:8-9. Verse 8 articulates both the psalmist's connection to the source of life and the faith on which it is founded. Like a long-lived olive tree growing on the temple grounds, the psalmist's life is firmly rooted in God's love (see Pss 1:3; 92:12-15; Jer 17:5-8, 11). In explicit contrast to those who trust their own ill-gotten gain (v. 7), the psalmist trusts God's steadfast love "forever and ever" (v. 8; see also v. 1 and note "forever" in v. 5). Thus, while the life of the wicked is characterized by greed (vv. 2-4, 7), the life of the psalmist is characterized by gratitude to God (v. 9*ab*). The psalmist's relationship to others involves not exploitation (see v. 7) but witness (v. 9*cd*). The term "faithful"/"saints" (חסיד *ḥāsîd*) is from the same root as "steadfast love," and it may be translated "the steadfastly loving [or loved] ones." In short, trust in God's steadfast love creates a community shaped by God's character or "name" (see Ps 54:6, where "good" is associated with God's "name"; elsewhere God is described as "good" in association with God's steadfast love, as in Pss 100:5; 106:1; 107:1; 118:1, 29; 136:1; 145:8-9). The verb in v. 9*cd* means "to wait for," "to hope" (קוה *qāwâ*; see Pss 25:3, 5, 21; 27:14; 37:34; 40:1; 130:5). The community of God's people is eschatological. It lives, surrounded by opposition from mighty ones, not by what it sees but by what it believes and hopes for. In doing so, it experiences already the abundant life that is greater than any earthly treasure or possession (see Matt 6:19-21; Luke 12:13-21).

REFLECTIONS

The words of Psalm 52 would be appropriate in various settings, ranging from the life of David to the post-exilic era to the contemporary scene. In other words, the central issue with which Psalm 52 deals is a perennial one: the nature of enduring security, wealth, and power. The temptation to live for ourselves at the expense of others is both as ancient as humanity itself (see Genesis 4) and as contemporary as today's date. Mays describes the depiction of the "mighty one" in vv. 1-4 as follows: "The portrait is that of a person who turns human capacities and possession into the basis of his existence."[217] This, of course, is precisely what much of contemporary society consistently presses us to do—to ground our lives in nothing but ourselves and our possessions (see Commentary on Psalms 1; 2; 49).

In other words, contemporary culture confronts us with the same alternatives that we find in Psalm 52. We can choose to live for ourselves, or we can choose to live for God. We can

217. James L. Mays, *Psalms,* Interpretation (Louisville: John Knox, 1994) 205.

trust ourselves and our own resources, or we can entrust our lives and futures to God. The choice is not an easy one.

Psalm 52 is a reminder that there has always been hostility to the gospel. And, of course, the psalmist—whether we think in terms of David or of some unknown post-exilic poet—is not the only faithful servant to be threatened by rich and powerful opponents. We need only consider, for instance, Amos (see Amos 7:10-17), Jeremiah (see Jer 26:10-19; 38:1-13), and Jesus. Those who are called to follow Jesus can expect opposition as well (see Mark 8:34). The alternatives presented in Psalm 52 are still very real, and the psalmist's words and example are a timely witness for those of us who live in circumstances in which trusting God will be both increasingly difficult and increasingly important.

PSALM 53:1-6, NO ONE DOES GOOD

NIV

Psalm 53

For the director of music. According to *mahalath.*[a] A *maskil*[b] of David.

[1]The fool says in his heart,
  "There is no God."
They are corrupt, and their ways are vile;
  there is no one who does good.

[2]God looks down from heaven
  on the sons of men
to see if there are any who understand,
  any who seek God.
[3]Everyone has turned away,
  they have together become corrupt;
there is no one who does good,
  not even one.

[4]Will the evildoers never learn—
  those who devour my people as men eat
    bread
  and who do not call on God?
[5]There they were, overwhelmed with dread,
  where there was nothing to dread.
God scattered the bones of those who
    attacked you;
  you put them to shame, for God despised
    them.

[6]Oh, that salvation for Israel would come out
    of Zion!
  When God restores the fortunes of his people,
  let Jacob rejoice and Israel be glad!

[a] Title: Probably a musical term   [b] Title: Probably a literary or musical term

NRSV

Psalm 53

To the leader: according to Mahalath. A Maskil of David.

[1] Fools say in their hearts, "There is no God."
  They are corrupt, they commit
    abominable acts;
  there is no one who does good.

[2] God looks down from heaven on humankind
  to see if there are any who are wise,
  who seek after God.

[3] They have all fallen away, they are all alike
    perverse;
  there is no one who does good,
  no, not one.

[4] Have they no knowledge, those evildoers,
  who eat up my people as they eat bread,
  and do not call upon God?

[5] There they shall be in great terror,
  in terror such as has not been.
For God will scatter the bones of the ungodly;[a]
  they will be put to shame,[b] for God has
    rejected them.

[6] O that deliverance for Israel would come
    from Zion!
  When God restores the fortunes of his people,
  Jacob will rejoice; Israel will be glad.

[a] Cn Compare Gk Syr: Heb *him who encamps against you*   [b] Gk: Heb *you have put (them) to shame*

COMMENTARY

Psalm 53 is nearly identical to Psalm 14, with the exception of 53:5 (cf. 14:5-6). The superscription of Psalm 53 is longer than that of Psalm 14; the noun translated "acts" (עול *'āwel*) in 53:1 differs from the noun in the corresponding position in Ps 14:1 (עלילה *'ălîlâ*); and the opening verbs of 53:3 and 14:3 differ. The divine name also differs in Psalms 14 and 53, since Psalm 53 is part of the Elohistic Psalter (Psalms 42–83; see Introduction). The two versions of essentially the same psalm were apparently parts of separate collections that were both included in the book of Psalms.

The opening line of Ps 53:5 is the same as 14:5, but then the two psalms diverge briefly.

Whereas 14:5-6 affirms God's presence with the righteous who find their refuge in God, Ps 53:5 develops the concept of "terror" (פחד *paḥad*). There are textual problems with v. 5 (see the NRSV notes); however, its apparent purpose is to portray God's judgment upon the "evildoers" mentioned in v. 4 (see Ps 141:7). This difference in Psalm 53 makes it a particularly suitable companion to Psalm 52, which also portrays God's judgment upon the wicked (see 52:5). Likewise, the content of Ps 14:5-6 has specific connections with its particular context, especially with Ps 12:5-7. (For further commentary, as well as Reflections, see Psalm 14.)

PSALM 54:1-7, SURELY, GOD IS MY HELPER

NIV

Psalm 54

For the director of music. With stringed instruments. A *maskil*[a] of David. When the Ziphites had gone to Saul and said, "Is not David hiding among us?"

[1]Save me, O God, by your name;
   vindicate me by your might.
[2]Hear my prayer, O God;
   listen to the words of my mouth.

[3]Strangers are attacking me;
   ruthless men seek my life—
   men without regard for God.   *Selah*

[4]Surely God is my help;
   the Lord is the one who sustains me.

[5]Let evil recoil on those who slander me;
   in your faithfulness destroy them.

[6]I will sacrifice a freewill offering to you;
   I will praise your name, O LORD,
      for it is good.
[7]For he has delivered me from all my troubles,
   and my eyes have looked in triumph on
      my foes.

a Title: Probably a literary or musical term

NRSV

Psalm 54

To the leader: with stringed instruments. A Maskil of David, when the Ziphites went and told Saul, "David is in hiding among us."

[1] Save me, O God, by your name,
      and vindicate me by your might.
[2] Hear my prayer, O God;
      give ear to the words of my mouth.

[3] For the insolent have risen against me,
      the ruthless seek my life;
   they do not set God before them.   *Selah*

[4] But surely, God is my helper;
      the Lord is the upholder of[a] my life.
[5] He will repay my enemies for their evil.
      In your faithfulness, put an end to them.

[6] With a freewill offering I will sacrifice to you;
      I will give thanks to your name, O LORD,
         for it is good.
[7] For he has delivered me from every trouble,
      and my eye has looked in triumph on my
         enemies.

a Gk Syr Jerome: Heb *is of those who uphold* or *is with those who uphold*

COMMENTARY

Psalm 54 is a prayer for help or individual lament/complaint. It opens with petition (vv. 1-2), followed by complaint (v. 3), affirmation of trust (vv. 4-5a), renewed petition (v. 5b), and vow to praise (v. 6) with accompanying reason (v. 7). Scholars disagree as to whether v. 7 indicates that the psalmist has already been delivered. It seems to do so, but it may allude to past deliverances that form the basis of the present confidence, or it may indicate that the psalmist is so sure of an anticipated deliverance that he or she can speak of it as already having occurred. The ambiguity has theological significance (see Reflections).

Attention is drawn to v. 3c by the *Selah* following it, as well as by the fact that it is the third part of the only three-part line in the poem. Regardless of whether v. 3c is a later addition, as several scholars suggest, its present position serves to set up the sharply contrasting affirmation in v. 4a. Verse 4 is the middle line of the psalm, and, perhaps not coincidentally, it contains the central theological assertion: "God is my helper." It is significant, too, that v. 4 is surrounded by references in vv. 3 and 5 to those who oppose the psalmist. Structurally speaking, the affirmation comes in the midst of opposition. Experientially speaking, the same is true.

The superscription assigns the prayer to David (see 1 Sam 23:19) at a point when Saul "had come out to seek his life" (1 Sam 23:15 NRSV; cf. Ps 54:3). As with other such superscriptions (see Psalms 3; 51; Introduction), this one should be taken illustratively rather than historically. The editors of the psalter recognized the appropriateness of Psalm 54 for that particular moment in David's life; however, the prayer is also appropriate for and was certainly used in a variety of circumstances. Several commentators suggest that it may have been used by persecuted persons seeking refuge in the Temple (see Psalms 5; 7), while Gerstenberger maintains that it was "rooted in small-group ritual and employed in order to save and rehabilitate suffering group members."[218] On the other hand, several scholars approach Psalm 54 as a communal prayer of the embattled post-exilic community. In short, the characteristic

inability to define a precise origin and setting testifies to the open-endedness and adaptability of the prayer.

54:1-2. The opening petition is a frequent one in Psalms (see Pss 3:7; 6:4; 7:1). The appeal to God's "name" is often interpreted as evidence of a late Deuteronomistic name theology (see Deut 12:5, 11, 21; 1 Kgs 8:16-20). While this is possible (see "name" also in v. 6), it perhaps more simply indicates an appeal to God's fundamental character, which includes both "might" (v. 1b; see also Pss 21:13; 65:6; 66:7; 71:18; 80:2; 89:13; and esp. 106:8) and "faithfulness" (v. 6; see also Exod 34:6; Pss 40:11-12; 57:3; 85:10-11; 86:15). The petition for God to "vindicate" is used less frequently (see Ps 7:9), but God is elsewhere described using this particular word as one who judges or sets things right as a manifestation of divine sovereignty (see Pss 9:8; 50:4; 96:10). In essence, the psalmist's appeal in v. 1 demonstrates that she or he trusts that the power and purposes of God are greater than the power and purposes of the enemy, a conviction that is reinforced in vv. 4-5, 7. Thus the psalmist asks God to hear and to give ear (v. 2; see Pss 17:1; 39:12; 84:8; and esp. 143:1, where these requests are linked to God's faithfulness).

54:3-5. In v. 3a, the NIV follows the Hebrew, a reading that is often cited by those who emphasize the communal dimension of the prayer, since the word "strangers" (זרים *zārîm*) usually designates foreign enemies (see Isa 1:7; Hos 7:9; 8:7; cf. Ps 109:11). The NRSV follows several manuscripts that read a similar word that means "insolent" (זדים *zēdîm*; on enemies rising, see Ps 3:1). The same word occurs in Ps 86:14, as does the Hebrew word translated "ruthless" here (עריצים *'ārîṣîm*; "ruffians" in 86:14 NRSV). In both verses, the ruthless, failing to attend to God, seek the psalmist's life (see also Pss 35:4; 38:12; 40:14; 63:9; 70:2). The editors of the psalter apparently had v. 3b in mind in linking Psalm 54 with David (see 1 Sam 23:15), but others also had their lives threatened by enemies—Elijah (1 Kgs 19:10, 14), Jeremiah (see Jer 11:21), the people of Jerusalem (Jer 21:7), Jesus. Thus v. 3b is another reminder of the adaptability of Psalm 54.

---

218. Gerstenberger, *Psalms*, 222.

Verses 3c and 4a provide a sharp contrast between the enemies and the psalmist. That contrast is made even more emphatic by the alliteration of "strangers" (zārîm) and "helper" (עזר 'ōzēr). The psalmist entrusts her or his life to God (see God as "help"/"helper" in Pss 10:14; 22:19). The syntax of v. 4b is difficult, but the translations seem to capture the proper sense (see Pss 3:5; 37:17, 24; 51:12; 119:116; 145:14). Again, the psalmist's life depends on God. God will deal with the psalmist's opponents, who in v. 5a are literally called "watchers" (שורר šôrēr; see the same Hebrew word in Pss 5:8; 27:11; 56:2; 59:10; 92:11). The appeal in v. 5b is based on God's character— "faithfulness"—just as the same petition in Ps 143:12 is based on God's steadfast love. The issue is not so much personal revenge as it is the psalmist's conviction that God wills to do justice, to give life, to set things right (see v. 1). If God does not deal with the enemies, then God's will is thwarted.

54:6-7. In apparent anticipation of the enactment of the divine will, the psalmist promises in v. 6 a "freewill offering" (see 2 Chr 31:14; Ezra 3:5; Ezek 46:12). The motive is gratitude for the manifestation of God's character (see "name" in v. 1; see also Pss 44:8; 52:9; 99:3; 138:2; 142:7). Although it is not clear whether deliverance has already occurred or is still anticipated, it is clear that the psalmist entrusts the future to God. The phrase "in triumph" is not in the Hebrew text (see also Pss 59:10; 118:7). While it may be an acceptable interpretive translation, it may also be too suggestive of the element of personal revenge. The real point is that God has or will set things right as the psalmist requested in v. 1.

REFLECTIONS

On the basis of vv. 5 and 7, the psalmist is sometimes understood as vengeful and vindictive. Weiser, for instance, says of the psalmist, "Human self-will and man's low instincts of vindictiveness and gloating retain their power over his thoughts."[219] Such a conclusion, however, overlooks the fact that the psalmist does not personally seek revenge but appeals to God's character and will to give life and to enact justice among human beings. In situations of injustice and oppression, in order for things to be set right, oppressors must be opposed. It is precisely this for which the psalmist prays. In short, the psalmist is not necessarily being vengeful but simply realistic. As Marvin Tate concludes: "The message of the psalm is clear enough: the Name of Yahweh will not fail the suppliant in a time of crisis. The enemies will not prevail. Yahweh will make a necessary connection between act and consequence, and the power of ruthless foes will be turned back against themselves."[220]

In essence, the psalmist demonstrates the same faith and prays the same way Jesus taught his disciples: "your will be done, on earth as it is in heaven . . . deliver us from the evil one" (Matt 6:10, 13 NIV). The perspective of the Lord's prayer is eschatological, as is that of Psalm 54—that is, the psalmist prayed and Christians pray in the midst of opposition and suffering. Yet, to affirm that "God is my helper," entrusting life and future to God, is already to be in touch with the source of enduring life and strength.

This tension between "already" and "not yet" makes the ambiguity of v. 7 theologically significant for us. In other words, persons who live in dependence upon God will experience the life that God intends, yet always in a world where brokenness and pain and disobedience are real. It is theologically appropriate that we not try to resolve the ambiguity of v. 7, for it reminds Christian readers of the truth that the cross and the resurrection are experienced not as separate but as simultaneous realities (see Commentary on Psalms 13; 22; Introduction).

219. Artur Weiser, *The Psalms,* OTL, trans. H. Hartwell (Philadelphia: Westminster, 1962) 416.
220. Marvin E. Tate, *Psalms 51–100,* WBC 20 (Dallas: Word, 1990) 49.

PSALM 55:1-23, CAST YOUR BURDENS ON THE LORD

NIV

Psalm 55

For the director of music. With stringed
instruments. A *maskil*[a] of David.

[1]Listen to my prayer, O God,
  do not ignore my plea;
[2] hear me and answer me.
My thoughts trouble me and I am distraught
[3] at the voice of the enemy,
  at the stares of the wicked;
for they bring down suffering upon me
  and revile me in their anger.

[4]My heart is in anguish within me;
  the terrors of death assail me.
[5]Fear and trembling have beset me;
  horror has overwhelmed me.
[6]I said, "Oh, that I had the wings of a dove!
  I would fly away and be at rest—
[7]I would flee far away
  and stay in the desert;   *Selah*
[8]I would hurry to my place of shelter,
  far from the tempest and storm."

[9]Confuse the wicked, O Lord, confound their
    speech,
  for I see violence and strife in the city.
[10]Day and night they prowl about on its walls;
  malice and abuse are within it.
[11]Destructive forces are at work in the city;
  threats and lies never leave its streets.

[12]If an enemy were insulting me,
  I could endure it;
if a foe were raising himself against me,
  I could hide from him.
[13]But it is you, a man like myself,
  my companion, my close friend,
[14]with whom I once enjoyed sweet fellowship
  as we walked with the throng at the
    house of God.

[15]Let death take my enemies by surprise;
  let them go down alive to the grave,[b]
  for evil finds lodging among them.

a Title: Probably a literary or musical term   b15 Hebrew *Sheol*

NRSV

Psalm 55

To the leader: with stringed instruments. A
Maskil of David.

[1] Give ear to my prayer, O God;
  ` do not hide yourself from my supplication.
[2] Attend to me, and answer me;
  I am troubled in my complaint.
I am distraught [3]by the noise of the enemy,
  because of the clamor of the wicked.
For they bring[a] trouble upon me,
  and in anger they cherish enmity against
    me.

[4] My heart is in anguish within me,
  the terrors of death have fallen upon me.
[5] Fear and trembling come upon me,
  and horror overwhelms me.
[6] And I say, "O that I had wings like a dove!
  I would fly away and be at rest;
[7] truly, I would flee far away;
  I would lodge in the wilderness;   *Selah*
[8] I would hurry to find a shelter for myself
  from the raging wind and tempest."

[9] Confuse, O Lord, confound their speech;
  for I see violence and strife in the city.
[10] Day and night they go around it
  on its walls,
and iniquity and trouble are within it;
[11] ruin is in its midst;
oppression and fraud
  do not depart from its marketplace.

[12] It is not enemies who taunt me—
  I could bear that;
it is not adversaries who deal insolently
    with me—
  I could hide from them.
[13] But it is you, my equal,
  my companion, my familiar friend,
[14] with whom I kept pleasant company;

a Cn Compare Gk: Heb *they cause to totter*

NIV

¹⁶But I call to God,
   and the LORD saves me.
¹⁷Evening, morning and noon
   I cry out in distress,
   and he hears my voice.
¹⁸He ransoms me unharmed
   from the battle waged against me,
   even though many oppose me.
¹⁹God, who is enthroned forever,
   will hear them and afflict them—   *Selah*
men who never change their ways
   and have no fear of God.

²⁰My companion attacks his friends;
   he violates his covenant.
²¹His speech is smooth as butter,
   yet war is in his heart;
his words are more soothing than oil,
   yet they are drawn swords.

²²Cast your cares on the LORD
   and he will sustain you;
he will never let the righteous fall.
²³But you, O God, will bring down the wicked
   into the pit of corruption;
bloodthirsty and deceitful men
   will not live out half their days.

But as for me, I trust in you.

NRSV

   we walked in the house of God with the
      throng.
¹⁵ Let death come upon them;
   let them go down alive to Sheol;
   for evil is in their homes and in their
      hearts.

¹⁶ But I call upon God,
   and the LORD will save me.
¹⁷ Evening and morning and at noon
   I utter my complaint and moan,
   and he will hear my voice.
¹⁸ He will redeem me unharmed
   from the battle that I wage,
   for many are arrayed against me.
¹⁹ God, who is enthroned from of old,   *Selah*
   will hear, and will humble them—
because they do not change,
   and do not fear God.

²⁰ My companion laid hands on a friend
   and violated a covenant with me[a]
²¹ with speech smoother than butter,
   but with a heart set on war;
with words that were softer than oil,
   but in fact were drawn swords.

²² Cast your burden[b] on the LORD,
   and he will sustain you;
he will never permit
   the righteous to be moved.

²³ But you, O God, will cast them down
   into the lowest pit;
the bloodthirsty and treacherous
   shall not live out half their days.
But I will trust in you.

[a] Heb lacks *with me*   [b] Or *Cast what he has given you*

COMMENTARY

Although this prayer for help contains typical features of the individual lament/complaint—petition (vv. 1-2*a*, 9*a*, 15), complaint (vv. 2*b*-8, 9*b*-11, 12-14, 20-21), expression of trust (vv. 16-19, 22-23)—it is also "astonishingly unique."[221] Not only are there many unusual words and difficult

expressions, but also the movement of the poem seems abrupt and disorderly, to the extent that Kraus even suggests that vv. 1-18*a* and vv. 18*b*-23 are two separate poems that were joined because of the prominent theme of betrayal by a friend (vv. 12-14, 20-21).[222] It seems preferable, how-

221. Erhard S. Gerstenberger, *Psalms, Part 1, with an Introduction to Cultic Poetry,* Forms of the OT Literature 14 (Grand Rapids: Eerdmans, 1988) 223.

222. H.-J. Kraus, *Psalms 1–59: A Commentary,* trans. H. C. Oswald (Minneapolis: Augsburg, 1988) 519-20.

ever, to view the structural irregularity as an apt representation of the chaotic conditions that prevail in the life of the psalmist.

Several attempts have been made to specify what these conditions may have been. It has been suggested that the psalm articulates the experience of exile, either of an individual or of the people, who find themselves in a strange and hostile city. Because of the military imagery and the betrayal theme, Psalm 55 is sometimes associated with the betrayal of David by Ahithophel as part of Absalom's revolt (see 2 Sam 15:31). While such proposals provide interesting background for the reading of Psalm 55, they remain very speculative. The theme of betrayal by friends also occurs in other prayers (see Pss 31:11; 35:12-15; 38:11; 41:9; 88:8, 18), and it is simply not possible to identify precisely the situations behind these prayers. Besides, Psalm 55 and other prayers were preserved and transmitted because of their ability to function liturgically and devotionally in a variety of times and places (see Reflections below). They articulate universal human experiences of opposition (vv. 2-3), danger (vv. 10-11), fear (vv. 4-5), and betrayal (vv. 12-14, 20-21), as well as assurance (vv. 16-19) and trust (vv. 22-23). As Gerstenberger suggests, Psalm 55 "summarizes liturgically the archetypal expressions of an ultimate anxiety in the face of death that is regularly experienced in situations of extreme danger."[223]

55:1-5. The psalm begins with four imperatives: "Give ear" (see Pss 5:1; 17:1), "do not hide" (see Ps 10:1), "attend" (see Pss 5:2; 17:1), "answer" (see Pss 27:7; 86:1). Having requested God's attention, the psalmist immediately shares his or her troubling "thoughts"/"complaint" (see v. 18; Pss 64:1; 142:3). The "enemy" (v. 3; see v. 12) causes trouble "to totter" upon the psalmist (v. 3; see the NRSV note), but in the end the psalmist realizes that God will not allow "the righteous to totter" (v. 22, author's trans.). But for now the complaint continues in vv. 4-5, where the language suggests precisely the opposite of deliverance. "Terrors" (v. 4) and "trembling" (v. 5) are what the Egyptians experienced as a result of opposing God (see Exod 15:15-16), and over-

whelming horror is what Ezekiel promises as a result of God's judgment (see Ezek 7:18).

55:6-11. It is understandable that the psalmist wants to escape (vv. 6-8). Speaking for God apparently, Jeremiah voices a similar sentiment in Jer 9:2-3; Jer 9:4-8 warns about betrayal by neighbors and kin, and Jer 9:9-10 announces a punishment from which the birds flee (see also Jer 4:25). Thus Jeremiah 9 recalls the content and movement of Psalm 55. The wilderness is seen as a place of refuge that contrasts with the violent city that is mentioned in vv. 9-11 (cf. Ezek 17:23; 31:13, where nesting birds are an image of safety). The wicked elsewhere are associated with violence (Pss 7:16; 11:5; 18:48; 27:12; 73:6; 74:20) and strife (Pss 18:43; 31:20), as well as with the other personified problems in vv. 10-11. For instance, the words the NRSV translates as "iniquity," "trouble," "oppression," and "fraud" all occur in Ps 10:7 to describe the speech of the wicked ("mischief" = "trouble" and "deceit" = "fraud"), who disrupt life in the villages (Ps 10:8). In Psalm 55, the city is characterized by "destructive forces" (v. 11), a condition elsewhere caused by the wicked (cf. Pss 5:9; 52:2, 7). The psalmist's plea in v. 9a recalls Gen 11:1-9 and the city of Babel (see esp. Gen 11:7, 9). The wicked threaten both the psalmist and God.

55:12-15. Verses 12-14 introduce a new dimension to the problem. The generally chaotic conditions of vv. 2b-5, 9-11 are accompanied by personal betrayal. Beginning with the personal pronoun "you," v. 13 designates the betrayer with three more terms that emphasize former intimacy. As suggested above, the theme of betrayal occurs in several other psalms and prophetic texts (in addition to Jer 9:4-8, see Isa 3:5; Jer 20:10; Mic 7:5-6). The shift from "you" in v. 13 to "them" in v. 15 returns the focus to the larger problem. Apparently, the disruption of intimate relationships is a part of the larger societal breakdown. Verse 15, which essentially tells the enemies to "Go to hell," recalls Numbers 16, where Korah and his company "go down alive into Sheol" (Num 16:30 NRSV; see also Num 16:33), which represents the realm and power of death (see Pss 18:5; 88:3; 116:3).

55:16-19. In the face of circumstances that are deadly (v. 4) and destructive (vv. 9-11),

223. Gerstenberger, *Psalms,* 224.

terrible and terrifying (v. 5), the psalmist looks to God for life (see "save"/"deliver" in Pss 3:7; 6:4; 7:1; 31:16; 54:1; 57:3). The emphatic personal pronoun "I" begins v. 16, effectively contrasting the psalmist with the treacherous "you" of v. 13. The psalmist is constantly in communication with God (v. 17a) in the confidence that God "will hear" (vv. 17, 19) and "redeem" (v. 12; see also Pss 26:11; 31:5; 34:22; 44:26; 69:18). The word for "unharmed" (בשלום *bĕšālôm*) in v. 18 is more literally translated "in peace," and suits the military imagery (see "battle" in v. 18 and "war" in v. 21). It was the responsibility of a monarch to establish peace; thus God's sovereignty is affirmed in v. 19 (see "enthroned"/"sits" in Pss 2:4; 9:7; 29:10; 102:12). The phrase "humble them" or "afflict them" (יענם *ya'ănēm*) is similar in sound to "answer me" (עני *'ănēnî*) in v. 2. God's answer will involve opposition to oppressors. Verse 19 makes explicit what was implied in vv. 9-11: The enemies of the psalmist are also opponents of God. Verses 16-19 profess the eschatological faith that pervades the book of Psalms: The power of God is ultimately greater than the power of the wicked. Although it may appear otherwise for now, God rules the world (see Psalm 2; Introduction).

55:20-23. On the basis of this conviction, despite human faithlessness and unreliability (vv. 20-21), the psalmist can invite others, including contemporary readers, to "Cast your burden on the LORD" (v. 22a). While it is possible to construe v. 22a as the sarcastic words of the enemy addressed to the psalmist (see v. 21), it is more likely that it should be understood as the psalmist's encouraging word to others, and this is certainly the way v. 22 has been appropriated in the history of its interpretation. The invitation is followed by an affirmation of God's care for the righteous. The pronoun "he" is emphatic; *God* will provide. Amid the chaos caused by the wicked, God offers stability. The righteous will not "totter" (see above on v. 3; see also "be moved"/"shake"/"fall"/"slipped" in Pss 13:5; 16:8; 17:4; 62:2, 6). The correlate occurs in v. 23, which recalls v. 15. Again, the personal pronoun "you" is emphatic; *God* will deal with the wicked, who are here described as "bloodthirsty" (see Pss 5:6; 26:9; 59:2; 139:19). "Treachery" represents the same Hebrew word as "fraud" in v. 11. The psalmist's difficult experience has clearly shown that human beings cannot be trusted, but it apparently has served to solidify the psalmist's trust in God (see Pss 4:5; 13:5; Introduction). Life and future belong with God.

REFLECTIONS

1. In a notable sermon, preached shortly after the death of his son, William Sloan Coffin pointed to the impossibility of using the Bible to explain tragedies: "As the grief that once seemed unbearable begins to turn now to bearable sorrow the truths in the 'right' biblical passages are beginning, once again, to take hold: 'Cast thy burden upon the LORD and he shall strengthen thee.' "[224]

Coffin's citation of v. 22a as a "right" biblical passage is testimony to the ability of Psalm 55 to function as a powerful prayer and affirmation of faith, regardless of the exact situation in which it originated and was used. In other words, human life is lived now as it was then, amid persistent opposition. Whatever the cause—whatever or whoever the enemy happens to be—we know from experience the realities of anguish, death, fear, horror, violence, oppression, betrayal. It is not surprising that 1 Pet 5:7 quotes v. 22a as the author exhorts those who are suffering (see 1 Pet 4:13, 19; 5:10).

2. Indeed, the complaint sections at several points sound strikingly contemporary. For instance, our cities are still full of violence and strife (v. 9). As Psalm 55 suggests, too, the generally chaotic conditions of our society are reflected in our difficulty in maintaining personal relationships. The experience of personal betrayal is not new, but it is particularly prevalent among us (see Luke 22:48). Psalm 55 may help us to acknowledge that reality and begin to

---

224. Quoted in Thomas G. Long, "Preaching About Suffering," *Journal for Preachers* 15/2 (Lent 1992) 14.

PSALM 55:1-23 REFLECTIONS

address it. Pastor Stephen P. McCutchan made this suggestion as he narrated the thoughts of a recently betrayed spouse who entered the Sunday service as the congregation was "invited to pray Psalm 55 slowly, pausing after each verse as the choir intoned the refrain, 'Cast your burden on the Lord, and God will sustain you.' " The woman's thoughts in part are as follows:

> How could the psalmist have known so long ago the deep anger that betrayal generates? How could the psalmist have understood that unless such anger is released to God, it will surely destroy either victim or victimizer? And now the congregation knew too. The unbearable pain was being borne by a larger body than hers. She felt the deeper anger that she had wrestled with alone and the relief that it was no longer hers alone.

McCutchan points out that psalms like this one encourage us to acknowledge our own pain and that of others and thus "to emerge from isolation." If they were used regularly in worship, "it might encourage people to consider worship as the appropriate place to cast their burden upon the Lord."[225] In short, Psalm 55 can still function as a faithful prayer and as a powerful profession of the faith that the sustaining power of God is ultimately greater than the power of human sin and its painful effects.

225. Stephen P. McCutchan, "A Parable in Liturgy," *Reformed Liturgy and Music* 26 (Summer 1992) 139-40.

PSALM 56:1-13, IN GOD I TRUST

NIV

Psalm 56

For the director of music. To ˻the tune of˼ "A Dove on Distant Oaks." Of David. A *miktam.*[a] When the Philistines had seized him in Gath.

[1]Be merciful to me, O God, for men hotly
    pursue me;
  all day long they press their attack.
[2]My slanderers pursue me all day long;
  many are attacking me in their pride.

[3]When I am afraid,
  I will trust in you.
[4]In God, whose word I praise,
  in God I trust; I will not be afraid.
  What can mortal man do to me?

[5]All day long they twist my words;
  they are always plotting to harm me.
[6]They conspire, they lurk,
  they watch my steps,
  eager to take my life.
[7]On no account let them escape;
  in your anger, O God, bring down the
    nations.

a Title: Probably a literary or musical term

NRSV

Psalm 56

To the leader: according to The Dove on Far-off Terebinths. Of David. A Miktam, when the Philistines seized him in Gath.

[1] Be gracious to me, O God, for people
    trample on me;
  all day long foes oppress me;
[2] my enemies trample on me all day long,
  for many fight against me.
O Most High, [3]when I am afraid,
  I put my trust in you.
[4] In God, whose word I praise,
  in God I trust; I am not afraid;
  what can flesh do to me?

[5] All day long they seek to injure my cause;
  all their thoughts are against me for evil.
[6] They stir up strife, they lurk,
  they watch my steps.
As they hoped to have my life,
[7] so repay[a] them for their crime;
  in wrath cast down the peoples, O God!

a Cn: Heb *rescue*

NIV

⁸Record my lament;
      list my tears on your scroll^a—
      are they not in your record?

⁹Then my enemies will turn back
      when I call for help.
      By this I will know that God is for me.
¹⁰In God, whose word I praise,
      in the LORD, whose word I praise—
¹¹in God I trust; I will not be afraid.
      What can man do to me?

¹²I am under vows to you, O God;
      I will present my thank offerings to you.
¹³For you have delivered me^b from death
      and my feet from stumbling,
      that I may walk before God
      in the light of life.^c

a8 Or / put my tears in your wineskin   b13 Or my soul   c13 Or the land of the living

NRSV

⁸ You have kept count of my tossings;
      put my tears in your bottle.
      Are they not in your record?
⁹ Then my enemies will retreat
      in the day when I call.
      This I know, that^a God is for me.
¹⁰ In God, whose word I praise,
      in the LORD, whose word I praise,
¹¹ in God I trust; I am not afraid.
      What can a mere mortal do to me?

¹² My vows to you I must perform, O God;
      I will render thank offerings to you.
¹³ For you have delivered my soul from death,
      and my feet from falling,
      so that I may walk before God
      in the light of life.

a Or because

COMMENTARY

While v. 13 suggests that Psalm 56 could be viewed as a song of thanksgiving that looks back upon and narrates former distress, it is more likely that the psalm is a prayer for help or an individual lament/complaint. Such prayers regularly turn to expressions of trust and praise, thus making it difficult to determine whether deliverance has occurred or is anticipated. This ambiguity has theological significance (see Commentary on Psalm 54). In any case, it is clear that expressions of trust predominate in Psalm 56 (vv. 3-4, 8-11). These expressions follow sections of petition and complaint (vv. 1-2, 5-8), and the psalm concludes with the promise to make a thank offering in response to deliverance (vv. 12-13).

The superscription connects the psalm with David's presence in Gath (see 1 Sam 21:10-14). As with similar superscriptions, it is likely that this one should be taken illustratively rather than historically, and it is certain that the prayer was used in various settings. The titles in the LXX and the Targum, for instance, offer the setting as being "for the people far removed from the sanctuary." In other words, like many other prayers in the psalter, Psalm 56 would have served as an appro-priate communal prayer in the exilic and post-exilic eras. Some scholars suggest that it may have been used by any persecuted person who sought comfort and found encouragement by entrusting her or his life to God. As with other prayers, the inability to specify the origin and setting of Psalm 56 suggests its adaptability to a variety of situations. Illustrative of the flexibility of the prayer is Prothero's report that during the English civil war, an imprisoned Charles I used Ps 56:1-2 to answer the taunts of his captors, whose insults in turn were drawn from Ps 52:1.[226] While this may not be the most edifying illustration, it demonstrates the dynamic nature of the prayers in the psalter.

The opening petition is a frequent one in Psalms (see Pss 4:1; 6:2), as is the situation of opposition by enemies. As usual, the precise nature of the circumstances is unclear. The Hebrew root that the NIV translates "attack"/"attacking" (לחם lāḥam, vv. 1-2) suggests a military setting. The repeated word "trample" (שאף šā'ap, vv. 1-2), on the other hand, could indicate socioeconomic

226. Rowland E. Prothero, *The Psalms in Human Life and Experience* (New York: E. P. Dutton, 1903) 183.

abuse (see Ps 57:3; Amos 2:7; 8:4), and the word "oppress" (לחץ *lāḥaṣ*, v. 1) could indicate either (see Exod 3:9; 22:21; 23:9; Judg 2:18; 4:3; Ps 106:42; Amos 6:14). The military imagery is probably metaphorical, but in any case, the vocabulary is open-ended enough to be appropriate in a variety of settings. As a comparison of the NIV with the NRSV suggests, the textual problem at the end of v. 2 has been approached differently. The syntax is difficult. The last word in v. 2 is a noun that means "height" (מרום *mārôm*). While the NIV construes its grammatical function as an adverb and gives it a figurative sense, the NRSV interprets it as a reference to God and suggests that it belongs to the beginning of the next line, where it functions as a vocative.

The exact situation behind the complaint is no clearer in vv. 5-7. Whereas petition led to complaint in vv. 1-2, the complaint in vv. 5-6 culminates in petition in v. 7, which would be particularly appropriate as a communal prayer. Whatever the problem is, it is a constant one, as the repeated phrase "all day long" indicates (vv. 1-2, 5). As the NIV suggests, the noun in v. 5*a* is literally "words" (דברים *dĕbārîm*), but the verb usually means "to hurt," "to grieve" and is unusual in Psalms (see Ps 78:40). More typical is the complaint in v. 6 about the enemies' "thoughts" or "plotting" (see "devise," "plan," "conceive," or "plot" in Pss 10:2; 21:11; 35:4, 20; 36:3; 52:2; 140:2, 4 NRSV; in 140:2, the verb the NRSV translates as "stir up strife" in v. 6 also occurs). Verse 6 suggests the vigilance with which the enemies seek to destroy the psalmist's life ("lurk" occurs in Ps 10:8; see "watch" in the superscription of Psalm 59 and in 71:10). The word "hoped" (קוה *qāwâ*) in v. 6*c* is elsewhere a theologically significant word that usually indicates trust in and reliance upon God (see "wait [for]" in Pss 25:3, 5, 21; 27:14; 37:34; 40:1 NRSV). Whereas the faithful place their hope in God, the psalmist's opponents find hope only in exploiting other people. Thus v. 7 is not so much a request for revenge as it is a plea that God set things right (see Ps 55:23; see also Commentary on Psalm 54).

What is clear about the opposition described in vv. 1-2, 5-7 is that it evokes fear in the psalmist (see "afraid" in vv. 3-4, 11). In contrast to the enemies, who seek security in taking advantage of others, the psalmist trusts God. Indeed, each occurrence of the word "afraid" (ירא *yārē'*) is accompanied by the word "trust" (בטח *bāṭaḥ*), effectively and emphatically contrasting these two possible responses to threat (see Pss 4:5; 13:5; Introduction). The arrangement of the key terms in vv. 3-4 is chiastic (see Introduction): "afraid"/"trust"/"word"/"trust"/"not afraid." The movement is from fear to being unafraid, and it is a movement that takes place structurally and existentially through trust, with the focal point being God's word. The psalmist's praising of God's word here is unique in the OT, but it is clearly important, as the repetition in v. 10 indicates. The "word" may consist of the whole body of tradition concerning God's relationship with God's people—that is, what we would call Scripture. More specifically, however, it seems to refer to the "word" delivered elsewhere in situations of distress: "Do not fear, for I am with you" (Isa 41:10 NRSV; see also Exod 14:13; Josh 10:25; Ps 49:16; Isa 40:9; 41:13-14; 43:5; Jer 30:10).

In other words, the psalmist professes that true security is a divine gift rather than a human achievement. The fundamental mistake of the wicked is their belief that they can make it on their own, that they can find hope in exploiting others (v. 6; see Isa 47:10). The psalmist knows better. Because security is ultimately a gift from God, no human action can take it away. This affirmation is made by means of the similar questions (vv. 4, 11) that conclude the two expressions of trust (vv. 3-4, 8-11). In a sense, the psalmist knows all too well what others can "do to me"—trample, oppress, fight, plot, conspire, lurk (vv. 1-2, 5-6). But in a deeper sense, the psalmist knows that her or his life is known by God (v. 8, reading the verb in v. 8*a* with the NRSV as an indicative, the subject of which is an emphatic *you*; on "tears," see Ps 6:6; on God's keeping a "record," see Ps 40:7). And the psalmist knows "that God is for me" (v. 9). Essentially the same affirmation occurs in Ps 118:6 (NIV, "with me"; NRSV, "on my side"; see also 118:7), where it is accompanied by the same question as in vv. 4, 11 and followed by an affirmation of the proper object of human trust—God, not humans, even the most powerful humans (118:8-9).

The fact that the psalmist trusts God makes irrelevant the scholarly discussion of whether deliverance from the current distress has already occurred (see v. 13; see Commentary on Psalm 54). Even if it has, a new threat is inevitably on the horizon. The point is that, regardless of outward circumstances, the psalmist has been transformed by trust. While current or future opposition may cause fear, the psalmist will always be able to say, "I will not be afraid" (vv. 4, 11). This ability is not an act of human bravery or courage but a result of the conviction that the life God offers is beyond the reach of human threat (vv. 4, 11). Thus, in the face of every threat, the psalmist will be able to live with gratitude (v. 12; see also Pss 50:14, 23; 107:22; 116:17). To "walk before God" (v. 13), or more literally, "to the face of God," means an unfading source of light (see Job 33:30; see "light" in Pss 4:6; 27:1; 43:3; 89:15) and life (see Pss 116:8-9; 36:9).

REFLECTIONS

Psychologists and theologians alike tell us that we must believe in something. A perennial human question is not *whether* we shall trust but *what* or *whom* we shall trust. It is this question that Psalm 56 helps us to address. A persistent temptation, of course, is to trust ourselves, our abilities or achievements, our resources, as do the psalmist's opponents (see also Pss 49:5-6; 52:7-8; 62:10; Isa 47:10). In this regard, it is particularly significant that the word "hoped" (v. 6) is used to summarize the purposes of the enemy. They stake their lives and futures on what *they* can do at the expense of other people; they trust themselves. In contrast, the psalmist trusts God and God's promises.

Psalm 56 does not suggest that God suddenly or even eventually removes the conditions that cause the psalmist to be afraid. What it and the other prayers teach us is that human life is always lived under threat, in the midst of opposition, either from ourselves or from others or from some external circumstance. The good news, however, is that because God is for us (see v. 9), we can say with the psalmist, "I am not afraid" (vv. 4, 11). Long before Franklin D. Roosevelt said it, and in a far more profound sense, the psalmist knew that the only thing to fear is fear itself.

The psalmist's affirmation of a trust that moves the self from "afraid" to "not afraid" suggests that the opposite of faith is not so much doubt as it is fear. Jesus seemed to reinforce this conclusion when he said to Jairus in a moment of great distress, "Do not fear, only believe" (Mark 5:36 NRSV). Such a response is possible, according to Psalm 56, because we both are known by God (v. 8) and know that God is for us. Again, Jesus also encouraged his followers not to fear for the same reason: God knows, and God cares (see Luke 12:4-7; see also Reflections on Psalm 27).

The NT writers saw and heard in the life, death, and resurrection of Jesus the same good news proclaimed by Psalm 56. In considering that human life is always lived amid opposition—"the sufferings of this present time" (Rom 8:18 NRSV)—the apostle Paul affirmed, "If God is for us, who can be against us?" (Rom 8:31 NIV). To be sure, Paul was aware of and had experienced the things that human enemies can do (see Rom 8:35), but he was convinced that nothing could separate us from God (Rom 8:38-39). Such is the trust that enables us not to be afraid.

The final phrase of Psalm 56 cannot help reminding Christian readers of Jesus' words in John 8:12, "I am the light of the world. Whoever follows me will never walk in darkness but will have the light of life" (NRSV). Again, Jesus did not promise his followers a life free of threat (see John 15:18-25; 16:33; 17:14-15), but he did promise a peace greater than the world can give, a peace that means ultimately living unafraid (see John 14:27). This peace is the real subject of Psalm 56.

PSALM 57:1-11, BE EXALTED, O GOD, ABOVE THE HEAVENS

NIV

Psalm 57

For the director of music. ⌊To the tune of⌋ "Do Not Destroy." Of David. A *miktam.*[a] When he had fled from Saul into the cave.

[1]Have mercy on me, O God, have mercy on me,
    for in you my soul takes refuge.
I will take refuge in the shadow of your wings
    until the disaster has passed.
[2]I cry out to God Most High,
    to God, who fulfills ⌊his purpose⌋ for me.
[3]He sends from heaven and saves me,
    rebuking those who hotly pursue me; *Selah*
    God sends his love and his faithfulness.

[4]I am in the midst of lions;
    I lie among ravenous beasts—
men whose teeth are spears and arrows,
    whose tongues are sharp swords.

[5]Be exalted, O God, above the heavens;
    let your glory be over all the earth.

[6]They spread a net for my feet—
    I was bowed down in distress.
They dug a pit in my path—
    but they have fallen into it
        themselves.   *Selah*

[7]My heart is steadfast, O God,
    my heart is steadfast;
    I will sing and make music.
[8]Awake, my soul!
    Awake, harp and lyre!
    I will awaken the dawn.

[9]I will praise you, O Lord, among the nations;
    I will sing of you among the peoples.
[10]For great is your love, reaching to the
        heavens;
    your faithfulness reaches to the skies.

[11]Be exalted, O God, above the heavens;
    let your glory be over all the earth.

[a] Title: Probably a literary or musical term

NRSV

Psalm 57

To the leader: Do Not Destroy. Of David. A Miktam, when he fled from Saul, in the cave.

[1] Be merciful to me, O God, be merciful to me,
    for in you my soul takes refuge;
    in the shadow of your wings I will take refuge,
    until the destroying storms pass by.
[2] I cry to God Most High,
    to God who fulfills his purpose for me.
[3] He will send from heaven and save me,
    he will put to shame those who trample
        on me.   *Selah*
    God will send forth his steadfast love and
        his faithfulness.

[4] I lie down among lions
    that greedily devour[a] human prey;
    their teeth are spears and arrows,
    their tongues sharp swords.

[5] Be exalted, O God, above the heavens.
    Let your glory be over all the earth.

[6] They set a net for my steps;
    my soul was bowed down.
They dug a pit in my path,
    but they have fallen into it themselves.
                Selah

[7] My heart is steadfast, O God,
    my heart is steadfast.
I will sing and make melody.
[8]   Awake, my soul!
Awake, O harp and lyre!
    I will awake the dawn.
[9] I will give thanks to you, O Lord, among
        the peoples;
    I will sing praises to you among the nations.
[10] For your steadfast love is as high as the heavens;
    your faithfulness extends to the clouds.

[11] Be exalted, O God, above the heavens.
    Let your glory be over all the earth.

[a] Cn: Heb *are aflame for*

COMMENTARY

Like Psalm 56, Psalm 57 is a prayer for help or an individual complaint/lament, in which the element of trust is prominent. Immediately following the opening petition (v. 1a), the psalmist expresses trust in God (vv. 1b-3). The complaint is voiced in vv. 4 and 6, separated by the first occurrence of the refrain, which also concludes the psalm (vv. 5, 11). Verses 7-10 begin with a statement of loyalty (v. 7ab), continue with a promise to praise God (vv. 7c-9), and conclude with an expression of trust (v. 10) that features the same attributes of God as in v. 3: steadfast love and faithfulness.

The superscription of Psalm 57 associates the prayer with a crisis in David's life (see 1 Sam 22:1; 24:3). As with other such superscriptions (see Psalms 3; 51; 56; Introduction), this one should be taken illustratively rather than historically. The actual circumstances of the origin and use of Psalm 57 are unknown. Relying primarily on v. 4, several scholars suggest that this psalm may originally have been the prayer of a falsely accused person who sought asylum in the Temple (see v. 1; see also Psalms 5; 7; Introduction). Others detect evidence for the use of Psalm 57 in a night vigil (see v. 8; see also Psalm 17). Gerstenberger concludes more generally that Psalm 57 was probably "used in a communal situation such as synagogal worship for the suffering person."[227] As with other prayers, the very variety of proposals is indicative of the adaptability of Psalm 57 and its ability to function in a variety of settings.

57:1-3. Although the NRSV obscures it, this psalm begins with the same petition as does Psalm 56 (see also Pss 4:1; 6:2); even more quickly than Psalm 56, Psalm 57 moves to an expression of trust. Although the word "trust" (בטח *bāṭaḥ*) is not used, the repeated term "refuge" (חסה *ḥsh*) clearly communicates this concept (see Commentary on Psalm 2; see also 2:12; 7:1; Introduction). That is, the psalmist depends on God for life and future. The phrase "shadow of your wings" may be an allusion to the winged creatures who at-

tended the ark, God's earthly throne, and who elsewhere announce a message similar to the refrain of Ps 57:5, 11 (see Isa 6:1-3). This may indicate an original temple setting, but it is also possible that the phrase is purely metaphorical (see Pss 17:8; 36:7; 63:7). At any rate, the psalmist trusts that his or her life is secure with God (v. 2; see also Ps 138:8, where the same affirmation occurs, as here, in the context of a celebration of God's steadfast love, faithfulness, glory, and saving power). God will "save" (v. 3; see Pss 3:7; 6:4; 7:1) the psalmist from the enemy (see Ps 56:1-2). The repetition of "send" in v. 3 suggests that God's saving action is a manifestation of God's essential character and purpose for humanity (see Exod 34:6-7; Introduction; "steadfast love" and "faithfulness" are also paired in v. 10; Pss 25:10; 40:10-11; 61:7; 85:10; 89:14; 115:1; 138:2). The psalmist affirms, in effect, that the love of God is the most powerful force in the universe. The enemies may attempt to enact their purposes, which include opposition to the psalmist, but God's purposes will prevail.

57:4-6. The actual complaint comes in vv. 4 and 6. It is not unusual that the enemies are described as ravenous beasts (v. 4; see Pss 7:2; 10:9; 17:12; 22:12-13, 16, 20-21; 34:10; 35:17; 58:6; 59:6-7, 14-15; 68:30; 91:13). The references to weapons reinforce their violent purposes (see Pss 11:2; 64:3; 91:5) in preparation for v. 6, where the enemies have "set a net" (see Pss 9:15; 10:9; 25:15; 140:5; cf. Lam 1:13) and have "dug a pit" (see Pss 7:15; 9:15; 119:85; Jer 18:22) in order that the psalmist be "bowed down" (see Pss 145:14; 146:8). Unexpectedly, the first occurrence of the refrain interrupts the complaint. The effect is to set the appeal to God, which at least implicitly is an affirmation of God's sovereignty (see the NIV's "exalt" in Exod 15:2; Pss 99:5, 9; 145:1 and "glory" in Pss 24:7-10; 29:1-3, 9; 96:3, 7; 97:6; 145:11, both of which occur in the context of the proclamation of God's reign), in the midst of a section that implies the sovereignty of the wicked. In short, as is always the case in the psalter and in Scripture as a whole, the sovereignty of God is asserted amid opposition. The proclamation is eschatological and calls for a

227. Erhard S. Gerstenberger, *Psalms, Part 1, with an Introduction to Cultic Poetry,* Forms of the OT Literature 14 (Grand Rapids: Eerdmans, 1988) 232.

decision (see Commentary on Psalm 2; Introduction).

57:7-11. The psalmist's decision is clear. In the midst of opposition, the psalmist takes a stand with God. As was the opening petition, so the psalmist's complaint is followed by an expression of trust (vv. 7-10), which lends the final occurrence of the refrain an added dimension (v. 11; vv. 7-11 occur in nearly identical form in Ps 108:1-5). The repetition in v. 7*ab* emphasizes the psalmist's loyalty to God; the decision is firm (cf. Ps 112:8, where the same idea is expressed with different words; cf. also Ps 78:37). Trust is accompanied by praise (v. 7*c*), to which the psalmist poetically summons his or her own self (v. 8*a*, lit., "my glory"; see "soul" in Pss 7:5; 16:9; 30:12 NRSV) as well as the instruments of praise (v. 8*b*; see also Ps 33:2). The phrase "awake the dawn" could suggest several things. It may express simply the psalmist's eagerness and intent to get an early start in praising God. Such eagerness may have been related to the belief that a new day promises God's help (see Pss 46:5; 59:16; 90:14; 143:8). It is also possible that v. 8*c* is an allusion to a beneficent Canaanite god "Dawn" (see Isa 14:12).

In any case, one need not be able to state precisely what v. 8*c* means in order to appreciate its lyric quality. Like all good poetry, it evokes a variety of images and possibilities.

In any case, it is clear from v. 9 that the psalmist intends his or her praise to be heard not only by God but also by others, perhaps precisely by those who represented the threat described in vv. 3-4, 6. Recalling v. 3, v. 10 again asserts that God's loving purposes pervade the cosmos (see Ps 36:5), providing a fitting introduction to the refrain in v. 11. Coming immediately after the psalmist's expression of trust and intent to praise, the refrain serves this time to emphasize the psalmist's recognition of God's cosmic sovereignty (note that v. 11 represents the fourth occurrence of "heaven[s]"; see vv. 3, 5, 10). Opposition or no opposition, the psalmist already experiences the new world of God's rule. Such a conclusion renders moot the scholarly debate about whether Psalm 57 anticipates deliverance or celebrates a deliverance that has already occurred (see Commentary on Psalms 54; 56). In either case, the psalmist finds security by entrusting his or her life to God.

REFLECTIONS

Psalm 57 articulates the remarkable conviction that God's steadfast love and faithfulness are the pervasive, fundamental realities in the universe (vv. 3, 10; see Commentary on Psalms 19; 36). It would have been easy for the psalmist to conclude otherwise (vv. 1, 3*b*, 4, 6). Similarly, it would be easy for us to conclude otherwise as we look out upon a world full of hatred and hostility and that seems bent on destroying itself.

But this is precisely the reason why Psalm 57 is such a crucial contemporary witness. It is a reminder that the rule of God has always been experienced and proclaimed amid opposition. The clearest reminder of this reality for Christians, of course, is the cross of Jesus Christ. Not surprisingly, Jesus taught his disciples both to proclaim the reign of God—"thine is the kingdom"—and to continue to pray for its coming—"thy kingdom come." In short, just as the psalmist is *"one who simultaneously possesses and yet expects,"*[228] so also are the followers of Jesus.

Indeed, the simultaneity of possession and expectation creates the possibility for Christians to be realistic about the world without becoming totally pessimistic. Because we trust that God ultimately rules the world and that God's purposes for us will finally be fulfilled (vv. 2-3, 5, 10-11), we dare to perceive the mystery of love where others can see only the misery of life. Because we trust that love is the basic reality in the universe, we are able in the face of evil, sin, and death not just to sigh resignedly but to sing rousingly enough to wake the dawn.

228. Artur Weiser, *The Psalms,* OTL, trans. H. Hartwell (Philadelphia: Westminster, 1962) 428.

PSALM 58:1-11, THERE IS A GOD WHO ESTABLISHES JUSTICE

NIV

Psalm 58

For the director of music. ⌊To the tune of⌋ "Do Not Destroy." Of David. A *miktam.*[a]

[1] Do you rulers indeed speak justly?
    Do you judge uprightly among men?
[2] No, in your heart you devise injustice,
    and your hands mete out violence on the earth.
[3] Even from birth the wicked go astray;
    from the womb they are wayward and speak lies.
[4] Their venom is like the venom of a snake,
    like that of a cobra that has stopped its ears,
[5] that will not heed the tune of the charmer,
    however skillful the enchanter may be.
[6] Break the teeth in their mouths, O God;
    tear out, O LORD, the fangs of the lions!
[7] Let them vanish like water that flows away;
    when they draw the bow, let their arrows be blunted.
[8] Like a slug melting away as it moves along,
    like a stillborn child, may they not see the sun.
[9] Before your pots can feel ⌊the heat of⌋ the thorns—
    whether they be green or dry—the wicked will be swept away.[b]
[10] The righteous will be glad when they are avenged,
    when they bathe their feet in the blood of the wicked.
[11] Then men will say,
    "Surely the righteous still are rewarded;
    surely there is a God who judges the earth."

[a] Title: Probably a literary or musical term   [b]9 The meaning of the Hebrew for this verse is uncertain.

NRSV

Psalm 58

To the leader: Do Not Destroy. Of David. A Miktam.

[1] Do you indeed decree what is right, you gods?[a]
    Do you judge people fairly?
[2] No, in your hearts you devise wrongs;
    your hands deal out violence on earth.

[3] The wicked go astray from the womb;
    they err from their birth, speaking lies.
[4] They have venom like the venom of a serpent,
    like the deaf adder that stops its ear,
[5] so that it does not hear the voice of charmers
    or of the cunning enchanter.

[6] O God, break the teeth in their mouths;
    tear out the fangs of the young lions, O LORD!
[7] Let them vanish like water that runs away;
    like grass let them be trodden down[b] and wither.
[8] Let them be like the snail that dissolves into slime;
    like the untimely birth that never sees the sun.
[9] Sooner than your pots can feel the heat of thorns,
    whether green or ablaze, may he sweep them away!

[10] The righteous will rejoice when they see vengeance done;
    they will bathe their feet in the blood of the wicked.
[11] People will say, "Surely there is a reward for the righteous;
    surely there is a God who judges on earth."

[a] Or *mighty lords*   [b] Cn: Meaning of Heb uncertain

COMMENTARY

Like the two immediately preceding Psalms, Psalm 58 expresses the conviction that God ultimately rules the world and that God's purposes will prevail (see vv. 10-11). Although not entirely unique, Psalm 58 is unusual in that it begins by directly addressing the perpetrators of evil rather than God (vv. 1-2). Verse 3 shifts to a third-person description of the wicked that continues through v. 5. Verses 6-9 are a prayer for justice, and vv. 10-11 articulate the assurance that justice will be done. Because of its unusual structure, Psalm 58 has been categorized in diverse ways. In view of the complaint (vv. 3-5) and prayer (vv. 6-9), it is possible to view this psalm as a modified prayer for help or as an individual or communal lament/complaint. Some scholars suggest, however, that Psalm 58 should be seen as a prophetic judgment speech (see vv. 1-2), perhaps delivered by a cultic prophet and aimed at oppressing nations, or as communal instruction, which originated among disaffected elements in the post-exilic community and was directed at unjust community leaders. Certainty is impossible.

58:1-2. Certainty is also elusive in v. 1 in the attempt to identify precisely the apparent addressee. The meaning of the Hebrew word אֵלֶם (*'ēlem*) is uncertain. It may mean "silence" or "when you speak, justice is silent."[229] This translation leaves the identity of the addressee unsettled. Most translations emend the word slightly and construe it as a vocative. The identity of the addressee, though, is still unsettled, because the emendation involved can mean either "gods" or "mighty ones," including human beings. The NRSV and the NIV represent the two most frequently adopted solutions. The NIV's translation is probably to be preferred, since v. 3 clearly has human beings in view and since Psalm 52 also begins by addressing a wicked, powerful human being (the NRSV's "mighty one" in Ps 52:1 is a different Hebrew word [גִּבּוֹר *gibbôr*] that clearly designates a human being). If the NRSV's translation is correct, then Psalm 58 has a clearer affinity with Psalm 82, in which God accuses the gods of injustice.

229. See Robert G. Bratcher and William D. Reyburn, *A Translator's Handbook on the Book of Psalms* (New York: United Bible Societies, 1991) 516; the authors present seven major proposals for construing v. 1.

In any case, the question in v. 1 has to do with whether righteousness and justice are being done. These concepts are frequently paired in the speeches of the prophets, who did not hesitate to call to account the leaders of their nation and of other nations as well (see Amos 5:7, 24; Mic 3:1, 8-9). The enthronement psalms indicate that righteousness and justice are the hallmarks of God's reign (see Pss 96:13; 98:9; the NRSV's "fairly" in v. 1 also occurs in Pss 96:10; 98:9, where it is rendered as "equity"), and Ps 58:1 suggests that they should characterize human governance as well. But v. 2 indicates that they do not. Instead, there are "wrongs" (see Pss 7:3; 37:1; 43:1, "unjust"; 53:2, "abominable acts"; 82:2, "unjustly") and "violence" (see Pss 7:16; 11:5; 27:12; 55:9; 73:6; Jer 6:7; 20:8; Amos 3:10; 6:3; Mic 6:12). In short, the governance of the wicked (see vv. 3-5) is a reign of terror, the antithesis of the reign of God. Despite the reality of wickedness, the psalmist stakes his or her life and future on the reality of God's rule, the affirmation of which climactically concludes Psalm 58 (vv. 10-11; note the recurrence of the concepts of righteousness and justice in v. 11).

58:3-5. It is likely that the addressees in vv. 1-2 are human beings, and they are designated "wicked" in v. 3. Whereas persons who look to God for help are aware of God's presence "from birth" and "from the womb" (see Ps 22:10), the wicked have never known God, according to the psalmist. The hyperbole is intensified as the psalmist claims that the wicked are, in effect, born liars (see "lies" in Pss 4:2; 5:6). Verses 4-5 indicate that these persons' incorrigible behavior has destructive consequences (see Ps 140:3; Jer 8:17).

58:6-9. The hyperbolic intensity continues in these verses as the psalmist turns to God. Lest the prayer sound unnecessarily brutal, one must realize that the "teeth" (v. 6) of the wicked represent their weapons, the means by which they carry out their violence (v. 2) and destruction (see Pss 3:7; 57:4; 124:6). As in Ps 57:4 (although a different Hebrew word is used here), the enemies are portrayed as ravening lions. The prayer in v. 6 is not a request for personal revenge but a petition for protection. In effect, it is a prayer for the justice and righteousness that v. 1 has suggested are God's will, and this is confirmed by v. 11. There are problems with the vocabulary of vv. 7-9 (cf. v. 7b NIV and NRSV), but it is clear enough that the images in these verses communicate the heart of the matter; the psalmist prays for the disappearance of all that opposes God's will for human life. The request is indicative of the psalmist's loyalty to God and God's ways, and it is in keeping with Ps 1:4-6 and its affirmation that wickedness will not endure.

58:10-11. Indeed, the psalmist moves from the prayer of vv. 6-9 to precisely this affirmation. The main characters are the same as in Ps 1:4-6: the righteous, the wicked, and God. Verses 10-11 must be heard in close relationship to vv. 1-2. Verse 10 affirms that the apparent sovereignty of the wicked (vv. 1-2) will be put to an end. Thus "violence on earth" (v. 2) will be replaced by the work of a God "who establishes justice on earth" (v. 11 author's trans.). As the repetition of "earth" suggests, the real issue is this: Who rules the world? For the wicked, they themselves are the only authority (see Pss 3:2; 10:4, 11; 73:11); but v. 11 asserts God's rule. The role of judging or establishing justice is elsewhere closely associated with God's reign (see Pss 9:7-8; 11:4-7; 96:13; 98:9). The imagery of v. 10b is harsh, but it is a typical ancient Near Eastern symbol for defeat of oppressors (see Deut 32:42-43; Ps 68:23), and it is an apt reminder that oppressors do not simply give up without a fight. The establishment of justice for the oppressed means the experience of judgment for the oppressors—the wicked. As suggested above concerning v. 6, the issue is not personal revenge. As Mays points out: "The notion of 'vengeance' (v. 10) is a feature of the vision of God as ruler. The term does not mean vindictive revenge; it refers to an action to do justice and restore order where the regular and responsible institutions of justice have failed."[230]

It is revealing, too, that the righteous do not carry out the vengeance but are witnesses to it. Vengeance belongs to God (see Deut 32:35; Ps 94:1), not to humans (see Lev 19:18). The word "reward" (פְּרִי *pĕrî*, v. 11) is literally "fruit"; thus living in dependence upon God will ultimately bear fruit (see Ps 1:3). As Mays suggests, the reward of the righteous is "not some sort of earned payoff, but the knowledge of the vindication of God's reign in spite of the power and arrogance of injustice."[231]

230. James L. Mays, *Psalms,* Interpretation (Louisville: John Knox, 1994) 212.
231. Ibid., 212.

REFLECTIONS

1. As is the case throughout the book of Psalms and throughout the Bible, the proclamation of God's reign is eschatological; it is proclaimed amid circumstances that seem to deny it—the power of the wicked (vv. 1-2; see Commentary on Psalm 2; Introduction). It was no different for Jesus. The "reward" for his proclamation of God's reign was a cross, and he promised his followers the same (see Mark 8:34). Yet, Jesus taught that to live in dependence upon God, which is the essence of being righteous (see Commentary on Psalm 1), is the fullest possible experience of life (see Mark 8:35). In short, the reward of the righteous is living, in dependence upon God, the life that God intends. To assert that "there is a God who establishes justice on earth" (v. 11 author's trans.) is to profess, in essence, that right makes might. To be sure, worldly wisdom is just the opposite—might makes right. But the righteous know with the apostle Paul that "God's weakness is stronger than human strength" (1 Cor 1:25 NRSV). So the righteous dare to assert in the face of the powers of evil (vv. 1-2) that God rules the world (vv. 10-11).

What the righteous assert, they also pray for, and Jesus taught his disciples to pray in the same way. Although it may sound offensive at first hearing, the prayer for justice in vv. 6-9 is, in essence, what Christians pray in the Lord's prayer: "thy will be done on earth as it is in heaven . . . deliver us from evil." Verses 6-9 are likely to sound less offensive when one realizes that the psalmist does not enact revenge but submits the complaint to God for action.

2. Other dimensions of vv. 6-9 are also quite positive. As Tate points out: "The imprecatory elements in the psalms are also evocative, challenging the reader to identify with oppressed and suffering people, even though the reader may be quite comfortable. . . . The language of these psalms evokes in us an awareness of the terrible wickedness that is in the world."[232] In other words, Psalm 58 can serve to remind us that our world is every bit as violent and unjust as that of ancient Israel. It may also serve to remind us that we bear some responsibility for the state of the world. Or, as Tate puts it: "The imprecatory psalms are likely to convict us of our own guilt. When we ask for divine judgment on our enemies, we are liable to an identity switch: We are often the enemies!"[233] Especially if wickedness in the psalms is understood essentially as self-centeredness and self-sufficiency (see Commentary on Psalm 1), we are all in danger of standing among the wicked.

Psalm 58 may be particularly relevant in view of Kraus's comment: "The psalmsinger suffers under a corrupt world order."[234] So do we; in some cases, perhaps, we must admit that we are the beneficiaries of a corrupt world order. In either case, the conviction that God will ultimately establish justice on earth is of greatest consequence. It calls us simultaneously to both joy and repentance, as did Jesus (see Mark 1:14-15).

232. Marvin E. Tate, *Psalms 51–100,* WBC 20 (Dallas: Word, 1990) 89.
233. Ibid., 90.
234. H.-J. Kraus, *Psalms 1–59: A Commentary,* trans. H. C. Oswald (Minneapolis: Augsburg, 1988) 537.

PSALM 59:1-17, THE GOD WHO SHOWS ME STEADFAST LOVE

NIV

Psalm 59

For the director of music. ⌊To the tune of⌋ "Do Not Destroy." Of David. A *miktam.*[a] When Saul had sent men to watch David's house in order to kill him.

¹Deliver me from my enemies, O God;
    protect me from those who rise up against
        me.
²Deliver me from evildoers
    and save me from bloodthirsty men.

³See how they lie in wait for me!
    Fierce men conspire against me
    for no offense or sin of mine, O LORD.
⁴I have done no wrong, yet they are ready to
        attack me.
    Arise to help me; look on my plight!
⁵O LORD God Almighty, the God of Israel,
    rouse yourself to punish all the nations;
    show no mercy to wicked traitors.   *Selah*

a Title: Probably a literary or musical term

NRSV

Psalm 59

To the leader: Do Not Destroy. Of David. A Miktam, when Saul ordered his house to be watched in order to kill him.

¹ Deliver me from my enemies, O my God;
    protect me from those who rise up
        against me.
² Deliver me from those who work evil;
    from the bloodthirsty save me.

³ Even now they lie in wait for my life;
    the mighty stir up strife against me.
For no transgression or sin of mine, O LORD,
⁴   for no fault of mine, they run and make
        ready.

Rouse yourself, come to my help and see!
⁵   You, LORD God of hosts, are God of Israel.
Awake to punish all the nations;
    spare none of those who treacherously
        plot evil.   *Selah*

910

NIV

⁶They return at evening,
    snarling like dogs,
    and prowl about the city.
⁷See what they spew from their mouths—
    they spew out swords from their lips,
    and they say, "Who can hear us?"
⁸But you, O Lord, laugh at them;
    you scoff at all those nations.

⁹O my Strength, I watch for you;
    you, O God, are my fortress, ¹⁰my loving
        God.

God will go before me
    and will let me gloat over those who
        slander me.
¹¹But do not kill them, O Lord our shield,ᵃ
    or my people will forget.
In your might make them wander about,
    and bring them down.
¹²For the sins of their mouths,
    for the words of their lips,
    let them be caught in their pride.
For the curses and lies they utter,
¹³   consume them in wrath,
    consume them till they are no more.
Then it will be known to the ends of the
        earth
    that God rules over Jacob.   Selah

¹⁴They return at evening,
    snarling like dogs,
    and prowl about the city.
¹⁵They wander about for food
    and howl if not satisfied.
¹⁶But I will sing of your strength,
    in the morning I will sing of your love;
for you are my fortress,
    my refuge in times of trouble.

¹⁷O my Strength, I sing praise to you;
    you, O God, are my fortress, my loving
        God.

ᵃ11 Or *sovereign*

NRSV

⁶ Each evening they come back,
    howling like dogs
    and prowling about the city.
⁷ There they are, bellowing with their mouths,
    with sharp wordsᵃ on their lips—
    for "Who," they think,ᵇ "will hear us?"

⁸ But you laugh at them, O Lord;
    you hold all the nations in derision.
⁹ O my strength, I will watch for you;
    for you, O God, are my fortress.
¹⁰ My God in his steadfast love will meet me;
    my God will let me look in triumph on
        my enemies.

¹¹ Do not kill them, or my people may forget;
    make them totter by your power, and
        bring them down,
    O Lord, our shield.
¹² For the sin of their mouths, the words of
        their lips,
    let them be trapped in their pride.
For the cursing and lies that they utter,
¹³   consume them in wrath;
    consume them until they are no more.
Then it will be known to the ends of the
        earth
    that God rules over Jacob.   Selah

¹⁴ Each evening they come back,
    howling like dogs
    and prowling about the city.
¹⁵ They roam about for food,
    and growl if they do not get their fill.

¹⁶ But I will sing of your might;
    I will sing aloud of your steadfast love in
        the morning.
For you have been a fortress for me
    and a refuge in the day of my distress.
¹⁷ O my strength, I will sing praises to you,
    for you, O God, are my fortress,
    the God who shows me steadfast love.

ᵃHeb *with swords*   ᵇHeb lacks *they think*

COMMENTARY

Psalm 59 contains the typical elements of a prayer for help or lament/complaint. Scholars have long commented on the unusual structure of Psalm 59, but, in fact, the prayers for help show a variety of arrangements of the typical elements; and the arrangement of elements in Psalm 59 is actually quite symmetrical. In the two main sections (vv. 1-10, 11-17), initial petition and complaint (vv. 1-5, 11-13) are followed by an additional complaint, introduced by a refrain (vv. 6-7, 14-15). Both sections conclude with an expression of assurance (vv. 8-10, 16-17), in which vv. 9 and 17a are nearly identical and also feature the concept of steadfast love. In a sense, this repetitive structure, including refrains, reinforces the content of the first refrain—that is, the structural elements of the poem "return" (vv. 6, 14) just as the psalmist's enemies "return" every evening. Thus the persistence of the threat is emphasized, as is the psalmist's perseverance in living in dependence upon God's steadfast love in the midst of distress.

The precise circumstances of the poem's origin and ancient use are unrecoverable. The superscription associates the psalm with Saul's threats against David (see 1 Sam 19:11), but as with similar superscriptions (see Psalms 3; 51; 54; 56; 57; Introduction), this one should be taken illustratively rather than historically. Several scholars suggest that Psalm 59 could have been the prayer of a falsely accused person (see vv. 1-4a, 7, 12) who fled to the Temple for asylum (see vv. 9-10, 16-17), especially since it contains a brief protestation of innocence (vv. 3b-4a; see Psalms 5; 7; Introduction). There is evidence, too, that this psalm may have been edited for use—or at least could have been appropriately used in its final form—as a prayer of the oppressed post-exilic community (see vv. 5, 8, 13). Gerstenberger says of v. 13, "The passage reflects, in my opinion, the transition of personal complaint into the worship situation of the early Jewish community."[235] As with other prayers in the psalter, the variety of proposals for understanding the origin and setting of Psalm 59 is testimony to the open-endedness of its language and imagery, as well as to its adaptability to a variety of settings, including contemporary ones (see Reflections below).

59:1-10. 59:1-3. The psalm begins with a fourfold petition (vv. 1-2), emphatic by virtue of the repetition of "deliver" in vv. 1a and 2a and by the chiastic structure (see Introduction) of each verse. In Hebrew the verbs are the first and last words of each verse; that is, the poetic structure suggests that the psalmist's defense is to surround the enemies, who are given four different names (see "rise up"/"rising" in Ps 3:1; "bloodthirsty" in Ps 26:9; and "evil" again in v. 5), with pleas to God. This is particularly appropriate, since the enemies "surround" the city ("prowling" in vv. 6, 14 is more literally "surrounding"). The petition "protect" in v. 1b is from the same Hebrew root as "fortress" in vv. 9, 17. Thus the opening verse anticipates the climactic expressions of assurance. The plea for God to save is a frequent one (see Ps 3:7).

Verses 1-2 have implied the psalmist's complaint, which is explicit in vv. 3-4a. The enemies "lie in wait" (see Ps 10:9) and "stir up strife" (see Ps 56:6). This time the enemies are called "the mighty," which also anticipates the climactic expressions of assurance. The word "mighty" is from the same root as "might" (v. 16) and "strength" (vv. 9, 17). These latter occurrences give the designation in v. 3 a sarcastic ring. The enemies may appear mighty, but the psalmist takes a stand upon and celebrates God's might (see discussion of v. 9 below). Lest there be any question that the psalmist's misfortune is deserved, he or she emphatically affirms innocence by employing the three major Hebrew words for sin (see Commentary on Psalms 32; 51; the word rendered "fault" [עָוֹן 'āwōn] is usually translated "iniquity" or "guilt"). The word "sin" is repeated in v. 12; the blame for the psalmist's distress lies with the enemies.

59:4b-5b. Just as the psalmist surrounded the enemies with pleas in vv. 1-2, so also now he or she surrounds God (v. 5a) with petitions in v. 4b and v. 5b. The urgency is suggested by the initial petitions in v. 4b (see Pss 7:6; 35:23; 44:23) and v. 5b (see Pss 35:23; 44:23) that suggest God is asleep. If God will "see" (v. 4b), God will eventually also "cause me to *see* those watching me" (v. 10b author's trans.). In a sense, then, God's seeing will lead to a divine appearance for which the psalmist

235. Gerstenberger, *Psalms,* 238.

watches (v. 9a) and a revelation that exposes those who have had their evil eyes on the psalmist (v. 10b). In short, God's *seeing* will put all other seeing and watching in proper perspective. As suggested above, the focal point of vv. 4b-5 is v. 5a, where the pronoun "You" is emphatic and is followed by three additional designations: God's personal name (Yahweh); God's military name ("God of hosts" or "God of the armies" [אלהים צבאות *ĕlōhîm ṣĕbāʾôt*], which is apt for this conflict situation; see Commentary on Ps 24:7-10); and a relational phrase ("God of Israel" [אלהי ישראל *ĕlōhê yiśrāʾēl*]). The latter prepares for the mention of "the nations" in the next line (see also v. 8) and gives the psalm a corporate dimension. The final petition, "show no mercy," stands out by virtue of its position and its negative form. It is the opposite of the frequent petition the psalmists make on their own behalf: "be gracious"/"be merciful"/"have mercy" (see Pss 4:1; 56:1; 57:1).

59:6-7. The refrain in v. 6 portrays the enemies as aggressive dogs (cf. 1 Kgs 14:11; 16:4; Ps 22:16, 20; Isa 56:11; Jer 5:3), who surround the city (see Ps 55:9-10 NRSV, where personified "violence" and "strife" "go around," literally surround, the city). They "spew" (v. 7; see Ps 94:4) threatening words that are metaphorically described as "swords" (see Ps 57:4). Their question in v. 7c demonstrates their arrogance. Accountable to no one but themselves, the enemies display the essence of wickedness—autonomy, or literally, "a law unto oneself" (see Commentary on Psalm 1; see also the questions or conclusions of the wicked in Pss 10:4, 6, 11; 14:1; 35:25; 42:3, 10; 73:11).

59:8-10. But God hears! And God responds. Both of the verbs in v. 8 occur also in Psalm 2:4, which is fundamentally an assertion of God's sovereignty over rebellious peoples and nations (see Commentary on Psalm 2). In the face of the self-assertion of the enemies, the psalmist emphatically proclaims God's rule (the "you" that begins v. 8 is emphatic). The psalmist's trust in God's reign is expressed too by the vocative "O my strength," since "strength" elsewhere is closely associated with God's sovereignty (see Exod 15:2, 13; Pss 29:1, 11; 93:1; 96:6-7). Because God—not the enemies—rules the world, the psalmist looks to God for protection (see above on v. 1). The noun translated "fortress" (משגב *miśgāb*) in v. 9 occurs twice in Ps 9:9 ("stronghold") in the context of the assertion of God's rule (see Ps 9:7).

God's reign—indeed, God's very being—is characterized by steadfast love (see Exod 34:6-7; Pss 5:7; 13:5; 98:3; Introduction). Verse 10c suggests that God's loving purposes will ultimately prevail over the hateful devices of the enemies (see Ps 54:7b). The phrase "in triumph" is not in the Hebrew, and perhaps suggests too much an element of personal revenge, as does the NIV's interpretive translation "gloat." The real point is that God will set things right for God's people (see Commentary on Ps 58:6-9).

59:11-17. To be sure, the petitions in vv. 11-13 also seem to contain an element of vindictiveness, especially v. 11, which seems to suggest something like, "Let them twist in the wind awhile before cutting them down." But even this request seems to be motivated by the psalmist's desire to have the destiny of the wicked be a reminder of God's sovereignty, and v. 13 states this desire even more explicitly. The disappearance of the wicked will be testimony to God's rule (see Pss 22:27-28; 67:7; 98:3). As in the preceding verses, the psalmist celebrates God's protecting power (v. 11; see Ps 3:3). The occurrence of "mouths" and "lips" in v. 12 recalls v. 7, which portrayed the destructive speech of the wicked and their self-assertion. Both themes are elaborated upon in v. 12 with the mention of the pride of the wicked, which is especially manifested in their speech (see Ps 10:7).

Verse 14 is identical to v. 6. Whereas v. 6 was followed by a verse depicting the arrogance of the wicked, v. 14 introduces a verse that portrays the persistence of the wicked. The Hebrew root of "growl" (לין *lîn*) can also mean "lodge," "spend the night." In short, the wicked do not go away. Nevertheless, the psalmist lives under God's reign and, in the face of opposition, celebrates God's strength (v. 16; see also vv. 9, 17; cf. v. 3) and steadfast love (v. 16; see also vv. 10, 17) and protection (see also vv. 1, 9, 16-17; the Hebrew word translated "refuge" [מנוס *mānôs*] also occurs in Pss 18:2; 142:4). It is possible that morning was generally viewed as a time for receiving help or offering praise (v. 16; see Pss 46:5; 57:8; 90:14; 143:8). It is appropriate that the final word of the psalm is "steadfast love" (חסד *ḥesed*), for the psalmist stakes life and future on the divine sovereignty that is perfected in love.

REFLECTIONS

1. Several young people have told me that their attempts to live out their faith at school have resulted, in effect, in their being alienated from and verbally attacked by their classmates. The causes may seem small—befriending a person others have deemed unpopular or refusing to wear trendy clothes. We are likely to dismiss all of this as normal teenage "peer pressure." But the young people I have talked to were trying seriously to represent God's claim on their lives and their priorities—to live under God's rule. It is precisely this same kind of peer pressure that perpetuates the consumeristic, narcissistic culture that we live in, a culture that regularly encourages us to "look out for number one" and do whatever it takes, or at least whatever we can get away with, to succeed. What we end up with, to borrow the imagery of Psalm 59, is a dog-eat-dog world, a culture of cut-throat competition in which we're convinced that no one will look out for us if we don't look out for ourselves.

This is what we ordinarily call "the real world," and its philosophy is really not much different from that espoused by the psalmist's enemies in Psalm 59—do anything to get ahead. One commentator has described Ps 59:6-7 as "a picture of disgusting, self-seeking, and hateful activity."[236] Unfortunately, this description applies to much of what passes in our society for good business or the necessities of politics or perhaps peer pressure. In other words, the portrayal of the enemies in Psalm 59 puts us in touch with the way things still are among us. It reminds us of the evil in ourselves and in our society—the so-called real world (see Commentary on Psalm 58).

2. But Psalm 59 also reminds us of a deeper reality, an alternative world, which is driven not by the lust for power but by the power of love. This world is the world of God's reign, and Psalm 59 proclaims it as the authentic "real world." So did Jesus as he invited people to enter the reign of God (Mark 1:14-15). To be sure, the proclamation and embodiment of the reign of God do not make wickedness suddenly go away. Psalm 59—along with the cross of Jesus Christ—reminds us of the persistence of evil in self and society, but it also reminds us that we can confront that evil as transformed people.

In short, Psalm 59, like Psalms 2 and 56–58 and the whole psalter (see Introduction), is eschatological. It affirms the reign of God amid circumstances that seem to deny it; thus it calls us to decision, as Jesus did. Confronted by "the mighty" (v. 3) of the so-called real world, we profess to find true strength in God. Faced by the seemingly overwhelming forces of evil, we profess to be met by a God who comes to us in love. Tempted by a dog-eat-dog world to join those who live only for themselves and by their own resources, we profess to find a "fortress" in God, and we yield our lives to God in grateful praise (vv. 16-17).

236. F. Nötscher, quoted in Kraus, *Psalms 1–59,* 541.

PSALM 60:1-12, HUMAN HELP IS WORTHLESS

NIV

Psalm 60

For the director of music. To ⌊the tune of⌋ "The Lily of the Covenant." A *miktam*[a] of David. For teaching. When he fought Aram Naharaim[b] and Aram Zobah,[c] and when Joab

a Title: Probably a literary or musical term   *b* Title: That is, Arameans of Northwest Mesopotamia   *c* Title: That is, Arameans of central Syria

NRSV

Psalm 60

To the leader: according to the Lily of the Covenant. A Miktam of David; for instruction; when he struggled with Aram-naharaim and with Aram-zobah, and when Joab on his return killed twelve thousand Edomites in the Valley of Salt.

NIV

returned and struck down twelve thousand Edomites in the Valley of Salt.

¹You have rejected us, O God, and burst forth
upon us;
you have been angry—now restore us!
²You have shaken the land and torn it open;
mend its fractures, for it is quaking.
³You have shown your people desperate times;
you have given us wine that makes us
stagger.

⁴But for those who fear you, you have raised
a banner
to be unfurled against the bow.   *Selah*

⁵Save us and help us with your right hand,
that those you love may be delivered.
⁶God has spoken from his sanctuary:
"In triumph I will parcel out Shechem
and measure off the Valley of Succoth.
⁷Gilead is mine, and Manasseh is mine;
Ephraim is my helmet,
Judah my scepter.
⁸Moab is my washbasin,
upon Edom I toss my sandal;
over Philistia I shout in triumph."

⁹Who will bring me to the fortified city?
Who will lead me to Edom?
¹⁰Is it not you, O God, you who have rejected us
and no longer go out with our armies?
¹¹Give us aid against the enemy,
for the help of man is worthless.
¹²With God we will gain the victory,
and he will trample down our enemies.

NRSV

¹ O God, you have rejected us, broken our
defenses;
you have been angry; now restore us!
² You have caused the land to quake; you
have torn it open;
repair the cracks in it, for it is tottering.
³ You have made your people suffer hard things;
you have given us wine to drink that
made us reel.

⁴ You have set up a banner for those who
fear you,
to rally to it out of bowshot.*ᵃ*   *Selah*
⁵ Give victory with your right hand, and
answer us,*ᵇ*
so that those whom you love may be
rescued.

⁶ God has promised in his sanctuary:*ᶜ*
"With exultation I will divide up
Shechem,
and portion out the Vale of Succoth.
⁷ Gilead is mine, and Manasseh is mine;
Ephraim is my helmet;
Judah is my scepter.
⁸ Moab is my washbasin;
on Edom I hurl my shoe;
over Philistia I shout in triumph."

⁹ Who will bring me to the fortified city?
Who will lead me to Edom?
¹⁰ Have you not rejected us, O God?
You do not go out, O God, with our armies.
¹¹ O grant us help against the foe,
for human help is worthless.
¹² With God we shall do valiantly;
it is he who will tread down our foes.

ᵃGk Syr Jerome: Heb *because of the truth*   ᵇAnother reading is
me   ᶜOr *by his holiness*

COMMENTARY

Marvin Tate states at the beginning of his comments on Psalm 60: "This psalm is plagued with difficulties, and all interpretation is tentative."[237] Most scholars agree, however, that Psalm

60 is a communal lament/complaint. While it does not display the typical structure of such prayers, its structure is relatively clear. Verses 1-5 contain complaint accompanied by petition, the final one of which is "answer us" (v. 5). Quite

237. Marvin E. Tate, *Psalms 51–100,* WBC 20 (Dallas: Word, 1990) 103.

logically, vv. 6-8 offer an answer in the form of a divine address; however, the content of the answer—God owns all the peoples and nations—is problematic in view of the crisis described in vv. 1-5. Thus v. 9, which some scholars include with vv. 6-8 and others with vv. 10-12, raises a question that seems to suggest that Edom is particularly responsible for the crisis. In the light of vv. 6-8, the only possible answer to the questions in v. 9 is "God." But, as vv. 1-3 have made clear, God is the problem. Thus the final section of the poem renews the complaint (v. 10; see "rejected" in v. 1) and petition (v. 11; the NRSV's "help" [תשועה *tĕšû'â*] in v. 11*b* is the same Hebrew root as in the opening petition of v. 5*a*); the psalm concludes with an affirmation of faith that recalls vv. 6-8.

The inclusion of so many geographical terms, including the singling out of Edom, has proved particularly tantalizingly to scholars. That is to say, it seems that Psalm 60 could be dated fairly accurately, but such has not been the case. Taking the superscription seriously, and noting that vv. 6-8 describe roughly the core of David's empire, many scholars have dated the psalm to David's time. The editors responsible for the superscription apparently had 2 Samuel 8 in mind (see esp. 2 Sam 8:13-14), although all the details do not correspond (see 1 Chr 18:12-13). Other scholars have dated Psalm 60 as late as the Maccabean revolt, 800 years later than the previous proposal. Then, too, a strong case can be made for an early post-exilic date. G. S. Ogden, for instance, notes the verbal links between Psalm 60 and Isa 63:1-6 (cf. v. 9 with Isa 63:1; v. 11 with Isa 63:5; v. 12 with Isa 63:6); Ogden concludes that the two texts "belong in the same fundamental historical and liturgical context." More specifically, he comments that "Isa. 63:1-6 is a prophetic response to the lament ceremony in which Ps. 60 was sung to seek God's vengeance upon a treacherous neighbor."[238] But even if Ogden is correct, it is possible that Psalm 60 could have originated much earlier, in which case it would have been deemed particularly relevant to the early post-exilic generation. In short, certainty is impossible, and, as with other prayers, the very variety of proposals is testimony to the flexibility and adapt-

ability of the prayer. Further evidence in this regard is the fact that vv. 5-12 are essentially the same as Ps 108:6-13.

60:1-3. These verses make it clear that the people perceive their misfortune to be a result of God's anger (see Ps 79:5). God has "rejected us," a frequent theme in the communal complaints (see v. 10 and Pss 44:9, 23; 74:1; 77:7; 89:38 NIV). It implies God's judgment, as does the second verb in v. 1*a* (see "Broke[n] out" in Ps 106:29; 2 Sam 6:8 NIV). Ogden suggests that the petition at the end of v. 1 be rendered "return to us," thus appropriately implying God's absence (see v. 10).[239] Verse 2 uses the imagery of an earthquake, perhaps to suggest the magnitude of the crisis as well as the extent of destruction. The verbs that the NRSV translates "quake" (רעש *rā'aš*) and "tottering" (מוט *môṭ*) also occur in Ps 46:2-3 to portray a cosmic crisis. In Psalm 46, God offers protection during the crisis, but here God causes the crisis. All the people can do is plead for help, and like v. 1, v. 2 ends with a petition (lit., "heal"; see Deut 32:39; Jer 30:17). The noun "hard things" (v. 3) recalls enslavement in Egypt (see Exod 1:14; 6:9; Deut 26:6); that is, God has reversed the exodus and is acting as taskmaster over the people. The cup God offers is not for refreshment (see Ps 75:8; Jer 23:9; 25:15-16; Zech 12:2).

60:4-5. Verse 4*a* is problematic, since it seems to say, in apparent contradiction to vv. 1-3 and 5, that God has already offered divine help. Thus several scholars construe v. 4*a* as a petition, and this may be the best solution. As the NRSV note suggests, there are difficulties with v. 4*b* as well. Verse 5 clearly returns to petition. The first petition is translated more accurately by the NIV. When the plea "save" is heard in conjunction with "right hand," it calls to mind the exodus (see "save" in Exod 14:30; "right hand" in Exod 15:6, 12). A new exodus is needed. Both the NIV and the NRSV reverse the order of the two parts of v. 5. In Hebrew, the final word is the imperative "answer" (ענה *'ānâ*), which sets the stage for vv. 6-8.

60:6-8. The NIV more literally translates v. 6*a* with "God has spoken," but the NRSV's more interpretative translation captures the tone of the divine speech. Gerstenberger describes vv. 6-8 as

238. G. S. Ogden, "Psalm 60: Its Rhetoric, Form, and Function," *JSOT* 31 (1985) 93.

239. Ibid., 85.

"a homiletical device," or in effect, a brief sermon (see Ps 50:7-23).[240] The good news is that all peoples and lands belong to God. It is the prerogative of an owner or a victor to divide up the land (v. 6; see Exod 15:9; Josh 19:51). The names listed in vv. 6-7 are clearly Israelite places. Ephraim and Judah, designations for the northern and southern kingdoms, are paired and are assigned similar metaphors (see Gen 49:10, where the scepter is also associated with Judah). Traditional enemies are cited in v. 8. The metaphors in v. 8*ab* are not as transparent. They may be intended as insults, but perhaps the intention is simply to say that Moab is owned by God, like a personal possession, and that Edom has been acquired by transaction (see Ruth 4:7, where sandals were exchanged to confirm transactions). The word translated "shout in triumph" (רוע *rûa'*) can designate a signal to prepare for battle or the victor's joyful cry (see Jer 50:15). In short, God controls Philistia as well. In view of the above-mentioned recollections of the exodus, it is significant that the three places mentioned in v. 8 also are named in Exod 15:14-15. Their defeat by God (Exod 15:16) led to the people's possession of the land (Exod 15:17), all of which is a sign of God's reign (Exod 15:18). In the midst of a crisis that calls for a new exodus, vv. 6-8 effectively proclaim just that. As in the other prayers for help, individual and communal, the proclamation is eschatological. God's sovereignty is asserted amid circumstances that seem to deny it (note that vv. 6-8 are surrounded by complaint and petition in vv. 1-5, 10-12).

60:9-12. Verse 9 is another of the difficulties of Psalm 60. By singling out Edom from among the enemies listed in v. 8, however, the psalmist seems to indicate that Edom is heavily involved in the crisis described in vv. 1-3 and that God needs to lead someone to Edom to take corrective action. The problem with this, however, is that the real cause of the crisis described in vv. 1-3 is God! So v. 10*a* returns to the complaint of v. 1. The pronoun "you" is emphatic; God is the real problem. Like the concluding petition of v. 1, v. 10*b* suggests God's absence. It will do no good for anyone to go anywhere if God does not accompany the forces (see Num 14:42-45; Judg 4:14-15, which articulate this aspect of the theology of holy war). All that is left is for the people to ask for God's "help" (v. 11*a*; see this Hebrew root for "help" [עזר *'zr*] in Pss 22:19; 38:22), while denying the utility of all human "help" (see Ps 146:3), or as the word is often translated elsewhere, "salvation" (see Ps 40:10; Isa 45:17; 46:13). Despite current appearances, the people continue to trust God and to entrust their lives and future to God. With God's help, they will "do valiantly" (v. 12*a*; see Num 24:18; Ps 118:15-16). The God who rejected them will also be the God who finally deals with their oppressors (see Ps 44:5; Isa 63:6). The God who wounded will be the God who heals (see Deut 32:39 and discussion above on v. 2).

240. Erhard S. Gerstenberger, *Psalms, Part 1, with an Introduction to Cultic Poetry,* Forms of the OT Literature 14 (Grand Rapids: Eerdmans, 1988) 240.

REFLECTIONS

At first sight, a psalm so closely tied to ancient military conflict and Israel's theology of holy war (v. 10) might seem to offer our contemporary era nothing edifying "for instruction" (see superscription). In fact, it might seem to reinforce in a dangerous way the all too pervasive temptation to equate national policy with God's will and to claim God as our ally in every cause. But a close reading of Psalm 60 subverts this possible approach. In fact, as Kraus points out, Psalm 60 is the prayer of a congregation that "trusts the sole efficacy of its God."[241] It is precisely this recognition of the inadequacy of human initiative and help that undercuts any temptation toward military triumphalism in the name of God (see Reflections on Psalm 20).

To put it somewhat differently, we must take seriously that Psalm 60 is the prayer of suffering and oppressed persons (see v. 3). Their prayer is not that of the powerful, who seek

241. H.-J. Kraus, *Psalms 60–150: A Commentary,* trans. H. C. Oswald (Minneapolis: Augsburg, 1989) 6.

to claim God's sanction to enforce the status quo. Rather, their prayer is the desperate plea of those who turn to God as the only possible hope in an apparently hopeless situation (v. 11). As Tate puts it, "the psalm is a stark reminder that the limits of human power are easily reached and that salvation is God's work."[242] In other words, the assertion of God's sovereignty (vv. 6-8, 12) relativizes all human claims to sovereignty.

The proclamation of the good news in Psalm 60 is eschatological, as it is throughout the psalter and throughout the Bible (see Psalms 2; 56–59; Introduction). As we proclaim God's reign, God's defeat of oppression and oppressors (vv. 6-8, 12), we also pray for it and await it (vv. 1-5, 10-11). In an era in which political, social, ethnic, economic, and religious conflicts desperately threaten the security of people's lives and the well-being of the world, our hope is not that we can somehow manage to pull things together; instead, our only real hope is in the reality of a God who lovingly claims all peoples and nations (see vv. 5, 6-8) and who cares for the future of the whole world, beginning with the suffering and the oppressed.

242. Tate, *Psalms 51–100*, 108.

PSALM 61:1-8, THE ROCK HIGHER THAN I

NIV

Psalm 61

For the director of music. With stringed instruments. Of David.

¹Hear my cry, O God;
   listen to my prayer.

²From the ends of the earth I call to you,
   I call as my heart grows faint;
   lead me to the rock that is higher than I.
³For you have been my refuge,
   a strong tower against the foe.

⁴I long to dwell in your tent forever
   and take refuge in the shelter of your
      wings.   *Selah*
⁵For you have heard my vows, O God;
   you have given me the heritage of those
      who fear your name.

⁶Increase the days of the king's life,
   his years for many generations.
⁷May he be enthroned in God's presence
      forever;
   appoint your love and faithfulness to
      protect him.

⁸Then will I ever sing praise to your name
   and fulfill my vows day after day.

NRSV

Psalm 61

To the leader: with stringed instruments.
Of David.

¹ Hear my cry, O God;
   listen to my prayer.
² From the end of the earth I call to you,
   when my heart is faint.

Lead me to the rock
   that is higher than I;
³ for you are my refuge,
   a strong tower against the enemy.

⁴ Let me abide in your tent forever,
   find refuge under the shelter of your
      wings.   *Selah*
⁵ For you, O God, have heard my vows;
   you have given me the heritage of those
      who fear your name.

⁶ Prolong the life of the king;
   may his years endure to all generations!
⁷ May he be enthroned forever before God;
   appoint steadfast love and faithfulness to
      watch over him!

⁸ So I will always sing praises to your name,
   as I pay my vows day after day.

COMMENTARY

Psalm 61 is usually classified as a prayer for help or an individual lament/complaint. Typical elements are present: petition (vv. 1, 2c, 4, 6-7), followed in each case by an affirmation of trust (vv. 3, 5) or promise to praise (v. 8), as well as a brief complaint (v. 2ab). Some scholars suggest on the basis of vv. 5 and 8 that the psalmist's prayer has already been answered, but this is not clear. Finally, however, this matter is not crucial. The pervasiveness of petition suggests that the psalmist will live constantly under some kind of threat, yet the affirmations in vv. 3 and 5 (see also "rock" in v. 2 and "refuge" in v. 4) indicate that the psalmist already experiences God as a present and enduring source of security (see Commentary on Psalms 54; 56; 57).

The circumstances of the origin and ancient use of Psalm 61 are unclear. Taking v. 2 literally, some suggest that the psalmist prayed in exile. On the basis of vv. 2c-5, others propose that the psalmist seeks asylum in the Temple from persecution of some sort (see Psalms 5; 7; Introduction). Noteworthy, too, is the prayer for the king in vv. 6-7 (see Pss 28:8; 63:11; 84:9). Do these verses indicate that the original speaker was the king? Or is the psalmist, having prayed for self (vv. 1, 2c, 4), now praying for the king? Verses 6-7 seem to indicate a pre-exilic origin for Psalm 61. If this is true, the psalm would almost certainly have been used in the post-exilic era as a communal prayer for help, in which case the prayer for the king would have been understood messianically or perhaps symbolically as a prayer for the future of the whole people. In any case, the reference to the king has presumably not prevented Psalm 61 from serving as a prayer for help or an expression of trust for generations of God's people over the centuries.

61:1-3. The opening petitions are commonly used in Psalms (see 5:2; 17:1; 86:6). Verse 2a need not be understood geographically. It is just as likely that it suggests metaphorically a situation of extremity, a conclusion reinforced by v. 2b (see "faint" in the superscription of Psalm 102 and Pss 77:3; 107:5; 142:3; 143:4 NRSV). The source of the problem is not clear, although faintness elsewhere is caused by hunger and thirst and perse-cution by enemies (see v. 3). In any case, the psalmist needs help and knows that her or his own resources are not sufficient (see Ps 60:11). As the petition and accompanying affirmation suggest (vv. 2c-3), God is the only source of help. The psalmist prays to be led (see Ps 23:3). God, or perhaps God's Temple, is the "rock" (צור *ṣûr*; see Pss 27:5; 31:2) that is "higher than I" (ירום ממני *yārûm mimmennî*; see Pss 113:4; 138:6; Isa 57:15). God is also a "refuge" (מחסה *maḥseh*; see Pss 2:12; 5:11; 14:6; 46:1; 62:7-8; Introduction) and a "strong tower" (מגדל-עז *migdal-'ōz*; see Prov 18:10). These three concepts—rock, refuge, strength—also occur together in Ps 62:7b ("my mighty rock" is literally "rock of my strength").

61:4-5. The request in v. 4a apparently involves entrance into the Temple (see Ps 15:1a), although the imagery can certainly be taken as a symbol of God's presence. Indeed, it is possible that the author intended it to be metaphorical. The same can be said of v. 4b, which repeats "refuge" from v. 3 and which may allude to the winged creatures associated with the ark (see Pss 17:8; 57:1; 63:7). Verse 5 is sometimes cited as evidence of God's removal of the distress articulated in v. 2. To be sure, the psalmist's vow or promise has been heard (see Pss 22:25; 50:14; 56:12; 65:1; 66:13; 116:14, 18), and the psalmist has been given "the heritage of those who fear your name." But exactly what this means is unclear. The root of the noun "heritage" (ירש *yāraš*) almost always designates possession of land, but this too may be heard symbolically. To possess the land meant to have the resources necessary to sustain life, and v. 5b would then affirm the psalmist's conviction that God has given him or her life (see Commentary on Psalm 37, esp. the discussion on vv. 9, 11, 22, 29, 34). Thus v. 5b may serve as the basis for the petitions in Psalm 61, not necessarily as an indication that the distress is past.

61:6-8. As suggested above, it is not clear whether vv. 6-7 indicate that Psalm 61 was originally the king's prayer. In any case, vv. 6-7a are similar to Ps 72:15, 17 (see also Pss 21:4; 89:29, 36-37), and v. 7b recalls other royal psalms. Psalm 89, for instance, features God's steadfast love and faithfulness, which are specifically said to accompany the king (see vv. 24, 33; see also Ps 21:7). In short, the king depends on God for life and future just as all people do, which is fitting, since the king was the symbolic representative of the whole people. In fact, vv. 6-7 may well have been understood in the post-exilic era as a prayer for the whole people of God, especially since it appears that the promises attached to the Davidic dynasty were transferred to the people as a whole (see Isa 55:1-3; cf. Ps 72:10-11, 15-17; see also Ps 105:15; Introduction). Verse 8 recalls v. 5 by way of repeating the words "vows" and "name." The phrase "day after day" also recalls v. 6 (lit., "Days upon days of the king may you increase"), and the repetition of "day(s)" may form an envelope structure for the final section. The repetition suggests at least that the continuing life of the king/people/psalmist will be lived joyfully and faithfully. In the final analysis, then, Psalm 61 invites readers of every generation to the faith and joy that derives from the conviction that life is sustained and secured by God's loving and faithful presence.

REFLECTIONS

1. Like the other prayers for help, Psalm 61 juxtaposes petition and trust in a manner that suggests they are simultaneous rather than sequential. The effect is to convey a perspective that is eschatological; the psalmist proclaims and entrusts the self to God's sovereign providence in the midst of circumstances that seem to deny God's sovereignty. Such a perspective always calls for decision, and the psalmist's decision is clear. He or she both possesses (vv. 5, 8) and simultaneously awaits (vv. 1-4) the aid of God (see Commentary on Psalms 54; 56; 57; 58; 59). This dynamic also characterized the preaching of Jesus, who taught that the kingdom of God was both to be entered immediately and to be yet awaited. In other words, Christians are simultaneously both people of the cross and people of the resurrection (see Commentary on Psalms 13; 22).

2. The distinctiveness of Psalm 61 may well lie, as Tate suggests, "in its metaphorical richness," the value of which is to "assist us to incorporate our own experience into the experience of prayer."[243] The "rock . . . higher than I" is a particularly striking and evocative image. The Hebrew root of the word "higher" is used in conjunction with God's sovereignty in Pss 99:2 and 145:1; thus the metaphor may be particularly pertinent in a culture that encourages one to make human potential and human achievement the highest measure of security. In short, it is especially important that this metaphor put us in touch with a presence and a power beyond ourselves and that it invite us and assist us to experience a source of security beyond our own achievement and potential. That source is God, to be sure, but it is also significant that the psalmist looks to God's sanctuary where the whole people gathered for worship. Bellinger concludes that Psalm 61 serves to "press us toward the *community at worship as the context for searching out genuine hope of protection.*"[244] In short, Psalm 61 encourages faith in God rather than in self, a reality that will be experienced communally and not in isolation.

This encouragement is not just a challenge to a thoroughly secular and individualistic society; it is also good news. One of the great ironies of our time is that its remarkable demonstration of human potential and achievement has left the human race anxious and on the brink of despair. But perhaps this is a perennial human condition, as Dahood suggests on the basis of v. 2: "The psalmist is here describing the human condition in existentialist terms: man constantly stands at the edge of the abyss, and only divine assistance can prevent his falling into it."[245] If this be the case, then the good news of Psalm 61 is for all seasons: We are not

243. Ibid., 116.
244. W. H. Bellinger, Jr., *A Hermeneutic of Curiosity and Readings of Psalm 61,* Studies in OT Interpretation 1 (Macon, Ga.: Mercer University Press, 1995) 114.
245. Mitchell Dahood, *Psalms II (51–100),* AB 17 (Garden City, N.Y.: Doubleday, 1968) 84. Dahood translates the beginning of v. 3 as: "From the brink of the nether world."

alone, for there is a presence and a power higher than we, which is ultimately made known to us as love and faithfulness. If we can manage to trust this good news, we shall undoubtedly join the psalmist and "always sing praises" to God's name (v. 8).

PSALM 62:1-12, TRUST IN GOD AT ALL TIMES

NIV

Psalm 62

For the director of music. For Jeduthun.
A psalm of David.

¹My soul finds rest in God alone;
  my salvation comes from him.
²He alone is my rock and my salvation;
  he is my fortress, I will never be shaken.

³How long will you assault a man?
  Would all of you throw him down—
  this leaning wall, this tottering fence?
⁴They fully intend to topple him
  from his lofty place;
  they take delight in lies.
With their mouths they bless,
  but in their hearts they curse.   *Selah*

⁵Find rest, O my soul, in God alone;
  my hope comes from him.
⁶He alone is my rock and my salvation;
  he is my fortress, I will not be shaken.
⁷My salvation and my honor depend on God[a];
  he is my mighty rock, my refuge.
⁸Trust in him at all times, O people;
  pour out your hearts to him,
  for God is our refuge.   *Selah*

⁹Lowborn men are but a breath,
  the highborn are but a lie;
if weighed on a balance, they are nothing;
  together they are only a breath.
¹⁰Do not trust in extortion
  or take pride in stolen goods;
though your riches increase,
  do not set your heart on them.

¹¹One thing God has spoken,
  two things have I heard:
that you, O God, are strong,

a7 Or / *God Most High is my salvation and my honor*

NRSV

Psalm 62

To the leader: according to Jeduthun. A Psalm
of David.

¹ For God alone my soul waits in silence;
  from him comes my salvation.
² He alone is my rock and my salvation,
  my fortress; I shall never be shaken.

³ How long will you assail a person,
  will you batter your victim, all of you,
  as you would a leaning wall, a tottering
    fence?
⁴ Their only plan is to bring down a person
  of prominence.
  They take pleasure in falsehood;
they bless with their mouths,
  but inwardly they curse.   *Selah*

⁵ For God alone my soul waits in silence,
  for my hope is from him.
⁶ He alone is my rock and my salvation,
  my fortress; I shall not be shaken.
⁷ On God rests my deliverance and my honor;
  my mighty rock, my refuge is in God.

⁸ Trust in him at all times, O people;
  pour out your heart before him;
  God is a refuge for us.   *Selah*

⁹ Those of low estate are but a breath,
  those of high estate are a delusion;
in the balances they go up;
  they are together lighter than a breath.
¹⁰ Put no confidence in extortion,
  and set no vain hopes on robbery;
  if riches increase, do not set your heart
    on them.

¹¹ Once God has spoken;

NIV	NRSV
12 and that you, O Lord, are loving. Surely you will reward each person according to what he has done.	twice have I heard this: that power belongs to God, 12 and steadfast love belongs to you, O Lord. For you repay to all according to their work.

COMMENTARY

Psalm 62 makes an excellent companion to Psalm 61 (see discussion above on the repetition of "rock," "refuge," and "strong" from Ps 61:2-3 in Ps 62:7*b,* plus note "steadfast love" in 61:7 and 62:12), and it also anticipates the content and tone of Psalm 63 (see "power" in 62:11 and 63:2; "steadfast love" in 62:12 and 63:3; and "soul" in 62:1, 5 and 63:1, 5, 8). Indeed, Kraus notes "a certain interrelation of these three psalms."[246] Whether intended or coincidental, Psalms 61–63 form a sort of trilogy of trust with Psalm 62 at the center. In fact, Psalm 62 is most frequently categorized as a song of confidence or trust. The direct address of the enemies in v. 3 and the description of them in v. 4 suggest circumstances similar to those underlying the prayers for help (see also Pss 6:8-9; 52:1-5; 55:12-14). Some scholars suggest that the psalmist was sick (see Psalms 6; 38; Introduction); some suggest that the psalmist was persecuted and had fled to the Temple for asylum (see Psalms 5; 7; 61); and some even classify the psalm as a prayer for help. But God is not directly addressed until v. 12, and even here there is not a petition but an expression of trust. The whole psalm has the character of a profession of faith with an explicitly instructional intent (vv. 8-10).

The most striking structural feature of Psalm 62 is the similarity of vv. 1 and 5 and the nearly exact equivalence of vv. 2 and 6. Taking this repetition as a structural clue, one may divide the psalm into three sections: (1) vv. 1-4, expression of trust followed by address to and description of the enemies, (2) vv. 5-10, expression of trust followed by address to the "people," and (3) vv. 11-12, (the basis for trust and concluding prayer). Some scholars suggest two main sections: (1) vv.

1-7 and (2) vv. 8-12. Either proposal can be justified; in fact, the structure may move at more than one level. For instance, without necessarily contradicting the previous proposals, it is possible to view v. 7 as the center and turning point. It is at or very near the structural center of the poem, preceded and followed by eight lines. Two key words in v. 7 have already occurred in vv. 1-6 (see "salvation" in vv. 1, 2, 6 and "rock" in vv. 2, 6 NIV), and neither occurs again after v. 7. Verse 7 also anticipates vv. 8-12. Two key words in v. 7 recur in vv. 8-12 (see "refuge" [מחסה *maḥseh*] in v. 8 and "power" [עז *'ōz*] in v. 11, which is the same Hebrew word as "mighty" in v. 7), and neither has occurred in vv. 1-6. In short, v. 7 functions as a structural and theological center, culminating the profession of faith in vv. 1-6 and serving as the foundation for the didactic call to decision in vv. 8-10 as well as the conclusion in vv. 11-12.

62:1-7. If it is permissible on some level to construe v. 7 as the central poetic line, then the similar professions of faith in vv. 1-2 and vv. 5-6 surround the address to and description of the enemies in vv. 3-4. The psalmist's trouble is real, but it exists only in the midst of—it is circumscribed by—the psalmist's faith. Verses 1-6 thus move from faith to faith. Despite opposition, the psalmist will not "be shaken" (vv. 2, 6; see Ps 13:4 and NRSV "moved" in Pss 15:5; 16:8; 21:7; 30:6; 112:6; cf. 10:6). The opposite of being "shaken" is being "still unto God," as Weiser renders vv. 1*a,* 5*a.*[247] The NIV's translation is more helpful than that of the NRSV at this point, and the NIV also accurately maintains the imperative in v. 5*a.* As the NRSV suggests, however, patient waiting could be an aspect of the

---

246. Kraus, *Psalms 60–150,* 8.

247. Artur Weiser, *The Psalms,* OTL, trans. H. Hartwell (Philadelphia: Westminster, 1962) 445.

psalmist's inner repose (see Pss 4:4; 37:7; 131:2). The psalmist can be calm, because he or she trusts in God alone. In biblical terms, salvation (vv. 1*b*, 2*a*; see vv. 6-7) means life, and God is the source (v. 1*b*) as well as the protector and guarantor (v. 2; see "rock" in Pss 19:14; 28:1; 31:2; 61:2; see also "fortress" in Pss 46:7, 11 [NRSV, "refuge"]; 59:9, 16-17). The Hebrew particle with which the psalm actually begins occurs five times as the first word in poetic lines in vv. 1-6 ("alone" in vv. 1-2, 5-6 and "only" in v. 4). This repetition emphasizes the alternatives, between which the psalmist has chosen and calls others, including the reader, to choose—that is, to live by trusting "God alone" or to live as if one's "only plan" were the destruction of other people.

The repetition of the particle that links vv. 1-2, 5-6 to vv. 3-4 also serves to emphasize that the threat to the psalmist is real and continuing. The ongoing reality of threat is also indicated by the subtle difference between vv. 1 and 5; "salvation" in v. 1 has been replaced by "hope" in v. 5 (see the noun in Pss 9:18; 71:5, as well as the verb translated "wait for" [קוה *qāwâ*] in Pss 27:14; 37:9; 39:7). The faith of the psalmist is not something attained after the crisis has passed. Rather, that faith endures throughout the ongoing threat. Verses 1-2, 5-6 are also linked to vv. 3-4 by the imagery of motion. The psalmist is "still" (v. 1) and not "shaken" (v. 2), even though the opponents are trying to "topple" the psalmist (v. 4) like a "tottering fence" (v. 3). As usual, the precise nature of the threat and identity of the opponents are unclear. Deceit is involved (see Pss 4:2; 5:6; 58:3; 109:28). Beyond this, however, one can only conclude that the threat is serious and ongoing. The phrase "How long . . . ?" suggests the duration of the crisis. The NRSV's "batter your victim" is more literally "kill," "murder" (רצח *rāṣaḥ*; see Exod 20:13). The language may be metaphorical, as the NRSV implies, but its intensity serves to indicate the urgency of the crisis. The psalmist's movement from faith to faith apparently leads through the valley of the shadow of death. The call to decision in vv. 8-10 must be heard in this context.

As already indicated, v. 7 both culminates the profession of faith in vv. 1-6 and anticipates the call to decision in vv. 8-10. Here the psalmist professes that everything he or she is and has

depends on God—life itself (NIV, "salvation"; see vv. 1-2, 5-6), substance and reputation ("honor" or "glory" can denote both material wealth and reputation; see Pss 3:3; 4:2), sustaining strength ("mighty rock" or "rock of my strength"), security ("refuge"; see Ps 2:12; Introduction). The structure of v. 7 reinforces this all-encompassing profession. The two prepositional phrases—"on God" and "in God"—begin and conclude the verse. All references to the psalmist are in between. Structurally and theologically, the reality of God encompasses the psalmist.

62:8-10. In this call to decision, the psalmist commands what he or she has experienced (cf. "my refuge" in v. 7 and "our refuge" in v. 8). To take refuge in God means to trust God, and "trust" (בטח *bāṭaḥ*) is the first verb in both v. 8 and v. 10 (see Pss 4:5; 9:10; Introduction); it introduces the positive alternative in v. 8 and the negative alternative in v. 10. To "pour out your heart" means to pray, especially prayers of petition in distress (see 1 Sam 1:15; Lam 2:19). In short, the psalmist calls others to trust God and pray. This advice seems rather weak in view of the alternative introduced by the second occurrence of "trust" in v. 10. Verse 10 indicates that the psalmist's opponents trust their own resources, whether honestly or dishonestly gained. For the psalmist, to trust in the self is a lie (v. 9; see also v. 4). In other words, trust in oneself is finally ineffective; it amounts to "a breath" (v. 9; the same Hebrew root lies behind "set no vain hopes" in v. 10). Human achievement, honest or dishonest, cannot secure life (see Pss 49:16-17; 52:7; 60:11).

62:11-12. These verses articulate the foundation of the psalmist's faith. In affirming that "power belongs to God" (v. 11), the psalmist asserts that God rules the world (see "power" or "strength" in Exod 15:2, 13; Pss 29:1, 11; 93:1, passages that explicitly proclaim God's reign). It is revealing that the first direct address to God is a celebration of God's steadfast love (v. 12*a*); that is, the psalmist trusts that God's sovereign purposes will ultimately be experienced as love (see Exod 15:13, where "steadfast love" and "strength" are also linked; see also Ps 98:1-3). The verb in the final assertion (v. 12*b*) is a form of the Hebrew root from which is derived the familiar word *shalom*, "peace." Perhaps v. 12*b* should be rendered, "For you will give peace to all according to their work," which allows for a more nuanced understanding. This conclusion obviously does not mean that God rewards the faithful with an easy and materially prosperous life. The psalmist's own experience is testimony to that. What v. 12*a* does suggest is that the way one lives affects one's destiny. For instance, life is "a lie" (v. 9) for those who live by "lies" (v. 4). In other words, v. 12*b* teaches that there are different kinds of peace or repayment or reward. Psalm 62 commends the rewarding experience of finding refuge in God alone (see Commentary on Psalms 1; 2).

REFLECTIONS

1. Like the psalter as a whole, the perspective of Psalm 62 is eschatological. It affirms God's power or reign amid circumstances that seem to deny it (vv. 3-4; see Commentary on Psalms 2; 56; 57; 58; 59; 60; 61; Introduction), and thus it calls for decision. Unlike many other psalms, the call for decision in Psalm 62 is explicit (vv. 8-10), and it is as applicable and relevant to contemporary readers as it was to the psalmist's ancient contemporaries. The vocabulary of the psalm encourages us to hear its call to decision in a variety of ways. For instance, the repetition of "trust" and "heart" in vv. 8 and 10 enables us to hear the call to decision as: Where do we set our heart? Where is our ultimate loyalty? In whom or in what do we trust? In whom or in what do we seek security?

The psalmist's choice is clear: Trust in God at all times. But the alternative seems so much more concrete and compelling: Trust your own resources; trust your own buying power; trust whatever you can get your hands on. The psalmist rejects this alternative as "but a breath" (v. 9), suggesting other ways to word the call to decision: What is real and enduring? Are those who get ahead unjustly really deluding themselves? What kind of life is truly "abundant" life (see John 10:10-11)? The psalmist takes a stand on God's power and love, seeking peace in God, and thus suggesting again a way to put the call to decision: What is true power, and who are the truly powerful? What is peace, and where do we seek it and find it? I can envision the psalmist singing the final verse of the hymn "They Cast Their Nets in Galilee":

> The peace of God, it is no peace,
> but strife closed in the sod.
> Yet . . . [people] pray for just one thing—
> The marvelous peace of God.[248]

To decide to seek the peace of God clearly involves also a decision about the pursuit of power. As the psalmist knew, and as Jesus and Paul knew as well, to seek the peace of God will be to experience "power . . . made perfect in weakness" (2 Cor 12:9 NRSV).

2. The prominence of the call to decision in Psalm 62 reminds us that Jesus' preaching clearly involved a similar call (see Mark 1:14-15). The reality of God's reign means the creation of a new world with new priorities and values. Like the psalmist, Jesus calls people to trust and to follow (see Mark 1:17). Not surprisingly, Jesus and his followers found opposition at every turn, as did the psalmist. Jesus' enemies sought to topple him. Jesus' response was a perfect embodiment of the psalmist's call to decision; he trusted God at all times, and he prayed (see Mark 14:32-36). It seemed like a weak alternative to the disciples (see Mark 8:31-33), and it led to a cross. But the cross and the resurrection have created a whole new world (see Acts 17:6)—a world in which to be powerful is to become like a child (Mark 10:13-16), to be great is to be the servant of all (Mark 9:33-37), to know peace is to bear a cross (Mark 8:34), to experience abundant life is to give oneself away (Mark 8:35). In short,

---

248. William Alexander Percy, "They Cast Their Nets in Galilee" in *The Hymnbook* (Richmond, Va.: Presbyterian Church in the U.S., UPCUSA, and the Reformed Church in America, 1955) 355 (#421).

Psalm 62 presents alternative paths to peace or repayment or reward (see v. 12b). Jesus said of the hypocrites who gave alms only to be seen and praised by others: "They have received their reward" (Matt 6:2 NRSV). Presumably, their reward is not the life and peace that Jesus offers. For the psalmist, peace is found in trust and prayer. This peace is by no means incompatible with suffering, but "surpasses all understanding" (Phil 4:7 NRSV), for it is not "as the world gives" (John 14:27 NRSV).

3. Psalm 62 recognizes that one of the greatest hindrances to entering and finding peace in the new world of God's reign is wealth (v. 10). It still is today. The psalmist's honor and wealth are in God (v. 7), but that is not the case with the opponents. It is significant that much of the vocabulary of Psalm 62 relates explicitly or implicitly to making money. Balances in v. 9 can be used to weigh money as well as people (see Jer 32:10). Extortion and robbery are obviously ways to get money, and v. 10 goes on to mention riches. The word "repay" (שלם *šalēm*) in v. 12 can mean to repay money (see 2 Kgs 4:7; Ps 37:21), and "work" (מעשה *maʿăśeh*, v. 12) can mean the activity by which one earns money (Gen 46:33). The preponderance of this imagery reminds us that money is one of the greatest obstacles to living under God's rule (see Mark 10:17-27, esp. v. 23; Luke 12:15; 1 Tim 6:7-10). To be sure, the problem is not money itself; rather, wealth lures us into thinking we are autonomous, *self*-ruled. Psalm 62 thus gives us an opportunity to reflect upon the question of how our "work" actually does "repay" us. Does God have anything to do with our work? What would it mean if our work were carried out with a primary awareness of God's claim upon us and upon our world? These and similar questions are vitally important in a culture that regularly discourages us from locating our life and substance in God (v. 7). To be sure, it is difficult for most of us even to imagine being countercultural, but then again, "all things are possible with God" (Mark 10:27 NIV).[249]

249. Portions of the above treatment of Psalm 62 appear in substantially the same form in McCann, "Psalm 62:5-12: Psalm for The Third Sunday After Epiphany," *No Other Foundation* 11/1 (Summer 1990) 43-48.

PSALM 63:1-11, YOUR LOVE IS BETTER THAN LIFE

NIV

Psalm 63

A psalm of David. When he was in the Desert of Judah.

¹O God, you are my God,
  earnestly I seek you;
my soul thirsts for you,
  my body longs for you,
in a dry and weary land
  where there is no water.

²I have seen you in the sanctuary
  and beheld your power and your glory.
³Because your love is better than life,

NRSV

Psalm 63

A Psalm of David, when he was in the Wilderness of Judah.

¹ O God, you are my God, I seek you,
  my soul thirsts for you;
my flesh faints for you,
  as in a dry and weary land where there is no water.
² So I have looked upon you in the sanctuary,
  beholding your power and glory.
³ Because your steadfast love is better than life,
  my lips will praise you.

NIV

my lips will glorify you.
⁴I will praise you as long as I live,
     and in your name I will lift up my hands.
⁵My soul will be satisfied as with the richest
          of foods;
     with singing lips my mouth will praise you.

⁶On my bed I remember you;
     I think of you through the watches of the
          night.
⁷Because you are my help,
     I sing in the shadow of your wings.
⁸My soul clings to you;
     your right hand upholds me.

⁹They who seek my life will be destroyed;
     they will go down to the depths of the
          earth.
¹⁰They will be given over to the sword
     and become food for jackals.

¹¹But the king will rejoice in God;
     all who swear by God's name will praise him,
     while the mouths of liars will be silenced.

NRSV

⁴ So I will bless you as long as I live;
     I will lift up my hands and call on your
          name.

⁵ My soul is satisfied as with a rich feast,ᵃ
     and my mouth praises you with joyful lips
⁶ when I think of you on my bed,
     and meditate on you in the watches of
          the night;
⁷ for you have been my help,
     and in the shadow of your wings I sing
          for joy.
⁸ My soul clings to you;
     your right hand upholds me.

⁹ But those who seek to destroy my life
     shall go down into the depths of the earth;
¹⁰ they shall be given over to the power of
          the sword,
     they shall be prey for jackals.
¹¹ But the king shall rejoice in God;
     all who swear by him shall exult,
     for the mouths of liars will be stopped.

ᵃHeb *with fat and fatness*

COMMENTARY

Scholars have offered a bewildering variety of proposals for classifying Psalm 63: song of praise (see v. 4), song of thanksgiving (see v. 5, a possible allusion to the meal that accompanied thanksgiving sacrifices), individual lament/complaint (see the complaint implied in vv. 1, 9-11), song of trust (see vv. 7-8), royal psalm (v. 11), and psalm for a night vigil (see v. 6). Each of these proposals entails, of course, a different understanding of the origin and ancient use of the psalm. What seems clear is that the psalmist has sought an experience of God's presence (v. 1; see Ps 27:4, 8 where the Hebrew verb translated "seek" is different from but conveys the same idea as the one used here), which the psalmist describes in terms of seeing God in the Temple (see "beholding" in v. 2 and "behold" in 27:4 NRSV). This description can be taken more or less literally. Several scholars, for instance, suggest that the psalmist spent the night at the Temple await-

ing an answer to prayer at dawn. Mark Smith even suggests that v. 2 describes a solar theophany; that is, the psalmist "looked upon" God when the sun arose over the Mount of Olives and illuminated the Temple, which faces east (see Ezek 43:1-5, as well as Psalms 11; 17; 27; 42–43, which Smith also associates with solar theophanies).[250] On the other hand, the description in vv. 1-2 can be taken metaphorically. The editors of the psalter, for instance, associated Psalm 63 with David's experience in the wilderness, perhaps associating v. 9 with Saul's attempts to kill David (see 1 Sam 23:14; 24:2).

What we must conclude from this variety of proposals for the origin and use of Psalm 63 is that it is suitable for use in a variety of settings. Regardless of how, where, and when it originated, it continued to function powerfully for generations

250. Mark S. Smith, *Psalms: The Divine Journey* (New York: Paulist, 1987) 54.

of Jews and Christians over the centuries (see Reflections below). In other words, more important than the categorization and possible original settings for Psalm 63 is the psalmist's claim that his or her life depends on God. As Smith concludes, "These words belong to a person who, thanks to God, is at rest and peace within."[251] In short, Psalm 63 articulates an experience that many persons from many places and times have had or can have as a result of their relationship to God. Psalm 63 is fundamentally about life and its true source. This fact is suggested by the fourfold occurrence of the Hebrew word נֶפֶשׁ (nepeš), which is translated "soul" (vv. 1, 5, 8) and "life" (v. 9), but which means fundamentally "vitality," "being"; in some contexts, it may even connote "appetite," a nuance that would be especially appropriate in vv. 1, 5. In the face of a threat on his or her life (v. 9), the psalmist finds sustenance, satisfaction, and security in the experience of God's presence. As the key word in Psalm 63, "soul"/"life" in vv. 1, 5, and 9 marks the beginning of the three sections of the psalm.

63:1-4. In v. 1, the psalmist expresses need in terms of thirst, a universal human necessity that can lead to faintness (see Isa 29:8). The only solution in this case is to see God (v. 2; see Ps 42:2, where the psalmist's soul "thirsts" and where the apparent solution is to "behold the face of God"). "Power" and "glory" are elsewhere associated with God's sovereignty; in Ps 29:1, the Hebrew words occur together but are there translated "strength" and "glory." The word for "power" also recalls Ps 62:11, where it was followed immediately by "steadfast love" (62:12). The same is true here (v. 3; see Commentary on Psalm 62 on the links among Psalms 61–63). The psalmist's entrusting of life to God's rule is expressed in a remarkable and memorable way in v. 3. "Steadfast love" is a primary feature of God's character as a forgiving and redeeming God (see Exod 15:13; 34:6-7; and Ps 5:7, where steadfast love is associated with entering God's house; see also Ps 61:7; Introduction). In other words, the psalmist recognizes that human life depends ultimately on God's faithfulness. The appropriate response is unending praise (vv. 3b-4a; see "bless" in Pss 16:7; 26:12; 34:1; 103:20-22), the joyful

yielding of the whole self to God, and prayer, the humble entrusting of life and future to God (v. 4b; see Pss 28:2; 134:2; and 62:8, where different terms articulate a call to continual trust and prayer).

63:5-8. Whereas thirst symbolized the psalmist's need in v. 1, that need is hunger in v. 5. The psalmist's whole being is "satisfied" (see Pss 81:16; 107:9; 132:15; and especially 17:15, where satisfaction is derived from "beholding" God's face, and 65:4, where being satisfied involves entering the Temple). "Mouth" and "lips," ordinary organs for eating, here become instruments of praise as well. In the light of v. 2, v. 6 could suggest that the psalmist spent the night in the Temple, and "your wings" in v. 7 may allude to the creatures that attended the ark (see Pss 17:8; 36:7; 57:1). But such conclusions remain speculative, and it is not necessary to take the imagery so literally. Verse 6 may be a way of emphasizing that the psalmist constantly, even throughout the night, remembers and meditates on God (see Ps 1:2, where meditation on God's instruction is to be continual, day and night). The experience described is sacramental; that is, the memory of God's help (Pss 22:19; 27:9; 40:17; 46:1) is inseparable from the current experience of God's real presence. Verse 8 articulates the immediacy and intimacy of the psalmist's relatedness to God (see Gen 2:24; see also Deut 10:20; 11:22; 30:20). It also reaffirms the psalmist's dependence upon God (see Ps 41:12; Isa 42:1). The joy in the experience is emphasized by the repetition in vv. 5b, 7.

63:9-11. The joyfulness of vv. 5-8 is even more striking after the transition to the final section, which indicates that it is not superficial cheeriness but a profound joy that endures ongoing threat to the *nepeš* (see Heb 12:2). As one whose life is sought by enemies, the psalmist joins the good company of Moses (Exod 4:19), David (1 Sam 20:1; 22:13; 23:15; 2 Sam 4:9; 16:11), Elijah (1 Kgs 19:10, 14), and Jeremiah (Jer 11:21) in the OT (see also Pss 35:4; 38:12; 54:3), and Jesus in the NT (see Mark 11:18). In these cases, the one threatened with death is given life, and so it is in Psalm 63. The psalmist finds sustenance and life in God's presence while the enemies "go down" to the realm devoid of God's presence (v. 9; see also Pss 86:13; 88:6). Whereas the psalmist's hunger is satisfied (v. 5), the opponents will

251. Ibid., 62.

become food for jackals (v. 10). The contrast between the destiny of the psalmist and that of the enemies is emphasized by the alliteration between the Hebrew words for "stopped" (סכר *sākar,* v. 11) and "seek" (שחר *šāḥar,* v. 1). The psalmist seeks God and lives; the enemies seek the lives of others and will be stopped. To seek God is to know the truth (v. 11*b*; "swear" and "satisfied" are also linked by alliteration), but to live at the expense of others

is to live a lie and ultimately to invite destruction. The mention of the king in v. 11 leads some scholars to conclude that he should be understood as the speaker throughout. While this is possible (see Ps 61:6-7), it is also possible to see the king as being representative or exemplary of the person who seeks God; it is clear that v. 11 did nothing to restrict the use of Psalm 63 by all kinds of persons in many places and times.

REFLECTIONS

1. The contrast between the uses of the word "mouth" in vv. 5 and 11 is significant. While the mouths of the enemies "will be stopped," the psalmist's mouth is open in joyful praise. The psalmist's open mouth seems to symbolize his or her orientation to God throughout the psalm: thirsting for God, hungering for God, praising God, praying to God. The open mouth indicates openness to God, which means life. In sharp contrast, the mouths of the enemies are closed so that they are unable to praise God, incapable of being satisfied, and unable to live, since to be closed to God is to be dead. The psalmist thus serves as a model of those who, in Jesus' words, "strive first for the kingdom of God" and find that "all these things [food, water, clothing] will be given . . . as well" (Matt 6:33 NRSV; see also Isa 55:1-9; Matt 5:6).

This remarkable openness to God is strikingly expressed in v. 3. It articulates the faith stance that persons in times past tried to elicit with a question reportedly asked to candidates for the ordained ministry in Calvinist churches: "Are you willing to be damned for the glory of God?" That this question now sounds so silly to us may be an indication of how difficult it is for persons in a self-centered culture to understand the intimacy of relatedness to God described in Psalm 63. Mays comments that:

> Trust becomes for a moment pure adoration that leaves the self behind as any participant in the reason for adoration. In the interpretation of patristic times this confession was associated with martyrs who valued God more than life and gave up their lives rather than deny their testimony. But in a salvation religion there is always the danger for all believers to take the value of their own lives as the primary reason to trust God. This verse leads us in prayer to the point of devotion to God alone that must be the goal of all true faith.[252]

Psalm 63 thus illumines Jesus' call to a discipleship that involves self-denial and cross-bearing (Mark 8:34), but that finally constitutes life as God intends (Mark 8:35-37).

This life is possible in the presence of what Charles Wesley called "Love Divine, All Loves Excelling," and of which he wrote words that recall Psalm 63:

> Come, Almighty to deliver,
> Let us all thy life receive;
> Suddenly return and never,
> Nevermore thy temples leave.
> Thee we would be always blessing,
> Serve thee as thy hosts above,
> Pray and praise thee without ceasing,
> Glory in thy perfect love.

The final phrase of the hymn aptly describes the kind of self-denial voiced by v. 3: "lost in wonder, love, and praise."

252. James L. Mays, *Psalms,* Interpretation (Louisville: John Knox, 1994) 218.

2. Perhaps in continuity with its ancient Israelite use, or because the verb "seek" in v. 1 apparently meant originally "to look for dawn," Psalm 63 has been used from earliest Christian times as a morning psalm. Given its widespread use and its eloquent and powerful expression of faith in God, it is not surprising that it has been a favorite of persons as varied in time and place as John Chrysostom, Thomas à Kempis, and Theodore Beza, who, in keeping with v. 6, regularly recited the psalm at night.[253] This history of use is testimony to the adaptability of the psalms and their ability to transcend the circumstances of their origin and to be perennially available to express the praises, prayers, and piety of the people of God.

253. See Rowland E. Prothero, *The Psalms in Human Life and Experience* (New York: E. P. Dutton, 1903) 77, 141.

PSALM 64:1-10, WHAT GOD HAS DONE

Psalm 64

For the director of music. A psalm of David.

¹Hear me, O God, as I voice my complaint;
  protect my life from the threat of the enemy.
²Hide me from the conspiracy of the wicked,
  from that noisy crowd of evildoers.

³They sharpen their tongues like swords
  and aim their words like deadly arrows.
⁴They shoot from ambush at the innocent man;
  they shoot at him suddenly, without fear.

⁵They encourage each other in evil plans,
  they talk about hiding their snares;
  they say, "Who will see them*ª*?"
⁶They plot injustice and say,
  "We have devised a perfect plan!"
  Surely the mind and heart of man are cunning.

⁷But God will shoot them with arrows;
  suddenly they will be struck down.
⁸He will turn their own tongues against them
  and bring them to ruin;
  all who see them will shake their heads in
    scorn.

⁹All mankind will fear;
  they will proclaim the works of God
  and ponder what he has done.
¹⁰Let the righteous rejoice in the LORD
  and take refuge in him;
  let all the upright in heart praise him!

ª5 Or us

Psalm 64

To the leader. A Psalm of David.

¹ Hear my voice, O God, in my complaint;
  preserve my life from the dread enemy.
² Hide me from the secret plots of the wicked,
  from the scheming of evildoers,
³ who whet their tongues like swords,
  who aim bitter words like arrows,
⁴ shooting from ambush at the blameless;
  they shoot suddenly and without fear.
⁵ They hold fast to their evil purpose;
  they talk of laying snares secretly,
  thinking, "Who can see us?ª
⁶ Who can search out our crimes?*ᵇ*
  We have thought out a cunningly conceived
    plot."
  For the human heart and mind are deep.

⁷ But God will shoot his arrow at them;
  they will be wounded suddenly.
⁸ Because of their tongue he will bring them
    to ruin;*ᶜ*
  all who see them will shake with horror.
⁹ Then everyone will fear;
  they will tell what God has brought about,
  and ponder what he has done.

¹⁰ Let the righteous rejoice in the LORD
  and take refuge in him.
  Let all the upright in heart glory.

ª Syr: Heb them   ᵇ Cn: Heb They search out crimes   ᶜ Cn: Heb They will bring him to ruin, their tongue being against them

COMMENTARY

Psalm 64 shows the characteristic features of a prayer for help or individual lament/complaint. Petition (vv. 1-2) is followed by complaint, which takes the form of a description of the enemy (vv. 3-6). Verses 7-9 consist of an affirmation of faith in God's activity, and v. 10 calls for joyful trust and praise. As usual, it is impossible to determine the precise circumstances of origin and use. To be sure, destructive speech is employed to threaten the psalmist. But how and by whom? It is possible that the persecuted psalmist has sought refuge in the Temple from persecution or false accusation (see Psalms 5; 7; 61; Introduction), and it is possible that Psalm 64 was used in some sort of restoration ritual within a family or small-group setting. We simply do not know. As Tate judiciously suggests, "In any case, the psalm is a literary entity, apparently without any strong ties to a specific ancient context. The text generates its own context in interaction with the reader."[254]

64:1-2. The psalmist characterizes this prayer as a complaint (v. 1a), and it apparently arises out of a frightening, threatening situation (v. 1b). The need to be hidden (v. 2a) reinforces the urgency of the threat (see 2 Kgs 11:2; Pss 17:8; 27:5; 31:20; Jer 36:26). The word that the NRSV translates "secret plots" (סוד sôd) usually designates consultation for good purposes, but clearly not in this case (see also Ps 83:3). The NIV's translation of v. 2b is probably more accurate, and by suggesting a sort of mob scene as opposed to a quiet conspiracy, it makes v. 2b a more all-encompassing request.

64:3-6. Verse 3 is similar to Pss 57:4 and 140:3, which suggest that the wicked use words as weapons. The bow-and-arrow imagery of v. 3b continues into v. 4. The word "ambush" in v. 4 is from the same Hebrew root (סתר str) as "hide" in v. 2; thus the wicked do their own sort of hiding, but the psalmist desires to be hidden by God. The wicked may shoot (see Ps 11:2), but the psalmist trusts that God shoots back (see v. 7). In short, the psalmist entrusts his or her life to God. Such trust is the real essence of being blameless or innocent (see Commentary on Psalms

15; 18). In contrast to the psalmist's dependence upon God, the wicked trust their own plans (v. 5a). They are convinced that they can do things secretly (v. 5b); the question in v. 5c further indicates their belief that they are autonomous (see Commentary on Psalm 1) and thus are accountable to no one (see Ps 10:13). Therefore, they continue to pursue "injustice" (v. 6a; see also Ps 58:2 NIV), convinced that they can do so with impunity (v. 6b) because of their own human capacities (v. 6c). Verse 6ab is made emphatic by the threefold repetition of a Hebrew root (חפש ḥpś) translated "plot," "devised," or "plan," and v. 6c prepares for the rest of the psalm. The word "heart" (לב lēb) anticipates the final line of the psalm, and the affirmation of human capacity sharply contrasts with the psalmist's focus on God, which begins in v. 7.

64:7-9. The shift at v. 7 is also marked by a reference to God in the third person, which gives the affirmation of faith in vv. 7-9 a sort of instructional tone. The repetition in vv. 7-10 of several words from vv. 3-6 serves to sharpen further the contrast between the psalmist's faith in God and wicked persons' faith in themselves. For instance, the words "shoot," "arrow," and "suddenly" in v. 7 recall vv. 3-4. God has arrows, too (see Ps 7:12-13). Thus the irony is that those who "shoot suddenly" will be "wounded suddenly." Verse 8a is difficult, but the word "tongue" (לשון lāšôn) recalls v. 3. Again, what the wicked perceive as their strength will be the cause of their undoing. The word "see" (ראה rā'â) in v. 8b recalls the question in v. 5b; that is, those who thought they could not be seen will become a public spectacle. Those who improperly had no fear (v. 4b) will engender a proper fear in others (v. 9a), and the crowning irony is that the lives of those who fancied themselves all-powerful will end up leading others to proclaim and wisely recognize God's powerful activity (v. 9bc).

64:10. The reversal between vv. 7-9 and vv. 3-6 is matched by the reversal between v. 10 and vv. 1-2. The psalmist's complaint has become an invitation for others to "rejoice" and "glory" (see Ps 34:2). The righteous (see Pss 1:5-6; 97:11) and the "upright in heart" (see Pss 7:10; 11:2; 32:11;

---

254. Marvin E. Tate, *Psalms 51–100*, WBC 20 (Dallas: Word, 1990) 133.

36:10; 94:15; 97:11) are those who live in dependence upon God rather than self. As the psalter has suggested from the beginning, to take refuge in God is the true source of happiness and joy (see Ps 2:12; Introduction). As with the other prayers for help, the movement from complaint to praise is not sequential or chronological; indeed, trust in God allows the psalmist to experience God's protection and to rejoice amid ongoing threat and the continuing reality of evil. In short, the perspective is eschatological, summoning readers in every time and place to trust and to have joy in the midst of human self-assertion that threatens both individuals and the security of our society and the world.

REFLECTIONS

The talk of swords and arrows and snares, as well as the portrayal of God's taking direct retributive action against the wicked, makes Psalm 64 seem rather far-removed from our contemporary world. Tate proposes, however, that it is more relevant than we might care to realize: "The psalm communicates a sense of anxiety and perplexity about the nature of human society that is at home in every generation. The supposed sophistication of modern society is not immune to deep awareness of destructive forces which threaten to reduce our semi-ordered world to chaos."[255]

In fact, the bold affirmation of human capacity and autonomy in vv. 5*b*-6 characterizes the way that most people, including Christians, routinely operate. Individual decision making and public policy making rarely include consideration of anything beyond our own interests. Although we may not be quite as crass as the wicked are in v. 5*b*, we seldom make accountability to God and others a major factor in our deliberations. This, of course, goes a long way toward explaining the existence of the "destructive forces" that Tate mentions—poverty and the unrest it breeds, oppression of women and minorities and the hostility it generates, warfare to protect ethnic claims or national interests and the chaos it produces, and so on. In a real sense, Psalm 64 calls us to recognize and to confess the evil within ourselves and our society.

It is also a call to faith—not to trust our own inclinations or capacities but to entrust our abilities and destiny to God. The structure of the psalm belies any facile understanding of divine retribution. For Christians, of course, the cross is a constant reminder that God does not exercise power by suddenly eliminating all evil and opposition. Rather, God's power is made perfect in weakness (see 1 Cor 1:25; 2 Cor 12:9-10). For Christians, the resurrection is the sign of God's victory, but we are called to live as people of the cross as well as of the resurrection (see Commentary on Psalms 13; 22; Introduction). Like the psalmist, we shall always find ourselves pleading and complaining as we confront the reality of evil (vv. 1-6), but because we ultimately trust God's power rather than human power (vv. 7-9), we shall also find that even now joy is possible (v. 10). We trust that evil is sowing the seeds of its own destruction, and we greet signs of evil's unraveling as what God has done (v. 9). Indeed, trusting God rather than self, we find the joy that liberates us for praise.

255. Ibid., 135.

PSALM 65:1-13, YOU CROWN THE YEAR WITH YOUR BOUNTY

NIV

Psalm 65

For the director of music. A psalm of David.
A song.

[1] Praise awaits[a] you, O God, in Zion;
    to you our vows will be fulfilled.
[2] O you who hear prayer,
    to you all men will come.
[3] When we were overwhelmed by sins,
    you forgave[b] our transgressions.
[4] Blessed are those you choose
    and bring near to live in your courts!
We are filled with the good things of your
        house,
    of your holy temple.

[5] You answer us with awesome deeds of
        righteousness,
    O God our Savior,
the hope of all the ends of the earth
    and of the farthest seas,
[6] who formed the mountains by your power,
    having armed yourself with strength,
[7] who stilled the roaring of the seas,
    the roaring of their waves,
    and the turmoil of the nations.
[8] Those living far away fear your wonders;
    where morning dawns and evening fades
    you call forth songs of joy.

[9] You care for the land and water it;
    you enrich it abundantly.
The streams of God are filled with water
    to provide the people with grain,
    for so you have ordained it.[c]
[10] You drench its furrows
    and level its ridges;
you soften it with showers
    and bless its crops.
[11] You crown the year with your bounty,
    and your carts overflow with abundance.

a1 Or *befits*; the meaning of the Hebrew for this word is uncertain.
b3 Or *made atonement for*   c9 Or *for that is how you prepare the land*

NRSV

Psalm 65

To the leader. A Psalm of David. A Song.

[1] Praise is due to you,
    O God, in Zion;
and to you shall vows be performed,
[2] O you who answer prayer!
To you all flesh shall come.
[3] When deeds of iniquity overwhelm us,
    you forgive our transgressions.
[4] Happy are those whom you choose and
        bring near
    to live in your courts.
We shall be satisfied with the goodness of
        your house,
    your holy temple.

[5] By awesome deeds you answer us with
        deliverance,
    O God of our salvation;
you are the hope of all the ends of the earth
    and of the farthest seas.
[6] By your[a] strength you established the
        mountains;
    you are girded with might.
[7] You silence the roaring of the seas,
    the roaring of their waves,
    the tumult of the peoples.
[8] Those who live at earth's farthest bounds
        are awed by your signs;
you make the gateways of the morning and
        the evening shout for joy.

[9] You visit the earth and water it,
    you greatly enrich it;
the river of God is full of water;
    you provide the people with grain,
    for so you have prepared it.
[10] You water its furrows abundantly,
    settling its ridges,
softening it with showers,
    and blessing its growth.

a Gk Jerome: Heb *his*

NIV

¹²The grasslands of the desert overflow;
   the hills are clothed with gladness.
¹³The meadows are covered with flocks
   and the valleys are mantled with grain;
   they shout for joy and sing.

NRSV

¹¹ You crown the year with your bounty;
   your wagon tracks overflow with richness.
¹² The pastures of the wilderness overflow,
   the hills gird themselves with joy,
¹³ the meadows clothe themselves with flocks,
   the valleys deck themselves with grain,
   they shout and sing together for joy.

COMMENTARY

Psalm 65 is usually categorized as a song of praise or a communal song of thanksgiving, and it is frequently associated with the autumn harvest festival. It is possible, however, to construe the verbs in vv. 3-5, 10 in an imperative sense, and on that basis several commentators interpret the psalm as a prayer for the rain that will produce an abundant harvest.

Although it is sometimes suggested that vv. 9-13 were originally an independent poem, there are clearly unifying features in the final form of Psalm 65. God is addressed directly throughout the psalm, and each section describes in a different way the reasons why God deserves to be praised (v. 1). Verses 1-4 center on God's answering of prayer (v. 2a), which means forgiveness (v. 3) and the ability to approach God's house (v. 4). Verses 5-8 recall more generally God's saving and creating activity, and vv. 9-13 offer a specific example of God's "awesome deeds" (v. 5) or "signs" (v. 8)—the provision of rain that makes the earth bountiful. Both the second and the third sections conclude with various elements of creation's offering the praise "due to you" (v. 1a).

65:1-4. The psalm begins in a striking way. The phrase "to you" begins the first two poetic lines (vv. 1a, 1c), and a similar phrase also begins the third poetic line (v. 2b). The effect is to make God the emphatic center of attention from the beginning, and this effect is reinforced by the emphatic pronoun in v. 3b, "you forgive." Verse 1a seems to read, literally, "To you silence is praise," perhaps a case of hyperbole, but it is probably better, as the NRSV and the NIV have done, to follow the reading of several ancient versions. God deserves praise, and people should keep their promises to God (that is, fulfill their

vows; see Pss 22:25; 61:8; 66:13; 116:12-14, 17-18). This is the case, because God has heard their prayers and apparently has responded favorably (v. 2). This has been the case, despite the people's willful rebellion, which is suggested by the word "transgression" (פשע *peša‘*, v. 3). The NIV note suggests that the word translated "forgave" here (כפר *kipper*) is not the one usually used. It occurs elsewhere in the Psalms only in 78:38 and 79:9, but it is much more frequently used in Exodus and Leviticus in the context of people's engaging in ritual activity to effect atonement. The striking thing here is that God makes the atonement. As suggested above, the focus remains emphatically on God. Here God's gracious initiative is primary. Sinful people do not simply decide to approach God with their rituals. Rather, people are chosen (see Pss 33:12; 78:68) and brought near by God. The verb "bring near" (קרב *qārab*) is often used in the context of bringing offerings (see Lev 3:7, 12). In effect, God brings the people to God's own self as an offering. If the people offer anything, it is their gratitude, possibly in the form of a thanksgiving sacrifice. The payment of vows (v. 1b) often took the form of a thanksgiving offering (see Ps 116:17-18), and the ritual involved a communal meal, which may be alluded to in v. 4. In any case, literally or figuratively or both, the people "shall be satisfied" in God's house (note "Zion" in v. 1 and "courts," "house," and "temple" in v. 4). God is the gracious host who invites people in to live and to eat at God's table (see Pss 22:26; 23:5-6; 36:8; 63:5; Matt 26:26-29).

65:5-8. The mention of "all flesh" in v. 2 has anticipated the broadening of perspective in vv. 5-8. Although God has a specific place to which people are invited, God's influence and power extend to "the ends of the earth" (v. 5; see v. 8, where "bounds" translates the same Hebrew root [קצה *qsh*] as "ends"). The mention of God's "awesome deeds" recalls the exodus (see Exod 15:11), when God proved to be the "God of our salvation" (v. 5; see Exod 15:2), and after which God's everlasting reign was proclaimed (Exod 15:18). God's sovereignty is implicit in v. 5, for "righteousness" elsewhere designates God's royal policy (see Pss 96:13; 97:6; 98:9). The exodus was a public event that was not simply for Israel's benefit but was intended to fulfill God's creational purposes (see Commentary on Psalms 33; 66). Thus it is not surprising that the "power" God revealed to Pharaoh (Exod 9:16) is mentioned in v. 6 as that which "formed the mountains." The chaotic waters and the unruly peoples are also subject to God's sovereignty (v. 7; see Ps 46:10, where God is exalted over the nations and the earth, which 46:3, 6 have described using the same root that is translated "tumult" [המה *hmh*] in 65:7). Just as God provided for the invited guests in vv. 1-4, so also God is the "security of all the ends of the earth" (v. 5 author's trans.). Thus the creation joins in praising God in recognition of God's gracious rule (v. 8).

65:9-13. Here the psalmist offers a specific example of the way God provides satisfaction (v. 4) and security (v. 5): by sending the rain that makes the earth fruitful and productive. Mays comments that we have here a remarkable poetic portrayal of God as a "cosmic farmer" who carefully tends and waters the earth (vv. 9-10) so that it produces abundantly (vv. 11-13).[256] The word "bounty" (טובה *ṭôbâ*, v. 11) is from the same root as "goodness" (v. 4). Both in God's place and throughout the earth, God is the gracious provider. The verb in v. 11*a* suggests that God, the cosmic ruler, gives the earth royal treatment (see "crown" in Pss 8:5; 103:4). In recognition of God's rule and God's role in sharing the benefits of God's sovereignty, the created elements again offer their joyful praise (v. 13*c*; see v. 8). The verb "shout" (רוע *rûa'*) specifically designates elsewhere the acclamation of God's reign (see Ps 47:1; see also Pss 95:1-2; 98:4, 6). As Kraus concludes, "The psalm fits best in the situation of the prostration before the creator and king of the world . . . who is enthroned on Zion and is worshiped in hymnic adoration (Pss. 95:6; 96:9; 99:5, 9)."[257] Psalm 65 is thus another affirmation of the theological heart of the psalter: God reigns! (See Psalms 2; 93; 95–99; Introduction.) It is also a reminder to us that we praise God, as also we live, in partnership with heaven and earth and all creation (see esp. vv. 8, 13; see also Psalms 8; 104; 143).

256. Mays, *Psalms,* 220.
257. H.-J. Kraus, *Psalms 60–150: A Commentary,* trans. H. C. Oswald (Minneapolis: Augsburg, 1989) 28.

REFLECTIONS

It is frequently suggested that vv. 9-13 have a polemical thrust, that the role of the Canaanite fertility God, Baal, is clearly occupied by Israel's God (see Hos 2:8, 16-20). Throughout Psalm 65, attention is directed clearly and often emphatically to God rather than to the gods or to human achievement. By worshiping Baal, the Canaanites—and frequently the Israelites—sought to secure by their own efforts a prosperous agricultural year. While we contemporary folk are not tempted to worship Baal, we are lured by Baalism's basic appeal (see Reflections on Psalm 29). In terms of security, we are convinced that we either do have or should have things under control. As for prosperity, we are generally convinced that we have earned it. From this perspective, of course, praise is due not to God but to ourselves. In short, we exalt ourselves, and the results are humbling. As Brueggemann puts it, "the loss of wonder, the inability to sing songs of praise about the reliability of life, is both a measure and a cause of our profanation of life."[258]

Psalm 65 is often read at observances of the national Thanksgiving holiday in the United States, a setting that clearly raises the issue of to whom our praise and gratitude are due. What

258. Walter Brueggemann, *The Message of the Psalms: A Theological Commentary* (Minneapolis: Augsburg, 1984) 136.

Reinhold Niebuhr wrote about a community Thanksgiving service in 1927 is still true today: "Thanksgiving becomes increasingly the business of congratulating the Almighty upon his most excellent co-workers, ourselves. . . . The Lord who was worshiped was not the Lord of Hosts, but the spirit of Uncle Sam, given a cosmic eminence for the moment which the dear old gentleman does not deserve."[259]

Thus the polemical thrust of Psalm 65 is still relevant. It reminds us that neither we nor the government of the United States (nor any other country) rules the world. God rules the world. To direct our praise and gratitude toward anything or anyone less will finally mean either self-congratulation or a misguided patriotism—idolatry, in either case.

If we were less idolatrous about our national life, we might even be able to do what Israel did in v. 3: admit publicly that we are sometimes wrong! As Brueggemann says of v. 3:

> Let us not miss the dramatic claim. The whole people (together with the king, presumably) concedes its guilt and celebrates its forgiveness. Such a scene is nearly unthinkable in our public life. . . .
>
> . . . Psalm 65 reflects a public imagination capable of a troubled spirit, not so full of self, but able to reflect on its life in light of the majesty of God, a community forgiven and therefore ready to begin afresh.[260]

Obviously, this posture is a far cry from the frequently heard slogan "My country, right or wrong." Citizenship in the reign of God allows persons to look beyond mere national security to the one who is the security of all the ends of the earth (see v. 5).

259. Reinhold Niebuhr, *Leaves from the Notebook of a Tamed Cynic* (San Francisco: Harper & Row, 1980) 147-48.
260. Brueggemann, *The Message of the Psalms,* 135.

PSALM 66:1-20, GOD HAS KEPT US AMONG THE LIVING

NIV	NRSV
Psalm 66	**Psalm 66**
For the director of music. A song. A psalm.	To the leader. A Song. A Psalm.
¹Shout with joy to God, all the earth!	¹ Make a joyful noise to God, all the earth;
² Sing the glory of his name;	² sing the glory of his name;
make his praise glorious!	give to him glorious praise.
³Say to God, "How awesome are your deeds!	³ Say to God, "How awesome are your deeds!
So great is your power	Because of your great power, your
that your enemies cringe before you.	enemies cringe before you.
⁴All the earth bows down to you;	⁴ All the earth worships you;
they sing praise to you,	they sing praises to you,
they sing praise to your name." *Selah*	sing praises to your name." *Selah*
⁵Come and see what God has done,	⁵ Come and see what God has done:
how awesome his works in man's behalf!	he is awesome in his deeds among
⁶He turned the sea into dry land,	mortals.
they passed through the waters on foot—	⁶ He turned the sea into dry land;
come, let us rejoice in him.	they passed through the river on foot.

NIV

⁷He rules forever by his power,
    his eyes watch the nations—
    let not the rebellious rise up
        against him.   *Selah*

⁸Praise our God, O peoples,
    let the sound of his praise be heard;
⁹he has preserved our lives
    and kept our feet from slipping.
¹⁰For you, O God, tested us;
    you refined us like silver.
¹¹You brought us into prison
    and laid burdens on our backs.
¹²You let men ride over our heads;
    we went through fire and water,
    but you brought us to a place of
        abundance.

¹³I will come to your temple with burnt
        offerings
    and fulfill my vows to you—
¹⁴vows my lips promised and my mouth spoke
    when I was in trouble.
¹⁵I will sacrifice fat animals to you
    and an offering of rams;
    I will offer bulls and goats.   *Selah*

¹⁶Come and listen, all you who fear God;
    let me tell you what he has done for me.
¹⁷I cried out to him with my mouth;
    his praise was on my tongue.
¹⁸If I had cherished sin in my heart,
    the Lord would not have listened;
¹⁹but God has surely listened
    and heard my voice in prayer.
²⁰Praise be to God,
    who has not rejected my prayer
    or withheld his love from me!

NRSV

There we rejoiced in him,
⁷   who rules by his might forever,
    whose eyes keep watch on the nations—
    let the rebellious not exalt
        themselves.   *Selah*

⁸ Bless our God, O peoples,
    let the sound of his praise be heard,
⁹ who has kept us among the living,
    and has not let our feet slip.
¹⁰ For you, O God, have tested us;
    you have tried us as silver is tried.
¹¹ You brought us into the net;
    you laid burdens on our backs;
¹² you let people ride over our heads;
    we went through fire and through water;
    yet you have brought us out to a spacious
        place.[a]

¹³ I will come into your house with burnt
        offerings;
    I will pay you my vows,
¹⁴ those that my lips uttered
    and my mouth promised when I was in
        trouble.
¹⁵ I will offer to you burnt offerings of fatlings,
    with the smoke of the sacrifice of rams;
    I will make an offering of bulls and goats.
                                        Selah

¹⁶ Come and hear, all you who fear God,
    and I will tell what he has done for me.
¹⁷ I cried aloud to him,
    and he was extolled with my tongue.
¹⁸ If I had cherished iniquity in my heart,
    the Lord would not have listened.
¹⁹ But truly God has listened;
    he has given heed to the words of my
        prayer.

²⁰ Blessed be God,
    because he has not rejected my prayer
    or removed his steadfast love from me.

[a] Cn Compare Gk Syr Jerome Tg: Heb *to a saturation*

COMMENTARY

Psalm 66 follows nicely upon Psalm 65. In fact, the same verb ("shout" [רוע *rûa'*]) appears in Pss 65:13c and 66:1a. Psalm 65 had proclaimed God to be the security of all the ends of the earth (v. 5), and Psalm 66 begins by bidding all the earth to praise God. Like Psalm 65, Psalm 66 is an eloquent affirmation that God rules the world (see esp. vv. 1-7), and, like Psalm 65, it is usually classified as a communal song of thanksgiving. It is easy to picture the use of Psalm 66 in a liturgical setting, but much more difficult to identify this setting with any certainty. Because of the allusions to the exodus and perhaps to the crossing of the Jordan (see vv. 1-7, esp. v. 6), Kraus suggests that the psalm may have been used at Gilgal in a festival commemorating these events (see Joshua 3–4; Psalm 114).[261] Other scholars, however, citing vv. 13-15, suggest the use of the psalm accompanying the offering of a sacrifice in the Temple.

These divergent directions, plus the shift from first-person plural to singular in v. 13, have led some scholars to question the unity of Psalm 66. But there are parallels and verbal links between vv. 1-12 and vv. 13-20, indicating that they should be heard as a whole. Furthermore, when the unity of the psalm is maintained, an important theological lesson is to be learned (see Reflections).

66:1-12. The psalm opens with an invitation to all the earth to praise God (v. 1), and reports that this praise does occur (v. 4). The mention of God's "name" (vv. 2, 4) is suggestive of God's character. Human beings worship God because of who God is, which is revealed by what God does (v. 3; see "cringe" in Pss 18:44; 81:15)—i.e., God rules the world. One should not be surprised, then, that the vocabulary of the invitations to praise frequently occurs in contexts explicitly affirming God's reign: "make a joyful noise"/"shout with joy" (v. 1; see Pss 95:1-2; 98:4, 6; 100:1); "glory" (v. 2; see Pss 24:7-10; 29:1-3, 9; 96:3, 7-8; 145:5, 11-12); "power"/"strength" (v. 3; see Exod 15:2, 13; Pss 29:1, 11; 93:1; 96:6-7); "worships"/"bows down" (v. 4; see Pss 95:6; 99:5); "sing praises" (v. 4; see Pss 47:6-7; 98:4-5). Since God rules the world, all the earth is God's congregation (see also v. 7).

Like vv. 1-4, vv. 5-7 begin with a plural imperative, suggesting that the addressee is still "all the earth" (see the similar invitations in Ps 46:9). The focus is again on God's activity (v. 5), which is described again as "awesome" (vv. 3, 5), the same adjective used of God's activity in delivering Israel from Egypt (Exod 15:11; see also 47:2; 65:6; 96:4; 99:3; 145:6, where it occurs in contexts that explicitly proclaim God's reign). The exodus comes into even sharper focus in v. 6 (cf. Exod 14:16, 22, 29). Especially in view of vv. 1-4, it is important to realize that the exodus was ultimately not just for Israel's benefit but for the enactment of God's will for all the earth. As Terence Fretheim suggests:

> While the liberation of Israel is the focus of God's activity, it is not the ultimate purpose. The deliverance of Israel is ultimately for the sake of all creation (see 9:16). The issue for God is finally not that God's name be made known in Israel but that it be declared to the entire earth. God's purpose in these events is creation-wide. What is at stake is God's mission for the world, for as 9:29 and 19:5 put it, "All the earth is God's" (cf. 8:22; 9:14). Hence the *public character* of these events is an important theme throughout.[262]

As in the book of Exodus, here all the earth is summoned to "come and see" (v. 5). God's activity is not just for Israel but for all people! God intends that the nations (v. 7) will recognize God's reign (see "rules" in Pss 22:28; 59:13; 103:19). Those who "see" (v. 5) God's sovereign, creationwide purposes, will not exalt themselves but will join Moses and the Israelites in exalting God (Exod 15:2; see discussion of v. 17 below).

Another plural imperative begins v. 8, and the repetition of "praise" (see v. 2) also reminds us that all the earth is invited to "bless our God" (see v. 20, another link between vv. 1-12 and 13-20). As in vv. 1-7, the focus of God's activity is on Israel, but the deliverance related in vv. 9-12 is again paradigmatic and is thus cause for all people to praise God. The deliverance involves rescue from death (v. 9a). In this sense, it is like the exodus, but the vocabulary in vv. 9-12 is not

261. H.-J. Kraus, *Psalms 60–150: A Commentary,* trans. H. C. Oswald (Minneapolis: Augsburg, 1989) 36.

262. Terence Fretheim, *Exodus,* Interpretation (Louisville: John Knox, 1991) 13.

specifically reminiscent of the exodus. God has not allowed the people to "slip" or to "be moved" (v. 9*b*; see also Pss 16:8; 17:5; 38:16; 55:22; 94:18; 121:3). The specific distress being faced is not described. Whatever it may have been, Israel is so sure of God's sovereignty that the trouble cannot be given a non-theological explanation. Thus the people affirm that God has "tested us" and "tried us" (v. 10). Tests and trials need not evoke the concept of punishment; indeed, they most frequently suggest that God is examining a person for the purpose of vindicating him or her (see Job 23:10; Pss 11:4-5; 17:3; 26:2; 139:23; Jer 12:3; Zech 13:9). In any case, the emphasis in vv. 10-11 is on God's deliverance of the people, made clear by the fact that vv. 9 and 12*c* envelope the description of distress.[263] Verse 12*b* is similar to Isa 43:2, which is a reminder that Isaiah 40–55 portrays the deliverance from exile as a new exodus. While v. 12*b* may be taken as a historical clue to the date of the psalm, also it indicates that Israel understood that "the exodus recurs again and again, in new circumstances."[264]

66:13-20. While the shift that occurs at v. 13

263. See John Bracke, "Psalm 66:8-20: Psalm for the Sixth Sunday of Easter," *No Other Foundation* 13/2 (Winter 1992–93) 42.
264. Walter Brueggemann, *The Message of the Psalms: A Theological Commentary* (Minneapolis: Augsburg, 1984) 138.

can be taken as a sign of discontinuity, it can also be construed as the psalmist's presentation of her or his life as a witness to God's recurring activity in new circumstances of delivering persons from death to life. As in vv. 8-12, the exact nature of the trouble (v. 14) is not specified, but the deliverance from it is given a public character. The psalmist invites others to "come and hear" (v. 16) about God's activity, echoing what the whole people had done (v. 5). In keeping with the people's counsel to the nations (v. 7), the psalmist has not been rebellious (v. 18). It is not so much a matter that this prayer has merited attention but that the psalmist has opened the self to God's recurring activity. In any case, God has "listened" (v. 19) and has not removed "steadfast love from me" (v. 20). As did vv. 5-7, so vv. 19-20 recall the exodus (see "listen" in Exod 3:7 and "steadfast love" in Exod 15:13). For the psalmist, the old, old story of deliverance has become the new, new song. The psalmist joins Moses and all Israel in exalting God (cf. v. 17 with Exod 15:2). Thus the psalmist's life is an example of heeding the counsel of v. 7. As the nations have been invited to do (v. 8), the psalmist declares God "blessed" (v. 20) on account of who God is and what God does—steadfastly loving (see Exod 34:6-7; Introduction) in the fulfillment of God's creational purposes for all the earth (vv. 1, 4).

REFLECTIONS

Rowland Prothero has written the following about John Bunyan's use of Psalm 66: "In his *Grace Abounding to the Chief of Sinners,* which bears the motto, 'Come and hear all ye that fear God, and I will declare what he hath done for my soul' [Ps 66:16], he has recorded, with a pen of iron and in letters of fire, his own passage from death to life."[265] Psalm 66 is about this "passage from death to life" (see esp. v. 9), so much so that the LXX and the Vulgate even provide this psalm with the title "Psalm of the resurrection," and it is still associated liturgically with the season of Easter. In the exodus (vv. 5-7), in recurring exoduses in new circumstances (vv. 8-12), and in individual experiences of deliverance (vv. 13-20), God is at work bringing life out of death. For Christians, of course, the ultimate paradigm of God's life-giving activity is found in the death and resurrection of Jesus (see Commentary on Psalm 118).

Just as Christians affirm participation in the paradigmatic death and resurrection of Jesus (see Rom 6:1-11), so also the psalmist affirms participation in the paradigmatic event of exodus. Finally, what God has done for all God's people (v. 5) is inseparable from what God has done for the individual (v. 16), and vice versa. Such is the lesson of Psalm 66 when it is read as a whole. As Brueggemann puts it, "This psalm shows the move from communal affirmation to individual appreciation, which is what we always do in biblical faith."[266]

265. Rowland E. Prothero, *The Psalms in Human Life and Experience* (New York: E. P. Dutton, 1903) 185.
266. Walter Brueggemann, *The Message of the Psalms: A Theological Commentary* (Minneapolis: Augsburg, 1984) 138.

PSALM 67:1-7, THAT GOD'S WAYS MAY BE KNOWN ON EARTH

NIV

Psalm 67

For the director of music. With stringed instruments. A psalm. A song.

¹May God be gracious to us and bless us
    and make his face shine upon us,   *Selah*
²that your ways may be known on earth,
    your salvation among all nations.

³May the peoples praise you, O God;
    may all the peoples praise you.

⁴May the nations be glad and sing for joy,
    for you rule the peoples justly
    and guide the nations of the earth.   *Selah*
⁵May the peoples praise you, O God;
    may all the peoples praise you.

⁶Then the land will yield its harvest,
    and God, our God, will bless us.
⁷God will bless us,
    and all the ends of the earth will fear him.

NRSV

Psalm 67

To the leader: with stringed instruments.
A Psalm. A Song.

¹ May God be gracious to us and bless us
    and make his face to shine upon us, *Selah*
² that your way may be known upon earth,
    your saving power among all nations.
³ Let the peoples praise you, O God;
    let all the peoples praise you.

⁴ Let the nations be glad and sing for joy,
    for you judge the peoples with equity
    and guide the nations upon earth.   *Selah*
⁵ Let the peoples praise you, O God;
    let all the peoples praise you.

⁶ The earth has yielded its increase;
    God, our God, has blessed us.
⁷ May God continue to bless us;
    let all the ends of the earth revere him.

COMMENTARY

Psalm 67 has ordinarily been classified either as a communal song of thanksgiving, possibly associated with a harvest festival (see v. 6), or as a prayer for God's blessing (vv. 1, 7). Perhaps it is both. In any case, its universal perspective fits well with that of Psalms 65–66. An earlier generation of scholars associated Psalm 67 with the annual celebration of God's enthronement. While it is clear that the central v. 4 asserts God's sovereignty, it is not clear that we can be very certain about the precise origin and ancient setting of the psalm. It would have been appropriate on a number of occasions, especially as a benediction. The traditional Jewish practice, for instance, was to recite it at the end of every sabbath.[267]

The psalm is usually divided into three parts (vv. 1-3, 4-5, 6-7), the first two of which end with an identical refrain. It is also possible, however, to discern a chiastic structure (see Introduction) that focuses attention on v. 4:

A		vv. 1-2	blessing and the knowledge of God among "all nations"
	B	v. 3	refrain
	C	v. 4	central profession of God's sovereignty
	B′	v. 5	refrain
A′		vv. 6-7	blessing and the reverence of God by "all the ends of the earth"

267. Marvin E. Tate, *Psalms 51–100*, WBC 20 (Dallas: Word, 1990) 155.

Verses 1-2, 6-7 feature the concept of blessing, which is somehow to involve "all" (vv. 2, 7; note too the repetition of "earth" in vv. 2, 6-7). The chiastic structure has the literary effect of surrounding the assertion of God's sovereignty (v. 4) with the acclamation of "all the peoples" (vv. 3, 5); that is, structure reinforces theological content, for the sovereign God deserves to be surrounded with praise. Verse 4 can be construed as a three-part poetic line, the only one of the poem; this, too, serves to set it apart.

67:1-2. In addition to the frequent petition that God "be gracious" (see Pss 4:1; 6:2), v. 1 introduces the thematic concept of blessing (see vv. 6-7; see also Pss 5:12; 28:9; 29:11). Verse 1 clearly recalls the so-called Aaronic or Priestly Benediction in Num 6:22-27. There as here, God's blessing is inseparable from God's presence or "face" (Num 6:26; see also Pss 4:6; 31:16; 80:3, 7, 19; 119:135) and ultimately from a knowledge of God's "way(s)" (v. 2; see also Ps 119:135, where the request that God's "face shine" is accompanied by the request that God "teach me") and from God's "salvation" (v. 2; see also Ps 80:3, 7, 19, where "let your face shine" is to result in being "saved").

While Israel is the primary object of God's blessing ("us" is the actual object in each case), it is clear that God intends the blessing somehow to be shared by "all" (vv. 2, 7; see also vv. 3, 5). Psalm 72 in particular portrays what blessing involves: "peace"/"prosperity" (שלום *šālôm*, vv. 3, 7) accompanied by "justice" and "righteousness" (72:1-2, 6-7; cf. "judge," which could be rendered "establish justice," in v. 4). As in Psalm 67, the blessings experienced by the king and his people (72:15) are to involve ultimately "all nations" (72:17; cf. 67:2).

67:3-5. As suggested above, the central profession of God's sovereignty is surrounded and set off by the refrain (vv. 3, 5). This central structural feature makes the fundamental profession that represents the theological heart of the book of Psalms: God rules the world (see Psalms 2; 93–99; Introduction). Judging or establishing justice is the primary responsibility of a monarch, human or divine (see Pss 9:8; 72:1-7; 96:13; 97:2; 98:9; 99:4; see "equity" in 9:8; 96:10; 98:9; 99:4). Only a sovereign God can "guide the nations upon earth" (see Exod 15:13, 18, where the celebration of God's guidance of Israel culminates in the proclamation of God's reign). This central profession of God's sovereignty underlies the request for a blessing that will have worldwide effects. This theme of universality is evident in the refrain. The verb translated "praise" (ידה *ydh*) is often translated "give thanks"; thus the psalmist's wish is that all the peoples acknowledge with gratitude God's rule. The word "all" (כל *kōl*, vv. 3, 5 as well as vv. 2, 7) emphasizes the universal perspective, as does the sevenfold occurrence of the words "peoples"/"nations," one occurrence for each of the poetic half-lines in vv. 3-5.

67:6-7. The psalm returns to the theme of blessing (cf. v. 6 with Lev 26:4), and the theme of universality is given its most comprehensive statement. The phrase "ends of the earth" occurs also in Pss 2:8 and 72:8 (see also Isa 52:7-10), both of which suggest that the sovereignty of God is exercised through God's chosen agent, the king (messiah). Even so, it is ultimately God who is to be revered or feared (v. 7; see Ps 2:11).

REFLECTIONS

The theme of blessing and the universal perspective of Psalm 67 recall Gen 12:1-3, the promise of blessing to Abraham and Sarah and their descendants, a blessing that will somehow involve "all the families of the earth" (Gen 12:3 NRSV). The promise is echoed throughout the OT (see Exod 9:16; Ps 22:27-28; Isa 2:2-4; 19:23-24; 49:5-7), including Psalm 67, and in the NT as well, where the apostle Paul cited it as support for his leadership in taking the gospel to the ends of the earth and for opening the church to all nations (see Gal 3:6-8, 28; Rev 22:1-5). As Kraus suggests concerning the message of Psalm 67, "The community of God here learns how to break away from all narrowness in the reception of salvation."[268]

In our contemporary world, plagued by injustice and divided by extremes of poverty and

268. Kraus, *Psalms 60–150,* 42.

wealth, it is crucial that we hear the message of Psalm 67: God rules the world and intends blessing for all the world's people. This means that God wills justice for all (v. 4), including the equitable distribution of the earth's "harvest" (v. 6). It is crucial, too, that we hear the message of Psalm 67 in a contemporary world that is torn by racial, ethnic, and national exclusivism and strife. In short, Psalm 67 can assist us, in the words of Cain Hope Felder, as we "engage the new challenge to recapture the ancient biblical vision of racial and ethnic pluralism as shaped by the Bible's own universalism."[269] The psalm reminds us that God so loves the whole world (John 3:16), and that God's choice of a particular people is so that the world may know (John 17:23; see Ps 67:2).

269. Cain Hope Felder, *Stony the Road We Trod: African American Biblical Interpretation*, ed. Cain Hope Felder (Minneapolis: Fortress, 1991) ix.

PSALM 68:1-35, MY GOD, MY KING!

NIV

Psalm 68

For the director of music. Of David. A psalm. A song.

[1] May God arise, may his enemies be scattered;
  may his foes flee before him.
[2] As smoke is blown away by the wind,
  may you blow them away;
as wax melts before the fire,
  may the wicked perish before God.
[3] But may the righteous be glad
  and rejoice before God;
  may they be happy and joyful.

[4] Sing to God, sing praise to his name,
  extol him who rides on the clouds[a]—
his name is the LORD—
  and rejoice before him.
[5] A father to the fatherless, a defender of
    widows,
  is God in his holy dwelling.
[6] God sets the lonely in families,[b]
  he leads forth the prisoners with singing;
  but the rebellious live in a sun-scorched
    land.

[7] When you went out before your people, O
    God,
  when you marched through the wasteland,
                                    Selah

a4 Or / prepare the way for him who rides through the deserts
b6 Or the desolate in a homeland

NRSV

Psalm 68

To the leader. Of David. A Psalm. A Song.

[1] Let God rise up, let his enemies be
    scattered;
  let those who hate him flee before him.
[2] As smoke is driven away, so drive them
    away;
  as wax melts before the fire,
  let the wicked perish before God.
[3] But let the righteous be joyful;
  let them exult before God;
  let them be jubilant with joy.

[4] Sing to God, sing praises to his name;
  lift up a song to him who rides upon the
    clouds[a]—
his name is the LORD—
  be exultant before him.

[5] Father of orphans and protector of widows
  is God in his holy habitation.
[6] God gives the desolate a home to live in;
  he leads out the prisoners to prosperity,
  but the rebellious live in a parched land.

[7] O God, when you went out before your
    people,
  when you marched through the
    wilderness,   *Selah*

aOr cast up a highway for him who rides through the deserts

NIV

⁸the earth shook,
    the heavens poured down rain,
before God, the One of Sinai,
    before God, the God of Israel.
⁹You gave abundant showers, O God;
    you refreshed your weary inheritance.
¹⁰Your people settled in it,
    and from your bounty, O God, you
        provided for the poor.

¹¹The Lord announced the word,
    and great was the company of those who
        proclaimed it:
¹²"Kings and armies flee in haste;
    in the camps men divide the plunder.
¹³Even while you sleep among the campfires,ᵃ
    the wings of ⌐my⌐ dove are sheathed with
        silver,
    its feathers with shining gold."
¹⁴When the Almightyᵇ scattered the kings in
        the land,
    it was like snow fallen on Zalmon.

¹⁵The mountains of Bashan are majestic
        mountains;
    rugged are the mountains of Bashan.
¹⁶Why gaze in envy, O rugged mountains,
    at the mountain where God chooses to
        reign,
    where the Lᴏʀᴅ himself will dwell forever?
¹⁷The chariots of God are tens of thousands
    and thousands of thousands;
    the Lord ⌐has come⌐ from Sinai into his
        sanctuary.
¹⁸When you ascended on high,
    you led captives in your train;
    you received gifts from men,
even fromᶜ the rebellious—
    that you,ᵈ O Lᴏʀᴅ God, might dwell
        there.

¹⁹Praise be to the Lord, to God our Savior,
    who daily bears our burdens.   *Selah*
²⁰Our God is a God who saves;
    from the Sovereign Lᴏʀᴅ comes escape
        from death.

²¹Surely God will crush the heads of his
        enemies,

ᵃ13 Or *saddlebags*   ᵇ14 Hebrew *Shaddai*   ᶜ18 Or *gifts for men,*
/ *even*   ᵈ18 Or *they*

NRSV

⁸ the earth quaked, the heavens poured down
        rain
    at the presence of God, the God of Sinai,
    at the presence of God, the God of Israel.
⁹ Rain in abundance, O God, you showered
        abroad;
    you restored your heritage when it
        languished;
¹⁰ your flock found a dwelling in it;
    in your goodness, O God, you provided
        for the needy.

¹¹ The Lord gives the command;
    great is the company of thoseᵃ who bore
        the tidings:
¹²   "The kings of the armies, they flee, they
        flee!"
    The women at home divide the spoil,
¹³   though they stay among the sheepfolds—
    the wings of a dove covered with silver,
    its pinions with green gold.
¹⁴ When the Almightyᵇ scattered kings there,
    snow fell on Zalmon.

¹⁵ O mighty mountain, mountain of Bashan;
    O many-peaked mountain, mountain of
        Bashan!
¹⁶ Why do you look with envy,
    O many-peaked mountain,
    at the mount that God desired for his abode,
    where the Lᴏʀᴅ will reside forever?

¹⁷ With mighty chariotry, twice ten thousand,
    thousands upon thousands,
    the Lord came from Sinai into the holy
        place.ᶜ
¹⁸ You ascended the high mount,
    leading captives in your train
    and receiving gifts from people,
    even from those who rebel against the Lᴏʀᴅ
        God's abiding there.
¹⁹ Blessed be the Lord,
    who daily bears us up;
    God is our salvation.   *Selah*
²⁰ Our God is a God of salvation,
    and to Gᴏᴅ, the Lord, belongs escape
        from death.

ᵃOr *company of the women*   ᵇTraditional rendering of Heb *Shad-*
dai   ᶜCn: Heb *The Lord among them Sinai in the holy* (place)

NIV

the hairy crowns of those who go on in
their sins.

²²The Lord says, "I will bring them from Bashan;
I will bring them from the depths of the sea,

²³that you may plunge your feet in the blood
of your foes,
while the tongues of your dogs have
their share."

²⁴Your procession has come into view, O God,
the procession of my God and King into
the sanctuary.

²⁵In front are the singers, after them the
musicians;
with them are the maidens playing
tambourines.

²⁶Praise God in the great congregation;
praise the Lord in the assembly of Israel.

²⁷There is the little tribe of Benjamin, leading
them,
there the great throng of Judah's princes,
and there the princes of Zebulun and of
Naphtali.

²⁸Summon your power, O God*a*;
show us your strength, O God, as you
have done before.

²⁹Because of your temple at Jerusalem
kings will bring you gifts.

³⁰Rebuke the beast among the reeds,
the herd of bulls among the calves of the
nations.
Humbled, may it bring bars of silver.
Scatter the nations who delight in war.

³¹Envoys will come from Egypt;
Cush*b* will submit herself to God.

³²Sing to God, O kingdoms of the earth,
sing praise to the Lord,   *Selah*

³³to him who rides the ancient skies above,
who thunders with mighty voice.

³⁴Proclaim the power of God,
whose majesty is over Israel,
whose power is in the skies.

³⁵You are awesome, O God, in your sanctuary;
the God of Israel gives power and strength
to his people.

Praise be to God!

a28 Many Hebrew manuscripts, Septuagint and Syriac; most Hebrew
manuscripts *Your God has summoned power for you*   *b31* That is,
the upper Nile region

NRSV

²¹ But God will shatter the heads of his enemies,
the hairy crown of those who walk in
their guilty ways.

²² The Lord said,
"I will bring them back from Bashan,
I will bring them back from the depths of
the sea,

²³ so that you may bathe*a* your feet in blood,
so that the tongues of your dogs may
have their share from the foe."

²⁴ Your solemn processions are seen,*b* O God,
the processions of my God, my King, into
the sanctuary—

²⁵ the singers in front, the musicians last,
between them girls playing tambourines:

²⁶ "Bless God in the great congregation,
the Lord, O you who are of Israel's
fountain!"

²⁷ There is Benjamin, the least of them, in the
lead,
the princes of Judah in a body,
the princes of Zebulun, the princes of
Naphtali.

²⁸ Summon your might, O God;
show your strength, O God, as you have
done for us before.

²⁹ Because of your temple at Jerusalem
kings bear gifts to you.

³⁰ Rebuke the wild animals that live among
the reeds,
the herd of bulls with the calves of the
peoples.
Trample*c* under foot those who lust after
tribute;
scatter the peoples who delight in war.*d*

³¹ Let bronze be brought from Egypt;
let Ethiopia*e* hasten to stretch out its
hands to God.

³² Sing to God, O kingdoms of the earth;
sing praises to the Lord,   *Selah*

³³ O rider in the heavens, the ancient heavens;
listen, he sends out his voice, his mighty
voice.

a Gk Syr Tg: Heb *shatter*   *b* Or *have been seen*   *c* Cn: Heb
Trampling   *d* Meaning of Heb of verse 30 is uncertain
e Or *Nubia*; Heb *Cush*

NRSV

34 Ascribe power to God,
    whose majesty is over Israel;
    and whose power is in the skies.
35 Awesome is God in his[a] sanctuary,
    the God of Israel;
    he gives power and strength to his
        people.

Blessed be God!

[a] Gk: Heb *from your*

COMMENTARY

Psalm 68 is generally known as the most difficult of all the psalms to interpret. It contains fifteen words that occur nowhere else in the OT as well as numerous other rare words. As Tate puts it, "The difficulties of interpreting Ps 68 are almost legendary."[270] Not surprisingly, opinions diverge widely concerning the structure and movement of the psalm. At one extreme, some scholars conclude that Psalm 68 has no discernible unity or regularity of structure, while at the other extreme, some discern a regular pattern of strophes and stanzas. The truth probably lies somewhere in between. The unity of the psalm is suggested by the obvious correspondence between v. 4 and vv. 32-33, which provide a bracket around the psalm. Furthermore, while there are no verbal links, vv. 34-35 celebrate the power that God is invited to manifest in vv. 1-3. The "righteous" (v. 3) correspond to "his people" (v. 35), who have been given "power and strength" (v. 35) and thus finally have good reason to "be jubilant with joy" (v. 3).

This psalm is often divided into three major sections (vv. 1-10, 11-23, 24-35), which are sometimes associated with the place featured in each: Sinai (v. 8), Bashan (vv. 15, 22), and Jerusalem (v. 29). An alternative is to view vv. 1-3 as an introduction, followed by two major sections (vv. 4-18, 19-35), each of which consists of four smaller sections (vv. 4-6, 7-10, 11-14, 15-18 and vv. 19-23, 24-27, 28-31, 32-35). The movement of vv. 4-18 proceeds geographically. Alluding to

270. Tate, *Psalms 51–100,* 170.

the exodus, vv. 4-6 describe the kind of God revealed in that event. Verses 7-10 recall Sinai and the provision made by God for the people in the wilderness. Verses 11-14 recall the entry into and conquest of the land, which meant God completed the journey of accompanying the people from Sinai to Jerusalem, bypassing other mountains that might have provided a home for God (vv. 15-18; see Exod 15:1-18, which also moves from exodus to God's choice of Zion). The repetition of "blessed" (ברוך *bārûk,* vv. 19, 35) provides an envelope for the second major section, in which God's victorious presence in Jerusalem is proclaimed (vv. 19-23), celebrated liturgically (vv. 24-27), invoked in prayer (vv. 28-31), and proclaimed again in the form of an invitation for all the earth to recognize God's sovereignty (vv. 32-35).

The origin and ancient use of Psalm 68 are also disputed. It has been identified as a victory hymn (cf. vv. 7-8 with Judg 5:4-5) as well as a communal song of thanksgiving. It finally celebrates God's reign from Jerusalem (see vv. 24, 32-35) and gives several indications of liturgical use (see the mention of God's abode or sanctuary in vv. 5, 16-18, 24, 29, 35). Verse 1 recalls Num 10:35, suggesting a possible association with the ark, which may have been involved in processional celebrations of God's reign (vv. 24-27; see Pss 24:7-10; 132:8). While there is no solid evidence for Mowinckel's theory of an annual enthronement festival, it is likely that Israel celebrated liturgically God's sovereignty on some occasion. What is clearer than reconstructed cultic settings, however, is the actual literary content with its proclamation of the victory and reign of God. Thus Psalm 68, along with Psalms 65–67, is another voice that proclaims the message that pervades the psalter: God reigns (see Psalms 2; 93–99; Introduction).

68:1-3. As mentioned above, v. 1 recalls Num 10:35, suggesting an association of Psalm 68 with the ark. Verse 1 thus prepares for the remainder of the psalm, which will portray God in battle as the divine warrior. The conflict is framed in vv. 2-3 in terms that recall Psalm 1, in which the righteous are promised life and "the way of the wicked will perish" (1:6). The transience of the wicked is also associated elsewhere with smoke (Ps 37:20) and the melting of wax (Ps 12:10). Later in the psalm, the righteous will rejoice (vv. 19-20, 24-27), but they will also pray for help (vv. 28-31). Thus Psalm 68 is another reminder that righteousness consists essentially in living in dependence upon God (see Commentary on Psalm 1).

68:4-18. 68:4-6. In anticipation of the victory that will be described in vv. 5-18, v. 4 invites the righteous to sing and to praise (see Exod 15:1-2). It also introduces the ancient Near Eastern mythic background, which is prominent in Psalm 68 along with the outline of Israel's basic story—exodus, Sinai/wilderness, conquest/possession of Jerusalem. In Canaanite literature, it was Baal "who rides upon the clouds." But here, Yahweh is specifically named (see also Deut 33:26; Ps 18:9-13; Isa 19:1; see below on vv. 32-33). The specificity of the expression "his name is the LORD" is indicative of a polemical thrust (see Exod 15:3). "Name" is also suggestive of character, which is in view in vv. 5-6. The intent here is polemical as well; Yahweh fulfills the ancient Near Eastern ideal of the king as protector of and provider for the poor (see Pss 10:14, 18; 94:6; 113:7-9; 146:9). Verses 4-6 also seem to allude to the exodus (cf. v. 4 with Exod 15:1-3; the verb "leads out" [יצא *yāṣā*'] in v. 6 is often used of the exodus), which would be especially appropriate in view of the more specific allusions to the wilderness and to Sinai in vv. 7-10.

68:7-10. The verb "went out" in v. 7*a* is the same Hebrew root as "leads out" in v. 6, again recalling the exodus. Verse 7*b* specifically mentions "the wilderness" (see Deut 32:10; Pss 78:40; 106:14), and v. 8 mentions Sinai. Verses

7-8 also recall the possession of the land, since they are nearly identical to Judg 5:4-5, a portion of the Song of Deborah. Furthermore, the word "heritage" (נחלה *naḥălâ*, v. 9) occurs frequently in Joshua; it can designate either the land or the people (see Deut 32:9; the NRSV's "restore" in v. 9 and "provided" in v. 10 translate the same Hebrew verb [כון *kûn*], which also occurs in Deut 32:6 as "established"). Yahweh, not Baal, provides renewing rain for the land and its people. The "you" in the final clause of v. 10 is emphatic. In short, God did everything necessary for the welfare of the people.

68:11-14. These verses are difficult, but they seem to allude to the military actions described in Numbers–Judges as part of Israel's entry into Canaan (and perhaps more specifically the battle against Sisera in Judges 5; see Judg 5:19). The expression "bore the tidings" (v. 11) came into Greek as "gospel," "good news"; elsewhere, the good news has to do with God's reign (see Ps 96:2; Isa 52:7). By scattering the kings (vv. 12, 14), God proves to be the true sovereign. Dividing the spoil (v. 12) indicates victory (see Judg 5:30). Verse 13 is obscure, as a comparison of the NIV and the NRSV makes clear. It may mean that despite Israel's inactivity (v. 13*a*), the victory has been won. The dove may refer to a jeweled object captured in battle (part of the spoils, perhaps even a statue of Astarte, who was represented by a dove); it may designate Israel (see Ps 74:19; Hos 7:11; 11:11), who has captured the wealth of the opposing kings; or it may indicate the release of birds to celebrate a victory.[271] Verse 14*b* is also obscure. The location of Zalmon is unknown; this verse is best understood metaphorically rather than geographically or historically.

68:15-18. The completion of God's journey from Sinai (v. 17) is related here. Victorious over all opposition, God ascends to the chosen place of residence to receive universal acclaim (v. 18; see Ps 47:5-9), even from "the rebellious" (see v. 6). Although some scholars suggest that vv. 17-18 may not have referred originally to Zion, they clearly do in the final form of the psalm (see v. 29; Ps 132:13-14). In choosing Zion, God apparently passed over other prime locations (vv. 15-16). Bashan was known for its luxuriance and

271. Ibid., 178-79.

desirability (Jer 22:20). Mount Hermon (elevation 9,000 feet) could be the particular mountain behind the references in vv. 15-16, but the real point is that Zion is the place "where the LORD will reside forever" (v. 16c).

68:19-35. 68:19-23. Because God is enthroned in Zion, the celebration can begin (see "Bless[ed]" in vv. 26, 35; Pss 28:6; 31:21, and esp. 66:8, 20, where it is associated with preservation of life). Like v. 4, vv. 19-20 recall the victory song that begins in Exod 15:1-3 (see esp. "salvation" in Exod 15:2). The verb "escape" is the same root as "leads out" (v. 6) and "went out" (v. 7), and it is often used specifically of the exodus, which was an escape from death. The mythic background and polemical thrust are evident in v. 20 as well. The Hebrew word for "death" (מות māwet) is the equivalent of Mot (מות môt), the Canaanite god of death, whom Baal defeated yearly to ensure fertility of the land. Here it is Israel's God, not Baal, who defeats death. And as vv. 21-23 suggest, God defeats all other enemies as well (see vv. 1-3, 11-14, 30-31; Num 24:8; 1 Kgs 21:19, 23-24; Pss 58:10; 110:5). In short, Israel's God is sovereign.

68:24-27. Not surprisingly, God is addressed as King in v. 24 (see Pss 5:2; 44:4; 47:6; 74:12; 84:3), which describes a liturgical celebration of God's reign (see Pss 24:7-10; 42:4; 132:8-9, 13-14), complete with singing, music, and percussion (v. 25; see also Exod 15:20-21; Pss 33:3; and esp. 149:2-3, where God is also addressed as King). Verse 26 can be understood as a quotation of the singers, who address God as Israel's "fountain" or source of life (see vv. 6, 20; Ps 36:10; Jer 2:13; 17:13). The four tribes listed in v. 27 are apparently intended to represent all of Israel (see Judg 5:14, where Benjamin is also in the lead).

68:28-31. It is significant that this section shifts to petition. The sovereignty of God is not questioned, but present circumstances apparently call for a new manifestation of God's "power" (עז 'ōz, v. 28). The imperative "show your strength" in v. 28b represents the same Hebrew root (עזז 'zz) as the noun "power" in v. 28a; that root will recur four more times ("mighty" in v. 33b, "power" twice in v. 34 and in v. 35). It frequently occurs in the context of proclamations of God's

reign (see "strength" in Exod 15:13; Pss 29:1, 11; 93:1; 96:6-7). In short, it is clear from vv. 28-31 that God's reign does not go unopposed. The verb in v. 29 should probably be heard as a jussive, "let the kings bear gifts"; that is, it, too, is petitionary, and a tension exists between v. 18 and v. 29. As the NRSV note indicates, v. 30 is problematic. It is clear enough, however, that it requests God to deal with powerful opponents, who are symbolized as beasts (see Pss 22:12-13, 16, 20-21; 17:12; 57:4; 58:6; 59:6, 14; 74:12-14; 89:10). The mention of reeds may indicate Egypt, which is named in v. 31, but the real intent seems to be to ask God to subject all opponents, including those from the farthest reaches, which is what Cush probably represents (see Zeph 3:10).

68:32-35. Congruent with this conclusion concerning vv. 28-31, v. 32 addresses the broadest possible invitation to recognize God's sovereignty (cf. v. 4). Verse 33 also recalls v. 4. God's voice is probably meant to be understood as thunder. In the ancient Near East, thunder was associated with Baal, the god of the storm (see also v. 9 concerning rain). In Psalm 29, as here, it is a sign that Yahweh is to be greeted as sovereign. Like Psalm 29, v. 34 invites recognition of God's rule over the earthly and heavenly realms (see also "majesty" in Deut 33:26). Awesomeness is an attribute of God as sovereign (v. 35; see also Exod 15:11; Pss 47:2; 65:5; 66:3, 5; 96:4; 99:3). Like Psalm 29 as well (see vv. 9-11), v. 35 situates God in the divine sanctuary, which seems to refer to God's heavenly and earthly abodes, and it envisions God sharing God's power with the people (see 29:11).

It is revealing that the six occurrences of the Hebrew root meaning "strength," "power," "might" occur in the final eight verses after the people's need has been expressed in petition (see also vv. 1-3). In other words, as is always the case, the proclamation of God's rule occurs amid circumstances that seem to deny it (see Psalm 2; Introduction). The perspective is eschatological. As such, Psalm 68 finally calls readers in every generation to live in dependence upon a God whose sovereignty is revealed not in sheer force but in the power of compassion, which some might mistake for weakness (see vv. 4-6; see also 1 Cor 1:25; 2 Cor 12:9).

REFLECTIONS

1. As long ago and far away as Psalm 68 seems in many respects, it deals with a perennial theological issue: how to talk about a transcendent God in human terms. Commenting on the movement of God from Sinai to Jerusalem in this psalm, Mays states that it represents "the coming of the reign of God in time and space."[272] Such particularity is scandalous, but it is not unusual to Christians. The preaching of the historical Jesus apparently featured precisely this claim. Jesus proclaimed that the kingdom of God was present in human time and space, and he invited people to enter it (Mark 1:14-15). Jesus' followers were convinced that he had not only rightly proclaimed the reign of God, but had also fully embodied God's wisdom and power in such a way that to enter the realm of God meant to do so through Jesus. In short, God was in Christ, and so Jesus is Lord. The particularity was transferred from a place— Jerusalem—to a person—Jesus. But the particularity is no less concrete or scandalous.

2. Psalm 68 and the psalter as a whole illustrate what is clear from the NT as well—namely, the proclamation of the reign of God in space and time is always eschatological. The reign of God is never fully manifested; it is always opposed. The people of Israel and Jerusalem were regularly assaulted; Jesus was crucified. Or, to put it in slightly different terms, the proclamation of God's reign is always polemical. For the psalmist, to say that Yahweh is sovereign means that Baal is not. For first-century Christianity, to say that Jesus is Lord meant that Caesar is not. For contemporary Christians, to say that God rules the world and that Jesus is Lord is to deny ultimacy and ultimate allegiance to a host of other claims—national security, political parties, economic systems, ethnic heritage, job, family, self. Indeed, the underlying temptation represented by Baalism is perhaps more prevalent than ever—that is, to conclude that human beings can manipulate the deity and thus ensure security by our own efforts (see Commentary on Psalms 29; 65). By its polemical proclamation of the reign of God, Psalm 68 undercuts the gospel of human progress. Ultimately, salvation is to be found in submission to God rather than in the assertion of self (see vv. 19-20).

The eschatological, polemical dimension of Psalm 68 is crucial, for it puts the militaristic image of God as divine warrior in a particular perspective. The fact that Psalm 68 begins and finally returns to petition (vv. 1-3, 28-31) indicates that God does not simply step in and wipe out God's opponents, a lesson that is reinforced by the cross of Jesus Christ. To be sure, God fights back against God's enemies (vv. 1-2), against those "who delight in war" (v. 3c). But God fights in an unexpected way—with love and compassion. For worldly strategists, might makes right. But for God the divine warrior, right makes might. Mays concludes of this psalm:

> In spite of its militant character and victorious confidence, such is not its spirit. There is a self-understanding and self-description in the psalm's measures that belies such a reading. The uses assigned to the power of the LORD as divine warrior are crucial. The God who dwells in his holy habitation as victor is father of orphans and protector of widows, who gives the desolate a home and liberates prisoners (vv. 5-6). . . .
>
> . . . The song belongs to the lowly, who in the midst of the powers of this world remember and hope for the victory of God.[273]

In short, Psalm 68 calls us not to triumphalism but to the humble enactment of God's justice that is born of compassion for the needy (v. 10; see also vv. 5-6).

3. Thus the biblical description of life is very different from what our culture portrays as the so-called good life. For the psalmist, life is not the achievement of our own ends but dependence upon God and openness to God's ways (vv. 19-20). In this regard, the liturgical

---

272. James L. Mays, *Psalms,* Interpretation (Louisville: John Knox, 1994) 228.
273. Ibid., 228-29.

dimension of Psalm 68 is instructive. In worship, we say who rules the world and thus to whom we belong. Worship in the spirit of Psalm 68 will not simply be something that reinforces cultural values. Rather, as J. David Pleins suggests on the basis of Psalm 68, "The words we use in worship must open us to the God of justice and awaken us to the world's desperate need for hope and genuine social change."[274]

4. To be an advocate of justice and hope in a desperate, broken world requires a motivation and a source of energy beyond ourselves. The good news is that God gives power and strength to God's people (v. 35). Christians understand this finally to be nothing less than the power of the resurrection (see the use of Ps 68:18 in Eph 4:8), and thus Psalm 68 is appropriately associated with the season of Easter. To trust in and represent the claims of God's reign in a desperate, broken world will mean, as it always has, that we will encounter opposition. Appropriately, therefore, John Knox concluded the Scots Confession with a prayer that begins with Ps 68:1 and alludes to vv. 32 and 35 as well: "Arise, O Lord, and let thine enemies be confounded; let them flee from thy presence that hate thy godly name. Give thy servants strength to speak thy word with boldness, and let all nations cleave to the true knowledge of thee. Amen."[275]

274. J. David Pleins, *The Psalms: Songs of Tragedy, Hope, and Justice* (Maryknoll, N.Y.: Orbis, 1993) 95.
275. Cited in Mays, *Psalms,* 229.

PSALM 69:1-36, FOR YOUR SAKE I HAVE BORNE REPROACH

NIV

Psalm 69

For the director of music. To the tune of "Lilies." Of David.

¹Save me, O God,
   for the waters have come up to my neck.
²I sink in the miry depths,
   where there is no foothold.
I have come into the deep waters;
   the floods engulf me.
³I am worn out calling for help;
   my throat is parched.
My eyes fail,
   looking for my God.
⁴Those who hate me without reason
   outnumber the hairs of my head;
many are my enemies without cause,
   those who seek to destroy me.
I am forced to restore
   what I did not steal.
⁵You know my folly, O God;
   my guilt is not hidden from you.

NRSV

Psalm 69

To the leader: according to Lilies.
Of David.

¹ Save me, O God,
   for the waters have come up to my neck.
² I sink in deep mire,
   where there is no foothold;
I have come into deep waters,
   and the flood sweeps over me.
³ I am weary with my crying;
   my throat is parched.
My eyes grow dim
   with waiting for my God.

⁴ More in number than the hairs of my head
   are those who hate me without cause;
many are those who would destroy me,
   my enemies who accuse me falsely.
What I did not steal
   must I now restore?
⁵ O God, you know my folly;

NIV

⁶May those who hope in you
   not be disgraced because of me,
   O Lord, the LORD Almighty;
 may those who seek you
   not be put to shame because of me,
   O God of Israel.
⁷For I endure scorn for your sake,
   and shame covers my face.
⁸I am a stranger to my brothers,
   an alien to my own mother's sons;
⁹for zeal for your house consumes me,
   and the insults of those who insult you fall
      on me.
¹⁰When I weep and fast,
   I must endure scorn;
¹¹when I put on sackcloth,
   people make sport of me.
¹²Those who sit at the gate mock me,
   and I am the song of the drunkards.

¹³But I pray to you, O LORD,
   in the time of your favor;
 in your great love, O God,
   answer me with your sure salvation.
¹⁴Rescue me from the mire,
   do not let me sink;
 deliver me from those who hate me,
   from the deep waters.
¹⁵Do not let the floodwaters engulf me
   or the depths swallow me up
   or the pit close its mouth over me.
¹⁶Answer me, O LORD, out of the goodness of
      your love;
   in your great mercy turn to me.
¹⁷Do not hide your face from your servant;
   answer me quickly, for I am in trouble.
¹⁸Come near and rescue me;
   redeem me because of my foes.

¹⁹You know how I am scorned, disgraced and
      shamed;
   all my enemies are before you.
²⁰Scorn has broken my heart
   and has left me helpless;
 I looked for sympathy, but there was
      none,
   for comforters, but I found none.
²¹They put gall in my food
   and gave me vinegar for my thirst.

NRSV

 the wrongs I have done are not hidden
   from you.

⁶ Do not let those who hope in you be put
   to shame because of me,
   O Lord GOD of hosts;
 do not let those who seek you be
   dishonored because of me,
   O God of Israel.
⁷ It is for your sake that I have borne
   reproach,
   that shame has covered my face.
⁸ I have become a stranger to my kindred,
   an alien to my mother's children.

⁹ It is zeal for your house that has consumed me;
   the insults of those who insult you have
      fallen on me.
¹⁰ When I humbled my soul with fasting,ᵃ
   they insulted me for doing so.
¹¹ When I made sackcloth my clothing,
   I became a byword to them.
¹² I am the subject of gossip for those who sit
      in the gate,
   and the drunkards make songs about me.

¹³ But as for me, my prayer is to you, O LORD.
   At an acceptable time, O God,
   in the abundance of your steadfast love,
      answer me.
 With your faithful help ¹⁴rescue me
   from sinking in the mire;
 let me be delivered from my enemies
   and from the deep waters.
¹⁵ Do not let the flood sweep over me,
   or the deep swallow me up,
   or the Pit close its mouth over me.

¹⁶ Answer me, O LORD, for your steadfast love
      is good;
   according to your abundant mercy, turn
      to me.
¹⁷ Do not hide your face from your servant,
   for I am in distress—make haste to
      answer me.
¹⁸ Draw near to me, redeem me,
   set me free because of my enemies.

ᵃGk Syr: Heb *I wept, with fasting my soul,* or *I made my soul mourn with fasting*

NIV

²²May the table set before them become a
    snare;
  may it become retribution and^a a trap.
²³May their eyes be darkened so they cannot
    see,
  and their backs be bent forever.
²⁴Pour out your wrath on them;
  let your fierce anger overtake them.
²⁵May their place be deserted;
  let there be no one to dwell in their tents.
²⁶For they persecute those you wound
  and talk about the pain of those you hurt.
²⁷Charge them with crime upon crime;
  do not let them share in your salvation.
²⁸May they be blotted out of the book of life
  and not be listed with the righteous.

²⁹I am in pain and distress;
  may your salvation, O God, protect me.

³⁰I will praise God's name in song
  and glorify him with thanksgiving.
³¹This will please the LORD more than an ox,
  more than a bull with its horns and hoofs.
³²The poor will see and be glad—
  you who seek God, may your hearts live!
³³The LORD hears the needy
  and does not despise his captive people.

³⁴Let heaven and earth praise him,
  the seas and all that move in them,
³⁵for God will save Zion
  and rebuild the cities of Judah.
  Then people will settle there and possess it;
³⁶ the children of his servants will inherit it,
  and those who love his name will dwell
    there.

^a22 Or snare / and their fellowship become

NRSV

¹⁹ You know the insults I receive,
  and my shame and dishonor;
  my foes are all known to you.
²⁰ Insults have broken my heart,
  so that I am in despair.
  I looked for pity, but there was none;
  and for comforters, but I found none.
²¹ They gave me poison for food,
  and for my thirst they gave me vinegar
    to drink.

²² Let their table be a trap for them,
  a snare for their allies.
²³ Let their eyes be darkened so that they
    cannot see,
  and make their loins tremble continually.
²⁴ Pour out your indignation upon them,
  and let your burning anger overtake them.
²⁵ May their camp be a desolation;
  let no one live in their tents.
²⁶ For they persecute those whom you have
    struck down,
  and those whom you have wounded,
    they attack still more.^a
²⁷ Add guilt to their guilt;
  may they have no acquittal from you.
²⁸ Let them be blotted out of the book of the
    living;
  let them not be enrolled among the
    righteous.
²⁹ But I am lowly and in pain;
  let your salvation, O God, protect me.

³⁰ I will praise the name of God with a song;
  I will magnify him with thanksgiving.
³¹ This will please the LORD more than an ox
  or a bull with horns and hoofs.
³² Let the oppressed see it and be glad;
  you who seek God, let your hearts revive.
³³ For the LORD hears the needy,
  and does not despise his own that are in
    bonds.

³⁴ Let heaven and earth praise him,
  the seas and everything that moves in
    them.
³⁵ For God will save Zion
  and rebuild the cities of Judah;

^a Gk Syr: Heb recount the pain of

NRSV

and his servants shall live[c] there and possess it;
36   the children of his servants shall inherit it,
      and those who love his name shall live
        in it.

[a]Syr: Heb *and they shall live*

COMMENTARY

Similar in many ways to Psalm 22, Psalm 69 is one of the longest and most impressive of the prayers for help or individual laments/complaints. Like Psalm 22, its first extended section (vv. 1-29) consists of alternating petition (vv. 1a, 6, 13-18, 22-25, 27-28, 29b) and complaint (vv. 1b-5, 7-12, 19-21, 26, 29a). And as the intensity of Psalm 22 is created in part by a sort of doubling (vv. 1-11, 12-21a), so it is with Psalm 69. Leslie C. Allen points out that the first major section consists of two smaller sections that are roughly parallel.[276] Allen's results can be summarized as follows:

Verses 1-13b		Verses 13c-29	
v. 1	Save me	v. 13d	your sure salvation
	waters	v. 14	do not let me sink
v. 2	I sink		deliver . . . from
	miry depths		deep waters
	deep waters	v. 15	do not let . . .
	floods		engulf me
	engulf me		floodwaters
v. 4	those who		depths
	hate me	v. 14	those who hate me
	my enemies	v. 18	my foes
v. 5	you know	v. 19	you know
v. 6	not be		
	disgraced		
	not be put		
	to shame		scorned
v. 7	scorn		disgraced
	shame		shamed
v. 9	insults of		
	those who		
	insult you	v. 20	scorn
v. 10	scorn		
v. 11	when I		
	put on	v. 21	they put
v. 13a	but I	v. 29	[but] I am

276. Leslie C. Allen, "The Value of Rhetorical Criticism in Psalm 69," *JBL* 105 (1986) 577-82. See the similar table in Marvin E. Tate, *Psalms 51–100,* WBC 20 (Dallas: Word, 1990) 193. Tate also summarizes additional details of Allen's analysis.

Obviously, the correspondence is not exact. Notably, vv. 22-28 are not represented at all. Even so, the parallels are too striking to be coincidental, and the doubling creates an impressive intensity. As in Psalm 22 as well, the promise to praise is especially outstanding after the prolonged complaint. It also consists of two parts (vv. 30-33, 34-36), the first of which is especially reminiscent of Ps 22:22-27. It is possible that vv. 34-36 were added to an original form of Psalm 69 to make it more explicitly relevant to the post-exilic situation.

As is usually the case, the circumstances that have given rise to the complaint are unclear, as is the identity of the enemies. Some scholars hypothesize terminal illness (see vv. 1-3, 26), which others interpret as a sign of sinfulness and as warrant to alienate (v. 8) and persecute the psalmist (v. 26). Other scholars suggest that the psalmist has been falsely accused (v. 4). But the language of the complaints is metaphorical, hyperbolic, and stereotypical. Tate recognizes, citing Psalm 69 that, "the probability of the usage of psalms in multiple contexts is high."[277] More accessible than reconstructed original settings for the psalm, and more important as well, is the psalmist's assertion that suffering is intimately related to God—even caused by God (v. 26)—so that the further suffering inflicted by others is for God's sake (vv. 7, 9-11). While this claim does not completely clarify the circumstances and characters involved, it does suggest larger literary settings in which Psalm 69 should be heard—the book of Job, Isaiah 53, the book of Jeremiah, the accounts of Jesus' passion (see Reflections below).

69:1-13b. 69:1-3. The opening petition links

277. Tate, *Psalms 51–100,* 196.

v. 1 to the beginning of the second section of complaint (v. 13cd), forms with v. 29 an envelope around the whole complaint, and also links the complaint to vv. 30-36 (see v. 35). To be saved (see Pss 3:2, 7, 8; 6:4) means to live, and the psalmist appears headed for death. She or he is about to go under (see Job 22:11; Pss 18:16; 32:6; 66:12; 144:7; Isa 43:2; Lam 3:54). The word translated "neck" in v. 1 (נפשׁ nepeš), which is usually translated "soul" or "life," seems to have meant originally "neck" or "throat." At any rate, the psalmist asks God to save her or his neck. Nearly sunk (v. 2) in a "mire" (see Ps 40:2) of "depths" (v. 2a; see Exod 15:5; Ps 88:6; Jonah 2:3), there is no touching bottom. "Waters" (מים mayim) occurs in both vv. 1 and 2, and a second Hebrew word for "deep"/"depths" (מעמקים ma'ămaqqîm) occurs in v. 2c (see Ps 130:1; Isa 51:10). The psalmist is about to be swept away (see v. 15; Ps 124:4). All she or he can do is appeal to God and wait (see Pss 31:24; 38:15), which has been done, but time is rapidly running out (v. 3; see Ps 6:6).

69:4-5. In addition to the actual threat, the psalmist must contend with people who make the situation worse (see "without cause" in Ps 35:7, 19). Verse 4 does not necessarily suggest that the psalmist has literally been accused of stealing. Rather, the psalmist suggests that she or he cannot make up for something that she or he has not done. In other words, there is no pleading guilty when one is actually innocent. Verse 5 indicates that the psalmist is willing to admit that she or he is not perfect. The point is that *God* knows the psalmist's shortcomings (the first "you" in v. 5 is emphatic), yet the psalmist is perfectly willing to rest the case with a loving and merciful God (see vv. 13, 16). In short, the problem is not that God condemns the psalmist. The problem is that other people condemn the psalmist. Job's friends come immediately to mind.

69:6-13b. Verse 6 indicates that the psalmist feels in some sense exemplary. The word "hope" (קוה qāwâ, v. 6) is essentially synonymous with "waiting" in v. 3. If the psalmist's suffering in waiting has produced only an adverse reaction (v. 4), then other God seekers could receive the same kind of discouraging treatment in their time of need. The psalmist thus prays that this will not happen. Verse 7 introduces a key word in the

psalm, "reproach" (חרפה ḥerpâ), which will be repeated five more times (NRSV, "insult[s]"/ "insulted" in vv. 10, 11, 19, 20; see also Pss 31:11; 109:25; Jer 20:8). The psalmist suffers the insults of others not because she or he is unfaithful but precisely because she or he *is faithful* (see Ps 22:7-8). The NRSV's "dishonored" (v. 6) and "shame" (v. 7) represent the same Hebrew root (כלם klm; see Ps 4:2). Verse 8 describes what was perhaps the epitome of shame in ancient cultures: alienation from one's family (see Job 19:13, 15; Pss 38:11; 88:8, 18; Jer 12:6). It also illustrates the cruelty of a strict application of the doctrine of retribution. Suffering that is viewed as punishment from God justifies exclusion of the sufferer, thus compounding the plight. Verses 9-12 reinforce the unfairness of the situation. The faithful psalmist, the one who has entrusted life and future to God, is insulted (vv. 9-10), belittled (v. 11; see Ps 44:14), and taunted (see Job 30, esp. vv. 9-15). Nevertheless, the psalmist stands firm, looking to God in prayer (v. 13ab). The concluding line of this section (vv. 1-13b) should probably be translated "for a time of favor" (see Pss 5:12; 30:5, 7; 106:4; Isa 49:8).[278]

69:13c-29. 69:13c-18. The first section of complaint has documented that human character cannot be trusted, so the second begins with a focus on the character of God, beginning with the one attribute that is the most fundamental: steadfast love (v. 13c; see also v. 16; Exod 34:6-7; Pss 5:7; 13:5; 86:15; Introduction). As is often the case, "steadfast love" is paired with "faithfulness" (v. 13d; see Exod 34:6; Pss 25:10; 40:10-11; Lam 3:22-23), and it is associated with "mercy" (v. 16; see Exod 34:6; Pss 86:15; 103:4). As suggested above the vocabulary of vv. 13c-15 parallels vv. 1-2, but goes beyond it as well. In effect, the psalmist asks not to be treated like an enemy of God—for instance, not to be swallowed up (see Exod 15:12; Num 16:30, 32, 34; Ps 124:3-4). Rather, like Job (31:5), the psalmist wants God to answer (vv. 13, 16-17). Indeed, the psalmist dares to ask to see God's face (the verb "turn" [פנה pānâ] in v. 16b and the noun "face" [פנים pānîm] in v. 17a are from the same Hebrew root; see Pss 22:24; 27:9; 102:1). The psalmist is postured as one whose life depends solely on God,

278. See ibid., 187, 189.

and thus appropriately refers to self in prayer as "your servant" (see Exod 14:31; Job 1:8; 2:3; Pss 19:11, 13; note also Pss 27:9; 31:16, where servanthood is associated with God's face). Because the psalmist belongs to God, God is in a position to "redeem" (גאל *gāʾal*, v. 18), an act customarily carried out by one's next of kin (see Lev 25:25; for God as redeemer, see Exod 15:13; Job 19:25; Isa 41:14; 43:14). This relational term recalls v. 8. Human kin have abandoned the psalmist, but she or he trusts God to act as next-of-kin (see discussion of 19:14 in Commentary on Psalm 19). The verb "set free" (פדה *pādâ*) is also frequently translated "redeem" (see Pss 26:11; 31:5; Jer 15:21).

69:19-21. Just as God knows the psalmist's shortcomings (v. 5), so also God knows all that the enemies have inflicted upon the psalmist (v. 19; see Jer 15:15). Insults (vv. 19-20; see vv. 7, 9) have broken the psalmist's heart (Ps 147:3) and have led to despair (see Jer 15:18). The psalmist has found no human relief. The Hebrew roots of "pity" (נוד *nûd*) and "comforters" (נחם *nḥm*, v. 20) occur in Job 2:11 to designate what Job's friends came to do. They were not successful, and the psalmist's experience recalls that of Job—nothing but bitterness from the human side (v. 21; see Mark 15:23; on the image, see Jer 8:14; 9:15; 23:15).

69:22-29. Thus the extended petition against the enemies (vv. 22-28) is understandable from a psychological point of view. In terms of the structure of the psalm, vv. 22-28 are roughly parallel to vv. 8-12, which describe how the psalmist has been mistreated. Thus, in essence, the psalmist simply asks for the opponents to experience what they have inflicted on others. Even so, the issue is not primarily personal revenge (see Psalms 35; 58; 109). Rather, from a theological point of view, the issue is justice or righteousness. The NRSV's "acquittal" (צדקה *ṣĕdāqâ*) in v. 27 is more literally translated "righteousness." In other words, the psalmist asks God to set things right. Again, the basic appeal is to God's character as loving, faithful, and compassionate. God wills justice for the poor, the lowly, and the oppressed (see Exod 3:7; Pss 9:18; 10:17-18; 68:4-6), and the psalmist is "lowly" and "in pain" (v. 29; see Exod 3:7; Job 2:13; Ps 39:3). Instead of exercising compassion, however, the opponents respond with persecution

and attack (v. 26). Thus, for God's will to be enacted, they must be opposed. In effect, then, the psalmist prays, "thy will be done." By their actions, the opponents invite God's wrath (v. 24). In fact, they have already removed themselves from the company of the living and the roll of the righteous, for life and righteousness in biblical terms consist of dependence upon God (v. 28; see Exod 32:32-33; Ps 139:16; Dan 12:1; see also Commentary on Psalm 1).

69:30-33. The transition from petition/complaint to praise at v. 30 is characteristic of the prayers for help. It is possible to explain the shift psychologically or cultically, but the theological significance lies in the effect of the final form of the psalm—the juxtaposition of complaint and praise (see Commentary on Psalms 13; 22; 31; Introduction). In the book of Psalms, to live is to praise God, and to praise God is to live. Thus, even though the psalmist remains threatened and persecuted, he or she lives by entrusting life and future to God. The perspective is eschatological. The psalmist continues to wait and pray for the enactment of God's will, and yet she or he already lives amid adversity by the power of God. This witness serves to magnify God (see "magnify" in Ps 34:3 and "great" in Pss 35:27; 40:16; 70:4). God's greatness elsewhere is associated with God's sovereignty (see Pss 47:2; 95:3; 99:2-3); that is, the experience of God's power is finally not incompatible with suffering (see Reflections below). The thanksgiving in v. 30 could take the form of a sacrifice, but apparently does not in this case (v. 31). Rather, the psalmist offers her or his life as a witness to God's character (see "name" in v. 30) and as a witness to others. The NRSV's "oppressed" (ענוים *ʿănāwîm*) in v. 32 is from the same Hebrew root as "lowly" in v. 29. Again, the psalmist's life is somehow exemplary (see v. 6). Other people in the same condition will see; they will share in the joy, and they, too, will live (v. 32; see Ps 22:26), knowing that, as is the case for all those "in bonds" (see Pss 68:6; 79:11; 102:20; 107:10; Lam 3:34), God is on their side (v. 33; see Pss 9:18; 12:5; 22:24; 35:10; 140:12).

69:34-36. These verses may be a later addition, yet they are linked closely to the preceding verses. All creation joins the psalmist in praise (vv. 30, 34). God's saving work extends to other people as well (v. 35; see vv. 1, 13d, 29; in relation to Zion, see v. 9), and other "servants" (v. 36; see v. 17) will participate in God's gift of life, which is made possible by God's character, or "name" (vv. 30, 36).

REFLECTIONS

Theological reflection on Psalm 69 is assisted by the "liturgical-theological profile" that Mays compiles of the psalmist and that is summarized in seven points: (1) The psalmist identifies herself or himself as God's "servant" (v. 17; see v. 36) and one of the "lowly" (v. 29; see v. 32). (2) The psalmist views her or his suffering as deriving from God (v. 26), perhaps because of the behavior mentioned in v. 5. (3) The psalmist waits amid suffering for God's saving action (vv. 1, 3, 13d, 29). (4) The psalmist waits with humble but fervent devotion to God and to God's house (vv. 9-11). (5) The psalmist is insulted, derided, and alienated because of this fervent waiting (vv. 8, 10-11, 19-21). (6) The psalmist, therefore, bears reproach that is actually directed to God (vv. 7, 9). (7) The psalmist is a representative figure, both in the condition of affliction and in being saved by God (vv. 29, 32-33).[279]

Mays further suggests that while this profile discourages identification with any one particular historical figure, it clearly calls to mind several persons or groups: Jeremiah (see especially the so-called Confessions in 11:18-20; 15:15-18; 17:14-18), the lamenting voice in Lamentations 3, the afflicted community of Psalm 44 (see vv. 22, 24), the Suffering Servant of Isaiah 53, and Job. Although precision and certainty are impossible, it is likely that all of these texts have been informed and shaped in one way or another by the experience of exile. Mays concludes: "Out of the anguish of the exile and its aftermath an understanding of affliction that goes beyond punishment and fits into the saving purpose of the LORD began to emerge. Psalm 69 is one piece of the pattern."[280]

For Christians, the ultimate piece in this emerging pattern is the cross of Jesus Christ. While Psalm 69 should not be interpreted as prophetic in a predictive sense, it is not surprising that this psalm was used several times by those who told and interpreted the story of Jesus' life, death, and resurrection. Like the psalmist, Jesus was persecuted not for being faithless but for being faithful (cf. v. 9 with John 2:17; v. 4 with John 15:25). Jesus was rejected by his own (see v. 8), mocked and insulted (see vv. 7, 9, 19-20), and received bitter treatment at human hands (cf. v. 21 with Matt 27:34; Mark 15:23; Luke 23:36; John 19:29-30). The familiarity of the psalm in the early church is indicated by the fact that even the petitions against the enemies (vv. 22-28) were cited in an attempt to explain the rejection of Jesus (cf. vv. 22-23 with Rom 11:9-10; v. 24 with Rev 16:1; v. 25 with Acts 1:20). The concluding verses of Psalm 69 also anticipate the joy and promise of new life that came with the resurrection of Jesus (see esp. v. 32).

Like the other prayers for help (see Reflections on Psalms 13; 22; 31), Psalm 69 finally communicates God's intimate, incarnational involvement with the lowly and the oppressed. The juxtaposition of complaint/petition and praise creates an eschatological perspective; that is, the psalmist lives, and the people of God will always live, in perpetual and painful waiting (see vv. 3, 6) that is simultaneously joyful assurance and life (vv. 30-36; see Matt 5:10-11). In other words, suffering and glory, pain and joy, crucifixion and resurrection are ultimately inseparable realities for God's people and for God's own self. God's sovereignty is ultimately the power of love and compassion (see vv. 13, 16).

279. Mays, *Psalms*, 230-32.
280. Ibid., 232.

PSALM 70:1-5, O LORD, DO NOT DELAY!

NIV

Psalm 70

For the director of music. Of David. A petition.

¹Hasten, O God, to save me;
  O LORD, come quickly to help me.
²May those who seek my life
  be put to shame and confusion;
may all who desire my ruin
  be turned back in disgrace.
³May those who say to me, "Aha! Aha!"
  turn back because of their shame.
⁴But may all who seek you
  rejoice and be glad in you;
may those who love your salvation always say,
  "Let God be exalted!"
⁵Yet I am poor and needy;
  come quickly to me, O God.
You are my help and my deliverer;
  O LORD, do not delay.

NRSV

Psalm 70

To the leader. Of David, for the memorial offering.

¹ Be pleased, O God, to deliver me.
  O LORD, make haste to help me!
² Let those be put to shame and confusion
  who seek my life.
Let those be turned back and brought to
    dishonor
  who desire to hurt me.
³ Let those who say, "Aha, Aha!"
  turn back because of their shame.

⁴ Let all who seek you
  rejoice and be glad in you.
Let those who love your salvation
  say evermore, "God is great!"
⁵ But I am poor and needy;
  hasten to me, O God!
You are my help and my deliverer;
  O LORD, do not delay!

COMMENTARY

Psalm 70 is almost identical to Ps 40:13-17. Some scholars think that Psalm 70 was an independent poem that was adapted for use as a conclusion to Psalm 40, while others view Psalm 40 as the older work and suggest that Psalm 70 was formed by borrowing the conclusion of Psalm 40. Certainty is not possible. It is interesting, though perhaps coincidental, that Ps 40:13-17 and Psalm 70 occur very near the ends of Books I and II. In fact, if Psalms 70 and 71 were originally meant to be one psalm (note that Psalm 71 lacks a superscription), then Ps 40:13-17 and Psalm 70 would be parts of the next-to-the-last psalm in both Books I and II.

The literary links between Psalms 70 and 71 reinforce the possibility that they were originally one psalm, or at least that someone intended them to be read as companions (cf. 70:1b, 5b with 71:12b; 70:2 with 71:10, 13; 70:1a with 71:2; 70:4c with 71:19c). In addition, the Hebrew word translated "memorial offering" (הזכיר *hazkîr*) in the superscription of Psalm 70 (see also the superscription of Psalm 38), is a causative form of the verb "remember" (זכר *zākar*), which occurs in a similar form in 71:16b. Psalm 70 also has affinities with Psalm 69. In both, for instance, the psalmist identifies herself or himself as "lowly"/"poor" (69:29; 70:5; the Hebrew word is the same), and the word "needy" (אביון *'ebyôn*) occurs in 69:33 and 70:5. Both psalms also feature the concept of "salvation" (69:1, 13cd, 29, 35; 70:4), the response to which is similar in each case ("magnify" in 69:30 and "great" in 70:4 represent the same Hebrew root [גדל *gādal*]).

The major difference between Ps 40:13-17 and Psalm 70 is found in a comparison of 40:17b and

70:5*b*. The word "thought" (חשב *ḥāšab*) in 40:17*b* recalls 40:5, while "hasten" (חוש *ḥûš*) in 70:5*b* recalls 70:1*b*. In short, the divergent content is appropriate in each case to its own context.

REFLECTIONS

Psalm 70 is traditionally used during Holy Week. In this setting, the quotation of the enemies in v. 3, "Aha, Aha!" (cf. Ps 35:21, 25), recalls the mocking words that onlookers directed to the crucified Jesus (see Mark 15:29). This liturgical setting is another reminder of the adaptability of the prayers for help to a variety of circumstances, and it is testimony, too, to the Christian conviction that Jesus ultimately embodied the role of the faithful sufferer who fully entrusts life and future to God (see Commentary on Psalms 22; 31; 41; 69). In other words, Jesus revealed the shape of God's sovereignty—greatness that is constituted by the power of suffering love (v. 4). (For further commentary and Reflections, see Psalm 40.)

PSALM 71:1-24, I WILL HOPE CONTINUALLY

NIV

Psalm 71

¹In you, O Lord, I have taken refuge;
   let me never be put to shame.
²Rescue me and deliver me in your righteousness;
   turn your ear to me and save me.
³Be my rock of refuge,
   to which I can always go;
 give the command to save me,
   for you are my rock and my fortress.
⁴Deliver me, O my God, from the hand of the
      wicked,
   from the grasp of evil and cruel men.

⁵For you have been my hope, O Sovereign
      Lord,
   my confidence since my youth.
⁶From birth I have relied on you;
   you brought me forth from my mother's
      womb.
   I will ever praise you.
⁷I have become like a portent to many,
   but you are my strong refuge.
⁸My mouth is filled with your praise,
   declaring your splendor all day long.

⁹Do not cast me away when I am old;
   do not forsake me when my strength is
      gone.

NRSV

Psalm 71

¹ In you, O Lord, I take refuge;
   let me never be put to shame.
² In your righteousness deliver me and rescue
      me;
   incline your ear to me and save me.
³ Be to me a rock of refuge,
   a strong fortress,ᵃ to save me,
   for you are my rock and my fortress.

⁴ Rescue me, O my God, from the hand of
      the wicked,
   from the grasp of the unjust and cruel.
⁵ For you, O Lord, are my hope,
   my trust, O Lord, from my youth.
⁶ Upon you I have leaned from my birth;
   it was you who took me from my
      mother's womb.
My praise is continually of you.

⁷ I have been like a portent to many,
   but you are my strong refuge.
⁸ My mouth is filled with your praise,
   and with your glory all day long.
⁹ Do not cast me off in the time of old
      age;

ᵃ Gk Compare 31.3: Heb *to come continually you have commanded*

NIV

10For my enemies speak against me;
  those who wait to kill me conspire
      together.
11They say, "God has forsaken him;
  pursue him and seize him,
  for no one will rescue him."
12Be not far from me, O God;
  come quickly, O my God, to help me.
13May my accusers perish in shame;
  may those who want to harm me
  be covered with scorn and disgrace.

14But as for me, I will always have hope;
  I will praise you more and more.
15My mouth will tell of your righteousness,
  of your salvation all day long,
  though I know not its measure.
16I will come and proclaim your mighty acts,
      O Sovereign Lord;
  I will proclaim your righteousness, yours
      alone.
17Since my youth, O God, you have taught me,
  and to this day I declare your marvelous
      deeds.
18Even when I am old and gray,
  do not forsake me, O God,
  till I declare your power to the next
      generation,
  your might to all who are to come.

19Your righteousness reaches to the skies, O
      God,
  you who have done great things.
  Who, O God, is like you?
20Though you have made me see troubles,
      many and bitter,
  you will restore my life again;
  from the depths of the earth
  you will again bring me up.
21You will increase my honor
  and comfort me once again.

22I will praise you with the harp
  for your faithfulness, O my God;
  I will sing praise to you with the lyre,
  O Holy One of Israel.
23My lips will shout for joy
  when I sing praise to you—
  I, whom you have redeemed.
24My tongue will tell of your righteous acts

NRSV

  do not forsake me when my strength is
      spent.
10 For my enemies speak concerning me,
  and those who watch for my life consult
      together.
11 They say, "Pursue and seize that person
  whom God has forsaken,
  for there is no one to deliver."

12 O God, do not be far from me;
  O my God, make haste to help me!
13 Let my accusers be put to shame and
      consumed;
  let those who seek to hurt me
  be covered with scorn and disgrace.
14 But I will hope continually,
  and will praise you yet more and more.
15 My mouth will tell of your righteous acts,
  of your deeds of salvation all day long,
  though their number is past my
      knowledge.
16 I will come praising the mighty deeds of
      the Lord God,
  I will praise your righteousness, yours
      alone.

17 O God, from my youth you have taught me,
  and I still proclaim your wondrous deeds.
18 So even to old age and gray hairs,
  O God, do not forsake me,
  until I proclaim your might
  to all the generations to come.[a]
  Your power 19and your righteousness,
      O God,
  reach the high heavens.

  You who have done great things,
  O God, who is like you?
20 You who have made me see many troubles
      and calamities
  will revive me again;
  from the depths of the earth
  you will bring me up again.
21 You will increase my honor,
  and comfort me once again.

22 I will also praise you with the harp
  for your faithfulness, O my God;

a Gk Compare Syr: Heb *to a generation, to all that come*

NIV

all day long,
for those who wanted to harm me
have been put to shame and confusion.

NRSV

I will sing praises to you with the lyre,
O Holy One of Israel.
23 My lips will shout for joy
when I sing praises to you;
my soul also, which you have rescued.
24 All day long my tongue will talk of your
righteous help,
for those who tried to do me harm
have been put to shame, and disgraced.

COMMENTARY

Psalm 71 contains the typical elements of a prayer for help or individual lament/complaint: petition (vv. 1-4, 7a, 9, 12-13, 18), complaint (vv. 10-11), and expressions of trust (vv. 5-6, 7b, 17, 20-21) and praise (vv. 8, 14-16, 19, 22-24). It has numerous similarities to other prayers for help and is even sometimes viewed as a collage of quotations from other psalms, especially Psalm 22 (cf. v. 6 with 22:9-10; v. 12 with 22:11, 19; v. 18b with 22:30-31) and Psalm 31 (cf. vv. 1-3 with 31:1-3; v. 9b with 31:10; v. 13 with 31:17), but others as well (cf. v. 12b with 38:12 and 40:13; v. 13 with 35:4, 26; v. 19 with 36:6; v. 24 with 35:28). There are also several verbal links to Psalm 70, and it is possible that Psalms 70 and 71 were originally a single psalm (see Commentary on Psalm 70). Besides Psalm 43, Psalm 71 is the only psalm in Book II without a superscription.

Although Psalm 71 contains all the typical elements of a prayer for help, its arrangement of them is unique. For example, this psalm moves from petition/complaint to trust/praise, as is typical for this genre, but the psalm does so *three* times:

vv. 1-4	petition
vv. 5-8	trust/praise
vv. 9-13	petition/complaint
vv. 14-17	trust/praise
v. 18	petition
vv. 19-24	trust/praise

This movement is significant. Without minimizing the reality of distress and opposition, the psalmist displays pervasive faith and hope (v. 14a) and

persistent praise (v. 6c; note the NRSV's "continually" in vv. 6c, 14a). The effect, in Kraus's words, is that "the psalm radiates tremendous assurance."[281]

71:1-4. This assurance is articulated in the opening words of the psalm. To "take refuge" in God may be related to the ancient practice of seeking asylum from accusers or persecutors in the Temple (see vv. 4, 10-11, 13; 1 Kgs 1:49-53; Psalms 5; 7; Introduction); however, the language may well be metaphorical. Some scholars suggest that the psalmist was ill (see v. 20) or was suffering the setbacks of old age (see vv. 9, 18), but this language may be metaphorical. What is clear is that, regardless of the circumstances, the psalmist's life depends on God. It is this dependence upon God that "refuge" communicates (see Pss 2:12; 5:11; 7:1; Introduction). It is reinforced by the series of imperatives in v. 2—"deliver" (see Ps 22:5, 9), "rescue" (see v. 4; Ps 7:2), and "save" (see Pss 3:2; 6:4; 7:1). The same word for "refuge" (מחסה *maḥseh*) recurs in v. 7, and the four nouns in v. 3 also communicate the psalmist's trust in God—"rock" (צור *ṣûr*; see Pss 18:2, 31, 46; 19:14, 28:1; 31:2), "refuge" (a different Hebrew word from that in vv. 1, 7; see also Ps 27:1; cf. Ps 31:2, although the Hebrew word in 71:2 actually differs slightly and means "dwelling place"); a second Hebrew word translated "rock" (סלע *sela'*; see Pss 18:2; 31:3; 42:9); and "fortress" (מצודה *mĕṣûdâ*; see Pss 18:2; 31:3). The NRSV suggests a fifth noun (v. 3b; see NRSV note); the

---

281. H.-J. Kraus, *Psalms 60–150: A Commentary,* trans. H. C. Oswald (Minneapolis: Augsburg, 1989) 73.

NIV has tried to render this difficult phrase more literally.

The psalmist's assurance and appeal rest on the foundation of God's righteousness (v. 2), which becomes the major theme of the psalm (see vv. 15-16, 19, 24). The word "righteousness" (צדקה *ṣĕdāqâ*) designates what God wills and enacts as ruler of the world, and it involves justice and equitable treatment for the oppressed (see Pss 9:7-9; 96:13; 97:2, 6, 10-12; 98:9). As a victim of injustice and cruelty (v. 4), the psalmist trusts that God will set things right by shaming those who seek to shame the psalmist (see "shame" in vv. 1, 13, 24). In short, the psalmist trusts that God—not the wicked—rules the world (v. 4). Although v. 24 gives the impression that God has already shamed the wicked, it is not specified whether the wicked have actually experienced a reversal of fortunes or whether the psalmist speaks with a certainty of God's help that allows the psalmist to envision it as already having occurred. In any case, it is clear that trust in God's righteous reign exists amid opposition for most of the psalm. In other words, the wicked (v. 4)—those who view themselves as self-sufficient rather than dependent on God—are a persistent reality (see Commentary on Psalm 1). Thus, as usual, the perspective is eschatological. God's rule is trusted and proclaimed amid powerful and persistent opposition (see Psalm 2; Introduction).

71:5-8. Verse 5 begins with the personal pronoun "you," which also occurs in vv. 3, 6-7 and focuses attention emphatically upon God. The psalmist's confidence is not self-confidence; it derives from "hope" (v. 5; see Ps 9:18) and "trust" (see Pss 4:8; 16:9; 40:4; 65:6). Verses 5-6 also introduce the theme of youth (vv. 5, 17) and old age (vv. 9, 18). While the language may be metaphorical, it expresses the psalmist's conviction that he or she has belonged to God from the day of birth and will always belong to God (see Ps 22:9-10; note especially that the word "trust" (בטח *bāṭaḥ*) occurs in 22:9, as the NIV makes clear). The proper response to God's sustaining care ("leaned" in v. 6*a* suggests sustenance; see "sustains" in Ps 3:5) is praise (vv. 6*c*, 8*a*, 14*b*; see vv. 16, 22-23, where different Hebrew words for "praise" occur). For those who know their lives belong to God, praise is not just an occasional liturgical act. Rather, it is a life-style offered con-

tinually (v. 6*c*; see also v. 14 as well as the phrase "all day long" in vv. 8, 15, 24), even in the midst of adversity.

The meaning of "portent" (מופת *môpēt*) in v. 7*a* is unclear. The verse may articulate the psalmist's complaint that the suffering is so great that others see it as a warning (see Deut 28:46). The word for "portent" usually designates something more positive, however, often the exodus (see "wonders" in Exod 7:3; Deut 4:34; 6:22). Thus v. 7*a* could suggest that the psalmist's example of trust amid adversity is an encouraging sign to others. Perhaps the ambiguity is intentional, or at least appropriate. As Tate suggests, "Some members of the community would have seen the supplicant as a 'sign' of God's providential care; others would have understood his or her condition as a divine judgment."[282] In any case, the psalmist apparently intends to be a public witness to God's reign by praising God and testifying to God's "glory" (v. 8; see "beauty" in Ps 96:6 NRSV, a verse that also contains the word "strong"/"strength" [עז *'ōz*], found in 71:7). This intent is another major theme of the psalm (see vv. 15-19, 24).

71:9-13. The psalmist returns to petition and complaint. Verse 9 anticipates v. 18 (see also Ps 31:10), and the verb "forsake" (עזב *'āzab*) also prepares for vv. 10-11. Verse 11, which recalls Ps 3:2, indicates that some people interpret the psalmist's suffering as a sign of divine punishment. But even though the psalmist cannot understand the suffering apart from God's causation (see v. 20), he or she does not interpret it as punishment. Thus the appeal to God is persistent. Verse 12 recalls Pss 22:19 and 70:1, 6, and "shame" in v. 13 recalls v. 1 and anticipates v. 24 (see also Pss 31:17; 70:2). This look backward and forward at the center of the psalm is appropriate, and it seems to mark a turning point. Whereas vv. 1-13 consist of two sections of petition/complaint (vv. 1-4, 9-13) surrounding an expression of trust and praise, vv. 14-24 consist of two expressions of trust and praise (vv. 14-17, 19-24) surrounding a brief petition (v. 18). The movement is toward assurance.

71:14-18. In a real sense, v. 14 states the psalmist's perspective throughout the psalm:

282. Marvin E. Tate, *Psalms 51–100*, WBC 20 (Dallas: Word, 1990) 214.

continual hope and praise (see vv. 6, 8, 15-17, 22-24). The Hebrew word for "hope" (יחל *yḥl*) in v. 14 differs from the one in v. 5, but they are essentially synonymous and occur elsewhere in the same context, often with one or the other of them being translated "wait" (see Ps 130:5, 7). Like v. 14, v. 15 recalls v. 8 (see "mouth"); and like v. 13, v. 15 recalls the beginning of the psalm (see "righteousness" and "save" in v. 2) and its conclusion (see "righteous" and "all day long" in v. 24). The effect is to focus attention on v. 14 as a kind of theological center. As vv. 15-17 suggest, continual hope inevitably issues in witness to God's righteous (vv. 15, 17), life-giving activity. The NRSV's "praise" (אזכיר *ʾazkîr*) in v. 16*b* is more literally, "cause to remember" (see Ps 77:11). The psalmist's role as witness is reinforced by the verb "proclaim" (נגד *ngd*) in v. 17. Even the petition in v. 18 is supported by the psalmist's desire to share the story. The verb *nāgad* is repeated, and the psalmist's stated concern is not for self-preservation but for the transmission of the faith.

71:19-24. At the heart of the psalmist's faith is the conviction that, despite appearances, God ultimately rules the world. The psalmist's proclamation focuses on God's righteousness (vv. 15-16, 19, 24) and "mighty acts"/"might" (vv. 16, 18), both of which are associated elsewhere with God's sovereignty (on "righteousness," see discussion above on v. 2; on "might," see Ps 145:4, 11-12 NIV). God's ability to do "great things" is also an attribute of God's sovereignty (v. 19; see Pss 47:2; 70:4; 95:3). In short, there is *no one* like God. Indeed, God's rule is so pervasive that the psalmist cannot help attributing his or her suffering to God (v. 20; see Deut 32:39), but does so in the confidence that God finally wills life (see "revive" in 69:32) and wholeness. The word "honor" (גדולה *gĕdûllâ*) in v. 21 is from the same root as "great things" in v. 19; thus the psalmist trusts that God's greatness is ultimately put at the service of human greatness. This in itself is a source of continual hope and "comfort" (see Ps 23:4). Thus the psalm ends with a crescendo of praise directed at God's faithfulness (see Exod 34:6; Ps 138:2; see esp. Pss 57:8-10 and 92:2-3, where harp and lyre are involved) and accompanied by another statement of resolve to be a constant witness to God's righteousness (v. 21; see Ps 35:28). The verb "tell" (הגה *hāgâ*) in v. 24 recalls the beginning of the psalter (in 1:2 *hgh* is translated as "meditate"), where it is made clear that what one meditates upon is crucial. In other words, the verb describes the orientation of one's whole existence, and the psalmist is consistently oriented to God and to God's righteousness. Precisely this orientation makes life possible and enables the psalmist to "hope continually" (v. 14).

REFLECTIONS

1. The psalmist's constant orientation to God and to God's righteousness recalls the words of Jesus as he spoke about the sustaining care of God: "But strive first for the kingdom of God and his righteousness, and all these things will be given to you as well" (Matt 6:33 NRSV; cf. Ps 71:5-6). Jesus knew that persons who strive for the kingdom of God will face adversity (see Matt 5:10-11), but he trusted and taught others to trust that God's providence is sufficient. The psalmist knew that same trust, and he or she, too, was committed to teaching it to others (vv. 17-18). Like Jesus, the psalmist lived with adversity (vv. 10-11), but the psalmist also lived in constant trust and hope that issued in praise (vv. 5-6, 14-17, 19-24). The structure of Psalm 71 represents the reality that faith lives amid adversity. Praise is not the celebration of the powerful and the prosperous; rather, it is the language and the life-style of those who know at all times and in every circumstance that their lives belong to God and that their futures depend on God.

2. Because of the psalmist's trust, hope, and faithful witness in the midst of threat and suffering, and perhaps because of the similarities between Psalm 71 and Psalms 22 and 31, Psalm 71 has customarily been associated with Jesus' passion and traditionally is used during Holy Week. It is also traditionally used during the season of Epiphany, for which the theme of the proclamation of God's righteousness (vv. 15-19, 24) makes it very appropriate. The psalmist also does the equivalent of what Christians customarily do during the season of Epiphany: We remember our baptisms. To remember our baptisms is to profess to the world that God claims us at birth and that we shall always belong to God (see vv. 5-6). In our *self*-centered, achievement-oriented culture, that simple profession is remarkable and radical. It means that we view life not as a reward to be achieved but as a gift to be received (see vv. 20-21). Thus praise becomes a life-long response and calling, from birth to old age. To praise God is to do as the psalmist did, even in the face of adversity—to look back and say "it was you who took me from my mother's womb" (v. 6) and to look forward and say, "You will . . . comfort me once again" (v. 21). As A. Hale Schroer has put it, "Praise is to declare even when the evidence seems stacked against it that this is God's world. . . . Praise is the posture of Epiphany for it keeps us open to the new ways God is manifesting Godself in our world."[283]

3. Although having grown old, the psalmist expects new things; indeed, the psalmist is intent on proclaiming God's deeds to "generations to come" (v. 18). Commentators have speculated that the psalmist was a member of one of the temple guilds, and thus was a specialist in writing songs for religious use. In our day and time, however, we cannot afford to leave the educational task to specialists. All who belong to God are called to praise God continually (v. 6) in joyful gratitude for God's faithfulness and righteousness (vv. 22-24), to witness to all the generations to come (v. 18) that ultimately nothing "will be able to separate us from the love of God" (Rom 8:39 NRSV).

283. A. Hale Schroer, "Having Confidence in God," *No Other Foundation* 9/2 (Winter 1988) 16.

PSALM 72:1-20, MAY RIGHTEOUSNESS FLOURISH AND PEACE ABOUND

NIV	NRSV
Psalm 72	Psalm 72
Of Solomon.	Of Solomon.
¹Endow the king with your justice, O God, the royal son with your righteousness.	¹ Give the king your justice, O God, and your righteousness to a king's son.
²He will[a] judge your people in righteousness, your afflicted ones with justice.	² May he judge your people with righteousness, and your poor with justice.
³The mountains will bring prosperity to the people, the hills the fruit of righteousness.	³ May the mountains yield prosperity for the people, and the hills, in righteousness.
⁴He will defend the afflicted among the people and save the children of the needy; he will crush the oppressor.	⁴ May he defend the cause of the poor of the people, give deliverance to the needy, and crush the oppressor.
⁵He will endure[b] as long as the sun, as long as the moon, through all generations.	⁵ May he live[a] while the sun endures, and as long as the moon, throughout all generations.
⁶He will be like rain falling on a mown field, like showers watering the earth.	

a2 Or *May he*; similarly in verses 3-11 and 17   b5 Septuagint; Hebrew *You will be feared*

aGk: Heb *may they fear you*

NIV

⁷In his days the righteous will flourish;
　　prosperity will abound till the moon is no
　　more.

⁸He will rule from sea to sea
　　and from the River*ᵃ* to the ends of the
　　earth.*ᵇ*
⁹The desert tribes will bow before him
　　and his enemies will lick the dust.
¹⁰The kings of Tarshish and of distant shores
　　will bring tribute to him;
　the kings of Sheba and Seba
　　will present him gifts.
¹¹All kings will bow down to him
　　and all nations will serve him.

¹²For he will deliver the needy who cry out,
　　the afflicted who have no one to help.
¹³He will take pity on the weak and the needy
　　and save the needy from death.
¹⁴He will rescue them from oppression and
　　violence,
　for precious is their blood in his sight.

¹⁵Long may he live!
　　May gold from Sheba be given him.
　May people ever pray for him
　　and bless him all day long.
¹⁶Let grain abound throughout the land;
　　on the tops of the hills may it sway.
　Let its fruit flourish like Lebanon;
　　let it thrive like the grass of the field.
¹⁷May his name endure forever;
　　may it continue as long as the sun.

　All nations will be blessed through him,
　　and they will call him blessed.

¹⁸Praise be to the LORD God, the God of Israel,
　　who alone does marvelous deeds.
¹⁹Praise be to his glorious name forever;
　　may the whole earth be filled with his
　　glory.
　　　Amen and Amen.

²⁰This concludes the prayers of David son of
　　Jesse.

ᵃ8 That is, the Euphrates　　*ᵇ8 Or the end of the land*

NRSV

⁶ May he be like rain that falls on the mown
　　grass,
　　like showers that water the earth.
⁷ In his days may righteousness flourish
　　and peace abound, until the moon is
　　no more.

⁸ May he have dominion from sea to sea,
　　and from the River to the ends of the earth.
⁹ May his foes*ᵃ* bow down before him,
　　and his enemies lick the dust.
¹⁰ May the kings of Tarshish and of the isles
　　render him tribute,
　may the kings of Sheba and Seba
　　bring gifts.
¹¹ May all kings fall down before him,
　　all nations give him service.

¹² For he delivers the needy when they call,
　　the poor and those who have no helper.
¹³ He has pity on the weak and the needy,
　　and saves the lives of the needy.
¹⁴ From oppression and violence he redeems
　　their life;
　and precious is their blood in his sight.

¹⁵ Long may he live!
　　May gold of Sheba be given to him.
　May prayer be made for him continually,
　　and blessings invoked for him all day long.
¹⁶ May there be abundance of grain in the land;
　　may it wave on the tops of the mountains;
　　may its fruit be like Lebanon;
　and may people blossom in the cities
　　like the grass of the field.
¹⁷ May his name endure forever,
　　his fame continue as long as the sun.
　May all nations be blessed in him;*ᵇ*
　　may they pronounce him happy.

¹⁸ Blessed be the LORD, the God of Israel,
　　who alone does wondrous things.
¹⁹ Blessed be his glorious name forever;
　　may his glory fill the whole earth.
　　　Amen and Amen.

²⁰ The prayers of David son of Jesse are ended.

ᵃ Gn: Heb those who live in the wilderness　　*ᵇ Or bless themselves
by him*

COMMENTARY

As v. 1 suggests, Psalm 72 originated as a prayer for the king. The attribution to Solomon is understandable (cf. v. 15 with 1 Kgs 10:10, and vv. 1-4 with the emphasis on Solomon's justice in 1 Kings 3, esp. v. 28); it is possible that the psalm was actually written for Solomon. We simply cannot date the psalm with any certainty, but it is likely that it was written for use at the coronation of Davidic kings in Jerusalem, in which case it would have been used repeatedly, along with the other royal psalms (see esp. Psalms 2; 18; 20–21; 45; 89; 110; 132; Introduction). Obviously, Psalm 72 continued to be used after the disappearance of the monarchy. Such ongoing use was possible, because what Psalm 72 prays for ultimately is the enactment of *God's* reign and *God's* will for the world. Thus the way was open for Psalm 72 to be interpreted eschatologically within Judaism and Christianity (see Reflections below).

After the initial imperative, the psalm continues with a series of verbs that can be construed either as indicatives (NIV) or as petitions (NRSV). The ambiguity is appropriate, since Psalm 72 probably functioned both as a charge to and a prayer for the new king. The psalm is usually divided as follows: vv. 1-7, vv. 8-14, vv. 15-17, vv. 18-20. Verses 18-19 serve both as an appropriate conclusion to the psalm and as a doxology for Book II, and v. 20 marks the conclusion of the collection that started with Psalm 51. It is significant that royal psalms (Psalms 2; 72; 89) appear at the seams of the psalter; they focus attention on God's reign at crucial points, and they lead up to the climactic proclamation of God's reign (Psalms 93; 95–99) that forms the theological heart of the psalter (see Introduction).

72:1-7. Verse 1 clearly marks the beginning of Psalm 72 as a prayer, and it introduces the two key words and concepts: justice and righteousness. Roland E. Murphy argues that the grammatical structure of v. 1 and subsequent verses serves as a clue to the programmatic significance of v. 1; that is, every section of the poem is to be heard in relation to v. 1.[284] But even apart from this

grammatical clue, it is clear that v. 1 has overarching significance. Everything said about or wished for the king depends ultimately on *God's* justice (the Hebrew word מִשְׁפָּטִים [*mišpāṭîm*] is plural, but the singular sense is appropriate, since the purpose of God's "judgments" is to enact justice) and *God's* righteousness. Justice and righteousness are first and foremost characteristic of God's reign (see Pss 96:13; 97:2, 6; 98:9; 99:4; 146:7); they describe God's royal policy, or in more theological terms, God's will. In short, the role of the king is to enact God's rule. The crucial significance of justice and righteousness for God, and thus for the king, is reinforced by repetition in vv. 1-7. The word "righteousness" (צֶדֶק *ṣedeq*) occurs in vv. 1-3 as well as in v. 7, where it marks the conclusion of the first section. The word "justice" occurs in v. 2; the verb "defend" (שָׁפַט *šāpaṭ*) in v. 4 represents the same Hebrew root, while "judge" (דִין *dîn*) in v. 2 is a synonym (see Pss 7:8; 9:8; 96:10). Syntax enters the picture as well; the chiastic structure (see Introduction) of vv. 1-2 has the effect of literarily surrounding the king and his people with justice.

When God's will is done—when justice and righteousness are enacted—the result is *shalom* (v. 3 [NRSV, "prosperity"]; v. 7 [NRSV, "peace"]). The shape of *shalom* is suggested in vv. 2-7. It has primarily to do with the condition of the poor and of the needy (for "poor," see vv. 2, 4; see v. 12; see also Commentary on Psalm 9, esp. discussion of 9:18; and Psalm 10; for "needy," see v. 4; see also vv. 12-13). In fact, the *only* stated responsibility of the king in vv. 2-7 or vv. 12-14 is to establish justice for the oppressed, to "save" the needy (v. 4; see v. 13). Such salvation was what God did in the exodus (see Exod 15:2, 18), and this function is the measure of royalty, whether human or divine (see Psalm 82). The significance of justice and righteousness is further indicated by the mention of the cosmic elements in vv. 3, 5-7; only in the presence of justice and righteousness does the whole world operate as God intends (see Pss 36:5-6; 82:5; and the involvement of cosmic elements as well in Psalms 93, 96–99). Both the NIV and the NRSV follow the LXX in v. 5*a*, thus maintaining the focus on

---

284. Roland E. Murphy, *A Study of Psalm 72* (Washington, D.C.: Catholic University Press, 1948) 6-14.

the earthly king. The Hebrew reading (see NIV and NRSV notes) has the advantage of grounding the king's work even more explicitly in God's reign.

72:8-14. Whereas vv. 5 and 7 envision the extension of the king's rule in time, vv. 8-11 envision its extension in space.[285] The river in v. 8 may be the Euphrates, or it may refer to the mythical river that flowed from God's throne in Jerusalem (see discussion of Ps 46:4 above). Tarshish is usually located in Spain (see Gen 10:4; 1 Kgs 10:22; Ps 48:7; Jer 10:9; Jonah 1:3); the isles probably refer to Mediterranean locales or perhaps to generally distant places; Sheba designates an area in the southern Arabian peninsula (see Isa 60:6; Jer 6:20; Ezek 27:22-25); and Seba may refer to generally the same area (see Gen 10:7; 1 Chr 1:9; Isa 43:3; 45:14; Joel 3:8).[286] In any case, vv. 8-11 envision the king's sovereignty as encompassing the whole world—all its rulers and all its people. The phrase "ends of the earth" recalls Psalm 2 (v. 8), which also describes the king's universal dominion over the other kings and nations. The words "bow down" (שחה šāḥâ) and "serve" (עבד ʿābad) in v. 11 designate responses ordinarily reserved for God (see Ps 2:11). Thus they are another reminder that the king's purpose is to enact God's reign.

The conjunction "for" (כי kî), which begins v. 12, connects universal political dominion not to clever strategy or to superior military might, as one might expect, but to the king's care for the oppressed. The vocabulary of vv. 12-14 recalls v. 4. And as v. 4 already began to suggest, the king does what is ordinarily attributed to God: He "delivers" when people cry out (see Exod 2:23); he "saves" (see Exod 15:2); he redeems (see Exod 15:13). He values the lives of those entrusted to his care (v. 14b; see Ps 116:15).

72:15-17. Given the correlation between the king's action and God's will, the acclamation "Long may he live!" (v. 15) is essentially a prayer that God enact God's will. As vv. 1-7 have already shown, the poet sees a connection between the work of the king and the operation of the cosmos—agricultural productivity and human productivity (v. 16). Verse 17 connects the rule of the king with the promise to Abraham in Gen 12:1-3. Scholars have traditionally dated the Yahwist (J) source in the Pentateuch, to which Gen 12:1-3 probably belongs, to the time of Solomon; Wolff even suggests that it was written to encourage the monarchy to be something other than simply self-serving.[287] While this conclusion may be tenuous, and while the evidence is too slim to make a historical connection between Gen 12:1-3 and Psalm 72, it is at least clear that Psalm 72 views the ultimate purpose of the monarchy in terms of the fulfillment of God's purposes for the whole creation (see Ps 47:8-9; Isa 2:2-4; 19:23-25).

72:18-20. As suggested above, vv. 18-19 seem to serve as the concluding doxology for Book II, but they also form a very appropriate theological conclusion to Psalm 72. That is to say, they make it explicit that praise for the king's activity belongs ultimately to God, for God alone is the real actor. The word "glorious"/"glory" (כבוד kābôd, v. 19) is often associated with God's reign (see Pss 29:1-3, 9; 24:7-10). In short, vv. 18-19 are a reminder that only God is ultimately sovereign and that the king's rule derives from and is intended to be a representation of God's reign.

Verse 20 originally may have marked the conclusion of the Davidic collection, Psalms 51–72. However, in the final form of the psalter, it also serves to mark the division between Books II and III (see Introduction).

---

285. See Robert Alter, *The Art of Biblical Poetry* (New York: Basic Books, 1985) 129-33.
286. See Tate, *Psalms 51–100,* 221.

287. Hans Walter Wolff, "The Kerygma of the Yahwist," in *The Vitality of Old Testament Traditions* (Atlanta: John Knox, 1975) 41-66.

REFLECTIONS

Perhaps the most obvious observation to make about Psalm 72 is the disparity between its portrayal of the king and the actual behavior of the kings of Israel and Judah. To be sure, such a disparity could tempt one to dismiss this psalm as part and parcel of ancient Near Eastern political propaganda (it does show marked similarities to other ancient documents, such as the Code of Hammurabi). But such a view would overlook the theological dimension of Psalm 72 in its role as Scripture. The disparity between Psalm 72 and the actual monarchy represents the disparity that always exists between the will of God and every attempt to implement the will of God concretely in space and time. The same disparity is evident, for instance, when we call the church "the body of Christ" and then observe the actual behavior of the church.

In other words, the disparity invites an eschatological understanding of Psalm 72. Even after the final failure and disappearance of the monarchy, Psalm 72 continued to be read and heard as a proclamation of God's reign and a portrayal of God's royal policy—God's will—for the world. By the time the psalm took its place in the psalter, it almost certainly was already understood messianically. For some Jews in the post-exilic era, Psalm 72 probably expressed the longing for the historical restoration of the monarchy by a king who would finally get things right. For a later generation of Jews who would become Christians, Psalm 72 expressed the conviction that Jesus was that messiah, that king. They saw in Jesus one who proclaimed the reign of God (Mark 1:14-15) and embodied it in a ministry to the poor and the needy. They were convinced that Jesus' birth signaled peace on earth (Luke 2:14; see Commentary on Psalm 29) and that Jesus left peace with his disciples (John 14:27). And these disciples went out and invited all nations (that is, the Gentiles) to find their blessing in Jesus (see Galatians 3, esp. vv. 8-9, 27-29). While Psalm 72 is not specifically quoted in the NT, its association with the seasons of Advent and Epiphany is testimony to the Christian conviction that Jesus ultimately fulfilled the vision of the king portrayed in Psalm 72. When Christians pray this prayer through Jesus Christ, they are still asking essentially what Jews are asking when they pray this prayer messianically: "Thy kingdom come, thy will be done on earth as it is in heaven."

It is important, too, in the contemporary use of Psalm 72 that we not forget the similarities between it and other ancient Near Eastern expressions of the desire for justice, righteousness, and peace. As Patrick D. Miller points out, the vision of peace expressed in Psalm 72 is universal and still calls for actualization:

> The potential of this shared vision for providing spiritual "weapons" in the struggle for peace was not realized in those days and has not been even until now. It still may be, however, that the wishes and hopes expressed in this psalm have their greatest possibility for actualization as they are joined with similar hopes, wishes, and prayers articulated by sisters and brothers of other religions and uttered in the hearing of all the human governments that rule our lives for good or ill, peace or war, righteousness or injustice, blessing or curse.[288]

In other words, Psalm 72 finally calls us as citizens of God's realm to remind every human ruler, politician, and government that "the way to peace and well-being is found only when power assumes responsibility for justice and is clothed in compassion, regarding as precious and valuable the life of every citizen in the land."[289] Or, to use the key word in Psalm 72, *right* makes might! The cruciform power of love, weak though it seems, is ultimately the greatest power in the world (see 1 Cor 1:25; 2 Cor 12:9).

288. Patrick D. Miller, "Power, Justice, and Peace: An Exegesis of Psalm 72," *Faith and Mission* 4/1 (1986) 66.
289. Ibid., 69.

BOOK III

PSALM 73:1-28, IT IS GOOD TO BE NEAR GOD

BOOK III

Psalms 73–89

Psalm 73

A psalm of Asaph.

¹Surely God is good to Israel,
to those who are pure in heart.
²But as for me, my feet had almost slipped;
I had nearly lost my foothold.
³For I envied the arrogant
when I saw the prosperity of the wicked.

⁴They have no struggles;
their bodies are healthy and strong.ᵃ
⁵They are free from the burdens common to man;
they are not plagued by human ills.
⁶Therefore pride is their necklace;
they clothe themselves with violence.
⁷From their callous hearts comes iniquityᵇ;
the evil conceits of their minds know no limits.
⁸They scoff, and speak with malice;
in their arrogance they threaten oppression.
⁹Their mouths lay claim to heaven,
and their tongues take possession of the earth.
¹⁰Therefore their people turn to them
and drink up waters in abundance.ᶜ
¹¹They say, "How can God know?
Does the Most High have knowledge?"

¹²This is what the wicked are like—
always carefree, they increase in wealth.

ᵃ4 With a different word division of the Hebrew; Masoretic Text *struggles at their death; / their bodies are healthy*   ᵇ7 Syriac (see also Septuagint); Hebrew *Their eyes bulge with fat*   ᶜ10 The meaning of the Hebrew for this verse is uncertain.

BOOK III

(Psalms 73–89)

Psalm 73

A Psalm of Asaph.

¹ Truly God is good to the upright,ᵃ
to those who are pure in heart.
² But as for me, my feet had almost stumbled;
my steps had nearly slipped.
³ For I was envious of the arrogant;
I saw the prosperity of the wicked.

⁴ For they have no pain;
their bodies are sound and sleek.
⁵ They are not in trouble as others are;
they are not plagued like other people.
⁶ Therefore pride is their necklace;
violence covers them like a garment.
⁷ Their eyes swell out with fatness;
their hearts overflow with follies.
⁸ They scoff and speak with malice;
loftily they threaten oppression.
⁹ They set their mouths against heaven,
and their tongues range over the earth.

¹⁰ Therefore the people turn and praise them,ᵇ
and find no fault in them.ᶜ
¹¹ And they say, "How can God know?
Is there knowledge in the Most High?"
¹² Such are the wicked;
always at ease, they increase in riches.
¹³ All in vain I have kept my heart clean
and washed my hands in innocence.

ᵃOr *good to Israel*   ᵇCn: Heb *his people return here*   ᶜCn: Heb *abundant waters are drained by them*

NIV

¹³Surely in vain have I kept my heart pure;
in vain have I washed my hands in
innocence.
¹⁴All day long I have been plagued;
I have been punished every morning.

¹⁵If I had said, "I will speak thus,"
I would have betrayed your children.
¹⁶When I tried to understand all this,
it was oppressive to me
¹⁷till I entered the sanctuary of God;
then I understood their final destiny.

¹⁸Surely you place them on slippery ground;
you cast them down to ruin.
¹⁹How suddenly are they destroyed,
completely swept away by terrors!
²⁰As a dream when one awakes,
so when you arise, O Lord,
you will despise them as fantasies.

²¹When my heart was grieved
and my spirit embittered,
²²I was senseless and ignorant;
I was a brute beast before you.

²³Yet I am always with you;
you hold me by my right hand.
²⁴You guide me with your counsel,
and afterward you will take me into glory.
²⁵Whom have I in heaven but you?
And earth has nothing I desire besides you.
²⁶My flesh and my heart may fail,
but God is the strength of my heart
and my portion forever.

²⁷Those who are far from you will perish;
you destroy all who are unfaithful to you.
²⁸But as for me, it is good to be near God.
I have made the Sovereign LORD my refuge;
I will tell of all your deeds.

NRSV

¹⁴ For all day long I have been plagued,
and am punished every morning.

¹⁵ If I had said, "I will talk on in this way,"
I would have been untrue to the circle of
your children.
¹⁶ But when I thought how to understand this,
it seemed to me a wearisome task,
¹⁷ until I went into the sanctuary of God;
then I perceived their end.
¹⁸ Truly you set them in slippery places;
you make them fall to ruin.
¹⁹ How they are destroyed in a moment,
swept away utterly by terrors!
²⁰ They are^a like a dream when one awakes;
on awaking you despise their phantoms.

²¹ When my soul was embittered,
when I was pricked in heart,
²² I was stupid and ignorant;
I was like a brute beast toward you.
²³ Nevertheless I am continually with you;
you hold my right hand.
²⁴ You guide me with your counsel,
and afterward you will receive me with
honor.^b
²⁵ Whom have I in heaven but you?
And there is nothing on earth that I
desire other than you.
²⁶ My flesh and my heart may fail,
but God is the strength^c of my heart and
my portion forever.

²⁷ Indeed, those who are far from you will perish;
you put an end to those who are false to
you.
²⁸ But for me it is good to be near God;
I have made the Lord GOD my refuge,
to tell of all your works.

^aCn: Heb *Lord*   ^bOr *to glory*   ^cHeb *rock*

COMMENTARY

Given the apparent intentionality to the shaping of the psalter, it is not surprising that Psalm 73, which begins Book III, recalls the very beginning of the psalter. The wicked are prominent charac-

ters in Psalm 73 (see esp. vv. 3, 12) as they are in Psalm 1 (vv. 1, 5-6). The conclusion of Psalm 73 also echoes Psalm 1 (see "perish" in 1:6; 73:27), and it recalls Psalm 2 by way of the repetition of "refuge" in Pss 2:12 and 73:28. In fact, Psalm 73 is a sort of summary of what the reader of the psalter would have learned after beginning with Psalms 1 and 2 and moving through the songs and prayers of Psalms 3–72; that is, happiness or goodness has to do, not with material prosperity and success, but with the assurance of God's presence in the midst of threat and suffering. Quite properly, Brueggemann suggests that Psalm 73 plays a crucial role in the movement from Psalm 1 to Psalm 150: "Thus, I suggest that in the canonical structuring of the Psalter, Psalm 73 stands at its center in a crucial role. Even if the Psalm is not literally in the center, I propose that it is central theologically as well as canonically."[290] At a prominent point in the psalter, Psalm 73 reinforces the central message already offered in Psalms 1–72: that goodness means to live not in dependence upon oneself but in taking refuge in God (Pss 2:12; 73:28). The highest good is to be near God (v. 28).

This message would have been particularly relevant during the years following the exile. Thus it is significant that, even though the psalm narrates the experience of an individual "I," it has "Israel" in view from the beginning (see v. 1 NIV, which follows the Hebrew text). Not coincidentally, Psalm 73 introduces a book that is dominated by communal psalms of lament/complaint (Psalms 74; 79; 80; 83; and at least elements of 85 and 89). It seems likely that the experience of the "I" was offered, or at least was eventually understood, as a model for the whole people in confronting the prosperity of the wicked (see Commentary on Psalm 74).

The circumstances of the actual origin and ancient use of Psalm 73 are unclear. Because of the apparently instructional intent, many scholars classify it as a wisdom psalm. But others consider it a song of thanksgiving, a lament/complaint, a song of trust, or a royal psalm. There is also a wide range of opinion concerning the original setting of the psalm. The discussion usually focuses on v. 17, which apparently mentions the Temple and may indicate a cultic setting. If so, it is not clear what may have happened in the Temple to change the psalmist's mind—perhaps a priestly oracle of salvation, some sort of festal

presentation, a Levitical sermon, or some kind of mystical experience. We simply cannot be sure. In any case, Psalm 73 finally has the character of a profession of faith, and it could easily have been used for religious instruction, for liturgy, or for both.

What is much clearer is that the structure of Psalm 73 reinforces the conclusion that the psalmist underwent a remarkable transformation of perspective. While scholars offer a variety of proposals, it seems best to divide the psalm into three major sections, each beginning with the same Hebrew particle (אַךְ 'ak):

(1) vv. 1-12		the problem (12 lines)
	vv. 1-3	the plight of the psalmist (3 lines)
	vv. 4-12	the prosperity of the wicked (9 lines)
(2) vv. 13-17		the turning point
(3) vv. 18-28		the solution (12 lines)
	vv. 18-20	the plight of the wicked (3 lines)
	vv. 21-28	the prosperity of the psalmist (9 lines)

As the outline suggests, the division on the basis of a stylistic criterion yields a symmetry that highlights the reversal of the psalmist's perspective. The central section (vv. 13-17) serves as the turning point. This section includes the much-discussed v. 17, but, as suggested below, v. 15 may be just as crucial. It is the actual mid-point of the psalm; it represents the first instance of direct address to God, and it is linked conceptually to v. 1 and by repetition to v. 28, both of which are key verses, linked to each other by the repetition of "good."[291]

73:1-12. The psalm begins with the rehearsal of what sounds like a traditional affirmation of faith (v. 1a; see Ps 24:4). But the psalmist immediately professes doubt (v. 2) that is caused by the prosperity or peace (שָׁלוֹם šālôm) of the wicked (see Ps 1:6). The statement of v. 2 will be elaborated upon in vv. 13-14, but first comes an extended description of the wicked (vv. 4-12). It emphasizes that their pretentious (vv. 6a, 9) and

290. Walter Brueggemann, "Bounded by Obedience and Praise: The Psalms as Canon," *JSOT* 50 (1991) 81.

291. See J. Clinton McCann, Jr., "Psalm 73: A Microcosm of Old Testament Theology," in *The Listening Heart: Essays in Wisdom and the Psalms in Honor of Roland E. Murphy, O. Carm.*, ed. K. G. Hogland, E. F. Huwiler, J. T. Glass, R. W. Lee, JSOTSup 58 (Sheffield: JSOT, 1987) 247-51.

oppressive (vv. 6b, 8) life-style is lived with impunity (vv. 4-5, 7, 9, 12). Verse 10 is difficult, but it seems to suggest that the wicked attract followers from among God's own people. The Hebrew of v. 10a can be read literally, "Therefore, his people turn away from here." These converts experience the apparent rewards described in vv. 4-5, 7, and they join the wicked in asserting their own self-sufficiency apart from God (v. 11; see Pss 3:2; 10:4, 11; 35:21, 25; 42:3, 10). The psalmist, too, seems almost to have yielded to this temptation, as the next section indicates.

73:13-17. The occurrence of "heart" (לבב *lēbāb*) in v. 13 recalls v. 1 (see also v. 7) and anticipates v. 26. Like v. 1, v. 13 recalls Ps 24:4 ("innocence" [נקיון *niqqāyôn*] in v. 13 is the same as "clean" in 24:4). The psalmist is having trouble seeing the purpose of remaining faithful (see vv. 2-3). Whereas the wicked are "not plagued" (v. 5), the psalmist is constantly "plagued" (v. 14). To use the key word found in vv. 1, 28, we can paraphrase vv. 13-14 in the form of a question: "What good is it to be faithful to God?" While v. 15 does not answer this question, it does mark a turning point that is at least as significant as v. 17. It is important that v. 15 marks the psalmist's first direct address to God. Apparently, the encounter with God also renews the psalmist's awareness of God's family. The psalmist realizes that if he or she were to keep on talking the way expressed in vv. 13-14, then it would be a betrayal of God's family—that is, Israel (see v. 1). What brings the psalmist through the crisis of faith, then, is apparently his or her identity as a member of God's people. This sense of identity, of belonging to God and thus belonging to God's people, is subsequently solidified in worship (vv. 16-17). But the psalmist would never have gotten as far as the Temple (the word "sanctuary" [מקדשים *miqdāšîm*] in v. 17 is actually plural but nonetheless seems to indicate the Temple) if he or she had not already decided to remain faithful (v. 15). Thus what actually happened in the Temple—which is irrecoverable anyway—is less important than the sense of solidarity expressed in v. 15.

73:18-28. That vv. 13-17 have, indeed, been the turning point of the psalm is indicated by the structure and content of the final section. Whereas formerly the psalmist was on slippery ground (vv.

1-3) and the wicked were secure (vv. 4-12), now the wicked are on slippery ground (vv. 18-20) and the psalmist is secure (vv. 21-28). The reversal involves not a change in outward circumstances but a change of understanding. The psalmist now realizes that the apparent prosperity of the wicked is not true peace at all. Consequently, the psalmist has discovered a true and lasting peace that is not "as the world gives" (John 14:27 NRSV). This peace is founded on the simple but profound good news that God is present (see Pss 23:4; 46:7, 11). This good news is emphasized by the repetition in Hebrew of the prepositional phrase "with you" (עמך *'immāk* in vv. 22-23; *'imměkā* in v. 25). Although the psalmist had been a "beast *toward you*" (v. 22; lit., "with you"), his or her behavior had not caused separation from God: "Nevertheless I am continually *with you*" (v. 23; see Ps 139:10). A third occurrence of the phrase is found in v. 25b, which reads literally, "and *with you* I have no desire on earth." The two occurrences of "heart" in v. 26 recall vv. 1 and 13. More fundamental than the traditional notions of being pure in heart (v. 1) and keeping one's heart clean (v. 13)—which apparently were associated with entering the Temple, the sphere of God's presence (see Ps 24:3-4)—is the assurance that God is always present and thus the enduring "strength of my heart" (lit., "rock of my heart"; see Ps 19:14). The word "portion" (חלק *ḥēleq*) elsewhere designates the share that every Israelite was supposed to have in the land and that, therefore, meant access to life and future (see Josh 15:13; 19:9). The psalmist now knows an even greater portion: God's own self (see Num 18:20; Ps 119:57; Lam 3:24), which promises life and future.

Verse 24 also articulates the good news of God's presence (see Ps 23:3), and v. 24b is often interpreted as a promise of life and future that transcends the boundary of death. Many scholars hear v. 24b as an allusion to the assumptions of Enoch and Elijah (Gen 5:24; 2 Kgs 2:11; see also Ps 49:15), and Dahood even contends that "the psalmist finds the solution to the inconsistencies of this life in the final reward of the righteous after death."[292] The precise meaning of v. 24b is unclear, and most interpreters find no evidence

---

292. Mitchell Dahood, *Psalms II (51–100),* AB 17 (Garden City, N.Y.: Doubleday, 1968) 195.

here for a developed doctrine of resurrection; however, v. 24*b* clearly pushes the boundaries of the usual Israelite conception of life and death (see discussions on Pss 22:29; 49:15 above).

Verses 27-28 underscore the significance of God's presence. Death is essentially alienation from God (v. 27; see Ps 1:6). The phrase "But as for me" (v. 28) recalls the psalmist's precarious position in v. 2, while the repetition of "good" recalls v. 1. Now it is clear what "God is good to Israel" really means. It does not mean the material prosperity and ease enjoyed by the wicked (vv. 4-12). Rather, the essential goodness of life is to be near God (see Deut 4:7; 30:14;

Pss 75:1; 145:18), to make God one's refuge (see Pss 2:12; 46:1; Introduction). The psalmist now knows the truth, and the truth has set him or her free "to tell of all your works" (v. 28*c*). This final phrase of the psalm recalls the central verse. Both refer to God in the second person, and the verb "tell" in v. 8 is the same as "talk" in v. 15. The psalmist's talk has changed from self-pity (vv. 13-14) to praise (v. 28). No longer focused on the self, the psalmist affirms that he or she belongs to God (vv. 23-28) and thus belongs in the circle of God's children (v. 15). This nearness to God is the essence of goodness, happiness (see Pss 1:1; 2:12), assurance, and life.

REFLECTIONS

Given the psalmist's initial dilemma (vv. 2-3) and the elaboration of it in vv. 13-14, we must reflect on the concept of reward and punishment. The psalmist almost lost faith, because he or she thought that good behavior should be materially rewarded; but it was not (vv. 13-14). What the psalmist came to realize is that true goodness, happiness, and peace consist of a different kind of reward—the experience of God's presence (vv. 23-28). In a sense, faithful behavior (vv. 1, 13) is its own reward; it is rewarding, not because it earns God's favor, but because it derives from and expresses the power and presence of God in our lives, individually (vv. 25-26, 28) and corporately (v. 15). The psalmist knew already the happiness Jesus would proclaim, "Blessed are the pure in heart, for they will see God" (Matt 5:8 NIV; see Ps 73:1, 28).

This experience of God's power and presence—in effect, this seeing God—finally convinced the psalmist that faithfulness was not in vain. While Psalm 73 probably does not embody a doctrine of resurrection, Christian readers cannot help being reminded that for the apostle Paul the resurrection of Jesus was the assurance that his labor in this life was not in vain (1 Cor 15:58; cf. Ps 73:13-14). The powerful testimony to God's power and presence in Psalm 73 also anticipates Paul's affirmation that nothing "in all creation, will be able to separate us from the love of God in Christ Jesus our Lord" (Rom 8:39 NRSV). This assurance is for our living and for our dying. Paul's words in Rom 14:7-8 (NRSV) capture the spirit and good news of Psalm 73: "We do not live to ourselves, and we do not die to ourselves. If we live, we live to the Lord, and if we die, we die to the Lord; so then, whether we live or whether we die, we are the Lord's."

PSALM 74:1-23, DO NOT FORGET YOUR AFFLICTED PEOPLE

NIV	NRSV
Psalm 74	Psalm 74
A *maskil*[a] of Asaph.	A Maskil of Asaph.
[1]Why have you rejected us forever, O God?	[1] O God, why do you cast us off forever?
[a] Title: Probably a literary or musical term	

NIV

Why does your anger smolder against the
sheep of your pasture?
²Remember the people you purchased of old,
the tribe of your inheritance, whom you
redeemed—
Mount Zion, where you dwelt.
³Turn your steps toward these everlasting ruins,
all this destruction the enemy has brought
on the sanctuary.

⁴Your foes roared in the place where you met
with us;
they set up their standards as signs.
⁵They behaved like men wielding axes
to cut through a thicket of trees.
⁶They smashed all the carved paneling
with their axes and hatchets.
⁷They burned your sanctuary to the ground;
they defiled the dwelling place of your
Name.
⁸They said in their hearts, "We will crush
them completely!"
They burned every place where God was
worshiped in the land.
⁹We are given no miraculous signs;
no prophets are left,
and none of us knows how long this will
be.

¹⁰How long will the enemy mock you, O God?
Will the foe revile your name forever?
¹¹Why do you hold back your hand, your right
hand?
Take it from the folds of your garment and
destroy them!

¹²But you, O God, are my king from of old;
you bring salvation upon the earth.
¹³It was you who split open the sea by your
power;
you broke the heads of the monster in the
waters.
¹⁴It was you who crushed the heads of
Leviathan
and gave him as food to the creatures of
the desert.
¹⁵It was you who opened up springs and
streams;
you dried up the ever flowing rivers.
¹⁶The day is yours, and yours also the night;

NRSV

Why does your anger smoke against the
sheep of your pasture?
² Remember your congregation, which you
acquired long ago,
which you redeemed to be the tribe of
your heritage.
Remember Mount Zion, where you came
to dwell.
³ Direct your steps to the perpetual ruins;
the enemy has destroyed everything in
the sanctuary.

⁴ Your foes have roared within your holy
place;
they set up their emblems there.
⁵ At the upper entrance they hacked
the wooden trellis with axes.ᵃ
⁶ And then, with hatchets and hammers,
they smashed all its carved work.
⁷ They set your sanctuary on fire;
they desecrated the dwelling place of
your name,
bringing it to the ground.
⁸ They said to themselves, "We will utterly
subdue them";
they burned all the meeting places of
God in the land.

⁹ We do not see our emblems;
there is no longer any prophet,
and there is no one among us who
knows how long.
¹⁰ How long, O God, is the foe to scoff?
Is the enemy to revile your name forever?
¹¹ Why do you hold back your hand;
why do you keep your hand inᵇ your bosom?

¹² Yet God my King is from of old,
working salvation in the earth.
¹³ You divided the sea by your might;
you broke the heads of the dragons in
the waters.
¹⁴ You crushed the heads of Leviathan;
you gave him as foodᶜ for the creatures
of the wilderness.
¹⁵ You cut openings for springs and torrents;
you dried up ever-flowing streams.

ᵃCn Compare Gk Syr: Meaning of Heb uncertain   ᵇCn: Heb *do
you consume your right hand from*   ᶜHeb *food for the people*

NIV

you established the sun and moon.
17It was you who set all the boundaries of the
    earth;
    you made both summer and winter.

18Remember how the enemy has mocked you,
    O LORD,
    how foolish people have reviled your name.
19Do not hand over the life of your dove to
    wild beasts;
    do not forget the lives of your afflicted
    people forever.
20Have regard for your covenant,
    because haunts of violence fill the dark
    places of the land.
21Do not let the oppressed retreat in disgrace;
    may the poor and needy praise your name.

22Rise up, O God, and defend your cause;
    remember how fools mock you all day long.
23Do not ignore the clamor of your adversaries,
    the uproar of your enemies, which rises
    continually.

NRSV

16 Yours is the day, yours also the night;
    you established the luminaries*a* and the
    sun.
17 You have fixed all the bounds of the earth;
    you made summer and winter.

18 Remember this, O LORD, how the enemy
    scoffs,
    and an impious people reviles your name.
19 Do not deliver the soul of your dove to the
    wild animals;
    do not forget the life of your poor
    forever.

20 Have regard for your*b* covenant,
    for the dark places of the land are full of
    the haunts of violence.
21 Do not let the downtrodden be put to
    shame;
    let the poor and needy praise your name.
22 Rise up, O God, plead your cause;
    remember how the impious scoff at you
    all day long.
23 Do not forget the clamor of your foes,
    the uproar of your adversaries that goes
    up continually.

*a*Or *moon*; Heb *light*   *b*Gk Syr: Heb *the*

COMMENTARY

Psalm 74 is a communal lament/complaint that confronts in corporate terms the same problem faced by the individual in Psalm 73: the apparent triumph of the wicked. Not surprisingly, there are several literary links between Psalms 73 and 74, including the name "Asaph" in the superscription, "sanctuary" in 73:17 and 74:7, "violence" in 73:6 and 74:20, "right hand" in 73:23 and 74:11, and "ruin(s)" in 73:18 and 74:3 (the only two occurrences of the plural form in the OT). These links suggest that Psalms 73 and 74 should be heard together, and they reinforce the impression that Psalm 73 offers a model for the whole people in confronting the prosperity of the wicked (see Commentary on Psalm 73). It is probably not coincidental that Psalms 42–44 open Book II in the same way that Psalms 73–74 open Book III

(see Commentary on Psalms 42–43; 44). The pattern of an "I" psalm (Psalms 42–43; 73) followed by a communal lament (Psalms 44; 74) provides a context for reading the rest of the psalms in Books II and III. It would have made both books not only particularly suited for addressing the situation following the exile, but also suited for ongoing use by the perpetually threatened people of God (see Introduction).

The rejection and destruction described in vv. 1-11 are usually associated with the fall of Jerusalem to the Babylonians in 587 BCE, although Psalm 74 has sometimes been dated as late as the Maccabean era. In particular, the lament over the absence of a prophet (v. 9) seems congruent with 1 Macc 4:46; 9:27; and 14:41. However, this feature could apply to an earlier setting as well (see Lam 2:9), and an earlier origin is more likely, in which case the psalm would have taken on renewed significance during the Maccabean era as well as during other crises throughout the centuries. In fact, the post-exilic community lived under constant threat and domination, as do the people of God in every age, and Psalm 74 has the ability to speak in a variety of times and places (see Reflections below).

The psalm is usually divided into three major sections: (1) vv. 1-11, (2) vv. 12-17, (3) vv. 18-23. The questions in vv. 1, 10-11 provide an inclusio[293] for the first section (see esp. "why" in vv. 1, 11), which also consists of petition (vv. 2-3) and more direct complaint that describes the destruction of the Temple (vv. 4-9). Verses 12-17 shift to praise of God as king and of God's past activity on behalf of Israel and the whole creation. Verses 18-23 return to petition with accompanying complaints that serve as motivation for God to take renewed action against opponents of God's reign and thus on behalf of God's afflicted people.

74:1-11. 74:1-3. The opening questions in v. 1 attribute the current crisis to God's anger. The language is typical of other complaints, both individual and communal (see "cast off"/"reject" in Pss 43:2; 44:9, 23; 60:1, 10; 88:14; 89:38; on smoking anger, see Deut 29:20; Pss 18:8; 80:4). Elsewhere, too, the people are called God's sheep (see Pss 79:13; 95:7; 100:3; Ezek 34:31). The first petition, "Remember," will recur twice more (vv. 18, 22; see also Exod 2:24; 32:13; Pss 25:6-7; 98:3). The vocabulary of v. 2 recalls the Song of the Sea and the exodus, in which God originally "acquired" the people (see Exod 15:16), having redeemed them from slavery (see Exod 15:13) to bring them to Mount Zion (see Exod 15:17; note "inheritance" in Exod 15:17 and Ps 74:2 NIV). Verse 2 also anticipates vv. 12-17, where the exodus will be poetically described (see "of old" in vv. 2, 12). The Song of the Sea culminates in the proclamation of God's reign "forever" (Exod 15:18), but the only "forever" perceived by the people in Psalm 74 involves rejection and ruin (see "forever"/"everlasting"/"perpetual" in vv. 1, 3, 10, 19). In other words, it appears that God's

opponents, rather than God, are sovereign. They have destroyed God's sanctuary.

74:4-11. Verses 4-9 describe the destruction in some detail. Roaring to signal their victory (see Ps 22:13; Jer 2:15), God's opponents also install in the Temple signs of their own rule (see "emblems" in vv. 4, 9 NRSV). Interpreting v. 5 is difficult, but along with v. 6, it seems to describe one of the means of destruction (see "carved" in 1 Kgs 6:29). Verses 7-8 mention another means: fire. The variety of synonyms for the Temple in vv. 4-8 emphasizes the point that the opponents have completely prevailed in Jerusalem and beyond. The NRSV's "meeting places" (מוֹעֲדִים *môʿădîm*) in v. 8 is the plural of "holy place" (מוֹעֵד *môʿēd*) in v. 4, and the Hebrew word may designate other holy sites outside Jerusalem, perhaps forerunners of the synagogue (see 1 Macc 3:46). In short, there is no sign of God's rule anywhere (v. 9*a*). A comparison of the NIV and the NRSV translations of v. 9*a* reveals two possible senses of the Hebrew word usually translated "sign" (אוֹת *ʾôt*). It can designate either a physical emblem, such as a flag (see "ensigns" in Num 2:2 NRSV) or a revelatory action of God. In either sense, there is no visible sign of God and no prophets to deliver a word from God (v. 9*b*; see Lam 2:9). In short, no one knows anything, including how long God will be absent (v. 9*c*). All that is left to do is ask, and the questions in vv. 10-11 thus reveal a remarkable depth of faith. They reveal that the people still trust God and God's sovereignty, despite a total lack of evidence for God's rule. Thus the perspective is eschatological. God's rule is assumed and asserted in the midst of powerful opposition that certainly seems to prevail. In other words, the question is not *whether* God is powerful (see v. 11; see also "right hand" in Exod 15:6, 12) but *when* God will show God's power—"How long?" (see Pss 79:5; 89:46). In the meantime, God's foes will continue to "scoff" (v. 10; see vv. 18, 22; see also "taunt"/"scorn"/ "reproach"/"insult" in Pss 22:6; 31:11; 42:10; 44:13, 16; 55:12; 69:9-10; 89:41) and "revile" (v. 10; see "renounce" in Ps 10:3, 13).

74:12-17. The sovereignty of God, which is asserted implicitly in the questions of vv. 10-11, is explicitly proclaimed in v. 12 (see Pss 5:2; 10:16; Introduction). As in the exodus, to which the following verses will allude, God's activity

---

293. Inclusio is a technical term for a biblical passage in which the opening expression, phrase, or idea is repeated, paraphrased, or in some other way returned to at the end.

involves salvation (see Exod 15:2). Verse 13*a* describes the event more or less as a historical phenomenon that reveal's God's might, an attribute elsewhere associated with royal sovereignty (see "strength" in Exod 15:13; Pss 29:1; 93:1; 96:6). The description, however, immediately spills over into the realm of the mythic in vv. 13*b*-14. The sea itself, as well as the "dragons" (see Gen 1:21; Job 7:12; Ps 148:7; Isa 27:1; 51:9) and Leviathan (see Job 3:8; 41:1; Ps 104:26; Isa 27:1), represent the chaotic forces over which God is sovereign. In some ancient Near Eastern creation stories, the supreme deity defeats a monster and uses its body parts to fashion the universe. Such mythic imagery lies in the background of vv. 13-14 (see also Pss 77:16-19; 89:9-11; 93:3-4; 104:5-9; 114:1-6; Isa 51:9-11). The emphasis on creation is even clearer in v. 15 ("cut" [בקע *bāqaʿ*] is the same verb as "divide" in Exod 14:16; see also Ps 104:10), v. 16 (see Gen 1:14-16), and v. 17 (see Gen 8:22; Ps 104:9). In short, God is ruler of the cosmos (note "earth" in vv. 12 and 17, forming an inclusio for the section). The merging of exodus and creation imagery suggests that God's creative activity is in itself salvific and that God's activity in the exodus was not simply on behalf of Israel but involved the fulfillment of God's purposes for the whole creation (see esp. Exod 9:16; see also Commentary on Psalms 33; 65; 66). Both God's saving and creating work, which should not finally be separated, are testimony to God's reign. The sevenfold occurrence of the Hebrew pronoun "you" (אתה *ʾattâ*) in vv. 13-17 is emphatic, perhaps corresponding to the seven-headed chaos monster in some ancient Near Eastern myths, but in any case suggesting that God alone is sovereign.

74:18-23. The proclamation of God's universal sovereignty in vv. 12-17 serves as the basis for the petitions in the next passage. Twice God is asked to "remember" (vv. 18, 22) and "not forget" (vv. 19, 23). It was the special calling of a king to provide for the poor (vv. 19, 21) and the needy (v. 21; see Pss 72:1-7, 12-14; 82:1-4), and the final section serves to remind God of this responsibility in view of the apparent triumph of the wicked and their arrogant behavior (vv. 18, 22-23; see v. 10). In other words, the "cause" of the poor and needy is *God's* cause as well (v. 22*a*; see Ps 43:1; Lam 3:58). Thus God can reasonably be asked to "rise up" (v. 22; see Pss 3:7; 9:19; 10:12) against those who have arisen against God (v. 23; the NRSV's "adversaries" [קמים *qāmîm*] is more literally, "those who arise"). Verses 19-20 are notoriously difficult and have given rise to a variety of translations and interpretations. Both the NIV and the NRSV translate the Hebrew literally, which is probably the best alternative in this case. The word "dove" (תור *tôr*) probably designates Israel in its current poverty or affliction. The mention of covenant also serves to recall God's past actions and the relationship God had established with the people (see Exod 24:1-8; Ps 44:17). Given the people's faith in God's cosmic sovereignty (vv. 12-17), the petitions in vv. 18-23 function finally as an affirmation of the people's trust that God will "not forget the life of your poor forever" (v. 19; see Ps 9:18).

REFLECTIONS

It is particularly significant that Psalm 74—the voice of suffering faith—contains not only the complaints and petitions that one might expect (vv. 1-11, 18-23) but also a rousing, hymnic affirmation of God's sovereignty (vv. 12-17). The paradox is instructive, for it reinforces the eschatological perspective that is present throughout the psalter and the entire Bible (see Introduction). That is to say, the reign of God is always proclaimed amid circumstances that seem to deny it: the destruction of the Temple and, in a later time, an executioner's cross. In the worst of times, when the forces of evil seem to prevail, the people of God profess their faith in a cosmic sovereign whose power seems to be no power at all, whose "power is made perfect in weakness" (2 Cor 12:9 NRSV; see 1 Cor 1:25). Of course, faith in a God who exercises sovereignty in this way profoundly affects one's understanding of suffering. Not surprisingly, the exile, out of which Psalm 74 seems to have arisen, produced several profoundly new expressions of the role of suffering in the life of the faithful—Isaiah 40–55, the book of Job, and certain psalms (see Commentary on Psalm 44).

As several commentators recognize, Psalm 74 has important ecclesiological implications, and these implications are related to the new understanding of the role of suffering. Mays comments:

> As for the self-understanding of the congregation in this prayer, is it of no importance that they have learned to think of themselves as the lowly [vv. 19-21]? This may be a form of the transformation worked in the character of the congregation by judgment for which Jeremiah and Ezekiel looked (Jer 31:33; Ezek 36:26). "Blessed are the poor in spirit . . . the meek . . . " (Matt. 5:3, 5).[294]

In other words, Psalm 74 anticipates Jesus' eschatological proclamation of the reign of God (Mark 1:14-15) and his invitation to be disciples, not by the avoidance of suffering but by taking up a cross (Mark 8:34). As in Psalm 74, the life of faith will be lived amid constant scoffing and continual opposition (vv. 10, 18, 22-23), as was Jesus' life.

It is interesting that Psalm 74 contains no confession of the sins that led to the destruction of the Temple and the exile. But in a sense, once the Temple had been destroyed and the people's "penalty . . . paid" (Isa 40:2 NRSV), confession of sin became irrelevant. The real issue then became the one that is at the heart of Psalm 74: Who is sovereign? Can the foes who carried out the destruction of the Temple be put in their place? Can God ultimately enact God's purposes for the whole creation? The voice of suffering faith in Psalm 74 dares to answer yes. In the face of dominant evil, then and now, such an affirmative answer appears foolish. But Psalm 74 asserts that the real foolishness is to deny the character and power of Israel's God (see vv. 18, 22). Then and now, the people of God assert that "God's foolishness is wiser than human wisdom" (1 Cor 1:25 NRSV), and so we continue to pray and to trust that God will not forget the lives of the poor and the needy, among whom we must always include ourselves.

294. James L. Mays, *Psalms,* Interpretation (Louisville: John Knox, 1994) 247-48.

PSALM 75:1-10, GOD SAYS TO THE ARROGANT, "DO NOT BOAST"

NIV	NRSV
Psalm 75	Psalm 75
For the director of music. ∟To the tune of⌐ "Do Not Destroy." A psalm of Asaph. A song.	To the leader: Do Not Destroy. A Psalm of Asaph. A Song.
¹We give thanks to you, O God, we give thanks, for your Name is near; men tell of your wonderful deeds.	¹ We give thanks to you, O God; we give thanks; your name is near. People tell of your wondrous deeds.
²You say, "I choose the appointed time; it is I who judge uprightly.	² At the set time that I appoint I will judge with equity.
³When the earth and all its people quake, it is I who hold its pillars firm. *Selah*	³ When the earth totters, with all its inhabitants, it is I who keep its pillars steady. *Selah*
⁴To the arrogant I say, 'Boast no more,' and to the wicked, "Do not lift up your horns.	⁴ I say to the boastful, "Do not boast,"

NIV

⁵Do not lift your horns against heaven;
  do not speak with outstretched neck.'"

⁶No one from the east or the west
  or from the desert can exalt a man.
⁷But it is God who judges:
  He brings one down, he exalts another.
⁸In the hand of the LORD is a cup
  full of foaming wine mixed with spices;
he pours it out, and all the wicked of the
    earth
  drink it down to its very dregs.

⁹As for me, I will declare this forever;
  I will sing praise to the God of Jacob.
¹⁰I will cut off the horns of all the wicked,
  but the horns of the righteous will be
    lifted up.

NRSV

and to the wicked, "Do not lift up your
    horn;
⁵ do not lift up your horn on high,
  or speak with insolent neck."

⁶ For not from the east or from the west
  and not from the wilderness comes lifting
    up;
⁷ but it is God who executes judgment,
  putting down one and lifting up another.
⁸ For in the hand of the LORD there is a cup
  with foaming wine, well mixed;
he will pour a draught from it,
  and all the wicked of the earth
  shall drain it down to the dregs.
⁹ But I will rejoice*ᵃ* forever;
  I will sing praises to the God of Jacob.

¹⁰ All the horns of the wicked I will cut off,
  but the horns of the righteous shall be
    exalted.

ᵃGk: Heb *declare*

COMMENTARY

Given the linguistic links between Psalms 73 and 74 (see Commentary on Psalm 74), it is interesting that Ps 75:1 clearly recalls Ps 73:28 (see "near" and "tell" in both verses). In addition, in the divine speech (vv. 2-5), God addresses "the arrogant" (v. 4), who were the source of the problem in Psalm 73 (see 73:3; the only other occurrence of this word in the psalter is 5:5; see also "the wicked" in 73:3, 12; 75:4, 8, 10). While there are no striking verbal links between Psalms 74 and 75 (but see "name" in 74:10, 18; 75:1), it is almost as if 75:2-5, 10 is a direct response to the petitions in 74:18-23; Psalm 75 develops the proclamation of God's sovereignty that is found in Psalm 74, portraying God as savior (vv. 2, 7, 10; see Ps 74:12-13) and cosmic creator and ruler (v. 3; see Ps 74:14-17). Thus, even if the sequence of Psalms 73–75 is coincidental, there are literary and conceptual links that suggest their coherence (see Introduction, concerning the shape of Book III).

Because of the existence and content of the

divine speech in vv. 2-5, 10, Psalm 75 is frequently labeled a prophetic judgment speech (see Psalm 82). It begins, however, like a song of praise (v. 1), and the response to the divine speech (vv. 6-8) is a profession of faith that has a didactic character. Verse 9 recites the psalmist's promise that results from the faith expressed in vv. 6-8. Despite the variety of forms, Psalm 75 is clearly a unit. The promise in v. 9, for instance, clearly recalls v. 1, even though the vocabulary of praise and proclamation differs. Furthermore, both the divine speech and the response focus on God's establishment of justice (see the forms of "judge" in vv. 2, 7), especially as this involves dealing with the apparent power (see "horn" in vv. 4-5, 10) of the wicked (vv. 4, 8, 10). Unity is provided by the sixfold occurrence of a Hebrew root (רום *rûm*) translated "lifting up" (vv. 4-7), "high" (v. 5), and "exalted" (v. 10).

75:1. The word "name" (שֵׁם *šēm*) suggests God's character and presence, and as in Ps 73:28 the experience of nearness to God is accompanied by proclamation of God's activity (see also Deut 4:7; 30:14; Ps 145:18). The Hebrew word translated as "wondrous deeds" (נפלאות *niplā'ôt*) elsewhere designates the exodus (Exod 3:20; 34:10), the crossing of the Jordan (Josh 3:5), and other acts of deliverance. In Psalms, giving thanks and proclamation of God's wondrous deeds often go together (see Pss 9:1; 26:7).

75:2-5. As the NIV more clearly suggests with its insertion of "You say" and its use of quotation marks, v. 2 marks the beginning of the divine speech that runs through v. 5. In the light of v. 1, the word for "set time"/"appointed time" (מועד *mô'ēd*) could be an echo of the exodus event (see Exod 9:5). It also occurs in Hab 2:3, where, as in Psalm 75, it involves divine judgment upon arrogant opponents (see 2:1-5)—namely, the Babylonians. Scholars often note other similarities between Habakkuk and Psalm 75 (see the concern for justice for the wicked in Hab 1:4, 12-13; cf. Hab 2:15-16 with Ps 75:8). And if Psalms 74–75 are read together, there is even more reason to think of the Babylonians as "the wicked," since they destroyed the Temple in 587 BCE. Of course, the possible historical connection between Psalm 75 and Habakkuk remains elusive, but Habakkuk provides an illustrative context for hearing Psalm 75 without limiting its application or usefulness to that particular historical setting (see Reflections below).

In any case, what God will eventually do is establish justice, which will mean judgment upon God's opponents. God's will to "judge with equity" is elsewhere associated with the proclamation of God's reign (see Pss 9:8; 96:10; 98:9; 99:4). In short, God will exercise sovereignty on a cosmic scale (v. 3). When the world is threatened with chaos, God holds things together (see

Psalm 46). The second "I" in v. 2 (אני *'ănî*) and the "I" in v. 3 (אנכי *'ānōkî*) are emphatic in Hebrew; therefore, *God* and no other rules the world. This means that powerful human beings, who think that they rule the world (see Pss 10:3-4; 94:4-7), must be told not to boast (v. 4*a*) and must be warned not to exert their power (v. 4*b*; see "horn" in Jer 48:25). The NRSV's "on high" (v. 5) sometimes designates heaven. In other words, God warns the arrogant and the wicked not to oppose God's own sovereignty (see 1 Sam 2:3; Pss 2:10-11; 66:7).

75:6-8. Repeating key words from vv. 2-5, the response to the divine speech recognizes that God alone establishes justice (v. 7*a*; see also v. 2) and that God alone has the power to put down and to lift up (vv. 6, 7*b*; see also vv. 4-5; 1 Sam 2:7-8, 10; Pss 113:5-7; 147:6). Verse 8 portrays this divine activity with the metaphor of a cup from which the wicked drink (see Ps 11:6; Isa 51:17; Jer 25:15; 49:12; Ezek 23:32-34; Hab 2:15-16; Rev 14:10; 16:19; 18:6; cf. Pss 23:5; 116:13; Mark 14:23-25).

75:9-10. The response of vv. 6-8 is personalized in v. 9. In contrast to the wicked, who exalt themselves, the psalmist praises God. As a comparison of the NIV and the NRSV makes clear, the verb in v. 9*a* is attested differently. The Hebrew makes sense, although an object needs to be supplied, and it also has the effect of making v. 9 a closer parallel to v. 1. The "I" in v. 10*a* could be understood as the psalmist, but the activity described is better attributed to God, especially in view of vv. 6-8. Thus v. 10 returns to the divine speech of vv. 2-5. (On the contrast of the wicked and the righteous and their respective futures, see Commentary on Psalm 1.)

REFLECTIONS

Like Psalm 1 and many other psalms, Psalm 75 portrays the righteous as those who live in dependence upon God and the wicked as those who live by self-assertion, and it contrasts the outcomes of these two ways of living. Just as Psalm 2 and many others, so also Psalm 75 asserts that the futures of the righteous and the wicked differ, because God rules the world. As is regularly the case in the book of Psalms, Psalm 75 does not precisely identify the wicked except by their boasting and self-centeredness. When Psalm 75 is read in the context of Psalm 74 and the book of Habakkuk, it is possible to identify the wicked as the Babylonians. Such an identification would have made Psalm 75 a particularly useful resource for facing the crisis of exile and its aftermath, and there is reason to think that Book III of the psalter was shaped with this in mind (see Introduction). But the psalm itself looks beyond this specific identification to "all the wicked of the earth" (v. 8).

If the wicked are understood as nations that take selfish pride in being world powers—perhaps even superpowers—then the problem of the wicked is just as real today as it was in the sixth century BCE. United States intervention in global conflicts may sometimes be morally healthy and helpful, but it also may serve as an excuse to protect national interests at any cost. Among all nations, there is a persistent temptation to identify as the will of God what simply seems to promote selfish concerns and goals, which are often given the high-sounding label of "national security."

If, on the other hand, the wicked are understood as powerful individuals who pride themselves on being self-sufficient, then the problem of the wicked is still just as real today as ever. Indeed, our culture generally teaches us to strive for autonomy and self-sufficiency, to look out for ourselves and our own above all else (see Commentary on Psalm 1).

In short, however wickedness is viewed, the truth is that it is well-represented in us and in our institutions at all levels, including nation and church. Thus, when Psalm 75 proclaims the rule of God, which will bring to justice "all the wicked of the earth," the message is eschatological. That is to say, as always, in Psalms and in the preaching of Jesus, the reign of God is proclaimed amid powerful opposition (see vv. 4-5; see also Commentary on Psalm 2; Introduction). And as always, the proclamation calls for a decision. Indeed, Psalm 75 invites the same commitment that Jesus invited when he said, "All who exalt themselves will be humbled, and all who humble themselves will be exalted" (Matt 23:12 NRSV; cf. Ps 75:7, 10). Psalm 75 reminds us that in God's reign, worldly values are turned upside down (see 1 Sam 2:1-10; Luke 1:46-55; 1 Cor 1:26-31). What this reversal means, as the apostle Paul recognized, is this: "Let the one who boasts, boast in the Lord" (1 Cor 1:31 NRSV; cf. Ps 34:2; 2 Cor 11:16-32; 12:1-10).

PSALM 76:1-12, GOD INDEED IS AWESOME

NIV

Psalm 76

For the director of music. With stringed instruments. A psalm of Asaph. A song.

[1]In Judah God is known;
his name is great in Israel.
[2]His tent is in Salem,
his dwelling place in Zion.
[3]There he broke the flashing arrows,
the shields and the swords, the weapons of
war.   *Selah*

[4]You are resplendent with light,
more majestic than mountains rich with
game.
[5]Valiant men lie plundered,
they sleep their last sleep;

NRSV

Psalm 76

To the leader: with stringed instruments. A Psalm of Asaph. A Song.

[1] In Judah God is known,
his name is great in Israel.
[2] His abode has been established in Salem,
his dwelling place in Zion.
[3] There he broke the flashing arrows,
the shield, the sword, and the weapons
of war.   *Selah*

[4] Glorious are you, more majestic
than the everlasting mountains.[a]
[5] The stouthearted were stripped of their spoil;

[a] Gk: Heb *the mountains of prey*

NIV

not one of the warriors
    can lift his hands.
⁶At your rebuke, O God of Jacob,
    both horse and chariot lie still.
⁷You alone are to be feared.
    Who can stand before you when you are
        angry?
⁸From heaven you pronounced judgment,
    and the land feared and was quiet—
⁹when you, O God, rose up to judge,
    to save all the afflicted of the land.   *Selah*
¹⁰Surely your wrath against men brings you
      praise,
    and the survivors of your wrath are
      restrained.ᵃ

¹¹Make vows to the Lᴏʀᴅ your God and fulfill
      them;
    let all the neighboring lands
    bring gifts to the One to be feared.
¹²He breaks the spirit of rulers;
    he is feared by the kings of the earth.

ᵃ10 Or Surely the wrath of men brings you praise, / and with the remainder of wrath you arm yourself

NRSV

    they sank into sleep;
  none of the troops
    was able to lift a hand.
⁶ At your rebuke, O God of Jacob,
    both rider and horse lay stunned.

⁷ But you indeed are awesome!
    Who can stand before you
      when once your anger is roused?
⁸ From the heavens you uttered judgment;
    the earth feared and was still
⁹ when God rose up to establish judgment,
    to save all the oppressed of the earth.
                          Selah

¹⁰ Human wrath serves only to praise you,
    when you bind the last bit of yourᵃ
      wrath around you.
¹¹ Make vows to the Lᴏʀᴅ your God, and
      perform them;
    let all who are around him bring gifts
    to the one who is awesome,
¹² who cuts off the spirit of princes,
    who inspires fear in the kings of the
      earth.

ᵃ Heb lacks your

COMMENTARY

Because of the celebration of Zion as God's dwelling place and the site of God's victory (vv. 2-3), Psalm 76 has been traditionally classified as a song of Zion (see Psalms 46; 48; 84; 87; 122). Although scholars have sometimes tried to tie the victory to a specific historical incident—e.g., David's taking of Jerusalem (2 Sam 5:6-10) or the deliverance of Jerusalem from Sennacherib in 701 ʙᴄᴇ (2 Kgs 19:35; Isa 36:1–37:38)—the present literary setting of Psalm 76 discourages such attempts. That is to say, when Psalm 76 is heard in the context of Psalm 74 (see also Pss 78:67–79:13), it clearly has an eschatological thrust. It asserts God's power and sovereignty, but it does so in a context where opposition and defeat are evident. While it may allude to Zion's past, it is more about the future that God will create for the people and for the earth. As Mays suggests,

"the psalm is more about the resident of Zion than about Zion itself."²⁹⁵

The psalm falls into four sections. Verses 1-3 introduce God's greatness and association with Zion. Verses 4-6 describe how God's power affects God's opponents. Verses 7-9 proclaim the purpose of God's power: justice for all (see "judgment" in vv. 8-9 NRSV; two different Hebrew words are represented). Alluding to the opposition (v. 10), the final section also describes God's power (v. 12) and invites recognition of and response to God's sovereignty (v. 11). The key word in vv. 7-12 is "feared" (ירא *yārēʾ*, vv. 7-8, 11-12).

76:1-3. The opening line already suggests a focus on God's sovereignty. It recalls another song of Zion in which "the great King . . . has shown

295. Ibid., 250.

himself a sure defense" (Ps 48:2-3; "shown" [ידע yāda'] represents the same verb used in 76:1). The verb "known" (yāda') is a reminder that the purpose of the exodus, also a demonstration of God's reign (Exod 15:18), was that the Egyptians "know that I am the LORD" (Exod 14:4 NRSV). God's greatness is elsewhere an attribute of God's sovereignty (Ps 95:3); as in v. 2, it is explicitly associated with God's residence in Zion (see Pss 48:2-3; 99:2-3). The words used for Zion are used elsewhere to designate a lion's den or lair, and they may suggest that God is being portrayed as divine warrior in the form of a mighty lion. Such an image would be congruent with other passages where God "roars from Zion" (see Jer 25:30; Joel 3:16; Amos 1:2). In any case, God uses God's power to destroy the implements of war (v. 3; cf. Ps 46:9-10, another song of Zion; see also Isa 2:4; Mic 4:3). The word "there" (שמה šāmmâ) seems to refer to Zion, but the description of God's activity recalls God's work in a variety of settings, especially the exodus (see v. 6). Thus the reader is reminded that Zion refers in Psalm 76 not just to a specific place, but also functions as a symbol of God's sovereignty in all times and places (see Commentary on Psalm 48).

76:4-6. The opening word of v. 4 is derived from the Hebrew root that means "light" (אור 'ôr); it is frequently associated with God's presence (see "light"/"shine" in Num 6:25; Pss 4:6; 27:1; 31:16). The Hebrew pronoun "you" focuses attention on God, and it anticipates the beginning of the next section where "you" actually occurs twice in v. 7a. The adjective "majestic" (אדיר 'addîr) also describes God in Ps 8:1, 9, as well as in 93:4 in the context of the proclamation of God's reign. The metaphor of God as a lion in vv. 1-3 makes the Hebrew of v. 4b more understandable. Verses 5-6 recall v. 3 in that God's intervention ends the battle. Verse 6 recalls the exodus with its mention of "horse and rider" (see Exod 15:1). The power of God's "rebuke" is indicative of God's sovereignty and was also manifest in the exodus, especially in God's command of the sea (see Pss 18:15; 104:7; Isa 50:2).

76:7-9. Although not obvious in translation, the opening verbs of vv. 1, 4, and 7 are the same Hebrew form (niphal participle), drawing even further attention to God and the divine attributes. As suggested above, v. 7a represents the first of four occurrences of the root "fear" (yārē'), and not surprisingly, it, too, is explicitly associated elsewhere with God's reign (see "awesome"/"to be feared"/"to be revered" in Exod 15:11; Pss 47:2; 96:4; 99:3; 145:6). God's royal policy as cosmic sovereign is expressed here, as elsewhere, as justice (vv. 8-9; see Ps 96:10, 13 where the two Hebrew words occur in the context of the proclamation of God's reign). God's justice will be worldwide (see vv. 8-9; see also v. 12). Verse 8 suggests that the result of God's justice will be peace (see Zech 1:11; see also Ps 46:10). The conditions for peace in biblical terms include provision for the lives of the oppressed (see "afflicted"/"poor"/"meek" in Pss 9:9, 12, 18; 10:12, 17-18; 74:19, 21), the prototypical example of which is the exodus (see "save"/"salvation" in Exod 14:30; 15:2; Pss 6:4; 7:1; Isa 11:4).

76:10-12. The sense of v. 10 is elusive, as a comparison of the NIV with the NRSV suggests. The verb "praise" (תודה tôdâ) in v. 10 is often rendered "give thanks." A noun form of the root means "thanksgiving offering," and such offerings were apparently accompanied by the making and performance of vows (see Ps 116:17-18). By perhaps suggesting that even human wrath or recalcitrance eventually ends up honoring the sovereign God, v. 10 may provide the background for the explicit invitation in v. 11 to recognize and respond to God's claim on the whole world (v. 12; see Pss 2:10-11; 48:4-6).

REFLECTIONS

At first sight, it may seem that the particularity of a song of Zion like Psalm 76 would make contemporary application very difficult. However, Zion functions in Psalm 76 as a symbol of God's sovereignty in all times and places (see Commentary on Psalms 46; 48). As is always the case, the assertion of God's reign is eschatological; it is made in the presence of powerful opposition (see Commentary on Psalm 2; Introduction). In fact, no one in the ancient world would have known this any better than the residents of Jerusalem, which was just as much a source of contention then as it is now.

Nevertheless, there arose in Judah what is often called the doctrine of the inviolability of Zion, the conviction that Jerusalem could not be destroyed because it was God's dwelling place. Needless to say, this doctrine required major reformulation after the destruction of Jerusalem in 587 BCE (see Commentary on Psalm 74). In all likelihood, however, the doctrine of Zion's inviolability was never intended to be taken literally; rather, it was to function symbolically. As J. David Pleins suggests, "the Zion image is far more dynamic: God's presence in Zion launches a new era in which warfare comes to an end." Pleins also points out that this "dramatic interpretation" of Zion is articulated also in Isa 2:2-4 and Mic 4:1-3, and he concludes:

> For the psalmists and these prophets, Zion is the image of the power of God's transformative peace in the face of war. The weaker doctrine of inviolability might leave one thinking that peace stops at Zion's walls. The sentiment that rings so clearly in the hymns of Zion and in Isaiah and Micah is that Zion is the starting point of a new way of living and worshiping in a world filled with war. The image of Zion broadens the definition of security to encompass not only city walls and towers, but also divine presence, the breaking of the bow, and hope for an end to war.[296]

In other words, Psalm 76 is finally an invitation to live under God's sovereignty (v. 11), to adopt God's values and God's ways (vv. 8-9). But to stand for justice and peace in a world filled with war and injustice requires a particular understanding of sovereignty. God's sovereignty is exercised not as sheer force but as the power of love. The world does not understand this kind of power, but it is power nonetheless (see 1 Cor 1:25). The invitation in v. 11 is ultimately an invitation to respond to God's love. William C. Placher declares that God's strength is finally God's very vulnerability. He concludes, "We worship God, then, not intimidated by sheer divine power, but because, in the face of a love that reaches literally beyond our human imagination, we are 'lost in wonder, love, and praise.' "[297] As children of God, we are inevitably peacemakers (see Matt 5:9), for we dare to tell the world of and commit our lives to a power that is greater than weapons and generals and princes and prime ministers and presidents (see vv. 3, 6, 12)—the power of God's love symbolized by Zion and made known ultimately in the cross of Jesus Christ, whom Christians profess was and is the new earthly locus of God's presence and power (see Commentary on Psalm 48).

296. J. David Pleins, *The Psalms: Songs of Tragedy, Hope, and Justice* (Maryknoll, N.Y.: Orbis, 1993) 122-23.
297. William C. Placher, "Narratives of a Vulnerable God," *The Princeton Seminary Bulletin* 14/2 (1993) 149.

PSALM 77:1-20, GOD'S FOOTPRINTS WERE UNSEEN

NIV	NRSV
Psalm 77	Psalm 77
For the director of music. For Jeduthun. Of Asaph. A psalm.	To the leader: according to Jeduthun. Of Asaph. A Psalm.
¹I cried out to God for help; I cried out to God to hear me. ²When I was in distress, I sought the Lord; at night I stretched out untiring hands and my soul refused to be comforted. ³I remembered you, O God, and I groaned;	¹ I cry aloud to God, aloud to God, that he may hear me. ² In the day of my trouble I seek the Lord; in the night my hand is stretched out without wearying; my soul refuses to be comforted.

NIV

I mused, and my spirit grew faint. *Selah*
⁴You kept my eyes from closing;
 I was too troubled to speak.
⁵I thought about the former days,
 the years of long ago;
⁶I remembered my songs in the night.
 My heart mused and my spirit inquired:

⁷"Will the Lord reject forever?
 Will he never show his favor again?
⁸Has his unfailing love vanished forever?
 Has his promise failed for all time?
⁹Has God forgotten to be merciful?
 Has he in anger withheld his
  compassion?" *Selah*

¹⁰Then I thought, "To this I will appeal:
 the years of the right hand of the Most
  High."
¹¹I will remember the deeds of the Lord;
 yes, I will remember your miracles of long
  ago.
¹²I will meditate on all your works
 and consider all your mighty deeds.

¹³Your ways, O God, are holy.
 What god is so great as our God?
¹⁴You are the God who performs miracles;
 you display your power among the peoples.
¹⁵With your mighty arm you redeemed your
  people,
 the descendants of Jacob and Joseph. *Selah*

¹⁶The waters saw you, O God,
 the waters saw you and writhed;
 the very depths were convulsed.
¹⁷The clouds poured down water,
 the skies resounded with thunder;
 your arrows flashed back and forth.
¹⁸Your thunder was heard in the whirlwind,
 your lightning lit up the world;
 the earth trembled and quaked.
¹⁹Your path led through the sea,
 your way through the mighty waters,
 though your footprints were not seen.
²⁰You led your people like a flock
 by the hand of Moses and Aaron.

NRSV

³ I think of God, and I moan;
 I meditate, and my spirit faints. *Selah*

⁴ You keep my eyelids from closing;
 I am so troubled that I cannot speak.
⁵ I consider the days of old,
 and remember the years of long ago.
⁶ I commune^a with my heart in the night;
 I meditate and search my spirit:^b
⁷ "Will the Lord spurn forever,
 and never again be favorable?
⁸ Has his steadfast love ceased forever?
 Are his promises at an end for all time?
⁹ Has God forgotten to be gracious?
 Has he in anger shut up his
  compassion?" *Selah*
¹⁰ And I say, "It is my grief
 that the right hand of the Most High has
  changed."

¹¹ I will call to mind the deeds of the Lord;
 I will remember your wonders of old.
¹² I will meditate on all your work,
 and muse on your mighty deeds.
¹³ Your way, O God, is holy.
 What god is so great as our God?
¹⁴ You are the God who works wonders;
 you have displayed your might among the
  peoples.
¹⁵ With your strong arm you redeemed your
  people,
 the descendants of Jacob and Joseph. *Selah*

¹⁶ When the waters saw you, O God,
 when the waters saw you, they were afraid;
 the very deep trembled.
¹⁷ The clouds poured out water;
 the skies thundered;
 your arrows flashed on every side.
¹⁸ The crash of your thunder was in the
  whirlwind;
 your lightnings lit up the world;
 the earth trembled and shook.
¹⁹ Your way was through the sea,
 your path, through the mighty waters;
 yet your footprints were unseen.
²⁰ You led your people like a flock
 by the hand of Moses and Aaron.

^a Gk Syr. Heb *My music*   ^b Syr Jerome: Heb *my spirit searches*

COMMENTARY

The first ten verses of Psalm 77 have the character of a lament/complaint or prayer for help, but God is not addressed directly except in v. 4. It is as if the psalmist has become so discouraged that prayer has become impossible (see v. 4b) and has given way to anguished meditation (v. 6; note the past tenses in vv. 1-6 NIV). The meditation culminates in the wrenching questions of vv. 7-9 and the apparently hopeless conclusion in v. 10. Verses 11-20 are so unexpected after vv. 1-10 that some scholars conclude that vv. 1-10 and vv. 11-20 should be considered separate psalms; however, a common vocabulary unifies the two sections. Most notably, the psalmist continues to remember (v. 11; see also vv. 3, 5-6) and to meditate (v. 12; see also vv. 3, 6). John Kselman argues that the two occurrences of the Hebrew "my voice" in v. 1 are matched by the two references to God's "voice" (NIV, "thunder") in vv. 17-18 and that a further mark of unity is the repetition of "hand" in vv. 3, 20. He also detects a chiastic structure (see Introduction) in vv. 8-20 that cuts across the usual division of the psalm between vv. 10 and 11. In his view, vv. 8-9 raise questions that are answered in vv. 16-20, the conclusion of v. 10 is answered in vv. 14-15, and attention is thereby focused on vv. 11-13, which celebrate God's incomparable greatness.[298] While it is difficult finally to deny the distinct division between vv. 1-10 and 11-20, Kselman's insights certainly contribute to the understanding of the unity of Psalm 77, and it is possible that the structure and movement of the psalm should be understood on more than one level.

77:1-3. The nature of the "trouble" or "distress" in v. 2 is not specified. Given the magnitude of the crisis and the literary placement of Psalm 77 (see Commentary on Psalms 73; 74; Introduction), many scholars conclude that the psalmist voices questions and doubts raised by the exile. This is a sound conclusion, but it is also clear that the usefulness of Psalm 77 is not limited to this setting. It has continued to articulate the fears and

the faith of the people of God throughout the centuries (see Reflections below).

The urgency of the situation is indicated in v. 1 by the repetition in Hebrew of the phrase "my voice unto God" (קוֹלִי אֶל־אֱלֹהִים *qôlî ʾel-ʾĕlōhîm*). The verb in v. 1a is used elsewhere in situations of grave distress (see Exod 14:10, 25; Deut 26:7; Josh 24:7; Pss 88:1; 107:6, 28). The psalmists elsewhere affirm that those who seek God will be answered and satisfied (see Pss 9:10; 22:26; 34:4, 10), but the constant seeking in Psalm 77 (see "day" and "night"), including unceasing prayer, has led only to the conclusion that no comfort is possible (see Gen 37:35; Jer 31:15)—another indication of the severity of the situation. Whereas remembrance of God elsewhere puts the psalmist in touch with God's loving care (see Ps 42:6-8), such is not the case here—at least not at first (cf. v. 3 with v. 11). Memory leads only to moaning (see Pss 42:5, 11; 43:5; see also Ps 55:17, where "moan" is accompanied by "complaint," which also occurs in 77:3 as "meditate"), and meditation leads only to further weakness (see Pss 107:5; 142:3; 143:4; Lam 2:12, 19).

77:4-10. Verse 4 describes characteristic signs of depression: inability to sleep and unspeakable distress. All the psalmist can do is think (see Ps 73:16), apparently about more auspicious times in the past (v. 5; see Ps 42:4). But the psalmist's sleepless nights and searching spirit (v. 6) produce no resolution, only agonizing questions that strike at the very heart of the biblical faith (vv. 7-9). The verb "spurn"/"reject" (זנח *zānaḥ*) occurs frequently in complaints (see Pss 43:2; 44:9, 23; 60:1, 10; 74:1), and v. 7a directly calls into question the affirmation of Lam 3:31 (see also "steadfast love" and "compassion" in Ps 77:8-9; Lam 3:32 NRSV). Indicative of the seriousness of the doubt are the references to time in vv. 7-8—"forever" (vv. 7-8; two different Hebrew words [לְעוֹלָמִים *lĕʿôlāmîm*, v. 7; לָנֶצַח *lāneṣaḥ*, v. 8]) and "for all time" (לְדֹר וָדֹר *lĕdōr wādōr*, v. 8). Perhaps even more indicative is the particular choice of vocabulary in vv. 8-9, which contain three of the key words from God's self-revelation in Exod 34:6: "steadfast love" (חסד *ḥesed*; see Introduction), "gracious" (חנות *ḥannôt*), and "compassion"

298. John Kselman, "Psalm 77 and the Book of Exodus," *Journal of the Ancient Near Eastern Society of Columbia University* 15 (1983) 51-58; see the summary in Marvin E. Tate, *Psalms 51–100*, WBC 20 (Dallas: Word, 1990) 272-73.

(רחמים *raḥămîm*; "merciful" in Exod 34:6). In short, the psalmist questions God's fundamental character, or, as v. 10 summarizes the crisis of faith, the psalmist is "sick" (a more literal translation of the verb) that God has apparently "changed" (see Ps 89:34; Mal 3:6).

77:11-20. Although the psalmist is apparently again remembering and meditating in vv. 11-12 (see vv. 3, 5-6), the result is remarkably different. Verse 11*b* shifts to direct address, which perhaps is not coincidental (see Reflections below). In any case, the psalmist comes to a new awareness of God and of God's "way" (vv. 13, 19). The words "wonders" (פלא *pele*') in v. 11 and "holy" (קדש *qōdeš*) in v. 13 call to mind the exodus (see Exod 15:11), and between the two references to God's "way" lies a hymnic celebration that is full of allusions to the exodus, especially to the song in Exod 15:1-18, which celebrates the crossing of the sea (see "great" in v. 13 and "might" in Exod 15:16; "wonders" in v. 14 and Exod 15:11; "might"/"strength" in v. 14 and Exod 15:2, 13; "arm" in v. 15 and Exod 15:16; "redeemed" in v. 15 and Exod 15:13; "waters" and "deep[s]" in v. 16 and Exod 15:8; "trembled" in vv. 16, 18 and Exod 15:14; see also "sea" and "mighty waters" in v. 19 and Exod 15:10). The words "might"/"strength" (עז *'ōz*) and "great" (גדול *gādôl*) also occur frequently elsewhere in the context of explicit proclamations of God's sovereignty (see Pss 29:1-3, 9; 48:2; 95:3; 96:6-7; 99:2-3; see also Exod 15:18). In other words, the psalmist finally affirms that God reigns and that God is powerfully present. Verses 16-18 recall not only the exodus but also other accounts of God's appearing (see Pss 18:7-15; 114:3-8), and the vocabulary and shepherd imagery of v. 20 are associated elsewhere with both God's sovereignty and God's gracious presence (see Exod 15:13; Ps 23:3; Ezek 34:12).

Particularly significant are the affirmations about God's "way" that frame the retelling of the exodus story. God's way is "holy" (v. 13), and God's "footprints were unseen" (v. 19), suggesting the otherness and mystery of God. The latter phrase is particularly important because it has no parallel in Exod 15:1-18. What the psalmist apparently realizes in the process of recalling the exodus in the light of the experience recounted in vv. 1-10 is that God's way is not always clearly visible or comprehensible in terms of human ways (see Isa 55:8-9). As Tate suggests, the psalmist learns that God has God's "own schedule and often the faithful must endure the anguish of waiting."[299] Psalm 77, then, like the psalter as a whole (see Commentary on Psalm 2; Introduction), is eschatological; it affirms God's rule in circumstances that make it appear that God does not reign.

299. Tate, *Psalms 51–100*, 276.

REFLECTIONS

For the psalmist, the transition from despair to hope seems instantaneous, which raises the question of how to account for this sudden transition. Brueggemann has suggested that the transition marked by vv. 11-12 involves "a shift from 'I' to 'Thou.'" Thus the shift to direct address in v. 11*b* is of crucial significance, and it is reinforced when the affirmation of v. 14*a* begins with an emphatic pronoun, "you." Thus begins the remembrance of the exodus, which "takes the mind off the hopelessness of self." Brueggemann proposes that this transition is not an achievement of the individual psalmist. Rather, the psalmist takes part in a communal process of remembering. As Brueggemann concludes, "Everything depends on having the public, canonical memory available which becomes in this moment of pain a quite powerful, personal hope."[300]

As Mays points out, the recital of the exodus story in worship evokes God's presence: "The LORD is there in the recital as the God whose right hand has not changed. The hymn [vv. 13-19] does what praise and confession are meant to do—to represent the God of revelation as the reality and subject of truth in the face of all circumstances and contrary experience."[301]

300. Walter Brueggemann, *Israel's Praise: Doxology Against Idolatry and Ideology* (Philadelphia: Fortress, 1988) 138, 140.
301. James L. Mays, *Psalms*, Interpretation (Louisville: John Knox, 1994) 253.

For Mays as for Brueggemann, the psalmist is still in the midst of "the day of trouble" (v. 2). What has changed is the psalmist, not the circumstance. No longer merely an isolated self (see v. 6), the psalmist is one of "your people" (vv. 15, 20) and is nurtured by the community's canonical memory.

Most commentators, including Brueggemann and Mays, interpret Ps 77:13-19 as genuine praise. Tate, however, disagrees; he considers these verses to be the psalmist's continued "anguished meditation." Thus the questions of vv. 7-9 are left open for the reader to answer. For Tate, although vv. 11-20 provide the basis for answering no to the questions of vv. 7-9, "the decision is ours."[302] Thus, like the psalter as a whole, Psalm 77 issues a call to decision. In every age, the people of God are called to proclaim and to embody the reign of God in the midst of circumstances that make it appear that God does not reign. Tate's perspective also raises the question of whether the movement from vv. 1-10 to vv. 11-20 need be understood sequentially. At the least, the presence of vv. 1-10 invites the honest expression of our doubts and fears. Indeed, in a broken and sinful world, there is a sense in which a mature faith cannot exist apart from doubt.[303] In any case, Psalm 77 reminds us that we are people of memory and of hope. Faith is no guarantee against the possibility of despair, but even amid despair, the faithful will remember that God has been our help in ages past and will be our hope for years to come.

302. Marvin E. Tate, *Psalms 51–100,* WBC 20 (Dallas: Word, 1990) 275-76.
303. See Paul Tillich, *Dynamics of Faith* (New York: Harper & Row, 1957) 1-29, esp. 16-22.

PSALM 78:1-72, TRUSTING IN GOD

NIV	NRSV
Psalm 78	Psalm 78
A *maskil*[a] of Asaph.	A Maskil of Asaph.

[1]O my people, hear my teaching;
    listen to the words of my mouth.
	[1] Give ear, O my people, to my teaching;
	    incline your ears to the words of my
	        mouth.

[2]I will open my mouth in parables,
    I will utter hidden things, things from of
        old—
	[2] I will open my mouth in a parable;
	    I will utter dark sayings from of old,

[3]what we have heard and known,
    what our fathers have told us.
	[3] things that we have heard and known,
	    that our ancestors have told us.

[4]We will not hide them from their children;
    we will tell the next generation
the praiseworthy deeds of the LORD,
    his power, and the wonders he has done.
	[4] We will not hide them from their children;
	    we will tell to the coming generation
	the glorious deeds of the LORD, and his
	        might,
	    and the wonders that he has done.

[5]He decreed statutes for Jacob
    and established the law in Israel,
which he commanded our forefathers
    to teach their children,
	[5] He established a decree in Jacob,
	    and appointed a law in Israel,
	which he commanded our ancestors
	    to teach to their children;

[6]so the next generation would know them,
    even the children yet to be born,
	[6] that the next generation might know them,
	    the children yet unborn,

a Title: Probably a literary or musical term

NIV

and they in turn would tell their children.
⁷Then they would put their trust in God
and would not forget his deeds
but would keep his commands.
⁸They would not be like their forefathers—
a stubborn and rebellious generation,
whose hearts were not loyal to God,
whose spirits were not faithful to him.

⁹The men of Ephraim, though armed with
bows,
turned back on the day of battle;
¹⁰they did not keep God's covenant
and refused to live by his law.
¹¹They forgot what he had done,
the wonders he had shown them.
¹²He did miracles in the sight of their fathers
in the land of Egypt, in the region of Zoan.
¹³He divided the sea and led them through;
he made the water stand firm like a wall.
¹⁴He guided them with the cloud by day
and with light from the fire all night.
¹⁵He split the rocks in the desert
and gave them water as abundant as the
seas;
¹⁶he brought streams out of a rocky crag
and made water flow down like rivers.

¹⁷But they continued to sin against him,
rebelling in the desert against the Most
High.
¹⁸They willfully put God to the test
by demanding the food they craved.
¹⁹They spoke against God, saying,
"Can God spread a table in the desert?
²⁰When he struck the rock, water gushed out,
and streams flowed abundantly.
But can he also give us food?
Can he supply meat for his people?"
²¹When the LORD heard them, he was very
angry;
his fire broke out against Jacob,
and his wrath rose against Israel,
²²for they did not believe in God
or trust in his deliverance.
²³Yet he gave a command to the skies above
and opened the doors of the heavens;
²⁴he rained down manna for the people to eat,
he gave them the grain of heaven.
²⁵Men ate the bread of angels;

NRSV

and rise up and tell them to their children,
⁷   so that they should set their hope in God,
and not forget the works of God,
but keep his commandments;
⁸ and that they should not be like their
ancestors,
a stubborn and rebellious generation,
a generation whose heart was not steadfast,
whose spirit was not faithful to God.

⁹ The Ephraimites, armed with[a] the bow,
turned back on the day of battle.
¹⁰ They did not keep God's covenant,
but refused to walk according to his law.
¹¹ They forgot what he had done,
and the miracles that he had shown them.
¹² In the sight of their ancestors he worked
marvels
in the land of Egypt, in the fields of Zoan.
¹³ He divided the sea and let them pass
through it,
and made the waters stand like a heap.
¹⁴ In the daytime he led them with a cloud,
and all night long with a fiery light.
¹⁵ He split rocks open in the wilderness,
and gave them drink abundantly as from
the deep.
¹⁶ He made streams come out of the rock,
and caused waters to flow down like
rivers.

¹⁷ Yet they sinned still more against him,
rebelling against the Most High in the
desert.
¹⁸ They tested God in their heart
by demanding the food they craved.
¹⁹ They spoke against God, saying,
"Can God spread a table in the
wilderness?
²⁰ Even though he struck the rock so that
water gushed out
and torrents overflowed,
can he also give bread,
or provide meat for his people?"

²¹ Therefore, when the LORD heard, he was
full of rage;
a fire was kindled against Jacob,

ᵃHeb armed with shooting

NIV

he sent them all the food they could eat.

²⁶He let loose the east wind from the heavens
and led forth the south wind by his power.

²⁷He rained meat down on them like dust,
flying birds like sand on the seashore.

²⁸He made them come down inside their camp,
all around their tents.

²⁹They ate till they had more than enough,
for he had given them what they craved.

³⁰But before they turned from the food they
craved,
even while it was still in their mouths,

³¹God's anger rose against them;
he put to death the sturdiest among them,
cutting down the young men of Israel.

³²In spite of all this, they kept on sinning;
in spite of his wonders, they did not
believe.

³³So he ended their days in futility
and their years in terror.

³⁴Whenever God slew them, they would seek
him;
they eagerly turned to him again.

³⁵They remembered that God was their Rock,
that God Most High was their Redeemer.

³⁶But then they would flatter him with their
mouths,
lying to him with their tongues;

³⁷their hearts were not loyal to him,
they were not faithful to his covenant.

³⁸Yet he was merciful;
he forgave their iniquities
and did not destroy them.
Time after time he restrained his anger
and did not stir up his full wrath.

³⁹He remembered that they were but flesh,
a passing breeze that does not return.

⁴⁰How often they rebelled against him in the
desert
and grieved him in the wasteland!

⁴¹Again and again they put God to the test;
they vexed the Holy One of Israel.

⁴²They did not remember his power—
the day he redeemed them from the
oppressor,

⁴³the day he displayed his miraculous signs in
Egypt,
his wonders in the region of Zoan.

NRSV

his anger mounted against Israel,

²² because they had no faith in God,
and did not trust his saving power.

²³ Yet he commanded the skies above,
and opened the doors of heaven;

²⁴ he rained down on them manna to eat,
and gave them the grain of heaven.

²⁵ Mortals ate of the bread of angels;
he sent them food in abundance.

²⁶ He caused the east wind to blow in the
heavens,
and by his power he led out the south
wind;

²⁷ he rained flesh upon them like dust,
winged birds like the sand of the seas;

²⁸ he let them fall within their camp,
all around their dwellings.

²⁹ And they ate and were well filled,
for he gave them what they craved.

³⁰ But before they had satisfied their craving,
while the food was still in their mouths,

³¹ the anger of God rose against them
and he killed the strongest of them,
and laid low the flower of Israel.

³² In spite of all this they still sinned;
they did not believe in his wonders.

³³ So he made their days vanish like a breath,
and their years in terror.

³⁴ When he killed them, they sought for him;
they repented and sought God earnestly.

³⁵ They remembered that God was their rock,
the Most High God their redeemer.

³⁶ But they flattered him with their mouths;
they lied to him with their tongues.

³⁷ Their heart was not steadfast toward him;
they were not true to his covenant.

³⁸ Yet he, being compassionate,
forgave their iniquity,
and did not destroy them;
often he restrained his anger,
and did not stir up all his wrath.

³⁹ He remembered that they were but flesh,
a wind that passes and does not come
again.

⁴⁰ How often they rebelled against him in the
wilderness
and grieved him in the desert!

NIV

⁴⁴He turned their rivers to blood;
　they could not drink from their streams.
⁴⁵He sent swarms of flies that devoured them,
　and frogs that devastated them.
⁴⁶He gave their crops to the grasshopper,
　their produce to the locust.
⁴⁷He destroyed their vines with hail
　and their sycamore-figs with sleet.
⁴⁸He gave over their cattle to the hail,
　their livestock to bolts of lightning.
⁴⁹He unleashed against them his hot anger,
　his wrath, indignation and hostility—
　a band of destroying angels.
⁵⁰He prepared a path for his anger;
　he did not spare them from death
　but gave them over to the plague.
⁵¹He struck down all the firstborn of Egypt,
　the firstfruits of manhood in the tents of
　　Ham.
⁵²But he brought his people out like a flock;
　he led them like sheep through the desert.
⁵³He guided them safely, so they were unafraid;
　but the sea engulfed their enemies.
⁵⁴Thus he brought them to the border of his
　　holy land,
　to the hill country his right hand had taken.
⁵⁵He drove out nations before them
　and allotted their lands to them as an
　　inheritance;
　he settled the tribes of Israel in their
　　homes.

⁵⁶But they put God to the test
　and rebelled against the Most High;
　they did not keep his statutes.
⁵⁷Like their fathers they were disloyal and
　　faithless,
　as unreliable as a faulty bow.
⁵⁸They angered him with their high places;
　they aroused his jealousy with their idols.
⁵⁹When God heard them, he was very angry;
　he rejected Israel completely.
⁶⁰He abandoned the tabernacle of Shiloh,
　the tent he had set up among men.
⁶¹He sent ⌐the ark of⌐ his might into captivity,
　his splendor into the hands of the enemy.
⁶²He gave his people over to the sword;
　he was very angry with his inheritance.
⁶³Fire consumed their young men,

NRSV

⁴¹ They tested God again and again,
　and provoked the Holy One of Israel.
⁴² They did not keep in mind his power,
　or the day when he redeemed them from
　　the foe;
⁴³ when he displayed his signs in Egypt,
　and his miracles in the fields of Zoan.
⁴⁴ He turned their rivers to blood,
　so that they could not drink of their
　　streams.
⁴⁵ He sent among them swarms of flies, which
　　devoured them,
　and frogs, which destroyed them.
⁴⁶ He gave their crops to the caterpillar,
　and the fruit of their labor to the locust.
⁴⁷ He destroyed their vines with hail,
　and their sycamores with frost.
⁴⁸ He gave over their cattle to the hail,
　and their flocks to thunderbolts.
⁴⁹ He let loose on them his fierce anger,
　wrath, indignation, and distress,
　a company of destroying angels.
⁵⁰ He made a path for his anger;
　he did not spare them from death,
　but gave their lives over to the plague.
⁵¹ He struck all the firstborn in Egypt,
　the first issue of their strength in the
　　tents of Ham.
⁵² Then he led out his people like sheep,
　and guided them in the wilderness like a
　　flock.
⁵³ He led them in safety, so that they were
　　not afraid;
　but the sea overwhelmed their enemies.
⁵⁴ And he brought them to his holy hill,
　to the mountain that his right hand had
　　won.
⁵⁵ He drove out nations before them;
　he apportioned them for a possession
　and settled the tribes of Israel in their
　　tents.

⁵⁶ Yet they tested the Most High God,
　and rebelled against him.
　They did not observe his decrees,
⁵⁷ but turned away and were faithless like
　　their ancestors;
　they twisted like a treacherous bow.

NIV

and their maidens had no wedding songs;
64their priests were put to the sword,
and their widows could not weep.

65Then the Lord awoke as from sleep,
as a man wakes from the stupor of wine.
66He beat back his enemies;
he put them to everlasting shame.
67Then he rejected the tents of Joseph,
he did not choose the tribe of Ephraim;
68but he chose the tribe of Judah,
Mount Zion, which he loved.
69He built his sanctuary like the heights,
like the earth that he established forever.
70He chose David his servant
and took him from the sheep pens;
71from tending the sheep he brought him
to be the shepherd of his people Jacob,
of Israel his inheritance.
72And David shepherded them with integrity of
heart;
with skillful hands he led them.

NRSV

58 For they provoked him to anger with their
high places;
they moved him to jealousy with their
idols.
59 When God heard, he was full of wrath,
and he utterly rejected Israel.
60 He abandoned his dwelling at Shiloh,
the tent where he dwelt among mortals,
61 and delivered his power to captivity,
his glory to the hand of the foe.
62 He gave his people to the sword,
and vented his wrath on his heritage.
63 Fire devoured their young men,
and their girls had no marriage song.
64 Their priests fell by the sword,
and their widows made no lamentation.
65 Then the Lord awoke as from sleep,
like a warrior shouting because of wine.
66 He put his adversaries to rout;
he put them to everlasting disgrace.

67 He rejected the tent of Joseph,
he did not choose the tribe of Ephraim;
68 but he chose the tribe of Judah,
Mount Zion, which he loves.
69 He built his sanctuary like the high heavens,
like the earth, which he has founded
forever.
70 He chose his servant David,
and took him from the sheepfolds;
71 from tending the nursing ewes he brought
him
to be the shepherd of his people Jacob,
of Israel, his inheritance.
72 With upright heart he tended them,
and guided them with skillful hand.

COMMENTARY

Along with Psalms 105, 106, and 136, Psalm 78 is usually classified as a historical psalm. There is good reason for this designation, since Psalm 78 consists largely of a recital of crucial elements of Israel's story, but the label may be misleading. The recital in Psalm 78 is not history the way that we ordinarily understand it in the modern world—a recounting of names, events, and dates as accurately and objectively as possible. Rather, Psalm 78 is a creative retelling of Israel's story, and it has a particular purpose. In the broadest sense, the purpose is to teach (v. 1), but not simply in the sense of imparting information. Rather, the psalmist's teaching is intended to inspire hope and obedience in the hearers and, indeed, in all subsequent generations (vv. 6-8). In other words, this kind of history is as much or more concerned with the present and the future as it is with the past.

The same is true of the other historical psalms. Borrowing a phrase from Martin Buber's commentary on a Hebrew root (פלא *pl'*) that appears four times in Psalm 78 (see "wonders," "miracles," "marvels" in vv. 4, 11-12, 32), Brueggemann proposes that the purpose of the historical psalms be understood in terms of "abiding astonishment." By recalling God's formative activity in the past, "they seek to make available to subsequent generations the experience and power of the initial astonishment which abides with compelling authority." As is especially the case with Psalm 78, which continues the story up through God's choice of Zion and David (see vv. 67-72), the lesson suggests that every historical moment "is to be perceived in the same modes and categories of astonishment." By re-creating and perpetuating a sense of awe and wonder in the hearers, the teacher intends to evoke a response that will involve *"obedience, petition, gratitude,* and *new political possibility."* [304] The teacher intends anything but an objective recital. Rather, he or she intends the hearers and readers in every generation to respond with their whole lives to a subject matter that is supremely important: God and God's claim upon the world (see Reflections below).

Proposed dates for the origin of Psalm 78 range all the way from the time of David to the postexilic era. Several scholars contend that v. 67 reflects the destruction of the northern kingdom in 722 BCE, and they also suggest that the origin of Psalm 78 would be particularly understandable in the time of Hezekiah, especially after the deliverance of Jerusalem from the Assyrians in 701. Certainty is impossible, however, and arguments can be made for the appropriateness of the use of Psalm 78 in a variety of circumstances. In any case, regardless of when the psalm originated, it would have been put to continuous use, and in the post-exilic era, for instance, Zion could have functioned symbolically and the references to David would have increasingly been understood messianically.

Scholars disagree on the literary structure and movement of Psalm 78 as well. Several outlines have been proposed, but one of the most helpful and widely accepted is that of R. J. Clifford, who divides the psalm into an introduction (vv. 1-11) and two recitals (vv. 12-39, vv. 40-72). Each recital follows a similar pattern—description of God's gracious activity (vv. 12-16, 40-55), rebellion of the people (vv. 17-20, 56-58), God's anger and punishment (vv. 21-32, 59-64), restoration of relationship by God (vv. 33-39, 65-72).[305] The paragraph divisions in the NIV and the NRSV indicate that it is perhaps better to extend the introduction only through v. 8. At any rate, Clifford's proposal has the advantage of highlighting God's graciousness as much or more than Israel's sinfulness, thus inviting the reader's attention more to constructive possibilities for response than to the criticism of Israel's past.

78:1-8. The psalmist's didactic intent is evident from the beginning. He or she describes the poem in terms that are at home in Israel's wisdom literature—"teaching" (see Prov 1:8*b*), "parable(s)" (see Prov 1:6), "hidden things" (see Prov 1:6). The latter two terms also occur in Ps 49:4. The word here translated "parable(s)" (משל *māšāl*) connotes literally a comparison, and it communicates the psalmist's desire for the psalm's hearers to compare themselves to their ancestors in order not to make the same mistakes (see "be like" in v. 8). The repetition in vv. 3-8 emphasizes knowing (v. 3; see v. 5, where "teach" is literally "cause to know" [הודיע *hôdîa'*]; see also v. 6) and telling (vv. 3-4, 6; see also Deut 6:20-25; Pss 44:1; 73:28; 79:13), an ongoing process that involves "ancestors" (vv. 3, 5, 8) and "children" (vv. 4-6) from generation to generation (vv. 4, 6, 8). The content of the proclamation involves God's "praiseworthy deeds" (v. 4; see Ps 79:13), God's "power"/"might" (v. 4; see vv. 26, 61), and the "wonders" God has done (v. 4; see vv. 11-12, 32). The latter two words especially recall the exodus (see "wonders" in Exod 3:20; 15:11; and "strength" in Exod 15:2, 13), an event that led soon after to Sinai, which is recalled in Ps 78:5 and is also to be proclaimed. In short, every generation is to know God's sovereignty and

---

304. Walter Brueggemann, *Abiding Astonishment: Psalms, Modernity, and the Making of History* (Louisville: Westminster John Knox, 1991) 34.

305. R. J. Clifford, "In Zion and David a New Beginning: An Interpretation of Psalm 78," in *Traditions in Transformation,* ed. F. M. Cross (Winona Lake: Eisenbrauns, 1981) 127-29.

God's sovereign claim, not simply as a matter of information but as a matter of life-saving hope (v. 4; see "confidence" in Prov 3:26). Interestingly, the ancestors who told their children the right things (v. 3) were apparently not able to do the right things (v. 8). Knowledge does not guarantee faithfulness; the ancestors were "stubborn" (see Jer 5:23; Hos 4:16), "rebellious" (see vv. 17, 40, 56; Jer 5:23), not steadfast (see v. 37), and "not unfaithful" (see vv. 22, 32, 37), as the rest of the psalm makes clear.

78:9-39. 78:9-16. The first recital probably starts in v. 9, meaning that vv. 9-11 would correspond with vv. 40-42 and that both recitals begin by noting the people's unfaithfulness before describing God's gracious activity. If v. 9 refers to a specific episode, the allusion is now lost to us. It is perhaps best to construe it as an indication of Israel's characteristic behavior, as is the case with v. 10 (see v. 37). The people do precisely what the ongoing process described in vv. 1-8 was designed to prevent—they forget (see v. 7) God's wondrous activity (see v. 4). So vv. 12-16 recite what God has done. Zoan (v. 2) is not mentioned in the book of Exodus but is often identified with Rameses (Exod 1:22). The NIV's "wonders" (v. 11) and "miracles" (v. 12) represent the same Hebrew root (*pl'*; see Exod 15:11), and the event in view is clearly the exodus (see Exod 14:21-29; 15:8; cf. Josh 3:13, 16). Verses 14-16 move on to God's provision for the people in the wilderness (see Exod 13:21-22; 17:1-6; Num 20:10-13), which remains the focus through the remainder of the first recital.

78:17-20. Recalling v. 8, v. 17 introduces the section describing the people's sinfulness (see v. 32; see also Deut 9:16) and rebellion (see also vv. 40, 56; Num 20:24; 27:14; Deut 9:7, 23-24). Israel tested God at Massah (a name derived from the verb "test" [נסה *nissâ*] in Exod 17:2, 7; see also v. 41; Num 14:22; Deut 6:16; Ps 95:8-9) by demanding water (see also Exod 15:22-25). God responded by providing water from a rock (see vv. 15, 20; Exod 17:6; Num 20:10-11), having already provided bread and meat (Exod 16:4-36, esp. v. 12) in response to the people's complaints (vv. 18, 20; see also Exod 16:1-3; Num 11:4-6).

78:21-32. Verse 21 introduces God's angry response to the people's faithlessness (see vv. 8, 32, 37) and lack of trust in God's "deliverance"

or "salvation" (v. 22; see Exod 15:2; Ps 3:8). But the bulk of vv. 21-32 is still devoted to God's gracious activity (vv. 23-29; see also Exod 16:13-36; Num 11:7-9, 31-32) before the section returns to God's wrath (vv. 30-31; see also Num 11:33-34) and notes again the people's sinfulness (v. 32).

78:33-39. The boundary between sections is fuzzy, but the final verses of the first recital mention again God's punishment of the people (v. 33) and their faithlessness (vv. 34-37) before concluding with a proclamation of God's grace (vv. 38-39). The vocabulary and content of v. 38 are reminiscent of the golden calf incident in Exodus 32–34, one of the major episodes in the wilderness (see "compassionate"/"merciful" in Exod 33:19; 34:6; "iniquity" in 34:7, 9; "restrained" in 32:12; "anger" in 32:10-12). At the conclusion of the golden calf episode, God reveals God's self to be a forgiving God, yet one who "by no means clears the guilty" (Exod 34:7). The same tension is evident in Psalm 78 (see Reflections below).

78:40-72. 78:40-55. The second recital also begins by recalling the people's rebellion (v. 40; see also vv. 8, 17, 56) and their testing of God (v. 41; see also vv. 18, 56). Verse 42 contains the third occurrence of the verb "remember" (זכר *zākar*, vv. 35, 39, 42). Just as God's faithfulness—not the people's—is crucial for the continuation of the story, so also God's memory is determinative (v. 39). As if to stimulate the people's failed memory, the psalmist again returns to recital (vv. 42*b*-55). Edward L. Greenstein comments that "through the rhetoric adopted by the psalmist for jogging the people's recollection, he exercises their memory by exercising his own."[306] The prominence of memory in Psalm 78 recalls Psalm 77, in which remembering is at first ineffectual (vv. 3, 6) but eventually becomes a stimulus to praise (v. 11). Although the juxtaposition of Psalms 77 and 78 may be coincidental, it is as if the psalmist wants to instruct future generations with Psalm 78 in how and what to remember, so that remembering will be an effective and powerful source of hope and obedience (see vv. 7-8).

Like the first, the second recital begins with

---

306. Edward L. Greenstein, "Mixing Memory and Design: Reading Psalm 78," *Prooftexts: A Journal of Jewish Literary History* 10/2 (1990) 209.

the mention of Egypt and Zoan (v. 43; see also v. 12); however, the emphasis now is on the plagues, which elsewhere are called "signs" (see Exod 7:3; 8:23; 10:1-2) and "miracles" (see "wonders" in Exod 7:3; 11:9-10). The plagues are rehearsed in vv. 44-51—water turned to blood (v. 44; see Exod 7:17-21; Ps 105:29); flies (v. 45a; see Exod 8:20-24; Ps 105:31); frogs (v. 45b; see Exod 8:1-7; Ps 105:30); locusts (v. 46; see Exod 10:1-20; Ps 105:34-35); hail (vv. 47-48; see Exod 9:18-26; Ps 105:32-33; Ps 78:48 may also recall the death of the cattle in Exod 9:1-7); and the death of the firstborn (vv. 49-50; see also Exod 11:1–12:30; Ps 105:36). Obviously, the order of the plagues differs in Psalm 78 from the Exodus account, but this matters little since the psalmist's concern is less with the past than with the present and the future. The recital continues with brief references to the crossing of the sea and guidance in the wilderness (vv. 52-53; see also v. 13) as well as to the entry into Canaan and possession of the land (vv. 54-55).

78:56-72. The response of the people is again to test God (see vv. 18, 41), to rebel (see vv. 17, 40), and to disobey (see v. 5). The form of their disobedience this time is one that was manifest after entry into the land (see vv. 54-55)—idolatry (v. 58). Again, God responds with wrath (v. 59; see v. 21), abandoning Shiloh (v. 60; see also Josh 18:1; 1 Sam 1:3; Jer 7:12), which probably housed the symbolic seat of the divine power, the ark (v. 61; see also 1 Sam 4:1-22). With God's having left them, the people are easy prey for their opponents (vv. 62-64, which may allude to the defeat of the Israelites by the Philistines in 1 Sam 4:10-11). But a compassionate and forgiving God (see v. 38) will not be content finally to abandon the people, so God awakes (v. 65; see also Pss 35:23; 44:23) and effects a reversal of fortunes, which may be intended to mean the victories of Saul and David against the Philistines (v. 66).

Given the historical references and probable allusions in vv. 60-66, and given the fact that Shiloh was in Ephraimite territory, v. 67 may be an allusion to God's abandonment of Shiloh and eventual move to Jerusalem (vv. 68-69) and the establishment of the Davidic dynasty (vv. 70-72). Verses 67-72 may have originated and functioned as a theological rationale for the priority of Zion and David. After 722 BCE, however, it is likely that v. 67 came to be heard as an allusion to the destruction of the northern kingdom. And after the destruction of Jerusalem in 587 BCE, an event that the shape of Book III seems to reflect (see Psalms 74; 79; Introduction), it is likely that the names "Zion" and "David" functioned primarily as religious symbols that communicated God's gracious commitment to the people in the past (2 Sam 7:15) and the promise of ongoing compassion and forgiveness in the future. Indeed, the primary purpose of the historical recitals seems to be the creation of a community that, despite its own failures and faithlessness, will live in hope (v. 7) as a result of the faithfulness and forgiveness of God (v. 38). In fact, this may be the solution to the psalmist's riddle (v. 2), which by inference can be stated as follows: "How can the recollection of a history of failure lead to a future of hope?"

REFLECTIONS

The shape of the recitals in Psalm 78 preserves a pattern that pervades the entire biblical story of the sovereign God who lives in the tension between justice and mercy—that is, gracious acts of God are followed by human disobedience, which in turn creates destructive consequences and necessitates God's gracious forgiveness and restoration if the story of God and God's people is to continue (see Genesis 6–9; Exodus 32–34, the shape of the prophetic books in their final form; see Commentary on Psalms 99; 103). For Christians, this pattern that portrays God's dilemma is stamped most clearly and decisively in the shape of a cross, which demonstrated just how far God is willing to go to forgive and to reclaim sinful humanity. For Christians, to recite Psalm 78 is to confess our own sinfulness and to profess our conviction that we are saved not by our merit or efforts but by the grace of God. Psalm 78 thus invites humility, gratitude, and the exercise of power in the form of love, not of force.

In highlighting the importance of teaching, knowing, and telling the story of the wonders

God has done (vv. 1-8), Psalm 78 is a lesson in the crucial importance of religious education and evangelism. It is true in every era that the faith of the people of God is only one generation away from extinction. Psalm 78 invites us to share the good news, and it reminds us that our own children are an essential place to start (see Deut 6:4-9, 20-25; Josh 4:1-7). To be sure, Psalm 78 is also a reminder that knowledge does not guarantee faithfulness; however, it insists that knowing the story is the foundation for faith and hope and life. The church in recent years and throughout its history has often been so self-absorbed and preoccupied with institutional maintenance that it has forgotten what God has done (v. 11) and has failed to tell the old, old story that is so full of new possibilities for responding with gratitude and service to God's persistent and amazing grace.

PSALM 79:1-13, THE NATIONS SAY, "WHERE IS THEIR GOD?"

NIV

Psalm 79

A psalm of Asaph.

¹O God, the nations have invaded your
    inheritance;
  they have defiled your holy temple,
  they have reduced Jerusalem to rubble.
²They have given the dead bodies of your
    servants
  as food to the birds of the air,
  the flesh of your saints to the beasts of the
    earth.
³They have poured out blood like water
  all around Jerusalem,
  and there is no one to bury the dead.
⁴We are objects of reproach to our neighbors,
  of scorn and derision to those around us.

⁵How long, O LORD? Will you be angry
    forever?
  How long will your jealousy burn like fire?
⁶Pour out your wrath on the nations
  that do not acknowledge you,
 on the kingdoms
  that do not call on your name;
⁷for they have devoured Jacob
  and destroyed his homeland.
⁸Do not hold against us the sins of the fathers;
  may your mercy come quickly to meet us,
  for we are in desperate need.

⁹Help us, O God our Savior,

NRSV

Psalm 79

A Psalm of Asaph.

¹ O God, the nations have come into your
    inheritance;
  they have defiled your holy temple;
  they have laid Jerusalem in ruins.
² They have given the bodies of your servants
  to the birds of the air for food,
  the flesh of your faithful to the wild
    animals of the earth.
³ They have poured out their blood like water
  all around Jerusalem,
  and there was no one to bury them.
⁴ We have become a taunt to our neighbors,
  mocked and derided by those around us.

⁵ How long, O LORD? Will you be angry
    forever?
  Will your jealous wrath burn like fire?
⁶ Pour out your anger on the nations
  that do not know you,
 and on the kingdoms
  that do not call on your name.
⁷ For they have devoured Jacob
  and laid waste his habitation.

⁸ Do not remember against us the iniquities
  of our ancestors;
  let your compassion come speedily to
    meet us,

NIV

for the glory of your name;
deliver us and forgive our sins
for your name's sake.
¹⁰Why should the nations say,
"Where is their God?"
Before our eyes, make known among the
nations
that you avenge the outpoured blood of
your servants.
¹¹May the groans of the prisoners come before
you;
by the strength of your arm
preserve those condemned to die.

¹²Pay back into the laps of our neighbors seven
times
the reproach they have hurled at you,
O Lord.
¹³Then we your people, the sheep of your
pasture,
will praise you forever;
from generation to generation
we will recount your praise.

NRSV

for we are brought very low.
⁹ Help us, O God of our salvation,
for the glory of your name;
deliver us, and forgive our sins,
for your name's sake.
¹⁰ Why should the nations say,
"Where is their God?"
Let the avenging of the outpoured blood of
your servants
be known among the nations before our
eyes.

¹¹ Let the groans of the prisoners come before
you;
according to your great power preserve
those doomed to die.
¹² Return sevenfold into the bosom of our
neighbors
the taunts with which they taunted you,
O Lord!
¹³ Then we your people, the flock of your
pasture,
will give thanks to you forever;
from generation to generation we will
recount your praise.

COMMENTARY

Psalm 79 is one of several communal laments or prayers for help (see Psalms 74; 80; 83–85; 89) that give Book III the appearance of having been decisively shaped by the experience of exile (see also Psalms 77; 81; Introduction). The juxtaposition of Pss 78:67-72 and 79:1-5 is especially jarring (see "inheritance" in Pss 78:62, 71; 79:1), and it suggests that the traditional Zion-David theology had to be reformulated in the light of the exile, just as the exile necessitated more generally a rethinking of the role of suffering in the life of the faithful (see Commentary on Psalms 44; 73; 74; 76). For other links between Psalms 78 and 79, see below.

As already suggested, most scholars relate the catastrophe described in this psalm to the destruction of Jerusalem by the Babylonians and the beginning of the exile (587 BCE). Some scholars, however, speculate that some other event accounts for the origin of Psalm 79, perhaps even the desecration of the Temple by Antiochus IV Epiphanes in the second century BCE. Portions of vv. 2-3 appear in the second-century 1 Maccabees as a comment on the murder of sixty faithful Jews (1 Macc 7:17). In that text, however, Psalm 79 is cited as "the word that was written" (1 Macc 7:16 NRSV), suggesting a much earlier origin for the psalm. It is most likely, then, that Psalm 79 was written as a response to the events of 587 BCE and that it was particularly relevant in later times as well, including the Maccabean era and beyond (see Reflections below).

While scholars propose several ways to outline the structure of Psalm 79, the most cogent and helpful is as follows: vv. 1-5, vv. 6-12, v. 13. As Mays points out, the complaint and petitions follow a " 'they, we, you' pattern" that highlights the major actors—the nations, the people, God—

"and keeps the focus on the painful problem of this three-sided relationship."[307] Verses 1-5 voice the complaint; the focus moves from the nations (vv. 1-3) to the people (v. 4) to God (v. 5). Verse 6 initiates a series of petitions with accompanying reasons; the focus, especially of the reasons, again moves from the nations (vv. 6-7) to the people (v. 8) to God (v. 9). Verse 10b initiates a second series of petitions with a similar movement; and the effect is to center attention on the question in v. 10a, which Mays calls "the climax and theological theme of the psalm."[308] Verse 13 concludes the psalm with the people's promise of perpetual gratitude and praise.

79:1-5. Verses 1-3 describe in graphic detail the desecration and destruction suffered by Jerusalem and its people at the hands of the nations (the repeated "they" of vv. 1-3; see Ps 74:4-7; Lam 1:10). The words "defiled" (טמא ṭāmēʾ) and "holy" (קדשׁ qōdeš) are used elsewhere for ritual purity or cleanness. God's place—the focus of Israel's purity—has become unclean; Jerusalem is in ruins (see Jer 26:18; Mic 3:12). The use of "your inheritance" in v. 1a in conjunction with the Temple in v. 1b recalls Exod 15:17-18, which affirms that the people will be "planted . . . on the mountain of your inheritance" (NIV) and that God "will reign forever and ever" (NRSV). When Ps 79:1 is heard in the light of Exod 15:17-18, the theological issue becomes clearer: The destruction of Jerusalem calls God's sovereignty into question. The nations are not alone in asking, "Where is God?" (v. 10; see also Pss 42:3, 10; 115:2). As Tate suggests, Psalm 79 echoes Israel's "deepest doubts and fears."[309]

The very entrance of the nations into the Temple was defilement enough, but the impurity is made worse by the presence of unburied bodies (see 2 Kgs 23:16), which bespeaks the ignominy of defeat and even divine punishment (see Deut 28:26; 2 Sam 21:10; Jer 7:33). In this regard, although v. 3 says the nations have poured out the blood of the faithful (see v. 10), the imagery could only have recalled Ezek 22:1-12, suggesting that the nations are simply completing a process that a corrupt people set in motion (see the

admission of sin in vv. 8-9, an element that is unusual in the communal laments).

The language of v. 4 appears frequently in other complaints. Just as the individual sufferer is sometimes a "taunt" (see also Pss 22:6; 31:11; 69:7), so also are the whole people (Ps 44:13) or their representative, the king (see Ps 89:41; see also 89:50, where the verb appears and where the king is called "your servant," as are the people in Ps 79:2, 10). What is particularly interesting is that v. 4 anticipates v. 12, which suggests that the taunts against the people are really taunts against God. So what is at stake is not just the people's reputation but also God's "name" (v. 9)—that is, God's reputation or character. God's anger or "jealousy" (v. 5) is mentioned elsewhere in the context of covenant making, where it is clear that God wants Israel's exclusive allegiance (see Exod 20:5; 34:14; Deut 4:24; 5:9; 6:15; Josh 24:19). God the lover wants Israel to love no other gods (see Ps 78:58). God's jealousy, therefore, is ultimately a manifestation of God's love. Having experienced the tough side of God's love, the people will appeal in v. 8 to the side of God's love that is experienced as "compassion" or "mercy" (רחמים raḥămîm). For now, the question is, "How long?" (see Pss 6:3; 13:1-2; 89:46).

79:6-12. If God is angry at the people, God should also be angry at the nations for their treatment of Jerusalem and its people (vv. 6-7; see Jer 10:25). Upon those who have "poured out" blood (v. 3), God should "pour out . . . anger" (v. 6; see "outpoured" in v. 10; see also Ezek 36:18). The people do not claim to be innocent (vv. 8-9). Rather, having been "brought very low" (v. 8; see also Pss 116:6; 142:6), they appeal to God's compassion for the lowly, God's "mercy" or "motherly compassion" (see Commentary on Psalm 25, esp. the discussion of vv. 6-7). God willingly forgives sinners, as evidenced in Exod 34:6, where God's character is described as merciful after God has forgiven the people, even after they had constructed and worshiped another god (see Exod 32:1-14). The words "mercy"/"merciful" (רחום raḥûm) and "forgive" (כפר kipper) also occur together in Ps 78:38, which rehearses at length "the iniquities of our ancestors" (79:8). That is to say, the good news of God's faithfulness and forgiveness proclaimed in Psalm 78 is also the basis of the appeal in Psalm 79. Given the appeal

307. James L. Mays, *Psalms,* Interpretation (Louisville: John Knox, 1994) 260.
308. Ibid.
309. Marvin E. Tate, *Psalms 51–100,* WBC 20 (Dallas: Word, 1990) 301.

to God's fundamental character in v. 8, the two occurrences of "name" in v. 9 are readily comprehensible. In effect, the people suggest that God's delivering them from their distress would be an opportunity for God's character to be proved to the nations (v. 9; see also Exod 9:16). The nations, who do not know God (v. 6), will come to know God if God will act to avenge Israel (v. 10; see also Ps 94:1; Ezek 25:14). Thus the form of the requests in v. 9 does not simply mask the people's selfish concern (see "help" in Ps 22:19). Rather, as they "waive the right of all self-help,"[310] they subordinate their well-being to the request that God be glorified (see Ps 115:1). The request to be delivered "for your name's sake" (v. 9) may suggest the people's humble recognition of their sin as well as their concern for God's reputation, even above their own (see Ezek 36:21-23). Or, as v. 12 suggests, when the nations ask, "Where is their God?" (v. 10a; see also Ps 115:2), it is not just a taunt against the people but one against God as well.

The people's apparently genuine need (vv. 1-3, 8b), as well as their willingness to entrust themselves fully to God's help and to seek first God's glory, puts the petitions of vv. 10b, 12 in a particular light. That is, these verses are not simply selfish requests for personal revenge. Rather,

they ask God to set right things that are obviously wrong (vv. 1-3), both for the people (v. 10; see vv. 2-3) and for God (v. 12; see also v. 1). Verses 10b, 12 realistically realize that when the lowly are liberated, then their oppressors must be judged. This is precisely the way God has always operated, as the allusion to the exodus in v. 11 recalls (see "strength of your arm," which also occurs in Exod 15:16). There, too, God saved people (see v. 9; Exod 15:2) who were prisoners and doomed to die (see Ps 102:20; Zech 9:11). And, as Psalm 79 suggests as well, God acted both for the sake of the people (Exod 3:7-8) and for the sake of God's name (Exod 9:16).

79:13. The word "then" (ו wa-) at the beginning of v. 13 is misleading; it appears too much as if Israel is simply trying to cut a deal with God. If the Hebrew conjunction is translated simply as "and," v. 13 becomes the people's affirmation that they will always be grateful for God's compassion and that they will witness to God's praiseworthy deeds (see Ps 78:4). In the light of vv. 1-5, this is a remarkable promise. But biblical faith *is* remarkable! It is about a God who will not tolerate unfaithfulness (v. 5), but whose deep compassion will not let go of unfaithful people (v. 8). It is about a people who suffer miserably, although due to their own unfaithfulness (vv. 8-9), but who continue to pray to live (vv. 8-9) and live to praise (v. 13).

310. H.-J. Kraus, *Psalms 60–150: A Commentary,* trans. H. C. Oswald (Minneapolis: Augsburg, 1989) 135.

REFLECTIONS

Despite its origin in a specific ancient event, Psalm 79 continued and continues to be useful to the people of God. Psalm 79 is alluded to in Rev 16:6; it was cited by Jerome in response to the invasion of Rome by the Visigoths; it was frequently on the lips of Christians as they died in the religious conflicts of sixteenth- and seventeenth-century Europe, and it was and is used by Jews on the ninth of Ab, which commemorates the destruction of Jerusalem, and in weekly services as well. As Mays suggests, "In all these ways the psalm continues to voice the prayer of those who raise the question, 'Why should the nations say, Where is your God?' "[311]

As suggested above, this question articulated not just the taunts of the nations but also the doubts and fears of God's people. And as we look around ourselves and see a broken world haunted by monstrous evil, we still ask the question, "Where is God?" As we do, we can be instructed by Psalm 79 and its insistence that suffering be seen in the perspective of faith. The psalmist never loses sight of the harsh realities facing the people of God (vv. 1-5). But the psalmist likewise never loses hope. As Brueggemann concludes: "Biblical faith is not romantic.

311. Mays, *Psalms,* 262; see also Rowland E. Prothero, *The Psalms in Human Life and Experience* (New York: E. P. Dutton, 1903) 31, 146-47.

It reckons with evil, and it knows that evil strikes at all that is crucial and most precious. Nevertheless it does affirm."[312]

The temptation was and is to view the suffering of the faithful as a sign of God's weakness—God no longer rules—or as a sign of God's punishment—God is forever angry. But in the face of catastrophic suffering, the psalmist continues to affirm. Such affirmation in the faith of contrary signs is eschatological (see Commentary on Psalms 2; 74; Introduction). It opens the way for a new understanding of God's sovereignty as power made perfect in weakness (see 2 Cor 12:9). It opens the way to the claim that God's love will ultimately be experienced as compassion, not jealousy. It opens the way to an embrace of suffering as something other than an indication of alienation from God (see Commentary on Psalms 44; 74). In short, the psalmist's affirmation in the face of adversity prepares the way for a time when a cross—the emblem of suffering and shame—will become a symbol of power and grace, the ultimate answer to the question, "Where is God?"

312. Walter Brueggemann, *The Message of the Psalms: A Theological Commentary* (Minneapolis: Augsburg, 1984) 74.

PSALM 80:1-19, RESTORE US, O GOD

NIV	NRSV
Psalm 80	**Psalm 80**
For the director of music. To ˌthe tune ofˌ "The Lilies of the Covenant." Of Asaph. A psalm.	To the leader: on Lilies, a Covenant. Of Asaph. A Psalm.
¹Hear us, O Shepherd of Israel, you who lead Joseph like a flock; you who sit enthroned between the cherubim, shine forth ² before Ephraim, Benjamin and Manasseh. Awaken your might; come and save us.	¹ Give ear, O Shepherd of Israel, you who lead Joseph like a flock! You who are enthroned upon the cherubim, shine forth ² before Ephraim and Benjamin and Manasseh. Stir up your might, and come to save us!
³Restore us, O God; make your face shine upon us, that we may be saved.	³ Restore us, O God; let your face shine, that we may be saved.
⁴O Lᴏʀᴅ God Almighty, how long will your anger smolder against the prayers of your people? ⁵You have fed them with the bread of tears; you have made them drink tears by the bowlful. ⁶You have made us a source of contention to our neighbors, and our enemies mock us.	⁴ O Lᴏʀᴅ God of hosts, how long will you be angry with your people's prayers? ⁵ You have fed them with the bread of tears, and given them tears to drink in full measure. ⁶ You make us the scorn[a] of our neighbors; our enemies laugh among themselves.
⁷Restore us, O God Almighty; make your face shine upon us,	⁷ Restore us, O God of hosts;

^aSyr: Heb *strife*

NIV

that we may be saved.

⁸You brought a vine out of Egypt;
    you drove out the nations and planted it.
⁹You cleared the ground for it,
    and it took root and filled the land.
¹⁰The mountains were covered with its shade,
    the mighty cedars with its branches.
¹¹It sent out its boughs to the Sea,ᵃ
    its shoots as far as the River.ᵇ

¹²Why have you broken down its walls
    so that all who pass by pick its grapes?
¹³Boars from the forest ravage it
    and the creatures of the field feed on it.
¹⁴Return to us, O God Almighty!
    Look down from heaven and see!
  Watch over this vine,
¹⁵   the root your right hand has planted,
    the sonᶜ you have raised up for yourself.

¹⁶Your vine is cut down, it is burned with fire;
    at your rebuke your people perish.
¹⁷Let your hand rest on the man at your right
    hand,
    the son of man you have raised up for
    yourself.
¹⁸Then we will not turn away from you;
    revive us, and we will call on your name.

¹⁹Restore us, O Lᴏʀᴅ God Almighty;
    make your face shine upon us,
    that we may be saved.

a11 Probably the Mediterranean   *b11* That is, the Euphrates
c15 Or *branch*

NRSV

    let your face shine, that we may be saved.

⁸ You brought a vine out of Egypt;
    you drove out the nations and planted it.
⁹ You cleared the ground for it;
    it took deep root and filled the land.
¹⁰ The mountains were covered with its shade,
    the mighty cedars with its branches;
¹¹ it sent out its branches to the sea,
    and its shoots to the River.
¹² Why then have you broken down its walls,
    so that all who pass along the way pluck
      its fruit?
¹³ The boar from the forest ravages it,
    and all that move in the field feed on it.

¹⁴ Turn again, O God of hosts;
    look down from heaven, and see;
  have regard for this vine,
¹⁵   the stock that your right hand planted.ᵃ
¹⁶ They have burned it with fire, they have
      cut it down;ᵇ
    may they perish at the rebuke of your
      countenance.
¹⁷ But let your hand be upon the one at your
      right hand,
    the one whom you made strong for
      yourself.
¹⁸ Then we will never turn back from you;
    give us life, and we will call on your
      name.

¹⁹ Restore us, O Lᴏʀᴅ God of hosts;
    let your face shine, that we may be saved.

a Heb adds from verse 17 *and upon the one whom you made strong
for yourself*   *b* Cn: Heb *it is cut down*

COMMENTARY

A communal lament like Psalm 79, Psalm 80 also continues the flock/shepherd imagery from Pss 77:20; 78:70-72; and 79:13. Like Psalm 79, too, Psalm 80 bases its appeal on the good news of God's faithfulness and forgiveness that is proclaimed in Psalm 78 (see below on the refrain, esp. v. 14). The flock/shepherd imagery culminates in Psalm 80 with the opening address of God as "Shepherd of Israel"; despite a sordid past (Psalm 78) and a devastating present (Psalm 79), Israel still addresses God as its sovereign, its hope for light and life.

There is disagreement among scholars about the calamity that lies behind the origin of Psalm 80. The mention of Ephraim and Manasseh in v. 2 has led several scholars to conclude that it was produced in the northern kingdom, perhaps during the final years before the conquest of Samaria by the Assyrians in 721 BCE. The LXX's superscription, "Concerning the Assyrians," may support this view. Certainty is impossible, however, and proposed dates of origin range from the tenth to the second centuries BCE. It is likely that if Psalm 80 did not actually originate as a response to exile, it was placed in its present literary context to function as such (see Commentary on Psalms 73; 74; 79; Introduction). In any case, as Mays puts it, "Whatever the original historical setting, the psalm in its continued use belongs to the repertoire of the afflicted people of God on their way through the troubles of history."[313] The structure and movement of Psalm 80 are dominated by the occurrence of a refrain (vv. 3, 7, 19; see also v. 14). After the opening plea (vv. 1-2) and initial complaint (vv. 4-6), each of which is followed by the refrain, vv. 8-13 present a historical allegory or parable. A variation of the refrain (v. 14) marks a return to petition, which culminates in the final occurrence of the refrain.

80:1-2. A series of imperatives that indicate the dimensions of the problem opens the psalm. In the psalms, the directive to "give ear" often accompanies the object "my prayer" (Pss 17:1; 55:1; 86:6; cf. 84:8; 141:1-2). The need for this plea suggests that the people believe that God is inattentive (see v. 4). The verb "shine forth" (יפע yp‘) is the language of theophany, and it is used to describe the appearance of God on mountains (Deut 33:2; Ps 50:2). The plea suggests that the people also believe that God is absent (see Ps 94:1). Two additional pleas in v. 2 convey the urgency of the situation. God seems to be asleep (see Ps 44:23). Since to be saved in OT terms means to remain alive (see Pss 3:8; 6:4), if God remains inattentive, inactive, and absent, the people will face death (see v. 18). The truly remarkable thing about these pleas in vv. 1-2 is that they are addressed to the same God who is perceived to be inattentive, inactive, and even absent, expressing a belief that even if God is the problem, nonetheless God is the solution. In spite of God's inattention and inaction, therefore, the people address God in the most exalted of terms. The appellation "shepherd," a royal title (see 2 Sam

7:7; Ezek 34:1-16; Ps 78:70-72), and the designation of God as the one "enthroned upon the cherubim" (see 1 Sam 4:4; 2 Sam 6:2; Ps 99:1) emphasize God's sovereignty. The imagery is associated elsewhere with the ark, God's earthly throne, a symbol of God's presence and power (see Commentary on Ps 24:7-10). Despite appearances to the contrary, the people still affirm that God reigns supreme.

80:3. This verse, which continues the series of imperatives, is related thematically to vv. 1-2. It is notable, however, because it contains the first occurrence of the refrain. The plea "Restore us" (השיבנו hăšîbēnû; more lit., "cause us to return") has several dimensions of meaning that are appropriate for Psalm 80. The word is used elsewhere to describe God's bringing the people back from exile (see 1 Kgs 8:34; Jer 27:22; cf. Dan 9:25). The word may also denote repentance, literally "causing people to return" to God (see Neh 9:26; Lam 5:21), as well as causing persons to return to life (2 Sam 12:23; Job 33:30). The plea "let your face shine" communicates much the same thing as "shine forth"; it is a request that God "be present for us." In Num 6:24-26, this phrase is paralleled by the terms "bless," "keep," "be gracious," and "give peace" (see also Pss 4:6; 31:16; 67:1).

80:4-6. The problems implied by vv. 1-3 come to the fore in vv. 4-6. The poignant question, "How long?" characteristic of both individual and communal complaints (see Pss 13:1-2; 74:10; 79:5; 94:3), sets the mood. God is angry with the people's prayers (lit., "smokes against"; see Deut 29:20; Ps 74:1) and refuses to listen to them (see v. 1). Like v. 4, v. 5 also recalls v. 1. Just as a shepherd feeds the flock, so also the king as shepherd should feed the people (see Ezek 34:1-16). The complaint of v. 5 becomes more poignant in the light of both the refrain, "let your face shine," and the existence in the Temple of the "bread of the face" (or "bread of the Presence"; see Exod 25:30; 1 Sam 21:16; 1 Kgs 7:48). In the present situation, the bread of God's face, symbolic of God's sustaining presence, has been replaced by the "bread of tears" (see Ps 42:3). The complaint is concluded in v. 6 with characteristic language. The NRSV's "laugh" represents the same Hebrew word (לעג lā‘ag) that the NRSV translates as "mocked" in Ps 79:4 and "derision" in Ps 44:13; both are communal laments. The NRSV's "scorn" is more accurately "source of contention," which is a preferable translation in view of the similarity between the refrain and the priestly benediction in Num 6:24-26. The same Hebrew verb translated "give" (שׂים śîm) in the phrase "give you peace" (Num 6:26) is rendered "made" in the phrase "made us a source of contention" (v. 6). Thus the people experience the opposite of the priestly benediction.

80:7. With the exception of the longer divine name, the refrain of v. 7 is identical to v. 3. The effect of the repetition is to express the urgency of the plea that pervades the psalm. The following allegory of the vine serves to remind God of past actions on Israel's behalf, and such recollections are typical in communal prayers for help (see Exod 32:11-12; Pss 44:1-8; 74:2, 12-17).

80:8-11. These verses are a brief review of Israel's history, starting with the exodus (v. 8a; "ordered . . . to set out" in Exod 15:22 NRSV translates the same verb as "brought . . . out" [נסע nāsa']), moving to the conquest (v. 8b; see "drove out" in Josh 24:12, 18; Ps 78:55), and concluding with the growth and culmination of the Davidic empire, which stretched from the Mediterranean Sea to the Euphrates River (vv. 9-11). The metaphor of the vine indicates careful planning, preparation, and patient nurturing, which makes possible growth and fruitfulness. Thus the metaphor appropriately represents the commitment that God shows to God's people (see Isa 5:1-7; Jer 2:21; 6:9; Ezek 17:1-10; 19:10-14; Hos 10:1; 14:7; John 15:11; and see the use of "plant" even when the vine image is absent, as in Exod 15:17; Ps 44:2).

80:12-13. These verses continue the allegory, exploring the question of why, after all of the careful planting and nurture, God would break down the walls around the vineyard (see Isa 5:5; Ps 89:40) and allow the vine to be devoured (see Ps 89:41). The question recalls the previous question, "How long?" (v. 4). The word "feed" (רעה rā'â, v. 13) is particularly poignant as it recalls v. 1, where the word for "shepherd" (רעה rō'ēh) is literally translated "feeder." God, who traditionally has been the one to feed Israel, is allowing Israel to be devoured.

80:14-18. The poignant question in v. 12 receives no answer. Instead, the psalmist renews the petition, "Turn again" or "Repent, O God of

hosts" (v. 14a). The sequence is not surprising, however, if one considers such passages as Exod 32:11-12 and Isa 5:1-7. Following Israel's apostasy, Moses twice asks "Why?" before requesting that God "turn" (Exod 32:12). Thus the renewed request in Ps 80:14 implies that the answer to the question in v. 12 is that God is punishing Israel for its sin. This view is reinforced by the people's promise in v. 18a, which also implies that the people have sinned previously, although there is no direct confession of sin. The people's sin, as well as the placement and construction of v. 14, makes clear that the initiative for restoration rests exclusively with God. The reader might expect the refrain again at v. 14; instead, "turn" is a different form of the same Hebrew verb translated "restore" in vv. 3, 7, 19. This seemingly intentional variation draws attention to v. 14 and, coupled with the absence of any confession of sin by the people, makes the message clear: There can be no life (v. 18) or future for God's people without *God's* repentance. The fourfold imperative in v. 14 serves to emphasize the need for God, not the people, to act. Just as in both major episodes of the exodus event, the deliverance from Egypt and the forgiveness following the golden calf episode, God's activity was determinative, so also now God must "turn," "see" (Exod 3:7), and "have regard for" Israel (Exod 3:16; 4:31).

The petition in v. 17 reinforces v. 14. To have God's hand upon one is to experience deliverance and protection (see Ezra 8:31). The phrases "one at your right hand" and "the one whom you made strong" are sometimes understood as references to a king or a future king. The Hebrew word translated "one whom" is literally "son of a human" (בן־אדם ben-'ādām). This expression probably refers to Israel (Israel is elsewhere referred to as a son; see Hos 11:1; see also Gen 49:22, where Joseph, represented by a plant, is called a "son of a fruit-bearer," or "fruitful bough"; note also the repetition of "right hand" and "son" in vv. 15, 17).

80:19. The final petition, the refrain in v. 19, differs from vv. 3, 7 by the inclusion of the more personal divine name, Yahweh. Verse 19 indicates that the promises of v. 18 are not just Israel's attempt to bribe God; rather, Israel has already been calling on God's name throughout the psalm in deathly circumstances. Thus, even while Israel pleads for life, the very plea itself indicates that life is, at least in some sense, already a present possession.

REFLECTIONS

John Calvin introduced his comment on Psalm 80 with the following words: "This is a sorrowful prayer, in which the faithful beseech God that he would be graciously pleased to succour his afflicted Church."[314] Psalm 80 is, indeed, "a sorrowful prayer," but as Calvin implies, it is surely an act of faith and hope. In short, Psalm 80 is eschatological (see Commentary on Psalm 2; Introduction). Amid calamitous circumstances, which seem to belie their affirmation, the people of God dare to affirm that God reigns (vv. 1-2). That was an act of faith, and because the people trusted God to transform their circumstances and restore them, this act of faith was also an act of hope (see Rom 8:24-25; Heb 11:1).

In the exilic and post-exilic eras, the people of God may have envisioned their future restoration primarily in political terms—that is, the restoration of statehood and monarchy (see v. 17, which many commentators suggest refers to a present or future king, and which was apparently read messianically within Judaism). If so, that hope was disappointed, and the royal vision was pushed further into the future (see Mic 5:2-5a) and was later claimed by and for Jesus (see Matt 2:6, which quotes Mic 5:2). As a king was supposed to do, Jesus embodied both the experience of his people (see John 15:1-11 in relation to Ps 80:8-13) and the reign of God. His crowning glory appeared to be a God-forsaken exile—a cross. In an act of faith and hope not unlike that of Psalm 80, the followers of Jesus dare to affirm that in Jesus the light of God shines and that through Jesus we are restored and have life. Like those who prayed Psalm 80 long ago, Christians dare to see and expect the reign of God where others see only chaos and expect nothing.

The conviction that one confronts God in every circumstance, both good and bad, lies at the heart of the ancient Israelite prayers for help. This conviction is the ultimate paradox of the laments (see Commentary on Psalms 13; 22). The language and imagery of Psalm 80 suggest that the people think that God is inattentive and inactive, if not entirely absent. At the same time, they seem to belie this position by continuing to address God and by attributing their present circumstances to God's action (see vv. 5-6). The belief that God is in some way confronted in suffering and death as well as for prosperity and life is a remarkable affirmation—especially in a time when the pious are apt to view suffering as evidence of alienation from God, and secular folk are loath to attribute their prosperity and life to God. Psalm 80 is traditionally associated with the season of Advent, the celebration of God's coming and continuing presence. There is no better way to express belief in the reality of God's sovereignty than to address God out of our individual and corporate afflictions and to continue looking to God as the only source of light and life.

Advent is a season of preparation and repentance, and lest we be tempted to focus on our own efforts in these matters, Psalm 80 proclaims that our lives ultimately depend on God's gracious willingness to repent (see v. 14). So does the birth, life, death, and resurrection of Jesus. What human repentance amounts to, at best, is turning to accept the loving embrace of the God who gives us life. As Jesus indicated in his extension of the image of the vine, "apart from me you can do nothing" (John 15:5 NRSV; see also Phil 1:6).

314. John Calvin, *Commentary on the Book of Psalms,* Calvin Translation Society, 5 vols. (Grand Rapids: Baker, 1981) V:3:295.

PSALM 81:1-16, IF MY PEOPLE WOULD ONLY LISTEN TO ME!

NIV

Psalm 81

For the director of music. According to *gittith*.[a]
Of Asaph.

¹Sing for joy to God our strength;
    shout aloud to the God of Jacob!
²Begin the music, strike the tambourine,
    play the melodious harp and lyre.
³Sound the ram's horn at the New Moon,
    and when the moon is full, on the day of
        our Feast;
⁴this is a decree for Israel,
    an ordinance of the God of Jacob.
⁵He established it as a statute for Joseph
    when he went out against Egypt,
    where we heard a language we did not
        understand.[b]

⁶He says, "I removed the burden from their
        shoulders;
    their hands were set free from the basket.
⁷In your distress you called and I rescued you,
    I answered you out of a thundercloud;
    I tested you at the waters of
        Meribah.   *Selah*

⁸"Hear, O my people, and I will warn you—
    if you would but listen to me, O Israel!
⁹You shall have no foreign god among you;
    you shall not bow down to an alien god.
¹⁰I am the LORD your God,
    who brought you up out of Egypt.
    Open wide your mouth and I will fill it.

¹¹"But my people would not listen to me;
    Israel would not submit to me.
¹²So I gave them over to their stubborn hearts
    to follow their own devices.

¹³"If my people would but listen to me,
    if Israel would follow my ways,
¹⁴how quickly would I subdue their enemies
    and turn my hand against their foes!

---

a Title: Probably a musical term   b5 Or / and we heard a voice we
had not known

NRSV

Psalm 81

To the leader: according to The Gittith.
Of Asaph.

¹ Sing aloud to God our strength;
    shout for joy to the God of Jacob.
² Raise a song, sound the tambourine,
    the sweet lyre with the harp.
³ Blow the trumpet at the new moon,
    at the full moon, on our festal day.
⁴ For it is a statute for Israel,
    an ordinance of the God of Jacob.
⁵ He made it a decree in Joseph,
    when he went out over[a] the land of
        Egypt.

I hear a voice I had not known:
⁶ "I relieved your[b] shoulder of the burden;
    your[b] hands were freed from the basket.
⁷ In distress you called, and I rescued you;
    I answered you in the secret place of
        thunder;
    I tested you at the waters of
        Meribah.   *Selah*
⁸ Hear, O my people, while I admonish you;
    O Israel, if you would but listen to me!
⁹ There shall be no strange god among you;
    you shall not bow down to a foreign god.
¹⁰ I am the LORD your God,
    who brought you up out of the land of
        Egypt.
    Open your mouth wide and I will fill it.

¹¹ "But my people did not listen to my voice;
    Israel would not submit to me.
¹² So I gave them over to their stubborn
        hearts,
    to follow their own counsels.
¹³ O that my people would listen to me,
    that Israel would walk in my ways!
¹⁴ Then I would quickly subdue their enemies,
    and turn my hand against their foes.

---

a Or *against*   b Heb *his*

NIV

15Those who hate the LORD would cringe
    before him,
    and their punishment would last forever.
16But you would be fed with the finest of
    wheat;
    with honey from the rock I would satisfy
    you."

NRSV

15 Those who hate the LORD would cringe
    before him,
    and their doom would last forever.
16 I would feed you[a] with the finest of the
    wheat,
    and with honey from the rock I would
    satisfy you."

aCn Compare verse 16b: Heb *he would feed him*

COMMENTARY

Often categorized as a prophetic exhortation, Psalm 81 may more helpfully be labeled a liturgical sermon (see Psalms 50; 95), in which the preacher delivers the word of God (cf. vv. 6-16 with Ps 50:7-23). As in Psalm 50, the sermon in Psalm 81 divides into two parts (vv. 5c-10, 11-16) preceded by an introduction. Verses 1-5b clearly suggest a liturgical setting, seemingly the beginning of one of Israel's festal celebrations (see vv. 3-5b), and it is possible that the sermon was preached on one of Israel's holy days. Joyous praise marks the beginning of the festival (vv. 1-2). The reference to blowing "the trumpet at the new moon" (v. 3) accords with the proscriptions in Lev 23:23-24 and Num 29:1-6 regarding the first day of the seventh month (sometimes called the Festival of Trumpets). The conviction of the people for their faithlessness (vv. 8, 11-13) would also be an appropriate rite for the Day of Atonement. The references to the opening of the Decalogue (vv. 9-10b) and the harvest (vv. 10c, 16) would be appropriate for the Feast of Booths or Tabernacles. Since all of these observances were held in the seventh month (see Lev 23:26-36; Num 29:7-39), Psalm 81 originally may have been related to this festal season.

Following two communal complaints and placed in the midst of Book III, which recalls the crisis of exile (see Commentary on Psalms 73; 74; 79; 80; Introduction), Psalm 81 serves both as an explanation for the people's suffering (vv. 11-12) and as a hopeful, encouraging word if Israel will but listen and respond (vv. 8-10, 13-16). Beyond its possible original festal setting and its literary setting, Psalm 81 can function as a call to commitment at all times and in all places.

81:1-5b. Psalm 81 begins like a song of praise instead of a sermon. In the light of the joyous season, people are encouraged to "sing aloud" (רנן *rnn*; see Ps 145:7; see also 5:11; 67:4; 95:1; 96:12; 98:4; 149:5), to "shout for joy" (רוע *rûa*'; see also Pss 95:1-2; 98:4, 6; 100:1), and to "raise a song" (שאו־זמרה *śĕʾû-zimrâ*; see Exod 15:2; Pss 33:2; 47:6-7; 95:2; 98:4-5) with instrumental accompaniment (see Exod 15:20; 2 Sam 6:5; Pss 33:2-3; 149:3; 150:3-4). Although this type of joyful praise was appropriate for a festival, the same invitations occur often in contexts that make clear that what is really being celebrated is the reign of God over all creation. It should not be surprising, then, that many of the psalms cited above either contain the exclamation "The LORD is king!" (Ps 96:10) or in some other way address God as king (Pss 5:2; 47:2, 7-8; 95:3; 98:6; 145:1; 149:2). Furthermore, the song of praise in Exodus 15 culminates in the affirmation of God's reign (v. 18), and 2 Sam 6:2 states that God is "enthroned on the cherubim" (NRSV). When the psalmist invites the people to celebrate God's sovereignty (vv. 1-2), the psalmist anticipates one of the main themes of the sermon that follows: Only Yahweh is God (see esp. vv. 9-10). As noted above, blowing the trumpet may signal the beginning of a festal day (v. 3), but a trumpet blast was also the way to greet a king, either human (see 1 Kgs 1:34, 39) or divine (see Pss 47:5; 98:6). Worship always involves the recognition and celebration of God's claim upon the world.

81:5c-10. Verse 5c is problematic, but it should probably be understood as the immediate introduction to the sermon. The preacher is claiming to be delivering *God's* word rather than the preacher's own words, a statement that may be similar to the contemporary "Listen for the Word of God." In any case, God speaks in the first person for the remainder of the psalm, first reminding the people of their gracious deliverance from slavery in Egypt (vv. 6c-7a; the Hebrew word translated "burden" [סבל *sēbel*] is found in Exod 1:11; 2:11; 5:4-5; 6:6) and then of further gracious dealings during the wilderness wanderings. Verse 7b seems to allude to Sinai; the phrase "secret place of thunder" may be meant to recall the cloud engulfing the mountain (see Exod 19:16; note also the mention of a trumpet blast in this verse). Verse 7c recalls the incident at Meribah, although the preacher seems to be giving Israel the benefit of the doubt, for Meribah is remembered elsewhere as a place where Israel tested God (see Exod 17:7; Ps 95:8). The recalling of the journey to Sinai (v. 7c) and of Sinai itself (v. 7b) would be an appropriate anticipation of the clear recollection of the Decalogue in vv. 9-10. Following v. 9, which is a rephrasing of the first commandment (Exod 20:3; Deut 5:7; see also Jer 2:4-13), v. 10 is an almost direct quotation of the prologue of the Decalogue (Exod 20:2; Deut 5:6).

A central motif of the first section of the sermon is God's desire that the people hear—"listen to me!" (v. 8; the same Hebrew root [שמע *šā ma'*] lies behind both "hear" and "listen"). Since God had heard the people's cries for deliverance in Egypt (Exod 3:7), it is reasonable that now they obey the command to hear God (see Deut 6:4; Ps 95:7). Indeed, abundance awaits their hearing (v. 10c). The two key elements of vv. 6-10—God's desire to be heard and the promise of abundance—will recur in the second section of the sermon (vv. 13, 16). The choice belongs to the people.

81:11-16. The second part of the sermon starts by stating the people's response to God's call to hear; they "did not listen" (v. 11; see also vv. 8, 13). God's reaction is to give them exactly what they have chosen: their own "stubborn hearts" and "their own counsels" (see Jer 7:24, where these terms are used in the context of the prophet's condemnation of the people; see vv. 6, 26). In effect, God's desire to supply good things, to "fill" and to "satisfy" (v. 16) the people has been thwarted by their refusal to accept God's gracious actions. God's pain is like that of a rejected lover. The occurrence of "hear"/"listen" in v. 13 is an urgent repetition of God's desire. The setbacks the people experience are the result of their own choice not to listen, and not the result of God's will. God wills abundance, not just manna in the wilderness, but the "finest of wheat" (v. 16; see also Ps 147:14), and not just water from the rock (Exod 17:6-7), but honey (see Deut 32:13-14).

In view of the preceding psalms, it is especially noticeable that each time the key word "hear"/"listen" appears, the people are addressed as "my people" (vv. 8, 11, 13). Psalm 80, for instance, has suggested that the people's future depends ultimately on God's repentance. Similarly, Psalm 81 suggests that even in the absence of the people's choice to listen to and to follow God (vv. 8, 13), they are still "my people." The people will live finally by grace, by God's compassion and willingness to forgive (see Pss 78:38; 79:8).

REFLECTIONS

1. Citing Abraham Heschel, Tate reflects on the theological significance of Psalm 81: "The divine pathos of Yahweh is expressed in v. 14 [English v. 13]. . . . Yahweh is not a God of abstract absoluteness, who holds himself aloof from the world. He is moved and affected by what his people do or do not do. He has a dynamic relationship with his people, his family, and their welfare."[315] Thus, in the absence of the people's response, God begs and pleads that they listen. So important was hearing that this imperative was constantly put before the people, followed by Israel's fundamental profession of faith. The formulation is known as the Shema, "Hear, O Israel: The LORD is our God, the LORD alone" (Deut 6:4 NRSV). It captures the message of Psalm 81.

---

315. Tate, *Psalms 51–100,* 327.

---

2. The repeated admonition to "hear"/"listen" to God calls to mind for Christian readers the story of Jesus' transfiguration (Mark 9:1-8). Both Psalm 81 and the NT transfiguration story recall the events at Sinai: the "mountain" (v. 2), the presence of Moses, the cloud (v. 7). The divine voice in the transfiguration story identifies Jesus as "my Son," the bearer of the divine will, and says, "Listen to him" (v. 7). Jesus proclaimed the reign of God and invited people to enter it (Mark 1:14-15; see also Ps 81:1-3). We are bombarded today by more competing voices than any other generation in the history of the world. In this din of voices vying for our attention and allegiance, Psalm 81 calls us to discern the pained but persistent voice of the one who says simply, "Follow me" (Mark 1:17 NRSV; cf. Ps 80:13*b*; John 10:4).

3. Listening to God is crucial. Psalm 81 thus becomes, in Mays's words, "a paradigm for what should happen in every religious festival."[316] Its emphatic call to hear/listen is a reminder, too, that the revelation of God is not a static entity confined to the past. Rather, it is a dynamic process that continues in the present as God is moved and affected by what God's people do (see Reflections on Psalm 119). It is still the role of preaching, teaching, and pastoral care to challenge people to hear and to respond to God's exclusive claim upon their lives. Listening to God is still at the heart of what it means to be the people of God.

316. James L. Mays, *Psalms,* Interpretation (Louisville: John Knox, 1994) 268.

PSALM 82:1-8, SHOW JUSTICE TO THE WEAK

NIV	NRSV
Psalm 82	Psalm 82
A psalm of Asaph.	A Psalm of Asaph.
¹God presides in the great assembly; he gives judgment among the "gods":	¹ God has taken his place in the divine council; in the midst of the gods he holds judgment:
²"How long will you*a* defend the unjust and show partiality to the wicked? *Selah*	² "How long will you judge unjustly and show partiality to the wicked? *Selah*
³Defend the cause of the weak and fatherless; maintain the rights of the poor and oppressed.	³ Give justice to the weak and the orphan; maintain the right of the lowly and the destitute.
⁴Rescue the weak and needy; deliver them from the hand of the wicked.	⁴ Rescue the weak and the needy; deliver them from the hand of the wicked."
⁵"They know nothing, they understand nothing. They walk about in darkness; all the foundations of the earth are shaken.	⁵ They have neither knowledge nor understanding, they walk around in darkness; all the foundations of the earth are shaken.
⁶"I said, 'You are "gods"; you are all sons of the Most High.'	⁶ I say, "You are gods, children of the Most High, all of you;
⁷But you will die like mere men; you will fall like every other ruler."	
⁸Rise up, O God, judge the earth, for all the nations are your inheritance.	

a2 The Hebrew is plural.

NRSV

7 nevertheless, you shall die like mortals,
    and fall like any prince."[a]

8 Rise up, O God, judge the earth;
    for all the nations belong to you!

[a] Or fall as one man, O princes

COMMENTARY

As if to supply a rationale for Ps 81:9, Psalm 82 portrays the death of all other gods. In so doing, it offers a clear picture of the ancient Near Eastern polytheistic culture that formed Israel's religious background. In Canaanite religion, the high god El convened the council of the gods (see this concept also in 1 Kgs 22:19-23; Job 1:6-12; and perhaps Ps 58:1-2). In v. 1, Israel's God has displaced El and convenes what proves to be an extraordinary meeting. Israel's God proceeds to put the gods on trial (see the trial metaphor also in Isa 3:13-15; Hos 4:1-3; Mic 6:1-5). After the gods are indicted and charged (vv. 2-4), the case against them is summarized in v. 5, and the sentence is announced (vv. 6-7). The psalmist then pleads for God to claim the dominion once held by the gods and to rule justly (v. 8). In short, the council of the gods is permanently adjourned, and so Psalm 82 affirms again the message that forms the theological heart of the book of Psalms: God rules the world (see Psalms 2; 29; 47; 93; 95–99; Introduction).

82:1-4. The key issue in the trial of the gods is the way they "judge" (שׁפט *šāpaṭ*, v. 2) or administer "justice" (v. 3; note the two other occurrences of the same Hebrew root—"holds judgment" in v. 1 and "judge" in v. 8). Acting as both prosecutor and judge, God accuses the gods of judging unjustly and showing partiality (v. 2). The inadequacy of such behavior is apparent in Leviticus 19, part of the Holiness Code, as well. There God commands the people of Israel to "not render an unjust judgment" and to "not be partial" (Lev 19:15 NRSV). Indeed, Lev 19:2 exhorts, "You shall be holy, for I the LORD your God am holy" (NRSV). Thus injustice among humans, and certainly among the gods, violates the very nature of divinity and the divine will for the world.

The importance of justice in the human realm is emphasized in vv. 3-4. The series of imperatives functions not to exhort the gods but to indict them. As the series unfolds, it becomes clear that justice is a matter of ordering the human community. In v. 3, "give justice" and "maintain the right" are parallel, just as the nouns "justice" and "righteousness" are frequently parallel (see Amos 5:7, 24; 6:12). Justice and righteousness are not just abstract principles or ideals; rather, they have to do with the very concrete matter of how human beings relate. For the God of Israel, the criterion of justice involves what is done for the weak, the orphaned, the destitute, the needy (see Pss 9:7-9, 18; 10:17-18; 68:5-6; 113:7; 146:7-9). Not surprisingly, justice and righteousness also appear as parallels in the psalms that proclaim God's reign or describe the reign of God's earthly agent, the king (see Pss 72:1-2; 97:2; 99:4; see also 96:10, 13; 98:9). Here again, the establishment of justice and righteousness is the measure of divinity and of human life as God intends it.

Verse 4 allows even more specificity. Justice and righteousness involve the very concrete matter of how power is distributed in the human community, and thus the matter of who has access to life. In biblical terms, only persons whose lives are threatened need to be rescued or delivered. For instance, the psalmists often plead in life-threatening situations for God to rescue them from the wicked (see Pss 17:13; 71:2, 4). The verb "deliver" (נצל *nṣl*) is used to describe what God did to save the Israelites "from the hand of the Egyptians" (Exod 18:9-10 NIV). The word "hand" describes "grasp," or more to the point, "power." The gods should have delivered the weak and needy from the power of the wicked

(v. 4), but it was precisely the wicked to whom the gods have been partial (v. 2). For the God of Israel, things are right in the human community when power is distributed in a way that all persons, especially the powerless, have access to the resources that enable them to live.

82:5. The speaker in v. 5 could be interpreted as the psalmist acting as narrator, but it is more likely that God continues to speak here. The "they" in v. 5 refers to the gods, and the case against them is summarized. The result of their ignorance and failure is disastrous. The shaking of "all the foundations of the earth" represents a worst-case scenario. In the ancient view of the world, the mountains were the foundations that held up the sky and held back the waters from flooding dry land. The shaking of the foundations meant that the whole creation was threatened by the return of chaos (see Isa 24:18-19; Ps 46:1-3). In short, v. 5 suggests that injustice destroys the world! Where injustice exists, the world—at least

the world as God intends it—falls apart. L. K. Handy argues that v. 5 is the structural center of Psalm 82, and its claim is certainly of central importance.[317]

82:6-7. Because the gods have failed to do justice, they are guilty of destroying human life and community as God intends them. Thus they deserve to die (vv. 6-7).

82:8. The death of the gods opens the way for God's reign of justice, for which the psalmist prays in v. 8 (see "rise up" in Pss 3:7; 9:19; 10:12). Having affirmed God's sovereignty, the psalmist also prays for and awaits God's rule; that is, the perspective is eschatological (see Commentary on Psalm 2; Introduction). But the psalmist is sure of the outcome. The final "you" is an emphatic pronoun; *God* rules the nations and the cosmos.

317. L. K. Handy, "Sounds, Words, and Meanings in Psalm 82," *JSOT* 47 (1990) 62-63.

REFLECTIONS

Psalm 82 raises the question of how we are to hear such an overtly mythological text in our very different world. The first step is to approach the psalm as a poetic expression of faith rather than a literal description of a trial in heaven. The truth of the psalm's message lies in its ability to illumine reality, which it does in a remarkable way—so much so that in our day, and with our distance from the ancient Near Eastern worldview, it is possible for us to appreciate the psalmist's conviction that injustice destroys the world. Indeed, we see it happening all around us—in our cities and neighborhoods, in our schools and churches and homes. That the foundations of the earth are still shaking reinforces that Psalm 82 does not literally describe the death of the gods, but instead denies ultimacy to any claim on our lives other than God's claim. The apostle Paul said it well in 1 Cor 8:5-6: "Indeed, even though there may be so-called gods in heaven or on earth—as in fact there are many gods and many lords—yet for us there is one God, the Father, from whom are all things and for whom we exist, and one Lord, Jesus Christ, through whom are all things and through whom we exist" (NRSV). Paul also refers to these so-called gods as "the rulers and authorities" (Eph 3:10; Col 2:15; see RSV "the principalities and powers"). These "rulers and authorities" are still with us in diverse forms—wherever and whenever anyone benefits from denying the God-given humanity of others. As Mays suggests, "As long as nations and their peoples do not see the reign of God as the reality that determines their way and destiny, there will be other gods who play that role."[318]

While such gods are still with us, Psalm 82 affirms, in Paul's words, that "for us there is one God." J. P. M. Walsh argues that the Canaanite polytheistic system elevated economic survival to ultimacy at the expense of compassion.[319] Thus the religion of the gods legitimated

318. Mays, *Psalms,* 271.
319. J. P. M. Walsh, *The Mighty from Their Thrones: Power in the Biblical Tradition* (Philadelphia: Fortress, 1987) see esp. chap. 2.

a hierarchical social system in which those at the top prospered and those at the bottom suffered. The religion of the one God, the God of Israel, countered by affirming that God's very nature is compassion. The faith of Israel was founded on the conviction that the one God hears the cries of victims and acts to deliver them from death to life (see Exod 3:7). The followers of the one God became an alternative community on the ancient Near Eastern scene. For them, the gods were dead.

For Christians, all rulers and authorities other than the one God have been dethroned; the gods are dead. We profess to live solely under the rule of God, which Jesus announced and embodied in a ministry of justice and righteousness, directed especially to the weak and to the needy. (See John 8:34-38, where Jesus cites Ps 82:6 in defense of his claim to be one with God on the basis of doing God's works; the sense of the argument depends on the Jewish custom of understanding "gods" in 82:6 as the people of Israel rather than divine beings.) We cannot help hearing the plea of v. 8 in terms of the prayer Jesus taught his disciples: "Your kingdom come. Your will be done, *on earth* as it is in heaven" (Matt 6:10 NRSV, italics added).

PSALM 83:1-18, LET YOUR ENEMIES KNOW

NIV

Psalm 83

A song. A psalm of Asaph.

¹O God, do not keep silent;
  be not quiet, O God, be not still.
²See how your enemies are astir,
  how your foes rear their heads.
³With cunning they conspire against your
    people;
  they plot against those you cherish.
⁴"Come," they say, "let us destroy them as a
    nation,
  that the name of Israel be remembered no
    more."
⁵With one mind they plot together;
  they form an alliance against you—
⁶the tents of Edom and the Ishmaelites,
  of Moab and the Hagrites,
⁷Gebal,ᵃ Ammon and Amalek,
  Philistia, with the people of Tyre.
⁸Even Assyria has joined them
  to lend strength to the descendants
    of Lot.   *Selah*

⁹Do to them as you did to Midian,
  as you did to Sisera and Jabin at the river
    Kishon,
¹⁰who perished at Endor

NRSV

Psalm 83

A Song. A Psalm of Asaph.

¹ O God, do not keep silence;
  do not hold your peace or be still, O God!
² Even now your enemies are in tumult;
  those who hate you have raised their
    heads.
³ They lay crafty plans against your people;
  they consult together against those you
    protect.
⁴ They say, "Come, let us wipe them out as
    a nation;
  let the name of Israel be remembered no
    more."
⁵ They conspire with one accord;
  against you they make a covenant—
⁶ the tents of Edom and the Ishmaelites,
  Moab and the Hagrites,
⁷ Gebal and Ammon and Amalek,
  Philistia with the inhabitants of Tyre;
⁸ Assyria also has joined them;
  they are the strong arm of the children
    of Lot.   *Selah*

⁹ Do to them as you did to Midian,
  as to Sisera and Jabin at the Wadi Kishon,

NIV

and became like refuse on the ground.
[11]Make their nobles like Oreb and Zeeb,
all their princes like Zebah and Zalmunna,
[12]who said, "Let us take possession
of the pasturelands of God."

[13]Make them like tumbleweed, O my God,
like chaff before the wind.
[14]As fire consumes the forest
or a flame sets the mountains ablaze,
[15]so pursue them with your tempest
and terrify them with your storm.
[16]Cover their faces with shame
so that men will seek your name, O LORD.

[17]May they ever be ashamed and dismayed;
may they perish in disgrace.
[18]Let them know that you, whose name is the
LORD—
that you alone are the Most High over all
the earth.

a7 That is, Byblos

NRSV

[10] who were destroyed at En-dor,
who became dung for the ground.
[11] Make their nobles like Oreb and Zeeb,
all their princes like Zebah and Zalmunna,
[12] who said, "Let us take the pastures of God
for our own possession."

[13] O my God, make them like whirling dust,[a]
like chaff before the wind.
[14] As fire consumes the forest,
as the flame sets the mountains ablaze,
[15] so pursue them with your tempest
and terrify them with your hurricane.
[16] Fill their faces with shame,
so that they may seek your name, O LORD.
[17] Let them be put to shame and dismayed
forever;
let them perish in disgrace.
[18] Let them know that you alone,
whose name is the LORD,
are the Most High over all the earth.

aOr a tumbleweed

COMMENTARY

Psalm 83 is one of several communal complaints/laments or prayers for help in Book III, which seems to have been shaped by the corporate afflictions of exile (see Psalms 74; 79; 80; Introduction). While Book III clearly reflects the experience of suffering, it also articulates the experience of God's nearness (see Ps 73:28) and a hope deriving from trust in God's sovereignty (see Pss 74:12-17; 76:7-9; 82:8). Psalm 83 does the same thing. Following the opening petition (v. 1), which already implies a crisis, the threat is described (vv. 2-5) and the enemies are named (vv. 6-8). Petition resumes in v. 9. Verses 9-12 appeal to past instances of help, while vv. 13-18 ask for vengeance upon the enemies that will demonstrate God's universal sovereignty (v. 18).

Whether Psalm 83 actually originated as a response to exile is not certain. If so, it is striking that the list of peoples and countries in vv. 6-8 does not include Babylon. Some commentators take the mention of Assyria as a primary clue to dating the psalm between the ninth and seventh

centuries BCE; however, the name may have been intended to function symbolically, and thus many commentators suggest a post-exilic origin for the psalm. Certainty is impossible. Israel lived under persistent threat, and the psalm would have been a timely prayer at many critical points, but especially during the exile and beyond.

83:1. The threefold opening plea recalls similar petitions in other prayers for help (see Pss 28:1; 35:22; 109:1), and God's saving presence is elsewhere described as God's not keeping silence (see Ps 50:3; Isa 62:1-2, 6-7). The NRSV preserves the chiastic structure (see Introduction) of the verse, with "God" being the first and last word. While perhaps coincidental, this structure itself may imply the confidence that God surrounds the psalmist's pleas even as hostile nations apparently gather to surround Israel (vv. 6-8).

83:2-5. These verses describe the crisis. The enemies are first designated as God's enemies, and, as threatening foes are described elsewhere, here too they are "in tumult" (v. 2; see also Ps

46:6; Jer 6:22) as they assert their own sovereignty (see the idiom of raising the head in Judg 8:28). Verses 2-3 are reminiscent of Psalm 2, and the NRSV's "plans" (סוד *sôd*) in v. 3 represents a Hebrew root that is similar to the one that appears as "take counsel together" in Ps 2:2. As the NIV indicates, the verb "plot" (יעץ *yāʿaṣ*) occurs in vv. 3*b*, 5*a*. Elsewhere, it is God who plots or makes plans against nations (see Isa 19:17; Jer 49:20), but here the nations assert themselves against God and God's people. Between the repeated verb in vv. 3*b*, 5*a*, v. 4 indicates the enemies' intent to obliterate Israel (see Jer 11:19).

83:6-8. The list of enemies in these verses is unusual in the book of Psalms (but see Ps 60:6-8), and its exact origin and purpose remain elusive. The names in vv. 6-7 occur elsewhere in the OT—e.g., Edom (Pss 60:9; 137:7; Isa 34:5-6; 63:1; Ezek 35:1-15); the Ishmaelites (Gen 17:20; 25:18; 37:25-28); Moab (Judg 3:12-30; 1 Sam 14:47; 2 Sam 8:12; 2 Kgs 3:4-24); the Hagrites (1 Chr 5:10, 19-20); Ammon and Amalek (Exod 17:8-15; Judg 3:13; 1 Samuel 15; 2 Kgs 24:2; Jer 41:15); Gebal (Ezek 27:9; see "Giblites" in Josh 13:5; 1 Kgs 5:18, possibly ancient Byblos); Philistia (Exod 15:14; 1 Samuel 4-6; 14; 17; Ps 60:8); Tyre (Isaiah 23; Ezekiel 27–28; Amos 1:9-10). Assyria was a persistent enemy, especially powerful in the eighth and seventh centuries, to which several scholars date Psalm 83. Given the comprehensive and probably hyperbolic character of the list, however, it is likely that Assyria functions as a symbol or stereotypical example of a world power (see Ezra 6:22; Lam 5:6; Zech 10:10). The mention of Edom first may suggest an exilic origin, since Edom was often targeted as a major foe shortly after the exile (see Ps 137:7; Obadiah); however, Edom also was a frequent foe. Tate suggests "the possibility that the peoples listed form a rough circle around Israel, beginning in the south, up the Transjordan region, over to Tyre (and Gebal), and back down the coast to Philistia."[320] In any case, the effect of vv. 6-8 is to indicate that Israel needs major assistance.

83:9-12. The remainder of the psalm indicates to whom Israel looks for help. Verses 9-12 recall

outstanding instances of God's deliverance of the people, focusing on the book of Judges. The narrative in Judges 6–8 goes to great lengths to emphasize that the victory over Midian was a result not of Gideon's leadership but of God's leadership (cf. Judg 8:28 with Ps 83:2*b*). The defeat of Sisera and Jabin (vv. 9*b*-10) recalls Judges 4–5 (on v. 10*b*, see Jer 8:2; 9:22). Verse 11 returns the focus to Midian (see Judg 7:25; 8:15). The story in Judges 6–8 does not record the words (v. 12) attributed to the figures mentioned in v. 11; however, v. 12 recalls v. 4, and the intent seems to be to indicate that the current crisis is on the magnitude of the ancient ones.

83:13-18. The severity of the opposition explains perhaps the vehemence of the prayer as it continues in vv. 13-18. The imagery of v. 13 is similar to that of Ps 1:4; Isa 17:13; 40:24; 41:2; Jer 13:24. Verse 14 recalls Ps 97:3; Isa 10:17-18; 47:14, and the imagery of v. 16 is also used elsewhere to describe God's wrath (see Isa 29:6; Jer 29:13; Hos 8:7; Amos 1:14). The words "terrify" (v. 15) and "dismayed" (v. 17) translate the same Hebrew root (בהל *bāhal*) that is used elsewhere to assert God's sovereignty over enemies of God and the people (see Exod 15:15, which also mentions Edom and Moab; Pss 2:5; 48:5). The verb "perish" (אבד *ʾābad*) also recalls Ps 2:12, where it occurs after the kings and rulers of the nations have been warned to subject themselves to God's rule.

While the petitions in vv. 9-18 are shockingly violent (although we hardly live in a less violent world!), vv. 16 and 18 suggest that the ultimate purpose of God is not to destroy but to reconcile (note the repeated "name" linking the two verses). The personal pronoun "you" provides emphasis on God's sovereign claims (v. 18*a*) and recalls the final verse of Psalm 82 as well (see "earth" also in Pss 82:8; 83:18). What God wills is that all the earth "know"—that is, recognize who truly rules the world (see Exod 5:2; 7:5; 14:4, 18; 1 Kgs 8:43; Ps 79:6, 10; see also Exod 9:16). The result will be a reign of justice and righteousness that characterizes God's rule as opposed to the rule of autonomous nations or the rule of the gods (see Psalm 82; Isa 2:1-4; Mic 4:1-3). Such constitutes the will of God.

320. Marvin E. Tate, *Psalms 51–100*, WBC 20 (Dallas: Word, 1990) 347.

REFLECTIONS

Psalm 83 is eschatological; its real purpose is to pray for and express trust in the fulfillment of God's reign over all the earth (v. 18) in the midst of opposition (see Commentary on Psalm 2; Introduction). To be sure, the prayer for deliverance from violent oppressors uses the language and imagery of violence. This in itself constitutes a valuable lesson, for it illustrates how persons are likely to respond when they have been victimized (see vv. 4, 12; see also Reflections on Psalms 109; 137). Verses 16 and 18 suggest, however, that the violent imagery is hyperbolic and that the real desire of God's people and God's own self is to enact God's reign of righteousness and justice. This is especially the case when Psalm 83 is heard in conjunction with Psalm 82. But as Psalm 82 also recognizes, God's will for justice and righteousness does not go unopposed. Thus both Psalms 82 and 83 very realistically recognize that oppressors do not give up without a fight. Pharoah, for instance, did not easily bend to the Israelites' request for liberation (see Exodus 1–15). Similarly, political equality for African Americans was achieved only by a long and costly struggle, and the white minority government of South Africa did not agree to dismantle apartheid without a prolonged and bitter fight.

Because of this recognition, the metaphor of God as divine warrior is appealed to by threatened people (see Exodus 1–15; Deuteronomy 32; Pss 66:3; 68:1, 21; 74:4, 18-23; 89:10). While the metaphor is understandable in the context of violent oppression, it can nonetheless be dangerous. Mays comments: "It is of course venturesome and dangerous for the people of God to see those who threaten them as enemies of God and to invoke God's vengeance against them. Such prayers can easily become the language of a self-serving, blind ideology."[321] This warning means that Psalm 83 finally calls the people of God themselves to humility—to humble enactment of God's ways of justice and righteousness.

Some may suggest that the violent imagery of Psalm 83 and its prayer for vengeance render it unusable for Christians. Properly warned, however, the church can hear this psalm as a cogent reminder that the reign of God and the divine purposes have never gone and never go unopposed. Israel knew this, of course, as did Jesus, Paul, and the early church. We should know it, too, for the contemporary world is hardly less inclined to violence than was the ancient world or more inclined to enact God's will for justice, righteousness, and peace. As Mays concludes: "Modern history is punctuated with attempts by secularized powers to dispossess the people of the LORD in both synagogue and church. Psalm 83 is in the psalter as the prayer of his people whose existence is the work of his reign and who leave the vengeance to God (see Psalm 94)."[322] In short, in our world of violence and oppression, we still pray as Psalms 82–83 suggest and as Jesus taught us: "Your kingdom come. Your will be done" (Matt 6:10 NRSV).

321. Mays, *Psalms,* 273.
322. Ibid., 273.

PSALM 84:1-12, HAPPY ARE THOSE WHOSE STRENGTH IS IN YOU

NIV	NRSV
Psalm 84	Psalm 84
For the director of music. According to *gittith.*[a] Of the Sons of Korah. A psalm.	To the leader: according to The Gittith. Of the Korahites. A Psalm.
a Title: Probably a musical term	¹ How lovely is your dwelling place,

NIV

¹How lovely is your dwelling place,
   O LORD Almighty!
²My soul yearns, even faints,
   for the courts of the LORD;
my heart and my flesh cry out
   for the living God.

³Even the sparrow has found a home,
   and the swallow a nest for herself,
   where she may have her young—
a place near your altar,
   O LORD Almighty, my King and my God.
⁴Blessed are those who dwell in your house;
   they are ever praising you.   *Selah*

⁵Blessed are those whose strength is in you,
   who have set their hearts on pilgrimage.
⁶As they pass through the Valley of Baca,
   they make it a place of springs;
   the autumn rains also cover it with pools.*ᵃ*
⁷They go from strength to strength,
   till each appears before God in Zion.

⁸Hear my prayer, O LORD God Almighty;
   listen to me, O God of Jacob.   *Selah*
⁹Look upon our shield,*ᵇ* O God;
   look with favor on your anointed one.

¹⁰Better is one day in your courts
   than a thousand elsewhere;
I would rather be a doorkeeper in the house
      of my God
   than dwell in the tents of the wicked.
¹¹For the LORD God is a sun and shield;
   the LORD bestows favor and honor;
no good thing does he withhold
   from those whose walk is blameless.

¹²O LORD Almighty,
   blessed is the man who trusts in you.

ᵃ6 Or blessings   ᵇ9 Or sovereign

NRSV

   O LORD of hosts!
² My soul longs, indeed it faints
   for the courts of the LORD;
my heart and my flesh sing for joy
   to the living God.

³ Even the sparrow finds a home,
   and the swallow a nest for herself,
   where she may lay her young,
at your altars, O LORD of hosts,
   my King and my God.
⁴ Happy are those who live in your house,
   ever singing your praise.   *Selah*

⁵ Happy are those whose strength is in you,
   in whose heart are the highways to Zion.*ᵃ*
⁶ As they go through the valley of Baca
   they make it a place of springs;
   the early rain also covers it with pools.
⁷ They go from strength to strength;
   the God of gods will be seen in Zion.

⁸ O LORD God of hosts, hear my prayer;
   give ear, O God of Jacob!   *Selah*
⁹ Behold our shield, O God;
   look on the face of your anointed.

¹⁰ For a day in your courts is better
   than a thousand elsewhere.
I would rather be a doorkeeper in the
      house of my God
   than live in the tents of wickedness.
¹¹ For the LORD God is a sun and shield;
   he bestows favor and honor.
No good thing does the LORD withhold
   from those who walk uprightly.
¹² O LORD of hosts,
   happy is everyone who trusts in you.

ᵃHeb lacks to Zion

COMMENTARY

Psalm 84 is perhaps the most expressive and beautiful of all the songs of Zion (see Psalms 46; 48; 76; 87; 122). Like the others, it may originally have been recited or sung by pilgrims as they made their way toward, arrived at, or walked about Jerusalem. Verse 1 seems to offer the psalm-ist's enthusiastic response upon first seeing the city or the Temple, an experience that the psalm-ist reflects on in v. 2. Verses 3-4 are linked by the repetition of the word "home"/"house" (בית *bayit*), which may derive from the psalmist's contemplation of the happiness of the priests and other cultic personnel who resided in the Temple. The word "happy" (אשרי 'ašrê) becomes a key word in the psalm (see vv. 4, 5, 12), and vv. 5-7 extend the experience to the pilgrims who will see God in Zion. Verses 8-9 consist of petition. Verse 10 shifts from direct address of God to reference to God in the third person; and with v. 11, the psalm has the character of a profession of faith. The profession is made explicit in the concluding verse, which at least implicitly invites others to share in the psalmist's experience of God. The two initial and concluding sections (vv. 1-4, 8-12) each consist of seven poetic lines. While this may be coincidental, the effect is to focus attention on vv. 5-7 as the central unit, thus highlighting the experience of the pilgrim. It may not be coincidental that v. 5 begins with the word "happy," which is featured in the concluding verses of the surrounding sections. By the end of the poem, the beatitudes in vv. 4-5, 12 have constructed a compelling portrait of a faithful follower of God.

The canonical placement of Psalm 84 is worthy of note. It occurs immediately following a psalm that concludes both the Asaph psalms (Psalms 50; 73–83; see Introduction) and the Elohistic psalter (Psalms 42–83). Even though Psalms 84–85 and 87–88 are psalms of Korah (see also Psalms 42–49, the beginning of the Elohistic psalter), they do not significantly change the character of Book III. Psalms 84 and 87, both songs of Zion, recall Psalm 76, and each is sandwiched between complaints that effectively call for deeper understanding—that is, how should the enthusiastic hope and trust of the Zion songs be understood in view of the stark realities voiced in the complaints? This question, prompted by the ordering of psalms in Book III (see Commentary on Psalms 73; 74; 78; 79; 80; Introduction), encourages an eschatological understanding of Psalm 84. In short, its use was not restricted to ancient pilgrims to Jerusalem. Rather, it effectively articulates the experience of generations of pilgrims, who, trusting God (v. 12), have "seen" God (v. 7) in various times and places and have derived from their experience of God a strength that transforms them and their lives (vv. 5-7; see Reflections below).

84:1-4. The translation "lovely" (ידידות yĕdîdôt) in v. 1 is adequate, because the psalmist's experience involves visual admiration of Zion, but the experience creates a bond between person and place that might be better expressed with the

word "beloved" (see the Hebrew word translated here as "dwelling place" [משכנות miškānôt] in Pss 43:3; 46:4; 132:5, 7). The title "LORD of hosts" is associated elsewhere with the ark, God's earthly throne (see Commentary on Psalm 24, esp. the discussion of vv. 7-10), and it occurs elsewhere in contexts where God is addressed as "King" (v. 3; see also Ps 48:8; Isa 6:5). Verse 2a further communicates the power of the place (see "courts" also in v. 10; Pss 65:4; 96:8; 100:4; 116:19; 135:2; Isa 1:12; 62:9), for which the psalmist "longs" (see Gen 31:30, where Jacob longs for his father's house, and note "home"/"house" in Ps 84:3-4) and "faints" (see "fail" in Ps 73:26; 119:81). As v. 2b indicates, the place derives its power from the presence of "the living God" (see Ps 42:2, where longing for God is also eloquently expressed but with different vocabulary and imagery). The verb in v. 2b usually indicates a joyful cry (see Pss 5:11; 67:4; 95:1; 96:12; 98:4), but it occasionally has a more plaintive sense (see Lam 2:19).

As Gen 31:30 suggests, longing is what one naturally feels for home. In other words, the psalmist is homesick for the true home: God's house. The sight of birds nesting within the temple complex (v. 3) and of the cultic officials at work leads the psalmist to reflect upon the appropriateness of literally finding a "home" in the Temple (see Pss 23:5-6; 27:4). The address of God as "my King," along with the repetition of the phrase "LORD of hosts" from v. 1 (see also vv. 8, 12), suggests that the psalmist's praise is not ultimately of the place but of God. The experience of the particular place puts the psalmist in touch with God's sovereignty over all places (see Commentary on Psalm 48).

84:5-7. The transformational power of Jerusalem is evident in the affirmations of vv. 5-7. The noun "strength" (עז 'ōz) indicates elsewhere an attribute of the sovereign God (see Exod 15:13; Pss 29:1; 93:1; 96:6-7), but it is also regularly imparted to God's people (see Exod 15:2; Pss 29:11; 68:35; 81:1; 86:16). Here the psalmist apparently claims that God bestows strength upon those traveling to Jerusalem, although the sense of v. 5b is uncertain (see NRSV note and cf. NRSV and NIV). Verse 6 also seems to connote transformation, although the precise sense is again unclear. "Baca" [בכא] is usually taken as a proper noun. Its location is unknown, but apparently it was a dry place, to which the pilgrims bring relief. The word is similar to the word בכי (běkî), which means "tears," in which case another sort of transformation is suggested. The mention of springs and rain may imply a connection with pilgrimage to the Feast of Tabernacles, which is associated elsewhere with rain (see Zech 14:16-19). Such a conclusion is uncertain, however, and it is possible to read the whole verse symbolically. The final form of the Hebrew text actually encourages this, since it has vocalized a set of consonants that could mean "pools" (ברכה běrēkôt) so that they mean "blessings" (běrākôt). In short, wherever the pilgrims go, they bring blessings. Enlivened and empowered by the vision of God's awaiting them (v. 8; see "saw"/"seen" in Ps 48:5, 8) or perhaps by the hope of being seen by God (see v. 9), the pilgrims gain strength (the Hebrew words differ in vv. 5 and 7; see also 1 Sam 2:4). They themselves are transformed.

84:8-12. Verses 8-9 move to petition, and apparently the pilgrim prays for the king. The word "shield" (מגן māgēn) which is used of God in v. 12 (see also Ps 3:3), can also be used of human rulers (see Ps 47:9), and the word "anointed" refers even more clearly to the king (see Ps 2:2). In the post-exilic era, the "anointed" (משיח māšîaḥ) could also have referred to the high priest (see Num 3:3). In either case, it would have been natural for those visiting Jerusalem to pray for the leaders of the people (see Ps 61:6-7).

Verses 10-11 again return to the psalmist's own experience (see vv. 1-4; note "courts" in v. 2 and "home"/"house" in vv. 3-4). The poetic hyperbole in v. 10*a* expresses the same longing as in v. 2. In v. 10*b,* "doorkeeper" probably does not refer to the office of that description (see 2 Kgs

12:9), but to anyone waiting to enter the Temple. Kraus translates as follows, "I would rather lie on the threshold at the house of my God than live in the tents of the wicked."[323] The "tents of the wicked" need not refer to a specific place, but to any place characterized by self-serving rather than to the service of God (see discussion of "the wicked" in Commentary on Psalm 1). To await entrance into God's house, by contrast, means to be one "whose walk is blameless" (v. 11). It is significant that precisely this kind of person is mentioned in Ps 15:2 in response to the question in 15:1, "Who may dwell on your holy hill?" To walk blamelessly does not mean absolute perfection but humble dependence upon God for life. Or, as v. 12 suggests, it means ultimately to trust God (see Ps 40:4 and the essentially synonymous beatitudes in Pss 2:12; 34:8*b*). Verse 11 articulates the content of this trust as the psalmist affirms God's providing "favor" and "honor" (see Prov 3:34-35, where these two words also occur together)—everything necessary for the sustenance of life. The same Hebrew word (טוב ṭôb) underlies "better" (v. 10) and "good thing" (v. 11), thus framing the two verses. The confidence expressed is not in a retributional scheme whereby good things are guaranteed as a reward. Neither is the happiness promised a facile or carefree cheeriness. Rather, happiness consists of taking refuge in God (see Pss 2:12; 73:28; note 84:5, 7), and the repetition of "good" recalls the affirmation of Ps 73:28 that ultimate goodness is to be near God (see also Ps 63:3). In a word, this is also the message that pervades Psalm 84.

323. H.-J. Kraus, *Psalms 1–59: A Commentary,* trans. H. C. Oswald (Minneapolis: Augsburg, 1988) 166.

REFLECTIONS

1. One of the most beautiful of contemporary musical arrangements of the psalms is "How Lovely, Lord," a metrical paraphrase of Psalm 84 by Arlo D. Duba that has been set to music by Hal H. Hopson (*Merle's Tune*). The auspicious wedding of text and tune captures movingly both the psalmist's longing for communion with God and the experience of well-being that results from encountering the living God. In other words, although our symbols for and understandings of God's presence in space and time may differ from those of the ancient psalmist, Psalm 84 can continue to function effectively and powerfully.

2. Citing Jon Levenson's conclusion that in Psalm 84 "physical ascent is also a spiritual ascent," Tate suggests that the pilgrimage experience described in Psalm 84 is sacramental—"visible actions become the means of grace and revelation of the presence of God."[324] For Christians, the visible actions may differ, but we still regularly engage in visible actions that we profess to be means of grace, modes of experiencing God's real presence and of finding our true home. For instance, we come regularly to what forms the centerpiece of any real home: a table. But for us, this is the Lord's table, where we eat and drink with Christ and with one another as a sign of our belonging. At the Lord's table we not only remember but are also re-membered; that is, we profess to receive a strength that derives not from ourselves but from God (see vv. 5, 7). In essence, as Psalm 23 suggests as well, church is home (see Commentary on Psalm 23, esp. discussion of vv. 5-6).

And so we go to church to profess that our lives are not our own but are lived under God's sovereign claim (see vv. 3-4; see also Reflections on Psalms 46; 100). We go to church to profess that insofar as we are powerful people, our strength derives not from ourselves but from God (see vv. 5, 7). We go to church to profess that our worthiness, insofar as we have any, derives not from what we manage to accomplish but from what God bestows (vv. 10-11). We go to church to profess that happiness is not the ceaseless pursuit of material well-being that our culture promotes but the entrusting of our lives and futures to God (see v. 12). As Mays suggests:

> Every visit to a temple or church or meeting of believers is in a profound sense a pilgrimage. We "go" [see v. 7 and the same Hebrew word translated "walk" in v. 11], not just for practical or personal reasons; we go theologically. Christians have read and sung Psalm 84 and through it praised the God to whom we "go" in different ways.[325]

Psalm 84 thus proclaims the good news that our destination, daily and eternally, lies in God. This good news contains the transforming power by which we profess to find strength, value, and life itself (see Commentary on Psalm 48).

324. Marvin E. Tate, *Psalms 51-100*, WBC 20 (Dallas: Word, 1990) 362; see Jon D. Levenson, *Sinai and Zion: An Entry into the Jewish Bible* (San Francisco: Harper & Row, 1985) 178.
325. James L. Mays, *Psalms*, Interpretation (Louisville: John Knox, 1994) 275.

PSALM 85:1-13, SURELY GOD'S SALVATION IS NEAR

Psalm 85

For the director of music. Of the Sons of Korah. A psalm.

¹You showed favor to your land, O LORD;
  you restored the fortunes of Jacob.
²You forgave the iniquity of your people
  and covered all their sins.   *Selah*
³You set aside all your wrath
  and turned from your fierce anger.

⁴Restore us again, O God our Savior,
  and put away your displeasure toward us.

Psalm 85

To the leader. Of the Korahites. A Psalm.

¹ LORD, you were favorable to your land;
  you restored the fortunes of Jacob.
² You forgave the iniquity of your people;
  you pardoned all their sin.   *Selah*
³ You withdrew all your wrath;
  you turned from your hot anger.

⁴ Restore us again, O God of our salvation,
  and put away your indignation toward us.
⁵ Will you be angry with us forever?

NIV

⁵Will you be angry with us forever?
    Will you prolong your anger through all
        generations?
⁶Will you not revive us again,
    that your people may rejoice in you?
⁷Show us your unfailing love, O LORD,
    and grant us your salvation.

⁸I will listen to what God the LORD will say;
    he promises peace to his people, his
        saints—
    but let them not return to folly.
⁹Surely his salvation is near those who fear
        him,
    that his glory may dwell in our land.

¹⁰Love and faithfulness meet together;
    righteousness and peace kiss each other.
¹¹Faithfulness springs forth from the earth,
    and righteousness looks down from heaven.
¹²The LORD will indeed give what is good,
    and our land will yield its harvest.
¹³Righteousness goes before him
    and prepares the way for his steps.

NRSV

Will you prolong your anger to all
        generations?
⁶ Will you not revive us again,
    so that your people may rejoice in you?
⁷ Show us your steadfast love, O LORD,
    and grant us your salvation.

⁸ Let me hear what God the LORD will speak,
    for he will speak peace to his people,
    to his faithful, to those who turn to him
        in their hearts.ᵃ
⁹ Surely his salvation is at hand for those
        who fear him,
    that his glory may dwell in our land.

¹⁰ Steadfast love and faithfulness will meet;
    righteousness and peace will kiss each
        other.
¹¹ Faithfulness will spring up from the ground,
    and righteousness will look down from
        the sky.
¹² The LORD will give what is good,
    and our land will yield its increase.
¹³ Righteousness will go before him,
    and will make a path for his steps.

ᵃ Gk: Heb *but let them not turn back to folly*

COMMENTARY

Another of the communal prayers for help or laments/complaints that give Book III a particular character (see Psalms 74; 79; 80; 83; 89; Introduction), Psalm 85 is known primarily for its striking portrayal of God's promise of peace and salvation in vv. 8-13. The promise is delivered in the midst of current distress (vv. 4-7) that has followed a more favorable time (vv. 1-3). This sequence means that Psalm 85 makes especially good sense as a corporate prayer for help in the early post-exilic era. Indeed, the phrase "restored the fortunes" (שוב שבית *šûb šĕbît*, v. 1), is often used to describe Israel's return from exile (see Jer 30:3, 18; 31:23; 33:7, 11; Ezek 39:25). Furthermore, the prophet of the exile proclaimed that God had forgiven the people (Isa 40:1-2; see also Ps 85:2-3) and brought them home; but the glorious vision of Isaiah 40–55 did not materialize.

The prophet Haggai lamented the people's failure to rebuild the Temple, and using the same verb as in Ps 85:1*a* ("showed favor" [רצה *rāṣâ*]), he suggests that this failure accounts for the lack of God's favor in the early restoration era (520 BCE; see Hag 1:8). Perhaps not coincidentally, the deficiencies Haggai detected are the very things promised in Ps 85:8-13. The "glory" of God did not dwell in the Temple (see Hag 2:7, 9; cf. Ps 85:9). The land yielded no crops (Hag 1:10; cf. Ps 85:12). There was no peace (Hag 2:9; cf. Ps 85:8, 10). In short, Psalm 85 may well have originated as a prayer of the people amid the disappointing circumstances of the early post-exilic era (see also Zech 1:12-17). The people had recently been restored (v. 1), but they soon found themselves again in need of restoration (v. 4; see also Ps 80:3, 7, 14, 19).

85:1-7. In terms of the above scenario, the relatively rapid change of fortune that necessitated the petitions of vv. 4-7 is not really surprising in the light of Israel's history. For instance, shortly after the deliverance from Egypt, the people's idolatry necessitated Moses' prayer that God "turn from your fierce anger" (Exod 32:12 NIV; see also Ps 85:3, 5). Moses' petition is accompanied by his reminder to God of the promise of land (Exod 32:13; see Ps 85:8-13, and note especially the mention of "land"/"ground" in vv. 1, 9, 11-12). God does indeed "turn" (שוב šûb; see Ps 85:3; the same Hebrew verb also underlies "restore[d]" in vv. 1, 4 and "again" in v. 6), allowing the people to live and finally revealing the divine character to consist of steadfast love and faithfulness (Exod 34:6; see also Ps 85:7, 10-11). The pronoun "you" in v. 6a is emphatic; it is God who must give life (see Ps 80:18).

The affinities between Psalm 85 and Exodus 32–34 do not necessarily indicate another historical setting for Psalm 85, but they do demonstrate that Psalm 85 is an appropriate prayer for a variety of circumstances. While the phrase "restored the fortunes" suggests the likelihood of a post-exilic prayer, it can indicate more generally any "reversal of Yahweh's judgment."[326] Like Psalm 126, which also contains the phrase in v. 1 and then petitions for further restoration (Ps 126:4; see also 85:4), Psalm 85 is perpetually appropriate for the people of God. That is to say, the people of God always stand in need of salvation (note how "salvation" in vv. 4, 7 frames the section of petition; see also v. 9; Exod 15:2; Pss 24:5; 25:5; 27:1, 9; 51:14; 95:1; 118:25).

85:8-13. The gifts prayed for in vv. 4, 7—

steadfast love and salvation—are promised in vv. 8-13. An individual voice, perhaps that of a prophet or liturgical preacher (see Commentary on Psalms 50; 81), delivers the good news of peace (v. 8ab) and calls for a response (v. 8c). God's "salvation is at hand" (v. 9), and steadfast love is one of the four personified attributes in v. 10. In a sense, the gifts are conditional; God's salvation will be experienced by those who fear God (v. 9; see also v. 8c; Commentary on Psalm 103). But in a deeper sense, the remarkable description in vv. 10-13 exceeds any possibility of human merit or accomplishment. The focus is clearly on God's character and activity. Steadfast love (vv. 7, 10) and faithfulness (vv. 10-11) are at the heart of God's character (Exod 34:6-7; see also Pss 25:10; 40:10-11; 57:3; 61:7; 86:15; 89:14; 115:1; 138:2; Introduction). Righteousness (vv. 10, 13) is the fundamental policy that God wills and enacts as sovereign of the universe (see Pss 96:13; 97:2; 98:9), and the result is "peace" (שלום šālôm; vv. 8, 10; see also Pss 29:11; 35:27; Isa 60:17; Ezek 34:25). God's character and activity will fill the universe, from ground to sky (v. 11; see also Ps 36:5-6). The repetition of "righteousness" (צדק ṣedeq) emphasizes the point: God *will* set things right. The vivid poetic description affirms, in essence, that God will be with and for the people; God's "glory," symbolic of God's presence, will "dwell in our land" (v. 9; see also Exod 33:18, 33; Ps 97:6; Isa 40:5; 60:1-2; Ezek 43:2). And, as previous psalms have made clear, the experience of God's presence is the essence of "what is good" (v. 12; see also Pss 73:28; 84:10-11). For similar descriptions of God's presence and its effects, see Pss 43:3; 89:14; Isa 32:16-18; 45:8; 58:8-9.

326. John Bracke, "*šûb šebût*: A Reappraisal," *ZAW* 97 (1985) 242.

Reflections

It is a revealing observation about Psalm 85 that it was a major inspiration both to the contemplative Thomas à Kempis, who relied on it heavily in the third book of *The Imitation of Christ,* and to the militant activist Oliver Cromwell, who found it "instructive and significant" as he proclaimed his intent that seventeenth-century England embody the reign of God on earth.[327] In other words, Psalm 85, especially vv. 8-13, captures the reality that Christians *already* know and experience in Jesus Christ, but that exists amid the ongoing brokenness of

327. See Rowland E. Prothero, *The Psalms in Human Life and Experience* (New York: E. P. Dutton, 1903) 76-77, 190, 196.

the world and the sinfulness of persons and of our society. Thus, as Mays points out: "The vision has an eschatological reach. It needs the coming of God himself to realize it fully (vv. 9, 13). The psalm therefore is a judgment on any easy satisfaction with life under the conditions created by human character and a summons to look for and pray for the time and life created by the character of God."[328]

For Christians, of course, the birth of Jesus Christ was the very coming of God, and his ministry was an embodiment of love, righteousness, faithfulness, and peace (see John 1:16-17; 14:27; Rom 1:16-17; 1 Cor 1:30). In short, we already know and experience salvation in Christ. But Christ promised to come again, and Christ taught disciples to continue to pray, "Your kingdom come. Your will be done on earth as it is in heaven" (Matt 6:10 NRSV). Thus Christians also live perpetually awaiting salvation—between the already and the not yet. It is always appropriate that we pray with the psalmist, "Restore us again" (v. 4).

With good reason, Psalm 85 has been traditionally associated with the season of Advent. While Advent is a season of awaiting the celebration of the birth of Jesus, its focus is even more clearly on the second coming of Christ. Thus, by its nature, Advent encourages us both to celebrate salvation and to pray for salvation, as does Psalm 85 (see Commentary on Psalm 126).

328. Mays, *Psalms*, 277-78.

PSALM 86:1-17, YOU ALONE ARE GOD

NIV

Psalm 86

A prayer of David.

[1]Hear, O LORD, and answer me,
  for I am poor and needy.
[2]Guard my life, for I am devoted to you.
  You are my God; save your servant
  who trusts in you.
[3]Have mercy on me, O Lord,
  for I call to you all day long.
[4]Bring joy to your servant,
  for to you, O Lord,
  I lift up my soul.

[5]You are forgiving and good, O Lord,
  abounding in love to all who call to you.
[6]Hear my prayer, O LORD;
  listen to my cry for mercy.
[7]In the day of my trouble I will call to you,
  for you will answer me.

[8]Among the gods there is none like you,
    O Lord;
  no deeds can compare with yours.
[9]All the nations you have made
  will come and worship before you, O Lord;

NRSV

Psalm 86

A Prayer of David.

[1] Incline your ear, O LORD, and answer me,
  for I am poor and needy.
[2] Preserve my life, for I am devoted to you;
  save your servant who trusts in you.
  You are my God; [3]be gracious to me,
    O Lord,
  for to you do I cry all day long.
[4] Gladden the soul of your servant,
  for to you, O Lord, I lift up my soul.
[5] For you, O Lord, are good and forgiving,
  abounding in steadfast love to all who
    call on you.
[6] Give ear, O LORD, to my prayer;
  listen to my cry of supplication.
[7] In the day of my trouble I call on you,
  for you will answer me.

[8] There is none like you among the gods,
    O Lord,
  nor are there any works like yours.
[9] All the nations you have made shall come

NIV

they will bring glory to your name.
[10]For you are great and do marvelous deeds;
you alone are God.

[11]Teach me your way, O LORD,
and I will walk in your truth;
give me an undivided heart,
that I may fear your name.
[12]I will praise you, O Lord my God, with all
my heart;
I will glorify your name forever.
[13]For great is your love toward me;
you have delivered me from the depths of
the grave.[a]

[14]The arrogant are attacking me, O God;
a band of ruthless men seeks my life—
men without regard for you.
[15]But you, O Lord, are a compassionate and
gracious God,
slow to anger, abounding in love and
faithfulness.
[16]Turn to me and have mercy on me;
grant your strength to your servant
and save the son of your maidservant.[b]
[17]Give me a sign of your goodness,
that my enemies may see it and be put to
shame,
for you, O LORD, have helped me and
comforted me.

[a]13 Hebrew Sheol   [b]16 Or save your faithful son

NRSV

and bow down before you, O Lord,
and shall glorify your name.
[10] For you are great and do wondrous things;
you alone are God.
[11] Teach me your way, O LORD,
that I may walk in your truth;
give me an undivided heart to revere
your name.
[12] I give thanks to you, O Lord my God, with
my whole heart,
and I will glorify your name forever.
[13] For great is your steadfast love toward me;
you have delivered my soul from the
depths of Sheol.

[14] O God, the insolent rise up against me;
a band of ruffians seeks my life,
and they do not set you before them.
[15] But you, O Lord, are a God merciful and
gracious,
slow to anger and abounding in steadfast
love and faithfulness.
[16] Turn to me and be gracious to me;
give your strength to your servant;
save the child of your serving girl.
[17] Show me a sign of your favor,
so that those who hate me may see it
and be put to shame,
because you, LORD, have helped me and
comforted me.

COMMENTARY

Psalm 86 stands out in Book III as one of only two individual complaints or prayers for help (see Psalm 88) and the only psalm attributed to David. This, plus the fact that it seems to interrupt a small Korah collection (Psalms 84–85; 87–88), seems to suggest intentional placement; however, the exact reasons are unclear. Given that Book III seems to reflect the experience of the exile and its aftermath (see Commentary on Psalms 73; 74; 85; Introduction), we can at least say that the individual prayer in Psalm 86 would have been a very appropriate one on behalf of the whole people, since Psalm 86 recalls a narrative context in which the people disobeyed and were forgiven (Exodus 32–34).

Because it alludes so often to other psalms and key biblical texts (cf. v. 1b with Pss 40:17; 69:29; 109:22; cf. v. 4b with Pss 25:1; 143:8; cf. v. 11a with Pss 27:11; 143:8; cf. v. 14 with Ps 54:3; cf. vv. 5, 15 with Exod 34:6), the originality of Psalm 86 and the creativity of its author have sometimes been questioned. Psalm 86 demonstrates, however, a unique structure, including the sixfold repetition of the Hebrew pronoun "you" that functions as a structuring device. While it is possible simply to divide the psalm into two (vv. 1-13, 14-17) or three sections (vv. 1-7, 8-13,

14-17), several scholars have detected a chiastic arrangement on some scale (see Introduction). At the simplest level, the complaints and petitions in vv. 1-7 and vv. 14-17 (see esp. vv. 7, 14) surround the hymnic affirmation of vv. 8-13. On a more elaborate scale, G. Giavini has suggested the following outline:

A vv. 1-4 (see "your servant" in vv. 2, 4)
  B vv. 5-6 (see "abounding in steadfast love," v. 5)
    C v. 7 (complaint)
      D vv. 8-10 (see "glorify your name" in v. 9)
        E v. 11 (central verse; note especially "your name")
      D′ vv. 12-13 (see "glorify your name," v. 12)
    C′ v. 14 (complaint)
  B′ v. 15 (see "abounding in steadfast love")
A′ vv. 16-17 (see "your servant," v. 16)[329]

The effect of this structure is to focus attention on the center of the psalm, thus highlighting the concept of God's name (vv. 9, 11-12) or character. The focus on God's character is reinforced by the vocabulary of Psalm 86, which is strongly reminiscent of God's self-revelation in Exod 34:6-7. It is further reinforced by the sixfold repetition of the Hebrew pronoun "you," referring to God (vv. 2, 5, 10, 15, 17). As Brueggemann points out, these occurrences also show a chiastic arrangement. The pronouns in vv. 2 and 17 claim God as belonging to or acting on behalf of the psalmist (note the nearly synonymous verbs for "save" [יָשַׁע *yš*ʿ] in v. 2 and "helped" [עָזַר ʿ*āzar*] in v. 17). The pronouns in vv. 5 and 15 are each accompanied by the title "Lord" as well as by a creedal statement recalling Exod 34:6. At the center is the double occurrence of "you" in v. 10, which proclaims God's exclusive sovereignty.[330] While the structural proposals differ slightly in details, they are similar enough to warrant the conclusion that the poet was intent upon focusing the reader's attention on the center of the psalm—v. 10 or v. 11, or perhaps the two together.

329. See Tate, *Psalms 51–100,* 377-78.
330. Walter Brueggemann, *The Message of the Psalms: A Theological Commentary* (Minneapolis: Augsburg, 1984) 62-63.

86:1-7. Immediately following the opening plea (see Ps 17:5), the psalmist includes herself or himself among those for whom God has special concern (see Ps 9:9, 18; 10:12; 82:2-3). The word "devoted" (חָסִיד *ḥāsîd*) in v. 2 is from the same Hebrew root as the word "steadfast love" (חֶסֶד *ḥesed,* vv. 5, 13, 15), suggesting that the psalmist's identity is bound up with God's identity. In essence, the psalmist belongs to God, an identity also suggested by the repeated phrase "your servant" (vv. 2, 4, 16). Only God can "save" (see Pss 3:8; 6:4)—that is, give life—so the psalmist entrusts her or his life to God (v. 2*b*; see Pss 4:5; 9:10; Introduction). Or, as the final phrase in v. 4*b* could be translated, "I offer you my life" (see Commentary on Psalm 25, esp. discussion of v. 1; see also Ps 143:8).

The psalmist's life is secure with God because of the way God is. So the focus in vv. 1-7 is not only on the psalmist's identity but also on God's identity, as suggested by the first two occurrences of the emphatic "you" (vv. 2*b,* 5*a*). Petitions in vv. 3, 6 appeal to one crucial attribute of God that is mentioned in Exod 34:6: mercy (see "gracious" in Exod 33:19; 34:6). Other key aspects of God's identity are clustered in Ps 86:5—goodness (see Exod 33:19; Pss 54:11; 85:12), willingness to forgive (see Exod 34:9), abundant steadfast love (see Exod 34:6-7; Ps 5:7; Introduction). Because God is merciful, good, forgiving, and loving, the psalmist appeals to God for life, and by v. 7, the repeated verb "answer" (עָנָה ʿ*ānâ*; see v. 1) indicates the psalmist's growing assurance.

86:8-13. The focus is even more clearly on God's identity in vv. 8-13, beginning with a proclamation of the incomparability of God's being (v. 8*a*; see also Exod 15:11; Ps 35:10) and activity (v. 8*b*; see also Deut 3:24). Verse 9 indicates that the nations recognize God's sovereignty and respond appropriately, bowing down (see "bow down" or "worship" in Pss 29:2; 95:6; 96:9; 99:5, 9—all psalms that proclaim God's reign) and glorifying (see Ps 29:1-2, 9). Verse 10, with its two occurrences of the emphatic "you," represents the culmination of the psalmist's proclamation about God. The word "great" (גָּדוֹל *gādôl*) is elsewhere associated with the recognition of God's reign (see Pss 47:2; 95:3; 99:2-3; 145:3), and "wondrous things" (נִפְלָאוֹת *niplā*ʾ*ôt*) recalls the exodus (see Exod 3:20; 15:11; 34:10; Ps 77:13-15), the paradigmatic demonstration of God's rule (see Exod 15:18). Brueggemann translates the phrase in v. 10a with "doing impossibilities"; the sovereign God can make things new.[331] The final phrase of v. 10 summarizes the theme that began in v. 8: God alone (see Ps 83:18).

It was the prerogative and responsibility of monarchs to lead persons into participation in the realm of peace that was supposed to result from their reign (see Pss 72:1-7; 85:8-13), and so the psalmist requests such direction in v. 11a. Having offered the self to God (see v. 4), the psalmist is open to God's instruction (see Commentary on Psalm 1; the verb "teach" [ירה yārâ] here represents the same Hebrew root as the noun for "instruction" [תורה tôrâ] in 1:2). Not surprisingly, in both of the other instances where the psalmist lifts up the soul to God, the context focuses on God's steadfast love and contains both the psalmist's profession of trust in God and a request to be taught by God (see Pss 25:1-2, 4-6, 10; 143:8, 10, 12). The word "truth" (אמת ʾĕmet) in v. 11 is the same as "faithfulness" in v. 15. Again (on "devoted," see above discussion of v. 2), the psalmist desires life and identity to be shaped by God's will and God's way. In other words, the psalmist gladly submits to God's sovereign rule. Undivided allegiance belongs not to self but to God (see "individual heart" and "whole heart" in vv. 11-12 NRSV; see "all your heart" in Deut 6:5 and "one heart" in Jer 32:39). The psalmist embodies personally the response of the nations (cf. vv. 9b, 12b). Life is gladly submitted to God, because the psalmist trusts that God's sovereign character—God's name (vv. 9, 11-12)—is ultimately manifested as love that leads to life (v. 13; see also Pss 30:3; 56:13).

86:14-17. Psalm 86 manifests the same tension that is evident in the other individual prayers for help. While v. 13 implies that the psalmist has been delivered, v. 14 returns to complaint and vv. 16-17 to petition (see vv. 1-7). As usual, the precise nature of the trouble is unclear, except to say that the psalmist is opposed by people who are also opponents of God (v. 14; see above on Ps 54:3). The first petition in v. 16 could be translated "Face me" (see Pss 25:16; 69:16). The petitions to "be gracious" and to "save" recall vv. 2-3, as does the phrase "your servant" (see also v. 4). "Strength" regularly characterizes God (see Exod 15:13; Pss 29:1; 93:1; 96:6-7), and the psalmist desires to live by God's provision (see Exod 15:2; Pss 81:1; 84:5). The psalmist's description of self in v. 16c may be intended to emphasize the psalmist's long-standing dependence upon God—that is, to the point of servanthood's being an inherited status (see Ps 116:16 GNB: "[Save me because] I serve you just as my mother did"). The "sign" in v. 17a seems to be the deliverance that the psalmist prays for and anticipates—that is, God's help (see Pss 10:14; 22:19; 30:10; 54:4) and comfort (see Pss 23:4; 71:21).

In any case, as the psalmist prays for and awaits God's help, she or he remains convinced of God's sovereignty, which will finally be revealed as love. In the midst of both series of petitions and complaints (vv. 1-7, 14-17) is an affirmation of faith that recalls the very heart of Israel's faith (vv. 5, 15). In fact, v. 15 reproduces Exod 34:6 almost exactly. As Brueggemann concludes about Psalm 86: "In the midst of the darkness, in the season of disorientation, Yahweh is affirmed, known to be the one who abides, who is not intimidated or alienated by the disorientation. The creedal claims of Yahweh are still credible in the darkness, perhaps especially credible here."[332]

331. Ibid., 63.

332. Ibid.

REFLECTIONS

1. Although the word *righteous* is not used in Psalm 86, the psalmist's words illustrate the essence of what it means to be righteous: to entrust one's life and future to God in openness to God's direction and instruction (see vv. 2, 4, 10; see also Commentary on Psalm 1). Such trust does not guarantee a life free of troubles and opposition (see vv. 7, 14); yet in the midst of such opposition, the psalmist somehow knows, experiences, and proclaims God's goodness, mercy, faithfulness, and love (vv. 5, 15). Truly, the psalmist knew what it meant to be justified by faith—to be rightly related to God by completely entrusting life and future to God. In terms of the psalmist's self-description, he or she was "your servant" (vv. 2, 4, 16), and on the basis of the psalmist's experience (vv. 7, 14) we must conclude that he or she was a suffering servant. In this sense, then, the psalmist's witness anticipates the life and ministry of Jesus, who, entrusting life unreservedly to God, proclaimed God's faithfulness and love amid persistent opposition. For Christians, the life, death, and resurrection of Jesus represent the ultimate sign of something that the psalmist had already discovered: For the faithful, suffering and glory are finally inseparable (see Commentary on Psalms 13; 22). In the apostle Paul's words, nothing in all creation "will be able to separate us from the love of God" (Rom 8:39 NRSV; see also Ps 86:5, 15).

2. As several commentators point out, the nature of the psalmist's witness also makes her or his words a model of prayer.

> Prayer is the utterance of an identity that is lived out. It is not mere language but brings to expression the role of servant adopted in existence. . . .
> Prayer is the voice of dependence [see v. 1]. . . .
> Prayer is the voice of trust [see v. 2]. . . .
> Prayer is not only a plea for life, it is a submission of life. The servant can serve only one master (see Matt. 6:19-34). Prayer is the voice of commitment [see vv. 11-12].[333]

In teaching his disciples to pray, Jesus also taught them to submit their lives—"thy will be done." As in the psalmist's case, such submission is possible, because we trust that God rules the world—"thine is the kingdom, the power, and the glory forever." Like the psalmist, we attempt to live out our faith in a broken world that opposes us and opposes God. This reality means we wait as we pray—"thy kingdom come."

333. Mays, *Psalms,* 280.

PSALM 87:1-7, THIS ONE WAS BORN IN ZION

NIV	NRSV
Psalm 87	Psalm 87
Of the Sons of Korah. A psalm. A song.	Of the Korahites. A Psalm. A Song.

¹He has set his foundation on the holy mountain;
²   the LORD loves the gates of Zion
    more than all the dwellings of Jacob.
³Glorious things are said of you,
  O city of God: *Selah*
⁴"I will record Rahab*ᵃ* and Babylon
  among those who acknowledge me—
Philistia too, and Tyre, along with Cush*ᵇ*—
  and will say, 'This*ᶜ* one was born in Zion.'"
 	
⁵Indeed, of Zion it will be said,
  "This one and that one were born in her,
	¹ On the holy mount stands the city he founded;
	² the LORD loves the gates of Zion
	    more than all the dwellings of Jacob.
	³ Glorious things are spoken of you,
	  O city of God. *Selah*
	
	⁴ Among those who know me I mention
	    Rahab and Babylon;
	  Philistia too, and Tyre, with Ethiopia*ᵃ*—
	  "This one was born there," they say.
	
	⁵ And of Zion it shall be said,
	  "This one and that one were born in it";

ᵃ4 A poetic name for Egypt ᵇ4 That is, the upper Nile region *ᶜ4 Or "O Rahab and Babylon, / Philistia, Tyre and Cush, / I will record concerning those who acknowledge me: / 'This*	*ᵃOr Nubia; Heb Cush*

NIV

and the Most High himself will establish
    her."
⁶The LORD will write in the register of the
    peoples:
    "This one was born in Zion."   *Selah*
⁷As they make music they will sing,
    "All my fountains are in you."

NRSV

for the Most High himself will establish
    it.
⁶ The LORD records, as he registers the
    peoples,
    "This one was born there."   *Selah*

⁷ Singers and dancers alike say,
    "All my springs are in you."

COMMENTARY

Psalm 87 is known for its many interpretive difficulties, and scholars and translators have often resorted to rearranging the text in an attempt to achieve a smoother reading. Kraus, for instance, suggests the following sequence: vv. 2, 1*b*, 5*b*, 7, 3, 6*a*, 4*b*/6*b*, 4*a*, 5*a*.[334] The NEB's alteration is less radical: vv. 1-2, 4-5, 6, 7, 3. The REB has returned to the traditional ordering of the verses, as have most recent commentators, and this clearly is the best policy. Even so, the comment by Booij is not unusual: "I think the question of what Ps lxxxvii essentially means to say can be answered only tentatively."[335]

While caution is in order, it is safe to say that Psalm 87 is a song of Zion (see Psalms 46; 48; 76; 84; 122). Like other songs of Zion, it asserts that Jerusalem is God's city (vv. 1-3; see Pss 46:4-5; 48:1; 76:2; 122:1-2). As such, Jerusalem has worldwide significance (vv. 3-7). The other songs of Zion suggest this as well when they relate God's residence in Zion to God's sovereignty over all the earth, including kings and nations (see Pss 46:6, 10; 48:2, 4-8; 76:8-9, 12; see also Isa 2:2-4; 45:22; Mic 4:1-3; Zech 2:10-11). To be sure, the striking imagery that Psalm 87 employs to assert Jerusalem's worldwide significance gives the psalm a poetic power that makes it unique.

As noted above, the structure of Psalm 87 has been much debated. The simplest proposal is to divide the psalm according to its two major themes: (1) vv. 1-2, Zion as God's city, (2) vv. 3-7, Zion's worldwide significance. A case can be made for taking v. 3 with vv. 1-2 (see the NRSV, and note the placement of the first *selah*); however, Mark Smith argues convincingly that the adverbs and prepositional phrases in vv. 3-7 are the clues to discerning a chiasm (see Introduction) that focuses on v. 5:

A "in you" (v. 3; NIV and NRSV, "of you")
  B "there" (v. 4; NIV, "in Zion")
    C "in her" (v. 5; NRSV, "in it")
  B′ "there" (v. 6; NIV, "in Zion")
A′ "in you" (v. 7)

As Smith concludes, "Theme and structure are one: God's establishment of Zion is a central fact of the divine order on earth."[336] It is possible, too, that the structure moves at more than one level, so it is not necessary to view varying proposals as mutually exclusive.

In its place in the psalter, Psalm 87 can be understood as an illustration of Ps 86:9. At the same time, however, the larger literary context of Book III suggests that the songs of Zion (Psalms 76; 84; 87; see also 78:67-72) be heard in the light of the communal prayers for help and their laments over the destruction of Jerusalem (see Psalms 74; 79; 80; 83; 85; 89). In other words, the context encourages the reader to construe Psalm 87 eschatologically and to hear its claims for Jerusalem symbolically.

87:1-2. The syntax of v. 1 is problematic, but essentially v. 1 affirms that Jerusalem is God's city (see "foundations" in Ezra 3:11; Isa 44:28). Elsewhere, too, the site is called a holy mountain or

334. H.-J. Kraus, *Psalms 60–150: A Commentary,* trans. H. C. Oswald (Minneapolis: Augsburg, 1989) 185.

335. T. Booij, "Some Observations on Psalm LXXXVII," *VT* 37 (1987) 22.

336. Mark Smith, "The Structure of Psalm LXXXVII," *VT* 38 (1988) 357-58.

hill (see Pss 2:6; 3:4; 15:1; 24:3; 48:1; 78:54). Verse 2 recalls Ps 78:68-69 (note "founded" in 78:69 in relation to 87:1; see also Ps 132:13). The exact phrase "gates of Zion" (שערי ציון ša'ărê ṣiyyôn) is unique, but the gates of the city are mentioned elsewhere (see Pss 9:14; 24:7, 9; 122:2). The mention of the gates, along with the singers and dancers in v. 7, has led some scholars to propose that Psalm 87 was used originally as part of a processional liturgy (see 2 Samuel 6; Pss 24:3-10; 68:24-27). This is certainly possible, but the origin and ancient use are elusive.

87:3-7. Just as God's name is glorified (see Ps 86:9, 12), so also are "glorious things" said about God's place (see Isa 62:2; Lam 1:8; Hag 2:3). In other words, the city itself makes God known (see Psalms 48; 122). Thus the ambiguity concerning the speaker in vv. 4-5 is appropriate; it could be the personified city, or it could be God. To know the city is to know God, and vice versa. Elsewhere, the stated purpose of God's acts of deliverance is that people will "know that I am the LORD" (Exod 14:4 NRSV; see also Exod 9:16; 10:2; Pss 46:10; 59:13; 100:3). In these contexts, to know God means to recognize God's sovereignty and to live under God's rule. What is striking about the list of nations that know God—and thus count Jerusalem as their hometown (see "born" in vv. 4-6)—is that it consists of traditional enemies. Rahab elsewhere designates Egypt (see Isa 30:7), a major opponent, as was Babylon; but the other three nations were enemies as well (on Philistia and Tyre, see Ps 83:7; on Ethiopa, see Isa 20:3, 5; 37:9; Jer 46:9; Ezek 30:4; Nah 3:9).

The quotation in v. 4c is sometimes interpreted as something that individual Jews in the diaspora may have said as a matter of honor; however, it should not be taken so literally. Rather, v. 4 should be understood in the light of v. 6 (see the chiastic structure outlined above) as the beginning of God's roll call of the peoples (on God's keeping records, see Exod 32:32-33; Pss 69:28; 139:16; Dan 7:10; Rev 20:12). In other words, the nations call Jerusalem their home (v. 4), because the God of Zion claims them as God's own people (v. 6; note that vv. 4c and 6b are identical). Actually, this perspective should not be as surprising as many commentators find it, for it is a recurrent claim that God's choice of Abraham and Israel meant that "in you all the families of the earth shall be blessed" (Gen 12:3 NRSV). This claim follows from God's worldwide sovereignty, which is proclaimed throughout the psalter (see Psalm 2; Introduction) and is in view in Ps 87:5 in the title "Most High" (עליון 'elyôn). The prophetic books also regularly assert God's claim upon all the peoples and nations. Psalm 87 is particularly reminiscent of Isa 19:18-25 (see esp. Isa 19:23-25; see also Isa 2:2-4; Jer 1:10; Mic 4:1-3; Zeph 3:9-13; Zech 9:20-23).

The syntax of v. 7 is difficult. The Hebrew lacks the verb "say," but it is reasonable to conclude that the psalm ends with a quotation of the worshipers whom God gathers in Jerusalem as God's own people. In other words, the psalm concludes with a sample of the "glorious things" spoken about Zion (note the chiastic structure in which vv. 3 and 7 correspond). The word "springs" (מעינות ma'yānôt) elsewhere describes sources of water that God provides to sustain life (see Pss 104:10; 114:8), and Joel 4:18 even poetically depicts the spring as flowing from God's house (see Isa 12:3; Pss 36:9; 46:4, although the Hebrew vocabulary differs in these cases). In Prov 5:16, "springs" is part of a larger metaphor bespeaking intimacy and relatedness. In other words, persons who gather to worship God acknowledge their belonging to God and profess that the sovereign God is the sole source of their life and well-being.

REFLECTIONS

1. Kraus entitles his comment on Psalm 87 "Zion I Call Mother."[337] This is also how he translates v. 5a, based on the LXX of v. 5a, which actually contains the Greek word for "mother" (μήτηρ mētēr). Although the Hebrew text does not explicitly call Jerusalem

337. Kraus, *Psalms 60–150*, 184.

"mother," the image is a helpful interpretation of the birth metaphor in vv. 4-6, for it captures the message that all nations and peoples are God's children (see above on Gen 12:1-3, Isa 19:23-25). Jerusalem—a specific place—became the symbol for God's sovereignty over all places, times, and peoples (see Commentary on Psalm 48; see also Gal 4:26; Heb 11:10; 12:22-24; Revelation 21–22).

The simple message that all people are God's children has sweeping and profound implications, including political and religious ones. In view of Psalm 87, it is not surprising and somehow appropriate that Jerusalem is a sacred place for Jews, Christians, and Muslims. Unfortunately, these groups have often treated each other as enemies, instead of allowing their very diversity to be a reminder that Jerusalem symbolizes a God who welcomes and claims all peoples and nations. If we must somehow view each other as opponents, then Psalm 87 at least calls for us to view the others as "fraternal opponents."[338] In other words, at the very least, Psalm 87 calls us, as Jesus called his followers, to love our enemies (see Matt 5:43). To take Psalm 87 seriously, then, would have a profound impact on the international policy of the nations of our world. The dehumanization of other people—a tactic that feeds hostility and warfare—cannot claim God's approval. The only permissible goal of "Christian soldiers" is love, for God claims all peoples as God's children. God so loves the world!

2. The structural embodiment of this good news was made in the early church by the welcoming of all the nations—the Gentiles (see Matt 28:19-20; Luke 24:47). The theological rationale was that God had "broken down the dividing wall, that is, the hostility between us" (Eph 2:14 NRSV), so that there are no longer "strangers to the covenants of promise" (Eph 2:12 NRSV). To be sure, the author of Ephesians is not specifically citing Psalm 87, but the universal perspective of Psalm 87 is surely akin to what the author discerns in Jesus Christ. In fact, the church as an inclusive community is described as "a holy temple in the Lord; in whom you are built together spiritually into a dwelling place for God" (Eph 2:21-22 NRSV).

3. Johanna W. H. Bos points out that Psalm 87 has traditionally been used as a baptismal psalm in Dutch Calvinist congregations.[339] And how appropriate it is! Not only does Psalm 87 anticipate the gathering of the nations on the Day of Pentecost (see Acts 2, esp. vv. 8-11, 37-39), but it also reminds us of the essential good news that baptism proclaims. In short, our fundamental identity is not one that we eventually achieve; rather, it is one with which we are born and that we share with every other human being. We are children of God.

4. The ability of Zion to function symbolically, thus proclaiming God's sovereign claim upon all places and times and peoples, is evident in the frequent use by Christians of John Newton's hymn "Glorious Things of Thee Are Spoken." The hymn departs from Ps 87:3, capturing well the symbolic dimension of the psalm. In short, this ancient song of Zion continues to articulate the Christian conviction of God's gracious claim upon the whole world.

---

338. This expression is used by Pinchas Lapide to characterize the relationship of Jews and Christians. See Karl Rahner and Pinchas Lapide, *Encountering Jesus—Encountering Judaism: A Dialogue,* trans. Davis Perkins (New York: Crossroad, 1987) 109.
339. Johanna W. H. Bos, "Psalm 87," *Int.* 47 (1993) 281.

PSALM 88:1-18, THE DARKNESS IS MY CLOSEST FRIEND

NIV

Psalm 88

A song. A psalm of the Sons of Korah. For the director of music. According to *mahalath leannoth.*[a] A *maskil*[b] of Heman the Ezrahite.

[1]O LORD, the God who saves me,
    day and night I cry out before you.
[2]May my prayer come before you;
    turn your ear to my cry.

[3]For my soul is full of trouble
    and my life draws near the grave.[c]
[4]I am counted among those who go down to
        the pit;
    I am like a man without strength.
[5]I am set apart with the dead,
    like the slain who lie in the grave,
whom you remember no more,
    who are cut off from your care.

[6]You have put me in the lowest pit,
    in the darkest depths.
[7]Your wrath lies heavily upon me;
    you have overwhelmed me with all your
        waves.   *Selah*
[8]You have taken from me my closest friends
    and have made me repulsive to them.
I am confined and cannot escape;
[9]   my eyes are dim with grief.

I call to you, O LORD, every day;
    I spread out my hands to you.
[10]Do you show your wonders to the dead?
    Do those who are dead rise up and praise
        you?   *Selah*
[11]Is your love declared in the grave,
    your faithfulness in Destruction[d]?
[12]Are your wonders known in the place of
        darkness,
    or your righteous deeds in the land of
        oblivion?

[13]But I cry to you for help, O LORD;

NRSV

Psalm 88

A Song. A Psalm of the Korahites. To the leader: according to Mahalath Leannoth. A Maskil of Heman the Ezrahite.

[1] O LORD, God of my salvation,
    when, at night, I cry out in your
        presence,
[2] let my prayer come before you;
    incline your ear to my cry.

[3] For my soul is full of troubles,
    and my life draws near to Sheol.
[4] I am counted among those who go down to
        the Pit;
    I am like those who have no help,
[5] like those forsaken among the dead,
    like the slain that lie in the grave,
like those whom you remember no more,
    for they are cut off from your hand.
[6] You have put me in the depths of the Pit,
    in the regions dark and deep.
[7] Your wrath lies heavy upon me,
    and you overwhelm me with all your
        waves.   *Selah*

[8] You have caused my companions to shun
        me;
    you have made me a thing of horror to
        them.
I am shut in so that I cannot escape;
[9]   my eye grows dim through sorrow.
Every day I call on you, O LORD;
    I spread out my hands to you.
[10] Do you work wonders for the dead?
    Do the shades rise up to praise you? *Selah*
[11] Is your steadfast love declared in the grave,
    or your faithfulness in Abaddon?
[12] Are your wonders known in the darkness,
    or your saving help in the land of
        forgetfulness?

[13] But I, O LORD, cry out to you;

---

[a] Title: Possibly a tune, "The Suffering of Affliction"   [b] Title: Probably a literary or musical term   [c]3 Hebrew *Sheol*   [d]11 Hebrew *Abaddon*

NIV

in the morning my prayer comes before
you.
[14]Why, O LORD, do you reject me
and hide your face from me?
[15]From my youth I have been afflicted and
close to death;
I have suffered your terrors and am in
despair.
[16]Your wrath has swept over me;
your terrors have destroyed me.
[17]All day long they surround me like a flood;
they have completely engulfed me.
[18]You have taken my companions and loved
ones from me;
the darkness is my closest friend.

NRSV

in the morning my prayer comes before
you.
[14] O LORD, why do you cast me off?
Why do you hide your face from me?
[15] Wretched and close to death from my
youth up,
I suffer your terrors; I am desperate.[a]
[16] Your wrath has swept over me;
your dread assaults destroy me.
[17] They surround me like a flood all day long;
from all sides they close in on me.
[18] You have caused friend and neighbor to
shun me;
my companions are in darkness.

[a]Meaning of Heb uncertain

COMMENTARY

Psalm 88 is classified as a prayer for help or an individual lament/complaint, but it has several features that make it distinctive, chief of which is the extent and severity of the complaint, which occupies virtually the whole psalm. Petition is limited to v. 2, and there is no explicit profession of trust or vow to praise.

Scholars have often insisted that the origin of the complaint in Psalm 88 can be traced to the psalmist's apparently terminal illness (see Commentary on Psalms 6; 38; 41). To be sure, the psalm is pervaded by vocabulary associated with death, but it is not necessary to conclude that sickness definitely accounts for the origin of the psalm, nor is it necessary to limit the psalm's relevance to situations of illness. The language is metaphorical and stereotypical enough to express other life-threatening situations. For instance, the history of interpretation of Psalm 88 reflects the opinion of both Jewish and Christian interpreters that this psalm was used as an exilic or post-exilic prayer to articulate the plight of the whole people. This use would be in keeping with the conclusion that the character of Book III has been shaped by the experience of the exile and its aftermath (see Commentary on Psalms 73; 74; 79; 80; Introduction), and it would make Psalm 88 an especially fitting anticipation of Psalm 89 (cf. v. 3 with Ps 89:48; vv. 7, 14a with Ps 89:38; v. 14b with Ps

89:46a; v. 11 with Ps 89:49; vv. 8, 18 with Ps 89:41, 50).

The structure of Psalm 88 is governed primarily by the three instances of the psalmist's crying out or calling to God (vv. 1, 9b, 13). Three different Hebrew words for "cry"/"call" (צעק ṣāʿaq, v. 1; קרא qārāʾ, v. 9b; שוע šwʿ, v. 13) are used, as if to indicate that the psalmist has exhausted every approach. To be noted, too, is that each of the psalmist's cries is accompanied by a chronological reference. In other words, every possible approach, at every possible moment, has been tried, and the result is "darkness," which is literally the final word of the psalm. Each section of the psalm contains a form of the Hebrew root for "darkness" (חשך ḥōšek, vv. 6, 12, 18). Darkness thus pervades both the psalm and the psalmist's experience.

88:1-2. Although Psalm 88 is pervaded by and ends in darkness, it begins with the psalmist addressing God as the one "who saves me" (see Exod 15:2; Pss 68:19-20; 89:26). The psalmist knows that God has traditionally responded when threatened persons "cry out" to God (see Exod 3:7, 9; Deut 26:7; Josh 24:7; Pss 9:12; 77:1; 107:6, 28). Thus the very fact that the psalmist bothers to make an appeal to God is indicative of an underlying trust in God's fundamental character, which the psalmist will also specifically refer to in vv. 10-12. In short, the psalmist's prayer (see also v. 13) is an act of faith and hope.

88:3-8. These verses are an indication that faithful, hopeful prayer need not sound "positive." The psalmist's complaint is bitterly and brutally honest. The bitterness is evident in v. 3*a*, where the Hebrew idiom employed (lit., "my soul is satisfied with" [שבעה נפשי ב *śābĕ'â napšî bĕ*-]) often communicates something good (see Pss 63:5; 65:4), but here the only thing that the psalmist has enough of is trouble. The words "Sheol" (שאול *šĕ'ôl*, v. 3*b*) and "Pit" (בור *bôr*, v. 4) indicate that the trouble is life-threatening (see Pss 6:5; 28:1; 30:3; 143:7). Indeed, the psalmist is apparently treated as one who is as good as dead (vv. 4-5). It is interesting that the verb "cut off" (גזר *gāzar*) is also used in the climactic Servant Song in Deutero-Isaiah to describe the plight of the servant (see Isa 53:8). The servant is often identified as the whole people, and this connection may have something to do with the use of Psalm 88 as a corporate prayer in the exilic and post-exilic eras. The verb is also used of the exiled and suffering people in Ezek 37:11 (see also "grave"/"graves" in Ps 88:5, 11; Ezek 37:12) and in Lam 3:54, where it is followed in Lam 3:55 by the same phrase used in Ps 88:6: "depths of the pit."

Verse 5 anticipates the shift in v. 6 to direct accusation of God. God has put the psalmist in the Pit (cf. v. 4). Since v. 1 has already alluded to the exodus (see "my salvation" in Exod 15:2 and "cry" in Exod 3:7, 9), it is not surprising to hear allusions to the exodus in vv. 6-9*a*; but this time they are in a negative direction. The word "deep" (מצלות *mĕṣôlôt*, v. 6*b*) designates the place where God put the Egyptians (Exod 15:5). Whereas God caused the Israelites to escape from Egypt (see "brought . . . out" in Exod 18:1; 20:2), the psalmist cannot escape (v. 8). Thus the psalmist remains in affliction (v. 9*a*; see Exod 3:7 NRSV, "sufferings"; 4:31 NRSV, "misery"; Deut 26:7), the state out of which the enslaved Israelites also cried to God. Apparently abandoned by God, the psalmist is also deserted by friends (v. 18; see Pss 31:11; 38:11; Job 19:13; 30:10; Jer 11:18-19; 12:6).

88:9-12. But the psalmist's prayer is constant. The phrase "every day" in v. 9*b* could also be rendered "all day long," and v. 9*c* describes the posture of prayer. The prayer in vv. 10-12 indicates that faithful, hopeful prayer need not be devoid of questioning. Like the opening address to God in v. 1, the questions in vv. 10-12 recall God's fundamental character. The repeated "wonders" (vv. 10, 12) again recalls the exodus (see Exod 3:20; 15:11; Pss 77:11; 78:12), and "steadfast love" and "faithfulness" (v. 11) recall God's self-revelation to Moses in Exod 34:6-7 (see Pss 5:7; 13:5; Introduction; see also Exod 34:10). The word the NIV translates as "righteous deeds" (אמונות *'ĕmûnôt*) denotes the work that God does as sovereign of the universe (see Ps 98:2). The question, however, is whether God can manifest God's characteristic being and activity with the dead (v. 10; see also Job 26:5; Isa 14:9; 26:14) or within the realm of the dead—"the grave" (v. 11*a*; see v. 5), Abaddon (v. 11*b*; see Job 26:6; 28:22; 31:12), "darkness" (v. 12*a*; see vv. 6, 18; Ps 143:3; Lam 3:6), "the land of oblivion" (cf. Job 10:21). The intended answer to the questions in vv. 10-12 is no, but the very questions themselves reveal the psalmist's implicit faith and hope. The questions are sometimes viewed as the psalmist's selfish appeal to God's own self-interest; however, it is better to view them as indicative of the psalmist's love of life and as an appeal to a God whom the psalmist knows as one who wills and works for life for God's people (see Commentary on Psalm 30, esp. discussion on v. 9).

88:13-18. The questions in vv. 10-12 are framed in general terms, but v. 13 begins with the emphatic Hebrew pronoun "I" (אני *'ănî*), thus focusing attention on the psalmist's own plight and cry (see Exod 2:23; Pss 18:6; 22:24). Not surprisingly, therefore, the questions in v. 14 are framed very personally. The verbs in both questions are characteristic of other prayers for help (on v. 14*a*, see "cast off"/"reject"/"spurn" [זנח *zānaḥ*] in Pss 43:2; 44:9, 23; 60:1, 10; 74:1; 77:7; 89:38; on v. 14*b*, see Job 13:24; Pss 13:1; 27:9; 30:7; 44:24; 69:17; 102:2; 143:7). In a word, they sum up the psalmist's situation; she or he has cried out in affliction, but God has not responded. Thus the psalmist remains "afflicted" (v. 15*a*; see v. 9), and the psalm concludes with an unremitting complaint. The psalmist experiences the "terrors" that God elsewhere inflicts on God's enemies (v. 15*b*; see Exod 15:16; Job 9:34; 13:21). The psalmist knows not God's salvation but the wrath God elsewhere shows to enemies (v. 16*a*; see Exod 15:7; Ps 2:5); the psalmist is under attack by God just as Job perceived himself to be (v. 16*b*; see Job 6:4). The psalmist is completely overwhelmed (v. 17; see also v. 7; Job 22:11; Ps 69:1). The psalm ends with another reminder of the psalmist's complete alienation (v. 18*a*; see also v. 8) and with the pitiful statement that "the darkness is my closest friend" (see the NIV, which makes better sense of the difficult Hebrew syntax than does the NRSV).

REFLECTIONS

1. The psalmist's situation is similar in many ways to that of the servant of Isaiah 53 and of Job; like Isaiah 53 and the book of Job, Psalm 88 prompts a re-evaluation of suffering, both human and divine (see Commentary on Psalms 8; 44). The theological problems and possibilities are posed most sharply, perhaps, by the two verses that conclude each of the psalmist's complaints (vv. 8, 18). God has caused the psalmist's suffering and isolation (as the NRSV's "caused . . . to shun" suggests, the Hebrew verb is a causative form). In short, God is the problem (see also vv. 6-7, 14, 16-17). But God is also the solution! The psalmist's prayer itself is evidence that she or he is convinced that even life's worst moments somehow have to do with God. So the psalmist's cries continue to arise out of the depths (see Ps 130:1).

2. Two statements by Brueggemann help to define the primary theological issue: "Psalm 88 is an embarrassment to conventional faith" and "Psalm 88 shows us what the cross is about: *faithfulness* in scenes of complete *abandonment.*"[340] These statements may sound contradictory, until we realize that there was and is nothing conventional about the cross, "a stumbling block to Jews and foolishness to Gentiles" (1 Cor 1:23 NRSV). To be sure, Psalm 88 is not a prediction of Jesus' suffering, but it serves to articulate the same experience that Jesus would live out. Facing the cross, Jesus' soul was "full of troubles" (v. 3; see Mark 14:33-34). He was shunned even by those closest to him (vv. 8, 18; see Mark 14:50). As it turned out, his closest friend was darkness (v. 18; see Mark 15:33). Like the psalmist, who out of the darkness still appealed constantly to God, Jesus was faithful and hopeful. In the midst of abandonment, his cry was still, "My God, my God" (see Mark 15:34, which quotes Ps 22:1 but which is also reminiscent of Ps 88:1). In other words, from the Christian point of view, Psalm 88 not only provides us words to articulate the pain of life's worst moments, but it also offers testimony to the extremes to which God was willing to go to demonstrate faithful love for humanity. Just as the psalmist in Psalm 88 suffered, so also God's Son suffered life's worst for us. That is what the cross is finally about; it shows us how much God loves the world. And there is nothing conventional about that kind of love, for it is neither fair nor just. Sheer grace is always a scandal. It is precisely this scandal that prompts the re-evaluation of the conventional view that suffering is a sign of God's punishment or a sign of alienation from God. Because God in Christ claimed the suffering of the psalmist in Psalm 88, we are invited to view suffering in a new way—invited, in fact, to take up a cross and follow Jesus (Mark 8:34), who in turn followed the way of the psalmist (see Commentary on Psalm 22).

3. The exceptional, extreme character of Psalm 88 makes it a valuable theological resource at all times, but especially perhaps when we have trouble perceiving any ecstasy at all accompanying our agony (see Commentary on Psalm 13). In his novel *Sophie's Choice,* William Styron depicts the main character, Stingo, returning to New York to confront a terrible tragedy. Stingo and an African American woman sitting beside him on the train begin to read the Bible, a "prescription for my torment," as Stingo puts it:

---

340. Walter Brueggemann, *The Message of the Psalms: A Theological Commentary* (Minneapolis: Augsburg, 1984) 78, 81.

"Psalm Eighty-eight," I would suggest. To which she would reply, "Dat is some fine psalm." . . . We read aloud through Wilmington, Chester, and past Trenton, turning from time to time to Ecclesiastes and Isaiah. After a while we tried the Sermon on the Mount, but somehow it didn't work for me; the grand old Hebrew woe seemed more cathartic, so we went back to Job.[341]

To read Psalm 88 may well be cathartic, but it is more. It is also faithful and instructive. To read Psalm 88 is to remind ourselves that even when we stand in utter darkness, we do not stand alone. We stand with the psalmist of old. We stand with Christ on the cross. To cry into the darkness, "O LORD, God of my salvation" (v. 1) is an act of solidarity with the communion of saints. It is indeed an act of faith and hope that God's will for life is greater than the reality of death.

341. William Styron, *Sophie's Choice* (Toronto: Bantam Books, 1979) 614-15; Brueggemann calls attention to Styron's use of Psalm 88 in *The Message of the Psalms*, 81.

PSALM 89:1-52, LORD, WHERE IS YOUR STEADFAST LOVE OF OLD?

NIV

Psalm 89

A *maskil*[a] of Ethan the Ezrahite.

[1] I will sing of the LORD's great love forever;
with my mouth I will make your faithfulness
known through all generations.
[2] I will declare that your love stands firm
forever,
that you established your faithfulness in
heaven itself.

[3] You said, "I have made a covenant with my
chosen one,
I have sworn to David my servant,
[4] I will establish your line forever
and make your throne firm through all
generations.'"   *Selah*

[5] The heavens praise your wonders, O LORD,
your faithfulness too, in the assembly of
the holy ones.
[6] For who in the skies above can compare
with the LORD?
Who is like the LORD among the heavenly
beings?
[7] In the council of the holy ones God is greatly
feared;
he is more awesome than all who
surround him.

a Title: Probably a literary or musical term

NRSV

Psalm 89

A Maskil of Ethan the Ezrahite.

[1] I will sing of your steadfast love, O LORD,[a]
forever;
with my mouth I will proclaim your
faithfulness to all generations.
[2] I declare that your steadfast love is
established forever;
your faithfulness is as firm as the
heavens.

[3] You said, "I have made a covenant with my
chosen one,
I have sworn to my servant David:
[4] "I will establish your descendants forever,
and build your throne for all
generations.'"   *Selah*

[5] Let the heavens praise your wonders,
O LORD,
your faithfulness in the assembly of the
holy ones.
[6] For who in the skies can be compared to
the LORD?
Who among the heavenly beings is like
the LORD,
[7] a God feared in the council of the holy ones,

a Gk: Heb *the steadfast love of the LORD*

NIV

⁸O LORD God Almighty, who is like you?
    You are mighty, O LORD, and your
        faithfulness surrounds you.

⁹You rule over the surging sea;
    when its waves mount up, you still them.
¹⁰You crushed Rahab like one of the slain;
    with your strong arm you scattered your
        enemies.
¹¹The heavens are yours, and yours also the earth;
    you founded the world and all that is in it.
¹²You created the north and the south;
    Tabor and Hermon sing for joy at your
        name.
¹³Your arm is endued with power;
    your hand is strong, your right hand
        exalted.

¹⁴Righteousness and justice are the foundation
        of your throne;
    love and faithfulness go before you.
¹⁵Blessed are those who have learned to
        acclaim you,
    who walk in the light of your presence,
        O LORD.
¹⁶They rejoice in your name all day long;
    they exult in your righteousness.
¹⁷For you are their glory and strength,
    and by your favor you exalt our horn.ᵃ
¹⁸Indeed, our shieldᵇ belongs to the LORD,
    our king to the Holy One of Israel.

¹⁹Once you spoke in a vision,
    to your faithful people you said:
"I have bestowed strength on a warrior;
    I have exalted a young man from among
        the people.
²⁰I have found David my servant;
    with my sacred oil I have anointed him.
²¹My hand will sustain him;
    surely my arm will strengthen him.
²²No enemy will subject him to tribute;
    no wicked man will oppress him.
²³I will crush his foes before him
    and strike down his adversaries.
²⁴My faithful love will be with him,
    and through my name his hornᶜ will be
        exalted.

a17 Horn here symbolizes strong one.   b18 Or sovereign   c24 Horn here symbolizes strength.

NRSV

    great and awesomeᵃ above all that are
        around him?
⁸ O LORD God of hosts,
    who is as mighty as you, O LORD?
    Your faithfulness surrounds you.
⁹ You rule the raging of the sea;
    when its waves rise, you still them.
¹⁰ You crushed Rahab like a carcass;
    you scattered your enemies with your
        mighty arm.
¹¹ The heavens are yours, the earth also is
        yours;
    the world and all that is in it—you have
        founded them.
¹² The north and the southᵇ—you created
        them;
    Tabor and Hermon joyously praise your
        name.
¹³ You have a mighty arm;
    strong is your hand, high your right hand.
¹⁴ Righteousness and justice are the foundation
        of your throne;
    steadfast love and faithfulness go before
        you.
¹⁵ Happy are the people who know the festal
        shout,
    who walk, O LORD, in the light of your
        countenance;
¹⁶ they exult in your name all day long,
    and extolᶜ your righteousness.
¹⁷ For you are the glory of their strength;
    by your favor our horn is exalted.
¹⁸ For our shield belongs to the LORD,
    our king to the Holy One of Israel.

¹⁹ Then you spoke in a vision to your faithful
        one, and said:
"I have set the crownᵈ on one who is
        mighty,
    I have exalted one chosen from the
        people.
²⁰ I have found my servant David;
    with my holy oil I have anointed him;
²¹ my hand shall always remain with him;
    my arm also shall strengthen him.
²² The enemy shall not outwit him,
    the wicked shall not humble him.

ᵃGk Syr: Heb greatly awesome   ᵇOr Zaphon and Yamin
ᶜCn: Heb are exalted in   ᵈCn: Heb help

NIV

25I will set his hand over the sea,
his right hand over the rivers.
26He will call out to me, 'You are my Father,
my God, the Rock my Savior.'
27I will also appoint him my firstborn,
the most exalted of the kings of the earth.
28I will maintain my love to him forever,
and my covenant with him will never fail.
29I will establish his line forever,
his throne as long as the heavens endure.

30"If his sons forsake my law
and do not follow my statutes,
31if they violate my decrees
and fail to keep my commands,
32I will punish their sin with the rod,
their iniquity with flogging;
33but I will not take my love from him,
nor will I ever betray my faithfulness.
34I will not violate my covenant
or alter what my lips have uttered.
35Once for all, I have sworn by my holiness—
and I will not lie to David—
36that his line will continue forever
and his throne endure before me like the
sun;
37it will be established forever like the moon,
the faithful witness in the sky."   *Selah*

38But you have rejected, you have spurned,
you have been very angry with your
anointed one.
39You have renounced the covenant with your
servant
and have defiled his crown in the dust.
40You have broken through all his walls
and reduced his strongholds to ruins.
41All who pass by have plundered him;
he has become the scorn of his neighbors.
42You have exalted the right hand of his foes;
you have made all his enemies rejoice.
43You have turned back the edge of his
sword
and have not supported him in battle.
44You have put an end to his splendor
and cast his throne to the ground.
45You have cut short the days of his youth;
you have covered him with a mantle of
shame.   *Selah*

NRSV

23 I will crush his foes before him
and strike down those who hate him.
24 My faithfulness and steadfast love shall be
with him;
and in my name his horn shall be exalted.
25 I will set his hand on the sea
and his right hand on the rivers.
26 He shall cry to me, 'You are my Father,
my God, and the Rock of my salvation!'
27 I will make him the firstborn,
the highest of the kings of the earth.
28 Forever I will keep my steadfast love for
him,
and my covenant with him will stand
firm.
29 I will establish his line forever,
and his throne as long as the heavens
endure.
30 If his children forsake my law
and do not walk according to my
ordinances,
31 if they violate my statutes
and do not keep my commandments,
32 then I will punish their transgression with
the rod
and their iniquity with scourges;
33 but I will not remove from him my
steadfast love,
or be false to my faithfulness.
34 I will not violate my covenant,
or alter the word that went forth from
my lips.
35 Once and for all I have sworn by my
holiness;
I will not lie to David.
36 His line shall continue forever,
and his throne endure before me like the
sun.
37 It shall be established forever like the moon,
an enduring witness in the skies."   *Selah*

38 But now you have spurned and rejected him;
you are full of wrath against your
anointed.
39 You have renounced the covenant with
your servant;
you have defiled his crown in the dust.
40 You have broken through all his walls;

NIV

[46] How long, O Lord? Will you hide yourself
forever?
How long will your wrath burn like fire?
[47] Remember how fleeting is my life.
For what futility you have created all men!
[48] What man can live and not see death,
or save himself from the power of the
grave[a]?   Selah
[49] O Lord, where is your former great love,
which in your faithfulness you swore to
David?
[50] Remember, Lord, how your servant has[b] been
mocked,
how I bear in my heart the taunts of all
the nations,
[51] the taunts with which your enemies have
mocked, O Lord,
with which they have mocked every step
of your anointed one.

[52] Praise be to the Lord forever!
Amen and Amen.

a48 Hebrew *Sheol*   b50 Or *your servants have*

NRSV

you have laid his strongholds in ruins.
[41] All who pass by plunder him;
he has become the scorn of his neighbors.
[42] You have exalted the right hand of his foes;
you have made all his enemies rejoice.
[43] Moreover, you have turned back the edge
of his sword,
and you have not supported him in battle.
[44] You have removed the scepter from his
hand,[a]
and hurled his throne to the ground.
[45] You have cut short the days of his youth;
you have covered him with shame. *Selah*

[46] How long, O Lord? Will you hide yourself
forever?
How long will your wrath burn like fire?
[47] Remember how short my time is—[b]
for what vanity you have created all
mortals!
[48] Who can live and never see death?
Who can escape the power of
Sheol?   *Selah*

[49] Lord, where is your steadfast love of old,
which by your faithfulness you swore to
David?
[50] Remember, O Lord, how your servant is
taunted;
how I bear in my bosom the insults of
the peoples,[c]
[51] with which your enemies taunt, O Lord,
with which they taunted the footsteps of
your anointed.

[52] Blessed be the Lord forever.
Amen and Amen.

a Cn: Heb *removed his cleanness*   b Meaning of Heb uncertain
c Cn: Heb *bosom all of many peoples*

COMMENTARY

A major interpretive issue for Psalm 89 is its unity, which many scholars have questioned on form-critical grounds. Because it deals with the Davidic king, Psalm 89 is ordinarily classified as a royal psalm, but it is clearly composed of varied kinds of material. Verses 1-2, 5-18 have a hymnic character; vv. 3-4, 19-37 are presented as an oracle from God (see esp. vv. 3, 19); and vv. 38-51 have the character of a lament, with vv. 38-45 narrating the circumstances behind the complaint and petition, which are voiced directly in vv. 46-51. Verse 52 is a doxology that closes Book III. Despite this diversity, there are compelling reasons to consider Psalm 89 as a unit, and most recent commentators have taken this approach. A primary indication in this regard is the repetition that links the three sections, especially the repetition of "steadfast love" (חסד *ḥesed*, vv. 1-2, 14, 24, 28, 33, 49) and the forms of a Hebrew root usually translated "faithfulness" (vv. 1-2, 5, 8, 14, 24, 28, 33, 37, 49). One of the effects achieved by this and other instances of repetition is to portray the reign of the Davidic king (vv. 19-37) in the same terms used to describe the reign of God (vv. 5-18). This effect is not accidental, and it demonstrates the unity of Psalm 89. It also sets the stage for the striking reversal that occurs at v. 38, and thus it contributes to the reader's appreciation of the magnitude of the crisis described in vv. 38-51. In short, the failure of the monarchy seems to bespeak the very failure of God.

The seriousness of this crisis raises the question of the origin and ancient use of Psalm 89. For other royal psalms, it makes sense that the psalm would have been used at the coronation of a king or possibly at an annual celebration of the king's reign (see Commentary on Psalms 2; 72), but this does not seem as likely for Psalm 89 because of vv. 38-51. In an attempt to surmount this difficulty, an earlier generation of scholars suggested that vv. 38-51 do not describe an actual historical setback. Rather, they were part of an annual ritual humiliation of the king that was enacted as a reminder that the king's sovereignty was derived from God. This view, however, is very unlikely. There is no evidence for such a ritual, and the intensity of vv. 38-51 indicates a real, not contrived, crisis of faith. The most likely precipitating event was the destruction of Jerusalem in 587 BCE and the consequent disappearance of the Judean monarchy.

To be sure, it is possible that Psalm 89 originated earlier than 587 BCE following the defeat of a Judean king. The likelihood of this possibility is increased by vv. 47-51, in which a surviving king seems to speak. Of course, this may be an exilic or post-exilic literary device, and finally the origin and ancient use of Psalm 89 remain elusive. What is more accessible is the literary context of Psalm 89 in Book III. Given that Book III seems to have been decisively shaped by the experience of exile and its aftermath (see Commentary on Psalms 73; 74; 79; 80; Introduction), it is especially likely that Psalm 89 eventually would have been read and heard as an articulation of the theological crisis posed by the exile. As Gerald Wilson suggests, the appearance of royal psalms (Psalms 2; 72; 89) at the seams of the psalter suggests a shaping of Books I–III that both encourages an articulation of the theological questions raised by the exile and anticipates the "answer" offered by Books IV–V: God reigns (see Introduction; see also Reflections below).

Actually, Psalm 89 itself contains this answer in vv. 5-18, but the linkage of the sovereignty of God and the sovereignty of the earthly king required re-evaluation of both concepts in the light of the exile. Psalm 89 is a piece of this process of re-evaluation that led to an eschatological understanding of both God's reign (see Commentary on Psalm 2; see also Reflections below) and the concept of an earthly king. The latter eventually developed into the expectation of an anointed one (messiah)—a hope that was open-ended enough to allow the suffering of the anointed one (see vv. 50-51) to be understood in some circles as an essential aspect of his work (see Reflections below).

89:1-4. Verses 1-2 introduce the two key words in Psalm 89: "steadfast love" and "faithfulness." The pattern of repetition between vv. 1-2 and vv. 3-4 immediately links God's steadfast love and faithfulness to the origin and continuity of the Davidic dynasty. The repetition is captured more clearly by the NIV. God's love will be proclaimed "forever" (v. 1), and David's throne is "forever" (v. 4). God's faithfulness will be made known, and the Davidic throne will last "through all generations" (vv. 1, 4). God's love is "firm," as is David's throne (vv. 2, 4), and God "established" the divine faithfulness as God "will establish" David's line (vv. 2, 4). The content of vv. 1-2 will be developed in vv. 5-18, while the content of vv. 3-4 will be developed in vv. 19-37 (see "covenant" in vv. 28, 34; "chosen" in v. 19; "sworn" in v. 35; "my servant David" in v. 20; "establish"/"sustain"/"remain" in vv. 21, 37; "descendants"/"line" in vv. 30, 36; "throne" in vv. 29, 36).

89:5-18. Verses 5-14 celebrate God's sovereignty, and vv. 15-18 describe the appropriate recognition of and response to God's rule.

89:5-8. The background of ancient Near Eastern polytheism is evident in vv. 5-8, which are reminiscent of Psalm 82, in which God convenes the council of the gods and condemns the gods to die. That is not the case here, but Israel's God is clearly preeminent (for the concept of a divine council, see 1 Kgs 22:19; Jer 23:22; Psalms 29; 82; 97:7, 9). The title "LORD God of hosts" may also reflect God's sovereignty over other divinities as well as earthly beings; it is associated elsewhere with God's reign (see Ps 24:7-10; Isa 6:1-5). In any case, the heavens are to praise God for God's "wonders," which elsewhere demonstrate God's sovereignty (see Exod 15:11; Pss 9:1; 88:10, 12). The gods are to praise God for God's faithfulness (vv. 5, 8; see also vv. 1-2, and note the gods' unfaithfulness in Psalm 82). Verses 6-8a are in the form of questions, although their rhetorical effect is to affirm God's incomparable sovereignty (see Exod 15:11; Pss 18:31; 35:10; 71:19; Mic 7:18; see also Ps 86:8-10).

89:9-14. Lest any doubt be implied by the questions of vv. 6-8a, vv. 9-14 offer a rousing affirmation of God's cosmic rule. The most obvious rhetorical feature is the fivefold repetition of the emphatic Hebrew pronoun "you" (vv. 9a, 9b, 10a, 11b, 12a), which focuses attention on God's activity: *"You* rule . . . *you* stilled them . . . " and so on. In addition, the pronominal suffix "your(s)" occurs nine times in vv. 9-14, occupying the first position in the poetic line in vv. 11, 13. Content reinforces style. God asserts divine rule (see Pss 22:28; 66:7; 103:19; Isa 40:10) over the cosmic waters (v. 9; see Ps 65:7; Mark 4:41). The name "Rahab" (v. 10) recalls both God's victory over Egypt at the exodus (see Ps 87:4; Isa 30:7) and God's cosmic conquest of the forces of chaos. Myth and history are merged in the assertion of God's reign (see Exod 15:4-8, 10, 18; Ps 74:12-15). The mention of "mighty arm" (vv. 10, 13) and "right hand" (v. 13) also recalls the song in Exodus 15 that culminates in the proclamation of God's rule (see Exod 15:6, 12, 16, 18). God's rule in history is evidence of God's cosmic power. The whole world belongs to God (v. 11; see Pss 24:1-2; 93:1), and God's creation will join in recognizing God's sovereignty (v. 12; see Pss

96:11-13; 97:6; 98:7-9). Mount Tabor and Mount Hermon could simply represent well-known mountains, but it is likely that they were associated with worship of the gods (see Judg 3:3; Hos 5:1), so their praise of God would have added significance (see the NRSV's note on v. 12; see also commentary on Ps 48:2 for the possible significance of Zaphon in this regard as well). The climactic reference to God's throne in v. 14a also bespeaks God's reign, the basic policies of which are righteousness and justice (see Psalm 97:2b; see also Pss 82:1-4; 93:2; 96:13; 98:9). Verse 14b returns to the particular themes of Psalm 89, but these, too, are elsewhere characteristic of God's sovereignty (see Ps 98:3; see also Ps 33:3-4).

89:15-18. These verses describe the appropriate response to God's sovereignty. Verses 15-16 seem to depict a liturgical celebration. Happiness results from submission to God (see commentaries on Pss 1:1; 2:12), and it is enacted in the liturgy. In keeping with the focus of vv. 5-14, it is significant that a festal shout specifically accompanies God's enthronement in Ps 47:5 (see also Ps 33:3). The "shouts of joy" also have a liturgical context in Ps 27:6, where they occur in conjunction with a celebration of God as light (27:1) and with a desire to seek God's "countenance" or "presence"—more literally, God's "face" (פנים *pānîm*, 27:8-9). People join the created order in praising God's "name" (v. 16; see v. 12)—a particularly appropriate designation, since it calls to mind God's character, which is in view not only in v. 16b but throughout the psalm as well. Verse 17a, in which the "you" is again emphatic (see above on vv. 9a, 9b, 10a, 11b, 12a), may affirm that God is the glory (see Ps 71:8; Isa 46:13) and strength (see Ps 84:7) of the people (on "horn," see v. 25; Pss 75:10; 92:11). On the other hand, "strength" (עז *'ōz*) and "horn" (קרן *qeren*, v. 17), along with "shield" (מגן *māgēn*, v. 18a; see also Ps 47:9), may refer to the earthly king. In either case, vv. 17-18, which start with the same Hebrew particle and seem to belong together, mark the shift of focus to the earthly sovereign, who will be featured in vv. 19-37.

89:19-37. The word "vision" (חזיון *ḥizzāyôn*) in v. 19 recalls the word that Nathan delivered to David in 2 Sam 7:4-17 concerning the future of the Davidic house. The addressee here is unclear, since Hebrew manuscripts disagree as to singular (see NRSV) or plural (see NIV). The difference is immaterial, for what is crucial is the content, which affects both king and people. Every aspect of the promise to David and his descendants is covered in vv. 19-37. Verses 19-20 recall 2 Sam 7:8, which in turn recalls the story of God's choice of David and the anointing of David by Samuel in 1 Samuel 16 (see "anoint[ed]" in 1 Sam 16:3, 12-13; see "chose[n]" in 2 Sam 16:18; 1 Kgs 11:34). Verses 21-27 recall primarily 2 Sam 7:9-11a, which promises God's help against enemies; however, v. 24 is similar to 2 Sam 7:15, and vv. 26-27 recall 2 Sam 7:14. To be noted is that the mention of the sea in v. 25 recalls v. 9; the claim is that the king participates in the exercise of God's sovereignty, even on the cosmic scale. Verses 28-37 correspond primarily to 2 Sam 7:11b-16, the provision for a Davidic line. "Steadfast love" is mentioned twice more (vv. 28, 33; see also v. 24; 2 Sam 7:15), and the emphasis is on the eternity of the promise (see "forever" in vv. 28-29, 36-37; 2 Sam 7:13, 16). Both texts make provision for punishment but never for removal of steadfast love (cf. Ps 89:30-33 with 2 Sam 7:14-15). Actually, Psalm 89 is even more emphatic about the promise than is 2 Samuel 7. The psalm explicitly names God's promise a "covenant" (vv. 28, 34; see also vv. 3, 39). Moreover, that covenant will not be violated (v. 34); God has sworn it (v. 35a; see v. 3), and God will not lie (v. 35b). To the contrary, one of God's prominent attributes is "faithfulness" (v. 33), a word that does not occur in 2 Samuel 7. Because God is faithful, the Davidic throne will be like the sun; and like the moon, it will be a "faithful witness in the sky" (v. 37; see "skies" in v. 6). Again, the metaphor suggests that the Davidic dynasty is an enduring structure of God's cosmic rule.

89:38-52. The emphasis on God's faithfulness throughout Psalm 89—as well as the insistent claims concerning the reliability of God's word (vv. 34-35) and the exalted status of the Davidic throne (vv. 25-27, 29, 36-37)—makes the transition at v. 38 all the more unexpected and remarkable. Verses 38-45 describe the occurrence of the unthinkable. This is not just punishment; this is rejection (see "reject"/"cast off"/"spurn" in Pss

43:2; 44:23; 77:7; 88:14, and esp. 74:1, which links conceptually the fate of Jerusalem with the fate of the Davidic king). The supposedly inviolable covenant has been broken (v. 39; see also vv. 3, 28, 34). The king's enemies are triumphant (vv. 40-43; cf. vv. 21-24). The eternal throne has been cast down (v. 44; cf. vv. 29, 36). The emphasis on "forever" has been replaced by a note of transience (v. 45a), and glory (v. 17) has become shame (v. 45b).

In vv. 46-52, the king prays. The question in v. 46a is typical of other complaints (see Pss 13:1; 44:24; 69:17; 88:14; 102:2; 143:7). In terms of v. 46b, Ps 103:9 affirms that God's anger is not forever, but time is running out for the king, as vv. 47-48 suggest. The climactic question is the one in v. 49, which employs for the seventh time each of the two key words in the psalm. The number seven often symbolizes completion, and Psalm 89 had earlier described God as completely loving and faithful. But not now! As if to emphasize a final time the incongruity between the promise to David and the present reality, the word "taunt[ed]" (חרף *ḥārap*) is used three times in vv. 50-51 (see also "scorn" [חרפה *ḥerpâ*] in v. 41). In terms of the shape of the psalter, it is significant that the king's final appeal also recalls Psalm 74 and its final appeal on behalf of the people. There, too, God is asked to remember "how the enemy scoffs" (v. 18; "scoffs" is the same verb translated "taunt[ed]" in 89:50-51; see also Ps 74:10, 22). In other words, Psalms 74 and 89 provide a sort of frame for Book III. This frame suggests that Book III invites the reader to consider the question of God's sovereignty in view of the destruction of Jerusalem (Psalm 74; see Psalm 79) and the disappearance of the Davidic monarchy (Psalm 89), as well as the attendant humbling of God's people (Psalms 80; 83; 85). Given its place as the final word in Book III, it is significant that Psalm 89 does not, as Tate points out, answer the question: "The perplexity and hurt are not resolved in this psalm; the matter is left open."[342] It is precisely this openness that calls for further theological reflection.

---

342. Marvin E. Tate, *Psalms 51–100*, WBC 20 (Dallas: Word, 1990) 429.

REFLECTIONS

Psalm 89 may have originated before 587 and the actual disappearance of the monarchy. If that is so, it certainly came to be read as a commentary on the events of 587, and it is extremely interesting and significant that the editors of the psalter chose to retain it and to give it a prominent place. It virtually forces the reader of the psalms to reflect upon the nature of God's reign, especially in the light of the destruction of God's city, the captivity of God's people, and the disappearance of the earthly agent of God's rule. The open-ended conclusion of Psalm 89 has crucial implications for understanding the shape of the psalter. It invites the reader to look for a solution to the dilemma in the following psalms, especially Book IV and its explicit affirmation of God's reign (Psalms 93; 95–99) in a context that is clearly Mosaic rather than Davidic. In fact, Psalm 90 is the only psalm attributed to Moses, the man who proclaimed God's rule *before* there even existed a monarchy, a temple, or a land (see Introduction; Commentary on Psalm 90).

In other words, the book of Psalms does not abandon the conviction that God rules the world. In fact, this message pervades the psalms, from Psalms 1–2 onward (see Commentary on Psalm 2; Introduction). But the persistent juxtaposition of this claim with psalms like 89 (and other communal and individual complaints) means that the assertion of God's rule is to be heard eschatologically. In short, God always rules amid opposition, which means that it does not appear that God reigns. God's sovereignty is a strength made perfect in weakness. The apparent incongruity between God's sovereignty and the prosperity of the wicked calls the reader to decide: Will I acknowledge God's rule and live under God's claim in fundamental dependence upon God? Or will I choose to be self-rooted and to live in fundamental dependence upon myself? In the psalter's own terms, the choice is between righteousness and wickedness (see Commentary on Psalms 1; 2). The lack of resolution in Psalm 89 contributes to the eschatological orientation of the psalter.

What then can be said of the Davidic monarchy, which is tied so closely in Psalm 89 to God's rule? The response to this question must be carefully nuanced. It is tempting to conclude that Psalm 89 points ultimately to the conclusion that the monarchy was a mistake. But if so, it is a mistake for which God bears major responsibility. While the narrative sources in 1 Samuel 8–12 reflect the ambiguity surrounding the monarchy, it was ultimately given divine sanction (see 1 Samuel 16; 2 Samuel 7; Psalm 2). Positively, it was an attempt to implement very concretely *God's* policies of justice and righteousness. In this sense, its purpose can be described as *incarnational*—an attempt to embody in the lives of real people, places, and times the will of God for the world. To be sure, in actual practice, the monarchy failed to accomplish this purpose. From this perspective, one may view it as a divine experiment that failed—a mistake. But because the language and conceptuality of the monarchy expressed so clearly God's purposes for the world, this language and conceptuality were retained.

The intentional retention of the language and conceptuality of the monarchy after the disappearance of the actual institution obviously called for reinterpretation. The reinterpretations differed then and still differ now. In some circles, the privileges and responsibilities of the monarch were apparently transferred to the whole people (see Pss 105:15; 144:9-15; 149:6-9; Isa 55:3-5; 61:1-3). Some Jews looked for a restoration of the monarchy as a political institution and looked for an anointed one (messiah) who would effect such a restoration; some Jews are still looking and waiting. Some Jews are less literal about the expectation of a messiah; they see the Jewish people as agents of God's rule, and they work toward the fulfillment of God's purposes and a messianic age. Christians claimed the language and conceptuality of monarchy for Jesus of Nazareth, who was hailed as Jesus Messiah or, to use the Greek equivalent, Jesus Christ. They viewed the triumph of the king's enemies (vv. 41-42), the king's suffering (v.

45), and the taunts of others (vv. 50-51) as essential aspects of the messiah's work (see the passion narratives in the Gospels). In short, Jesus incarnated the re-evaluation of sovereignty that is called for by the open-endedness of Psalm 89. In this sense, Psalm 89 is properly read as a text for Advent.

But even while seeing in Jesus a kind of completion to the open-endedness of Psalm 89, Christians would do well to continue to read the psalm as testimony to the difficulty of embodying concretely in space and time the justice and righteousness that God wills for the world. In this sense, Psalm 89 may function finally as a call to humility, for the church—the body of Christ—often does no better than the monarchy did in furthering God's will in and for the world (see Reflections on Psalm 72). Thus the church, too, is only a provisional institution, at least in the sense that it lives not by its own sufficiency or merit but by the steadfast love and faithfulness of God. As in Psalm 89, these fundamental realities are ones that we simultaneously celebrate (vv. 1-2) and await (v. 49).

BOOK IV

PSALM 90:1-17, HAVE COMPASSION ON YOUR SERVANTS

NIV

BOOK IV

Psalms 90–106

Psalm 90

A prayer of Moses the man of God.

¹Lord, you have been our dwelling place
throughout all generations.
²Before the mountains were born
or you brought forth the earth and the
world,
from everlasting to everlasting you are God.

³You turn men back to dust,
saying, "Return to dust, O sons of men."
⁴For a thousand years in your sight
are like a day that has just gone by,
or like a watch in the night.
⁵You sweep men away in the sleep of death;
they are like the new grass of the
morning—
⁶though in the morning it springs up new,
by evening it is dry and withered.

⁷We are consumed by your anger
and terrified by your indignation.
⁸You have set our iniquities before you,
our secret sins in the light of your presence.
⁹All our days pass away under your wrath;
we finish our years with a moan.
¹⁰The length of our days is seventy years—
or eighty, if we have the strength;
yet their span* is but trouble and sorrow,
for they quickly pass, and we fly away.

a10 Or yet the best of them

NRSV

BOOK IV

(Psalms 90–106)

Psalm 90

A Prayer of Moses, the man of God.

¹ Lord, you have been our dwelling place*ᵃ*
in all generations.
² Before the mountains were brought forth,
or ever you had formed the earth and
the world,
from everlasting to everlasting you are God.

³ You turn us*ᵇ* back to dust,
and say, "Turn back, you mortals."
⁴ For a thousand years in your sight
are like yesterday when it is past,
or like a watch in the night.

⁵ You sweep them away; they are like a
dream,
like grass that is renewed in the morning;
⁶ in the morning it flourishes and is renewed;
in the evening it fades and withers.

⁷ For we are consumed by your anger;
by your wrath we are overwhelmed.
⁸ You have set our iniquities before you,
our secret sins in the light of your
countenance.

⁹ For all our days pass away under your wrath;
our years come to an end*ᶜ* like a sigh.

*ᵃ Another reading is our refuge   ᵇ Heb humankind   ᶜ Syr: Heb
we bring our years to an end*

NIV

11Who knows the power of your anger?
　　For your wrath is as great as the fear that
　　　is due you.
12Teach us to number our days aright,
　　that we may gain a heart of wisdom.

13Relent, O LORD! How long will it be?
　　Have compassion on your servants.
14Satisfy us in the morning with your unfailing
　　love,
　　that we may sing for joy and be glad all
　　　our days.
15Make us glad for as many days as you have
　　afflicted us,
　　for as many years as we have seen trouble.
16May your deeds be shown to your servants,
　　your splendor to their children.

17May the favora of the Lord our God rest
　　upon us;
　　establish the work of our hands for us—
　　yes, establish the work of our hands.

a17 Or beauty

NRSV

10 The days of our life are seventy years,
　　or perhaps eighty, if we are strong;
　　even then their spana is only toil and
　　　trouble;
　　they are soon gone, and we fly away.

11 Who considers the power of your anger?
　　Your wrath is as great as the fear that is
　　　due you.
12 So teach us to count our days
　　that we may gain a wise heart.

13 Turn, O LORD! How long?
　　Have compassion on your servants!
14 Satisfy us in the morning with your
　　steadfast love,
　　so that we may rejoice and be glad all
　　　our days.
15 Make us glad as many days as you have
　　afflicted us,
　　and as many years as we have seen evil.
16 Let your work be manifest to your servants,
　　and your glorious power to their children.
17 Let the favor of the Lord our God be upon us,
　　and prosper for us the work of our
　　　hands—
　　O prosper the work of our hands!

a Cn Compare Gk Syr Jerome Tg: Heb pride

COMMENTARY

Psalm 90 is the only psalm attributed to Moses. This alone might indicate its significance, but this is especially the case since Psalm 90 opens Book IV of the psalter. Book III is heavily weighted with prayers that lament the destruction of Jerusalem, and Psalm 89 concludes Book III with the announcement of God's rejection of the covenant with David and with the anguished questions of vv. 46 and 49. Thus it seems more than coincidental that Book IV immediately takes the reader back to the time of Moses, when there was no land or Temple or monarchy. Indeed, Book IV can be characterized as a Moses-book, and in response to the crisis of exile and its aftermath, it offers the "answer" that pervades the psalter and forms its theological heart: God reigns! (See Introduction.) In short, even without land, Tem-

ple, and monarchy, relatedness to God is still possible, as it was in the time of Moses.

Thus the superscription of Psalm 90 should be taken seriously—not as an indication of Mosaic authorship, but as a clue to read Psalm 90 in the context of the stories about Moses in the Pentateuch. For instance, D. N. Freedman notes the similarity between Ps 90:13 and Exod 32:12, where Moses tells God to "turn" or "repent" from God's anger; Freedman considers it likely "that the composer of the psalm based it on the episode in Exodus 32 and imagined in poetic form how Moses may have spoken in the circumstances of Exodus 32."343 The superscription in the Targum

343. David Noel Freedman, "Other Than Moses . . . Who Asks (or Tells) God to Repent?" Bible Review 1 (Winter 1985) 59.

supports Freedman's conclusion; it reads, "A prayer of Moses the prophet, when the people of Israel sinned in the desert." Given the canonical placement of Psalm 90, however, it is more likely that the editors of the psalter intended for readers to hear this psalm as a poetic imagining of how Moses might have spoken to the monumental crisis posed by the loss of land, Temple, and monarchy. In any case, it is important to attempt to hear Psalm 90 as an imagined prayer of Moses. (Further connections between Psalm 90 and the Pentateuch will be noted below.)

This is not the way interpretation of Psalm 90 has been approached in recent years. It has sometimes been classified as a communal lament/prayer for help, a categorization that is at least congruent with its placement in the psalter. Several commentators note that vv. 13-15 in particular indicate a prolonged period of distress, which the exile certainly represented. Psalm 90, however, has more often been viewed as a wisdom psalm, a poetic meditation on the transience of human life (see esp. vv. 3-10). To be sure, this approach has merit, and it should not be ignored. Proponents of this approach have virtually ignored the attribution to Moses, however, and it is not necessary to do so. In a sense, Moses' problem was time—namely, his time was too short. One of the most incredibly surprising aspects of the whole biblical story is that the illustrious Moses dies before entering the promised land. The reason given is that God was "angry" with Moses (see Deut 3:26, where the word "angry" [עבר 'ābar] is from the same Hebrew root as "wrath" [עברה 'ebrâ] in Ps 90:9, 11). Moses thus became a paradigm for Israel's existence and human existence. We always come up short, in terms of time, intentions, and accomplishments. What initially seems like a depressing message, however, is actually an encouraging one. If the great Moses came up short, then perhaps it is not such a disaster that we do too. Moses' death was a reminder that God, not Moses, would lead the people into the land (see Deut 31:3; 32:52). *Our* time, therefore, is not all there is to measure. *God's* time is primary, and as Psalm 90 suggests, our time must be measured finally in terms of God's time. The focus on time in this psalm will be elaborated upon below.

The structure of Psalm 90 can be outlined in several ways, but the simplest division is this: vv. 1-2, vv. 3-6, vv. 7-12, vv. 13-17. Verses 1-2 focus primarily on God, while vv. 3-6 focus on humanity. Verses 7-12 then explore the matter of human transience. The word "anger" in vv. 7, 11 provides an envelope structure for this section, suggesting that v. 12 is really a sort of transition. The tone of vv. 13-17 is markedly more hopeful than the preceding verses.

90:1-2. Although Psalm 90 focuses primarily on time, it begins with an affirmation involving place as well. As a response to exile, v. 1 is a particularly pertinent and powerful affirmation: God is really the only "dwelling place" that counts (see "refuge" in Ps 71:3; see also Ps 91:9). Indeed, such has always been the case—"in all generations." This phrase directs attention to the passage of time, as do the two verbs in v. 2, each of which is used elsewhere to speak of childbirth (see NIV). Here God is portrayed not as Mother Earth, but as mother of the earth.

Verses 1-2 already make the crucial juxtaposition of human time ("all generations") and God's time ("everlasting to everlasting"). The chiastic structure (see Introduction) of the two verses is striking, especially considering that the use of the Hebrew pronoun "you" in vv. 1-2 is often used for emphasis:

A "Lord, *you* . . ." (God)
  B "all generations" (time)
    C "mountains" (space)
    C′ "earth and the world" (space)
  B′ "everlasting to everlasting" (time)
A′ "*you* are God" (God)

The literary structure makes a theological point. The divine "You" is all-encompassing of time and space. Human life and the life of the world find their origin and destiny in God.

90:3-6. The vocabulary of vv. 3-6 continues to call to mind the passage of time—"back to dust" (v. 3), "children" (v. 3; NRSV, "mortals"; NIV, "sons"), "years" (v. 4), "yesterday" (v. 4), "watch in the night" (v. 4), "morning" (vv. 5-6), "evening" (v. 6). Verse 3 is usually taken to be an allusion to Gen 3:19, and it may be, even though the Hebrew words for "dust" differ in the two verses. The Hebrew word in Ps 90:3 (דכא dakkā') appears to mean something like "crushed," "pulverized (particle)," perhaps suggesting the crushing weight of time upon human existence. On the other hand, the meaning of v. 3 may not be quite so negative. The Hebrew root elsewhere means "contrite" (see Ps 51:17; Isa 57:15); the servant in Isaiah 53 is "crushed" (vv. 5, 10), but will still effect God's will for the benefit of other people. Similarly, God's command to humans to "turn back" may not be as cruel as it sounds; the imperative could also be translated, "Repent." To be sure, v. 3 is unremittingly realistic about human finitude and transience, but it anticipates the good news of v. 13, where the same Hebrew word (שוב šûb) is used to call upon God to "turn" or "repent."

The poetic structure of vv. 4-6 emphasizes the reality of human transience. In v. 4, which Alter contends "is one of the most exquisite uses of intraverset focusing in the Bible" (a verset is what Alter calls one component of a poetic line, and the focusing involves the increasingly smaller units of time in each component of v. 4), the movement from God's time to human time highlights the juxtaposition already begun in vv. 1-2.[344] For God, a thousand years are like three hours! The focusing in v. 4 leads directly into vv. 5-6, the chiastic structure (see Introduction) of which re-creates the progression of a day:

A v. 5a	"like a dream" (night)
B v. 5b	morning
B' v. 6a	morning
A' v. 6b	evening

Poetic structure imitates the inexorable passage of time, which is what Psalm 90 is about (see Isa 40:6-8).

90:7-12. 90:7-11. Like v. 3, vv. 7-11 are often interpreted in the light of Genesis 2–3. Indeed, both Psalm 90 and Genesis 2–3 do make a connection between sin and death, but the connection is difficult to define precisely. In Genesis 2–3, for instance, it is not at all clear that the humans would have lived forever even if they had not sinned. According to the text, the punishment for sin was not physical death but banishment from the garden (Gen 3:23). It is entirely possible to conclude that physical death was always a part of God's plan for humanity. From this perspective, then, the question for Psalm 90 is this: If death

is not simply punishment for sin, what does Psalm 90 mean by associating human transience with the anger and wrath of God in vv. 7, 9, 11? Mays's perspective is helpful:

> The wrath of God is a linguistic symbol for the divine limits and pressure placed against human resistance to his sovereignty. . . . Eternity belongs to the sovereign deity of the LORD as God . . . Death is the final and ultimate "no" that cancels any pretension to autonomy from the human side.[345]

In biblical terms, death means fundamentally to be alienated from God. In this sense, sin always results directly in death. The first humans sinned; they alienated themselves from God, and so do we. Therefore, the limitation of physical death becomes a problem. If we accepted our lives and our allotted time as gifts from God, and if we entrusted the future of our lives and the life of the world to God, then physical death would be no problem. It could be accepted as part of God's plan. But in the presence of sin, human transience is a problem. Normal human limits are experienced as wrath (see vv. 7, 9). Failing to trust God, we fear physical death, and the fear of death itself becomes "death-serving."[346] That is, it motivates us to further self-assertion and thus further alienates us from God. Thus, while sin and death are related, the relationship is not necessarily causal. Sin does not cause physical death. Rather, sin involves alienation from God, which makes physical death a problem. And when physical death is feared, then it becomes necessary to conclude that death causes sin!

The words "anger" (אף 'ap, vv. 7, 11) and "consume" (כלה kālâ) also call to mind a Mosaic context as background for hearing vv. 7-11 (see Exod 32:10-12). When the people's sin evoked God's anger and God's threat to consume the people, Moses prayed that God "turn"/"repent" (Exod 32:12; see Ps 90:13). In Exodus 32, the people's sinfulness and God's anger were not the final words. God repented, eventually revealing the divine self to be gracious, merciful, faithful and steadfastly loving (see Exod 34:6-7; see also Ps 90:14). This is also the direction in which

344. Robert Alter, *The Art of Biblical Poetry* (New York: Basic Books, 1985) 127.

345. James L. Mays, *Psalms*, Interpretation (Louisville: John Knox, 1994) 292.
346. See Douglas John Hall, *God and Human Suffering: An Exercise in the Theology of the Cross* (Minneapolis: Augsburg, 1986) 62.

Psalm 90 moves. The despair of vv. 7-11 moves toward hope (vv. 13-17), and the transition occurs in v. 12.

90:12. If God's wrath and the reality of transience were all that could be said of human life, it would be insufferably sadistic of God to "teach us to count our days" (v. 12). But v. 12 is obviously meant to be hopeful and encouraging. God is not implored to teach us how oppressive life is, but to teach us how to accept our allotted time as a *gift.* If v. 12 is heard in the Mosaic context of the story of gathering manna in the wilderness (see below on v. 14), v. 12 may even be paraphrased, "teach us to live day by day," as the Israelites had to do in the wilderness when manna was received daily. When this is done—when life is accepted as a gift and entrusted daily to God—then a "heart of wisdom" is gained, and physical death is no longer a problem. Human transience—the reality of death as part of God's plan—becomes not an occasion for despair but an opportunity for prayer.

90:13-17. 90:13. While the entire psalm has been addressed to God, the prayer takes an obviously different direction in v. 13. The first imperative recalls v. 3, where "turn" was used twice. There God's turning seemed to contribute to human transience, but v. 13 suggests that God's turning can take a different form. Verse 13 is not a request to undo human transience, for that is part of God's plan. Rather, v. 13 is a request for God to forgive human sinfulness, which alienates us from God and makes finitude a problem. The request is a bold one! God is being asked to do what human beings consistently fail to do: to turn or repent. The alienation caused by *human* sinfulness must be overcome by *God's* turning toward humanity, which is precisely what God's steadfast love (v. 14) is all about. Verses 13-14 especially recall Exodus 32–34, where Moses boldly requests God to repent (Exod 32:12), and God does (Exod 32:14), revealing that God's fundamental character involves steadfast love, which takes concrete form in the forgiveness of sins (Exod 34:6-7).

Verse 13 also has a connection with the Song of Moses in Deuteronomy 32, where Moses affirms that God will "have compassion on his servants" (v. 36). The verb translated "have compassion" (נחם *nḥm*) in v. 13 and Deut 32:36 also

occurs in Exod 32:12, 14. In fact, Exod 32:12, 14 and Deut 32:36 represent two of the four times in the Pentateuch where God is the subject of this verb. Interestingly, one other occasion is Gen 6:6-7, where God is "sorry" that God created humankind. The shift in the sense of the verb (signaled by a different form of the Hebrew verb) from the beginning to the end of the Pentateuch is revealing. It is as if the use of this verb signals a shift in God's dealing with humanity; the same sort of behavior that grieved God in the beginning now moves God to compassion. The psalmist appeals to God's compassion in Ps 90:13 as Moses had also appealed in the Pentateuch. In terms of the suggestion that Psalm 90 imagines Moses' words for the exilic situation, it is also significant that the verb in question is a key word in other texts that address the exile. For instance, Isa 40:1 starts with this verb, "Comfort, comfort my people"; the prophet is commissioned to proclaim what Moses prays for in Exodus 32 and Deuteronomy 32 and Psalm 90: God's compassion upon the people in the form of the forgiveness of sins (see also Isa 49:13; 51:3, 12).

90:14-17. The request in v. 14 also calls to mind a Mosaic context, the wilderness episode in Exodus 16, where the people were indeed satisfied in the morning (see Exod 16:8, 12; the NRSV translates the verb as "your fill"). To be sure, the satisfaction is different in the two cases. In Ps 90:14, it involves steadfast love, which, as suggested already, has strong Mosaic connections (see Exod 34:6-7). The plea of v. 14 is also particularly appropriate for the exilic situation, especially in the light of Psalm 89, where "steadfast love" occurs seven times, culminating in the crucial question of v. 49 (see Commentary on Psalm 89). For a new wilderness experience—the exile— Psalm 90 offers Moses as intercessor.

Whether the situation is the Babylonian exile and its aftermath or contemporary experiences of alienation and despair, Psalm 90 finally affirms that God's faithfulness in the face of human unfaithfulness is redemptive. In particular, God redeems time. Verses 13-17, like vv. 1-12, are still a prayer about time, but the perspective on time has been remarkably transformed. Whereas previously the passage of time could be perceived only as "toil and trouble" (v. 10), now there are new possibilities. Because God is faithful, "morning" can "satisfy" (v. 14) rather than mark a fleeting moment on the way to our demise (cf. vv. 5-6; see also Lam 3:19-24). Because God is faithful, "days" and "years" can bring gladness rather than tedium (v. 5; cf. vv. 9-10). The occurrence of the word "children" (בנים *bānîm*) in v. 16 recalls v. 3, and again the perspective has been transformed. Whereas children in v. 3 are involved in the dissolution of life, in v. 16 they represent the continuity of human life. There will be a future! And as has always been the case, that future belongs first to God. It is God's work that humans need to perceive (v. 16) and upon which human life depends. The word "splendor" (הדר *hādār*) in v. 16 occurs frequently elsewhere in the context of the proclamation of God's reign (see Pss 29:4; 96:6; 145:5). In short, what humans need to perceive is that God reigns; God is "Lord" (v. 1), and humans are God's "servants" (v. 16; see v. 13).

To be sure, humans also have work to do (see Ps 8:5, where God bestows splendor upon humanity; NIV and NRSV, "honor"), but "the work of our hands" is finally the object of God's activity—God must "establish" it (v. 17). While Psalm 90 ends with this plea, the clear implication is that God will turn, satisfy, make glad, manifest God's own work and establish humanity's work, as God did in answer to Moses' intercession in Exodus 32–34. Indeed, Ps 91:16 affirms that God will act (see Commentary on Psalm 91). In the wilderness, God's possibilities were not thwarted by human sinfulness; in the exile, God's possibilities were not thwarted by human sinfulness. The conclusion of Psalm 90 suggests that God's purposes will never finally be thwarted by human sinfulness. That is our hope and the hope of the world, as Isaac Watts's paraphrase of Psalm 90 captures so well: "O God, our help in ages past, our hope for years to come."

REFLECTIONS

Because Psalm 90 is in itself a sort of theological reflection, the commentary has already begun the process of reflection; however, there is more to be said. The priority of God's activity and the priority of God's time reshape human activity and human time.[347] Our days and years are not simply moments to be endured on the way to oblivion; our efforts are not simply fleeting and futile. Because God is eternal and faithful and eternally faithful in turning toward humanity, our allotted time becomes something meaningful, purposeful, joyful, enduring.

1. In the final analysis, Psalm 90 functions like the songs of praise as a call to decision. We are called to entrust ourselves and our allotted time to God with the assurance that, grounded in God's work and God's time, our lives and labors participate in the eternal (see John 3:16-17, where trust in God's forgiving love results in "eternal life"). Psalm 90 is finally, therefore, not an act of futility but an act of faith. And it is also an act of hope. Without having to see it happen, the psalmist trusts that God can and will satisfy and make glad and manifest God's work and establish the work of our hands (vv. 14-17). And Psalm 90 is also an act of love. The psalmist's trust puts him or her in communion with past generations who found a dwelling place in God (v. 1) and with future generations, the children, to whom the work of God will be manifest (v. 16). For the psalmist, sin and death are inevitable realities. But so are forgiveness and life! Psalm 90 is a profession of faith that invites us and instructs us to live the only way it makes any sense whatsoever to live—in faith and in hope and in love. The words of Reinhold Niebuhr provide an excellent summary of the good news of Psalm 90:

> Nothing that is worth doing can be achieved in our lifetime; therefore we must be saved by hope. Nothing which is true or beautiful or good makes complete sense in any immediate context of history; therefore we must be saved by faith. Nothing we do, however virtuous, can be accomplished alone; therefore we are saved by love. No virtuous act is quite as virtuous from the

347. See Alter, *The Art of Biblical Poetry*, 129.

standpoint of our friend or foe as it is from our standpoint. Therefore we must be saved by the final form of love which is forgiveness.[348]

2. Because Psalm 90 moves from despair to hope, it is quite appropriate for what is probably its most frequent contemporary setting in life: funeral services. To be sure, these services of worship confront us starkly with our finitude, as does Psalm 90 (see vv. 3-11). But the funeral service is not a witness to human mortality; it is a witness to the redemptive power of God, as is Psalm 90 (see vv. 13-17). This is not to say that the author of Psalm 90 possessed a doctrine of resurrection. Rather, trusting God's sovereignty (vv. 1-2, 16), the psalmist was empowered to entrust life and future to God, which is what the resurrection also invites people to do. The psalmist trusted that God's redeeming love was greater than human sinfulness and human finitude. Christians articulate this same trust by affirming faith in the resurrection. For us, the resurrection, above all else, makes God's work manifest (see v. 16). And the resurrection assures us that God establishes the work of our hands. In the words of the apostle Paul: "You know that in the Lord your labor is not in vain" (1 Cor 15:58 NRSV).

348. Reinhold Niebuhr, *The Irony of American History* (New York: Charles Scribner's Sons, 1952) 63.

PSALM 91:1-16, THE SHELTER OF THE MOST HIGH

NIV

Psalm 91

[1]He who dwells in the shelter of the Most
    High
  will rest in the shadow of the Almighty.[a]
[2]I will say[b] of the LORD, "He is my refuge and
    my fortress,
  my God, in whom I trust."

[3]Surely he will save you from the fowler's
    snare
  and from the deadly pestilence.
[4]He will cover you with his feathers,
  and under his wings you will find refuge;
  his faithfulness will be your shield and
    rampart.
[5]You will not fear the terror of night,
  nor the arrow that flies by day,
[6]nor the pestilence that stalks in the darkness,
  nor the plague that destroys at midday.
[7]A thousand may fall at your side,
  ten thousand at your right hand,
  but it will not come near you.
[8]You will only observe with your eyes
  and see the punishment of the wicked.

a1 Hebrew Shaddai   b2 Or He says

NRSV

Psalm 91

[1] You who live in the shelter of the Most
    High,
  who abide in the shadow of the
    Almighty,[a]
[2] will say to the LORD, "My refuge and my
    fortress;
  my God, in whom I trust."
[3] For he will deliver you from the snare of
    the fowler
  and from the deadly pestilence;
[4] he will cover you with his pinions,
  and under his wings you will find refuge;
  his faithfulness is a shield and buckler.
[5] You will not fear the terror of the night,
  or the arrow that flies by day,
[6] or the pestilence that stalks in darkness,
  or the destruction that wastes at noonday.

[7] A thousand may fall at your side,
  ten thousand at your right hand,
  but it will not come near you.
[8] You will only look with your eyes

aTraditional rendering of Heb Shaddai

NIV

⁹If you make the Most High your dwelling—
  even the LORD, who is my refuge—
¹⁰then no harm will befall you,
  no disaster will come near your tent.
¹¹For he will command his angels concerning
    you
  to guard you in all your ways;
¹²they will lift you up in their hands,
  so that you will not strike your foot
    against a stone.
¹³You will tread upon the lion and the cobra;
  you will trample the great lion and the
    serpent.
¹⁴"Because he loves me," says the LORD, "I will
    rescue him;
  I will protect him, for he acknowledges my
    name.
¹⁵He will call upon me, and I will answer him;
  I will be with him in trouble,
  I will deliver him and honor him.
¹⁶With long life will I satisfy him
  and show him my salvation."

NRSV

and see the punishment of the wicked.

⁹ Because you have made the LORD your refuge,ᵃ
  the Most High your dwelling place,
¹⁰ no evil shall befall you,
  no scourge come near your tent.

¹¹ For he will command his angels concerning you
  to guard you in all your ways.
¹² On their hands they will bear you up,
  so that you will not dash your foot
    against a stone.
¹³ You will tread on the lion and the adder,
  the young lion and the serpent you will
    trample under foot.

¹⁴ Those who love me, I will deliver;
  I will protect those who know my name.
¹⁵ When they call to me, I will answer them;
  I will be with them in trouble,
  I will rescue them and honor them.
¹⁶ With long life I will satisfy them,
  and show them my salvation.

ᵃCn: Heb *Because you, LORD, are my refuge; you have made*

COMMENTARY

Psalm 91 consists of an eloquent profession of faith (vv. 1-13) followed by a divine speech that confirms the faith of the psalmist (vv. 14-16). Verse 1 states the theme of the psalm, and in v. 2 the psalmist directs personal profession to God. The profession continues in vv. 3-13 as testimony offered to an unidentified "you," with the exception of v. 9a, which in Hebrew reads, "Indeed, you, O LORD, [are] my refuge." This direct address to God matches v. 2; Tate suggests that v. 9a does double duty, both forming with v. 2 an envelope around vv. 3-8 and initiating a second section of the psalmist's testimony (vv. 9-13).[349]

With good reason, Psalm 91 is ordinarily classified as a psalm of confidence or trust. Scholars disagree, however, concerning its ancient origin and use. Some suggest that the testimony arises from a person who had sought refuge in the Temple from persecutors (see below on vv. 3-4; see also Psalms 5; 17; Introduction). Others propose that the psalmist offered thankful testimony after recovery from a serious illness (see vv. 5-7; see also Psalms 6; 38). More specifically in this regard, one scholar even suggests that Psalm 91 may have been the verbal accompaniment to the purification rituals prescribed in Leviticus 14 for restoration of persons into the community.[350] Still others contend that Psalm 91 originated and was used as a liturgy for entrance to the Temple (see Psalms 15; 24), or that it should be viewed as a liturgy used by the king before a battle, or that it can be traced to testimony offered by a recent convert to Yahwism. The very variety of these proposals indicates that the language and imagery of Psalm 91 are open-ended enough to be relevant

---

349. Marvin E. Tate, *Psalms 51–100,* WBC 20 (Dallas: Word, 1990) 449, 453.

350. See Herbert J. Levine, *Sing Unto God a New Song: A Contemporary Reading of the Psalms* (Bloomington: Indiana University Press, 1995) 67-68.

and powerful in many situations; indeed, Psalm 91 has served throughout the centuries and continues to serve as a source of encouragement and strength for the people of God (see Reflections below).

More accessible than the ancient origin and use of Psalm 91 is its literary setting. A. F. Kirkpatrick argued long ago that Psalms 90–92 belong together and that Psalm 91 responds with assurance to Israel's voice out of exile (Psalm 90).[351] This proposal is congruent with the interpretation of Psalm 90 offered above and with the conclusion that Book IV responds to the crisis of exile portrayed in Books I–III, especially Book III and Psalm 89 in particular (see Commentary on Psalms 73; 74; 79; 80; 89; Introduction). The relationship between Psalms 90 and 91 is established by the occurrence of the relatively rare word "dwelling place" (מעון *māʿôn*) in Pss 90:1 and 91:9. Even more striking is that two of the concluding petitions of Ps 90:13-17 are explicitly answered in Ps 91:16, where God promises to "satisfy" (see Ps 90:14) and to "show" (see Ps 90:16). The promise of satisfaction with "length of days" (author's trans.) is particularly apt after Psalm 90 and its focus on human transience (see "days" in Ps 90:9-10, 12, 15).

91:1-2. Verse 1, the syntax of which is better captured by the NIV, summarizes the message of the psalm: God provides security. The word "shelter" (סתר *sēter*) occurs also in Pss 27:5; 31:20; and 61:4, and "shadow" (צל *ṣēl*) occurs in Pss 17:8; 36:7; 57:1; and 63:7. These words often occur in conjunction with and are virtually synonymous with those in v. 2: "fortress" (מצודה *mĕṣûdâ*; see Pss 18:2; 31:2-3; 71:3; 144:2) and the more frequent "refuge" (מחסה *maḥseh*), which is repeated in vv. 4 and 9 ("refuge" is a key word throughout the psalter; see Pss 2:12; 5:11; 11:1; 14:6; 16:1; 17:7; 31:3; 36:7; 51:1; 61:3-4; 63:7; Introduction). The four nouns in vv. 1-2 express metaphorically what the psalmist affirms directly in v. 2b: God is worthy of trust (see Pss 4:5; 9:10; Introduction). The noun "refuge," especially when it is associated with God's "wings" (v. 4; see Ruth 2:12; Pss 17:8; 36:7; 57:1; 63:7), originally may have referred to the practice of seeking sanctuary from persecutors in the Temple (see 1 Kgs 1:49-53) or to Israel's experience of finding security in worship. If either is the case, the image was broadened to mean the entrusting of one's whole self and life to God in every circumstance.

91:3-13. These verses affirm the effectiveness of trusting God in every circumstance, even the very worst. Brueggemann points out that God provides the psalmist both a "safe place" (vv. 1-2, 9-10) and a "safe journey" (vv. 3-6, 11-13); God's protection is effective everywhere.[352] Verses 5-6 assure the reader that God will protect him or her at all times as well—"night," "day," "darkness," "noonday." In addition, every manner of danger and difficulty is covered in vv. 3-13 (see Exod 23:27-29 for a possible source of some of the imagery)—surprise attack (v. 3a; see also Pss 124:7; 140:5; 141:9; 142:3), disease (see "pestilence" in vv. 3, 6), demonic powers (see vv. 5-6, which may refer to such entities), violence and war (v. 7 and perhaps v. 5a; see "arrow" in Pss 11:2; 57:4; 64:3), wicked enemies (v. 8), wild animals (v. 13; see Pss 35:17; 58:4, 6). It is not essential that we be able to identify precisely all the references and allusions in vv. 3-13. The poetic hyperbole and allusion are meant more to evoke than to specify; thus the psalmist affirms that no place, no time, no circumstance that befalls us is beyond God's ability to protect us. God's "angels" or messengers will "guard you in *all* your ways" (v. 11; see also Exod 23:20). God's faithfulness (v. 4) knows no bounds, an especially timely affirmation if Psalm 91 joins Psalm 90 in responding to Psalm 89 (see Commentary on Psalm 89, esp. discussion of v. 49; see also Ps 5:12 for the image of covering with a shield).

91:14-16. The comprehensiveness of the psalmist's profession of trust (vv. 1-13) is matched by a more compact but equally comprehensive divine promise of protection in vv. 14-16. Seven first-person verbs surround a verbless clause in v. 15b (the number seven often symbolizes comprehensiveness or completion). It contains an emphatic personal pronoun: "with him [am] *I* in trouble" (author's trans.). The only other use of the emphatic pronoun in this psalm is in the pivotal v. 9a, in which the Hebrew pronoun refers to God. Using the two emphatic pronouns and

351. A. F. Kirkpatrick, *The Book of Psalms* (Cambridge: Cambridge University Press, 1951) 553-54.

352. Walter Brueggemann, *The Message of the Psalms: A Theological Commentary* (Minneapolis: Augsburg, 1984) 156.

the seven first-person verbs, the psalmist locates the source of life in God alone.

The Hebrew verb translated "love" (חשק *ḥāšaq*) in v. 14*a* connotes as well "to be attached to," "to be connected with." The verb "know" (ידע *yāda*, NRSV) in v. 14*b* also conveys the intimacy of relation to God. Rather than suggesting that God's deliverance and protection are a reward for loving God, then, v. 14 suggests that relation to God *is* deliverance—it is life. In Ps 9:10, those who know God's name "put their trust" in God, and this is also the case here (see v. 2). It is they who experience God as protector (see Ps 9:9, where the two occurrences of "stronghold" [משגב *miśgāb*] represent the same Hebrew root as protect in Ps 91:14; see also Ps 20:2). The mention of God's "name" may recall vv. 1-2, where the psalmist moves from more general names for God to the more personal "Yahweh" (or "LORD"). In any case, vv. 14-16 describe the life of one who has entrusted the whole self to God. Such trust constitutes life, which is the meaning of deliver-ance and rescue and salvation (see Exod 15:2; Pss 3:2, 7-8; 13:5). It may seem unusual for God to "honor" human beings (see 1 Sam 2:30; Ps 8:5), but this action, too, bespeaks the closeness of the relationship God promises. The perspective is thoroughly God-centered; in this regard it is significant that the psalm ends with the divine speech. As John Bracke concludes: "While the psalm's first word was of human trust, the psalmist reserves the last word for God. . . . By ending the psalm in God's word of promise, the psalmist points to the ultimate ground of human confidence, security, and hope. We are finally grounded in God's sovereign power and promise."[353] Thus Psalm 91 finally invites the reader to follow the psalmist's example of trust (v. 2), in the assurance that those who humble themselves will be exalted (v. 15; see Luke 18:14).

353. John Bracke, "Psalm 91:1-10: Psalm for the Third Sunday After Pentecost," *No Other Foundation* 10 (Winter 1989–90) 50.

REFLECTIONS

1. The sheer eloquence and comprehensiveness of the psalmist's affirmation of faith make Psalm 91 powerful. These same attributes, however, can also be a source of misunderstanding. For instance, many Jews and Christians have copied passages of the psalm and worn them in amulets to magically ward off danger; indeed, vv. 11-13 have been used to support the notion that guardian angels protect us from harm.[354] Illustrating such misuses of the psalm, in Luke 4:9-12 the devil quotes Ps 91:11-12 to tempt Jesus to jump from the pinnacle of the Temple, but Jesus refuses to claim God's promise of protection for his own benefit. For Jesus says, to do so would be to test rather than to trust God (see also Matt 4:5-7). We should not use Psalm 91 as a magical guarantee against danger, threat, or difficulty. Rather, this psalm is a reminder to us that nothing "will be able to separate us from the love of God" (Rom 8:39 NRSV). Neither Jesus nor the apostle Paul sought to avoid danger or difficulty at the expense of being faithful, and Jesus warned his followers not to abuse the promised power of God (see Luke 10:19; cf. Ps 91:13). In fact, Jesus' and Paul's faithfulness to God and to God's purposes impelled them into dangerous situations (see 1 Cor 6:4-10); when Jesus did claim the assurance of the psalms, it was *from the cross* (see Luke 23:46, where Jesus quotes Ps 31:5). Jesus' life, death, and resurrection demonstrate the self-denial and humble trust (see Ps 91:2) that lead to being exalted by God (see Ps 91:15).

2. Psalm 91 is traditionally used at the beginning of Lent, and its thoroughly God-centered perspective makes it appropriate for this season. It warns us not to reduce Lenten disciplines to trivial, self-help schemes. Genuine self-denial begins with the kind of radical affirmation of trust that is found in Psalm 91.

354. See James L. Mays, *Psalms,* Interpretation (Louisville: John Knox, 1994) 297.

PSALM 92:1-15, BUT YOU, O LORD, ARE EXALTED FOREVER!

NIV

Psalm 92

A psalm. A song. For the Sabbath day.

¹It is good to praise the LORD
   and make music to your name, O Most
      High,
²to proclaim your love in the morning
   and your faithfulness at night,
³to the music of the ten-stringed lyre
   and the melody of the harp.

⁴For you make me glad by your deeds, O LORD;
   I sing for joy at the works of your hands.
⁵How great are your works, O LORD,
   how profound your thoughts!
⁶The senseless man does not know,
   fools do not understand,
⁷that though the wicked spring up like grass
   and all evildoers flourish,
   they will be forever destroyed.

⁸But you, O LORD, are exalted forever.

⁹For surely your enemies, O LORD,
   surely your enemies will perish;
   all evildoers will be scattered.
¹⁰You have exalted my horn[a] like that of a
      wild ox;
   fine oils have been poured upon me.
¹¹My eyes have seen the defeat of my
      adversaries;
   my ears have heard the rout of my wicked
      foes.

¹²The righteous will flourish like a palm tree,
   they will grow like a cedar of Lebanon;
¹³planted in the house of the LORD,
   they will flourish in the courts of our God.
¹⁴They will still bear fruit in old age,
   they will stay fresh and green,
¹⁵proclaiming, "The LORD is upright;
   he is my Rock, and there is no wickedness
      in him."

a10 *Horn* here symbolizes strength.

NRSV

Psalm 92

A Psalm. A Song for the Sabbath Day.

¹ It is good to give thanks to the LORD,
   to sing praises to your name, O Most High;
² to declare your steadfast love in the
      morning,
   and your faithfulness by night,
³ to the music of the lute and the harp,
   to the melody of the lyre.
⁴ For you, O LORD, have made me glad by
      your work;
   at the works of your hands I sing for joy.

⁵ How great are your works, O LORD!
   Your thoughts are very deep!
⁶ The dullard cannot know,
   the stupid cannot understand this:
⁷ though the wicked sprout like grass
   and all evildoers flourish,
   they are doomed to destruction forever,
⁸   but you, O LORD, are on high forever.
⁹ For your enemies, O LORD,
   for your enemies shall perish;
   all evildoers shall be scattered.

¹⁰ But you have exalted my horn like that of
      the wild ox;
   you have poured over me[a] fresh oil.
¹¹ My eyes have seen the downfall of my enemies;
   my ears have heard the doom of my evil
      assailants.

¹² The righteous flourish like the palm tree,
   and grow like a cedar in Lebanon.
¹³ They are planted in the house of the LORD;
   they flourish in the courts of our God.
¹⁴ In old age they still produce fruit;
   they are always green and full of sap,
¹⁵ showing that the LORD is upright;
   he is my rock, and there is no
      unrighteousness in him.

a Syr: Meaning of Heb uncertain

COMMENTARY

Psalm 92 is the only psalm assigned to a specific day—the sabbath. Given the overwhelming significance of the sabbath in the Pentateuch (see, e.g., Exod 20:8-11; Deut 5:12-15) and in the history of Israel and Judaism, it is not surprising that the sabbath should be singled out in this way. Rabbinic sources confirm the use of Psalm 92 in the Temple on the sabbath following the daily offering, but they also cite Psalms 24; 48; 81; 82; 93; and 94 for use on the other six days of the week. Since the superscriptions of none of these other psalms reflect such use, Nahum M. Sarna concludes that the unique superscription of Psalm 92 "must be indicative of deliberate selection for the Sabbath day, prior to, and independent of, the other six."[355]

This is not to say that Psalm 92 was written for use on the sabbath. At some point, though one cannot with certainty say why, the psalm was deemed appropriate for such use. God's "works" (vv. 4-5) may refer to the creation, with which the sabbath was also associated (see Gen 2:1-3; Exod 20:8-11; see also v. 9, which may reflect the mythic notion of creation by God's combat with the forces of chaos). But there are other reasons for linking the psalm to the sabbath: Psalm 92 reflects God's will for the righteous ordering of human society (see vv. 7, 11, 12-15), and the sabbath was associated with the proper treatment of human beings (see Exod 23:12; Deut 5:12-15); and the sabbath day was devoted to praising God (vv. 1-3) and gathering for worship (v. 13). One might even see a link in that the name "Yahweh" ("LORD") occurs seven times in the psalm, and the sabbath was the seventh day.[356]

Psalm 92 is usually categorized as an individual song of thanksgiving, and in vv. 1-3 the psalmist at least implicitly invites others to share in thanksgiving; vv. 4, 10-11 may be construed as a description of the psalmist's deliverance, also typical of thanksgiving songs. It is unclear, however, whether one should translate the verbs in vv. 10-11 in the past tense or the future tense. Has the psalmist already been exalted and the enemies

defeated, or do these events still lie in the future? This uncertainty brings to light another major aspect of Psalm 92: its concern is not just with the individual psalmist (vv. 10-11) but more generally with the life and future of the righteous (vv. 12-15) and the wicked (vv. 7, 9). Because the psalmist recognizes that the wicked flourish, at least for a time (v. 7), and because a strong case can be made for translating the verbs in vv. 10-11 in the future tense (as in v. 9), it is best to approach Psalm 92 not so much as a celebration of a particular deliverance, but as affirmation of the sovereignty of God and the deliverance of God's people.

Indeed, the structure of Psalm 92 focuses attention on God's sovereignty. The very middle verse (v. 8; note how the NIV sets it apart) further stands out by virtue of the emphatic pronoun "you." To affirm that God is "on high forever" is to affirm that God rules the world (see Ps 93:4, which contains the phrase "on high" and which initiates a series of psalms that proclaim God's reign; see the same Hebrew root in Pss 99:5, 9; 145:1). Tate even suggests that v. 8 is the pivotal verse in a chiastic structure (see Introduction) in which vv. 1-3 correspond with vv. 12-15 (joyful celebration of God's character; see "proclaim"/"proclaiming" in vv. 2, 15 NIV), vv. 4-6 with vv. 10-11 (the work of God), and v. 7 with v. 9 (both are three-part lines dealing with the wicked).[357] This proposal may be too elaborate; however, it does have the advantage of suggesting that Psalm 92 is not simply a typical song of thanksgiving, and it thus allows for the didactic tone that scholars often detect (see vv. 5-7, 12-15, which are especially reminiscent of Psalms 1; 37; and 73, which also have a didactic character).

As suggested above, Ps 92:8 anticipates Ps 93:4 and the subsequent series of psalms proclaiming God's reign (Psalms 95–99); it also is linked literarily to the two preceding psalms (see Commentary on Psalms 90; 91). Psalm 92:1-4 especially recalls Psalm 90 with the mention of proclaiming God's "steadfast love in the morning" (v. 2; see also 90:14). The word "faithfulness"

---

355. Nahum M. Sarna, "The Psalm for the Sabbath Day (Ps 92)," *JBL* 81 (1962) 156.
356. See ibid., 157-68.

357. Tate, *Psalms 51–100,* 464; Tate relies on the insights of R. M. Davidson.

(אמונה 'ĕmûnâ) in v. 2 recalls Ps 91:4, and all three psalms are concerned with day and night (90:4-6; 91:5-6; 92:2). Furthermore, 92:4 answers the requests of 90:14-15; in both cases, joy and gladness are associated with God's work (90:1b, 92:4). In part, this work has to do with God's opposition to the wicked (see Pss 91:8; 92:11). Thus Psalm 92 joins Psalms 90–91, as well as the subsequent psalms in Book IV, as a response to the theological crisis posed by the exile and especially articulated in Book III (see Commentary on Psalms 73; 74; 79; 80; 89; Introduction).

92:1-6. Both verbs in v. 1 occur also in Ps 7:17, which immediately follows an affirmation of the downfall of the wicked (7:12-16; see also 92:7, 9, 11). Verses 1-2, as well as the reference to musical instruments in v. 3 (see Ps 33:2), support an original liturgical setting for Psalm 92 (see above on the superscription).

As in the hymns, the offering of praise is supported by reasons for praise (vv. 4-6). The Hebrew word translated "work" (פעל *pōʿal,* v. 4a; NIV, "deeds") usually designates God's saving work on behalf of the people (see Deut 32:4; Pss 44:1; 90:16; 95:9; Isa 5:12). The word "works" in vv. 4b, 5a also refers often to God's saving activity (see Josh 24:31; Judg 2:7, 10; Ps 33:4), but it refers as well to God's activity in creation (see Pss 8:3; 19:1; 103:22; 104:24). Either nuance is appropriate, for both God's creating and saving activities testify ultimately to God's universal sovereignty. The word "great" (גדל *gādal*) is also associated frequently with the proclamation of God's reign (see Pss 47:2; 95:3; 96:4; 99:2). Thus vv. 4-5 anticipate the pivotal v. 8. Although the NIV and the NRSV link v. 6 syntactically to v. 7, it can also be understood in relation to vv. 4-5; that is, the recognition of God's sovereignty constitutes true understanding (see Job 28:28; Ps 111:10; Prov 1:7; 9:10).

92:7-9. It is both structurally and theologically significant that v. 8 is surrounded by two verses that focus on "evildoers" (vv. 7, 9; the "doers"

component of this compound word is the same as "work" in v. 4a NRSV, thus contrasting God and the wicked). In terms of the structure of the psalm and of the reality of the psalmist's world, the affirmation of God's rule is made in the midst of evil. Thus the perspective is eschatological (see Psalm 2; Introduction). Appearances seem to deny God's reign, for the evildoers flourish (v. 7; see also vv. 12-13). But, the psalmist affirms, they shall perish (v. 9; see also Pss 1:6; 37:20; 73:27).

92:10-15. The Hebrew verb forms do not change between vv. 9 and 10, so it is likely that the verbs in vv. 10-11 should be translated in the future tense (and probably those in vv. 12-14 as well). The correlate of the wicked person's perishing is described by the psalmist first in personal terms (v. 10) and then more generally. The psalmist will be "exalted" (see Ps 75:7). The wicked will flourish, but only briefly, "like grass"; the righteous will flourish like trees that are planted in God's garden (cf. v. 7 with vv. 12-13; see also Ps 1:3; Jer 17:7-8). The righteous are able to take root, grow, and be fruitful, because God is both their foundation and their constant source of nourishment. Whereas the righteous trust God, the wicked trust themselves (see Jer 17:5, 7). Psalm 92 affirms that trust in self alone is illusory and ultimately leads to destruction (vv. 7, 9, 11). But trust in God brings true understanding (v. 6) and connects one to the unfailing source of life (see Commentary on Psalm 1, esp. discussion of v. 3). The integrity, vitality, and joy of the righteous (vv. 4, 12-14)—who exist *even now* amid the flourishing of evil—offer testimony to God's character (v. 15; see also v. 2). God is "upright" (see Deut 32:4; Pss 25:8; 33:4), and unlike other so-called authorities, God does "no unrighteousness" (see Ps 58:2; 82:2). The life of the righteous also testifies to God's strength (see "rock" in Deut 32:4; Pss 19:14; 28:1; 31:2; 73:26; 95:1), for the righteous have discovered that trusting God is precisely what constitutes life.

REFLECTIONS

1. The eschatological perspective of Psalm 92 is in keeping with the orientation of the whole psalter (see Commentary on Psalm 2; Introduction), but Psalm 92 is especially reminiscent of Psalms 1; 37; and 73. Its message that trusting oneself alone is illusory and destructive offers a sobering warning to a generation that generally "cannot understand this" (v. 6). As much or more than any generation before in the history of the world, we are inclined to trust our own intelligence, strength, and technology more than we trust God or each other. From the perspective of Psalm 92, the irony is that the more sophisticated and self-sufficient we think we are, the more stupid and more insecure we actually are. A renewed sense of the greatness of God's works, of the stunning depth of God's design for the cosmos, and of the breadth of God's sovereign claim upon humankind, is urgently needed (see vv. 5-9).

2. As with Psalms 1–2; 37; 73; and many others, the eschatological affirmation of God's rule challenges us to find our security in God rather than in ourselves, which suggests another dimension to Psalm 92 as a sabbath song. According to the Heidelberg Catechism, the Fourth Commandment requires that one "cease from my evil works all the days of my life, allow the Lord to work in me through his spirit, and thus begin in this life the eternal sabbath" (Question 103). In recognizing and yielding to God's rule (Ps 92:8), we experience at once "the eternal sabbath," the peace God intends and will bring about (vv. 4, 12-15; see also Isa 55:10-13).

3. The theme of proclaiming makes Psalm 92 especially appropriate for Epiphany (see vv. 2, 15). What is to be proclaimed gets at the very heart of God's character—steadfast love and faithfulness (v. 2; see also Exod 34:6-7; Pss 89:50; 98:3; 138:2; Introduction), as well as God's righteousness (v. 15). The proclamation is to be made throughout every day (see "morning" and "night" in v. 2) and throughout a lifetime (see "old age" in v. 14). It involves both liturgical activity (see vv. 3, 13) and style of life (see v. 14). By their worship and by their work, the people of God proclaim that their lives and futures belong not to themselves but to God. Indeed, the content of this proclamation is the essence of being "righteous" (v. 12; see also Commentary on Psalm 1). This message was liberating good news to ancient exiles, and it is still liberating good news to contemporary persons captivated by themselves, alienated from God, and isolated from one another.

PSALM 93:1-5, GOD HAS ESTABLISHED THE WORLD

NIV	NRSV
Psalm 93	Psalm 93
¹The LORD reigns, he is robed in majesty; the LORD is robed in majesty and is armed with strength. The world is firmly established; it cannot be moved.	¹ The LORD is king, he is robed in majesty; the LORD is robed, he is girded with strength. He has established the world; it shall never be moved;
²Your throne was established long ago; you are from all eternity.	² your throne is established from of old; you are from everlasting.
³The seas have lifted up, O LORD, the seas have lifted up their voice; the seas have lifted up their pounding waves.	³ The floods have lifted up, O LORD, the floods have lifted up their voice; the floods lift up their roaring.
⁴Mightier than the thunder of the great waters, mightier than the breakers of the sea—	⁴ More majestic than the thunders of mighty waters,

NIV

the Lord on high is mighty.

⁵Your statutes stand firm;
holiness adorns your house
for endless days, O Lord.

NRSV

more majestic than the waves*ᵃ* of the sea,
majestic on high is the Lord!

⁵ Your decrees are very sure;
holiness befits your house,
O Lord, forevermore.

ᵃ Cn: Heb *majestic are the waves*

COMMENTARY

Psalm 93 is the first in a collection of enthronement psalms (Psalms 93; 95–99; on the apparent intrusion of Psalm 94, see Introduction and Commentary on Psalm 94), which forms the theological heart of the psalter (see Introduction). To be sure, its fundamental claim—"the Lord is king" (v. 1)—pervades the psalter; there have already been other enthronement psalms (see Psalms 29; 47). The strength of this collection, however, is impressive, and it comes at a crucial point in the psalter in response to the theological crisis articulated by Book III (see Commentary on Psalms 73; 74; 79; 80; 89; 90; Introduction).

The origin and ancient setting of the enthronement psalms are much debated. While there is no solid evidence for Mowinckel's view that they were used at a New Year festival where God was annually enthroned, it is entirely likely they were used in some liturgical setting (see Commentary on Psalm 47). There are affinities between the enthronement psalms and the poetry of Isaiah 40–55 (see Isa 52:7-10; see also Commentary on Psalm 96), but the direction of the influence is unclear. In their present setting, the enthronement psalms do seem to respond to the same crisis to which Isaiah 40–55 is directed: the exile. Their literary context in the psalter also gives the enthronement psalms an eschatological orientation; they assert the reign of God in the face of circumstances that seem to deny it (see Commentary on Psalm 2; Introduction). It is finally not possible or necessary to view as mutually exclusive the cultic, historical, and eschatological approaches to Psalm 93 and the other enthronement psalms (see Commentary on Psalm 96).

While the enthronement psalms share much in common, each one is unique. Psalm 93, for instance, features God's role as creator and the attendant ancient Near Eastern mythic background. Verses 1-2 describe poetically the reality of God's kingship, while vv. 3-4 use the image of water to portray the response. Verse 5, which at first sight may appear unrelated to vv. 1-4, then addresses the privilege and responsibility that fall to a monarch to order justly and rightly the lives of those subject to his or her rule.

The translation of the Hebrew verb form in the opening affirmation has been the subject of prolonged debate. Several scholars have defended the translation "has become king," and this rendering fits nicely their view of an annual enthronement or re-enthronement of God. This translation is grammatically possible, but so is the present tense, which is preferable in view of the affirmation in vv. 1c-2 that God has *always* been king. Verse 1 continues with a figurative description of God's royal garments (see Isa 51:9, where the NIV's "clothe" and the NRSV's "put on" represent the same verb as "is robed" [לבש *lābaš*] here, and where "strength" is also involved; see also Ps 104:1; Isa 59:17). First is "majesty" (גאות *gē'ût*) which interestingly in view of vv. 3-4, is used of waters in Ps 46:3 and of the sea in Ps 89:9. But God has subdued the chaotic waters (vv. 3-4) and thus demonstrated God's sovereignty. It is significant, too, that God's majesty is also celebrated in the Song of the Sea in Exodus 15 (see Exod 15:7), where God defeats not only the Egyptians (a historical foe), but also the waters (v. 8). The whole episode is a demonstration of God's strength (vv. 2, 13), and the song culminates in the proclamation of God's reign (v. 18). The song in Exodus 15 is also framed by a verbal form of the root that appears in 93:1 as "majesty" (see Exod 15:1, 21).

93:1-2. To be "girded" usually denotes preparedness for battle, as the NIV more clearly suggests (see Pss 18:32, 39; 65:6). As in Exodus 15, "strength" is elsewhere associated with the proclamation of God's reign (see Pss 29:1; 96:6-7). In short, the depiction of God's royal attire as "majesty" and "strength" amounts to the portrayal of the king as divine warrior. Verse 1c follows logically from this portrayal, since creation in the ancient Near East was often viewed as a battle between God and the forces of chaos—the sea or the waters or the deep (see Ps 74:12-17). In this battle, God has proven victorious; so chaos is ordered, and the world is "established" as solid and immovable (see Pss 24:1-2; 96:10; see also 46:5, where Zion is the solid point in the chaotic swirl described in 46:1-3; see also 15:5; 16:8, where individuals will not be moved on account of God's presence). The verb "established" (כון *kûn*) links vv. 1 and 2, and thus provides another conceptual tie between God's sovereignty and the ordered existence of the world (see other references to God's throne in Pss 47:8; 89:14; 97:2; 103:19). Verse 2 shifts to direct address of God; in a case of unusual syntax, the last word in the line is the Hebrew pronoun "you," which emphatically focuses attention directly on God.

93:3-4. That the cosmic battle with chaos lies in the background of vv. 1-2 is confirmed in vv. 3-4 with the mention of "floods" (see Ps 98:8), "waters," and "the sea." The threefold occurrence of "floods" and "lift up" may be intended to suggest the repetitive motion of large bodies of water. In any case, the sound of the waters ("voice" in v. 3 and "thunder[s]" in v. 4 are the same Hebrew word [קול *qôl*]) seems to be viewed poetically as their way of paying homage to God (see Isa 24:14). The NIV's "pounding," however, may point in a different direction. The form is difficult, but the word seems to derive from a root that means "to crush." Its appearance in Ps 94:5

may suggest that the noise of the sea indicates its hostile intent. If so, however, God's power is greater, as v. 4 makes clear. The repeated "majestic" (v. 4) occurs in Exod 15:10, where it also describes "waters" ("the sea" also is present in this verse). The affirmation is that God's majesty/might is greater than that of the chaotic waters, which were actually personified as gods in Canaanite literature. Thus God rules the world (see "majestic" also in Pss 8:1, 9; 76:5; and see "on high" in Pss 7:7; 68:18 NIV).

93:5. As suggested above, the movement from vv. 1-4 to v. 5 is not unnatural. The affirmation of v. 5a is virtually identical to that of Ps 19:7b; like Psalm 93, Psalm 19 also moves from creation to God's instruction (cf. vv. 1-6 with vv. 7-14). In fact, the exodus narrative, to which Psalm 93 alludes, makes a similar movement from the proclamation of God's sovereignty (Exod 15:1-21, esp. v. 18) to Sinai and the proclamation of God's will (Exodus 19–24). God's decrees are "sure" (אמן *'āman*), which translates the Hebrew root that lies behind the noun "faithfulness." That is, God's will embodies faithfulness. It was precisely God's faithfulness that the exile called into question (see Ps 89:49), and Psalm 93 is part of the response that Book IV provides: God reigns, and God's will is faithful (see Pss 92:2; 98:3).

God's "house" in v. 5 is apparently the Temple. Elsewhere, too, the Temple (or Zion or God's throne) is called "holy" (see Pss 2:6; 3:4; 5:7; 11:4; 15:1; 24:3; 47:8). Holiness in its root sense connotes unapproachability, so it is significant that holiness here has to do with the communication and enactment of God's will—that is, God's will to *relate*. The same complex of ideas recurs in Psalm 99, where the repeated assertion is that God is holy (vv. 3, 5, 9), but where God has again communicated God's decrees (v. 7) for the relational purpose of enacting justice and righteousness (v. 4). Such was and is the true calling of the powerful, divine and human (see Commentary on Psalms 72; 82).

REFLECTIONS

1. The probability that Psalm 93 was placed literarily to respond to events that called into question God's faithfulness and love (see Ps 89:49) is significant, for rampant evil in our world still raises similar questions in people's minds. In other words, the affirmation that God reigns is eschatological; it is always made amid circumstances that seem to deny it—exile, evil, alienation, sin, suffering, death. Yet, Psalm 93 joins the psalter as a whole in asserting unequivocally and enthusiastically that God alone rules the world and that God's purposes can be trusted. In short, the real and fundamental truth about the world is simply this: God reigns. The disparity between this proclamation and the so-called real world calls for a decision. Weiser, noting that Psalm 93 offers through the eyes of faith a very particular view of God and the world, says that "He is the God who was, who is and who is to come, and before whose reality the barriers of time disappear so that what happened long ago and what will come to pass in the future both simultaneously call for a decision at the present moment."[358] In fact, this decision is the same one Jesus called for when he announced the presence of God's reign and invited people to enter it (Mark 1:14-15). Of course, to most of his contemporaries, Jesus seemed out of touch with the "real world," and his cross was an offense. But again, the reign of God is always proclaimed amid circumstances that seem to deny it.

2. The certainty that Psalm 93 was used liturgically in some setting is also significant, for it suggests that worship affords us the opportunity to affirm that we trust that God rules the world. It is an exceedingly difficult affirmation to make. On the one hand, the very existence of monstrous evil in the world leads many Christians to attribute equal, if not superior, power to the devil (which, of course, offers a convenient excuse for our own failings). This, in turn, raises a second source of difficulty. Our culture teaches us essentially that there is no need to talk about God anyway; God is a projection either of our own guilt or of our own will to power, and it is really we who are in control of the world and of our destinies for good or ill. Because of these two different but persistent temptations, it is crucial that our worship incorporate the fundamental message of Psalm 93: God reigns.

This astounding good news has profound consequences. It means that we belong fundamentally not to ourselves, but to God. And so does the world. The ecological implications alone are staggering, not to mention the social, economic, and political ones! (See Commentary on Psalms 2; 8; 29; 47.) But Christians profess that the place to start is by following the one who invites people to enter God's reign by denying self and taking up a cross (Mark 8:34). Jesus' disciples thought it was a strange way to acknowledge God's sovereignty, and the world still thinks it strange! All of this suggests that the most important thing we can do, repeatedly in our worship and work, is to affirm God's fundamental claim upon our lives and our world—God reigns. In the words of Hauerwas and Willimon: "We would like a church that again asserts that God, not nations, rules the world, that the boundaries of God's kingdom transcend those of Caesar, and that the main political task of the church is the formation of people who see clearly the cost of discipleship and are willing to pay the price."[359]

358. Artur Weiser, *The Psalms,* OTL, trans. H. Hartwell (Philadelphia: Westminster, 1962) 618.
359. Stanley Hauerwas and William H. Willimon, *Resident Aliens: Life in the Christian Colony* (Nashville: Abingdon, 1989) 48.

PSALM 94:1-23, JUSTICE WILL RETURN

NIV	NRSV
Psalm 94	Psalm 94
[1]O LORD, the God who avenges, O God who avenges, shine forth.	[1] O LORD, you God of vengeance, you God of vengeance, shine forth!

NIV

²Rise up, O Judge of the earth;
   pay back to the proud what they deserve.
³How long will the wicked, O LORD,
   how long will the wicked be jubilant?

⁴They pour out arrogant words;
   all the evildoers are full of boasting.
⁵They crush your people, O LORD;
   they oppress your inheritance.
⁶They slay the widow and the alien;
   they murder the fatherless.
⁷They say, "The LORD does not see;
   the God of Jacob pays no heed."

⁸Take heed, you senseless ones among the
      people;
   you fools, when will you become wise?
⁹Does he who implanted the ear not hear?
   Does he who formed the eye not see?
¹⁰Does he who disciplines nations not punish?
   Does he who teaches man lack knowledge?
¹¹The LORD knows the thoughts of man;
   he knows that they are futile.

¹²Blessed is the man you discipline, O LORD,
   the man you teach from your law;
¹³you grant him relief from days of trouble,
   till a pit is dug for the wicked.
¹⁴For the LORD will not reject his people;
   he will never forsake his inheritance.
¹⁵Judgment will again be founded on
      righteousness,
   and all the upright in heart will follow it.

¹⁶Who will rise up for me against the wicked?
   Who will take a stand for me against
      evildoers?
¹⁷Unless the LORD had given me help,
   I would soon have dwelt in the silence of
      death.
¹⁸When I said, "My foot is slipping,"
   your love, O LORD, supported me.
¹⁹When anxiety was great within me,
   your consolation brought joy to my soul.

²⁰Can a corrupt throne be allied with you—
   one that brings on misery by its decrees?
²¹They band together against the righteous
   and condemn the innocent to death.
²²But the LORD has become my fortress,
   and my God the rock in whom I take
      refuge.

NRSV

² Rise up, O judge of the earth;
   give to the proud what they deserve!
³ O LORD, how long shall the wicked,
   how long shall the wicked exult?

⁴ They pour out their arrogant words;
   all the evildoers boast.
⁵ They crush your people, O LORD,
   and afflict your heritage.
⁶ They kill the widow and the stranger,
   they murder the orphan,
⁷ and they say, "The LORD does not see;
   the God of Jacob does not perceive."

⁸ Understand, O dullest of the people;
   fools, when will you be wise?
⁹ He who planted the ear, does he not hear?
   He who formed the eye, does he not see?
¹⁰ He who disciplines the nations,
   he who teaches knowledge to humankind,
      does he not chastise?
¹¹ The LORD knows our thoughts,ᵃ
   that they are but an empty breath.

¹² Happy are those whom you discipline,
      O LORD,
   and whom you teach out of your law,
¹³ giving them respite from days of trouble,
   until a pit is dug for the wicked.
¹⁴ For the LORD will not forsake his people;
   he will not abandon his heritage;
¹⁵ for justice will return to the righteous,
   and all the upright in heart will follow it.

¹⁶ Who rises up for me against the wicked?
   Who stands up for me against evildoers?
¹⁷ If the LORD had not been my help,
   my soul would soon have lived in the
      land of silence.
¹⁸ When I thought, "My foot is slipping,"
   your steadfast love, O LORD, held me up.
¹⁹ When the cares of my heart are many,
   your consolations cheer my soul.
²⁰ Can wicked rulers be allied with you,
   those who contrive mischief by statute?
²¹ They band together against the life of the
      righteous,
   and condemn the innocent to death.

ᵃHeb the thoughts of humankind

NIV

23He will repay them for their sins
    and destroy them for their wickedness;
    the Lord our God will destroy them.

NRSV

22 But the Lord has become my stronghold,
    and my God the rock of my refuge.
23 He will repay them for their iniquity
    and wipe them out for their wickedness;
    the Lord our God will wipe them out.

COMMENTARY

Mays suggests that the message of Psalm 94 is captured in the familiar hymn "This Is My Father's World": "Though the wrong seems oft so strong, God is the ruler yet."[360] Thus, even though Psalm 94 does not directly say that God reigns, it reinforces the proclamation explicit in Psalms 93; 95–99. Psalm 94 also recalls Psalm 92; both psalms are concerned with the lives and futures of the righteous (92:12; 94:21) and the wicked (92:7; 94:3, 13), the latter described twice in each psalm as evildoers (92:7, 9; 94:4, 16). Both psalms have an instructional intent (cf. 92:6 with 94:8); they share several items of vocabulary (see the NRSV's "steadfast love," 92:2; 94:18; "upright," 92:15; 94:15; "rock" 92:15; 94:22), and they both reinforce the explicit proclamation of God's reign. The similarity suggests that the apparent intrusion of Psalm 94 into the series of enthronement psalms (93; 95–99) may serve the purpose of binding this collection more explicitly to Psalms 90–92, which open Book IV (see Introduction).[361]

Psalm 94 is often categorized as a communal lament or prayer for help; however, this designation applies well only to vv. 1-7. Verses 8-15 are addressed not to God but to foolish people (vv. 8-11) and to the righteous (vv. 12-15). Verses 16-23 consist of direct address to God (vv. 18-21), framed by references to God in the third person that have the character of professions of faith (vv. 16-17, 22-23). The structure is usually outlined according to the above divisions: vv. 1-7, vv. 8-15, vv. 16-23. Several scholars, however, suggest a chiastic arrangement (see Introduction), in which

vv. 1-2 are an introduction, vv. 3-7 correspond to vv. 20-23, vv. 8-11 to 16-19, and vv. 12-15 form the focal point.[362] While the first proposal is simpler, the second has the advantage of highlighting a unit that seems to summarize the message of the psalm. The two proposals need not be viewed as mutually exclusive.

94:1-7. As the juxtaposition of the major concepts in vv. 1-2 suggests, vengeance has to do with God's establishment of justice. Elsewhere, too, God is characterized as a "God of vengeance" (see Deut 32:35, 41, 43; Pss 58:10; 79:10; Jer 51:6; Ezek 25:12, 14, 17), and it is especially significant that Ps 99:8 describes God as avenging the people's wrongs as part of the exercise of God's reign (see 99:1). God's role as judge—God's establishment of justice—also belongs to the exercise of God's rule (see Pss 9:7-8; 96:13; 97:2; 98:9; 99:4). The plea that God "shine forth" uses the language of theophany (see Deut 33:2; Pss 50:2; 80:1), and it reveals the psalmist's trust that when God appears, God will set things right. That is to say, God will deal with the wicked (v. 3), who are elsewhere characterized by pride or arrogance (v. 2; see also Pss 10:2; 31:18, 23; 36:11; 73:6). The same Hebrew root behind "proud" (גאה g'h) underlies the translation "majesty" in Ps 93:1, thus linking the two psalms in a way that suggests the wicked assert their own sovereignty while the psalmist requests God to make known God's sovereignty.

The wicked are characterized by arrogant speech (v. 4; see also Pss 31:18; 59:7; 73:8; 75:5) as well as oppressive behavior (v. 5; see also Exod 1:11, 12; 2 Sam 7:10; the psalmists often used this Hebrew root [ענה 'ānâ] to complain of being afflicted, poor, or oppressed, as in Ps 10:2, 9).

360. James L. Mays, *Psalms,* Interpretation (Louisville: John Knox, 1994) 302.
361. See Gerald H. Wilson, "Shaping the Psalter: A Consideration of Editorial Linkage in the Book of Psalms," in *The Shape and Shaping of the Psalter,* ed. J. C. McCann, Jr., JSOTSup 159 (Sheffield: JSOT, 1993) 75-76.

362. See Marvin E. Tate, *Psalms 51–100,* WBC 20 (Dallas: Word, 1990) 486.

The verb "crush" (דכא *dākā'*) also appears to be related to the word that designates the activity of the floods in Ps 93:3, thus providing another link between the two psalms and tying the activity of the wicked to the chaotic forces that God orders in the role of sovereign. Verse 6 illustrates the oppressive behavior of the wicked; they afflict precisely those for whom God has particular concern (see Exod 22:20-23; Pss 68:5-6; 146:9). Verse 7 illustrates the arrogant speech of the wicked; they view themselves as completely autonomous, accountable to no one, not even God (see Pss 10:4, 11; 14:1; 53:1; 73:11).

94:8-11. Using the same verb that the wicked have just used in v. 7*b*, the psalmist in v. 8*a* calls them to attention (the verb is more literally "understand," as in 8*a* NRSV; see also Ps 92:6). The imperative is followed by a question in v. 8*b*, which recalls Ps 2:10 (see also Ps 14:1), where being wise also involved recognizing God's sovereignty (see 2:11). In Psalm 73, the psalmist describes himself or herself as dull or senseless (v. 22) when he or she failed to "know" (v. 22; see Ps 94:10) or to "understand" (v. 17) God and God's dealings with the wicked. The psalmist eventually reached the proper understanding (vv. 17-20; 27; as the NIV suggests, the verb in Ps 73:27*b* is the same as in 94:23), and it is the same knowledge that the psalmist also seeks to impart in Psalm 94. The question in v. 8*b* is followed by a series of questions, which really function as affirmations. God is not oblivious, as the wicked had claimed (v. 7). God does hear and see (v. 9), and God does respond (v. 10). The verb "disciplines" (יסר *yissēr*, v. 10*a*) also recalls Ps 2:10, thus offering another reminder that the real issue is who is sovereign. The wicked claim that they are, but the psalmist claims that God is. God "teaches knowledge" (v. 10, because God "knows" (v. 11). Verse 11 should be heard in relation to v. 7. It is not an abstract affirmation of God's omniscience, but an affirmation that the arrogantly stated intentions of the wicked will come to nothing (see Ps 39:11). God will deal with humanity's evil "thoughts" (see Gen 6:5). In short, God is sovereign.

94:12-15. Whereas vv. 8-11 have recalled Psalm 2, vv. 12-15 recall Psalm 1. The beatitude in v. 12 contains two key words from Ps 1:1-2: "happy" and "law," or better, "instruction." The

vocabulary of v. 12 also recalls that of vv. 8-11 (see "discipline" and "teaches" in v. 10). The crucial claim is that happiness derives not from pursuing one's own intentions, as the wicked do, but from being instructed by God (see Commentary on Psalm 1). Such openness to God's instruction does not offer immunity from trouble (v. 13*a*), but it does provide "respite" or "relief" while the wicked pursue their evil intentions (v. 13*b*; on a pit for the wicked, see Pss 7:15; 9:15; 35:8). In Isa 32:17, the Hebrew root of "respite" is used to designate one of the results of God's reign (see Isa 32:1) of justice and righteousness—"quietness" for God's people. The "respite" in Psalm 94 is also tied conceptually to "justice" and to "righteousness" (v. 15; see the NIV, which follows the Hebrew text, while the NRSV follows a variant reading). Justice and righteousness are the hallmarks of God's reign (see Pss 96:13; 97:2; 98:9; 99:4). God's "heritage," God's people, may suffer affliction (see v. 5; see also Ps 34:19), but because God is sovereign and not the wicked, God's people will not be forsaken (v. 14). The "upright in heart" are the ones who experience life as God intends it (see Pss 7:10; 32:11; 36:10; 64:10; 97:11).

94:16-19. The questions of v. 16 (see Pss 9:19; 10:12) are answered in v. 17. It is God who helps (see Pss 22:19; 27:9; 38:22; 40:13, 17; 46:2). The "land of silence" (v. 17*b*; see also Ps 115:17) designates Sheol, the realm of the dead. Verse 18 returns to direct address; it and the following verses express gratitude and trust. The verb translated "slipping" (נטה *nātâ*) is used often in expressions of both threat and confidence (see also "moved"/"shaken" in Pss 13:4; 15:5; 16:8; 30:6; 38:1). God is a solid support for the psalmist (see Pss 18:35), as God is also the solid support for the world (see Ps 93:1). It is a matter of God's character, which is expressed in a word by "steadfast love" (see Pss 5:7; 13:5; Introduction; in the more immediate context, see 90:14; 92:2; 98:3; 100:5; 103:4, 8, 11, 17; 106:1, 45).

94:20-23. Verse 20 is difficult. The NIV offers a more literal reading of v. 20*a*, which the NRSV has rendered more interpretively. Verses 20-21 recall vv. 5-7 and seem to suggest that the oppressive, deadly activity of the wicked is institutionalized. But in the face of such ingrained evil, the psalmist asserts trust in God (vv. 22-23). God is the psalmist's source of protection (see "strong-hold"/"fortress" in Pss 9:9; 18:2; 62:2, 6) and strength (see "rock" in Pss 31:2; 62:7; 92:16; 95:1)—in short, the psalmist's "refuge" (מחסה *mahseh*) a word that also recalls Psalm 2 (see Pss 2:12; 5:11; 7:1; Introduction). As for the wicked, God "will return upon them their iniquity" (v. 23*a*, author's trans.). Thus the wicked suffer from delusions of grandeur (see v. 7); they are actually sowing the seeds of their own destruction (see Pss 7:15-16; 73:27).

REFLECTIONS

It does not appear that God reigns, for the wicked prosper, and crime does pay. The psalmist does not deny appearances (vv. 3-7, 13, 20-21), but neither does he or she waver from the conviction that God rules (vv. 1-2, 8-15) and that God is the help and hope of God's people (vv. 16-19, 22-23). In short, the perspective is eschatological. God's reign is proclaimed amid circumstances that seem to deny it, and the reader is thus called to decision—either to choose the self-assertion of the wicked or to find happiness (v. 12) and consolation (v. 19) and refuge (v. 22) in God (see Reflections on Psalms 1; 2; 93; Introduction).

As Mays suggests, the psalmist has the conviction of a prophet and the voice of a pastor. Like the prophets, the psalmist calls God to deal with injustice (vv. 1-2) and announces punishment for the wicked (v. 23). But it is even more evident in Psalm 94 that "the psalmist had a pastoral calling to encourage and support the discouraged and hurt in their life as the people of God."[363] That calling is still a timely one. We are still familiar with the arrogance and oppression that derive from self-assertion (vv. 3-7), and it is still discouraging and hurtful. So Psalm 94 can perhaps serve as a model for contemporary pastors, who are called upon not to deny appearances (vv. 3-7) or to acquiesce with institutionalized oppression (vv. 20-21), but to find ways of honestly encouraging and supporting God's people. In a world that teaches and rewards self-assertion (see Commentary on Psalm 1) and is usually content to acquiesce with oppression, the pastoral task seems like an insurmountable one. As Psalm 94 suggests, it must be rooted in the proclamation that God reigns, and it must involve the invitation to live under God's rule as the first step toward the pursuit of the elusive goal of being "happy" (v. 12). This proclamation and invitation were, after all, the essence of Jesus' ministry as well (see Mark 1:14-15).

Part of the difficulty of such a task involves the issue of how to preach judgment without being judgmental, and how to preach vengeance with being vengeful (see vv. 1-2). The psalmist apparently avoided the pitfalls of this dilemma by holding firmly to the conviction that *God* is judge and that consequently, "Vengeance is mine" (Deut 32:35 NRSV; see also Rom 12:19; Heb 10:30). For those who are convinced that preaching must refrain from any mention of judgment and vengeance, Psalm 94 is a reminder that it is not possible. In a world of oppression and institutionalized evil, to preach the judgment and vengeance of God is to profess our hope and our conviction that God rules the world and that "justice will return" (v. 15).

363. Mays, *Psalms,* 304.

PSALM 95:1-11, LISTEN TO GOD'S VOICE

NIV

Psalm 95

¹Come, let us sing for joy to the LORD;
  let us shout aloud to the Rock of our
    salvation.
²Let us come before him with thanksgiving
  and extol him with music and song.
³For the LORD is the great God,
  the great King above all gods.
⁴In his hand are the depths of the earth,
  and the mountain peaks belong to him.
⁵The sea is his, for he made it,
  and his hands formed the dry land.

⁶Come, let us bow down in worship,
  let us kneel before the LORD our Maker;
⁷for he is our God
  and we are the people of his pasture,
    the flock under his care.

 Today, if you hear his voice,
⁸ do not harden your hearts as you did at
      Meribah,ᵃ
    as you did that day at Massahᵇ in the
        desert,
⁹where your fathers tested and tried me,
  though they had seen what I did.
¹⁰For forty years I was angry with that
      generation;
  I said, "They are a people whose hearts go
      astray,
    and they have not known my ways."
¹¹So I declared on oath in my anger,
  "They shall never enter my rest."

ᵃ8 *Meribah* means *quarreling.*   ᵇ8 *Massah* means *testing.*

NRSV

Psalm 95

¹ O come, let us sing to the LORD;
  let us make a joyful noise to the rock of
    our salvation!
² Let us come into his presence with
      thanksgiving;
  let us make a joyful noise to him with
      songs of praise!
³ For the LORD is a great God,
  and a great King above all gods.
⁴ In his hand are the depths of the earth;
  the heights of the mountains are his also.
⁵ The sea is his, for he made it,
  and the dry land, which his hands have
      formed.

⁶ O come, let us worship and bow down,
  let us kneel before the LORD, our Maker!
⁷ For he is our God,
  and we are the people of his pasture,
    and the sheep of his hand.

 O that today you would listen to his voice!
⁸ Do not harden your hearts, as at Meribah,
    as on the day at Massah in the
        wilderness,
⁹ when your ancestors tested me,
  and put me to the proof, though they
      had seen my work.
¹⁰ For forty years I loathed that generation
  and said, "They are a people whose
      hearts go astray,
    and they do not regard my ways."
¹¹ Therefore in my anger I swore,
  "They shall not enter my rest."

COMMENTARY

Psalm 95 is often categorized as an enthronement psalm, because it begins (vv. 1-7b) with a song of praise to God, the "great King" (v. 3), and because it adjoins a collection of similar psalms (Psalms 93; 96–99). The unique conclusion to Psalm 95 (vv. 7c-11), however, has led some scholars to label it a prophetic exhortation or a liturgy of divine judgment. Actually, vv. 1-7b are somewhat unusual as well. The typical elements of a song of praise are present—invitation to praise (vv. 1-2, 6) and reasons for praise (vv. 3-5, 7ab)—but they appear twice. In fact, some scholars detect three separate invitations (vv. 1, 2, 6), each of which they associate with a different liturgical movement. Taken together, in these scholars' view, the three movements constitute a processional that would have culminated with entrance through the temple gates or into the Temple (vv. 6-7ab), at which time the prophetic exhortation would have been heard. If this scenario is correct, then Psalm 95 has strong affinities with Psalm 24, which also celebrates God's role as creator (cf. 24:1-2 with 95:4-5) in the context of hailing God as king (cf. 24:7-10 with 95:3) and could easily have originated or been used as a liturgy for entrance into the Temple (see Commentary on Psalm 24).

The literary or liturgical movement from praise to the hearing of God's word also makes Psalm 95 similar to Psalms 50 and 81, especially the latter (cf. 81:8, 13 with 95:7c). Indeed, Psalms 50; 81; and 95 have often been viewed as festival psalms, but there is no consensus on their precise liturgical setting. While there is no solid evidence for an annual enthronement festival in conjunction with the New Year (see Introduction), it is likely that Psalm 95 would have been used in some liturgical setting, perhaps the Feast of Booths. At some point, its use would have been adapted for worship in the synagogues; rabbinic sources associate its use with the beginning of the sabbath. In keeping with this Jewish usage, Psalm 95 was and is used in Christian liturgy as a call to worship. Scholarly views of vv. 7c-11 vary in accordance with the way one views the setting and ancient use of the psalm. These verses can be construed as an oracle delivered by a cultic prophet, but it is probably more accurate to view them as representative of a Levitical sermon (see Commentary on Psalms 50; 81).

As part of the enthronement collection that occupies a prominent place in Book IV, Psalm 95 participates in the response to the theological crisis raised by the shape and content of Books I–III (see Commentary on Psalms 73; 74; 79; 80; 89; 90; 93; Introduction). Psalm 95:8 also contributes to the character of Book IV as a Moses-book (see Psalm 90; Introduction), and it is possible that Psalms 95 and 100 are intended to serve as a frame around Psalms 96–99, the core of the

enthronement collection (cf. 95:1-2, 6 with 100:1-2, 4; 95:7ab with 100:3).[364]

95:1-2. The invitations in vv. 1-2 anticipate the explicit proclamation of God's kingship in v. 3. The repeated "make a joyful noise" indicates an appropriate way to respond to God's sovereignty (see Pss 47:1; 66:1; 81:1; 98:4, 6). The other Hebrew roots used in vv. 1-2 also occur in explicit proclamations of God's rule (for the NRSV's "let us sing," see Pss 96:12; 98:4, 8; for "songs of praise," see Pss 47:6; 98:4-5). The "thanksgiving" in v. 2 could mean a sacrifice that accompanies other expressions of gratitude, or it could indicate the non-sacrificial expressions themselves (see Pss 50:14, 23; 100:3; see also the title to Psalm 100). In any case, the thanksgiving is to be presented to God's "face" (see Ps 27:8-9). The metaphor of God as a rock is a frequent one in the psalms (see Pss 31:2; 62:2, 6; 89:26; 92:15; 94:22).

95:3-5. Reasons for praise follow in vv. 3-5. Verse 3 assumes the polytheistic background of the ancient Near East (see Pss 82:1; 96:4; 97:9), but Yahweh is preeminent among the gods—the "great King" (see Ps 47:2; greatness is frequently associated with God's sovereignty, as in Pss 96:4; 99:2). God's sovereignty extends throughout the cosmos. The repetition of "his hand(s)" in vv. 4a, 5b has the literary effect of surrounding all the elements of the cosmos with references to God's hands. Structure reinforces content; that is, the whole world is in God's hands (see Pss 24:1-2; 138:7-8).

95:6-7b. Verse 6 again invites actions that were appropriate for greeting a king. The first verb (שחה šāḥâ) means more literally "bow down" (see 1 Sam 24:8; 2 Sam 14:4, 22; 1 Kgs 1:31 for earthly kings; Pss 29:2; 96:9; 99:5 for God), which is also the meaning of the second verb (see 2 Chr 7:3; 29:29; Pss 22:29; 72:9). It is followed in several instances by the noun "knees" (see 1 Kgs 8:54; Isa 45:23), thus anticipating the third verb, which in other conjugations of the root means "to bless" (ברך bārak; see Pss 96:2; 100:4; 145:1). The address of God as "our Maker" recalls the verb "made" (עשה ʿāśâ) in v. 5a, and the repetition highlights the two possible senses of

364. See Tate, *Psalms 51–100*, 475; D. M. Howard, Jr., *The Structure of Psalms 93–100* (Ann Arbor, Mich.: University Microfilms, 1986) 78, 134, 174-76, 207-8.

"made." It can mean God's salvific activity (v. 6: God made Israel by way of the exodus, which is already alluded to in v. 5 and will be again in v. 9; see Pss 100:3; 118:24), as well as God's activity in creation (v. 5). Indeed, ultimately the two senses are inseparable, for the making of Israel was for the purpose of enacting God's creational purposes (see Commentary on Psalms 33; 66). In this regard, it should be noted that "sea" in v. 5 not only recalls creation but also is reminiscent of Exod 15:1, 8, and "dry land" calls to mind both creation (see Gen 1:9, 10) and exodus as well (see Exod 14:16, 22, 29; 15:19). Appropriately, just as God holds the world in God's hands (vv. 4a, 5b), so also Israel represents "the sheep of his hand" (v. 7b). In the ancient Near East, kings were known as the shepherds of their people (see Jer 23:1-4; Ezek 34:1-10), so it is especially fitting that this metaphor appears in a psalm that celebrates God's kingship (see also Pss 23:1; 74:1; 79:13; 80:1; 100:3; Ezek 34:11-16). The "great God" (v. 3) is "our God" (v. 7a).

95:7c. Verse 7c is really a transitional verse. Sheep are supposed to listen to the voice of their shepherd (see John 10:3-5, 14, 16), so v. 7c could be considered the culmination of vv. 1-7. But v. 7c also introduces the issue illustrated negatively in vv. 8-11. The three-part poetic line of v. 7 also has the effect of isolating, and thus emphasizing, v. 7c as a call to attention and obedience (see Ps 81:8, 13). The word translated "listen" in v. 7c often has the sense of "obey," especially in Deuteronomy. The emphasis on "today"—on reactualizing the past—is also characteristic of Deuteronomy (see 4:40; 5:3; 6:6; 7:11).

95:8-11. These verses recall places and events in the wilderness shortly after Israel had been "made" ('āśâ, Exodus 1–14; see the Hebrew root of "made" in Exod 14:31 [NRSV, "did"; NIV, "displayed"]) and God's reign proclaimed (Exod 15:1-21, esp. v. 18). Meribah and Massah are mentioned together in Exod 17:1-7 (see also Massah in Deut 6:16; 9:22; Meribah in Num 20:13, 24; Pss 81:7; 106:32; and both in Deut 33:8), which could be considered the text for the sermon in vv. 8-11. Exodus 17:1-7 does not say that the people hardened their hearts, although the Hebrew root translated "hardened" (קשׁה qāšâ) is used elsewhere to characterize the behavior of the people in the wilderness. In a different form, it appears as the first element in the term "stiff-necked" (see Exod 32:9; 33:3, 5; 34:9). Against the background of these references to the book of Exodus, "my work" in v. 9 certainly refers to the exodus itself (see Pss 44:1; 77:12). Thus, the whole exodus event and the people's response lie in the background of vv. 8-11. In the book of Exodus, the sequence of deliverance (Exodus 1–14) and proclamation of God's reign (Exod 15:1-21) should have led to immediate obedience, but instead it led to immediate complaining and testing of God (Exod 17:1-7; see also Exod 15:22-27). The people even ask, "Is the LORD among us or not?" (Exod 17:7 NRSV). Against this background, Psalm 95 says, in effect, "Do not repeat that mistake." In other words, in your place and time—your today (v. 7c)—listen to God's voice. In response to the proclamation of God's reign (v. 3), submit instead of rebelling (v. 6), and obey instead of complaining (v. 7c). Verses 10-11 conclude the sermon with a reminder of past consequences for disobedience—namely, God's displeasure (see Num 14:33-35) and failure to enter the land (see "rest" in Deut 12:9; see also Num 10:33)—which is intended to serve as a warning for the present. The call for a decision in response to God's reign is an urgent matter—indeed, a matter of life and death.

REFLECTIONS

1. The message that pervades the psalter is explicit in Psalm 95: God reigns. As the shape and content of the book of Psalms demonstrate, the proclamation of God's reign is eschatological; it is always made in circumstances that seem to deny it (see Commentary on Psalms 2; 29; 47; 93; Introduction). It is revealing that in Psalm 95 it is not the forces of chaos that resist God's claim (as in Psalm 93), nor is it the wicked or the nations (as in Psalm 94). Rather, God's own people resist God's claim. This situation is significant, for it reveals something crucial about how God exercises sovereignty. God does not coerce obedience; God invites obedience. God warns that the consequences of disobedience are severe, but God refuses to be an enforcer. It leaves God in the vulnerable position of having to implore the people to obey (v. 7c), but such is the price of integrity and of love.

2. God's invitation to obedience is particularly clear in Psalm 95. The proclamation of God's reign always calls for a decision, but that call for decision is highlighted by the structure and movement of Psalm 95 (see esp. v. 7c). As with Psalm 93, it is significant that the call to decision appears in an explicitly liturgical context. Thus this psalm teaches us about worship. In worship, we profess who is sovereign, and we actualize today the reality of God's claim upon us. To be sure, worship has something to do with the past, but it also clearly has to do with the present. Worship really is a "service" in the sense that we act out our servanthood, our submission to the God whom we profess rules the world and our lives. Worship is a matter of word and deed (see Matt 7:21-23).

3. There is a rabbinic tale that culminates in a reference to Psalm 95:7c and emphasizes the significance of its call to decision. Rabbi Yoshua Ben Levi finds the prophet Elijah and asks him when the Messiah will come. Elijah tells the rabbi where to find the Messiah so that he can address the question to him.

> "Peace be unto you, my master and teacher."
> The Messiah answered, "Peace unto you, son of Levi."
> He asked, "When is the master coming?"
> "Today," he answered.
> Rabbi Yoshua returned to Elijah, who asked, "What did he tell you?"
> "He indeed has deceived me, for he said, 'Today I am coming' and he has not come."
> Elijah said, "This is what he told you: 'Today if you would listen to my voice.' "[365]

The reign of God represented in the tale by the coming of the Messiah is experienced as a decision made *today*. While the eschatological character of God's reign means that we await its full manifestation, it also means that we can enter and live in God's realm right now, as Jesus proclaimed (Mark 1:14-15).

4. The author of Hebrews, who claimed Jesus as Messiah, used Ps 95:7c-11 as the text for a Christian sermon (Heb 3:7–4:13). That author heard in Psalm 95 encouragement to persevere in trust and obedience (see 3:12-14), based on the assurance that God's rest is still available for the people of God (see 4:1-3, 6-7, 9-11). Thus, in keeping with the intent of Psalm 95, the author uses it to call to decision and accountability the people of his or her "today."

---

365. Cited in Henri J. M. Nouwen, *The Wounded Healer* (Garden City, N.Y.: Image Books, 1972) 94-95; see also 71-72. The story is from the tractate *Sanhedrin*.

PSALM 96:1-13, GOD IS COMING TO ESTABLISH JUSTICE

NIV	NRSV
Psalm 96	Psalm 96
¹Sing to the LORD a new song; sing to the LORD, all the earth. ²Sing to the LORD, praise his name;	¹ O sing to the LORD a new song; sing to the LORD, all the earth. ² Sing to the LORD, bless his name;

NIV

proclaim his salvation day after day.
³Declare his glory among the nations,
his marvelous deeds among all peoples.

⁴For great is the LORD and most worthy of
praise;
he is to be feared above all gods.
⁵For all the gods of the nations are idols,
but the LORD made the heavens.
⁶Splendor and majesty are before him;
strength and glory are in his sanctuary.

⁷Ascribe to the LORD, O families of nations,
ascribe to the LORD glory and strength.
⁸Ascribe to the LORD the glory due his name;
bring an offering and come into his courts.
⁹Worship the LORD in the splendor of his^a
holiness;
tremble before him, all the earth.

¹⁰Say among the nations, "The LORD reigns."
The world is firmly established, it cannot
be moved;
he will judge the peoples with equity.
¹¹Let the heavens rejoice, let the earth be glad;
let the sea resound, and all that is in it;
¹²   let the fields be jubilant, and everything in
them.
Then all the trees of the forest will sing for joy;
¹³   they will sing before the LORD, for he comes,
he comes to judge the earth.
He will judge the world in righteousness
and the peoples in his truth.

^a9 Or LORD with the splendor of

NRSV

tell of his salvation from day to day.
³ Declare his glory among the nations,
his marvelous works among all the
peoples.
⁴ For great is the LORD, and greatly to be
praised;
he is to be revered above all gods.
⁵ For all the gods of the peoples are idols,
but the LORD made the heavens.
⁶ Honor and majesty are before him;
strength and beauty are in his sanctuary.

⁷ Ascribe to the LORD, O families of the peoples,
ascribe to the LORD glory and strength.
⁸ Ascribe to the LORD the glory due his name;
bring an offering, and come into his courts.
⁹ Worship the LORD in holy splendor;
tremble before him, all the earth.

¹⁰ Say among the nations, "The LORD is king!
The world is firmly established; it shall
never be moved.
He will judge the peoples with equity."
¹¹ Let the heavens be glad, and let the earth
rejoice;
let the sea roar, and all that fills it;
¹²   let the field exult, and everything in it.
Then shall all the trees of the forest sing for
joy
¹³   before the LORD; for he is coming,
for he is coming to judge the earth.
He will judge the world with righteousness,
and the peoples with his truth.

COMMENTARY

Psalm 96 is part of an impressive collection of enthronement psalms (Psalms 93; 95–99) that are strategically placed in Book IV to respond to the theological questions raised by Book III, especially Psalm 89 (see Psalms 73–74; 79–80; 89; 93; Introduction). In proclaiming God's reign, Psalm 96 shows the typical structure of a song of praise; that is, invitations to praise (vv. 1-3, 7-10a, 11-12a) are followed by reasons for praise (vv. 4-6, 10b, 12b-13), which together describe the nature and consequences of God's rule.

The ancient origin and use of enthronement psalms have been the subject of extensive scholarly debate, which can be summarized briefly by considering the primary options for identifying the "new song" in Ps 96:1a: (1) The new song perhaps should be understood as Psalm 96 itself as it was sung in the Temple upon the occasion of the re-enthronement of God at an annual New Year festival (see 1 Chr 16:23-33, where most of Psalm 96 appears as part of the praises accompanying David's movement of the ark to Jerusalem).

Actually, there is almost no solid evidence for such a festival; however, it is certain that God's rule was regularly proclaimed anew in some setting; a liturgical song like Psalm 96 would have re-actualized for the present moment for the present worshipers the reality of God's reign. Thus Psalm 96 itself could be viewed as the new song, insofar as "it is the evocation of an alternative reality that comes into play in the very moment of the liturgy."[366] (2) The "new song" may also be understood as the response to a historical event, such as the return of the exiles from Babylonian captivity. In this regard, it is significant that Isaiah 40–55, which originated as a response to exile, also invites the people to "sing to the LORD a new song" (Isa 42:10 NRSV) in response to the "new thing" (Isa 43:19; see 42:9) that God is doing in returning the exiles to their land. Just as the exodus of old was celebrated in a song proclaiming God's reign (see Exod 15:1-21, esp. v. 18), so also a new exodus should be accompanied by a new song. The relationship between Psalm 96 and Isaiah 40–55 is reinforced by several other parallels. Both texts are concerned with the proclamation of "good tidings" or "good news" (Isa 40:9; 41:27; 42:7; the same Hebrew [בשׂר *biśśar*] root underlies "proclaim" in Ps 96:2*b*) involving the reign of God (Ps 96:10; Isa 52:7), the proper response to which is singing for joy (Ps 96:12; Isa 52:8). And in both texts, God's purpose is justice (Ps 96:10, 13; Isa 42:1, 3-4) for the earth and its peoples (Ps 96:7, 10, 13; Isa 42:1; 45:22-23; 49:1-6; 52:10; 55:4-5). While a relationship between Psalm 96 and Isaiah 40–55 is clear, it is not clear which text originated first or even whether one text directly influenced the other. (3) The new song may be sung not so much in celebration of what God has done or is doing but in anticipation of what God will do. Especially in v. 13, it seems that God's coming is still in the future, as is God's establishment of justice and righteousness. In this view, the new song would have an eschatological orientation.

In actuality, the above three options are not mutually exclusive. The liturgical celebration of God's reign in the present is related to experience of God in the past, and both the past and present dimensions lead to the anticipation of a transformed future. In other words, a liturgical or historical reading of Psalm 96 will also inevitably have an eschatological dimension (see below on v. 13 and Reflections).

96:1-3. Of the six imperatives in vv. 1-3, three invite the people to "sing" (שׁיר *šîr*, vv. 1-2*a*; see also Exod 15:1, 21; Pss 13:6; 27:6; 33:3; 104:33), a joyful response to God that involves but goes beyond simple speech. As suggested above, the new song (see Pss 40:4; 98:1; 144:9; Isa 42:10), as well as the very act of singing, recall the song that Moses, Miriam, and the people sang after deliverance from Egypt (Exod 15:1-21). Allusion to the past is accompanied by actualization in the present and anticipation of the future. God was, is, and will be king. The directing of the invitation to "all the earth" (v. 1; see also v. 9) bespeaks the cosmic scope of God's rule, and it anticipates the further invitations to and reasons for praise in vv. 10-13 (see also Pss 97:1; 98:4; 99:1). The fundamental sense of "bless" (ברך *bārak,* v. 2) seems to be to kneel in homage (see Ps 95:6; see Pss 100:4; 145:1, 21, where blessing God's name is involved; see also 16:7; 26:12). The invitation to recognize God's sovereignty is accompanied by the invitation to communicate it to others. The Hebrew root of the verb "proclaim" (*biśśar,* v. 2) came into Greek as the word usually translated "good news," "gospel";[367] Mays rightly observes that Psalm 96 "has a definite evangelical cast." *Biśśar* is most frequent in Isaiah 40–55 (see 40:9; 41:27; 52:7; see also Ps 40:9; Isa 60:6; 61:1). The good news has to do with God's life-giving work; the word "salvation" (ישׁועה *yěšûʿâ*) again recalls the exodus (see Exod 15:2; Pss 3:2, 7-8; 98:1-3). Also to be declared (see Pss 44:1; 73:28; 78:3-4) are God's "glory," which bespeaks God's sovereignty (see Pss 24:7-10; 29:1-3, 9; 97:6) and God's "marvelous works." The latter once more recalls the exodus as well as the subsequent series of God's acts of deliverance (see Exod 3:20; 15:11; Josh 3:5; Judg 6:13; Pss 9:1; 26:7; 77:11, 14; 78:4, 11-12, 43; 98:1).

96:4-6. The reasons for praise begin with God's greatness (see Pss 47:2; 48:1; 70:4; 77:13; 86:10; 95:3; 99:2-3; 138:5), an attribute that means God's sovereignty is exclusive (see Exod 20:3; Pss 86:10; 95:3). Other so-called gods are

---

366. Walter Brueggemann, *The Message of the Psalms: A Theological Commentary* (Minneapolis: Augsburg, 1984) 144.

367. James L. Mays, *Psalms,* Interpretation (Louisville: John Knox, 1994) 308.

but idols (see Ps 97:7). Whereas vv. 1-3 had recalled the exodus, v. 5 points to creation as evidence of God's rule (see Commentary on Psalm 95; see also 97:6). While vv. 4-5 seem to partake of the ancient Near Eastern concept of a council of the gods (see Ps 82:1), v. 6 perhaps moves toward the de-divination of these gods by surrounding God with only the divine attributes themselves. These attributes are elsewhere explicitly associated with sovereignty—"honor"/"splendor" (see Pss 21:5; 45:3; 145:5), "majesty" (see Pss 21:5; 29:4; 45:3; 145:5), "strength" (see Exod 15:2, 13; Pss 29:1; 93:1), and "beauty"/"glory" (see 1 Chr 29:11).

96:7-10a. Perhaps also in the direction of de-divination of the gods, vv. 7-9 take up the invitation of Ps 29:1-2, but it is addressed this time not to "heavenly beings" (29:1) but to "families of the peoples." The invitation of Ps 29:1-2 is expanded in 96:7-9 (see vv. 8b, 9b; on "tremble," see Pss 97:4; 29:9), and apparently what is envisioned is a procession of the nations to Jerusalem (see Isa 2:2-3; Mic 4:1-2; Zech 8:20-23). What is at stake is the universal recognition of and proclamation of God's reign (v. 10a; see Pss 93:1; 97:1; 99:1).

96:10b-13. What God's cosmic rule means is stated in v. 10bc: stability for the world (see Ps 93:1) and justice for all the world's peoples. The whole cosmos participates in and celebrates God's just ordering of the world (vv. 11-12; see also Pss 97:6; 98:7-8). The Hebrew word translated "judge" (דין dîn) in v. 10c is different from the one translated the same way in v. 13 (שפט šāpaṭ), but they are essentially synonymous, and both designate the prerogative and responsibility of a sovereign. In short, a king is to establish justice and righteousness (see Ps 72:1-2, where the root in Ps 96:10 appears as "judge" in v. 2, and the root in 96:13 appears as "justice" in vv. 1-2). It is precisely the failure to establish justice and righteousness that indicts the gods (see Ps 82:1-4) and threatens the earth with chaotic instability (see Ps 82:5, where "shaken" [מוט môṭ] is the same word as "moved" in Ps 96:10), and the establishment of justice and righteousness is the hallmark of God's reign (see Pss 97:2; 98:9; 99:4). God's justice and righteousness mean "equity" (see Pss 9:8; 98:9; 99:4) rather than partiality (see Ps 82:2), faithfulness (v. 13; see also Pss 89:49; 92:2 for a different form of the same Hebrew root) rather than neglect (see Ps 82:3-4).

As the NIV suggests, the references to God's coming in v. 13 can be understood in a present as well as a future sense. The ambiguity is appropriate. Israel affirmed God's just and righteous rule as a present reality, and yet the experience of God's justice and righteousness was for Israel and is for us always in the midst of ongoing injustice and brokenness. In short, the affirmation of God's reign, here as always, is eschatological.

REFLECTIONS

1. Psalm 96 articulates the good news that forms the theological heart of the book of Psalms: God reigns (see Psalms 2; 29; 47; 65–68; 93; 95; 97–99; Introduction). Because God rules the world, it is not sufficient to gather a congregation less than "all the earth" (vv. 1, 9). This includes humans, to be sure (see v. 7), but it also includes "the heavens," "the earth" itself, "the sea," "the field," and "all the trees" (vv. 11-12). The ecumenical and inter-faith implications are profound; we are somehow partners with all the "families of the peoples" (v. 7). The ecological implications are staggering; we humans are somehow partners with oceans and trees and soil and air in glorifying God. The destiny of humankind and the destiny of the earth are inseparable. We—people, plants, and even inanimate entities—are all in this together (see Ps 150:6; Hos 4:1-3; see also Psalms 8; 104).

2. The invitation to praise in Ps 96:7-9 is essentially the same as that in Ps 29:1-2, except that the invitation in 96:7 is extended to the "families of the peoples" rather than to the "heavenly beings." This difference suggests at least that God's sovereignty is to be effective on earth as well as in heaven. To hear Psalms 96 and 29 together is to be taught to pray, in effect, "thy kingdom come, thy will be done on earth as it is in heaven." Like Psalm 96, the perspective of the Lord's Prayer is eschatological. Reciting it, we both affirm the present reality of God's reign—"thine is the kingdom"—and pray for the coming of God's reign—"thy kingdom come."

3. The emphasis in vv. 2-3 on proclaiming the good news makes Psalm 96 especially appropriate for Epiphany. Psalm 96 is also traditionally used on Christmas Day. This use articulates the Christian conviction that Jesus' birth manifests God's rule (see Psalms 29; 97; 98). Not surprisingly, the basic message of Psalm 96 is the same as that proclaimed by Jesus: God reigns. And like the preaching of Jesus, Psalm 96 calls for a decision; it invites us to submit ourselves to God's sovereignty, to enter the reign of God (see Mark 1:14-15). The shape of the psalter makes it clear that the sovereignty of God is asserted in the face of opposition (see Introduction), and so it was with the preaching of Jesus and the proclamation of the early church. In the face of severe persecution came this proclamation:

> "The kingdom of the world has become
> the kingdom of our Lord and of his Christ,
> and he will reign for ever and ever." (Rev 11:15 NIV)

Such an assertion is, as Brueggemann says of Psalm 96, "an act of profound hope." But, he adds, it is also "more than hope."[368] The conviction that God rules the world empowers us even now, in the face of old injustice and brokenness, to defy such realities as we live under God's claim and sing "a new song" (v. 1; see Rev 5:9; 14:3).

368. Brueggemann, *The Message of the Psalms,* 145.

PSALM 97:1-12, REJOICE THAT THE LORD REIGNS

NIV

Psalm 97

¹The LORD reigns, let the earth be glad;
  let the distant shores rejoice.
²Clouds and thick darkness surround him;
  righteousness and justice are the
    foundation of his throne.
³Fire goes before him
  and consumes his foes on every side.
⁴His lightning lights up the world;
  the earth sees and trembles.
⁵The mountains melt like wax before the LORD,
  before the Lord of all the earth.
⁶The heavens proclaim his righteousness,
  and all the peoples see his glory.

⁷All who worship images are put to shame,
  those who boast in idols—
  worship him, all you gods!

⁸Zion hears and rejoices

NRSV

Psalm 97

¹ The LORD is king! Let the earth rejoice;
  let the many coastlands be glad!
² Clouds and thick darkness are all around
    him;
  righteousness and justice are the
    foundation of his throne.
³ Fire goes before him,
  and consumes his adversaries on every
    side.
⁴ His lightnings light up the world;
  the earth sees and trembles.
⁵ The mountains melt like wax before the
    LORD,
  before the Lord of all the earth.

⁶ The heavens proclaim his righteousness;
  and all the peoples behold his glory.
⁷ All worshipers of images are put
    to shame,

NIV

and the villages of Judah are glad
  because of your judgments, O LORD.
⁹For you, O LORD, are the Most High over all
    the earth;
  you are exalted far above all gods.

¹⁰Let those who love the LORD hate evil,
  for he guards the lives of his faithful ones
  and delivers them from the hand of the
    wicked.
¹¹Light is shed upon the righteous
  and joy on the upright in heart.
¹²Rejoice in the LORD, you who are righteous,
  and praise his holy name.

NRSV

those who make their boast in worthless
    idols;
  all gods bow down before him.
⁸ Zion hears and is glad,
  and the towns[a] of Judah rejoice,
  because of your judgments, O God.
⁹ For you, O LORD, are most high over all the
    earth;
  you are exalted far above all gods.

¹⁰ The LORD loves those who hate[b] evil;
  he guards the lives of his faithful;
  he rescues them from the hand of the
    wicked.
¹¹ Light dawns[c] for the righteous,
  and joy for the upright in heart.
¹² Rejoice in the LORD, O you righteous,
  and give thanks to his holy name!

COMMENTARY

Like the other enthronement psalms (see Psalms 29; 47; 93; 95–96; 98–99), Psalm 97 features the affirmation that forms the theological heart of the psalter: God reigns (see Introduction). It shares much of the vocabulary and themes of the other enthronement psalms; Tate even considers Psalms 96 and 97 to be "twin-psalms."[369] Even so, Psalm 97 is unique. The first section (vv. 1-5) is written in the style of a theophany (a description of God's appearing), as if to portray the coming of God mentioned in Ps 96:13. Verses 6-9 present the response to and consequences of God's appearing. Verses 6-7 show a chiastic structure (see Introduction), moving from the heavenly realm (v. 6a) to the earthly sphere (vv. 6b-7ab) and back to the heavenly (v. 7c). Verse 8 focuses on the response of God's own people as it shifts to more intimate direct address of God, and v. 9 asserts again God's sovereignty over the earthly (v. 9a) and heavenly realms (v. 9b). The occurrence of "earth" (ארץ 'eres) in v. 9a is the fourth one in the psalm (see vv. 1, 4-5). The occurrences in vv. 1, 4-5 form an envelope structure for the

369. See Marvin E. Tate, *Psalms 51–100*, WBC 20 (Dallas: Word, 1990) 508.

first section; however, it is possible to construe the occurrences in vv. 1, 9 as an envelope for a larger section consisting of vv. 1-9. In either case, vv. 10-12 form the final section, the effect of which is to extend the invitation to respond to the readers of the psalm in every generation.

Another unique aspect of Psalm 97 is the way that the themes of joy/gladness and righteousness are unifying features. To be sure, these themes occur in other enthronement psalms (see joy/gladness in Ps 96:11, and righteousness in Pss 96:13; 98:9; 99:4), but here they are pervasive. Rejoicing is for the earth (v. 1), for God's own people (v. 8), for all the upright/righteous (vv. 11-12; see also "glad" in vv. 1, 8). The theme of rejoicing occurs in every section of the psalm, as does the theme of righteousness (vv. 2, 6, 11-12). The first two occurrences refer to God's righteousness, and the final two suggest that those who submit themselves to God's rule will derive their character from God's character. Because God rules, there is the possibility that people can be righteous too.

The origin and ancient use of the enthronement psalms have been and are the subject of extensive scholarly debate (see Commentary on Psalms 29; 47; 93; 95–96; Introduction). Regardless of the conclusions one reaches on these matters, however, the final form of the psalter suggests that Psalm 97 and the others should be heard eschatologically (see Reflections below). The final form of the psalter also suggests that Psalm 97, as part of the collection including Psalms 93–99, participates in the response to the theological crisis of exile that is articulated by Books I–III (see Commentary on Psalms 89; 90; Introduction).

97:1-5. In v. 1, the earth (see Pss 96:1, 9, 11; 98:4; 99:1) and "the distant shores" (see Ps 72:10; Isa 41:5; 42:4, 10; 49:1; 51:5) are the first invited to respond to the proclamation of God's rule, making it immediately evident that God's reign has cosmic significance. God's appearance is surrounded by manifestations of the natural order—dark clouds (v. 2), lightning (vv. 3-4*a*), and thunder that shakes the earth (vv. 4*b*-5; see also Pss 29:3-9; 96:9). The same poetic imagery is used elsewhere in the OT to depict God's appearing (see Exod 13:21-22; 19:6-20; 20:18-21; 24:16-17; Pss 18:7-15; 50:3; Mic 1:4; Hab 3:3-12). Yet the psalm also affirms God's relatedness to humankind in suggesting that righteousness and justice are the foundational principles of God's rule (see Ps 89:14; see also 96:13; 98:9; 99:4). God's will for the right ordering of human society is embodied in the very structure of the cosmos; this suggests that in the presence of the injustice perpetrated by the gods (see vv. 7, 9), the very existence of the world is threatened (see also Pss 82:5; 93:1; 96:10).

97:6. A comparison of the NIV and the NRSV suggests that v. 6 can be understood as related more closely to vv. 1-5 (NIV) or to vv. 7-9 (NRSV). In contrast to v. 1, where the earth was called upon to respond, v. 6 is the response of the heavens to God's appearing. "The heavens" and "the earth" designate the whole cosmos (see Gen 1:1); therefore, the whole universe responds to God's reign. It is significant that the heavens proclaim God's "righteousness" (צֶדֶק *sedeq*), a term used frequently to describe God's will for human relatedness (see Ps 50:6; cf. Ps 19:1). As in v. 2, the psalmist links God's rule of the cosmos with the right ordering of humankind (see v. 6*b*). In beholding God's "glory," we also confront God's presence (see Exod 16:7, 10; 24:16-17; 33:18, 22)

and are invited to acknowledge God's sovereignty (see Pss 24:7-10; 29:1-3, 9; 96:3, 7-8).

97:7-9. In v. 7, the psalmist recognizes that not all persons do acknowledge God's sovereignty; rather, such persons are "put to shame" as their gods "bow down before" the true God (see Pss 95:3; 96:4). Like the heavens and the earth, God's people—Zion and Judah—celebrate God's "acts of justice" (v. 8). Thus God's people are in tune with the cosmos. As the focus narrows to God's own people, the form of address becomes more intimate. The direct address of God continues in v. 9, and it is accentuated by the appearance of the Hebrew pronoun "you" (אתה *'attâ*). The phrase "most high" (עליון *'elyôn*) and the word "exalted" (נעלית *na'ǎlêtā*) translate the same Hebrew root, emphasizing the affirmation that God rules both the earthly and the heavenly realms. This same Hebrew root also occurs at two crucial points in Psalm 47 (see vv. 5, 9), another enthronement psalm.

97:10-12. The reader should follow the NIV translation of v. 10 (see NRSV note). Here the worshipers are directly addressed, as are the readers of Psalm 97 in every generation. Those who recognize God's rule are called upon to hate evil. The prophets, persistent advocates of justice and righteousness, made the same appeal (see Amos 5:15; Mic 3:2). In any generation, those who hate evil out of allegiance to God's rule will face opposition from "the wicked." The appearance of "the wicked" in this psalm is a reminder that, like the other enthronement psalms and the psalter as a whole, Psalm 97 is eschatological; it proclaims God's rule in circumstances in which one may think that God does *not* rule (see Commentary on Psalms 1; 2). Those who are "faithful" (v. 10), "righteous" (vv. 11-12), and "upright in heart" (v. 11; see also Pss 7:10; 94:15) will not go unopposed, but God will guard and ultimately deliver them from the power of the wicked (see Ps 82:4). God rules, not the wicked. Light, another cosmic element that is used as a symbol for God's presence and protection (see Pss 4:6; 27:1; 43:3; Mic 7:8), "is sown for the righteous" (v. 11; see the NRSV note). Thus people who live by God's rule instead of by self-will are at one with the universe as God intends it. The righteous can rejoice that, despite the wickedness around them, it is possible to be joyous (vv. 11-12; see also vv. 1, 8). The righteous are invited to acknowledge with gratitude "the remembrance of his holiness" (author's trans.; see above on Ps 30:4; note also that Psalms 93 and 99 conclude with the mention of God's holiness). The good news is that God's holiness connotes not unapproachability but the willingness of the "most high" God (v. 9) to enact justice and righteousness on earth as it is in heaven.

REFLECTIONS

1. Psalm 97 is honest. It acknowledges the reality of evil and the power of the wicked, who oppose God's rule (v. 10). But behind this view of the so-called real world, the psalmist discerns and celebrates an even deeper and more profound reality: God reigns (v. 1). Like the other enthronement psalms, then, Psalm 97 is eschatological; it is an act of hope. Mays puts it as follows: "The psalm's proclamation of God's reign offers the righteous hope in their opposition to evil. When the kingdom of God is proclaimed, the righteous take courage."[370] In this sense, then, Psalm 97 is also more than an act of hope. It is the proclamation of and participation in a new reality in which joy and gladness are possible even *now* in the midst of evil.

Not surprisingly—since Jesus' fundamental message was identical to that of Psalm 97 (see Mark 1:14-15)—Jesus also invited his followers amid opposition and persecution to "rejoice and be glad" (Matt 5:12; cf. Ps 97:1, 12). This invitation makes sense only for those who acknowledge God's reign and accept the invitation to live under God's rule (see "kingdom of heaven" in Matt 4:17; 5:3, 10, 19-20).

2. Like Psalm 96, Psalm 97 is traditionally used on Christmas Day, and appropriately so, as Brueggemann suggests: "In Christmas the Church does not simply celebrate the birth of a wondrous baby. Through that birth we celebrate the cosmic reality that God has entered the process of the world in a decisive way that changes everything toward life. That entry of God into the process of the world is the premise of the poem in Psalm 97."[371] Christmas is also known as the festival of the *incarnation*; so involved is God in the process of the world that "the Word became flesh and lived among us" (John 1:14 NRSV). Jesus incarnated what it means to love God, to hate evil, to enact justice and righteousness. It landed him on a cross, but Jesus affirmed that this difficult way is the way that leads to life (see Matt 7:13-14; see also Mark 8:34-35).

In what we Christians profess is the ultimate demonstration of God's sovereignty, Jesus arose. God delivered him from the power of the wicked (see Ps 97:10), and light shone into what appeared to be utter darkness (Ps 97:11; see also Mark 16:2; John 1:4-5). Appropriately, Psalm 97 is also used during the season of Easter. From cradle to cross to empty tomb, God's incarnational entry into the process of the world still invites our joyful pursuit of justice and righteousness—our submission to the God we love and our opposition to the evil God calls us to hate (see Rom 12:9). To hear Psalm 97 is to make Christmas and Easter and any season "a time to reflect on the transformation wrought by God and the ethical possibility offered us in that transformation."[372] Such reflection promises a radiant joy that will not fade (v. 11).

370. Mays, *Psalms*, 312.
371. Walter Brueggemann, "Psalm 97: Psalm for Christmas Day," *No Other Foundation* 7 (Winter 1986) 3.
372. Ibid., 6.

PSALM 98:1-9, JOY TO THE WORLD

Psalm 98

A psalm.

[1]Sing to the LORD a new song,
for he has done marvelous things;
his right hand and his holy arm
have worked salvation for him.
[2]The LORD has made his salvation known
and revealed his righteousness to the
nations.
[3]He has remembered his love
and his faithfulness to the house of Israel;
all the ends of the earth have seen
the salvation of our God.

[4]Shout for joy to the LORD, all the earth,
burst into jubilant song with music;
[5]make music to the LORD with the harp,
with the harp and the sound of singing,
[6]with trumpets and the blast of the ram's
horn—
shout for joy before the LORD, the King.

[7]Let the sea resound, and everything in it,
the world, and all who live in it.
[8]Let the rivers clap their hands,
let the mountains sing together for joy;
[9]let them sing before the LORD,
for he comes to judge the earth.
He will judge the world in righteousness
and the peoples with equity.

Psalm 98

A Psalm.

[1] O sing to the LORD a new song,
for he has done marvelous things.
His right hand and his holy arm
have gotten him victory.
[2] The LORD has made known his victory;
he has revealed his vindication in the
sight of the nations.
[3] He has remembered his steadfast love and
faithfulness
to the house of Israel.
All the ends of the earth have seen
the victory of our God.

[4] Make a joyful noise to the LORD, all the
earth;
break forth into joyous song and sing
praises.
[5] Sing praises to the LORD with the lyre,
with the lyre and the sound of melody.
[6] With trumpets and the sound of the horn
make a joyful noise before the King, the
LORD.

[7] Let the sea roar, and all that fills it;
the world and those who live in it.
[8] Let the floods clap their hands;
let the hills sing together for joy
[9] at the presence of the LORD, for he is coming
to judge the earth.
He will judge the world with righteousness,
and the peoples with equity.

COMMENTARY

Similar in many ways to the other enthronement psalms, especially Psalm 96 (cf. 96:1a with 98:1a; 96:11b with 98:7a; 96:13 with 98:9), Psalm 98 is nonetheless unique. The first section (vv. 1-3), for instance, features an occurrence of the word "salvation" (יֵשׁע $y\check{s}^{\prime}$) in each verse, and this section primarily elaborates reasons for praise that allude to God's saving activity on behalf of Israel (vv. 1-3). The middle section (vv. 4-6) consists entirely of invitation to praise, framed by the imperative "Make a joyful noise" in vv. 4a, 6b. The invitation continues in vv. 7-8, but it is directed to elements of the created order. The word "righteousness" (צדק $\d{s}edeq$) in the subsequent section (v. 9) recalls v. 2, thus linking the whole creation and "the house of Israel" (v. 3) as spheres for God's work of setting things right—that is, "salvation."

On the possible origin and ancient use of the enthronement psalms, see the Commentary on Psalms 29; 47; 93; 95; 96; and the Introduction. As for its present literary setting as part of a collection of enthronement psalms (Psalms 93; 95–99), Psalm 98 participates in the response of Book IV to the theological crisis articulated in Book III, especially in Ps 89:38-51 (see Commentary on Psalms 73; 74; 79; 80; 89; Introduction). In particular, v. 3 sounds as if it could be a direct response to the question of Ps 89:49 (see also "remember" in Pss 89:47, 50; 98:3). In addition, the recollection of the exodus in Ps 98:1-3 fits the characterization of Book IV as a Moses-book (see Psalm 90; Introduction), and the similarity between Ps 98:1-3 and Isa 52:7-10 also reinforces other indications that Book IV has been shaped in part to respond to the crisis of exile and its aftermath (see Psalms 89; 90; Introduction). Even so, as Tate suggests, "The psalm encompasses the whole range of Yahweh's victories."[373] That is to say, while it may recall the exodus and celebrate the new exodus from Babylon, Psalm 98 and its affirmation of God's reign had, and still has, ongoing significance for the people of God (see Reflections below).

98:1-3. Verse 1 is itself a brief song of praise, with an invitation (v. 1a; on "new song," see Ps 96:1) and reasons for praise. Every major item of vocabulary recalls Exodus 15: "song" (see Exod 15:1, 21), "marvelous things" (see Exod 15:11), "right hand" (see Exod 15:6, 12), "holy arm" (see Exod 15:11, 16), "salvation" (see Exod 15:2). The stated purpose of the exodus was that the Egyptians might know God's sovereignty (see Exod 7:5; 8:10; 9:14; 14:4, 18). Thus Ps 98:2 is also reminiscent of the exodus, and v. 3 recalls Exod 9:16, which suggests that the ultimate purpose of the exodus was to make God manifest "through all the earth." As suggested above, vv. 1-3 are also similar to Isa 52:7-10 (cf. Ps 98:3b with Isa 52:10b), and more generally, the universalistic perspective of Psalm 98 is like that of Isaiah 40–55 (see Commentary on Psalm 96). Psalm 98

thus reinforces the analogy drawn in Isaiah 40–55 between the exodus and the return of the exiles from Babylon. In effect, both events are revelatory of God's basic character, which is best summarized by the word pair "steadfast love and faithfulness" (see Exod 34:6-7; Pss 25:10; 86:15; 89:2, 14, 24, 49; 92:2; 100:5; Introduction; see also "remember" in Exod 2:24). Because the perspective of Psalm 98 is finally eschatological (see v. 9), it invites its readers to extend the analogy as they discern manifestations of God's reign that result in justice and righteousness for the world (see Reflections below).

98:4-6. The universal perspective opened up in vv. 1-3 is reflected also in the invitation in v. 4 addressed to "all the earth" (see Pss 96:1, 9; 97:1; 100:1). Each invited action is an appropriate way to acknowledge God's sovereignty and to pay joyful, enthusiastic homage—"make a joyful noise" (see Pss 47:1; 95:1-2), sing a "joyous song" (see Pss 95:1; 96:12; Isa 52:8), "sing praises" (see Pss 47:6-7; 149:3a). The human voice is to be accompanied by full instrumentation (see Pss 33:2-3; 47:5; 149:3; 150:3).

98:7-8. But a human choir and its instrumental accompaniment are not sufficient response to God's reign. The whole creation will respond (vv. 7-8; see also Ps 96:11-12). In ancient Near Eastern creation accounts, the sea and the "floods" represent chaotic forces that oppose in battle the sovereignty of the supreme creator-God (see Ps 93:3-4). Thus vv. 7-8 call to mind the image of God as divine warrior, who subjected hostile forces to create the world (vv. 7-8) as well as to create and re-create God's people (vv. 1-3; the NRSV assumes this background with its decision to use "victory" instead of "salvation"). Psalm 98 is a witness, therefore, to a God whose choice of a particular people, and whose activity on their behalf, are for the ultimate purpose of fulfilling God's purposes for the whole creation (see Gen 12:1-3; Isa 2:2-4; 19:19-25; 42:5-9; 49:6; see also Commentary on Psalms 33; 65; 66; 93).

98:9. This verse points to the same conclusion (see Ps 96:13). God's coming is to establish justice for "the earth" and to set things right (see v. 2) for "the world." It is no mere local action that is envisioned. God's equitable treatment (see "equity" in Pss 9:8; 96:10; 99:4) includes not just *a* people but *the* peoples. God so loves the world.

373. Tate, *Psalms 51–100*, 524.

REFLECTIONS

Psalm 98 proclaims exuberantly the message that pervades and forms the theological heart of the psalter: God reigns (see Introduction). Like other enthronement psalms, Psalm 98 presents justice and righteousness as the essence of the worldwide policy that God wills and enacts (vv. 2, 9). Psalm 98 also makes it clear that this policy is motivated by God's faithfulness and love (v. 3). In short, the good news is that God rules the universe with faithfulness and love, and the ecumenical, ecological, economic, social, and political implications of this message are profound (see Reflections on Psalms 29; 47; 93; 95; 96; 97; 99; see also Psalms 2; 19; 65–68).

Although the enemies of God are not explicitly mentioned in Psalm 98, they are implied, and the larger literary context of the psalter makes it clear that the assertion of God's sovereignty never goes unopposed. In short, Psalm 98 is eschatological. Its eschatological orientation (see Commentary on Psalm 2; Introduction), as well as the way it draws an analogy between the exodus and the return from exile, encouraged the people of God to continue to apply it analogically and to use it to profess their conviction that God reigns. For instance, the early Christians, who knew that Jesus proclaimed the reign of God (see Mark 1:14-15), also saw in Jesus the ultimate embodiment of God's reign. They experienced in Jesus a king/messiah who lovingly and faithfully enacted justice and righteousness for all people; they experienced his ministry as salvation; and they sang Psalm 98 as a song about Jesus. In response to the announcement of Jesus' birth, Mary interpreted the upcoming event as God's "remembrance of his mercy" (Luke 1:54 NRSV; see also Ps 98:3).[374]

Appropriately, then, Psalm 98 is traditionally used on Christmas Day (see also Psalms 96–97). Such use affirms the Christian conviction that the birth of Jesus Christ belongs with exodus and return from exile in the sequence of God's marvelous doings (v. 1). In fact, although they may not recognize it as such, most Christians are probably familiar with Psalm 98 primarily in the metrical version through Isaac Watts's hymn "Joy to the World." To sing Psalm 98 to greet the birth of Jesus affirms that this event had and has cosmic significance (see Commentary on Psalm 29); it changed and changes the world. To be sure, it seems strange that the birth of a humble baby should signal God's cosmic rule, but the strangeness is a hint of things to come. This baby would finally enact from a cross God's sovereign claim upon the world. The cross of Christ reveals a strength made perfect in weakness (see 2 Cor 12:9), and so it is appropriate that Psalm 98 is traditionally used at the Easter Vigil and during the season of Easter. This rhythm of liturgical use is a reminder that the incarnation, the crucifixion, and the resurrection together proclaim the good news that God so loves the world and that together they portray a divine sovereignty manifest, not as sheer force, but as sheer love.

374. See Mays, *Psalms*, 314.

PSALM 99:1-9, THE LORD OUR GOD IS HOLY

NIV	NRSV
Psalm 99	Psalm 99
¹The LORD reigns, let the nations tremble; he sits enthroned between the cherubim,	¹ The LORD is king; let the peoples tremble! He sits enthroned upon the cherubim; let the earth quake!

NIV

let the earth shake.
²Great is the LORD in Zion;
he is exalted over all the nations.
³Let them praise your great and awesome
name—
he is holy.

⁴The King is mighty, he loves justice—
you have established equity;
in Jacob you have done
what is just and right.
⁵Exalt the LORD our God
and worship at his footstool;
he is holy.

⁶Moses and Aaron were among his priests,
Samuel was among those who called on
his name;
they called on the LORD
and he answered them.
⁷He spoke to them from the pillar of cloud;
they kept his statutes and the decrees he
gave them.

⁸O LORD our God,
you answered them;
you were to Israelᵃ a forgiving God,
though you punished their misdeeds.ᵇ
⁹Exalt the LORD our God
and worship at his holy mountain,
for the LORD our God is holy.

ᵃ8 Hebrew *them*   ᵇ8 Or / *an avenger of the wrongs done to them*

NRSV

² The LORD is great in Zion;
he is exalted over all the peoples.
³ Let them praise your great and awesome
name.
Holy is he!
⁴ Mighty King,ᵃ lover of justice,
you have established equity;
you have executed justice
and righteousness in Jacob.
⁵ Extol the LORD our God;
worship at his footstool.
Holy is he!

⁶ Moses and Aaron were among his priests,
Samuel also was among those who called
on his name.
They cried to the LORD, and he answered
them.
⁷ He spoke to them in the pillar of cloud;
they kept his decrees,
and the statutes that he gave them.

⁸ O LORD our God, you answered them;
you were a forgiving God to them,
but an avenger of their wrongdoings.
⁹ Extol the LORD our God,
and worship at his holy mountain;
for the LORD our God is holy.

ᵃ Cn: Heb *And a king's strength*

COMMENTARY

Psalm 99 is the conclusion of a collection of enthronement psalms (Psalm 93, 95–99) that form the theological heart of the psalter and appear to be strategically placed to respond to the crisis articulated in Book III, especially Ps 89:38-51 and its lament over the failure of the Davidic covenant (see Commentary on Psalms 73; 74; 79; 80; 89; Introduction). Book IV responds to Book III by proclaiming God's reign and by offering a pre-Davidic, Mosaic perspective—a reminder that Moses proclaimed the reign of God (Exod 15:18) before there was land, Temple, or monarchy. In this regard, it is crucial that Book IV begins with

the only psalm attributed to Moses (Psalm 90), and it is significant that Psalm 99, the climactic enthronement psalm, explicitly mentions Moses and Aaron (v. 6; see also Pss 103:7; 105:26; 106:16, 23, 32), as well as Samuel, who opposed the formation of the monarchy on the grounds that only God could properly be considered Israel's king (see 1 Sam 8:1-18).

It is revealing, too, that there are numerous verbal links between Psalm 99 and Exod 15:1-18, the song of praise that Moses and the Israelites sang after being delivered from Egypt. Both songs celebrate God's reign (v. 1; Exod 15:18). In both,

God is to be "exalted" (vv. 2, 5, 9; Exod 15:2), because God is "great" (vv. 2-3; see "might" in Exod 15:16 NRSV), "awesome" (v. 3; Exod 15:11), "mighty" (v. 4; see "strength" in Exod 15:2, 13), and "holy" (vv. 3, 5, 9; Exod 15:11, 13). In both songs, people "tremble" (v. 1; Exod 15:14), and in both, God is established in God's own place (vv. 1-2, 5, 9; Exod 15:13, 17). It seems as if Psalm 99 intentionally recalls Exod 15:1-18 as a way of affirming for a later generation—discouraged by events like those described in Book III—that God *still* reigns. In the context of the book of Psalms, and in the context of the world as we know it, this affirmation is made in the face of opposition to God's reign. That is to say, it is eschatological, and it calls every generation to make the decision to live under God's rule (see Psalm 2; Introduction). On the possible origin and ancient use of Psalm 99 and the other enthronement psalms, see the Commentary on Psalms 29; 47; 93; 95; 96; and the Introduction.

While Psalm 99 has much in common with the other enthronement psalms, including the theme of holiness (see Pss 29:2; 47:8; 93:5; 96:9; 97:12; 98:1), it is unique in its use of the theme of holiness as a pervasive structuring concept. The phrase "Holy is he!" in vv. 3, 5 divides the psalm into three sections: vv. 1-3, vv. 4-5, vv. 6-9. Verses 5 and 9 are nearly identical, and v. 9 has two more occurrences of the key word "holy" (קדוש *qādôš*). Holiness, in its fundamental sense, designates the awesome presence of God that evoked fear and required human beings to keep their distance or to approach God only after making special preparations or taking special precautions (see Exod 19:7-25, esp. v. 23; 20:18-21). This fundamental sense is reflected in Ps 99:1-3; the presence of God causes people to "tremble" and the earth to "quake" (v. 1; see also Exod 19:16; 20:18, although the Hebrew words translated "trembled" are both different from the one in Ps 99:1; the same observation also applies to Pss 96:9; 97:4). As the psalm proceeds, however, holiness is defined in very different terms. Rather than keeping humans at a distance, God relates to them, doing justice and righteousness (v. 4), answering cries (vv. 6, 8), and both forgiving and holding accountable (v. 8).

99:1-3. In addition to reflecting the fundamental sense of holiness, vv. 1-3 introduce the striking claim that while God's sovereignty is universal, it is focused "in Zion" (v. 2). God's enthronement "upon the cherubim" (v. 1) also indicates the centrality of Jerusalem. The reference is apparently to the ark, which was understood symbolically as God's throne (see Ps 80:1). The particularity of v. 1 continues throughout the psalm. God's "footstool" is another reference to the ark (v. 5; see also 1 Chr 28:2; Ps 132:7), and God's "holy mountain" is Zion (v. 9; see also Pss 2:6; 15:1; 43:3; 48:1). In short, Jerusalem is the earthly locus of the presence and power of God (see Psalms 46; 48; 76; 84; 87; 122), who is nonetheless a cosmic sovereign (see "awesome" in Ps 47:2 and "great" in Pss 47:2; 95:3; 96:4).

99:4-5. By insisting on the particularity of Zion, vv. 1-3 have already begun to suggest that the holy God is not entirely separable from human places and matters. Verses 4-5 now indicate just how intimate God's involvement actually is. As the NRSV note suggests, v. 4a is somewhat problematic, but it can be construed as follows: "The strength of a king (is to be) one who loves justice" (see Ps 72:1-2). The implication is that God loves justice, for God does "justice and righteousness" (see Pss 9:7-8; 96:13; 97:2; 98:9; see "equity" in Pss 9:8; 96:10; 98:9). In other words, God is not enthroned above the struggle for rightly ordered human relatedness; rather, God is intimately involved in it. The shift to direct address of God in v. 4 reinforces this message, and the personal pronoun provides emphasis: "*you* have done. . . ." As the prophetic books make clear, justice and righteousness have to do with the concrete, daily realities of human existence and relatedness, especially provision for the poor and needy (see Amos 5:7-13, 21-24; Mic 3:1-12; 6:6-8). Indeed, as Psalm 82 suggests, doing justice and righteousness is the fundamental criterion of divinity. For God, holiness ultimately means not transcendence but immanence, not inseparability but involvement.

99:6-9. These verses portray even more clearly the tension between transcendence and immanence. In other words, for the holy God to be involved with humankind means that God has a problem. What Moses, Aaron, and Samuel called on God about was the people's sinfulness (see Exod 32:7-14; Num 16:20-22; 1 Sam 7:5-11). The "pillar of cloud" (v. 7; see also Exod 13:21-22;

14:19, 24; 33:9-10; Num 12:5; 14:14) represented God's presence with the people throughout the exodus and wilderness experience. Although v. 7 indicates that the people "kept his decrees . . . and statutes," the wilderness was actually characterized by distrust, complaining, and disobedience (see v. 8) that necessitated intercession by Moses and Aaron. God "answered" (vv. 6, 8), and that answer inevitably involved forgiveness (note the shift to direct address of God in v. 8 and another emphatic "you" in v. 8a). Only by God's grace did the people continue to exist (v. 8b), but

God continued to demand the people's obedience (v. 8c). Herein lies God's problem: how to be both a forgiving God and "an avenger of their wrongdoings." Verse 8 portrays the same tension that is evident in God's self-revelation to Moses in Exod 34:6-7. God's holiness ultimately involves not God's avoidance of sin and sinners but God's willingness to bear the burden of sin (v. 8; the Hebrew word translated "forgiving" [נשא *nāśāʾ*] means lit. "to bear," "to carry") and to love sinners.

REFLECTIONS

What has been said about the other enthronement psalms applies to Psalm 99 (see Reflections on Psalms 29; 47; 93; 95; 96; 97; 98); however, it is fitting that the final enthronement psalm brings into sharpest focus the issue of the nature of God's sovereignty. A popular notion of sovereignty equates it with the fundamental sense of holiness—that is, absolute freedom, transcendence, and unapproachability. Thus it is significant that Psalm 99 pushes toward a redefinition of holiness in the direction of involvement and committed, forgiving love.

1. In a word, the theology of Psalm 99 is *incarnational* (see Commentary on Psalm 97). God is involved with a particular place (vv. 1-2, 5, 9) and with particular people (vv. 6-8) in the struggle for justice and righteousness (v. 4). Christians affirm a scandalous particularity that is analogous. Replacing Zion and the Temple (see Mark 13:1-2; 14:58; 15:29), Jesus became the earthly locus of God's presence and power, the focus and revelation of God's glory (see John 1:14-18). The incarnation of Jesus is the ultimate redefinition of holiness: God resides in human flesh! Psalm 99, however, evidences already the redefinition of God's holiness, which culminates in the incarnation. And in the tension represented in v. 8 between God's forgiving and God's holding accountable, it is not difficult to discern the shape of a cross. God's sovereignty is manifested ultimately in suffering love, a manner that appears to the world to be weakness (see 1 Cor 1:22-25; 2 Cor 12:9).

2. Psalm 99 is used traditionally on Transfiguration Sunday. The association of Psalm 99 with the transfiguration may be due to the Gospel accounts' mention of Moses and the cloud (see Matt 17:1-8; Mark 9:2-9; Luke 9:28-36), but there is a deeper connection. The transfiguration is a scene that partakes of the fundamental sense of holiness; Jesus is set apart and unapproachable, and the disciples are terrified. In each Gospel, however, the transfiguration follows immediately Jesus' first announcement that he must go to Jerusalem to suffer, die, and be raised. Like Psalm 99, this juxtaposition pushes toward a redefinition of holiness and sovereignty in the direction of committed involvement and suffering love. Defying the conventional notion of holiness and the worldly definition of royal power, God is the Holy One who is persistently present in our midst (see Hos 11:9). Because the Holy One is committed to being with us and enacting justice and righteousness among us, it is fitting that Jesus taught us to pray, "hallowed be thy name; thy kingdom come, thy will be done, *on earth* as it is in heaven."

PSALM 100:1-5, KNOW THAT THE LORD IS GOD

NIV

Psalm 100

A psalm. For giving thanks.

¹Shout for joy to the LORD, all the earth.
² Worship the LORD with gladness;
come before him with joyful songs.
³Know that the LORD is God.
It is he who made us, and we are his[a];
we are his people, the sheep of his pasture.

⁴Enter his gates with thanksgiving
and his courts with praise;
give thanks to him and praise his name.
⁵For the LORD is good and his love endures
forever;
his faithfulness continues through all
generations.

a3 Or *and not we ourselves*

NRSV

Psalm 100

A Psalm of thanksgiving.

¹ Make a joyful noise to the LORD, all the
earth.
² Worship the LORD with gladness;
come into his presence with singing.

³ Know that the LORD is God.
It is he that made us, and we are his;[a]
we are his people, and the sheep of his
pasture.

⁴ Enter his gates with thanksgiving,
and his courts with praise.
Give thanks to him, bless his name.

⁵ For the LORD is good;
his steadfast love endures forever,
and his faithfulness to all generations.

aAnother reading is *and not we ourselves*

COMMENTARY

Although Psalm 100 is not ordinarily considered a part of the collection of enthronement psalms (Psalms 93; 95–99), it has many affinities with this collection. Given the similarity between Psalms 95 and 100 (cf. Pss 95:7 with 100:3), one can reasonably conclude that they are intended to form a frame around Psalms 96–99, which seem to form the core of the collection.[375] In any case, Psalm 100 shares much of the vocabulary of the preceding psalms (see references below), and it certainly serves admirably as a conclusion to the preceding collection, regardless of whether it was intended to do so. (On the literary placement of the collection and the role of Psalms 93–100 and Book IV as a whole, see Commentary on Psalms 90; 93; 99; Introduction). It is not clear exactly how to construe the superscription. The Hebrew

word rendered "thanksgiving" (תודה *tôdâ*) can designate an actual sacrifice, but it can also denote liturgical expressions of gratitude that apparently served as substitutes for sacrifice (see Ps 50:14, 23). The word recurs in v. 4 (see also Ps 95:2), and the same root in verbal form also occurs in v. 4 (see Ps 97:12). Thus the origin and ancient use of Psalm 100 are unclear, but it is certain that Psalm 100 would have been used in some liturgical setting (see "gates" and "courts" in v. 4), perhaps in conjunction with Psalms 93; 95–99. (See Commentary on Psalm 96 for the possible origin and use of the enthronement psalms.)

In a sense, Psalm 100 demonstrates the typical structure of a song of praise: invitation to praise (vv. 1-4), followed by reasons for praise (v. 5). In this case, the invitation is predominant. Within this apparently regular structure, however, v. 3 stands out. Like vv. 1, 2, 4, it begins with an imperative, but the invited action is different. It

375. See Marvin E. Tate, *Psalms 51–100,* WBC 20 (Dallas: Word, 1990) 535.

invites the hearer to "know" something that underlies all action, and it is followed immediately by instruction about God and God's people. Furthermore, v. 3 is the central verse in the psalm; the imperative in v. 3 is the central one in a series of seven (there are three imperatives in vv. 1-2 and three in v. 4). In short, while all the songs of praise are implicitly instructional (note the reasons for praise), the structure and content of Psalm 100 focus attention on v. 3, which gives the psalm an explicitly instructional quality.

100:1-2. In keeping with the perspective of the enthronement psalms and other songs of praise, the invitation in v. 1 is addressed to "all the earth" (see Pss 66:1; 96:1, 9; 97:1; 98:3; 99:1). The underlying rationale is that a cosmic sovereign deserves nothing less than a cosmic response. To "make a joyful noise" is an appropriate way to acknowledge and to greet a monarch (see Pss 95:1-2; 98:4, 6). To summon any congregation less than "all the earth" is to misunderstand the identity of Israel's God.

The imperative "worship" (עבד 'ābad) in v. 2 also bespeaks God's sovereignty. While the Hebrew root can mean "worship," this translation probably does not convey satisfactorily the comprehensiveness of the term. The word means to orient one's whole life and existence to a sovereign master, to be the servant or slave of a monarch. The word always occurs in the psalter in relation to a royal figure, either human or divine (see Pss 2:11; 18:43; 22:30; 72:11; 97:7; 102:22).[376] The imagery of royalty also includes the imperative to "come into his presence" (see 1 Kgs 1:28, 32), as well as to "bless" in v. 4 (see "kneel" in Ps 95:6; see also Ps 96:2). The inseparability of service and sovereignty is also clear in other contexts. For instance, the culminating affirmation of the people following the exodus is "the LORD will reign forever and ever" (Exod 15:18 NRSV). This proclamation of God's sovereignty is congruent with the stated goal of the exodus that the people may "serve" God (see Exod 4:23; 7:16; 8:20; 9:1, 13; 10:3; 12:31). Thus it is probably not coincidental that one of the only two occurrences of the imperative "Serve the LORD" is in Ps 100:2, immediately following the explicit proclamation of God's reign in Psalms

93; 95–99. In terms of the shape of the psalter, it is revealing that the other occurrence is in Ps 2:11. In short, Psalm 100 and the other songs of praise are fundamentally about precisely what Psalm 2 suggests the whole psalter will be about: the reign of God (see Introduction).

100:3-5. As suggested above, the lone imperative in v. 3 stands out; Psalm 100 explicitly intends to teach. A literal translation of v. 3 makes the nature of the teaching even clearer:

> Know that YHWH, he (is) God,
> He made us, and not we,
>   his people (are we) and the sheep of his
>   pasture.

The clustering of personal pronouns and pronominal suffixes in v. 3 is striking, as is their sequence: "he . . . he . . . us . . . we . . . his . . . his." This arrangement dramatically suggests that the question of human identity must begin and end with God. This is what the psalm intends for us to "know." As Mays points out, v. 3 is a variation on what Zimmerli identified as the "recognition formula" ("and you will know that I am Yahweh"), which always follows a description of God's activity (see Ezek 5:13; 6:7; see also Exod 7:5; 8:10; 9:14; 14:4, 18; see above on Ps 98:2).[377] Here the imperative introduces a description of God's activity. There is a rich ambiguity in the word "made" (עשה 'āśâ); it could refer to God's creation of the world and all living things (see Pss 95:5; 104:24), or it could refer to God's "making" or electing Israel as God's own people (see Deut 32:6, 15; 44:2; see above on Ps 95:6, where the same ambiguity is present). The ambiguity is appropriate, for Israel could never tell the story of its election apart from an understanding of God's intention for "all the earth" (v. 1; see Commentary on Psalms 33; 65; 66; 93; 98). The reasons for praise in v. 5 also point in both directions. The word "good" (טוב ṭôb) recalls the recurrent evaluation of God's creative activity in Genesis 1, while "steadfast love" (חסד ḥesed) and "faithfulness" (אמונה 'ĕmûnâ) recall God's self-revelation to Moses (see Exod 34:6-7; Introduction) immediately prior to the reestablishment of a covenant with the people (see Exod 34:10).

Verse 5 also recalls Ps 98:3, where steadfast

---

376. See James L. Mays, "Worship, World, and Power," *Int.* 23 (1969) 321.

377. Ibid., 319.

love and faithfulness to Israel are mentioned in the context of the proclamation of God's reign (see also Pss 86:15; 89:2, 14, 49; 92:2; 117:2). The same proclamation is implicit in Psalm 100, and it is reinforced by the sheep/shepherd imagery in v. 3. In the ancient Near East, kings were known as the shepherds of their people (see Ezek 34:1-10). Psalm 100 wants us to know that God is shepherd both of God's people and of the whole cosmos (see Pss 23:1; 74:1; 80:1; 95:7; Ezek 34:11-16). The only proper response is joyful gratitude and praise (vv. 1-2, 4; see also Pss 95:1-2; 96:11; 97:1, 8, 12; 98:4-6) that bespeaks the offering of one's whole self in service (v. 2) to the ruler of the world.

REFLECTIONS

1. Psalm 100 is perhaps the most familiar of the songs of praise. Mays observes: "Were the statistics known, Psalm 100 would probably prove to be the song most often chanted from within the history that runs from the Israelite temple on Mount Zion to the synagogues and churches spread across the earth."[378]

Psalm 100 is certainly the banner hymn of the Reformed tradition. A metrical version of the psalm, "All People That on Earth Do Dwell," was composed by William Kethe, a friend of John Knox, in 1561. The tune by Louis Bourgeois, musical composer for John Calvin, became known as *Old Hundreth,* even though it was originally composed for a paraphrase of Psalm 134.[379] *Old Hundredth* is now the tune that accompanies words that many Christian congregations know simply as "The Doxology" (lit., "the word of glory/praise").

2. The appeal of Psalm 100 may lie in part in its brevity and simplicity, as well as in its explicitly instructional tone. The lesson itself is remarkably simple yet deeply profound: God rules the world, and consequently we belong to God. This message lies not only at the heart of the book of Psalms but also at the heart of Jesus' preaching and of the whole of Scripture (see Commentary on Psalms 29; 47; 93; 95–99). In a quite different context, the apostle Paul taught essentially the same lesson: "Or do you not *know* that your body is a temple of the Holy Spirit within you, which you have from God, and that *you are not your own?* For you were bought with a price; therefore *glorify God* in your body" (2 Cor 6:19-20 NRSV, italics added).

We are not our own! This is a difficult lesson to hear and to get across in a culture that encourages us to be "self-made" men and women. Most of us seem to believe the popular saying, "It's *my* life to live." The Bible insists, however, that our lives are not simply our own to live. Genuine life is found in submission to God. In biblical terms, to live is to praise God, and to praise God is to live. As Claus Westermann puts it, to praise anything or anyone other than God "must disturb and finally destroy life itself."[380]

From this perspective, Psalm 100 is an "act of sanity," as Brueggemann calls it:

> Obviously our world is at the edge of insanity and we with it. Inhumaneness is developed as a scientific enterprise. Greed is celebrated as economic advance. Power runs unbridled to destructiveness.
>
> In a world like this one, our psalm is an act of sanity, whereby we may be "reclothed in our rightful minds" (cf. Mark 5:15). . . . Life is no longer self-grounded without thanks but rooted in thanks.[381]

---

378. Ibid., 316.
379. See Rowland E. Prothero, *The Psalms in Human Life and Experience* (New York: E. P. Dutton, 1903) 114.
380. Claus Westermann, *Praise and Lament in the Psalms,* trans. K. R. Crim and R. N. Soulen (Atlanta: John Knox, 1965/1981) 161.
381. Walter Brueggemann, "Psalm 100," *Int.* 39 (1985) 67.

Brueggemann cites Geoffrey Wainwright, who has pointed out what is undoubtedly true: "The world is not an easy place in which to live doxologically."[382] But as difficult as it may be, to live doxologically is of paramount importance, for to praise anything or anyone other than God "must disturb and finally destroy life itself." At this point, Psalm 100 offers essentially the same instruction as Psalms 1–2. To be happy means submission to God—openness to God's instruction (1:2) and primary dependence on God rather than self (2:12). To be wicked is to be an autonomous self, and "a wicked life leads only to ruin" (Ps 1:6).[383]

Because the Reformed tradition has so treasured Psalm 100, it is fitting that its essential instruction is contained in the first question and answer of the Westminster Shorter Catechism:

Question: What is the chief end of humankind?
Answer: The chief end of humankind is to glorify God and enjoy God forever.

382. Geoffrey Wainwright, *Doxology* (New York: Oxford University Press, 1980) 425; see Brueggemann, "Psalm 100," 69.
383. The translation is that of Gary Chamberlain, *The Psalms: a New Translation for Prayer and Worship* (Nashville: The Upper Room, 1984) 26.

PSALM 101:1-8, I WILL SING OF YOUR LOVE AND JUSTICE

NIV

Psalm 101

Of David. A psalm.

¹I will sing of your love and justice;
   to you, O LORD, I will sing praise.
²I will be careful to lead a blameless life—
   when will you come to me?

I will walk in my house
   with blameless heart.
³I will set before my eyes
   no vile thing.

The deeds of faithless men I hate;
   they will not cling to me.
⁴Men of perverse heart shall be far from me;
   I will have nothing to do with evil.

⁵Whoever slanders his neighbor in secret,
   him will I put to silence;
whoever has haughty eyes and a proud heart,
   him will I not endure.

⁶My eyes will be on the faithful in the land,
   that they may dwell with me;
he whose walk is blameless
   will minister to me.

⁷No one who practices deceit
   will dwell in my house;

NRSV

Psalm 101

Of David. A Psalm.

¹ I will sing of loyalty and of justice;
   to you, O LORD, I will sing.
² I will study the way that is blameless.
   When shall I attain it?

I will walk with integrity of heart
   within my house;
³ I will not set before my eyes
   anything that is base.

I hate the work of those who fall away;
   it shall not cling to me.
⁴ Perverseness of heart shall be far from me;
   I will know nothing of evil.

⁵ One who secretly slanders a neighbor
   I will destroy.
A haughty look and an arrogant heart
   I will not tolerate.

⁶ I will look with favor on the faithful in the land,
   so that they may live with me;
whoever walks in the way that is blameless

NIV

no one who speaks falsely
    will stand in my presence.
⁸Every morning I will put to silence
    all the wicked in the land;
I will cut off every evildoer
    from the city of the LORD.

NRSV

    shall minister to me.

⁷ No one who practices deceit
    shall remain in my house;
no one who utters lies
    shall continue in my presence.

⁸ Morning by morning I will destroy
    all the wicked in the land,
cutting off all evildoers
    from the city of the LORD.

COMMENTARY

Psalm 101 has always been something of an enigma to commentators. It is best viewed as a royal psalm in which the king was the original speaker. The king's question in v. 2, which the NIV translates more accurately, is primary for considering the origin, ancient use, and literary setting of Psalm 101. Without the question, Psalm 101 would make good sense as a pledge or oath of office that the king might have recited at his coronation, following the assumption of office (see Psalm 2) and perhaps appropriate ceremonial prayers (see Psalm 72). Indeed, it is possible that the psalm was written and used for this purpose, but the question in v. 2 seems inappropriate. If it is not considered a later addition or emended somehow, it has the force of a plea for help and gives the rest of the psalm the character of a complaint (see the questions in Pss 42:2; 119:82, 84 and the similar "How long?" in Pss 6:3; 74:10; 94:3). That is to say, the king professes his loyalty and good behavior as a basis for asking when he will experience God's presence and favor—a reasonable question in view of Ps 18:20-30, another royal psalm (see Ps 18:25, where "loyal" and "blameless" occur as in Ps 101:1-2). In fact, in view of the similarities between Psalms 18 and 101, Leslie Allen categorizes Psalm 101 as a royal complaint and concludes:

Psalm 18 looks back to God's intervention in response to the king's appeal and testimonial, and gives thanks that he was delivered from a situation of distress. Psalm 101 is set at an earlier stage in royal experience.[384]

384. Leslie C. Allen, *Psalms 101–150*, WBC 21 (Waco, Tex.: Word, 1983) 6.

While this conclusion makes sense chronologically, it raises questions about the literary placement of Psalms 18 and 101: If Psalm 101 reflects an earlier stage of royal experience, why is it placed after Psalm 18? Then, too, since Psalm 89 suggests the failure of the covenant with David and the disappearance of the monarchy (see Commentary on Psalm 89; Introduction), why are there any royal psalms at all in Books IV and V (see Psalms 110; 144)? Assuming the placement is not simply haphazard, one can respond that in its current literary setting, the royal complaint in Psalm 101 is a response to the destruction of the monarchy, as are Psalms 90–100 (see Commentary on Psalms 90; 93; Introduction). The voice of an imagined future king says, in effect, "I shall do everything right," implying that the monarchy should be restored; the question in v. 2 thus asks when the restoration will occur. The cogency of this approach is strengthened by the juxtaposition of Psalm 101 with 102, which, while it starts out as an individual prayer (perhaps still to be heard as the voice of a king?), suddenly in v. 12 becomes an expression of hope for the restoration of Zion, the seat of the monarchy (cf. 101:2 with 102:13), as well as an expression of hope for the return of the exiles (vv. 18-22). Thus Psalms 101–102 together address the three key elements of the crisis of exile—loss of monarchy, Zion/Temple, and land. This loss is documented in Book III, to which Book IV responds (see Psalm 90; Introduction), and Psalms 101–102 can be construed as a part of that response. Even if this proposal is incorrect, it is clear that as years passed without the restoration of the monarchy, Psalm 101 would have been read either messianically or perhaps as a recital of what God intends for the whole people, as well as for faithful individuals (see Reflections below).

Scholars offer a wide variety of proposals for understanding the structure and movement of Psalm 101, probably because the frequent repetitions point in several directions. The complexity may suggest that the structure moves on more than one level. Verses 1-2a introduce what the whole psalm is about, which can be summarized with the key word "blameless"/"integrity" (תמים tāmîm, vv. 2ab, 6). Many commentators take vv. 2b-4 as the next section (the king's own behavior), and vv. 5-8 as the final section (the king's enforcement of integrity). This makes sense, but the sevenfold listing of negative behaviors in vv. 3-5 also suggests that vv. 2b-5 form a coherent unit that begins and ends with the word "heart" (לבב lēbāb, vv. 2b, 5b; see also v. 4). In this view, vv. 6-8 form the final section, which begins and ends with the word "land" (ארץ 'ereṣ, vv. 6a, 8a). The two sections are characterized by four repeated terms or phrases that occur in the same order in each: "blameless"/"integrity" (vv. 2b, 6b), "in my house" (vv. 2b, 7a), "before my eyes"/"in my presence" (vv. 3a, 7b; see "eyes" in vv. 5b, 6a NIV), and "destroy" (vv. 5a, 8a).

A further structural feature is a chiastic pattern of repetition (see Introduction) that also links the two sections (my literal translations):[385]

A v. 3a "before my eyes"
  B v. 3a "*speech* of worthlessness"
    C v. 3b "those *doing* crooked (things)"
      D v. 5b "haughtiness of *eyes*"
      D' v. 6a "my *eyes* (are upon)"
    C' v. 7a "those *doing* deceit"
  B' v. 7b "those *speaking* lies"
A' v. 7b "before my eyes"

The word "eyes" (עינים 'ēnayim) lies on the boundaries and at the center of the chiastic pattern, thus suggesting that the king sees all (vv. 3a, 7b) but watches out for "the faithful" (v. 6a) in contrast to the arrogant. Each poetic line at the center of the pattern is linked by repetition to

<hr/>

385. See John S. Kselman, "Psalm 101: Royal Confession and Divine Oracle," *JSOT* 33 (1985) 47.

the verse that either opens or concludes each major section of the poem but does not figure in the pattern (see "heart" in vv. 5b, 2b, and see "land" in vv. 6a, 8a). Again, the effect is to contrast integrity with arrogance (vv. 2b, 5b) and faithfulness with wickedness (vv. 6a, 8a). The king chooses and supports God's values—the way of integrity, which embodies loyalty and justice (vv. 1-2a).

101:1-2a. Singing indicates celebration (see Pss 47:6; 96:1; 98:1, 4-5), and what the king celebrates are the characteristics of God's reign. The word translated "loyalty" (חסד ḥesed) is usually rendered "steadfast love" in the NRSV; it characterizes God's very being (see Exod 34:6-7; Pss 5:7; 13:5; Introduction) as well as the way God exercises sovereignty (see Pss 89:1-2, 14; 98:3), including the way God relates to the king, the earthly agent of God's rule (see Pss 18:25; 18:50; 21:7; 89:24, 28, 33, 49; 2 Sam 7:15). The word "justice" (משפט mišpāṭ) also describes the policy that God wills and enacts as sovereign (see Pss 9:7-8; 89:14; 96:13; 97:2; 98:9; 99:4), as well as what God intends for the earthly king to will and enact (see Ps 72:1-2, 4). Similarly, blamelessness or integrity is rooted in God's character, as Psalm 18 makes clear. God's way is one of integrity (18:30), and God deals with integrity with those who have dealt likewise with God (18:25), and this includes the king (18:23). God's integrity or blamelessness involves God's faithfulness and dependability; human integrity or blamelessness means not moral perfection but the commitment to live according to the priorities of and in dependence upon God (see Commentary on Psalms 15; 18). The king implies this commitment in v. 1 and indicates it more explicitly in v. 2a. The verb translated "study"/"be careful" (שכל śākal) recalls Ps 2:10, where it is used as a warning to all kings of the earth to "be wise"—that is, to serve God (see Ps 100:2).

Having made this commitment, the king asks when he can expect the treatment promised in Ps 18:25. This question in its current literary setting may once have functioned as a plea for restoration of the monarchy; in any case, it gives the psalm a future orientation. Other interpreters view the question in v. 2 as evidence of the king's ritual humiliation in an annual cultic drama or as a general plea for assurance or as the king's request for the kind of revelation that Solomon received in a dream in 1 Kings 3.[386]

101:2b-5. After the reaffirmation to pursue integrity (v. 2*b*), vv. 3-5 offer a list of seven things that the king will avoid or abolish. Seven is often symbolic of completeness, and this symbolism would be very appropriate in a psalm in which a key word is "integrity" (תמים *tāmîm*), the Hebrew root of which means "to be complete, whole." In other words, the king completely avoids evil. There is a similar list of seven in Prov 6:16-19, and several scholars detect the influence of the wisdom literature here. This is not unlikely, but several of the negative behaviors are also mentioned elsewhere in the psalms. For instance, "vile thing" in v. 3*a* occurs as "vile disease" in 41:8, and "perverse(ness)" in v. 4*a* occurs in Ps 18:26. This word occurs also in Prov 10:9; 11:20, where it is explicitly the opposite of "integrity"/"blameless." Perversity or crookedness, along with arrogance (v. 5*b*; see also Ps 138:6), forms the primary contrast to the integrity that the king advocates and embodies. Silencing or destroying the wicked (v. 5*a*; see also v. 8*a*) is something ordinarily reserved for God (see Pss 54:6; 94:23), but the king is to be the agent of God's rule (see Ps 18:40). The list of behaviors in vv. 3-5 is reminiscent of Psalm 15 (see 15:3-5), where the issue of entrance to the Temple begins with integrity or blamelessness (see 15:1-2*a*). Kraus even suggests that Psalm 101 casts the king in the role of "the guardian of the Torah of the [temple] gate."[387]

101:6-8. Using much of the same vocabulary as vv. 2*b*-5, vv. 6-8 drive home the point. The king will support and surround himself with people of integrity. The gatekeeping function of the king is called to mind again by the mention of "deceit" (רמיה *rěmiyyâ*) in v. 7*a*, since deceitfulness also disqualifies one from entering the Temple in Ps 24:4. Given what could be considered the redundancy of vv. 2*b*-5 and vv. 6-8, Kselman suggests that vv. 6-8 be considered a divine oracle delivered to the king by a cultic prophet—the answer, as it were, to the king's question in v. 2 about God's coming to him.[388] To be sure, this is a possible construal of vv. 6-8, since what may be intended as divine speech can occur with no introduction (Kselman cites Ps 32:8-9). Kselman's proposal has the advantage of emphasizing clearly the ideal that the earthly king be the embodiment of divine sovereignty, but this is clear enough from Psalm 101 without Kselman's proposal, which remains highly speculative. The king pursues God's way of integrity, which is embodied in love and justice.

386. See Th. Booij, "Psalm CI 2—'When Wilt Thou Come to Me?'" *VT* 38 (1988) 460.

387. H.-J. Kraus, *Psalms 60–150: A Commentary,* trans. H. C. Oswald (Minneapolis: Augsburg, 1989) 279.
388. Kselman, "Psalm 101," 52-57.

REFLECTIONS

1. Psalm 101 may have originated as a king's oath of office, and it was probably placed in Book IV to serve as a hopeful plea in the aftermath of exile. Even so, Psalm 101 has the potential to speak to and be useful for the people of God in a variety of circumstances. With the disappearance of the monarchy and the eventual realization that it would never be reinstituted, Psalm 101 could at least be understood as an articulation of the values that God wills to be concretely embodied among humans—love, justice, integrity. Furthermore, the psalm is implicitly a profession of faith in God's sovereignty. The psalmist begins by affirming God's steadfast love and justice, aspects of God's reign, and the psalmist makes a commitment to pursue love and justice, even in the apparent absence of God (see the question in v. 2*a*). In short, the psalmist depends ultimately not on his or her good behavior but on God's coming.

2. Because the early Christians saw in Jesus a representation of God's values and a commitment to pursue love and justice even in the apparent absence of God—the cross (see Mark 15:34, quoting Ps 22:1)—they heard Psalm 101 as Jesus' instruction to the faithful in all times and places. In a sense, the psalm has been democratized, as Mays suggests, although he also recognizes that it remains especially pertinent for those who govern:

The psalm teaches that it is not enough for those who lead to live by the legalities and govern by codes. It is the character of the governor and the character of those in his government that really determine what the effect of their governing is on the governed. In this the psalm is radical, but history is replete with examples that prove it is right. The psalm also teaches that conduct depends on character and character is shaped by ultimate commitments. It would insist that "you cannot be good without God," a lesson for more than rulers.[389]

In a society where the word *politician* has become almost synonymous with *crooked* and where much speech—for instance, advertising—is designed to mislead, the invitation of Psalm 101 is particularly timely: that we speak and embody the truth in love as a witness to God's claim upon our lives and our world (see Eph 4:15).

389. James L. Mays, *Psalms,* Interpretation (Louisville: John Knox, 1994) 322.

PSALM 102:1-28, GOD HEARS THE PRAYER OF THE DESTITUTE

NIV	NRSV
Psalm 102	**Psalm 102**
A prayer of an afflicted man. When he is faint and pours out his lament before the LORD.	A prayer of one afflicted, when faint and pleading before the LORD.

¹Hear my prayer, O LORD;
   let my cry for help come to you.
²Do not hide your face from me
   when I am in distress.
Turn your ear to me;
   when I call, answer me quickly.
	¹ Hear my prayer, O LORD;
	   let my cry come to you.
	² Do not hide your face from me
	   in the day of my distress.
	Incline your ear to me;
	   answer me speedily in the day when I call.

³For my days vanish like smoke;
   my bones burn like glowing embers.
⁴My heart is blighted and withered like grass;
   I forget to eat my food.
⁵Because of my loud groaning
   I am reduced to skin and bones.
⁶I am like a desert owl,
   like an owl among the ruins.
⁷I lie awake; I have become
   like a bird alone on a roof.
⁸All day long my enemies taunt me;
   those who rail against me use my name as
     a curse.
⁹For I eat ashes as my food
   and mingle my drink with tears
¹⁰because of your great wrath,
   for you have taken me up and thrown me
     aside.
	³ For my days pass away like smoke,
	   and my bones burn like a furnace.
	⁴ My heart is stricken and withered like grass;
	   I am too wasted to eat my bread.
	⁵ Because of my loud groaning
	   my bones cling to my skin.
	⁶ I am like an owl of the wilderness,
	   like a little owl of the waste places.
	⁷ I lie awake;
	   I am like a lonely bird on the housetop.
	⁸ All day long my enemies taunt me;
	   those who deride me use my name for a
	     curse.
	⁹ For I eat ashes like bread,
	   and mingle tears with my drink,
	¹⁰ because of your indignation and anger;

NIV

[11]My days are like the evening shadow;
   I wither away like grass.

[12]But you, O LORD, sit enthroned forever;
   your renown endures through all
      generations.
[13]You will arise and have compassion on Zion,
   for it is time to show favor to her;
   the appointed time has come.
[14]For her stones are dear to your servants;
   her very dust moves them to pity.
[15]The nations will fear the name of the LORD,
   all the kings of the earth will revere your
      glory.
[16]For the LORD will rebuild Zion
   and appear in his glory.
[17]He will respond to the prayer of the destitute;
   he will not despise their plea.

[18]Let this be written for a future generation,
   that a people not yet created may praise
      the LORD:
[19]"The LORD looked down from his sanctuary
      on high,
   from heaven he viewed the earth,
[20]to hear the groans of the prisoners
   and release those condemned to death."
[21]So the name of the LORD will be declared in
      Zion
   and his praise in Jerusalem
[22]when the peoples and the kingdoms
   assemble to worship the LORD.

[23]In the course of my life[a] he broke my
      strength;
   he cut short my days.
[24]So I said:
   "Do not take me away, O my God, in the
      midst of my days;
   your years go on through all generations.
[25]In the beginning you laid the foundations of
      the earth,
   and the heavens are the work of your
      hands.
[26]They will perish, but you remain;
   they will all wear out like a garment.
Like clothing you will change them
   and they will be discarded.
[27]But you remain the same,

a23 Or By his power

NRSV

for you have lifted me up and thrown
      me aside.
[11] My days are like an evening shadow;
   I wither away like grass.

[12] But you, O LORD, are enthroned forever;
   your name endures to all generations.
[13] You will rise up and have compassion on
      Zion,
   for it is time to favor it;
   the appointed time has come.
[14] For your servants hold its stones dear,
   and have pity on its dust.
[15] The nations will fear the name of the LORD,
   and all the kings of the earth your
      glory.
[16] For the LORD will build up Zion;
   he will appear in his glory.
[17] He will regard the prayer of the destitute,
   and will not despise their prayer.

[18] Let this be recorded for a generation to
      come,
   so that a people yet unborn may praise
      the LORD:
[19] that he looked down from his holy height,
   from heaven the LORD looked at the earth,
[20] to hear the groans of the prisoners,
   to set free those who were doomed to
      die;
[21] so that the name of the LORD may be
      declared in Zion,
   and his praise in Jerusalem,
[22] when peoples gather together,
   and kingdoms, to worship the LORD.

[23] He has broken my strength in midcourse;
   he has shortened my days.
[24] "O my God," I say, "do not take me away
   at the midpoint of my life,
you whose years endure
   throughout all generations."

[25] Long ago you laid the foundation of the
      earth,
   and the heavens are the work of your
      hands.
[26] They will perish, but you endure;
   they will all wear out like a garment.

NIV	NRSV
and your years will never end. ²⁸The children of your servants will live in your presence; their descendants will be established before you."	You change them like clothing, and they pass away; ²⁷ but you are the same, and your years have no end. ²⁸ The children of your servants shall live secure; their offspring shall be established in your presence.

COMMENTARY

Psalm 102 begins like an individual prayer for help or lament/complaint (vv. 1-11), but then it makes a sudden shift. A brief ascription of praise is followed by an expression of hope for and confidence in the restoration of Zion (vv. 12-17) and of hope for the return of the exiles (vv. 18-22). Verses 23-24 return the focus to individual complaint and plea, but then vv. 25-28 again shift to praise, followed by an expression of confidence in the people's future. The presence of both individual and corporate material has been particularly problematic for form critics. As Allen states, "A bewildering multiplicity of interpretations have been offered for this complex psalm."[390]

It is possible, for instance, to conclude that the king was the original individual speaker (see Psalm 101) and that he spoke on behalf of the whole people. Or perhaps the prayer of an individual, seemingly one who was sick, served as the basis for post-exilic additions to create a corporate prayer. Or perhaps an individual in the post-exilic era simply included a prayer for the nation in the midst of his or her prayers for self. Certainty concerning the origin and ancient use of Psalm 102 remains elusive. What should be noted is that the character of Psalm 102 is quite appropriate for its present literary setting in Book IV, which serves as a response to the crisis of exile and its aftermath, and is presented in Book III (see Commentary on Psalms 73; 74; 79; 80; 89; Introduction). Like Psalm 90, which it recalls at several points (see vv. 4, 10-11, 23-28), Psalm 102 grounds hope for the future in God's eternity.

390. Leslie C. Allen, *Psalms 101–150*, WBC 21 (Waco, Tex.: Word, 1983) 11.

And like the enthronement psalms, which serve as the core of Book IV (see Psalms 93; 95–99), Psalm 102 is a proclamation of God's reign (see esp. vv. 12, 15-16). Psalms 101–102 together deal with the three crucial aspects of the exilic crisis—loss of monarchy, Temple/Zion, and land (see Commentary on Psalm 101)—by grounding hope in God's coming (101:2) and God's enduring presence (102:26-28).

The superscription is one of the very few that accurately describes the actual content of the following psalm. The state of affliction applies to both sections—Zion's need (vv. 12-17) as well as that of the individual (vv. 1-11, 23-24)—and the word "afflicted"/"poor"/"oppressed"/"weak" (עני *ʿānî*) is used frequently in the psalms to designate a category of people whom God is particularly committed to helping (see Pss 9:12, 18; 10:2, 9, 12; 25:16; 35:10; 37:14; 74:19, 21; 86:1; see also Exod 3:7, 17; 4:3). The sufferers in the psalms also describe themselves elsewhere as "faint" (see Pss 61:2; 77:3; 142:3; 143:4; 107:5; see also Lam 2:11-12, 19, which describe the effects of the destruction that led to exile), and they describe their prayers as "lament" or "complaint" (see Pss 55:2; 64:1; and esp. 142:2, which uses the idiom of pouring out the complaint).

102:1-2. As is often the case, the prayer begins with petition that God hear (v. 1*a*), and the prayer is more specifically designated a "cry for help" (v. 1*b*; see also Exod 2:23; Pss 18:6; 34:15; 39:12; 145:19; Lam 3:56). The petitions in v. 2 are typical as well: "Do not hide your face" (see Pss 13:1; 27:9; 69:17; 88:14; 143:7); "Incline your ear" (Ps 17:6); "answer . . . quickly" (see Pss 69:17; 143:7). The repetition of "day" in v. 2

introduces the theme of time (see "days" in vv. 3, 11, 23-24 NIV); the psalmist will eventually discover hope for fleeting human life in God's eternity (see "years" in vv. 24, 27; see also Psalm 90).

102:3-11. These verses are the complaint proper, marked by an envelope structure formed by the repetition of "days" (vv. 3, 11) as well as "wither(ed)" and "grass" (vv. 4, 11). The psalmist portrays the brevity of life with the metaphors of smoke (see Ps 37:20; Hos 13:3) and withering grass (see Ps 90:5-6; Isa 40:6-8). These metaphors—as well as the mention of burning bones (v. 3*b*; see also Pss 6:2; 31:10; and esp. Lam 1:13, where the pain expressed involves Jerusalem's destruction), a stricken heart (v. 4*a*; see also 1 Sam 5:12; Isa 53:4), an apparent loss of appetite (v. 4*b*; see the NIV's more literal translation), and perhaps a loss of weight (v. 5; see Job 19:20)—often lead scholars to conclude that the psalmist was gravely ill (see Psalms 6; 38; 88). To be sure, this is possible. Sickness elsewhere leads to isolation and alienation (vv. 6-7; see also Pss 38:11; 88:8, 18) and persecution (v. 8; see also Pss 6:8; 38:12, 16, 19-20), which in turn causes feelings of humiliation and grief (v. 9; see "ashes" in Isa 6:3; Lam 3:16; see "tears"/"weeping" in Pss 6:8; 42:3; 80:5). Disease is also attributed to God's anger (v. 10; see Pss 6:1; 38:1-2; 88:7; see also Pss 90:7-11, where human transience is associated with God's anger). But it is possible, too, that the language and imagery were intended to be metaphorical, or at least came to be understood metaphorically. Similar imagery in Lamentations (see references above) supports this conclusion, as does the juxtaposition of vv. 3-11 with vv. 12-17. That is, vv. 3-11 were certainly capable of being heard as an articulation of the pain, alienation, grief, and despair of exile (cf. v. 10*b* with Deut 29:28, where the same vocabulary is used to describe what happened with the destruction of Jerusalem). The exile apparently made Israel particularly aware of the general frailty and transience of human existence (see Ps 90:5-11; Isa 40:6-8; on the simile of the shadow, see Job 8:9; 14:2; Pss 109:23; 144:4). Thus the transition marked by v. 12 may not be quite so abrupt and problematic as it first seems.

102:12-17. In fact, v. 12 seems intended to play off of vv. 3-11. The focus on the psalmist is shifted dramatically to God as both v. 12 and v. 13 begin with the emphatic Hebrew pronoun "you," and the name Yahweh (LORD) occurs for the first time since v. 1. Whereas human transience was the subject of vv. 3-11, v. 12 affirms God's eternity (see "forever" and "all generations"). In keeping with the dominant emphasis of Book IV (see Psalms 93; 95–99), v. 12 also proclaims God's sovereignty (see "sits"/"enthroned" in Pss 2:4; 9:7; 29:10). Because God is eternally sovereign, God's "name"—literally, "remembrance" (זכר *zēker*)—will always endure. The same word occurs in Ps 111:4 (see also Exod 3:15; Ps 97:12), where the accompanying affirmation is that God is "gracious and compassionate." The same two Hebrew roots occur in Ps 102:13 ("compassion" [רחם *rḥm*] and "favor" [חנן *ḥnn*]) to describe God's anticipated action toward Zion, and they get at the essence of God's character revealed to Moses after the episode of the golden calf (see Exod 34:6). This allusion implies that the psalmist's hope is grounded in the earlier exodus event, which also aimed at manifesting God's universal sovereignty (Exod 9:16; 15:18; see also Ps 102:15; Isa 40:5; 66:18) and was celebrated as the first step in God's and the people's movement to Zion (Exod 15:17; see also Ps 102:16; Isa 45:13; 60:10). The two occurrences of "prayer" in v. 17 recall the superscription and v. 1, suggesting again that the hope expressed in vv. 12-16 is somehow related to vv. 1-11.

102:18-22. While the hope expressed in vv. 12-17 alludes to the exodus, the vocabulary of vv. 12-17 also is reminiscent of the way Isaiah 40–55 anticipates the return from exile, and the return of the exiles is even more clearly in view in vv. 18-22. The theme of time is again evident in v. 18 as the psalmist anticipates a future for God's people (see Pss 22:30-31; 90:13-17). It will be because God "looked down," as God had "looked down" to defeat the Egyptians (Exod 14:24) and as God was regularly requested to do to ensure the life of the people (see Deut 26:15; Ps 113:5-6). This looking down will be to liberate prisoners, who elsewhere also are the beneficiaries of God's saving work (see Pss 68:6; 69:33; 107:10). In Ps 79:11, which is very similar to v. 20, the prisoners seem to be precisely the victims of the destruction of Jerusalem and the subsequent exile (see also Isa 49:9; 61:1; Lam 3:34; Zech 9:11). In short, the return of the exiles to a restored Zion (vv. 12-17) will be the prelude to the universal recognition of God's sovereignty (vv. 21-22; the word "worship" [עבד ʿābad] suggests more literally to "serve" a superior; see Isa 66:18-23).

102:23-24. These verses return the focus to the psalmist, as in vv. 1-11. The fact that the individual prayer encloses vv. 12-22 suggests again that the two sections should not be sharply separated. Someone—the original author or an editor—intended them to be read together. In view of the explicit address of exilic concerns in vv. 12-22, it is significant that v. 23b recalls Ps 89:45a, which is in a section of lament over the failure of the Davidic dynasty. In Ps 89:46 the voice of an apparently deposed Davidic king inquires how long God will hide God's face (see Ps 102:2) and be angry (see Ps 102:10). The king then asks God to remember his own (and human) transience (89:47-48; see also 102:3-4, 11) and to remember the taunts of his enemies (89:50-51; see also 102:8). These similarities may be coinci-

dental, but they increase the likelihood that the individual voice in Psalm 102 should be heard as a Davidic king, albeit a deposed one (see Psalm 101), or at least that the individual complaint in Psalm 102 be heard in relation to the exile.

102:25-28. Verse 24b already shifts the focus back to God, where it remains in vv. 25-28. Two occurrences of the emphatic "you" (vv. 26a, 27a) match those in vv. 12-13. Whereas vv. 12-13 alluded to the exodus, vv. 26-28 look to God's creative activity as a sign of God's enduring sovereignty (on v. 25, see Pss 24:1-2; 104:5; on v. 26, see Ps 104:6). God's enduring "years" (vv. 24b, 27) contrast with the psalmist's "days" (vv. 2, 3, 8, 11) and are the hope of God's people. The language of v. 28—"children," "your servants," "established"—recalls Ps 90:13-17, where essentially the same hope is expressed. As eternal sovereign, God is in a position to "establish" things, and God does—the work of human hands (Ps 90:17), the world (Ps 93:1), and the future of God's people (102:28).

REFLECTIONS

1. In the face of exile and subsequent crises throughout the generations, the people of God have found hope and strength in the conviction that because God reigns, the future can be entrusted to God. Psalm 102 is the fifth of the church's seven Penitential Psalms (see also Psalms 6; 32; 38; 51; 130; 143). It contains no explicit confession of sin, although one may be implied in v. 10. But the Penitential Psalms are about more than confession of sin; they are ultimately testimony to God's grace. This is certainly the case with Psalm 102. The future of Zion, which symbolizes the future of the people, depends on God's compassion and favor (v. 13)—or as these Hebrew roots are translated elsewhere, God's mercy and grace.

2. This message is reinforced if the psalm is heard as a plea out of exile or out of the despair of the early post-exilic era. While Israel viewed the exile as deserved punishment, Israel also concluded at some point that enough was enough (see Isa 40:1-2). At that point, the reality of exile became viewed as an opportunity for God to perform a new exodus (see Isa 49:8-26)—to have "compassion on Zion" (Ps 102:13; see also Isa 49:13, 15). That v. 13 recalls Exod 34:6 is significant, because God revealed God's nature as merciful and gracious after the people had sinned by worshiping the golden calf. This episode proved to be paradigmatic of Israel's whole history; Israel proved constantly disobedient, making it necessary for God to bear the burden of their sin. In short, the ongoing existence of Israel was testimony to God's mercy and grace. The church professes to be heir to Israel's story, and its history certainly demonstrates that it continues to live not by its own merit or worthiness but by the grace of God.

In Psalm 102, Zion is the symbol of God's willingness to be concretely present in space and time with a particular people (see Commentary on Psalms 46; 48; 76; 84; 87; 122). For the church, the symbolism of Zion has been transferred to Jesus (see Heb 1:10-12, which views Ps 102:25-27 as testimony to Jesus' lordship). For Christians, Jesus' life, death, and resurrection are the ultimate demonstration of God's reign, which takes the form of mercy and grace. Jesus is the seal of God's constancy (see Heb 13:18; cf. Ps 102:27), and the church professes to find its hope in these words of Jesus, which make essentially the same promise for the future as Ps 102:28: "I am with you always, to the end of the age" (Matt 28:20 NRSV). The good news for individuals (vv. 1-11, 23-24) and for the whole church (vv. 12-22) is that by the grace of God we are indeed "established in your presence" (v. 28).

PSALM 103:1-22, BLESS THE LORD, O MY SOUL

NIV

Psalm 103

Of David.

¹Praise the LORD, O my soul;
  all my inmost being, praise his holy name.
²Praise the LORD, O my soul,
  and forget not all his benefits—
³who forgives all your sins
  and heals all your diseases,
⁴who redeems your life from the pit
  and crowns you with love and compassion,
⁵who satisfies your desires with good things
  so that your youth is renewed like the
    eagle's.

⁶The LORD works righteousness
  and justice for all the oppressed.

⁷He made known his ways to Moses,
  his deeds to the people of Israel:
⁸The LORD is compassionate and gracious,
  slow to anger, abounding in love.
⁹He will not always accuse,
  nor will he harbor his anger forever;
¹⁰he does not treat us as our sins deserve
  or repay us according to our iniquities.
¹¹For as high as the heavens are above the
    earth,
  so great is his love for those who fear him;
¹²as far as the east is from the west,
  so far has he removed our transgressions
    from us.
¹³As a father has compassion on his children,
  so the LORD has compassion on those who
    fear him;
¹⁴for he knows how we are formed,
  he remembers that we are dust.

NRSV

Psalm 103

Of David.

¹ Bless the LORD, O my soul,
  and all that is within me,
  bless his holy name.
² Bless the LORD, O my soul,
  and do not forget all his benefits—
³ who forgives all your iniquity,
  who heals all your diseases,
⁴ who redeems your life from the Pit,
  who crowns you with steadfast love and
    mercy,
⁵ who satisfies you with good as long as you
    liveᵃ
  so that your youth is renewed like the
    eagle's.

⁶ The LORD works vindication
  and justice for all who are oppressed.
⁷ He made known his ways to Moses,
  his acts to the people of Israel.
⁸ The LORD is merciful and gracious,
  slow to anger and abounding in steadfast
    love.
⁹ He will not always accuse,
  nor will he keep his anger forever.
¹⁰ He does not deal with us according to our
    sins,
  nor repay us according to our iniquities.
¹¹ For as the heavens are high above the earth,
  so great is his steadfast love toward those
    who fear him;
¹² as far as the east is from the west,
  so far he removes our transgressions from us.

ᵃ Meaning of Heb uncertain

NIV

¹⁵As for man, his days are like grass,
he flourishes like a flower of the field;
¹⁶the wind blows over it and it is gone,
and its place remembers it no more.
¹⁷But from everlasting to everlasting
the Lord's love is with those who fear him,
and his righteousness with their children's
children—
¹⁸with those who keep his covenant
and remember to obey his precepts.

¹⁹The Lord has established his throne in heaven,
and his kingdom rules over all.

²⁰Praise the Lord, you his angels,
you mighty ones who do his bidding,
who obey his word.
²¹Praise the Lord, all his heavenly hosts,
you his servants who do his will.
²²Praise the Lord, all his works
everywhere in his dominion.

Praise the Lord, O my soul.

NRSV

¹³ As a father has compassion for his children,
so the Lord has compassion for those
who fear him.
¹⁴ For he knows how we were made;
he remembers that we are dust.

¹⁵ As for mortals, their days are like grass;
they flourish like a flower of the field;
¹⁶ for the wind passes over it, and it is gone,
and its place knows it no more.
¹⁷ But the steadfast love of the Lord is from
everlasting to everlasting
on those who fear him,
and his righteousness to children's
children,
¹⁸ to those who keep his covenant
and remember to do his commandments.

¹⁹ The Lord has established his throne in the
heavens,
and his kingdom rules over all.
²⁰ Bless the Lord, O you his angels,
you mighty ones who do his bidding,
obedient to his spoken word.
²¹ Bless the Lord, all his hosts,
his ministers that do his will.
²² Bless the Lord, all his works,
in all places of his dominion.
Bless the Lord, O my soul.

COMMENTARY

Psalm 103 is one of the most familiar and beloved of all the psalms. One of its most frequent words is "all" (כל *kōl*, vv. 1-3, 6, 19, 21-22), for Psalm 103 intends to be comprehensive. It affirms that God, who rules over all and does all good things for all persons in need, is to be praised in all places by all creatures and things with all of their being. Although not an acrostic, its twenty-two lines—the number of letters in the Hebrew alphabet—also suggest the psalmist's intent to say it all.

Scholars disagree on the categorization of Psalm 103 and its original setting. Some label it an individual song of thanksgiving that celebrates the psalmist's recovery from a serious illness (see vv.

3-5). The liturgical setting of the thanksgiving ceremony would have included the invitation to others to praise God (vv. 1-22), as well as testimony to God's character (vv. 6-19), which has been revealed in the psalmist's experience. Other scholars suggest that Psalm 103 is a song of praise, celebrating not a specific deliverance but God's general activity (vv. 3-5 or 3-6) and character (vv. 5 or 6-18 or 19) as reasons for praise. As a hymn, Psalm 103 could well have been used at large festal gatherings. Some scholars, however, view it as a late imitation of hymnic forms, and thus they suggest that it may have been used in small gatherings of the pious. Certainty on these matters is not possible.

The structure of Psalm 103 is often outlined as follows: vv. 1-5, vv. 6-18, vv. 19-22. The first and last lines are identical, thus forming an envelope structure, which can be expanded to vv. 1-2, 20-22, all of which contain the verb "bless" (ברך *bārak*) in the imperative. Many scholars further divide vv. 6-18 into three sections on the basis of style and content: vv. 6-10, vv. 11-14 (note the symmetrical pattern of the opening words of each verse, "For . . . as . . . As . . . for"), vv. 15-18. The criteria, however, are ambiguous. For instance, "works" in v. 6 is a participle, as are all the verbal forms in vv. 3-5*a*. One could argue, therefore, that v. 6 should not be separated from vv. 1-5. On the other hand, the participle in v. 6 is the only one that has a subject ("LORD") with it, so perhaps this variation signals the beginning of a new section, or perhaps v. 6 is meant to be transitional. The same could be said of v. 19. On the one hand, it seems to belong with vv. 20-22 (see "all" in vv. 19, 21-22; plus "rules" in v. 19 and "dominion" in v. 22 translate the same Hebrew root [משל *mšʾl*]); however, the syntax of vv. 15*a* and 19*a* is similar, perhaps suggesting that the psalmist's intent is to contrast human instability with divine stability. Again, v. 19 may be transitional.[391]

Only recently have scholars confronted the question of the literary placement of Psalm 103. If Book IV is a response to the crisis of exile elaborated in Book III (see Commentary on Psalms 73; 74; 79; 80; 89; 90; Introduction), then Psalm 103 is extremely well-placed. In fact, Psalm 101 and especially Psalm 102 (see vv. 12-22) have just rehearsed the problem again—loss of monarchy, Zion/Temple, and land. In this literary context, it is possible to hear Psalm 103 as the praise anticipated in Ps 102:15, 18, 21-22 (see "name" in 102:15, 21; 103:1). Part of the strategy of Book IV is to return the reader to the perspective of the Mosaic era, in which the reign of God was celebrated without land, Temple, or monarchy (see Psalm 90; Introduction), and Psalm 103 is congruent with this perspective (see v. 7). In particular, Ps 103:8-10 recalls God's self-revelation to Moses in Exod 33:12–34:7 (cf. esp. Exod 34:6 with Ps 103:8), and two key words from

this episode become key words in Psalm 103: "steadfast love" (חסד *ḥesed*, vv. 4, 8, 11, 17) and "mercy"/"compassion" (vv. 4, 8, 13). Of course, the good news of God's love and compassion, manifest in God's willingness to forgive, is precisely what the exiles needed to hear (see vv. 9-13; see Commentary on Psalm 89, esp. discussion of v. 49). Not coincidentally, it seems, Psalm 103 is reminiscent of the prophetic preaching found in Isaiah 40–66 (cf. v. 5 with Isa 40:31; v. 9 with Isa 57:16; v. 11 with Isa 55:9; vv. 15-16 with Isa 40:6-8; see also "steadfast love" in Isa 54:10; 55:3; 63:7; and "mercy"/"compassion"/"pity" in Isa 49:10, 13; 54:7-8, 10; 55:7; 60:10; 63:7). Furthermore, like the prophet of the exile (see Isa 52:7-10) and like the core of Book IV of the psalter (see Psalms 93; 95–99), Psalm 103 proclaims God's universal sovereignty (see vv. 19-22). This theme will also be continued in Psalm 104, which is verbally linked to Psalm 103 by its opening and concluding invitation.

103:1-5. These verses have the form of a hymn—invitation to praise (vv. 1-2), followed by reasons for praise (vv. 3-5). The word "bless" (*bārak*) seems to have meant originally to bend the knee before—that is, to bow in homage to one's sovereign (see Pss 16:7; 26:12; 34:1; 63:4; 95:6; 96:2; 100:4; 145:1, 21). The psalmist, in effect, invites his or her whole self to bless God and God's "name," which is suggestive of God's essence or character (see vv. 8-13, where the subject is specifically God's character). In other words, the psalmist owes his or her whole life to God, and this is exactly what vv. 3-5 will say. The word "benefits" (גמול *gĕmûl*) in v. 2 almost always elsewhere indicates a negative consequence—God's recompense or retribution (the same root underlies "repay" in v. 10). Its use here makes the content of vv. 3-5 all the more pleasantly surprising. God's recompense is first of all forgiveness! It is significant that this particular word for "forgiveness" (סלח *sālaḥ*) ties Psalm 103 to the literary contexts mentioned above; it occurs in both Exod 34:9 and Isa 55:7. Similarly, several of the other "benefits," which could be understood simply as individual terms, are reminiscent of what God has done (and will do again) for the whole people, especially in reference to the periods of exodus and return from exile—healing (see Exod 15:26; Deut 32:39; Isa 57:18-19; Jer 30:17;

391. For a more detailed discussion, see T. M. Willis, " 'So Great Is His Steadfast Love': A Rhetorical Analysis of Psalm 103," *Biblica* 72 (1991) 525-37.

33:6), redeeming (Exod 6:6; 15:13; Pss 74:2; 77:15; Isa 43:1; 44:22-23; see esp. Isa 51:10, where the people are called "the redeemed," and 51:14, where "the Pit" is a metaphor for the threat represented by the oppression of exile), and satisfying (see Exod 16:8, 12; Isa 58:11; Jer 31:14; see also "goodness" in Exod 33:19). In Lam 5:16, the exile is characterized as the crown "fallen from our head" as a result of sin and iniquity (see Lam 5:7). To this situation, Ps 103:4*b* (along with vv. 3, 8-13) would offer a fitting response.

103:6. This transitional verse presents a climactic description of what God has done and will do again. "Righteousness" and "justice" are what the sovereign God wills and works to enact for all humanity (see Pss 9:7-8; 89:14; 96:13; 97:2; 98:9; 99:4). These words are not used specifically to describe the exodus, but they are found frequently in Isaiah 40–55 to designate God's work in returning the exiles (see esp. Isa 51:1-8 NIV, where "justice" occurs in vv. 4-5 and "righteousness" in vv. 1, 5-6, 8). The Hebrew root of "oppressed" (עשׁק 'āšaq) in v. 6 also occurs in Isa 52:4, where it is applied to the Egyptian captivity as well as to the more recent exile, and in Isa 54:14, where the removal of oppression is designated as "righteousness."

103:7-18. While v. 6 belongs with vv. 3-5, it also anticipates vv. 7-10 and vv. 11-18. What God works to enact implies the nature of God's character, which is described more fully in vv. 8-18. Elsewhere, too, "righteousness" is associated with the attributes of God listed in v. 8 (see Pss 85:10-13; 89:14; 98:3, 9; 111:3-4; 116:5). Verse 8 quotes Exod 34:6 (see also Pss 86:15*b*; Introduction), but the whole golden calf episode (Exod 32:1–34:9) is in the background, especially its conclusion, beginning at Exod 33:12 (see "know"/"known" in Exod 33:13; Ps 103:7 NIV). The people's idolatry provoked God's anger (see Exod 32:7-14), but the episode culminates in Exod 34:6-7, thus illustrating the affirmations of v. 9 (see also Jer 3:5, 12) and vv. 10-18. God forgives "sins," "iniquities," and "transgressions" (vv. 10, 12; see also Exod 34:7). Two of the attributes in Exod 34:6 get further attention: "steadfast love" (vv. 11, 17) and God's "mercy" or fatherly "compassion" (רחם *rāḥam,* v. 13; see also Exod 33:19; and see above on Ps 25:6 for

an explanation of why the Hebrew root fundamentally suggests motherly compassion).

The revelation of God's steadfast love and compassion in Exodus 32–34 required *God's* repentance or change of mind (see Exod 32:12-14), and Moses concludes the episode by reminding God of the nature of the people with whom God must deal (Exod 34:9). The whole episode is reminiscent of Genesis 6–9, where God's realization about human nature prompts the promise never again to destroy all creatures (cf. Gen 6:5 with 8:21). Psalm 103:14 also recalls the opening chapters of Genesis, and in Psalm 103, as in Genesis 6–9 and Exodus 32–34, God's willingness to forgive is tied to God's realization about human nature. To the sinful, transient creature (vv. 14-16; also see Pss 89:47; 90:3-11; 102:3-4, 11; Isa 40:6-8), God continually shows God's steadfast love and righteousness (v. 17; see also v. 6). The mention of steadfast love in v. 17 means that there is one occurrence for each major division of the poem, except vv. 19-22.

While the structure of Psalm 103 communicates the pervasiveness of God's steadfast love, there seems to be a qualification. Three times the psalmist reserves steadfast love or compassion for those who fear God (vv. 11, 13, 17; see also Pss 25:14; 33:18; 34:7, 9; 85:9; 111:5; 115:11; 145:19; 147:11), and righteousness is reserved for those who are obedient (v. 18; see also Exod 20:6). There seems to be a contradiction: How is it "mercy" if finally it is deserved? And what need is there for forgiveness? This contradiction, or better perhaps, tension, represents the inevitable dilemma for God, who both wills and demands justice and righteousness and yet who loves and is committed to relationship with sinful people. This tension is present already in Genesis 6–9, and it is clearly expressed in Exod 34:6-7, where the affirmation of God's willingness to forgive is followed immediately by the announcement that God "does not leave the guilty unpunished." It cannot be otherwise for God, who is both just and merciful (see above on Ps 99:6-9; see also Reflections below).

103:19-22. As in Psalms 90; 102; and Isa 40:6-8, where the experience of God's wrath awakens an acute sense of human transience, the solution is to be found in the affirmation of both God's transcendence and God's immanence—

God's eternity and unbounded sovereignty (Ps 103:19-22; see also Pss 90:1-2; 102:12, 25-27; Isa 40:8; 55:8-11) as well as God's compassionate love, which is manifested in forgiveness (Ps 103:6-18; see also Pss 90:13-17; 102:13; Isa 40:1-2; 55:1-7). The concluding verses of Psalm 103 recall both the opening verses of the psalm and other psalms that proclaim God's reign. For instance, v. 19 echoes Ps 93:2, and along with v. 22, it anticipates Ps 145:10-13. Because God's sovereignty is "over all" (v. 19), all beings (the ancient Near Eastern notion of a divine council of attendants is in view here as in Pss 29:1-2; 82:1; 97:7,

9; 148:2) and all things are invited to praise God (see Pss 96:11-12; 98:7-8; 148:1-12). The sequence of invitations concludes by focusing attention again on the individual psalmist. In other words, one puts oneself in tune with the whole cosmic order by acknowledging God's reign and by joining all beings in conforming to God's word and will (see vv. 18, 21, where the NRSV's "do" links human behavior with that of the heavenly beings). The cosmic dimension of God's reign and the significance of conformity to it are evident in Psalm 104, to which Psalm 103 is linked (see 104:1, 35).

REFLECTIONS

Psalm 103 is a good place to start when talking with persons who perceive God in the OT to be simply a God of wrath and judgment. In fact, in his *Elements of Old Testament Theology,* Claus Westermann begins his discussion of God's compassion with an interpretation of Psalm 103. Westermann recognizes the tension between God's justice and God's mercy, and he addresses it as follows:

> The poet has no intention of contesting God's activity in wrath. But he makes a distinction. God's activity in wrath is limited; God's goodness knows no boundaries (v. 17). . . . The same is true of sin and its forgiveness. If God compensated man commensurate with the way he sins, then one might despair. But here too, God is inconsistent; his forgiving goodness is immeasurable. One might even say that the entire Psalm deals with the incomprehensible excess of God's goodness.[392]

As Weiser puts it, the poet "has been granted an insight into the heart of the majesty of God, and what he has found there is grace."[393]

The immeasurability of God's grace does not dissolve the tension between God's radical demand for obedience and God's willingness to forgive. This is the dilemma with which God, as a loving parent (v. 13), must always live, and it is one that human parents know as well. It cannot be otherwise for God, else grace would be cheap (see Rom 6:1). For Christians, God's dilemma is in sharpest focus on the cross of Jesus Christ. Christian theology has traditionally interpreted the cross as an event to satisfy God's demand for justice, but the satisfaction is made by the offering of God's own self, *not* by human obedience—"while we still were sinners Christ died for us" (Rom 5:8 NRSV). The cross thus seems to compromise God's justice at the same time that it seems to compromise God's sovereignty. Such is the mystery of sovereignty and the miracle of grace, which for all the world looks like weakness (see 1 Cor 1:25; 2 Cor 12:9). But Psalm 103 knows better (see Reflections on Psalm 99).

The mystery and the miracle do not mean that grace is cheap, as Psalm 103 also recognizes. On the contrary, the cross indicates the great cost to God, and the cross demands our whole lives as well (see Mark 8:34-35; see also Ps 103:1, 11, 13, 17, 22). Yet for us self-centered, sinful people who know that even our very best is not enough, our hope is finally not in our ability to measure up but in the immeasurable, incomprehensible excess of God's goodness. We dare to profess that the ruling power in the universe (v. 19) is One who treats us like a loving father, a compassionate mother (see Isa 49:15). Such love demands our soul, our life, our all.

392. Claus Westermann, *Elements of Old Testament Theology,* trans. D. W. Stott (Atlanta: John Knox, 1982) 139.
393. Artur Weiser, *The Psalms,* OTL, trans. H. Hartwell (Philadelphia: Westminster, 1962) 663.

PSALM 104:1-35, GOD AS CREATOR AND PROVIDER

NIV

Psalm 104

¹Praise the LORD, O my soul.

O LORD my God, you are very great;
    you are clothed with splendor and majesty.
²He wraps himself in light as with a garment;
    he stretches out the heavens like a tent
³   and lays the beams of his upper chambers
        on their waters.
He makes the clouds his chariot
    and rides on the wings of the wind.
⁴He makes winds his messengers,ᵃ
    flames of fire his servants.

⁵He set the earth on its foundations;
    it can never be moved.
⁶You covered it with the deep as with a
      garment;
    the waters stood above the mountains.
⁷But at your rebuke the waters fled,
    at the sound of your thunder they took to
      flight;
⁸they flowed over the mountains,
    they went down into the valleys,
    to the place you assigned for them.
⁹You set a boundary they cannot cross;
    never again will they cover the earth.

¹⁰He makes springs pour water into the ravines;
    it flows between the mountains.
¹¹They give water to all the beasts of the field;
    the wild donkeys quench their thirst.
¹²The birds of the air nest by the waters;
    they sing among the branches.
¹³He waters the mountains from his upper
      chambers;
    the earth is satisfied by the fruit of his
      work.
¹⁴He makes grass grow for the cattle,
    and plants for man to cultivate—
    bringing forth food from the earth:
¹⁵wine that gladdens the heart of man,
    oil to make his face shine,

ᵃ4 Or *angels*

NRSV

Psalm 104

¹ Bless the LORD, O my soul.

    O LORD my God, you are very great.
You are clothed with honor and majesty,
²   wrapped in light as with a garment.
You stretch out the heavens like a tent,
³   you set the beams of yourᵃ chambers on
      the waters,
you make the clouds yourᵃ chariot,
    you ride on the wings of the wind,
⁴ you make the winds yourᵃ messengers,
    fire and flame yourᵃ ministers.

⁵ You set the earth on its foundations,
    so that it shall never be shaken.
⁶ You cover it with the deep as with a
      garment;
    the waters stood above the mountains.
⁷ At your rebuke they flee;
    at the sound of your thunder they take
      to flight.
⁸ They rose up to the mountains, ran down
      to the valleys
    to the place that you appointed for them.
⁹ You set a boundary that they may not pass,
    so that they might not again cover the
      earth.

¹⁰ You make springs gush forth in the valleys;
    they flow between the hills,
¹¹ giving drink to every wild animal;
    the wild asses quench their thirst.
¹² By the streamsᵇ the birds of the air have
      their habitation;
    they sing among the branches.
¹³ From your lofty abode you water the
      mountains;
    the earth is satisfied with the fruit of
      your work.

¹⁴ You cause the grass to grow for the cattle,
    and plants for people to use,ᶜ

ᵃ Heb *his*   ᵇ Heb *By them*   ᶜ Or *to cultivate*

NIV

and bread that sustains his heart.
¹⁶The trees of the LORD are well watered,
the cedars of Lebanon that he planted.
¹⁷There the birds make their nests;
the stork has its home in the pine trees.
¹⁸The high mountains belong to the wild goats;
the crags are a refuge for the coneys.ª

¹⁹The moon marks off the seasons,
and the sun knows when to go down.
²⁰You bring darkness, it becomes night,
and all the beasts of the forest prowl.
²¹The lions roar for their prey
and seek their food from God.
²²The sun rises, and they steal away;
they return and lie down in their dens.
²³Then man goes out to his work,
to his labor until evening.

²⁴How many are your works, O LORD!
In wisdom you made them all;
the earth is full of your creatures.
²⁵There is the sea, vast and spacious,
teeming with creatures beyond number—
living things both large and small.
²⁶There the ships go to and fro,
and the leviathan, which you formed to
frolic there.

²⁷These all look to you
to give them their food at the proper time.
²⁸When you give it to them,
they gather it up;
when you open your hand,
they are satisfied with good things.
²⁹When you hide your face,
they are terrified;
when you take away their breath,
they die and return to the dust.
³⁰When you send your Spirit,
they are created,
and you renew the face of the earth.

³¹May the glory of the LORD endure forever;
may the LORD rejoice in his works—
³²he who looks at the earth, and it trembles,
who touches the mountains, and they
smoke.
³³I will sing to the LORD all my life;
I will sing praise to my God as long as I live.

ª18 That is, the hyrax or rock badger

NRSV

to bring forth food from the earth,
¹⁵   and wine to gladden the human heart,
oil to make the face shine,
and bread to strengthen the human heart.
¹⁶ The trees of the LORD are watered
abundantly,
the cedars of Lebanon that he planted.
¹⁷ In them the birds build their nests;
the stork has its home in the fir trees.
¹⁸ The high mountains are for the wild goats;
the rocks are a refuge for the coneys.
¹⁹ You have made the moon to mark the
seasons;
the sun knows its time for setting.
²⁰ You make darkness, and it is night,
when all the animals of the forest come
creeping out.
²¹ The young lions roar for their prey,
seeking their food from God.
²² When the sun rises, they withdraw
and lie down in their dens.
²³ People go out to their work
and to their labor until the evening.

²⁴ O LORD, how manifold are your works!
In wisdom you have made them all;
the earth is full of your creatures.
²⁵ Yonder is the sea, great and wide,
creeping things innumerable are there,
living things both small and great.
²⁶ There go the ships,
and Leviathan that you formed to sport
in it.

²⁷ These all look to you
to give them their food in due season;
²⁸ when you give to them, they gather it up;
when you open your hand, they are filled
with good things.
²⁹ When you hide your face, they are
dismayed;
when you take away their breath, they die
and return to their dust.
³⁰ When you send forth your spirit,ª they are
created;
and you renew the face of the ground.

³¹ May the glory of the LORD endure forever;

ª Or your breath

NIV

³⁴May my meditation be pleasing to him,
 as I rejoice in the LORD.
³⁵But may sinners vanish from the earth
 and the wicked be no more.

 Praise the LORD, O my soul.

 Praise the LORD.ᵃ

ᵃ35 Hebrew *Hallelu Yah*; in the Septuagint this line stands at the beginning of Psalm 105.

NRSV

 may the LORD rejoice in his works—
³² who looks on the earth and it trembles,
 who touches the mountains and they
 smoke.
³³ I will sing to the LORD as long as I live;
 I will sing praise to my God while I have
 being.
³⁴ May my meditation be pleasing to him,
 for I rejoice in the LORD.
³⁵ Let sinners be consumed from the earth,
 and let the wicked be no more.
 Bless the LORD, O my soul.
 Praise the LORD!

COMMENTARY

Linked to Psalm 103 by the only occurrences in the psalter of the invitation "Bless the LORD, O my soul" (103:1, 22; 104:1, 35), Psalm 104 is an eloquent poetic elaboration on the cosmic reign of God that is proclaimed in Ps 103:19-22. Psalm 103 asserts that God "rules over all" (v. 19), and Psalm 104 agrees (see "all" in vv. 24, 27), exquisitely depicting how all God's "works" (Pss 103:22; 104:24a) effectively bless God simply by taking their rightful place in an intricate ecosystem that originated with and constantly depends on its sovereign Maker. In fact, the Hebrew root of "works" (עשׂה *'āśâ*) is the key word in Psalm 104, occurring five more times—"make(s)"/"made" in vv. 4, 19, 24b and "work(s)" in vv. 13, 31. Thus Psalm 104 focuses on creation, whereas Psalm 103 had given more attention to God's saving mercy and love (vv. 4, 8, 11, 13, 17). But together the two psalms are another reminder that God's creating work and God's saving work (see "works" in Ps 103:6) are finally inseparable; God's activity on behalf of Israel was toward the enactment of God's purposes for the whole creation (see Commentary on Psalms 33; 65; 66; 93; 95; 98). Together, then, Psalms 103–104 affirm God's cosmic sovereignty in response to the theological crisis articulated in Psalms 101–102 (see Commentary on Psalms 101; 102; 103). And in concert with Psalms 93; 95–99, Psalms 103–104 contribute to the response of Book IV to the theological issues raised in Book III (see Commentary on Psalms 73; 74; 79; 80; 89; 90; Introduction).

Scholars have traditionally debated at length the origin of and influences on Psalm 104. It is obviously reminiscent of Genesis 1, but there is no warrant for attempting to discern a seven-day structure in Psalm 104 or even for positing direct literary influence in either direction. Such is possible, of course; but if anything, Psalm 104 appears to be an exuberant poetic reflection on the evaluation of creation that is found in Gen 1:31: "it was very good" (NRSV). Psalm 104 is also similar in some ways to Psalm 8, but the affirmation of the exalted status of the human creature (see Ps 8:4-8) is absent in Psalm 104, in which the human is one among many creatures that depend on God for life. In addition, there are striking similarities between Psalm 104 and the Egyptian hymn of Amenhotep IV to Aten, the sun disc. While direct literary influence cannot be ruled out entirely, it is more likely that the similarities can be traced to the common stock of cosmological ideas that were extant in the ancient Near East. Psalm 104 actually reflects the influence of a variety of ancient Near Eastern materials, including Egyptian lists of cosmological phenomena and Canaanite accounts in which creation is the result of a battle among the gods and the subsequent ordering of the forces of a watery chaos (see below on vv. 1-9). In each case, these ideas have been adopted and stamped with

Israel's faith in the exclusive sovereignty of Yahweh. The elements of the cosmos are objects of God's action, not gods in themselves (see vv. 2-9, 19, 26); it is clear throughout that God "made them all" (v. 24).

The structure of Psalm 104 can be perceived in several ways. Attention to stylistic detail suggests division as follows:

vv. 1-4	God and the heavens
vv. 5-13	God and the earth (see "earth" in vv. 5, 13)
vv. 14-23	God and people (see "people" in vv. 14, 23 NRSV; the same Hebrew root also appears in vv. 14, 23 NIV as "cultivate" and "labor")
vv. 24-30	"all" God's works (see "all" in vv. 24, 27)
vv. 31-35	conclusion: God's joy (v. 31) and human joy (v. 34)

Allen even suggests that this outline constitutes a concentric structure that focuses attention on vv. 14-23, and he notes that the key word "work(s)"/"made" appears in either the first or the last verse of each section (vv. 4, 13, 24*ab*, 31), except for the central section, where it occurs in the middle (v. 19).[394] This may be coincidental, however, and the actual content of the sections tends to overlap considerably. The focus shifts from heaven (vv. 2-4) to earth (vv. 5-6) to waters (vv. 7-10) to wild animals (v. 11) to birds (v. 12) to earth again (v. 13) to plants that feed animals and people (vv. 14-15) to trees (v. 16) to birds (v. 17) to wild animals (v. 18) to heavenly bodies (vv. 19-20*a*) to wild animals (vv. 20*b*-22) to people again (v. 23). It is as if the psalmist cannot quite control an effusive, joyful flow of observations and words that culminate in the exclamation of v. 24*a*, only to overflow again in vv. 25-26 before the psalmist is able to manage a conclusion that expresses what has been evident throughout: All creatures depend on God for sustenance and for life itself (vv. 27-30). An even more reasoned response is represented by the psalmist's wishes and promises in vv. 31-35. It is possible also, as

Mays suggests, to consider vv. 1-9 under the rubric of creation and vv. 10-23 under the rubric of providence, both of which are in view in the summary observations of vv. 24-30 before the actual conclusion.[395]

104:1-4. These verses affirm God's sovereignty. To say that God is great is to say, in effect, that God reigns supreme, for greatness is frequently associated with sovereignty (see Pss 47:2; 48:2; 95:3; 96:4). This more abstract profession is reinforced with the metaphor of God's clothing (vv. 1*b*-2*a*) and the description of God's activity (vv. 2*b*-4). God wears "honor"/"splendor" and "majesty," the attributes of royalty (see Pss 21:5; 45:3; 96:6; 145:5), as well as "light." Light is regularly associated with God's presence (see Pss 4:6; 27:1; 43:3; 44:3), sometimes in the context of language and imagery that affirm God's sovereignty (see Pss 76:4 in connection with 76:1; 89:15 in connection with 89:14). "Light" also indicates the cosmic dimension of God's rule (see Gen 1:3). The description of God's activity begins in vv. 2*b*-3*a* with God's establishing a dwelling place. The word translated "tent" (יריעה *yĕrî'â*) seems to mean more specifically the curtain of a tent, and by far the majority of its uses designate the curtain of the tabernacle (see Exod 26:2). With this dimension of the word in the background, v. 2*b* then suggests that God's real house is not the Temple but the universe (see 2 Sam 7:6; 1 Kgs 8:27), which is only appropriate for a cosmic sovereign. The verb in "set the beams" (קרה *qārâ*) and the noun in "upper chambers" (עליה *'aliyyâ*, see v. 13) in v. 3*a* are architectural terms. That God builds God's house upon the "waters" suggests also the mythic background of a created order resulting from the divine warrior's defeat of the chaotic waters (see Pss 74:12-15; 93:3-4). The mythic background is even clearer in vv. 3*b*-4. In the Canaanite worldview, Baal, god of the storm, rode the clouds and commanded the winds (vv. 3*b*-4*a*) and the lightning. But here Baal has been dethroned and his forces de-divinized. Yahweh reigns, and God asserts sovereignty over elements that have resulted from God's own creative work (see Pss 18:15; 29:3-9; 68:4; 97:1-5; Isa 19:1; cf. Job 22:14).

104:5-13. As suggested above, v. 5 seems to

394. Leslie C. Allen, *Psalms 101–150,* WBC 21 (Waco, Tex.: Word, 1983) 31-32.

395. James L. Mays, *Psalms,* Interpretation (Louisville: John Knox, 1994) 332-35.

start a new section, either a major unit (vv. 5-13) or at least a subdivision of vv. 1-9. In any case, God's creative work is still in view. It results in a stable world. As were vv. 3b-4, v. 5 is at least implicitly polemical. According to Ps 82:5, the rule of the gods resulted in the shaking of the earth's foundations, but the work of the truly sovereign God holds the world together (see Pss 24:1-2; 93:1; 96:10). The mythic background is again evident in vv. 6-9. God controls "the deep" (see Gen 1:2; Exod 15:8; Pss 33:7; 77:16). The waters obey God's voice (v. 7; see "rebuke" in Job 26:11; Pss 18:15; 76:6) and perform God's will for them (v. 8). The NRSV's "appointed" (יסד *yāsad*) in v. 8 is the same Hebrew root as "set" in v. 5; thus earth and the waters are under God's rule. The chaotic forces have been tamed (v. 9a; see also Job 38:8-11, although the vocabulary differs), and the earth is safe (v. 9b; see also Gen 9:11, although again the vocabulary differs).

The occurrence of "earth" in v. 9 may mark a subdivision of the larger vv. 5-13 (see "earth" also in vv. 5, 13). In any case, God's control of water is still the subject (v. 10), and under God's rule, water becomes not a threat to but a sustainer of life (vv. 11-13a). The NIV's "give water" (v. 11a) and "waters" (v. 13a) represent the same Hebrew verb (שקה *šqh*). God provides for animate and inanimate things alike; the earth has what it needs. This theme of God's providence will be echoed by the repetitions of "satisfied" in v. 16 ("watered abundantly") and v. 28.

104:14-23. Human beings enter the picture for the first time in v. 14, and the words "people" (אדם *ʾādām*) and "cultivate"/"labor" (עבדה *ʾăbōdâ*/פעל *pāʾal*) in vv. 14, 23 may form an envelope structure for this section. The subject is still God's provision. By way of plants, God provides "food" (לחם *leḥem,* v. 14; "bread" in v. 15 translates the same Hebrew word), but more as well. Plants also yield wine—a source of pleasure as well as sustenance (see Sir 31:27-28)—and oil, the purpose of which is not clear here. The use of oil occurs elsewhere in contexts that suggest hospitality, honor, and joy (see Pss 23:5; 45:7; 92:10; Luke 7:46). God "satisfies" not just people but trees—God's trees! (v. 16)—which in turn provide hospitality for animals (vv. 17-18; see also v. 12; Prov 30:26).

Each creature has not only its place but also its

appropriate time, according to God's design and implementation (vv. 19-23). Perhaps it is not coincidental that the key word "made" occurs in v. 19 with its object "the moon." The moon and the sun were widely regarded as deities. It is possible that the sun played a legitimate part in Israelite worship at some point (see Commentary on Psalm 63), and whether legitimate or not, worship of the sun apparently occurred rather frequently (see Jer 8:1-2; 19:13; Ezek 8:16). But here the sun simply serves God's purpose of ordering the lives of the creatures.

104:24-30. Containing two occurrences of the key word "works"/"made," v. 24 is an exclamatory summary of vv. 1-23. *Everything* derives from God. The heavens, the earth, plants, animals, people—God made them all, and the whole creation is a witness to God's wisdom (see Prov 3:19; 8:22-31; Jer 10:21). The word "wisdom" (חכמה *ḥokmâ*) can mean not only knowledge, but also technical skill in construction (see Exod 31:3, 6). Both senses are appropriate here (see above on vv. 2b-3a); God is both architect and artisan. The exclamation overflows into a further observation about the sea, which perhaps not coincidentally is called great as God was called great in v. 1. In the Canaanite view, the sea was a god who represented chaotic power. Psalm 104 has already suggested that God orders the chaotic waters into life-giving rivers and springs (vv. 6-13). Verses 25-26 affirm that even the mighty and mysterious oceans are subject to God (see Ps 29:10; Isa 51:9-10). The "great" living thing (v. 25) that resides in the sea is Leviathan (v. 26), a version of the divine chaos-monster known in other ancient Near Eastern sources. Here Leviathan is a creature who simply plays in the water. Or is Leviathan, in effect, God's water toy? The grammar is ambiguous, but in either case, Leviathan has been rendered harmless (see Job 41:1-11; Ps 74:12-15; Isa 27:1; 51:9-10).

The "all" in v. 27 refers to the "all" in v. 24. Every creature, human and otherwise, depends on God. Food is a gift from God (see "give" in vv. 27b, 28a). The description of the creatures gathering their food recalls Israel's gathering of manna in the wilderness (see Exodus 16). In both instances, God satisfies (v. 28; see also vv. 13, 16; Exod 16:8, 12). Verses 27-28 occur in a similar form in Ps 145:15-16. Psalm 145 brings together the perspectives of Psalms 103–104, and it may be significant that the concluding psalms of the psalter explicitly recall Book IV (see Introduction and Commentary on Psalms 145; 146 for further similarities between them and Psalms 103–104).

God provides not only food but also the very breath of life itself (vv. 29-30). The words "breath" and "spirit" (the capitalization in the NIV should be avoided) are the same Hebrew word (רוח *rûaḥ*). The vocabulary—"breath"/"spirit," "dust," "created," "ground"—recalls Genesis 1–2. The breath of the creatures is not identical to God's breath, but God is responsible for giving life to the creatures (see Gen 1:2; 2:7; Job 34:14-15; Ps 146:4). Verses 29-30 also suggest that God's creating is an ongoing process. God's breath brings new creatures into being (v. 30*a*); God's "face" (v. 29) serves to "renew the face of the ground" (v. 30*b*).

104:31-35. Just as vv. 1-30 have asserted God's sovereignty, so also the psalmist's first wish is for the eternity of God's rule. Elsewhere, "glory" is associated with both God's rule (see Pss 24:7-10; 29:1-3, 9-11; 145:1, 5, 12; Isa 6:1-5) and God's presence (see Exod 24:16-17; 33:18, 22; Pss 26:8; 102:16; Ezek 10:4, 18; 43:4-5), each of which is manifested in God's ongoing creation of the world—in God's works (v. 31). Verse 32 is the language of theophany—God's appearing (see Exod 19:18)—and the psalmist hopes that God's appearing will afford God joy (v. 31*b*). This also seems to be the thrust of v. 35; the psalmist wants no one to interfere with the operation of the world as God intends it (see Pss 145:20; 146:9; see also Reflections below). The psalmist is certainly committed to that end, responding to God with unceasing praise (v. 33), which involves the yielding of the whole self to God in liturgy and life. The psalmist hopes that his or her meditation—seemingly a reference to the preceding poem—will be an acceptable offering to God (see Ps 19:14) and an indication that the psalmist intends to enjoy God forever (v. 34*b*). Thus the psalmist's joy reflects the joy of his or her creator (v. 31), just as the psalmist intends his or her life to reflect what God intends for the life of the whole creation.

REFLECTIONS

1. Thousands of years before smog, acid rain, global warming, and the so-called butterfly effect—the awareness that a butterfly flapping its wings has at least some tiny physical impact on the environment on the other side of the planet—the poet who wrote Psalm 104 was an environmentalist. The psalmist knew about the intricate interconnectedness and subtle interdependence of air, soil, water, plants, and animals, including humans. The psalmist knew the truth revealed in the etymological connection between the Hebrew word for "humanity" (אדם *'ādām*) and the word for "ground" (אדמה *'ădāmâ*): Human beings really are creatures of the earth. The origin and destiny of humankind is inextricably tied to the origin and destiny of the earth. The same truth is revealed in the etymological connection between the English word *human* and the Latin word *humus,* "soil." But, as it were, we have forgotten our roots, both etymological and physical.

Of course, the psalmist's awareness was grounded not in etymology, not in a knowledge of physical sciences like botany, zoology, geology, hydrology, and meteorology. Rather, the psalmist's awareness was grounded in *theology.* The psalmist was convinced of the profound interdependence of air, soil, water, and all living things, because he or she believed that *everything* derived from and was ultimately dependent upon God: "the Lord God made them all," as a familiar hymn also puts it ("All Things Bright and Beautiful"). "Nature," as we often call it today, is not divine, but it is sacred. It does not and cannot exist apart from God and God's renewing breath. Because for the psalmist life derives from God, it follows that our lives belong to God (see Psalm 100). Because for the psalmist we live in God's world, it follows that everything we do has an effect on God's world and thus on God. Ecology and theology are inseparable.

2. The psalmist's environmental consciousness is of a different sort from that of most contemporary folk. To be sure, regardless of what motivates it, any concern for the environment is better than none at all. Still, it is important to realize that much of our concern for the future of the earth is motivated by our desire to maintain our current standard of living without trashing things so terribly or depleting natural resources so severely that we cannot pass the same style of life on to our children. In other words, our primary concern is ourselves, and our major motivation is fear. While this kind of environmental consciousness may be better than none at all, our efforts to "save" the earth are surely misguided and doomed to failure as long as the focus is on ourselves and our motivation is fear.

The psalmist demonstrates another way. For the psalmist, relating to the world—in our terms, perhaps, an environmental consciousness—begins with praising God. The motivation is not fear but rejoicing in the Lord (vv. 33-34). Praise involves the acknowledgment of God's sovereignty and the commitment to live under God's rule (see vv. 1-4, 33-34). Taking the psalmist as an example, we would have to conclude that concern for the environment begins with praising God. To be sure, this sounds hopelessly simplistic, scientifically and technologically naive. But such a starting point—and its underlying conviction that the world belongs to God—is the only thing that will dislodge our arrogant assumption that *we* can *save* the world, as if it were ours to save! In biblical terms, salvation means life, and in biblical terms, the world does not need to be saved. God has already done that! Psalm 104 affirms that God has made every arrangement and provision for the life of the world. The only problem will be if someone disrupts God's design and destroys the delicate balance God has put in place. For the contemporary world, v. 35 may be the key verse in the psalm. To paraphrase a famous line: We have seen the wicked, and it is us!

The environmental crisis will be addressed by nothing short of praising God, exalting God, and humbling ourselves (see Commentary on Psalm 8). It may be telling that Psalm 104 uses the phrase "trees of the Lord" (v. 16) but not "people of the Lord." In a profound sense, Psalm 104 puts us humans in our place—with springs and hills and trees and creeping things. If our motivation for facing our own future and the future of the earth were to glorify God, we might even have the humility to ask ourselves what it would really mean to live in partnership with a tree or with a wild goat or with the thousands of species whose disappearance causes hardly a ripple of attention, primarily because we are convinced that nature exists to serve humanity. Quite simply, Psalm 104 asserts that this is not the case. Rather, to serve God will mean ultimately to serve God's creation (see Gen 2:15, where the vocation of the human in the garden of Eden should be translated "to *serve* it and keep it"). Psalm 104 counsels praise of and rejoicing in the Lord, but it cannot help adding its own word of warning that may evoke in us legitimate fear, especially since the warnings of our scientists give a whole new dimension of meaning to the scenario of "sinners [being] consumed from the earth" (v. 35). As for us, we can do no better than the psalmist's own response to this scenario: "Bless the Lord, O my soul./ Praise the Lord [הללו־יה *halĕllû-yāh,* "Hallelujah"]!" As Mays asks concerning this first instance of *Hallelujah* in the psalter: "Could a more appropriate place be found?"[396]

3. Psalm 104 is traditionally used on the Day of Pentecost to celebrate the gift of God's Spirit, which gave new life to a discouraged and dispirited band of disciples (Acts 2), who then went about "turning the world upside down" (Acts 17:6 NRSV). At first glance, it may seem as if the spirit of God in Psalm 104 (v. 30) has little to do with Pentecost, the celebration of the coming of God's Holy Spirit. But the spirit of God in Psalm 104 is associated with ongoing creation and renewal (v. 30), which is also what Pentecost is about. To use Psalm 104 on Pentecost is to affirm that God is the source of all life—the physical life of the world,

---

396. Mays, *Psalms,* 336.

the eternal life offered in Christ, the life of the church—and, indeed, that these spheres of life are finally inseparable. Psalm 104 is a reminder also that, like all of God's creations, the church lives by the power of God's renewing Spirit, not by its own ability, merit, or ingenuity. The church exists, like all of God's works, to praise the Lord (v. 35).

PSALM 105:1-45, ALL GOD'S WONDERFUL WORKS

NIV

Psalm 105

[1]Give thanks to the LORD, call on his name;
  make known among the nations what he
    has done.
[2]Sing to him, sing praise to him;
  tell of all his wonderful acts.
[3]Glory in his holy name;
  let the hearts of those who seek the LORD
    rejoice.
[4]Look to the LORD and his strength;
  seek his face always.

[5]Remember the wonders he has done,
  his miracles, and the judgments he
    pronounced,
[6]O descendants of Abraham his servant,
  O sons of Jacob, his chosen ones.
[7]He is the LORD our God;
  his judgments are in all the earth.

[8]He remembers his covenant forever,
  the word he commanded, for a thousand
    generations,
[9]the covenant he made with Abraham,
  the oath he swore to Isaac.
[10]He confirmed it to Jacob as a decree,
  to Israel as an everlasting covenant:
[11]"To you I will give the land of Canaan
  as the portion you will inherit."

[12]When they were but few in number,
  few indeed, and strangers in it,
[13]they wandered from nation to nation,
  from one kingdom to another.
[14]He allowed no one to oppress them;
  for their sake he rebuked kings:
[15]"Do not touch my anointed ones;
  do my prophets no harm."

[16]He called down famine on the land

NRSV

Psalm 105

[1] O give thanks to the LORD, call on his name,
  make known his deeds among the
    peoples.
[2] Sing to him, sing praises to him;
  tell of all his wonderful works.
[3] Glory in his holy name;
  let the hearts of those who seek the LORD
    rejoice.
[4] Seek the LORD and his strength;
  seek his presence continually.
[5] Remember the wonderful works he has done,
  his miracles, and the judgments he has
    uttered,
[6] O offspring of his servant Abraham,[a]
  children of Jacob, his chosen ones.

[7] He is the LORD our God;
  his judgments are in all the earth.
[8] He is mindful of his covenant forever,
  of the word that he commanded, for a
    thousand generations,
[9] the covenant that he made with Abraham,
  his sworn promise to Isaac,
[10] which he confirmed to Jacob as a statute,
  to Israel as an everlasting covenant,
[11] saying, "To you I will give the land of
    Canaan
  as your portion for an inheritance."

[12] When they were few in number,
  of little account, and strangers in it,
[13] wandering from nation to nation,
  from one kingdom to another people,
[14] he allowed no one to oppress them;
  he rebuked kings on their account,
[15] saying, "Do not touch my anointed ones;

[a]Another reading is *Israel* (compare 1 Chr 16.13)

NIV

and destroyed all their supplies of food;
[17] and he sent a man before them—
Joseph, sold as a slave.
[18] They bruised his feet with shackles,
his neck was put in irons,
[19] till what he foretold came to pass,
till the word of the LORD proved him true.
[20] The king sent and released him,
the ruler of peoples set him free.
[21] He made him master of his household,
ruler over all he possessed,
[22] to instruct his princes as he pleased
and teach his elders wisdom.

[23] Then Israel entered Egypt;
Jacob lived as an alien in the land of Ham.
[24] The LORD made his people very fruitful;
he made them too numerous for their foes,
[25] whose hearts he turned to hate his people,
to conspire against his servants.
[26] He sent Moses his servant,
and Aaron, whom he had chosen.
[27] They performed his miraculous signs among
them,
his wonders in the land of Ham.
[28] He sent darkness and made the land dark—
for had they not rebelled against his words?
[29] He turned their waters into blood,
causing their fish to die.
[30] Their land teemed with frogs,
which went up into the bedrooms of their
rulers.
[31] He spoke, and there came swarms of flies,
and gnats throughout their country.
[32] He turned their rain into hail,
with lightning throughout their land;
[33] he struck down their vines and fig trees
and shattered the trees of their country.
[34] He spoke, and the locusts came,
grasshoppers without number;
[35] they ate up every green thing in their land,
ate up the produce of their soil.
[36] Then he struck down all the firstborn in their
land,
the firstfruits of all their manhood.
[37] He brought out Israel, laden with silver and
gold,
and from among their tribes no one
faltered.

NRSV

do my prophets no harm."

[16] When he summoned famine against the land,
and broke every staff of bread,
[17] he had sent a man ahead of them,
Joseph, who was sold as a slave.
[18] His feet were hurt with fetters,
his neck was put in a collar of iron;
[19] until what he had said came to pass,
the word of the LORD kept testing him.
[20] The king sent and released him;
the ruler of the peoples set him free.
[21] He made him lord of his house,
and ruler of all his possessions,
[22] to instruct[a] his officials at his pleasure,
and to teach his elders wisdom.

[23] Then Israel came to Egypt;
Jacob lived as an alien in the land of
Ham.
[24] And the LORD made his people very fruitful,
and made them stronger than their foes,
[25] whose hearts he then turned to hate his
people,
to deal craftily with his servants.
[26] He sent his servant Moses,
and Aaron whom he had chosen.
[27] They performed his signs among them,
and miracles in the land of Ham.
[28] He sent darkness, and made the land dark;
they rebelled[b] against his words.
[29] He turned their waters into blood,
and caused their fish to die.
[30] Their land swarmed with frogs,
even in the chambers of their kings.
[31] He spoke, and there came swarms of flies,
and gnats throughout their country.
[32] He gave them hail for rain,
and lightning that flashed through their
land.
[33] He struck their vines and fig trees,
and shattered the trees of their country.
[34] He spoke, and the locusts came,
and young locusts without number;
[35] they devoured all the vegetation in their
land,

[a] Gk Syr Jerome: Heb *to bind*   [b] Cn Compare Gk Syr: Heb *they did not rebel*

NIV

38Egypt was glad when they left,
because dread of Israel had fallen on them.
39He spread out a cloud as a covering,
and a fire to give light at night.
40They asked, and he brought them quail
and satisfied them with the bread of
heaven.
41He opened the rock, and water gushed out;
like a river it flowed in the desert.

42For he remembered his holy promise
given to his servant Abraham.
43He brought out his people with rejoicing,
his chosen ones with shouts of joy;
44he gave them the lands of the nations,
and they fell heir to what others had toiled
for—
45that they might keep his precepts
and observe his laws.

Praise the LORD.a

a45 Hebrew *Hallelu Yah*

NRSV

and ate up the fruit of their ground.
36 He struck down all the firstborn in their
land,
the first issue of all their strength.

37 Then he brought Israela out with silver and
gold,
and there was no one among their tribes
who stumbled.
38 Egypt was glad when they departed,
for dread of them had fallen upon it.
39 He spread a cloud for a covering,
and fire to give light by night.
40 They asked, and he brought quails,
and gave them food from heaven in
abundance.
41 He opened the rock, and water gushed out;
it flowed through the desert like a river.
42 For he remembered his holy promise,
and Abraham, his servant.

43 So he brought his people out with joy,
his chosen ones with singing.
44 He gave them the lands of the nations,
and they took possession of the wealth of
the peoples,
45 that they might keep his statutes
and observe his laws.
Praise the LORD!

a Heb *them*

COMMENTARY

Like Psalms 78; 106; and 136, Psalm 105 is usually classified as a historical psalm. As in the others, the recital of history in Psalm 105 is a selective and creative retelling of Israel's story. Psalm 105 is sometimes labeled a didactic hymn, and its purpose may be to educate. But if so, the subject matter is not just names, places, and events out of Israel's past. Rather, the real subject matter is praise (vv. 1-6) and obedience (v. 45). In other words, the psalmist's intent in retelling the old story is to evoke the people's grateful and faithful response to God's choice (see "chosen" in vv. 6, 26, 43) to be related to them (see "covenant" in vv. 8-10), a choice supported by the

"wonderful works" (vv. 2, 5) that God has done on their behalf (vv. 12-43). Thus the psalm is not primarily about the past. Rather, it is about the present and the future (see Commentary on Psalm 78, especially Brueggemann's observations about the historical psalms).

In form, Psalm 105 may be considered a song of praise, with vv. 1-6 constituting the invitation to praise and vv. 7-45 giving the reasons. In content, Psalm 105 is similar to Psalm 136 in that both psalms focus exclusively on what God has done. This is in sharp contrast to Psalms 78 and 106, which recount at length the people's unfaithful response. Of course, the juxtaposition of

Psalms 105 and 106 makes the contrast particularly obvious, an effect apparently intended by the editors of the psalter. The two should be read together. On the one hand, Psalm 105 makes the people's faithlessness look all the more grievous. But on the other hand, Psalm 106 makes God's grace look all the more amazing (see esp. 106:45). This too may well have been the intent of the editors of the psalter, especially since the conclusion of Psalm 106 apparently situates the people in exile. The hope for the exiles lay in the possibility that God would again hear their cry and turn away from wrath, as God had repeatedly done in the story, which is told in two different ways in Psalms 105–106.

The intent of Psalms 105–106 to address the crisis of exile is in keeping with the apparent purpose of Book IV (see Commentary on Psalms 90; 93; 94; 95; 96; 97; 98; 99; 101; 102; Introduction) to respond to the theological crisis of exile elaborated in Book III (see Psalms 73–74; 79–80; 89; Introduction). This does not necessarily mean that Psalm 105 was written in the exilic or post-exilic era, but in addition to its connection with Psalm 106, several features of Psalm 105 would support such a conclusion. For instance, due to the loss of the land, possession of the land was a preeminent exilic concern (see vv. 11, 44). It was natural, therefore, to look back behind the failed Davidic covenant (see Commentary on Psalm 89; Introduction) to the covenant with Abraham (vv. 9-10). The prophet of the exile does the same thing (see Isa 41:8; 51:1-2), apparently transferring the notion of a Davidic covenant to the people as a whole (see Isa 55:3). A similar move may be suggested by Ps 105:15, where the people are referred to with a term often applied to the Davidic kings: "my anointed" (משיחי *měšîḥāy*; see Pss 2:6; 18:50; 20:6). In addition, the chronicler assigns the use of Ps 105:1-11 to Asaph upon the occasion of David's transfer of the ark to Jerusalem (1 Chr 16:8-18). It is generally thought that the chronicler reflects the concerns and practices of his own era more so than those of earlier periods, and this may indicate the currency of Psalm 105 in the post-exilic setting. In any case, the usefulness of Psalm 105 was not limited to whatever circumstances may have occasioned its origin and ancient use. It continued and can still continue to call the people of God to grateful praise and faithful obedience.

105:1-6. The same imperative opens Psalms 105–107, suggesting that the relationship between Psalms 105 and 106 should be extended (see Commentary on Psalm 107; see also Pss 44:8; 97:12; 100:4). The psalmists affirm elsewhere that God makes known God's own deeds (see Pss 77:14*b*; 98:2; 103:7; 106:8), and the people are called upon to join God in this public witness (v. 1*b*; see also Pss 78:5; 145:12). God's "deeds" are testimony to God's sovereignty (see Ps 9:11), which is appropriately greeted with singing and praise (see Pss 96:1; 98:1, 5). "Wonderful works" (vv. 3*a*, 5*a*) recalls the exodus as well as other saving manifestations of God's sovereignty (see Exod 3:20; 15:11; Josh 3:5; Pss 77:11, 14; 78:4, 11-12, 32; 106:7, 22), thus anticipating what the psalmist will remember (see v. 5) and tell (v. 26; the root is the same as "meditation" [שיח *śîaḥ*] in Ps 104:34) in vv. 12-45. The word "miracles" (מופת *môpēt*) in v. 5 refers often to the plagues (see Exod 7:3; 11:9-10; Ps 78:43), an aspect of the demonstration of God's sovereignty over Pharaoh that will also be featured in Psalm 105 (see v. 27). The word "judgments" (משפטים *mišpāṭîm*, vv. 5-7), or better "acts of justice," designates the policy God wills and enacts as cosmic ruler (see Pss 96:13; 97:2; 98:9; 99:4).

Another appropriate response to the demonstration of God's sovereignty is invited in v. 3*a*. The word "glory" (התהללו *hithāllû*) represents the Hebrew root that, in a more frequent conjugation of the verb, means "to praise" (הלל *hillēl*, see 104:35). In this form, it has the nuance of "boast," which is proper only if directed to God (see Pss 34:2; 106:5; Isa 41:16; 45:25; cf. Ps 75:5). The phrase "his holy name" (שם קדשו *šēm qādšô*, v.3*a*; see Pss 106:47 and 97:12, where a different Hebrew word underlies "name") recalls v. 1*a*; "name" directs attention to the character of God revealed in God's "wonderful works." Two different Hebrew verbs underlie the three occurrences of "seek" [בקש *biqqēš*; דרש *dāraš*] in vv. 3*b*-4 (cf. v. 4*a* NIV). To seek God's "face" may suggest to approach God in worship (see Pss 24:6; 27:8), perhaps indicating a cultic setting for the psalm. More broadly, however, to seek God means to entrust one's whole existence to God in recognition of God's sovereign claim (see Pss 9:10; 34:5, 10; 40:16; 69:6). God's "strength" bespeaks God's sovereignty (Pss 29:1; 96:6), but it is also a gift shared with God's people (see Pss 29:11; 68:35; 84:5; 86:16). Thus the act of remembering (v. 5c; see also Pss 77:11; 106:7), which Psalm 105 itself represents, is a fundamental first step toward participation in the paradox of being strong by yielding the self in order to be God's servant (v. 6a; see also v. 42), which is what the sovereign God intends the "chosen ones" to be (v. 6b; see also vv. 26, 43).

105:7-11. Before the actual rehearsing of God's "wonderful works" in vv. 12-45, vv. 7-11 lay the foundation for God's action on behalf of Israel: the covenant with Abraham, Isaac, and Jacob, involving the promise of the land (see Gen 12:1-3; 15:1-19, esp. vv. 18-19; 17:1-14, esp. vv. 2, 7-8; 24:7; 26:3; 28:13; 35:12; 50:24; see also Deut 1:8; 4:31; 8:1). The "he" that begins v. 7 is emphatic, and God is the subject of every verb in vv. 7-11. Verse 8 is especially reminiscent of Exod 2:24, where God remembers the covenant just prior to initiating the series of events that lead to the exodus (see also Exod 6:2-5; Ps 106:45). The covenant is termed an "everlasting covenant" (v. 10) elsewhere only in sources that are generally considered exilic or post-exilic (see Gen 9:16; 17:7; Isa 55:3; 61:8; Jer 32:40; Ezek 16:60; 37:26), except perhaps 2 Sam 23:5.

105:12-25. These verses recall the wanderings of the patriarchs and matriarchs, who are called "strangers" (or "alien") in Gen 19:9; 26:3; 35:27. Verse 14 may have in view the stories in which Sarah is threatened by Abraham's deception (Gen 12:10-20; 20:1-7; cf. Gen 26:6-11). Abraham is called a prophet in Gen 20:7 (see above on v. 15). Both prophets and kings ("anointed ones") were known as God's servants, the primary identification of the whole people in Psalm 105 (vv. 6, 25, 42; see also "slave" in v. 17). Verses 16-22 summarize the story of Joseph (Genesis 37–50), whose unlikely release from captivity and rise to power might have been a particularly encouraging example to the exilic and post-exilic generations. Jacob/Israel arrived in Egypt toward the conclusion of the Joseph story (v. 23; see Genesis 46). The people remained there and prospered (v. 24; see Exod 1:1-7), provoking the hatred of the Egyptians (v. 25; Exod 1:7-22).

105:26-38. Here the psalmist rehearses the rest of the exodus story (Exod 2:1–15:21), focusing primarily on the plagues (v. 27; see also Ps 78:43)—darkness (v. 28; v. 28 should probably be translated in accordance with the NRSV note, understanding the subject as personified darkness;[397] see Exod 10:21-29), waters to blood (v. 29; see Exod 7:14-25; Ps 78:44), frogs (v. 30; see Exod 8:1-15; Ps 78:45b), flies and gnats (v. 32; see Exod 8:16-32; Ps 78:45a), hail and lightning (vv. 32-33; see Exod 9:13-35; Ps 78:47-48), locusts (vv. 34-35; see Exod 10:1-20; Ps 78:46), and death of the firstborn (v. 36; see Exod 11:1-10; 12:29-32; Pss 78:51; 135:8; 136:10). The number and order of the plagues differ in Psalm 105 from both Exod 7:14–12:32 and Ps 78:44-51, perhaps reflecting a different tradition and illustrating that the poet's purpose was not historical accuracy. Verses 37-38 recall Exod 12:33-36.

105:39-44. The cloud and fire led the people even before the crossing of the sea (see Exod 13:21-22; 14:24) and continued with them into the wilderness (see Num 9:15-16; 14:4), which is also the setting for v. 40 (see Exod 16:13; Num 11:31-32) and v. 41 (see Exod 17:1-7; Num 20:2-13). Verse 42 recalls v. 8 ("promise" [דבר *dābār*] in v. 42 is more literally "word"), and v. 43 perhaps looks back over the whole exodus/wilderness story ("brought out" is often used of the exodus; see Exod 18:1–20:2) in anticipation of the recollection of the entry into the land in v. 44. Verse 43, however, is similar to the description of the return from exile in Deutero-Isaiah (see Isa 55:12), who saw the return as a new exodus. Verse 43 is probably another indication that Psalms 105–106 were intended to address the crisis of exile.

105:45. Along with vv. 1-6, v. 45 indicates the real purpose of the psalm: to evoke praise and obedience. Verses 1-6 point to God's sovereignty, and it was the responsibility of a sovereign to establish justice, righteousness, and peace among his or her servant people (see Pss 72:1-7; 82:1-4; 106:3). It is to this end that v. 45 is directed (see Deut 26:16-19; Ps 78:7). Verse 45 also prepares the reader to hear Psalm 106, which will document at length the people's failure to respond to God's "wonderful works" (Pss 105:2, 5; 106:7, 22).

397. Th. Booij, "The Role of Darkness in Psalm CV 28," *VT* 39 (1989) 211-12.

REFLECTIONS

A familiar hymn asks the question, "Why should the wonders He hath wrought be lost in silence and forgot?" (Isaac Watts, "Bless O My Soul! the Living God"). In answer to this question, Psalm 105 resoundingly proclaims, "They shouldn't!" Rather, the people of God are called upon to "make known . . . tell . . . remember" (vv. 1-2, 6). By asserting God's sovereignty and inviting people to praise and obey God (vv. 1-6, 45), Psalm 105 subverts every human claim to power and privilege (see Commentary on Psalm 78). In other words, the primary identity of God's people is that of servant (see vv. 6, 26, 42), and the good news is that persons who submit their lives to God's claim will be strong (v. 4; see also Mark 8:35; Luke 18:14).

By focusing exclusively on God's activity, including God's choice of a people (vv. 6, 26, 43) and the establishment of a covenant with them (vv. 8-10), Psalm 105 articulates the priority of God's grace. God does call for obedience, but only *after* God's choice of the people and the performance of "wonderful works." In this regard, Psalm 105 is like the Pentateuch, which is featured in the psalm. That is, exodus precedes Sinai; deliverance precedes demand; grace comes first. God's choice precedes all human choices.

Not only is grace the first word, but as the juxtaposition of Psalms 105 and 106 affirms, grace is the final word as well (see Commentary on Psalm 106). Even after a long and sordid history of faithlessness and disobedience, God will still remember the covenant God made with the people (Ps 106:45; see also 105:8, 42), and God will act "for their sake" (106:45). Thus, by telling the story of God's "wonderful works," Psalms 105–106 not only rehearse the past but also anticipate the future. For Christians, God's "wonderful works"—the story of God's acting "for their sake"—continues in Jesus Christ. He is taken to be the ultimate sign of the good news already evident in Psalms 105–106: the priority and perseverance of God's amazing grace (see Rom 3:24; 5:1-2; 6:14-15).

PSALM 106:1-48, OUT OF GREAT LOVE, GOD RELENTED

NIV	NRSV
Psalm 106	**Psalm 106**
[1]Praise the LORD.[a]	[1] Praise the LORD!
Give thanks to the LORD, for he is good;	O give thanks to the LORD, for he is good;
his love endures forever.	for his steadfast love endures forever.
[2]Who can proclaim the mighty acts of the LORD	[2] Who can utter the mighty doings of the LORD,
or fully declare his praise?	or declare all his praise?
[3]Blessed are they who maintain justice,	[3] Happy are those who observe justice,
who constantly do what is right.	who do righteousness at all times.
[4]Remember me, O LORD, when you show favor to your people,	[4] Remember me, O LORD, when you show favor to your people;
come to my aid when you save them,	help me when you deliver them;

a1 Hebrew Hallelu Yah; also in verse 48

NIV

⁵that I may enjoy the prosperity of your
    chosen ones,
  that I may share in the joy of your nation
  and join your inheritance in giving praise.

⁶We have sinned, even as our fathers did;
  we have done wrong and acted wickedly.
⁷When our fathers were in Egypt,
  they gave no thought to your miracles;
  they did not remember your many kindnesses,
  and they rebelled by the sea, the Red Sea.ᵃ
⁸Yet he saved them for his name's sake,
  to make his mighty power known.
⁹He rebuked the Red Sea, and it dried up;
  he led them through the depths as through
    a desert.
¹⁰He saved them from the hand of the foe;
  from the hand of the enemy he redeemed
    them.
¹¹The waters covered their adversaries;
  not one of them survived.
¹²Then they believed his promises
  and sang his praise.

¹³But they soon forgot what he had done
  and did not wait for his counsel.
¹⁴In the desert they gave in to their craving;
  in the wasteland they put God to the test.
¹⁵So he gave them what they asked for,
  but sent a wasting disease upon them.

¹⁶In the camp they grew envious of Moses
  and of Aaron, who was consecrated to the
    Lord.
¹⁷The earth opened up and swallowed Dathan;
  it buried the company of Abiram.
¹⁸Fire blazed among their followers;
  a flame consumed the wicked.

¹⁹At Horeb they made a calf
  and worshiped an idol cast from metal.
²⁰They exchanged their Glory
  for an image of a bull, which eats grass.
²¹They forgot the God who saved them,
  who had done great things in Egypt,
²²miracles in the land of Ham
  and awesome deeds by the Red Sea.
²³So he said he would destroy them—
  had not Moses, his chosen one,

ᵃ7 Hebrew *Yam Suph*; that is, Sea of Reeds; also in verses 9 and
22

NRSV

⁵ that I may see the prosperity of your
    chosen ones,
  that I may rejoice in the gladness of your
    nation,
  that I may glory in your heritage.

⁶ Both we and our ancestors have sinned;
  we have committed iniquity, have done
    wickedly.
⁷ Our ancestors, when they were in Egypt,
  did not consider your wonderful works;
  they did not remember the abundance of
    your steadfast love,
  but rebelled against the Most Highᵃ at
    the Red Sea.ᵇ
⁸ Yet he saved them for his name's sake,
  so that he might make known his mighty
    power.
⁹ He rebuked the Red Sea,ᵇ and it became dry;
  he led them through the deep as through
    a desert.
¹⁰ So he saved them from the hand of the foe,
  and delivered them from the hand of the
    enemy.
¹¹ The waters covered their adversaries;
  not one of them was left.
¹² Then they believed his words;
  they sang his praise.

¹³ But they soon forgot his works;
  they did not wait for his counsel.
¹⁴ But they had a wanton craving in the
    wilderness,
  and put God to the test in the desert;
¹⁵ he gave them what they asked,
  but sent a wasting disease among them.

¹⁶ They were jealous of Moses in the camp,
  and of Aaron, the holy one of the Lord.
¹⁷ The earth opened and swallowed up Dathan,
  and covered the faction of Abiram.
¹⁸ Fire also broke out in their company;
  the flame burned up the wicked.

¹⁹ They made a calf at Horeb
  and worshiped a cast image.
²⁰ They exchanged the glory of Godᶜ

ᵃCn Compare 78.17, 56: Heb *rebelled at the sea*   ᵇOr *Sea of
Reeds*   ᶜCompare Gk Mss: Heb *exchanged their glory*

NIV

stood in the breach before him
    to keep his wrath from destroying them.

24Then they despised the pleasant land;
    they did not believe his promise.
25They grumbled in their tents
    and did not obey the LORD.
26So he swore to them with uplifted hand
    that he would make them fall in the desert,
27make their descendants fall among the nations
    and scatter them throughout the lands.

28They yoked themselves to the Baal of Peor
    and ate sacrifices offered to lifeless gods;
29they provoked the LORD to anger by their
        wicked deeds,
    and a plague broke out among them.
30But Phinehas stood up and intervened,
    and the plague was checked.
31This was credited to him as righteousness
    for endless generations to come.
32By the waters of Meribah they angered the
        LORD,
    and trouble came to Moses because of
        them;
33for they rebelled against the Spirit of God,
    and rash words came from Moses' lips.a

34They did not destroy the peoples
    as the LORD had commanded them,
35but they mingled with the nations
    and adopted their customs.
36They worshiped their idols,
    which became a snare to them.
37They sacrificed their sons
    and their daughters to demons.
38They shed innocent blood,
    the blood of their sons and daughters,
    whom they sacrificed to the idols of Canaan,
    and the land was desecrated by their blood.
39They defiled themselves by what they did;
    by their deeds they prostituted themselves.

40Therefore the LORD was angry with his people
    and abhorred his inheritance.
41He handed them over to the nations,
    and their foes ruled over them.
42Their enemies oppressed them
    and subjected them to their power.
43Many times he delivered them,

a33 Or *against his spirit, / and rash words came from his lips*

NRSV

    for the image of an ox that eats grass.
21 They forgot God, their Savior,
    who had done great things in Egypt,
22 wondrous works in the land of Ham,
    and awesome deeds by the Red Sea.a
23 Therefore he said he would destroy them—
    had not Moses, his chosen one,
    stood in the breach before him,
    to turn away his wrath from destroying
        them.

24 Then they despised the pleasant land,
    having no faith in his promise.
25 They grumbled in their tents,
    and did not obey the voice of the LORD.
26 Therefore he raised his hand and swore to
        them
    that he would make them fall in the
        wilderness,
27 and would disperseb their descendants
        among the nations,
    scattering them over the lands.

28 Then they attached themselves to the Baal
        of Peor,
    and ate sacrifices offered to the dead;
29 they provoked the LORD to anger with their
        deeds,
    and a plague broke out among them.
30 Then Phinehas stood up and interceded,
    and the plague was stopped.
31 And that has been reckoned to him as
        righteousness
    from generation to generation forever.

32 They angered the LORDc at the waters of
        Meribah,
    and it went ill with Moses on their
        account;
33 for they made his spirit bitter,
    and he spoke words that were rash.

34 They did not destroy the peoples,
    as the LORD commanded them,
35 but they mingled with the nations
    and learned to do as they did.
36 They served their idols,

aOr *Sea of Reeds*   bSyr Compare Ezek 20.23: Heb *cause to fall*
cHeb *him*

NIV

but they were bent on rebellion
and they wasted away in their sin.

⁴⁴But he took note of their distress
when he heard their cry;
⁴⁵for their sake he remembered his covenant
and out of his great love he relented.
⁴⁶He caused them to be pitied
by all who held them captive.

⁴⁷Save us, O LORD our God,
and gather us from the nations,
that we may give thanks to your holy name
and glory in your praise.

⁴⁸Praise be to the LORD, the God of Israel,
from everlasting to everlasting.
Let all the people say, "Amen!"

Praise the LORD.

NRSV

which became a snare to them.
³⁷ They sacrificed their sons
and their daughters to the demons;
³⁸ they poured out innocent blood,
the blood of their sons and daughters,
whom they sacrificed to the idols of Canaan;
and the land was polluted with blood.
³⁹ Thus they became unclean by their acts,
and prostituted themselves in their doings.

⁴⁰ Then the anger of the LORD was kindled
against his people,
and he abhorred his heritage;
⁴¹ he gave them into the hand of the nations,
so that those who hated them ruled over
them.
⁴² Their enemies oppressed them,
and they were brought into subjection
under their power.
⁴³ Many times he delivered them,
but they were rebellious in their purposes,
and were brought low through their iniquity.
⁴⁴ Nevertheless he regarded their distress
when he heard their cry.
⁴⁵ For their sake he remembered his covenant,
and showed compassion according to the
abundance of his steadfast love.
⁴⁶ He caused them to be pitied
by all who held them captive.

⁴⁷ Save us, O LORD our God,
and gather us from among the nations,
that we may give thanks to your holy name
and glory in your praise.

⁴⁸ Blessed be the LORD, the God of Israel,
from everlasting to everlasting.
And let all the people say, "Amen."
Praise the LORD!

COMMENTARY

Like Psalm 105, with which it should be heard, Psalm 106 rehearses Israel's story, but it includes a very different series of episodes. To be sure, the psalmist is aware of the "wonderful works" that are featured in Psalm 105 (see 106:7, 22; see also 105:2, 5), but what the psalmist tells about are Israel's reprehensible works, the result of not remembering God's work (vv. 7, 13, 21) and consequently not trusting God's word (see v. 24b; cf. v. 12). Whereas God remembers God's word and the covenant it bespeaks (Pss 105:8, 42; 106:45), the people constantly forget, and their forgetfulness leads to a history of faithlessness that is costly to the people (vv. 40-43) and painful for their spurned lover—God. Indeed, only the abundance of God's steadfast love has kept the story going (vv. 1, 7, 45; see Introduction) and serves as the basis for the hopeful appeal in v. 47.

Verse 47 situates the people and the psalm in the exilic or post-exilic era. This is in keeping with the whole of Book IV (see Commentary on Psalms 90; 93; 101; 102; Introduction), which confronts and responds to the theological crisis of exile that is presented in Book III (see Commentary on Psalms 73; 74; 79; 80; 89; Introduction). The pattern presented in Psalms 105–106—God's "wonderful works," followed by the people's disobedience, followed by God's compassion (see vv. 43-46)—was the only hope the exiles had. While concluding Book IV, Psalm 106 also anticipates the opening of Book V. Psalms 106 and 107 begin the same way, and Psalm 107 recounts precisely the experience for which Ps 106:47 prays (see "gather[ed]" in 106:47; 107:3; see also Commentary on Psalm 107, which also features several other words from Psalm 106, including "steadfast love" and "wonderful works").

Scholars cannot agree on the proper form-critical categorization of Psalm 106. Thus it is variously viewed as a song of praise (see vv. 1-2), a communal lament or prayer for help (see vv. 4-5, 47), a liturgy of penitence (see vv. 6-7), and a sermon, as well as its more frequent designation as a historical psalm. Like the other historical psalms (see Psalms 78; 105; 136), the purpose of Psalm 106 is not to impart information about the past. Rather, it is to invite gratitude, faithfulness, and obedience in the present as the prelude to a transformed future (see Commentary on Psalm 78). Psalm 106 grounds the hope for a transformed future, however, not in the people's willingness or ability to be faithful and obedient but in God's abundant love. Thus it finally has the character of a profession of faith in God and God's compassionate, faithful, forgiving love.

106:1-3. Actually, v. 1 is itself a basic profession of faith (see 2 Chr 5:13; 7:3; Pss 107:1; 118:1, 29; 136:1; Introduction), as well as an invitation to praise (see the return to the vocabulary of praise in v. 47). While in the form of a question, v. 2 is actually an affirmation that no one is capable of adequately praising God. Verse 3 suggests that in the absence of this capability, what we are called upon to do, for our own sake as well as God's, is to conform to God's will—justice and righteousness (see Deut 16:19-20; Pss 96:10, 13; 97:2; 98:9; 99:4; Mic 6:8). Happiness is to be found not in acting selfishly but in doing what God intends (see Ps 1:1-2). Of course, most of the rest of the psalm documents Israel's failure in precisely this regard.

106:4-5. But before turning to the confession of sin and accompanying recital, the poet or worship leader voices in vv. 4-5 an individual petition that points to the end of the psalm and its hopeful conclusion (see "remember" in vv. 4, 45; "people" in vv. 4, 40; "deliver"/"save" in vv. 4, 47; "glory"/"praise" in vv. 5, 47; "heritage" in vv. 5, 40). The brief prayer also recalls v. 1 ("good" in v. 1 and "prosperity" in v. 5 are the same Hebrew root [טוב *ṭôb*]), and the mention of "saving"/"delivering" (ישע *yāša'*) becomes thematic (see also vv. 8, 10, 21). The designation "chosen ones" is a link to Psalm 105 (see 105:6, 26, 43), as is the word "glory" (see 105:3).

106:6. This verse introduces both the first historical episode and the penitent character of the whole psalm. It contains three of the major Hebrew roots that convey "sin" (see Commentary on Psalms 32; 51). Verse 6a reads, literally, "We have sinned with our ancestors," perhaps recalling Exod 20:6; 34:7, which suggest that the parents' sins have ongoing effects (cf. Jer 31:27-30; Ezek 18:1-4). While the subsequent recital will focus on the past, the psalmist demonstrates from the beginning the same concern evident in the book of Deuteronomy: to actualize the experience of past generations for the present generation. The extended confession of sin also recalls the Deuteronomistic speech placed on the lips of Solomon in 1 Kgs 8:33-40, 46-53; from the perspective of its imagined tenth-century BCE setting, it anticipates the people's sin and the loss of land, both of which are presupposed in Psalm 106 (see also Neh 9:9-37; Isa 63:7–64:12; Dan 9:3-19).

106:7-12. Although the Song of the Sea celebrates God's "wonderful works" (see Exod 15:11), Psalm 106 is correct to trace the people's failure of memory and faith all the way back to Egypt (v. 7; see Exod 14:10-12). "Consider" (שׂכל

šākal) in v. 7 means more literally "to be wise," and the beginning of the psalter defines wisdom as recognition of God's sovereignty (see Ps 2:10). Israel's foolish self-reliance—their rebellion (see vv. 33, 43; see also Pss 78:8, 17, 40, 56; 107:11)—does not prevent God's acting for God's own sake (v. 8; see "know" in Exod 14:18). Verses 9-11 briefly rehearse the sea crossing (see Exod 14:21-29; cf. v. 28 with Exod 14:28), and v. 12 correctly recalls Israel's initial belief (see Exod 14:31) and praise in song (Exod 15:1-21).

106:13-15. The "soon" in v. 13 is an understatement. Only three verses after the conclusion of the Song of the Sea, the people are already complaining (Exod 15:24). The psalmist may have this episode in view, as well as several other similar scenes in the wilderness, especially Num 11:4-34 (cf. Ps 106:14a with Num 11:4; see also Exodus 16). Verse 14b also recalls Exod 17:1-7 (see "tested" in v. 7). Verse 15a recognizes that God did provide water, manna, and quail; the difficult v. 15b, if the NIV and the NRSV are followed, recalls Num 11:33. Verse 15b can be construed more positively as conveying God's provision for the people: "he cast out (the) leanness in their throat." That vv. 13-15 recall several episodes should not be surprising. The psalmist does not follow the canonical order of events and is not intent upon accurate historical presentation.

106:16-23. Verses 16-18 offer a summary of the rebellion in Num 16:1-35 (see esp. Num 16:1-3, 30-35). The omission of Korah is surprising and perhaps indicates that the psalmist was working with a different or earlier form of the tradition. Verses 19-23 recall the beginning of the golden calf episode in Exod 32:1-14. In addition, v. 20 is similar to Hos 4:17 and Jer 2:11. Later in the psalm, there will be an allusion to the conclusion of the golden calf episode, in which God "showed compassion" (v. 45; see also Exod 32:14) or "relented," ultimately revealing God's self as a God of abundant "steadfast love" and pity/mercy (Exod 34:6; see also Ps 106:45-46).

106:24-27. These verses are a summary of Num 14:1-25, where the people refuse to accept the report of those sent to spy on the promised land (cf. v. 24 with Num 14:11; v. 25 with Num 14:22; Deut 1:27). As v. 26 suggests, the people's grumbling was the catalyst for God's decision that the wilderness generation would not enter the land (see Num 14:22-23; Deut 1:34). Like the golden calf episode, the spies episode also ends with Moses' appeal for God's forgiveness, based on God's steadfast love (cf. Exod 34:6b-7 with Num 14:18-19; see Ps 106:45). Verse 27 draws an analogy between the consequences experienced by the wilderness generation and the present experience of the people (see v. 47; Lev 26:33; Ezek 20:23).

106:28-33. These verses cite the episode described in Num 25:1-13 (see Hos 9:10). Numbers 25:2 does not associate the sacrifices with ones "offered to the dead" (Ps 106:28); however, there is some evidence that the worship of the Canaanite gods was associated with funeral observances—the *marzeaḥ* feast seemingly alluded to in Jer 16:6-9 and Amos 6:4-7.[398] Verses 32-33 summarize Exod 17:1-7 (see also Num 20:2-13). The NIV is closer to the Hebrew text in v. 33a, but the Hebrew words for "rebel" (מרה *mārâ*; see vv. 7, 43) and "bitter" (מרר *mārar*) are similar, and many translators go with the NRSV translation.

106:34-39. These verses turn to the people's disobedience after they had entered the land—syncretism and idolatry (vv. 34-35; see Num 33:50-56; Deut 7:1-6; 13:6-18; 17:2-7; 20:16-18; 32:15-18), including child sacrifice (vv. 37-38; see Lev 18:21; Deut 12:31; 2 Kgs 16:3; 21:6; 23:10; Jer 7:31; 19:5). The verb in "be unclean" (טמא *ṭāmē*, v. 39) is used often in Leviticus of temporary ritual impurity, but the prophets also use it to describe the results of Israel's idolatry (see "defile"/"pollute" Jer 2:7, 23; Ezek 20:30-31, 43; Hos 5:3; 6:10). The verb "to prostitute" (זנה *zānâ*) is used the same way (see "prostitute"/"play the whore" in Exod 34:15-16; Deut 31:16; Jer 2:20; 3:1; Ezek 23:3, 19; Hos 4:10; 5:3).

106:40-46. These verses are particularly reminiscent of the Deuteronomistic pattern repeated several times in the book of Judges (see Judg 2:11-13; "moved to pity" in Judg 2:18 NRSV is the same verb as "showed compassion" in Ps 106:45), but they could well describe the vicissitudes of Israelite and Judean history recounted in the books of Judges through 2 Kings. As v. 44

---

398. See Neil H. Richardson, "Psalm 106: Yahweh's Succouring Love Saves from the Death of a Broken Covenant," in *Love and Death in the Ancient Near East,* ed. J. H. Marks and R. M. Good (Guilford, Conn.: Four Quarters, 1987) 198.

reminds the reader, the pattern is related to the exodus (see Exod 3:7). But after the exodus, the problem became not just external oppression but the internal faithlessness that is described at length in vv. 13-39. In the book of Exodus, the question became, "Will God put up with this rebellious people?" (see Exod 32:7-10). The answer is yes, not because the people ever do any better, but because God is steadfastly loving and merciful (see Exod 34:6-7), the attributes celebrated in vv. 45-46. God's character—not their own—was the people's only hope, especially in exile and beyond (v. 47). The word "name" (שֵׁם *šēm*) in v. 47 often stands for character, and its occurrence at the end of the sorry story in vv. 6-46 is another reminder that God's holiness consists finally not in God's separation from sin and sinners but in God's bearing the burden of sin and forgiving sinners (see Commentary on Psalms 99; 103).

106:47-48. While Ps 105:1-11 opened with the prayer offered on David's behalf in 1 Chr 16:7-36, Ps 106:47-48 provides its conclusion (1 Chr 16:35-36). This envelope structure is an appropriate reflection in the chronicler's work of the reality of the exile and its aftermath. It is interesting that v. 48, the doxology concluding Book IV, occurs also in 1 Chr 16:36. This seems to suggest that the divisions of the psalter were already in place, unless one concludes that the doxologies in the psalms occur coincidentally and have no editorial significance (see Introduction).

REFLECTIONS

1. Whereas Psalm 105 affirmed the priority of God's grace (see Commentary on Psalm 105), Psalm 106 proclaims the perseverance of God's grace. This good news is clearly what Israel needed to hear in the midst of the exile and its aftermath; but, as Psalm 106 demonstrates, this good news had been evident from the beginning and throughout Israel's history (see esp. vv. 8, 43). Indeed, there would have been no story to rehearse, apart from the way God is—steadfastly loving, ceaselessly compassionate, abundantly merciful (vv. 45-46). Israel was saved by grace!

2. This good news did not stop with Israel's story. The apostle Paul saw in v. 20 not only a comment on Israel's character but also a comment on the character of all humanity (see Rom 1:23). To be sure, Paul could cite episodes from Israel's wilderness experience as "examples for us" (1 Cor 10:6; cf. 1 Cor 10:5, 7-11 with Ps 106:19-23, 28-31), in order to encourage Christians to be obedient. Paul knew, however, that humankind is fundamentally sinful (see Rom 1:18-28; 3:9-20; 7:14-25). And Paul proclaimed ultimately that we are justified by God's grace (Rom 3:24-26; 5:1-2)—"while we still were sinners Christ died for us" (Rom 5:8 NRSV). Humankind is saved by grace!

3. Lest Israel's story sound too bad to be true, Christians should be reminded that the same basic story was played out by Jesus' disciples. In the Gospels, especially in Mark, the disciples are incredibly foolish (see Mark 8:31-33; 9:30-37; 10:32-44) and incurably faithless (see Mark 14:50, 66-72). Yet these same disciples are later empowered to be the church (see John 20:19-23; Acts 2). The church was created by grace. And lest we look askance at Jesus' disciples and the early church, we need only remind ourselves of the many sorry chapters from the annals of church history, or of the many embarrassing realities that characterize the contemporary church—racism, sexism, greed, cultural accommodation, disunity, reluctance to proclaim the good news and to embody it in selfless love for all people and all creation. Indeed, some have proclaimed the beginning of the post-Christian era, noting that the church is awash in an overwhelming sea of cultural influences—a contemporary exile perhaps. If so, then Psalm 106 may be even more timely than ever, "Save us, O LORD our God,/ and gather us from among the nations,/ that we may give thanks to your holy name/ and glory in your praise" (v. 47).

Self-centered as we are, and priding ourselves on being powerful people, we are likely to want to respond to the current crisis by trying to program our way out of it—in short, trusting ourselves instead of entrusting ourselves to God. But praise is about trusting God. Mays points out:

> The voice of trusting praise is the sound and sign of a people restored by the LORD's salvation (vv. 12, 47). The litmus test for the spiritual health of the people of the LORD is the integrity and actuality of their praise, whether they "remember the abundance of the LORD's steadfast love" (v. 7) or forget his deed and let themselves be determined by dangers or desires or the ways of the nations.[399]

The current crisis facing the church is not really new; it is simply another chapter in the ongoing story told in Psalm 106. Now, as then, the best possible news is that God loves us steadfastly (see Commentary on Psalms 32; 51). We are saved by grace! "Praise the LORD!" (vv. 1, 48).

399. James L. Mays, *Psalms,* Interpretation (Louisville: John Knox, 1994) 342.

PSALMS 107–150

BOOK V

PSALM 107:1-43, CONSIDER THE STEADFAST LOVE OF GOD

NIV

BOOK V

Psalms 107–150

Psalm 107

[1] Give thanks to the LORD, for he is good;
his love endures forever.
[2] Let the redeemed of the LORD say this—
those he redeemed from the hand of the
foe,
[3] those he gathered from the lands,
from east and west, from north and south.[a]

[4] Some wandered in desert wastelands,
finding no way to a city where they could
settle.
[5] They were hungry and thirsty,
and their lives ebbed away.
[6] Then they cried out to the LORD in their
trouble,
and he delivered them from their distress.
[7] He led them by a straight way
to a city where they could settle.
[8] Let them give thanks to the LORD for his
unfailing love
and his wonderful deeds for men,
[9] for he satisfies the thirsty
and fills the hungry with good things.

[10] Some sat in darkness and the deepest gloom,
prisoners suffering in iron chains,
[11] for they had rebelled against the words of God
and despised the counsel of the Most High.
[12] So he subjected them to bitter labor;

a3 Hebrew *north and the sea*

NRSV

BOOK V

(Psalms 107–150)

Psalm 107

[1] O give thanks to the LORD, for he is good;
for his steadfast love endures forever.
[2] Let the redeemed of the LORD say so,
those he redeemed from trouble
[3] and gathered in from the lands,
from the east and from the west,
from the north and from the south.[a]

[4] Some wandered in desert wastes,
finding no way to an inhabited town;
[5] hungry and thirsty,
their soul fainted within them.
[6] Then they cried to the LORD in their trouble,
and he delivered them from their distress;
[7] he led them by a straight way,
until they reached an inhabited town.
[8] Let them thank the LORD for his steadfast
love,
for his wonderful works to humankind.
[9] For he satisfies the thirsty,
and the hungry he fills with good things.

[10] Some sat in darkness and in gloom,
prisoners in misery and in irons,
[11] for they had rebelled against the words of
God,
and spurned the counsel of the Most
High.

a Cn: Heb *sea*

NIV

they stumbled, and there was no one to
    help.
13Then they cried to the Lord in their trouble,
    and he saved them from their distress.
14He brought them out of darkness and the
    deepest gloom
    and broke away their chains.
15Let them give thanks to the Lord for his
    unfailing love
    and his wonderful deeds for men,
16for he breaks down gates of bronze
    and cuts through bars of iron.

17Some became fools through their rebellious
    ways
    and suffered affliction because of their
    iniquities.
18They loathed all food
    and drew near the gates of death.
19Then they cried to the Lord in their trouble,
    and he saved them from their distress.
20He sent forth his word and healed them;
    he rescued them from the grave.
21Let them give thanks to the Lord for his
    unfailing love
    and his wonderful deeds for men.
22Let them sacrifice thank offerings
    and tell of his works with songs of joy.

23Others went out on the sea in ships;
    they were merchants on the mighty waters.
24They saw the works of the Lord,
    his wonderful deeds in the deep.
25For he spoke and stirred up a tempest
    that lifted high the waves.
26They mounted up to the heavens and went
    down to the depths;
    in their peril their courage melted away.
27They reeled and staggered like drunken men;
    they were at their wits' end.
28Then they cried out to the Lord in their
    trouble,
    and he brought them out of their distress.
29He stilled the storm to a whisper;
    the waves of the sea were hushed.
30They were glad when it grew calm,
    and he guided them to their desired haven.
31Let them give thanks to the Lord for his
    unfailing love
    and his wonderful deeds for men.

NRSV

12 Their hearts were bowed down with hard
    labor;
    they fell down, with no one to help.
13 Then they cried to the Lord in their trouble,
    and he saved them from their distress;
14 he brought them out of darkness and gloom,
    and broke their bonds asunder.
15 Let them thank the Lord for his steadfast
    love,
    for his wonderful works to humankind.
16 For he shatters the doors of bronze,
    and cuts in two the bars of iron.

17 Some were sick[a] through their sinful ways,
    and because of their iniquities endured
    affliction;
18 they loathed any kind of food,
    and they drew near to the gates of death.
19 Then they cried to the Lord in their trouble,
    and he saved them from their distress;
20 he sent out his word and healed them,
    and delivered them from destruction.
21 Let them thank the Lord for his steadfast
    love,
    for his wonderful works to humankind.
22 And let them offer thanksgiving sacrifices,
    and tell of his deeds with songs of joy.

23 Some went down to the sea in ships,
    doing business on the mighty waters;
24 they saw the deeds of the Lord,
    his wondrous works in the deep.
25 For he commanded and raised the stormy wind,
    which lifted up the waves of the sea.
26 They mounted up to heaven, they went
    down to the depths;
    their courage melted away in their
    calamity;
27 they reeled and staggered like drunkards,
    and were at their wits' end.
28 Then they cried to the Lord in their trouble,
    and he brought them out from their
    distress;
29 he made the storm be still,
    and the waves of the sea were hushed.
30 Then they were glad because they had quiet,
    and he brought them to their desired haven.

a Cn: Heb *fools*

NIV

³²Let them exalt him in the assembly of the
people
and praise him in the council of the elders.

³³He turned rivers into a desert,
flowing springs into thirsty ground,
³⁴and fruitful land into a salt waste,
because of the wickedness of those who
lived there.
³⁵He turned the desert into pools of water
and the parched ground into flowing
springs;
³⁶there he brought the hungry to live,
and they founded a city where they could
settle.
³⁷They sowed fields and planted vineyards
that yielded a fruitful harvest;
³⁸he blessed them, and their numbers greatly
increased,
and he did not let their herds diminish.

³⁹Then their numbers decreased, and they
were humbled
by oppression, calamity and sorrow;
⁴⁰he who pours contempt on nobles
made them wander in a trackless waste.
⁴¹But he lifted the needy out of their affliction
and increased their families like flocks.
⁴²The upright see and rejoice,
but all the wicked shut their mouths.

⁴³Whoever is wise, let him heed these things
and consider the great love of the Lord.

NRSV

³¹ Let them thank the Lord for his steadfast
love,
for his wonderful works to humankind.
³² Let them extol him in the congregation of
the people,
and praise him in the assembly of the
elders.

³³ He turns rivers into a desert,
springs of water into thirsty ground,
³⁴ a fruitful land into a salty waste,
because of the wickedness of its
inhabitants.
³⁵ He turns a desert into pools of water,
a parched land into springs of water.
³⁶ And there he lets the hungry live,
and they establish a town to live in;
³⁷ they sow fields, and plant vineyards,
and get a fruitful yield.
³⁸ By his blessing they multiply greatly,
and he does not let their cattle decrease.

³⁹ When they are diminished and brought low
through oppression, trouble, and sorrow,
⁴⁰ he pours contempt on princes
and makes them wander in trackless
wastes;
⁴¹ but he raises up the needy out of distress,
and makes their families like flocks.
⁴² The upright see it and are glad;
and all wickedness stops its mouth.
⁴³ Let those who are wise give heed to these
things,
and consider the steadfast love of the
Lord.

COMMENTARY

Psalm 107 opens Book V with what appears to
be a direct response to the concluding plea of
Book IV (see "gather[ed]" in Pss 106:47; 107:3).
Psalm 107 also features in an impressive way one
of the key words in Psalm 106 and the psalter as
a whole: "steadfast love" (חסד ḥesed; see Ps
106:1, 7, 45; Introduction). The word occurs in
the first and last verses of Psalm 107 (note that
106:1 and 107:1 are identical), and it occurs in

the second of the psalm's two refrains (vv. 8, 15,
21, 31). There are still more literary and conceptual
links between Psalms 106 and 107—"wonderful
works" (106:7, 22; 107:8, 15, 21, 24, 31), "rebel"
(106:7, 33, 43; 107:11), "redeemed" (106:10;
107:2), "counsel" (106:13; 107:11), "subjected"
(106:42; 107:12), "distress"/"trouble" (106:44;
107:2, 6, 13, 19, 28), "iniquity" (106:43; 107:17).
Indeed, Psalm 107 can be regarded as further

illustration of the pattern evident throughout Psalm 106 and summarized in 106:43-46. In other words, Book V begins in a manner that suggests that the editors of the psalter intended it, like Book IV (see Commentary on Psalms 90; 93; Introduction), to serve as a response to Book III and its elaboration of the theological crisis of exile and its aftermath (see Commentary on Psalms 73; 74; 79; 80; 89; Introduction). Psalm 107, for instance, serves as a pointed response to the question raised in Ps 89:49: "Lord, where is your steadfast love of old?"

Psalm 107 is usually categorized as an individual song of thanksgiving, based on v. 1, the second refrain (vv. 8, 15, 21, 31), and the expansion of this refrain in vv. 22, 32. It may have been used as a congregational liturgy (v. 32) accompanying a thanksgiving sacrifice offered in the Temple (v. 22). Most scholars who propose this idea, however, also suggest that an original core of Psalm 107 (vv. 1, 4-32) has been expanded by the addition of vv. 2-3, 33-43 in order to explicitly address the exilic or post-exilic era. This conclusion is congruent with that suggested above concerning the canonical placement of Psalm 107.

In considering the structure of Psalm 107, it is helpful to think of it as a sermon on God's steadfast love, beginning with an invitation for congregational response (vv. 1-3), followed by four narrative illustrations (vv. 4-9, 10-16, 17-22, 23-32), and concluding with a hymnlike summary based on the four illustrations (vv. 33-42) and an admonition to continue to attend to the message about God's steadfast love (v. 43). The whole psalm effectively conveys what God's steadfast love is all about: compassion for people in need, including forgiveness, since the distress in two instances is the result of human sinfulness (see vv. 11, 17). Jorge Mejía suggests that the four illustrations are arranged chiastically (see Introduction). Arguing that the desert and the sea are symbolic of chaos, Mejía concludes that "two acts of salvation from sin [vv. 10-16, 17-22] are framed by two acts of salvation from chaos [vv. 4-9, 23-32]." The result, especially in the light of the addition of vv. 33-43, is "a fairly complete theology of salvation."[400]

107:1-3. Verse 1 not only ties Psalm 107

conceptually to Psalm 106, but also introduces its major theme: steadfast love. Verse 2 introduces the countertheme: trouble. Each of these key words is featured in one of the refrains. Given the definition of "the redeemed" as those "gathered" from exile, it is not surprising that the post-exilic generations were known elsewhere as "The Redeemed of the Lord" (Isa 62:12; see also Isa 43:1; 44:22-23; 48:20; 52:9).

107:4-9. While these verses may be read as the experience of any person or group, the reader may also find allusions to Israel's experience of exodus/wilderness and return from exile. Each involves wandering (see "go astray" in Ps 95:10; Isa 35:8 NRSV) in a "desert" (see Exod 15:22; 16:1; Isa 40:3) or "wastelands" (see Deut 32:10; Ps 78:40; Isa 43:19-20). Each involves hunger (see Exod 26:3; Isa 49:10) and thirst (Exod 17:3; Isa 41:17), which are filled or satisfied by God (see Exod 16:12; Isa 55:2). Each involves God's leading the way (see Exod 3:18; 5:3; Isa 11:15; 48:17), and each may be described or anticipated as "wonderful works" (see Exod 3:20; 15:11; Mic 7:15). In short, even if vv. 4-9 originated in the experience of some people (v. 4), these verses were easily adaptable to corporate experiences of deliverance, such as exodus and return from exile. The verb "cried" (צעק *ṣāʿaq*, v. 6) is particularly reminiscent of the exodus (see Exod 3:7, 9; 14:10; Deut 26:7), but it is not limited to that experience (see also Judg 3:9, 15; 6:6-7; Neh 9:4; Ps 142:5). In fact, the people's crying out is always a feature of the experience of salvation, as its repetition in Psalm 107 suggests. As Mays puts it:

What sets the *hesed* ["steadfast love"] of the LORD in motion in every case is the cry to the LORD in trouble. The psalm sees the *hesed* of the LORD manifest in salvation completely in this way. It elevates the prayer for help, the voice of dependence on God, to the central place in the relation to God.[401]

107:10-16. These verses could describe anyone's experience of oppression. See "darkness," for instance, in Pss 18:28; 143:3; Isa 9:2; Mic 7:8, and see "gloom" in Ps 23:4 (NIV, "shadow of death"; NRSV, "darkest"); Isa 9:2. But both of

400. Jorge Mejía, "Some Observations on Psalm 107," *Biblical Theology Bulletin* 5 (1975) 58, 66.

401. James L. Mays, *Psalms,* Interpretation (Louisville: John Knox, 1994) 347; see also Richard N. Boyce, *The Cry to God in the Old Testament,* SBLDS 103 (Atlanta: Scholars Press, 1985) 68-69.

these words are used also of exile (see "darkness" in Isa 42:7; 49:9; Jer 13:16; Lam 3:2; and see "gloom" in Ps 44:19; Jer 13:16). Similarly, the word "prisoners" (אסירים 'ăsîrîm) need not designate the condition of the exiles (see Ps 68:6), but it can (see Isa 49:9; Lam 3:34; Zech 9:11; and perhaps Pss 79:11; 102:20), as can the word "misery" (עני 'ŏnî; see v. 17 NIV and NRSV, "affliction"; v. 41 NRSV, "distress"; see also Ps 44:24; Lam 1:3, 7; 3:19). The attribution of the oppression to rebellion (v. 11) is also appropriate for the exile, and v. 11 also recalls Psalm 106 (see vv. 7, 13, 33, 43), reinforcing the conclusion that Psalm 107 also intends to address the exilic crisis and its aftermath by presenting the same pattern that pervades Psalm 106. In keeping with God's character, God helps those who have "no one to help" (v. 12; see also Ps 22:11 and Commentary on Psalm 3). God is steadfastly loving.

107:17-22. A comparison of the NIV with the NRSV of v. 17a reveals that the NIV retains the Hebrew text. Because of the description in v. 18 and the mention of healing in v. 20, however, many translators emend the text in the direction of the NRSV. This is not necessary, nor is it advisable in the light of the mention of "wise" in v. 43. Even if sickness is the subject of vv. 17-22, sickness elsewhere is associated with disobedience (see Psalms 6; 38), which in turn is elsewhere a manifestation of foolishness (see Prov 1:7; Isa 19:11; Jer 4:22). It is possible that the imagery of sickness is a metaphorical description of an urgent, life-threatening situation (see "gates of death" in Ps 9:13; cf. Isa 38:10, however, where sickness is the problem). In any case, it is God who heals, literally (see 2 Kgs 20:5) or figuratively (see Jer 3:22; Hos 6:1; 11:3; 14:5). In fact, the figurative use of the verb can portray the forgiveness that enables return from exile (see Isa 57:18-19; Jer 33:6). Again, even if vv. 17-22 originated as a general description of deliverance, these verses were easily adaptable to the return from exile. The means of God's deliverance is God's "word" (see Isa 40:8; 55:11). In contrast to the first two illustrations, the concluding verse of this one is an invitation for response (see v. 32). The delivered are to proclaim publicly what God has done (see Ps 73:28c).

107:23-32. "Works" in v. 22 recurs in v. 24a. God's "works" are seen by sailors at sea. While the previous three illustrations have affinities with

other material in the psalms, nowhere else in the psalter is there a description of deliverance from distress at sea (see Jonah 1–2; the words "deep" and "depths" in Ps 107:24, 26 also occur in Jonah 2:3, 5). This scenario, however, gives the psalmist the opportunity to assert God's ability to deliver even from hostile cosmic forces, which are symbolized by "the sea," "the deep" and "the depths," "the storm," and "the waves" (see v. 29 and above commentaries on Pss 74:12-15; 93:3-4; see also Gen 1:2; Exod 15:5, 8; Matt 8:23-27; Mark 4:35-41). The phrase "were at their wits' end" (v. 27b) is more literally, "all their wisdom was swallowed up," perhaps another allusion to Jonah (see Jonah 1:17). In any case, "wisdom" anticipates v. 43. True wisdom is to cry out to God, to acknowledge one's utter dependence upon God and to know that God's steadfast love is sufficient for even the worst possible scenario (see Commentary on Psalm 46). The appropriate response to this good news is praise, which is a public liturgical response that bespeaks the yielding of one's life to God (v. 32; see also Ps 106:47). To "extol" or "exalt" God involves the fundamental recognition of God's sovereignty, which is manifest in God's acts of deliverance like those illustrated in Psalm 107 (see Exod 15:2; Pss 99:5, 9; 145:1).

107:33-43. Many scholars consider this section to be an exilic or post-exilic updating of an original core of the psalm (vv. 4-32). This proposal is strengthened by the fact that portions of vv. 33-43 are based on previous verses (cf. v. 36a with vv. 5, 9; v. 36b with vv. 4, 7; v. 40 with v. 4; v. 41 with vv. 10, 17). On the other hand, all good poets and storytellers regularly employ repetition. In any case, vv. 33-43 are reminiscent of other exilic material (cf. v. 33a with Isa 50:2; v. 35 with Isa 41:18), and they serve as an apt poetic description of the return from exile (see vv. 2-3). Earthly sovereigns are made subject to the sovereignty of God (v. 40; see also Pss 47:9; 118:9; 146:3) as part of God's great reversal of fortunes (v. 41; see also 1 Sam 2:8; Pss 113:7; 146:8). Those who acknowledge God's sovereignty—"the upright" (v. 42a; see also Pss 11:7; 33:1)—can rejoice as injustice is thwarted (see Pss 52:6-7; 58:10-11; 63:11).

It may be coincidental, but just as the first psalm in Book IV portrayed wisdom as humble, daily dependence upon God (see Ps 90:12), so also Ps 107:43a asserts that wisdom consists of heeding the lesson of the preceding illustrations: Those who renounce self-sufficency and cry to God will be the beneficiaries of God's "wonderful works," which reveal God's enduring steadfast love (v. 43b; see vv. 1, 8, 15, 21, 31). Such was the only hope for exiles, as it had been Israel's only hope throughout its history (see Psalm 106). It is our hope as well (see Reflections).

REFLECTIONS

The probability that vv. 4-32 originated in the experience of some and were claimed by the whole people (or simply the fact that vv. 4-32 apply to a variety of experiences) is theologically significant, for it suggests that Scripture is a "living word that it is not exhausted in an ancient situation nor does it require repetition of history to become valid again, but runs freely, challenging a new generation of believers to see a fresh correspondence between word and experience." [402] To put it differently, the four illustrations in vv. 4-32 not only apply to a variety of ancient settings, including the crisis of exile and its aftermath, but also became "open paradigms." [403] Psalm 107 suggests, therefore, that there are certain typical things we can count on as we look for fresh correspondences between our experience and God's word and work. For instance, the four narrative illustrations assert the essential weakness, neediness, and sinfulness of humanity. Persons who are "wise" and "heed these things" (v. 43) will realize that there is never a time when they are not in "trouble" (vv. 2, 6, 13, 19, 28). Thus, crying out to God, living in dependence upon God, is not simply an emergency measure but a way of life (see Commentary on Psalms 1; 2; 3).

This message is diametrically opposed to what much of contemporary North American culture teaches people. In modern culture, maturity is often measured by how *self*-sufficient we are. We are taught that we earn what we have (see vv. 4-9); we are taught that we must pull ourselves up by our bootstraps when we are down (see vv. 10-16); we are taught that wisdom is getting ahead in whatever way we can manage without getting caught (see vv. 17-22); we are taught that our security results from careful planning, investment, and management (see vv. 23-32). In short, we are taught to be self-made persons—no need to cry to God for help, and consequently no need to thank God for anything. Seldom, if ever, does it occur to us that human life depends on God.

Thus the message of Psalm 107 is simple but radical: There is ultimately no such thing as self-sufficiency, for human life depends on God. The good news is that we can depend on God. God is good (v. 1), and God shares God's goodness (v. 9). God loves us with a steadfast love, and Christians profess that this love is manifested in the life, death, and resurrection of Jesus Christ. Thus it is not surprising that Jesus does the same kinds of things that God does in the four narrative illustrations: feeding the hungry in the wilderness (Mark 6:30-44; 8:1-10; see Luke 1:53), liberating those bound by demonic powers (Mark 1:21-28; 3:20-27; Luke 4:16-21), healing and forgiving the sick (Mark 2:1-12), stilling storms at sea (Matt 8:23-27; Mark 4:35-41). Jesus called people to acknowledge and to live under God's sovereignty (see Mark 1:14-15), to renounce self-sufficiency and to walk the way of the cross in dependence upon God (see Mark 8:34-35). Indeed, as Paul recognized, the cross is precisely the sign that God chooses the foolish, the weak, the low, and the despised—that is, the very kind of people featured in the four narrative illustrations in Psalm 107. Using one of the key words in Psalm 107, Paul proclaims that the cross is "the power of God and the wisdom of God" (1 Cor 1:24 NRSV; see Ps 107:43). This kind of wisdom means that no one should "boast in the presence of God" (1 Cor 1:29 NRSV). Rather, the fundamental attitude and activity of the faithful will

402. Leslie C. Allen, *Psalms 101–150*, WBC 21 (Waco, Tex.: Word, 1983) 65.
403. Mays, *Psalms*, 346.

be gratitude for God's goodness and steadfast love. It is precisely this that Psalm 107 encourages and invites: "O give thanks to the LORD" (v. 1; see vv. 8, 15, 21, 31; see also Commentary on Psalm 50). The invitation to humble gratitude makes Psalm 107 appropriate for the season of Lent and for all seasons.

PSALM 108:1-13, WITH GOD WE SHALL DO VALIANTLY

NIV

Psalm 108

A song. A psalm of David.

¹My heart is steadfast, O God;
    I will sing and make music with all my
        soul.
²Awake, harp and lyre!
    I will awaken the dawn.
³I will praise you, O LORD, among the nations;
    I will sing of you among the peoples.
⁴For great is your love, higher than the
        heavens;
    your faithfulness reaches to the skies.
⁵Be exalted, O God, above the heavens,
    and let your glory be over all the earth.

⁶Save us and help us with your right hand,
    that those you love may be delivered.
⁷God has spoken from his sanctuary:
    "In triumph I will parcel out Shechem
    and measure off the Valley of Succoth.
⁸Gilead is mine, Manasseh is mine;
    Ephraim is my helmet,
    Judah my scepter.
⁹Moab is my washbasin,
    upon Edom I toss my sandal;
    over Philistia I shout in triumph."

¹⁰Who will bring me to the fortified city?
    Who will lead me to Edom?
¹¹Is it not you, O God, you who have rejected
        us
    and no longer go out with our armies?
¹²Give us aid against the enemy,
    for the help of man is worthless.
¹³With God we will gain the victory,
    and he will trample down our enemies.

NRSV

Psalm 108

A Song. A Psalm of David.

¹ My heart is steadfast, O God, my heart is
        steadfast;ᵃ
    I will sing and make melody.
    Awake, my soul!ᵇ
² Awake, O harp and lyre!
    I will awake the dawn.
³ I will give thanks to you, O LORD, among
        the peoples,
    and I will sing praises to you among the
        nations.
⁴ For your steadfast love is higher than the
        heavens,
    and your faithfulness reaches to the
        clouds.

⁵ Be exalted, O God, above the heavens,
    and let your glory be over all the earth.
⁶ Give victory with your right hand, and
        answer me,
    so that those whom you love may be
        rescued.

⁷ God has promised in his sanctuary:ᶜ
    "With exultation I will divide up
        Shechem,
    and portion out the Vale of Succoth.
⁸ Gilead is mine; Manasseh is mine;
    Ephraim is my helmet;
    Judah is my scepter.
⁹ Moab is my washbasin;
    on Edom I hurl my shoe;
    over Philistia I shout in triumph."

ᵃHeb Mss Gk Syr: MT lacks *my heart is steadfast*   ᵇCompare 57.8: Heb *also my soul*   ᶜOr *by his holiness*

NRSV

¹⁰ Who will bring me to the fortified city?
   Who will lead me to Edom?
¹¹ Have you not rejected us, O God?
   You do not go out, O God, with our
   armies.
¹² O grant us help against the foe,
   for human help is worthless.
¹³ With God we shall do valiantly;
   it is he who will tread down our foes.

COMMENTARY

Psalm 108 has apparently been composed by the joining of Ps 57:7-11 (Ps 108:1-5) and Ps 60:5-12 (Ps 108:6-13). While scholars agree that Psalms 57 and 60 represent the earlier versions of this material, they have reached no consensus concerning the reason for the use of portions of Psalms 57 and 60 to create Psalm 108. Kraus even suggests that it is "difficult, indeed almost impossible," to discern the reasons for and intent of the new composition.[404]

While there is clearly no room for absolute certainty, it is possible to find good reasons for the composition and current placement of Psalm 108 in the light of the intent of Books IV and V to respond to the crisis of exile and its aftermath (see Commentary on Psalms 90; 107; Introduction). Psalm 107 celebrates God's redemption of the people and the return from exile (vv. 2-3), calling for grateful praise in response to God's steadfast love (vv. 1, 8, 15, 21-22, 31-32). Ps 57:7-11—now Ps 108:1-5—supplies precisely that. The verb "give thanks" (ידה $y\bar{a}d\hat{a}$) from Ps 107:1, 8, 15, 21, 31 recurs in Ps 108:3. Then, too, the word "steadfast love" (חסד $\d{h}esed$), which accompanies each occurrence of "give thanks" in Psalm 107, is the stated reason for praise in Ps 108:4. This verse can also be viewed as a direct response to Ps 89:49, the question with which Book III leaves the reader. Furthermore, "be exalted" (Ps 108:5) recalls Ps 107:32. Again, Ps 108:1-5 articulates the praise that Psalm 107 invites, and given the celebration of the return from exile, it is especially fitting that the praise is

offered "among the peoples, and . . . nations" (v. 3). In Psalm 57, vv. 7-11 immediately follow an announcement that the psalmist has been delivered from enemies (57:6). Given the introduction (vv. 2-3) and conclusion (vv. 39-42) of Psalm 107, these verses have found a similar setting in Psalm 108—they offer exuberant praise and thanksgiving in response to God's steadfast love.

The skillful joining of portions of Psalms 57 and 60 is indicated by the fact that vv. 5-6 of Psalm 108 form a section of petition consisting of the last verse of the quotation from Psalm 57 (57:11) and the first verse from the quotation from Psalm 60 (60:5). The repetition of "glory" (v. 1, NIV and NRSV "soul"; v. 5) marks the beginning of the first two sections of the psalm (vv. 1-4, 5-6) and also signals the shift of attention from the psalmist's activity to God's activity. Following vv. 1-6, there is an oracle (vv. 7-9), a complaint (vv. 10-11), a further petition (v. 12), and an expression of trust (v. 13). In other words, following praise in celebration of deliverance (vv. 1-4), there is renewed complaint and petition for deliverance (vv. 10-12). This sequence is unusual but not entirely unique (see Psalms 40; 118; 126), but what is of particular interest here is that the sequence fits exactly the situation involved in the return from exile and subsequent events. Whereas the return itself was cause for celebration (vv. 1-4; see Psalm 107; Isaiah 40–55), the actual conditions following the return were far from ideal (see Isaiah 56–66; Haggai; Zechariah 1–8). In short, further help was needed and further petition became necessary as well, and Ps 60:5-12—now Ps 108:6-13—supplies precisely that. It seems to

---

404. H.-J. Kraus, *Psalms 60–150: A Commentary,* trans. H. C. Oswald (Minneapolis: Augsburg, 1989) 333.

have been chosen because of its focus on Edom, which apparently rejoiced over and perhaps participated in the defeat of Jerusalem that led to the exile (see Ps 137:7; Obadiah 10–14) and therefore was a target of hostility in the exilic and post-exilic eras (see Obadiah 15–21). (For more detailed comment on Psalm 108, see the Commentary on Psalms 57; 60.)

REFLECTIONS

1. As was the case with Psalm 107, Psalm 108 illustrates the dynamic life and use of the psalms. In Allen's words, "The combination of earlier psalms illustrates the vitality of older scriptures as they were appropriated and applied to new situations in the experience of God's people."[405] In this case, Psalms 57 and 60 were brought together to form Psalm 108 as a response to the post-exilic situation. But Psalm 108 remains vital and applicable to the life of the people of God. By following initial praise with ongoing petition, Psalm 108 teaches us that the people of God never live beyond trouble and the need for God's help (see Commentary on Psalm 107). In a word, the perspective of Psalm 108, like that of the psalter as a whole, is eschatological, for it simultaneously celebrates and asks for God's help (see Commentary on Psalms 2; 57; 60; 93; 95; 96; 97; 98; 99; Introduction). Renouncing human help, it affirms that human life and the life of God's people depend finally on God (vv. 12-13).

2. One is tempted to conclude that in addition to the reasons suggested above, Ps 57:7-11 was chosen to begin Psalm 108 on account of its splendid poetry; indeed, this could have been a consideration. In any case, the continuing artistic appeal of these verses is demonstrated by Leonard Bernstein's choice of Ps 108:2 to open the first movement of his *Chichester Psalms*. Bernstein juxtaposes Ps 108:2 with Psalm 100, another psalm that articulates both dependence upon God (100:3) and gratitude for God's steadfast love and faithfulness (100:4-5; see 108:3-4). Bernstein's work is testimony, too, to the vitality of the psalms as scripture and to their ability to be applied creatively to new situations in the life of God's people.

405. Allen, *Psalms 101–150*, 70.

PSALM 109:1-31, GOD SAVES THOSE WHO ARE NEEDY

NIV	NRSV
Psalm 109	Psalm 109
For the director of music. Of David. A psalm.	To the leader. Of David. A Psalm.

¹O God, whom I praise,
  do not remain silent,
²for wicked and deceitful men
  have opened their mouths against me;
  they have spoken against me with lying
    tongues.
³With words of hatred they surround me;
  they attack me without cause.
⁴In return for my friendship they accuse me,
  but I am a man of prayer.
	¹ Do not be silent, O God of my praise.
	² For wicked and deceitful mouths are
	    opened against me,
	  speaking against me with lying tongues.
	³ They beset me with words of hate,
	  and attack me without cause.
	⁴ In return for my love they accuse me,
	  even while I make prayer for them.[a]
	⁵ So they reward me evil for good,

	ª Syr: Heb *I prayer*

NIV

⁵They repay me evil for good,
and hatred for my friendship.

⁶Appoint*ᵃ* an evil man*ᵇ* to oppose him;
let an accuser*ᶜ* stand at his right hand.
⁷When he is tried, let him be found guilty,
and may his prayers condemn him.
⁸May his days be few;
may another take his place of leadership.
⁹May his children be fatherless
and his wife a widow.
¹⁰May his children be wandering beggars;
may they be driven*ᵈ* from their ruined
homes.
¹¹May a creditor seize all he has;
may strangers plunder the fruits of his
labor.
¹²May no one extend kindness to him
or take pity on his fatherless children.
¹³May his descendants be cut off,
their names blotted out from the next
generation.
¹⁴May the iniquity of his fathers be
remembered before the LORD;
may the sin of his mother never be blotted
out.
¹⁵May their sins always remain before the LORD,
that he may cut off the memory of them
from the earth.

¹⁶For he never thought of doing a kindness,
but hounded to death the poor
and the needy and the brokenhearted.
¹⁷He loved to pronounce a curse—
may it*ᵉ* come on him;
he found no pleasure in blessing—
may it be*ᶠ* far from him.
¹⁸He wore cursing as his garment;
it entered into his body like water,
into his bones like oil.
¹⁹May it be like a cloak wrapped about him,
like a belt tied forever around him.
²⁰May this be the LORD's payment to my
accusers,
to those who speak evil of me.

²¹But you, O Sovereign LORD,

ᵃ6 Or ⌐They say:⌐ "Appoint (with quotation marks at the end of verse 19) ᵇ6 Or the Evil One ᶜ6 Or let Satan ᵈ10 Septuagint; Hebrew sought ᵉ17 Or curse, / and it has ᶠ17 Or blessing, / and it is

NRSV

and hatred for my love.

⁶ They say,*ᵃ* "Appoint a wicked man against
him;
let an accuser stand on his right.
⁷ When he is tried, let him be found guilty;
let his prayer be counted as sin.
⁸ May his days be few;
may another seize his position.
⁹ May his children be orphans,
and his wife a widow.
¹⁰ May his children wander about and beg;
may they be driven out of*ᵇ* the ruins they
inhabit.
¹¹ May the creditor seize all that he has;
may strangers plunder the fruits of his toil.
¹² May there be no one to do him a kindness,
nor anyone to pity his orphaned children.
¹³ May his posterity be cut off;
may his name be blotted out in the
second generation.
¹⁴ May the iniquity of his father*ᶜ* be
remembered before the LORD,
and do not let the sin of his mother be
blotted out.
¹⁵ Let them be before the LORD continually,
and may his*ᵈ* memory be cut off from the
earth.
¹⁶ For he did not remember to show kindness,
but pursued the poor and needy
and the brokenhearted to their death.
¹⁷ He loved to curse; let curses come on him.
He did not like blessing; may it be far
from him.
¹⁸ He clothed himself with cursing as his
coat,
may it soak into his body like water,
like oil into his bones.
¹⁹ May it be like a garment that he wraps
around himself,
like a belt that he wears every day."

²⁰ May that be the reward of my accusers
from the LORD,
of those who speak evil against my life.
²¹ But you, O LORD my Lord,
act on my behalf for your name's sake;

ᵃHeb lacks They say ᵇGk: Heb and seek ᶜCn: Heb fathers ᵈGk: Heb their

NIV

deal well with me for your name's sake;
   out of the goodness of your love, deliver
   me.
[22]For I am poor and needy,
   and my heart is wounded within me.
[23]I fade away like an evening shadow;
   I am shaken off like a locust.
[24]My knees give way from fasting;
   my body is thin and gaunt.
[25]I am an object of scorn to my accusers;
   when they see me, they shake their heads.

[26]Help me, O LORD my God;
   save me in accordance with your love.
[27]Let them know that it is your hand,
   that you, O LORD, have done it.
[28]They may curse, but you will bless;
   when they attack they will be put to
   shame,
   but your servant will rejoice.
[29]My accusers will be clothed with disgrace
   and wrapped in shame as in a cloak.

[30]With my mouth I will greatly extol the LORD;
   in the great throng I will praise him.
[31]For he stands at the right hand of the needy
   one,
   to save his life from those who condemn
   him.

NRSV

because your steadfast love is good,
   deliver me.
[22] For I am poor and needy,
   and my heart is pierced within me.
[23] I am gone like a shadow at evening;
   I am shaken off like a locust.
[24] My knees are weak through fasting;
   my body has become gaunt.
[25] I am an object of scorn to my accusers;
   when they see me, they shake their
   heads.

[26] Help me, O LORD my God!
   Save me according to your steadfast love.
[27] Let them know that this is your hand;
   you, O LORD, have done it.
[28] Let them curse, but you will bless.
   Let my assailants be put to shame;[a] may
   your servant be glad.
[29] May my accusers be clothed with dishonor;
   may they be wrapped in their own
   shame as in a mantle.
[30] With my mouth I will give great thanks to
   the LORD;
   I will praise him in the midst of the
   throng.
[31] For he stands at the right hand of the needy,
   to save them from those who would
   condemn them to death.

[a] Gk: Heb *They have risen up and have been put to shame*

COMMENTARY

Hermann Gunkel considered Psalm 109 to be the only pure psalm of imprecation in the psalter, and many commentators note its peculiar character.[406] While it begins and ends with elements that are typical of a prayer for help or individual lament/complaint—petition (vv. 1a, 20-21, 26-29), complaint (vv. 1b-5, 22-25), vow to praise and profession of trust (vv. 30-31)—the verses in between (vv. 6-19) constitute what Brueggemann aptly calls a "song of hate."[407] Lest Psalm 109 be too quickly dismissed as nothing but an expression of desire for unlimited revenge, it is important to consider the context of vv. 6-19. Verses 1-5 suggest that the psalmist, although innocent, has been put on trial. Several scholars assert that the trial would have taken place in the Temple before priestly judges (see Commentary on Psalms 5; 7; see also Exod 22:8; Deut 17:8-13; 1 Kgs 8:31-32). Whether the psalm actually records the psalmist's prayer in such a setting or whether such a setting should be interpreted metaphorically is unclear. In either case, it is crucial to hear the psalmist's words as those of an unjustly accused person; in short,

406. Hermann Gunkel, *The Psalms*, trans. T. M. Herner, FBBS 19 (Philadelphia: Fortress, 1967) 35.
407. Walter Brueggemann, *The Message of the Psalms: A Theological Commentary* (Minneapolis: Augsburg, 1984) 83.

the psalmist comes to God as one who is "poor and needy" (v. 22; see vv. 16, 31).

A major interpretive issue, reflected in a comparison of v. 6 in the NIV and the NRSV, is whether vv. 6-19 should be understood as the words of the psalmist against the accusers (NIV), or whether they should be construed as the psalmist's quotation of what the accusers have said about him or her (NRSV; NIV note). Since the psalmist has been referring to a plurality of accusers (vv. 2-5), the switch to the singular in v. 6 seems to support the NRSV. Furthermore, if v. 6 begins the words of the accusers, then v. 31 would be an eminently fitting reply by the psalmist. Whereas the enemies wish for an accuser to stand on the psalmist's right (v. 6), the psalmist professes that it is God who "stands at the right hand of the needy" (v. 31). On the other hand, there is nothing in the text to indicate specifically that vv. 6-19 are the words of the accusers; it is entirely possible that the psalmist switches to the singular simply to address more specifically the last accuser who pointed the finger at him or her. Certainty is not possible, and commentators are divided almost equally on the issue. In either case, it should be noted that the option chosen by the NRSV does not remove the necessity of confronting the psalmist's desire for vengeance, because in v. 20 the psalmist claims the "song of hate" as an expression of his or her own desire for the accusers (even if it was the accusers who originally uttered the words). In the comments below, I shall follow the NIV's decision on this matter.

The placement of Psalm 109 may be entirely coincidental, but its major concept—steadfast love (vv. 21, 26; "kindness," vv. 12, 16 NIV and NRSV)—is also one that is featured prominently in Psalm 107 (vv. 1, 8, 15, 21, 31, 43) and appears in Psalm 108 as well (v. 3). Anticipating deliverance, the psalmist vows in v. 30 to do exactly what Psalm 107 enjoins: to give thanks to God (107:1, 8, 15, 21, 31) and to praise God publicly (107:32). In effect, the psalmist's anticipated deliverance in Psalm 109 can be added to the four narrative illustrations of God's saving love in Psalm 107 (vv. 4-32). Then, too, the psalmist, while vehemently expressing the desire for vengeance, apparently leaves the actual activity to God, as in Psalm 108 (vv. 21, 26-27, 31; see Ps 108:12-13). Furthermore, it may not be coinci-

dental that the grounding of vengeance in God's love for the poor and needy (vv. 21-22) follows immediately the mention of Edom in Ps 108:10. If Psalm 109, like Psalms 107 and 108, is intended to address the post-exilic situation (see Introduction), then desire for vengeance against Edom would have been a major issue (see Ps 108:10; Obadiah 15-21; see also Ps 137:8-9, where the desire for vengeance is directed against Babylon, but apparently intended for Edom as well, as 137:7 suggests). It would have been important to articulate and ground this desire carefully, especially since Israel also remembered Edom as a brother (see Gen 25:30; see Ps 109:4-5). Whether intended or not, Psalm 109 could have this effect.

109:1-5. After a brief initial petition (v. 1; see Pss 28:1; 35:22; 83:1), the psalmist voices the complaint that he or she has been falsely accused. Although the phrase "deceitful mouths" is unique in the psalter, the psalmists frequently complain about deceitful persons and their speech (see Pss 5:6; 10:7; 35:20; 36:4), which is sometimes specifically described as "lying" (see Pss 27:12; 31:18; 101:7). This latter term often refers to testimony offered in court, so it may be particularly apt here (see Deut 19:18). In any case, the enemies' hateful words are not justified (v. 3; see Pss 35:7, 19; 69:4). The occurrence of "without cause" in Lam 3:52 is particularly interesting, because there a prayer upon the destruction of Jerusalem is voiced by an "I," who makes some of the same complaints and appeals as in Psalm 109. This indicates that Psalm 109 may have been understood corporately, especially following Psalms 107–108. The Hebrew root underlying "accuse(r)" in vv. 4, 6 (שָׂטַן *śāṭan,* see also vv. 20, 29) later became used of a superhuman adversary or accuser—Satan (see NIV note; 1 Chr 21:1; Zech 3:1)—but the word in v. 4 simply designates an accusing witness (see Pss 38:20; 71:13). The enemies' accusations are even harder to take, because the psalmist has shown them not hatred but love (vv. 4-5).

109:6-19. Verses 4-5 describe a situation that cannot get any worse. Thus in v. 6 the psalmist asks for redress, suggesting in effect that the accusers get a dose of their own medicine. As they have proven themselves "wicked" (v. 2), so let the wicked get after them (v. 6*a*). As they have accused (v. 4), so let an accuser stand on their right—the position of closeness and help (v. 6*b*; see v. 31). Verse 6 could be understood as a request for due process, but v. 7 leaves due process behind. In other words, there is really no need for a trial, because the enemies are clearly "guilty" (רשע *rāšā*, v. 7*a*, which translates the same Hebrew word as "wicked" in vv. 2, 6). Verse 7*b* also attempts to turn the tables on the accusers; just as the psalmist's prayer has been to no avail (v. 4*b*), so also let the enemies' prayer "miss the mark" (the fundamental sense of the NRSV's "sin").

In other words, the psalmist has put the enemies on trial (vv. 6-7), and vv. 8-19 can thus be understood as the sentence that a representative enemy deserves. The psalmist's desire for vengeance covers all the bases, to say the least. Not only is the enemy the direct target (vv. 8, 11-12, 17-19), but also are his wife (v. 9), his children (vv. 9-10, 12), his posterity and any future remembrance of his name (v. 13), and even his ancestors (v. 14). The hyperbole would be comic were it not for the utter seriousness of the psalmist's request—let the enemy be annihilated. Even so, it is important to notice that the psalmist's request is in accordance with what most persons, then and now, would say is only fair—the punishment should fit the crime (see Exod 21:23-24; Lev 24:19-20; and esp. Deut 19:18*b*-19, 21). In particular, the enemy deserves no kindness (v. 12, or "steadfast love"), because he showed no kindness (v. 16). The enemy deserves to be impoverished (vv. 8-11), because he mistreated the poor and the needy (v. 16; see Ps 10:2). The enemy deserves to be cursed, because he cursed others (vv. 17-19, 28-29; see Ps 62:4). In short, the enemy deserves to die (v. 8), because he pursued others to their death (vv. 16, 31; see "pursue"/"persecute" in Pss 7:1; 31:15; 35:3; 119:84, 86, 157, 161; 142:6; 143:3).

109:20-31. The case against the accusers is summarized in v. 20, and in v. 21, the psalmist turns his or her case over to God. The "you" that begins v. 21 is emphatic, introducing the contrast between the character of the accusers and the character of God, who can be trusted to act in accordance with the divine character—"for your name's sake" (see Ps 23:3). If any one word describes God's character, it is "steadfast love" (חסד *ḥesed*; see Exod 34:6-7; Pss 5:7; 13:5; 103:4, 8, 11, 17; 107:1; Introduction). So the psalmist entrusts the self to God. Whereas the accusers showed no steadfast love (or kindness), God's steadfast love is "good" (v. 21; see also v. 26.) Whereas the accusers pursued the poor and the needy, God can be trusted to "deliver" them (v. 21), to "help" them (v. 26), to "save" them (v. 26). Whereas the accusers cursed, God can be trusted to bless (v. 28; see Gen 12:3; 5:12; 29:11). In other words, the psalmist professes the faith that pervades the psalter: God will hear the cries of the oppressed, and God will act (see Pss 9:18; 10:17-18; 11:7; 12:5; 14:5-6; 17:13-15; 107:39-43; 108:12-13). So the psalmist stresses his or her oppression and neediness (v. 22*a*; see Pss 35:10; 40:17; 70:6; 74:21; 86:1) in language reminiscent of other prayers for help— "pierced"/"wounded" (v. 22*b*; see Ps 69:26; Isa 53:5), "like a shadow" (v. 23*a*; see Job 17:7; Ps 102:11), "weak" knees (v. 24*a*; see Pss 31:10; 107:12; see also Isa 35:3-4, where this condition evokes God's vengeance against the perpetrators), "an object of scorn" that turns people's heads (v. 25; see Pss 22:6-7).

Recalling v. 21, the "you" in v. 27 is again emphatic; it is *God* who effects the great reversal of fortunes. (The NRSV's "act" [עשה *'āśâ*] in v. 21 and "done" in v. 27 are the same Hebrew verb, and both verses also mention God's steadfast love; note also the reversal in Ps 107:39-43.) There is another emphatic "you" in v. 28—*God* will bless, despite the enemies' curses. God's purposes will not be thwarted. Those who sought to shame the psalmist will themselves be ashamed (vv. 28-29; see Ps 35:26), and the psalmist will respond with joy (v. 28*b*), gratitude (v. 30*a*), praise (v. 30*b*), and trust in the God who loves and saves the oppressed (v. 31).

REFLECTIONS

1. In recent years at least, Psalm 109 has been largely ignored in Christian liturgy; in fact, it is often criticized as being morally inferior. This is a very interesting response, because most

Christians seem to support what underlies the psalmist's expression of desire for vengeance in vv. 6-19—that is, that the punishment should fit the crime. Indeed, most Christians seem to support the death penalty for capital offenses. It would seem, therefore, that Psalm 109 should not present much of a problem. Yet, most Christians seem to think the psalmist's sentiments are somehow "unchristian," especially in the light of Jesus' admonition to love enemies, turn the other cheek, go the second mile. The psalmist does not measure up. The disparity between the standard we affirm (and legislatively embody in our legal system) and the standard to which we hold the psalmist is the initial clue to what Christians can learn from Psalm 109. If we are honest, we must conclude that the psalm teaches us about ourselves. *We* are vengeful people. As Brueggemann puts it:

> The real theological problem, I submit, is not that vengeance is *there* in the Psalms, but that it is *here* in our midst. And that it is there and here only reflects how attuned the Psalter is to what goes on among us. Thus, we may begin with a recognition of the acute correspondence between what is *written there* and what is *practiced here.* The Psalms do "tell it like it is" with us.[408]

2. Psalm 109 not only tells it like it is with us, but it also tells us how it is with the world. The psalmist had been victimized, and when persons become victims, they are bound to react with rage. C. S. Lewis says that Psalm 109 shows "the natural result of injuring a human being."[409] When persons are treated unjustly, we can expect them to lash out. We can expect them to express vehemently the desire for an end to the violence that has made them a victim. In other words, we can expect them to demand justice (the word "tried" in v. 7 could be translated "brought to justice"). When we hear Psalm 109 as a victim's appeal for justice, then "what we thought was a poisonous yearning for vengeance sounds more like a just claim submitted to the real judge."[410]

3. The psalmist's submission to God of rage, hurt, and demand for justice is not only to be expected, but it is also to be accepted as a sign of health. At this point, Psalm 109 teaches a basic principle of pastoral care: Anger is the legitimate response to abuse and victimization, and appropriate anger must be expressed. Such catharsis is healing. What Psalm 109 represents, however, is not merely a therapeutic movement. Rather, this is *theological* catharsis as well. The anger is expressed, but it is expressed in prayer and thereby submitted to God. While it is not explicit, we may assume that the psalmist's submission of anger to God in prayer was sufficient (see vv. 21, 27). This angry, honest prayer thus removes the necessity for the psalmist to take actual revenge upon the enemy. It seems that the psalmist honors God's affirmation in Deut 32:35, "Vengeance is mine" (NRSV; see also Psalm 94). Thus this vehement, violent-sounding prayer is, in fact, an act of nonviolence.

4. In the final analysis, then, Psalm 109 teaches us not only about ourselves and the world but also about God. It suggests that evil, injustice, and oppression must be confronted, opposed, hated because God hates them (see Psalm 82). From this perspective, the psalmist's desire for vengeance amounts to a desire for justice and righteousness in self and society—"Your will be done." God wills not victimization of persons but compassion for persons, as the fourfold occurrence of "steadfast love" indicates (vv. 12, 16, 21, 26). The psalmist's enemies had failed to embody God's fundamental character and will—"steadfast love." Thus their actions led to death for others instead of life. The psalmist grounds this appeal for help precisely in God's steadfast love (vv. 21, 26) and his or her own oppression and neediness (v. 22; see v. 31; cf. v. 16). The psalmist affirms that God's steadfast love means judgment upon victimizers for the sake of the victims—the poor and the needy. Psalm 109 thus teaches us who God is, what

408. Walter Brueggemann, *Praying the Psalms* (Winona, Minn.: St. Mary's, 1982) 68.
409. C. S. Lewis, *Reflections on the Psalms* (New York: Harcourt, Brace and Co., 1958) 24.
410. Walter Brueggemann, "Psalm 109: Three Times 'Steadfast Love,' " *Word and World* 5 (1985) 154.

God wills and does, and what God would have us do. To be instructed by Psalm 109 is to take our stand with God, which means we shall stand with the poor and the needy as well (see v. 31).

5. To be sure, there is nothing morally inferior or unchristian about Psalm 109 as instruction. But what about Psalm 109 as a prayer? Can it be a Christian prayer? Most North American Christians have never been so completely victimized as the psalmist had been, so perhaps they will not need to pray this prayer for themselves. But can Psalm 109 then be a prayer for others? In speaking about the psalms as prayers, Mays suggests this possibility:

> Could the use of these prayers remind us and bind us to all those in the worldwide church who are suffering in faith and for the faith? All may be well in our place. There may be no trouble for the present that corresponds to the tribulations described in the psalms. But do we need to do more than call the roll of such places as El Salvador, South Africa, and Palestine to remember that there are sisters and brothers whose trials could be given voice in our recitation of the psalms? The old church believed that it was all the martyrs who prayed as they prayed the psalmic prayers.
>
> Would it be possible to say them for the sake of and in the name of the fellow Christians known to us? We do make intercessions for them, but perhaps these psalms can help us do more than to simply, prayerfully wish grace and help for them, can help us to find words to represent their hurt, alienation, failure, and discouragement. . . .
>
> The apostle said "If one member suffers, all suffer together" (1 Cor. 12:26) and he also said "Bear one another's burdens." Can these prayers become a way of doing that?[411]

Yes, they can. To pray Psalm 109 is a commitment to bear one another's burdens, to stand in solidarity and in suffering with the abused, the victimized, and the oppressed, because that is where God stands (v. 31).

6. Psalm 109 has not always been ignored by the Christian church. Not surprisingly, given the similarities between Psalm 109 and other texts that figure more prominently in the story of Jesus' passion (cf. v. 2 with Ps 31:18; v. 3 with Ps 69:4; v. 22*b* with Ps 69:26; Isa 53:5; v. 24*a* with Ps 31:10; v. 25 with Ps 22:6-7), Psalm 109 was also seen as a reflection of the suffering of Jesus, who was also victimized by accusers and their hateful, deceitful words. Evidence in this regard is Acts 1:20, which cites Ps 109:8 to describe Judas's fate. As Allen says of Psalm 109: "Behind its use in Acts 1:20 lies an understanding of the psalm, as in the case of so many psalms of innocent suffering, whereby it found its loudest echo in the experience of Jesus. From this perspective Judas became the fitting heir of its curse, as history's archetype of wanton infidelity."[412] Like Psalm 109, Jesus' life and death are testimony to the good news that God stands with the poor and the needy.

411. James L. Mays, *The Lord Reigns: A Theological Handbook to the Psalms* (Louisville: Westminster John Knox, 1994) 52-53.
412. Leslie C. Allen, *Psalms 101–150*, WBC 21 (Waco, Tex.: Word, 1983) 78.

PSALM 110:1-7, SIT AT MY RIGHT HAND

NIV	NRSV
Psalm 110	Psalm 110
Of David. A psalm.	Of David. A Psalm.
[1]The LORD says to my Lord: "Sit at my right hand	[1] The LORD says to my lord, "Sit at my right hand

NIV

until I make your enemies
a footstool for your feet."

²The LORD will extend your mighty scepter
from Zion;
you will rule in the midst of your enemies.
³Your troops will be willing
on your day of battle.
Arrayed in holy majesty,
from the womb of the dawn
you will receive the dew of your youth.ª

⁴The LORD has sworn
and will not change his mind:
"You are a priest forever,
in the order of Melchizedek."

⁵The Lord is at your right hand;
he will crush kings on the day of his wrath.
⁶He will judge the nations, heaping up the
dead
and crushing the rulers of the whole earth.
⁷He will drink from a brook beside the wayᵇ;
therefore he will lift up his head.

ª3 Or / your young men will come to you like the dew
ᵇ7 Or / The One who grants succession will set him in authority

NRSV

until I make your enemies your footstool."

² The LORD sends out from Zion
your mighty scepter.
Rule in the midst of your foes.
³ Your people will offer themselves willingly
on the day you lead your forces
on the holy mountains.ª
From the womb of the morning,
like dew, your youthᵇ will come to you.
⁴ The LORD has sworn and will not change
his mind,
"You are a priest forever according to the
order of Melchizedek."ᶜ

⁵ The Lord is at your right hand;
he will shatter kings on the day of his
wrath.
⁶ He will execute judgment among the
nations,
filling them with corpses;
he will shatter heads
over the wide earth.
⁷ He will drink from the stream by the path;
therefore he will lift up his head.

ªAnother reading is *in holy splendor*   ᵇCn: Heb *the dew of your
youth*   ᶜOr *forever, a rightful king by my edict*

COMMENTARY

Commentators generally agree that Psalm 110 is a royal psalm (see Psalms 2; 18; 20–21; 45; 72; 89; 101; 132; 144), but that is where the agreement ends. Most scholars suggest that Psalm 110 was probably used originally at the coronation of Judean kings (see vv. 1, 4; see Psalms 2; 72), but some conclude that Psalm 110 was written to be used either in preparation for a battle or to celebrate the king's victory in battle (see vv. 2-3, 5-7; see Psalms 18; 20–21; 144). Proposed dates for Psalm 110 range over a period of 800 years, from the time of David to the Maccabean era.

Obviously, those who date the psalm in the post-exilic era do not associate its original use with the actual monarchy. Rather, they suggest that the psalm was composed to express messianic hopes. Certainty on matters of date and original use is impossible. It is likely that Psalm 110 existed before the exile, but it is clear that the disappearance of the monarchy in 587 BCE would have necessitated a reinterpretation of the psalm. Indeed, its close proximity to Psalms 107–108 (see Commentary on Psalms 107; 108; Introduction) also encourages the reader to hear Psalm 110 in the light of the exile. That Psalm 110 did survive suggests that it was understood as articulating hope for the future—perhaps hope for a literal restoration of the monarchy or for continued existence of the whole people as God's chosen or anointed ones (see Ps 105:15). In any case, Psalm 110 would have been understood as an affirmation of the trust that God continues to manifest God's reign in some concrete way among God's people. Concluding that the placement of Psalm

110 probably reflects how the editors of the psalter construed it, Mays suggests that "it is a sequel to Psalm 89 and its lament over the rejected Messiah. It is a prophetic voice repeating and affirming the promises of Psalm 2 that the LORD will claim the nations through the Messiah. Until God has defeated his enemies, the Messiah is 'seated on the right hand.' "[413]

This trusting hope obviously was rather open-ended, as witnessed by the fact that the early Christians heard Psalm 110 as testimony to Jesus as Messiah (see Reflections below).

Discernment of the structure of Psalm 110 is hindered by the difficulty of understanding vv. 3, 7. As Mays says about these two verses, "For the purposes of preaching and teaching, it is best to admit that the perspicuity of Scripture is missing here."[414] Nevertheless, it is simplest to divide Psalm 110 into two sections: vv. 1-3, vv. 4-7. Each section then begins with an oracle, perhaps uttered originally by a cultic prophet ("says" occurs mostly in the prophetic books), followed by elaboration in subsequent verses. Unfortunately, the climactic verses of each section are the very ones that are so difficult to understand.

110:1-3. The repetition of "right hand" (ימין *yāmîn*) in Pss 109:31 and 110:1 may be coincidental; however, the juxtaposition is interesting. Psalm 109 concludes by affirming that God stands at the right hand of the oppressed (see also 110:5), presumably including the whole people in their time of need (see Ps 107:2-3, 39-43). Psalm 110 begins by affirming that the king—the representative of the whole people (or perhaps the whole people is now understood as a corporate anointed one in view of Ps 105:15)—is to sit at the right hand of God. In other words, the two psalms together portray a mutuality, an intimate relationship, between God and God's needy people. God offers protection from enemies (Ps 110:1-3, 5-6; see also 107:39-41; 108:12-13; 109:26-27, 31), and the people offer themselves as partners in the embodiment of God's reign in the world.

As suggested above, the oracular announcement of v. 1 may originally have played a part in the coronation of the king. The predominant theme in vv. 1-3 is God's subjugation of the

king's enemies, a theme that also plays a major role in Psalm 2 (see vv. 1-5, 8-11). The word "footstool" (הדם רגלים *hădōm roglayim*) is ordinarily used of God's footstool, probably the ark, which served symbolically as God's earthly throne (see Pss 99:5; 132:7). It is even possible that the king's coronation involved a visit to the ark, to stand symbolically at God's right hand. In any case, the allusion to God's reign is appropriate, since the earthly king (and/or people) ultimately represented God's reign in the world (see Commentary on Psalm 2). While "mighty scepter" (v. 2*a*; see Jer 48:17) bespeaks the king's royal authority, and while the king is enjoined to have dominion or to exercise royal rule (v. 2*b*; the NRSV accurately translates the Hebrew; see "dominion" in Ps 72:8 and "ruled" in Ezek 34:4 NRSV), it is actually God who initiates the action in v. 2. Although quite problematic, v. 3 also seems to promise God's provision of willing warriors.

110:4. Like v. 3, v. 4 has its share of uncertainties as well. Like v. 1, it is an oracle, but it is not clear who is speaking. While some scholars suggest that the newly crowned king now addresses the high priest, it is more likely that the addressee is still the king. That he is called a priest is surprising perhaps, but not too unusual. The king officiated at liturgical functions (see 1 Kings 8); Melchizedek (king of pre-Israelite Jerusalem) is identified in Gen 14:18 as both priest and king (if, indeed, Melchizedek here is intended to be a proper name; see the NRSV note). The priestly designation also would have presented no problem for a post-exilic understanding of the whole people as God's anointed one (see Exod 19:6). If the NRSV note is followed, the stress would again be on God's initiative. The word "rightful" (צדק *ṣedeq*) is usually translated "righteousness," and it is both a fundamental aspect of God's reign (see Pss 96:13; 97:2; 98:9; 99:4) and of what God wills for the earthly king (see Pss 45:4, 7; 72:1-2, 7).

110:5-6. Repeating "right hand" (see v. 1; Ps 109:31), v. 5 reiterates the intimate relationship between God and the king/people. The "he" in vv. 5*b*, 6*ab* is apparently God. Even more clearly than in vv. 1-2, vv. 5*b*-6 recall the holy war traditions in which God does all the fighting on behalf of the people. God deals with opponents of the divine reign, establishing justice (v. 6*a*), which in this case means judgment upon oppressors (see Pss 9:8*b*; 96:10*b*, where the same word for judgment is used). The NRSV's "shatter" oc-

413. James L. Mays, *Psalms,* Interpretation (Louisville: John Knox, 1994) 353.
414. Ibid., 352.

curs in both vv. 5 and 6. In another royal psalm, the king does the shattering of the enemies after being instructed by God (see "struck down" in Ps 18:38a NRSV), but in Ps 110:5-6 the initiative even more exclusively belongs to God. The brutal imagery reflects the standard ancient Near Eastern practice of warfare, or at least of describing literarily one's preeminence in battle (see 2 Kgs 8:12; Ps 137:9; Hos 10:14; Nah 3:30).

110:7. The "he" that begins v. 7 apparently should be understood as the king. The significance of the action involved is not clear. It may indicate that the battle is over and that the king can pause and drink now that the victory is won (see the image of lifting up the head in Pss 3:3; 27:6). Or there may be some ritual significance behind v. 7, perhaps related to coronation. (See 1 Kgs 1:38-40, where Solomon's anointing takes place beside a stream, although it is not clear that the stream itself played any part in the ritual.)

REFLECTIONS

1. It is likely that Psalm 110 was already understood messianically when it found its place in the psalter—that is, it was viewed as an expression of the trust that God would manifest God's sovereign claim upon the world. Because the actual monarchy had disappeared, the messiah's role as an agent of God's sovereignty was not clear. To state the matter more positively, the hope was open-ended, and different groups within Judaism drew different conclusions. By the first century CE, for instance, Josephus could claim the Roman Emperor Vespasian as the fulfillment of Jewish messianic hopes. Many other Jews drew almost precisely the opposite conclusion; the messiah would arise to throw off Roman oppression. Still others were convinced that God's sovereign claim upon the world had been truly proclaimed and embodied by Jesus of Nazareth, whom they hailed as Jesus Messiah or, in its Greek equivalent, Jesus Christ.

Not surprisingly, Psalm 110 entered the first-century CE debate concerning the identity of the Messiah (see Matt 22:42-45; Mark 12:35-37; Luke 20:41-44). For Christians, the matter was settled, and they thus claimed Psalm 110 as testimony to Jesus' messiahship. In fact, Psalm 110 is the most frequently used psalm in the New Testament. It was used by the first-century Christians to affirm their faith that the life, death, and resurrection of Jesus were and are the ultimate demonstration of the concrete manifestation of God's sovereignty in the world. Thus it is Jesus to whom God must finally have addressed the words "sit at my right hand" (see Matt 26:64; Mark 14:62; Luke 22:69; Acts 2:34-35; 7:55-56; Rom 8:34; Eph 1:20; Col 3:1; Heb 1:3, 13; 8:1; 10:12; 1 Pet 3:22). Christians continue to make this affirmation every time they recite the Apostles' Creed: "I believe . . . in Jesus Christ, who . . . sitteth on the right hand of God."

2. What slips so easily off our tongues without a thought is actually a profoundly radical affirmation. The Christian appropriation of Psalm 110 "holds the enthronement of Jesus in relation to the question of political power in the world."[415] Jesus threatened then and threatens now politics as usual. After all, he was not crucified for spouting innocuous religious niceties. Rather, Jesus subverted both the power of Roman legions and the authority of Jewish tradition when he announced the simple good news that God rules the world (see Mark 1:14-15). This radical good news allowed tax collectors, sinners, lepers, prostitutes, children, women, and men to sit down and eat at the same table in the realm of God. Thus Psalm 110 is no mere artifact of ancient political propaganda. Rather, in relation to Jesus Messiah, it is a world-transforming challenge to every form of politics and power that does not begin with submission of the self to God's claim. Jesus, messiah and priest (see Heb 5:6; 7:17, 21), guarantees all people access to God. Those who would deny such grace and its claims set themselves up as enemies of the reign of God; the exalted will be humbled. Persons who accept such grace and submit to its claims open themselves to abundant life; the humble will be exalted (see Psalms 113; 115).

415. Ibid., 354.

PSALM 111:1-10, GREAT ARE THE WORKS OF THE LORD

PSALM 111:1-10

NIV

Psalm 111[a]

[1]Praise the LORD.[b]

I will extol the LORD with all my heart
in the council of the upright and in the
assembly.

[2]Great are the works of the LORD;
they are pondered by all who delight in
them.

[3]Glorious and majestic are his deeds,
and his righteousness endures forever.

[4]He has caused his wonders to be remembered;
the LORD is gracious and compassionate.

[5]He provides food for those who fear him;
he remembers his covenant forever.

[6]He has shown his people the power of his
works,
giving them the lands of other nations.

[7]The works of his hands are faithful and just;
all his precepts are trustworthy.

[8]They are steadfast for ever and ever,
done in faithfulness and uprightness.

[9]He provided redemption for his people;
he ordained his covenant forever—
holy and awesome is his name.

[10]The fear of the LORD is the beginning of
wisdom;
all who follow his precepts have good
understanding.
To him belongs eternal praise.

[a]This psalm is an acrostic poem, the lines of which begin with the successive letters of the Hebrew alphabet.   [b]1 Hebrew Hallelu Yah

NRSV

Psalm 111

[1] Praise the LORD!
I will give thanks to the LORD with my
whole heart,
in the company of the upright, in the
congregation.

[2] Great are the works of the LORD,
studied by all who delight in them.

[3] Full of honor and majesty is his work,
and his righteousness endures forever.

[4] He has gained renown by his wonderful
deeds;
the LORD is gracious and merciful.

[5] He provides food for those who fear him;
he is ever mindful of his covenant.

[6] He has shown his people the power of his
works,
in giving them the heritage of the nations.

[7] The works of his hands are faithful and just;
all his precepts are trustworthy.

[8] They are established forever and ever,
to be performed with faithfulness and
uprightness.

[9] He sent redemption to his people;
he has commanded his covenant forever.
Holy and awesome is his name.

[10] The fear of the LORD is the beginning of
wisdom;
all those who practice it[a] have a good
understanding.
His praise endures forever.

[a]Gk Syr: Heb them

COMMENTARY

Psalms 111 and 112 belong together. Each is an acrostic; that is, each poetic line (each half-verse in English) begins with a successive letter of the Hebrew alphabet. In form, Psalm 111 can be categorized as a song of praise. An invitation to praise (v. 1a) and a statement of intention (v.

1bc) are followed by reasons for praise, the theme of which is stated in vv. 2-3—God's work (see "works" [מעשׂים ma'ăśîm] in vv. 2, 6-7; the same root occurs as "gained" in v. 4 NRSV, and a synonym occurs as "work" in v. 3 NRSV), which bespeaks God's sovereignty (see below on v. 3).

God's saving work from exodus to entry into the land is reviewed in vv. 4-6, and God's work of instructing the people and establishing the covenant is covered in vv. 7-10. The key word used four times of God's work (vv. 2, 4, 6, 7) is used twice more in vv. 8, 10 to describe the people's response ("performed" and "practice"). Performing God's precepts is summed up in the phrase "fear of the LORD" (v. 10), which then becomes the point of departure for Psalm 112. Whereas Psalm 111 focuses primarily on God's work, Psalm 112 focuses on human response and consists of a description of the happiness of those who fear the Lord. What is remarkable is that the same thing is said of both God and those who fear God: Their "righteousness endures forever" (Pss 111:3; 112:3, 9). In other ways, too, the character and life of those who fear God conform to God's own character and life (cf. 112:2*b* with 111:1*c*; 112:4*b* with 111:4*b*; 112:5*b* with 111:7*a*; 112:6*b* with 111:4*a*; 112:7*b* with 111:1*a*; 112:9*a* with 111:5*a*). Indeed, in the most profound sense, this is the reward of fearing God (see Commentary on Psalm 1).

The individual voice in Psalm 111 joins the ones in Pss 108:3 and 109:30 in giving thanks to God (v. 1*b*), as Psalm 107 had enjoined (see 107:1, 8, 15, 21, 31). If the opening psalms in Book V are read sequentially, the effect of Psalms 111–112 is to put the return from exile (Psalms 107–108) in line with all God's saving work on behalf of the oppressed (Psalm 109) and in particular with the classical historical sequence of exodus through entry into the land (Psalms 111–112). Psalm 113 initiates a series of psalms that again celebrate God's saving work in general (Psalms 113; 115; 116; 117) and the exodus in particular (Psalms 114; 118). Perhaps not coincidentally, the culminating Psalm 118 recalls Psalm 107 (cf. Pss 118:1, 29 with 107:1), and it has the effect of putting even anticipated future deliverances in sequence with the exodus (see Commentary on Psalm 118). Also not coincidental, perhaps, is the fact that the vocabulary of Psalms 111–112 anticipates Psalm 119 as well.

111:1. The psalmist offers thanks with the "whole heart" (v. 1*b*; see Ps 86:11-12, where the phrase also occurs in the context of fearing God; see also Pss 9:1; 119:2, 10; 138:1). Praise involves the whole person, and it is the essence of true

security (see Ps 112:7-8). Praise is intensely personal but not private; it is offered in the gathered congregation of God's people (v. 1*c*). The word "congregation" (עדה *'ēdâ*) recalls Ps 1:5 and is the first of several verbal and conceptual links between Psalms 111–112 and Psalms 1–2. The "upright" (ישרים *yěšārîm*; see v. 8; Pss 112:2, 4) are the same as the "righteous" (צדיקים *ṣaddîqîm*) in Ps 1:5-6 (see Ps 112:6).

111:2-3. The next link, in fact, occurs in v. 2: "delight" (see Pss 1:2; 112:1; 119:35). Those who delight in God's works, which include God's instruction (see 111:7), study them (see "seek"/"sought" in Ps 119:2, 10, 45). Verses 2-3 bespeak God's sovereignty. Greatness is an attribute of a monarch (see Pss 47:2; 48:1; 95:3), as are "honor and majesty" (see Ps 96:6), and "righteousness" describes the royal policy God wills and enacts (see Pss 96:13; 97:2; 98:9; 99:4). It was the prerogative and responsibility of a sovereign to follow up acts of deliverance with measures to enact justice and righteousness among his or her subjects. God's "works" include both of these spheres—deliverance (vv. 4-6) and establishment of the conditions for justice (vv. 7-10).

111:4-6. While the word "wonderful deeds" (נפלאות *niplā'ôt*) in v. 4*a* does not refer exclusively to the exodus, it often describes the exodus (see Exod 3:20; 15:11; Ps 77:11, 14). The word that the NIV translates "to be remembered" (זכר *zēker*) also recalls the climactic plague (see Exod 12:14; see also Ps 112:6*b*), and the words "gracious and merciful" (חנון ורחום *ḥannûn wěraḥûm*, v. 4*b*) are reminiscent of Exod 34:6, God's self-revelation to Moses following the golden calf episode (see also Ps 112:4*b*). Verse 5*a* maintains the focus on the wilderness (see Exodus 16; Numbers 11), and v. 5*b* recalls Exod 2:24 as well as Exod 34:10, 27. The word "power" (כח *kōaḥ*) in v. 6*a* recalls Exod 9:16; 15:6; as v. 6*b* suggests, the ultimate result of the exodus was the possession of the land. Verse 6*b* also recalls Ps 2:8. It is revealing, perhaps, that the promise made to the king in Ps 2:8 is now articulated in terms of the whole people (see Commentary on Psalms 105, esp. v. 15; 110).

111:7-10. Verse 7*a* could actually serve as a climactic summary of vv. 4-6 or as an introduction to vv. 7*b*-10. Perhaps it is intentionally transitional, linking conceptually God's saving works (see v. 6) and God's works that take the form of instruction (see v. 2, where both meanings seem to be present). The word "justice" (משפט *mišpāṭ*; NIV and NRSV, "just") also points backward and forward. Along with righteousness (v. 3), it is a fundamental aspect of God's sovereignty (see Pss 96:13; 97:2; 98:9; 99:4). God's saving work establishes justice for the oppressed (see vv. 4-6), and God's "precepts" (פקודים *piqqûdîm*) are intended to enable God's people to maintain justice. The word "precepts" is not used frequently in the psalter (see elsewhere only Pss 19:8; 103:18 NIV; 119); it is synonymous with God's instruction.

The words "faithful" (אמת *ʾĕmet*) and "trustworthy" (נאמנים *neʾĕmānîm*) in v. 7 are from the same Hebrew root. God relates faithfully to God's people (see Exod 34:6), and God expects faithfulness in return (v. 8b)—both God's work of redemption (v. 9; see Deut 7:8; 13:5; Pss 25:22; 78:42) and the people's work of obedience (see "performed" in v. 8 and "practice" in v. 10) are integral to the covenant that God intends. In addition to the repetition of "works"/"performed"/"practice" (vv. 2, 6-8, 10) and "faithful(ness)" (vv. 7-8), the repetition represented by "awesome" (נורא *nôrāʾ*, v. 9) and "fear" (יראה *yirʾâ*, v. 10) stresses the mutuality of the covenant. God's awesomeness derives from God's sovereignty (see Exod 15:11; Pss 47:2; 76:7; 96:4; 99:3; note also the pairing with holiness in Ps 99:3 as in 111:9). Here, as elsewhere, God's awesomeness and holiness are not intended to keep people at a distance (see Commentary on Psalm 99). Rather, God's awesomeness calls forth the people's "fear of the LORD" (see Pss 2:11; 25:12, 14; 34:9)—their recognition of God's reign issues in praise (v. 10c; see v. 1a) and obedience (see the NRSV note for v. 10, where "them," i.e., "precepts," is the object of "practice"). Precisely such yielding of the self to God's claim constitutes wisdom and understanding (see Deut 4:5-6; Job 28:28; Prov 1:7; 9:10). It also constitutes true happiness, according to Psalm 112, which takes 111:10 as its point of departure.

REFLECTIONS

1. Psalm 111 begins and ends with praise. The only action involving the psalmist is the expression of intent to give public thanks to God with the whole being (v. 1). This complete dedication of the self to God, of course, is the essence of praise. As such, it inevitably involves obedience. This posture toward God—praise, gratitude, obedience—is captured by the phrase "fear of the LORD." It is the fundamental human "work"—not a "work" in the sense of a meritorious accomplishment but in the sense of human vocation or calling in response to God's grace. While "fear of the LORD" clearly involves performance and practice (vv. 8, 10), the structure and movement of Psalm 111 make it clear that human works (vv. 8, 10) are evoked by God's works (vv. 4-6). In terms of the history of Israel, exodus precedes Sinai. In short, grace is prior. Salvation is a gift to which God's people make grateful response with their whole hearts. Praise, therefore, is both liturgy (v. 1) and life-style (vv. 8, 10).

2. Indeed, praise is the foundation of the psalmist's epistemology—true knowledge begins with grateful praise and obedience! The psalmist's closing affirmation is a radical challenge to our ways of knowing and our definitions of knowledge. From the scientific point of view, for instance, the acquisition of knowledge requires the shedding of all values and commitments in order to try to become completely objective. Reaction to scientism leads in precisely the opposite direction—to the claim that knowledge does not exist apart from subjective human experience. The psalmist's affirmation contradicts both of these perspectives. True knowledge—wisdom—is not grounded in ourselves but in God, and it involves the embrace of God's commitments and values. Thus wisdom will take concrete shape in righteousness, grace, and mercy (see vv. 3-4), and those who fear the Lord (Ps 112:1), therefore, will be "gracious, merciful, and righteous" (Ps 112:4; see Commentary on Psalm 112). For Christians, the One who perfectly embodied God's character and values also is professed as "the wisdom of God" (1 Cor 1:24 NRSV).

PSALM 112:1-10, HAPPY ARE THOSE WHO FEAR THE LORD

NIV

Psalm 112[a]

[1]Praise the LORD.[b]

Blessed is the man who fears the LORD,
who finds great delight in his commands.

[2]His children will be mighty in the land;
the generation of the upright will be
blessed.

[3]Wealth and riches are in his house,
and his righteousness endures forever.

[4]Even in darkness light dawns for the upright,
for the gracious and compassionate and
righteous man.[c]

[5]Good will come to him who is generous and
lends freely,
who conducts his affairs with justice.

[6]Surely he will never be shaken;
a righteous man will be remembered
forever.

[7]He will have no fear of bad news;
his heart is steadfast, trusting in the LORD.

[8]His heart is secure, he will have no fear;
in the end he will look in triumph on his
foes.

[9]He has scattered abroad his gifts to the poor,
his righteousness endures forever;
his horn[d] will be lifted high in honor.

[10]The wicked man will see and be vexed,
he will gnash his teeth and waste away;
the longings of the wicked will come to
nothing.

aThis psalm is an acrostic poem, the lines of which begin with the
successive letters of the Hebrew alphabet.   b1 Hebrew Hallelu Yah
c4 Or / ,for the LORD, is gracious and compassionate and righteous
d9 Horn here symbolizes dignity.

NRSV

Psalm 112

[1] Praise the LORD!
Happy are those who fear the LORD,
who greatly delight in his commandments.

[2] Their descendants will be mighty in the
land;
the generation of the upright will be
blessed.

[3] Wealth and riches are in their houses,
and their righteousness endures forever.

[4] They rise in the darkness as a light for the
upright;
they are gracious, merciful, and righteous.

[5] It is well with those who deal generously
and lend,
who conduct their affairs with justice.

[6] For the righteous will never be moved;
they will be remembered forever.

[7] They are not afraid of evil tidings;
their hearts are firm, secure in the LORD.

[8] Their hearts are steady, they will not be
afraid;
in the end they will look in triumph on
their foes.

[9] They have distributed freely, they have
given to the poor;
their righteousness endures forever;
their horn is exalted in honor.

[10] The wicked see it and are angry;
they gnash their teeth and melt away;
the desire of the wicked comes
to nothing.

COMMENTARY

Psalm 112 clearly belongs with Psalm 111. Both psalms begin with the same phrase, and both are acrostic poems. Furthermore, Psalm 112 offers a more developed description of those who fear

the Lord (see Pss 111:10; 112:1). The remarkable thing is that the same is said of both God and those who fear God: Their "righteousness endures forever" (Pss 111:3; 112:3, 9; see Commentary on Psalm 111 for other verbal links between Psalms 111 and 112).

As suggested above, Psalms 111–112 recall Psalms 1–2. For instance, if its opening invitation is viewed as a sort of superscription (see Pss 111:1; 113:1), Psalm 112 begins and ends with exactly the same words that open and close Psalm 1: "happy" and "perish" ("come[s] to nothing," 112:10). In addition, Psalms 1 and 112 feature the same characters—"the righteous" (1:5; 112:6) and "the wicked" (1:1, 5-6; 112:10). Indeed, Psalms 111–112 are a sort of mirror image of Psalms 1–2. Whereas Psalm 1 portrays the life of the righteous and Psalm 2 grounds it in the sovereignty of God (see esp. Ps 2:12), Psalms 111–112 reverse the pattern. Psalm 111 asserts the sovereignty of God as the foundation for the life of the righteous. It is as if Psalms 111–112 serve as reinforcement for Psalms 1–2 after the prosperity of the wicked—including the crucial reality of exile and its aftermath—has been clearly confronted and articulated in the preceding psalms (note the preponderance of complaints in Books I–III, and see esp. Psalms 42–43; 73; 74; 89–90; 105–108; see also Introduction).

Discussion of the structure of Psalm 112 usually focuses on its acrostic pattern; most translations, including the NIV and the NRSV, give no indication of structural divisions. This may be the best policy, but several scholars suggest that the identical vv. 3b, 9b, as well as the similar v. 6, divide Psalm 112 into three equal sections, each of which focuses on the life of the righteous and its outcome. Verse 10 shifts the focus to the life of the wicked and its outcome as the psalm concludes.

112:1-3. As in Ps 1:1-2, happiness in Ps 112:1 is associated with "delight." In Ps 1:1-2, it was delight in God's "instruction" (or "law"); here it is delight in God's commandments. In both cases, therefore, happiness has to do not with self-fulfillment but with the orientation of life to God's purposes. Fear is essentially the recognition of God's sovereignty that leads to the entrusting of life and future to God (see "fear" in Ps 2:11 and "happy" in Ps 2:12). Despite what vv. 2-3 seem to suggest, such happiness does not consist essentially of material reward or of a life free of trouble and opposition (see Ps 49:6; Prov 3:16; 8:18; 13:7). Rather, such happiness consists of being

right with God, a condition that neither "bad news" (v. 7a) nor opposition (v. 8b) can ever dislodge (vv. 3b, 6a, 9b). In short, trusting God (see v. 7b) is true might (v. 2; see Ps 37:11; Matt 5:5) and true wealth (v. 3; see Ps 49:5-7). Happiness is not a reward that is earned but is the experience of being connected to God (see Commentary on Psalms 1; 2).

112:4-6. Those who fear God, who trust God and whose lives are oriented to God's purposes, become like God. Like God, they are sources of light for others (v. 4a; see Pss 27:1; 36:9). Their character embodies God's character (v. 4b; see Ps 111:4b), including gracious provision for others (v. 5a; the NRSV's "deal generously" is the same Hebrew root as "gracious" [חנון ḥannûn] in v. 4b; see Pss 37:26; 111:5a) and the establishment of justice (v. 5b; see Ps 111:7a). Fearing God means entrusting life to God and embodying God's values and purposes, and it provides a stability that is both effective in the present (v. 6a; see Pss 15:5; 16:8; see Commentary on Psalm 1) and enduring forever (v. 6b; see Ps 111:4a).

112:7-10. Verses 7-8 make it clear that the happiness of the righteous is no facile, carefree existence. The righteous are not immune from bad news and opposition. Rather, because they fear God, they need not fear evil (see Ps 23:4; "evil" in Ps 23:4 and "bad news" [שמועה רעה rā'â šĕmû'â] in Ps 112:7a NIV have the same Hebrew root). The imagery of stability that is present in v. 6 continues in vv. 7-8 (see Commentary on Psalm 1). The repeated "heart(s)" [לב lēb] in vv. 7-8 recalls Ps 111:1. The grateful, faithful heart is the secure heart. Faith triumphs over fear and foe (v. 8; see Pss 54:7b; 59:10; 118:7). Those who humble themselves (v. 9a) will be exalted (v. 9c; see Pss 75:10; 92:10).

Verse 8b suggests that the perspective of Psalms 111–112, like that of Psalms 1–2, is eschatological. That is to say, the reign of God and the consequent security of the righteous are asserted in the midst of ongoing opposition. Thus the disagreement between translation of the verb tenses in vv. 9c-10 is appropriate. As the NRSV suggests, the exaltation of the righteous and the demise of the wicked are *already* a reality, but as the NIV suggests, this reality is a process that is not yet complete. The reign of God is always both now and yet to come. The purposes of the wicked will not endure (see Pss 1:5; 37:12-13); their desires will ultimately perish (see Pss 1:6; 10:3). Thus those who know this and who align them-selves with God's purposes—in short, those who fear God—are truly wise (Ps 111:10) and genu-inely happy (Ps 112:1).

REFLECTIONS

In a secular culture, where wisdom is divorced from faithfulness and where happiness is often viewed superficially as material prosperity and ease, it is crucial to hear Psalms 111–112. They are a vivid reminder that faithfulness to God and to God's purposes is not a guarantee of success and security as the world defines these concepts. Happiness and security are derived not by conformity to the standards of the world but by transforming ourselves to be like God. In a similar world-negating stance, Jesus pronounced happy those whom the world would consider unfortunate and most likely to be unhappy (see Matt 5:3-11). This teaching, of course, appears in the context of Jesus' proclamation of the reign of God (see Matt 4:17; 5:3, 10, 20; 6:33). Jesus, too, was an eschatological preacher, announcing the reign of God amid persistent opposition and demonstrating God's sovereignty most clearly on a cross (see Commentary on Psalms 1; 2).

Such a stance is indeed countercultural, a witness to the transforming power of God. This perspective accounts for the psalmist's remarkable attribution to the righteous of God's own characteristics (see esp. Ps 112:3b, 4, 5b, 6b, 9b). As Mays says of Psalm 112, "Its composer believes so profoundly that the works of God take shape in the life of the righteous that for the psalmist the commendation of the latter becomes also the praise of God.[416] This perspective recalls not only Jesus' beatitudes but also the apostle Paul's admonition to his readers to "join in imitating me" (Phil 3:17 NRSV). This admonition is not the arrogant self-assertion of an egomaniac but the bold challenge of one who was convinced that "it is no longer I who live, but it is Christ who lives in me" (Gal 2:20 NRSV). In short, like the psalmist, Paul was convinced that by the transforming mercy of God (see Rom 12:1-2), the works of God take shape in the life of the righteous. For Paul, this is no cause for boasting, except insofar as one boasts in God (see 1 Cor 1:31). The transformed lives of the righteous become the praise of God.

416. James L. Mays, *Psalms*, Interpretation (Louisville: John Knox, 1994) 361.

PSALM 113:1-9, WHO IS LIKE THE LORD OUR GOD?

NIV	NRSV
Psalm 113	**Psalm 113**
¹Praise the LORD.ᵃ	¹ Praise the LORD!
Praise, O servants of the LORD, praise the name of the LORD.	Praise, O servants of the LORD; praise the name of the LORD.
²Let the name of the LORD be praised, both now and forevermore.	² Blessed be the name of the LORD from this time on and forevermore.
³From the rising of the sun to the place where it sets,	³ From the rising of the sun to its setting the name of the LORD is to be praised.
ᵃ1 Hebrew *Hallelu Yah*; also in verse 9	⁴ The LORD is high above all nations,

NIV

the name of the LORD is to be praised.

4The LORD is exalted over all the nations,
    his glory above the heavens.
5Who is like the LORD our God,
    the One who sits enthroned on high,
6who stoops down to look
    on the heavens and the earth?

7He raises the poor from the dust
    and lifts the needy from the ash heap;
8he seats them with princes,
    with the princes of their people.
9He settles the barren woman in her home
    as a happy mother of children.

Praise the LORD.

NRSV

and his glory above the heavens.

5 Who is like the LORD our God,
    who is seated on high,
6 who looks far down
    on the heavens and the earth?
7 He raises the poor from the dust,
    and lifts the needy from the ash heap,
8 to make them sit with princes,
    with the princes of his people.
9 He gives the barren woman a home,
    making her the joyous mother of children.
Praise the LORD!

COMMENTARY

Psalm 113 is a song of praise that Jews and Christians have given "a special place in their repertoire of praise."[417] For Jews, it begins the Egyptian *Hallel* (Psalms 113–118; *Hallel* means "praise," as in the phrase, *Hallelu-yah,* "Praise the LORD!"), a collection used at all major festivals but especially at the beginning and conclusion of the Passover. For Christians, Psalm 113 is used for the celebration of Easter. While the association of Psalm 113 with Psalms 114–118 is traditional (see *Hallelu-yah* in Pss 113:1, 9; 115:18; 116:19; 117:2), it is often overlooked that the phrase *Hallelu-yah* also links Psalm 113 to Psalms 111–112 (see 111:1; 112:1). To be sure, Psalm 113 is an appropriate introduction to Psalms 114–118 and their theme of deliverance, especially exodus (see Psalms 114; 118). But it is also an appropriate culmination to Psalms 111–112. Like Psalm 111, it articulates God's sovereignty (see below on vv. 1-4; see also 111:2-6, esp. v. 4, which recalls the exodus), and it offers an especially appropriate response to the exclamation of 111:9*c* (see "name" in 111:9*c*; 113:1-3). Furthermore, like Psalms 111–112, Psalm 113 asserts that God's power is manifested in gracious, compassionate provision for the poor (see Pss 111:4-5*a*; 112:9*a*; 113:7-9; the words "poor" in 112:9*a* and "needy"

417. Peter Craigie, "Psalm 113," *Int.* 39 (1985) 70.

in 113:7*b* represent the same Hebrew word [אביון *'ebyôn*]). This theme also ties Psalm 113 to Psalm 107, which begins Book V (see esp. 107:39-42). Thus Psalm 113, as well as the *Hallel* collection it initiates, also would have served as an appropriate response to the crisis of exile and its aftermath (see Commentary on Psalm 107, esp. vv. 2-3; Introduction). As such, it is also testimony to God's enduring character and typical activity (see Psalms 107; 118; and Reflections below).

While it is clear that Psalm 113 was (and is) used liturgically, its origin and original setting are uncertain. Psalm 113 shows striking similarities with the Song of Hannah in 1 Sam 2:1-11 (cf. esp. Ps 113:5 with 1 Sam 2:2; Ps 113:9 with 1 Sam 2:5*b*; Ps 113:7-8 with 1 Sam 2:7-8); however, the similarities do not allow a certain dating of the psalm. Scholars disagree also on how to describe the structure and movement of Psalm 113. As the NIV suggests, it is possible to divide the psalm into three sections (apart from the opening and closing *Hallelu-yah*): (1) vv. 1-3, which function as a call to praise and are bound together by the repetition of "praise" (vv. 1, 3) and "name"; (2) vv. 4-6, which focus on God's identity as reason for praise; and (3) vv. 7-9, which focus on God's activity as reason for praise. On the other hand, as the NRSV suggests, it is possible to conclude that the question in v. 5

begins a new section, in which case the psalm consists of vv. 1-4 and vv. 5-9. It is possible that the structure moves at more than one level. For instance, it is possible that v. 5, the center line of the poem, serves as a sort of pivot. Each of vv. 1-5*a* contains the divine name "Yahweh" ("LORD"), culminating in the question of God's identity in v. 5*a*. Beginning with v. 5*b*, the rest of the psalm is intended to answer the central question. After v. 5*a*, there are no further occurrences of the divine name (except the final *Hallelu-yah*). Instead, God's identity is described in terms of God's activity. Verses 5*b*-9 are bound grammatically by the fact that each of the six verbal forms is *hiphil,* a causative form of the verb. A more literal translation captures the effect: God "makes God's self high in order to sit" (v. 5*b*), "makes God's self low in order to see" (v. 6*a*), "causes the poor to arise" (v. 7*a*), "makes exalted the needy . . . to cause them to sit with princes" (vv. 7*b*-8*a*), "makes a home" (v. 9*a*). In short, God is active. God's character is known, and God is to be praised (vv. 1-5*a*), because God makes particular things happen (vv. 5*b*-9).

113:1-4. Beginning with the designation "servants" (v. 1), vv. 1-3 bespeak God's sovereignty. "Servants" are persons who are subject to a sovereign master (see "serve" in Pss 2:11; "worship" in 100:2), and the appropriate response of servants is to submit their whole selves—that is, to praise (see vv. 1, 3*b*) or to bless (v. 2*a*; see Pss 96:2; 100:4; 145:1, 21). The occurrence of "name" in each of vv. 1-3 suggests not only the mode of God's presence but also the issue of God's character. Verse 4 reinforces the conclusion that God is to be praised because of God's sovereign character. God is "exalted" or "high above

all nations"—that is, sovereign on earth (v. 4*a*; see "exalt" in the context of the proclamation of God's reign in Pss 99:5, 9; 145:1 NIV). And God's "glory," a word elsewhere explicitly associated with God's reign (see Pss 29:1-3, 9; 96:3, 7-8; 97:6), is also "above the heavens" (v. 4*b*).

113:5-9. After the central question of v. 5*a,* which also explicitly raises the issue of God's character (see Exod 15:11; Pss 35:10; 86:8; Mic 7:18), vv. 5*b*-9 make it clear that God's sovereignty—God's "aboveness" or "highness" (v. 4)—is manifest in a very particular way. To be sure, God's enthronement is real (v. 5*b*; see also Ps 2:4), but God "makes God's self low to look upon the heavens and the earth" (v. 6 author's trans.). Note that the same two spheres of God's sovereignty are present in v. 6 as in v. 4—earth and the heavens—but God exercises God's sovereignty from below! The immediate consequence is that God "raises the poor" and "lifts the needy" (v. 7). The occurrence of the same Hebrew root in vv. 4 and 7 is particularly revealing (see "exalted" in v. 4*a* and "lifts" in v. 7*b* NIV); the exalted one has chosen to be humbled, and the humbled are thus exalted.

Another crucial dimension of God's activity is indicated by the repetition of the Hebrew root (יָשַׁב *yāšab*) that the NIV translates "sits enthroned" in v. 5*b*, "seats" in v. 8*a*, and "settles" in v. 9*a*. God gives a home to the homeless. Again, the exalted God is involved in the activity of exalting the humbled. Because Israel's God exercises sovereignty from below in order to exalt the poor and the needy (vv. 6-9), Israel's God is like no other (see v. 5*a*; see Commentary on Psalm 82). Therefore, this God deserves enduring and unlimited praise (vv. 1-3).

REFLECTIONS

1. Psalm 113 is testimony to who God is, revealed by what God does. Not surprisingly, therefore, Psalm 113 is similar to other biblical psalms, especially the Song of Hannah in 1 Sam 2:1-11 and Mary's song, the Magnificat, in Luke 1:46-55. Like Psalm 113, both of these songs celebrate God's exaltation of those who are humbled (see 1 Sam 2:4-5, 7-8; Luke 1:48, 51-53). The apostle Paul also detected God at work in the same way in Jesus Christ (see Phil 2:5-11) and in the formation of the church (see 1 Cor 1:26-29). The Gospels suggest that Jesus and the disciples would have sung Psalm 113 at their last supper (see Mark 14:26), and Jesus' teaching affirms the pattern evident in Psalm 113: The humble will be exalted (see Luke 18:14).

2. Especially when heard in sequence with Psalm 112, which suggests that human character and activity are to conform to God's character and activity, Psalm 113 is an invitation to the people of God to join God at God's work in the world on behalf of the poor and the needy. At the same time, however, Psalm 113 is a warning against the persistent temptation to leave God out of the picture. As Hauerwas and Willimon put it: "Most of our social activism is formed on the presumption that God is superfluous to the formation of a world of peace with justice. Fortunately, we are powerful people who, because we live in a democracy, are free to use our power. It is all up to us."[418]

The nature and subtlety of this temptation is portrayed movingly by Flannery O'Connor in her story "The Lame Shall Enter First." In the story, Sheppard, a well-intentioned City Recreation Director, goes to great lengths to assist a lame juvenile delinquent, Johnson. Sheppard takes the boy into his home, gets corrective shoes for him, attempts to give him every possible advantage. In a conversation with Johnson, Sheppard's son Norton says of his father:

> "He's good," he mumbled. "He helps people."
> "Good!" Johnson said savagely. He thrust his head forward. "Listen here," he hissed. "I don't care if he's good or not. He ain't *right*!"

What Johnson means becomes clear as the story unfolds. When Johnson refuses to cooperate easily with Sheppard's helpfulness, Sheppard initiates the following exchange:

> "I'm stronger than you are. I'm stronger than you are and I'm going to save you. The good will triumph."
> "Not when it ain't true," the boy said, "Not when it ain't right."
> "My resolve isn't shaken," Sheppard replied. "I'm going to save you. . . ."
> Johnson thrust his head forward. "Save yourself," he hissed. "Nobody can save me but Jesus."

Johnson finally sums up Sheppard's motivation with the conclusion: "He thinks he's God."[419] Thus he illuminates the temptation to which Sheppard has yielded. For Sheppard, God is superfluous. In his view, it was all up to him. His actions, well-intentioned as they are, are fundamentally selfish. He may be good, but he is not right.

As a powerful testimony to the sovereignty and transcendence of God (vv. 4-5), Psalm 113 is also a powerful warning against the temptation to conclude, "It is all up to us." Psalm 113 affirms that God's character is known in God's activity; God makes things happen. To be sure, God's people may, indeed must, join God at God's work in the world. But as Hauerwas and Willimon point out, "The moment that life is formed on the presumption that we are not participants in *God's* continuing history of creation and redemption, we are acting on unbelief rather than faith."[420] In the final analysis, Psalm 113 encourages faith—submission to God's reign that is manifest in praise and participation in God's continuing story of creation and redemption.

418. Stanley Hauerwas and William H. Willimon, *Resident Aliens: Life in the Christian Colony* (Nashville: Abingdon, 1989) 36.
419. Flannery O'Connor, *The Complete Stories* (New York: Farrar, Straus, and Giroux, 1971) 454, 474, 480.
420. Hauerwas and Willimon, *Resident Aliens,* 36-37, italics added.

PSALM 114:1-8, TREMBLE, O EARTH, AT THE PRESENCE OF THE LORD

NIV	NRSV
Psalm 114	Psalm 114
¹When Israel came out of Egypt,	¹ When Israel went out from Egypt,

NIV

the house of Jacob from a people of
    foreign tongue,
²Judah became God's sanctuary,
    Israel his dominion.

³The sea looked and fled,
    the Jordan turned back;
⁴the mountains skipped like rams,
    the hills like lambs.

⁵Why was it, O sea, that you fled,
    O Jordan, that you turned back,
⁶you mountains, that you skipped like rams,
    you hills, like lambs?

⁷Tremble, O earth, at the presence of the Lord,
    at the presence of the God of Jacob,
⁸who turned the rock into a pool,
    the hard rock into springs of water.

NRSV

the house of Jacob from a people of
    strange language,
² Judah became God'sᵃ sanctuary,
    Israel his dominion.

³ The sea looked and fled;
    Jordan turned back.
⁴ The mountains skipped like rams,
    the hills like lambs.

⁵ Why is it, O sea, that you flee?
    O Jordan, that you turn back?
⁶ O mountains, that you skip like rams?
    O hills, like lambs?

⁷ Tremble, O earth, at the presence of the
    LORD,
    at the presence of the God of Jacob,
⁸ who turns the rock into a pool of water,
    the flint into a spring of water.

ᵃ Heb *his*

COMMENTARY

While Psalm 114 is usually categorized as a song of praise, it is a distinctive one. There is no invitation to praise, except perhaps v. 7, which is addressed not to persons but to the earth. Most of the psalm could be considered an elaboration of reasons for praise, but they are not simply listed in the usual manner following an invitation to praise. Rather, Psalm 114 consists of a series of poetic allusions to the basic elements of Israel's story: exodus (vv. 1, 3*a,* 5*a*), God's provision in the wilderness (v. 8), the crossing of the Jordan to enter the promised land (vv. 3*b,* 5*b*), and the choice of the people and their establishment in the land (v. 2).

The exuberant tone of Psalm 114 suggests liturgical use; we know that Psalms 113–118 were eventually used at the major festivals, including Passover, for which the allusions to the exodus make Psalm 114 particularly fitting (see Commentary on Psalm 113). When Psalm 114 originated, and how and where it may have been used originally, we do not know. In its present literary setting, it serves to put the exodus and

entry into the land (see also Ps 111:4-6) in sequence with the return from exile (see Psalms 107–108) and other divine acts of deliverance (see Psalms 109; 115–116). The sequence of Psalms 107–118 would have served as a hopeful response to the exile and its aftermath (see Commentary on Psalm 107; Introduction). Beyond that, however, the sequence serves to encourage the oppressed people of God in any age, as well as to give them words to articulate their faith in and praise for God's ongoing story with God's people (see Commentary on Psalm 118).

As both the NIV and the NRSV indicate, the structure of Psalm 114 is best described as four pairs of poetic lines. Verses 1-2 lay out the movement from exodus to settlement in the land, and vv. 3-4 are a poetic commentary on these events. Using the same vocabulary as vv. 3-4, vv. 5-6 ask the questions to which vv. 7-8 offer a response. In so doing, vv. 7-8 highlight the crucial concept that accounts for Israel's election, deliverance, and establishment in the land: the presence of God (see below on v. 7).

114:1-2. The verb in "went out" (יצא *yāṣā'*, v. 1*a*) is used frequently of the exodus (see "bring out" in Exod 3:10-12; 14:11; 18:1; 20:2). The phrase "strange language" (לעז *lō'ēz*, v. 1*b*) is unique, but similar phrases are used elsewhere to designate Israel's opponents (see Deut 28:49; Isa 33:19; Jer 5:15). The precise sense of v. 2 is unclear, but it appears to mean that God has chosen Judah both as God's own people and as the place of God's dwelling. The movement from exodus to God's dwelling place is also present in the song the people sang immediately following the crossing of the sea (see Exod 15:1-18, esp. vv. 13, 17, where "holy" and "sanctuary" represent the same word as "sanctuary" [קדש *qōdeš*] in Ps 114:2). The sanctuary was the place where God's presence could be experienced most immediately, so v. 2 perhaps anticipates v. 7. In Exodus 15, the mention of the sanctuary (v. 17) is juxtaposed with the affirmation of God's reign (v. 18). Both concepts are present in Ps 114:2 as well. The word "dominion" (ממשלה *memšālâ*) represents a different Hebrew root than does "reign" (ממלכה *mamlākâ*), but they are essentially synonymous and occur together in Ps 145:13.

114:3-4. Verse 3*a* is clearly recognizable as a poetic description of the parting of the waters that allowed the people's crossing of the sea (see Exodus 14, esp. vv. 21-29). In Exod 14:25, 27, it is not the sea but the Egyptians who flee. That fleeing is here attributed to the sea is indicative of a mythic dimension already present in Exodus 14; thus God's deliverance of the Israelites by commanding the sea indicates God's sovereignty not only over Pharaoh but also over all chaotic forces, including cosmic ones (see above on Pss 74:12-17; 77:16-19). The ultimate implication is that God's creative work (see Ps 104:7) and God's saving work are united. The exodus is an enactment of God's creational purposes (see Commentary on Psalms 33; 65; 66). Verse 3*b* alludes to

the people's crossing of the Jordan and subsequent entry into the land (see Josh 3:1-17), an event perceived as analogous to the exodus (see Josh 4:23-24). Although not as clear, v. 4 may be a poetic allusion to Sinai (see Exodus 19). In any case, it is a poetic description of the effects of God's appearing. Elsewhere, too, God's appearing affects the mountains and hills (see Hab 3:6), even causing them to "skip" (see Ps 29:6, which is part of a description that culminates in the affirmation of God's cosmic sovereignty).

114:5-8. Verses 1-4 do not explicitly mention God (see the NRSV note in v. 2). Thus the questions in vv. 5-6 build toward the climactic v. 7. The events described and alluded to in vv. 1-4 happened because of "the presence of the LORD." The Hebrew syntax gives this phrase the emphatic position in the line, and the repetition of "presence of" has the poetic effect of surrounding the imperative with the two references to God's presence. Poetic structure reinforces content, for the poet intends to affirm that the whole earth is pervaded by God's presence and thus is subject to God's sovereignty. The appropriate response to God's sovereign presence is indicated by the imperative "tremble" (חולי *ḥûlî*). This is precisely what the earth does in Ps 97:4*b* in response to God's appearing as king (see 97:1-4*a*). The same verb also describes the effects of God's appearing in Pss 29:8-9; 77:16. Apparently, the verb implies a mixture of fear and joy in response to the awesome presence and power of God. The mention of water in v. 8 alludes to God's provision for the people in the wilderness (see Exod 17:1-7; Num 20:2-13; Deut 8:15). As in v. 3, water is involved, although in a different form and context. Even so, the event alluded to in v. 8 is another indication of God's cosmic sovereignty, manifested in gracious provision for human need (see Commentary on Psalm 113).

REFLECTIONS

Psalm 114 is a poetic affirmation of the faith that lies at the heart of the whole Bible: the God who rules the cosmos is made known in space and time for the purpose of properly ordering the world and the human community. Indeed, this affirmation is made in Psalm 113, as well as in Psalm 115, with which Psalm 114 belongs in some manuscript traditions; whereas

Psalm 114 invites the earth to tremble (v. 7), Psalm 115 invites the specifically human response of trust (see 115:9-11).

The specific events in view in Psalm 114 constitute the basics of Israel's story: exodus, provision in the wilderness, entry into the land as God's people. But the fundamental trust articulated in Psalm 114—that the sovereign God reveals God's self concretely in space and time—contributed to the discernment of an ongoing story of God with the world. The return from exile was understood as a new exodus; later, the early Christians perceived the cosmic God at work in quite ordinary events, like the birth of a child (see Commentary on Psalm 29, to which Luke 2:13-14, like Psalm 114, has affinities), as well as scandalously concrete events, like the cross. Consequently, as Mays concludes concerning Psalm 114: "The church has read and sung the psalm in the light of what happened in Judah and Israel through Jesus Christ. It sees in his death and resurrection yet another and a climactic theophany of the divine rule in which the Presence assumes a new relation to people and place."[421]

421. Mays, *Psalms*, 365.

PSALM 115:1-18, TRUST IN THE LORD

NIV	NRSV
Psalm 115	Psalm 115

[1]Not to us, O LORD, not to us
    but to your name be the glory,
    because of your love and faithfulness.
	[1] Not to us, O LORD, not to us, but to your
	    name give glory,
	    for the sake of your steadfast love and
	    your faithfulness.

[2]Why do the nations say,
    "Where is their God?"
	[2] Why should the nations say,
	    "Where is their God?"

[3]Our God is in heaven;
    he does whatever pleases him.
	[3] Our God is in the heavens;
	    he does whatever he pleases.

[4]But their idols are silver and gold,
    made by the hands of men.
	[4] Their idols are silver and gold,
	    the work of human hands.

[5]They have mouths, but cannot speak,
    eyes, but they cannot see;
	[5] They have mouths, but do not speak;
	    eyes, but do not see.

[6]they have ears, but cannot hear,
    noses, but they cannot smell;
	[6] They have ears, but do not hear;
	    noses, but do not smell.

[7]they have hands, but cannot feel,
    feet, but they cannot walk;
    nor can they utter a sound with their
        throats.
	[7] They have hands, but do not feel;
	    feet, but do not walk;
	    they make no sound in their throats.

[8]Those who make them will be like them,
    and so will all who trust in them.
	[8] Those who make them are like them;
	    so are all who trust in them.

[9]O house of Israel, trust in the LORD—
    he is their help and shield.
	[9] O Israel, trust in the LORD!
	    He is their help and their shield.

[10]O house of Aaron, trust in the LORD—
    he is their help and shield.
	[10] O house of Aaron, trust in the LORD!
	    He is their help and their shield.

[11]You who fear him, trust in the LORD—
    he is their help and shield.
	[11] You who fear the LORD, trust in the LORD!
	    He is their help and their shield.

[12]The LORD remembers us and will bless us:	

NIV

He will bless the house of Israel,
he will bless the house of Aaron,
¹³he will bless those who fear the LORD—
small and great alike.

¹⁴May the LORD make you increase,
both you and your children.
¹⁵May you be blessed by the LORD,
the Maker of heaven and earth.

¹⁶The highest heavens belong to the LORD,
but the earth he has given to man.
¹⁷It is not the dead who praise the LORD,
those who go down to silence;
¹⁸it is we who extol the LORD,
both now and forevermore.

Praise the LORD.ᵃ

ᵃ18 Hebrew *Hallelu Yah*

NRSV

¹² The LORD has been mindful of us; he will
bless us;
he will bless the house of Israel;
he will bless the house of Aaron;
¹³ he will bless those who fear the LORD,
both small and great.

¹⁴ May the LORD give you increase,
both you and your children.
¹⁵ May you be blessed by the LORD,
who made heaven and earth.

¹⁶ The heavens are the LORD's heavens,
but the earth he has given to human
beings.
¹⁷ The dead do not praise the LORD,
nor do any that go down into silence.
¹⁸ But we will bless the LORD
from this time on and forevermore.
Praise the LORD!

COMMENTARY

Not surprisingly, since Psalms 114 and 115 are a single psalm in some textual traditions, Psalm 115 portrays the human equivalent of the earth's trembling at the sovereign presence of God (see Ps 114:7)—namely, humble submission (v. 1), trust (vv. 9-11), assurance (vv. 12-13), and praise (vv. 3, 16-18). These elements, plus the presence of complaint (v. 2) and petition (vv. 14-15), make Psalm 115 difficult to classify. Verses 9-13 suggest the probability of liturgical use (see Commentary on Psalms 113; 114), and the polemic against idolatry (vv. 4-8; see also v. 2) may indicate a post-exilic origin (see Isa 40:18-20; 44:9-20). While certainty concerning origin and original use is impossible, it is clear that Psalm 115 is congruent with the apparent purpose of Book V to address the crisis of exile and its aftermath (see Commentary on Psalms 107; 108; 111; Introduction).

Because of its variety of elements, Psalm 115 is subject to a diversity of structural proposals, usually based on division by content. Attempting to take stylistic criteria seriously and noting a cluster of repeated words toward the beginning and end of the psalm (see "not" in vv. 1, 17; "does"/"made"/"make" in vv. 3-4, 15 NIV; "human" in vv. 4, 16 NRSV; "heaven(s)" in vv. 3, 15-16), Allen proposes the following divisions, which have a particular symmetry:

A		vv. 1-4
	B	vv. 5-8
		C′ vv. 9-11
	B′	vv. 12-13
A′		vv. 14-18

In this view, vv. 9-11 and vv. 12-13 also correspond by virtue of the repetition between and within the two sections.[422] Although perhaps coincidental, vv. 9-11 stand at almost the exact structural center of the poem, thus emphasizing the repeated term "trust" (בטח *bāṭaḥ*).

115:1-2. The unusual syntax of v. 1a emphasizes the opening negation, which suggests the people's recognition that "glory" belongs properly to the sovereign God (see Pss 29:1-3, 9; 79:9). Even so, God's glory will include the manifesta-

422. Leslie C. Allen, *Psalms 101–150*, WBC 21 (Waco, Tex.: Word, 1983) 109-10.

tion of God's basic character (v. 1*b*; see Exod 34:6; Pss 89:49; 92:2; 108:4; Introduction), and thus will be of help to God's people (see vv. 9-13) amid the hostility of the nations (v. 2; see Pss 42:3, 10; 79:9-10).

115:3-8. This assurance is reinforced in v. 3. Neither v. 3*a* nor v. 16, which it anticipates, should be understood geographically. God is not restricted to "the heavens"; rather, the heavens symbolize God's cosmic sovereignty (see Ps 113:4-5). Verse 3*b* articulates this sovereignty as well; it should be heard in the light of v. 1*b*. That is, it does not intend to say that God is whimsical but that God has the power to enact God's faithful, loving purposes. In contrast, the idols of the nations have no power (vv. 4-8; see Ps 135:15-18). The contrast is emphasized by the repetition of the Hebrew root "do," "make" (עשׂה '*āśâ*) in vv. 3-4, 8 (see also v. 15). That is, while God *makes* things happen, the idols are *made* by people. Those who make and trust in idols, the psalmist asserts, become like the idols (v. 8; see Ps 97:7; Isa 45:16-17). In other words, those who presume to make their gods will find themselves powerless as well, or at least limited to the power that they themselves can muster. In short, those who exalt themselves will be humbled (see Psalm 113).

115:9-11. The illusion of trusting in idols leads the psalmist to encourage trust in God (see Pss 4:5; 9:10; 25:2; 62:8; Introduction). Such trust puts people in touch with a source of help beyond themselves (see "help and shield" in Ps 33:20, where these concepts are also associated with trusting God). It is possible that different groups are represented in vv. 9-11 (see Ps 135:19-

20), perhaps the worshiping congregation (v. 9) and the priests (v. 10). Scholars sometimes suggest on the basis of late sources that those "who fear the LORD" are proselytes, but it is more likely that this phrase is a designation for the whole people (see v. 13; Ps 112:1).

115:12-15. God's remembrance of the people is a crucial element in experiences of deliverance (see Gen 9:15; Exod 2:24; 32:13; Pss 9:12; 74:2, 18, 22), and the people express the confidence that God remembers and therefore "will bless" (vv. 12-13; see Pss 5:12; 29:11; 67:1, 6-7; 107:38). The mention of "small and great alike" (v. 13; see Jer 31:34) makes it clear that the people have not earned the blessing, for unlike the worshipers of idols, they live in dependence upon God rather than self. The request for blessing in vv. 14-15 also reinforces this perspective. While the nations "make" idols (v. 8), God's people look to the "Maker of heaven and earth" (v. 15).

115:16-18. The transcendence of God is also in view in v. 16. To be sure, human beings also have a God-given sphere of influence (v. 16; see Commentary on Psalm 8). But as vv. 17-18 suggest, the earth is not a realm for unbridled human self-assertion but for praising (v. 17; see Pss 6:5; 30:9; 88:10) and blessing God (v. 18; see Pss 103:1-2, 20-22; 104:1, 35). The "we" in v. 18 is emphatic, as if the community of God's people wants to distinguish itself as sharply as possible from those who make and trust in other gods. Appropriately, the psalm concludes with the people's promise to offer unlimited praise to the God whose sovereignty is unlimited (see Ps 113:2).

REFLECTIONS

Psalm 115 begins and ends with an emphatic focus on the community—"us" (v. 1) and "we" (v. 18)—but in each case, the community looks beyond itself. In its intent to glorify and bless God (vv. 1, 18), the community denies itself (see Mark 8:34); it renounces reliance upon itself and its own resources and places its trust in God (vv. 9-11). Such humbling of self, it trusts, will be its exaltation (vv. 12-15; see Luke 18:14).

Trust in God sets the community apart from those who make and worship idols. As Mays points out, the polemic in vv. 4-8 "is hardly an accurate and fair description of the religions of the nations around Israel who made images to be representations and symbols of the person and presence of their deities."[423] Even so, the exaggeration is not without a point. The polemic

423. James L. Mays, *Psalms,* Interpretation (Louisville: John Knox, 1994) 366.

is grounded in the first and second commandments, which state Israel's conviction that no material image can properly represent God. The inevitable tendency of the use of human-made images is to limit God. In effect, people create gods in their own image, and the human self becomes preeminent (see v. 8). It is important to note, too, that because the polemic is part of the liturgy of the congregation, it also serves to remind the community of the persistent temptation toward the idolatrous self-centeredness that it professes to renounce.

The presence of the polemic in vv. 4-8 may well indicate the exilic or post-exilic origin of the psalm—that is, a period of domination by the nations (see v. 2). In any case, Allen reaches the following conclusion, "Psalm 115 is a stirring lesson to the people of God in every age concerning survival in an alien, hostile environment."[424] As such, it can be a particularly valuable resource for the contemporary church, which confronts a culture that is increasingly alien and hostile. To be sure, the hostility may not always be overt, but much in modern North American culture systematically teaches self-groundedness and self-centeredness; it assigns primary importance to enjoying ourselves rather than to glorifying God (see Commentary on Psalms 1; 100).

In such a culture, it is an increasingly radical act to profess faith in God—to say the Apostles' Creed, to which Ps 115:15*b* has contributed a crucial phrase (see also Gen 14:19, 22; Pss 121:2; 124:8; 134:3). To profess faith in God, "Maker of heaven and earth," is to affirm that we intend to live first and finally to God's glory rather than to our own (see v. 1). It is to affirm that we live by trusting God rather than ourselves (see vv. 9-11). In such a culture, it is also an increasingly radical act to pray as the community prays, to say the concluding line of the Lord's Prayer, which is reminiscent of Ps 115:1: "For thine is the kingdom and the power and the glory forever. Amen."

424. Leslie C. Allen, *Psalms 101–150*, WBC 21 (Waco, Tex.: Word, 1983) 111.

PSALM 116:1-19, I WILL LIFT UP THE CUP OF SALVATION

NIV	NRSV
Psalm 116	**Psalm 116**
¹I love the LORD, for he heard my voice; 　he heard my cry for mercy. ²Because he turned his ear to me, 　I will call on him as long as I live. ³The cords of death entangled me, 　the anguish of the grave*ᵃ* came upon me; 　I was overcome by trouble and sorrow. ⁴Then I called on the name of the LORD: 　"O LORD, save me!" ⁵The LORD is gracious and righteous; 　our God is full of compassion. ⁶The LORD protects the simplehearted; 　when I was in great need, he saved me. ⁷Be at rest once more, O my soul,	¹ I love the LORD, because he has heard 　my voice and my supplications. ² Because he inclined his ear to me, 　therefore I will call on him as long as I 　live. ³ The snares of death encompassed me; 　the pangs of Sheol laid hold on me; 　I suffered distress and anguish. ⁴ Then I called on the name of the LORD: 　"O LORD, I pray, save my life!" ⁵ Gracious is the LORD, and righteous; 　our God is merciful. ⁶ The LORD protects the simple; 　when I was brought low, he saved me. ⁷ Return, O my soul, to your rest,

*ᵃ*3 Hebrew *Sheol*

NIV

for the Lord has been good to you.

⁸For you, O Lord, have delivered my soul
from death,
my eyes from tears,
my feet from stumbling,
⁹that I may walk before the Lord
in the land of the living.
¹⁰I believed; therefore*ᵃ* I said,
"I am greatly afflicted."
¹¹And in my dismay I said,
"All men are liars."

¹²How can I repay the Lord
for all his goodness to me?
¹³I will lift up the cup of salvation
and call on the name of the Lord.
¹⁴I will fulfill my vows to the Lord
in the presence of all his people.

¹⁵Precious in the sight of the Lord
is the death of his saints.
¹⁶O Lord, truly I am your servant;
I am your servant, the son of your
maidservant*ᵇ*;
you have freed me from my chains.

¹⁷I will sacrifice a thank offering to you
and call on the name of the Lord.
¹⁸I will fulfill my vows to the Lord
in the presence of all his people,
¹⁹in the courts of the house of the Lord—
in your midst, O Jerusalem.

Praise the Lord.*ᶜ*

*ᵃ10 Or believed even when   ᵇ16 Or servant, your faithful son
ᶜ19 Hebrew Hallelu Yah*

NRSV

for the Lord has dealt bountifully with
you.

⁸ For you have delivered my soul from death,
my eyes from tears,
my feet from stumbling.
⁹ I walk before the Lord
in the land of the living.
¹⁰ I kept my faith, even when I said,
"I am greatly afflicted";
¹¹ I said in my consternation,
"Everyone is a liar."

¹² What shall I return to the Lord
for all his bounty to me?
¹³ I will lift up the cup of salvation
and call on the name of the Lord,
¹⁴ I will pay my vows to the Lord
in the presence of all his people.

¹⁵ Precious in the sight of the Lord
is the death of his faithful ones.
¹⁶ O Lord, I am your servant;
I am your servant, the child of your
serving girl.
You have loosed my bonds.
¹⁷ I will offer to you a thanksgiving sacrifice
and call on the name of the Lord.
¹⁸ I will pay my vows to the Lord
in the presence of all his people,
¹⁹ in the courts of the house of the Lord,
in your midst, O Jerusalem.

Praise the Lord!

COMMENTARY

Psalm 116 is a song of thanksgiving (see Psalms 30; 32; 34). It is clear from vv. 1-2 that the psalmist's prayer for help has been answered (see also vv. 6*b*, 7*b*, 8-9, 12, 16*c*). The psalmist can now look back on the former threat (vv. 3-4, 8, 10-11, 15), celebrate God's goodness and the deliverance God has effected (vv. 5-6*a*, 7), profess devotion to God (vv. 1*a*, 2*b*, 16*ab*), and make a public response of gratitude in the Temple (vv. 12-14, 17-19). While the traditional elements of a song of thanksgiving are present, they seem to be presented in no particular order; scholars disagree on the structure of the psalm. In fact, the LXX and the Vulgate transmit vv. 1-9 and vv. 10-19 as two separate psalms. Even so, there are clear indications of the unity of Psalm 116—for instance, the repetition of "call" in vv. 2, 4, 13, 17; the repetition of "death" in vv. 3, 8, 15; and the repetition of "bountifully"/"bounty" in vv. 7, 12.

Taking the repetition in vv. 13*b*-14 and 17*b*-18 as a major clue, Allen divides Psalm 116 into three sections: vv. 1-7, vv. 8-14, vv. 15-19.[425] Each section looks back to the former distress (see vv. 3-4, 8, 10-11, 15; note esp. "death" in each section), and if v. 7*a* is properly construed as a statement of the psalmist's intent to go to the Temple, as Mays suggests, then each section also concludes with what Mays calls "a performance statement"—the psalmist's promise to respond gratefully to God (vv. 7, 13-14, 17-19).[426] The psalm was probably originally used by an individual as an expression of gratitude and faith following deliverance from some life-threatening distress, perhaps sickness (see Psalms 6; 38), but the language is open-ended enough to apply to a variety of crises. It was apparently performed at the Temple (v. 19) and accompanied by sacrifice (vv. 13, 17). At some point, Psalm 116 became a part of the *Hallel* collection (Psalms 113–118), which was used at Passover, and it also became associated by Christians with the Lord's supper (see Reflections below). Its theme of deliverance is in keeping with the thrust of Book V (see Psalms 107; 109; 111; 113–115; 118; on the purpose of Book V, see Commentary on Psalms 107; 111; Introduction).

116:1-4. The beginning of Psalm 116 is unique (see Ps 18:1, where a different Hebrew verb is translated "love"), and the psalmists only rarely speak elsewhere of loving God (see Pss 5:11; 31:23; 40:16). As subsequent verses indicate, the psalmist's love for God grows out of the realization that God has saved his or her life (v. 4). As elsewhere in the psalms, death is described in conjunction with a place, Sheol, the realm of the dead (v. 3). Sheol is sometimes portrayed as a place beyond even God's reach (see Pss 6:5; 30:9; 88:3-7, 10-13), but at other times, Sheol is viewed as a sort of power that invades life and from which God can rescue (see Pss 30:3; 49:15; 56:13; 86:13; see also Ps 139:8). As Mays points out, there is a tension between these points of view.[427] The tension may be testimony to the diversity of Israelite views of life and death, or perhaps to the development of differing perspectives over time (see Commentary on Psalms 22;

425. Ibid., 114-15.
426. Mays, *Psalms,* 369.
427. Ibid., 370.

49). In any case, the psalmist is convinced that he or she is alive because of what God has done. Thus what the psalmist did in the time of distress—call on God's name (v. 4)—has become a life-long commitment (v. 2). To love someone is to be in constant conversation with him or her.

116:5-7. Love also motivates one to communicate enthusiastically to others the character of the beloved (v. 5). The word "name" (שֵׁם *šēm*) in v. 4 has already suggested the importance of God's character, and the words "gracious" (חנון *ḥannûn*) and "merciful" (מרחם *měrahēm*) are used elsewhere to describe God's fundamental character (see Exod 34:6; Pss 86:15; 111:4). The word "righteous" (צדיק *ṣaddîq*), too, describes what God fundamentally is and wills (see Pss 9:8; 96:13; 97:2; 98:9; 99:4); it does not usually occur in conjunction with "gracious" and "merciful," but it is certainly an appropriate grouping (see Ps 111:3-4). Motivated by compassion, impelled by grace, God sets things right for "the simple" (v. 6*a*)—that is, the powerless—and those "brought low" (v. 6*b*; see Ps 79:8, where Israel appeals to God's "mercy"/"compassion" when "brought very low"; see also Ps 142:7). God helps those who cannot help themselves (see Psalms 3; 107; 109; 113; 118). This is the bounty (vv. 7*b*, 12) the psalmist has experienced (v. 6*b*) and to which he or she intends to respond (v. 7*a*; cf. Ps 95:11).

116:8-11. Verse 8 rehearses the deliverance. The threat of death is elsewhere symbolized by "tears" (see Pss 6:6; 39:12; 56:8) and "stumbling" (see Ps 56:13). The psalmist does not stumble but walks (v. 9*a*); the psalmist does not die but remains "in the land of the living" (v. 9*b*; see Pss 27:13; 52:5; 142:5; Isa 38:11; 53:8; Jer 11:19). In looking back over this experience, the psalmist recalls articulating the severity of the affliction (v. 10; see Ps 31:22). But the psalmist's words are not indicative of resignation or despair. In the light of v. 10, v. 11 should be viewed not so much as evidence that the psalmist has been the victim of deceit but that he or she did not place hope in human help (see Ps 62:9).

116:12-14. Recalling v. 7, v. 12 raises the question of an appropriate expression of gratitude. It was apparently customary to accompany public expressions of gratitude with sacrifices, and the "cup of salvation" (v. 13) seems originally to have been some form of sacrificial offering (see Exod

29:40; Num 28:7). In good times (vv. 13*b*, 17*b*; see v. 2) as well as in bad (v. 4), the psalmist calls upon the name of God. The material and verbal expressions of gratitude fulfill the vow the psalmist would have made as part of a prayer for help during the time of distress (vv. 14, 18; see Pss 22:25; 61:5, 8; 65:1).

116:15-19. The NIV and the NRSV make v. 15 sound as if God welcomes the death of the faithful, but the whole point of the psalm is that God wills life and works to make life a reality. Thus the Hebrew word translated "precious" (יקר *yāqār*) should be understood in the sense of "costly." Because God does *not* welcome the death of the faithful, the psalmist professes em-

phatically his or her relatedness to God as servant (v. 16*ab*; see above on Ps 86:16), and recalls again God's intervention to deliver (v. 16*c*; see Ps 107:14). Like the previous two sections, the final one concludes with a performance statement. Verses 17*b*-18 are identical to vv. 13*b*-14, but v. 17*a* cites a different sacrificial act than does v. 13*a*: "a thanksgiving sacrifice" (see Lev 7:12; 22:29; Pss 27:6; 107:22). Verse 19 specifies the public setting as the Temple (see "courts" in Pss 65:4; 84:2, 10; 96:8; 100:4; 135:2), and the final *Hallelu-yah* links Psalm 116 to the rest of the *Hallel* collection (see Commentary on Psalm 113).

REFLECTIONS

1. Like other songs of thanksgiving, as well as songs of praise and prayers for help, Psalm 116 is testimony to the gracious character and righteous purposes of God. Contrary to conventional worldly wisdom, the psalmist asserts that God helps those who cannot help themselves (see Commentary on Psalm 3). Psalm 116 thus invites, not self-reliance, but dependence upon God—in short, trust (vv. 2, 10; see Ps 115:9-11; see also Commentary on Psalms 1; 2). Genuine faith in God inevitably involves loving God (v. 1); as the psalmist's life demonstrates, love of God is manifested in witness to God's character (vv. 5-6), gratitude (vv. 12-14, 17-19), and humble service (v. 16). Such faith is also manifested in the ability to endure every affliction (v. 10; see Ps 34:19; see also 2 Cor 4:8 and note that Ps 116:10 is alluded to in 2 Cor 4:13).

2. Although originating apparently for use by an individual in response to deliverance by God, Psalm 116 eventually came to be used in wider liturgical settings. The exact reason why Psalm 116 became part of the *Hallel* collection is not known. Perhaps it was because of its theme of deliverance from death (see Pss 115:17; 118:17-18), or if the *Hallel* collection had an original connection with Passover, perhaps Psalm 116 was chosen because of its mention of a cup (v. 13). In any case, the Passover meal involves the lifting up and blessing of four cups of wine; rabbinic sources connect the reading of Psalms 115–118 with the fourth cup. Thus the lifting of "the cup of salvation" (v. 13) would have come to be understood in this setting as a celebration of the exodus (see Psalms 114; 118). The Passover liturgy encourages the reactualization of the exodus by every subsequent generation.

3. Jesus, of course, reactualized the Passover meal in a way that transformed its significance for Christians. Not surprisingly, Psalm 116 became associated by Christians with the Lord's supper, which is also known as the eucharist—that is, thanksgiving. In particular, Psalm 116 is traditionally the psalm for Holy Thursday. In this liturgical setting, Christians are encouraged to hear the psalmist's experience as an anticipation of Jesus' faithful suffering (v. 10) and ultimate deliverance from death in the resurrection (vv. 3-4, 8-9, 16). Jesus' lifting of the cup and his new interpretation of it (see Matt 26:27-28; Mark 14:23-24; Luke 22:20; 1 Cor 10:10; 11:25) point to his own death as the sacrifice (v. 17) and to a new dimension of the affirmation of what it means for him and for his followers to be delivered from death into "the land of the living" (v. 9).

PSALM 117:1-2, PRAISE THE LORD, ALL YOU NATIONS

NIV

Psalm 117

¹Praise the LORD, all you nations;
    extol him, all you peoples.
²For great is his love toward us,
    and the faithfulness of the LORD endures
        forever.

Praise the LORD.ᵃ

ᵃ2 Hebrew *Hallelu Yah*

NRSV

Psalm 117

¹ Praise the LORD, all you nations!
    Extol him, all you peoples!
² For great is his steadfast love toward us,
    and the faithfulness of the LORD endures
        forever.
Praise the LORD!

COMMENTARY

Although the shortest of all the psalms, Psalm 117 manages to demonstrate in two verses the typical structure of a song of praise: invitation to praise (v. 1) and reasons for praise (v. 2). For all its brevity and typicality, Psalm 117 makes a claim that is long on significance and anything but routine. The claim is simple but breathtaking: Praising God is the proper vocation and goal of human life!

The invitation in v. 1 points to this claim. It is extended not to Israel or to Judah or to some group of the faithful, but to "all you nations" and "all you peoples." Underlying this invitation is the conviction that the God of Israel is the God who rules the world. Not surprisingly, the psalms that explicitly proclaim God's reign also address their invitations to praise to a universal audience (see Pss 47:1; 96:1, 7, 9, 11-12; 97:1; 98:4, 7-8; 99:1-3; 100:1). Praise is what God intends for everybody. Because God rules the world, God's congregation must include all peoples and nations along with all creatures and all creation (see Pss 148:1-4, 7-12; 150:6).

Given the universality of the invitation, one might expect the accompanying reasons to depart from the opening chapters of the book of Genesis

(see Pss 86:9; 150:6), but the reasons for praise recall instead the book of Exodus. The words "steadfast love" (חסד *ḥesed*) and "faithfulness" (אמת *ʾĕmet*) are two of the key words in God's self-revelation to Moses, which forms the culmination of the golden calf episode (see Exod 34:6; see also Pss 25:10; 36:5; 40:10; 57:10; 85:10; 86:15; 89:14; 92:2; 98:3; 100:5; 108:4; 138:2; Introduction). The recollection of this narrative context is important, because by this point in the story, God is clearly aware that the creation of humankind and the choice of a particular people leave God no other option than to be related to a sinful humanity. By recalling Exodus 34:6, therefore, Psalm 117 grounds the reasons for praising God in God's fundamental identity. Because God is steadfastly loving and forever faithful, God can do no other than love the world and its sinful inhabitants. In relation to the sovereignty of God, implied in v. 1, the word translated "great" (גבר *gābar*) in v. 2 is particularly interesting (see Ps 103:11). The Hebrew root is often used to indicate the power of a military conqueror. Here it also affirms that God conquers the world, but that God does so by the power of faithful love.

REFLECTIONS

1. Psalm 117 communicates the good news that God loves the world, all nations and peoples (see Psalms 19; 87; John 3:16-17), and that God rules the world with the power of faithful love (see John 16:33). Thus it also teaches that human life is incomprehensible apart from God and from God's love for the world. To praise God is to understand and affirm that genuine life consists ultimately in submission to God rather than assertion of self. In our world, which seems either unable or unwilling to praise God, the message of Psalm 117 is crucial (see Commentary on Psalms 8; 100).

2. Like every affirmation of God's rule, explicit or implicit, Psalm 117 must be heard eschatologically (see Commentary on Psalms 2; 93–99; Introduction). As Mays puts it: "The call to the nations reaches toward an eschatological horizon when nationality and race shall be comprehended and healed in a larger unity that can be constituted only by the faith spoken in praise of God." [428] To live under God's rule, to live eschatologically, means that God's future affects the human present. On the basis of the eschatological horizon glimpsed in Psalm 117, for instance, the apostle Paul insisted that the Christian church be open to the Gentiles, to the nations (see Paul's citation of Ps 117:1 in Rom 15:11).

3. In our age, in which the church transcends the barriers of race and nation, Psalm 117 invites us perhaps to conversation with persons of other faiths or of no faith at all. William C. Placher suggests that Christians enter such dialogue to represent the truth we perceive but also to learn from other traditions and practices. The success of such conversations should not be measured by the goal of conversion, but simply by the effort to speak honestly and listen carefully to a variety of persons, who, as Psalm 117 suggests, are also children of God. [429]

428. Ibid., 372-73.
429. William C. Placher, *Unapologetic Theology: A Christian Voice in a Pluralistic Conversation* (Louisville: Westminster John Knox, 1989) 115-18, 143-49. Placher does not cite Psalm 117, but it would support his appeal to texts like Gen 1:26 and Acts 17:23 (p. 116).

PSALM 118:1-29, THIS IS THE DAY ON WHICH THE LORD HAS ACTED

NIV	NRSV
Psalm 118	**Psalm 118**
¹Give thanks to the LORD, for he is good; his love endures forever.	¹ O give thanks to the LORD, for he is good; his steadfast love endures forever!
²Let Israel say: "His love endures forever." ³Let the house of Aaron say: "His love endures forever." ⁴Let those who fear the LORD say: "His love endures forever."	² Let Israel say, "His steadfast love endures forever." ³ Let the house of Aaron say, "His steadfast love endures forever." ⁴ Let those who fear the LORD say, "His steadfast love endures forever."
⁵In my anguish I cried to the LORD, and he answered by setting me free. ⁶The LORD is with me; I will not be afraid. What can man do to me?	⁵ Out of my distress I called on the LORD; the LORD answered me and set me in a broad place.

NIV

⁷The LORD is with me; he is my helper.
    I will look in triumph on my enemies.

⁸It is better to take refuge in the LORD
    than to trust in man.
⁹It is better to take refuge in the LORD
    than to trust in princes.

¹⁰All the nations surrounded me,
    but in the name of the LORD I cut them off.
¹¹They surrounded me on every side,
    but in the name of the LORD I cut them off.
¹²They swarmed around me like bees,
    but they died out as quickly as burning
        thorns;
    in the name of the LORD I cut them off.

¹³I was pushed back and about to fall,
    but the LORD helped me.
¹⁴The LORD is my strength and my song;
    he has become my salvation.

¹⁵Shouts of joy and victory
    resound in the tents of the righteous:
    "The LORD's right hand has done mighty
        things!
¹⁶   The LORD's right hand is lifted high;
    the LORD's right hand has done mighty things!"

¹⁷I will not die but live,
    and will proclaim what the LORD has done.
¹⁸The LORD has chastened me severely,
    but he has not given me over to death.

¹⁹Open for me the gates of righteousness;
    I will enter and give thanks to the LORD.
²⁰This is the gate of the LORD
    through which the righteous may enter.
²¹I will give you thanks, for you answered me;
    you have become my salvation.

²²The stone the builders rejected
    has become the capstone;
²³the LORD has done this,
    and it is marvelous in our eyes.
²⁴This is the day the LORD has made;
    let us rejoice and be glad in it.

²⁵O LORD, save us;
    O LORD, grant us success.
²⁶Blessed is he who comes in the name of the
        LORD.
    From the house of the LORD we bless you.ᵃ

ᵃ26 The Hebrew is plural.

NRSV

⁶ With the LORD on my side I do not fear.
    What can mortals do to me?
⁷ The LORD is on my side to help me;
    I shall look in triumph on those who
        hate me.
⁸ It is better to take refuge in the LORD
    than to put confidence in mortals.
⁹ It is better to take refuge in the LORD
    than to put confidence in princes.

¹⁰ All nations surrounded me;
    in the name of the LORD I cut them off!
¹¹ They surrounded me, surrounded me on
        every side;
    in the name of the LORD I cut them off!
¹² They surrounded me like bees;
    they blazedᵃ like a fire of thorns;
    in the name of the LORD I cut them off!
¹³ I was pushed hard,ᵇ so that I was falling,
    but the LORD helped me.
¹⁴ The LORD is my strength and my might;
    he has become my salvation.

¹⁵ There are glad songs of victory in the tents
        of the righteous:
    "The right hand of the LORD does valiantly;
¹⁶   the right hand of the LORD is exalted;
    the right hand of the LORD does valiantly."
¹⁷ I shall not die, but I shall live,
    and recount the deeds of the LORD.
¹⁸ The LORD has punished me severely,
    but he did not give me over to death.

¹⁹ Open to me the gates of righteousness,
    that I may enter through them
    and give thanks to the LORD.

²⁰ This is the gate of the LORD;
    the righteous shall enter through it.

²¹ I thank you that you have answered me
    and have become my salvation.
²² The stone that the builders rejected
    has become the chief cornerstone.
²³ This is the LORD's doing;
    it is marvelous in our eyes.
²⁴ This is the day that the LORD has made;
    let us rejoice and be glad in it.ᶜ

ᵃ Gk: Heb *were extinguished*   ᵇ Gk Syr Jerome: Heb *You pushed
me hard*   ᶜ Or *in him*

NIV

²⁷The LORD is God,
    and he has made his light shine upon us.
With boughs in hand, join in the festal
        procession
    up^a to the horns of the altar.

²⁸You are my God, and I will give you thanks;
    you are my God, and I will exalt you.

²⁹Give thanks to the LORD, for he is good;
    his love endures forever.

^{a}27 Or *Bind the festal sacrifice with ropes / and take it*

NRSV

²⁵ Save us, we beseech you, O LORD!
    O LORD, we beseech you, give us success!

²⁶ Blessed is the one who comes in the name
        of the LORD.^{a}
    We bless you from the house of the LORD.
²⁷ The LORD is God,
    and he has given us light.
Bind the festal procession with branches,
    up to the horns of the altar.^{b}

²⁸ You are my God, and I will give thanks to
        you;
    you are my God, I will extol you.

²⁹ O give thanks to the LORD, for he is good,
    for his steadfast love endures forever.

^{a}Or *Blessed in the name of the LORD is the one who comes*
^{b}Meaning of Heb uncertain

COMMENTARY

As the opening and closing verses might suggest, Psalm 118 is ordinarily categorized as a song of thanksgiving. Like others of this type (see Psalms 30; 34; 116), it recounts (see vv. 5-18) and publicly celebrates an experience of deliverance (vv. 19-28). But Psalm 118 is unique. While the speaker for most of the psalm is an individual "I" (vv. 5-21), the distress recounted seems to suggest a crisis of national proportions (see esp. vv. 10-14). This has led many scholars to conclude that the "I" is the king speaking on behalf of the people, but certainty is elusive. The speaker actually shifts to the plural in vv. 23-27, leading scholars to disagree as to whether the song should be viewed as individual, communal, or both. Further complicating the interpretive task is the fact that Psalm 118 is especially reminiscent of the celebration of the exodus and return from exile, plus the psalm shifts to petition at v. 25 before concluding with thanksgiving again.

All of these features of Psalm 118 must be considered in addressing the question of its original use and setting. It seems that some sort of liturgical procession, perhaps culminating in a thank offering, originally lay behind vv. 19-28.

And it seems that some sort of national victory or deliverance was the focus of the original celebration, perhaps led by the king (see Commentary on Psalms 18; 20-21). But it is difficult to be any more specific than this.

What is more certain is that Psalm 118 is the concluding psalm of the *Hallel* collection (Psalms 113–118), which came to be used at Passover (see Commentary on Psalm 113). In this setting, its recollection of the exodus is especially significant (see Psalm 114). But its allusion to the return from exile and the shift to petition in v. 25 suggest that both exodus and deliverance from exile served as bases for hope that future deliverance would also occur. This gives Psalm 118 an open-endedness that would have made it particularly relevant to the post-exilic era, during which the aftermath of exile persisted and the people continued to be dominated by the nations. Indeed, this feature of Psalm 118 makes its placement in Book V readily understandable. Book V begins by establishing a post-exilic perspective (see Ps 107:2-3) and by commending consideration of God's steadfast love (see 107:43). Not coincidentally perhaps, Psalm 118 begins and ends with the same verse that opens Book V (107:1), suggesting the possibility that Psalms 107–118 together offer a perspective from which to face the reality of continuing oppression: recollection of God's past activity as a basis for petition and grateful trust in God's future activity on behalf of the people (see Commentary on Psalms 107; 108; 111; Introduction). The open-endedness of Psalm 118 is also evident in the way that the early Christian church heard it and understood its speaker and subject to be Jesus (see Reflections below).

118:1-4. The opening and concluding invitations (vv. 1-4, 29) provide a framework for the recital (vv. 5-18) and celebration of deliverance (vv. 19-28). Each verse of the framework features the word "steadfast love" (see Pss 106:1; 107:1; 136:1), a word that describes the very essence of God's character that is revealed in acts of deliverance like those described and alluded to in Psalm 118 (see Exod 15:13; 34:6; Introduction). Verses 2-4 anticipate the communal dimension, which is explicitly present in vv. 23-27 (on the three different addressees, see Pss 115:9-11; 135:19-20). The communal dimension is also evident in vv. 1, 29. The other three psalms that begin with this same verse conclude by associating their theme of deliverance with the situation of the whole people following the return from exile (see Pss 106:44-47; 107:33-41; 136:23-24).

118:5-18. The recital in vv. 5-18 can be divided into three sections: vv. 5-9, vv. 10-14, vv. 15-18. Verse 5 offers a succinct account of the deliverance. The Hebrew root of the noun "distress" (מצר *mēṣar,* v. 5*a*) has the sense of "restricted," "narrow," "tight." When the psalmist was in a tight spot, God gave space (v. 5*b*; see "broad place" in Pss 18:19; 31:8 NRSV). Verses 6-9 relate what the psalmist has learned from the whole experience. "On my side" (לי *lî,* vv. 6*a,* 7*a*) is more literally "for me." The psalmist's knowledge that God is "for me" (see Pss 56:9; 124:1-2; Rom 8:31) meant that the psalmist need not fear other people (see Ps 56:4, 11), even enemies (v. 7*b*; see Pss 54:7*b*; 59:10*b*; 112:8*b*). The psalmist has experienced God's help (v. 7*a*; see v. 13; Pss 10:14; 22:19; 37:40; 115:9-11; 121:2; 124:8; 146:5), and so the psalmist can affirm what the psalmists elsewhere assert makes for genuine happiness: taking refuge in God (see Pss 2:12; 34:8; Introduction), trusting God (see

Ps 84:12) rather than even the most powerful humans.

Verses 10-12 again recount the deliverance. The word "surrounded" (סבב *sābab*) links these verses (see Pss 17:11; 22:12), but the description of the distress is intensified with each recounting. Even so, each verse ends with the identical phrase; that is, God's help remains constant amid the growing threat. The verb "cut off" (מול *mûl*) is used most frequently of circumcision, an especially interesting nuance given that the threat comes from the nations. At the crucial moment, God helps (v. 13), just as God did at the exodus, which is recalled very specifically in v. 14. In fact, v. 14 quotes Exod 15:2*ab,* a portion of the song that Moses and the Israelites sang immediately after crossing the sea (see also Isa 12:2*cd,* where the same affirmation occurs in a context that presents it as celebration of return from exile and dispersion).

The words "salvation" (v. 14) and "victory" (v. 15) represent the same Hebrew word (ישועה *yĕšû'â;* see also vv. 21, 25), and the allusions to the exodus continue in vv. 15-18. The three occurrences of "right hand" (ימין *yāmîn*) in vv. 15*b*-16 recall the three occurrences in Exod 15:6, 12 (see also Isa 41:10 in the context of God's returning the exiles). The word "exalted" (רוממה *rômēmâ,* v. 16*a*) again recalls Exod 15:2 (see below on v. 28). The Hebrew root (עשה *'āśâ*) represented by "does" (vv. 15-16) and "deeds" (v. 17) also occurs in v. 6 and v. 24. The effect of the repetition is to contrast human deeds, which threaten the psalmist and the people with death, with God's deeds, which offer life (vv. 17-18; see Pss 115:17; 116:8-9). The mention of punishment/chastening/disciplining in v. 18*a* indicates that the psalmist or the people interpret the distress as God's doing as well (see v. 13*a;* see NRSV note), but there is no specific indication of wrongdoing (see Pss 6:1; 38:1; 94:12; Jer 30:11; 31:18; see also Ps 2:10).

118:19-29. Verses 19-28 have several features of a public worship service, including indications of alternating voices and a liturgical procession (vv. 19-20, 26-27). This section is framed by the individual speaker's expression of intent to "give thanks" (vv. 19, 28; see vv. 1, 29). Verse 28 clearly recalls Exod 15:2*cd* (see above on v. 14; and see v. 16, where "exalt" is the same as "extol" in v. 28). Thus the speaker again suggests that the present deliverance is analogous to the exodus. He or she apparently intends to enter the temple gates to make the appropriate expression of gratitude (see "gates" in Pss 24:7, 9; 100:4; Jer 7:2). Verse 20 appears to be a response to v. 19 by a priest or some temple official (see 1 Chr 16:42). As is the case throughout the psalms, "the righteous" are not persons who have proven themselves worthy (see v. 18) but those who acknowledge that they owe their lives and futures to God (see vv. 8-9; see also Commentary on Psalm 1). Indeed, this is precisely what the psalmist gratefully acknowledges in v. 21 (see "answered" in v. 5 and "salvation"/"save" in vv. 14-15, 25).

Verse 22 seems to be a congregational response that interprets the psalmist's experience of deliverance from death to life; it would have served in the post-exilic era to interpret the experience of the people as well (see Isa 28:16; Jer 51:26). The shift to a plural speaker is clear in vv. 23-27. The reversal of fortunes is unambiguously attributed to God, and the vocabulary of vv. 23-24 continues to recall the exodus as a prototype. The root of "marvelous" (פלא pālā') in v. 23b occurs as "wonders" in Exod 15:11, and the focus on "the day on which the LORD has acted" (v. 24a NEB) recalls the crossing of the sea (see Exod 14:13).

The shift to petition in v. 25 is unexpected. The plea "Save us, we beseech you" is a real and urgent petition (cf. Mark 11:9-10, where the similar "Hosanna" appears to have been a celebrative cry; see also Reflections below). The psalm's earlier testimony (vv. 5-18, 21), though written in the first-person singular, is the basis for prayer in the midst of communal distress. As psalmist and people had been saved in the past

(vv. 5, 13-14, 15-18, 21), so now the people need to be saved again. The plea for "success" is not a request for abundant material prosperity but an appeal to God to provide resources for life amid the current threat (on "prosper," see commentary on Ps 1:3). The petition in v. 25 orients the psalm to the future as well as to the past and thus gives the psalm an open-endedness that is evident in the history of its use.

The blessing and affirmation of vv. 26-27 recall vv. 19-20 ("comes" [בוא bô'] in v. 26 is the same verb as "enter" in vv. 19-20), but they should also be heard in the context of the petition of v. 25. The "one who comes in the name of the LORD" represents the possibility of blessing in the midst of the current threat (v. 26), and the present crisis does not diminish the people's trust that "the LORD is God" or their memory of God's past faithfulness in giving light (v. 27; see "light"/ "shine" in Pss 4:6; 27:1; 31:16; 67:1). Thus v. 27 seems to express the people's confidence in God's illuminating presence in the midst of their current need. In any case, the people are apparently intent upon celebrating even during the moment of threat, although the precise nature and significance of the activity described in v. 27b are unclear (see NIV and NRSV notes). The mention of "branches" may suggest an origin in or allusion to the Feast of Tabernacles (see Lev 23:40).

In v. 28, the psalmist echoes in an emphatic and very personal way the communal affirmation of v. 27a: "My God (are) you " (v. 28a, author's trans.). The psalmist also reaffirms the intent to give thanks (see vv. 1, 19, 21), again alludes to the exodus (see Exod 15:2cd), and invites the community to participate in giving thanks (v. 29; see v. 1; Pss 106:1; 107:1; 136:1).

REFLECTIONS

The failure of Psalm 118 to identify the speaker in vv. 5-18, 28 contributed to the open-endedness of the psalm. So did its juxtaposition of clear allusions to past saving events—exodus and return from exile—with the petition for help in v. 25. Regardless of the circumstances of its origin and original use, Psalm 118 became a part of the *Hallel* collection, which was used at Passover, a recollection of the exodus and an anticipation of God's continuing presence and ongoing help (see Commentary on Psalms 113; 114; 115; 116; 117).

1. The same factors that contribute to the open-endedness of Psalm 118—in particular, the movement from thanksgiving to petition back to thanksgiving in vv. 19-29—also make it, in

Brueggemann's words, "a model for evangelical prayer."[430] Praise and petition join in affirming God's sovereignty and the persistent reality of human need. As Mays indicates, Psalm 118, which serves as a model for prayer, suggests too that human need and God's saving activity "are not tied to a particular historical occasion or social setting or festival, but are read as functions of the canon." To view this psalm in the context of the biblical canon "opens the psalm to use and interpretation in later and other times by the community for whom the canon of scripture is the guide to faith and life."[431]

2. Thus the early Christian community identified the speaker in vv. 5-18, 28 as Jesus. According to the Gospels, when Jesus entered Jerusalem shortly before his crucifixion, he was greeted by a crowd in a manner reminiscent of Psalm 118. In Mark 11:9, the first part of the greeting consists of Ps 118:25a, 26a. The use of Psalm 118 at this point is not really surprising, since Jesus enters Jerusalem during the week of Passover. But this observation does not exhaust the significance of Mark's use of Psalm 118. Verses 22-23 were understood within first-century Judaism to refer to the Messiah.[432] In fact, Matt 21:42 cites these verses to suggest that Jesus is the rejected Messiah (see also Luke 20:17; Acts 4:11-12). In the story of Jesus' entry into Jerusalem, the Gospel writers have extended the messianic interpretation to vv. 25-26. Mark 11:10 and Matt 21:9 make this clear by mentioning "the kingdom of our father David" (NRSV) and "Son of David" respectively, while the parallel accounts in Luke and John record that the crowd addresses Jesus as "King" (Luke 23:38; John 12:13). For all the Gospel writers, Psalm 118 is a means of understanding and articulating the significance of Jesus.

In other words, by articulating the significance of Jesus through Psalm 118, the Gospel writers profess that the life, death, and resurrection of Jesus are an extension of God's saving activity in the exodus and return from exile. Psalm 118 has become in Christian liturgical tradition not just a psalm for Palm/Passion Sunday, which celebrates Jesus' entry into Jerusalem, but also for Easter Sunday. For Christians, Easter is above all "the day on which the Lord has acted" (v. 24 NEB). God was active in the exodus; God was active in returning exiles; God was active in the life, death, and resurrection of Jesus. So the Gospel writers affirm in their use of Psalm 118. As a traditional call to worship, v. 24 is a reminder to Christians that every Sunday is a celebration of the resurrection, the Lord's Day, the day on which the Lord has acted and is still active. Thus Psalm 118 can be seen as a focal point for discerning the continuity between the Old and the New Testament witnesses that God is "for us" (see vv. 6-7; Rom 8:31) and that God's "steadfast love endures forever" (vv. 1-4, 29; see Rom 8:38-39).

3. Not surprisingly, the special appeal that Psalm 118 had for the Gospel writers has continued throughout centuries of Christian interpretation. Martin Luther, for instance, viewed Psalm 118 as "My own beloved psalm."[433] Not surprisingly either, v. 17 has been heard by Christian interpreters as an affirmation both of the resurrection of Jesus and of believers. That is to say, in view of the extension of God's saving activity to include Jesus Christ, Christians hear v. 17 with a fuller sense. Luther, for instance, called v. 17 "a masterpiece," and concluded that "all the saints have sung this verse and will continue to sing it to the end."[434] Given the rich historical allusions and open-endedness of the psalm, as well as the history and currency of its use in Judaism and Christianity, one might make the same conclusion of Psalm 118 as a whole—all the saints have sung it and will sing it to the end.

430. Walter Brueggemann, "Psalm 118:19-29: Psalm for Palm Sunday," *No Other Foundation* 10 (Winter 1989–90) 16.
431. James L. Mays, "Psalm 118 in the Light of Canonical Analysis," in *Canon, Theology, and Old Testament Interpretation,* ed. G. M. Tucker, D. L. Petersen, R. R. Wilson (Philadelphia: Fortress, 1988) 310.
432. See H.-J. Kraus, *Theology of the Psalms,* trans. Keith Crim (Minneapolis: Augsburg, 1986) 196.
433. Quoted in Ronald M. Hals, "Psalm 118," *Int.* 37 (1983) 277.
434. See ibid., 280. These quotes and the previous one are from Luther's *Works,* Vol. 14: *Selected Psalms III,* ed. J. Pelikan (St. Louis: Concordia, 1958) 45, 87.

PSALM 119:1-176, HOW I LOVE YOUR INSTRUCTION

NIV

Psalm 119[a]

א Aleph

[1]Blessed are they whose ways are blameless,
  who walk according to the law of the LORD.
[2]Blessed are they who keep his statutes
  and seek him with all their heart.
[3]They do nothing wrong;
  they walk in his ways.
[4]You have laid down precepts
  that are to be fully obeyed.
[5]Oh, that my ways were steadfast
  in obeying your decrees!
[6]Then I would not be put to shame
  when I consider all your commands.
[7]I will praise you with an upright heart
  as I learn your righteous laws.
[8]I will obey your decrees;
  do not utterly forsake me.

ב Beth

[9]How can a young man keep his way pure?
  By living according to your word.
[10]I seek you with all my heart;
  do not let me stray from your commands.
[11]I have hidden your word in my heart
  that I might not sin against you.
[12]Praise be to you, O LORD;
  teach me your decrees.
[13]With my lips I recount
  all the laws that come from your mouth.
[14]I rejoice in following your statutes
  as one rejoices in great riches.
[15]I meditate on your precepts
  and consider your ways.
[16]I delight in your decrees;
  I will not neglect your word.

ג Gimel

[17]Do good to your servant, and I will live;
  I will obey your word.
[18]Open my eyes that I may see

[a]This psalm is an acrostic poem; the verses of each stanza begin with the same letter of the Hebrew alphabet.

NRSV

Psalm 119

[1] Happy are those whose way is blameless,
  who walk in the law of the LORD.
[2] Happy are those who keep his decrees,
  who seek him with their whole heart,
[3] who also do no wrong,
  but walk in his ways.
[4] You have commanded your precepts
  to be kept diligently.
[5] O that my ways may be steadfast
  in keeping your statutes!
[6] Then I shall not be put to shame,
  having my eyes fixed on all your
    commandments.
[7] I will praise you with an upright heart,
  when I learn your righteous ordinances.
[8] I will observe your statutes;
  do not utterly forsake me.

[9] How can young people keep their way pure?
  By guarding it according to your word.
[10] With my whole heart I seek you;
  do not let me stray from your
    commandments.
[11] I treasure your word in my heart,
  so that I may not sin against you.
[12] Blessed are you, O LORD;
  teach me your statutes.
[13] With my lips I declare
  all the ordinances of your mouth.
[14] I delight in the way of your decrees
  as much as in all riches.
[15] I will meditate on your precepts,
  and fix my eyes on your ways.
[16] I will delight in your statutes;
  I will not forget your word.

[17] Deal bountifully with your servant,
  so that I may live and observe your word.
[18] Open my eyes, so that I may behold
  wondrous things out of your law.
[19] I live as an alien in the land;

NIV

wonderful things in your law.
[19] I am a stranger on earth;
    do not hide your commands from me.
[20] My soul is consumed with longing
    for your laws at all times.
[21] You rebuke the arrogant, who are cursed
    and who stray from your commands.
[22] Remove from me scorn and contempt,
    for I keep your statutes.
[23] Though rulers sit together and slander me,
    your servant will meditate on your decrees.
[24] Your statutes are my delight;
    they are my counselors.

ד Daleth

[25] I am laid low in the dust;
    preserve my life according to your word.
[26] I recounted my ways and you answered me;
    teach me your decrees.
[27] Let me understand the teaching of your
        precepts;
    then I will meditate on your wonders.
[28] My soul is weary with sorrow;
    strengthen me according to your word.
[29] Keep me from deceitful ways;
    be gracious to me through your law.
[30] I have chosen the way of truth;
    I have set my heart on your laws.
[31] I hold fast to your statutes, O Lord;
    do not let me be put to shame.
[32] I run in the path of your commands,
    for you have set my heart free.

ה He

[33] Teach me, O Lord, to follow your decrees;
    then I will keep them to the end.
[34] Give me understanding, and I will keep your
        law
    and obey it with all my heart.
[35] Direct me in the path of your commands,
    for there I find delight.
[36] Turn my heart toward your statutes
    and not toward selfish gain.
[37] Turn my eyes away from worthless things;
    preserve my life according to your word.[a]
[38] Fulfill your promise to your servant,
    so that you may be feared.

a37 Two manuscripts of the Masoretic Text and Dead Sea Scrolls; most
manuscripts of the Masoretic Text *life in your way*

NRSV

do not hide your commandments from
    me.
[20] My soul is consumed with longing
    for your ordinances at all times.
[21] You rebuke the insolent, accursed ones,
    who wander from your commandments;
[22] take away from me their scorn and
        contempt,
    for I have kept your decrees.
[23] Even though princes sit plotting against me,
    your servant will meditate on your
        statutes.
[24] Your decrees are my delight,
    they are my counselors.

[25] My soul clings to the dust;
    revive me according to your word.
[26] When I told of my ways, you answered me;
    teach me your statutes.
[27] Make me understand the way of your
        precepts,
    and I will meditate on your wondrous
        works.
[28] My soul melts away for sorrow;
    strengthen me according to your word.
[29] Put false ways far from me;
    and graciously teach me your law.
[30] I have chosen the way of faithfulness;
    I set your ordinances before me.
[31] I cling to your decrees, O Lord;
    let me not be put to shame.
[32] I run the way of your commandments,
    for you enlarge my understanding.

[33] Teach me, O Lord, the way of your statutes,
    and I will observe it to the end.
[34] Give me understanding, that I may keep
        your law
    and observe it with my whole heart.
[35] Lead me in the path of your commandments,
    for I delight in it.
[36] Turn my heart to your decrees,
    and not to selfish gain.
[37] Turn my eyes from looking at vanities;
    give me life in your ways.
[38] Confirm to your servant your promise,
    which is for those who fear you.
[39] Turn away the disgrace that I dread,
    for your ordinances are good.

NIV

³⁹Take away the disgrace I dread,
    for your laws are good.
⁴⁰How I long for your precepts!
    Preserve my life in your righteousness.

ו Waw

⁴¹May your unfailing love come to me, O LORD,
    your salvation according to your promise;
⁴²then I will answer the one who taunts me,
    for I trust in your word.
⁴³Do not snatch the word of truth from my
        mouth,
    for I have put my hope in your laws.
⁴⁴I will always obey your law,
    for ever and ever.
⁴⁵I will walk about in freedom,
    for I have sought out your precepts.
⁴⁶I will speak of your statutes before kings
    and will not be put to shame,
⁴⁷for I delight in your commands
    because I love them.
⁴⁸I lift up my hands to^a your commands, which
        I love,
    and I meditate on your decrees.

ז Zayin

⁴⁹Remember your word to your servant,
    for you have given me hope.
⁵⁰My comfort in my suffering is this:
    Your promise preserves my life.
⁵¹The arrogant mock me without restraint,
    but I do not turn from your law.
⁵²I remember your ancient laws, O LORD,
    and I find comfort in them.
⁵³Indignation grips me because of the wicked,
    who have forsaken your law.
⁵⁴Your decrees are the theme of my song
    wherever I lodge.
⁵⁵In the night I remember your name, O LORD,
    and I will keep your law.
⁵⁶This has been my practice:
    I obey your precepts.

ח Heth

⁵⁷You are my portion, O LORD;
    I have promised to obey your words.
⁵⁸I have sought your face with all my heart;
    be gracious to me according to your promise.

^a48 Or for

NRSV

⁴⁰ See, I have longed for your precepts;
    in your righteousness give me life.

⁴¹ Let your steadfast love come to me, O LORD,
    your salvation according to your promise.
⁴² Then I shall have an answer for those who
        taunt me,
    for I trust in your word.
⁴³ Do not take the word of truth utterly out
        of my mouth,
    for my hope is in your ordinances.
⁴⁴ I will keep your law continually,
    forever and ever.
⁴⁵ I shall walk at liberty,
    for I have sought your precepts.
⁴⁶ I will also speak of your decrees before
        kings,
    and shall not be put to shame;
⁴⁷ I find my delight in your commandments,
    because I love them.
⁴⁸ I revere your commandments, which I love,
    and I will meditate on your statutes.

⁴⁹ Remember your word to your servant,
    in which you have made me hope.
⁵⁰ This is my comfort in my distress,
    that your promise gives me life.
⁵¹ The arrogant utterly deride me,
    but I do not turn away from your law.
⁵² When I think of your ordinances from of
        old,
    I take comfort, O LORD.
⁵³ Hot indignation seizes me because of the
        wicked,
    those who forsake your law.
⁵⁴ Your statutes have been my songs
    wherever I make my home.
⁵⁵ I remember your name in the night, O LORD,
    and keep your law.
⁵⁶ This blessing has fallen to me,
    for I have kept your precepts.

⁵⁷ The LORD is my portion;
    I promise to keep your words.
⁵⁸ I implore your favor with all my heart;
    be gracious to me according to your
        promise.
⁵⁹ When I think of your ways,
    I turn my feet to your decrees;

NIV

⁵⁹I have considered my ways
and have turned my steps to your statutes.
⁶⁰I will hasten and not delay
to obey your commands.
⁶¹Though the wicked bind me with ropes,
I will not forget your law.
⁶²At midnight I rise to give you thanks
for your righteous laws.
⁶³I am a friend to all who fear you,
to all who follow your precepts.
⁶⁴The earth is filled with your love, O LORD;
teach me your decrees.

ט Teth

⁶⁵Do good to your servant
according to your word, O LORD.
⁶⁶Teach me knowledge and good judgment,
for I believe in your commands.
⁶⁷Before I was afflicted I went astray,
but now I obey your word.
⁶⁸You are good, and what you do is good;
teach me your decrees.
⁶⁹Though the arrogant have smeared me with
lies,
I keep your precepts with all my heart.
⁷⁰Their hearts are callous and unfeeling,
but I delight in your law.
⁷¹It was good for me to be afflicted
so that I might learn your decrees.
⁷²The law from your mouth is more precious
to me
than thousands of pieces of silver and gold.

י Yodh

⁷³Your hands made me and formed me;
give me understanding to learn your
commands.
⁷⁴May those who fear you rejoice when they
see me,
for I have put my hope in your word.
⁷⁵I know, O LORD, that your laws are righteous,
and in faithfulness you have afflicted me.
⁷⁶May your unfailing love be my comfort,
according to your promise to your servant.
⁷⁷Let your compassion come to me that I may
live,
for your law is my delight.
⁷⁸May the arrogant be put to shame for
wronging me without cause;

NRSV

⁶⁰ I hurry and do not delay
to keep your commandments.
⁶¹ Though the cords of the wicked ensnare me,
I do not forget your law.
⁶² At midnight I rise to praise you,
because of your righteous ordinances.
⁶³ I am a companion of all who fear you,
of those who keep your precepts.
⁶⁴ The earth, O LORD, is full of your steadfast
love;
teach me your statutes.

⁶⁵ You have dealt well with your servant,
O LORD, according to your word.
⁶⁶ Teach me good judgment and knowledge,
for I believe in your commandments.
⁶⁷ Before I was humbled I went astray,
but now I keep your word.
⁶⁸ You are good and do good;
teach me your statutes.
⁶⁹ The arrogant smear me with lies,
but with my whole heart I keep your
precepts.
⁷⁰ Their hearts are fat and gross,
but I delight in your law.
⁷¹ It is good for me that I was humbled,
so that I might learn your statutes.
⁷² The law of your mouth is better to me
than thousands of gold and silver pieces.

⁷³ Your hands have made and fashioned me;
give me understanding that I may learn
your commandments.
⁷⁴ Those who fear you shall see me and
rejoice,
because I have hoped in your word.
⁷⁵ I know, O LORD, that your judgments are
right,
and that in faithfulness you have
humbled me.
⁷⁶ Let your steadfast love become my comfort
according to your promise to your servant.
⁷⁷ Let your mercy come to me, that I may live;
for your law is my delight.
⁷⁸ Let the arrogant be put to shame,
because they have subverted me with guile;
as for me, I will meditate on your
precepts.
⁷⁹ Let those who fear you turn to me,

NIV

but I will meditate on your precepts.
⁷⁹May those who fear you turn to me,
those who understand your statutes.
⁸⁰May my heart be blameless toward your
decrees,
that I may not be put to shame.

‏כ‎ Kaph

⁸¹My soul faints with longing for your salvation,
but I have put my hope in your word.
⁸²My eyes fail, looking for your promise;
I say, "When will you comfort me?"
⁸³Though I am like a wineskin in the smoke,
I do not forget your decrees.
⁸⁴How long must your servant wait?
When will you punish my persecutors?
⁸⁵The arrogant dig pitfalls for me,
contrary to your law.
⁸⁶All your commands are trustworthy;
help me, for men persecute me without
cause.
⁸⁷They almost wiped me from the earth,
but I have not forsaken your precepts.
⁸⁸Preserve my life according to your love,
and I will obey the statutes of your
mouth.

‏ל‎ Lamedh

⁸⁹Your word, O LORD, is eternal;
it stands firm in the heavens.
⁹⁰Your faithfulness continues through all
generations;
you established the earth, and it endures.
⁹¹Your laws endure to this day,
for all things serve you.
⁹²If your law had not been my delight,
I would have perished in my affliction.
⁹³I will never forget your precepts,
for by them you have preserved my life.
⁹⁴Save me, for I am yours;
I have sought out your precepts.
⁹⁵The wicked are waiting to destroy me,
but I will ponder your statutes.
⁹⁶To all perfection I see a limit;
but your commands are boundless.

‏מ‎ Mem

⁹⁷Oh, how I love your law!
I meditate on it all day long.

NRSV

so that they may know your decrees.
⁸⁰ May my heart be blameless in your statutes,
so that I may not be put to shame.

⁸¹ My soul languishes for your salvation;
I hope in your word.
⁸² My eyes fail with watching for your promise;
I ask, "When will you comfort me?"
⁸³ For I have become like a wineskin in the
smoke,
yet I have not forgotten your statutes.
⁸⁴ How long must your servant endure?
When will you judge those who
persecute me?
⁸⁵ The arrogant have dug pitfalls for me;
they flout your law.
⁸⁶ All your commandments are enduring;
I am persecuted without cause; help me!
⁸⁷ They have almost made an end of me on
earth;
but I have not forsaken your precepts.
⁸⁸ In your steadfast love spare my life,
so that I may keep the decrees of your
mouth.

⁸⁹ The LORD exists forever;
your word is firmly fixed in heaven.
⁹⁰ Your faithfulness endures to all generations;
you have established the earth, and it
stands fast.
⁹¹ By your appointment they stand today,
for all things are your servants.
⁹² If your law had not been my delight,
I would have perished in my misery.
⁹³ I will never forget your precepts,
for by them you have given me life.
⁹⁴ I am yours; save me,
for I have sought your precepts.
⁹⁵ The wicked lie in wait to destroy me,
but I consider your decrees.
⁹⁶ I have seen a limit to all perfection,
but your commandment is exceedingly
broad.

⁹⁷ Oh, how I love your law!
It is my meditation all day long.
⁹⁸ Your commandment makes me wiser than
my enemies,
for it is always with me.

NIV

⁹⁸Your commands make me wiser than my
enemies,
for they are ever with me.
⁹⁹I have more insight than all my teachers,
for I meditate on your statutes.
¹⁰⁰I have more understanding than the elders,
for I obey your precepts.
¹⁰¹I have kept my feet from every evil path
so that I might obey your word.
¹⁰²I have not departed from your laws,
for you yourself have taught me.
¹⁰³How sweet are your words to my taste,
sweeter than honey to my mouth!
¹⁰⁴I gain understanding from your precepts;
therefore I hate every wrong path.

נ Nun

¹⁰⁵Your word is a lamp to my feet
and a light for my path.
¹⁰⁶I have taken an oath and confirmed it,
that I will follow your righteous laws.
¹⁰⁷I have suffered much;
preserve my life, O LORD, according to
your word.
¹⁰⁸Accept, O LORD, the willing praise of my
mouth,
and teach me your laws.
¹⁰⁹Though I constantly take my life in my
hands,
I will not forget your law.
¹¹⁰The wicked have set a snare for me,
but I have not strayed from your precepts.
¹¹¹Your statutes are my heritage forever;
they are the joy of my heart.
¹¹²My heart is set on keeping your decrees
to the very end.

ס Samekh

¹¹³I hate double-minded men,
but I love your law.
¹¹⁴You are my refuge and my shield;
I have put my hope in your word.
¹¹⁵Away from me, you evildoers,
that I may keep the commands of my God!
¹¹⁶Sustain me according to your promise, and I
will live;
do not let my hopes be dashed.
¹¹⁷Uphold me, and I will be delivered;
I will always have regard for your decrees.

NRSV

⁹⁹ I have more understanding than all my
teachers,
for your decrees are my meditation.
¹⁰⁰ I understand more than the aged,
for I keep your precepts.
¹⁰¹ I hold back my feet from every evil way,
in order to keep your word.
¹⁰² I do not turn away from your ordinances,
for you have taught me.
¹⁰³ How sweet are your words to my taste,
sweeter than honey to my mouth!
¹⁰⁴ Through your precepts I get understanding;
therefore I hate every false way.

¹⁰⁵ Your word is a lamp to my feet
and a light to my path.
¹⁰⁶ I have sworn an oath and confirmed it,
to observe your righteous ordinances.
¹⁰⁷ I am severely afflicted;
give me life, O LORD, according to your
word.
¹⁰⁸ Accept my offerings of praise, O LORD,
and teach me your ordinances.
¹⁰⁹ I hold my life in my hand continually,
but I do not forget your law.
¹¹⁰ The wicked have laid a snare for me,
but I do not stray from your precepts.
¹¹¹ Your decrees are my heritage forever;
they are the joy of my heart.
¹¹² I incline my heart to perform your statutes
forever, to the end.

¹¹³ I hate the double-minded,
but I love your law.
¹¹⁴ You are my hiding place and my shield;
I hope in your word.
¹¹⁵ Go away from me, you evildoers,
that I may keep the commandments of
my God.
¹¹⁶ Uphold me according to your promise, that
I may live,
and let me not be put to shame in my
hope.
¹¹⁷ Hold me up, that I may be safe
and have regard for your statutes
continually.
¹¹⁸ You spurn all who go astray from your
statutes;
for their cunning is in vain.

NIV

118You reject all who stray from your decrees,
for their deceitfulness is in vain.
119All the wicked of the earth you discard like
dross;
therefore I love your statutes.
120My flesh trembles in fear of you;
I stand in awe of your laws.

ע Ayin

121I have done what is righteous and just;
do not leave me to my oppressors.
122Ensure your servant's well-being;
let not the arrogant oppress me.
123My eyes fail, looking for your salvation,
looking for your righteous promise.
124Deal with your servant according to your love
and teach me your decrees.
125I am your servant; give me discernment
that I may understand your statutes.
126It is time for you to act, O Lord;
your law is being broken.
127Because I love your commands
more than gold, more than pure gold,
128and because I consider all your precepts right,
I hate every wrong path.

פ Pe

129Your statutes are wonderful;
therefore I obey them.
130The unfolding of your words gives light;
it gives understanding to the simple.
131I open my mouth and pant,
longing for your commands.
132Turn to me and have mercy on me,
as you always do to those who love your
name.
133Direct my footsteps according to your word;
let no sin rule over me.
134Redeem me from the oppression of men,
that I may obey your precepts.
135Make your face shine upon your servant
and teach me your decrees.
136Streams of tears flow from my eyes,
for your law is not obeyed.

צ Tsadhe

137Righteous are you, O Lord,
and your laws are right.

NRSV

119 All the wicked of the earth you count as
dross;
therefore I love your decrees.
120 My flesh trembles for fear of you,
and I am afraid of your judgments.

121 I have done what is just and right;
do not leave me to my oppressors.
122 Guarantee your servant's well-being;
do not let the godless oppress me.
123 My eyes fail from watching for your
salvation,
and for the fulfillment of your righteous
promise.
124 Deal with your servant according to your
steadfast love,
and teach me your statutes.
125 I am your servant; give me understanding,
so that I may know your decrees.
126 It is time for the Lord to act,
for your law has been broken.
127 Truly I love your commandments
more than gold, more than fine gold.
128 Truly I direct my steps by all your precepts;[a]
I hate every false way.

129 Your decrees are wonderful;
therefore my soul keeps them.
130 The unfolding of your words gives light;
it imparts understanding to the simple.
131 With open mouth I pant,
because I long for your commandments.
132 Turn to me and be gracious to me,
as is your custom toward those who love
your name.
133 Keep my steps steady according to your
promise,
and never let iniquity have dominion
over me.
134 Redeem me from human oppression,
that I may keep your precepts.
135 Make your face shine upon your servant,
and teach me your statutes.
136 My eyes shed streams of tears
because your law is not kept.

137 You are righteous, O Lord,
and your judgments are right.

a Gk Jerome: Meaning of Heb uncertain

NIV

138The statutes you have laid down are
    righteous;
    they are fully trustworthy.
139My zeal wears me out,
    for my enemies ignore your words.
140Your promises have been thoroughly tested,
    and your servant loves them.
141Though I am lowly and despised,
    I do not forget your precepts.
142Your righteousness is everlasting
    and your law is true.
143Trouble and distress have come upon me,
    but your commands are my delight.
144Your statutes are forever right;
    give me understanding that I may live.

ק Qoph

145I call with all my heart; answer me, O LORD,
    and I will obey your decrees.
146I call out to you; save me
    and I will keep your statutes.
147I rise before dawn and cry for help;
    I have put my hope in your word.
148My eyes stay open through the watches of
    the night,
    that I may meditate on your promises.
149Hear my voice in accordance with your love;
    preserve my life, O LORD, according to
    your laws.
150Those who devise wicked schemes are near,
    but they are far from your law.
151Yet you are near, O LORD,
    and all your commands are true.
152Long ago I learned from your statutes
    that you established them to last forever.

ר Resh

153Look upon my suffering and deliver me,
    for I have not forgotten your law.
154Defend my cause and redeem me;
    preserve my life according to your promise.
155Salvation is far from the wicked,
    for they do not seek out your decrees.
156Your compassion is great, O LORD;
    preserve my life according to your laws.
157Many are the foes who persecute me,
    but I have not turned from your statutes.
158I look on the faithless with loathing,
    for they do not obey your word.

NRSV

138 You have appointed your decrees in
    righteousness
    and in all faithfulness.
139 My zeal consumes me
    because my foes forget your words.
140 Your promise is well tried,
    and your servant loves it.
141 I am small and despised,
    yet I do not forget your precepts.
142 Your righteousness is an everlasting
    righteousness,
    and your law is the truth.
143 Trouble and anguish have come upon me,
    but your commandments are my delight.
144 Your decrees are righteous forever;
    give me understanding that I may live.

145 With my whole heart I cry; answer me,
    O LORD.
    I will keep your statutes.
146 I cry to you; save me,
    that I may observe your decrees.
147 I rise before dawn and cry for help;
    I put my hope in your words.
148 My eyes are awake before each watch of
    the night,
    that I may meditate on your promise.
149 In your steadfast love hear my voice;
    O LORD, in your justice preserve my life.
150 Those who persecute me with evil purpose
    draw near;
    they are far from your law.
151 Yet you are near, O LORD,
    and all your commandments are true.
152 Long ago I learned from your decrees
    that you have established them forever.

153 Look on my misery and rescue me,
    for I do not forget your law.
154 Plead my cause and redeem me;
    give me life according to your promise.
155 Salvation is far from the wicked,
    for they do not seek your statutes.
156 Great is your mercy, O LORD;
    give me life according to your justice.
157 Many are my persecutors and my adversaries,
    yet I do not swerve from your decrees.
158 I look at the faithless with disgust,
    because they do not keep your commands.

NIV

¹⁵⁹See how I love your precepts;
    preserve my life, O LORD, according to
        your love.
¹⁶⁰All your words are true;
    all your righteous laws are eternal.

ש Sin and Shin

¹⁶¹Rulers persecute me without cause,
    but my heart trembles at your word.
¹⁶²I rejoice in your promise
    like one who finds great spoil.
¹⁶³I hate and abhor falsehood
    but I love your law.
¹⁶⁴Seven times a day I praise you
    for your righteous laws.
¹⁶⁵Great peace have they who love your law,
    and nothing can make them stumble.
¹⁶⁶I wait for your salvation, O LORD,
    and I follow your commands.
¹⁶⁷I obey your statutes,
    for I love them greatly.
¹⁶⁸I obey your precepts and your statutes,
    for all my ways are known to you.

ת Taw

¹⁶⁹May my cry come before you, O LORD;
    give me understanding according to your
        word.
¹⁷⁰May my supplication come before you;
    deliver me according to your promise.
¹⁷¹May my lips overflow with praise,
    for you teach me your decrees.
¹⁷²May my tongue sing of your word,
    for all your commands are righteous.
¹⁷³May your hand be ready to help me,
    for I have chosen your precepts.
¹⁷⁴I long for your salvation, O LORD,
    and your law is my delight.
¹⁷⁵Let me live that I may praise you,
    and may your laws sustain me.
¹⁷⁶I have strayed like a lost sheep.
    Seek your servant,
        for I have not forgotten your commands.

NRSV

¹⁵⁹ Consider how I love your precepts;
    preserve my life according to your
        steadfast love.
¹⁶⁰ The sum of your word is truth;
    and every one of your righteous
        ordinances endures forever.

¹⁶¹ Princes persecute me without cause,
    but my heart stands in awe of your
        words.
¹⁶² I rejoice at your word
    like one who finds great spoil.
¹⁶³ I hate and abhor falsehood,
    but I love your law.
¹⁶⁴ Seven times a day I praise you
    for your righteous ordinances.
¹⁶⁵ Great peace have those who love your law;
    nothing can make them stumble.
¹⁶⁶ I hope for your salvation, O LORD,
    and I fulfill your commandments.
¹⁶⁷ My soul keeps your decrees;
    I love them exceedingly.
¹⁶⁸ I keep your precepts and decrees,
    for all my ways are before you.

¹⁶⁹ Let my cry come before you, O LORD;
    give me understanding according to your
        word.
¹⁷⁰ Let my supplication come before you;
    deliver me according to your promise.
¹⁷¹ My lips will pour forth praise,
    because you teach me your statutes.
¹⁷² My tongue will sing of your promise,
    for all your commandments are right.
¹⁷³ Let your hand be ready to help me,
    for I have chosen your precepts.
¹⁷⁴ I long for your salvation, O LORD,
    and your law is my delight.
¹⁷⁵ Let me live that I may praise you,
    and let your ordinances help me.
¹⁷⁶ I have gone astray like a lost sheep; seek
        out your servant,
    for I do not forget your commandments.

COMMENTARY

Simply by virtue of its length, Psalm 119 is impressive and imposing, perhaps even intimidating. Leslie Allen aptly calls it "a literary monument raised in honor of Yahweh's revelation . . . to Israel."[435] As is the case with any imposing structure, some people like Psalm 119, and some people do not. Leopold Sabourin, for instance, reflects the opinion of many commentators when he describes Psalm 119: "Tedious repetitions, poor thought-sequence, apparent lack of inspiration reflect the artificiality of the composition."[436] In contrast, Dahood detects "a freshness of thought and a felicity of expression" throughout the psalm.[437]

To be sure, Psalm 119 is repetitive, but repetition is not necessarily tedious. By "artificiality," Sabourin means the acrostic structure of Psalm 119, comprising twenty-two sections, one for each letter of the Hebrew alphabet (see NIV). Each poetic line in the first section begins with the letter *Aleph* (א), each line in the second section begins with *Beth* (ב) and so on. This kind of repetition is accompanied by another: the repeated use of eight Hebrew terms that designate God's revelation. The frequent use of eight terms may explain why each section contains eight verses; however, not every verse contains one of these terms. The first and most frequently used (twenty-five occurrences, at least once in every section except vv. 9-16) is *torah* (v. 1*b*; NIV and NRSV, "law"), which should be translated "teaching" or "instruction" or "law" (see Commentary on Psalm 1). The other seven can be considered synonyms of *torah* (תורה *tôrâ*; for the nuances of each term, see below). In order of their first appearance in the psalm, they are as follows: "decrees" (or "statutes," עדת *'ēdōt*, v. 20, twenty-three occurrences), "precepts" (פקודים *piqqûdîm*, v. 4, twenty-one occurrences), "statutes" (or "decrees," חקים *huqqîm*, v. 5, twenty-two occurrences), "command(ments)" (מצות *miṣwōt*, v. 6, twenty-two occurrences), "ordinances" (משפטים *mišpāṭîm*, v. 7 NRSV; NIV, "laws"; twenty-two

occurrences, usually plural, but singular in vv. 84, 121, 132 where it is translated differently), "word" (דבר *dābār*, v. 9, twenty-two occurrences), "promise" (אמרה *'imrâ*, v. 11, nineteen occurrences). With the exception of vv. 3, 37, 90, and 122, every line in Psalm 119 contains one of these eight words.

When commentators consider this repetition tedious, they are missing the point. Psalm 119 is more artistic than artificial. As a literary artist, the psalmist intended the structure of the poem to reinforce its theological content. In short, *torah*— God's revelatory instruction—is pervasive and all-encompassing. It applies to everything from A to Z, or in Hebrew, *Aleph* to *Taw*. As Westermann recognizes, "If a person succeeds in reading this psalm's 176 verses one after the other at one sitting, the effect is overwhelming."[438] This is precisely the effect the psalmist intended! For the psalmist, the importance of God's instruction is overwhelming. It applies to everything at every moment, and apart from it, there is nothing worthy to be called life (see Commentary on Psalm 19). This being the case, the proper stance toward God is constant openness to God's instruction (see Commentary on Psalm 1); Jon Levenson suggests that the repetition in Psalm 119 is intended to create a psychological condition—the proper state of mind and heart—which is conducive to concentration upon God and thus openness to God's revelation:

> It seems likely that the psalm was written to serve as an inducement for the kind of revelation and illumination for which it petitions. Its high degree of regularity and repetition can have a mesmerizing effect upon those who recite it, with the octad of synonyms functioning like a mantra and providing a relaxing predictability while banishing thoughts that distract from the object of contemplation. If the goal of the author was to create the psychic conditions conducive to the spiritual experience he seeks, then those commentators who wish the psalm were shorter have missed the point of it . . . there are liturgies that are best short, and others, like Psalm 119, that work only if they are long.[439]

435. Leslie C. Allen, *Psalms 101–150,* WBC 21 (Waco, Tex.: Word, 1983) 141.
436. Leopold Sabourin, *The Psalms: Their Origin and Meaning* (New York: Alba House, 1994) 381.
437. Mitchell Dahood, *Psalms III (101–150),* AB 17*a* (Garden City, N.Y.: Doubleday, 1970) 172.

438. Claus Westermann, *The Psalms: Structure, Content, and Message,* trans. R. D. Gehrke (Minneapolis: Augsburg, 1980) 117.
439. Jon Levenson, "The Sources of Torah: Psalm 119 and the Modes of Revelation in Second Temple Judaism," in *Ancient Israelite Religion,* ed. P. D. Miller, Jr., P. D. Hanson, S. D. McBride (Philadelphia: Fortress, 1987) 566.

The psalmist's concept of *torah* is an expansive one. While Psalm 119 has several verbal and conceptual affinities with the book of Deuteronomy and the Deuteronomistic history, including the importance of obedience to God's commandments, it is striking that the psalmist never considers *torah* to be simply a body of legislation, Mosaic or otherwise, and certainly not a book—that is, not the Pentateuch or an emerging core of the Pentateuch. In this regard, the psalmist seems to have more in common with how *torah* was understood by the prophets or wisdom teachers. Levenson summarizes: "We have seen that the author of Psalm 119 recognizes three sources of *tôrâ*: (1) received tradition, passed on most explicitly by teachers (vv. 99-100) but including perhaps some sacred books now in the Hebrew Bible, (2) cosmic or natural law (vv. 89-91), and (3) unmediated divine teaching (e. g., vv. 26-29)."[440] In short, while oral and written tradition were very significant for the psalmist, he or she remained open to God's ongoing instruction, to God's further revelation, to new experiences of the divine Word. This openness has profound implications for current discussions of the inspiration of and authority of Scripture as a written word (see Reflections below).

While Psalm 119 demonstrates affinities with Deuteronomy, with wisdom materials, and with the prophets (especially Jeremiah), it is not possible to identify the psalmist easily with any particular figure, body of material, or perspective. Will Soll argues that Psalm 119 makes sense as a prayer of the exiled King Jehoiachin for the restoration of the Davidic monarchy.[441] But Levenson points out that the psalmist's concept of *torah* is quite similar to that of Ben Sira, who taught and wrote some four hundred years after Jehoiachin.[442] This disparity points to the difficulty, if not the impossibility, of recovering the circumstances of the origin and original use of Psalm 119. It probably originated during the post-exilic era, but what is more recoverable is the setting implied by the content of the psalm itself. Mays suggests

on the basis of Psalm 119 (as well as Psalms 1 and 19, which also highlight the concept of *torah*) that the setting for *all* the Psalms is "a type of piety . . . that used the entire book as prayer and praise." This torah piety was characterized by "faithfulness through study and obedience and hope through prayer and waiting."[443]

The identification of the setting of Psalm 119 as a type of piety explains why the psalm would have been an appropriate prayer for Jehoiachin or Jeremiah or Ben Sira or Israel in exile/dispersion. While the psalmist does not claim to be perfect (see v. 176), it is clear that he or she is committed to obedience. Even so, the psalmist is scorned and persecuted (vv. 22-23, 42, 51, 61, 69, 84-87, 95, 110, 121, 134, 141, 150, 157, 161) and experiences sorrow and affliction (vv. 28, 50, 71, 75, 92, 107, 153). Thus the psalmist lives in waiting as a suffering servant (see vv. 17, 23, 38, 49, 65, 76, 84, 91, 122, 124, 125, 135). In other words, the perspective of Psalm 119 is eschatological. Life is entrusted to the sovereign God in circumstances that seem to belie God's sovereignty (see Commentary on Psalms 1; 2; Introduction).

The eschatological dimension of Psalm 119 makes it a fitting anchor for Book V, which, along with Book IV, responds to the crisis of exile and its aftermath by proclaiming God's sovereignty, by recalling past deliverance, and by praying for future deliverance (see Commentary on Psalms 107; 111; 118; Introduction). Psalm 119 also clearly recalls Psalms 1–2 (cf. 119:1 with 1:1; 2:12), which from the beginning of the psalter commend openness to God's instruction and the entrusting of life and future to God. The eschatological dimension of Psalm 119 also gives the psalm the character of a prayer for help or individual lament/complaint, and some commentators classify it as such. Most commentators, however, consider Psalm 119 a torah psalm, along with Psalms 1 and 19. In a sense, Psalm 119 belongs in a class by itself. Because of its length, it contains elements of all types of psalms. This in itself is appropriate, since Psalm 119 articulates so eloquently and powerfully the torah-piety that pervades the whole psalter.

The acrostic pattern of Psalm 119 is its most prominent structural feature and some would say

440. Ibid., 570.

441. Will Soll, *Psalm 119: Matrix, Form, and Setting*, CBQMS 23 (Washington, D.C.: Catholic Biblical Association, 1991) 152-54.

442. Jon Levenson, "The Sources of Torah: Psalm 119 and the Modes of Revelation in Second Temple Judaism," in *Ancient Israelite Religion*, ed. P. D. Miller, Jr., P. D. Hanson, S. D. McBride (Philadelphia: Fortress, 1987) 567-68.

443. James L. Mays, "The Place of the Torah-Psalms in the Psalter," *JBL* 106 (1987) 12.

its only organizing principle. Indeed, some scholars suggest that Psalm 119 would make as much sense read backward as it does forward. Soll, however, detects a larger coherence. He suggests the following divisions designated by the letters of the Hebrew alphabet, featured in each eight-verse section:

I. *Aleph-Bêt* (vv. 1-16): Prologue
II. *Gîmel-Wāw* (vv. 17-48)
III. *Zayin-Yôd* (vv. 49-80)
IV. *Kaph-Sāmek* (vv. 81-120): central section
V. *'Ayin-Ṣādê* (vv. 121-144)
VI. *Qôph-Tāw* (vv. 145-176): Concluding section

In Soll's view, Psalm 119 is an individual lament, and it shows the characteristic movement of such prayers—from complaint and petition (vv. 17-24) to praise and assurance (vv. 169-176), with the turning point coming at vv. 89-96. This turning point, which Soll considers the zenith of the poem, occurs in the central division immediately following the section that Soll identifies as the "nadir" of the poem (vv. 81-88). Soll recognizes that complaint and petition continue to occur after the central division, but he attributes this to the length of the poem, suggesting that the basic movement from complaint/petition to praise is recapitulated in each division, as in Psalm 31.[444] While Soll finds significantly more coherence in Psalm 119 than do most other commentators, his proposal is a welcome corrective to those who assert that Psalm 119 shows no coherence or logical movement. After all, it only makes sense that the psalmist's careful artistry would extend beyond the measure of the individual poetic line or section.

119:1-8. It is not surprising that Psalm 119 uses several items of vocabulary from Psalms 1 and 19. In fact, every word of v. 1 occurs in either Psalm 1 or Psalm 19. It is clear that the blamelessness (see Ps 19:13) involved is not moral perfection, for the psalmist later confesses, "I have strayed like a lost sheep" (v. 176, lit., "perishing sheep"; "perish" [אבד *'ābad*] is the same word used to describe the way of the wicked in Ps 1:6!). Likewise, the psalmist's being "happy" (see Pss 1:1; 2:12) must involve something very different from simply reaping material benefits for obedience. Somehow, the psalmist's happiness

cannot be incompatible with the persecution, scorn, sorrow, and affliction he or she experiences. In short, happiness has to do with entrusting life to God, which means constant openness to God's life-giving *torah* (see Pss 1:2; 19:7).

Subsequent verses introduce other terms for God's revelation. Verse 2 is reminiscent of Deuteronomy, where God's "decrees" (see Ps 19:7) are to be heard and kept (see Deut 4:45; 6:17, 20) and where God is to be sought wholeheartedly (see Deut 4:29; Ps 119:10). Verse 3 is unusual in that it does not contain one of the eight major synonyms. Rather, God's "ways" indicate God's revelation in this case (see also vv. 15, 37), and the image of walking in God's ways is again reminiscent of Deuteronomy, occurring often in parallel with keeping God's commandments (see Deut 8:6; 10:12-13; 11:22; see Ps 119:6). While "precepts" (*piqqûdîm*, v. 4) occurs elsewhere only in the psalms (see 19:8; 103:18; 111:7), "statutes" (*huqqîm*, vv. 5, 8) and "ordinances" (*mišpāṭîm*, v. 7) again recall Deuteronomy and other portions of the Pentateuch (see Exod 18:16; Deut 6:1; 7:11). The word "ordinances" is the plural of a noun usually translated "justice" (see vv. 121, 156), a reminder that the purpose of God's instruction is to order rightly (see "righteous" or "right" in vv. 7, 62, 75, 106, 121, 137, 164) the human community (see Pss 97:2; 99:4). While the repeated terms in Psalm 119 can and certainly do elsewhere suggest written formulations of God's will, and while the psalmist may have such written codes in mind, the obedience he or she seeks should not be understood as a simple matter of following a set of rules. Verses 1-8 communicate the sense that the psalmist continually seeks God, which means seeking new and deeper understandings of how God intends justice and righteousness to be enacted in the world. This seems clear as well in vv. 9-16.

119:9-16. The question of cleanness or purity in v. 9*a* (see Ps 73:13; Prov 20:9) is answered by reference to another of the eight synonyms: "word" (*dābār*). While *torah* seems to be the most important of the eight (vv. 9-16 is the only section in which it does not occur), "word" seems to be next in line. Not only does it provide an envelope structure for the second introductory section (vv. 9, 16), but it also appears in the first

444. Soll, *Psalm 119*, 90-111.

line of fully half of the psalm's twenty-two sections. While "word" can suggest written revelation (see Exod 34:27-28; Deut 4:13), it also designates God's communication beyond any current written formulation (see 1 Kgs 6:11; 13:20; Jer 1:4; Ezek 1:3) and thus suggests a dynamic revelatory power that will not finally be thwarted (see Ps 33:6; Isa 40:8; 55:11). The psalmist apparently is open to both God's past and future revelation.

Verse 11 introduces the final of the eight synonyms and the one that occurs least often. The noun is derived from a verb that means "to say," "to utter" (אמר 'āmar), and it never clearly designates a written formulation of God's revelation, except perhaps in Deut 33:9 (see "word"/"speak"/"promise" in Deut 32:2; Pss 12:6; 105:19; 138:2; 147:15; Prov 30:5; Isa 5:24; 28:23; 32:9). For this reason, perhaps, the word is usually translated "promise" in Psalm 119 (of the nineteen occurrences, the NIV uses "promise" thirteen times and the NRSV fourteen times; otherwise, they use "word," except for "command" in v. 158 NRSV). In the psalmist's mind, "word" (vv. 9, 16) and "promise" appear to be associated, perhaps because they are the most dynamic of the eight synonyms. Of the nineteen occurrences of "promise," eight occur in verses immediately preceding or following occurrences of "word" (see vv. 41-42, 49-50, 57-58, 81-82, 89-140, 147-148, 161-162, 169-170). Another six occur within two verses of "word" (see vv. 9, 11; 65, 67; 74, 76; 101, 103; 114, 116; 158, 160), and only five times does "promise" occur any further apart from "word" (vv. 38, 123, 133, 154, 172).

Verse 11 is reminiscent of Jer 31:33, a verse in which God promises to write "instruction" on the people's hearts. In short, God will teach the people directly (see Jer 31:34), a conviction also evident in Ps 119:12 and throughout the psalm. The implication is that the psalmist has more to learn and that God has more to reveal.

119:17-24. While vv. 1-8 have hinted that the psalmist lives under threat (see vv. 6a, 8b), vv. 17-24 clearly have the character of a complaint. The section begins with petition (vv. 17-18) and moves to complaint (v. 19); it also introduces a regular feature of the prayers for help—the enemies (vv. 21-23; see Pss 22:6; 31:11; 44:13). The desire to see "wondrous things" (v. 18; see vv. 27, 129; Exod 3:20; 15:11) suggests the need for deliverance, as does the psalmist's description of his or her "alien" status (see v. 54), an allusion perhaps to the plights of Abraham (see Gen 13:4) and Moses (see Exod 2:22; 18:3). Verse 23a also calls to mind the plight of Jeremiah (see Jeremiah 36–38). Princes and kings regularly employed advisers and counselors, but the psalmist professes to be advised by God's revelation. Verses 23-24 perhaps anticipate v. 46, where the psalmist dares to speak before kings, because he or she looks to a higher authority. The plight described in vv. 17-24 is one with which the exilic and post-exilic generations could have readily identified, but it is also one that regularly confronts the people of God (see Reflections below).

119:25-32. The complaint continues. Verse 25 communicates urgency, for "dust" is associated elsewhere with death (see Ps 22:15, 29). Life resides in God's "word" (see v. 17, where "live" [חיה ḥāyâ] represents the same Hebrew word as "revive" in v. 25 NRSV). "Grief"/"sorrow" in v. 28 is also frequently associated with death (see Gen 42:38; 44:31; Pss 31:10; 116:3), and again it is God's word that offers strength ("strengthen" [קימני qayyĕmēnî] in v. 28b is lit., "cause me to stand," which is reminiscent of the literal meaning of "resurrection," which is "to stand up again"). As in vv. 9-16, God is the teacher (see vv. 26-27, 29), and God's teaching means life. Thus, while the psalmist's "soul clings to the dust" (v. 25), he or she is expressing the intent to cling to God's revelation (v. 31). God's word is life (see Commentary on Psalms 1; 19).

119:33-40. The marked difference between vv. 33-40 and vv. 17-32 supports Soll's contention of a logical movement in Psalm 119. Verses 33-40 are dominated by petition. In fact, each of the first seven lines begins with a *hipil* imperative. As suggested above (see vv. 12, 26), God is the teacher (v. 33; the Hebrew verb "to teach" [ירה yārâ] underlies the noun *torah,* which occurs in v. 34). God is the primary actor, and the psalmist's actions are in response to God's previous activity. The psalmist prays that God's instruction permeate his or her whole being (v. 34) and that he or she not be distracted by "selfish gain" (v. 36; see Exod 18:21; 1 Sam 8:3; Prov 1:19; 15:27; Isa 56:11; Jer 6:13; 22:17) or "worthless things" (v.

37), a word that sometimes implies idolatry (see Ps 31:6). In other words, only God is sovereign—not the self or other gods. Both "servant" and "fear" in v. 38 suggest further the psalmist's recognition of God's claim and rule. Those who deny God's sovereignty may "scorn" the psalmist (see v. 22; "disgrace" in v. 39 is from the same Hebrew root), but the psalmist remains oriented to God (v. 40) and convinced that only God can "give me life" (vv. 37, 40; see also vv. 17, 24). As the imploring stance in vv. 33-40 makes clear, life is a gift to be received rather than a reward to be earned.

119:41-48. The movement in Psalm 119 continues, since vv. 41-48 have a different tone from vv. 33-40. Petition recurs (vv. 41, 43a), but the dominant note is assurance (vv. 42a, 45), based on trust (v. 42b; see Pss 4:5; 9:10) and hope (v. 43b; see vv. 49, 74, 80, 114, 147; "wait" in Ps 31:24) and manifested in freedom (v. 45a; lit., "in a broad place"; see Ps 118:5), courage (v. 46), and joy (v. 47). Verses 46 and 48b recall v. 23, thus highlighting the movement from complaint to trust—or at least the juxtaposition of the two—that is characteristic of Psalm 119 and establishes its eschatological perspective. The occurrence of "steadfast love" in v. 41 is the first of seven (see vv. 64, 76, 88, 124, 149, 159). Its appearance here and throughout the psalm is eminently appropriate. To trust God's word (v. 42) is to trust God's very self, the essence of which God revealed to be steadfast love (see Exod 34:6; Pss 5:7; 13:5; Introduction). The psalmist may still be taunted (v. 42; "taunt" is the same Hebrew word as NRSV "scorn" in v. 22 and "disagree" in v. 39), but lives joyfully by trusting the truth that sets people free.

119:49-56. According to Soll's outline, vv. 49-56 initiate the next major division (vv. 49-80), which is characterized by retrospection. This direction is set by the three occurrences of the verb "remember" (זכר zākar) at the beginning of vv. 49, 52, 55. Remembrance does not suddenly eliminate suffering (see vv. 50-51) or the existence of the wicked (v. 53). As is always the case, memory is inseparable from hope (v. 49b; see above on v. 43); together, they are a source of comfort (vv. 50a, 52b).

Levenson says that v. 54b, which reads literally "in the house of my sojourning" (the same He-

brew root as "alien" in v. 19 NRSV) "implies an identification of the *persona* of the psalmist with a homeless Israel, trusting in an unfulfilled promise."[445] This kind of identification reinforces the conclusion that Psalm 119 would have been particularly meaningful to the exilic and post-exilic generations, but it also makes Psalm 119 forever timely. It is always the case that the faithful live inevitably by hope. The image of home/homeless also provides a link between vv. 49-56 and v. 57, which begins the next section.

119:57-64. Perhaps the most meaningful profession that a homeless Israel could make is that "the LORD is my portion" (v. 57a). The word "portion" (חלק ḥēleq) designates elsewhere the allotment of land that each Israelite, except the priests and Levites, was supposed to have (see Num 18:20; Josh 15:13; 18:7; 19:9). To entrust one's life and future to God—in effect, to have God as one's "portion"— is to never be without a home (see Pss 16:5; 73:26; 142:5; Lam 3:24) and, furthermore, never without a community (see v. 63). This means praise is possible at all times (v. 62), even in distress (v. 61). To have God as one's "portion" means that nothing—not time, not place, not circumstance—can separate one from God's steadfast love (v. 64; see above on v. 41; see also Rom 8:38-39).

119:65-72. This good news is articulated in vv. 65-72, in which the key word is "good" (טוב ṭôb, vv. 65 [NRSV, "well"] 66, 68, 71, 72 [NRSV, "better"; NIV, "precious"]; in fact, each of these verses begins with the word "good"). God's goodness is celebrated amid current affliction (vv. 67, 71). In view of v. 67, it seems that the affliction could well have been interpreted formerly as divine punishment (see v. 75). If so, however, it can be no longer. The psalmist is now faithful and obedient, even though the affliction persists. The motivation, therefore, cannot be fear of retribution, but the conviction that genuine life is found in openness to God's instruction and reliance upon God's help. No amount of material reward can truly constitute life (v. 72; see Ps 19:10; Luke 12:15).

119:73-80. This section begins with the psalmist's profession that, in effect, he or she belongs to God; life is in God's hands. This, plus

445. Levenson, "The Sources of Torah," 568.

the affirmation of God's righteousness (see v. 7), becomes the basis for the petitions in vv. 76-80. Verse 75 recalls vv. 67, 71 and seems to reinforce the conclusion that the psalmist viewed the current affliction as justifiable punishment (see Ps 51:4). This, of course, would provide another analogy between the *persona* of the psalmist and Israel, which was persistently deserving of punishment (see Commentary on Psalm 51). Or, to state it from the other side, Israel consistently stood in need of God's steadfast love (v. 76) and mercy/compassion (v. 77). Only God could comfort (v. 76; see vv. 50, 52; Isa 40:1-2). Fortunately, steadfast love and mercy/compassion lie at the very heart of God's character (see Exod 34:6-7; Introduction). As the psalmist recognizes, his or her life depended on it (v. 77; see vv. 17, 25, 37, 40, 50, 88, 93, 116, 154, 156, 159, 175), and so did Israel's life. In the context of this understanding, to be "blameless" (v. 80) can ultimately mean nothing other than to be forgiven (see v. 1; Pss 15:2; 18:25; 19:13; 37:18). As in other psalms in which the psalmist has been forgiven or anticipates forgiveness, the psalmist also anticipates being an example, a teacher, or a witness to encourage others (vv. 74, 79; see Pss 32:8-9; 51:13).

119:81-88. According to Soll's outline, vv. 81-88 begin the central division of the psalm (vv. 81-120). The petition of vv. 76-80 gives way to the most extended and bitter complaint in the psalm—its nadir. Indicative of the urgency of this section is the threefold occurrence of the verb meaning "to fail," "to be finished," "to be spent" (see "languishes" in v. 81; "fail" in v. 82; "made an end" in v. 87; see also v. 123; Pss 31:10; 69:3; 73:26). The questions in vv. 82, 84 also contribute to the sense of urgency, as does the departure from the psalmist's regular pattern in v. 84; the NRSV's "judge" represents the singular of the word that is usually plural ("ordinances"). While the singular occurs also in vv. 121, 132, 149, it does stand out. The questions in v. 84 are essentially a plea for help. The petition is direct in vv. 86*b*, 88*a* (see "persecute" in vv. 84*b*, 86*b*, linking the questions and the direct petition), but its abbreviated statement gives the impression of an urgent shout (see the punctuation at the end of v. 86 NRSV).

As is the case throughout the psalm, the psalm-

ist looks to God for life (v. 88; see above on v. 77) and comfort (v. 88*b*; see above on v. 76). He or she continues to live in hope (v. 81), but vv. 81-88 portray very clearly the psalmist's existence as a suffering servant. Not surprisingly, v. 85 recalls Jer 18:20, 22, the prayer of another servant who suffered precisely because he was an instrument of God's word.

119:89-96. From its nadir, Psalm 119 moves to its zenith. Complaint has given way to a profession of faith in God's sovereignty for all time (vv. 89*a*, 90*a*), in all places (vv. 89*b*, 90*a*), and over "all things" (v. 91). The profession is highlighted by the uniqueness of v. 90, which does not contain one of the eight synonyms. Rather, the word "faithfulness" (אמונה *'ĕmûnâ*) occurs instead (see v. 75). Often paired with the word "steadfast love" (חסד *ḥesed,* see v. 88; Pss 25:10; 57:3; 85:10; 98:3), it communicates the way in which God exercises sovereignty—with faithful love that issues in forgiveness (see Exod 34:6-7; Introduction). Thus the psalmist, who would have perished (v. 92; "misery" is the same root as "humbled" in vv. 67, 71, 75), remains alive (v. 93; see above on v. 77). Verse 94*a* articulates again the psalmist's conviction that his or her life belongs to God. The petition and renewal of complaint (v. 95), following the marvelous affirmation of vv. 89-93, indicate that there will never be a time when the psalmist will be self-sufficient. He or she will always depend on God. Verse 96 returns to the expansive perspective of vv. 89-91. The meaning of the word translated "perfection" (תכלה *tiklâ*) is not entirely clear, but v. 96 could be paraphrased as follows: "I am weak, but you are strong." In short, it seems to be another profession of dependence upon God.

119:97-104. Following the zenith of the psalm, it is appropriate that vv. 97-104 are effusive in their expression of love for and joy in *torah* (see esp. vv. 97, 103), as well as in their description of the effects of God's instruction (see esp. vv. 98-100, 104). Verses 97-104 stand in the middle of what Soll identifies as the central division of the psalm (vv. 81-120), so perhaps they should be considered the real focal point of the psalm. The exclamations in vv. 97, 103 are downright sensual. The psalmist is in love with God's revelation (v. 97*a*; see vv. 47-48, 113, 119, 127,

132, 159, 163, 165, 167). As is always the case with a beloved person or thing, the psalmist has God's revelation always in mind (v. 97*b*). The word "meditate" (שׂיח *śîaḥ*) occurs several times in Psalm 119 (see also vv. 15, 23, 27, 48, 78, 99, 148), but this is the only place where the meditation is "all day long" (see also the chronological references in vv. 55, 62, 147-148, 164). Thus v. 97 is reminiscent of Ps 1:1-2 (although the Hebrew words translated "meditate" are different), where those who meditate on God's instruction are pronounced "happy." The psalmist in Psalm 119 exemplifies such happiness; it is not a superficial cheeriness (see vv. 81-88) but the happiness of a person who is in love with the one who truly offers life. Not surprisingly, v. 103 employs the sensual language of the Song of Solomon (see 2:3; 4:11; 5:1, 16; 7:9; see also Ps 19:10; Prov 24:13-14). The psalmist has an emotional attachment to God's word that is indicative of his or her love for and commitment to God.

The wisdom tradition is drawn upon in vv. 98-100 to describe the benefits of God's instruction ("wiser," v. 98; "insight," v. 99; and "understanding," v. 100; see v. 104; Pss 2:10; 14:2; 19:7; 94:8; Hos 14:9). Instructed by God (see v. 102), the psalmist need not fear the foe (v. 98) or be intimidated by the friend (vv. 99-100). The authority figures in the psalmist's life—"teachers" and "the elders"—are subordinated to God's ultimate authority. This theme is paralleled in Deut 4:6, where Moses tells the people that obedience to the "statutes and ordinances" (Deut 4:5) they are receiving "will show your wisdom and understanding to the nations" (NIV). Thus "this entire law" (Deut 4:8 NRSV) is to govern the people's existence. The psalmist's wisdom is a personal witness and example of what it means to hear and to heed God's instruction.

The correlate of loving God's *torah* (v. 97) is hating "every false way" (v. 104; see vv. 29, 128). The psalmist had complained about being the victim of falsehood (see v. 86). In other words, the psalmist hates what works toward death, and he or she loves what works toward life: God's revelation.

119:105-112. As if to indicate again that human life never stands beyond threat, or beyond need for God's help, vv. 105-112 return to com-

plaint and petition (see esp. vv. 107, 110; see above on v. 94). But this section starts with the memorable profession of v. 105. God's revelation is the truly reliable guide to life (see v. 130; Prov 6:23). It is not surprising, since God's word reveals God's very self, that the word "light" (אור *ʾôr*) is used as a metaphor for both (see Pss 4:6; 27:1). As is the case throughout the psalm, eloquent expressions of trust like v. 105 are juxtaposed with forthright complaint. "Afflicted" (v. 107*a*) recalls vv. 67, 71, 75, and 92, and the petition "give me life" (v. 107*b*) pervades the psalm (see above on v. 77). After the complaint of v. 110 (see Pss 91:3; 124:7; 140:5; 142:3), v. 111 offers another expression of trust that recalls v. 57. Like "portion" in v. 57, the word "heritage" (נחלה *naḥălâ*) designates the allotment of land that each Israelite, except the priests and Levites, was supposed to have (see "inheritance" in Josh 11:23; 14:3). This inheritance was precious, because land represented access to life and a future (see 1 Kgs 21:3). In v. 111, the psalmist affirms that God's revelation itself guarantees a future.

119:113-120. The final section of the central division of the psalm, these verses articulate primarily loyalty and trust. This section uses words and themes from earlier in the psalm—"love" (vv. 113, 119; see vv. 47-48, 97) and "hope" (יחל *yāḥal,* v. 114; see v. 43; the word translated "hope" [שׂבר *śābar*] in v. 116 differs and recurs in v. 166). But it also introduces new vocabulary—"hiding place" (v. 114*a*; see "cover" in Ps 27:5 and "shelter" in Pss 31:20; 91:1) and "shield" (see Ps 3:3). Amid the expressions of trust, the presence of opposition is evident (vv. 113, 115, 118-119), and as always, it is necessary to pray for life (v. 116; see above on v. 77). The NRSV's "judgments" in v. 120*b* translates the word usually rendered as "ordinances"; the NIV of v. 120*b* is more helpful.

119:121-128. This section is the first of three in the fifth major division of the psalm. Like the other divisions, it moves generally from complaint (vv. 121-128) to petition (vv. 129-136) to affirmation (vv. 137-144), but each section contains all three of these elements. The petitions in vv. 121-122 imply the complaint (see "oppress" in each verse; see also v. 134), which is voiced directly in v. 123*a* (see v. 82). The word "just" (משפט *mišpaṭ*) in v. 121 is the singular of the word the NRSV translates as "ordinances" (see vv. 84, 132). Verse 122 is the most irregular in the psalm. It contains none of the eight major synonyms, nor a variant form of one of them (as in v. 121), nor even a substitute as in vv. 3, 37, 90. This irregularity perhaps replicates the disorientation caused by the reality of oppression. In any case, the psalmist appeals to God's loving character (v. 124; see above on v. 41) and for a benefit celebrated earlier (v. 125; see v. 100). While v. 126 recaptures some of the urgency of vv. 81-88, v. 128 indicates that the psalmist has not become totally disoriented as he or she waits. Furthermore, the psalmist already experiences a reward (v. 127; see v. 72; Ps 19:10) that is greater than the material wealth oppressors might gain by their dishonest ways (v. 128; see v. 104): the love of God's revelation, which constitutes life.

119:129-136. The tone of vv. 127-128 continues in vv. 129-130. Verse 129 recalls v. 18; v. 130*a* recalls v. 105; and v. 130*b* recalls v. 100 at the same time that it seems to respond to v. 125. The imagery of vv. 131, 136 portrays again the necessity of waiting—that is, the eschatological dimension—and thus vv. 131, 136 serve as an appropriate frame for the petitions in vv. 132-135. The NRSV's "custom" (v. 132) represents the singular of the more frequent plural translated "ordinances" (see vv. 84, 121). More literally, the psalmist asserts that it is God's "justice" to be gracious. This assertion reinforces the psalmist's conviction that his or her life depends ultimately on God's mercy and love (see above on vv. 76-77). The subsequent petitions indicate that the psalmist entrusts life to God, depending on God for guidance (v. 133), liberation from oppression (v. 134; see vv. 121-122), and illumination (v. 135; "Make . . . shine" [האר *hā'er*] is the same Hebrew root as "light" in v. 130; see also v. 105; Num 6:25; Pss 4:6; 31:16; 67:1).

119:137-144. Occurring five times (vv. 137, 138, 142, 142, 144), the key word is this section is "righteous(ness) (צדק *ṣdq*); the word "right" (ישׁ *yāšār*) in v. 137 is from a different Hebrew root. God is "righteous" (vv. 137, 142; see Pss 7:9, 11; 11:7; 116:5), and God's "decrees are righteous" (v. 144; see v. 138 as well as vv. 7, 62, 75, 106, 160). The word "righteousness" is used elsewhere to describe the policy that God wills and enacts as ruler of the universe (see Pss

89:14; 96:13; 97:2, 6; 98:9; 99:4). In keeping with the conviction of God's universal reign (see above on vv. 89-91), the psalmist proclaims that God's righteousness is "everlasting"/"forever" (vv. 142, 144). As in v. 75, righteousness is inextricably associated with God's faithfulness (vv. 138, 142; "truth" [אמת *'ĕmet*] represents a word usually translated "faithful").

As a servant (v. 140), one who recognizes God's sovereignty, the psalmist is bothered by the same thing that bothers God: disloyalty. The word "zeal" (קנאה *qînâ'*), used to describe the psalmist's response to the people's forgetting "your words" (v. 139), is also used to describe God as a "jealous" God who will tolerate no rival (see Exod 20:5; 34:14; Deut 4:24; 6:15; Ps 79:5). Others may forget, but the psalmist does not (v. 141; see vv. 16, 61, 83, 93, 109, 153; Deut 4:23; 26:13).

At the same time proclaiming loyalty to God, the psalmist is also complaining about troubles (see vv. 141, 143). The juxtaposition of the proclamation of God's righteousness and the psalmist's complaint reminds us once again of the psalmist's eschatological perspective. While "delight" is a present reality (v. 143*b*; see vv. 24, 47, 70, 77, 92, 174), so are "trouble and anguish" (v. 143*a*). God and God's will are righteous, but not everything in the world is yet right. God and God's servants are opposed (vv. 139, 141). Thus the psalmist is inevitably a suffering servant, delighting already in God and in God's will, but constantly awaiting the consummation of God's reign. Appropriately, this section ends with a petition that indicates again the psalmist's dependence upon God for life and future (v. 144; see above on v. 77).

119:145-152. Like the other major divisions of the psalm, vv. 145-176 recapitulate the movement from complaint (vv. 145-152) and petition (vv. 153-160) to affirmation (vv. 161-168) and praise (vv. 169-176). Again, however, all these elements are interspersed in each section. Verses 145-152 begin with vocabulary that is typical of complaint (see "call" in vv. 145, 146; "save me" in v. 146; "cry for help" in v. 147). The chronological references in vv. 147-148 emphasize that the psalmist is in constant conversation with God (see vv. 55, 62, 97, 164). As always, the psalmist looks to God's steadfast love (v. 149*a*; see vv. 41, 76) and justice (v. 149*b*; see vv. 132, 156) for life (see v. 77). And as always, this is necessary because of the presence of opposition (v. 150; see "persecute" in vv. 84, 86 as well as in the next two sections in vv. 157, 161). Verses 150-151 play on the opposites "near" (vv. 150*a*, 151*a*) and "far" (v. 150*b*). The complaint of v. 150 issues in the emphatic affirmation of v. 151: "you are near." In the final analysis, God's nearness is all that the psalmist needs and all that really matters (see Ps 73:28). Verse 152 seems to be a response to the plea of v. 125, since the psalmist here affirms that he or she long "has known" (a more literal translation) God's decrees.

119:153-160. This section begins with and is dominated by petition (see vv. 153*a*, 154*a*), especially the one that pervades the psalm: "give me life" (vv. 154, 156, 159; see above on v. 77). This plea is associated in vv. 156, 159 with God's mercy/compassion and steadfast love (see vv. 76-77), as well as with God's justice (v. 156*b*; see vv. 132, 149). As affirmed throughout, God's justice ultimately takes the form of merciful love. Verse 160 again associates God's faithfulness (see NIV, "true"; NRSV, "truth"), another attribute regularly associated with God's mercy and love (see Exod 34:6-7), with God's righteousness (see vv. 75, 142). The righteousness God intends will be effected ultimately by God's faithful love.

119:161-168. Although this section starts with complaint (see vv. 23, 150, 157), it moves quickly to expressions of joy (v. 162) and commitment (v. 163; see vv. 104, 128). The word "praise" (הלל *hillēl*) is relatively rare in Psalm 119, but its occurrence in v. 164 anticipates the two occurrences in the final section (vv. 171,

175). It is not clear whether the "seven times" is meant literally or whether it is figurative for something like "all day long" (see v. 97). The eschatological perspective of the psalm is again evident; the one persecuted without cause (v. 161) knows simultaneously "great peace" (v. 165*a*) and security (v. 165*b*). The faithful life inevitably involves both hope (v. 166; see v. 116; Ps 146:5) and the present experience of God (v. 168*b*; see v. 151*a*).

119:169-176. The final section contains several pleas that by this point are familiar: pleas for understanding (v. 169*b*; see v. 100, 125), for grace (v. 170; "supplication" [תחנה *tĕhinnâ*] represents the same root as "be gracious" in vv. 58, 132), for help (vv. 173, 175; see v. 86), as well as the all-embracing plea for life (v. 175; see vv. 17, 25, 37, 40, 77, 88, 107, 116, 144, 149, 154, 156, 159). The psalmist anticipates and promises praise (vv. 171, 175), but it is striking, especially in view of all the expressions of loyalty and obedience throughout the psalm (see v. 176*b*), that the psalmist includes in the final verse another plea for help that follows what sounds like a confession of sin. The word "lost" (אבד *'ōbēd*) is more literally "perishing." Thus, just as Ps 119:1 was reminiscent of the first verse of Psalm 1, so also Ps 119:176 recalls the final verse of Psalm 1. But—and this is the remarkable thing—in Ps 1:6, it is the wicked who are to perish! The final verse of Psalm 119 is, therefore, a final reminder of what the psalmist has affirmed all along: The faithful are saved by grace. Their lives and their futures belong to God (see Luke 15:1-7).

REFLECTIONS

1. Like Psalm 1, Psalm 119 has often received bad scholarly press. Not infrequently, it has been criticized not only as artificial and tedious, but also as the product of a self-righteous psalmist who exhibits the legalism that supposedly characterized post-exilic Judaism. The charges against Psalm 119 should be dropped. They are not fair to either the psalm or the psalmist—or to Judaism. To be sure, the psalmist exhibits an unmistakable torah piety. The psalmist is thoroughly devoted to God's word and is intent upon a faithfulness to God that includes obedience. But the psalmist shows no trace of legalism or self-righteousness. Rather, the psalmist is thoroughly aware of his or her own failings, of the need for grace and mercy, of dependence upon God for life and future. It is likely that the psalmist's view of God's torah, "instruction," included recognition of written sources of revelation that constituted the core of a developing canon of Scripture. But, as Levenson points out, "Psalm 119 lacks any trace of book consciousness," and the psalmist is open to a variety of sources of the revelation of God's word and will, including "unmediated divine teaching." [446] In short, the psalmist is open in the broadest sense to God's instruction.

2. If there is no trace of book consciousness in Psalm 119, neither is there any trace of the psalmist's commitment to a rigid retributional scheme. In this regard, the final verse of the psalm is particularly striking. While it reaffirms the psalmist's loyalty to God and commitment to obedience, it also employs language used elsewhere to describe the wicked. It leaves the psalmist utterly dependent on God's grace. Furthermore, the psalmist has repeatedly appealed to God's steadfast love and mercy—to divine attributes that manifest themselves in forgiveness (see Exod 34:6-7). Also, the psalmist's regular juxtaposition of complaint and profession of trust indicates that he or she could not support a simple retributional scheme. While the psalmist admits wrongdoing, the psalmist must also have considered himself or herself more deserving than those who are described as the wicked, the insolent, the arrogant, evildoers, "my oppressors," and "my persecutors." Yet, it is precisely the psalmist who *is* persecuted and oppressed. In a word, he or she is a suffering servant, "who waits and looks for Yahweh's effective word of power." [447] The perspective is eschatological. The sovereignty of God and God's word is upheld amid circumstances that seem to deny it.

3. The psalmist clearly reminds us of figures like Jeremiah and Elijah, who suffered as a result of their faithfulness to God's word and will. Christian readers of Psalm 119 will also inevitably be reminded of Jesus. The psalmist's commitment to discerning the word of God and doing the will of God anticipates the life and ministry of Jesus, who even as a boy is depicted "among the teachers" (Luke 2:46; see Luke 2:42-51; note esp. "understanding" in v. 47 and "wisdom" in v. 52; cf. Ps 119:98-100). Jesus upheld the *torah* (see Matt 5:17-20), but he was not bound to specific formulations (see Matt 12:1-8; 15:1-20). Rather, he sought to extend the *torah* to represent God's sovereign claim upon all of human life (see Matt 5:21-48). The psalmist was no legalist, and neither was Jesus. Rather, both the psalmist and Jesus were open to God's instruction in a variety of forms—Scripture, tradition, and ongoing events and experiences that reveal God's way and represent God's claim upon humanity and the world. By constantly affirming that he or she lives by the word of God, the psalmist anticipates Jesus' articulation of the motive for his faithful, hopeful obedience to God (Matt 4:4; see also Deut 8:3):

> "One does not live by bread alone,
> but by every word that comes
> from the mouth of God."

4. This kind of torah piety has profound implications for the life of the church in the world. For instance, in a scientifically oriented and education-obsessed culture, Psalm 119 has radical epistemological implications. That is to say, it points to generally unacceptable conclusions about what we know and how we know it, for it asserts that true knowledge is not achieved through detachment and objectivity. Rather, wisdom grows from passionate involvement with God and commitment of one's whole self to God (see 1 Cor 1:18–2:16). In short, Psalm 119 claims that as people of God, we believe in order to understand (see Commentary on Psalm 111).

This claim, of course, should not be understood to be anti-intellectual or anti-scientific. Rather, it is an invitation for us to recognize the inevitable limits of human knowledge, human power, and human technology. It is an invitation to accept the biblical claim that human life is finally a gift of God and that it depends ultimately on God. The proper human prayer is the one that pervades Psalm 119: "Give me life."

446. Jon Levenson, "The Sources of Torah: Psalm 119 and the Modes of Revelation in Second Temple Judaism," in *Ancient Israelite Religion*, ed. P. D. Miller, Jr., P. D. Hanson, S. D. McBride (Philadelphia: Fortress, 1987) 565, 570.

447. H.-J. Kraus, *Psalms 60–150: A Commentary,* trans. H. C. Oswald (Minneapolis: Augsburg, 1989) 420.

5. The claim of Psalm 119 is certainly not a warrant to retreat into a narrow view of the inerrancy of Scripture, a position that amounts to making the Bible an idol. While the psalmist included written formulations as one source of God's Word, he or she by no means limited God's revelation to written sources. The psalmist's openness to God's Word has profound implications for understanding Scripture as the Word of God. While Scripture is to be honored as a source of God's revelation, it is always to be heard in conversation with the theological tradition of the church and within the context of the contemporary place and time. Apart from such a hearing, God's ability to speak to God's people is anchored entirely in the past, and there is no possibility of God's continuing to reveal God's self. In short, Scripture is not a dead letter but a dynamic, living word. It is to be read and heard and proclaimed in openness to the Holy Spirit—what Levenson might call "unmediated divine teaching"—who leads the church to discern the Word of God for our place and time.

PSALMS 120–134, SONGS OF ASCENTS

OVERVIEW

Psalm 120 is the first of fifteen consecutive psalms that bear the title "A Song of Ascents." While certainty is not possible, it is likely that this collection was originally used by pilgrims on their way to Jerusalem or as part of a festal celebration in Jerusalem. Each psalm is relatively short (except Psalm 132) and thus capable of being memorized, and a variety of types and themes is represented. The noun translated "ascents" (מעלות *maʿălôt*) is from a Hebrew root meaning "to go up" (עלה *ʿālâ*); as Ps 122:4 points out, it was decreed that "the tribes go up" regularly to Jerusalem (see Deut 16:16; see also 1 Kgs 12:28; Ps 24:3; Isa 2:3). The noun can also mean "steps" or "stairs," and it is elsewhere used for the steps of the Temple (Ezek 40:6) and the steps to the city of David (Neh 3:15; 12:37).

The likelihood that Psalms 120–134 were used by pilgrims on the journey to Jerusalem or during a celebration in Jerusalem is increased by the frequent references to Jerusalem and Zion (see Psalms 122; 125–126; 128–129; 132–134). Also, the alternation between singular and plural references to the people suggests group participation, as do the frequent liturgical elements, such as invitations for response (124:1; 129:1; 130:7; 131:3), professions of faith (121:2; 124:8; 134:3), and benedictions (125:5; 128:5-6; 134:3). These elements also represent verbal links among the psalms that suggest the unity of the collection.

Even if some of these elements are redactional, as several scholars suggest, this in itself suggests that an editor provided further indications of unity to a collection that he or she already recognized as a unit.

Scholars frequently observe that Psalms 120–134 deal often with matters of daily life—place of residence (120:5-6), routine activities (121:8; 127:2; 128:2), the importance of spouse and children (128:3-4), as well as larger family and friends (122:8; 133:1). This, too, increases the likelihood that the collection was originally used by ordinary persons on the way to or upon arrival at Jerusalem. The juxtaposition of psalms reflecting daily concerns with those reflecting national concerns (Psalms 123–126; 130–132; 134) also makes sense in the context of festal celebrations, where individuals and families from all over would have been brought together by loyalties that transcended the personal and familial.

Several scholars also detect evidence of a pilgrimage orientation in the shape of the collection, especially the beginning and end. Psalm 120:5, for instance, has the effect of locating the speaker outside Jerusalem and even outside the land, even though the geographical references may have been intended metaphorically. The imagery of Psalm 121 makes especially good sense in the context of a journey—seeing mountains in the distance (v. 1), the concern with stumbling and with safety in general (vv. 3-4), the need for protection from the heat of the sun and the dangers of darkness (vv. 5-6), the mention of departure and entrance (v. 8). The joyful tone of Psalm 122 gives the impression of just having arrived at Jerusalem, and Psalm 134 would have served well as a benediction upon departure. To be sure, this arrangement may be coincidental, but in conjunction with the above considerations, the shape of the collection increases the likelihood of its use by pilgrims.

Psalm 120:1-7, I Am for Peace

NIV

Psalm 120

A song of ascents.

¹I call on the LORD in my distress,
  and he answers me.
²Save me, O LORD, from lying lips
  and from deceitful tongues.

³What will he do to you,
  and what more besides, O deceitful tongue?
⁴He will punish you with a warrior's sharp
    arrows,
  with burning coals of the broom tree.

⁵Woe to me that I dwell in Meshech,
  that I live among the tents of Kedar!
⁶Too long have I lived
  among those who hate peace.
⁷I am a man of peace;
  but when I speak, they are for war.

NRSV

Psalm 120

A Song of Ascents.

¹ In my distress I cry to the LORD,
  that he may answer me:
² "Deliver me, O LORD,
  from lying lips,
  from a deceitful tongue."

³ What shall be given to you?
  And what more shall be done to you,
  you deceitful tongue?
⁴ A warrior's sharp arrows,
  with glowing coals of the broom tree!

⁵ Woe is me, that I am an alien in Meshech,
  that I must live among the tents of Kedar.
⁶ Too long have I had my dwelling
  among those who hate peace.
⁷ I am for peace;
  but when I speak,
  they are for war.

COMMENTARY

The psalm's location of the speaker outside the land (metaphorically, at least) and in a situation of hostility (vv. 6-8) may also explain the placement of the Songs of Ascents in Book V; at least it makes their perspective congruent with that established in Psalms 107–118 as well as in Psalm 119. Along with Book IV, Book V seems to respond to the theological crisis of exile that continued into the post-exilic era of dispersion; and Psalm 107 begins Book V by establishing this setting (see also 106:47). Especially when Psalms 107 and 108 are read together, the impression

left is that the return from exile has not solved the problem; the people still need help. This is also the message suggested by Psalm 118, which is linked verbally to Psalm 107 (see 107:1; 118:1, 29). While alluding to exodus and return from exile, Psalm 118 concludes with a petition for salvation; that is, the people still need help. Psalm 119 leads to the same conclusion. While the psalmist clearly celebrates God's presence and power as mediated through God's instruction, the psalmist still needs help. Indeed, the imagery at several points portrays the psalmist as an exile or alien who finds a place only in God's revelation (see vv. 19, 54, 57, 111). Not surprisingly, then, Psalm 120 also portrays the psalmist as an alien; furthermore, vv. 1-2 preserve in brief the same pattern evident in Psalm 118: recollection of past deliverance (v. 1; the verbs should be rendered in the past tense) that serves as the basis for petition in the midst of a new crisis (v. 2; see Commentary on Psalm 118 on the transition from v. 24 to v. 25; and on Psalm 126 on the transition from v. 3 to v. 4).

The question of how to translate the tenses of the verbs in vv. 1, 5-6 is the most debated one in the psalm. It is possible to render them all in the past tense and thus to conclude that the crisis lies completely in the past. In this case, v. 2 can be considered a quote from a past prayer, and Psalm 120 can be construed as a song of thanksgiving.[448] Although both the NIV and the NRSV use present tenses in v. 1, both also suggest that the crisis is current and that Psalm 120 is a lament/complaint or prayer for help. While there is clearly room for disagreement, this seems to be the most reasonable conclusion; it also makes Psalm 120 congruent with the perspective of the preceding psalms.

120:1-4. Elsewhere, too, the psalmists relate the experience of God's answering a prayer out of distress (v. 1; see Ps 118:5). The description of the new distress is also a familiar one in the psalms (v. 2; see Pss 31:18; 52:2-3; 64:8; 109:2; the word translated "lying" [שֶׁקֶר *šeqer*] in v. 2 also occurs as "false[hood]" or "lies" in Ps 119:29, 69, 104, 128, 163). In v. 3, the "deceitful tongue" is personified and addressed with a question, which is answered in v. 4. Verses 3-4 express poetically the psalmist's conviction that the enemies will eventually be brought to justice. The

psalmist petitions God for the same judgment upon enemies in Ps 140:10 (see also Prov 25:22). These enemies have shown themselves with their tongues and lips (140:3; cf. 120:2) to be proponents of war (140:2; cf. 120:7), and the petition for judgment upon them is followed by a profession of faith in God's execution of justice for the victimized (140:12). Verses 3-4 profess this same faith.

120:5-7. These verses elaborate upon the distress that has already been articulated in v. 2. Because most scholars locate Meshech significantly to the north of Israel and Kedar to the south, it is likely that the two names were intended as metaphors for "those who hate peace" (v. 6; see Meshech in Ezek 32:26; 38:2-4; 39:1-3; and Kedar in Isa 21:16-17). The Hebrew verb forms in vv. 5-6 would ordinarily be translated with English past tenses. If this is done, however, the verbs should be understood to indicate a current situation of long-standing rather than a situation that no longer exists. The psalmist's attempts to be conciliatory have been met only with hostility (v. 7; see Ps 109:2-5). Verses 6-7 anticipate the theme of peace in 122:6-8, a link that perhaps supports the detection of a pilgrim sequence involving Psalms 120–122.

Another noteworthy feature of vv. 5-7 is what scholars often call stairlike repetition. That is, the verb "live" (שָׁכַן *šā kan*) in v. 5*b* recurs in v. 6*a*, and the noun "peace" (שָׁלוֹם *šā lôm*) in v. 6*b* recurs in v. 7*a*. Thus the repetition leads the reader along step by step as up a flight of stairs. This pattern of repetition is particularly appropriate for a poem labeled "A Song of Ascents," or "A Song of the Steps." Not coincidentally, it seems, this pattern of repetition occurs frequently in Psalms 120–134 (see, e.g., 121:1*b*-2*a*, 3*b*-4, 7*b*-8*a*; 122:4*ab*, 5).

448. See ibid, 422-25.

REFLECTIONS

The juxtaposition of deliverance recalled (v. 1) with ongoing petition (v. 2) and complaint (vv. 5-7) is characteristic of Book V, and it would have been particularly meaningful to the post-exilic generations. More generally, this juxtaposition is in line with the eschatological perspective of the whole psalter—indeed, the whole Bible. God's establishment of justice for the victimized is both affirmed on the basis of past experience (vv. 1, 3-4) and prayed for and awaited (vv. 2, 5-7). As Allen correctly recognizes, Psalm 120 not only would have been particularly meaningful for Jews in dispersion, but it also expresses a perspective that is characteristic of Scripture generally: "The psalm hovers between divine promise and fulfillment, like so much of the Bible."[449]

In short, Psalm 120 leaves the people of God between "already" and "not yet." So does Jesus' proclamation of the eschatological reign of God, which is now a reality (Mark 1:14-15) but which is experienced amid persistent opposition from the world, as Jesus' own cross so clearly demonstrates. This "betweenness" is evident also in the teaching of Jesus, in which "Blessed are the peacemakers" is followed immediately by "Blessed are those who are persecuted for righteousness' sake" (Matt 5:10 NRSV). In short, the experience of the psalmist (vv. 6-7) proves to be the persistent experience of the people of God. The peace God gives is real, but it is not a peace that the world recognizes or accepts (see John 14:27). Thus the church will always, in a real sense, lead an alien existence; it will always be in the world but not of the world (see John 17:14-18; 1 Pet 1:1-2; 2:11-12). Its efforts for peace and reconciliation will be met with hostility, because they threaten the ways of the world.

It is still true, and examples abound. In the United States during the 1950s and 1960s and in South Africa in the 1980s and 1990s, legislation ending racial segregation and apartheid came only after an extended and often violent struggle. Christians of various nations who promote and work for world peace are frequently labeled unpatriotic, and those who side with the victimized are often dismissed as bleeding hearts. To be for peace is to invite a battle (v. 7); to follow Jesus is to bear a cross (see Mark 8:34).

449. Leslie C. Allen, *Psalms 101–150*, WBC 21 (Waco, Tex.: Word, 1983) 150.

Psalm 121:1-8, God's Protective Care

<table>
<tr><td>NIV</td><td>NRSV</td></tr>
<tr><td>Psalm 121</td><td>Psalm 121</td></tr>
<tr><td>A song of ascents.</td><td>A Song of Ascents.</td></tr>
<tr><td>

¹I lift up my eyes to the hills—
  where does my help come from?
²My help comes from the LORD,
  the Maker of heaven and earth.

³He will not let your foot slip—
  he who watches over you will not slumber;
⁴indeed, he who watches over Israel
  will neither slumber nor sleep.

⁵The LORD watches over you—
  the LORD is your shade at your right hand;
⁶the sun will not harm you by day,
  nor the moon by night.

⁷The LORD will keep you from all harm—
  he will watch over your life;
⁸the LORD will watch over your coming and
    going
  both now and forevermore.

</td><td>

¹ I lift up my eyes to the hills—
  from where will my help come?
² My help comes from the LORD,
  who made heaven and earth.

³ He will not let your foot be moved;
  he who keeps you will not slumber.
⁴ He who keeps Israel
  will neither slumber nor sleep.

⁵ The LORD is your keeper;
  the LORD is your shade at your right hand.
⁶ The sun shall not strike you by day,
  nor the moon by night.

⁷ The LORD will keep you from all evil;
  he will keep your life.
⁸ The LORD will keep
  your going out and your coming in
  from this time on and forevermore.

</td></tr>
</table>

COMMENTARY

The second of the Songs of Ascents (Psalms 120–134), Psalm 121 is an eloquent profession of faith in God's providence and protection. The circumstances of the psalm's origin are unknown. Noting the military significance of mountains or hills (v. 1; see 1 Kgs 20:23), Anthony R. Ceresko proposes that Psalm 121 may have originated as a prayer or profession of a warrior, and that it was reread as a pilgrimage psalm when it became a part of the ascents collection (see Overview of Psalms 120–134).[450] James Limburg, on the other hand, suggests that the psalm originated as a "farewell liturgy," in which vv. 1-2 should be heard as the words of one who is about to depart and vv. 3-8 are the response of one who is staying behind.[451] In any case, Psalm 121 is in an auspicious position, if, as is likely, Psalms 120–134 form a collection that was used by pilgrims on their way to or upon arrival at Jerusalem. Its language and imagery are readily understood in terms of a journey—seeing mountains in the distance (v. 1), the concern with stumbling and safety in general (vv. 3-4), the need for protection from the heat of the sun and the dangers of darkness (vv. 5-6), and the mention of departure and entrance (v. 8). It is even possible that the sequence of Psalms 120–122 is intended to re-create the movement from dispersion (120:5-7) by way of a journey (Psalm 121) to the gates of Jerusalem (122:1-2). The dialogical character of Psalm 121 would have made it suitable for an exchange between priest and pilgrim upon arrival at Jerusalem or perhaps in preparation for departure home. In any case, vv. 7-8 expand the journey concept to the whole of life. Thus the usefulness of Psalm 121 has transcended the circumstances of its origin as well as its ancient role as a pilgrim song (see Reflections below).

The structure of Psalm 121 is disputed. A few scholars suggest dividing it into three sections: vv. 1-2, vv. 3-5, vv. 6-8. Most prefer four two-verse sections. A prominent stylistic feature is the stair-like or steplike repetition that occurs in vv. 1-2, vv. 3-4, and vv. 7-8 (see Commentary on Psalm

120, esp. discussion of vv. 5-7). This pattern is especially appropriate for a psalm about a journey, which in ancient times would literally have proceeded step by step. Even more prominent perhaps is the sixfold occurrence of the word "keep" (שמר *šāmar*, vv. 3, 4, 5, 7*ab*, 8). The pervasiveness of this key word matches the pervasiveness of God's protecting presence.

121:1-2. Verse 1 is sometimes translated as a statement, but it is better rendered as a question that is answered in v. 2. The exact referent of "hills" is not clear. "Hills" could indicate simply an unspecified destination, as in the contemporary idiom, "head for the hills." If the speaker were on a journey, "hills" could refer to elevated terrain in the distance that perhaps promises a difficult climb and possible danger. In the context of the Songs of Ascents, the hills in the distance might be intended to include Mount Zion, a symbol not of danger but of divine help (see Deut 33:7, 26, 29; Pss 22:19; 33:20; 54:4; 63:7; 70:1, 5; 115:9-11; 124:8), since it is the place where the cosmic God (see v. 2*b*) sits upon an earthly throne (see Pss 48:1-2; 125:1-2; 132:8, 13-14). Psalm 123 also begins with the psalmist lifting up his or her eyes, and there it is specifically to the cosmic God. The similarity between 121:1 and 123:1 may support the conclusion that we should construe 121:1 as an indication of the psalmist's looking toward Zion. In any case, it is significant that the Lord is identified both very personally—"my help"—and cosmicly. The phrase "Maker of heaven and earth" both anticipates the expansive conclusion to the psalm in vv. 7-8 and provides one of the threads of unity for the collection (see Pss 124:8; 134:3; see above on Ps 115:15).

121:3-4. The image in v. 3*a* is obviously appropriate for a person traveling on foot. The traveler could literally "slip," but the image also functions metaphorically. For instance, the same image is used in Ps 66:9*b* in parallel with God's activity to preserve people "among the living" (see also "moved"/"shaken" in Pss 16:8; 55:22; 62:2, 6; 112:6). The verb "moved" (מוט *môt*) recurs in Ps 125:1*b*, where it communicates the stability of Mount Zion, which is to be a symbol of the people's security (see 125:1*a*, 2). The verbal links

450. Anthony R. Ceresko, "Psalm 121: Prayer of a Warrior?" *Biblica* 70 (1989) 501-5.
451. James Limburg, "Psalm 121: A Psalm for Sojourners," *Word & World* 5 (1985) 183.

between Psalms 121 and 125 increase the probability that "hills" in 121:1 should be understood to include Mount Zion (cf. 121:8 with 125:2c). Verse 3b contains the first occurrence of "keep" (šāmar). This word recalls God's protection of the whole people following the exodus during the journey to the promised land (see Num 6:24; Josh 24:17). Both it and the verb "slumber" (נום nûm) create the steplike repetition in vv. 3-4, which affirm God's eternal vigilance. The addition of "sleep" (ישׁן yāšēn) in v. 4 intensifies the assurance. God will definitely not do what the people sometimes fear God might be doing (see Ps 44:23).

121:5-6. Ceresko points out that v. 5a is preceded and followed by exactly the same number of syllables and that it is the center of the psalm.[452] Thus structure serves to reinforce the repetition of "keep" to emphasize the psalm's central theological affirmation. Not surprisingly, the subject—"the LORD"—is in the emphatic position. Verse 5b introduces another metaphor, which occurs in Ps 91:1 (see "shadow"), another psalm that celebrates God's protecting presence (note, too, that "guard" in Ps 91:11 is the same verb rendered "keep" in Psalm 121; see also "day" and "night" in Pss 91:5; 121:6; as well as "foot" in 91:12; 121:3). The metaphor of God as shadow occurs most often in the phrase "shadow of your wings" (see Pss 17:8; 36:8; 57:1; 63:7), an image that may derive from the winged creatures that decorated the ark in the Temple. Thus

v. 5b may hint at the destination of the pilgrim's journey—Jerusalem—while at the same time affirming that the God who resides in Zion is also present on the journey. Especially for the traveler on foot, the sun could be deadly (see Isa 49:10), and people in antiquity apparently believed moonlight to be harmful, a notion evident in Matt 4:24; 17:15, where "epileptic(s)" literally means "moonstruck" (the English word *lunatic* derives from the Latin word for "moon"). In any case, vv. 5-6 again affirm God's constant vigilance. God is always in a position to help (see "right hand" in Ps 109:31).

121:7-8. These verses each begin with the subject—"the LORD"—in the emphatic position, thus recalling v. 5. The emphatic and expansive character of vv. 7-8 is also communicated by three more occurrences of "keep," each of which broadens the scope of God's protection. Verse 7a indicates that vv. 3-7 have merely been illustrative. God will protect from "all evil," because the psalmist's very life is the real object of God's care. Verse 8 culminates this movement by making it clear that the real journey on which the psalmist has embarked is the journey of life. Every departure and arrival will be under God's care (see Deut 28:6)—now and forever (see Pss 125:2; 131:3). No place, no time, no circumstance will be able to separate the psalmist from God's loving care (see Rom 8:38-39). The direction of vv. 7-8 points to the adaptability of Psalm 121 to a variety of settings and provides a textual grounding for the psalm's ongoing use throughout the human journey of many centuries.

452. Ceresko, "Psalm 121," 499.

REFLECTIONS

1. Although short in length, Psalm 121 has been long on influence. It has contributed a phrase to the Apostles' Creed (v. 2b; see also Pss 115:5; 124:8; 134:3), and, except for Psalm 23, with which it shares the same fundamental message, Psalm 121 is probably recited from memory as often as any other in the psalter when people of faith reach for words of assurance amid the trials and turmoil of their life journey. Like the folk song, which moves from God's "got the whole world in his hands" to God's "got you and me, sister/brother, in his hands," Psalm 121 affirms that the sovereign ruler of the cosmos has a personal concern for the lives of all God's people (v. 2).

2. In keeping with what was perhaps its original use, Psalm 121 has remained a psalm for travelers. Upon the morning of his departure from England to do missionary work in Africa, David Livingstone is said to have read Psalm 121.[453] But Psalm 121 finally has in view all of

453. See Rowland E. Prothero, *The Psalms in Human Life and Experience* (New York: E. P. Dutton, 1903) 264.

life as a journey. Thus it is appropriate that it has been traditionally used in the Evangelical Lutheran Church as part of the baptismal liturgy and that it is used by many traditions in funeral services. From birth to death and beyond, Psalm 121 is a psalm for the journey of life.

3. James Limburg calls Psalm 121 "A Psalm for Sojourners."[454] Not only does this title explain why Psalm 121 would have been particularly meaningful to dispersed post-exilic generations (see above on Pss 119:19, 54, 57, 111; 120:5-7), but it also serves to remind every generation of God's people that while the earth is our home, because God made it, it is housing each of us only temporarily (see Ps 39:12). This reality is not an excuse to grab all the gusto we can get on our one time around (see Luke 12:13-21), but an invitation to live fully in the present on the basis of a promise. Like Abraham and Sarah, we are called to live as sojourners, as people always on the way (see Gen 47:9; Heb 11:9-10). With good reason, the early church was known as "the Way" (see Acts 9:2; 19:23; 22:4; 24:22). In the Gospel of Mark, to be a disciple is to follow Jesus "on the way" (see Mark 8:27; 9:33; 10:52). Jesus characterizes his own existence as that of a sojourn rather than a settled existence (see Luke 9:57-62), and Jesus' instructions to those he sent out do not allow for the implements or provisions of a settled existence (see Mark 6:7-13). While this orientation may have an other-worldly thrust, it does not lend itself to a pie-in-the-sky-by-and-by escapism. For Jesus, the unsettledness he advocated led to a radical undermining of the social arrangements that supported power and privilege and that his contempories sought to maintain by claiming divine sanction.[455] Thus Jesus' journey led finally to a cross, but the good news is that God was there too, keeping his life. And as we follow Jesus on that way (Mark 8:34), God is our keeper as well.

454. Limburg, "Psalm 121," 180, 186-87.
455. See John Dominic Crossan, *Jesus: A Revolutionary Biography* (San Francisco: Harper, 1994) 102-22.

Psalm 122:1-9, The Peace of Jerusalem

NIV	NRSV
Psalm 122	Psalm 122
A song of ascents. Of David.	A Song of Ascents. Of David.

[1] I rejoiced with those who said to me,
    "Let us go to the house of the LORD."
[2] Our feet are standing
    in your gates, O Jerusalem.
	[1] I was glad when they said to me,
	    "Let us go to the house of the LORD!"
	[2] Our feet are standing
	    within your gates, O Jerusalem.

[3] Jerusalem is built like a city
    that is closely compacted together.
[4] That is where the tribes go up,
    the tribes of the LORD,
to praise the name of the LORD
    according to the statute given to Israel.
[5] There the thrones for judgment stand,
    the thrones of the house of David.
	[3] Jerusalem—built as a city
	    that is bound firmly together.
	[4] To it the tribes go up,
	    the tribes of the LORD,
	as was decreed for Israel,
	    to give thanks to the name of
	        theLORD.
	[5] For there the thrones for judgment were set
	        up,
	    the thrones of the house of David.

[6] Pray for the peace of Jerusalem: "May those who love you be secure. [7] May there be peace within your walls	

NIV

and security within your citadels."
8For the sake of my brothers and friends,
    I will say, "Peace be within you."
9For the sake of the house of the LORD our
        God,
    I will seek your prosperity.

NRSV

6 Pray for the peace of Jerusalem:
    "May they prosper who love you.
7 Peace be within your walls,
    and security within your towers."
8 For the sake of my relatives and friends
    I will say, "Peace be within you."
9 For the sake of the house of the LORD our
        God,
    I will seek your good.

COMMENTARY

Psalm 122, the third of the Songs of Ascents (see Overview on Psalms 120–134), is the only psalm in the collection that is explicitly a pilgrimage song. However, the sequence of Psalms 120–122 may be intentional. The sequence moves the psalmist from dispersion (120:5-7) by way of a journey (Psalm 121) to Jerusalem (122:1-2). Because it locates the speaker(s) in Jerusalem, or at least focuses the reader's attention squarely on Jerusalem, Psalm 122 is usually categorized as a song of Zion (see Psalms 46; 48; 76; 84; 87). Its attention to the architectural features of the city is particularly reminiscent of Psalm 48 (see "the house of the LORD" in vv. 1, 9; "gates" in v. 2; "thrones" in v. 5; "walls" and "towers" in v. 7).

Scholars propose various structural outlines for Psalm 122, but most favor the threefold division followed by the NIV and the NRSV. Verses 1-2 describe the setting. They are followed by two sections, each of which begins with a reference to Jerusalem and contains four poetic lines. Attention to other features of the psalm, however, yields a different division, and it is legitimate to analyze the structure and movement of the psalm at more than one level. For instance, references to "the house of the LORD" encompass the psalm (vv. 1, 9), as if to say that the beginning and end, the motivation and destination, of the ascent to Jerusalem is the Temple, God's house. At the same time, there is a focusing of attention on the center of the psalm by means of a chiastic structure (see Introduction) and the repetition of the word "house":

A vv. 1-2 the psalmist, his or her
    companions ("I"/"us"), and "the house
    of the LORD"
  B vv. 3-4 Jerusalem
    C v. 5 "house of David"
  B′ vv. 6-7 Jerusalem
A′ vv. 8-9 the psalmist, companions, and
    "the house of the LORD"

There were two houses in Jerusalem—"the house of the LORD" and "the house of David"—just as Jerusalem was known as both "the city of God" and "the city of David." The structure of Psalm 122 calls attention to both houses. While "the house of David" is central, its position in the psalm and thus its authority are encompassed by "the house of the LORD." In other words, the power of the Davidic house is derivative. The three occurrences of the key word "house" (vv. 1, 5, 9) recall the narrative of 2 Samuel 7 in which "house" is also a key word. 2 Samuel 7 makes it clear that David did not build God a house (that is, a temple); rather, God built David a house (that is, a dynasty). Thus the reign of the Davidic house is but an agency of God's reign, and the fundamental purpose of the Davidic administration is to enact the fundamental purpose of God's rule: justice (v. 5; see Ps 48:11). The psalms that explicitly proclaim God's reign also portray God's royal policy as "justice" (see Pss 96:10, 13; 97:2, 8; 98:9; 99:4; see also 82:1-3, 8). The structure of Psalm 122 suggests what other psalms also indicate: The Davidic reign is to manifest God's reign (see Psalms 2; 72). To experience Jerusalem is ultimately to experience the reality of God's reign and God's purposes for the world (see Ps 123:1).

122:1-2. These verses make it clear that the pilgrimage to Jerusalem was indeed a special experience. Verse 1 apparently reflects the typical invitation for a pilgrimage (see 1 Sam 14:11; Isa 2:3; Jer 31:6), and v. 1 seems to convey the sense of joy and excitement that would have accompanied a pilgrim's arrival. Since the verb in v. 2 would ordinarily be translated by an English past tense ("were" instead of "are"), however, some scholars conclude that Psalm 122 looks back over the whole experience after the pilgrim has returned home. While this is possible, vv. 6-9 also convey an immediacy that suggests the speaker's presence in Jerusalem. But the chronological issue is not crucial; the centrality of Jerusalem is evident in either case.

122:3-4. The word "Jerusalem" ends v. 2 and begins v. 3, representing another case of the steplike repetition that characterizes the Songs of Ascents (see Pss 120:5-7; 121:1-4, 7-8). The translation and sense of v. 3 are problematic. Both the NIV and the NRSV suggest an observation concerning Jerusalem's architectural quality, and this makes good sense in the context of a pilgrimage that involves the celebration of that particular place (see Commentary on Psalm 48, esp. discussion of vv. 12-14). The word translated "bound"/"compacted" (חבר *ḥābar*), however, is never used elsewhere of buildings. Rather, it is used of human compacts or alliances (see "allied" in Ps 94:20). Thus it is possible that it is not so much Jerusalem's architecture that is being praised but Jerusalem's ability to bring people together. Thus, the NEB translates v. 3*b*: "where people come together in unity." This too makes good sense, especially in view of v. 4, which describes the gathering of the tribes (cf. Exod 23:14-7; Deut 16:16; 1 Kgs 12:28). It is conceivable that the ambiguity is intended as a play on the possible senses of the verb. At any rate, v. 4 maintains the focus on Jerusalem. The NRSV's "it" is literally "there" (שם *šām*), a word that occurs regularly in the songs of Zion (see Pss 48:6; 76:3; 87:4; 132:17; 133:3). The repetition of "tribes" continues the steplike pattern.

122:5. While certain features of the psalm point to the centrality of v. 5, it is also true that v. 5 is not to be sharply separated from vv. 3-4. The word "there" recurs in v. 5, and the mention of "the name of the LORD" in v. 4 perhaps antici-

pates v. 5 and its focus on justice, a central attribute of God's "name" or character. The repeated plural "thrones" (כסאות *kis'ôt*), another instance of the steplike pattern, has been puzzling to commentators. It is probably a figurative way of saying that the Davidic house and its bureaucracy were responsible for justice in the city and throughout the land (see 2 Sam 8:15; 15:2-6; Isa 1:21-23; Mic 3:9-12).

122:6-9. Justice, which the Davidic house was to enact in accordance with God's reign, was supposed to result in *shalom*, "peace" (see Pss 29:10-11; 72:3, 7), which is the key word in vv. 6-8. Continuing the steplike pattern, it occurs once in each verse; the Hebrew root is also a component of the name "Jerusalem," which may mean "possession of peace" or "foundation of peace." The Hebrew word for "pray" (שאל *šā'al*, v. 6) and the word translated "secure"/"security" (שלוה *šalwâ*, v. 7) both contain the first two consonants of the root of "peace." This makes for what is probably the most striking example of alliteration in the whole psalter; the effect is to emphasize even further the concept of "peace."

The psalmist's invitation in v. 6*a* and his or her prayer for Jerusalem and those who live in it (vv. 6*b*-7) clearly imply that Jerusalem is not peaceful. In fact, Jerusalem has always been one of the most contested and conflicted cities in the world. Especially in the post-exilic era, during which it is likely that the Songs of Ascents were collected, Jerusalem existed in anything but "security" (v. 7*b*; see "prosper" in Lam 1:5; see also Neh 1:3; Jer 15:5). Yet, for the pilgrim who experiences conflict outside of Jerusalem (see Ps 120:5-7), Jerusalem is the consummate sign and symbol of peace. How can this be? Is the psalmist nostalgically recalling the former glory of Davidic and Solomonic times, or is the psalmist simply engaging in patriotic wishful thinking? So some might conclude, but on a deeper level, the psalmist's prayers for the peace of Jerusalem, as well as the commitment to seek its good (v. 9), are indicative of the recognition of God's reign and the intent to live under God's rule. Such recognition and commitment do not represent facile optimism or merely patriotic wishful thinking. Rather, the psalmist's motivation and conviction are eschatological. For the psalmist, to enter Jerusalem *really does* mean to enter a new world. The joy is real

(v. 1). To live for God's sake (v. 9) and for the sake of others (v. 8) is to experience, to embody, and to extend the justice that God intends as ruler of the world. This life-style, this commitment, *is* reality. To be sure, the same old so-called realities will still be present—hatred and war (see Ps 120:5-7), trouble and turmoil (see Neh 1:3)—but they will no longer be determinative. To enter Jerusalem, to acknowledge God's reign and to commit oneself to live under it is to be trans-formed and enabled to live in an extraordinary manner in the ordinary world of daily reality that is frequently reflected in the Songs of Ascents (see Overview on Psalms 120–134 and the Reflections below). The transformation of the pilgrim may be represented by the movement from v. 1 to vv. 8-9. While the psalmist articulates in v. 1 the benefit Jerusalem can have on the self, the focus in vv. 8-9 is on what the psalmist can do for the benefit of others and of God.

REFLECTIONS

1. Given the ongoing unrest in the Middle East and the uneasiness of peace accords that have been reached, the psalmist's invitation in v. 6*a* is remarkably contemporary in its literal sense. Yet even as we pray for the peace of Jerusalem, it is crucial to realize that Jerusalem represents in the psalms not just a place but a symbol of God's presence in space and time. Ironically, much of the ongoing controversy surrounding Jerusalem stems from the failure to discern its symbolic function; the city has often been viewed only as a *place* to be possessed rather than a symbol of the concrete presence in the world of a God who *cannot* ultimately be possessed and whose presence certainly cannot be limited to a particular place (as Psalm 121 proclaims!). To enter Jerusalem is ultimately to experience the reality of God's reign and to be transformed to represent God's just purposes in God's world. In short, to enter Jerusalem is to live eschatologically, because God's claim and God's purposes are always opposed (see Commentary on Psalms 48; 84).

What it means to enter Jerusalem, to live eschatologically, to live under God's reign, is illustrated powerfully by one of Walker Percy's characters, Will Barrett, in the novel *The Second Coming*. Will's father had committed suicide when Will was a young man, and Will's own life has been a persistent battle with a voice inside him (his father's voice perhaps) that tells him to do the same. The voice knows what the so-called real world is like:

> Come, what else is there [except suicide]? What other end if you don't make the end? Make your own bright end in the darkness of this dying world, this foul and feckless place, where you know as well as I that nothing ever really works, that you were never once yourself and never will be or he himself or she herself and certainly never once we ourselves together. Come, close it out before it closes you out because believe me life does no better job with dying than with living. Close it out. At least you can do that, not only not lose but win, with one last splendid gesture defeat the whole foul feckless world.[456]

Will's answer to the voice is a simple no, based on an experience of genuine love between him and another human being, which he takes as a sign that "the Lord is here."[457]

What the psalmist saw in Jerusalem was, in effect, a sign that "the Lord is here," amid the dark, daily realities of a dying world, a frustrating world where nothing ever really works out completely right and we are never all that we can be. Walker Percy does not take the story of Will Barrett beyond his discovery of the sign, but the reader assumes that Will discontinues his frantic search for the second coming of Christ and begins to live in the new world created by the good news that "the Lord is here." As for the psalmist, this good news is also transformational, enabling people to live in an extraordinary manner among the often dark and difficult daily realities of the world.

456. Walker Percy, *The Second Coming* (New York: Ivy Books, 1980) 307.
457. Ibid., 328.

2. Psalm 122 is appropriately used by the church during the season of Advent. Advent maintains a dual focus on Christ's second coming and Christ's first coming—his birth—and so it effectively celebrates the good news that "the Lord is here" and will be here forever. Indeed, for the Gospel writers, Jesus represents what the Temple had symbolized; Jesus is the new locus of God's revelation in space and time (see Mark 13:1-2; 14:58; 15:29). Because this is the case, the Christian reader cannot help hearing Psalm 122 in the light of Jesus' reaction as he made a final pilgrimage to Jerusalem. When Jesus "saw the city, he wept over it," because it was evident to him from his own reception that the people did not recognize "the things that make for peace!" (Luke 19:41-42 NRSV). Tellingly, Jesus moves directly to the Temple, where he pronounces it a means of fleeing from justice rather than furthering the just purposes of God's reign (Luke 19:45-46). As Mays concludes concerning a Christian hearing of Psalm 122:

> When we return to the psalm from this scene in Luke we have to read it and sing it tutored by his [Jesus'] questions. As we pray for the peace of church and city, have we recognized the things that make for peace? Do we know that unless we go with him the pilgrimage toward peace will find no Jerusalem?[458]

Thus, as the good news always does, Psalm 122 leaves us with a challenge that is appropriate for Advent and for all seasons.[459]

458. James L. Mays, *Psalms,* Interpretation (Louisville: John Knox, 1994) 394.
459. Portions of the above treatment of Psalm 122 appear in substantially the same form in J. Clinton McCann, Jr., "Preaching on Psalms for Advent," *Journal for Preachers* 16/1 (Advent 1992) 11-16.

Psalm 123:1-4, Our Eyes Look to the Lord

NIV	NRSV
Psalm 123	Psalm 123
A song of ascents.	A Song of Ascents.
¹I lift up my eyes to you, / to you whose throne is in heaven.	¹ To you I lift up my eyes, / O you who are enthroned in the heavens!
²As the eyes of slaves look to the hand of / their master, / as the eyes of a maid look to the hand of / her mistress, / so our eyes look to the LORD our God, / till he shows us his mercy.	² As the eyes of servants / look to the hand of their master, / as the eyes of a maid / to the hand of her mistress, / so our eyes look to the LORD our God, / until he has mercy upon us.
³Have mercy on us, O LORD, have mercy on / us, / for we have endured much contempt.	³ Have mercy upon us, O LORD, have mercy / upon us, / for we have had more than enough of / contempt.
⁴We have endured much ridicule from the / proud, / much contempt from the arrogant.	⁴ Our soul has had more than its fill / of the scorn of those who are at ease, / of the contempt of the proud.

COMMENTARY

Fourth among the Songs of Ascents (see Overview on Psalms 120–134), Psalm 123 is the first complete prayer in the collection (see Ps 120:2, a brief petition characteristic of the prayers for help; portions of 122:6-8 also could be construed as prayer). The opening profession of trust begins in the first-person singular (v. 1a) but concludes in the plural (v. 2b), and the accompanying petition (v. 3a) and complaint (vv. 3b-4) are also in the plural. Thus Psalm 123 is traditionally categorized as a communal lament/complaint or prayer for help.

The shift from singular to plural makes sense in the context of a pilgrimage (see Commentary on Psalms 120; 121; 122), during which individuals or small groups of travelers became part of a much larger group upon their arrival at Jerusalem. Psalms 120–122 seem to form an intended sequence, moving the pilgrim from dispersion (120:5-7) by way of a journey (Psalm 121) to Jerusalem (Psalm 122). Psalm 123 makes sense as the culmination of this sequence; that is, if Ps 120:5-7 describes the conflicted circumstances of those dwelling in dispersion, then it makes sense that the first thing they would do upon arrival at Jerusalem (Psalm 122) is to look to God (123:1-2) and ask for help (123:3-4). Indeed, the complaint in vv. 3-4 portrays a situation similar to that described in 120:5-7, although there are no verbal links. As several scholars observe, the situation certainly sounds like that of the post-exilic era (see, e.g., Neh 2:19; 4:4, where "ridiculed" and "despised" represent the same Hebrew root as "contempt" in Ps 123:3-4; "scorn" in 123:4 also occurs in Neh 2:19; 4:1 as "mocked"). This means that Psalm 123 is consistent with the character of Book V, which from the beginning (see Ps 107:2-3) appears to be a response to the theological crisis and the need for help that persisted even after the return from exile (see Commentary on Psalms 107; 108; 111; 118; 120; Introduction).

123:1. The NRSV preserves the Hebrew word order of v. 1a. The phrase "to you" is in the emphatic position, suggesting the psalmist's complete orientation to God. To lift up the eyes can indicate arrogance (see 2 Kgs 19:22; cf. Ps 131:1),

but that is clearly not the case here (see Ps 141:8). Rather, God is viewed and addressed as cosmic sovereign (v. 1b; see "sits"/"enthroned" in Pss 2:4; 9:7; 29:10; see also 11:4; 115:3). Thus Ps 123:1 reinforces the direction that is implied in Psalm 122; to enter Jerusalem is to acknowledge God's sovereignty and commit oneself to live under God's rule.

123:2. The two metaphors in v. 2 clearly portray the humble dependence that characterizes the psalmist's approach to God. Because God is sovereign (v. 1), God's people are in the position of "servants" (see Pss 34:22; 69:35-36; 79:2, 10; 86:2, 4, 16; 90:13, 16; 113:1; 116:16) of their "master" or "mistress." The word translated "master" (אדון 'ādôn) is used frequently of God elsewhere (usually translated "Lord"; see Ps 97:5b), but the feminine imaging of God here is striking, although not unprecedented (see Isa 66:13; Hos 11:4; see also Commentary on Psalm 131). The repetition of "eyes" (עינים 'ênayim), which occurs in each of the four poetic lines in vv. 1-2, is another instance of the steplike pattern that characterizes the Songs of Ascents (see Pss 120:5-7; 121:1-4, 7-8; 122:2-5). This pattern of repetition also cuts across the two sections of Psalm 123; "mercy" at the end of v. 2 occurs twice more in v. 3a.

123:3. The double petition "have mercy" (חנן ḥānan, v. 3a) has the emphatic literary effect of surrounding the Lord with pleas for help. The petition is a frequent one in the psalms, often translated "be gracious" (see Pss 4:1; 6:2; 9:13; 25:16; 26:11; 27:7). While it may imply the specific need and desire for forgiveness, it more generally is an indication that the psalmist or the people depend on God for life itself. The Hebrew verb recalls Exod 34:6 (see also Exod 33:19), where God reveals the divine self to be fundamentally gracious. In this case, God's grace does specifically involve forgiveness (see Exod 34:7), but it includes more broadly God's willingness to be present with the people to make life possible (see Exod 34:9).

123:4. The need in Psalm 123 is stated in terms of the people's experience of "contempt" (vv. 3b, 4b) and "ridicule" (v. 4a). The particular situation is not known precisely, but it makes sense to hear the complaint in the narrative context of the post-exilic book of Nehemiah (see Neh 2:19; 4:1, 4). Similar complaints also appear in other psalms, where the psalmists or people are victims of contempt (Pss 31:18; 119:22; "pride" in Ps 31:18 is also from the same root as "proud" [נָאוֹן *gāʾôn*] in 123:4*b*) and ridicule (see Pss 22:7; 44:13; 79:4). The similarity of the complaint in Ps 123:3-4 to those in 44:13; 79:4 is particularly suggestive, since Psalm 79 laments the destruction of Jerusalem and since Psalm 44 is also a communal complaint that follows a prayer that apparently belongs to a person who is absent from Jerusalem (Psalm 42) and who states his or her intention to make a pilgrimage to Jerusalem

(Psalm 43). Thus the similarity of Psalm 123 to Psalms 44; 79 would support the hearing of Psalm 123 in a post-exilic context. The "proud"/"arrogant" also appear as opponents of God and/or the psalmist in Pss 94:2; 140:5. Not surprisingly, the complaint continues the steplike pattern of repetition (see "endured much" in vv. 3*b*, 4*a* as well as "contempt" in vv. 3*b*, 4*b*).

As is more common with the communal complaints than the individual complaints, Psalm 123 ends with the complaint itself. While praise has been implied and trust expressed in vv. 1-2, there is no concluding movement in this direction. What Psalm 123 may lack, however, Psalm 124 will supply.

REFLECTIONS

1. While Psalm 123 makes sense in the historical context of the post-exilic era, it also has affinities with prayers for help that originated and were used in circumstances that simply cannot be determined. This in itself suggests the appropriateness of Psalm 123 for a variety of settings. John Calvin, for instance, unable to determine the authorship of and historical circumstances behind Psalm 123, concluded that its real importance is that it "calls upon us to have recourse to God, whenever wicked men unrighteously and proudly persecute, not one or two of the faithful, but the whole body of the Church."[460] In other words, Psalm 123 can be the prayer of the people of God in every generation.

2. North American Christians in particular may never have experienced persecution or "contempt" on account of their faith. If this is the case, it is because we have not faithfully proclaimed and embodied the radical good news that God so loves the whole world and intends it to be rightly ordered so that all may know life and peace (see Commentary on Psalms 31; 120). It was precisely because he proclaimed and embodied this good news that Jesus ended up on a cross, and he calls people to follow him (Mark 8:34). Insofar as it is faithful, the church will win no popularity contests judged by the standards of the world. While the church is called to be in the world, it can never be of the world (see John 17:14-18). Thus Psalm 123 calls the church to the kind of humble servanthood that lives in utter dependence upon the sovereign God (see vv. 1-2) and that will inevitably be like Jesus' suffering servanthood (see Commentary on Psalm 44). Paradoxically, only at the point that we know the contempt of the world can we know the grace and peace that overcomes the world (see John 16:33). It is for this grace and peace that Psalm 123 prays. And in so doing, it may begin to teach us self-centered folk to turn away from ourselves long enough to be able to say that "our eyes look to the LORD our God" (v. 2).

460. Quoted in H.-J. Kraus, *Psalms 60–150: A Commentary,* trans. H. C. Oswald (Minneapolis: Augsburg, 1989) 437.

Psalm 124:1-8, If the Lord Were Not for Us . . .

NIV

Psalm 124

A song of ascents. Of David.

¹If the LORD had not been on our side—
　let Israel say—
²if the LORD had not been on our side
　when men attacked us,
³when their anger flared against us,
　they would have swallowed us alive;
⁴the flood would have engulfed us,
　the torrent would have swept over us,
⁵the raging waters
　would have swept us away.

⁶Praise be to the LORD,
　who has not let us be torn by their teeth.
⁷We have escaped like a bird
　out of the fowler's snare;
　the snare has been broken,
　and we have escaped.
⁸Our help is in the name of the LORD,
　the Maker of heaven and earth.

NRSV

Psalm 124

A Song of Ascents. Of David.

¹ If it had not been the LORD who was on
　　our side
　—let Israel now say—
² if it had not been the LORD who was on
　　our side,
　when our enemies attacked us,
³ then they would have swallowed us up
　　alive,
　when their anger was kindled against us;
⁴ then the flood would have swept us away,
　the torrent would have gone over us;
⁵ then over us would have gone
　the raging waters.

⁶ Blessed be the LORD,
　who has not given us
　as prey to their teeth.
⁷ We have escaped like a bird
　from the snare of the fowlers;
　the snare is broken,
　and we have escaped.

⁸ Our help is in the name of the LORD,
　who made heaven and earth.

COMMENTARY

Psalm 124 is the fifth of the Songs of Ascents (see Overview on Psalms 120–134). While its position following Psalm 123 may be coincidental, the sequence is an auspicious one. Psalm 123 is a prayer for help in the face of hostility and opposition, while Psalm 124 reports deliverance from enemies and publicly proclaims that help comes from the Lord (v. 8). In fact, v. 8 represents the entire people's affirmation of what an individual traveler had professed in Ps 121:2, suggesting the possibility that the sequence of Psalms 120–124 is intentional. In any case, the sequence in

its current form seems to say that the individual faith professed in Ps 121:2 is confirmed by the pilgrim's arrival at Jerusalem, where his or her voice is joined with that of all Israel (see 124:2). In other words, just as Psalm 123 recalls Psalm 120, so also Psalm 124 recalls Psalm 121. In the midst of opposition, individual or corporate, God is the one who helps. Along with Psalms 120–123, Psalm 124 would have been an effective response to the realities of the post-exilic era. Thus it is in keeping with the apparent intent of

Book V (see Commentary on Psalms 107; 108; 111; 120; Introduction).

Psalm 124 consists of three sections. Verses 1-5 consist of what can be rendered as one long conditional sentence with two if clauses (vv. 1-2) and three then clauses (the NRSV more accurately conveys the fact that each of vv. 3-5 begins with the same Hebrew word). Verses 6-7 offer praise for the deliverance described in vv. 1-5, while at the same time offering another metaphor for the deliverance. Verse 8 concludes with a profession of trust.

124:1-5. Verses 1a, 2a can be translated more literally as, "If God had not been *for us."* Both the syntax and the content recall Ps 94:17, and the particular phrase "for us" recalls Ps 118:6. Verse 2b can be translated more literally as, "when humans rose *against us"* (see "rise" in Ps 3:1 NIV). In short, vv. 1-2 set up a contrast between the power of God and the power of humans, a contrast that is also present in Ps 118:6 (see the NRSV's "mortals"; see also Pss 9:19-20; 56:4, 11). The real issue is "help" (עזר *ʿēzer*). Whose help is ultimately effective? The answer present in vv. 1-5 and vv. 6-7 is given memorable expression in v. 8 (note "help" also in Pss 94:17; 118:7; see also Psalm 3, although the Hebrew word behind "help" in 3:2 differs from the one in Pss 94:17; 118:7; 124:8). As suggested above, the apparently liturgical invitation in v. 1b makes sense in the context of a festal gathering attended by pilgrims (see also Ps 129:1b).

Without God's help, the hostile actions of other humans would have resulted in the people's demise. Verses 3-5 do not specifically identify the disaster that would have occurred. The verb "swallow" (בלע *bālaʿ*) is used in Jer 51:34 to describe Babylon's defeat of Zion (see Jer 51:35). Verses 3-5 certainly make good sense as a description of what the Babylonian exile could well have been: the end of God's people. Whether such specificity is intended here, however, is not clear. The verb "swallow" is used in a variety of other contexts as well (see Exod 15:12; Num 16:30, 32, 34; Jonah 1:17). Similarly, the water imagery in vv. 4-5 is used to describe the threat to Jerusalem (see Isa 28:17, where "overwhelms" is

the same as "swept . . . away" in Ps 124:4a), and the prophet of the exile promises that waters will not "overwhelm" (Isa 43:2 NRSV) the people on their return from Babylon to Jerusalem. But again, the particular verb in v. 4a and the general image is used elsewhere of either unspecified or clearly different threats of chaos (see Pss 42:7; 69:1-2; Jonah 2:3, 5); God's sovereignty over the chaotic waters is affirmed elsewhere as well (see Pss 74:12-15; 89:9-10; 93:3-4). "Us" (נפש *nepeš*) in vv. 4b, 5 translates a Hebrew word that is usually translated "soul" but seems to have originally meant "neck," a translation that would be appropriate here (see Ps 69:1). The NRSV preserves the chiastic poetic structure (see Introduction) of vv. 4-5; it visually represents the threat, as the two occurrences of "waters" (vv. 4a, 5b) surround the two occurrences of "us" (vv. 4b, 5a).

124:6-7. Verse 6a offers praise to God for being "for us" (see "bless" in Pss 28:6; 31:21; 103:1-2, 20-22; 104:1, 35; 115:18), and v. 6b introduces another image for the deliverance (see Job 29:17; Pss 3:8; 57:4; 58:6). Just as the chiastic structure of vv. 4-5 represented the threat, so also the chiastic structure of v. 7 visually represents the escape. The two occurrences of "we have escaped" (see Isa 49:25) surround the two occurrences of "snare" (see Pss 64:5; 91:3; 140:5; 141:9). The people are no longer trapped. Rather, as Kraus translated the final phrase of v. 7, "we are free!"[461] The "we" that begins v. 7 translates the "us"/"our neck" that was surrounded in vv. 4-5, and the "we" in the final phrase of v. 7 is the emphatic personal pronoun. Thus poetic structure, the pattern of repetition, and the effective choice of personal pronoun combine to reinforce the good news: "We are free!"

124:8. This verse climactically affirms the answer to the question implied in vv. 1-2: Where or who is our help? It is no mere earthbound mortal, but the cosmic sovereign "who made heaven and earth" (see Pss 121:2; 134:3; see also 115:15; 146:6).

461. Ibid., 439.

REFLECTIONS

The affirmation in v. 8 has perhaps been made so familiar by traditional use that we fail to grasp its profound and radical implications. To profess that God is our fundamental help means to profess that we are not sufficient to create and secure our own lives and futures. In short, we need help. Of course, this is something that most people are hesitant to say or even to admit, for it undercuts one of the primary principles that seems to drive our individual lives as well as our social and economic institutions—namely, "God helps those who help themselves." Psalm 125 teaches just the opposite; God helps those who *cannot* help themselves (see Commentary on Psalm 3). Apart from this teaching, it is not possible to speak with any integrity about what lies at the heart of the biblical message: the grace of God (see Psalm 123). Indeed, discipleship and servanthood (see Ps 123:2) really begin with the profession that we owe our very lives to God (see Mark 8:34-35).

The fundamental trust that God secures our lives and futures—that God is "for us" (vv. 1-2) and is "our help" (v. 8)—is what empowered Israel to claim the role of suffering servant in the post-exilic era (see Commentary on Psalm 44); it is what empowered Jesus to bear a cross as a suffering servant; and it is what has empowered, does empower, and will empower the church to continue to serve even when it means suffering at the hand of those who oppose God's reign and God's will (v. 2). As the apostle Paul put it with his words and embodied with his sufferings, "If God is for us, who can be against us?" (Rom 8:31 NIV).

Psalm 125:1-5, Those Who Trust in the Lord

NIV

Psalm 125

A song of ascents.

¹Those who trust in the LORD are like Mount
    Zion,
  which cannot be shaken but endures
    forever.
²As the mountains surround Jerusalem,
  so the LORD surrounds his people
  both now and forevermore.

³The scepter of the wicked will not remain
  over the land allotted to the righteous,
for then the righteous might use
  their hands to do evil.

⁴Do good, O LORD, to those who are good,
  to those who are upright in heart.
⁵But those who turn to crooked ways
  the LORD will banish with the evildoers.

Peace be upon Israel.

NRSV

Psalm 125

A Song of Ascents.

¹ Those who trust in the LORD are like Mount
    Zion,
  which cannot be moved, but abides
    forever.
² As the mountains surround Jerusalem,
  so the LORD surrounds his people,
  from this time on and forevermore.

³ For the scepter of wickedness shall not rest
  on the land allotted to the righteous,
so that the righteous might not stretch out
  their hands to do wrong.

⁴ Do good, O LORD, to those who are good,
  and to those who are upright in their
    hearts.
⁵ But those who turn aside to their own
    crooked ways
  the LORD will lead away with evildoers.
Peace be upon Israel!

COMMENTARY

Psalm 125 is the sixth of the Songs of Ascents (see Overview on Psalms 120–134). While it is not possible to demonstrate conclusively that the sequence is intentional, it is possible to detect a pattern in the opening psalms of the collection. The first three psalms have the effect of moving an individual pilgrim from dispersion (Psalm 120) by way of a safe journey (Psalm 121) to Jerusalem (Psalm 122). The next three psalms approximate this same movement, but they do so in the plural rather than the singular. Psalm 123 articulates the contempt that was evident in Ps 120:5-7; Psalm 124 expresses trust in God's help, as did Psalm 121 (cf. 121:2 and 124:8, as well as 121:8 and 124:2); and like Psalm 122, Psalm 125 focuses on Jerusalem and concludes with petition aimed at the establishment of peace. To be sure, this pattern may be coincidental, but at least it suggests that Psalm 125 fits comfortably in the context of the Songs of Ascents. That is to say, it makes sense to conclude that it was originally used by pilgrims on the way to or upon arrival at Jerusalem.

Like Psalm 123, Psalm 125 is usually classified as a communal lament/complaint or prayer for help, and it begins with an expression of trust (vv. 1-2). Verse 3 continues the expression of trust but concludes with a clause that implies complaint and petition. The petition is explicit in v. 4. Verse 5 returns to trust in the form of a warning, and the psalm concludes with a declaration of peace. Scholars frequently suggest, especially on the basis of v. 3, that Psalm 125 reflects the people's domination by the nations in the post-exilic era. This makes good sense and also makes Psalm 125 congruent with its immediate context in the Songs of Ascents and with the larger context of Book V (see Psalms 107–108; 111; 118; 120; Introduction); however, the usefulness of Psalm 125 and its ability to speak for and to the people of God are not limited to an ancient setting. It continues to reflect both the faith and the struggle of the people of God in every generation (see Reflections below).

125:1-2. While the word "trust" (בטח *bāṭaḥ*) has not occurred in the Songs of Ascents until Ps 125:1*a*, the concept has been clearly portrayed in the preceding psalms (see Pss 121:1-8; 123:1-2; 124:1-5, 8). In fact, v. 1*b* explicitly recalls Ps 121:3 (see Pss 16:8; 55:22), and the stability of those who entrust their lives to God is a central theme throughout the psalter (see "trust" in Pss 4:5; 9:10; see the related theme of "refuge" in Ps 2:12; Introduction). The use of geological imagery also is characteristic of the psalter. The metaphor of God as rock may derive from the prominence of Zion (see above on Pss 18:2, 46; 31:2), but here Zion is a simile for the people's stability, which, of course, derives from God (v. 2). Verse 2 makes it easy to picture pilgrims in Jerusalem looking out toward the surrounding mountains (see Ps 121:1) and then interpreting the panoramic view as a metaphor for God's eternal protection (see Pss 121:8; 131:3). The repetition of "surround(s)" continues the steplike pattern that characterizes the Songs of Ascents (see Pss 120:5-7; 121:1-4, 7-8; 122:4-8; 123:1-2).

125:3. The Hebrew particle (כִּי *kî*) that begins this verse should probably be translated "surely" rather than "for" (note that the NIV simply omits it). While v. 3 continues the expression of trust, it does seem to stand apart from vv. 1-2. Carol Bechtel Reynolds even suggests that "the entire psalm seems to pivot on this verse," the conclusion of which should be translated with the KJV, "lest the righteous put forth their hands unto iniquity."[462] In other words, v. 3 implies that the wicked do wield authority in the land and that their persistent influence tempts the righteous to adopt their ways (see Ps 73:10). Because the Hebrew word translated "land allotted" occurs frequently in the book of Joshua as the land is being settled (see Josh 15:1; 17:1), scholars frequently conclude that v. 3 reflects the situation of the post-exilic era, when the people and the land were dominated by other nations. This is a reasonable conclusion, especially since other Songs of Ascents seem to reflect the same situation (see Pss 120:5-7; 123:3-4). The interpretive significance of v. 3, however, should not be limited to the ancient setting. The effect of v. 3, especially in the light of the petition in v. 4, is to give the psalm an eschatological orientation; it

---

462. Carol Bechtel Reynolds, "Psalm 125," *Int.* 48 (1994) 273.

suggests that the people of God always live amid circumstances that make it appear that the wicked are in control (see Commentary on Psalms 2; 93; 96; 97; 98; 99; Introduction).

125:4-5. The reality of wickedness makes necessary the petition in v. 4. God's "doing good" is elsewhere associated with the people's possession of and prosperity in the land, so the verb may reinforce the conclusion that Psalm 125 originated amid the oppression of the post-exilic era (see Deut 8:16; 28:63; 30:5; see also Mic 2:7). But in keeping with the broader relevance of Psalm 125, it should be noted that the contrast between "the righteous"/the "good"/"the upright" and "the wicked"/"those who turn aside"/"the evildoers" is introduced in Psalm 1 and pervades the psalter.

The real issue is this: Who rules the world? While it appears that the wicked rule (note that "scepter" or "rod" in v. 3 occurs often in contexts where the subject is sovereignty, as in Judg 5:14; Pss 2:9; 45:6; Isa 14:5), the expressions of trust in vv. 1-2, 3*a*, 5 indicate the psalmist's conviction that God reigns. Thus it is fitting that the final line of the psalm declares "Peace," which describes the conditions that prevail when God's sovereign rule is recognized and enacted (see Pss 29:10-11; 72:3, 7). In longing for peace (Ps 120:7), in praying for peace (Ps 122:6-7), in declaring peace (Pss 122:8; 125:5; 128:6), the psalmists identify themselves as faithful citizens of the reign of God.

REFLECTIONS

The peace derived from service (see Ps 123:2) under God's sovereignty is no ordinary peace. It surpasses all understanding (see Phil 4:7), and it is greater than the world can ever give (see John 14:27). Like the peace Jesus left with his disciples, so the peace the psalmist declares is experienced amid opposition from the world, the apparent sovereignty of the wicked (v. 3). Thus, as the NT also makes clear, the faith of the people of God (v. 1) is inseparable from hope (see Rom 8:24-25; Heb 11:1). In short, the people of God always live eschatologically, proclaiming God's rule in the face of wickedness, attempting to embody the peace that God offers in the midst of a hostile world (see Commentary on Psalms 2; 31; 120; Introduction).

The opposition to God's rule is as evident in the contemporary era as it was in the post-exilic era. Thus Psalm 125 continues to speak to and for the people of God. In his essay "Are We Afraid of Peace?" Elie Wiesel addresses the ongoing opposition to the peace that God wills for the world:

> Though temporary in nature, war seems to last forever. In the service of death, it mocks the living. It allows men to do things that in normal times they have no right to do: to indulge in cruelty. A collective as well as individual gratification of unconscious impulses, war may be too much a part of human behavior to be eliminated—ever.[463]

In a similar direction, Reinhold Niebuhr reminds us that moral people are far more inclined to do immoral things—like indulging in cruelty—in the name of their society or nation.[464] And the characters in novelist Walker Percy's novels constantly confront the reader with the observation that human beings do not seem to tolerate very well the ordinariness of daily life: "War is better than Monday morning."[465]

Given these trenchant and realistic assessments of human nature, we can begin to appreciate the profound importance of Ps 125:3. Because the dynamic of evil seems to have a subtle way of luring the righteous, it is all the more important that human hostility and cruelty be identified, named for what they are, and opposed. It is crucial that the people of God, who know a more excellent way, be just as faithfully determined as the psalmist that evil not prevail (v. 3*a*), that they pray for God's goodness (v. 4), and that they display the psalmist's confident courage in

---

463. Elie Wiesel, *From the Kingdom of Memory: Reminiscences* (New York: Summit Books, 1990) 225.
464. See Reinhold Niebuhr, *Moral Man and Immoral Society: A Study in Ethics and Politics* (New York: Charles Scribner's Sons, 1960).
465. Walker Percy, *The Last Gentleman* (New York: Ivy Books, 1966) 74.

declaring a peace that opposes the declaration of war and every other impulse toward cruelty (v. 5; see Ps 120:5-7).

Psalm 126:1-6, Restore Our Fortunes, O Lord

NIV

Psalm 126

A song of ascents.

[1]When the LORD brought back the captives to[a]
Zion,
we were like men who dreamed.[b]
[2]Our mouths were filled with laughter,
our tongues with songs of joy.
Then it was said among the nations,
"The LORD has done great things for them."
[3]The LORD has done great things for us,
and we are filled with joy.

[4]Restore our fortunes,[c] O LORD,
like streams in the Negev.
[5]Those who sow in tears
will reap with songs of joy.
[6]He who goes out weeping,
carrying seed to sow,
will return with songs of joy,
carrying sheaves with him.

[a]1 Or LORD restored the fortunes of   [b]1 Or men restored to health
[c]4 Or Bring back our captives

NRSV

Psalm 126

A Song of Ascents.

[1] When the LORD restored the fortunes of
Zion,[a]
we were like those who dream.
[2] Then our mouth was filled with laughter,
and our tongue with shouts of joy;
then it was said among the nations,
"The LORD has done great things for
them."
[3] The LORD has done great things for us,
and we rejoiced.

[4] Restore our fortunes, O LORD,
like the watercourses in the Negeb.
[5] May those who sow in tears
reap with shouts of joy.
[6] Those who go out weeping,
bearing the seed for sowing,
shall come home with shouts of joy,
carrying their sheaves.

[a]Or brought back those who returned to Zion

COMMENTARY

Psalm 126 is the seventh of the Song of Ascents (see Overview on Psalms 120–134). Given the unifying features of the collection and even the possibility of the intentional arrangement of Psalms 120–125 (see Commentary on Psalm 125), it is not surprising that Psalm 126 reflects the perspective of the preceding psalms—that is, the people have experienced God's deliverance in the past (Ps 126:1-3; see Pss 120:1; 124:1-7), but now confronted with another crisis in the present, they petition God for help (Ps 126:4-5; see 120:2; 122:6-7; 123:3-4; 125:4) and profess their trust in God's help (Ps 126:6; see Pss 121:1-8; 123:1-2;

124:8; 125:1-2, 5). Of course, this construal of the psalm depends on a translation similar to that provided by the NIV and the NRSV, and the translation of the verb tenses in Psalm 126 is often disputed. For instance, some translate all the verbs in vv. 1-3 (as well as those in vv. 5-6) in the future tense, thus making the psalm consistently a prayer for help. Others translate all the verbs in vv. 4-6 (as well as those in vv. 1-3) in the past tense, thus making the psalm consistently a song of thanksgiving. Such strategies appear to be forced attempts to remove the tension between vv. 1-3 and vv. 4-6, but it is precisely this tension that is reflected in Psalms 120–125 and that gives Psalm 126 its continuing theological relevance to the people of God in every generation.

Historically speaking, the tension between vv. 1-3 and vv. 4-6 makes very good sense in the post-exilic era. The likelihood of a post-exilic origin for Psalm 126 is increased by the appearance of the phrase the NRSV translates as "restored the fortunes" in v. 1a. While this more general sense is preferable, it is likely that the phrase refers to the return of the exiles from Babylon to Jerusalem (see Deut 30:3; Jer 30:3, 18; 32:44; Ezek 39:25). This glorious pilgrimage ran up against hard historical realities. The vision of Isaiah 40–55 did not materialize, and soon the disillusioned people found themselves again in need of restoration (see the books of Ezra; Nehemiah; Haggai; and Zechariah). The same phrase that occurs in Ps 126:1, 4 also occurs in Ps 85:1 (see also the verb in 85:4); Psalms 85 and 126 share the same movement, and they can be reasonably understood in the same historical context (see Commentary on Psalm 85). Even so, it is not necessary to tie Psalm 126 inextricably to a specific historical occasion. The phrase "restored the fortunes" can refer more generally to any reversal of God's judgment, and it is clear that Psalm 126 has continued to speak to and for the people of God throughout the centuries (see Reflections below).

126:1-3. It is easy to imagine how the return of the captives from Babylon would have been like a dream come true (v. 1b), especially in the light of the exalted interpretation of this event by Isaiah 40–55 as a second exodus, God's "new thing" (Isa 43:19). While there is support in the ancient versions for an alternate reading of v. 1b (see the NIV note), the Hebrew makes perfectly good sense (see Isa 29:7-8; Joel 2:28; Acts 12:9). The return to Jerusalem was also a source of great joy (v. 2ab), and joy becomes the dominant note of the psalm (see "songs of joy" [רִנָּה rinnâ] in vv. 2, 5-6). Not surprisingly, the Hebrew root of "songs of joy" occurs frequently in Isaiah 40–55 to describe the appropriate response to the return from exile (see Isa 44:23; 48:20; 49:13), but it is also used more generally to portray the appropriate emotion for approaching the house of God (see Ps 42:4) and for worship in response to divine deliverance (see Pss 47:1; 118:15). The joyful tone is reinforced by the mention of "laughter"

(v. 2a; see Job 8:21) and by the verb "rejoice" in v. 3b (the root is different from the one behind "songs of joy").

According to Isaiah 40–55, the return from exile was to be universally proclaimed (see Isa 41:1; 48:20); indeed, it was effected by God's use of other nations (see Isa 45:1-7) so that God's people might become "a light to the nations" (Isa 42:6 NRSV). Again, this background helps to make sense of what the nations say in v. 2cd, especially since the nations usually are portrayed as saying something quite different (see Pss 79:10; 115:2; see above on Pss 120:5-7; 123:3-4). Continuing the steplike pattern of repetition that characterizes the Songs of Ascents, the people echo what the nations have observed (see Joel 2:20-21).

126:4-6. The retrospective look of vv. 1-3 is left behind in vv. 4-6, which have the present need in view. The recollection of v. 1a in v. 4a sharpens the contrast between past and present, as do the occurrences of "tears" (v. 5) and "weeping" as antonyms to "songs of joy" (vv. 5-6; cf. v. 2). But the present is not without hope. The image of the "streams in the Negev" (v. 4b) communicates both the people's neediness and their confidence in God. While often dry, even today these stream beds can suddenly become rushing torrents when the seasonal rains arrive. So the simile used here functions to convey not only the people's current dryness but also their expectation of the life-giving deliverance of God. In Ps 42:1, as well, the need for God is represented in terms of the desire for "streams of water"; Joel 3:18 depicts future deliverance by using the same imagery.

The imagery shifts to sowing and reaping in vv. 5-6 (see Amos 9:13-15, where similar agricultural imagery depicts future deliverance). That the people "sow in tears" and go out "weeping" is often interpreted as a reflection of ancient Near Eastern rituals of mourning for a dead fertility god, whose burial is represented by the sowing of seeds into the ground. While such a background is possible, it is just as important to observe that sowing is always an act of anticipation and hope. The mention of tears and weeping in this case may simply emphasize the urgency of the need already articulated in v. 4, and thus the fervency of the people's hope. Appeals for help from God are made elsewhere in the OT with "tears" and "weeping" (see

2 Kgs 20:5; Pss 39:12; 42:3; 56:8; Jer 9:1, 18; 13:17; 31:16; Lam 1:16; 2:18; Joel 2:17). Just as the people's need is real, so also is their hope real. Like v. 6, v. 5 can also be translated with an indicative force. The repetition of "songs of joy" in vv. 5-6 is emphatic; there will be a joyful harvest.

REFLECTIONS

1. While Psalm 126 makes good sense against the background of the post-exilic era, its relevance and use are much broader. Concerning the key phrase, "restored the fortunes," Kraus maintains that it can be properly understood as "an expression for a historical change to a new state of affairs for all things."[466] In other words, v. 1 articulates the remembrance of a past deliverance that evokes laughter and joy among God's people. Similarly, the prayer in v. 4 is perpetually appropriate for the faithful—both individuals and the whole people. No matter how often we proclaim that God "has done great things for us" (v. 3; see also v. 2), we will still find ourselves in need of God's help and renewed deliverance (see Commentary on Psalms 123; 125). Thus Psalm 126 reminds us that we live in the hope of God's help, always remembering what God has done in the past (vv. 1-3; see also Psalm 124) and always anticipating what God will do in the future (vv. 4-6; see Isa 43:19; 65:17; Rev 21:5; see Commentary on Psalms 2; 93; 96; 97; 98; 99; Introduction).

2. Given the several similarities between Psalm 126 and the book of Joel (in addition to the references cited above, cf. Ps 126:1, 4 with Joel 3:1), Walter Beyerlin argues that the author(s) of Psalm 126 actually used the book of Joel as a source in the attempt to address the disappointing circumstances that prevailed in Judah following the return from exile.[467] Even without this possible historical connection, however, it is instructive to read the book of Joel alongside Psalm 126. Like the psalm, Joel moves from an articulation of need (1:2–2:17) to the promise of God's response (2:18–3:21). Thus Psalm 126 and Joel join in proclaiming the good news that God will ultimately provide for God's people. This theme, along with the harvest imagery, makes Psalm 126 an appropriate reading for Thanksgiving Day.

3. Psalm 126 is also appropriately associated with the seasons of Advent and Lent, because it communicates the reality that the people of God always live by both memory and hope. During Advent and Lent, we remember the humble and humbling circumstances of Jesus' birth and death; yet we do so in the joyful hope represented by his resurrection and the promise of the renewal of all things. The hopeful, joyful tone of Psalm 126 points to the possibility that dreaming in v. 1 involves not simply the incredulous response to a divine act of deliverance but the suggestion that every divine act of deliverance evokes a joyous vision of the future out of which the people of God live (see Joel 2:28 and its use in Acts 2:17). The joyful tone of the hymn "Bringing in the Sheaves," based on Psalm 126, suggests the effect of living as a visionary, through which anticipated joy becomes a present reality even amid the distressing circumstances that lead us to pray, "Restore our fortunes, O LORD." In other words, "Blessed are those who mourn, for they will be comforted" (Matt 5:4 NRSV).

466. H.-J. Kraus, *Psalms 60–150: A Commentary,* trans. H. C. Oswald (Minneapolis: Augsburg, 1989) 450.
467. Walter Beyerlin, *We Are Like Dreamers,* trans. D. Livingston (Edinburgh: T. and T. Clark, 1982) 41-58.

Psalm 127:1-5, Unless the Lord Builds the House

NIV

Psalm 127

A song of ascents. Of Solomon.

[1]Unless the LORD builds the house,
its builders labor in vain.
Unless the LORD watches over the city,
the watchmen stand guard in vain.
[2]In vain you rise early
and stay up late,
toiling for food to eat—
for he grants sleep to[a] those he loves.

[3]Sons are a heritage from the LORD,
children a reward from him.
[4]Like arrows in the hands of a warrior
are sons born in one's youth.
[5]Blessed is the man
whose quiver is full of them.
They will not be put to shame
when they contend with their enemies in
the gate.

[a]2 Or eat— / for while they sleep he provides for

NRSV

Psalm 127

A Song of Ascents. Of Solomon.

[1] Unless the LORD builds the house,
those who build it labor in vain.
Unless the LORD guards the city,
the guard keeps watch in vain.
[2] It is in vain that you rise up early
and go late to rest,
eating the bread of anxious toil;
for he gives sleep to his beloved.[a]

[3] Sons are indeed a heritage from the LORD,
the fruit of the womb a reward.
[4] Like arrows in the hand of a warrior
are the sons of one's youth.
[5] Happy is the man who has
his quiver full of them.
He shall not be put to shame
when he speaks with his enemies in the
gate.

[a]Or for he provides for his beloved during sleep

COMMENTARY

Psalm 127 is the eighth of the Songs of Ascents (see Overview on Psalms 120–134). The eighth position represents the middle of the collection, but it is not clear how much significance should be attached to the shape of the collection. It does seem to be the case, though, that while expressing trust in God's help (Psalms 121; 124), Psalms 120–126 articulate primarily the ongoing need of the people in a hostile environment (see Pss 120:5-7; 122:6-9; 123:3-4; 125:3-5; 126:4-6). While Psalm 127 continues to articulate the importance of trusting God and living in dependence upon God (see esp. vv. 1-2), it introduces the possibility of happiness (v. 5). This vocabulary is picked up in Ps 128:1-2, which also seems to offer assurance in response to the petition of 125:4 ("Do good" in Ps 125:4 and "go well" in 128:2 translate the same Hebrew root). Psalm 128 also introduces the concept of blessing as applied to humanity (v. 5), a concept that does not occur in this sense in Psalms 120–126 (cf. Ps 126:6) but recurs several times in subsequent psalms (Pss 129:8; 132:15; 133:3; 134:3). Psalms 130–131 encourage hope (130:7; 131:3), and Psalm 132 is an encouraging word about Jerusalem. All in all, then, the tone of Psalms 128–134 is more upbeat than that of Psalms 120–126, and the people's opponents are seldom in view (see only Psalm 129). If anything, what threatens the people are their own misplaced priorities (127:1-2), sinfulness (130:3), and pride (131:1). Hence, Psalm 127 does seem to represent something of a turning point. Its function in this regard may be marked by the unique attribution of the psalm to Solomon.

Earlier generations of scholars had difficulty

perceiving the unity of Psalm 127, and they often concluded that it was composed of two independent wisdom sayings (vv. 1-2 and vv. 3-5). Recent scholarship has detected a unity between the two parts on a structural and a conceptual level. For instance, on the structural level, the verb "build(s)" (בנה *bānâ*) in v. 1 begins with the same two Hebrew letters that form the word "sons" (בנים *bānîm*) in vv. 3-4, thus signaling a unity. On the conceptual level, to build a house can refer not only literally to the physical construction of an edifice, but also figuratively to the establishment of a family. This latter sense is in view in vv. 3-5; in both vv. 1-2 and vv. 3-5, the ultimate accomplishment belongs to God.

Verses 1-2 display the steplike pattern of repetition that is characteristic of the Songs of Ascents (see Pss 120:5-7; 121:1-4, 7-8; 122:4-8; 123:1-2), as the words or phrases "Unless the LORD," "build(s)," "guard(s)," and "vain" are repeated. Three activities are described as "vain"—that is, ultimately purposeless and worthless—without God's involvement. As suggested above, building a house could include several things, from physical construction of a house (Gen 33:17; Deut 8:12) or the Temple (2 Sam 7:13) to having children (Deut 25:9; Ruth 4:11). When God builds a house, the reference is to the establishment of a priestly or royal dynasty (see 1 Sam 2:35; 2 Sam 7:27), a direction that points toward vv. 3-5. Guarding or keeping is a characteristic activity of God (see Num 6:24; Pss 25:20; 34:20; 86:2; 97:10; 116:6; 121:3-5, 7-8). Patrick D. Miller points out that the reference to "the city" is "richly ambiguous": "It may be Jerusalem, or it may be any city, that is, the city of those who sing this song."[468] The third activity involves excessive work, which is accompanied by needless anxiety. Although the sense of v. 2*d* is not entirely clear (see NIV and NRSV notes), the message is that God ultimately provides what humans need without their excessive striving. While the word "sleep" (שנא *šēnā'*) is well-attested (see Pss 3:5; 4:8), J. A. Emerton suggests an emendation that yields a word meaning "glory" or "honor" or "wealth."[469] In either case, the sense is that pro-

vision for human life is a result, not of extraordinary human effort, but of the grace of God. As Miller suggests, we should hear in v. 2 an echo of Gen 3:17-19, although v. 2 is really "a counterword to Gen 3:17-19," in that it promises provision beyond what human beings can manage to produce.[470]

Even if building a house (v. 1) is not heard in the sense of establishing a family, there is a connection between vv. 1-2 and vv. 3-5. All the activities cited are ordinary necessities of life— securing a home (v. 2*ab*), establishing a safe neighborhood (v. 1*cd*), working for a living (v. 2), having children (vv. 3-5). Each activity can, of course, be approached simply in terms of human effort and accomplishment, but the psalmist insists that each be viewed in relation to God. In the case of children, they are God's gift. The word "heritage" (נחלה *naḥălâ*) often refers to God's gift of land (see "inheritance" in Josh 14:3), which represented access to life and a future. Here, children represent much the same thing, and it is God who gives them (see Gen 15:1, where "reward" involves the promise of children in Abram's future; see also Gen 30:2, where "the fruit of the womb" is God's prerogative to give). They represent strength (v. 4) and apparently a security that comes from sheer numbers, although the precise sense of v. 5 is unclear (the NIV's "they" translates the Hebrew accurately). The city gate functioned like a courthouse (see Deut 21:19; 25:7; Amos 5:12), and perhaps a person with a large family had guaranteed allies in settling disputes.

Given the central position of Psalm 127 in the Songs of Ascents, it is probable that its context affected the way the community heard and construed "house," "city," and "sons." As pilgrimage songs (see Overview on Psalms 120–134), Psalms 120–134 show particular interest in the Temple (see Pss 122:1, 9; 134:1), Jerusalem (see Pss 122:2-3, 6-9; 125:1-2; 126:1; 129:5; 132:13), and the Davidic dynasty (Pss 122:5; 132:1-5, 10-12). Thus it is likely that "the house" (v. 1) was construed as the Temple or perhaps the Davidic dynasty, that "the city" (v. 1) was understood to be Jerusalem, and that the "sons" (vv. 3-4) were taken to be royal descendants. Perhaps Ps 127:2 was even heard in the light of the words attrib-

468. Patrick D. Miller, Jr., *Interpreting the Psalms* (Philadelphia: Fortress, 1986) 133.

469. J. A. Emerton, "The Meaning of *šēnā'* [שנא] in Psalm cxxvii 2," *VT* 24 (1974) 15-31.

470. Miller, *Interpreting the Psalms*, 133-34.

uted to David in Ps 132:3-5; that is, David's determined attempt to build God a house actually resulted in God's building David a house (see 2 Samuel 7). In any case, this reading of Psalm 127 probably accounts for the attribution of Psalm 127 to Solomon, who carried out numerous building projects, including the Temple (see 1 Kgs 3:1-2; 7:1-11; 8:13; 9:1). Given that Solomon's motives may not have been the purest—he spent thirteen years building his own palace and only seven years on the Temple (see 1 Kgs 6:38; 7:1)—and that his policies led to the split of the kingdom (see 1 Kgs 5:13; 12:1-16), it is perhaps proper to view Solomon in some sense as a negative example. Thus without God's involvement, human efforts and achievements, even those as great as Solomon's, are finally fleeting and empty.

REFLECTIONS

1. Given that Psalms 120–134 are probably a pilgrimage collection, it is not surprising that several psalms reflect the realities of daily living, such as work and family (see Psalms 122; 127; 133). The effect of grounding such realities in the will of God and of construing them ultimately as the work of God is to give the ordinary realities of life an extraordinary significance. That is to say, God cares about the so-called routine matters, such as home, community, work, and family.

While making this affirmation, Psalm 127 is also an insistent challenge to a purely secular reading of human experience. While some people need to be reminded that home, community, work, and family are not simply necessities to be tolerated, other people need to be reminded that neither are these realms of experience the be-all and end-all of human existence. Having a nice house may be part of the American dream, but it does not necessarily fulfill the will of God (see Luke 9:57-62). Having a crime-free neighborhood does little good if we have nothing to live for except our possessions, and making a living means nothing if we do not know what life is really all about (see Luke 12:15). Family can become an idolatrous means of escaping God's will if it is defined too narrowly (see Mark 3:31-35; see also Commentary on Psalm 133). As Miller concludes, "The word of the psalm is that unless such enterprises become God's enterprises as those who build, watch, and labor seek the will and way of God and invoke God's presence and purpose in these activities, then there is an emptiness to them."[471] Or worse, there is a demonic, destructive side to them when these activities become means of expressing self-sufficiency rather than dependence upon God (see Commentary on Psalms 1; 121) and means of pursuing greed rather than generosity. In the final analysis, Psalm 127 functions as an invitation to entrust our lives to God and so not to be anxious about our lives, but to pursue God's claim upon us and strive to embody God's will (see Matt 6:25-34).

2. The corporate construal of Psalm 127, signaled by the attribution to Solomon, reminds us that what applies to our individual lives also applies to our lives as a community of God's people. As Mays concludes, "Unless the LORD builds the church, they labor in vain who build it."[472] Quite properly, Psalm 127 is widely used in liturgies of dedication of new church buildings. The subtle temptation is to make even church buildings into monuments to human achievement. Psalm 127 opposes the pervasive temptation to take personal credit for God's activity among us.

---

471. Ibid., 137.
472. James L. Mays, *Psalms,* Interpretation (Louisville: John Knox, 1994) 402.

Psalm 128:1-6, You Shall Be Happy

NIV

Psalm 128

A song of ascents.

¹Blessed are all who fear the LORD,
who walk in his ways.
²You will eat the fruit of your labor;
blessings and prosperity will be yours.
³Your wife will be like a fruitful vine
within your house;
your sons will be like olive shoots
around your table.
⁴Thus is the man blessed
who fears the LORD.

⁵May the LORD bless you from Zion
all the days of your life;
may you see the prosperity of Jerusalem,
⁶ and may you live to see your children's
children.

Peace be upon Israel.

NRSV

Psalm 128

A Song of Ascents.

¹ Happy is everyone who fears the LORD,
who walks in his ways.
² You shall eat the fruit of the labor of your
hands;
you shall be happy, and it shall go well
with you.

³ Your wife will be like a fruitful vine
within your house;
your children will be like olive shoots
around your table.
⁴ Thus shall the man be blessed
who fears the LORD.

⁵ The LORD bless you from Zion.
May you see the prosperity of Jerusalem
all the days of your life.
⁶ May you see your children's children.
Peace be upon Israel!

COMMENTARY

Psalm 128 is the ninth of the Songs of Ascents (see Overview on Psalms 120–134). Although scholars continue to debate whether there is an intentionality to the shape of the collection, it seems that Psalm 127 represents a sort of turning point. In any case, it is clear that Psalm 128 should be heard as a companion to Psalm 127. The two psalms are linked by the occurrences of "happy" in 127:5 and 128:1-2; verbal links also highlight the fact that both psalms deal with the subjects of work (see "eating"/"eat" in 127:2; 128:2) and family (see "sons"/"children" in 127:3-4; 128:3, 6). Both psalms affirm that fruitfulness of family (see 127:3; 128:3; "fruit" in 128:2 is a different Hebrew word) and of work derives from God.

The NIV follows the usual structural division of Psalm 128: vv. 1-4 and vv. 5-6. In this view,

the word "fear(s)" serves to mark the beginning and end of the first section. Allen divides the psalm into vv. 1-3 and vv. 4-6, suggesting that the beginning of each section is marked by the word "fear(s)" and that both sections display the same movement from third person (vv. 1, 4) to direct address (vv. 2-3, 5-6) while repeating the major concept of each section (see "happy" in vv. 1-2, "blessing" in vv. 4-5).[473] The NRSV offers yet another proposal: vv. 1-2, vv. 3-4, vv. 5-6. In this view, vv. 1-2 focus on the happiness derived from work; vv. 3-4 focus on the blessings of family; and vv. 5-6 put both within the context of God's blessing from Zion (see "prosperity" in vv. 2, 5 NIV and "children" in vv. 3, 6 NRSV). In short, several structural proposals can be justified, de-

473. Leslie C. Allen, *Psalms 101–150,* WBC 21 (Waco, Tex.: Word, 1983) 184.

pending on which clues one considers most important.

128:1. The psalm begins with a beatitude that is very similar to Ps 112:1 and recalls Ps 1:1-2. Although, like Psalm 112, Psalm 128 seems to suggest that happiness consists largely of material reward—the benefits of one's work (v. 2) and a large family (v. 3)—the matter is clearly not so simple or superficial. To fear the Lord means fundamentally to recognize God's sovereignty and so to entrust life and future to God (see Pss 2:11; 25:14; 31:19; 33:18; 34:9, 11; 60:4; 112:1; 115:11, 13; 118:4). It is to orient one's whole life to God's ways rather than one's own ways (v. 1*b*; see Deut 8:6; 10:12, where walking in God's ways is also parallel to fearing God; see also Ps 119:3). While the psalmist properly maintains that such orientation of one's life affects what one experiences in life, he or she does not intend to advocate a mechanistic system of rewards or punishment, as the literary context of Psalm 128 makes clear (see Pss 120:5-7; 123:3-4; 126:4-6). Rather, as in Psalms 1–2, happiness is ultimately the connecting of one's life to the true source of life: God.

128:2-4. The inability to enjoy the fruit of one's own labor was a traditional sign of God's disfavor (see Deut 28:33; Pss 78:46; 109:11), as was barrenness (see Gen 30:1-2; 1 Sam 1:5). Similarly, fruitfulness of work (v. 1) and of family (v. 3) was understood as God's blessing (v. 4; see Ps 115:13). The psalms regularly make it clear that faithfulness to God does not guarantee such blessings in any mechanistic way (see Pss 3:1; 34:19). For instance, the petition in Ps 125:4 ("Do good" represents the same Hebrew root as "well" [טוֹב *ţôb*] in 128:2) implicitly indicates that the faithful frequently stand in need. Even so, Ps 128:1-4 encourages the faithful to view the so-called ordinary daily benefits of life in relation to God. Those who fear God will know a blessedness that endures in all circumstances.

128:5-6. These verses are sometimes construed as a priestly benediction (see Num 6:24-26; Ps 134:3). While it is easy to imagine the blessing of the people by a priest within the context of a pilgrimage to Jerusalem (see Overview on Psalms 120–134), the ancient setting of Psalm 128 remains uncertain. What is clearer is that the mention of Zion in v. 5 connects Psalm 128 to its literary context (see Pss 122:1-2, 6-9; 125:1-2; 126:1; 129:5; 132:13; 134:3), as does the theme of blessing (see Pss 129:8; 132:15; 133:3; 134:3) and the proclamation of peace that concludes the psalm (see Pss 120:7; 122:6-9; 125:5). The proclamation of peace is appropriate by those who fear God, who live under God's rule, since it describes the conditions that prevail when God's sovereignty is recognized and enacted (see above on Ps 125:5).

REFLECTIONS

Claus Westermann distinguishes between God's activity in saving—extraordinary moments that involve deliverance from death to life—and God's activity in blessing—God's ongoing provision for the ordinary necessities of daily life.[474] While this distinction can be pressed too far, it can also be helpful. And in these terms, Psalm 128 articulates a theology of blessing as it celebrates the daily realms of work and family as gifts of God. In this regard, it is similar to Psalm 127. Together, the two psalms resist our persistent tendency to view the world purely in secular terms (see Commentary on Psalm 127).

The possible danger of a theology of blessing is that people are tempted to turn it into a mechanistic system of reward and punishment. The immediate literary context of Psalm 128 and its larger canonical context resist this tendency. For instance, when Psalm 128 is heard in conjunction with Psalm 125 (cf. Pss 125:5 with 128:6), the proclamation of peace must be understood eschatologically; peace always exists amid the hostility of those who do not fear the Lord (see Commentary on Psalm 125). This does not make it any less real, but the peace God gives surpasses all human understanding (see Phil 4:7), for it is not "as the world gives"

---

474. Claus Westermann, *Elements of Old Testament Theology,* trans. D. W. Stott (Atlanta: John Knox, 1982) 35-117.

(John 14:27 NRSV). In this context, the experience of the blessing and peace of God is cause not for self-congratulation but for gratitude (see Commentary on Psalms 50; 67).

Psalm 129:1-8, God Has Cut the Cords of the Wicked

NIV	NRSV
Psalm 129	**Psalm 129**
A song of ascents.	A Song of Ascents.
¹They have greatly oppressed me from my youth— let Israel say— ²they have greatly oppressed me from my youth, but they have not gained the victory over me. ³Plowmen have plowed my back and made their furrows long. ⁴But the LORD is righteous; he has cut me free from the cords of the wicked. ⁵May all who hate Zion be turned back in shame. ⁶May they be like grass on the roof, which withers before it can grow; ⁷with it the reaper cannot fill his hands, nor the one who gathers fill his arms. ⁸May those who pass by not say, "The blessing of the LORD be upon you; we bless you in the name of the LORD."	¹ "Often have they attacked me from my youth" —let Israel now say— ² "often have they attacked me from my youth, yet they have not prevailed against me. ³ The plowers plowed on my back; they made their furrows long." ⁴ The LORD is righteous; he has cut the cords of the wicked. ⁵ May all who hate Zion be put to shame and turned backward. ⁶ Let them be like the grass on the housetops that withers before it grows up, ⁷ with which reapers do not fill their hands or binders of sheaves their arms, ⁸ while those who pass by do not say, "The blessing of the LORD be upon you! We bless you in the name of the LORD!"

COMMENTARY

Psalm 129 is the tenth of the Songs of Ascents (see Overview on Psalms 120–134). It has been categorized in several ways by scholars—communal lament/complaint, communal thanksgiving, and communal song of assurance. In any case, the invitation for the people's participation in v. 1 recalls Ps 124:1 (see also Ps 118:2-4), and the openings of the two psalms relate a similar story of threat and deliverance ("attacked" in 124:1-2 and 129:1-2 translates two different Hebrew words). The pattern of an individual voice joined by the voice of the community makes good sense if the Songs of Ascents were originally used by pilgrims on the way to or upon arrival at Jerusa-lem (see Commentary on Psalms 120; 124). So does the focus on Zion (v. 5), which is frequent in the collection (see Pss 122:6-9; 125:1-2; 126:1; 132:13; 134:3).

The NIV follows the usual division of the psalm into two roughly equal sections. Several scholars suggest, however, a division into vv. 1-3 and vv. 4-8, since the first-person perspective extends only through v. 3 (note that the NRSV includes vv. 1-3 in quotation marks, although it indicates no structural divisions at all). Of course, it would be possible to extend the quotation at least through v. 4. Allen, for instance, suggests that vv. 2-4 can be understood as the speech of a personified Zion.

He finds support for this proposal in Micah's prophecy that Zion will be "plowed" (see Mic 3:12), and he notes that a personified Zion also speaks elsewhere (see Isa 49:14; Jer 4:31; Lam 1:9).[475] In short, as is often the case, the structure and movement of Psalm 129 can be described on more than one level, depending on which clues are taken to be the most important (see Commentary on Psalm 128).

129:1-4. A comparison of the NIV with the NRSV shows that the adverb at the beginning of vv. 1-2 can be construed to indicate either the frequency of the opposition or its severity. In either case, vv. 1-2 recall the occurrences of the same adverb used earlier in the collection, where it also suggests both length and severity of opposition (see Pss 120:6; 123:4). Thus vv. 1-2 articulate the reality of the persistent opposition, which has been and is being experienced by the people of God and which is described figuratively in v. 3 (see Isa 51:23). Even so, the people have continued to exist (v. 2*b*); as v. *1a* indicates, their ongoing existence is testimony not to their own achievement but to God's righteousness (see Pss 7:9, 11; 11:7). The attribution of righteousness to God occurs often in the context of the proclamation of God's sovereignty (see Pss 9:7-8; 96:13; 97:2; 98:9; 99:4); the mention of "cords" in v. 4*b* also raises the issue of sovereignty (see Ps 2:3; see also 46:9, where God "cuts" the spear). The

affirmation of God's sovereignty (v. 4) in the context of persistent opposition (vv. 1-3) means that Psalm 129 shares the eschatological perspective that characterizes the Songs of Ascents (see Commentary on Psalms 120; 123; 124; 126) and that pervades the psalter (see Commentary on Psalms 2; 46; 93; 96; 97; 98; 99; Introduction).

129:5-8. The mention of Zion in v. 5 probably recalls the original pilgrimage setting of Psalm 129. It also is a reminder that opposition to God's people was also opposition to God, since Zion was God's place (see Commentary on Psalms 46; 48; 76; 84; 87; 122). Verses 5-8 may be construed as a wish or a prayer, in which case they recall the petitions in Pss 123:3; 125:4; 126:4-6. On the other hand, the verbs can be translated with an indicative sense, in which case vv. 5-8 would have the character either of a prophecy concerning Zion's future or of a further expression of trust in God's sovereignty (see v. 4; Pss 121:3-4; 124:8; 125:5). In either case, the perspective is still eschatological, for it assumes the existence of those who hate Zion and who constantly assail the people of God (vv. 1-2). It is not clear how to construe v. 8. The NIV and the NRSV include both v. 8*b* and v. 8*c* in the quote of the saying, which the wicked will not hear; however, it is possible that v. 8*c* should be heard as a concluding benediction offered by or for the people of God (see Pss 128:5-6; 134:3).

475. Allen, *Psalms 101–150,* 189.

REFLECTIONS

From its earliest to its latest chapters—from the struggles of the patriarchs and matriarchs to the embattled generations of the post-exilic era—the story of God's people is one of persistent opposition. This reality, of course, is another way of articulating an eschatological perspective; God's sovereignty is always opposed. Thus the people of God experience the opposition directed at God. Inevitably, Israel lived by both memory and hope (see Psalms 77; 126). Jesus, too, invited his followers to live eschatologically, to enter God's reign (Mark 1:14-15) by taking "up their cross" (see Mark 8:34). It will always be so. Insofar as they faithfully embody God's claim, the people of God will experience the hostility of the world (see John 17:11-19; see also Commentary on Psalms 31; 120; 125).

The juxtaposition of Psalms 129 and 130 is fortunate. Lest the people of God be tempted to self-righteousness by their suffering for God's sake, Psalm 130 is an eloquent reminder that the opposition to God is internal as well as external. The history of Israel may be one single passion narrative, but it is also one singularly marked by Israel's persistent faithlessness and disobedience (see Commentary on Psalms 51; 78; 106). The people of God live ultimately by the grace of a steadfastly loving God, who is willing to bear opposition from all sides, including Israel and the church (see Ps 130:7-8).

Psalm 130:1-8, Out of the Depths

NIV

Psalm 130

A song of ascents.

NRSV

Psalm 130

A Song of Ascents.

NIV

¹Out of the depths I cry to you, O Lord;
² O Lord, hear my voice.
Let your ears be attentive
to my cry for mercy.

³If you, O Lord, kept a record of sins,
O Lord, who could stand?
⁴But with you there is forgiveness;
therefore you are feared.

⁵I wait for the Lord, my soul waits,
and in his word I put my hope.
⁶My soul waits for the Lord
more than watchmen wait for the morning,
more than watchmen wait for the morning.

⁷O Israel, put your hope in the Lord,
for with the Lord is unfailing love
and with him is full redemption.
⁸He himself will redeem Israel
from all their sins.

NRSV

¹ Out of the depths I cry to you, O Lord.
² Lord, hear my voice!
Let your ears be attentive
to the voice of my supplications!

³ If you, O Lord, should mark iniquities,
Lord, who could stand?
⁴ But there is forgiveness with you,
so that you may be revered.

⁵ I wait for the Lord, my soul waits,
and in his word I hope;
⁶ my soul waits for the Lord
more than those who watch for the
morning,
more than those who watch for the
morning.

⁷ O Israel, hope in the Lord!
For with the Lord there is steadfast love,
and with him is great power to redeem.
⁸ It is he who will redeem Israel
from all its iniquities.

COMMENTARY

Psalm 130 is the eleventh of the Songs of Ascents (see Overview on Psalms 120–134). While it is not certain that the arrangement of the collection is intentional (see Commentary on Psalm 127), the juxtaposition of Psalms 129 and 130 serves an important purpose: to address any temptation toward self-righteousness by reminding the people that, although they suffer for God's sake at the hands of oppressors (see Ps 129:1-2), they must also confront their own "iniquities" (Ps 130:3, 8; see Reflections on Psalm 129). Quite appropriately, Psalm 131 begins with a profession of humility; not coincidentally, Ps 131:3 recalls Ps 130:7.

Psalm 130 is usually categorized as an individual lament/complaint or prayer for help. It starts in typical fashion (vv. 1-2), but the question in v. 3 makes it clear that "the depths" have something to do with the psalmist's own sinfulness (see Psalms 32; 51). The psalmist's affirmation in v. 4 responds to his or her own question. It also prepares for the profession of faith in vv. 5-6, which are no longer addressed directly to God. This shift prepares for the psalmist's direct address to Israel (v. 7a), which is followed by another profession of faith (vv. 7b-8) that focuses clearly on the character of God and amounts to nothing short of a proclamation of the good news that lies at the heart of the whole Bible. While vv. 7-8 are often viewed as a later addition to an earlier portion of the psalm, they are linked to vv. 1-6 by the repetition of "iniquities" (vv. 3, 8) and "hope" (vv. 5, 7), as well as by similar syntactical uses of the preposition "with" (vv. 4, 7), each occurrence of which communicates a crucial aspect of God's character. Furthermore, the movement from individual to communal perspectives is characteristic of the Songs of Ascents (see Psalms 121–124; 129; 131).

130:1-4. In a real sense, the memorable opening phrase of Psalm 130 expresses the location or condition from which all the laments arise; the psalm is often known simply by the Latin rendering of this phrase, *de profundis*. The word "depths" (מעמקים *ma'ămaqqîm*) names the chaotic forces that confront human life with destruction, devastation, and death, and that are regularly symbolized by water (see NRSV, "deep waters" in Ps 69:2, 14). The exodus is described as being evoked by the people's crying out to God (see Exod 3:7, 9), and the prophet of the exile recalls the exodus as God's making "the depths of the sea a way for the redeemed to cross over" (Isa 51:10 NRSV). Given this pattern, it is crucial that the psalmist cries out to God, asking for a sort of personal exodus and perhaps encouraging Israel to anticipate a new exodus as well (see vv. 7-8). The repetition of "voice" (vv. 1-2) demonstrates the steplike pattern that is characteristic of the Songs of Ascents (see Pss 120:5-7; 121:1-4, 7-8; 122:4-5, 6-8; 123:1-4). The final word in v. 2 (תחנון *taḥănûn*) can mean more generally "supplications," but as the NIV suggests, the root contains the nuance of "mercy." This nuance is particularly appropriate here, since v. 3 makes it clear that the destructive forces confronting the psalmist are to be traced in part to his or her own sinfulness (see also v. 8).

In concert with the vocabulary of vv. 3-4 and vv. 7-8, "cry for mercy" in v. 2 recalls God's self-revelation to Moses in Exodus 34, an episode that brings to a culmination the story of the people's disobedience in making the golden calf (see Exod 32:1-14). There God reveals the divine self to be "gracious" (Exod 34:6; the same root lies behind the NIV's "cry for mercy" in Ps 130:2) and "abounding in steadfast love" (Exod 34:6 NRSV; see Exod 34:7; Ps 130:7), and these at-

tributes are manifested concretely in God's forgiveness (see Exod 34:9; Ps 130:4) of the people's "iniquity" (Exod 34:7, 9; see the plural in Ps 130:3, 8). God's willingness to forgive makes possible the renewal of the covenant and thus the continuation of the "awesome thing" that God will do with God's people (Exod 34:10; the *niphal* of the same Hebrew root [ירא *yārē'*] appears in Ps 130:4 as "may be revered"). Thus the psalmist's question (see Ps 143:2) and response in vv. 3-4 constitute an eloquent affirmation of God's essential character, and the echoes of Exodus 34 prepare for the direct address of Israel in v. 7. Apparently because of the unusual form of the verb in v. 4*b*, but perhaps because the translators had a different text, the LXX of v. 4*b* reads, "according to your law." This reading contains the profound theological insight that God's law is ultimately grace; it might also serve to call further attention to the allusions to Exodus 34, which is part of "the law," or the Torah. The Hebrew, however, is to be preferred.

130:5-6. The syntax of these verses is unusual. For instance, v. 6*a* has no verb, and the word "waits" has to be supplied from v. 5. Furthermore, the apparent redundancy of v. 6*bc* leads some translators to omit v. 6*c*. The repetition in v. 6*bc*, however, draws out the poetic line; thus it reproduces literally the effect of waiting (see Ps 5:3, although the verb the NRSV translates "watch" differs). Furthermore, this steplike pattern of repetition is characteristic of the Songs of Ascents (see above on vv. 1-2), and it is evident as well in the repetition of "wait(s)" (קוה *qwh*, v. 5) and "my soul" (vv. 5*a*, 6*a*). The psalmist can "watch" (v. 6*bc*) with anticipation, because God does not "watch iniquities" (v. 3, author's trans.). This instance of repetition thus calls attention again to the character of God. The psalmist's waiting is based on the conviction that God is fundamentally gracious and forgiving. Waiting is the persistent posture of God's servants (note the servant-master relationship implied by the address of God as "Lord" in vv. 1*b*, 3*b*, 6*a*), whose own sinfulness appears to belie God's sovereignty and who also experience the destructive effects of the sinfulness of others (see Ps 129:1-2). In short, the psalmist's waiting articulates the eschatological perspective that pervades the psalter, which regularly proclaims God's sovereignty among persons and in circumstances that seem to deny it (see Psalms 2; 13; 93; 96–99; 126; Introduction). In the midst of their troubles, self-imposed or inflicted by others, the psalmists wait and encourage others to wait as well (see Pss 25:3, 5, 21; 27:14; 37:34; 52:9; see also the NRSV note). The verb "hope" (יחל *yḥl*) is synonymous with "wait" (see Isa 51:5, where they occur together; see also Pss 31:24; 33:18, 22; 71:14; Lam 3:21, 24). Because God's Word relates and represents God's grace, to hope in God's Word is to hope in God, as v. 7 will suggest (see Pss 119:74, 81, 114, 147).

130:7-8. As elsewhere, the psalmist's faith and hope impel him or her to encourage others to be faithful and hopeful (v. 7*a*; see Pss 22:22-23; 27:14; 31:23-24; 32:8-11; 34:3, 5, 8-14; 51:13-14; 131:3). The repetition of "hope" connects the conclusion of the psalm to vv. 5-6, and the recurrence of the preposition "with" (עם *ʿim*) links the final profession of faith to the earlier one in v. 4, while at the same time suggesting that the experience of God's forgiveness and love and redemption is nothing less than the experience of God's own presence (v. 4, for instance, can be construed to mean that people experience forgiveness when they are "with you"). As suggested above, the focus is on God's character. Israel's future does not depend on its own worthiness or ability to save itself but on God's faithful love and ability to redeem. The words "steadfast love" (v. 7) and "iniquities" (v. 8) recall Exodus 34, which narrates this same good news. The psalmists regularly celebrate God's steadfast love in songs of praise (see Pss 33:5, 18, 22; 98:3; 100:5; 103:4, 8, 11, 17; 117:2) and appeal to God's steadfast love in prayers for help (see Pss 25:6-7; 31:7, 16, 21; 32:10; 51:1; Introduction).

It may be coincidental, but the word "great" (הרבה *harbēh*) in v. 7 represents the same Hebrew root as "greatly" in Ps 129:1-2. Even if coincidental, this verbal link encourages a sequential reading of the two psalms, and it suggests that the greatness of the opposition to Israel is more than matched by the greatness of God's will and ability to redeem. The repetition of "redeem," as well as the adjective "all" (v. 8), make the final profession impressively comprehensive (see Ps 25:22, and note "wait" in 25:3, 5, 21). No sin or setback will be of sufficient depth to separate God's people from God's amazing grace and faithful love (see Rom 8:38-39).

REFLECTIONS

1. The power of Psalm 130 has been evident throughout the centuries of its use. Given its honest confrontation of sinfulness (vv. 3, 8) and the psalmist's humble professions of dependence on God's mercy (vv. 4-8), it is understandable that Psalm 130 became by the fifth century one of the church's seven penitential psalms (see Psalms 6; 32; 38; 51; 102; 143), an ecclesiastical grouping that perhaps originated with Augustine. Not surprisingly, Psalm 130 was one of Martin Luther's favorites; one of Luther's most well-known hymns is his metrical version of this psalm. Another of the early Reformers, Theodore Beza, is said to have died with the words of Ps 130:3 on his lips.[476] It is also said that John Wesley heard Psalm 130 performed as an anthem on May 24, 1738, at St. Paul's Cathedral. According to R. E. Prothero, "the psalm was one of the influences that attuned his [Wesley's] heart to receive that assurance of his salvation by faith, which the evening of the same day brought to him in the room at Aldersgate Street."[477] By Wesley's own account, his heart was "strangely warmed," not unlike, perhaps, those two disciples on the Emmaus road, who felt their "hearts burning within" them as Jesus interpreted to them what was written about him "in the law of Moses, the prophets, and the psalms" (Luke 24:32, 44 NRSV).

2. This is not to say that the psalms are predictions of Jesus, but psalms like 130 certainly do testify to the kind of God whose presence in "the depths" would ultimately be expressed by the death of Jesus on a cross. After all, the really striking thing about Psalm 130 is the

476. See Rowland E. Prothero, *The Psalms in Human Life and Experience* (New York: E. P. Dutton, 1903) 141.
477. Ibid., 230.

psalmist's conviction that God is somehow present in the depths, or is at least within earshot. This is the paradox of the prayer, since the depths represent the forces of all that oppose God and since the psalmist's own turning away from God is at least partially responsible for his or her present despair. The good news is that God will not so easily be rejected; God's presence and power can be, must be reckoned with in every human experience—even in the depths, even on a cross! At this point, it may be helpful to distinguish, as Terence Fretheim does, among varying intensifications of God's presence. As he puts it, "The Old Testament language of absence (e.g., 'hide,' 'withdraw,' 'forsake,' etc.) always entails presence at some level of intensification, albeit diminished." [478] In any case, the psalmist's cry from the depths *to God* articulates the conviction that led Israel to cry out from bondage in Egypt and from exile in Babylon, and that led Jesus to cry out to God from the cross—no place or circumstance is beyond the reach of God's forgiving, loving, redeeming presence and power (see Commentary on Psalms 13; 22; 69; 139).

3. This conviction has profound implications for understanding God and ourselves. It means, as Miller suggests, that God "is subject to being moved, responsive, affected by the human cries out of the depths." [479] This kind of God opens the divine self to the vulnerability of being in relationship with a sinful humanity. God's sovereignty, therefore, cannot be the exercise of sheer force but the power of committed love. For the people of God, it means that we shall live not only with the destructive effects of our own sinfulness (vv. 3, 8) but also with the suffering we experience from others when we do manage to be faithful and obedient (see Ps 129:1-2). In other words, the faithful life inevitably involves waiting upon the Lord and hoping in God's word. Because God's "power is made perfect in weakness" (2 Cor 12:9 NRSV), we, empowered by faith and hope, are able to say with the apostle Paul, "Whenever I am weak, then I am strong" (2 Cor 12:10 NRSV; see Isa 40:30-31).

478. Terence Fretheim, *The Suffering of God: An Old Testament Perspective* (Philadelphia: Fortress, 1984) 65.
479. Patrick D. Miller, Jr., *Interpreting the Psalms* (Philadelphia: Fortress, 1986) 140.

Psalm 131:1-3, Like the Weaned Child That Is with Me

NIV	NRSV
Psalm 131	**Psalm 131**
A song of ascents. Of David.	A Song of Ascents. Of David.

¹My heart is not proud, O LORD,
    my eyes are not haughty;
I do not concern myself with great matters
    or things too wonderful for me.
²But I have stilled and quieted my soul;
    like a weaned child with its mother,
    like a weaned child is my soul within me.
 	
³O Israel, put your hope in the LORD
    both now and forevermore.
	¹ O LORD, my heart is not lifted up,
	    my eyes are not raised too high;
	I do not occupy myself with things
	    too great and too marvelous for me.
	² But I have calmed and quieted my soul,
	    like a weaned child with its mother;
	    my soul is like the weaned child that is
	        with me.[a]
	
	³ O Israel, hope in the LORD
	    from this time on and forevermore.

ᵃOr *my soul within me is like a weaned child*

COMMENTARY

Psalm 131 is the twelfth of the Songs of Ascents (see Overview on Psalms 120–134). The repetition of the exhortation to hope (Pss 130:7; 131:3) indicates that Psalms 130 and 131 should be read together. Furthermore, Psalm 130 calls for a posture of humility that Ps 131:1-2 eloquently expresses. The metaphor of a child with its mother is not unexpected in a collection that may have derived from or been used by groups of pilgrims on their way to Jerusalem (see Overview on Psalms 120–134) and that displays elsewhere a concern with families and children (see Pss 122:8; 127:3-5; 128:3, 6; 133:1). Even so, v. 2 is striking, because a straightforward translation of v. 2c (see NRSV) suggests that the psalmist is almost certainly a woman. Several scholars even suggest that Psalm 131 may have originally been uttered by a woman as she carried her young child along the way to Jerusalem, perhaps even up the steps toward the Temple. While it is difficult to be too confident about such specific proposals, it is clear that the imagery in v. 2 involves the experience of a mother and child; most likely, the psalm was authored by a mother on the basis of her own experience of comforting children. Other songs and prayers were, of course, written and spoken by women in various contexts (see Exod 15:20-21; 1 Sam 2:1-10; Jdt 16:1-7; Luke 1:47-55).

131:1. The psalm begins with a series of three negatives that eschew pride and arrogance. The word "heart" (לב *lēb*, which could also be translated "mind") in the first clause suggests internal matters; the psalmist is free of destructive pride and haughty thoughts (see 1 Sam 2:3; 2 Chr 26:16; 32:25; Pss 101:5; 138:6; Prov 16:5; 18:12; Ezek 28:2, 5, 17; Hos 13:6). The word "eyes" (עינים *ʿênayim*) in v. 1b suggests external things; raised or haughty eyes are associated in Prov 6:16-19 with destructive behaviors (see Prov 21:4; Isa 2:11; 5:15). In other words, the psalmist affirms that in both thought and deed, she has been humble. The words the NIV translates as "great matters" and "things too wonderful" are ordinarily understood to designate arrogant, self-centered pursuits that the psalmist properly avoided. This may be the correct interpretation, but Miller points out that these words elsewhere refer almost exclusively to God's great and wonderful works. Therefore, he suggests that the third clause of v.

1 may well indicate the "inappropriateness on the part of the woman and mother to care about and bother with theology," and he considers it likely that v. 1 is "an indication of the role restrictions placed upon women in the patriarchal structure of Israelite society."[480] Indeed, this restriction may account, at least in part, for the struggle implied in v. 2—that is, the woman's need to find a calmness of soul, a peace of mind and heart, that is denied her by her social setting.

131:2. The woman finds peace in her acceptance by and dependence upon God. The grammatical construction that begins v. 2 is emphatic. Despite restrictive circumstances—ones that perhaps made humility as much coercion as choice—the psalmist affirms that she *really has* found a certain equilibrium (the first verb in v. 2 seems to mean literally "to be even," "to be smooth") and security with God, like her child (a member, of course, of another devalued class in the ancient world as well as the modern world) has found with her. The child is not an infant but a "weaned child." Having once found acceptance and satisfaction (the Hebrew root of "weaned child" [גמל *gml*] means fundamentally to "deal fully with") and nurture at the mother's breast, the weaned child returns for comfort and security to the mother's loving embrace.

131:3. As Mays points out, "Verse 2 prepares for and interprets verse 3."[481] In short, the image of the loving, comforting mother embracing her needy child portrays Israel's hope (see Deut 1:31; Isa 66:13; Jer 31:20; Hos 11:1-9). The vulnerable God (see Commentary on Psalm 130), whose choices are restricted by the rebellious stance of the wicked (see Ps 129:1-2) and by the iniquities of God's own people (see Ps 130:3, 8), will finally do nothing other than lovingly embrace God's children, including both the victims of pain and those who by their iniquities have inflicted pain upon other people and upon God. Such incomprehensible love and amazing grace are the hope of Israel and of the world (see Ps 130:7)—then, now, and forever (see Pss 121:8; 125:2).

480. Patrick D. Miller, *They Cried to the Lord: The Form and Theology of Biblical Prayer* (Minneapolis: Fortress, 1994) 240.
481. James L. Mays, *Psalms,* Interpretation (Louisville: John Knox, 1994) 408.

REFLECTIONS

1. Remarkable in its beauty and its brevity, Psalm 131 performs the valuable service of eloquently enlarging the stock of metaphors that most people ordinarily use for understanding God—God is the loving, compassionate, comforting mother, who, although regularly pained and aggrieved and fatigued by her own children, welcomes them back into her arms and bears them up along a difficult way (see above on Ps 25:6). As for the human side, Psalm 131 commends the style of life that the psalms regularly describe as "righteous" and "happy"—utter trust in and childlike dependence upon God for life and future (see Commentary on Psalms 1; 2). Thus, for the Christian reader, Psalm 131 cannot help being a reminder that Jesus performed the mother's role of Psalm 131 as he took children into his arms and commended them as models for entrance into the reign of God (Matt 18:1-4; Mark 9:33-37; 10:13-16).

2. Consider further the probability that as a woman in a patriarchal society, the psalmist's humility was in some sense forced upon her (see above on v. 1). That the psalmist's experience of oppression impelled her to seek and find comfort with God should in no sense be taken as justification for oppression. Rather, Psalm 131 gives us a glimpse of the beginnings of women's experience of equality in God's sight. It is no coincidence that as he proclaimed and embodied the reign of God, Jesus readily accepted and befriended women and children (see Mark 9:33-37; 10:13-16; 15:40-41; John 20:11-18). Therefore, it is not surprising that in a remarkable reversal of social practices in the ancient Near Eastern world, women were among the leaders of the early church (see Acts 18:26; Rom 16:1, 3; 1 Cor 16:19). In short, as she experienced the liberating acceptance of God, the humble and humbled psalmist experienced the revolutionary, hopeful good news that to be set free by God means never to be a slave again to human masters. The only proper master of humans is God, the recognition of whose sovereignty creates, not patterns of human domination, but a community of sisters and brothers who are *mutually* servants, each of the other (see Mark 10:41-45; Gal 3:28).

Psalm 132:1-18, For the Lord Has Chosen Zion

NIV

Psalm 132

A song of ascents.

¹O Lord, remember David
    and all the hardships he endured.

²He swore an oath to the Lord
    and made a vow to the Mighty One of
        Jacob:
³"I will not enter my house
    or go to my bed—
⁴I will allow no sleep to my eyes,
    no slumber to my eyelids,
⁵till I find a place for the Lord,
    a dwelling for the Mighty One of Jacob."

⁶We heard it in Ephrathah,

NRSV

Psalm 132

A Song of Ascents.

¹ O Lord, remember in David's favor
    all the hardships he endured;
² how he swore to the Lord
    and vowed to the Mighty One of Jacob,
³ "I will not enter my house
    or get into my bed;
⁴ I will not give sleep to my eyes
    or slumber to my eyelids,
⁵ until I find a place for the Lord,
    a dwelling place for the Mighty One of
        Jacob."

⁶ We heard of it in Ephrathah;

NIV

we came upon it in the fields of Jaar[a][b]
[7]"Let us go to his dwelling place;
   let us worship at his footstool—
[8]arise, O LORD, and come to your resting place,
   you and the ark of your might.
[9]May your priests be clothed with
      righteousness;
   may your saints sing for joy."

[10]For the sake of David your servant,
   do not reject your anointed one.

[11]The LORD swore an oath to David,
   a sure oath that he will not revoke:
"One of your own descendants
   I will place on your throne—
[12]if your sons keep my covenant
   and the statutes I teach them,
then their sons will sit
   on your throne for ever and ever."

[13]For the LORD has chosen Zion,
   he has desired it for his dwelling:
[14]"This is my resting place for ever and ever;
   here I will sit enthroned, for I have
      desired it—
[15]I will bless her with abundant provisions;
   her poor will I satisfy with food.
[16]I will clothe her priests with salvation,
   and her saints will ever sing for joy.

[17]"Here I will make a horn[c] grow for David
   and set up a lamp for my anointed one.
[18]I will clothe his enemies with shame,
   but the crown on his head will be
      resplendent."

[a]6 That is, Kiriath Jearim   [b]6 Or heard of it in Ephrathah, / we
found it in the fields of Jaar. (And no quotes around verses 7-9)
[c]17 Horn here symbolizes strong one, that is, king.

NRSV

we found it in the fields of Jaar.
[7] "Let us go to his dwelling place;
   let us worship at his footstool."

[8] Rise up, O LORD, and go to your resting
      place,
   you and the ark of your might.
[9] Let your priests be clothed with
      righteousness,
   and let your faithful shout for joy.
[10] For your servant David's sake
   do not turn away the face of your
      anointed one.

[11] The LORD swore to David a sure oath
   from which he will not turn back:
"One of the sons of your body
   I will set on your throne.
[12] If your sons keep my covenant
   and my decrees that I shall teach them,
their sons also, forevermore,
   shall sit on your throne."

[13] For the LORD has chosen Zion;
   he has desired it for his habitation:
[14] "This is my resting place forever;
   here I will reside, for I have desired it.
[15] I will abundantly bless its provisions;
   I will satisfy its poor with bread.
[16] Its priests I will clothe with salvation,
   and its faithful will shout for joy.
[17] There I will cause a horn to sprout up for
      David;
   I have prepared a lamp for my anointed
      one.
[18] His enemies I will clothe with disgrace,
   but on him, his crown will gleam."

COMMENTARY

The thirteenth of the Songs of Ascents (Psalms 120–134), Psalm 132 stands out in the collection, because it is noticeably longer than the others. Its length seems to signal its special importance. The Songs of Ascents probably originally served as a collection used by pilgrims on the way to or upon arrival at Jerusalem (see Overview on Psalms 120–134), and Psalm 132 impressively articulates the theological rationale for making the pilgrimage—namely, Zion is God's chosen place (vv. 13-14; see Pss 122:1-2, 9; 125:1-2; 126:1; 128:5; 129:5; 133:3; 134:3), as well as the site of the Davidic throne (see Commentary on Psalm 122, esp. vv. 4-5).

The connection between Zion and the Davidic dynasty is implied in Psalm 122 and perhaps in Psalm 127 (see the superscription), but Psalm 132 clearly articulates the connection (see also Ps 78:67-72). For this reason, Psalm 132 especially recalls 2 Sam 6:1-19, the account of David's bringing of the ark to Jerusalem (see Ps 132:1-10), and 2 Samuel 7, Nathan's announcement that David would not build a house for God but that God would build a house for David (see Ps 132:11-12, 17-18). The precise relationship between 2 Samuel 6–7 and Psalm 132 is not clear, and opinions vary widely. Some scholars conclude that Psalm 132 is very early, to be dated to the time of Solomon. In short, they suggest that the chronicler's account of Solomon's use of Ps 132:8-9 (see 2 Chr 6:41) at the dedication of the Temple is essentially accurate historically, in which case Psalm 132 pre-dates the final form of 2 Samuel 6–7. The chronicler's account is a post-exilic retelling of Israel's story, however, and the chronicler's use of Psalm 132 may suggest its late origin. Thus some scholars conclude that the psalm originated as a poetic rendering of the material in 2 Samuel 6–7 for the purpose of expressing hope for the post-exilic generations.

The latter view is more likely, especially considering the place of Psalm 132 in the psalter. Psalm 89, the final psalm in Book III, rehearses at length the rejection of the Davidic dynasty; Books IV–V seem to have been shaped to respond to the crisis of exile and its aftermath, which included the ongoing loss of the monarchy (see Commentary on Psalms 89; 90; 107; Introduction). In this regard, "all the hardships" (v. 1) of David may refer not only to the trouble he took to rescue the ark but also to the apparent rejection of the Davidic dynasty, recounted in Psalm 89. Furthermore, vv. 17-18 seem to suggest that no king currently is in place; perhaps not coincidentally, the word "disgrace" (בשׁת *bōšet*) in 132:18*a* recalls Ps 89:45, where the disgrace belongs to David and the pronouncement concerning David's "crown" in 132:18*b* reverses the reality stated in Ps 89:39. In any case, Psalm 132 would eventually have been understood in the context of the realities of the post-exilic era, and these realities are articulated very well in the immediate context of the Songs of Ascents—namely, the subjugation of God's people by their enemies (see Pss 123:3-4;

126:4-6; 129:1-2) and the people's acute awareness of their own iniquities (see Ps 130:3, 8). As Allen suggests, the placement of Psalm 132 encourages the reader to hear it as an articulation of the hope called for in Pss 130:7; 131:3. Thus the references to David are to be heard messianically; they are a way of symbolizing concretely the hope for the future of God's people.[482]

The structure of Psalm 132 is that of a prayer (vv. 1-10) and a response to the prayer (vv. 11-18). The content and movement of the first section are paralleled in the second. Verses 1-5 are David's vow to God, while vv. 11-12 are God's vow to David (see "swore" in vv. 2, 11). After vv. 6-7 report the discovery of the ark, v. 8 appears to invite the Lord to accompany the ark to "your resting place." Verses 13-15 correspond to vv. 6-8 as they report the Lord's acceptance of the invitation and God's blessing of Zion (see "resting place" in vv. 8, 14). The prayer for priest and people in v. 9 is answered in v. 16, and the prayer for David in v. 10 is answered in vv. 17-18. The repetition represented by the NRSV's "turn away" (v. 10) and "turn back" (v. 11) serves as a hinge between the two main sections.

132:1-10. The imperative "remember" (זכור *zĕkôr*) in v. 1 recalls Ps 89:47, 50 where the rejected anointed one makes the same plea. The Hebrew word translated "hardships" also recalls Psalm 89. The same word appears in the promise that no one "will oppress" (v. 22) the anointed one, but Ps 132:1 seems to assume, in accordance with Ps 89:38-51, that the anointed one has indeed been oppressed. As the NIV suggests, v. 1 should not be linked so closely with v. 2; that is, the word "hardships" (ענות *'ūnôt*) suggests something more severe than the efforts of David described in vv. 3-5.

The vow recorded in vv. 3-5 does not appear elsewhere. These verses seem to be an imaginative poetic rendering of the kind of sentiments David expresses in 2 Sam 7:1-2; however, the remainder of the psalm shows no interest in David's specific concern, which is so evident in 2 Samuel 7—that is, the building of a house for the Lord. In fact, vv. 6-7 allude more clearly to 2 Samuel 6, the account of the bringing of the ark to Jerusalem. The precise sense of vv. 6-7,

---

482. See Leslie C. Allen, *Psalms 101–150*, WBC 21 (Waco, Tex.: Word, 1983) 209.

however, is elusive. For instance, it is not clear what the antecedent of "it" is supposed to be. Is it the ark (see v. 8)? Or is it David's oath (vv. 3-5)? Furthermore, it is not entirely clear that "Ephrathah" and "Jaar" are intended to designate specific geographical places; even if they are, the precise locations are unknown. The most frequent conclusion is that the first term refers to the environs of Bethlehem, David's home, and that the second is a poetic designation of Kiriath-jearim, where the ark is located in 1 Sam 6:19–7:2. Thus vv. 6-7 seem to have in view David's movement of the ark from Kiriath-jearim to Jerusalem (cf. 1 Sam 7:1 and 2 Sam 6:3). But who are the "we" of v. 6 and the "us" of v. 7? This, too, is unclear, but the most compelling suggestion is offered by Elizabeth F. Huwiler, who concludes that vv. 6-7 both recall David's story and articulate the current experience of worshipers in Jerusalem—for instance, pilgrims who are on the way to or have arrived at Jerusalem (see Overview on Psalms 120–134). As she puts it: "The 'we,' the voice of the worshiping community, functions both to bring the David story from the historical past into the liturgical present and to transport the congregants from current worship setting into that same historical past."[483]

In other words, vv. 6-7 may indicate that pilgrims to Jerusalem understood their journey as being analogous to David's earlier journey to Jerusalem with the ark; they, too, are accompanied by the presence of God (see Psalm 121). At the same time, of course, they would have realized that God had already taken up the divine residence in Jerusalem (see Pss 99:5; 122:1).

Verse 8 can also be understood as both an allusion to the past and a present petition. With an eye to the past, v. 8 would be heard as a poetic invitation to God to join David on the journey to Jerusalem. The grammatical construction of v. 8 actually makes this sense unlikely, however (there is no "and go" or "and come" in the Hebrew of v. 8a); since, from the perspective of present worshipers, God is already present in Zion, v. 8 can also be heard as a request for God to protect or deliver Zion. This is the more usual sense of

"rise up" (קום *qûm*, v. 8a; see Ps 3:7). Verse 8a could thus be translated, "Rise up, O LORD, for the sake of your resting place." This construal would also be congruent with the frequent role of the ark in protecting or delivering God's people (see Num 10:35).[484] It also puts the request in v. 8 more in line with those of vv. 9-10, especially v. 10, which sounds like a plea for protection or deliverance. The references in vv. 1, 10 to David and to David's apparent need provide an envelope structure for the first section.

132:11-18. As suggested above, David's oath to God (vv. 2-5) is matched by God's oath to David (vv. 11-12). In general terms, vv. 11-12 again recall 2 Samuel 7, but with glaring exceptions. For instance, the key word in 2 Samuel 7—"house" (see Commentary on Psalm 122)—is missing in Psalm 132. Furthermore, 2 Samuel 7 does not use the word "covenant" (ברית *bĕrît*) to describe the promise to David. This word more clearly recalls Psalm 89 (see vv. 3, 28, 34, 39). Psalm 132:11-18 would have made especially good sense in view of the exile and its aftermath, during which the monarchy remained extinct but Zion was recovered. The conditional sentence in v. 12 would have served to explain the disappearance of the monarchy—the Davidic descendants disobeyed God. Verses 13-16 focus on the aspects of the pre-exilic era that were recovered—Jerusalem (including a rebuilt Temple), the priesthood, and an identity as God's people. Of particular interest is the clear emphasis on God's initiative. *God,* not David, "has chosen Zion" (v. 13); the repetition of "desired" (vv. 13b, 14b) reinforces the point. In v. 15, God promises to do what David himself did in 2 Sam 6:19.

Just as references to David envelope vv. 1-10, so also promises to David provide an envelope for vv. 11-18 (see vv. 11-12, 17-18). The language of v. 17 strongly implies that the monarchy no longer exists (see Ezek 29:21, where the image of a horn sprouting suggests the restoration of something that has been destroyed; see also 2 Sam 2:17, where "lamp" represents the possibility of a future). Thus the psalm concludes on a note of hope, but it is open-ended enough to have been understood in several ways as the post-exilic era unfolded. Some, no doubt, looked toward a literal

483. Elizabeth F. Huwiler, "Patterns and Problems in Psalm 132," in *The Listening Heart: Essays in Wisdom and the Psalms in Honor of Roland E. Murphy,* O. Carm., ed. K. G. Hogland, E. F. Huwiler, J. T. Glass, R. W. Lee, JSOTSup 58 (Sheffield: JSOT, 1987) 207.

484. See ibid., 204.

restoration of the Davidic monarchy. Others seem to have applied the Davidic ideology to the people as a whole (see Pss 105:15; 149:5-9; Isa 55:3). Still later, the early Christians would claim to see in Jesus of Nazareth the fulfillment not only of the Davidic hope but also of the Zion theology as well. Thus Jesus would be proclaimed both a son of David (see Matt 1:2) and the one whom God had chosen for the divine habitation (see John 1:14).

REFLECTIONS

1. Because of its focus on both David and Zion, Psalm 132 has traditionally been classified as either a royal psalm or a song of Zion (or both). Like other royal psalms (see Psalms 2; 18; 20–21; 45; 72; 89; 110; 144; Introduction) and songs of Zion (see Psalms 46; 48; 76; 84; 87; 122; Introduction), Psalm 132 articulates Israel's conviction that the rule of God was manifested concretely in the world of people, space, and time (see Reflections on the above-listed psalms). The traditional use of Psalm 132 on the Sunday that celebrates the Reign of Christ is a reminder that Christianity has not abandoned the scandalous particularity of the royal psalms and the Zion songs, or the inevitable connection between David and Zion. Rather, Jesus has been proclaimed preeminently as *the* royal son (see Ps 2:7), who both proclaimed and concretely embodied God's justice and righteousness (see Ps 72:1). Furthermore, the incarnation of Jesus presents him as the successor of what Zion symbolized—the earthly locus of God's presence and power (see Mark 13:1-2; 14:58; 15:29; see also Commentary on Psalms 48; 122).

2. As Mays suggests, Ps 132:1 is particularly worthy of note in view of the larger canonical context. He notes that where the NIV and the NRSV translate "all the hardships," the Jewish Publication Society translates "his great self-denial." He then further observes:

> His [David's] self-denial served the dwelling of the LORD in the midst of his people. A resonance sets in with another poem that speaks of one who took the form of a servant, and, being found in human form, humbled himself, and in his obedience unto death (Phil. 2:6-8) has become God with us and God for us, the presence and power of the kingdom of God. The need for a Messiah who keeps the covenant and promise of horn and lamp for David to appear in Zion are fulfilled in him.[485]

485. Mays, *Psalms*, 412.

Psalm 133:1-3, In Praise of Unity Among God's People

NIV

Psalm 133

A song of ascents. Of David.

¹How good and pleasant it is
  when brothers live together in unity!
²It is like precious oil poured on the head,
  running down on the beard,
running down on Aaron's beard,
  down upon the collar of his robes.
³It is as if the dew of Hermon
  were falling on Mount Zion.
For there the LORD bestows his blessing,
  even life forevermore.

NRSV

Psalm 133

A Song of Ascents.

¹ How very good and pleasant it is
  when kindred live together in unity!
² It is like the precious oil on the head,
  running down upon the beard,
on the beard of Aaron,
  running down over the collar of his robes.
³ It is like the dew of Hermon,
  which falls on the mountains of Zion.
For there the LORD ordained his blessing,
  life forevermore.

COMMENTARY

Psalm 133 is the fourteenth of the Songs of Ascents (Psalms 120–134). Given the probable origin and use of the collection by pilgrims on the way to or upon arrival at Jerusalem (see Overview on Psalms 120–134), it is not surprising that Psalm 133 is akin to several other Songs of Ascents in its use of the imagery of family (v. 1; see Pss 122:8; 127:3-5; 128:3, 6; 131:2). But as in the others, family concerns are set within the larger context of God's whole people (v. 3; see Pss 122:6-8; 128:3-6; 131:2-3). Adele Berlin even argues that the main theme of Psalm 133 is "the reunification of the country"—that is, "the dew of Hermon," representing the people of the northern kingdom, is to flow down upon Zion, the center of the southern kingdom.[486] While absolute certainty is elusive, it is clear that the focal point of Psalm 133 is finally not on local families but on Zion (v. 3), which is the rallying point and gathering place for God's larger family (see Pss 122:4; 125:1-2; 126:1). The pilgrims gathered there to receive God's blessing (v. 3). Not coincidentally, it is precisely the climactic themes of Zion and blessing that link Psalm 133 closely with Psalms 132 (see vv. 13-15) and 134 (see v. 3).

Verse 1 may have circulated at one time as a proverbial saying. In any case, it introduces the concept of unity or harmony; v. 1 itself does view family on a local level. The only other occurrence of the expression "when kindred live together" is in Deut 25:5, where the concern is with the responsibilities attendant upon members of an extended family in order to provide for and perpetuate the family. As Deut 25:5-10 makes clear, and as everyone knows from experience, harmony does not always prevail within extended families. When it does, v. 1 asserts, it is "good and pleasant" (see Ps 135:3, where the same two adjectives describe God; Ps 147:1, where they describe what it is like to praise God; see also Ps 128:2, 5).

The effect of the similes of oil and dew in vv. 2-3 is to broaden significantly the focus of v. 1. The Hebrew repetition represented by "good" (טוב *ṭôb,* v. 1)/"precious" (*ṭôb,* v. 2) links vv. 1 and

486. Adele Berlin, "On the Interpretation of Psalm 133," in *Directions in Hebrew Poetry,* ed. Elaine R. Follis, JSOTSup 40 (Sheffield: JSOT, 1987) 145.

2. The steplike pattern is characteristic of the Songs of Ascents (see Pss 120:5-7; 121:1-4, 7-8; 122:6-8). An even more noticeable instance is evident in vv. 2-3, where the verb "to go down" (ירד *yārad*) occurs three times in an identical form (NIV, "running down," twice in v. 2, and "falling" in v. 3). This repetition re-creates literarily and visually the effect of oil or dew slowly flowing downward, as does the repetition of "beard" (זקן *zāqān*). The question remains, of course, as to what the two similes intend to communicate. The pouring of oil over the head seems to have been an act of hospitality, signaling joy and relatedness (see Pss 23:5; 92:10; 141:5), as well as an official act of consecrating kings and priests. Both senses would be appropriate here, but the mention of Aaron especially calls to mind the latter (see Exod 28:41). Insofar as v. 2 looks back to v. 1 (note the repetition in vv. 1-2), the message would be that family unity is a joyful, even a holy, thing.

It is likely, however, that the poet intended v. 2 to look forward to v. 3 as much as or more than backward to v. 1 (note the repetition of "running down"/"falling"). The allusion to Aaron's consecration has already served to begin to broaden the focus beyond the local extended family, and the mention of Zion in v. 3 goes even further in this direction. Mount Hermon, located in the north some 200 kilometers from Jerusalem, was known for its abundant dew. In other words, the abundance of outlying areas properly belongs with Zion. While this may be, as Berlin suggests, an appeal for national unity, it serves clearly also to shift the focus from the local family to the whole people. The shift is completed by "there"—Zion—in v. 3. The word "blessing" (see Pss 128:4-5; 132:15; 134:3) gathers up the meaning of the phrase "good and pleasant" from v. 1, but by the end of the poem it is clear that the ultimate goodness that God intends is the gathering of God's larger family, the whole people of God. When God's people gather in Jerusalem, God's place, they experience their true family and home, for they are in touch with the true source of their life— God's presence. As Mays concludes: "It is this abundant life, which Israel can receive only in its unity, and only from the Presence at this place that is the *summum bonum* [that is, "the greatest good"; see v. 1]. The life that the Lord gives his people in their unity is the supreme family value."[487]

487. James L. Mays, *Psalms*, Interpretation (Louisville: John Knox, 1994) 414.

REFLECTIONS

1. Psalm 133 reflects an obvious concern in ancient Israel that is a perennial concern in every culture: family values. The family is a crucial institution. It affects everyone, for good or ill. By its very nature, it can be the place where one experiences and learns intimacy, love, and growth, or it can be the place where one experiences and learns resentment, abuse, and destructive behavior. Clearly, v. 1 commends the former, but the expansive perspective of vv. 2-3 puts the consideration of family values in the larger context of the relationship between God and God's people. The effect is to relativize the importance of the individual family; it cannot be in any unqualified sense the most important institution in a society.

The teachings and actions of Jesus move in the same direction as does Psalm 133, and they serve to bring into focus the radical implications of this direction. In the Gospel of Mark, for instance, when Jesus' mother and brothers come to see him, he looks at those around him and says, "Here are my mother and my brothers! Whoever does the will of God is my brother and sister and mother" (Mark 3:35-36 NRSV). In short, the most important sphere of relatedness is defined as the larger family of God's people (see also Luke 11:27-28; 12:51-53). John Dominic Crossan captures eloquently the radical implications of Jesus' words and deeds, ones that are in keeping with the direction of Psalm 133:

> The family is society in miniature, the place where we first and most deeply learn how to love and be loved, hate and be hated, help and be helped, abuse and be abused. It is not just a center of domestic serenity; since it involves power, it invites the abuse of power, and it is at that precise point that Jesus attacks it. His ideal group is, contrary to Mediterranean and indeed most human familial reality, an open one equally accessible to all under God. It is the Kingdom of God, and it negates that terrible abuse of power that is power's dark specter and lethal shadow.[488]

As Crossan rightly recognizes, "most human familial reality" has not considered the critique of Jesus and Psalm 133. In other words, a focus on the family may well serve to do nothing other than reinforce cultural patterns that regularly exploit women and marginalize children (see Commentary on Psalm 131). Indeed, if the discussion of family values begins and ends with the individual family, apart from the vision and experience of God's larger family, open and accessible to all, then such values will inevitably promote exploitation and abuse.

2. The church's use of Psalm 133 has upheld the psalm's portrayal of God's family as the true definition of familial reality and the true source of blessing and life. While Augustine surely oversimplified the matter, he attributes the origin of monasteries and their brotherhoods to Psalm 133. To be sure, these family orders engendered problems of their own, but they were grounded in the affirmation of a family structure that transcends that of the biological family. The traditional association of Psalm 133 with the Lord's supper makes the same affirmation, for the Lord's supper brings the whole people of God to a family table where all profess their unworthiness and yet all are welcome. Some traditions also suggest the use of Psalm 133 in services of Christian unity, in which "the psalm is a witness that God is at work building a family that transcends all the given and instituted barriers that separate and diminish life."[489] Thus Psalm 133 affirms that life derives ultimately from God's ordaining and blessing

488. John Dominic Crossan, *Jesus: A Revolutionary Biography* (San Francisco: HarperCollins, 1994) 60.
489. Mays, *Psalms*, 414.

and in communion with the whole body of God's people. This profession radically undercuts our pervasive tendency to conclude that life derives from human effort and achievement and that we can successfully manage it on our own (see Commentary on Psalms 1; 2). Psalm 133 is, therefore, an appropriate psalm for the season of Easter, during which we especially celebrate the reality of a life-giving power that both transcends and transforms human efforts and human structures: the resurrection of Jesus. To profess the resurrection is to take our place in God's family, and it is thus to receive an identity that prevents our making an idol of human familial reality in any of its various cultural forms.

Psalm 134:1-3, May the Lord Bless You from Zion

NIV	NRSV
Psalm 134	Psalm 134
A song of ascents.	A Song of Ascents.
¹Praise the LORD, all you servants of the LORD who minister by night in the house of the LORD. ²Lift up your hands in the sanctuary and praise the LORD. ³May the LORD, the Maker of heaven and earth, bless you from Zion.	¹ Come, bless the LORD, all you servants of the LORD, who stand by night in the house of the LORD! ² Lift up your hands to the holy place, and bless the LORD. ³ May the LORD, maker of heaven and earth, bless you from Zion.

COMMENTARY

Psalm 134 is the final Song of Ascents (Psalms 120–134). Given the probable origin and use of the collection among pilgrims on their way to or after arrival at Jerusalem (see Overview on Psalms 120–134), it is evident that Psalm 134 forms a fitting conclusion. After Psalm 133 has celebrated the unity of the gathered people of God in Zion, Psalm 134 addresses the gathered congregation, inviting them to do what they had come to Jerusalem to do: praise the Lord (vv. 1-2). Verse 3, then, has the character of a benediction, which would have effectively sent the people forth with what they had come to Jerusalem to receive: the blessing of God.

While the original cultic setting must remain speculative, it is clear that Psalm 134 has close connections with its literary context, including both the preceding Songs of Ascents and the following psalms, especially Psalm 135. For instance, the congregation is portrayed elsewhere as

blessing the Lord (see Ps 124:6); it is described earlier as standing in the house of the Lord (see Ps 122:1-2). The blessing of the people by God is also a theme of the Songs of Ascents (see Ps 128:5, where the blessing is also "from Zion"; 132:15 and 133:3, where the blessing is "there"—in Zion), and God is twice described earlier as "Maker of heaven and earth" (v. 3; see also Pss 121:2; 124:8). The possibility that Psalms 135–137 form an appendix to the Songs of Ascents is suggested by the fact that Ps 135:1-2 also address the people as "servants of the LORD" as they "stand in the house of the LORD." The conclusion of Psalm 135 (vv. 19-21) also recalls Psalm 134 as it invites all the people to "bless the LORD!" and as it repeats the phrase "from Zion" (although this time it is the Lord who is blessed "from Zion"; cf. Ps 134:3).

The verb "bless" (ברך *bārak*) occurs in three of the four poetic lines of Psalm 134. The two imperatives to "bless" (vv. 1a, 2b), addressed to the whole congregation, form an envelope for vv. 1-2, which are structured chiastically (see Introduction)—that is, the two imperatives surround two references to the Temple (vv. 1b, 2a). The people thus surround God with blessing. The final poetic line repeats the word "bless," but the direction is reversed—from God to people. The repetition clearly communicates the mutuality of blessing, and this mutuality points to the remarkable theological claim of the psalm (see Reflections below).

The Hebrew root that the NRSV regularly translates as "bless" (bārak) originally meant more literally "to kneel," as in paying homage to a superior (see above on Ps 95:6; see also Pss 16:7; 26:12; 34:1; 63:4; 103:1-2, 22; 115:18; 135:19-20; 145:1, 10). Thus the characterization of the gathered worshipers as servants is especially appropriate in this context (see Pss 31:16; 34:22; 35:27; 113:1; 135:1, 14); it is not necessary to view the imperative as addressed exclusively to priests. The lifting up of the hands could indicate a gesture of praise (see Ps 63:4, where the same gesture is also parallel to "bless"); but it could also indicate the posture of intercessory prayer (see Ps 28:2; Lam 2:19). In either case, the posture indicates loyalty to and dependence upon God.

In terms of the possible original setting and use of Psalm 134, v. 3 makes good sense as a priestly benediction (see Num 6:23-25; Deut 21:5; 2 Sam 2:20; Ps 118:26), pronounced as the pilgrims prepare to leave Jerusalem on the night before they set out (see Isa 30:29). As such, it recalls the affirmation of God's cosmic sovereignty that the pilgrims perhaps made on the journey to (see Ps 121:2) and upon arrival at Jerusalem (see Ps 124:8, where the affirmation also follows the people's blessing of God). More significant, however, are the theological implications of the mutuality of blessing between God and the people, a mutuality that bespeaks the genuine relatedness between God and the people, based ultimately in God's redeeming love (see Ps 130:7-8).

REFLECTIONS

The double call to "bless the LORD," the characterization of the people as servants, and the description of God as "maker of heaven and earth" communicate clearly the people's conviction of God's sovereignty and thus of their dependence upon God (see Commentary on Psalms 1; 2). It is to be expected that the people kneel before God—that is, bless God. What is striking, however, is the mutuality of blessing that is anticipated in v. 3. Thus there is a sense in which God will kneel before the people! In other words, God will voluntarily take on the servant role that properly belongs to the people. This mutuality, which ultimately means God's willingness to be vulnerable, results from God's risky choice of Zion (see Ps 132:13-14) and from God's choice to take on the responsibility of providing for Zion's people (see Ps 132:15-18). What promises blessing for God's people promises suffering for God, for the very people committed to blessing God regularly end up burdening God with their iniquities (see Ps 130:3, 8). In short, the mutuality between God and God's people means ultimately that God reveals the divine character to be essentially forgiving and steadfastly loving (see Ps 130:4, 7). Such love explains how a persistently sinful people can dare to anticipate that the cosmic God will bless them from Zion. Such love, in other words, is their only hope (see Pss 130:7; 131:3), a hope that Christians profess to be sealed in Jesus' incarnation of God in the form of a servant (see Phil 2:5-11).

PSALM 135:1-21, YOUR NAME, O LORD, ENDURES FOREVER

NIV

Psalm 135

[1] Praise the LORD.[a]

Praise the name of the LORD;
    praise him, you servants of the LORD,
[2] you who minister in the house of the LORD,
    in the courts of the house of our God.

[3] Praise the LORD, for the LORD is good;
    sing praise to his name, for that is pleasant.
[4] For the LORD has chosen Jacob to be his own,
    Israel to be his treasured possession.

[5] I know that the LORD is great,
    that our Lord is greater than all gods.
[6] The LORD does whatever pleases him,
    in the heavens and on the earth,
    in the seas and all their depths.
[7] He makes clouds rise from the ends of the
        earth;
    he sends lightning with the rain
    and brings out the wind from his
        storehouses.

[8] He struck down the firstborn of Egypt,
    the firstborn of men and animals.
[9] He sent his signs and wonders into your
        midst, O Egypt,
    against Pharaoh and all his servants.
[10] He struck down many nations
    and killed mighty kings—
[11] Sihon king of the Amorites,
    Og king of Bashan
    and all the kings of Canaan—
[12] and he gave their land as an inheritance,
    an inheritance to his people Israel.

[13] Your name, O LORD, endures forever,
    your renown, O LORD, through all
        generations.
[14] For the LORD will vindicate his people
    and have compassion on his servants.

[15] The idols of the nations are silver and gold,
    made by the hands of men.

[a] 1 Hebrew Hallelu Yah; also in verses 3 and 21

NRSV

Psalm 135

[1] Praise the LORD!
    Praise the name of the LORD;
    give praise, O servants of the LORD,
[2] you that stand in the house of the LORD,
    in the courts of the house of our God.
[3] Praise the LORD, for the LORD is good;
    sing to his name, for he is gracious.
[4] For the LORD has chosen Jacob for himself,
    Israel as his own possession.

[5] For I know that the LORD is great;
    our Lord is above all gods.
[6] Whatever the LORD pleases he does,
    in heaven and on earth,
    in the seas and all deeps.
[7] He it is who makes the clouds rise at the
        end of the earth;
    he makes lightnings for the rain
    and brings out the wind from his
        storehouses.

[8] He it was who struck down the firstborn of
        Egypt,
    both human beings and animals;
[9] he sent signs and wonders
    into your midst, O Egypt,
    against Pharaoh and all his servants.
[10] He struck down many nations
    and killed mighty kings—
[11] Sihon, king of the Amorites,
    and Og, king of Bashan,
    and all the kingdoms of Canaan—
[12] and gave their land as a heritage,
    a heritage to his people Israel.

[13] Your name, O LORD, endures forever,
    your renown, O LORD, throughout all ages.
[14] For the LORD will vindicate his people,
    and have compassion on his servants.

[15] The idols of the nations are silver and gold,
    the work of human hands.

NIV

¹⁶They have mouths, but cannot speak,
   eyes, but they cannot see;
¹⁷they have ears, but cannot hear,
   nor is there breath in their mouths.
¹⁸Those who make them will be like them,
   and so will all who trust in them.

¹⁹O house of Israel, praise the LORD;
   O house of Aaron, praise the LORD;
²⁰O house of Levi, praise the LORD;
   you who fear him, praise the LORD.
²¹Praise be to the LORD from Zion,
   to him who dwells in Jerusalem.

   Praise the LORD.

NRSV

¹⁶ They have mouths, but they do not speak;
   they have eyes, but they do not see;
¹⁷ they have ears, but they do not hear,
   and there is no breath in their mouths.
¹⁸ Those who make them
   and all who trust them
   shall become like them.

¹⁹ O house of Israel, bless the LORD!
   O house of Aaron, bless the LORD!
²⁰ O house of Levi, bless the LORD!
   You that fear the LORD, bless the LORD!
²¹ Blessed be the LORD from Zion,
   he who resides in Jerusalem.
   Praise the LORD!

COMMENTARY

Although the Songs of Ascents conclude with Psalm 134, it is as if the editors of the psalter intended for Psalms 135–136 to articulate the praise invited by Ps 134:1-2. For instance, like Ps 134:1, Ps 135:1 addresses the worshipers as "servants," and "stand" in Ps 135:2 also recalls Ps 134:1. Furthermore, Ps 135:19-21 uses the key word "bless" (ברך *bārak*) from Psalm 134. Similar themes and concerns connect Psalms 135 and 136 (cf. 135:5 with 136:2-3; 135:8-12 with 136:10-22), prompting several scholars to suggest that Psalms 135–136 (and perhaps Psalm 137, since, like the Songs of Ascents, it features Zion) form an appendix to the Songs of Ascents.

It is perhaps not coincidental that Psalms 135–136 also recall Psalms 111–118, which precede Psalm 119 and the Ascents collection. For instance, the opening and concluding *hallelu-yah* of Psalm 135 occurs also in Pss 111:1; 112:1; 113:1, 9; 115:18; 116:19; 117:2. And at several points, Psalm 135 clearly recalls Psalm 115 (cf. 135:6 with 115:3; 135:15-18 with 115:4-8; 135:19-20 with 115:9-11). As for Psalm 136, v. 1 is identical to Ps 118:1, 29. The central theme of Psalm 135—God's universal sovereignty, especially over the gods—is congruent with the apparent purpose of Books IV–V to respond to the crisis of exile and its aftermath (see Commentary on Psalms 90; 93; 95; 96; 97; 98; 99; 107; Introduction). In this regard, too, it may be especially significant that Psalm 135 alludes to several crucial Pentateuchal texts (cf. Ps 135:5 with Exod 18:11; v. 13 with Exod 3:15; v. 14 with Deut 32:36) and summarizes in vv. 7-12 the movement from creation to exodus to entry into the land. In short, despite appearances to the contrary, God rules the world.

Psalm 135 is a hymn or song of praise, but its structure can be outlined in several ways. The fivefold division of the NIV and the NRSV is compelling. As Allen points out, the elements are concentric; that is, vv. 1-4 correspond to vv. 19-21 (invitations to and reasons for praise), and vv. 5-7 correspond to vv. 15-18 (polemic against idols and God's sovereignty).[490] The effect is to focus on vv. 8-14 as the central section; it illustrates the divine sovereignty (vv. 5-7, 15-18) that makes praising and blessing God the appropriate response (vv. 1-4, 19-21).

135:1-4. The imperative "praise" occurs three times in v. 1 and once in v. 3 (see Pss 22:23; 107:1; 148:1-5; 150:1-6). The word "name" (שׁם *šēm*) also occurs in vv. 1 and 3. Connoting "reputation" or "character," it becomes a key word in Psalm 135, occurring again in v. 13. In essence, the whole psalm is a defense of God's character or reputation, especially over against the

490. Leslie C. Allen, *Psalms 101–150*, WBC 21 (Waco, Tex.: Word, 1983) 226.

gods (see vv. 5, 15-18). God is fundamentally "good" (see Pss 100:5; 106:1; 107:1; 118:1, 29). The syntax of v. 3*b* is ambiguous, but it is syntactically possible to construe the adjective as descriptive of God (see the same ambiguity in Ps 147:1). As v. 4 suggests, God's identity and thus reputation are bound up with God's choice of Israel (see Exod 19:5; Deut 7:7-11). Thus the movement from vv. 1-3 to v. 4 anticipates the movement from v. 13 to v. 14. True to the divine character (v. 13), God will set things right for God's chosen people (v. 14), as opposed to those who make and trust in idols (v. 18).

135:5-7. Verse 5 recalls Jethro's profession of faith in the Lord in the light of the exodus (see Exod 18:11). The issue raised by the bondage in Egypt was "Who is sovereign?" The exodus revealed the Lord's sovereignty (see Exod 15:18). Not surprisingly, God is frequently described as "great" in contexts that explicitly proclaim God's reign (see Pss 47:2; 95:3; 96:4; 99:2). The title "Lord" also communicates sovereignty; its correlate, "servants," occurs in vv. 1, 14. The sphere of God's sovereignty is unlimited, encompassing every dimension of the three-storied universe as it was portrayed in ancient Near Eastern cosmology—heaven, earth, depths (v. 6; see Ps 115:3). The elements of the most impressive and powerful natural phenomenon—the thunderstorm—are under God's control (v. 7; see Exod 19:16; Jer 10:13; 51:16; see also Commentary on Psalm 29). Control of these phenomena was regularly attributed to the Canaanite god Baal, so v. 7 is clearly polemical. That is, it is another way of affirming that "our LORD is above all gods" (v. 5). The NRSV's "does" in v. 6 and the second "makes" in v. 7 translate the same Hebrew root (עשׂה *'āśâ*), which recurs as "work" in v. 15 and "make" in v. 18. The effect of this repetition is to contrast even more sharply the true God who *makes* things happen as opposed to the idols, which are *made* by humans.

135:8-14. The vocabulary of v. 5 has already alluded to the exodus, the culmination of which involved God's "wind" (v. 7; see Exod 14:21; 15:10) driving back the "seas" and the "deeps" (v. 6; see Exod 14:21-22; 15:4, 8, 10), so that God could lead the people to Sinai, where "clouds" and "lightning" awaited them (v. 7; see Exod 19:16; see also Commentary on Psalms 19;

33; 65; 66 for more on the importance of discerning a unity between creation and exodus). In short, vv. 5-7 have amply prepared for the specific focus on the climactic plague in v. 8 (see Exod 13:29-32; Pss 78:51; 105:36; 136:10) and then for the summary of God's actions against Pharaoh in v. 9 (see Exod 4:8-9, 21; Deut 4:34; 26:8; Pss 78:43; 105:27). Pharaoh's people are called "servants" (v. 9), recalling v. 1 and anticipating v. 14, thus sharpening the focus on the issue of sovereignty. The verb "struck down" (נכה *nkh*) is repeated in v. 10 (see Ps 136:17) as vv. 10-11 continue the recital that culminates with Israel's possession of the land (v. 12; see also Ps 136:21-22). God's defeat of two persons identified by the title "king" (v. 11*ab*; see Sihon and Og in Num 21:21-35; see also Ps 136:17-20), and indeed God's defeat of "all the kingdoms of Canaan" (v. 11*c*), further emphasize God's reign. The central section of the psalm culminates in vv. 13-14. The exodus and subsequent victories demonstrate God's enduring "name" and "renown" (see Exod 3:15, where the same two nouns occur). In short, God's actions reveal the content of God's character as one who will set things right for the oppressed and have compassion for people (see Deut 32:36).

135:15-18. In striking contrast to the wondrous activity of God, the idols do absolutely nothing (note the series of negations in vv. 16-17; see also Ps 115:4-7). Verses 15-18 are framed by the occurrences of "work" (v. 15) and "make" (v. 18), which recall "does" and "makes" in vv. 6-7. The idols do not create, because they have been created. The final negation (v. 17*b*) involves "breath" or "wind," thus recalling v. 7. The "wind" serves God's command, but the idols have no "wind"—no vital power. As v. 18 suggests, the real issue is trust (see Ps 115:8-11). Those who trust their lives to nothing will experience nothingness, whereas those who entrust their lives to the sovereign God will participate in God's enduring future (vv. 12-14).

135:19-21. Thus it is appropriate that God's people "bless the LORD!" (vv. 19-21). The word "bless" (*bārak*) appears originally to have meant "to kneel," as in acknowledging the sovereignty of another (see above on Ps 134:1-2). The repetition effectively makes the point: God eminently deserves the people's allegiance and praise. The different designations in vv. 19-20 may indicate different groups of worshipers (such as priests in v. 19*b,* temple personnel in v. 20*a*), or they may all be designations for the whole assembly (see above on Pss 115:9-11; 118:2-4). The phrase "from Zion" in v. 21 recalls Ps 134:3, but the blessing here moves in the opposite direction. Thus Psalms 134–135 together portray the mutu-ality of blessing that is already evident in Psalm 134. By the end of Psalm 135, the movement has been from praise (vv. 1-4) to praise (vv. 19-21; note especially the opening and closing *hallelu-yah*), the fitting response to the God who is "above all gods" (v. 5) and whose name "endures forever" (v. 13).

REFLECTIONS

Psalm 135 articulates again the conviction that pervades the book of Psalms: God reigns! This conviction, of course, is intimately connected to the first two of the Ten Command-ments—no other gods and, in particular, no human-made idols (see Exod 20:3-4). This conviction is always polemical and always pertinent. Israel's immediate inclination was precisely to make an idol and to worship other gods (see Exod 32:1-6), and this inclination seems to be an inevitable human tendency. To be sure, contemporary forms of idolatry may be more subtle but hardly less crass. Idolatry is finally an elevation of the human self to the status of God, and we are masters of that art. The word *masters* characterizes the way we tend to see ourselves. By virtue of our sophisticated scientific knowledge and incredible technological achievements, we are inclined to view ourselves as masters of the universe rather than servants of a universal God.

This confusion is a dangerous one, indeed a deadly one, for to place ultimate trust in ourselves is to consign our destiny to nothingness (v. 18). What, after all, have we accomplished with our amazing scientific discoveries and dazzling technological achievements? *We have created* a situation in which it appears that the future of human civilization hangs in a delicate nuclear and ecological balance. If we can manage not to blow ourselves away suddenly, we appear to be in danger of slowly poisoning the earth and ourselves to death. The irony is that the more powerful we become, the less secure the human future seems to be.

The current situation is obviously complex, and there will be no simple solutions. Indeed, there will be no solutions at all apart from our relinquishment of the seemingly inevitable drive to be masters of the universe. Given the history of humankind, ancient and modern, there is little room for optimism in this regard. But the Bible, including Psalm 135, dares to affirm that there is room for hope—not in ourselves, but in God. Hope for the world will begin not with scientific knowledge but with what the psalmist knows: "The LORD is great . . . above all gods" (v. 5), including ourselves. That kind of knowledge begins and ends where Psalm 135 begins and ends: with praise, the yielding of the human self to God in liturgy and in life. To praise God (vv. 1-3), to bless God (vv. 19 20), means that we shall not be masters of the universe but servants of a universal master. It will mean considering first not what we desire but what "the LORD pleases" (v. 6)—"thy will be done."

The current endangered state of the earth and its peoples is a reminder that the proclamation of God's reign is eschatological; it always is made amid circumstances and people (including ourselves) who deny it. Thus God's sovereignty is what the world considers a strange form of power, not sheer force but the force of suffering love. To praise the Lord is to choose, as Jesus showed, to be a suffering servant. It means that we shall live by faith, not trusting ourselves (v. 18) but entrusting life and future to the God whose name "endures forever" (v. 13; see Commentary on Psalms 8; 100; 104; 115).

PSALM 136:1-26, GOD'S STEADFAST LOVE ENDURES FOREVER

NIV

Psalm 136

¹Give thanks to the LORD, for he is good.
> *His love endures forever.*

²Give thanks to the God of gods.
> *His love endures forever.*

³Give thanks to the Lord of lords:
> *His love endures forever.*

⁴to him who alone does great wonders,
> *His love endures forever.*

⁵who by his understanding made the heavens,
> *His love endures forever.*

⁶who spread out the earth upon the waters,
> *His love endures forever.*

⁷who made the great lights—
> *His love endures forever.*

⁸the sun to govern the day,
> *His love endures forever.*

⁹the moon and stars to govern the night;
> *His love endures forever.*

¹⁰to him who struck down the firstborn of
Egypt
> *His love endures forever.*

¹¹and brought Israel out from among them
> *His love endures forever.*

¹²with a mighty hand and outstretched arm;
> *His love endures forever.*

¹³to him who divided the Red Seaᵃ asunder
> *His love endures forever.*

¹⁴and brought Israel through the midst of it,
> *His love endures forever.*

¹⁵but swept Pharaoh and his army into the Red
Sea;
> *His love endures forever.*

¹⁶to him who led his people through the
desert,
> *His love endures forever.*

¹⁷who struck down great kings,
> *His love endures forever.*

¹⁸and killed mighty kings—
> *His love endures forever.*

ᵃ13 Hebrew *Yam Suph*; that is, Sea of Reeds; also in verse 15

NRSV

Psalm 136

¹ O give thanks to the LORD, for he is good,
for his steadfast love endures forever.

² O give thanks to the God of gods,
for his steadfast love endures forever.

³ O give thanks to the Lord of lords,
for his steadfast love endures forever;

⁴ who alone does great wonders,
for his steadfast love endures forever;

⁵ who by understanding made the heavens,
for his steadfast love endures forever;

⁶ who spread out the earth on the waters,
for his steadfast love endures forever;

⁷ who made the great lights,
for his steadfast love endures forever;

⁸ the sun to rule over the day,
for his steadfast love endures forever;

⁹ the moon and stars to rule over the night,
for his steadfast love endures forever;

¹⁰ who struck Egypt through their firstborn,
for his steadfast love endures forever;

¹¹ and brought Israel out from among them,
for his steadfast love endures forever;

¹² with a strong hand and an outstretched arm,
for his steadfast love endures forever;

¹³ who divided the Red Seaᵃ in two,
for his steadfast love endures forever;

¹⁴ and made Israel pass through the midst of it,
for his steadfast love endures forever;

¹⁵ but overthrew Pharaoh and his army in the
Red Sea,ᵇ
for his steadfast love endures forever;

¹⁶ who led his people through the wilderness,
for his steadfast love endures forever;

¹⁷ who struck down great kings,
for his steadfast love endures forever;

¹⁸ and killed famous kings,
for his steadfast love endures forever;

¹⁹ Sihon, king of the Amorites,

ᵃOr *Sea of Reeds*

NIV

¹⁹Sihon king of the Amorites

His love endures forever.

²⁰and Og king of Bashan—

His love endures forever.

²¹and gave their land as an inheritance,

His love endures forever.

²²an inheritance to his servant Israel;

His love endures forever.

²³to the One who remembered us in our low estate

His love endures forever.

²⁴and freed us from our enemies,

His love endures forever.

²⁵and who gives food to every creature.

His love endures forever.

²⁶Give thanks to the God of heaven.

His love endures forever.

NRSV

for his steadfast love endures forever;

²⁰ and Og, king of Bashan,

for his steadfast love endures forever;

²¹ and gave their land as a heritage,

for his steadfast love endures forever;

²² a heritage to his servant Israel,

for his steadfast love endures forever.

²³ It is he who remembered us in our low estate,

for his steadfast love endures forever;

²⁴ and rescued us from our foes,

for his steadfast love endures forever;

²⁵ who gives food to all flesh,

for his steadfast love endures forever;

²⁶ O give thanks to the God of heaven,

for his steadfast love endures forever.

COMMENTARY

Psalm 136 is clearly related to Psalm 135, with which it seems to form an appendix to the Songs of Ascents (see Commentary on Psalm 135). Both are songs of praise, and both begin by citing the Lord's goodness as a basic reason for praise (135:3; 136:1). Furthermore, Ps 136:2-3 recalls Ps 135:5, and Ps 136:5-9 can be viewed as an expansion of Ps 135:6-7, while 136:10-22 are an extended version of 135:8-12. Because of its expanded recital of God's "great wonders" (v. 4), Psalm 136 is often categorized along with Psalms 78; 105–106 as a historical psalm. This label is helpful so long as it is clear that these psalms are not merely objective rehearsals of Israel's story. Each of these four psalms features the Hebrew word translated "wonders" (נפלאות *nipla'ôt*) in 136:4 (although the translations of it differ; see Pss 78:4, 11-12, 32; 105:2, 5; 106:7, 22). Borrowing from Martin Buber's reflection on this Hebrew word, Brueggemann suggests that the historical psalms be viewed under the rubric of "abiding astonishment." Their focus is not so much on the past as on the present as they seek to evoke a response of *"obedience, petition, gratitude,* and *new political possibility."* [491] In short, Psalm 136 articulates God's claim upon

the world, and it calls for the reader's response (see Commentary on Psalms 78; 105; 106).

The most obvious feature of Psalm 136 is the identical refrain that concludes every verse. Psalm 136:1 itself forms a brief hymn that occurs several times elsewhere (see 1 Chr 16:34; Pss 106:1; 107:1; 118:1, 29). Nearly identical but briefer formulations occur in 2 Chr 5:13; 7:3; 20:21; and Ezra 3:11, where the context indicates that they were used by the congregation as liturgical responses during worship services. Thus the concluding portion of an apparently standard liturgical formula forms the refrain of Psalm 136, which consequently bears the mark of a responsorial liturgy. That is, the congregation probably sang the refrain in response to a leader's singing of the first part of every verse. While absolute certainty is not possible, Psalm 136 more than any other psalm demonstrates the probability of responsorial liturgical use. The precise setting of its ancient use remains elusive.

When Psalm 136 is considered as a literary product in its current placement within the psalter, the effect of the refrain is to give an explicitly theological dimension to this recital of Israel's story. As suggested above, the rehearsal is not meant to be objective. Rather, by way of the

491. Walter Brueggemann, *Abiding Astonishment: Psalms, Modernity, and the Making of History* (Louisville: Westminster John Knox, 1991) 34.

refrain, the psalmist affirms that every aspect and moment of Israel's story—from creation (vv. 5-9) to exodus (vv. 10-15) to wilderness journey (vv. 16-20) to possession of the land (vv. 21-22) to the present moment (vv. 23-24), including the daily meal (v. 25)—is pervaded by and dependent upon God's steadfast love. As several scholars suggest, vv. 23-24 seem to take the story beyond the exile to the return from Babylon. This would make Psalm 136 congruent with the perspective of the Songs of Ascents and with the apparent purpose of Books IV–V to respond to the crisis of exile and its aftermath (see Commentary on Psalms 90; 107; 120; Introduction). In any case, Israel's fundamental response is to be gratitude (vv. 1-3, 26; see Reflections below).

While it is obvious that the refrain is the most important structural feature of Psalm 136, scholars disagree in their discernment of an outline of the psalm. As suggested above, structural divisions could be made by content (creation, exodus, etc.). Attention to grammatical forms, however, yields a different outline. For instance, following the introductory imperatives (vv. 1-3), the subsequent reasons for praise are introduced in several lines by a preposition followed by a participle. If this pattern marks structural divisions, they would be as follows: vv. 4, 5, 6, 7-9, 10-12, 13-15, 16, 17-22. A different pattern exists in vv. 23-25 before v. 26 returns to an imperative. Such irregularity might aptly represent the irregularity of Israel's history; however, many scholars are intent on finding a more symmetrical structure. Several propose, for instance, four major sections. Each of the first two, vv. 1-9 and vv. 10-18, consist of three triads of verses, and the final two sections, vv. 19-22 and vv. 23-26, consist of four verses each. Jacob Bazak even suggests that regular geometric patterns are formed by the small divisions as well as the whole.[492] Obviously, the scholarly proposals differ markedly. Because they attend to different criteria in each case, they need not be considered mutually exclusive. More significant, in any case, are the refrain and its claim that the origin and history of the world and of Israel are inextricably tied to the love of God.

136:1-9. The titles for God in vv. 2-3 (see also

v. 26) recall Ps 135:5. Again, the issue is sovereignty, and exclusive sovereignty is reserved for Israel's God (see Psalm 82). Israel's God alone does the "great wonders" (v. 4) that are recounted in vv. 5-22. Unlike the other historical psalms, God's "wonders" in this case include creation (vv. 5-9). In other words, as in the Pentateuch, Israel here professes that its story begins with creation. The affirmation is a crucial one, for it suggests that Israel's specific story is part of God's wondrous and comprehensive purpose for the whole cosmos. God's steadfast love lies behind and accounts for the origin of the world. Actually, the recital does not really conclude until v. 25, which returns to the creational perspective of vv. 5-9. This conceptual envelope means that the recital of Israel's story is surrounded by affirmations of God's love for the world and all its creatures. That is, God's steadfast love is also responsible for God's providence for all creation (see Pss 33:5; 36:5-9). God has the whole world in God's hands! (See Commentary on Psalm 19; see also Psalms 33; 65–66; 135; 145–146, which also insist that the creation of the world and the origin of Israel are parts of the same story.)

Verse 4 is linked to vv. 5-9 by repetition of the verb "does"/"made" (עשׂה 'āśâ, vv. 4-5, 7; see also Ps 135:6-7, 15, 18). The verb makes clear that God's character, the essence of which is steadfast love, is made known by God's creating, redeeming, sustaining activity. Verse 5 calls to mind Prov 3:19, and, of course, it and vv. 6-9 are reminiscent of Genesis 1. The verb "spread out" (רקע rāqaʿ, v. 6) appears as the noun "expanse" in Gen 1:14-15, 17 (see Isa 42:5). Also, "the great lights" (v. 7) are mentioned in Gen 1:16, where their function is also described in a manner similar to Ps 136:8-9 (Gen 1:16 does not name them "sun" and "moon," however; see also Ps 148:3-4). The effect of vv. 5-9 is to affirm that God's wisdom and God's power are ultimately motivated by and are manifestations of God's love.

136:10-22. In one sense, the focus narrows in vv. 10-22 (see Exod 12:29–15:21; Num 21:21-35; Josh 12:1-6; Pss 78:12-16, 23-30, 51-55; 105:26-45; 106:8-12; 135:8-12), but the refrain effectively communicates that in another crucial sense the focus remains as broad as it was in vv. 5-9. In other words, the story of Israel's deliverance from Egypt (that is, from death) and entry

492. Jacob Bazak, "The Geometric-Figurative Structure of Psalm CXXXVI," *VT* 35 (1985) 129-38.

into the land (that is, into life) is still the story of the fulfillment of God's creational purposes. To be sure, the particularity is scandalous, and many persons find it particularly problematic that God "struck down great kings" (v. 17) and "killed famous kings" (v. 18) like Sihon and Og (vv. 19-20; see Ps 135:10-11). To many people, this does not seem to be very loving, but the stark realism indicates that God's love is not simply sentimental. God's creational purposes, God's will to grant life to the threatened and the disposessed (see vv. 23-24), cannot finally be opposed with impunity. Egypt and Pharaoh found this out (vv. 10, 15); other famous kings found this out (vv. 17-20); and, to put this dynamic in proper perspective, God's own people and their kings found this out, too—the exile saw the destruction of the monarchy, the death of many persons, and the dispersal of God's people (see Psalm 137).

136:23-26. While it is possible that vv. 23-24 refer simply to the exodus and subsequent events recounted in vv. 10-22, it is likely that they carry the story further by reflecting the return from exile. To be sure, they would certainly have been understood this way in the post-exilic era. In other words, opposition from neither great and famous kings nor from God's own chosen people could thwart God's steadfastly loving purposes. God remains at work, doing what God had done previously—turning things around for the oppressed (see Exod 2:24). Lest God's activity be perceived too narrowly, v. 25 is a reminder that God's work is for the benefit of "all flesh" (see above on vv. 5-9; see also Pss 104:14-15, 27-28; 145:15-16; 146:7; 147:9). God so loves the world.

In view of the fact that vv. 10-22 in particular have described God's work on earth, it is significant that v. 26 addresses God as "the God of heaven" (see vv. 5, 7-9). Thus v. 26, which recalls vv. 1-3, is a final reminder that Israel professes its God to be the cosmic ruler of the universe.

REFLECTIONS

1. As Bratcher and Reyburn point out, the word "steadfast love" is "the one word which more than any other expresses Yahweh's attitude toward his people."[493] But more than that, according to Psalm 136, steadfast love characterizes the attitude of God toward the whole cosmos, including the earth and all its features and all its creatures. There can be no more profoundly good news than this—that God's attitude toward the world and God's motivation for action are summarized by steadfast love. This concept, of course, is crucial throughout the book of Psalms and elsewhere in the OT (see, e.g., Exod 34:6-7; Pss 5:7; 13:5; 23:6; 25:6-7, 10; 33:5, 18, 22; 103:4, 8, 11, 17; Introduction). As Exod 34:6-7 makes eminently clear, steadfast love inevitably involves God's grace. Thus Psalm 136 ultimately affirms that the origin, continuity, and destiny of the cosmos are dependent upon the grace of God.

2. This expansive profession of faith is crucial for construing the scandalous particularity of vv. 10-22, lest these verses be dismissed simply as ancient nationalistic propaganda or be misused to support the notion that God is partial to one particular group of people. Particularity is necessary and desirable, but any construal of God's will is misguided if it fails to take into account God's love for the whole creation (vv. 5-9) and God's intention to provide for "all flesh" (v. 25). In other words, Psalm 136 proclaims that God rules the world. Thus it joins the other historical psalms as "determined challenges to the autonomy of reason and the autonomy of power."[494] The gratitude to which Ps 136:1-3, 26 invite us will take the form of humble submission of our wills to the will of God. Our lives and the life of the world will be received as loving, gracious gifts of God. Psalm 136 calls us to live in dependence not upon ourselves but upon God (see Commentary on Psalms 1; 2).

493. Robert G. Bratcher and William D. Reyburn, *A Translator's Handbook on the Book of Psalms* (New York: United Bible Societies, 1991) 1108.

494. Brueggemann, *Abiding Astonishment,* 44.

3. The use of Psalm 136 at the Easter Vigil is an illustration of the reality that this historical psalm continues to speak to people in and concerning the present. Its use in this liturgical context also affirms the Christian conviction that God's steadfast love continued and continues to be manifested in the life, death, and resurrection of Jesus. Like Psalm 136, Jesus announced God's claim upon the whole world, and he invited people to enter God's reign (see Mark 1:14-15). Jesus proclaimed, represented, and embodied God's amazing grace and the incomparable good news that God steadfastly and eternally loves and provides for the world (see John 3:16-17). Noting the movement of Psalm 136 from God's creation of the cosmos (vv. 5-9) to God's provision of daily bread (v. 25), Mays concludes:

> That brings the story down to every meal and makes the recitation of the LORD's mighty works a preface to every blessing said over the food we eat. It becomes apparent here why our LORD taught us to pray for the coming of the reign of God and the gift of daily bread in one short prayer. They are both part of the continuum of God's mighty works. All of history and each day of living are contained in the story of the LORD's steadfast love.[495]

495. James L. Mays, *Psalms,* Interpretation (Louisville: John Knox, 1994) 421.

PSALM 137:1-9, BY THE RIVERS OF BABYLON

Psalm 137

[1]By the rivers of Babylon we sat and wept
   when we remembered Zion.
[2]There on the poplars
   we hung our harps,
[3]for there our captors asked us for songs,
   our tormentors demanded songs of joy;
   they said, "Sing us one of the songs of
      Zion!"

[4]How can we sing the songs of the LORD
   while in a foreign land?
[5]If I forget you, O Jerusalem,
   may my right hand forget ⌐its skill⌐.
[6]May my tongue cling to the roof of my mouth
   if I do not remember you,
if I do not consider Jerusalem
   my highest joy.

[7]Remember, O LORD, what the Edomites did
   on the day Jerusalem fell.
"Tear it down," they cried,
   "tear it down to its foundations!"

[8]O Daughter of Babylon, doomed to
      destruction,
   happy is he who repays you
   for what you have done to us—

Psalm 137

[1] By the rivers of Babylon—
   there we sat down and there we wept
   when we remembered Zion.
[2] On the willows[a] there
   we hung up our harps.
[3] For there our captors
   asked us for songs,
   and our tormentors asked for mirth, saying,
   "Sing us one of the songs of Zion!"

[4] How could we sing the LORD's song
   in a foreign land?
[5] If I forget you, O Jerusalem,
   let my right hand wither!
[6] Let my tongue cling to the roof of my mouth,
   if I do not remember you,
if I do not set Jerusalem
   above my highest joy.

[7] Remember, O LORD, against the Edomites
   the day of Jerusalem's fall,
   how they said, "Tear it down! Tear it down!
   Down to its foundations!"
[8] O daughter Babylon, you devastator![b]

[a]Or *poplars*   [b]Or *you who are devastated*

NIV	NRSV

⁹he who seizes your infants
    and dashes them against the rocks.
	Happy shall they be who pay you back
	    what you have done to us!
	⁹ Happy shall they be who take your little
	    ones
	    and dash them against the rock!

COMMENTARY

H.-J. Kraus calls Psalm 137 "the only psalm in the psalter that can be dated reliably."[496] If it was not composed in Babylon during the exile (587–539 BCE), it must have originated shortly after the return to Judah, when the pain of exile was still fresh in the minds and hearts of the people. It is quite possible that it was written by a member of the Levitical guilds, which were responsible for music and singing in the Temple (see 2 Chr 25:1-8; Ezra 2:40-42).

The combination of first-person plural and singular voices, the focus on Jerusalem, and even the length of the psalm make it similar to the Songs of Ascents (Psalms 120–134). Given the similarities between Psalms 134 and 135, as well as Psalms 135 and 136, it is likely that Psalms 135–137 form a sort of appendix to the Songs of Ascents (see Commentary on Psalms 135; 136). In view of Pss 135:12 and 136:21-22, the sense of loss and grief articulated by Psalm 137 is all the more acute. The clearly exilic or early post-exilic perspective of Psalm 137 is congruent with the apparent purpose of the Songs of Ascents and of Books IV–V to respond to the crisis of exile and its aftermath (see Commentary on Psalms 90; 107; 120; Introduction).

The structure of Psalm 137 is debated, but most scholars suggest three divisions. Those suggested by the NIV and the NRSV are acceptable, but it is probably better to combine v. 4 with vv. 1-3. According to this view of the psalm, vv. 1-4 express the exiles' grief, and vv. 7-9 express the exiles' rage and desire for revenge. In between, at the literary and conceptual heart of the poem, vv. 5-6 focus on the crucial activity of remembering. This central concept links vv. 5-6 to vv. 1-4, in which the exiles remember Jerusalem (v. 1),

496. H.-J. Kraus, *Psalms 60–150: A Commentary,* trans. H. C. Oswald (Minneapolis: Augsburg, 1989) 501.

and to vv. 7-9, in which the Lord is called upon to remember Jerusalem as well (v. 7). Thus the importance of memory is pervasive, both literarily and conceptually. For the exiles, remembering Zion means faithfulness to God's place and to God's ongoing purposes. It is an act of resistance; "in a foreign land" (v. 4), they could not sing, but they could and must and did remember.

137:1-4. Babylon was nothing like home for the exiles, and the psalmist expresses the painful reality of remembering Zion in vv. 1-4. The geographical strangeness of the land, with its system of canals between the Tigris and the Euphrates—the "rivers of Babylon"—may have exacerbated the grief when Jerusalem was remembered. Of course, things were only made worse by their captors' sarcastic invitation (v. 3), the effect of which was to ask, "Where is your God?" (see Pss 42:3, 10; 79:10). There was nothing to do but weep, for singing was out of the question in their present location (vv. 2, 4; see Lam 1:2, 16, where the personified Jerusalem weeps at the devastation of exile, and note Lam 1:7, where Jerusalem also "remembers"; see also Ps 42:3). The "LORD's song" (v. 4) would perhaps have been one of the joyful "songs of Zion" (v. 3; see Commentary on Psalms 46; 48; 76; 84; 87; 122). They could be sung only in Jerusalem, the Lord's place, and not in Babylon.

137:5-6. Although the people could not sing in Babylon, they could remember their homeland. The chiastic structure of vv. 5-6a emphasizes this crucial activity:

A   *If I forget you,* O Jerusalem,
　B   *let my right hand* wither!
　B′   Let *my tongue* cling to the roof
　　　　of my mouth,
A′   *if I do not remember you,*

Addressing the personified Jerusalem as "you" in vv. 5-6, the individual voice asserts that if Jerusalem is not remembered, then music and song will become impossible *forever*. The withered right hand will not be able to pluck the strings of the harp (see v. 2), and the paralyzed tongue will not be able to sing. As painful as it is for the people to remember Jerusalem (v. 1), it would be more painful for them not to remember, for these memories offer hope, indeed life, amid the pain (vv. 1-4) and devastation of exile (vv. 7-9).

137:7-9. The people's request for God to remember them (v. 7) is a plea for God to share in their suffering. Whereas the psalmist expresses that pain as grief in vv. 1-4, the psalmist voices that grief as anger and outrage in vv. 7-9. The anger is directed first at Edom (v. 7), which apparently took particular advantage of Jerusalem's misfortune at the hands of the Babylonians (see the book of Obadiah, esp. vv. 10-14; Ezek 35:5-15; see also Lam 1:20-22; 3:64). Not surprisingly, since it was the Babylonians who destroyed Jerusalem and took the people into exile, the psalm concludes by addressing a personified Babylon (cf. the personification of Jerusalem in vv.

5-6). While vv. 8-9 shock our sensibilities, and rightfully so, it is necessary to point out that they merely express a sentiment that most Americans would claim; this is clear in v. 8. The Babylonian conquest of Judah certainly involved the deaths of many Judeans, including children, who represent the future of a people. Verse 9 suggests that the Babylonians deserve the same. As Kraus suggests concerning v. 9, it should be understood not only as the expression of a particular individual but also as "a reference to the cruelty of ancient warfare generally,"[497] the typical practices of which are reflected in 2 Kgs 8:12; Isa 13:16; Hos 10:14; Nah 3:10 (see also Revelation 18, esp. vv. 6, 20-24, for another expression of the desire for revenge against "Babylon"). Thus, in view of the cultural context, the wish expressed in vv. 8-9 represents a principle that most Americans routinely espouse: The punishment should fit the crime. Those who have deprived others of a future deserve no future themselves (see Commentary on Psalm 109).

497. Ibid., 504.

REFLECTIONS

1. Perhaps because it is a psalm about singing ("songs"/"song" is used five times in vv. 3-4), Psalm 137, with the omission of vv. 7-9, has often been set to music and used in worship services. The psalm in its entirety, however, including its shocking conclusion, has much to teach us about prayer, about ourselves, and about God. One thing it teaches us, for instance, is the lesson that in extreme situations, grief and anger are both inevitable and inseparable. The worst possible response to monstrous evil is to feel nothing. What *must* be felt—by the victims and on behalf of the victims—are grief, rage, outrage. In the absence of these feelings, evil becomes an acceptable commonplace. In other words, to forget is to submit to evil, to wither and die; to remember is to resist, to be faithful, and to live again.

From this perspective, the psalmist's outburst in vv. 8-9 is both a psychological and a theological necessity. The psalmist is motivated toward revenge out of loyalty to Jerusalem—indeed, loyalty to God! John Bright claims of the psalmist, "It would not be too much to say that he hated so because he loved so." [498] Yet, there is no evidence that the psalmist did act out the expressed desire for revenge. Rather, the psalmist expresses these feelings to God in prayer (v. 7) and apparently leaves them with God. Thus the cycle of violence is broken by the psalmist's honesty with God (see Commentary on Psalm 109).

Psalm 137 as a whole, then, is an "invitation to a kind of prayer that is passionate in its utter honesty." [499] To pray is to offer ourselves and our desires—anger as well as grief—to God and to know that God loves us as we are. This aspect of Psalm 137 represents "a drive

498. John Bright, *The Authority of the Old Testament* (Grand Rapids: Baker, 1975) 237.
499. James S. Lowery, "By the Waters of Babylon," *Journal for Preachers* 15/3 (1992) 29.

toward incarnation"; God chooses to be revealed through people "of like passions with ourselves."[500] We must acknowledge that we are no less vengeful than the psalmist was. But the good news is that God loves us and chooses to use us anyway. Thus Psalm 137 points ultimately to forgiveness. It is even possible that the psalmist's cathartic expression of vengeance represents a first step toward forgiving the victimizers. Similarly, after proclaiming God's forgiveness of the sins that led to the exile (Isa 40:1-2), Isaiah proclaims God's word that the mission of exilic and post-exilic Israel is to be "a light to the nations, that my salvation may reach to the end of the earth" (Isa 49:6 NRSV). The desire for revenge gives way to a mission to save. Hate has been replaced by hope.

2. In our time, Psalm 137 cannot help reminding us of the Holocaust, the monstrous victimization of the Jewish people during World War II. Holocaust survivor Elie Wiesel has dedicated his life to making sure the world remembers what happened. Wiesel says frequently that he can tolerate the memory of silence but not the silence of memory. In other words, the Holocaust can be remembered in unutterable horror—silence. But it *must* be remembered. To remember is painful; grief is always painful. To remember is unsettling; anger always unsettles. But to remember is also to resist the same thing's happening again. To remember is to choose to live and to be faithful to God's purpose of life for all people.

Given the mention of "little ones" in v. 9, it is especially revealing to consider Elie Wiesel's special concern for children. It is, perhaps, a clue to the ultimate direction and significance of remembering in Psalm 137—namely, grief and rage energize a memory that eventually takes the form of compassion. Although it is not explicit, we may assume that the psalmist's submission of anger to God obviates the need for actual revenge upon the enemy. It is encouraging, at least, to think that Wiesel's life provides support for this assumption. His remembrance of victimization, a remembrance sustained certainly by grief and rage, is now expressed as compassion for the vulnerable and as faithfulness to God's purpose of life for all God's children. Consider Wiesel's own words:

> When I see a child, any child, I have tears in my eyes [see Ps 137:1]. Especially my own, especially Jewish children, but any children. . . . We [Holocaust survivors] want to caress our children 24 hours a day. We want to shelter them, to show them nothing but joy and beauty. And yet we want them to know. . . .
>
> When I speak of life, I mean, children. To me, nothing is more sacred, nothing more divine, than a child's life. There are two absolutes, life and death. I choose life.[501]

For survivors of victimization, ancient or modern, to express grief and outrage is to live. If Wiesel's life can be taken as evidence, such expression is a necessary first step in a lifelong process of remembrance, which ultimately issues in a compassion for others that is grounded in God's compassion for all.

3. A psalm about remembrance that both expresses the pain of death and harbors hope for life cannot help reminding Christians of the Lord's supper and Jesus' words, "Do this in remembrance of me" (Luke 22:19). Remembering Jesus' self-sacrifice is painful, for it must recall his death. But in remembering there is hope, for "you proclaim the Lord's death until he comes" (1 Cor 11:26). The final stanza of Ewald Bash's metrical paraphrase of Psalm 137 captures this sense of hope:

> Let Thy cross be benediction
> For men bound in tyranny;
> By the power of resurrection
> Loose them from captivity.[502]

500. Bright, *The Authority of the Old Testament,* 236.
501. "Elie Wiesel and the Two Who Saved His Life," *The St. Louis Post-Dispatch,* October 5, 1988, E6.
502. Ewald Bash, "By the Babylonian Rivers," in *The Worshipbook* (Philadelphia: Westminster, 1978) no. 328.

Remembrance, which is at the heart of Psalm 137, is also at the heart of the Christian faith. In a profound sense, Psalm 137 can be a Christian prayer. It can be prayed as an act of honesty about our own vengefulness; it can be prayed for victims, for those in captivity, and for ourselves, since we know that we are inevitably both victims and victimizers. As we pray and reflect upon Psalm 137, we remember and are retaught the pain of exile, the horror of war, the truth about ourselves, the terror of despair and death, the loneliness of a cross. But as we pray and reflect upon Psalm 137, we are also taught to submit our frailty and finitude to God; we begin a journey that transforms grief and anger into compassion; we affirm that life is lived and promised in the midst of death; and we anticipate and celebrate a resurrection power that frees us from captivity.

PSALM 138:1-8, THANKSGIVING AND PRAISE FOR GOD'S DELIVERANCE

NIV

Psalm 138

Of David.

[1]I will praise you, O LORD, with all my heart;
    before the "gods" I will sing your praise.
[2]I will bow down toward your holy temple
    and will praise your name
    for your love and your faithfulness,
  for you have exalted above all things
    your name and your word.
[3]When I called, you answered me;
    you made me bold and stouthearted.

[4]May all the kings of the earth praise you,
        O LORD,
    when they hear the words of your mouth.
[5]May they sing of the ways of the LORD,
    for the glory of the LORD is great.

[6]Though the LORD is on high, he looks upon
        the lowly,
    but the proud he knows from afar.
[7]Though I walk in the midst of trouble,
    you preserve my life;
  you stretch out your hand against the anger
        of my foes,
    with your right hand you save me.
[8]The LORD will fulfill ⌐his purpose⌐ for me;
    your love, O LORD, endures forever—
    do not abandon the works of your hands.

NRSV

Psalm 138

Of David.

[1] I give you thanks, O LORD, with my whole
        heart;
    before the gods I sing your praise;
[2] I bow down toward your holy temple
    and give thanks to your name for your
        steadfast love and your faithfulness;
    for you have exalted your name and your
        word
    above everything.[a]
[3] On the day I called, you answered me,
    you increased my strength of soul.[b]

[4] All the kings of the earth shall praise you,
        O LORD,
    for they have heard the words of your
        mouth.
[5] They shall sing of the ways of the LORD,
    for great is the glory of the LORD.
[6] For though the LORD is high, he regards the
        lowly;
    but the haughty he perceives from far away.

[7] Though I walk in the midst of trouble,
    you preserve me against the wrath of my
        enemies;

[a]Cn: Heb you have exalted your word above all your name
[b]Syr Compare Gk Tg: Heb you made me arrogant in my soul with strength

NRSV

you stretch out your hand,
and your right hand delivers me.
8 The LORD will fulfill his purpose for me;
your steadfast love, O LORD, endures
forever.
Do not forsake the work of your hands.

COMMENTARY

Psalm 138 has traditionally been classified as an individual song of thanksgiving, and v. 2 has often been taken as a clue to its original setting and use. Having been delivered from distress (v. 3), the psalmist has come to the Temple to offer praise (vv. 1-2), perhaps along with a sacrifice of thanksgiving. While this proposal is plausible, it does not fully address the uniqueness of Psalm 138, nor does it explain a fundamental ambiguity; it seems that the psalmist has already been delivered (v. 3a), but the psalmist continues to pray for deliverance. This ambiguity opens the way to a theological approach to Psalm 138 (see Reflections below).

The attempt to discern the original setting and use of Psalm 138 also fails to take into account the possible significance of its present literary placement. One of the unique features of Psalm 138—the psalmist's offering of praise not simply before the congregation of Israel but also "before the gods" (v. 1)—recalls Pss 135:5 and 136:2-3. There are additional connections to Psalms 135–136 as well. For instance, the psalmist's praise is directed to God's "name" (v. 2; see Ps 135:1, 3), and both psalms proclaim God's greatness (see 135:5; 138:5). Furthermore, in giving thanks to God (vv. 2-3), the psalmist does precisely what Ps 136:1-3, 26 invite, and the psalmist is grateful for God's "steadfast love" (vv. 2, 8; v. 8 especially recalls the refrain of Psalm 136). Given the connections between Psalm 138 and Psalms 135–136, and considering as well the intervening Psalm 137, it is reasonable to conclude with Mays that Psalm 138 "can be understood as a general song of praise by the restored community in the postexilic period, written under the influence of the prophets whose words are gathered in Isaiah

40–66"[503] (see below for similarities to Isaiah 40–66).

Especially in its present literary context, then, the message of Psalm 138 is in keeping with the apparent purposes of Books IV–V to address the crisis of exile and its aftermath (see Commentary on Psalms 90; 107; 120; Introduction). While conclusive proof is not possible, it seems that Psalm 138 serves as a sort of transition between the Songs of Ascents (Psalms 120–134), including their appendix (Psalms 135–137), and the subsequent Davidic collection (Psalms 138–145). This collection draws to a close with a psalm that also sounds like the praise (see 144:1-10) and prayer (see 144:11-15) of the post-exilic community. Psalm 145 then recalls Psalm 138 as it explicitly asserts God's sovereignty and celebrates God's steadfast love. In between Psalms 138 and 144–145 are five psalms characterized by complaint and petition for deliverance from the wicked. This placement of Psalms 139–143 in Book V, including their framing by Psalms 138 and 144–145, encourages a corporate reading of these psalms by the post-exilic community. While these psalms may have originated as individual prayers, they certainly were capable of speaking to the crisis of the exile and its aftermath in keeping with the response of Book V (see Commentary on Psalms 107; 108; Introduction).

The structural divisions indicated by the NRSV are to be preferred. In vv. 1-3, the psalmist describes his or her own approach to and relationship with God. The focus shifts to "the kings of the earth" in vv. 4-6, although, as the NIV suggests, it is possible to relate v. 6 more closely to vv. 7-8. Perhaps it is intended to be transitional.

503. Mays, *Psalms*, 424.

In any case, vv. 7-8 clearly focus again on the psalmist and God.

138:1-3. The first section of the psalm begins with the psalmist presenting his or her whole self to God in thanks—"with my whole heart" (v. 1*a*; see 1 Kgs 8:23; Pss 9:1; 119:2, 10, 34, 58, 69, 145; Jer 3:10; 24:7). The unique v. 1*b* has a polemical tone, which is perhaps best captured by a literal translation that yields the contemporary idiom "in your face." The psalmist offers praise "in the face of the gods," almost contemptuously denying them sovereignty (see Pss 58:1-2; 82:1). For the psalmist to "bow down toward your holy temple [or palace]" is to profess that God alone is sovereign, the sole provider for his or her life (v. 2*a*; see also v. 7).

The psalmist is able to present his or her whole life to God, because the psalmist trusts that it is God's character to manifest "steadfast love" (חסד *ḥesed*) and "faithfulness" (אמת *ĕmet*, v. 2*b*; the word "name" can connote character or reputation). These two words are used in God's self-revelation to Moses (Exod 34:6-7), and they became part of a basic profession of Israel's faith (see Introduction). They are paired frequently in the psalms as the basis for an appeal to God for help (see 40:11-12; 115:1-2), or as a profession of trust (see 57:2; 85:10-13). God's dependability is also emphasized in v. 2*c*. The Hebrew is difficult (see NRSV note), but could perhaps be translated interpretively as "your promises surpass even your fame" (NJB). However God's "word" is construed—as God's revelation generally or as God's promises in written form (see Ps 119:11, 38, 41)—it is apparently perceived by the psalmist as a very personal address (v. 3*a*). Again, v. 3*b* is difficult, but it appears to be the psalmist's affirmation that he or she is strengthened. God's word gives life (see Deut 8:3; Matt 4:4).

138:4-6. The second section of the psalm (vv. 4-6) suggests that the psalmist's experience is universal (see the NRSV as opposed to the NIV, which construes vv. 4-5 as petition). Somehow, "all the kings of the earth" have been reached by God's "words" (אמרה *imrâ*, v. 4; see "word" in v. 2), and they join the psalmist in giving thanks to God ("praise" in v. 4 translates the same Hebrew verb as "give thanks" in vv. 1-2). Verse 5*a* asserts that the kings yield their sovereignty in recognition of God's sovereignty (see Isa 49:7; 52:15). They celebrate "the ways of the LORD"

rather than exercising their own wills. This is precisely what Psalm 2 at the beginning of the psalter admonished the kings of the earth to do in order not to perish (2:10-12). For the kings of the earth as for the psalmist, the word of God gives life.

Not surprisingly, "glory" (כבוד *kābôd*, v. 5*b*) elsewhere is associated with the recognition and celebration of God's reign (see Isa 6:1-8; Pss 24:7-10; 29:1-3, 9-11; 97:1, 6; 145:10-13; see also Isa 40:5), as is the word "great" (גדול *gādôl*; see Pss 47:2; 48:1; 95:3; 135:5; the same Hebrew root also appears in 138:2 as "exalted"). Lest the kings of the earth or anyone else misunderstand, however, the nature of God's strange sovereignty is clarified in v. 6, which is reminiscent of 1 Sam 2:1-10 and Ps 113:4-9 (see also Isa 57:15). Verse 6 thus articulates the topsy-turvy values that prevail in the reign of God (see Reflections below).

138:7-8. As the NIV division of the psalm suggests, v. 6 at least prepares for the return to the psalmist's personal situation in vv. 7-8. Those who relinquish self-sufficiency and commit themselves to the reign of God will undoubtedly experience trouble and have enemies (v. 7). The psalmist affirms that God "gives me life" in the midst of the struggle, not beyond it. Deliverance/salvation/life (see Ps 3:2, 7-8) is both a present reality and yet something that awaits fulfillment (v. 8*a*; see Ps 57:2-3, where the same affirmation is made in the context of trust in God's steadfast love and faithfulness). As in v. 2, the psalmist's ability to entrust life and future to God is grounded in God's steadfast love (v. 8*b*). The "not yet" dimension of deliverance is evident in the final petition (v. 8*c*). The Hebrew word translated "forsake" (רפה *rāpâ*) more literally means "to let fall," "to drop," a meaning that is appropriate in a context that refers to hands three times (vv. 7-8). The petition thus implicitly affirms the psalmist's trust that he or she is in God's hands. The "works of your hands" (v. 8*c*) certainly includes the psalmist (see Job 14:15, where an individual person is so designated). But the phrase should also be understood more inclusively, especially in the light of the affirmation of God's sovereignty in vv. 4-5. In terms of the post-exilic hearing of the psalm, the phrase can designate the whole people (see Isa 64:8), and God's "works" elsewhere includes all the creatures and, indeed, the whole creation (see Ps 104:24). God—not the gods (v. 1)—rules the world.

REFLECTIONS

1. The final petition of Psalm 138 implicitly affirms what Christians affirm with the singing of a well-known folk song: God's "got the whole world in his hands." Like the psalmist, we make this affirmation in the midst of all kinds of trouble, opposition, and apparent evidence to the contrary. In other words, the proclamation that God rules the world is eschatological (see Commentary on Psalms 2; 65; 66; 67; 93; 95; 96; 97; 98; 99; Introduction). Amid the "not yetness" of our lives and our world, it is our way of professing our trust that God will fulfill God's purposes for us and for our world.

The eschatological perspective of Psalm 138 means that we shall always live in the midst of the fundamental ambiguity that characterizes the psalm. That is to say, we shall always find ourselves simultaneously professing God's deliverance (v. 3) and praying for God's deliverance (v. 8c)—"thine is the kingdom" and "thy kingdom come." The apparent ambiguity is actually a representation of the reality of the life of faith. As faithful people, we know that experiences of grace do not alter our essential and perpetual neediness. Psalm 138 thus ultimately teaches us about and calls us to fundamental dependence upon God. Such dependence upon God rather than upon ourselves or the gods of our own making (see v. 1b) enables us to live in the present with assurance (v. 7; see Ps 23:4), offering our whole selves and lives to God (v. 1a).

2. Verse 6 is a particular reminder that to acknowledge God's reign and to live in dependence upon God means a transformation of what and whom the world generally values. Hannah's song (1 Sam 2:1-10), which v. 6 recalls, is taken up by Mary in anticipation of the birth of Jesus (see Luke 1:46-55, esp. vv. 51-53). Jesus embodied God's strange sovereignty and world-transforming values, distancing himself from the proud and powerful in favor of the lowly. Jesus showed us what it means to live in fundamental dependence upon God, to offer one's "whole heart" gratefully to God.

3. The profession that God rules the world is clearly appropriate for the season of Epiphany, with which Psalm 138 is associated. Like all proclamations of God's rule, Psalm 138 calls us to decision. It invites us to join the psalmist and the kings of the earth in praising God and offering ourselves to God with our "whole heart."

PSALM 139:1-24, SEARCH ME, O GOD, AND KNOW MY HEART

NIV	NRSV
Psalm 139	Psalm 139
For the director of music. Of David. A psalm.	To the leader. Of David. A Psalm.

¹O Lord, you have searched me
    and you know me.
	¹ O Lord, you have searched me and known
	    me.

²You know when I sit and when I rise;
    you perceive my thoughts from afar.
	² You know when I sit down and when I
	    rise up;
	    you discern my thoughts from far away.

³You discern my going out and my lying down; you are familiar with all my ways.	³ You search out my path and my lying down,

NIV

⁴Before a word is on my tongue
   you know it completely, O Lᴏʀᴅ.

⁵You hem me in—behind and before;
   you have laid your hand upon me.
⁶Such knowledge is too wonderful for me,
   too lofty for me to attain.

⁷Where can I go from your Spirit?
   Where can I flee from your presence?
⁸If I go up to the heavens, you are there;
   if I make my bed in the depths,ᵃ you are
      there.
⁹If I rise on the wings of the dawn,
   if I settle on the far side of the sea,
¹⁰even there your hand will guide me,
   your right hand will hold me fast.

¹¹If I say, "Surely the darkness will hide me
   and the light become night around me,"
¹²even the darkness will not be dark to you;
   the night will shine like the day,
   for darkness is as light to you.

¹³For you created my inmost being;
   you knit me together in my mother's
      womb.
¹⁴I praise you because I am fearfully and
      wonderfully made;
   your works are wonderful,
   I know that full well.
¹⁵My frame was not hidden from you
   when I was made in the secret place.
   When I was woven together in the depths of
      the earth,
¹⁶   your eyes saw my unformed body.
   All the days ordained for me
      were written in your book
      before one of them came to be.

¹⁷How precious toᵇ me are your thoughts,
      O God!
   How vast is the sum of them!
¹⁸Were I to count them,
   they would outnumber the grains of sand.
   When I awake,
   I am still with you.

¹⁹If only you would slay the wicked, O God!
   Away from me, you bloodthirsty men!
²⁰They speak of you with evil intent;

ᵃ8 Hebrew *Sheol*   ᵇ17 Or *concerning*

NRSV

   and are acquainted with all my ways.
⁴ Even before a word is on my tongue,
      O Lᴏʀᴅ, you know it completely.
⁵ You hem me in, behind and before,
   and lay your hand upon me.
⁶ Such knowledge is too wonderful for me;
   it is so high that I cannot attain it.

⁷ Where can I go from your spirit?
   Or where can I flee from your presence?
⁸ If I ascend to heaven, you are there;
   if I make my bed in Sheol, you are there.
⁹ If I take the wings of the morning
   and settle at the farthest limits of the sea,
¹⁰ even there your hand shall lead me,
   and your right hand shall hold me fast.
¹¹ If I say, "Surely the darkness shall cover me,
   and the light around me become night,"
¹² even the darkness is not dark to you;
   the night is as bright as the day,
   for darkness is as light to you.

¹³ For it was you who formed my inward parts;
   you knit me together in my mother's
      womb.
¹⁴ I praise you, for I am fearfully and
      wonderfully made.
   Wonderful are your works;
   that I know very well.
¹⁵   My frame was not hidden from you,
   when I was being made in secret,
      intricately woven in the depths of the
         earth.
¹⁶ Your eyes beheld my unformed substance.
   In your book were written
      all the days that were formed for me,
      when none of them as yet existed.
¹⁷ How weighty to me are your thoughts,
      O God!
   How vast is the sum of them!
¹⁸ I try to count them—they are more than
      the sand;
   I come to the endᵃ—I am still with you.

¹⁹ O that you would kill the wicked, O God,
   and that the bloodthirsty would depart
      from me—
²⁰ those who speak of you maliciously,

ᵃOr *I awake*

NIV

your adversaries misuse your name.
²¹Do I not hate those who hate you, O LORD,
    and abhor those who rise up against you?
²²I have nothing but hatred for them;
    I count them my enemies.

²³Search me, O God, and know my heart;
    test me and know my anxious thoughts.
²⁴See if there is any offensive way in me,
    and lead me in the way everlasting.

NRSV

and lift themselves up against you for
    evil!ᵃ
²¹ Do I not hate those who hate you, O LORD?
    And do I not loathe those who rise up
        against you?
²² I hate them with perfect hatred;
    I count them my enemies.
²³ Search me, O God, and know my heart;
    test me and know my thoughts.
²⁴ See if there is any wickedᵇ way in me,
    and lead me in the way everlasting.ᶜ

ᵃ Cn: Meaning of Heb uncertain   ᵇ Heb hurtful   ᶜ Or the ancient way. Compare Jer 6.16

COMMENTARY

The key word in Psalm 139 is "know(n)"/ "knowledge" (vv. 1-2, 4, 6, 14, and twice in v. 23). It may be entirely coincidental that it occurs seven times—the number indicating fullness or completion—but such a pattern appropriately reinforces the message that the psalmist is fully and completely known by God. This message pervades the first eighteen verses of the psalm, and it serves as the foundation for the petitions and affirmations in vv. 19-24. Scholars frequently suggest that these concluding verses offer a clue to the origin of Psalm 139. It is possible that the psalmist had been accused of idolatry and that the appeal in vv. 23-24 serves as the psalmist's affirmation of innocence (see Psalms 7; 17; 26). In any case, the psalmist's assurance of being known by God and of belonging inseparably to God transcends the particular circumstances of the psalm's origin. It has communicated good news to persons in all places and times. Indeed, the literary placement of Psalm 139 suggests the possibility that it served to express both the assurance and the wishes of the post-exilic community (see Commentary on Psalm 138; Introduction).

While Psalm 139 has been analyzed structurally in a variety of ways, the simplest conclusion is that represented by the NRSV. Verses 1-6 focus on God's knowledge of the psalmist's actions, thoughts, and words. The question in v. 7 introduces a new section, and the response in vv. 8-12 affirms God's knowledge of the psalmist in the form of an inescapable presence. Verses 13-18 trace God's intimate knowledge of the psalmist to God's creative activity. The shift that takes place at v. 19 is signaled by the introduction of "the wicked" and "bloodthirsty," who are enemies of the psalmist and of God; vv. 19-24 effectively contrast the rebellious behavior of those enemies with the psalmist's loyalty to God.

139:1-6. The very first word of the psalm is the divine name "Yahweh," and the first word of v. 2 is the emphatic Hebrew pronoun "you." While vv. 1-6 are often described as a statement of God's omniscience, what really matters about God to the psalmist is that the divine "you" knows "me." Four of the seven occurrences of the word "know" (ידע *yāda'*) are in vv. 1-6, and both verbs in v. 1 recur in v. 23, indicating that the psalmist desires to be and is fully known by God. As Patrick D. Miller puts it, "From beginning to end it is 'I' and 'you.' "[504] Verses 2-4 make it clear that God knows the psalmist fully—deeds (vv. 2*a*, 3; see "way[s]" in vv. 3, 24), thoughts (v. 2*b*), and words before they are even spoken (v. 4). "Such knowledge," which the psalmist describes as "too wonderful" (v. 5; see Ps 131:1), could easily be perceived as threatening. Indeed, there seems to be some ambivalence in the psalmist's mind. For instance, the verb in the phrase "hem me in" (צור *ṣûr*, v. 5) can have the sense

504. Patrick D. Miller, Jr., *Interpreting the Psalms* (Philadelphia: Fortress, 1986) 144.

of "besiege," "confine" as well as "protect." Ambivalence would be understandable, for it is risky "to dismiss the deceptive coverings under which most men take refuge," as John Calvin describes the psalmist's posture.[505] To be fully known is to be completely vulnerable, but on the whole, the psalmist certainly celebrates as good news the marvelous and mysterious reality that his or her life is accessible to God in every way and at every moment.

139:7-12. From the beginning of the Bible, the word "spirit" (רוח *rûaḥ,* or "wind"/"breath") is a way of indicating God's presence (see Gen 1:2; see also the proximity of "spirit" and "presence," or more literally "face," in Isa 63:9-10). Indeed, the mention of "heaven," "morning," and "sea" recalls God's creative activity (see below on vv. 13-14). While vv. 7-12 are often construed as a statement of God's omnipresence, the crucial thing for the psalmist is that God's presence is inescapable. Again, the "I" and "you" are pre-eminent; again, there is a possible ambivalence. For instance, the word "flee" (ברח *bāraḥ,* v.7) usually indicates an attempt to get away from (see Amos 9:2-4, which is similar to vv. 7-12 and where God's inescapable presence is clearly bad news). But again, the conviction of God's presence is fundamentally good news for the psalmist (cf. Job 23:8-10), who is convinced that God will "lead me, and . . . hold me" (v. 10; see Ps 73:23-24). In a case of enthusiastic poetic outreach (see above on Pss 22:29-31; 49:15), the psalmist affirms that God is "there" even "in Sheol" (v. 8), an affirmation that contradicts the more usual view of Sheol as a realm beyond God's reach (see Job 17:12-16; Pss 6:5; 30:3, 9; 88:3-7). There seems to be a mythic background to v. 9, but in any case, the imagery communicates a situation of extremity. The word "dark(ness)" (חשך *ḥōšek*), which occurs four times in vv. 11-12, is associated elsewhere with the forces of chaos and death (see Job 12:22; 17:12-13; Pss 23:4; 88:6, 12, 18). But the forces of darkness are dispelled by God's light (see John 1:5). Light is elsewhere associated with God's "presence" or "face"/"countenance," so vv. 11-12 recall v. 7 (see also Num 6:25-26; Pss 4:6; 27:1, 8-9; 44:3; 89:15). But aside from alluding to other texts, vv. 11-12 communicate by their poetic beauty the pervasive brilliance of God's presence.

139:13-18. Like v. 2, v. 13 begins with the emphatic Hebrew pronoun "you." In short, God's activity is emphasized, and vv. 13-18 are an eloquent presentation of the biblical view that human life is not simply a natural, biological occurrence but is the result of the will and work of a benevolent creator. The verb translated "formed" (קנה *qānâ*) in v. 13 is used elsewhere of God's gracious activity of constituting the whole people (Exod 15:16; Ps 74:2; Deut 32:6). God's creation of Israel is also proclaimed elsewhere as one of God's wonderful works (v. 14; see Exod 3:20; 15:11; Pss 77:11, 14). That the same language is used here to describe God's creation of an individual human being affirms God's loving care for every person (see Ps 138:8; Matt 6:26). As for the mode of creation, the psalmist does not use the more familiar image of God as potter (see Gen 2:7; Jer 18:11) but the more unusual metaphor of God as weaver. The psalmist has been "knit together" (v. 13; see Job 10:11).

Verses 15-16*a* seem to move in a different direction as it appears that God is portrayed as more an observer of a process, the details of which are unclear. It is possible that "depths of the earth" (v. 15*b*) is a metaphor for the womb, or perhaps v. 15 alludes to ancient Near Eastern mythic material in which human beings originated from below the earth. If so, according to v. 16, God is ultimately in control of even this process. Yet another alternative is that the poet intends to say that God is not just an observer. Rather, in keeping with the weaver image of v. 13, God is the one who has "intricately woven" (v. 15) the psalmist together. Certainty is elusive. The Hebrew word that the NRSV translates "my un-formed substance" (גלמי *gōlmî*) occurs only here in the OT. The NIV proposes a more specific rendering, and some translators even use "embryo." Such specificity is probably misleading, since we do not know the precise background of the imagery in vv. 15-16*a* or the real meaning of the word. In any case, it is clear that the poetic, evocative language of vv. 15-16*a* does not answer the kind of question that is often posed in contemporary debates over abortion—that is, when does human life begin?

---

505. John Calvin, *Commentary on the Book of Psalms,* Calvin Translation Society, 5 vols. (Grand Rapids: Baker, 1981) VI:5:206.

At the same time, the fundamental affirmation of vv. 13-18 is certainly relevant to any consideration of ethical questions. In other words, both v. 13 and vv. 15-16a are congruent with the affirmation in v. 14a, where the psalmist says that she or he is "fearfully and wonderfully made." The psalmist knows (v. 14b; cf. the RSV, which reads the conclusion of v. 14 as another statement that God knows the psalmist) that each human life belongs to God in every aspect—past (vv. 13-16a; see Jer 1:5) and future (v. 16b; on God's "book," see Exod 32:32-33; Ps 69:28; Mal 3:16), as well as present (see below on vv. 23-24a). Whereas God knows human thoughts (v. 2), humans cannot begin to comprehend God's thoughts (v. 17). Because the Hebrew verb in v. 18b means "awake" (קיץ qîs), some scholars propose that the psalmist spent the night in the Temple as protection from accusers or to await an answer to prayer (see Commentary on Psalm 73). While this is possible, it is finally not really important. What matters is the psalmist's realization that she or he is always "with you" (see Ps 73:23a). Thus v. 18 serves to summarize the affirmation of vv. 7-12, while v. 17 recalls vv. 1-6 (see esp. v. 6). The psalmist's origin and destiny lie with God.

139:19-24. Whereas in v. 14 the psalmist properly responds with gratitude to God's creative activity (the verb translated "praise" is the same one translated "give thanks" in Ps 138:1, 3), his or her response in vv. 19-22 seems quite different. Commentators have often concluded that these verses do not really belong with vv. 1-18; liturgical use of the psalm has often omitted these verses, apparently because of their direct request for revenge. In their present place, however, vv. 19-22 join vv. 23-24 as the culmination of the psalm. They articulate the way things always are; people who belong to God (vv. 1-18) and who try to live as God intends (vv. 23-24) will always be opposed by those who oppose God (see Pss 26:9; 55:23; 59:2). While vv. 19-20 inevitably sound like a request for personal revenge, their import is much broader and deeper; they request that God set things right in the world; in other words, "thy will be done." As in other psalms that contain requests for vengeance, the matter is apparently entrusted to and left with God rather than taken into human hands (see Commentary on Psalms 58; 109; 137). Similarly, the hatred expressed in vv. 21-22 is not simply a matter of personal feeling but the psalmist's way of saying that he or she opposes those who oppose God, in effect, "I am on the LORD's side" (see Pss 26:5; 31:6; 119:158).

The psalmist's oath of loyalty is sealed by vv. 23-24, where in language recalling vv. 1-3, the psalmist lays himself or herself open to God's examination. Having been searched (v. 1), the psalmist wants to be continually searched. Having been known (vv. 1-2, 4), the psalmist wants to be continually known. Having been seen (v. 16), the psalmist wants to be continually seen. Having experienced God's leading (see v. 10), the psalmist wants to be continually led. In short, by the end of the psalm, there is no hint of ambivalence. The psalmist fully entrusts her or his life to God, for now (vv. 23-24a) and forever (v. 24b), secure in the conviction that he or she has been, is being, and will be "fully known" (1 Cor 13:12).

REFLECTIONS

1. Explicitly theological concepts like omniscience and omnipresence are often applied by interpreters to Psalm 139. Almost inevitably these terms will fail to do justice to the psalm, since the psalmist did not intend to articulate systematically a doctrine of God. Rather, the psalmist affirms that God *knows me* and that God is *with me.* Similarly, the discussion of Psalm 139 in terms of the doctrine of predestination will inevitably be misleading if this doctrine is heard in its classical sense; however, the word *predestination* may be appropriately applied to Psalm 139 if it is understood fundamentally as an affirmation that our lives derive from God, belong to God, and find their true destination in God's purposes. In Romans, the apostle Paul suggests that to be "predestined" (8:29) means essentially that nothing "in all creation, will be able to separate us from the love of God in Christ Jesus our Lord" (8:39 NRSV). While obviously not appropriating the message through Jesus Christ as Paul was, the psalmist knew essentially the same good news about God. Although unable to comprehend God's thoughts (vv. 17-18), the psalmist is sure of one thing: "I am still with you" (v. 18*b*). This assurance that God is Emmanuel ("God-with-us"; see Matt 1:23; 28:20) enables the psalmist to entrust her or his life and future to God, inviting God's searching gaze (v. 23) in openness to God's "way everlasting" (v. 24). Such trust means, in effect, that the psalmist displays what Psalm 1 calls "happy"—an openness to God's instruction that derives from the assurance that God *"knows* the way of the righteous" (1:6*a* RSV; see Commentary on Psalms 1; 2).

2. Not surprisingly, Psalm 1 affirms exactly what the psalmist prays for in 139:19: "The way of the wicked will perish" (1:6*b*). The affirmation and the prayer are evidence that the perspective of the psalter is pervasively eschatological; it affirms God's claim on the world (see Psalms 2; 93; 95–99; 145–146; 148) and on every individual life at the same time that it acknowledges the existence of the wicked and their opposition to God and to God's people (vv. 19-20). This perspective means that the faithful in all times and in all places will find themselves doing precisely what the psalmist does in Psalm 139—professing that they belong to God, entrusting their lives and futures to God on the basis of the experience of God's pervasive presence, and praying for God to set things right. For this reason, to be sure, Psalm 139 is a profoundly important theological resource, although, as Miller suggests, "it may translate into the poetic expression of Francis Thompson's 'The Hound of Heaven' as easily as or better than into a systematic theological expression."[506] In short, God actively pursues us and will not let us get away (see above on Ps 23:6). The presence of such love invites both fierce loyalty (vv. 19-22) and sweet surrender (vv. 23-24).

506. Miller, *Interpreting the Psalms,* 144.

PSALM 140:1-13, A CRY FOR PROTECTION FROM VIOLENCE

NIV

Psalm 140

For the director of music. A psalm of David.

[1]Rescue me, O LORD, from evil men;
  protect me from men of violence,
[2]who devise evil plans in their hearts
  and stir up war every day.
[3]They make their tongues as sharp as a
    serpent's;
  the poison of vipers is on their lips.   *Selah*

[4]Keep me, O LORD, from the hands of the
    wicked;
  protect me from men of violence
  who plan to trip my feet.
[5]Proud men have hidden a snare for me;
  they have spread out the cords of their
    net

NRSV

Psalm 140

To the leader. A Psalm of David.

[1] Deliver me, O LORD, from evildoers;
  protect me from those who are
    violent,
[2] who plan evil things in their minds
  and stir up wars continually.
[3] They make their tongue sharp as a snake's,
  and under their lips is the venom of
    vipers.   *Selah*

[4] Guard me, O LORD, from the hands of the
    wicked;
  protect me from the violent
  who have planned my downfall.
[5] The arrogant have hidden a trap for me,

NIV

and have set traps for me along my
    path.   *Selah*
⁶O Lᴏʀᴅ, I say to you, "You are my God."
    Hear, O Lᴏʀᴅ, my cry for mercy.
⁷O Sovereign Lᴏʀᴅ, my strong deliverer,
    who shields my head in the day of battle—
⁸do not grant the wicked their desires, O Lᴏʀᴅ;
    do not let their plans succeed,
    or they will become proud.   *Selah*

⁹Let the heads of those who surround me
    be covered with the trouble their lips have
        caused.
¹⁰Let burning coals fall upon them;
    may they be thrown into the fire,
    into miry pits, never to rise.
¹¹Let slanderers not be established in the land;
    may disaster hunt down men of violence.

¹²I know that the Lᴏʀᴅ secures justice for the
        poor
    and upholds the cause of the needy.
¹³Surely the righteous will praise your name
    and the upright will live before you.

NRSV

and with cords they have spread a net,ᵃ
along the road they have set snares for
    me.   *Selah*

⁶ I say to the Lᴏʀᴅ, "You are my God;
    give ear, O Lᴏʀᴅ, to the voice of my
        supplications."
⁷ O Lᴏʀᴅ, my Lord, my strong deliverer,
    you have covered my head in the day
        of battle.
⁸ Do not grant, O Lᴏʀᴅ, the desires of the wicked;
    do not further their evil plot.ᵇ   *Selah*

⁹ Those who surround me lift up their heads;ᶜ
    let the mischief of their lips overwhelm
        them!
¹⁰ Let burning coals fall on them!
    Let them be flung into pits, no more to rise!
¹¹ Do not let the slanderer be established in
        the land;
    let evil speedily hunt down the violent!

¹² I know that the Lᴏʀᴅ maintains the cause
        of the needy,
    and executes justice for the poor.
¹³ Surely the righteous shall give thanks to
        your name;
    the upright shall live in your presence.

ᵃOr *they have spread cords as a net*   ᵇHeb adds *they are exalted*
ᶜCn Compare Gk: Heb *those who surround me are uplifted in
head*; Heb divides verses 8 and 9 differently

COMMENTARY

Psalm 140 is ordinarily categorized as a prayer for help or individual lament/complaint. The occurrences of *Selah* after vv. 3, 5, and 8 suggest a fourfold division of the psalm, but scholars often conclude that vv. 12-13 should be separated from vv. 9-11. Still others prefer a threefold division (vv. 1-5, 6-11, 12-13) or a different fourfold structure (vv. 1-5, vv. 6-8, vv. 9-11, vv. 12-13). As Allen points out, it is certainly possible that there is "more than one artistic scheme in the psalm."[507] He detects, for instance, a chiastic arrangement (see Introduction) of terms in vv. 1-11, as follows:

507. Leslie C. Allen, *Psalms 101–150,* WBC 21 (Waco, Tex.: Word, 1983) 267.

v. 1	"evil(doers)," "violent"
v. 3	"lips"
v. 4	"wicked"
v. 8	"wicked"
v. 9	"lips"
v. 11	"evil," "violent"

The effect is to focus attention toward the center, which Allen identifies as vv. 6-7. He also points out that the phrase "in the day of battle" (v. 7) recalls "wars every day" from v. 2. At the same time, "head" in v. 7 anticipates "heads" in v. 9. Again, the effect is to focus attention toward the center of the psalm. Thus the psalmist's petitions for protection against and deliverance from the violent (vv. 1-5, 8-11) surround the psalmist's profession of trust in God (vv. 6-7). This profession also anticipates and is tied conceptually to the conclusion of the psalm (vv. 12-13).

In an attempt to arrive at the origin and ancient use of Psalm 140, scholars often suggest that the psalmist was falsely accused and that he or she came to the Temple to seek vindication and help from God (see Commentary on Psalms 5; 7; 139). While this is possible, certainty is elusive. In the present literary setting, the petitions in Psalm 140 can be understood as an elaboration of Ps 139:19-22 (see Pss 139:19; 140:4, 8), and the assurance expressed in Psalm 140 corresponds with Ps 139:1-18 (see Pss 139:7; 140:13; note also the emphatic pronoun "you" in Pss 139:2, 13; 140:6). Psalm 140 also anticipates the similar prayers in Psalms 141–143 (see Commentary on Psalm 141), and Psalms 139–143 are framed by psalms that make good sense as testimony and petition offered by the post-exilic community (Psalms 138; 144–145). This framing may have provided literary encouragement to the post-exilic community to hear the individual expressions of petition and profession in Psalms 138–145 as pertinent to the whole community. If so, then Psalms 138–145 would be congruent with the purpose of Book V to address the ongoing crisis of the exile and its aftermath (see Commentary on Psalms 107–108; 111; 118; Introduction).

140:1-5. The opening petitions are typical of the prayers for help (see Pss 6:4; 25:21; 40:11), as are the descriptions of the perpetrators (see the first, lit., "a man of evil," in Ps 10:15; see "violent"/"violence" in Gen 6:11, 13; Pss 7:16; 11:5; 55:9; 72:14; 73:6). The further description of the violent in v. 2a recalls Ps 35:4, 20, where the NRSV's "devise" and "conceive" translate the Hebrew verb rendered "plan[ned]" (חשׁב *ḥāšab*) in Ps 140:2, 4. Verse 2b is reminiscent of Pss 56:6; 59:3; 120:7. Three of the four words in v. 3a contain an "sh" sound, thus creating the onomatopoeic effect of a snake hissing (see Ps 58:4). The mention of "tongue" (see v. 11) and "lips" (see v. 9) in v. 3 suggests verbal violence (see Pss 57:4; 64:3; 73:8).

Verbal abuse is inevitably part of a larger pattern of destructive activity, and this is indicated in vv. 4-5. The word "hands" (ידים *yādayim*) in

v. 4a connotes "grasp" or "power" (see Ps 82:4). Verse 4b repeats v. 1b; the violent do not stop at verbal abuse. They have "planned" (v. 4c; see also v. 2) to bring the psalmist down. The NIV's translation of v. 4c is more literal and conveys how the imagery of v. 4 carries into v. 5, which also indicates that violent speech (v. 3) is accompanied by violent action (see Pss 9:15; 10:9; 31:4; 37:6; 64:5; 141:9; 142:3). Verse 5 also introduces another designation of the enemies—the "proud" or "arrogant" (see Pss 94:2; 123:4).

140:6-7. While it would appear from vv. 1-5 that the violent are in control, the psalmist affirms in the central section of the psalm (vv. 6-7) that God is sovereign. The title "Lord" in v. 7 indicates a sovereign master, and the Hebrew root translated "strong" (עז *'ōz*) is regularly associated with God's reign (see Pss 29:1; 93:1; 96:6-7; 99:4). In Exod 15:2, as here, it appears in conjunction with God's saving activity (see "salvation" in Exod 15:2; the phrase in Ps 140:8 is more literally "strength of my salvation"); the song in Exodus 15 also culminates in the proclamation of God's reign (v. 18). Furthermore, the sovereign God is "my Lord" (v. 7) and "my God" (v. 6). The appearance of the Hebrew pronoun "you" in v. 6 emphasizes the point. Like the psalm as a whole, which juxtaposes petition and profession, so do vv. 6-7. The petition in v. 6b is followed by profession in v. 7b (see Pss 5:11 and 91:4, where God also covers the psalmist). In short, the psalmist simultaneously celebrates and prays for deliverance; the perspective is eschatological (see Reflections below).

140:8-11. Petition is resumed in v. 8. The "desires of the wicked" involve violence, oppression, and destruction (see vv. 1-5, 9, 11; see also Pss 10:3; 112:10)—that is, the antithesis of "justice" (v. 12). Their behavior is further described in vv. 8-11 as an "evil plot" (v. 8b; see Gen 11:6; Pss 31:13; 37:12), "mischief" (v. 9b; see Pss 7:14, 16; 10:7; 55:10), and "slander" (v. 11a, lit., "a man of tongue," recalling v. 3). The psalmist's prayer in vv. 8-11 is not a request for personal revenge. Rather, the psalmist asks that God set things right. Of course, "justice for the poor" (v. 12) will necessarily mean judgment upon the victimizers. Repeating the words "evil" (see vv. 1-2) and "violent" (see vv. 1, 4), v. 11b requests simply that the violent experience the results they intend to inflict upon others. Again, the matter is not revenge but justice (see Commentary on Psalms 109; 137; 139).

140:12-13. These verses state positively what the psalmist has prayed for in vv. 8-11. Verses 6-7 have asserted God's sovereignty, and vv. 12-13 present the royal policy that God wills and enacts—justice. The word the NRSV translates "cause" (דין *dîn*) in v. 12*a* appears elsewhere in contexts that explicitly proclaim God's rule (see Pss 9:4 in the context of 9:7; 96:10). So does the word "justice"/"judge" (משפט *mišpāṭ*; see Pss

96:13; 97:2; 98:9; 99:4; see also "presence of the LORD" in 98:9). The beneficiaries of God's justice are those who are the victims of the violent: the "poor" and the "needy" (see Commentary on Psalms 9; 10; 82; 109). These same persons can also be called "the righteous" (see Commentary on Psalm 1) or "the upright" (see Pss 33:1; 111:1; 112:2, 4). They depend for life not on themselves but on God. Thus their fundamental posture is gratitude to God (v. 13*a*; see Ps 138:1-2), and their "salvation" (v. 7) is to "live in your presence" (v. 13*b*; see Pss 23:6; 27:4; 73:28).

REFLECTIONS

As is the case throughout the book of Psalms, the juxtaposition of petition and profession of faith in Psalm 140 creates an eschatological perspective. That is, the reign of God is proclaimed amid circumstances that appear to deny it (see Commentary on Psalms 2; 13; 22; 138; Introduction). It was, of course, no different for Jesus, whose proclamation of and embodiment of the reign of God (see Mark 1:14-15) led him to a cross.

1. While Psalm 140 represents a theological perspective that pervades the psalter, indeed, the whole Bible, many people might question the appropriateness of Psalm 140 as a Christian prayer on account of the petitions in vv. 8-11. As suggested above, however, the issue in vv. 8-11 is not personal revenge but justice for the victimized. If we are not victimized to the point that we feel the need to pray as the psalmist does in Psalm 140, then we should pray Psalm 140 on behalf of others who are victims (see Reflections on Psalm 109). If we prayed Psalm 140 on behalf of others, we would perhaps be reminded of some of the stark realities of our culture—the frequency of spousal and child abuse, for instance. In our midst, there are millions who daily need to pray literally, "Protect me from those who are violent" (vv. 1*b*, 4*b*).

2. But there is a further dimension to the use of Psalm 140 as a contemporary prayer. In Rom 3:13, Paul quotes Ps 140:3*b* to support his claim that all people "are under the power of sin" (Rom 3:9 NRSV). From this perspective, Psalm 140 becomes a prayer requesting that we be delivered *from ourselves!* That is to say, Psalm 140 forces us to consider that all of us are victimizers. For instance, most contemporary persons give at least implicit approval to a culture that all but glorifies violence. Even children watch violence daily on television, and violence is a staple of adult entertainment. When we seek solutions to domestic and international problems, those solutions frequently amount to fighting violence with violence. In short, violence is not just a problem for and with *other* people; it is a problem for and with *all of us* (see Commentary on Psalm 109). Many philosophers convincingly argue that violence, hostility, and war are inevitable human realities, for peace is simply too boring and too costly in the so-called real world (see Commentary on Psalms 120; 125). In the face of such conclusions, Psalm 140 is ultimately a reminder that, as people of God, we profess that the true real world is the world of God's reign (vv. 6-7), and it is a confirmation of the faithfulness of the contemporary slogan "If you want peace, work for justice." Violence will never effectively be fought with violence. It will only effectively be answered with the justice that God wills and works to enact (see vv. 12-13).

PSALM 141:1-10, DELIVER ME FROM WICKEDNESS

NIV

Psalm 141

A psalm of David.

¹O LORD, I call to you; come quickly to me.
  Hear my voice when I call to you.
²May my prayer be set before you like incense;
  may the lifting up of my hands be like the
    evening sacrifice.

³Set a guard over my mouth, O LORD;
  keep watch over the door of my lips.
⁴Let not my heart be drawn to what is evil,
  to take part in wicked deeds
with men who are evildoers;
  let me not eat of their delicacies.

⁵Let a righteous manᵃ strike me—it is a
    kindness;
  let him rebuke me—it is oil on my head.
  My head will not refuse it.

Yet my prayer is ever against the deeds of
    evildoers;
⁶ their rulers will be thrown down from the
    cliffs,
  and the wicked will learn that my words
    were well spoken.
⁷⌐They will say,⌐ "As one plows and breaks up
    the earth,
  so our bones have been scattered at the
    mouth of the grave.ᵇ"

⁸But my eyes are fixed on you, O Sovereign
    LORD;
  in you I take refuge—do not give me over
    to death.
⁹Keep me from the snares they have laid for
    me,
  from the traps set by evildoers.
¹⁰Let the wicked fall into their own nets,
  while I pass by in safety.

ᵃ5 Or *Let the Righteous One*   ᵇ7 Hebrew *Sheol*

NRSV

Psalm 141

A Psalm of David.

¹ I call upon you, O LORD; come quickly to
    me;
  give ear to my voice when I call to you.
² Let my prayer be counted as incense before
    you,
  and the lifting up of my hands as an
    evening sacrifice.

³ Set a guard over my mouth, O LORD;
  keep watch over the door of my lips.
⁴ Do not turn my heart to any evil,
  to busy myself with wicked deeds
in company with those who work iniquity;
  do not let me eat of their delicacies.

⁵ Let the righteous strike me;
  let the faithful correct me.
Never let the oil of the wicked anoint my head,ᵃ
  for my prayer is continuallyᵇ against their
    wicked deeds.
⁶ When they are given over to those who
    shall condemn them,
  then they shall learn that my words were
    pleasant.
⁷ Like a rock that one breaks apart and
    shatters on the land,
  so shall their bones be strewn at the
    mouth of Sheol.ᶜ

⁸ But my eyes are turned toward you,
  O GOD, my Lord;
  in you I seek refuge; do not leave me
    defenseless.
⁹ Keep me from the trap that they have laid
    for me,
  and from the snares of evildoers.
¹⁰ Let the wicked fall into their own nets,
  while I alone escape.

ᵃ Gk: Meaning of Heb uncertain   ᵇ Cn: Heb *for continually and
my prayer*   ᶜ Meaning of Heb of verses 5-7 is uncertain

COMMENTARY

Like Psalms 140 and 142, with which it has several similarities, Psalm 141 is ordinarily classified as an individual lament/complaint or prayer for help. As is typical, the psalmist prays for deliverance from specific threats (v. 9), but less typically, the psalmist also prays for deliverance from the temptation represented by the very existence of the wicked and their apparent prosperity (vv. 3-5).

While the origin and ancient use of Psalm 141 are uncertain, it is evident that it continues the focus on the wicked that is present in Psalms 139–140. In this regard, the verbal links between Psalms 140 and 141 are significant—see "wicked" in Pss 140:4, 8 and 141:4, 10 (see also 139:19); "righteous" in 140:13 and 141:5; "guard" in 140:4 and "guard"/"keep" in 141:3, 9; "lips" in 140:3, 9 and 141:3; "evil" in 140:1-2, 11 and 141:4, 5; "my Lord" in 140:7 and 141:8; and "trap(s)," "net(s)," and "snares" in 140:5 and 141:9-10. Psalm 141 also anticipates Psalm 142, especially by way of the repetition of the important word "refuge" (חסה ḥāsâ) in 141:8 and 142:5 (see also "voice" in 141:1 and 142:1; "righteous" in 141:5 and 142:7; "trap" in 141:9 and 142:3). In short, it appears that Psalms 140–142, or perhaps 139–143, form the core of the Davidic collection, which includes Psalms 138–145. Framed by Psalms 138 and 144–145, this Davidic collection makes especially good sense against the background of the post-exilic era (see Psalms 138–140; 144). Thus Psalm 141 participates in the response of Book V to the ongoing crisis of exile and its aftermath (see Commentary on Psalms 107; 108; 111; 118; 140; Introduction). This crisis involved not only the need for protection against powerful enemies (see Psalm 140) but also the persistent temptation to conclude, in effect, "If you can't beat them, join them." It is to this temptation that Psalm 141 is particularly addressed (see Commentary on Psalm 125, esp. discussion of v. 3). Of course, the seductive power of evil is a perennial temptation, so Psalm 141 remains a timely prayer for the people of God (see Reflections below).

Psalm 141 is outlined by scholars in a variety of ways. This variety stems in part perhaps from the textual difficulties in vv. 5-7 (see NRSV notes). Pointing out that vv. 5-7 have been "understood and translated in the most diverse ways possible," Bratcher and Reyburn conclude that these verses are "extremely obscure, not to say unintelligible."[508] Artur Weiser even chooses to leave vv. 5c-7 untranslated on the grounds that they are finally incomprehensible (see below for a literal translation).[509] In any case, the NIV and the NRSV offer two different fourfold divisions of the psalm. Some scholars prefer a division in two sections (vv. 1-5, vv. 6-10), while others suggest three (vv. 1-2, vv. 3-6, vv. 7-10). On the basis of content, it is also possible to divide the psalm into vv. 1-2, vv. 3-7, vv. 8-10. In vv. 1-2, the psalmist requests to be heard. Verses 3-7 focus on the psalmist and the wicked. Verses 3-5b request help to oppose temptation, while vv. 5c-7 may be a profession of trust in God's justice or perhaps a complaint. Verses 8-10 begin with a profession of trust, which is followed by petition for deliverance.

141:1-2. The language of v. 1 is typical. The "call" to God indicates prayer (see Ps 4:1, 3), which is mentioned specifically in v. 2. The two occurrences of "I call" surround two more pleas— "come quickly" (see Pss 22:19; 38:22; 40:13) and "give ear" (see Pss 55:1; 86:6; 143:1). Verse 2b depicts a posture of prayer (see Pss 28:2; 63:4; 134:2). This verse may indicate an original cultic setting, but it is often taken as indication of the spiritualization of sacrifice (on "evening sacrifice," see 2 Kgs 16:15; Ezra 9:4-5; Dan 9:21). In Ezra 9:5, though, Ezra prays immediately following the evening sacrifice, a sequence that would make good sense in terms of v. 2. In any case, there is simply not enough evidence here to suggest a movement to replace sacrifice by prayer (see Commentary on Psalm 50). As Mays succinctly concludes, "Word and sacrament are not at odds here."[510]

141:3-5b. The vocabulary of these verses recalls Psalm 140. Whereas Psalm 140 contains the

508. Robert G. Bratcher and William D. Reyburn, *A Translator's Handbook on the Book of Psalms* (New York: United Bible Societies, 1991) 1142, 1144.

509. Artur Weiser, *The Psalms,* OTL, trans. H. Hartwell (Philadelphia: Westminster, 1962) 811.

510. James L. Mays, *Psalms,* Interpretation (Louisville: John Knox, 1994) 431.

psalmist's prayer for deliverance from the destructive "lips" of the wicked (vv. 3, 9), here the psalmist prays that her or his own "lips" be kept from destructive behavior (v. 3b). Whereas the psalmist prayed in Psalm 140 for deliverance from "evil" (see vv. 1-2), here the prayer is that she or he be prevented from joining the wicked in their "evil" (v. 4). The psalmist desires to be counted among "the righteous" (v. 5a), even if this means being disciplined by their rebuke (v. 5b). The NIV translation of v. 5a is more literal, and the word rendered "kindness" is the same word the NRSV ordinarily translates as "steadfast love." In short, the psalmist will welcome the loving correction of his or her brothers and sisters. The NIV also attempts a more literal translation of the difficult v. 5b, connecting it more closely to v. 5a than does the NRSV (see the NRSV note). While faithfulness is clearly a matter of proper speech in v. 3, the issue is broader in v. 4 and includes even what is eaten. While the vocabulary differs, v. 4 recalls Daniel 1, where Daniel's faithfulness is also a matter of refusing to eat the king's royal food (see Dan 1:8-18). While Psalm 141 should not be connected historically to the book of Daniel, Daniel 1 does provide a narrative illustration of the logic of Ps 140:4; it may also illustrate how Psalm 141 would have been an important resource in facing the ongoing crises of the post-exilic era. In any case, the petition of v. 4 amounts fundamentally to what Jesus taught his disciples to pray: "Lead us not into temptation, but deliver us from evil."

141:5c-7. Although v. 5c is again difficult (see the NRSV note), it seems to be the psalmist's affirmation that her or his intent is congruent with what the psalmist has just prayed for in vv. 3-5b. The textual difficulties are multiplied in vv. 6-7, which read literally:

v. 6   Their judges were thrown
              down into the hands of
              the rock,
          and they heard
              my words, for they were
              pleasing.

v. 7   Like one clearing and
              plowing the earth,
          our bones have been
              scattered at the mouth
              of Sheol.

While these verses appear to make no sense, the scholarly proposals amount to little more than speculation. It may do just as well to try to make sense of the Hebrew as it appears. Although certainty is impossible, vv. 6-7 may be a highly poetic complaint. That is, those who could have served to punish the wicked (v. 6a) and reward the psalmist for his or her pleasing words (v. 6b; "pleasing" [נעם nāʿēm] is from the same root as "delicacies" in v. 4) have been brutally dealt with (v. 6a). Thus the psalmist and his or her associates have been effectively driven into the ground (v. 7a) and are as good as dead (v. 7b; see "Sheol" in Pss 30:3; 55:15; 116:3). In contrast to this attempt at a literal reading, the NIV and the NRSV turn vv. 6-7 into the psalmist's affirmation that God will ultimately deal with the wicked, in which case vv. 6-7 anticipate v. 10. Construing vv. 6-7 as a complaint, however, seems to make more sense of the Hebrew particle at the beginning of v. 8, which both the NIV and the NRSV render in an adversative sense.

141:8-10. In other words, despite the brutal treatment of those who seek justice (v. 6) and despite the resulting setback expressed by the psalmist (v. 7), the psalmist affirms, "But my eyes are turned toward you" (v. 8a; see Ps 123:1). Whereas it appears that the wicked are sovereign, the psalmist addresses God as "my Lord" (v. 8a; see Ps 140:7). Whereas the wicked appear to prosper and promote evil with impunity (v. 6), the psalmist refuses to join the wicked and chooses instead to "seek refuge" in God (v. 8b). That is, the psalmist resists the seductive temptation of wickedness and professes to live in dependence upon God (see Pss 2:12; 5:11; Introduction). The petition in v. 8b could be rendered more literally "do not leave my life naked." Nakedness elsewhere is indicative of punishment and even recalls the plight of the destroyed Jerusalem (see Lam 1:8; Ezek 16:37; 23:10, 29). Petition continues in v. 9 (see Ps 140:5; 142:3), and the corollary of God's defense of the vulnerable is God's destruction of the wicked (v. 10; see Ps 1:6). Like other requests for the destruction of the wicked (see Pss 7:9-11, 15-16; 12:3-4; 17:13-14; 58:6-9; 109:6-19; 137:8-9; 139:19-22), v. 10 is the psalmist's way of pleading for God to set things right, in effect, a way of praying, "Thy will be done."

REFLECTIONS

Because of the reference to an "evening sacrifice" in v. 2, Psalm 141 was used from earliest Christian times as an evening prayer, and it still is. Its contemporary use is appropriate, indeed very timely, in a culture that surrounds us with both subtle and blatant temptations to do evil. People are taught to use speech as a weapon to intimidate, as a tool to get ahead and to get their own way (see v. 3). Millions of dollars are spent daily by advertisers who want to convince us to "eat . . . their delicacies" (v. 4) or to drink the coolest beverage or to drive the hottest car. In short, we are bombarded daily with messages that both subliminally and overtly assert that life does consist in the abundance of possessions (see Luke 12:15) and that happiness consists of getting what we want and accomplishing what we desire. The "American dream" amounts essentially to having the power and the resources so as to be answerable to no one but ourselves.

In biblical terms, however, this is the essence of wickedness, from which the psalmist prays to be delivered (vv. 3-5b; see Commentary on Psalms 1; 2). For the psalmist, the pursuit of happiness involves not material abundance or unbridled self-assertion (vv. 3-4) but the fundamental orientation of life to God (v. 8a). Rejecting the temptations of the wicked and their outward prosperity, the psalmist prays for and apparently finds the strength to live in humble dependence upon God (v. 8b). Thus the psalmist can articulate the intention to live as part of a community of loving discipline (v. 5a) rather than as an isolated self. Even so, it is revealing that the psalmist continues to pray for help (vv. 8b-10), including the request that she or he not be left exposed to the pervasive enticements of the wicked (v. 8b). The psalmist's example is instructive, and it reinforces Jesus' instruction that his disciples constantly need to pray, "Thy will be done; . . . lead us not into temptation, but deliver us from evil."

PSALM 142:1-7, NO ONE CARES FOR ME

NIV

Psalm 142

A *maskil*[a] of David. When he was in the cave. A prayer.

[1]I cry aloud to the LORD;
   I lift up my voice to the LORD for mercy.
[2]I pour out my complaint before him;
   before him I tell my trouble.
[3]When my spirit grows faint within me,
   it is you who know my way.
In the path where I walk
   men have hidden a snare for me.
[4]Look to my right and see;
   no one is concerned for me.

[a]Title: Probably a literary or musical term

NRSV

Psalm 142

A Maskil of David. When he was in the cave. A Prayer.

[1] With my voice I cry to the LORD;
   with my voice I make supplication to the LORD.
[2] I pour out my complaint before him;
   I tell my trouble before him.
[3] When my spirit is faint,
   you know my way.

In the path where I walk
   they have hidden a trap for me.
[4] Look on my right hand and see—
   there is no one who takes notice of me;

NIV

I have no refuge;
    no one cares for my life.

⁵I cry to you, O LORD;
    I say, "You are my refuge,
    my portion in the land of the living."
⁶Listen to my cry,
    for I am in desperate need;
rescue me from those who pursue me,
    for they are too strong for me.
⁷Set me free from my prison,
    that I may praise your name.

Then the righteous will gather about me
    because of your goodness to me.

NRSV

no refuge remains to me;
    no one cares for me.

⁵ I cry to you, O LORD;
    I say, "You are my refuge,
    my portion in the land of the living."
⁶ Give heed to my cry,
    for I am brought very low.

Save me from my persecutors,
    for they are too strong for me.
⁷ Bring me out of prison,
    so that I may give thanks to your name.
The righteous will surround me,
    for you will deal bountifully with me.

COMMENTARY

An individual lament/complaint or prayer for help, Psalm 142 is linked verbally to Psalm 141. Its vocabulary also anticipates Psalm 143 (see "supplication[s]" in Pss 142:1; 143:1; "spirit grows faint" in 142:3; 143:4; "save me" in 142:6; 143:9; "pursue[s]" in 142:6; 143:3; and perhaps "refuge" in 142:5; 143:9, but see the NRSV note). It makes sense to view Psalm 142 as part of the core of the Davidic collection (Psalms 139–143) framed by Psalms 138 and 144–145, which would have been especially appropriate for the post-exilic community. Thus Psalm 142 participates in the response of Book V to the ongoing crisis of exile and its aftermath (see Commentary on Psalms 107; 108; 111; 118; 138; 140; 141; Introduction).

Whether Psalm 142 originated as a response to the exile or to the post-exilic situation is unclear, since the origin and ancient use of Psalm 142 are unknown. What is clearer is that Psalm 142 would have been an appropriate exilic or post-exilic prayer, although its usefulness cannot be limited to that setting (see Reflections below). Indeed, the superscription suggests a narrative context within David's life as the background for hearing Psalm 142 (see 1 Sam 22:1; 24:3-4). It recalls the superscription of Psalm 57, which also features the concept of "refuge" (see v. 1). The superscription should not be understood histori-

cally but as illustrative of a narrative context for hearing the psalm (see Commentary on Psalms 3; 7; 18; 34; 51; 52; 56; 57). The appearance in Book V of a Davidic collection, especially one that includes a royal psalm (Psalm 144), reinforces the necessity to reinterpret the traditional Davidic theology (see Commentary on Psalms 89; 110; 132; 144; Introduction).

The structure of Psalm 142 can be outlined in several ways, as the difference between the NIV and the NRSV indicates. Allen suggests a division into vv. 1-4 and vv. 5-7, based on the pattern of repetition between these two sections (see "I cry" in vv. 1, 5; the emphatic pronoun "you" [אתה 'attâ] in vv. 3, 5; and "me" [נפש nepeš] in vv. 4, 7).[511] Still another possibility is to divide the psalm into vv. 1-3a, vv. 3b-5, vv. 6-7. In this case, each section begins with complaint or petition and moves toward assurance (vv. 3a, 5, 7b). In short, as is often the case, various proposals can be justified, depending on the criteria one chooses to emphasize. It is possible that the structure and movement operate at more than one level, so the various proposals need not be considered mutually exclusive.

142:1-3a. Although the Hebrew root translated "cry" (זעק zā'aq) in vv. 1, 5 does not occur

511. Leslie C. Allen, *Psalms 101–150*, WBC 21 (Waco, Tex.: Word, 1983) 276-77.

often in the psalms (see Pss 22:5; 107:13, 19), it is an important theological word. For instance, it recalls the exodus (see Exod 2:23); it is a crucial part of the pattern in the book of Judges (see Judg 3:9, 15; 6:6-7); indeed, it became understood as a typical element in God's dealing with God's people (see Neh 9:28). The very act of crying out to God bespoke the trust that God hears and that God cares; this trust is evident in the movement toward assurance in each of three sections of Psalm 142. This trust was particularly necessary during the aftermath of the exile, and it is significant that the word "cry" occurs twice in Psalm 107 (see Ps 107:13, 19; a nearly identical variant also occurs in Ps 107:6, 28), the first psalm in Book V. As the NIV suggests, the verb in v. 1b derives from a root that means "to be merciful," "to be gracious" (see Pss 4:1; 6:2; 9:13). It is God's mercy upon which the psalmist depends, and his or her assurance is communicated effectively by the chiastic structure of v. 2. The two occurrences of the prepositional phrase "before him" (lit., "to his face") surround the two words that describe the psalmist's situation—"complaint" (see Pss 55:2; 64:1; and the superscription of Psalm 102, where the words "pour out" and "faint" also occur) and "trouble." In other words, the psalmist's problem is encompassed by God's presence, and this assurance is stated explicitly in v. 3a. Needy and weak (see Pss 61:2; 77:3; 107:5; 143:4; Lam 2:12), the psalmist is assured of God's presence. The "you" in v. 3b is emphatic; the psalmist is sure that God knows. Such knowledge is not simply informational but relational (see Ps 139:1-2, 4, 23).

142:3b-5. The complaint becomes specific in the second section of the psalm. The psalmist is targeted by enemies (v. 3b; see Pss 140:5; 141:9), and there is no one in the traditional position for helping—at the "right hand" (v. 4a; see Ps 109:6, 31). In the struggle against the enemies, the psalmist has no one to turn to (v. 4b, 4d) and no place to hide (v. 4c). Verse 4c reads literally, "a refuge perishes from me"; this same expression occurs also in Job 11:20; Jer 25:35; and Amos 2:14. In short, the situation appears to be hopeless.

But for the psalmist, faith is "the conviction of

things not seen" (Heb 11:1 NRSV; see 142:4a). So the psalmist emphatically says to God, *"You are my refuge"* (v. 5b). The appearance of the Hebrew pronoun recalls v. 3a. The Hebrew words translated "refuge" differ in vv. 4 and 5 (מנוס *mānôs*, v. 4; מחסה *maḥseh*, v. 5). The latter is the more frequently used one and is present from the beginning of the psalter. In the worst possible circumstance, the psalmist can affirm what Ps 2:12 presents as true happiness: entrusting life and future completely to God (see also Pss 5:11; 7:1; 141:8; Introduction). Although not seen, God's help is as dependable and tangible as the "portion" of land that was intended to represent every Israelite's stake in life and in the future (v. 5c; see Num 18:20; Pss 16:5; 73:26; 119:57; Lam 3:24). The psalmist is faced with death, but God offers life (see Ps 27:13).

142:6-7. The beginning of the final section of the psalm again returns to petition and complaint. The request to be heard (v. 6a; see Ps 5:1) is accompanied by complaint (v. 6b; see Pss 79:8; 116:6), as is the first request for deliverance (v. 6cd; see Ps 18:17). A second request for deliverance is made in v. 7a. The act of bringing out is what God did in delivering the people from Egypt (see Exod 18:1; 20:2) and from exile (see Ezek 20:34, 41; 34:13). The psalmist asks for a personal exodus from "prison." To be sure, some commentators take this word literally and find in it a clue to the original setting of the psalm (see Lev 24:12; Num 15:34), but it is likely that the word should be heard metaphorically and certainly came to be understood that way. In Isa 42:7, it seems to designate the exile (see also Ps 88:8; Lam 3:7); this dimension of meaning would be especially appropriate for the placement of Psalm 142 in Book V. Whereas the first request for deliverance was accompanied by complaint, the second is supported by the psalmist's promise to praise God (v. 7b). Perhaps not coincidentally, the wording recalls Ps 138:1-2, the beginning of the present Davidic collection. In view of the complaint in v. 4 of total isolation from help, it is fitting that the psalmist states the final assurance in vv. 7cd in terms of being surrounded by the "righteous" (see Pss 140:13; 141:5). This company of friends, helpers, and fellow worshipers will be a sign of God's bountiful treatment of the psalmist (see Pss 13:6; 116:7; 119:17). Similar gatherings are depicted in the conclusions of other prayers for help or songs of thanksgiving (see Pss 22:22-26; 116:14, 17-19).

REFLECTIONS

Like the other complaints or prayers for help, Psalm 142 portrays the simultaneity of trouble and assurance. It is thus another reminder of the inseparability of complaint and praise; to put it in explicitly Christian terms, Psalm 142 represents the inseparability of cross and resurrection (see Commentary on Psalms 13; 22; 69). Jesus invited his followers both to take up their crosses and to go forth empowered by the resurrection (see Matt 16:24; 28:19-20). These are not separate invitations. Rather, the resurrection offers both assurance for the difficult present and promise for the future. Inevitably, therefore, like the psalmist, Christians live by a power we cannot see (see v. 4)—we live by faith and by hope (see Rom 8:24-25; Heb 11:1). We live in fundamental dependence upon God, and so, despite appearances, we shall never be alone (John 14:18-19).

Living by a power that cannot be seen (v. 4) means that Christians have a unique epistemology, a unique way of knowing (see Commentary on Psalms 111; 119). For the world and perhaps especially in our scientifically oriented culture, "seeing is believing." But for us, as for the psalmist, the opposite is true—believing is seeing! Trusting God, we know and experience the very power of God (see John 20:29). Thus things are not as they appear. Apparent weakness is strength (see 1 Cor 1:25; 2 Cor 12:9), for instance, and those with no visible means of support actually have an ever-present refuge in God (v. 5) and in the community of God's people (v. 7).

This assurance, however, is not meant to be an excuse simply to dismiss the needy with pious reminders that their help is in God (see James 1:14-17). Most Christians are fortunate enough to have sufficient power and resources at their disposal so that they may never need to pray v. 4 literally. But this verse should be a reminder to us of the pain of the world, especially in places where plenty of persons are reduced to the status of non-persons. Psalm 142 affirms that God hears persons whom nobody else bothers to hear, and that God cares for those whom nobody else appears to care for (v. 4d)—the homeless, the destitute, the low, and the despised. In a nearly incomprehensible statement for most of us, Jesus even said, "Happy are you destitute, for yours is the kingdom of God" (Luke 6:20, author's trans.). This is no romanticizing of poverty. Rather, it is a powerful affirmation of what Psalm 142 also affirms: God helps those who cannot help themselves (see Commentary on Psalm 3)! From this perspective, Psalm 142 is ultimately a warning to the wealthy, the privileged, the self-sufficient. Although it may appear that they have no advocates at their "right hand" (see v. 4a), the needy find that God stands at their right hand (see Ps 109:31). This is precisely what the psalmist knew (v. 5), and her or his knowledge calls us to renounce self-sufficiency for dependence upon God, and thereby to renounce isolation from the needy for solidarity with the needy (which now includes us!). In short, Psalm 142 calls us "righteous" folk to "surround" and be surrounded by our needy brothers and sisters as a sign of our mutual dependence on God's bounty (v. 7cd).

PSALM 143:1-12, NO ONE LIVING IS RIGHTEOUS BEFORE YOU

NIV

Psalm 143

A psalm of David.

[1]O LORD, hear my prayer,
    listen to my cry for mercy;
in your faithfulness and righteousness
    come to my relief.
[2]Do not bring your servant into judgment,
    for no one living is righteous before you.

[3]The enemy pursues me,
    he crushes me to the ground;
he makes me dwell in darkness
    like those long dead.
[4]So my spirit grows faint within me;
    my heart within me is dismayed.

[5]I remember the days of long ago;
    I meditate on all your works
    and consider what your hands have done.
[6]I spread out my hands to you;
    my soul thirsts for you like a parched
        land.   *Selah*

[7]Answer me quickly, O LORD;
    my spirit fails.
Do not hide your face from me
    or I will be like those who go down to
        the pit.
[8]Let the morning bring me word of your
        unfailing love,
    for I have put my trust in you.
Show me the way I should go,
    for to you I lift up my soul.
[9]Rescue me from my enemies, O LORD,
    for I hide myself in you.
[10]Teach me to do your will,
    for you are my God;
may your good Spirit
    lead me on level ground.

[11]For your name's sake, O LORD, preserve my
        life;
    in your righteousness, bring me out of
        trouble.

NRSV

Psalm 143

A Psalm of David.

[1] Hear my prayer, O LORD;
    give ear to my supplications in your
        faithfulness;
    answer me in your righteousness.
[2] Do not enter into judgment with your
        servant,
    for no one living is righteous before you.

[3] For the enemy has pursued me,
    crushing my life to the ground,
    making me sit in darkness like those long
        dead.
[4] Therefore my spirit faints within me;
    my heart within me is appalled.

[5] I remember the days of old,
    I think about all your deeds,
    I meditate on the works of your hands.
[6] I stretch out my hands to you;
    my soul thirsts for you like a parched
        land.   *Selah*

[7] Answer me quickly, O LORD;
    my spirit fails.
Do not hide your face from me,
    or I shall be like those who go down to
        the Pit.
[8] Let me hear of your steadfast love in the
        morning,
    for in you I put my trust.
Teach me the way I should go,
    for to you I lift up my soul.

[9] Save me, O LORD, from my enemies;
    I have fled to you for refuge.[a]
[10] Teach me to do your will,
    for you are my God.
Let your good spirit lead me
    on a level path.

[a]One Heb Ms Gk: MT *to you I have hidden*

NIV

¹²In your unfailing love, silence my enemies;
    destroy all my foes,
for I am your servant.

NRSV

¹¹ For your name's sake, O LORD, preserve my
    life.
    In your righteousness bring me out of
    trouble.
¹² In your steadfast love cut off my enemies,
    and destroy all my adversaries,
    for I am your servant.

COMMENTARY

Linked literarily to Psalm 142, Psalm 143 joins Psalms 139–142 as the core of the Davidic collection, framed by Psalms 138 and 144–145. Its current placement means that Psalm 143 participates in the response of Book V to the exile and its aftermath (see Commentary on Psalms 107; 108; 138; 140; Introduction), but this is not to say that it originated with that purpose in mind. While Psalm 143 can be classified as an individual lament/complaint or prayer for help, the circumstances of its origin and original use are unknown. Because of the reference to "morning" in v. 8, some scholars have suggested that the psalm was prayed as part of a ritual that involved the psalmist's spending the night in the Temple to await God's answer. This remains speculative, however, and it is likely that the open-endedness of the imagery contributed to the use of Psalm 143 in a variety of ways and circumstances throughout the generations (see Reflections below).

As Allen points out, the pattern of some of the repetition in Psalm 143 suggests a division into two major sections: vv. 1-6 and vv. 7-12. For instance, "answer" occurs in v. 1 and again in v. 7; "not" occurs in vv. 2, 7; "before you"/"your face" (the same word in Hebrew) also occurs in vv. 2, 7; "in your righteousness" is found in vv. 1, 11; and "your servant" occurs in vv. 2, 12.[512] As the NIV and the NRSV suggest, these major sections can be subdivided. Verses 1-6 move from petition (vv. 1-2) to complaint (vv. 3-4) to a sort of profession of loyalty and desire for God (vv. 5-6). Verses 7-12 form an extended series of petitions. They may be treated as a single unit or divided into three parts (NRSV) or into two parts

(see the NIV's break after v. 10). Still another alternative is to construe the emphatic "you" in v. 10 and the emphatic "I" in v. 12 as an envelope structure, in which case the subdivisions are vv. 7-9 and vv. 10-12.

143:1-2. The requests to be heard in v. 1*ab* are typical (see "hear my prayer" in Ps 4:1; see "give ear" in Pss 5:1; 86:6; 140:6; 141:1). "Cry for mercy" (חנן *ḥānan*) in v. 1*b* (see Pss 28:2, 6; 31:22) already suggests that the psalmist's plea will be based on God's character. The underlying Hebrew root occurs as "gracious" in Exod 34:6—God's self-revelation to Moses—as does the root of "faithfulness" (אמן *'mn*). The phrase "in your righteousness" in v. 1*c* anticipates not only v. 12 but also v. 2. The words "righteous(ness)" and "justice" (v. 2 reads lit., "Do not enter into justice") often occur in the same context to indicate God's character in action—God's sovereign will (see Pss 89:14; 96:13; 97:2). What is striking about v. 2*a* is that the psalmist does not want justice! What she or he needs is mercy, because "no one living is righteous" (v. 2*b*). The theological implication is clear: In attempting to set things right among human beings, God's will must ultimately be manifested as grace. In prayers of complaint about pursuers, it is more frequently the case that the psalmist proclaims innocence or righteousness (see Psalms 17; 26). But this is not the case in v. 2, which Kraus characterizes as "most remarkable."[513] Interestingly, v. 2*b* is not the personal confession of sin one might expect following v. 2*a* but an appeal to the sinfulness of all humanity (see Ps 39:11; cf. 39:7; see also

512. Ibid., 283-84.

513. H.-J. Kraus, *Psalms 60–150: A Commentary,* trans. H. C. Oswald (Minneapolis: Augsburg, 1989) 536.

130:3). It later serves well Paul's argument in Rom 3:20 (see also Gal 2:16; Reflections below).

143:3-4. Verse 3 introduces two more terms that are repeated throughout the psalm: "enemy"/"enemies" (איב 'ōyēb; see vv. 9, 12) and "me"/"my" (נפש nepeš, vv. 3, 11-12; "soul" in vv. 6, 8), which means fundamentally "vitality," "life." In the light of v. 2, it seems that the general unrighteousness of humanity is manifested when some persons ("the enemy") threaten the lives of others (in this case, the psalmist). The psalmist has already identified herself or himself as a "servant" (v. 2; see also v. 12), and v. 3 makes it clear that the psalmist is a suffering servant, ("pursued"; see Ps 142:6) and, like the suffering servant in the book of Isaiah, crushed (see Isa 53:5, 10; see also Ps 94:5; Lam 3:34). The phrase "in darkness" also describes the condition of the people in exile in Isaiah 40–55 and Lamentations (see Isa 42:16; Lam 3:6), as does the verb "faints" (see Lam 2:11-12, 19; see above on Ps 142:3). As suggested above, this does not mean that Psalm 143 originated as a response to the exile or to conditions in the post-exilic era, but it does suggest that the post-exilic community could easily have found in Psalm 143 the language to articulate its complaint.

143:5-6. The language of vv. 5-6 clearly recalls Psalm 77, in which the psalmist also complains that "my spirit faints" (Pss 77:3; 143:4) and stretches his or her hands to God in the posture of prayer (Pss 77:2; 143:6; see also Exod 9:29, 33; Ps 141:2; Lam 1:17). There, too, the psalmist remembers (77:3, 11 NIV) and meditates (77:12 NIV) and considers (77:3, 12; the translation is "mused" in v. 3 NIV); as in Psalm 143, these activities are directed to "the days of old" (77:5; see Isa 63:9, 11) and to God's "works" (77:12) and to what God has "done"/"performs" (Ps 77:14; 143:5). The allusions are most likely to the exodus. Thus the psalmist's longing in v. 6b (see Ps 63:1) is for an analogous deliverance from deadly threats, and her or his prayer would have been and has been found to be appropriate amid a variety of crises, personal and corporate.

143:7-9. The first plea in v. 7 recalls v. 1 as it opens the second major section, and "spirit" recalls v. 4 (see "fails" in Pss 31:10; 73:26). Although the psalmist realizes that no living person is righteous before God's face (v. 2, "before

you"), she or he also pleads that God not hide God's face (see Pss 13:1; 22:24; 27:9; 69:17; 88:14; 102:2), lest she or he die (see Pss 28:1; 30:3). In other words, the psalmist obviously trusts that God is steadfastly loving, an attribute that means God shows compassion for the afflicted and willingness to forgive the sinful (see Exod 34:6-7; Pss 5:7; 13:5; 25:6-7, 10; 86:5, 13, 15; 138:2, 8; Introduction). Thus, although both sinful (v. 2) and afflicted (vv. 3-4), the psalmist can confidently entrust the whole self to this kind of God. The plea that God "teach me" (v. 8) is indicative of the psalmist's total dedication of the self to God, as is the statement that concludes v. 8. The verb translated "lift up" (נשא nāśāʾ) is used elsewhere of offering sacrifices, and the statement could also be translated "to you I offer my life." The same formulation also occurs in Pss 25:1; 86:4; just as in Psalm 143, so also in Psalms 25 and 86 the psalmist appeals to God's steadfast love (25:6-7, 10; 86:5, 13, 15) and prays to be taught by God (25:4-5; 86:11). The same depth of trust is expressed in v. 9, in which the petition is again followed by a statement of confidence. The NIV of v. 9b attempts to read the Hebrew more literally (see NRSV note), although the NRSV's "refuge" has some manuscript support and would certainly be appropriate in this context (see Pss 2:12; 5:11; 141:8; 142:5; Introduction).

143:10-12. As suggested above, these verses are set off by the complementary affirmations in vv. 10b and 12c (see Ps 86:2, 14, 16). Verse 10 begins with another request for God's teaching (the Hebrew verbs differ in vv. 8 and 10, as the NIV suggests). Because the psalmist belongs to God, she or he desires to know God's "will" (see Pss 40:8; 103:21) and to experience the leading (see Pss 23:3; 31:3; 73:24; 139:10) of God's "good spirit" (see Neh 9:20, where the "good spirit" also plays an educational role) toward "level ground" (see Pss 26:12; 27:11). As the beginning of v. 11 indicates again, the issue is fundamentally one of God's character (see Pss 23:3; 25:11). God is righteous (v. 11b) and steadfastly loving (v. 12), attributes that have already been mentioned in such a way as to demonstrate that they involve God's grace (see vv. 2, 8). As vv. 11-12 indicate, for God to set things right will involve both life for the psalmist (v. 11a; see Pss 80:18; 119:37, 77) and destruction of the enemies (v. 12; see Pss 1:6; 54:7; 73:27; 94:23; 101:5, 8). The psalmist's plea is not a matter of personal revenge but of God's will for righteousness and justice. The oppressors do not yield themselves as servants to God's will as the psalmist does (see vv. 2, 10, 12). Thus the psalmist's personal exodus (see "bring me out" in v. 11; Exod 18:1; 20:2) will necessarily involve the same treatment of oppressors as in Israel's exodus from Egypt—that is, their decision to cut themselves off from God and God's will means ultimately that they choose their own destruction (see Commentary on Psalms 58; 94; 139; 141).

In the final analysis, Psalm 143 demonstrates the tension that pervades the psalter and the whole Bible: God demands submission to God's will but is ultimately gracious (see Commentary on Psalms 99; 103). While the psalmist is well aware that she or he does not completely embody God's will (v. 2), the psalmist at least affirms that she or he belongs to God (v. 8) and is open to God's will and to God's guidance (vv. 8, 10). In a word, the psalmist sees herself or himself not as the master of her or his own destiny but as God's "servant" (v. 12c). To be God's "servant" is to profess to live finally by the grace of the Master.

REFLECTIONS

1. While the circumstances of its origin and original use are unknown, Psalm 143 provides an apt commentary on and prayer for use by post-exilic Israel. The exile, after all, was understood to be a result of the people's own sinfulness (see v. 2a). But the prophets proclaimed that Israel's sins had been forgiven (see Isa 40:1-4). Thus the protracted suffering of the people in the post-exilic era was viewed in terms of the disobedience of the nations, as evidence of the general unrighteousness of humankind (v. 2b). It is clear that the exile and its aftermath forced Israel to rethink many things, including the nature of suffering and sin and their complex interrelatedness (see Commentary on Psalms 44; 89).

2. While Psalm 143 seems to have assisted Israel to rethink and express its theology in the post-exilic era, it clearly served such a purpose for the apostle Paul. In Rom 3:20, Paul cites Ps 143:2 in support of his conclusion that all "are under the power of sin" (Rom 3:9 NRSV). For Paul, therefore, as for the psalmist, God's activity of setting things right—including the justification of humanity—is finally a manifestation of God's grace. Paul's insight, of course, led to a radical re-formation of the shape of the people of God. Not surprisingly, Psalm 143 later became one of the church's Penitential Psalms, a grouping that can perhaps be traced to Augustine (see Psalms 6; 32; 38; 51; 102; 130). While Psalm 143 does not contain a direct, personal confession of sin, it clearly does assert the sinfulness of humankind. It also eloquently articulates the basis for penitence: the conviction that God is steadfastly loving and that we can therefore offer our whole selves to God (v. 8). Such trust leads to transformed lives that are lived in openness to God's instruction (vv. 8, 10) and that manifest concretely the fruits of repentance. Not surprisingly again, Martin Luther's fresh hearing of the psalms, of Paul, and of Augustine contributed mightily to another radical re-formation of the shape of the people of God in the sixteenth century and beyond.

3. Psalm 143 is assigned for liturgical use as part of the Easter vigil. In this setting, the psalmist's example of suffering servanthood can be an apt and powerful reminder of the life, ministry, death, and resurrection of Jesus, as well as a reminder of Jesus' call for disciples to follow him by taking up their crosses. This kind of discipleship will be possible, however, only as we trust in the ultimate power of God that is manifested as faithful, forgiving love. As an embodiment of God's power and, indeed, God's very character and being, Jesus revealed the depth of God's love and the lengths that God is willing to go to on behalf of sinful humanity. The good news is that God is ultimately the exemplar of suffering servanthood!

In the face of such love, perhaps we may find the motivation and the courage to confront our own individual sinfulness and the corporate sinfulness of humankind. Both dimensions are important, but in our time and place, the latter is crucial. As Douglas John Hall points out: "Most people in the churches seem still, despite half a century of serious and critical reflection on the subject, to think of sin in rather crudely moralistic terms—in terms, to be explicit, of *private* morality, with special emphasis on private *sexual* morality."[514] Hall calls for the church to reexamine its tradition of thinking about sin, including rediscovery of the awareness of the corporate and tragic dimensions of human sinfulness. Our psalmist certainly knew of her or his shortcomings (v. 2*a*), but the psalmist also knew about the corporate sin of humankind (v. 2*b*). Perhaps the psalmist's prayer can begin to put us in touch with the terrible truth about ourselves in order that we may, like the psalmist, rest our case on the wonderful truth about God and God's amazing grace (see Commentary on Psalms 32; 51).

514. Douglas John Hall, *God and Human Suffering: An Exercise in the Theology of the Cross* (Minneapolis: Augsburg, 1986) 77-78.

PSALM 144:1-15, HAPPY ARE THE PEOPLE WHOSE GOD IS THE LORD

NIV

Psalm 144

Of David.

[1]Praise be to the LORD my Rock,
  who trains my hands for war,
  my fingers for battle.
[2]He is my loving God and my fortress,
  my stronghold and my deliverer,
 my shield, in whom I take refuge,
  who subdues peoples[a] under me.

[3]O LORD, what is man that you care for him,
  the son of man that you think of him?
[4]Man is like a breath;
  his days are like a fleeting shadow.

[5]Part your heavens, O LORD, and come down;
  touch the mountains, so that they smoke.
[6]Send forth lightning and scatter ⌊the enemies⌋;
  shoot your arrows and rout them.
[7]Reach down your hand from on high;
  deliver me and rescue me
 from the mighty waters,
  from the hands of foreigners
[8]whose mouths are full of lies,

a2 Many manuscripts of the Masoretic Text, Dead Sea Scrolls, Aquila, Jerome and Syriac; most manuscripts of the Masoretic Text subdues my people

NRSV

Psalm 144

Of David.

[1] Blessed be the LORD, my rock,
  who trains my hands for war, and my
    fingers for battle;
[2] my rock[a] and my fortress,
  my stronghold and my deliverer,
 my shield, in whom I take refuge,
  who subdues the peoples[b] under me.

[3] O LORD, what are human beings that you
    regard them,
  or mortals that you think of them?
[4] They are like a breath;
  their days are like a passing shadow.

[5] Bow your heavens, O LORD, and come down;
  touch the mountains so that they smoke.
[6] Make the lightning flash and scatter them;
  send out your arrows and rout them.
[7] Stretch out your hand from on high;
  set me free and rescue me from the
    mighty waters,

a With 18.2 and 2 Sam 22.2: Heb my steadfast love
b Heb Mss Syr Aquila Jerome: MT my people

NIV

⁹I will sing a new song to you, O God;
   on the ten-stringed lyre I will make music
      to you,
¹⁰to the One who gives victory to kings,
   who delivers his servant David from the
      deadly sword.

¹¹Deliver me and rescue me
   from the hands of foreigners
whose mouths are full of lies,
   whose right hands are deceitful.

¹²Then our sons in their youth
   will be like well-nurtured plants,
and our daughters will be like pillars
   carved to adorn a palace.
¹³Our barns will be filled
   with every kind of provision.
Our sheep will increase by thousands,
   by tens of thousands in our fields;
¹⁴   our oxen will draw heavy loads.ᵃ
There will be no breaching of walls,
   no going into captivity,
   no cry of distress in our streets.

¹⁵Blessed are the people of whom this is true;
   blessed are the people whose God is the
      LORD.

a14 Or our chieftains will be firmly established

NRSV

   from the hand of aliens,
⁸ whose mouths speak lies,
   and whose right hands are false.

⁹ I will sing a new song to you, O God;
   upon a ten-stringed harp I will play to
      you,
¹⁰ the one who gives victory to kings,
   who rescues his servant David.
¹¹ Rescue me from the cruel sword,
   and deliver me from the hand of aliens,
whose mouths speak lies,
   and whose right hands are false.

¹² May our sons in their youth
   be like plants full grown,
our daughters like corner pillars,
   cut for the building of a palace.
¹³ May our barns be filled,
   with produce of every kind;
may our sheep increase by thousands,
   by tens of thousands in our fields,
¹⁴   and may our cattle be heavy with young.
May there be no breach in the walls,ᵃ no
      exile,
   and no cry of distress in our streets.

¹⁵ Happy are the people to whom such
      blessings fall;
   happy are the people whose God is the
      LORD.

a Heb lacks in the walls

COMMENTARY

Psalm 144 has proved to be quite an enigma to form critics. Because of the numerous similarities to Psalm 18 (cf. vv. 1-2 to Ps 18:1-2, 34, 46-47; v. 5 to Ps 18:9; v. 6 to Ps 18:14; v. 7 to Ps 18:16, 44-45; and v. 10 to the superscription of Psalm 18), Psalm 144 has traditionally been categorized as a royal psalm. At the same time, however, form critics have recognized that this label really does not fit. In particular, the shift from singular to plural speaker in vv. 12-14 is anomalous if Psalm 144 were intended for actual use as a liturgy for kings.

What is puzzling and problematic from a form-critical perspective, however, makes more sense when one considers the placement of Psalm 144 within the psalter. As the final Davidic collection in the psalter (Psalms 138–145) draws to a close, Psalm 144 offers, in effect, a rereading of Psalm 18. It is significant that this rereading reflects the realities of the exile and its aftermath. This is especially the case in vv. 12-14, but this perspective is reinforced by the fact that Ps 144:5-7 has transformed the affirmations of Ps 18:9, 14, 16, 44-45 into petitions. It is particularly noticeable that the "aliens" (בני־נכר *běnê-nēkār,* vv. 7, 11) whom God had dealt with on the king's behalf in Ps 18:44-45 are precisely the problem in Psalm 144. Again, this situation accurately portrays the perennial reality of the post-exilic era (see the same Hebrew term in Neh 9:2; Isa 56:3, 6; 60:10; 61:5; 62:8; Ezek 44:7, 9). As Mays concludes concerning the use in Psalm 144 of Ps 18:44-45: "The composer of Psalm 144 must have found in these verses a promise for his own time . . . . By re-praying Psalm 18 in a new version, he appealed to the LORD to do for his people what the LORD had done for his servant David."[515] As Mays implies, and as Allen also asserts, Psalm 144 reflects a situation in which the Davidic monarchy had disappeared and in which the promises formerly attached to the monarchy had been transferred to the people as a whole (see Isa 55:3-5 and Commentary on Psalms 105; 110; 132; 149; Introduction).[516]

The perspective of Psalm 144 is thus congruent with that of Books IV-V, which respond to the failure of the Davidic covenant that is articulated in the concluding psalm of Book III, Psalm 89 (see above on Psalms 89; 90; 107; Introduction). In the face of the failure of human monarchs, the people realized that their true and ultimate hope lay in God's sovereignty. Thus, it is not surprising that the phrase "new song" in v. 9 recalls Psalms 96 and 98, both of which explicitly proclaim God's reign. But v. 9 even more clearly recalls Ps 33:2*b*-3*a.* Furthermore, v. 15*b* recalls Ps 33:12*a.* Psalm 33 also asserts God's sovereign claim over all the world and its peoples; and in view of the re-reading of Psalm 18 in Psalm 144, it is not surprising to find these recollections of another psalm from Book I. Indeed, there is still at least one more clear indication that the psalmist was re-reading Book I—namely, v. 3 recalls Ps 8:4. The answer in v. 4 to the question in v. 3 obviously departs from the direction of Psalm 8, but it is very much in keeping with exilic and post-exilic expressions of the awareness of the transience of human life (see Isa 40:6-8). Not coincidentally perhaps, Ps 89:47-48 also articulate an awareness of human transience as the prelude to an appeal for God's help. The same movement

is present in Psalm 144, where vv. 3-4 are followed by the petitions of vv. 5-8.

The implicit affirmation of God's sovereignty in Psalm 144 is followed by the explicit affirmation in Ps 145:1, which addresses God as "King." Thus, it seems that Psalms 144–145 form a pair which participates with Psalm 138 in framing the prayers in Psalms 139–143 that form the core of the final Davidic collection in the Psalter (see above on Psalm 138). The effect is to highlight the appropriateness of the individual prayers in Psalms 139–143 for expressing the communal plight of the exilic and post-exilic eras.

144:1-11. As suggested above, the shift of persons in v. 12 serves to divide Psalm 144 into two major sections (see NRSV). As NRSV indicates, it makes sense to further divide vv. 1-11 into sections of praise (vv. 1-2), reflection (vv. 3-4), petition (vv. 5-8), and further praise and petition (vv. 9-10). NIV and NRSV disagree on the construal of the role of v. 11. As I have suggested, NRSV takes it as the conclusion to the first major section; but NIV interprets v. 11 as a petition which initiates the second major section of the psalm. The NIV's construal apparently envisions the speaker in vv. 11-14 as an imaginary Davidic descendent (see above on Ps 89:46-51). In any case, the situation presupposed is still the one which prevailed in the post-exilic era.

As suggested above, vv. 1-2 recall Ps 18:1-2, 34, 46-47. The major departure from the vocabulary of Psalm 18 is the first word in v. 2—"my steadfast love" (חסד *hesed;* see NRSV note). NIV has stayed with the Hebrew at this point, but NRSV has chosen to harmonize Ps 144:2 with Ps 18:2. This choice is understandable, but the NIV is to be preferred. After all, the psalmist's use of Psalm 18 is not slavish. The word "steadfast love" represents a creative departure from Psalm 18; and it both recalls the occurrences of "steadfast love" in Psalm 138 (vv. 2, 8) and anticipates the occurrence in Psalm 145 (v. 8). Thus, the three psalms that frame the core of the Davidic collection (Psalms 139–143) all contain the word "steadfast love" (see also Ps 143:8, 12), effectively linking the collection to the beginning of Book V (see Pss 107:1, 8, 15, 21, 31, 43; 108:4; 109:12, 16, 21, 26; Introduction). The word "refuge" in v. 2 links Psalm 144 to the core of the Davidic collection (see Pss 141:8; 142:5), and it also

515. James L. Mays, *Psalms,* Interpretation (Louisville: John Knox, 1994) 436.
516. Leslie C. Allen, *Psalms 101–150,* WBC 21 (Waco: Word, 1983) 290.

represents what is a key word from the beginning and throughout the Psalter (see Ps 2:12; Introduction). Psalm 2 is also a royal psalm which proclaims God's sovereignty over "the peoples" (Ps 2:1).

But Psalm 2 also recognizes that "the peoples" and their rulers are rebellious, and the transition from vv. 1-2 to vv. 3-4 of Psalm 144 suggests that the rebellious peoples have clearly gained the upper hand. Verses 3-4 recall not Psalm 2 but Psalm 89, another royal psalm but one which recounts the rejection of the Davidic line (see Ps 89:38-51, especially vv. 46-48). Thus, the affirmations found in yet another royal psalm, Psalm 18, have become petitions in Ps 144:5-7 (cf. Ps 18:9, 14, 16, 44-45). The allusions to Psalm 18 in Ps 144:5-7 are drawn from the theophany section (Ps 18:7-15) and from descriptions of the king's deliverance from threat, including "foreigners" or "aliens" (Pss 18:44-45; cf. 144:7, 11). In effect, Psalm 144 requests a new divine appearance and a new deliverance, to which the proper response will be a "new song" (v. 9). Verses 9-10 indicate that the post-exilic community has not given up on the sovereignty of God, despite the dominance of those who are their enemies and God's enemies. As is the case from the beginning and throughout the psalter, the perspective is eschatological; that is, the sovereignty of God is asserted and trusted amid circumstances that seem to deny it (see above on Psalms 2; 65–67; 93; 95–99; 138; Introduction).

144:12-15. The people are left in waiting, anticipating the fulfillment described in vv. 12-14 (see Deut 8:12-13; 28:4). Verse 15 reinforces the conclusion suggested above that Psalm 144 represents a re-reading of Psalm 18 that applies to the whole people the promises formerly attached to the Davidic dynasty. Verse 15 also indicates that happiness is a present possibility even as the people await deliverance, for happiness ultimately involves belonging to God. Not coincidentally, Psalm 33, to which Ps 144:15 alludes (cf. 144:15*b* with 33:12*a*), also leaves the people hoping and waiting (see 33:18-22), as well as praying for God's steadfast love (33:22; see Ps 144:2). The double beatitude in v. 15 also recalls Pss 1:1; 2:12. Amid the existence and apparent prosperity of the wicked, true happiness involves an openness to God that seeks and finds refuge in the sovereign God.

REFLECTIONS

1. Although Psalm 144 would have had special relevance to the post-exilic community, it portrays the position which the people of God perpetually occupy. Like the psalmist, Jesus accompanied his proclamation of God's reign with the announcement that even now happiness belongs to the poor and the persecuted (see Matt 5:3-12). Such happiness consists fundamentally of recognizing God's sovereignty and accepting the invitation to live in the new world of God's reign—that is, of belonging to God. We continue to announce God's claim upon the world amid circumstances that seem to deny it. In short we continue to live eschatologically—in waiting.

2. The process of the composition of Psalm 144 has theological significance. As Mays concludes concerning Psalm 144:

> This psalm, then, is an illustration of the practice of using psalms to compose hymns and prayers, combining earlier material into new compositions for new needs .... Revising the material of Psalms for new hymns and prayers is a practice that continues to this day. By it the power and beauty of psalmic material continuously make a canonical contribution to worship.[517]

Psalm 144 is thus an invitation to treat the Psalms not as historical artifacts but as living words which can continue both to address us with God's claim upon our lives and our world and to express our hopes and fears, our praises and prayers.

517. Mays, *Psalms,* 437.

PSALM 145:1-21, GOD IS GREAT AND GOOD

<table>
<tr><td>

NIV

Psalm 145[a]

A psalm of praise. Of David.

[1] I will exalt you, my God the King;
I will praise your name for ever and ever.
[2] Every day I will praise you
and extol your name for ever and ever.

[3] Great is the LORD and most worthy of praise;
his greatness no one can fathom.
[4] One generation will commend your works to
another;
they will tell of your mighty acts.
[5] They will speak of the glorious splendor of
your majesty,
and I will meditate on your wonderful
works.[b]
[6] They will tell of the power of your awesome
works,
and I will proclaim your great deeds.
[7] They will celebrate your abundant goodness
and joyfully sing of your righteousness.

[8] The LORD is gracious and compassionate,
slow to anger and rich in love.
[9] The LORD is good to all;
he has compassion on all he has made.
[10] All you have made will praise you, O LORD;
your saints will extol you.
[11] They will tell of the glory of your kingdom
and speak of your might,
[12] so that all men may know of your mighty acts
and the glorious splendor of your kingdom.
[13] Your kingdom is an everlasting kingdom,
and your dominion endures through all
generations.

The LORD is faithful to all his promises
and loving toward all he has made.[c]
[14] The LORD upholds all those who fall
and lifts up all who are bowed down.

</td><td>

NRSV

Psalm 145

Praise. Of David.

[1] I will extol you, my God and King,
and bless your name forever and ever.
[2] Every day I will bless you,
and praise your name forever and ever.
[3] Great is the LORD, and greatly to be praised;
his greatness is unsearchable.

[4] One generation shall laud your works to
another,
and shall declare your mighty acts.
[5] On the glorious splendor of your majesty,
and on your wondrous works, I will
meditate.
[6] The might of your awesome deeds shall be
proclaimed,
and I will declare your greatness.
[7] They shall celebrate the fame of your
abundant goodness,
and shall sing aloud of your
righteousness.

[8] The LORD is gracious and merciful,
slow to anger and abounding in steadfast
love.
[9] The LORD is good to all,
and his compassion is over all that he
has made.

[10] All your works shall give thanks to you,
O LORD,
and all your faithful shall bless you.
[11] They shall speak of the glory of your
kingdom,
and tell of your power,
[12] to make known to all people your[a] mighty
deeds,
and the glorious splendor of your[b]
kingdom.
[13] Your kingdom is an everlasting kingdom,
and your dominion endures throughout
all generations.

</td></tr>
</table>

[a] This psalm is an acrostic poem, the verses of which (including verse 13b) begin with the successive letters of the Hebrew alphabet.
[b] 5 Dead Sea Scrolls and Syriac (see also Septuagint); Masoretic Text *On the glorious splendor of your majesty / and on your wonderful works I will meditate* [c] 13 One manuscript of the Masoretic Text, Dead Sea Scrolls and Syriac (see also Septuagint); most manuscripts of the Masoretic Text do not have the last two lines of verse 13.

[a] Gk Jerome Syr: Heb *his* [b] Heb *his*

NIV

¹⁵The eyes of all look to you,
and you give them their food at the proper
time.
¹⁶You open your hand
and satisfy the desires of every living thing.

¹⁷The LORD is righteous in all his ways
and loving toward all he has made.
¹⁸The LORD is near to all who call on him,
to all who call on him in truth.
¹⁹He fulfills the desires of those who fear him;
he hears their cry and saves them.
²⁰The LORD watches over all who love him,
but all the wicked he will destroy.

²¹My mouth will speak in praise of the LORD.
Let every creature praise his holy name
for ever and ever.

NRSV

The LORD is faithful in all his words,
and gracious in all his deeds.ᵃ
¹⁴ The LORD upholds all who are falling,
and raises up all who are bowed down.
¹⁵ The eyes of all look to you,
and you give them their food in due
season.
¹⁶ You open your hand,
satisfying the desire of every living thing.
¹⁷ The LORD is just in all his ways,
and kind in all his doings.
¹⁸ The LORD is near to all who call on him,
to all who call on him in truth.
¹⁹ He fulfills the desire of all who fear him;
he also hears their cry, and saves them.
²⁰ The LORD watches over all who love him,
but all the wicked he will destroy.

²¹ My mouth will speak the praise of the LORD,
and all flesh will bless his holy name
forever and ever.

ᵃ These two lines supplied by Q Ms Gk Syr

COMMENTARY

Psalm 145 is the only psalm identified by its superscription as "Praise" (NRSV). This uniqueness is appropriate, since Psalm 145 concludes the final Davidic collection in the Psalter (see above on Psalm 138). It is even possible that the Psalter originally ended with Psalm 145. But even as the Psalter now stands, Psalm 145 is, in the words of Gerald Wilson, "the 'climax' of the fifth book of the Psalter, with the final *hallel* (Pss 146–150) drawing its impetus from 145:21."[518] Given the apparent intention of Book V to address the crisis of exile and its aftermath (see above on Psalms 107–108; Introduction), and given the post-exilic perspective reflected in Psalm 144, it is especially significant that this climactic psalm features from its beginning the kingship of the Lord (see NIV, which translates v. 1a more accurately). In so doing, it not only recalls the theological heart of the psalter in Book IV (see above on Psalms 93–99; Introduction); but it also, as Wilson sug-

gests, anticipates the explicit proclamation of God's reign in Pss 146:10; 149:2. In view of the disappearance of the monarchy and the accompanying theological crisis, it is highly significant that this climactic Davidic psalm asserts God's comprehensive sovereignty in such an emphatic way.

The proclamation of God's sovereignty is made emphatic by the fourfold repetition of the Hebrew root of "king" (מלך *mlk,* v. 1) in vv. 11-13. In fact, in the Hebrew word order, the word "kingdom" (מלכות *malkût*) occurs three times in succession—once at the end of v. 12 and twice at the beginning of v. 13. This repetition is particularly noticeable since it occurs near the center of the poem. In fact, Barnabas Lindars suggests that vv. 10-13 form the central panel of Psalm 145 (see below). This means that vv. 11, 12, and 13a are the central poetic lines. Reading from the bottom upward, the first Hebrew letters of each of these poetic lines combine to spell מלך (*mlk*), the Hebrew root from which the words "king"

518. Gerald H. Wilson, *The Editing of the Hebrew Psalter,* SBLDS 76 (Chico, Calif.: Scholars Press, 1985) 225.

(*melek*) and "kingdom" (*malkût*) are derived.[519] While this circumstance may be coincidental, it was probably intended by the clever poet who carefully structured Psalm 145. Its effect is to further emphasize the message that God is king.

That the poet intended to structure Psalm 145 carefully is suggested by its acrostic pattern (see above on Psalms 25; 34; 37; 111; 112; 119). The major Hebrew textual tradition does not contain a poetic line beginning with the letter *nûn* (נ, "n," a circumstance that would have called attention to the *mlk* sequence mentioned above), but both NIV and NRSV have supplied the missing line as v. 13*b* on the basis of strong manuscript evidence, including the appearance of the *nûn* line in a Hebrew text from Qumran (see NIV and NRSV notes). The acrostic pattern also serves to reinforce the message of Psalm 145. It suggests completeness or comprehensiveness, and thus it is appropriate for a psalm which proclaims and praises God's comprehensive sovereignty. In this regard too, it is significant that the word "all"/"every" occurs seventeen times!

While the acrostic pattern is the most obvious structural feature of Psalm 145, it is likely that other features also exist that serve to divide the psalm into sections. The traditional observation has been that Psalm 145 is composed of four sections: vv. 1-3, vv. 4-9, vv. 10-13*a*, vv. 13*b*-21. In this view, the first three sections consist of announcements of praise (vv. 1-2, 4-7, 10-12) followed by descriptions of God's character (vv. 3, 8-9, 13*a*). The final section reverses this pattern. An extended description of God's character (vv. 13*b*-20) is followed by a brief but climactic announcement of praise (v. 21). This proposal has the advantage of identifying clearly the alternation between praise and reasons for praise, and it also calls attention to the expansive progression in the first three sections from the individual psalmist's praise (vv. 1-2) to the praise of "All your works" (v. 10 NRSV). This movement is highlighted also in v. 21, which combines the perspective of the individual with that of "all flesh" (NRSV).

Attention to other features of Psalm 145, however, yields a different structural proposal. Lindars, for instance, notes the repetition which links vv. 1-2, 21 (see "bless" in vv. 1-2, 21 NRSV; "praise"

in vv. 2, 21 NRSV; "forever and ever" in vv. 1, 21); and he concludes that these verse stand apart as a framework for the psalm. Verse 3 then belongs with vv. 4-6, and the words "Great" (v. 3) and "greatness" (vv. 3, 6 NRSV) form an envelope for this section. The words "goodness" (v. 7) and "good" (v. 9) do the same thing for vv. 7-9. The central section consists of vv. 10-13; it is bounded by a double envelope (see NRSV "works" and "deeds," which translate the same Hebrew word; see also "faithful" in v. 10 and "gracious" in v. 13 NRSV, which translate the same Hebrew root). The beginning of the central section is tied to the framework of the poem by means of the repetition of "bless" (NRSV), and this section features the concept of kingship which is introduced in v. 1 (see above). According to Lindars, vv. 14-16 form a three-line section corresponding to vv. 7-9, and v. 17-20 form a four-line section corresponding to vv. 3-6, thus providing symmetry for the poem and focusing attention toward the center.[520] Lindars's proposal and the traditional proposal need not be considered as mutually exclusive. Rather, it is possible to view the structure and movement of Psalm 145 on more than one level. Each proposal highlights different, but equally important, aspects of the poem.

145:1-6. The word "praise" (תהלה *tĕhillâ*) in the title sets the tone for the whole psalm (see vv. 2-3, 21). As the psalmist addresses "my God the King" (v. 1 NIV), he or she announces three actions, each of which communicates the recognition of God's sovereignty: "extol"/"exalt" (see Exod 15:2 in relation to 15:18; Ps 99:5, 9), "bless" (NRSV; see Ps 96:2 in relation to 96:10), and "praise" (see Ps 22:26 in relation to 22:28 where the NRSV's "dominion" is from the same root as "King"/"kingdom" in 145:1, 11-13). The mention of God's "name" in vv. 1-2 anticipates the attention which will subsequently be directed to God's character (vv. 3, 8-9), including God's activity (see "works"/"made"/"deeds"/"doings" in vv. 4, 9, 10, 13, 17 NRSV; "fulfills" in v. 19 also translates the same Hebrew root).

The attribute of greatness is regularly associated with God's reign (vv. 3, 6; see Pss 47:2; 95:3; 99:2 and especially 48:1; 96:4). So are the words

519. Barnabas Lindars, "The Structure of Psalm CXLV," *VT* 29 (1989) 26-28.

520. Ibid., 25-29.

in the phrase "glorious splendor of your majesty" in v. 5 (see vv. 11-12; the same three words occur in Ps 96:6-7 as the NRSV's "honor," "majesty," and "glory"). While God's greatness is finally "unsearchable" (NRSV; see Job 5:9; 9:10; 36:26; Isa 40:28), there is much that can be seen and understood—God's "works" (vv. 4, 9, 10, 13, 17, 19; see above), "mighty acts" (see "mighty" and "mighty acts" in vv. 11-12 NIV; and see Pss 106:2; 150:2), "wondrous works" (v. 5 NRSV; see Exod 3:20; 15:11; Pss 9:1; 26:7; 77:11, 14; 78:4; 106:22), and "awesome deeds" (v. 6 NRSV; see Exod 15:11; Pss 47:2; 66:3, 5; 68:35; 76:7; 106:22). As is always the case, the reality of God's reign is good news that must be and is communicated (see NRSV "declare" in v. 4; "meditate," which can also connote telling, in v. 5; "tell" in vv. 6, 11 NIV; "proclaim" in v. 6 NIV; "speak" in vv. 11, 21 NIV; "make known" in v. 12 NRSV).

145:7-9. God's activity reveals God's character, to which vv. 7-9 direct attention. NRSV "fame" (v. 7) is more literally "remembrance"; it is associated elsewhere with God's activity and character (see NRSV "name" in Pss 30:4; 97:12; "renown" in 111:4). As in God's revelation to Moses, so here God's goodness (vv. 7, 9; see Exod 33:19; Pss 25:7; 27:13; 100:5; 106:1; 107:1; 118:1) takes the form of grace, mercy/compassion, and steadfast love (vv. 8-9; see Exod 34:6-7; Pss 25:6-7; 86:15; 103:8; Introduction). In short, it is God's gracious love which finally yields "righteousness" (v. 7), one of the hallmarks of God's reign (see Pss 89:14; 96:13; 97:2; 98:9; 99:4). The repeated "compassionate" in vv. 8-9 (NIV) underscores the astounding message—God's power is manifest as motherly love (see above on Psalm 25; 131). The two occurrences of "all" in v. 9 anticipate the expansive perspective of vv. 10-21, which contain fourteen more occurrences of "all"/"every" (see above).

145:10-13. The psalmist and the generations are joined by "All your works" in expressing thankful praise (v. 10; see Psalm 148). This is only appropriate, since "all" God "has made" has been the recipient of God's motherly compassion (v. 9; "made" in v. 9 and "works" in v. 10 are the same Hebrew word). The experience of God's gracious love produces witnesses to God's sovereignty, to God's particular way of exercising power. The word "kingdom" occurs four times in

vv. 11-13. God's sovereignty is central both structurally and theologically (see above). Its spatial and temporal reach is unlimited (vv. 12-13a; see Dan 4:3). Its character is unwavering; in word and deed, God's power is manifest as faithful love (v. 13b; NRSV's "faithful" and "gracious" represent the Hebrew roots behind the word-pair "steadfast love and faithfulness" in Exod 34:6; see Introduction).

145:14-20. These verses provide concrete illustrations of the divine activity which reveals God's grace, compassion, and love. In this sense, Lindars is correct to correlate vv. 14-16 with vv. 7-9 and vv. 17-20 with vv. 3-6; however, vv. 14-20 lack the verbal clues that would clearly distinguish vv. 14-16 from vv. 17-20. But Lindars admits that throughout Psalm 145, the sections overlap. In this case, for instance, vv. 14-16 and vv. 18-20 seem to surround the central v. 17, in which "righteous" (NIV) recalls v. 7 and "loving" (NIV) recalls vv. 8, 10, and 13b. In any case, vv. 14-17 assert that God shows steadfast love by upholding or sustaining the threatened (v. 14a; see Pss 3:5; 37:17, 24; 54:4), by lifting up the oppressed (v. 14b; see Ps 146:8), and by providing for all creatures (vv. 15-16; see Ps 104:27-28). Without contradicting this universalistic perspective, vv. 18-20 focus more narrowly on those who explicitly recognize God's sovereignty—those who "call on" (v. 18), "fear" (v. 19a; see 22:23; 25:12, 14; 103:11, 13, 17; 112:1), "cry" to (v. 19b; see Exod 2:23; Pss 18:6; 34:15; 39:12; 40:1), and "love" God (v. 20a; see Pss 31:23; 116:1). They will experience God's presence (v. 18; see Pss 34:18; 75:1), provision (v. 19), and protection (v. 20a; see NRSV "keep" in Ps 121:3-5, 7-8).

In short, those who acknowledge God's sovereignty experience salvation or life (v. 19b; see above on Ps 3:2, 7-8), while the wicked are destroyed (v. 20b). Verse 20b in particular seems to contradict v. 9 and the universalistic perspective of vv. 10-17. The sharp distinction between the wicked and those who love God recalls Psalm 1, and what applies to Psalm 1 applies to Psalm 145 as well. That is, the happiness or prosperity of the righteous (see Ps 1:1, 3) is not so much a reward as it is their experience of being connected to the true source of life—God. Similarly, the destruction of the wicked is not so much a punishment as it is the result of their own choice to cut themselves off from the source of life. The compassionate God does not will to destroy the wicked (see Ps 145:9), but their own autonomy leads to their ruin (see above on Psalms 1–2).

145:21. The psalmist's choice is clear. She or he "will speak the praise of the LORD" (v. 21*a* NRSV; see the superscription and vv. 2-3). It is the vocation that the psalmist envisions for "all flesh" (v. 21*b* NRSV). Thus v. 21 prepares for the crescendo of praise which follows in Psalms 146–150, culminating in the similar verse which concludes the psalter (150:6). To praise God—that is, to acknowledge one's own insufficiency and the sovereignty of God's loving purposes—is ultimately the only mode of being that truly constitutes life (see Commentary on Psalms 8; 100; 103–104).

REFLECTIONS

As Mays points out concerning Psalm 145, "the Talmud showed its estimate of the psalm's worth by saying, 'Every one who repeats the *Tehillah* of David thrice a day may be sure that he is a child of the world to come' (*Berakot*, 4b)."[521] To repeat Psalm 145 is to confess the insufficiency of self and the sovereignty of God. It is, in a real sense, to live in a different world—not in an escapist sense, but in the sense that God's claims, values, and priorities inevitably put us at odds with a prevailing culture that promotes autonomy (see Commentary on Psalms 1; 2). In other words, Psalm 145 invites us to live in the world of God's reign, the world where the fundamental reality and pervasive power is the gracious, compassionate, faithful love of God. It is to life in this world that Jesus also invites his followers, reminding them that the decision to enter involves repentance (Mark 1:14-15) and the denial of self in order to experience true self-fulfillment (Mark 8:34-35). As Jesus reminds his followers, and as Psalm 145 also asserts, the world of God's reign is a topsy-turvy world where the poor and the persecuted are happy, where the humble are exalted, and where the last are first (see Ps 145:14-20; Matt 5:3-11; Mark 8:33-37; 10:41-45; Luke 18:9-14). To live in this world is to live eschatologically (see Commentary on Psalms 2; 93; 95; 96; 97; 98; 99); amid the wicked and their opposition to God (see v. 20*b*), those who love God dare to live by God's claim, under God's watchful care, and into God's promising future.

Not only do classical Jewish sources recognize the value of Psalm 145, but so do Christian ones. Augustine, for instance, opens his *Confessions* by quoting Ps 145:3 (see also Pss 48:1; 96:4). In his opening paragraph, Augustine claims that because human beings are God's creation, they cannot experience contentment apart from praising God, "because you made us for yourself and our hearts find no peace until they rest in you."[522] As Augustine recognized, the psalmist knew this great truth; and Psalm 145 invites us and "all flesh" to know it as well. What's more, Psalm 145 invites us to live by this truth, and to join all creation in making known to all people the good news that God's power is manifest in gracious, compassionate love (vv. 7-13; see Matt 28:18-20, John 17:20-23, and above on Psalms 8, 100, 103 104, 117).

521. James L. Mays, *Psalms*, Interpretation (Louisville: John Knox, 1994) 437.
522. Augustine, *Confessions*, trans. R. S. Pine-Coffin (New York: Penguin Books, 1979) 21.

PSALM 146:1-10, JUSTICE FOR THE OPPRESSED

<table>
<tr><td>

NIV

Psalm 146

[1]Praise the LORD.[a]

Praise the LORD, O my soul.
[2] I will praise the LORD all my life;
    I will sing praise to my God as long as I
        live.

[3]Do not put your trust in princes,
    in mortal men, who cannot save.
[4]When their spirit departs, they return to the
        ground;
    on that very day their plans come to
        nothing.

[5]Blessed is he whose help is the God of Jacob,
    whose hope is in the LORD his God,
[6]the Maker of heaven and earth,
    the sea, and everything in them—
    the LORD, who remains faithful forever.
[7]He upholds the cause of the oppressed
    and gives food to the hungry.
The LORD sets prisoners free,
[8] the LORD gives sight to the blind,
the LORD lifts up those who are bowed down,
    the LORD loves the righteous.
[9]The LORD watches over the alien
    and sustains the fatherless and the widow,
    but he frustrates the ways of the wicked.

[10]The LORD reigns forever,
    your God, O Zion, for all generations.

Praise the LORD.

[a]1 Hebrew *Hallelu Yah*; also in verse 10

</td><td>

NRSV

Psalm 146

[1] Praise the LORD!
    Praise the LORD, O my soul!
[2] I will praise the LORD as long as I live;
    I will sing praises to my God all my life
        long.

[3] Do not put your trust in princes,
    in mortals, in whom there is no help.
[4] When their breath departs, they return to
        the earth;
    on that very day their plans perish.

[5] Happy are those whose help is the God of
        Jacob,
    whose hope is in the LORD their God,
[6] who made heaven and earth,
    the sea, and all that is in them;
who keeps faith forever;
[7] who executes justice for the oppressed;
    who gives food to the hungry.

The LORD sets the prisoners free;
[8] the LORD opens the eyes of the blind.
The LORD lifts up those who are bowed
        down;
    the LORD loves the righteous.
[9] The LORD watches over the strangers;
    he upholds the orphan and the widow,
    but the way of the wicked he brings to
        ruin.

[10] The LORD will reign forever,
    your God, O Zion, for all generations.
Praise the LORD!

</td></tr>
</table>

COMMENTARY

Psalm 146 is the first in a series of hymns or songs of praise (Psalms 146–150), all opening and closing with "Praise the LORD!" (*Hallelu-yah*), that brings the book of Psalms to a conclusion with a crescendo of praise. Psalm 145, especially v. 21, has prepared for Psalms 146–150, including an-

ticipation of several themes that are present in Psalm 146 as well as in Psalms 147–150. For instance, like Psalm 145, Psalm 146 recalls both the beginning of the psalter (Psalms 1–2) and the theological heart of the psalter (Psalms 93; 95–99). In particular, Psalm 146 is explicitly instructional (vv. 3-5), recalling Psalm 1, which orients the reader to hear the entire collection as *torah*, "instruction" (Ps 1:2; NIV and NRSV, "law"). The content of the instruction in Psalm 146 is essentially the same as that of Psalm 2: Trust God, not human rulers. Because human rulers and their plans perish (v. 4; see also Pss 1:6; 2:12), "happy" are those who entrust their lives to God (v. 5; see also Pss 1:1; 2:12). The message of Psalm 2 anticipates the theological heart of the psalter: The Lord reigns (see Psalms 93; 95–99; Introduction); thus it is not surprising that this message is echoed clearly at the conclusion of the psalter, including Ps 146:10 (see also Pss 145:1, 11-13; 149:2). The contrast between "the righteous" (v. 8) and "the way of the wicked" (v. 9) also explicitly recalls Ps 1:5-6. This contrast pervades the psalter (see Commentary on Psalms 1–2; Introduction), and again, it is not surprising that it is clearly echoed as the psalter concludes (see also Pss 145:20; 147:6; and the same contrast presented in different terms in 149:5-9).

The NIV's divisions reflect the traditional structural analysis of Psalm 146. Following the initial *hallelu-yah*, vv. 1-2 introduce the psalm by both inviting and announcing praise. Verses 3-4 offer instruction concerning what praise means: exclusive loyalty to and trust in God rather than human rulers. The beatitude in v. 5 initiates a section that continues with an extended series of participial phrases (vv. 6-9a) and is rounded off by a return to finite verb forms in v. 9bc. The NRSV's division between v. 7ab and v. 7c marks the point where the participles begin to be accompanied by a subject, "the LORD" (vv. 7c-9a). Returning to the political vocabulary of vv. 3-4 (see "princes"), v. 10 offers a climactic concluding affirmation of God's eternal reign, followed by the final *hallelu-yah*.

John Kselman proposes an alternative structural analysis. Paying particular attention to the didactic dimension of the psalm, he proposes a chiastic structure in which vv. 1-2 correspond to v. 10; vv. 3-4 correspond to vv. 8c-9, both of which Kselman labels "Wisdom"; and vv. 5-8b form the central section, which Kselman calls "God Creator and Redeemer."[523] Kselman's proposal has the advantage of highlighting the instructional intent

of Psalm 146 (vv. 3-4, 8c-9). Given the participial series in vv. 6-9a, it seems unlikely that a division should be made between v. 8b and v. 8c; however, the words "righteous" (צדיקם *ṣaddîqîm*) in v. 8c and "wicked" (רשעים *rěšā'îm*) in v. 9c form a conceptual envelope that lends support to Kselman's analysis. In the final analysis, it is not necessary to view the traditional proposal and Kselman's proposal as mutually exclusive. As is often the case, attention to varying stylistic criteria yields alternative proposals that may be equally legitimate and helpful in calling attention to the various features of a poem.

146:1-4. As is typical for a song of praise, v. 1 begins with an invitation in the imperative, although it is unusual that it is addressed to "my soul." This happens elsewhere only in Pss 103:1, 22 and 104:1, 35. Not coincidentally perhaps, v. 2 is also reminiscent of Psalm 104 (see v. 33), a psalm that eloquently portrays God's cosmic sovereignty over "the heavens" (v. 2), "the earth" (v. 4), and "the sea" (v. 25). These same three realms will be mentioned in Ps 146:6. Praise—the offering of the whole self to God in worship and work—is the lifelong vocation of the human creature in response to God's cosmic sovereignty and thus God's comprehensive claim on human life and the life of the world (see Reflections; see also Psalms 8; 100; 103; 104; 145; 150).

The antithesis of praising God is trusting oneself or trusting human agencies and institutions in place of God. It is precisely this that the psalmist warns against in v. 3 (see Ps 118:8-9; Jer 17:5-7; see also Pss 9:10; 25:2; Introduction). Thus, while all the songs of praise are implicitly instructional, Psalm 146 is very explicitly so (see above on Ps 100:3). The Hebrew play on words in vv. 3-4 emphasizes the transience of human life and human "help" (v. 3b); that is, "mortals" (אדם *'ādām*, v. 3) soon revert to "the earth" (אדמה *'ādāmâ*, v. 4). As the NIV suggests, the NRSV's "help" is often translated "salvation" or "deliverance." This word is key in Psalm 3 (see vv. 2, 7-8), and thus Psalm 146 recalls Psalm 3 as well as Psalms 1–2. As suggested above, "perish" (v. 4) recalls Pss 1:6; 2:12, where "the way of the wicked" (1:6; see 146:9) and the way of those who refuse to "serve the LORD" (2:11) will "perish." In the book of Psalms and the Bible as a whole, wickedness is essentially a matter of trust. It involves the deci-

523. John S. Kselman, "Psalm 146 in Its Context," *CBQ* 50 (1988) 591.

sion to trust someone or something other than God, and the results are empty and destructive, as vv. 4, 9 suggest (see above on Kselman's structural proposal, which posits a correspondence between vv. 3-4 and vv. 8c-9). Given the recollection of Psalm 104 in vv. 1-2, it is not surprising that v. 4 is reminiscent of Ps 104:29. This common feature of vv. 1-2, 4 is another link between Psalm 146 and Psalm 145, in which vv. 15-16 recall Ps 104:27-28 (see below on Ps 147:8-9).

146:5-10. In Ps 40:4, as in Psalm 146, happiness is also a matter of whom one trusts (see Jer 17:7). In Ps 33:20-21, confidence in God's help is articulated as "trust" (see also the beatitude in Ps 33:12). Thus, the beatitude in v. 5 is not unexpected. In fact, as the final beatitude in the psalter, it effectively summarizes all the others (see 1:2; 2:12; Introduction). As the whole sweep of the psalter makes clear, happiness is not the absence of pain and trouble but the presence of a God who cares about human hurt and who acts on behalf of the afflicted and the oppressed. The series of participial phrases in vv. 6-9a portrays precisely such a God. Verse 6 cites Israel's two basic traditions, which are finally inseparable (see Commentary on Psalms 33; 65; 66)—God is creator (v. 6a; see Genesis 1–2; Psalms 8; 104), and God is deliverer (v. 6b; see Exod 34:6, the self-revelation of God that forms the real culmination of the exodus story). Verse 7a represents what Brueggemann calls "the main claim for Yahweh" (see Ps 103:6, where the nearly identical claim is the climactic element in a series of participles).[524] Not surprisingly, v. 7a features the

concept of "justice," which elsewhere characterizes the royal policy or will of the sovereign God (see Pss 89:14; 96:13; 97:2; 98:9; 99:4). The remainder of the participial series tells how God exercises sovereignty—namely, by loving service on behalf of persons in need. Verses 7b-9a offer concrete illustrations involving those whom God helps—"the hungry" (see Ps 107:9; Isa 58:7), "prisoners" (see Isa 61:1), "the blind" (see Isa 42:7), the "bowed down" (see Ps 145:14), "the alien" (see Exod 23:9; Ps 94:6; Jer 7:6). While it may seem that "the righteous" (v. 8c) do not belong in this series, we must remember that it is precisely "the righteous" in the psalter who are constantly besieged, assaulted, and oppressed (see Ps 34:19). Verse 9bc returns to the use of finite verbs, but the affirmation is the same: God helps the needy (see Pss 68:5; 94:6; Jer 7:6; 22:3) and opposes "the way of the wicked" (see Pss 1:6; 145:20; 147:6).

In view of v. 10, which explicitly affirms the eternal reign of God (see Exod 15:18; Pss 29:10; 96:10; 97:1; 99:1; 145:1, 13), vv. 6-9 come into focus all the more clearly as a policy statement for the kingdom of God. The sovereign God stands for and works for justice, not simply as an abstract principle but as an embodied reality—provision for basic human needs, liberation from oppression, empowerment for the disenfranchised and dispossessed. Whereas in v. 1 the psalmist invites her or his own self to praise God, the psalmist addresses Zion in v. 10. The proper response—individually and corporately—to God's sovereign claim on the world is simply this, "Praise the LORD!"

---

524. Walter Brueggemann, "Psalm 146: Psalm for the Nineteenth Sunday after Pentecost," *No Other Foundation* 8/1 (Summer 1987) 28.

REFLECTIONS

1. Since it introduces the final collection of the psalter, it is fitting that Psalm 146 recalls Psalms 1–3 in such a way that it summarizes the fundamental message of the book. Like Psalm 1, Psalm 146 pronounces "happy" those whose lives are completely oriented to God. Like Psalm 2, Psalm 146 asserts God's sovereign claim on the world. Like Psalm 3, Psalm 146 makes it clear that God's help does not mean a carefree existence for the righteous. In other words, by characterizing "the righteous" as being oppressed and hungry and imprisoned and so on (vv. 7-9), Psalm 146 conveys the eschatological perspective of the psalter: God's reign is proclaimed amid circumstances that seem to deny it (see Psalms 2; 93; 95–99; Introduction).

2. The eschatological proclamation of God's reign calls for a decision. To use a key term employed by Psalm 146, the issue is this: Whom shall we *trust?* The question is as timely and crucial now as it ever has been. To trust in "princes" and "mortals" is a perennial and pervasive temptation, especially in a thoroughly secularized society like ours. Human help seems so compelling and immediate and effective. Self-help schemes abound, and the credo of our culture has virtually become, "God helps those who help themselves" (see Commentary on Psalm 3). Such a credo, however, results inevitably not in praise of God but in self-congratulation. The results are ruinous (v. 9*c*). As Claus Westermann puts it: "The praise of God occupied for Israel is actually the place where 'faith [that is, *trust*] in God' stands for us . . . the directing of this praise to a man, an idea, or an institution must disturb and finally destroy life itself."[525]

3. Psalm 146 is, therefore, an urgent call to praise—indeed, a call to life (see Commentary on Psalm 100). In biblical terms, to praise God is to live, and to live is to praise God. Praise is thus both liturgy and life-style; the two are inseparable. Brueggemann makes this clear as he reflects upon Psalm 146, taking "sing praise" in v. 2 as a point of departure:

> Israel holds doxology against the powerful staying force of the rulers of this age. Israel sings, and we never know what holy power is unleashed by such singing. Israel sings, and we never know what human imagination is authorized by such singing. One reason we may not sing is that such hope is intellectually outrageous. Another reason we may not sing is that such an alternative is too subversive. But the Church and Israel do sing! This singing is our vocation, our duty, and our delight. We name this staggering name—and the world becomes open again, especially for those on whom it had closed in such deathly ways—the prisoners, the blind, the sojourner, the widow, the orphan. The world is sung open. Against this Holy One and this song, death cannot close the world into injustice again.[526]

4. By way of its call to praise (v. 1) and its instruction (vv. 3-4) and proclamation of God's reign (v. 10), Psalm 146 anticipates Jesus' preaching of the reign of God (see Mark 1:14-15), as well as Jesus' teaching about happiness (see Matt 5:3-11) and his enactment of God's will in a ministry of justice, feeding, liberation, healing, and compassion (see Matt 11:2-6; Luke 4:16-21). As the church faces the same kind of opposition to God's values and policies that Jesus faced, Psalm 146 is an encouragement to God's people to sing and to pray as Jesus taught, affirming "thine is the kingdom" even as we pray, "thy kingdom come, thy will be done on earth as it is in heaven."

525. Claus Westermann, *Praise and Lament in the Psalms,* trans. K. R. Crim and R. N. Soulen (Atlanta: John Knox, 1981) 155, 160-61.
526. Walter Brueggemann, "Psalm 146. Psalm for the Nineteenth Sunday After Pentecost," *No Other Foundation* 8/1 (Summer 1987) 29.

PSALM 147:1-20, GOD SENDS OUT GOD'S WORD

NIV	NRSV
Psalm 147	Psalm 147

[1]Praise the LORD.[a]
 	
How good it is to sing praises to our God,
 how pleasant and fitting to praise him!
[2]The LORD builds up Jerusalem;
	[1] Praise the LORD!
	 How good it is to sing praises to our God;
	  for he is gracious, and a song of praise is
	  fitting.
	[2] The LORD builds up Jerusalem;
	  he gathers the outcasts of Israel.

[a]1 Hebrew *Hallelu Yah;* also in verse 20	

NIV

he gathers the exiles of Israel.
³He heals the brokenhearted
    and binds up their wounds.
⁴He determines the number of the stars
    and calls them each by name.
⁵Great is our Lord and mighty in power;
    his understanding has no limit.
⁶The LORD sustains the humble
    but casts the wicked to the ground.

⁷Sing to the LORD with thanksgiving;
    make music to our God on the harp.
⁸He covers the sky with clouds;
    he supplies the earth with rain
    and makes grass grow on the hills.
⁹He provides food for the cattle
    and for the young ravens when they call.

¹⁰His pleasure is not in the strength of the
        horse,
    nor his delight in the legs of a man;
¹¹the LORD delights in those who fear him,
    who put their hope in his unfailing love.

¹²Extol the LORD, O Jerusalem;
    praise your God, O Zion,
¹³for he strengthens the bars of your gates
    and blesses your people within you.
¹⁴He grants peace to your borders
    and satisfies you with the finest of wheat.

¹⁵He sends his command to the earth;
    his word runs swiftly.
¹⁶He spreads the snow like wool
    and scatters the frost like ashes.
¹⁷He hurls down his hail like pebbles.
    Who can withstand his icy blast?
¹⁸He sends his word and melts them;
    he stirs up his breezes, and the waters
        flow.

¹⁹He has revealed his word to Jacob,
    his laws and decrees to Israel.
²⁰He has done this for no other nation;
    they do not know his laws.

    Praise the LORD.

NRSV

³ He heals the brokenhearted,
    and binds up their wounds.
⁴ He determines the number of the stars;
    he gives to all of them their names.
⁵ Great is our Lord, and abundant in power;
    his understanding is beyond measure.
⁶ The LORD lifts up the downtrodden;
    he casts the wicked to the ground.

⁷ Sing to the LORD with thanksgiving;
    make melody to our God on the lyre.
⁸ He covers the heavens with clouds,
    prepares rain for the earth,
    makes grass grow on the hills.
⁹ He gives to the animals their food,
    and to the young ravens when they cry.
¹⁰ His delight is not in the strength of the horse,
    nor his pleasure in the speed of
        a runner;ᵃ
¹¹ but the LORD takes pleasure in those who
        fear him,
    in those who hope in his steadfast love.

¹² Praise the LORD, O Jerusalem!
    Praise your God, O Zion!
¹³ For he strengthens the bars of your gates;
    he blesses your children within you.
¹⁴ He grants peaceᵇ within your borders;
    he fills you with the finest of wheat.
¹⁵ He sends out his command to the earth;
    his word runs swiftly.
¹⁶ He gives snow like wool;
    he scatters frost like ashes.
¹⁷ He hurls down hail like crumbs—
    who can stand before his cold?
¹⁸ He sends out his word, and melts them;
    he makes his wind blow, and the waters
        flow.
¹⁹ He declares his word to Jacob,
    his statutes and ordinances to Israel.
²⁰ He has not dealt thus with any other nation;
    they do not know his ordinances.
    Praise the LORD!

ᵃHeb legs of a person   ᵇOr prosperity

COMMENTARY

Psalm 147 is a hymn or song of praise that is part of the final collection in the psalter (Psalms 146–150), each psalm of which begins and ends with *hallelu-yah.* In several ways, Psalm 147 follows well upon Psalm 146. In fact, v. 1 seems to serve as much as an evaluation of the preceding psalm as it does an introduction to the rest of Psalm 147 (see 142:6; 147:1). Furthermore, Ps 147:6 recalls Ps 146:9, and more generally, Psalm 147 focuses alternately upon the two conceptually distinct but ultimately inseparable spheres that are introduced in Ps 146:6: creation and deliverance (see Commentary on Psalm 146 and below on the structure of Psalm 147). Besides recalling Psalm 146, Psalm 147 also anticipates Psalms 148 and 149, each of which will concentrate on one of the two alternating spheres in Psalm 147. Psalm 148 invites all creation to praise God, while Psalm 149 extends the invitation to Israel (see esp. 149:2, 5).

Given the establishment of a post-exilic perspective from the beginning of Book V (see Ps 107:2-3), it is not surprising that the concluding collection also clearly articulates this perspective. In particular, Ps 147:2-3, 12-14 conveys the same good news that was announced in the exilic and post-exilic eras. The Greek and Latin textual traditions associate Psalm 147 with Haggai and Zechariah, although scholars are more inclined to associate it with the time of Nehemiah. The psalm also has affinities with the material in Isaiah 40–66. All of this suggests the post-exilic origin of this psalm, although precision is not possible. In any case, its placement reinforces the conclusion that Book V was shaped in response to the ongoing crisis of the post-exilic era (see Psalms 107; 108; 111; 120; 137; 138; 149; Introduction).

Psalm 147 is usually divided into three sections: vv. 1-6, vv. 7-11, vv. 12-20. The beginning of each section is marked by an imperative. In the Greek and Latin traditions, vv. 12-20 actually constitute a separate psalm; some commentators have even suggested that three separate psalms have been joined to form Psalm 147. But the unity of Psalm 147 is evident. Not only is it bounded by *hallelu-yah,* but also each section gives attention to both creation (vv. 4-5, 8-10, 15-18) and deliverance (vv. 2-3, 6, 11, 13-14, 19-20). In fact, the first and last sections show a similar pattern— deliverance (vv. 2-3, 6 and vv. 13-14, 19-20) encompasses creation (vv. 4-5 and vv. 15-18). Thus the very noticeable juxtaposition of vv. 18-19, marked by the repetition of "word," is simply the climactic instance of a pattern that characterizes the whole poem (see Ps 146:6-7).

147:1-6. After the initial *hallelu-yah,* v. 1 offers an observation about praise that is unusual but not entirely unique (see Ps 92:1). As a comparison of the NIV with the NRSV suggests, the conclusion of v. 1 is ambiguous. The adjective "fitting" (נאוה *nā'wâ*) certainly seems to describe the act of praising God (see Ps 33:1), but does the adjective "gracious"/"pleasant" (נעים *nā'îm*) describe God or the act of praising God? The same ambiguity is present in Ps 135:3; in all likelihood, it is intentional. James Kugel even suggests that v. 1 is an instance of "strangeifying"—that is, using language in an unusual way for special effect and to pose an interpretive challenge.[527] Thus it is appropriate that different possibilities are offered for construing v. 1.

Reasons for praise follow in vv. 2-6. Verse 2 in particular suggests an exilic or post-exilic perspective. In these eras, Jerusalem was rebuilt (v. 2*a*; see Neh 12:27), and the exiles or "outcasts" were gathered (v. 2*b*; see Deut 30:4; Neh 1:9; Isa 11:12; 56:8; Jer 30:17; Ezek 34:16; Mic 4:6). The language and imagery of v. 3 are also used elsewhere of God's redemptive handling of the exiles, who are characterized elsewhere as "brokenhearted" (see Isa 61:1), whom God "heals" (see Ps 107:20; Isa 57:18-19; Jer 30:17) and "binds up" (Isa 61:1; Ezek 34:16). The same can be said of v. 6*a* (see also Isa 61:1). Verses 2-3, 6 encompass vv. 4-5, which cite God's creative activity as reason for praise. Similar juxtaposition of God's creative and redemptive activity is found frequently in Isaiah 40–66 (see Isa 40:28; 41:14; 45:18-21), which can be dated to the exilic and early post-exilic eras. In fact, vv. 4-5 are very similar to Isa 40:26. The word "great" (גדול *gādôl*)

---

527. James L. Kugel, *The Idea of Biblical Poetry* (New Haven: Yale University Press, 1981) 92.

in v. 5*a* is expressive of sovereignty (see Pss 48:1; 95:3; 96:4; 99:2; Jer 10:6-7), as is the word "power" (כח *kōaḥ* ; see Exod 9:16; Ps 29:4; Jer 10:10-12). In the face of the stark realities of the exilic and post-exilic eras—including the loss of the Davidic monarchy—the prophet of the exile proclaimed the sovereignty of God (see Isa 52:7). The book of Psalms appears to have been shaped to offer the same response (see Commentary on Psalms 2; 89; 90; 93; 94; 95; 96; 97; 98; 99; 107; Introduction), and it is appropriate that the concluding collection returns explicitly to this proclamation (see Pss 146:10; 149:2). The NRSV's "number" (v. 4*a*) and "measure" (v. 5*b*) translate the same Hebrew root (ספר *sāpar*), thus providing an envelope structure for these two verses and emphasizing the message that God's "understanding" exceeds human comprehension (see Isa 40:28; see a similar idea in Ps 139:17-18, where "count" in v. 18*a* represents the same Hebrew root as "number" and "measure" in 147:4-5).

147:7-11. The return to imperatives in v. 7 marks the beginning of the second section. The verb translated "sing" (ענה *ʿānâ*) is unusual in the psalms (see only Ps 119:172). Its very infrequency may call attention to Israel's deliverance from Egypt, since it is used to introduce Miriam's song in response to the sea crossing (Exod 15:21), a song that follows immediately the proclamation of God's reign in Exod 15:18. To sing "with thanksgiving" is an appropriate response to God's sovereignty (see the title to and v. 4 of Psalm 100). The second imperative, "make melody," also indicates an appropriate response to God's sovereignty (see Ps 149:3; see also v. 1; Pss 47:6-7; 98:5). The lyre is specifically involved in such responses in Pss 98:5; 149:3 (see also Ps 33:2). As is often the case, the assertion of God's sovereignty in vv. 8-9 is at least implicitly polemical (see Pss 96:5; 97:7). Here God does what the Canaanites routinely attributed to Baal—sending the rain that provided growth for plants and food for animals (see Commentary on Psalms 29; 104). Verses 8-9 especially recall Ps 104:14, 27. Psalms 145 and 146 also recall Psalm 104 (see Pss 145:5, 15-16; 146:1-2, 4), thus providing a further link between Psalms 145–147 and increasing the likelihood that these concluding psalms are relatively late and were written in part as artistic anthologies of earlier psalms. In this regard, v. 10 recalls Ps

33:16-17 and v. 11 even more clearly recalls Ps 33:18. God does not need impressive displays of human power; rather, God is pleased when persons yield themselves to the divine rule (see Pss 25:12, 14; 33:18; 103:11, 13, 17). Because God's sovereignty consists of the power of faithful love (see Pss 5:7; 25:6-7, 10; 33:5, 18, 22; 103:4, 8, 11, 17; Introduction) rather than sheer force, God's people will live inevitably by hope and in waiting (see Pss 25:3, 5, 21; 33:18, 22). The repetition of "pleasure" in vv. 10*b*, 11*a* anticipates Ps 149:4 and also recalls another exilic text, Isa 42:1.

147:12-20. Two more imperatives in v. 12 mark the beginning of the final section. The mention of Jerusalem recalls v. 2, as does the content of v. 13*a* (see Neh 3:3, 6, 13). Jerusalem was the place where God's blessing was sought (v. 13*b*; see Pss 129:8; 132:15; 133:3; 134:3) and peace was anticipated (v. 14*a*; see Pss 125:5; 128:6; Isa 60:17). Verse 14*b* recalls Ps 81:16. Verse 15 introduces the word that provides conceptual unity for the rest of the poem: God's "word" (see vv. 18-19; see also Pss 33:4, 6; 107:20). As in the conclusion to the preceding section (vv. 10-11), vv. 15-20 appear to have been influenced by Psalm 33 (see esp. 33:4-9), in which God's "word" also indicates and enacts God's sovereignty (see also Genesis 1; Isa 40:8; 55:10-11). God is sovereign over the "earth" (v. 15*a*; see Pss 146:6; 148:7-10) and all the forces that are still impressive to modern people but would have been especially impressive and important to ancient folk—snow and frost (v. 16; see Job 38:29; Isa 55:10), hail (v. 17*a*; see Job 37:10; 38:29), cold (v. 17*b*; Job 37:9). The mention of God's "word" in v. 18*a* makes it clear that these phenomena cannot be subsumed simply under the category of meteorology. For the psalmist, because God rules the world, even the weather is a theological matter! Thus, while "wind" in v. 18*b* is a proper translation, we should hear in it another nuance. The word is רוח (*rûaḥ*), often translated "spirit." As in Gen 1:2 and Exod 14:21, the wind is not simply a meteorological phenomenon. It somehow contains and conveys the power, presence, and purpose of Israel's personal God. Verse 19 reveals the personal dimension of the divine word. God's word— formerly addressed to snow and hail and wind—is now addressed to Israel. To know God's word is to know God's will and, indeed, God's very self. The NRSV's "ordinances" (מִשְׁפָּטִים *mišpāṭîm*, vv. 19b, 20b) could more literally be translated "justices," and God's establishment of justice is a hallmark of God's reign (see Pss 89:14; 96:13; 97:2; 98:9; 99:4; 146:7; 149:9). The word God sends out marks God's sovereign claim on the earth and everything in it (vv. 15-18; see Ps 148:7-8), including Israel (vv. 19-20) and ultimately all the earth's rulers and peoples (see Ps 148:11-12).

REFLECTIONS

Verses 15-20, especially the juxtaposition of vv. 18-19, convey in a particularly clear way a crucial theological insight: the ultimate inseparability of creation and redemption. To put the matter in slightly different terms, God's dealing with a particular people—Israel and the church—is for the fulfillment of God's purposes for all creation. To be sure, this conviction is not unique to Psalm 147. It is evident in Israel's choice to begin its story with creation rather than with exodus, and it is evident in the sweep of the biblical witness from the OT to the NT in the direction of "a new heaven and a new earth" (Rev 21:1 NRSV) and "the healing of the nations" (Rev 22:2 NRSV). Furthermore, this insight is conveyed in several other psalms as well (see Commentary on Psalms 19; 33; 65; 66; 96; 97; 98; 99).

Even so, Psalm 147 articulates this conviction in a striking way that brings home its remarkable significance. The force that drives the universe, producing rain and snow and heat and cold (vv. 15-18), is not just something we observe and experience but *someone* we know (vv. 19-20). At the heart of the biblical faith is the astounding claim that the power that has strewn the stars into their courses (v. 4) is the same power that—or better, *who*—"heals the brokenhearted" (v. 3), "lifts up the downtrodden" (v. 6), and declares an intelligible, personal, life-giving word to Israel (vv. 19-20). In short, our trust—indeed, our only hope—is that the power behind the universe has a personal face that is turned toward us in "steadfast love" (v. 11b). Although this word will not be used until the NT, Psalm 147 articulates the *incarnation* of God's word (see John 1:1, 14). The cosmic God is personally, intimately, inextricably involved in the lives and futures of human beings. With good reason, Psalm 147 is regularly used during the season of Christmas, the Festival of the Incarnation. The only proper and fitting response to the good news of God's incarnational involvement with the world is to stand in awe (v. 11a) and to sing the words that convey the grateful offering of our lives, "Praise the LORD!"

PSALM 148:1-14, LET THEM PRAISE THE NAME OF THE LORD

NIV	NRSV
Psalm 148	Psalm 148
¹Praise the LORD.ᵃ	¹ Praise the LORD!
Praise the LORD from the heavens, praise him in the heights above.	Praise the LORD from the heavens; praise him in the heights!
²Praise him, all his angels,	² Praise him, all his angels; praise him, all his host!

ᵃ1 Hebrew *Hallelu Yah*; also in verse 14

NIV

praise him, all his heavenly hosts.
[3]Praise him, sun and moon,
    praise him, all you shining stars.
[4]Praise him, you highest heavens
    and you waters above the skies.
[5]Let them praise the name of the LORD,
    for he commanded and they were created.
[6]He set them in place for ever and ever;
    he gave a decree that will never pass away.

[7]Praise the LORD from the earth,
    you great sea creatures and all ocean
        depths,
[8]lightning and hail, snow and clouds,
    stormy winds that do his bidding,
[9]you mountains and all hills,
    fruit trees and all cedars,
[10]wild animals and all cattle,
    small creatures and flying birds,
[11]kings of the earth and all nations,
    you princes and all rulers on earth,
[12]young men and maidens,
    old men and children.

[13]Let them praise the name of the LORD,
    for his name alone is exalted;
    his splendor is above the earth and the
        heavens.
[14]He has raised up for his people a horn,[a]
    the praise of all his saints,
    of Israel, the people close to his heart.

Praise the LORD.

[a]14 *Horn* here symbolizes strong one, that is, king.

NRSV

[3] Praise him, sun and moon;
    praise him, all you shining stars!
[4] Praise him, you highest heavens,
    and you waters above the heavens!

[5] Let them praise the name of the LORD,
    for he commanded and they were created.
[6] He established them forever and ever;
    he fixed their bounds, which cannot be
        passed.[a]

[7] Praise the LORD from the earth,
    you sea monsters and all deeps,
[8] fire and hail, snow and frost,
    stormy wind fulfilling his command!

[9] Mountains and all hills,
    fruit trees and all cedars!
[10] Wild animals and all cattle,
    creeping things and flying birds!
[11] Kings of the earth and all peoples,
    princes and all rulers of the earth!
[12] Young men and women alike,
    old and young together!

[13] Let them praise the name of the LORD,
    for his name alone is exalted;
    his glory is above earth and heaven.
[14] He has raised up a horn for his people,
    praise for all his faithful,
    for the people of Israel who are close to
        him.

Praise the LORD!

[a]Or *he set a law that cannot pass away*

COMMENTARY

Psalm 148 is the third in a collection of hymns or songs of praise, each bounded by *hallelu-yah*, that concludes the psalter (see Commentary on Psalm 146). Of the two alternating spheres of God's activity in Psalm 147—creation and deliverance—Psalm 148 focuses on the former as it calls all creation to praise God. Only in v. 14 does Psalm 148 turn to the sphere of deliverance, thus anticipating the focus of Psalm 149 (see 148:14; 149:1, 5, 9). Although neither Psalm 147 nor

Psalm 148 contains the word "reign" or "king," they are bounded by two psalms that do (see Pss 146:10; 149:2), and the effect of both Psalms 147 and 148 is to articulate God's universal sovereignty (see below on v. 13). Thus Psalm 148 participates in the final collection's recalling of the theological heart of the psalter: God reigns (see Commentary on Psalms 93; 95; 96; 97; 98; 99; Introduction). And thereby it contributes to the response of Books IV–V to the theological crisis of the exilic and post-exilic eras (see Commentary on Psalms 90; 107; Introduction).

In a sense, Psalm 148 displays the typical structure of a song of praise—invitation to praise followed by reasons for praise. But in this case, the invitation is greatly elaborated, thus anticipating Psalm 150. Every half-line of the psalm up through v. 4a, for instance, begins with an imperative summons to praise. The invitation is resumed in v. 5a with a jussive verbal form ("Let them praise"), and then reasons for praise follow in vv. 5b-6. The return to the imperative in v. 7a marks the beginning of the second section of the poem. Whereas vv. 1-6 focus on praise "from the heavens" (v. 1), vv. 7-14 focus on praise "from the earth" (v. 7). As in the first section, a jussive invitation to praise (v. 13a, which is identical to v. 5a) immediately precedes the reasons for praise in vv. 13b-14. By the end of the psalm, the word "praise" (הלל hillēl) has occurred eleven times as a verb and once as a noun (v. 14). This impressive repetition in itself suggests the inclusivity of praise, which Psalm 148 invites. The intent to be inclusive—indeed, universal—is reinforced by the prepositional phrases in vv. 1, 7 (see also NRSV, "above earth and heaven" in v. 13) and by the repetition of "all" in vv. 2-3, 7, 9-11, 14. Then, of course, there is the actual listing of beings (heavenly and earthly) and things (animate and inanimate) that are invited to praise God. The effect of the structure and stylistic features of Psalm 148 is even more inclusive than the climactic final verse of the psalter, for in Psalm 148 it is not just a matter of "everything that breathes" praising God (150:6). Rather, it is also a matter of everything that is praising God.

148:1-6. In the first section, God is to be praised "from the heavens" (v. 1) by the beings and objects that inhabit the heavens (vv. 2-3), as well as by the heavens themselves (v. 4a, lit., "heaven of heavens"; see Ps 19:1). As will be the case in the second section, praise is invited from both the animate and inanimate spheres—"angels" (v. 2a; see Ps 103:20) and God's "host" (v. 2b; see Pss 24:10; 103:21) as well as sun and moon and stars (v. 3; see Pss 8:3; 19:4-6; 136:8-9; 147:4). The list is reminiscent of Genesis 1–2—"heavens" (see Gen 1:1; 2:1), "host" (see Gen 2:1), "stars" (see Gen 1:16). All the heavenly beings and bodies are to praise God's "name" (vv.

5a, 13)—that is, God's essential character and purposes, which represent God's very self (see Pss 8:1, 10; 23:3; 29:2; 135:1, 3, 13). The character and purposes of God are revealed in what God has done as creator, and such is the focus of the reasons for praise in vv. 5b-6. The verb "created" (ברא bārā') recalls Gen 1:1–2:4, as does the mode of creation by speech, although the verb "command" (צוה ṣiwwâ) does not occur in Gen 1:1–2:4 (see also Job 38:10; Pss 33:6-9; 104:5-9; Prov 8:29).

148:7-13. The second section invites praise "from the earth" by beings, objects, and elements in this realm, both animate and inanimate. Not unexpectedly, v. 8 recalls Ps 147:15-18, both in terms of the elements of creation involved and of the creative power of God's "word." The list again is reminiscent of Genesis 1–2—"earth" (see Gen 1:1; 2:1, 4; the phrase "earth and heaven" occurs only in Gen 2:4b and Ps 147:13); "sea monsters" (see Gen 1:21); "deeps" (see Gen 1:2); "fruit trees" (see Gen 1:11); "wild animals and all cattle, creeping things and flying birds" (see Gen 1:21, 24-25). As in Genesis 1, the culminating focus in Psalm 148 is on humanity (see vv. 11-12). Those whom human beings recognize as sovereign are to acknowledge the ultimate sovereignty of God (v. 11), as are all general categories of people (v. 12). Verse 11 recalls Ps 2:1-2, 10-12, which at the beginning of the psalter calls for recognition of God's sovereignty (see also Ps 149:5-9). Quite appropriately, the reasons for praise in v. 13b proclaim God's sovereignty. The word "exalted" (שגב śāgab) occurs elsewhere in the context of the proclamation of God's kingship (see Isa 33:5 in the context of 33:17-22), and the word "glory" (הוד hôd) regularly describes royalty, both human (see Pss 21:5; 45:3) and divine (see Pss 96:6; 145:5). In keeping with the two divisions of the psalm, v. 13b affirms that God's sovereignty is over "earth and heaven." In short, God rules the cosmos.

148:14. This verse continues the reasons for praise, but it moves in a different direction. The cosmic God has chosen to fulfill the divine purposes through a particular people. To "raise up a horn" seems to mean to protect or to strengthen (see Pss 75:10; 89:17, 24; 92:10; 112:9). The two occurrences of this image in Psalm 89 are particularly interesting, because Psalm 89 concludes Book III with a rehearsal of the failure of the Davidic covenant, to which Books IV–V offer a response (see Commentary on Psalms 89; 90; 107; Introduction). That the concluding collection of Book V returns to this image may be more than coincidental. It is as if Ps 148:14 asserts a reinstatement—*not* of the Davidic king, however (see Ps 89:24), but of the whole people, "all his faithful" (see Ps 89:17). Interestingly in this regard, "the faithful" play the key role in Psalm 149, which reserves for them the role assigned to the king in Psalm 2 (see below on Ps 149:5-9). Thus Psalms 148–149 offer further warrant to conclude that the Davidic theology was transferred in the post-exilic era to the whole people (see Commentary on Psalms 105; 110; 132; 144; Introduction).

It is unclear what is meant precisely by the phrase "praise for all his faithful" in v. 14. In view of the placement of Psalm 148 in Book V, it seems to suggest, along with the preceding horn imagery, the reinstatement of God's people represented by the return from exile and reoccupation of Jerusalem (see Ps 147:2-3, 12-14). But the noun "praise" cannot help recalling the eleven verbal occurrences that have preceded in vv. 1-13. In short, Israel is one among many participants in the cosmic praising of God; its unique role, per-

haps, is to articulate intelligibly the unspoken praise of the rest of creation (see Ps 19:1-4). Terence Fretheim suggests, although the exact meaning is elusive, that v. 14 recalls Ps 22:3 and that it perhaps should be construed as follows:

> God has made God's people strong, indeed has made them a praise in the earth, for the purposes of the universal praise of God.... Just as the various other creatures show forth the praise of God by being what they are as God's creatures, so Israel having been made what it now is by God, shows forth God's praise by being who they are, the redeemed people of God.... God's people in every age are called upon to continue showing forth the praise of God because of what they have been made by God. In this way they will join with that vast chorus of God's nonhuman creatures in honor of God and in witness to God.[528]

Because God rules the cosmos, God's praise is incomplete without the participation of every voice, human and nonhuman, in heaven and in earth and in all creation.

528. Terence E. Fretheim, "Nature's Praise of God in the Psalms," *Ex Auditu* 3 (1987) 29-30.

REFLECTIONS

1. While the songs of praise generally push toward universality (see Pss 67:1-7; 100:1; 103:20-22; 117:1; Introduction), Psalm 148 takes inclusivity to the limit, surpassing even the final climactic verse of the psalter (150:6). The inclusivity of the invitation to praise God has profound implications that demonstrate the inseparability of theology and ecology (see Commentary on Psalms 8; 96; 98; 104). We human beings, we people of God, are partners in praising God with a multitude of other living beings and inanimate things as well. For this reason, Psalm 148 recalls not only Gen 1:1–2:4, but also Genesis 9. In Genesis 9 the covenant after the flood is established not just with Noah and his descendents (Gen 9:9) but also with "every living creature" (Gen 9:10, 12, 15-16), indeed, with "the earth" (Gen 9:13). This covenant, along with the all-inclusive invitation to praise in Psalm 148, suggests that the human vocation of "dominion" (Gen 1:26, 28) involves not just a stewardship *of* creation but a partnership *with* creation. Francis of Assisi had it right when, on the basis of Psalm 148, he composed his *Canticle of the Sun,* in which he addresses the sun and wind and fire as brother, and the moon and waters and earth as sister. Psalm 148 is not a call to pantheism, but on the basis of Psalm 148, we must speak of a "symbiosis in praise" involving humans and nature; we can hear in Psalm 148 "an implicit call to human beings to relate to the natural orders in such a way that nature's praise might show forth with greater clarity."[529] In short, human beings are called to exercise their God-given "dominion" or sovereignty in the same way that God exercises power: as a servant. To so fulfill our vocation is to praise God by, in effect, imitating God.

529. Ibid., 28-29. Fretheim also calls attention to two contemporary hymns that capture the message of Psalm 148: "Let All Things Now Living" and "Earth and All Stars."

2. Several other hymns that proclaim God's reign also invite heaven and earth and the beings and objects therein to praise God (see Pss 29:1; 96:11-12; 97:1; 98:4, 7-8). Indeed, the movement of Psalm 148 is similar to that of Psalm 29; the praise of heavenly beings (Pss 29:1-2, 9; 148:2-4) is accompanied by a prayer for or the affirmation of God's strengthening or blessing of God's people (Pss 29:11; 148:14). The same movement is also found in Luke 2:13-14, where heavenly beings proclaim both God's glory and peace on earth. The angels' song communicates Luke's conviction that the birth of Jesus represents God's enthronement, God's cosmic sovereignty. Its parallel movement with Psalm 148 suggests the appropriateness of Psalm 148 for the season of Christmas. The church affirms that Jesus the Christ not only announced but also embodied the cosmic reign of God in a ministry of suffering servanthood. But for this very reason, Jesus is to be exalted, so that "at the name of Jesus every knee should bend, in heaven and on earth and under the earth" (Phil 2:10 NRSV; cf. Ps 148:13). One of the church's cherished Christmas hymns, "Joy to the World," is a paraphrase of Psalm 98, another hymn that proclaims God's reign and invites universal recognition in praise. To greet Jesus as Lord is to recognize God's sovereign claim on our lives and on the whole created order, and it is to commit ourselves to exercise God-given sovereignty over the earth as God demonstrated divine sovereignty in Jesus—the power of suffering servanthood. Thus Psalm 148 is a psalm for Christmas and for Easter and for all seasons.

PSALM 149:1-9, THE JUSTICE THAT IS WRITTEN

NIV

Psalm 149

[1]Praise the LORD.[a]

Sing to the LORD a new song,
  his praise in the assembly of the saints.
[2]Let Israel rejoice in their Maker;
  let the people of Zion be glad in their King.
[3]Let them praise his name with dancing
  and make music to him with tambourine
    and harp.
[4]For the LORD takes delight in his people;
  he crowns the humble with salvation.
[5]Let the saints rejoice in this honor
  and sing for joy on their beds.

[6]May the praise of God be in their mouths
  and a double-edged sword in their hands,
[7]to inflict vengeance on the nations
  and punishment on the peoples,
[8]to bind their kings with fetters,
  their nobles with shackles of iron,
[9]to carry out the sentence written against them.
  This is the glory of all his saints.

Praise the LORD.

a1 Hebrew *Hallelu Yah*; also in verse 9

NRSV

Psalm 149

[1] Praise the LORD!
Sing to the LORD a new song,
  his praise in the assembly of the faithful.
[2] Let Israel be glad in its Maker;
  let the children of Zion rejoice in their
    King.
[3] Let them praise his name with dancing,
  making melody to him with tambourine
    and lyre.
[4] For the LORD takes pleasure in his people;
  he adorns the humble with victory.
[5] Let the faithful exult in glory;
  let them sing for joy on their couches.
[6] Let the high praises of God be in their
    throats
  and two-edged swords in their hands,
[7] to execute vengeance on the nations
  and punishment on the peoples,
[8] to bind their kings with fetters
  and their nobles with chains of iron,
[9] to execute on them the judgment decreed.
  This is glory for all his faithful ones.
Praise the LORD!

COMMENTARY

Psalm 149 is the fourth in a collection of hymns or songs of praise, each bounded by *hallelu-yah*, that concludes the psalter (see Commentary on Psalm 146). The psalm begins like a typical song of praise—invitation to praise (vv. 1-3), followed by reasons for praise (v. 4). The renewed invitation to praise in v. 5 is also not unusual, but then vv. 6-9 offer "an unparalleled departure" from the typical form.[530] These verses have been an enigma to scholars and somewhat difficult for readers who are offended by the psalmist's call for vengeance. The uniqueness of Psalm 149 has given rise to a variety of proposals for understanding its origin and ancient use, including the suggestion that vv. 6-9 indicate its use accompanying a sword dance at a victory celebration or perhaps a cultic celebration of God's kingship (see vv. 2-3). Read figuratively, however, vv. 6-9 represent a radical call for the faithful to enact and to embody the reign of God, which is celebrated in vv. 1-4, thus making Psalm 149 particularly appropriate for use on All Saints Day (see Reflections below).

That "an unparalleled departure" should characterize the penultimate psalm in the psalter is probably not coincidental. In short, the uniqueness of Psalm 149 invites careful consideration of its placement within the book. For instance, vv. 6-9 recall Psalm 2, where the concern is also with rebellious "nations" and "peoples" (Ps 2:1; cf. 149:7) and "kings" (Ps 2:2, 10; cf. 149:8). Psalm 2 is ultimately an affirmation of God's sovereignty (see Commentary on Psalm 2, esp. discussion of vv. 10-12; Introduction), and so is Psalm 149. Both assert that those who attempt to exercise their own sovereignty (see Ps 2:3) will be called to account (Pss 2:8-12; 149:7-9; note "iron" in 2:8; 149:8). Thus, whereas Psalm 2 anticipates the theological heart of the psalter, Psalm 149 clearly recalls it—namely, Psalms 93; 95–99 and their affirmation of God's reign (see Introduction). The invitation in Ps 149:1 to sing "a new song" echoes Pss 96:1; 98:1, and 149:2 addresses God as "King" (see Pss 95:3; 97:1; 99:4).

Book IV, of which Psalms 93–99 form the core, responds to the crisis of exile that is articulated in Psalm 89. As Psalm 89 makes clear, a major aspect of this crisis was the disappearance of the Davidic monarchy. Besides proclaiming *God's* kingship (see Commentary on Psalms 90; 93; 95; 96; 97; 98; 99), the response of Book IV moves in the direction of transferring the Davidic theology from the monarchy to the whole people (see Commentary on Psalm 105). Thus the royal psalms became appropriated messianically—that is, as affirmation of God's sovereignty that is and will be made manifest through the whole people rather than through the Davidic monarchy (see Introduction). This kind of appropriation is especially clear in the final royal psalm in the psalter, Psalm 144 (see also Psalms 110; 132 in Book V), to which Psalm 149 is linked by the repetition of "new song" (144:9; 149:1). In a real sense, then, Psalm 149 completes the movement of transferring the Davidic theology to the whole people, since after asserting God's sovereignty (vv. 1-3), it assigns to the "faithful" the task of concretely implementing God's sovereignty in the world, a task Psalm 2 assigns to the monarchy. Not surprisingly, the faithful will be addressed several times in Psalm 149 in royal terms (see below on vv. 4-5, 9).[531]

Since Psalm 149 participates fully in the psalter's response to the crisis of the exilic and post-exilic eras, it is also not surprising that it has many affinities with Isaiah 40–66 (see Commentary on Psalms 96; 98). In particular, Allen cites six verbal links between Psalm 149 and Isaiah 61: "humble"/"oppressed" (Ps 149:4; Isa 61:1); "pleasure"/"favor" (Ps 149:4; Isa 61:2); "vengeance" (Ps 149:7; Isa 61:2); "crowns" (Ps 149:4), which occurs twice in Isa 61:3 as "crown of beauty" and "splendor" (NIV); "Zion" (Ps 149:2; Isa 61:3); and "judgment"/"justice" (Ps 149:9; Isa 61:8). In addition, he sees parallels between Psalm 149 and Isa 45:14; 46:13; 60:1-3, 9, 11-12, 14; 66:14-16, 18-21. Contending that Psalms 96; 98 partake of the same tradition as Isaiah 40–66, Allen concludes: "It is difficult to avoid the conclusion that

---

530. Leslie C. Allen, *Psalms 101–150*, WBC 21 (Waco, Tex.: Word, 1983) 319.

531. I am indebted to the insights of Gary Martindale, "Vengeance, the Tie That Binds: An Intratextual Reading of Psalm 149," unpublished paper presented to the Society of Biblical Literature, Nov. 21, 1994, Chicago, IL.; and Rich Brzowsky, "Exegesis and Reflection: Psalm 149," unpublished paper, Eden Seminary, May 18, 1993.

like Pss 96-98 this psalm is building upon the motifs of the future victory of Yahweh over the nations and of the exaltation of Israel. The psalm appears to have emanated from a similar tradition to that of Pss 96–98 and to develop its themes."[532] While, as Allen suggests, there is a future dimension involved, Psalm 149 is eschatological in a more fundamental sense; it proclaims God's present sovereignty amid ongoing opposition by nations and their kings (see Commentary on Psalms 2; 93; 96; 97; 98; 99; Introduction).

Scholars have reached no consensus concerning the structure of Psalm 149. Some suggest a three-fold division: vv. 1-3, vv. 4-6, vv. 7-9. But most favor a division into two sections, with the break occurring either between vv. 4 and 5 or between vv. 5 and 6 (see NIV). Interestingly, Psalm 149 is one of the few psalms for which the NRSV suggests no divisions. Observing that v. 5 seems to go equally well with vv. 1-4 or vv. 6-9, Anthony R. Ceresko argues that v. 5 should be understood as a "pivot" or hinge.[533] Furthermore, v. 5 is precisely the central poetic line, and along with vv. 1 and 9, it contains one of the three occurrences of "faithful," thus providing a further mark of symmetry.

Ceresko argues convincingly that the conceptual unity of Psalm 149 lies in its allusions to two crucial historical events: the exodus (vv. 1-4) and the possession of the land (vv. 6-9). For instance, "Maker" [עֹשֵׂה 'ōśeh] in v. 2 probably refers not to creation but to God's formation of Israel as a people (see Pss 95:6; 100:3), and the constitutive event was the exodus (the Hebrew root of "Maker" occurs in Exod 14:31). The people's immediate response was to sing (Exod 15:1), and the "new song" of Ps 149:1 probably alludes to the Song of the Sea in Exod 15:1-21. Other verbal links make this interpretation plausible: "praise" (Ps 149:1; Exod 15:11), "dancing" and "tambourine" (Ps 149:3; Exod 15:20), and "victory" (Ps 149:4; Exod 15:2). In addition, the word "reign" (מָלַךְ mālak) in the climactic Exod 15:18 represents the same Hebrew root as "King" (melek) in Ps 149:2. In short, both the Song of the Sea in Exodus 15 and the "new song" called for in Ps 149:1 are celebrations of God's sovereignty.

532. Allen, Psalms 101–150, 319-20.
533. Anthony R. Ceresko, "Psalm 149: Poetry, Themes (Exodus and Conquest), and Social Function," Biblica 67 (1986) 185.

149:1-4. While these verses are reminiscent of the exodus, the psalmist's assertion of God's sovereignty in a new context also recalls Isaiah, the prophet of the exile (see Isa 43:15; 52:7; see above on other parallels with Isaiah 40–66). The prophet interpreted God's ongoing commitment to the people as a new exodus (see Isa 43:1-7), a "new thing" (Isa 43:19; see also Isa 42:9; 48:6). The appropriate response would thus be "a new song" (Ps 149:1; Isa 42:10). The affirmation that God "takes pleasure in" the people (v. 4a; see Ps 147:10-11) further recalls Isa 42:1, where the servant—who should almost certainly be understood as the whole people—has a mission to establish justice among the nations (see also Isa 42:3-4, 6; see below on Ps 149:9). Like vv. 6-9, the mission of the servant in Isa 42:1-9 casts the whole people in the role formerly assigned to the monarchy. In this regard, it is significant that v. 4b asserts that God "crowns the humble." The Hebrew root behind "crowns" (פָּאַר pā'ar) is associated elsewhere with royalty (see Exod 8:9; Esth 1:4), including the Davidic monarchy (see Zech 12:7). Even more significantly, it occurs as a verb in Isa 55:5 to describe what God has done for the whole people; that this occurrence comes immediately after Isa 55:3 suggests the transfer of the Davidic promise to the whole people (see also Isa 60:9). In short, v. 4b is further evidence for the transfer of the Davidic theology to the whole people.

149:5. The same can be said of v. 5a, where "glory" is also a word that is regularly associated with sovereignty, both human (see Pss 8:5; 21:5a) and divine (see Pss 24:7-10; 29:1-2, 9; 96:3, 7-8). To be sure, v. 5a invites a recognition of God's sovereignty (see Ps 96:4), so "glory" could refer primarily to God's glory. In view of v. 9, however, it seems that the glory is at least shared by the people, an interpretation the NIV makes more explicit. Singing for joy (v. 5b) also describes elsewhere the proper response to God's reign (see Pss 96:12; 98:8). What it means for the people to celebrate God's rule "on their beds" is not clear. Several emendations are often suggested, but they have no manuscript support. The phrase is sometimes taken as evidence that the ancient worshipers spent the night in the Temple (see Pss 27:4; 139:18) or that they were being called to prostrate themselves as an act of obeisance. Another possibility is that v. 5*b* exhorts the people to recognize God's sovereignty in every sphere of their existence, public as well as private (see "on their beds" in Mic 2:1).

149:6-9. These verses continue to invite the recognition of God's reign (v. 6*a*) as well as to suggest the people's participation in God's reign (vv. 6*b*-9). The NRSV's "high praises" (v. 6*a*) is from a root that elsewhere describes the response to God's sovereignty (see Pss 99:5, 9; 145:1). Verse 6*b* begins, however, to suggest the people's participation. "Vengeance" ordinarily belongs to God (see Deut 32:35; Ps 94:1), but v. 7 indicates the people's role. They are now assigned the part formerly played by the Davidic kings (vv. 7-8; cf. Ps 2:9). This sharing in the enactment of God's reign in order to establish justice (v. 9*a*; see also Pss 96:13; 97:2; 98:9; 99:4; 146:7) is the people's "glory" (v. 9*b*). Thus v. 9*b* recalls v. 5*a*, although the two words the NRSV translates "glory" differ. The word in v. 9*b* is also regularly associated with sovereignty, including God's sovereignty (see Pss 29:4; 96:6). More interesting here, however, is that the faithful possess the glory formerly reserved for the Davidic kings (see Pss 21:5; 45:3). It is they who share in the responsibility for justice—not the Davidic kings (cf. Ps 72:1-2).

In the NIV and the NRSV, it is almost inevitable that vv. 6*b*-9 sound triumphalistic, perhaps dangerously so (see Reflections below). It is important to remember that in the book of Psalms, vengeance always serves the purpose of justice (see, e.g., Psalms 94; 109). A different translation of v. 9*a* will also help to avert triumphalist tendencies. For instance, v. 9*a* could be rendered, "to enact among them the justice which is written." This translation means that the actions of God's people can never be self-serving or simply punitive but must constructively serve the establishment of justice (see Isa 42:1-4). The proposed translation raises the question, of course, of what precisely is the "justice written." In terms of the shape of the book of Psalms, it may well refer to the affirmations found earlier in the book that the sovereign God wills justice and righteousness (see Pss 96:13; 97:2; 98:9; 99:4). God's justice and righteousness always encompass all peoples and, indeed, all things, as Psalms 96–99 suggest and as the immediately preceding psalms have made clear (see esp. Pss 145:10-13; 146:7; 148:11-12). When Psalm 149 is heard in this literary context, vv. 6-9 may even take on an ironic ring, especially insofar as Psalm 149 recalls Psalm 2. That is to say, the whole people have displaced the kings as partner in God's sovereignty, because *their own kings* have been brought to justice! That is to say, the monarchy disappeared with the exile (see Psalm 89).

In the larger canonical context, the "justice written" may refer to earlier traditions, perhaps the book of Judges, in accordance with Ceresko's suggestion that vv. 6-9 allude to the narratives of Israel's possession of the land. In this perspective, vv. 6-9 recall Judg 3:16-23, where Ehud uses "a double-edged sword" (Judg 3:16 NIV) to kill King Eglon of Moab as part of Israel's consolidation of its settlement in the land (see also Num 31:2-3, another episode in the possession of the land). If Psalm 149 does allude to the book of Judges, one must note that Judges credits Israel's victories to God, and not to Israel or to its leaders. Like the book of Judges, then, Psalm 149 is ultimately an affirmation of God's sovereignty—only God is king (see Judg 9:7-20).

REFLECTIONS

1. As suggested in the Commentary, vv. 6-9 may sound dangerously triumphalistic—a call to violence against the enemies of God. Indeed, Psalm 149 has been used to promote violence. Prothero points out that Psalm 149 was cited by Caspar Schopp as he called Roman Catholic princes to a holy war against the Protestants; the result was the Thirty Years War. And Thomas Müntzer appealed to Psalm 149 to incite the German peasants to revolt.[534] There is no question that the military imagery of vv. 6-9 is problematic and even positively dangerous if taken literally as a call to arms.

But vv. 6-9 should not be taken literally. Rather, their theological thrust is to assert God's

534. Rowland E. Prothero, *The Psalms in Human Life and Experience* (New York: E. P. Dutton, 1903) 115.

universal sovereignty and to invite God's people to join God at God's work in the world. That work, as the whole book of Psalms makes clear, consists fundamentally of justice (see v. 9) and righteousness (see Psalms 96–99), the result of which is peace (see Ps 72:3, 7). Thus, again when understood figuratively, vv. 6-9 are a profoundly theological call to discipleship. To be sure, the military imagery will always require careful interpretation, but its value is to convey the reality that the faithful will always face opposition insofar as they really do represent and work to enact God's justice and righteousness in the world (see Eph 6:10-17). In short, the proclamation of God's sovereignty is eschatological; it is always made in the midst of opposition and circumstances that seem to deny it (see Psalms 2; 93; 96–99; Introduction).

Because the proclamation of God's reign is always eschatological, the call to discipleship is a call to bear a cross (Mark 8:34). Entrance into the reign of God invites opposition, as Jesus' life and death demonstrate. The faithful life will always involve a struggle, a battle. In this sense, the people of God will always be "Christian soldiers," but they will always be waging peace instead of war (see Eph 6:15). As John Calvin concludes concerning Psalm 149, citing Eph 6:17, "As to the Church collective, the sword now put into our hand is of another kind, that of the word and spirit."[535] To proclaim that God rules the world is to invite opposition from those who want to claim power for themselves, as Israel knew, and as the early Christians knew, and as is still true today. As Hauerwas and Willimon put it, we live in a "world [which] has declared war upon the gospel in the most subtle of ways."[536] The battle will mean for us what it meant for exilic and post-exilic Israel, which discovered its identity as a servant (see above on Isa 42:1-9), and what it meant for Jesus: suffering. The good news is that such suffering is our "glory" (Ps 149:9; see Rom 8:17).

2. Not surprisingly, since it arose in a situation in which the church was being persecuted by the Roman Empire, the Revelation to John draws upon many of the concepts present in Psalm 149 and in related passages, such as Psalms 96; 98; and Isaiah 40–66. Although it appeared that Rome ruled the world and that Caesar was Lord, the church dared to proclaim that God was still sovereign (see Rev 11:15). Because God rules the world, the faithful can "sing a new song" (see Rev 5:9; 14:3). The Revelation is less a vision of the future than it is a profession of faith about the present—God reigns. And as in Psalm 149, the author is convinced that the faithful reign with God (see Rev 4:10; 22:5) toward the end of fulfilling God's purpose of drawing in all nations and peoples and kings (see Rev 21:24-26; 22:2), and indeed all creation (see Rev 21:1). What greater glory could there be for us than God's permitting us to participate in enacting among all peoples and nations the justice, righteousness, and peace God wills for all creatures and all creation? The only possible response from all the saints is "Praise the Lord!"

535. John Calvin, *Commentary on the Book of Psalms,* Calvin Translation Society, 5 vols. (Calvin's Commentaries, vols. IV-VI; Grand Rapids, Mich.: Baker, rep. 1981) VI:5:316.
536. Stanley Hauerwas and William H. Willimon, *Resident Aliens: Life in the Christian Colony* (Nashville: Abingdon, 1989) 152.

PSALM 150:1-6, PRAISE THE LORD!

NIV

Psalm 150

¹Praise the LORD.ᵃ

Praise God in his sanctuary;
    praise him in his mighty heavens.
²Praise him for his acts of power;
    praise him for his surpassing greatness.
³Praise him with the sounding of the trumpet,
    praise him with the harp and lyre,
⁴praise him with tambourine and dancing,
    praise him with the strings and flute,
⁵praise him with the clash of cymbals,
    praise him with resounding cymbals.

⁶Let everything that has breath praise the LORD.

Praise the LORD.

ᵃ1 Hebrew *Hallelu Yah*; also in verse 6

NRSV

Psalm 150

¹ Praise the LORD!
Praise God in his sanctuary;
    praise him in his mighty firmament!ᵃ
² Praise him for his mighty deeds;
    praise him according to his surpassing
    greatness!

³ Praise him with trumpet sound;
    praise him with lute and harp!
⁴ Praise him with tambourine and dance;
    praise him with strings and pipe!
⁵ Praise him with clanging cymbals;
    praise him with loud clashing cymbals!
⁶ Let everything that breathes praise the LORD!
Praise the LORD!

ᵃOr *dome*

COMMENTARY

With a rousing and uninterrupted invitation to praise, Psalm 150 concludes the final collection of the psalter (Psalms 146–150) and the psalter itself. Every half-line begins with an imperative form of the verb "praise" (הלל *hillēl*), except the final one, which puts the subject first—"everything that breathes"—and switches to a jussive form of the verb ("Let everything . . . praise"). The uniqueness of Psalm 150 is fitting for its placement. Not only does v. 6 recall Ps 145:21 and thus provide a cosmicly oriented envelope around the final collection, but also the psalm serves as an appropriate doxology to conclude Book V (see Pss 41:13; 72:19; 89:52; 106:48) and the whole psalter. Just as Psalm 149 is an apt counterpart to Psalm 2 (see Commentary on Psalm 149), so also is Psalm 150 for Psalms 1 and 2. From the beginning, the psalter has commended openness to God's instruction (Psalm 1) and recognition of God's sovereignty (Psalm 2). Praise is the offering of one's whole life and self to God, and Psalm 150 is an enthusiastic invitation to all creatures to yield themselves to God (see also Psalm 148). Thus the whole psalter moves toward its

climactic crescendo of *hallelu-yah* psalms (Psalms 146–150), and Psalm 150 provides the final, breath-taking and breath-claiming note. Although the prayers for help actually outnumber the songs of praise along the way, the book of Psalms is aptly known in Hebrew as תהלים (*tĕhillîm*, "Praises").

Scholars often divide Psalm 150 into vv. 1-2, vv. 3-5, and v. 6. What sets vv. 1-2 apart is that the summons here at least implies what is usually an explicit feature of the songs of praise—that is, reasons for praise. Verses 3-5 are unified by their references to musical instruments, and v. 6 provides the conclusion. In other words, Psalm 150 tells who is to be praised (v. 1), why God is to be praised (v. 2), how God is to be praised (vv. 3-5), and who is to offer the praise (v. 6).[537]

150:1-2. These verses suggest reasons for praising God by way of their vocabulary, which elsewhere in the psalter is associated with God's reign. God's sovereignty is the fundamental af-

537. James L. Mays, *Psalms*, Interpretation (Louisville: John Knox, 1994) 450.

firmation that pervades the psalter (see Psalms 2; 5; 93; 95–99; Introduction), and it is especially prominent in Psalms 145–149 (see 145:1, 11-13; 146:10; 149:2). Although the Hebrew root for "to reign" or "to be king" (מלך *mālak*) does not occur in Psalm 150, the vocabulary of vv. 1-2 affirms God's rule. For instance, "sanctuary" (v. 1) elsewhere designates where God dwells as king. God's throne is there (see Ps 11:4, where "holy" represents the same word as "sanctuary" here), and God is explicitly greeted as "my king" as God enters "into the sanctuary" (Ps 68:24). It is not clear whether the sanctuary here should be understood as God's heavenly abode or the earthly Temple. Perhaps both senses are intended (cf. Pss 11:4; 68:24). As Kraus suggests, "At the holy place heaven and earth touch each other."[538] The word "firmament" (רקיע *rāqîaʿ*) suggests heaven, but it is not clear whether v. 1*a* and v. 1*b* should be construed as completely parallel.

The Hebrew roots behind the words "mighty" (עז *ʿōz*, v. 1*b*) and "mighty deeds" (גבורה *gĕbûrâ*, v. 2*a*) occur together as the phrase "strong and mighty" in Ps 24:8 to describe God as "King of glory." The word "mighty" occurs often in the context of the proclamation of God's reign (see Ps 99:4; see "strength" in 29:1; 93:1; 96:6 NRSV), as does the root behind "greatness" (גדל *gādal*, v. 2*b*; see Pss 47:2; 48:1; 95:3; 99:2; see also 147:5). In short, all creatures are summoned to praise God, because God rules the world.

150:3-5. Praise involves all aspects and spheres of life, including liturgy. In this section, worship of God in the Temple is in view, and music is featured. Every section of the orchestra—horns, strings, pipes, percussion—is invited to join in a symphony of praise. Given the direction to which the vocabulary of vv. 1-2 points—that is, toward the proclamation of God's sovereignty—it is significant that elsewhere the sound of the

trumpet announces God's reign (see Pss 47:5-7; 98:6). Furthermore, several of the instruments in vv. 3-5 are involved in the liturgy of 2 Samuel 6, where the ark on which God is "enthroned" (v. 2) is brought to Jerusalem (see, e.g., 2 Sam 6:5; 1 Chr 13:8; 15:28; 2 Chr 5:13; Neh 12:27; Pss 33:2-3; 68:24-25; 149:3). As is still often the case in more contemporary symphonic arrangements, the loud clash of the cymbals marks a climactic moment. The repetition of "cymbals" in v. 5*a* provides emphasis, preparing the way for the mention in v. 6 of the only thing that can surpass the praise of the full temple orchestra: the uplifted voice of every creature!

150:6. In addition to its final position, the switch in syntax and verbal form makes this verse emphatic. As it makes clear, the symphony of praise must ultimately include all creatures. The songs of praise regularly push toward universality, inviting "all you nations" (Ps 117:1) and "all the earth" (Ps 100:1) and indeed everything in heaven and on earth (Psalm 148) to praise God. Along with Ps 145:21 and Psalm 148, v. 6 is the ultimate extension of that invitation. The word "breath" (נשמה *nĕšāmâ*) recalls the creation of the world and of human life (Gen 2:7) as well as the flood story, in which the destiny of human and animal life went awry (Gen 7:22). Against this background, Psalm 150 proclaims that the proper goal of every creature is praise—life shaped by God's claim and lived under God's rule. As Mays puts it: "No other use of breath could be more right and true to life than praise of the LORD. No other sound could better speak the gratitude of life than praise of the LORD."[539] The final verse of the psalter is an eloquent reminder of the book's pervasive message: To praise God is to live, and to live is to praise God (see Commentary on Psalms 8; 100; 103; 104; 145).

538. H.-J. Kraus, *Psalms 1–59: A Commentary,* trans. H. C. Oswald (Minneapolis: Augsburg, 1988) 570.

539. Mays, *Psalms,* 451.

REFLECTIONS

Psalm 150 clearly indicates that the praises of God's people are meant to be sung to the accompaniment of musical instruments. Indeed, Israel and the church have always sung and still sing the psalms as well as other songs of praise and prayer. As Mays says of Psalm 150: "It is a witness to the power of music, its amazing potential for evoking beauty and feeling and for carrying vision beyond the range of words into the realm of imagination. That we sing the praise of God is no accidental custom."[540]

A concrete illustration of the power of music is the version of Psalm 150 performed by Duke Ellington. Jazz historian Stanley Dance describes the response to Ellington's rendition:

> In Barcelona, in the ancient Church of Santa Maria del Mar, the enthusiasm was such that the congregation burst into the aisles to participate in the finale, "Praise God and Dance" [Psalm 150]. The music and the message of the concert seemed to transcend language barriers without difficulty.[541]

Dance's comment touches upon two complementary concepts that are important for reflecting on Psalm 150: music and message. Precisely because music is powerful and can transcend barriers without difficulty, it is an appropriate medium for conveying the message about the sovereignty of God, whose claim transcends all the barriers that separate peoples from one another and humans from other creatures and the whole creation (see Psalm 148). By virtue of its vocabulary, which richly alludes to God's reign (vv. 1-2), by its call for full and enthusiastic musical accompaniment (vv. 3-5), and by its final invitation to every creature (v. 6), Psalm 150 "expresses a lyrical self-abandonment, an utter yielding of self, without vested interest, calculation, desire, or hidden agenda."[542]

Such "lyrical self-abandonment" is precisely what Jesus called for in response to the reign of God (see Mark 1:14-15; 8:34-36). The resurrection is the validation of Jesus' claim that to lose one's life for the sake of the gospel is to save it (Mark 8:35). Thus the use of Psalm 150 during the season of Easter puts us in touch with Jesus' claim. In concert with Jesus' life, death, and resurrection, Psalm 150 and the psalter as a whole invite and commend "lyrical self-abandonment" in liturgy and in every moment of life (see Ps 1:1-2). Indeed, God wills that our worship and work become inseparable, symphonic expressions of our response to the simple but marvelously profound invitation, "Praise the LORD!"

---

540. Ibid., 450.

541. From the album cover of Duke Ellington's *Sacred Sounds,* The Prestige Series, P-24045. See James Limburg, *Psalms for Sojourners* (Minneapolis: Augsburg, 1986) 91-92.

542. Walter Brueggemann, "Bounded by Obedience and Praise: The Psalms as Canon," *JSOT* 50 (1991) 67.

TRANSLITERATION SCHEMA

HEBREW AND ARAMAIC TRANSLITERATION

Consonants:

א	=	'	ט	=	*ṭ*	פ or ף	=	*p*
ב	=	*b*	י	=	*y*	צ or ץ	=	*ṣ*
ג	=	*g*	כ or ך	=	*k*	ק	=	*q*
ד	=	*d*	ל	=	*l*	ר	=	*r*
ה	=	*h*	מ or ם	=	*m*	שׂ	=	*ś*
ו	=	*w*	נ or ן	=	*n*	שׁ	=	*š*
ז	=	*z*	ס	=	*s*	ת	=	*t*
ח	=	*ḥ*	ע	=	'

Masoretic Pointing:

Pure-long			Tone-long			Short			Composite *shewa*		
הָ	=	*â*	ָ	=	*ā*	ַ	=	*a*	ֲ	=	*ă*
ֵי or ֶי	=	*ê*	ֵ	=	*ē*	ֶ	=	*e*	ֱ or ֳ	=	*ĕ*
ִי or ִ	=	*î*				ִ	=	*i*			
ֹ or וֹ	=	*ô*	ֹ	=	*ō*	ָ	=	*o*	ֳ	=	*ŏ*
ֻ or וּ	=	*û*				ֻ	=	u			

GREEK TRANSLITERATION

α	=	*a*	ι	=	*i*	ρ	=	*r*
β	=	*b*	κ	=	*k*	σ or ς	=	*s*
γ	=	*g*	λ	=	*l*	τ	=	*t*
δ	=	*d*	μ	=	*m*	υ	=	*y*
ε	=	*e*	ν	=	*n*	φ	=	*ph*
ζ	=	*z*	ξ	=	*x*	χ	=	*ch*
η	=	*ē*	ο	=	*o*	ψ	=	*ps*
θ	=	*th*	π	=	*p*	ω	=	*ō*

INDEX OF EXCURSUSES, MAPS, CHARTS, AND ILLUSTRATIONS

ABBREVIATIONS

General

BCE	Before the Common Era
CE	Common Era
c.	circa
cent.	century
cf.	compare
chap(s).	chapter(s)
esp.	especially
lit.	literally
ll.	lines
LXX	Septuagint
MS(S)	manuscript(s)
MT	Masoretic Text
n(n).	note(s)
OL	Old Latin
NT	New Testament
OT	Old Testament
pl(s).	plate(s)
v(v).	verse(s)

Names of Biblical Books (with the Apocrypha)

Gen	Nah	1–4 Kgdms	John
Exod	Hab	Add Esth	Acts
Lev	Zeph	Bar	Rom
Num	Hag	Bel	1–2 Cor
Deut	Zech	1–2 Esdr	Gal
Josh	Mal	4 Ezra	Eph
Judg	Ps (Pss)	Jdt	Phil
1–2 Sam	Job	Ep Jer	Col
1–2 Kgs	Prov	1–4 Macc	1–2 Thess
Isa	Ruth	Pr Azar	1–2 Tim
Jer	Cant	Pr Man	Titus
Ezek	Eccl	Sir	Phlm
Hos	Lam	Sus	Heb
Joel	Esth	Tob	Jas
Amos	Dan	Wis	1–2 Pet
Obad	Ezra	Matt	1–3 John
Jonah	Neh	Mark	Jude
Mic	1–2 Chr	Luke	Rev

Names of Pseudepigraphical and Early Patristic Books

1-2-3 Enoch	Ethiopic, Slavonic, Hebrew *Enoch*
Jub.	*Jubilees*

Names of Dead Sea Scrolls and Related Texts

CD	Cairo (Genizah text of the) *Damascus* (*Document*)
Q	Qumran
1QH	*Hôdāyôt* (*Thanksgiving Hymns*) from Qumran Cave 1
1QpHab	*Pesher on Habakkuk* from Qumran Cave 1
1QM	*Milḥāmāh* (*War Scroll*)
1QS	*Serek hayyahad* (*Rule of the Community, Manual of Discipline*)
1QSa	Appendix A (*Rule of the Congregation*) to 1QS

4QMMT	*Miqsat Ma' aseh Torah* from Qumran Cave 4
11QTemple	*Temple Scroll* from Qumran Cave 11

Orders and Tractates in Mishnaic and Related Literature

To distinguish the same-named tractates in the Mishna, Tosepta, Babylonian Talmud, and Jerusalem Talmud, *m., t., b.,* or *y.* precedes the title of the tractate.

ʾAbot	ʾAbot
B. Bat.	Baba Batra
b. Git.	Gittin
Sanh.	Sanhedrin
Yoma	Yoma (= Kippurim)

Other Rabbinic Works

Pesiq. R.	Pesiqta Rabbati

Commonly Used Periodicals, Reference Works, and Serials

AB	Anchor Bible
ABD	Anchor Bible Dictionary
ANEP	J. B. Pritchard (ed.), Ancient Near East in Pictures
ANET	J. B. Pritchard (ed.), Ancient Near Eastern Texts
AJSL	American Journal of Semitic Languages and Literature
BA	Biblical Archaeologist
BibOr	Biblica et orientalia
BJS	Brown Judaic Studies
BSO(A)S	Bulletin of the School of Oriental (and African) Studies
BZAW	Beihefte zur ZAW
CBQ	Catholic Biblical Quarterly
CBQMS	Catholic Biblical Quarterly—Monograph Series
CP	Classical Philology
EPRO	Etudes préliminaires aux religions orientales dans l'empire Romain
ExpTim	Expository Times
FBBS	Facet Books, Biblical Series
FRLANT	Forschungen zur Religion und Literatur des Alten und Neuen Testaments
GNB	Good News Bible
HAR	Hebrew Annual Review
HBC	J. L. Mays, et al. (eds.), Harper's Bible Commentary
HBT	Horizons in Biblical Theology
HSM	Harvard Semitic Monographs
HTR	Harvard Theological Review
HUCA	Hebrew Union College Annual
ICC	International Critical Commentary
IDB	G. A. Buttrick (ed.), Interpreter's Dictionary of the Bible
IDBSup	Supplementary volume to IDB
Int.	Interpretation
JBL	Journal of Biblical Literature
JJS	Journal of Jewish Studies
JQR	Jewish Quarterly Review
JSOT	Journal for the Study of the Old Testament
JSOTSup	Journal for the Study of the Old Testament—Supplement Series
JSP	Journal for the Study of the Pseudepigrapha
JSS	Journal of Semitic Studies
KJV	King James Version
KAT	Kommentar zum Alten Testament
NAB	New American Bible
NCB	New Century Bible
NEB	New English Bible
NIB	New Interpreter's Bible
NICOT	New International Commentary on the Old Testament
NIV	New International Version
NJB	H. Wansbrough (ed.), New Jerusalem Bible
NRSV	New Revised Standard Version
OTL	Old Testament Library
OTS	Oudtestamentische Studiën
RB	Revue biblique
REB	Revised English Bible
ResQ	Restoration Quarterly

RSV	Revised Standard Version
SBL	Society of Biblical Literature
SBLDS	SBL Dissertation Series
SJLA	Studies in Judaism in Late Antiquity
SR	*Studies in Religion/Sciences religieuses*
SSN	Studia semitica neerlandica
TDOT	G. J. Botterweck and II. Ringgren (eds.), *Theological Dictionary of the Old Testament*
TNK	Tanakh
TToday	*Theology Today*
VT	*Vetus Testamentum*
VTSup	Vetus Testamentum, Supplements
WBC	Word Biblical Commentary
WMANT	Wissenschaftliche Monographien zum Alten und Neuen Testament
ZAH	*Zeitschrift für Althebraistik*
ZAW	*Zeitschrift für die alttestamentliche Wissenschaft*